Cities Ranked & Rated

More than 400 Metropolitan Areas Evaluated in the U.S. & Canada

2nd Edition

Bert Sperling & Peter Sander

Wiley Publishing, Inc.

Published by:

Wiley Publishing, Inc.

111 River St.
Hoboken, NJ 07030-5774

Editors: Marc Nadeau and Michael Kelly
Production Editor: Suzanna R. Thompson
Cartographer: Guy Ruggiero
Photo Editor: Richard Fox
Anniversary Logo Design: Richard Pacifico
Interior Designer: Marie Kristine Parial-Leonardo
Production by Wiley Indianapolis Composition Services

ISBN 978-0-470-06864-9

For information on our other products and services or to obtain technical support, please contact our Customer Care Department within the U.S. at 800/762-2974, outside the U.S. at 317/572-3993 or fax 317/572-4002.

Wiley also publishes its books in a variety of electronic formats. Some content that appears in print may not be available in electronic formats.

Manufactured in the United States of America

5   4   3   2   1

Contents

Tables

Maps

Acknowledgments

Once again, I'd like to recognize the Frommer's/Wiley team, led by publisher Mike Spring, for having the vision and perseverance to bring the *Cities Ranked & Rated* series to reality. There are many, many others—friends, professional colleagues, real estate professionals, acquaintances, and even family members—who have offered help and insight along the way. If you're reading this, you know who you are. Of course, my family, wife Jennifer and boys Julian and Jonathan, deserve a piece of the action, contributing both inspiration and notable patience throughout, making many sacrifices especially during precious summer breaks as I toiled away. Of course, it isn't all bad—research for *Cities Ranked & Rated* has taken us everywhere from the barren steppes east of El Paso, Texas, to cool places like Château Frontenac in Québec City, Québec, and hundreds of places in between. Finally, my parents, Jerry and Betty Sander, must be recognized for dispensing with the Disneyland trips in favor of adventurous land travels, bringing me the rich experience of visiting 38 states and 5 provinces—before my 18th birthday—with numerous discussions about what it would be like to live in each.

—Peter Sander

I'm very thankful for the opportunity to help people make one of the most important decisions in life—finding a new home. I really believe that there are wonderful aspects to all places, even those that may be challenged by a lagging economy or a natural disaster. I would not have been able to do any of this without the support and guidance of my wife, Gretchen. Creating a career where none existed previously has been challenging, and at times, lonely. Gretchen has been steadfast in her belief in our work, and that good things will come from doing good. I could not have done any of this without her help and support. Thanks also to my sons Bert and Ted, who are now off on their own careers after contributing several years to our endeavor. Their work was invaluable, and I'll always remember our time together. I'd also like to thank my associates, Adam DuVander and Al Olsen, whose work has enabled our studies and information to reach millions of people. Finally, I'd like to acknowledge the contributions of people all over the country who have shared experiences about their hometowns. Thanks to them, I can pass along their insights to help others throughout the country.

—Bert Sperling

An Invitation to the Reader

In this book, we've compiled many facts that provide insights into living and working in different metro areas. But there's much more to know, and we'd like your help. You are an expert in your own city or neighborhood. Please take some time to share your observations or experiences to let others know what it's like to live in your hometown. You can enter your information online at the *Cities Ranked & Rated* website at www.bestplaces.net/CRAR or at www.frommers.com, or you can write to:

Cities Ranked & Rated, 2nd Edition
Wiley Publishing, Inc. • 111 River St. • Hoboken, NJ 07030-5774

About the Authors

Peter Sander is a professional author, researcher, and consultant in the fields of location reference, business, and personal finance. He has written 15 books including *Cities Ranked & Rated, Best Places to Raise Your Family, Value Investing For Dummies, Personal Finance for Entrepreneurs, The 250 Personal Finance Questions Everyone Should Ask, Everything Personal Finance,* and *Niche and Get Rich.* His educational background includes an MBA in Logistics Management from Indiana University and a B.A. in Urban Affairs and Administration from Miami University of Ohio, and professional training and examination as a Certified Financial Planner (CFP®). His career includes 20 years as a marketing and logistics specialist for a major high-tech firm. He has appeared on *NBC Today, CNBC, CNNfn,* and *Fox News* and has been a frequent radio guest and commentator about location issues across the U.S. and Canada. Originally from Cincinnati, Ohio, and now living in Granite Bay, California, he has traveled in all 50 U.S. states.

For more than 20 years, **Bert Sperling** has helped people find their own best place to live, work, play, and retire. In addition to this book, he coauthored *Best Places to Raise Your Family* (Wiley Publishing, Inc., 2006), also with Peter Sander. Bert appears regularly in the national media to discuss his studies, which cover a broad range of topics, including "Best Places for Seniors," "Best Places to Retire," "Most Stressful Cities," "Best Cities for Dating," "Most Fiscally Fit Cities," "America's Healthiest Cities," "Most Drivable Cities," "Best and Worst Cities for Fleas," "Most Romantic Cities," "Most Photogenic Cities," "Best Places to Buy a Second Home," "Best Cities for Teens," "Best Cities for Sleep," "Best Cities for Family Fun," "Adventure Cities," "Riskiest Places for ID Theft," "America's Migraine Hot Spots," and many others. His firm's free website, www.bestplaces.net, provides insight and guidance to nearly a million visitors each month, and its content is found on the websites of MSN, CNN-Money, AOL, Yahoo!, eBay, the *Wall Street Journal,* and AARP, among others. Bert was born in Brooklyn, New York, and has lived in such diverse places as Kodiak, Alaska; Carmel Valley, California; Key West, Florida; Long Island, New York; and Oslo, Norway. He currently makes his home in Portland and Depoe Bay, Oregon, with his wife Gretchen and their faithful English bull terrier, Molly.

Introduction

For some of you, the grass always seems greener somewhere else. You lie awake at night in constant need to scratch that itch: "Now, what if I lived somewhere else? Would I find enough to do? Could I find work? Could I afford the place? Would my kids get what they need? Would I be safe and healthy?" The list of questions is endless. People are naturally curious about places to live—including their own. Some may decide to move if they can find a better place, while others have to move for career or family reasons and want to know more about what they are getting into. Still others just like to browse, perhaps looking for a city that suits their own long-term personal or financial plan. Regardless of the reason, the sheer complexity of factors that makes one place better than another makes the evaluation rich and challenging.

Numerous features, good stuff, bad stuff, and an assortment of items more a matter of personal preference determine what makes a city *your* best place to live. Living in a dream home in the suburbs of a large city might involve a 1½-hour commute to work or a high cost of living—or both. A more "ideal" place may be a bucolic burg with tree-lined streets, a short walk to work, and affordable necessities, but the location could be a 1-hour airplane flight from a symphony or surgical hospital or even a good bookstore. Another place may be a beach paradise that comes with the downsides of crowds and standing in line to pay 30% more than the rest of the country for recreational activities. Rumors fly about places with lower taxes—maybe no income or sales tax at all. Real estate flyers show glowing photos of attractive, well-built homes on large, wooded lots in nice neighborhoods at apparent bargain prices. Some places have reputations for great nightlife, restaurants, theater, or activities for children.

But what is the truth in these stories? How do these cities really stack up against one another? And how can people weigh the pros and cons to determine the best fit for their chosen lifestyle and financial means? *Cities Ranked & Rated*, 2nd Edition, is designed and presented to answer these questions with up-to-date facts and interpretation of those facts to help readers find their ideal place to live.

What Is *Cities Ranked & Rated?*

Simply put, *Cities Ranked & Rated* as a series is designed to compare places to live. Books in this series offer a rich set of comparative facts and figures on North American cities—both in the U.S. and Canada. *Cities Ranked & Rated*, 2nd Edition, covers 375 U.S. cities and 27 in Canada. Comparisons start with the facts, which are then blended with a subjective assessment of a place's image, character, and overall quality of life to determine each city's rank in relation to the others. *Cities Ranked & Rated* editions cover cities from a broad perspective, while others, like *Best Places to Raise Your Family* (Wiley Publishing, Inc., 2006) look at places through the eyes of a single demographic group, in that case, families with children or couples planning to have children some day.

Cities Ranked & Rated books are valuable resources to help with the following challenges:

- *Immediate voluntary (or involuntary) relocation:* Many are looking to relocate to somewhere better suited to their immediate needs, tastes, and financial means. Others make career-change or migration decisions based on job opportunities. A move may involve a life-stage change, such as graduation from college, marriage, arrival of children, or retirement. Statistically, by a slim margin, job or career issues were the number one reason cited for relocation in the early part of the decade, while more recently, family-oriented reasons have barely taken over. See the sidebar "Moving: The Reasons Why," later in this introduction, for more details.

- *Long-term planning: Cities Ranked & Rated* can help to build a career, financial, or retirement plan that eventually, if not immediately, results in a move to an ideal place. By studying and comparing places as they are today, readers can track what happens with those places as their plans unfold.

- *Business relocation/site selection:* Entrepreneurs are interested in the business and tax climates of different places, both for their business and for prospective employees. *Cities Ranked & Rated* is not only handy for business climate but also as a tool to find out where people—customers—are going and why they're going there. While *Cities Ranked & Rated* isn't intended as a substitute for detailed market research, it is a good place to start.

- *Curiosity and reference: Cities Ranked & Rated* provides statistics and analyses in an accessible package not available in one place anywhere else. People wanting to learn more about an area can use it as a reference.

Cities Ranked & Rated is not a "study." Many studies emerge from periodicals, universities, and other sources, usually on a small cross-section of the "best places" theme. Examples include "Best Places to Retire" (*Money*), "Best Places to Be Single" (Forbes.com), and "Most Literate Cities" (Central Connecticut State University). While these studies are usually of high quality, and many use the same data used in *Cities Ranked & Rated,* they are limited in scope, covering perhaps 40 or 50 different places, and rely on smaller sets of facts. If you share common characteristics or interests with one of these groups, these articles give an interesting if less complete take on the "best place" question.

Cities Ranked & Rated is, most emphatically, not a travel guide. Travel books cover restaurants, lodging, and temporal points of interest and things to do in a place. While you may go out of your way while traveling to see an ancient burial site or a place where Abraham Lincoln once slept, these features would not necessarily influence your decision to *live* in a place.

What Makes a Best Place Best?

Particularly for those looking to relocate, *Cities Ranked & Rated,* 2nd Edition, is about choices and alternatives. If every U.S. resident was looking for the same thing in a place and had the same best place in mind, there would be 300 million people living there, and it wouldn't be a best place much longer. What makes the choice intriguing is that everyone has different goals, needs, aspirations, and interests. People are in different life stages and desire different lifestyles. The choice is not *just* about lifestyle—otherwise most would choose to live in Beverly Hills or the Hamptons in Long Island—it is also about *means,* the financial considerations and prospects for those who live there.

Boiled down, most people consider four broad categories when evaluating a place: economy, cost of living, climate, and character. Economy refers to the economic health and vitality of a place, and the ability to turn that health into personal or family income. Cost of living, as the name suggests, refers to what it costs to live there, including the cost of basic housing and necessities such as food, utilities, and transportation as well as local tax burden. It may surprise some, but according to the U.S. Census, climate is far from the primary reason most people decide to relocate. But it probably does play a role in deciding *where* to relocate. Character, the broadest, most nebulous, and most personally unique category, covers an area's look and feel and personality as well as specific activities and services available locally. It also covers such negatives as crime and health problems.

The evaluation process of *Cities Ranked & Rated* relies on the following 10 categories to determine score and rank for each place:

Economy & Jobs	Crime
Cost of Living	Transportation
Climate	Leisure
Education	Arts & Culture
Health & Healthcare	Quality of Life

Chapter 3 includes an in-depth explanation of these categories and their components, and explains how each is built into the ranking process.

What's Changed Since the First Edition?

The first edition of *Cities Ranked & Rated* was released in March 2004. It's fair to ask: Why do a second edition? Do places really change that fast? Do I really need to spend $25 for an update?"

The answer is: yes and no. In some ways, places change quite rapidly—witness the rapid escalation in residential real estate prices, mainly in coastal regions and around larger cities, during the most recent 3-year period. In some ways, change is more measured, perhaps more of an *evolution,* but we've seen an inexorable march along the evolutionary path. For instance, we've seen a substantial rise in commute times as residents move farther and farther away from cities into distant suburbs and exurbs. There has been—partially in response to such long commutes—an escalation of commercial development and employment in these exurbs and so-called "boomburghs"—large secondary downtown cores near major urban centers such as Bellevue, Washington; Alexandria, Virginia; and the Galleria area outside Houston. There are signs that this evolution may come full circle, as cities plan more center-city high-rises and other residential facilities, including mixed-use and so-called "New Urbanist" developments within their boundaries. Recent escalations in the cost and time consumed in commuting, as well as healthcare and housing costs, motivate us to look at new facts—or weigh some of the existing ones more heavily. We examine more closely the dynamic between city and suburbs in our subjective Quality of Life appraisal.

While much is changing, some things hardly change, if at all. Aside from the gradual effects of global warming, climate remains virtually unchanged. We bring these constants forward into the new edition.

While our design objective is to keep our essential approach unchanged, giving continuity from one edition to the next, there are some important changes, most of which serve to make *Cities Ranked & Rated,* 2nd Edition, a more complete and useful treatment. Among them:

- *New and changing places:* In this edition we incorporate full treatment of the 44 so-called "emerging" metro areas from the first edition—metro areas that had made the list just prior to the first edition's release. Those areas are now included in the main ranking of 375 places. Many areas grew or were split into segments; for example, the Boston area is now treated as three areas: Boston–Quincy, Cambridge–Newton–Framingham, and Essex County. The new alignment allows more precise analysis of key sectors of an area. See chapter 1 for a full explanation of cities rated and how they have evolved.

- *New analysis:* We have added several data fields to the presentation of area facts, including political alignment, religious observance, job mix, buying power, and housing affordability, as well as additional commute time detail. We have adjusted the ranking model to weight certain factors, such as healthcare costs, educational attainment, commute times, and future job growth a little (not a lot) more heavily, reflecting lifestyle concerns of our times. Finally, many of our metro areas are so large that readers may seek some detail below the radar—what parts of town or even neighborhoods to set sights on. In our *Best Places to Raise Your Family,* we developed the tools to "take places apart" into individual neighborhoods, and have added some of this knowledge and wisdom in this edition. Chapter 3 explains these changes.

- *New rankings:* Ultimately, the purpose of *Cities Ranked & Rated* is to present a composite snapshot of a place, a blend of specific facts, and our interpretation of those facts about each place. From these composites we do a ranking as a comparison of how places stack up and as a guideline—not an absolute truth—for you to use as a comparison tool. In this edition, we adjusted the model slightly as mentioned above. The resulting ranking was not unlike the first edition in that the top and bottom places were quite diverse in terms of size, region of the country, and overall character. But the ranking is hardly identical—only three places occurring in the top 10 in the first edition remained there in this one. As in the first edition, a number of college towns are found near the top of the list—some old faces, some new ones. Larger cities such as Portland, Oregon, and Indianapolis, Indiana, rose, while other larger areas such as Denver, Minneapolis–St Paul, and even New York, fell in the rankings due to the "3 Cs"—cost, commute, and crime. Chapter 2 gives more detail on ranking results.

Data Sources

The facts used and compared in *Cities Ranked & Rated,* 2nd Edition, come from an assortment of public and private sources widely used in demographic and market research. While the Internet has evolved, and a considerable amount of the information is available for free—the hard part is knowing where to find it and how to assemble it into a practical and usable package.

As an example, the National Climatic Data Center (NCDC), a branch of the National Oceanic and Atmospheric Administration (NOAA) of the U.S. Department of Commerce, publishes vast amounts of climate and weather statistics, all available, and most of it online, for free. However, they include up to 70 years of monthly weather observations for 18,000 weather stations around the United States. *Cities Ranked & Rated,* 2nd Edition, distills this ocean of detail into what's important to know for the 375 U.S. places in this book.

Among the major U.S. data sources are:

- U.S. Census Bureau for population and demographics, commute statistics, and commercial activity
- Bureau of Labor Statistics for economy, employment, and cost of living
- National Climatic Data Center for climate and weather
- Department of Education, National Center for Education Statistics for education
- Centers for Disease Control and Prevention for health
- Claritas, Inc., a private market data services provider

And among those used for Canada:

- Statistics Canada for population, demographics, economic, crime, and education
- Environment Canada for climate data

Additional data comes from published sources and from industry associations and trade groups, like the American Medical Association, National Association or Realtors, National Association of Insurance Commissioners, or the Association of American Museums. In discussing attributes, chapter 3 details specific data sources, which can also be found in Table 5.1.

Data Timeliness

Most of the data in this book is compiled from government and public agency sources. These agencies collect mountains of data, particularly from the decennial (every 10 years) U.S. Census. Follow-up surveys and projections are developed and posted by these agencies, but they often lag natural time due to the sheer volume of processing required to compile and present the date.

The most recent "core" U.S. Census was taken in 2000, so you might rightfully question the validity of these facts today in 2006 and beyond. The U.S. Census is rapidly evolving its data collection model into an annual update based on annual statistical surveys. Each year the census does the American Community Survey, and our facts are largely based on the 2005 survey published in 2006. Eventually, the U.S. Census plans to migrate away from the decennial census altogether and replace it with the continuous updates, much as many manufacturers and warehouse operators have reduced or done away with most or all physical inventories in favor of a statistical sampling, or "cycle counting," approach.

Where possible *Cities Ranked & Rated* acquires and presents the most up-to-date facts available for a topic. Recent changes, such as those undertaken by the U.S. Census, have made more frequent updates available. Where an official update isn't available, we are often able to plug holes with private sources, including facts available through research firms such as Claritas.

Unfortunately, our publication cycle did not match well with the Canadian Census, which is updated every 5 years, most recently in 2001 and 2006. While the 2006 update suggests refresh facts would be available, it is in fact the date that Census Canada takes the census, not the date the results are presented, so these results weren't available at the time of our compilation.

Online Research

Bert Sperling, one of the co-creators of this book, has been analyzing livable cities for more than 25 years, and is responsible for many of the best-known studies and articles on the subject. His website, www.bestplaces.net, includes additional data and detail not included in *Cities Ranked & Rated,* 2nd Edition, and can be used as a companion tool for the book. The website features thousands of city and neighborhood profiles built on data similar to that presented in this book, and tools that allow head-to-head comparison using your personal criteria and weightings.

In addition to www.bestplaces.net, readers may have already discovered numerous other online sources. They may also have discovered that online content can be inconsistent, complex, and overly "salesy" at times. That said, the following types of websites can be helpful when researching a place:

- *City website:* Most cities and towns have their own site. These are largely administrative in nature, with information on garbage collection, road closures, and other mostly irrelevant topics. But more and more, the better ones have sections describing the city, its history, its economy and infrastructure, and recognition received in other rating studies. Occasionally, county sites serve this purpose.

- *Chamber of Commerce:* Most places we examine have a chamber of commerce with their own website. The goal and orientation of these organizations is to attract business and commerce to an area. Some are loaded with sales hype but few facts, and some concentrate on industrial parks and other potential business locations in the area.

- *Convention and Visitors Bureau:* Most larger cities have a convention and visitors bureau oriented to attracting events and meetings. Many of these sites are filled with information on accommodations, restaurants, and entertainment attractions more suited to a travel guide, and most only show a good face for an area and little real information about it.

- *Realtor sites:* Obviously oriented to selling property, these sites may have some information directed toward potential relocation candidates. Most have pictures of homes, which give a good idea not only of home value but also of the character and appearance of local residences. Some have fact sets or subsets similar to those presented in *Cities Ranked & Rated,* but we find that outside of specific real estate information most are incomplete and out of date.

- *Satellite and mapping tools:* Pictures are worth a thousand words, and the advent of satellite visual and mapping tools such as Google Earth give us new insight into the infrastructure, layout, and appearance of a place. Data-interconnected mapping tools such as Microsoft MapPoint help connect place with important facts, such as demographics, home prices, and educational attainment, down to the zip-code level.

- *Local evangelists:* Finally, some people love their place so much that they want to share their insight and experience with the world. Some do it using their own website or blog, which can be uncovered on a Google search. Wikipedia, the online shared encyclopedia, is a good repository of well-organized locally created facts and commentary, although some must be taken with a grain of salt.

U.S. Postal Codes

The tables in this book use the two-letter postal codes assigned and used by the U.S. Postal Service. See Table 0.1 for a guide to the abbreviations.

TABLE 0.1 U.S. STATES & POSTAL CODES
As assigned by the U.S. Postal Service

Alaska	AK	Hawaii	HI	Maine	ME	New Jersey	NJ	South Dakota	SD
Alabama	AL	Iowa	IA	Michigan	MI	New Mexico	NM	Tennessee	TN
Arkansas	AR	Idaho	ID	Minnesota	MN	Nevada	NV	Texas	TX
Arizona	AZ	Illinois	IL	Missouri	MO	New York	NY	Utah	UT
California	CA	Indiana	IN	Mississippi	MS	Ohio	OH	Virginia	VA
Colorado	CO	Kansas	KS	Montana	MT	Oklahoma	OK	Vermont	VT
Connecticut	CT	Kentucky	KY	North Carolina	NC	Oregon	OR	Washington	WA
Delaware	DE	Louisiana	LA	North Dakota	ND	Pennsylvania	PA	Wisconsin	WI
Florida	FL	Massachusetts	MA	Nebraska	NE	Rhode Island	RI	West Virginia	WV
Georgia	GA	Maryland	MD	New Hampshire	NH	South Carolina	SC	Wyoming	WY

Moving: The Reasons Why

Roughly 40 million U.S. residents contemplate an immediate move each year. On average, about one in seven people move each year. Or put another way, the average U.S. resident moves once every 7 years. This figure has remained fairly constant over the years, although it has fallen off a bit since the boom years of the late 1990s. Of the one out of seven that move, some 40% of those move to a different state or county, a figure that has grown slightly over the years. In particular, the percentage of movers moving out of state has grown from a steady 15% to 16% of all movers to 19% to 20%, suggesting that while there are fewer moves, a higher percentage are done over a long distance and have the purpose of making a major economic or lifestyle change.

We've also seen a slight shift in the reasons given for moving. In 2001, the leading reason given for an intercounty move was "job or career related," explaining some 31% of all moves, while "personal and family" was cited 25.6% of the time and "housing related" was given 27.6% of the time. In 2003 (unfortunately, the most recent Census mobility data published to date), the pattern had shifted: Career and jobs dropped to 27.9% while housing increased to 30.8% and personal and family increased to 28.3%. We interpret the message as being (1) family considerations have become more important, (2) the disparity in housing prices across the country is making itself felt, and (3) people are more able to work anywhere and work *from* anywhere than ever before.

We're anxious to see how these trends evolve. We also believe that *Cities Ranked & Rated*, 2nd Edition, in light of current trends, is more valuable than ever before.

part

I

Finding Your Best Place to Live

chapter 1

The Places

deally, *Cities Ranked & Rated,* 2nd Edition, would examine *all* places to live in the U.S. and Canada; however, the resulting book would be too thick (and expensive) to serve anyone's purpose well. So, as in the first edition, we limit our task to the places where *most* of the population tends to congregate and where most economic and cultural activity occurs—that is, within the major population centers in the U.S. and Canada. *Cities Ranked & Rated,* 2nd Edition, examines more than 400 places to live—375 in the United States and 27 in Canada. The 375 U.S. places are classified as Metropolitan Statistical Areas, or MSAs, defined shortly. According to the latest U.S. Census population estimates, MSAs represent just under 84% of the total U.S. population. The 27 Canadian population centers, identified by Statistics Canada as Census Metropolitan Areas, or CMAs, are similarly defined but have a higher population threshold than U.S. MSAs and cover 65% of the Canadian population.

U.S. Metropolitan Statistical Areas (MSAs)

Metropolitan Statistical Areas, or MSAs, are defined by the U.S. Office of Management and Budget (OMB), an arm of the U.S. Executive Branch, primarily for the twin purposes of statistical analysis and budget allocation. U.S. government agencies such as the Census Bureau and Bureau of Labor Statistics use these definitions in various ways to collect and classify their information. The terms "MSA," "metropolitan area," and "metro area" are used interchangeably throughout this book.

Definition

The definition for a Metropolitan Statistical Area, last refined in 2003, is ". . . [a place] *that has at least one urbanized area of 50,000 or more population, plus adjacent territory that has a high degree of social integration with the core as measured by commuting ties*" (OMB, June 2003).

MSAs are typically defined as one, and sometimes more than one, urban core, along with the county or group of counties in which it, or they, sit. An MSA can cross state lines, and many do. The relationship between urban cores and counties can be one to one, one to many, many to one, or many to many, as the following examples illustrate:

- One core to one county (Altoona, Pennsylvania, and Blair County)

- One core to many counties (Amarillo, Texas, and Armstrong, Carson, Potter, and Randall counties)

- Many cores to one county (Fort Collins–Loveland, Colorado, and Larimer County)

- Many cores to many counties (Pensacola–Ferry Pass–Brent, Florida, and Escambia and Santa Rosa counties)

If a county is integrated with an urban core, the *entire* county is included, regardless of size and content. Ordinarily this is logical, but it produces odd situations in the West where large, empty areas are classified as part of an MSA. Examples include the Mojave Desert in San Bernardino County (part of the MSA of Riverside–San Bernardino–Ontario, CA) and much of the Grand Canyon in Coconino County (part of the Flagstaff, AZ, MSA). Aside from perhaps evoking a smile, such situations don't much affect the ranking and evaluation of these places.

U.S. OMB definitions also include eight cities in Puerto Rico that are not included in this book.

MSA Naming Conventions

The name of an MSA is derived from the "principal cities" that OMB defines in each area, usually the largest or most prominent urban cores if an MSA has more than one city. If the MSA name has multiple principal cities, it is constructed in descending order of population of each principal city. Thus the MSA name "Virginia Beach–Norfolk–Newport

Abbreviated Names

It is not easy to simplify a book like *Cities Ranked & Rated*, 2nd Edition, but we do use shortened MSA names in this book's maps to simplify presentation. So, for example, Virginia Beach–Norfolk–Newport News becomes "Virginia Beach" in maps. Likewise, Palm Bay–Melbourne–Titusville becomes "Palm Bay."

News, VA-NC," is constructed as such because Virginia Beach is the largest principal city in the area. In the first edition, this metro area was called "Norfolk–Virginia Beach–Newport News, VA-NC," but Virginia Beach has outgrown Norfolk over the past 3 years, hence the name change.

As in the Virginia Beach area, several MSAs have multiple states listed after the name. This is due to the fact that some portion of the designated area extends across state lines. For example, the Virginia Beach area includes one county in extreme northeastern North Carolina.

Some MSAs may include a principal city and the name of the county in which it lies; typically this naming occurs when the city and county governments are merged as one, as in Louisville–Jefferson County, KY-IN, or Lexington–Fayette, KY. Some MSAs, such as Rockingham County–Strafford County, NH, are defined exclusively by county name.

In the first edition, metro areas in New England were not defined by county but by another OMB definition known as "NECTAs," or New England City and Town Areas. The boundaries followed townships, a typically stronger level of government and administration in that region. The latest definitions have changed to include counties. This creates some geographically large MSAs, especially in Connecticut, where counties tend to be large. This change does simplify data gathering and mapping, so we have followed it.

The most recent set of MSA names was announced by OMB in December 2005 and is the basis for our list.

Compiling Our List

Generally we follow the OMB set of MSAs as defined. But in the interest of simplicity and clarity, we did make a few adjustments to the list.

OMB lists 361 MSAs in the U.S. proper, excluding the 8 in Puerto Rico. To that list we added 29 *Metropolitan Divisions*. Metropolitan Divisions are designated splits of very large MSAs, such as Boston, New York, San Francisco,

and Chicago, all having a population of more than 2.5 million. OMB splits these large MSAs, where it makes sense, into Metropolitan Divisions (MD). For example, the Boston area is split into four MDs: Boston–Quincy, Cambridge–Newton–Framingham, Essex County, and Rockingham County–Strafford County in New Hampshire. Because these regions within a large metro area can vary considerably, we felt that presenting these larger MSAs in their narrower Metropolitan Division splits gives readers more to work with when researching the areas discussed in this book. This is especially true where the geographic divide between MDs is significant, as with San Francisco and the Oakland/East Bay areas of California. So we added 29 MDs to the list of 361, giving 390, and subtracted the 11 "mother" MSAs from the list, since covering them would now be redundant. Result: a list of 379 MSAs.

Then we noted some OMB splits that we didn't quite agree with. For example, OMB split the Greensboro–Winston-Salem–High Point, NC, metro area into three MSAs (Greensboro–High Point, Winston-Salem, and the third for Burlington, NC). We didn't see the rationale for this change, so didn't follow it. We also didn't follow the OMB's split of the Biloxi–Gulfport–Pascagoula, MS, area into two areas, so we recombined those. Finally, OMB combined Bergen County, NJ, into the New York–White Plains, NY, Metropolitan Division. We see Bergen County as sufficiently separate from New York's core, including Manhattan and the other boroughs and White Plains, to cover separately, so we have. That brought us from 379 MSAs, recombining 5 and splitting 1, to a conveniently round number of 375 MSAs, which is our final list, and it is shown in Table 1.3 and used throughout the book.

Splits & Merges

Those familiar with the first edition of *Cities Ranked & Rated* (published in 2004) may notice that familiar names, such as Danbury, CT; Galveston, TX; and Lowell, MA, have disappeared. A few others, such as Napa, CA, and

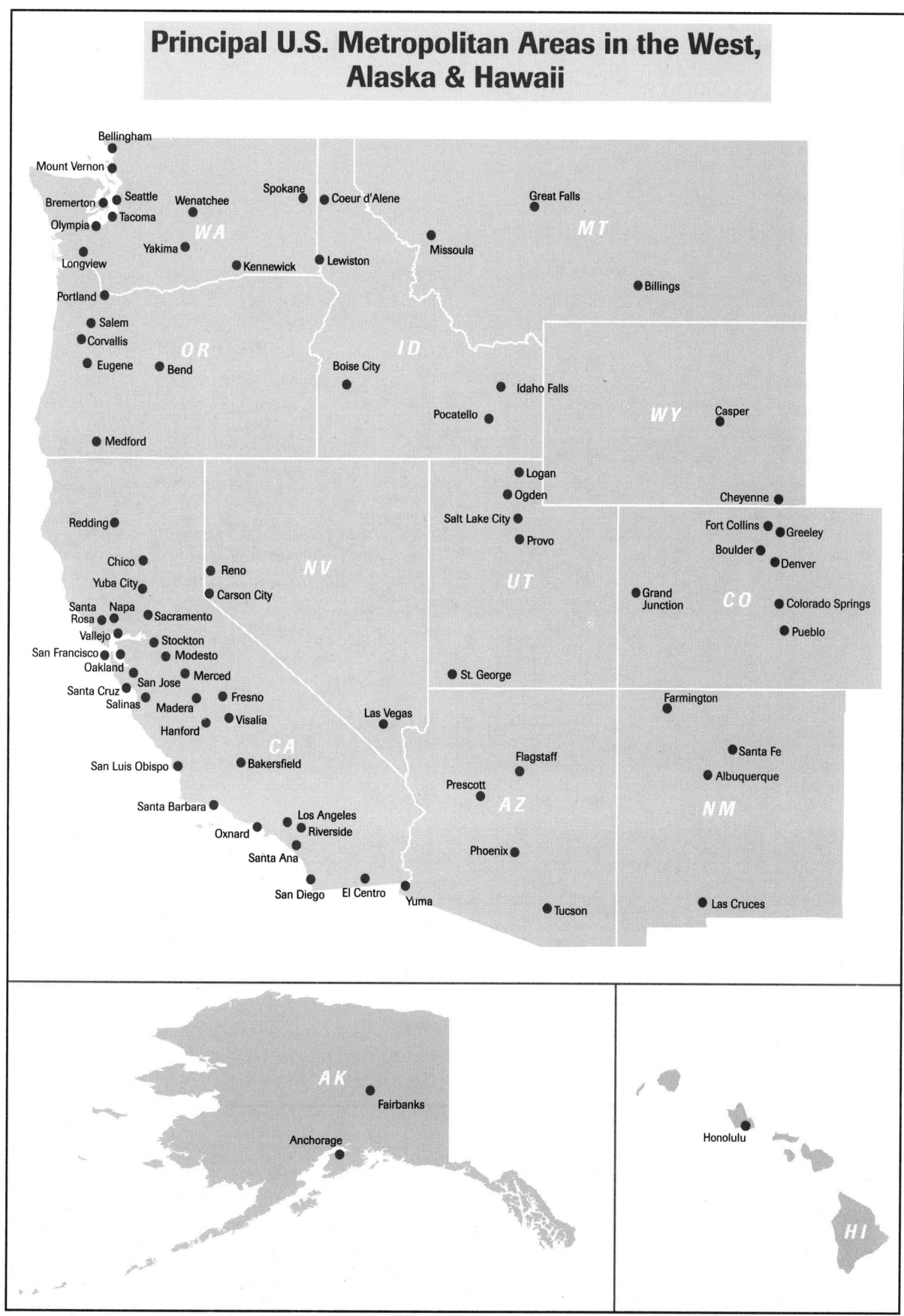

Principal U.S. Metropolitan Areas in the West, Alaska & Hawaii

Principal U.S. Metropolitan Areas in the Central Region

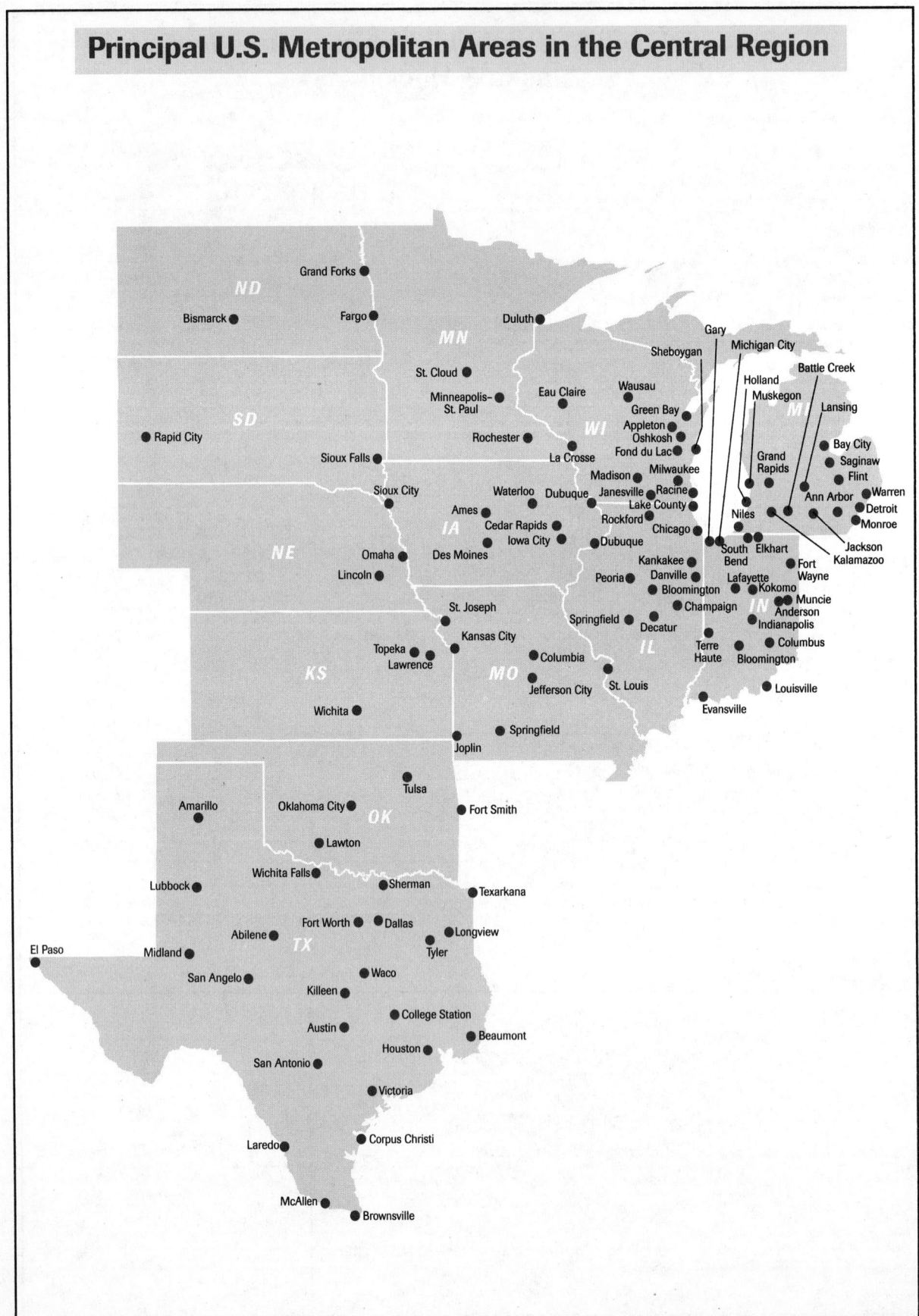

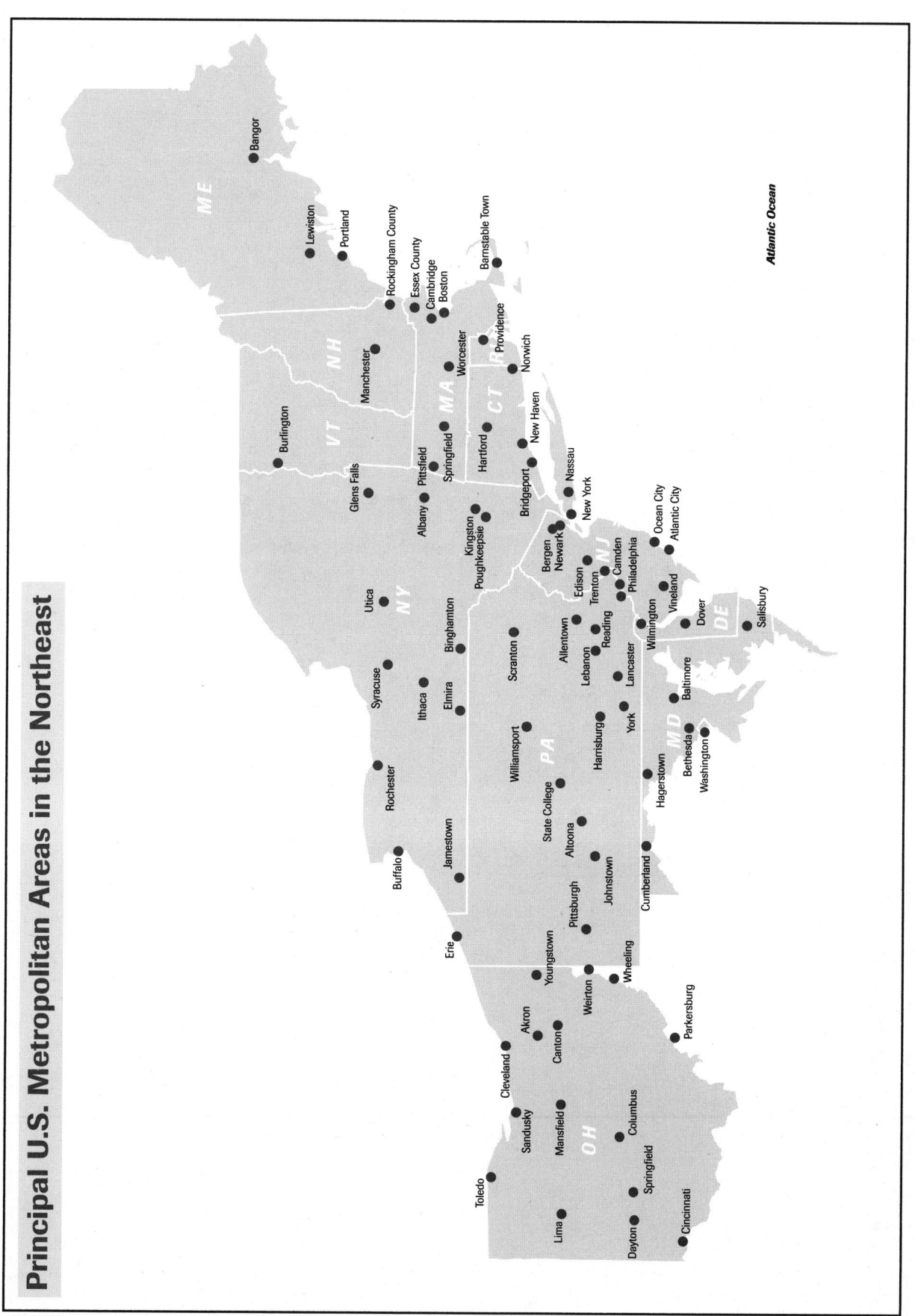

Principal U.S. Metropolitan Areas in the Northeast

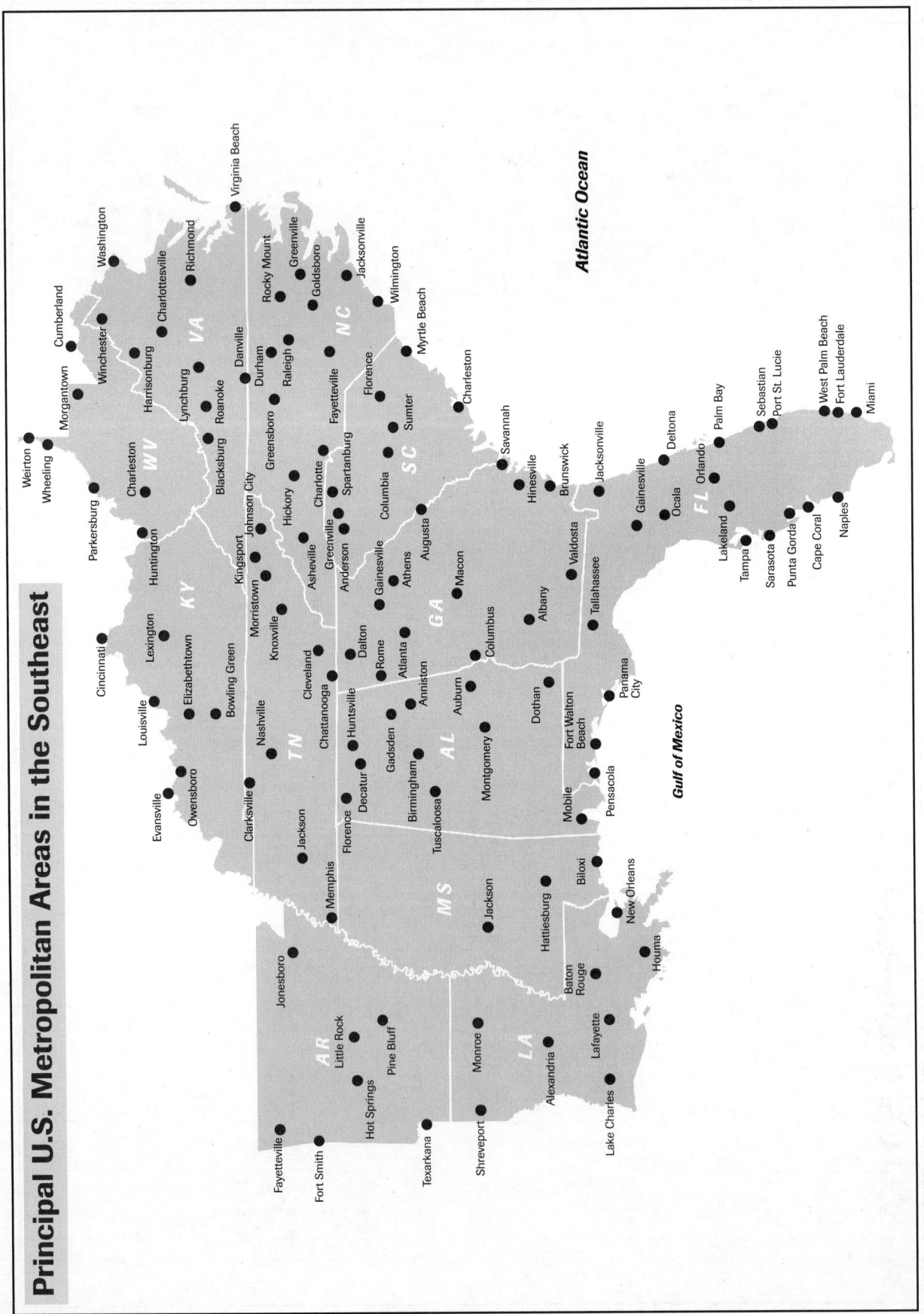

Principal U.S. Metropolitan Areas in the Southeast

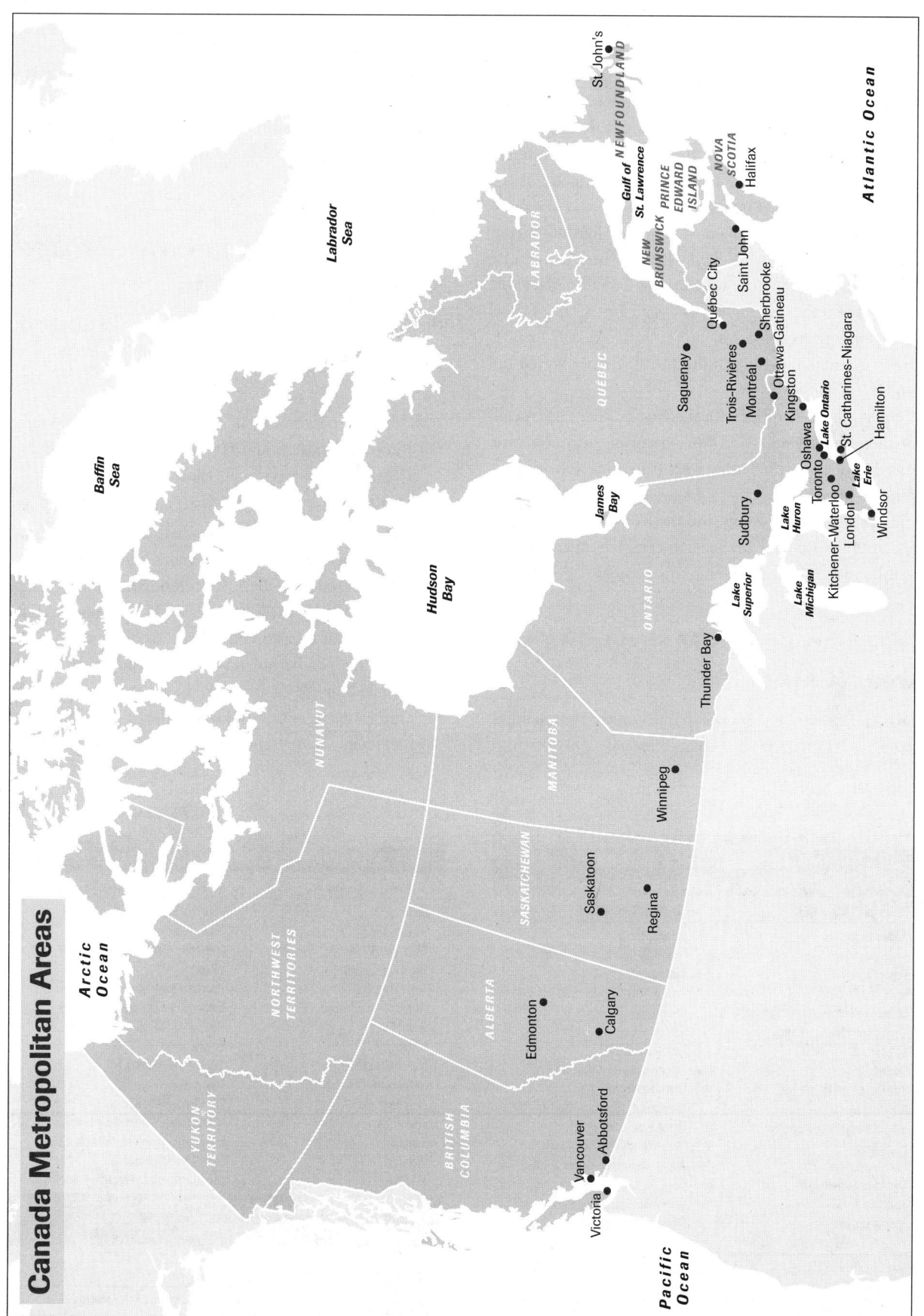

Canada Metropolitan Areas

Anderson, IN, may have been part of another MSA in the first edition. Due to population changes and other factors, several metro areas were redefined or realigned in OMB's 2005 revision. Table 1.1 lists 17 metro areas "gained" as a result of splitting from other metro areas. For example, Napa, CA, was split from the 2003 Napa–Vallejo–Fairfield, CA, metro area. Table 1.2 lists 15 metro areas "lost" by being merged into nearby metro areas. For example, Galveston, TX, was merged into the Houston–Sugar Land–Baytown, TX, MSA. Table 1.2 also lists two MSAs that shrunk in population or otherwise failed to meet the criteria this time: Jamestown, NY, and Enid, OK. These merges and splits are all included in the "base" of 361 MSAs mentioned above and the list of 375 we ended up with.

Finally, those familiar with the first edition may recall so-called "emerging" MSAs—a group of smaller metro areas that just qualified as we were compiling that edition. By necessity, we gave these 44 areas abbreviated treatment. They are now included in the 375 metro areas covered in this edition. They receive complete analysis and are fully integrated into the ranking process.

Canadian Census Metropolitan Areas (CMAs)

Canadian government officials define Census Metropolitan Areas, or CMAs, as an urban core of 100,000 and surrounding areas "with a high degree of social and economic interaction" with the core areas. Aside from the different population threshold, the Canadian approach differs from the United States in that once an area is designated a CMA, it always remains so, regardless of subsequent population declines. There are 27 CMAs in Canada.

What's Included in *Cities Ranked & Rated,* 2nd Edition?

The complex and shifting definitions may be frustrating, so for clarity, here is a summary of what's included in *Cities Ranked & Rated,* 2nd Edition:

- 375 U.S. Metropolitan Statistical Areas based on 2005 definitions and classifications, including 29 Metropolitan Divisions (Table 1.3)
- 27 Canada Census Metropolitan Areas (Table 1.4). Due to inherent difficulties with data comparisons with not quite "apples-to-apples" data, and the relatively few readers considering migration between countries, Canadian CMAs are presented in chapter 6 in an abbreviated fashion and are likewise not included in the U.S. rankings. Canadian CMAs are ranked among themselves and an estimate is made of where they would rank among U.S. metropolitan areas.

TABLE 1.1 METRO AREAS GAINED FROM SPLITS

METRO AREAS ONCE PART OF LARGER METRO AREAS

2006 METRO AREA	2003 METRO AREA
Anderson, IN	Indianapolis, IN
Anderson, SC	Greenville–Spartanburg–Anderson, SC
Battle Creek, MI	Kalamazoo–Battle Creek, MI
Bay City, MI	Saginaw–Bay City–Midland, MI
Bethesda–Gaithersburg–Frederick, MD	Washington, DC-MD-VA-WV
Cambridge–Newton–Framingham, MA	Boston, MA
Camden, NJ	Phildadelphia, PA-NJ
Durham, NC	Raleigh–Durham–Chapel Hill, NC
Holland–Grand Haven, MI	Grand Rapids, MI
Johnson City, TN	Johnson City–Bristol–Kingsport, TN
Muskegon–Norton Shores, MI	Grand Rapids, MI
Napa, CA	Napa–Vallejo–Fairfield, CA
Neenah–Oshkosh, WI	Appleton–Neenah–Oshkosh, WI
Ogden–Clearfield, UT	Salt Lake City–Ogden, UT
Spartanburg, SC	Greenville–Spartanburg–Anderson, SC
Springfield, OH	Dayton–Springfield, OH
Warren–Troy–Farmington Hills, MI	Detroit, MI

Source: Office of Management and Budget, *Cities Ranked & Rated* analysis, 2006

TABLE 1.2 METRO AREAS LOST THROUGH MERGER OR CHANGE

METRO AREAS LOST THROUGH MERGER

2003 METRO AREA	MERGED INTO 2006 METRO AREA
Brazoria, TX	Houston–Sugar Land–Baytown, TX
Brockton, MA	Boston–Quincy, MA
Danbury, CT	Bridgeport–Stamford–Norwalk, CT
Fitchburg–Leominster, MA	Worcester, MA
Galveston, TX	Houston–Sugar Land–Baytown, TX
Hamilton–Middletown, OH	Cincinnati–Middletown, OH-KY-IN
Jersey City, NJ	Newark–Union, NJ
Lowell, MA	Essex County, MA
Manchester, NH	Manchester–Nashua, NH
Monmouth–Ocean, NJ	Edison, NJ
New Bedford, MA	Providence–New Bedford–Fall River, MA
Sharon, PA	Youngstown–Warren–Boardman, OH-PA
Stamford–Norwalk, CT	Bridgeport–Stamford–Norwalk, CT
Waterbury, CT	New Haven–Milford, CT
Yolo, CA	Sacramento–Arden-Arcade–Roseville, CA

METRO AREAS LOST THROUGH POPULATION DECLINE

Enid, OK	
Jamestown, NY	

Source: Office of Management and Budget, *Cities Ranked & Rated* analysis, 2006

TABLE 1.3 PRINCIPAL U.S. METROPOLITAN STATISTICAL AREAS

METRO AREA & INCLUDED COUNTIES	2005 POPULATION	5-YEAR GROWTH	15-YEAR GROWTH
Abilene, TX	**157,871**	**-1.5%**	**6.9%**
Taylor County, TX	125,015	-1.2%	4.5%
Jones County, TX	19,837	-4.6%	20.3%
Callahan County, TX	13,019	0.9%	9.8%
Akron, OH	**704,288**	**1.3%**	**7.1%**
Summit County, OH	548,117	1.0%	6.4%
Portage County, OH	156,171	2.7%	9.5%
Albany, GA	**162,356**	**3.4%**	**16.6%**
Dougherty County, GA	95,660	-0.4%	-0.7%
Lee County, GA	29,480	19.1%	81.4%
Worth County, GA	21,841	-0.6%	10.6%
Terrell County, GA	10,843	-1.2%	1.8%
Baker County, GA	4,532	11.2%	25.4%
Albany–Schenectady–Troy, NY	**848,411**	**2.8%**	**5.3%**
Albany County, NY	299,833	1.8%	2.5%
Saratoga County, NY	213,983	6.7%	18.0%
Rensselaer County, NY	154,951	1.6%	0.3%
Schenectady County, NY	147,914	0.9%	-0.9%
Schoharie County, NY	31,730	0.5%	-0.5%
Albuquerque, NM	**782,916**	**7.4%**	**32.2%**
Bernalillo County, NM	594,358	6.8%	23.7%
Sandoval County, NM	103,095	14.7%	62.8%
Valencia County, NM	68,563	3.6%	51.6%
Torrance County, NM	16,900	-0.1%	64.3%
Alexandria, LA	**147,275**	**1.5%**	**-1.1%**
Rapides Parish, LA	128,243	1.5%	-2.5%
Grant Parish, LA	19,032	1.8%	8.6%
Allentown–Bethlehem–Easton, PA-NJ	**781,787**	**5.6%**	**14.0%**
Lehigh County, PA	324,967	4.1%	11.6%
Northampton County, PA	284,092	6.4%	15.0%
Warren County, NJ	111,957	9.3%	22.1%
Carbon County, PA	60,771	3.3%	7.2%
Altoona, PA	**126,446**	**-2.1%**	**-3.1%**
Blair County, PA	126,446	-2.1%	-3.1%
Amarillo, TX	**237,241**	**4.8%**	**21.1%**
Potter County, TX	118,059	4.0%	20.6%
Randall County, TX	110,584	6.0%	23.3%
Carson County, TX	6,525	0.1%	-0.8%
Armstrong County, TX	2,073	-3.5%	2.6%
Ames, IA	**84,569**	**5.7%**	**13.9%**
Story County, IA	84,569	5.7%	13.9%
Anchorage, AK	**350,175**	**9.9%**	**34.9%**
Anchorage Municipality, AK	278,203	6.9%	22.9%
Matanuska–Susitna Borough, AK	71,972	21.3%	81.4%
Anderson, IN	**130,198**	**-2.4%**	**-0.4%**
Madison County, IN	130,198	-2.4%	-0.4%
Anderson, SC	**173,780**	**4.9%**	**19.7%**
Anderson County, SC	173,780	4.9%	19.7%
Ann Arbor, MI	**345,128**	**6.9%**	**22.0%**
Washtenaw County, MI	345,128	6.9%	22.0%
Anniston–Oxford, AL	**112,525**	**0.2%**	**-3.0%**
Calhoun County, AL	112,525	0.2%	-3.0%
Appleton, WI	**214,903**	**6.6%**	**23.1%**
Outagamie County, WI	169,946	5.6%	20.9%
Calumet County, WI	44,957	10.6%	31.1%
Asheville, NC	**387,970**	**5.1%**	**26.3%**
Buncombe County, NC	215,997	4.7%	23.9%
Henderson County, NC	95,953	7.6%	37.6%
Haywood County, NC	56,114	3.9%	19.5%
Madison County, NC	19,906	1.4%	17.4%
Athens–Clarke County, GA	**175,323**	**5.7%**	**30.7%**
Clarke County, GA	104,762	3.2%	19.6%
Oconee County, GA	29,107	11.0%	65.2%
Madison County, GA	27,719	7.7%	31.7%
Oglethorpe County, GA	13,735	8.7%	40.7%

continued

TABLE 1.3 PRINCIPAL U.S. METROPOLITAN STATISTICAL AREAS *(CONTINUED)*			
METRO AREA & INCLUDED COUNTIES	**2005 POPULATION**	**5-YEAR GROWTH**	**15-YEAR GROWTH**
Atlanta–Sandy Springs–Marietta, GA	**4,765,845**	**13.2%**	**65.5%**
Fulton County, GA	818,251	0.3%	26.1%
Gwinnett County, GA	710,182	20.7%	101.2%
DeKalb County, GA	677,224	1.7%	24.1%
Cobb County, GA	668,057	9.9%	49.2%
Clayton County, GA	269,244	13.8%	47.9%
Cherokee County, GA	177,467	25.1%	96.7%
Henry County, GA	164,105	37.5%	179.4%
Forsyth County, GA	134,645	36.8%	205.4%
Paulding County, GA	108,331	32.6%	160.3%
Coweta County, GA	106,796	19.7%	98.3%
Douglas County, GA	106,768	15.8%	50.1%
Carroll County, GA	103,697	18.8%	45.2%
Fayette County, GA	102,316	12.1%	63.9%
Bartow County, GA	88,433	16.3%	58.2%
Newton County, GA	82,537	33.1%	97.4%
Rockdale County, GA	77,366	10.3%	43.0%
Walton County, GA	73,040	20.4%	89.3%
Spalding County, GA	61,572	5.4%	13.1%
Barrow County, GA	56,863	23.2%	91.3%
Pickens County, GA	28,676	24.8%	98.7%
Haralson County, GA	28,284	10.1%	28.8%
Butts County, GA	23,222	19.0%	51.5%
Meriwether County, GA	22,876	1.5%	2.1%
Dawson County, GA	19,826	23.9%	110.3%
Lamar County, GA	16,265	2.2%	24.8%
Pike County, GA	15,592	13.9%	52.5%
Jasper County, GA	13,081	14.5%	54.7%
Heard County, GA	11,129	1.1%	29.0%
Atlantic City, NJ	**269,202**	**6.6%**	**20.0%**
Atlantic County, NJ	269,202	6.6%	20.0%
Auburn–Opelika, AL	**121,703**	**5.7%**	**39.7%**
Lee County, AL	121,703	5.7%	39.7%
Augusta–Richmond County, GA-SC	**517,869**	**3.9%**	**21.3%**
Richmond County, GA	197,979	–0.9%	4.4%
Aiken County, SC	148,955	4.5%	23.2%
Columbia County, GA	101,366	13.5%	53.5%
Edgefield County, SC	24,765	0.7%	34.8%
Burke County, GA	23,217	4.4%	12.8%
McDuffie County, GA	21,587	1.7%	7.3%
Austin–Round Rock, TX	**1,415,324**	**14.0%**	**72.7%**
Travis County, TX	865,974	6.6%	50.2%
Williamson County, TX	320,551	28.2%	129.7%
Hays County, TX	122,335	25.4%	86.4%
Bastrop County, TX	69,758	20.8%	82.3%
Caldwell County, TX	36,706	14.0%	39.1%
Bakersfield, CA	**730,105**	**10.3%**	**34.3%**
Kern County, CA	730,105	10.3%	34.3%
Baltimore–Towson, MD	**2,644,882**	**3.9%**	**14.7%**
Baltimore County, MD	788,216	4.5%	13.9%
Baltimore city, MD	618,315	–5.0%	–16.0%
Anne Arundel County, MD	513,490	4.9%	20.2%
Howard County, MD	270,931	9.3%	44.6%
Harford County, MD	238,952	9.3%	31.2%
Carroll County, MD	169,064	12.0%	37.0%
Queen Anne's County, MD	45,914	13.2%	35.2%
Bangor, ME	**148,170**	**2.2%**	**1.1%**
Penobscot County, ME	148,170	2.2%	1.1%
Barnstable Town, MA	**232,462**	**4.6%**	**24.6%**
Barnstable County, MA	232,462	4.6%	24.6%
Baton Rouge, LA	**731,558**	**4.1%**	**19.9%**
East Baton Rouge Parish, LA	413,543	0.2%	8.8%
Livingston Parish, LA	106,620	16.1%	51.2%
Ascension Parish, LA	88,049	14.9%	51.3%
Iberville Parish, LA	32,493	–2.5%	4.7%
Pointe Coupee Parish, LA	22,544	–1.0%	0.0%
West Baton Rouge Parish, LA	21,774	0.8%	12.1%

METRO AREA & INCLUDED COUNTIES	2005 POPULATION	5-YEAR GROWTH	15-YEAR GROWTH
East Feliciana Parish, LA	21,033	−1.5%	9.5%
West Feliciana Parish, LA	15,311	1.3%	18.6%
St. Helena Parish, LA	10,191	−3.2%	3.2%
Battle Creek, MI	**139,193**	**0.9%**	**2.4%**
Calhoun County, MI	139,193	0.9%	2.4%
Bay City, MI	**109,184**	**−0.9%**	**−2.3%**
Bay County, MI	109,184	−0.9%	−2.3%
Beaumont–Port Arthur, TX	**384,524**	**−0.1%**	**6.7%**
Jefferson County, TX	249,311	−1.1%	4.1%
Orange County, TX	85,216	0.3%	5.8%
Hardin County, TX	49,997	4.0%	21.0%
Bellingham, WA	**180,122**	**8.0%**	**41.0%**
Whatcom County, WA	180,122	8.0%	41.0%
Bend, OR	**136,927**	**18.7%**	**82.7%**
Deschutes County, OR	136,927	18.7%	82.7%
Bergen–Passaic, NJ	**2,009,955**	**1.4%**	**9.7%**
Bergen County, NJ	903,206	2.2%	9.4%
Hudson County, NJ	605,015	−0.7%	9.4%
Passaic County, NJ	501,734	2.6%	10.7%
Bethesda–Gaithersburg–Frederick, MD	**1,158,319**	**8.4%**	**27.6%**
Montgomery County, MD	937,020	7.3%	22.9%
Frederick County, MD	221,299	13.3%	47.3%
Billings, MT	**144,970**	**4.4%**	**19.3%**
Yellowstone County, MT	135,112	4.5%	19.1%
Carbon County, MT	9,858	3.2%	22.0%
Biloxi–Gulfport–Pascagoula, MS	**405,766**	**2.4%**	**20.1%**
Harrison County, MS	189,444	−0.1%	14.6%
Jackson County, MS	134,950	2.7%	17.1%
Hancock County, MS	46,002	7.1%	44.8%
George County, MS	21,011	9.8%	26.0%
Stone County, MS	14,359	5.4%	33.6%
Binghamton, NY	**250,483**	**−0.7%**	**−5.3%**
Broome County, NY	198,698	−0.9%	−6.3%
Tioga County, NY	51,785	0.0%	−1.1%
Birmingham–Hoover, AL	**1,082,898**	**3.3%**	**17.7%**
Jefferson County, AL	656,922	−0.8%	0.8%
Shelby County, AL	167,044	16.6%	68.1%
St. Clair County, AL	70,473	8.9%	40.9%
Walker County, AL	69,829	−1.3%	3.2%
Blount County, AL	55,606	9.0%	41.7%
Chilton County, AL	41,493	4.8%	27.8%
Bibb County, AL	21,531	3.4%	29.5%
Bismarck, ND	**97,858**	**3.4%**	**17.1%**
Burleigh County, ND	72,770	4.8%	21.0%
Morton County, ND	25,088	−0.8%	5.9%
Blacksburg–Christiansburg–Radford, VA	**151,890**	**0.5%**	**8.8%**
Montgomery County, VA	86,096	2.9%	16.5%
Pulaski County, VA	34,363	−2.2%	−0.4%
Giles County, VA	16,761	0.6%	2.6%
Radford city, VA	14,670	−7.5%	−8.0%
Bloomington, IN	**181,149**	**3.2%**	**16.1%**
Monroe County, IN	124,467	3.2%	14.2%
Greene County, IN	33,349	0.6%	9.7%
Owen County, IN	23,333	7.1%	35.0%
Bloomington–Normal, IL	**159,689**	**6.2%**	**23.6%**
McLean County, IL	159,689	6.2%	23.6%
Boise City–Nampa, ID	**530,294**	**14.3%**	**66.7%**
Ada County, ID	334,704	11.2%	62.7%
Canyon County, ID	160,540	22.1%	78.2%
Gem County, ID	16,098	6.0%	35.9%
Owyhee County, ID	11,460	7.7%	36.6%
Boise County, ID	7,492	12.3%	113.5%
Boston–Quincy, MA	**1,821,563**	**0.5%**	**6.4%**
Suffolk County, MA	673,143	−2.4%	1.4%
Norfolk County, MA	655,243	0.8%	6.4%
Plymouth County, MA	493,177	4.3%	13.3%
Boulder, CO	**279,897**	**3.8%**	**34.0%**
Boulder County, CO	279,897	3.8%	34.0%

continued

TABLE 1.3 PRINCIPAL U.S. METROPOLITAN STATISTICAL AREAS *(CONTINUED)*

METRO AREA & INCLUDED COUNTIES	2005 POPULATION	5-YEAR GROWTH	15-YEAR GROWTH
Bowling Green, KY	**109,501**	**5.1%**	**25.9%**
Warren County, KY	97,542	5.4%	27.2%
Edmonson County, KY	11,959	2.7%	15.5%
Bremerton–Silverdale, WA	**242,681**	**4.6%**	**27.9%**
Kitsap County, WA	242,681	4.6%	27.9%
Bridgeport–Stamford–Norwalk, CT	**906,546**	**2.7%**	**9.5%**
Fairfield County, CT	906,546	2.7%	9.5%
Brownsville–Harlingen, TX	**378,542**	**12.9%**	**45.5%**
Cameron County, TX	378,542	12.9%	45.5%
Brunswick, GA	**97,758**	**5.1%**	**19.6%**
Glynn County, GA	71,400	5.7%	14.2%
Brantley County, GA	15,536	6.2%	40.3%
McIntosh County, GA	10,822	−0.2%	25.3%
Buffalo–Niagara Falls, NY	**1,156,286**	**−1.2%**	**−2.8%**
Erie County, NY	938,438	−1.2%	−3.1%
Niagara County, NY	217,848	−0.9%	−1.3%
Burlington–South Burlington, VT	**205,359**	**3.3%**	**16.3%**
Chittenden County, VT	149,901	2.3%	13.8%
Franklin County, VT	47,709	5.0%	19.3%
Grand Isle County, VT	7,749	12.3%	45.7%
Cambridge–Newton–Framingham, MA	**1,471,486**	**0.4%**	**5.2%**
Middlesex County, MA	1,471,486	0.4%	5.2%
Camden, NJ	**1,244,729**	**4.9%**	**10.8%**
Camden County, NJ	517,151	1.6%	2.8%
Burlington County, NJ	454,259	7.3%	15.0%
Gloucester County, NJ	273,319	7.3%	18.8%
Canton–Massillon, OH	**407,507**	**0.2%**	**3.5%**
Stark County, OH	377,490	−0.2%	2.7%
Carroll County, OH	30,017	4.1%	13.2%
Cape Coral–Fort Myers, FL	**518,281**	**17.6%**	**54.7%**
Lee County, FL	518,281	17.6%	54.7%
Carson City, NV	**56,679**	**8.0%**	**40.1%**
Carson City, NV	56,679	8.0%	40.1%
Casper, WY	**69,177**	**4.0%**	**13.0%**
Natrona County, WY	69,177	4.0%	13.0%
Cedar Rapids, IA	**244,910**	**3.2%**	**16.4%**
Linn County, IA	197,967	3.3%	17.3%
Benton County, IA	26,591	5.1%	18.6%
Jones County, IA	20,352	0.6%	4.7%
Champaign–Urbana, IL	**220,855**	**5.1%**	**9.0%**
Champaign County, IL	190,304	5.9%	10.0%
Piatt County, IL	16,527	1.0%	6.3%
Ford County, IL	14,024	−1.5%	−1.8%
Charleston, WV	**306,523**	**−0.9%**	**0.9%**
Kanawha County, WV	194,024	−3.0%	−6.5%
Putnam County, WV	53,908	4.5%	25.9%
Boone County, WV	25,942	1.6%	0.3%
Lincoln County, WV	22,296	0.9%	4.3%
Clay County, WV	10,353	0.2%	3.7%
Charleston–North Charleston, SC	**583,676**	**6.4%**	**15.6%**
Charleston County, SC	327,069	5.5%	10.9%
Berkeley County, SC	148,436	4.1%	15.3%
Dorchester County, SC	108,171	12.2%	30.2%
Charlotte–Gastonia–Concord, NC-SC	**1,484,570**	**11.9%**	**47.7%**
Mecklenburg County, NC	777,685	11.8%	52.1%
Gaston County, NC	194,090	2.0%	10.9%
York County, SC	184,267	11.9%	40.1%
Union County, NC	155,884	26.0%	85.1%
Cabarrus County, NC	147,552	12.6%	49.1%
Anson County, NC	25,092	−0.7%	6.9%
Charlottesville, VA	**185,936**	**7.8%**	**35.1%**
Albemarle County, VA	87,150	10.0%	28.1%
Charlottesville city, VA	41,394	−8.1%	2.6%
Fluvanna County, VA	24,939	24.4%	100.7%
Greene County, VA	17,357	13.9%	68.6%
Nelson County, VA	15,096	4.5%	18.1%

METRO AREA & INCLUDED COUNTIES	2005 POPULATION	5-YEAR GROWTH	15-YEAR GROWTH
Chattanooga, TN-GA	**490,543**	**3.1%**	**14.3%**
Hamilton County, TN	310,374	0.8%	8.7%
Walker County, GA	63,308	3.7%	8.6%
Catoosa County, GA	60,415	13.4%	42.3%
Marion County, TN	27,984	0.7%	12.8%
Dade County, GA	16,217	7.0%	23.1%
Sequatchie County, TN	12,245	7.7%	38.2%
Cheyenne, WY	**85,454**	**4.7%**	**16.8%**
Laramie County, WY	85,454	4.7%	16.8%
Chicago–Naperville–Joliet, IL	**7,883,317**	**4.0%**	**18.0%**
Cook County, IL	5,336,843	−0.7%	4.5%
DuPage County, IL	932,882	3.2%	19.3%
Will County, IL	625,727	24.6%	75.1%
Kane County, IL	480,048	18.8%	51.2%
McHenry County, IL	298,106	14.6%	62.7%
DeKalb County, IL	96,468	8.4%	23.8%
Kendall County, IL	72,724	33.3%	84.5%
Grundy County, IL	40,519	7.9%	25.3%
Chico, CA	**213,359**	**5.0%**	**17.2%**
Butte County, CA	213,359	5.0%	17.2%
Cincinnati–Middletown, OH-KY-IN	**2,063,586**	**3.3%**	**16.7%**
Hamilton County, OH	812,803	−3.8%	−6.2%
Butler County, OH	347,942	4.5%	19.4%
Warren County, OH	192,092	21.3%	68.6%
Clermont County, OH	189,380	6.4%	26.1%
Kenton County, KY	152,901	0.9%	7.7%
Boone County, KY	102,136	18.8%	77.4%
Campbell County, KY	87,577	−1.2%	4.4%
Dearborn County, IN	48,649	5.5%	25.3%
Brown County, OH	44,467	5.2%	27.2%
Grant County, KY	24,661	10.2%	56.7%
Franklin County, IN	23,114	4.3%	18.0%
Pendleton County, KY	15,430	7.2%	27.8%
Bracken County, KY	8,569	3.5%	10.3%
Gallatin County, KY	8,120	3.2%	50.6%
Ohio County, IN	5,745	2.2%	8.1%
Clarksville, TN-KY	**239,180**	**3.4%**	**29.8%**
Montgomery County, TN	144,602	7.3%	43.9%
Christian County, KY	68,548	−5.1%	−0.6%
Stewart County, TN	13,019	5.2%	37.3%
Trigg County, KY	13,011	3.3%	25.6%
Cleveland, TN	**107,613**	**3.5%**	**23.2%**
Bradley County, TN	91,391	3.9%	24.0%
Polk County, TN	16,222	1.1%	18.9%
Cleveland–Elyria–Mentor, OH	**2,136,729**	**−0.4%**	**2.7%**
Cuyahoga County, OH	1,350,482	−3.1%	−4.4%
Lorain County, OH	294,884	3.6%	8.8%
Lake County, OH	229,367	0.8%	6.4%
Medina County, OH	166,428	10.1%	36.0%
Geauga County, OH	95,568	5.1%	17.8%
Coeur d'Alene, ID	**121,824**	**12.1%**	**74.5%**
Kootenai County, ID	121,824	12.1%	74.5%
College Station–Bryan, TX	**200,336**	**8.4%**	**33.4%**
Brazos County, TX	166,651	9.3%	36.8%
Burleson County, TX	17,571	6.7%	29.0%
Robertson County, TX	16,114	0.7%	3.9%
Colorado Springs, CO	**581,424**	**8.2%**	**42.3%**
El Paso County, CO	558,804	8.1%	40.8%
Teller County, CO	22,620	10.0%	81.4%
Columbia, MO	**153,706**	**5.6%**	**26.3%**
Boone County, MO	143,771	6.1%	27.9%
Howard County, MO	9,935	−2.7%	3.2%
Columbia, SC	**683,285**	**5.6%**	**25.4%**
Richland County, SC	337,708	5.3%	18.2%
Lexington County, SC	231,667	7.2%	38.3%
Kershaw County, SC	55,401	5.2%	27.1%

continued

TABLE 1.3 PRINCIPAL U.S. METROPOLITAN STATISTICAL AREAS (CONTINUED)

METRO AREA & INCLUDED COUNTIES	2005 POPULATION	5-YEAR GROWTH	15-YEAR GROWTH
Fairfield County, SC	23,938	2.1%	7.4%
Saluda County, SC	19,074	−0.6%	15.6%
Calhoun County, SC	15,497	2.1%	21.5%
Columbus, GA-AL	**289,578**	**3.7%**	**10.2%**
Muscogee County, GA	185,915	−0.2%	3.7%
Russell County, AL	48,645	−2.2%	3.8%
Harris County, GA	27,000	13.9%	51.8%
Chattahoochee County, GA	20,839	40.0%	23.1%
Marion County, GA	7,179	0.5%	28.4%
Columbus, IN	**72,867**	**2.0%**	**14.5%**
Bartholomew County, IN	72,867	2.0%	14.5%
Columbus, OH	**1,701,266**	**6.0%**	**25.0%**
Franklin County, OH	1,096,456	2.6%	14.0%
Licking County, OH	153,110	5.2%	19.3%
Delaware County, OH	142,926	29.9%	113.5%
Fairfield County, OH	137,152	11.7%	32.5%
Pickaway County, OH	51,461	−2.4%	6.7%
Union County, OH	44,857	9.7%	40.3%
Madison County, OH	40,909	1.7%	10.3%
Morrow County, OH	34,395	8.7%	24.0%
Corpus Christi, TX	**408,480**	**1.3%**	**11.4%**
Nueces County, TX	316,246	0.8%	8.6%
San Patricio County, TX	68,186	1.6%	16.2%
Aransas County, TX	24,048	6.9%	34.4%
Corvallis, OR	**81,105**	**3.8%**	**14.5%**
Benton County, OR	81,105	3.8%	14.5%
Cumberland, MD-WV	**100,406**	**−1.6%**	**−1.3%**
Allegany County, MD	73,202	−2.3%	−2.4%
Mineral County, WV	27,204	0.5%	1.9%
Dallas–Plano–Irving, TX	**3,873,350**	**13.3%**	**58.6%**
Dallas County, TX	2,323,249	4.7%	25.4%
Collin County, TX	638,761	29.9%	141.9%
Denton County, TX	547,014	26.3%	99.5%
Ellis County, TX	130,182	16.9%	52.9%
Kaufman County, TX	86,341	21.1%	65.3%
Hunt County, TX	83,001	8.4%	29.0%
Rockwall County, TX	59,344	37.8%	131.8%
Delta County, TX	5,458	2.5%	12.4%
Dalton, GA	**130,386**	**8.7%**	**33.7%**
Whitfield County, GA	89,677	7.4%	23.8%
Murray County, GA	40,709	11.5%	55.7%
Danville, IL	**82,333**	**−1.9%**	**−6.7%**
Vermilion County, IL	82,333	−1.9%	−6.7%
Danville, VA	**107,592**	**−2.3%**	**0.3%**
Pittsylvania County, VA	61,399	−0.6%	10.3%
Danville city, VA	46,193	−4.6%	−12.9%
Davenport–Moline–Rock Island, IA-IL	**374,905**	**−0.3%**	**1.9%**
Scott County, IA	159,875	0.8%	5.9%
Rock Island County, IL	147,302	−1.4%	−1.0%
Henry County, IL	50,700	−0.6%	−0.9%
Mercer County, IL	17,028	0.4%	−1.5%
Dayton, OH	**846,389**	**−0.2%**	**0.7%**
Montgomery County, OH	550,137	−1.6%	−4.1%
Greene County, OH	152,859	3.4%	11.8%
Miami County, OH	100,981	2.1%	8.3%
Preble County, OH	42,412	0.2%	5.7%
Decatur, AL	**148,042**	**1.5%**	**12.6%**
Morgan County, AL	113,605	2.3%	13.6%
Lawrence County, AL	34,437	−1.1%	9.3%
Decatur, IL	**109,589**	**−4.5%**	**−6.5%**
Macon County, IL	109,589	−4.5%	−6.5%
Deltona–Daytona Beach–Ormond Beach, FL	**481,398**	**8.6%**	**29.9%**
Volusia County, FL	481,398	8.6%	29.9%
Denver–Aurora, CO	**2,350,559**	**8.9%**	**61.8%**
Denver County, CO	557,476	0.5%	19.3%
Arapahoe County, CO	527,393	8.1%	34.5%
Jefferson County, CO	526,947	0.4%	20.8%

METRO AREA & INCLUDED COUNTIES	2005 POPULATION	5-YEAR GROWTH	15-YEAR GROWTH
Adams County, CO	394,886	13.3%	53.0%
Douglas County, CO	245,311	39.6%	306.2%
Broomfield County, CO	43,832	12.2%	72.4%
Elbert County, CO	23,297	17.2%	141.5%
Park County, CO	16,932	16.6%	136.0%
Clear Creek County, CO	9,575	2.7%	25.7%
Gilpin County, CO	4,910	3.2%	59.9%
Des Moines–West Des Moines, IA	**512,416**	**6.6%**	**24.1%**
Polk County, IA	394,685	5.4%	20.6%
Dallas County, IA	48,665	19.4%	63.6%
Warren County, IA	42,678	4.9%	18.4%
Madison County, IA	14,723	5.0%	17.9%
Guthrie County, IA	11,665	2.7%	6.7%
Detroit–Livonia–Dearborn, MI	**2,014,262**	**−2.3%**	**−4.6%**
Wayne County, MI	2,014,262	−2.3%	−4.6%
Dothan, AL	**134,931**	**3.2%**	**12.2%**
Houston County, AL	92,932	4.7%	14.3%
Geneva County, AL	25,457	−1.2%	7.7%
Henry County, AL	16,542	1.4%	7.6%
Dover, DE	**138,324**	**9.2%**	**24.6%**
Kent County, DE	138,324	9.2%	24.6%
Dubuque, IA	**90,696**	**1.7%**	**5.0%**
Dubuque County, IA	90,696	1.7%	5.0%
Duluth, MN-WI	**274,430**	**−0.3%**	**2.2%**
St. Louis County, MN	197,010	−1.8%	−0.6%
Douglas County, WI	43,917	1.5%	5.2%
Carlton County, MN	33,503	5.8%	14.5%
Durham, NC	**456,036**	**7.2%**	**32.6%**
Durham County, NC	242,052	8.4%	33.1%
Orange County, NC	118,830	0.5%	27.1%
Chatham County, NC	57,705	17.0%	47.4%
Person County, NC	37,449	5.1%	24.1%
Eau Claire, WI	**153,621**	**3.6%**	**11.7%**
Eau Claire County, WI	95,711	2.8%	12.4%
Chippewa County, WI	57,910	4.9%	10.6%
Edison, NJ	**2,313,085**	**6.4%**	**22.2%**
Middlesex County, NJ	794,310	5.9%	18.2%
Monmouth County, NJ	639,747	4.0%	15.7%
Ocean County, NJ	561,292	9.9%	29.6%
Somerset County, NJ	317,736	6.8%	32.2%
El Centro, CA	**153,881**	**8.1%**	**40.8%**
Imperial County, CA	153,881	8.1%	40.8%
Elizabethtown, KY	**110,153**	**2.4%**	**9.2%**
Hardin County, KY	96,693	2.7%	8.4%
Larue County, KY	13,460	0.7%	15.2%
Elkhart–Goshen, IN	**191,890**	**5.0%**	**22.8%**
Elkhart County, IN	191,890	5.0%	22.8%
Elmira, NY	**90,057**	**−1.1%**	**−5.4%**
Chemung County, NY	90,057	−1.1%	−5.4%
El Paso, TX	**719,377**	**5.8%**	**21.6%**
El Paso County, TX	719,377	5.8%	21.6%
Erie, PA	**279,563**	**−0.5%**	**1.4%**
Erie County, PA	279,563	−0.5%	1.4%
Essex County, MA	**742,291**	**2.6%**	**10.8%**
Essex County, MA	742,291	2.6%	10.8%
Eugene–Springfield, OR	**334,865**	**3.7%**	**18.4%**
Lane County, OR	334,865	3.7%	18.4%
Evansville, IN-KY	**347,584**	**1.5%**	**7.5%**
Vanderburgh County, IN	172,087	0.1%	4.3%
Warrick County, IN	56,047	7.0%	24.8%
Henderson County, KY	45,321	1.1%	5.3%
Gibson County, IN	33,303	2.5%	4.4%
Posey County, IN	26,793	−1.0%	3.2%
Webster County, KY	14,033	−0.6%	0.6%
Fairbanks, AK	**84,771**	**2.3%**	**9.1%**
Fairbanks North Star Borough, AK	84,771	2.3%	9.1%

continued

TABLE 1.3 PRINCIPAL U.S. METROPOLITAN STATISTICAL AREAS (CONTINUED)

METRO AREA & INCLUDED COUNTIES	2005 POPULATION	5-YEAR GROWTH	15-YEAR GROWTH
Fargo, ND-MN	**181,586**	**4.2%**	**19.3%**
Cass County, ND	129,241	5.0%	25.6%
Clay County, MN	52,345	2.2%	3.8%
Farmington, NM	**126,259**	**10.9%**	**37.8%**
San Juan County, NM	126,259	10.9%	37.8%
Fayetteville, NC	**344,757**	**2.7%**	**18.3%**
Cumberland County, NC	305,120	0.7%	11.1%
Hoke County, NC	39,637	17.8%	73.4%
Fayetteville–Springdale–Rogers, AR-MO	**392,659**	**13.4%**	**66.3%**
Benton County, AR	181,028	18.0%	85.7%
Washington County, AR	175,005	11.0%	54.3%
McDonald County, MO	22,232	2.5%	31.3%
Madison County, AR	14,394	1.1%	23.9%
Flagstaff, AZ	**128,963**	**10.9%**	**33.5%**
Coconino County, AZ	128,963	10.9%	33.5%
Flint, MI	**444,915**	**2.0%**	**3.4%**
Genesee County, MI	444,915	2.0%	3.4%
Florence, SC	**198,117**	**2.6%**	**12.5%**
Florence County, SC	129,883	3.3%	13.6%
Darlington County, SC	68,234	1.2%	10.3%
Florence–Muscle Shoals, AL	**141,063**	**−1.3%**	**7.4%**
Lauderdale County, AL	86,704	−1.4%	8.8%
Colbert County, AL	54,359	−1.1%	5.2%
Fond du Lac, WI	**98,791**	**1.5%**	**9.7%**
Fond du Lac County, WI	98,791	1.5%	9.7%
Fort Collins–Loveland, CO	**270,414**	**7.5%**	**45.3%**
Larimer County, CO	270,414	7.5%	45.3%
Fort Lauderdale–Pompano Beach–Deerfield, FL	**1,750,486**	**7.9%**	**39.4%**
Broward County, FL	1,750,486	7.9%	39.4%
Fort Smith, AR-OK	**282,729**	**3.5%**	**21.1%**
Sebastian County, AR	118,070	2.6%	18.6%
Crawford County, AR	56,705	6.5%	33.4%
Le Flore County, OK	49,341	2.6%	14.0%
Sequoyah County, OK	40,485	3.9%	19.7%
Franklin County, AR	18,128	2.0%	21.7%
Fort Walton Beach–Crestview–Destin, FL	**183,733**	**7.8%**	**27.8%**
Okaloosa County, FL	183,733	7.8%	27.8%
Fort Wayne, IN	**404,263**	**3.6%**	**14.1%**
Allen County, IN	344,142	3.7%	14.4%
Whitley County, IN	32,061	4.4%	15.9%
Wells County, IN	28,060	1.7%	8.1%
Fort Worth–Arlington, TX	**1,913,563**	**11.9%**	**40.3%**
Tarrant County, TX	1,608,997	11.3%	37.5%
Johnson County, TX	145,389	14.7%	49.6%
Parker County, TX	103,523	17.0%	59.8%
Wise County, TX	55,654	14.1%	60.5%
Fresno, CA	**866,531**	**8.4%**	**29.8%**
Fresno County, CA	866,531	8.4%	29.8%
Gadsden, AL	**103,134**	**−0.3%**	**3.3%**
Etowah County, AL	103,134	−0.3%	3.3%
Gainesville, FL	**247,579**	**6.6%**	**30.0%**
Alachua County, FL	231,427	6.2%	27.4%
Gilchrist County, FL	16,152	11.9%	67.1%
Gainesville, GA	**163,158**	**17.1%**	**71.0%**
Hall County, GA	163,158	17.1%	71.0%
Gary, IN	**690,812**	**2.2%**	**8.0%**
Lake County, IN	489,503	1.0%	2.9%
Porter County, IN	155,303	5.8%	20.5%
Jasper County, IN	31,588	5.1%	26.6%
Newton County, IN	14,418	−1.0%	6.4%
Glens Falls, NY	**127,879**	**2.8%**	**8.0%**
Warren County, NY	65,513	3.5%	10.6%
Washington County, NY	62,366	2.2%	5.1%
Goldsboro, NC	**113,261**	**−0.1%**	**8.2%**
Wayne County, NC	113,261	−0.1%	8.2%

METRO AREA & INCLUDED COUNTIES	2005 POPULATION	5-YEAR GROWTH	15-YEAR GROWTH
Grand Forks, ND-MN	**95,087**	**−2.5%**	**−7.8%**
Grand Forks County, ND	64,321	−2.7%	−9.0%
Polk County, MN	30,766	−1.9%	−5.3%
Grand Junction, CO	**126,685**	**9.0%**	**36.0%**
Mesa County, CO	126,685	9.0%	36.0%
Grand Rapids–Wyoming, MI	**770,802**	**4.1%**	**19.4%**
Kent County, MI	596,841	3.9%	19.2%
Ionia County, MI	64,464	4.8%	13.0%
Barry County, MI	59,709	5.2%	19.3%
Newaygo County, MI	49,788	4.0%	30.3%
Great Falls, MT	**79,448**	**−1.1%**	**2.3%**
Cascade County, MT	79,448	−1.1%	2.3%
Greeley, CO	**221,957**	**22.7%**	**68.4%**
Weld County, CO	221,957	22.7%	68.4%
Green Bay, WI	**295,898**	**4.7%**	**21.5%**
Brown County, WI	237,532	4.7%	22.1%
Oconto County, WI	37,729	5.9%	24.8%
Kewaunee County, WI	20,637	2.2%	9.3%
Greensboro–Winston-Salem–High Point, NC	**1,253,347**	**4.8%**	**24.4%**
Guilford County, NC	439,457	4.4%	26.4%
Forsyth County, NC	323,173	5.6%	21.7%
Alamance County, NC	139,119	6.4%	28.6%
Randolph County, NC	137,371	5.3%	28.9%
Rockingham County, NC	92,916	1.1%	8.0%
Stokes County, NC	45,442	1.6%	22.2%
Davie County, NC	38,037	9.2%	36.5%
Yadkin County, NC	37,832	4.1%	24.1%
Greenville, NC	**161,770**	**5.9%**	**31.2%**
Pitt County, NC	141,216	5.5%	30.8%
Greene County, NC	20,554	8.3%	33.6%
Greenville, SC	**586,800**	**4.8%**	**24.3%**
Greenville County, SC	402,310	6.0%	25.8%
Pickens County, SC	113,896	2.8%	21.3%
Laurens County, SC	70,594	1.5%	21.0%
Hagerstown–Martinsburg, MD-WV	**245,404**	**10.5%**	**29.5%**
Washington County, MD	139,566	5.8%	15.0%
Berkeley County, WV	90,071	18.7%	52.0%
Morgan County, WV	15,767	5.5%	30.0%
Hanford–Corcoran, CA	**140,941**	**8.9%**	**38.9%**
Kings County, CA	140,941	8.9%	38.9%
Harrisburg–Carlisle, PA	**521,971**	**2.6%**	**10.2%**
Dauphin County, PA	254,445	1.1%	7.0%
Cumberland County, PA	223,017	4.4%	14.2%
Perry County, PA	44,509	2.1%	8.1%
Harrisonburg, VA	**113,343**	**4.8%**	**28.9%**
Rockingham County, VA	70,897	4.7%	23.3%
Harrisonburg city, VA	42,446	4.9%	38.2%
Hartford–West Hartford–East Hartford, CT	**1,192,119**	**3.8%**	**6.3%**
Hartford County, CT	878,867	2.5%	3.2%
Middlesex County, CT	164,374	6.0%	14.8%
Tolland County, CT	148,878	9.2%	15.7%
Hattiesburg, MS	**130,920**	**5.8%**	**21.1%**
Forrest County, MS	75,377	3.8%	10.3%
Lamar County, MS	43,212	10.6%	42.0%
Perry County, MS	12,331	1.6%	13.5%
Hickory–Lenoir–Morganton, NC	**353,336**	**3.4%**	**21.1%**
Catawba County, NC	148,669	4.9%	25.6%
Burke County, NC	90,097	1.1%	18.9%
Caldwell County, NC	79,186	2.3%	12.0%
Alexander County, NC	35,384	5.3%	28.5%
Hinesville–Fort Stewart, GA	**68,159**	**−5.0%**	**19.4%**
Liberty County, GA	57,226	−7.1%	8.5%
Long County, GA	10,933	6.1%	76.3%
Holland–Grand Haven, MI	**253,985**	**6.6%**	**35.3%**
Ottawa County, MI	253,985	6.6%	35.3%

continued

TABLE 1.3 PRINCIPAL U.S. METROPOLITAN STATISTICAL AREAS (CONTINUED)

METRO AREA & INCLUDED COUNTIES	2005 POPULATION	5-YEAR GROWTH	15-YEAR GROWTH
Honolulu, HI	**917,158**	**4.7%**	**9.7%**
Honolulu County, HI	917,158	4.7%	9.7%
Hot Springs, AR	**92,752**	**5.3%**	**26.4%**
Garland County, AR	92,752	5.3%	26.4%
Houma–Bayou Cane–Thibodaux, LA	**199,005**	**2.3%**	**8.9%**
Terrebonne Parish, LA	106,962	2.4%	10.3%
Lafourche Parish, LA	92,043	2.3%	7.2%
Houston–Sugar Land–Baytown, TX	**5,239,517**	**11.4%**	**42.4%**
Harris County, TX	3,687,104	8.4%	30.8%
Fort Bend County, TX	448,388	26.5%	98.9%
Montgomery County, TX	364,182	24.0%	99.9%
Galveston County, TX	274,342	9.7%	26.2%
Brazoria County, TX	271,909	12.5%	41.8%
Liberty County, TX	76,725	9.4%	45.5%
Waller County, TX	36,682	12.3%	56.8%
Chambers County, TX	29,663	14.0%	47.7%
Austin County, TX	26,461	12.2%	33.4%
San Jacinto County, TX	24,061	8.2%	47.0%
Huntington–Ashland, WV-KY-OH	**286,119**	**−0.9%**	**−0.7%**
Cabell County, WV	94,396	−2.5%	−2.5%
Lawrence County, OH	62,916	1.0%	1.7%
Boyd County, KY	49,494	−0.5%	−3.2%
Wayne County, WV	42,272	−1.5%	1.5%
Greenup County, KY	37,041	0.4%	0.8%
Huntsville, AL	**365,076**	**6.6%**	**24.6%**
Madison County, AL	295,774	6.9%	23.8%
Limestone County, AL	69,302	5.5%	28.0%
Idaho Falls, ID	**110,220**	**8.4%**	**24.2%**
Bonneville County, ID	89,425	8.4%	23.8%
Jefferson County, ID	20,795	8.6%	25.7%
Indianapolis–Carmel, IN	**1,626,173**	**7.4%**	**33.3%**
Marion County, IN	864,477	0.5%	8.4%
Hamilton County, IN	231,997	27.0%	113.0%
Johnson County, IN	126,479	9.8%	43.5%
Hendricks County, IN	125,196	20.3%	65.3%
Morgan County, IN	69,692	4.5%	24.6%
Hancock County, IN	61,297	10.7%	34.6%
Boone County, IN	50,869	10.3%	33.3%
Shelby County, IN	43,696	0.6%	8.4%
Putnam County, IN	37,039	2.8%	22.2%
Brown County, IN	15,431	3.2%	9.6%
Iowa City, IA	**138,941**	**5.5%**	**20.2%**
Johnson County, IA	117,386	5.7%	22.1%
Washington County, IA	21,555	4.3%	9.9%
Ithaca, NY	**103,641**	**7.4%**	**10.1%**
Tompkins County, NY	103,641	7.4%	10.1%
Jackson, MI	**164,114**	**3.6%**	**9.6%**
Jackson County, MI	164,114	3.6%	9.6%
Jackson, MS	**516,783**	**4.3%**	**20.4%**
Hinds County, MS	248,894	−0.8%	−2.2%
Rankin County, MS	128,965	11.8%	48.0%
Madison County, MS	82,226	10.1%	52.9%
Copiah County, MS	29,076	1.1%	5.4%
Simpson County, MS	27,622	−0.1%	15.3%
Jackson, TN	**110,597**	**3.0%**	**21.8%**
Madison County, TN	94,730	3.2%	21.5%
Chester County, TN	15,867	2.1%	23.8%
Jacksonville, FL	**1,243,108**	**10.9%**	**36.6%**
Duval County, FL	840,709	7.9%	24.9%
Clay County, FL	164,203	16.6%	54.9%
St. Johns County, FL	149,915	21.7%	78.8%
Nassau County, FL	64,426	11.7%	46.6%
Baker County, FL	23,855	7.2%	29.0%
Jacksonville, NC	**145,656**	**−3.1%**	**−2.8%**
Onslow County, NC	145,656	−3.1%	−2.8%
Janesville, WI	**155,268**	**1.9%**	**11.3%**
Rock County, WI	155,268	1.9%	11.3%

METRO AREA & INCLUDED COUNTIES	2005 POPULATION	5-YEAR GROWTH	15-YEAR GROWTH
Jefferson City, MO	**144,081**	**2.9%**	**19.8%**
Cole County, MO	73,206	2.5%	15.1%
Callaway County, MO	42,626	4.6%	29.9%
Moniteau County, MO	15,050	1.5%	22.4%
Osage County, MO	13,199	1.0%	9.8%
Johnson City, TN	**189,188**	**4.2%**	**18.1%**
Washington County, TN	111,648	4.2%	20.9%
Carter County, TN	59,745	5.3%	16.0%
Unicoi County, TN	17,795	0.7%	7.5%
Johnstown, PA	**148,204**	**-2.9%**	**-9.1%**
Cambria County, PA	148,204	-2.9%	-9.1%
Jonesboro, AR	**111,174**	**3.2%**	**19.5%**
Craighead County, AR	85,818	4.5%	24.5%
Poinsett County, AR	25,356	-1.0%	2.8%
Joplin, MO	**164,801**	**4.8%**	**22.2%**
Jasper County, MO	109,822	4.9%	21.4%
Newton County, MO	54,979	4.5%	23.7%
Kalamazoo–Portage, MI	**323,306**	**2.7%**	**10.2%**
Kalamazoo County, MI	244,064	2.3%	9.2%
Van Buren County, MI	79,242	3.9%	13.1%
Kankakee–Bradley, IL	**106,591**	**2.7%**	**10.7%**
Kankakee County, IL	106,591	2.7%	10.7%
Kansas City, MO-KS	**1,934,400**	**5.6%**	**20.7%**
Jackson County, MO	661,454	1.0%	4.5%
Johnson County, KS	502,205	11.3%	41.4%
Clay County, MO	198,776	8.0%	29.6%
Wyandotte County, KS	156,419	-0.9%	-3.4%
Cass County, MO	91,670	11.7%	43.7%
Platte County, MO	81,823	10.9%	41.4%
Leavenworth County, KS	72,674	5.8%	12.9%
Lafayette County, MO	32,927	-0.1%	5.9%
Miami County, KS	29,552	4.2%	25.9%
Franklin County, KS	25,900	4.5%	17.8%
Ray County, MO	24,217	3.7%	10.2%
Clinton County, MO	20,718	9.2%	24.8%
Bates County, MO	17,023	2.2%	13.3%
Linn County, KS	9,762	2.0%	18.3%
Caldwell County, MO	9,280	3.5%	10.7%
Kennewick–Richland–Pasco, WA	**216,153**	**12.8%**	**44.3%**
Benton County, WA	158,085	11.0%	40.4%
Franklin County, WA	58,068	17.7%	55.0%
Killeen–Temple–Fort Hood, TX	**348,803**	**5.6%**	**30.3%**
Bell County, TX	254,086	6.8%	33.0%
Coryell County, TX	74,580	-0.5%	16.1%
Lampasas County, TX	20,137	13.4%	48.9%
Kingsport–Bristol–Bristol, TN-VA	**301,138**	**0.9%**	**9.9%**
Sullivan County, TN	153,458	0.3%	6.9%
Hawkins County, TN	55,645	3.9%	24.9%
Washington County, VA	51,819	1.4%	13.0%
Scott County, VA	23,019	-1.6%	-0.8%
Bristol city, VA	17,197	-1.0%	-6.8%
Kingston, NY	**182,812**	**2.8%**	**10.6%**
Ulster County, NY	182,812	2.8%	10.6%
Knoxville, TN	**647,044**	**5.1%**	**21.6%**
Knox County, TN	398,623	4.3%	18.7%
Blount County, TN	114,071	7.8%	32.7%
Anderson County, TN	72,267	1.3%	5.9%
Loudon County, TN	42,831	9.6%	37.0%
Union County, TN	19,252	8.1%	40.6%
Kokomo, IN	**101,258**	**-0.3%**	**4.5%**
Howard County, IN	84,929	0.0%	5.1%
Tipton County, IN	16,329	-1.5%	1.3%
La Crosse, WI-MN	**129,118**	**1.8%**	**10.9%**
La Crosse County, WI	109,130	1.9%	11.5%
Houston County, MN	19,988	1.4%	8.1%

continued

TABLE 1.3 PRINCIPAL U.S. METROPOLITAN STATISTICAL AREAS (CONTINUED)

METRO AREA & INCLUDED COUNTIES	2005 POPULATION	5-YEAR GROWTH	15-YEAR GROWTH
Lafayette, IN	**187,749**	**5.2%**	**18.6%**
Tippecanoe County, IN	157,983	6.1%	21.0%
Carroll County, IN	20,686	2.6%	10.0%
Benton County, IN	9,080	−3.6%	−3.8%
Lafayette, LA	**246,790**	**3.2%**	**18.3%**
Lafayette Parish, LA	196,258	3.0%	19.1%
St. Martin Parish, LA	50,532	4.0%	14.9%
Lake Charles, LA	**194,173**	**0.3%**	**9.5%**
Calcasieu Parish, LA	184,553	0.5%	9.8%
Cameron Parish, LA	9,620	−3.7%	3.9%
Lake County–Kenosha County, IL-WI	**859,472**	**8.3%**	**33.5%**
Lake County, IL	701,900	8.9%	35.9%
Kenosha County, WI	157,572	5.3%	22.9%
Lakeland, FL	**523,502**	**8.2%**	**29.1%**
Polk County, FL	523,502	8.2%	29.1%
Lancaster, PA	**488,738**	**3.8%**	**15.6%**
Lancaster County, PA	488,738	3.8%	15.6%
Lansing–East Lansing, MI	**459,398**	**2.6%**	**6.8%**
Ingham County, MI	283,130	1.4%	0.4%
Eaton County, MI	107,310	3.5%	15.5%
Clinton County, MI	68,958	6.5%	19.1%
Laredo, TX	**223,790**	**15.9%**	**68.0%**
Webb County, TX	223,790	15.9%	68.0%
Las Cruces, NM	**186,522**	**6.8%**	**37.6%**
Dona Ana County, NM	186,522	6.8%	37.6%
Las Vegas–Paradise, NV	**1,667,216**	**21.2%**	**124.9%**
Clark County, NV	1,667,216	21.2%	124.9%
Lawrence, KS	**104,295**	**4.3%**	**27.5%**
Douglas County, KS	104,295	4.3%	27.5%
Lawton, OK	**114,348**	**−0.6%**	**2.6%**
Comanche County, OK	114,348	−0.6%	2.6%
Lebanon, PA	**124,033**	**3.1%**	**9.0%**
Lebanon County, PA	124,033	3.1%	9.0%
Lewiston, ID-WA	**58,928**	**1.7%**	**14.8%**
Nez Perce County, ID	38,213	2.1%	13.2%
Asotin County, WA	20,715	0.8%	17.7%
Lewiston–Auburn, ME	**107,449**	**3.5%**	**2.1%**
Androscoggin County, ME	107,449	3.5%	2.1%
Lexington–Fayette, KY	**429,410**	**5.3%**	**24.5%**
Fayette County, KY	270,386	3.8%	20.0%
Jessamine County, KY	42,649	9.2%	39.8%
Scott County, KY	38,423	16.2%	61.0%
Clark County, KY	34,384	3.7%	16.6%
Woodford County, KY	23,859	2.8%	19.6%
Bourbon County, KY	19,709	1.8%	2.5%
Lima, OH	**108,317**	**−0.1%**	**−1.3%**
Allen County, OH	108,317	−0.1%	−1.3%
Lincoln, NE	**283,001**	**6.1%**	**23.7%**
Lancaster County, NE	266,272	6.4%	24.6%
Seward County, NE	16,729	1.4%	8.3%
Little Rock–North Little Rock, AR	**636,868**	**4.5%**	**22.6%**
Pulaski County, AR	366,219	1.3%	4.7%
Faulkner County, AR	94,850	10.3%	58.1%
Saline County, AR	89,469	7.1%	39.4%
Lonoke County, AR	58,620	11.0%	49.3%
Grant County, AR	17,162	4.2%	23.0%
Perry County, AR	10,548	3.3%	32.4%
Logan, UT-ID	**110,632**	**7.7%**	**39.4%**
Cache County, UT	98,522	7.8%	40.4%
Franklin County, ID	12,110	6.9%	31.2%
Longview, TX	**199,966**	**3.1%**	**11.2%**
Gregg County, TX	115,213	3.4%	9.8%
Rusk County, TX	47,707	0.7%	9.1%
Upshur County, TX	37,046	5.0%	18.1%
Longview, WA	**96,262**	**3.6%**	**17.2%**
Cowlitz County, WA	96,262	3.6%	17.2%

METRO AREA & INCLUDED COUNTIES	2005 POPULATION	5-YEAR GROWTH	15-YEAR GROWTH
Los Angeles–Long Beach–Glendale, CA	**10,088,274**	**6.0%**	**13.8%**
Los Angeles County, CA	10,088,274	6.0%	13.8%
Louisville–Jefferson County, KY-IN	**1,203,842**	**3.8%**	**16.4%**
Jefferson County, KY	702,518	1.3%	5.7%
Clark County, IN	101,206	4.9%	15.3%
Floyd County, IN	71,074	0.4%	10.4%
Bullitt County, KY	66,627	8.8%	40.1%
Oldham County, KY	52,348	13.4%	57.4%
Nelson County, KY	40,639	8.4%	36.8%
Shelby County, KY	37,115	11.3%	49.5%
Harrison County, IN	36,367	5.9%	21.7%
Meade County, KY	28,076	6.6%	16.2%
Washington County, IN	27,710	1.8%	16.8%
Henry County, KY	15,807	5.0%	23.3%
Spencer County, KY	15,366	30.6%	125.9%
Trimble County, KY	8,989	10.6%	47.6%
Lubbock, TX	**259,577**	**4.0%**	**13.0%**
Lubbock County, TX	252,972	4.3%	13.6%
Crosby County, TX	6,605	−6.6%	−9.6%
Lynchburg, VA	**232,081**	**1.5%**	**14.2%**
Lynchburg city, VA	66,433	1.8%	0.5%
Bedford County, VA	62,740	3.9%	37.5%
Campbell County, VA	51,156	0.2%	7.7%
Amherst County, VA	31,792	−0.3%	11.2%
Appomattox County, VA	13,630	−0.5%	10.8%
Bedford city, VA	6,330	0.5%	3.8%
Macon–Warner Robins, GA	**353,400**	**6.4%**	**22.1%**
Bibb County, GA	154,623	0.5%	3.1%
Houston County, GA	125,293	13.1%	40.5%
Jones County, GA	26,416	11.7%	27.4%
Monroe County, GA	24,059	10.6%	40.6%
Crawford County, GA	12,588	0.7%	40.0%
Twiggs County, GA	10,421	−1.6%	6.3%
Madera, CA	**136,880**	**11.2%**	**55.4%**
Madera County, CA	136,880	11.2%	55.4%
Madison, WI	**534,567**	**6.5%**	**23.7%**
Dane County, WI	456,489	7.0%	24.4%
Columbia County, WI	54,572	4.0%	21.0%
Iowa County, WI	23,506	3.2%	16.7%
Manchester–Nashua, NH	**399,781**	**5.0%**	**19.0%**
Hillsborough County, NH	399,781	5.0%	19.0%
Mansfield, OH	**128,231**	**−0.5%**	**1.7%**
Richland County, OH	128,231	−0.5%	1.7%
McAllen–Edinburg–Mission, TX	**666,049**	**17.0%**	**73.7%**
Hidalgo County, TX	666,049	17.0%	73.7%
Medford, OR	**194,365**	**7.2%**	**32.8%**
Jackson County, OR	194,365	7.2%	32.8%
Memphis, TN-MS-AR	**1,256,461**	**4.7%**	**21.7%**
Shelby County, TN	911,599	1.6%	10.3%
DeSoto County, MS	132,348	23.5%	94.9%
Tipton County, TN	55,371	8.0%	47.4%
Crittenden County, AR	51,259	0.8%	2.6%
Marshall County, MS	35,765	2.2%	17.8%
Fayette County, TN	33,824	17.4%	32.3%
Tate County, MS	26,035	2.6%	21.5%
Tunica County, MS	10,260	11.2%	25.7%
Merced, CA	**236,401**	**12.3%**	**32.5%**
Merced County, CA	236,401	12.3%	32.5%
Miami–Miami Beach–Kendall, FL	**2,378,142**	**5.5%**	**22.8%**
Miami-Dade County, FL	2,378,142	5.5%	22.8%
Michigan City–La Porte, IN	**109,665**	**−0.4%**	**2.4%**
LaPorte County, IN	109,665	−0.4%	2.4%
Midland–Odessa, TX	**244,036**	**2.9%**	**8.3%**
Ector County, TX	124,541	2.8%	4.7%
Midland County, TX	119,495	3.0%	12.1%

continued

TABLE 1.3 PRINCIPAL U.S. METROPOLITAN STATISTICAL AREAS *(CONTINUED)*

METRO AREA & INCLUDED COUNTIES	2005 POPULATION	5-YEAR GROWTH	15-YEAR GROWTH
Milwaukee–Waukesha–West Allis, WI	**1,518,832**	**1.3%**	**7.6%**
Milwaukee County, WI	931,896	–0.9%	–2.9%
Waukesha County, WI	377,369	4.6%	23.8%
Washington County, WI	124,014	5.6%	30.1%
Ozaukee County, WI	85,553	3.9%	17.5%
Minneapolis–St. Paul–Bloomington, MN-WI	**3,138,324**	**6.2%**	**27.8%**
Hennepin County, MN	1,128,667	1.1%	9.3%
Ramsey County, MN	507,629	–0.7%	4.5%
Dakota County, MN	381,543	7.2%	38.6%
Anoka County, MN	318,916	7.0%	30.9%
Washington County, MN	219,483	9.1%	50.4%
Scott County, MN	113,717	27.1%	96.6%
Wright County, MN	108,258	20.3%	57.6%
Carver County, MN	81,985	16.8%	71.1%
Sherburne County, MN	79,458	23.3%	89.4%
St. Croix County, WI	74,560	18.1%	48.4%
Chisago County, MN	48,620	18.3%	59.3%
Pierce County, WI	38,554	4.8%	17.7%
Isanti County, MN	36,934	18.0%	42.5%
Missoula, MT	**99,890**	**4.3%**	**26.9%**
Missoula County, MT	99,890	4.3%	26.9%
Mobile, AL	**399,938**	**0.0%**	**5.6%**
Mobile County, AL	399,938	0.0%	5.6%
Modesto, CA	**504,411**	**12.8%**	**36.1%**
Stanislaus County, CA	504,411	12.8%	36.1%
Monroe, LA	**171,870**	**1.1%**	**5.6%**
Ouachita Parish, LA	148,783	1.0%	4.6%
Union Parish, LA	23,087	1.2%	11.6%
Monroe, MI	**152,801**	**4.7%**	**14.4%**
Monroe County, MI	152,801	4.7%	14.4%
Montgomery, AL	**355,235**	**2.8%**	**19.0%**
Montgomery County, AL	221,277	–1.0%	5.8%
Elmore County, AL	72,892	10.7%	48.1%
Autauga County, AL	47,761	9.4%	39.6%
Lowndes County, AL	13,305	–1.2%	5.1%
Morgantown, WV	**115,519**	**3.9%**	**10.7%**
Monongalia County, WV	85,590	4.5%	13.4%
Preston County, WV	29,929	2.0%	3.1%
Morristown, TN	**129,332**	**5.2%**	**29.9%**
Hamblen County, TN	59,208	1.9%	17.3%
Jefferson County, TN	48,308	9.1%	46.3%
Grainger County, TN	21,816	5.6%	27.6%
Mount Vernon–Anacortes, WA	**110,809**	**7.6%**	**39.3%**
Skagit County, WA	110,809	7.6%	39.3%
Muncie, IN	**116,688**	**–1.8%**	**–2.5%**
Delaware County, IN	116,688	–1.8%	–2.5%
Muskegon–Norton Shores, MI	**174,431**	**2.5%**	**9.7%**
Muskegon County, MI	174,431	2.5%	9.7%
Myrtle Beach–Conway–North Myrtle Beach, SC	**217,547**	**10.6%**	**51.0%**
Horry County, SC	217,547	10.6%	51.0%
Napa, CA	**133,051**	**7.1%**	**20.1%**
Napa County, CA	133,051	7.1%	20.1%
Naples–Marco Island, FL	**307,487**	**22.3%**	**102.2%**
Collier County, FL	307,487	22.3%	102.2%
Nashville–Davidson–Murfreesboro, TN	**1,398,214**	**7.0%**	**38.4%**
Davidson County, TN	570,088	0.0%	11.6%
Rutherford County, TN	211,702	16.3%	78.5%
Williamson County, TN	147,883	16.8%	82.5%
Sumner County, TN	142,396	9.2%	37.9%
Wilson County, TN	98,334	10.7%	45.3%
Robertson County, TN	59,762	9.8%	44.0%
Dickson County, TN	45,834	6.2%	30.7%
Cheatham County, TN	37,943	5.7%	39.8%
Hickman County, TN	23,733	6.4%	41.7%
Macon County, TN	21,249	4.2%	33.6%
Smith County, TN	18,410	3.9%	30.2%

METRO AREA & INCLUDED COUNTIES	2005 POPULATION	5-YEAR GROWTH	15-YEAR GROWTH
Cannon County, TN	13,352	4.1%	27.6%
Trousdale County, TN	7,528	3.7%	27.2%
Nassau–Suffolk, NY	**2,828,933**	**2.8%**	**8.6%**
Suffolk County, NY	1,487,601	4.8%	12.6%
Nassau County, NY	1,341,332	0.5%	4.2%
Newark–Union, NJ-PA	**2,159,686**	**3.0%**	**11.6%**
Essex County, NJ	798,103	0.6%	2.6%
Union County, NJ	531,611	1.7%	7.6%
Morris County, NJ	489,732	4.2%	16.2%
Sussex County, NJ	154,441	7.1%	18.2%
Hunterdon County, NJ	130,812	7.2%	21.7%
Pike County, PA	54,987	18.8%	96.3%
New Haven–Milford, CT	**850,873**	**3.3%**	**5.8%**
New Haven County, CT	850,873	3.3%	5.8%
New Orleans–Metairie–Kenner, LA	**1,321,402**	**0.7%**	**7.4%**
Orleans Parish, LA	462,861	−4.5%	−6.9%
Jefferson Parish, LA	452,618	−0.6%	1.0%
St. Tammany Parish, LA	215,837	12.8%	49.4%
St. Bernard Parish, LA	65,745	−2.2%	−1.3%
St. Charles Parish, LA	49,883	3.8%	17.5%
St. John the Baptist Parish, LA	45,682	6.1%	14.2%
Plaquemines Parish, LA	28,776	7.5%	12.5%
New York–White Plains, NY	**9,456,583**	**1.6%**	**10.8%**
Kings County, NY	2,472,995	0.3%	7.5%
Queens County, NY	2,223,275	−0.3%	13.9%
New York County, NY	1,576,353	2.5%	6.0%
Bronx County, NY	1,374,586	3.1%	14.2%
Westchester County, NY	945,910	2.4%	8.1%
Richmond County, NY	466,519	5.1%	23.1%
Rockland County, NY	295,771	3.1%	11.4%
Putnam County, NY	101,174	5.7%	20.5%
Niles–Benton Harbor, MI	**163,121**	**0.4%**	**1.1%**
Berrien County, MI	163,121	0.4%	1.1%
Norwich–New London, CT	**266,582**	**2.9%**	**4.6%**
New London County, CT	266,582	2.9%	4.6%
Oakland–Fremont–Hayward, CA	**2,500,934**	**4.6%**	**20.3%**
Alameda County, CA	1,484,803	2.8%	16.1%
Contra Costa County, CA	1,016,131	7.1%	26.4%
Ocala, FL	**291,640**	**12.6%**	**49.7%**
Marion County, FL	291,640	12.6%	49.7%
Ocean City, NJ	**101,848**	**−0.5%**	**7.1%**
Cape May County, NJ	101,848	−0.5%	7.1%
Ogden–Clearfield, UT	**476,959**	**7.8%**	**35.7%**
Davis County, UT	261,493	9.4%	39.1%
Weber County, UT	207,854	5.8%	31.3%
Morgan County, UT	7,612	6.8%	37.7%
Oklahoma City, OK	**1,150,837**	**5.1%**	**18.9%**
Oklahoma County, OK	683,728	3.5%	14.0%
Cleveland County, OK	225,651	8.5%	29.5%
Canadian County, OK	95,348	8.7%	28.1%
Grady County, OK	48,450	6.4%	16.1%
Logan County, OK	36,126	6.5%	24.5%
Lincoln County, OK	32,351	0.8%	10.7%
McClain County, OK	29,183	5.2%	28.0%
Olympia, WA	**224,064**	**8.1%**	**39.0%**
Thurston County, WA	224,064	8.1%	39.0%
Omaha–Council Bluffs, NE-IA	**806,108**	**5.2%**	**18.0%**
Douglas County, NE	483,365	4.3%	16.1%
Sarpy County, NE	136,973	11.7%	33.5%
Pottawattamie County, IA	88,928	1.4%	7.6%
Cass County, NE	25,762	5.9%	20.8%
Washington County, NE	20,150	7.3%	21.3%
Saunders County, NE	20,097	1.3%	9.9%
Harrison County, IA	15,707	0.3%	6.6%
Mills County, IA	15,126	4.0%	14.6%

continued

TABLE 1.3 PRINCIPAL U.S. METROPOLITAN STATISTICAL AREAS (CONTINUED)

METRO AREA & INCLUDED COUNTIES	2005 POPULATION	5-YEAR GROWTH	15-YEAR GROWTH
Orlando–Kissimmee, FL	**1,894,018**	**15.5%**	**57.0%**
Orange County, FL	1,008,469	12.5%	48.9%
Seminole County, FL	401,480	9.9%	39.6%
Lake County, FL	258,416	22.7%	69.9%
Osceola County, FL	225,653	30.8%	109.5%
Oshkosh–Neenah, WI	**159,972**	**2.0%**	**14.0%**
Winnebago County, WI	159,972	2.0%	14.0%
Owensboro, KY	**111,518**	**1.5%**	**6.6%**
Daviess County, KY	93,242	1.9%	6.9%
McLean County, KY	9,829	−1.1%	2.1%
Hancock County, KY	8,447	0.7%	7.4%
Oxnard–Thousand Oaks–Ventura, CA	**806,367**	**7.1%**	**20.5%**
Ventura County, CA	806,367	7.1%	20.5%
Palm Bay–Melbourne–Titusville, FL	**520,207**	**9.2%**	**30.4%**
Brevard County, FL	520,207	9.2%	30.4%
Panama City–Lynn Haven, FL	**158,050**	**6.6%**	**24.5%**
Bay County, FL	158,050	6.6%	24.5%
Parkersburg–Marietta–Vienna, WV-OH	**162,558**	**−1.3%**	**0.4%**
Wood County, WV	87,030	−1.1%	0.1%
Washington County, OH	62,332	−1.5%	0.1%
Pleasants County, WV	7,462	−0.7%	−1.1%
Wirt County, WV	5,734	−2.4%	10.4%
Pensacola–Ferry Pass–Brent, FL	**438,226**	**6.7%**	**31.2%**
Escambia County, FL	300,976	2.2%	14.7%
Santa Rosa County, FL	137,250	16.6%	67.4%
Peoria, IL	**366,035**	**−0.2%**	**2.2%**
Peoria County, IL	182,098	−0.7%	−0.4%
Tazewell County, IL	127,915	−0.4%	3.4%
Woodford County, IL	36,851	3.9%	12.9%
Marshall County, IL	13,046	−1.0%	1.6%
Stark County, IL	6,125	−3.3%	−6.3%
Philadelphia, PA	**3,888,163**	**1.2%**	**5.6%**
Philadelphia County, PA	1,464,886	−3.5%	−7.6%
Montgomery County, PA	779,879	4.0%	15.0%
Bucks County, PA	619,545	3.7%	14.5%
Delaware County, PA	555,502	0.8%	1.4%
Chester County, PA	468,351	8.0%	24.4%
Phoenix–Mesa–Scottsdale, AZ	**3,730,550**	**14.7%**	**66.7%**
Maricopa County, AZ	3,520,072	14.6%	65.9%
Pinal County, AZ	210,478	17.1%	80.9%
Pine Bluff, AR	**105,528**	**−1.7%**	**−1.1%**
Jefferson County, AR	82,394	−2.2%	−3.6%
Lincoln County, AR	14,328	−1.1%	4.7%
Cleveland County, AR	8,806	2.7%	13.2%
Pittsburgh, PA	**2,402,483**	**−1.1%**	**−2.2%**
Allegheny County, PA	1,252,246	−2.3%	−6.3%
Westmoreland County, PA	367,859	−0.6%	−0.7%
Washington County, PA	205,034	1.1%	0.2%
Butler County, PA	182,753	5.0%	20.2%
Beaver County, PA	177,882	−1.9%	−4.4%
Fayette County, PA	145,266	−2.3%	−0.1%
Armstrong County, PA	71,443	−1.3%	−2.8%
Pittsfield, MA	**132,926**	**−1.5%**	**−4.6%**
Berkshire County, MA	132,926	−1.5%	−4.6%
Pocatello, ID	**82,874**	**−0.3%**	**13.5%**
Bannock County, ID	75,567	0.0%	14.5%
Power County, ID	7,307	−3.1%	3.1%
Portland–South Portland–Biddeford, ME	**513,373**	**5.4%**	**16.6%**
Cumberland County, ME	273,765	3.1%	12.6%
York County, ME	202,507	8.4%	23.0%
Sagadahoc County, ME	37,101	5.4%	10.6%
Portland–Vancouver–Beaverton, OR-WA	**2,082,023**	**8.1%**	**39.3%**
Multnomah County, OR	687,569	4.1%	17.8%
Washington County, OR	490,503	10.1%	57.4%
Clark County, WA	391,644	13.4%	64.5%
Clackamas County, OR	364,388	7.7%	30.7%
Yamhill County, OR	90,889	6.9%	38.7%

METRO AREA & INCLUDED COUNTIES	2005 POPULATION	5-YEAR GROWTH	15-YEAR GROWTH
Columbia County, OR	46,776	7.4%	24.5%
Skamania County, WA	10,254	3.9%	23.7%
Port St. Lucie–Fort Pierce, FL	**360,929**	**13.1%**	**44.0%**
St. Lucie County, FL	222,422	15.4%	48.1%
Martin County, FL	138,507	9.3%	37.3%
Poughkeepsie–Newburgh–Middletown, NY	**668,899**	**7.7%**	**18.1%**
Orange County, NY	373,314	9.4%	21.3%
Dutchess County, NY	295,585	5.5%	13.9%
Prescott, AZ	**192,353**	**14.8%**	**78.6%**
Yavapai County, AZ	192,353	14.8%	78.6%
Providence–New Bedford–Fall River, RI-MA	**1,641,304**	**3.7%**	**8.8%**
Providence County, RI	647,709	4.2%	8.6%
Bristol County, MA	552,500	3.3%	9.1%
Kent County, RI	173,225	3.7%	7.5%
Washington County, RI	130,690	5.8%	18.8%
Newport County, RI	86,149	0.8%	−1.2%
Bristol County, RI	51,031	0.8%	4.4%
Provo–Orem, UT	**424,127**	**12.6%**	**57.4%**
Utah County, UT	415,233	12.7%	57.5%
Juab County, UT	8,894	8.0%	52.9%
Pueblo, CO	**150,748**	**6.6%**	**22.5%**
Pueblo County, CO	150,748	6.6%	22.5%
Punta Gorda, FL	**157,503**	**11.2%**	**41.9%**
Charlotte County, FL	157,503	11.2%	41.9%
Racine, WI	**192,488**	**1.9%**	**10.0%**
Racine County, WI	192,488	1.9%	10.0%
Raleigh–Cary, NC	**922,315**	**15.7%**	**70.7%**
Wake County, NC	724,965	15.5%	71.2%
Johnston County, NC	143,135	17.4%	76.1%
Franklin County, NC	54,215	14.7%	48.8%
Rapid City, SD	**118,211**	**4.8%**	**14.5%**
Pennington County, SD	93,243	5.3%	14.6%
Meade County, SD	24,968	2.9%	14.1%
Reading, PA	**390,857**	**4.6%**	**16.1%**
Berks County, PA	390,857	4.6%	16.1%
Redding, CA	**178,425**	**9.3%**	**21.3%**
Shasta County, CA	178,425	9.3%	21.3%
Reno–Sparks, NV	**388,876**	**13.4%**	**51.2%**
Washoe County, NV	385,274	13.5%	51.3%
Storey County, NV	3,602	6.0%	42.6%
Richmond, VA	**1,160,347**	**6.0%**	**25.5%**
Chesterfield County, VA	284,039	9.3%	35.5%
Henrico County, VA	278,300	6.1%	27.7%
Richmond city, VA	193,726	−2.1%	−4.5%
Hanover County, VA	96,841	12.2%	53.0%
Prince George County, VA	35,832	8.4%	30.3%
Petersburg city, VA	32,127	−4.8%	−16.1%
Louisa County, VA	28,753	12.2%	41.5%
Powhatan County, VA	25,799	15.3%	68.3%
Dinwiddie County, VA	25,402	3.5%	21.3%
Caroline County, VA	23,503	6.2%	22.3%
Hopewell city, VA	22,437	0.4%	−2.9%
Goochland County, VA	18,930	12.3%	33.7%
Colonial Heights city, VA	17,353	2.7%	8.0%
New Kent County, VA	15,419	14.5%	47.6%
King William County, VA	14,430	9.8%	32.2%
Amelia County, VA	12,142	6.5%	38.2%
Sussex County, VA	11,980	−4.2%	16.9%
Cumberland County, VA	9,395	4.2%	20.1%
Charles City County, VA	7,204	4.0%	14.6%
King and Queen County, VA	6,735	1.6%	7.1%
Riverside–San Bernardino–Ontario, CA	**3,753,368**	**15.4%**	**45.9%**
San Bernardino County, CA	1,909,875	11.7%	34.7%
Riverside County, CA	1,843,493	19.3%	57.5%
Roanoke, VA	**292,443**	**1.5%**	**10.3%**
Roanoke city, VA	92,509	−2.5%	−4.1%
Roanoke County, VA	88,343	3.0%	12.0%

continued

TABLE 1.3 PRINCIPAL U.S. METROPOLITAN STATISTICAL AREAS (CONTINUED)

METRO AREA & INCLUDED COUNTIES	2005 POPULATION	5-YEAR GROWTH	15-YEAR GROWTH
Franklin County, VA	49,971	5.7%	26.4%
Botetourt County, VA	31,759	4.1%	27.1%
Salem city, VA	24,692	−0.2%	2.0%
Craig County, VA	5,169	1.5%	17.6%
Rochester, MN	**176,606**	**8.0%**	**24.6%**
Olmsted County, MN	134,973	8.6%	26.8%
Wabasha County, MN	22,181	2.6%	12.3%
Dodge County, MN	19,452	9.7%	23.7%
Rochester, NY	**1,043,266**	**0.5%**	**4.1%**
Monroe County, NY	737,839	0.3%	3.3%
Ontario County, NY	103,446	3.2%	8.8%
Wayne County, NY	93,730	0.0%	5.2%
Livingston County, NY	64,696	0.6%	3.7%
Orleans County, NY	43,555	−1.4%	4.1%
Rockford, IL	**336,260**	**5.2%**	**20.1%**
Winnebago County, IL	287,521	3.3%	13.7%
Boone County, IL	48,739	16.6%	58.2%
Rockingham County–Strafford County, NH	**415,131**	**6.6%**	**18.6%**
Rockingham County, NH	294,970	6.3%	20.0%
Strafford County, NH	120,161	7.1%	15.3%
Rocky Mount, NC	**145,601**	**1.9%**	**10.3%**
Nash County, NC	90,880	4.0%	18.5%
Edgecombe County, NC	54,721	−1.6%	−3.2%
Rome, GA	**94,758**	**4.6%**	**16.6%**
Floyd County, GA	94,758	4.6%	16.6%
Sacramento–Arden-Arcade–Roseville, CA	**2,023,535**	**12.7%**	**38.0%**
Sacramento County, CA	1,362,572	11.4%	30.9%
Placer County, CA	300,906	21.1%	74.1%
Yolo County, CA	187,903	11.4%	33.2%
El Dorado County, CA	172,154	10.1%	36.6%
Saginaw–Saginaw Township North, MI	**209,037**	**−0.5%**	**−1.4%**
Saginaw County, MI	209,037	−0.5%	−1.4%
St. Cloud, MN	**177,225**	**6.0%**	**19.1%**
Stearns County, MN	138,897	4.3%	16.9%
Benton County, MN	38,328	12.0%	27.0%
St. George, UT	**110,515**	**22.3%**	**127.6%**
Washington County, UT	110,515	22.3%	127.6%
St. Joseph, MO-KS	**122,675**	**0.5%**	**6.7%**
Buchanan County, MO	84,511	−1.7%	1.7%
Andrew County, MO	16,964	2.9%	15.9%
DeKalb County, MO	13,100	13.0%	31.4%
Doniphan County, KS	8,100	−1.8%	−0.4%
St. Louis, MO-IL	**2,754,233**	**2.4%**	**10.1%**
St. Louis County, MO	1,011,308	−0.5%	1.8%
St. Louis city, MO	325,969	−6.4%	−17.8%
St. Charles County, MO	323,677	14.0%	52.0%
Madison County, IL	262,987	1.6%	5.5%
St. Clair County, IL	260,238	1.6%	−1.0%
Jefferson County, MO	210,884	6.5%	23.1%
Franklin County, MO	98,316	4.8%	22.0%
Macoupin County, IL	49,141	0.2%	3.1%
Lincoln County, MO	46,682	19.9%	61.6%
Clinton County, IL	36,498	2.7%	7.5%
Monroe County, IL	30,706	11.2%	36.9%
Warren County, MO	27,947	14.0%	43.1%
Washington County, MO	24,196	3.6%	18.7%
Jersey County, IL	22,472	3.7%	9.4%
Bond County, IL	18,111	2.7%	20.8%
Calhoun County, IL	5,101	0.3%	−4.2%
Salem, OR	**369,411**	**6.4%**	**32.9%**
Marion County, OR	302,931	6.4%	32.6%
Polk County, OR	66,480	6.6%	34.2%
Salinas, CA	**419,440**	**4.4%**	**17.9%**
Monterey County, CA	419,440	4.4%	17.9%
Salisbury, MD	**114,561**	**4.7%**	**17.3%**
Wicomico County, MD	88,953	5.1%	19.7%
Somerset County, MD	25,608	3.5%	9.2%

METRO AREA & INCLUDED COUNTIES	2005 POPULATION	5-YEAR GROWTH	15-YEAR GROWTH
Salt Lake City, UT	**1,023,434**	**5.8%**	**35.5%**
Salt Lake County, UT	938,047	4.4%	29.2%
Tooele County, UT	50,465	23.9%	89.7%
Summit County, UT	34,922	17.4%	125.0%
San Angelo, TX	**105,367**	**-0.4%**	**5.3%**
Tom Green County, TX	103,564	-0.4%	5.2%
Irion County, TX	1,803	1.8%	10.7%
San Antonio, TX	**1,863,789**	**9.0%**	**34.0%**
Bexar County, TX	1,501,149	7.8%	26.6%
Guadalupe County, TX	101,617	14.1%	56.6%
Comal County, TX	91,222	16.9%	76.0%
Atascosa County, TX	42,512	10.1%	39.2%
Medina County, TX	42,418	7.9%	55.3%
Wilson County, TX	37,074	14.4%	63.7%
Kendall County, TX	27,519	15.9%	88.6%
Bandera County, TX	20,278	14.9%	92.0%
San Diego–Carlsbad–San Marcos, CA	**2,998,625**	**6.6%**	**20.0%**
San Diego County, CA	2,998,625	6.6%	20.0%
Sandusky, OH	**78,374**	**-1.5%**	**1.9%**
Erie County, OH	78,374	-1.5%	1.9%
San Francisco–San Mateo–Redwood City, CA	**1,714,445**	**-1.0%**	**6.9%**
San Francisco County, CA	764,306	-1.6%	5.6%
San Mateo County, CA	703,110	-0.6%	8.2%
Marin County, CA	247,029	-0.1%	7.4%
San Jose–Sunnyvale–Santa Clara, CA	**1,764,054**	**1.6%**	**15.3%**
Santa Clara County, CA	1,706,595	1.4%	14.0%
San Benito County, CA	57,459	7.9%	56.6%
San Luis Obispo–Paso Robles, CA	**257,154**	**4.2%**	**18.5%**
San Luis Obispo County, CA	257,154	4.2%	18.5%
Santa Ana–Anaheim–Irvine, CA	**3,015,707**	**6.0%**	**25.1%**
Orange County, CA	3,015,707	6.0%	25.1%
Santa Barbara–Santa Maria, CA	**408,425**	**2.3%**	**10.4%**
Santa Barbara County, CA	408,425	2.3%	10.4%
Santa Cruz–Watsonville, CA	**254,222**	**-0.5%**	**10.7%**
Santa Cruz County, CA	254,222	-0.5%	10.7%
Santa Fe, NM	**139,921**	**8.2%**	**41.4%**
Santa Fe County, NM	139,921	8.2%	41.4%
Santa Rosa–Petaluma, CA	**472,121**	**2.9%**	**21.6%**
Sonoma County, CA	472,121	2.9%	21.6%
Sarasota–Bradenton–Venice, FL	**654,397**	**10.9%**	**33.9%**
Sarasota County, FL	357,389	9.6%	28.7%
Manatee County, FL	297,008	12.5%	40.3%
Savannah, GA	**309,709**	**6.2%**	**25.2%**
Chatham County, GA	236,781	2.0%	9.1%
Effingham County, GA	45,116	20.2%	75.6%
Bryan County, GA	27,812	18.8%	80.2%
Scranton–Wilkes-Barre, PA	**549,430**	**-2.0%**	**-4.5%**
Luzerne County, PA	311,770	-2.3%	-5.0%
Lackawanna County, PA	209,379	-1.8%	-4.4%
Wyoming County, PA	28,281	0.7%	0.7%
Seattle–Bellevue–Everett, WA	**2,444,743**	**4.4%**	**24.6%**
King County, WA	1,790,396	3.1%	18.8%
Snohomish County, WA	654,347	8.0%	40.5%
Sebastian–Vero Beach, FL	**124,365**	**10.1%**	**37.9%**
Indian River County, FL	124,365	10.1%	37.9%
Sheboygan, WI	**114,338**	**1.5%**	**10.1%**
Sheboygan County, WI	114,338	1.5%	10.1%
Sherman–Denison, TX	**118,041**	**6.7%**	**24.2%**
Grayson County, TX	118,041	6.7%	24.2%
Shreveport–Bossier City, LA	**380,050**	**1.2%**	**6.3%**
Caddo Parish, LA	250,028	-0.8%	0.7%
Bossier Parish, LA	103,735	5.5%	20.5%
De Soto Parish, LA	26,287	3.1%	3.7%
Sioux City, IA-NE-SD	**142,968**	**0.0%**	**9.6%**
Woodbury County, IA	103,022	-0.8%	4.8%
Dakota County, NE	20,640	1.9%	23.3%
Union County, SD	13,271	5.5%	30.2%
Dixon County, NE	6,035	-4.8%	-1.8%

continued

TABLE 1.3 PRINCIPAL U.S. METROPOLITAN STATISTICAL AREAS (CONTINUED)

METRO AREA & INCLUDED COUNTIES	2005 POPULATION	5-YEAR GROWTH	15-YEAR GROWTH
Sioux Falls, SD	**203,375**	**9.4%**	**37.3%**
Minnehaha County, SD	157,441	6.2%	27.2%
Lincoln County, SD	31,537	30.7%	104.4%
Turner County, SD	8,508	–3.9%	–0.8%
McCook County, SD	5,889	1.0%	3.5%
South Bend–Mishawaka, IN-MI	**318,102**	**0.5%**	**7.3%**
St. Joseph County, IN	266,659	0.4%	7.9%
Cass County, MI	51,443	0.7%	4.0%
Spartanburg, SC	**264,753**	**4.3%**	**16.7%**
Spartanburg County, SC	264,753	4.3%	16.7%
Spokane, WA	**436,631**	**4.5%**	**20.8%**
Spokane County, WA	436,631	4.5%	20.8%
Springfield, IL	**205,571**	**2.1%**	**8.5%**
Sangamon County, IL	192,948	2.1%	8.2%
Menard County, IL	12,623	1.1%	13.1%
Springfield, MA	**693,648**	**2.0%**	**3.1%**
Hampden County, MA	464,171	1.7%	1.7%
Hampshire County, MA	156,974	3.1%	7.1%
Franklin County, MA	72,503	1.4%	3.5%
Springfield, MO	**392,592**	**6.9%**	**36.0%**
Greene County, MO	248,843	3.5%	19.7%
Christian County, MO	64,861	19.5%	98.7%
Webster County, MO	33,906	9.2%	42.7%
Polk County, MO	28,632	6.1%	31.2%
Dallas County, MO	16,350	4.4%	29.3%
Springfield, OH	**142,815**	**–1.3%**	**–3.2%**
Clark County, OH	142,815	–1.3%	–3.2%
State College, PA	**144,311**	**6.3%**	**16.6%**
Centre County, PA	144,311	6.3%	16.6%
Stockton, CA	**650,102**	**15.3%**	**35.3%**
San Joaquin County, CA	650,102	15.3%	35.3%
Sumter, SC	**106,986**	**2.2%**	**4.2%**
Sumter County, SC	106,986	2.2%	4.2%
Syracuse, NY	**656,857**	**1.0%**	**–0.4%**
Onondaga County, NY	461,915	0.8%	–1.5%
Oswego County, NY	124,311	1.6%	2.1%
Madison County, NY	70,631	1.7%	2.2%
Tacoma, WA	**756,177**	**7.9%**	**29.0%**
Pierce County, WA	756,177	7.9%	29.0%
Tallahassee, FL	**340,298**	**6.3%**	**33.2%**
Leon County, FL	253,555	5.9%	31.7%
Gadsden County, FL	45,899	1.8%	11.7%
Wakulla County, FL	26,699	16.8%	88.0%
Jefferson County, FL	14,145	9.6%	25.2%
Tampa–St. Petersburg–Clearwater, FL	**2,592,782**	**8.5%**	**26.8%**
Hillsborough County, FL	1,110,497	11.2%	33.1%
Pinellas County, FL	935,269	1.5%	9.8%
Pasco County, FL	399,559	15.9%	42.1%
Hernando County, FL	147,457	12.7%	45.8%
Terre Haute, IN	**169,676**	**–0.7%**	**2.2%**
Vigo County, IN	104,257	–1.5%	–1.7%
Clay County, IN	26,982	1.6%	9.2%
Sullivan County, IN	21,910	0.7%	15.4%
Vermillion County, IN	16,527	–1.6%	–1.5%
Texarkana, TX-AR	**133,977**	**3.3%**	**11.5%**
Bowie County, TX	91,285	2.2%	11.8%
Miller County, AR	42,692	5.6%	11.0%
Toledo, OH	**661,740**	**0.4%**	**1.4%**
Lucas County, OH	453,814	–0.3%	–1.8%
Wood County, OH	123,889	2.3%	9.4%
Fulton County, OH	42,639	1.3%	10.8%
Ottawa County, OH	41,398	1.0%	3.4%
Topeka, KS	**227,273**	**1.2%**	**8.2%**
Shawnee County, KS	171,532	1.0%	6.6%
Jefferson County, KS	18,959	2.9%	19.2%
Osage County, KS	16,807	0.6%	10.2%

METRO AREA & INCLUDED COUNTIES	2005 POPULATION	5-YEAR GROWTH	15-YEAR GROWTH
Jackson County, KS	13,231	4.5%	14.8%
Wabaunsee County, KS	6,744	−2.0%	2.1%
Trenton–Ewing, NJ	**367,375**	**4.7%**	**12.8%**
Mercer County, NJ	367,375	4.7%	12.8%
Tucson, AZ	**924,462**	**9.6%**	**38.6%**
Pima County, AZ	924,462	9.6%	38.6%
Tulsa, OK	**887,968**	**3.4%**	**17.5%**
Tulsa County, OK	572,797	1.7%	13.8%
Rogers County, OK	80,070	13.3%	45.1%
Creek County, OK	69,278	2.8%	13.7%
Wagoner County, OK	63,826	11.0%	33.3%
Osage County, OK	45,492	2.4%	9.2%
Okmulgee County, OK	39,710	0.1%	8.8%
Pawnee County, OK	16,795	1.1%	7.8%
Tuscaloosa, AL	**195,626**	**1.9%**	**11.2%**
Tuscaloosa County, AL	167,428	1.5%	11.3%
Hale County, AL	18,324	6.6%	18.2%
Greene County, AL	9,874	−1.0%	−2.7%
Tyler, TX	**188,887**	**8.1%**	**24.8%**
Smith County, TX	188,887	8.1%	24.8%
Utica–Rome, NY	**297,934**	**−0.7%**	**−5.9%**
Oneida County, NY	234,415	−0.4%	−6.5%
Herkimer County, NY	63,519	−1.4%	−3.5%
Valdosta, GA	**123,938**	**3.7%**	**26.0%**
Lowndes County, GA	96,069	4.3%	26.4%
Brooks County, GA	16,175	−1.7%	5.0%
Lanier County, GA	7,535	4.1%	36.2%
Echols County, GA	4,159	10.8%	78.2%
Vallejo–Fairfield, CA	**417,749**	**5.9%**	**22.7%**
Solano County, CA	417,749	5.9%	22.7%
Victoria, TX	**113,803**	**1.9%**	**14.6%**
Victoria County, TX	85,622	1.8%	15.1%
Calhoun County, TX	20,913	1.3%	9.8%
Goliad County, TX	7,268	4.9%	21.5%
Vineland–Millville–Bridgeton, NJ	**151,111**	**3.2%**	**9.5%**
Cumberland County, NJ	151,111	3.2%	9.5%
Virginia Beach–Norfolk–Newport News, VA-NC	**1,645,236**	**4.7%**	**16.7%**
Virginia Beach city, VA	438,740	3.2%	11.6%
Norfolk city, VA	239,417	2.1%	−8.3%
Chesapeake city, VA	213,499	7.2%	40.5%
Newport News city, VA	182,061	1.1%	6.8%
Hampton city, VA	145,812	−0.4%	9.1%
Portsmouth city, VA	97,983	−2.6%	−5.7%
Suffolk city, VA	77,560	21.8%	48.8%
York County, VA	62,614	11.2%	47.6%
James City County, VA	55,792	16.0%	61.1%
Gloucester County, VA	36,736	5.6%	21.9%
Isle of Wight County, VA	32,293	8.6%	28.9%
Currituck County, NC	22,279	22.5%	62.2%
Williamsburg city, VA	12,304	2.6%	7.6%
Poquoson city, VA	11,839	2.4%	7.6%
Mathews County, VA	9,430	2.4%	13.0%
Surry County, VA	6,877	0.7%	11.9%
Visalia–Porterville, CA	**397,963**	**8.1%**	**27.6%**
Tulare County, CA	397,963	8.1%	27.6%
Waco, TX	**222,521**	**4.2%**	**17.7%**
McLennan County, TX	222,521	4.2%	17.7%
Warren–Troy–Farmington Hills, MI	**2,481,882**	**3.9%**	**16.9%**
Oakland County, MI	1,213,777	1.6%	12.0%
Macomb County, MI	824,751	4.6%	15.0%
Livingston County, MI	179,324	14.3%	55.1%
St. Clair County, MI	171,413	4.4%	17.7%
Lapeer County, MI	92,617	5.4%	23.9%
Washington–Arlington–Alexandria, DC-VA-MD-WV	**4,080,798**	**10.7%**	**37.0%**
Fairfax County, VA	1,022,168	5.4%	25.0%
Prince George's County, MD	854,309	6.6%	18.0%
District of Columbia, DC	556,900	−2.6%	−8.2%

continued

TABLE 1.3 PRINCIPAL U.S. METROPOLITAN STATISTICAL AREAS (CONTINUED)

METRO AREA & INCLUDED COUNTIES	2005 POPULATION	5-YEAR GROWTH	15-YEAR GROWTH
Prince William County, VA	347,267	23.7%	61.4%
Loudoun County, VA	246,754	45.5%	185.0%
Arlington County, VA	190,768	0.7%	11.6%
Charles County, MD	138,875	15.2%	37.3%
Alexandria city, VA	134,747	5.0%	20.8%
Stafford County, VA	118,596	28.3%	93.4%
Spotsylvania County, VA	116,333	28.7%	102.6%
Calvert County, MD	88,615	18.8%	72.5%
Fauquier County, VA	63,302	14.8%	30.1%
Jefferson County, WV	48,217	14.3%	34.2%
Manassas city, VA	38,017	8.2%	37.0%
Warren County, VA	34,770	10.1%	33.0%
Fairfax city, VA	23,397	8.8%	16.6%
Fredericksburg city, VA	20,862	8.2%	9.7%
Clarke County, VA	13,697	8.3%	13.2%
Manassas Park city, VA	12,268	19.2%	63.9%
Falls Church city, VA	10,936	5.4%	19.0%
Waterloo–Cedar Falls, IA	**161,638**	**–1.3%**	**1.9%**
Black Hawk County, IA	125,904	–1.6%	1.7%
Bremer County, IA	23,391	0.3%	2.5%
Grundy County, IA	12,343	–0.2%	2.6%
Wausau, WI	**128,677**	**2.3%**	**11.5%**
Marathon County, WI	128,677	2.3%	11.5%
Weirton–Steubenville, WV-OH	**127,280**	**–3.6%**	**–10.7%**
Jefferson County, OH	71,178	–3.7%	–11.4%
Hancock County, WV	31,351	–4.0%	–11.0%
Brooke County, WV	24,751	–2.7%	–8.3%
Wenatchee, WA	**103,216**	**4.0%**	**31.6%**
Chelan County, WA	68,874	3.4%	31.8%
Douglas County, WA	34,342	5.3%	31.1%
West Palm Beach–Boca Raton–Boynton Beach, FL	**1,250,845**	**10.6%**	**44.9%**
Palm Beach County, FL	1,250,845	10.6%	44.9%
Wheeling, WV-OH	**149,366**	**–2.5%**	**–6.1%**
Belmont County, OH	69,510	–1.0%	–2.2%
Ohio County, WV	45,193	–4.7%	–11.2%
Marshall County, WV	34,663	–2.4%	–7.2%
Wichita, KS	**587,939**	**3.0%**	**15.3%**
Sedgwick County, KS	467,192	3.2%	15.7%
Butler County, KS	62,011	4.3%	22.6%
Harvey County, KS	33,793	2.8%	8.9%
Sumner County, KS	24,943	–3.9%	–3.5%
Wichita Falls, TX	**151,127**	**–0.2%**	**7.7%**
Wichita County, TX	130,478	–0.9%	6.6%
Clay County, TX	11,589	5.3%	15.6%
Archer County, TX	9,060	2.3%	13.6%
Williamsport, PA	**117,917**	**–1.8%**	**–0.7%**
Lycoming County, PA	117,917	–1.8%	–0.7%
Wilmington, DE-MD-NJ	**683,379**	**5.1%**	**18.7%**
New Castle County, DE	522,152	4.4%	18.1%
Cecil County, MD	96,027	11.7%	34.6%
Salem County, NJ	65,200	1.4%	–0.1%
Wilmington, NC	**301,847**	**10.1%**	**51.6%**
New Hanover County, NC	171,719	7.1%	42.8%
Brunswick County, NC	85,469	16.9%	67.6%
Pender County, NC	44,659	8.7%	54.8%
Winchester, VA-WV	**113,613**	**10.4%**	**36.3%**
Frederick County, VA	66,756	12.7%	46.0%
Winchester city, VA	25,177	6.8%	14.7%
Hampshire County, WV	21,680	7.3%	31.4%
Worcester, MA	**787,489**	**4.9%**	**11.0%**
Worcester County, MA	787,489	4.9%	11.0%
Yakima, WA	**229,111**	**2.9%**	**21.3%**
Yakima County, WA	229,111	2.9%	21.3%
York–Hanover, PA	**401,753**	**5.2%**	**18.3%**
York County, PA	401,753	5.2%	18.3%

METRO AREA & INCLUDED COUNTIES	2005 POPULATION	5-YEAR GROWTH	15-YEAR GROWTH
Youngstown–Warren–Boardman, OH-PA	**589,541**	**–2.2%**	**–3.9%**
Mahoning County, OH	249,517	–3.1%	–5.8%
Trumbull County, OH	220,130	–2.2%	–3.4%
Mercer County, PA	119,894	–0.3%	–0.9%
Yuba City, CA	**150,706**	**8.3%**	**24.0%**
Sutter County, CA	86,381	9.4%	34.1%
Yuba County, CA	64,325	6.8%	10.5%
Yuma, AZ	**177,838**	**11.1%**	**66.4%**
Yuma County, AZ	177,838	11.1%	66.4%

Source: U.S. Census Bureau

TABLE 1.4 CANADIAN CENSUS METROPOLITAN AREAS			
2001 DESIGNATION			
CMA	2001 POPULATION	1996 POPULATION	CHANGE	PERCENTAGE CHANGE
---	---	---	---	---
Abbotsford, British Columbia	147,370	136,480	10,890	8.0%
Calgary, Alberta	951,395	821,628	129,767	15.8%
Saguenay, Québec	154,938	160,454	(5,516)	–3.4%
Edmonton, Alberta	937,845	862,597	75,248	8.7%
Halifax, Nova Scotia	359,183	342,966	16,217	4.7%
Hamgilton, Ontario	662,401	624,360	38,041	6.1%
Kingston, Ontario	146,838	144,528	2,310	1.6%
Kitchener–Waterloo, Ontario	414,284	382,940	31,344	8.2%
London, Ontario	432,451	416,546	15,905	3.8%
Montréal, Québec	3,426,350	3,326,447	99,903	3.0%
Oshawa, Ontario	296,298	268,773	27,525	10.2%
Ottawa–Gatineau, Ontario-Québec	1,063,664	998,718	64,946	6.5%
Québec City, Québec	682,757	671,889	10,868	1.6%
Regina, Saskatchewan	192,800	193,652	(852)	–0.4%
St. Catharines–Niagara, Ontario	377,009	372,406	4,603	1.2%
Saint John, New Brunswick	122,678	125,705	(3,027)	–2.4%
St. John's, Newfoundland and Labrador	172,918	174,051	(1,133)	–0.7%
Saskatoon, Saskatchewan	225,927	219,056	6,871	3.1%
Sherbrooke, Québec	153,811	149,569	4,242	2.8%
Sudbury, Ontario	155,601	165,618	(10,017)	–6.0%
Thunder Bay, Ontario	121,986	126,643	(4,657)	–3.7%
Toronto, Ontario	4,682,897	4,263,759	419,138	9.8%
Trois-Rivières, Québec	137,507	139,956	(2,449)	–1.7%
Vancouver, British Columbia	1,986,965	1,831,665	155,300	8.5%
Victoria, British Columbia	311,902	304,827	7,075	2.3%
Windsor, Ontario	307,877	286,811	21,066	7.3%
Winnipeg, Manitoba	671,274	667,093	4,181	0.6%

Source: Statistics Canada; *Canadian Global Almanac 2004*

chapter

The Rankings

I n chapter 5, *Cities Ranked & Rated*, 2nd Edition, we show scores and ranks for each of 373 U.S. metropolitan areas, or MSAs (as defined in chapter 1), and rank them in sequence from no. 1 (best) through no. 373 (worst).

Note: You may recall from chapter 1 that we defined 375 metro areas for evaluation and analysis. For scoring and ranking purposes, we decided to exclude New Orleans, LA, and Biloxi–Gulfport–Pascagoula, MS, due to the extreme effects and dislocations of the Hurricane Katrina disaster in 2005. These areas will no doubt change dramatically as they rebuild. Also, we couldn't be sure how much of or how well our fact base incorporated these issues. For that reason, the scoring and ranking might be misleading. So in chapter 5, we describe current and future prospects for these places, but do not show a data table, nor scores and ranks for these areas.

Rankings are based on an overall composite score, which is in turn based on scores developed from nine sets, or *categories,* of factual attributes and one subjective appraisal. Raw facts, or data, are grouped into a category score for such categories as Cost of Living and Arts & Culture. Then all categories are weighted according to the expected needs and interests of the typical individual citizen and family and blended into an area's overall score.

For the rankings of all 373 metropolitan areas, refer to Tables 2.4 and 2.5 at the end of this chapter. For just the highest and lowest ranked cities, see Tables 2.1 and 2.2 below.

About the *Cities Ranked & Rated* Model

As mentioned above, the *Cities Ranked & Rated* model produces a score and rank for each of the nine factual categories and a composite score and rank for the metropolitan area derived from those figures. At its core, the *Cities Ranked & Rated* scoring and ranking model is an adjustable points-based model. It awards points for good things and more points for better things; it awards fewer points or may even deduct points for bad things. The model weighs specific data and entire categories according to how much influence they are believed to have on the everyday life and long-term goals of a typical citizen or family. It also examines the *consistency* of scoring across the nine factual categories and the single subjective category, Quality of Life, and makes adjustments described shortly.

The model and factors used in *Cities Ranked & Rated,* 2nd Edition, is substantially unchanged from the first edition.

Category Point Scoring

Points are assigned to specific attributes within each of nine factual ranking categories. Once a point value is calculated,

the result is weighed by importance and accumulated inside the category. For example, points are assigned for having relatively few days with temperatures below 0°F. Points are also assigned for having relatively few thunderstorms. But since bitter cold weather is less desirable for most people than the occasional occurrence of thunderstorms, the "0°F" factor gets more weight, and consequently more points are assigned for a good score.

Points are calculated and assigned for each of the following categories:

1. Economy & Jobs
2. Cost of Living
3. Climate
4. Education
5. Health & Healthcare
6. Crime
7. Transportation
8. Leisure
9. Arts & Culture

TABLE 2.1 THE TOP 30 U.S. METROPOLITAN AREAS			
RANK	SCORE	METROPOLITAN AREA	STATE
1	100.0	Gainesville	FL
2	95.1	Bellingham	WA
3	95.0	Portland–Vancouver–Beaverton	OR-WA
4	93.9	Colorado Springs	CO
5	93.2	Ann Arbor	MI
6	92.8	Ogden–Clearfield	UT
7	90.5	Asheville	NC
8	89.8	Fort Collins–Loveland	CO
9	89.8	San Luis Obispo–Paso Robles	CA
10	89.6	Boise City–Nampa	ID
11	89.6	Santa Barbara–Santa Maria	CA
12	88.9	Logan	UT-ID
13	88.5	Provo–Orem	UT
14	87.3	Corvallis	OR
15	87.2	Durham	NC
16	86.8	Olympia	WA
17	86.8	Charlottesville	VA
18	85.7	Flagstaff	AZ
19	85.4	Indianapolis–Carmel	IN
20	85.3	Santa Fe	NM
21	85.1	Dover	DE
22	85.1	Oxnard–Thousand Oaks–Ventura	CA
23	84.8	Sebastian–Vero Beach	FL
24	84.3	Lexington–Fayette	KY
25	84.3	Lafayette	IN
26	84.2	Napa	CA
27	84.1	Salt Lake City	UT
28	84.0	Rockingham County–Strafford County	NH
29	83.8	Athens–Clarke County	GA
30	83.5	Richmond	VA

TABLE 2.2 THE BOTTOM 30 U.S. METROPOLITAN AREAS			
RANK	SCORE	METROPOLITAN AREA	STATE
344	23.8	Detroit–Livonia–Dearborn	MI
345	23.8	Morristown	TN
346	23.8	St. Joseph	MO-KS
347	23.8	Decatur	AL
348	23.8	Lake Charles	LA
349	23.8	Hattiesburg	MS
350	23.8	Stockton	CA
351	23.8	Houma–Bayou Cane–Thibodaux	LA
352	23.8	Dothan	AL
353	23.8	Rocky Mount	NC
354	23.8	Danville	IL
355	23.8	Jackson	TN
356	23.8	Victoria	TX
357	23.8	Florence–Muscle Shoals	AL
358	23.8	Weirton–Steubenville	WV-OH
359	23.8	Florence	SC
360	23.8	Elmira	NY
361	23.8	Pine Bluff	AR
362	23.8	Hanford–Corcoran	CA
363	14.4	Sumter	SC
364	14.2	Anniston–Oxford	AL
365	13.6	El Centro	CA
366	13.3	Alexandria	LA
367	12.7	Lafayette	LA
368	12.5	Farmington	NM
369	12.4	Monroe	LA
370	11.7	Merced	CA
371	10.9	Yuba City	CA
372	3.6	Visalia–Porterville	CA
373	0.0	Modesto	CA

The 10th category, Quality of Life (QOL), is subjective and considers physical setting, downtown core, overall appearance, heritage, and general livability.

Scoring Model Results

Once the data is "crunched" inside each category, a point score is accumulated for each of the nine factual categories and for the subjective Quality of Life rating for a total of 10 category scores for each metropolitan area. Each point total is converted to a 0–100 percentile scale to allow for easier comparison. The 10 category scores are then accumulated to reach the area's composite total score, which is also converted to a 0–100 scale. This is the score that is shown in the header of each metro area in chapter 5. That score is then used to determine the overall ranking for the metropolitan area, also shown in the MSA's header.

The model allows different category weightings. *Cities Ranked & Rated* weighs Cost of Living, Economy & Jobs, and Quality of Life slightly more than the other categories. This decision was based on the notion that these attributes have the most profound effect on daily life and long-term goals. Within the categories, we placed a slightly greater weight on attributes such as future job growth and healthcare cost. The weightings have been set to reflect, in our judgment, what is most important to the typical citizen or family.

Obviously, readers desire different lifestyles with different interests and means. Simulating results tailored to individual preferences can be done on the "Find Your Best Place" page on Sperling's BestPlaces website (www.bestplaces.net/fybp). While the model on the website isn't as comprehensive as this book, nor does it rank all 373 metropolitan areas side by side, it does provide some insight into how individual needs, interests, and tastes can be met.

Consistency Adjustment

In the *Cities Ranked & Rated* category scores, some individual cities excel in certain categories but score very poorly in others, while other cities sort of plod along, not being "best in class" in anything but being good overall. An example of the former is New York, which consistently rates at the top of the list in the categories of Arts & Culture, Education, and Leisure—but scores very low for Cost of Living and Economy & Jobs. Similarly, California cities score high for Climate, Leisure, and Arts & Culture,

				CATEGORY RANKINGS (0-100 SCALE)									
RANK	SCORE	METROPOLITAN AREA	STATE	ECONOMY & JOBS	COST OF LIVING	CLIMATE	EDUCATION	HEALTH & HEALTHCARE	CRIME	TRANSPORTATION	LEISURE	ARTS & CULTURE	QUALITY OF LIFE
71	73.4	Manchester–Nashua	NH	72	75	6	76	33	81	55	79	72	87
290	44.2	Mansfield	OH	12	66	20	9	76	66	82	15	48	39
342	23.8	McAllen–Edinburg–Mission	TX	93	88	78	0	12	28	19	14	30	2
34	82.3	Medford	OR	63	54	58	45	20	72	42	25	20	56
278	45.6	Memphis	TN-MS-AR	17	84	47	42	39	2	18	72	70	39
370	11.7	Merced	CA	2	9	92	2	8	21	64	45	2	17
250	49.0	Miami–Miami Beach–Kendall	FL	63	10	80	29	9	1	44	96	90	56

TABLE 2.3 RANKING REPORT SAMPLE

but fail miserably on Cost of Living and Transportation. Small Texas towns flourish on Cost of Living, but flounder on Arts & Culture and sometimes Education. Adjusting category weights, as was done with the individual data, doesn't work in these cases because such an adjustment would bias the model result across the board instead of penalizing or rewarding individual cities that excel or fall well below average.

To address this issue, a *consistency* factor is added to the determination of overall score. A city scoring consistently high—above the 60th percentile—in seven of nine data categories receives a bonus, while a city with a particularly poor individual category score—below the 20th percentile—receives a penalty against its total composite score. Therefore, a city like Los Angeles with mostly good scores but a few really poor ones will receive a penalty, just as in real life where the high cost of living or a 1-hour commute might taint an otherwise stellar appraisal of a place. Note that with this approach, one city can receive both a bonus and a penalty. When this happens, they cancel one another, either partially or completely.

Reading the Ranking Report

Tables 2.4 and 2.5 show the overall and category rankings for the 373 U.S. metropolitan areas included in chapter 5. To better understand how to read these tables, which are organized by rank and alphabetically, refer to Table 2.3, which includes seven cities from Table 2.5.

What follows is a rundown of the data in Table 2.3, reading from left to right.

- *Rank* is the position among the principal U.S. metropolitan areas. Manchester–Nashua, NH, the first city in the sample, ranks 71st out of 373 areas overall.

- *Score* is a composite of scores, on a 0–100 scale, from the 10 ranking categories, which are weighed according to importance and adjusted by the consistency factor. Manchester–Nashua scores 73.4 out of a possible 100; that is the basis for the ranking of 71.

- *Metropolitan Area* and *State* give the complete name of the Metropolitan Statistical Area (MSA) and the state or states in which it is located.

- *Category Rankings* show scores in the 10 individual ranking categories on a scale of 0–100.

Manchester–Nashua provides a good illustration of scoring and the concept of consistency. This area has seven categories—Economy & Jobs, Cost of Living, Education, Crime, Leisure, Arts & Culture, and Quality of Life—scoring at 60 or above on the 0–100 scale. As a result, it received a consistency bonus. However, the score for Climate (6) is below 20, so it also received a penalty. These adjustments largely cancel out, and the area retains a favorable score of 73.4 and rank of 71 among the 373 metropolitan areas. This composite score reflects the weighting of individual categories and consistency adjustments. Had it not been for the climate factor, Manchester–Nashua would have scored and ranked higher, and had it not been for the consistency factor, it would have scored and ranked lower.

Ranking Changes since 2004

Those familiar with the first edition of *Cities Ranked & Rated* are probably curious as to how the rankings changed from that edition. Like most things in life, some things change and some things stay the same, and the things that changed naturally had some effect on the ranking.

The majority of metro areas retained a similar ranking position to last time; areas ranked in the bottom 10%

tended to stay there; areas ranked in the middle tended to stay close to the middle. Some ranks, particularly in the lower half of the list, may appear lower than last time simply because there are more places on the list; the bottom of the list last time occurred at 331 while this time it is at 373.

New Boundaries

Some area ranks changed because of redefined boundaries rather than a pure improvement or deterioration of factors. This is particularly likely in larger cities, such as Boston, which are divided into new metro areas based on Metropolitan Divisions (see chapter 1 for an explanation of this new designation). Also, in New England, metro areas were redrawn according to county instead of township lines. So for example, Lawrence, MA-NH, which ranked 326 in the first edition, is now reconfigured as Essex County, MA, picking up nicer Cape May shoreline areas, and is now ranked 253. Area splits, such as Napa, CA, and Vallejo–Fairfield, CA, also resulted in large ranking shifts, in this case with the dramatic rise of Napa to 26 and fall of Vallejo–Fairfield to 320 from their previous combined rank of 78. Likewise, the relatively posh shoreline area of Lake County–Kenosha County, IL-WI, was split from the Chicago area, giving a rank of 41 for the former and dropping the rank of the big city (there were other factors too) to 258 from 155 in the first edition.

Winners & Losers

We saw a few smaller places shed the effects of "penalty" categories. Flagstaff, AZ, was our top-ranking gainer, shedding poor economy, arts, and healthcare scores to achieve a rank of 18, up from 244. Allentown–Bethlehem–Easton, PA made a similar transition to reach 39 from 202. On the downside we saw a number of larger cities get a bigger hit from the "3 Cs" (crime, cost of living, and commute), such as Minneapolis–St. Paul–Bloomington, MN-WI, dropping from 28 to 262 (also affected by climate, a fourth "C") and New York City (New York–White Plains, NY) dropping from 40 to 251. We saw widespread deterioration in these attributes for large cities; most did not fare as well in this edition, the notable exception being the Portland–Vancouver–Beaverton, OR-WA, area.

While these ranking declines are severe, they should be taken with a grain of salt, as most likely they just crossed one or more penalty thresholds. These places generally haven't become that much worse in reality, particularly for those more tolerant of the cost, commute, and crime issues.

Cost continued to hurt smaller areas in California and other parts of the West, particularly when combined with crime, economic issues, and low educational attainment. In fact, a number of smaller cities and towns, such as Fresno and Yuba City, CA, and Longview and Tyler, TX, as well as some more northerly areas such as La Crosse, WI-MN, continue to suffer from the "4 Es" that hurt many such small towns—economy, educational attainment, entertainment, and ethnic diversity. The California places suffer further because of the high costs; many especially in the Central Valley region are found near the bottom of our list.

College towns were strong in the last edition, and proved stronger in this one. Eight of the top 20 rankings are college towns, including Gainesville, FL, the highest ranked area overall. Most of these areas show strength in a majority of ranking categories, gaining still more through consistency adjustments. While the cost of living/housing in these areas is often a deterrent, it has risen more slowly than in many coastal and large city areas, helping such college towns rank more favorably.

TABLE 2.4 U.S. METROPOLITAN AREAS BY RANK

RANK	SCORE	METROPOLITAN AREA	STATE	ECONOMY & JOBS	COST OF LIVING	CLIMATE	EDUCATION	HEALTH & HEALTHCARE	CRIME	TRANSPORTATION	LEISURE	ARTS & CULTURE	QUALITY OF LIFE
1	100.0	Gainesville	FL	83	80	84	93	70	32	29	44	66	87
2	95.1	Bellingham	WA	97	59	82	64	27	37	72	66	59	96
3	95.0	Portland–Vancouver–Beaverton	OR-WA	75	22	78	92	22	60	32	87	89	96
4	93.9	Colorado Springs	CO	63	36	91	94	36	35	64	69	73	56
5	93.2	Ann Arbor	MI	74	32	38	97	86	66	63	81	78	91
6	92.8	Ogden–Clearfield	UT	92	33	29	71	71	93	41	89	79	91
7	90.5	Asheville	NC	32	45	66	61	83	86	57	43	55	96
8	89.8	Fort Collins–Loveland	CO	75	33	54	93	47	88	65	75	37	98
9	89.8	San Luis Obispo–Paso Robles	CA	44	4	98	74	37	91	25	75	70	98
10	89.6	Boise City–Nampa	ID	98	32	58	68	32	44	22	54	62	96
11	89.6	Santa Barbara–Santa Maria	CA	56	4	98	69	40	75	43	77	66	98
12	88.9	Logan	UT-ID	96	51	64	82	84	99	83	44	20	83
13	88.5	Provo–Orem	UT	97	47	55	90	61	69	64	78	52	87
14	87.3	Corvallis	OR	42	57	67	96	48	76	84	39	28	72
15	87.2	Durham	NC	58	28	63	90	94	22	38	66	84	73
16	86.8	Olympia	WA	94	54	44	80	31	63	30	82	55	93
17	86.8	Charlottesville	VA	66	19	71	82	99	91	80	40	64	98
18	85.7	Flagstaff	AZ	66	60	63	73	25	27	54	57	43	83
19	85.4	Indianapolis–Carmel	IN	59	74	48	73	23	45	65	74	89	73
20	85.3	Santa Fe	NM	84	14	94	75	26	24	23	55	59	98
21	85.1	Dover	DE	85	82	60	21	40	43	91	55	21	73
22	85.1	Oxnard–Thousand Oaks–Ventura	CA	52	1	97	57	28	89	88	91	71	73
23	84.8	Sebastian–Vero Beach	FL	46	58	66	37	62	38	78	29	23	73
24	84.3	Lexington–Fayette	KY	68	37	37	79	88	41	85	30	75	87
25	84.3	Lafayette	IN	35	95	48	68	54	82	74	42	51	73
26	84.2	Napa	CA	24	3	95	49	77	65	82	94	60	93
27	84.1	Salt Lake City	UT	91	26	29	74	58	20	32	90	82	87
28	84.0	Rockingham County–Strafford County	NH	81	62	29	83	26	95	35	92	94	56
29	83.8	Athens–Clarke County	GA	57	38	52	64	79	29	88	34	57	73
30	83.5	Richmond	VA	92	46	35	69	79	28	67	62	83	73
31	83.0	Greensboro–Winston-Salem–High Point	NC	67	42	59	56	53	45	76	62	69	38
32	82.5	Iowa City	IA	89	49	23	96	99	86	61	22	59	73
33	82.4	Columbus	IN	56	85	43	35	82	82	93	73	78	39
34	82.3	Medford	OR	63	54	58	45	20	72	42	25	20	56
35	82.1	St. Louis	MO-IL	32	32	36	85	28	45	24	85	96	56
36	81.9	Columbus	OH	53	27	41	86	32	35	26	73	91	56
37	81.7	Spokane	WA	70	66	28	80	35	47	36	56	47	87
38	81.6	Cincinnati–Middletown	OH-KY-IN	45	35	33	63	24	31	67	78	90	70
39	81.1	Allentown–Bethlehem–Easton	PA-NJ	47	21	32	63	39	54	93	67	77	70
40	80.8	Fargo	ND-MN	65	79	35	88	65	95	62	24	49	55
41	80.8	Lake County–Kenosha County	IL-WI	94	22	25	83	20	55	79	94	95	39
42	80.5	Wilmington	DE-MD-NJ	71	53	64	50	21	62	100	81	86	39
43	80.0	Wichita	KS	20	59	58	53	39	24	34	35	67	39
44	79.7	Louisville–Jefferson County	KY-IN	36	41	45	34	21	79	66	65	71	39
45	79.7	Ocean City	NJ	19	25	93	46	37	40	47	84	85	56
46	79.7	Des Moines–West Des Moines	IA	76	25	22	84	49	61	37	40	69	73
47	79.7	Winchester	VA-WV	95	50	68	20	91	97	58	83	90	93
48	79.5	Spartanburg	SC	54	72	50	28	24	28	56	36	60	39
49	79.5	State College	PA	33	77	40	86	88	98	48	30	44	73
50	79.0	Evansville	IN-KY	30	96	36	32	54	82	39	30	63	39
51	78.9	San Antonio	TX	87	83	89	50	27	12	22	69	68	70
52	78.5	Naples–Marco Island	FL	97	7	83	57	29	65	76	74	24	93
53	78.3	South Bend–Mishawaka	IN-MI	60	95	24	41	49	55	95	47	64	39
54	78.2	Atlanta–Sandy Springs–Marietta	GA	86	28	74	94	36	30	11	94	91	83
55	78.0	Abilene	TX	93	92	90	41	93	59	54	18	39	37
56	77.6	Bend	OR	94	40	66	66	25	84	47	63	8	98
57	77.1	Atlantic City	NJ	38	18	85	35	41	40	99	84	80	56

continued

TABLE 2.4 U.S. METROPOLITAN AREAS BY RANK (CONTINUED)

RANK	SCORE	METROPOLITAN AREA	STATE	ECONOMY & JOBS	COST OF LIVING	CLIMATE	EDUCATION	HEALTH & HEALTHCARE	CRIME	TRANSPORTATION	LEISURE	ARTS & CULTURE	QUALITY OF LIFE
58	77.0	San Jose–Sunnyvale–Santa Clara	CA	37	0	97	88	0	89	68	93	84	73
59	76.8	Santa Ana–Anaheim–Irvine	CA	67	0	98	79	16	86	83	98	79	56
60	76.8	Roanoke	VA	69	49	76	47	98	67	19	33	50	87
61	76.2	Coeur d'Alene	ID	99	29	65	47	22	71	26	65	5	93
62	76.1	Boulder	CO	57	9	54	98	45	80	81	85	71	96
63	75.9	Raleigh–Cary	NC	86	23	63	91	33	74	5	67	84	87
64	75.4	Reno–Sparks	NV	42	16	85	55	29	51	57	79	56	56
65	75.3	Punta Gorda	FL	96	56	83	26	52	68	38	45	2	56
66	75.1	Grand Junction	CO	30	52	71	51	92	58	44	51	16	87
67	75.0	Palm Bay–Melbourne–Titusville	FL	91	87	77	62	5	22	24	66	31	73
68	73.7	Eugene–Springfield	OR	39	51	65	68	7	65	70	67	49	83
69	73.5	Lewiston	ID-WA	65	49	70	49	86	85	78	33	18	56
70	73.4	Bethesda–Gaithersburg–Frederick	MD	68	5	41	93	44	86	49	92	96	91
71	73.4	Manchester–Nashua	NH	72	75	6	76	33	81	55	79	72	87
72	73.3	St. George	UT	100	37	55	54	82	100	56	32	3	69
73	72.8	San Francisco–San Mateo–Redwood City	CA	27	0	99	91	3	36	87	98	97	91
74	72.5	Pittsburgh	PA	17	48	27	91	30	84	33	83	95	87
75	72.3	Deltona–Daytona Beach–Ormond Beach	FL	85	68	78	38	2	37	28	63	41	39
76	72.3	Pueblo	CO	14	58	68	42	87	27	28	40	67	56
77	71.9	Bergen–Passaic	NJ	48	5	45	58	22	78	91	88	86	83
78	71.9	Madison	WI	31	18	20	95	65	94	59	50	58	98
79	71.8	Fayetteville–Springdale–Rogers	AR-MO	98	31	53	23	61	77	40	21	14	73
80	71.8	Greeley	CO	79	84	54	54	9	21	43	78	46	73
81	71.6	Trenton–Ewing	NJ	61	13	59	78	36	39	97	84	88	56
82	71.3	Salem	OR	32	48	67	45	19	25	31	65	38	56
83	71.1	San Diego–Carlsbad–San Marcos	CA	58	1	96	85	5	59	48	95	87	93
84	71.0	Dayton	OH	13	34	46	63	40	52	89	54	91	56
85	70.9	Charlotte–Gastonia–Concord	NC-SC	92	24	43	73	27	6	23	60	85	73
86	70.5	Bloomington	IN	5	76	49	65	38	86	51	50	49	70
87	70.5	Springfield	OH	15	35	46	28	48	63	86	51	87	56
88	70.3	Missoula	MT	78	79	18	81	73	55	58	45	25	93
89	70.3	Honolulu	HI	71	1	98	67	24	38	9	67	87	83
90	70.2	Nassau–Suffolk	NY	29	2	77	94	4	96	92	98	92	83
91	70.1	Savannah	GA	64	39	60	29	51	23	5	59	54	55
92	69.9	Prescott	AZ	86	21	97	49	18	79	61	20	12	83
93	69.8	Los Angeles–Long Beach–Glendale	CA	28	2	97	98	15	39	78	100	97	38
94	69.6	Greenville	SC	83	58	50	53	50	10	55	37	54	56
95	69.6	Hagerstown–Martinsburg	MD-WV	54	30	43	9	66	91	69	85	78	39
96	69.5	Lancaster	PA	51	63	32	21	12	83	98	53	21	73
97	69.2	Oakland–Fremont–Hayward	CA	45	1	99	90	0	35	30	96	89	39
98	69.1	Jackson	MS	25	70	51	55	76	51	3	20	74	39
99	69.1	Knoxville	TN	22	88	36	70	57	45	8	76	70	56
100	68.9	Lawrence	KS	44	37	31	95	30	43	57	16	50	73
101	68.8	Champaign–Urbana	IL	35	60	39	89	54	15	62	21	72	56
102	68.8	Appleton	WI	62	44	12	59	62	98	70	63	31	87
103	68.5	Austin–Round Rock	TX	97	62	88	92	33	11	12	50	75	96
104	68.4	Augusta–Richmond County	GA-SC	48	55	53	37	80	53	4	29	32	39
105	68.4	Harrisonburg	VA	90	37	17	36	74	58	81	24	28	87
106	68.4	Riverside–San Bernardino–Ontario	CA	79	6	96	25	6	31	72	97	86	56
107	68.3	Harrisburg–Carlisle	PA	55	74	33	58	76	93	98	71	64	17
108	68.0	Santa Rosa–Petaluma	CA	29	2	95	70	0	68	68	87	61	93
109	67.9	Cheyenne	WY	55	98	40	78	21	58	92	0	33	38
110	67.9	Columbia	SC	57	61	34	66	48	12	42	58	59	56
111	67.9	Greenville	NC	52	42	52	50	74	26	45	17	22	39

continued

RANK	SCORE	METROPOLITAN AREA	STATE	ECONOMY & JOBS	COST OF LIVING	CLIMATE	EDUCATION	HEALTH & HEALTHCARE	CRIME	TRANSPORTATION	LEISURE	ARTS & CULTURE	QUALITY OF LIFE
				CATEGORY SCORES (0-100 SCALE)									
112	67.8	Casper	WY	50	99	38	68	56	66	62	5	21	39
113	67.5	Grand Forks	ND-MN	22	82	35	72	97	54	73	15	41	39
114	67.5	Bismarck	ND	75	74	21	83	98	90	63	31	10	56
115	67.5	Columbia	MO	63	41	20	91	98	49	44	13	65	56
116	67.4	Macon–Warner Robins	GA	41	50	50	24	84	44	82	25	49	17
117	67.2	Fort Wayne	IN	53	87	41	43	46	59	32	38	76	17
118	67.2	Reading	PA	55	53	32	24	19	70	94	52	48	39
119	67.1	Bowling Green	KY	54	71	28	31	95	57	60	27	9	56
120	67.0	Toledo	OH	22	33	39	44	43	33	93	68	83	17
121	67.0	Sheboygan	WI	25	43	14	32	59	91	84	53	51	73
122	67.0	Tallahassee	FL	75	81	61	83	62	27	2	45	74	39
123	66.7	Mount Vernon–Anacortes	WA	87	47	91	51	50	20	27	14	6	93
124	66.6	Bloomington–Normal	IL	73	45	37	87	51	55	59	26	54	17
125	66.6	Peoria	IL	77	68	39	44	63	60	27	42	60	17
126	66.6	Waterloo–Cedar Falls	IA	51	43	28	58	91	75	69	17	55	39
127	66.5	Omaha–Council Bluffs	NE-IA	69	26	14	77	58	44	48	64	77	56
128	66.4	Auburn–Opelika	AL	39	63	23	70	47	50	91	38	8	56
129	66.3	Seattle–Bellevue–Everett	WA	80	14	81	95	11	47	24	99	88	91
130	66.2	Washington–Arlington–Alexandria	DC-VA-MD-WV	88	5	42	98	25	25	50	95	96	87
131	66.0	Rochester	MN	78	27	9	85	100	62	88	62	35	69
132	65.9	Dallas–Plano–Irving	TX	87	61	87	86	13	8	53	90	93	70
133	65.8	Fort Worth–Arlington	TX	91	72	87	62	14	17	57	80	81	73
134	65.6	Great Falls	MT	72	86	11	56	87	35	66	47	33	56
135	65.6	Cedar Rapids	IA	60	46	14	82	63	52	39	22	47	56
136	65.5	Fond du Lac	WI	34	50	26	33	78	96	66	25	5	39
137	65.4	Virginia Beach–Norfolk–Newport News	VA-NC	62	31	62	66	66	40	10	82	85	56
138	65.3	Billings	MT	70	78	6	70	72	74	51	34	36	73
139	65.3	Lincoln	NE	78	29	10	86	54	32	64	35	70	56
140	65.2	Holland–Grand Haven	MI	74	54	8	60	34	92	67	69	81	39
141	65.0	Redding	CA	58	16	96	38	28	68	28	51	27	2
142	64.7	Oshkosh–Neenah	WI	50	43	12	48	73	85	75	63	38	39
143	64.6	St. Cloud	MN	39	35	12	56	75	86	71	50	45	39
144	64.3	Tulsa	OK	59	32	79	59	31	11	21	60	57	39
145	63.8	Albuquerque	NM	74	29	85	62	22	3	14	71	76	83
146	63.6	Muskegon–Norton Shores	MI	51	48	7	31	49	41	54	68	80	39
147	63.4	Niles–Benton Harbor	MI	28	74	25	39	68	36	97	39	25	2
148	63.3	Bremerton–Silverdale	WA	89	44	81	75	16	51	4	83	25	73
149	63.2	Sarasota–Bradenton–Venice	FL	95	16	83	56	13	27	50	55	43	83
150	63.1	Denver–Aurora	CO	56	15	54	94	18	42	32	93	95	93
151	62.9	Las Cruces	NM	83	57	92	26	13	60	25	21	44	17
152	62.8	San Angelo	TX	70	95	93	35	94	28	51	18	32	2
153	62.8	Philadelphia	PA	24	12	64	97	12	48	99	94	98	70
154	62.5	Las Vegas–Paradise	NV	98	24	79	36	6	14	31	80	69	56
155	62.3	Orlando–Kissimmee	FL	96	40	83	74	5	18	27	85	68	39
156	62.3	Lakeland	FL	81	86	79	13	2	33	47	58	45	73
157	62.1	Rapid City	SD	80	90	4	66	68	69	52	44	26	39
158	61.8	Fort Lauderdale–Pompano Beach–Deerfield Beach	FL	83	11	80	50	8	36	59	82	67	56
159	61.5	Vineland–Millville–Bridgeton	NJ	20	24	85	2	45	14	80	74	63	39
160	61.4	Boston–Quincy	MA	9	10	30	99	29	46	68	98	100	91
161	61.4	Edison	NJ	55	6	59	89	7	95	90	92	79	73
162	61.4	Ocala	FL	90	94	84	7	10	41	60	47	20	39
163	61.3	Camden	NJ	72	9	64	60	14	64	98	93	98	39
164	61.3	New Haven–Milford	CT	5	8	75	69	31	79	98	91	83	39
165	61.2	El Paso	TX	67	73	88	5	42	29	20	27	52	15
166	61.1	Cambridge–Newton–Framingham	MA	30	18	30	99	8	83	70	97	99	83
167	61.1	Sherman–Denison	TX	89	94	87	45	69	40	74	34	4	2
168	61.0	Lubbock	TX	49	87	86	51	88	4	60	27	26	17

continued

TABLE 2.4 U.S. METROPOLITAN AREAS BY RANK (CONTINUED)

RANK	SCORE	METROPOLITAN AREA	STATE	ECONOMY & JOBS	COST OF LIVING	CLIMATE	EDUCATION	HEALTH & HEALTHCARE	CRIME	TRANSPORTATION	LEISURE	ARTS & CULTURE	QUALITY OF LIFE
169	60.9	Amarillo	TX	72	91	86	39	83	6	45	35	29	15
170	60.7	Tuscaloosa	AL	88	62	19	33	68	56	12	22	44	39
171	60.6	Barnstable Town	MA	21	7	67	96	16	71	50	63	63	72
172	60.5	Corpus Christi	TX	37	81	86	23	56	3	26	52	32	17
173	60.5	Baltimore–Towson	MD	48	17	42	87	51	14	90	95	95	73
174	60.4	Charleston–North Charleston	SC	81	34	57	55	42	10	6	79	66	83
175	60.4	College Station–Bryan	TX	79	93	69	79	74	19	94	12	27	39
176	60.3	Port St. Lucie–Fort Pierce	FL	91	35	66	30	29	64	16	41	19	73
177	59.8	Anderson	IN	19	87	48	15	47	72	73	71	91	56
178	59.6	Carson City	NV	20	19	72	35	75	61	63	43	4	56
179	59.4	Lynchburg	VA	64	68	71	36	97	81	13	29	35	17
180	59.2	Newark–Union	NJ-PA	24	4	58	85	17	53	94	90	93	39
181	59.2	Blacksburg–Christiansburg–Radford	VA	17	25	57	75	96	99	35	28	12	56
182	59.0	Pensacola–Ferry Pass–Brent	FL	82	92	70	48	23	47	2	69	30	17
183	58.7	Sacramento–Arden-Arcade–Roseville	CA	68	6	94	77	1	13	79	91	75	70
184	58.6	Gainesville	GA	90	29	57	8	48	57	55	81	78	17
185	58.6	Oklahoma City	OK	66	36	72	64	26	9	20	61	62	17
186	58.5	Brunswick	GA	68	82	68	30	79	8	20	27	14	39
187	58.3	Kingsport–Bristol–Bristol	TN-VA	5	99	56	20	80	73	6	44	43	39
188	58.2	Lebanon	PA	33	82	56	12	60	68	85	70	65	17
189	57.8	Ames	IA	65	31	18	98	85	93	76	12	42	83
190	57.8	Warren–Troy–Farmington Hills	MI	41	20	38	76	15	75	10	91	92	39
191	57.8	Johnson City	TN	20	97	56	23	99	69	17	43	39	17
192	57.7	Lawton	OK	52	56	77	44	43	12	72	25	23	2
193	57.6	Wilmington	NC	76	28	52	63	64	30	9	37	29	2
194	57.6	Kokomo	IN	99	93	48	34	80	48	72	9	35	17
195	57.6	Hickory–Lenoir–Morganton	NC	27	60	59	8	73	37	66	29	16	39
196	57.6	Little Rock–North Little Rock	AR	69	47	43	45	85	5	6	47	73	56
197	57.4	Ithaca	NY	39	10	9	99	72	99	74	48	42	93
198	57.1	West Palm Beach–Boca Raton–Boynton Beach	FL	86	9	65	59	7	20	74	83	73	73
199	57.1	Kansas City	MO-KS	41	26	18	87	35	11	22	77	92	73
200	57.1	Montgomery	AL	52	54	55	39	67	29	8	35	72	17
201	56.9	York–Hanover	PA	62	77	32	40	16	85	95	46	7	39
202	56.7	Sandusky	OH	27	69	51	32	67	70	96	2	31	17
203	56.2	Altoona	PA	12	91	40	11	90	50	79	31	36	39
204	56.2	Hinesville–Fort Stewart	GA	28	66	70	27	56	31	9	31	41	0
205	56.1	Springfield	IL	81	75	36	61	75	4	79	10	46	39
206	56.0	Wheeling	WV-OH	25	70	27	9	94	84	46	37	57	17
207	56.0	Kennewick–Richland–Pasco	WA	78	78	33	52	45	83	15	26	18	39
208	56.0	Bridgeport–Stamford–Norwalk	CT	10	4	76	87	1	89	94	89	88	73
209	56.0	Michigan City–La Porte	IN	23	94	24	10	70	56	93	82	81	17
210	55.9	Decatur	IL	59	96	37	16	61	34	46	9	29	39
211	55.9	Huntsville	AL	75	50	16	72	24	51	37	16	37	73
212	55.9	Tucson	AZ	44	20	95	65	89	9	11	77	74	70
213	55.9	Grand Rapids–Wyoming	MI	61	53	7	48	45	67	17	71	83	73
214	55.8	Columbus	GA-AL	9	51	47	27	85	34	89	23	38	17
215	55.8	Sioux Falls	SD	87	90	16	67	93	76	52	17	48	39
216	55.6	Santa Cruz–Watsonville	CA	18	2	99	77	1	43	38	89	75	87
217	55.6	Johnstown	PA	23	90	40	8	85	78	58	49	34	17
218	55.5	Springfield	MO	59	78	31	57	77	71	14	23	61	17
219	55.4	Chattanooga	TN-GA	22	90	21	21	82	7	4	54	72	56
220	54.8	Tampa–St. Petersburg–Clearwater	FL	84	43	82	60	6	9	39	86	67	73
221	54.8	Terre Haute	IN	8	96	49	37	71	21	37	11	44	17
222	54.7	Goldsboro	NC	12	65	61	22	66	23	41	28	21	0

continued

RANK	SCORE	METROPOLITAN AREA	STATE	ECONOMY & JOBS	COST OF LIVING	CLIMATE	EDUCATION	HEALTH & HEALTHCARE	CRIME	TRANSPORTATION	LEISURE	ARTS & CULTURE	QUALITY OF LIFE
223	54.3	Birmingham–Hoover	AL	27	38	22	46	50	19	0	49	71	39
224	54.2	Idaho Falls	ID	98	48	7	72	55	75	36	41	2	56
225	54.1	Eau Claire	WI	13	45	9	62	91	73	82	26	29	56
226	54.0	Sioux City	IA-NE-SD	40	44	25	33	70	37	69	12	48	17
227	54.0	Janesville	WI	14	40	21	41	78	77	97	28	34	17
228	53.8	Anchorage	AK	90	86	3	79	15	20	28	72	63	72
229	53.3	Duluth	MN-WI	18	46	3	71	69	77	33	74	58	73
230	53.3	Gary	IN	26	70	25	31	11	57	89	75	76	0
231	53.3	Portland–South Portland–Biddeford	ME	37	17	0	84	41	98	53	72	56	87
232	53.1	Kingston	NY	37	7	6	77	34	74	84	79	79	39
233	52.8	Davenport–Moline–Rock Island	IA-IL	35	39	14	53	59	22	34	37	61	17
234	52.6	Kalamazoo–Portage	MI	60	69	8	72	74	47	34	48	62	17
235	52.6	Albany–Schenectady–Troy	NY	36	11	2	95	42	87	36	75	85	55
236	52.5	Canton–Massillon	OH	38	71	11	28	38	25	91	32	56	17
237	52.4	Lansing–East Lansing	MI	47	56	5	81	79	66	75	56	68	17
238	52.2	Wausau	WI	21	41	13	40	65	90	48	5	24	56
239	52.2	Battle Creek	MI	29	67	8	40	87	23	87	49	55	17
240	51.9	Erie	PA	34	83	8	40	81	77	61	38	60	2
241	51.8	Pocatello	ID	93	51	1	60	94	81	59	41	8	39
242	51.2	Jackson	MI	49	74	5	33	56	61	60	32	31	17
243	51.2	Pittsfield	MA	1	22	2	76	66	94	73	53	55	39
244	50.9	Wenatchee	WA	1	57	77	43	86	69	86	19	40	56
245	50.7	Glens Falls	NY	33	21	2	60	81	81	13	55	35	39
246	50.3	Bangor	ME	4	28	0	55	58	91	21	36	62	72
247	49.4	Bakersfield	CA	39	20	93	5	10	38	21	66	33	17
248	49.1	Chico	CA	43	21	91	47	14	72	44	58	13	15
249	49.1	Cape Coral–Fort Myers	FL	95	35	82	36	17	25	4	72	17	69
250	49.0	Miami–Miami Beach–Kendall	FL	63	10	80	29	9	1	44	96	90	56
251	49.0	New York–White Plains	NY	9	3	45	100	2	50	99	99	99	87
252	48.9	Jacksonville	FL	93	80	74	59	10	10	0	86	65	56
253	48.7	Essex County	MA	7	13	31	87	5	73	56	96	98	93
254	48.6	Brownsville–Harlingen	TX	77	89	91	1	25	33	24	61	1	2
255	48.6	Midland–Odessa	TX	56	88	88	16	64	64	46	2	22	2
256	48.4	Houston–Sugar Land–Baytown	TX	82	60	56	78	10	14	14	86	87	70
257	48.4	Topeka	KS	32	55	41	47	68	42	47	19	10	17
258	48.1	Chicago–Naperville–Joliet	IL	8	13	24	97	9	33	85	99	97	91
259	48.0	Worcester	MA	6	12	30	84	17	90	52	97	99	39
260	47.7	Charleston	WV	16	82	81	27	55	32	0	20	53	17
261	47.5	Fort Walton Beach–Crestview–Destin	FL	98	100	70	67	44	82	13	41	6	2
262	47.2	Minneapolis–St. Paul–Bloomington	MN-WI	71	12	9	97	14	48	43	93	97	93
263	47.1	Longview	WA	80	64	80	25	33	24	85	8	14	2
264	47.0	Beaumont–Port Arthur	TX	39	92	69	18	47	16	80	51	45	17
265	46.8	Wichita Falls	TX	64	89	79	39	89	2	48	7	24	2
266	46.7	Providence–New Bedford–Fall River	RI-MA	6	8	31	65	12	76	77	89	90	73
267	46.6	Baton Rouge	LA	39	42	74	16	27	26	2	59	68	15
268	46.6	Yuma	AZ	21	45	90	0	27	39	41	60	11	0
269	46.6	Youngstown–Warren–Boardman	OH-PA	5	72	5	28	63	66	87	36	54	17
270	46.5	Monroe	MI	54	27	55	17	4	88	71	87	94	2
271	46.5	Shreveport–Bossier City	LA	34	71	74	31	89	7	17	32	50	2
272	46.3	Tacoma	WA	82	40	82	67	12	16	1	88	77	56
273	46.3	Fayetteville	NC	3	41	61	48	32	18	42	8	40	55
274	46.2	Killeen–Temple–Fort Hood	TX	66	95	69	53	52	52	30	6	2	2
275	46.2	Panama City–Lynn Haven	FL	94	60	71	38	31	14	20	46	15	2
276	45.9	Syracuse	NY	46	17	4	89	53	45	40	70	89	17
277	45.8	Yakima	WA	2	85	33	4	32	24	31	61	40	17
278	45.6	Memphis	TN-MS-AR	17	84	47	42	39	2	18	72	70	39
279	45.6	Muncie	IN	1	94	49	37	34	77	92	11	53	17

continued

RANK	SCORE	METROPOLITAN AREA	STATE	ECONOMY & JOBS	COST OF LIVING	CLIMATE	EDUCATION	HEALTH & HEALTHCARE	CRIME	TRANSPORTATION	LEISURE	ARTS & CULTURE	QUALITY OF LIFE
280	45.4	Milwaukee–Waukesha–West Allis	WI	15	15	12	71	43	44	97	80	93	56
281	45.3	Nashville–Davidson–Murfreesboro	TN	38	80	17	78	71	12	1	68	86	56
282	45.2	Jonesboro	AR	82	37	46	6	91	53	65	1	22	17
283	45.0	Green Bay	WI	16	30	13	52	78	88	39	43	17	83
284	44.9	Dalton	GA	67	62	44	1	75	60	89	23	8	17
285	44.7	Cleveland–Elyria–Mentor	OH	7	23	12	64	18	47	30	86	98	39
286	44.7	Albany	GA	31	51	62	10	83	59	27	8	28	0
287	44.6	Jacksonville	NC	17	66	52	22	55	98	21	21	0	2
288	44.4	Morgantown	WV	35	68	28	52	95	94	45	10	10	17
289	44.3	Parkersburg–Marietta–Vienna	WV-OH	13	63	45	27	58	72	33	4	37	2
290	44.2	Mansfield	OH	12	66	20	9	76	66	82	15	48	39
291	44.2	Elkhart–Goshen	IN	46	78	24	4	44	79	81	5	51	17
292	44.2	Rome	GA	51	59	44	5	90	35	77	4	22	2
293	44.1	Cleveland	TN	4	93	26	30	84	50	14	39	52	17
294	44.1	La Crosse	WI-MN	11	43	10	74	92	90	50	18	37	56
295	44.0	Myrtle Beach–Conway–North Myrtle Beach	SC	85	39	51	42	35	1	7	32	24	2
296	43.9	Rochester	NY	14	16	10	93	37	52	54	77	82	39
297	43.8	Elizabethtown	KY	12	73	21	21	60	89	17	46	58	17
298	43.7	Akron	OH	49	34	16	54	17	53	75	73	77	15
299	43.7	Rockford	IL	77	52	19	19	60	31	95	28	28	17
300	43.6	Buffalo–Niagara Falls	NY	10	19	11	71	36	67	53	70	81	37
301	43.5	Waco	TX	79	93	87	43	39	8	96	19	33	2
302	43.5	Racine	WI	8	33	13	34	61	74	96	59	51	17
303	43.4	Scranton–Wilkes-Barre	PA	6	67	15	24	78	64	71	57	42	17
304	43.0	Saginaw–Saginaw Township North	MI	24	84	15	22	56	4	70	56	52	17
305	42.8	Joplin	MO	28	79	27	20	63	43	35	6	19	2
306	42.4	Hartford–West Hartford–East Hartford	CT	13	14	1	89	38	39	95	64	94	39
307	42.4	Burlington–South Burlington	VT	11	21	0	90	81	62	16	60	40	73
308	42.2	Poughkeepsie–Newburgh–Middletown	NY	44	8	2	82	20	97	87	87	82	17
309	41.9	Binghamton	NY	10	24	4	75	77	97	43	40	46	17
310	41.9	Kankakee–Bradley	IL	50	76	6	12	41	68	90	68	39	2
311	41.0	Springfield	MA	4	20	1	92	41	21	90	62	74	17
312	40.8	Lewiston–Auburn	ME	20	30	0	26	52	94	6	36	13	56
313	38.4	Salinas	CA	2	0	100	19	3	29	81	81	47	56
314	37.6	Phoenix–Mesa–Scottsdale	AZ	84	18	90	81	3	5	12	97	82	56
315	36.7	Madera	CA	64	12	94	2	35	77	0	76	44	2
316	36.5	Salisbury	MD	36	31	84	14	93	5	77	16	4	73
317	36.4	Fresno	CA	31	11	89	17	6	22	16	78	43	39
318	35.5	Tyler	TX	70	91	75	52	77	6	32	16	13	17
319	35.4	Longview	TX	72	97	75	32	59	6	15	3	20	17
320	35.1	Vallejo–Fairfield	CA	53	3	95	46	0	9	18	95	58	39
321	35.0	Utica–Rome	NY	4	13	4	58	71	56	41	57	66	2
322	34.7	Hot Springs	AR	95	64	53	10	97	0	21	6	6	39
323	34.6	Mobile	AL	60	52	60	7	29	10	1	59	41	17
324	34.6	Cumberland	MD-WV	25	86	51	18	98	2	81	17	5	39
325	34.6	Danville	VA	0	99	60	2	87	80	38	3	36	2
326	34.2	Fort Smith	AR-OK	71	55	47	4	70	33	10	24	10	17
327	34.1	Anderson	SC	41	77	50	18	46	8	8	39	53	2
328	34.0	Owensboro	KY	43	83	37	18	57	96	40	4	16	2
329	33.7	Jefferson City	MO	29	67	19	25	90	95	66	5	3	17
330	33.6	Bay City	MI	8	85	15	15	53	93	23	52	47	17
331	33.6	Fairbanks	AK	58	81	29	80	11	17	56	42	11	2
332	33.5	Williamsport	PA	11	89	10	29	95	87	44	22	17	17
333	33.5	Clarksville	TN-KY	43	98	17	24	67	42	13	20	15	17

continued

RANK	SCORE	METROPOLITAN AREA	STATE	ECONOMY & JOBS	COST OF LIVING	CLIMATE	EDUCATION	HEALTH & HEALTHCARE	CRIME	TRANSPORTATION	LEISURE	ARTS & CULTURE	QUALITY OF LIFE
							CATEGORY SCORES (0-100 SCALE)						
334	33.3	Gadsden	AL	9	69	22	6	82	41	76	1	26	2
335	33.3	Flint	MI	16	56	23	43	18	17	29	76	64	2
336	33.1	Lima	OH	23	66	20	14	59	13	78	13	38	2
337	32.9	Valdosta	GA	48	65	72	16	95	32	29	2	5	2
338	32.9	Norwich–New London	CT	19	17	1	81	23	85	86	64	93	17
339	32.6	Dubuque	IA	50	47	3	20	80	92	74	12	18	17
340	23.8	Huntington–Ashland	WV-KY-OH	7	76	81	15	83	62	6	14	36	17
341	23.8	Laredo	TX	89	91	89	1	50	26	18	4	0	0
342	23.8	McAllen–Edinburg–Mission	TX	93	88	78	0	12	28	19	14	30	2
343	23.8	Texarkana	TX-AR	77	98	76	12	96	13	29	13	1	2
344	23.8	Detroit–Livonia–Dearborn	MI	0	14	39	29	4	5	36	90	94	17
345	23.8	Morristown	TN	47	98	26	14	86	49	1	9	4	17
346	23.8	St. Joseph	MO-KS	9	79	18	19	60	57	49	0	32	17
347	23.8	Decatur	AL	31	63	16	14	52	83	3	31	3	17
348	23.8	Lake Charles	LA	73	71	67	6	51	16	24	9	19	15
349	23.8	Hattiesburg	MS	15	72	62	41	72	63	10	13	17	17
350	23.8	Stockton	CA	36	5	92	12	1	1	36	56	34	2
351	23.8	Houma–Bayou Cane–Thibodaux	LA	26	70	73	0	46	19	12	54	1	2
352	23.8	Dothan	AL	62	73	47	6	97	54	16	1	7	2
353	23.8	Rocky Mount	NC	2	58	63	8	63	0	35	23	14	2
354	23.8	Danville	IL	33	97	42	13	55	16	52	2	15	2
355	23.8	Jackson	TN	3	89	35	44	91	1	62	0	11	17
356	23.8	Victoria	TX	83	97	86	13	89	18	15	1	27	2
357	23.8	Florence–Muscle Shoals	AL	44	77	17	11	72	80	7	33	13	17
358	23.8	Weirton–Steubenville	WV-OH	0	85	27	10	20	97	82	6	7	17
359	23.8	Florence	SC	60	59	34	9	67	0	54	7	12	2
360	23.8	Elmira	NY	1	25	5	51	96	56	51	3	16	2
361	23.8	Pine Bluff	AR	47	36	44	3	40	3	9	7	23	0
362	23.8	Hanford–Corcoran	CA	26	10	89	3	21	63	25	8	0	0
363	14.4	Sumter	SC	3	65	34	13	37	0	66	15	9	2
364	14.2	Anniston–Oxford	AL	6	64	22	5	69	13	85	11	9	17
365	13.6	El Centro	CA	74	8	68	0	8	71	63	0	1	0
366	13.3	Alexandria	LA	18	81	62	3	90	2	3	10	27	2
367	12.7	Lafayette	LA	43	73	73	7	64	18	4	18	12	2
368	12.5	Farmington	NM	88	39	72	16	2	46	2	14	6	17
369	12.4	Monroe	LA	14	55	75	17	93	7	19	10	30	17
370	11.7	Merced	CA	2	9	92	2	8	21	64	45	2	17
371	10.9	Yuba City	CA	44	15	94	10	9	29	9	48	0	2
372	3.6	Visalia–Porterville	CA	0	23	90	1	19	4	18	47	9	2
373	0.0	Modesto	CA	17	6	93	4	4	17	71	57	18	2

TABLE 2.5 U.S. METROPOLITAN AREAS BY ALPHABETICAL SEQUENCE WITH RANK

RANK	SCORE	METROPOLITAN AREA	STATE	ECONOMY & JOBS	COST OF LIVING	CLIMATE	EDUCATION	HEALTH & HEALTHCARE	CRIME	TRANSPORTATION	LEISURE	ARTS & CULTURE	QUALITY OF LIFE
55	78.0	Abilene	TX	93	92	90	41	93	59	54	18	39	37
298	43.7	Akron	OH	49	34	16	54	17	53	75	73	77	15
286	44.7	Albany	GA	31	51	62	10	83	59	27	8	28	0
235	52.6	Albany–Schenectady–Troy	NY	36	11	2	95	42	87	36	75	85	55
145	63.8	Albuquerque	NM	74	29	85	62	22	3	14	71	76	83
366	13.3	Alexandria	LA	18	81	62	3	90	2	3	10	27	2
39	81.1	Allentown–Bethlehem–Easton	PA-NJ	47	21	32	63	39	54	93	67	77	70
203	56.2	Altoona	PA	12	91	40	11	90	50	79	31	36	39
169	60.9	Amarillo	TX	72	91	86	39	83	6	45	35	29	15
189	57.8	Ames	IA	65	31	18	98	85	93	76	12	42	83
228	53.8	Anchorage	AK	90	86	3	79	15	20	28	72	63	72
177	59.8	Anderson	IN	19	87	48	15	47	72	73	71	91	56
327	34.1	Anderson	SC	41	77	50	18	46	8	8	39	53	2
5	93.2	Ann Arbor	MI	74	32	38	97	86	66	63	81	78	91
364	14.2	Anniston–Oxford	AL	6	64	22	5	69	13	85	11	9	17
102	68.8	Appleton	WI	62	44	12	59	62	98	70	63	31	87
7	90.5	Asheville	NC	32	45	66	61	83	86	57	43	55	96
29	83.8	Athens–Clarke County	GA	57	38	52	64	79	29	88	34	57	73
54	78.2	Atlanta–Sandy Springs–Marietta	GA	86	28	74	94	36	30	11	94	91	83
57	77.1	Atlantic City	NJ	38	18	85	35	41	40	99	84	80	56
128	66.4	Auburn–Opelika	AL	39	63	23	70	47	50	91	38	8	56
104	68.4	Augusta–Richmond County	GA-SC	48	55	53	37	80	53	4	29	32	39
103	68.5	Austin–Round Rock	TX	97	62	88	92	33	11	12	50	75	96
247	49.4	Bakersfield	CA	39	20	93	5	10	38	21	66	33	17
173	60.5	Baltimore–Towson	MD	48	17	42	87	51	14	90	95	95	73
246	50.3	Bangor	ME	4	28	0	55	58	91	21	36	62	72
171	60.6	Barnstable Town	MA	21	7	67	96	16	71	50	63	63	72
267	46.6	Baton Rouge	LA	39	42	74	16	27	26	2	59	68	15
239	52.2	Battle Creek	MI	29	67	8	40	87	23	87	49	55	17
330	33.6	Bay City	MI	8	85	15	15	53	93	23	52	47	17
264	47.0	Beaumont–Port Arthur	TX	39	92	69	18	47	16	80	51	45	17
2	95.1	Bellingham	WA	97	59	82	64	27	37	72	66	59	96
56	77.6	Bend	OR	94	40	66	66	25	84	47	63	8	98
77	71.9	Bergen–Passaic	NJ	48	5	45	58	22	78	91	88	86	83
70	73.4	Bethesda–Gaithersburg–Frederick	MD	68	5	41	93	44	86	49	92	96	91
138	65.3	Billings	MT	70	78	6	70	72	74	51	34	36	73
309	41.9	Binghamton	NY	10	24	4	75	77	97	43	40	46	17
223	54.3	Birmingham–Hoover	AL	27	38	22	46	50	19	0	49	71	39
114	67.5	Bismarck	ND	75	74	21	83	98	90	63	31	10	56
181	59.2	Blacksburg–Christiansburg–Radford	VA	17	25	57	75	96	99	35	28	12	56
86	70.5	Bloomington	IN	5	76	49	65	38	86	51	50	49	70
124	66.6	Bloomington–Normal	IL	73	45	37	87	51	55	59	26	54	17
10	89.6	Boise City–Nampa	ID	98	32	58	68	32	44	22	54	62	96
160	61.4	Boston–Quincy	MA	9	10	30	99	29	46	68	98	100	91
62	76.1	Boulder	CO	57	9	54	98	45	80	81	85	71	96
119	67.1	Bowling Green	KY	54	71	28	31	95	57	60	27	9	56
148	63.3	Bremerton–Silverdale	WA	89	44	81	75	16	51	4	83	25	73
208	56.0	Bridgeport–Stamford–Norwalk	CT	10	4	76	87	1	89	94	89	88	73
254	48.6	Brownsville–Harlingen	TX	77	89	91	1	25	33	24	61	1	2
186	58.5	Brunswick	GA	68	82	68	30	79	8	20	27	14	39
300	43.6	Buffalo–Niagara Falls	NY	10	19	11	71	36	67	53	70	81	37
307	42.4	Burlington–South Burlington	VT	11	21	0	90	81	62	16	60	40	73
166	61.1	Cambridge–Newton–Framingham	MA	30	18	30	99	8	83	70	97	99	83
163	61.3	Camden	NJ	72	9	64	60	14	64	98	93	98	39
236	52.5	Canton–Massillon	OH	38	71	11	28	38	25	91	32	56	17
249	49.1	Cape Coral–Fort Myers	FL	95	35	82	36	17	25	4	72	17	69
178	59.6	Carson City	NV	20	19	72	35	75	61	63	43	4	56

continued

RANK	SCORE	METROPOLITAN AREA	STATE	ECONOMY & JOBS	COST OF LIVING	CLIMATE	EDUCATION	HEALTH & HEALTHCARE	CRIME	TRANSPORTATION	LEISURE	ARTS & CULTURE	QUALITY OF LIFE
							CATEGORY SCORES (0–100 SCALE)						
112	67.8	Casper	WY	50	99	38	68	56	66	62	5	21	39
135	65.6	Cedar Rapids	IA	60	46	14	82	63	52	39	22	47	56
101	68.8	Champaign–Urbana	IL	35	60	39	89	54	15	62	21	72	56
260	47.7	Charleston	WV	16	82	81	27	55	32	0	20	53	17
174	60.4	Charleston–North Charleston	SC	81	34	57	55	42	10	6	79	66	83
85	70.9	Charlotte–Gastonia–Concord	NC-SC	92	24	43	73	27	6	23	60	85	73
17	86.8	Charlottesville	VA	66	19	71	82	99	91	80	40	64	98
219	55.4	Chattanooga	TN-GA	22	90	21	21	82	7	4	54	72	56
109	67.9	Cheyenne	WY	55	98	40	78	21	58	92	0	33	38
258	48.1	Chicago–Naperville–Joliet	IL	8	13	24	97	9	33	85	99	97	91
248	49.1	Chico	CA	43	21	91	47	14	72	44	58	13	15
38	81.6	Cincinnati–Middletown	OH-KY-IN	45	35	33	63	24	31	67	78	90	70
333	33.5	Clarksville	TN-KY	43	98	17	24	67	42	13	20	15	17
293	44.1	Cleveland	TN	4	93	26	30	84	50	14	39	52	17
285	44.7	Cleveland–Elyria–Mentor	OH	7	23	12	64	18	47	30	86	98	39
61	76.2	Coeur d'Alene	ID	99	29	65	47	22	71	26	65	5	93
175	60.4	College Station–Bryan	TX	79	93	69	79	74	19	94	12	27	39
4	93.9	Colorado Springs	CO	63	36	91	94	36	35	64	69	73	56
115	67.5	Columbia	MO	63	41	20	91	98	49	44	13	65	56
110	67.9	Columbia	SC	57	61	34	66	48	12	42	58	59	56
214	55.8	Columbus	GA-AL	9	51	47	27	85	34	89	23	38	17
33	82.4	Columbus	IN	56	85	43	35	82	82	93	73	78	39
36	81.9	Columbus	OH	53	27	41	86	32	35	26	73	91	56
172	60.5	Corpus Christi	TX	37	81	86	23	56	3	26	52	32	17
14	87.3	Corvallis	OR	42	57	67	96	48	76	84	39	28	72
324	34.6	Cumberland	MD-WV	25	86	51	18	98	2	81	17	5	39
132	65.9	Dallas–Plano–Irving	TX	87	61	87	86	13	8	53	90	93	70
284	44.9	Dalton	GA	67	62	44	1	75	60	89	23	8	17
354	23.8	Danville	IL	33	97	42	13	55	16	52	2	15	2
325	34.6	Danville	VA	0	99	60	2	87	80	38	3	36	2
233	52.8	Davenport–Moline–Rock Island	IA-IL	35	39	14	53	59	22	34	37	61	17
84	71.0	Dayton	OH	13	34	46	63	40	52	89	54	91	56
347	23.8	Decatur	AL	31	63	16	14	52	83	3	31	3	17
210	55.9	Decatur	IL	59	96	37	16	61	34	46	9	29	39
75	72.3	Deltona–Daytona Beach–Ormond Beach	FL	85	68	78	38	2	37	28	63	41	39
150	63.1	Denver–Aurora	CO	56	15	54	94	18	42	32	93	95	93
46	79.7	Des Moines–West Des Moines	IA	76	25	22	84	49	61	37	40	69	73
344	23.8	Detroit–Livonia–Dearborn	MI	0	14	39	29	4	5	36	90	94	17
352	23.8	Dothan	AL	62	73	47	6	97	54	16	1	7	2
21	85.1	Dover	DE	85	82	60	21	40	43	91	55	21	73
339	32.6	Dubuque	IA	50	47	3	20	80	92	74	12	18	17
229	53.3	Duluth	MN-WI	18	46	3	71	69	77	33	74	58	73
15	87.2	Durham	NC	58	28	63	90	94	22	38	66	84	73
225	54.1	Eau Claire	WI	13	45	9	62	91	73	82	26	29	56
161	61.4	Edison	NJ	55	6	59	89	7	95	90	92	79	73
365	13.6	El Centro	CA	74	8	68	0	8	71	63	0	1	0
297	43.8	Elizabethtown	KY	12	73	21	21	60	89	17	46	58	17
291	44.2	Elkhart–Goshen	IN	46	78	24	4	44	79	81	5	51	17
360	23.8	Elmira	NY	1	25	5	51	96	56	51	3	16	2
165	61.2	El Paso	TX	67	73	88	5	42	29	20	27	52	15
240	51.9	Erie	PA	34	83	8	40	81	77	61	38	60	2
253	48.7	Essex County	MA	7	13	31	87	5	73	56	96	98	93
68	73.7	Eugene–Springfield	OR	39	51	65	68	7	65	70	67	49	83
50	79.0	Evansville	IN-KY	30	96	36	32	54	82	39	30	63	39
331	33.6	Fairbanks	AK	58	81	29	80	11	17	56	42	11	2
40	80.8	Fargo	ND-MN	65	79	35	88	65	95	62	24	49	55
368	12.5	Farmington	NM	88	39	72	16	2	46	2	14	6	17
273	46.3	Fayetteville	NC	3	41	61	48	32	18	42	8	40	55
79	71.8	Fayetteville–Springdale–Rogers	AR-MO	98	31	53	23	61	77	40	21	14	73
18	85.7	Flagstaff	AZ	66	60	63	73	25	27	54	57	43	83

continued

TABLE 2.5 U.S. METROPOLITAN AREAS BY ALPHABETICAL SEQUENCE WITH RANK (CONTINUED)

RANK	SCORE	METROPOLITAN AREA	STATE	ECONOMY & JOBS	COST OF LIVING	CLIMATE	EDUCATION	HEALTH & HEALTHCARE	CRIME	TRANSPORTATION	LEISURE	ARTS & CULTURE	QUALITY OF LIFE
335	33.3	Flint	MI	16	56	23	43	18	17	29	76	64	2
359	23.8	Florence	SC	60	59	34	9	67	0	54	7	12	2
357	23.8	Florence–Muscle Shoals	AL	44	77	17	11	72	80	7	33	13	17
136	65.5	Fond du Lac	WI	34	50	26	33	78	96	66	25	5	39
8	89.8	Fort Collins–Loveland	CO	75	33	54	93	47	88	65	75	37	98
158	61.8	Fort Lauderdale–Pompano Beach–Deerfield Beach	FL	83	11	80	50	8	36	59	82	67	56
326	34.2	Fort Smith	AR-OK	71	55	47	4	70	33	10	24	10	17
261	47.5	Fort Walton Beach–Crestview–Destin	FL	98	100	70	67	44	82	13	41	6	2
117	67.2	Fort Wayne	IN	53	87	41	43	46	59	32	38	76	17
133	65.8	Fort Worth–Arlington	TX	91	72	87	62	14	17	57	80	81	73
317	36.4	Fresno	CA	31	11	89	17	6	22	16	78	43	39
334	33.3	Gadsden	AL	9	69	22	6	82	41	76	1	26	2
1	100.0	Gainesville	FL	83	80	84	93	70	32	29	44	66	87
184	58.6	Gainesville	GA	90	29	57	8	48	57	55	81	78	17
230	53.3	Gary	IN	26	70	25	31	11	57	89	75	76	0
245	50.7	Glens Falls	NY	33	21	2	60	81	81	13	55	35	39
222	54.7	Goldsboro	NC	12	65	61	22	66	23	41	28	21	0
113	67.5	Grand Forks	ND-MN	22	82	35	72	97	54	73	15	41	39
66	75.1	Grand Junction	CO	30	52	71	51	92	58	44	51	16	87
213	55.9	Grand Rapids–Wyoming	MI	61	53	7	48	45	67	17	71	83	73
134	65.6	Great Falls	MT	72	86	11	56	87	35	66	47	33	56
80	71.8	Greeley	CO	79	84	54	54	9	21	43	78	46	73
283	45.0	Green Bay	WI	16	30	13	52	78	88	39	43	17	83
31	83.0	Greensboro–Winston-Salem–High Point	NC	67	42	59	56	53	45	76	62	69	38
111	67.9	Greenville	NC	52	42	52	50	74	26	45	17	22	39
94	69.6	Greenville	SC	83	58	50	53	50	10	55	37	54	56
95	69.6	Hagerstown–Martinsburg	MD-WV	54	30	43	9	66	91	69	85	78	39
362	23.8	Hanford–Corcoran	CA	26	10	89	3	21	63	25	8	0	0
107	68.3	Harrisburg–Carlisle	PA	55	74	33	58	76	93	98	71	64	17
105	68.4	Harrisonburg	VA	90	37	17	36	74	58	81	24	28	87
306	42.4	Hartford–West Hartford–East Hartford	CT	13	14	1	89	38	39	95	64	94	39
349	23.8	Hattiesburg	MS	15	72	62	41	72	63	10	13	17	17
195	57.6	Hickory–Lenoir–Morganton	NC	27	60	59	8	73	37	66	29	16	39
204	56.2	Hinesville–Fort Stewart	GA	28	66	70	27	56	31	9	31	41	0
140	65.2	Holland–Grand Haven	MI	74	54	8	60	34	92	67	69	81	39
89	70.3	Honolulu	HI	71	1	98	67	24	38	9	67	87	83
322	34.7	Hot Springs	AR	95	64	53	10	97	0	21	6	6	39
351	23.8	Houma–Bayou Cane–Thibodaux	LA	26	70	73	0	46	19	12	54	1	2
256	48.4	Houston–Sugar Land–Baytown	TX	82	60	56	78	10	14	14	86	87	70
340	23.8	Huntington–Ashland	WV-KY-OH	7	76	81	15	83	62	6	14	36	17
211	55.9	Huntsville	AL	75	50	16	72	24	51	37	16	37	73
224	54.2	Idaho Falls	ID	98	48	7	72	55	75	36	41	2	56
19	85.4	Indianapolis–Carmel	IN	59	74	48	73	23	45	65	74	89	73
32	82.5	Iowa City	IA	89	49	23	96	99	86	61	22	59	73
197	57.4	Ithaca	NY	39	10	9	99	72	99	74	48	42	93
242	51.2	Jackson	MI	49	74	5	33	56	61	60	32	31	17
98	69.1	Jackson	MS	25	70	51	55	76	51	3	20	74	39
355	23.8	Jackson	TN	3	89	35	44	91	1	62	0	11	17
252	48.9	Jacksonville	FL	93	80	74	59	10	10	0	86	65	56
287	44.6	Jacksonville	NC	17	66	52	22	55	98	21	21	0	2
227	54.0	Janesville	WI	14	40	21	41	78	77	97	28	34	17
329	33.7	Jefferson City	MO	29	67	19	25	90	95	66	5	3	17
191	57.8	Johnson City	TN	20	97	56	23	99	69	17	43	39	17
217	55.6	Johnstown	PA	23	90	40	8	85	78	58	49	34	17

continued

RANK	SCORE	METROPOLITAN AREA	STATE	ECONOMY & JOBS	COST OF LIVING	CLIMATE	EDUCATION	HEALTH & HEALTHCARE	CRIME	TRANSPORTATION	LEISURE	ARTS & CULTURE	QUALITY OF LIFE
282	45.2	Jonesboro	AR	82	37	46	6	91	53	65	1	22	17
305	42.8	Joplin	MO	28	79	27	20	63	43	35	6	19	2
234	52.6	Kalamazoo–Portage	MI	60	69	8	72	74	47	34	48	62	17
310	41.9	Kankakee–Bradley	IL	50	76	6	12	41	68	90	68	39	2
199	57.1	Kansas City	MO-KS	41	26	18	87	35	11	22	77	92	73
207	56.0	Kennewick–Richland–Pasco	WA	78	78	33	52	45	83	15	26	18	39
274	46.2	Killeen–Temple–Fort Hood	TX	66	95	69	53	52	52	30	6	2	2
187	58.3	Kingsport–Bristol–Bristol	TN-VA	5	99	56	20	80	73	6	44	43	39
232	53.1	Kingston	NY	37	7	6	77	34	74	84	79	79	39
99	69.1	Knoxville	TN	22	88	36	70	57	45	8	76	70	56
194	57.6	Kokomo	IN	99	93	48	34	80	48	72	9	35	17
294	44.1	La Crosse	WI-MN	11	43	10	74	92	90	50	18	37	56
25	84.3	Lafayette	IN	35	95	48	68	54	82	74	42	51	73
367	12.7	Lafayette	LA	43	73	73	7	64	18	4	18	12	2
348	23.8	Lake Charles	LA	73	71	67	6	51	16	24	9	19	15
41	80.8	Lake County–Kenosha County	IL-WI	94	22	25	83	20	55	79	94	95	39
156	62.3	Lakeland	FL	81	86	79	13	2	33	47	58	45	73
96	69.5	Lancaster	PA	51	63	32	21	12	83	98	53	21	73
237	52.4	Lansing–East Lansing	MI	47	56	5	81	79	66	75	56	68	17
341	23.8	Laredo	TX	89	91	89	1	50	26	18	4	0	0
151	62.9	Las Cruces	NM	83	57	92	26	13	60	25	21	44	17
154	62.5	Las Vegas–Paradise	NV	98	24	79	36	6	14	31	80	69	56
100	68.9	Lawrence	KS	44	37	31	95	30	43	57	16	50	73
192	57.7	Lawton	OK	52	56	77	44	43	12	72	25	23	2
188	58.2	Lebanon	PA	33	82	56	12	60	68	85	70	65	17
69	73.5	Lewiston	ID-WA	65	49	70	49	86	85	78	33	18	56
312	40.8	Lewiston–Auburn	ME	20	30	0	26	52	94	6	36	13	56
24	84.3	Lexington–Fayette	KY	68	37	37	79	88	41	85	30	75	87
336	33.1	Lima	OH	23	66	20	14	59	13	78	13	38	2
139	65.3	Lincoln	NE	78	29	10	86	54	32	64	35	70	56
196	57.6	Little Rock–North Little Rock	AR	69	47	43	45	85	5	6	47	73	56
12	88.9	Logan	UT-ID	96	51	64	82	84	99	83	44	20	83
319	35.4	Longview	TX	72	97	75	32	59	6	15	3	20	17
263	47.1	Longview	WA	80	64	80	25	33	24	85	8	14	2
93	69.8	Los Angeles–Long Beach–Glendale	CA	28	2	97	98	15	39	78	100	97	38
44	79.7	Louisville–Jefferson County	KY-IN	36	41	45	34	21	79	66	65	71	39
168	61.0	Lubbock	TX	49	87	86	51	88	4	60	27	26	17
179	59.4	Lynchburg	VA	64	68	71	36	97	81	13	29	35	17
116	67.4	Macon–Warner Robins	GA	41	50	50	24	84	44	82	25	49	17
315	36.7	Madera	CA	64	12	94	2	35	77	0	76	44	2
78	71.9	Madison	WI	31	18	20	95	65	94	59	50	58	98
71	73.4	Manchester–Nashua	NH	72	75	6	76	33	81	55	79	72	87
290	44.2	Mansfield	OH	12	66	20	9	76	66	82	15	48	39
342	23.8	McAllen–Edinburg–Mission	TX	93	88	78	0	12	28	19	14	30	2
34	82.3	Medford	OR	63	54	58	45	20	72	42	25	20	56
278	45.6	Memphis	TN-MS-AR	17	84	47	42	39	2	18	72	70	39
370	11.7	Merced	CA	2	9	92	2	8	21	64	45	2	17
250	49.0	Miami–Miami Beach–Kendall	FL	63	10	80	29	9	1	44	96	90	56
209	56.0	Michigan City–La Porte	IN	23	94	24	10	70	56	93	82	81	17
255	48.6	Midland–Odessa	TX	56	88	88	16	64	64	46	2	22	2
280	45.4	Milwaukee–Waukesha–West Allis	WI	15	15	12	71	43	44	97	80	93	56
262	47.2	Minneapolis–St. Paul–Bloomington	MN-WI	71	12	9	97	14	48	43	93	97	93
88	70.3	Missoula	MT	78	79	18	81	73	55	58	45	25	93
323	34.6	Mobile	AL	60	52	60	7	29	10	1	59	41	17
373	0.0	Modesto	CA	17	6	93	4	4	17	71	57	18	2
369	12.4	Monroe	LA	14	55	75	17	93	7	19	10	30	17
270	46.5	Monroe	MI	54	27	55	17	4	88	71	87	94	2

continued

TABLE 2.5 U.S. METROPOLITAN AREAS BY ALPHABETICAL SEQUENCE WITH RANK (CONTINUED)

RANK	SCORE	METROPOLITAN AREA	STATE	ECONOMY & JOBS	COST OF LIVING	CLIMATE	EDUCATION	HEALTH & HEALTHCARE	CRIME	TRANSPORTATION	LEISURE	ARTS & CULTURE	QUALITY OF LIFE
200	57.1	Montgomery	AL	52	54	55	39	67	29	8	35	72	17
288	44.4	Morgantown	WV	35	68	28	52	95	94	45	10	10	17
345	23.8	Morristown	TN	47	98	26	14	86	49	1	9	4	17
123	66.7	Mount Vernon–Anacortes	WA	87	47	91	51	50	20	27	14	6	93
279	45.6	Muncie	IN	1	94	49	37	34	34	77	92	11	53	17
146	63.6	Muskegon–Norton Shores	MI	51	48	7	31	49	41	54	68	80	39
295	44.0	Myrtle Beach–Conway–North Myrtle Beach	SC	85	39	51	42	35	1	7	32	24	2
26	84.2	Napa	CA	24	3	95	49	77	65	82	94	60	93
52	78.5	Naples–Marco Island	FL	97	7	83	57	29	65	76	74	24	93
281	45.3	Nashville–Davidson–Murfreesboro	TN	38	80	17	78	71	12	1	68	86	56
90	70.2	Nassau–Suffolk	NY	29	2	77	94	4	96	92	98	92	83
164	61.3	New Haven–Milford	CT	5	8	75	69	31	79	98	91	83	39
251	49.0	New York–White Plains	NY	9	3	45	100	2	50	99	99	99	87
180	59.2	Newark–Union	NJ-PA	24	4	58	85	17	53	94	90	93	39
147	63.4	Niles–Benton Harbor	MI	28	74	25	39	68	36	97	39	25	2
338	32.9	Norwich–New London	CT	19	17	1	81	23	85	86	64	93	17
97	69.2	Oakland–Fremont–Hayward	CA	45	1	99	90	0	35	30	96	89	39
162	61.4	Ocala	FL	90	94	84	7	10	41	60	47	20	39
45	79.7	Ocean City	NJ	19	25	93	46	37	40	47	84	85	56
6	92.8	Ogden–Clearfield	UT	92	33	29	71	71	93	41	89	79	91
185	58.6	Oklahoma City	OK	66	36	72	64	26	9	20	61	62	17
16	86.8	Olympia	WA	94	54	44	80	31	63	30	82	55	93
127	66.5	Omaha–Council Bluffs	NE-IA	69	26	14	77	58	44	48	64	77	56
155	62.3	Orlando–Kissimmee	FL	96	40	83	74	5	18	27	85	68	39
142	64.7	Oshkosh–Neenah	WI	50	43	12	48	73	85	75	63	38	39
328	34.0	Owensboro	KY	43	83	37	18	57	96	40	4	16	2
22	85.1	Oxnard–Thousand Oaks–Ventura	CA	52	1	97	57	28	89	88	91	71	73
67	75.0	Palm Bay–Melbourne–Titusville	FL	91	87	77	62	5	22	24	66	31	73
275	46.2	Panama City–Lynn Haven	FL	94	60	71	38	31	14	20	46	15	2
289	44.3	Parkersburg–Marietta–Vienna	WV-OH	13	63	45	27	58	72	33	4	37	2
182	59.0	Pensacola–Ferry Pass–Brent	FL	82	92	70	48	23	47	2	69	30	17
125	66.6	Peoria	IL	77	68	39	44	63	60	27	42	60	17
153	62.8	Philadelphia	PA	24	12	64	97	12	48	99	94	98	70
314	37.6	Phoenix–Mesa–Scottsdale	AZ	84	18	90	81	3	5	12	97	82	56
361	23.8	Pine Bluff	AR	47	36	44	3	40	3	9	7	23	0
74	72.5	Pittsburgh	PA	17	48	27	91	30	84	33	83	95	87
243	51.2	Pittsfield	MA	1	22	2	76	66	94	73	53	55	39
241	51.8	Pocatello	ID	93	51	1	60	94	81	59	41	8	39
231	53.3	Portland–South Portland–Biddeford	ME	37	17	0	84	41	98	53	72	56	87
3	95.0	Portland–Vancouver–Beaverton	OR-WA	75	22	78	92	22	60	32	87	89	96
176	60.3	Port St. Lucie–Fort Pierce	FL	91	35	66	30	29	64	16	41	19	73
308	42.2	Poughkeepsie–Newburgh–Middletown	NY	44	8	2	82	20	97	87	87	82	17
92	69.9	Prescott	AZ	86	21	97	49	18	79	61	20	12	83
266	46.7	Providence–New Bedford–Fall River	RI-MA	6	8	31	65	12	76	77	89	90	73
13	88.5	Provo–Orem	UT	97	47	55	90	61	69	64	78	52	87
76	72.3	Pueblo	CO	14	58	68	42	87	27	28	40	67	56
65	75.3	Punta Gorda	FL	96	56	83	26	52	68	38	45	2	56
302	43.5	Racine	WI	8	33	13	34	61	74	96	59	51	17
63	75.9	Raleigh–Cary	NC	86	23	63	91	33	74	5	67	84	87
157	62.1	Rapid City	SD	80	90	4	66	68	69	52	44	26	39
118	67.2	Reading	PA	55	53	32	24	19	70	94	52	48	39
141	65.0	Redding	CA	58	16	96	38	28	68	28	51	27	2
64	75.4	Reno–Sparks	NV	42	16	85	55	29	51	57	79	56	56
30	83.5	Richmond	VA	92	46	35	69	79	28	67	62	83	73

continued

RANK	SCORE	METROPOLITAN AREA	STATE	CATEGORY SCORES (0-100 SCALE)									
				ECONOMY & JOBS	COST OF LIVING	CLIMATE	EDUCATION	HEALTH & HEALTHCARE	CRIME	TRANSPORTATION	LEISURE	ARTS & CULTURE	QUALITY OF LIFE
106	68.4	Riverside–San Bernardino–Ontario	CA	79	6	96	25	6	31	72	97	86	56
60	76.8	Roanoke	VA	69	49	76	47	98	67	19	33	50	87
131	66.0	Rochester	MN	78	27	9	85	100	62	88	62	35	69
296	43.9	Rochester	NY	14	16	10	93	37	52	54	77	82	39
299	43.7	Rockford	IL	77	52	19	19	60	31	95	28	28	17
28	84.0	Rockingham County–Strafford County	NH	81	62	29	83	26	95	35	92	94	56
353	23.8	Rocky Mount	NC	2	58	63	8	63	0	35	23	14	2
292	44.2	Rome	GA	51	59	44	5	90	35	77	4	22	2
183	58.7	Sacramento–Arden-Arcade–Roseville	CA	68	6	94	77	1	13	79	91	75	70
304	43.0	Saginaw–Saginaw Township North	MI	24	84	15	22	56	4	70	56	52	17
143	64.6	St. Cloud	MN	39	35	12	56	75	86	71	50	45	39
72	73.3	St. George	UT	100	37	55	54	82	100	56	32	3	69
346	23.8	St. Joseph	MO-KS	9	79	18	19	60	57	49	0	32	17
35	82.1	St. Louis	MO-IL	32	32	36	85	28	45	24	85	96	56
82	71.3	Salem	OR	32	48	67	45	19	25	31	65	38	56
313	38.4	Salinas	CA	2	0	100	19	3	29	81	81	47	56
316	36.5	Salisbury	MD	36	31	84	14	93	5	77	16	4	73
27	84.1	Salt Lake City	UT	91	26	29	74	58	20	32	90	82	87
152	62.8	San Angelo	TX	70	95	93	35	94	28	51	18	32	2
51	78.9	San Antonio	TX	87	83	89	50	27	12	22	69	68	70
83	71.1	San Diego–Carlsbad–San Marcos	CA	58	1	96	85	5	59	48	95	87	93
202	56.7	Sandusky	OH	27	69	51	32	67	70	96	2	31	17
73	72.8	San Francisco–San Mateo–Redwood City	CA	27	0	99	91	3	36	87	98	97	91
58	77.0	San Jose–Sunnyvale–Santa Clara	CA	37	0	97	88	0	89	68	93	84	73
9	89.8	San Luis Obispo–Paso Robles	CA	44	4	98	74	37	91	25	75	70	98
59	76.8	Santa Ana–Anaheim–Irvine	CA	67	0	98	79	16	86	83	98	79	56
11	89.6	Santa Barbara–Santa Maria	CA	56	4	98	69	40	75	43	77	66	98
216	55.6	Santa Cruz–Watsonville	CA	18	2	99	77	1	43	38	89	75	87
20	85.3	Santa Fe	NM	84	14	94	75	26	24	23	55	59	98
108	68.0	Santa Rosa–Petaluma	CA	29	2	95	70	0	68	68	87	61	93
149	63.2	Sarasota–Bradenton–Venice	FL	95	16	83	56	13	27	50	55	43	83
91	70.1	Savannah	GA	64	39	60	29	51	23	5	59	54	55
303	43.4	Scranton–Wilkes-Barre	PA	6	67	15	24	78	64	71	57	42	17
129	66.3	Seattle–Bellevue–Everett	WA	80	14	81	95	11	47	24	99	88	91
23	84.8	Sebastian–Vero Beach	FL	46	58	66	37	62	38	78	29	23	73
121	67.0	Sheboygan	WI	25	43	14	32	59	91	84	53	51	73
167	61.1	Sherman–Denison	TX	89	94	87	45	69	40	74	34	4	2
271	46.5	Shreveport–Bossier City	LA	34	71	74	31	89	7	17	32	50	2
226	54.0	Sioux City	IA-NE-SD	40	44	25	33	70	37	69	12	48	17
215	55.6	Sioux Falls	SD	87	90	16	67	93	76	52	17	48	39
53	78.3	South Bend–Mishawaka	IN-MI	60	95	24	41	49	55	95	47	64	39
48	79.5	Spartanburg	SC	54	72	50	28	24	28	56	36	60	39
37	81.7	Spokane	WA	70	66	28	80	35	47	36	56	47	87
205	56.1	Springfield	IL	81	75	36	61	75	4	79	10	46	39
311	41.0	Springfield	MA	4	20	1	92	41	21	90	62	74	17
218	55.5	Springfield	MO	59	78	31	57	77	71	14	23	61	17
87	70.5	Springfield	OH	15	35	46	28	48	63	86	51	87	56
49	79.5	State College	PA	33	77	40	86	88	98	48	30	44	73
350	23.8	Stockton	CA	36	5	92	12	1	1	36	56	34	2
363	14.4	Sumter	SC	3	65	34	13	37	0	66	15	9	2
276	45.9	Syracuse	NY	46	17	4	89	53	45	40	70	89	17

continued

TABLE 2.5 U.S. METROPOLITAN AREAS BY ALPHABETICAL SEQUENCE WITH RANK (CONTINUED)

RANK	SCORE	METROPOLITAN AREA	STATE	ECONOMY & JOBS	COST OF LIVING	CLIMATE	EDUCATION	HEALTH & HEALTHCARE	CRIME	TRANSPORTATION	LEISURE	ARTS & CULTURE	QUALITY OF LIFE
272	46.3	Tacoma	WA	82	40	82	67	12	16	1	88	77	56
122	67.0	Tallahassee	FL	75	81	61	83	62	27	2	45	74	39
220	54.8	Tampa–St. Petersburg–Clearwater	FL	84	43	82	60	6	9	39	86	67	73
221	54.8	Terre Haute	IN	8	96	49	37	71	21	37	11	44	17
343	23.8	Texarkana	TX-AR	77	98	76	12	96	13	29	13	1	2
120	67.0	Toledo	OH	22	33	39	44	43	33	93	68	83	17
257	48.4	Topeka	KS	32	55	41	47	68	42	47	19	10	17
81	71.6	Trenton–Ewing	NJ	61	13	59	78	36	39	97	84	88	56
212	55.9	Tucson	AZ	44	20	95	65	89	9	11	77	74	70
144	64.3	Tulsa	OK	59	32	79	59	31	11	21	60	57	39
170	60.7	Tuscaloosa	AL	88	62	19	33	68	56	12	22	44	39
318	35.5	Tyler	TX	70	91	75	52	77	6	32	16	13	17
321	35.0	Utica–Rome	NY	4	13	4	58	71	56	41	57	66	2
337	32.9	Valdosta	GA	48	65	72	16	95	32	29	2	5	2
320	35.1	Vallejo–Fairfield	CA	53	3	95	46	0	9	18	95	58	39
356	23.8	Victoria	TX	83	97	86	13	89	18	15	1	27	2
159	61.5	Vineland–Millville–Bridgeton	NJ	20	24	85	2	45	14	80	74	63	39
137	65.4	Virginia Beach–Norfolk–Newport News	VA-NC	62	31	62	66	66	40	10	82	85	56
372	3.6	Visalia–Porterville	CA	0	23	90	1	19	4	18	47	9	2
301	43.5	Waco	TX	79	93	87	43	39	8	96	19	33	2
190	57.8	Warren–Troy–Farmington Hills	MI	41	20	38	76	15	75	10	91	92	39
130	66.2	Washington–Arlington–Alexandria	DC-VA-MD-WV	88	5	42	98	25	25	50	95	96	87
126	66.6	Waterloo–Cedar Falls	IA	51	43	28	58	91	75	69	17	55	39
238	52.2	Wausau	WI	21	41	13	40	65	90	48	5	24	56
358	23.8	Weirton–Steubenville	WV-OH	0	85	27	10	20	97	82	6	7	17
244	50.9	Wenatchee	WA	1	57	77	43	86	69	86	19	40	56
198	57.1	West Palm Beach–Boca Raton–Boynton Beach	FL	86	9	65	59	7	20	74	83	73	73
206	56.0	Wheeling	WV-OH	25	70	27	9	94	84	46	37	57	17
43	80.0	Wichita	KS	20	59	58	53	39	24	34	35	67	39
265	46.8	Wichita Falls	TX	64	89	79	39	89	2	48	7	24	2
332	33.5	Williamsport	PA	11	89	10	29	95	87	44	22	17	17
42	80.5	Wilmington	DE-MD-NJ	71	53	64	50	21	62	100	81	86	39
193	57.6	Wilmington	NC	76	28	52	63	64	30	9	37	29	2
47	79.7	Winchester	VA-WV	95	50	68	20	91	97	58	83	90	93
259	48.0	Worcester	MA	6	12	30	84	17	90	52	97	99	39
277	45.8	Yakima	WA	2	85	33	4	32	24	31	61	40	17
201	56.9	York–Hanover	PA	62	77	32	40	16	85	95	46	7	39
269	46.6	Youngstown–Warren–Boardman	OH-PA	5	72	5	28	63	66	87	36	54	17
371	10.9	Yuba City	CA	44	15	94	10	9	29	9	48	0	2
268	46.6	Yuma	AZ	21	45	90	0	27	39	41	60	11	0

The Categories

The rankings presented in chapter 2 start the journey toward understanding what places are best and why. Gainesville, Bellingham, and Portland probably *are* better places to live for most people than Pensacola, Yakima, and Medford. But there's still a lot more to know.

While by itself the ranking helps to build a general impression of an area, comparing specific facts and attributes provides a much richer understanding of a place, what it costs, and what it has to offer. What is the experience of those living there, and can an individual or family "make it"—that is, prosper financially—there? What are the good and bad features of a place, and how do they trade off? What is the weather like, and how many below-zero nights are there? What about home prices? How do they compare with national averages and other cities? What about cost of living? Home prices? Education? Healthcare? Commute times? Availability and quality of museums? This chapter helps answer those questions by enriching understanding of the facts used in this book to determine the quality of a place and its ranking.

Specifically, this chapter explains the format and content for metropolitan area fact tables developed for chapter 5, covering U.S. metro areas. Many of the explanations also apply to tables for Canada Metropolitan Areas in chapter 6, and the introduction to that chapter addresses any differences that are not obvious. This chapter clarifies the definition, origin, and significance of individual facts while also pointing out important trends observed in overall categories. Further, in this chapter we present *highlight tables* for important fact categories, showing best and worst, most and least, highest and lowest, and other notable extracts. For example, there are listings of cities with the most and fewest cloudy days, highest and lowest cost of living, and highest and lowest job growth.

Reading the Facts

Depending on what we are trying to explain or compare, or what kind of fact is being presented, *Cities Ranked & Rated* presents the figures in different ways. An explanation and clarification of terms upfront will help avoid confusion.

Means, Medians & Averages

Most figures in the metropolitan area fact tables are presented as a statistic for the area, followed by, to its right, a figure representing a U.S. average where such an average is meaningful. Figures are presented either as absolute numbers, percentages, or dollars—whichever makes the most sense for the item and category.

The terms *mean, median,* and *average* occur frequently both in tables and in the discussion that follows in this chapter. Essentially *mean* and *average* are the same thing and are used interchangeably. A mean (or average) is the *arithmetic* average of all data in a set, that is, all figures are added and divided by the total number of figures. An average population growth of all U.S. metropolitan areas of

1.6% doesn't tell us *how many* areas grew at a higher or lower rate than the national average. A limited number of cities growing at a much higher rate may raise the average.

A *median,* on the other hand, is a common statistical representation of data designed to balance the effects of unusual pockets of data far removed from an average. A median population growth of all U.S. metropolitan areas of 1.6% would mean that exactly half of the metropolitan areas were higher and half were lower. Such data as home prices are commonly represented as a median, otherwise a few expensive homes would distort the representative single figure.

Scores, Ratings & Indexes

Just as we did in the first edition, *Cities Ranked & Rated,* 2nd Edition, makes consistent use of three different presentation formats to present metro area facts. Some of these formats are designed to present a bigger picture by grouping multiple facts and occasionally combining them with subjective assessments. Understanding the nature and differences among the formats will enhance the value you get from our presentation.

- A *score* is an accumulation of points converted to a 0–100 scale, with 0 being the lowest or worst and 100 being the highest or best. Points are usually accumulated as a sum of several variables. For example, the air-quality score is compiled from individual measures of particulates, volatile organic compounds, ozone, and other combustion byproducts. The raw score is converted to a 0–100 scale to facilitate comparison among metro areas by indicating where an individual area stacks up against the highest and lowest levels observed for the attribute. An area with an air-quality score of 100 is the best among the 375 metro areas. An area with a 90 is good and, in rough figures, 90% as good as the best area. An area with a score of 20 has relatively dirty air. Air quality, water quality, and pollen/allergy attributes are presented as scores, as are the composite figures for the 10 major ranking categories—Economy & Jobs, Cost of Living, Climate, Education, Health & Healthcare, Crime, Transportation, Leisure, Arts & Culture, and Quality of Life. An area with a 100 for Arts & Culture is best, a 0 is worst, and so forth. ***Note:*** SAT and ACT scores, reported in the Education category, represent true test scores, not 0–100 scale-based scores as we define them here.

- A *rating* is a more qualitative assessment of an attribute presented on a 1–10 scale, with 1 being the lowest or worst and 10 being the highest or best. In the Leisure and Arts & Culture categories, ratings are used to represent a blend of quantitative and subjective assessments. Ratings incorporate "hard" facts such as the number, size, and cost of available facilities with "soft" assessments of quality, accessibility, and proximity. Ratings are used to evaluate such attributes as restaurants, professional sports, performing arts, and museums.

- An *index* compares a quantifiable attribute measured against a national average or norm. Using 100 to represent the average or norm, an individual index is less than 100 for area attributes less than the average or norm and greater than 100 for attributes greater than the norm. The actual figure indicates the percentage difference: 140 is 40% higher than the average; 83 is 17% lower than the average. Cost of living figures are among those presented as an index. Indexes are useful in comparing areas with each other. Suppose the Cost of Living (COL) Index for Area A is 120 and for Area B is

80. The comparative quotient of 120 over 80, or 1.50, suggests that A is actually 50% more expensive than B. Using real numbers, the Fort Lauderdale–Pompano Beach–Deerfield Beach, Florida, area has a COL Index of 129.4, meaning it is 29.4% more expensive than the national average. Fort Smith, Arkansas, on the other hand, has a COL index of 76.2, making it 23.8% cheaper than the national average. Thus, in round numbers Fort Lauderdale is almost 70% (129.4/76.2) more expensive than Fort Smith.

To summarize:

- *Scores* are 0–100 and based mainly on quantitative data.
- *Ratings* are 1–10 and are a mix of quantitative and subjective influences.
- *Indexes* are quantitative comparisons with an average or norm represented by 100.

Use of Data for Ranking & Scoring

Not all facts presented in this book are used to determine metropolitan area scores and ranks. Some information is shown only to indicate more fully the character of a place. Population, for example, doesn't get a score and isn't factored into the overall ranking. Because high and low population density can indicate different things, and may be a matter of personal preference rather than a universally accepted element of area quality, this data point is informational only. Likewise, personal incomes and population numbers above and below certain income levels are interesting to know, but *Cities Ranked & Rated* doesn't place a comparative value judgment on a place strictly because of these factors.

Only facts that are clearly driven by the nature and characteristic of an area and that can be easily qualified as *good* or *bad* are used in the rankings. Employment data, for example, is used for scoring and ranking in the Economy & Jobs category. This data is one of the purest indicators of a strong economy and whether a job, a better job, or income growth might be available for a resident. Even the economic health of those *not* in the traditional job market, such as

TABLE 3.1 NET GAIN OR LOSS IN POPULATION BY REGION			
1990–2004			
	NORTHEAST	MIDWEST	SOUTH	WEST
1990–2000	–3,144,570	–730,087	3,801,093	73,564
2000–2004	–987,262	–644,792	1,411,172	220,882

Source: U.S. Census Bureau

Population

TABLE 3.2 SAMPLE POPULATION DATA FROM GAINESVILLE, FL								
DEMOGRAPHICS	AREA	U.S. AVG	ETHNIC COMPOSITION	AREA	U.S. AVG	RESIDENT PROFILE	AREA	U.S. AVG
Population	247,579		White	72.4%	79.0%	Single	44.8%	32.4%
Population density per sq. mile	202.4	358.5	Black	20.1%	10.5%	Married	40.9%	52.7%
Population growth	30.0%	21.1%	Asian	3.7%	2.7%	Divorced/separated	14.3%	14.9%
Median age	31.6	36.1	Hispanic	5.7%	10.6%	Married with children	17.0%	23.7%
Percent democrat	54.4%	44.5%	Religious observance	34.1%	48.9%	Single with children	8.6%	9.1%
Percent republican	44.7%	54.5%	Diversity measure	49.1	40.1	Over age 65	10.3%	12.9%

self-employed or retired people, is ultimately affected by an area's job and job-growth picture. In addition, employment and job growth not only *make* an area better, they often occur *because* an area is better. Therefore, such a fact can be a double-edged indicator of an area's prospects.

Population

The Population category covers the total population of an area along with population density and growth, ethnic composition, marital and family status, and religious observance of residents.

Overall Population Trends

The most notable trend is the continuing migration of the U.S. population toward the South and West, the South in particular. Table 3.1 shows the total *net* migration (those moving in *less* those moving out) for the 15-year period, 1990–2004.

Better climate and the persistently low costs of living, housing, and doing business have drawn people and jobs to the South and, aside from the larger California and other coastal cities, to the West. Historically, no factor has greater influence on these population shifts than the continued expansion of air-conditioning and climate-control technology. Without it, places like Phoenix, Houston, Atlanta, Las Vegas, and Sacramento would be largely unbearable in summer, particularly for those in commerce and industry.

Additionally, the population concentration in coastal areas has grown. According to the 2000 U.S. Census, more than 148 million people, or 53% of the population, live along the oceans or the Gulf of Mexico. Projections at that time called for a 50% growth in coastal populations over the next 12 years. Aside from the obvious recreational opportunities, people are lured by the more moderate climates and—in most cases—physical beauty. For many years, new immigrants from other nations tended to settle along the coasts. However, that trend, most likely due to costs and greater tolerance of diversity in inland locations, has diminished, and more immigrants are seeking their first U.S. residence in inland locations. Additionally, higher coastal living costs have begun to lead more longtime U.S.

residents inland; so, although coastal population growth continues, it does so at a diminished rate.

Population Attributes

Many *Cities Ranked & Rated*, 2nd Edition, population attributes are based on the 2000 U.S. Census published in 2001. Total population figures have been updated through 2005 by the U.S. Census Annual Population Survey.

Table 3.2 shows the Population table exactly as presented in chapter 5 for Gainesville, Florida.

- *Population* is the 2005 U.S. Census estimated Metropolitan Statistical Area (MSA) population, including the urban core and surrounding county or counties. See chapter 1 for an explanation of the MSA designation.

- *Population density* is the number of people *per square mile* in an area. The average density for a U.S. metropolitan area is 1,261.4 people. This number ranges from under 100 in places with large county areas such as Flagstaff, Arizona, and in smaller cities such as Grand Junction, Colorado, and Pine Bluff, Arkansas, to more than 20,000 per square mile in New York City. The size of the county surrounding the core urban area influences reported density. For more on density and crowding, see the "Growth and Sprawl" sidebar at the end of this section.

- *Population growth* represents the area's population increase or decrease in the 1990–2005 period as a percentage. The population of Las Vegas, Nevada, has more than doubled, while that of Weirton–Steubenville, West Virginia-Ohio, has declined almost 11% during the period. The average metro area population growth is 21.1%.

- *Median age* indicates the median years of age for the area's population. For Gainesville, Florida, the median age is 32.3 years, meaning that half the population is younger than 32.3 and half is older. The U.S. median age of 36.5 (2006 estimate) is evidence that the population of Gainesville is, on average, slightly younger than the country as a whole.

Growth & Sprawl

You'll see it over and over as a negative as you examine the metro areas presented in chapter 5—*growth and sprawl*. Indeed, one of the defining characteristics of the American urban and especially suburban landscape over the last 50 years is the tendency for cities to spread farther and farther into the surrounding countryside. The driving forces for individuals and families are fairly obvious and include the ubiquity of the automobile and the desire for affordable housing in pleasant surroundings. Other factors include the avoidance of inner-city crime and the pursuit of newer, better schools. But the causes don't just lie with individual needs and desires. In many jurisdictions the insatiable thirst for annexation and local sales tax revenue have put expansion at the top of the agenda for many large and smaller cities, particularly in states like Texas, Colorado, Virginia, and others that have, consciously or unconsciously, created a favorable environment for such expansion.

Sprawl has been a concern since the advent of the interstate highway system, and for most of us, it isn't news. But recent escalations in housing costs and expanding job markets on the urban periphery have caused, in our view, a growth explosion. Developers and homebuilders are now large corporations buying huge tracts of land, bringing not just a dozen new homes but, in some cases, tens of thousands in a single development. While the singularity of these developers lends itself to some degree of planning and coordination in the result, we feel it brings monotony and stress in addition to the obvious effects of size.

Entertainment venues aren't local but are national chains. The result is a grinding sameness not only within the area but across the country. Drive from Los Angeles to Jacksonville, Florida, and you'll hardly know what state or city you're in. Beyond the sameness are the obvious effects of growth and sprawl— long commutes, poor air quality, high transportation costs—and the severity of these effects is clearly on the rise. For example, the average commute time across the U.S., estimated at 22.6 minutes in 2000, has grown to 27.4 minutes, and 1-hour-plus commutes have become almost a standard feature in major metro areas. Such commutes make a large dent in quality of life, and in part explain why rankings of larger cities trended downward in this edition.

Sprawl seems ubiquitous, yet we still see it worse in some places than others. Climates are most favorable where few geographic constraints exist, where local laws accommodate or even promote it, and where big is thought to be best. Texas has become a poster child for aggressive growth; annexation-driven Houston now has a third beltway and a second downtown with little end in sight. We see large outbreaks in other cities in the Southwest, including Phoenix, Albuquerque, Denver, and smaller surrounding cities. California continues to have sprawl problems, but they have become moderated in coastal areas by mountainous geography, moving inland to places such as Riverside County and Sacramento. Larger Midwestern cities, some quite in check for many years, are threatened by sprawl issues more than ever— Cincinnati and Minneapolis–St Paul come to mind. Those looking to avoid massive sprawl and cookie-cutter development should look to the Pacific Northwest, New England, New Jersey, and other parts of the Northeast and mid-Atlantic.

If you see "growth and sprawl" listed as a "con" for a metro area in chapter 5, assume that long commutes, air-quality issues, unattractive infrastructure, and a degree of stress aren't far behind.

- *Percent Democrat* and *Percent Republican* shows the percentage that voted Democratic or Republican in the 2004 presidential election. Independent votes are not included.

- *White, Black, Asian,* and *Hispanic* shows the percentage of these ethnic groups in an area. These figures can add up to more than 100% because groups overlap. The most common overlap occurs between white (a large and inclusive *race*) and Hispanic (an ethnic group with a common cultural or national origin).

- *Religious observance* is the percent of the population that regularly attends religious services, taken from a 2000 survey conducted by the Glenmary Research Center. The range across the U.S. is surprisingly high, led by metro areas in the Mormon-dominated Salt Lake Valley and some parts of the upper

Midwest with figures as high as 90% observant. Smaller towns in the Pacific Northwest tend to show the lowest figures, dropping as low as 23%.

- *Diversity measure* is a calculation furnished by Sperling's BestPlaces (www.bestplaces.net). It represents the probability that the next person you meet "on the street" is of an ethnic origin other than your own. This is the best measure of overall diversity, as "person A" who encounters someone else on the street represents *all* races and ethnic groups, not just the white majority group. A high score indicates a high probability of meeting someone unlike yourself. Results range from a low of 6% in Altoona, Pennsylvania, to a high of 84% in the Los Angeles area. In Los Angeles, the measure indicates that there is an 84% chance that the next person met is of a different ethnicity. The average percentage across U.S. metro areas is 40.3%.

- *Single, Married,* and *Divorced/Separated* show the percentage of individuals in an area with these profiles.

- *Married with children* and *Single with children* show the percentage of families of either marital status with one or more children. A high presence of families with children *may* indicate that an area is well suited for children. In this case, schools may be better, more activities may exist for children, and crime may be lower. Interestingly, the married-with-children statistic is lowest in Florida cities, where the presence of retirees drives the figure below 20% in most areas, and 9 of the lowest 10 cities in the U.S. are in that state. At the same time, Texas border towns and areas of Utah lead the list with Provo, Utah, highest at just over 43%. The U.S. average is just under 29%.

- *Percent over age 65* is the percentage of the population in that age group. The highest concentrations, not surprisingly, are in Florida with Punta Gorda highest at 35%, while the lowest occur in an assortment of military, border, and college towns, ranging from 5% upward.

Population Highlights, Tables 3.3–3.10

TABLE 3.3 LARGEST & SMALLEST METROPOLITAN AREAS			
BY POPULATION			
LARGEST METRO AREAS	**POPULATION**	**SMALLEST METRO AREAS**	**POPULATION**
Los Angeles–Long Beach–Glendale, CA	10,088,274	Carson City, NV	56,679
New York–White Plains, NY	9,456,583	Lewiston, ID	58,928
Chicago–Naperville–Joliet, IL	7,883,317	Hinesville–Fort Stewart, GA	68,159
Houston–Sugar Land–Baytown, TX	5,239,517	Casper, WY	69,177
Atlanta–Sandy Springs–Marietta, GA	4,765,845	Columbus, IN	72,867
Washington–Arlington–Alexandria, DC-VA-MD-WV	4,080,798	Sandusky, OH	78,374
Philadelphia, PA	3,888,163	Great Falls, MT	79,448
Dallas–Plano–Irving, TX	3,873,350	Corvallis, OR	81,105
Riverside–San Bernardino–Ontario, CA	3,753,368	Danville, IL	82,333
Phoenix–Mesa–Scottsdale, AZ	3,730,550	Pocatello, ID	82,874
Minneapolis–St. Paul–Bloomington, MN-WI	3,138,324	Ames, IA	84,569
Santa Ana–Anaheim–Irvine, CA	3,015,707	Fairbanks, AK	84,771
San Diego–Carlsbad–San Marcos, CA	2,998,625	Cheyenne, WY	85,454
Nassau–Suffolk, NY	2,828,933	Elmira, NY	90,057
St. Louis, MO	2,754,233	Dubuque, IA	90,696
Baltimore–Towson, MD	2,644,882	Hot Springs, AR	92,752
Tampa–St. Petersburg–Clearwater, FL	2,592,782	Rome, GA	94,758
Oakland–Fremont–Hayward, CA	2,500,934	Grand Forks, ND	95,087
Warren–Troy–Farmington Hills, MI	2,481,882	Longview, WA	96,262
Seattle–Bellevue–Everett, WA	2,444,743	Brunswick, GA	97,758
Pittsburgh, PA	2,402,483	Bismarck, ND	97,858
Miami–Miami Beach–Kendall, FL	2,378,142	Fond du Lac, WI	98,791
Denver–Aurora, CO	2,350,559	Missoula, MT	99,890
Edison, NJ	2,313,085	Cumberland, MD	100,406
Newark–Union, NJ-PA	2,159,686	Kokomo, IN	101,258
Cleveland–Elyria–Mentor, OH	2,136,729	Ocean City, NJ	101,848
Portland–Vancouver–Beaverton, OR-WA	2,082,023	Gadsden, AL	103,134
Cincinnati–Middletown, OH-KY-IN	2,063,586	Wenatchee, WA	103,216
Sacramento–Arden-Arcade–Roseville, CA	2,023,535	Ithaca, NY	103,641
Detroit–Livonia–Dearborn, MI	2,014,262	Lawrence, KS	104,295

Source: U.S. Census Bureau, 2005 Population Survey

TABLE 3.4 FASTEST GROWING METROPOLITAN AREAS BY POPULATION, 1990–2005

METRO AREA	PERCENTAGE GROWTH
St. George, UT	127.6%
Las Vegas–Paradise, NV	124.9%
Naples–Marco Island, FL	102.2%
Bend, OR	82.7%
Prescott, AZ	78.6%
Coeur d'Alene, ID	74.5%
McAllen–Edinburg–Mission, TX	73.7%
Austin–Round Rock, TX	72.7%
Gainesville, GA	71.0%
Raleigh–Cary, NC	70.7%
Greeley, CO	68.4%
Laredo, TX	68.0%
Phoenix–Mesa–Scottsdale, AZ	66.7%
Boise City–Nampa, ID	66.7%
Yuma, AZ	66.4%
Fayetteville–Springdale–Rogers, AR-MO	66.3%
Atlanta–Sandy Springs–Marietta, GA	65.5%
Denver–Aurora, CO	61.8%
Dallas–Plano–Irving, TX	58.6%
Provo–Orem, UT	57.4%
Orlando–Kissimmee, FL	57.0%
Madera, CA	55.4%
Cape Coral–Fort Myers, FL	54.7%
Wilmington, NC	51.6%
Reno–Sparks, NV	51.2%
Myrtle Beach–Conway–North Myrtle Beach, SC	51.0%
Ocala, FL	49.7%
Charlotte–Gastonia–Concord, NC-SC	47.7%
Riverside–San Bernardino–Ontario, CA	45.9%
Brownsville–Harlingen, TX	45.5%

Source: U.S. Census Bureau, 2005 Population Survey

TABLE 3.5 DECLINING & SLOWEST GROWING METROPOLITAN AREAS BY POPULATION, 1990–2005

METRO AREA	PERCENTAGE GROWTH
Weirton–Steubenville, WV-OH	−10.7%
Johnstown, PA	−9.1%
Grand Forks, ND	−7.8%
Danville, IL	−6.7%
Decatur, IL	−6.5%
Wheeling, WV	−6.1%
Utica–Rome, NY	−5.9%
Elmira, NY	−5.4%
Binghamton, NY	−5.3%
Detroit–Livonia–Dearborn, MI	−4.6%
Pittsfield, MA	−4.6%
Scranton–Wilkes-Barre, PA	−4.5%
Youngstown–Warren–Boardman, OH-PA	−3.9%
Springfield, OH	−3.2%
Altoona, PA	−3.1%
Anniston–Oxford, AL	−3.0%
Jacksonville, NC	−2.8%
Buffalo–Niagara Falls, NY	−2.8%
Muncie, IN	−2.5%
Bay City, MI	−2.3%
Pittsburgh, PA	−2.2%
Saginaw–Saginaw Township North, MI	−1.4%
Lima, OH	−1.3%
Cumberland, MD	−1.3%
Pine Bluff, AR	−1.1%
Alexandria, LA	−1.1%
Huntington–Ashland, WV-KY-OH	−0.7%
Williamsport, PA	−0.7%
Syracuse, NY	−0.4%
Anderson, IN	−0.4%

Source: U.S. Census Bureau, 2005 Population Survey

TABLE 3.6 POPULATION DENSITY

MOST CROWDED METRO AREAS	PERSONS PER SQUARE MILE	LEAST CROWDED METRO AREAS	SQUARE MILE
New York–White Plains, NY	26,516.5	Flagstaff, AZ	6.9
San Francisco–San Mateo–Redwood City, CA	8,007.5	Fairbanks, AK	11.5
Philadelphia, PA	5,077.2	Casper, WY	13.0
Boston–Quincy, MA	5,043.0	Wenatchee, WA	22.0
Chicago–Naperville–Joliet, IL	4,290.0	Farmington, NM	22.9
Newark–Union, NJ-PA	3,881.7	Prescott, AZ	23.7
Santa Ana–Anaheim–Irvine, CA	3,820.2	Rapid City, SD	28.0
Detroit–Livonia–Dearborn, MI	3,279.7	Great Falls, MT	29.4
Washington–Arlington–Alexandria, DC-VA-MD-WV	3,151.0	Cheyenne, WY	31.8
Nassau–Suffolk, NY	3,075.9	Yuma, AZ	32.3
Baltimore–Towson, MD	2,606.3	Duluth, MN	32.8
Milwaukee–Waukesha–West Allis, WI	2,580.1	Grand Forks, ND	35.3
Los Angeles–Long Beach–Glendale, CA	2,484.3	Bismarck, ND	36.5
Cleveland–Elyria–Mentor, OH	2,093.5	El Centro, CA	36.9
Virginia Beach–Norfolk–Newport News, VA-NC	1,990.4	Grand Junction, CO	38.1
Dallas–Plano–Irving, TX	1,811.8	Missoula, MT	38.4
Cambridge–Newton–Framingham, MA	1,787.0	Lewiston, ID	40.6
Oakland–Fremont–Hayward, CA	1,768.6	Idaho Falls, ID	42.4
Tampa–St. Petersburg–Clearwater, FL	1,758.0	Bangor, ME	43.6
Trenton–Ewing, NJ	1,626.1	Bend, OR	45.4
Houston–Sugar Land–Baytown, TX	1,617.3	St. George, UT	45.5
Edison, NJ	1,612.9	Redding, CA	47.1
Bethesda–Gaithersburg–Frederick, MD	1,593.5	Billings, MT	48.1
Fort Worth–Arlington, TX	1,590.0	Las Cruces, NM	49.0
Honolulu, HI	1,529.2	Yakima, WA	53.3
St. Louis, MO	1,528.2	Greeley, CO	55.6
Minneapolis–St. Paul–Bloomington, MN-WI	1,487.4	Reno–Sparks, NV	60.3
Essex County, MA	1,482.6	Pocatello, ID	62.4
New Orleans, LA	1,466.7	Pueblo, CO	63.1
Fort Lauderdale–Pompano Beach–Deerfield Beach, FL	1,452.2	Mount Vernon–Anacortes, WA	63.9

Source: U.S. Census Bureau, 2005 Population Survey

TABLE 3.7 DEMOCRATS & REPUBLICANS
AREAS WITH HIGHEST VOTING PERCENTAGE DEMOCRAT & REPUBLICAN IN 2004 ELECTION

METRO AREAS MOST DEMOCRATIC	PERCENTAGE	METRO AREAS MOST REPUBLICAN	PERCENTAGE
San Francisco–San Mateo–Redwood City, CA	76.1%	Provo–Orem, UT	85.8%
Pittsfield, MA	73.1%	Logan, UT	82.6%
Santa Cruz–Watsonville, CA	73.0%	St. George, UT	81.0%
New York–White Plains, NY	72.0%	Idaho Falls, ID	79.0%
Santa Fe, NM	71.1%	Midland–Odessa, TX	78.6%
Oakland–Fremont–Hayward, CA	69.9%	Amarillo, TX	78.5%
Detroit–Livonia–Dearborn, MI	69.4%	Gainesville, GA	78.2%
Santa Rosa–Petaluma, CA	67.2%	Fort Walton Beach–Crestview–Destin, FL	77.6%
Boulder, CO	66.3%	Abilene, TX	76.9%
Duluth, MN	64.9%	San Angelo, TX	75.5%
Boston–Quincy, MA	64.2%	Ogden–Clearfield, UT	75.3%
Ithaca, NY	64.2%	Lubbock, TX	75.2%
Fort Lauderdale–Pompano Beach–Deerfield Beach, FL	64.2%	Dothan, AL	74.2%
Cambridge–Newton–Framingham, MA	64.0%	Dalton, GA	72.9%
Madison, WI	63.8%	Tyler, TX	72.5%
Springfield, MA	63.6%	Wichita Falls, TX	72.1%
San Jose–Sunnyvale–Santa Clara, CA	63.6%	Holland–Grand Haven, MI	71.6%
Philadelphia, PA	63.5%	Panama City–Lynn Haven, FL	71.2%
Ann Arbor, MI	63.5%	Longview, TX	71.1%
Durham, NC	63.1%	Joplin, MO	71.1%
Los Angeles–Long Beach–Glendale, CA	63.1%	Cleveland, TN	70.7%
Washington–Arlington–Alexandria, DC-VA-MD-WV	62.2%	Elkhart–Goshen, IN	70.0%
Chicago–Naperville–Joliet, IL	61.9%	Jacksonville, NC	69.5%
Seattle–Bellevue–Everett, WA	61.8%	Sherman–Denison, TX	69.3%
Trenton–Ewing, NJ	61.3%	Pensacola–Ferry Pass–Brent, FL	69.1%
Providence–New Bedford–Fall River, RI-MA	61.1%	Victoria, TX	68.7%
Pine Bluff, AR	60.9%	Hattiesburg, MS	68.6%
Bethesda–Gaithersburg–Frederick, MD	60.9%	Rapid City, SD	67.9%
Burlington–South Burlington, VT	60.8%	Williamsport, PA	67.9%
Tallahassee, FL	60.8%	College Station–Bryan, TX	67.8%

Source: State Elections Divisions, 2006

TABLE 3.8 PERCENT RELIGIOUSLY OBSERVANT
PERCENTAGE OF POPULATION SELF-DECLARED AS RELIGIOUSLY OBSERVANT

METRO AREAS MOST OBSERVANT	PERCENTAGE	METRO AREAS LEAST OBSERVANT	PERCENTAGE
Provo–Orem, UT	89.8%	Medford, OR	22.2%
Logan, UT	85.6%	Corvallis, OR	22.6%
Johnstown, PA	81.6%	Hinesville–Fort Stewart, GA	23.1%
Lafayette, LA	80.8%	Redding, CA	23.9%
Appleton, WI	79.5%	Eugene–Springfield, OR	24.5%
Bismarck, ND	79.3%	Jacksonville, NC	25.8%
Dubuque, IA	78.3%	Ithaca, NY	26.5%
Las Cruces, NM	77.4%	Bend, OR	26.9%
Idaho Falls, ID	76.6%	Muncie, IN	27.3%
St. George, UT	75.1%	Olympia, WA	27.4%
Houma–Bayou Cane–Thibodaux, LA	75.1%	Chico, CA	27.4%
Ogden–Clearfield, UT	74.9%	Reno–Sparks, NV	27.7%
Cambridge–Newton–Framingham, MA	73.6%	Bremerton–Silverdale, WA	28.3%
Laredo, TX	73.6%	Grand Junction, CO	28.6%
Sheboygan, WI	72.3%	Yuba City, CA	28.6%
Owensboro, KY	71.9%	Lawrence, KS	29.1%
Green Bay, WI	71.8%	Bellingham, WA	29.4%
Nassau–Suffolk, NY	71.8%	Prescott, AZ	29.7%
Buffalo–Niagara Falls, NY	71.0%	Tacoma, WA	29.8%
Wausau, WI	70.8%	Morgantown, WV	29.8%
Bridgeport–Stamford–Norwalk, CT	70.1%	Charleston, WV	30.6%
Amarillo, TX	69.5%	Flagstaff, AZ	30.9%
St. Cloud, MN	68.4%	Greenville, NC	31.4%
Gadsden, AL	68.3%	Madera, CA	31.6%
Fond du Lac, WI	67.7%	Longview, WA	31.9%
Salt Lake City, UT	67.7%	Coeur d'Alene, ID	32.0%
Victoria, TX	67.7%	Dover, DE	32.1%
Pittsfield, MA	67.1%	Santa Rosa–Petaluma, CA	32.2%
La Crosse, WI	66.6%	Missoula, MT	32.4%
Dothan, AL	66.5%	Portland–Vancouver–Beaverton, OR-WA	33.0%

Source: Glenmary Research Center, 2000

TABLE 3.9 DIVERSITY MEASURE
PROBABILITY NEXT PERSON MET OF DIFFERENT ETHNIC ORIGIN

MOST DIVERSE METRO AREAS	PERCENTAGE	LEAST DIVERSE METRO AREAS	PERCENTAGE
Los Angeles–Long Beach–Glendale, CA	84%	Altoona, PA	6%
Fresno, CA	82%	Parkersburg–Marietta–Vienna, WV-OH	7%
Stockton, CA	81%	Bangor, ME	8%
Hanford–Corcoran, CA	81%	Kingsport–Bristol–Bristol, TN-VA	8%
Merced, CA	81%	Huntington–Ashland, WV-KY-OH	10%
Salinas, CA	80%	Dubuque, IA	10%
Riverside–San Bernardino–Ontario, CA	79%	Portland–South Portland–Biddeford, ME	10%
Visalia–Porterville, CA	79%	Wheeling, WV	10%
Bakersfield, CA	79%	Lewiston–Auburn, ME	10%
San Jose–Sunnyvale–Santa Clara, CA	78%	Rockingham County–Strafford County, NH	10%
Madera, CA	78%	Eau Claire, WI	10%
Vallejo–Fairfield, CA	77%	Scranton–Wilkes-Barre, PA	10%
Oakland–Fremont–Hayward, CA	77%	Johnstown, PA	11%
New York–White Plains, NY	76%	Bismarck, ND	11%
Santa Ana–Anaheim–Irvine, CA	75%	Glens Falls, NY	12%
Yakima, WA	75%	Burlington–South Burlington, VT	12%
Modesto, CA	75%	Weirton–Steubenville, WV-OH	12%
El Centro, CA	74%	St. Cloud, MN	12%
Yuma, AZ	74%	Williamsport, PA	12%
Albuquerque, NM	74%	Duluth, MN	12%
Houston–Sugar Land–Baytown, TX	74%	La Crosse, WI	13%
San Diego–Carlsbad–San Marcos, CA	73%	Cumberland, MD	13%
Honolulu, HI	73%	Johnson City, TN	13%
Oxnard–Thousand Oaks–Ventura, CA	73%	Fond du Lac, WI	13%
Miami–Miami Beach–Kendall, FL	72%	Owensboro, KY	13%
Las Cruces, NM	72%	Springfield, MO	14%
Santa Fe, NM	72%	Monroe, MI	14%
San Antonio, TX	71%	Coeur d'Alene, ID	14%
Santa Barbara–Santa Maria, CA	71%	Barnstable Town, MA	14%
Farmington, NM	70%	Cedar Rapids, IA	14%

Source: Sperling's BestPlaces, 2006

TABLE 3.10 FAMILIES WITH CHILDREN
PERCENTAGE OF HOUSEHOLDS WITH ONE OR MORE CHILDREN UNDER 19 PRESENT

METRO AREAS WITH MOST FAMILIES WITH CHILDREN	PERCENTAGE	METRO AREAS WITH FEWEST FAMILIES WITH CHILDREN	PERCENTAGE
Provo–Orem, UT	43.2%	Punta Gorda, FL	12.0%
Laredo, TX	41.8%	Sarasota–Bradenton–Venice, FL	14.3%
McAllen–Edinburg–Mission, TX	39.0%	Sebastian–Vero Beach, FL	15.1%
Logan, UT	38.4%	Cape Coral–Fort Myers, FL	15.6%
Ogden–Clearfield, UT	37.7%	Ocala, FL	15.9%
Hinesville–Fort Stewart, GA	35.5%	Deltona–Daytona Beach–Ormond Beach, FL	16.2%
Brownsville–Harlingen, TX	34.3%	Naples–Marco Island, FL	16.5%
Idaho Falls, ID	34.1%	Prescott, AZ	16.8%
El Centro, CA	33.7%	Port St. Lucie–Fort Pierce, FL	17.0%
Lake County–Kenosha County, IL-WI	32.8%	Gainesville, FL	17.0%
El Paso, TX	32.8%	Hot Springs, AR	17.4%
Hanford–Corcoran, CA	32.8%	West Palm Beach–Boca Raton–Boynton Beach, FL	17.6%
Salt Lake City, UT	32.7%	Myrtle Beach–Conway–North Myrtle Beach, SC	17.6%
Holland–Grand Haven, MI	32.6%	Barnstable Town, MA	17.7%
Merced, CA	32.5%	Tampa–St. Petersburg–Clearwater, FL	17.9%
Jacksonville, NC	32.4%	Ithaca, NY	18.2%
Visalia–Porterville, CA	31.7%	Wilmington, NC	18.3%
Oxnard–Thousand Oaks–Ventura, CA	31.0%	Ocean City, NJ	18.4%
Killeen–Temple–Fort Hood, TX	30.9%	San Francisco–San Mateo–Redwood City, CA	18.4%
Fairbanks, AK	30.5%	Palm Bay–Melbourne–Titusville, FL	18.5%
St. George, UT	30.4%	Tallahassee, FL	18.7%
Nassau–Suffolk, NY	30.0%	Chico, CA	18.7%
Appleton, WI	29.9%	Pittsfield, MA	18.8%
Riverside–San Bernardino–Ontario, CA	29.8%	Danville, VA	18.8%
Modesto, CA	29.8%	Blacksburg–Christiansburg–Radford, VA	18.9%
Salinas, CA	29.8%	Muncie, IN	19.1%
Clarksville, TN	29.7%	Detroit–Livonia–Dearborn, MI	19.1%
Kennewick–Richland–Pasco, WA	29.7%	Weirton–Steubenville, WV-OH	19.2%
Bakersfield, CA	29.3%	New York–White Plains, NY	19.4%
Madera, CA	29.2%	Lakeland, FL	19.4%

Source: U.S. Census American Community Survey, 2005

Economy & Jobs

The Economy & Jobs category includes specific information on personal and household income, employment, job mix, and the largest employing industries in an area.

Overall Employment Trends

Although some questions exist about how the statistics are collected and presented, largely based on the number of people actively seeking employment, overall employment trends have been favorable since the 2001–2003 recession. The well-publicized national unemployment rate has dropped to 4.7% from 6.1% in mid-2003. Within those figures, we see a continuation of a migration away from manufacturing jobs toward more jobs in the service sector. More disturbing, in our view, is the growth of construction and other real estate–related employment, which might include mortgage lending and individuals engaged in producing real estate transactions—realtors, escrow officers, and the like. The recent real estate boom brought a rapid rise in this area and in retail associated the growth and sprawl this construction has produced.

Unfortunately, much of this employment and the prosperity brought to certain areas appears temporary, as the boom cools and as it is supported largely through funds borrowed as long-term mortgages. Areas without deep manufacturing or research roots and that have experienced rapid rises in real estate–related employment, such as Sacramento, Phoenix, and Las Vegas, might be especially vulnerable, and we have called out this vulnerability in our analysis of these places. We are also concerned about the aggressive growth in healthcare employment, which, while steady and relatively high paying, tends to extract wealth from an area more than it creates. Bottom line: We prefer areas with a balanced employment base among manufacturing, government, and service activities and that produce goods and services that can be sold outside the area.

Economy & Jobs Attributes

The Economy & Jobs category is divided into *Income*, *Employment*, and *Largest Employing Industry*. Income and employment data come from the U.S. Department of Labor Bureau of Labor Statistics, the U.S. Census Bureau including the U.S. Economic Census, and Claritas, Inc., a large private supplier of market and demographic data.

Table 3.11 shows the Economy & Jobs table for Bellingham, Washington.

Income

Of the following data points, only *Household income growth* is included in scoring and ranking.

- *Per capita income* is the average annual dollar income for every man, woman, and child in the U.S. population in 2000. Metropolitan area and national averages are shown.

- *Household income* is the average annual 2005 dollar income per U.S. household, defined as a home with more than one member. Household income is the best single indicator of the economic status of an average family, and taken together with cost of living, gives a picture of a family's standard of living. We'll offer this more complete picture in the upcoming "Cost of Living" section. Areas with a relatively large difference between per capita and household income probably have more two-earner households. These figures range from a low of $28,000 to $32,000 annually in Texas border towns to more than $93,000 in San Jose, California, with a U.S. average of $44,614. It should be noted that some college towns, like top-ranked Gainesville, Florida, show relatively low median household incomes due to high student populations.

- *Household income < $25K* and *Household income > $75K* are 2005 figures expressed as percentages of the total population that indicate income distribution. Areas with a high percentage below $25K are disadvantaged; likewise, areas with a high percentage above $75K indicate wealth and a higher standard of living. Note that these figures are not absolute indicators of standard of living because cost of living varies widely between areas. Again, figures for college towns, where underemployed students mix with highly paid academics and administrators, may be misleading.

- *Household income growth* is the percentage change in household incomes over the 2002–2006 period.

TABLE 3.11 SAMPLE ECONOMY & JOBS DATA FROM BELLINGHAM, WA

INCOME	AREA	U.S. AVG	EMPLOYMENT	AREA	U.S. AVG	EMPLOYING INDUSTRIES		
Per capita income	$22,543	$23,235	Unemployment rate	4.8%	4.7%	Largest: Manufacturing		
Household income	$44,430	$46,414	Recent job growth	5.5%	1.3%			
Household income ‹ $25K	26.9%	26.2%	Projected future job growth	27.6%	11.5%	Percent manufacturing	13.5%	15.4%
Household income › $75K	23.7%	25.4%	White collar	57.1%	57.8%	Percent public sector	15.2%	15.7%
Household income growth	11.1%	13.6%	Blue collar	23.6%	25.2%	Percent construction	10.1%	9.9%

$
Economy
& Jobs

Score: 97.1
Rank: 12

Figures above national averages tell of a strong economy and an improving job mix, while figures below national averages may indicate economic challenges ahead for the average family. Income growth averages over 13% for the 5-year period; the range is wide, from the high single digits in Rust Belt areas such as Rockford, Illinois, and Kokomo, Indiana, to the high teens in several California locations and some prosperous new-economy cities such as Boston, Salt Lake City, and San Francisco.

Employment

The following facts are collected to give a picture of area employment level and mix as an indicator of quality and sustainability of employment in an area. Employment level includes current unemployment rates and recent and projected future job growth. In this edition, particularly owing to our concerns about boom employment in construction and real estate noted above, we place a little more emphasis on future job-growth projections and suggest you do the same. As also noted earlier, we feel the employment mix in an area is important, and offer some facts, including the percentage of job *types*—white collar, blue collar, and service—and key employing industry segments including manufacturing, construction, and the public sector.

- *Unemployment rate* is the standard figure provided by the Bureau of Labor Statistics and frequently reported in the media. Representing the percentage of active job seekers without a job, the figure excludes all of those not seeking employment, whether they have gone back to school or given up their search. Because of this, the number may understate the true amount of economic dislocation in an area. It may also be affected by surges of new job seekers, such as college students looking for work at the beginning of summer. Regardless, it is a relevant indicator of the economy in a local area, particularly when examined over time. The figures are from August 2006 when the U.S. average unemployment rate was 4.7%.

- *Recent job growth* shows the percentage growth in total jobs from August 2005 through August 2006. The figure reveals the recent economic health of an area.

- *Projected future job growth*, a projection through 2010 calculated by Sperling's BestPlaces, is based on recent job growth and other economic indicators present in an area. Like any growth projection, it is subject to error depending on the economy as a whole and dynamics within a particular area. The calculation is especially revealing when first compared to national averages and then compared

between metropolitan areas. Average metro area projected job growth is 11.5%, compared to 15.4% coming out of the 2001–2003 recession as reported in the first edition of *Cities Ranked & Rated*. But several areas, notably in the Great Lakes region and upstate New York, have negative projections, while retirement and construction boom towns such as St. George, Utah; Coeur d'Alene, Idaho; and Las Vegas hold the top spots with projections as high as 52%. Most other strong areas are in the Southwest and are either retirement and construction boom centers or border towns adjacent to Mexico.

- *White collar* represents the percentage of the employment base considered executive, managerial, technical, sales, clerical, administrative, or of such professional specialties as law, medicine, or education. These jobs generally require a college education or specific, academically oriented skills. Typically these jobs are salaried, not hourly. A comparatively high percentage of white-collar workers indicates higher-paying jobs, greater affluence, and a higher educational base for the population.

- *Blue collar* represents the percentage in the trades and labor sector who perform manual labor and earn an hourly wage, including such professions as production operators, repair technicians, transportation workers, construction trades and laborers, and agricultural workers, to name a few. These professions are less likely to require a 4-year college education, and workers are more likely to receive lower compensation than those in white-collar jobs, but some are quite skilled and are paid well.

Employing Industries

The nature and mix of employing industries in an area will not only tell a lot about the mix of available jobs but also about the economic stability and even the character of a place. An area with a strong manufacturing presence is likely to have a different character than one dominated by construction and service businesses or one where public sector jobs pull the largest weight. Taken together with employment mix—blue collar, white collar, and service—the picture of local employment becomes clearer. We can't give a complete picture of an area's economic mix in a few facts and descriptions, but with the following we try to give a sense of what readers can expect to find and a sense of how balanced an area's economy tends to be. Readers are encouraged to research the U.S. Economic Census (see the upcoming sidebar, "Taking the Economic Pulse: The U.S. Economic Census") and contact local chamber of commerce organizations to find out more about industry and job mix. The better organizations have lists of largest employers and largest employing industries on their websites.

As stated earlier in this section, a balance among employing industry sectors suggests stability and long-term economic viability.

- *Largest employing industry* is based on NAICS (North American Industry Classification System) codes from the U.S. Economic Census. The data represent the largest industry in the area by number of people employed.

- *Percent manufacturing employment* represents the percentage of area employment in the manufacturing sector, which comprises, as described by the U.S. Census, "... establishments engaged in the mechanical, physical, or chemical transformation of materials, substances, or components into new products." Most such activity occurs in typical manufacturing plants, but the census goes on to add that it can include such activities as baking, candy making, and tailoring. The strongest manufacturing concentrations are found in small towns in the Midwest and South, with Dalton, Georgia, leading the way at

almost 36%. Lower concentrations are in college towns and in other high-end employment centers.

- *Percent public sector employment* covers a broad assortment of public entities and job classifications including traditional government bodies but also military and education and healthcare as delivered by the public sector. Areas with high public sector employment are stable but are not always prosperous and are usually not high-growth areas. Places with high military concentrations (such as Lawton, Oklahoma), large areas of public land nearby (Fairbanks, Alaska), and smaller towns with large public universities and university hospitals (College Station, Texas) are high in this list.

- *Percent construction employment* represents the construction sector including engineering, actual construction trades, site preparation, and some repair and upgrading activities. Our interest in construction employment stems from the typically temporal nature of this activity and the fact is it largely supported by borrowed funds. Areas with highest construction employment are boom towns such as St. George, Utah, and Prescott, Arizona, as well as—unfortunately—hurricane-stricken areas along the Gulf Coast.

Economy & Jobs Highlights, Tables 3.12–3.19

TABLE 3.12 MEDIAN HOUSEHOLD INCOME			
MEDIAN COMBINED ANNUAL GROSS HOUSEHOLD INCOME			
METRO AREAS WITH HIGHEST HOUSEHOLD INCOME	INCOME	METRO AREAS WITH LOWEST HOUSEHOLD INCOME	INCOME
San Jose–Sunnyvale–Santa Clara, CA	$93,503	McAllen–Edinburg–Mission, TX	$28,677
Bethesda–Gaithersburg–Frederick, MD	$86,410	Brownsville–Harlingen, TX	$30,296
Nassau–Suffolk, NY	$81,775	Morgantown, WV	$32,712
San Francisco–San Mateo–Redwood City, CA	$79,975	Laredo, TX	$32,731
Bridgeport–Stamford–Norwalk, CT	$79,096	Huntington–Ashland, WV-KY-OH	$33,432
Washington–Arlington–Alexandria, DC-VA-MD-WV	$78,879	College Station–Bryan, TX	$33,504
Lake County–Kenosha County, IL-WI	$76,164	Johnstown, PA	$33,828
Cambridge–Newton–Framingham, MA	$75,771	Las Cruces, NM	$34,143
Oakland–Fremont–Hayward, CA	$72,781	Wheeling, WV	$34,195
Edison, NJ	$71,689	Auburn–Opelika, AL	$34,475
Oxnard–Thousand Oaks–Ventura, CA	$70,833	Alexandria, LA	$34,570
Santa Ana–Anaheim–Irvine, CA	$69,764	Jonesboro, AR	$34,589
Newark–Union, NJ-PA	$69,730	Danville, VA	$34,654
Trenton–Ewing, NJ	$69,514	Cumberland, MD	$34,726
Boulder, CO	$69,148	Gadsden, AL	$34,883
Vallejo–Fairfield, CA	$68,961	El Paso, TX	$35,116
Santa Cruz–Watsonville, CA	$68,923	Johnson City, TN	$35,321
Warren–Troy–Farmington Hills, MI	$68,472	Pine Bluff, AR	$35,380
Santa Rosa–Petaluma, CA	$67,322	Gainesville, FL	$35,575
Minneapolis–St. Paul–Bloomington, MN-WI	$66,602	Valdosta, GA	$35,716
Rockingham County–Strafford County, NH	$65,330	Lubbock, TX	$35,758
Denver–Aurora, CO	$64,927	Hattiesburg, MS	$35,826
Anchorage, AK	$63,784	Weirton–Steubenville, WV-OH	$36,036
Boston–Quincy, MA	$63,653	Fort Smith, AR	$36,179
Napa, CA	$63,508	Hot Springs, AR	$36,267
Bergen–Passaic, NJ	$63,096	Blacksburg–Christiansburg–Radford, VA	$36,272
Manchester–Nashua, NH	$62,986	Anniston–Oxford, AL	$36,316
Camden, NJ	$62,119	Ocala, FL	$36,373
Essex County, MA	$62,088	Kingsport–Bristol–Bristol, TN-VA	$36,436
Poughkeepsie–Newburgh–Middletown, NY	$62,051	Morristown, TN	$36,473

Source: Claritas, Inc., from U.S. Census, 2006

Taking the Economic Pulse: The U.S. Economic Census

The U.S. Economic Census collects and organizes vast amounts of information about business and industry and tabulates it by state, county, metro area, and city. Unfortunately, it isn't easy to do a high-level assessment of economic and industry mix by metro area. The U.S. Census Economic Census portal (www.census.gov/main/www/cen2000.html) is set up to pull reports by state and then industry. This helps to understand the statewide picture for a particular industry, but you must pull a lot of reports to get a read on the complete makeup of a metro area. The most current data offered is from 2002, although economic data doesn't change very fast for most places and most industries. A new economic census survey will refresh the data in 2007, but full results may not be published for some time after that. We expect the economic census data, over time, to expand coverage and become more accessible and easier to use for those who like to get a good read on an area's economy.

TABLE 3.13 HOUSEHOLD INCOME GROWTH			
PERCENTAGE OF GROWTH FROM 2002 TO 2006			
METRO AREAS WITH HIGHEST GROWTH	PERCENTAGE	METRO AREAS WITH LOWEST GROWTH	PERCENTAGE
Houma–Bayou Cane–Thibodaux, LA	19.2%	Columbus, IN	8.1%
Santa Rosa–Petaluma, CA	19.0%	Rockford, IL	8.2%
Santa Cruz–Watsonville, CA	18.4%	Kokomo, IN	8.3%
Vallejo–Fairfield, CA	18.3%	Flint, MI	8.5%
Fort Collins–Loveland, CO	18.3%	Atlantic City, NJ	9.0%
Napa, CA	18.2%	Elkhart–Goshen, IN	9.1%
Yuma, AZ	18.1%	Saginaw–Saginaw Township North, MI	9.4%
Cape Coral–Fort Myers, FL	17.8%	Erie, PA	9.5%
Casper, WY	17.8%	Holland–Grand Haven, MI	9.5%
Hanford–Corcoran, CA	17.6%	Janesville, WI	9.5%
Salinas, CA	17.6%	Decatur, IL	9.6%
Lafayette, LA	17.6%	Springfield, OH	9.7%
Goldsboro, NC	17.4%	Fort Wayne, IN	9.8%
Oakland–Fremont–Hayward, CA	17.4%	Danville, VA	9.8%
San Francisco–San Mateo–Redwood City, CA	17.4%	Monroe, MI	9.8%
Lawrence, KS	17.3%	York–Hanover, PA	9.8%
Essex County, MA	17.3%	Michigan City–La Porte, IN	10.0%
San Diego–Carlsbad–San Marcos, CA	17.2%	Rochester, NY	10.2%
Pueblo, CO	17.2%	Seattle–Bellevue–Everett, WA	10.2%
Killeen–Temple–Fort Hood, TX	17.0%	Lynchburg, VA	10.3%
Boston–Quincy, MA	16.9%	Danville, IL	10.3%
San Luis Obispo–Paso Robles, CA	16.7%	Hickory–Lenoir–Morganton, NC	10.4%
Salt Lake City, UT	16.7%	Lancaster, PA	10.5%
Wenatchee, WA	16.7%	Lima, OH	10.5%
Missoula, MT	16.6%	Toledo, OH	10.5%
Lawton, OK	16.6%	Jackson, MI	10.5%
Jacksonville, NC	16.5%	Las Vegas–Paradise, NV	10.5%
Laredo, TX	16.5%	Reading, PA	10.6%
Flagstaff, AZ	16.4%	Sandusky, OH	10.6%
Santa Fe, NM	16.4%	Kalamazoo–Portage, MI	10.7%

Source: Claritas, Inc., from U.S. Census, 2006

TABLE 3.14 UNEMPLOYMENT RATES
PERCENTAGE OF ELIGIBLE WORKFORCE

METRO AREAS WITH HIGHEST UNEMPLOYMENT	PERCENTAGE	METRO AREAS WITH LOWEST UNEMPLOYMENT	PERCENTAGE
Yuma, AZ	21.3%	Fargo, ND	2.5%
El Centro, CA	17.3%	Iowa City, IA	2.7%
Detroit–Livonia–Dearborn, MI	9.9%	Winchester, VA	2.8%
Flint, MI	9.5%	Idaho Falls, ID	2.8%
Merced, CA	9.2%	Fort Walton Beach–Crestview–Destin, FL	2.8%
Visalia–Porterville, CA	8.9%	Bismarck, ND	2.8%
Saginaw–Saginaw Township North, MI	8.6%	Rochester, MN	2.9%
Danville, VA	8.6%	Harrisonburg, VA	2.9%
Janesville, WI	8.5%	Honolulu, HI	2.9%
Sumter, SC	8.5%	Charlottesville, VA	3.0%
Yuba City, CA	8.4%	Ames, IA	3.0%
Hanford–Corcoran, CA	8.3%	Gainesville, FL	3.1%
Hickory–Lenoir–Morganton, NC	8.3%	Sioux Falls, SD	3.1%
Muskegon–Norton Shores, MI	8.0%	Madison, WI	3.2%
Rocky Mount, NC	7.9%	Cape Coral–Fort Myers, FL	3.2%
Florence, SC	7.9%	Burlington–South Burlington, VT	3.2%
Fresno, CA	7.9%	Billings, MT	3.3%
Niles–Benton Harbor, MI	7.8%	Sarasota–Bradenton–Venice, FL	3.3%
Bakersfield, CA	7.8%	Grand Forks, ND	3.3%
Weirton–Steubenville, WV-OH	7.8%	St. Cloud, MN	3.3%
Monroe, MI	7.7%	Minneapolis–St. Paul–Bloomington, MN-WI	3.3%
Modesto, CA	7.7%	Fayetteville–Springdale–Rogers, AR-MO	3.3%
McAllen–Edinburg–Mission, TX	7.7%	Rapid City, SD	3.3%
Jackson, MI	7.4%	Auburn–Opelika, AL	3.4%
Battle Creek, MI	7.4%	Ithaca, NY	3.4%
Bay City, MI	7.3%	Bethesda–Gaithersburg–Frederick, MD	3.5%
Stockton, CA	7.3%	Panama City–Lynn Haven, FL	3.5%
Pine Bluff, AR	7.3%	Casper, WY	3.5%
Spartanburg, SC	7.2%	Tallahassee, FL	3.5%
Brownsville–Harlingen, TX	7.2%	Huntsville, AL	3.5%

Source: U.S. Bureau of Labor Statistics, August 2006

TABLE 3.15 RECENT JOB GROWTH
PERCENTAGE GROWTH FROM AUGUST 2005 TO AUGUST 2006

METRO AREAS WITH HIGHEST JOB GROWTH	PERCENTAGE	METRO AREAS WITH LOWEST JOB GROWTH	PERCENTAGE
Coeur d'Alene, ID	9.2%	Wenatchee, WA	−3.1%
El Centro, CA	9.0%	Green Bay, WI	−2.2%
Kokomo, IN	8.6%	Cleveland, TN	−2.1%
St. George, UT	8.2%	Jackson, TN	−1.9%
Idaho Falls, ID	6.6%	Yakima, WA	−1.7%
Yuma, AZ	6.6%	Eau Claire, WI	−1.6%
Hot Springs, AR	6.6%	Muncie, IN	−1.4%
Fayetteville–Springdale–Rogers, AR-MO	6.5%	Elmira, NY	−1.3%
Cape Coral–Fort Myers, FL	6.2%	Racine, WI	−1.3%
Abilene, TX	5.9%	Burlington–South Burlington, VT	−1.3%
Sarasota–Bradenton–Venice, FL	5.8%	Danville, VA	−1.2%
Boise City–Nampa, ID	5.8%	Wausau, WI	−1.1%
Fort Walton Beach–Crestview–Destin, FL	5.8%	La Crosse, WI	−1.1%
McAllen–Edinburg–Mission, TX	5.7%	Knoxville, TN	−1.0%
Winchester, VA	5.7%	Bloomington, IN	−1.0%
Panama City–Lynn Haven, FL	5.7%	Rochester, NY	−0.7%
Naples–Marco Island, FL	5.6%	Cleveland–Elyria–Mentor, OH	−0.7%
Orlando–Kissimmee, FL	5.5%	Nashville–Davidson–Murfreesboro, TN	−0.7%
Bellingham, WA	5.5%	Memphis, TN	−0.7%
Punta Gorda, FL	5.4%	Pittsfield, MA	−0.7%
Port St. Lucie–Fort Pierce, FL	5.3%	Madison, WI	−0.6%
Tuscaloosa, AL	5.0%	Sheboygan, WI	−0.6%
Sherman–Denison, TX	4.8%	Detroit–Livonia–Dearborn, MI	−0.6%
Harrisonburg, VA	4.7%	Biloxi, MS	−0.6%
Pocatello, ID	4.6%	Gadsden, AL	−0.6%
Lakeland, FL	4.6%	Wichita, KS	−0.6%
Provo–Orem, UT	4.6%	Youngstown–Warren–Boardman, OH-PA	−0.5%
Las Vegas–Paradise, NV	4.5%	Rocky Mount, NC	−0.5%
Farmington, NM	4.5%	Kingsport–Bristol–Bristol, TN-VA	−0.4%
Texarkana, TX	4.5%	Johnson City, TN	−0.4%

Source: U.S. Bureau of Labor Statistics, August 2006

TABLE 3.16 PROJECTED FUTURE JOB GROWTH
PERCENTAGE GROWTH PROJECTED FROM 2005 TO 2010

METRO AREAS WITH BEST JOB OUTLOOK	PERCENTAGE	METRO AREAS WITH WORST JOB OUTLOOK	PERCENTAGE
St. George, UT	52.9%	Elmira, NY	−5.9%
Coeur d'Alene, ID	45.6%	Danville, VA	−5.5%
Las Vegas–Paradise, NV	41.0%	Detroit–Livonia–Dearborn, MI	−5.0%
El Centro, CA	34.5%	Weirton–Steubenville, WV-OH	−4.3%
McAllen–Edinburg–Mission, TX	33.2%	Pittsfield, MA	−4.2%
Fayetteville–Springdale–Rogers, AR-MO	32.9%	Utica–Rome, NY	−2.8%
Naples–Marco Island, FL	32.7%	Muncie, IN	−2.4%
Provo–Orem, UT	32.0%	Binghamton, NY	−1.9%
Punta Gorda, FL	30.8%	Scranton–Wilkes-Barre, PA	−1.4%
Bend, OR	30.8%	Springfield, MA	−1.2%
Prescott, AZ	30.8%	New Haven–Milford, CT	−0.7%
Yuma, AZ	30.3%	Buffalo–Niagara Falls, NY	−0.6%
Laredo, TX	29.9%	Rochester, NY	−0.3%
Boise City–Nampa, ID	29.5%	Fayetteville, NC	−0.3%
Logan, UT	28.5%	Youngstown–Warren–Boardman, OH-PA	−0.1%
Austin–Round Rock, TX	28.1%	Bangor, ME	−0.1%
Farmington, NM	27.8%	Springfield, OH	−0.1%
Bellingham, WA	27.6%	Williamsport, PA	0.2%
Las Cruces, NM	26.1%	Cleveland–Elyria–Mentor, OH	0.3%
Orlando–Kissimmee, FL	26.0%	Grand Forks, ND	0.6%
Olympia, WA	25.5%	Anniston–Oxford, AL	0.7%
Sarasota–Bradenton–Venice, FL	24.9%	Danville, IL	0.9%
Idaho Falls, ID	24.8%	Kingsport–Bristol–Bristol, TN-VA	0.9%
Brownsville–Harlingen, TX	24.6%	Hartford–West Hartford–East Hartford, CT	0.9%
Santa Fe, NM	24.5%	Norwich–New London, CT	1.0%
Cape Coral–Fort Myers, FL	24.5%	Dayton, OH	1.1%
Fort Walton Beach–Crestview–Destin, FL	23.7%	Bay City, MI	1.1%
Pocatello, ID	23.5%	Bridgeport–Stamford–Norwalk, CT	1.1%
Myrtle Beach–Conway–North Myrtle Beach, SC	23.3%	Lima, OH	1.2%
Phoenix–Mesa–Scottsdale, AZ	22.9%	Racine, WI	1.6%

Source: Sperling's BestPlaces, 2006

TABLE 3.17 MANUFACTURING EMPLOYMENT
PERCENTAGE EMPLOYED IN MANUFACTURING INDUSTRIES

METRO AREAS WITH HIGHEST MANUFACTURING EMPLOYMENT	PERCENTAGE	METRO AREAS WITH LOWEST MANUFACTURING EMPLOYMENT	PERCENTAGE
Dalton, GA	35.7%	Bethesda–Gaithersburg–Frederick, MD	5.4%
Hickory–Lenoir–Morganton, NC	34.2%	Santa Fe, NM	6.5%
Elkhart–Goshen, IN	32.6%	Washington–Arlington–Alexandria, DC-VA-MD-WV	6.7%
Morristown, TN	29.5%	Gainesville, FL	7.2%
Sheboygan, WI	29.3%	Tallahassee, FL	7.2%
Danville, VA	28.5%	Barnstable Town, MA	7.5%
Cleveland, TN	27.6%	Ithaca, NY	7.5%
Kokomo, IN	26.8%	Boulder, CO	7.5%
Janesville, WI	26.4%	San Francisco–San Mateo–Redwood City, CA	7.6%
Mansfield, OH	25.9%	Naples–Marco Island, FL	7.9%
Muskegon–Norton Shores, MI	25.7%	Ocean City, NJ	8.0%
Fort Smith, AR	25.7%	Springfield, IL	8.3%
Decatur, AL	25.4%	West Palm Beach–Boca Raton–Boynton Beach, FL	8.3%
Lima, OH	25.4%	Cambridge–Newton–Framingham, MA	8.4%
Fond du Lac, WI	25.1%	Charlottesville, VA	8.5%
Columbus, IN	24.7%	Honolulu, HI	8.8%
Spartanburg, SC	24.5%	Ames, IA	8.9%
Monroe, MI	24.1%	Santa Cruz–Watsonville, CA	9.0%
Anderson, SC	24.0%	Boston–Quincy, MA	9.1%
Gainesville, GA	23.9%	Atlantic City, NJ	9.1%
Joplin, MO	23.7%	Punta Gorda, FL	9.1%
Battle Creek, MI	23.6%	Las Vegas–Paradise, NV	9.1%
Rocky Mount, NC	23.5%	Cape Coral–Fort Myers, FL	9.2%
Sandusky, OH	23.4%	Fort Lauderdale–Pompano Beach–Deerfield Beach, FL	9.2%
Michigan City–La Porte, IN	23.4%	Fort Walton Beach–Crestview–Destin, FL	9.2%
Sumter, SC	23.2%	Tucson, AZ	9.2%
Lebanon, PA	23.2%	Nassau–Suffolk, NY	9.3%
Danville, IL	23.1%	Bridgeport–Stamford–Norwalk, CT	9.3%
Anniston, AL	23.0%	Austin–Round Rock, TX	9.4%
Gadsden, AL	22.9%	Sebastian–Vero Beach, FL	9.5%

Source: Claritas, Inc. from U.S. Economic Census, 2006

TABLE 3.18 PUBLIC SECTOR EMPLOYMENT

PERCENTAGE EMPLOYED IN THE PUBLIC SECTOR, INCLUDING EDUCATION, 2005

METRO AREAS WITH HIGHEST PUBLIC SECTOR EMPLOYMENT	PERCENTAGE	METRO AREAS WITH LOWEST PUBLIC SECTOR EMPLOYMENT	PERCENTAGE
Tallahassee, FL	35.9%	Elkhart–Goshen, IN	6.6%
Ames, IA	33.4%	Lancaster, PA	7.2%
Olympia, WA	32.3%	Appleton, WI	7.5%
Gainesville, FL	31.1%	Holland–Grand Haven, MI	8.2%
Fairbanks, AK	30.7%	Fort Wayne, IN	8.4%
College Station–Bryan, TX	30.0%	Dubuque, IA	8.5%
Springfield, IL	29.8%	Grand Rapids–Wyoming, MI	8.6%
Jefferson City, MO	29.6%	Warren–Troy–Farmington Hills, MI	8.7%
Iowa City, IA	29.5%	Sheboygan, WI	8.9%
Hinesville–Fort Stewart, GA	28.2%	Monroe, MI	8.9%
Flagstaff, AZ	28.0%	Columbus, IN	9.0%
El Centro, CA	28.0%	Sioux Falls, SD	9.0%
Bremerton–Silverdale, WA	27.5%	Reading, PA	9.0%
Blacksburg–Christiansburg–Radford, VA	27.3%	Rockford, IL	9.1%
Hanford–Corcoran, CA	26.8%	Niles–Benton Harbor, MI	9.2%
Lawton, OK	26.7%	South Bend–Mishawaka, IN-MI	9.3%
Champaign–Urbana, IL	26.5%	Kokomo, IN	9.3%
Charlottesville, VA	26.4%	Wausau, WI	9.4%
Cheyenne, WY	26.2%	Naples–Marco Island, FL	9.4%
Jacksonville, NC	25.6%	San Jose–Sunnyvale–Santa Clara, CA	9.4%
Columbia, MO	25.6%	York–Hanover, PA	9.5%
Athens–Clarke County, GA	25.5%	Joplin, MO	9.5%
Las Cruces, NM	25.4%	Rochester, MN	9.5%
Corvallis, OR	25.3%	Green Bay, WI	9.6%
Morgantown, WV	25.3%	Flint, MI	9.6%
Washington–Arlington–Alexandria, DC-VA-MD-WV	24.6%	Dalton, GA	9.7%
Killeen–Temple–Fort Hood, TX	24.4%	Bridgeport–Stamford–Norwalk, CT	9.7%
Alexandria, LA	23.5%	Canton–Massillon, OH	9.7%
Albany–Schenectady–Troy, NY	23.5%	Muskegon–Norton Shores, MI	9.7%
Fayetteville, NC	23.3%	Pittsburgh, PA	9.8%

Source: Claritas, Inc. from U.S. Economic Census, 2006

TABLE 3.19 CONSTRUCTION EMPLOYMENT

PERCENTAGE OF EMPLOYMENT IN CONSTRUCTION & RELATED TRADES

METRO AREAS WITH HIGHEST CONSTRUCTION EMPLOYMENT	PERCENTAGE	METRO AREAS WITH LOWEST CONSTRUCTION EMPLOYMENT	PERCENTAGE
Farmington, NM	17.3%	Ithaca, NY	5.5%
Houma–Bayou Cane–Thibodaux, LA	14.2%	Ann Arbor, MI	5.8%
Victoria, TX	14.2%	San Francisco–San Mateo–Redwood City, CA	5.9%
Jacksonville, NC	14.0%	Trenton–Ewing, NJ	6.0%
Lake Charles, LA	13.9%	Cambridge–Newton–Framingham, MA	6.1%
Wilmington, NC	13.8%	Boulder, CO	6.2%
Biloxi, MS	13.7%	Bethesda–Gaithersburg–Frederick, MD	6.3%
St. George, UT	13.7%	Corvallis, OR	6.3%
Fairbanks, AK	13.6%	Ames, IA	6.4%
Beaumont–Port Arthur, TX	13.4%	Iowa City, IA	6.7%
Casper, WY	13.3%	Champaign–Urbana, IL	6.7%
Cape Coral–Fort Myers, FL	13.3%	State College, PA	6.7%
Winchester, VA	13.2%	New York–White Plains, NY	6.7%
Myrtle Beach–Conway–North Myrtle Beach, SC	13.2%	San Jose–Sunnyvale–Santa Clara, CA	6.8%
Coeur d'Alene, ID	13.2%	Gainesville, FL	6.9%
Prescott, AZ	13.2%	Bergen–Passaic, NJ	6.9%
Bend, OR	13.0%	Columbia, MO	7.0%
Monroe, MI	12.9%	Rochester, NY	7.0%
Hinesville–Fort Stewart, GA	12.9%	Boston–Quincy, MA	7.0%
Longview, TX	12.8%	Milwaukee–Waukesha–West Allis, WI	7.1%
Corpus Christi, TX	12.8%	Bloomington–Normal, IL	7.1%
Greeley, CO	12.8%	Santa Ana–Anaheim–Irvine, CA	7.2%
Decatur, AL	12.7%	Buffalo–Niagara Falls, NY	7.2%
Gainesville, GA	12.7%	Philadelphia, PA	7.3%
Midland–Odessa, TX	12.6%	Hartford–West Hartford–East Hartford, CT	7.3%
Naples–Marco Island, FL	12.6%	Essex County, MA	7.3%
Punta Gorda, FL	12.5%	Madison, WI	7.4%
Hot Springs, AR	12.5%	Binghamton, NY	7.4%
Brunswick, GA	12.5%	Elmira, NY	7.4%
McAllen–Edinburg–Mission, TX	12.5%	Tallahassee, FL	7.5%

Source: Claritas, Inc. from U.S. Economic Census, 2006

Cost of Living

The Cost of Living category displays overall cost of living and its key components as compared to U.S. averages and expected income levels. Components include taxes, housing, and necessities such as food, utilities, transportation, healthcare, and miscellaneous expenses.

For most people, cost of living (COL) is one of the most critical elements in determining standard of living and even the lifestyle of an individual or family unit. The range of cost of living among places is surprisingly high, with areas in the south-central United States running 25% below national averages, while places on the East and West coasts run as much as *twice* the national average. But understanding the factors that drive cost of living is critical to seeing the overall picture. Particularly in big cities and coastal areas, housing costs are the biggest factor, followed by taxes. Housing costs vary considerably within regions, metropolitan areas, and even among the local assortment of housing choices. The impact of taxes varies by area and individual circumstances because each locality taxes income (income tax), consumption (sales tax), and wealth (property tax) differently. Housing and tax costs thus depend on *where* you are and *who* you are.

Cost of Living Trends

Fortunately, federal government policy and a weak economy have kept inflation tame in the period since 2000. As a result, overall cost of living has remained fairly stable nationally. Through mid-2006, the total Consumer Price Index, or CPI, for all items except housing rose a total of 18.4% since 2000, or only 2.9% per year on a compounded basis. This is the good news. There are two items of bad news. First, due mainly to energy costs, the rate of cost increase has increased in 2004 and 2005; annual increases, which ranged in the 2.5% to 3.0% range in the early part of the decade, rose to 3.4% in 2004–2005 and 3.8% in 2005–2006. As costly energy has a disproportionate impact on suburban dwellers of large cities, this is particularly concerning for that group. But even bigger is the story of home prices. Low interest rates, continued growth in household formation, favorable tax policy, higher building and land development costs, and concerns about the stock market brought an almost unprecedented boom in resale home values between 2000 and 2005, with the national median rising from $139,300 to a high of $231,000 during 2005, a 66% increase. There is some good news on the home price front, however, as prices moderated in 2006 to a figure closer to $220,000. On an annual compound rate basis, home prices have climbed 8.8% a year, a striking comparison to the 2.9% rate of inflation growth overall—more than double the annual inflation rate. Additionally, there is a strong geographic disparity among these increases, with coastal locations showing still stronger home price increases. California and some desirable Northeast locations led the way; there was a boom in Florida prices during 2004 and 2005 that has now moderated due in part to hurricane concerns. Obviously, those who already own a home and those who want to buy one experience this trend differently. If planning to move to a "hot" area, look out. Likewise, those sensitive to cost-of-living factors need to keep track of changes in tax policy, and, because of recent upheaval in the energy markets, the Utilities Index.

Cost of Living Attributes

Cost of Living is divided into *Indexes & Taxes*, *Housing*, and *Necessities*. Table 3.20 shows the Cost of Living table for the metropolitan area of Portland–Vancouver–Beaverton, Oregon-Washington.

Indexes & Taxes

■ *Cost of Living Index*, captured in the second quarter of 2006, is a composite of all cost factors, including housing and other necessities, expressed as an index against a national average of 100. The figure, derived from data obtained by the Bureau of Labor Statistics and frequently quoted in the media, is an important standard and barometer of comparative area performance. Quite interesting is the dispersion of U.S. metro areas around the

TABLE 3.20 SAMPLE COST OF LIVING TABLE FROM PORTLAND–VANCOUVER–BEAVERTON, OR-WA								
INDEXES & TAXES	AREA	U.S. AVG	**HOUSING**	AREA	U.S. AVG	**NECESSITIES**	AREA	U.S. AVG
Cost of Living Index	110.6	100.0	Median home price	$283,400	$220,000	Food Index	100.7	100.0
Buying Power Index	109.2	109.3	Home price appreciation	58.5%	10.1%	Housing Index	105.0	100.0
Income tax rate	8.96%	4.70%	Median rent	$737	$709	Utilities Index	80.1	100.0
Sales tax rate	1.48%	6.58%	Homes owned	59.9%	62.3%	Transportation Index	108.1	100.0
Property tax rate	$11.34	$12.00	Home price ratio	5.3	4.2	Healthcare Index	122.5	100.0
						Miscellaneous cost Index	104.3	100.0

Cost of Living
Score: 22.7
Rank: 288

national average of 100. It turns out that, of 375 metro areas, only 114 of them have COL indexes higher than 100, that is, are more expensive than the national average. Fully 261 areas are cheaper than average, and 211 of these are more than 10% cheaper (COL Index of 90 or less). The largest group of metro areas, 158 in all, lie between 80% and 90% of the national average. Table 3.21 shows the COL Index breakdown for U.S. metro areas.

- *Buying Power Index* (BPI), designed by *Cities Ranked & Rated,* compares metro area incomes to metro area cost of living, and, bottom line, indicates the potential for long-term financial prosperity in an area. An area with high incomes looks attractive on the surface, but an income level 20% higher than national averages simply disappears when living costs are also 20% higher; the BPI shows where real incomes are sufficient or insufficient to meet local living costs. The Buying Power Index is calculated as a ratio of metro area median household income, normalized against national averages, to the cost of living, which is also so normalized. The BPI is also presented as an index compared to the national average. Families looking toward long-term financial goals should find places with a high BPI, which indicates a better chance to build net worth over time because incomes are high relative to costs. National results vary widely, with the highest Buying Power Index at 154 in Warren–Troy–Farmington Hills, Michigan, and the lowest at 60.7 in New York City. Generally, areas in Texas and the Midwest have high BPIs, while those in California and on the East Coast are low. Of particular note are California Central Valley towns such as Merced, Stockton, Modesto, and Fresno, with relatively low incomes driven down in part by a strong agricultural presence but with persistently high living costs, thus the low BPI. Many of these cities fared poorly in our rankings.

- *Income tax rate, Sales tax rate,* and *Property tax rate* are compiled by Sperling's BestPlaces from several sources, including the Commerce Clearing House, Federation of Tax Administrators, and the District of Columbia Tax Rates and Tax Burdens study. Because tax rates are more complex than meets the eye—total tax paid depending not only on *rate,* but also on *basis,* the amount to which the rate applies—*Cities Ranked & Rated* shows approximate tax rates at the metropolitan area level for the sake of comparison. To learn more about a

TABLE 3.21 COST OF LIVING INDEX RANGES

COL INDEX	NUMBER OF METRO AREAS
>120	46
110–120	31
100–110	37
90–100	50
80–90	153
70–80	58

particular area, readers should take a close look at local laws. For a more complete look at tax policy and its effects, see "Taxation" in chapter 4.

- *Income tax rate* is the approximate state income tax rate, with local income taxes added in where known. The reported figure represents the highest marginal rate for the area and may not be representative of what an individual or family with average income would pay.

- *Sales tax rate* shows the state base sales tax rate, with local general sales taxes and special tax surcharges (for schools, transit projects, and so on) added in where known. When an area has multiple sales tax rates, the one paid by the majority of the population is shown.

- *Property tax rate* shows the average dollar amount paid per $1,000 property valuation in an area. Note that both statutory rates and valuations vary widely among and even within areas; these figures are averages.

Housing

Housing price data is compiled by Sperling's BestPlaces from an assortment of sources, including the National Association of Realtors, Freddie Mac, and the U.S. Census Bureau.

- *Median home price* shows the price for an average home in the area based on mid-2006 sales. (Recall that median means half the homes sold for more, half for less.) The "average home in the area" can vary considerably from a one-bedroom apartment in Manhattan to a three-bedroom detached home on a suburban half-acre with a garage and basement. Of course, location, style, quality, uniqueness, and special features will cause a specific home or even a neighborhood to deviate considerably from the averages. The range among metropolitan areas is extremely wide, with median prices well over $600,000 in California areas and Honolulu, Hawaii, and over $700,000 in the most desirable

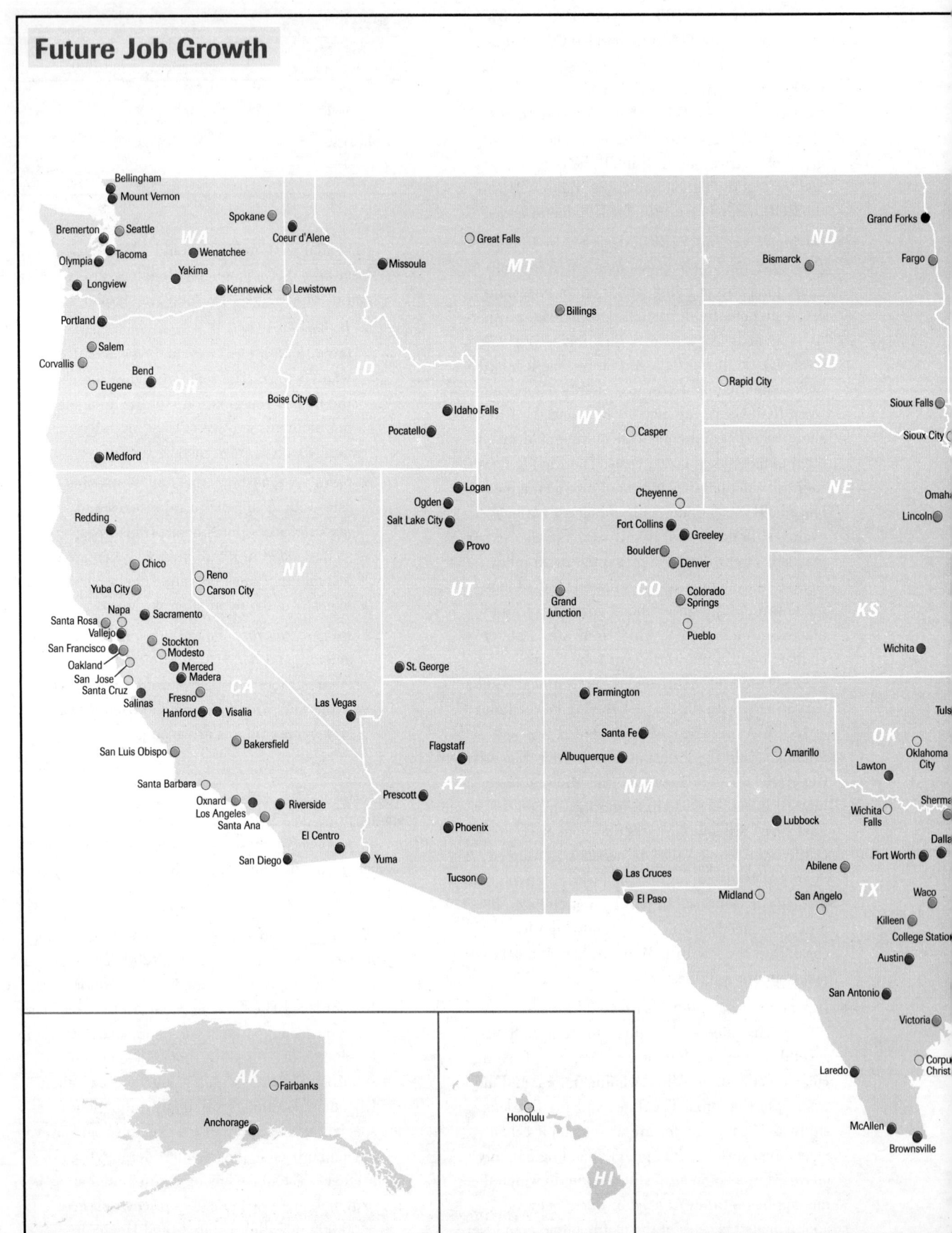

Future Job Growth

Future Job Growth in Principal MSAs Grouped by Quintiles

- ● *Highest 20%*
- ○
- ○ *Middle 20%*
- ●
- ● *Lowest 20%*

Cheapest & Most Expensive Cities

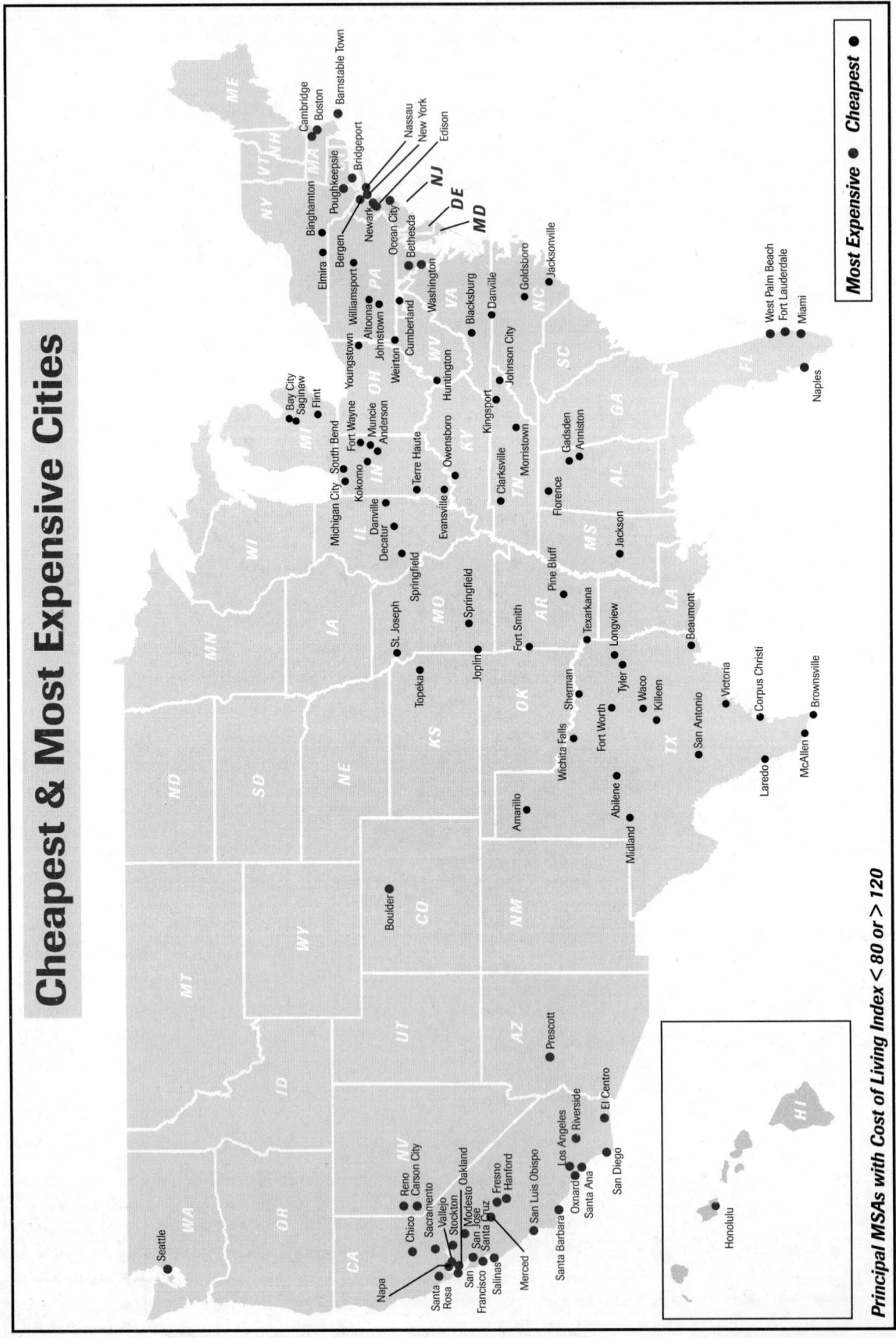

Most Expensive ● Cheapest ●

Principal MSAs with Cost of Living Index < 80 or > 120

Big City Bargains

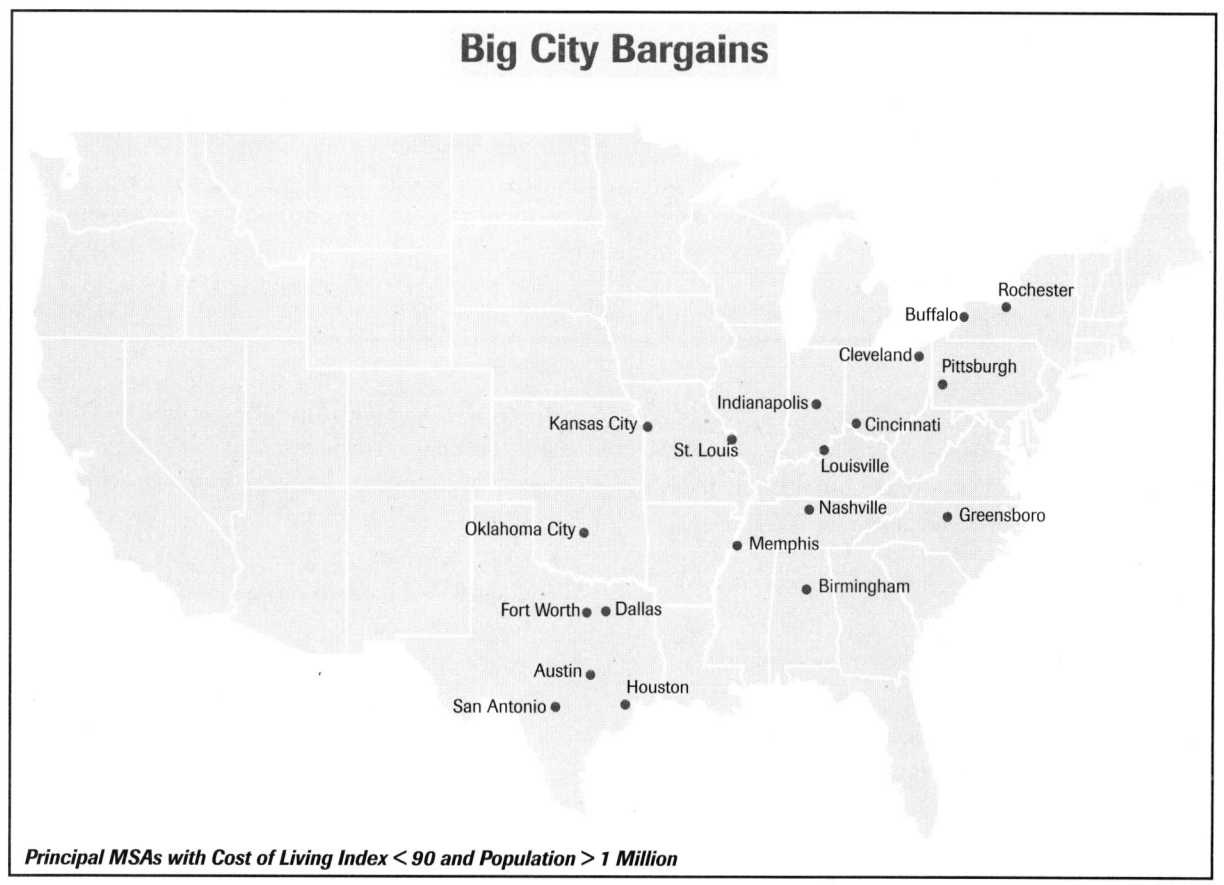

Principal MSAs with Cost of Living Index < 90 and Population > 1 Million

coastal California areas. Smaller Midwestern towns and some in Texas and the South still have median home prices below $100,000. In fact, as a telling statistic, the number of metro areas with median home prices under $100,000 dropped from 92 in the first edition to 24 in this one.

■ *Home price appreciation* shows the growth in median home prices from 2002 through 2006. The recent surges in California and Florida real estate prices are telling: Of the top 30 gainers nationwide, 17 are in California and 12 are in Florida. Not surprisingly, especially with recent auto industry malaise, the weakest appreciation figures are found in the Midwest and some parts of the South.

■ *Median rent*, like home prices, reflects rental cost for an average unit in an area.

■ *Homes owned* shows the percentage of households living in a purchased home. The highest levels of home ownership are in stable small towns like Owensboro, Kentucky, and York, Pennsylvania, with ownership rates over 75%, while the lowest are in areas like Jersey City, New Jersey, where affordability is an issue, or in military towns with more population transience.

■ *Home price ratio* (HPR) compares home prices to typical household incomes in the area and is a quick measure of affordability. Specifically, a metro area HPR is the median home price divided by the median household income for the area. A median home price of $180,000 taken against a median household income of $60,000 would produce an HPR of 3.0. Naturally, it makes sense to use HPR figures to compare areas, but do they tell you whether a place is affordable? In fact, yes, they do. If you run through the math, using conventional financing (20% down, 80% loan) and an interest rate of 6%, and a housing payment of 28% of gross income, a typical family will qualify for such a conventional loan if the HPR is 4.86 or lower. So in rough numbers HPRs of 5 or lower are affordable, while ratios in the 9 and 10 range are quite out of sight for "average" families in an area. Indeed, we see a wide disparity, from rock-bottom ratios under 2 in some fairly depressed areas like Danville, Illinois, and Flint, Michigan, as well as the more prosperous Fort Worth, Texas, to ratios over 9 in California, New York City, and Honolulu. Generally, if an area has an HPR under 3, housing values are attractive.

Is Strong Home Appreciation a Good Thing?

On the surface, the merit of home price appreciation depends on whether one owns or plans to buy. Sustainability is another issue—just because home prices have been "hot" for the past 5 years doesn't mean they'll stay high in the future. *Cities Ranked & Rated* continues to take the position that *some* appreciation is good. If nothing else, it tells something about the growth and overall prospects for an area's future. Home price appreciation was included in rankings but did not receive a heavy weighting.

Necessities

The Bureau of Labor Statistics calculates indexes for the following components of the overall Cost of Living Index. Data shown is from the second quarter of 2006.

- *Food Index* includes a standard "basket" of food purchased in the area.

- *Housing Index* measures the cost of acquiring (purchasing or renting) and maintaining a home.

- *Utilities Index* includes the average cost (price times usage) of major utilities, mainly electricity and heating fuels.

- *Transportation Index* includes most costs of driving an automobile, including the vehicle itself, fuel, repairs, insurance, licensing, parking, and public transit.

- *Healthcare Index* includes the cost of physician, clinical, and hospital services, as well as medications and supplies.

- *Miscellaneous Cost Index* includes a variety of items needed to support daily living, including clothing, durable goods, and an assortment of services, such as personal care and financial services.

Cost of Living Highlights, Tables 3.22–3.26

TABLE 3.22 COST OF LIVING INDEX			
METRO AREAS WITH HIGHEST COL INDEX	**COL INDEX**	**METRO AREAS WITH LOWEST COL INDEX**	**COL INDEX**
San Francisco–San Mateo–Redwood City, CA	200.9	Texarkana, TX	71.3
San Jose–Sunnyvale–Santa Clara, CA	194.8	Anderson, IN	73.2
Salinas, CA	191.5	Danville, VA	73.4
Santa Ana–Anaheim–Irvine, CA	186.5	Altoona, PA	74.3
New York–White Plains, NY	177.6	Decatur, IL	74.3
Honolulu, HI	177.5	Longview, TX	74.4
Santa Rosa–Petaluma, CA	176.5	Youngstown–Warren–Boardman, OH-PA	74.4
Oxnard–Thousand Oaks–Ventura, CA	175.0	Victoria, TX	74.7
Santa Cruz–Watsonville, CA	173.4	McAllen–Edinburg–Mission, TX	74.9
Oakland–Fremont–Hayward, CA	171.9	Clarksville, TN	75.3
San Diego–Carlsbad–San Marcos, CA	170.5	Laredo, TX	75.3
Cambridge–Newton–Framingham, MA	169.3	Kingsport–Bristol–Bristol, TN-VA	75.4
Napa, CA	163.8	Muncie, IN	75.7
Los Angeles–Long Beach–Glendale, CA	163.2	Evansville, IN	76.0
Vallejo–Fairfield, CA	163.1	Morristown, TN	76.0
Bridgeport–Stamford–Norwalk, CT	160.7	Danville, IL	76.1
Nassau–Suffolk, NY	157.1	Flint, MI	76.2
Bergen–Passaic, NJ	151.5	Fort Smith, AR	76.2
San Luis Obispo–Paso Robles, CA	151.4	Johnson City, TN	76.3
Santa Barbara–Santa Maria, CA	149.9	Joplin, MO	76.5
Stockton, CA	147.9	Killeen–Temple–Fort Hood, TX	76.5
Newark–Union, NJ-PA	144.5	Waco, TX	76.6
Washington–Arlington–Alexandria, DC-VA-MD-WV	140.6	Bay City, MI	76.9
Barnstable Town, MA	139.5	Kokomo, IN	76.9
Bethesda–Gaithersburg–Frederick, MD	139.5	South Bend–Mishawaka, IN-MI	76.9
Naples–Marco Island, FL	138.5	Goldsboro, NC	77.1
Modesto, CA	137.1	Owensboro, KY	77.1
Edison, NJ	136.8	Saginaw–Saginaw Township North, MI	77.1
West Palm Beach–Boca Raton–Boynton Beach, FL	134.4	Elmira, NY	77.2
Boston–Quincy, MA	134.2	Gadsden, AL	77.2

Note: U.S. average: 100

Source: U.S. Bureau of Labor Statistics/Sperling's BestPlaces, 2006

TABLE 3.23 BUYING POWER INDEX (BPI)
MEDIAN HOUSEHOLD INCOME/COST OF LIVING, SHOWN AS AN INDEX

METRO AREAS WITH HIGHEST BUYING POWER	BPI	METRO AREAS WITH LOWEST BUYING POWER	BPI
Warren–Troy–Farmington Hills, MI	154	New York–White Plains, NY	60.7
Appleton, WI	150	El Centro, CA	64.4
Fort Worth–Arlington, TX	149	Los Angeles–Long Beach–Glendale, CA	64.9
Indianapolis–Carmel, IN	149	Chico, CA	65.7
Holland–Grand Haven, MI	147	Salinas, CA	66.5
Atlanta–Sandy Springs–Marietta, GA	147	Miami–Miami Beach–Kendall, FL	69.9
Lake County–Kenosha County, IL-WI	145	Merced, CA	70.6
Dallas–Plano–Irving, TX	143	Stockton, CA	70.8
Ogden–Clearfield, UT	141	San Diego–Carlsbad–San Marcos, CA	72.5
Austin–Round Rock, TX	141	Honolulu, HI	73.0
Kokomo, IN	140	San Luis Obispo–Paso Robles, CA	73.3
Springfield, IL	139	Prescott, AZ	73.7
Rochester, MN	139	Modesto, CA	74.0
Fond du Lac, WI	137	Fresno, CA	74.3
Sheboygan, WI	137	Hanford–Corcoran, CA	74.7
Monroe, MI	137	Yuba City, CA	76.3
Raleigh–Cary, NC	136	Madera, CA	77.6
Racine, WI	136	Redding, CA	78.5
Kansas City, MO	136	Riverside–San Bernardino–Ontario, CA	79.9
Salt Lake City, UT	135	Santa Rosa–Petaluma, CA	80.2
Wausau, WI	135	Santa Ana–Anaheim–Irvine, CA	80.4
Houston–Sugar Land–Baytown, TX	134	Santa Barbara–Santa Maria, CA	80.7
Flint, MI	134	Visalia–Porterville, CA	81.0
Oshkosh–Neenah, WI	134	Gainesville, FL	81.7
Cincinnati–Middletown, OH-KY-IN	133	Fort Lauderdale–Pompano Beach–Deerfield Beach, FL	81.7
Anderson, IN	133	Yuma, AZ	81.7
Des Moines–West Des Moines, IA	133	Morgantown, WV	82.2
Lansing–East Lansing, MI	133	Bakersfield, CA	82.6
South Bend–Mishawaka, IN-MI	133	Santa Cruz–Watsonville, CA	82.6
Fort Wayne, IN	132	Carson City, NV	82.7

Note: U.S. average: 100

Source: Calculation based on U.S. Bureau of Labor Statistics data, 2006

TABLE 3.24 MEDIAN HOME PRICES
FOR AVERAGE HOME IN AREA, 2006 Q2

METRO AREAS WITH MOST EXPENSIVE HOMES	HOME PRICE	METRO AREAS WITH LEAST EXPENSIVE HOMES	HOME PRICE
San Francisco–San Mateo–Redwood City, CA	$751,900	Danville, IL	$65,200
San Jose–Sunnyvale–Santa Clara, CA	$748,200	Altoona, PA	$73,500
Salinas, CA	$744,700	Youngstown–Warren–Boardman, OH-PA	$78,700
Santa Ana–Anaheim–Irvine, CA	$726,200	Terre Haute, IN	$81,600
Oxnard–Thousand Oaks–Ventura, CA	$660,900	Anderson, IN	$82,500
Honolulu, HI	$640,000	Flint, MI	$82,500
San Diego–Carlsbad–San Marcos, CA	$613,100	Decatur, IL	$85,300
Santa Rosa–Petaluma, CA	$603,000	Pine Bluff, AR	$86,800
Santa Cruz–Watsonville, CA	$601,500	Elmira, NY	$87,300
Cambridge–Newton–Framingham, MA	$599,800	Weirton–Steubenville, WV-OH	$88,100
Los Angeles–Long Beach–Glendale, CA	$576,300	Saginaw–Saginaw Township North, MI	$90,500
Oakland–Fremont–Hayward, CA	$572,400	Danville, VA	$92,200
New York–White Plains, NY	$549,200	McAllen–Edinburg–Mission, TX	$92,200
Napa, CA	$538,700	Texarkana, TX	$92,400
Vallejo–Fairfield, CA	$534,800	Binghamton, NY	$92,800
San Luis Obispo–Paso Robles, CA	$513,200	Johnstown, PA	$94,600
Santa Barbara–Santa Maria, CA	$499,700	Bay City, MI	$94,700
Bridgeport–Stamford–Norwalk, CT	$495,500	Sioux City, IA	$95,200
Nassau–Suffolk, NY	$478,000	Brownsville–Harlingen, TX	$95,800
Stockton, CA	$461,500	Muncie, IN	$96,500
Bethesda–Gaithersburg–Frederick, MD	$451,600	Buffalo–Niagara Falls, NY	$96,800
Naples–Marco Island, FL	$451,100	Michigan City–La Porte, IN	$97,900
Newark–Union, NJ-PA	$443,800	Morristown, TN	$99,600
Washington–Arlington–Alexandria, DC-VA-MD-WV	$443,400	Wheeling, WV	$99,700
Bergen–Passaic, NJ	$437,000	Cumberland, MD	$100,000
West Palm Beach–Boca Raton–Boynton Beach, FL	$410,400	South Bend–Mishawaka, IN-MI	$100,600
Barnstable Town, MA	$406,300	Fort Worth–Arlington, TX	$100,800
Modesto, CA	$398,900	Waco, TX	$101,000
Riverside–San Bernardino–Ontario, CA	$395,700	Sherman–Denison, TX	$101,100
Edison, NJ	$393,600	Clarksville, TN	$101,200

MEDIAN HOME PRICES BY REGION

Northeast	$295,800
Midwest	$167,200
South	$199,000
West	$350,900

Notes: 2006 Q2 median U.S. home price: $220,000

Source: National Association of Realtors, 2006

TABLE 3.25 HOME PRICE RATIO
MEDIAN HOME PRICE/MEDIAN HOUSEHOLD INCOME
Conventional Qualifying Ratio 4.86 at 6% interest rate

LEAST AFFORDABLE METRO AREAS	RATIO	MOST AFFORDABLE METRO AREAS	RATIO
Salinas, CA	13.1	Danville, IL	1.7
Los Angeles–Long Beach–Glendale, CA	12.2	Flint, MI	1.8
New York–White Plains, NY	11.4	Anderson, IN	1.9
San Diego–Carlsbad–San Marcos, CA	11.1	Fort Worth–Arlington, TX	1.9
Honolulu, HI	11.1	Youngstown–Warren–Boardman, OH-PA	2.0
Santa Ana–Anaheim–Irvine, CA	10.9	Altoona, PA	2.0
San Luis Obispo–Paso Robles, CA	10.4	Decatur, IL	2.1
San Francisco–San Mateo–Redwood City, CA	10.1	Terre Haute, IN	2.1
Stockton, CA	9.9	Elmira, NY	2.1
Oxnard–Thousand Oaks–Ventura, CA	9.7	Saginaw–Saginaw Township North, MI	2.1
El Centro, CA	9.6	Michigan City–La Porte, IN	2.1
Santa Rosa–Petaluma, CA	9.5	Kokomo, IN	2.2
Miami–Miami Beach–Kendall, FL	9.4	Sandusky, OH	2.2
Santa Cruz–Watsonville, CA	9.4	Sioux City, IA	2.2
Santa Barbara–Santa Maria, CA	9.3	Fort Wayne, IN	2.2
San Jose–Sunnyvale–Santa Clara, CA	8.8	Bay City, MI	2.2
Modesto, CA	8.8	South Bend–Mishawaka, IN-MI	2.2
Napa, CA	8.8	Buffalo–Niagara Falls, NY	2.2
Chico, CA	8.8	Indianapolis–Carmel, IN	2.3
Merced, CA	8.6	Topeka, KS	2.3
Prescott, AZ	8.6	Springfield, IL	2.3
Cambridge–Newton–Framingham, MA	8.5	Binghamton, NY	2.3
Vallejo–Fairfield, CA	8.4	Appleton, WI	2.3
Riverside–San Bernardino–Ontario, CA	8.3	Wichita, KS	2.3
Oakland–Fremont–Hayward, CA	8.3	Evansville, IN	2.4
Hanford–Corcoran, CA	8.2	Rochester, NY	2.4
Naples–Marco Island, FL	8.1	Rockford, IL	2.4
West Palm Beach–Boca Raton–Boynton Beach, FL	8.1	Sherman–Denison, TX	2.4
Fort Lauderdale–Pompano Beach–Deerfield Beach, FL	8.0	Peoria, IL	2.4
Carson City, NV	7.7	Clarksville, TN	2.4

Source: Calculation based on National Association of Realtors, U.S. Census data, 2006

TABLE 3.26 HOME PRICE APPRECIATION
5-YEAR GROWTH IN MEDIAN HOME PRICES, 2002–2006

METRO AREAS WITH HIGHEST APPRECIATION	PERCENTAGE GROWTH	METRO AREAS WITH LOWEST APPRECIATION	PERCENTAGE GROWTH
Bakersfield, CA	171.2%	Lafayette, IN	12.1%
Fresno, CA	164.9%	Youngstown–Warren–Boardman, OH-PA	13.8%
Riverside–San Bernardino–Ontario, CA	157.1%	Sioux City, IA	14.7%
Modesto, CA	155.5%	Memphis, TN	14.7%
Merced, CA	155.2%	Kokomo, IN	15.7%
Port St. Lucie–Fort Pierce, FL	153.5%	Victoria, TX	15.8%
Miami–Miami Beach–Kendall, FL	150.3%	Jonesboro, AR	16.1%
Los Angeles–Long Beach–Glendale, CA	150.2%	Canton–Massillon, OH	16.2%
Naples–Marco Island, FL	149.0%	Springfield, OH	16.2%
Punta Gorda, FL	148.3%	Akron, OH	16.3%
Fort Lauderdale–Pompano Beach–Deerfield Beach, FL	145.7%	Fort Wayne, IN	16.7%
Ocean City, NJ	145.4%	Dayton, OH	16.8%
Madera, CA	143.7%	Springfield, IL	17.0%
Yuba City, CA	143.6%	Columbus, IN	17.1%
Cape Coral–Fort Myers, FL	141.8%	Toledo, OH	17.2%
West Palm Beach–Boca Raton–Boynton Beach, FL	141.2%	Rocky Mount, NC	17.4%
Santa Barbara–Santa Maria, CA	140.8%	Ogden–Clearfield, UT	17.4%
Visalia–Porterville, CA	138.4%	Warren–Troy–Farmington Hills, MI	17.5%
Hanford–Corcoran, CA	134.8%	Greensboro–Winston-Salem–High Point, NC	18.0%
Sarasota–Bradenton–Venice, FL	132.7%	Danville, VA	18.1%
Sacramento–Arden-Arcade–Roseville, CA	131.5%	Decatur, AL	18.1%
Palm Bay–Melbourne–Titusville, FL	130.8%	Erie, PA	18.4%
Santa Ana–Anaheim–Irvine, CA	130.8%	Owensboro, KY	18.4%
Chico, CA	129.5%	Jackson, TN	18.4%
Oxnard–Thousand Oaks–Ventura, CA	128.8%	Goldsboro, NC	18.5%
Stockton, CA	126.9%	Austin–Round Rock, TX	18.5%
Fort Walton Beach–Crestview–Destin, FL	125.7%	Cleveland–Elyria–Mentor, OH	18.6%
Sebastian–Vero Beach, FL	125.0%	Raleigh–Cary, NC	18.7%
Redding, CA	123.8%	Anderson, IN	19.2%
Deltona–Daytona Beach–Ormond Beach, FL	122.7%	Bloomington–Normal, IL	19.3%

Source: National Association of Realtors/Sperling's BestPlaces, 2006

The Difference between Climate & Weather

The difference between *climate* and *weather* may be confusing to some. Generally, climate is the *cause* and weather is the *effect*. Climate is the result of a set of physical factors, including latitude, altitude, water presence, wind direction, nearby landforms, seasons, and natural atmospheric patterns. Although there can be minor variations in atmospheric patterns and wind direction, most of these factors are fixed, and therefore, climate is fixed. Weather, on the other hand, is the result of the daily interaction of these phenomena, and can vary considerably from one day to the next and even one minute to the next. Weather describes the events—rain, snow, heat, cold, clouds, sun—that occur, while climate speaks to the permanent physical phenomena that govern weather on a daily basis.

Climate

Although most don't cite climate as the primary reason to relocate, it is almost certainly taken into consideration. Climatology—the study of climate—is extremely complex and fairly technical in nature. *Cities Ranked & Rated* presents data on the key components of climate—temperature, precipitation, cloud cover, humidity, and hazards—to provide an image of what a place is like most of the year.

Climate Drivers

Specific factors unique to a place determine the kind of climate present.

- *Latitude* represents the north–south location of a place. In general, places farther south are warmer and have less seasonal effect, while those farther north are colder and have more pronounced seasonal changes. Differences in sun angle mean larger seasonal changes and greater variety in length of day for places farther north. Places in the northern United States and Canada have summer days 15 to 18 hours long and winter days 6 to 9 hours long. Places farther south see much smaller seasonal differences.

- *Altitude*, like latitude, can have a profound effect on climate. Less dense air at higher altitudes allows greater heat loss and less water content (that is, humidity). The general rule: Temperatures average 5°F lower for every 1,000 feet in elevation, although many other factors enter into temperature differences. Aside from temperature and humidity, altitude is also a consideration for those with health problems. Thinner air means less oxygen, increased fatigue, and greater strain on the human circulatory system. Elevation is given in the opening box of each city in chapter 5.

- *Nearby water*—and the size, location, and temperature of that water—can have a strong impact on local climates. Water retains heat and provides moisture. Areas near water receive significant temperature moderation. A shoreline city can see winter low temperatures 5°F, 10°F, even 20°F warmer than areas just a few miles inland; likewise, summer highs may be 5°F to 20°F cooler, depending on local wind direction and water temperature. So Baltimore has more moderate temperatures than Hagerstown, Maryland, and Seattle more so than Yakima, Washington. Water moderates no matter the latitude, but the effects are more pronounced when the wind direction is onshore. Places to the lee or downwind from bodies of water receive the effects of its moisture, particularly when dramatic differences between water and air temperature are present. Nowhere is this more true than upstate New York or northern Indiana, where moisture and temperature differences create impressive "lake effect" snows from Lake Erie and Lake Michigan, respectively. Both of these phenomena can work on a smaller scale, as observed in Burlington, Vermont, on Lake Champlain.

- *Wind direction* significantly affects climate. The prevailing wind direction across the middle latitudes of North America is west to east; however, local variations exist due to landforms, upper air and storm patterns, and water. Prevailing wind direction is the main reason that coastal New England cities do not enjoy the same temperature moderation as those in the Pacific Northwest. A mid-Atlantic/Caribbean phenomenon known as the "Bermuda High" circulates warm, moist Gulf of Mexico air from the southwest to the northeast in the summer, giving high heat and humidity in the southeast and spreading into the central United States and Canada. Cold,

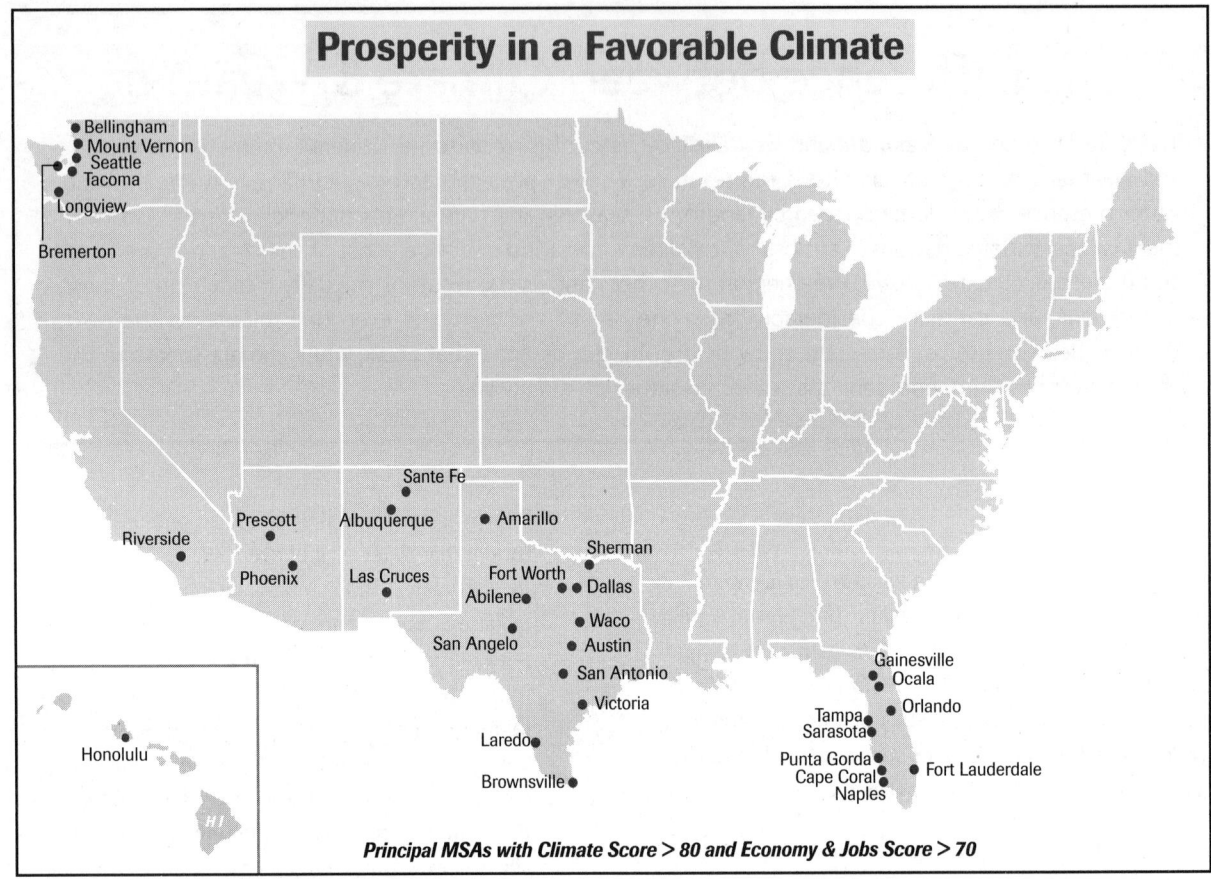

Prosperity in a Favorable Climate

Principal MSAs with Climate Score > 80 and Economy & Jobs Score > 70

dry winds from the northwest and Canada bring cold spells and strong temperature fluctuations. Prevailing winter winds in much of the central part of the continent are from the northwest.

■ *Landforms,* such as mountains and valleys, often greatly influence local climate. First, where mountain ranges block prevailing winds, a rain shadow occurs, creating drier and less humid climates than places just a few miles upwind. Sheltered by the Cascade Range, Yakima, Washington, for example, is one of the 10 driest metro areas in the United States, with 8 inches of precipitation annually, while Seattle, just 150 miles west, gets five times as much rain with three times as many cloudy days. Effects are less pronounced for cities shadowed by the Appalachians. Second, mountains also shelter places from cold, winter air invading from the north. Valleys can trap warm or cold air, reducing winds and temperature changes, but keep a cold chill or a hot spell firmly in place. Finally, areas downwind from large mountain barriers can experience rapid and prolonged winter warming atypical of the region and latitude when downslope winds compress and become warmer. These so-called

chinook winds occur on the Front Range of the Rocky Mountains as far north as Edmonton, Alberta.

■ *Storm tracks* strongly affect the climates of places in their path. Due to the Earth's rotation and the presence of solar energy, rivers of air continuously circulate the planet at high speeds in the upper elevations of the atmosphere. Known as jet streams, these currents cause atmospheric mixing and determine the direction and speed of storms. Where these currents flow is a matter of land and water location, seasons, and some cyclical fluctuation. The typical storm track for the continental United States is west to east, entering the continent in the Pacific Northwest, sweeping across the Rockies, and bending south into the southern Great Plains, then swinging back northeast more or less along the Ohio River Valley and into New England. The pattern fluctuates in shape and strength and tends to move farther south in winter and farther north in summer. Areas commonly on or near storm tracks—Oklahoma City, Oklahoma; Evansville, Indiana; Cleveland, Ohio; and Albany, New York—tend to see greater swings in weather and strong storms.

Long Summer Evenings

Those who enjoy long summer evenings to play golf, enjoy a backyard barbecue, or sit at a sidewalk cafe should look for a place that (1) is farther north, (2) sits at the western edge of a time zone, and (3) practices daylight saving time (most places do, except Hawaii and Arizona). Best bets are Michigan, Minnesota, Montana, Washington, and naturally, Alaska.

Climate Zones

Climate experts divide land areas into climate zones, each indicative of the prevailing climate type in that area. Zones define seasonal patterns, temperature ranges, and precipitation, among other characteristics. *Subtropical* climates have persistent hot, humid summers and mild winters. *Continental* climates are influenced by vast land areas with little water, and thus have strong seasonal patterns, rapid changes, and extreme temperatures. *Steppe* or *semi-arid* climates are higher, drier versions of continental climates, with variable summers, cold winters, and little rain. *Arid* climates are hot and dry, with fewer than 10 inches of precipitation per year. *Marine* climates are found mainly near coastlines, and have less extreme temperatures and are often quite wet. Finally, the *Mediterranean* climate has long, clear, rainless summers and cool, wet winters. See Table 4.5 in chapter 4 for more detail on climate zones.

Climate Attributes

The combined attributes of temperature, precipitation, comfort factors, and hazards define a climate. Each of these breaks down into several individual variables. The data source is the U.S. National Climatic Data Center

(NCDC) section of the National Oceanic and Atmospheric Administration (NOAA) arm of the Department of Commerce. Most data represents annual averages calculated over as many as 70 years of monthly and daily data observations.

Table 3.27 shows the Climate table for the metropolitan area of Colorado Springs, Colorado.

Temperature

Temperature attributes indicate average temperatures for the periods given.

- *Average January low* is the average minimum temperature for each day during January. Not surprisingly, average minimums are below zero in North Dakota and parts of Minnesota and in the mid-50s in Florida.

- *Average July high* is the average maximum temperature for each day during the month of July. These averages range from the mid-60s in Alaska and on the northern California coast to just under 100°F in central Texas and Oklahoma to over 100°F in Phoenix and Yuma, Arizona, and Las Vegas.

TABLE 3.27 SAMPLE CLIMATE TABLE FROM COLORADO SPRINGS, CO

Climate

Score: 91.2
Rank: 34

TEMPERATURE	AREA	U.S. AVG	PRECIPITATION	AREA	U.S. AVG	COMFORTS & HAZARDS	AREA	U.S. AVG
Average January low	16.1	26.2	Annual inches precipitation	16.0	37.7	July relative humidity	49%	66%
Average July high	84.4	87.4	Annual inches snowfall	40.0	7.0	Annual days mostly sunny	249	208
Annual days > 90°F	15	38	Annual days precipitation	87	109	Annual days with thunderstorms	59	39
Annual days < 32°F	162	89	Annual days rain > 0.5 inches	8	22	Tornado risk score	18	18
Annual days < 0°F	7	6	Annual days snow > 1.5 inches	9	6	Hurricane risk score	0	13

TEMPERATURE

PRECIPITATION

DAYS OF CLOUDS & PRECIPITATION

The Profound Effect of Altitude

Altitude-related temperature profiles gave us our favorite piece of trivia in the first edition. The metropolitan area with the most days (nights, actually) observed with temperatures below 32°F wasn't in Minnesota, North Dakota, or Maine, but instead was in Flagstaff, Arizona! At an altitude of nearly 7,000 feet, Flagstaff experiences temperatures of 32°F or below 210 days a year. Now in this edition, Fairbanks, Alaska, has become a principal metro area, and takes the crown at 225 days. Still, Flagstaff will surprise most even at no. 2.

- *Annual days > 90°F* is the average number of days per year where the high temperature exceeds 90°F. Places in central California and the desert Southwest top the list with over 100 and up to 164 days, which is almost 1 day in 2.

- *Annual days < 32°F* is the number of days per year with a low temperature below freezing. Topping the list, with as many as 225 days, are higher latitude and higher elevation locations such as Fairbanks and Anchorage, Alaska, and Flagstaff and Prescott, Arizona.

- *Annual days < 0°F* is the number of days (nights, actually) with a low temperature below zero. Bitter cold places include the likely suspects—Grand Forks and Fargo, North Dakota, and Duluth, Minnesota—with 50+ below-zero days per year.

Precipitation

Precipitation attributes indicate the amount and kind of rain and snow.

- *Annual inches precipitation* represents rain and snow combined. On average, 10 to 12 inches of snow equal 1 inch of rain. The U.S. range is 4 inches to 67 inches per year, with Las Vegas the lowest and Gulf Coast cities typically the highest.

- *Annual inches snowfall* is total inches of measurable snowfall each year.

- *Annual days precipitation* is the average number of days per year with at least some measurable rain or snow. Together with *Annual inches precipitation*, this forms a clear climate picture. Cities in the Pacific Northwest, such as Bellingham, Washington, and in the eastern Great Lakes, such as Erie, Pennsylvania, have high numbers of days with rain, but relatively moderate rainfall totals. This means they receive frequent light rain and drizzle.

Cities in the South have high rainfall totals and relatively moderate days of precipitation, indicating heavy downpours. Annual days precipitation ranges from the 30s in the desert Southwest to the 180s in the eastern Great Lakes.

- *Annual days rain > 0.5 inches* shows the number of days with significant rain each year.

- *Annual days snow > 1.5 inches* shows the number of days with significant snowfall accumulation.

Comforts & Hazards

Such factors as presence of sunshine, humidity, and stormy weather combine with temperature to make a place more or less comfortable.

- *July relative humidity* is the moisture content of the air relative to temperature. As air temperature changes, the amount of moisture it can hold also changes. Relative humidity is measured as the amount of moisture present as a percentage of the total amount the air can hold at that temperature. Technical details aside, greater humidity means less comfort. This measure is taken in July when high humidity degrades comfort the most. The most humid places are on the Gulf Coast and up the Atlantic seaboard with 75% to 80% relative humidity; the Rocky Mountains and desert Southwest are driest with 30% to 50% readings.

- *Annual days mostly sunny.* The NCDC tracks the number of days that are sunny or minimally cloudy. Combined with precipitation factors, a complete climate picture forms. Because of marine moisture, Pacific Northwest and Great Lakes cities tend to be cloudy, but the precipitation totals aren't that high. Michigan cities in particular are extremely cloudy, but not extremely wet. Not surprisingly, desert Southwest and California cities

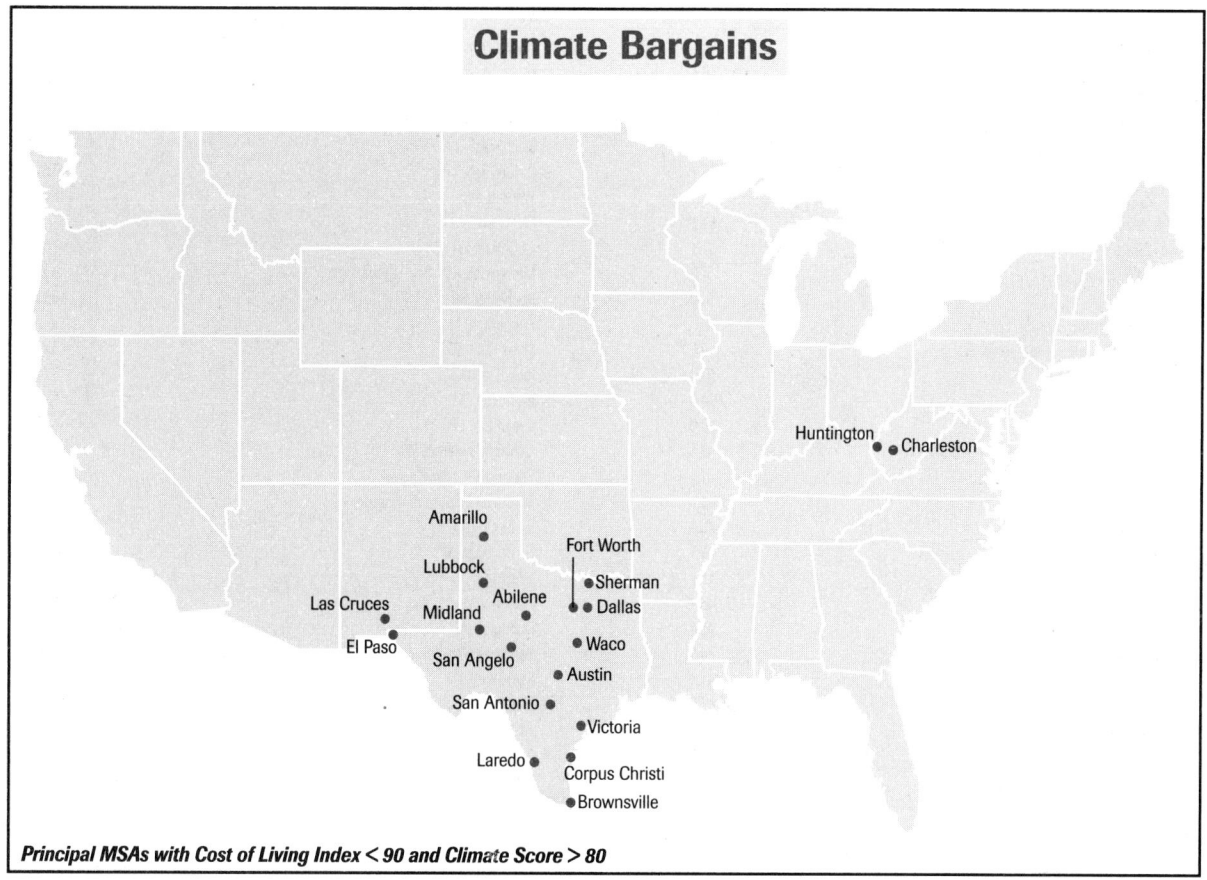

Climate Bargains

Principal MSAs with Cost of Living Index < 90 and Climate Score > 80

are the sunniest and the driest. Sunny day totals range from the 130s in Anchorage, Seattle, and Portland to 300 for Las Vegas.

- *Annual days with thunderstorms* shows the average number of days each year with thunder and lightning present.

- *Tornado risk score* and *Hurricane risk score* reflect the probability and severity of tornados, on a 0–100 scale, based on prevailing meteorological or geophysical patterns and the history of that locality and nearby areas. A place may have a high score even if it has yet to record a damaging tornado or hurricane. Calculations come from Sperling's BestPlaces.

Charts

Three charts present important climate elements. The first shows average daily temperatures in each month of the year, with average daily minimums and maximums. The second shows annual precipitation, rain and snow, in inches. The third shows annual cloudy days and rainy days.

Climate Rankings

The Climate ranking, which takes all of the category's attributes into consideration, is based on desirable ranges. For example, too much rain or no rain at all is undesirable. *Cities Ranked & Rated* defines a desirable range for rainfall of 20 inches to 30 inches per year. Areas falling within this range receive maximum points. Areas outside the range get reduced points, which are further reduced the farther away the number falls. Table 3.28 shows the desirable ranges used in the rankings.

TABLE 3.28 DESIRABLE RANGES FOR CLIMATE ATTRIBUTES

ATTRIBUTE	DESIRABLE RANGE
January low	30°F–60°F
July high	72°F–82°F
Annual days > 90°F	3–10
Annual day < 32°F	0–30
Annual days < 0°F	0
Annual inches precipitation	20–30
Annual inches snowfall	0–24
Annual days precipitation	50–100
July relative humidity	50%–70%
Annual days mostly sunny	250–300

Source: *Cities Ranked & Rated* determination

Climate Highlights, Tables 3.29–3.36

TABLE 3.29 WINTER TEMPERATURES
AVERAGE JANUARY LOWS (°F)

METRO AREAS WITH WARMEST WINTERS	°F	METRO AREAS WITH COOLEST WINTERS	°F
Honolulu, HI	65.3	Fairbanks, AK	−19.3
Fort Lauderdale–Pompano Beach–Deerfield Beach, FL	58.7	Fargo, ND	−3.6
Miami–Miami Beach–Kendall, FL	58.7	Grand Forks, ND	−3.0
Sebastian–Vero Beach, FL	56.0	St. Cloud, MN	−1.4
Port St. Lucie–Fort Pierce, FL	55.9	Bismarck, ND	−1.1
West Palm Beach–Boca Raton–Boynton Beach, FL	55.9	Duluth, MN	−0.6
Cape Coral–Fort Myers, FL	52.3	Wausau, WI	3.1
Naples–Marco Island, FL	52.3	Eau Claire, WI	3.2
Punta Gorda, FL	52.3	La Crosse, WI	3.2
Brownsville–Harlingen, TX	51.0	Minneapolis–St. Paul–Bloomington, MN-WI	3.2
Lakeland, FL	51.0	Rochester, MN	3.2
Sarasota–Bradenton–Venice, FL	50.1	Anchorage, AK	3.5
Tampa–St. Petersburg–Clearwater, FL	50.1	Sioux Falls, SD	3.7
Gainesville, FL	50.0	Iowa City, IA	5.0
Ocala, FL	50.0	Appleton, WI	6.9
Orlando–Kissimmee, FL	50.0	Green Bay, WI	6.9
Deltona–Daytona Beach–Ormond Beach, FL	47.6	Oshkosh–Neenah, WI	6.9
Palm Bay–Melbourne–Titusville, FL	47.6	Waterloo–Cedar Falls, IA	6.9
Corpus Christi, TX	46.1	Burlington–South Burlington, VT	7.6
San Diego–Carlsbad–San Marcos, CA	45.8	Sioux City, IA	7.7
Biloxi, MS	45.5	Fond du Lac, WI	7.9
Los Angeles–Long Beach–Glendale, CA	45.4	Janesville, WI	8.2
Oxnard–Thousand Oaks–Ventura, CA	45.4	Madison, WI	8.2
Santa Ana–Anaheim–Irvine, CA	45.4	Dubuque, IA	9.0
Jacksonville, FL	44.5	Kankakee–Bradley, IL	10.0
Riverside–San Bernardino–Ontario, CA	44.4	Rapid City, SD	10.0
El Centro, CA	44.0	Bangor, ME	10.2
McAllen–Edinburg–Mission, TX	43.6	Ames, IA	11.0
Houma–Bayou Cane–Thibodaux, LA	43.5	Great Falls, MT	11.0
New Orleans, LA	43.5	Lewiston–Auburn, ME	11.0

Source: U.S. National Climatic Data Center

TABLE 3.30 SUMMER TEMPERATURES
AVERAGE JULY HIGHS (°F)

METRO AREAS WITH HOTTEST SUMMERS	°F	METRO AREAS WITH COOLEST SUMMERS	°F
El Centro, CA	107.0	Anchorage, AK	65.6
Phoenix–Mesa–Scottsdale, AZ	104.8	Oakland–Fremont–Hayward, CA	69.7
Yuma, AZ	104.8	Fairbanks, AK	72.4
Las Vegas–Paradise, NV	103.9	Salinas, CA	73.6
St. George, UT	101.6	San Francisco–San Mateo–Redwood City, CA	73.6
College Station–Bryan, TX	99.2	Santa Cruz–Watsonville, CA	73.6
Killeen–Temple–Fort Hood, TX	99.2	Mount Vernon–Anacortes, WA	73.7
Wichita Falls, TX	99.2	San Luis Obispo–Paso Robles, CA	73.9
Lawton, OK	99.1	Santa Barbara–Santa Maria, CA	73.9
Bakersfield, CA	99.1	Bellingham, WA	75.1
Tucson, AZ	98.3	Bremerton–Silverdale, WA	75.1
Fresno, CA	98.2	Seattle–Bellevue–Everett, WA	75.1
Visalia–Porterville, CA	98.2	Tacoma, WA	75.1
Hanford–Corcoran, CA	98.0	Los Angeles–Long Beach–Glendale, CA	75.8
Redding, CA	98.0	Oxnard–Thousand Oaks–Ventura, CA	75.8
Madera, CA	98.0	Santa Ana–Anaheim–Irvine, CA	75.8
Chico, CA	96.5	Duluth, MN	76.4
Waco, TX	96.2	Wausau, WI	77.0
Dallas–Plano–Irving, TX	96.1	San Diego–Carlsbad–San Marcos, CA	77.3
Sherman–Denison, TX	96.1	Erie, PA	77.4
Austin–Round Rock, TX	95.9	Bangor, ME	77.5
Laredo, TX	95.9	Longview, WA	77.7
San Antonio, TX	95.9	Lewiston–Auburn, ME	78.0
Fort Worth–Arlington, TX	95.5	Olympia, WA	78.4
Abilene, TX	95.3	Binghamton, NY	78.5
Midland–Odessa, TX	95.0	San Jose–Sunnyvale–Santa Clara, CA	78.6
San Angelo, TX	95.0	Elmira, NY	79.0
El Paso, TX	94.9	Portland–Vancouver–Beaverton, OR-WA	79.0
Corpus Christi, TX	94.8	Portland–South Portland–Biddeford, ME	79.1
Merced, CA	94.7	Buffalo–Niagara Falls, NY	79.5

Source: U.S. National Climatic Data Center

TABLE 3.31 TEMPERATURE EXTREMES
NUMBER OF DAYS PER YEAR WITH EXTREME TEMPERATURES

METRO AREA	DAYS > 90°F	METRO AREA	DAYS < 32°F	METRO AREA	DAYS < 0°F
El Centro, CA	179	Fairbanks, AK	225	Fairbanks, AK	116
Phoenix–Mesa–Scottsdale, AZ	164	Flagstaff, AZ	210	Bismarck, ND	56
Yuma, AZ	164	Prescott, AZ	210	Grand Forks, ND	55
Tucson, AZ	139	Anchorage, AK	192	Fargo, ND	54
Las Vegas–Paradise, NV	131	Reno–Sparks, NV	189	Duluth, MN	51
St. George, UT	113	Duluth, MN	187	St. Cloud, MN	46
Laredo, TX	111	Bismarck, ND	186	Anchorage, AK	41
San Antonio, TX	111	Casper, WY	183	Wausau, WI	38
Hanford–Corcoran, CA	111	Cheyenne, WY	183	Eau Claire, WI	34
Bakersfield, CA	110	Fargo, ND	181	La Crosse, WI	34
San Angelo, TX	109	Grand Forks, ND	180	Minneapolis–St. Paul–Bloomington, MN-WI	34
Madera, CA	107	Carson City, NV	178	Rochester, MN	34
Fresno, CA	107	St. Cloud, MN	178	Sioux Falls, SD	33
Visalia–Porterville, CA	107	Sioux Falls, SD	171	Rapid City, SD	31
Cape Coral–Fort Myers, FL	106	Wausau, WI	170	Waterloo–Cedar Falls, IA	31
Naples–Marco Island, FL	106	Rapid City, SD	169	Appleton, WI	29
Punta Gorda, FL	106	Missoula, MT	167	Green Bay, WI	29
College Station–Bryan, TX	106	Idaho Falls, ID	166	Oshkosh–Neenah, WI	29
Killeen–Temple–Fort Hood, TX	106	Pocatello, ID	166	Iowa City, IA	29
Wichita Falls, TX	106	Janesville, WI	164	Burlington–South Burlington, VT	28
Victoria, TX	105	Madison, WI	164	Great Falls, MT	28
Waco, TX	105	Boulder, CO	163	Janesville, WI	25
Gainesville, FL	104	Denver–Aurora, CO	163	Madison, WI	25
Ocala, FL	104	Fort Collins–Loveland, CO	163	Fond du Lac, WI	25
Orlando–Kissimmee, FL	104	Greeley, CO	163	Missoula, MT	24
El Paso, TX	103	Fond du Lac, WI	163	Casper, WY	22
Brownsville–Harlingen, TX	102	Appleton, WI	163	Cheyenne, WY	22
McAllen–Edinburg–Mission, TX	101	Green Bay, WI	163	Sioux City, IA	22
Austin–Round Rock, TX	101	Oshkosh–Neenah, WI	163	Billings, MT	18
Redding, CA	98	Burlington–South Burlington, VT	163	Dubuque, IA	18

Source: U.S. National Climatic Data Center

TABLE 3.32 ANNUAL INCHES PRECIPITATION
AVERAGE TOTAL PRECIPITATION (RAIN & SNOWMELT) IN INCHES

WETTEST METRO AREAS	INCHES	DRIEST METRO AREAS	INCHES
Mobile, AL	67.0	El Centro, CA	3.0
Fort Walton Beach–Crestview–Destin, FL	64.2	Las Vegas–Paradise, NV	4.0
Panama City–Lynn Haven, FL	64.2	Bakersfield, CA	6.0
Pensacola–Ferry Pass–Brent, FL	64.2	Reno–Sparks, NV	7.0
Valdosta, GA	63.3	Phoenix–Mesa–Scottsdale, AZ	7.0
Port St. Lucie–Fort Pierce, FL	62.1	Yuma, AZ	7.0
West Palm Beach–Boca Raton–Boynton Beach, FL	62.1	Hanford–Corcoran, CA	7.4
Sebastian–Vero Beach, FL	62.0	Kennewick–Richland–Pasco, WA	8.0
Albany, GA	62.0	Yakima, WA	8.0
Tallahassee, FL	62.0	Albuquerque, NM	8.0
Fort Lauderdale–Pompano Beach–Deerfield Beach, FL	60.0	Las Cruces, NM	8.0
Miami–Miami Beach–Kendall, FL	60.0	El Paso, TX	8.0
Biloxi, MS	59.0	Farmington, NM	8.2
Houma–Bayou Cane–Thibodaux, LA	57.0	St. George, UT	8.4
New Orleans, LA	57.0	Wenatchee, WA	8.9
Lake Charles, LA	55.5	Grand Junction, CO	9.0
Beaumont–Port Arthur, TX	55.1	San Diego–Carlsbad–San Marcos, CA	9.0
Baton Rouge, LA	54.1	Fresno, CA	10.0
Lafayette, LA	54.1	Visalia–Porterville, CA	10.0
Greenville, NC	54.0	Carson City, NV	10.5
Jacksonville, NC	54.0	Madera, CA	10.6
Myrtle Beach–Conway–North Myrtle Beach, SC	54.0	Fairbanks, AK	10.8
Wilmington, NC	54.0	Tucson, AZ	11.0
Alexandria, LA	54.0	Idaho Falls, ID	11.3
Auburn–Opelika, AL	54.0	Pueblo, CO	11.9
Jacksonville, FL	54.0	Casper, WY	12.0
Cape Coral–Fort Myers, FL	54.0	Cheyenne, WY	12.0
Naples–Marco Island, FL	54.0	Pocatello, ID	12.0
Punta Gorda, FL	54.0	Boise City–Nampa, ID	12.0
Cleveland, TN	53.3	San Luis Obispo–Paso Robles, CA	12.0

Source: U.S. National Climatic Data Center

TABLE 3.33 SNOWIEST METROPOLITAN AREAS
METRO AREAS BY ANNUAL INCHES SNOWFALL

METRO AREA	INCHES	METRO AREA	INCHES
Syracuse, NY	109.0	Grand Rapids–Wyoming, MI	77.0
Utica–Rome, NY	109.0	Holland–Grand Haven, MI	77.0
Ithaca, NY	107.0	Kalamazoo–Portage, MI	77.0
Flagstaff, AZ	99.0	Muskegon–Norton Shores, MI	77.0
Bangor, ME	95.0	Portland–South Portland–Biddeford, ME	74.0
Buffalo–Niagara Falls, NY	90.0	Pittsfield, MA	73.0
Rochester, NY	88.4	Harrisonburg, VA	71.0
Binghamton, NY	86.0	Albany–Schenectady–Troy, NY	71.0
Erie, PA	83.6	Glens Falls, NY	71.0
Elmira, NY	82.0	Poughkeepsie–Newburgh–Middletown, NY	71.0
Casper, WY	81.0	Lewiston–Auburn, ME	71.0
Cheyenne, WY	81.0	Anchorage, AK	70.0
Burlington–South Burlington, VT	79.0	Fairbanks, AK	67.8
Duluth, MN	78.0	Kingston, NY	63.0
Battle Creek, MI	77.0	Great Falls, MT	63.0

Source: U.S. National Climatic Data Center

TABLE 3.34 ANNUAL DAYS OF PRECIPITATION
AVERAGE NUMBER OF DAYS OF MEASURABLE PRECIPITATION EACH YEAR

METRO AREAS WITH MOST DAYS	DAYS	METRO AREAS WITH FEWEST DAYS	DAYS
Erie, PA	188	El Centro, CA	16
Wausau, WI	185	Las Vegas–Paradise, NV	24
Rochester, NY	182	Phoenix–Mesa–Scottsdale, AZ	34
Youngstown–Warren–Boardman, OH-PA	181	Yuma, AZ	34
Bay City, MI	181	Riverside–San Bernardino–Ontario, CA	35
Saginaw–Saginaw Township North, MI	181	Los Angeles–Long Beach–Glendale, CA	35
Harrisonburg, VA	174	Oxnard–Thousand Oaks–Ventura, CA	35
Longview, WA	174	Santa Fe, NM	36
Ithaca, NY	170	Bakersfield, CA	36
Syracuse, NY	168	Santa Ana–Anaheim–Irvine, CA	40
Utica–Rome, NY	168	San Diego–Carlsbad–San Marcos, CA	41
Canton–Massillon, OH	168	Hanford–Corcoran, CA	43
Buffalo–Niagara Falls, NY	168	Fresno, CA	44
Tacoma, WA	164	Visalia–Porterville, CA	44
Binghamton, NY	163	El Paso, TX	45
Olympia, WA	163	Madera, CA	45
Bellingham, WA	160	San Luis Obispo–Paso Robles, CA	45
Bremerton–Silverdale, WA	160	Santa Barbara–Santa Maria, CA	45
Seattle–Bellevue–Everett, WA	160	Napa, CA	47
Elmira, NY	159	Santa Rosa–Petaluma, CA	47
Jackson, MI	156	Vallejo–Fairfield, CA	47
Lansing–East Lansing, MI	156	San Jose–Sunnyvale–Santa Clara, CA	47
Cleveland–Elyria–Mentor, OH	156	Reno–Sparks, NV	49
Williamsport, PA	156	Carson City, NV	50
Mount Vernon–Anacortes, WA	155	Tucson, AZ	50
Morgantown, WV	154	Merced, CA	52
Burlington–South Burlington, VT	153	Modesto, CA	52
Akron, OH	153	Stockton, CA	52
Scranton–Wilkes-Barre, PA	153	Las Cruces, NM	53
Lima, OH	152	Midland–Odessa, TX	53

Source: U.S. National Climatic Data Center

TABLE 3.35 SUMMER HUMIDITY
AVERAGE JULY RELATIVE HUMIDITY AS A PERCENT

MOST HUMID METRO AREAS	RELATIVE HUMIDITY	LEAST HUMID METRO AREAS	RELATIVE HUMIDITY
Beaumont–Port Arthur, TX	79%	St. George, UT	19%
Deltona–Daytona Beach–Ormond Beach, FL	78%	El Centro, CA	20%
Palm Bay–Melbourne–Titusville, FL	78%	Carson City, NV	20%
Lake Charles, LA	78%	Hanford–Corcoran, CA	24%
Corpus Christi, TX	77%	Madera, CA	24%
Asheville, NC	77%	Logan, UT	24%
Houston–Sugar Land–Baytown, TX	77%	Bend, OR	25%
Alexandria, LA	77%	Idaho Falls, ID	26%
Houma–Bayou Cane–Thibodaux, LA	77%	Wenatchee, WA	28%
New Orleans, LA	77%	Las Vegas–Paradise, NV	29%
Biloxi, MS	77%	Farmington, NM	29%
Oakland–Fremont–Hayward, CA	76%	Lewiston, ID	29%
Brownsville–Harlingen, TX	76%	Coeur d'Alene, ID	31%
Bay City, MI	76%	Prescott, AZ	33%
Saginaw–Saginaw Township North, MI	76%	Phoenix–Mesa–Scottsdale, AZ	36%
Barnstable Town, MA	76%	Yuma, AZ	36%
Charleston–North Charleston, SC	76%	Flagstaff, AZ	36%
Cape Coral–Fort Myers, FL	76%	Tucson, AZ	38%
Naples–Marco Island, FL	76%	El Paso, TX	39%
Punta Gorda, FL	76%	Albuquerque, NM	43%
Albany, GA	76%	Grand Junction, CO	47%
Tallahassee, FL	76%	Longview, WA	47%
Salinas, CA	75%	Las Cruces, NM	49%
San Francisco–San Mateo–Redwood City, CA	75%	Fairbanks, AK	49%
Santa Cruz–Watsonville, CA	75%	Casper, WY	49%
Victoria, TX	75%	Cheyenne, WY	49%
Elmira, NY	75%	Colorado Springs, CO	49%
Jackson, MS	75%	Reno–Sparks, NV	50%
Hattiesburg, MS	75%	Pueblo, CO	50%
Greenville, NC	75%	Mount Vernon–Anacortes, WA	51%

Source: U.S. National Climatic Data Center

TABLE 3.36 SUNSHINE
AVERAGE ANNUAL DAYS MOSTLY SUNNY

CLOUDIEST METRO AREAS	DAYS	SUNNIEST METRO AREAS	DAYS
Fairbanks, AK	125	Las Vegas–Paradise, NV	300
Anchorage, AK	131	Phoenix–Mesa–Scottsdale, AZ	295
Mount Vernon–Anacortes, WA	133	Yuma, AZ	295
Tacoma, WA	136	El Paso, TX	294
Bellingham, WA	136	Prescott, AZ	293
Bremerton–Silverdale, WA	136	Flagstaff, AZ	290
Seattle–Bellevue–Everett, WA	136	Tucson, AZ	287
Olympia, WA	137	Las Cruces, NM	287
Portland–Vancouver–Beaverton, OR-WA	137	Napa, CA	285
Binghamton, NY	151	Santa Rosa–Petaluma, CA	285
Elmira, NY	151	Vallejo–Fairfield, CA	285
Longview, WA	152	San Luis Obispo–Paso Robles, CA	285
Corvallis, OR	153	Santa Barbara–Santa Maria, CA	285
Missoula, MT	158	Albuquerque, NM	283
Eugene–Springfield, OR	158	Santa Fe, NM	283
Buffalo–Niagara Falls, NY	159	Bakersfield, CA	281
Salem, OR	159	El Centro, CA	277
Pittsburgh, PA	161	Farmington, NM	276
Weirton–Steubenville, WV-OH	161	Yuba City, CA	276
Wheeling, WV	161	Chico, CA	276
Burlington–South Burlington, VT	161	Madera, CA	271
Erie, PA	161	Fresno, CA	271
Battle Creek, MI	163	Visalia–Porterville, CA	271
Grand Rapids–Wyoming, MI	163	Riverside–San Bernardino–Ontario, CA	268
Holland–Grand Haven, MI	163	Lubbock, TX	267
Kalamazoo–Portage, MI	163	San Diego–Carlsbad–San Marcos, CA	267
Muskegon–Norton Shores, MI	163	Amarillo, TX	265
Bay City, MI	163	Sacramento–Arden-Arcade–Roseville, CA	265
Saginaw–Saginaw Township North, MI	163	Salinas, CA	265
Ithaca, NY	164	San Francisco–San Mateo–Redwood City, CA	265

Source: U.S. National Climatic Data Center

Education

The Education category encompasses both primary/secondary schooling and post-secondary—college and postgraduate—schooling for younger and older adults. The importance of education is obvious for individuals and families with school-age children. But beyond that, the availability and quality of educational resources goes a long way toward defining the quality of life of everyone in an area.

Although recent legislation and trends appear to be having a positive effect, large gaps still exist in the quality of public, primary, and secondary education among schools, nationally and locally. Unfortunately, quality of primary and secondary education has been notoriously difficult to assess. School comparisons have generally been based on *process* measures, such as investment (expenditures), numbers of schools and teachers, and student-teacher ratios, not *results* measures.

Recent legislation and trends have brought on a greater use of testing—some standardized and some not—to determine student achievement and school performance, but these programs are still in the implementation phase. The No Child Left Behind Act (NCLB) passed in 2002 has defined a long road toward implementing full school accountability on some 42 different standards, including test results and "adequate yearly progress" toward academic goals. The debate rages on as to whether this program is properly conceived and funded, and whether it delivers the intended results or something altogether different. But many feel that, even if testing were fully implemented and successfully executed, because education involves experiences beyond academics and testing, these newer assessments will never be adequate.

Although in our sister volume *Best Places to Raise Your Family* (Wiley Publishing, Inc.) we made an ambitious attempt to look more closely at educational testing and results, we still find it extraordinarily difficult to read the facts to determine whether a school, or school system, really effectively delivers a quality education. It is particularly difficult the larger the area gets—undoubtedly, New York or Dallas or Dayton, Ohio, have some great schools and some bad ones—how do you assign a composite rating for an area based on hundreds of test scores for each individual school, grade, and subject?

Over time, we have found—and some important studies confirm—that the two best predictors of whether schools in an area are good are (1) the level of educational attainment of the parents and (2) teacher salaries. *Educational attainment* refers to the average maximum level of education reached by individuals in an area; when a substantial portion of the population has achieved a 4-year college or university or even postgraduate degree, the population is considered educated. Educated populaces not only indicate the presence of good local education but also tend to make good local education *happen*. Educated individuals tend to gravitate to places with strong education resources, and then support them through volunteerism, parent involvement and advocacy, and even by voting for tax levies. We think an educated population—high levels of educational attainment compared to national averages—is the single best indicator of good schools and educational processes in an area.

On the notion that the best teachers flock to locations that pay more and have been on the job longest, we would also look at teacher salaries—especially as adjusted for or compared to local living costs—as a good indicator. Unfortunately we don't have a good source of composite teacher salary information by metro area, but those of you doing a deeper drill-down into a school system or district are encouraged to look at salaries as well.

Education Trends

The famed and somewhat controversial No Child Left Behind program continues to set today's pattern for primary and secondary public education. We appreciate creator and present Secretary of Education Margaret Spelling's admonition that "what gets measured gets done." And for better or for worse, there has been an undeniable and highly visible emphasis on testing and achieving good classroom-wide test results in individual schools. As the "law of unintended consequences" might suggest, not all is good; teachers, motivated by fear for their jobs, have tended to "teach to the tests" in many instances, and worse, give up on students who seem to have no prospect of moving class scores higher (in an ironic juxtaposition of what the program was intended to do in the first place). And millions of dollars have been spent on compliance and reporting, with some favorable impact but with the inevitable outcome of producing some reporting that seems too complex for even the educators, not to mention the educated, to understand.

In apparent homage to states rights, NCLB allows states to custom-build their own testing and appraisal programs. A guideline is set for what is to be tested and that testing must be fully implemented by the 2012–13 school year, but no guidelines exist for how or to what standard testing is to be done. The result is a complex and uncoordinated patchwork of tests and testing standards. In one state, average scores for a particular grade and subject might exceed 90%, while a neighboring state administers a different test with a different degree of difficulty to a different grade, resulting in average scores in the 30% to 40% range, making it largely impossible to compare places. It is possible to examine trends within states, but the data is barely sufficient to do so. Some states, instead of reporting the often excessive bundle of actual scores or averages, simply assign A through F "grades" (Florida) or numeric performance ratings (California'a API, or Academic Performance Index). Such ratings are helpful for rating schools within a state.

Despite these complexities and shortcomings, we still see some improvement in educational delivery and results. For years, and long before NCLB, the National Assessment of Education Progress, known informally as the "Nation's Report Card" and administered by the U.S. Department of Education, has given aggregate performance results in reading and math and more recently science. Unlike NCLB, the results are not tabulated by school and aren't used to measure school performance. At an aggregate level there has been a sizable improvement in math scores particularly at the 4th-grade level (67% proficient in 2000 to 79% proficient in 2005), with lesser improvements in 8th-grade math and 4th-grade reading scores. Curiously, 8th-grade reading scores have remained unchanged (see Table 4.20 in chapter 4 for U.S. and state-by-state results). NCLB and other testing have shown that solid achievement early—in 3rd and 4th grades—usually leads to solid achievement later on, so good achievement sown here will be reaped in higher grade levels later on.

The higher education landscape has experienced more gradual change. One enduring trend is the increased cost of higher education, aggravated recently by persistent and growing state budget deficits. According to the College Board, 4-year private institutions have an average 2006–07 tuition of $22,218, up 5.9% from the year before, while 4-year public school tuition is $5,836, up 6.3%, and 2-year public school tuition is $2,272, up 4.1%.

Higher-education enrollment rates are increasing, particularly for students just out of high school. While high school graduation rates have increased only from 85% in 1972 to about 90% in 2004, the percentage of high school students going straight to college has risen from 49% to 67% during that same period. Fifty-eight percent of 25- to 29-year-olds have completed some college education, up from 34% in the early '70s. College enrollment overall is growing at a faster rate, up some 21% from 1994 to 2004, and the growth rate is still faster (25%) for women. Women now outnumber men at many college campuses, particularly in graduate programs.

Education Attributes

Cities Ranked & Rated presents data in the categories of *Attainment, Public Schools,* and *Higher Education.* All attributes except SAT/ACT scores are used in scoring and ranking. For reasons given above, *Cities Ranked & Rated* assigns the highest weightings to 4-year college and graduate degree attainment.

Table 3.37 shows the Education table for the metropolitan area of Ann Arbor, Michigan.

Attainment

Attainment represents student learning as reflected in the attainment of various levels of education. College degree attainment reflects the *highest* level attained. Facts come from the U.S. Census population surveys, reflecting 2005 figures.

- *High school degree* shows the percentage of the population completing high school and earning a diploma. In the United States, the 2004 overall high school completion rate approaches 90% but large variations exist among metropolitan areas. The percentage range is in the mid-50s to low-60s in the rural south, Texas border towns, and large inner city areas such as Los Angeles and Newark, New Jersey, up to the low to mid-90s in college towns such as Ann Arbor, Michigan; Corvallis, Oregon; and Ames, Iowa.

TABLE 3.37 SAMPLE EDUCATION TABLE FROM ANN ARBOR, MI								
ACHIEVEMENT	**AREA**	**U.S. AVG**	**PUBLIC SCHOOLS**	**AREA**	**U.S. AVG**	**HIGHER EDUCATION**	**AREA**	**U.S. AVG**
High school degree	91.5%	82.7%	Expenditures per pupil	$6,960	$5,686	No. 2-year colleges	1	4
2-year college degree	6.1%	6.4%	Student/teacher ratio	19.4	16.7	No. 4-year colleges/universities	6	6
4-year college degree	24.5%	15.7%	Attending public school	90.5%	90.1%	No. highly ranked universities	1	1
Graduate/professional degree	23.4%	8.9%	State SAT score	1151	1021			
			State ACT score	21.5*	20.9			

Education
Score: 97.1
Rank: 12

- *2-year college degree* attainment ranges from 2.5% to 11% among metropolitan areas. There is no real pattern other than that both high and low figures tend to be in small towns. Figures are probably driven by the relative availability of 2-year and 4-year programs and the local job market.

- *4-year college degree* attainment ranges widely from 5% to 35% among metropolitan areas. The highest percentages tend to be in college towns, wealthier areas such as Orange County, California, and Naples, Florida, and high-tech centers such as San Francisco and the Research Triangle cities of North Carolina. Lower figures occur in working-class or agricultural towns such as Dalton, Georgia; Visalia–Porterville, California; and Lima, Ohio.

- *Graduate/professional degree* attainment is similar to 4-year degrees, with 25% to 40% rates in college towns and 2% to 3% in working-class towns. It can be assumed that these individuals also have a 4-year degree; they are not included in the 4-year facts just presented. Table 3.39 combines 4-year and graduate attainment, perhaps the best indicator of an educated population.

Public Schools

Facts in the first three categories below come from the National Center for Education Statistics in the U.S. Department of Education. SAT and ACT scores come from College Board, Inc., and American College Testing Service, Inc.

- *Expenditures per pupil* is widely used, although its meaning has been diluted by numerous changes and inconsistencies in calculation (for instance, does it include administrative costs?) and an increased emphasis on achievement and results.

Nevertheless, there are notable differences, ranging from $10,000 to $12,000 per student per year in big Eastern cities to $3,000 to $5,000 in small, Midwestern and Southern towns, with Utah at the bottom. To some degree these figures reflect cost of living through teacher salaries.

- *Student/teacher ratio*, like *Expenditures per pupil*, has seen changes and inconsistencies in calculation; however, it is still a benchmark for school districts and metropolitan areas. Lower figures in large inner cities or small towns can be misleading because the presence of special educators distorts figures by their abundance in inner cities or by the relative lack of students in smaller towns. The higher ratios are from 22 to 30 and appear in the South, Southern California, and in some larger cities. Interestingly, ratios in Texas have dropped considerably since the last edition, leaving us unsure if it's a matter of policy or a change in reporting. Lower figures of 10 to 12 occur in smaller towns and some college towns, and Tennessee and Massachusetts do not report the figures at all.

- *Attending public school* is the percentage of total elementary and secondary students enrolled in public schools. A lower percentage reflects greater parental apathy about public schools, although there are other significant factors, such as household affluence, strength of religious affiliations, and the availability of parochial and private schools. This statistic ranges from the mid-70% range in Dubuque, Iowa, and education-ravaged New Orleans to the high 90s in many places in the intermountain West and South.

- *State SAT score* and *State ACT score* are state averages, with an asterisk (*) denoting the test

Doing Your Homework on Schools

The facts presented here are a place to start, but clearly, if primary and secondary schools are a big factor in your best place, it's worth doing some homework to find out more. Particularly since the advent of No Child Left Behind, mountains of data are collected about each school and school district. Most is published on school websites, but you have to find the site, and comparing schools is difficult. One of our favorite resources is the pioneering nonprofit portal GreatSchools.net (www.greatschools.net), which offers comprehensive profiles, including test scores and parent reviews, for some 120,000 schools nationwide in a reasonably easy-to-use construct designed for use by parents seeking to learn more about school performance.

emphasized in that state. See "Education" in chapter 4 for details on SAT and ACT scores and their correct interpretation.

Higher Education

These facts outline the higher education *resources*—the number and quality of colleges and universities in an area. The presence of such facilities tells something of the educational opportunity, climate, and amenities available in an area. Interestingly, higher education facilities are present in all but 5 of the 375 metro areas. Facts on 2-year and 4-year colleges come from the National Center for Education Statistics. *No. highly ranked universities* data comes from the Princeton Review, a popular college rating service.

- *No. 2-year colleges:* Most cities have at least some 2-year college presence, ranging from a single college to dozens in larger urban areas.

- *No. 4-year colleges/universities:* The definition of 4-year colleges and universities is fairly broad and includes branch campuses of larger universities. All but 33 metro areas have at least some recognized 4-year college presence. There are 10 or more in 57 metro areas.

- *No. highly ranked universities:* This measure counts the number of educational institutions judged by the Princeton Review facilities as having selective admissions standards based on test score requirements and percentage of applicants admitted. This statistic is fairly selective: 196 metro areas have no such facilities, 87 have one, and 66 have two or three. Los Angeles has the most with 11.

Education Highlights, Tables 3.38–3.42

TABLE 3.38 HIGH SCHOOL GRADUATION RATE			
PERCENTAGE OF POPULATION WITH HIGH SCHOOL DIPLOMA, 2005			
METRO AREAS WITH HIGHEST GRADUATION RATE	PERCENTAGE	METRO AREAS WITH LOWEST GRADUATION RATE	PERCENTAGE
Ames, IA	93.8%	McAllen–Edinburg–Mission, TX	50.6%
Corvallis, OR	93.2%	Laredo, TX	53.7%
Boulder, CO	92.7%	Brownsville–Harlingen, TX	55.8%
Lawrence, KS	92.6%	El Centro, CA	58.8%
Fort Collins–Loveland, CO	92.5%	Visalia–Porterville, CA	61.6%
Iowa City, IA	92.0%	Dalton, GA	62.0%
Colorado Springs, CO	91.8%	Merced, CA	63.3%
Fairbanks, AK	91.8%	Madera, CA	64.9%
Barnstable Town, MA	91.8%	Yuma, AZ	65.5%
Ann Arbor, MI	91.5%	El Paso, TX	66.2%
Madison, WI	91.5%	Houma–Bayou Cane–Thibodaux, LA	67.1%
Ithaca, NY	91.5%	Fresno, CA	67.2%
Missoula, MT	91.0%	Salinas, CA	67.6%
Provo–Orem, UT	91.0%	Danville, VA	67.8%
Bloomington–Normal, IL	91.0%	Miami–Miami Beach–Kendall, FL	68.2%
Bremerton–Silverdale, WA	90.8%	Yakima, WA	68.3%
Minneapolis–St. Paul–Bloomington, MN–WI	90.7%	Vineland–Millville–Bridgeton, NJ	68.4%
Champaign–Urbana, IL	90.5%	Bakersfield, CA	68.5%
Lincoln, NE	90.4%	Morristown, TN	68.5%
Logan, UT	90.4%	Hanford–Corcoran, CA	68.9%
Cedar Rapids, IA	90.0%	Los Angeles–Long Beach–Glendale, CA	69.4%
Rochester, MN	90.0%	Gainesville, GA	70.1%
Fargo, ND	89.9%	Modesto, CA	70.2%
Anchorage, AK	89.9%	Las Cruces, NM	70.2%
Seattle–Bellevue–Everett, WA	89.9%	Hickory–Lenoir–Morganton, NC	70.4%
Bethesda–Gaithersburg–Frederick, MD	89.8%	Rome, GA	71.4%
Ogden–Clearfield, UT	89.5%	Stockton, CA	71.7%
Olympia, WA	89.4%	Rocky Mount, NC	71.8%
Rockingham County–Strafford County, NH	89.3%	Cleveland, TN	71.9%
Spokane, WA	89.2%	Florence, SC	71.9%

Source: Claritas, Inc. from U.S. Census American Community Survey, 2005

TABLE 3.39 COMBINED COLLEGE & GRADUATE DEGREE ATTAINMENT
PERCENTAGE OF POPULATION WITH 4-YEAR OR GRADUATE DEGREE AS HIGHEST LEVEL OF ATTAINMENT

METRO AREAS WITH MOST DEGREES	PERCENTAGE	METRO AREAS WITH FEWEST DEGREES	PERCENTAGE
Boulder, CO	69.3%	El Centro, CA	10.4%
Bethesda–Gaithersburg–Frederick, MD	69.2%	Hanford–Corcoran, CA	10.6%
Ithaca, NY	68.6%	Merced, CA	10.8%
Ann Arbor, MI	66.9%	Dalton, GA	10.8%
Corvallis, OR	60.2%	Danville, VA	11.1%
Ames, IA	58.4%	Visalia–Porterville, CA	11.5%
Lawrence, KS	58.1%	Vineland–Millville–Bridgeton, NJ	11.7%
Cambridge–Newton–Framingham, MA	56.0%	Madera, CA	11.9%
Iowa City, IA	55.9%	Yuma, AZ	12.0%
San Francisco–San Mateo–Redwood City, CA	54.8%	Weirton–Steubenville, WV-OH	12.1%
Columbia, MO	53.1%	Morristown, TN	12.2%
Durham, NC	50.5%	Danville, IL	12.3%
Fort Collins–Loveland, CO	49.5%	Houma–Bayou Cane–Thibodaux, LA	12.5%
Washington–Arlington–Alexandria, DC-VA-MD-WV	48.4%	Mansfield, OH	12.7%
Bridgeport–Stamford–Norwalk, CT	48.2%	Yuba City, CA	12.9%
San Jose–Sunnyvale–Santa Clara, CA	47.7%	Hinesville–Fort Stewart, GA	13.0%
Charlottesville, VA	47.2%	McAllen–Edinburg–Mission, TX	13.0%
State College, PA	46.2%	Longview, WA	13.1%
Raleigh–Cary, NC	46.1%	Fort Smith, AR	13.1%
Madison, WI	45.1%	Farmington, NM	13.5%
Gainesville, FL	45.0%	Cumberland, MD	13.6%
Bloomington–Normal, IL	45.0%	Gadsden, AL	13.6%
Santa Fe, NM	44.9%	Hickory–Lenoir–Morganton, NC	13.6%
Austin–Round Rock, TX	44.4%	Johnstown, PA	13.7%
Champaign–Urbana, IL	44.3%	Lima, OH	13.7%
Seattle–Bellevue–Everett, WA	44.2%	Bakersfield, CA	13.7%
Burlington–South Burlington, VT	42.8%	Ocala, FL	13.7%
Tallahassee, FL	42.2%	Brownsville–Harlingen, TX	13.8%
Boston–Quincy, MA	42.0%	Rocky Mount, NC	13.8%
Lake County–Kenosha County, IL-WI	41.2%	Muskegon–Norton Shores, MI	13.9%

Source: Claritas, Inc. from U.S. Census American Community Survey, 2005

TABLE 3.40 PUBLIC SCHOOL INVESTMENT
ANNUAL EXPENDITURES PER STUDENT

METRO AREAS WITH HIGHEST EXPENDITURES	AMOUNT	METRO AREAS WITH LOWEST EXPENDITURES	AMOUNT
Nassau–Suffolk, NY	$11,864	St. George, UT	$3,444
Ocean City, NJ	$10,496	Logan, UT	$3,713
Kingston, NY	$10,495	Provo–Orem, UT	$3,728
Ithaca, NY	$10,189	Ogden–Clearfield, UT	$3,785
Newark–Union, NJ-PA	$9,590	Jackson, MS	$3,848
Trenton–Ewing, NJ	$9,513	Salt Lake City, UT	$3,920
Glens Falls, NY	$9,372	Hattiesburg, MS	$4,024
Vineland–Millville–Bridgeton, NJ	$9,030	Jacksonville, NC	$4,146
Edison, NJ	$8,864	Hot Springs, AR	$4,175
Bridgeport–Stamford–Norwalk, CT	$8,819	Biloxi, MS	$4,181
Poughkeepsie–Newburgh–Middletown, NY	$8,542	Monroe, LA	$4,237
Buffalo–Niagara Falls, NY	$8,535	Hinesville–Fort Stewart, GA	$4,240
Norwich–New London, CT	$8,494	Montgomery, AL	$4,293
Camden, NJ	$8,492	Decatur, IL	$4,300
Albany–Schenectady–Troy, NY	$8,452	Fayetteville–Springdale–Rogers, AR-MO	$4,303
Atlantic City, NJ	$8,319	Morristown, TN	$4,305
New York–White Plains, NY	$8,311	Mobile, AL	$4,323
Hartford–West Hartford–East Hartford, CT	$8,265	Lafayette, LA	$4,325
Rochester, NY	$8,254	Jonesboro, AR	$4,339
Elmira, NY	$8,013	Houma–Bayou Cane–Thibodaux, LA	$4,342
Utica–Rome, NY	$7,984	Joplin, MO	$4,343
Pittsfield, MA	$7,975	Anniston–Oxford, AL	$4,348
New Haven–Milford, CT	$7,851	Springfield, MO	$4,355
Syracuse, NY	$7,818	Oklahoma City, OK	$4,428
Fairbanks, AK	$7,804	Cleveland, TN	$4,464
Bethesda–Gaithersburg–Frederick, MD	$7,762	Boise City–Nampa, ID	$4,471
Cambridge–Newton–Framingham, MA	$7,667	Johnson City, TN	$4,472
Boston–Quincy, MA	$7,654	Idaho Falls, ID	$4,484
Binghamton, NY	$7,645	Alexandria, LA	$4,486
Milwaukee–Waukesha–West Allis, WI	$7,247	Sioux Falls, SD	$4,492

Source: U.S. National Center for Education Statistics, 2005

TABLE 3.41 STUDENT/TEACHER RATIO
AVERAGE CLASS SIZE

METRO AREAS WITH BEST RATIOS	RATIO	METRO AREAS WITH WORST RATIOS	RATIO
Bismarck, ND	10.2	Yuma, AZ	29.3
Pittsfield, MA	11.0	Jacksonville, NC	27.4
Ocean City, NJ	11.7	Bethesda–Gaithersburg–Frederick, MD	27.2
Casper, WY	12.1	Owensboro, KY	24.0
Harrisonburg, VA	12.2	Clarksville, TN	23.7
Rapid City, SD	12.3	Hot Springs, AR	22.5
Charlottesville, VA	12.5	Bowling Green, KY	22.2
Abilene, TX	12.7	Santa Ana–Anaheim–Irvine, CA	22.2
Worcester, MA	12.8	Fayetteville–Springdale–Rogers, AR-MO	22.2
Vineland–Millville–Bridgeton, NJ	13.1	Louisville–Jefferson County, KY-IN	22.0
Lincoln, NE	13.1	Modesto, CA	22.0
College Station–Bryan, TX	13.2	Dover, DE	22.0
Sherman–Denison, TX	13.3	Oxnard–Thousand Oaks–Ventura, CA	21.8
Victoria, TX	13.3	Little Rock–North Little Rock, AR	21.8
Durham, NC	13.4	St. George, UT	21.7
Cheyenne, WY	13.4	Los Angeles–Long Beach–Glendale, CA	21.7
San Angelo, TX	13.4	Seattle–Bellevue–Everett, WA	21.6
St. Joseph, MO	13.4	Fort Lauderdale–Pompano Beach–Deerfield Beach, FL	21.5
Lubbock, TX	13.4	Yakima, WA	21.3
Jefferson City, MO	13.4	Jonesboro, AR	21.0
La Crosse, WI	13.5	Ogden–Clearfield, UT	20.9
Duluth, MN	13.7	Riverside–San Bernardino–Ontario, CA	20.9
Sioux City, IA	13.8	Santa Cruz–Watsonville, CA	20.9
Wichita Falls, TX	13.8	Elizabethtown, KY	20.8
Kingsport–Bristol–Bristol, TN-VA	13.8	Oakland–Fremont–Hayward, CA	20.7
Billings, MT	13.9	Lexington–Fayette, KY	20.7
Danville, IL	13.9	Portland–Vancouver–Beaverton, OR-WA	20.7
Longview, TX	14.0	Merced, CA	20.7
Greenville, NC	14.0	Vallejo–Fairfield, CA	20.7
Ithaca, NY	14.0	Monroe, MI	20.7

No data reported for TN, MA

Source: U.S. National Center for Education Statistics, 2005

TABLE 3.42 PUBLIC SCHOOL UTILIZATION
PERCENTAGE OF STUDENTS ATTENDING PUBLIC SCHOOL

METRO AREAS WITH HIGHEST % IN PUBLIC SCHOOL	PERCENTAGE	METRO AREAS WITH LOWEST % IN PUBLIC SCHOOL	PERCENTAGE
Logan, UT	99.6%	New Orleans, LA	74.5%
Lawton, OK	98.7%	Dubuque, IA	75.0%
Provo–Orem, UT	98.6%	Philadelphia, PA	77.1%
Madera, CA	98.4%	San Francisco–San Mateo–Redwood City, CA	77.3%
Greeley, CO	97.9%	Wilmington, DE	79.1%
McAllen–Edinburg–Mission, TX	97.9%	Baton Rouge, LA	79.4%
Abilene, TX	97.8%	Jefferson City, MO	80.4%
Idaho Falls, ID	97.7%	Lafayette, LA	80.9%
Morristown, TN	97.6%	Honolulu, HI	81.0%
Wenatchee, WA	97.5%	New York–White Plains, NY	81.0%
Hinesville–Fort Stewart, GA	97.5%	Milwaukee–Waukesha–West Allis, WI	81.1%
Farmington, NM	97.5%	Trenton–Ewing, NJ	81.2%
Dalton, GA	97.4%	Louisville–Jefferson County, KY-IN	81.7%
Flagstaff, AZ	97.4%	Lancaster, PA	81.7%
Las Cruces, NM	97.3%	Mobile, AL	81.8%
Ogden–Clearfield, UT	97.2%	Cincinnati–Middletown, OH-KY-IN	82.3%
Glens Falls, NY	97.2%	Bergen–Passaic, NJ	82.4%
Blacksburg–Christiansburg–Radford, VA	97.2%	Scranton–Wilkes-Barre, PA	82.6%
Sherman–Denison, TX	97.1%	Santa Fe, NM	82.7%
Killeen–Temple–Fort Hood, TX	97.1%	Jackson, TN	82.7%
Ames, IA	97.1%	Bethesda–Gaithersburg–Frederick, MD	82.8%
Ithaca, NY	97.0%	Erie, PA	83.2%
Wichita Falls, TX	96.9%	St. Louis, MO	83.2%
St. George, UT	96.8%	Baltimore–Towson, MD	83.5%
Jonesboro, AR	96.8%	South Bend–Mishawaka, IN-MI	83.5%
Casper, WY	96.7%	Fort Wayne, IN	83.5%
Decatur, AL	96.7%	Wheeling, WV	83.8%
Roanoke, VA	96.6%	Cleveland–Elyria–Mentor, OH	83.9%
Visalia–Porterville, CA	96.6%	Appleton, WI	84.1%
Hickory–Lenoir–Morganton, NC	96.6%	Edison, NJ	84.2%

Source: U.S. National Center for Education Statistics, 2005

Health & Healthcare

Health and healthcare have become an important issue for increasing numbers of people. Why? The aging population means more health problems and increased health risks. The cost of healthcare continues to far outpace inflation. Plus, expectations for good health are rising, particularly as life expectancy continues to grow and as aging adults pursue active lives.

Much like education, healthcare services can be difficult to evaluate, as it is easier to appraise the quantity than the quality of services delivered. The number of physicians or hospital beds in an area measures the quantity of healthcare service available, but it doesn't speak to its effectiveness or value delivered. Nonetheless, knowing that the infrastructure exists can be reassuring.

Health & Healthcare Trends

Health, healthcare, and health consciousness have improved gradually in the United States during the past century. Total life expectancy for the average U.S. citizen has gone from 47.3 years in 1900 to 77.3 years in 2002. Heart disease death rates have dropped by almost half since the 1950s. However, notable changes have occurred in the healthcare system and related costs. New treatments, fancy drugs, and the increasing depth of treatments for complex diseases like cancer have, in part, driven healthcare costs rapidly higher. Skyrocketing costs have led to a dramatic increase in managed care (for example, health maintenance organizations, or HMOs), outpatient treatment, preventative medicine, and alternative treatments.

In this edition we place additional ranking weight on healthcare costs. Why? Because the decline in full-coverage insurance offered by employers and the growth of the self-employed and uninsured expose more and more individuals and families to the price of healthcare, increasing the influence on healthcare decisions. Additionally, high healthcare costs can greatly influence an area's attractiveness to employers and especially business employers, thus trickling down rapidly into employment growth and stability and ultimately quality of life.

Health & Healthcare Attributes

Cities Ranked & Rated takes a two-pronged approach to examining health and healthcare. The first approach looks at hazards that cause health problems. The second examines healthcare services and their costs. All attributes figure into the Health and Healthcare scoring and ranking. Air quality, incidence of disease and allergies, and availability of doctors and hospital beds get the highest weighting.

Table 3.43 shows the Health & Healthcare table for the metropolitan area of Ogden–Clearfield, Utah.

Hazards & Illnesses

Cities Ranked & Rated presents data on those health hazards that affect the greatest number of people. Sources for this information include the U.S. Environmental Protection Agency and Centers for Disease Control and Prevention (U.S. Department of Health and Human Services), with calculations by Sperling's BestPlaces.

- *Air-quality score* is a complex composite measure of several air pollutants, including particulates, ozone, volatile organic compounds, and various combustion byproducts on a 0–100 scale, with 100 being the highest or best. Not surprisingly, Los Angeles receives a 1.0, as does San Diego. Detroit and Farmington, New Mexico, also score at the bottom, while Tucson, Arizona; Carson City, Nevada; and several smaller cities in Virginia score near the top, as do many smaller cities nationwide. When looking at these numbers, keep in mind the score isn't just about what the air *looks* like, it is about chemical composition. Areas on or near storm tracks, with high altitude, or with a high degree of atmospheric circulation and change tend to score better, while areas with greater stagnation and higher concentrations of polluting industry or automobile traffic tend to score low.

- *Water-quality score* refers to the quality of runoff and groundwater—not necessarily the quality of drinking water. It reflects both natural minerals and man-made pollutants, such as agricultural and

TABLE 3.43 SAMPLE HEALTH & HEALTHCARE TABLE FROM OGDEN–CLEARFIELD, UT

Health & Healthcare
Score: 71.1
Rank: 109

HAZARDS & ILLNESSES	AREA	U.S. AVG	HEALTHCARE	AREA	U.S. AVG
Air-quality score	39	37	Physicians per capita	139.8	244.2
Water-quality score	60	52	Hospital beds per capita	273.6	420.0
Pollen/allergy score	60	61	No. teaching hospitals	2	3
Cancer mortality per capita	104.8	201.9	Cost per doctor visit	$70	$77
Depression days per month	3.3	3.5	Cost per dental visit	$56	$70
Stress score	16	50			

mine waste. The score, presented on a 0–100 scale, is much more evenly distributed than air quality. Better areas are in Texas, Florida, and the Colorado Front Range, while the worst areas tend to be in industrial eastern and Midwestern cities.

- *Pollen/allergy score* is significant to the estimated 38% of all U.S. citizens who suffer from the effects of one or more airborne allergies. The score, on a 0–100 scale (100 being best), is a composite of multiple allergy types, including grass, tree pollen, and mold allergies. Better areas tend to be the California coast, Texas, and some mountain locations, while the worst are in the upper Midwest.

- *Cancer mortality per capita* shows an age-weighted number of cancer deaths per 100,000 person-years. This unusual but universally accepted measure accounts for both size and age of a population in determining the rate. In other words, areas with a high incidence of cancer among relatively younger people will get a higher (worse) figure than an area with the same incidence among a relatively older population. Ranges are from a low of 114.1 in Provo–Orem, Utah, to 207.1 in Jersey City, New Jersey. Areas with high concentrations of chemical industries are notably higher. Data is from the Centers for Disease Control and Prevention.

- *Depression days per month* shows the results of a National Centers for Disease Control and Prevention survey performed in each area. The survey question: "Now thinking about your mental health, which includes stress, depression, and problems with emotions, for how many days in the past 30 days was your mental health not good?" Answers range from 0.5 days per month in San Angelo, Texas, to 6.7 days in Charlottesville, Virginia. There is no clear discernable pattern, although college towns and areas with little to do and/or cloudy weather appear to have more depression days. This statistic is included in the stress score explained above.

- *Stress score* is a composite of eight measures contributing to our feelings of stress calculated by Sperling's BestPlaces based on a concept originally appearing in *Psychology Today*. The eight factors include divorce rate, commute time, unemployment rate, total crime rate, suicide rate, alcohol use rate, days feeling depressed, and cloudy days. The score is presented on a 0–100 scale, with 100 being most stressful and 0 being most stress-free. Places such as Tacoma, Washington; Detroit and Flint, Michigan; and Mobile, Alabama, tend to score as more stressful, with combinations of challenging climates, unemployment, crime, and other factors, while upper Midwest cities such as Dubuque, Iowa, and Bismarck, North Dakota, are least stressful. Sources include the National Centers for Disease Control and Prevention, Bureau of Labor Statistics, FBI, National Climatic Data Center, Census Bureau, and National Vital Statistics Program.

Healthcare

Physician data comes from the American Medical Association. Information on hospitals comes from the U.S. Department of Health and Human Services. Doctor, dentist, and daily hospital room costs are from a 2006 survey by the American Chamber of Commerce Research Association. We also advise readers to review the Healthcare Index component of the Cost of Living Index in the Cost of Living section of the fact table, and offer a highlight table showing best and worst areas below.

- *Physicians per capita* refers to the total number per 100,000 residents of accredited physicians, generalists, and specialists in an area. It is important to remember that this attribute does not directly translate into availability of medical services because many of these professionals do not treat patients directly. Because of the presence of the Mayo Clinic, Rochester, Minnesota, has far and away the largest number of physicians per capita (1,386 per 100,000 residents), followed by many college towns with teaching hospitals such as Iowa City, Iowa, and Columbia, Missouri. Most cities—about 200 of the 375 metro areas—fall into the 150 to 250 physicians per 100,000 range. At the low end are south Texas, the California Central Valley, and an assortment of small mostly Southern towns.

- *Hospital beds per capita,* presented as a rate of number of beds per 100,000 residents, is a figure that's declining in importance with the increase in outpatient services. Nevertheless, the number indicates the availability of hospital facilities in a more general sense. Rochester, Minnesota; college towns; and a few military towns make the top of the list, while an assortment of mostly small towns and towns close to other large metropolitan areas are at the bottom. Napa, California, is actually no. 1 owing to a large veterans' care facility in the area.

- *No. teaching hospitals* represents the number of hospitals that are accredited to train physicians, a fact suggesting the breadth and depth of staff, available services, and overall quality. Large cities tend to have the highest number, with New York leading the field with 64, Chicago second with 57, Philadelphia with 51, Los Angeles with 48, and so forth. Only 75 metropolitan areas do not have a teaching hospital.

- *Cost per doctor visit* and *Cost per dental visit* are based on average dollars billed per incident, not

including prescription medicine or other services, obtained from the American Chamber of Commerce Research Association in the first quarter of 2006. The range of these costs is striking. Doctor visits range from about $50 in smaller places in the South and Midwest to $100 to $115 in California, Alaska, and other coastal areas with generally higher living costs. Dental visits have a slightly larger range and a similar geography, although places in the Pacific Northwest for some reason migrate to the top of the cost list in this category.

Health & Healthcare Highlights, Tables 3.44–3.50

TABLE 3.44 AIR QUALITY			
COMPOSITE OF PARTICULATES, VOLATILE ORGANIC COMPOUNDS & OZONE, REPRESENTED AS 0–100 SCORE			
METRO AREAS WITH DIRTIEST AIR	SCORE	METRO AREAS WITH CLEANEST AIR	SCORE
Detroit–Livonia–Dearborn, MI	1	Tucson, AZ	89
Farmington, NM	1	Carson City, NV	82
Los Angeles–Long Beach–Glendale, CA	1	Winchester, VA	72
San Diego–Carlsbad–San Marcos, CA	1	Danville, VA	71
Santa Ana–Anaheim–Irvine, CA	2	Lynchburg, VA	70
Phoenix–Mesa–Scottsdale, AZ	3	Charlottesville, VA	70
Miami–Miami Beach–Kendall, FL	5	Cumberland, MD	68
Fort Lauderdale–Pompano Beach–Deerfield Beach, FL	8	Roanoke, VA	66
Houston–Sugar Land–Baytown, TX	8	Cleveland, TN	63
Seattle–Bellevue–Everett, WA	9	Wenatchee, WA	62
Las Cruces, NM	9	Lewiston, ID	62
Chicago–Naperville–Joliet, IL	10	Morristown, TN	62
San Jose–Sunnyvale–Santa Clara, CA	11	Elmira, NY	62
Cambridge–Newton–Framingham, MA	11	Salisbury, MD	62
West Palm Beach–Boca Raton–Boynton Beach, FL	11	Glens Falls, NY	61
Riverside–San Bernardino–Ontario, CA	12	Blacksburg–Christiansburg–Radford, VA	61
Las Vegas–Paradise, NV	12	Harrisonburg, VA	60
Mobile, AL	12	Elizabethtown, KY	60
Bakersfield, CA	13	Hagerstown–Martinsburg, MD-WV	59
Fresno, CA	13	St. George, UT	59
Dallas–Plano–Irving, TX	14	Johnson City, TN	59
Oakland–Fremont–Hayward, CA	14	Hinesville–Fort Stewart, GA	59
Nassau–Suffolk, NY	14	Athens–Clarke County, GA	59
Buffalo–Niagara Falls, NY	15	Jackson, TN	57
Deltona–Daytona Beach–Ormond Beach, FL	15	St. Joseph, MO	57
Eugene–Springfield, OR	15	Huntington–Ashland, WV-KY-OH	57
San Antonio, TX	15	Dalton, GA	57
Tampa–St. Petersburg–Clearwater, FL	16	Jefferson City, MO	56
Fort Worth–Arlington, TX	16	Bloomington, IN	56
Salt Lake City, UT	16	Virginia Beach–Norfolk–Newport News, VA-NC	56

Source: Sperling's BestPlaces

TABLE 3.45 WATER QUALITY

COMPOSITE INDEX OF WATERSHED QUALITY, REPRESENTED AS 0–100 SCORE

METRO AREAS WITH DIRTIEST WATER	SCORE	METRO AREAS WITH CLEANEST WATER	SCORE
Hanford–Corcoran, CA	1	Panama City–Lynn Haven, FL	100
Huntsville, AL	6	Boulder, CO	100
Philadelphia, PA	7	Pueblo, CO	100
Camden, NJ	8	San Angelo, TX	100
Muncie, IN	10	Hot Springs, AR	100
Indianapolis–Carmel, IN	10	College Station–Bryan, TX	99
Lafayette, LA	12	Fort Collins–Loveland, CO	99
Essex County, MA	13	Abilene, TX	99
Atlantic City, NJ	13	Tallahassee, FL	98
Edison, NJ	14	Blacksburg–Christiansburg–Radford, VA	97
Wilmington, DE	15	Dothan, AL	97
Newark–Union, NJ-PA	16	Binghamton, NY	96
Madera, CA	16	Clarksville, TN	95
Louisville–Jefferson County, KY-IN	17	Williamsport, PA	94
Baton Rouge, LA	18	Colorado Springs, CO	93
Lancaster, PA	20	Tuscaloosa, AL	93
Flint, MI	20	Johnson City, TN	93
Merced, CA	20	Lynchburg, VA	93
Weirton–Steubenville, WV-OH	20	Kingsport–Bristol–Bristol, TN-VA	92
Rockingham County–Strafford County, NH	20	State College, PA	92
Decatur, IL	20	Altoona, PA	92
Sheboygan, WI	20	Jonesboro, AR	92
Yuma, AZ	20	Anniston–Oxford, AL	91
Sandusky, OH	20	Fort Worth–Arlington, TX	91
Ocean City, NJ	20	Fort Walton Beach–Crestview–Destin, FL	90
Pocatello, ID	20	Laredo, TX	90
Vineland–Millville–Bridgeton, NJ	20	Johnstown, PA	90
Boston–Quincy, MA	20	Morristown, TN	90
Sioux Falls, SD	20	Raleigh–Cary, NC	90
Toledo, OH	21	Denver–Aurora, CO	87

Source: Sperling's BestPlaces

TABLE 3.46 CANCER MORTALITY RATES

REPORTED CASES PER 100,000 PERSON YEARS (AGE WEIGHTED)

METRO AREAS WITH HIGHEST RATES	CASES	METRO AREAS WITH LOWEST RATES	CASES
Panama City–Lynn Haven, FL	291.8	Logan, UT	98.2
Jacksonville, FL	289.0	St. George, UT	98.2
Charleston, WV	286.9	Provo–Orem, UT	100.2
Fort Walton Beach–Crestview–Destin, FL	282.7	Fairbanks, AK	103.6
Gainesville, FL	273.3	Ogden–Clearfield, UT	104.8
Tallahassee, FL	272.0	Salt Lake City, UT	108.5
Deltona–Daytona Beach–Ormond Beach, FL	271.4	Anchorage, AK	114.9
Pensacola–Ferry Pass–Brent, FL	270.9	McAllen–Edinburg–Mission, TX	116.0
Ocala, FL	268.9	Brownsville–Harlingen, TX	120.1
Palm Bay–Melbourne–Titusville, FL	267.0	Laredo, TX	121.4
Philadelphia, PA	266.6	Boulder, CO	130.7
Huntington–Ashland, WV-KY-OH	262.4	Santa Fe, NM	131.3
Morgantown, WV	260.1	Yuma, AZ	134.8
Tampa–St. Petersburg–Clearwater, FL	259.9	San Jose–Sunnyvale–Santa Clara, CA	136.9
Bangor, ME	259.7	Fort Collins–Loveland, CO	137.2
Altoona, PA	259.4	Idaho Falls, ID	138.3
Erie, PA	258.0	El Paso, TX	143.3
Weirton–Steubenville, WV-OH	253.7	Greeley, CO	143.7
Orlando–Kissimmee, FL	252.9	Colorado Springs, CO	143.8
Pittsburgh, PA	252.0	Denver–Aurora, CO	146.0
Lakeland, FL	250.6	Austin–Round Rock, TX	146.5
Scranton–Wilkes-Barre, PA	249.2	Salinas, CA	147.3
Sebastian–Vero Beach, FL	248.6	Santa Cruz–Watsonville, CA	147.3
Port St. Lucie–Fort Pierce, FL	245.7	Santa Barbara–Santa Maria, CA	147.8
Lewiston–Auburn, ME	245.4	Bethesda–Gaithersburg–Frederick, MD	148.0
Atlantic City, NJ	245.0	Santa Ana–Anaheim–Irvine, CA	149.3
Mobile, AL	243.9	Pueblo, CO	150.7
Fort Smith, AR	243.7	Hanford–Corcoran, CA	152.0
Portland–South Portland–Biddeford, ME	243.3	San Antonio, TX	152.5
Wheeling, WV	242.7	Los Angeles–Long Beach–Glendale, CA	152.8

Source: Centers for Disease Control and Prevention, 2004

TABLE 3.47 PHYSICIANS PER CAPITA
NUMBER OF PHYSICIANS PER 100,000 RESIDENTS

METRO AREAS WITH THE MOST PHYSICIANS	PHYSICIANS	METRO AREAS WITH THE FEWEST PHYSICIANS	PHYSICIANS
Rochester, MN	1,386.4	Hinesville–Fort Stewart, GA	54
Iowa City, IA	927.8	El Centro, CA	74
Durham, NC	857.2	Hanford–Corcoran, CA	82
Ann Arbor, MI	809.3	Monroe, MI	86
Charlottesville, VA	801.1	Madera, CA	90
Columbia, MO	702.5	Laredo, TX	95
Gainesville, FL	668.5	Merced, CA	96
Morgantown, WV	660.3	McAllen–Edinburg–Mission, TX	102
Bethesda–Gaithersburg–Frederick, MD	552.6	Yuma, AZ	104
Boston–Quincy, MA	548.9	Visalia–Porterville, CA	109
Burlington–South Burlington, VT	492.8	Brownsville–Harlingen, TX	121
Greenville, NC	491.6	Jackson, MI	123
San Francisco–San Mateo–Redwood City, CA	488.2	Holland–Grand Haven, MI	127
Cambridge–Newton–Framingham, MA	438.0	Anderson, IN	128
Springfield, IL	429.5	Elkhart–Goshen, IN	129
Nassau–Suffolk, NY	427.4	Provo–Orem, UT	130
Lexington–Fayette, KY	425.2	Bakersfield, CA	131
Madison, WI	421.6	Stockton, CA	131
Philadelphia, PA	419.1	Decatur, AL	131
New Haven–Milford, CT	412.2	Greeley, CO	133
Shreveport–Bossier City, LA	407.0	Jacksonville, NC	134
Johnson City, TN	397.9	Logan, UT	135
New Orleans, LA	393.5	Houma–Bayou Cane–Thibodaux, LA	137
New York–White Plains, NY	390.6	Sumter, SC	137
Charleston–North Charleston, SC	386.4	Morristown, TN	137
La Crosse, WI	379.7	Clarksville, TN	137
Baltimore–Towson, MD	377.4	Cleveland, TN	138
Little Rock–North Little Rock, AR	375.9	Rocky Mount, NC	139
Augusta–Richmond County, GA-SC	373.2	Las Cruces, NM	139
Lubbock, TX	368.9	Ogden–Clearfield, UT	140

Source: American Medical Association, 2005

TABLE 3.48 HOSPITAL BEDS PER CAPITA
NUMBER OF HOSPITAL BEDS PER 100,000 RESIDENTS

METRO AREAS WITH THE MOST HOSPITAL BEDS	NO. BEDS	METRO AREAS WITH THE FEWEST HOSPITAL BEDS	NO. BEDS
Napa, CA	2,359.2	Hinesville–Fort Stewart, GA	71.9
Wheeling, WV	1,055.8	Prescott, AZ	110.2
Lynchburg, VA	1,052.0	Greeley, CO	117.1
Great Falls, MT	998.1	Hanford–Corcoran, CA	118.5
Rome, GA	975.1	Bellingham, WA	119.4
Lubbock, TX	970.4	Monroe, MI	126.3
Rochester, MN	918.4	Bremerton–Silverdale, WA	134.7
Goldsboro, NC	879.4	Farmington, NM	137.0
Alexandria, LA	873.9	Santa Fe, NM	137.9
Bowling Green, KY	853.0	St. George, UT	138.4
Dothan, AL	832.3	El Centro, CA	139.7
Jackson, TN	809.2	Holland–Grand Haven, MI	157.9
Elmira, NY	801.7	Santa Cruz–Watsonville, CA	159.3
San Angelo, TX	789.6	Jacksonville, NC	161.3
Columbia, MO	789.2	Vallejo–Fairfield, CA	162.3
Monroe, LA	788.4	Norwich–New London, CT	164.3
Iowa City, IA	778.0	Merced, CA	166.2
Grand Forks, ND	764.6	Salinas, CA	167.1
Pueblo, CO	758.2	Bend, OR	168.7
Morgantown, WV	754.0	Yuma, AZ	172.6
Wichita Falls, TX	753.7	Colorado Springs, CO	172.7
Bismarck, ND	735.8	Lawrence, KS	174.5
Florence–Muscle Shoals, AL	713.9	Dover, DE	175.0
Weirton–Steubenville, WV-OH	709.5	Flagstaff, AZ	177.6
Victoria, TX	707.4	Naples–Marco Island, FL	179.5
Texarkana, TX	682.2	Boulder, CO	182.6
Buffalo–Niagara Falls, NY	677.3	Barnstable Town, MA	183.3
Johnstown, PA	674.7	Stockton, CA	184.7
Hot Springs, AR	670.6	Bethesda–Gaithersburg–Frederick, MD	185.4
Springfield, IL	669.4	Fort Collins–Loveland, CO	186.4

Source: U.S. Department of Health and Human Services (DHHS), 2005

TABLE 3.49 HEALTHCARE COST INDEX

AREAS WITH HIGHEST HEALTHCARE COSTS	INDEX	AREAS WITH LOWEST HEALTHCARE COSTS	INDEX
New York–White Plains, NY	172.8	Nashville–Davidson–Murfreesboro, TN	82.6
Santa Rosa–Petaluma, CA	168.1	Jackson, MS	82.8
San Francisco–San Mateo–Redwood City, CA	166.9	Mobile, AL	83.9
Fairbanks, AK	165.3	Gadsden, AL	84.2
Nassau–Suffolk, NY	164.0	Johnson City, TN	84.5
Napa, CA	162.4	Morristown, TN	84.8
Vallejo–Fairfield, CA	161.9	Fort Smith, AR	85.7
Anchorage, AK	158.7	Kingsport–Bristol–Bristol, TN-VA	85.8
Santa Cruz–Watsonville, CA	156.0	Decatur, IL	86.3
Oakland–Fremont–Hayward, CA	154.7	Winchester, VA	86.6
Bridgeport–Stamford–Norwalk, CT	154.5	Hattiesburg, MS	86.7
San Jose–Sunnyvale–Santa Clara, CA	154.2	Goldsboro, NC	87.3
Yuba City, CA	153.8	Williamsport, PA	87.7
Chico, CA	152.1	San Antonio, TX	87.8
Sacramento–Arden-Arcade–Roseville, CA	150.8	Provo–Orem, UT	87.8
Stockton, CA	147.4	Jacksonville, FL	87.8
Bergen–Passaic, NJ	141.6	Memphis, TN	87.9
Modesto, CA	136.8	Charleston, WV	88.1
Albany–Schenectady–Troy, NY	136.5	Florence–Muscle Shoals, AL	88.1
Providence–New Bedford–Fall River, RI-MA	134.4	Youngstown–Warren–Boardman, OH-PA	88.1
Pittsfield, MA	131.9	Chattanooga, TN	88.3
Poughkeepsie–Newburgh–Middletown, NY	130.6	Salt Lake City, UT	88.3
Boston–Quincy, MA	130.4	Bismarck, ND	88.3
Barnstable Town, MA	130.1	Albany, GA	88.5
Kingston, NY	129.9	Jonesboro, AR	88.8
El Centro, CA	129.9	Cumberland, MD	88.8
Bremerton–Silverdale, WA	129.8	Dothan, AL	88.9
San Diego–Carlsbad–San Marcos, CA	129.6	Victoria, TX	89.1
Minneapolis–St. Paul–Bloomington, MN-WI	129.4	Jackson, TN	89.1
Edison, NJ	128.0	Knoxville, TN	89.2

Note: U.S. average: 100

Source: U.S. Bureau of Labor Statistics/Sperling's BestPlaces, 2006

TABLE 3.50 DOCTOR FEES
AVERAGE COST PER ROUTINE OFFICE VISIT

MOST EXPENSIVE DOCTOR VISITS	COST	LEAST EXPENSIVE DOCTOR VISITS	COST
Anchorage, AK	$115	St. Joseph, MO	$42
Boston–Quincy, MA	$112	Auburn–Opelika, AL	$51
Bend, OR	$111	Johnstown, PA	$51
Los Angeles–Long Beach–Glendale, CA	$111	Florence–Muscle Shoals, AL	$53
San Jose–Sunnyvale–Santa Clara, CA	$110	Joplin, MO	$54
Stockton, CA	$110	Mobile, AL	$54
Fairbanks, AK	$109	Tuscaloosa, AL	$55
Providence–New Bedford–Fall River, RI-MA	$108	Gadsden, AL	$57
Eau Claire, WI	$107	Dothan, AL	$58
Eugene–Springfield, OR	$105	Sherman–Denison, TX	$58
Bowling Green, KY	$104	Kankakee–Bradley, IL	$60
Salinas, CA	$104	Lakeland, FL	$60
Miami–Miami Beach–Kendall, FL	$103	New Orleans, LA	$60
Oxnard–Thousand Oaks–Ventura, CA	$103	Tampa–St. Petersburg–Clearwater, FL	$60
Rochester, MN	$103	Birmingham–Hoover, AL	$61
Wausau, WI	$103	Lebanon, PA	$61
Napa, CA	$102	Little Rock–North Little Rock, AR	$61
Santa Ana–Anaheim–Irvine, CA	$102	Pensacola–Ferry Pass–Brent, FL	$61
Visalia–Porterville, CA	$102	Reading, PA	$61
Barnstable Town, MA	$101	Akron, OH	$62
Bakersfield, CA	$100	Danville, IL	$62
Essex County, MA	$100	Hot Springs, AR	$62
New York–White Plains, NY	$100	Huntsville, AL	$62
Santa Cruz–Watsonville, CA	$100	McAllen–Edinburg–Mission, TX	$62
Seattle–Bellevue–Everett, WA	$100	State College, PA	$62
Vallejo–Fairfield, CA	$100	Allentown–Bethlehem–Easton, PA	$63
Hartford–West Hartford–East Hartford, CT	$99	College Station–Bryan, TX	$63
Portland–Vancouver–Beaverton, OR-WA	$99	Danville, VA	$63
Champaign–Urbana, IL	$98	Jackson, MS	$63
Great Falls, MT	$98	Jacksonville, FL	$63

Source: American Chamber of Commerce Research Association, 2005

Crime

Particularly for those who have been victims, the incidence of serious crime is a major consideration when examining a place. The Federal Bureau of Investigation (U.S. Department of Justice) keeps close tabs on violent and nonviolent crime rates and efforts toward law enforcement.

Numerous doctorate degrees have been conferred on studies of crime and its causes. True cause and effect will probably never be known, but there are some interesting correlations and geographic relationships. First, crime appears to be influenced by the economy and particularly the job market for fairly obvious reasons. Second, there is a relationship to climate. Areas with warm—extremely warm—climates tend to have higher crime rates. Miami, Florida; Memphis, Tennessee; and Pine Bluff, Arkansas, have high rates of violent crime, and total crime rates have been highest in states such as Arizona, New Mexico, South Carolina, Texas, and Florida. Reasons are sketchy, but it may have to do with opportunity (more favorable weather to execute crimes), temperament, and stress, or population compositions and the presence of economically disadvantaged groups in these areas. Third, population age is a factor—the older the population, the lower the crime rates. Finally, crime is (as can be expected) reduced by more and better law enforcement.

Crime Trends

The 1990s saw a dramatic decline in overall crime rates, led by a strong economy but getting an assist from an aging population and improved enforcement driven in part by technology. Rates for violent crime dropped nearly 32% for the 10-year period ending in 2005, while rates for property crime dropped by a bit over 25%. But with the economic turn, rates began to tick up slightly in 2001, leveling off in 2002 and staying steady. Then from 2004 to 2006, the first significant increases were reported in several years, with a 2.5% increase in overall violent crime and a 4.8% increase in murders reported in 2005 drawing particular attention. Researchers are still studying the reasons, but many point to an "echo boom"—children of baby boomers coming of age—a spread of city crime patterns into smaller cities, and a resurgence in gang and drug-related activity. Also, while the overall economy has been improving, differences between "haves" and "have-nots" have also been growing.

Crime
Score: 86.9
Rank: 48

TABLE 3.51 SAMPLE CRIME TABLE FROM ASHEVILLE, NC		
CRIME	AREA	U.S. AVG
Violent crime rate	257.1	465.5
Change in violent crime rate	-1.9%	-2.2%
Property crime rate	3,268.3	3,517.1
Change in property crime rate	0.1%	-2.1%

Crime Attributes

The data in this section comes from the U.S. Department of Justice Federal Bureau of Investigation Uniform Crime Reports. Statistics are only kept for reported and more serious crimes. Routine traffic violations, trespassing, or disorderly conduct don't count. Total nonviolent crimes typically run about 8 to 10 times the rate of violent crimes, although the mix can vary in different places. All crime facts are used in scoring and ranking.

Table 3.51 shows the Crime table for the metropolitan area of Asheville, North Carolina.

- *Violent crime rate* is the combined incidence of murder, rape, robbery, and assault per 100,000 residents per year.

- *Change in violent crime rate* reflects the percentage growth or decrease in the rates for violent crime during the period from 2001 to 2005.

- *Property crime rate,* or nonviolent crime rate, is the combined incidence of burglary, theft, and auto theft.

- *Change in property crime* reflects the percentage growth or decrease in the rates for property crime during the period from 2001 to 2005.

TABLE 3.52 VIOLENT CRIME RATES

REPORTED INCIDENTS OF MURDER, FORCIBLE RAPE, ROBBERY & ASSAULT PER 100,000 RESIDENTS

METRO AREAS WITH HIGHEST VIOLENT CRIME RATES	INCIDENTS	METRO AREAS WITH LOWEST VIOLENT CRIME RATES	INCIDENTS
Florence, SC	1,286.4	Logan, UT	67.1
Detroit–Livonia–Dearborn, MI	1,250.7	Bangor, ME	82.7
Memphis, TN	1,196.8	Sheboygan, WI	107.4
Shreveport–Bossier City, LA	1,078.5	State College, PA	108.0
Saginaw–Saginaw Township North, MI	1,037.6	Bismarck, ND	109.9
Miami–Miami Beach–Kendall, FL	989.1	Provo–Orem, UT	110.7
Jackson, TN	989.0	Appleton, WI	111.6
Alexandria, LA	983.0	Ithaca, NY	115.9
Fairbanks, AK	960.1	Harrisonburg, VA	117.8
Sumter, SC	939.6	Rockingham County–Strafford County, NH	117.9
Springfield, IL	917.2	Fargo, ND	120.7
Stockton, CA	909.4	Lewiston–Auburn, ME	122.0
Salisbury, MD	906.4	Eau Claire, WI	125.4
Lubbock, TX	904.5	Fond du Lac, WI	126.1
Vineland–Millville–Bridgeton, NJ	899.6	Burlington–South Burlington, VT	129.3
Nashville–Davidson–Murfreesboro, TN	894.1	Corvallis, OR	134.4
Gainesville, FL	867.4	Portland–South Portland–Biddeford, ME	139.5
Little Rock–North Little Rock, AR	863.5	Columbus, IN	144.4
Myrtle Beach–Conway–North Myrtle Beach, SC	860.5	Lewiston, ID	146.9
Flint, MI	859.1	Jacksonville, NC	147.3
Texarkana, TX	847.6	La Crosse, WI	147.7
Charleston–North Charleston, SC	843.7	Grand Forks, ND	148.2
Albuquerque, NM	838.9	Wausau, WI	148.8
Charlotte–Gastonia–Concord, NC-SC	837.7	Terre Haute, IN	151.2
Baltimore–Towson, MD	837.1	Anderson, IN	152.3
Orlando–Kissimmee, FL	821.4	Manchester–Nashua, NH	153.8
Tallahassee, FL	819.7	Elizabethtown, KY	160.5
Pine Bluff, AR	799.9	Lancaster, PA	172.2
Battle Creek, MI	767.4	Edison, NJ	172.4
Anchorage, AK	753.7	Owensboro, KY	172.7

Source: U.S. Department of Justice Federal Bureau of Investigation Uniform Crime Reports, 2005

TABLE 3.53 PROPERTY CRIME RATES

REPORTED INCIDENTS OF BURGLARY, THEFT & AUTO THEFT PER 100,000 RESIDENTS

METRO AREAS WITH HIGHEST PROPERTY CRIME RATES	INCIDENTS	METRO AREAS WITH LOWEST PROPERTY CRIME RATES	INCIDENTS
Hot Springs, AR	7,601.9	Harrisonburg, VA	1,559.0
Mount Vernon–Anacortes, WA	7,469.3	Rockingham County–Strafford County, NH	1,599.4
Yakima, WA	7,017.4	Nassau–Suffolk, NY	1,680.2
Myrtle Beach–Conway–North Myrtle Beach, SC	6,862.0	Fond du Lac, WI	1,824.5
Corpus Christi, TX	6,296.1	Wheeling, WV	1,837.0
Longview, WA	6,087.7	Logan, UT	1,854.9
Memphis, TN	6,085.8	Elizabethtown, KY	1,859.9
Springfield, OH	6,031.1	Edison, NJ	1,875.7
Anniston–Oxford, AL	5,920.2	Poughkeepsie–Newburgh–Middletown, NY	1,880.1
Laredo, TX	5,767.6	Wausau, WI	1,880.6
Little Rock–North Little Rock, AR	5,767.2	Weirton–Steubenville, WV-OH	1,889.2
Florence, SC	5,733.4	Cambridge–Newton–Framingham, MA	1,904.0
Wichita Falls, TX	5,723.5	Holland–Grand Haven, MI	1,906.9
Pueblo, CO	5,674.8	Rochester, MN	1,966.5
Jackson, TN	5,607.8	New York–White Plains, NY	1,967.9
Stockton, CA	5,587.4	Pittsfield, MA	1,969.4
Fayetteville, NC	5,560.4	Kingston, NY	1,974.3
Fairbanks, AK	5,557.4	Lake County–Kenosha County, IL-WI	1,980.1
Waco, TX	5,523.7	State College, PA	2,000.9
Pine Bluff, AR	5,518.1	Lynchburg, VA	2,002.6
Lubbock, TX	5,509.7	Worcester, MA	2,004.4
Eugene–Springfield, OR	5,501.4	Erie, PA	2,013.9
Columbus, GA	5,468.6	Manchester–Nashua, NH	2,036.0
Topeka, KS	5,467.1	Oxnard–Thousand Oaks–Ventura, CA	2,083.1
Modesto, CA	5,418.0	Essex County, MA	2,101.7
Seattle–Bellevue–Everett, WA	5,359.1	Naples–Marco Island, FL	2,110.9
Amarillo, TX	5,349.6	Oshkosh–Neenah, WI	2,122.1
San Antonio, TX	5,346.9	Lebanon, PA	2,123.1
Oklahoma City, OK	5,345.4	Jacksonville, NC	2,128.8
San Angelo, TX	5,327.9	Williamsport, PA	2,131.9

Source: U.S. Department of Justice Federal Bureau of Investigation Uniform Crime Reports, 2005

TABLE 3.54 CHANGE IN VIOLENT CRIME RATES
PERCENTAGE OF INCREASE OR DECREASE, 2001–2005

METRO AREAS WITH GREATEST INCREASE	PERCENTAGE	METRO AREAS WITH GREATEST DECREASE	PERCENTAGE
Dubuque, IA	35.9%	Wheeling, WV	−33.4%
Boulder, CO	32.6%	Bowling Green, KY	−30.0%
Florence–Muscle Shoals, AL	31.3%	Johnstown, PA	−26.8%
Des Moines–West Des Moines, IA	31.3%	Corvallis, OR	−25.7%
Oshkosh–Neenah, WI	30.8%	Monroe, LA	−25.0%
Pittsfield, MA	29.3%	Wichita Falls, TX	−24.4%
Fairbanks, AK	28.1%	Lawrence, KS	−24.1%
Youngstown–Warren–Boardman, OH-PA	28.0%	Victoria, TX	−23.8%
Fond du Lac, WI	26.7%	Great Falls, MT	−21.2%
Detroit–Livonia–Dearborn, MI	26.1%	Rome, GA	−20.7%
Decatur, IL	24.8%	Canton–Massillon, OH	−20.4%
Bismarck, ND	23.9%	Sumter, SC	−20.1%
Sandusky, OH	23.7%	El Paso, TX	−19.3%
Janesville, WI	23.7%	Charleston, WV	−18.8%
Glens Falls, NY	23.4%	Iowa City, IA	−18.7%
Bend, OR	23.0%	Parkersburg–Marietta–Vienna, WV-OH	−18.5%
Casper, WY	22.7%	Terre Haute, IN	−18.2%
Jefferson City, MO	22.5%	Biloxi, MS	−17.4%
Huntsville, AL	22.5%	Yuma, AZ	−16.8%
Albany–Schenectady–Troy, NY	22.1%	Harrisonburg, VA	−16.7%
Fayetteville–Springdale–Rogers, AR-MO	21.7%	Athens–Clarke County, GA	−16.6%
Binghamton, NY	21.6%	Houma–Bayou Cane–Thibodaux, LA	−16.4%
Hattiesburg, MS	21.4%	Danville, VA	−16.4%
Brunswick, GA	21.2%	Danville, IL	−16.4%
Johnson City, TN	21.1%	Muncie, IN	−16.1%
St. Joseph, MO	20.7%	Mount Vernon–Anacortes, WA	−15.8%
Kingston, NY	20.1%	Eau Claire, WI	−15.7%
Duluth, MN	19.8%	Shreveport–Bossier City, LA	−15.7%
Blacksburg–Christiansburg–Radford, VA	19.4%	South Bend–Mishawaka, IN-MI	−15.7%
Ithaca, NY	18.9%	Ocean City, NJ	−15.6%

Source: U.S. Department of Justice Federal Bureau of Investigation Uniform Crime Reports

TABLE 3.55 CHANGE IN PROPERTY CRIME RATES
PERCENTAGE OF INCREASE OR DECREASE, 2001–2005

METRO AREAS WITH GREATEST INCREASE	PERCENTAGE	METRO AREAS WITH GREATEST DECREASE	PERCENTAGE
Missoula, MT	50.2%	Brunswick, GA	−34.0%
Glens Falls, NY	41.1%	Spokane, WA	−29.4%
Anderson, IN	23.1%	Tucson, AZ	−24.6%
Ithaca, NY	22.3%	Lake County–Kenosha County, IL-WI	−23.3%
Blacksburg–Christiansburg–Radford, VA	22.0%	Las Cruces, NM	−21.8%
Parkersburg–Marietta–Vienna, WV-OH	19.9%	Mobile, AL	−19.1%
Huntsville, AL	19.8%	New Orleans, LA	−18.4%
Pueblo, CO	18.8%	Provo–Orem, UT	−16.1%
Jonesboro, AR	17.9%	Lafayette, LA	−15.7%
Yakima, WA	15.7%	Houma–Bayou Cane–Thibodaux, LA	−15.6%
Jefferson City, MO	14.2%	Victoria, TX	−15.6%
Charlottesville, VA	14.1%	Sumter, SC	−15.3%
Youngstown–Warren–Boardman, OH-PA	13.6%	Lawrence, KS	−15.1%
Kokomo, IN	13.4%	Pocatello, ID	−14.6%
Billings, MT	12.7%	Washington–Arlington–Alexandria, DC-VA-MD-WV	−14.1%
Minneapolis–St. Paul–Bloomington, MN-WI	12.5%	Clarksville, TN	−13.6%
Eugene–Springfield, OR	12.1%	Columbia, SC	−13.5%
Anchorage, AK	12.0%	St. Joseph, MO	−13.4%
Fayetteville–Springdale–Rogers, AR-MO	11.8%	Carson City, NV	−13.3%
Dothan, AL	11.7%	Erie, PA	−13.2%
Elmira, NY	11.7%	Panama City–Lynn Haven, FL	−13.2%
Pittsfield, MA	11.3%	Burlington–South Burlington, VT	−13.1%
Mount Vernon–Anacortes, WA	10.4%	Eau Claire, WI	−12.9%
Hickory–Lenoir–Morganton, NC	10.3%	Hot Springs, AR	−12.6%
Altoona, PA	10.3%	Sioux City, IA	−12.6%
Rome, GA	10.2%	Great Falls, MT	−12.4%
Santa Cruz–Watsonville, CA	10.1%	Napa, CA	−12.2%
Johnstown, PA	9.9%	Hinesville–Fort Stewart, GA	−12.2%
El Centro, CA	9.0%	Duluth, MN	−12.1%
Topeka, KS	8.7%	Chico, CA	−11.6%

Source: U.S. Department of Justice Federal Bureau of Investigation Uniform Crime Reports

America's Most Drivable Cities

Is driving a pleasurable and relaxing experience in most cities? Are traffic jams, rough roads, and high costs a perpetual nightmare? In 2003, Sperling's BestPlaces teamed up with the automotive supply retailer Pep Boys to study these issues. They arrived at these conclusions:

- Small Texas cities do well. Corpus Christi, Texas, took top honors among the 70 cities studied, followed closely by Beaumont–Port Arthur and Brownsville. These areas have the lowest gas prices, short travel times, and low traffic flow. Florida cities, such as Fort Myers and Pensacola, also score well.

- Los Angeles, not surprisingly, rates as the least drivable, with the longest travel times in the nation (which include, but are not exclusive to commute times). San Francisco, with congestion and high gas prices, is second worst, followed by Chicago, Denver, and Boston.

- Cities in the Northeast tend to rank poorly. Philadelphia, Hartford, and New York City all rank in the bottom 20.

- The most drivable *large* city is Atlanta.

- The northern California cities of San Francisco, San Jose, and Oakland have the highest gas prices outside of Hawaii.

- Detroit, Fresno, and Sacramento have the roughest roads.

Some of the least drivable cities, such as Chicago, New York, Boston, and San Francisco, have made up for their shortcomings with excellent public transportation facilities. Others, such as Los Angeles, are behind the curve and likely to remain there for some time.

Transportation

Transportation is usually where the true impact of crowding or isolation in an area is most felt. Gauging all daily activity around the avoidance of rush hour (even on weekends), having to drive 350 miles to get to the nearest airport with suitable (and affordable) air service, or commuting 2 hours a day by automobile into a crowded urban core (with $30 per day parking) all indicate failures in transportation service that ultimately affect lifestyle. *Cities Ranked & Rated* presents all the factors—commute times, how people commute to work, availability and utilization of public transportation, intercity transport services, and automobile costs—that come into play. As the duration of commute times and related stress and expense grows, this edition places a slightly heavier weighting on commute times. We also have added a figure for the percentage of commutes longer than 60 minutes to give light to worst-case scenarios in an area.

Transportation Trends

Since 1960, the number of motor vehicle registrations and the average driving distance from home to work both *tripled,* while U.S. population increased 60%. There are more than 220 million motor vehicles in the United States and more drivers are spending more time on the road than ever before. Road infrastructure, on the other hand, grew only 11% during the 40-year period, while vehicle miles have *quadrupled.* Result: more traffic and traffic jams and longer commute times almost everywhere, both urban and rural. Commute times have stretched out in most urban areas as suburban growth continues and major arteries into cities become more clogged.

Public transportation infrastructure and use have also grown, but problems with utilization persist as far-flung suburban infrastructures, nurtured by the automobile, make it less practical as an alternative. Nationwide, we are seeing more ambitious mass transit infrastructure projects, especially light rail and some heavy rail corridors. Commute rail services have expanded in the Northeast and major California cities as one might expect, but now Denver and Dallas have enjoyed major expansions and even more moderately sized places such as Nashville, Tennessee, are jumping on the bandwagon. Federal dollars and the availability of abandoned or underutilized rail corridors have helped. Still, mass transit use has stayed steady at only about 4.7% of all commutes made in the U.S.

Getting Paid to *Not* Drive

Want to add a few bucks to your paycheck? Bike to work. Or take a ferry or walk or get dropped off. In Seattle, biotech giant Amgen spends more than $1 million a year on incentives to get people out of their automobiles. Each of the company's 1,000 employees is eligible for a monthly $50 gift certificate at locally headquartered outdoor wares giant REI for biking, walking, or being dropped off, or $25 for car pooling. And in return, Amgen gets recognition for being one of the area's 250 "Best Job Sites for Commuters." Such a designation is to be expected for green-friendly Seattle, but does it reach out elsewhere? Turns out the answer is a resounding "yes." The "Best Workplaces for Commuters" program is a nascent but growing joint program administered by the Environmental Protection Agency and the U.S. Department of Transportation. To qualify for the list, an employer must (1) employ someone to tell commuters about benefits; (2) provide a way for employees to get home in an emergency; (3) offer a "key commuter benefit," including a reward, transit subsidy, or telecommuting program; and (4) offer at least three supporting benefits, such as showers or dry cleaning services. In addition to Seattle's Puget Sound region, 13 other major regions and metro areas have already released Best Workplaces lists, including Phoenix, Houston, and the Triangle Research region in North Carolina. For the complete list of participating regions, see www.bwc.gov.

As a result, most cities face a transportation crunch. Worse yet, they face a Catch-22 dilemma, where the most expedient solution of building more roads (if even geographically possible) is met with more urban sprawl and, regrettably, an even greater demand for transportation. Federal transportation investments are still centered on highways and intercity air travel infrastructure and operations, but there is some light on the horizon as federal and some state agencies get serious about motivating employers to create and even incentivize commute-friendly environments (see the "Getting Paid to *Not* Drive" sidebar above). Perhaps as a result of these programs and higher gas prices, we saw in 2005 the first decline—albeit small—in single-occupant-vehicle commutes in years, from 78.2% to 77.0%.

As municipalities, urban planners, and architects embrace the commute problem, there may be some hope for more transportation-efficient infrastructure. Although it can exacerbate sprawl, we also see more infrastructure locating closer to residential areas and away from downtown areas and traditional commercial zones—even into integrated mixed-use developments—giving shorter commutes and improving quality of life. In some areas, such as Emeryville, California, in the Oakland–Fremont–Hayward area, newer commercial zones are coming on line at major public transportation hubs. Such improvements, however, remain the exception rather than the rule.

We haven't said much about *intercity* transportation. Indeed, not much has changed since the last edition, except that air service has generally become less available and more expensive. The happy exception continues to be discount carriers such as Southwest, JetBlue, ATA, and AirTran, which are concentrated in different parts of the country but have expanded into almost national systems. One interesting trend is the emergence of secondary airports as simple, convenient, and inexpensive access points to larger urban areas, in particular with Southwest Airlines. Manchester, New Hampshire, and Providence, Rhode Island, give access to the Boston area and New England; Islip to New York City; Baltimore to the Washington, D.C. area; Ontario and Burbank to the Los Angeles area; and the southside Midway Airport to Chicago. We expect this trend to continue.

Transportation Attributes

Transportation attributes are subdivided into intracity or intercity services and automobile costs. The time spent commuting, the availability of alternatives, and dependence on cars all determine the transportation picture, particularly in larger cities. Most transportation data comes from the U.S. Department of Transportation and the 2005 U.S. Census American Community Survey. Airport and rail information comes from carriers and local industry associations and is processed by Sperling's BestPlaces. Scoring and ranking uses commute times, available mass transit service, and air and rail departures. Commute times and mass transit get the highest weighting, while air and rail get moderate and light weightings, respectively.

A Streetcar Named Desire

The presence of light rail transit systems on the urban/suburban scene has been growing steadily for the past 20 years. Light rail represents a combination of two older technologies: streetcars, which for 75 years furnished the chief public transportation in urban areas, and interurban lines, which mainly connected suburban towns to urban areas. Although the systems are expensive and one might rightfully be concerned about the benefit received for the cost, we look at light rail not only as a convenience but also as a more global commitment to providing solid transit alternatives in an area. According to the American Public Transportation Association, 20 metro areas already have light rail systems, and some 37 more have systems underway or on the drawing board. We especially applaud close integration with regional airports, and look forward to system expansion and expanded integration with other forms of transit.

Cities with existing light rail systems are the following:

Baltimore, MD	Los Angeles, CA	St. Louis, MO
Boston, MA	Minneapolis, MN	Salt Lake City, UT
Buffalo, NY	Newark, NJ	San Diego, CA
Cleveland, OH	Philadelphia, PA	San Francisco, CA
Dallas, TX	Pittsburgh, PA	San Jose, CA
Denver, CO	Portland, OR	Tacoma, WA
Houston, TX	Sacramento, CA	

Cities with light rail systems in planning stages or under construction are:

Albuquerque, NM	El Paso, TX	Orlando, FL
Atlanta, GA	Fort Worth, TX	Phoenix, AZ
Austin, TX	Grand Canyon, AZ	Raleigh, NC
Bangor, ME	Jacksonville, FL	Richmond, VA
Birmingham, AL	Louisville, KY	Rochester, NY
Charleston, SC	Madison, WI	San Antonio, TX
Charlotte, NC	Miami, FL	Seattle, WA
Chicago, IL	Milwaukee, WI	Spokane, WA
Cincinnati, OH	New York, NY	Tampa, FL
Columbus, OH	Norfolk, VA	Tucson, AZ
Corpus Christi, TX	Oceanside, CA	Washington, DC
Detroit, MI	Orange, CA	

Table 3.56 shows the Transportation table for the metropolitan area of Fort Collins–Loveland, Colorado.

Commute

- *Average commute time* is the average one-way commute in minutes. The worst places tend to be larger East and West urban areas and suburban complexes surrounding them. Naturally, the best places are smaller towns, such as Cedar Falls–Waterloo, Idaho; Grand Forks, North Dakota; and Rochester, Minnesota.

- *Commute > 60 minutes* is the percentage of one-way commutes taking longer than 1 hour. Large, dense

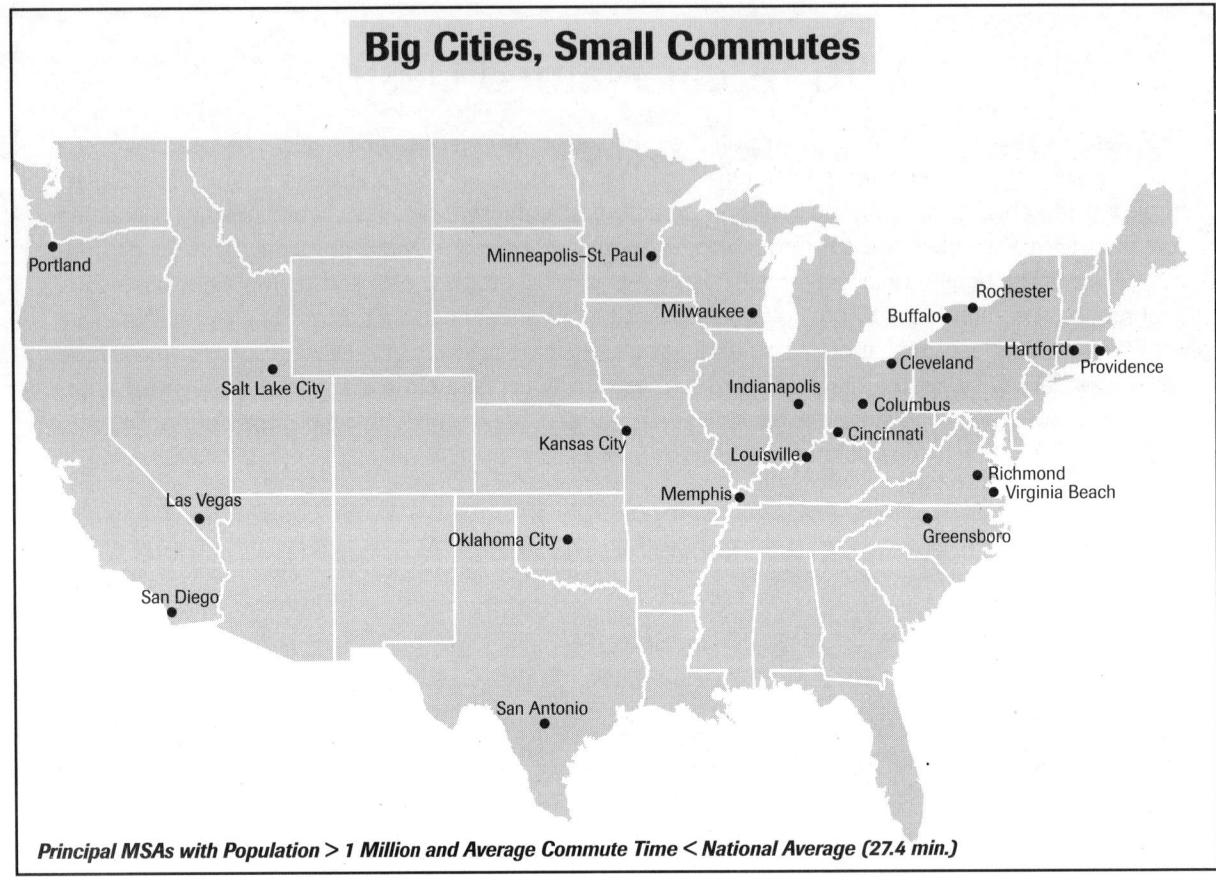

Big Cities, Small Commutes

Portland

Minneapolis–St. Paul •

Milwaukee •

Rochester

Buffalo •

Cleveland •

Hartford • • Providence

Salt Lake City •

Indianapolis •

Columbus •

Cincinnati •

Kansas City •

Louisville •

Las Vegas •

Richmond •

Memphis •

• Virginia Beach

Oklahoma City •

Greensboro •

San Diego •

San Antonio •

Principal MSAs with Population > 1 Million and Average Commute Time < National Average (27.4 min.)

urban areas, particularly where more than one mode of transport is used as in the New York area, tend to be longest. There are some individual neighborhoods in these areas where 50 percent or more individuals may have a commute of 1 hour or longer.

■ *Commute by auto* shows the percentage of all commutes done by automobile with a single driver (not a carpool). Not surprisingly, New York has the lowest percentage of such single-occupant vehicle (SOV) commutes at 51.2% and a number of college towns follow suit. Small towns in the Midwest and South tend to have the highest percentages.

■ *Commute by mass transit* shows the utilization of scheduled public transport services, including bus, subway, rail, and ferry. This statistic has the

most meaning in medium and large cities and in commuter suburbs.

■ *Work at home* shows the percentage of those who avoid a commute either as self-employed workers or telecommuters sponsored by their firms. Recognizing the impact on local infrastructure and work productivity, some companies and governmental jurisdictions have implemented progressive telecommute programs, but these are in the early stages. Interestingly, the highest work-at-home percentages tend to be in smaller Western cities and cities in the upper Midwest, but none exceed 8% of the workforce. The lowest tend to be in smaller cities in the South with percentages in the 1% to 2% range.

TABLE 3.56 SAMPLE TRANSPORTATION TABLE FROM FORT COLLINS–LOVELAND, CO

Transportation

Score: 65.2
Rank: 131

COMMUTE	AREA	U.S. AVG	INTERCITY SERVICES	AREA	U.S. AVG	AUTOMOTIVE	AREA	U.S. AVG
Average commute time	23.3	27.4	Major airports within 60 miles	1	1	Insurance, annual premium	$1,323	$1,432
Percent commutes > 60 mins.	6.0%	5.9%	Size of regional airport	Large	Large	Gas, cost per gallon	$2.46	$2.49
Commute by auto	77.9%	78.9%	Daily airline activity	812	686	Daily vehicle miles per capita	21.5	24.0
Commute by mass transit	0.8%	1.9%	Amtrak service	No	No			
Work at home	5.2%	3.1%						
Mass transit miles per capita	0.79	1.87						

■ *Mass transit miles per capita* indicates the availability of public transportation in the area. This figure represents the number of vehicle miles traveled by all types of transit vehicles—whether full or empty—per person.

Transport Services

■ *Number of major airports within 60 miles* shows the number of airports designated by the Federal Aviation Administration as a "hub" or "major" airport within that driving distance.

■ *Size of regional airport* profiles the airport and air service available in or near a metropolitan area. "Large" indicates a large airport with multiple terminals serving as service hubs for one or more carriers and connecting hubs for commuter aircraft. "Medium" indicates a medium airport that may have multiple terminals, usually served by four or more carriers, and a connecting hub for commuter aircraft. "Small" indicates a small airport characterized by a single terminal that might be served by two or three carriers, with full-sized jet service usually available.

■ *Daily airline activity* reflects the average number of passenger aircraft arriving and departing the area's airport(s) per day. The "area" includes all airports within a 100-mile radius. Leaders, as might be expected, are the larger regional and national hubs such as Chicago, New York, Atlanta, and Los Angeles.

■ *Amtrak service* is a yes/no indicator of whether the metro area has intercity Amtrak service. A total of 169 metropolitan areas have no Amtrak service at all, while many cities, mostly on the Northeast Corridor, have more than 10 departures per day.

Automotive

■ *Insurance, annual premium* represents the 2006 average annual cost of full-coverage auto insurance for an average automobile and a clean driving record, as tabulated by the National Association of Insurance Commissioners. The figure indicates the complexity, difficulty, and dependence on driving in an area, as rates are typically higher in cities with higher accident rates. Decidedly higher auto insurance rates occur on the East Coast and Southern California with many rates over $1,700 per year per vehicle. Smaller cities and towns in the Midwest are generally the least expensive at $800 to $900 a year.

■ *Gas, cost per gallon* is the average cost for a gallon of unleaded gasoline (summer 2006). While gas prices fluctuate considerably, this indicator is useful as a comparative measure between areas.

■ *Daily vehicle miles per capita* measures the 2004 average daily vehicular mileage per person in the metropolitan area, as supplied by the Federal Highway Administration in 2006. Factors include not only driving distances and urban sprawl but also the concentration of retirees in the area and the climate (which may facilitate walking). The lowest averages, not surprisingly, occur in college towns and smaller towns in the Midwest; the college town of Morgantown, West Virginia, is the lowest among metro areas at 3.8 miles driven per day. Longer distances occur in New York–area satellite metros and in an unpatterned assortment of other places. California cities have lower averages than might be expected due to the number of retirees and agricultural workers; it's safe to assume that without these influences, the average California driver drives long distances.

TABLE 3.57 COMMUTE TIMES
AVERAGE ONE-WAY COMMUTE IN MINUTES

METRO AREAS WITH LONGEST COMMUTES	MINUTES	METRO AREAS WITH SHORTEST COMMUTES	MINUTES
New York–White Plains, NY	40.7	Grand Forks, ND	16.8
Washington–Arlington–Alexandria, DC-VA-MD-WV	36.0	Dubuque, IA	17.2
Bethesda–Gaithersburg–Frederick, MD	35.8	Great Falls, MT	17.7
Oakland–Fremont–Hayward, CA	35.3	Lewiston, ID	17.8
Nassau–Suffolk, NY	35.2	Bismarck, ND	18.0
Edison, NJ	34.6	Fargo, ND	18.1
Chicago–Naperville–Joliet, IL	34.4	Casper, WY	18.1
Vallejo–Fairfield, CA	34.0	Cheyenne, WY	18.1
Bergen–Passaic, NJ	33.9	Waterloo–Cedar Falls, IA	18.2
Atlanta–Sandy Springs–Marietta, GA	33.9	Lawton, OK	18.6
Newark–Union, NJ-PA	33.7	Sheboygan, WI	18.6
Bremerton–Silverdale, WA	33.2	Ames, IA	18.7
Riverside–San Bernardino–Ontario, CA	33.0	St. George, UT	18.7
Poughkeepsie–Newburgh–Middletown, NY	33.0	Bloomington–Normal, IL	18.8
Boston–Quincy, MA	33.0	Lubbock, TX	18.9
Miami–Miami Beach–Kendall, FL	32.7	Missoula, MT	18.9
Baltimore–Towson, MD	32.1	Pocatello, ID	19.0
San Francisco–San Mateo–Redwood City, CA	32.1	Abilene, TX	19.1
Lake County–Kenosha County, IL-WI	31.9	Rapid City, SD	19.2
Los Angeles–Long Beach–Glendale, CA	31.8	San Angelo, TX	19.2
Houston–Sugar Land–Baytown, TX	31.6	Fairbanks, AK	19.3
Philadelphia, PA	31.5	Logan, UT	19.4
Stockton, CA	31.4	Sioux City, IA	19.4
Tacoma, WA	31.0	Champaign–Urbana, IL	19.5
Dallas–Plano–Irving, TX	30.3	Rochester, MN	19.6
Camden, NJ	30.3	Corvallis, OR	19.6
Santa Cruz–Watsonville, CA	30.3	Oshkosh–Neenah, WI	19.6
Bridgeport–Stamford–Norwalk, CT	30.1	Sioux Falls, SD	19.6
Honolulu, HI	30.1	Wichita Falls, TX	19.6
Cambridge–Newton–Framingham, MA	29.9	Wenatchee, WA	19.7

Source: U.S. Census American Community Survey, 2005

TABLE 3.58 COMMUTES BY AUTO
PERCENTAGE OF SINGLE-OCCUPANT VEHICLE (SOV) COMMUTES

METRO AREAS WITH MOST SOV COMMUTES	PERCENTAGE	METRO AREAS WITH FEWEST SOV COMMUTES	PERCENTAGE
Monroe, MI	88.2%	New York–White Plains, NY	31.2%
Sandusky, OH	88.2%	San Francisco–San Mateo–Redwood City, CA	57.0%
Warren–Troy–Farmington Hills, MI	88.0%	Ithaca, NY	60.4%
Bay City, MI	87.4%	Honolulu, HI	61.5%
Youngstown–Warren–Boardman, OH-PA	86.1%	Bergen–Passaic, NJ	63.1%
Canton–Massillon, OH	86.1%	Boston–Quincy, MA	64.2%
Holland–Grand Haven, MI	86.0%	Jacksonville, NC	66.0%
Florence–Muscle Shoals, AL	86.0%	Bremerton–Silverdale, WA	66.2%
Saginaw–Saginaw Township North, MI	86.0%	Washington–Arlington–Alexandria, DC-VA-MD-WV	67.0%
Akron, OH	85.7%	State College, PA	67.2%
Decatur, AL	85.5%	Oakland–Fremont–Hayward, CA	68.1%
Kingsport–Bristol–Bristol, TN-VA	85.4%	Philadelphia, PA	68.5%
Weirton–Steubenville, WV-OH	85.4%	Salinas, CA	68.6%
Owensboro, KY	85.3%	Flagstaff, AZ	68.6%
Anniston–Oxford, AL	85.3%	Chicago–Naperville–Joliet, IL	68.8%
Kokomo, IN	85.2%	Santa Barbara–Santa Maria, CA	69.3%
Lima, OH	85.1%	Santa Cruz–Watsonville, CA	69.3%
Dothan, AL	84.8%	Iowa City, IA	69.4%
Knoxville, TN	84.8%	Los Angeles–Long Beach–Glendale, CA	70.3%
Mansfield, OH	84.8%	Seattle–Bellevue–Everett, WA	70.5%
Toledo, OH	84.8%	Boulder, CO	70.8%
Evansville, IN	84.7%	Corvallis, OR	71.1%
Flint, MI	84.7%	Bethesda–Gaithersburg–Frederick, MD	71.3%
Oshkosh–Neenah, WI	84.7%	Newark–Union, NJ-PA	71.5%
Wichita, KS	84.6%	Santa Fe, NM	71.6%
Columbus, IN	84.6%	Champaign–Urbana, IL	71.6%
Gadsden, AL	84.5%	Eugene–Springfield, OR	71.9%
Decatur, IL	84.5%	Laredo, TX	72.1%
York–Hanover, PA	84.4%	Ames, IA	72.3%
Dayton, OH	84.3%	Cambridge–Newton–Framingham, MA	72.3%

Source: U.S. Census American Community Survey, 2005

TABLE 3.59 AUTO INSURANCE PREMIUMS
AVERAGE ANNUAL COST FOR AN AVERAGE AUTOMOBILE

METRO AREAS WITH HIGHEST PREMIUMS	COST	METRO AREAS WITH LOWEST PREMIUMS	COST
Detroit–Livonia–Dearborn, MI	$2,279	Iowa City, IA	$825
Newark–Union, NJ-PA	$1,977	Bangor, ME	$840
Los Angeles–Long Beach–Glendale, CA	$1,812	Bismarck, ND	$845
Philadelphia, PA	$1,798	Jackson, TN	$845
Santa Ana–Anaheim–Irvine, CA	$1,733	Cleveland, TN	$879
Trenton–Ewing, NJ	$1,707	Fargo, ND	$880
San Diego–Carlsbad–San Marcos, CA	$1,701	Idaho Falls, ID	$881
New York–White Plains, NY	$1,647	Ames, IA	$885
Warren–Troy–Farmington Hills, MI	$1,633	Dubuque, IA	$885
Tampa–St. Petersburg–Clearwater, FL	$1,616	Grand Forks, ND	$894
Edison, NJ	$1,615	Waterloo–Cedar Falls, IA	$897
Miami–Miami Beach–Kendall, FL	$1,558	Oshkosh–Neenah, WI	$901
Camden, NJ	$1,521	Rapid City, SD	$901
Boston–Quincy, MA	$1,519	Johnson City, TN	$903
Phoenix–Mesa–Scottsdale, AZ	$1,499	Pocatello, ID	$906
Sacramento–Arden-Arcade–Roseville, CA	$1,484	La Crosse, WI	$910
Modesto, CA	$1,480	Janesville, WI	$911
Cambridge–Newton–Framingham, MA	$1,467	Morristown, TN	$911
Honolulu, HI	$1,460	Clarksville, TN	$912
Las Vegas–Paradise, NV	$1,457	Kingsport–Bristol–Bristol, TN-VA	$912
New Orleans, LA	$1,414	Wausau, WI	$917
Oakland–Fremont–Hayward, CA	$1,396	Lewiston–Auburn, ME	$921
Fort Lauderdale–Pompano Beach–Deerfield Beach, FL	$1,385	Cedar Rapids, IA	$925
Essex County, MA	$1,378	Eau Claire, WI	$925
Bergen–Passaic, NJ	$1,373	St. George, UT	$925
Atlanta–Sandy Springs–Marietta, GA	$1,361	Danville, VA	$926
Stockton, CA	$1,358	Sioux City, IA	$929
New Haven–Milford, CT	$1,357	Fond du Lac, WI	$930
Bridgeport–Stamford–Norwalk, CT	$1,343	Roanoke, VA	$934
Denver–Aurora, CO	$1,340	Portland–South Portland–Biddeford, ME	$937

Source: National Association of Insurance Commissioners, 2006

TABLE 3.60 DRIVING MILES
AVERAGE MILES DRIVEN PER PERSON PER DAY

METRO AREAS WITH MOST MILES DRIVEN	MILES	METRO AREAS WITH LEAST MILES DRIVEN	MILES
Asheville, NC	49.1	Morgantown, WV	3.8
Decatur, AL	47.9	Merced, CA	10.0
Jackson, MS	44.7	Hinesville–Fort Stewart, GA	11.1
Hickory–Lenoir–Morganton, NC	42.0	Laredo, TX	12.5
Ocala, FL	41.6	Lebanon, PA	12.9
Poughkeepsie–Newburgh–Middletown, NY	40.3	Lewiston, ID	13.3
Santa Fe, NM	38.1	Yuba City, CA	13.3
Gadsden, AL	37.7	Chico, CA	13.4
Tulsa, OK	37.0	Racine, WI	13.5
Pensacola–Ferry Pass–Brent, FL	36.9	Corvallis, OR	13.7
Binghamton, NY	36.7	Grand Forks, ND	14.0
Cumberland, MD	36.6	Ames, IA	14.3
Dothan, AL	36.5	Napa, CA	14.3
Sherman–Denison, TX	36.2	Oakland–Fremont–Hayward, CA	14.4
Barnstable Town, MA	36.0	Jacksonville, NC	14.6
Birmingham–Hoover, AL	35.6	Great Falls, MT	14.6
Port St. Lucie–Fort Pierce, FL	35.6	San Angelo, TX	14.7
Greensboro–Winston-Salem–High Point, NC	35.3	Madera, CA	14.8
Houston–Sugar Land–Baytown, TX	35.2	Sheboygan, WI	14.9
Kingsport–Bristol–Bristol, TN-VA	35.0	Ithaca, NY	14.9
Las Cruces, NM	34.8	Salinas, CA	15.0
Punta Gorda, FL	34.7	Lake County–Kenosha County, IL-WI	15.1
Chattanooga, TN	34.2	El Centro, CA	15.4
Dover, DE	34.1	Modesto, CA	15.6
Cape Coral–Fort Myers, FL	33.6	Sandusky, OH	15.8
Jacksonville, FL	33.5	Santa Rosa–Petaluma, CA	15.9
Indianapolis–Carmel, IN	33.5	Visalia–Porterville, CA	16.0
Jackson, TN	33.1	Coeur d'Alene, ID	16.0
Knoxville, TN	32.7	Bismarck, ND	16.1
Monroe, MI	32.6	Parkersburg–Marietta–Vienna, WV-OH	16.1

Source: U.S. Department of Transportation Federal Highway Administration, 2004

Leisure

With the apparently hectic pace of life experienced by most people, the concept of spare time would seem to be an afterthought. In reality, most of the Western world has more spare time than ever before. The availability of activities therefore plays a significant role in determining an ideal place to live. *Cities Ranked & Rated* covers two categories, Leisure and Arts & Culture.

Leisure considers a cross section of shopping, entertainment, and outdoor recreation activities that broadly reflect the mix, quantity, and quality of leisure assets in an area. We know that recreation and arts tastes are individual, so our approach assumes that areas strong in a diverse set of activities are more likely to have specific activities of individual interest. For example, attributes such as nightlife and fishing can to some extent be inferred from other facts such as restaurant concentration, presence of college arts, and the presence of water.

Leisure Trends

The infinite variety of leisure forms leads to about as many leisure trends. This section highlights those trends that broadly impact the landscape and quality of life in an area.

Dining

The locally owned family restaurant continues to be in decline, especially in larger urban and suburban areas. New restaurant construction is generally for chains such as Applebee's, Joe's Crab Shack, P.F. Chang's, or cookie-cutter fast-food joints. Local legends such as Kansas City barbecue and Chicago-style pizza and steakhouses continue to flourish, and recent trends toward back-to-basics "comfort foods" have stemmed the tide a bit. *Cities Ranked & Rated* examines the restaurants in an area as they are rated by travel publications and other industry sources.

Shopping

Shopping has evolved dramatically and in hand with urban sprawl. The abundance of retail can be a double-edged sword—too much or too little reduces the quality of life. Forty years ago, shopping started to migrate from downtown areas to shopping malls, many of which led the charge toward the suburbanization of major cities. In the 1960s and 1970s, big malls prevailed, then high rents, traffic, and overdependence on department stores led to the proliferation of strip malls in the 1980s, and then to "big box" retailers and warehouse clubs—with super-sized buying and pricing power—in the 1990s. Today, many urban landscapes are dotted with partially vacant, poorly performing malls, while big-box complexes line freeway interchanges and cause massive traffic headaches as people drive from one store to another. Most recently, we've seen a deeper proliferation of the big-box format into smaller towns and cities.

Planning can combat these negative effects. Some places insist that retail developments include well-planned street access and parking, and conform to design standards consistent with local architecture. Many cities in the South and Midwest, such as Atlanta and Columbus, Ohio, have such practices, while some states in the West, such as California, Arizona, and Nevada, often allow developers to build whatever they please, leading to an ugly, formless jumble of nondescript buildings and parking lots.

To once again attract customers, shopping malls are getting bigger and becoming entertainment destinations with contained amusement parks, movie theaters, and entertainment restaurants like Rainforest Cafe. The massive 400-store Mall of America in Minneapolis–St. Paul leads this trend in the U.S. In some places, such as Houston's Sugar Land to the southwest and the Woodlands to the north, the mall has evolved into an artificial streetscape, a new small town but populated with chain stores, some even with mixed-use (residential second floor) spaces built in. We like the idea even if a bit fake and despite the potential to bring traditional downtown parking problems back into play. Finally, the advent of the outlet mall continues to shape the shopping environment, particularly in small towns. Often "outlet" stores are no more than a clever way for manufacturers to bypass retailers. Once located far outside urban areas to protect retailers, many of these malls are opening on urban fringes (such as Vallejo–Fairfield, California), which once again leads to sprawl and traffic.

What does this all mean? Areas with the right mix of well-planned shopping, with traditional and modern venues, are desirable. The continued building of large, traffic-choked complexes of big boxes and strip malls—unvarying assortments of New York Stock Exchange companies seeming to sell the same things—while downtown areas sit unused spells trouble for the future. Look for places that restrict and control development, reuse older buildings, and preserve local businesses bringing variety to the shopping landscape. There's no dominant example, but we see more of this in the Pacific Northwest, upper Midwest, and New England than in other places.

Spectator Sports

Spectator sports continue the boom enjoyed for most of the past 50 years. While major league sports have become mainstays of big cities, more franchises are being created in smaller cities, particularly in the South, like

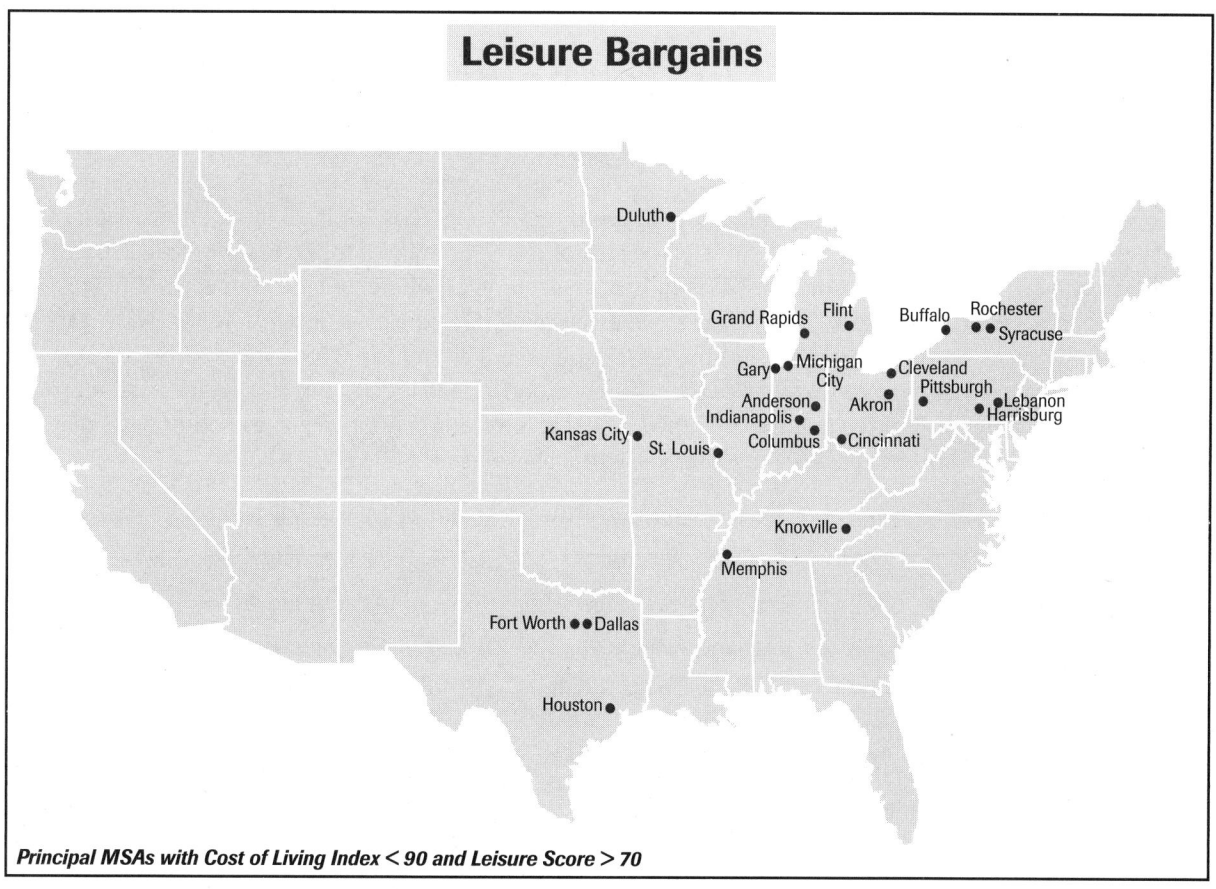

Leisure Bargains

Principal MSAs with Cost of Living Index < 90 and Leisure Score > 70

Jacksonville, Florida; Nashville, Tennessee; and Charlotte, North Carolina. Perhaps more interesting is the growth of minor league sports, particularly baseball and hockey, in places like Fresno, California, and the metropolitan area of Greensboro–Winston-Salem–High Point, North Carolina. The popularity of collegiate sports in college towns is legendary, but the appeal is spreading to wider segments of the population, particularly in states like Alabama and Kentucky, which lack major league teams. Finally, we applaud NASCAR for placing many smaller metro areas such as Dover, Delaware; Florence, South Carolina; and Anniston, Alabama, on the national sports map.

Outdoor Recreation

After booming in the 1990s, golf has leveled off, but will probably continue to grow modestly as baby boomers retire. But although tempered by the recent real estate slowdown, planned golf communities—especially in Florida, Arizona, and Texas—continue to be the biggest growth area in golf today.

Park systems in most places are under strain, both at the national and local level. Improved automobile and transportation infrastructures and increased leisure time have made parks more accessible. Meanwhile, funding continues to suffer as government agencies are forced to cut back. The predictable result is crowding, reduced quality in some cases, and higher entrance fees. National parks in California have been known to close completely to new entrants on holiday weekends, and accommodations, including campsites, must be reserved up to a year in advance. The rule of thumb is that any national park within a weekend drive of a major city is likely to be overcrowded in the high season. As urban sprawl continues, some county and larger city parks once part of the countryside are now becoming true city and suburban treasures, with large areas for recreation, entertainment, water parks, zoos, and preserved history where local funding allows. Of course, New York's Central Park is the original example. The Hamilton County Park District in Cincinnati, Ohio, serves as an excellent modern-day example.

Leisure Attributes

Cities Ranked & Rated examines available activities in or near a place. Ratings are expressed either on a 1–10 scale (1 worst, 10 best) based on availability, proximity, and quality of facilities in the area or as specific numbers when that approach is more meaningful, as in the number of Starbucks. In the ranking process, areas that have a

Take Me Out to the Ball Game

Throughout the book we present facts about overall cost of living. But what about the cost of entertainment and leisure? Sure, it's baked into the Cost of Living Index at some level. But is it possible to capture and know the cost of movie tickets, Big Macs, and greens fees in hundreds of places around the country? Not really. So as we often do, we found a proxy: the cost of taking a family of four to a major league baseball game. Now, we know major league baseball isn't available everywhere, but we thought the figures, captured in a recent *New York Times* article, were revealing. Of particular interest is the wide gap between the most expensive (Boston) and the least expensive (Kansas City). Now, you may be thinking that high player salaries might drive some of the difference, and indeed it does. But in most markets ticket prices are only about half of the figure that follows. The rest is refreshments, parking, and other costs that have nothing to do with the team, win or lose. The national average is $172.

Boston Red Sox	$288	Toronto Blue Jays	$183	Minnesota Twins	$149
Chicago Cubs	$219	San Diego Padres	$180	Arizona Diamondbacks	$148
New York Yankees	$209	Los Angeles Dodgers	$175	Atlanta Braves	$146
St. Louis Cardinals	$207	Oakland Athletics	$170	Colorado Rockies	$141
New York Mets	$207	Washington Nationals	$170	Pittsburgh Pirates	$139
San Francisco Giants	$202	Detroit Tigers	$163	Los Angeles Angels	$134
Philadelphia Phillies	$194	Baltimore Orioles	$159	Texas Rangers	$134
Houston Astros	$192	Cleveland Indians	$158	Milwaukee Brewers	$132
Chicago White Sox	$191	Cincinnati Reds	$157	Tampa Bay Devil Rays	$130
Seattle Mariners	$186	Florida Marlins	$154	Kansas City Royals	$120

broad and diverse set of amenities—good restaurants, skiing, and parks—will rate higher than an area located next to a ski resort but that has nothing else.

These attributes come from a variety of data sources, which can be trade associations for a sport or leisure form, corporate sources, industry marketing information sources such as Claritas, Inc., or selected travel guides. National park data and inland water information come from the National Park Service and National Oceanic and Atmospheric Administration, respectively. All information is processed and rated by Sperling's BestPlaces.

Table 3.61 shows the Leisure table for San Luis Obispo–Paso Robles, California.

Dining & Shopping

- *Restaurant rating* is a 1–10 rating of restaurants in the area mainly considering quality and availability as compiled by travel guides and other industry sources.

- *Outlet mall score* rates outlet malls in and near the metro area by number of malls, number of stores, and distance from the metro area. Highest scores are best, but unlike other *Cites Ranked & Rated* scores, this score is not shown on a 1–100 scale.

- *No. Starbucks* is the number of Starbucks retail outlets in an area. The figure is indicative of the overall quality of retail establishments.

TABLE 3.61 SAMPLE LEISURE TABLE FROM SAN LUIS OBISPO–PASO ROBLES, CA

Leisure

Score: 75.1
Rank: 93

DINING & SHOPPING	AREA	U.S. AVG	ENTERTAINMENT	AREA	U.S. AVG	OUTDOOR ACTIVITIES	AREA	U.S. AVG
Restaurant rating	1	2	Professional sports rating	2	4	Golf-course rating	3	4
No. outlet malls	58	42	College sports rating	4	4	Ski-area rating	10	3
No. Starbucks	11	13	Zoo/aquarium rating	2	3	Sq. miles inland water	2	4
No. warehouse clubs	1	2	Amusement park rating	1	3	Miles of coastline	77.3	10.7
			Botanical garden arboretum rating	1	4	National Park rating	10	3

Are Golf Courses Headed for the Rough?

Throughout the 1980s and 1990s, expanded leisure time and an upwardly mobile but slowly aging demographic led to a boom in golf course design and development, culminating in a total of some 280 new golf courses arriving on the scene in 2001. That trend, however, has reversed, according to figures from the National Golf Foundation (NGF). The NGF cites increased prices, diminished numbers of golfers with a full day to allocate to the sport, and hard times in economically sensitive areas such as auto-dependent Michigan. Add to that pressure to redevelop golf courses into housing tracts and shopping centers and a growing feeling that golf is exclusive and not appropriate for corporate events in today's diversity-conscious society, and the result is as predictable as a bad lie in the rough. In 2006, the number of courses closing exceeded the number opening for the first time in years.

- *No. warehouse clubs* tallies the number of Costco, Sam's Club, and BJ's stores in an area. The figure is indicative of the availability of large-scale discount shopping.

Entertainment

- *Professional sports rating* is a 1–10 rating for professional baseball, football, basketball, and hockey teams, including both major league and minor league teams. New York leads this category. Its suburban communities share the rating because people will usually travel a commute distance for these events.

- *College sports rating* rates collegiate sports at all levels on a 1–10 scale. Not surprisingly, college towns and some big cities rate high. Collegiate sports are available in all but 77 metropolitan areas.

- *Zoo/aquarium rating* is a 1–10 rating covering animal parks of all types, including marine parks with a high degree of animal activity. High ratings go to an assortment of big cities and areas near warm water. There are 13 areas with a 9 or 10 rating and 179 areas with no noted presence.

- *Amusement park rating* covers amusement parks based on number, proximity, and quality of facilities on a 1–10 scale. There are 22 areas rated 9 or 10 and 248 areas with no noted presence.

- *Botanical garden/arboretum rating* represents formal gardens, conservatories, and other botanical facilities on a 1–10 scale.

Outdoor Activities

- *Golf course rating* rates public and private golf courses based on number, quality, and cost on a 1–10 scale. Some areas on the "leaderboard"

might surprise in this area, including Detroit, Philadelphia, and Winchester, Virginia, along with more expected entrants such as Phoenix, Las Vegas, and Tampa–St. Petersburg–Clearwater. Among smaller places, Myrtle Beach, South Carolina, and Jacksonville, Florida, are leaders.

- *Ski-area rating* takes into account that no metropolitan areas have skiing within their boundaries, so the 1–10 scale rating necessarily considers proximity. No surprises at the top of the list: Denver, Salt Lake City, and Reno. As popularity grows and snowmaking technology improves, even places like Atlanta get a small rating. There are 148 places with no facilities whatsoever, mostly in predictable places in the South.

- *Sq. miles inland water* is the measured amount of water in square miles. Inland water refers to completely enclosed bodies of water, not ocean bays or inlets. High on the list are cities in southern Louisiana, northern Minnesota, and Florida. Only 21 areas have no noted inland water.

- *Miles of coastline* represents the number of miles of coastline bordering the entire metropolitan area. Coastline usually refers to ocean coastline, but can also include the Great Lakes. Highest coastline ratings occur on islands: Nassau–Suffolk, New York (Long Island), and Honolulu, Hawaii. There are 279 places with no coastline.

- *National Park rating* is a 1–10 scale rating of the availability, proximity, and quality of nearby National Parks and National Forests. The highest ratings occur in western cities at the base of the Sierra Nevada, Rocky, and Cascade mountain ranges and areas in Arizona that border large areas of public land. There are 153 places with no noted national park resources.

Leisure Highlights

TABLE 3.62 METROPOLITAN AREAS WITH HIGHLY RATED RECREATIONAL FACILITIES					
RATED ON A 1–10 SCALE					
AMUSEMENT PARKS	RATING	ZOOS/AQUARIUMS	RATING	GOLF COURSES	RATING
Los Angeles–Long Beach–Glendale, CA	10	Los Angeles–Long Beach–Glendale, CA	10	Los Angeles–Long Beach–Glendale, CA	10
Santa Ana–Anaheim–Irvine, CA	10	Chicago–Naperville–Joliet, IL	10	Chicago–Naperville–Joliet, IL	10
Chicago–Naperville–Joliet, IL	10	Atlanta–Sandy Springs–Marietta, GA	10	New York–White Plains, NY	10
Minneapolis–St. Paul–Bloomington, MN–WI	10	San Diego–Carlsbad–San Marcos, CA	10	Bethesda–Gaithersburg–Frederick, MD	10
Orlando–Kissimmee, FL	10	New York–White Plains, NY	10	Washington–Arlington–Alexandria, DC-VA-MD-WV	10
San Jose–Sunnyvale–Santa Clara, CA	10	Baltimore–Towson, MD	10	Winchester, VA	10
St. Louis, MO	10	Bethesda–Gaithersburg–Frederick, MD	10	Cleveland–Elyria–Mentor, OH	10
Harrisburg–Carlisle, PA	10	Washington–Arlington–Alexandria, DC-VA-MD-WV	10	Camden, NJ	10
Lebanon, PA	10	Winchester, VA	10	Philadelphia, PA	10
Atlanta–Sandy Springs–Marietta, GA	10	Minneapolis–St. Paul–Bloomington, MN–WI	9	Detroit–Livonia–Dearborn, MI	10
Miami–Miami Beach–Kendall, FL	9	St. Louis, MO	9	Monroe, MI	10
Tampa–St. Petersburg–Clearwater, FL	9	Gainesville, GA	9	Nassau–Suffolk, NY	10
Virginia Beach–Norfolk–Newport News, VA-NC	9	Lake County–Kenosha County, IL-WI	9	Riverside–San Bernardino–Ontario, CA	10
San Diego–Carlsbad–San Marcos, CA	9	Miami–Miami Beach–Kendall, FL	8	West Palm Beach–Boca Raton–Boynton Beach, FL	10
Santa Cruz–Watsonville, CA	9	Virginia Beach–Norfolk–Newport News, VA-NC	8	Newark–Union, NJ-PA	10
Napa, CA	9	Seattle–Bellevue–Everett, WA	8	Warren–Troy–Farmington Hills, MI	10
Vallejo–Fairfield, CA	9	Cleveland–Elyria–Mentor, OH	8	Lake County–Kenosha County, IL-WI	9
Fort Worth–Arlington, TX	9	Boston–Quincy, MA	8	Atlanta–Sandy Springs–Marietta, GA	9
Akron, OH	9	Cambridge–Newton–Framingham, MA	8	Minneapolis–St. Paul–Bloomington, MN–WI	9
Louisville–Jefferson County, KY-IN	9	Essex County, MA	8	Gainesville, GA	9
San Antonio, TX	9	Worcester, MA	8	Boston–Quincy, MA	9
Lake County–Kenosha County, IL-WI	9	Atlantic City, NJ	8	Cambridge–Newton–Framingham, MA	9
Sacramento–Arden-Arcade–Roseville, CA	8	Ocean City, NJ	8	Essex County, MA	9
Houston–Sugar Land–Baytown, TX	8	Chattanooga, TN	8	Worcester, MA	9
Seattle–Bellevue–Everett, WA	8	Philadelphia, PA	8	Pittsburgh, PA	9
Knoxville, TN	8	Pittsburgh, PA	8	Tampa–St. Petersburg–Clearwater, FL	9
Richmond, VA	8	Phoenix–Mesa–Scottsdale, AZ	8	Kingston, NY	9
Fresno, CA	8	San Francisco–San Mateo–Redwood City, CA	8	Poughkeepsie–Newburgh–Middletown, NY	9
Madera, CA	8	Bridgeport–Stamford–Norwalk, CT	8	Edison, NJ	9
Portland–Vancouver–Beaverton, OR-WA	8	New Haven–Milford, CT	8	Rochester, MN	9

Source: Sperling's BestPlaces

Arts & Culture

The Arts & Culture category encompasses fine arts, humanities, science, and history through cultural media, performing arts, and museums. These assets serve the twin purposes of providing intellectually stimulating entertainment and education for families and children. An area with strong cultural assets usually also has good educational ones, a strong sense of tradition and heritage, and finer entertainment options. Furthermore, strong cultural assets tend to attract other assets, thus improving an area's overall quality of life. This fact is not lost on local governments and chambers of commerce, many of which will aggressively pursue such amenities with funding when they can.

Arts & Culture Trends

More than ever, the major issue facing most performing arts is funding. Fiscal health is generally not a problem for the best-known entities, such as the New York Philharmonic or the quasi-public Smithsonian Institution. Beyond that, almost every cultural asset faces the same issues:

increasing costs, recession-driven declines in contributions and public support, and declining endowments. Possibly following the example set by the Bill and Melinda Gates Foundation, people have recently favored human service causes at the expense of the arts with their charitable intentions. Institutions at the fringe in small to medium-size cities and those dependent on large amounts of unionized talent, such as symphony orchestras, are having the hardest time. Most orchestras and many local theaters cover only half of their costs through ticket sales, and many went bankrupt or teetered on the brink through the 1990s and into 2003. Fortunately, for the moment, there are no major crises in the news.

Public radio and television are still holding their own, but stations must resort to more creative (and more commercial-like) activities in the face of competition from satellite and cable TV networks and satellite radio. Stations energetically sell program sponsorships to corporations and produce sponsored shows for networks, public and private. Some rent out their studios for income.

Live theater continues to thrive in pockets, and in some areas, it depends on the quality of the venue as much as

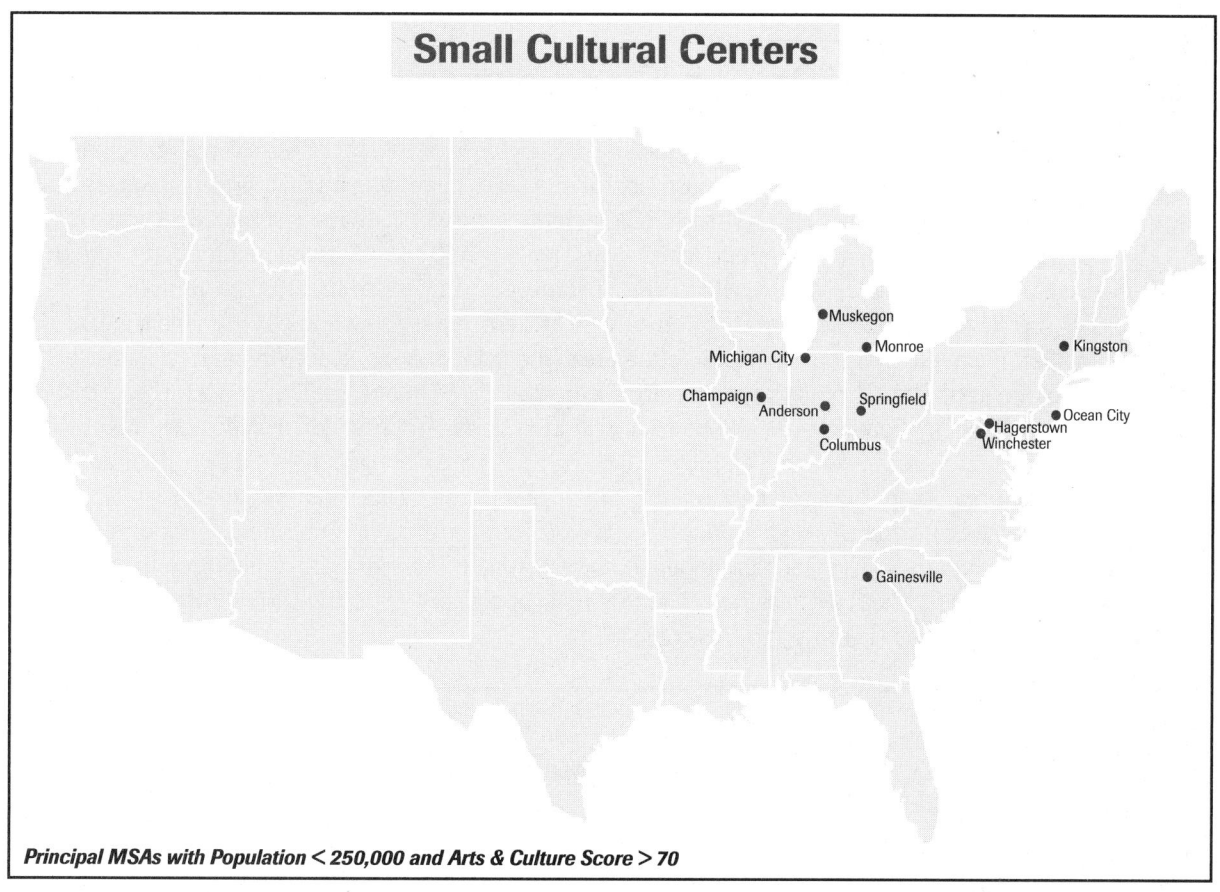

Small Cultural Centers

Principal MSAs with Population < 250,000 and Arts & Culture Score > 70

the quality of the product to attract regular audiences. University arts programs, including theater, music, and dance, are doing more outreach into local communities, especially in larger cities. University performing arts programs feature not only indigenous talent from the student body but also touring acts from the United States and abroad. Helping these programs remain viable are low overhead and the use of campus facilities, plus the fact that residents not affiliated with the university find college campuses to be pleasant evening destinations.

Good museums continue to see funding and attendance and are trending toward more frequently changing and traveling exhibits. According to the American Association of Museums, there are an estimated 16,000 museums in the United States, which receive more than 850 million visits per year, more than all the country's professional baseball, football, and basketball sporting events combined. Museums address several topics: art, history, natural history, science, technology, children's interests, and the military. Art museums have traditionally formed the largest category, with more than 200 listings in the United States. But children's museums, with hands-on activities and educational features, are the fastest-growing segment, with more than 200 listed in the United States. *Cities Ranked*

& Rated breaks out ratings for art, science, and children's museums because these are the most likely types of museums to be patronized repeatedly by area residents.

Another trend among museums is the employment of scientific marketing techniques to research and identify local markets in the population, and to tailor exhibits (and, of course, fundraising) accordingly. Many museums are adding more interactive and "fun" exhibits to provide greater entertainment along with educational value. An increasing number of museums are located in smaller towns and in museum parks and complexes away from city centers; one example is Balboa Park in San Diego, California.

By museum type, American median annual museum attendance, including zoos and arboretums, breaks down as follows, according to the American Association of Museums:

- Zoo: 520,935
- Science/technology museum: 183,417
- Arboretum/botanic garden: 119,575
- Children's/youth museum: 85,088
- Natural history/anthropology: 64,768
- Art museum: 61,312

Does It Pay to Support the Arts?

Public funding of arts and cultural assets always sparks a lively debate—do arts investments really drive the economic prosperity of a region, or is it just "art for arts sake" benefiting a small minority? Recently, the Colorado Business Committee for the Arts (CBCA) gave their answer to that question. CBCA commissions a periodic study to evaluate the effectiveness of a 0.1% "Scientific and Cultural Facilities" tax added into sales taxes that generates some $38 million in annual revenue distributed to 300 organizations. Their conclusion: The 14.1 million people attending Denver-area arts amenities spent some $785 million, including $334 million from "cultural tourists" outside the area. The total economic activity was estimated at $1.4 billion including all capital outlays and operating expenses, up from $461 million in 1992. The 10,800 employed collect $96 million in wages and pay $16 million in taxes. And none of this includes the economic benefits of businesses and other employers moving to the area, bringing higher-paying jobs and a more educated population. Not to mention the brand new Daniel Libeskind–designed Denver Art Museum's contribution to the city skyline. Not a bad payoff for a small tax commitment. Yet, not everyone agrees. Local free-market think tank Independence Institute President Jon Caldara commented: "I'm glad that working families have less money so that rich yuppies can go to the Denver Symphony tax-subsidized." Well, everyone is entitled to their opinion.

- General museum: 49,983
- Nature center: 40,500
- Specialized museum: 32,000
- Historic house/site: 16,000
- History museum: 15,000

Arts & Culture Attributes

Arts & Culture is divided into three areas: *Media & Libraries*, *Performing Arts*, and *Museums*. Since most people attend performing arts as a special occasion, rating points are usually given for available amenities up to 100 miles away unless that distance contains a significant geographic or transportation barrier. Most attributes are compiled by Sperling's BestPlaces, mainly from cultural association publications. Library and university arts data come from the National Center for Education Statistics, U.S. Department of Education. All values are used in scoring and ranking.

Table 3.63 shows the Arts & Culture table for Boise City–Nampa, Idaho.

Media & Libraries

- *Arts radio rating* covers both "listener-supported" stations usually affiliated with National Public Radio (NPR) and private stations broadcasting classical music, jazz, or noncommercial talk formats, all rated on a 1–10 scale. Large cities typically score well, but others such as Grand Rapids–Wyoming, Michigan, and Albany, New York, also have good ratings.

- *No. public libraries* is the total number library facilities in an area, including branches. Notables for their size include Cincinnati–Middletown, Ohio-Kentucky-Indiana (with 92 libraries); Rochester, New York (71); and Columbus, Ohio (53). Smaller towns with lower incomes and less education have fewer facilities.

- *Library volumes per capita* is the actual number of books available per citizen in the area. Bangor, Maine, and Fort Wayne, Indiana, are two of the top three areas on this list.

TABLE 3.63 SAMPLE ARTS & CULTURE TABLE FROM BOISE CITY–NAMPA, ID								
MEDIA & LIBRARIES	AREA	U.S. AVG	**PERFORMING ARTS**	AREA	U.S. AVG	**MUSEUMS**	AREA	U.S. AVG
Arts radio rating	8	3	Classical music rating	3	4	Overall museum rating	5	5
No. public libraries	24	27	Ballet/dance rating	3	3	Art museum rating	5	5
Library volumes per capita	2.40	2.78	Professional theater rating	1	3	Science museum rating	5	5
			University arts programs rating	5	5	Children's museum rating	1	3

Arts & Culture

Score: 62.3
Rank: 141

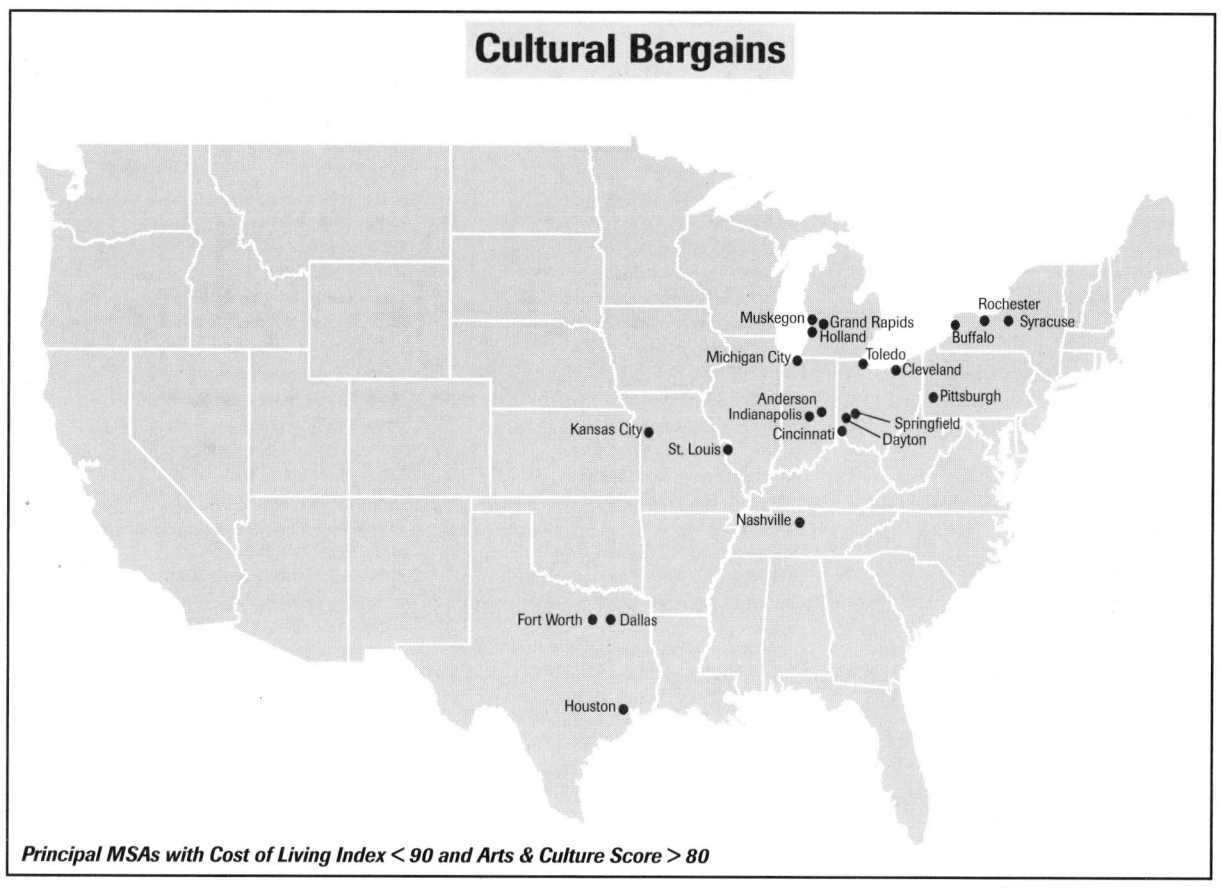

Cultural Bargains

Principal MSAs with Cost of Living Index < 90 and Arts & Culture Score > 80

Performing Arts

- *Classical music rating* covers traditional symphony and opera companies in or near an area. The number of musicians, frequency of performances, and overall quality and critical acclaim all figure into the rating on a 1–10 scale. Large cities score well, as do communities in close proximity to large cities or cities with major classical music assets.

- *Ballet/dance rating* covers traditional ballet and dance companies in a manner similar to classical music, rated on a 1–10 scale.

- *Professional theater rating* covers traditional theater companies but not dinner theaters or traveling shows, rated on a 1–10 scale.

- *University arts programs rating* covers classical music, dance, theater, and international programs sponsored by local colleges and universities, all rated on a 1–10 scale.

Museums

- *Overall museum rating* recognizes the number and quality of all museums in—or near—an area on a 1–10 scale. Not surprisingly, New York and Washington, D.C., top the list, but Buffalo, New York; Detroit, Michigan; and Richmond, Virginia, are up there as well. There are only nine areas with no noted museum presence. The next three attributes single out the types of museums of most interest to long-term residents of an area (in contrast to historical museums, which typically appeal more to the traveler).

- *Art museum rating* covers museums designated as art museums by the American Association of Museums, rated on a 1–10 scale.

- *Science museum rating* covers museums designated as science museums by the American Association of Museums, rated on a 1–10 scale.

- *Children's museum rating* covers museums designated as children's museums by the American Association of Museums, rated on a 1–10 scale.

TABLE 3.64 METROPOLITAN AREAS WITH HIGHLY RATED MUSEUMS
RATED ON A 1–10 SCALE

ART MUSEUMS	RATING	SCIENCE MUSEUMS	RATING	CHILDREN'S MUSEUMS	RATING
Baltimore–Towson, MD	10	Baltimore–Towson, MD	10	Chicago–Naperville–Joliet, IL	10
Boston–Quincy, MA	10	Chicago–Naperville–Joliet, IL	10	Los Angeles–Long Beach–Glendale, CA	10
Bridgeport–Stamford–Norwalk, CT	10	Houston–Sugar Land–Baytown, TX	10	New York–White Plains, NY	10
Camden, NJ	10	Los Angeles–Long Beach–Glendale, CA	10	Washington–Arlington–Alexandria, DC-VA-MD-WV	10
Chicago–Naperville–Joliet, IL	10	Minneapolis–St. Paul–Bloomington, MN-WI	10	Riverside–San Bernardino–Ontario, CA	10
Detroit–Livonia–Dearborn, MI	10	New Haven–Milford, CT	10	Virginia Beach–Norfolk–Newport News, VA-NC	10
Houston–Sugar Land–Baytown, TX	10	New York–White Plains, NY	10	St. Louis, MO	10
Los Angeles–Long Beach–Glendale, CA	10	Philadelphia, PA	10	Seattle–Bellevue–Everett, WA	10
Minneapolis–St. Paul–Bloomington, MN-WI	10	Pittsburgh, PA	10	Cincinnati–Middletown, OH-KY-IN	10
New Haven–Milford, CT	10	Poughkeepsie–Newburgh–Middletown, NY	10	Fort Worth–Arlington, TX	10
New York–White Plains, NY	10	San Francisco–San Mateo–Redwood City, CA	10	Oakland–Fremont–Hayward, CA	10
Philadelphia, PA	10	Washington–Arlington–Alexandria, DC-VA-MD-WV	10	Hartford–West Hartford–East Hartford, CT	10
Pittsburgh, PA	10	Atlanta–Sandy Springs–Marietta, GA	10	Baltimore–Towson, MD	9
Poughkeepsie–Newburgh–Middletown, NY	10	Columbus, OH	10	Houston–Sugar Land–Baytown, TX	9
St. Louis, MO	10	Indianapolis–Carmel, IN	10	Minneapolis–St. Paul–Bloomington, MN-WI	9
San Francisco–San Mateo–Redwood City, CA	10	Riverside–San Bernardino–Ontario, CA	10	Philadelphia, PA	9
Santa Fe, NM	10	San Diego–Carlsbad–San Marcos, CA	10	San Francisco–San Mateo–Redwood City, CA	9
Seattle–Bellevue–Everett, WA	10	San Jose–Sunnyvale–Santa Clara, CA	10	Atlanta–Sandy Springs–Marietta, GA	9
Washington–Arlington–Alexandria, DC-VA-MD-WV	10	Santa Ana–Anaheim–Irvine, CA	10	Columbus, OH	9
Wilmington, DE	10	Trenton–Ewing, NJ	10	Indianapolis–Carmel, IN	9
Worcester, MA	10	Virginia Beach–Norfolk–Newport News, VA-NC	10	San Jose–Sunnyvale–Santa Clara, CA	9
Albany–Schenectady–Troy, NY	9	Edison, NJ	10	Bethesda–Gaithersburg–Frederick, MD	9
Ann Arbor, MI	9	Essex County, MA	10	Boston–Quincy, MA	9
Atlanta–Sandy Springs–Marietta, GA	9	Napa, CA	10	Bridgeport–Stamford–Norwalk, CT	9
Cambridge–Newton–Framingham, MA	9	Oxnard–Thousand Oaks–Ventura, CA	10	Ann Arbor, MI	9
Cincinnati–Middletown, OH-KY-IN	9	Bethesda–Gaithersburg–Frederick, MD	10	Cambridge–Newton–Framingham, MA	9
Cleveland–Elyria–Mentor, OH	9	Kingston, NY	10	Dallas–Plano–Irving, TX	9
Columbus, OH	9	Santa Cruz–Watsonville, CA	10	Nassau–Suffolk, NY	9
Dallas–Plano–Irving, TX	9	Boston–Quincy, MA	9	Newark–Union, NJ-PA	9
Denver–Aurora, CO	9	Bridgeport–Stamford–Norwalk, CT	9	Bergen–Passaic, NJ	9

Source: Sperling's BestPlaces

Finding Refuge among the Trees

A lot can be said for the visual benefits of tree-lined streets and the appeal and apparent cleanliness of a place with lots of trees. Some cities take their trees quite seriously, and spend lots of time and money planting and caring for their trees. For example, in Sacramento, California, such tree consciousness has completely changed the look in an otherwise barren, flatland valley. Calgary, Alberta has a similar story. The U.S. Forest Service (USFS) publishes a periodic count of trees per capita (now, how would you like to have that job?). The top 20 cities in the 2004 survey, which includes cities in Canada and Chile (hard to say why the USFS went to Santiago!) are listed below:

1. Moorestown, NJ (part of Camden MSA): 31.4
2. Morgantown, WV: 24.6
3. Atlanta, GA: 22.6
4. Calgary, Alberta: 13.5
5. Woodbridge, NJ (part of Edison MSA): 9.8
6. Syracuse, NY: 5.9
7. Freehold, NJ (part of Edison MSA): 4.4
8. Sacramento, CA: 4.3
9. Baltimore, MD: 4.0
10. Oakland, CA: 4.0
11. Washington, DC: 3.4
12. Toronto, Ontario: 3.0
13. Minneapolis, MN: 2.6
14. Boston, MA: 2.0
15. Chicago, IL: 1.4
16. Philadelphia, PA: 1.4
17. Santiago, Chile: 1.2
18. San Francisco, CA: 0.9
19. New York, NY: 0.7
20. Jersey City, NJ (part of Newark–Union MSA): 0.6

America's Most Literate Cities

Central Connecticut State University released its 2005 ranking of 69 U.S. cities based on the following variables contributing to literacy: the origination and circulation of local published materials such as periodicals and newspapers, the availability and quality of libraries, the presence of booksellers, and the overall level of educational attainment. A more literate city reads more—not better—than a less literate city. One interesting trend emerges: Less reading seems to occur in Sun Belt cities and California and Texas in particular. Incidentally, this is the same study previously published by the University of Wisconsin-Whitewater by the same researchers.

The top 10 cities, in order, are:

1. Seattle, WA
2. Minneapolis, MN
3. Washington, DC
4. Atlanta, GA
5. San Francisco, CA

6. Denver, CO
7. Boston, MA
8. Pittsburgh, PA
9. Cincinnati, OH
10. St. Paul, MN

The 10 worst (of 69 metropolitan areas studied) are:

59. Riverside, CA (tie)
59. Los Angeles, CA (tie)
61. Long Beach, CA
62. Santa Ana, CA
63. Fresno, CA
64. San Antonio, TX

65. Bakersfield, CA
66. Anaheim, CA
67. Corpus Christi, TX
68. El Paso, TX
69. Stockton, TX

Quality of Life

We have determined a combined score for each metropolitan area based on the perceived overall quality of life. The score is included in scoring and ranking, but is not shown in individual city tables. Refer to Tables 2.4 and 2.5 in chapter 2 for the Quality of Life scores for each metropolitan area.

By their very nature, the factors determining this score are difficult to quantify. They are based mainly on perception, personal experience, and anecdotes from others who have spent time in these places. Features considered include the following:

- *Physical attractiveness:* This includes both the physical setting and overall appearance of the area itself. Included is the attractiveness and functionality of the downtown core. We believe these factors influence initial impressions and long-term satisfaction in an area. The effects of a pancake-flat, windswept, nondescript landscape with dirty air and little vegetation are far different from that of attractive, well-kept, tree-lined streets with good buildings and a pristine mountain, valley river, or lakeside setting. Cities such as Boulder, Colorado; Corvallis, Oregon; and Burlington, Vermont, do well in this regard, while some larger cities such as Pittsburgh, Pennsylvania, and Chattanooga, Tennessee, are improving.

- *Heritage:* A city that knows its roots and tries to preserve its physical and cultural heritage is usually more physically attractive as well as genuine in character. These cities are almost invariably better places to live. Metropolitan areas with well-preserved historic districts and public buildings include Charlottesville and Winchester, Virginia; Boston, Massachusetts; Portland, Maine; and Santa Fe, New Mexico.

■ *Overall ease of living:* The most subjective element in this subjective category, ease of living incorporates crowdedness, attitude and friendliness of people, and simplicity of infrastructure. In essence, it considers the "stress factor." Issues with places such as Los Angeles, San Francisco, and New York are obvious, and these cities score poorly, while cities in the South—even the workaholic New South—tend to score high.

chapter 4

The States

Which states have the most people? The biggest governments? The most growth? The best employment and income opportunities? The most favorable tax climate? The best educational system? Evaluating information at the state level can shed a useful comparative light on U.S. places. Many state-level facts and attributes shape the nature of individual places within the state and identify important structural characteristics found in those places. Some of these elements help to provide a more complete image of the state, while others, such as tax policy, have a direct effect on day-to-day life.

How *Cities Ranked & Rated* Compares States

Cities Ranked & Rated takes a high-level, comparative approach to evaluating states. Complete factual descriptions of each state are purposely left out due to space and easy access elsewhere. In addition, many attributes vary considerably within the state and make more sense to examine at a local level. This chapter does include analysis and comparisons touching across some of the most interesting aspects of population, physical environment, economics, taxes, politics, law, and education. They offer insight into a state's character and how it might align to an individual's interests. Moreover, many indicate something beyond face value. For example, drunk driving laws say something about the ability—and willingness—of a state legislature to involve itself in ensuring personal safety.

Some statewide attributes may not apply to a particular city under examination. For example, the state of Oregon may have an average per capita income just under $30,000, but that figure is much higher in the Portland area. Likewise, the political landscape of Georgia may not well describe that of Atlanta, nor does the tax burden in Bridgeport necessarily describe all of Connecticut. Therefore, when examining specific places, it's important not to stop at the state level—this would be like ending a shopping trip at the selection of a store.

Where it serves a purpose, we will also draw comparisons to facts presented in the 2004 edition. That, of course, won't be everywhere, for many facts, like climate, don't change a lot over the course of 3 years.

Much of this information can be found in an almanac or at U.S. government websites, and some attributes may already be familiar—for instance, that California is number one in population and that Massachusetts tends to vote Democratic. However, *Cities Ranked & Rated* presents this material in such a way as to make easy comparisons and to show *leaders and laggards* among the states for each attribute. Most tables are sorted by *attribute*—not by state—a different approach from most reference resources. There are two columns, one for states that *exceed* the U.S. average for an attribute, and one for states *below* that average. This approach will become clearer with examples that follow.

Overall Rankings

Table 4.1 shows a comparison of the average ranks of the metropolitan areas in chapter 5 by state for states that have more than one metro area. The table doesn't rank individual states *per se*, but highlights which states contain areas with consistently better ratings. When viewing the table, keep in mind that ranks for individual cities in the state may differ widely from the averages, and all states have an assortment of high- and low-ranked cities. Note also that these averages are straight arithmetic averages, not weighted by population, so a "good" or "bad" metropolitan area will have equal influence on a state average regardless of size. Comparing to 2004, the states of New Hampshire, New Jersey, and Utah in particular were strong gainers in average area ranking, while Minnesota, Virginia, and New Mexico lost ground.

TABLE 4.1 AVERAGE METRO AREA SCORE & RANK BY STATE

	SORT BY STATE			SORT BY RANK	
STATE	AVERAGE SCORE	AVERAGE RANK	STATE	AVERAGE SCORE	AVERAGE RANK
AK	43.7	280	UT	85.5	26
AL	40.7	274	DE	82.8	32
AR	44.5	261	NH	78.7	50
AZ	59.1	181	OR	79.0	51
CA	51.2	200	CO	77.5	64
CO	77.5	64	ND	72.0	89
CT	48.1	254	WY	67.9	111
DE	82.8	32	NJ	68.0	115
FL	63.6	155	MT	67.1	120
GA	58.7	183	VA	68.2	120
ID	69.1	121	ID	69.1	121
IA	61.5	166	NE	65.9	133
IL	55.2	203	KS	65.8	133
IN	65.6	142	IN	65.6	142
KS	65.8	133	NC	63.3	153
KY	61.8	162	FL	63.6	155
LA	25.6	334	WA	64.2	156
MA	51.9	232	KY	61.8	162
MD	54.9	196	PA	61.2	166
ME	53.5	221	IA	61.5	166
MI	52.5	225	NM	56.1	171
MN	57.8	191	OK	60.2	174
MO	56.4	200	AZ	59.1	181
MS	46.4	224	GA	58.7	183
MT	67.1	120	SD	58.9	186
NC	63.3	153	OH	57.8	190
ND	72.0	89	MN	57.8	191
NE	65.9	133	MD	54.9	196
NH	78.7	50	MO	56.4	200
NJ	68.0	115	CA	51.2	200
NM	56.1	171	WI	56.3	202
NV	56.7	203	NV	56.7	203
NY	46.9	263	IL	55.2	203
OH	57.8	190	ME	53.5	221
OK	60.2	174	TX	51.2	221
OR	79.0	51	SC	49.2	221
PA	61.2	166	MS	46.4	224
SC	49.2	221	MI	52.5	225
SD	58.9	186	MA	51.9	232
TN	45.7	258	CT	48.1	254
TX	51.2	221	TN	45.7	258
UT	85.5	26	AR	44.5	261
VA	68.2	120	NY	46.9	263
WA	64.2	156	AL	40.7	274
WI	56.3	202	AK	43.7	280
WV	40.0	290	WV	40.0	290
WY	67.9	111	LA	25.6	334

Note: For states with more than one metro area, scores represent an arithmetic average of all metro areas in the state.

Population

With regards to population, state characteristics can fall far short of indicating the true nature of a metropolitan area. San Francisco is very different from Bakersfield, California; Detroit from Kalamazoo, Michigan; and Boston from Pittsfield, Massachusetts. But the variations in

TABLE 4.2 2004 STATE POPULATIONS

MOST POPULOUS			LEAST POPULOUS		
STATE	POPULATION	RANK	STATE	POPULATION	RANK
CA	34,501,130	1	SC	4,063,011	26
TX	21,325,018	2	OR	3,472,867	27
NY	19,011,376	3	OK	3,460,097	28
FL	16,396,515	4	CT	3,425,074	29
IL	12,482,301	5	IA	2,923,179	30
PA	12,287,150	6	MS	2,858,029	31
OH	11,373,541	7	KS	2,694,641	32
MI	9,990,817	8	AR	2,692,090	33
NJ	8,484,431	9	UT	2,269,769	34
GA	8,383,915	10	NV	2,106,074	35
NC	8,186,268	11	NM	1,829,146	36
VA	7,187,734	12	WV	1,801,916	37
MA	6,379,304	13	NE	1,713,235	38
IN	6,114,745	14	ID	1,321,006	39
WA	5,987,973	15	ME	1,286,670	40
TN	5,740,021	16	NH	1,259,181	41
MO	5,627,707	17	HI	1,224,398	42
WI	5,401,906	18	RI	1,058,920	43
MD	5,375,136	19	MT	904,433	44
AZ	5,307,331	20	DE	796,195	45
MN	4,972,294	21	SD	756,600	46
LA	4,465,430	22	AK	634,892	47
AL	4,464,356	23	ND	634,448	48
CO	4,417,714	24	VT	613,090	49
KY	4,065,556	25	WY	494,423	50

Total U.S. population: 293,101,811; District of Columbia not included
Source: U.S. Census Bureau

population and especially population growth among states are nonetheless interesting.

Tables 4.2, 4.3, and 4.4 present three state views: population, population density, and population growth. The facts work together to define the states in terms of crowding (or uncrowding) now and in the future. At the same time, population growth figures reveal the aggregate decisions of those who've chosen to move from one state to another, although it doesn't reveal the rationale for their choices or the effects on quality of life that result.

Table 4.2 shows 2004 state population estimates from the U.S. Census Bureau in order from largest to smallest. The population dominance of California, Texas, and New York is no surprise. However, of note is that the top seven states now comprise 48% of the U.S. population, up from 45% in 2001. As will be seen in the growth figures, population is not only concentrating in the more populous states but is also moving south and west.

In terms of crowding, total population figures mean more when looked at against land area, that is, as *population density*, shown in Table 4.3. The smaller East Coast and New England states are generally more dense and crowded, as expected. But much of the impact on quality of life has to do with how areas manage growth and crowding, and some states, most notably New Jersey in recent

TABLE 4.3 2004 STATE POPULATION DENSITY NUMBER OF RESIDENTS PER SQUARE MILE

ABOVE U.S. AVERAGE		BELOW U.S. AVERAGE	
STATE	RESIDENTS	STATE	RESIDENTS
NJ	1175.6	MO	83.5
RI	1041.3	WV	75.4
MA	818.2	VT	67.2
CT	722.9	MN	64.1
MD	572.3	MS	61.9
DE	425.4	AR	52.9
NY	407.2	IA	52.9
FL	322.7	OK	51.3
OH	280.1	AZ	50.6
PA	276.9	CO	44.4
CA	230.2	ME	42.7
IL	228.8	OR	37.5
HI	196.6	KS	33.4
VA	186.5	UT	29.1
MI	178.5	NE	22.7
NC	175.4	NV	21.3
IN	173.9	ID	16.8
GA	153.4	NM	15.7
NH	144.9	SD	10.2
TN	143.2	ND	9.2
SC	139.4	MT	6.4
KY	104.7	WY	5.2
LA	104.2	AK	1.2
WI	101.5		
WA	93.2		
AL	89.3		
TX	86.0		

Note: U.S. average: 83.6 per square mile
Source: U.S. Census Bureau

TABLE 4.4 2004 STATE POPULATION GROWTH

ABOVE U.S. AVERAGE		BELOW U.S. AVERAGE	
STATE	CHANGE FROM 2001	STATE	CHANGE FROM 2001
NV	10.9%	TN	2.8%
AZ	8.2%	MN	2.6%
FL	6.1%	WY	2.4%
ID	5.5%	ME	2.4%
TX	5.5%	CT	2.3%
UT	5.3%	MO	2.3%
DE	4.4%	AR	2.2%
NC	4.3%	RI	2.1%
CO	4.2%	IN	2.0%
GA	4.1%	NE	2.0%
NM	4.1%	WI	2.0%
CA	4.0%	KY	2.0%
VA	3.8%	SD	1.9%
NJ	3.8%	IL	1.9%
WA	3.6%	OK	1.8%
MT	3.6%	MS	1.6%
OR	3.5%	KS	1.5%
MD	3.4%	AL	1.5%
SC	3.3%	VT	1.4%
AK	3.2%	MI	1.2%
NH	3.2%	NY	1.1%
HI	3.1%	LA	1.1%
AL	1.5%	IA	1.1%
		PA	1.0%
		OH	0.8%
		WV	0.7%
		MA	0.6%
		ND	0.0%

Note: U.S. average: 3.1%
Source: U.S. Census Bureau

years, have made great strides to plan land use and manage encroaching development. While some growth management may make the populated areas still *more* dense, the approach creates open space. Likewise, California is shown as no. 11 on the density list. When one realizes that as much as two-thirds of California is made up of uninhabitable desert or mountain areas, the inhabited areas in California become as dense as all but a small handful of states.

Population growth, shown in Table 4.4, is a good indicator of a state's future. Growth has a two-pronged effect: (1) it improves the local economy and (2) it attracts still more people due to the perception of success in the area. But population increases also tend to be a leading indicator of problems—crime, commute times, air quality, cost of living, cost of housing—as well as opportunity.

For a host of reasons, including both physical and tax climate, states such as Nevada and Arizona have seen exceptional growth in recent years, and the growth rates are accelerating. Florida, Idaho, Texas, and Utah round out the top six—the path west and south is obvious. Infrastructure in those states has become sufficient to support a complete set of economic activities, and both

areas have become popular retirement spots. These states tend to have pro-growth attitudes and policies, catering to new business and residential development.

Physical Environment

At the state level, it's hard to make generalizations beyond climate in terms of physical environment. We do feel that the attractiveness of physical setting does influence the quality of life; however, that is mainly a local, not statewide, characteristic. Here we examine and describe the type of climate generally found in each state, though again the climate can vary greatly by specific location, especially in Western states.

Because of local variations in topography and proximity to water—factors that can greatly influence weather conditions—climate is most meaningfully discussed at the metropolitan level. However, climate zones can give an idea of general statewide conditions. Table 4.5 shows the predominant zone in each state where most of the population is located. These zones are not absolute: States like Kansas and Michigan sit across zone boundaries;

TABLE 4.5 MAJOR U.S. CLIMATE ZONES		
LOWER 48 STATES		
CLIMATE TYPE	DESCRIPTION	STATES
Humid Subtropical (no dry season)	Hot, humid summer days are influenced by Gulf of Mexico moisture. Winters are mild. Precipitation arrives as frequent thunderstorms, steady periods of rain in all seasons, and minimal snow.	AR, AL, DE, FL, GA, KY, LA, MS, OK, NC, SC, TN, TX, VA, WV
Humid Continental (hot summer)	Four definite seasons experience changeable weather, with alternating influence between warm, moist, Gulf of Mexico air and cooler, drier air from the northwest. Hot summer periods, often in the 90s, are intermittently moderated by advancing cold fronts. Winters alternate between below freezing and just above freezing, with occasional colder snaps. Precipitation is variable and occasionally heavy during periods of change.	CT, IA, IL, IN, KS, MD, MO, NE, NJ, OH, PA, RI
Humid Continental (warm summer)	Four definite seasons have changeable weather and normally cool days with occasional periods of warmer weather year-round. Summers temperatures rarely exceed 90°F. Winter typically remains below freezing with occasional bitter cold snaps. Summer precipitation arrives mainly as thundershowers. Winter precipitation is mainly snow, which may remain on the ground all season.	MA, ME, MI, MN, ND, NH, NY, SD, VT, WI
Steppe (semiarid)	This higher altitude climate, typically found at elevations greater than 3,000 feet, is characterized by plenty of sunshine and strong diurnal temperature variations. Long, warm, summer days have low humidity; cool evenings often require a jacket. Winters are cool and dry. Precipitation arrives mainly as summer thundershowers and winter snow often associated with advancing frontal systems. Snow may be heavy.	CO, ID, MT, NM, NV, UT, WY
Desert (mostly arid)	Precipitation totals less than 10 inches per year. The air and ground are dry at all times. Temperatures are generally hot, with over 100°F common in summer. Winter highs reach the 60s and 70s, sometimes higher. Low humidity means cool, summer evenings and winter nights often below freezing. Precipitation is scarce and often occurs in scattered, heavy downpours.	AZ
Marine West Coast	Strong and persistent flow of moist marine air from the Pacific governs the climate. Marine influence keeps temperatures in a tight range year-round, with few summer or winter extremes. Persistent moisture flows make clouds and drizzly rain a constant possibility. Occasional stronger storm systems with wind and heavier rain occur. Freezing temperatures and snow are relatively uncommon for the latitude.	OR, WA
Mediterranean	A strong seasonal pattern brings warm, very dry summers followed by cool, wet winters. Virtually all precipitation arrives from November through May, although annual amounts may equal locations in the East or Midwest. Summers are warm near the coast to quite hot inland, with cloudless days and very low humidity the norm. Ocean-borne, rain-free stratus clouds may move in from the Pacific. Winters are the most humid, with frequent cloudy and foggy conditions and drizzle, with an occasional heavier storm.	CA

California, Washington, and Idaho have significant Alpine subzones in mountainous areas; and large states such as Texas stretch across multiple zones.

Economy

This section presents a comparative overview of the private economy (personal income) and public economy (government size) in each state. In this edition we've strengthened our take on state economic drivers by including an analysis of state employment mix, and have refreshed our unique analysis of state dependence on tourism.

Per Capita Income

Table 4.6 shows per capita income by state. As a high-level average, this table illustrates what the typical resident earns per year as gross income. The gap between top and bottom is large but has stayed about the same since 2001, and most states retain a similar position. The numbers reflect each state's job types, education levels, lifestage mix, and more. The large number of retirees living in Florida brings that state's average down, and states with a mainly rural or farm economy tend to be lower. Interestingly, a large number of states are below the

national average, while relatively few are above it, but substantially so. Still, one doesn't necessarily become wealthy by living in Connecticut, Massachusetts, or New Jersey. Cost of living and taxes in those states tend to be high. In fact, awareness of the cost of living in those states serves to drive incomes higher, as people are reluctant to live and work there unless paid more.

Those considering a move should look at the per capita and especially the household incomes in the local metro area, and measure those incomes against the cost of living in that area. These numbers are presented in chapter 5 with each metro area. In addition, we offer the Buying Power Index as a way to appraise whether local incomes, on average, compare favorably with local costs. See the explanation of this unique *Cities Ranked & Rated* calculation in chapter 3.

Size of State Government

Tables 4.7 and 4.8 give a sense of the size of state government, and, reading between the lines, government involvement in income redistribution and daily living in general. Table 4.7 shows total state expenditures, provided by the U.S. Census Bureau and current through 2004. Table 4.8 puts this number into better perspective

TABLE 4.6
2004 PER CAPITA INCOME BY STATE

ABOVE U.S. AVERAGE		BELOW U.S. AVERAGE	
STATE	INCOME	STATE	INCOME
CT	$45,398	VT	$32,770
MA	$41,801	WI	$32,157
NJ	$41,332	HI	$32,150
MD	$39,247	MI	$31,954
NY	$38,228	FL	$31,455
NH	$37,040	ND	$31,398
CO	$36,083	NE	$31,339
DE	$35,961	OH	$31,322
MN	$35,861	SD	$30,856
VA	$35,477	KS	$30,811
WA	$35,299	MO	$30,608
CA	$35,019	IA	$30,569
AK	$34,454	ME	$30,566
IL	$34,351	TX	$30,222
WY	$34,306	IN	$30,094
RI	$33,733	GA	$30,051
NV	$33,405	TN	$30,005
PA	$33,348	OR	$29,971
		NC	$29,246
		AZ	$28,442
		OK	$28,089
		AL	$27,795
		KY	$27,709
		LA	$27,581
		SC	$27,172
		ID	$27,098
		MT	$26,857
		UT	$26,606
		NM	$26,191
		WV	$25,872
		AR	$25,725
		MS	$24,650

Note: U.S. average: $32,925
Source: U.S. Department of Commerce

TABLE 4.7
2004 STATE GOVERNMENT EXPENDITURES
TOTAL ANNUAL EXPENDITURES IN BILLIONS

ABOVE U.S. AVERAGE		BELOW U.S. AVERAGE	
STATE	AMOUNT	STATE	AMOUNT
CA	$204.4	MD	$24.6
NY	$127.5	IN	$23.1
TX	$76.4	MO	$21.6
PA	$57.4	SC	$21.0
OH	$56.4	TN	$21.0
FL	$56.3	CT	$20.7
IL	$51.3	AZ	$19.6
MI	$51.0	KY	$19.1
NJ	$44.9	LA	$18.7
NC	$34.4	AL	$18.5
MA	$32.7	OR	$18.0
WA	$32.6	CO	$17.7
GA	$32.5	OK	$15.1
VA	$29.2	MS	$13.5
MN	$28.9	IA	$13.1
WI	$27.7	AR	$12.1
		KS	$10.9
		NM	$10.7
		UT	$10.3
		WV	$10.0
		AK	$8.1
		NV	$7.8
		HI	$7.6
		NE	$6.8
		ME	$6.7
		RI	$6.0
		ID	$5.4
		NH	$5.3
		DE	$4.9
		MT	$4.4
		VT	$3.9
		WY	$3.2
		ND	$3.1
		SD	$2.9

Note: U.S. average: $27.2 billion per state per year
Source: U.S. Census Bureau

by showing expenditures per capita, which are calculated by dividing by 2004 U.S. Census population estimates.

The tables illustrate a sizable discrepancy between states on budget size, and, by extension, government size. The numbers give an idea of the sheer size of California's budget, which is approaching twice the size of the next largest state, New York, and has risen some 19% since 2001. However, on a per capita basis, California ranks only no. 8, but this too has risen since its no. 12 ranking in 2001. A look at total and per capita expenditures together brings New York to the top of the big government list. Notably, Texas and Florida have the lowest per capita state expenditures. These states have no state income tax, and generally pursue a path of small government and low involvement.

Note: Tables 4.7 and 4.8 reflect expenditures only, not revenues. They do not indicate that state's tax "take," and many of these expenditures are financed by incoming federal funds and directed by federal programs. That is why

(besides the small population) Alaska shows such a high per capita figure, having a proportionally large number of federal programs administered by the state. Other states with low populations and large public assets, like Wyoming and Hawaii, similarly reflect large per capita expenditures.

State Employment Mix

New for this edition, Table 4.9 shows the mix of jobs in each state for what we think are the three most indicative categories: government, manufacturing, and construction. Each category tells a story on its own, and the mix says something about the quality and stability of employment in the state. High levels of government employment suggest stability but also suggest oversized government or an economy that can't get along without government support.

TABLE 4.8 2004 PER CAPITA STATE EXPENDITURES			
ABOVE U.S. AVERAGE		BELOW U.S. AVERAGE	
STATE	AMOUNT	STATE	AMOUNT
AK	$14,250	NJ	$4,670
NY	$5,607	ME	$4,647
WY	$5,547	KY	$4,642
VT	$5,498	PA	$4,642
HI	$5,415	MA	$4,602
CT	$5,350	SC	$4,568
DE	$5,311	MI	$4,476
CA	$5,084	MD	$4,462
MN	$5,053	WI	$4,460
NM	$5,015	OR	$4,450
RI	$4,950	IA	$4,449
WV	$4,941	ND	$4,439
WA	$4,700	AR	$4,430
		UT	$4,359
		OK	$4,314
		MT	$4,263
		OH	$4,210
		MS	$4,198
		LA	$4,157
		AL	$4,101
		NH	$4,093
		NC	$4,080
		IL	$4,055
		KS	$4,020
		ID	$3,961
		VA	$3,955
		NE	$3,929
		CO	$3,890
		SD	$3,786
		MO	$3,771
		GA	$3,749
		IN	$3,724
		TN	$3,597
		AZ	$3,514
		NV	$3,486
		TX	$3,456
		FL	$3,313

Note: U.S. average: $4,683 per person per year
Source: U.S. Census Bureau

TABLE 4.9 STATE EMPLOYMENT MIX PERCENTAGE OF EMPLOYMENT, 2005			
STATE	% GOVERNMENT	% MANUFACTURING	% CONSTRUCTION
AK	26.7%	11.7%	5.9%
AL	18.8%	15.4%	5.4%
AR	17.7%	17.2%	4.5%
AZ	16.9%	7.1%	8.5%
CA	18.5%	10.4%	6.0%
CO	16.9%	5.9%	7.2%
CT	14.7%	11.8%	4.3%
DE	14.2%	8.0%	6.4%
FL	14.2%	5.1%	6.7%
GA	16.6%	11.2%	5.1%
HI	20.5%	2.6%	5.4%
IA	16.9%	15.2%	4.7%
ID	19.5%	10.2%	7.3%
IL	14.5%	11.8%	4.6%
IN	14.6%	19.2%	5.2%
KS	19.5%	13.2%	5.0%
KY	17.2%	14.6%	4.8%
LA	19.9%	7.8%	6.1%
MA	12.9%	9.7%	4.5%
MD	18.4%	5.4%	7.0%
ME	17.5%	9.9%	5.2%
MI	16.0%	15.4%	4.4%
MN	15.5%	12.7%	4.8%
MO	16.1%	11.5%	5.1%
MS	21.5%	10.8%	4.4%
MT	21.3%	4.6%	6.1%
NC	17.1%	14.8%	4.4%
ND	22.3%	7.3%	5.4%
NE	17.4%	13.6%	5.3%
NH	14.7%	12.6%	4.9%
NJ	16.0%	8.1%	4.1%
NM	25.3%	4.4%	6.6%
NV	12.0%	3.8%	10.9%
NY	17.6%	6.8%	3.8%
OH	15.0%	15.1%	4.2%
OK	21.0%	9.4%	4.2%
OR	17.2%	12.3%	5.3%
PA	13.4%	11.9%	4.5%
RI	13.5%	11.1%	4.3%
SC	18.5%	14.4%	6.1%
SD	19.7%	10.1%	5.6%
TN	15.3%	15.1%	4.4%
TX	17.6%	9.2%	5.7%
UT	18.0%	10.3%	7.0%
VA	18.1%	8.2%	6.6%
VT	18.0%	12.1%	5.9%
WA	19.4%	9.7%	6.2%
WI	14.9%	17.6%	4.7%
WV	19.5%	8.4%	5.2%
WY	25.4%	3.5%	7.9%
US Average	17.7%	10.6%	5.6%

Source: U.S. Department of Labor, 2005

High levels of manufacturing imply an economy producing more than it consumes, normally a sign of strength, but in these times, a sign of vulnerability as manufacturing dislocations and offshoring continue. Finally, high levels of construction suggest growth but also suggest vulnerability, as construction is cyclical and highly dependent on borrowed funds. We prefer states with balance across all three components or a bias towards manufacturing.

Dependence on Tourism

Dependence on tourism, shown in Table 4.10, is the total amount spent on travel and tourism divided by the state's total Gross Domestic Product, or GDP. This indicator shows two things. First, states with a high dependence on tourism experience amplified cycles compared to the economy as a whole. That is, when the U.S. and world economies are strong, tourism increases, and the resulting economic boom is usually stronger than experienced in other neighboring economies. On the flip side, economies of tourism-dependent states may suffer proportionately more during downturns, although in some notable cases like California, tourism has actually reduced the shock.

Second, this piece of information reveals something about the nature and quality of life in an area. A fifth of Nevada's economy comes from tourism, and local residents who aren't serving tourists spend most of their time trying to avoid them. Similarly, high levels of tourists add a crowding factor, particularly in certain seasons. Plus, they may cause the arrival of services and amenities, such as motel strips, souvenir shops, wax museums, and other "tourist sprawl," not particularly attractive to local residents. This is not to say that living in a state depending on tourism is all bad—but it is good to know where a state rates.

Taxation

When comparing states, it is important to look at the complete tax picture, and the tax laws are so different and complex among the states that this becomes quite challenging. Different states tax different things at different rates in different ways, so "apples-to-apples" comparisons can be elusive. As an example, the state of Oregon publishes a 9% marginal (applied to every incremental dollar of earnings) tax rate, which appears high and in fact rates the state as the third highest in this category. But on closer examination, one finds that Oregonians can deduct federal income taxes against adjusted gross income (AGI)—the basis for applying the tax—reducing the effective rate to something less than 7% for most residents. Likewise, many states apply a flat rate to every dollar earned, while others, looking to tax the rich and help the poor, apply higher rates to higher levels of income, a concept known as "progressivity." Sales tax rates not only vary by nominal state rate, but many states allow the addition of local surcharges and differ in terms of what's taxed—some tax groceries and drugs, and some do not. Property tax is a patchwork of different rates, basis calculations, and rules.

It's handy to keep the following in mind when comparing state taxes:

- **Assume states are more similar than they appear.** States need to raise revenue, one way or another. Oregon and Montana are noted for high income tax rates, but have no sales tax. Washington and Texas have no income tax, but have among the highest sales tax rates. California has high income and sales taxes, and relatively low property tax rates—but the high basis still raises plenty of tax dollars.

- **Understand that different tax structures affect different lifestyles differently.** Some states aim the bulk of their taxation at income, some at consumption, still others at wealth as rep-

TABLE 4.10 STATE DEPENDENCE ON TOURISM
TOURIST REVENUE AS PERCENT OF STATE GDP, 2004

AT OR ABOVE U.S. AVERAGE		BELOW U.S. AVERAGE	
STATE	PERCENTAGE	STATE	PERCENTAGE
NV	19.4%	IA	4.0%
HI	15.0%	MD	4.0%
MT	7.6%	KY	4.0%
FL	7.2%	AL	4.0%
MS	7.1%	CA	4.0%
WY	7.0%	OK	3.9%
NM	6.7%	KS	3.8%
VT	6.3%	NC	3.8%
LA	6.0%	WV	3.6%
SC	5.3%	CT	3.6%
NH	5.2%	TX	3.6%
SD	5.1%	MN	3.5%
ND	5.1%	NJ	3.5%
ID	5.1%	WI	3.4%
AR	5.0%	RI	3.3%
TN	4.9%	PA	3.2%
ME	4.6%	MI	3.2%
AZ	4.6%	MA	3.1%
CO	4.6%	WA	3.1%
MO	4.5%	NY	3.1%
UT	4.5%	OH	3.0%
OR	4.5%	IN	2.5%
VA	4.3%	DE	2.0%
GA	4.3%		
AK	4.1%		
NE	4.1%		
IL	4.1%		

Note: U.S. average: 4.1%
Source: *The World Almanac and Book of Facts*, 2006

resented by property ownership. A self-employed person with healthy income and modest needs may want to live in Washington or Texas; a retired person with modest income might do better in Oregon or Delaware; and all four states might play out differently depending on their housing situation. A working family might do okay in Connecticut or New Jersey—until they decide to buy an expensive home in a nice neighborhood.

- **Look at total tax burden.** Comparing rates, basis, and progressivity is a good place to start, but to identify the differences—and how a certain lifestyle will be ultimately taxed—examine the total tax burden. See the section below about the District of Columbia study for comparative total tax burdens by state.

- **Research further the states under consideration.** Individual state websites provide access to state information. Income tax booklets and other literature can be ordered. For a comprehensive and well-updated Web source, the Federation of Tax Administrators, a nonprofit organization, is recommended (www.taxadmin.org).

Tax Talk

At the end of the day, taxpayers should always focus on their tax burden, that is, the *amount* of tax dollars they pay. That amount depends on two things: *basis* and *rate*. Basis is the amount on which the tax is paid—adjusted gross income, property value, or amount of a sale. The rate is the percentage applicable to the basis to determine the tax. It's far too common to pay attention to the tax rate alone, and doing so can lead to erroneous conclusions. For example, California's famed Proposition 13 reduced residential property tax rates to a nominal 1 percent, but taken against the high property value *basis,* dollars paid can be as high or higher than other states or counties quoting a higher rate. Further, as many have experienced, property tax rates have stayed fairly constant or even declined in many jurisdictions, but assessors have been busy reassessing, and raising, basis.

State Income Tax

Table 4.11 is sorted by top marginal rates (the top bracket on an income basis), with states above the 6.4% U.S. average marginal rate (for states that have income tax) on the left, and those below that rate on the right. Also shown are the tax rates at the intermediate basis levels of $50,000 and $100,000. These rates and basis levels are based on "married filing jointly" filing status.

To help interpret the table, consider California as an example. The table shows that California has a 9.3% marginal tax rate on a top marginal bracket of $82,953. That is, every dollar earned above $82,953 is taxed at 9.3%. Each state has a different bracket and rate structure below the top rate—for examples, see the marginal rates at $50,000 and $100,000 income levels. (Amounts on the table are $50,001 and $100,001, because many states draw bracket lines at the round figure.) States listed with a top marginal rate but no top income bracket charge a flat rate for all brackets. The progressive states begin to show (New Jersey, at 2.45% for $50,000 rising to 6.37% at $150,000), as do the less progressive (Kentucky, 6% at all but the lowest levels). Colorado, Massachusetts, Michigan, Indiana, Illinois, and Pennsylvania have flat rates—that is, the same percentage applies regardless of income level or bracket. Even this picture may be incomplete because of additional income basis adjustments and tax credits lurking below the surface.

The seven states with no income tax—Alaska, Florida, Nevada, South Dakota, Texas, Washington, and Wyoming—are particularly noteworthy. Among residents of these states, differences in taxes can be thousands of dollars per year for high-income individuals and families. It is advisable to watch for changes in this status.

Finally, we have noted changes in tax rates, brackets, and methodology at the bottom of the table. There is a faint general trend towards reducing state income tax bite, or at least to index brackets to inflation to reduce the likelihood of encountering the highest rates. Naturally, we applaud these actions.

State Sales Tax

Table 4.12 shows comparative *base* sales tax rates—the state-legislated tax to which local levies are often added depending on state law. The table also indicates whether food and medication are included in the tax base—an important consideration especially for large families or older individuals. Keep in mind too that some states tax the sales of big-ticket items, such as automobiles, while others don't. What is *not* shown are the local add-ons, which can be substantial in some otherwise-favorable states such as Colorado. Table 4.13 in the District of Columbia study below sheds some light on this.

The table illustrates that there's no geographic or socio-economic pattern to who has high rates and who does not. In general, states with higher sales tax have lower income tax (exception: California), and the five states with no sales tax (1) face deep internal struggles to keep it that way, and (2) tend to have higher income tax (exceptions: Alaska and New Hampshire). We have seen four states increase sales taxes recently, while none have been lowered. There is also a trend towards using temporary sales tax increases, some over long periods, to finance public works projects like transit, sports stadiums, or downtown redevelopment.

TABLE 4.11 2005 STATE INCOME TAXES
SORTED BY TOP MARGINAL RATE FOR MARRIED FILING JOINTLY

STATE	TOP MARGINAL RATE	TOP INCOME BRACKET	MARGINAL RATE AT AGI $50,001	MARGINAL RATE AT AGI $100,001	STATE	TOP MARGINAL RATE	TOP INCOME BRACKET	MARGINAL RATE AT AGI $50,001	MARGINAL RATE AT AGI $100,001
CA	9.30%	$82,953	8.00%	9.30%	NJ	6.37%	$150,000	2.45%	6.37%
OR	9.00%	$13,000	9.00%	9.00%	GA	6.00%	$10,000	6.00%	6.00%
VT	9.00%	$178,651	7.20%	8.50%	KY	6.00%	$8,000	6.00%	6.00%
IA	8.98%	$57,106	7.92%	8.98%	LA	6.00%	$50,000	6.00%	6.00%
ME	8.50%	$35,450	8.50%	8.50%	MO	6.00%	$9,000	6.00%	6.00%
HI	8.25%	$80,000	7.60%	8.25%	NM	6.00%	$24,001	6.00%	6.00%
NC	8.25%	$200,000	7.00%	7.75%	DE	5.95%	$60,000	5.55%	5.95%
MN	7.85%	$115,511	7.05%	7.05%	VA	5.75%	$17,000	5.75%	5.75%
ID	7.80%	$45,153	7.80%	7.80%	ND	5.54%	$326,481	3.92%	3.92%
NY	7.25%	$40,000	6.85%	6.85%	MA	5.30%	-	5.30%	5.30%
OH	7.18%	$200,000	4.98%	5.69%	AZ	5.04%	$300,000	3.74%	4.72%
AR	7.00%	$28,500	7.00%	7.00%	AL	5.00%	$6,000	5.00%	5.00%
SC	7.00%	$12,651	7.00%	7.00%	CT	5.00%	$20,000	5.00%	5.00%
UT	7.00%	$8,627	7.00%	7.00%	MS	5.00%	$10,000	5.00%	5.00%
MT	6.90%	$3,900	6.90%	6.90%	MD	4.75%	$3,000	4.75%	4.75%
NE	6.84%	$46,750	6.84%	6.84%	CO	4.63%	-	4.63%	4.63%
WI	6.75%	$176,771	6.50%	6.50%	MI	3.90%	-	3.90%	3.90%
OK	6.65%	$10,000	6.65%	6.65%	IN	3.40%	-	3.40%	3.40%
WV	6.50%	$60,000	6.00%	6.50%	PA	3.07%	-	3.07%	3.07%
KS	6.45%	$60,000	6.25%	6.45%	IL	3.00%	-	3.00%	3.00%

STATES WITH INCOME TAX TIED TO BASIS OTHER THAN EARNED INCOME

RI: 25% of federal income tax
TN: 6% on dividends and interest only
NH: 5% on dividends and interest only

STATES WITH NO INCOME TAX

AK, FL, NV, SD, TX, WA, WY

CHANGES 2002–2005

Increased brackets: AR, CA, IA, ID, ME, MN, ND, OR, SC, UT, WI, WV
New top brackets: NJ, NY
New graduated tax system: VT
Graduated rates increased: NE, CT
Graduated rates lowered: OH, MT
Flat rate increased: PA
Flat rate lowered: MI, OK

Notes: U.S. average (among states with income tax) for 2002 is 6.4%. There is fairly wide variation in the base Adjusted Gross Income (AGI) on which the income tax is levied. For example, Oregon allows federal income taxes to be deducted from state AGI, making the effective top marginal rate closer to 7.0%. See local tax documents and websites.

Source: *The World Almanac and Book of Facts, 2006; CCH Tax Guide*

District of Columbia Tax Rates & Tax Burdens Study

There is a lot of interest among state legislators, policy-makers, and tax authorities in comparative impact of taxation. The government of the District of Columbia has gone the distance to research and publish the annual study *Tax Rates and Tax Burdens in the District of Columbia— A Nationwide Comparison* (known here as the "D.C. study"), a hallmark research piece. The study examines tax burdens for the *largest* city in each of the 50 states. The study estimates basis and applies currently researched rates to that basis, including many of the subtleties of sales tax surcharges, income adjustments, and property valuation. If the study has a weakness, it is that it only calibrates on the largest city—the total burden in New York may exceed that in Binghamton because of

a different basis, and often, different rates. As a cautionary note, this information is presented as a way to compare *states*. The situation in a given metropolitan area, or even part of that area, may be different.

State Sales Tax Detail

Table 4.13 from the D.C. study presents a deeper picture of sales tax beyond Table 4.12 by providing a glimpse of local surcharges to the state general sales tax. This table illuminates states that have chosen to push taxation down to a self-determined local level. Colorado, for example, has a low general tax rate of 2.9%, but an additional 3.5% is added in the Denver area, followed by another 0.8% transit levy, bringing the effective rate to 7.2%. In general, the largest cities in a state are most likely to have supplemental sales, school, and especially transit taxes.

TABLE 4.12 STATE SALES TAXES
JANUARY 2006 BASE SALES TAX RATE, BEFORE LOCAL SURCHARGES

ABOVE U.S. AVERAGE		BASIS			BELOW U.S. AVERAGE		BASIS		
STATE	BASE SALES TAX RATE	INCLUDE FOOD?	INCLUDE RX DRUGS?	INCLUDE NON-RX DRUGS?	STATE	BASE SALES TAX RATE	INCLUDE FOOD?	INCLUDE RX DRUGS?	INCLUDE NON-RX DRUGS?
CA	7.25%	No	No	Yes	KS	5.30%	Yes	No	Yes
MS	7.00%	Yes	No	Yes	AR	5.13%	No	No	Yes
RI	7.00%	No	No	No	IA	5.00%	No	No	Yes
TN	7.00%	6.00%	No	Yes	ID	5.00%	Yes	No	Yes
MN	6.50%	No	No	No	MA	5.00%	No	No	Yes
NV	6.50%	No	No	No	MD	5.00%	No	No	No
WA	6.50%	No	No	Yes	ME	5.00%	No	No	Yes
IL	6.25%	1.00%	1.00%	1.00%	ND	5.00%	No	No	Yes
TX	6.25%	No	No	No	NM	5.00%	No	No	Yes
CT	6.00%	No	No	No	SC	5.00%	Yes	No	Yes
FL	6.00%	No	No	No	VA	5.00%	2.5%	No	No
IN	6.00%	No	No	Yes	WI	5.00%	No	No	Yes
KY	6.00%	No	No	Yes	UT	4.75%	Yes	No	Yes
MI	6.00%	No	No	Yes	NC	4.50%	No	No	Yes
NJ	6.00%	No	No	No	OK	4.50%	Yes	No	Yes
PA	6.00%	No	No	No	MO	4.23%	1.23%	No	Yes
VT	6.00%	No	No	No	AL	4.00%	Yes	No	Yes
WV	6.00%		No	Yes	GA	4.00%	No	No	Yes
AZ	5.60%	No	No	Yes	HI	4.00%	Yes	No	Yes
NE	5.50%	No	No	Yes	LA	4.00%	No	No	Yes
OH	5.50%	No	No	Yes	NY	4.00%	No	No	No
					SD	4.00%	Yes	No	Yes
					WY	4.00%	Yes	No	Yes
					CO (*)	2.90%	No	No	Yes

STATES WITH NO SALES TAX

AK, DE, MT, NH, OR

CHANGES SINCE 2003

Increased base rates: AR, OH, VA, VT

Notes: U.S. average (among states with sales tax): 5.34%. For basis, a percentage figure indicates that the item is taxed at the rate shown. (*) indicates local taxes are significant, generally 4% or higher.
Source: Federation of Tax Administrators

Property Tax

With the exception of a few states, property tax defies a broad state-level comparison. Rates can vary widely with few state guidelines, and state exemptions and local assessment can lead to large variations in basis. States like Ohio allow localities to determine residential rates based on the industrial base in the locality; that is, residents pay what the industrial base doesn't. As a result, residents in areas with a lot of industry pay relatively little, while residents in areas with little industry might pay a lot. A different system exists in California, where the rate (determined by Proposition 13) is consistent statewide (save for a few minor local district levies voted in), but the *basis* is determined by purchase price and can vary greatly. This means that in an inflating real estate environment, extreme tax variations exist from one parcel of property to another, depending on when it was last sold. As these examples illustrate, predicting exact property tax liabilities in a specific area is difficult. The property tax rates given in chapter 5 for the metropolitan areas are

a "finger in the air" to determine, comparatively, which way the wind blows.

Table 4.14 from the D.C. study shows tax rates in each of the largest cities, and how the approach to property assessment influences the basis. The rate and the basis work together to determine the total tax, and many localities use a fraction—often a small fraction—of a property's appraised value (or transaction value) to determine tax. The evolution of this system is unclear, but the political desire to avoid the impression of a drastic wealth tax, or recognition that most people only "own" a small portion of their residence net of the mortgage, may have played a part. That said, states with a low assessment level, such as Arizona, Oklahoma, or North Dakota, tend to have higher tax rates. The "effective rate"—both factors taken together—is shown at the far right. Again—every state is different, and a true apples-to-apples comparison is challenging.

What you end up paying in property tax not only depends on rate and basis but also on special exemptions and rate reductions put in place by state or local law. Most

TABLE 4.13 STATE & LOCAL GENERAL SALES TAX RATES BY STATE, 2004
LARGEST CITY, EACH STATE

CITY	STATE	TOTAL RATE	STATE	CITY	COUNTY	SCHOOL	TRANSIT
Memphis	TN	9.25	7.0		2.25		
New Orleans	LA	9.0	4.0	3.5		1.5	
Seattle	WA	8.8	6.5	0.85	0.25		1.2
Chicago	IL	8.75	6.25	1.0	0.75		0.75
New York City	NY	8.625	4.25	4.125			0.25
Los Angeles	CA	8.50	6.25	1.0	0.25		1.0
Oklahoma City	OK	8.375	4.5	3.875			
Houston	TX	8.25	6.25	1.0			1.0
Phoenix	AZ	8.1	5.6	1.8	0.7		
Birmingham	AL	8.0	4.0	3.0	1.0		
Little Rock	AR	7.5	6.0	0.5	1.0		
Charlotte	NC	7.5	4.5		2.5		0.5
Las Vegas	NV	7.5	2.0		3.0	2.25	
Denver	CO	7.2	2.9	3.5			0.8
Jacksonville	FL	7.0	6.0		0.5		0.5
Atlanta	GA	7.0	4.0		1.0	1.0	1.0
Minneapolis	MN	7.0	6.5	0.5			
Jackson	MS	7.0	7.0				
Omaha	NE	7.0	5.5	1.5			
Philadelphia	PA	7.0	6.0		1.0		
Providence	RI	7.0	7.0				
Kansas City	MO	6.975	4.225	1.5	0.750		0.5
Albuquerque	NM	6.75	5.0	1.50	0.25		
Columbus	OH	6.75	6.0		0.5		0.25
Salt Lake City	UT	6.6	4.75	1.0	0.35		0.5
Wichita	KS	6.3	5.3		1.0		
Bridgeport	CT	6.0	6.0				
Des Moines	IA	6.0	5.0			1.0	
Louisville	KY	6.0	6.0				
Detroit	MI	6.0	6.0				
Fargo	ND	6.0	5.0	1.0			
Newark	NJ	6.0	6.0				
Sioux Falls	SD	6.0	4.0	2.0			
Boise	ID	6.0	6.0				
Burlington	VT	6.0	6.0				
Charleston	WV	6.0	6.0				
Cheyenne	WY	6.0	4.0		2.0		
Washington	DC	5.75	5.75				
Milwaukee	WI	5.6	5.0		0.6		
Indianapolis	IN	5.0	5.0				
Boston	MA	5.0	5.0				
Baltimore	MD	5.0	5.0				
Portland	ME	5.0	5.0				
Columbia	SC	5.0	5.0				
Virginia Beach	VA	5.0	4.0	1.0			
Honolulu	HI	4.0	4.0				
Unweighted Average		**6.72**	**5.24**				
Median		**6.75**	**5.24**				

Source: District of Columbia Tax Rates and Tax Burdens Study, 2004

TABLE 4.14 RESIDENTIAL PROPERTY TAX RATES, 2004
LARGEST CITY, EACH STATE

CITY	STATE	NOMINAL RATE PER $100	ASSESSMENT LEVEL	EFFECTIVE RATE PER $100
Houston	TX	$2.99	100.0%	$2.99
Providence	RI	$2.97	100.0%	$2.97
Indianapolis	IN	$2.78	100.0%	$2.78
Bridgeport	CT	$3.90	70.0%	$2.73
Philadelphia	PA	$8.26	32.0%	$2.64
Manchester	NH	$2.64	100.0%	$2.64
Milwaukee	WI	$2.63	96.8%	$2.54
Baltimore	MD	$2.46	100.0%	$2.46
Newark	NJ	$2.43	94.7%	$2.30
Des Moines	IA	$4.56	48.5%	$2.21
Portland	ME	$2.68	82.0%	$2.20
Omaha	NE	$2.21	94.0%	$2.08
Jacksonville	FL	$2.02	98.0%	$1.98
Fargo	ND	$48.41	3.9%	$1.89
Detroit	MI	$6.71	27.8%	$1.86
Columbia	SC	$46.10	4.0%	$1.84
Chicago	IL	$7.88	22.1%	$1.74
New Orleans	LA	$17.40	10.0%	$1.74
Memphis	TN	$7.27	23.8%	$1.73
Boise	ID	$1.78	97.3%	$1.73
Atlanta	GA	$4.29	40.0%	$1.72
Jackson	MS	$17.09	10.0%	$1.71
Anchorage	AK	$1.63	100.0%	$1.63
Sioux Falls	SD	$1.84	85.0%	$1.56
Billings	MT	$1.94	80.0%	$1.55
Burlington	VT	$2.28	67.6%	$1.54
Salt Lake City	UT	$1.53	99.0%	$1.51
Columbus	OH	$4.91	30.3%	$1.49
Portland	OR	$2.23	64.2%	$1.43
Wilmington	DE	$2.71	51.2%	$1.39
Little Rock	AR	$6.90	20.0%	$1.38
Phoenix	AZ	$13.21	10.0%	$1.32
Wichita	KS	$11.43	11.5%	$1.31
Minneapolis	MN	$1.48	88.6%	$1.31
Albuquerque	NM	$3.80	33.3%	$1.27
Los Angeles	CA	$1.25	100.0%	$1.25
Boston	MA	$1.23	100.0%	$1.23
Oklahoma City	OK	$10.91	11.0%	$1.20
Kansas City	MO	$6.30	19.0%	$1.20
New York City	NY	$14.46	8.0%	$1.16
Charlotte	NC	$1.18	95.8%	$1.13
Louisville	KY	$1.23	90.0%	$1.10
Las Vegas	NV	$3.12	35.0%	$1.09
Virginia Beach	VA	$1.22	88.7%	$1.08
Seattle	WA	$1.09	94.1%	$1.03
Washington	DC	$0.96	100.0%	$0.96
Charleston	WV	$1.47	60.0%	$0.88
Birmingham	AL	$6.95	10.0%	$0.70
Cheyenne	WY	$7.11	9.5%	$0.68
Denver	CO	$6.69	8.0%	$0.53
Honolulu	HI	$0.38	100.0%	$0.38
Unweighted Average		**$6.29**	**59.3%**	**$1.62**
Median				**$1.54**

Source: District of Columbia Tax Rates and Tax Burdens Study, 2004

are so-called "homestead" or homeowner exemptions given for owner-occupied residences, but there are more creative versions, such as some set up for older residents, tied to age, with the assumption being that older residents don't use the school system and thus shouldn't fully fund it. The latest release of the D.C. tax study identifies some of these exemptions, which are figured into Table 4.15 and the Estimated Total Tax Burden tables to follow.

Estimated Total Tax Burden

Tables 4.16, 4.17, and 4.18 pull it all together—sales tax, property tax, and state income tax—for the major cities at three different household income levels: $50,000,

TABLE 4.15 PROPERTY TAX EXEMPTIONS & RATE REDUCTIONS			
LARGEST CITY, EACH STATE			
CITY	STATE	EXEMPTION OR TAX REDUCTION AMOUNT	BASIS OF TAX REDUCTION OR EXEMPTION
Birmingham	AL	$4,000	Assessed value-homestead
Little Rock	AR	$300 credit against homestead for homeowners	Tax credit
Phoenix	AZ	35% exemption on school tax rates up to $500	Assessed value
Los Angeles	CA	$7,000 exemption	Assessed value
Washington	DC	$30,000 exemption	Assessed value-homestead
Jacksonville	FL	$25,000 exemption	Assessed value
Atlanta	GA	$15,000 exemption	Assessed value
Honolulu	HI	$40,000 exemption (below age 55)	Assessed value
Boise	ID	50% up to $50,000 exemption	Assessed value-improvements
Chicago	IL	$5,000 exemption	Equalized assessed value
Indianapolis	IN	15% credit and $6,000 exemption	Assessed value-homestead
Wichita	KS	$20,000 school levy exemption	Assessed value
Louisville	KY	$26,800 homestead exemption	Assessed value
Des Moines	IA	$4,850 exemption credit on 1st $4,800 taxable value	Assessed value-homestead
New Orleans	LA	$7,500 exemption	Assessed value
Boston	MA	20% residential exemption	Assessed value
Detroit	MI	Homestead property exempt from basic local school operating millage	Taxable value
Jackson	MS	$300 exemption	Assessed value
Billings	MT	31.4% homestead exemption	Market value
Albuquerque	NM	$2,000 household head exemption, $2,000 veteran exemption	Taxable value
New York City	NY	$30,000	Full value-residential school property taxes
Columbus	OH	12.5% tax rollback	Assessed value
Oklahoma City	OK	$1,000 exemption	Assessed value-homestead
Providence	RI	33.35%	Assessed value
Columbia	SC	30.0% school district credit	Property tax relief fund
Houston	TX	20% exemption on value plus $15,000 exemption	Assessed value-school district only
Salt Lake City	UT	45% residential	Taxable value exemption
Milwaukee	WI	School levy credit: $0.118 per $100 market value	Tax credit; equalized assessed value

Source: District of Columbia Tax Rates and Tax Burdens Study, 2004

$100,000, and $150,000. Each table includes a figure for auto tax, which represents registration, sales taxes at purchase, and property taxes related to the ownership of a car.

From the tables, the relatively high tax burdens for East Coast cities, particularly Bridgeport, Connecticut; Newark, New Jersey; and Providence, Rhode Island, are apparent. Property tax is the category that moves these three to the top. Through these tables one can readily separate the high tax states (Connecticut, Minnesota, and New Jersey) from the low tax states (Florida, South Dakota, and Wyoming). Also interesting is the migration of California (Los Angeles) from 15th place at the $50,000 level to 4th place on the $150,000 income list, reflecting the more progressive nature of the state's tax policy. Indianapolis, on the other hand, is 9th on the $50,000 list while placing 17th on the $150,000 list, indicating a better environment for high income earners.

The average state and local tax burden is about 10% of income, plus or minus 6% depending on the state and individual income situation. For example, it's worth noting the wide disparity between the highest and lowest states at each income level, with tax burdens ranging from 3% to 4% in the lowest tax states to over 15% in the highest. That disparity makes total state and local tax burden

worth a look, especially for higher income individuals and families.

Note: The figures presented in Tables 4.13 through 4.18 may not agree with those presented at the metropolitan area level in chapter 5, due to local variation in tax laws and differences in the timing of collection of tax data.

Education

In most circles education is taken to be a state's first responsibility. Indeed, education is the largest item on the whole in state budgets, running about 40% of expenditures on average. Numerous published studies reference aspects of the education process, such as expenditures, pupil-teacher ratios, class size, square feet of facilities, and library books. Chapter 5 includes data for some of these attributes at the metro area level.

Brought on to a large degree by the 2002 No Child Left Behind Act, considerable energy is now aimed at academic achievement and the performance metrics and testing required to measure it. This area continues to evolve rapidly. Measuring educational results is, in practice, extremely difficult, and while we feel the intentions of the 2002 act are good, the implementation thus far leaves a

TABLE 4.16 ESTIMATED TAX BURDEN, $50,000 TOTAL HOUSEHOLD INCOME, 2004
For a hypothetical family of four
LARGEST CITY, EACH STATE

RANK	CITY	STATE	TAXES				BURDEN	
			INCOME	PROPERTY	SALES	AUTO	AMOUNT	PERCENT
1	Philadelphia	PA	$3,146	$2,131	$728	$232	$6,237	12.5%
2	New York City	NY	$2,479	$2,579	$915	$171	$6,143	12.3%
3	Newark	NJ	$616	$4,448	$731	$168	$5,962	11.9%
4	Bridgeport	CT	$500	$4,052	$811	$456	$5,819	11.6%
5	Baltimore	MD	$2,242	$2,398	$824	$217	$5,681	11.4%
6	Providence	RI	$967	$3,128	$781	$612	$5,489	11.0%
7	Portland	OR	$3,004	$2,203	$0	$191	$5,398	10.8%
8	Detroit	MI	$2,564	$1,749	$727	$212	$5,253	10.5%
9	Indianapolis	IN	$1,892	$2,390	$809	$129	$5,221	10.4%
10	Milwaukee	WI	$1,612	$2,484	$766	$245	$5,107	10.2%
11	Portland	ME	$1,340	$2,731	$621	$264	$4,956	9.9%
12	Atlanta	GA	$1,381	$2,366	$971	$231	$4,949	9.9%
13	Chicago	IL	$1,145	$2,303	$1,108	$310	$4,865	9.7%
14	Louisville	KY	$2,949	$908	$764	$232	$4,854	9.7%
15	Los Angeles	CA	$154	$3,380	$849	$336	$4,719	9.4%
16	Columbus	OH	$2,261	$1,394	$835	$224	$4,715	9.4%
17	Boston	MA	$1,993	$2,124	$391	$206	$4,713	9.4%
18	Salt Lake City	UT	$1,938	$1,414	$962	$294	$4,607	9.2%
19	Washington	DC	$2,185	$1,342	$811	$245	$4,584	9.2%
20	Des Moines	IA	$1,466	$1,702	$908	$334	$4,410	8.8%
21	Kansas City	MO	$1,983	$1,093	$961	$350	$4,387	8.8%
22	Omaha	NE	$1,169	$1,929	$944	$284	$4,325	8.7%
23	Charlotte	NC	$1,770	$1,339	$857	$249	$4,215	8.4%
24	Minneapolis	MN	$1,495	$1,684	$748	$233	$4,160	8.3%
25	Oklahoma City	OK	$1,741	$1,020	$1,132	$204	$4,096	8.2%
26	Burlington	VT	$974	$2,197	$722	$180	$4,073	8.1%
27	Virginia Beach	VA	$1,695	$1,252	$832	$277	$4,056	8.1%
28	Little Rock	AR	$1,576	$999	$1,151	$296	$4,021	8.0%
29	Honolulu	HI	$1,923	$1,138	$601	$280	$3,941	7.9%
30	Birmingham	AL	$2,303	$405	$979	$247	$3,933	7.9%
31	Charleston	WV	$1,697	$935	$854	$373	$3,858	7.7%
32	Albuquerque	NM	$963	$1,643	$1,069	$165	$3,840	7.7%
33	Jackson	MS	$1,002	$1,228	$1,074	$498	$3,802	7.6%
34	Boise	ID	$1,429	$1,142	$865	$234	$3,670	7.3%
35	Columbia	SC	$1,490	$1,094	$689	$367	$3,641	7.3%
36	New Orleans	LA	$1,225	$1,044	$1,177	$162	$3,607	7.2%
37	Fargo	ND	$577	$2,046	$737	$206	$3,566	7.1%
38	Seattle	WA	$0	$2,146	$1,038	$377	$3,561	7.1%
39	Manchester	NH	$0	$3,015	$316	$187	$3,518	7.0%
40	Wilmington	DE	$1,757	$1,534	$0	$170	$3,461	6.9%
41	Denver	CO	$1,289	$916	$911	$279	$3,395	6.8%
42	Wichita	KS	$1,364	$790	$842	$338	$3,335	6.7%
43	Phoenix	AZ	$809	$1,100	$1,205	$207	$3,321	6.6%
44	Houston	TX	$0	$2,041	$1,063	$190	$3,295	6.6%
45	Memphis	TN	$0	$1,668	$1,339	$213	$3,219	6.4%
46	Sioux Falls	SD	$0	$1,541	$1,083	$201	$2,826	5.7%
47	Billings	MT	$1,290	$1,181	$0	$299	$2,770	5.5%
48	Las Vegas	NV	$0	$1,485	$751	$361	$2,596	5.2%
49	Anchorage	AK	$0	$2,055	$0	$86	$2,142	4.3%
50	Jacksonville	FL	$0	$880	$859	$216	$1,956	3.9%
51	Cheyenne	WY	$0	$739	$989	$210	$1,938	3.9%
Average			$1,531	$1,775	$874	$260	$4,161	8.3%
Median			$1,381	$1,643	$842	$233	$4,073	8.1%

Source: District of Columbia Tax Rates and Tax Burdens Study, 2004

lot to be desired. Pundits are quick to point out the lack of funding to go along with the additional assessment and bureaucracy created around it. We see bigger problems. One is the wide variation in testing standards among states. Another is the unleashing of a variety of unintended consequences including "teaching to the test" and working hardest to raise performance of the best students, not the weakest, in order to manipulate results. A third is

TABLE 4.17 ESTIMATED TAX BURDEN, $100,000 TOTAL HOUSEHOLD INCOME, 2004
For a hypothetical family of four
LARGEST CITY, EACH STATE

RANK	CITY	STATE	TAXES				BURDEN	
			INCOME	PROPERTY	SALES	AUTO	AMOUNT	PERCENT
1	Bridgeport	CT	$4,158	$7,699	$1,540	$1,154	$14,551	14.6%
2	New York City	NY	$7,239	$5,212	$1,738	$302	$14,491	14.5%
3	Philadelphia	PA	$7,291	$4,050	$1,383	$410	$13,133	13.1%
4	Providence	RI	$2,843	$5,944	$1,484	$1,912	$12,183	12.2%
5	Baltimore	MD	$5,527	$4,557	$1,565	$392	$12,041	12.0%
6	Newark	NJ	$1,865	$8,451	$1,388	$310	$12,014	12.0%
7	Portland	ME	$4,766	$5,189	$1,181	$754	$11,890	11.9%
8	Los Angeles	CA	$2,781	$6,501	$1,613	$851	$11,745	11.7%
9	Portland	OR	$7,036	$4,185	$0	$334	$11,555	11.6%
10	Atlanta	GA	$3,715	$5,074	$1,844	$629	$11,262	11.3%
11	Milwaukee	WI	$4,471	$4,803	$1,455	$437	$11,167	11.2%
12	Detroit	MI	$5,838	$3,323	$1,382	$467	$11,010	11.0%
13	Washington	DC	$5,791	$2,810	$1,541	$412	$10,553	10.6%
14	Indianapolis	IN	$4,092	$4,678	$1,538	$227	$10,535	10.5%
15	Columbus	OH	$5,866	$2,650	$1,587	$402	$10,504	10.5%
16	Louisville	KY	$6,358	$2,021	$1,452	$562	$10,393	10.4%
17	Omaha	NE	$3,950	$3,665	$1,793	$759	$10,166	10.2%
18	Boston	MA	$4,643	$4,036	$778	$612	$10,068	10.1%
19	Charlotte	NC	$5,107	$2,545	$1,628	$733	$10,013	10.0%
20	Chicago	IL	$2,523	$4,731	$2,104	$576	$9,934	9.9%
21	Columbia	SC	$4,381	$3,159	$1,310	$972	$9,821	9.8%
22	Salt Lake City	UT	$4,711	$2,686	$1,827	$585	$9,808	9.8%
23	Des Moines	IA	$3,777	$3,433	$1,726	$738	$9,673	9.7%
24	New Orleans	LA	$3,808	$3,157	$2,236	$470	$9,671	9.7%
25	Boise	ID	$4,580	$2,947	$1,644	$423	$9,595	9.6%
26	Minneapolis	MN	$4,348	$3,260	$1,422	$418	$9,449	9.4%
27	Little Rock	AR	$4,389	$2,167	$2,187	$698	$9,441	9.4%
28	Kansas City	MO	$4,665	$2,076	$1,826	$868	$9,435	9.4%
29	Charleston	WV	$4,857	$1,776	$1,622	$884	$9,138	9.1%
30	Jackson	MS	$3,114	$2,603	$2,041	$1,303	$9,061	9.1%
31	Albquerque	NM	$3,513	$3,191	$2,031	$297	$9,031	9.0%
32	Honolulu	HI	$4,973	$2,296	$1,141	$501	$8,911	8.9%
33	Burlington	VT	$2,988	$4,174	$1,371	$325	$8,859	8.9%
34	Virginia Beach	VA	$4,142	$2,379	$1,580	$621	$8,723	8.7%
35	Oklahoma City	OK	$4,451	$1,692	$2,150	$377	$8,670	8.7%
36	Wichita	KS	$3,934	$1,738	$1,600	$846	$8,118	8.1%
37	Birmingham	AL	$4,663	$1,014	$1,860	$569	$8,106	8.1%
38	Wilmington	DE	$4,618	$2,914	$0	$299	$7,831	7.8%
39	Denver	CO	$3,346	$1,740	$1,730	$793	$7,609	7.6%
40	Phoenix	AZ	$2,144	$2,540	$2,290	$608	$7,582	7.6%
41	Billings	MT	$4,476	$2,244	$0	$759	$7,479	7.5%
42	Fargo	ND	$1,769	$3,888	$1,401	$354	$7,412	7.4%
43	Seattle	WA	$0	$4,078	$1,971	$882	$6,932	6.9%
44	Manchester	NH	$0	$5,729	$601	$514	$6,844	6.8%
45	Houston	TX	$0	$4,153	$2,020	$345	$6,518	6.5%
46	Memphis	TN	$30	$3,169	$2,545	$387	$6,130	6.1%
47	Sioux Falls	SD	$0	$2,928	$2,057	$364	$5,349	5.3%
48	Las Vegas	NV	$0	$2,821	$1,426	$710	$4,957	5.0%
49	Jacksonville	FL	$0	$2,573	$1,633	$382	$4,588	4.6%
50	Anchorage	AK	$0	$3,905	$0	$158	$4,063	4.1%
51	Cheyenne	WY	$0	$1,404	$1,879	$667	$3,951	4.0%
Average			$4,171	$3,529	$1,662	$595	$9,254	9.3%
Median			$4,142	$3,169	$1,600	$562	$9,449	9.4%

Source: District of Columbia Tax Rates and Tax Burdens Study, 2004

TABLE 4.18 ESTIMATED TAX BURDEN, $150,000 TOTAL HOUSEHOLD INCOME, 2004
For a hypothetical family of four

			TAXES				BURDEN	
RANK	CITY	STATE	INCOME	PROPERTY	SALES	AUTO	AMOUNT	PERCENT
1	New York City	NY	$12,302	$7,553	$2,469	$310	$22,635	15.1%
2	Bridgeport	CT	$6,925	$10,941	$2,189	$1,310	$21,364	14.2%
3	Philadelphia	PA	$10,936	$5,755	$1,965	$421	$19,077	12.7%
4	Los Angeles	CA	$6,516	$9,275	$2,292	$965	$19,048	12.7%
5	Newark	NJ	$4,487	$12,009	$1,973	$316	$18,785	12.5%
6	Providence	RI	$5,450	$8,447	$2,109	$2,329	$18,335	12.2%
7	Portland	ME	$8,239	$7,374	$1,678	$830	$18,120	12.1%
8	Baltimore	MD	$8,668	$6,476	$2,224	$402	$17,769	11.8%
9	Portland	OR	$11,271	$5,947	$0	$344	$17,562	11.7%
10	Atlanta	GA	$6,013	$7,482	$2,621	$724	$16,839	11.2%
11	Milwaukee	WI	$7,305	$6,865	$2,068	$449	$16,687	11.1%
12	Columbus	OH	$10,026	$3,765	$2,255	$412	$16,458	11.0%
13	Detroit	MI	$9,063	$4,723	$1,963	$628	$16,377	10.9%
14	Washington	DC	$9,612	$4,114	$2,189	$412	$16,327	10.9%
15	Omaha	NE	$6,994	$5,207	$2,547	$877	$15,626	10.4%
16	Louisville	KY	$9,830	$3,010	$2,063	$632	$15,536	10.4%
17	Indianapolis	IN	$6,292	$6,712	$2,185	$234	$15,423	10.3%
18	Columbia	SC	$7,247	$4,994	$1,861	$1,113	$15,215	10.1%
19	Boise	ID	$7,662	$4,552	$2,337	$433	$14,984	10.0%
20	Charlotte	NC	$8,178	$3,616	$2,314	$806	$14,914	9.9%
21	Boston	MA	$7,293	$5,735	$1,124	$681	$14,833	9.9%
22	New Orleans	LA	$6,102	$5,036	$3,177	$486	$14,802	9.9%
23	Minneapolis	MN	$7,384	$4,709	$2,021	$414	$14,528	9.7%
24	Little Rock	AR	$7,329	$3,206	$3,108	$780	$14,423	9.6%
25	Chicago	IL	$3,916	$6,888	$2,990	$585	$14,380	9.6%
26	Des Moines	IA	$5,993	$4,971	$2,452	$802	$14,219	9.5%
27	Salt Lake City	UT	$7,238	$3,816	$2,562	$594	$14,210	9.5%
28	Kansas City	MO	$7,527	$2,950	$2,595	$987	$14,059	9.4%
29	Burlington	VT	$5,729	$5,932	$1,949	$333	$13,943	9.3%
30	Charleston	WV	$8,105	$2,523	$2,305	$989	$13,922	9.3%
31	Albuquerque	NM	$6,131	$4,567	$2,886	$304	$13,887	9.3%
32	Honlulu	HI	$8,239	$3,327	$1,621	$513	$13,700	9.1%
33	Oklahoma City	OK	$7,055	$2,939	$3,056	$371	$13,421	8.9%
34	Jackson	MS	$5,199	$3,826	$2,900	$1,484	$13,409	8.9%
35	Virginia Beach	VA	$6,559	$3,381	$2,246	$678	$12,863	8.6%
36	Wichita	KS	$6,654	$2,580	$2,274	$921	$12,429	8.3%
37	Billings	MT	$8,388	$3,189	$0	$796	$12,373	8.2%
38	Wilmington	DE	$7,636	$4,141	$0	$308	$12,085	8.1%
39	Birmingham	AL	$6,846	$1,556	$2,643	$632	$11,677	7.8%
40	Phoenix	AZ	$3,625	$3,821	$3,254	$671	$11,371	7.6%
41	Fargo	ND	$3,316	$5,525	$1,991	$363	$11,194	7.5%
42	Denver	CO	$5,304	$2,473	$2,459	$862	$11,098	7.4%
43	Seattle	WA	$0	$5,796	$2,801	$984	$9,581	6.4%
44	Manchester	NH	$10	$8,141	$853	$570	$9,574	6.4%
45	Houston	TX	$0	$6,030	$2,763	$352	$9,145	6.1%
46	Memphis	TN	$150	$4,503	$3,616	$395	$8,664	5.8%
47	Sioux Falls	SD	$0	$4,161	$2,924	$372	$7,457	5.0%
48	Las Vegas	NV	$0	$4,009	$2,027	$771	$6,806	4.5%
49	Jacksonville	FL	$0	$4,077	$2,320	$393	$6,791	4.5%
50	Anchorage	AK	$0	$5,550	$0	$161	$5,711	3.8%
51	Cheyenne	WY	$0	$1,996	$2,671	$744	$5,410	3.6%
Average			$6,926	$5,101	$2,359	$652	$13,903	9.3%
Median			$6,846	$4,709	$2,274	$594	$14,219	9.5%

Source: District of Columbia Tax Rates and Tax Burdens Study, 2004

State Taxes & College Costs

Everyone knows about the rapidly rising costs of college. And anyone familiar with the federal tax system knows that helping taxpayers finance college education is a top federal priority, leading to an assortment of tax credits and deductions and tax-preferred savings tools such as education IRAs and so-called qualified "529" savings plans. But what about the states? Which states seem to care the most about helping their residents finance college costs? It turns out that there are breaks, and they vary all over the map. A number of states not only exempt 529 plan gains from taxation (as does the federal government) but also allow residents to deduct their contributions. There are some 31 states allowing some deduction, adding to the seven that have no state income tax in the first place. The breakdown is interesting:

- States allowing deductions for contributions to their own 529 plan:
  - Unlimited deduction: CO, NM, SC, WV
  - Deduction with large limits: ($5–$10K): AR, CT, IL, MI, MS, MO, NY, OK, PA
  - Deduction with lower limits: (0–$5K): DC, GA, ID, IA, KS, LA, ME, MD, MT, NE, NC, OH, OR, RI, UT, WI
  - Credit: IN, VT
  - No state income tax: AK, FL, NV, NH, SD, TN, TX
- States allowing deductions for *any* 529 plan: PA, ME, KS

Our hats go off to those states with large deductions and especially to Pennsylvania, which permits a large deduction for funds going into any state plan. And we wonder when some of the others—California, Minnesota, New Jersey, and Massachusetts, for example—might get on the bandwagon.

overemphasis on facts and scores at the expense of less tangible educational processes and subjects like art and music.

In short, the process is still maturing and evolving. We take a closer look at No Child Left Behind, including its results and shortcomings, in our *Best Places to Raise Your Family* (Wiley Publishing, 2006) and also encourage a look at GreatSchools.net (www.greatschools.net), a website devoted to collecting and tabulating school-level test score information.

Here in *Cities Ranked & Rated*, we examine some of the higher level outputs of the educational process at the state level, including statewide SAT scores, aggregate testing from the National Assessment of Educational Progress, and implementation status for No Child Left Behind programs and processes.

SAT Scores

The SAT, or Scholastic Aptitude Test, administered by the College Board, is viewed as a standard bellwether for college admissions skills and aptitude. For many, it reflects the degree of preparation that students receive through

their primary and secondary education. However, the College Board itself warns against comparing states by score, as important differences exist in the way tests are used and administered among states. Some state schools require the SAT, while others require its cousin, the ACT (American College Test), which is generally considered a less stringent test and is seldom used by more selective schools. For that and other reasons, participation in the SAT can vary greatly by state. In states that depend on the ACT, the SAT is taken mainly by students seeking admission to more selective schools. As a result, states emphasizing the ACT may achieve higher SAT test scores because fewer students take it and those that do tend to be more advanced.

Table 4.19 shows verbal, math, and composite (verbal plus math) scores in 1990 and 2005, and the change in composite scores during this period. The table is sorted in descending order of percentage growth in the composite score. Considering the College Board advice, readers should (1) focus on change in scores and (2) make sure participation is comparable among states. Change in scores is less significant in states with lower participation. States

	1990			2005				
STATE	**VERBAL**	**MATH**	**COMPOSITE**	**VERBAL**	**MATH**	**COMPOSITE**	**CHANGE, 1990 TO 2005**	**% GRADS TAKING SAT**
IL	542	547	1089	594	605	1199	10.1%	10%
MO	548	541	1089	588	588	1176	8.0%	7%
MI	529	534	1063	568	579	1147	7.9%	10%
WI	552	559	1111	592	599	1191	7.2%	6%
MN	552	558	1110	592	597	1189	7.1%	11%
NC	478	470	948	499	511	1010	6.5%	74%
SC	475	467	942	494	499	993	5.4%	64%
CO	533	534	1067	560	560	1120	5.0%	26%
MA	503	498	1001	520	527	1047	4.6%	86%
GA	478	473	951	497	496	993	4.4%	75%
AL	545	534	1079	567	559	1126	4.4%	10%
IN	486	486	972	504	508	1012	4.1%	66%
WA	513	511	1024	532	534	1066	4.1%	56%
KS	566	563	1129	585	588	1173	3.9%	9%
VT	507	493	1000	521	517	1038	3.8%	67%
LA	551	537	1088	565	562	1127	3.6%	8%
AR	545	532	1077	563	552	1115	3.5%	6%
MS	552	528	1080	564	554	1118	3.5%	4%
OK	553	542	1095	570	563	1133	3.5%	7%
VA	501	496	997	516	514	1030	3.3%	67%
ND	579	578	1157	590	605	1195	3.3%	4%
OH	526	522	1048	539	543	1082	3.2%	29%
CT	506	496	1002	517	517	1034	3.2%	88%
TN	558	544	1102	572	563	1135	3.0%	16%
OR	515	509	1024	526	528	1054	2.9%	59%
NE	559	562	1121	574	579	1153	2.9%	8%
KY	548	541	1089	561	559	1120	2.8%	12%
IA	584	588	1172	596	608	1204	2.7%	5%
NJ	495	498	993	503	517	1020	2.7%	85%
US AVG	**500**	**501**	**1001**	**508**	**520**	**1028**	**2.7%**	**49%**
AK	514	501	1015	523	519	1042	2.7%	52%
SD	580	570	1150	589	589	1178	2.4%	5%
CA	494	508	1002	504	522	1026	2.4%	50%
NY	489	496	985	497	511	1008	2.3%	92%
ME	501	490	991	509	505	1014	2.3%	75%
RI	498	488	986	503	505	1008	2.2%	72%
NH	518	510	1028	525	525	1050	2.1%	81%
HI	480	505	985	514	490	1004	1.9%	61%
ID	542	524	1066	544	542	1086	1.9%	21%
MD	506	502	1008	511	515	1026	1.8%	71%
PA	497	490	987	501	503	1004	1.7%	75%
TX	490	489	979	493	502	995	1.6%	54%
AZ	521	520	1041	526	530	1056	1.4%	33%
WY	534	538	1072	544	543	1087	1.4%	12%
FL	495	493	988	498	498	996	0.8%	65%
NM	554	546	1100	558	547	1105	0.5%	13%
UT	566	555	1121	566	557	1123	0.2%	7%
WV	520	514	1034	523	511	1034	0.0%	20%
NV	511	511	1022	508	513	1021	−0.1%	39%
DE	510	496	1006	503	502	1005	−0.1%	74%
MT	540	542	1082	540	540	1080	−0.2%	31%

TABLE 4.19 SAT SCORES BY STATE
VERBAL, MATH, COMPOSITE, 1990 & 2005, SORTED BY PERCENT CHANGE

Source: The College Board

TABLE 4.20 MATH & READING ACHIEVEMENT BY STATE
PERCENT OF STUDENTS SCORING AT OR ABOVE BASIC PROFICIENCY
Sorted by state

STATE	MATH GRADE 4 2000	2005	READING GRADE 4 2000	2005	MATH GRADE 8 2000	2005	READING GRADE 8 2000	2005
AK	na	77	na	53	na	69	na	70
AL	57	66	56	53	52	53	67	63
AR	56	77	54	58	52	69	68	70
AZ	58	70	51	52	62	64	72	65
CA	52	71	48	50	52	57	63	60
CO	na	81	69	69	na	70	76	75
CT	77	84	76	71	72	70	81	74
DE	na	84	53	73	na	72	64	80
FL	na	82	53	65	na	65	67	66
GA	58	76	54	58	55	62	68	67
HI	55	73	45	56	52	53	59	88
ID	71	86	na	69	71	73	na	76
IL	66	74	na	62	68	68	na	75
IA	78	85	67	67	na	75	na	79
IN	78	84	na	64	76	74	na	73
KS	76	88	70	66	77	77	81	78
KY	60	75	62	65	63	64	74	75
LA	57	74	44	53	48	59	63	64
MA	79	91	70	80	76	78	79	83
MD	61	79	58	65	65	66	70	69
ME	74	84	72	71	76	74	83	81
MI	72	79	62	63	70	68	na	73
MN	78	88	69	71	80	79	81	80
MO	72	79	61	67	67	68	75	76
MS	45	69	47	48	41	52	62	60
MT	73	85	72	71	80	80	83	82
NC	76	83	58	62	70	72	74	68
ND	75	89	na	72	77	81	na	83
NE	67	80	na	68	74	75	na	80
NH	na	89	75	74	na	77	na	80
NJ	na	86	na	68	na	74	na	80
NM	51	65	51	51	50	53	71	62
NV	60	72	51	52	58	60	70	63
NY	67	81	62	69	68	70	76	75
OH	73	84	na	69	75	74	na	78
OK	69	79	66	60	64	63	80	72
OR	65	80	58	62	71	72	78	74
PA	na	82	na	72	na	69	na	77
RI	67	76	64	62	64	63	76	71
SC	60	81	53	57	55	71	66	67
SD	na	86	na	80	na	70	na	82
TN	60	74	57	59	53	61	71	71
TX	77	87	59	64	68	72	74	69
UT	70	83	62	68	68	71	77	73
VA	73	83	62	72	67	75	78	78
VT	73	87	na	72	75	78	na	79
WA	na	84	64	70	na	75	76	75
WI	na	84	72	67	na	76	79	77
WV	68	75	60	61	62	60	75	67
WY	73	87	64	71	79	76	76	81
US AVG	67	79	58	62	65	68	71	71

Source: National Assessment of Education Progress (NAEP)–National Center for Education Statistics

TABLE 4.21 MATH & READING ACHIEVEMENT BY GRADE 8 MATH PROFICIENCY
PERCENT OF STUDENTS SCORING AT OR ABOVE BASIC PROFICIENCY
Sorted by grade 8 math proficiency

STATE	MATH GRADE 4 2000	2005	READING GRADE 4 2000	2005	MATH GRADE 8 2000	2005	READING GRADE 8 2000	2005
ND	75	89	na	72	77	81	na	83
MT	73	85	72	71	80	80	83	82
MN	78	88	69	71	80	79	81	80
MA	79	91	70	80	76	78	79	83
VT	73	87	na	72	75	78	na	79
KS	76	88	70	66	77	77	81	78
NH	na	89	75	74	na	77	na	80
WI	na	84	72	67	na	76	79	77
WY	73	87	64	71	79	76	76	81
IA	78	85	67	67	na	75	na	79
NE	67	80	na	68	74	75	na	80
VA	73	83	62	72	67	75	78	78
WA	na	84	64	70	na	75	76	75
IN	78	84	na	64	76	74	na	73
ME	74	84	72	71	76	74	83	81
NJ	na	86	na	68	na	74	na	80
OH	73	84	na	69	75	74	na	78
ID	71	86	na	69	71	73	na	76
DE	na	84	53	73	na	72	64	80
NC	76	83	58	62	70	72	74	68
OR	65	80	58	62	71	72	78	74
TX	77	87	59	64	68	72	74	69
SC	60	81	53	57	55	71	66	67
UT	70	83	62	68	68	71	77	73
CO	na	81	69	69	na	70	76	75
CT	77	84	76	71	72	70	81	74
NY	67	81	62	69	68	70	76	75
SD	na	86	na	80	na	70	na	82
AK	na	77	na	53	na	69	na	70
AR	56	77	54	58	52	69	68	70
PA	na	82	na	72	na	69	na	77
IL	66	74	na	62	68	68	na	75
MI	72	79	62	63	70	68	na	73
MO	72	79	61	67	67	68	75	76
US AVG	67	79	58	62	65	68	71	71
MD	61	79	58	65	65	66	70	69
FL	na	82	53	65	na	65	67	66
AZ	58	70	51	52	62	64	72	65
KY	60	75	62	65	63	64	74	75
OK	69	79	66	60	64	63	80	72
RI	67	76	64	62	64	63	76	71
GA	58	76	54	58	55	62	68	67
TN	60	74	57	59	53	61	71	71
NV	60	72	51	52	58	60	70	63
WV	68	75	60	61	62	60	75	67
LA	57	74	44	53	48	59	63	64
CA	52	71	48	50	52	57	63	60
AL	57	66	56	53	52	53	67	63
HI	55	73	45	56	52	53	59	88
NM	51	65	51	51	50	53	71	62
MS	45	69	47	48	41	52	62	60

Source: National Assessment of Education Progress (NAEP)–National Center for Education Statistics

TABLE 4.22 NO CHILD LEFT BEHIND IMPLEMENTATION STATUS, 2005
STATES NOT IN FULL COMPLIANCE WITH ACADEMIC STANDARDS OR BASIC ASSESSMENT REQUIREMENTS

	READING STANDARDS	MATH STANDARDS	SCIENCE STANDARDS	ANNUAL READING ASSESSMENTS	ANNUAL MATH ASSESSMENTS	ANNUAL SCIENCE ASSESSMENTS	REPORT CARD
IA				P	P	P	P
MI	P	P					
NE	P	P					P
NH			P			P	
NY	P						P
PA	P	P				P	
RI						P	P
WI	P	P					

STATES WITH STANDARDS & ASSESSMENTS IN PLACE, BUT HAVE REPORT CARD ONLY PARTIALLY IN PLACE

AL	CA	ID	MN	NJ	SC	UT
AR	GA	MA	MT	NM	SD	VT
AZ	HI	ME	ND	OK	TX	WV

Source: Education Commission of the States

TABLE 4.23 NO CHILD LEFT BEHIND IMPLEMENTATION COMPLIANCE, 2005
STATES FULLY IN COMPLIANCE WITH ACADEMIC STANDARDS & BASIC ASSESSMENT REQUIREMENTS

AK	IL	MD	OH	VA
CO	IN	MS	OR	WA
CT	KS	NC	SD	WY
FL	KY	NV	TN	

Source: Education Commission of the States

such as North and South Carolina, Georgia, Indiana, and Washington have high participation, while South Dakota, Wisconsin, and Tennessee are low. As such, the composite score growth in North and South Carolina scores are probably most telling.

National Assessment of Educational Process

Since 1969, each year thousands of schools across the country administer federally standardized tests to 4th, 8th, and 12th graders to measure academic progress in a variety of subjects, most notably math, reading, and science. Unlike No Child Left Behind, where the objective is to measure specific school performance and performance of specific student groups, the National Assessment of Educational Process (NAEP) strives for a higher-level educational assessment. As such, NAEP scores are probably more telling about a state educational performance, while No Child Left Behind tells more about a specific school or neighborhood in which the school is located. As such, we now include NAEP results in *Cities Ranked & Rated*.

Tables 4.20 and 4.21 show NAEP scores by state in a way that allows comparison of scores in 2000 and 2005. Table 4.20 sorts results by state. Table 4.21 sorts on 8th-grade math proficiency, which was found to be highest in North Dakota, Montana, and Minnesota. Overall U.S. figures show growth in math proficiency, while results in reading proficiency have been mixed. States in the South have shown the largest improvements. Another interesting trend: Scores among 4th graders have shown more rapid improvement, suggesting that recent educational focus is working where it counts most—when kids are younger—while today's 8th graders are the product of the educational past.

No Child Left Behind Status

As No Child Left Behind (NCLB) moves forward towards its goal of bringing 100% of students up to the "proficient" level on state tests by the 2013–14 school year, it makes sense today to keep track of how states are doing against major goals. Among the 40-plus NCLB requirements are the establishment of standards, annual assessments against those standards, and creating a so-called "report card" to disseminate the results. Table 4.22 shows progress against these standards, and as we see from the table, most states are getting close to getting these programs in place, if they haven't gotten there already. Table 4.23 lists the 19 states fully in compliance with assessment requirements. Readers wishing to learn more about NCLB progress may go to the Education Commission of the States website at www.ecs.org, while those wishing to see test results at a school or school district level, as mentioned earlier, can check out www.greatschools.net.

Politics

Political party affiliation and voting behavior are among the most outward signs of an area's political character. Table 4.24 displays the party of the state governor and also shows voting results by party for the 2004 presidential election and Congressional representation current as of the 2006 midterm elections.

The table divides states into four groups:

- **Democrat/Democrat** states voted Democratic in the 2004 election *and* have a majority or equality Democratic representation in Congress. Whether or not they have a Democratic governor was not considered. Within this category, states are sorted according to the percentage of Democratic presidential vote; that is, Rhode Island had the strongest presidential Democratic majority.

- **Democrat/Republican** represents states that voted for the Democratic presidential candidate, but sent a majority of Republican representatives to Congress.

- **Republican/Democrat** states voted Republican for president but sent an equal or majority number of Democrats to Congress.

- **Republican/Republican** states voted consistently Republican for both president and Congress. Wyoming and Utah lead this group with the highest percentage presidential Republican vote.

The table shows the strength of a state's party commitment. States such as Rhode Island, Massachusetts, New York, and many Southern states approach national- and state-level politics quite differently, consistently electing Democrats to serve at the national level but Republicans to serve in the statehouse—or vice versa. Some states, such as California and Pennsylvania, have a reputation of voting differently at different levels to achieve sort of a "check and balance" in their leadership.

Safety & Safety Consciousness

Out of many possible variables, this section looks at drunk driving laws and highway fatalities, which together give a sense of a state's social, political, and legal environment. In this edition, we combine two tables published in the 2004 edition of this book into Table 4.25. This table, titled "Traffic Deaths and Alcohol Involvement, and Alcohol Laws," summarizes traffic deaths, deaths related to alcohol, and the Insurance Information Institute's 2003 evaluation of state drunk driving laws carried over from this book's preceding edition.

Highway Fatalities

Grim as they might be, highway fatality statistics can be construed as a result of state law, state spending, infrastructure, and social attitudes about safety. A surprisingly wide variation exists among states. States in the South and West tend to fare poorly. But to be fair, experts suggest that states with a largely rural character and a high percentage of two-lane roads will have greater fatalities because accidents under these circumstances, while similar in number, tend to produce more fatalities. The numbers, while supporting this argument, still suggest room for improvement in some states.

State Drunk Driving Laws

All states have cracked down on drunk drivers, but some have gone further than others. Table 4.25 shows the Insurance Information Institute's appraisal of more than 25 parameters of state law on drunk driving, from definitions and determinations of drunkenness to legal remedies and special clauses for minors and repeat offenders. The report groups states into four categories, with the accompanying characteristics:

- **Good (G):** Blood alcohol concentration (BAC) limit 0.08%, zero percent BAC for drivers under 21, sobriety checkpoints permitted, license revocation of at least 30 days

- **Acceptable (A):** BAC limit 0.08%, at least one additional provision from the "Good" category

- **Marginal (M):** Zero percent BAC for drivers under 21, sobriety checkpoints permitted

- **Poor (P):** One or none of the provisions listed in the "Good" category

TABLE 4.24 STATE PARTY LINES
Voting behavior for 2004 presidential election
Party affiliation in U.S. House of Representatives & governorships as of January 2007

DEMOCRAT/DEMOCRAT
States voting Democrat in 2004 with equal or Democratic majority representation following 2006 election

STATE	2004 PRESIDENTIAL VOTE PERCENT OF TOTAL VOTE		REPRESENTATIVES IN CONGRESS			GOVERNOR
	DEMOCRAT	REPUBLICAN	DEMOCRAT	REPUBLICAN	TOTAL	PARTY
MA	62.7%	37.3%	10	0	10	D
RI	60.6%	39.4%	2	0	2	R
VT	60.3%	39.7%	1	0	1	I
NY	59.3%	40.7%	23	6	29	D
MD	56.6%	43.4%	6	2	8	D
CT	55.3%	44.7%	4	1	5	R
IL	55.2%	44.8%	10	9	19	D
CA	55.0%	45.0%	34	19	53	R
ME	54.6%	45.4%	2	0	2	D
HI	54.4%	45.6%	2	0	2	R
WA	53.7%	46.3%	6	3	9	D
NJ	53.4%	46.6%	7	6	13	D
OR	52.1%	47.9%	4	1	5	D
MN	51.8%	48.2%	5	3	8	R
PA	51.3%	48.7%	11	8	19	D
NH	50.7%	49.3%	2	0	2	D
WI	50.2%	49.8%	5	3	8	D

DEMOCRAT/REPUBLICAN
States voting Democrat in 2004 with Republican majority representation following 2006 election

STATE	2004 PRESIDENTIAL VOTE PERCENT OF TOTAL VOTE		REPRESENTATIVES IN CONGRESS			GOVERNOR
	DEMOCRAT	REPUBLICAN	DEMOCRAT	REPUBLICAN	TOTAL	PARTY
DE	53.9%	46.1%	0	1	1	D
MI	51.7%	48.3%	6	9	15	D

REPUBLICAN/DEMOCRAT
States voting Republican in 2004 with Democratic majority representation following 2006 election

STATE	2004 PRESIDENTIAL VOTE PERCENT OF TOTAL VOTE		REPRESENTATIVES IN CONGRESS			GOVERNOR
	DEMOCRAT	REPUBLICAN	DEMOCRAT	REPUBLICAN	TOTAL	PARTY
ND	36.2%	63.8%	1	0	1	R
SD	39.0%	61.0%	1	0	1	R
IN	39.6%	60.4%	5	4	9	R
TN	43.2%	56.8%	5	4	9	D
WV	43.5%	56.5%	2	1	3	D
NC	43.7%	56.3%	7	6	13	D
AR	45.0%	55.0%	3	1	4	D
CO	47.6%	52.4%	4	3	7	D
IA	49.7%	50.3%	3	2	5	D

REPUBLICAN/REPUBLICAN
States voting Republican in 2004 with equal or Republican majority representation following 2006 election

STATE	2004 PRESIDENTIAL VOTE PERCENT OF TOTAL VOTE		REPRESENTATIVES IN CONGRESS			GOVERNOR
	DEMOCRAT	REPUBLICAN	DEMOCRAT	REPUBLICAN	TOTAL	PARTY
UT	26.6%	73.4%	1	2	3	R
WY	29.7%	70.3%	0	1	1	D
ID	30.7%	69.3%	0	2	2	R
NE	33.1%	66.9%	0	3	3	R
OK	34.4%	65.6%	1	4	5	D
AK	36.8%	63.2%	0	1	1	R
AL	37.1%	62.9%	2	5	7	R
KS	37.1%	62.9%	2	2	4	D
TX	38.5%	61.5%	13	19	32	R
MT	39.5%	60.5%	0	1	1	D
KY	40.0%	60.0%	2	4	6	R
MS	40.1%	59.9%	2	2	4	R
SC	41.4%	58.6%	2	4	6	R
GA	41.6%	58.4%	6	7	13	R
LA	42.7%	57.3%	2	5	7	D
FL	44.4%	55.6%	9	16	25	R
AZ	44.7%	55.3%	4	4	8	D
VA	45.9%	54.1%	3	8	11	D
MO	46.4%	53.6%	4	5	9	R
NV	48.7%	51.3%	1	2	3	R
OH	48.9%	51.1%	7	11	18	D
NM	49.6%	50.4%	1	2	3	D

Source: *The World Almanac and Book of Facts, 2006; The House of Representatives Official Page.*

TABLE 4.25 TRAFFIC DEATHS & ALCOHOL INVOLVEMENT & ALCOHOL LAWS

STATE	2004 TOTAL TRAFFIC DEATHS	2004 ALCOHOL-RELATED DEATHS PER 100,000	PERCENT ALCOHOL-RELATED	STATE DRUNK DRIVING LAW RATING (*)
AK	101	31	31%	Good
AL	1,154	442	38%	Good
AR	704	276	39%	Acceptable
AZ	1,150	435	38%	Good
CA	4,120	1,643	40%	Good
CO	665	259	39%	Acceptable
CT	291	127	44%	Acceptable
DE	134	51	38%	Acceptable
FL	3,244	1,222	38%	Good
GA	1,634	525	32%	Good
HI	142	65	46%	Good
IA	390	110	28%	Acceptable
ID	260	93	36%	Acceptable
IL	1,356	604	45%	Acceptable
IN	947	299	32%	Acceptable
KS	461	148	32%	Good
KY	964	308	32%	Acceptable
LA	904	414	46%	Good
MA	476	203	43%	Acceptable
MD	643	286	45%	Acceptable
ME	194	70	36%	Acceptable
MI	1,159	430	37%	Poor
MN	567	184	32%	Acceptable
MO	1,130	449	40%	Good
MS	900	341	38%	Acceptable
MT	229	106	46%	Poor
NC	1,557	553	35%	Acceptable
ND	100	39	39%	Acceptable
NE	254	92	36%	Good
NH	171	59	35%	Good
NJ	731	270	37%	Poor
NM	521	211	40%	Acceptable
NV	395	152	39%	Acceptable
NY	1,493	587	39%	Acceptable
OH	1,286	492	38%	Acceptable
OK	774	278	36%	Acceptable
OR	456	199	44%	Acceptable
PA	1,490	614	41%	Marginal
RI	83	42	50%	Poor
SC	1,046	464	44%	Marginal
SD	197	86	44%	Acceptable
TN	1,288	519	40%	Acceptable
TX	3,583	1,642	46%	Acceptable
UT	296	72	24%	Good
VA	925	359	39%	Acceptable
VT	98	32	32%	Good
WA	563	246	44%	Acceptable
WI	792	358	45%	Acceptable
WV	411	136	33%	Acceptable
WY	164	59	36%	Acceptable
National	42,636	16,694	39%	

(*) As rated by the Insurance Information Institute (2003)
Source: MADD/National Highway Traffic Safety Administration, 2005

part

II

Evaluating the Cities

chapter 5

U.S. Metropolitan Areas

Earlier chapters set the stage for the in-depth look at each of the 375 metropolitan areas found in this chapter. *Cities Ranked & Rated*, 2nd Edition, presents each metro area in alphabetical order with a header containing identifying characteristics, scores, and ranks for the area as a whole and for each category, a narrative description, and complete fact tables. The narrative highlights and interprets important facts and trends and gives an overview of the qualities, appearance, and climate of the place. Explanations of attributes shown in the fact tables can be found in chapter 3, as well as in Table 5.1 (p. 146).

Area Profiles

Cities Ranked & Rated employs a set of simple phrases in each area header to describe the role and general nature of a place and the dominant city or cities contained within. Most of these phrases are standard, such as "college town" and "capital city," but a few are unique to a particular area or are a combination of several profiles, such as "mid-size city/college town." Sometimes we use the word "complex" to identify an area with multiple centers or principal cities, for example, "small city complex." The logic will make more sense as you review the narratives in this chapter; the more commonly used area profiles are described below.

National Center

A national center is a large urban area recognized both nationally and internationally as a leading center for government, commerce, industry, education, services, and the arts. Population generally exceeds eight million, with an exception given for Washington, D.C., at five million. Numerous satellite cities, ethnically concentrated neighborhoods, and large areas of suburbs characterize a national center. A vibrant downtown, often containing architectural and historic landmarks, is attractive as a working and tourist destination. The ethnic mix and cost-of-living profile in the city are quite different from surrounding areas. A complete transportation network and services, such as air, rail, and public transport, are available. The airport serves as an international gateway for passengers and freight, and the city is a world center for

entire industries, as Los Angeles is for movies and entertainment and New York is for book publishing. Foreign countries use the city as a base for their U.S. operations. Major universities, world-renowned arts and cultural assets, and extensive restaurants and nightlife round out the available amenities.

Examples:

Chicago–Naperville–Joliet, IL

Los Angeles–Long Beach–Glendale, CA

New York–White Plains, NY

Washington–Arlington–Alexandria, DC-VA-MD-WV

Regional Center

This major city, or collection of cities, with a large surrounding area usually has a population greater than two million and serves as a multistate hub for economic and commercial activity, services, and amenities. A large and vibrant downtown is surrounded by neighborhoods and suburbs, often reflecting the population mix of the region. The cost-of-living profile is usually high compared to surrounding areas. Generally the area is a business center, providing banking and financial services for the region, with offices for national and multinational companies designed to service the region and an assortment of smaller businesses. Also supporting the region are major air and transport services. The city is a destination for shopping, healthcare, and many specialized services and amenities.

Examples:

Atlanta–Sandy Springs–Marietta, GA

Dallas–Plano–Irving, TX

Miami–Miami Beach–Kendall, FL

Minneapolis–St. Paul–Bloomington, MN

Seattle–Bellevue–Everett, WA

Large City

A self-sufficient city, with a moderately sized surrounding area, consists of an area population greater than one million and may rise to as much as five million for more populous areas not having the characteristics of a regional center, such as Philadelphia. Often a state's largest city, it serves its own needs and those of a moderately large, generally in-state area. Typical large cities have a well-developed downtown core, with distinct neighborhoods and suburbs, and often reflect the ethnic mix and cultural flavor of the surrounding area. Commercial activities, education, healthcare, transportation, arts, recreation, and other amenities are available, and residents generally don't feel the need to go elsewhere for them.

Examples:

Buffalo–Niagara Falls, NY

Cincinnati–Middletown, OH-KY-IN

Tampa–St. Petersburg–Clearwater, FL (a good example of a large city complex)

Pittsburgh, PA

Portland–Vancouver–Beaverton, OR-WA

St Louis, MO-IL

Small City & Mid-Size City

These areas have elements of a big-city and a small-town experience and feel. Typically small city areas have a population ranging from 100,000 to 250,000, while "mid-size" areas have 250,000 to 1 million. These metro areas typically serve a few counties outside the immediate area, but the area is always smaller than the state as a whole. Generally the city has a small-scale downtown with multi-story commercial buildings and a few distinct neighborhoods, and getting around is easy. Cost of living is typically much lower than in larger cities. Some cities have diverse commercial and industrial bases, while others are subject to the economical vulnerability of a single industry. Typically some large-city amenities, including healthcare, air service, and culture and arts, are available, but some residents consider the quality to be inadequate. Residents *occasionally* go to a nearby "large city"

or "regional center" for services and amenities such as air service, shopping, or arts. The city may contain strong "college town" or "capital city" elements.

Mid-size city examples:

Akron, OH

Chattanooga, TN-GA

Colorado Springs, CO

Fresno, CA

Omaha–Council Bluffs, NE-IA

Roanoke, VA

Small city examples:

Abilene, TX

Battle Creek, MI

Fargo, ND-MN

Johnstown, PA

Lynchburg, VA

Pittsfield, MA

Waco, TX

Small Town

Normally with a population less than 100,000, the small town area is laid out around a central business district, usually in a rectangular grid pattern with tree-lined streets and abundant sidewalks. The more attractive small towns have walkable central-business districts with stores, restaurants, and commercial buildings, and on-street parking. Some or all buildings have a historic look and feel. Residential areas generally have well-kept older homes, some with historic or architectural interest, with newer construction farther from the center of town. New developments, including shopping malls, strip centers, and franchise outlets, are usually on the outskirts of town along highway and bypass strips. Most industry is light and located on the outskirts. While most of today's small towns have some modern cookie-cutter development, the better ones repurpose older buildings and keep downtown areas functional. Occasionally we classify a metro area with a population of more than 100,000 as a small town if the principal city has a small town character and is well below 100,000 in population.

Examples:

Columbus, IN

Great Falls, MT

Harrisonburg, VA

Lewiston, ID–WA

Muncie, IN

Owensboro, KY

Salisbury, MD

Wenatchee, WA

Military Town

This place has a strong military presence with one or more military bases located nearby and a large portion of the town's economy tied to the military. Areas of low-cost and base housing are near commercial districts that support the needs of military personnel and their families. Lower income, low cost of living, few cultural amenities, and shopping oriented toward the lower-income ranges characterize the area. The economy may be steady, although turnover among residents and the percentage of rental housing may be high. Investment and infrastructure may deteriorate in towns vulnerable to base closings, although this is less of a threat than it was in the 1990s. Entertainment and nightlife is often oriented toward young men, although family-entertainment amenities sometimes exist. Some military towns, such as Fairfield, California, have been encroached upon by advancing suburbs and have lost most of their military town character.

Examples:

Jacksonville, NC

Lawton, OK

Pensacola–Ferry Pass–Brent, FL

College Town

One or more colleges or universities dominate the economy and local infrastructure. There is usually a large and often parklike campus, with historic buildings and a generally attractive appearance, in or adjacent to the central town area. A mix of relatively young, lower income, transient students; relatively higher income, more educated faculty; and institution employees live here. Cost of living, especially housing costs, tends to be high. Overall educational attainment is very high, and these areas tend to have exceptional primary and secondary schools in addition to the college or university; often there are ties between the schools. There may be important healthcare and healthcare-research facilities, both in the private and public sector. If there is any industry, it is usually located on the outskirts of town away from the student areas, and often has a strong research or new-economy component. The often walkable town areas support the commercial

and recreational needs of the students and faculty alike, with nightlife, interesting restaurants, and small stores that sell books, supplies, and other items for the young market. The university provides a number of cultural amenities such as museums and performing arts including traveling acts. Often there is considerable historic interest. College sports provide entertainment and often become a local obsession. Some towns (such as Tuscaloosa, Alabama) are "pure" college towns, while others (such as Austin, Texas) have a significant college-town element mixed into a larger community.

Examples:

Boulder, CO

Charlottesville, VA

Iowa City, IA

Lawrence, KS

State College, PA

Capital City

Capital cities contain the center of state government. Whether government dominates the local economy and infrastructure depends on the size of the capital city. In smaller capitals such as Olympia, Washington, or Dover, Delaware, the governmental element tends to dominate, whereas it is only a player among many in larger capitals such as Atlanta, Georgia, or Denver, Colorado. State governments generally bring attractive, permanent buildings, often in parklike settings (particularly the Capitol building itself), and stable employment. The stability of the employment base extends from the government payroll itself to other enterprises performing services for the government. The government and its sphere of enterprises are generally industries with high-paying, white-collar jobs. Capital cities often have museums and items of historical interest pertaining to the state. A small city that is both state capital and home to a large state university brings especially pleasing infrastructure and amenities; examples include Madison, Wisconsin; Austin, Texas; and Lansing, Michigan.

Examples:

Albany–Schenectady–Troy, NY

Carson City, NV

Harrisburg–Carlisle, PA

Indianapolis–Carmel, IN

Jackson, MS

Salem, OR

Tallahassee, FL

Beach Town

Many towns in coastal areas in the East and South have a typical "beach town" look and feel. There is usually a wide beach, separated from the rest of the city by a wide boulevard running parallel to the coast. On the immediate inland side of the boulevard one often finds high-rise hotels and residential buildings with intermittent clusters of smaller commercial buildings, usually containing locally owned restaurants and shops catering to tourists. There are nice walking areas and even classic board-walks. The area where local residents live and do business is farther inland and often older and less attractive than the beach area. Some beach towns have the beach and commercial strip on a barrier island. The local economy varies within the town, with wealthier and more expensive enclaves near the beach and lower income areas and less expensive housing inland. Crime is often a problem, perhaps due to income disparities and the abundance of tourists. Because of rugged coastal geography, the typical "beach town" format is less common on the West Coast, although some examples exist within the Los Angeles area.

Examples:

Atlantic City, NJ

Fort Walton Beach–Crestview–Destin, FL

Myrtle Beach–Conway–North Myrtle Beach, SC

West Palm Beach–Boca Raton–Boynton Beach, FL

Suburban Complex

The area is a large collection of suburbs and suburban towns usually outside and adjacent to a much larger city. Some exist mainly as a residential or bedroom community for the larger city or urban area, but many, like the Orange County (Santa Ana–Anaheim–Irvine) area of California, have evolved into economically self-sufficient entities, as commercial activity has become centered in these areas. The character is mainly suburban, predominated by large areas of single- and multifamily housing, and dotted with small older town centers and newer retail malls and "big-box" retail complexes. Some of these areas, especially on the East Coast, are very attractive and even historic, with well-spaced smaller towns and suburban facilities. Others are large, endless, and monotonous monuments to urban sprawl with little real sense of place. Minor entertainment establishments are available locally as a matter of convenience, but there is usually little in the way of cultural stimulation—that role is reserved for the larger city. These areas are connected to the main city center by a well-developed network of commuting routes, many of which are served by public transit. These areas are close enough to the main city to enjoy many of its services and amenities, such as air transport, professional sports teams, and cultural assets.

Examples:

Edison, NJ

Essex County, MA

Lake County–Kenosha County, IL-WI

Nassau–Suffolk, NY

Santa Ana–Anaheim–Irvine, CA

Vallejo–Fairfield, CA

Warren–Troy–Farmington Hills, MI

TABLE 5.1 U.S. METROPOLITAN AREAS: DATA DESCRIPTIONS & SOURCES

FIELD NAME	DESCRIPTION	SOURCE	DATE
POPULATION			
DEMOGRAPHICS			
Population	Total residents in metropolitan area	Claritas, Inc.—updated from U.S. Census	2005
Population density per sq. mile	Total residents per square mile in area	Claritas, Inc.—updated from U.S. Census	2005
Population growth	Growth in metro area population, 1990–2005	Claritas, Inc.—updated from U.S. Census	2005
Median age	Median age in years	Claritas, Inc.—updated from U.S. Census	2005
Percent Democrat	Percent voting Democratic in 2004 Presidential election	Compiled from state elections divisions	2005
Percent Republican	Percent voting Republican in 2004 Presidential election	Compiled from state elections divisions	2005
ETHNIC COMPOSITION			
White	Percentage of population surveyed as Caucasian	Claritas, Inc.—updated from U.S. Census	2005
Black	Percentage of population surveyed as African-American	Claritas, Inc.—updated from U.S. Census	2005
Asian	Percentage of population surveyed of Asian origin	Claritas, Inc.—updated from U.S. Census	2005
Hispanic	Percentage of population surveyed of Hispanic origin	Claritas, Inc.—updated from U.S. Census	2005
Religious observance	Percentage of population regularly attending religious services	Glenmary Research Center	2000
Diversity measure	Probability that next person met is ethnicity other than your own	Sperling's BestPlaces	2005

FIELD NAME	DESCRIPTION	SOURCE	DATE

POPULATION (cont.)

RESIDENT PROFILE

Single	Percentage of population surveyed as single	Claritas, Inc.—updated from U.S. Census	2005
Married	Percentage of population surveyed as married	Claritas, Inc.—updated from U.S. Census	2005
Divorced/separated	Percentage of population surveyed as divorced or separated	Claritas, Inc.—updated from U.S. Census	2005
Married with children	Percent of population surveyed as married with one or more children	Claritas, Inc.—updated from U.S. Census	2005
Single with children	Percentage of population surveyed as single with one or more children	Claritas, Inc.—updated from U.S. Census	2005
Percent over age 65	Percentage of population over age of 65	Claritas, Inc.—updated from U.S. Census	2005

ECONOMY & JOBS

INCOME

Per capita income	Average annual gross income for every U.S. citizen of all ages	Claritas, Inc.—updated from U.S. Census	2005
Household income	Average annual gross income for every U.S. household	Claritas, Inc.—updated from U.S. Census	2005
Household income ‹ $25K	Percentage of households with annual gross income less than $25,000	Claritas, Inc.—updated from U.S. Census	2005
Household income › $75K	Percentage of households with annual gross income over $75,000	Claritas, Inc.—updated from U.S. Census	2005
Household income growth	Percentage of growth in average household income, 2002–2006	Claritas, Inc.—updated from U.S. Census	2005

EMPLOYMENT

Unemployment rate	Percentage of active job seekers without a job, August 2006	Bureau of Labor Statistics	2006
Recent job growth	Percentage of job growth or decline, August 2005–August 2006	Bureau of Labor Statistics	2006
Projected future job growth	Percentage of projected job growth or decline through 2010	Sperling's BestPlaces	2006
White collar	Percentage of workers in executive/managerial/professional/technical/sales/clerical positions	Bureau of Labor Statistics	2005
Blue collar	Percentage of workers in production/repair/transportation/construction/labor/agriculture positions	Bureau of Labor Statistics	2005

EMPLOYING INDUSTRIES

Largest employing industry	Industry with the largest employment base in area	Claritas, Inc.	2005
Percent manufacturing	Percentage employed in manufacturing job classifications	Claritas, Inc.—updated from U.S. Census	2005
Percent public sector	Percent employed in public sector job classifications	Claritas, Inc.—updated from U.S. Census	2005
Percent construction	Percent employed in construction job classifications	Claritas, Inc.—updated from U.S. Census	2005

COST OF LIVING

INDEXES & TAXES

Cost of Living Index	Total cost of living as an index against national average, second quarter 2006; 100 as average	Bureau of Labor Statistics	2006
Buying Power Index	Household income divided by Cost of Living Index, versus national average; 100 as average	*Cities Ranked & Rated* calculation	2006
Income tax rate	Highest marginal combined state and local rate	Sperling's BestPlaces	2006
Sales tax rate	Most commonly paid total state and local sales tax rate	Sperling's BestPlaces	2006
Property tax rate	Average dollar amount paid per $1,000 in property	Sperling's BestPlaces	2006

HOUSING

Median home price	Median selling price for the average home type in the area, second quarter 2006	National Association of Realtors	2006
Home price appreciation	Growth in home prices, 2002–2006	National Association of Realtors/Sperling's BestPlaces	2006
Median rent	Median rental price for typical rental unit in the area, first half of 2006	U.S. Census	2006
Homes owned	Percentage of households owning home	Claritas, Inc.—updated from U.S. Census	2006
Home price ratio	Median home price/Median household income	*Cities Ranked & Rated* calculation	2006

NECESSITIES

Food Index	Purchased food (groceries) cost against national average, second quarter 2006; 100 as average	Bureau of Labor Statistics	2006
Housing Index	Purchase/rent and upkeep cost against national average, second quarter 2006; 100 as average	Bureau of Labor Statistics	2006
Utilities Index	Gas and electricity cost against national average, second quarter 2006; 100 as average	Bureau of Labor Statistics	2006
Transportation Index	Automotive and other costs against national average, second quarter 2006; 100 as average	Bureau of Labor Statistics	2006
Healthcare Index	Health and health insurance cost against national average, second quarter 2006; 100 as average	Bureau of Labor Statistics	2006
Miscellaneous Cost Index	Other costs against national average, second quarter 2006; 100 as average	Bureau of Labor Statistics	2006

FIELD NAME	DESCRIPTION	SOURCE	DATE
CLIMATE			
TEMPERATURE			
Average January low	January daily low temperature, 70-year average	NOAA/National Climatic Data Center	2005
Average July high	July daily high temperature, 70-year average	NOAA/National Climatic Data Center	2005
Annual days > 90°F	Average days per year where temperature exceeds 90°F	NOAA/National Climatic Data Center	2005
Annual days < 32°F	Average days per year where temperature drops below freezing, 32°F	NOAA/National Climatic Data Center	2005
Annual days < 0°F	Average days per year where temperature drops below 0°F	NOAA/National Climatic Data Center	2005
PRECIPITATION	2005		
Annual inches precipitation	Annual total precipitation (snow or rain), equivalent water inches, 70-year average	NOAA/National Climatic Data Center	2005
Annual inches snowfall	Annual snowfall in inches, 70-year average	NOAA/National Climatic Data Center	2005
Annual days precipitation	Average days per year with measurable precipitation	NOAA/National Climatic Data Center	2005
Annual days rain > 0.5 inches	Average days per year recording over 0.5 inches of equivalent precipitation	NOAA/National Climatic Data Center	2005
Annual days snow > 1.5 inches	Average days per year recording 1.5 inches or more of snow	NOAA/National Climatic Data Center	2005
COMFORT & HAZARDS	2005		
July relative humidity	Average percentage relative humidity recorded during July	NOAA/National Climatic Data Center	2005
Annual days mostly sunny	Average days per year with mostly sun or partly cloudy	NOAA/National Climatic Data Center	2005
Annual days with thunderstorms	Average days per year with observed thunderstorms	NOAA/National Climatic Data Center	2005
Tornado risk score	Calculated likelihood and severity of tornadoes; 1–100 scale	Sperling's BestPlaces	2005
Hurricane risk score	Calculated likelihood and severity of hurricanes; 1–100 scale	Sperling's BestPlaces	2005
EDUCATION			
ACHIEVEMENT			
High school degree	Percentage of population surveyed with high school diploma	Claritas, Inc.—updated from U.S. Census	2005
2-year college degree	Percentage of population surveyed with 2-year degree or trade school certificate	Claritas, Inc.—updated from U.S. Census	2005
4-year college degree	Percentage of population surveyed with 4-year college/university degree	Claritas, Inc.—updated from U.S. Census	2005
Graduate/professional degree	Percentage of population surveyed with graduate or professional degree	Claritas, Inc.—updated from U.S. Census	2005
PUBLIC SCHOOLS			
Expenditures per pupil	Dollars spent for public education divided by number of students	National Center for Education Statistics	2005
Student/teacher ratio	Ratio showing number of students per teacher in public schools	National Center for Education Statistics	2005
Attending public school	Percentage of total students in area attending public school	National Center for Education Statistics	2005
State SAT score	Average state SAT score; asterisk denotes state emphasis over ACT	College Board/American College Testing Service	2006
State ACT score	Average state ACT score; asterisk denotes state emphasis over SAT	College Board/American College Testing Service	2006
HIGHER EDUCATION			
No. 2-year colleges	Number of 2-year colleges and trade schools	National Center for Education Statistics	2005
No. 4-year colleges/universities	Number of 4-year colleges, universities, and branch campuses	National Center for Education Statistics	2005
No. highly ranked universities	Number of colleges and universities with selective admission standards	National Center for Education Statistics/ Princeton Review study	2005
HEALTH & HEALTHCARE			
HAZARDS & ILLNESSES			
Air-quality score	Composite of particulates, ozone, and volatile organic compounds; 1–100 scale	Sperling's BestPlaces	2005
Water-quality score	Natural and man-made pollutants in runoff and ground water; 1–100 scale	Sperling's BestPlaces	2005
Pollen/allergy score	Composite of grass, tree, and mold allergens; 1–100 scale	Sperling's BestPlaces	2005
Cancer mortality per capita	Death rate attributable from cancer or cancer-related causes; 1–100 scale	National Centers for Disease Control and Prevention	2004
Depression days per month	Number of days reported by survey with stress or depression	Sperling's BestPlaces	2005
Stress score	Composite of eight stress factors shown as 1–100 score	Sperling's BestPlaces	2005
HEALTHCARE			
Physicians per capita	Number of accredited generalists and specialists per 100,000 people	American Medical Association	2005
Hospital beds per capita	Number of hospital beds per 100,000 people	U.S. Department of Health and Human Services	2005
No. teaching hospitals	Number of hospitals accredited to teach or train physicians	U.S. Department of Health and Human Services	2005
Cost per doctor visit	Average dollar cost per doctor visit	American Chamber of Commerce Research Association	2006
Cost per dental visit	Average dollar cost per dentist visit	American Chamber of Commerce Research Association	2006
CRIME			
Violent crime rate	Number of murder, rape, robbery, and assault crimes per 100,000 people	FBI Uniform Crime Reports	2005
Change in violent crime rate	Change in violent crime rate, 2001–2005	FBI Uniform Crime Reports	2005
Property crime rate	Number of burglaries, thefts, and auto thefts per 100,000 people	FBI Uniform Crime Reports	2005
Change in property crime rate	Change in property crime rate, 2001–2005	FBI Uniform Crime Reports	2005

FIELD NAME	DESCRIPTION	SOURCE	DATE
TRANSPORTATION			
COMMUTE			
Average commute time	Average number of minutes per one-way commute to work	Claritas, Inc.—updated from U.S. Census	2005
Percent commutes › 60 minutes	Percentage of one-way commutes taking longer than 60 minutes	Claritas, Inc.—updated from U.S. Census	2005
Commute by auto	Percentage of workers commuting as single driver in vehicle	Claritas, Inc.—updated from U.S. Census	2005
Commute by mass transit	Percentage of workers commuting by scheduled public transit	Claritas, Inc.—updated from U.S. Census	2005
Work at home	Percentage of workers working at home	Claritas, Inc.—updated from U.S. Census	2005
Mass transit miles per capita	Number of transit vehicle miles available per person per day	Urban Mass Transit Association	2004
INTERCITY SERVICES			
Major airports within 60 miles	Number of airports designated as "hub" or "major" within 60 miles	Federal Aviation Administration	2004
Size of regional airport	Federal Aviation Administration airport type: large, medium, small hub, or non-hub	Federal Aviation Administration	2004
Daily airline activity	Average number of passenger aircraft departing per day	Federal Aviation Administration	2004
Amtrak service	Yes if Amtrak service, No if none	Sperling's BestPlaces/Amtrak	2004
AUTOMOTIVE			
Insurance, annual premium	Average insurance premium	National Association of Insurance Commissioners	2006
Gas, cost per gallon	Average cost per gallon of regular unleaded gas, summer 2006	American Automobile Association	2006
Daily vehicle miles per capita	Average daily road miles per person per day	Federal Highway Administration	2004
LEISURE			
DINING & SHOPPING			
Restaurant rating	Availability and quality of restaurants; 1–10 scale	Sperling's BestPlaces	2005
Outlet mall score	Proximity of outlet malls and number of stores in those malls	Claritas, Inc.	2005
No. Starbucks	Number of Starbucks retail stores	Sperling's BestPlaces/Starbucks, Inc.	2006
No. warehouse clubs	Number of Costco, Sam's Club, and BJ's stores	Sperling's BestPlaces/Warehouse club sources	2006
ENTERTAINMENT			
Professional sports rating	Availability of professional major- and minor-league spectator sports; 1–10 scale	Sperling's BestPlaces	2005
College sports rating	Availability of college sports teams; 1–10 scale	Sperling's BestPlaces	2005
Zoo/aquarium rating	Availability of zoos, aquariums, and animal parks; 1–10 scale	Sperling's BestPlaces	2005
Amusement park rating	Availability, quality, and proximity of traditional amusement parks; 1–10 scale	Sperling's BestPlaces	2005
Botanical garden/arboretum rating	Availability of botanical gardens, arboretums, and conservatories; 1–10 scale	Sperling's BestPlaces	2004
OUTDOOR ACTIVITIES			
Golf-course rating	Availability, quality, and cost of public and private golf courses; 1–10 scale	Sperling's BestPlaces	2005
Ski-area rating	Availability, quality, proximity, and cost of ski areas; 1–10 scale	Sperling's BestPlaces	2005
Sq. miles inland water	Square miles of nearby inland freshwater including lakes and streams	Sperling's BestPlaces	2004
Miles of coastline	Miles of ocean or Great Lakes coastline adjacent to area	Sperling's BestPlaces	2004
National Park rating	Availability, quality, and proximity of national parks and forests; 1–10 scale	Sperling's BestPlaces	2005
ARTS & CULTURE			
MEDIA & LIBRARIES			
Arts radio rating	Availability of radio stations (NPR or private) with classical, jazz, or news format; 1–10 scale	Sperling's BestPlaces	2004
No. public libraries	Number of library facilities including branches	Sperling's BestPlaces/National Center for Education Statistics	2004
Library volumes per capita	Number of volumes per 100,000 residents	Sperling's BestPlaces/National Center for Education Statistics	2004
PERFORMING ARTS			
Classical music rating	Availability and quality of symphony, chamber, or opera organizations and venues; 1–10 scale	Sperling's BestPlaces/Symphony Magazine	2004
Ballet/dance rating	Availability and quality of ballet and dance organizations and venues; 1–10 scale	Sperling's BestPlaces/Sterns Ballet/Dance Directory	2004
Professional theater rating	Availability of theater venues registered with Sterns Theater Directory; 1–10 scale	Sperling's BestPlaces/Sterns Theater Directory	2004
University arts programs rating	Availability of arts programs associated with or sponsored by local university; 1–10 scale	Sperling's BestPlaces/National Center for Education Statistics	2004
MUSEUMS			
Overall museum rating	Availability and quality of all museums; 1–10 scale	Sperling's BestPlaces/American Association of Museums	2004
Art museum rating	Availability and quality of art museums; 1–10 scale	Sperling's BestPlaces/American Association of Museums	2004
Science museum rating	Availability and quality of science museums; 1–10 scale	Sperling's BestPlaces/American Association of Museums	2004
Children's museum rating	Availability and quality of children's museums; 1–10 scale	Sperling's BestPlaces/American Association of Museums	2004

Abilene, TX

Score: 78.0 Rank: 55 2004 rank: 32

Profile: Small city
Location: North-central Texas, 185 miles west of Dallas
Elevation: 1,790 feet
Time zone: Central Standard Time

PRO	CON
Cost of living	Isolation
Small-town atmosphere	Recreation
Historic/cultural interest	Low incomes

Abilene is a former watering hole and junction where the Chisholm Trail met the railroad. Today the area is largely supported by agriculture but also has some minor manufacturing, three small colleges and universities, and nearby Dyess Air Force Base. The city has a good set of arts and cultural amenities for a town its size, and has been recognized for its use of the arts to preserve and revitalize its historic downtown district. Good residential areas surround Abilene, with the strongest lying south and southwest of the city. Cost of living at 80 is very attractive, and the summer climate is better than most areas of Texas. Regional air service closes the gap somewhat, but otherwise it's a long haul to other cities. Abilene has a good balance of qualities and represents typical, small-town Texas life.

To the north and west lie the southern Great Plains, and to the south is the Texas Hill Country. Cattle, occasional crops, and low hills to the south and west dot the mainly level and treeless landscape. The climate is variable. Summers are hot and generally dry, with periods of thunderstorms more likely in late spring and early fall. In winter, northerly cold air battles moist warm air from the south; sudden below-freezing temperatures and wind mix with intermittent periods of mild weather. First freeze is early November; last is late April.

Population

DEMOGRAPHICS	AREA	U.S. AVG	ETHNIC COMPOSITION	AREA	U.S. AVG	RESIDENT PROFILE	AREA	U.S. AVG
Population	157,871		White	80.6%	79.0%	Single	29.9%	32.4%
Population density per sq. mile	57.5	358.5	Black	6.3%	10.5%	Married	53.1%	52.7%
Population growth	6.9%	21.1%	Asian	1.1%	2.7%	Divorced/separated	16.9%	14.9%
Median age	33.7	36.1	Hispanic	19.4%	10.6%	Married with children	24.9%	23.7%
Percent Democrat	22.6%	44.5%	Religious observance	65.8%	48.9%	Single with children	9.1%	9.1%
Percent Republican	76.9%	54.5%	Diversity measure	53.8	40.1	Percent over age 65	13.2%	12.9%

Economy & Jobs
Score: 93.0
Rank: 27

INCOME	AREA	U.S. AVG	EMPLOYMENT	AREA	U.S. AVG	EMPLOYING INDUSTRIES	AREA	U.S. AVG
Per capita income	$18,273	$23,235	Unemployment rate	4.2%	4.7%	Largest: Healthcare & Social Assistance		
Household income	$37,069	$46,414	Recent job growth	5.9%	1.3%			
Household income < $25K	32.9%	26.2%	Projected future job growth	14.9%	11.5%	Percent manufacturing	11.8%	15.4%
Household income > $75K	16.3%	25.4%	White collar	56.7%	57.8%	Percent public sector	17.7%	15.7%
Household income growth	11.2%	13.6%	Blue collar	22.6%	25.2%	Percent construction	10.8%	9.9%

Cost of Living
Score: 92.5
Rank: 29

INDEXES & TAXES	AREA	U.S. AVG	HOUSING	AREA	U.S. AVG	NECESSITIES	AREA	U.S. AVG
Cost of Living Index	80.0	100.0	Median home price	$125,300	$220,000	Food Index	86.8	100.0
Buying Power Index	103.9	100.0	Home price appreciation	22.3%	10.1%	Housing Index	47.0	100.0
Income tax rate	0.00%	4.70%	Median rent	$549	$709	Utilities Index	99.2	100.0
Sales tax rate	8.25%	6.58%	Homes owned	58.8%	62.3%	Transportation Index	96.0	100.0
Property tax rate	$15.95	$12.00	Home price ratio	3.4	4.2	Healthcare Index	92.6	100.0
						Miscellaneous Cost Index	97.0	100.0

Climate
Score: 90.4
Rank: 37

TEMPERATURE	AREA	U.S. AVG	PRECIPITATION	AREA	U.S. AVG	COMFORTS & HAZARDS	AREA	U.S. AVG
Average January low	31.7	26.2	Annual inches precipitation	24.0	37.7	July relative humidity	59%	66%
Average July high	95.3	87.4	Annual inches snowfall	5.0	7.0	Annual days mostly sunny	246	208
Annual days > 90°F	89	38	Annual days precipitation	65	109	Annual days with thunderstorms	42	39
Annual days < 32°F	56	89	Annual days rain > 0.5 inches	16	22	Tornado risk score	42	18
Annual days < 0°F	0	6	Annual days snow > 1.5 inches	2	6	Hurricane risk score	2	13

TEMPERATURE

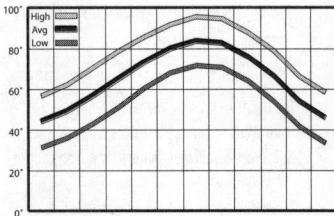

PRECIPITATION

DAYS OF CLOUDS & PRECIPITATION

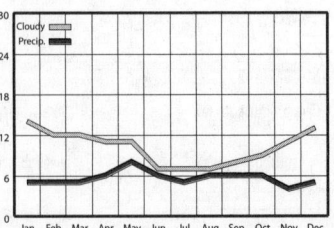

Education
Score: 41.4
Rank: 220

ACHIEVEMENT	AREA	U.S. AVG	PUBLIC SCHOOLS	AREA	U.S. AVG	HIGHER EDUCATION	AREA	U.S. AVG
High school degree	79.2%	82.7%	Expenditures per pupil	$5,467	$5,686	No. 2-year colleges	0	4
2-year college degree	5.3%	6.4%	Student/teacher ratio	12.7	16.7	No. 4-year colleges/universities	3	6
4-year college degree	13.3%	15.7%	Attending public school	97.8%	90.1%	No. highly ranked universities	0	1
Graduate/professional degree	6.7%	8.9%	State SAT score	997*	1021			
			State ACT score	20.3	20.9			

Health & Healthcare
Score: 93.3
Rank: 26

HAZARDS & ILLNESSES	AREA	U.S. AVG	HEALTHCARE	AREA	U.S. AVG	CRIME	AREA	U.S. AVG
Air-quality score	49	37	Physicians per capita	183.2	244.2	Violent crime rate	397.2	465.5
Water-quality score	99	52	Hospital beds per capita	463.7	420.0	Change in violent crime rate	9.8%	-2.2%
Pollen/allergy score	78	61	No. teaching hospitals	0	3	Property crime rate	3,845.5	3,517.1
Cancer mortality per capita	174.3	201.9	Cost per doctor visit	$71	$77	Change in property crime rate	-5.6%	-2.1%
Depression days per month	4.3	3.5	Cost per dental visit	$56	$70			
Stress score	34	50						

Crime
Score: 59.9
Rank: 151

Transportation
Score: 54.3
Rank: 171

COMMUTE	AREA	U.S. AVG	INTERCITY SERVICES	AREA	U.S. AVG	AUTOMOTIVE	AREA	U.S. AVG
Average commute time	19.1	27.4	Major airports within 60 miles	0	1	Insurance, annual premium	$1,040	$1,432
Percent commutes > 60 mins.	3.3%	5.9%	Size of regional airport	None	Large	Gas, cost per gallon	$2.50	$2.49
Commute by auto	80.9%	78.9%	Daily airline activity	22	686	Daily vehicle miles per capita	25.8	24.0
Commute by mass transit	0.4%	1.9%	Amtrak service	No	No			
Work at home	2.3%	3.1%						
Mass transit miles per capita	0.41	1.87						

Leisure
Score: 19.0
Rank: 302

DINING & SHOPPING	AREA	U.S. AVG	ENTERTAINMENT	AREA	U.S. AVG	OUTDOOR ACTIVITIES	AREA	U.S. AVG
Restaurant rating	1	2	Professional sports rating	2	4	Golf-course rating	2	4
Outlet mall score	0	42	College sports rating	5	4	Ski-area rating	1	3
No. Starbucks	1	13	Zoo/aquarium rating	3	3	Sq. miles inland water	2	4
No. warehouse clubs	0	2	Amusement park rating	1	3	Miles of coastline	0.0	10.7
			Botanical garden/ arboretum rating	5	4	National Park rating	1	3

Arts & Culture
Score: 39.6
Rank: 226

MEDIA & LIBRARIES	AREA	U.S. AVG	PERFORMING ARTS	AREA	U.S. AVG	MUSEUMS	AREA	U.S. AVG
Arts radio rating	1	3	Classical music rating	2	4	Overall museum rating	4	5
No. public libraries	8	27	Ballet/dance rating	1	3	Art museum rating	5	5
Library volumes per capita	2.22	2.78	Professional theater rating	1	3	Science museum rating	5	5
			University arts programs rating	7	5	Children's museum rating	5	3

Akron, OH

Score: 43.7   Rank: 298   2004 rank: 140

Profile: Mid-size industrial city
Location: Northeastern Ohio, 40 miles south of Cleveland
Elevation: 1,027 feet
Time zone: Eastern Standard Time

PRO	CON
Revitalizing economy	Entertainment
Nearby recreation	Cloudy, wet climate
Close to Cleveland	Industrial landscape

Akron is an industrial city, and the center of the U.S. rubber industry. The area once produced more than half the tires made in the United States, in addition to manufacturing other rubber, plastic, and chemical products. Although the majority of production has shifted south and overseas, Akron remains a corporate center for tire companies, including Goodyear, Uniroyal-Goodrich, and GenCorp. The city has a strong pro-business climate and a strategic location to many U.S. markets, and is slowly increasing its service-economy base. Physically and in many other ways the city lacks interest, and although some of the industrial effects of past years are gone, it still has some depressed areas and air-quality issues. Annual local events commanding national attention are the National Soap Box Derby and the PGA golf tournaments at

Firestone Country Club. For a town its size Akron does have some arts presence. The University of Akron and nearby Kent State University add some college flavor. Cost of living and housing are reasonable. Nearby Cleveland offers many amenities and services not locally present.

The rolling to hilly terrain reaches its highest elevation at 1,300 feet. Many small lakes provide water for industry and recreation, and the landscape is a mix of open terrain and wooded areas. Because of the terrain, winter temperatures and snowfall vary considerably over the area, with more snow in the north. In between the late springs and pleasant autumns, summers are moderately warm and quite humid. Fog is common, especially in the fall. First freeze is mid-October; last is late April.

Population

DEMOGRAPHICS	AREA	U.S. AVG		ETHNIC COMPOSITION	AREA	U.S. AVG		RESIDENT PROFILE	AREA	U.S. AVG
Population	704,288			White	85.1%	79.0%		Single	33.3%	32.4%
Population density per sq. mile	778.1	358.5		Black	11.2%	10.5%		Married	53.1%	52.7%
Population growth	7.1%	21.1%		Asian	1.6%	2.7%		Divorced/separated	13.6%	14.9%
Median age	37.7	36.1		Hispanic	0.9%	10.6%		Married with children	22.1%	23.7%
Percent Democrat	55.9%	44.5%		Religious observance	44.3%	48.9%		Single with children	8.7%	9.1%
Percent Republican	43.7%	54.5%		Diversity measure	27.2	40.1		Percent over age 65	13.5%	12.9%

Economy & Jobs
Score: 49.2
Rank: 191

INCOME	AREA	U.S. AVG		EMPLOYMENT	AREA	U.S. AVG		EMPLOYING INDUSTRIES	AREA	U.S. AVG
Per capita income	$25,409	$23,235		Unemployment rate	5.4%	4.7%		Largest: Manufacturing		
Household income	$47,915	$46,414		Recent job growth	1.1%	1.3%				
Household income < $25K	24.1%	26.2%		Projected future job growth	9.5%	11.5%		Percent manufacturing	17.0%	15.4%
Household income > $75K	27.2%	25.4%		White collar	60.2%	57.8%		Percent public sector	11.8%	15.7%
Household income growth	12.1%	13.6%		Blue collar	25.2%	25.2%		Percent construction	8.2%	9.9%

Cost of Living
Score: 34.8
Rank: 244

INDEXES & TAXES	AREA	U.S. AVG		HOUSING	AREA	U.S. AVG		NECESSITIES	AREA	U.S. AVG
Cost of Living Index	86.6	100.0		Median home price	$123,400	$220,000		Food Index	105.4	100.0
Buying Power Index	124.0	100.0		Home price appreciation	16.3%	10.1%		Housing Index	61.3	100.0
Income tax rate	6.96%	4.70%		Median rent	$722	$709		Utilities Index	125.1	100.0
Sales tax rate	6.86%	6.58%		Homes owned	66.8%	62.3%		Transportation Index	101.5	100.0
Property tax rate	$13.10	$12.00		Home price ratio	2.6	4.2		Healthcare Index	109.8	100.0
								Miscellaneous Cost Index	99.8	100.0

Climate
Score: 16.3
Rank: 312

TEMPERATURE	AREA	U.S. AVG		PRECIPITATION	AREA	U.S. AVG		COMFORTS & HAZARDS	AREA	U.S. AVG
Average January low	18.6	26.2		Annual inches precipitation	35.0	37.7		July relative humidity	71%	66%
Average July high	82.6	87.4		Annual inches snowfall	48.0	7.0		Annual days mostly sunny	171	208
Annual days > 90°F	7	38		Annual days precipitation	153	109		Annual days with thunderstorms	40	39
Annual days < 32°F	128	89		Annual days rain > 0.5 inches	21	22		Tornado risk score	13	18
Annual days < 0°F	5	6		Annual days snow > 1.5 inches	10	6		Hurricane risk score	2	13

TEMPERATURE

PRECIPITATION

DAYS OF CLOUDS & PRECIPITATION

Education
Score: 54.5
Rank: 171

ACHIEVEMENT	AREA	U.S. AVG		PUBLIC SCHOOLS	AREA	U.S. AVG		HIGHER EDUCATION	AREA	U.S. AVG
High school degree	85.9%	82.7%		Expenditures per pupil	$5,790	$5,686		No. 2-year colleges	6	4
2-year college degree	5.2%	6.4%		Student/teacher ratio	17.6	16.7		No. 4-year colleges/universities	4	6
4-year college degree	16.4%	15.7%		Attending public school	88.4%	90.1%		No. highly ranked universities	1	1
Graduate/professional degree	8.3%	8.9%		State SAT score	1079	1021				
				State ACT score	21.5*	20.9				

Health & Healthcare
Score: 17.1
Rank: 309

HAZARDS & ILLNESSES	AREA	U.S. AVG		HEALTHCARE	AREA	U.S. AVG		CRIME	AREA	U.S. AVG
Air-quality score	29	37		Physicians per capita	272.0	244.2		Violent crime rate	266.4	465.5
Water-quality score	31	52		Hospital beds per capita	378.1	420.0		Change in violent crime rate	-3.0%	-2.2%
Pollen/allergy score	64	61		No. teaching hospitals	6	3		Property crime rate	3,662.1	3,517.1
Cancer mortality per capita	224.7	201.9		Cost per doctor visit	$62	$77		Change in property crime rate	-2.9%	-2.1%
Depression days per month	4.5	3.5		Cost per dental visit	$71	$70				
Stress score	56	50								

Crime
Score: 53.7
Rank: 173

Transportation
Score: 75.4
Rank: 93

COMMUTE	AREA	U.S. AVG		INTERCITY SERVICES	AREA	U.S. AVG		AUTOMOTIVE	AREA	U.S. AVG
Average commute time	25.1	27.4		Major airports within 60 miles	2	1		Insurance, annual premium	$1,491	$1,432
Percent commutes > 60 mins.	4.6%	5.9%		Size of regional airport	Large	Large		Gas, cost per gallon	$2.46	$2.49
Commute by auto	85.7%	78.9%		Daily airline activity	1150	686		Daily vehicle miles per capita	22.3	24.0
Commute by mass transit	1.3%	1.9%		Amtrak service	Yes	No				
Work at home	2.6%	3.1%								
Mass transit miles per capita	1.34	1.87								

DINING & SHOPPING	AREA	U.S. AVG	ENTERTAINMENT	AREA	U.S. AVG	OUTDOOR ACTIVITIES	AREA	U.S. AVG
Restaurant rating	1	2	Professional sports rating	6	4	Golf-course rating	8	4
Outlet mall score	0	42	College sports rating	5	4	Ski-area rating	2	3
No. Starbucks	8	13	Zoo/aquarium rating	4	3	Sq. miles inland water	3	4
No. warehouse clubs	3	2	Amusement park rating	9	3	Miles of coastline	0.0	10.7
			Botanical garden/			National Park rating	3	3
			arboretum rating	7	4			

Leisure
Score: 73.8
Rank: 98

MEDIA & LIBRARIES	AREA	U.S. AVG	PERFORMING ARTS	AREA	U.S. AVG	MUSEUMS	AREA	U.S. AVG
Arts radio rating	4	3	Classical music rating	6	4	Overall museum rating	7	5
No. public libraries	35	27	Ballet/dance rating	4	3	Art museum rating	8	5
Library volumes per capita	3.81	2.78	Professional theater rating	5	3	Science museum rating	8	5
			University arts programs rating	8	5	Children's museum rating	2	3

Arts & Culture
Score: 77.5
Rank: 84

Albany, GA

Score: 44.7 Rank: 286 2004 rank: 255

Profile: Small agricultural/industrial town
Location: Southwest Georgia in a mostly agricultural region about 80 miles north of Tallahassee, Florida
Elevation: 200 feet
Time zone: Eastern Standard Time

PRO	CON
Cost of living	Summer heat
Small-town atmosphere	Entertainment
Mild winters	Isolation

Albany is a commercial center for the pecan and peanut farming area of southwest Georgia. A fairly robust economy and the availability of services make this clean, quiet town livable, if not intellectually stimulating. Low cost of living, economic incentives, and a favorable location have made it a minor manufacturing center, with Procter & Gamble, Miller Brewing, and Merck among blue-chip employers. Downtown is plain but has undergone some redevelopment on the Flint River waterfront, bringing in minor entertainment and cultural amenities. Downsides include persistent summer heat and limited cultural and advanced educational opportunities.

The city sits in a plain at the junction of the Flint River and several smaller rivers. The mostly level terrain contains large peanut farms and plantations and a few stands of trees. Summers are very warm and humid with the inland temperatures more extreme than those in the Florida Panhandle to the south. Afternoon thunderstorms are common, but periods of extended dry heat also occur. Winter often includes long periods of rain and cloudiness. Because of the flat terrain, local floods are possible. Although temperatures are usually mild, freezing occurs every winter. First freeze is early December; last is mid-February.

DEMOGRAPHICS	AREA	U.S. AVG	ETHNIC COMPOSITION	AREA	U.S. AVG	RESIDENT PROFILE	AREA	U.S. AVG
Population	162,356		White	48.5%	79.0%	Single	36.1%	32.4%
Population density per sq. mile	84.0	358.5	Black	49.3%	10.5%	Married	47.2%	52.7%
Population growth	16.6%	21.1%	Asian	0.8%	2.7%	Divorced/separated	16.7%	14.9%
Median age	33.6	36.1	Hispanic	1.2%	10.6%	Married with children	21.7%	23.7%
Percent Democrat	47.4%	44.5%	Religious observance	38.8%	48.9%	Single with children	14.3%	9.1%
Percent Republican	52.2%	54.5%	Diversity measure	45.8	40.1	Percent over age 65	11.3%	12.9%

Population

INCOME	AREA	U.S. AVG	EMPLOYMENT	AREA	U.S. AVG	EMPLOYING INDUSTRIES	AREA	U.S. AVG
Per capita income	$19,317	$23,235	Unemployment rate	6.3%	4.7%	Largest: Manufacturing		
Household income	$38,404	$46,414	Recent job growth	1.4%	1.3%			
Household income < $25K	34.4%	26.2%	Projected future job growth	9.1%	11.5%	Percent manufacturing	18.1%	15.4%
Household income > $75K	20.2%	25.4%	White collar	54.3%	57.8%	Percent public sector	21.5%	15.7%
Household income growth	12.7%	13.6%	Blue collar	28.3%	25.2%	Percent construction	10.2%	9.9%

Economy & Jobs
Score: 31.6
Rank: 256

INDEXES & TAXES	AREA	U.S. AVG	HOUSING	AREA	U.S. AVG	NECESSITIES	AREA	U.S. AVG
Cost of Living Index	81.1	100.0	Median home price	$120,500	$220,000	Food Index	95.9	100.0
Buying Power Index	106.1	100.0	Home price appreciation	28.9%	10.1%	Housing Index	52.3	100.0
Income tax rate	6.00%	4.70%	Median rent	$557	$709	Utilities Index	94.6	100.0
Sales tax rate	7.00%	6.58%	Homes owned	56.8%	62.3%	Transportation Index	92.5	100.0
Property tax rate	$13.16	$12.00	Home price ratio	3.1	4.2	Healthcare Index	88.7	100.0
						Miscellaneous Cost Index	100.1	100.0

Cost of Living
Score: 51.3
Rank: 179

Climate
Score: 62.3
Rank: 140

TEMPERATURE	AREA	U.S. AVG	PRECIPITATION	AREA	U.S. AVG	COMFORTS & HAZARDS	AREA	U.S. AVG
Average January low	41.0	26.2	Annual inches precipitation	62.0	37.7	July relative humidity	76%	66%
Average July high	90.6	87.4	Annual inches snowfall	0.0	7.0	Annual days mostly sunny	233	208
Annual days > 90°F	87	38	Annual days precipitation	119	109	Annual days with thunderstorms	86	39
Annual days < 32°F	36	89	Annual days rain > 0.5 inches	38	22	Tornado risk score	24	18
Annual days < 0°F	0	6	Annual days snow > 1.5 inches	0	6	Hurricane risk score	38	13

TEMPERATURE

PRECIPITATION

DAYS OF CLOUDS & PRECIPITATION

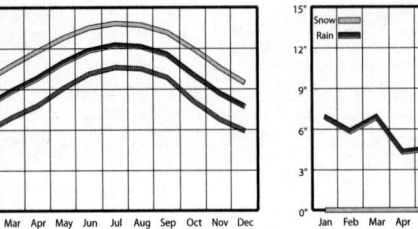
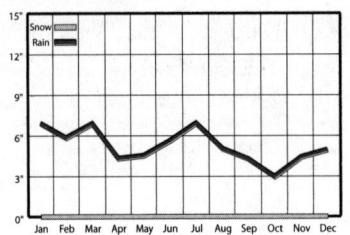
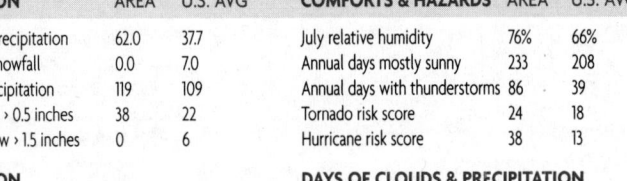

Education
Score: 10.7
Rank: 333

ACHIEVEMENT	AREA	U.S. AVG	PUBLIC SCHOOLS	AREA	U.S. AVG	HIGHER EDUCATION	AREA	U.S. AVG
High school degree	73.8%	82.7%	Expenditures per pupil	$5,551	$5,686	No. 2-year colleges	2	4
2-year college degree	4.7%	6.4%	Student/teacher ratio	16.0	16.7	No. 4-year colleges/universities	1	6
4-year college degree	10.3%	15.7%	Attending public school	95.4%	90.1%	No. highly ranked universities	0	1
Graduate/professional degree	5.7%	8.9%	State SAT score	990*	1021			
			State ACT score	20.2	20.9			

Health & Healthcare
Score: 83.2
Rank: 64

Crime
Score: 59.4
Rank: 152

HAZARDS & ILLNESSES	AREA	U.S. AVG	HEALTHCARE	AREA	U.S. AVG	CRIME	AREA	U.S. AVG
Air-quality score	53	37	Physicians per capita	185.1	244.2	Violent crime rate	374.8	465.5
Water-quality score	60	52	Hospital beds per capita	448.4	420.0	Change in violent crime rate	-9.9%	-2.2%
Pollen/allergy score	60	61	No. teaching hospitals	1	3	Property crime rate	4,057.2	3,517.1
Cancer mortality per capita	181.5	201.9	Cost per doctor visit	$69	$77	Change in property crime rate	-6.4%	-2.1%
Depression days per month	2.9	3.5	Cost per dental visit	$69	$70			
Stress score	41	50						

Transportation
Score: 27.0
Rank: 274

COMMUTE	AREA	U.S. AVG	INTERCITY SERVICES	AREA	U.S. AVG	AUTOMOTIVE	AREA	U.S. AVG
Average commute time	22.2	27.4	Major airports within 60 miles	0	1	Insurance, annual premium	$1,288	$1,432
Percent commutes > 60 mins.	3.6%	5.9%	Size of regional airport	Small	Large	Gas, cost per gallon	$2.40	$2.49
Commute by auto	79.4%	78.9%	Daily airline activity	69	686	Daily vehicle miles per capita	28.9	24.0
Commute by mass transit	0.8%	1.9%	Amtrak service	No	No			
Work at home	1.7%	3.1%						
Mass transit miles per capita	0.81	1.87						

Leisure
Score: 8.8
Rank: 340

DINING & SHOPPING	AREA	U.S. AVG	ENTERTAINMENT	AREA	U.S. AVG	OUTDOOR ACTIVITIES	AREA	U.S. AVG
Restaurant rating	1	2	Professional sports rating	2	4	Golf-course rating	1	4
Outlet mall score	12	42	College sports rating	4	4	Ski-area rating	1	3
No. Starbucks	0	13	Zoo/aquarium rating	1	3	Sq. miles inland water	2	4
No. warehouse clubs	1	2	Amusement park rating	1	3	Miles of coastline	0.0	10.7
			Botanical garden/ arboretum rating	1	4	National Park rating	1	3

Arts & Culture
Score: 28.1
Rank: 268

MEDIA & LIBRARIES	AREA	U.S. AVG	PERFORMING ARTS	AREA	U.S. AVG	MUSEUMS	AREA	U.S. AVG
Arts radio rating	1	3	Classical music rating	3	4	Overall museum rating	2	5
No. public libraries	13	27	Ballet/dance rating	1	3	Art museum rating	3	5
Library volumes per capita	3.23	2.78	Professional theater rating	1	3	Science museum rating	1	5
			University arts programs rating	3	5	Children's museum rating	1	3

Albany–Schenectady–Troy, NY

Score: 52.6 **Rank:** 235 **2004 rank:** 240

Profile: Capital-city complex
Location: East-central New York, along the Hudson River 160 miles north of New York City
Elevation: 292 feet
Time zone: Eastern Standard Time

PRO	CON
Diverse economy	Harsh winters
Educated population	Entertainment
Nearby recreation	Cost of living

The Albany area includes six counties, the cities of Troy and Schenectady, and the historic Saratoga Springs area to the north. An assortment of commercial and state government activities support this capital city. Downtown Albany is modern with a number of historic sites and an attractive waterfront. There is an assortment of mostly small arts and cultural amenities throughout the metropolitan area. Schenectady is an older industrial center known once for producing railroad locomotives and known past and present as a major center for the General Electric Company. Downtown Schenectady has benefited from a large renewal investment and has become a minor entertainment destination. The Rensselaer Polytechnic Institute in Troy brings some college-town flavor to that city. At 109.2 the cost of living is moderately high for what's available, though not as high as the urban areas to the south. The area is at best a mixed bag of steady and declining economic interests and population, but with the right set of improvements and gradual recognition as an alternative to bigger East Coast cities, may be on the improvement track.

The city of Albany is located on a gently rolling valley floor on the west bank of the Hudson River, 8 miles south of the confluence of the Mohawk and Hudson rivers. The area's elevation rises from sea level at the Hudson to 1,500 feet, 11 miles west of Albany. East of the Hudson, the terrain rises more sharply into the Berkshires of western Massachusetts. In warmer seasons, temperatures rise sharply by day, but fall rapidly after sunset; nights are relatively cool. Periods of oppressive heat occasionally extend a week or more. Winters are cold and sometimes severe, with lows frequently below 10°F. Most precipitation comes from summer thunderstorms; almost 6 feet of snow falls each winter. Albany tends to get more sunshine than other places in the state. First freeze is end of September; last is early May.

DEMOGRAPHICS	AREA	U.S. AVG	ETHNIC COMPOSITION	AREA	U.S. AVG	RESIDENT PROFILE	AREA	U.S. AVG
Population	848,411		White	86.8%	79.0%	Single	35.3%	32.4%
Population density per sq. mile	301.1	358.5	Black	7.4%	10.5%	Married	50.6%	52.7%
Population growth	5.3%	21.1%	Asian	2.8%	2.7%	Divorced/separated	14.1%	14.9%
Median age	38.4	36.1	Hispanic	3.4%	10.6%	Married with children	21.5%	23.7%
Percent Democrat	52.5%	44.5%	Religious observance	55.0%	48.9%	Single with children	8.8%	9.1%
Percent Republican	45.4%	54.5%	Diversity measure	28.3	40.1	Percent over age 65	13.9%	12.9%

Population

INCOME	AREA	U.S. AVG	EMPLOYMENT	AREA	U.S. AVG	EMPLOYING INDUSTRIES	AREA	U.S. AVG
Per capita income	$26,406	$23,235	Unemployment rate	4.1%	4.7%	Largest: Healthcare & Social Assistance		
Household income	$50,438	$46,414	Recent job growth	1.8%	1.3%			
Household income < $25K	22.7%	26.2%	Projected future job growth	5.7%	11.5%	Percent manufacturing	10.8%	15.4%
Household income > $75K	29.8%	25.4%	White collar	67.1%	57.8%	Percent public sector	23.5%	15.7%
Household income growth	14.3%	13.6%	Blue collar	18.3%	25.2%	Percent construction	7.6%	9.9%

Economy & Jobs
Score: 36.9
Rank: 236

INDEXES & TAXES	AREA	U.S. AVG	HOUSING	AREA	U.S. AVG	NECESSITIES	AREA	U.S. AVG
Cost of Living Index	109.2	100.0	Median home price	$193,000	$220,000	Food Index	116.7	100.0
Buying Power Index	103.5	100.0	Home price appreciation	71.3%	10.1%	Housing Index	83.0	100.0
Income tax rate	7.13%	4.70%	Median rent	$752	$709	Utilities Index	149.4	100.0
Sales tax rate	8.00%	6.58%	Homes owned	59.2%	62.3%	Transportation Index	111.1	100.0
Property tax rate	$22.71	$12.00	Home price ratio	3.8	4.2	Healthcare Index	136.7	100.0
						Miscellaneous Cost Index	119.3	100.0

Cost of Living
Score: 11.8
Rank: 329

Climate
Score: 2.7
Rank: 363

TEMPERATURE	AREA	U.S. AVG
Average January low	12.5	26.2
Average July high	83.9	87.4
Annual days > 90°F	8	38
Annual days > 32°F	155	89
Annual days < 0°F	17	6

PRECIPITATION	AREA	U.S. AVG
Annual inches precipitation	33.0	37.7
Annual inches snowfall	71.0	7.0
Annual days precipitation	135	109
Annual days rain > 0.5 inches	23	22
Annual days snow > 1.5 inches	13	6

COMFORTS & HAZARDS	AREA	U.S. AVG
July relative humidity	71%	66%
Annual days mostly sunny	182	208
Annual days with thunderstorms	28	39
Tornado risk score	6	18
Hurricane risk score	7	13

TEMPERATURE

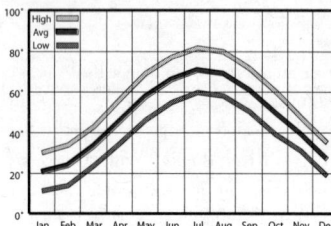

PRECIPITATION

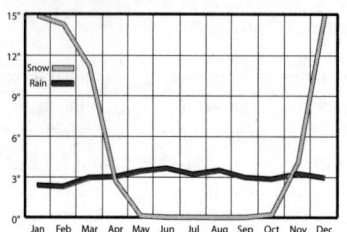

DAYS OF CLOUDS & PRECIPITATION

Education
Score: 96.0
Rank: 16

ACHIEVEMENT	AREA	U.S. AVG
High school degree	86.2%	82.7%
2-year college degree	10.0%	6.4%
4-year college degree	16.3%	15.7%
Graduate/professional degree	13.0%	8.9%

PUBLIC SCHOOLS	AREA	U.S. AVG
Expenditures per pupil	$8,452	$5,686
Student/teacher ratio	15.0	16.7
Attending public school	90.3%	90.1%
State SAT score	1003*	1021
State ACT score	22.6	20.9

HIGHER EDUCATION	AREA	U.S. AVG
No. 2-year colleges	10	4
No. 4-year colleges/universities	14	6
No. highly ranked universities	5	1

Health & Healthcare
Score: 42.2
Rank: 215

HAZARDS & ILLNESSES	AREA	U.S. AVG
Air-quality score	40	37
Water-quality score	66	52
Pollen/allergy score	41	61
Cancer mortality per capita	213.8	201.9
Depression days per month	3.1	3.5
Stress score	12	50

HEALTHCARE	AREA	U.S. AVG
Physicians per capita	306.0	244.2
Hospital beds per capita	367.7	420.0
No. teaching hospitals	7	3
Cost per doctor visit	$85	$77
Cost per dental visit	$83	$70

Crime
Score: 87.7
Rank: 46

CRIME	AREA	U.S. AVG
Violent crime rate	365.7	465.5
Change in violent crime rate	22.1%	-2.2%
Property crime rate	2,662.1	3,517.1
Change in property crime rate	3.8%	-2.1%

Transportation
Score: 36.1
Rank: 236

COMMUTE	AREA	U.S. AVG
Average commute time	24.5	27.4
Percent commutes > 60 mins.	4.1%	5.9%
Commute by auto	79.8%	78.9%
Commute by mass transit	3.2%	1.9%
Work at home	3.0%	3.1%
Mass transit miles per capita	3.17	1.87

INTERCITY SERVICES	AREA	U.S. AVG
Major airports within 60 miles	1	1
Size of regional airport	Medium	Large
Daily airline activity	340	686
Amtrak service	Yes	No

AUTOMOTIVE	AREA	U.S. AVG
Insurance, annual premium	$1,717	$1,432
Gas, cost per gallon	$2.62	$2.49
Daily vehicle miles per capita	28.9	24.0

Leisure
Score: 75.9
Rank: 90

DINING & SHOPPING	AREA	U.S. AVG
Restaurant rating	1	2
Outlet mall score	27	42
No. Starbucks	7	13
No. warehouse clubs	5	2

ENTERTAINMENT	AREA	U.S. AVG
Professional sports rating	3	4
College sports rating	10	4
Zoo/aquarium rating	1	3
Amusement park rating	5	3
Botanical garden/ arboretum rating	5	4

OUTDOOR ACTIVITIES	AREA	U.S. AVG
Golf-course rating	7	4
Ski-area rating	7	3
Sq. miles inland water	5	4
Miles of coastline	0.0	10.7
National Park rating	2	3

Arts & Culture
Score: 85.8
Rank: 54

MEDIA & LIBRARIES	AREA	U.S. AVG
Arts radio rating	10	3
No. public libraries	60	27
Library volumes per capita	3.59	2.78

PERFORMING ARTS	AREA	U.S. AVG
Classical music rating	5	4
Ballet/dance rating	5	3
Professional theater rating	6	3
University arts programs rating	6	5

MUSEUMS	AREA	U.S. AVG
Overall museum rating	8	5
Art museum rating	9	5
Science museum rating	9	5
Children's museum rating	8	3

Albuquerque, NM

Score: 63.8 Rank: 145 2004 rank: 45

Profile: Mid-size city/college town
Location: Near the center of New Mexico
Elevation: 5,314 feet
Time zone: Mountain Standard Time

PRO
Year-round climate
Attractive setting
Arts and culture

CON
Crime rate
Urban sprawl
Economic cycles

Albuquerque, located at the crossroads of the state's travel routes, is the largest city in New Mexico. Clear, sunny, dry days; an attractive mountain landscape; and a mostly healthy economy attract new residents from around the country. The area also has a favorable tax climate, and the state's fiscal health is among the best in the country. The area is a hub for transportation and warehousing, as well as research-oriented activities that are centered on the giant Sandia Laboratories nuclear research facility south of town. With more than 100 mostly small- and medium-size tech-related companies, the area has experienced some vulnerability to tech industry economic cycles. Albuquerque boasts a modern downtown and an excellent historic district with shops, restaurants, and entertainment venues. The town sprawls in all directions from the city core; managing growth, sprawl, congestion, and air quality are among the area's biggest challenges. Crime, and particularly violent crime, is another challenge, which clearly hurts the area's ranking in this edition. More upscale neighborhoods lie to the northeast, while more middle-class areas spread west and also south towards the large Kirtland Air Force Base. The University of New Mexico brings a strong college presence to downtown. There are a number of arts organizations, and the area, with its mix of Native American and Hispanic heritage, has a unique cultural flavor, though many consider the cultural offerings in Santa Fe, 60 miles north, to be superior. Within a day's drive are interesting historic and archaeological sites and mountain areas to the east.

The Albuquerque metro area is largely situated in the Rio Grande Valley and on the mesas and piedmont slopes rising on either side of the valley floor. The Sandia and Manzano mountains rise abruptly from the eastern edge of the city with Tijeras Canyon separating the two ranges. West of the city the land gradually rises to the Continental Divide, some 90 miles away. More than three-fourths of daylight hours have sunshine, even in winter. Average summer temperatures are high, with warm days up to 90°F, low humidity, and cool nights. Winter temperatures usually reach the 50s, but can fail to rise above freezing on a few days. Precipitation is adequate only for native vegetation. Snow in the city is light and infrequent, but the mountains get enough for skiing. Most annual precipitation comes from afternoon summer thundershowers, which peak during August. Winter and spring windstorms may bring dust. First freeze is mid-October; last is early May.

DEMOGRAPHICS	AREA	U.S. AVG	ETHNIC COMPOSITION	AREA	U.S. AVG	RESIDENT PROFILE	AREA	U.S. AVG
Population	782,916		White	68.2%	79.0%	Single	33.4%	32.4%
Population density per sq. mile	84.3	358.5	Black	2.5%	10.5%	Married	50.5%	52.7%
Population growth	32.2%	21.1%	Asian	1.9%	2.7%	Divorced/separated	16.1%	14.9%
Median age	35.9	36.1	Hispanic	43.4%	10.6%	Married with children	22.6%	23.7%
Percent Democrat	50.0%	44.5%	Religious observance	54.3%	48.9%	Single with children	10.7%	9.1%
Percent Republican	48.8%	54.5%	Diversity measure	74.1	40.1	Percent over age 65	11.6%	12.9%

Score: 74.1 Rank: 97

INCOME	AREA	U.S. AVG	EMPLOYMENT	AREA	U.S. AVG	EMPLOYING INDUSTRIES	AREA	U.S. AVG
Per capita income	$23,528	$23,235	Unemployment rate	5.9%	4.7%	Largest: Healthcare & Social Assistance		
Household income	$45,380	$46,414	Recent job growth	3.4%	1.3%			
Household income < $25K	26.0%	26.2%	Projected future job growth	19.2%	11.5%	Percent manufacturing	9.9%	15.4%
Household income > $75K	25.3%	25.4%	White collar	64.7%	57.8%	Percent public sector	18.9%	15.7%
Household income growth	16.3%	13.6%	Blue collar	19.4%	25.2%	Percent construction	9.5%	9.9%

Score: 29.4 Rank: 263

INDEXES & TAXES	AREA	U.S. AVG	HOUSING	AREA	U.S. AVG	NECESSITIES	AREA	U.S. AVG
Cost of Living Index	94.8	100.0	Median home price	$185,400	$220,000	Food Index	107.5	100.0
Buying Power Index	107.3	100.0	Home price appreciation	30.4%	10.1%	Housing Index	64.4	100.0
Income tax rate	7.10%	4.70%	Median rent	$746	$709	Utilities Index	97.2	100.0
Sales tax rate	6.56%	6.58%	Homes owned	63.4%	62.3%	Transportation Index	100.6	100.0
Property tax rate	$8.03	$12.00	Home price ratio	4.1	4.2	Healthcare Index	106.7	100.0
						Miscellaneous Cost Index	97.0	100.0

Climate
Score: 85.8
Rank: 54

TEMPERATURE	AREA	U.S. AVG
Average January low	23.5	26.2
Average July high	92.2	87.4
Annual days > 90°F	61	38
Annual days < 32°F	123	89
Annual days < 0°F	1	6

PRECIPITATION	AREA	U.S. AVG
Annual inches precipitation	8.0	37.7
Annual inches snowfall	11.0	7.0
Annual days precipitation	59	109
Annual days rain > 0.5 inches	2	22
Annual days snow > 1.5 inches	3	6

COMFORTS & HAZARDS	AREA	U.S. AVG
July relative humidity	43%	66%
Annual days mostly sunny	283	208
Annual days with thunderstorms	43	39
Tornado risk score	9	18
Hurricane risk score	1	13

TEMPERATURE

PRECIPITATION

DAYS OF CLOUDS & PRECIPITATION

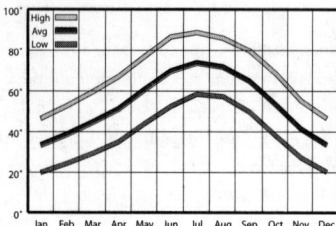
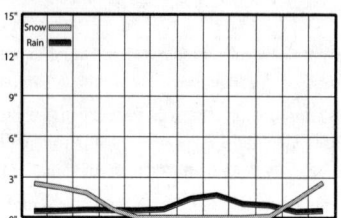

Education
Score: 62.8
Rank: 140

ACHIEVEMENT	AREA	U.S. AVG
High school degree	84.0%	82.7%
2-year college degree	6.0%	6.4%
4-year college degree	16.5%	15.7%
Graduate/professional degree	11.7%	8.9%

PUBLIC SCHOOLS	AREA	U.S. AVG
Expenditures per pupil	$4,673	$5,686
Student/teacher ratio	16.0	16.7
Attending public school	90.0%	90.1%
State SAT score	1106	1021
State ACT score	20.1*	20.9

HIGHER EDUCATION	AREA	U.S. AVG
No. 2-year colleges	5	4
No. 4-year colleges/universities	9	6
No. highly ranked universities	0	1

Health & Healthcare
Score: 22.2
Rank: 290

HAZARDS & ILLNESSES	AREA	U.S. AVG
Air-quality score	19	37
Water-quality score	47	52
Pollen/allergy score	74	61
Cancer mortality per capita	168.5	201.9
Depression days per month	3.8	3.5
Stress score	91	50

HEALTHCARE	AREA	U.S. AVG
Physicians per capita	306.2	244.2
Hospital beds per capita	288.4	420.0
No. teaching hospitals	4	3
Cost per doctor visit	$77	$77
Cost per dental visit	$73	$70

	CRIME	AREA	U.S. AVG
Crime	Violent crime rate	838.9	465.5
Score: 3.5	Change in violent crime rate	-0.5%	-2.2%
Rank: 360	Property crime rate	4,914.4	3,517.1
	Change in property crime rate	1.8%	-2.1%

Transportation
Score: 14.7
Rank: 320

COMMUTE	AREA	U.S. AVG
Average commute time	25.6	27.4
Percent commutes > 60 mins.	4.8%	5.9%
Commute by auto	77.9%	78.9%
Commute by mass transit	1.1%	1.9%
Work at home	3.9%	3.1%
Mass transit miles per capita	1.15	1.87

INTERCITY SERVICES	AREA	U.S. AVG
Major airports within 60 miles	1	1
Size of regional airport	Medium	Large
Daily airline activity	184	686
Amtrak service	Yes	No

AUTOMOTIVE	AREA	U.S. AVG
Insurance, annual premium	$1,733	$1,432
Gas, cost per gallon	$2.54	$2.49
Daily vehicle miles per capita	26.3	24.0

Leisure
Score: 71.1
Rank: 108

DINING & SHOPPING	AREA	U.S. AVG
Restaurant rating	1	2
Outlet mall score	0	42
No. Starbucks	20	13
No. warehouse clubs	4	2

ENTERTAINMENT	AREA	U.S. AVG
Professional sports rating	3	4
College sports rating	4	4
Zoo/aquarium rating	6	3
Amusement park rating	5	3
Botanical garden/ arboretum rating	1	4

OUTDOOR ACTIVITIES	AREA	U.S. AVG
Golf-course rating	3	4
Ski-area rating	10	3
Sq. miles inland water	1	4
Miles of coastline	0.0	10.7
National Park rating	5	3

Arts & Culture
Score: 76.7
Rank: 87

MEDIA & LIBRARIES	AREA	U.S. AVG
Arts radio rating	7	3
No. public libraries	35	27
Library volumes per capita	2.68	2.78

PERFORMING ARTS	AREA	U.S. AVG
Classical music rating	5	4
Ballet/dance rating	6	3
Professional theater rating	1	3
University arts programs rating	5	5

MUSEUMS	AREA	U.S. AVG
Overall museum rating	8	5
Art museum rating	8	5
Science museum rating	8	5
Children's museum rating	8	3

Alexandria, LA

Score: 13.3 Rank: 366 2004 rank: 321

Profile: Small city
Location: Center of Louisiana
Elevation: 118 feet
Time zone: Central Standard Time

PRO	CON
Cost of living	Crime rate
Healthcare	Arts and culture
Air quality	Unattractive downtown

Alexandria, located at the center of the state's major transportation routes, is a nondescript Southern city. During the Civil War, Federal forces wiped out most antebellum buildings, and today the city lacks historic charm. The downtown area is a mix of decline and modest renewal. The nearby Kisatchie National Forest provides some recreational opportunities. Economically, the area is supported mainly by public sector and healthcare industries, with some forest product and basic industries as well. The area did get some economic benefit—and hardship—from a modest refugee migration because of the 2005 hurricanes farther south. Healthcare resources are very good for the size of town. While cost of living is the second lowest in the state, the area suffers from high crime, a low high-school graduation rate, and a lack of things to do—hence the low overall rating.

The mainly level terrain supports agriculture beyond the town's sprawl. Forests of mixed hardwood and pine grow in and around the city. Summer months are still, warm, and humid with a few days above 100°F. Winters are mild with occasional cold snaps. Rain is abundant, with greater amounts in late spring and less in late summer; isolated showers and thunderstorms can persist for days. Winter ice storms and occasional snowfalls occur.

Population

DEMOGRAPHICS	AREA	U.S. AVG
Population	147,275	
Population density per sq. mile	74.8	358.5
Population growth	-1.1%	21.1%
Median age	36.0	36.1
Percent Democrat	33.6%	44.5%
Percent Republican	65.1%	54.5%

ETHNIC COMPOSITION	AREA	U.S. AVG
White	68.2%	79.0%
Black	28.5%	10.5%
Asian	0.9%	2.7%
Hispanic	1.7%	10.6%
Religious observance	61.8%	48.9%
Diversity measure	46.3	40.1

RESIDENT PROFILE	AREA	U.S. AVG
Single	33.6%	32.4%
Married	50.2%	52.7%
Divorced/separated	16.3%	14.9%
Married with children	23.0%	23.7%
Single with children	11.6%	9.1%
Percent over age 65	13.3%	12.9%

Economy & Jobs
Score: 19.0
Rank: 303

INCOME	AREA	U.S. AVG
Per capita income	$18,770	$23,235
Household income	$34,570	$46,414
Household income < $25K	36.9%	26.2%
Household income > $75K	17.3%	25.4%
Household income growth	15.9%	13.6%

EMPLOYMENT	AREA	U.S. AVG
Unemployment rate	6.4%	4.7%
Recent job growth	2.3%	1.3%
Projected future job growth	5.7%	11.5%
White collar	56.1%	57.8%
Blue collar	23.8%	25.2%

EMPLOYING INDUSTRIES	AREA	U.S. AVG
Largest: Healthcare & Social Assistance		
Percent manufacturing	12.1%	15.4%
Percent public sector	23.5%	15.7%
Percent construction	11.7%	9.9%

Cost of Living
Score: 81.6
Rank: 70

INDEXES & TAXES	AREA	U.S. AVG
Cost of Living Index	82.0	100.0
Buying Power Index	94.5	100.0
Income tax rate	4.00%	4.70%
Sales tax rate	7.13%	6.58%
Property tax rate	$4.37	$12.00

HOUSING	AREA	U.S. AVG
Median home price	$126,000	$220,000
Home price appreciation	27.3%	10.1%
Median rent	$501	$709
Homes owned	63.0%	62.3%
Home price ratio	3.6	4.2

NECESSITIES	AREA	U.S. AVG
Food Index	91.2	100.0
Housing Index	54.9	100.0
Utilities Index	97.0	100.0
Transportation Index	99.5	100.0
Healthcare Index	91.5	100.0
Miscellaneous Cost Index	99.4	100.0

Climate
Score: 62.6
Rank: 139

TEMPERATURE	AREA	U.S. AVG
Average January low	36.7	26.2
Average July high	91.8	87.4
Annual days > 90°F	75	38
Annual days < 32°F	43	89
Annual days < 0°F	0	6

PRECIPITATION	AREA	U.S. AVG
Annual inches precipitation	54.0	37.7
Annual inches snowfall	1.0	7.0
Annual days precipitation	106	109
Annual days rain > 0.5 inches	35	22
Annual days snow > 1.5 inches	0	6

COMFORTS & HAZARDS	AREA	U.S. AVG
July relative humidity	77%	66%
Annual days mostly sunny	219	208
Annual days with thunderstorms	69	39
Tornado risk score	23	18
Hurricane risk score	29	13

TEMPERATURE

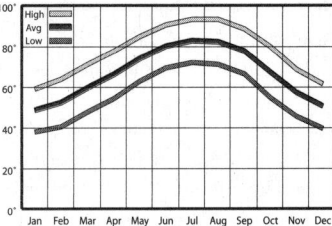

PRECIPITATION

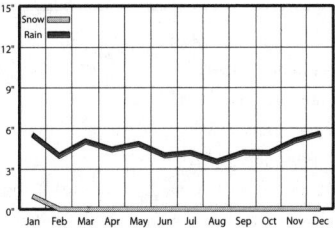

DAYS OF CLOUDS & PRECIPITATION

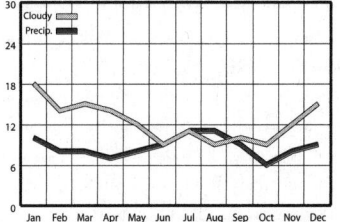

Education
Score: 3.7
Rank: 359

ACHIEVEMENT	AREA	U.S. AVG	PUBLIC SCHOOLS	AREA	U.S. AVG	HIGHER EDUCATION	AREA	U.S. AVG
High school degree	74.5%	82.7%	Expenditures per pupil	$4,486	$5,686	No. 2-year colleges	1	4
2-year college degree	3.6%	6.4%	Student/teacher ratio	16.2	16.7	No. 4-year colleges/universities	2	6
4-year college degree	10.0%	15.7%	Attending public school	89.3%	90.1%	No. highly ranked universities	0	1
Graduate/professional degree	5.6%	8.9%	State SAT score	1141	1021			
			State ACT score	20.1*	20.9			

Health & Healthcare
Score: 90.6
Rank: 36

HAZARDS & ILLNESSES	AREA	U.S. AVG	HEALTHCARE	AREA	U.S. AVG	CRIME	AREA	U.S. AVG
Air-quality score	43	37	Physicians per capita	250.2	244.2	Violent crime rate	983.0	465.5
Water-quality score	47	52	Hospital beds per capita	873.9	420.0	Change in violent crime rate	6.1%	-2.2%
Pollen/allergy score	67	61	No. teaching hospitals	2	3	Property crime rate	4,786.7	3,517.1
Cancer mortality per capita	220.6	201.9	Cost per doctor visit	$76	$77	Change in property crime rate	-7.3%	-2.1%
Depression days per month	3.1	3.5	Cost per dental visit	$65	$70			
Stress score	80	50						

Crime **Score:** 2.7 **Rank:** 363

Transportation
Score: 3.7
Rank: 359

COMMUTE	AREA	U.S. AVG	INTERCITY SERVICES	AREA	U.S. AVG	AUTOMOTIVE	AREA	U.S. AVG
Average commute time	25.5	27.4	Major airports within 60 miles	0	1	Insurance, annual premium	$1,553	$1,432
Percent commutes > 60 mins.	7.3%	5.9%	Size of regional airport	None	Large	Gas, cost per gallon	$2.46	$2.49
Commute by auto	78.7%	78.9%	Daily airline activity	22	686	Daily vehicle miles per capita	24.4	24.0
Commute by mass transit	1.2%	1.9%	Amtrak service	No	No			
Work at home	2.4%	3.1%						
Mass transit miles per capita	1.21	1.87						

Leisure
Score: 10.7
Rank: 333

DINING & SHOPPING	AREA	U.S. AVG	ENTERTAINMENT	AREA	U.S. AVG	OUTDOOR ACTIVITIES	AREA	U.S. AVG
Restaurant rating	1	2	Professional sports rating	2	4	Golf-course rating	1	4
Outlet mall score	3	42	College sports rating	1	4	Ski-area rating	1	3
No. Starbucks	0	13	Zoo/aquarium rating	1	3	Sq. miles inland water	2	4
No. warehouse clubs	1	2	Amusement park rating	1	3	Miles of coastline	0.0	10.7
			Botanical garden/arboretum rating	1	4	National Park rating	5	3

Arts & Culture
Score: 27.0
Rank: 272

MEDIA & LIBRARIES	AREA	U.S. AVG	PERFORMING ARTS	AREA	U.S. AVG	MUSEUMS	AREA	U.S. AVG
Arts radio rating	1	3	Classical music rating	3	4	Overall museum rating	2	5
No. public libraries	15	27	Ballet/dance rating	1	3	Art museum rating	4	5
Library volumes per capita	3.12	2.78	Professional theater rating	1	3	Science museum rating	1	5
			University arts programs rating	1	5	Children's museum rating	1	3

Allentown–Bethlehem–Easton, PA

Score: 81.1 Rank: 39 2004 rank: 202

Profile: Mid-size-city complex
Location: East-central Pennsylvania (along I-78) 20 miles west of the New Jersey border
Elevation: 264 feet
Time zone: Eastern Standard Time

PRO
Strategic location
Affordable housing
Attractive downtown

CON
Economic cycles
Some unattractive areas
Entertainment

The cities of Allentown, Bethlehem, and Easton have a strong industrial and working-class heritage, anchored by the enormous Bethlehem Steel Works. The gigantic 500-acre mill complex, abandoned 20 years ago, is still a formidable presence just south of downtown Bethlehem, and is likely to evolve—at least in part—to a preserved national park site celebrating our industrial heritage. The rest of the area is a center for mostly old-economy manufacturing with the Lucent Technologies spinoff Agere adding a not-too-prosperous high-tech element. Binney & Smith, known worldwide as the maker of Crayola crayons, has its factory in Easton.

But these legacy industries are no longer the whole story. The area is strategically located 90 miles west of the New York area and even closer to many prosperous and busy areas in New Jersey. Combined with higher

education facilities in Bethlehem, notably Lehigh University, the area is starting to draw people seeking a slower pace of life, lower cost of living, and a distinct city with a strong sense of place. Bethlehem brought workers into the area from central Europe, and the area (including Easton) has a distinct German and Moravian architecture and feel. Downtown Bethlehem is clean, attractive, and walkable, with small businesses, historic interest, some arts amenities, and a minor college town feel. Stately older homes lie just east of downtown, with more rural and attractive homes farther east and north. Allentown is the largest and plainest of the three cities, with large numbers of good older homes available to be fixed up or modified. Cost of living has risen to 108.6 but homes average $243,400, with a home price ratio of 4.8—attractive for an area so close to more expensive areas. There is some commuter bus service toward

New York, and we expect these services to expand into rail service some day. As a combined result of all of these forces, the area is attracting more small businesses, individual entrepreneurs, and telecommuters needing the big cities only occasionally. As reflected in the ranking, we feel this area is on an upward path.

The three cities are located about 12 miles apart in the Lehigh River Valley between mountain ridges running southwest to northeast.

Summers are hot and can be uncomfortably humid. Winters are comparatively mild with the numerous mountain ridges providing some shelter from cold air and winds from the north. Temperatures above 100°F or below 0°F are infrequent. Summer thunderstorms are often heavy. Snowfall is variable, and cool air trapped in the valley can cause freezing rain. Snowmelt and spring rains create a flood threat. First freeze is mid-October; the last is late April.

Population

DEMOGRAPHICS	AREA	U.S. AVG	ETHNIC COMPOSITION	AREA	U.S. AVG	RESIDENT PROFILE	AREA	U.S. AVG
Population	781,787		White	88.7%	79.0%	Single	32.0%	32.4%
Population density per sq. mile	535.7	358.5	Black	3.2%	10.5%	Married	55.2%	52.7%
Population growth	14.0%	21.1%	Asian	2.1%	2.7%	Divorced/separated	12.8%	14.9%
Median age	39.4	36.1	Hispanic	8.4%	10.6%	Married with children	23.7%	23.7%
Percent Democrat	48.5%	44.5%	Religious observance	60.5%	48.9%	Single with children	7.4%	9.1%
Percent Republican	50.6%	54.5%	Diversity measure	32.3	40.1	Percent over age 65	15.3%	12.9%

Economy & Jobs
Score: 47.1
Rank: 199

INCOME	AREA	U.S. AVG	EMPLOYMENT	AREA	U.S. AVG	EMPLOYING INDUSTRIES	AREA	U.S. AVG
Per capita income	$25,174	$23,235	Unemployment rate	5.0%	4.7%	Largest: Healthcare & Social Assistance		
Household income	$50,897	$46,414	Recent job growth	2.3%	1.3%			
Household income < $25K	22.5%	26.2%	Projected future job growth	7.0%	11.5%	Percent manufacturing	17.2%	15.4%
Household income > $75K	29.6%	25.4%	White collar	59.2%	57.8%	Percent public sector	10.1%	15.7%
Household income growth	12.4%	13.6%	Blue collar	26.4%	25.2%	Percent construction	9.2%	9.9%

Cost of Living
Score: 21.7
Rank: 292

INDEXES & TAXES	AREA	U.S. AVG	HOUSING	AREA	U.S. AVG	NECESSITIES	AREA	U.S. AVG
Cost of Living Index	108.6	100.0	Median home price	$243,400	$220,000	Food Index	101.9	100.0
Buying Power Index	105.0	100.0	Home price appreciation	64.5%	10.1%	Housing Index	84.5	100.0
Income tax rate	3.62%	4.70%	Median rent	$828	$709	Utilities Index	120.4	100.0
Sales tax rate	6.00%	6.58%	Homes owned	67.5%	62.3%	Transportation Index	112.7	100.0
Property tax rate	$18.19	$12.00	Home price ratio	4.8	4.2	Healthcare Index	105.1	100.0
						Miscellaneous Cost Index	108.1	100.0

Climate
Score: 32.4
Rank: 252

TEMPERATURE	AREA	U.S. AVG	PRECIPITATION	AREA	U.S. AVG	COMFORTS & HAZARDS	AREA	U.S. AVG
Average January low	19.8	26.2	Annual inches precipitation	42.5	37.7	July relative humidity	71%	66%
Average July high	85.4	87.4	Annual inches snowfall	32.2	7.0	Annual days mostly sunny	206	208
Annual days > 90°F	16	38	Annual days precipitation	133	109	Annual days with thunderstorms	33	39
Annual days < 32°F	127	89	Annual days rain > 0.5 inches	26	22	Tornado risk score	16	18
Annual days < 0°F	2	6	Annual days snow > 1.5 inches	8	6	Hurricane risk score	11	13

TEMPERATURE

PRECIPITATION

DAYS OF CLOUDS & PRECIPITATION

Education
Score: 63.1
Rank: 139

ACHIEVEMENT	AREA	U.S. AVG	PUBLIC SCHOOLS	AREA	U.S. AVG	HIGHER EDUCATION	AREA	U.S. AVG
High school degree	81.5%	82.7%	Expenditures per pupil	$6,641	$5,686	No. 2-year colleges	8	4
2-year college degree	6.8%	6.4%	Student/teacher ratio	17.9	16.7	No. 4-year colleges/universities	8	6
4-year college degree	14.1%	15.7%	Attending public school	87.7%	90.1%	No. highly ranked universities	4	1
Graduate/professional degree	7.9%	8.9%	State SAT score	993*	1021			
			State ACT score	21.8	20.9			

Health & Healthcare
Score: 39.8
Rank: 224

Crime
Score: 54.8
Rank: 170

HAZARDS & ILLNESSES	AREA	U.S. AVG	HEALTHCARE	AREA	U.S. AVG	CRIME	AREA	U.S. AVG
Air-quality score	38	37	Physicians per capita	261.9	244.2	Violent crime rate	298.9	465.5
Water-quality score	48	52	Hospital beds per capita	413.9	420.0	Change in violent crime rate	15.0%	-2.2%
Pollen/allergy score	60	61	No. teaching hospitals	7	3	Property crime rate	2,551.8	3,517.1
Cancer mortality per capita	234.9	201.9	Cost per doctor visit	$63	$77	Change in property crime rate	-2.0%	-2.1%
Depression days per month	3.5	3.5	Cost per dental visit	$50	$70			
Stress score	38	50						

Transportation
Score: 93.3
Rank: 26

COMMUTE	AREA	U.S. AVG	INTERCITY SERVICES	AREA	U.S. AVG	AUTOMOTIVE	AREA	U.S. AVG
Average commute time	27.3	27.4	Major airports within 60 miles	3	1	Insurance, annual premium	$1,414	$1,432
Percent commutes > 60 mins.	9.3%	5.9%	Size of regional airport	Large	Large	Gas, cost per gallon	$2.46	$2.49
Commute by auto	82.1%	78.9%	Daily airline activity	2168	686	Daily vehicle miles per capita	22.2	24.0
Commute by mass transit	1.3%	1.9%	Amtrak service	No	No			
Work at home	2.6%	3.1%						
Mass transit miles per capita	1.27	1.87						

Leisure
Score: 67.9
Rank: 120

DINING & SHOPPING	AREA	U.S. AVG	ENTERTAINMENT	AREA	U.S. AVG	OUTDOOR ACTIVITIES	AREA	U.S. AVG
Restaurant rating	1	2	Professional sports rating	6	4	Golf-course rating	6	4
Outlet mall score	8	42	College sports rating	3	4	Ski-area rating	4	3
No. Starbucks	1	13	Zoo/aquarium rating	2	3	Sq. miles inland water	3	4
No. warehouse clubs	3	2	Amusement park rating	7	3	Miles of coastline	0.0	10.7
			Botanical garden/			National Park rating	3	3
			arboretum rating	1	4			

Arts & Culture
Score: 77.8
Rank: 83

MEDIA & LIBRARIES	AREA	U.S. AVG	PERFORMING ARTS	AREA	U.S. AVG	MUSEUMS	AREA	U.S. AVG
Arts radio rating	5	3	Classical music rating	6	4	Overall museum rating	7	5
No. public libraries	32	27	Ballet/dance rating	4	3	Art museum rating	7	5
Library volumes per capita	2.59	2.78	Professional theater rating	7	3	Science museum rating	4	5
			University arts programs rating	9	5	Children's museum rating	2	3

Altoona, PA

Score: 56.2 **Rank:** 203 **2004 rank:** 112

Profile: Small city
Location: South-central Pennsylvania along the main Allegheny Mountain ridge
Elevation: 1,320 feet
Time zone: Eastern Standard Time

PRO
Cost of living
Nearby mountains
Historic interest

CON
Isolation
Weak economy
Low ethnic diversity

Altoona is a historic railroad town and transportation gateway. Its roots are as a company town for the Pennsylvania Railroad, still a major artery today. But after the railroad ceased to be an independent entity, the town's shops and facilities, which once employed 15,000, went into permanent decline. Its role as a transportation gateway likewise declined when the Pennsylvania Turnpike bypassed the area by 50 miles. A modest amount of light industry has taken the railroad's place, and Interstate 99 now connects the area with the major east-west turnpike. Entertainment amenities include a minor league baseball team and railroad-heritage sights, such as the Altoona Railroader's Memorial Museum and Horseshoe Curve, both destinations for train buffs worldwide. The small but enterprising Altoona Symphony Orchestra was rated a Leading Small Community Symphony by the American Symphony

Orchestra League and has received other national accolades. The area scores relatively consistently across all categories. Although far from big-city amenities and services, the area has a low cost of living (74.3) and the second-lowest median home prices in the country with a self-sufficient, small-town character. Altoona also serves as a gateway to the Allegheny Mountain region. The area's economic challenges account for much of Altoona's ranking drop.

Altoona is located in a narrow valley along the main Allegheny ridge, which runs west of town from southwest to northeast. A series of lower parallel ridges rises to the east. Summer days can be warm and humid with occasional relief from the northwest. Air-mass collisions can produce significant snow in winter. Weather can change rapidly at all times of the year. First freeze is early October; last is early May.

Population

DEMOGRAPHICS	AREA	U.S. AVG	ETHNIC COMPOSITION	AREA	U.S. AVG	RESIDENT PROFILE	AREA	U.S. AVG
Population	126,446		White	97.5%	79.0%	Single	34.1%	32.4%
Population density per sq. mile	240.5	358.5	Black	1.2%	10.5%	Married	53.2%	52.7%
Population growth	-3.1%	21.1%	Asian	0.5%	2.7%	Divorced/separated	12.7%	14.9%
Median age	40.8	36.1	Hispanic	0.4%	10.6%	Married with children	21.0%	23.7%
Percent Democrat	33.4%	44.5%	Religious observance	55.9%	48.9%	Single with children	8.1%	9.1%
Percent Republican	66.0%	54.5%	Diversity measure	5.8	40.1	Percent over age 65	17.6%	12.9%

Economy & Jobs
Score: 12.0
Rank: 328

INCOME	AREA	U.S. AVG	EMPLOYMENT	AREA	U.S. AVG	EMPLOYING INDUSTRIES	AREA	U.S. AVG
Per capita income	$19,020	$23,235	Unemployment rate	5.3%	4.7%	Largest: Healthcare & Social Assistance		
Household income	$36,676	$46,414	Recent job growth	0.0%	1.3%			
Household income < $25K	33.4%	26.2%	Projected future job growth	2.5%	11.5%	Percent manufacturing	19.5%	15.4%
Household income > $75K	14.8%	25.4%	White collar	51.9%	57.8%	Percent public sector	11.5%	15.7%
Household income growth	11.6%	13.6%	Blue collar	30.4%	25.2%	Percent construction	10.9%	9.9%

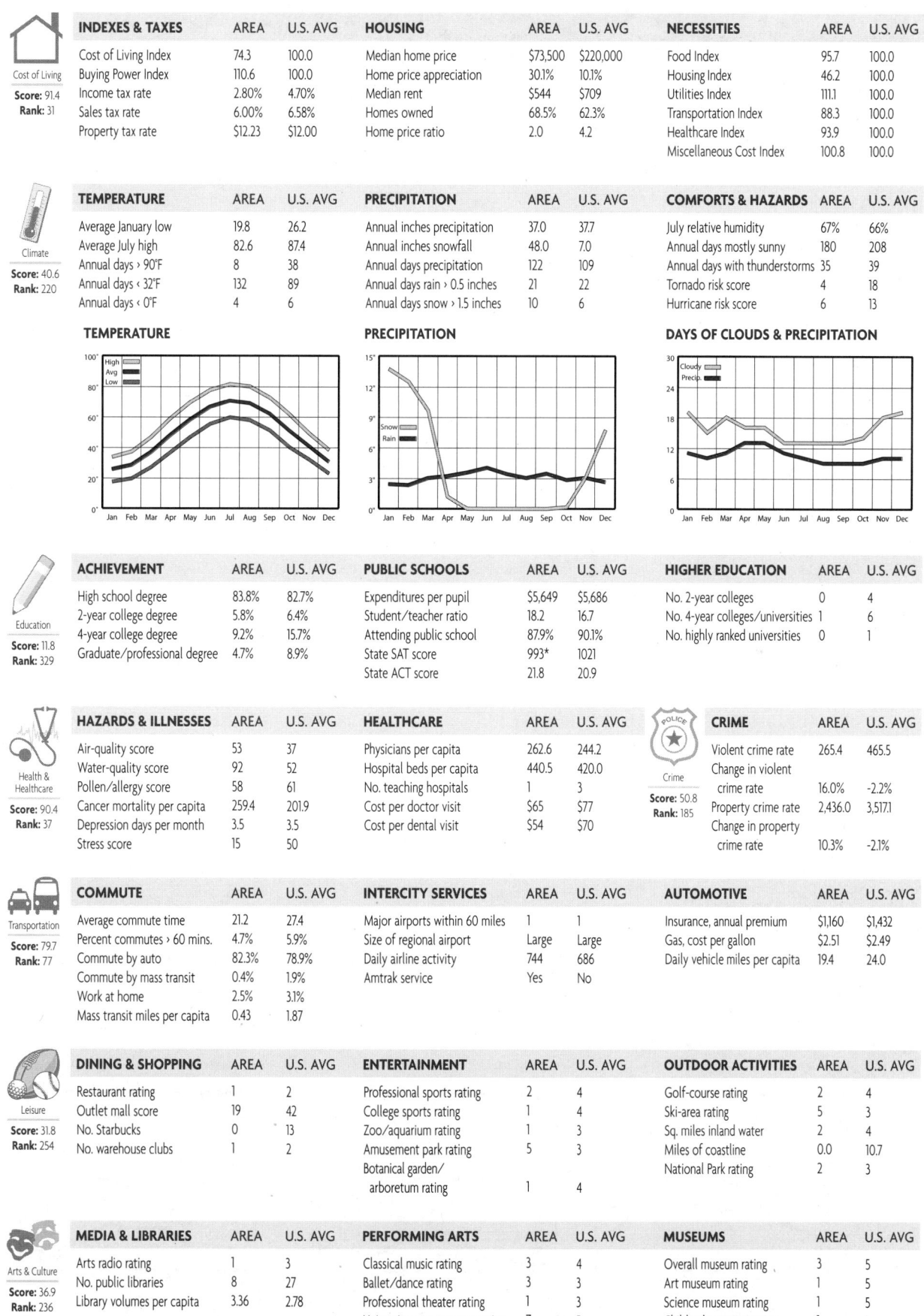

Cost of Living — Score: 91.4, Rank: 31

INDEXES & TAXES	AREA	U.S. AVG
Cost of Living Index	74.3	100.0
Buying Power Index	110.6	100.0
Income tax rate	2.80%	4.70%
Sales tax rate	6.00%	6.58%
Property tax rate	$12.23	$12.00

HOUSING	AREA	U.S. AVG
Median home price	$73,500	$220,000
Home price appreciation	30.1%	10.1%
Median rent	$544	$709
Homes owned	68.5%	62.3%
Home price ratio	2.0	4.2

NECESSITIES	AREA	U.S. AVG
Food Index	95.7	100.0
Housing Index	46.2	100.0
Utilities Index	111.1	100.0
Transportation Index	88.3	100.0
Healthcare Index	93.9	100.0
Miscellaneous Cost Index	100.8	100.0

Climate — Score: 40.6, Rank: 220

TEMPERATURE	AREA	U.S. AVG
Average January low	19.8	26.2
Average July high	82.6	87.4
Annual days > 90°F	8	38
Annual days < 32°F	132	89
Annual days < 0°F	4	6

PRECIPITATION	AREA	U.S. AVG
Annual inches precipitation	37.0	37.7
Annual inches snowfall	48.0	7.0
Annual days precipitation	122	109
Annual days rain > 0.5 inches	21	22
Annual days snow > 1.5 inches	10	6

COMFORTS & HAZARDS	AREA	U.S. AVG
July relative humidity	67%	66%
Annual days mostly sunny	180	208
Annual days with thunderstorms	35	39
Tornado risk score	4	18
Hurricane risk score	6	13

Education — Score: 11.8, Rank: 329

ACHIEVEMENT	AREA	U.S. AVG
High school degree	83.8%	82.7%
2-year college degree	5.8%	6.4%
4-year college degree	9.2%	15.7%
Graduate/professional degree	4.7%	8.9%

PUBLIC SCHOOLS	AREA	U.S. AVG
Expenditures per pupil	$5,649	$5,686
Student/teacher ratio	18.2	16.7
Attending public school	87.9%	90.1%
State SAT score	993*	1021
State ACT score	21.8	20.9

HIGHER EDUCATION	AREA	U.S. AVG
No. 2-year colleges	0	4
No. 4-year colleges/universities	1	6
No. highly ranked universities	0	1

Health & Healthcare — Score: 90.4, Rank: 37

HAZARDS & ILLNESSES	AREA	U.S. AVG
Air-quality score	53	37
Water-quality score	92	52
Pollen/allergy score	58	61
Cancer mortality per capita	259.4	201.9
Depression days per month	3.5	3.5
Stress score	15	50

HEALTHCARE	AREA	U.S. AVG
Physicians per capita	262.6	244.2
Hospital beds per capita	440.5	420.0
No. teaching hospitals	1	3
Cost per doctor visit	$65	$77
Cost per dental visit	$54	$70

Crime — Score: 50.8, Rank: 185

CRIME	AREA	U.S. AVG
Violent crime rate	265.4	465.5
Change in violent crime rate	16.0%	-2.2%
Property crime rate	2,436.0	3,517.1
Change in property crime rate	10.3%	-2.1%

Transportation — Score: 79.7, Rank: 77

COMMUTE	AREA	U.S. AVG
Average commute time	21.2	27.4
Percent commutes > 60 mins.	4.7%	5.9%
Commute by auto	82.3%	78.9%
Commute by mass transit	0.4%	1.9%
Work at home	2.5%	3.1%
Mass transit miles per capita	0.43	1.87

INTERCITY SERVICES	AREA	U.S. AVG
Major airports within 60 miles	1	1
Size of regional airport	Large	Large
Daily airline activity	744	686
Amtrak service	Yes	No

AUTOMOTIVE	AREA	U.S. AVG
Insurance, annual premium	$1,160	$1,432
Gas, cost per gallon	$2.51	$2.49
Daily vehicle miles per capita	19.4	24.0

Leisure — Score: 31.8, Rank: 254

DINING & SHOPPING	AREA	U.S. AVG
Restaurant rating	1	2
Outlet mall score	19	42
No. Starbucks	0	13
No. warehouse clubs	1	2

ENTERTAINMENT	AREA	U.S. AVG
Professional sports rating	2	4
College sports rating	1	4
Zoo/aquarium rating	1	3
Amusement park rating	5	3
Botanical garden/arboretum rating	1	4

OUTDOOR ACTIVITIES	AREA	U.S. AVG
Golf-course rating	2	4
Ski-area rating	5	3
Sq. miles inland water	2	4
Miles of coastline	0.0	10.7
National Park rating	2	3

Arts & Culture — Score: 36.9, Rank: 236

MEDIA & LIBRARIES	AREA	U.S. AVG
Arts radio rating	1	3
No. public libraries	8	27
Library volumes per capita	3.36	2.78

PERFORMING ARTS	AREA	U.S. AVG
Classical music rating	3	4
Ballet/dance rating	3	3
Professional theater rating	1	3
University arts programs rating	7	5

MUSEUMS	AREA	U.S. AVG
Overall museum rating	3	5
Art museum rating	1	5
Science museum rating	1	5
Children's museum rating	1	3

Amarillo, TX

Score: 60.9 **Rank:** 169 **2004 rank:** 229

Profile: Small city
Location: North Texas in center of Texas Panhandle
Elevation: 3,604 feet
Time zone: Central Standard Time

PRO	CON
Cost of living	Isolation
Low unemployment	Unattractive setting
Cool, dry climate	Crime rate

Set in the middle of the rugged plains of the Texas Panhandle, Amarillo is a true "cow town" of cowboys and ranch life, with some color left over from its glory days as a watering hole on legendary Route 66. Today the area is accessible by modern transportation, and modern heating and air-conditioning have tamed the harsh plains environment. These changes have led to population growth and buildup of the downtown area, but other than steakhouses and a few museums and historic sites, cultural amenities outside the native Western culture are about as scarce as trees. Along with agriculture and food processing, there is some primarily defense-related manufacturing and some other basic industries. The area has a small-town feel and low cost of living, but the downside is a wide-open, featureless space far across the plains from anywhere else.

The Spaniards named Amarillo, which means "yellow" in Spanish, for a dry clay soil in the mostly flat, empty, high plains area. The climate offers dramatic temperature variations and high winds. Summer days are warm to hot with low humidity; evenings are pleasant. Winters are changeable, with alternating mild air from the south and cold blasts that can drive temperatures below zero from the northwest. The area is generally sunny and dry with periods of spring and summer thunderstorms and winter snowstorms. Some years droughts occur and dust is a problem. First freeze is early November; last is late April.

Population

DEMOGRAPHICS	AREA	U.S. AVG	ETHNIC COMPOSITION	AREA	U.S. AVG	RESIDENT PROFILE	AREA	U.S. AVG
Population	237,241		White	78.3%	79.0%	Single	28.0%	32.4%
Population density per sq. mile	64.8	358.5	Black	5.6%	10.5%	Married	53.9%	52.7%
Population growth	21.1%	21.1%	Asian	1.7%	2.7%	Divorced/separated	18.2%	14.9%
Median age	34.1	36.1	Hispanic	21.6%	10.6%	Married with children	24.4%	23.7%
Percent Democrat	21.0%	44.5%	Religious observance	69.5%	48.9%	Single with children	9.7%	9.1%
Percent Republican	78.5%	54.5%	Diversity measure	53.9	40.1	Percent over age 65	12.0%	12.9%

Economy & Jobs
Score: 73.0
Rank: 101

INCOME	AREA	U.S. AVG	EMPLOYMENT	AREA	U.S. AVG	EMPLOYING INDUSTRIES	AREA	U.S. AVG
Per capita income	$20,440	$23,235	Unemployment rate	4.0%	4.7%	Largest: Healthcare & Social Assistance		
Household income	$40,399	$46,414	Recent job growth	2.5%	1.3%			
Household income ‹ $25K	30.2%	26.2%	Projected future job growth	11.5%	11.5%	Percent manufacturing	14.3%	15.4%
Household income › $75K	20.1%	25.4%	White collar	55.7%	57.8%	Percent public sector	15.5%	15.7%
Household income growth	12.3%	13.6%	Blue collar	25.1%	25.2%	Percent construction	10.8%	9.9%

Cost of Living
Score: 91.4
Rank: 32

INDEXES & TAXES	AREA	U.S. AVG	HOUSING	AREA	U.S. AVG	NECESSITIES	AREA	U.S. AVG
Cost of Living Index	78.8	100.0	Median home price	$118,600	$220,000	Food Index	92.4	100.0
Buying Power Index	114.9	100.0	Home price appreciation	22.3%	10.1%	Housing Index	44.2	100.0
Income tax rate	0.00%	4.70%	Median rent	$575	$709	Utilities Index	91.4	100.0
Sales tax rate	8.24%	6.58%	Homes owned	61.5%	62.3%	Transportation Index	101.0	100.0
Property tax rate	$16.06	$12.00	Home price ratio	2.9	4.2	Healthcare Index	92.5	100.0
						Miscellaneous Cost Index	93.3	100.0

Climate
Score: 86.6
Rank: 51

TEMPERATURE	AREA	U.S. AVG	PRECIPITATION	AREA	U.S. AVG	COMFORTS & HAZARDS	AREA	U.S. AVG
Average January low	22.5	26.2	Annual inches precipitation	20.0	37.7	July relative humidity	55%	66%
Average July high	91.4	87.4	Annual inches snowfall	14.0	7.0	Annual days mostly sunny	265	208
Annual days › 90°F	63	38	Annual days precipitation	67	109	Annual days with thunderstorms	48	39
Annual days › 32°F	108	89	Annual days rain › 0.5 inches	13	22	Tornado risk score	44	18
Annual days ‹ 0°F	2	6	Annual days snow › 1.5 inches	5	6	Hurricane risk score	0	13

TEMPERATURE

PRECIPITATION

DAYS OF CLOUDS & PRECIPITATION

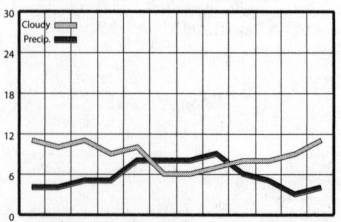

Education
Score: 39.0
Rank: 229

ACHIEVEMENT	AREA	U.S. AVG	PUBLIC SCHOOLS	AREA	U.S. AVG	HIGHER EDUCATION	AREA	U.S. AVG
High school degree	80.1%	82.7%	Expenditures per pupil	$4,671	$5,686	No. 2-year colleges	1	4
2-year college degree	6.2%	6.4%	Student/teacher ratio	15.6	16.7	No. 4-year colleges/universities	1	6
4-year college degree	14.0%	15.7%	Attending public school	94.6%	90.1%	No. highly ranked universities	0	1
Graduate/professional degree	7.0%	8.9%	State SAT score	997*	1021			
			State ACT score	20.3	20.9			

Health & Healthcare
Score: 83.7
Rank: 62

HAZARDS & ILLNESSES	AREA	U.S. AVG	HEALTHCARE	AREA	U.S. AVG	CRIME	AREA	U.S. AVG
Air-quality score	45	37	Physicians per capita	261.6	244.2	Violent crime rate	676.3	465.5
Water-quality score	61	52	Hospital beds per capita	591.0	420.0	Change in violent crime rate	4.8%	-2.2%
Pollen/allergy score	71	61	No. teaching hospitals	3	3	Property crime rate	5,349.6	3,517.1
Cancer mortality per capita	165.9	201.9	Cost per doctor visit	$71	$77	Change in property crime rate	1.6%	-2.1%
Depression days per month	5.1	3.5	Cost per dental visit	$60	$70			
Stress score	52	50						

Crime
Score: 7.0
Rank: 347

Transportation
Score: 45.7
Rank: 204

COMMUTE	AREA	U.S. AVG	INTERCITY SERVICES	AREA	U.S. AVG	AUTOMOTIVE	AREA	U.S. AVG
Average commute time	20.1	27.4	Major airports within 60 miles	0	1	Insurance, annual premium	$1,285	$1,432
Percent commutes > 60 mins.	3.3%	5.9%	Size of regional airport	Small	Large	Gas, cost per gallon	$2.43	$2.49
Commute by auto	81.8%	78.9%	Daily airline activity	39	686	Daily vehicle miles per capita	21.0	24.0
Commute by mass transit	0.4%	1.9%	Amtrak service	No	No			
Work at home	2.5%	3.1%						
Mass transit miles per capita	0.36	1.87						

Leisure
Score: 35.8
Rank: 239

DINING & SHOPPING	AREA	U.S. AVG	ENTERTAINMENT	AREA	U.S. AVG	OUTDOOR ACTIVITIES	AREA	U.S. AVG
Restaurant rating	1	2	Professional sports rating	3	4	Golf-course rating	2	4
Outlet mall score	0	42	College sports rating	3	4	Ski-area rating	1	3
No. Starbucks	2	13	Zoo/aquarium rating	1	3	Sq. miles inland water	3	4
No. warehouse clubs	0	2	Amusement park rating	5	3	Miles of coastline	0.0	10.7
			Botanical garden/ arboretum rating	1	4	National Park rating	4	3

Arts & Culture
Score: 29.9
Rank: 262

MEDIA & LIBRARIES	AREA	U.S. AVG	PERFORMING ARTS	AREA	U.S. AVG	MUSEUMS	AREA	U.S. AVG
Arts radio rating	1	3	Classical music rating	3	4	Overall museum rating	5	5
No. public libraries	10	27	Ballet/dance rating	3	3	Art museum rating	4	5
Library volumes per capita	3.55	2.78	Professional theater rating	1	3	Science museum rating	5	5
			University arts programs rating	1	5	Children's museum rating	6	3

Ames, IA

Score: 57.8 Rank: 189 2004 rank: not ranked

Profile: College town
Location: Central Iowa, 25 miles north of Des Moines
Elevation: 921 feet
Time zone: Central Standard Time

PRO	CON
College-town amenities	Outdoor recreation
Cost of living	Low diversity
Steady employment	Harsh winters

Home to land-grant Iowa State University, Ames is a pleasant college town a short distance north of Des Moines along Interstate 35. Downtown is typical of most small college towns: clean, attractive, and containing a variety of independent small businesses. The economic base is steady, anchored by the university and other state agencies and an assortment of mostly agricultural, pharmaceutical, and biotech-related manufacturing and research facilities for companies such as 3M, BASF, Ball Plastics, and Boehringer Ingelheim. The U.S. Department of Agriculture National Animal Disease Center makes its home in Ames. Most residents work locally and commutes are very short—the shortest on average in the U.S. Educational attainment is high; schools are strong and have won national recognition. The cost of living at 88.5 is reasonable for the profile. The city has a strong parks and recreation system, but outdoor activities are generally not abundant in the surrounding area. Ames has a solid Midwestern feel, but some may not find enough to do in the area nor in Des Moines to the south.

The terrain is mainly flat to slightly rolling and agricultural, with the Skunk River flowing through town in a shallow valley. Summers are warm and humid with frequent showers and thunderstorms, some heavy. Winter brings mostly cold, dry air from the north with short periods of precipitation, mainly snow. Below zero temperatures, strong winds, and bitter wind chills occur occasionally. First freeze is early October; last is early May.

Population

DEMOGRAPHICS	AREA	U.S. AVG
Population	84,569	
Population density per sq. mile	147.6	358.5
Population growth	13.9%	21.1%
Median age	29.7	36.1
Percent Democrat	52.2%	44.5%
Percent Republican	46.6%	54.5%

ETHNIC COMPOSITION	AREA	U.S. AVG
White	89.6%	79.0%
Black	1.8%	10.5%
Asian	6.5%	2.7%
Hispanic	1.6%	10.6%
Religious observance	51.0%	48.9%
Diversity measure	21.8	40.1

RESIDENT PROFILE	AREA	U.S. AVG
Single	46.0%	32.4%
Married	44.8%	52.7%
Divorced/separated	9.3%	14.9%
Married with children	22.3%	23.7%
Single with children	4.8%	9.1%
Percent over age 65	10.0%	12.9%

Economy & Jobs
Score: 65.2
Rank: 131

INCOME	AREA	U.S. AVG
Per capita income	$22,853	$23,235
Household income	$45,871	$46,414
Household income < $25K	26.5%	26.2%
Household income > $75K	25.6%	25.4%
Household income growth	13.4%	13.6%

EMPLOYMENT	AREA	U.S. AVG
Unemployment rate	3.0%	4.7%
Recent job growth	2.3%	1.3%
Projected future job growth	8.1%	11.5%
White collar	68.2%	57.8%
Blue collar	15.2%	25.2%

EMPLOYING INDUSTRIES	AREA	U.S. AVG
Largest: Manufacturing		
Percent manufacturing	8.9%	15.4%
Percent public sector	33.4%	15.7%
Percent construction	6.4%	9.9%

Cost of Living
Score: 31.3
Rank: 256

INDEXES & TAXES	AREA	U.S. AVG
Cost of Living Index	88.5	100.0
Buying Power Index	116.2	100.0
Income tax rate	6.68%	4.70%
Sales tax rate	7.00%	6.58%
Property tax rate	$13.10	$12.00

HOUSING	AREA	U.S. AVG
Median home price	$161,800	$220,000
Home price appreciation	23.1%	10.1%
Median rent	$682	$709
Homes owned	56.4%	62.3%
Home price ratio	3.5	4.2

NECESSITIES	AREA	U.S. AVG
Food Index	90.5	100.0
Housing Index	50.1	100.0
Utilities Index	113.7	100.0
Transportation Index	98.7	100.0
Healthcare Index	102.7	100.0
Miscellaneous Cost Index	95.8	100.0

Climate
Score: 18.2
Rank: 305

TEMPERATURE	AREA	U.S. AVG
Average January low	11.0	26.2
Average July high	86.0	87.4
Annual days > 90°F	26	38
Annual days < 32°F	137	89
Annual days < 0°F	16	6

PRECIPITATION	AREA	U.S. AVG
Annual inches precipitation	31.8	37.7
Annual inches snowfall	33.0	7.0
Annual days precipitation	106	109
Annual days rain > 0.5 inches	21	22
Annual days snow > 1.5 inches	10	6

COMFORTS & HAZARDS	AREA	U.S. AVG
July relative humidity	60%	66%
Annual days mostly sunny	203	208
Annual days with thunderstorms	50	39
Tornado risk score	5	18
Hurricane risk score	1	13

TEMPERATURE

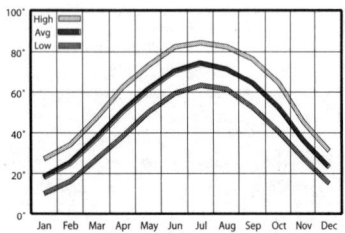

PRECIPITATION

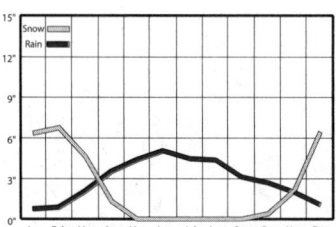

DAYS OF CLOUDS & PRECIPITATION

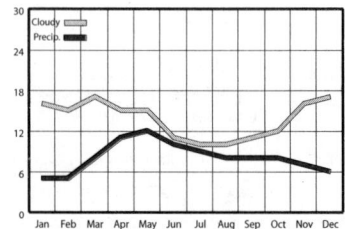

Education
Score: 98.1
Rank: 8

ACHIEVEMENT	AREA	U.S. AVG
High school degree	93.8%	82.7%
2-year college degree	6.9%	6.4%
4-year college degree	25.9%	15.7%
Graduate/professional degree	20.9%	8.9%

PUBLIC SCHOOLS	AREA	U.S. AVG
Expenditures per pupil	$5,442	$5,686
Student/teacher ratio	15.9	16.7
Attending public school	97.1%	90.1%
State SAT score	1215	1021
State ACT score	22.1*	20.9

HIGHER EDUCATION	AREA	U.S. AVG
No. 2-year colleges	1	4
No. 4-year colleges/universities	1	6
No. highly ranked universities	0	1

Health & Healthcare
Score: 85.8
Rank: 54

HAZARDS & ILLNESSES	AREA	U.S. AVG
Air-quality score	54	37
Water-quality score	61	52
Pollen/allergy score	40	61
Cancer mortality per capita	187.0	201.9
Depression days per month	2.1	3.5
Stress score	1	50

HEALTHCARE	AREA	U.S. AVG
Physicians per capita	189.1	244.2
Hospital beds per capita	329.9	420.0
No. teaching hospitals	0	3
Cost per doctor visit	$74	$77
Cost per dental visit	$66	$70

Crime
Score: 93.0
Rank: 27

CRIME	AREA	U.S. AVG
Violent crime rate	187.1	465.5
Change in violent crime rate	-6.6%	-2.2%
Property crime rate	2,750.0	3,517.1
Change in property crime rate	-2.6%	-2.1%

Transportation
Score: 76.2
Rank: 90

COMMUTE	AREA	U.S. AVG
Average commute time	18.7	27.4
Percent commutes > 60 mins.	2.2%	5.9%
Commute by auto	72.3%	78.9%
Commute by mass transit	3.9%	1.9%
Work at home	3.5%	3.1%
Mass transit miles per capita	3.89	1.87

INTERCITY SERVICES	AREA	U.S. AVG
Major airports within 60 miles	0	1
Size of regional airport	Small	Large
Daily airline activity	164	686
Amtrak service	No	No

AUTOMOTIVE	AREA	U.S. AVG
Insurance, annual premium	$885	$1,432
Gas, cost per gallon	$2.41	$2.49
Daily vehicle miles per capita	14.3	24.0

DINING & SHOPPING	AREA	U.S. AVG	ENTERTAINMENT	AREA	U.S. AVG	OUTDOOR ACTIVITIES	AREA	U.S. AVG
Restaurant rating	1	2	Professional sports rating	1	4	Golf-course rating	2	4
Outlet mall score	22	42	College sports rating	7	4	Ski-area rating	1	3
No. Starbucks	0	13	Zoo/aquarium rating	1	3	Sq. miles inland water	1	4
No. warehouse clubs	1	2	Amusement park rating	1	3	Miles of coastline	0.0	10.7
			Botanical garden/ arboretum rating	2	4	National Park rating	2	3

Leisure
Score: 12.0
Rank: 327

MEDIA & LIBRARIES	AREA	U.S. AVG	PERFORMING ARTS	AREA	U.S. AVG	MUSEUMS	AREA	U.S. AVG
Arts radio rating	2	3	Classical music rating	2	4	Overall museum rating	2	5
No. public libraries	11	27	Ballet/dance rating	1	3	Art museum rating	5	5
Library volumes per capita	4.49	2.78	Professional theater rating	1	3	Science museum rating	3	5
			University arts programs rating	5	5	Children's museum rating	1	3

Arts & Culture
Score: 42.2
Rank: 216

Anchorage, AK

Score: 53.8 Rank: 228 2004 rank: 160

Profile: Regional center
Location: At the head of Cook Inlet in extreme south-central Alaska
Elevation: 132 feet
Time zone: Alaska Standard Time

PRO	CON
Attractive setting	Dreary winters
Outdoor recreation	Healthcare
Strong employment	Earthquake risk

Anchorage is the largest city and main regional center for the frontier state of Alaska. Most of the state's commercial and industrial activity occurs here. Because of rebuilding after an earthquake in 1964 and the recent influx of oil money, the city is quite modern. The area has a strong, growing economy, with high incomes, no sales or income taxes, and a modest state-paid royalty from oil income, all of which is offset by a high cost of living (115.5) caused by geographic isolation. Downtown is clean, attractive, and modern with nice waterfront areas and a large new performing arts center. The best residential neighborhoods lie to the south. The climate is moderate, despite the latitude, but cloud cover—Anchorage is one of the cloudiest places in the country, with only 131 annual days of sunshine—combined with short winter days make the area unattractive to many people. When the weather cooperates, beautiful scenery is close at hand and the outdoor recreational opportunities are among the best in the country.

Anchorage is located in a stunning landscape with mountains and abundant water. The city itself is in a valley with terrain rising gradually to the east and marshes interspersed with glacial moraines and small streams. On the far eastern horizon, the Chugach Mountains rise abruptly to elevations up to 10,000 feet. The much higher Alaska Range, including Mount McKinley, lies 150 to 200 miles to the north. Snowcapped peaks are visible most of the year.

The Alaska Range acts as a barrier against very cold air from the north. Summer high temperatures average 60°F with lows near 50°F. During July and August, 2 out of every 3 days are cloudy and 1 out of 3 has rain, but the days are up to 19 hours long. The brief autumn ends in October, with snow becoming more frequent during that month. Winter extends from mid-October through early April, with temperatures dropping below zero on clear days and reaching the 30s on mild, cloudy ones, and 70 to 90 inches of snowfall per season. January highs are near 20°F with lows near 5°F. First freeze is early September; last is early June.

DEMOGRAPHICS	AREA	U.S. AVG	ETHNIC COMPOSITION	AREA	U.S. AVG	RESIDENT PROFILE	AREA	U.S. AVG
Population	350,175		White	73.4%	79.0%	Single	30.5%	32.4%
Population density per sq. mile	13.3	358.5	Black	5.1%	10.5%	Married	52.8%	52.7%
Population growth	34.9%	21.1%	Asian	5.7%	2.7%	Divorced/separated	16.7%	14.9%
Median age	33.6	36.1	Hispanic	5.9%	10.6%	Married with children	28.2%	23.7%
Percent Democrat	34.7%	44.5%	Religious observance	35.3%	48.9%	Single with children	11.2%	9.1%
Percent Republican	62.3%	54.5%	Diversity measure	50.0	40.1	Percent over age 65	6.5%	12.9%

Population

INCOME	AREA	U.S. AVG	EMPLOYMENT	AREA	U.S. AVG	EMPLOYING INDUSTRIES	AREA	U.S. AVG
Per capita income	$27,890	$23,235	Unemployment rate	5.3%	4.7%	Largest: Healthcare & Social Assistance		
Household income	$61,586	$46,414	Recent job growth	4.2%	1.3%			
Household income < $25K	16.0%	26.2%	Projected future job growth	19.1%	11.5%	Percent manufacturing	9.7%	15.4%
Household income > $75K	38.6%	25.4%	White collar	63.3%	57.8%	Percent public sector	21.8%	15.7%
Household income growth	12.7%	13.6%	Blue collar	21.0%	25.2%	Percent construction	11.3%	9.9%

Economy & Jobs
Score: 90.4
Rank: 37

Cost of Living
Score: 86.9
Rank: 50

INDEXES & TAXES	AREA	U.S. AVG	HOUSING	AREA	U.S. AVG	NECESSITIES	AREA	U.S. AVG
Cost of Living Index	115.5	100.0	Median home price	$226,300	$220,000	Food Index	124.2	100.0
Buying Power Index	119.5	100.0	Home price appreciation	56.8%	10.1%	Housing Index	86.8	100.0
Income tax rate	0.00%	4.70%	Median rent	$912	$709	Utilities Index	98.5	100.0
Sales tax rate	0.00%	6.58%	Homes owned	57.6%	62.3%	Transportation Index	107.1	100.0
Property tax rate	$14.46	$12.00	Home price ratio	3.7	4.2	Healthcare Index	159.2	100.0
						Miscellaneous Cost Index	123.3	100.0

Climate
Score: 3.5
Rank: 360

TEMPERATURE	AREA	U.S. AVG	PRECIPITATION	AREA	U.S. AVG	COMFORTS & HAZARDS	AREA	U.S. AVG
Average January low	3.5	26.2	Annual inches precipitation	14.0	37.7	July relative humidity	71%	66%
Average July high	65.6	87.4	Annual inches snowfall	70.0	7.0	Annual days mostly sunny	131	208
Annual days > 90°F	12	38	Annual days precipitation	113	109	Annual days with thunderstorms	1	39
Annual days < 32°F	192	89	Annual days rain > 0.5 inches	6	22	Tornado risk score	0	18
Annual days < 0°F	41	6	Annual days snow > 1.5 inches	17	6	Hurricane risk score	0	13

TEMPERATURE

PRECIPITATION

DAYS OF CLOUDS & PRECIPITATION

Education
Score: 79.7
Rank: 77

ACHIEVEMENT	AREA	U.S. AVG	PUBLIC SCHOOLS	AREA	U.S. AVG	HIGHER EDUCATION	AREA	U.S. AVG
High school degree	89.9%	82.7%	Expenditures per pupil	$7,104	$5,686	No. 2-year colleges	0	4
2-year college degree	8.1%	6.4%	Student/teacher ratio	17.7	16.7	No. 4-year colleges/universities	3	6
4-year college degree	17.3%	15.7%	Attending public school	94.2%	90.1%	No. highly ranked universities	0	1
Graduate/professional degree	9.3%	8.9%	State SAT score	1034*	1021			
			State ACT score	21.1	20.9			

Health & Healthcare
Score: 15.2
Rank: 316

Crime
Score: 20.6
Rank: 297

HAZARDS & ILLNESSES	AREA	U.S. AVG	HEALTHCARE	AREA	U.S. AVG	CRIME	AREA	U.S. AVG
Air-quality score	28	37	Physicians per capita	256.2	244.2	Violent crime rate	753.7	465.5
Water-quality score	45	52	Hospital beds per capita	219.6	420.0	Change in violent crime rate	-6.5%	-2.2%
Pollen/allergy score	57	61	No. teaching hospitals	1	3	Property crime rate	4,276.1	3,517.1
Cancer mortality per capita	114.9	201.9	Cost per doctor visit	$115	$77	Change in property crime rate	12.0%	-2.1%
Depression days per month	3.1	3.5	Cost per dental visit	$106	$70			
Stress score	99	50						

Transportation
Score: 28.1
Rank: 270

COMMUTE	AREA	U.S. AVG	INTERCITY SERVICES	AREA	U.S. AVG	AUTOMOTIVE	AREA	U.S. AVG
Average commute time	24.8	27.4	Major airports within 60 miles	1	1	Insurance, annual premium	$1,569	$1,432
Percent commutes > 60 mins.	8.1%	5.9%	Size of regional airport	Medium	Large	Gas, cost per gallon	$2.36	$2.49
Commute by auto	73.4%	78.9%	Daily airline activity	328	686	Daily vehicle miles per capita	17.2	24.0
Commute by mass transit	1.7%	1.9%	Amtrak service	No	No			
Work at home	4.3%	3.1%						
Mass transit miles per capita	1.67	1.87						

Leisure
Score: 72.7
Rank: 102

DINING & SHOPPING	AREA	U.S. AVG	ENTERTAINMENT	AREA	U.S. AVG	OUTDOOR ACTIVITIES	AREA	U.S. AVG
Restaurant rating	1	2	Professional sports rating	3	4	Golf-course rating	1	4
Outlet mall score	0	42	College sports rating	3	4	Ski-area rating	6	3
No. Starbucks	3	13	Zoo/aquarium rating	3	3	Sq. miles inland water	4	4
No. warehouse clubs	4	2	Amusement park rating	1	3	Miles of coastline	87.6	10.7
			Botanical garden/arboretum rating	1	4	National Park rating	9	3

Arts & Culture
Score: 63.9
Rank: 135

MEDIA & LIBRARIES	AREA	U.S. AVG	PERFORMING ARTS	AREA	U.S. AVG	MUSEUMS	AREA	U.S. AVG
Arts radio rating	6	3	Classical music rating	4	4	Overall museum rating	6	5
No. public libraries	14	27	Ballet/dance rating	3	3	Art museum rating	7	5
Library volumes per capita	2.48	2.78	Professional theater rating	10	3	Science museum rating	7	5
			University arts programs rating	1	5	Children's museum rating	6	3

Anderson, IN

Score: 59.8 **Rank:** 177 **2004 rank:** not ranked

Profile: Small industrial town
Location: 50 miles northeast of Indianapolis along I-69
Elevation: 875 feet
Time zone: Eastern Standard Time

PRO	CON
Cost of housing	Employment and economy
Small-town feel	Recreation
Close to Indianapolis	Low educational attainment

In June 2006 the City of Anderson proudly announced that "[f]or the first time in 10 years, Anderson's employment statistics show an increase." This gives you an idea of where this small, Midwestern, manufacturing-oriented city has been, and perhaps where it's going. Anderson has been a center for small- to medium-size manufacturing facilities primarily tied to the automotive industry. Manufacturing employs more than 20% of the workforce, twice the national average. Downtown is clean but mostly plain and nondescript. Residential and industrial areas surround the town, with simple and attractively priced homes. Median home prices remain below $100,000, a rarity these days, and cost of living is 73.2, second lowest in the U.S.; in fact, home prices

relative to income, as measured by its home price ratio of 1.9, is third best in the country. The area is only 50 miles from downtown Indianapolis—just 30 miles from the capital city's growing northeastern suburbs—so eventually Anderson could benefit from Indianpolis's growth. In any case, having Indianapolis and its many amenities nearby is definitely a plus.

The terrain surrounding Anderson is mainly flat and agricultural with little in the way of interest for outdoor recreation. Summers are warm and humid with few extremes. Winters are variable with occasional periods of extreme cold and snow, but generally precipitation is a mix of rain and snow. First freeze is mid- to late October; the last is late April.

Population

DEMOGRAPHICS	AREA	U.S. AVG	ETHNIC COMPOSITION	AREA	U.S. AVG	RESIDENT PROFILE	AREA	U.S. AVG
Population	130,198		White	89.5%	79.0%	Single	28.3%	32.4%
Population density per sq. mile	288.0	358.5	Black	7.9%	10.5%	Married	54.1%	52.7%
Population growth	-0.4%	21.1%	Asian	0.5%	2.7%	Divorced/separated	17.5%	14.9%
Median age	38.3	36.1	Hispanic	1.7%	10.6%	Married with children	20.3%	23.7%
Percent Democrat	39.9%	44.5%	Religious observance	37.0%	48.9%	Single with children	9.5%	9.1%
Percent Republican	59.3%	54.5%	Diversity measure	22.0	40.1	Percent over age 65	15.3%	12.9%

Economy & Jobs
Score: 19.8
Rank: 300

INCOME	AREA	U.S. AVG	EMPLOYMENT	AREA	U.S. AVG	EMPLOYING INDUSTRIES	AREA	U.S. AVG
Per capita income	$22,385	$23,235	Unemployment rate	6.5%	4.7%	Largest: Manufacturing		
Household income	$43,505	$46,414	Recent job growth	1.0%	1.3%			
Household income < $25K	26.3%	26.2%	Projected future job growth	1.6%	11.5%	Percent manufacturing	22.2%	15.4%
Household income > $75K	22.5%	25.4%	White collar	51.0%	57.8%	Percent public sector	10.6%	15.7%
Household income growth	11.8%	13.6%	Blue collar	32.2%	25.2%	Percent construction	10.0%	9.9%

Cost of Living
Score: 87.4
Rank: 48

INDEXES & TAXES	AREA	U.S. AVG	HOUSING	AREA	U.S. AVG	NECESSITIES	AREA	U.S. AVG
Cost of Living Index	73.2	100.0	Median home price	$82,500	$220,000	Food Index	94.2	100.0
Buying Power Index	133.2	100.0	Home price appreciation	19.2%	10.1%	Housing Index	43.9	100.0
Income tax rate	4.10%	4.70%	Median rent	$604	$709	Utilities Index	94.8	100.0
Sales tax rate	6.00%	6.58%	Homes owned	69.4%	62.3%	Transportation Index	99.1	100.0
Property tax rate	$8.92	$12.00	Home price ratio	1.9	4.2	Healthcare Index	93.9	100.0
						Miscellaneous Cost Index	91.1	100.0

Climate
Score: 48.4
Rank: 191

TEMPERATURE	AREA	U.S. AVG	PRECIPITATION	AREA	U.S. AVG	COMFORTS & HAZARDS	AREA	U.S. AVG
Average January low	19.7	26.2	Annual inches precipitation	39.0	37.7	July relative humidity	73%	66%
Average July high	85.4	87.4	Annual inches snowfall	21.0	7.0	Annual days mostly sunny	191	208
Annual days > 90°F	15	38	Annual days precipitation	122	109	Annual days with thunderstorms	45	39
Annual days < 32°F	122	89	Annual days rain > 0.5 inches	27	22	Tornado risk score	33	18
Annual days < 0°F	7	6	Annual days snow > 1.5 inches	7	6	Hurricane risk score	4	13

TEMPERATURE

PRECIPITATION

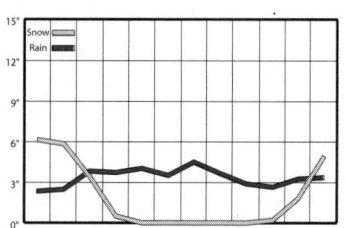

DAYS OF CLOUDS & PRECIPITATION

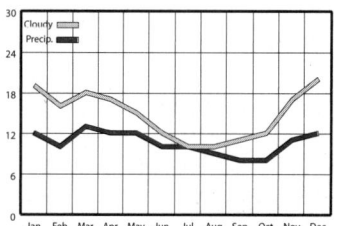

	ACHIEVEMENT	AREA	U.S. AVG	PUBLIC SCHOOLS	AREA	U.S. AVG	HIGHER EDUCATION	AREA	U.S. AVG
Education	High school degree	80.0%	82.7%	Expenditures per pupil	$6,051	$5,686	No. 2-year colleges	1	4
Score: 15.5	2-year college degree	6.0%	6.4%	Student/teacher ratio	17.9	16.7	No. 4-year colleges/universities	1	6
Rank: 315	4-year college degree	8.8%	15.7%	Attending public school	92.8%	90.1%	No. highly ranked universities	0	1
	Graduate/professional degree	5.5%	8.9%	State SAT score	1007*	1021			
				State ACT score	21.7	20.9			

	HAZARDS & ILLNESSES	AREA	U.S. AVG	HEALTHCARE	AREA	U.S. AVG		CRIME	AREA	U.S. AVG
Health & Healthcare	Air-quality score	45	37	Physicians per capita	128.1	244.2		Violent crime rate	152.3	465.5
Score: 47.1	Water-quality score	27	52	Hospital beds per capita	427.8	420.0	Crime	Change in violent crime rate	-8.2%	-2.2%
Rank: 198	Pollen/allergy score	71	61	No. teaching hospitals	0	3	**Score:** 72.2	Property crime rate	3,189.9	3,517.1
	Cancer mortality per capita	208.5	201.9	Cost per doctor visit	$72	$77	**Rank:** 104	Change in property crime rate	23.1%	-2.1%
	Depression days per month	5.2	3.5	Cost per dental visit	$74	$70				
	Stress score	94	50							

	COMMUTE	AREA	U.S. AVG	INTERCITY SERVICES	AREA	U.S. AVG	AUTOMOTIVE	AREA	U.S. AVG
Transportation	Average commute time	25.6	27.4	Major airports within 60 miles	2	1	Insurance, annual premium	$1,010	$1,432
Score: 73.8	Percent commutes > 60 mins.	6.2%	5.9%	Size of regional airport	Large	Large	Gas, cost per gallon	$2.46	$2.49
Rank: 99	Commute by auto	81.8%	78.9%	Daily airline activity	1284	686	Daily vehicle miles per capita	26.8	24.0
	Commute by mass transit	0.5%	1.9%	Amtrak service	No	No			
	Work at home	2.6%	3.1%						
	Mass transit miles per capita	0.50	1.87						

	DINING & SHOPPING	AREA	U.S. AVG	ENTERTAINMENT	AREA	U.S. AVG	OUTDOOR ACTIVITIES	AREA	U.S. AVG
Leisure	Restaurant rating	1	2	Professional sports rating	7	4	Golf-course rating	7	4
Score: 71.9	Outlet mall score	22	42	College sports rating	5	4	Ski-area rating	4	3
Rank: 105	No. Starbucks	1	13	Zoo/aquarium rating	7	3	Sq. miles inland water	2	4
	No. warehouse clubs	0	2	Amusement park rating	1	3	Miles of coastline	0.0	10.7
				Botanical garden/arboretum rating	6	4	National Park rating	1	3

	MEDIA & LIBRARIES	AREA	U.S. AVG	PERFORMING ARTS	AREA	U.S. AVG	MUSEUMS	AREA	U.S. AVG
Arts & Culture	Arts radio rating	7	3	Classical music rating	7	4	Overall museum rating	5	5
Score: 91.2	No. public libraries	7	27	Ballet/dance rating	6	3	Art museum rating	7	5
Rank: 34	Library volumes per capita	4.22	2.78	Professional theater rating	8	3	Science museum rating	3	5
				University arts programs rating	8	5	Children's museum rating	4	3

Anderson, SC

Score: 34.1 Rank: 327 2004 rank: 80

Profile: Small city
Location: Northwest South Carolina 15 miles east of Georgia border
Elevation: 770 feet
Time zone: Eastern Standard Time

PRO
Growing economy
Nearby college town
Cost of living

CON
Hot, humid summers
Unattractive downtown
Crime rate

Anderson is one of the three small cities making up the old metro area triumvirate of Greenville–Spartanburg–Anderson, SC, the center of South Carolina's so-called "Upstate" economic region. Anderson is the westernmost of the three, which were split into distinct MSAs in 2005. The Upstate region, formerly known for textiles and agriculture, has become one of the more prosperous manufacturing regions in the South. Led by BMW, which is actually located in nearby Greer between Greenville and Spartanburg, and Michelin in Spartanburg, the area has gained prominence in manufacturing auto parts, plastics, chemicals, and other fabricated products and materials. Such small manufacturing has become Anderson's mainstay. Of the three cities, Anderson has been the least prosperous, at least until recently, and the downtown area has that old declining Southern textile town appearance, but we expect that to improve gradually. There are some nice neighborhoods with old,

historic but affordable homes. A number of amenities are nearby, including the college town of Clemson just 20 miles away and water recreation at Hartwell Lake on the Georgia border. About 25 miles to the northeast, Greenville also offers a lot of cultural life and services. For bigger city services, Charlotte, North Carolina, is about 100 miles northeast along Interstate 85. Cost of living is an attractive 80.5. The drop in ranking reflects the city's separation from the larger tri-city metro area.

Located on the eastern slope of the southern Appalachian Mountains, Anderson is in gently rolling country about 30 miles southeast of the higher mountains ridges. The mountains usually protect the area from the brunt of northern cold air. Summers are warm and muggy with frequent thunderstorms. Winters are pleasant, with below-freezing daytime temperatures only a few times a year. Rainfall is abundant and spread throughout the year. A few small snowfalls or episodes of freezing rain may occur each year.

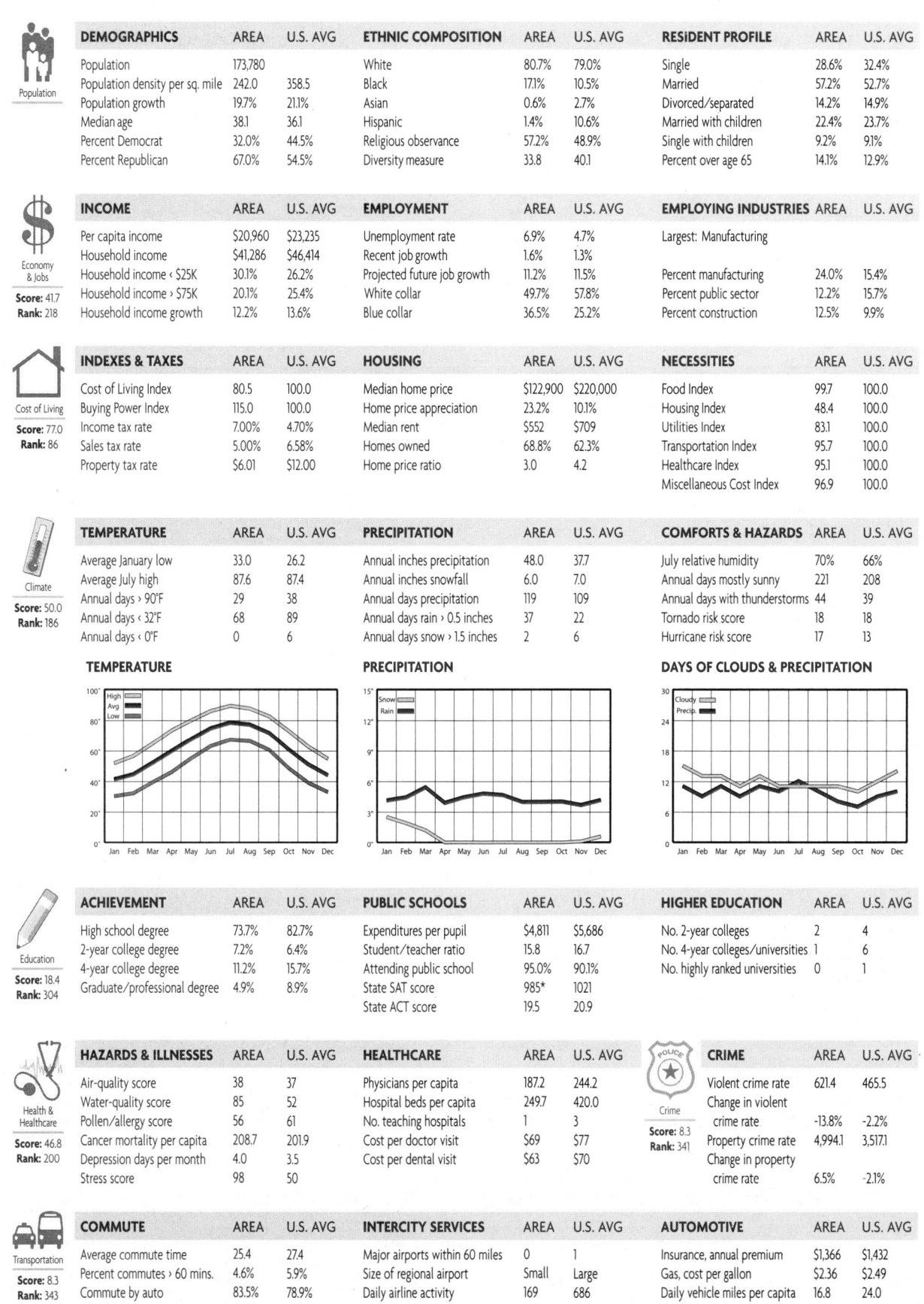

DEMOGRAPHICS	AREA	U.S. AVG
Population	173,780	
Population density per sq. mile	242.0	358.5
Population growth	19.7%	21.1%
Median age	38.1	36.1
Percent Democrat	32.0%	44.5%
Percent Republican	67.0%	54.5%

ETHNIC COMPOSITION	AREA	U.S. AVG
White	80.7%	79.0%
Black	17.1%	10.5%
Asian	0.6%	2.7%
Hispanic	1.4%	10.6%
Religious observance	57.2%	48.9%
Diversity measure	33.8	40.1

RESIDENT PROFILE	AREA	U.S. AVG
Single	28.6%	32.4%
Married	57.2%	52.7%
Divorced/separated	14.2%	14.9%
Married with children	22.4%	23.7%
Single with children	9.2%	9.1%
Percent over age 65	14.1%	12.9%

Population

INCOME	AREA	U.S. AVG
Per capita income	$20,960	$23,235
Household income	$41,286	$46,414
Household income < $25K	30.1%	26.2%
Household income > $75K	20.1%	25.4%
Household income growth	12.2%	13.6%

EMPLOYMENT	AREA	U.S. AVG
Unemployment rate	6.9%	4.7%
Recent job growth	1.6%	1.3%
Projected future job growth	11.2%	11.5%
White collar	49.7%	57.8%
Blue collar	36.5%	25.2%

EMPLOYING INDUSTRIES	AREA	U.S. AVG
Largest: Manufacturing		
Percent manufacturing	24.0%	15.4%
Percent public sector	12.2%	15.7%
Percent construction	12.5%	9.9%

Economy & Jobs
Score: 41.7
Rank: 218

INDEXES & TAXES	AREA	U.S. AVG
Cost of Living Index	80.5	100.0
Buying Power Index	115.0	100.0
Income tax rate	7.00%	4.70%
Sales tax rate	5.00%	6.58%
Property tax rate	$6.01	$12.00

HOUSING	AREA	U.S. AVG
Median home price	$122,900	$220,000
Home price appreciation	23.2%	10.1%
Median rent	$552	$709
Homes owned	68.8%	62.3%
Home price ratio	3.0	4.2

NECESSITIES	AREA	U.S. AVG
Food Index	99.7	100.0
Housing Index	48.4	100.0
Utilities Index	83.1	100.0
Transportation Index	95.7	100.0
Healthcare Index	95.1	100.0
Miscellaneous Cost Index	96.9	100.0

Cost of Living
Score: 77.0
Rank: 86

TEMPERATURE	AREA	U.S. AVG
Average January low	33.0	26.2
Average July high	87.6	87.4
Annual days > 90°F	29	38
Annual days < 32°F	68	89
Annual days < 0°F	0	6

PRECIPITATION	AREA	U.S. AVG
Annual inches precipitation	48.0	37.7
Annual inches snowfall	6.0	7.0
Annual days precipitation	119	109
Annual days rain > 0.5 inches	37	22
Annual days snow > 1.5 inches	2	6

COMFORTS & HAZARDS	AREA	U.S. AVG
July relative humidity	70%	66%
Annual days mostly sunny	221	208
Annual days with thunderstorms	44	39
Tornado risk score	18	18
Hurricane risk score	17	13

Climate
Score: 50.0
Rank: 186

TEMPERATURE
PRECIPITATION
DAYS OF CLOUDS & PRECIPITATION

ACHIEVEMENT	AREA	U.S. AVG
High school degree	73.7%	82.7%
2-year college degree	7.2%	6.4%
4-year college degree	11.2%	15.7%
Graduate/professional degree	4.9%	8.9%

PUBLIC SCHOOLS	AREA	U.S. AVG
Expenditures per pupil	$4,811	$5,686
Student/teacher ratio	15.8	16.7
Attending public school	95.0%	90.1%
State SAT score	985*	1021
State ACT score	19.5	20.9

HIGHER EDUCATION	AREA	U.S. AVG
No. 2-year colleges	2	4
No. 4-year colleges/universities	1	6
No. highly ranked universities	0	1

Education
Score: 18.4
Rank: 304

HAZARDS & ILLNESSES	AREA	U.S. AVG
Air-quality score	38	37
Water-quality score	85	52
Pollen/allergy score	56	61
Cancer mortality per capita	208.7	201.9
Depression days per month	4.0	3.5
Stress score	98	50

HEALTHCARE	AREA	U.S. AVG
Physicians per capita	187.2	244.2
Hospital beds per capita	249.7	420.0
No. teaching hospitals	1	3
Cost per doctor visit	$69	$77
Cost per dental visit	$63	$70

CRIME	AREA	U.S. AVG
Violent crime rate	621.4	465.5
Change in violent crime rate	-13.8%	-2.2%
Property crime rate	4,994.1	3,517.1
Change in property crime rate	6.5%	-2.1%

Health & Healthcare
Score: 46.8
Rank: 200

Crime
Score: 8.3
Rank: 341

COMMUTE	AREA	U.S. AVG
Average commute time	25.4	27.4
Percent commutes > 60 mins.	4.6%	5.9%
Commute by auto	83.5%	78.9%
Commute by mass transit	0.3%	1.9%
Work at home	1.6%	3.1%
Mass transit miles per capita	0.30	1.87

INTERCITY SERVICES	AREA	U.S. AVG
Major airports within 60 miles	0	1
Size of regional airport	Small	Large
Daily airline activity	169	686
Amtrak service	No	No

AUTOMOTIVE	AREA	U.S. AVG
Insurance, annual premium	$1,366	$1,432
Gas, cost per gallon	$2.36	$2.49
Daily vehicle miles per capita	16.8	24.0

Transportation
Score: 8.3
Rank: 343

Leisure

Score: 39.8
Rank: 224

DINING & SHOPPING	AREA	U.S. AVG	ENTERTAINMENT	AREA	U.S. AVG	OUTDOOR ACTIVITIES	AREA	U.S. AVG
Restaurant rating	1	2	Professional sports rating	3	4	Golf-course rating	5	4
Outlet mall score	59	42	College sports rating	5	4	Ski-area rating	1	3
No. Starbucks	0	13	Zoo/aquarium rating	3	3	Sq. miles inland water	2	4
No. warehouse clubs	1	2	Amusement park rating	1	3	Miles of coastline	0.0	10.7
			Botanical garden/ arboretum rating	6	4	National Park rating	1	3

Arts & Culture

Score: 53.2
Rank: 175

MEDIA & LIBRARIES	AREA	U.S. AVG	PERFORMING ARTS	AREA	U.S. AVG	MUSEUMS	AREA	U.S. AVG
Arts radio rating	1	3	Classical music rating	6	4	Overall museum rating	4	5
No. public libraries	9	27	Ballet/dance rating	3	3	Art museum rating	5	5
Library volumes per capita	1.92	2.78	Professional theater rating	1	3	Science museum rating	3	5
			University arts programs rating	3	5	Children's museum rating	1	3

Ann Arbor, MI

Score: 93.2 Rank: 5 2004 rank: 6

Profile: College town
Location: Southeast Michigan, 40 miles west of Detroit
Elevation: 664 feet
Time zone: Eastern Standard Time

PRO	CON
College-town amenities	Home prices
Educated population	Cost of living
Healthcare	Winter climate

Ann Arbor is an important cultural center for Michigan. The University of Michigan and its campus dominate the scene both physically and culturally. The downtown has a pleasant small-town atmosphere with college-style restaurants, shopping, and entertainment, plus a couple of large medical complexes. Many amenities, including spectator sports and museums, are provided by the university. Live music is abundant. The population's educational attainment is among the top five nationwide. The area has a noted literary tradition, indirectly evidenced by the national bookseller Borders Group, which makes its headquarters locally. Beyond the university, economic activity is healthy, with a mix of industries and research and development activities, many in the pharmaceutical and medical technology fields. The area has tight planning and growth controls—for example, corner con-

venience stores are relatively hard to find—which maintains the small college town feel but also drives up costs. Complex traffic arrangements make some parts of the city hard to get around. Nearby Detroit provides services and transportation not available in the immediate area. Crime rates are among the lowest in the state. However, home prices are the state's highest and cost of living is above the national average.

The city is located on the banks of the Huron River on a mostly level plain. Summers are warm and humid but seldom unbearably hot, with occasional rain and thundershowers and mostly cool, pleasant evenings. Winters are a mix of cold, rain, snow, and sleet, although the nearby Great Lakes moderate the worst of the cold. The contrast of lake-effect moisture and cooler temperatures produces cloudy periods in all seasons, particularly fall and winter. First freeze is mid-October; last is late April.

Population

DEMOGRAPHICS	AREA	U.S. AVG	ETHNIC COMPOSITION	AREA	U.S. AVG	RESIDENT PROFILE	AREA	U.S. AVG
Population	345,128		White	75.6%	79.0%	Single	41.4%	32.4%
Population density per sq. mile	486.2	358.5	Black	12.1%	10.5%	Married	46.6%	52.7%
Population growth	22.0%	21.1%	Asian	8.0%	2.7%	Divorced/separated	12.0%	14.9%
Median age	33.2	36.1	Hispanic	2.8%	10.6%	Married with children	22.2%	23.7%
Percent Democrat	63.5%	44.5%	Religious observance	33.4%	48.9%	Single with children	7.0%	9.1%
Percent Republican	35.5%	54.5%	Diversity measure	43.9	40.1	Percent over age 65	8.6%	12.9%

Economy & Jobs

Score: 74.6
Rank: 96

INCOME	AREA	U.S. AVG	EMPLOYMENT	AREA	U.S. AVG	EMPLOYING INDUSTRIES	AREA	U.S. AVG
Per capita income	$31,059	$23,235	Unemployment rate	4.8%	4.7%	Largest: Healthcare & Social Assistance		
Household income	$58,860	$46,414	Recent job growth	2.5%	1.3%			
Household income < $25K	20.1%	26.2%	Projected future job growth	11.2%	11.5%	Percent manufacturing	9.9%	15.4%
Household income > $75K	38.2%	25.4%	White collar	70.5%	57.8%	Percent public sector	17.7%	15.7%
Household income growth	13.2%	13.6%	Blue collar	15.6%	25.2%	Percent construction	5.8%	9.9%

Cost of Living

Score: 32.9
Rank: 251

INDEXES & TAXES	AREA	U.S. AVG	HOUSING	AREA	U.S. AVG	NECESSITIES	AREA	U.S. AVG
Cost of Living Index	104.0	100.0	Median home price	$247,600	$220,000	Food Index	102.9	100.0
Buying Power Index	126.9	100.0	Home price appreciation	24.5%	10.1%	Housing Index	85.8	100.0
Income tax rate	4.40%	4.70%	Median rent	$934	$709	Utilities Index	97.1	100.0
Sales tax rate	6.00%	6.58%	Homes owned	58.3%	62.3%	Transportation Index	101.3	100.0
Property tax rate	$14.86	$12.00	Home price ratio	4.2	4.2	Healthcare Index	103.5	100.0
						Miscellaneous Cost Index	97.9	100.0

Climate
Score: 38.2
Rank: 230

TEMPERATURE	AREA	U.S. AVG
Average January low	17.3	26.2
Average July high	83.4	87.4
Annual days > 90°F	11	38
Annual days < 32°F	139	89
Annual days < 0°F	7	6

PRECIPITATION	AREA	U.S. AVG
Annual inches precipitation	32.0	37.7
Annual inches snowfall	39.0	7.0
Annual days precipitation	133	109
Annual days rain > 0.5 inches	19	22
Annual days snow > 1.5 inches	9	6

COMFORTS & HAZARDS	AREA	U.S. AVG
July relative humidity	72%	66%
Annual days mostly sunny	185	208
Annual days with thunderstorms	33	39
Tornado risk score	31	18
Hurricane risk score	3	13

TEMPERATURE

PRECIPITATION

DAYS OF CLOUDS & PRECIPITATION

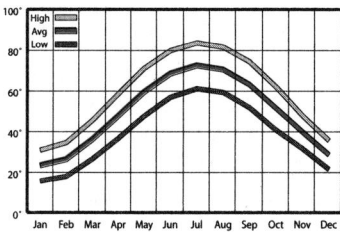

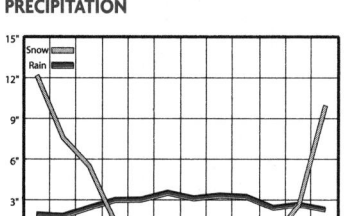

Education
Score: 97.1
Rank: 12

ACHIEVEMENT	AREA	U.S. AVG
High school degree	91.5%	82.7%
2-year college degree	6.1%	6.4%
4-year college degree	24.5%	15.7%
Graduate/professional degree	23.4%	8.9%

PUBLIC SCHOOLS	AREA	U.S. AVG
Expenditures per pupil	$6,960	$5,686
Student/teacher ratio	19.4	16.7
Attending public school	90.5%	90.1%
State SAT score	1151	1021
State ACT score	21.5*	20.9

HIGHER EDUCATION	AREA	U.S. AVG
No. 2-year colleges	1	4
No. 4-year colleges/universities	6	6
No. highly ranked universities	1	1

Health & Healthcare
Score: 86.1
Rank: 53

HAZARDS & ILLNESSES	AREA	U.S. AVG
Air-quality score	35	37
Water-quality score	44	52
Pollen/allergy score	58	61
Cancer mortality per capita	185.0	201.9
Depression days per month	2.6	3.5
Stress score	17	50

HEALTHCARE	AREA	U.S. AVG
Physicians per capita	809.3	244.2
Hospital beds per capita	479.0	420.0
No. teaching hospitals	3	3
Cost per doctor visit	$72	$77
Cost per dental visit	$71	$70

Crime
Score: 66.6
Rank: 126

CRIME	AREA	U.S. AVG
Violent crime rate	344.4	465.5
Change in violent crime rate	7.3%	-2.2%
Property crime rate	2,992.9	3,517.1
Change in property crime rate	3.2%	-2.1%

Transportation
Score: 63.9
Rank: 136

COMMUTE	AREA	U.S. AVG
Average commute time	24.6	27.4
Percent commutes > 60 mins.	4.4%	5.9%
Commute by auto	76.6%	78.9%
Commute by mass transit	3.1%	1.9%
Work at home	3.6%	3.1%
Mass transit miles per capita	3.05	1.87

INTERCITY SERVICES	AREA	U.S. AVG
Major airports within 60 miles	1	1
Size of regional airport	Large	Large
Daily airline activity	846	686
Amtrak service	Yes	No

AUTOMOTIVE	AREA	U.S. AVG
Insurance, annual premium	$1,641	$1,432
Gas, cost per gallon	$2.54	$2.49
Daily vehicle miles per capita	27.6	24.0

Leisure
Score: 81.8
Rank: 68

DINING & SHOPPING	AREA	U.S. AVG
Restaurant rating	1	2
Outlet mall score	126	42
No. Starbucks	4	13
No. warehouse clubs	1	2

ENTERTAINMENT	AREA	U.S. AVG
Professional sports rating	8	4
College sports rating	10	4
Zoo/aquarium rating	2	3
Amusement park rating	5	3
Botanical garden/ arboretum rating	8	4

OUTDOOR ACTIVITIES	AREA	U.S. AVG
Golf-course rating	7	4
Ski-area rating	5	3
Sq. miles inland water	3	4
Miles of coastline	0.0	10.7
National Park rating	1	3

Arts & Culture
Score: 78.9
Rank: 79

MEDIA & LIBRARIES	AREA	U.S. AVG
Arts radio rating	8	3
No. public libraries	12	27
Library volumes per capita	2.80	2.78

PERFORMING ARTS	AREA	U.S. AVG
Classical music rating	4	4
Ballet/dance rating	6	3
Professional theater rating	1	3
University arts programs rating	8	5

MUSEUMS	AREA	U.S. AVG
Overall museum rating	9	5
Art museum rating	9	5
Science museum rating	9	5
Children's museum rating	9	3

Anniston–Oxford, AL

Score: 14.2 **Rank:** 364 **2004 rank:** 323

Profile: Small-town complex/military town
Location: Northeast Alabama between Birmingham and Atlanta, Georgia
Elevation: 630 feet
Time zone: Central Standard Time

PRO	CON
Cost of living	Crime rates
Cost of housing	Arts and culture
Nearby mountains	Entertainment

Anniston is an unremarkable town now known for the Anniston Army Depot and the Talladega Superspeedway, both nearby. The army depot is the mainstay of the economy, and nearby Talladega Mountain provides recreation opportunities. At one time, the area was a planned company town, and later a health resort, and there is still some historic interest in town. Oxford is a smaller town south of Anniston located on the east-west Interstate 20, and its location on the freeway has brought some new development and commercial growth. At 78.6, the cost of living profile is attractive, but is overshadowed in overall ranking and scoring by the relative lack of other features and amenities.

Anniston is located in a wooded valley of the Appalachian Foothills just to the west of Talladega Mountain (actually a 60-mile long ridge, not a single mountain). Cheaha Mountain, about 15 miles south, is the highest point in the state at 2,400 feet. Four distinct seasons include long, warm, humid summers and mild winters with occasional cold snaps, ice storms, and snow. First freeze is mid-November; last is mid-March.

Population

DEMOGRAPHICS	AREA	U.S. AVG	ETHNIC COMPOSITION	AREA	U.S. AVG	RESIDENT PROFILE	AREA	U.S. AVG
Population	112,525		White	77.4%	79.0%	Single	29.6%	32.4%
Population density per sq. mile	184.9	358.5	Black	19.6%	10.5%	Married	54.7%	52.7%
Population growth	-3.0%	21.1%	Asian	0.8%	2.7%	Divorced/separated	15.7%	14.9%
Median age	37.9	36.1	Hispanic	1.9%	10.6%	Married with children	20.7%	23.7%
Percent Democrat	33.3%	44.5%	Religious observance	64.3%	48.9%	Single with children	8.6%	9.1%
Percent Republican	65.9%	54.5%	Diversity measure	38.6	40.1	Percent over age 65	14.6%	12.9%

Economy & Jobs
Score: 6.7
Rank: 348

INCOME	AREA	U.S. AVG	EMPLOYMENT	AREA	U.S. AVG	EMPLOYING INDUSTRIES	AREA	U.S. AVG
Per capita income	$20,023	$23,235	Unemployment rate	4.2%	4.7%	Largest: Manufacturing		
Household income	$36,316	$46,414	Recent job growth	-0.3%	1.3%			
Household income < $25K	35.2%	26.2%	Projected future job growth	0.7%	11.5%	Percent manufacturing	23.0%	15.4%
Household income > $75K	17.0%	25.4%	White collar	50.7%	57.8%	Percent public sector	18.0%	15.7%
Household income growth	14.3%	13.6%	Blue collar	34.2%	25.2%	Percent construction	11.2%	9.9%

Cost of Living
Score: 64.2
Rank: 134

INDEXES & TAXES	AREA	U.S. AVG	HOUSING	AREA	U.S. AVG	NECESSITIES	AREA	U.S. AVG
Cost of Living Index	78.6	100.0	Median home price	$115,100	$220,000	Food Index	96.4	100.0
Buying Power Index	103.6	100.0	Home price appreciation	30.4%	10.1%	Housing Index	49.8	100.0
Income tax rate	5.00%	4.70%	Median rent	$493	$709	Utilities Index	94.6	100.0
Sales tax rate	10.00%	6.58%	Homes owned	64.4%	62.3%	Transportation Index	86.6	100.0
Property tax rate	$3.27	$12.00	Home price ratio	3.2	4.2	Healthcare Index	91.4	100.0
						Miscellaneous Cost Index	96.9	100.0

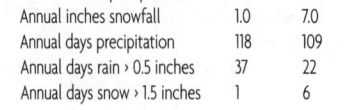
Climate
Score: 22.7
Rank: 288

TEMPERATURE	AREA	U.S. AVG	PRECIPITATION	AREA	U.S. AVG	COMFORTS & HAZARDS	AREA	U.S. AVG
Average January low	34.0	26.2	Annual inches precipitation	53.0	37.7	July relative humidity	72%	66%
Average July high	90.0	87.4	Annual inches snowfall	1.0	7.0	Annual days mostly sunny	210	208
Annual days > 90°F	39	38	Annual days precipitation	118	109	Annual days with thunderstorms	58	39
Annual days < 32°F	60	89	Annual days rain > 0.5 inches	37	22	Tornado risk score	24	18
Annual days < 0°F	0	6	Annual days snow > 1.5 inches	1	6	Hurricane risk score	19	13

TEMPERATURE

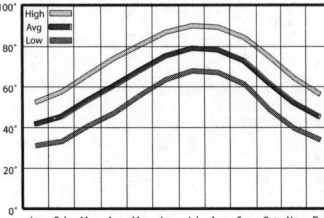

PRECIPITATION

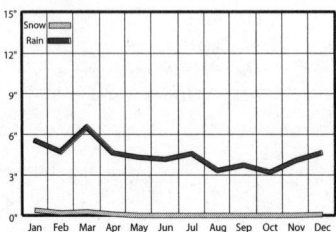

DAYS OF CLOUDS & PRECIPITATION

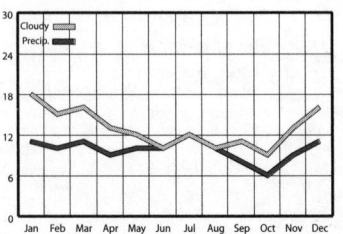

Education
Score: 5.6
Rank: 352

ACHIEVEMENT	AREA	U.S. AVG	PUBLIC SCHOOLS	AREA	U.S. AVG	HIGHER EDUCATION	AREA	U.S. AVG
High school degree	74.3%	82.7%	Expenditures per pupil	$4,348	$5,686	No. 2-year colleges	0	4
2-year college degree	5.1%	6.4%	Student/teacher ratio	17.4	16.7	No. 4-year colleges/universities	1	6
4-year college degree	9.1%	15.7%	Attending public school	91.9%	90.1%	No. highly ranked universities	0	1
Graduate/professional degree	6.5%	8.9%	State SAT score	1126	1021			
			State ACT score	20.2*	20.9			

Health & Healthcare
Score: 69.3
Rank: 116

HAZARDS & ILLNESSES	AREA	U.S. AVG	HEALTHCARE	AREA	U.S. AVG	CRIME	AREA	U.S. AVG
Air-quality score	44	37	Physicians per capita	173.2	244.2	Violent crime rate	668.8	465.5
Water-quality score	91	52	Hospital beds per capita	415.9	420.0	Change in violent crime rate	2.9%	-2.2%
Pollen/allergy score	65	61	No. teaching hospitals	0	3	Property crime rate	5,920.2	3,517.1
Cancer mortality per capita	239.6	201.9	Cost per doctor visit	$65	$77	Change in property crime rate	8.1%	-2.1%
Depression days per month	5.3	3.5	Cost per dental visit	$44	$70			
Stress score	79	50						

Crime
Score: 13.4
Rank: 323

Transportation
Score: 85.0
Rank: 57

COMMUTE	AREA	U.S. AVG	INTERCITY SERVICES	AREA	U.S. AVG	AUTOMOTIVE	AREA	U.S. AVG
Average commute time	25.0	27.4	Major airports within 60 miles	1	1	Insurance, annual premium	$1,202	$1,432
Percent commutes > 60 mins.	6.1%	5.9%	Size of regional airport	Large	Large	Gas, cost per gallon	$2.45	$2.49
Commute by auto	85.3%	78.9%	Daily airline activity	1575	686	Daily vehicle miles per capita	32.0	24.0
Commute by mass transit	0.5%	1.9%	Amtrak service	Yes	No			
Work at home	1.7%	3.1%						
Mass transit miles per capita	0.51	1.87						

Leisure
Score: 11.5
Rank: 330

DINING & SHOPPING	AREA	U.S. AVG	ENTERTAINMENT	AREA	U.S. AVG	OUTDOOR ACTIVITIES	AREA	U.S. AVG
Restaurant rating	1	2	Professional sports rating	2	4	Golf-course rating	2	4
Outlet mall score	28	42	College sports rating	2	4	Ski-area rating	1	3
No. Starbucks	1	13	Zoo/aquarium rating	1	3	Sq. miles inland water	2	4
No. warehouse clubs	0	2	Amusement park rating	1	3	Miles of coastline	0.0	10.7
			Botanical garden/arboretum rating	1	4	National Park rating	3	3

Arts & Culture
Score: 9.6
Rank: 337

MEDIA & LIBRARIES	AREA	U.S. AVG	PERFORMING ARTS	AREA	U.S. AVG	MUSEUMS	AREA	U.S. AVG
Arts radio rating	1	3	Classical music rating	3	4	Overall museum rating	2	5
No. public libraries	5	27	Ballet/dance rating	1	3	Art museum rating	1	5
Library volumes per capita	1.96	2.78	Professional theater rating	6	3	Science museum rating	5	5
			University arts programs rating	3	5	Children's museum rating	1	3

Appleton, WI

Score: 68.8 Rank: 102 2004 rank: 117

Profile: Small city
Location: Northeastern Wisconsin along north shore of Lake Winnebago
Elevation: 755 feet
Time zone: Central Standard Time

PRO	CON
Cost of living	Cold winters
Outdoor recreation	Educational attainment
Low crime rate	Low ethnic diversity

Lake Winnebago is the primary source for the Fox River, which ultimately reaches Lake Michigan at Green Bay. The so-called "Fox Cities"—Appleton, Neenah, Oshkosh, and Fond du Lac—surround the lake, and the area, known as the Fox River Valley, is a prosperous forest products, papermaking, and manufacturing region. Appleton is the largest and most diverse of the Fox Cities. Downtown Appleton—clean, attractive, and active—sits right at the lake, with livable city neighborhoods spreading especially east and northeast until reaching farmland outside the city. Lawrence University, a highly rated liberal arts school, adds a college town element. Blue collar and white collar elements mix well in this town. Cost of living is low and standards of living are high: The Buying Power Index is second highest in the U.S.

Future job-growth projections have been healthy for the manufacturing area as companies discover the strong local labor force. That said, the future of the paper industry has been a concern. Nearby water, state parks, and the vast forested areas of upstate Wisconsin provide above average recreation opportunities, both summer and winter.

The Fox Cities sit in a mostly level valley plain surrounded by areas of low rolling and densely wooded hills. Summers are pleasantly warm and sometimes humid, with occasional hot spells and cool evenings. Most summer precipitation arrives as thunderstorms from May through September. Winters are harsh and cold, although the coldest days are often sunny and dry. Most winter precipitation comes as snow with persistent snow cover. First freeze is early October; last is mid-May.

Population

DEMOGRAPHICS	AREA	U.S. AVG	ETHNIC COMPOSITION	AREA	U.S. AVG	RESIDENT PROFILE	AREA	U.S. AVG
Population	214,903		White	93.5%	79.0%	Single	29.2%	32.4%
Population density per sq. mile	223.8	358.5	Black	0.6%	10.5%	Married	60.6%	52.7%
Population growth	23.1%	21.1%	Asian	2.6%	2.7%	Divorced/separated	10.3%	14.9%
Median age	36.0	36.1	Hispanic	2.1%	10.6%	Married with children	29.9%	23.7%
Percent Democrat	43.8%	44.5%	Religious observance	79.5%	48.9%	Single with children	6.5%	9.1%
Percent Republican	55.1%	54.5%	Diversity measure	16.0	40.1	Percent over age 65	11.1%	12.9%

Economy & Jobs
Score: 62.6
Rank: 141

INCOME	AREA	U.S. AVG	EMPLOYMENT	AREA	U.S. AVG	EMPLOYING INDUSTRIES	AREA	U.S. AVG
Per capita income	$25,753	$23,235	Unemployment rate	4.2%	4.7%	Largest: Manufacturing		
Household income	$56,896	$46,414	Recent job growth	-0.1%	1.3%			
Household income < $25K	15.8%	26.2%	Projected future job growth	12.5%	11.5%	Percent manufacturing	22.0%	15.4%
Household income > $75K	31.4%	25.4%	White collar	54.5%	57.8%	Percent public sector	7.5%	15.7%
Household income growth	13.3%	13.6%	Blue collar	32.0%	25.2%	Percent construction	10.0%	9.9%

Cost of Living
Score: 44.7
Rank: 206

INDEXES & TAXES	AREA	U.S. AVG	HOUSING	AREA	U.S. AVG	NECESSITIES	AREA	U.S. AVG
Cost of Living Index	85.3	100.0	Median home price	$131,900	$220,000	Food Index	95.7	100.0
Buying Power Index	149.5	100.0	Home price appreciation	27.9%	10.1%	Housing Index	50.5	100.0
Income tax rate	6.93%	4.70%	Median rent	$604	$709	Utilities Index	114.4	100.0
Sales tax rate	5.00%	6.58%	Homes owned	71.8%	62.3%	Transportation Index	99.9	100.0
Property tax rate	$20.04	$12.00	Home price ratio	2.3	4.2	Healthcare Index	101.1	100.0
						Miscellaneous Cost Index	100.8	100.0

Climate
Score: 12.6
Rank: 326

TEMPERATURE	AREA	U.S. AVG	PRECIPITATION	AREA	U.S. AVG	COMFORTS & HAZARDS	AREA	U.S. AVG
Average January low	6.9	26.2	Annual inches precipitation	27.0	37.7	July relative humidity	73%	66%
Average July high	80.7	87.4	Annual inches snowfall	43.0	7.0	Annual days mostly sunny	192	208
Annual days > 90°F	7	38	Annual days precipitation	120	109	Annual days with thunderstorms	35	39
Annual days < 32°F	163	89	Annual days rain > 0.5 inches	16	22	Tornado risk score	16	18
Annual days < 0°F	29	6	Annual days snow > 1.5 inches	11	6	Hurricane risk score	0	13

TEMPERATURE

PRECIPITATION

DAYS OF CLOUDS & PRECIPITATION

Education
Score: 59.1
Rank: 154

ACHIEVEMENT	AREA	U.S. AVG	PUBLIC SCHOOLS	AREA	U.S. AVG	HIGHER EDUCATION	AREA	U.S. AVG
High school degree	88.0%	82.7%	Expenditures per pupil	$6,084	$5,686	No. 2-year colleges	2	4
2-year college degree	8.7%	6.4%	Student/teacher ratio	15.5	16.7	No. 4-year colleges/universities	1	6
4-year college degree	16.5%	15.7%	Attending public school	84.1%	90.1%	No. highly ranked universities	1	1
Graduate/professional degree	5.8%	8.9%	State SAT score	1188	1021			
			State ACT score	22.2*	20.9			

Health & Healthcare
Score: 62.8
Rank: 140

Crime
Score: 98.9
Rank: 5

HAZARDS & ILLNESSES	AREA	U.S. AVG	HEALTHCARE	AREA	U.S. AVG	CRIME	AREA	U.S. AVG
Air-quality score	47	37	Physicians per capita	162.6	244.2	Violent crime rate	111.6	465.5
Water-quality score	34	52	Hospital beds per capita	188.9	420.0	Change in violent crime rate	17.2%	-2.2%
Pollen/allergy score	30	61	No. teaching hospitals	2	3	Property crime rate	2,142.4	3,517.1
Cancer mortality per capita	193.0	201.9	Cost per doctor visit	$89	$77	Change in property crime rate	-3.2%	-2.1%
Depression days per month	3.4	3.5	Cost per dental visit	$68	$70			
Stress score	7	50						

Transportation
Score: 70.3
Rank: 112

COMMUTE	AREA	U.S. AVG	INTERCITY SERVICES	AREA	U.S. AVG	AUTOMOTIVE	AREA	U.S. AVG
Average commute time	20.2	27.4	Major airports within 60 miles	1	1	Insurance, annual premium	$965	$1,432
Percent commutes > 60 mins.	2.6%	5.9%	Size of regional airport	Medium	Large	Gas, cost per gallon	$2.55	$2.49
Commute by auto	84.3%	78.9%	Daily airline activity	373	686	Daily vehicle miles per capita	25.7	24.0
Commute by mass transit	0.7%	1.9%	Amtrak service	No	No			
Work at home	3.5%	3.1%						
Mass transit miles per capita	0.65	1.87						

Leisure
Score: 63.6
Rank: 136

DINING & SHOPPING	AREA	U.S. AVG	ENTERTAINMENT	AREA	U.S. AVG	OUTDOOR ACTIVITIES	AREA	U.S. AVG
Restaurant rating	1	2	Professional sports rating	4	4	Golf-course rating	4	4
Outlet mall score	0	42	College sports rating	4	4	Ski-area rating	2	3
No. Starbucks	3	13	Zoo/aquarium rating	1	3	Sq. miles inland water	10	4
No. warehouse clubs	1	2	Amusement park rating	1	3	Miles of coastline	0.0	10.7
			Botanical garden/			National Park rating	1	3
			arboretum rating	5	4			

Arts & Culture
Score: 31.8
Rank: 255

MEDIA & LIBRARIES	AREA	U.S. AVG	PERFORMING ARTS	AREA	U.S. AVG	MUSEUMS	AREA	U.S. AVG
Arts radio rating	1	3	Classical music rating	2	4	Overall museum rating	3	5
No. public libraries	12	27	Ballet/dance rating	1	3	Art museum rating	3	5
Library volumes per capita	3.27	2.78	Professional theater rating	1	3	Science museum rating	2	5
			University arts programs rating	2	5	Children's museum rating	1	3

Asheville, NC

Score: 90.5 Rank: 7 2004 rank: 8

Profile: Mid-size city
Location: Far western North Carolina, 30 miles southeast of Tennessee border, near Great Smoky Mountains National Park
Elevation: 2,207 feet
Time zone: Eastern Standard Time

PRO	CON
Attractive setting	Home prices
Attractive downtown	Air service
Nearby mountains	Winter cold

Asheville lies at the foot of the Great Smoky Mountains, the highest portion of the Appalachian Range. The town is an eastern equivalent of the many mountain resort towns that dot the American West, particularly in the Rocky Mountains. Originally settled in the 1850s as a health resort, Asheville has an interesting history—in the late 1800s and especially the 1920s, the area was a popular retreat for wealthy vacationers, including eight presidents and many well-known industrialists. Today the area has an active economy and serves both as a getaway from summer heat in the nearby lowlands and as a travel destination for many East Coast travelers. Although Asheville has some manufacturing interests, led by GE Lighting Systems, the economy is largely supported by the hospitality, education, and healthcare sectors. The area attracts educated young professionals, artisans, and active retirees. The attractive downtown offers a mix of modern and Art Deco buildings and an assortment of trendy restaurants and live-entertainment venues. Several resorts and planned communities surround the city, especially to the north and west. The city has controlled urban sprawl better than many of its type. At most times of the year, except winter, tourists can make the area feel crowded. Overall, the area scores well in most categories with no major downsides, hence the high ranking.

The city of Asheville sprawls along both banks of the French Broad River, near the center of the French Broad Basin. Mountain ridges to the east and west flank the entire valley with peaks from 2,000 feet to 4,400 feet above the valley floor. At the Carolina-Tennessee border, 25 miles northwest, the relatively high Appalachian/Great Smoky Mountain ridge blocks the northern end of the valley. The Blue Ridge rises about 30 miles south. Summers are warm and humid, but the elevation and nearby mountains cause some cooling, particularly in the evenings. The high mountains to the northwest block precipitation and cold fronts in the winter. Precipitation in Asheville, particularly northwest of the immediate city, is the lowest in North Carolina. Significant snowfall is uncommon. Heavy Gulf rains can cause flooding in the river valley. First freeze is late October; last is mid-April.

Population

DEMOGRAPHICS	AREA	U.S. AVG	ETHNIC COMPOSITION	AREA	U.S. AVG	RESIDENT PROFILE	AREA	U.S. AVG
Population	387,970		White	91.0%	79.0%	Single	28.2%	32.4%
Population density per sq. mile	190.8	358.5	Black	5.0%	10.5%	Married	56.6%	52.7%
Population growth	26.3%	21.1%	Asian	0.8%	2.7%	Divorced/separated	15.2%	14.9%
Median age	40.8	36.1	Hispanic	4.0%	10.6%	Married with children	19.7%	23.7%
Percent Democrat	44.6%	44.5%	Religious observance	57.5%	48.9%	Single with children	7.2%	9.1%
Percent Republican	54.8%	54.5%	Diversity measure	23.0	40.1	Percent over age 65	17.7%	12.9%

Economy & Jobs
Score: 32.6
Rank: 251

INCOME	AREA	U.S. AVG	EMPLOYMENT	AREA	U.S. AVG	EMPLOYING INDUSTRIES	AREA	U.S. AVG
Per capita income	$22,778	$23,235	Unemployment rate	4.8%	4.7%	Largest: Healthcare & Social Assistance		
Household income	$40,852	$46,414	Recent job growth	0.6%	1.3%			
Household income < $25K	28.8%	26.2%	Projected future job growth	8.5%	11.5%	Percent manufacturing	17.6%	15.4%
Household income > $75K	19.4%	25.4%	White collar	54.3%	57.8%	Percent public sector	13.3%	15.7%
Household income growth	12.5%	13.6%	Blue collar	28.9%	25.2%	Percent construction	11.3%	9.9%

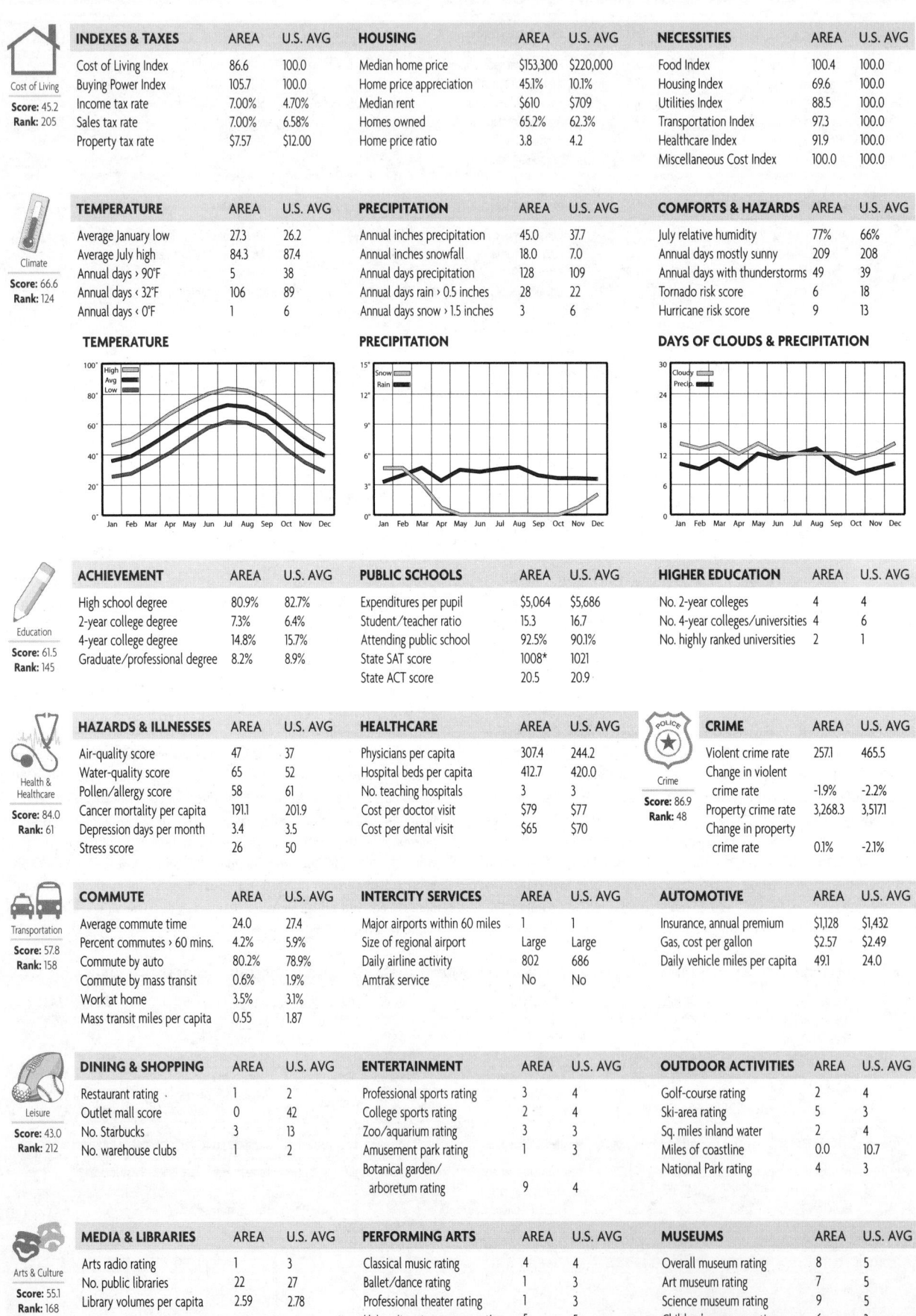

Cost of Living
Score: 45.2
Rank: 205

INDEXES & TAXES	AREA	U.S. AVG
Cost of Living Index	86.6	100.0
Buying Power Index	105.7	100.0
Income tax rate	7.00%	4.70%
Sales tax rate	7.00%	6.58%
Property tax rate	$7.57	$12.00

HOUSING	AREA	U.S. AVG
Median home price	$153,300	$220,000
Home price appreciation	45.1%	10.1%
Median rent	$610	$709
Homes owned	65.2%	62.3%
Home price ratio	3.8	4.2

NECESSITIES	AREA	U.S. AVG
Food Index	100.4	100.0
Housing Index	69.6	100.0
Utilities Index	88.5	100.0
Transportation Index	97.3	100.0
Healthcare Index	91.9	100.0
Miscellaneous Cost Index	100.0	100.0

Climate
Score: 66.6
Rank: 124

TEMPERATURE	AREA	U.S. AVG
Average January low	27.3	26.2
Average July high	84.3	87.4
Annual days > 90°F	5	38
Annual days < 32°F	106	89
Annual days < 0°F	1	6

PRECIPITATION	AREA	U.S. AVG
Annual inches precipitation	45.0	37.7
Annual inches snowfall	18.0	7.0
Annual days precipitation	128	109
Annual days rain > 0.5 inches	28	22
Annual days snow > 1.5 inches	3	6

COMFORTS & HAZARDS	AREA	U.S. AVG
July relative humidity	77%	66%
Annual days mostly sunny	209	208
Annual days with thunderstorms	49	39
Tornado risk score	6	18
Hurricane risk score	9	13

TEMPERATURE (High / Avg / Low, Jan–Dec)

PRECIPITATION (Snow / Rain, Jan–Dec)

DAYS OF CLOUDS & PRECIPITATION (Cloudy / Precip., Jan–Dec)

Education
Score: 61.5
Rank: 145

ACHIEVEMENT	AREA	U.S. AVG
High school degree	80.9%	82.7%
2-year college degree	7.3%	6.4%
4-year college degree	14.8%	15.7%
Graduate/professional degree	8.2%	8.9%

PUBLIC SCHOOLS	AREA	U.S. AVG
Expenditures per pupil	$5,064	$5,686
Student/teacher ratio	15.3	16.7
Attending public school	92.5%	90.1%
State SAT score	1008*	1021
State ACT score	20.5	20.9

HIGHER EDUCATION	AREA	U.S. AVG
No. 2-year colleges	4	4
No. 4-year colleges/universities	4	6
No. highly ranked universities	2	1

Health & Healthcare
Score: 84.0
Rank: 61

HAZARDS & ILLNESSES	AREA	U.S. AVG
Air-quality score	47	37
Water-quality score	65	52
Pollen/allergy score	58	61
Cancer mortality per capita	191.1	201.9
Depression days per month	3.4	3.5
Stress score	26	50

HEALTHCARE	AREA	U.S. AVG
Physicians per capita	307.4	244.2
Hospital beds per capita	412.7	420.0
No. teaching hospitals	3	3
Cost per doctor visit	$79	$77
Cost per dental visit	$65	$70

Crime
Score: 86.9
Rank: 48

CRIME	AREA	U.S. AVG
Violent crime rate	257.1	465.5
Change in violent crime rate	-1.9%	-2.2%
Property crime rate	3,268.3	3,517.1
Change in property crime rate	0.1%	-2.1%

Transportation
Score: 57.8
Rank: 158

COMMUTE	AREA	U.S. AVG
Average commute time	24.0	27.4
Percent commutes > 60 mins.	4.2%	5.9%
Commute by auto	80.2%	78.9%
Commute by mass transit	0.6%	1.9%
Work at home	3.5%	3.1%
Mass transit miles per capita	0.55	1.87

INTERCITY SERVICES	AREA	U.S. AVG
Major airports within 60 miles	1	1
Size of regional airport	Large	Large
Daily airline activity	802	686
Amtrak service	No	No

AUTOMOTIVE	AREA	U.S. AVG
Insurance, annual premium	$1,128	$1,432
Gas, cost per gallon	$2.57	$2.49
Daily vehicle miles per capita	49.1	24.0

Leisure
Score: 43.0
Rank: 212

DINING & SHOPPING	AREA	U.S. AVG
Restaurant rating	1	2
Outlet mall score	0	42
No. Starbucks	3	13
No. warehouse clubs	1	2

ENTERTAINMENT	AREA	U.S. AVG
Professional sports rating	3	4
College sports rating	2	4
Zoo/aquarium rating	3	3
Amusement park rating	1	3
Botanical garden/arboretum rating	9	4

OUTDOOR ACTIVITIES	AREA	U.S. AVG
Golf-course rating	2	4
Ski-area rating	5	3
Sq. miles inland water	2	4
Miles of coastline	0.0	10.7
National Park rating	4	3

Arts & Culture
Score: 55.1
Rank: 168

MEDIA & LIBRARIES	AREA	U.S. AVG
Arts radio rating	1	3
No. public libraries	22	27
Library volumes per capita	2.59	2.78

PERFORMING ARTS	AREA	U.S. AVG
Classical music rating	4	4
Ballet/dance rating	1	3
Professional theater rating	1	3
University arts programs rating	5	5

MUSEUMS	AREA	U.S. AVG
Overall museum rating	8	5
Art museum rating	7	5
Science museum rating	9	5
Children's museum rating	6	3

Athens—Clarke County, GA

Score: 83.8   Rank: 29   2004 rank: 34

Profile: College town
Location: Northeast Georgia, about 70 miles east of Atlanta
Elevation: 802 feet
Time zone: Eastern Standard Time

PRO	CON
College-town amenities	Home prices
Nightlife	Property crime
Educated population	Air service

Athens is a clean, attractive, and progressive town with a distinct Southern flair. The local University of Georgia is the centerpiece of the area's economy. Athens is noted as a center for pop music—REM and the B-52's are from here—and the entertainment scene includes plenty of live music. Other arts and cultural amenities emanate from the university. The area has some interesting architecture and building projects, including a 10-year-old Victorian-look Classic Center, which is used as a convention center and concert hall. Like many college towns, especially in the South, Athens is attractive to young people and active retirees alike. Home prices are high for a small Georgia town, and air service requires a trip to Atlanta, but overall liv-

ing costs are reasonable (89.0). Jobs center on university-related activities, healthcare, and a modest high-tech industry. While not excelling in any category, Athens is consistently good across the board, and an attractive place to live overall.

Athens is located on the Piedmont Plateau. Terrain is rolling to hilly with elevations ranging from 600 feet to 850 feet. Summers are warm and somewhat humid, but not as hot as other areas in the state. Highs reach 90°F only 19 days a year on average compared to a state average of 60 days. Winters are not severe but have short cold spells. Thunderstorms occur year-round, and spring storms may be severe. Snowfall is infrequent, but freezing rain and ice storms occur.

Population

DEMOGRAPHICS	AREA	U.S. AVG
Population	175,323	
Population density per sq. mile	170.0	358.5
Population growth	30.7%	21.1%
Median age	31.6	36.1
Percent Democrat	45.8%	44.5%
Percent Republican	52.9%	54.5%

ETHNIC COMPOSITION	AREA	U.S. AVG
White	74.0%	79.0%
Black	19.5%	10.5%
Asian	2.2%	2.7%
Hispanic	5.8%	10.6%
Religious observance	35.6%	48.9%
Diversity measure	45.3	40.1

RESIDENT PROFILE	AREA	U.S. AVG
Single	41.7%	32.4%
Married	43.7%	52.7%
Divorced/separated	14.6%	14.9%
Married with children	20.2%	23.7%
Single with children	8.7%	9.1%
Percent over age 65	9.3%	12.9%

Economy & Jobs
Score: 57.5
Rank: 160

INCOME	AREA	U.S. AVG
Per capita income	$20,749	$23,235
Household income	$38,984	$46,414
Household income < $25K	34.7%	26.2%
Household income > $75K	21.3%	25.4%
Household income growth	12.1%	13.6%

EMPLOYMENT	AREA	U.S. AVG
Unemployment rate	4.3%	4.7%
Recent job growth	1.7%	1.3%
Projected future job growth	12.8%	11.5%
White collar	58.9%	57.8%
Blue collar	24.5%	25.2%

EMPLOYING INDUSTRIES	AREA	U.S. AVG
Largest: Healthcare & Social Assistance		
Percent manufacturing	16.0%	15.4%
Percent public sector	25.5%	15.7%
Percent construction	8.4%	9.9%

Cost of Living
Score: 38.5
Rank: 230

INDEXES & TAXES	AREA	U.S. AVG
Cost of Living Index	89.0	100.0
Buying Power Index	98.2	100.0
Income tax rate	6.00%	4.70%
Sales tax rate	7.00%	6.58%
Property tax rate	$9.47	$12.00

HOUSING	AREA	U.S. AVG
Median home price	$157,800	$220,000
Home price appreciation	31.0%	10.1%
Median rent	$665	$709
Homes owned	54.1%	62.3%
Home price ratio	4.0	4.2

NECESSITIES	AREA	U.S. AVG
Food Index	101.3	100.0
Housing Index	66.4	100.0
Utilities Index	93.2	100.0
Transportation Index	102.0	100.0
Healthcare Index	103.7	100.0
Miscellaneous Cost Index	98.5	100.0

Climate
Score: 52.9
Rank: 175

TEMPERATURE	AREA	U.S. AVG
Average January low	33.4	26.2
Average July high	89.5	87.4
Annual days > 90°F	48	38
Annual days < 32°F	54	89
Annual days < 0°F	0	6

PRECIPITATION	AREA	U.S. AVG
Annual inches precipitation	50.6	37.7
Annual inches snowfall	1.7	7.0
Annual days precipitation	112	109
Annual days rain > 0.5 inches	33	22
Annual days snow > 1.5 inches	2	6

COMFORTS & HAZARDS	AREA	U.S. AVG
July relative humidity	72%	66%
Annual days mostly sunny	218	208
Annual days with thunderstorms	52	39
Tornado risk score	25	18
Hurricane risk score	28	13

TEMPERATURE

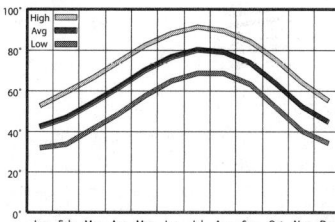

PRECIPITATION

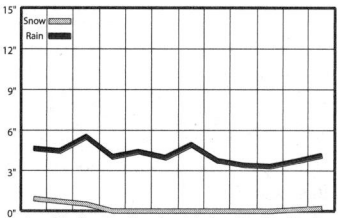

DAYS OF CLOUDS & PRECIPITATION

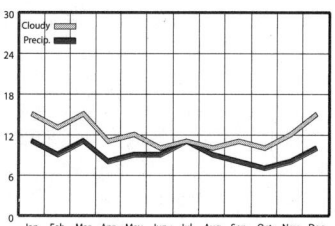

ACHIEVEMENT	AREA	U.S. AVG	PUBLIC SCHOOLS	AREA	U.S. AVG	HIGHER EDUCATION	AREA	U.S. AVG
High school degree	79.6%	82.7%	Expenditures per pupil	$5,522	$5,686	No. 2-year colleges	1	4
2-year college degree	3.9%	6.4%	Student/teacher ratio	14.6	16.7	No. 4-year colleges/universities	1	6
4-year college degree	18.1%	15.7%	Attending public school	89.8%	90.1%	No. highly ranked universities	1	1
Graduate/professional degree	15.1%	8.9%	State SAT score	990*	1021			
			State ACT score	20.2	20.9			

Education
Score: 64.4
Rank: 134

HAZARDS & ILLNESSES	AREA	U.S. AVG	HEALTHCARE	AREA	U.S. AVG	CRIME	AREA	U.S. AVG
Air-quality score	59	37	Physicians per capita	207.3	244.2	Violent crime rate	280.0	465.5
Water-quality score	60	52	Hospital beds per capita	410.7	420.0	Change in violent crime rate	-16.6%	-2.2%
Pollen/allergy score	63	61	No. teaching hospitals	0	3	Property crime rate	4,172.1	3,517.1
Cancer mortality per capita	166.0	201.9	Cost per doctor visit	$68	$77	Change in property crime rate	-8.9%	-2.1%
Depression days per month	3.3	3.5	Cost per dental visit	$70	$70			
Stress score	16	50						

Health & Healthcare
Score: 79.4
Rank: 78

Crime
Score: 29.9
Rank: 261

COMMUTE	AREA	U.S. AVG	INTERCITY SERVICES	AREA	U.S. AVG	AUTOMOTIVE	AREA	U.S. AVG
Average commute time	23.8	27.4	Major airports within 60 miles	1	1	Insurance, annual premium	$1,454	$1,432
Percent commutes > 60 mins.	6.2%	5.9%	Size of regional airport	Large	Large	Gas, cost per gallon	$2.45	$2.49
Commute by auto	77.7%	78.9%	Daily airline activity	1499	686	Daily vehicle miles per capita	27.8	24.0
Commute by mass transit	1.5%	1.9%	Amtrak service	No	No			
Work at home	2.5%	3.1%						
Mass transit miles per capita	1.48	1.87						

Transportation
Score: 88.5
Rank: 44

DINING & SHOPPING	AREA	U.S. AVG	ENTERTAINMENT	AREA	U.S. AVG	OUTDOOR ACTIVITIES	AREA	U.S. AVG
Restaurant rating	1	2	Professional sports rating	2	4	Golf-course rating	1	4
Outlet mall score	170	42	College sports rating	8	4	Ski-area rating	1	3
No. Starbucks	1	13	Zoo/aquarium rating	1	3	Sq. miles inland water	1	4
No. warehouse clubs	1	2	Amusement park rating	1	3	Miles of coastline	0.0	10.7
			Botanical garden/arboretum rating	5	4	National Park rating	2	3

Leisure
Score: 34.5
Rank: 244

MEDIA & LIBRARIES	AREA	U.S. AVG	PERFORMING ARTS	AREA	U.S. AVG	MUSEUMS	AREA	U.S. AVG
Arts radio rating	1	3	Classical music rating	6	4	Overall museum rating	5	5
No. public libraries	8	27	Ballet/dance rating	5	3	Art museum rating	6	5
Library volumes per capita	2.04	2.78	Professional theater rating	1	3	Science museum rating	7	5
			University arts programs rating	5	5	Children's museum rating	1	3

Arts & Culture
Score: 57.2
Rank: 160

Atlanta–Sandy Springs–Marietta, GA   Score: 78.2 Rank: 54 2004 rank: 7

Profile: Regional center
Location: North-central Georgia at the southern tip of the Appalachian Mountains
Elevation: 1,034 feet
Time zone: Eastern Standard Time

PRO
Excellent housing
Entertainment
Education

CON
Growth and sprawl
Traffic and commutes
Summer heat

The large, energetic, and cosmopolitan Atlanta is a booming regional center for the growing and increasingly prosperous American South. Originally, Atlanta was founded as a transportation crossroads, as railroads converged on its end-of-the-mountains location and radiated in all directions. Today's Atlanta still plays that role, both for ground and air transport, as it originates more flights than any city except Chicago. But more generally, Atlanta has boomed, first as home to such giants as Coca-Cola and Delta Airlines, and more recently as a vital regional and headquarters business center for large corporations. Home offices for Home Depot, UPS, CNN, and Bellsouth are in the area, and almost any company you can think of has an operation here, and some are quite large. Culturally, Atlanta sits at the crossroads between the Old and New South, as old economy and agrarian interests mingle with modern corporate America and numerous technology and research interests. Atlanta has a rich diversity of socioeconomic backgrounds, and is full of northerners drawn by the booming economy, pleasant climate, activities, and cultural diversity. Some locals call it the "northernmost Southern city," but—make no mistake—despite the corporate towers and fast pace, Atlanta retains its Southern roots, which become more apparent the farther you go outside the Interstate 285 beltway, known locally as the "Perimeter." Atlanta's economy continues to grow as more businesses expand operations in the area and more people move here for employment. The future employment picture looks bright, with future job growth projected at over 20%, an astounding figure for such a large city.

The commercial downtown is modern, but not as impressive as most large American cities. It has undergone several renewals, with the development of the notable "Underground" many years ago, which has faded from the limelight somewhat, but more recently with the growth of residential towers, some new parks, and a new aquarium complex. But the real story is suburban growth: The city has spread primarily to the north and northeast into the wooded areas of Dekalb, Cobb, and Cherokee counties, where the most desirable residential neighborhoods are found. Most new commercial development is also north along the Interstate 285 beltway. The regions to the east and south are more industrial, while the west is a mix. Some suburbs are inside the Perimeter ("ITP") around the upscale Buckhead, more are outside it in suburbs such as Sandy Springs, Dunwoody, Roswell, and Norcross and Marietta (a 2006 All-America City Award winner), spread along the major radii running north across and outside the Perimeter ("OTP"). The sprawl is going still farther north, beyond Marietta to Kennesaw, beyond Roswell to the more upscale Alpharetta, and so forth. Most people commute to somewhere along the Perimeter, not downtown. Traffic to and from the Perimeter and on the Perimeter has become a major problem, a concern we had in the last edition. Since then, average commute times have risen 10%, and some 12% of commutes take more than an hour, a figure only found in the New York and Los Angeles areas otherwise. Commuter rail transit has come on line with an airport linkage, but the multidirectional nature of traffic flows is hard to conquer. Traffic and commutes are a big problem and one of the chief reasons Atlanta has fallen from a robust no. 7 ranking to its present position.

While traffic has grown, more than many other cities, Atlanta is planned with a certain element of common sense. Main arteries such as Peachtree Street, for example, have collector and access roads that aid the flow of traffic. Housing is still one of Atlanta's most attractive features. The area has some of the highest quality residential properties anywhere per dollar spent, particularly for a city of this size. Nice family-style homes are affordable thanks to inexpensive labor, materials, and business costs. Generous, well-built houses on attractive wooded lots are the rule, not the exception. The area looks more attractive than most, but some areas are starting to get crowded and overbuilt.

There is plenty to do in Atlanta and surrounding areas, with an abundance of rich cultural amenities and nightlife; the list is too long to share here. Atlanta has some of the country's best restaurants, and eateries in general are plentiful and reasonably priced, and professional sport franchises are an obsession even if performance has been spotty. Atlanta is a particularly strong choice for families and career-minded middle class seeking good single-family housing in a lively big-city environment. But those residents must increasingly be willing to tolerate the side effects of rapid growth.

Physically, Atlanta is located in a transition zone between forested hills to the north and more level agricultural areas to the south. Summer temperatures are warm but moderated by elevation. There may be prolonged periods of late summer heat. Winters are mild with short cold spells. Active precipitation occurs during spring with thunderstorms, some severe, lasting into July, with frequent dry periods into late summer and fall. Most winter precipitation is rain with occasional snowfall. Ice storms and freezing rain with newsworthy damage and travel disruption occur 2 out of every 3 years. First freeze is mid-November; last is late March.

DEMOGRAPHICS	AREA	U.S. AVG	ETHNIC COMPOSITION	AREA	U.S. AVG	RESIDENT PROFILE	AREA	U.S. AVG
Population	4,765,845		White	61.6%	79.0%	Single	32.5%	32.4%
Population density per sq. mile	569.0	358.5	Black	28.9%	10.5%	Married	52.2%	52.7%
Population growth	65.5%	21.1%	Asian	3.8%	2.7%	Divorced/separated	15.3%	14.9%
Median age	33.9	36.1	Hispanic	8.1%	10.6%	Married with children	26.6%	23.7%
Percent Democrat	44.1%	44.5%	Religious observance	44.0%	48.9%	Single with children	9.7%	9.1%
Percent Republican	55.2%	54.5%	Diversity measure	54.2	40.1	Percent over age 65	8.0%	12.9%

Population

INCOME	AREA	U.S. AVG	EMPLOYMENT	AREA	U.S. AVG	EMPLOYING INDUSTRIES	AREA	U.S. AVG
Per capita income	$28,214	$23,235	Unemployment rate	5.5%	4.7%	Largest: Professional, Scientific & Technical Services		
Household income	$59,507	$46,414	Recent job growth	2.1%	1.3%			
Household income < $25K	17.4%	26.2%	Projected future job growth	20.5%	11.5%	Percent manufacturing	12.2%	15.4%
Household income > $75K	36.7%	25.4%	White collar	65.1%	57.8%	Percent public sector	12.3%	15.7%
Household income growth	13.7%	13.6%	Blue collar	22.6%	25.2%	Percent construction	10.4%	9.9%

Economy & Jobs
Score: 86.9
Rank: 50

INDEXES & TAXES	AREA	U.S. AVG	HOUSING	AREA	U.S. AVG	NECESSITIES	AREA	U.S. AVG
Cost of Living Index	90.9	100.0	Median home price	$173,900	$220,000	Food Index	99.6	100.0
Buying Power Index	146.7	100.0	Home price appreciation	21.6%	10.1%	Housing Index	64.0	100.0
Income tax rate	6.00%	4.70%	Median rent	$774	$709	Utilities Index	92.1	100.0
Sales tax rate	6.67%	6.58%	Homes owned	65.0%	62.3%	Transportation Index	103.0	100.0
Property tax rate	$9.66	$12.00	Home price ratio	2.9	4.2	Healthcare Index	104.4	100.0
						Miscellaneous Cost Index	99.0	100.0

Cost of Living
Score: 28.9
Rank: 266

Climate
Score: 74.9
Rank: 94

TEMPERATURE	AREA	U.S. AVG
Average January low	33.4	26.2
Average July high	86.5	87.4
Annual days > 90°F	19	38
Annual days < 32°F	59	89
Annual days < 0°F	0	6

PRECIPITATION	AREA	U.S. AVG
Annual inches precipitation	48.0	37.7
Annual inches snowfall	2.0	7.0
Annual days precipitation	116	109
Annual days rain > 0.5 inches	33	22
Annual days snow > 1.5 inches	1	6

COMFORTS & HAZARDS	AREA	U.S. AVG
July relative humidity	70%	66%
Annual days mostly sunny	219	208
Annual days with thunderstorms	50	39
Tornado risk score	26	18
Hurricane risk score	19	13

TEMPERATURE

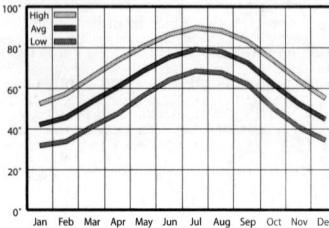

PRECIPITATION

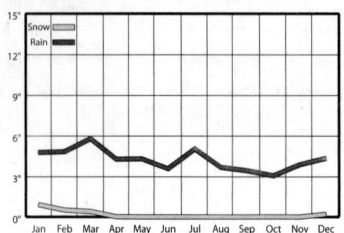

DAYS OF CLOUDS & PRECIPITATION

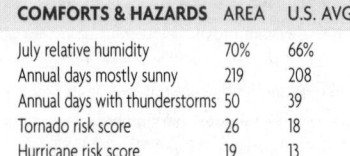

Education
Score: 94.4
Rank: 22

ACHIEVEMENT	AREA	U.S. AVG
High school degree	83.3%	82.7%
2-year college degree	5.7%	6.4%
4-year college degree	20.7%	15.7%
Graduate/professional degree	9.8%	8.9%

PUBLIC SCHOOLS	AREA	U.S. AVG
Expenditures per pupil	$5,512	$5,686
Student/teacher ratio	16.3	16.7
Attending public school	92.1%	90.1%
State SAT score	990*	1021
State ACT score	20.2	20.9

HIGHER EDUCATION	AREA	U.S. AVG
No. 2-year colleges	26	4
No. 4-year colleges/universities	32	6
No. highly ranked universities	5	1

Health &
Healthcare
Score: 36.6
Rank: 236

HAZARDS & ILLNESSES	AREA	U.S. AVG
Air-quality score	31	37
Water-quality score	48	52
Pollen/allergy score	63	61
Cancer mortality per capita	161.1	201.9
Depression days per month	3.6	3.5
Stress score	78	50

HEALTHCARE	AREA	U.S. AVG
Physicians per capita	211.0	244.2
Hospital beds per capita	242.6	420.0
No. teaching hospitals	11	3
Cost per doctor visit	$80	$77
Cost per dental visit	$74	$70

Crime
Score: 30.7
Rank: 259

CRIME	AREA	U.S. AVG
Violent crime rate	492.0	465.5
Change in violent crime rate	-5.7%	-2.2%
Property crime rate	4,115.2	3,517.1
Change in property crime rate	-2.6%	-2.1%

Transportation
Score: 11.5
Rank: 332

COMMUTE	AREA	U.S. AVG
Average commute time	33.9	27.4
Percent commutes > 60 mins.	12.2%	5.9%
Commute by auto	77.5%	78.9%
Commute by mass transit	3.3%	1.9%
Work at home	3.4%	3.1%
Mass transit miles per capita	3.26	1.87

INTERCITY SERVICES	AREA	U.S. AVG
Major airports within 60 miles	1	1
Size of regional airport	Large	Large
Daily airline activity	1423	686
Amtrak service	Yes	No

AUTOMOTIVE	AREA	U.S. AVG
Insurance, annual premium	$2,186	$1,432
Gas, cost per gallon	$2.40	$2.49
Daily vehicle miles per capita	31.5	24.0

Leisure
Score: 94.4
Rank: 22

DINING & SHOPPING	AREA	U.S. AVG
Restaurant rating	8	2
Outlet mall score	174	42
No. Starbucks	91	13
No. warehouse clubs	17	2

ENTERTAINMENT	AREA	U.S. AVG
Professional sports rating	7	4
College sports rating	6	4
Zoo/aquarium rating	10	3
Amusement park rating	10	3
Botanical garden/ arboretum rating	9	4

OUTDOOR ACTIVITIES	AREA	U.S. AVG
Golf-course rating	9	4
Ski-area rating	1	3
Sq. miles inland water	4	4
Miles of coastline	0.0	10.7
National Park rating	2	3

Arts & Culture
Score: 91.7
Rank: 32

MEDIA & LIBRARIES	AREA	U.S. AVG
Arts radio rating	9	3
No. public libraries	140	27
Library volumes per capita	1.76	2.78

PERFORMING ARTS	AREA	U.S. AVG
Classical music rating	7	4
Ballet/dance rating	9	3
Professional theater rating	10	3
University arts programs rating	10	5

MUSEUMS	AREA	U.S. AVG
Overall museum rating	10	5
Art museum rating	9	5
Science museum rating	10	5
Children's museum rating	9	3

Atlantic City, NJ

Score: 77.1   **Rank:** 57   **2004 rank:** 123

Profile: Beach and resort city
Location: Southern New Jersey shore
Elevation: 10 feet
Time zone: Eastern Standard Time

PRO	CON
Entertainment	Tourist impact
Nearby beaches	Cost of living
Favorable climate	Arts and culture

Atlantic City lies on a barrier island on the south coast of New Jersey. Once a popular resort area for residents of New York and Philadelphia (the street names in the board game "Monopoly" are taken from downtown streets), the city went into decline after World War II as better travel and transportation services made other destinations accessible. The return of legalized gambling in the late 1970s was a partially successful attempt to revive the earlier prominence. Today the shore area thrives. The Boardwalk is both a historic gem and a good, if somewhat crowded, place to spend a morning or afternoon. The large high-rise casino properties rise abruptly on the other side of the Boardwalk. Inland from the casinos is a small featureless downtown, and most other parts of the city remain run-down. The economy depends almost entirely on tourism. Cost of living and housing are low for New Jersey but high relative to incomes and U.S. averages. Areas along the coast to the south towards Ocean City and Cape May are more attractive, prosperous, and livable, and retain more of their historic feel.

Surrounding terrain is mainly flat and composed of tidal marshes and beach sand. Summers are relatively cooler and winters milder than elsewhere at the same latitude. During the warm season, sea breezes in the late morning and afternoon keep temperatures in the 80s. Precipitation is moderate and well distributed through the year. Tropical storms or hurricanes occasionally bring heavy rain. Most winter precipitation comes from coastal storms ("noreasters"), which create a rain/snow mix. Large snow accumulations and ice storms are far less common than nearby inland locations. First freeze is late October; last is mid-April.

Population

DEMOGRAPHICS	AREA	U.S. AVG	ETHNIC COMPOSITION	AREA	U.S. AVG	RESIDENT PROFILE	AREA	U.S. AVG
Population	269,202		White	67.5%	79.0%	Single	36.1%	32.4%
Population density per sq. mile	479.8	358.5	Black	16.9%	10.5%	Married	47.2%	52.7%
Population growth	20.0%	21.1%	Asian	5.8%	2.7%	Divorced/separated	16.7%	14.9%
Median age	37.7	36.1	Hispanic	13.7%	10.6%	Married with children	21.1%	23.7%
Percent Democrat	52.5%	44.5%	Religious observance	40.6%	48.9%	Single with children	10.6%	9.1%
Percent Republican	46.6%	54.5%	Diversity measure	62.4	40.1	Percent over age 65	13.6%	12.9%

Economy & Jobs

Score: 38.2
Rank: 231

INCOME	AREA	U.S. AVG	EMPLOYMENT	AREA	U.S. AVG	EMPLOYING INDUSTRIES	AREA	U.S. AVG
Per capita income	$23,296	$23,235	Unemployment rate	5.1%	4.7%	Largest: Accommodations & Food Services		
Household income	$47,878	$46,414	Recent job growth	0.8%	1.3%			
Household income < $25K	23.9%	26.2%	Projected future job growth	8.3%	11.5%	Percent manufacturing	9.1%	15.4%
Household income > $75K	26.5%	25.4%	White collar	51.5%	57.8%	Percent public sector	14.4%	15.7%
Household income growth	9.0%	13.6%	Blue collar	17.8%	25.2%	Percent construction	8.7%	9.9%

Cost of Living

Score: 18.4
Rank: 304

INDEXES & TAXES	AREA	U.S. AVG	HOUSING	AREA	U.S. AVG	NECESSITIES	AREA	U.S. AVG
Cost of Living Index	110.2	100.0	Median home price	$257,300	$220,000	Food Index	104.0	100.0
Buying Power Index	97.4	100.0	Home price appreciation	109.1%	10.1%	Housing Index	85.8	100.0
Income tax rate	2.91%	4.70%	Median rent	$964	$709	Utilities Index	124.5	100.0
Sales tax rate	6.00%	6.58%	Homes owned	55.9%	62.3%	Transportation Index	108.1	100.0
Property tax rate	$23.27	$12.00	Home price ratio	5.4	4.2	Healthcare Index	99.7	100.0
						Miscellaneous Cost Index	106.8	100.0

Climate

Score: 85.3
Rank: 56

TEMPERATURE	AREA	U.S. AVG	PRECIPITATION	AREA	U.S. AVG	COMFORTS & HAZARDS	AREA	U.S. AVG
Average January low	24.0	26.2	Annual inches precipitation	46.0	37.7	July relative humidity	73%	66%
Average July high	84.7	87.4	Annual inches snowfall	16.0	7.0	Annual days mostly sunny	204	208
Annual days > 90°F	16	38	Annual days precipitation	112	109	Annual days with thunderstorms	25	39
Annual days < 32°F	15	89	Annual days rain > 0.5 inches	26	22	Tornado risk score	5	18
Annual days < 0°F	1	6	Annual days snow > 1.5 inches	4	6	Hurricane risk score	25	13

TEMPERATURE

PRECIPITATION

DAYS OF CLOUDS & PRECIPITATION

ACHIEVEMENT	AREA	U.S. AVG	PUBLIC SCHOOLS	AREA	U.S. AVG	HIGHER EDUCATION	AREA	U.S. AVG
High school degree	78.4%	82.7%	Expenditures per pupil	$8,319	$5,686	No. 2-year colleges	1	4
2-year college degree	5.5%	6.4%	Student/teacher ratio	14.1	16.7	No. 4-year colleges/universities	1	6
4-year college degree	12.9%	15.7%	Attending public school	90.9%	90.1%	No. highly ranked universities	1	1
Graduate/professional degree	5.9%	8.9%	State SAT score	1011*	1021			
			State ACT score	21.8	20.9			

Education Score: 35.8 Rank: 241

HAZARDS & ILLNESSES	AREA	U.S. AVG	HEALTHCARE	AREA	U.S. AVG	CRIME	AREA	U.S. AVG
Air-quality score	43	37	Physicians per capita	231.6	244.2	Violent crime rate	516.2	465.5
Water-quality score	13	52	Hospital beds per capita	620.0	420.0	Change in violent crime rate	-2.8%	-2.2%
Pollen/allergy score	60	61	No. teaching hospitals	2	3	Property crime rate	3,994.3	3,517.1
Cancer mortality per capita	245.0	201.9	Cost per doctor visit	$67	$77	Change in property crime rate	-1.5%	-2.1%
Depression days per month	3.5	3.5	Cost per dental visit	$87	$70			
Stress score	75	50						

Health & Healthcare Score: 42.0 Rank: 216

Crime Score: 40.4 Rank: 223

COMMUTE	AREA	U.S. AVG	INTERCITY SERVICES	AREA	U.S. AVG	AUTOMOTIVE	AREA	U.S. AVG
Average commute time	25.5	27.4	Major airports within 60 miles	4	1	Insurance, annual premium	$1,867	$1,432
Percent commutes > 60 mins.	6.6%	5.9%	Size of regional airport	Large	Large	Gas, cost per gallon	$2.32	$2.49
Commute by auto	73.8%	78.9%	Daily airline activity	2532	686	Daily vehicle miles per capita	26.5	24.0
Commute by mass transit	7.3%	1.9%	Amtrak service	No	No			
Work at home	2.0%	3.1%						
Mass transit miles per capita	7.33	1.87						

Transportation Score: 99.7 Rank: 2

DINING & SHOPPING	AREA	U.S. AVG	ENTERTAINMENT	AREA	U.S. AVG	OUTDOOR ACTIVITIES	AREA	U.S. AVG
Restaurant rating	1	2	Professional sports rating	8	4	Golf-course rating	6	4
Outlet mall score	48	42	College sports rating	3	4	Ski-area rating	3	3
No. Starbucks	3	13	Zoo/aquarium rating	8	3	Sq. miles inland water	6	4
No. warehouse clubs	2	2	Amusement park rating	6	3	Miles of coastline	53.2	10.7
			Botanical garden/ arboretum rating	1	4	National Park rating	3	3

Leisure Score: 84.5 Rank: 58

MEDIA & LIBRARIES	AREA	U.S. AVG	PERFORMING ARTS	AREA	U.S. AVG	MUSEUMS	AREA	U.S. AVG
Arts radio rating	8	3	Classical music rating	7	4	Overall museum rating	3	5
No. public libraries	15	27	Ballet/dance rating	5	3	Art museum rating	6	5
Library volumes per capita	3.42	2.78	Professional theater rating	5	3	Science museum rating	1	5
			University arts programs rating	3	5	Children's museum rating	1	3

Arts & Culture Score: 80.7 Rank: 73

Auburn–Opelika, AL

Score: 66.4 Rank: 128 2004 rank: 192

Profile: College-town complex
Location: East-central Alabama near Georgia border
Elevation: 658 feet
Time zone: Central Standard Time

PRO	CON
College-town amenities	Crime rate
Historic interest	Growth and sprawl
Strong economy	Hot, humid summers

Auburn, home to Auburn University, the largest in Alabama, is a typical small college town with an inviting campus and attractive historic buildings in a nicely laid-out downtown. Standout features include high educational attainment, with over 29% of residents holding 4-year or graduate degrees and unemployment at a low 3.4%—both among the best in the state. While the Cost of Living Index is a very modest 85.7, attractive for a college town, home prices are relatively high for the region but still reasonable with respect to incomes and on a national scale. The economy was once driven by agriculture, primarily cotton, and then the university. Today Auburn has a stronger commercial and industrial component, mainly small businesses and manufacturing. The business-friendly town of Opelika, 7 miles northeast, is considerably more industrial, with distribution centers, automotive parts manufacturers, and a Uniroyal plant, among others. Opelika has had some crime and education issues, and some residents live in Auburn and work in Opelika. The greater numbers discovering Auburn's small-town lifestyle, low costs, and advantages of living in a college town have driven strong growth and created some sprawl issues, and there is a comprehensive and innovative development plan to address them. The area is a bit isolated, but services and amenities in Atlanta are 110 miles away.

The town sits in an area of gently rolling, wooded hills and level, open plain at the geologic end of the Appalachian range. Summers are warm, still, and humid with many days in the 90s and frequent thunderstorms. Winters are mild and wet with a few cold periods caused by northerly air masses. First freeze is early November; last is late March.

Population

DEMOGRAPHICS	AREA	U.S. AVG	ETHNIC COMPOSITION	AREA	U.S. AVG	RESIDENT PROFILE	AREA	U.S. AVG
Population	121,703		White	73.0%	79.0%	Single	43.5%	32.4%
Population density per sq. mile	199.9	358.5	Black	23.4%	10.5%	Married	44.6%	52.7%
Population growth	39.7%	21.1%	Asian	1.9%	2.7%	Divorced/separated	11.9%	14.9%
Median age	30.3	36.1	Hispanic	1.6%	10.6%	Married with children	21.0%	23.7%
Percent Democrat	36.4%	44.5%	Religious observance	34.6%	48.9%	Single with children	8.6%	9.1%
Percent Republican	62.7%	54.5%	Diversity measure	43.0	40.1	Percent over age 65	8.6%	12.9%

Economy & Jobs
Score: 39.6
Rank: 222

INCOME	AREA	U.S. AVG	EMPLOYMENT	AREA	U.S. AVG	EMPLOYING INDUSTRIES	AREA	U.S. AVG
Per capita income	$19,346	$23,235	Unemployment rate	3.4%	4.7%	Largest: Manufacturing		
Household income	$34,475	$46,414	Recent job growth	0.7%	1.3%			
Household income < $25K	40.2%	26.2%	Projected future job growth	9.1%	11.5%	Percent manufacturing	15.2%	15.4%
Household income > $75K	19.3%	25.4%	White collar	59.8%	57.8%	Percent public sector	20.8%	15.7%
Household income growth	11.4%	13.6%	Blue collar	24.2%	25.2%	Percent construction	9.0%	9.9%

Cost of Living
Score: 63.1
Rank: 138

INDEXES & TAXES	AREA	U.S. AVG	HOUSING	AREA	U.S. AVG	NECESSITIES	AREA	U.S. AVG
Cost of Living Index	85.7	100.0	Median home price	$145,300	$220,000	Food Index	98.2	100.0
Buying Power Index	90.2	100.0	Home price appreciation	36.9%	10.1%	Housing Index	61.1	100.0
Income tax rate	5.10%	4.70%	Median rent	$546	$709	Utilities Index	95.9	100.0
Sales tax rate	8.00%	6.58%	Homes owned	56.0%	62.3%	Transportation Index	98.3	100.0
Property tax rate	$5.00	$12.00	Home price ratio	4.2	4.2	Healthcare Index	96.6	100.0
						Miscellaneous Cost Index	95.9	100.0

Climate
Score: 23.3
Rank: 286

TEMPERATURE	AREA	U.S. AVG	PRECIPITATION	AREA	U.S. AVG	COMFORTS & HAZARDS	AREA	U.S. AVG
Average January low	33.2	26.2	Annual inches precipitation	54.0	37.7	July relative humidity	70%	66%
Average July high	91.3	87.4	Annual inches snowfall	0.5	7.0	Annual days mostly sunny	214	208
Annual days > 90°F	42	38	Annual days precipitation	117	109	Annual days with thunderstorms	65	39
Annual days < 32°F	65	89	Annual days rain > 0.5 inches	37	22	Tornado risk score	21	18
Annual days < 0°F	0	6	Annual days snow > 1.5 inches	1	6	Hurricane risk score	28	13

TEMPERATURE

PRECIPITATION

DAYS OF CLOUDS & PRECIPITATION

Education
Score: 70.6
Rank: 111

ACHIEVEMENT	AREA	U.S. AVG	PUBLIC SCHOOLS	AREA	U.S. AVG	HIGHER EDUCATION	AREA	U.S. AVG
High school degree	82.3%	82.7%	Expenditures per pupil	$4,834	$5,686	No. 2-year colleges	0	4
2-year college degree	6.5%	6.4%	Student/teacher ratio	15.2	16.7	No. 4-year colleges/universities	1	6
4-year college degree	16.2%	15.7%	Attending public school	95.3%	90.1%	No. highly ranked universities	0	1
Graduate/professional degree	13.9%	8.9%	State SAT score	1126	1021			
			State ACT score	20.2*	20.9			

Health & Healthcare
Score: 47.9
Rank: 196

Crime
Score: 50.5
Rank: 186

HAZARDS & ILLNESSES	AREA	U.S. AVG	HEALTHCARE	AREA	U.S. AVG	CRIME	AREA	U.S. AVG
Air-quality score	49	37	Physicians per capita	148.0	244.2	Violent crime rate	398.5	465.5
Water-quality score	73	52	Hospital beds per capita	246.5	420.0	Change in violent crime rate	-13.3%	-2.2%
Pollen/allergy score	60	61	No. teaching hospitals	0	3	Property crime rate	4,326.1	3,517.1
Cancer mortality per capita	225.3	201.9	Cost per doctor visit	$51	$77	Change in property crime rate	-0.2%	-2.1%
Depression days per month	4.1	3.5	Cost per dental visit	$49	$70			
Stress score	5	50						

Transportation
Score: 91.2
Rank: 34

COMMUTE	AREA	U.S. AVG	INTERCITY SERVICES	AREA	U.S. AVG	AUTOMOTIVE	AREA	U.S. AVG
Average commute time	21.9	27.4	Major airports within 60 miles	1	1	Insurance, annual premium	$1,033	$1,432
Percent commutes > 60 mins.	3.5%	5.9%	Size of regional airport	Large	Large	Gas, cost per gallon	$2.44	$2.49
Commute by auto	84.1%	78.9%	Daily airline activity	1423	686	Daily vehicle miles per capita	31.5	24.0
Commute by mass transit	0.6%	1.9%	Amtrak service	No	No			
Work at home	1.8%	3.1%						
Mass transit miles per capita	0.58	1.87						

DINING & SHOPPING	AREA	U.S. AVG	ENTERTAINMENT	AREA	U.S. AVG	OUTDOOR ACTIVITIES	AREA	U.S. AVG
Restaurant rating	1	2	Professional sports rating	2	4	Golf-course rating	3	4
Outlet mall score	26	42	College sports rating	6	4	Ski-area rating	1	3
No. Starbucks	1	13	Zoo/aquarium rating	1	3	Sq. miles inland water	4	4
No. warehouse clubs	0	2	Amusement park rating	1	3	Miles of coastline	0.0	10.7
			Botanical garden/			National Park rating	4	3
			arboretum rating	6	4			

Leisure
Score: 38.8
Rank: 228

MEDIA & LIBRARIES	AREA	U.S. AVG	PERFORMING ARTS	AREA	U.S. AVG	MUSEUMS	AREA	U.S. AVG
Arts radio rating	1	3	Classical music rating	3	4	Overall museum rating	3	5
No. public libraries	2	27	Ballet/dance rating	1	3	Art museum rating	3	5
Library volumes per capita	1.47	2.78	Professional theater rating	1	3	Science museum rating	3	5
			University arts programs rating	5	5	Children's museum rating	1	3

Arts & Culture
Score: 8.8
Rank: 340

Augusta–Richmond County, GA-SC

Score: 68.4 **Rank:** 104 **2004 rank:** 164

Profile: Mid-size city
Location: Georgia–South Carolina border along the Savannah River
Elevation: 136 feet
Time zone: Eastern Standard Time

PRO	CON
Historic interest	Isolation
Cost of living	Entertainment
Healthcare	Arts and culture

Those familiar with professional golf know Augusta. The city emerged after the turn of the 19th century as a winter escape for Northerners. Resorts and country clubs, including the heralded Augusta National Country Club, opened at that time. During most of the year, Augusta is a tranquil Southern city with varied small industry and commercial activity. In April, the Masters golf tournament brings worldwide attention and crowds. People with nicer homes rent them to visiting dignitaries and executives (and receive a tax break thanks to a federal tax loophole seemingly designed for this event). Besides golf, the city offers history and architectural interest, and even a minor league ice hockey team. Cost of living at 85.2 (aside from Masters week) is low for the state and reasonable for this type of town. Downtown is plain with a few historic buildings, and a recent revitalization effort brought some

riverfront arts and entertainment amenities and a monthly festival. But the area is generally quiet and additional entertainment and cultural amenities and air service are available in Columbia, South Carolina, 70 miles northeast, and Atlanta, 150 miles west.

Augusta is located along the Savannah River between the Piedmont Plateau and the Coastal Plain. The city is in a narrow river plain with wooded rolling hills up to 200 feet on all sides. Lowland is swampy, especially to the southeast. Summers are hot and humid with thundershowers; strong storms can occur especially in spring. Because the Appalachian Mountains shield the city from extreme cold and storms from the northwest, winters are mild with rare measurable snow. Ice storms are less common than in Atlanta.

DEMOGRAPHICS	AREA	U.S. AVG	ETHNIC COMPOSITION	AREA	U.S. AVG	RESIDENT PROFILE	AREA	U.S. AVG
Population	517,869		White	60.8%	79.0%	Single	32.9%	32.4%
Population density per sq. mile	157.9	358.5	Black	34.9%	10.5%	Married	50.6%	52.7%
Population growth	21.3%	21.1%	Asian	1.5%	2.7%	Divorced/separated	16.6%	14.9%
Median age	35.2	36.1	Hispanic	2.2%	10.6%	Married with children	23.9%	23.7%
Percent Democrat	41.7%	44.5%	Religious observance	42.9%	48.9%	Single with children	12.0%	9.1%
Percent Republican	57.6%	54.5%	Diversity measure	48.5	40.1	Percent over age 65	11.4%	12.9%

Population

INCOME	AREA	U.S. AVG	EMPLOYMENT	AREA	U.S. AVG	EMPLOYING INDUSTRIES	AREA	U.S. AVG
Per capita income	$21,254	$23,235	Unemployment rate	6.5%	4.7%	Largest: Manufacturing		
Household income	$43,414	$46,414	Recent job growth	2.0%	1.3%			
Household income < $25K	29.3%	26.2%	Projected future job growth	10.4%	11.5%	Percent manufacturing	17.1%	15.4%
Household income > $75K	23.2%	25.4%	White collar	55.8%	57.8%	Percent public sector	21.6%	15.7%
Household income growth	12.2%	13.6%	Blue collar	28.0%	25.2%	Percent construction	10.9%	9.9%

Economy & Jobs
Score: 48.1
Rank: 195

INDEXES & TAXES	AREA	U.S. AVG	HOUSING	AREA	U.S. AVG	NECESSITIES	AREA	U.S. AVG
Cost of Living Index	85.2	100.0	Median home price	$137,500	$220,000	Food Index	105.2	100.0
Buying Power Index	114.2	100.0	Home price appreciation	30.8%	10.1%	Housing Index	57.8	100.0
Income tax rate	6.00%	4.70%	Median rent	$585	$709	Utilities Index	97.8	100.0
Sales tax rate	6.62%	6.58%	Homes owned	63.8%	62.3%	Transportation Index	95.8	100.0
Property tax rate	$8.50	$12.00	Home price ratio	3.2	4.2	Healthcare Index	95.0	100.0
						Miscellaneous Cost Index	96.8	100.0

Cost of Living
Score: 55.1
Rank: 167

Climate
Score: 53.7
Rank: 172

TEMPERATURE	AREA	U.S. AVG
Average January low	34.0	26.2
Average July high	90.8	87.4
Annual days > 90°F	63	38
Annual days < 32°F	59	89
Annual days < 0°F	0	6

PRECIPITATION	AREA	U.S. AVG
Annual inches precipitation	43.0	37.7
Annual inches snowfall	1.3	7.0
Annual days precipitation	107	109
Annual days rain > 0.5 inches	29	22
Annual days snow > 1.5 inches	1	6

COMFORTS & HAZARDS	AREA	U.S. AVG
July relative humidity	72%	66%
Annual days mostly sunny	217	208
Annual days with thunderstorms	55	39
Tornado risk score	8	18
Hurricane risk score	34	13

TEMPERATURE

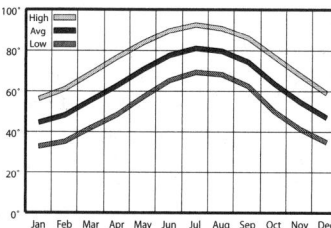

PRECIPITATION

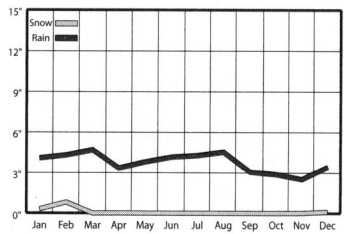

DAYS OF CLOUDS & PRECIPITATION

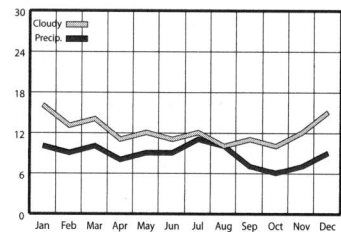

Education
Score: 37.2
Rank: 236

ACHIEVEMENT	AREA	U.S. AVG
High school degree	78.7%	82.7%
2-year college degree	6.6%	6.4%
4-year college degree	13.4%	15.7%
Graduate/professional degree	7.3%	8.9%

PUBLIC SCHOOLS	AREA	U.S. AVG
Expenditures per pupil	$4,812	$5,686
Student/teacher ratio	16.1	16.7
Attending public school	92.3%	90.1%
State SAT score	990*	1021
State ACT score	20.2	20.9

HIGHER EDUCATION	AREA	U.S. AVG
No. 2-year colleges	3	4
No. 4-year colleges/universities	5	6
No. highly ranked universities	0	1

Health &
Healthcare
Score: 80.5
Rank: 74

HAZARDS & ILLNESSES	AREA	U.S. AVG
Air-quality score	43	37
Water-quality score	76	52
Pollen/allergy score	62	61
Cancer mortality per capita	195.3	201.9
Depression days per month	4.0	3.5
Stress score	96	50

HEALTHCARE	AREA	U.S. AVG
Physicians per capita	373.2	244.2
Hospital beds per capita	408.8	420.0
No. teaching hospitals	2	3
Cost per doctor visit	$66	$77
Cost per dental visit	$66	$70

Crime
Score: 53.2
Rank: 175

CRIME	AREA	U.S. AVG
Violent crime rate	392.3	465.5
Change in violent crime rate	2.9%	-2.2%
Property crime rate	4,518.5	3,517.1
Change in property crime rate	2.3%	-2.1%

Transportation
Score: 4.3
Rank: 354

COMMUTE	AREA	U.S. AVG
Average commute time	26.0	27.4
Percent commutes > 60 mins.	5.4%	5.9%
Commute by auto	80.3%	78.9%
Commute by mass transit	0.7%	1.9%
Work at home	1.7%	3.1%
Mass transit miles per capita	0.69	1.87

INTERCITY SERVICES	AREA	U.S. AVG
Major airports within 60 miles	0	1
Size of regional airport	Small	Large
Daily airline activity	169	686
Amtrak service	No	No

AUTOMOTIVE	AREA	U.S. AVG
Insurance, annual premium	$1,569	$1,432
Gas, cost per gallon	$2.38	$2.49
Daily vehicle miles per capita	22.9	24.0

Leisure
Score: 29.1
Rank: 264

DINING & SHOPPING	AREA	U.S. AVG
Restaurant rating	1	2
Outlet mall score	19	42
No. Starbucks	1	13
No. warehouse clubs	1	2

ENTERTAINMENT	AREA	U.S. AVG
Professional sports rating	3	4
College sports rating	2	4
Zoo/aquarium rating	1	3
Amusement park rating	1	3
Botanical garden/ arboretum rating	1	4

OUTDOOR ACTIVITIES	AREA	U.S. AVG
Golf-course rating	4	4
Ski-area rating	1	3
Sq. miles inland water	3	4
Miles of coastline	0.0	10.7
National Park rating	2	3

Arts & Culture
Score: 32.4
Rank: 253

MEDIA & LIBRARIES	AREA	U.S. AVG
Arts radio rating	1	3
No. public libraries	28	27
Library volumes per capita	1.45	2.78

PERFORMING ARTS	AREA	U.S. AVG
Classical music rating	3	4
Ballet/dance rating	3	3
Professional theater rating	1	3
University arts programs rating	5	5

MUSEUMS	AREA	U.S. AVG
Overall museum rating	5	5
Art museum rating	5	5
Science museum rating	7	5
Children's museum rating	1	3

Austin–Round Rock, TX

Score: 68.5 **Rank:** 103 **2004 rank:** 22

Profile: Capital city/college town
Location: West-central Texas northwest of San Antonio
Elevation: 570 feet
Time zone: Central Standard Time

PRO	CON
Entertainment	Growth and sprawl
Economy	Cost of housing
College-town amenities	Summer heat

The Austin area continues to be regarded by most as the best place to live in Texas, with a strong economy, good education, attractive housing, a relatively pleasant climate, and plenty to do. Highlights include the University of Texas, an important music scene, and a large high-tech industry, including Dell, Inc. in Round Rock, 20 miles north. The 50,000-student university is located on a large campus north of downtown. The walkable downtown preserves a small-town Texas feel and is packed with nightclubs and music venues, including the famous "Drag" and the Warehouse District. Music is mostly rock 'n' roll, "hard" country, and blues. Entertainment and cultural amenities are plentiful, as is outdoor recreation not too far west in the so-called Hill Country. The town is growing rapidly, with a 72% population increase since 1990, the highest increase nationwide for a larger city aside from Las Vegas. Growth is spreading mainly north, towards Round Rock and Pflugerville, accompanied by plenty of middle-class housing, large areas of more upscale housing to the west among the hills and towards Lake Travis, and growing issues related to increased sprawl and traffic.

The cost of living, while low on a national scale, is highest in Texas, but home prices, high by state standards, are low by national standards and are a good value. The area continues to be a magnet for business and particularly high-tech and small business start-ups. The list of names with facilities in town could form a NASDAQ high-tech stock index. Incomes are very high relative to cost of living (Buying Power Index is 140.5), and the area has one of the highest expected job-growth rates in the country.

The downtown area sits in a low basin with mostly flat land to the east and hilly areas with limestone outcroppings to the west, separated by a river flowing through town. Summers are hot and moderately humid with most days in the 90s and many evenings in the 70s. Winters are mild with an occasional cold snap. Precipitation is scattered through the year with peaks in late spring and early fall. Moist air and storms from the Gulf can bring heavy rain for days at a time. Winter brings lighter but steady rains. The hills shelter the area from the destructive storms that happen to the north.

DEMOGRAPHICS	AREA	U.S. AVG	ETHNIC COMPOSITION	AREA	U.S. AVG	RESIDENT PROFILE	AREA	U.S. AVG
Population	1,415,324		White	70.9%	79.0%	Single	34.3%	32.4%
Population density per sq. mile	335.1	358.5	Black	7.4%	10.5%	Married	50.6%	52.7%
Population growth	72.7%	21.1%	Asian	4.0%	2.7%	Divorced/separated	15.1%	14.9%
Median age	32.3	36.1	Hispanic	29.1%	10.6%	Married with children	25.7%	23.7%
Percent Democrat	48.7%	44.5%	Religious observance	44.5%	48.9%	Single with children	8.0%	9.1%
Percent Republican	49.5%	54.5%	Diversity measure	67.9	40.1	Percent over age 65	7.4%	12.9%

Population

INCOME	AREA	U.S. AVG	EMPLOYMENT	AREA	U.S. AVG	EMPLOYING INDUSTRIES	AREA	U.S. AVG
Per capita income	$27,686	$23,235	Unemployment rate	4.3%	4.7%	Largest: Professional, Scientific & Technical Services		
Household income	$55,915	$46,414	Recent job growth	3.7%	1.3%			
Household income < $25K	19.4%	26.2%	Projected future job growth	28.1%	11.5%	Percent manufacturing	9.4%	15.4%
Household income > $75K	34.8%	25.4%	White collar	68.5%	57.8%	Percent public sector	18.2%	15.7%
Household income growth	13.4%	13.6%	Blue collar	18.9%	25.2%	Percent construction	9.5%	9.9%

Economy & Jobs
Score: 97.3
Rank: 11

INDEXES & TAXES	AREA	U.S. AVG	HOUSING	AREA	U.S. AVG	NECESSITIES	AREA	U.S. AVG
Cost of Living Index	89.2	100.0	Median home price	$176,700	$220,000	Food Index	86.7	100.0
Buying Power Index	140.5	100.0	Home price appreciation	18.5%	10.1%	Housing Index	67.2	100.0
Income tax rate	0.00%	4.70%	Median rent	$836	$709	Utilities Index	91.9	100.0
Sales tax rate	8.14%	6.58%	Homes owned	58.1%	62.3%	Transportation Index	95.3	100.0
Property tax rate	$17.48	$12.00	Home price ratio	3.2	4.2	Healthcare Index	106.0	100.0
						Miscellaneous Cost Index	102.6	100.0

Cost of Living
Score: 62.8
Rank: 139

Climate
Score: 88.8
Rank: 43

TEMPERATURE	AREA	U.S. AVG
Average January low	39.3	26.2
Average July high	95.9	87.4
Annual days > 90°F	101	38
Annual days < 32°F	23	89
Annual days < 0°F	0	6

PRECIPITATION	AREA	U.S. AVG
Annual inches precipitation	33.0	37.7
Annual inches snowfall	1.0	7.0
Annual days precipitation	82	109
Annual days rain > 0.5 inches	18	22
Annual days snow > 1.5 inches	1	6

COMFORTS & HAZARDS	AREA	U.S. AVG
July relative humidity	67%	66%
Annual days mostly sunny	231	208
Annual days with thunderstorms	41	39
Tornado risk score	31	18
Hurricane risk score	17	13

TEMPERATURE

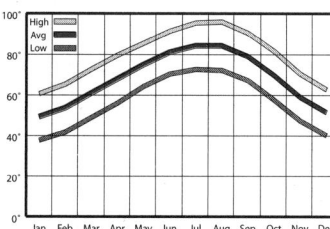

PRECIPITATION

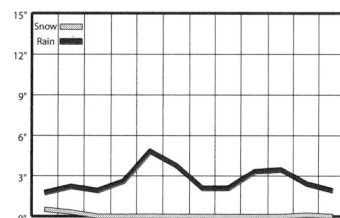

DAYS OF CLOUDS & PRECIPITATION

Education
Score: 92.2
Rank: 30

ACHIEVEMENT	AREA	U.S. AVG
High school degree	85.0%	82.7%
2-year college degree	5.6%	6.4%
4-year college degree	24.2%	15.7%
Graduate/professional degree	12.1%	8.9%

PUBLIC SCHOOLS	AREA	U.S. AVG
Expenditures per pupil	$5,256	$5,686
Student/teacher ratio	14.6	16.7
Attending public school	94.7%	90.1%
State SAT score	997*	1021
State ACT score	20.3	20.9

HIGHER EDUCATION	AREA	U.S. AVG
No. 2-year colleges	7	4
No. 4-year colleges/universities	11	6
No. highly ranked universities	2	1

Health & Healthcare
Score: 33.2
Rank: 249

HAZARDS & ILLNESSES	AREA	U.S. AVG
Air-quality score	26	37
Water-quality score	81	52
Pollen/allergy score	76	61
Cancer mortality per capita	146.5	201.9
Depression days per month	3.1	3.5
Stress score	57	50

HEALTHCARE	AREA	U.S. AVG
Physicians per capita	195.4	244.2
Hospital beds per capita	206.9	420.0
No. teaching hospitals	3	3
Cost per doctor visit	$78	$77
Cost per dental visit	$67	$70

Crime
Score: 11.5
Rank: 330

CRIME	AREA	U.S. AVG
Violent crime rate	346.2	465.5
Change in violent crime rate	-5.0%	-2.2%
Property crime rate	4,134.2	3,517.1
Change in property crime rate	-1.8%	-2.1%

Transportation
Score: 12.3
Rank: 329

COMMUTE	AREA	U.S. AVG
Average commute time	28.5	27.4
Percent commutes > 60 mins.	6.5%	5.9%
Commute by auto	77.2%	78.9%
Commute by mass transit	2.2%	1.9%
Work at home	3.6%	3.1%
Mass transit miles per capita	2.21	1.87

INTERCITY SERVICES	AREA	U.S. AVG
Major airports within 60 miles	2	1
Size of regional airport	Medium	Large
Daily airline activity	372	686
Amtrak service	Yes	No

AUTOMOTIVE	AREA	U.S. AVG
Insurance, annual premium	$1,150	$1,432
Gas, cost per gallon	$2.44	$2.49
Daily vehicle miles per capita	26.6	24.0

Leisure
Score: 50.8
Rank: 183

DINING & SHOPPING	AREA	U.S. AVG
Restaurant rating	1	2
Outlet mall score	0	42
No. Starbucks	37	13
No. warehouse clubs	4	2

ENTERTAINMENT	AREA	U.S. AVG
Professional sports rating	3	4
College sports rating	9	4
Zoo/aquarium rating	1	3
Amusement park rating	1	3
Botanical garden/ arboretum rating	5	4

OUTDOOR ACTIVITIES	AREA	U.S. AVG
Golf-course rating	4	4
Ski-area rating	1	3
Sq. miles inland water	4	4
Miles of coastline	0.0	10.7
National Park rating	1	3

Arts & Culture
Score: 75.7
Rank: 91

MEDIA & LIBRARIES	AREA	U.S. AVG
Arts radio rating	5	3
No. public libraries	44	27
Library volumes per capita	2.38	2.78

PERFORMING ARTS	AREA	U.S. AVG
Classical music rating	4	4
Ballet/dance rating	8	3
Professional theater rating	1	3
University arts programs rating	8	5

MUSEUMS	AREA	U.S. AVG
Overall museum rating	7	5
Art museum rating	8	5
Science museum rating	7	5
Children's museum rating	7	3

Bakersfield, CA

Score: 49.4 **Rank:** 247 **2004 rank:** 282

Profile: Mid-size city
Location: South-central California, at the southern end of the Central Valley
Elevation: 492 feet
Time zone: Pacific Standard Time

PRO	CON
Mild winters	Summer heat
Low rainfall	High unemployment
Cost of living	Air quality

Bakersfield is a quiet agricultural and industrial town located in one of the driest inhabited areas of California. Irrigated agriculture, mostly cotton, orchard crops, and grapes, lies to the north, and a large oil industry supported by nearby fields operates in and around the city. There isn't much to do, but the area is becoming a refuge for Southern Californians looking to escape the high costs and bustle of the L.A. Basin, which starts about 80 miles and across a mountain range south. The area is also picking up businesses looking for an inexpensive location with Southern California access, thus the economy is improving after years of malaise. But those moving in will need to trust their air conditioners: Summer heat can be relentless, with temperatures frequently ranging from 105°F to 110°F. Air quality also can be a problem in the deep valley. The downtown is plain, but has a new riverfront park. The nicer neighborhoods lie west towards the Bakersfield campus of California State University, and some new retail and housing development is coming in especially west of town. Some recreation is available in the southern Sierra Nevada just to the east and north, and downtown Los Angeles is about 2 hours away.

Bakersfield is partially surrounded by a horseshoe-shaped rim of mountains with an open side to the northwest and the crest at an average distance of 40 miles. Summers are cloudless with 100°F readings and very low humidity. Winters are mild but fairly humid with frequent fog that usually burns off but can last for weeks.

Population

DEMOGRAPHICS	AREA	U.S. AVG	ETHNIC COMPOSITION	AREA	U.S. AVG	RESIDENT PROFILE	AREA	U.S. AVG
Population	730,105		White	58.9%	79.0%	Single	30.8%	32.4%
Population density per sq. mile	89.7	358.5	Black	5.9%	10.5%	Married	50.3%	52.7%
Population growth	34.3%	21.1%	Asian	3.6%	2.7%	Divorced/separated	19.0%	14.9%
Median age	31.0	36.1	Hispanic	42.7%	10.6%	Married with children	29.3%	23.7%
Percent Democrat	32.5%	44.5%	Religious observance	43.7%	48.9%	Single with children	12.9%	9.1%
Percent Republican	66.5%	54.5%	Diversity measure	78.5	40.1	Percent over age 65	9.3%	12.9%

Economy & Jobs
Score: 39.6
Rank: 223

INCOME	AREA	U.S. AVG	EMPLOYMENT	AREA	U.S. AVG	EMPLOYING INDUSTRIES	AREA	U.S. AVG
Per capita income	$17,691	$23,235	Unemployment rate	7.8%	4.7%	Largest: Healthcare & Social Assistance		
Household income	$40,519	$46,414	Recent job growth	2.5%	1.3%			
Household income < $25K	31.5%	26.2%	Projected future job growth	18.0%	11.5%	Percent manufacturing	13.4%	15.4%
Household income > $75K	22.3%	25.4%	White collar	50.6%	57.8%	Percent public sector	20.7%	15.7%
Household income growth	14.3%	13.6%	Blue collar	24.3%	25.2%	Percent construction	10.9%	9.9%

Cost of Living
Score: 20.3
Rank: 297

INDEXES & TAXES	AREA	U.S. AVG	HOUSING	AREA	U.S. AVG	NECESSITIES	AREA	U.S. AVG
Cost of Living Index	110.0	100.0	Median home price	$256,700	$220,000	Food Index	111.3	100.0
Buying Power Index	82.6	100.0	Home price appreciation	171.2%	10.1%	Housing Index	122.1	100.0
Income tax rate	6.00%	4.70%	Median rent	$646	$709	Utilities Index	112.1	100.0
Sales tax rate	7.25%	6.58%	Homes owned	56.6%	62.3%	Transportation Index	105.5	100.0
Property tax rate	$10.69	$12.00	Home price ratio	6.3	4.2	Healthcare Index	117.0	100.0
						Miscellaneous Cost Index	103.2	100.0

Climate
Score: 93.9
Rank: 24

TEMPERATURE	AREA	U.S. AVG	PRECIPITATION	AREA	U.S. AVG	COMFORTS & HAZARDS	AREA	U.S. AVG
Average January low	37.4	26.2	Annual inches precipitation	6.0	37.7	July relative humidity	52%	66%
Average July high	99.1	87.4	Annual inches snowfall	0.0	7.0	Annual days mostly sunny	281	208
Annual days > 90°F	110	38	Annual days precipitation	36	109	Annual days with thunderstorms	3	39
Annual days > 32°F	11	89	Annual days rain > 0.5 inches	2	22	Tornado risk score	1	18
Annual days < 0°F	0	6	Annual days snow > 1.5 inches	0	6	Hurricane risk score	0	13

TEMPERATURE

PRECIPITATION

DAYS OF CLOUDS & PRECIPITATION

ACHIEVEMENT	AREA	U.S. AVG	PUBLIC SCHOOLS	AREA	U.S. AVG	HIGHER EDUCATION	AREA	U.S. AVG
High school degree	68.5%	82.7%	Expenditures per pupil	$5,509	$5,686	No. 2-year colleges	5	4
2-year college degree	6.4%	6.4%	Student/teacher ratio	18.7	16.7	No. 4-year colleges/universities	1	6
4-year college degree	9.2%	15.7%	Attending public school	96.0%	90.1%	No. highly ranked universities	0	1
Graduate/professional degree	4.5%	8.9%	State SAT score	1019*	1021			
			State ACT score	21.6	20.9			

Education
Score: 5.1
Rank: 354

HAZARDS & ILLNESSES	AREA	U.S. AVG	HEALTHCARE	AREA	U.S. AVG	CRIME	AREA	U.S. AVG
Air-quality score	13	37	Physicians per capita	131.0	244.2	Violent crime rate	527.1	465.5
Water-quality score	42	52	Hospital beds per capita	221.2	420.0	Change in violent crime rate	-14.0%	-2.2%
Pollen/allergy score	54	61	No. teaching hospitals	2	3	Property crime rate	4,593.5	3,517.1
Cancer mortality per capita	173.0	201.9	Cost per doctor visit	$100	$77	Change in property crime rate	4.3%	-2.1%
Depression days per month	4.0	3.5	Cost per dental visit	$76	$70			
Stress score	81	50						

Health & Healthcare
Score: 10.2
Rank: 335

Crime
Score: 38.8
Rank: 229

COMMUTE	AREA	U.S. AVG	INTERCITY SERVICES	AREA	U.S. AVG	AUTOMOTIVE	AREA	U.S. AVG
Average commute time	24.6	27.4	Major airports within 60 miles	1	1	Insurance, annual premium	$1,672	$1,432
Percent commutes > 60 mins.	7.4%	5.9%	Size of regional airport	Medium	Large	Gas, cost per gallon	$2.72	$2.49
Commute by auto	74.2%	78.9%	Daily airline activity	168	686	Daily vehicle miles per capita	17.6	24.0
Commute by mass transit	1.3%	1.9%	Amtrak service	Yes	No			
Work at home	2.7%	3.1%						
Mass transit miles per capita	1.31	1.87						

Transportation
Score: 21.9
Rank: 292

DINING & SHOPPING	AREA	U.S. AVG	ENTERTAINMENT	AREA	U.S. AVG	OUTDOOR ACTIVITIES	AREA	U.S. AVG
Restaurant rating	1	2	Professional sports rating	3	4	Golf-course rating	3	4
Outlet mall score	41	42	College sports rating	6	4	Ski-area rating	5	3
No. Starbucks	15	13	Zoo/aquarium rating	1	3	Sq. miles inland water	3	4
No. warehouse clubs	2	2	Amusement park rating	1	3	Miles of coastline	0.0	10.7
			Botanical garden/ arboretum rating	1	4	National Park rating	10	3

Leisure
Score: 66.0
Rank: 127

MEDIA & LIBRARIES	AREA	U.S. AVG	PERFORMING ARTS	AREA	U.S. AVG	MUSEUMS	AREA	U.S. AVG
Arts radio rating	5	3	Classical music rating	3	4	Overall museum rating	5	5
No. public libraries	26	27	Ballet/dance rating	1	3	Art museum rating	5	5
Library volumes per capita	1.43	2.78	Professional theater rating	1	3	Science museum rating	5	5
			University arts programs rating	1	5	Children's museum rating	7	3

Arts & Culture
Score: 33.2
Rank: 250

Baltimore–Towson, MD

Score: 60.5   Rank: 173   2004 rank: 179

Profile: Large city
Location: East-central Maryland along Chesapeake Bay, 40 miles northeast of Washington, D.C.
Elevation: 32 feet
Time zone: Eastern Standard Time

PRO
Historic preservation
Attractive suburbs
Arts and culture

CON
Violent crime rate
Growth and sprawl
Long commutes

Baltimore is a diverse and complete East Coast city—though considered by some to be the less attractive sister of Washington, D.C. Baltimore surrounds a major inland port on the upper portion of the Chesapeake Bay, with prosperous shipping, transportation, and manufacturing industries among others. Many areas of the city, particularly downtown, have experienced a vast renewal with a strong emphasis on historic preservation. The restored waterfront adjacent to downtown is now a commercial and leisure destination with excellent museums, a first-class aquarium, and plenty more to do. Urban residential areas close to downtown are known for their row houses, many dating back to the 18th century, spreading for miles and full of character and historic interest. Some, like the Federal Hill neighborhood and others adjacent

on the South Baltimore Peninsula just southeast of the waterfront area, have been nicely reclaimed and inhabited by higher income professionals, while others in other directions are classic run-down zones of urban blight. Baltimore is indeed a city of such contrasts, with a mix of attractive and leading-edge neighborhoods and some of the worst urban decay on the East Coast, with socioeconomic disparity, crime, drugs, education issues, and all the other things that accompany such neglect in those parts of town.

Transportation has always been one of the city's strengths. Baltimore is one of the few East Coast destinations of discount carrier Southwest Airlines. Train service and interstate highways make Washington, New York, and other cities along the Northeast Corridor easily accessible.

Cost of living and housing, while high by U.S. standards, are moderate for the region at large. Leisure activities are plentiful, and the town is big on sports, particularly the Baltimore Orioles baseball and Baltimore Ravens football teams. Camden Yards (next to the historic Baltimore and Ohio Railroad freight station just past the right-field wall), exemplifies Baltimore's tradition and vitality, and has become an urban sports icon that other major-league cities have imitated.

Neighborhoods surrounding Baltimore are very attractive, particularly west, southwest, and some southeast of the city. Many spread into areas of horse farms in gently rolling, wooded countryside. Columbia is a planned community to the southwest, offering abundant residential space integrated with small suburban town centers, parks, and commercial/industrial areas. Columbia's strategic location places it near the airport and commute lines heading south into the greater Washington area. But many of these suburbs are so far out that commute distances are long and sprawl and growth issues are large even though the population isn't growing that fast.

The area is situated on the Chesapeake Bay in a largely level, open plain where several rivers converge to form the Patapsco Bay. The Appalachians rise about 50 miles to the west, beyond areas of modest hills and farmland. Summer brings warm, humid days. Winters are cold but tempered by the ocean and mountains. Snow does occur, but snowfall is generally light except during large spring storms. Some freezing rain and sleet occur each year. Summer precipitation is mainly showers and thunderstorms, and late season Atlantic hurricanes can bring heavy rains. First freeze is late October; last is mid-April.

Population

DEMOGRAPHICS	AREA	U.S. AVG	ETHNIC COMPOSITION	AREA	U.S. AVG	RESIDENT PROFILE	AREA	U.S. AVG
Population	2,644,882		White	67.0%	79.0%	Single	35.6%	32.4%
Population density per sq. mile	1013.7	358.5	Black	26.9%	10.5%	Married	49.6%	52.7%
Population growth	14.7%	21.1%	Asian	3.3%	2.7%	Divorced/separated	14.8%	14.9%
Median age	37.3	36.1	Hispanic	2.2%	10.6%	Married with children	22.4%	23.7%
Percent Democrat	54.0%	44.5%	Religious observance	44.3%	48.9%	Single with children	9.9%	9.1%
Percent Republican	44.7%	54.5%	Diversity measure	41.1	40.1	Percent over age 65	12.2%	12.9%

Economy & Jobs
Score: 48.7
Rank: 193

INCOME	AREA	U.S. AVG	EMPLOYMENT	AREA	U.S. AVG	EMPLOYING INDUSTRIES	AREA	U.S. AVG
Per capita income	$28,598	$23,235	Unemployment rate	5.0%	4.7%	Largest: Healthcare & Social Assistance		
Household income	$58,837	$46,414	Recent job growth	1.6%	1.3%			
Household income < $25K	19.8%	26.2%	Projected future job growth	7.9%	11.5%	Percent manufacturing	10.2%	15.4%
Household income > $75K	36.4%	25.4%	White collar	67.0%	57.8%	Percent public sector	20.4%	15.7%
Household income growth	13.4%	13.6%	Blue collar	18.5%	25.2%	Percent construction	8.3%	9.9%

Cost of Living
Score: 17.6
Rank: 307

INDEXES & TAXES	AREA	U.S. AVG	HOUSING	AREA	U.S. AVG	NECESSITIES	AREA	U.S. AVG
Cost of Living Index	110.2	100.0	Median home price	$285,100	$220,000	Food Index	96.6	100.0
Buying Power Index	119.7	100.0	Home price appreciation	102.5%	10.1%	Housing Index	119.0	100.0
Income tax rate	7.49%	4.70%	Median rent	$998	$709	Utilities Index	114.5	100.0
Sales tax rate	5.00%	6.58%	Homes owned	64.3%	62.3%	Transportation Index	103.1	100.0
Property tax rate	$13.50	$12.00	Home price ratio	4.8	4.2	Healthcare Index	96.2	100.0
						Miscellaneous Cost Index	99.5	100.0

Climate
Score: 42.5
Rank: 214

TEMPERATURE	AREA	U.S. AVG	PRECIPITATION	AREA	U.S. AVG	COMFORTS & HAZARDS	AREA	U.S. AVG
Average January low	24.9	26.2	Annual inches precipitation	40.0	37.7	July relative humidity	67%	66%
Average July high	86.7	87.4	Annual inches snowfall	22.0	7.0	Annual days mostly sunny	205	208
Annual days > 90°F	31	38	Annual days precipitation	112	109	Annual days with thunderstorms	26	39
Annual days < 32°F	100	89	Annual days rain > 0.5 inches	25	22	Tornado risk score	14	18
Annual days < 0°F	0	6	Annual days snow > 1.5 inches	4	6	Hurricane risk score	14	13

TEMPERATURE

PRECIPITATION

DAYS OF CLOUDS & PRECIPITATION

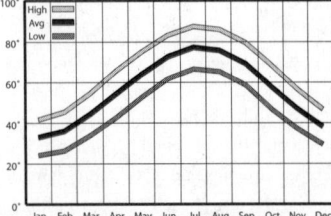

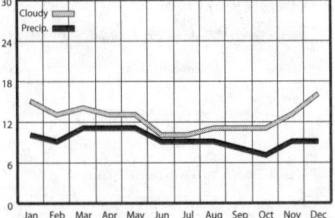

Education
Score: 87.4
Rank: 47

ACHIEVEMENT	AREA	U.S. AVG	PUBLIC SCHOOLS	AREA	U.S. AVG	HIGHER EDUCATION	AREA	U.S. AVG
High school degree	82.4%	82.7%	Expenditures per pupil	$6,618	$5,686	No. 2-year colleges	8	4
2-year college degree	5.5%	6.4%	Student/teacher ratio	18.2	16.7	No. 4-year colleges/universities	21	6
4-year college degree	17.7%	15.7%	Attending public school	83.5%	90.1%	No. highly ranked universities	7	1
Graduate/professional degree	12.0%	8.9%	State SAT score	1012*	1021			
			State ACT score	21.4	20.9			

HAZARDS & ILLNESSES	AREA	U.S. AVG	HEALTHCARE	AREA	U.S. AVG	CRIME	AREA	U.S. AVG
Air-quality score	33	37	Physicians per capita	377.4	244.2	Violent crime rate	837.1	465.5
Water-quality score	50	52	Hospital beds per capita	485.8	420.0	Change in violent crime rate	-5.5%	-2.2%
Pollen/allergy score	65	61	No. teaching hospitals	18	3	Property crime rate	3,467.6	3,517.1
Cancer mortality per capita	211.1	201.9	Cost per doctor visit	$83	$77	Change in property crime rate	-5.3%	-2.1%
Depression days per month	3.4	3.5	Cost per dental visit	$77	$70			
Stress score	56	50						

Health & Healthcare
Score: 51.1
Rank: 184

Crime
Score: 14.7
Rank: 318

COMMUTE	AREA	U.S. AVG	INTERCITY SERVICES	AREA	U.S. AVG	AUTOMOTIVE	AREA	U.S. AVG
Average commute time	32.1	27.4	Major airports within 60 miles	4	1	Insurance, annual premium	$1,998	$1,432
Percent commutes > 60 mins.	10.7%	5.9%	Size of regional airport	Large	Large	Gas, cost per gallon	$2.54	$2.49
Commute by auto	74.9%	78.9%	Daily airline activity	2266	686	Daily vehicle miles per capita	23.9	24.0
Commute by mass transit	6.6%	1.9%	Amtrak service	Yes	No			
Work at home	3.1%	3.1%						
Mass transit miles per capita	6.62	1.87						

Transportation
Score: 90.6
Rank: 36

DINING & SHOPPING	AREA	U.S. AVG	ENTERTAINMENT	AREA	U.S. AVG	OUTDOOR ACTIVITIES	AREA	U.S. AVG
Restaurant rating	3	2	Professional sports rating	9	4	Golf-course rating	8	4
Outlet mall score	144	42	College sports rating	5	4	Ski-area rating	2	3
No. Starbucks	29	13	Zoo/aquarium rating	10	3	Sq. miles inland water	9	4
No. warehouse clubs	12	2	Amusement park rating	5	3	Miles of coastline	94.0	10.7
			Botanical garden/ arboretum rating	9	4	National Park rating	3	3

Leisure
Score: 96.0
Rank: 16

MEDIA & LIBRARIES	AREA	U.S. AVG	PERFORMING ARTS	AREA	U.S. AVG	MUSEUMS	AREA	U.S. AVG
Arts radio rating	8	3	Classical music rating	9	4	Overall museum rating	10	5
No. public libraries	80	27	Ballet/dance rating	7	3	Art museum rating	10	5
Library volumes per capita	3.61	2.78	Professional theater rating	10	3	Science museum rating	10	5
			University arts programs rating	10	5	Children's museum rating	9	3

Arts & Culture
Score: 96.0
Rank: 16

Bangor, ME

Score: 50.3   Rank: 246   2004 rank: 127

Profile: Small city/college town
Location: Central Maine along the Penobscot River, about 30 miles north of the Atlantic Ocean
Elevation: 110 feet
Time zone: Eastern Standard Time

PRO
Attractive setting
Outdoor recreation
Nearby university

CON
Harsh winters
Isolation
Low job growth

Bangor is the gateway to the "north country" and a fairly prosperous lumber, paper, and shipping center and the navigable terminus of the Penobscot River in east-central Maine. The areas to the north are wooded wilderness. The rugged shore area is 30 miles to the south, and the "Down East" coast to the northeast is a vast, unpopulated area of classic New England coastline with fishing and other recreational sites. Acadia National Park is on an island 40 miles to the south. Old Town, on a river island 10 miles north, is home to the University of Maine and the Old Town Canoe Company, a business befitting to the area. The economy has generally made the transition to service industries faster than most of the state, but that isn't saying much and employment is still an issue. Downtown is clean, attractive, walkable, and somewhat historic. In part due to the college presence, the area does have some small but well-regarded arts amenities, including what is thought to be the nation's longest continuously performing symphony orchestra. Bangor is isolated from many city amenities and services—some residents travel to Canadian cities such as Saint John in New Brunswick and Québec City or Montréal in Québec. For those who can find employment and tolerate the long, hard winter, Bangor is a good choice.

Bangor lies in a river valley near sea level. The surrounding area is hilly and wooded with a mix of deciduous and coniferous forests. Summers are warm and pleasant, normally not uncomfortably hot, and feature cool evenings. Winters are cold, often brutally, and windy when cold air masses descend from the northwest. Below-zero temperatures and snow cover are common. Spring comes slowly with frequent freezes. Precipitation is moderate and spread throughout the year, although fall tends to be the driest and most pleasant. First freeze is early October; last is early May.

Population

DEMOGRAPHICS	AREA	U.S. AVG	ETHNIC COMPOSITION	AREA	U.S. AVG	RESIDENT PROFILE	AREA	U.S. AVG
Population	148,170		White	96.5%	79.0%	Single	32.8%	32.4%
Population density per sq. mile	43.6	358.5	Black	0.5%	10.5%	Married	52.6%	52.7%
Population growth	1.1%	21.1%	Asian	0.9%	2.7%	Divorced/separated	14.7%	14.9%
Median age	38.8	36.1	Hispanic	0.7%	10.6%	Married with children	21.2%	23.7%
Percent Democrat	49.2%	44.5%	Religious observance	33.7%	48.9%	Single with children	8.8%	9.1%
Percent Republican	49.1%	54.5%	Diversity measure	8.0	40.1	Percent over age 65	13.6%	12.9%

Economy & Jobs
Score: 4.5
Rank: 356

INCOME	AREA	U.S. AVG	EMPLOYMENT	AREA	U.S. AVG	EMPLOYING INDUSTRIES	AREA	U.S. AVG
Per capita income	$20,828	$23,235	Unemployment rate	5.1%	4.7%	Largest: Healthcare & Social Assistance		
Household income	$39,218	$46,414	Recent job growth	0.6%	1.3%			
Household income < $25K	31.8%	26.2%	Projected future job growth	-0.1%	11.5%	Percent manufacturing	15.2%	15.4%
Household income > $75K	18.7%	25.4%	White collar	56.6%	57.8%	Percent public sector	16.6%	15.7%
Household income growth	14.4%	13.6%	Blue collar	25.0%	25.2%	Percent construction	9.9%	9.9%

Cost of Living
Score: 28.3
Rank: 268

INDEXES & TAXES	AREA	U.S. AVG	HOUSING	AREA	U.S. AVG	NECESSITIES	AREA	U.S. AVG
Cost of Living Index	98.6	100.0	Median home price	$168,400	$220,000	Food Index	103.8	100.0
Buying Power Index	89.2	100.0	Home price appreciation	57.3%	10.1%	Housing Index	64.0	100.0
Income tax rate	8.50%	4.70%	Median rent	$654	$709	Utilities Index	151.7	100.0
Sales tax rate	5.00%	6.58%	Homes owned	61.0%	62.3%	Transportation Index	105.8	100.0
Property tax rate	$12.79	$12.00	Home price ratio	4.3	4.2	Healthcare Index	111.4	100.0
						Miscellaneous Cost Index	105.4	100.0

Climate
Score: 0.0
Rank: 373

TEMPERATURE	AREA	U.S. AVG	PRECIPITATION	AREA	U.S. AVG	COMFORTS & HAZARDS	AREA	U.S. AVG
Average January low	10.2	26.2	Annual inches precipitation	43.0	37.7	July relative humidity	72%	66%
Average July high	77.5	87.4	Annual inches snowfall	95.0	7.0	Annual days mostly sunny	205	208
Annual days > 90°F	4	38	Annual days precipitation	135	109	Annual days with thunderstorms	18	39
Annual days < 32°F	155	89	Annual days rain > 0.5 inches	28	22	Tornado risk score	0	18
Annual days < 0°F	16	6	Annual days snow > 1.5 inches	17	6	Hurricane risk score	13	13

TEMPERATURE

PRECIPITATION

DAYS OF CLOUDS & PRECIPITATION

Education
Score: 55.1
Rank: 169

ACHIEVEMENT	AREA	U.S. AVG	PUBLIC SCHOOLS	AREA	U.S. AVG	HIGHER EDUCATION	AREA	U.S. AVG
High school degree	85.8%	82.7%	Expenditures per pupil	$5,869	$5,686	No. 2-year colleges	2	4
2-year college degree	7.8%	6.4%	Student/teacher ratio	15.4	16.7	No. 4-year colleges/universities	4	6
4-year college degree	13.0%	15.7%	Attending public school	92.3%	90.1%	No. highly ranked universities	0	1
Graduate/professional degree	7.5%	8.9%	State SAT score	1002*	1021			
			State ACT score	22.3	20.9			

Health & Healthcare
Score: 58.6
Rank: 156

Crime
Score: 91.2
Rank: 34

HAZARDS & ILLNESSES	AREA	U.S. AVG	HEALTHCARE	AREA	U.S. AVG	CRIME	AREA	U.S. AVG
Air-quality score	29	37	Physicians per capita	290.5	244.2	Violent crime rate	82.7	465.5
Water-quality score	60	52	Hospital beds per capita	471.8	420.0	Change in violent crime rate	16.8%	-2.2%
Pollen/allergy score	34	61	No. teaching hospitals	1	3	Property crime rate	2,854.6	3,517.1
Cancer mortality per capita	259.7	201.9	Cost per doctor visit	$81	$77	Change in property crime rate	-8.6%	-2.1%
Depression days per month	3.9	3.5	Cost per dental visit	$74	$70			
Stress score	36	50						

Transportation
Score: 21.4
Rank: 294

COMMUTE	AREA	U.S. AVG	INTERCITY SERVICES	AREA	U.S. AVG	AUTOMOTIVE	AREA	U.S. AVG
Average commute time	22.6	27.4	Major airports within 60 miles	0	1	Insurance, annual premium	$840	$1,432
Percent commutes > 60 mins.	5.3%	5.9%	Size of regional airport	None	Large	Gas, cost per gallon	$2.48	$2.49
Commute by auto	79.5%	78.9%	Daily airline activity	43	686	Daily vehicle miles per capita	24.5	24.0
Commute by mass transit	0.8%	1.9%	Amtrak service	No	No			
Work at home	3.8%	3.1%						
Mass transit miles per capita	0.84	1.87						

DINING & SHOPPING	AREA	U.S. AVG	ENTERTAINMENT	AREA	U.S. AVG	OUTDOOR ACTIVITIES	AREA	U.S. AVG
Restaurant rating	1	2	Professional sports rating	2	4	Golf-course rating	2	4
Outlet mall score	0	42	College sports rating	3	4	Ski-area rating	7	3
No. Starbucks	1	13	Zoo/aquarium rating	1	3	Sq. miles inland water	3	4
No. warehouse clubs	1	2	Amusement park rating	1	3	Miles of coastline	0.0	10.7
			Botanical garden/ arboretum rating	2	4	National Park rating	1	3

Leisure
Score: 36.4
Rank: 237

MEDIA & LIBRARIES	AREA	U.S. AVG	PERFORMING ARTS	AREA	U.S. AVG	MUSEUMS	AREA	U.S. AVG
Arts radio rating	5	3	Classical music rating	3	4	Overall museum rating	3	5
No. public libraries	24	27	Ballet/dance rating	1	3	Art museum rating	2	5
Library volumes per capita	7.57	2.78	Professional theater rating	1	3	Science museum rating	5	5
			University arts programs rating	5	5	Children's museum rating	1	3

Arts & Culture
Score: 62.6
Rank: 140

Barnstable Town, MA

Score: 60.6 Rank: 171 2004 rank: 75

Profile: Resort-town complex
Location: Central portion of Cape Cod
Elevation: 60 feet
Time zone: Eastern Standard Time

PRO
Nearby coastline
Educated population
Pleasant summers

CON
Cost of living and housing
Tourist impact
Low ethnic diversity

Barnstable is the commercial center and gateway to Cape Cod. The towns along Cape Cod are typical New England coastal towns with attractive commercial and residential areas and seaside wharves. The considerable fishing industry and tourist market support a large assortment of restaurants and local entertainment. Surrounding Cape Cod is an outdoor recreation and entertainment paradise. Educational attainment at all levels is among the highest in the state. Not surprisingly because of tourist appeal and relatively constrained land for building, cost of living and housing are highest in the state, and home prices have grown somewhat faster than elsewhere in Massachusetts. The economy, supported mostly by service and hospitality industries, isn't very well balanced. Jobs in this sector don't pay enough to afford most of the avail-

able housing, so the economy is dependent on wealth arriving from elsewhere. All these factors have combined to lower the area's ranking by nearly 100 places. The area is crowded with tourists at certain times of the year, but escape from the crowds is possible and off seasons are nice. Those who can handle the high costs and the periodically damp marine climate will do well in the area.

The Barnstable area is located on the mostly flat coastal plain of Cape Cod with beaches to the north. Summers are warm but not hot, with more prevalent sunshine than the rest of the state. Other seasons are highly variable with frequent fog, rain, and snow. The area has far fewer rainy days and far less snow than the rest of the state. First freeze is end of October; last is mid-April.

DEMOGRAPHICS	AREA	U.S. AVG	ETHNIC COMPOSITION	AREA	U.S. AVG	RESIDENT PROFILE	AREA	U.S. AVG
Population	232,462		White	94.1%	79.0%	Single	29.7%	32.4%
Population density per sq. mile	587.8	358.5	Black	1.9%	10.5%	Married	55.2%	52.7%
Population growth	24.6%	21.1%	Asian	0.9%	2.7%	Divorced/separated	15.1%	14.9%
Median age	45.2	36.1	Hispanic	1.5%	10.6%	Married with children	17.7%	23.7%
Percent Democrat	54.6%	44.5%	Religious observance	42.9%	48.9%	Single with children	6.6%	9.1%
Percent Republican	44.3%	54.5%	Diversity measure	14.1	40.1	Percent over age 65	23.2%	12.9%

Population

INCOME	AREA	U.S. AVG	EMPLOYMENT	AREA	U.S. AVG	EMPLOYING INDUSTRIES	AREA	U.S. AVG
Per capita income	$29,855	$23,235	Unemployment rate	3.6%	4.7%	Largest: Healthcare & Social Assistance		
Household income	$52,837	$46,414	Recent job growth	0.2%	1.3%			
Household income < $25K	21.0%	26.2%	Projected future job growth	8.4%	11.5%	Percent manufacturing	7.5%	15.4%
Household income > $75K	31.4%	25.4%	White collar	62.6%	57.8%	Percent public sector	14.5%	15.7%
Household income growth	15.0%	13.6%	Blue collar	18.5%	25.2%	Percent construction	11.0%	9.9%

Economy & Jobs
Score: 21.4
Rank: 293

INDEXES & TAXES	AREA	U.S. AVG	HOUSING	AREA	U.S. AVG	NECESSITIES	AREA	U.S. AVG
Cost of Living Index	139.5	100.0	Median home price	$406,300	$220,000	Food Index	110.1	100.0
Buying Power Index	84.9	100.0	Home price appreciation	87.4%	10.1%	Housing Index	103.9	100.0
Income tax rate	5.95%	4.70%	Median rent	$1,003	$709	Utilities Index	128.1	100.0
Sales tax rate	5.00%	6.58%	Homes owned	50.2%	62.3%	Transportation Index	115.6	100.0
Property tax rate	$10.54	$12.00	Home price ratio	7.7	4.2	Healthcare Index	130.6	100.0
						Miscellaneous Cost Index	113.5	100.0

Cost of Living
Score: 7.2
Rank: 346

Climate
Score: 67.4
Rank: 121

TEMPERATURE	AREA	U.S. AVG	PRECIPITATION	AREA	U.S. AVG	COMFORTS & HAZARDS	AREA	U.S. AVG
Average January low	21.6	26.2	Annual inches precipitation	45.0	37.7	July relative humidity	76%	66%
Average July high	81.7	87.4	Annual inches snowfall	36.0	7.0	Annual days mostly sunny	211	208
Annual days > 90°F	5	38	Annual days precipitation	79	109	Annual days with thunderstorms	14	39
Annual days < 32°F	110	89	Annual days rain > 0.5 inches	30	22	Tornado risk score	8	18
Annual days < 0°F	0	6	Annual days snow > 1.5 inches	16	6	Hurricane risk score	21	13

TEMPERATURE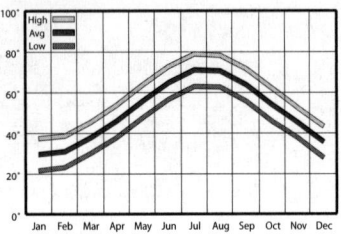

PRECIPITATION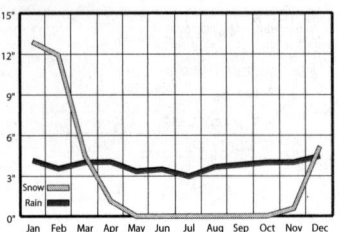

DAYS OF CLOUDS & PRECIPITATION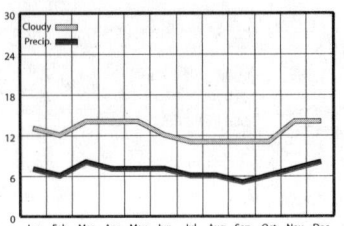

Education
Score: 96.8
Rank: 13

ACHIEVEMENT	AREA	U.S. AVG	PUBLIC SCHOOLS	AREA	U.S. AVG	HIGHER EDUCATION	AREA	U.S. AVG
High school degree	91.8%	82.7%	Expenditures per pupil	$7,223	$5,686	No. 2-year colleges	1	4
2-year college degree	8.9%	6.4%	Student/teacher ratio	0.0	16.7	No. 4-year colleges/universities	2	6
4-year college degree	20.5%	15.7%	Attending public school	93.8%	90.1%	No. highly ranked universities	0	1
Graduate/professional degree	13.0%	8.9%	State SAT score	1037*	1021			
			State ACT score	23	20.9			

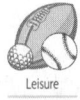
Health & Healthcare
Score: 16.3
Rank: 312

HAZARDS & ILLNESSES	AREA	U.S. AVG	HEALTHCARE	AREA	U.S. AVG	CRIME	AREA	U.S. AVG
Air-quality score	39	37	Physicians per capita	250.5	244.2	Violent crime rate	406.1	465.5
Water-quality score	40	52	Hospital beds per capita	183.3	420.0	Change in violent crime rate	11.6%	-2.2%
Pollen/allergy score	62	61	No. teaching hospitals	1	3	Property crime rate	2,342.9	3,517.1
Cancer mortality per capita	214.0	201.9	Cost per doctor visit	$101	$77	Change in property crime rate	-2.1%	-2.1%
Depression days per month	3.0	3.5	Cost per dental visit	$90	$70			
Stress score	32	50						

Crime
Score: 71.4
Rank: 108

COMMUTE	AREA	U.S. AVG	INTERCITY SERVICES	AREA	U.S. AVG	AUTOMOTIVE	AREA	U.S. AVG
Average commute time	25.7	27.4	Major airports within 60 miles	1	1	Insurance, annual premium	$1,601	$1,432
Percent commutes > 60 mins.	9.7%	5.9%	Size of regional airport	Large	Large	Gas, cost per gallon	$2.47	$2.49
Commute by auto	81.4%	78.9%	Daily airline activity	902	686	Daily vehicle miles per capita	36.0	24.0
Commute by mass transit	1.5%	1.9%	Amtrak service	No	No			
Work at home	5.1%	3.1%						
Mass transit miles per capita	1.45	1.87						

Transportation
Score: 50.8
Rank: 185

DINING & SHOPPING	AREA	U.S. AVG	ENTERTAINMENT	AREA	U.S. AVG	OUTDOOR ACTIVITIES	AREA	U.S. AVG
Restaurant rating	3	2	Professional sports rating	5	4	Golf-course rating	1	4
Outlet mall score	63	42	College sports rating	1	4	Ski-area rating	6	3
No. Starbucks	2	13	Zoo/aquarium rating	4	3	Sq. miles inland water	3	4
No. warehouse clubs	1	2	Amusement park rating	1	3	Miles of coastline	25.2	10.7
			Botanical garden/ arboretum rating	4	4	National Park rating	1	3

Leisure
Score: 63.9
Rank: 134

MEDIA & LIBRARIES	AREA	U.S. AVG	PERFORMING ARTS	AREA	U.S. AVG	MUSEUMS	AREA	U.S. AVG
Arts radio rating	1	3	Classical music rating	4	4	Overall museum rating	7	5
No. public libraries	35	27	Ballet/dance rating	1	3	Art museum rating	7	5
Library volumes per capita	5.38	2.78	Professional theater rating	1	3	Science museum rating	8	5
			University arts programs rating	2	5	Children's museum rating	1	3

Arts & Culture
Score: 63.1
Rank: 138

Baton Rouge, LA

Score: 46.6 **Rank:** 267 **2004 rank:** 295

Profile: Mid-size capital city/industrial city/college town
Location: Southeast Louisiana along the Mississippi River north of the Mississippi Delta
Elevation: 64 feet
Time zone: Central Standard Time

PRO	CON
College-town amenities	Hot, humid summers
Historic interest	Crime rate
Future job growth	Uncertain future

Before Hurricane Katrina, Baton Rouge was a staid but fairly unattractive, ordinary city with a diverse economic and cultural base as state capital, petrochemical industry center, and college town. Hurricane Katrina brought as many as 800,000 refugees of all socioeconomic strata into the city. Some obviously fled temporarily, but a sizable number, estimated at some 60,000 to 100,000, seeking the area's relative geographic and economic stability, will stay. In part stimulated by growth and need and in part by designation as a tax-incentive rich Federal Gulf Opportunity Zone, or "GO Zone," the local economy is booming, especially with smaller business start-ups and construction. The long-term impact on the area's population, economy, and amenities remains unclear.

Baton Rouge lies about 30 miles up the Mississippi River from New Orleans and 65 miles from the coast. A rich past as an ocean port, center for antebellum commerce, and Louisiana's colorful political history adds spice to the local character. There are many points of interest along the shady streets with their gracious old homes. There is plenty to do:

Two universities (Louisiana State and Southern) bring an assortment of cultural amenities, and the active and renovated Mississippi waterfront area has restaurants, theaters, and historic buildings. Downsides include hot summer weather, poor air quality, the high crime rate typical of most of the state, and some ugly urban sprawl towards the east. The long-term effects—both good and bad—of the Katrina migration certainly bear watching.

The area is near the first evident relief north of the broad, flat delta plain extending to the south. Lush wet forests of evergreen, live oak, and magnolia trees grow in the area. Especially to the west lie areas of mixed agricultural use, sugar plantations, and marshland, with areas of woodland and pine forest to the north. Summer months are muggy with clouds, light winds, and abundant rainfall, but seldom exceed 100°F. Showers occur every 1 in 2 days during summer. Winter months are normally mild with a few cold spells, lengthy periods of rain, and a few nights with below-freezing temperatures. It rarely stays below freezing during the day.

Population

DEMOGRAPHICS	AREA	U.S. AVG	ETHNIC COMPOSITION	AREA	U.S. AVG	RESIDENT PROFILE	AREA	U.S. AVG
Population	731,558		White	62.3%	79.0%	Single	36.0%	32.4%
Population density per sq. mile	181.5	358.5	Black	34.3%	10.5%	Married	48.8%	52.7%
Population growth	19.9%	21.1%	Asian	1.6%	2.7%	Divorced/separated	15.2%	14.9%
Median age	33.6	36.1	Hispanic	2.0%	10.6%	Married with children	24.4%	23.7%
Percent Democrat	41.2%	44.5%	Religious observance	52.1%	48.9%	Single with children	11.2%	9.1%
Percent Republican	57.8%	54.5%	Diversity measure	46.7	40.1	Percent over age 65	10.1%	12.9%

Economy & Jobs
Score: 39.6
Rank: 224

INCOME	AREA	U.S. AVG	EMPLOYMENT	AREA	U.S. AVG	EMPLOYING INDUSTRIES	AREA	U.S. AVG
Per capita income	$21,095	$23,235	Unemployment rate	6.3%	4.7%	Largest: Construction		
Household income	$42,586	$46,414	Recent job growth	1.4%	1.3%			
Household income < $25K	30.4%	26.2%	Projected future job growth	13.4%	11.5%	Percent manufacturing	13.2%	15.4%
Household income > $75K	24.4%	25.4%	White collar	59.5%	57.8%	Percent public sector	19.8%	15.7%
Household income growth	13.7%	13.6%	Blue collar	25.1%	25.2%	Percent construction	11.9%	9.9%

Cost of Living
Score: 42.5
Rank: 215

INDEXES & TAXES	AREA	U.S. AVG	HOUSING	AREA	U.S. AVG	NECESSITIES	AREA	U.S. AVG
Cost of Living Index	94.4	100.0	Median home price	$172,300	$220,000	Food Index	104.9	100.0
Buying Power Index	101.1	100.0	Home price appreciation	27.9%	10.1%	Housing Index	55.4	100.0
Income tax rate	4.00%	4.70%	Median rent	$735	$709	Utilities Index	119.5	100.0
Sales tax rate	8.88%	6.58%	Homes owned	64.0%	62.3%	Transportation Index	105.0	100.0
Property tax rate	$3.30	$12.00	Home price ratio	4.0	4.2	Healthcare Index	96.2	100.0
						Miscellaneous Cost Index	103.7	100.0

Climate
Score: 74.3
Rank: 96

TEMPERATURE	AREA	U.S. AVG	PRECIPITATION	AREA	U.S. AVG	COMFORTS & HAZARDS	AREA	U.S. AVG
Average January low	40.5	26.2	Annual inches precipitation	54.1	37.7	July relative humidity	74%	66%
Average July high	91.2	87.4	Annual inches snowfall	1.8	7.0	Annual days mostly sunny	218	208
Annual days > 90°F	83	38	Annual days precipitation	108	109	Annual days with thunderstorms	70	39
Annual days < 32°F	25	89	Annual days rain > 0.5 inches	36	22	Tornado risk score	31	18
Annual days < 0°F	0	6	Annual days snow > 1.5 inches	1	6	Hurricane risk score	42	13

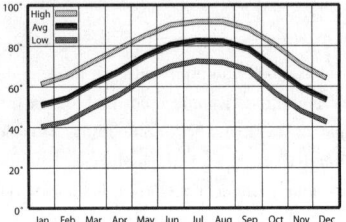

TEMPERATURE — **PRECIPITATION** — **DAYS OF CLOUDS & PRECIPITATION**

Education
Score: 16.6
Rank: 309

ACHIEVEMENT	AREA	U.S. AVG	PUBLIC SCHOOLS	AREA	U.S. AVG	HIGHER EDUCATION	AREA	U.S. AVG
High school degree	79.8%	82.7%	Expenditures per pupil	$4,591	$5,686	No. 2-year colleges	19	4
2-year college degree	2.8%	6.4%	Student/teacher ratio	16.5	16.7	No. 4-year colleges/universities	4	6
4-year college degree	14.9%	15.7%	Attending public school	79.4%	90.1%	No. highly ranked universities	0	1
Graduate/professional degree	8.0%	8.9%	State SAT score	1141	1021			
			State ACT score	20.1*	20.9			

Health & Healthcare
Score: 27.8
Rank: 268

Crime
Score: 26.7
Rank: 274

HAZARDS & ILLNESSES	AREA	U.S. AVG	HEALTHCARE	AREA	U.S. AVG	CRIME	AREA	U.S. AVG
Air-quality score	28	37	Physicians per capita	181.9	244.2	Violent crime rate	719.2	465.5
Water-quality score	18	52	Hospital beds per capita	479.7	420.0	Change in violent crime rate	13.7%	-2.2%
Pollen/allergy score	76	61	No. teaching hospitals	2	3	Property crime rate	4,723.3	3,517.1
Cancer mortality per capita	205.7	201.9	Cost per doctor visit	$85	$77	Change in property crime rate	-7.0%	-2.1%
Depression days per month	3.0	3.5	Cost per dental visit	$66	$70			
Stress score	78	50						

Transportation
Score: 2.7
Rank: 363

COMMUTE	AREA	U.S. AVG	INTERCITY SERVICES	AREA	U.S. AVG	AUTOMOTIVE	AREA	U.S. AVG
Average commute time	27.9	27.4	Major airports within 60 miles	1	1	Insurance, annual premium	$1,900	$1,432
Percent commutes > 60 mins.	6.7%	5.9%	Size of regional airport	Medium	Large	Gas, cost per gallon	$2.47	$2.49
Commute by auto	82.1%	78.9%	Daily airline activity	259	686	Daily vehicle miles per capita	25.6	24.0
Commute by mass transit	0.9%	1.9%	Amtrak service	No	No			
Work at home	2.1%	3.1%						
Mass transit miles per capita	0.90	1.87						

Leisure
Score: 59.6
Rank: 151

DINING & SHOPPING	AREA	U.S. AVG	ENTERTAINMENT	AREA	U.S. AVG	OUTDOOR ACTIVITIES	AREA	U.S. AVG
Restaurant rating	3	2	Professional sports rating	2	4	Golf-course rating	3	4
Outlet mall score	42	42	College sports rating	9	4	Ski-area rating	1	3
No. Starbucks	6	13	Zoo/aquarium rating	4	3	Sq. miles inland water	5	4
No. warehouse clubs	0	2	Amusement park rating	2	3	Miles of coastline	0.0	10.7
			Botanical garden/arboretum rating	6	4	National Park rating	1	3

Arts & Culture
Score: 68.2
Rank: 119

MEDIA & LIBRARIES	AREA	U.S. AVG	PERFORMING ARTS	AREA	U.S. AVG	MUSEUMS	AREA	U.S. AVG
Arts radio rating	1	3	Classical music rating	6	4	Overall museum rating	6	5
No. public libraries	42	27	Ballet/dance rating	3	3	Art museum rating	5	5
Library volumes per capita	3.05	2.78	Professional theater rating	1	3	Science museum rating	7	5
			University arts programs rating	8	5	Children's museum rating	4	3

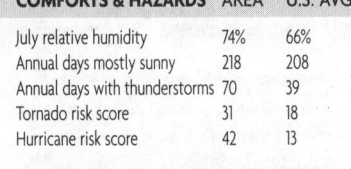

Battle Creek, MI

Score: 52.2 **Rank:** 239 **2004 rank:** 237

Profile: Small city
Location: Southwestern Michigan, midway between Detroit and Chicago along I-94
Elevation: 830 feet
Time zone: Eastern Standard Time

PRO	CON
Cost of living	Entertainment
Community feel	Clouds and rain
Nearby recreation	Crime rates

In the 1890s, two brothers named Kellogg figured out a way to turn corn and wheat into flakes for breakfast cereal, and the rest is history. Battle Creek is known worldwide as the capital of the breakfast cereal industry, and is headquarters for the Kellogg Corporation as well as the Post division of Kraft and the cereal division of Ralston Purina. Not surprisingly, breakfast food and related manufacturing industries are the center of Battle Creek's economy today. A large family entertainment mall and aquatic center gives an otherwise unremarkable downtown a bit of a recreational spark. Naturally, there's a museum celebrating the cereal industry, but beyond a few other minor cultural amenities, there isn't a lot to do. The city was represented in a combined MSA with Kalamazoo in the previous edition of this book.

The terrain is mainly flat with farmland and areas of deciduous hardwood forest particularly to the southwest. Summers are warm but not too hot and moderately humid. Winters are cold, wet, and snowy with the most extreme cold tempered by Lake Michigan and the harshest winds moderated by the hills to the northwest. Still, prevailing winds bring significant cloudiness and precipitation. Winter snow cover is common. First freeze is mid-October; last is late April.

Population

DEMOGRAPHICS	AREA	U.S. AVG	ETHNIC COMPOSITION	AREA	U.S. AVG	RESIDENT PROFILE	AREA	U.S. AVG
Population	139,193		White	83.5%	79.0%	Single	31.9%	32.4%
Population density per sq. mile	196.4	358.5	Black	10.8%	10.5%	Married	51.9%	52.7%
Population growth	2.4%	21.1%	Asian	1.3%	2.7%	Divorced/separated	16.3%	14.9%
Median age	37.2	36.1	Hispanic	3.4%	10.6%	Married with children	20.7%	23.7%
Percent Democrat	47.7%	44.5%	Religious observance	33.0%	48.9%	Single with children	10.7%	9.1%
Percent Republican	51.2%	54.5%	Diversity measure	33.6	40.1	Percent over age 65	13.8%	12.9%

Economy & Jobs
Score: 29.1
Rank: 265

INCOME	AREA	U.S. AVG	EMPLOYMENT	AREA	U.S. AVG	EMPLOYING INDUSTRIES	AREA	U.S. AVG
Per capita income	$21,567	$23,235	Unemployment rate	7.4%	4.7%	Largest: Manufacturing		
Household income	$43,138	$46,414	Recent job growth	1.3%	1.3%			
Household income < $25K	27.4%	26.2%	Projected future job growth	7.2%	11.5%	Percent manufacturing	23.6%	15.4%
Household income > $75K	21.6%	25.4%	White collar	50.9%	57.8%	Percent public sector	13.0%	15.7%
Household income growth	10.8%	13.6%	Blue collar	32.0%	25.2%	Percent construction	8.4%	9.9%

Cost of Living
Score: 67.9
Rank: 121

INDEXES & TAXES	AREA	U.S. AVG	HOUSING	AREA	U.S. AVG	NECESSITIES	AREA	U.S. AVG
Cost of Living Index	83.5	100.0	Median home price	$124,100	$220,000	Food Index	100.4	100.0
Buying Power Index	115.8	100.0	Home price appreciation	22.1%	10.1%	Housing Index	47.9	100.0
Income tax rate	4.40%	4.70%	Median rent	$610	$709	Utilities Index	89.5	100.0
Sales tax rate	6.00%	6.58%	Homes owned	67.6%	62.3%	Transportation Index	103.9	100.0
Property tax rate	$14.32	$12.00	Home price ratio	2.9	4.2	Healthcare Index	97.1	100.0
						Miscellaneous Cost Index	101.1	100.0

Climate
Score: 8.6
Rank: 341

TEMPERATURE	AREA	U.S. AVG	PRECIPITATION	AREA	U.S. AVG	COMFORTS & HAZARDS	AREA	U.S. AVG
Average January low	16.0	26.2	Annual inches precipitation	32.0	37.7	July relative humidity	73%	66%
Average July high	83.3	87.4	Annual inches snowfall	77.0	7.0	Annual days mostly sunny	163	208
Annual days > 90°F	11	38	Annual days precipitation	144	109	Annual days with thunderstorms	37	39
Annual days < 32°F	149	89	Annual days rain > 0.5 inches	19	22	Tornado risk score	19	18
Annual days < 0°F	8	6	Annual days snow > 1.5 inches	21	6	Hurricane risk score	2	13

TEMPERATURE

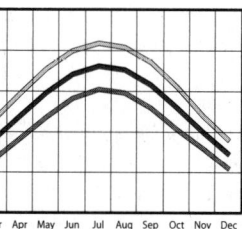

PRECIPITATION

DAYS OF CLOUDS & PRECIPITATION

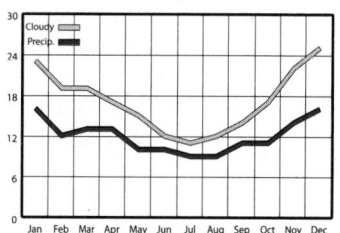

Education
Score: 40.6
Rank: 223

ACHIEVEMENT	AREA	U.S. AVG	PUBLIC SCHOOLS	AREA	U.S. AVG	HIGHER EDUCATION	AREA	U.S. AVG
High school degree	83.4%	82.7%	Expenditures per pupil	$5,970	$5,686	No. 2-year colleges	1	4
2-year college degree	7.8%	6.4%	Student/teacher ratio	18.3	16.7	No. 4-year colleges/universities	1	6
4-year college degree	10.6%	15.7%	Attending public school	93.9%	90.1%	No. highly ranked universities	1	1
Graduate/professional degree	5.6%	8.9%	State SAT score	1151	1021			
			State ACT score	21.5*	20.9			

Health & Healthcare
Score: 87.7
Rank: 47

HAZARDS & ILLNESSES	AREA	U.S. AVG	HEALTHCARE	AREA	U.S. AVG	CRIME	AREA	U.S. AVG
Air-quality score	48	37	Physicians per capita	170.7	244.2	Violent crime rate	767.4	465.5
Water-quality score	72	52	Hospital beds per capita	533.1	420.0	Change in violent crime rate	13.2%	-2.2%
Pollen/allergy score	42	61	No. teaching hospitals	0	3	Property crime rate	4,099.0	3,517.1
Cancer mortality per capita	209.5	201.9	Cost per doctor visit	$69	$77	Change in property crime rate	-6.8%	-2.1%
Depression days per month	4.9	3.5	Cost per dental visit	$69	$70			
Stress score	91	50						

Crime
Score: 23.5
Rank: 286

Transportation
Score: 88.0
Rank: 46

COMMUTE	AREA	U.S. AVG	INTERCITY SERVICES	AREA	U.S. AVG	AUTOMOTIVE	AREA	U.S. AVG
Average commute time	21.5	27.4	Major airports within 60 miles	1	1	Insurance, annual premium	$1,425	$1,432
Percent commutes > 60 mins.	4.0%	5.9%	Size of regional airport	Large	Large	Gas, cost per gallon	$2.54	$2.49
Commute by auto	82.5%	78.9%	Daily airline activity	1098	686	Daily vehicle miles per capita	27.7	24.0
Commute by mass transit	0.9%	1.9%	Amtrak service	Yes	No			
Work at home	2.8%	3.1%						
Mass transit miles per capita	0.89	1.87						

Leisure
Score: 49.7
Rank: 187

DINING & SHOPPING	AREA	U.S. AVG	ENTERTAINMENT	AREA	U.S. AVG	OUTDOOR ACTIVITIES	AREA	U.S. AVG
Restaurant rating	1	2	Professional sports rating	3	4	Golf-course rating	3	4
Outlet mall score	62	42	College sports rating	2	4	Ski-area rating	5	3
No. Starbucks	0	13	Zoo/aquarium rating	5	3	Sq. miles inland water	3	4
No. warehouse clubs	0	2	Amusement park rating	1	3	Miles of coastline	0.0	10.7
			Botanical garden/ arboretum rating	2	4	National Park rating	1	3

Arts & Culture
Score: 55.6
Rank: 166

MEDIA & LIBRARIES	AREA	U.S. AVG	PERFORMING ARTS	AREA	U.S. AVG	MUSEUMS	AREA	U.S. AVG
Arts radio rating	1	3	Classical music rating	3	4	Overall museum rating	6	5
No. public libraries	7	27	Ballet/dance rating	3	3	Art museum rating	4	5
Library volumes per capita	2.85	2.78	Professional theater rating	1	3	Science museum rating	3	5
			University arts programs rating	7	5	Children's museum rating	1	3

Bay City, MI

Score: 33.6 **Rank:** 330 **2004 rank:** 219

Profile: Small industrial city
Location: Eastern Michigan at the head of Saginaw Bay
Elevation: 595 feet
Time zone: Eastern Standard Time

PRO	CON
Historic downtown	Industrial landscape
Nearby recreation	Educational attainment
Cost of living	Cloudy, wet climate

Bay City is part of a tri-city area that includes Saginaw and Midland generally located on the Saginaw Bay, forms the "thumb" of Michigan's "hand." Bay City is a natural Great Lakes port and center for shipping, and has a vast industrial presence in the automotive, chemical, forest products, and other basic industries. Industry leaders include General Motors, Dow Chemical, and Dow Corning, the latter two situated in nearby Midland. The region's early industrial history and prosperity brought a then-attractive and now-historic downtown and waterfront that is well preserved today. The city has three historic districts and several museums and attractions related to its history, and won a "Great American Main Street" award in 1999 from the National Trust for Historic Preservation. The area has a strong sense of community.

Areas outside the city and especially north are well known for outdoor recreation, both on land and water. Cost of living is very low at 76.9.

The Saginaw River meanders gently through Bay City, and then flows 2 miles into Saginaw Bay. The terrain is mainly level to gently rolling with a mix of agriculture and dense forests. Summers are humid but moderate in temperature, seldom reaching 100°F. Winters are cold with frequent snow and rain/snow mixes. Moisture from the Great Lakes produces significant snows and snow cover is prevalent through winter. Most precipitation occurs in late spring, summer, and early fall. The lake effect generates clouds year-round, making the area one of the cloudiest places in the nation. First freeze is early October; last is early May.

Population

DEMOGRAPHICS	AREA	U.S. AVG
Population	109,184	
Population density per sq. mile	245.8	358.5
Population growth	-2.3%	21.1%
Median age	39.6	36.1
Percent Democrat	54.4%	44.5%
Percent Republican	44.6%	54.5%

ETHNIC COMPOSITION	AREA	U.S. AVG
White	94.7%	79.0%
Black	1.3%	10.5%
Asian	0.5%	2.7%
Hispanic	4.1%	10.6%
Religious observance	59.7%	48.9%
Diversity measure	17.2	40.1

RESIDENT PROFILE	AREA	U.S. AVG
Single	32.6%	32.4%
Married	55.1%	52.7%
Divorced/separated	12.3%	14.9%
Married with children	22.0%	23.7%
Single with children	8.5%	9.1%
Percent over age 65	15.1%	12.9%

Economy & Jobs
Score: 8.3
Rank: 342

INCOME	AREA	U.S. AVG
Per capita income	$22,406	$23,235
Household income	$42,873	$46,414
Household income < $25K	27.9%	26.2%
Household income > $75K	23.2%	25.4%
Household income growth	10.9%	13.6%

EMPLOYMENT	AREA	U.S. AVG
Unemployment rate	7.3%	4.7%
Recent job growth	-0.1%	1.3%
Projected future job growth	1.1%	11.5%
White collar	53.5%	57.8%
Blue collar	28.9%	25.2%

EMPLOYING INDUSTRIES	AREA	U.S. AVG
Largest: Manufacturing		
Percent manufacturing	18.0%	15.4%
Percent public sector	10.9%	15.7%
Percent construction	10.9%	9.9%

Cost of Living
Score: 85.0
Rank: 57

INDEXES & TAXES	AREA	U.S. AVG
Cost of Living Index	76.9	100.0
Buying Power Index	125.0	100.0
Income tax rate	4.40%	4.70%
Sales tax rate	6.00%	6.58%
Property tax rate	$15.16	$12.00

HOUSING	AREA	U.S. AVG
Median home price	$94,700	$220,000
Home price appreciation	22.4%	10.1%
Median rent	$546	$709
Homes owned	75.4%	62.3%
Home price ratio	2.2	4.2

NECESSITIES	AREA	U.S. AVG
Food Index	103.5	100.0
Housing Index	38.5	100.0
Utilities Index	75.6	100.0
Transportation Index	97.6	100.0
Healthcare Index	96.2	100.0
Miscellaneous Cost Index	98.2	100.0

Climate
Score: 15.2
Rank: 315

TEMPERATURE	AREA	U.S. AVG
Average January low	16.5	26.2
Average July high	83.8	87.4
Annual days > 90°F	16	38
Annual days < 32°F	147	89
Annual days < 0°F	5	6

PRECIPITATION	AREA	U.S. AVG
Annual inches precipitation	29.0	37.7
Annual inches snowfall	47.0	7.0
Annual days precipitation	181	109
Annual days rain > 0.5 inches	31	22
Annual days snow > 1.5 inches	10	6

COMFORTS & HAZARDS	AREA	U.S. AVG
July relative humidity	76%	66%
Annual days mostly sunny	163	208
Annual days with thunderstorms	38	39
Tornado risk score	8	18
Hurricane risk score	2	13

TEMPERATURE

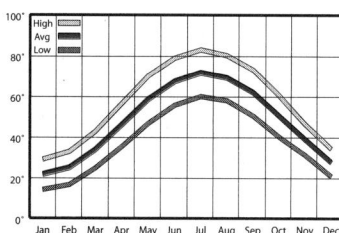

PRECIPITATION

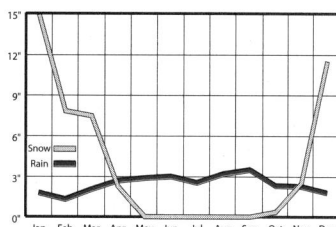

DAYS OF CLOUDS & PRECIPITATION

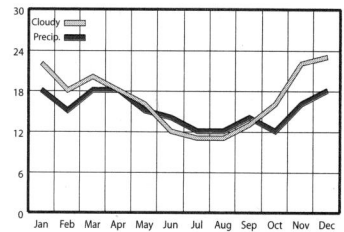

Education
Score: 15.2
Rank: 316

ACHIEVEMENT	AREA	U.S. AVG
High school degree	82.4%	82.7%
2-year college degree	8.0%	6.4%
4-year college degree	9.7%	15.7%
Graduate/professional degree	4.4%	8.9%

PUBLIC SCHOOLS	AREA	U.S. AVG
Expenditures per pupil	$6,024	$5,686
Student/teacher ratio	20.5	16.7
Attending public school	86.7%	90.1%
State SAT score	1151	1021
State ACT score	21.5*	20.9

HIGHER EDUCATION	AREA	U.S. AVG
No. 2-year colleges	1	4
No. 4-year colleges/universities	1	6
No. highly ranked universities	0	1

Health & Healthcare
Score: 53.5
Rank: 175

HAZARDS & ILLNESSES	AREA	U.S. AVG
Air-quality score	41	37
Water-quality score	30	52
Pollen/allergy score	47	61
Cancer mortality per capita	200.2	201.9
Depression days per month	4.0	3.5
Stress score	67	50

HEALTHCARE	AREA	U.S. AVG
Physicians per capita	160.8	244.2
Hospital beds per capita	372.8	420.0
No. teaching hospitals	1	3
Cost per doctor visit	$72	$77
Cost per dental visit	$69	$70

Crime
Score: 93.6
Rank: 24

CRIME	AREA	U.S. AVG
Violent crime rate	280.2	465.5
Change in violent crime rate	-1.1%	-2.2%
Property crime rate	2,685.1	3,517.1
Change in property crime rate	6.5%	-2.1%

Transportation
Score: 23.3
Rank: 288

COMMUTE	AREA	U.S. AVG
Average commute time	23.2	27.4
Percent commutes > 60 mins.	5.0%	5.9%
Commute by auto	87.4%	78.9%
Commute by mass transit	0.6%	1.9%
Work at home	2.7%	3.1%
Mass transit miles per capita	0.63	1.87

INTERCITY SERVICES	AREA	U.S. AVG
Major airports within 60 miles	0	1
Size of regional airport	Small	Large
Daily airline activity	175	686
Amtrak service	No	No

AUTOMOTIVE	AREA	U.S. AVG
Insurance, annual premium	$1,402	$1,432
Gas, cost per gallon	$2.54	$2.49
Daily vehicle miles per capita	25.4	24.0

Leisure
Score: 52.1
Rank: 178

DINING & SHOPPING	AREA	U.S. AVG
Restaurant rating	1	2
Outlet mall score	108	42
No. Starbucks	0	13
No. warehouse clubs	0	2

ENTERTAINMENT	AREA	U.S. AVG
Professional sports rating	2	4
College sports rating	4	4
Zoo/aquarium rating	2	3
Amusement park rating	1	3
Botanical garden/ arboretum rating	3	4

OUTDOOR ACTIVITIES	AREA	U.S. AVG
Golf-course rating	5	4
Ski-area rating	4	3
Sq. miles inland water	2	4
Miles of coastline	39.9	10.7
National Park rating	2	3

Arts & Culture
Score: 47.9
Rank: 195

MEDIA & LIBRARIES	AREA	U.S. AVG
Arts radio rating	1	3
No. public libraries	5	27
Library volumes per capita	2.75	2.78

PERFORMING ARTS	AREA	U.S. AVG
Classical music rating	4	4
Ballet/dance rating	1	3
Professional theater rating	1	3
University arts programs rating	3	5

MUSEUMS	AREA	U.S. AVG
Overall museum rating	3	5
Art museum rating	2	5
Science museum rating	1	5
Children's museum rating	1	3

Beaumont–Port Arthur, TX

Score: 47.0 **Rank:** 264 **2004 rank:** 183

Profile: Small-city complex
Location: Extreme southeast Texas near Gulf Coast and Louisiana border
Elevation: 16 feet
Time zone: Central Standard Time

PRO	CON
Cost of living	Hot, humid summers
Revitalized downtown	Industrial landscape
Outdoor recreation	Uncertain hurricane effects

The towns of Beaumont and Port Arthur are located 20 miles apart in extreme southeast Texas. Port Arthur is located on Sabine Lake, a body of water deep enough to support ocean shipping and connected to the Gulf by a canal. Beaumont is inland. The area's destiny changed in 1901 when the first oil well blew in the nearby Spindletop field, and it changed again in September 2005 when Hurricane Rita swept through the area. The 1901 event turned the area from a quiet lumber and port town into a thriving oil and gas economy, with one of the largest concentrations of oil refineries, oil, and petrochemical-related businesses in the state. The heavy industry and gentle decline of some of that industry took its toll on the city and its environs, but renewal programs in recent years put some life back into the cities, especially the downtown areas. Low living costs and nearby outdoor recreation opportunities brought some people back into the area. These folks found a small-town life and cost environment (COL index is 79.5) while being close enough to Houston to benefit from its big-city amenities. Then the hurricane hit and did some major damage to the city's infrastructure, nearby housing, and the economy. Recovery is under way, aided by federal relief programs, but full long-term effects on the population, economy, and quality of life are unclear.

The area is located on a flat coastal plain with mostly treeless areas near the coast giving way to large pine forests moving inland. Sea breezes usually prevent summer temperature extremes. The Gulf and evenly distributed rainfall give the area the highest relative humidity in the nation. Cloudy, rainy weather is most common in the winter. Heavy rainfall occurs during thunderstorms and infrequent tropical storms. Slower-moving storms bring longer periods of rain in spring and fall. Fog occurs especially in winter and spring.

Population

DEMOGRAPHICS	AREA	U.S. AVG
Population	384,524	
Population density per sq. mile	178.5	358.5
Population growth	6.7%	21.1%
Median age	36.1	36.1
Percent Democrat	44.7%	44.5%
Percent Republican	54.9%	54.5%

ETHNIC COMPOSITION	AREA	U.S. AVG
White	66.9%	79.0%
Black	25.4%	10.5%
Asian	2.1%	2.7%
Hispanic	9.2%	10.6%
Religious observance	64.3%	48.9%
Diversity measure	52.2	40.1

RESIDENT PROFILE	AREA	U.S. AVG
Single	29.5%	32.4%
Married	51.6%	52.7%
Divorced/separated	18.8%	14.9%
Married with children	23.2%	23.7%
Single with children	10.7%	9.1%
Percent over age 65	13.4%	12.9%

Economy & Jobs
Score: 39.3
Rank: 227

INCOME	AREA	U.S. AVG
Per capita income	$20,045	$23,235
Household income	$40,339	$46,414
Household income < $25K	31.9%	26.2%
Household income > $75K	21.8%	25.4%
Household income growth	12.9%	13.6%

EMPLOYMENT	AREA	U.S. AVG
Unemployment rate	7.1%	4.7%
Recent job growth	2.4%	1.3%
Projected future job growth	8.6%	11.5%
White collar	53.7%	57.8%
Blue collar	29.4%	25.2%

EMPLOYING INDUSTRIES	AREA	U.S. AVG
Largest: Manufacturing		
Percent manufacturing	16.0%	15.4%
Percent public sector	15.6%	15.7%
Percent construction	13.4%	9.9%

Cost of Living
Score: 92.2
Rank: 30

INDEXES & TAXES	AREA	U.S. AVG
Cost of Living Index	79.5	100.0
Buying Power Index	113.7	100.0
Income tax rate	0.00%	4.70%
Sales tax rate	7.99%	6.58%
Property tax rate	$16.53	$12.00

HOUSING	AREA	U.S. AVG
Median home price	$114,200	$220,000
Home price appreciation	23.5%	10.1%
Median rent	$593	$709
Homes owned	64.2%	62.3%
Home price ratio	2.8	4.2

NECESSITIES	AREA	U.S. AVG
Food Index	90.4	100.0
Housing Index	52.3	100.0
Utilities Index	96.5	100.0
Transportation Index	99.3	100.0
Healthcare Index	100.8	100.0
Miscellaneous Cost Index	98.7	100.0

Climate
Score: 69.3
Rank: 114

TEMPERATURE	AREA	U.S. AVG
Average January low	42.4	26.2
Average July high	92.0	87.4
Annual days › 90°F	84	38
Annual days ‹ 32°F	18	89
Annual days ‹ 0°F	0	6

PRECIPITATION	AREA	U.S. AVG
Annual inches precipitation	55.1	37.7
Annual inches snowfall	0.5	7.0
Annual days precipitation	104	109
Annual days rain › 0.5 inches	32	22
Annual days snow › 1.5 inches	0	6

COMFORTS & HAZARDS	AREA	U.S. AVG
July relative humidity	79%	66%
Annual days mostly sunny	217	208
Annual days with thunderstorms	64	39
Tornado risk score	64	18
Hurricane risk score	55	13

TEMPERATURE

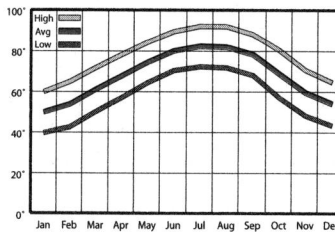

PRECIPITATION

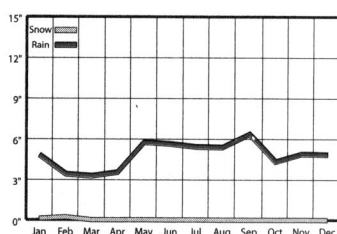

DAYS OF CLOUDS & PRECIPITATION

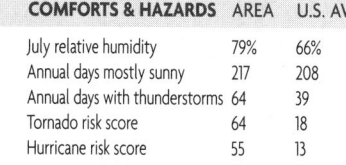

Education
Score: 18.7
Rank: 302

ACHIEVEMENT	AREA	U.S. AVG
High school degree	78.8%	82.7%
2-year college degree	5.3%	6.4%
4-year college degree	10.6%	15.7%
Graduate/professional degree	4.2%	8.9%

PUBLIC SCHOOLS	AREA	U.S. AVG
Expenditures per pupil	$5,190	$5,686
Student/teacher ratio	14.6	16.7
Attending public school	95.6%	90.1%
State SAT score	997*	1021
State ACT score	20.3	20.9

HIGHER EDUCATION	AREA	U.S. AVG
No. 2-year colleges	3	4
No. 4-year colleges/universities	1	6
No. highly ranked universities	0	1

Health & Healthcare
Score: 47.6
Rank: 197

HAZARDS & ILLNESSES	AREA	U.S. AVG
Air-quality score	24	37
Water-quality score	68	52
Pollen/allergy score	71	61
Cancer mortality per capita	181.6	201.9
Depression days per month	4.0	3.5
Stress score	89	50

HEALTHCARE	AREA	U.S. AVG
Physicians per capita	159.2	244.2
Hospital beds per capita	516.7	420.0
No. teaching hospitals	3	3
Cost per doctor visit	$71	$77
Cost per dental visit	$60	$70

Crime
Score: 16.3
Rank: 313

CRIME	AREA	U.S. AVG
Violent crime rate	547.0	465.5
Change in violent crime rate	4.2%	-2.2%
Property crime rate	4,498.0	3,517.1
Change in property crime rate	-2.1%	-2.1%

Transportation
Score: 80.2
Rank: 75

COMMUTE	AREA	U.S. AVG
Average commute time	23.4	27.4
Percent commutes › 60 mins.	4.6%	5.9%
Commute by auto	83.2%	78.9%
Commute by mass transit	0.6%	1.9%
Work at home	1.7%	3.1%
Mass transit miles per capita	0.63	1.87

INTERCITY SERVICES	AREA	U.S. AVG
Major airports within 60 miles	2	1
Size of regional airport	Large	Large
Daily airline activity	963	686
Amtrak service	Yes	No

AUTOMOTIVE	AREA	U.S. AVG
Insurance, annual premium	$1,211	$1,432
Gas, cost per gallon	$2.44	$2.49
Daily vehicle miles per capita	26.4	24.0

Leisure
Score: 51.1
Rank: 182

DINING & SHOPPING	AREA	U.S. AVG
Restaurant rating	1	2
Outlet mall score	1	42
No. Starbucks	1	13
No. warehouse clubs	1	2

ENTERTAINMENT	AREA	U.S. AVG
Professional sports rating	3	4
College sports rating	2	4
Zoo/aquarium rating	1	3
Amusement park rating	1	3
Botanical garden/ arboretum rating	5	4

OUTDOOR ACTIVITIES	AREA	U.S. AVG
Golf-course rating	3	4
Ski-area rating	1	3
Sq. miles inland water	6	4
Miles of coastline	31.9	10.7
National Park rating	5	3

Arts & Culture
Score: 45.5
Rank: 204

MEDIA & LIBRARIES	AREA	U.S. AVG
Arts radio rating	1	3
No. public libraries	20	27
Library volumes per capita	3.04	2.78

PERFORMING ARTS	AREA	U.S. AVG
Classical music rating	4	4
Ballet/dance rating	3	3
Professional theater rating	1	3
University arts programs rating	4	5

MUSEUMS	AREA	U.S. AVG
Overall museum rating	5	5
Art museum rating	5	5
Science museum rating	6	5
Children's museum rating	1	3

Bellingham, WA

Score: 95.1 **Rank:** 2 **2004 rank:** 38

Profile: Small city
Location: East shore of Puget Sound along I-5 in extreme northwest Washington, 25 miles south of Canadian border
Elevation: 68 feet
Time zone: Pacific Standard Time

PRO	CON
Attractive setting	Clouds and rain
Pleasant summers	Economic cycles
Nearby recreation	Some crime issues

Bellingham is a lush, green, rapidly growing, and typically Pacific Northwest city about halfway between Seattle and Vancouver. Its legacy, still in force to a degree, is as a thriving lumber and paper-mill town and seaport for outbound forest products. Today, the beautiful setting, climate, and relatively low costs for a West Coast location are bringing many migrants to the area. The economy is making the transition from cyclical basic industries to a more steady new-economy flavor. Residents may work locally, make the lengthy commute (likely in carpools) to Seattle and especially its northern suburbs, or telecommute or run small businesses serving clients in the larger cities. The community also has a strong and growing base of retirees. The city is also an important passenger gateway to Alaska and the San Juan Islands to the west. Downtown is clean and functional, while the secondary Fairhaven downtown district a few miles south at the ferry departure is a nicely preserved Victorian historic district. Western Washington University brings a college-town element. Some areas, notably north of the downtown, have a more working-class flavor, but the Lynden area, farther north almost at the Canadian border, is growing fast. Bigger city amenities are available to the south in Seattle and to the north in Vancouver,

British Columbia. Home prices are high on a national scale but are moderate for the state and especially the coast. While summers are very pleasant, other periods are among the cloudiest and rainiest in the United States. For those tolerant of these negatives and looking for a historic small town in a beautiful setting, Bellingham continues to be a good option and is worth of its no. 2 ranking.

Bellingham sits in a narrow and mainly level coastal plain along the Puget Sound. To the east and north the land rises sharply to low plateaus with mixed coniferous forests and cleared land. To the south the area is hilly with dense coniferous forests. The San Juan Islands rise dramatically from the Puget Sound to the west, and the 11,000-foot Mount Baker punctuates the sky 25 miles east. The pleasantly cool summers are the sunniest, driest time of year, albeit with some clouds and rain. The rest of the year is cloudy more often than not, with periods of mostly light rain. The good news: The rains are seldom torrential and it seldom turns to snow. Winters are damp and chilly but not cold; unlike most areas at this latitude, there are no days below zero and days below 20°F are rare. First freeze is early October; last is May 1.

DEMOGRAPHICS	AREA	U.S. AVG	ETHNIC COMPOSITION	AREA	U.S. AVG	RESIDENT PROFILE	AREA	U.S. AVG
Population	180,122		White	87.5%	79.0%	Single	34.4%	32.4%
Population density per sq. mile	85.0	358.5	Black	0.8%	10.5%	Married	51.7%	52.7%
Population growth	41.0%	21.1%	Asian	3.3%	2.7%	Divorced/separated	13.9%	14.9%
Median age	35.0	36.1	Hispanic	5.7%	10.6%	Married with children	22.3%	23.7%
Percent Democrat	53.4%	44.5%	Religious observance	29.4%	48.9%	Single with children	8.0%	9.1%
Percent Republican	44.6%	54.5%	Diversity measure	31.3	40.1	Percent over age 65	12.1%	12.9%

INCOME	AREA	U.S. AVG	EMPLOYMENT	AREA	U.S. AVG	EMPLOYING INDUSTRIES	AREA	U.S. AVG
Per capita income	$22,543	$23,235	Unemployment rate	4.8%	4.7%	Largest: Manufacturing		
Household income	$44,430	$46,414	Recent job growth	5.5%	1.3%			
Household income < $25K	26.9%	26.2%	Projected future job growth	27.6%	11.5%	Percent manufacturing	13.5%	15.4%
Household income > $75K	23.7%	25.4%	White collar	57.1%	57.8%	Percent public sector	15.2%	15.7%
Household income growth	11.1%	13.6%	Blue collar	23.6%	25.2%	Percent construction	10.1%	9.9%

Economy & Jobs
Score: 97.1
Rank: 12

INDEXES & TAXES	AREA	U.S. AVG	HOUSING	AREA	U.S. AVG	NECESSITIES	AREA	U.S. AVG
Cost of Living Index	99.2	100.0	Median home price	$213,400	$220,000	Food Index	103.5	100.0
Buying Power Index	100.4	100.0	Home price appreciation	83.1%	10.1%	Housing Index	84.2	100.0
Income tax rate	0.00%	4.70%	Median rent	$741	$709	Utilities Index	67.3	100.0
Sales tax rate	8.30%	6.58%	Homes owned	55.4%	62.3%	Transportation Index	110.4	100.0
Property tax rate	$11.34	$12.00	Home price ratio	4.8	4.2	Healthcare Index	118.8	100.0
						Miscellaneous Cost Index	104.4	100.0

Cost of Living
Score: 59.1
Rank: 153

Climate
Score: 82.4
Rank: 67

TEMPERATURE	AREA	U.S. AVG
Average January low	33.0	26.2
Average July high	75.1	87.4
Annual days > 90°F	3	38
Annual days < 32°F	32	89
Annual days < 0°F	0	6

PRECIPITATION	AREA	U.S. AVG
Annual inches precipitation	39.0	37.7
Annual inches snowfall	15.0	7.0
Annual days precipitation	160	109
Annual days rain > 0.5 inches	24	22
Annual days snow > 1.5 inches	2	6

COMFORTS & HAZARDS	AREA	U.S. AVG
July relative humidity	74%	66%
Annual days mostly sunny	136	208
Annual days with thunderstorms	7	39
Tornado risk score	0	18
Hurricane risk score	0	13

TEMPERATURE

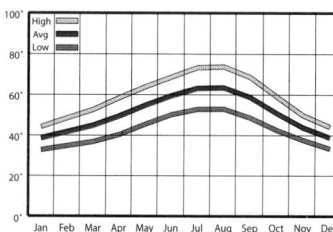

PRECIPITATION

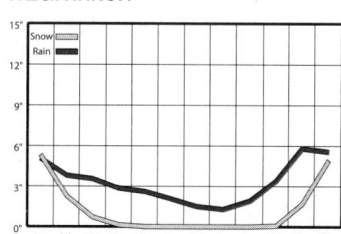

DAYS OF CLOUDS & PRECIPITATION

Education
Score: 64.2
Rank: 135

ACHIEVEMENT	AREA	U.S. AVG
High school degree	87.5%	82.7%
2-year college degree	7.3%	6.4%
4-year college degree	18.4%	15.7%
Graduate/professional degree	8.9%	8.9%

PUBLIC SCHOOLS	AREA	U.S. AVG
Expenditures per pupil	$5,349	$5,686
Student/teacher ratio	19.6	16.7
Attending public school	89.9%	90.1%
State SAT score	1059*	1021
State ACT score	22.9	20.9

HIGHER EDUCATION	AREA	U.S. AVG
No. 2-year colleges	4	4
No. 4-year colleges/universities	1	6
No. highly ranked universities	0	1

Health & Healthcare
Score: 27.3
Rank: 271

HAZARDS & ILLNESSES	AREA	U.S. AVG
Air-quality score	33	37
Water-quality score	60	52
Pollen/allergy score	48	61
Cancer mortality per capita	173.3	201.9
Depression days per month	3.4	3.5
Stress score	45	50

HEALTHCARE	AREA	U.S. AVG
Physicians per capita	223.7	244.2
Hospital beds per capita	119.4	420.0
No. teaching hospitals	0	3
Cost per doctor visit	$82	$77
Cost per dental visit	$83	$70

Crime
Score: 37.4
Rank: 234

CRIME	AREA	U.S. AVG
Violent crime rate	229.5	465.5
Change in violent crime rate	-6.2%	-2.2%
Property crime rate	5,215.6	3,517.1
Change in property crime rate	-1.1%	-2.1%

Transportation
Score: 72.7
Rank: 103

COMMUTE	AREA	U.S. AVG
Average commute time	22.2	27.4
Percent commutes > 60 mins.	5.1%	5.9%
Commute by auto	76.1%	78.9%
Commute by mass transit	1.9%	1.9%
Work at home	5.0%	3.1%
Mass transit miles per capita	1.94	1.87

INTERCITY SERVICES	AREA	U.S. AVG
Major airports within 60 miles	1	1
Size of regional airport	Large	Large
Daily airline activity	698	686
Amtrak service	Yes	No

AUTOMOTIVE	AREA	U.S. AVG
Insurance, annual premium	$1,322	$1,432
Gas, cost per gallon	$2.70	$2.49
Daily vehicle miles per capita	19.2	24.0

Leisure
Score: 66.6
Rank: 125

DINING & SHOPPING	AREA	U.S. AVG
Restaurant rating	1	2
Outlet mall score	0	42
No. Starbucks	10	13
No. warehouse clubs	1	2

ENTERTAINMENT	AREA	U.S. AVG
Professional sports rating	2	4
College sports rating	5	4
Zoo/aquarium rating	1	3
Amusement park rating	1	3
Botanical garden/ arboretum rating	1	4

OUTDOOR ACTIVITIES	AREA	U.S. AVG
Golf-course rating	1	4
Ski-area rating	8	3
Sq. miles inland water	5	4
Miles of coastline	0.0	10.7
National Park rating	10	3

Arts & Culture
Score: 59.9
Rank: 150

MEDIA & LIBRARIES	AREA	U.S. AVG
Arts radio rating	5	3
No. public libraries	11	27
Library volumes per capita	3.32	2.78

PERFORMING ARTS	AREA	U.S. AVG
Classical music rating	3	4
Ballet/dance rating	3	3
Professional theater rating	1	3
University arts programs rating	4	5

MUSEUMS	AREA	U.S. AVG
Overall museum rating	4	5
Art museum rating	6	5
Science museum rating	4	5
Children's museum rating	5	3

Bend, OR

Score: 77.6 Rank: 56 2004 rank: not ranked

Profile: Small resort city
Location: Central Oregon, just east of the Cascade Range
Elevation: 3,623 feet
Time zone: Pacific Standard Time

PRO	CON
Attractive setting	Cost of living and housing
Outdoor recreation	Arts and culture
Pleasant climate	Isolation

Bend is an artsy resort community in the high Oregon desert just east of the Cascade Range and the Mount Bachelor ski area. To Oregon, it is what Aspen is to Colorado or Truckee/Lake Tahoe is to California—with a fairly upscale clientele, several nearby resort communities, and an attractive small downtown. Quite obviously Bend has been discovered for its recreation opportunities, climate, and small-town atmosphere, and has grown rapidly (by nearly 83% from 1990 to 2005) as a retreat for retirees, young people, and self-employed or small-business workers with only occasional need for a bigger city. This rapid growth aggravates the downsides of increasing living and housing costs and has brought some areas of unattractive sprawl. The private industry base is fairly small and jobs outside of the public sector or tourist industry are hard to find; that said, overall job-growth projections are strong.

The 160-mile drive to Portland is difficult, particularly in winter. But for now, Bend remains a highly desirable and relatively affordable address by West Coast standards.

Bend is in an attractive setting located at the western edge of the high plateau area that comprises much of central Oregon. The Cascade Range lies just west. Bend sits at the transition between coniferous forest and a high sagebrush desert, with several broad creek valleys moving west from the town into the mountains. The climate is semi-arid with an abundance of sunshine and a wide range between daytime and nighttime temperatures. Summer thundershowers and occasional winter rain and snows provide most of the moisture. Snow cover is generally light but much heavier to the west in the mountains.

Population

DEMOGRAPHICS	AREA	U.S. AVG	ETHNIC COMPOSITION	AREA	U.S. AVG	RESIDENT PROFILE	AREA	U.S. AVG
Population	136,927		White	94.1%	79.0%	Single	25.4%	32.4%
Population density per sq. mile	45.4	358.5	Black	0.4%	10.5%	Married	60.2%	52.7%
Population growth	82.7%	21.1%	Asian	1.0%	2.7%	Divorced/separated	14.5%	14.9%
Median age	38.3	36.1	Hispanic	4.4%	10.6%	Married with children	23.8%	23.7%
Percent Democrat	42.1%	44.5%	Religious observance	26.9%	48.9%	Single with children	8.3%	9.1%
Percent Republican	56.4%	54.5%	Diversity measure	18.8	40.1	Percent over age 65	13.5%	12.9%

Economy & Jobs
Score: 94.9
Rank: 20

INCOME	AREA	U.S. AVG	EMPLOYMENT	AREA	U.S. AVG	EMPLOYING INDUSTRIES	AREA	U.S. AVG
Per capita income	$25,423	$23,235	Unemployment rate	5.5%	4.7%	Largest: Healthcare & Social Assistance		
Household income	$47,866	$46,414	Recent job growth	4.4%	1.3%			
Household income < $25K	21.6%	26.2%	Projected future job growth	30.8%	11.5%	Percent manufacturing	12.6%	15.4%
Household income > $75K	26.5%	25.4%	White collar	58.3%	57.8%	Percent public sector	12.5%	15.7%
Household income growth	14.4%	13.6%	Blue collar	25.6%	25.2%	Percent construction	13.0%	9.9%

Cost of Living
Score: 40.4
Rank: 222

INDEXES & TAXES	AREA	U.S. AVG	HOUSING	AREA	U.S. AVG	NECESSITIES	AREA	U.S. AVG
Cost of Living Index	102.2	100.0	Median home price	$229,000	$220,000	Food Index	101.2	100.0
Buying Power Index	105.0	100.0	Home price appreciation	80.2%	10.1%	Housing Index	85.4	100.0
Income tax rate	9.00%	4.70%	Median rent	$700	$709	Utilities Index	87.4	100.0
Sales tax rate	0.00%	6.58%	Homes owned	60.6%	62.3%	Transportation Index	100.9	100.0
Property tax rate	$11.40	$12.00	Home price ratio	4.8	4.2	Healthcare Index	124.0	100.0
						Miscellaneous Cost Index	104.5	100.0

Climate
Score: 66.8
Rank: 123

TEMPERATURE	AREA	U.S. AVG	PRECIPITATION	AREA	U.S. AVG	COMFORTS & HAZARDS	AREA	U.S. AVG
Average January low	21.6	26.2	Annual inches precipitation	44.2	37.7	July relative humidity	25%	66%
Average July high	82.0	87.4	Annual inches snowfall	32.6	7.0	Annual days mostly sunny	194	208
Annual days > 90°F	15	38	Annual days precipitation	77	109	Annual days with thunderstorms	10	39
Annual days < 32°F	54	89	Annual days rain > 0.5 inches	3	22	Tornado risk score	1	18
Annual days < 0°F	4	6	Annual days snow > 1.5 inches	6	6	Hurricane risk score	0	13

TEMPERATURE

PRECIPITATION

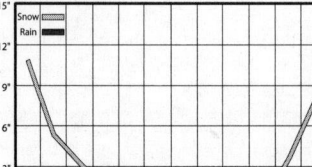

DAYS OF CLOUDS & PRECIPITATION

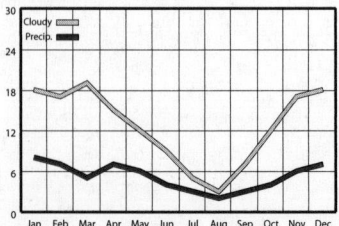

ACHIEVEMENT	AREA	U.S. AVG	PUBLIC SCHOOLS	AREA	U.S. AVG	HIGHER EDUCATION	AREA	U.S. AVG
High school degree	88.6%	82.7%	Expenditures per pupil	$6,080	$5,686	No. 2-year colleges	2	4
2-year college degree	7.8%	6.4%	Student/teacher ratio	20.7	16.7	No. 4-year colleges/universities	1	6
4-year college degree	17.4%	15.7%	Attending public school	93.9%	90.1%	No. highly ranked universities	0	1
Graduate/professional degree	7.9%	8.9%	State SAT score	1052*	1021			
			State ACT score	22.4	20.9			

Education
Score: 66.8
Rank: 125

HAZARDS & ILLNESSES	AREA	U.S. AVG	HEALTHCARE	AREA	U.S. AVG	CRIME	AREA	U.S. AVG
Air-quality score	34	37	Physicians per capita	230.9	244.2	Violent crime rate	213.6	465.5
Water-quality score	60	52	Hospital beds per capita	168.7	420.0	Change in violent crime rate	23.0%	-2.2%
Pollen/allergy score	53	61	No. teaching hospitals	1	3	Property crime rate	4,384.9	3,517.1
Cancer mortality per capita	194.8	201.9	Cost per doctor visit	$111	$77	Change in property crime rate	-2.6%	-2.1%
Depression days per month	3.3	3.5	Cost per dental visit	$83	$70			
Stress score	34	50						

Health & Healthcare
Score: 25.7
Rank: 277

Crime
Score: 84.5
Rank: 59

COMMUTE	AREA	U.S. AVG	INTERCITY SERVICES	AREA	U.S. AVG	AUTOMOTIVE	AREA	U.S. AVG
Average commute time	20.2	27.4	Major airports within 60 miles	0	1	Insurance, annual premium	$1,159	$1,432
Percent commutes > 60 mins.	3.2%	5.9%	Size of regional airport	Small	Large	Gas, cost per gallon	$2.49	$2.49
Commute by auto	75.5%	78.9%	Daily airline activity	51	686	Daily vehicle miles per capita	20.2	24.0
Commute by mass transit	0.8%	1.9%	Amtrak service	No	No			
Work at home	6.6%	3.1%						
Mass transit miles per capita	0.77	1.87						

Transportation
Score: 47.6
Rank: 197

DINING & SHOPPING	AREA	U.S. AVG	ENTERTAINMENT	AREA	U.S. AVG	OUTDOOR ACTIVITIES	AREA	U.S. AVG
Restaurant rating	2	2	Professional sports rating	1	4	Golf-course rating	6	4
Outlet mall score	0	42	College sports rating	1	4	Ski-area rating	10	3
No. Starbucks	6	13	Zoo/aquarium rating	1	3	Sq. miles inland water	3	4
No. warehouse clubs	1	2	Amusement park rating	1	3	Miles of coastline	0.0	10.7
			Botanical garden/ arboretum rating	8	4	National Park rating	8	3

Leisure
Score: 63.4
Rank: 137

MEDIA & LIBRARIES	AREA	U.S. AVG	PERFORMING ARTS	AREA	U.S. AVG	MUSEUMS	AREA	U.S. AVG
Arts radio rating	2	3	Classical music rating	2	4	Overall museum rating	3	5
No. public libraries	5	27	Ballet/dance rating	1	3	Art museum rating	1	5
Library volumes per capita	2.64	2.78	Professional theater rating	2	3	Science museum rating	5	5
			University arts programs rating	1	5	Children's museum rating	1	3

Arts & Culture
Score: 8.0
Rank: 343

Bergen–Passaic, NJ

Score: 71.9   Rank: 77   2004 rank: 176

Profile: Suburban complex
Location: Northeastern corner of New Jersey, adjacent to New York State, and across the lower Hudson from New York City
Elevation: 72 feet
Time zone: Eastern Standard Time

PRO	CON
Close to New York City	Cost of living and housing
Attractive residential areas	Long commutes
Low crime	Low employment growth

The Bergen–Passaic area is one of the few where we chose to depart from the U.S. Office of Management and Budget (OMB) definitions of MSAs. Why? Because OMB lumped it together with New York City and its in-state suburbs. We thought that was wrong, because, although right across the river, we feel this area has a unique and decidedly less urban character and somewhat different economic factors deserving separate treatment. So we retained the Bergen–Passaic definition used in the first edition of this book.

Bergen County is a complex patchwork of commercial and residential activity, with more than 100 villages and towns spread along major transportation corridors and between those corridors moving west from the Hudson River. Many of these small towns have an upscale, rural char-

acter surprising for their proximity to New York City. Only four of these communities—Teaneck, Paramus, Bergenfield, and Paterson—have populations exceeding 25,000. The northern part of Bergen County is particularly pleasant, with mature, wooded residential areas and attractive, functional small-town centers. There is good rail service to New York, and good recreational opportunities lie to the north and west. Primary and secondary education in most locales is particularly strong. Moving south toward Paramus and Passaic, the area has a more middle-class feel, with suburbs, shopping malls, and a variety of commercial/industrial establishments. There are areas of poverty and urban decay around Paterson and other larger, older settlements. Several corporations have their headquarters here, including Union Camp, Toys "R" Us, and Becton, Dickinson and Company. It's also a favorite location for U.S. subsidiaries of European companies. The cost of living and housing are among the highest in New Jersey and nation,

The area starts at the east with high, densely wooded bluffs overlooking the Hudson River across from Upper Manhattan, the Bronx, and Yonkers. Most of the area is rolling to hilly and heavily wooded, with a few flat and heavily developed areas and a series of straight valleys serving as transportation corridors. The area is warm and humid in the summer; afternoon thundershowers are common. Winters are cool and wet, receiving both snow and rain. Heavy snows do occur, particularly with coastal "noreaster" storms, and freezing rain once or twice a winter is common. Below-zero temperatures are not common. Spring is variable and wet, while fall is pleasant usually with at least one period of Indian summer. First freeze is mid-October; last is late April.

Population

DEMOGRAPHICS	AREA	U.S. AVG	ETHNIC COMPOSITION	AREA	U.S. AVG	RESIDENT PROFILE	AREA	U.S. AVG
Population	2,009,955		White	65.0%	79.0%	Single	37.5%	32.4%
Population density per sq. mile	4305.9	358.5	Black	9.6%	10.5%	Married	48.9%	52.7%
Population growth	9.7%	21.1%	Asian	9.6%	2.7%	Divorced/separated	13.6%	14.9%
Median age	37.7	36.1	Hispanic	26.6%	10.6%	Married with children	23.9%	23.7%
Percent Democrat	57.4%	44.5%	Religious observance	64.7%	48.9%	Single with children	8.0%	9.1%
Percent Republican	41.9%	54.5%	Diversity measure	68.4	40.1	Percent over age 65	13.3%	12.9%

Economy & Jobs

Score: 48.4
Rank: 194

INCOME	AREA	U.S. AVG	EMPLOYMENT	AREA	U.S. AVG	EMPLOYING INDUSTRIES	AREA	U.S. AVG
Per capita income	$30,648	$23,235	Unemployment rate	4.2%	4.7%	Largest: Finance & Insurance		
Household income	$61,021	$46,414	Recent job growth	2.1%	1.3%			
Household income < $25K	20.2%	26.2%	Projected future job growth	10.4%	11.5%	Percent manufacturing	13.8%	15.4%
Household income > $75K	39.7%	25.4%	White collar	66.2%	57.8%	Percent public sector	11.8%	15.7%
Household income growth	13.7%	13.6%	Blue collar	20.7%	25.2%	Percent construction	6.9%	9.9%

Cost of Living

Score: 5.6
Rank: 352

INDEXES & TAXES	AREA	U.S. AVG	HOUSING	AREA	U.S. AVG	NECESSITIES	AREA	U.S. AVG
Cost of Living Index	151.5	100.0	Median home price	$437,000	$220,000	Food Index	121.9	100.0
Buying Power Index	90.3	100.0	Home price appreciation	92.0%	10.1%	Housing Index	148.4	100.0
Income tax rate	2.45%	4.70%	Median rent	$1,160	$709	Utilities Index	137.1	100.0
Sales tax rate	6.00%	6.58%	Homes owned	51.6%	62.3%	Transportation Index	119.4	100.0
Property tax rate	$23.00	$12.00	Home price ratio	7.2	4.2	Healthcare Index	150.3	100.0
						Miscellaneous Cost Index	120.8	100.0

Climate

Score: 45.7
Rank: 201

TEMPERATURE	AREA	U.S. AVG	PRECIPITATION	AREA	U.S. AVG	COMFORTS & HAZARDS	AREA	U.S. AVG
Average January low	24.3	26.2	Annual inches precipitation	41.5	37.7	July relative humidity	65%	66%
Average July high	85.6	87.4	Annual inches snowfall	28.4	7.0	Annual days mostly sunny	207	208
Annual days > 90°F	20	38	Annual days precipitation	129	109	Annual days with thunderstorms	25	39
Annual days < 32°F	87	89	Annual days rain > 0.5 inches	26	22	Tornado risk score	14	18
Annual days < 0°F	0	6	Annual days snow > 1.5 inches	5	6	Hurricane risk score	17	13

TEMPERATURE

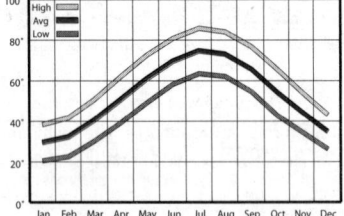

PRECIPITATION

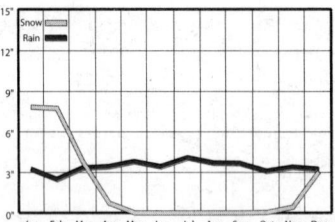

DAYS OF CLOUDS & PRECIPITATION

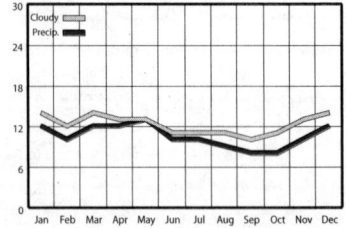

Education

Score: 58.0
Rank: 158

ACHIEVEMENT	AREA	U.S. AVG	PUBLIC SCHOOLS	AREA	U.S. AVG	HIGHER EDUCATION	AREA	U.S. AVG
High school degree	78.3%	82.7%	Expenditures per pupil	$6,576	$5,686	No. 2-year colleges	6	4
2-year college degree	4.4%	6.4%	Student/teacher ratio	15.2	16.7	No. 4-year colleges/universities	9	6
4-year college degree	19.3%	15.7%	Attending public school	82.4%	90.1%	No. highly ranked universities	2	1
Graduate/professional degree	10.8%	8.9%	State SAT score	1011*	1021			
			State ACT score	21.8	20.9			

Health & Healthcare

Score: 23.0
Rank: 287

Crime

Score: 78.9
Rank: 80

HAZARDS & ILLNESSES	AREA	U.S. AVG	HEALTHCARE	AREA	U.S. AVG	CRIME	AREA	U.S. AVG
Air-quality score	24	37	Physicians per capita	316.9	244.2	Violent crime rate	401.3	465.5
Water-quality score	33	52	Hospital beds per capita	375.0	420.0	Change in violent crime rate	-6.9%	-2.2%
Pollen/allergy score	62	61	No. teaching hospitals	8	3	Property crime rate	2,285.6	3,517.1
Cancer mortality per capita	204.7	201.9	Cost per doctor visit	$70	$77	Change in property crime rate	-4.4%	-2.1%
Depression days per month	3.5	3.5	Cost per dental visit	$83	$70			
Stress score	37	50						

Transportation Score: 91.7 Rank: 32	COMMUTE	AREA	U.S. AVG	INTERCITY SERVICES	AREA	U.S. AVG	AUTOMOTIVE	AREA	U.S. AVG
	Average commute time	32.5	27.4	Major airports within 60 miles	4	1	Insurance, annual premium	$2,234	$1,432
	Percent commutes > 60 mins.	12.9%	5.9%	Size of regional airport	Large	Large	Gas, cost per gallon	$2.34	$2.49
	Commute by auto	63.1%	78.9%	Daily airline activity	2696	686	Daily vehicle miles per capita	23.1	24.0
	Commute by mass transit	17.1%	1.9%	Amtrak service	No	No			
	Work at home	2.5%	3.1%						
	Mass transit miles per capita	6.30	1.87						

Leisure Score: 88.8 Rank: 43	DINING & SHOPPING	AREA	U.S. AVG	ENTERTAINMENT	AREA	U.S. AVG	OUTDOOR ACTIVITIES	AREA	U.S. AVG
	Restaurant rating	1	2	Professional sports rating	10	4	Golf-course rating	9	4
	Outlet mall score	23	42	College sports rating	8	4	Ski-area rating	5	3
	No. Starbucks	26	13	Zoo/aquarium rating	6	3	Sq. miles inland water	6	4
	No. warehouse clubs	6	2	Amusement park rating	5	3	Miles of coastline	0.0	10.7
				Botanical garden/ arboretum rating	7	4	National Park rating	3	3

Arts & Culture Score: 86.4 Rank: 52	MEDIA & LIBRARIES	AREA	U.S. AVG	PERFORMING ARTS	AREA	U.S. AVG	MUSEUMS	AREA	U.S. AVG
	Arts radio rating	4	3	Classical music rating	7	4	Overall museum rating	10	5
	No. public libraries	110	27	Ballet/dance rating	8	3	Art museum rating	8	5
	Library volumes per capita	3.59	2.78	Professional theater rating	8	3	Science museum rating	9	5
				University arts programs rating	10	5	Children's museum rating	9	3

Bethesda–Gaithersburg–Frederick, MD

Score: 73.4 Rank: 70 2004 rank: 26

Profile: Suburban complex
Location: North and northwest of the District of Columbia
Elevation: 303 feet
Time zone: Eastern Standard Time

PRO
Employment and incomes
Education
Attractive housing

CON
Cost of living and housing
Growth and sprawl
Long commutes

The bulk of the Bethesda–Gaithersburg–Frederick metro area really represents, and is known to most locals, as Montgomery County, a large and prosperous county adjacent to the northern "corner" border of Washington, D.C. Frederick County is just to the north. Much of the economic activity and residential core lies along Interstate 270 heading northwest and the heavily traveled Interstate 495 beltway that circles Washington. The area includes not only the three communities named but also such Washington suburbs as Silver Spring, Chevy Chase, and Rockville, as well as the town of Germantown farther north. For the most part, this area, and especially the central and western Montgomery County portions, is affluent, with high incomes, an abundance of high-paying jobs, and excellent education. On the whole, this is the most affluent part of the greater Washington area.

The list of corporate residents is lengthy and concentrated in the Rockville and Gaithersburg areas, with numerous high-tech, biotech, and high-level government contractors occupying endless concrete and glass buildings mainly along Interstate 270. Many federal government agencies also have offices, and many corporations, if they don't produce in the area, have an office to serve the region and manage government affairs. Incomes are high, but so is cost of living. The COL index of 139.5 and median home price at $451,600 are far higher than most other metro areas and even the rest of the Washington metro area. However, the high median incomes give a relatively strong Buying Power Index of 128.4.

Geographically, the area is large, and as a generalization, is wooded and mostly residential with attractive homes on large lots being the standard. The towns themselves, especially Gaithersburg and Frederick to the north, have interesting and well-preserved old historic cores. Frederick, in fact, received a Great American Main Street Award in 2005 for its preservation efforts. The Montgomery County school system has an excellent reputation, and local educational attainment levels are among the highest anywhere, providing a strong educational context. While Washington itself serves as the primary cultural center for the region, amenities are growing in the suburbs, and many never travel to Washington except for special occasions. For those who do travel into the District, public transportation facilities are excellent, but if you don't use them and it's rush hour, look out. Growth and urban sprawl, and their impacts on transportation, air quality, and overall quality of life are at the top of this area's agenda.

The Bethesda–Gaithersburg–Frederick area lies in a zone of gently rolling hills predominantly covered with thick deciduous trees. There are flat, agricultural valleys especially moving north towards Frederick. Summers are warm and humid with occasional hot, sticky spells and thunderstorms. Winters are cold but not severe. Precipitation is uniformly distributed throughout the year. Normal winter snowfall is moderate, but the storm track and moisture can align at times to produce very heavy snowfall; snows of 25 inches or more do occur. First freeze is early November; last is April 1.

Population

DEMOGRAPHICS	AREA	U.S. AVG	ETHNIC COMPOSITION	AREA	U.S. AVG	RESIDENT PROFILE	AREA	U.S. AVG
Population	1,158,319		White	68.1%	79.0%	Single	31.3%	32.4%
Population density per sq. mile	999.9	358.5	Black	12.4%	10.5%	Married	56.0%	52.7%
Population growth	27.6%	21.1%	Asian	11.0%	2.7%	Divorced/separated	12.6%	14.9%
Median age	37.9	36.1	Hispanic	10.8%	10.6%	Married with children	28.3%	23.7%
Percent Democrat	60.9%	44.5%	Religious observance	51.7%	48.9%	Single with children	7.2%	9.1%
Percent Republican	37.9%	54.5%	Diversity measure	58.0	40.1	Percent over age 65	11.4%	12.9%

Economy & Jobs
Score: 68.7
Rank: 118

INCOME	AREA	U.S. AVG	EMPLOYMENT	AREA	U.S. AVG	EMPLOYING INDUSTRIES	AREA	U.S. AVG
Per capita income	$38,876	$23,235	Unemployment rate	3.5%	4.7%	Largest: Professional, Scientific & Technical Services		
Household income	$79,883	$46,414	Recent job growth	2.0%	1.3%			
Household income < $25K	10.6%	26.2%	Projected future job growth	11.3%	11.5%	Percent manufacturing	5.4%	15.4%
Household income > $75K	52.7%	25.4%	White collar	76.3%	57.8%	Percent public sector	21.4%	15.7%
Household income growth	15.1%	13.6%	Blue collar	11.7%	25.2%	Percent construction	6.3%	9.9%

Cost of Living
Score: 5.1
Rank: 354

INDEXES & TAXES	AREA	U.S. AVG	HOUSING	AREA	U.S. AVG	NECESSITIES	AREA	U.S. AVG
Cost of Living Index	139.5	100.0	Median home price	$451,600	$220,000	Food Index	103.6	100.0
Buying Power Index	128.4	100.0	Home price appreciation	115.2%	10.1%	Housing Index	173.6	100.0
Income tax rate	9.45%	4.70%	Median rent	$1,286	$709	Utilities Index	98.8	100.0
Sales tax rate	5.00%	6.58%	Homes owned	68.4%	62.3%	Transportation Index	105.7	100.0
Property tax rate	$11.53	$12.00	Home price ratio	5.7	4.2	Healthcare Index	107.9	100.0
						Miscellaneous Cost Index	103.8	100.0

Climate
Score: 42.0
Rank: 216

TEMPERATURE	AREA	U.S. AVG	PRECIPITATION	AREA	U.S. AVG	COMFORTS & HAZARDS	AREA	U.S. AVG
Average January low	27.7	26.2	Annual inches precipitation	39.0	37.7	July relative humidity	64%	66%
Average July high	88.2	87.4	Annual inches snowfall	16.0	7.0	Annual days mostly sunny	207	208
Annual days > 90°F	37	38	Annual days precipitation	111	109	Annual days with thunderstorms	29	39
Annual days < 32°F	75	89	Annual days rain > 0.5 inches	27	22	Tornado risk score	12	18
Annual days < 0°F	0	6	Annual days snow > 1.5 inches	4	6	Hurricane risk score	13	13

TEMPERATURE

PRECIPITATION

DAYS OF CLOUDS & PRECIPITATION

Education
Score: 93.6
Rank: 25

ACHIEVEMENT	AREA	U.S. AVG	PUBLIC SCHOOLS	AREA	U.S. AVG	HIGHER EDUCATION	AREA	U.S. AVG
High school degree	89.8%	82.7%	Expenditures per pupil	$7,762	$5,686	No. 2-year colleges	3	4
2-year college degree	5.0%	6.4%	Student/teacher ratio	27.2	16.7	No. 4-year colleges/universities	6	6
4-year college degree	25.5%	15.7%	Attending public school	82.8%	90.1%	No. highly ranked universities	1	1
Graduate/professional degree	24.2%	8.9%	State SAT score	1012*	1021			
			State ACT score	21.4	20.9			

Health & Healthcare
Score: 44.9
Rank: 207

Crime
Score: 86.4
Rank: 52

HAZARDS & ILLNESSES	AREA	U.S. AVG	HEALTHCARE	AREA	U.S. AVG	CRIME	AREA	U.S. AVG
Air-quality score	24	37	Physicians per capita	552.6	244.2	Violent crime rate	255.4	465.5
Water-quality score	50	52	Hospital beds per capita	185.4	420.0	Change in violent crime rate	-0.3%	-2.2%
Pollen/allergy score	68	61	No. teaching hospitals	3	3	Property crime rate	2,302.2	3,517.1
Cancer mortality per capita	148.0	201.9	Cost per doctor visit	$91	$77	Change in property crime rate	-0.5%	-2.1%
Depression days per month	2.8	3.5	Cost per dental visit	$83	$70			
Stress score	11	50						

Transportation
Score: 49.5
Rank: 190

COMMUTE	AREA	U.S. AVG	INTERCITY SERVICES	AREA	U.S. AVG	AUTOMOTIVE	AREA	U.S. AVG
Average commute time	35.8	27.4	Major airports within 60 miles	3	1	Insurance, annual premium	$2,016	$1,432
Percent commutes > 60 mins.	14.0%	5.9%	Size of regional airport	Large	Large	Gas, cost per gallon	$2.54	$2.49
Commute by auto	71.3%	78.9%	Daily airline activity	1722	686	Daily vehicle miles per capita	27.7	24.0
Commute by mass transit	10.2%	1.9%	Amtrak service	Yes	No			
Work at home	4.7%	3.1%						
Mass transit miles per capita	10.24	1.87						

DINING & SHOPPING	AREA	U.S. AVG	ENTERTAINMENT	AREA	U.S. AVG	OUTDOOR ACTIVITIES	AREA	U.S. AVG
Restaurant rating	3	2	Professional sports rating	9	4	Golf-course rating	10	4
Outlet mall score	108	42	College sports rating	9	4	Ski-area rating	2	3
No. Starbucks	42	13	Zoo/aquarium rating	10	3	Sq. miles inland water	8	4
No. warehouse clubs	2	2	Amusement park rating	2	3	Miles of coastline	0.0	10.7
			Botanical garden/ arboretum rating	9	4	National Park rating	4	3

Leisure
Score: 92.5
Rank: 29

MEDIA & LIBRARIES	AREA	U.S. AVG	PERFORMING ARTS	AREA	U.S. AVG	MUSEUMS	AREA	U.S. AVG
Arts radio rating	9	3	Classical music rating	10	4	Overall museum rating	8	5
No. public libraries	27	27	Ballet/dance rating	9	3	Art museum rating	7	5
Library volumes per capita	2.97	2.78	Professional theater rating	10	3	Science museum rating	10	5
			University arts programs rating	10	5	Children's museum rating	9	3

Arts & Culture
Score: 96.5
Rank: 13

Billings, MT
Score: 65.3 **Rank:** 138 **2004 rank:** 106

Profile: Small city
Location: South-central Montana along the Yellowstone River
Elevation: 3,570 feet
Time zone: Mountain Standard Time

PRO	CON
Nearby mountains	Harsh winters
Water recreation	Isolation
Pleasant summers	Low ethnic diversity

Montana's largest city, Billings is a growing cultural and business center for a large area in Montana and northern Wyoming. Since the days of Lewis and Clark, it has also served as a transportation gateway between the plains to the east and the mountain areas to the west. The area is characterized by the dramatic landscape to the west, pleasant summer weather, and a strong Western flavor. Not unlike other mountain towns such as Boise, Spokane, and Reno, the combination of local services, small-town flavor, setting, and recreational opportunities draws some permanent migrants, retirees, and seasonal population, and provides some employment servicing these groups. The economy otherwise is supported by forest products, mineral, and petroleum industries with an assortment of business interests typically found in a city serving a large rural geography. The surroundings are eye-catching, but the city and its suburbs are generally not. Downtown is plain and uninspiring, with most suburbs, also fairly plain, spreading up the side of the Yellowstone Valley to the northwest. Downsides include winter cold and the 500-plus mile trip to Denver, the nearest big city.

The area is situated in the Yellowstone River valley between the Great Plains and the Rocky Mountains. The Yellowstone River, a world-class fly-fishing stream, bisects the city, and the surrounding countryside is mainly dry bluffs, rolling plains, and irrigated farmland. To the west, the land rises and becomes more rugged towards the Absaroka Range with peaks exceeding 11,000 feet. The summer season is warm with abundant sunshine and low humidity. Nights are cool from altitude and cool mountain breezes. Winters are cold and sometimes windy but with mild periods. Spring brings wide fluctuations with periods of cool, cloudy, rainy days. Falls vary in length; some last into December, others end in September. First freeze averages late September but can occur in late August; last freeze is mid-May but can be as late as the end of June.

DEMOGRAPHICS	AREA	U.S. AVG	ETHNIC COMPOSITION	AREA	U.S. AVG	RESIDENT PROFILE	AREA	U.S. AVG
Population	144,970		White	92.1%	79.0%	Single	30.0%	32.4%
Population density per sq. mile	31.0	358.5	Black	0.5%	10.5%	Married	55.0%	52.7%
Population growth	19.3%	21.1%	Asian	0.7%	2.7%	Divorced/separated	15.0%	14.9%
Median age	38.3	36.1	Hispanic	3.8%	10.6%	Married with children	22.7%	23.7%
Percent Democrat	36.3%	44.5%	Religious observance	47.9%	48.9%	Single with children	8.5%	9.1%
Percent Republican	61.8%	54.5%	Diversity measure	21.0	40.1	Percent over age 65	13.9%	12.9%

Population

INCOME	AREA	U.S. AVG	EMPLOYMENT	AREA	U.S. AVG	EMPLOYING INDUSTRIES	AREA	U.S. AVG
Per capita income	$22,573	$23,235	Unemployment rate	3.3%	4.7%	Largest: Healthcare & Social Assistance		
Household income	$42,314	$46,414	Recent job growth	2.4%	1.3%			
Household income < $25K	28.8%	26.2%	Projected future job growth	14.3%	11.5%	Percent manufacturing	11.4%	15.4%
Household income > $75K	21.0%	25.4%	White collar	60.7%	57.8%	Percent public sector	12.3%	15.7%
Household income growth	16.2%	13.6%	Blue collar	20.6%	25.2%	Percent construction	9.3%	9.9%

Economy & Jobs
Score: 70.1
Rank: 113

INDEXES & TAXES	AREA	U.S. AVG	HOUSING	AREA	U.S. AVG	NECESSITIES	AREA	U.S. AVG
Cost of Living Index	84.6	100.0	Median home price	$127,700	$220,000	Food Index	98.8	100.0
Buying Power Index	112.1	100.0	Home price appreciation	46.7%	10.1%	Housing Index	55.6	100.0
Income tax rate	10.00%	4.70%	Median rent	$598	$709	Utilities Index	103.4	100.0
Sales tax rate	0.00%	6.58%	Homes owned	65.9%	62.3%	Transportation Index	99.7	100.0
Property tax rate	$12.98	$12.00	Home price ratio	3.0	4.2	Healthcare Index	103.9	100.0
						Miscellaneous Cost Index	99.4	100.0

Cost of Living
Score: 78.3
Rank: 82

Climate
Score: 6.7
Rank: 348

TEMPERATURE	AREA	U.S. AVG
Average January low	12.5	26.2
Average July high	85.6	87.4
Annual days > 90°F	28	38
Annual days < 32°F	152	89
Annual days < 0°F	18	6

PRECIPITATION	AREA	U.S. AVG
Annual inches precipitation	14.0	37.7
Annual inches snowfall	56.0	7.0
Annual days precipitation	95	109
Annual days rain > 0.5 inches	8	22
Annual days snow > 1.5 inches	15	6

COMFORTS & HAZARDS	AREA	U.S. AVG
July relative humidity	55%	66%
Annual days mostly sunny	206	208
Annual days with thunderstorms	29	39
Tornado risk score	7	18
Hurricane risk score	0	13

TEMPERATURE

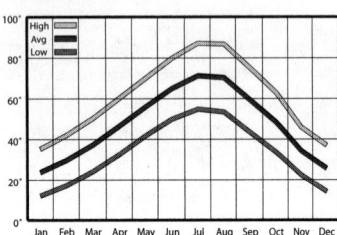

PRECIPITATION

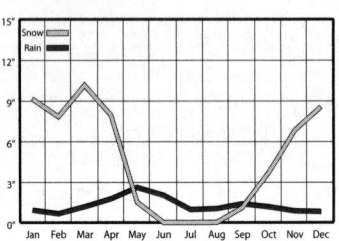

DAYS OF CLOUDS & PRECIPITATION

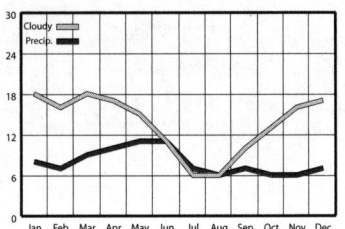

Education
Score: 70.9
Rank: 110

ACHIEVEMENT	AREA	U.S. AVG
High school degree	88.6%	82.7%
2-year college degree	5.5%	6.4%
4-year college degree	19.3%	15.7%
Graduate/professional degree	7.5%	8.9%

PUBLIC SCHOOLS	AREA	U.S. AVG
Expenditures per pupil	$6,452	$5,686
Student/teacher ratio	13.9	16.7
Attending public school	93.5%	90.1%
State SAT score	1083	1021
State ACT score	21.9*	20.9

HIGHER EDUCATION	AREA	U.S. AVG
No. 2-year colleges	1	4
No. 4-year colleges/universities	3	6
No. highly ranked universities	0	1

Health & Healthcare
Score: 72.5
Rank: 104

HAZARDS & ILLNESSES	AREA	U.S. AVG
Air-quality score	35	37
Water-quality score	38	52
Pollen/allergy score	27	61
Cancer mortality per capita	207.8	201.9
Depression days per month	3.6	3.5
Stress score	23	50

HEALTHCARE	AREA	U.S. AVG
Physicians per capita	307.2	244.2
Hospital beds per capita	410.4	420.0
No. teaching hospitals	2	3
Cost per doctor visit	$96	$77
Cost per dental visit	$72	$70

Crime
Score: 74.3
Rank: 96

CRIME	AREA	U.S. AVG
Violent crime rate	218.7	465.5
Change in violent crime rate	9.7%	-2.2%
Property crime rate	4,603.6	3,517.1
Change in property crime rate	12.7%	-2.1%

Transportation
Score: 51.1
Rank: 184

COMMUTE	AREA	U.S. AVG
Average commute time	19.9	27.4
Percent commutes > 60 mins.	3.9%	5.9%
Commute by auto	80.6%	78.9%
Commute by mass transit	1.0%	1.9%
Work at home	4.6%	3.1%
Mass transit miles per capita	1.03	1.87

INTERCITY SERVICES	AREA	U.S. AVG
Major airports within 60 miles	0	1
Size of regional airport	Small	Large
Daily airline activity	80	686
Amtrak service	No	No

AUTOMOTIVE	AREA	U.S. AVG
Insurance, annual premium	$1,071	$1,432
Gas, cost per gallon	$2.32	$2.49
Daily vehicle miles per capita	16.5	24.0

Leisure
Score: 34.8
Rank: 243

DINING & SHOPPING	AREA	U.S. AVG
Restaurant rating	1	2
Outlet mall score	0	42
No. Starbucks	2	13
No. warehouse clubs	1	2

ENTERTAINMENT	AREA	U.S. AVG
Professional sports rating	2	4
College sports rating	2	4
Zoo/aquarium rating	1	3
Amusement park rating	1	3
Botanical garden/ arboretum rating	1	4

OUTDOOR ACTIVITIES	AREA	U.S. AVG
Golf-course rating	2	4
Ski-area rating	7	3
Sq. miles inland water	3	4
Miles of coastline	0.0	10.7
National Park rating	1	3

Arts & Culture
Score: 36.6
Rank: 237

MEDIA & LIBRARIES	AREA	U.S. AVG
Arts radio rating	1	3
No. public libraries	5	27
Library volumes per capita	2.45	2.78

PERFORMING ARTS	AREA	U.S. AVG
Classical music rating	3	4
Ballet/dance rating	1	3
Professional theater rating	1	3
University arts programs rating	5	5

MUSEUMS	AREA	U.S. AVG
Overall museum rating	3	5
Art museum rating	5	5
Science museum rating	3	5
Children's museum rating	1	3

Biloxi–Gulfport–Pascagoula, MS

Score: not ranked **Rank:** not ranked **2004 rank:** 293

Profile: Coastal-city/beach-town complex
Location: Mississippi Gulf Coast
Elevation: 15 feet
Time zone: Central Standard Time

PRO	CON
Beaches	Hurricane impact
Winter climate	Tourist sprawl
Entertainment	Arts and culture

While Hurricane Katrina triggered the well-known and catastrophic flood in New Orleans, it scored an even more direct hit on the Mississippi Gulf Coast towns of Biloxi, Gulfport, and to a lesser extent, Pascagoula to the east. It was a knockout punch. The full destructive force of high winds and a remarkable storm surge inundated Biloxi, leaving some 90% of buildings along the coast destroyed. Most of Biloxi's economy and especially its recent growth was tied to beachfront enterprises, including a new set of casinos that had sprung up during the 1990s. These casinos and most of the tourism industry on which the town depends were literally washed away, but some larger ones have come back on line recently, and a recent law change will allow casinos to be on land, not just on floating watercraft. Biloxi is by some accounts already the third-largest U.S. gambling destination behind Las Vegas and Atlantic City, and the storm and rebirth are likely to bring the casino industry even further onto center stage. Because it isn't clear how much of our fact base includes Katrina effects, and because so much is in transition with an uncertain future outcome, we decline to rank this metro area in this edition of *Cities Ranked & Rated*.

All three cities lie at the base of the narrow Gulf extension of the state of Mississippi. Biloxi is more commercial, Gulfport is more of a residential beach community, and Pascagoula is more industrial with shipyards, oil refineries, and other heavier industries. Much of this coastal area had developed as a second-class beach resort for travelers, mostly from the South and Midwest, looking for an alternative to Florida. Prior to Katrina, most of the beach development was fairly unattractive, with miles of commercial strips and new casinos that didn't add much to the physical attractiveness of the area. There were some older historic districts of interest in the downtown areas, but there was little in the way of intellectual stimulation. It is possible—likely, in fact—that the redeveloped area will be better planned, more cohesive, and more attractive. That said, casinos and related hospitality are likely to become more dominant at the expense of some of the local flavor. Biloxi was also a center for the shrimping and fishing industries and has many good restaurants, activities, and museums related to the seafood trade, and it is likely this role will continue. Current employment is bolstered by reconstruction efforts, but the long-term effects of Katrina are far from clear. The tax base is weak and it is unclear how it will recover. Property insurance considerations are likely to hamper residential reconstruction efforts, and it may force some development to back away from the shore, not altogether a bad outcome. At this writing, the entire area is a "wait and see."

The surrounding area is a flat coastal plain with barrier islands and peninsulas, and pine forests beginning north of town. The area is considerably influenced by the Gulf of Mexico. Summers are warm and humid but less so than inland. Sea breezes usually keep temperatures reasonable, particularly in late afternoon and evening. There may be a few cold snaps but they seldom persist and freezes are infrequent. Summer thundershowers are frequent. Given the location and local topography, hurricanes are a continuing threat; Hurricane Camille in 1969 gave a preview to the 2005 Katrina disaster.

DEMOGRAPHICS	AREA	U.S. AVG	ETHNIC COMPOSITION	AREA	U.S. AVG	RESIDENT PROFILE	AREA	U.S. AVG
Population	405,766		White	74.8%	79.0%	Single	30.3%	32.4%
Population density per sq. mile	149.8	358.5	Black	20.1%	10.5%	Married	52.7%	52.7%
Population growth	20.1%	21.1%	Asian	2.3%	2.7%	Divorced/separated	17.0%	14.9%
Median age	35.5	36.1	Hispanic	2.2%	10.6%	Married with children	23.7%	23.7%
Percent Democrat	32.5%	44.5%	Religious observance	52.4%	48.9%	Single with children	11.0%	9.1%
Percent Republican	66.7%	54.5%	Diversity measure	41.8	40.1	Percent over age 65	11.9%	12.9%

INCOME	AREA	U.S. AVG	EMPLOYMENT	AREA	U.S. AVG	EMPLOYING INDUSTRIES	AREA	U.S. AVG
Per capita income	$20,259	$23,235	Unemployment rate	6.0%	4.7%	Largest: Manufacturing		
Household income	$41,779	$46,414	Recent job growth	-0.6%	1.3%			
Household income < $25K	28.6%	26.2%	Projected future job growth	9.5%	11.5%	Percent manufacturing	13.9%	15.4%
Household income > $75K	20.4%	25.4%	White collar	52.1%	57.8%	Percent public sector	17.0%	15.7%
Household income growth	14.5%	13.6%	Blue collar	27.6%	25.2%	Percent construction	13.7%	9.9%

Score: - **Rank:** -

INDEXES & TAXES	AREA	U.S. AVG	HOUSING	AREA	U.S. AVG	NECESSITIES	AREA	U.S. AVG
Cost of Living Index	85.2	100.0	Median home price	$137,100	$220,000	Food Index	96.4	100.0
Buying Power Index	109.9	100.0	Home price appreciation	38.2%	10.1%	Housing Index	48.6	100.0
Income tax rate	5.00%	4.70%	Median rent	$629	$709	Utilities Index	106.6	100.0
Sales tax rate	7.00%	6.58%	Homes owned	63.6%	62.3%	Transportation Index	95.8	100.0
Property tax rate	$8.51	$12.00	Home price ratio	3.3	4.2	Healthcare Index	89.5	100.0
						Miscellaneous Cost Index	98.7	100.0

Score: - **Rank:** -

Climate

Score: -
Rank: -

TEMPERATURE	AREA	U.S. AVG
Average January low	45.5	26.2
Average July high	89.6	87.4
Annual days > 90°F	52	38
Annual days < 32°F	11	89
Annual days < 0°F	0	6

PRECIPITATION	AREA	U.S. AVG
Annual inches precipitation	59.0	37.7
Annual inches snowfall	0.0	7.0
Annual days precipitation	75	109
Annual days rain > 0.5 inches	37	22
Annual days snow > 1.5 inches	0	6

COMFORTS & HAZARDS	AREA	U.S. AVG
July relative humidity	77%	66%
Annual days mostly sunny	219	208
Annual days with thunderstorms	94	39
Tornado risk score	30	18
Hurricane risk score	57	13

TEMPERATURE

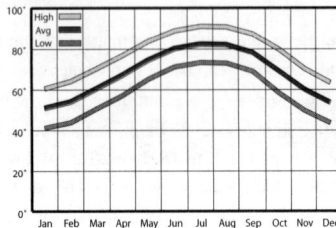

PRECIPITATION

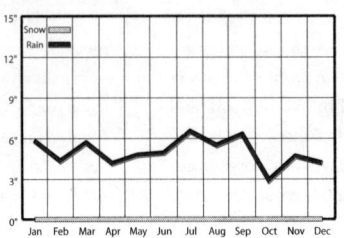

DAYS OF CLOUDS & PRECIPITATION

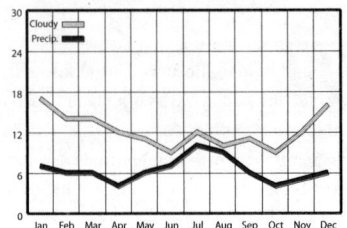

Education

Score: -
Rank: -

ACHIEVEMENT	AREA	U.S. AVG
High school degree	79.6%	82.7%
2-year college degree	7.5%	6.4%
4-year college degree	10.8%	15.7%
Graduate/professional degree	6.1%	8.9%

PUBLIC SCHOOLS	AREA	U.S. AVG
Expenditures per pupil	$4,181	$5,686
Student/teacher ratio	17.3	16.7
Attending public school	92.3%	90.1%
State SAT score	1097	1021
State ACT score	18.8*	20.9

HIGHER EDUCATION	AREA	U.S. AVG
No. 2-year colleges	2	4
No. 4-year colleges/universities	0	6
No. highly ranked universities	0	1

Health & Healthcare

Score: -
Rank: -

HAZARDS & ILLNESSES	AREA	U.S. AVG
Air-quality score	35	37
Water-quality score	54	52
Pollen/allergy score	77	61
Cancer mortality per capita	222.4	201.9
Depression days per month	4.7	3.5
Stress score	100	50

HEALTHCARE	AREA	U.S. AVG
Physicians per capita	221.1	244.2
Hospital beds per capita	406.9	420.0
No. teaching hospitals	0	3
Cost per doctor visit	$64	$77
Cost per dental visit	$70	$70

Crime

Score: -
Rank: -

CRIME	AREA	U.S. AVG
Violent crime rate	254.8	465.5
Change in violent crime rate	-17.4%	-2.2%
Property crime rate	4,134.2	3,517.1
Change in property crime rate	-10.8%	-2.1%

Transportation

Score: -
Rank: -

COMMUTE	AREA	U.S. AVG
Average commute time	26.5	27.4
Percent commutes > 60 mins.	7.0%	5.9%
Commute by auto	79.6%	78.9%
Commute by mass transit	0.4%	1.9%
Work at home	2.1%	3.1%
Mass transit miles per capita	0.41	1.87

INTERCITY SERVICES	AREA	U.S. AVG
Major airports within 60 miles	1	1
Size of regional airport	Medium	Large
Daily airline activity	184	686
Amtrak service	Yes	No

AUTOMOTIVE	AREA	U.S. AVG
Insurance, annual premium	$1,226	$1,432
Gas, cost per gallon	$2.48	$2.49
Daily vehicle miles per capita	27.9	24.0

Leisure

Score: -
Rank: -

DINING & SHOPPING	AREA	U.S. AVG
Restaurant rating	1	2
Outlet mall score	78	42
No. Starbucks	0	13
No. warehouse clubs	1	2

ENTERTAINMENT	AREA	U.S. AVG
Professional sports rating	3	4
College sports rating	1	4
Zoo/aquarium rating	2	3
Amusement park rating	7	3
Botanical garden/ arboretum rating	2	4

OUTDOOR ACTIVITIES	AREA	U.S. AVG
Golf-course rating	3	4
Ski-area rating	1	3
Sq. miles inland water	3	4
Miles of coastline	30.3	10.7
National Park rating	5	3

Arts & Culture

Score: -
Rank: -

MEDIA & LIBRARIES	AREA	U.S. AVG
Arts radio rating	5	3
No. public libraries	22	27
Library volumes per capita	1.76	2.78

PERFORMING ARTS	AREA	U.S. AVG
Classical music rating	1	4
Ballet/dance rating	1	3
Professional theater rating	1	3
University arts programs rating	1	5

MUSEUMS	AREA	U.S. AVG
Overall museum rating	5	5
Art museum rating	4	5
Science museum rating	1	5
Children's museum rating	1	3

Binghamton, NY

Score: 41.9 **Rank:** 309 **2004 rank:** 241

Profile: Small city
Location: South-central New York, 10 miles north of Pennsylvania border
Elevation: 1,590 feet
Time zone: Eastern Standard Time

PRO	CON
Cost of living	Climate
Central location	Entertainment
Low crime rates	Economy

Binghamton is a diversified manufacturing center and transportation gateway to other areas of upstate New York. Manufacturers are varied and led today by IBM. The town itself is quiet and unremarkable, and offers little to do, although there is a good set of performing arts amenities. The central location is near several areas of interest: The Finger Lakes and Ithaca to the northwest, where Cornell University provides cultural amenities; New York City to the southeast; and the Adirondacks to the northeast. The climate can be depressing, as Binghamton has the greatest number of cloudy days (214) per year of any city outside the Pacific Northwest, and ranks 14th highest in the U.S. for days of precipitation. That precipitation combined with the narrow valley river confluence can bring flooding, as it did during a prolonged period of rain in June 2006. Cost of living and particularly the cost of

housing are very low, especially for the region, but recent economic performance is weak at best.

Binghamton is in a comparatively narrow valley at the confluence of the Susquehanna and Chenango rivers. Within a 5-mile radius, hills rise to an elevation of 1,600 feet. Summers are warm, but temperatures and humidity seldom become oppressing. Daytime temperatures rise rapidly but get up to 90°F only a few days each month. Summer evenings are typically cool. Winters are cold but not severe with daytime highs in the 20s and 30s and lows in the mid-teens to 20s. A few subzero readings occur each winter. Snowfall is moderate and much higher in the surrounding hills. The cloudiness and valley fogs arise from proximity to Lake Ontario and nearby landforms combined with the storm track location. First freeze is early October; last is early May.

Population

DEMOGRAPHICS	AREA	U.S. AVG	ETHNIC COMPOSITION	AREA	U.S. AVG	RESIDENT PROFILE	AREA	U.S. AVG
Population	250,483		White	91.0%	79.0%	Single	34.7%	32.4%
Population density per sq. mile	204.4	358.5	Black	3.4%	10.5%	Married	51.4%	52.7%
Population growth	-5.3%	21.1%	Asian	2.9%	2.7%	Divorced/separated	14.0%	14.9%
Median age	39.2	36.1	Hispanic	2.4%	10.6%	Married with children	20.8%	23.7%
Percent Democrat	48.3%	44.5%	Religious observance	51.8%	48.9%	Single with children	8.6%	9.1%
Percent Republican	49.5%	54.5%	Diversity measure	20.6	40.1	Percent over age 65	16.1%	12.9%

Economy & Jobs
Score: 10.4
Rank: 334

INCOME	AREA	U.S. AVG	EMPLOYMENT	AREA	U.S. AVG	EMPLOYING INDUSTRIES	AREA	U.S. AVG
Per capita income	$21,592	$23,235	Unemployment rate	5.0%	4.7%	Largest: Manufacturing		
Household income	$40,615	$46,414	Recent job growth	0.2%	1.3%			
Household income < $25K	30.2%	26.2%	Projected future job growth	-1.9%	11.5%	Percent manufacturing	15.6%	15.4%
Household income > $75K	20.5%	25.4%	White collar	60.7%	57.8%	Percent public sector	18.0%	15.7%
Household income growth	11.7%	13.6%	Blue collar	23.0%	25.2%	Percent construction	7.4%	9.9%

Cost of Living
Score: 24.6
Rank: 281

INDEXES & TAXES	AREA	U.S. AVG	HOUSING	AREA	U.S. AVG	NECESSITIES	AREA	U.S. AVG
Cost of Living Index	78.9	100.0	Median home price	$92,800	$220,000	Food Index	97.6	100.0
Buying Power Index	115.4	100.0	Home price appreciation	34.1%	10.1%	Housing Index	44.9	100.0
Income tax rate	7.13%	4.70%	Median rent	$574	$709	Utilities Index	125.2	100.0
Sales tax rate	8.25%	6.58%	Homes owned	62.2%	62.3%	Transportation Index	97.5	100.0
Property tax rate	$23.31	$12.00	Home price ratio	2.3	4.2	Healthcare Index	90.3	100.0
						Miscellaneous Cost Index	98.6	100.0

Climate
Score: 4.8
Rank: 355

TEMPERATURE	AREA	U.S. AVG	PRECIPITATION	AREA	U.S. AVG	COMFORTS & HAZARDS	AREA	U.S. AVG
Average January low	15.2	26.2	Annual inches precipitation	37.0	37.7	July relative humidity	74%	66%
Average July high	78.5	87.4	Annual inches snowfall	86.0	7.0	Annual days mostly sunny	151	208
Annual days > 90°F	2	38	Annual days precipitation	163	109	Annual days with thunderstorms	31	39
Annual days < 32°F	147	89	Annual days rain > 0.5 inches	22	22	Tornado risk score	3	18
Annual days < 0°F	8	6	Annual days snow > 1.5 inches	18	6	Hurricane risk score	5	13

TEMPERATURE

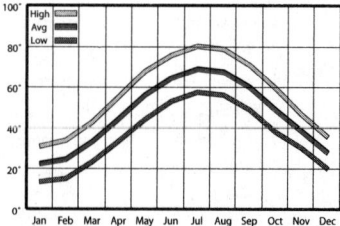

PRECIPITATION

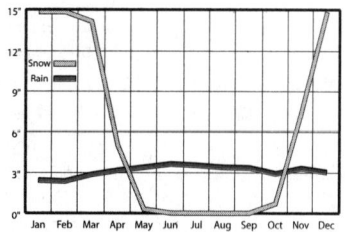

DAYS OF CLOUDS & PRECIPITATION

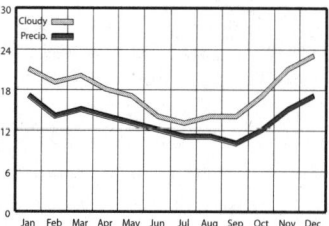

Education
Score: 75.7
Rank: 92

ACHIEVEMENT	AREA	U.S. AVG	PUBLIC SCHOOLS	AREA	U.S. AVG	HIGHER EDUCATION	AREA	U.S. AVG
High school degree	84.0%	82.7%	Expenditures per pupil	$7,645	$5,686	No. 2-year colleges	1	4
2-year college degree	10.0%	6.4%	Student/teacher ratio	14.3	16.7	No. 4-year colleges/universities	2	6
4-year college degree	12.5%	15.7%	Attending public school	94.4%	90.1%	No. highly ranked universities	1	1
Graduate/professional degree	9.7%	8.9%	State SAT score	1003*	1021			
			State ACT score	22.6	20.9			

Health & Healthcare
Score: 77.3
Rank: 86

HAZARDS & ILLNESSES	AREA	U.S. AVG	HEALTHCARE	AREA	U.S. AVG	CRIME	AREA	U.S. AVG
Air-quality score	46	37	Physicians per capita	236.8	244.2	Violent crime rate	173.1	465.5
Water-quality score	96	52	Hospital beds per capita	406.8	420.0	Change in violent crime rate	21.6%	-2.2%
Pollen/allergy score	55	61	No. teaching hospitals	3	3	Property crime rate	2,500.1	3,517.1
Cancer mortality per capita	210.1	201.9	Cost per doctor visit	$75	$77	Change in property crime rate	4.7%	-2.1%
Depression days per month	3.6	3.5	Cost per dental visit	$63	$70			
Stress score	11	50						

Crime
Score: 97.9
Rank: 9

Transportation
Score: 43.3
Rank: 212

COMMUTE	AREA	U.S. AVG	INTERCITY SERVICES	AREA	U.S. AVG	AUTOMOTIVE	AREA	U.S. AVG
Average commute time	21.7	27.4	Major airports within 60 miles	0	1	Insurance, annual premium	$1,539	$1,432
Percent commutes > 60 mins.	3.8%	5.9%	Size of regional airport	Small	Large	Gas, cost per gallon	$2.56	$2.49
Commute by auto	79.9%	78.9%	Daily airline activity	129	686	Daily vehicle miles per capita	36.7	24.0
Commute by mass transit	2.2%	1.9%	Amtrak service	No	No			
Work at home	2.6%	3.1%						
Mass transit miles per capita	2.25	1.87						

Leisure
Score: 40.4
Rank: 222

DINING & SHOPPING	AREA	U.S. AVG	ENTERTAINMENT	AREA	U.S. AVG	OUTDOOR ACTIVITIES	AREA	U.S. AVG
Restaurant rating	1	2	Professional sports rating	3	4	Golf-course rating	3	4
Outlet mall score	0	42	College sports rating	6	4	Ski-area rating	4	3
No. Starbucks	1	13	Zoo/aquarium rating	2	3	Sq. miles inland water	2	4
No. warehouse clubs	1	2	Amusement park rating	1	3	Miles of coastline	0.0	10.7
			Botanical garden/ arboretum rating	2	4	National Park rating	1	3

Arts & Culture
Score: 46.5
Rank: 200

MEDIA & LIBRARIES	AREA	U.S. AVG	PERFORMING ARTS	AREA	U.S. AVG	MUSEUMS	AREA	U.S. AVG
Arts radio rating	1	3	Classical music rating	5	4	Overall museum rating	4	5
No. public libraries	20	27	Ballet/dance rating	1	3	Art museum rating	4	5
Library volumes per capita	2.34	2.78	Professional theater rating	1	3	Science museum rating	5	5
			University arts programs rating	4	5	Children's museum rating	4	3

Birmingham–Hoover, AL

Score: 54.3   Rank: 223   2004 rank: 218

Profile: Mid-size city
Location: North-central Alabama, about 300 miles north of the Gulf of Mexico
Elevation: 618 feet
Time zone: Central Standard Time

PRO
Diversifying economy
Mild winters
Arts and culture

CON
Summer heat and humidity
Crime rates
Air service

Birmingham is one of the South's most misunderstood cities. A former steel and manufacturing center once known as the "Pittsburgh of the South," Birmingham is still thought by many outsiders to combine the grittiness of this legacy with some of the other more unsavory images of the Old South. But the truth is far different: Birmingham has experienced a major economic turnaround, and while not quite as far along as noted Southern stars such as Charlotte, Raleigh-Durham, and Atlanta, the area has come a long way, drawing young educated workers and their families looking for alternatives to these other booming Southern centers. The steel industry is still evident but has transitioned into higher value-add manufacturing enterprises supporting the South's growing automotive assembly industry, which surrounds the city in places such as Tuscaloosa, Lincoln, and Montgomery in Alabama, and Spring Hill and Smyrna in Tennessee. Beyond this industry, the economy has moved decidedly toward more new-economy enterprises in research, medicine, banking, finance, and technology. Nice older (and some newer) suburban neighborhoods have grown mainly south of the city towards Vestavia Hills and Hoover. The area scores relatively well in healthcare, arts, and the economy, and poorly in air service and climate.

Birmingham is located in a valley within a hilly area in the Appalachian foothills. Ridges rise to 600 feet above the valley floor, with a mix of open land and forest. Summers are long, hot, and humid with frequent thunderstorms. Winters are mild. Total annual rainfall is among the highest in the United States.

DEMOGRAPHICS	AREA	U.S. AVG	ETHNIC COMPOSITION	AREA	U.S. AVG	RESIDENT PROFILE	AREA	U.S. AVG
Population	1,082,898		White	68.7%	79.0%	Single	31.2%	32.4%
Population density per sq. mile	204.4	358.5	Black	28.3%	10.5%	Married	53.6%	52.7%
Population growth	17.7%	21.1%	Asian	1.0%	2.7%	Divorced/separated	15.2%	14.9%
Median age	37.0	36.1	Hispanic	2.3%	10.6%	Married with children	23.3%	23.7%
Percent Democrat	35.9%	44.5%	Religious observance	56.7%	48.9%	Single with children	8.9%	9.1%
Percent Republican	63.4%	54.5%	Diversity measure	42.2	40.1	Percent over age 65	12.9%	12.9%

Score: 27.5
Rank: 271

INCOME	AREA	U.S. AVG	EMPLOYMENT	AREA	U.S. AVG	EMPLOYING INDUSTRIES	AREA	U.S. AVG
Per capita income	$24,186	$23,235	Unemployment rate	3.9%	4.7%	Largest: Healthcare & Social Assistance		
Household income	$45,083	$46,414	Recent job growth	0.1%	1.3%			
Household income ‹ $25K	28.1%	26.2%	Projected future job growth	7.7%	11.5%	Percent manufacturing	14.0%	15.4%
Household income › $75K	25.5%	25.4%	White collar	61.9%	57.8%	Percent public sector	13.5%	15.7%
Household income growth	16.0%	13.6%	Blue collar	24.9%	25.2%	Percent construction	10.9%	9.9%

Score: 38.8
Rank: 229

INDEXES & TAXES	AREA	U.S. AVG	HOUSING	AREA	U.S. AVG	NECESSITIES	AREA	U.S. AVG
Cost of Living Index	89.2	100.0	Median home price	$169,700	$220,000	Food Index	94.8	100.0
Buying Power Index	113.3	100.0	Home price appreciation	32.1%	10.1%	Housing Index	61.1	100.0
Income tax rate	5.84%	4.70%	Median rent	$590	$709	Utilities Index	100.9	100.0
Sales tax rate	8.65%	6.58%	Homes owned	66.1%	62.3%	Transportation Index	96.1	100.0
Property tax rate	$4.97	$12.00	Home price ratio	3.8	4.2	Healthcare Index	91.4	100.0
						Miscellaneous Cost Index	100.6	100.0

TEMPERATURE	AREA	U.S. AVG	PRECIPITATION	AREA	U.S. AVG	COMFORTS & HAZARDS	AREA	U.S. AVG
Average January low	34.1	26.2	Annual inches precipitation	53.0	37.7	July relative humidity	72%	66%
July high	90.3	87.4	Annual inches snowfall	1.0	7.0	Annual days mostly sunny	210	208
Annual days › 90°F	39	38	Annual days precipitation	118	109	Annual days with thunderstorms	58	39
Annual days ‹ 32°F	60	89	Annual days rain › 0.5 inches	36	22	Tornado risk score	72	18
Annual days ‹ 0°F	0	6	Annual days snow › 1.5 inches	2	6	Hurricane risk score	18	13

Score: 22.5
Rank: 289

TEMPERATURE

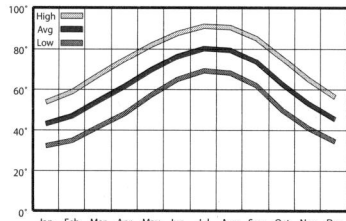

PRECIPITATION

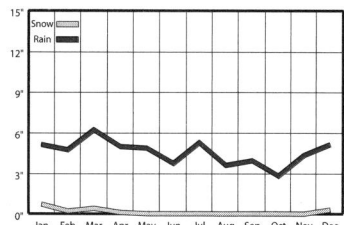

DAYS OF CLOUDS & PRECIPITATION

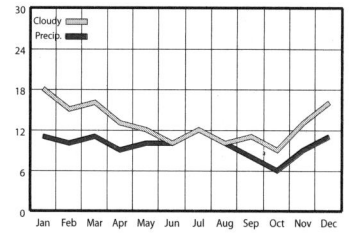

ACHIEVEMENT	AREA	U.S. AVG	PUBLIC SCHOOLS	AREA	U.S. AVG	HIGHER EDUCATION	AREA	U.S. AVG
High school degree	79.1%	82.7%	Expenditures per pupil	$4,864	$5,686	No. 2-year colleges	5	4
2-year college degree	5.5%	6.4%	Student/teacher ratio	15.5	16.7	No. 4-year colleges/universities	9	6
4-year college degree	15.1%	15.7%	Attending public school	90.7%	90.1%	No. highly ranked universities	1	1
Graduate/professional degree	8.0%	8.9%	State SAT score	1126	1021			
			State ACT score	20.2*	20.9			

Score: 46.3
Rank: 202

HAZARDS & ILLNESSES	AREA	U.S. AVG	HEALTHCARE	AREA	U.S. AVG	CRIME	AREA	U.S. AVG
Air-quality score	21	37	Physicians per capita	324.1	244.2	Violent crime rate	621.3	465.5
Water-quality score	81	52	Hospital beds per capita	537.4	420.0	Change in violent crime rate	7.4%	-2.2%
Pollen/allergy score	68	61	No. teaching hospitals	10	3	Property crime rate	4,373.8	3,517.1
Cancer mortality per capita	215.9	201.9	Cost per doctor visit	$61	$77	Change in property crime rate	-1.4%	-2.1%
Depression days per month	3.8	3.5	Cost per dental visit	$78	$70			
Stress score	68	50						

Score: 50.5
Rank: 186

Score: 19.8
Rank: 300

COMMUTE	AREA	U.S. AVG	INTERCITY SERVICES	AREA	U.S. AVG	AUTOMOTIVE	AREA	U.S. AVG
Average commute time	29.1	27.4	Major airports within 60 miles	0	1	Insurance, annual premium	$1,388	$1,432
Percent commutes › 60 mins.	7.0%	5.9%	Size of regional airport	Small	Large	Gas, cost per gallon	$2.45	$2.49
Commute by auto	83.4%	78.9%	Daily airline activity	152	686	Daily vehicle miles per capita	35.6	24.0
Commute by mass transit	0.7%	1.9%	Amtrak service	Yes	No			
Work at home	2.1%	3.1%						
Mass transit miles per capita	0.70	1.87						

Score: 0.0
Rank: 373

Leisure
Score: 49.2
Rank: 189

DINING & SHOPPING	AREA	U.S. AVG	ENTERTAINMENT	AREA	U.S. AVG	OUTDOOR ACTIVITIES	AREA	U.S. AVG
Restaurant rating	1	2	Professional sports rating	2	4	Golf-course rating	6	4
Outlet mall score	40	42	College sports rating	4	4	Ski-area rating	1	3
No. Starbucks	10	13	Zoo/aquarium rating	6	3	Sq. miles inland water	3	4
No. warehouse clubs	2	2	Amusement park rating	1	3	Miles of coastline	0.0	10.7
			Botanical garden/ arboretum rating	8	4	National Park rating	2	3

Arts & Culture
Score: 71.1
Rank: 108

MEDIA & LIBRARIES	AREA	U.S. AVG	PERFORMING ARTS	AREA	U.S. AVG	MUSEUMS	AREA	U.S. AVG
Arts radio rating	6	3	Classical music rating	3	4	Overall museum rating	8	5
No. public libraries	70	27	Ballet/dance rating	3	3	Art museum rating	7	5
Library volumes per capita	2.45	2.78	Professional theater rating	1	3	Science museum rating	8	5
			University arts programs rating	8	5	Children's museum rating	9	3

Bismarck, ND

Score: 67.5   **Rank:** 114   **2004 rank:** 195

Profile: Capital city
Location: Central North Dakota
Elevation: 1,697 feet
Time zone: Central Standard Time

PRO	CON
Capital-city amenities	Cold winters
Low crime	Entertainment
Cost of living	Low ethnic diversity

The name Bismarck comes from an attempt to attract German capital during the late 19th century for railroad building and other enterprises. Located along the Missouri River near where Lewis and Clark made their famous winter camp, this capital is an agriculture and transportation center for the state. There is some energy industry and a strong healthcare presence, along with some manufacturing led by construction equipment maker Bobcat. The downtown and the area along the Missouri River are clean and pleasant but plain and quiet with lots of parks and attractive waterfront areas. The suburbs spread east from the Missouri River. Bismarck has among the lowest cost of living and crime rates for a capital city.

Bismarck is on the east bank of the Missouri River in a shallow basin surrounded by low-lying hills. Seasonal temperature ranges are extreme and typical of the northern Great Plains. Summers are warm with few hot, humid days. Most annual precipitation falls in the summer as thunderstorms. Winters tend to be long and very cold but with plenty of mild days. Snow has been reported in all months except July and August. Because of low moisture, snowfalls are usually modest; however, the combination of strong winds and low temperatures can produce severe blizzards. Blowing and drifting snow is a frequent hazard. Sunshine is abundant, both summer and winter. First freeze is late September; last is mid-May.

Population

DEMOGRAPHICS	AREA	U.S. AVG	ETHNIC COMPOSITION	AREA	U.S. AVG	RESIDENT PROFILE	AREA	U.S. AVG
Population	97,858		White	95.0%	79.0%	Single	32.0%	32.4%
Population density per sq. mile	27.5	358.5	Black	0.3%	10.5%	Married	57.3%	52.7%
Population growth	17.1%	21.1%	Asian	0.5%	2.7%	Divorced/separated	10.8%	14.9%
Median age	37.2	36.1	Hispanic	0.7%	10.6%	Married with children	25.6%	23.7%
Percent Democrat	30.5%	44.5%	Religious observance	79.3%	48.9%	Single with children	7.5%	9.1%
Percent Republican	67.8%	54.5%	Diversity measure	11.0	40.1	Percent over age 65	13.4%	12.9%

Economy & Jobs
Score: 75.9
Rank: 90

INCOME	AREA	U.S. AVG	EMPLOYMENT	AREA	U.S. AVG	EMPLOYING INDUSTRIES	AREA	U.S. AVG
Per capita income	$23,353	$23,235	Unemployment rate	2.8%	4.7%	Largest: Healthcare & Social Assistance		
Household income	$46,149	$46,414	Recent job growth	1.8%	1.3%			
Household income ‹ $25K	25.0%	26.2%	Projected future job growth	14.5%	11.5%	Percent manufacturing	10.3%	15.4%
Household income › $75K	23.2%	25.4%	White collar	61.1%	57.8%	Percent public sector	18.1%	15.7%
Household income growth	14.8%	13.6%	Blue collar	19.7%	25.2%	Percent construction	9.4%	9.9%

Cost of Living
Score: 74.3
Rank: 97

INDEXES & TAXES	AREA	U.S. AVG	HOUSING	AREA	U.S. AVG	NECESSITIES	AREA	U.S. AVG
Cost of Living Index	84.7	100.0	Median home price	$128,600	$220,000	Food Index	101.5	100.0
Buying Power Index	122.1	100.0	Home price appreciation	35.2%	10.1%	Housing Index	59.5	100.0
Income tax rate	3.92%	4.70%	Median rent	$536	$709	Utilities Index	109.2	100.0
Sales tax rate	5.74%	6.58%	Homes owned	67.3%	62.3%	Transportation Index	99.7	100.0
Property tax rate	$16.37	$12.00	Home price ratio	2.8	4.2	Healthcare Index	87.9	100.0
						Miscellaneous Cost Index	99.0	100.0

Climate
Score: 21.7
Rank: 292

TEMPERATURE	AREA	U.S. AVG
Average January low	-1.1	26.2
July high	83.9	87.4
Annual days > 90°F	20	38
Annual days < 32°F	186	89
Annual days < 0°F	56	6

PRECIPITATION	AREA	U.S. AVG
Annual inches precipitation	17.0	37.7
Annual inches snowfall	39.0	7.0
Annual days precipitation	101	109
Annual days rain > 0.5 inches	9	22
Annual days snow > 1.5 inches	9	6

COMFORTS & HAZARDS	AREA	U.S. AVG
July relative humidity	64%	66%
Annual days mostly sunny	199	208
Annual days with thunderstorms	17	39
Tornado risk score	9	18
Hurricane risk score	0	13

TEMPERATURE

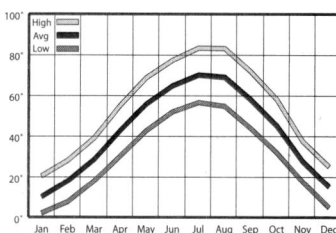

PRECIPITATION

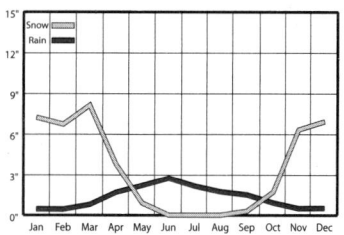

DAYS OF CLOUDS & PRECIPITATION

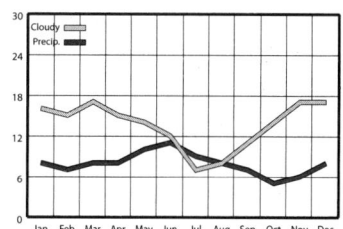

Education
Score: 83.4
Rank: 63

ACHIEVEMENT	AREA	U.S. AVG
High school degree	86.1%	82.7%
2-year college degree	11.4%	6.4%
4-year college degree	19.3%	15.7%
Graduate/professional degree	6.3%	8.9%

PUBLIC SCHOOLS	AREA	U.S. AVG
Expenditures per pupil	$5,785	$5,686
Student/teacher ratio	10.2	16.7
Attending public school	90.9%	90.1%
State SAT score	1227	1021
State ACT score	21.4*	20.9

HIGHER EDUCATION	AREA	U.S. AVG
No. 2-year colleges	3	4
No. 4-year colleges/universities	2	6
No. highly ranked universities	0	1

Health & Healthcare
Score: 98.1
Rank: 8

HAZARDS & ILLNESSES	AREA	U.S. AVG
Air-quality score	51	37
Water-quality score	60	52
Pollen/allergy score	43	61
Cancer mortality per capita	219.6	201.9
Depression days per month	2.6	3.5
Stress score	3	50

HEALTHCARE	AREA	U.S. AVG
Physicians per capita	291.2	244.2
Hospital beds per capita	735.8	420.0
No. teaching hospitals	2	3
Cost per doctor visit	$83	$77
Cost per dental visit	$67	$70

Crime
Score: 90.6
Rank: 36

CRIME	AREA	U.S. AVG
Violent crime rate	109.9	465.5
Change in violent crime rate	23.9%	-2.2%
Property crime rate	2,202.9	3,517.1
Change in property crime rate	2.0%	-2.1%

Transportation
Score: 63.6
Rank: 137

COMMUTE	AREA	U.S. AVG
Average commute time	18.0	27.4
Percent commutes > 60 mins.	3.3%	5.9%
Commute by auto	82.1%	78.9%
Commute by mass transit	0.4%	1.9%
Work at home	4.7%	3.1%
Mass transit miles per capita	0.42	1.87

INTERCITY SERVICES	AREA	U.S. AVG
Major airports within 60 miles	0	1
Size of regional airport	None	Large
Daily airline activity	25	686
Amtrak service	No	No

AUTOMOTIVE	AREA	U.S. AVG
Insurance, annual premium	$845	$1,432
Gas, cost per gallon	$2.44	$2.49
Daily vehicle miles per capita	16.1	24.0

Leisure
Score: 31.0
Rank: 257

DINING & SHOPPING	AREA	U.S. AVG
Restaurant rating	1	2
Outlet mall score	0	42
No. Starbucks	3	13
No. warehouse clubs	0	2

ENTERTAINMENT	AREA	U.S. AVG
Professional sports rating	2	4
College sports rating	1	4
Zoo/aquarium rating	2	3
Amusement park rating	1	3
Botanical garden/ arboretum rating	1	4

OUTDOOR ACTIVITIES	AREA	U.S. AVG
Golf-course rating	2	4
Ski-area rating	1	3
Sq. miles inland water	6	4
Miles of coastline	0.0	10.7
National Park rating	3	3

Arts & Culture
Score: 10.4
Rank: 334

MEDIA & LIBRARIES	AREA	U.S. AVG
Arts radio rating	1	3
No. public libraries	5	27
Library volumes per capita	2.93	2.78

PERFORMING ARTS	AREA	U.S. AVG
Classical music rating	3	4
Ballet/dance rating	1	3
Professional theater rating	1	3
University arts programs rating	2	5

MUSEUMS	AREA	U.S. AVG
Overall museum rating	5	5
Art museum rating	1	5
Science museum rating	3	5
Children's museum rating	1	3

Blacksburg–Christiansburg–Radford, VA

Score: 59.2   **Rank:** 181   **2004 rank:** not ranked

Profile: Small-town/college-town complex
Location: Southwestern Virginia, 30 miles southwest of Roanoke
Elevation: 2,080 feet
Time zone: Eastern Standard Time

PRO	CON
Attractive setting	Low job growth
Cost of living	Isolation
College town amenities	Arts and culture

This tri-city area, really a cluster of several small towns, is best known as home of the 25,000-student, 2,600-acre campus of the Virginia Polytechnic Institute (better known as Virginia Tech). Blacksburg, population 40,000, is the largest of the small triangle of towns that includes Christiansburg, Radford, Merrimac, and Fairlawn. The area, and Blacksburg in particular, combines small-town feel and college-town amenities with a mountain setting, outdoor recreation, and proximity to Roanoke and its excellent arts, commerce, and healthcare amenities. Virginia Tech is known for its sports programs, bringing much excitement especially in fall and winter. Virginia Tech is not the only game in town, however; the state-supported, 10,000-student Radford University brings a college presence to Radford as well. While some big-city services and amenities are missing, the blend of available features and cost of living are attractive. Some might not like the isolation, particularly from air services, characteristic of many western Virginia locations.

The location along the Appalachian and Blue Ridge mountains, in an area known as the Virginia Highlands, is comprised of a series of southwest-to-northeast low mountain ridges separated by narrow valleys. The mountains provide a natural barrier to winter cold from the northwest and from the most severe effects of Atlantic tropical storms. Summers are warm and humid but mountain air and elevation bring relatively cool evenings. Winters are generally mild but feature snow each winter, producing significant accumulations if conditions are right. Flooding can be an issue with narrow valleys and summer thunderstorms or approaching storms from the Atlantic mainly in fall. First freeze is late October; last is mid-April.

DEMOGRAPHICS	AREA	U.S. AVG	ETHNIC COMPOSITION	AREA	U.S. AVG	RESIDENT PROFILE	AREA	U.S. AVG
Population	151,890		White	91.3%	79.0%	Single	41.2%	32.4%
Population density per sq. mile	141.2	358.5	Black	4.3%	10.5%	Married	45.7%	52.7%
Population growth	8.8%	21.1%	Asian	2.4%	2.7%	Divorced/separated	13.0%	14.9%
Median age	32.6	36.1	Hispanic	1.4%	10.6%	Married with children	18.9%	23.7%
Percent Democrat	42.8%	44.5%	Religious observance	35.6%	48.9%	Single with children	6.3%	9.1%
Percent Republican	56.1%	54.5%	Diversity measure	18.5	40.1	Percent over age 65	11.4%	12.9%

INCOME	AREA	U.S. AVG	EMPLOYMENT	AREA	U.S. AVG	EMPLOYING INDUSTRIES	AREA	U.S. AVG
Per capita income	$19,649	$23,235	Unemployment rate	3.9%	4.7%	Largest: Manufacturing		
Household income	$36,272	$46,414	Recent job growth	1.2%	1.3%			
Household income < $25K	35.7%	26.2%	Projected future job growth	2.5%	11.5%	Percent manufacturing	17.3%	15.4%
Household income > $75K	18.0%	25.4%	White collar	56.6%	57.8%	Percent public sector	27.3%	15.7%
Household income growth	12.6%	13.6%	Blue collar	26.5%	25.2%	Percent construction	9.2%	9.9%

Economy & Jobs — **Score:** 17.9 **Rank:** 306

INDEXES & TAXES	AREA	U.S. AVG	HOUSING	AREA	U.S. AVG	NECESSITIES	AREA	U.S. AVG
Cost of Living Index	79.6	100.0	Median home price	$138,600	$220,000	Food Index	94.1	100.0
Buying Power Index	102.1	100.0	Home price appreciation	42.7%	10.1%	Housing Index	75.6	100.0
Income tax rate	5.75%	4.70%	Median rent	$566	$709	Utilities Index	72.9	100.0
Sales tax rate	5.00%	6.58%	Homes owned	57.5%	62.3%	Transportation Index	86.4	100.0
Property tax rate	$6.58	$12.00	Home price ratio	3.8	4.2	Healthcare Index	91.4	100.0
						Miscellaneous Cost Index	93.5	100.0

Cost of Living — **Score:** 25.9 **Rank:** 276

Climate
Score: 57.2
Rank: 159

TEMPERATURE	AREA	U.S. AVG
Average January low	25.0	26.2
July high	86.4	87.4
Annual days > 90°F	31	38
Annual days < 32°F	90	89
Annual days < 0°F	0	6

PRECIPITATION	AREA	U.S. AVG
Annual inches precipitation	40.6	37.7
Annual inches snowfall	24.0	7.0
Annual days precipitation	120	109
Annual days rain > 0.5 inches	26	22
Annual days snow > 1.5 inches	5	6

COMFORTS & HAZARDS	AREA	U.S. AVG
July relative humidity	54%	66%
Annual days mostly sunny	205	208
Annual days with thunderstorms	38	39
Tornado risk score	1	18
Hurricane risk score	1	13

TEMPERATURE

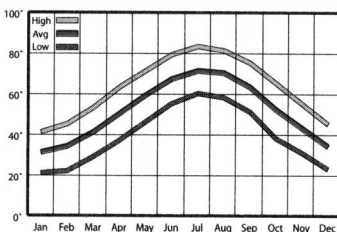

PRECIPITATION

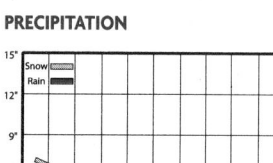

DAYS OF CLOUDS & PRECIPITATION

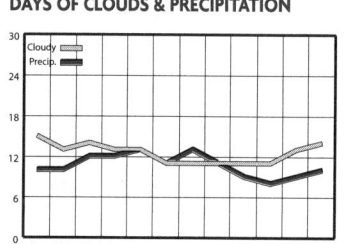

Education
Score: 75.4
Rank: 93

ACHIEVEMENT	AREA	U.S. AVG
High school degree	80.6%	82.7%
2-year college degree	6.3%	6.4%
4-year college degree	14.5%	15.7%
Graduate/professional degree	14.3%	8.9%

PUBLIC SCHOOLS	AREA	U.S. AVG
Expenditures per pupil	$5,436	$5,686
Student/teacher ratio	14.3	16.7
Attending public school	97.2%	90.1%
State SAT score	1025*	1021
State ACT score	21.1	20.9

HIGHER EDUCATION	AREA	U.S. AVG
No. 2-year colleges	1	4
No. 4-year colleges/universities	4	6
No. highly ranked universities	1	1

Health & Healthcare
Score: 96.3
Rank: 15

HAZARDS & ILLNESSES	AREA	U.S. AVG
Air-quality score	61	37
Water-quality score	97	52
Pollen/allergy score	55	61
Cancer mortality per capita	184.5	201.9
Depression days per month	4.2	3.5
Stress score	9	50

HEALTHCARE	AREA	U.S. AVG
Physicians per capita	167.4	244.2
Hospital beds per capita	316.7	420.0
No. teaching hospitals	0	3
Cost per doctor visit	$65	$77
Cost per dental visit	$61	$70

Crime
Score: 99.2
Rank: 4

CRIME	AREA	U.S. AVG
Violent crime rate	195.4	465.5
Change in violent crime rate	19.4%	-2.2%
Property crime rate	2,675.7	3,517.1
Change in property crime rate	22.0%	-2.1%

Transportation
Score: 35.8
Rank: 241

COMMUTE	AREA	U.S. AVG
Average commute time	22.1	27.4
Percent commutes > 60 mins.	4.0%	5.9%
Commute by auto	79.3%	78.9%
Commute by mass transit	1.7%	1.9%
Work at home	2.5%	3.1%
Mass transit miles per capita	1.74	1.87

INTERCITY SERVICES	AREA	U.S. AVG
Major airports within 60 miles	0	1
Size of regional airport	Small	Large
Daily airline activity	173	686
Amtrak service	No	No

AUTOMOTIVE	AREA	U.S. AVG
Insurance, annual premium	$984	$1,432
Gas, cost per gallon	$2.38	$2.49
Daily vehicle miles per capita	20.0	24.0

Leisure
Score: 28.1
Rank: 268

DINING & SHOPPING	AREA	U.S. AVG
Restaurant rating	2	2
Outlet mall score	0	42
No. Starbucks	3	13
No. warehouse clubs	0	2

ENTERTAINMENT	AREA	U.S. AVG
Professional sports rating	1	4
College sports rating	5	4
Zoo/aquarium rating	2	3
Amusement park rating	1	3
Botanical garden/ arboretum rating	1	4

OUTDOOR ACTIVITIES	AREA	U.S. AVG
Golf-course rating	2	4
Ski-area rating	1	3
Sq. miles inland water	2	4
Miles of coastline	0.0	10.7
National Park rating	5	3

Arts & Culture
Score: 12.3
Rank: 327

MEDIA & LIBRARIES	AREA	U.S. AVG
Arts radio rating	1	3
No. public libraries	8	27
Library volumes per capita	2.48	2.78

PERFORMING ARTS	AREA	U.S. AVG
Classical music rating	2	4
Ballet/dance rating	1	3
Professional theater rating	1	3
University arts programs rating	3	5

MUSEUMS	AREA	U.S. AVG
Overall museum rating	2	5
Art museum rating	4	5
Science museum rating	1	5
Children's museum rating	1	3

Bloomington, IN

Score: 70.5   **Rank:** 86   **2004 rank:** 29

Profile: College town
Location: South-central Indiana, 45 miles south of Indianapolis
Elevation: 928 feet
Time zone: Eastern Standard Time

PRO	CON
College-town atmosphere	Housing cost
Attractive setting	Recent employment declines
Nearby recreation	Low ethnic diversity

Bloomington is a true college town, with a large and attractive campus to the northeast of downtown; an area of shops, restaurants, and nightlife serving the student community; and a typically Midwestern town square with a courthouse at the center. Indiana University, founded in 1820 and currently serving some 35,000 students, provides a variety of culture and entertainment and is the dominant factor in the local economy and character. Sports, particularly basketball, are a local obsession. The university is also home to one of the top music schools in the nation. Educational attainment here is among the highest in the state, crime is low, the economy is steady, and attitudes are progressive. Compared to other Indiana cities, housing is in relatively short supply and expensive, and some arriving from other places may find good jobs in short supply. Nearby Lake Monroe, the Hoosier National Forest, and Brown County State Park provide good outdoor recreation; the adventurous can swim in abandoned limestone quarries.

The area is mostly deciduous wooded hills crisscrossed by creek drainages. Summers are warm and humid with frequent thundershowers, but with diminished severity compared to areas to the north. The area is far enough south of Lake Michigan to avoid much of its snows and bitter cold. First freeze is mid-October; last is late April.

DEMOGRAPHICS	AREA	U.S. AVG	ETHNIC COMPOSITION	AREA	U.S. AVG	RESIDENT PROFILE	AREA	U.S. AVG
Population	181,149		White	92.6%	79.0%	Single	40.9%	32.4%
Population density per sq. mile	137.1	358.5	Black	1.9%	10.5%	Married	46.7%	52.7%
Population growth	16.1%	21.1%	Asian	3.0%	2.7%	Divorced/separated	12.4%	14.9%
Median age	32.5	36.1	Hispanic	1.5%	10.6%	Married with children	19.8%	23.7%
Percent Democrat	47.4%	44.5%	Religious observance	33.6%	48.9%	Single with children	6.9%	9.1%
Percent Republican	51.4%	54.5%	Diversity measure	16.3	40.1	Percent over age 65	11.1%	12.9%

Economy & Jobs
Score: 5.9
Rank: 351

INCOME	AREA	U.S. AVG	EMPLOYMENT	AREA	U.S. AVG	EMPLOYING INDUSTRIES	AREA	U.S. AVG
Per capita income	$20,836	$23,235	Unemployment rate	5.1%	4.7%	Largest: Manufacturing		
Household income	$38,627	$46,414	Recent job growth	-1.0%	1.3%			
Household income < $25K	32.8%	26.2%	Projected future job growth	5.6%	11.5%	Percent manufacturing	15.2%	15.4%
Household income > $75K	20.7%	25.4%	White collar	57.6%	57.8%	Percent public sector	21.0%	15.7%
Household income growth	14.1%	13.6%	Blue collar	25.2%	25.2%	Percent construction	10.0%	9.9%

Cost of Living
Score: 76.2
Rank: 90

INDEXES & TAXES	AREA	U.S. AVG	HOUSING	AREA	U.S. AVG	NECESSITIES	AREA	U.S. AVG
Cost of Living Index	89.8	100.0	Median home price	$151,800	$220,000	Food Index	104.6	100.0
Buying Power Index	96.4	100.0	Home price appreciation	25.1%	10.1%	Housing Index	56.5	100.0
Income tax rate	3.90%	4.70%	Median rent	$623	$709	Utilities Index	92.4	100.0
Sales tax rate	6.00%	6.58%	Homes owned	56.7%	62.3%	Transportation Index	97.0	100.0
Property tax rate	$9.09	$12.00	Home price ratio	3.9	4.2	Healthcare Index	102.2	100.0
						Miscellaneous Cost Index	108.7	100.0

Climate
Score: 49.2
Rank: 189

TEMPERATURE	AREA	U.S. AVG	PRECIPITATION	AREA	U.S. AVG	COMFORTS & HAZARDS	AREA	U.S. AVG
Average January low	19.7	26.2	Annual inches precipitation	39.0	37.7	July relative humidity	73%	66%
July high	85.4	87.4	Annual inches snowfall	21.0	7.0	Annual days mostly sunny	191	208
Annual days > 90°F	15	38	Annual days precipitation	122	109	Annual days with thunderstorms	45	39
Annual days < 32°F	122	89	Annual days rain > 0.5 inches	25	22	Tornado risk score	15	18
Annual days < 0°F	7	6	Annual days snow > 1.5 inches	6	6	Hurricane risk score	4	13

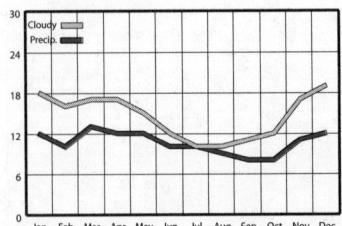

TEMPERATURE

PRECIPITATION

DAYS OF CLOUDS & PRECIPITATION

Education
Score: 65.2
Rank: 131

ACHIEVEMENT	AREA	U.S. AVG	PUBLIC SCHOOLS	AREA	U.S. AVG	HIGHER EDUCATION	AREA	U.S. AVG
High school degree	85.1%	82.7%	Expenditures per pupil	$5,644	$5,686	No. 2-year colleges	1	4
2-year college degree	5.2%	6.4%	Student/teacher ratio	17.8	16.7	No. 4-year colleges/universities	1	6
4-year college degree	16.0%	15.7%	Attending public school	92.3%	90.1%	No. highly ranked universities	0	1
Graduate/professional degree	14.9%	8.9%	State SAT score	1007*	1021			
			State ACT score	21.7	20.9			

Health & Healthcare
Score: 38.2
Rank: 230

HAZARDS & ILLNESSES	AREA	U.S. AVG	HEALTHCARE	AREA	U.S. AVG	CRIME	AREA	U.S. AVG
Air-quality score	56	37	Physicians per capita	188.3	244.2	Violent crime rate	185.4	465.5
Water-quality score	30	52	Hospital beds per capita	216.9	420.0	Change in violent crime rate	10.6%	-2.2%
Pollen/allergy score	73	61	No. teaching hospitals	0	3	Property crime rate	2,693.7	3,517.1
Cancer mortality per capita	212.1	201.9	Cost per doctor visit	$69	$77	Change in property crime rate	6.2%	-2.1%
Depression days per month	3.4	3.5	Cost per dental visit	$66	$70			
Stress score	32	50						

Crime
Score: 86.6
Rank: 51

Transportation
Score: 51.3
Rank: 183

COMMUTE	AREA	U.S. AVG	INTERCITY SERVICES	AREA	U.S. AVG	AUTOMOTIVE	AREA	U.S. AVG
Average commute time	24.5	27.4	Major airports within 60 miles	2	1	Insurance, annual premium	$1,000	$1,432
Percent commutes > 60 mins.	7.9%	5.9%	Size of regional airport	Medium	Large	Gas, cost per gallon	$2.50	$2.49
Commute by auto	75.3%	78.9%	Daily airline activity	547	686	Daily vehicle miles per capita	20.7	24.0
Commute by mass transit	1.2%	1.9%	Amtrak service	No	No			
Work at home	3.5%	3.1%						
Mass transit miles per capita	1.22	1.87						

Leisure
Score: 50.0
Rank: 186

DINING & SHOPPING	AREA	U.S. AVG	ENTERTAINMENT	AREA	U.S. AVG	OUTDOOR ACTIVITIES	AREA	U.S. AVG
Restaurant rating	1	2	Professional sports rating	2	4	Golf-course rating	7	4
Outlet mall score	53	42	College sports rating	6	4	Ski-area rating	4	3
No. Starbucks	3	13	Zoo/aquarium rating	1	3	Sq. miles inland water	3	4
No. warehouse clubs	1	2	Amusement park rating	1	3	Miles of coastline	0.0	10.7
			Botanical garden/arboretum rating	2	4	National Park rating	1	3

Arts & Culture
Score: 49.5
Rank: 189

MEDIA & LIBRARIES	AREA	U.S. AVG	PERFORMING ARTS	AREA	U.S. AVG	MUSEUMS	AREA	U.S. AVG
Arts radio rating	1	3	Classical music rating	3	4	Overall museum rating	3	5
No. public libraries	9	27	Ballet/dance rating	1	3	Art museum rating	6	5
Library volumes per capita	3.69	2.78	Professional theater rating	1	3	Science museum rating	5	5
			University arts programs rating	5	5	Children's museum rating	1	3

Bloomington–Normal, IL

Score: 66.6   Rank: 124   2004 rank: 42

Profile: Mid-size-city complex
Location: North-central Illinois, 100 miles southwest of Chicago
Elevation: 662 feet
Time zone: Central Standard Time

PRO	CON
Small-town atmosphere	Entertainment
Stable economy	Air service
Educated population	Unattractive landscape

Bloomington and sister city Normal are a typical Illinois "prairie" town pair near the center of the state. However, the campuses of Illinois State University and Illinois Wesleyan University, with their college-town flavor, add a unique element and a few amenities. The troubled Mitsubishi Motors is the largest manufacturer, but the insurance and financial services and agricultural interests steady the economy. State Farm Insurance makes its headquarters in Bloomington and is by far the largest employer. The city is clean and quiet, with an educated population and a large annual Shakespeare festival. Living is simple and stress-free, but some might not find enough to do. Commutes are among the shortest in the country, rates for property crime are low, and air quality is excellent. The area scores consistently well in all categories, resulting in a relatively high ranking.

The terrain is a typically flat, agricultural Illinois prairie with few topographic features. Summers are warm and humid with pleasant weather in June and September. Most precipitation falls as thunderstorms in the summer, and drops off in the winter with a mix of rain and snow. First freeze is late October; last is late April.

Population

DEMOGRAPHICS	AREA	U.S. AVG	ETHNIC COMPOSITION	AREA	U.S. AVG	RESIDENT PROFILE	AREA	U.S. AVG
Population	159,689		White	87.1%	79.0%	Single	36.7%	32.4%
Population density per sq. mile	134.9	358.5	Black	6.6%	10.5%	Married	49.9%	52.7%
Population growth	23.6%	21.1%	Asian	3.1%	2.7%	Divorced/separated	13.4%	14.9%
Median age	31.9	36.1	Hispanic	3.4%	10.6%	Married with children	24.4%	23.7%
Percent Democrat	41.7%	44.5%	Religious observance	44.2%	48.9%	Single with children	7.2%	9.1%
Percent Republican	57.6%	54.5%	Diversity measure	28.7	40.1	Percent over age 65	9.7%	12.9%

Economy & Jobs
Score: 73.8
Rank: 99

INCOME	AREA	U.S. AVG	EMPLOYMENT	AREA	U.S. AVG	EMPLOYING INDUSTRIES	AREA	U.S. AVG
Per capita income	$26,140	$23,235	Unemployment rate	4.1%	4.7%	Largest: Finance & Insurance		
Household income	$53,412	$46,414	Recent job growth	1.9%	1.3%			
Household income ‹ $25K	21.4%	26.2%	Projected future job growth	13.9%	11.5%	Percent manufacturing	10.5%	15.4%
Household income › $75K	32.2%	25.4%	White collar	66.1%	57.8%	Percent public sector	13.8%	15.7%
Household income growth	13.6%	13.6%	Blue collar	17.6%	25.2%	Percent construction	7.1%	9.9%

Cost of Living
Score: 46.0
Rank: 202

INDEXES & TAXES	AREA	U.S. AVG	HOUSING	AREA	U.S. AVG	NECESSITIES	AREA	U.S. AVG
Cost of Living Index	91.3	100.0	Median home price	$151,000	$220,000	Food Index	97.5	100.0
Buying Power Index	131.1	100.0	Home price appreciation	19.3%	10.1%	Housing Index	70.2	100.0
Income tax rate	3.00%	4.70%	Median rent	$644	$709	Utilities Index	107.6	100.0
Sales tax rate	6.25%	6.58%	Homes owned	63.2%	62.3%	Transportation Index	104.8	100.0
Property tax rate	$19.55	$12.00	Home price ratio	2.8	4.2	Healthcare Index	99.9	100.0
						Miscellaneous Cost Index	109.7	100.0

Climate
Score: 38.0
Rank: 231

TEMPERATURE	AREA	U.S. AVG	PRECIPITATION	AREA	U.S. AVG	COMFORTS & HAZARDS	AREA	U.S. AVG
Average January low	15.7	26.2	Annual inches precipitation	35.0	37.7	July relative humidity	72%	66%
July high	85.5	87.4	Annual inches snowfall	23.0	7.0	Annual days mostly sunny	197	208
Annual days › 90°F	17	38	Annual days precipitation	111	109	Annual days with thunderstorms	49	39
Annual days ‹ 32°F	132	89	Annual days rain › 0.5 inches	24	22	Tornado risk score	39	18
Annual days ‹ 0°F	11	6	Annual days snow › 1.5 inches	6	6	Hurricane risk score	2	13

TEMPERATURE

PRECIPITATION

DAYS OF CLOUDS & PRECIPITATION

Education
Score: 87.2
Rank: 49

ACHIEVEMENT	AREA	U.S. AVG	PUBLIC SCHOOLS	AREA	U.S. AVG	HIGHER EDUCATION	AREA	U.S. AVG
High school degree	91.0%	82.7%	Expenditures per pupil	$4,863	$5,686	No. 2-year colleges	1	4
2-year college degree	5.8%	6.4%	Student/teacher ratio	16.6	16.7	No. 4-year colleges/universities	2	6
4-year college degree	26.0%	15.7%	Attending public school	89.2%	90.1%	No. highly ranked universities	1	1
Graduate/professional degree	11.1%	8.9%	State SAT score	1200	1021			
			State ACT score	20.5*	20.9			

Health & Healthcare
Score: 51.3
Rank: 183

Crime
Score: 55.1
Rank: 169

HAZARDS & ILLNESSES	AREA	U.S. AVG	HEALTHCARE	AREA	U.S. AVG	CRIME	AREA	U.S. AVG
Air-quality score	40	37	Physicians per capita	184.9	244.2	Violent crime rate	497.4	465.5
Water-quality score	40	52	Hospital beds per capita	365.7	420.0	Change in violent crime rate	8.6%	-2.2%
Pollen/allergy score	49	61	No. teaching hospitals	0	3	Property crime rate	2,812.6	3,517.1
Cancer mortality per capita	189.4	201.9	Cost per doctor visit	$86	$77	Change in property crime rate	1.8%	-2.1%
Depression days per month	2.4	3.5	Cost per dental visit	$67	$70			
Stress score	4	50						

Transportation
Score: 59.1
Rank: 153

COMMUTE	AREA	U.S. AVG	INTERCITY SERVICES	AREA	U.S. AVG	AUTOMOTIVE	AREA	U.S. AVG
Average commute time	18.8	27.4	Major airports within 60 miles	0	1	Insurance, annual premium	$1,004	$1,432
Percent commutes › 60 mins.	2.9%	5.9%	Size of regional airport	None	Large	Gas, cost per gallon	$2.50	$2.49
Commute by auto	80.2%	78.9%	Daily airline activity	26	686	Daily vehicle miles per capita	26.0	24.0
Commute by mass transit	1.1%	1.9%	Amtrak service	Yes	No			
Work at home	3.2%	3.1%						
Mass transit miles per capita	1.07	1.87						

DINING & SHOPPING	AREA	U.S. AVG	ENTERTAINMENT	AREA	U.S. AVG	OUTDOOR ACTIVITIES	AREA	U.S. AVG
Restaurant rating	1	2	Professional sports rating	2	4	Golf-course rating	2	4
Outlet mall score	44	42	College sports rating	4	4	Ski-area rating	2	3
No. Starbucks	2	13	Zoo/aquarium rating	3	3	Sq. miles inland water	2	4
No. warehouse clubs	0	2	Amusement park rating	1	3	Miles of coastline	0.0	10.7
			Botanical garden/ arboretum rating	1	4	National Park rating	1	3

Leisure
Score: 26.2
Rank: 275

MEDIA & LIBRARIES	AREA	U.S. AVG	PERFORMING ARTS	AREA	U.S. AVG	MUSEUMS	AREA	U.S. AVG
Arts radio rating	1	3	Classical music rating	6	4	Overall museum rating	4	5
No. public libraries	14	27	Ballet/dance rating	1	3	Art museum rating	2	5
Library volumes per capita	3.88	2.78	Professional theater rating	1	3	Science museum rating	1	5
			University arts programs rating	8	5	Children's museum rating	2	3

Arts & Culture
Score: 54.5
Rank: 169

Boise City–Nampa, ID   Score: 89.6   Rank: 10   2004 rank: 68

Profile: Mid-size capital city
Location: Southwestern Idaho, on a river plain at the base of the Boise Mountains
Elevation: 2,868 feet
Time zone: Mountain Standard Time

PRO	CON
Attractive setting	Growth and sprawl
Outdoor recreation	Economic cycles
Mild climate	Entertainment

Boise is the capital, largest city, and cultural center of Idaho. The clean, attractive, yet somewhat plain downtown is framed by mountains to the northeast and irrigated agricultural plains to the west. The economy is a diverse blend of agriculture, agricultural processing, light manufacturing, and high-tech industries, including Micron Technology (semiconductors), Hewlett-Packard, and J.R. Simplot (agriculture and french-fry fame). The presence of state government rounds out the economic picture. More recently, the mountains, pleasant climate, and low costs relative to other West Coast locations have brought a strong surge of migrants, many from California, and the typical construction, real estate, and service businesses that emerge from such migration. Considerable recent job growth has resulted from this migration.

Outdoor recreation is abundant, with excellent fishing, hiking, bicycling, and other activities, particularly in the Boise National Forest just to the northeast. Bogus Basin offers an after-work ski opportunity 20 miles away. In town, the historic commercial area west of downtown has been revitalized and serves as a destination with a well-attended farmer's market. Boise State University adds some college life, but entertainment and nightlife are not the city's strong suits. Residential areas have begun to sprawl into agricultural lands to the west towards Eagle and Nampa, resulting in suburban sprawl and concerns about traffic and water supply, although many of these suburbs are more attractive than other Western counterparts. Cost of living is growing (at 105.0) but is still reasonable especially for the region.

The Boise Mountains, which rise 5,000 feet to 8,000 feet, are covered with a mix of sagebrush and chaparral, giving way to ridges of fir, spruce, and pine at the summits. To the south and west, the land is generally level with benches defined by former flows of the Boise and Snake rivers. Summer offers low humidity and generally pleasant days, punctuated by an occasional thunderstorm or heat wave from the south. Temperatures over 100°F occur nearly every year. Winters are mostly mild with periods of clouds and brisk, stormy weather. Occasional cold spells drop temperatures to 10°F or lower with periodic snow and fog. Most precipitation occurs in the winter. First freeze is early October; last is early May.

DEMOGRAPHICS	AREA	U.S. AVG	ETHNIC COMPOSITION	AREA	U.S. AVG	RESIDENT PROFILE	AREA	U.S. AVG
Population	530,294		White	88.4%	79.0%	Single	27.0%	32.4%
Population density per sq. mile	45.0	358.5	Black	0.6%	10.5%	Married	58.0%	52.7%
Population growth	66.7%	21.1%	Asian	1.7%	2.7%	Divorced/separated	15.0%	14.9%
Median age	33.5	36.1	Hispanic	10.3%	10.6%	Married with children	28.8%	23.7%
Percent Democrat	32.6%	44.5%	Religious observance	42.5%	48.9%	Single with children	8.4%	9.1%
Percent Republican	66.2%	54.5%	Diversity measure	33.9	40.1	Percent over age 65	10.1%	12.9%

Population

INCOME	AREA	U.S. AVG	EMPLOYMENT	AREA	U.S. AVG	EMPLOYING INDUSTRIES	AREA	U.S. AVG
Per capita income	$22,552	$23,235	Unemployment rate	3.6%	4.7%	Largest: Manufacturing		
Household income	$48,094	$46,414	Recent job growth	5.8%	1.3%			
Household income < $25K	22.7%	26.2%	Projected future job growth	29.5%	11.5%	Percent manufacturing	13.3%	15.4%
Household income > $75K	25.7%	25.4%	White collar	59.8%	57.8%	Percent public sector	14.5%	15.7%
Household income growth	13.9%	13.6%	Blue collar	23.6%	25.2%	Percent construction	10.3%	9.9%

Economy & Jobs
Score: 98.4
Rank: 7

Cost of Living
Score: 32.6
Rank: 252

INDEXES & TAXES	AREA	U.S. AVG	HOUSING	AREA	U.S. AVG	NECESSITIES	AREA	U.S. AVG
Cost of Living Index	105.0	100.0	Median home price	$269,000	$220,000	Food Index	95.8	100.0
Buying Power Index	102.7	100.0	Home price appreciation	50.6%	10.1%	Housing Index	63.3	100.0
Income tax rate	8.20%	4.70%	Median rent	$692	$709	Utilities Index	75.4	100.0
Sales tax rate	6.00%	6.58%	Homes owned	69.4%	62.3%	Transportation Index	100.9	100.0
Property tax rate	$10.61	$12.00	Home price ratio	5.6	4.2	Healthcare Index	111.6	100.0
						Miscellaneous Cost Index	99.6	100.0

Climate
Score: 58.3
Rank: 155

TEMPERATURE	AREA	U.S. AVG	PRECIPITATION	AREA	U.S. AVG	COMFORTS & HAZARDS	AREA	U.S. AVG
Average January low	21.4	26.2	Annual inches precipitation	12.0	37.7	July relative humidity	57%	66%
July high	90.5	87.4	Annual inches snowfall	21.0	7.0	Annual days mostly sunny	214	208
Annual days > 90°F	43	38	Annual days precipitation	91	109	Annual days with thunderstorms	15	39
Annual days < 32°F	124	89	Annual days rain > 0.5 inches	3	22	Tornado risk score	4	18
Annual days < 0°F	2	6	Annual days snow > 1.5 inches	5	6	Hurricane risk score	0	13

TEMPERATURE

PRECIPITATION

DAYS OF CLOUDS & PRECIPITATION

Education
Score: 68.2
Rank: 120

ACHIEVEMENT	AREA	U.S. AVG	PUBLIC SCHOOLS	AREA	U.S. AVG	HIGHER EDUCATION	AREA	U.S. AVG
High school degree	85.7%	82.7%	Expenditures per pupil	$4,471	$5,686	No. 2-year colleges	5	4
2-year college degree	6.8%	6.4%	Student/teacher ratio	18.1	16.7	No. 4-year colleges/universities	6	6
4-year college degree	17.5%	15.7%	Attending public school	94.3%	90.1%	No. highly ranked universities	1	1
Graduate/professional degree	7.6%	8.9%	State SAT score	1088	1021			
			State ACT score	21.4*	20.9			

Health & Healthcare
Score: 32.1
Rank: 253

Crime
Score: 44.7
Rank: 207

HAZARDS & ILLNESSES	AREA	U.S. AVG	HEALTHCARE	AREA	U.S. AVG	CRIME	AREA	U.S. AVG
Air-quality score	30	37	Physicians per capita	201.3	244.2	Violent crime rate	314.8	465.5
Water-quality score	24	52	Hospital beds per capita	217.4	420.0	Change in violent crime rate	-0.2%	-2.2%
Pollen/allergy score	45	61	No. teaching hospitals	3	3	Property crime rate	3,085.2	3,517.1
Cancer mortality per capita	166.2	201.9	Cost per doctor visit	$80	$77	Change in property crime rate	2.0%	-2.1%
Depression days per month	3.5	3.5	Cost per dental visit	$75	$70			
Stress score	21	50						

Transportation
Score: 22.7
Rank: 290

COMMUTE	AREA	U.S. AVG	INTERCITY SERVICES	AREA	U.S. AVG	AUTOMOTIVE	AREA	U.S. AVG
Average commute time	22.9	27.4	Major airports within 60 miles	0	1	Insurance, annual premium	$998	$1,432
Percent commutes > 60 mins.	3.2%	5.9%	Size of regional airport	Small	Large	Gas, cost per gallon	$2.33	$2.49
Commute by auto	79.5%	78.9%	Daily airline activity	112	686	Daily vehicle miles per capita	22.6	24.0
Commute by mass transit	0.6%	1.9%	Amtrak service	No	No			
Work at home	4.3%	3.1%						
Mass transit miles per capita	0.56	1.87						

Leisure
Score: 54.5
Rank: 170

DINING & SHOPPING	AREA	U.S. AVG	ENTERTAINMENT	AREA	U.S. AVG	OUTDOOR ACTIVITIES	AREA	U.S. AVG
Restaurant rating	1	2	Professional sports rating	3	4	Golf-course rating	2	4
Outlet mall score	26	42	College sports rating	4	4	Ski-area rating	10	3
No. Starbucks	13	13	Zoo/aquarium rating	1	3	Sq. miles inland water	2	4
No. warehouse clubs	1	2	Amusement park rating	1	3	Miles of coastline	0.0	10.7
			Botanical garden/ arboretum rating	1	4	National Park rating	2	3

Arts & Culture
Score: 62.3
Rank: 141

MEDIA & LIBRARIES	AREA	U.S. AVG	PERFORMING ARTS	AREA	U.S. AVG	MUSEUMS	AREA	U.S. AVG
Arts radio rating	8	3	Classical music rating	3	4	Overall museum rating	5	5
No. public libraries	24	27	Ballet/dance rating	3	3	Art museum rating	5	5
Library volumes per capita	2.40	2.78	Professional theater rating	1	3	Science museum rating	5	5
			University arts programs rating	5	5	Children's museum rating	1	3

Boston–Quincy, MA

Score: 61.4   **Rank:** 160   **2004 rank:** 71

Profile: Regional center/capital city
Location: Central Massachusetts coast at the head of Boston Bay
Elevation: 29 feet
Time zone: Eastern Standard Time

PRO	CON
Historic interest	Cost of living
Arts and culture	Traffic and sprawl
Education	Economic cycles

Boston is widely viewed as the intellectual and historic capital of the United States. It is a cosmopolitan city with a complete set of services, a broad range of amenities, and a rich tradition and culture almost unmatched in the rest of the country. The metro area defined as Boston–Quincy actually includes downtown and areas mostly south of city into Norfolk and Plymouth counties. Suburbs to the west and northwest are covered in the Cambridge–Newton–Framingham metro area (p. 243); northern suburbs to New Hampshire are covered in the Essex County MSA (p. 341).

Boston has a modern, attractive, and completely walkable downtown. It is dotted with Revolutionary-period historic sites along the Freedom Trail and preserved old streetscapes mixed in with modern commercial office buildings. The layout is interesting, and not at all on a typical grid—there are surprises around every corner. Areas near the waterfront are filled with attractions, including the historic Faneuil Hall marketplace, an excellent aquarium, numerous shops and restaurants, and the historic North End. Downtown, a world-class financial center, bustles with business and government workers and tourists at most times of day, most times of the year. Smart Bostonians learn to take the train—a day of waterfront parking costs $29. In fact, Boston, necessitated by geography and the spread of suburbs all around, has an excellent and well-used commuter rail system; anyone planning to work downtown is well served to get familiar with it. As a general rule, arts and culture amenities in downtown Boston and the entire area are exceptional, and most, like the Boston Pops and the Museum of Fine Arts, are well known beyond the city limits. Boston's affinity for professional sports hardly needs mention, and the fact that 36,000-seat Fenway Park still exists well illustrates the area's devotion to tradition. Education, at all levels, is excellent in the Boston area. Area public schools are nationally recognized; people move to the area just for the schools. Boston has the largest number of highly ranked universities in the country.

That tradition goes well beyond the limits of downtown, where living accommodations are either expensive high-rises or the posh historical gem of Beacon Hill just west of the main downtown business district. Suburban Boston is really a series of old towns, set up and distanced in the days of horseback a few miles apart. These towns, some along main corridors, some connected by roads following old Indian trails that seem to wind endlessly through the woods and past one stately home after another, are generally preserved as much as possible in their original form. Each neighborhood has its own little town center, clean, functional, accessible, and dominated by local businesses. Homes are well preserved and on large lots, and few sprawling "maze" subdivisions are found—most developments are a single street off of one of the thoroughfares. You won't find very many Tuscan villas in the Boston area; people take their style and architectural heritage very seriously, and Boston is a virtual museum of American residential architecture, both in the older inner city and more rural suburbs. The result: Housing is expensive, but it is a good value.

Interstate 95, the innermost of the city's two beltways and better known locally as Route 128, became famous in the 1980s as a location for high-tech companies, an industry which today centers on biotech and emerging technologies. Commutes to these areas generally require a car, and traffic and long commutes are a concern. The employment picture in recent years has been mixed, partly due to rollover in start-up firms and to high business costs. The latter seems to affect businesses such as textiles and shipbuilding the hardest. There are still several industrial areas, but industry and manufacturing do not define the future. Businesses with a stronger research and development component are more likely to prosper.

The Boston-Quincy metro area starts downtown, where living accommodations are either expensive high-rises or the posh historical gem of Beacon Hill just west of the main downtown business district. Older, more working class neighborhoods lie south in Quincy, Braintree, and Dedham, mixed in with commercial areas. From there, living choices lie primarily along three corridors. The Interstate 95 corridor, farthest west and south of the inner beltway, is the fastest growing area, especially out towards Foxboro and beyond. Excellent family communities can be found in and around Westwood, Sharon, and Attleboro. The State Route 24 corridor to the east is more commercial but also has good residential areas: Randolph, Avon, and the old mill town of Brockton. Finally, areas south and west of State Route 3 offer excellent housing and good values—the Hanovers and the Pembrokes are classic with lots of small lakes adding to the scenery. Proximity to the Atlantic Ocean also brings somewhat cooler summer evenings.

Boston's positives—education, arts, entertainment, historic interest, housing—are unquestionably among the tops in the U.S. But it's expensive, fast-paced, and has a challenging climate, and many find it stressful. For those able to deal with these shortcomings, it is hard to do better. But the declining ranking reflects high cost of living, a hardy climate, congestion, and loss of some of its more promising areas northeast and northwest when the metro area was split.

Boston is located in a basin where the Charles River enters the Boston Bay and Atlantic Ocean. It is relatively level with land rising in all directions. Storm tracks, latitude, and the coastal location work together to guarantee changing weather patterns and significant precipitation. Hot summer afternoons are frequently relieved by locally celebrated sea breezes, particularly close to shore. Winter cold is moderated by the relatively warm ocean. Summer precipitation comes mainly as intermittent showers and thunderstorms. Passing storms, particularly coastal "noreasters," produce heavy rain and snow especially in winter. Snow on the ground is prevalent with occasional thaws. Fog can be expected all times of year. First freeze is early November; last is early April—but add a month to each end in inland suburban locations.

Population

DEMOGRAPHICS	AREA	U.S. AVG
Population	1,821,563	
Population density per sq. mile	1627.8	358.5
Population growth	6.4%	21.1%
Median age	36.9	36.1
Percent Democrat	64.2%	44.5%
Percent Republican	34.6%	54.5%

ETHNIC COMPOSITION	AREA	U.S. AVG
White	75.5%	79.0%
Black	11.0%	10.5%
Asian	5.6%	2.7%
Hispanic	7.8%	10.6%
Religious observance	64.6%	48.9%
Diversity measure	44.5	40.1

RESIDENT PROFILE	AREA	U.S. AVG
Single	41.5%	32.4%
Married	45.4%	52.7%
Divorced/separated	13.0%	14.9%
Married with children	21.4%	23.7%
Single with children	8.1%	9.1%
Percent over age 65	12.5%	12.9%

Economy & Jobs
Score: 9.9 Rank: 335

INCOME	AREA	U.S. AVG
Per capita income	$31,736	$23,235
Household income	$61,281	$46,414
Household income < $25K	20.8%	26.2%
Household income > $75K	39.9%	25.4%
Household income growth	16.9%	13.6%

EMPLOYMENT	AREA	U.S. AVG
Unemployment rate	4.9%	4.7%
Recent job growth	0.3%	1.3%
Projected future job growth	3.6%	11.5%
White collar	69.0%	57.8%
Blue collar	16.1%	25.2%

EMPLOYING INDUSTRIES	AREA	U.S. AVG
Largest: Finance & Insurance		
Percent manufacturing	9.1%	15.4%
Percent public sector	13.2%	15.7%
Percent construction	7.0%	9.9%

Cost of Living
Score: 10.4 Rank: 334

INDEXES & TAXES	AREA	U.S. AVG
Cost of Living Index	134.2	100.0
Buying Power Index	102.4	100.0
Income tax rate	5.95%	4.70%
Sales tax rate	5.00%	6.58%
Property tax rate	$11.77	$12.00

HOUSING	AREA	U.S. AVG
Median home price	$372,500	$220,000
Home price appreciation	61.3%	10.1%
Median rent	$1,335	$709
Homes owned	55.3%	62.3%
Home price ratio	6.1	4.2

NECESSITIES	AREA	U.S. AVG
Food Index	112.5	100.0
Housing Index	135.7	100.0
Utilities Index	126.2	100.0
Transportation Index	115.0	100.0
Healthcare Index	130.3	100.0
Miscellaneous Cost Index	111.8	100.0

Climate
Score: 30.5 Rank: 259

TEMPERATURE	AREA	U.S. AVG
Average January low	22.5	26.2
July high	81.4	87.4
Annual days > 90°F	12	38
Annual days < 32°F	99	89
Annual days < 0°F	1	6

PRECIPITATION	AREA	U.S. AVG
Annual inches precipitation	43.0	37.7
Annual inches snowfall	42.0	7.0
Annual days precipitation	128	109
Annual days rain > 0.5 inches	29	22
Annual days snow > 1.5 inches	15	6

COMFORTS & HAZARDS	AREA	U.S. AVG
July relative humidity	67%	66%
Annual days mostly sunny	205	208
Annual days with thunderstorms	19	39
Tornado risk score	10	18
Hurricane risk score	19	13

TEMPERATURE

PRECIPITATION

DAYS OF CLOUDS & PRECIPITATION

Education
Score: 99.2 Rank: 4

ACHIEVEMENT	AREA	U.S. AVG
High school degree	85.3%	82.7%
2-year college degree	6.9%	6.4%
4-year college degree	21.0%	15.7%
Graduate/professional degree	13.9%	8.9%

PUBLIC SCHOOLS	AREA	U.S. AVG
Expenditures per pupil	$7,654	$5,686
Student/teacher ratio	0.0	16.7
Attending public school	86.3%	90.1%
State SAT score	1037*	1021
State ACT score	23	20.9

HIGHER EDUCATION	AREA	U.S. AVG
No. 2-year colleges	17	4
No. 4-year colleges/universities	38	6
No. highly ranked universities	6	1

Health & Healthcare
Score: 29.4 Rank: 263

HAZARDS & ILLNESSES	AREA	U.S. AVG
Air-quality score	27	37
Water-quality score	20	52
Pollen/allergy score	67	61
Cancer mortality per capita	232.9	201.9
Depression days per month	3.4	3.5
Stress score	49	50

HEALTHCARE	AREA	U.S. AVG
Physicians per capita	548.9	244.2
Hospital beds per capita	599.9	420.0
No. teaching hospitals	22	3
Cost per doctor visit	$112	$77
Cost per dental visit	$99	$70

Crime
Score: 46.5 Rank: 199

CRIME	AREA	U.S. AVG
Violent crime rate	592.7	465.5
Change in violent crime rate	-1.0%	-2.2%
Property crime rate	2,690.5	3,517.1
Change in property crime rate	-7.0%	-2.1%

Transportation
Score: 68.7 Rank: 118

COMMUTE	AREA	U.S. AVG
Average commute time	33.0	27.4
Percent commutes > 60 mins.	11.9%	5.9%
Commute by auto	64.2%	78.9%
Commute by mass transit	17.4%	1.9%
Work at home	2.8%	3.1%
Mass transit miles per capita	17.39	1.87

INTERCITY SERVICES	AREA	U.S. AVG
Major airports within 60 miles	2	1
Size of regional airport	Large	Large
Daily airline activity	1278	686
Amtrak service	Yes	No

AUTOMOTIVE	AREA	U.S. AVG
Insurance, annual premium	$2,433	$1,432
Gas, cost per gallon	$2.43	$2.49
Daily vehicle miles per capita	22.9	24.0

DINING & SHOPPING	AREA	U.S. AVG	ENTERTAINMENT	AREA	U.S. AVG	OUTDOOR ACTIVITIES	AREA	U.S. AVG
Restaurant rating	6	2	Professional sports rating	9	4	Golf-course rating	9	4
Outlet mall score	181	42	College sports rating	10	4	Ski-area rating	7	3
No. Starbucks	55	13	Zoo/aquarium rating	8	3	Sq. miles inland water	7	4
No. warehouse clubs	7	2	Amusement park rating	7	3	Miles of coastline	39.8	10.7
			Botanical garden/			National Park rating	2	3
			arboretum rating	9	4			

Leisure
Score: 98.4
Rank: 7

MEDIA & LIBRARIES	AREA	U.S. AVG	PERFORMING ARTS	AREA	U.S. AVG	MUSEUMS	AREA	U.S. AVG
Arts radio rating	10	3	Classical music rating	10	4	Overall museum rating	10	5
No. public libraries	103	27	Ballet/dance rating	8	3	Art museum rating	10	5
Library volumes per capita	7.14	2.78	Professional theater rating	10	3	Science museum rating	9	5
			University arts programs rating	10	5	Children's museum rating	9	3

Arts & Culture
Score: 100.0
Rank: 1

Boulder, CO

Score: 76.1   **Rank:** 62   **2004 rank:** 142

Profile: College-town/suburban complex
Location: 25 miles northwest of Denver at the base of the Rocky Mountain Front Range
Elevation: 5,332 feet
Time zone: Mountain Standard Time

PRO	CON
College-town atmosphere	Cost of living and housing
Attractive downtown	Traffic and sprawl
Educational attainment	Economic cycles

Boulder, home to the University of Colorado, is a lively and classic college town, with liberal politics, alternative social lifestyles and attitudes, and an assortment of trendy small businesses, restaurants, galleries, and entertainment venues. There is plenty to do in this bicycle-friendly town, which has a pedestrian mall downtown and outdoor recreation in the nearby mountains. The area has the highest combined 4-year and graduate degree attainment rate in the nation. Some larger business and government research facilities add to the area's economy, and a sizeable high-tech belt is found toward Denver.

Part of the Boulder story is the set of small towns nearby that have exploded into large but generally well-planned and attractively priced suburbs positioned well to take advantage of what both Boulder and Denver have to offer. Longmont, a 2006 winner of an All-American City Award, is historically an agricultural town to the northeast currently experiencing a major housing boom. The towns of Louisville and Lafayette are also good examples. Located near the four-lane U.S. 36 corridor toward Denver, these former coal-mining towns have excellent housing and schools and plenty of nearby employment. Louisville received top honors in our *Best Places to Raise Your Family* (Wiley Publishing, 2006). Boulder would get a still higher ranking if it weren't for its Cost of Living Index (126.0), by far the highest in Colorado. Housing prices follow suit. High-tech dislocations created an employment dip in the early part of the decade but job trends are on the upswing.

Boulder lies in a shallow valley just at the foot of the Rockies, with surrounding areas of gently rolling grassland plateaus with occasional lakes and reservoirs. The surrounding suburbs occupy some of this higher ground, giving excellent views but also some exposure to inclement climate. Summer days are warm and sunny with low humidity and occasional thunderstorms, which can be heavy. Periods of extreme temperatures in winter are short, with the mountains providing some shielding from the worst and windiest cold weather. Large or persistent snow accumulations are uncommon, but occasional heavy snows, particularly in fall and spring, can disrupt transportation. First freeze is early October; last is late April.

DEMOGRAPHICS	AREA	U.S. AVG	ETHNIC COMPOSITION	AREA	U.S. AVG	RESIDENT PROFILE	AREA	U.S. AVG
Population	279,897		White	86.6%	79.0%	Single	35.8%	32.4%
Population density per sq. mile	384.1	358.5	Black	0.9%	10.5%	Married	50.2%	52.7%
Population growth	34.0%	21.1%	Asian	3.9%	2.7%	Divorced/separated	14.0%	14.9%
Median age	34.5	36.1	Hispanic	12.2%	10.6%	Married with children	23.6%	23.7%
Percent Democrat	66.3%	44.5%	Religious observance	47.2%	48.9%	Single with children	6.8%	9.1%
Percent Republican	32.4%	54.5%	Diversity measure	40.6	40.1	Percent over age 65	8.3%	12.9%

Population

INCOME	AREA	U.S. AVG	EMPLOYMENT	AREA	U.S. AVG	EMPLOYING INDUSTRIES	AREA	U.S. AVG
Per capita income	$34,021	$23,235	Unemployment rate	4.7%	4.7%	Largest: Prof & tech svcs.		
Household income	$64,976	$46,414	Recent job growth	1.8%	1.3%			
Household income < $25K	17.0%	26.2%	Projected future job growth	13.3%	11.5%	Percent manufacturing	7.5%	15.4%
Household income > $75K	42.5%	25.4%	White collar	73.9%	57.8%	Percent public sector	14.9%	15.7%
Household income growth	16.3%	13.6%	Blue collar	13.8%	25.2%	Percent construction	6.2%	9.9%

Economy & Jobs
Score: 57.2
Rank: 161

Cost of Living
Score: 9.1
Rank: 339

INDEXES & TAXES	AREA	U.S. AVG
Cost of Living Index	126.0	100.0
Buying Power Index	115.6	100.0
Income tax rate	5.00%	4.70%
Sales tax rate	8.16%	6.58%
Property tax rate	$6.69	$12.00

HOUSING	AREA	U.S. AVG
Median home price	$373,200	$220,000
Home price appreciation	23.6%	10.1%
Median rent	$1,041	$709
Homes owned	62.6%	62.3%
Home price ratio	5.7	4.2

NECESSITIES	AREA	U.S. AVG
Food Index	113.5	100.0
Housing Index	113.4	100.0
Utilities Index	84.9	100.0
Transportation Index	105.9	100.0
Healthcare Index	117.3	100.0
Miscellaneous Cost Index	97.0	100.0

Climate
Score: 54.5
Rank: 169

TEMPERATURE	AREA	U.S. AVG
Average January low	16.2	26.2
July high	87.4	87.4
Annual days > 90°F	32	38
Annual days < 32°F	163	89
Annual days < 0°F	10	6

PRECIPITATION	AREA	U.S. AVG
Annual inches precipitation	16.0	37.7
Annual inches snowfall	60.0	7.0
Annual days precipitation	88	109
Annual days rain > 0.5 inches	8	22
Annual days snow > 1.5 inches	14	6

COMFORTS & HAZARDS	AREA	U.S. AVG
July relative humidity	53%	66%
Annual days mostly sunny	246	208
Annual days with thunderstorms	35	39
Tornado risk score	27	18
Hurricane risk score	0	13

TEMPERATURE

PRECIPITATION

DAYS OF CLOUDS & PRECIPITATION

Education
Score: 98.7
Rank: 6

ACHIEVEMENT	AREA	U.S. AVG
High school degree	92.7%	82.7%
2-year college degree	5.7%	6.4%
4-year college degree	31.6%	15.7%
Graduate/professional degree	21.3%	8.9%

PUBLIC SCHOOLS	AREA	U.S. AVG
Expenditures per pupil	$5,207	$5,686
Student/teacher ratio	17.0	16.7
Attending public school	87.6%	90.1%
State SAT score	1122	1021
State ACT score	20.3*	20.9

HIGHER EDUCATION	AREA	U.S. AVG
No. 2-year colleges	2	4
No. 4-year colleges/universities	4	6
No. highly ranked universities	1	1

Health & Healthcare
Score: 45.2
Rank: 206

HAZARDS & ILLNESSES	AREA	U.S. AVG
Air-quality score	35	37
Water-quality score	100	52
Pollen/allergy score	84	61
Cancer mortality per capita	130.7	201.9
Depression days per month	2.7	3.5
Stress score	38	50

HEALTHCARE	AREA	U.S. AVG
Physicians per capita	291.8	244.2
Hospital beds per capita	182.6	420.0
No. teaching hospitals	1	3
Cost per doctor visit	$84	$77
Cost per dental visit	$69	$70

Crime
Score: 80.5
Rank: 74

CRIME	AREA	U.S. AVG
Violent crime rate	400.7	465.5
Change in violent crime rate	32.6%	-2.2%
Property crime rate	3,162.8	3,517.1
Change in property crime rate	-3.7%	-2.1%

Transportation
Score: 81.8
Rank: 68

COMMUTE	AREA	U.S. AVG
Average commute time	24.3	27.4
Percent commutes > 60 mins.	5.2%	5.9%
Commute by auto	70.8%	78.9%
Commute by mass transit	4.7%	1.9%
Work at home	6.5%	3.1%
Mass transit miles per capita	4.69	1.87

INTERCITY SERVICES	AREA	U.S. AVG
Major airports within 60 miles	2	1
Size of regional airport	Large	Large
Daily airline activity	887	686
Amtrak service	No	No

AUTOMOTIVE	AREA	U.S. AVG
Insurance, annual premium	$1,486	$1,432
Gas, cost per gallon	$2.43	$2.49
Daily vehicle miles per capita	21.1	24.0

Leisure
Score: 85.8
Rank: 53

DINING & SHOPPING	AREA	U.S. AVG
Restaurant rating	3	2
Outlet mall score	244	42
No. Starbucks	9	13
No. warehouse clubs	1	2

ENTERTAINMENT	AREA	U.S. AVG
Professional sports rating	8	4
College sports rating	5	4
Zoo/aquarium rating	2	3
Amusement park rating	2	3
Botanical garden/arboretum rating	6	4

OUTDOOR ACTIVITIES	AREA	U.S. AVG
Golf-course rating	3	4
Ski-area rating	10	3
Sq. miles inland water	3	4
Miles of coastline	0.0	10.7
National Park rating	7	3

Arts & Culture
Score: 71.9
Rank: 105

MEDIA & LIBRARIES	AREA	U.S. AVG
Arts radio rating	4	3
No. public libraries	8	27
Library volumes per capita	4.12	2.78

PERFORMING ARTS	AREA	U.S. AVG
Classical music rating	5	4
Ballet/dance rating	6	3
Professional theater rating	3	3
University arts programs rating	6	5

MUSEUMS	AREA	U.S. AVG
Overall museum rating	7	5
Art museum rating	7	5
Science museum rating	6	5
Children's museum rating	4	3

Bowling Green, KY

Score: 67.1   **Rank:** 119   **2004 rank:** not ranked

Profile: Small town/college town
Location: Western Kentucky, 120 miles south of Louisville
Elevation: 496 feet
Time zone: Central Standard Time

PRO	CON
Historic interest	Isolation
College-town amenities	Economic cycles
Nearby national park	Hot, humid summers

Bowling Green, located 20 miles north of the Tennessee border along Interstate 65, has a diverse economic and cultural base. Best known as the city where the Chevrolet Corvette is built, this pleasant, small town is also home to the 15,000 students of Western Kentucky University. Other prominent employers include Holley Performance Products (carburetors) and Fruit of the Loom, and the town is a center for a wide and diverse agricultural region. Downtown is modest and attractive with a classic main street and numerous historic homes and Civil War sites. The city won a 2006 National Trust for Historic Preservation "Dozen Distinctive Locations" award for 2006. Cost of living and housing are attractive on a regional and national scale. The university, the third largest in the state, does bring some college-town amenities and feel. Mammoth Cave National Park, one of a few national parks in the region, is located 30 miles northeast. Healthcare facilities are above average for a city of its size. The area is popular for business due to its central location among an assortment of larger cities— Louisville, Lexington, Nashville, Evansville, Indianapolis, St. Louis. Nashville is closest at 60 miles, but that may not be close enough to bigger-city services for some.

The Bowling Green area is gently rolling with a mix of deciduous woods and agricultural land. Summers can experience strong climate shifts and occasional strong storms. Snow is infrequent but may be heavy when it occurs. Fall is the driest, and for many, the most pleasant season. First freeze is late October; last is in mid-April.

DEMOGRAPHICS	AREA	U.S. AVG	ETHNIC COMPOSITION	AREA	U.S. AVG	RESIDENT PROFILE	AREA	U.S. AVG
Population	109,501		White	87.1%	79.0%	Single	32.4%	32.4%
Population density per sq. mile	129.2	358.5	Black	8.0%	10.5%	Married	53.4%	52.7%
Population growth	25.9%	21.1%	Asian	1.5%	2.7%	Divorced/separated	14.2%	14.9%
Median age	34.2	36.1	Hispanic	3.0%	10.6%	Married with children	23.0%	23.7%
Percent Democrat	35.8%	44.5%	Religious observance	50.7%	48.9%	Single with children	8.3%	9.1%
Percent Republican	63.5%	54.5%	Diversity measure	27.5	40.1	Percent over age 65	11.2%	12.9%

Score: 54.3
Rank: 172

INCOME	AREA	U.S. AVG	EMPLOYMENT	AREA	U.S. AVG	EMPLOYING INDUSTRIES	AREA	U.S. AVG
Per capita income	$20,764	$23,235	Unemployment rate	5.4%	4.7%	Largest: Manufacturing		
Household income	$39,376	$46,414	Recent job growth	1.9%	1.3%			
Household income < $25K	32.2%	26.2%	Projected future job growth	12.8%	11.5%	Percent manufacturing	18.7%	15.4%
Household income > $75K	20.1%	25.4%	White collar	55.9%	57.8%	Percent public sector	15.9%	15.7%
Household income growth	12.9%	13.6%	Blue collar	27.6%	25.2%	Percent construction	8.9%	9.9%

Score: 71.1
Rank: 109

INDEXES & TAXES	AREA	U.S. AVG	HOUSING	AREA	U.S. AVG	NECESSITIES	AREA	U.S. AVG
Cost of Living Index	83.8	100.0	Median home price	$134,700	$220,000	Food Index	105.6	100.0
Buying Power Index	105.3	100.0	Home price appreciation	21.8%	10.1%	Housing Index	63.3	100.0
Income tax rate	6.00%	4.70%	Median rent	$591	$709	Utilities Index	91.8	100.0
Sales tax rate	6.00%	6.58%	Homes owned	60.2%	62.3%	Transportation Index	91.1	100.0
Property tax rate	$5.89	$12.00	Home price ratio	3.4	4.2	Healthcare Index	92.2	100.0
						Miscellaneous Cost Index	96.1	100.0

Score: 28.3
Rank: 267

TEMPERATURE	AREA	U.S. AVG	PRECIPITATION	AREA	U.S. AVG	COMFORTS & HAZARDS	AREA	U.S. AVG
Average January low	28.0	26.2	Annual inches precipitation	47.4	37.7	July relative humidity	59%	66%
July high	90.0	87.4	Annual inches snowfall	11.0	7.0	Annual days mostly sunny	210	208
Annual days > 90°F	51	38	Annual days precipitation	119	109	Annual days with thunderstorms	54	39
Annual days < 32°F	76	89	Annual days rain > 0.5 inches	32	22	Tornado risk score	3	18
Annual days < 0°F	1	6	Annual days snow > 1.5 inches	3	6	Hurricane risk score	1	13

TEMPERATURE

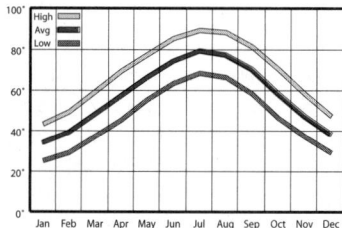

PRECIPITATION

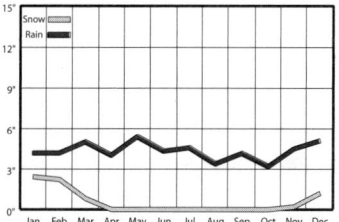

DAYS OF CLOUDS & PRECIPITATION

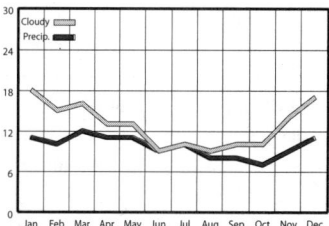

Education	ACHIEVEMENT	AREA	U.S. AVG	PUBLIC SCHOOLS	AREA	U.S. AVG	HIGHER EDUCATION	AREA	U.S. AVG
	High school degree	78.8%	82.7%	Expenditures per pupil	$5,186	$5,686	No. 2-year colleges	3	4
Score: 31.3	2-year college degree	4.6%	6.4%	Student/teacher ratio	22.2	16.7	No. 4-year colleges/universities	1	6
Rank: 258	4-year college degree	13.8%	15.7%	Attending public school	94.8%	90.1%	No. highly ranked universities	0	1
	Graduate/professional degree	9.5%	8.9%	State SAT score	1124	1021			
				State ACT score	20.6*	20.9			

Health & Healthcare	HAZARDS & ILLNESSES	AREA	U.S. AVG	HEALTHCARE	AREA	U.S. AVG	CRIME	AREA	U.S. AVG
	Air-quality score	56	37	Physicians per capita	228.8	244.2	Violent crime rate	314.2	465.5
	Water-quality score	67	52	Hospital beds per capita	853.0	420.0	Change in violent crime rate	-30.0%	-2.2%
Score: 95.5	Pollen/allergy score	69	61	No. teaching hospitals	0	3	Property crime rate	3,434.1	3,517.1
Rank: 18	Cancer mortality per capita	229.3	201.9	Cost per doctor visit	$104	$77	Change in property crime rate	-1.7%	-2.1%
	Depression days per month	4.1	3.5	Cost per dental visit	$61	$70			
	Stress score	56	50						

Score: 57.8 Rank: 158 (Crime)

Transportation	COMMUTE	AREA	U.S. AVG	INTERCITY SERVICES	AREA	U.S. AVG	AUTOMOTIVE	AREA	U.S. AVG
	Average commute time	23.0	27.4	Major airports within 60 miles	2	1	Insurance, annual premium	$1,128	$1,432
Score: 60.7	Percent commutes > 60 mins.	5.2%	5.9%	Size of regional airport	Medium	Large	Gas, cost per gallon	$2.46	$2.49
Rank: 148	Commute by auto	79.9%	78.9%	Daily airline activity	492	686	Daily vehicle miles per capita	26.5	24.0
	Commute by mass transit	0.5%	1.9%	Amtrak service	No	No			
	Work at home	2.7%	3.1%						
	Mass transit miles per capita	0.51	1.87						

Leisure	DINING & SHOPPING	AREA	U.S. AVG	ENTERTAINMENT	AREA	U.S. AVG	OUTDOOR ACTIVITIES	AREA	U.S. AVG
	Restaurant rating	1	2	Professional sports rating	1	4	Golf-course rating	3	4
Score: 27.0	Outlet mall score	4	42	College sports rating	3	4	Ski-area rating	2	3
Rank: 272	No. Starbucks	1	13	Zoo/aquarium rating	2	3	Sq. miles inland water	2	4
	No. warehouse clubs	0	2	Amusement park rating	1	3	Miles of coastline	0.0	10.7
				Botanical garden/ arboretum rating	1	4	National Park rating	6	3

Arts & Culture	MEDIA & LIBRARIES	AREA	U.S. AVG	PERFORMING ARTS	AREA	U.S. AVG	MUSEUMS	AREA	U.S. AVG
	Arts radio rating	1	3	Classical music rating	2	4	Overall museum rating	4	5
Score: 9.9	No. public libraries	4	27	Ballet/dance rating	1	3	Art museum rating	2	5
Rank: 336	Library volumes per capita	1.63	2.78	Professional theater rating	1	3	Science museum rating	3	5
				University arts programs rating	4	5	Children's museum rating	1	3

Bremerton–Silverdale, WA

Score: 63.3   Rank: 148   2004 rank: 44

Profile: Small-town/suburban complex
Location: West shore of Puget Sound opposite of Seattle
Elevation: 125 feet
Time zone: Pacific Standard Time

PRO
Attractive setting
Nearby recreation
Close to Seattle

CON
Clouds and rain
Cost of living
Long ferry commutes

The Bremerton–Silverdale metropolitan area represents a group of island communities across Puget Sound's main channel. Bremerton is the largest city, with seaport and shipbuilding activities, but the character of the area outside of the city and on other islands is mainly suburban and rural, with small towns and commuter communities on Bainbridge Island and Vashon Island, among others. Bremerton itself has suffered some economic decline in its major industries, and the downtown area experienced some decay but has also undergone some revitalization; the result is a mixed bag. Silverdale is a residential and shopping area just north. Ferry service to Seattle takes about an hour with relatively infrequent sailings 1½ hours apart, so commutes must be well planned. Seattle offers some of the finest big-city amenities available in the country, and the last ferry departure at 12:50am enables locals to take advantage of them in off hours. Most communities have attractive housing in wooded settings. Most of the region has a livable small-town atmosphere with excellent outdoor recreation and a pleasant—if wet—climate.

The area is a series of level to slightly hilly islands and inlets with dense coniferous forest. Summers are cool and mainly dry. The rest of the year is a mix of clouds, light rain, and an occasional snow, although the water-level location makes snow uncommon. First freeze is early October; last is end of April.

DEMOGRAPHICS	AREA	U.S. AVG	ETHNIC COMPOSITION	AREA	U.S. AVG	RESIDENT PROFILE	AREA	U.S. AVG
Population	242,681		White	83.8%	79.0%	Single	27.5%	32.4%
Population density per sq. mile	612.8	358.5	Black	2.7%	10.5%	Married	56.7%	52.7%
Population growth	27.9%	21.1%	Asian	5.1%	2.7%	Divorced/separated	15.8%	14.9%
Median age	36.6	36.1	Hispanic	4.7%	10.6%	Married with children	26.9%	23.7%
Percent Democrat	51.3%	44.5%	Religious observance	28.3%	48.9%	Single with children	9.0%	9.1%
Percent Republican	46.9%	54.5%	Diversity measure	35.6	40.1	Percent over age 65	11.1%	12.9%

Economy & Jobs
Score: 89.6
Rank: 40

INCOME	AREA	U.S. AVG	EMPLOYMENT	AREA	U.S. AVG	EMPLOYING INDUSTRIES	AREA	U.S. AVG
Per capita income	$26,088	$23,235	Unemployment rate	5.2%	4.7%	Largest: Healthcare & Social Assistance		
Household income	$54,189	$46,414	Recent job growth	3.8%	1.3%			
Household income < $25K	19.0%	26.2%	Projected future job growth	22.0%	11.5%	Percent manufacturing	10.3%	15.4%
Household income > $75K	31.6%	25.4%	White collar	59.8%	57.8%	Percent public sector	27.5%	15.7%
Household income growth	15.7%	13.6%	Blue collar	22.2%	25.2%	Percent construction	11.9%	9.9%

Cost of Living
Score: 44.4
Rank: 208

INDEXES & TAXES	AREA	U.S. AVG	HOUSING	AREA	U.S. AVG	NECESSITIES	AREA	U.S. AVG
Cost of Living Index	108.1	100.0	Median home price	$255,500	$220,000	Food Index	107.3	100.0
Buying Power Index	112.4	100.0	Home price appreciation	69.0%	10.1%	Housing Index	87.6	100.0
Income tax rate	0.00%	4.70%	Median rent	$782	$709	Utilities Index	86.2	100.0
Sales tax rate	8.60%	6.58%	Homes owned	62.8%	62.3%	Transportation Index	111.5	100.0
Property tax rate	$12.20	$12.00	Home price ratio	4.7	4.2	Healthcare Index	129.1	100.0
						Miscellaneous Cost Index	100.7	100.0

Climate
Score: 81.6
Rank: 70

TEMPERATURE	AREA	U.S. AVG	PRECIPITATION	AREA	U.S. AVG	COMFORTS & HAZARDS	AREA	U.S. AVG
Average January low	33.0	26.2	Annual inches precipitation	39.0	37.7	July relative humidity	74%	66%
July high	75.1	87.4	Annual inches snowfall	15.0	7.0	Annual days mostly sunny	136	208
Annual days > 90°F	3	38	Annual days precipitation	160	109	Annual days with thunderstorms	7	39
Annual days < 32°F	32	89	Annual days rain > 0.5 inches	26	22	Tornado risk score	0	18
Annual days < 0°F	0	6	Annual days snow > 1.5 inches	2	6	Hurricane risk score	0	13

TEMPERATURE

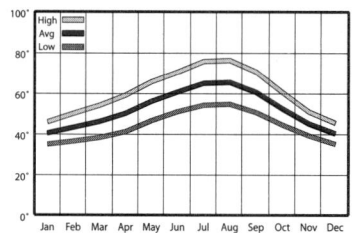

PRECIPITATION

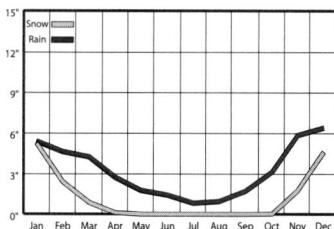

DAYS OF CLOUDS & PRECIPITATION

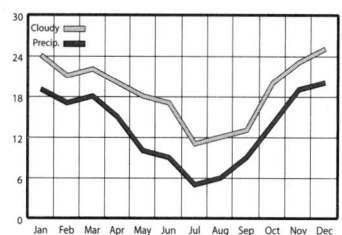

Education
Score: 75.9
Rank: 91

ACHIEVEMENT	AREA	U.S. AVG	PUBLIC SCHOOLS	AREA	U.S. AVG	HIGHER EDUCATION	AREA	U.S. AVG
High school degree	90.8%	82.7%	Expenditures per pupil	$5,431	$5,686	No. 2-year colleges	1	4
2-year college degree	9.1%	6.4%	Student/teacher ratio	20.5	16.7	No. 4-year colleges/universities	1	6
4-year college degree	17.0%	15.7%	Attending public school	94.9%	90.1%	No. highly ranked universities	0	1
Graduate/professional degree	8.4%	8.9%	State SAT score	1059*	1021			
			State ACT score	22.9	20.9			

Health & Healthcare
Score: 16.0
Rank: 313

HAZARDS & ILLNESSES	AREA	U.S. AVG	HEALTHCARE	AREA	U.S. AVG	CRIME	AREA	U.S. AVG
Air-quality score	41	37	Physicians per capita	203.1	244.2	Violent crime rate	420.4	465.5
Water-quality score	40	52	Hospital beds per capita	134.7	420.0	Change in violent crime rate	-3.2%	-2.2%
Pollen/allergy score	48	61	No. teaching hospitals	0	3	Property crime rate	2,878.6	3,517.1
Cancer mortality per capita	192.1	201.9	Cost per doctor visit	$88	$77	Change in property crime rate	1.9%	-2.1%
Depression days per month	3.5	3.5	Cost per dental visit	$92	$70			
Stress score	97	50						

Crime
Score: 51.1
Rank: 184

Transportation
Score: 4.0
Rank: 358

COMMUTE	AREA	U.S. AVG	INTERCITY SERVICES	AREA	U.S. AVG	AUTOMOTIVE	AREA	U.S. AVG
Average commute time	33.2	27.4	Major airports within 60 miles	1	1	Insurance, annual premium	$1,464	$1,432
Percent commutes > 60 mins.	18.6%	5.9%	Size of regional airport	Large	Large	Gas, cost per gallon	$2.45	$2.49
Commute by auto	66.2%	78.9%	Daily airline activity	698	686	Daily vehicle miles per capita	17.6	24.0
Commute by mass transit	8.8%	1.9%	Amtrak service	No	No			
Work at home	4.7%	3.1%						
Mass transit miles per capita	8.81	1.87						

Leisure

Score: 83.4
Rank: 62

DINING & SHOPPING	AREA	U.S. AVG	ENTERTAINMENT	AREA	U.S. AVG	OUTDOOR ACTIVITIES	AREA	U.S. AVG
Restaurant rating	1	2	Professional sports rating	7	4	Golf-course rating	3	4
Outlet mall score	0	42	College sports rating	2	4	Ski-area rating	10	3
No. Starbucks	6	13	Zoo/aquarium rating	2	3	Sq. miles inland water	7	4
No. warehouse clubs	1	2	Amusement park rating	3	3	Miles of coastline	30.8	10.7
			Botanical garden/ arboretum rating	6	4	National Park rating	7	3

Arts & Culture

Score: 25.4
Rank: 278

MEDIA & LIBRARIES	AREA	U.S. AVG	PERFORMING ARTS	AREA	U.S. AVG	MUSEUMS	AREA	U.S. AVG
Arts radio rating	3	3	Classical music rating	3	4	Overall museum rating	8	5
No. public libraries	9	27	Ballet/dance rating	5	3	Art museum rating	6	5
Library volumes per capita	1.95	2.78	Professional theater rating	3	3	Science museum rating	7	5
			University arts programs rating	2	5	Children's museum rating	6	3

Bridgeport–Stamford–Norwalk, CT   Score: 56.0   Rank: 208   2004 rank: 145

Profile: Large city
Location: Southwestern Connecticut along Long Island Sound, 50 miles northeast of New York City
Elevation: 7 feet
Time zone: Eastern Standard Time

PRO	CON
Diverse economy	Cost of living
Close to New York City	Long commutes
Good climate for region	Some blighted areas

The most recent MSA designations created some major shifts in Connecticut, where metro areas are more closely aligned by county borders than by the towns and townships of the old New England structure. As a result, two important and highly diverse metro areas, Danbury and Stamford–Norwalk, were merged into this now very large and complex Bridgeport area. Formerly a whaling port, Bridgeport itself grew up as an industrial and manufacturing center known for large machinery and brass products. Some of this heavy industry remains, but general industrial decline has left considerable areas of blight. The area's story is far more complex today. In combination with other centers along the Long Island Sound and major commute lines, the area has emerged into a major corporate center for headquarters and financial operations. Surrounding cities such as Fairfield, Stratford, and Trumbull provide a variety of suburban living environments and are within commuting distance of New York. Closer to New York, Stamford, Norwalk, and Greenwich bring some additional older industrial infrastructure and corporate functions but more importantly areas of very attractive and affluent commuter suburbs. Danbury is an attractive smaller city with a diverse commercial base, low crime, attractive rural areas nearby, and again, proximity to New York but a bit outside practical commute distance.

Smaller classic New England–style towns, such as Newtown, lie between Danbury and the shore mainly east and south, offering excellent residential opportunities. The economy, needless to say, is diverse and offers a lot of high-paying jobs, especially for those willing to make a lengthy commute. The affluence, high property values, and high property tax rates, which are among the highest in the nation, make the area challenging for migrants or younger families starting out, although other taxes are relatively modest. Many older sections, especially near Bridgeport, are industrial with low educational attainment and high crime, while most of these issues are avoided farther inland.

Sea breezes and the proximity of the Long Island Sound tend to moderate temperatures both in summer and winter, and also to reduce winter snows for areas along the shore. Summer temperatures may be 5°F to 10°F lower than nearby inland locations, and winter snowfalls average 10 inches less. Summers are warm and humid, while winters are variable and might be punctuated with heavy "noreaster" snowstorms. Short periods of bitter cold can occur, but are usually shorter in duration than their counterparts in more northerly, inland locations. High tides and large coastal Atlantic storms can create flooding in low-lying areas. First freeze is end of October; last is mid-April.

Population

DEMOGRAPHICS	AREA	U.S. AVG	ETHNIC COMPOSITION	AREA	U.S. AVG	RESIDENT PROFILE	AREA	U.S. AVG
Population	906,546		White	77.9%	79.0%	Single	33.1%	32.4%
Population density per sq. mile	1448.6	358.5	Black	10.1%	10.5%	Married	54.3%	52.7%
Population growth	9.5%	21.1%	Asian	3.9%	2.7%	Divorced/separated	12.6%	14.9%
Median age	38.7	36.1	Hispanic	13.3%	10.6%	Married with children	26.7%	23.7%
Percent Democrat	51.4%	44.5%	Religious observance	70.1%	48.9%	Single with children	7.4%	9.1%
Percent Republican	47.3%	54.5%	Diversity measure	52.1	40.1	Percent over age 65	13.3%	12.9%

Economy & Jobs

Score: 11.0
Rank: 332

INCOME	AREA	U.S. AVG	EMPLOYMENT	AREA	U.S. AVG	EMPLOYING INDUSTRIES	AREA	U.S. AVG
Per capita income	$41,727	$23,235	Unemployment rate	5.0%	4.7%	Largest: Finance & Insurance		
Household income	$73,944	$46,414	Recent job growth	0.4%	1.3%			
Household income ‹ $25K	15.7%	26.2%	Projected future job growth	1.1%	11.5%	Percent manufacturing	9.3%	15.4%
Household income › $75K	49.3%	25.4%	White collar	70.2%	57.8%	Percent public sector	9.7%	15.7%
Household income growth	13.3%	13.6%	Blue collar	16.9%	25.2%	Percent construction	7.6%	9.9%

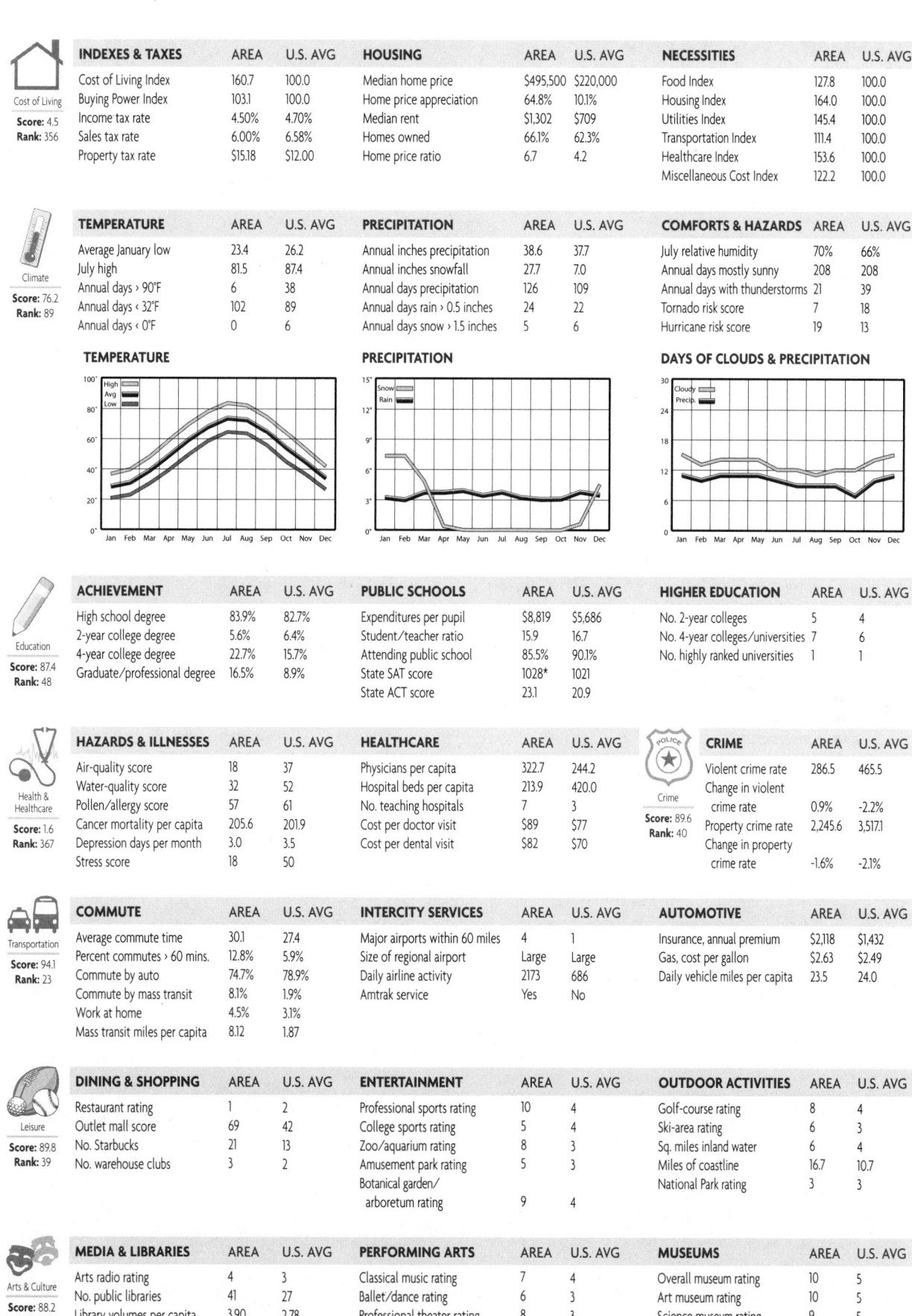

Cost of Living
Score: 4.5
Rank: 356

INDEXES & TAXES	AREA	U.S. AVG	HOUSING	AREA	U.S. AVG	NECESSITIES	AREA	U.S. AVG
Cost of Living Index	160.7	100.0	Median home price	$495,500	$220,000	Food Index	127.8	100.0
Buying Power Index	103.1	100.0	Home price appreciation	64.8%	10.1%	Housing Index	164.0	100.0
Income tax rate	4.50%	4.70%	Median rent	$1,302	$709	Utilities Index	145.4	100.0
Sales tax rate	6.00%	6.58%	Homes owned	66.1%	62.3%	Transportation Index	111.4	100.0
Property tax rate	$15.18	$12.00	Home price ratio	6.7	4.2	Healthcare Index	153.6	100.0
						Miscellaneous Cost Index	122.2	100.0

Climate
Score: 76.2
Rank: 89

TEMPERATURE	AREA	U.S. AVG	PRECIPITATION	AREA	U.S. AVG	COMFORTS & HAZARDS	AREA	U.S. AVG
Average January low	23.4	26.2	Annual inches precipitation	38.6	37.7	July relative humidity	70%	66%
July high	81.5	87.4	Annual inches snowfall	27.7	7.0	Annual days mostly sunny	208	208
Annual days > 90°F	6	38	Annual days precipitation	126	109	Annual days with thunderstorms	21	39
Annual days < 32°F	102	89	Annual days rain > 0.5 inches	24	22	Tornado risk score	7	18
Annual days < 0°F	0	6	Annual days snow > 1.5 inches	5	6	Hurricane risk score	19	13

TEMPERATURE   **PRECIPITATION**   **DAYS OF CLOUDS & PRECIPITATION**

Education
Score: 87.4
Rank: 48

ACHIEVEMENT	AREA	U.S. AVG	PUBLIC SCHOOLS	AREA	U.S. AVG	HIGHER EDUCATION	AREA	U.S. AVG
High school degree	83.9%	82.7%	Expenditures per pupil	$8,819	$5,686	No. 2-year colleges	5	4
2-year college degree	5.6%	6.4%	Student/teacher ratio	15.9	16.7	No. 4-year colleges/universities	7	6
4-year college degree	22.7%	15.7%	Attending public school	85.5%	90.1%	No. highly ranked universities	1	1
Graduate/professional degree	16.5%	8.9%	State SAT score	1028*	1021			
			State ACT score	23.1	20.9			

Health & Healthcare
Score: 1.6
Rank: 367

Crime
Score: 89.6
Rank: 40

HAZARDS & ILLNESSES	AREA	U.S. AVG	HEALTHCARE	AREA	U.S. AVG	CRIME	AREA	U.S. AVG
Air-quality score	18	37	Physicians per capita	322.7	244.2	Violent crime rate	286.5	465.5
Water-quality score	32	52	Hospital beds per capita	213.9	420.0	Change in violent crime rate	0.9%	-2.2%
Pollen/allergy score	57	61	No. teaching hospitals	7	3	Property crime rate	2,245.6	3,517.1
Cancer mortality per capita	205.6	201.9	Cost per doctor visit	$89	$77	Change in property crime rate	-1.6%	-2.1%
Depression days per month	3.0	3.5	Cost per dental visit	$82	$70			
Stress score	18	50						

Transportation
Score: 94.1
Rank: 23

COMMUTE	AREA	U.S. AVG	INTERCITY SERVICES	AREA	U.S. AVG	AUTOMOTIVE	AREA	U.S. AVG
Average commute time	30.1	27.4	Major airports within 60 miles	4	1	Insurance, annual premium	$2,118	$1,432
Percent commutes > 60 mins.	12.8%	5.9%	Size of regional airport	Large	Large	Gas, cost per gallon	$2.63	$2.49
Commute by auto	74.7%	78.9%	Daily airline activity	2173	686	Daily vehicle miles per capita	23.5	24.0
Commute by mass transit	8.1%	1.9%	Amtrak service	Yes	No			
Work at home	4.5%	3.1%						
Mass transit miles per capita	8.12	1.87						

Leisure
Score: 89.8
Rank: 39

DINING & SHOPPING	AREA	U.S. AVG	ENTERTAINMENT	AREA	U.S. AVG	OUTDOOR ACTIVITIES	AREA	U.S. AVG
Restaurant rating	1	2	Professional sports rating	10	4	Golf-course rating	8	4
Outlet mall score	69	42	College sports rating	5	4	Ski-area rating	6	3
No. Starbucks	21	13	Zoo/aquarium rating	8	3	Sq. miles inland water	6	4
No. warehouse clubs	3	2	Amusement park rating	5	3	Miles of coastline	16.7	10.7
			Botanical garden/ arboretum rating	9	4	National Park rating	3	3

Arts & Culture
Score: 88.2
Rank: 45

MEDIA & LIBRARIES	AREA	U.S. AVG	PERFORMING ARTS	AREA	U.S. AVG	MUSEUMS	AREA	U.S. AVG
Arts radio rating	4	3	Classical music rating	7	4	Overall museum rating	10	5
No. public libraries	41	27	Ballet/dance rating	6	3	Art museum rating	10	5
Library volumes per capita	3.90	2.78	Professional theater rating	8	3	Science museum rating	9	5
			University arts programs rating	8	5	Children's museum rating	9	3

Brownsville–Harlingen, TX

Score: 48.6   **Rank:** 254   **2004 rank:** 314

Profile: Small-border-city complex
Location: Extreme south Texas along the Rio Grande and Mexican border, 20 miles from the Gulf of Mexico
Elevation: 20 feet
Time zone: Central Standard Time

PRO	CON
Cost of living	Property crime
Nearby water recreation	Low educational attainment
Pleasant winters	Heat and humidity

Located at the extreme southern tip of Texas and the continental U.S., Brownsville is a thriving border town and minor resort area mainly serving wintering Texans. Gulf Coast beach areas about 20 miles east of town at the mouth of the Rio Grande, notably South Padre Island, are a favorite winter and spring-break destination. Brownsville anchors the subtropical Lower Rio Grande Valley, a vast area spreading 60 miles west and 30 miles north, a business-friendly area clustered with small towns, agriculture, and commercial and manufacturing interests tied to Mexico and free-trade status. Brownsville is a major trading center, international seaport, and *maquiladora* (border zone) manufacturing center for U.S. companies. While recent economic statistics are mixed with high unemployment, the region has undergone rapid growth recently as industries have located to take advantage of inexpensive labor, the North American Free Trade Agreement (NAFTA), and ocean shipping. Industry is diverse, with everything from food processing to petrochemicals to paper bags and hats. The city has a large Hispanic population and a sizable Hispanic middle class. The mix of Hispanic and Anglo cultures adds interest, but besides South Padre Island,

there isn't much to do, and the area is physically unappealing. There are few cultural or recreational amenities outside of watersports and cross-border shopping, and though home prices are reasonable, parts of the city have problems with traffic, unemployment, and substandard housing. Harlingen, a smaller city about 25 miles northwest in the Rio Grande Valley, has an Air Force base and is also an industrial and transportation center largely connected to Mexico and the free-trade market.

The surrounding country is mainly level agricultural land with marshy coastal areas to the east. October through April temperatures are mild with highs in the 70s and 80s. For the remainder of the year, highs are in the 90s with lows in the 70s. Hot, dry winds out of Mexico can yield temperatures of 100°F. Cold weather is infrequent and of short duration. The heaviest rains occur in late spring and again in early fall with some extended periods of cool rainy weather in winter. Torrential rains may accompany tropical storms or hurricanes that occasionally move over the area in summer or fall.

DEMOGRAPHICS	AREA	U.S. AVG	ETHNIC COMPOSITION	AREA	U.S. AVG	RESIDENT PROFILE	AREA	U.S. AVG
Population	378,542		White	80.0%	79.0%	Single	31.7%	32.4%
Population density per sq. mile	417.9	358.5	Black	0.4%	10.5%	Married	54.1%	52.7%
Population growth	45.5%	21.1%	Asian	0.5%	2.7%	Divorced/separated	14.2%	14.9%
Median age	28.8	36.1	Hispanic	86.3%	10.6%	Married with children	34.3%	23.7%
Percent Democrat	49.2%	44.5%	Religious observance	52.8%	48.9%	Single with children	11.7%	9.1%
Percent Republican	50.3%	54.5%	Diversity measure	49.0	40.1	Percent over age 65	10.9%	12.9%

INCOME	AREA	U.S. AVG	EMPLOYMENT	AREA	U.S. AVG	EMPLOYING INDUSTRIES	AREA	U.S. AVG
Per capita income	$12,584	$23,235	Unemployment rate	7.2%	4.7%	Largest: Healthcare & Social Assistance		
Household income	$30,296	$46,414	Recent job growth	4.1%	1.3%			
Household income < $25K	42.5%	26.2%	Projected future job growth	24.6%	11.5%	Percent manufacturing	15.7%	15.4%
Household income > $75K	13.8%	25.4%	White collar	52.9%	57.8%	Percent public sector	20.3%	15.7%
Household income growth	15.8%	13.6%	Blue collar	26.0%	25.2%	Percent construction	10.3%	9.9%

Score: 77.3
Rank: 86

INDEXES & TAXES	AREA	U.S. AVG	HOUSING	AREA	U.S. AVG	NECESSITIES	AREA	U.S. AVG
Cost of Living Index	78.1	100.0	Median home price	$95,800	$220,000	Food Index	86.1	100.0
Buying Power Index	86.9	100.0	Home price appreciation	23.3%	10.1%	Housing Index	39.9	100.0
Income tax rate	0.00%	4.70%	Median rent	$513	$709	Utilities Index	104.8	100.0
Sales tax rate	8.25%	6.58%	Homes owned	55.6%	62.3%	Transportation Index	100.4	100.0
Property tax rate	$18.58	$12.00	Home price ratio	3.2	4.2	Healthcare Index	106.7	100.0
						Miscellaneous Cost Index	101.7	100.0

Score: 89.3
Rank: 41

Climate
Score: 91.4
Rank: 33

TEMPERATURE	AREA	U.S. AVG
Average January low	51.0	26.2
July high	93.0	87.4
Annual days > 90°F	102	38
Annual days < 32°F	2	89
Annual days < 0°F	0	6

PRECIPITATION	AREA	U.S. AVG
Annual inches precipitation	25.0	37.7
Annual inches snowfall	0.0	7.0
Annual days precipitation	73	109
Annual days rain > 0.5 inches	16	22
Annual days snow > 1.5 inches	0	6

COMFORTS & HAZARDS	AREA	U.S. AVG
July relative humidity	76%	66%
Annual days mostly sunny	234	208
Annual days with thunderstorms	24	39
Tornado risk score	17	18
Hurricane risk score	46	13

TEMPERATURE

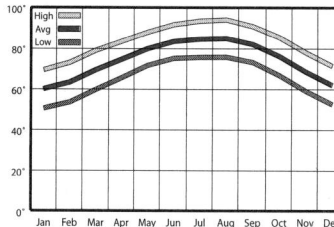

PRECIPITATION

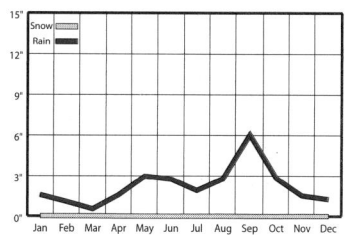

DAYS OF CLOUDS & PRECIPITATION

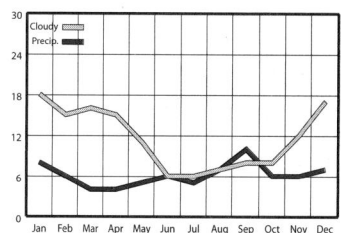

Education
Score: 1.1
Rank: 369

ACHIEVEMENT	AREA	U.S. AVG
High school degree	55.8%	82.7%
2-year college degree	4.4%	6.4%
4-year college degree	8.7%	15.7%
Graduate/professional degree	5.1%	8.9%

PUBLIC SCHOOLS	AREA	U.S. AVG
Expenditures per pupil	$5,274	$5,686
Student/teacher ratio	15.8	16.7
Attending public school	94.5%	90.1%
State SAT score	997*	1021
State ACT score	20.3	20.9

HIGHER EDUCATION	AREA	U.S. AVG
No. 2-year colleges	2	4
No. 4-year colleges/universities	1	6
No. highly ranked universities	0	1

Health & Healthcare
Score: 25.9
Rank: 276

HAZARDS & ILLNESSES	AREA	U.S. AVG
Air-quality score	29	37
Water-quality score	61	52
Pollen/allergy score	82	61
Cancer mortality per capita	120.1	201.9
Depression days per month	2.9	3.5
Stress score	33	50

HEALTHCARE	AREA	U.S. AVG
Physicians per capita	121.2	244.2
Hospital beds per capita	254.4	420.0
No. teaching hospitals	1	3
Cost per doctor visit	$79	$77
Cost per dental visit	$68	$70

Crime
Score: 33.2
Rank: 249

CRIME	AREA	U.S. AVG
Violent crime rate	479.7	465.5
Change in violent crime rate	2.7%	-2.2%
Property crime rate	5,026.2	3,517.1
Change in property crime rate	-7.3%	-2.1%

Transportation
Score: 24.9
Rank: 281

COMMUTE	AREA	U.S. AVG
Average commute time	22.3	27.4
Percent commutes > 60 mins.	3.8%	5.9%
Commute by auto	73.3%	78.9%
Commute by mass transit	0.7%	1.9%
Work at home	2.5%	3.1%
Mass transit miles per capita	0.71	1.87

INTERCITY SERVICES	AREA	U.S. AVG
Major airports within 60 miles	0	1
Size of regional airport	Small	Large
Daily airline activity	28	686
Amtrak service	No	No

AUTOMOTIVE	AREA	U.S. AVG
Insurance, annual premium	$1,212	$1,432
Gas, cost per gallon	$2.39	$2.49
Daily vehicle miles per capita	18.0	24.0

Leisure
Score: 61.8
Rank: 143

DINING & SHOPPING	AREA	U.S. AVG
Restaurant rating	1	2
Outlet mall score	0	42
No. Starbucks	1	13
No. warehouse clubs	2	2

ENTERTAINMENT	AREA	U.S. AVG
Professional sports rating	2	4
College sports rating	1	4
Zoo/aquarium rating	5	3
Amusement park rating	1	3
Botanical garden/ arboretum rating	9	4

OUTDOOR ACTIVITIES	AREA	U.S. AVG
Golf-course rating	2	4
Ski-area rating	1	3
Sq. miles inland water	10	4
Miles of coastline	30.6	10.7
National Park rating	4	3

Arts & Culture
Score: 1.3
Rank: 368

MEDIA & LIBRARIES	AREA	U.S. AVG
Arts radio rating	1	3
No. public libraries	8	27
Library volumes per capita	1.31	2.78

PERFORMING ARTS	AREA	U.S. AVG
Classical music rating	1	4
Ballet/dance rating	1	3
Professional theater rating	1	3
University arts programs rating	1	5

MUSEUMS	AREA	U.S. AVG
Overall museum rating	6	5
Art museum rating	1	5
Science museum rating	7	5
Children's museum rating	4	3

Brunswick, GA

Score: 58.5   **Rank:** 186   **2004 rank:** not ranked

Profile: Historic port and resort town
Location: Southeast Georgia, along the Atlantic Coast
Elevation: 10 feet
Time zone: Eastern Standard Time

PRO	CON
Nearby coastal areas	Rising housing costs
Attractive downtown	High crime rates
Recreation	Summer heat

Brunswick, a historic port town located halfway between the bigger-city services found in Savannah, Georgia, and Jacksonville, Florida, serves as a gateway to the "Golden Isles"—the resort islands of Jekyll and St. Simons. Brunswick itself is quaint and full of historic interest, but also functions as a major port of entry for automobiles and other commodities, and has a substantial fishing and shrimp industry and some remnants of a once-larger chemical industry. But the big "growth" industry is leisure and retirement. The islands, recognized leisure destinations for more than 100 years, offer a wide assortment of leisure and resort activities and living accommodations. The Cost of Living Index (82.3) and median home prices are moderate but the latter have grown rapidly, no doubt affected by the influx of retirees and expensive estates on Jekyll Island and elsewhere. Coastal areas offer excellent recreation, including boating, golf, and other resort activities.

Brunswick is located on a narrow coastal peninsula just east of Interstate 95 along the Intercoastal Waterway. Jekyll and St. Simons islands, both easily accessible by bridges, lie just east. Summers can be very hot and humid when sea breezes fail. Winters are generally pleasant with perhaps one or two colder periods each year. The area is vulnerable to tropical storms and hurricanes, but most Atlantic storms moving this far north tend to turn farther north into the Carolinas and farther up the East Coast.

Population

DEMOGRAPHICS	AREA	U.S. AVG	ETHNIC COMPOSITION	AREA	U.S. AVG	RESIDENT PROFILE	AREA	U.S. AVG
Population	97,758		White	74.2%	79.0%	Single	28.5%	32.4%
Population density per sq. mile	75.2	358.5	Black	23.1%	10.5%	Married	55.0%	52.7%
Population growth	19.6%	21.1%	Asian	0.5%	2.7%	Divorced/separated	16.5%	14.9%
Median age	37.4	36.1	Hispanic	2.8%	10.6%	Married with children	21.2%	23.7%
Percent Democrat	32.4%	44.5%	Religious observance	46.4%	48.9%	Single with children	10.4%	9.1%
Percent Republican	67.2%	54.5%	Diversity measure	41.4	40.1	Percent over age 65	13.9%	12.9%

Economy & Jobs
Score: 68.2
Rank: 120

INCOME	AREA	U.S. AVG	EMPLOYMENT	AREA	U.S. AVG	EMPLOYING INDUSTRIES	AREA	U.S. AVG
Per capita income	$22,426	$23,235	Unemployment rate	4.9%	4.7%	Largest: Healthcare & Social Assistance		
Household income	$41,143	$46,414	Recent job growth	2.3%	1.3%			
Household income < $25K	31.1%	26.2%	Projected future job growth	13.0%	11.5%	Percent manufacturing	14.5%	15.4%
Household income > $75K	22.5%	25.4%	White collar	53.0%	57.8%	Percent public sector	17.7%	15.7%
Household income growth	12.8%	13.6%	Blue collar	27.0%	25.2%	Percent construction	12.5%	9.9%

Cost of Living
Score: 82.1
Rank: 68

INDEXES & TAXES	AREA	U.S. AVG	HOUSING	AREA	U.S. AVG	NECESSITIES	AREA	U.S. AVG
Cost of Living Index	82.3	100.0	Median home price	$122,500	$220,000	Food Index	102.1	100.0
Buying Power Index	112.1	100.0	Home price appreciation	47.5%	10.1%	Housing Index	142.6	100.0
Income tax rate	6.00%	4.70%	Median rent	$540	$709	Utilities Index	89.4	100.0
Sales tax rate	6.27%	6.58%	Homes owned	58.5%	62.3%	Transportation Index	95.0	100.0
Property tax rate	$9.38	$12.00	Home price ratio	3.0	4.2	Healthcare Index	91.4	100.0
						Miscellaneous Cost Index	100.7	100.0

Climate
Score: 68.2
Rank: 118

TEMPERATURE	AREA	U.S. AVG	PRECIPITATION	AREA	U.S. AVG	COMFORTS & HAZARDS	AREA	U.S. AVG
Average January low	43.0	26.2	Annual inches precipitation	52.0	37.7	July relative humidity	59%	66%
July high	92.0	87.4	Annual inches snowfall	0.0	7.0	Annual days mostly sunny	210	208
Annual days > 90°F	83	38	Annual days precipitation	114	109	Annual days with thunderstorms	62	39
Annual days < 32°F	16	89	Annual days rain > 0.5 inches	31	22	Tornado risk score	2	18
Annual days < 0°F	0	6	Annual days snow > 1.5 inches	1	6	Hurricane risk score	6	13

TEMPERATURE

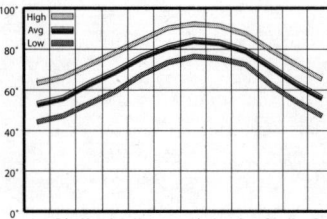

PRECIPITATION

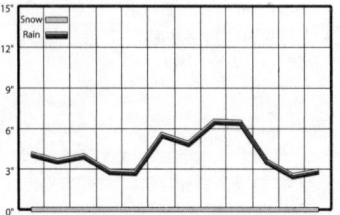

DAYS OF CLOUDS & PRECIPITATION

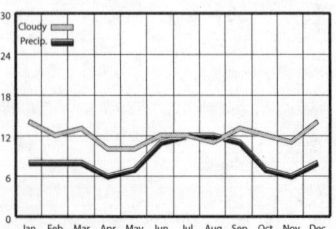

Education
Score: 30.5
Rank: 261

ACHIEVEMENT	AREA	U.S. AVG	PUBLIC SCHOOLS	AREA	U.S. AVG	HIGHER EDUCATION	AREA	U.S. AVG
High school degree	79.5%	82.7%	Expenditures per pupil	$5,535	$5,686	No. 2-year colleges	1	4
2-year college degree	5.6%	6.4%	Student/teacher ratio	14.9	16.7	No. 4-year colleges/universities	0	6
4-year college degree	12.2%	15.7%	Attending public school	92.9%	90.1%	No. highly ranked universities	0	1
Graduate/professional degree	7.3%	8.9%	State SAT score	990*	1021			
			State ACT score	20.2	20.9			

Health & Healthcare
Score: 79.1
Rank: 79

HAZARDS & ILLNESSES	AREA	U.S. AVG	HEALTHCARE	AREA	U.S. AVG	CRIME	AREA	U.S. AVG
Air-quality score	52	37	Physicians per capita	184.3	244.2	Violent crime rate	702.8	465.5
Water-quality score	60	52	Hospital beds per capita	476.7	420.0	Change in violent crime rate	21.2%	-2.2%
Pollen/allergy score	65	61	No. teaching hospitals	0	3	Property crime rate	4,515.7	3,517.1
Cancer mortality per capita	183.2	201.9	Cost per doctor visit	$65	$77	Change in property crime rate	-34.0%	-2.1%
Depression days per month	3.2	3.5	Cost per dental visit	$70	$70			
Stress score	67	50						

Crime
Score: 8.3
Rank: 342

Transportation
Score: 20.6
Rank: 298

COMMUTE	AREA	U.S. AVG	INTERCITY SERVICES	AREA	U.S. AVG	AUTOMOTIVE	AREA	U.S. AVG
Average commute time	24.6	27.4	Major airports within 60 miles	1	1	Insurance, annual premium	$1,244	$1,432
Percent commutes > 60 mins.	5.7%	5.9%	Size of regional airport	Medium	Large	Gas, cost per gallon	$2.48	$2.49
Commute by auto	79.3%	78.9%	Daily airline activity	194	686	Daily vehicle miles per capita	25.5	24.0
Commute by mass transit	0.5%	1.9%	Amtrak service	No	No			
Work at home	2.6%	3.1%						
Mass transit miles per capita	0.45	1.87						

Leisure
Score: 27.3
Rank: 271

DINING & SHOPPING	AREA	U.S. AVG	ENTERTAINMENT	AREA	U.S. AVG	OUTDOOR ACTIVITIES	AREA	U.S. AVG
Restaurant rating	1	2	Professional sports rating	1	4	Golf-course rating	5	4
Outlet mall score	60	42	College sports rating	2	4	Ski-area rating	1	3
No. Starbucks	0	13	Zoo/aquarium rating	2	3	Sq. miles inland water	2	4
No. warehouse clubs	0	2	Amusement park rating	1	3	Miles of coastline	9.0	10.7
			Botanical garden/ arboretum rating	1	4	National Park rating	4	3

Arts & Culture
Score: 14.7
Rank: 318

MEDIA & LIBRARIES	AREA	U.S. AVG	PERFORMING ARTS	AREA	U.S. AVG	MUSEUMS	AREA	U.S. AVG
Arts radio rating	1	3	Classical music rating	2	4	Overall museum rating	6	5
No. public libraries	8	27	Ballet/dance rating	1	3	Art museum rating	2	5
Library volumes per capita	1.84	2.78	Professional theater rating	1	3	Science museum rating	1	5
			University arts programs rating	1	5	Children's museum rating	1	3

Buffalo–Niagara Falls, NY

Score: 43.6 Rank: 300 2004 rank: 205

Profile: Large-city complex
Location: Western New York at eastern end of Lake Erie
Elevation: 706 feet
Time zone: Eastern Standard Time

PRO
Nearby recreation
Arts and culture
Pleasant summers

CON
Winter snow
Economy
Some unattractive areas

Buffalo's image is maligned by weather, areas of urban decay, rabid sports fans, and a strong working-class element. New York's second largest city is a major port and Rust Belt manufacturing center, although its industries are in various stages of decline. Heavy lake-effect snows make Buffalo the fifth snowiest metropolitan area in the country. Downtown is unremarkable but clean and improving, although there are many gritty areas around the city. But positive qualities do exist: Lake effects bring notably pleasant weather in spring, summer, and early fall, and there is a strong assortment of cultural amenities, historic districts, and architectural highlights with few crowds.

Buffalo has better-than-average shopping supported in part by Canadian citizens traveling across the border to avoid local taxes and high prices—although this comes and goes with fluctuations in the

dollar. Recently, the strength in the Canadian currency has expanded this influx. A number of old-economy industries have been lost; others such as auto-parts maker Delphi have been struggling. Yet, community spirit and strong state economic development programs have brought in some newer-economy businesses, notably biotech and medical technology companies; we'll see if these stick. The strong community feel spreads into the suburbs, and some, particularly north and east towards Amherst, offer excellent values. The city is fanatical about professional sports, with the Buffalo Bills, Sabres, and a few minor league teams as focal points. Niagara Falls is a special attraction, and there is a large wine-growing area to the east and another to the west. For a real cosmopolitan getaway, Toronto is 100 miles away. Bottom line: Buffalo is a city of trade-offs; for those able to take the winters and economic malaise, it offers numerous amenities at a reasonable cost, and while today's overall ranking is weak, its fortunes may at last be on the upswing.

Buffalo is located on the coastal plain of Lake Erie, where the Niagara River connects north to Lake Ontario. The reputation for bad weather comes from heavy localized lake-effect snows, but summers are among the sunniest, driest, and most pleasant in the Northeast. Winters are generally cloudy, cold, snowy, and changeable with frequent thaws and rain. Snow covers the ground more often than not from Christmas into early March. Because of the water, Buffalo warms more slowly in the spring, but the lake also inhibits spring and early summer thunderstorms. Temperatures seldom reach 90°F. First freeze is late September; last is May, but inland conditions are more extreme.

Population

DEMOGRAPHICS	AREA	U.S. AVG	ETHNIC COMPOSITION	AREA	U.S. AVG	RESIDENT PROFILE	AREA	U.S. AVG
Population	1,156,286		White	82.2%	79.0%	Single	36.4%	32.4%
Population density per sq. mile	737.8	358.5	Black	12.6%	10.5%	Married	49.6%	52.7%
Population growth	-2.8%	21.1%	Asian	1.7%	2.7%	Divorced/separated	14.0%	14.9%
Median age	39.3	36.1	Hispanic	3.5%	10.6%	Married with children	20.4%	23.7%
Percent Democrat	55.1%	44.5%	Religious observance	71.0%	48.9%	Single with children	9.2%	9.1%
Percent Republican	42.8%	54.5%	Diversity measure	35.2	40.1	Percent over age 65	15.8%	12.9%

Economy
& Jobs
Score: 10.7
Rank: 333

INCOME	AREA	U.S. AVG	EMPLOYMENT	AREA	U.S. AVG	EMPLOYING INDUSTRIES	AREA	U.S. AVG
Per capita income	$23,136	$23,235	Unemployment rate	5.7%	4.7%	Largest: Manufacturing		
Household income	$43,617	$46,414	Recent job growth	0.8%	1.3%			
Household income < $25K	29.0%	26.2%	Projected future job growth	-0.6%	11.5%	Percent manufacturing	15.3%	15.4%
Household income > $75K	24.3%	25.4%	White collar	61.6%	57.8%	Percent public sector	16.8%	15.7%
Household income growth	13.3%	13.6%	Blue collar	22.5%	25.2%	Percent construction	7.2%	9.9%

Cost of Living
Score: 19.3
Rank: 301

INDEXES & TAXES	AREA	U.S. AVG	HOUSING	AREA	U.S. AVG	NECESSITIES	AREA	U.S. AVG
Cost of Living Index	84.2	100.0	Median home price	$96,800	$220,000	Food Index	116.1	100.0
Buying Power Index	116.1	100.0	Home price appreciation	32.0%	10.1%	Housing Index	44.2	100.0
Income tax rate	7.13%	4.70%	Median rent	$616	$709	Utilities Index	123.0	100.0
Sales tax rate	8.25%	6.58%	Homes owned	61.3%	62.3%	Transportation Index	106.8	100.0
Property tax rate	$26.66	$12.00	Home price ratio	2.2	4.2	Healthcare Index	104.5	100.0
						Miscellaneous Cost Index	96.9	100.0

Climate
Score: 11.2
Rank: 331

TEMPERATURE	AREA	U.S. AVG	PRECIPITATION	AREA	U.S. AVG	COMFORTS & HAZARDS	AREA	U.S. AVG
Average January low	17.6	26.2	Annual inches precipitation	36.0	37.7	July relative humidity	73%	66%
July high	79.5	87.4	Annual inches snowfall	90.0	7.0	Annual days mostly sunny	159	208
Annual days > 90°F	2	38	Annual days precipitation	168	109	Annual days with thunderstorms	31	39
Annual days < 32°F	137	89	Annual days rain > 0.5 inches	22	22	Tornado risk score	8	18
Annual days < 0°F	5	6	Annual days snow > 1.5 inches	19	6	Hurricane risk score	4	13

TEMPERATURE

PRECIPITATION

DAYS OF CLOUDS & PRECIPITATION

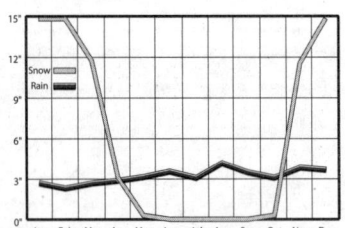

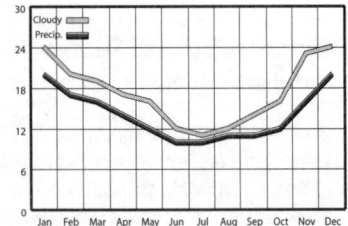

Education
Score: 71.9
Rank: 106

ACHIEVEMENT	AREA	U.S. AVG	PUBLIC SCHOOLS	AREA	U.S. AVG	HIGHER EDUCATION	AREA	U.S. AVG
High school degree	83.2%	82.7%	Expenditures per pupil	$8,535	$5,686	No. 2-year colleges	7	4
2-year college degree	9.6%	6.4%	Student/teacher ratio	15.5	16.7	No. 4-year colleges/universities	10	6
4-year college degree	13.9%	15.7%	Attending public school	85.8%	90.1%	No. highly ranked universities	1	1
Graduate/professional degree	9.6%	8.9%	State SAT score	1003*	1021			
			State ACT score	22.6	20.9			

Health &
Healthcare
Score: 36.1
Rank: 238

Crime
Score: 67.4
Rank: 123

HAZARDS & ILLNESSES	AREA	U.S. AVG	HEALTHCARE	AREA	U.S. AVG	CRIME	AREA	U.S. AVG
Air-quality score	15	37	Physicians per capita	297.2	244.2	Violent crime rate	515.7	465.5
Water-quality score	66	52	Hospital beds per capita	677.3	420.0	Change in violent crime rate	7.2%	-2.2%
Pollen/allergy score	57	61	No. teaching hospitals	10	3	Property crime rate	3,013.1	3,517.1
Cancer mortality per capita	216.2	201.9	Cost per doctor visit	$74	$77	Change in property crime rate	0.6%	-2.1%
Depression days per month	3.5	3.5	Cost per dental visit	$66	$70			
Stress score	26	50						

Transportation
Score: 53.2
Rank: 176

COMMUTE	AREA	U.S. AVG
Average commute time	23.0	27.4
Percent commutes > 60 mins.	3.2%	5.9%
Commute by auto	82.0%	78.9%
Commute by mass transit	3.4%	1.9%
Work at home	2.1%	3.1%
Mass transit miles per capita	3.39	1.87

INTERCITY SERVICES	AREA	U.S. AVG
Major airports within 60 miles	1	1
Size of regional airport	Medium	Large
Daily airline activity	297	686
Amtrak service	Yes	No

AUTOMOTIVE	AREA	U.S. AVG
Insurance, annual premium	$1,833	$1,432
Gas, cost per gallon	$2.56	$2.49
Daily vehicle miles per capita	19.9	24.0

Leisure
Score: 70.3
Rank: 111

DINING & SHOPPING	AREA	U.S. AVG
Restaurant rating	1	2
Outlet mall score	0	42
No. Starbucks	14	13
No. warehouse clubs	4	2

ENTERTAINMENT	AREA	U.S. AVG
Professional sports rating	6	4
College sports rating	4	4
Zoo/aquarium rating	5	3
Amusement park rating	1	3
Botanical garden/ arboretum rating	7	4

OUTDOOR ACTIVITIES	AREA	U.S. AVG
Golf-course rating	6	4
Ski-area rating	5	3
Sq. miles inland water	2	4
Miles of coastline	29.5	10.7
National Park rating	1	3

Arts & Culture
Score: 81.3
Rank: 71

MEDIA & LIBRARIES	AREA	U.S. AVG
Arts radio rating	1	3
No. public libraries	64	27
Library volumes per capita	2.74	2.78

PERFORMING ARTS	AREA	U.S. AVG
Classical music rating	7	4
Ballet/dance rating	1	3
Professional theater rating	10	3
University arts programs rating	9	5

MUSEUMS	AREA	U.S. AVG
Overall museum rating	8	5
Art museum rating	8	5
Science museum rating	7	5
Children's museum rating	2	3

Burlington–South Burlington, VT

Score: 42.4 **Rank:** 307 **2004 rank:** 232

Profile: College town
Location: Northwest Vermont along east shore of Lake Champlain
Elevation: 200 feet
Time zone: Eastern Standard Time

PRO	CON
College-town amenities	Harsh winters
Attractive downtown	Recent employment
Outdoor recreation	Cost of living

Burlington is the largest city in Vermont and its cultural and educational center. The University of Vermont and two smaller colleges bring a strong college-town feel, with culture, entertainment, and a youthful ambience. Downtown is pleasant, with lots of trees, historic streets and lakefront areas, and a pedestrian mall. The university is located on a bluff just east of town. The nearest big-city amenities are in Montréal, Québec, about 100 miles north. There is plenty of outdoor recreation at Lake Champlain and in the nearby Adirondacks and Green Mountains. As a college town, not surprisingly, there is a wide variety of housing and living environments available, and cost of living and housing are high by national standards, which when factored with the weak economy, cold winters, and cloudy wet climate, keeps scoring and ranking low. The area has a number of small businesses concentrated mainly in South Burlington, including forest products and food processing companies (notably ice cream maker Ben & Jerry's). But the area stops far short of being a major commercial or industrial center, and jobs may be scarce for those coming into the area without one. For those tolerant of the negatives, Burlington is an attractive place, and the current ranking may understate its potential lifestyle.

The town is located at the widest part of Lake Champlain. The highest Adirondacks lie 35 miles west while the foothills of the Green Mountains begin 10 miles to the east and southeast. The area is green and lush in summer and is known for beautiful fall seasons. The city is one of the cloudiest in the United States. During winter, temperatures along the lake's shore are often 5°F to 10°F warmer than at the airport 3½ miles inland. Summer weather is pleasant and few days exceed 90°F. This moderate summer heat gives way to a cooler but pleasant fall period, usually extending well into October. Cold Canadian air arrives in winter, but extended periods of bitter cold are unusual. First freeze is early October; last is mid-May.

Population

DEMOGRAPHICS	AREA	U.S. AVG
Population	205,359	
Population density per sq. mile	163.2	358.5
Population growth	16.3%	21.1%
Median age	36.8	36.1
Percent Democrat	60.8%	44.5%
Percent Republican	36.9%	54.5%

ETHNIC COMPOSITION	AREA	U.S. AVG
White	94.8%	79.0%
Black	0.8%	10.5%
Asian	1.9%	2.7%
Hispanic	1.0%	10.6%
Religious observance	43.7%	48.9%
Diversity measure	11.7	40.1

RESIDENT PROFILE	AREA	U.S. AVG
Single	34.9%	32.4%
Married	52.4%	52.7%
Divorced/separated	12.7%	14.9%
Married with children	25.1%	23.7%
Single with children	8.0%	9.1%
Percent over age 65	10.6%	12.9%

INCOME

INCOME	AREA	U.S. AVG
Per capita income	$26,060	$23,235
Household income	$53,407	$46,414
Household income < $25K	19.7%	26.2%
Household income > $75K	30.9%	25.4%
Household income growth	15.8%	13.6%

Economy & Jobs
Score: 11.2
Rank: 330

EMPLOYMENT	AREA	U.S. AVG
Unemployment rate	3.2%	4.7%
Recent job growth	-1.3%	1.3%
Projected future job growth	3.5%	11.5%
White collar	64.9%	57.8%
Blue collar	20.5%	25.2%

EMPLOYING INDUSTRIES	AREA	U.S. AVG
Largest: Manufacturing		
Percent manufacturing	12.6%	15.4%
Percent public sector	13.2%	15.7%
Percent construction	7.9%	9.9%

INDEXES & TAXES

INDEXES & TAXES	AREA	U.S. AVG
Cost of Living Index	116.3	100.0
Buying Power Index	102.9	100.0
Income tax rate	7.00%	4.70%
Sales tax rate	6.00%	6.58%
Property tax rate	$19.49	$12.00

Cost of Living
Score: 21.1
Rank: 294

HOUSING	AREA	U.S. AVG
Median home price	$289,200	$220,000
Home price appreciation	64.3%	10.1%
Median rent	$983	$709
Homes owned	63.7%	62.3%
Home price ratio	5.4	4.2

NECESSITIES	AREA	U.S. AVG
Food Index	107.0	100.0
Housing Index	78.2	100.0
Utilities Index	143.9	100.0
Transportation Index	104.2	100.0
Healthcare Index	105.2	100.0
Miscellaneous Cost Index	109.0	100.0

TEMPERATURE

TEMPERATURE	AREA	U.S. AVG
Average January low	7.6	26.2
July high	81.0	87.4
Annual days > 90°F	5	38
Annual days > 32°F	163	89
Annual days < 0°F	28	6

Climate
Score: 0.8
Rank: 370

PRECIPITATION	AREA	U.S. AVG
Annual inches precipitation	33.0	37.7
Annual inches snowfall	79.0	7.0
Annual days precipitation	153	109
Annual days rain > 0.5 inches	21	22
Annual days snow > 1.5 inches	17	6

COMFORTS & HAZARDS	AREA	U.S. AVG
July relative humidity	71%	66%
Annual days mostly sunny	161	208
Annual days with thunderstorms	25	39
Tornado risk score	0	18
Hurricane risk score	5	13

TEMPERATURE

PRECIPITATION

DAYS OF CLOUDS & PRECIPITATION

ACHIEVEMENT

ACHIEVEMENT	AREA	U.S. AVG
High school degree	88.6%	82.7%
2-year college degree	8.9%	6.4%
4-year college degree	21.8%	15.7%
Graduate/professional degree	13.3%	8.9%

Education
Score: 90.4
Rank: 37

PUBLIC SCHOOLS	AREA	U.S. AVG
Expenditures per pupil	$6,024	$5,686
Student/teacher ratio	15.3	16.7
Attending public school	89.2%	90.1%
State SAT score	1032*	1021
State ACT score	22.5	20.9

HIGHER EDUCATION	AREA	U.S. AVG
No. 2-year colleges	1	4
No. 4-year colleges/universities	4	6
No. highly ranked universities	1	1

HAZARDS & ILLNESSES

HAZARDS & ILLNESSES	AREA	U.S. AVG
Air-quality score	48	37
Water-quality score	72	52
Pollen/allergy score	44	61
Cancer mortality per capita	211.5	201.9
Depression days per month	3.0	3.5
Stress score	15	50

Health & Healthcare
Score: 81.3
Rank: 70

HEALTHCARE	AREA	U.S. AVG
Physicians per capita	492.8	244.2
Hospital beds per capita	273.7	420.0
No. teaching hospitals	1	3
Cost per doctor visit	$91	$77
Cost per dental visit	$65	$70

Crime
Score: 62.0
Rank: 141

CRIME	AREA	U.S. AVG
Violent crime rate	129.3	465.5
Change in violent crime rate	-5.7%	-2.2%
Property crime rate	2,520.8	3,517.1
Change in property crime rate	-13.1%	-2.1%

COMMUTE

COMMUTE	AREA	U.S. AVG
Average commute time	23.6	27.4
Percent commutes > 60 mins.	4.1%	5.9%
Commute by auto	75.5%	78.9%
Commute by mass transit	1.1%	1.9%
Work at home	4.6%	3.1%
Mass transit miles per capita	1.10	1.87

Transportation
Score: 16.6
Rank: 312

INTERCITY SERVICES	AREA	U.S. AVG
Major airports within 60 miles	0	1
Size of regional airport	Small	Large
Daily airline activity	69	686
Amtrak service	Yes	No

AUTOMOTIVE	AREA	U.S. AVG
Insurance, annual premium	$1,070	$1,432
Gas, cost per gallon	$2.46	$2.49
Daily vehicle miles per capita	24.0	24.0

DINING & SHOPPING

DINING & SHOPPING	AREA	U.S. AVG
Restaurant rating	1	2
Outlet mall score	0	42
No. Starbucks	4	13
No. warehouse clubs	1	2

Leisure
Score: 60.7
Rank: 147

ENTERTAINMENT	AREA	U.S. AVG
Professional sports rating	2	4
College sports rating	4	4
Zoo/aquarium rating	2	3
Amusement park rating	1	3
Botanical garden/ arboretum rating	1	4

OUTDOOR ACTIVITIES	AREA	U.S. AVG
Golf-course rating	1	4
Ski-area rating	8	3
Sq. miles inland water	8	4
Miles of coastline	0.0	10.7
National Park rating	1	3

Arts & Culture
Score: 40.6
Rank: 222

MEDIA & LIBRARIES	AREA	U.S. AVG	PERFORMING ARTS	AREA	U.S. AVG	MUSEUMS	AREA	U.S. AVG
Arts radio rating	1	3	Classical music rating	3	4	Overall museum rating	4	5
No. public libraries	34	27	Ballet/dance rating	1	3	Art museum rating	1	5
Library volumes per capita	3.48	2.78	Professional theater rating	1	3	Science museum rating	4	5
			University arts programs rating	8	5	Children's museum rating	2	3

Cambridge–Newton–Framingham, MA   Score: 61.1   Rank: 166   2004 rank: 71

Profile: Suburban complex
Location: On outer I-495 Boston beltway, 30 miles north of Boston and 5 miles south of the New Hampshire border
Elevation: 115 feet
Time zone: Eastern Standard Time

PRO	CON
Attractive setting	Cost of living
Attractive housing	Traffic and sprawl
Historic interest	Economic cycles

Although the three named communities all stretch along the Massachusetts Turnpike (I-90) due west from downtown Boston, the area as defined, Middlesex County, is really much larger and more diverse, and stretches all the way north to the New Hampshire border. Within this county lies an enormous assortment of large and small suburbs and even cities, with well-known Boston-area names such as Lowell, Chelmsford, Lexington, Concord, Arlington, Waltham, Woburn, and Acton all within this area. These cities, and the many, many smaller burgs in between, provide an immense set of choices for living. All, of course, are served well by the rich cultural and practical resources offered by the Boston area.

Most of these places are really old towns laid out a few miles apart, when a few miles apart was a long way before the automobile. Most are well preserved with attractive and functional historic cores with small shops; people use these downtown areas. For the most part, newer retail, fast-food, and similar establishments, where allowed at all, are well planned and controlled and kept visually in check with architectural standards consistent with the area. Homes are spread out along main roads, which crisscross the area in a way that fosters easily getting from one place to another (many are old Indian trails). Large mass-produced housing developments are uncommon; most homes are constructed one at a time or perhaps on a single street branching off a main thoroughfare. Homes are on large lots and typically not hidden by fences. As a result, home prices are high, but we think the value received is high for the amount paid.

Of course, Cambridge and other areas closer to Boston are more urban, crowded, and expensive. Cambridge is the home of Harvard University, Massachusetts Institute of Technology, and a number of first-class museums. By contrast, Lowell is a pre–Industrial Age mill town relic that, at least until recently, was a working-class stronghold. These contrasts run through the area; the socioeconomic strata of the Boston area make themselves quite clear on a neighborhood-by-neighborhood basis and they aren't hard to figure out. While on the subject of Lowell, by the way, it has become one of the best examples of preservation to be found anywhere. The acres of old mill buildings are still there, crowding the narrow streets and canals that once gave them life, but now they've been repurposed into quite an active area of residences, restaurants, and nightlife, anchored by the Lowell National Historical Park occupying several of the mills in the center of town.

Schools, healthcare, cultural activities, entertainment, and most services are excellent and readily available within the Middlesex County area, and naturally in the Boston area at large. Traffic is always an issue, although the area invests well in public transportation. Some of the larger high-tech players in the Route 128 corridor ran into some bumps, bringing some employment concerns, and Boston manufacturing businesses still struggle with high costs. And not everyone likes the climate. But the Boston area has a lot to offer, and this is one of the top areas to capitalize on it. The ranking suffers because of the economy, high costs (especially housing affordability), commute issues, and climate, but for many it's better than the ranking indicates. We also recommend a look at the eastern portions of Essex County towards Cape May and the "south shore" area south of Boston along Route 3.

The terrain is gently rolling to hilly, with small creek valleys and thick deciduous woods. Summers are moderate with an occasional hot, humid spell and thundershowers. Winters have frequent cold snaps and considerable snowfall, with occasional "noreaster" storms from the Atlantic. First freeze is mid-October; last is late April.

Population

DEMOGRAPHICS	AREA	U.S. AVG	ETHNIC COMPOSITION	AREA	U.S. AVG	RESIDENT PROFILE	AREA	U.S. AVG
Population	1,471,486		White	83.6%	79.0%	Single	37.8%	32.4%
Population density per sq. mile	1786.9	358.5	Black	3.7%	10.5%	Married	50.9%	52.7%
Population growth	5.2%	21.1%	Asian	7.9%	2.7%	Divorced/separated	11.3%	14.9%
Median age	38.1	36.1	Hispanic	4.9%	10.6%	Married with children	24.1%	23.7%
Percent Democrat	64.0%	44.5%	Religious observance	73.6%	48.9%	Single with children	6.0%	9.1%
Percent Republican	34.5%	54.5%	Diversity measure	35.9	40.1	Percent over age 65	12.9%	12.9%

Economy & Jobs
Score: 30.2
Rank: 261

INCOME	AREA	U.S. AVG	EMPLOYMENT	AREA	U.S. AVG	EMPLOYING INDUSTRIES	AREA	U.S. AVG
Per capita income	$36,501	$23,235	Unemployment rate	4.2%	4.7%	Largest: Prof & tech svcs.		
Household income	$70,217	$46,414	Recent job growth	0.4%	1.3%			
Household income ‹ $25K	16.2%	26.2%	Projected future job growth	2.6%	11.5%	Percent manufacturing	8.4%	15.4%
Household income › $75K	46.5%	25.4%	White collar	73.8%	57.8%	Percent public sector	11.6%	15.7%
Household income growth	15.4%	13.6%	Blue collar	14.5%	25.2%	Percent construction	6.1%	9.9%

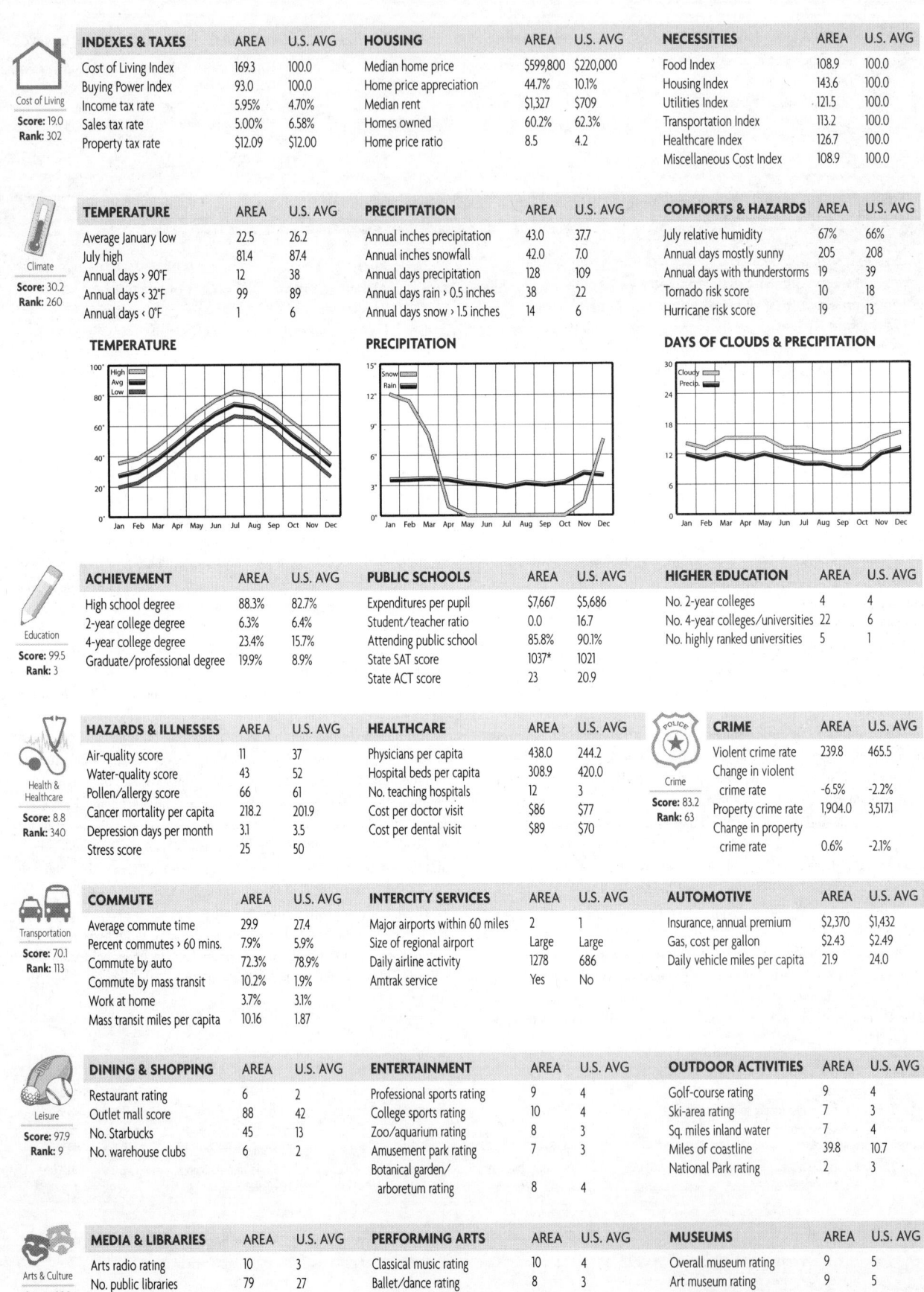

Cost of Living
Score: 19.0
Rank: 302

INDEXES & TAXES	AREA	U.S. AVG
Cost of Living Index	169.3	100.0
Buying Power Index	93.0	100.0
Income tax rate	5.95%	4.70%
Sales tax rate	5.00%	6.58%
Property tax rate	$12.09	$12.00

HOUSING	AREA	U.S. AVG
Median home price	$599,800	$220,000
Home price appreciation	44.7%	10.1%
Median rent	$1,327	$709
Homes owned	60.2%	62.3%
Home price ratio	8.5	4.2

NECESSITIES	AREA	U.S. AVG
Food Index	108.9	100.0
Housing Index	143.6	100.0
Utilities Index	121.5	100.0
Transportation Index	113.2	100.0
Healthcare Index	126.7	100.0
Miscellaneous Cost Index	108.9	100.0

Climate
Score: 30.2
Rank: 260

TEMPERATURE	AREA	U.S. AVG
Average January low	22.5	26.2
July high	81.4	87.4
Annual days > 90°F	12	38
Annual days < 32°F	99	89
Annual days < 0°F	1	6

PRECIPITATION	AREA	U.S. AVG
Annual inches precipitation	43.0	37.7
Annual inches snowfall	42.0	7.0
Annual days precipitation	128	109
Annual days rain > 0.5 inches	38	22
Annual days snow > 1.5 inches	14	6

COMFORTS & HAZARDS	AREA	U.S. AVG
July relative humidity	67%	66%
Annual days mostly sunny	205	208
Annual days with thunderstorms	19	39
Tornado risk score	10	18
Hurricane risk score	19	13

Education
Score: 99.5
Rank: 3

ACHIEVEMENT	AREA	U.S. AVG
High school degree	88.3%	82.7%
2-year college degree	6.3%	6.4%
4-year college degree	23.4%	15.7%
Graduate/professional degree	19.9%	8.9%

PUBLIC SCHOOLS	AREA	U.S. AVG
Expenditures per pupil	$7,667	$5,686
Student/teacher ratio	0.0	16.7
Attending public school	85.8%	90.1%
State SAT score	1037*	1021
State ACT score	23	20.9

HIGHER EDUCATION	AREA	U.S. AVG
No. 2-year colleges	4	4
No. 4-year colleges/universities	22	6
No. highly ranked universities	5	1

Health & Healthcare
Score: 8.8
Rank: 340

HAZARDS & ILLNESSES	AREA	U.S. AVG
Air-quality score	11	37
Water-quality score	43	52
Pollen/allergy score	66	61
Cancer mortality per capita	218.2	201.9
Depression days per month	3.1	3.5
Stress score	25	50

HEALTHCARE	AREA	U.S. AVG
Physicians per capita	438.0	244.2
Hospital beds per capita	308.9	420.0
No. teaching hospitals	12	3
Cost per doctor visit	$86	$77
Cost per dental visit	$89	$70

CRIME	AREA	U.S. AVG
Violent crime rate	239.8	465.5
Change in violent crime rate	-6.5%	-2.2%
Property crime rate	1,904.0	3,517.1
Change in property crime rate	0.6%	-2.1%

Crime
Score: 83.2
Rank: 63

Transportation
Score: 70.1
Rank: 113

COMMUTE	AREA	U.S. AVG
Average commute time	29.9	27.4
Percent commutes > 60 mins.	7.9%	5.9%
Commute by auto	72.3%	78.9%
Commute by mass transit	10.2%	1.9%
Work at home	3.7%	3.1%
Mass transit miles per capita	10.16	1.87

INTERCITY SERVICES	AREA	U.S. AVG
Major airports within 60 miles	2	1
Size of regional airport	Large	Large
Daily airline activity	1278	686
Amtrak service	Yes	No

AUTOMOTIVE	AREA	U.S. AVG
Insurance, annual premium	$2,370	$1,432
Gas, cost per gallon	$2.43	$2.49
Daily vehicle miles per capita	21.9	24.0

Leisure
Score: 97.9
Rank: 9

DINING & SHOPPING	AREA	U.S. AVG
Restaurant rating	6	2
Outlet mall score	88	42
No. Starbucks	45	13
No. warehouse clubs	6	2

ENTERTAINMENT	AREA	U.S. AVG
Professional sports rating	9	4
College sports rating	10	4
Zoo/aquarium rating	8	3
Amusement park rating	7	3
Botanical garden/ arboretum rating	8	4

OUTDOOR ACTIVITIES	AREA	U.S. AVG
Golf-course rating	9	4
Ski-area rating	7	3
Sq. miles inland water	7	4
Miles of coastline	39.8	10.7
National Park rating	2	3

Arts & Culture
Score: 99.2
Rank: 4

MEDIA & LIBRARIES	AREA	U.S. AVG
Arts radio rating	10	3
No. public libraries	79	27
Library volumes per capita	4.27	2.78

PERFORMING ARTS	AREA	U.S. AVG
Classical music rating	10	4
Ballet/dance rating	8	3
Professional theater rating	10	3
University arts programs rating	10	5

MUSEUMS	AREA	U.S. AVG
Overall museum rating	9	5
Art museum rating	9	5
Science museum rating	9	5
Children's museum rating	9	3

Camden, NJ

Score: 61.3   Rank: 163   2004 rank: 76

Profile: Industrial-city/suburban complex
Location: Southwest New Jersey across the Delaware River from Philadelphia
Elevation: 23 feet
Time zone: Eastern Standard Time

PRO	CON
Central location	Areas of urban decay
Access to Philadelphia	Long commutes
Cost of living	Economic cycles

Camden and its many suburbs lie east across the Delaware River from Philadelphia. Camden itself has always been a secondary transportation and industrial hub to the bigger city, and is in a decades-long period of decline. In its better years, in the early 20th century, it was actually a sort of leading-edge industrial center, serving as a cradle for the development of recorded music, being home to the Victor Talking Machine Company (later RCA Victor) and early recording studios. Those days are long gone, with RCA and even the manufacturing plant for native Fortune 500 company Campbell Soup now history (though Campbell still keeps its headquarters in Camden). Areas near the Delaware River are mostly run-down and plagued with crime, receiving the unwelcome moniker "America's Most Dangerous City" as measured by violent crime over the preceding three years. As you can see from the reported crime statistics, the area as a whole does not score that badly and there has been improvement. Some attempts at renewal, particularly along the waterfront, include a new aquarium and the Battleship *New Jersey* exhibit, but the inner parts of Camden have a long way to go.

The story gets better farther out in the Camden suburbs. This metro area actually covers not only Camden but also Burlington and Gloucester counties, reaching far into the well-preserved rural parts of central New Jersey. Along the New Jersey Turnpike and about 10 miles east of downtown Camden lies the suburb and township of Cherry Hill, recognized widely as a good locale in the Philly area and along the East Coast. Cherry Hill is an economic hub for south Jersey and features a number of prosperous newer-economy companies such as Subaru of America, Melitta Coffee, and Commerce Bancorp. Incomes are high, housing is attractive but reasonably priced, and buying power is high.

All together, the Camden area is a mixed bag, and newcomers will have to shop neighborhoods carefully. The area does have geographic advantages, with Philly's services and strong cultural amenities, and easy access 100 miles up the turnpike to New York. Coastal areas on the south Jersey shore are also within easy access. Cost of living, on the whole, is reasonable for such an East Coast location.

The Delaware Valley is broad and flat and stays that way with just a few low hills moving east. Summers are warm with periods of high humidity, occasionally cooled by sea breezes. Precipitation is fairly evenly distributed throughout the year, with the largest amounts coming in late summer as thunderstorms. Winter precipitation is a mix of rain and snow, and may become heavy when storms track up the Atlantic Coast.

DEMOGRAPHICS	AREA	U.S. AVG	ETHNIC COMPOSITION	AREA	U.S. AVG	RESIDENT PROFILE	AREA	U.S. AVG
Population	1,244,729		White	75.0%	79.0%	Single	34.1%	32.4%
Population density per sq. mile	920.9	358.5	Black	16.2%	10.5%	Married	52.8%	52.7%
Population growth	10.8%	21.1%	Asian	3.2%	2.7%	Divorced/separated	13.1%	14.9%
Median age	37.4	36.1	Hispanic	7.1%	10.6%	Married with children	25.9%	23.7%
Percent Democrat	56.8%	44.5%	Religious observance	52.1%	48.9%	Single with children	8.9%	9.1%
Percent Republican	42.5%	54.5%	Diversity measure	47.4	40.1	Percent over age 65	12.5%	12.9%

Score: 72.2 Rank: 105

INCOME	AREA	U.S. AVG	EMPLOYMENT	AREA	U.S. AVG	EMPLOYING INDUSTRIES	AREA	U.S. AVG
Per capita income	$28,040	$23,235	Unemployment rate	4.4%	4.7%	Largest: Healthcare & Social Assistance		
Household income	$60,808	$46,414	Recent job growth	3.2%	1.3%			
Household income < $25K	17.3%	26.2%	Projected future job growth	9.6%	11.5%	Percent manufacturing	12.1%	15.4%
Household income > $75K	38.4%	25.4%	White collar	65.5%	57.8%	Percent public sector	15.5%	15.7%
Household income growth	14.1%	13.6%	Blue collar	20.7%	25.2%	Percent construction	8.5%	9.9%

Score: 9.9 Rank: 336

INDEXES & TAXES	AREA	U.S. AVG	HOUSING	AREA	U.S. AVG	NECESSITIES	AREA	U.S. AVG
Cost of Living Index	106.5	100.0	Median home price	$219,600	$220,000	Food Index	105.8	100.0
Buying Power Index	128.0	100.0	Home price appreciation	86.9%	10.1%	Housing Index	69.6	100.0
Income tax rate	7.54%	4.70%	Median rent	$923	$709	Utilities Index	128.3	100.0
Sales tax rate	6.00%	6.58%	Homes owned	70.8%	62.3%	Transportation Index	113.7	100.0
Property tax rate	$26.75	$12.00	Home price ratio	3.6	4.2	Healthcare Index	103.5	100.0
						Miscellaneous Cost Index	111.1	100.0

Climate
Score: 65.0
Rank: 130

TEMPERATURE	AREA	U.S. AVG
Average January low	24.4	26.2
July high	86.8	87.4
Annual days > 90°F	19	38
Annual days < 32°F	101	89
Annual days < 0°F	0	6

PRECIPITATION	AREA	U.S. AVG
Annual inches precipitation	40.0	37.7
Annual inches snowfall	20.0	7.0
Annual days precipitation	116	109
Annual days rain > 0.5 inches	28	22
Annual days snow > 1.5 inches	6	6

COMFORTS & HAZARDS	AREA	U.S. AVG
July relative humidity	67%	66%
Annual days mostly sunny	205	208
Annual days with thunderstorms	27	39
Tornado risk score	20	18
Hurricane risk score	16	13

TEMPERATURE

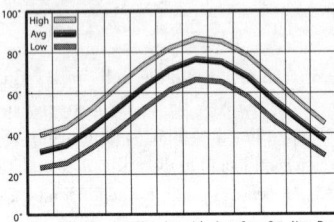

PRECIPITATION

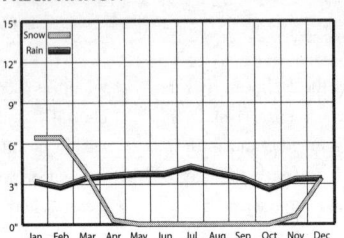

DAYS OF CLOUDS & PRECIPITATION

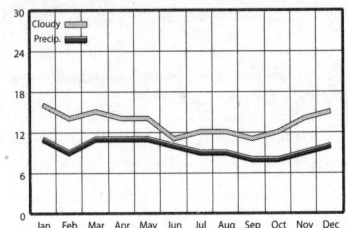

Education
Score: 61.0
Rank: 146

ACHIEVEMENT	AREA	U.S. AVG
High school degree	83.7%	82.7%
2-year college degree	6.3%	6.4%
4-year college degree	16.9%	15.7%
Graduate/professional degree	8.3%	8.9%

PUBLIC SCHOOLS	AREA	U.S. AVG
Expenditures per pupil	$8,492	$5,686
Student/teacher ratio	15.4	16.7
Attending public school	87.6%	90.1%
State SAT score	1011*	1021
State ACT score	21.8	20.9

HIGHER EDUCATION	AREA	U.S. AVG
No. 2-year colleges	4	4
No. 4-year colleges/universities	3	6
No. highly ranked universities	1	1

Health & Healthcare
Score: 14.2
Rank: 319

HAZARDS & ILLNESSES	AREA	U.S. AVG
Air-quality score	33	37
Water-quality score	8	52
Pollen/allergy score	64	61
Cancer mortality per capita	237.0	201.9
Depression days per month	3.6	3.5
Stress score	45	50

HEALTHCARE	AREA	U.S. AVG
Physicians per capita	288.5	244.2
Hospital beds per capita	317.6	420.0
No. teaching hospitals	7	3
Cost per doctor visit	$68	$77
Cost per dental visit	$88	$70

Crime
Score: 64.7
Rank: 133

CRIME	AREA	U.S. AVG
Violent crime rate	351.3	465.5
Change in violent crime rate	-11.5%	-2.2%
Property crime rate	2,519.6	3,517.1
Change in property crime rate	-6.9%	-2.1%

Transportation
Score: 98.7
Rank: 6

COMMUTE	AREA	U.S. AVG
Average commute time	30.3	27.4
Percent commutes > 60 mins.	10.1%	5.9%
Commute by auto	79.0%	78.9%
Commute by mass transit	5.3%	1.9%
Work at home	2.6%	3.1%
Mass transit miles per capita	5.27	1.87

INTERCITY SERVICES	AREA	U.S. AVG
Major airports within 60 miles	5	1
Size of regional airport	Large	Large
Daily airline activity	3044	686
Amtrak service	No	No

AUTOMOTIVE	AREA	U.S. AVG
Insurance, annual premium	$2,567	$1,432
Gas, cost per gallon	$2.51	$2.49
Daily vehicle miles per capita	22.8	24.0

Leisure
Score: 93.3
Rank: 26

DINING & SHOPPING	AREA	U.S. AVG
Restaurant rating	8	2
Outlet mall score	45	42
No. Starbucks	10	13
No. warehouse clubs	5	2

ENTERTAINMENT	AREA	U.S. AVG
Professional sports rating	10	4
College sports rating	6	4
Zoo/aquarium rating	8	3
Amusement park rating	6	3
Botanical garden/ arboretum rating	6	4

OUTDOOR ACTIVITIES	AREA	U.S. AVG
Golf-course rating	10	4
Ski-area rating	4	3
Sq. miles inland water	5	4
Miles of coastline	0.0	10.7
National Park rating	3	3

Arts & Culture
Score: 98.4
Rank: 7

MEDIA & LIBRARIES	AREA	U.S. AVG
Arts radio rating	10	3
No. public libraries	61	27
Library volumes per capita	2.92	2.78

PERFORMING ARTS	AREA	U.S. AVG
Classical music rating	10	4
Ballet/dance rating	9	3
Professional theater rating	10	3
University arts programs rating	10	5

MUSEUMS	AREA	U.S. AVG
Overall museum rating	10	5
Art museum rating	10	5
Science museum rating	7	5
Children's museum rating	4	3

Canton–Massillon, OH

Score: 52.5   **Rank:** 236   **2004 rank:** 278

Profile: Small-city complex
Location: Northeast Ohio, 60 miles south of Cleveland and 20 miles south of Akron
Elevation: 1,208 feet
Time zone: Eastern Standard Time

PRO
Cost of living and housing
Nearby recreation
Nearby city amenities

CON
Economic malaise
Low educational attainment
Cloudy, wet climate

In today's real estate market, homes anywhere for under $10,000 make headlines, and it just so happens that Canton recently made national news for just such an occurrence—a number of serviceable early-20th-century downtown fringe homes in that price range. It's certainly not the case that every home is this cheap, but it underscores the plight of Canton and many other downtrodden old-economy towns in northeastern Ohio. However, at these prices, we would be buyers, for the fortunes of many of these towns may be gradually reversing, and we see good value potential for patient residents.

Canton is the southernmost city in the industrial corridor stretching south from Cleveland in northeast Ohio. Massillon is almost a twin city just to the west. The area is a center of diverse manufacturing and a gateway to the large Appalachian foothills to the south and east. Manufacturers include Timken (roller bearings), Diebold (ATMs and banking systems), and the Hoover Company (vacuums). Admittedly, manufacturing has seen hard times (a large steel mill closed in 2000), and the turnaround is slow. The downtown area, though mostly unremarkable, has undergone an attractive core renewal that has brought some business back. Newer suburbs contain a good assortment of spacious homes with attractive settings and prices. The Pro Football Hall of Fame in Canton is one local attraction, and areas in the foothills yield recreation and some interesting historic industrial and agricultural areas, including the glassblowing and brick-making areas around Dover and New Philadelphia. Residents drive north toward Cleveland for cultural amenities and shopping.

The area has rolling-to-hilly terrain, which becomes more hilly moving south from the city. Valleys are open and agricultural, and the hills are mostly deciduous woods. Summers are moderately warm and quite humid, with late springs and pleasant fall periods. Temperature and snowfall vary considerably over the area, with more snow in the north. First freeze is mid-October; last is late April.

DEMOGRAPHICS	AREA	U.S. AVG	ETHNIC COMPOSITION	AREA	U.S. AVG	RESIDENT PROFILE	AREA	U.S. AVG
Population	407,507		White	90.5%	79.0%	Single	30.7%	32.4%
Population density per sq. mile	419.8	358.5	Black	6.7%	10.5%	Married	55.8%	52.7%
Population growth	3.5%	21.1%	Asian	0.7%	2.7%	Divorced/separated	13.5%	14.9%
Median age	39.2	36.1	Hispanic	0.9%	10.6%	Married with children	22.5%	23.7%
Percent Democrat	50.1%	44.5%	Religious observance	50.4%	48.9%	Single with children	8.2%	9.1%
Percent Republican	49.3%	54.5%	Diversity measure	18.9	40.1	Percent over age 65	15.4%	12.9%

Population

INCOME	AREA	U.S. AVG	EMPLOYMENT	AREA	U.S. AVG	EMPLOYING INDUSTRIES	AREA	U.S. AVG
Per capita income	$22,790	$23,235	Unemployment rate	5.8%	4.7%	Largest: Manufacturing		
Household income	$44,227	$46,414	Recent job growth	1.4%	1.3%			
Household income < $25K	25.8%	26.2%	Projected future job growth	6.3%	11.5%	Percent manufacturing	22.0%	15.4%
Household income > $75K	22.4%	25.4%	White collar	54.0%	57.8%	Percent public sector	9.7%	15.7%
Household income growth	11.9%	13.6%	Blue collar	30.7%	25.2%	Percent construction	8.7%	9.9%

Economy & Jobs
Score: 38.5
Rank: 230

INDEXES & TAXES	AREA	U.S. AVG	HOUSING	AREA	U.S. AVG	NECESSITIES	AREA	U.S. AVG
Cost of Living Index	82.2	100.0	Median home price	$114,400	$220,000	Food Index	104.0	100.0
Buying Power Index	120.6	100.0	Home price appreciation	16.2%	10.1%	Housing Index	47.9	100.0
Income tax rate	4.99%	4.70%	Median rent	$588	$709	Utilities Index	121.8	100.0
Sales tax rate	6.54%	6.58%	Homes owned	68.8%	62.3%	Transportation Index	94.6	100.0
Property tax rate	$10.95	$12.00	Home price ratio	2.6	4.2	Healthcare Index	98.3	100.0
						Miscellaneous Cost Index	96.8	100.0

Cost of Living
Score: 71.9
Rank: 106

Climate
Score: 11.5
Rank: 330

TEMPERATURE	AREA	U.S. AVG
Average January low	18.6	26.2
July high	82.6	87.4
Annual days > 90°F	7	38
Annual days < 32°F	128	89
Annual days < 0°F	6	6

PRECIPITATION	AREA	U.S. AVG
Annual inches precipitation	35.1	37.7
Annual inches snowfall	48.2	7.0
Annual days precipitation	168	109
Annual days rain > 0.5 inches	23	22
Annual days snow > 1.5 inches	11	6

COMFORTS & HAZARDS	AREA	U.S. AVG
July relative humidity	71%	66%
Annual days mostly sunny	171	208
Annual days with thunderstorms	40	39
Tornado risk score	8	18
Hurricane risk score	3	13

TEMPERATURE

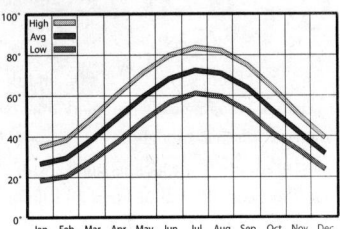

PRECIPITATION

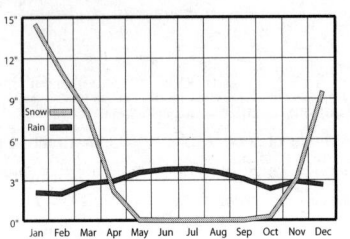

DAYS OF CLOUDS & PRECIPITATION

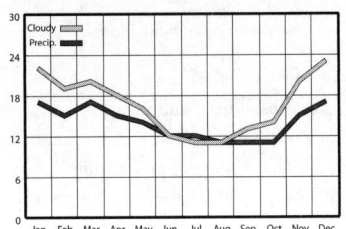

Education
Score: 28.6
Rank: 268

ACHIEVEMENT	AREA	U.S. AVG
High school degree	83.3%	82.7%
2-year college degree	5.2%	6.4%
4-year college degree	11.5%	15.7%
Graduate/professional degree	5.9%	8.9%

PUBLIC SCHOOLS	AREA	U.S. AVG
Expenditures per pupil	$4,974	$5,686
Student/teacher ratio	19.0	16.7
Attending public school	90.4%	90.1%
State SAT score	1079	1021
State ACT score	21.5*	20.9

HIGHER EDUCATION	AREA	U.S. AVG
No. 2-year colleges	7	4
No. 4-year colleges/universities	3	6
No. highly ranked universities	1	1

Health & Healthcare
Score: 38.5
Rank: 229

HAZARDS & ILLNESSES	AREA	U.S. AVG
Air-quality score	32	37
Water-quality score	33	52
Pollen/allergy score	63	61
Cancer mortality per capita	211.4	201.9
Depression days per month	3.3	3.5
Stress score	49	50

HEALTHCARE	AREA	U.S. AVG
Physicians per capita	221.4	244.2
Hospital beds per capita	585.8	420.0
No. teaching hospitals	4	3
Cost per doctor visit	$68	$77
Cost per dental visit	$62	$70

Crime
Score: 25.1
Rank: 280

CRIME	AREA	U.S. AVG
Violent crime rate	278.7	465.5
Change in violent crime rate	-20.4%	-2.2%
Property crime rate	3,978.4	3,517.1
Change in property crime rate	-0.8%	-2.1%

Transportation
Score: 92.0
Rank: 31

COMMUTE	AREA	U.S. AVG
Average commute time	23.6	27.4
Percent commutes > 60 mins.	4.9%	5.9%
Commute by auto	86.1%	78.9%
Commute by mass transit	1.0%	1.9%
Work at home	2.4%	3.1%
Mass transit miles per capita	1.02	1.87

INTERCITY SERVICES	AREA	U.S. AVG
Major airports within 60 miles	3	1
Size of regional airport	Large	Large
Daily airline activity	1420	686
Amtrak service	Yes	No

AUTOMOTIVE	AREA	U.S. AVG
Insurance, annual premium	$1,320	$1,432
Gas, cost per gallon	$2.45	$2.49
Daily vehicle miles per capita	18.9	24.0

Leisure
Score: 32.9
Rank: 249

DINING & SHOPPING	AREA	U.S. AVG
Restaurant rating	1	2
Outlet mall score	0	42
No. Starbucks	3	13
No. warehouse clubs	2	2

ENTERTAINMENT	AREA	U.S. AVG
Professional sports rating	3	4
College sports rating	2	4
Zoo/aquarium rating	1	3
Amusement park rating	1	3
Botanical garden/ arboretum rating	1	4

OUTDOOR ACTIVITIES	AREA	U.S. AVG
Golf-course rating	5	4
Ski-area rating	2	3
Sq. miles inland water	3	4
Miles of coastline	0.0	10.7
National Park rating	1	3

Arts & Culture
Score: 57.0
Rank: 161

MEDIA & LIBRARIES	AREA	U.S. AVG
Arts radio rating	1	3
No. public libraries	23	27
Library volumes per capita	3.96	2.78

PERFORMING ARTS	AREA	U.S. AVG
Classical music rating	4	4
Ballet/dance rating	3	3
Professional theater rating	1	3
University arts programs rating	5	5

MUSEUMS	AREA	U.S. AVG
Overall museum rating	7	5
Art museum rating	5	5
Science museum rating	7	5
Children's museum rating	8	3

Cape Coral–Fort Myers, FL

Score: 49.1   **Rank:** 249   **2004 rank:** 220

Profile: Mid-size-city complex
Location: Gulf Coast, 130 miles south of Tampa–St. Petersburg
Elevation: 31 feet
Time zone: Eastern Standard Time

PRO	CON
Winter climate	Tourist impact
Baseball spring training	Hurricane risk
Attractive downtown	Arts and culture

Fort Myers, on the southern Florida Gulf Coast, is a quiet city famous for its palm tree–lined streets. Not a typical beach town, it nonetheless maintains a tropical flavor, attracts some tourists, and is home to several baseball spring-training camps. It is also home to a large number of retirees. Offshore islands Sanibel and Captiva are more touristy, although both are restrained in development compared to other areas in the state. Cape Coral, just to the southwest, is a relatively large and new planned community even more popular with retirees, 115 square miles in all, located along canals and the waterfront. Although Fort Myers is better known, Cape Coral is actually the larger community. The whole area and Cape Coral in particular suffered damage during passing hurricanes Charley (2004) and Wilma (2005). The Florida climate is generally pleasant, but the southerly and slightly inland location of Fort Myers provides particularly nice and dry winter weather. But on the downside, the area is far from big-city amenities such as arts and culture, entertainment, and air service. While employment has been a concern at times, current and future projections are strong. The area is also spread out and growing, creating some sprawl-related problems.

Fort Myers is located on the south bank of the Caloosahatchee River about 15 miles inland from the Gulf of Mexico. The terrain is level and low with a mix of coastal plain and wet oak, magnolia, and evergreen forests. High temperatures generally range from the low 60s in winter to the low 80s in summer. Winters are mild with many bright warm days and moderately cool nights. Occasional cold snaps drop temperatures to the 30s, but rarely to the 20s. About two-thirds of annual precipitation occurs June through September, mostly as cooling late-afternoon thunderstorms. Late summer and fall tropical storms and hurricanes cause occasional torrential downpours, delivering perhaps 6 to 10 inches in 24 hours.

DEMOGRAPHICS	AREA	U.S. AVG	ETHNIC COMPOSITION	AREA	U.S. AVG	RESIDENT PROFILE	AREA	U.S. AVG
Population	518,281		White	85.0%	79.0%	Single	26.0%	32.4%
Population density per sq. mile	644.9	358.5	Black	7.5%	10.5%	Married	59.1%	52.7%
Population growth	54.7%	21.1%	Asian	1.1%	2.7%	Divorced/separated	14.9%	14.9%
Median age	44.2	36.1	Hispanic	13.2%	10.6%	Married with children	15.6%	23.7%
Percent Democrat	39.0%	44.5%	Religious observance	38.2%	48.9%	Single with children	6.8%	9.1%
Percent Republican	59.9%	54.5%	Diversity measure	43.7	40.1	Percent over age 65	24.0%	12.9%

Score: 95.7
Rank: 17

INCOME	AREA	U.S. AVG	EMPLOYMENT	AREA	U.S. AVG	EMPLOYING INDUSTRIES	AREA	U.S. AVG
Per capita income	$28,647	$23,235	Unemployment rate	3.2%	4.7%	Largest: Healthcare & Social Assistance		
Household income	$47,499	$46,414	Recent job growth	6.2%	1.3%			
Household income < $25K	22.1%	26.2%	Projected future job growth	24.5%	11.5%	Percent manufacturing	9.2%	15.4%
Household income > $75K	26.3%	25.4%	White collar	58.3%	57.8%	Percent public sector	11.5%	15.7%
Household income growth	17.8%	13.6%	Blue collar	22.5%	25.2%	Percent construction	13.3%	9.9%

Score: 35.3
Rank: 241

INDEXES & TAXES	AREA	U.S. AVG	HOUSING	AREA	U.S. AVG	NECESSITIES	AREA	U.S. AVG
Cost of Living Index	110.1	100.0	Median home price	$287,000	$220,000	Food Index	100.9	100.0
Buying Power Index	96.7	100.0	Home price appreciation	141.8%	10.1%	Housing Index	118.6	100.0
Income tax rate	0.00%	4.70%	Median rent	$757	$709	Utilities Index	99.2	100.0
Sales tax rate	6.00%	6.58%	Homes owned	59.2%	62.3%	Transportation Index	110.2	100.0
Property tax rate	$13.18	$12.00	Home price ratio	6.0	4.2	Healthcare Index	94.6	100.0
						Miscellaneous Cost Index	97.4	100.0

Score: 82.9
Rank: 65

TEMPERATURE	AREA	U.S. AVG	PRECIPITATION	AREA	U.S. AVG	COMFORTS & HAZARDS	AREA	U.S. AVG
Average January low	52.3	26.2	Annual inches precipitation	54.0	37.7	July relative humidity	76%	66%
July high	91.5	87.4	Annual inches snowfall	0.0	7.0	Annual days mostly sunny	264	208
Annual days > 90°F	106	38	Annual days precipitation	112	109	Annual days with thunderstorms	93	39
Annual days < 32°F	1	89	Annual days rain > 0.5 inches	32	22	Tornado risk score	52	18
Annual days < 0°F	0	6	Annual days snow > 1.5 inches	0	6	Hurricane risk score	80	13

TEMPERATURE

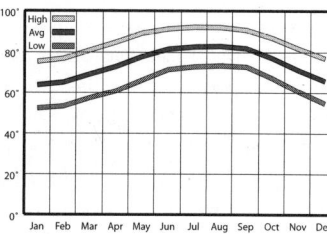

PRECIPITATION

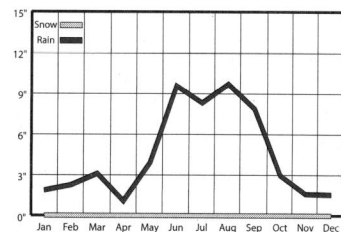

DAYS OF CLOUDS & PRECIPITATION

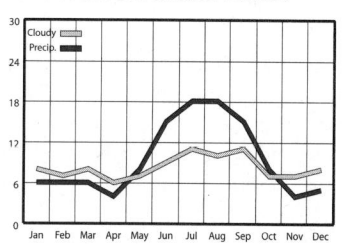

ACHIEVEMENT	AREA	U.S. AVG	PUBLIC SCHOOLS	AREA	U.S. AVG	HIGHER EDUCATION	AREA	U.S. AVG
High school degree	82.7%	82.7%	Expenditures per pupil	$5,763	$5,686	No. 2-year colleges	4	4
2-year college degree	6.1%	6.4%	Student/teacher ratio	18.9	16.7	No. 4-year colleges/universities	1	6
4-year college degree	13.7%	15.7%	Attending public school	89.8%	90.1%	No. highly ranked universities	0	1
Graduate/professional degree	7.7%	8.9%	State SAT score	993*	1021			
			State ACT score	20.3	20.9			

Education
Score: 36.9
Rank: 237

HAZARDS & ILLNESSES	AREA	U.S. AVG	HEALTHCARE	AREA	U.S. AVG	CRIME	AREA	U.S. AVG
Air-quality score	24	37	Physicians per capita	196.5	244.2	Violent crime rate	567.8	465.5
Water-quality score	59	52	Hospital beds per capita	354.4	420.0	Change in violent crime rate	-1.8%	-2.2%
Pollen/allergy score	72	61	No. teaching hospitals	0	3	Property crime rate	3,532.8	3,517.1
Cancer mortality per capita	229.5	201.9	Cost per doctor visit	$80	$77	Change in property crime rate	-2.7%	-2.1%
Depression days per month	3.3	3.5	Cost per dental visit	$74	$70			
Stress score	53	50						

Health & Healthcare
Score: 17.4
Rank: 308

Crime
Score: 25.4
Rank: 278

COMMUTE	AREA	U.S. AVG	INTERCITY SERVICES	AREA	U.S. AVG	AUTOMOTIVE	AREA	U.S. AVG
Average commute time	26.7	27.4	Major airports within 60 miles	1	1	Insurance, annual premium	$1,899	$1,432
Percent commutes > 60 mins.	5.9%	5.9%	Size of regional airport	Medium	Large	Gas, cost per gallon	$2.62	$2.49
Commute by auto	79.0%	78.9%	Daily airline activity	125	686	Daily vehicle miles per capita	33.6	24.0
Commute by mass transit	0.7%	1.9%	Amtrak service	No	No			
Work at home	3.6%	3.1%						
Mass transit miles per capita	0.72	1.87						

Transportation
Score: 4.3
Rank: 355

DINING & SHOPPING	AREA	U.S. AVG	ENTERTAINMENT	AREA	U.S. AVG	OUTDOOR ACTIVITIES	AREA	U.S. AVG
Restaurant rating	1	2	Professional sports rating	3	4	Golf-course rating	4	4
Outlet mall score	165	42	College sports rating	1	4	Ski-area rating	1	3
No. Starbucks	4	13	Zoo/aquarium rating	3	3	Sq. miles inland water	10	4
No. warehouse clubs	2	2	Amusement park rating	4	3	Miles of coastline	38.0	10.7
			Botanical garden/ arboretum rating	8	4	National Park rating	2	3

Leisure
Score: 72.2
Rank: 104

MEDIA & LIBRARIES	AREA	U.S. AVG	PERFORMING ARTS	AREA	U.S. AVG	MUSEUMS	AREA	U.S. AVG
Arts radio rating	1	3	Classical music rating	4	4	Overall museum rating	6	5
No. public libraries	14	27	Ballet/dance rating	1	3	Art museum rating	2	5
Library volumes per capita	2.26	2.78	Professional theater rating	1	3	Science museum rating	8	5
			University arts programs rating	2	5	Children's museum rating	7	3

Arts & Culture
Score: 17.9
Rank: 306

Carson City, NV

Score: 59.6   Rank: 178   2004 rank: not ranked

Profile: Capital city
Location: Extreme western Nevada, south of Reno
Elevation: 4,687 feet
Time zone: Pacific Standard Time

PRO
Nearby mountains
Year-round climate
Historic interest

CON
Unattractive sprawl
Cost of living and housing
Arts and culture

Carson City is one of the more unusual capital cities in the U.S. Served neither by an interstate highway nor a railroad, the small desert-mountain city is located just east of the main Sierra Nevada rise and Lake Tahoe. The booming city of Reno lies 30 miles to the north across a low mountain pass. Currently, the road to Reno is being widened and will become the city's first interstate, a spur from Interstate 80, when completed. Attractive residential areas are in the mountains and valleys 15 miles farther south into the Carson Valley toward the small agricultural centers of Minden and Gardnerville, but they are becoming expensive as more Californians move in. While "Carson" enjoys its attractive setting, the city itself is far from attractive. There is an assortment of small state government buildings, second-tier casinos, and unattractive desert sprawl mainly to the south and east and

particularly along a crowded commercial strip south of town. The city has some points of historical interest and a couple of museum "gems," including the Nevada State Railroad Museum, but few find the city itself a travel or residential destination of choice. All around Carson, however, there is plenty to do and plenty of historic interest. Lake Tahoe just west is a standout, and Virginia City and other mining centers in the vicinity offer above-average recreational opportunities. Areas south along U.S. 395 are rugged, wild, relatively unpopulated, and filled with hiking and fishing spots. The state and tourist industries anchor the employment base. But outside of retail there is little private industry in the immediate area. Some commute to the ever-growing Reno to the north, and this commute will likely get easier with the new interstate. Cost of living (127.6) and housing ($364,600) are high for what's available—and likely to get higher. While the surrounding areas are rich with attractions and the Carson Valley area south is excellent, the ranking may overstate the living experience for many.

Typically, towns of this genre in otherwise desirable locations get the message and set out to upgrade their infrastructure, and we expect Carson to do the same. It might be a diamond in the rough for those willing to take a chance. The city has recently adopted an extensive master plan, but the jury is still out on whether it will deal effectively with the negatives, or just allow future growth to overwhelm the relatively tight land space it controls. For those wanting a more certain outcome and

willing to pay more, we recommend a look further south into the Carson Valley.

Carson City is situated in a high and mainly dry desert valley, with the eastern flank of the Sierra and Lake Tahoe rising dramatically to the west, and dry desert hills, some quite high, rising to the east. Summer days are hot and dry with only occasional afternoon thundershowers; evenings are dry and cool. Hot spells will drive daytime temperatures over 100°F occasionally. Winters are mostly cool and dry but will bring dustings, though little in the way of heavy snow. Sunshine is abundant all year with most precipitation occurring in winter and spring, much like neighboring California.

Population

DEMOGRAPHICS	AREA	U.S. AVG	ETHNIC COMPOSITION	AREA	U.S. AVG	RESIDENT PROFILE	AREA	U.S. AVG
Population	56,679		White	85.2%	79.0%	Single	27.0%	32.4%
Population density per sq. mile	395.3	358.5	Black	1.5%	10.5%	Married	49.8%	52.7%
Population growth	40.1%	21.1%	Asian	1.6%	2.7%	Divorced/separated	23.2%	14.9%
Median age	38.9	36.1	Hispanic	16.1%	10.6%	Married with children	20.3%	23.7%
Percent Democrat	40.9%	44.5%	Religious observance	39.8%	48.9%	Single with children	9.5%	9.1%
Percent Republican	57.0%	54.5%	Diversity measure	46.5	40.1	Percent over age 65	15.5%	12.9%

Economy & Jobs
Score: 20.1
Rank: 299

INCOME	AREA	U.S. AVG	EMPLOYMENT	AREA	U.S. AVG	EMPLOYING INDUSTRIES	AREA	U.S. AVG
Per capita income	$23,521	$23,235	Unemployment rate	4.5%	4.7%	Largest: Manufacturing		
Household income	$47,061	$46,414	Recent job growth	-0.3%	1.3%			
Household income < $25K	23.7%	26.2%	Projected future job growth	9.8%	11.5%	Percent manufacturing	13.8%	15.4%
Household income > $75K	25.6%	25.4%	White collar	58.4%	57.8%	Percent public sector	23.1%	15.7%
Household income growth	12.6%	13.6%	Blue collar	23.1%	25.2%	Percent construction	9.2%	9.9%

Cost of Living
Score: 19.5
Rank: 300

INDEXES & TAXES	AREA	U.S. AVG	HOUSING	AREA	U.S. AVG	NECESSITIES	AREA	U.S. AVG
Cost of Living Index	127.6	100.0	Median home price	$364,600	$220,000	Food Index	116.7	100.0
Buying Power Index	82.7	100.0	Home price appreciation	105.5%	10.1%	Housing Index	111.1	100.0
Income tax rate	0.00%	4.70%	Median rent	$794	$709	Utilities Index	105.6	100.0
Sales tax rate	7.00%	6.58%	Homes owned	59.7%	62.3%	Transportation Index	103.3	100.0
Property tax rate	$7.28	$12.00	Home price ratio	7.7	4.2	Healthcare Index	119.8	100.0
						Miscellaneous Cost Index	100.3	100.0

Climate
Score: 72.5
Rank: 102

TEMPERATURE	AREA	U.S. AVG	PRECIPITATION	AREA	U.S. AVG	COMFORTS & HAZARDS	AREA	U.S. AVG
Average January low	20.9	26.2	Annual inches precipitation	10.5	37.7	July relative humidity	20%	66%
July high	88.9	87.4	Annual inches snowfall	21.2	7.0	Annual days mostly sunny	255	208
Annual days > 90°F	50	38	Annual days precipitation	50	109	Annual days with thunderstorms	14	39
Annual days < 32°F	178	89	Annual days rain > 0.5 inches	1	22	Tornado risk score	1	18
Annual days < 0°F	2	6	Annual days snow > 1.5 inches	4	6	Hurricane risk score	0	13

TEMPERATURE

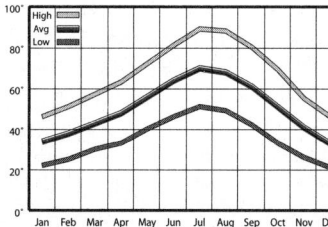

PRECIPITATION

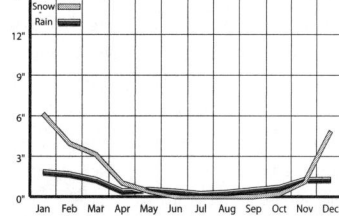

DAYS OF CLOUDS & PRECIPITATION

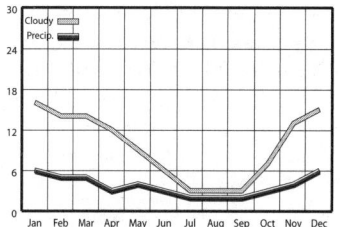

Education
Score: 35.3
Rank: 243

ACHIEVEMENT	AREA	U.S. AVG	PUBLIC SCHOOLS	AREA	U.S. AVG	HIGHER EDUCATION	AREA	U.S. AVG
High school degree	82.2%	82.7%	Expenditures per pupil	$5,191	$5,686	No. 2-year colleges	2	4
2-year college degree	6.7%	6.4%	Student/teacher ratio	17.3	16.7	No. 4-year colleges/universities	0	6
4-year college degree	11.9%	15.7%	Attending public school	93.6%	90.1%	No. highly ranked universities	0	1
Graduate/professional degree	6.6%	8.9%	State SAT score	1006*	1021			
			State ACT score	21.5	20.9			

HAZARDS & ILLNESSES	AREA	U.S. AVG		HEALTHCARE	AREA	U.S. AVG		CRIME	AREA	U.S. AVG
Air-quality score	82	37		Physicians per capita	256.7	244.2		Violent crime rate	507.8	465.5
Water-quality score	40	52		Hospital beds per capita	225.8	420.0		Change in violent crime rate	-0.1%	-2.2%
Pollen/allergy score	63	61		No. teaching hospitals	0	3		Property crime rate	2,502.9	3,517.1
Cancer mortality per capita	205.2	201.9		Cost per doctor visit	$86	$77		Change in property crime rate	-13.3%	-2.1%
Depression days per month	3.7	3.5		Cost per dental visit	$82	$70				
Stress score	62	50								

Health & Healthcare
Score: 75.4
Rank: 93

Crime
Score: 61.8
Rank: 144

COMMUTE	AREA	U.S. AVG		INTERCITY SERVICES	AREA	U.S. AVG		AUTOMOTIVE	AREA	U.S. AVG
Average commute time	19.7	27.4		Major airports within 60 miles	1	1		Insurance, annual premium	$1,622	$1,432
Percent commutes > 60 mins.	3.0%	5.9%		Size of regional airport	Medium	Large		Gas, cost per gallon	$2.62	$2.49
Commute by auto	77.7%	78.9%		Daily airline activity	123	686		Daily vehicle miles per capita	20.2	24.0
Commute by mass transit	0.6%	1.9%		Amtrak service	No	No				
Work at home	3.3%	3.1%								
Mass transit miles per capita	0.63	1.87								

Transportation
Score: 63.4
Rank: 138

DINING & SHOPPING	AREA	U.S. AVG		ENTERTAINMENT	AREA	U.S. AVG		OUTDOOR ACTIVITIES	AREA	U.S. AVG
Restaurant rating	1	2		Professional sports rating	1	4		Golf-course rating	3	4
Outlet mall score	34	42		College sports rating	1	4		Ski-area rating	8	3
No. Starbucks	2	13		Zoo/aquarium rating	1	3		Sq. miles inland water	2	4
No. warehouse clubs	1	2		Amusement park rating	1	3		Miles of coastline	0.0	10.7
				Botanical garden/ arboretum rating	1	4		National Park rating	6	3

Leisure
Score: 43.6
Rank: 210

MEDIA & LIBRARIES	AREA	U.S. AVG		PERFORMING ARTS	AREA	U.S. AVG		MUSEUMS	AREA	U.S. AVG
Arts radio rating	1	3		Classical music rating	2	4		Overall museum rating	3	5
No. public libraries	1	27		Ballet/dance rating	1	3		Art museum rating	3	5
Library volumes per capita	1.99	2.78		Professional theater rating	1	3		Science museum rating	6	5
				University arts programs rating	1	5		Children's museum rating	1	3

Arts & Culture
Score: 4.5
Rank: 356

Casper, WY

Score: 67.8 **Rank:** 112 **2004 rank:** 185

Profile: Small town
Location: East-central Wyoming on the eastern slope of the Rockies
Elevation: 5,237 feet
Time zone: Mountain Standard Time

PRO	CON
Small-town atmosphere	Wind and cold
Outdoor recreation	Isolation
Cost of living	Low ethnic diversity

Casper is a somewhat remote town supported mainly by the oil and gas industries (exploration, production, and refinement), and more recently by low-sulfur coal in the Powder River Basin to the north and east. Ranching and agriculture are also present. Employment is steady but not oriented toward growth. The city has a distinctly Western, almost boomtown feel, with a traditional downtown and suburban development encroaching upon the grasslands. In clear contrast to the surrounding bluffs, downtown and most residential areas have lots of trees. The area is noted for its wide-open spaces and friendliness.

Casper is located in the North Platte River Valley. The immediately surrounding country is mostly rolling and hilly grassland with flat prairies in each direction except toward the south, where Casper Mountain rises 3,500 feet above the valley floor. Summer days are warm, dry, and pleasant with cool evenings. Winters are variable with occasional outbreaks of windy cold. About 70% of annual precipitation occurs during late spring and summer mostly as thunderstorms. Monthly snowfall amounts are unusually uniform from November through February, a bit heavier in March and April. Snow has occurred as early as September and as late as early June. Wind is significant especially in winter and spring. First freeze is late September; last is late May.

DEMOGRAPHICS	AREA	U.S. AVG		ETHNIC COMPOSITION	AREA	U.S. AVG		RESIDENT PROFILE	AREA	U.S. AVG
Population	69,177			White	93.4%	79.0%		Single	29.0%	32.4%
Population density per sq. mile	13.0	358.5		Black	1.0%	10.5%		Married	54.5%	52.7%
Population growth	13.0%	21.1%		Asian	0.5%	2.7%		Divorced/separated	16.6%	14.9%
Median age	37.1	36.1		Hispanic	4.9%	10.6%		Married with children	22.1%	23.7%
Percent Democrat	30.8%	44.5%		Religious observance	43.9%	48.9%		Single with children	10.0%	9.1%
Percent Republican	67.1%	54.5%		Diversity measure	20.8	40.1		Percent over age 65	12.9%	12.9%

Population

Economy & Jobs — Score: 50.5 — Rank: 186

INCOME	AREA	U.S. AVG
Per capita income	$22,577	$23,235
Household income	$43,132	$46,414
Household income ‹ $25K	27.1%	26.2%
Household income › $75K	21.8%	25.4%
Household income growth	17.8%	13.6%

EMPLOYMENT	AREA	U.S. AVG
Unemployment rate	3.5%	4.7%
Recent job growth	2.2%	1.3%
Projected future job growth	9.2%	11.5%
White collar	58.3%	57.8%
Blue collar	25.2%	25.2%

EMPLOYING INDUSTRIES	AREA	U.S. AVG
Largest: Healthcare & Social Assistance		
Percent manufacturing	11.9%	15.4%
Percent public sector	16.1%	15.7%
Percent construction	13.3%	9.9%

Cost of Living — Score: 99.7 — Rank: 2

INDEXES & TAXES	AREA	U.S. AVG
Cost of Living Index	85.9	100.0
Buying Power Index	112.5	100.0
Income tax rate	0.00%	4.70%
Sales tax rate	5.00%	6.58%
Property tax rate	$5.89	$12.00

HOUSING	AREA	U.S. AVG
Median home price	$133,700	$220,000
Home price appreciation	64.8%	10.1%
Median rent	$512	$709
Homes owned	63.1%	62.3%
Home price ratio	3.1	4.2

NECESSITIES	AREA	U.S. AVG
Food Index	107.0	100.0
Housing Index	53.9	100.0
Utilities Index	106.3	100.0
Transportation Index	93.3	100.0
Healthcare Index	97.5	100.0
Miscellaneous Cost Index	99.9	100.0

Climate — Score: 38.8 — Rank: 228

TEMPERATURE	AREA	U.S. AVG
Average January low	34.3	26.2
July high	87.5	87.4
Annual days › 90°F	26	38
Annual days ‹ 32°F	183	89
Annual days ‹ 0°F	22	6

PRECIPITATION	AREA	U.S. AVG
Annual inches precipitation	12.0	37.7
Annual inches snowfall	81.0	7.0
Annual days precipitation	95	109
Annual days rain › 0.5 inches	5	22
Annual days snow › 1.5 inches	17	6

COMFORTS & HAZARDS	AREA	U.S. AVG
July relative humidity	49%	66%
Annual days mostly sunny	219	208
Annual days with thunderstorms	34	39
Tornado risk score	7	18
Hurricane risk score	0	13

TEMPERATURE

PRECIPITATION

DAYS OF CLOUDS & PRECIPITATION

Education — Score: 69.0 — Rank: 117

ACHIEVEMENT	AREA	U.S. AVG
High school degree	88.2%	82.7%
2-year college degree	9.0%	6.4%
4-year college degree	13.4%	15.7%
Graduate/professional degree	6.6%	8.9%

PUBLIC SCHOOLS	AREA	U.S. AVG
Expenditures per pupil	$5,439	$5,686
Student/teacher ratio	12.1	16.7
Attending public school	96.7%	90.1%
State SAT score	1103	1021
State ACT score	21.6*	20.9

HIGHER EDUCATION	AREA	U.S. AVG
No. 2-year colleges	1	4
No. 4-year colleges/universities	0	6
No. highly ranked universities	0	1

Health & Healthcare — Score: 57.0 — Rank: 161

HAZARDS & ILLNESSES	AREA	U.S. AVG
Air-quality score	34	37
Water-quality score	40	52
Pollen/allergy score	55	61
Cancer mortality per capita	190.6	201.9
Depression days per month	3.2	3.5
Stress score	20	50

HEALTHCARE	AREA	U.S. AVG
Physicians per capita	212.6	244.2
Hospital beds per capita	318.0	420.0
No. teaching hospitals	1	3
Cost per doctor visit	$69	$77
Cost per dental visit	$62	$70

Crime — Score: 66.8 — Rank: 124

CRIME	AREA	U.S. AVG
Violent crime rate	234.9	465.5
Change in violent crime rate	22.7%	-2.2%
Property crime rate	4,777.6	3,517.1
Change in property crime rate	-1.8%	-2.1%

Transportation — Score: 62.0 — Rank: 143

COMMUTE	AREA	U.S. AVG
Average commute time	18.1	27.4
Percent commutes › 60 mins.	3.7%	5.9%
Commute by auto	82.9%	78.9%
Commute by mass transit	0.4%	1.9%
Work at home	3.2%	3.1%
Mass transit miles per capita	0.41	1.87

INTERCITY SERVICES	AREA	U.S. AVG
Major airports within 60 miles	0	1
Size of regional airport	None	Large
Daily airline activity	26	686
Amtrak service	No	No

AUTOMOTIVE	AREA	U.S. AVG
Insurance, annual premium	$1,068	$1,432
Gas, cost per gallon	$2.26	$2.49
Daily vehicle miles per capita	25.4	24.0

Leisure — Score: 5.9 — Rank: 351

DINING & SHOPPING	AREA	U.S. AVG
Restaurant rating	1	2
Outlet mall score	0	42
No. Starbucks	0	13
No. warehouse clubs	1	2

ENTERTAINMENT	AREA	U.S. AVG
Professional sports rating	2	4
College sports rating	1	4
Zoo/aquarium rating	1	3
Amusement park rating	1	3
Botanical garden/arboretum rating	1	4

OUTDOOR ACTIVITIES	AREA	U.S. AVG
Golf-course rating	1	4
Ski-area rating	1	3
Sq. miles inland water	3	4
Miles of coastline	0.0	10.7
National Park rating	2	3

MEDIA & LIBRARIES	AREA	U.S. AVG	PERFORMING ARTS	AREA	U.S. AVG	MUSEUMS	AREA	U.S. AVG
Arts radio rating	1	3	Classical music rating	3	4	Overall museum rating	2	5
No. public libraries	3	27	Ballet/dance rating	1	3	Art museum rating	3	5
Library volumes per capita	3.24	2.78	Professional theater rating	1	3	Science museum rating	4	5
			University arts programs rating	1	5	Children's museum rating	1	3

Cedar Rapids, IA

Score: 65.6   Rank: 135   2004 rank: 207

Profile: Small city
Location: East-central Iowa, along Cedar River
Elevation: 594 feet
Time zone: Central Standard Time

PRO	CON
Attractive downtown	Harsh winters
Arts and culture	Recent job weakness
Cost of living	Entertainment

Cedar Rapids is a typically Midwestern agricultural and industrial hub, the center of which is built on an island at the "rapids" of the Cedar River. Downtown is modern in appearance, with attractive parks and waterfront areas. Arts and culture amenities are better than average for a small city, with a symphony and an art museum that holds the largest collection of works by native son Grant Wood. There are a couple of small colleges in town and some minor league sports. The Czech Village provides an interesting slice of cultural diversity. Nightlife and entertainment are somewhat lacking, but can be found in abundance in Iowa City 20 miles south. Some preferring the smaller rural town life and lower costs live here and work in that more prosperous city. The economy is supported by large agricultural producers (ADM, Quaker Oats, and Cargill, among others), and also by a handful of insurance firms, electrical equipment manufacturer Square D, and an assortment of high-tech firms along a corridor leading south toward Iowa City. The industrial presence is strong but the recent employment picture is fairly weak. Overall cost of living is attractive at 85.8.

The area around Cedar Rapids is mainly agricultural, with areas of wooded hills to the south. Summers are warm and fairly humid, with showers and thundershowers. Most precipitation falls during the summer months. Winters are cold and dry with brief snowstorms and occasional periods of extreme cold. First freeze is early October; last is late April.

DEMOGRAPHICS	AREA	U.S. AVG	ETHNIC COMPOSITION	AREA	U.S. AVG	RESIDENT PROFILE	AREA	U.S. AVG
Population	244,910		White	93.7%	79.0%	Single	30.5%	32.4%
Population density per sq. mile	121.9	358.5	Black	2.5%	10.5%	Married	57.2%	52.7%
Population growth	16.4%	21.1%	Asian	1.5%	2.7%	Divorced/separated	12.3%	14.9%
Median age	36.9	36.1	Hispanic	1.4%	10.6%	Married with children	24.5%	23.7%
Percent Democrat	53.8%	44.5%	Religious observance	58.2%	48.9%	Single with children	7.5%	9.1%
Percent Republican	45.5%	54.5%	Diversity measure	14.4	40.1	Percent over age 65	13.2%	12.9%

INCOME	AREA	U.S. AVG	EMPLOYMENT	AREA	U.S. AVG	EMPLOYING INDUSTRIES	AREA	U.S. AVG
Per capita income	$24,987	$23,235	Unemployment rate	4.1%	4.7%	Largest: Manufacturing		
Household income	$50,213	$46,414	Recent job growth	1.0%	1.3%			
Household income < $25K	20.6%	26.2%	Projected future job growth	9.1%	11.5%	Percent manufacturing	15.6%	15.4%
Household income > $75K	26.9%	25.4%	White collar	61.3%	57.8%	Percent public sector	10.3%	15.7%
Household income growth	11.5%	13.6%	Blue collar	24.1%	25.2%	Percent construction	8.4%	9.9%

INDEXES & TAXES	AREA	U.S. AVG	HOUSING	AREA	U.S. AVG	NECESSITIES	AREA	U.S. AVG
Cost of Living Index	85.8	100.0	Median home price	$133,400	$220,000	Food Index	89.9	100.0
Buying Power Index	131.2	100.0	Home price appreciation	20.5%	10.1%	Housing Index	51.0	100.0
Income tax rate	7.95%	4.70%	Median rent	$592	$709	Utilities Index	144.1	100.0
Sales tax rate	5.27%	6.58%	Homes owned	70.7%	62.3%	Transportation Index	96.5	100.0
Property tax rate	$12.99	$12.00	Home price ratio	2.7	4.2	Healthcare Index	91.5	100.0
						Miscellaneous Cost Index	98.6	100.0

Climate
Score: 15.0
Rank: 317

TEMPERATURE	AREA	U.S. AVG
Average January low	13.0	26.2
July high	85.2	87.4
Annual days > 90°F	22	38
Annual days < 32°F	136	89
Annual days < 0°F	16	6

PRECIPITATION	AREA	U.S. AVG
Annual inches precipitation	36.0	37.7
Annual inches snowfall	30.0	7.0
Annual days precipitation	112	109
Annual days rain > 0.5 inches	25	22
Annual days snow > 1.5 inches	9	6

COMFORTS & HAZARDS	AREA	U.S. AVG
July relative humidity	70%	66%
Annual days mostly sunny	202	208
Annual days with thunderstorms	47	39
Tornado risk score	15	18
Hurricane risk score	0	13

TEMPERATURE **PRECIPITATION** **DAYS OF CLOUDS & PRECIPITATION**

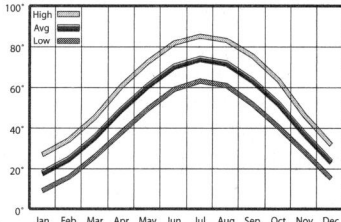
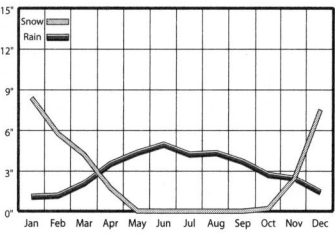
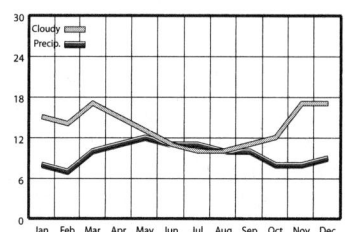

Education
Score: 82.9
Rank: 65

ACHIEVEMENT	AREA	U.S. AVG
High school degree	90.0%	82.7%
2-year college degree	9.1%	6.4%
4-year college degree	18.8%	15.7%
Graduate/professional degree	6.5%	8.9%

PUBLIC SCHOOLS	AREA	U.S. AVG
Expenditures per pupil	$5,115	$5,686
Student/teacher ratio	16.1	16.7
Attending public school	89.5%	90.1%
State SAT score	1215	1021
State ACT score	22.1*	20.9

HIGHER EDUCATION	AREA	U.S. AVG
No. 2-year colleges	4	4
No. 4-year colleges/universities	5	6
No. highly ranked universities	2	1

Health & Healthcare
Score: 63.9
Rank: 135

HAZARDS & ILLNESSES	AREA	U.S. AVG
Air-quality score	41	37
Water-quality score	67	52
Pollen/allergy score	45	61
Cancer mortality per capita	225.7	201.9
Depression days per month	3.0	3.5
Stress score	6	50

HEALTHCARE	AREA	U.S. AVG
Physicians per capita	165.6	244.2
Hospital beds per capita	382.2	420.0
No. teaching hospitals	2	3
Cost per doctor visit	$79	$77
Cost per dental visit	$88	$70

Crime
Score: 52.1
Rank: 180

CRIME	AREA	U.S. AVG
Violent crime rate	231.3	465.5
Change in violent crime rate	5.7%	-2.2%
Property crime rate	3,171.9	3,517.1
Change in property crime rate	-7.4%	-2.1%

Transportation
Score: 39.8
Rank: 225

COMMUTE	AREA	U.S. AVG
Average commute time	20.9	27.4
Percent commutes > 60 mins.	3.0%	5.9%
Commute by auto	81.5%	78.9%
Commute by mass transit	0.9%	1.9%
Work at home	3.7%	3.1%
Mass transit miles per capita	0.91	1.87

INTERCITY SERVICES	AREA	U.S. AVG
Major airports within 60 miles	0	1
Size of regional airport	Small	Large
Daily airline activity	58	686
Amtrak service	No	No

AUTOMOTIVE	AREA	U.S. AVG
Insurance, annual premium	$925	$1,432
Gas, cost per gallon	$2.50	$2.49
Daily vehicle miles per capita	22.7	24.0

Leisure
Score: 22.7
Rank: 288

DINING & SHOPPING	AREA	U.S. AVG
Restaurant rating	1	2
Outlet mall score	31	42
No. Starbucks	1	13
No. warehouse clubs	1	2

ENTERTAINMENT	AREA	U.S. AVG
Professional sports rating	3	4
College sports rating	3	4
Zoo/aquarium rating	1	3
Amusement park rating	1	3
Botanical garden/ arboretum rating	1	4

OUTDOOR ACTIVITIES	AREA	U.S. AVG
Golf-course rating	2	4
Ski-area rating	2	3
Sq. miles inland water	2	4
Miles of coastline	0.0	10.7
National Park rating	1	3

Arts & Culture
Score: 47.6
Rank: 196

MEDIA & LIBRARIES	AREA	U.S. AVG
Arts radio rating	1	3
No. public libraries	28	27
Library volumes per capita	3.34	2.78

PERFORMING ARTS	AREA	U.S. AVG
Classical music rating	4	4
Ballet/dance rating	1	3
Professional theater rating	1	3
University arts programs rating	6	5

MUSEUMS	AREA	U.S. AVG
Overall museum rating	4	5
Art museum rating	4	5
Science museum rating	5	5
Children's museum rating	5	3

Champaign–Urbana, IL

Score: 68.8   **Rank:** 101   **2004 rank:** 33

Profile: College-town complex
Location: East-central Illinois, 110 miles south of Chicago
Elevation: 662 feet
Time zone: Central Standard Time

PRO	CON
College-town atmosphere	Isolation
Cost of living	Harsh winters
Educated population	Outdoor recreation

Champaign–Urbana is an agricultural center as well as home to the University of Illinois. The clean agricultural region is well rounded by the university presence. The cities offer what one would expect from a large Big Ten university town: entertainment, top sporting events, good museums, and a mix of restaurants. The area has a strong economic base anchored by agriculture and the presence of a number of research and technology companies, some of which are affiliated with the university. The downtown is okay—it isn't as strongly connected to the university as in other college towns—but has been under redevelopment for several years. An attempt to preserve agricultural roots led to suburban enclaves being developed outside a belt of pre-

served farmland. Cost of living is reasonable for a major college town and the area features stable employment and low commute times. While entertainment and arts amenities are strong, there isn't much outdoor recreation. A recent decline in future job projections and some crime issues have brought the overall ranking decline.

The area is mainly level prairie surrounded by farmland. To the east the terrain starts to undulate, particularly near the Wabash River valley just east of the Indiana border. Summers are warm, humid, and intermittently wet; winters bring variety. Summer thunderstorms are common, and winter changes bring alternating periods of mildness and cold with snow cover. First freeze is late October; last is late April.

Population

DEMOGRAPHICS	AREA	U.S. AVG	ETHNIC COMPOSITION	AREA	U.S. AVG	RESIDENT PROFILE	AREA	U.S. AVG
Population	220,855		White	79.6%	79.0%	Single	41.6%	32.4%
Population density per sq. mile	114.9	358.5	Black	9.6%	10.5%	Married	46.2%	52.7%
Population growth	9.0%	21.1%	Asian	6.8%	2.7%	Divorced/separated	12.2%	14.9%
Median age	31.9	36.1	Hispanic	3.5%	10.6%	Married with children	20.4%	23.7%
Percent Democrat	48.0%	44.5%	Religious observance	44.0%	48.9%	Single with children	7.4%	9.1%
Percent Republican	50.8%	54.5%	Diversity measure	38.7	40.1	Percent over age 65	10.8%	12.9%

Economy & Jobs
Score: 35.6
Rank: 240

INCOME	AREA	U.S. AVG	EMPLOYMENT	AREA	U.S. AVG	EMPLOYING INDUSTRIES	AREA	U.S. AVG
Per capita income	$23,125	$23,235	Unemployment rate	4.4%	4.7%	Largest: Healthcare & Social Assistance		
Household income	$43,728	$46,414	Recent job growth	2.0%	1.3%			
Household income < $25K	28.7%	26.2%	Projected future job growth	4.1%	11.5%	Percent manufacturing	12.3%	15.4%
Household income > $75K	23.6%	25.4%	White collar	64.6%	57.8%	Percent public sector	26.5%	15.7%
Household income growth	13.9%	13.6%	Blue collar	19.0%	25.2%	Percent construction	6.7%	9.9%

Cost of Living
Score: 60.7
Rank: 147

INDEXES & TAXES	AREA	U.S. AVG	HOUSING	AREA	U.S. AVG	NECESSITIES	AREA	U.S. AVG
Cost of Living Index	89.0	100.0	Median home price	$143,500	$220,000	Food Index	96.8	100.0
Buying Power Index	110.1	100.0	Home price appreciation	33.5%	10.1%	Housing Index	65.1	100.0
Income tax rate	3.00%	4.70%	Median rent	$633	$709	Utilities Index	116.3	100.0
Sales tax rate	6.47%	6.58%	Homes owned	55.7%	62.3%	Transportation Index	103.3	100.0
Property tax rate	$17.68	$12.00	Home price ratio	3.3	4.2	Healthcare Index	98.2	100.0
						Miscellaneous Cost Index	103.6	100.0

Climate
Score: 39.3
Rank: 226

TEMPERATURE	AREA	U.S. AVG	PRECIPITATION	AREA	U.S. AVG	COMFORTS & HAZARDS	AREA	U.S. AVG
Average January low	15.7	26.2	Annual inches precipitation	35.0	37.7	July relative humidity	72%	66%
July high	85.5	87.4	Annual inches snowfall	23.0	7.0	Annual days mostly sunny	197	208
Annual days > 90°F	17	38	Annual days precipitation	111	109	Annual days with thunderstorms	49	39
Annual days < 32°F	132	89	Annual days rain > 0.5 inches	24	22	Tornado risk score	22	18
Annual days < 0°F	11	6	Annual days snow > 1.5 inches	5	6	Hurricane risk score	3	13

TEMPERATURE

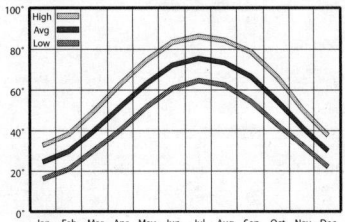

PRECIPITATION

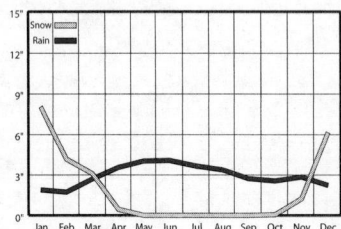

DAYS OF CLOUDS & PRECIPITATION

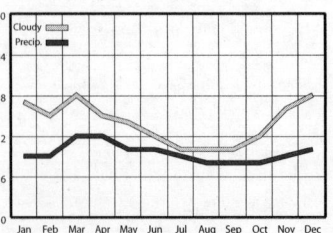

ACHIEVEMENT	AREA	U.S. AVG	PUBLIC SCHOOLS	AREA	U.S. AVG	HIGHER EDUCATION	AREA	U.S. AVG
High school degree	90.5%	82.7%	Expenditures per pupil	$4,708	$5,686	No. 2-year colleges	1	4
2-year college degree	7.2%	6.4%	Student/teacher ratio	15.3	16.7	No. 4-year colleges/universities	1	6
4-year college degree	18.0%	15.7%	Attending public school	89.8%	90.1%	No. highly ranked universities	1	1
Graduate/professional degree	17.9%	8.9%	State SAT score	1200	1021			
			State ACT score	20.5*	20.9			

Education
Score: 89.0
Rank: 42

HAZARDS & ILLNESSES	AREA	U.S. AVG	HEALTHCARE	AREA	U.S. AVG	CRIME	AREA	U.S. AVG
Air-quality score	44	37	Physicians per capita	244.7	244.2	Violent crime rate	702.4	465.5
Water-quality score	22	52	Hospital beds per capita	301.6	420.0	Change in violent crime rate	-1.6%	-2.2%
Pollen/allergy score	54	61	No. teaching hospitals	2	3	Property crime rate	3,364.1	3,517.1
Cancer mortality per capita	203.9	201.9	Cost per doctor visit	$98	$77	Change in property crime rate	5.9%	-2.1%
Depression days per month	2.9	3.5	Cost per dental visit	$66	$70			
Stress score	7	50						

Health & Healthcare
Score: 54.0
Rank: 173

Crime
Score: 15.5
Rank: 315

COMMUTE	AREA	U.S. AVG	INTERCITY SERVICES	AREA	U.S. AVG	AUTOMOTIVE	AREA	U.S. AVG
Average commute time	19.5	27.4	Major airports within 60 miles	0	1	Insurance, annual premium	$1,031	$1,432
Percent commutes > 60 mins.	2.9%	5.9%	Size of regional airport	None	Large	Gas, cost per gallon	$2.48	$2.49
Commute by auto	71.6%	78.9%	Daily airline activity	22	686	Daily vehicle miles per capita	20.1	24.0
Commute by mass transit	4.2%	1.9%	Amtrak service	Yes	No			
Work at home	3.9%	3.1%						
Mass transit miles per capita	4.16	1.87						

Transportation
Score: 62.8
Rank: 140

DINING & SHOPPING	AREA	U.S. AVG	ENTERTAINMENT	AREA	U.S. AVG	OUTDOOR ACTIVITIES	AREA	U.S. AVG
Restaurant rating	1	2	Professional sports rating	2	4	Golf-course rating	2	4
Outlet mall score	54	42	College sports rating	6	4	Ski-area rating	2	3
No. Starbucks	1	13	Zoo/aquarium rating	1	3	Sq. miles inland water	1	4
No. warehouse clubs	1	2	Amusement park rating	1	3	Miles of coastline	0.0	10.7
			Botanical garden/ arboretum rating	1	4	National Park rating	1	3

Leisure
Score: 21.9
Rank: 291

MEDIA & LIBRARIES	AREA	U.S. AVG	PERFORMING ARTS	AREA	U.S. AVG	MUSEUMS	AREA	U.S. AVG
Arts radio rating	8	3	Classical music rating	3	4	Overall museum rating	5	5
No. public libraries	22	27	Ballet/dance rating	1	3	Art museum rating	7	5
Library volumes per capita	4.78	2.78	Professional theater rating	1	3	Science museum rating	5	5
			University arts programs rating	5	5	Children's museum rating	1	3

Arts & Culture
Score: 72.7
Rank: 102

Charleston, WV

Score: 47.7   Rank: 260   2004 rank: 233

Profile: Capital city
Location: West-central West Virginia along Kanawha River
Elevation: 827 feet
Time zone: Eastern Standard Time

PRO	CON
Cost of living/housing	Heavy industry
Capital city amenities	Entertainment
Nearby water recreation	Isolation

Charleston is the state capital and government and commercial center of West Virginia. Hydrocarbon resources (coal, oil, and gas) and salt and brine deposits led to industrial growth as a center for chemicals and chemical-related industries, which stretch up the Kanawha Valley to the east. There are some modest cultural amenities and a nice performing arts center downtown. As you might expect for a capital city, the downtown area is clean but fairly plain. A new riverfront development plan is in the works. Some of the industrial areas are fairly gritty and can hurt air quality at times. White-water rafting on the Gawley and New rivers is the most prominent recreational feature. The economy is cyclical and current figures are fairly weak, but home prices and housing costs are attractive. Crime rates are moderately high, and air-service options are among the weakest in the country among capital cities.

Charleston lies at the junction of the Kanawha and Elk rivers in the western foothills of the Appalachian Mountains. The main urban and business areas have developed along the two river valleys, while some residential areas are in nearby valleys and on the surrounding deciduous-wooded hills. Winters can vary greatly from one season to the next. Summer and early fall are more consistent, with warm temperatures and hazy humidity and an occasional hot spell. Summer precipitation falls mainly as thundershowers. Most winters have two or three extended cold spells where temperatures stay below freezing. Snow falls, but only lingers on hilltops. First freeze is mid-October; last is late April.

Population

DEMOGRAPHICS	AREA	U.S. AVG	ETHNIC COMPOSITION	AREA	U.S. AVG	RESIDENT PROFILE	AREA	U.S. AVG
Population	306,523		White	92.6%	79.0%	Single	29.5%	32.4%
Population density per sq. mile	121.1	358.5	Black	4.8%	10.5%	Married	56.1%	52.7%
Population growth	0.9%	21.1%	Asian	0.9%	2.7%	Divorced/separated	14.4%	14.9%
Median age	40.7	36.1	Hispanic	0.5%	10.6%	Married with children	21.2%	23.7%
Percent Democrat	47.5%	44.5%	Religious observance	30.6%	48.9%	Single with children	7.8%	9.1%
Percent Republican	51.9%	54.5%	Diversity measure	14.5	40.1	Percent over age 65	15.6%	12.9%

Economy & Jobs
Score: 16.3
Rank: 312

INCOME	AREA	U.S. AVG	EMPLOYMENT	AREA	U.S. AVG	EMPLOYING INDUSTRIES	AREA	U.S. AVG
Per capita income	$22,370	$23,235	Unemployment rate	5.2%	4.7%	Largest: Healthcare & Social Assistance		
Household income	$38,592	$46,414	Recent job growth	0.5%	1.3%			
Household income < $25K	33.6%	26.2%	Projected future job growth	5.1%	11.5%	Percent manufacturing	13.2%	15.4%
Household income > $75K	20.2%	25.4%	White collar	59.9%	57.8%	Percent public sector	18.3%	15.7%
Household income growth	15.9%	13.6%	Blue collar	24.6%	25.2%	Percent construction	11.4%	9.9%

Cost of Living
Score: 82.4
Rank: 64

INDEXES & TAXES	AREA	U.S. AVG	HOUSING	AREA	U.S. AVG	NECESSITIES	AREA	U.S. AVG
Cost of Living Index	80.2	100.0	Median home price	$123,100	$220,000	Food Index	98.7	100.0
Buying Power Index	107.9	100.0	Home price appreciation	22.0%	10.1%	Housing Index	38.3	100.0
Income tax rate	6.00%	4.70%	Median rent	$555	$709	Utilities Index	76.7	100.0
Sales tax rate	6.00%	6.58%	Homes owned	68.1%	62.3%	Transportation Index	102.1	100.0
Property tax rate	$6.09	$12.00	Home price ratio	3.2	4.2	Healthcare Index	87.8	100.0
						Miscellaneous Cost Index	95.6	100.0

Climate
Score: 81.3
Rank: 71

TEMPERATURE	AREA	U.S. AVG	PRECIPITATION	AREA	U.S. AVG	COMFORTS & HAZARDS	AREA	U.S. AVG
Average January low	25.6	26.2	Annual inches precipitation	38.9	37.7	July relative humidity	71%	66%
July high	85.7	87.4	Annual inches snowfall	25.6	7.0	Annual days mostly sunny	166	208
Annual days > 90°F	17	38	Annual days precipitation	139	109	Annual days with thunderstorms	44	39
Annual days < 32°F	23	89	Annual days rain > 0.5 inches	27	22	Tornado risk score	0	18
Annual days < 0°F	2	6	Annual days snow > 1.5 inches	7	6	Hurricane risk score	5	13

TEMPERATURE

PRECIPITATION

DAYS OF CLOUDS & PRECIPITATION

Education
Score: 27.0
Rank: 273

ACHIEVEMENT	AREA	U.S. AVG	PUBLIC SCHOOLS	AREA	U.S. AVG	HIGHER EDUCATION	AREA	U.S. AVG
High school degree	77.4%	82.7%	Expenditures per pupil	$6,103	$5,686	No. 2-year colleges	8	4
2-year college degree	4.7%	6.4%	Student/teacher ratio	14.0	16.7	No. 4-year colleges/universities	2	6
4-year college degree	10.9%	15.7%	Attending public school	94.7%	90.1%	No. highly ranked universities	0	1
Graduate/professional degree	6.9%	8.9%	State SAT score	1029	1021			
			State ACT score	20.6*	20.9			

Health & Healthcare
Score: 55.6
Rank: 167

HAZARDS & ILLNESSES	AREA	U.S. AVG	HEALTHCARE	AREA	U.S. AVG	CRIME	AREA	U.S. AVG
Air-quality score	41	37	Physicians per capita	298.1	244.2	Violent crime rate	382.8	465.5
Water-quality score	55	52	Hospital beds per capita	473.7	420.0	Change in violent crime rate	-18.8%	-2.2%
Pollen/allergy score	60	61	No. teaching hospitals	1	3	Property crime rate	4,114.1	3,517.1
Cancer mortality per capita	286.9	201.9	Cost per doctor visit	$77	$77	Change in property crime rate	3.6%	-2.1%
Depression days per month	4.6	3.5	Cost per dental visit	$56	$70			
Stress score	93	50						

Crime
Score: 32.9
Rank: 251

Transportation
Score: 0.5
Rank: 371

COMMUTE	AREA	U.S. AVG	INTERCITY SERVICES	AREA	U.S. AVG	AUTOMOTIVE	AREA	U.S. AVG
Average commute time	27.5	27.4	Major airports within 60 miles	0	1	Insurance, annual premium	$1,211	$1,432
Percent commutes > 60 mins.	7.4%	5.9%	Size of regional airport	None	Large	Gas, cost per gallon	$2.53	$2.49
Commute by auto	81.0%	78.9%	Daily airline activity	65	686	Daily vehicle miles per capita	28.2	24.0
Commute by mass transit	1.5%	1.9%	Amtrak service	Yes	No			
Work at home	2.2%	3.1%						
Mass transit miles per capita	1.46	1.87						

DINING & SHOPPING	AREA	U.S. AVG	ENTERTAINMENT	AREA	U.S. AVG	OUTDOOR ACTIVITIES	AREA	U.S. AVG
Restaurant rating	1	2	Professional sports rating	3	4	Golf-course rating	3	4
Outlet mall score	0	42	College sports rating	2	4	Ski-area rating	1	3
No. Starbucks	1	13	Zoo/aquarium rating	1	3	Sq. miles inland water	3	4
No. warehouse clubs	1	2	Amusement park rating	1	3	Miles of coastline	0.0	10.7
			Botanical garden/ arboretum rating	1	4	National Park rating	1	3

Leisure
Score: 20.6
Rank: 295

MEDIA & LIBRARIES	AREA	U.S. AVG	PERFORMING ARTS	AREA	U.S. AVG	MUSEUMS	AREA	U.S. AVG
Arts radio rating	1	3	Classical music rating	4	4	Overall museum rating	4	5
No. public libraries	25	27	Ballet/dance rating	3	3	Art museum rating	7	5
Library volumes per capita	2.64	2.78	Professional theater rating	1	3	Science museum rating	6	5
			University arts programs rating	5	5	Children's museum rating	2	3

Arts & Culture
Score: 53.7
Rank: 173

Charleston–North Charleston, SC

Score: 60.4 Rank: 174 2004 rank: 63

Profile: Mid-size coastal city complex
Location: Southeastern South Carolina on the Atlantic Coast
Elevation: 48 feet
Time zone: Eastern Standard Time

PRO	CON
Historic interest	Air service
Cost of living	Tourist impact
Pleasant winters	Hot, humid summers

Charleston is a unique 300-year-old city with a fascinating historic tradition as an 18th-century seaport and business center, and location of the initial moments of the Civil War. History has left its imprint, particularly on the city center, where a large and beautifully preserved mainly residential historic district is popular with local residents and tourists, and has become more popular with wealthy "refugees" from northeastern cities. Today there is some small industry, but major industries and the old seaport are gone. The area is supported by tourism and is known as a good place for small business. To the northwest lie features of a typical Southern city, with areas of magnolia-lined streets, older homes, and commercial buildings, mixed in with some less attractive and impoverished areas. Those used to typical downtown skyscrapers won't find them here. Old plantation homes on large spreads lie to the south and west in varying conditions both near the water and farther inland; away from the coastal resorts these areas aren't doing well. The rapidly growing North Charleston is actually as big as Charleston and is the third largest city in the state. The layout is typically suburban with large areas of retail and commercial development; if Charleston represents the Old South, then North Charleston is the newer version.

Besides historic sites, Charleston has some minor cultural amenities and good seafood and Southern-style restaurants. The lifestyle is slow paced, pleasant, and dignified, but the city is relatively isolated from other big cities. There are a number of recreational opportunities and excellent golf courses, especially in the island areas to the south. At 97.6, overall cost of living is moderate for what is available, but there is a big difference in cost between the historic center and outlying areas. The growth in living costs since 2004 (was 80.5) explains in part the drop in ranking.

Charleston is a peninsula city bounded by two rivers, opening onto a spacious harbor. The terrain is generally level with gradual increases in elevation toward inland areas. Summer is warm and humid, but temperatures exceeding 100°F are infrequent and sea breezes keep coastal temperatures lower. Fall is pleasant with sun, rare temperature extremes, and long Indian summers. The December-to-February winter is mild with periods of steady rain and chances of snow flurries, but accumulation is rare. Winter low temperatures may be 10°F to 15°F higher on the peninsula than inland. Most winters have one cold spell, but temperatures below 20°F are unusual. Spring thunderstorms, some severe, and the occasional Atlantic hurricane punctuate precipitation patterns.

DEMOGRAPHICS	AREA	U.S. AVG	ETHNIC COMPOSITION	AREA	U.S. AVG	RESIDENT PROFILE	AREA	U.S. AVG
Population	583,676		White	63.6%	79.0%	Single	35.1%	32.4%
Population density per sq. mile	225.3	358.5	Black	31.7%	10.5%	Married	49.7%	52.7%
Population growth	15.6%	21.1%	Asian	1.7%	2.7%	Divorced/separated	15.2%	14.9%
Median age	34.9	36.1	Hispanic	2.4%	10.6%	Married with children	22.5%	23.7%
Percent Democrat	42.5%	44.5%	Religious observance	39.3%	48.9%	Single with children	10.8%	9.1%
Percent Republican	56.0%	54.5%	Diversity measure	51.6	40.1	Percent over age 65	11.0%	12.9%

Population

INCOME	AREA	U.S. AVG	EMPLOYMENT	AREA	U.S. AVG	EMPLOYING INDUSTRIES	AREA	U.S. AVG
Per capita income	$23,505	$23,235	Unemployment rate	5.0%	4.7%	Largest: Healthcare & Social Assistance		
Household income	$45,550	$46,414	Recent job growth	3.8%	1.3%			
Household income < $25K	26.2%	26.2%	Projected future job growth	17.9%	11.5%	Percent manufacturing	13.1%	15.4%
Household income > $75K	25.3%	25.4%	White collar	58.9%	57.8%	Percent public sector	19.9%	15.7%
Household income growth	15.8%	13.6%	Blue collar	24.5%	25.2%	Percent construction	11.4%	9.9%

Economy & Jobs
Score: 81.3
Rank: 71

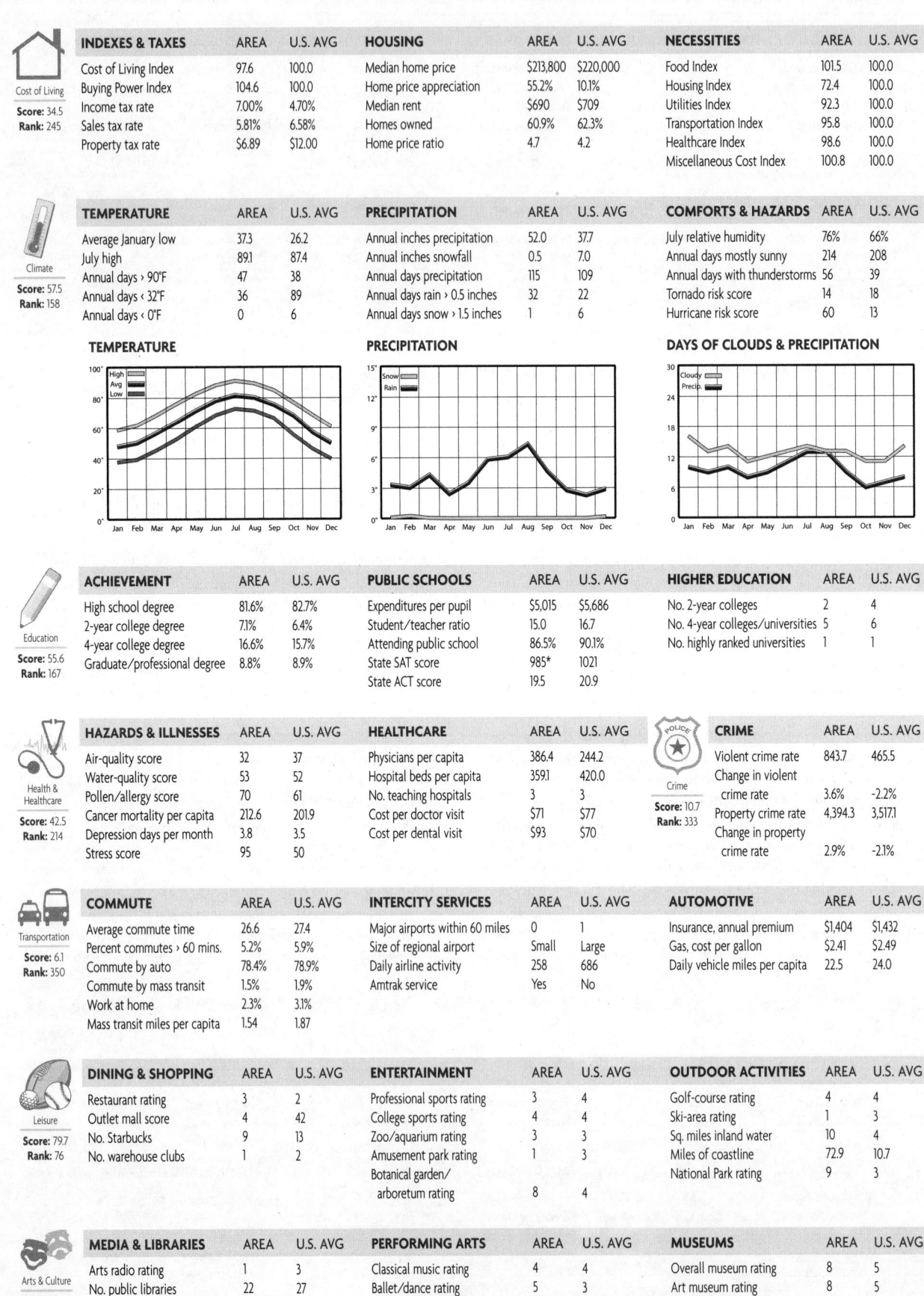

Cost of Living
Score: 34.5
Rank: 245

INDEXES & TAXES	AREA	U.S. AVG
Cost of Living Index	97.6	100.0
Buying Power Index	104.6	100.0
Income tax rate	7.00%	4.70%
Sales tax rate	5.81%	6.58%
Property tax rate	$6.89	$12.00

HOUSING	AREA	U.S. AVG
Median home price	$213,800	$220,000
Home price appreciation	55.2%	10.1%
Median rent	$690	$709
Homes owned	60.9%	62.3%
Home price ratio	4.7	4.2

NECESSITIES	AREA	U.S. AVG
Food Index	101.5	100.0
Housing Index	72.4	100.0
Utilities Index	92.3	100.0
Transportation Index	95.8	100.0
Healthcare Index	98.6	100.0
Miscellaneous Cost Index	100.8	100.0

Climate
Score: 57.5
Rank: 158

TEMPERATURE	AREA	U.S. AVG
Average January low	37.3	26.2
July high	89.1	87.4
Annual days > 90°F	47	38
Annual days < 32°F	36	89
Annual days < 0°F	0	6

PRECIPITATION	AREA	U.S. AVG
Annual inches precipitation	52.0	37.7
Annual inches snowfall	0.5	7.0
Annual days precipitation	115	109
Annual days rain > 0.5 inches	32	22
Annual days snow > 1.5 inches	1	6

COMFORTS & HAZARDS	AREA	U.S. AVG
July relative humidity	76%	66%
Annual days mostly sunny	214	208
Annual days with thunderstorms	56	39
Tornado risk score	14	18
Hurricane risk score	60	13

TEMPERATURE

PRECIPITATION

DAYS OF CLOUDS & PRECIPITATION

Education
Score: 55.6
Rank: 167

ACHIEVEMENT	AREA	U.S. AVG
High school degree	81.6%	82.7%
2-year college degree	7.1%	6.4%
4-year college degree	16.6%	15.7%
Graduate/professional degree	8.8%	8.9%

PUBLIC SCHOOLS	AREA	U.S. AVG
Expenditures per pupil	$5,015	$5,686
Student/teacher ratio	15.0	16.7
Attending public school	86.5%	90.1%
State SAT score	985*	1021
State ACT score	19.5	20.9

HIGHER EDUCATION	AREA	U.S. AVG
No. 2-year colleges	2	4
No. 4-year colleges/universities	5	6
No. highly ranked universities	1	1

Health & Healthcare
Score: 42.5
Rank: 214

HAZARDS & ILLNESSES	AREA	U.S. AVG
Air-quality score	32	37
Water-quality score	53	52
Pollen/allergy score	70	61
Cancer mortality per capita	212.6	201.9
Depression days per month	3.8	3.5
Stress score	95	50

HEALTHCARE	AREA	U.S. AVG
Physicians per capita	386.4	244.2
Hospital beds per capita	359.1	420.0
No. teaching hospitals	3	3
Cost per doctor visit	$71	$77
Cost per dental visit	$93	$70

Crime
Score: 10.7
Rank: 333

CRIME	AREA	U.S. AVG
Violent crime rate	843.7	465.5
Change in violent crime rate	3.6%	-2.2%
Property crime rate	4,394.3	3,517.1
Change in property crime rate	2.9%	-2.1%

Transportation
Score: 6.1
Rank: 350

COMMUTE	AREA	U.S. AVG
Average commute time	26.6	27.4
Percent commutes > 60 mins.	5.2%	5.9%
Commute by auto	78.4%	78.9%
Commute by mass transit	1.5%	1.9%
Work at home	2.3%	3.1%
Mass transit miles per capita	1.54	1.87

INTERCITY SERVICES	AREA	U.S. AVG
Major airports within 60 miles	0	1
Size of regional airport	Small	Large
Daily airline activity	258	686
Amtrak service	Yes	No

AUTOMOTIVE	AREA	U.S. AVG
Insurance, annual premium	$1,404	$1,432
Gas, cost per gallon	$2.41	$2.49
Daily vehicle miles per capita	22.5	24.0

Leisure
Score: 79.7
Rank: 76

DINING & SHOPPING	AREA	U.S. AVG
Restaurant rating	3	2
Outlet mall score	4	42
No. Starbucks	9	13
No. warehouse clubs	1	2

ENTERTAINMENT	AREA	U.S. AVG
Professional sports rating	3	4
College sports rating	4	4
Zoo/aquarium rating	3	3
Amusement park rating	1	3
Botanical garden/ arboretum rating	8	4

OUTDOOR ACTIVITIES	AREA	U.S. AVG
Golf-course rating	4	4
Ski-area rating	1	3
Sq. miles inland water	10	4
Miles of coastline	72.9	10.7
National Park rating	9	3

Arts & Culture
Score: 66.6
Rank: 125

MEDIA & LIBRARIES	AREA	U.S. AVG
Arts radio rating	1	3
No. public libraries	22	27
Library volumes per capita	2.41	2.78

PERFORMING ARTS	AREA	U.S. AVG
Classical music rating	4	4
Ballet/dance rating	5	3
Professional theater rating	1	3
University arts programs rating	8	5

MUSEUMS	AREA	U.S. AVG
Overall museum rating	8	5
Art museum rating	8	5
Science museum rating	7	5
Children's museum rating	1	3

Charlotte–Gastonia–Concord, NC

Score: 70.9   Rank: 85   2004 rank: 98

Profile: Mid-size city complex
Location: Southwest North Carolina along Catawba River near South Carolina border
Elevation: 769 feet
Time zone: Eastern Standard Time

PRO
Diverse economy
Educated population
Entertainment

CON
Crime rates
Growth and sprawl
Long commutes

Charlotte is a modern urban and financial center grown up dramatically from its previous agricultural and regional banking roots. Today the city is reputedly the headquarters for more banks than any city outside New York, and is the home to such financial heavyweights as BankAmerica and Wachovia, as well as Lowe's (home improvement retail) and specialty steel maker Nucor. A diverse commercial and industrial economy has developed around the financial industry. Downtown is a mix of contemporary skyscraper architecture and a number of well-preserved 19th-century neighborhoods. Charlotte isn't a world-class entertainment center—yet—but the city has a good collection of museums, shopping options, and especially sports teams. The city is home to the Carolina Panthers NFL team and was able to defy sports tradition by actually replacing a professional sports franchise it lost, the Charlotte Hornets NBA team (now the Bobcats). There is an active NASCAR racing circuit in the area, centered in the otherwise ordinary city of Concord, which is 20 miles northeast. The city has modern transportation amenities and even a few direct flights to Europe. Growth-related urban sprawl and related traffic problems are moderate to severe, but a light rail system is scheduled to open its first leg in 2007. Most attractive neighborhoods lie to the south toward the Interstate 485 beltway, with attractive Southern-style homes cut into wooded lots, many on golf courses, being a common find. Gastonia, 20 miles west, returns to the Old South, with decrepit old mills and a largely failed downtown area. Although climate, low costs, and familiar jobs make the area a favorite for Northeast migrants, the Charlotte area blends the New South with Southern-style friendliness, and it has its share of New South workaholics. These migrations have dramatically increased the area's diversity and reputation as a cosmopolitan center.

This city complex sits in the Carolina Piedmont, a transitional area of rolling country between the mountains to the west and the Coastal Plain to the east. Summers are warm, with days over 90°F, while winters are cool. Temperatures fall as low as freezing about 1 in 2 winter days. Winter weather is changeable, with occasional cold periods, but extreme cold is rare. Snow and snow accumulation are infrequent. Late summer and fall hurricanes can produce substantial rainfall but seldom damaging winds.

DEMOGRAPHICS	AREA	U.S. AVG	ETHNIC COMPOSITION	AREA	U.S. AVG	RESIDENT PROFILE	AREA	U.S. AVG
Population	1,484,570		White	69.1%	79.0%	Single	31.2%	32.4%
Population density per sq. mile	479.2	358.5	Black	23.4%	10.5%	Married	54.2%	52.7%
Population growth	47.7%	21.1%	Asian	2.5%	2.7%	Divorced/separated	14.6%	14.9%
Median age	34.9	36.1	Hispanic	7.0%	10.6%	Married with children	24.8%	23.7%
Percent Democrat	42.8%	44.5%	Religious observance	49.9%	48.9%	Single with children	8.7%	9.1%
Percent Republican	56.7%	54.5%	Diversity measure	51.8	40.1	Percent over age 65	9.9%	12.9%

Economy & Jobs
Score: 92.2
Rank: 30

INCOME	AREA	U.S. AVG	EMPLOYMENT	AREA	U.S. AVG	EMPLOYING INDUSTRIES	AREA	U.S. AVG
Per capita income	$27,603	$23,235	Unemployment rate	5.5%	4.7%	Largest: Finance & Insurance		
Household income	$54,288	$46,414	Recent job growth	4.1%	1.3%			
Household income < $25K	19.6%	26.2%	Projected future job growth	20.8%	11.5%	Percent manufacturing	15.4%	15.4%
Household income > $75K	32.1%	25.4%	White collar	62.4%	57.8%	Percent public sector	10.2%	15.7%
Household income growth	13.9%	13.6%	Blue collar	25.2%	25.2%	Percent construction	9.8%	9.9%

Cost of Living
Score: 24.3
Rank: 282

INDEXES & TAXES	AREA	U.S. AVG	HOUSING	AREA	U.S. AVG	NECESSITIES	AREA	U.S. AVG
Cost of Living Index	93.7	100.0	Median home price	$191,400	$220,000	Food Index	100.2	100.0
Buying Power Index	129.9	100.0	Home price appreciation	20.0%	10.1%	Housing Index	67.1	100.0
Income tax rate	7.00%	4.70%	Median rent	$704	$709	Utilities Index	92.1	100.0
Sales tax rate	7.14%	6.58%	Homes owned	64.5%	62.3%	Transportation Index	97.9	100.0
Property tax rate	$9.40	$12.00	Home price ratio	3.5	4.2	Healthcare Index	101.0	100.0
						Miscellaneous Cost Index	97.7	100.0

Climate
Score: 43.9
Rank: 209

TEMPERATURE	AREA	U.S. AVG
Average January low	32.1	26.2
July high	88.3	87.4
Annual days > 90°F	31	38
Annual days < 32°F	71	89
Annual days < 0°F	0	6

PRECIPITATION	AREA	U.S. AVG
Annual inches precipitation	43.0	37.7
Annual inches snowfall	6.0	7.0
Annual days precipitation	111	109
Annual days rain > 0.5 inches	28	22
Annual days snow > 1.5 inches	2	6

COMFORTS & HAZARDS	AREA	U.S. AVG
July relative humidity	69%	66%
Annual days mostly sunny	214	208
Annual days with thunderstorms	42	39
Tornado risk score	14	18
Hurricane risk score	24	13

TEMPERATURE

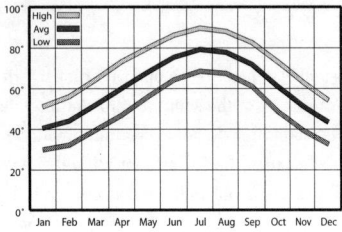

PRECIPITATION

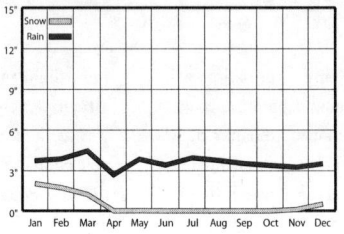

DAYS OF CLOUDS & PRECIPITATION

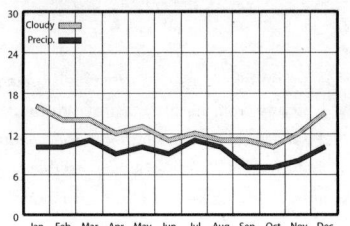

Education
Score: 73.8
Rank: 99

ACHIEVEMENT	AREA	U.S. AVG
High school degree	81.8%	82.7%
2-year college degree	6.9%	6.4%
4-year college degree	20.6%	15.7%
Graduate/professional degree	7.9%	8.9%

PUBLIC SCHOOLS	AREA	U.S. AVG
Expenditures per pupil	$4,998	$5,686
Student/teacher ratio	16.3	16.7
Attending public school	89.9%	90.1%
State SAT score	1008*	1021
State ACT score	20.5	20.9

HIGHER EDUCATION	AREA	U.S. AVG
No. 2-year colleges	10	4
No. 4-year colleges/universities	13	6
No. highly ranked universities	1	1

Health & Healthcare
Score: 27.0
Rank: 272

HAZARDS & ILLNESSES	AREA	U.S. AVG
Air-quality score	30	37
Water-quality score	61	52
Pollen/allergy score	68	61
Cancer mortality per capita	194.2	201.9
Depression days per month	3.3	3.5
Stress score	74	50

HEALTHCARE	AREA	U.S. AVG
Physicians per capita	209.6	244.2
Hospital beds per capita	268.6	420.0
No. teaching hospitals	5	3
Cost per doctor visit	$79	$77
Cost per dental visit	$76	$70

Crime
Score: 6.4
Rank: 349

CRIME	AREA	U.S. AVG
Violent crime rate	837.7	465.5
Change in violent crime rate	9.7%	-2.2%
Property crime rate	5,170.6	3,517.1
Change in property crime rate	-4.2%	-2.1%

Transportation
Score: 23.5
Rank: 286

COMMUTE	AREA	U.S. AVG
Average commute time	28.5	27.4
Percent commutes > 60 mins.	6.1%	5.9%
Commute by auto	81.2%	78.9%
Commute by mass transit	1.3%	1.9%
Work at home	2.9%	3.1%
Mass transit miles per capita	1.35	1.87

INTERCITY SERVICES	AREA	U.S. AVG
Major airports within 60 miles	1	1
Size of regional airport	Large	Large
Daily airline activity	915	686
Amtrak service	Yes	No

AUTOMOTIVE	AREA	U.S. AVG
Insurance, annual premium	$1,675	$1,432
Gas, cost per gallon	$2.49	$2.49
Daily vehicle miles per capita	28.8	24.0

Leisure
Score: 60.2
Rank: 149

DINING & SHOPPING	AREA	U.S. AVG
Restaurant rating	1	2
Outlet mall score	0	42
No. Starbucks	28	13
No. warehouse clubs	7	2

ENTERTAINMENT	AREA	U.S. AVG
Professional sports rating	5	4
College sports rating	2	4
Zoo/aquarium rating	2	3
Amusement park rating	5	3
Botanical garden/ arboretum rating	4	4

OUTDOOR ACTIVITIES	AREA	U.S. AVG
Golf-course rating	7	4
Ski-area rating	1	3
Sq. miles inland water	3	4
Miles of coastline	0.0	10.7
National Park rating	2	3

Arts & Culture
Score: 85.3
Rank: 56

MEDIA & LIBRARIES	AREA	U.S. AVG
Arts radio rating	8	3
No. public libraries	47	27
Library volumes per capita	2.24	2.78

PERFORMING ARTS	AREA	U.S. AVG
Classical music rating	8	4
Ballet/dance rating	3	3
Professional theater rating	1	3
University arts programs rating	8	5

MUSEUMS	AREA	U.S. AVG
Overall museum rating	8	5
Art museum rating	8	5
Science museum rating	9	5
Children's museum rating	3	3

Charlottesville, VA

Score: 86.8   **Rank:** 17   **2004 rank:** 1

Profile: College town
Location: West-central Virginia at base of Blue Ridge Mountains,
75 miles northeast of Richmond
Elevation: 480 feet
Time zone: Eastern Standard Time

PRO	CON
Historic interest	Rising home prices
College-town amenities	Air service
Attractive setting	Rapid growth

Charlottesville "had it going on" in 2004 when we gave it top ranking in the first edition of *Cities Ranked & Rated.* Being no. 1 is certainly a well-earned thrill, but it does, alas, tend to bring more people and more growth pressure to an area. That, in fact, is what we've seen in Charlottesville (and we recognize we aren't the *only* reason why!). Evidence: Median home prices have grown from $177,000 to $345,000 and have exhibited one of the fastest appreciation rates outside of desirable U.S. coastal areas. The Cost of Living Index has also gone "above par" to 117.6, the highest in the state except for some areas outside of Washington, D.C. So "CVille" is tops no longer, although it didn't fall far from its perch. Aside from these negatives we still see an attractive, intellectually stimulating, and prosperous city with a handle on its growth issues (which have also driven up prices as supply has lagged demand).

The city is one of many in Virginia set attractively in agricultural land against mountains, in this case the Blue Ridge. It is home to the dignified University of Virginia, which was founded and designed by Thomas Jefferson in the 18th century as an architectural model for a university. The city possesses a special mix of college-town and historic amenities. The commercial downtown area is separated from the campus and a small commercial area by a railroad grade; that small commercial area and the campus could star in any film about college life. Streets all through town, including the residential districts near campus, are shaded with abundant magnolias and other shade trees. Most of the town is easily accessed by foot or bicycle. Growth pressure has brought some relatively unappealing areas of commercial development mostly north and west but so far the city has resisted most unattractive sprawl. What commercial strips do exist are attractively laid out and avoid most of the hectic and crowded feel found in most areas. Farther north, excellent suburbs lie in well-planned communities, and the surrounding countryside is dotted with farms and some residential areas. The school brings an assortment of amenities and entertainment, and recreational opportunities are available in the nearby mountains and Shenandoah National Park. Washington, D.C., about 2 hours away, supplies any missing services and adds to the area's interest. The area *still* does well in all other categories. Mr. Jefferson would *still* be proud.

Charlottesville is located on a wooded plateau at the base of the Blue Ridge Mountains. Surrounding hills are mostly wooded and steep with areas of agriculture in the valleys. Summers are warm and humid but not excessively hot. Winters are generally mild with mountain shelter from severe storms and cold. Most of the heavier storms travel up the Atlantic Coast or arrive from the southwest bringing periods of unstable weather and thunderstorms in summer and mixed rain and snow in winter. Fall is usually dry and warm with beautiful color. First freeze is early October; last is early April.

Population

DEMOGRAPHICS	AREA	U.S. AVG	ETHNIC COMPOSITION	AREA	U.S. AVG	RESIDENT PROFILE	AREA	U.S. AVG
Population	185,936		White	81.7%	79.0%	Single	35.6%	32.4%
Population density per sq. mile	112.7	358.5	Black	13.1%	10.5%	Married	50.9%	52.7%
Population growth	35.1%	21.1%	Asian	2.6%	2.7%	Divorced/separated	13.6%	14.9%
Median age	35.8	36.1	Hispanic	2.6%	10.6%	Married with children	21.8%	23.7%
Percent Democrat	52.1%	44.5%	Religious observance	36.6%	48.9%	Single with children	7.8%	9.1%
Percent Republican	46.8%	54.5%	Diversity measure	34.3	40.1	Percent over age 65	12.7%	12.9%

Economy & Jobs
Score: 66.0
Rank: 128

INCOME	AREA	U.S. AVG	EMPLOYMENT	AREA	U.S. AVG	EMPLOYING INDUSTRIES	AREA	U.S. AVG
Per capita income	$26,975	$23,235	Unemployment rate	3.0%	4.7%	Largest: Healthcare & Social Assistance		
Household income	$50,569	$46,414	Recent job growth	2.4%	1.3%			
Household income < $25K	23.0%	26.2%	Projected future job growth	11.7%	11.5%	Percent manufacturing	8.5%	15.4%
Household income > $75K	29.4%	25.4%	White collar	66.9%	57.8%	Percent public sector	26.4%	15.7%
Household income growth	14.2%	13.6%	Blue collar	17.5%	25.2%	Percent construction	9.0%	9.9%

Cost of Living
Score: 19.8
Rank: 299

INDEXES & TAXES	AREA	U.S. AVG	HOUSING	AREA	U.S. AVG	NECESSITIES	AREA	U.S. AVG
Cost of Living Index	117.6	100.0	Median home price	$345,000	$220,000	Food Index	98.5	100.0
Buying Power Index	96.4	100.0	Home price appreciation	76.7%	10.1%	Housing Index	126.4	100.0
Income tax rate	5.75%	4.70%	Median rent	$792	$709	Utilities Index	89.5	100.0
Sales tax rate	5.00%	6.58%	Homes owned	60.4%	62.3%	Transportation Index	105.8	100.0
Property tax rate	$7.94	$12.00	Home price ratio	6.8	4.2	Healthcare Index	98.6	100.0
						Miscellaneous Cost Index	97.7	100.0

Climate
Score: 71.4
Rank: 106

TEMPERATURE	AREA	U.S. AVG	PRECIPITATION	AREA	U.S. AVG	COMFORTS & HAZARDS	AREA	U.S. AVG
Average January low	27.3	26.2	Annual inches precipitation	38.3	37.7	July relative humidity	69%	66%
July high	86.1	87.4	Annual inches snowfall	18.2	7.0	Annual days mostly sunny	218	208
Annual days > 90°F	19	38	Annual days precipitation	125	109	Annual days with thunderstorms	41	39
Annual days < 32°F	94	89	Annual days rain > 0.5 inches	28	22	Tornado risk score	13	18
Annual days < 0°F	1	6	Annual days snow > 1.5 inches	3	6	Hurricane risk score	15	13

TEMPERATURE

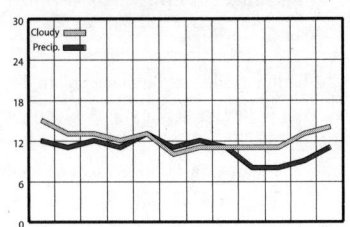

PRECIPITATION

DAYS OF CLOUDS & PRECIPITATION

Education
Score: 82.6
Rank: 66

ACHIEVEMENT	AREA	U.S. AVG	PUBLIC SCHOOLS	AREA	U.S. AVG	HIGHER EDUCATION	AREA	U.S. AVG
High school degree	83.0%	82.7%	Expenditures per pupil	$6,001	$5,686	No. 2-year colleges	1	4
2-year college degree	4.8%	6.4%	Student/teacher ratio	12.5	16.7	No. 4-year colleges/universities	1	6
4-year college degree	20.4%	15.7%	Attending public school	84.8%	90.1%	No. highly ranked universities	1	1
Graduate/professional degree	18.5%	8.9%	State SAT score	1025*	1021			
			State ACT score	21.1	20.9			

Health & Healthcare
Score: 99.5
Rank: 3

Crime
Score: 91.4
Rank: 33

HAZARDS & ILLNESSES	AREA	U.S. AVG	HEALTHCARE	AREA	U.S. AVG	CRIME	AREA	U.S. AVG
Air-quality score	70	37	Physicians per capita	801.1	244.2	Violent crime rate	288.3	465.5
Water-quality score	71	52	Hospital beds per capita	485.1	420.0	Change in violent crime rate	2.9%	-2.2%
Pollen/allergy score	63	61	No. teaching hospitals	1	3	Property crime rate	2,665.8	3,517.1
Cancer mortality per capita	166.1	201.9	Cost per doctor visit	$81	$77	Change in property crime rate	14.1%	-2.1%
Depression days per month	2.8	3.5	Cost per dental visit	$73	$70			
Stress score	13	50						

Transportation
Score: 80.7
Rank: 73

COMMUTE	AREA	U.S. AVG	INTERCITY SERVICES	AREA	U.S. AVG	AUTOMOTIVE	AREA	U.S. AVG
Average commute time	25.5	27.4	Major airports within 60 miles	2	1	Insurance, annual premium	$1,051	$1,432
Percent commutes > 60 mins.	5.2%	5.9%	Size of regional airport	Large	Large	Gas, cost per gallon	$2.46	$2.49
Commute by auto	74.1%	78.9%	Daily airline activity	1274	686	Daily vehicle miles per capita	23.7	24.0
Commute by mass transit	2.1%	1.9%	Amtrak service	Yes	No			
Work at home	5.0%	3.1%						
Mass transit miles per capita	2.06	1.87						

Leisure
Score: 40.1
Rank: 223

DINING & SHOPPING	AREA	U.S. AVG	ENTERTAINMENT	AREA	U.S. AVG	OUTDOOR ACTIVITIES	AREA	U.S. AVG
Restaurant rating	1	2	Professional sports rating	2	4	Golf-course rating	1	4
Outlet mall score	0	42	College sports rating	7	4	Ski-area rating	5	3
No. Starbucks	5	13	Zoo/aquarium rating	1	3	Sq. miles inland water	2	4
No. warehouse clubs	0	2	Amusement park rating	1	3	Miles of coastline	0.0	10.7
			Botanical garden/arboretum rating	1	4	National Park rating	4	3

Arts & Culture
Score: 64.7
Rank: 131

MEDIA & LIBRARIES	AREA	U.S. AVG	PERFORMING ARTS	AREA	U.S. AVG	MUSEUMS	AREA	U.S. AVG
Arts radio rating	8	3	Classical music rating	1	4	Overall museum rating	7	5
No. public libraries	9	27	Ballet/dance rating	1	3	Art museum rating	6	5
Library volumes per capita	3.01	2.78	Professional theater rating	1	3	Science museum rating	3	5
			University arts programs rating	4	5	Children's museum rating	4	3

Chattanooga, TN

Score: 55.4   **Rank:** 219   **2004 rank:** 210

Profile: Mid-size city
Location: Extreme southeast Tennessee at the Georgia border, along I-75 110 miles north of Atlanta
Elevation: 665 feet
Time zone: Eastern Standard Time

PRO	CON
Revitalized downtown	Crime rates
Cost of living	Arts and culture
Attractive setting	Hot, humid summers

The colorfully named Chattanooga is a transportation and historic gateway to the Deep South. It was a zone of contention in the latter stages of the Civil War, and history plays a big role in the city's conscience. For years it marched on as a nondescript Old South city with areas of urban decay in the old city center, as well as environmental and crime issues. An ambitious downtown redevelopment initiative, just completed with public and private support, has brought a lot of life back into the downtown area, both as a commercial and recreation destination. The 22-mile Tennessee River waterfront is now a park and features several museums and a nationally noted aquarium. These improve-

ments, the attractive mountain setting, favorable tax climate, and proximity of Atlanta services promise a stronger future. The area is still a bit weak on performing arts and some services, such as air service, and there are still some lingering economic and crime issues.

Chattanooga and the Tennessee Valley are located between the Cumberland Mountains to the west and the Appalachian Mountains to the east. The climate is moderate, characterized by cool winters and very warm summers. Winter weather is changeable with highly variable snowfall and occasional freezing rain. Spring and fall weather are particularly pleasant. First freeze is early November; last is late March.

DEMOGRAPHICS	AREA	U.S. AVG	ETHNIC COMPOSITION	AREA	U.S. AVG	RESIDENT PROFILE	AREA	U.S. AVG
Population	490,543		White	82.7%	79.0%	Single	29.0%	32.4%
Population density per sq. mile	234.8	358.5	Black	13.9%	10.5%	Married	55.3%	52.7%
Population growth	14.3%	21.1%	Asian	1.2%	2.7%	Divorced/separated	15.7%	14.9%
Median age	38.0	36.1	Hispanic	1.7%	10.6%	Married with children	21.9%	23.7%
Percent Democrat	38.0%	44.5%	Religious observance	52.2%	48.9%	Single with children	8.5%	9.1%
Percent Republican	61.3%	54.5%	Diversity measure	30.2	40.1	Percent over age 65	13.9%	12.9%

Population

INCOME	AREA	U.S. AVG	EMPLOYMENT	AREA	U.S. AVG	EMPLOYING INDUSTRIES	AREA	U.S. AVG
Per capita income	$22,421	$23,235	Unemployment rate	4.9%	4.7%	Largest: Manufacturing		
Household income	$42,069	$46,414	Recent job growth	-0.1%	1.3%			
Household income < $25K	29.0%	26.2%	Projected future job growth	5.3%	11.5%	Percent manufacturing	20.1%	15.4%
Household income > $75K	21.2%	25.4%	White collar	56.0%	57.8%	Percent public sector	13.2%	15.7%
Household income growth	12.3%	13.6%	Blue collar	30.1%	25.2%	Percent construction	10.0%	9.9%

Economy & Jobs
Score: 23.0
Rank: 288

INDEXES & TAXES	AREA	U.S. AVG	HOUSING	AREA	U.S. AVG	NECESSITIES	AREA	U.S. AVG
Cost of Living Index	84.4	100.0	Median home price	$142,300	$220,000	Food Index	100.0	100.0
Buying Power Index	111.7	100.0	Home price appreciation	32.7%	10.1%	Housing Index	48.6	100.0
Income tax rate	0.13%	4.70%	Median rent	$608	$709	Utilities Index	88.8	100.0
Sales tax rate	8.61%	6.58%	Homes owned	65.3%	62.3%	Transportation Index	94.2	100.0
Property tax rate	$9.31	$12.00	Home price ratio	3.4	4.2	Healthcare Index	88.7	100.0
						Miscellaneous Cost Index	101.9	100.0

Cost of Living
Score: 90.9
Rank: 35

TEMPERATURE	AREA	U.S. AVG	PRECIPITATION	AREA	U.S. AVG	COMFORTS & HAZARDS	AREA	U.S. AVG
Average January low	30.5	26.2	Annual inches precipitation	52.0	37.7	July relative humidity	72%	66%
July high	89.5	87.4	Annual inches snowfall	4.2	7.0	Annual days mostly sunny	213	208
Annual days > 90°F	49	38	Annual days precipitation	121	109	Annual days with thunderstorms	56	39
Annual days < 32°F	75	89	Annual days rain > 0.5 inches	37	22	Tornado risk score	10	18
Annual days < 0°F	0	6	Annual days snow > 1.5 inches	2	6	Hurricane risk score	11	13

Climate
Score: 21.9
Rank: 291

TEMPERATURE

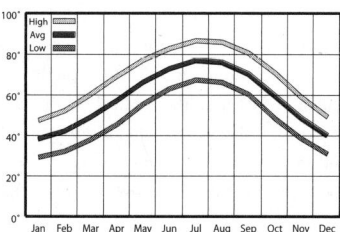

PRECIPITATION

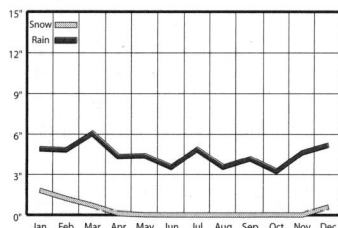

DAYS OF CLOUDS & PRECIPITATION

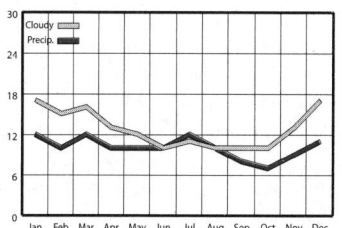

Education
Score: 21.7
Rank: 291

ACHIEVEMENT	AREA	U.S. AVG	PUBLIC SCHOOLS	AREA	U.S. AVG	HIGHER EDUCATION	AREA	U.S. AVG
High school degree	76.7%	82.7%	Expenditures per pupil	$4,685	$5,686	No. 2-year colleges	4	4
2-year college degree	5.6%	6.4%	Student/teacher ratio	16.2	16.7	No. 4-year colleges/universities	5	6
4-year college degree	12.9%	15.7%	Attending public school	85.6%	90.1%	No. highly ranked universities	1	1
Graduate/professional degree	6.5%	8.9%	State SAT score	1142	1021			
			State ACT score	20.7*	20.9			

Health & Healthcare
Score: 82.1
Rank: 68

HAZARDS & ILLNESSES	AREA	U.S. AVG	HEALTHCARE	AREA	U.S. AVG	CRIME	AREA	U.S. AVG
Air-quality score	41	37	Physicians per capita	250.2	244.2	Violent crime rate	589.2	465.5
Water-quality score	57	52	Hospital beds per capita	579.2	420.0	Change in violent crime rate	-3.5%	-2.2%
Pollen/allergy score	63	61	No. teaching hospitals	3	3	Property crime rate	4,622.8	3,517.1
Cancer mortality per capita	211.4	201.9	Cost per doctor visit	$86	$77	Change in property crime rate	-8.2%	-2.1%
Depression days per month	3.3	3.5	Cost per dental visit	$54	$70			
Stress score	84	50						

Crime
Score: 7.5
Rank: 344

Transportation
Score: 4.3
Rank: 356

COMMUTE	AREA	U.S. AVG	INTERCITY SERVICES	AREA	U.S. AVG	AUTOMOTIVE	AREA	U.S. AVG
Average commute time	25.8	27.4	Major airports within 60 miles	0	1	Insurance, annual premium	$974	$1,432
Percent commutes > 60 mins.	4.4%	5.9%	Size of regional airport	Small	Large	Gas, cost per gallon	$2.46	$2.49
Commute by auto	82.7%	78.9%	Daily airline activity	130	686	Daily vehicle miles per capita	34.2	24.0
Commute by mass transit	0.7%	1.9%	Amtrak service	No	No			
Work at home	2.1%	3.1%						
Mass transit miles per capita	0.72	1.87						

Leisure
Score: 54.0
Rank: 172

DINING & SHOPPING	AREA	U.S. AVG	ENTERTAINMENT	AREA	U.S. AVG	OUTDOOR ACTIVITIES	AREA	U.S. AVG
Restaurant rating	1	2	Professional sports rating	2	4	Golf-course rating	3	4
Outlet mall score	76	42	College sports rating	3	4	Ski-area rating	1	3
No. Starbucks	2	13	Zoo/aquarium rating	8	3	Sq. miles inland water	4	4
No. warehouse clubs	1	2	Amusement park rating	5	3	Miles of coastline	0.0	10.7
			Botanical garden/ arboretum rating	3	4	National Park rating	2	3

Arts & Culture
Score: 72.2
Rank: 104

MEDIA & LIBRARIES	AREA	U.S. AVG	PERFORMING ARTS	AREA	U.S. AVG	MUSEUMS	AREA	U.S. AVG
Arts radio rating	5	3	Classical music rating	5	4	Overall museum rating	8	5
No. public libraries	15	27	Ballet/dance rating	3	3	Art museum rating	6	5
Library volumes per capita	3.38	2.78	Professional theater rating	1	3	Science museum rating	5	5
			University arts programs rating	8	5	Children's museum rating	7	3

Cheyenne, WY

Score: 67.9   Rank: 109   2004 rank: 182

Profile: Capital city
Location: Southeast corner of Wyoming at junction of I-80 and I-25
Elevation: 6,115 feet
Time zone: Mountain Standard Time

PRO	CON
Small-town atmosphere	Arts and culture
Stable economy	Air service
Close to Denver	Winter cold

Cheyenne is the capital city and commercial center for the state of Wyoming. The gateway from the Great Plains from the advent of the transcontinental railroad, it still serves as a major ground transportation and agricultural center. The functional and attractive downtown core has a well-preserved historic Western feel. The city has a few museums, but many of the typical cultural amenities of a capital city are absent. That said, Cheyenne has a strong community feel, and it's known for being a friendly place; the area has more than its share of community events and entertainment, the Cheyenne Frontier Days rodeo being among the larger and more well known of these. Major employers include the state government, the Union Pacific Railroad, and several agriculture and energy-related industries. The employment base is more stable than most other cities in the region. A greater assortment of services and amenities are in Denver, 100 miles south.

The city is located on a broad plateau between the North and South Platte rivers. The surrounding country is mostly rolling prairie used primarily for grazing. The ground level rises rapidly to a north-south Rocky Mountain ridge approximately 9,000 feet in elevation about 30 miles west of the city. The Laramie Mountains block some cold air from the north, and winds from the northwest are "downslope" and produce a marked chinook, or warming effect, which is especially noticeable during the winter months. Winds from the north through east to south are upslope and may cause fog or low stratus clouds throughout the year. The terrain variation and wind direction play an important role in controlling the local temperature and weather. First freeze is mid-October; last is late April.

DEMOGRAPHICS	AREA	U.S. AVG	ETHNIC COMPOSITION	AREA	U.S. AVG	RESIDENT PROFILE	AREA	U.S. AVG
Population	85,454		White	87.5%	79.0%	Single	27.2%	32.4%
Population density per sq. mile	31.8	358.5	Black	3.0%	10.5%	Married	55.3%	52.7%
Population growth	16.8%	21.1%	Asian	1.2%	2.7%	Divorced/separated	17.5%	14.9%
Median age	36.2	36.1	Hispanic	11.8%	10.6%	Married with children	24.1%	23.7%
Percent Democrat	33.0%	44.5%	Religious observance	47.7%	48.9%	Single with children	9.0%	9.1%
Percent Republican	65.1%	54.5%	Diversity measure	39.1	40.1	Percent over age 65	12.0%	12.9%

Economy & Jobs
Score: 55.1
Rank: 169

INCOME	AREA	U.S. AVG	EMPLOYMENT	AREA	U.S. AVG	EMPLOYING INDUSTRIES	AREA	U.S. AVG
Per capita income	$23,306	$23,235	Unemployment rate	4.0%	4.7%	Largest: Healthcare & Social Assistance		
Household income	$45,750	$46,414	Recent job growth	2.4%	1.3%			
Household income < $25K	23.9%	26.2%	Projected future job growth	8.8%	11.5%	Percent manufacturing	13.4%	15.4%
Household income > $75K	23.2%	25.4%	White collar	59.2%	57.8%	Percent public sector	26.2%	15.7%
Household income growth	15.5%	13.6%	Blue collar	24.4%	25.2%	Percent construction	11.0%	9.9%

Cost of Living
Score: 98.4
Rank: 7

INDEXES & TAXES	AREA	U.S. AVG	HOUSING	AREA	U.S. AVG	NECESSITIES	AREA	U.S. AVG
Cost of Living Index	88.6	100.0	Median home price	$153,400	$220,000	Food Index	107.3	100.0
Buying Power Index	115.7	100.0	Home price appreciation	42.3%	10.1%	Housing Index	64.4	100.0
Income tax rate	0.00%	4.70%	Median rent	$633	$709	Utilities Index	103.2	100.0
Sales tax rate	6.00%	6.58%	Homes owned	64.8%	62.3%	Transportation Index	95.2	100.0
Property tax rate	$6.90	$12.00	Home price ratio	3.4	4.2	Healthcare Index	101.4	100.0
						Miscellaneous Cost Index	96.4	100.0

Climate
Score: 40.1
Rank: 223

TEMPERATURE	AREA	U.S. AVG	PRECIPITATION	AREA	U.S. AVG	COMFORTS & HAZARDS	AREA	U.S. AVG
Average January low	34.3	26.2	Annual inches precipitation	12.0	37.7	July relative humidity	49%	66%
July high	87.5	87.4	Annual inches snowfall	81.0	7.0	Annual days mostly sunny	217	208
Annual days > 90°F	26	38	Annual days precipitation	95	109	Annual days with thunderstorms	34	39
Annual days < 32°F	183	89	Annual days rain > 0.5 inches	6	22	Tornado risk score	16	18
Annual days < 0°F	22	6	Annual days snow > 1.5 inches	17	6	Hurricane risk score	0	13

TEMPERATURE

PRECIPITATION

DAYS OF CLOUDS & PRECIPITATION

Education
Score: 78.9
Rank: 80

ACHIEVEMENT	AREA	U.S. AVG	PUBLIC SCHOOLS	AREA	U.S. AVG	HIGHER EDUCATION	AREA	U.S. AVG
High school degree	89.1%	82.7%	Expenditures per pupil	$6,524	$5,686	No. 2-year colleges	2	4
2-year college degree	9.2%	6.4%	Student/teacher ratio	13.4	16.7	No. 4-year colleges/universities	0	6
4-year college degree	15.4%	15.7%	Attending public school	95.5%	90.1%	No. highly ranked universities	0	1
Graduate/professional degree	8.1%	8.9%	State SAT score	1103	1021			
			State ACT score	21.6*	20.9			

Health & Healthcare
Score: 21.4
Rank: 293

HAZARDS & ILLNESSES	AREA	U.S. AVG	HEALTHCARE	AREA	U.S. AVG	CRIME	AREA	U.S. AVG
Air-quality score	32	37	Physicians per capita	220.0	244.2	Violent crime rate	178.4	465.5
Water-quality score	36	52	Hospital beds per capita	224.7	420.0	Change in violent crime rate	-5.9%	-2.2%
Pollen/allergy score	69	61	No. teaching hospitals	1	3	Property crime rate	3,655.4	3,517.1
Cancer mortality per capita	193.8	201.9	Cost per doctor visit	$74	$77	Change in property crime rate	1.1%	-2.1%
Depression days per month	3.2	3.5	Cost per dental visit	$60	$70			
Stress score	19	50						

Transportation
Score: 92.2
Rank: 30

COMMUTE	AREA	U.S. AVG	INTERCITY SERVICES	AREA	U.S. AVG	AUTOMOTIVE	AREA	U.S. AVG
Average commute time	18.1	27.4	Major airports within 60 miles	1	1	Insurance, annual premium	$945	$1,432
Percent commutes > 60 mins.	3.7%	5.9%	Size of regional airport	Large	Large	Gas, cost per gallon	$2.33	$2.49
Commute by auto	80.3%	78.9%	Daily airline activity	812	686	Daily vehicle miles per capita	31.6	24.0
Commute by mass transit	0.4%	1.9%	Amtrak service	No	No			
Work at home	3.7%	3.1%						
Mass transit miles per capita	0.39	1.87						

Leisure
Score: 0.5
Rank: 371

DINING & SHOPPING	AREA	U.S. AVG	ENTERTAINMENT	AREA	U.S. AVG	OUTDOOR ACTIVITIES	AREA	U.S. AVG
Restaurant rating	1	2	Professional sports rating	2	4	Golf-course rating	1	4
Outlet mall score	11	42	College sports rating	1	4	Ski-area rating	1	3
No. Starbucks	1	13	Zoo/aquarium rating	1	3	Sq. miles inland water	2	4
No. warehouse clubs	1	2	Amusement park rating	1	3	Miles of coastline	0.0	10.7
			Botanical garden/ arboretum rating	3	4	National Park rating	1	3

Arts & Culture
Score: 33.7
Rank: 248

MEDIA & LIBRARIES	AREA	U.S. AVG	PERFORMING ARTS	AREA	U.S. AVG	MUSEUMS	AREA	U.S. AVG
Arts radio rating	1	3	Classical music rating	3	4	Overall museum rating	3	5
No. public libraries	3	27	Ballet/dance rating	1	3	Art museum rating	5	5
Library volumes per capita	3.50	2.78	Professional theater rating	1	3	Science museum rating	4	5
			University arts programs rating	1	5	Children's museum rating	1	3

Chicago–Naperville–Joliet, IL   Score: 48.1   Rank: 258   2004 rank: 155

Profile: National center
Location: Northeastern Illinois along Lake Michigan
Elevation: 623 feet
Time zone: Central Standard Time

PRO
Economic and cultural
    diversity
Arts and culture
Historic interest and
    preservation

CON
Harsh climate
Cost of living
Violent crime

A world-class commercial, industrial, and cultural city, Chicago functions as a major national center and as the major regional center for America's heartland. It originally emerged as a transport center for cargo headed west and agricultural products headed east by land and water. Although transportation technology has changed, the city's role has not. The city is the most important passenger and freight transport hub in the country, with the largest number of air departures and the most rail traffic in the nation. The commercial and manufacturing economy stands out both for its size and diversity. More than 30 Fortune 500 companies in an assortment of industries have headquarters here. Factories and warehouses extend for miles from the downtown area. Chicago is also a major center for small manufacturing and business. There is probably no more diverse an economy in the country.

The city grew up in America's Gilded Age and the prosperity spilled over into some of the finest neighborhoods and architectural statements in the country. Oak Park, where architect Frank Lloyd Wright started his original studio, is a museum of residential architecture. It is an attractive, typically Midwestern commuter enclave of square city blocks, stately homes with shaded streets, and a shopping area next to the rail station, which still functions as an important commuter terminal. This story is repeated frequently; for example, Riverside to the south is similar but with flowing curved streets and a parklike setting designed by Frederick Law Olmstead of Central Park fame. The city has an extraordinary sense of history and historic preservation. Many architectural styles, both commercial and residential, were invented and first used in Chicago, and the city goes out of its way to preserve them. The old 1880s elevated rail line continues to operate around the "Loop," the city's main business district. The former Navy Pier on Lake Michigan has been restored into a popular entertainment complex. The waterfront Soldier Field was recently renovated at great expense rather than replaced by a larger stadium with modern amenities. In short, the city is a living museum and monument to American urban history.

Chicago is also a city of neighborhoods. North side, west side, south side—each provides a set of neighborhoods to suit any taste and (mostly) any budget. Areas of older homes and "two-flats" have been restored into viable neighborhoods on major arteries in the inner suburbs. Along the lake and to the north are wealthier areas and the community of Evanston, home of Northwestern University. Areas become more typically middle class (but still with variety) to the northwest, west, and southwest. Like many large cities, Chicago has its sprawl and growth issues, and suburbs have overtaken many older farm communities and towns like Elgin and Aurora, and there is little in the way of geography to restrain the push. Naperville, due west and strategically located among the area's beltways, has become something of an exurb, with a strong commercial base attracting commuters from other neighborhoods in all directions. Joliet is an older industrial and transportation hub on the southwest side. The rest of the area map is a patchwork quilt of suburbs, one after the other, defined by rectangular grid arteries sliced through by radii mainly along rail commute routes emanating from the city. Choices are too numerous to cover in detail but the more popular suburbs typically lie towards the northwest. Some have pushed far out into old farmland, such as Cary, Algonquin, Geneva, and the more upscale Lake Zurich, while other quality neighborhoods lie closer in, such as Elk Grove Village and Schaumberg. Good neighborhoods also lie to the south and southwest side, although contrasts are stronger between the livable and more run-down areas; Hinsdale and Orland Park are more upscale picks on the southwest side.

In Chicago, location relative to major transportation routes is most important. Many endure hour-long commutes into the city and around its crowded beltways. The city has an excellent urban and suburban transportation network with an assortment of rail and bus services; nonetheless, traffic along arteries and beltways can be intense. A less typical urban problem is that Chicago's downtown and nearby neighborhoods have become so livable—and so many businesses have located on the urban fringe—that rush-hour traffic affects people commuting *out* of the city.

Chicago offers numerous amenities. Museums, notably The Art Institute of Chicago, and the performing arts are top quality. Sports are legendary—whether the teams win or lose—and Wrigley Field is another of those American urban icons. Few cities have more or better restaurants. Plus, the area has some of the best higher education in the country, and quality education is available at all levels in most neighborhoods.

Climate and the "C" factors typical of large city living—cost of living, crowdedness, crime, and commute—are the main negatives. Chicago's climate can be pleasant but downright miserable at times. The lakeside location, facing into the teeth of the storm track, and continental climate from the northwest produce cold, snow, wind, storms, humid heat, and weather changes invigorating for some but intolerable for others. Cost of living varies by neighborhood and lifestyle, but is accelerating after years as a relative bargain for a big city. The violent crime rate was well known even before the television show *ER* and is still a problem in some neighborhoods. There are still some grubby, run-down areas that would make some people think twice. These facts hurt the statistical appraisal of Chicago. But we think the area offers a rich and complete assortment of lifestyles, amenities, and opportunities for most people willing to make a few trade-offs; most shouldn't be discouraged by the low ranking.

Chicago is located on a level coastal plain generally less than 100 feet above the lake. Most land is open and almost completely flat with occasional areas of deciduous woods. The climate is continental with frequently changing weather and is invigorating to say the least. Although lake winds can be strong and channeled by downtown office buildings, the nickname "Windy City" is a bit of a misnomer as average wind through the year is not exceptional. That said, winter wind-chill factors can reach extreme proportions. Summers can be warm and breezy to hot and humid. Lake breezes may moderate downtown temperatures 10°F to 15°F but will only occasionally extend several miles inland. Summer precipitation comes mainly from thunderstorms and can be heavy. Winter precipitation may arrive as frontal systems from the west or heavy squalls off the lake. Fall and spring are changeable, and along with winter, can have long periods of precipitation. Half the summers have temperatures over 96°F; half the winters have temperatures as low as −15°F. First freeze is mid-October; last is late April.

Population

DEMOGRAPHICS	AREA	U.S. AVG	ETHNIC COMPOSITION	AREA	U.S. AVG	RESIDENT PROFILE	AREA	U.S. AVG
Population	7,883,317		White	63.3%	79.0%	Single	37.5%	32.4%
Population density per sq. mile	1708.3	358.5	Black	19.3%	10.5%	Married	48.9%	52.7%
Population growth	18.0%	21.1%	Asian	5.4%	2.7%	Divorced/separated	13.5%	14.9%
Median age	34.8	36.1	Hispanic	19.5%	10.6%	Married with children	24.9%	23.7%
Percent Democrat	61.9%	44.5%	Religious observance	56.7%	48.9%	Single with children	8.7%	9.1%
Percent Republican	37.4%	54.5%	Diversity measure	66.1	40.1	Percent over age 65	10.9%	12.9%

Economy & Jobs
Score: 8.6
Rank: 341

INCOME	AREA	U.S. AVG	EMPLOYMENT	AREA	U.S. AVG	EMPLOYING INDUSTRIES	AREA	U.S. AVG
Per capita income	$27,695	$23,235	Unemployment rate	6.7%	4.7%	Largest: Finance & Insurance		
Household income	$57,833	$46,414	Recent job growth	-0.4%	1.3%			
Household income < $25K	19.6%	26.2%	Projected future job growth	4.5%	11.5%	Percent manufacturing	14.6%	15.4%
Household income > $75K	36.7%	25.4%	White collar	64.5%	57.8%	Percent public sector	11.6%	15.7%
Household income growth	12.3%	13.6%	Blue collar	22.2%	25.2%	Percent construction	7.7%	9.9%

Cost of Living
Score: 13.9
Rank: 321

INDEXES & TAXES	AREA	U.S. AVG	HOUSING	AREA	U.S. AVG	NECESSITIES	AREA	U.S. AVG
Cost of Living Index	113.6	100.0	Median home price	$278,500	$220,000	Food Index	105.3	100.0
Buying Power Index	114.1	100.0	Home price appreciation	54.7%	10.1%	Housing Index	125.1	100.0
Income tax rate	3.00%	4.70%	Median rent	$932	$709	Utilities Index	107.1	100.0
Sales tax rate	8.05%	6.58%	Homes owned	61.4%	62.3%	Transportation Index	117.6	100.0
Property tax rate	$16.97	$12.00	Home price ratio	4.8	4.2	Healthcare Index	114.8	100.0
						Miscellaneous Cost Index	106.2	100.0

Climate
Score: 24.9
Rank: 280

TEMPERATURE	AREA	U.S. AVG	PRECIPITATION	AREA	U.S. AVG	COMFORTS & HAZARDS	AREA	U.S. AVG
Average January low	17.0	26.2	Annual inches precipitation	34.0	37.7	July relative humidity	67%	66%
July high	84.4	87.4	Annual inches snowfall	40.0	7.0	Annual days mostly sunny	197	208
Annual days > 90°F	21	38	Annual days precipitation	123	109	Annual days with thunderstorms	40	39
Annual days < 32°F	119	89	Annual days rain > 0.5 inches	22	22	Tornado risk score	40	18
Annual days < 0°F	7	6	Annual days snow > 1.5 inches	9	6	Hurricane risk score	2	13

TEMPERATURE

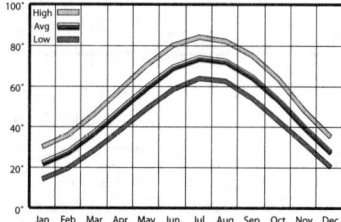

PRECIPITATION

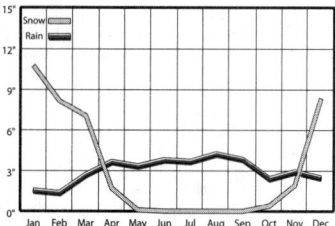

DAYS OF CLOUDS & PRECIPITATION

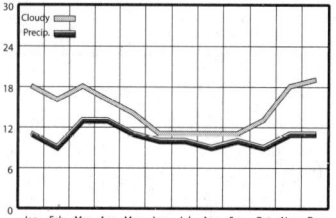

Education Score: 97.6 Rank: 10	ACHIEVEMENT	AREA	U.S. AVG	PUBLIC SCHOOLS	AREA	U.S. AVG	HIGHER EDUCATION	AREA	U.S. AVG
	High school degree	80.7%	82.7%	Expenditures per pupil	$5,923	$5,686	No. 2-year colleges	32	4
	2-year college degree	5.7%	6.4%	Student/teacher ratio	17.2	16.7	No. 4-year colleges/universities	82	6
	4-year college degree	18.6%	15.7%	Attending public school	86.1%	90.1%	No. highly ranked universities	6	1
	Graduate/professional degree	10.8%	8.9%	State SAT score	1200	1021			
				State ACT score	20.5*	20.9			

Health & Healthcare Score: 9.1 Rank: 339	HAZARDS & ILLNESSES	AREA	U.S. AVG	HEALTHCARE	AREA	U.S. AVG	CRIME	AREA	U.S. AVG
	Air-quality score	10	37	Physicians per capita	292.4	244.2	Violent crime rate	619.4	465.5
	Water-quality score	37	52	Hospital beds per capita	333.9	420.0	Change in violent crime rate	0.1%	-2.2%
	Pollen/allergy score	57	61	No. teaching hospitals	56	3	Property crime rate	3,292.0	3,517.1
	Cancer mortality per capita	203.4	201.9	Cost per doctor visit	$80	$77	Change in property crime rate	-4.3%	-2.1%
	Depression days per month	3.4	3.5	Cost per dental visit	$83	$70			
	Stress score	55	50				Crime Score: 34.0 Rank: 246		

Transportation Score: 85.8 Rank: 53	COMMUTE	AREA	U.S. AVG	INTERCITY SERVICES	AREA	U.S. AVG	AUTOMOTIVE	AREA	U.S. AVG
	Average commute time	34.4	27.4	Major airports within 60 miles	3	1	Insurance, annual premium	$1,946	$1,432
	Percent commutes > 60 mins.	13.8%	5.9%	Size of regional airport	Large	Large	Gas, cost per gallon	$2.56	$2.49
	Commute by auto	68.8%	78.9%	Daily airline activity	2083	686	Daily vehicle miles per capita	22.1	24.0
	Commute by mass transit	13.0%	1.9%	Amtrak service	Yes	No			
	Work at home	2.9%	3.1%						
	Mass transit miles per capita	13.03	1.87						

Leisure Score: 99.2 Rank: 4	DINING & SHOPPING	AREA	U.S. AVG	ENTERTAINMENT	AREA	U.S. AVG	OUTDOOR ACTIVITIES	AREA	U.S. AVG
	Restaurant rating	9	2	Professional sports rating	9	4	Golf-course rating	10	4
	Outlet mall score	200	42	College sports rating	9	4	Ski-area rating	4	3
	No. Starbucks	205	13	Zoo/aquarium rating	10	3	Sq. miles inland water	3	4
	No. warehouse clubs	21	2	Amusement park rating	10	3	Miles of coastline	32.6	10.7
				Botanical garden/arboretum rating	10	4	National Park rating	2	3

Arts & Culture Score: 97.3 Rank: 11	MEDIA & LIBRARIES	AREA	U.S. AVG	PERFORMING ARTS	AREA	U.S. AVG	MUSEUMS	AREA	U.S. AVG
	Arts radio rating	8	3	Classical music rating	10	4	Overall museum rating	10	5
	No. public libraries	272	27	Ballet/dance rating	10	3	Art museum rating	10	5
	Library volumes per capita	3.75	2.78	Professional theater rating	10	3	Science museum rating	10	5
				University arts programs rating	10	5	Children's museum rating	10	3

Chico, CA

Score: 49.1   Rank: 248   2004 rank: 281

Profile: Small town/college town
Location: Northern California, northeastern portion of the Central Valley at the foot of the Sierra range
Elevation: 230 feet
Time zone: Pacific Standard Time

PRO
Some college-town amenities
Mild winters
Nearby mountains

CON
Isolation
High unemployment
Low ethnic diversity

Chico is home to a major campus of the California State University system and a variety of agricultural activities. Nearby mountains, Lassen Volcanic National Park, and Lake Almanor offer outdoor recreation. "Chico State," as the school is known locally, brings a few college amenities to the area but it falls short of description as a classic college town. While summers can be unbearably hot and dry, winters are pleasant and many outdoor activities can be pursued throughout the year. The decline of the forest-products industry has led to unemployment, and the poor air service and 2½-hour drive to Sacramento are negatives. Agricultural processing, supporting a large area of fruit and orchard land to the southwest, is an economic mainstay. There are a number of retirement and resort communities in the mountains northeast—Paradise is

an example—and support of these communities adds to the Chico economy. On a California scale, housing, cost of living, and crime are all reasonable, but rankings are done on a national scale.

The immediate terrain is flat to gently rolling and agricultural. Immediately to the east, grassland and oak-studded foothills begin to rise. Mt. Lassen, an 11,000-foot dormant volcano, dominates the skyline to the northeast. Nearby are numerous steep canyons, notably the Feather River Canyon. Climate is typical Central Valley Mediterranean, with long, hot, dry summers and mild, moist winters. Summer days are usually cloudless and in the 90s or low 100s. Evenings may be cooled by mountain air or by "delta" breezes from the San Francisco Bay.

Population

DEMOGRAPHICS	AREA	U.S. AVG	ETHNIC COMPOSITION	AREA	U.S. AVG	RESIDENT PROFILE	AREA	U.S. AVG
Population	213,359		White	83.0%	79.0%	Single	36.3%	32.4%
Population density per sq. mile	130.1	358.5	Black	1.4%	10.5%	Married	47.8%	52.7%
Population growth	17.2%	21.1%	Asian	3.9%	2.7%	Divorced/separated	15.9%	14.9%
Median age	35.6	36.1	Hispanic	11.6%	10.6%	Married with children	18.7%	23.7%
Percent Democrat	44.1%	44.5%	Religious observance	27.4%	48.9%	Single with children	9.6%	9.1%
Percent Republican	53.7%	54.5%	Diversity measure	44.7	40.1	Percent over age 65	15.1%	12.9%

Economy & Jobs
Score: 43.6
Rank: 212

INCOME	AREA	U.S. AVG	EMPLOYMENT	AREA	U.S. AVG	EMPLOYING INDUSTRIES	AREA	U.S. AVG
Per capita income	$20,186	$23,235	Unemployment rate	6.6%	4.7%	Largest: Healthcare & Social Assistance		
Household income	$36,919	$46,414	Recent job growth	3.2%	1.3%			
Household income < $25K	34.5%	26.2%	Projected future job growth	15.3%	11.5%	Percent manufacturing	11.6%	15.4%
Household income > $75K	18.9%	25.4%	White collar	57.5%	57.8%	Percent public sector	19.3%	15.7%
Household income growth	15.6%	13.6%	Blue collar	20.9%	25.2%	Percent construction	9.3%	9.9%

Cost of Living
Score: 21.9
Rank: 290

INDEXES & TAXES	AREA	U.S. AVG	HOUSING	AREA	U.S. AVG	NECESSITIES	AREA	U.S. AVG
Cost of Living Index	126.0	100.0	Median home price	$324,300	$220,000	Food Index	120.1	100.0
Buying Power Index	65.7	100.0	Home price appreciation	129.5%	10.1%	Housing Index	81.6	100.0
Income tax rate	6.00%	4.70%	Median rent	$702	$709	Utilities Index	110.4	100.0
Sales tax rate	7.25%	6.58%	Homes owned	56.3%	62.3%	Transportation Index	114.7	100.0
Property tax rate	$8.67	$12.00	Home price ratio	8.8	4.2	Healthcare Index	152.5	100.0
						Miscellaneous Cost Index	103.7	100.0

Climate
Score: 92.0
Rank: 31

TEMPERATURE	AREA	U.S. AVG	PRECIPITATION	AREA	U.S. AVG	COMFORTS & HAZARDS	AREA	U.S. AVG
Average January low	35.7	26.2	Annual inches precipitation	26.0	37.7	July relative humidity	68%	66%
July high	96.5	87.4	Annual inches snowfall	0.6	7.0	Annual days mostly sunny	276	208
Annual days > 90°F	92	38	Annual days precipitation	62	109	Annual days with thunderstorms	7	39
Annual days > 32°F	36	89	Annual days rain > 0.5 inches	21	22	Tornado risk score	4	18
Annual days < 0°F	0	6	Annual days snow > 1.5 inches	0	6	Hurricane risk score	0	13

TEMPERATURE

PRECIPITATION

DAYS OF CLOUDS & PRECIPITATION

Education
Score: 47.1
Rank: 199

ACHIEVEMENT	AREA	U.S. AVG	PUBLIC SCHOOLS	AREA	U.S. AVG	HIGHER EDUCATION	AREA	U.S. AVG
High school degree	82.3%	82.7%	Expenditures per pupil	$4,803	$5,686	No. 2-year colleges	1	4
2-year college degree	7.8%	6.4%	Student/teacher ratio	19.2	16.7	No. 4-year colleges/universities	1	6
4-year college degree	15.1%	15.7%	Attending public school	94.5%	90.1%	No. highly ranked universities	0	1
Graduate/professional degree	7.0%	8.9%	State SAT score	1019*	1021			
			State ACT score	21.6	20.9			

Health & Healthcare
Score: 14.2
Rank: 320

HAZARDS & ILLNESSES	AREA	U.S. AVG	HEALTHCARE	AREA	U.S. AVG	CRIME	AREA	U.S. AVG
Air-quality score	33	37	Physicians per capita	189.6	244.2	Violent crime rate	350.8	465.5
Water-quality score	68	52	Hospital beds per capita	343.6	420.0	Change in violent crime rate	-0.4%	-2.2%
Pollen/allergy score	74	61	No. teaching hospitals	0	3			
Cancer mortality per capita	180.9	201.9	Cost per doctor visit	$91	$77	Property crime rate	3,421.5	3,517.1
Depression days per month	3.9	3.5	Cost per dental visit	$80	$70	Change in property crime rate	-11.6%	-2.1%
Stress score	80	50						

Crime
Score: 72.2
Rank: 105

Transportation
Score: 44.9
Rank: 206

COMMUTE	AREA	U.S. AVG	INTERCITY SERVICES	AREA	U.S. AVG	AUTOMOTIVE	AREA	U.S. AVG
Average commute time	22.0	27.4	Major airports within 60 miles	1	1	Insurance, annual premium	$1,677	$1,432
Percent commutes > 60 mins.	5.5%	5.9%	Size of regional airport	Medium	Large	Gas, cost per gallon	$2.61	$2.49
Commute by auto	74.4%	78.9%	Daily airline activity	144	686	Daily vehicle miles per capita	13.4	24.0
Commute by mass transit	1.1%	1.9%	Amtrak service	Yes	No			
Work at home	4.3%	3.1%						
Mass transit miles per capita	1.11	1.87						

DINING & SHOPPING	AREA	U.S. AVG	ENTERTAINMENT	AREA	U.S. AVG	OUTDOOR ACTIVITIES	AREA	U.S. AVG
Restaurant rating	1	2	Professional sports rating	2	4	Golf-course rating	1	4
Outlet mall score	42	42	College sports rating	5	4	Ski-area rating	10	3
No. Starbucks	4	13	Zoo/aquarium rating	1	3	Sq. miles inland water	2	4
No. warehouse clubs	1	2	Amusement park rating	1	3	Miles of coastline	0.0	10.7
			Botanical garden/ arboretum rating	1	4	National Park rating	6	3

Leisure
Score: 58.3
Rank: 156

MEDIA & LIBRARIES	AREA	U.S. AVG	PERFORMING ARTS	AREA	U.S. AVG	MUSEUMS	AREA	U.S. AVG
Arts radio rating	1	3	Classical music rating	3	4	Overall museum rating	3	5
No. public libraries	6	27	Ballet/dance rating	1	3	Art museum rating	2	5
Library volumes per capita	1.31	2.78	Professional theater rating	1	3	Science museum rating	4	5
			University arts programs rating	4	5	Children's museum rating	3	3

Arts & Culture
Score: 13.9
Rank: 321

Cincinnati—Middletown, OH-KY-IN

Score: 81.6   **Rank:** 38   **2004 rank:** 92

Profile: Large city
Location: Southwestern Ohio along the Ohio River and Kentucky/Indiana borders
Elevation: 550 feet
Time zone: Eastern Standard Time

PRO	CON
Arts and culture	Growth and sprawl
Entertainment	Declining downtown
Cost of living	Hot, humid summers

Cincinnati is a livable city at the crossroads—literally and figuratively—of north and south, east and west, and Old World and New World. Called by some the "northernmost Southern city," it is a transportation and cultural gateway between the industrial North and rural South dating back to Underground Railroad days. The area's largest industry and employer is Procter & Gamble, with a history that dates back to the city's early stockyards when soap was made from animal byproducts. Other companies also make soap and cosmetic products, while machine tools are another important industry. The area has experienced growth in financial services and in commercial and manufacturing facilities for overseas companies. There are some businesses supporting the auto industry, but the area's economy has been less susceptible to disruptions from that industry, and is in good shape for a Midwestern city.

German and Italian immigrants brought a distinctly European architectural and cultural flair still evident in certain areas. There are few tourist attractions but the city is a patchwork of interesting historic neighborhoods, including the San Francisco–like Mount Adams, an area overlooking the Ohio River with nightlife, restaurants, and cultural amenities; the planned historic gaslight village of Glendale; and the posh Indian Hill. These are intermingled with numerous plain subdivisions and industrial areas. The city has increasing urban-sprawl problems, with an unusually wide beltway and surrounding counties vying for new growth. Recently, growth of housing and commercial activities has exploded north of the Interstate 275 beltway toward Mason, Kings Mills, and Fairfield, creating traffic headaches and an exurban environment where residents of these areas commute to beltway commercial areas and seldom see the city. This isn't all that unusual in American urban history, but it's a big change for Cincinnati; and the downtown area, a long holdout against urban decay, is having problems. As if to confirm the trend, the metro area now includes the cities of Hamilton and Middletown to the north, mostly industrial centers but lying in the direction of growth.

Northern Kentucky areas surrounding Covington are also growing rapidly thanks to new highway access, and areas near the Ohio River on the Kentucky side have become a center for entertainment. While sprawl and distances threaten, and the area's hilly geography has always isolated some areas, most places in Cincinnati, including downtown, are easy to get to but commute times are growing. The most attractive suburbs lie north and east both inside and outside the beltway; names like Montgomery, Evendale, Blue Ash, Loveland, Kenwood, and yes, Mason should be on the radar of those looking at the area.

For a Midwestern city, Cincinnati has excellent and widely recognized cultural amenities, including the Cincinnati Symphony Orchestra, Cincinnati Pops, and the Cincinnati Art Museum. On the downside, racial tensions, inner-city crime, and landmark battles between conservative and progressive elements over arts and pornography have made national headlines. The city has a long major-league sports tradition that is more accessible and less expensive to attend—even when the teams are winning—than most cities. Beyond the city, Hamilton County has an outstanding park system. The city has a very attractive cost of living profile (COL index is 86.8) for what is offered. We're concerned about the downtown core; nonetheless, the city scores consistently well in all categories and the ranking has risen this time around.

The city itself is located in the narrow, relatively steep-sided valley of the Ohio River. The Mill Creek, Licking River, and Miami River valleys join the Ohio with broad tributary valleys giving way to hills and plateaus on both sides of the Ohio. Summers are warm and humid, in the high 80s and 90s but seldom reaching 100°F. Winters are moderately cold with periods of extensive cloudiness. Passing storms can create heavy spring and summer thunderstorms and winter snowfalls. Slow-moving systems can cause long rainy periods during all seasons. Heavy snow is fairly uncommon and usually melts within a few days. First freeze is late October; last is mid-April.

Population

DEMOGRAPHICS	AREA	U.S. AVG	ETHNIC COMPOSITION	AREA	U.S. AVG	RESIDENT PROFILE	AREA	U.S. AVG
Population	2,063,586		White	84.9%	79.0%	Single	32.3%	32.4%
Population density per sq. mile	469.2	358.5	Black	11.4%	10.5%	Married	54.2%	52.7%
Population growth	16.7%	21.1%	Asian	1.7%	2.7%	Divorced/separated	13.5%	14.9%
Median age	36.1	36.1	Hispanic	1.3%	10.6%	Married with children	24.9%	23.7%
Percent Democrat	37.7%	44.5%	Religious observance	44.5%	48.9%	Single with children	9.1%	9.1%
Percent Republican	61.8%	54.5%	Diversity measure	26.3	40.1	Percent over age 65	11.8%	12.9%

Economy & Jobs
Score: 45.7
Rank: 204

INCOME	AREA	U.S. AVG	EMPLOYMENT	AREA	U.S. AVG	EMPLOYING INDUSTRIES	AREA	U.S. AVG
Per capita income	$26,423	$23,235	Unemployment rate	5.1%	4.7%	Largest: Healthcare & Social Assistance		
Household income	$51,650	$46,414	Recent job growth	0.7%	1.3%			
Household income < $25K	22.1%	26.2%	Projected future job growth	9.0%	11.5%	Percent manufacturing	15.3%	15.4%
Household income > $75K	30.7%	25.4%	White collar	61.7%	57.8%	Percent public sector	10.8%	15.7%
Household income growth	13.6%	13.6%	Blue collar	24.2%	25.2%	Percent construction	8.9%	9.9%

Cost of Living
Score: 35.8
Rank: 239

INDEXES & TAXES	AREA	U.S. AVG	HOUSING	AREA	U.S. AVG	NECESSITIES	AREA	U.S. AVG
Cost of Living Index	86.8	100.0	Median home price	$149,100	$220,000	Food Index	98.3	100.0
Buying Power Index	133.4	100.0	Home price appreciation	25.5%	10.1%	Housing Index	58.3	100.0
Income tax rate	6.69%	4.70%	Median rent	$665	$709	Utilities Index	98.0	100.0
Sales tax rate	6.69%	6.58%	Homes owned	64.5%	62.3%	Transportation Index	97.1	100.0
Property tax rate	$12.00	$12.00	Home price ratio	2.9	4.2	Healthcare Index	95.3	100.0
						Miscellaneous Cost Index	100.3	100.0

Climate
Score: 33.4
Rank: 248

TEMPERATURE	AREA	U.S. AVG	PRECIPITATION	AREA	U.S. AVG	COMFORTS & HAZARDS	AREA	U.S. AVG
Average January low	24.3	26.2	Annual inches precipitation	40.0	37.7	July relative humidity	70%	66%
July high	86.6	87.4	Annual inches snowfall	19.0	7.0	Annual days mostly sunny	177	208
Annual days > 90°F	28	38	Annual days precipitation	131	109	Annual days with thunderstorms	50	39
Annual days < 32°F	98	89	Annual days rain > 0.5 inches	27	22	Tornado risk score	29	18
Annual days < 0°F	2	6	Annual days snow > 1.5 inches	5	6	Hurricane risk score	4	13

TEMPERATURE
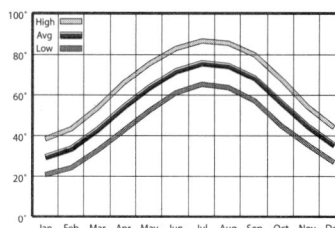

PRECIPITATION
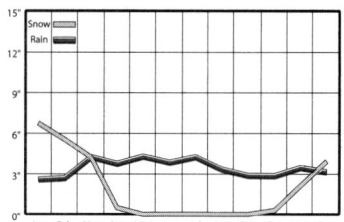

DAYS OF CLOUDS & PRECIPITATION
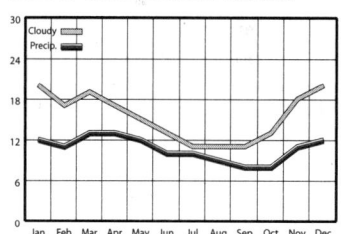

Education
Score: 63.4
Rank: 138

ACHIEVEMENT	AREA	U.S. AVG	PUBLIC SCHOOLS	AREA	U.S. AVG	HIGHER EDUCATION	AREA	U.S. AVG
High school degree	82.7%	82.7%	Expenditures per pupil	$5,444	$5,686	No. 2-year colleges	27	4
2-year college degree	6.1%	6.4%	Student/teacher ratio	18.9	16.7	No. 4-year colleges/universities	17	6
4-year college degree	16.1%	15.7%	Attending public school	82.3%	90.1%	No. highly ranked universities	2	1
Graduate/professional degree	8.7%	8.9%	State SAT score	1079	1021			
			State ACT score	21.5*	20.9			

Health & Healthcare
Score: 24.9
Rank: 280

Crime
Score: 31.8
Rank: 255

HAZARDS & ILLNESSES	AREA	U.S. AVG	HEALTHCARE	AREA	U.S. AVG	CRIME	AREA	U.S. AVG
Air-quality score	32	37	Physicians per capita	261.9	244.2	Violent crime rate	366.9	465.5
Water-quality score	33	52	Hospital beds per capita	277.9	420.0	Change in violent crime rate	1.8%	-2.2%
Pollen/allergy score	60	61	No. teaching hospitals	10	3	Property crime rate	3,675.9	3,517.1
Cancer mortality per capita	234.4	201.9	Cost per doctor visit	$69	$77	Change in property crime rate	0.1%	-2.1%
Depression days per month	4.4	3.5	Cost per dental visit	$66	$70			
Stress score	76	50						

Transportation
Score: 67.6
Rank: 122

COMMUTE	AREA	U.S. AVG	INTERCITY SERVICES	AREA	U.S. AVG	AUTOMOTIVE	AREA	U.S. AVG
Average commute time	26.6	27.4	Major airports within 60 miles	2	1	Insurance, annual premium	$1,476	$1,432
Percent commutes > 60 mins.	4.8%	5.9%	Size of regional airport	Large	Large	Gas, cost per gallon	$2.49	$2.49
Commute by auto	81.7%	78.9%	Daily airline activity	1157	686	Daily vehicle miles per capita	24.2	24.0
Commute by mass transit	2.7%	1.9%	Amtrak service	Yes	No			
Work at home	2.8%	3.1%						
Mass transit miles per capita	2.73	1.87						

DINING & SHOPPING	AREA	U.S. AVG	ENTERTAINMENT	AREA	U.S. AVG	OUTDOOR ACTIVITIES	AREA	U.S. AVG
Restaurant rating	3	2	Professional sports rating	6	4	Golf-course rating	7	4
Outlet mall score	29	42	College sports rating	5	4	Ski-area rating	2	3
No. Starbucks	25	13	Zoo/aquarium rating	6	3	Sq. miles inland water	3	4
No. warehouse clubs	8	2	Amusement park rating	8	3	Miles of coastline	0.0	10.7
			Botanical garden/ arboretum rating	9	4	National Park rating	1	3

Leisure
Score: 78.6
Rank: 80

MEDIA & LIBRARIES	AREA	U.S. AVG	PERFORMING ARTS	AREA	U.S. AVG	MUSEUMS	AREA	U.S. AVG
Arts radio rating	7	3	Classical music rating	8	4	Overall museum rating	9	5
No. public libraries	93	27	Ballet/dance rating	4	3	Art museum rating	9	5
Library volumes per capita	4.26	2.78	Professional theater rating	7	3	Science museum rating	9	5
			University arts programs rating	8	5	Children's museum rating	10	3

Arts & Culture
Score: 90.6
Rank: 36

Clarksville, TN-KY

Score: 33.5   Rank: 333   2004 rank: 215

Profile: Small city/military town
Location: Extreme northern Tennessee along Cumberland River at Kentucky border
Elevation: 605 feet
Time zone: Central Standard Time

PRO	CON
Cost of living	Educational attainment
Attractive downtown	Arts and culture
Close to Nashville	Hot, humid summers

Clarksville is a growing city with a well-preserved small-town feel. The nearby Fort Campbell Military Reservation is an economic mainstay, and an assortment of other business activity is located in what is considered a healthy business and labor climate. The downtown area is historic and attractive, and although a 1999 tornado caused significant damage, most of the scars have healed. Austin Peay State University supplies most of the cultural amenities and is the largest non-military employer. Cost of living (75.3) is the lowest in Tennessee, and the low median home price of $101,200 is an attraction. The city claims to be the third-fastest-growing city in the state behind Nashville and Memphis, and was highlighted by the U.S. Census as one of the 25 fastest-growing cities with populations exceeding 100,000. Growth has brought some new amenities to the area, including a new full-service hospital and a lot of new housing. The area offers a good choice of city, suburban, and rural living environments, and is close enough to Nashville (48 miles) to appeal to some telecommuters and small businesses looking for occasional access to that market. In the ranking process, Clarksville just missed a few minimum thresholds and is probably better than the ranking indicates.

The city lies in an area of gently rolling hills mostly in agricultural use with some areas of dense deciduous forest. Summers are long, warm, and humid with frequent thunderstorms. Winters and springs are variable with frequent shifts between cold and mild conditions with periods of rain and storms. Severe cold seldom occurs but snow is not uncommon and can be heavy. Likewise, spring storms can be severe. The first freeze is late October; last is in mid-April.

DEMOGRAPHICS	AREA	U.S. AVG	ETHNIC COMPOSITION	AREA	U.S. AVG	RESIDENT PROFILE	AREA	U.S. AVG
Population	239,180		White	72.5%	79.0%	Single	26.5%	32.4%
Population density per sq. mile	110.6	358.5	Black	20.0%	10.5%	Married	58.1%	52.7%
Population growth	29.8%	21.1%	Asian	1.9%	2.7%	Divorced/separated	15.5%	14.9%
Median age	31.7	36.1	Hispanic	3.7%	10.6%	Married with children	29.7%	23.7%
Percent Democrat	38.9%	44.5%	Religious observance	47.4%	48.9%	Single with children	9.8%	9.1%
Percent Republican	60.5%	54.5%	Diversity measure	46.3	40.1	Percent over age 65	9.7%	12.9%

Population

INCOME	AREA	U.S. AVG	EMPLOYMENT	AREA	U.S. AVG	EMPLOYING INDUSTRIES	AREA	U.S. AVG
Per capita income	$19,198	$23,235	Unemployment rate	6.2%	4.7%	Largest: Manufacturing		
Household income	$41,588	$46,414	Recent job growth	0.6%	1.3%			
Household income < $25K	26.5%	26.2%	Projected future job growth	14.9%	11.5%	Percent manufacturing	20.5%	15.4%
Household income > $75K	18.5%	25.4%	White collar	50.6%	57.8%	Percent public sector	20.5%	15.7%
Household income growth	15.4%	13.6%	Blue collar	31.4%	25.2%	Percent construction	11.0%	9.9%

Economy & Jobs
Score: 43.0
Rank: 213

INDEXES & TAXES	AREA	U.S. AVG	HOUSING	AREA	U.S. AVG	NECESSITIES	AREA	U.S. AVG
Cost of Living Index	75.3	100.0	Median home price	$101,200	$220,000	Food Index	91.7	100.0
Buying Power Index	123.8	100.0	Home price appreciation	21.1%	10.1%	Housing Index	44.4	100.0
Income tax rate	0.16%	4.70%	Median rent	$580	$709	Utilities Index	87.2	100.0
Sales tax rate	8.29%	6.58%	Homes owned	58.1%	62.3%	Transportation Index	95.8	100.0
Property tax rate	$8.42	$12.00	Home price ratio	2.4	4.2	Healthcare Index	89.6	100.0
						Miscellaneous Cost Index	96.0	100.0

Cost of Living
Score: 98.9
Rank: 5

Climate
Score: 17.4
Rank: 308

TEMPERATURE	AREA	U.S. AVG
Average January low	29.0	26.2
July high	90.2	87.4
Annual days > 90°F	37	38
Annual days < 32°F	75	89
Annual days < 0°F	1	6

PRECIPITATION	AREA	U.S. AVG
Annual inches precipitation	46.0	37.7
Annual inches snowfall	10.7	7.0
Annual days precipitation	119	109
Annual days rain > 0.5 inches	32	22
Annual days snow > 1.5 inches	2	6

COMFORTS & HAZARDS	AREA	U.S. AVG
July relative humidity	71%	66%
Annual days mostly sunny	210	208
Annual days with thunderstorms	55	39
Tornado risk score	7	18
Hurricane risk score	6	13

TEMPERATURE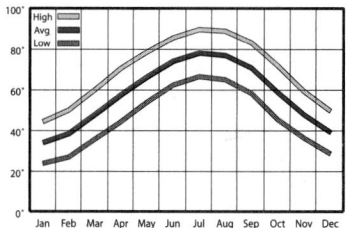

PRECIPITATION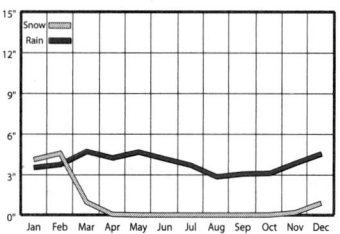

DAYS OF CLOUDS & PRECIPITATION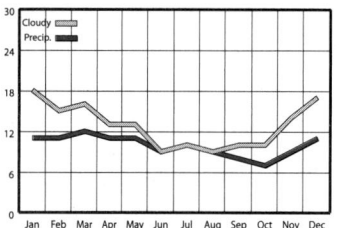

Education
Score: 24.6
Rank: 282

ACHIEVEMENT	AREA	U.S. AVG
High school degree	81.7%	82.7%
2-year college degree	6.8%	6.4%
4-year college degree	10.7%	15.7%
Graduate/professional degree	6.0%	8.9%

PUBLIC SCHOOLS	AREA	U.S. AVG
Expenditures per pupil	$4,492	$5,686
Student/teacher ratio	23.7	16.7
Attending public school	95.6%	90.1%
State SAT score	1142	1021
State ACT score	20.7*	20.9

HIGHER EDUCATION	AREA	U.S. AVG
No. 2-year colleges	5	4
No. 4-year colleges/universities	1	6
No. highly ranked universities	0	1

Health & Healthcare
Score: 67.9
Rank: 121

HAZARDS & ILLNESSES	AREA	U.S. AVG
Air-quality score	51	37
Water-quality score	95	52
Pollen/allergy score	68	61
Cancer mortality per capita	232.5	201.9
Depression days per month	3.8	3.5
Stress score	88	50

HEALTHCARE	AREA	U.S. AVG
Physicians per capita	137.3	244.2
Hospital beds per capita	372.5	420.0
No. teaching hospitals	0	3
Cost per doctor visit	$74	$77
Cost per dental visit	$57	$70

Crime
Score: 42.5
Rank: 215

CRIME	AREA	U.S. AVG
Violent crime rate	521.8	465.5
Change in violent crime rate	14.0%	-2.2%
Property crime rate	3,076.1	3,517.1
Change in property crime rate	-13.6%	-2.1%

Transportation
Score: 13.9
Rank: 323

COMMUTE	AREA	U.S. AVG
Average commute time	26.0	27.4
Percent commutes > 60 mins.	7.6%	5.9%
Commute by auto	79.7%	78.9%
Commute by mass transit	0.7%	1.9%
Work at home	2.1%	3.1%
Mass transit miles per capita	0.74	1.87

INTERCITY SERVICES	AREA	U.S. AVG
Major airports within 60 miles	1	1
Size of regional airport	Medium	Large
Daily airline activity	264	686
Amtrak service	No	No

AUTOMOTIVE	AREA	U.S. AVG
Insurance, annual premium	$912	$1,432
Gas, cost per gallon	$2.46	$2.49
Daily vehicle miles per capita	21.8	24.0

Leisure
Score: 20.3
Rank: 297

DINING & SHOPPING	AREA	U.S. AVG
Restaurant rating	1	2
Outlet mall score	8	42
No. Starbucks	2	13
No. warehouse clubs	0	2

ENTERTAINMENT	AREA	U.S. AVG
Professional sports rating	2	4
College sports rating	1	4
Zoo/aquarium rating	1	3
Amusement park rating	1	3
Botanical garden/arboretum rating	1	4

OUTDOOR ACTIVITIES	AREA	U.S. AVG
Golf-course rating	2	4
Ski-area rating	1	3
Sq. miles inland water	2	4
Miles of coastline	0.0	10.7
National Park rating	7	3

Arts & Culture
Score: 15.5
Rank: 315

MEDIA & LIBRARIES	AREA	U.S. AVG
Arts radio rating	1	3
No. public libraries	4	27
Library volumes per capita	1.30	2.78

PERFORMING ARTS	AREA	U.S. AVG
Classical music rating	4	4
Ballet/dance rating	1	3
Professional theater rating	1	3
University arts programs rating	3	5

MUSEUMS	AREA	U.S. AVG
Overall museum rating	8	5
Art museum rating	2	5
Science museum rating	1	5
Children's museum rating	1	3

Cleveland, TN

Score: 44.1   **Rank:** 293   **2004 rank:** not ranked

Profile: Small town
Location: Extreme southeast Tennessee, 30 miles northeast of Chattanooga
Elevation: 864 feet
Time zone: Eastern Standard Time

PRO	CON
Nearby recreation	Low educational attainment
Diverse economy	Recent employment declines
Small-town feel	Arts and culture

Cherokee, commerce, and Chattanooga—these might be the three "C's" best associated with this small town in southeast Tennessee. Add Christian, cardboard, and chemicals to the mix and the picture becomes more complete. Cleveland is a fairly nondescript, small Southern town located along Interstate 81 at the base of the Appalachian and Great Smoky mountains within long commute range of Chattanooga. The town is at the center of the so-called Cherokee Nation, which made its last encampment in nearby Red Clay State Historic Park before the famed Oklahoma relocation. The Cherokee heritage adds some historic interest, and nearby mountains and the Cherokee National Forest offer plenty of outdoor recreation, but there isn't much else to do. Chattanooga helps fill the gaps in amenities and cultural and recreational assets. The area has a diverse industrial base including chemicals, food processing,

machinery, furniture, and paper and cardboard products. Bigger names include Maytag, Georgia Pacific, Weyerhaeuser, Archer-Daniels-Midland, and the Olin Corporation, but as the statistics show, all has not been bright recently in the local economy. Lee University is affiliated with the Church of God of Prophecy, which is headquartered in this town of strong Protestant traditions.

The terrain is attractive with mostly deciduous-forested mountains nearby and especially to the east and south. Summers are very warm and humid. Winters are fairly mild but unpredictable, as the area is sheltered by the Cumberland Mountains to the northwest. But cold air arriving from the north can bring snow, and remnants of that cold air, overridden with warm moist air from the south, can produce freezing rain and ice storms. First freeze is early November; last is late March.

Population

DEMOGRAPHICS	AREA	U.S. AVG	ETHNIC COMPOSITION	AREA	U.S. AVG	RESIDENT PROFILE	AREA	U.S. AVG
Population	107,613		White	93.2%	79.0%	Single	25.8%	32.4%
Population density per sq. mile	140.9	358.5	Black	3.5%	10.5%	Married	58.8%	52.7%
Population growth	23.2%	21.1%	Asian	0.8%	2.7%	Divorced/separated	15.3%	14.9%
Median age	37.2	36.1	Hispanic	2.2%	10.6%	Married with children	24.0%	23.7%
Percent Democrat	28.6%	44.5%	Religious observance	60.3%	48.9%	Single with children	7.5%	9.1%
Percent Republican	70.7%	54.5%	Diversity measure	16.7	40.1	Percent over age 65	13.2%	12.9%

Economy & Jobs

Score: 4.8
Rank: 355

INCOME	AREA	U.S. AVG	EMPLOYMENT	AREA	U.S. AVG	EMPLOYING INDUSTRIES	AREA	U.S. AVG
Per capita income	$20,332	$23,235	Unemployment rate	5.3%	4.7%	Largest: Manufacturing		
Household income	$38,863	$46,414	Recent job growth	-2.1%	1.3%			
Household income < $25K	31.7%	26.2%	Projected future job growth	6.7%	11.5%	Percent manufacturing	27.6%	15.4%
Household income > $75K	18.0%	25.4%	White collar	47.5%	57.8%	Percent public sector	10.5%	15.7%
Household income growth	13.6%	13.6%	Blue collar	39.4%	25.2%	Percent construction	11.8%	9.9%

Cost of Living

Score: 93.9
Rank: 24

INDEXES & TAXES	AREA	U.S. AVG	HOUSING	AREA	U.S. AVG	NECESSITIES	AREA	U.S. AVG
Cost of Living Index	81.7	100.0	Median home price	$124,700	$220,000	Food Index	102.1	100.0
Buying Power Index	106.6	100.0	Home price appreciation	28.5%	10.1%	Housing Index	54.0	100.0
Income tax rate	0.00%	4.70%	Median rent	$549	$709	Utilities Index	81.5	100.0
Sales tax rate	9.25%	6.58%	Homes owned	65.4%	62.3%	Transportation Index	92.9	100.0
Property tax rate	$7.12	$12.00	Home price ratio	3.2	4.2	Healthcare Index	89.7	100.0
						Miscellaneous Cost Index	100.8	100.0

Climate

Score: 26.5
Rank: 274

TEMPERATURE	AREA	U.S. AVG	PRECIPITATION	AREA	U.S. AVG	COMFORTS & HAZARDS	AREA	U.S. AVG
Average January low	29.0	26.2	Annual inches precipitation	53.3	37.7	July relative humidity	56%	66%
July high	90.0	87.4	Annual inches snowfall	4.0	7.0	Annual days mostly sunny	207	208
Annual days > 90°F	48	38	Annual days precipitation	120	109	Annual days with thunderstorms	55	39
Annual days < 32°F	73	89	Annual days rain > 0.5 inches	37	22	Tornado risk score	3	18
Annual days < 0°F	0	6	Annual days snow > 1.5 inches	2	6	Hurricane risk score	1	13

TEMPERATURE

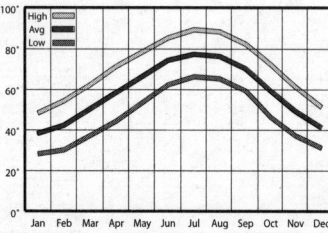

PRECIPITATION

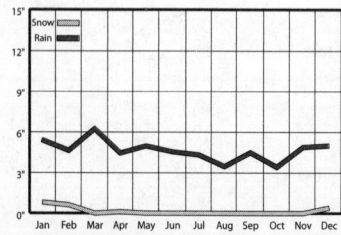

DAYS OF CLOUDS & PRECIPITATION

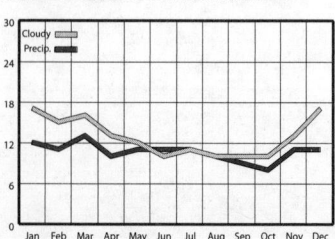

Education
Score: 30.7
Rank: 260

ACHIEVEMENT	AREA	U.S. AVG	PUBLIC SCHOOLS	AREA	U.S. AVG	HIGHER EDUCATION	AREA	U.S. AVG
High school degree	71.9%	82.7%	Expenditures per pupil	$4,464	$5,686	No. 2-year colleges	1	4
2-year college degree	5.5%	6.4%	Student/teacher ratio	0.0	16.7	No. 4-year colleges/universities	3	6
4-year college degree	9.5%	15.7%	Attending public school	95.7%	90.1%	No. highly ranked universities	1	1
Graduate/professional degree	5.2%	8.9%	State SAT score	1142	1021			
			State ACT score	20.7*	20.9			

Health & Healthcare
Score: 84.5
Rank: 59

HAZARDS & ILLNESSES	AREA	U.S. AVG	HEALTHCARE	AREA	U.S. AVG
Air-quality score	63	37	Physicians per capita	138.2	244.2
Water-quality score	55	52	Hospital beds per capita	294.6	420.0
Pollen/allergy score	63	61	No. teaching hospitals	0	3
Cancer mortality per capita	204.5	201.9	Cost per doctor visit	$71	$77
Depression days per month	3.5	3.5	Cost per dental visit	$58	$70
Stress score	87	50			

Crime
Score: 50.0
Rank: 187

CRIME	AREA	U.S. AVG
Violent crime rate	721.4	465.5
Change in violent crime rate	9.1%	-2.2%
Property crime rate	3,735.1	3,517.1
Change in property crime rate	-1.6%	-2.1%

Transportation
Score: 14.2
Rank: 321

COMMUTE	AREA	U.S. AVG	INTERCITY SERVICES	AREA	U.S. AVG	AUTOMOTIVE	AREA	U.S. AVG
Average commute time	23.8	27.4	Major airports within 60 miles	0	1	Insurance, annual premium	$879	$1,432
Percent commutes > 60 mins.	4.7%	5.9%	Size of regional airport	Small	Large	Gas, cost per gallon	$2.46	$2.49
Commute by auto	82.6%	78.9%	Daily airline activity	89	686	Daily vehicle miles per capita	29.7	24.0
Commute by mass transit	0.2%	1.9%	Amtrak service	No	No			
Work at home	2.3%	3.1%						
Mass transit miles per capita	0.17	1.87						

Leisure
Score: 39.0
Rank: 227

DINING & SHOPPING	AREA	U.S. AVG	ENTERTAINMENT	AREA	U.S. AVG	OUTDOOR ACTIVITIES	AREA	U.S. AVG
Restaurant rating	1	2	Professional sports rating	2	4	Golf-course rating	3	4
Outlet mall score	75	42	College sports rating	3	4	Ski-area rating	1	3
No. Starbucks	0	13	Zoo/aquarium rating	8	3	Sq. miles inland water	2	4
No. warehouse clubs	0	2	Amusement park rating	1	3	Miles of coastline	0.0	10.7
			Botanical garden/ arboretum rating	3	4	National Park rating	2	3

Arts & Culture
Score: 52.7
Rank: 176

MEDIA & LIBRARIES	AREA	U.S. AVG	PERFORMING ARTS	AREA	U.S. AVG	MUSEUMS	AREA	U.S. AVG
Arts radio rating	1	3	Classical music rating	5	4	Overall museum rating	6	5
No. public libraries	5	27	Ballet/dance rating	3	3	Art museum rating	3	5
Library volumes per capita	1.06	2.78	Professional theater rating	1	3	Science museum rating	1	5
			University arts programs rating	8	5	Children's museum rating	3	3

Cleveland–Elyria–Mentor, OH

Score: 44.7   Rank: 285   2004 rank: 264

Profile: Large city complex
Location: Northeast Ohio along Lake Erie
Elevation: 806 feet
Time zone: Eastern Standard Time

PRO
Arts and culture
Revitalized downtown
Attractive neighborhoods

CON
Industrial areas
Economic cycles
Cloudy, wet climate

Cleveland is a major industrial city and gateway with a storied past and an improving future. The city's industrial heritage is notable, with steel mills and shipping facilities along the waterfront and in the Cuyahoga River valley to the south. A number of factors—the decline of core industries in the '60s and '70s, the decay of the inner city, and pollution problems that culminated in the ignition of the river into a fiery inferno—gave the city a black eye from which it is still recovering, and the local nickname "Mistake on the Lake." A massive urban renewal program has cleaned up some of the industrial zones, created the entertainment-oriented "Flats" waterfront section, and brought new sports stadiums into the city. The spruced-up downtown has become a more attractive commercial center, although it's still not among the best. Some inner neighborhoods, particularly east, have begun to gentrify and

attract new business, but this is by no means universal. The I. M. Pei–designed Rock and Roll Hall of Fame and Museum is a major draw and cultural icon, and local sports enthusiasm is strong. There are a number of other nationally recognized amenities, some brought by strong and generous endowments funded by its industrial past. Healthcare facilities are nationally recognized, led by the Cleveland Clinic, and there is an emerging biotech and medical research industry. The Cleveland Symphony Orchestra is world class and is considered one of the "Big 5" orchestras in the U.S.

Like many large cities in the Rust Belt, Cleveland is a city of neighborhoods, with plain, working-class neighborhoods to the south and west and a mix of more affluent areas to the east and southeast, notably Shaker Heights, University Heights, and Chagrin Falls. The University

Circle area around Case Western Reserve University just east of town is noted for museums and cultural amenities. Some of these better residential areas offer fine homes on large, wooded lots for reasonable prices. Elyria is a middle-class suburb on the west side, while Mentor, middle class with more upscale areas near the lake and a strong commercial/retail presence, stretches along Lake Erie some 25 miles east of downtown. Good neighborhoods surround both, including the aptly if not creatively named Westlake on the west side near Elyria and Eastlake near Mentor.

With all of its efforts, Cleveland still has some troubled areas, with poverty, unemployment, low educational attainment, and some public school problems. Some areas of the city are quite unattractive, and the city still has a bit of an inferiority complex and image problem. Ask someone where they're from, and they're likely to say "Shaker Heights," "Elyria," "Parma," "Westlake," and not "Cleveland." That said, and perhaps for the same reasons, many are very loyal to their city and will evangelize at any opportunity. But the city's grimy past and rough winters trade off against numerous entertainment options and housing values continue to be a well-kept secret. For those willing to deal with the negatives and take a chance on an area with promise, the ranking may understate reality.

Cleveland has 31 miles of Lake Erie frontage. The surrounding terrain is generally level except for an abrupt ridge on the eastern edge of the city rising some 500 feet above the shore. The Cuyahoga River, which flows through a rather deep but narrow north-south valley, bisects the city. West to northerly winds blowing off Lake Erie moderate summer and winter temperatures. Summers are warm and humid with occasional days above 90°F. Winters are cold and cloudy with an average of 5 days below 0°F. Lake snow squalls can drop significant snowfall, particularly in the eastern half of the city. First freeze is early October; last is late April.

DEMOGRAPHICS	AREA	U.S. AVG	ETHNIC COMPOSITION	AREA	U.S. AVG	RESIDENT PROFILE	AREA	U.S. AVG
Population	2,136,729		White	75.3%	79.0%	Single	35.5%	32.4%
Population density per sq. mile	1066.0	358.5	Black	19.4%	10.5%	Married	50.5%	52.7%
Population growth	2.7%	21.1%	Asian	1.8%	2.7%	Divorced/separated	14.0%	14.9%
Median age	38.6	36.1	Hispanic	3.6%	10.6%	Married with children	21.1%	23.7%
Percent Democrat	60.1%	44.5%	Religious observance	53.7%	48.9%	Single with children	9.3%	9.1%
Percent Republican	39.4%	54.5%	Diversity measure	40.5	40.1	Percent over age 65	14.6%	12.9%

Score: 7.8
Rank: 344

INCOME	AREA	U.S. AVG	EMPLOYMENT	AREA	U.S. AVG	EMPLOYING INDUSTRIES	AREA	U.S. AVG
Per capita income	$25,506	$23,235	Unemployment rate	5.8%	4.7%	Largest: Healthcare & Social Assistance		
Household income	$48,077	$46,414	Recent job growth	-0.7%	1.3%			
Household income < $25K	24.7%	26.2%	Projected future job growth	0.3%	11.5%	Percent manufacturing	15.9%	15.4%
Household income > $75K	27.8%	25.4%	White collar	61.7%	57.8%	Percent public sector	11.9%	15.7%
Household income growth	11.2%	13.6%	Blue collar	23.8%	25.2%	Percent construction	7.9%	9.9%

Score: 23.3
Rank: 286

INDEXES & TAXES	AREA	U.S. AVG	HOUSING	AREA	U.S. AVG	NECESSITIES	AREA	U.S. AVG
Cost of Living Index	89.5	100.0	Median home price	$139,000	$220,000	Food Index	106.3	100.0
Buying Power Index	120.4	100.0	Home price appreciation	18.6%	10.1%	Housing Index	62.8	100.0
Income tax rate	6.99%	4.70%	Median rent	$702	$709	Utilities Index	126.2	100.0
Sales tax rate	7.53%	6.58%	Homes owned	64.9%	62.3%	Transportation Index	104.0	100.0
Property tax rate	$14.68	$12.00	Home price ratio	2.9	4.2	Healthcare Index	110.4	100.0
						Miscellaneous Cost Index	99.7	100.0

Score: 12.0
Rank: 328

TEMPERATURE	AREA	U.S. AVG	PRECIPITATION	AREA	U.S. AVG	COMFORTS & HAZARDS	AREA	U.S. AVG
Average January low	20.3	26.2	Annual inches precipitation	35.0	37.7	July relative humidity	72%	66%
July high	81.6	87.4	Annual inches snowfall	52.0	7.0	Annual days mostly sunny	168	208
Annual days > 90°F	8	38	Annual days precipitation	156	109	Annual days with thunderstorms	36	39
Annual days < 32°F	125	89	Annual days rain > 0.5 inches	21	22	Tornado risk score	14	18
Annual days < 0°F	5	6	Annual days snow > 1.5 inches	13	6	Hurricane risk score	2	13

TEMPERATURE

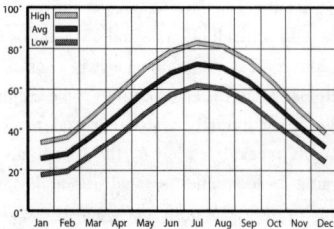

PRECIPITATION

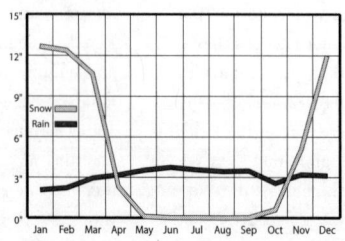

DAYS OF CLOUDS & PRECIPITATION

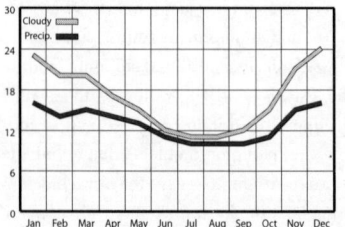

Education Score: 64.7 Rank: 133	ACHIEVEMENT	AREA	U.S. AVG	PUBLIC SCHOOLS	AREA	U.S. AVG	HIGHER EDUCATION	AREA	U.S. AVG
	High school degree	83.2%	82.7%	Expenditures per pupil	$6,605	$5,686	No. 2-year colleges	18	4
	2-year college degree	5.8%	6.4%	Student/teacher ratio	17.0	16.7	No. 4-year colleges/universities	19	6
	4-year college degree	15.3%	15.7%	Attending public school	83.9%	90.1%	No. highly ranked universities	2	1
	Graduate/professional degree	8.7%	8.9%	State SAT score	1079	1021			
				State ACT score	21.5*	20.9			

Health & Healthcare Score: 18.4 Rank: 304	HAZARDS & ILLNESSES	AREA	U.S. AVG	HEALTHCARE	AREA	U.S. AVG	CRIME Score: 47.6 Rank: 194	AREA	U.S. AVG
	Air-quality score	18	37	Physicians per capita	362.2	244.2	Violent crime rate	393.5	465.5
	Water-quality score	31	52	Hospital beds per capita	469.2	420.0	Change in violent crime rate	8.5%	-2.2%
	Pollen/allergy score	64	61	No. teaching hospitals	18	3	Property crime rate	3,437.7	3,517.1
	Cancer mortality per capita	226.0	201.9	Cost per doctor visit	$78	$77	Change in property crime rate	4.9%	-2.1%
	Depression days per month	3.7	3.5	Cost per dental visit	$68	$70			
	Stress score	72	50						

Transportation Score: 30.5 Rank: 259	COMMUTE	AREA	U.S. AVG	INTERCITY SERVICES	AREA	U.S. AVG	AUTOMOTIVE	AREA	U.S. AVG
	Average commute time	26.3	27.4	Major airports within 60 miles	1	1	Insurance, annual premium	$1,874	$1,432
	Percent commutes > 60 mins.	4.6%	5.9%	Size of regional airport	Medium	Large	Gas, cost per gallon	$2.46	$2.49
	Commute by auto	81.4%	78.9%	Daily airline activity	487	686	Daily vehicle miles per capita	21.7	24.0
	Commute by mass transit	4.2%	1.9%	Amtrak service	Yes	No			
	Work at home	2.7%	3.1%						
	Mass transit miles per capita	4.18	1.87						

Leisure Score: 86.1 Rank: 52	DINING & SHOPPING	AREA	U.S. AVG	ENTERTAINMENT	AREA	U.S. AVG	OUTDOOR ACTIVITIES	AREA	U.S. AVG
	Restaurant rating	3	2	Professional sports rating	8	4	Golf-course rating	10	4
	Outlet mall score	5	42	College sports rating	3	4	Ski-area rating	3	3
	No. Starbucks	32	13	Zoo/aquarium rating	8	3	Sq. miles inland water	2	4
	No. warehouse clubs	11	2	Amusement park rating	7	3	Miles of coastline	56.5	10.7
				Botanical garden/ arboretum rating	9	4	National Park rating	2	3

Arts & Culture Score: 98.7 Rank: 6	MEDIA & LIBRARIES	AREA	U.S. AVG	PERFORMING ARTS	AREA	U.S. AVG	MUSEUMS	AREA	U.S. AVG
	Arts radio rating	8	3	Classical music rating	10	4	Overall museum rating	10	5
	No. public libraries	110	27	Ballet/dance rating	8	3	Art museum rating	9	5
	Library volumes per capita	5.99	2.78	Professional theater rating	10	3	Science museum rating	9	5
				University arts programs rating	9	5	Children's museum rating	5	3

Coeur d'Alene, ID

Score: 76.2   Rank: 61   2004 rank: not ranked

Profile: Small resort town
Location: Northern Idaho, 25 miles east of Spokane, Washington
Elevation: 2,181 feet
Time zone: Pacific Standard Time

PRO	CON
Attractive setting	Crowding and sprawl
Nearby recreation	Cold winters
Close to Spokane	Low ethnic diversity

Coeur d'Alene, perched in a beautiful lakefront mountain setting, is becoming a favorite destination for retirees and many others fleeing other urban areas, especially on the Pacific Coast. There is plenty to do and the summer climate is particularly pleasant and fresh. Downtown is clean and vibrant but, save for the setting, not that interesting. Most residential and commercial areas spread into the relatively flat landscape to the north. Spokane to the west is close enough to provide amenities and services plus employment for those who need it. But there is plenty to do locally, with numerous recreation, entertainment, and minor arts amenities. The local construction boom, tourism, and some light commercial activity round out a healthy economic climate.

The 15-year growth rate of 74.5% should raise eyebrows—growth and crowding are having an impact on the area.

Coeur d'Alene sits on a small spit at the north end of a large lake of the same name. The setting is decidedly attractive, with lake views on three sides of downtown and mountains on all sides looking south. The high altitude and northern latitude keep the area green and lush most of the year. That latitude, and the open northern exposure, bring occasionally harsh winter weather, but the climate is more often influenced by moderate air flows from the Pacific to the west. Summers are sunny, dry, and nice.

Population

DEMOGRAPHICS	AREA	U.S. AVG	ETHNIC COMPOSITION	AREA	U.S. AVG	RESIDENT PROFILE	AREA	U.S. AVG
Population	121,824		White	95.3%	79.0%	Single	25.5%	32.4%
Population density per sq. mile	97.8	358.5	Black	0.3%	10.5%	Married	59.6%	52.7%
Population growth	74.5%	21.1%	Asian	0.7%	2.7%	Divorced/separated	15.0%	14.9%
Median age	37.0	36.1	Hispanic	2.7%	10.6%	Married with children	26.0%	23.7%
Percent Democrat	32.2%	44.5%	Religious observance	32.0%	48.9%	Single with children	8.9%	9.1%
Percent Republican	66.2%	54.5%	Diversity measure	14.1	40.1	Percent over age 65	13.1%	12.9%

Economy & Jobs

Score: 99.7
Rank: 2

INCOME	AREA	U.S. AVG	EMPLOYMENT	AREA	U.S. AVG	EMPLOYING INDUSTRIES	AREA	U.S. AVG
Per capita income	$20,566	$23,235	Unemployment rate	3.6%	4.7%	Largest: Healthcare & Social Assistance		
Household income	$43,004	$46,414	Recent job growth	9.2%	1.3%			
Household income < $25K	25.8%	26.2%	Projected future job growth	45.6%	11.5%	Percent manufacturing	13.6%	15.4%
Household income > $75K	20.0%	25.4%	White collar	55.3%	57.8%	Percent public sector	13.1%	15.7%
Household income growth	13.9%	13.6%	Blue collar	26.8%	25.2%	Percent construction	13.2%	9.9%

Cost of Living

Score: 29.9
Rank: 262

INDEXES & TAXES	AREA	U.S. AVG	HOUSING	AREA	U.S. AVG	NECESSITIES	AREA	U.S. AVG
Cost of Living Index	112.6	100.0	Median home price	$293,000	$220,000	Food Index	105.6	100.0
Buying Power Index	85.6	100.0	Home price appreciation	80.5%	10.1%	Housing Index	73.9	100.0
Income tax rate	8.20%	4.70%	Median rent	$646	$709	Utilities Index	75.3	100.0
Sales tax rate	6.50%	6.58%	Homes owned	66.6%	62.3%	Transportation Index	102.5	100.0
Property tax rate	$9.84	$12.00	Home price ratio	6.8	4.2	Healthcare Index	118.6	100.0
						Miscellaneous Cost Index	106.6	100.0

Climate

Score: 65.5
Rank: 128

TEMPERATURE	AREA	U.S. AVG	PRECIPITATION	AREA	U.S. AVG	COMFORTS & HAZARDS	AREA	U.S. AVG
Average January low	20.0	26.2	Annual inches precipitation	17.0	37.7	July relative humidity	31%	66%
July high	83.0	87.4	Annual inches snowfall	51.0	7.0	Annual days mostly sunny	176	208
Annual days > 90°F	18	38	Annual days precipitation	113	109	Annual days with thunderstorms	11	39
Annual days < 32°F	140	89	Annual days rain > 0.5 inches	7	22	Tornado risk score	1	18
Annual days < 0°F	10	6	Annual days snow > 1.5 inches	13	6	Hurricane risk score	0	13

TEMPERATURE

PRECIPITATION

DAYS OF CLOUDS & PRECIPITATION

Education

Score: 47.6
Rank: 197

ACHIEVEMENT	AREA	U.S. AVG	PUBLIC SCHOOLS	AREA	U.S. AVG	HIGHER EDUCATION	AREA	U.S. AVG
High school degree	87.4%	82.7%	Expenditures per pupil	$4,607	$5,686	No. 2-year colleges	2	4
2-year college degree	8.4%	6.4%	Student/teacher ratio	18.7	16.7	No. 4-year colleges/universities	0	6
4-year college degree	13.1%	15.7%	Attending public school	93.2%	90.1%	No. highly ranked universities	0	1
Graduate/professional degree	6.0%	8.9%	State SAT score	1088	1021			
			State ACT score	21.4*	20.9			

Health & Healthcare

Score: 22.7
Rank: 288

HAZARDS & ILLNESSES	AREA	U.S. AVG	HEALTHCARE	AREA	U.S. AVG	CRIME	AREA	U.S. AVG
Air-quality score	27	37	Physicians per capita	183.0	244.2	Violent crime rate	324.3	465.5
Water-quality score	48	52	Hospital beds per capita	244.6	420.0	Change in violent crime rate	17.0%	-2.2%
Pollen/allergy score	42	61	No. teaching hospitals	0	3	Property crime rate	3,385.7	3,517.1
Cancer mortality per capita	186.0	201.9	Cost per doctor visit	$72	$77	Change in property crime rate	-3.1%	-2.1%
Depression days per month	3.4	3.5	Cost per dental visit	$71	$70			
Stress score	39	50						

Crime Score: 71.7
Rank: 107

Transportation

Score: 26.5
Rank: 276

COMMUTE	AREA	U.S. AVG	INTERCITY SERVICES	AREA	U.S. AVG	AUTOMOTIVE	AREA	U.S. AVG
Average commute time	23.2	27.4	Major airports within 60 miles	1	1	Insurance, annual premium	$966	$1,432
Percent commutes > 60 mins.	4.8%	5.9%	Size of regional airport	Medium	Large	Gas, cost per gallon	$2.39	$2.49
Commute by auto	81.2%	78.9%	Daily airline activity	115	686	Daily vehicle miles per capita	16.0	24.0
Commute by mass transit	0.2%	1.9%	Amtrak service	No	No			
Work at home	4.3%	3.1%						
Mass transit miles per capita	0.23	1.87						

DINING & SHOPPING	AREA	U.S. AVG	ENTERTAINMENT	AREA	U.S. AVG	OUTDOOR ACTIVITIES	AREA	U.S. AVG
Restaurant rating	1	2	Professional sports rating	1	4	Golf-course rating	6	4
Outlet mall score	18	42	College sports rating	1	4	Ski-area rating	9	3
No. Starbucks	4	13	Zoo/aquarium rating	1	3	Sq. miles inland water	6	4
No. warehouse clubs	0	2	Amusement park rating	1	3	Miles of coastline	0.0	10.7
			Botanical garden/ arboretum rating	1	4	National Park rating	8	3

Leisure
Score: 65.5
Rank: 129

MEDIA & LIBRARIES	AREA	U.S. AVG	PERFORMING ARTS	AREA	U.S. AVG	MUSEUMS	AREA	U.S. AVG
Arts radio rating	1	3	Classical music rating	2	4	Overall museum rating	2	5
No. public libraries	8	27	Ballet/dance rating	1	3	Art museum rating	1	5
Library volumes per capita	2.07	2.78	Professional theater rating	2	3	Science museum rating	1	5
			University arts programs rating	1	5	Children's museum rating	1	3

Arts & Culture
Score: 5.1
Rank: 353

College Station–Bryan, TX

Score: 60.4   Rank: 175   2004 rank: 14

Profile: College town/small-town complex
Location: Southeast Texas halfway between Dallas and Houston
Elevation: 387 feet
Time zone: Central Standard Time

PRO	CON
College-town amenities	Summer heat
Educated population	Isolation
Cost of living	Crime rates

Bryan's town slogan, "The good life, Texas style," adopted in 2004, is apt for this typical and not-so-typical small-town pair. Bryan, a center for agriculture and light industry, is an average-size town with a revitalized core and some historic interest. Bryan has grown together with the more notable College Station, home to Texas A&M University, the fourth-largest university in the country with 45,000 students. As an A&M university, the school doesn't bring the assortment of arts and cultural amenities one finds in some college towns, but the sports teams are popular and there is an active entertainment scene. Cultural and service amenities can be found in Austin, although it is a difficult 100-mile drive. The town has a few historic districts, a more attractive setting, and more outdoor recreation opportunities than most Texas towns. Not surprisingly, educational attainment is high. Like most Texas towns—maybe more than most—the area has a good balance of features, with a low cost of living, very affordable housing, a strong economy, a pleasant small-town feel, and plenty to do. While crime rates aren't astronomical, they have become high enough to knock the area off its high perch from the 2004 edition, and the average July temperature of 99°F doesn't help.

The area contains level to gently rolling land with mixed agriculture and wooded areas. The Sam Houston National Forest begins about 30 miles east. The area endures warm to very hot summers, high humidity, and generally warm evenings. Winters are mild, but cold spells can drop temperatures below freezing at night. Most precipitation falls as rain and thunderstorms mainly in spring and early fall. Infrequent snowfall does occur.

DEMOGRAPHICS	AREA	U.S. AVG	ETHNIC COMPOSITION	AREA	U.S. AVG	RESIDENT PROFILE	AREA	U.S. AVG
Population	200,336		White	72.9%	79.0%	Single	43.8%	32.4%
Population density per sq. mile	95.1	358.5	Black	12.0%	10.5%	Married	42.6%	52.7%
Population growth	33.4%	21.1%	Asian	3.3%	2.7%	Divorced/separated	13.6%	14.9%
Median age	28.5	36.1	Hispanic	19.2%	10.6%	Married with children	21.0%	23.7%
Percent Democrat	31.2%	44.5%	Religious observance	50.3%	48.9%	Single with children	7.5%	9.1%
Percent Republican	67.8%	54.5%	Diversity measure	61.5	40.1	Percent over age 65	8.6%	12.9%

Population

INCOME	AREA	U.S. AVG	EMPLOYMENT	AREA	U.S. AVG	EMPLOYING INDUSTRIES	AREA	U.S. AVG
Per capita income	$18,717	$23,235	Unemployment rate	3.9%	4.7%	Largest: Healthcare & Social Assistance		
Household income	$33,504	$46,414	Recent job growth	3.6%	1.3%			
Household income < $25K	40.2%	26.2%	Projected future job growth	15.1%	11.5%	Percent manufacturing	10.8%	15.4%
Household income > $75K	19.9%	25.4%	White collar	61.8%	57.8%	Percent public sector	30.0%	15.7%
Household income growth	13.8%	13.6%	Blue collar	20.5%	25.2%	Percent construction	9.7%	9.9%

Economy & Jobs
Score: 79.9
Rank: 76

INDEXES & TAXES	AREA	U.S. AVG	HOUSING	AREA	U.S. AVG	NECESSITIES	AREA	U.S. AVG
Cost of Living Index	85.0	100.0	Median home price	$168,200	$220,000	Food Index	84.9	100.0
Buying Power Index	88.3	100.0	Home price appreciation	22.2%	10.1%	Housing Index	46.9	100.0
Income tax rate	0.00%	4.70%	Median rent	$714	$709	Utilities Index	86.2	100.0
Sales tax rate	8.25%	6.58%	Homes owned	46.5%	62.3%	Transportation Index	94.0	100.0
Property tax rate	$16.10	$12.00	Home price ratio	5.0	4.2	Healthcare Index	92.0	100.0
						Miscellaneous Cost Index	91.6	100.0

Cost of Living
Score: 93.0
Rank: 27

Climate

Score: 69.5
Rank: 113

TEMPERATURE	AREA	U.S AVG
Average January low	29.4	26.2
July high	99.2	87.4
Annual days > 90°F	106	38
Annual days < 32°F	70	89
Annual days < 0°F	0	6

PRECIPITATION	AREA	U.S AVG
Annual inches precipitation	25.0	37.7
Annual inches snowfall	1.5	7.0
Annual days precipitation	78	109
Annual days rain > 0.5 inches	16	22
Annual days snow > 1.5 inches	1	6

COMFORTS & HAZARDS	AREA	U.S AVG
July relative humidity	67%	66%
Annual days mostly sunny	231	208
Annual days with thunderstorms	49	39
Tornado risk score	9	18
Hurricane risk score	34	13

TEMPERATURE

PRECIPITATION

DAYS OF CLOUDS & PRECIPITATION

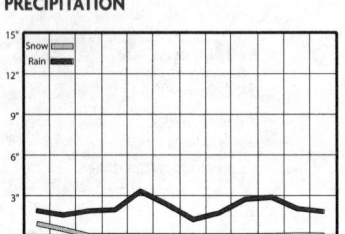

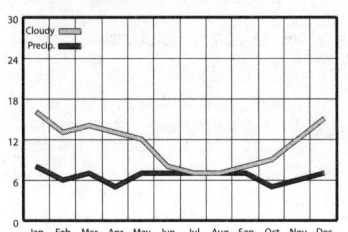

Education

Score: 79.9
Rank: 76

ACHIEVEMENT	AREA	U.S. AVG
High school degree	80.3%	82.7%
2-year college degree	4.6%	6.4%
4-year college degree	18.7%	15.7%
Graduate/professional degree	15.5%	8.9%

PUBLIC SCHOOLS	AREA	U.S. AVG
Expenditures per pupil	$5,422	$5,686
Student/teacher ratio	13.2	16.7
Attending public school	96.0%	90.1%
State SAT score	997*	1021
State ACT score	20.3	20.9

HIGHER EDUCATION	AREA	U.S. AVG
No. 2-year colleges	0	4
No. 4-year colleges/universities	2	6
No. highly ranked universities	1	1

Health & Healthcare

Score: 74.6
Rank: 96

Crime

Score: 19.3
Rank: 302

HAZARDS & ILLNESSES	AREA	U.S. AVG
Air-quality score	49	37
Water-quality score	99	52
Pollen/allergy score	75	61
Cancer mortality per capita	158.7	201.9
Depression days per month	3.6	3.5
Stress score	11	50

HEALTHCARE	AREA	U.S. AVG
Physicians per capita	195.6	244.2
Hospital beds per capita	245.6	420.0
No. teaching hospitals	2	3
Cost per doctor visit	$63	$77
Cost per dental visit	$60	$70

CRIME	AREA	U.S. AVG
Violent crime rate	508.3	465.5
Change in violent crime rate	-8.2%	-2.2%
Property crime rate	4,597.5	3,517.1
Change in property crime rate	-0.9%	-2.1%

Transportation

Score: 94.4
Rank: 22

COMMUTE	AREA	U.S. AVG
Average commute time	20.5	27.4
Percent commutes > 60 mins.	4.3%	5.9%
Commute by auto	76.8%	78.9%
Commute by mass transit	0.8%	1.9%
Work at home	2.7%	3.1%
Mass transit miles per capita	0.76	1.87

INTERCITY SERVICES	AREA	U.S. AVG
Major airports within 60 miles	3	1
Size of regional airport	Large	Large
Daily airline activity	1146	686
Amtrak service	No	No

AUTOMOTIVE	AREA	U.S. AVG
Insurance, annual premium	$1,087	$1,432
Gas, cost per gallon	$2.44	$2.49
Daily vehicle miles per capita	25.0	24.0

Leisure

Score: 12.8
Rank: 325

DINING & SHOPPING	AREA	U.S. AVG
Restaurant rating	1	2
Outlet mall score	0	42
No. Starbucks	2	13
No. warehouse clubs	0	2

ENTERTAINMENT	AREA	U.S. AVG
Professional sports rating	2	4
College sports rating	6	4
Zoo/aquarium rating	1	3
Amusement park rating	1	3
Botanical garden/ arboretum rating	1	4

OUTDOOR ACTIVITIES	AREA	U.S. AVG
Golf-course rating	1	4
Ski-area rating	1	3
Sq. miles inland water	2	4
Miles of coastline	0.0	10.7
National Park rating	1	3

Arts & Culture

Score: 27.5
Rank: 271

MEDIA & LIBRARIES	AREA	U.S. AVG
Arts radio rating	1	3
No. public libraries	5	27
Library volumes per capita	1.64	2.78

PERFORMING ARTS	AREA	U.S. AVG
Classical music rating	3	4
Ballet/dance rating	1	3
Professional theater rating	1	3
University arts programs rating	5	5

MUSEUMS	AREA	U.S. AVG
Overall museum rating	5	5
Art museum rating	5	5
Science museum rating	4	5
Children's museum rating	3	3

Colorado Springs, CO

Score: 93.9   **Rank:** 4   **2004 rank:** 18

Profile: Mid-size city
Location: Central Colorado at the base of the Front Range, 65 miles south of Denver
Elevation: 6,170 feet
Time zone: Mountain Standard Time

PRO	CON
Attractive setting	Growth and sprawl
Summer climate	Economic cycles
Educational attainment	Crime rates

Once known as a resort city, "The Springs" has a strong military presence and a growing commercial economy led by varying components of the high-tech industry. Several military installations, including the U.S. Air Force Academy and the Space Command, are located within or near the city. The surrounding prairie provides grazing land for cattle and sheep. Summer weather is notably pleasant and dry, with only 15 days above 90°F. The Rockies to the west and Denver to the north provide a broad range of outdoor recreation and other entertainment. The area has seen—and has been strained by—a dramatic population growth over the last 30 years. Some of the accompanying physical and infrastructure growth, especially in its suburbs mainly to the north, is unattractive in contrast with the existing landscape. The influx has also brought some crime problems. Employment growth slowed, in part due to the downturn in the high-tech industry, but seems on an uptrend once again. The climate and physical setting are nice, there is plenty to do, and it is an attractive place to live overall with few major negatives, hence the rank of 4.

Colorado Springs is located in relatively flat semiarid country on the eastern slope of the Rocky Mountains. Immediately to the west the mountains rise abruptly to heights ranging from 10,000 feet to 14,000 feet. Rolling prairie lies to the east. Uncomfortable extremes in summer and winter are rare and of short duration. Precipitation is relatively sparse, with more than 80% falling between April and September mostly as thunderstorms. Humidity is low and it can be windy. First freeze is early October; last is early May.

Population

DEMOGRAPHICS	AREA	U.S. AVG	ETHNIC COMPOSITION	AREA	U.S. AVG	RESIDENT PROFILE	AREA	U.S. AVG
Population	581,424		White	80.1%	79.0%	Single	27.5%	32.4%
Population density per sq. mile	216.7	358.5	Black	6.5%	10.5%	Married	58.0%	52.7%
Population growth	42.3%	21.1%	Asian	3.0%	2.7%	Divorced/separated	14.5%	14.9%
Median age	34.0	36.1	Hispanic	11.8%	10.6%	Married with children	28.3%	23.7%
Percent Democrat	32.0%	44.5%	Religious observance	36.6%	48.9%	Single with children	8.5%	9.1%
Percent Republican	66.8%	54.5%	Diversity measure	48.2	40.1	Percent over age 65	9.0%	12.9%

Economy & Jobs
Score: 63.4
Rank: 138

INCOME	AREA	U.S. AVG	EMPLOYMENT	AREA	U.S. AVG	EMPLOYING INDUSTRIES	AREA	U.S. AVG
Per capita income	$25,783	$23,235	Unemployment rate	5.5%	4.7%	Largest: Professional, Scientific & Technical Services		
Household income	$54,433	$46,414	Recent job growth	1.5%	1.3%			
Household income < $25K	18.1%	26.2%	Projected future job growth	17.2%	11.5%	Percent manufacturing	10.3%	15.4%
Household income > $75K	31.6%	25.4%	White collar	65.6%	57.8%	Percent public sector	14.7%	15.7%
Household income growth	15.9%	13.6%	Blue collar	20.0%	25.2%	Percent construction	9.7%	9.9%

Cost of Living
Score: 36.9
Rank: 236

INDEXES & TAXES	AREA	U.S. AVG	HOUSING	AREA	U.S. AVG	NECESSITIES	AREA	U.S. AVG
Cost of Living Index	97.3	100.0	Median home price	$218,300	$220,000	Food Index	105.1	100.0
Buying Power Index	125.4	100.0	Home price appreciation	33.1%	10.1%	Housing Index	77.8	100.0
Income tax rate	5.00%	4.70%	Median rent	$789	$709	Utilities Index	83.1	100.0
Sales tax rate	6.42%	6.58%	Homes owned	63.5%	62.3%	Transportation Index	97.8	100.0
Property tax rate	$5.79	$12.00	Home price ratio	4.0	4.2	Healthcare Index	110.4	100.0
						Miscellaneous Cost Index	93.3	100.0

Climate
Score: 91.2
Rank: 34

TEMPERATURE	AREA	U.S. AVG	PRECIPITATION	AREA	U.S. AVG	COMFORTS & HAZARDS	AREA	U.S. AVG
Average January low	16.1	26.2	Annual inches precipitation	16.0	37.7	July relative humidity	49%	66%
Average July high	84.4	87.4	Annual inches snowfall	40.0	7.0	Annual days mostly sunny	249	208
Annual days > 90°F	15	38	Annual days precipitation	87	109	Annual days with thunderstorms	59	39
Annual days < 32°F	162	89	Annual days rain > 0.5 inches	8	22	Tornado risk score	18	18
Annual days < 0°F	7	6	Annual days snow > 1.5 inches	9	6	Hurricane risk score	0	13

TEMPERATURE

PRECIPITATION

DAYS OF CLOUDS & PRECIPITATION

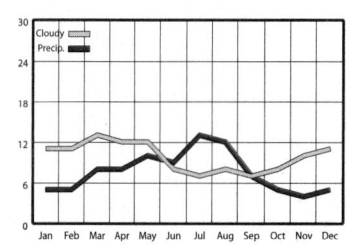

Education — Score: 94.9 Rank: 20

ACHIEVEMENT	AREA	U.S. AVG	PUBLIC SCHOOLS	AREA	U.S. AVG	HIGHER EDUCATION	AREA	U.S. AVG
High school degree	91.8%	82.7%	Expenditures per pupil	$5,188	$5,686	No. 2-year colleges	7	4
2-year college degree	9.6%	6.4%	Student/teacher ratio	16.3	16.7	No. 4-year colleges/universities	9	6
4-year college degree	20.7%	15.7%	Attending public school	93.7%	90.1%	No. highly ranked universities	2	1
Graduate/professional degree	11.8%	8.9%	State SAT score	1122	1021			
			State ACT score	20.3*	20.9			

Health & Healthcare — Score: 36.4 Rank: 237

HAZARDS & ILLNESSES	AREA	U.S. AVG	HEALTHCARE	AREA	U.S. AVG	CRIME	AREA	U.S. AVG
Air-quality score	28	37	Physicians per capita	196.0	244.2	Violent crime rate	477.5	465.5
Water-quality score	93	52	Hospital beds per capita	172.7	420.0	Change in violent crime rate	8.4%	-2.2%
Pollen/allergy score	64	61	No. teaching hospitals	1	3	Property crime rate	4,106.2	3,517.1
Cancer mortality per capita	143.8	201.9	Cost per doctor visit	$87	$77	Change in property crime rate	-3.1%	-2.1%
Depression days per month	3.3	3.5	Cost per dental visit	$75	$70			
Stress score	81	50						

Crime — Score: 35.8 Rank: 239

Transportation — Score: 64.2 Rank: 134

COMMUTE	AREA	U.S. AVG	INTERCITY SERVICES	AREA	U.S. AVG	AUTOMOTIVE	AREA	U.S. AVG
Average commute time	24.8	27.4	Major airports within 60 miles	2	1	Insurance, annual premium	$1,634	$1,432
Percent commutes > 60 mins.	5.2%	5.9%	Size of regional airport	Large	Large	Gas, cost per gallon	$2.48	$2.49
Commute by auto	78.4%	78.9%	Daily airline activity	887	686	Daily vehicle miles per capita	21.8	24.0
Commute by mass transit	0.8%	1.9%	Amtrak service	No	No			
Work at home	4.3%	3.1%						
Mass transit miles per capita	0.82	1.87						

Leisure — Score: 69.8 Rank: 112

DINING & SHOPPING	AREA	U.S. AVG	ENTERTAINMENT	AREA	U.S. AVG	OUTDOOR ACTIVITIES	AREA	U.S. AVG
Restaurant rating	1	2	Professional sports rating	3	4	Golf-course rating	3	4
Outlet mall score	73	42	College sports rating	4	4	Ski-area rating	10	3
No. Starbucks	18	13	Zoo/aquarium rating	5	3	Sq. miles inland water	2	4
No. warehouse clubs	2	2	Amusement park rating	1	3	Miles of coastline	0.0	10.7
			Botanical garden/ arboretum rating	3	4	National Park rating	5	3

Arts & Culture — Score: 73.5 Rank: 99

MEDIA & LIBRARIES	AREA	U.S. AVG	PERFORMING ARTS	AREA	U.S. AVG	MUSEUMS	AREA	U.S. AVG
Arts radio rating	5	3	Classical music rating	6	4	Overall museum rating	8	5
No. public libraries	17	27	Ballet/dance rating	1	3	Art museum rating	7	5
Library volumes per capita	1.94	2.78	Professional theater rating	1	3	Science museum rating	7	5
			University arts programs rating	8	5	Children's museum rating	1	3

Columbia, MO

Score: 67.5 Rank: 115 2004 rank: 189

Profile: College town
Location: North-central Missouri midway between St. Louis and Kansas City
Elevation: 887 feet
Time zone: Central Standard Time

PRO
College-town amenities
Educational attainment
Cost of living

CON
Isolation
Hot, humid summers
Summer doldrums

Columbia is home to the University of Missouri and two smaller colleges. The area has a distinct college-town feel and most of the amenities that you would expect in a college town. Columbia also has an economic base in the insurance and medical-technology industries. The downtown is clean and lively, and the population is friendly and progressive; some say it is the Midwest with just a slight hint of the South. For a town with this profile, Columbia features a low cost of living and promising future job-growth projections. There are plenty of recreational opportunities on and off campus, including a large state-of-the-art water park, but some complain things get pretty slow (and hot and sticky) in summers when the students leave town.

The area consists of gently rolling and partially wooded plains at the edge of the broad Missouri River Valley. Summer are hot and humid; temperatures can reach 100°F. Early summer rain is frequent and sometimes heavy. Winter temperatures and conditions are variable, with occasional cold spells alternating with mild days with temperatures rising into the 60s. Temperatures below 0°F occur, but not every winter. Snow falls every winter but snow cover rarely persists more than 3 weeks. First freeze is mid-October; last is mid-April.

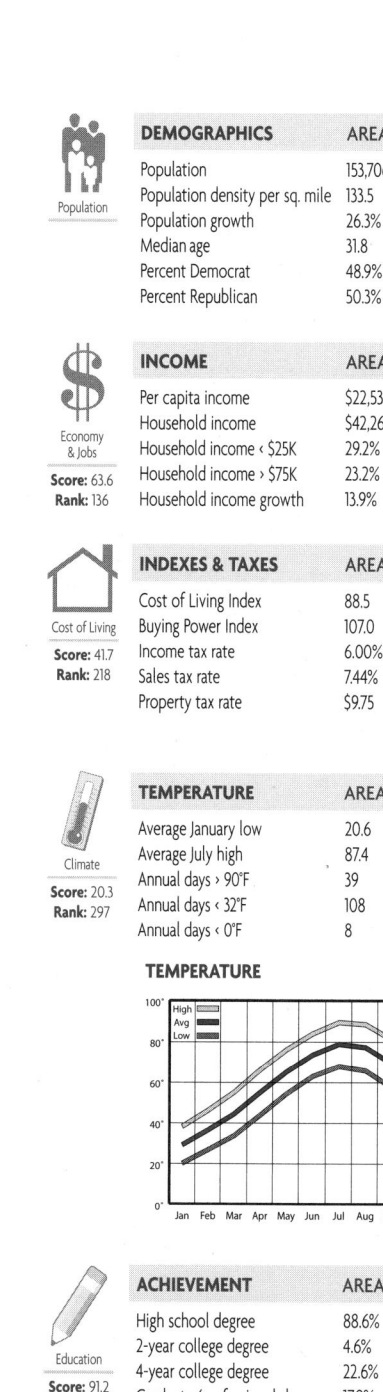

DEMOGRAPHICS	AREA	U.S. AVG
Population	153,706	
Population density per sq. mile	133.5	358.5
Population growth	26.3%	21.1%
Median age	31.8	36.1
Percent Democrat	48.9%	44.5%
Percent Republican	50.3%	54.5%

ETHNIC COMPOSITION	AREA	U.S. AVG
White	84.9%	79.0%
Black	8.5%	10.5%
Asian	3.3%	2.7%
Hispanic	1.9%	10.6%
Religious observance	41.7%	48.9%
Diversity measure	29.7	40.1

RESIDENT PROFILE	AREA	U.S. AVG
Single	39.6%	32.4%
Married	46.7%	52.7%
Divorced/separated	13.7%	14.9%
Married with children	21.5%	23.7%
Single with children	8.9%	9.1%
Percent over age 65	9.4%	12.9%

Economy & Jobs
Score: 63.6
Rank: 136

INCOME	AREA	U.S. AVG
Per capita income	$22,536	$23,235
Household income	$42,267	$46,414
Household income < $25K	29.2%	26.2%
Household income > $75K	23.2%	25.4%
Household income growth	13.9%	13.6%

EMPLOYMENT	AREA	U.S. AVG
Unemployment rate	3.9%	4.7%
Recent job growth	1.0%	1.3%
Projected future job growth	17.1%	11.5%
White collar	66.9%	57.8%
Blue collar	16.9%	25.2%

EMPLOYING INDUSTRIES	AREA	U.S. AVG
Largest: Healthcare & Social Assistance		
Percent manufacturing	9.9%	15.4%
Percent public sector	25.6%	15.7%
Percent construction	7.0%	9.9%

Cost of Living
Score: 41.7
Rank: 218

INDEXES & TAXES	AREA	U.S. AVG
Cost of Living Index	88.5	100.0
Buying Power Index	107.0	100.0
Income tax rate	6.00%	4.70%
Sales tax rate	7.44%	6.58%
Property tax rate	$9.75	$12.00

HOUSING	AREA	U.S. AVG
Median home price	$156,500	$220,000
Home price appreciation	29.1%	10.1%
Median rent	$582	$709
Homes owned	55.1%	62.3%
Home price ratio	3.7	4.2

NECESSITIES	AREA	U.S. AVG
Food Index	93.8	100.0
Housing Index	64.8	100.0
Utilities Index	93.5	100.0
Transportation Index	107.6	100.0
Healthcare Index	94.3	100.0
Miscellaneous Cost Index	100.5	100.0

Climate
Score: 20.3
Rank: 297

TEMPERATURE	AREA	U.S. AVG
Average January low	20.6	26.2
Average July high	87.4	87.4
Annual days > 90°F	39	38
Annual days < 32°F	108	89
Annual days < 0°F	8	6

PRECIPITATION	AREA	U.S. AVG
Annual inches precipitation	37.0	37.7
Annual inches snowfall	24.0	7.0
Annual days precipitation	109	109
Annual days rain > 0.5 inches	26	22
Annual days snow > 1.5 inches	6	6

COMFORTS & HAZARDS	AREA	U.S. AVG
July relative humidity	69%	66%
Annual days mostly sunny	191	208
Annual days with thunderstorms	51	39
Tornado risk score	22	18
Hurricane risk score	1	13

TEMPERATURE

PRECIPITATION

DAYS OF CLOUDS & PRECIPITATION

Education
Score: 91.2
Rank: 34

ACHIEVEMENT	AREA	U.S. AVG
High school degree	88.6%	82.7%
2-year college degree	4.6%	6.4%
4-year college degree	22.6%	15.7%
Graduate/professional degree	17.9%	8.9%

PUBLIC SCHOOLS	AREA	U.S. AVG
Expenditures per pupil	$4,661	$5,686
Student/teacher ratio	14.8	16.7
Attending public school	92.6%	90.1%
State SAT score	1178	1021
State ACT score	21.6*	20.9

HIGHER EDUCATION	AREA	U.S. AVG
No. 2-year colleges	0	4
No. 4-year colleges/universities	5	6
No. highly ranked universities	1	1

Health & Healthcare
Score: 98.9
Rank: 5

HAZARDS & ILLNESSES	AREA	U.S. AVG
Air-quality score	46	37
Water-quality score	60	52
Pollen/allergy score	55	61
Cancer mortality per capita	216.4	201.9
Depression days per month	2.7	3.5
Stress score	12	50

HEALTHCARE	AREA	U.S. AVG
Physicians per capita	702.5	244.2
Hospital beds per capita	789.2	420.0
No. teaching hospitals	2	3
Cost per doctor visit	$67	$77
Cost per dental visit	$59	$70

Crime
Score: 49.5
Rank: 190

CRIME	AREA	U.S. AVG
Violent crime rate	421.6	465.5
Change in violent crime rate	16.4%	-2.2%
Property crime rate	3,039.2	3,517.1
Change in property crime rate	3.6%	-2.1%

Transportation
Score: 44.1
Rank: 209

COMMUTE	AREA	U.S. AVG
Average commute time	20.2	27.4
Percent commutes > 60 mins.	2.7%	5.9%
Commute by auto	77.4%	78.9%
Commute by mass transit	0.6%	1.9%
Work at home	3.4%	3.1%
Mass transit miles per capita	0.64	1.87

INTERCITY SERVICES	AREA	U.S. AVG
Major airports within 60 miles	0	1
Size of regional airport	None	Large
Daily airline activity	12	686
Amtrak service	No	No

AUTOMOTIVE	AREA	U.S. AVG
Insurance, annual premium	$1,039	$1,432
Gas, cost per gallon	$2.33	$2.49
Daily vehicle miles per capita	23.8	24.0

Leisure	DINING & SHOPPING	AREA	U.S. AVG	ENTERTAINMENT	AREA	U.S. AVG	OUTDOOR ACTIVITIES	AREA	U.S. AVG
Score: 13.4	Restaurant rating	1	2	Professional sports rating	2	4	Golf-course rating	2	4
Rank: 323	Outlet mall score	0	42	College sports rating	5	4	Ski-area rating	1	3
	No. Starbucks	0	13	Zoo/aquarium rating	1	3	Sq. miles inland water	2	4
	No. warehouse clubs	1	2	Amusement park rating	1	3	Miles of coastline	0.0	10.7
				Botanical garden/ arboretum rating	1	4	National Park rating	1	3

Arts & Culture	MEDIA & LIBRARIES	AREA	U.S. AVG	PERFORMING ARTS	AREA	U.S. AVG	MUSEUMS	AREA	U.S. AVG
Score: 65.8	Arts radio rating	7	3	Classical music rating	3	4	Overall museum rating	2	5
Rank: 128	No. public libraries	5	27	Ballet/dance rating	1	3	Art museum rating	4	5
	Library volumes per capita	2.77	2.78	Professional theater rating	1	3	Science museum rating	4	5
				University arts programs rating	8	5	Children's museum rating	1	3

Columbia, SC

Score: 67.9   **Rank:** 110   **2004 Rank:** 50

Profile: College town/capital city
Location: Central South Carolina
Elevation: 225 feet
Time zone: Eastern Standard Time

PRO	CON
College-town amenities	Hot, humid summers
Historic interest	Air service
Cost of living	Crime rates

Columbia is the capital, the largest city, and the commercial, industrial, and educational hub for the state. The city is laid out in a traditional grid along the Congaree River with a number of historic buildings, although many of the older ones were destroyed in Sherman's famous march. Columbia is home to the University of South Carolina; the attractive and historic campus is in the south part of the downtown area and adds a dose of college-town feel, a few amenities, and sports-related entertainment. The downtown is clean and attractive, with entertainment near the campus and in a restored waterfront area. Beautiful older residential areas extend east with a clear antebellum imprint and good home values, but this isn't the part of town with the best reputation for education and safety. The best suburbs spread northwest towards Irmo and Lake Murray. The economy, while soft recently, is stable with a good future outlook. Cost of living at 84.7 is attractive, especially for what is available, and buying power is strong. While a bit far away for air service and other city amenities, Columbia does enjoy a good central location relative to Atlanta 200 miles west, Charleston and the coast 120 miles southeast, and the mountains northwest.

Columbia is located at a river confluence. Surrounding terrain is rolling and slopes gently from north to south. Long summers are prevalent with persistent warm and humid weather. Typically there are about 6 days over 100°F and midsummer thunderstorms are frequent. Fall is the most pleasant time of year, with relatively less rainfall and plenty of sun. Winters are mild, with occasional short cold outbreaks. Spring is variable, with occasional storms and cold snaps.

Population	DEMOGRAPHICS	AREA	U.S. AVG	ETHNIC COMPOSITION	AREA	U.S. AVG	RESIDENT PROFILE	AREA	U.S. AVG
	Population	683,285		White	61.2%	79.0%	Single	33.4%	32.4%
	Population density per sq. mile	184.6	358.5	Black	34.4%	10.5%	Married	50.1%	52.7%
	Population growth	25.4%	21.1%	Asian	1.5%	2.7%	Divorced/separated	16.4%	14.9%
	Median age	35.5	36.1	Hispanic	2.7%	10.6%	Married with children	22.8%	23.7%
	Percent Democrat	44.8%	44.5%	Religious observance	45.0%	48.9%	Single with children	10.4%	9.1%
	Percent Republican	54.2%	54.5%	Diversity measure	48.0	40.1	Percent over age 65	10.9%	12.9%

Economy & Jobs	INCOME	AREA	U.S. AVG	EMPLOYMENT	AREA	U.S. AVG	EMPLOYING INDUSTRIES	AREA	U.S. AVG
Score: 57.8	Per capita income	$23,405	$23,235	Unemployment rate	5.4%	4.7%	Largest: Healthcare & Social Assistance		
Rank: 159	Household income	$45,965	$46,414	Recent job growth	1.2%	1.3%			
	Household income < $25K	25.5%	26.2%	Projected future job growth	13.4%	11.5%	Percent manufacturing	13.4%	15.4%
	Household income > $75K	25.4%	25.4%	White collar	62.3%	57.8%	Percent public sector	21.6%	15.7%
	Household income growth	12.7%	13.6%	Blue collar	23.1%	25.2%	Percent construction	9.7%	9.9%

Cost of Living	INDEXES & TAXES	AREA	U.S. AVG	HOUSING	AREA	U.S. AVG	NECESSITIES	AREA	U.S. AVG
Score: 61.8	Cost of Living Index	84.7	100.0	Median home price	$145,100	$220,000	Food Index	101.3	100.0
Rank: 143	Buying Power Index	121.6	100.0	Home price appreciation	28.5%	10.1%	Housing Index	57.1	100.0
	Income tax rate	6.78%	4.70%	Median rent	$646	$709	Utilities Index	95.7	100.0
	Sales tax rate	5.45%	6.58%	Homes owned	64.5%	62.3%	Transportation Index	91.5	100.0
	Property tax rate	$7.64	$12.00	Home price ratio	3.2	4.2	Healthcare Index	93.1	100.0
							Miscellaneous Cost Index	96.5	100.0

Climate
Score: 34.8
Rank: 243

TEMPERATURE	AREA	U.S. AVG
Average January low	33.9	26.2
Average July high	92.0	87.4
Annual days > 90°F	64	38
Annual days < 32°F	60	89
Annual days < 0°F	0	6

PRECIPITATION	AREA	U.S. AVG
Annual inches precipitation	46.0	37.7
Annual inches snowfall	2.0	7.0
Annual days precipitation	111	109
Annual days rain > 0.5 inches	31	22
Annual days snow > 1.5 inches	1	6

COMFORTS & HAZARDS	AREA	U.S. AVG
July relative humidity	73%	66%
Annual days mostly sunny	223	208
Annual days with thunderstorms	54	39
Tornado risk score	24	18
Hurricane risk score	34	13

TEMPERATURE

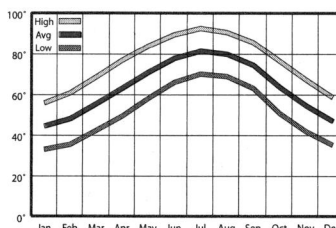

PRECIPITATION

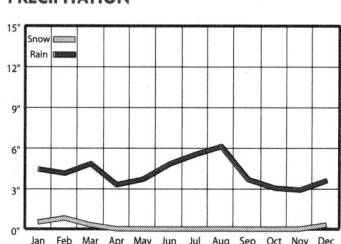

DAYS OF CLOUDS & PRECIPITATION

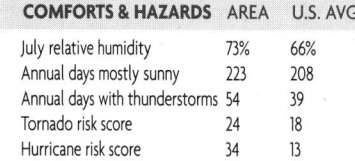

Education
Score: 66.3
Rank: 126

ACHIEVEMENT	AREA	U.S. AVG
High school degree	82.5%	82.7%
2-year college degree	7.5%	6.4%
4-year college degree	17.7%	15.7%
Graduate/professional degree	9.2%	8.9%

PUBLIC SCHOOLS	AREA	U.S. AVG
Expenditures per pupil	$5,572	$5,686
Student/teacher ratio	14.3	16.7
Attending public school	91.6%	90.1%
State SAT score	985*	1021
State ACT score	19.5	20.9

HIGHER EDUCATION	AREA	U.S. AVG
No. 2-year colleges	1	4
No. 4-year colleges/universities	7	6
No. highly ranked universities	0	1

Health & Healthcare
Score: 48.7
Rank: 193

HAZARDS & ILLNESSES	AREA	U.S. AVG
Air-quality score	32	37
Water-quality score	56	52
Pollen/allergy score	65	61
Cancer mortality per capita	207.4	201.9
Depression days per month	3.2	3.5
Stress score	85	50

HEALTHCARE	AREA	U.S. AVG
Physicians per capita	256.4	244.2
Hospital beds per capita	418.9	420.0
No. teaching hospitals	2	3
Cost per doctor visit	$75	$77
Cost per dental visit	$71	$70

Crime
Score: 12.3
Rank: 326

CRIME	AREA	U.S. AVG
Violent crime rate	725.9	465.5
Change in violent crime rate	-9.6%	-2.2%
Property crime rate	4,015.2	3,517.1
Change in property crime rate	-13.5%	-2.1%

Transportation
Score: 42.2
Rank: 216

COMMUTE	AREA	U.S. AVG
Average commute time	26.3	27.4
Percent commutes > 60 mins.	5.4%	5.9%
Commute by auto	79.3%	78.9%
Commute by mass transit	1.1%	1.9%
Work at home	2.3%	3.1%
Mass transit miles per capita	1.11	1.87

INTERCITY SERVICES	AREA	U.S. AVG
Major airports within 60 miles	1	1
Size of regional airport	Large	Large
Daily airline activity	871	686
Amtrak service	Yes	No

AUTOMOTIVE	AREA	U.S. AVG
Insurance, annual premium	$1,403	$1,432
Gas, cost per gallon	$2.38	$2.49
Daily vehicle miles per capita	23.8	24.0

Leisure
Score: 58.8
Rank: 154

DINING & SHOPPING	AREA	U.S. AVG
Restaurant rating	1	2
Outlet mall score	0	42
No. Starbucks	4	13
No. warehouse clubs	1	2

ENTERTAINMENT	AREA	U.S. AVG
Professional sports rating	3	4
College sports rating	6	4
Zoo/aquarium rating	7	3
Amusement park rating	1	3
Botanical garden/ arboretum rating	10	4

OUTDOOR ACTIVITIES	AREA	U.S. AVG
Golf-course rating	3	4
Ski-area rating	1	3
Sq. miles inland water	5	4
Miles of coastline	0.0	10.7
National Park rating	3	3

Arts & Culture
Score: 59.1
Rank: 153

MEDIA & LIBRARIES	AREA	U.S. AVG
Arts radio rating	1	3
No. public libraries	26	27
Library volumes per capita	3.02	2.78

PERFORMING ARTS	AREA	U.S. AVG
Classical music rating	3	4
Ballet/dance rating	3	3
Professional theater rating	1	3
University arts programs rating	8	5

MUSEUMS	AREA	U.S. AVG
Overall museum rating	8	5
Art museum rating	7	5
Science museum rating	8	5
Children's museum rating	5	3

Columbus, GA-AL

Score: 55.8   Rank: 214   2004 rank: 94

Profile: Small city/military town
Location: West-central Georgia on Georgia-Alabama border along Chattahoochee River
Elevation: 445 feet
Time zone: Eastern Standard Time

PRO	CON
Cost of living	Employment
Water recreation	Entertainment
Healthcare	Summer heat

Columbus, the third-largest city in Georgia, supports the large nearby Fort Benning Army base. The base occupies the better part of the county and dominates the economy and the local mindset. The area was once a textile producer but has modernized and diversified into financial services; headquarters for AFLAC (insurance) and Synovus, a regional banking conglomerate, are located here. Even with the transition, the employment picture is fairly bleak. The area has a number of museums, mostly of a military theme, and some historic interest and urban revitalization in this very Southern city, but there isn't a lot to do. Other services and amenities are available in Atlanta, 100 miles away.

The area is a mix of gently rolling, wooded hills and a level, open plain. Summers are warm and humid with most days in the 90s, a few into the 100s, and frequent thunderstorms. Occasional heavy rains originate from hurricanes in the Gulf of Mexico. Winters are mild with temperatures seldom below 20°F. Snow is rare. First freeze is early November; last is late March.

Population

DEMOGRAPHICS	AREA	U.S. AVG	ETHNIC COMPOSITION	AREA	U.S. AVG	RESIDENT PROFILE	AREA	U.S. AVG
Population	289,578		White	54.9%	79.0%	Single	35.3%	32.4%
Population density per sq. mile	149.5	358.5	Black	39.5%	10.5%	Married	47.2%	52.7%
Population growth	10.2%	21.1%	Asian	1.5%	2.7%	Divorced/separated	17.4%	14.9%
Median age	33.9	36.1	Hispanic	3.6%	10.6%	Married with children	23.7%	23.7%
Percent Democrat	48.3%	44.5%	Religious observance	44.0%	48.9%	Single with children	12.6%	9.1%
Percent Republican	51.2%	54.5%	Diversity measure	55.9	40.1	Percent over age 65	11.4%	12.9%

Economy & Jobs
Score: 9.9
Rank: 336

INCOME	AREA	U.S. AVG	EMPLOYMENT	AREA	U.S. AVG	EMPLOYING INDUSTRIES	AREA	U.S. AVG
Per capita income	$20,115	$23,235	Unemployment rate	6.9%	4.7%	Largest: Healthcare & Social Assistance		
Household income	$39,998	$46,414	Recent job growth	0.8%	1.3%			
Household income < $25K	31.1%	26.2%	Projected future job growth	5.6%	11.5%	Percent manufacturing	17.7%	15.4%
Household income > $75K	20.2%	25.4%	White collar	55.7%	57.8%	Percent public sector	18.8%	15.7%
Household income growth	14.9%	13.6%	Blue collar	28.0%	25.2%	Percent construction	10.3%	9.9%

Cost of Living
Score: 51.3
Rank: 180

INDEXES & TAXES	AREA	U.S. AVG	HOUSING	AREA	U.S. AVG	NECESSITIES	AREA	U.S. AVG
Cost of Living Index	83.6	100.0	Median home price	$136,200	$220,000	Food Index	98.5	100.0
Buying Power Index	107.2	100.0	Home price appreciation	31.8%	10.1%	Housing Index	58.8	100.0
Income tax rate	6.00%	4.70%	Median rent	$570	$709	Utilities Index	89.9	100.0
Sales tax rate	7.17%	6.58%	Homes owned	52.9%	62.3%	Transportation Index	99.2	100.0
Property tax rate	$7.97	$12.00	Home price ratio	3.4	4.2	Healthcare Index	94.0	100.0
						Miscellaneous Cost Index	99.0	100.0

Climate
Score: 47.6
Rank: 195

TEMPERATURE	AREA	U.S. AVG	PRECIPITATION	AREA	U.S. AVG	COMFORTS & HAZARDS	AREA	U.S. AVG
Average January low	35.9	26.2	Annual inches precipitation	51.0	37.7	July relative humidity	73%	66%
Average July high	90.8	87.4	Annual inches snowfall	0.5	7.0	Annual days mostly sunny	216	208
Annual days > 90°F	74	38	Annual days precipitation	111	109	Annual days with thunderstorms	58	39
Annual days < 32°F	46	89	Annual days rain > 0.5 inches	32	22	Tornado risk score	21	18
Annual days < 0°F	0	6	Annual days snow > 1.5 inches	0	6	Hurricane risk score	28	13

TEMPERATURE

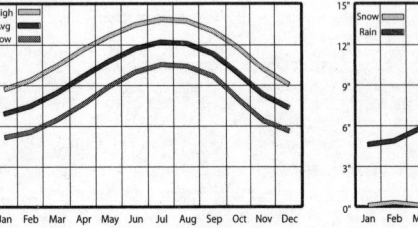

PRECIPITATION

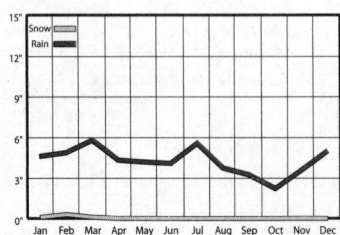

DAYS OF CLOUDS & PRECIPITATION

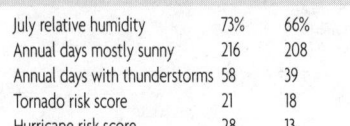
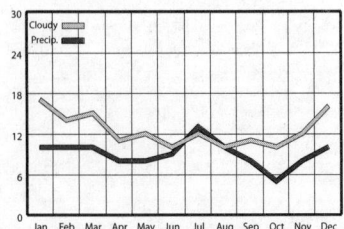

Education Score: 27.0 Rank: 274	ACHIEVEMENT	AREA	U.S. AVG	PUBLIC SCHOOLS	AREA	U.S. AVG	HIGHER EDUCATION	AREA	U.S. AVG
	High school degree	77.5%	82.7%	Expenditures per pupil	$5,157	$5,686	No. 2-year colleges	3	4
	2-year college degree	6.3%	6.4%	Student/teacher ratio	15.8	16.7	No. 4-year colleges/universities	3	6
	4-year college degree	11.9%	15.7%	Attending public school	91.2%	90.1%	No. highly ranked universities	0	1
	Graduate/professional degree	7.0%	8.9%	State SAT score	990*	1021			
				State ACT score	20.2	20.9			

Health & Healthcare Score: 85.0 Rank: 56	HAZARDS & ILLNESSES	AREA	U.S. AVG	HEALTHCARE	AREA	U.S. AVG	CRIME Score: 34.5 Rank: 244	AREA	U.S. AVG
	Air-quality score	51	37	Physicians per capita	220.7	244.2	Violent crime rate	422.1	465.5
	Water-quality score	62	52	Hospital beds per capita	579.8	420.0	Change in violent crime rate	7.2%	-2.2%
	Pollen/allergy score	60	61	No. teaching hospitals	1	3	Property crime rate	5,468.6	3,517.1
	Cancer mortality per capita	189.0	201.9	Cost per doctor visit	$68	$77	Change in property crime rate	6.9%	-2.1%
	Depression days per month	4.7	3.5	Cost per dental visit	$68	$70			
	Stress score	86	50						

Transportation Score: 89.6 Rank: 40	COMMUTE	AREA	U.S. AVG	INTERCITY SERVICES	AREA	U.S. AVG	AUTOMOTIVE	AREA	U.S. AVG
	Average commute time	23.0	27.4	Major airports within 60 miles	1	1	Insurance, annual premium	$1,785	$1,432
	Percent commutes > 60 mins.	4.5%	5.9%	Size of regional airport	Large	Large	Gas, cost per gallon	$2.44	$2.49
	Commute by auto	75.8%	78.9%	Daily airline activity	1423	686	Daily vehicle miles per capita	24.0	24.0
	Commute by mass transit	1.1%	1.9%	Amtrak service	No	No			
	Work at home	1.9%	3.1%						
	Mass transit miles per capita	1.09	1.87						

Leisure Score: 23.8 Rank: 283	DINING & SHOPPING	AREA	U.S. AVG	ENTERTAINMENT	AREA	U.S. AVG	OUTDOOR ACTIVITIES	AREA	U.S. AVG
	Restaurant rating	1	2	Professional sports rating	3	4	Golf-course rating	2	4
	Outlet mall score	20	42	College sports rating	5	4	Ski-area rating	1	3
	No. Starbucks	0	13	Zoo/aquarium rating	1	3	Sq. miles inland water	2	4
	No. warehouse clubs	1	2	Amusement park rating	1	3	Miles of coastline	0.0	10.7
				Botanical garden/ arboretum rating	10	4	National Park rating	1	3

Arts & Culture Score: 38.5 Rank: 230	MEDIA & LIBRARIES	AREA	U.S. AVG	PERFORMING ARTS	AREA	U.S. AVG	MUSEUMS	AREA	U.S. AVG
	Arts radio rating	1	3	Classical music rating	4	4	Overall museum rating	7	5
	No. public libraries	11	27	Ballet/dance rating	1	3	Art museum rating	7	5
	Library volumes per capita	2.18	2.78	Professional theater rating	1	3	Science museum rating	7	5
				University arts programs rating	1	5	Children's museum rating	1	3

Columbus, IN

Score: 82.4 **Rank:** 33 **2004 rank:** not ranked

Profile: Small town
Location: South-central Indiana, 50 miles south of Indianapolis along I-65
Elevation: 628 feet
Time zone: Eastern Standard Time

PRO	CON
Architectural interest	Entertainment
Nearby recreation	Economic cycles
Central location	Low ethnic diversity

This typical Midwestern town has a unique feature: A 1950s endowment from J. Irwin Miller, the owner of diesel-engine giant Cummins Engine Company, paid the fees to bring in renowned architects of the day to design local buildings. The result is a virtual museum of modern and postmodern architecture, with more than 50 noted architect-designed facilities mainly in the downtown area. Buildings from public schools to fire stations to churches and banks by the likes of Eliel and Eero Saarinen, Cesar Pelli, I. M. Pei, Richard Meier, and others provide visual surprises among mostly restored older buildings in its fairly typical Midwestern town layout. It works, and it's fun.

Cummins Engine is still the largest employer and powers the economy, and a number of smaller businesses have arrived, but employment statistics aren't that strong. The proximity to Indianapolis for businesses seeking access to this market and for some commuters is a plus. A recent decision by Honda Motor to locate a plant in Greensburg 18 miles east will also give a boost to the area. The cost of living and housing are reasonable. The enclosed downtown Commons Mall is a local destination. Brown County State Park, the college town of Bloomington, and Lake Monroe to the west provide entertainment that may be somewhat lacking locally. Those looking for city life and amenities have Indy and even Cincinnati, 70 miles east.

The terrain is mainly flat becoming gently rolling to the west and is mostly agricultural. Summers are warm and humid; winters bring variety. Precipitation occurs throughout the year with some periods of strong thunderstorms in spring and early summer. Snowfalls are light to moderate, but snow cover can be persistent in some winters. First freeze is mid- to late October; last is late April.

Population

DEMOGRAPHICS	AREA	U.S. AVG	ETHNIC COMPOSITION	AREA	U.S. AVG	RESIDENT PROFILE	AREA	U.S. AVG
Population	72,867		White	93.5%	79.0%	Single	24.4%	32.4%
Population density per sq. mile	179.1	358.5	Black	1.6%	10.5%	Married	61.0%	52.7%
Population growth	14.5%	21.1%	Asian	2.4%	2.7%	Divorced/separated	14.6%	14.9%
Median age	37.3	36.1	Hispanic	2.9%	10.6%	Married with children	25.8%	23.7%
Percent Democrat	32.2%	44.5%	Religious observance	51.2%	48.9%	Single with children	8.0%	9.1%
Percent Republican	67.0%	54.5%	Diversity measure	17.5	40.1	Percent over age 65	13.0%	12.9%

Economy & Jobs
Score: 56.1
Rank: 165

INCOME	AREA	U.S. AVG	EMPLOYMENT	AREA	U.S. AVG	EMPLOYING INDUSTRIES	AREA	U.S. AVG
Per capita income	$23,698	$23,235	Unemployment rate	4.7%	4.7%	Largest: Manufacturing		
Household income	$47,768	$46,414	Recent job growth	1.0%	1.3%			
Household income < $25K	22.9%	26.2%	Projected future job growth	6.5%	11.5%	Percent manufacturing	24.7%	15.4%
Household income > $75K	25.5%	25.4%	White collar	54.4%	57.8%	Percent public sector	9.0%	15.7%
Household income growth	8.1%	13.6%	Blue collar	32.3%	25.2%	Percent construction	7.6%	9.9%

Cost of Living
Score: 85.3
Rank: 54

INDEXES & TAXES	AREA	U.S. AVG	HOUSING	AREA	U.S. AVG	NECESSITIES	AREA	U.S. AVG
Cost of Living Index	85.4	100.0	Median home price	$139,700	$220,000	Food Index	99.4	100.0
Buying Power Index	125.4	100.0	Home price appreciation	17.1%	10.1%	Housing Index	49.3	100.0
Income tax rate	3.40%	4.70%	Median rent	$700	$709	Utilities Index	95.3	100.0
Sales tax rate	6.00%	6.58%	Homes owned	70.0%	62.3%	Transportation Index	93.8	100.0
Property tax rate	$9.05	$12.00	Home price ratio	2.9	4.2	Healthcare Index	99.5	100.0
						Miscellaneous Cost Index	98.7	100.0

Climate
Score: 43.3
Rank: 211

TEMPERATURE	AREA	U.S. AVG	PRECIPITATION	AREA	U.S. AVG	COMFORTS & HAZARDS	AREA	U.S. AVG
Average January low	18.0	26.2	Annual inches precipitation	40.2	37.7	July relative humidity	59%	66%
Average July high	85.0	87.4	Annual inches snowfall	25.0	7.0	Annual days mostly sunny	194	208
Annual days > 90°F	19	38	Annual days precipitation	127	109	Annual days with thunderstorms	43	39
Annual days < 32°F	119	89	Annual days rain > 0.5 inches	27	22	Tornado risk score	5	18
Annual days < 0°F	8	6	Annual days snow > 1.5 inches	6	6	Hurricane risk score	1	13

TEMPERATURE

PRECIPITATION

DAYS OF CLOUDS & PRECIPITATION

Education
Score: 35.6
Rank: 242

ACHIEVEMENT	AREA	U.S. AVG	PUBLIC SCHOOLS	AREA	U.S. AVG	HIGHER EDUCATION	AREA	U.S. AVG
High school degree	83.7%	82.7%	Expenditures per pupil	$5,230	$5,686	No. 2-year colleges	2	4
2-year college degree	6.2%	6.4%	Student/teacher ratio	19.8	16.7	No. 4-year colleges/universities	0	6
4-year college degree	13.5%	15.7%	Attending public school	88.4%	90.1%	No. highly ranked universities	0	1
Graduate/professional degree	8.4%	8.9%	State SAT score	1007*	1021			
			State ACT score	21.7	20.9			

Health & Healthcare
Score: 82.6
Rank: 65

HAZARDS & ILLNESSES	AREA	U.S. AVG	HEALTHCARE	AREA	U.S. AVG	CRIME	AREA	U.S. AVG
Air-quality score	56	37	Physicians per capita	240.5	244.2	Violent crime rate	144.4	465.5
Water-quality score	40	52	Hospital beds per capita	414.5	420.0	Change in violent crime rate	-3.5%	-2.2%
Pollen/allergy score	73	61	No. teaching hospitals	0	3	Property crime rate	3,951.5	3,517.1
Cancer mortality per capita	205.1	201.9	Cost per doctor visit	$69	$77	Change in property crime rate	5.1%	-2.1%
Depression days per month	3.1	3.5	Cost per dental visit	$74	$70			
Stress score	22	50						

Crime
Score: 82.4
Rank: 67

Transportation
Score: 93.9
Rank: 24

COMMUTE	AREA	U.S. AVG	INTERCITY SERVICES	AREA	U.S. AVG	AUTOMOTIVE	AREA	U.S. AVG
Average commute time	21.2	27.4	Major airports within 60 miles	3	1	Insurance, annual premium	$969	$1,432
Percent commutes > 60 mins.	4.8%	5.9%	Size of regional airport	Large	Large	Gas, cost per gallon	$2.50	$2.49
Commute by auto	84.6%	78.9%	Daily airline activity	1263	686	Daily vehicle miles per capita	20.5	24.0
Commute by mass transit	0.5%	1.9%	Amtrak service	No	No			
Work at home	2.7%	3.1%						
Mass transit miles per capita	0.50	1.87						

Leisure
Score: 73.3
Rank: 100

DINING & SHOPPING	AREA	U.S. AVG	ENTERTAINMENT	AREA	U.S. AVG	OUTDOOR ACTIVITIES	AREA	U.S. AVG
Restaurant rating	1	2	Professional sports rating	7	4	Golf-course rating	7	4
Outlet mall score	88	42	College sports rating	5	4	Ski-area rating	4	3
No. Starbucks	1	13	Zoo/aquarium rating	7	3	Sq. miles inland water	2	4
No. warehouse clubs	0	2	Amusement park rating	1	3	Miles of coastline	0.0	10.7
			Botanical garden/ arboretum rating	6	4	National Park rating	1	3

Arts & Culture
Score: 78.6
Rank: 80

MEDIA & LIBRARIES	AREA	U.S. AVG	PERFORMING ARTS	AREA	U.S. AVG	MUSEUMS	AREA	U.S. AVG
Arts radio rating	1	3	Classical music rating	7	4	Overall museum rating	4	5
No. public libraries	2	27	Ballet/dance rating	6	3	Art museum rating	6	5
Library volumes per capita	3.14	2.78	Professional theater rating	1	3	Science museum rating	3	5
			University arts programs rating	8	5	Children's museum rating	4	3

Columbus, OH

Score: 81.9   Rank: 36   2004 rank: 110

Profile: Capital city
Location: Geographic center of Ohio along Scioto River
Elevation: 833 feet
Time zone: Eastern Standard Time

PRO	CON
Diverse economy	Growth and sprawl
Excellent housing	Areas of urban decay
Educated population	Crime rates

Columbus, the capital of Ohio, is a well-blended mixture of government, industry, and the enormous Ohio State University. Downtown is fairly dull and many inner neighborhoods have been neglected, but efforts are underway to revive them and some people are moving back into the city. The university brings a strong intellectual and cultural base to the city, efforts that contributed to Columbus earning an All-America City Award in 2006. Many businesses are attracted to Columbus because of its central location relative to the rest of the country, an educated population, and good workforce. There is a strong high-tech presence, and big corporate names include The Limited and Abercrombie & Fitch (retail), Nationwide Insurance, Wendy's, and Cardinal Health. This diverse base brings more economic stability and growth than many of its Rust Belt neighbors.

Sprawling but attractive residential suburbs have emerged, especially to the northwest, starting with the high-end Upper Arlington just west of Ohio State, moving out to Hilliard along the Interstate 270 beltway, northwest to Dublin, and around the corner to Worthington and Westerville to the east. These areas have excellent housing, shopping, schools, golf courses, and civic amenities in a layout more spacious, wooded, and attractive than many similar cities in the region. Throughout the area, housing value per dollar spent is notably high, but

some of the transportation and air-quality effects of sprawl are starting to show. There is plenty of employment in commercial centers in and near these suburbs, although some areas became overbuilt in recent years. Cost of living is attractive at 90.6 for what is available, and the Buying Power Index of 128 is strong for a bigger city. Columbus hasn't graduated to the level of major-league sports, except with an NHL hockey franchise, but has a number of quality minor-league teams, and the Ohio State University football team is a local obsession. Professional sports and stronger cultural amenities are available in Cleveland to the north and Cincinnati to the south. The area has a good airport and discount air service, and the central location makes it popular with frequent business travelers. Columbus is one of a few cities used extensively for test marketing because of its statistically average American population.

The area is flat with four north–south stream valleys forming relatively deep, wooded gorges. Surrounding areas are mostly level plateaus of mixed open land and woods. Summers are warm and humid with little wind and occasional thundershowers. Winters are typical of the area and latitude with cold temperatures, rain, and snow. Occasionally, Atlantic winter storms will affect the area. Precipitation is distributed throughout the year with a little less in fall. Fog is common, especially in the valleys. First freeze is late October; last is mid-April.

Population

DEMOGRAPHICS	AREA	U.S. AVG	ETHNIC COMPOSITION	AREA	U.S. AVG	RESIDENT PROFILE	AREA	U.S. AVG
Population	1,701,266		White	80.0%	79.0%	Single	33.7%	32.4%
Population density per sq. mile	427.0	358.5	Black	13.5%	10.5%	Married	51.9%	52.7%
Population growth	25.0%	21.1%	Asian	3.1%	2.7%	Divorced/separated	14.4%	14.9%
Median age	34.9	36.1	Hispanic	2.2%	10.6%	Married with children	23.4%	23.7%
Percent Democrat	47.7%	44.5%	Religious observance	36.2%	48.9%	Single with children	9.2%	9.1%
Percent Republican	51.8%	54.5%	Diversity measure	35.1	40.1	Percent over age 65	10.3%	12.9%

Economy & Jobs
Score: 53.5
Rank: 175

INCOME	AREA	U.S. AVG	EMPLOYMENT	AREA	U.S. AVG	EMPLOYING INDUSTRIES	AREA	U.S. AVG
Per capita income	$26,569	$23,235	Unemployment rate	4.9%	4.7%	Largest: Finance & Insurance		
Household income	$51,736	$46,414	Recent job growth	1.3%	1.3%			
Household income < $25K	21.4%	26.2%	Projected future job growth	9.6%	11.5%	Percent manufacturing	13.5%	15.4%
Household income > $75K	30.3%	25.4%	White collar	64.8%	57.8%	Percent public sector	14.6%	15.7%
Household income growth	13.6%	13.6%	Blue collar	21.1%	25.2%	Percent construction	7.6%	9.9%

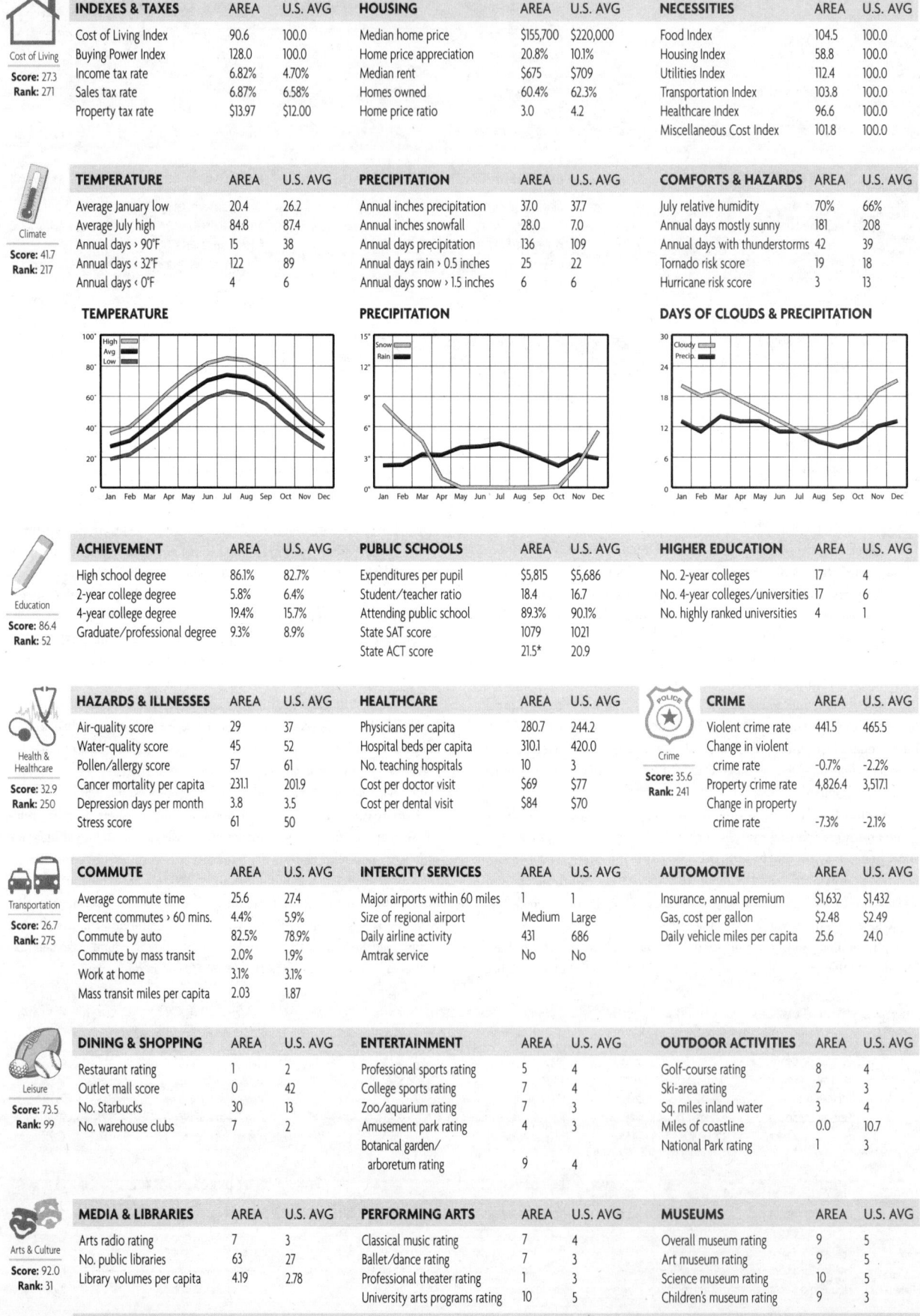

Cost of Living
Score: 27.3
Rank: 271

INDEXES & TAXES	AREA	U.S. AVG
Cost of Living Index	90.6	100.0
Buying Power Index	128.0	100.0
Income tax rate	6.82%	4.70%
Sales tax rate	6.87%	6.58%
Property tax rate	$13.97	$12.00

HOUSING	AREA	U.S. AVG
Median home price	$155,700	$220,000
Home price appreciation	20.8%	10.1%
Median rent	$675	$709
Homes owned	60.4%	62.3%
Home price ratio	3.0	4.2

NECESSITIES	AREA	U.S. AVG
Food Index	104.5	100.0
Housing Index	58.8	100.0
Utilities Index	112.4	100.0
Transportation Index	103.8	100.0
Healthcare Index	96.6	100.0
Miscellaneous Cost Index	101.8	100.0

Climate
Score: 41.7
Rank: 217

TEMPERATURE	AREA	U.S. AVG
Average January low	20.4	26.2
Average July high	84.8	87.4
Annual days > 90°F	15	38
Annual days < 32°F	122	89
Annual days < 0°F	4	6

PRECIPITATION	AREA	U.S. AVG
Annual inches precipitation	37.0	37.7
Annual inches snowfall	28.0	7.0
Annual days precipitation	136	109
Annual days rain > 0.5 inches	25	22
Annual days snow > 1.5 inches	6	6

COMFORTS & HAZARDS	AREA	U.S. AVG
July relative humidity	70%	66%
Annual days mostly sunny	181	208
Annual days with thunderstorms	42	39
Tornado risk score	19	18
Hurricane risk score	3	13

TEMPERATURE

PRECIPITATION

DAYS OF CLOUDS & PRECIPITATION

Education
Score: 86.4
Rank: 52

ACHIEVEMENT	AREA	U.S. AVG
High school degree	86.1%	82.7%
2-year college degree	5.8%	6.4%
4-year college degree	19.4%	15.7%
Graduate/professional degree	9.3%	8.9%

PUBLIC SCHOOLS	AREA	U.S. AVG
Expenditures per pupil	$5,815	$5,686
Student/teacher ratio	18.4	16.7
Attending public school	89.3%	90.1%
State SAT score	1079	1021
State ACT score	21.5*	20.9

HIGHER EDUCATION	AREA	U.S. AVG
No. 2-year colleges	17	4
No. 4-year colleges/universities	17	6
No. highly ranked universities	4	1

Health & Healthcare
Score: 32.9
Rank: 250

HAZARDS & ILLNESSES	AREA	U.S. AVG
Air-quality score	29	37
Water-quality score	45	52
Pollen/allergy score	57	61
Cancer mortality per capita	231.1	201.9
Depression days per month	3.8	3.5
Stress score	61	50

HEALTHCARE	AREA	U.S. AVG
Physicians per capita	280.7	244.2
Hospital beds per capita	310.1	420.0
No. teaching hospitals	10	3
Cost per doctor visit	$69	$77
Cost per dental visit	$84	$70

Crime
Score: 35.6
Rank: 241

CRIME	AREA	U.S. AVG
Violent crime rate	441.5	465.5
Change in violent crime rate	-0.7%	-2.2%
Property crime rate	4,826.4	3,517.1
Change in property crime rate	-7.3%	-2.1%

Transportation
Score: 26.7
Rank: 275

COMMUTE	AREA	U.S. AVG
Average commute time	25.6	27.4
Percent commutes > 60 mins.	4.4%	5.9%
Commute by auto	82.5%	78.9%
Commute by mass transit	2.0%	1.9%
Work at home	3.1%	3.1%
Mass transit miles per capita	2.03	1.87

INTERCITY SERVICES	AREA	U.S. AVG
Major airports within 60 miles	1	1
Size of regional airport	Medium	Large
Daily airline activity	431	686
Amtrak service	No	No

AUTOMOTIVE	AREA	U.S. AVG
Insurance, annual premium	$1,632	$1,432
Gas, cost per gallon	$2.48	$2.49
Daily vehicle miles per capita	25.6	24.0

Leisure
Score: 73.5
Rank: 99

DINING & SHOPPING	AREA	U.S. AVG
Restaurant rating	1	2
Outlet mall score	0	42
No. Starbucks	30	13
No. warehouse clubs	7	2

ENTERTAINMENT	AREA	U.S. AVG
Professional sports rating	5	4
College sports rating	7	4
Zoo/aquarium rating	7	3
Amusement park rating	4	3
Botanical garden/ arboretum rating	9	4

OUTDOOR ACTIVITIES	AREA	U.S. AVG
Golf-course rating	8	4
Ski-area rating	2	3
Sq. miles inland water	3	4
Miles of coastline	0.0	10.7
National Park rating	1	3

Arts & Culture
Score: 92.0
Rank: 31

MEDIA & LIBRARIES	AREA	U.S. AVG
Arts radio rating	7	3
No. public libraries	63	27
Library volumes per capita	4.19	2.78

PERFORMING ARTS	AREA	U.S. AVG
Classical music rating	7	4
Ballet/dance rating	7	3
Professional theater rating	1	3
University arts programs rating	10	5

MUSEUMS	AREA	U.S. AVG
Overall museum rating	9	5
Art museum rating	9	5
Science museum rating	10	5
Children's museum rating	9	3

Corpus Christi, TX

Score: 60.5   **Rank:** 172   **2004 rank:** 121

Profile: Mid-size city
Location: South Texas Gulf Coast, 140 miles southeast of San Antonio
Elevation: 44 feet
Time zone: Central Standard Time

PRO	CON
Nearby coastal areas	Crime rates
Cost of living	Isolation
Pleasant winters	Industrial landscape

Corpus Christi is a prosperous port town about 160 miles north of the Mexican border. It is a center for the petroleum and petrochemical industry, and a major shipping gateway on the Intracoastal Waterway. There is a military presence with two naval air stations in the vicinity, and a Texas A&M campus in town. The series of long barrier islands, particularly South Padre Island to the south, provide excellent beach, boating, and wildlife-viewing opportunities for tourists and residents alike. The local cultural amenities and museums in particular exceed what you might expect to find in such a town. Like many Texas coastal towns, the area has a good economy, low housing costs and cost of living (79.9), and a warm humid climate, but also brings some of the high crime rates found in other places along the Gulf.

Corpus Christi is located on Corpus Christi Bay, an inlet off the Gulf of Mexico. Summer days are consistent with highs ranging from the mid-80s to the mid-90s with moderating Gulf breezes late in the afternoon; 100°F temperatures are rare at the coast but common a few miles inland. Summer evenings and mornings are warm with lows seldom below 70°F. Winter months have the least rainfall and are quite mild with just a few days below freezing. Severe tropical storms occur about once every 10 years, with lesser storms once every 5 years. Snow falls an average of once every 2 years.

DEMOGRAPHICS	AREA	U.S. AVG	ETHNIC COMPOSITION	AREA	U.S. AVG	RESIDENT PROFILE	AREA	U.S. AVG
Population	408,480		White	73.3%	79.0%	Single	31.5%	32.4%
Population density per sq. mile	229.6	358.5	Black	3.2%	10.5%	Married	51.8%	52.7%
Population growth	11.4%	21.1%	Asian	1.2%	2.7%	Divorced/separated	16.7%	14.9%
Median age	34.2	36.1	Hispanic	55.9%	10.6%	Married with children	25.7%	23.7%
Percent Democrat	40.7%	44.5%	Religious observance	54.6%	48.9%	Single with children	10.8%	9.1%
Percent Republican	58.7%	54.5%	Diversity measure	69.7	40.1	Percent over age 65	11.9%	12.9%

Economy & Jobs
Score: 37.7
Rank: 232

INCOME	AREA	U.S. AVG	EMPLOYMENT	AREA	U.S. AVG	EMPLOYING INDUSTRIES	AREA	U.S. AVG
Per capita income	$19,563	$23,235	Unemployment rate	5.9%	4.7%	Largest: Healthcare & Social Assistance		
Household income	$40,855	$46,414	Recent job growth	1.5%	1.3%			
Household income < $25K	31.1%	26.2%	Projected future job growth	10.7%	11.5%	Percent manufacturing	12.0%	15.4%
Household income > $75K	21.7%	25.4%	White collar	56.6%	57.8%	Percent public sector	18.1%	15.7%
Household income growth	15.2%	13.6%	Blue collar	24.8%	25.2%	Percent construction	12.8%	9.9%

Cost of Living
Score: 81.0
Rank: 72

INDEXES & TAXES	AREA	U.S. AVG	HOUSING	AREA	U.S. AVG	NECESSITIES	AREA	U.S. AVG
Cost of Living Index	79.9	100.0	Median home price	$138,500	$220,000	Food Index	79.8	100.0
Buying Power Index	114.6	100.0	Home price appreciation	36.4%	10.1%	Housing Index	45.3	100.0
Income tax rate	0.00%	4.70%	Median rent	$687	$709	Utilities Index	102.1	100.0
Sales tax rate	8.25%	6.58%	Homes owned	56.2%	62.3%	Transportation Index	93.9	100.0
Property tax rate	$20.32	$12.00	Home price ratio	3.4	4.2	Healthcare Index	93.2	100.0
						Miscellaneous Cost Index	93.7	100.0

Climate
Score: 86.9
Rank: 50

TEMPERATURE	AREA	U.S. AVG	PRECIPITATION	AREA	U.S. AVG	COMFORTS & HAZARDS	AREA	U.S. AVG
Average January low	46.1	26.2	Annual inches precipitation	29.0	37.7	July relative humidity	77%	66%
Average July high	94.8	87.4	Annual inches snowfall	0.0	7.0	Annual days mostly sunny	222	208
Annual days > 90°F	96	38	Annual days precipitation	77	109	Annual days with thunderstorms	31	39
Annual days < 32°F	7	89	Annual days rain > 0.5 inches	18	22	Tornado risk score	43	18
Annual days < 0°F	0	6	Annual days snow > 1.5 inches	0	6	Hurricane risk score	39	13

TEMPERATURE

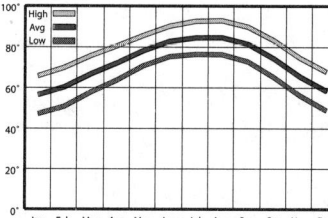

PRECIPITATION

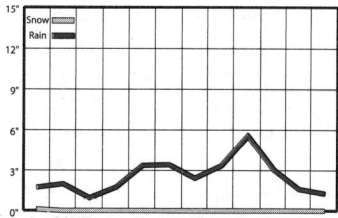

DAYS OF CLOUDS & PRECIPITATION

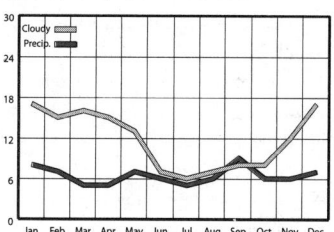

Education
Score: 23.8
Rank: 285

ACHIEVEMENT	AREA	U.S. AVG	PUBLIC SCHOOLS	AREA	U.S. AVG	HIGHER EDUCATION	AREA	U.S. AVG
High school degree	74.6%	82.7%	Expenditures per pupil	$5,295	$5,686	No. 2-year colleges	1	4
2-year college degree	5.6%	6.4%	Student/teacher ratio	15.0	16.7	No. 4-year colleges/universities	2	6
4-year college degree	11.8%	15.7%	Attending public school	95.5%	90.1%	No. highly ranked universities	0	1
Graduate/professional degree	6.5%	8.9%	State SAT score	997*	1021			
			State ACT score	20.3	20.9			

Health & Healthcare
Score: 56.1
Rank: 164

Crime
Score: 3.7
Rank: 359

HAZARDS & ILLNESSES	AREA	U.S. AVG	HEALTHCARE	AREA	U.S. AVG	CRIME	AREA	U.S. AVG
Air-quality score	27	37	Physicians per capita	220.6	244.2	Violent crime rate	601.7	465.5
Water-quality score	75	52	Hospital beds per capita	582.9	420.0	Change in violent crime rate	0.3%	-2.2%
Pollen/allergy score	84	61	No. teaching hospitals	3	3	Property crime rate	6,296.1	3,517.1
Cancer mortality per capita	169.6	201.9	Cost per doctor visit	$70	$77	Change in property crime rate	1.1%	-2.1%
Depression days per month	4.9	3.5	Cost per dental visit	$58	$70			
Stress score	83	50						

Transportation
Score: 26.2
Rank: 277

COMMUTE	AREA	U.S. AVG	INTERCITY SERVICES	AREA	U.S. AVG	AUTOMOTIVE	AREA	U.S. AVG
Average commute time	22.4	27.4	Major airports within 60 miles	0	1	Insurance, annual premium	$1,232	$1,432
Percent commutes > 60 mins.	3.9%	5.9%	Size of regional airport	Small	Large	Gas, cost per gallon	$2.39	$2.49
Commute by auto	76.7%	78.9%	Daily airline activity	42	686	Daily vehicle miles per capita	27.2	24.0
Commute by mass transit	1.4%	1.9%	Amtrak service	No	No			
Work at home	2.5%	3.1%						
Mass transit miles per capita	1.44	1.87						

Leisure
Score: 52.7
Rank: 176

DINING & SHOPPING	AREA	U.S. AVG	ENTERTAINMENT	AREA	U.S. AVG	OUTDOOR ACTIVITIES	AREA	U.S. AVG
Restaurant rating	1	2	Professional sports rating	3	4	Golf-course rating	2	4
Outlet mall score	0	42	College sports rating	2	4	Ski-area rating	1	3
No. Starbucks	1	13	Zoo/aquarium rating	1	3	Sq. miles inland water	10	4
No. warehouse clubs	1	2	Amusement park rating	1	3	Miles of coastline	25.0	10.7
			Botanical garden/ arboretum rating	2	4	National Park rating	1	3

Arts & Culture
Score: 32.9
Rank: 251

MEDIA & LIBRARIES	AREA	U.S. AVG	PERFORMING ARTS	AREA	U.S. AVG	MUSEUMS	AREA	U.S. AVG
Arts radio rating	5	3	Classical music rating	3	4	Overall museum rating	6	5
No. public libraries	14	27	Ballet/dance rating	3	3	Art museum rating	4	5
Library volumes per capita	1.65	2.78	Professional theater rating	1	3	Science museum rating	1	5
			University arts programs rating	3	5	Children's museum rating	1	3

Corvallis, OR

Score: 87.3   Rank: 14   2004 rank: 10

Profile: College town
Location: North-central Oregon in Willamette Valley, 80 miles south of Portland
Elevation: 282 feet
Time zone: Pacific Standard Time

PRO
Educated population
Nearby recreation
Attractive setting

CON
Cost of living
Clouds and rain
Housing quality

The Corvallis area includes the cities of Corvallis and Albany, 12 miles apart in the central part of the Willamette Valley. Corvallis is the home of Oregon State University, and while the university is a strong factor in the makeup and economy of the town, it isn't the whole story, and we've seen stronger college-town influence and amenities in other places. A large research facility makes Hewlett-Packard the largest private employer. Educational attainment and resources are notably strong. College sports provide entertainment, and nearby recreation in the mountains and coastal areas is excellent. Albany is mainly working class with employers in the timber, paper, and chemical industries. Although a large area is run-down and industrial, Corvallis has experienced some resurgence and has a nice historic downtown residen-

tial area. Corvallis is a "green" city in both senses; it has lush, green countryside and rigidly enforced no-growth policies, the latter of which curbs urban sprawl and preserves the surrounding area but also brings a residential supply-and-demand imbalance and high home prices. Overall, the area has a true small-town flavor with access to a wide and balanced set of amenities and a fairly pleasant climate devoid of extremes.

The level Willamette Valley is mainly agricultural. Large forested hills of the Coast Range rise just to the west of Corvallis, providing a nice backdrop, with smaller rolling hills covered by oaks and grassland north of Albany. Summers are usually warm, dry, and pleasant, with temperatures in the 70s or low 80s; one annual hot spell usually raises temperatures to about 100°F. Summer rains are infrequent. Fall, winter, and spring are marked with sequential periods of rain but there is little snow and few freezes. Although mountains to the west block the heaviest precipitation and winds, clouds and rain can last for days.

DEMOGRAPHICS	AREA	U.S. AVG
Population	81,105	
Population density per sq. mile	119.9	358.5
Population growth	14.5%	21.1%
Median age	33.2	36.1
Percent Democrat	58.0%	44.5%
Percent Republican	40.4%	54.5%

ETHNIC COMPOSITION	AREA	U.S. AVG
White	88.0%	79.0%
Black	0.9%	10.5%
Asian	5.6%	2.7%
Hispanic	5.3%	10.6%
Religious observance	22.6%	48.9%
Diversity measure	30.0	40.1

RESIDENT PROFILE	AREA	U.S. AVG
Single	39.9%	32.4%
Married	49.4%	52.7%
Divorced/separated	10.7%	14.9%
Married with children	22.2%	23.7%
Single with children	6.1%	9.1%
Percent over age 65	10.8%	12.9%

Economy & Jobs
Score: 42.5
Rank: 215

INCOME	AREA	U.S. AVG
Per capita income	$25,275	$23,235
Household income	$48,249	$46,414
Household income < $25K	26.2%	26.2%
Household income > $75K	30.0%	25.4%
Household income growth	15.2%	13.6%

EMPLOYMENT	AREA	U.S. AVG
Unemployment rate	5.3%	4.7%
Recent job growth	1.0%	1.3%
Projected future job growth	13.9%	11.5%
White collar	67.0%	57.8%
Blue collar	16.0%	25.2%

EMPLOYING INDUSTRIES	AREA	U.S. AVG
Largest: Manufacturing		
Percent manufacturing	9.7%	15.4%
Percent public sector	25.3%	15.7%
Percent construction	6.3%	9.9%

Cost of Living
Score: 57.5
Rank: 159

INDEXES & TAXES	AREA	U.S. AVG
Cost of Living Index	112.8	100.0
Buying Power Index	95.9	100.0
Income tax rate	9.00%	4.70%
Sales tax rate	0.00%	6.58%
Property tax rate	$10.04	$12.00

HOUSING	AREA	U.S. AVG
Median home price	$283,700	$220,000
Home price appreciation	35.3%	10.1%
Median rent	$721	$709
Homes owned	54.5%	62.3%
Home price ratio	5.9	4.2

NECESSITIES	AREA	U.S. AVG
Food Index	104.1	100.0
Housing Index	83.7	100.0
Utilities Index	92.7	100.0
Transportation Index	108.1	100.0
Healthcare Index	124.6	100.0
Miscellaneous Cost Index	104.6	100.0

Climate
Score: 67.6
Rank: 120

TEMPERATURE	AREA	U.S. AVG
Average January low	33.0	26.2
Average July high	81.6	87.4
Annual days > 90°F	9	38
Annual days < 32°F	50	89
Annual days < 0°F	0	6

PRECIPITATION	AREA	U.S. AVG
Annual inches precipitation	42.0	37.7
Annual inches snowfall	6.0	7.0
Annual days precipitation	145	109
Annual days rain > 0.5 inches	25	22
Annual days snow > 1.5 inches	1	6

COMFORTS & HAZARDS	AREA	U.S. AVG
July relative humidity	73%	66%
Annual days mostly sunny	153	208
Annual days with thunderstorms	5	39
Tornado risk score	2	18
Hurricane risk score	0	13

TEMPERATURE

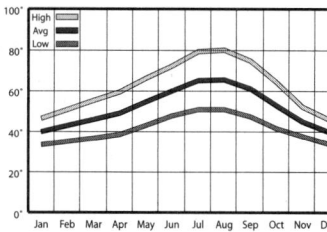

PRECIPITATION

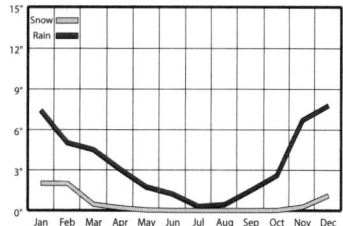

DAYS OF CLOUDS & PRECIPITATION

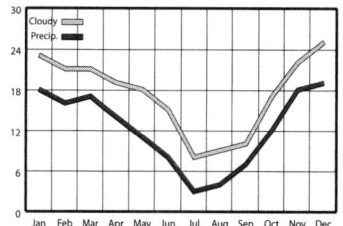

Education
Score: 96.3
Rank: 15

ACHIEVEMENT	AREA	U.S. AVG
High school degree	93.2%	82.7%
2-year college degree	7.3%	6.4%
4-year college degree	26.4%	15.7%
Graduate/professional degree	21.3%	8.9%

PUBLIC SCHOOLS	AREA	U.S. AVG
Expenditures per pupil	$5,569	$5,686
Student/teacher ratio	18.8	16.7
Attending public school	86.2%	90.1%
State SAT score	1052*	1021
State ACT score	22.4	20.9

HIGHER EDUCATION	AREA	U.S. AVG
No. 2-year colleges	1	4
No. 4-year colleges/universities	1	6
No. highly ranked universities	0	1

Health & Healthcare
Score: 48.9
Rank: 192

HAZARDS & ILLNESSES	AREA	U.S. AVG
Air-quality score	49	37
Water-quality score	59	52
Pollen/allergy score	60	61
Cancer mortality per capita	160.7	201.9
Depression days per month	2.8	3.5
Stress score	8	50

HEALTHCARE	AREA	U.S. AVG
Physicians per capita	281.1	244.2
Hospital beds per capita	201.0	420.0
No. teaching hospitals	0	3
Cost per doctor visit	$90	$77
Cost per dental visit	$79	$70

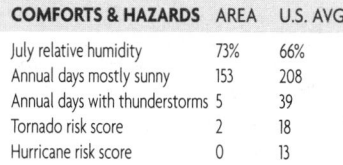

Crime
Score: 76.7
Rank: 88

CRIME	AREA	U.S. AVG
Violent crime rate	134.4	465.5
Change in violent crime rate	-25.7%	-2.2%
Property crime rate	3,754.5	3,517.1
Change in property crime rate	-3.2%	-2.1%

COMMUTE	AREA	U.S. AVG	INTERCITY SERVICES	AREA	U.S. AVG	AUTOMOTIVE	AREA	U.S. AVG
Average commute time	19.6	27.4	Major airports within 60 miles	1	1	Insurance, annual premium	$1,098	$1,432
Percent commutes > 60 mins.	3.9%	5.9%	Size of regional airport	Medium	Large	Gas, cost per gallon	$2.39	$2.49
Commute by auto	71.1%	78.9%	Daily airline activity	484	686	Daily vehicle miles per capita	13.7	24.0
Commute by mass transit	1.6%	1.9%	Amtrak service	No	No			
Work at home	4.3%	3.1%						
Mass transit miles per capita	1.57	1.87						

Transportation
Score: 84.2
Rank: 59

DINING & SHOPPING	AREA	U.S. AVG	ENTERTAINMENT	AREA	U.S. AVG	OUTDOOR ACTIVITIES	AREA	U.S. AVG
Restaurant rating	1	2	Professional sports rating	2	4	Golf-course rating	1	4
Outlet mall score	0	42	College sports rating	5	4	Ski-area rating	8	3
No. Starbucks	3	13	Zoo/aquarium rating	1	3	Sq. miles inland water	2	4
No. warehouse clubs	0	2	Amusement park rating	1	3	Miles of coastline	0.0	10.7
			Botanical garden/ arboretum rating	2	4	National Park rating	2	3

Leisure
Score: 39.6
Rank: 225

MEDIA & LIBRARIES	AREA	U.S. AVG	PERFORMING ARTS	AREA	U.S. AVG	MUSEUMS	AREA	U.S. AVG
Arts radio rating	1	3	Classical music rating	2	4	Overall museum rating	2	5
No. public libraries	4	27	Ballet/dance rating	1	3	Art museum rating	3	5
Library volumes per capita	3.62	2.78	Professional theater rating	1	3	Science museum rating	1	5
			University arts programs rating	4	5	Children's museum rating	1	3

Arts & Culture
Score: 28.6
Rank: 267

Cumberland, MD-WV

Score: 34.6   **Rank:** 324   **2004 rank:** 175

Profile: Small town
Location: Western Maryland in the western portion of the panhandle, between Pennsylvania and West Virginia
Elevation: 1,233 feet
Time zone: Eastern Standard Time

PRO	CON
Cost of living	Isolation
Attractive setting	Employment
Nearby mountains	Arts and culture

Cumberland has a history as a transportation center and gateway to the West. Originally, the Chesapeake and Ohio Canal met toll roads to the West there. Later came the railroads and the historic National Road—now U.S. 40. Cumberland is still a railroad town, with almost 1,000 employed by CSX, but that figure has declined significantly over the decades. Today the town has a small manufacturing base, some call centers, and a strong tourist economy, but employment trends are weak. There is a lot of historic interest in the old downtown, and it has been preserved and rehabilitated into a destination area. The low cost of living (77.5) relative to the Northeast region, quiet mountain setting with abundant outdoor recreational opportunities, and beautiful fall seasons are the area's main draws.

Cumberland is in a small valley, at a bend in the Potomac River, surrounded by deciduous forest and the Appalachian Mountains. Summers are calm, warm, and humid with occasional thundershowers. The mountains moderate winter storms, but periods of cold and snow with occasional freezing rain occur annually. First freeze is late October; last is early April.

DEMOGRAPHICS	AREA	U.S. AVG	ETHNIC COMPOSITION	AREA	U.S. AVG	RESIDENT PROFILE	AREA	U.S. AVG
Population	100,406		White	94.0%	79.0%	Single	30.8%	32.4%
Population density per sq. mile	133.3	358.5	Black	4.6%	10.5%	Married	51.9%	52.7%
Population growth	-1.3%	21.1%	Asian	0.5%	2.7%	Divorced/separated	17.4%	14.9%
Median age	39.6	36.1	Hispanic	0.7%	10.6%	Married with children	19.8%	23.7%
Percent Democrat	34.1%	44.5%	Religious observance	52.7%	48.9%	Single with children	7.5%	9.1%
Percent Republican	64.9%	54.5%	Diversity measure	12.7	40.1	Percent over age 65	17.4%	12.9%

Population

INCOME	AREA	U.S. AVG	EMPLOYMENT	AREA	U.S. AVG	EMPLOYING INDUSTRIES	AREA	U.S. AVG
Per capita income	$18,691	$23,235	Unemployment rate	6.1%	4.7%	Largest: Healthcare & Social Assistance		
Household income	$34,726	$46,414	Recent job growth	2.1%	1.3%			
Household income < $25K	36.5%	26.2%	Projected future job growth	3.0%	11.5%	Percent manufacturing	18.9%	15.4%
Household income > $75K	14.4%	25.4%	White collar	50.8%	57.8%	Percent public sector	20.8%	15.7%
Household income growth	12.3%	13.6%	Blue collar	30.0%	25.2%	Percent construction	11.1%	9.9%

Economy & Jobs
Score: 25.1
Rank: 280

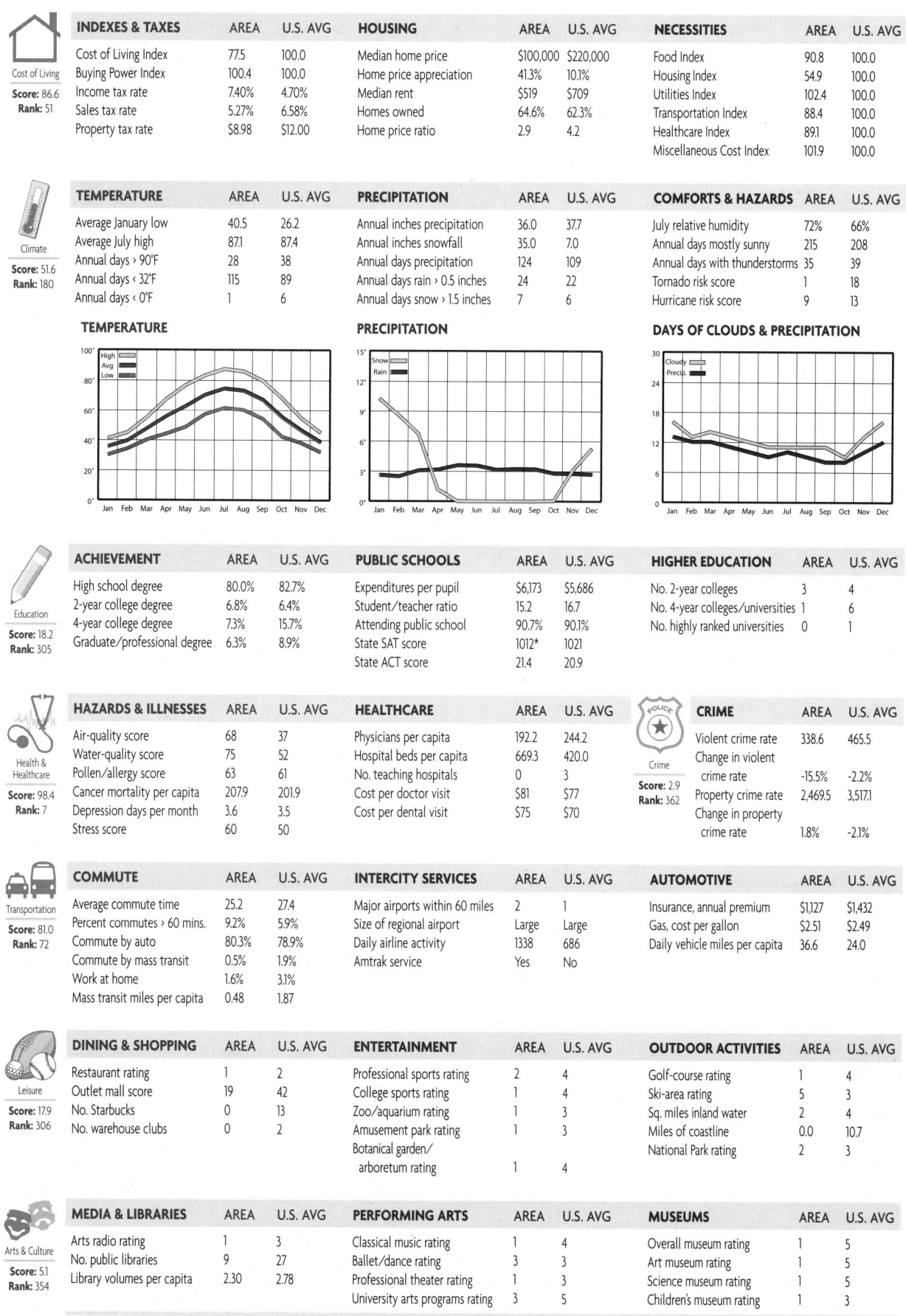

Cost of Living
Score: 86.6
Rank: 51

INDEXES & TAXES	AREA	U.S. AVG	HOUSING	AREA	U.S. AVG	NECESSITIES	AREA	U.S. AVG
Cost of Living Index	77.5	100.0	Median home price	$100,000	$220,000	Food Index	90.8	100.0
Buying Power Index	100.4	100.0	Home price appreciation	41.3%	10.1%	Housing Index	54.9	100.0
Income tax rate	7.40%	4.70%	Median rent	$519	$709	Utilities Index	102.4	100.0
Sales tax rate	5.27%	6.58%	Homes owned	64.6%	62.3%	Transportation Index	88.4	100.0
Property tax rate	$8.98	$12.00	Home price ratio	2.9	4.2	Healthcare Index	89.1	100.0
						Miscellaneous Cost Index	101.9	100.0

Climate
Score: 51.6
Rank: 180

TEMPERATURE	AREA	U.S. AVG	PRECIPITATION	AREA	U.S. AVG	COMFORTS & HAZARDS	AREA	U.S. AVG
Average January low	40.5	26.2	Annual inches precipitation	36.0	37.7	July relative humidity	72%	66%
Average July high	87.1	87.4	Annual inches snowfall	35.0	7.0	Annual days mostly sunny	215	208
Annual days > 90°F	28	38	Annual days precipitation	124	109	Annual days with thunderstorms	35	39
Annual days < 32°F	115	89	Annual days rain > 0.5 inches	24	22	Tornado risk score	1	18
Annual days < 0°F	1	6	Annual days snow > 1.5 inches	7	6	Hurricane risk score	9	13

TEMPERATURE

PRECIPITATION

DAYS OF CLOUDS & PRECIPITATION

Education
Score: 18.2
Rank: 305

ACHIEVEMENT	AREA	U.S. AVG	PUBLIC SCHOOLS	AREA	U.S. AVG	HIGHER EDUCATION	AREA	U.S. AVG
High school degree	80.0%	82.7%	Expenditures per pupil	$6,173	$5,686	No. 2-year colleges	3	4
2-year college degree	6.8%	6.4%	Student/teacher ratio	15.2	16.7	No. 4-year colleges/universities	1	6
4-year college degree	7.3%	15.7%	Attending public school	90.7%	90.1%	No. highly ranked universities	0	1
Graduate/professional degree	6.3%	8.9%	State SAT score	1012*	1021			
			State ACT score	21.4	20.9			

Health & Healthcare
Score: 98.4
Rank: 7

Crime
Score: 2.9
Rank: 362

HAZARDS & ILLNESSES	AREA	U.S. AVG	HEALTHCARE	AREA	U.S. AVG	CRIME	AREA	U.S. AVG
Air-quality score	68	37	Physicians per capita	192.2	244.2	Violent crime rate	338.6	465.5
Water-quality score	75	52	Hospital beds per capita	669.3	420.0	Change in violent crime rate	-15.5%	-2.2%
Pollen/allergy score	63	61	No. teaching hospitals	0	3	Property crime rate	2,469.5	3,517.1
Cancer mortality per capita	207.9	201.9	Cost per doctor visit	$81	$77	Change in property crime rate	1.8%	-2.1%
Depression days per month	3.6	3.5	Cost per dental visit	$75	$70			
Stress score	60	50						

Transportation
Score: 81.0
Rank: 72

COMMUTE	AREA	U.S. AVG	INTERCITY SERVICES	AREA	U.S. AVG	AUTOMOTIVE	AREA	U.S. AVG
Average commute time	25.2	27.4	Major airports within 60 miles	2	1	Insurance, annual premium	$1,127	$1,432
Percent commutes > 60 mins.	9.2%	5.9%	Size of regional airport	Large	Large	Gas, cost per gallon	$2.51	$2.49
Commute by auto	80.3%	78.9%	Daily airline activity	1338	686	Daily vehicle miles per capita	36.6	24.0
Commute by mass transit	0.5%	1.9%	Amtrak service	Yes	No			
Work at home	1.6%	3.1%						
Mass transit miles per capita	0.48	1.87						

Leisure
Score: 17.9
Rank: 306

DINING & SHOPPING	AREA	U.S. AVG	ENTERTAINMENT	AREA	U.S. AVG	OUTDOOR ACTIVITIES	AREA	U.S. AVG
Restaurant rating	1	2	Professional sports rating	2	4	Golf-course rating	1	4
Outlet mall score	19	42	College sports rating	1	4	Ski-area rating	5	3
No. Starbucks	0	13	Zoo/aquarium rating	1	3	Sq. miles inland water	2	4
No. warehouse clubs	0	2	Amusement park rating	1	3	Miles of coastline	0.0	10.7
			Botanical garden/ arboretum rating	1	4	National Park rating	2	3

Arts & Culture
Score: 5.1
Rank: 354

MEDIA & LIBRARIES	AREA	U.S. AVG	PERFORMING ARTS	AREA	U.S. AVG	MUSEUMS	AREA	U.S. AVG
Arts radio rating	1	3	Classical music rating	1	4	Overall museum rating	1	5
No. public libraries	9	27	Ballet/dance rating	3	3	Art museum rating	1	5
Library volumes per capita	2.30	2.78	Professional theater rating	1	3	Science museum rating	1	5
			University arts programs rating	3	5	Children's museum rating	1	3

Dallas–Plano–Irving, TX

Score: 65.9   Rank: 132   2004 rank: 95

Profile: Regional center
Location: Northeast Texas
Elevation: 596 feet
Time zone: Central Standard Time

PRO	CON
Entertainment	Growth and sprawl
Arts and culture	Unattractive physical setting
Diverse economy	Summer heat

Dallas is the eastern, larger half of the Dallas–Fort Worth "Metroplex." Dallas is what most people think of when they first think of Texas—big, busy, growing, cosmopolitan, rich, glitzy, and self-confident. Located topographically pretty much in the middle of nowhere, dozens of gleaming downtown skyscrapers tower above the level plains, while an assortment of neighborhoods and suburban commercial centers sprawl in all directions around the city core. It has far outgrown its beltway and is supported by a web of freeways going in all directions, a network almost without compare in other U.S. cities. Long commutes are common, thanks to the large population, growth rate, and urban sprawl, but most don't commute to the city itself. A rapidly developing rail-transit program is helping to cope, but Dallas is pretty much a "motor city."

Above all else, Dallas is a center for corporate America. Because of its central location relative to the rest of the nation, Dallas is a popular convention site and home to many corporate headquarters; if a company isn't headquartered here, it probably has a large regional office. Also contributing are the favorable business climate, the availability of educated workers, and the unspoken notion of being in the center of all things big. Although little oil is produced in the immediate area, Dallas' growth began with the east Texas oil boom, and petroleum continues to be a large factor in the local economy.

The strong economy and wealthy population have endowed the city with a collection of arts, cultural assets, and parks. The many cultural landmarks include theaters, the Dallas Museum of Art, the Meyerson Symphony Center, and the Frank Lloyd Wright–inspired Dallas Theater Center. Filling out the roster of major-league teams are the NFL Cowboys, MLB Rangers, NBA Mavericks, and NHL Stars, all drawing a strong local and national following. Dallas reputedly has more retail stores and restaurants per capita than any other place in the country. A few lakes exist to the north and east, but outdoor recreational opportunities in the surrounding flat plains are limited. Nonetheless, as the center of the nation's air-transport networks and the hub for American and Southwest airlines, Dallas provides numerous getaway opportunities; the city lags only behind Chicago, Los Angeles, and Atlanta in the number of available airline flights.

The extensive network of suburbs spreads in all directions but especially towards the northwest, north, and northeast. Supersized suburbs such as Plano, Irving, and Garland are bigger than many metro areas, each exceeding 200,000 in population. These middle- to upper-middle-class suburbs extend for miles with attractively priced, mostly large homes, large commercial centers, large employers, and even some corporate headquarters. Frito-Lay, for example, makes its home in Plano. When traveling in the area, it isn't always clear which suburb you're in—check the nearest water tower rising from the flat plain! Other more upscale, upcoming suburbs include Grapevine, Lewisville, Flower Mound, and Allen to the north and Mesquite to the east. What these suburbs have in common are good home values, strong schools, plenty of jobs, high incomes, a mostly featureless physical setting, and lots of sprawl and sprawl-related issues. It is suburban America for those who like things big.

The Dallas–Fort Worth Metroplex is approximately 250 miles north of the Gulf of Mexico. Terrain is flat to rolling, and largely devoid of natural trees. Annual precipitation varies considerably, ranging from less than 20 to more than 50 inches. Summer hot spells are broken into 3- to 5-day periods by thunderstorm activity. Summer daytime temperatures frequently exceed 100°F with occasional nights above 80°F. Winters are mild but north winds bring sudden temperature drops. Occasional periods of snowfall and extreme cold are rare and short-lived. First freeze is late November; last is mid-March.

DEMOGRAPHICS	AREA	U.S. AVG
Population	3,873,350	
Population density per sq. mile	693.1	358.5
Population growth	58.6%	21.1%
Median age	32.5	36.1
Percent Democrat	40.6%	44.5%
Percent Republican	58.7%	54.5%

ETHNIC COMPOSITION	AREA	U.S. AVG
White	64.2%	79.0%
Black	14.9%	10.5%
Asian	4.9%	2.7%
Hispanic	27.2%	10.6%
Religious observance	52.2%	48.9%
Diversity measure	68.8	40.1

RESIDENT PROFILE	AREA	U.S. AVG
Single	31.0%	32.4%
Married	53.1%	52.7%
Divorced/separated	15.8%	14.9%
Married with children	27.8%	23.7%
Single with children	9.2%	9.1%
Percent over age 65	7.7%	12.9%

Population

INCOME	AREA	U.S. AVG
Per capita income	$27,942	$23,235
Household income	$56,940	$46,414
Household income < $25K	18.9%	26.2%
Household income > $75K	35.4%	25.4%
Household income growth	12.9%	13.6%

EMPLOYMENT	AREA	U.S. AVG
Unemployment rate	5.1%	4.7%
Recent job growth	2.3%	1.3%
Projected future job growth	18.7%	11.5%
White collar	66.5%	57.8%
Blue collar	21.2%	25.2%

EMPLOYING INDUSTRIES	AREA	U.S. AVG
Largest: Professional, Scientific & Technical Services		
Percent manufacturing	11.5%	15.4%
Percent public sector	10.1%	15.7%
Percent construction	9.7%	9.9%

Economy & Jobs
Score: 88.0
Rank: 46

INDEXES & TAXES	AREA	U.S. AVG
Cost of Living Index	89.0	100.0
Buying Power Index	143.4	100.0
Income tax rate	0.00%	4.70%
Sales tax rate	8.25%	6.58%
Property tax rate	$18.94	$12.00

HOUSING	AREA	U.S. AVG
Median home price	$153,900	$220,000
Home price appreciation	20.1%	10.1%
Median rent	$798	$709
Homes owned	56.2%	62.3%
Home price ratio	2.7	4.2

NECESSITIES	AREA	U.S. AVG
Food Index	99.0	100.0
Housing Index	62.9	100.0
Utilities Index	95.0	100.0
Transportation Index	106.5	100.0
Healthcare Index	107.5	100.0
Miscellaneous Cost Index	98.6	100.0

Cost of Living
Score: 61.5
Rank: 144

Climate
Score: 87.4
Rank: 48

TEMPERATURE	AREA	U.S. AVG
Average January low	33.9	26.2
Average July high	96.1	87.4
Annual days > 90°F	88	38
Annual days < 32°F	39	89
Annual days < 0°F	0	6

PRECIPITATION	AREA	U.S. AVG
Annual inches precipitation	32.0	37.7
Annual inches snowfall	3.0	7.0
Annual days precipitation	79	109
Annual days rain > 0.5 inches	20	22
Annual days snow > 1.5 inches	1	6

COMFORTS & HAZARDS	AREA	U.S. AVG
July relative humidity	67%	66%
Annual days mostly sunny	233	208
Annual days with thunderstorms	46	39
Tornado risk score	44	18
Hurricane risk score	11	13

TEMPERATURE

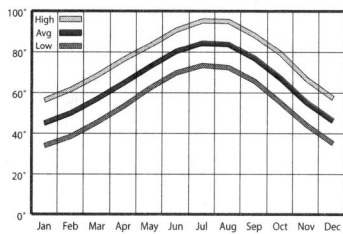

PRECIPITATION

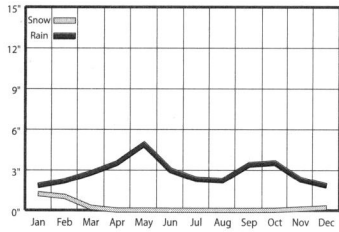

DAYS OF CLOUDS & PRECIPITATION

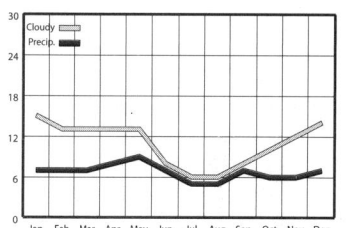

Education
Score: 86.9
Rank: 50

ACHIEVEMENT	AREA	U.S. AVG
High school degree	80.2%	82.7%
2-year college degree	5.5%	6.4%
4-year college degree	21.4%	15.7%
Graduate/professional degree	9.7%	8.9%

PUBLIC SCHOOLS	AREA	U.S. AVG
Expenditures per pupil	$5,068	$5,686
Student/teacher ratio	16.4	16.7
Attending public school	93.1%	90.1%
State SAT score	997*	1021
State ACT score	20.3	20.9

HIGHER EDUCATION	AREA	U.S. AVG
No. 2-year colleges	22	4
No. 4-year colleges/universities	19	6
No. highly ranked universities	3	1

Health & Healthcare
Score: 13.4
Rank: 322

HAZARDS & ILLNESSES	AREA	U.S. AVG
Air-quality score	14	37
Water-quality score	83	52
Pollen/allergy score	87	61
Cancer mortality per capita	161.2	201.9
Depression days per month	2.9	3.5
Stress score	75	50

HEALTHCARE	AREA	U.S. AVG
Physicians per capita	217.7	244.2
Hospital beds per capita	256.7	420.0
No. teaching hospitals	17	3
Cost per doctor visit	$88	$77
Cost per dental visit	$78	$70

Crime
Score: 8.0
Rank: 343

CRIME	AREA	U.S. AVG
Violent crime rate	591.0	465.5
Change in violent crime rate	-3.8%	-2.2%
Property crime rate	4,713.7	3,517.1
Change in property crime rate	-5.4%	-2.1%

Transportation
Score: 53.5
Rank: 175

COMMUTE	AREA	U.S. AVG
Average commute time	30.3	27.4
Percent commutes > 60 mins.	7.9%	5.9%
Commute by auto	78.0%	78.9%
Commute by mass transit	2.3%	1.9%
Work at home	3.2%	3.1%
Mass transit miles per capita	2.35	1.87

INTERCITY SERVICES	AREA	U.S. AVG
Major airports within 60 miles	2	1
Size of regional airport	Large	Large
Daily airline activity	1557	686
Amtrak service	Yes	No

AUTOMOTIVE	AREA	U.S. AVG
Insurance, annual premium	$1,445	$1,432
Gas, cost per gallon	$2.51	$2.49
Daily vehicle miles per capita	25.4	24.0

Leisure
Score: 90.4
Rank: 37

DINING & SHOPPING	AREA	U.S. AVG
Restaurant rating	5	2
Outlet mall score	0	42
No. Starbucks	107	13
No. warehouse clubs	16	2

ENTERTAINMENT	AREA	U.S. AVG
Professional sports rating	9	4
College sports rating	6	4
Zoo/aquarium rating	6	3
Amusement park rating	5	3
Botanical garden/ arboretum rating	10	4

OUTDOOR ACTIVITIES	AREA	U.S. AVG
Golf-course rating	8	4
Ski-area rating	1	3
Sq. miles inland water	7	4
Miles of coastline	0.0	10.7
National Park rating	1	3

Arts & Culture
Score: 93.3
Rank: 26

MEDIA & LIBRARIES	AREA	U.S. AVG
Arts radio rating	8	3
No. public libraries	98	27
Library volumes per capita	2.19	2.78

PERFORMING ARTS	AREA	U.S. AVG
Classical music rating	10	4
Ballet/dance rating	8	3
Professional theater rating	10	3
University arts programs rating	8	5

MUSEUMS	AREA	U.S. AVG
Overall museum rating	9	5
Art museum rating	9	5
Science museum rating	9	5
Children's museum rating	9	3

Dalton, GA

Score: 44.9   **Rank:** 284   **2004 rank:** not ranked

Profile: Small city
Location: North Georgia, 14 miles south of the Tennessee border
Elevation: 767 feet
Time zone: Eastern Standard Time

PRO	CON
Economy	Educational attainment
Nearby recreation	Entertainment
Historic interest	Arts and culture

Dalton, a typical Southern town along Interstate 75, is noted for its carpet industry. "Noted" actually understates the case a bit—there are reputedly more than 150 carpet mills and 100 carpet outlet stores, and the area ships more than half—some sources say up to 90%—of the world's manufactured carpets. Such a concentration has made Dalton a minor tourist attraction, with carpet buyers and lookers coming from all over, and yes, they do save money, even with freight. Aside from carpet, there is some chemical, plastic, and other manufacturing industries, and the area is known for its productive labor force and good labor relations. Downtown is older and typically Southern with a few historic buildings. There isn't a lot to do locally, but Chattanooga, Tennessee, is 20 miles north and Atlanta is 75 miles south. As the tax climate in Tennessee is more favorable, relatively few make the commute to Chattanooga. Healthcare resources, anchored by the Hamilton Medical Center, are above average for this type of town. There is some recreational activity in the nearby mountains and streams, and the Chickamauga battlefield park 15 miles northwest adds historic interest. Predictably, cost of living and housing are low in this small Southern city.

Dalton is located in a broad and mostly wooded valley surrounded by hilly and deciduous-wooded terrain. Summers can be hot, still, and sticky with occasional thunderstorms. Winters are variable with occasional cold snaps and periods of freezing rain or ice storms following them. Tropical moisture can produce steady rains at all times of the year, although most consider fall weather most pleasant. First freeze is early November; last is late March.

Population

DEMOGRAPHICS	AREA	U.S. AVG	ETHNIC COMPOSITION	AREA	U.S. AVG	RESIDENT PROFILE	AREA	U.S. AVG
Population	130,386		White	83.0%	79.0%	Single	25.6%	32.4%
Population density per sq. mile	205.5	358.5	Black	2.6%	10.5%	Married	58.3%	52.7%
Population growth	33.7%	21.1%	Asian	0.9%	2.7%	Divorced/separated	16.1%	14.9%
Median age	33.3	36.1	Hispanic	21.2%	10.6%	Married with children	28.8%	23.7%
Percent Democrat	26.5%	44.5%	Religious observance	46.2%	48.9%	Single with children	8.6%	9.1%
Percent Republican	72.9%	54.5%	Diversity measure	51.4	40.1	Percent over age 65	10.1%	12.9%

Economy & Jobs
Score: 67.6
Rank: 122

INCOME	AREA	U.S. AVG	EMPLOYMENT	AREA	U.S. AVG	EMPLOYING INDUSTRIES	AREA	U.S. AVG
Per capita income	$19,587	$23,235	Unemployment rate	5.1%	4.7%	Largest: Manufacturing		
Household income	$42,967	$46,414	Recent job growth	1.6%	1.3%			
Household income < $25K	26.4%	26.2%	Projected future job growth	15.3%	11.5%	Percent manufacturing	35.7%	15.4%
Household income > $75K	20.5%	25.4%	White collar	43.9%	57.8%	Percent public sector	9.7%	15.7%
Household income growth	11.2%	13.6%	Blue collar	45.5%	25.2%	Percent construction	9.8%	9.9%

Cost of Living
Score: 62.0
Rank: 142

INDEXES & TAXES	AREA	U.S. AVG	HOUSING	AREA	U.S. AVG	NECESSITIES	AREA	U.S. AVG
Cost of Living Index	84.8	100.0	Median home price	$144,200	$220,000	Food Index	99.7	100.0
Buying Power Index	113.6	100.0	Home price appreciation	34.2%	10.1%	Housing Index	64.9	100.0
Income tax rate	5.17%	4.70%	Median rent	$537	$709	Utilities Index	87.3	100.0
Sales tax rate	7.00%	6.58%	Homes owned	65.5%	62.3%	Transportation Index	93.1	100.0
Property tax rate	$7.08	$12.00	Home price ratio	3.4	4.2	Healthcare Index	91.2	100.0
						Miscellaneous Cost Index	101.7	100.0

Climate
Score: 44.1
Rank: 208

TEMPERATURE	AREA	U.S. AVG	PRECIPITATION	AREA	U.S. AVG	COMFORTS & HAZARDS	AREA	U.S. AVG
Average January low	29.0	26.2	Annual inches precipitation	53.3	37.7	July relative humidity	56%	66%
Average July high	90.0	87.4	Annual inches snowfall	4.0	7.0	Annual days mostly sunny	223	208
Annual days > 90°F	48	38	Annual days precipitation	120	109	Annual days with thunderstorms	55	39
Annual days < 32°F	73	89	Annual days rain > 0.5 inches	37	22	Tornado risk score	3	18
Annual days < 0°F	0	6	Annual days snow > 1.5 inches	2	6	Hurricane risk score	1	13

TEMPERATURE

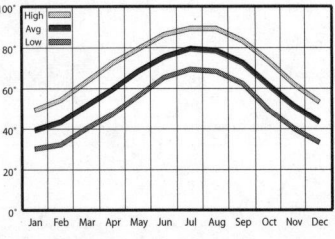

PRECIPITATION

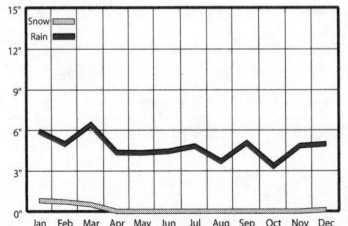

DAYS OF CLOUDS & PRECIPITATION

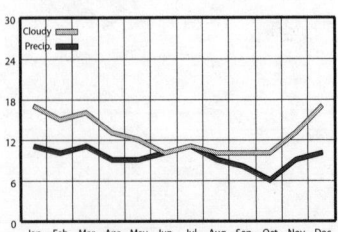

Education
Score: 1.3
Rank: 368

ACHIEVEMENT	AREA	U.S. AVG	PUBLIC SCHOOLS	AREA	U.S. AVG	HIGHER EDUCATION	AREA	U.S. AVG
High school degree	62.0%	82.7%	Expenditures per pupil	$5,120	$5,686	No. 2-year colleges	0	4
2-year college degree	3.7%	6.4%	Student/teacher ratio	15.6	16.7	No. 4-year colleges/universities	1	6
4-year college degree	6.8%	15.7%	Attending public school	97.4%	90.1%	No. highly ranked universities	0	1
Graduate/professional degree	4.0%	8.9%	State SAT score	990*	1021			
			State ACT score	20.2	20.9			

Health & Healthcare
Score: 75.7
Rank: 92

HAZARDS & ILLNESSES	AREA	U.S. AVG	HEALTHCARE	AREA	U.S. AVG	CRIME	AREA	U.S. AVG
Air-quality score	57	37	Physicians per capita	141.1	244.2	Violent crime rate	376.8	465.5
Water-quality score	66	52	Hospital beds per capita	270.7	420.0	Change in violent crime rate	6.0%	-2.2%
Pollen/allergy score	63	61	No. teaching hospitals	0	3	Property crime rate	4,546.5	3,517.1
Cancer mortality per capita	175.5	201.9	Cost per doctor visit	$64	$77	Change in property crime rate	6.3%	-2.1%
Depression days per month	3.4	3.5	Cost per dental visit	$68	$70			
Stress score	47	50						

Crime
Score: 60.4
Rank: 149

Transportation
Score: 89.0
Rank: 42

COMMUTE	AREA	U.S. AVG	INTERCITY SERVICES	AREA	U.S. AVG	AUTOMOTIVE	AREA	U.S. AVG
Average commute time	23.4	27.4	Major airports within 60 miles	1	1	Insurance, annual premium	$1,396	$1,432
Percent commutes > 60 mins.	3.7%	5.9%	Size of regional airport	Large	Large	Gas, cost per gallon	$2.46	$2.49
Commute by auto	78.0%	78.9%	Daily airline activity	1512	686	Daily vehicle miles per capita	29.7	24.0
Commute by mass transit	0.4%	1.9%	Amtrak service	No	No			
Work at home	1.6%	3.1%						
Mass transit miles per capita	0.44	1.87						

Leisure
Score: 23.8
Rank: 284

DINING & SHOPPING	AREA	U.S. AVG	ENTERTAINMENT	AREA	U.S. AVG	OUTDOOR ACTIVITIES	AREA	U.S. AVG
Restaurant rating	1	2	Professional sports rating	1	4	Golf-course rating	2	4
Outlet mall score	111	42	College sports rating	2	4	Ski-area rating	1	3
No. Starbucks	0	13	Zoo/aquarium rating	1	3	Sq. miles inland water	4	4
No. warehouse clubs	0	2	Amusement park rating	1	3	Miles of coastline	0.0	10.7
			Botanical garden/ arboretum rating	1	4	National Park rating	3	3

Arts & Culture
Score: 8.3
Rank: 342

MEDIA & LIBRARIES	AREA	U.S. AVG	PERFORMING ARTS	AREA	U.S. AVG	MUSEUMS	AREA	U.S. AVG
Arts radio rating	1	3	Classical music rating	2	4	Overall museum rating	4	5
No. public libraries	5	27	Ballet/dance rating	1	3	Art museum rating	7	5
Library volumes per capita	1.73	2.78	Professional theater rating	1	3	Science museum rating	1	5
			University arts programs rating	1	5	Children's museum rating	1	3

Danville, IL

Score: 23.9   Rank: 354   2004 rank: not ranked

Profile: Small town
Location: East-central Illinois, at the Indiana border
Elevation: 602 feet
Time zone: Central Standard Time

PRO	CON
Cost of living	Depressed economy
Small-town feel	Low educational attainment
Outdoor recreation	Arts and culture

Danville is a quiet, unremarkable, and economically challenged Midwestern community about 35 miles east of Champaign–Urbana along Interstate 74. The economy, once tied to agriculture and coal and clay mining, has diversified into many areas of manufacturing but is still bleak with high unemployment and low growth projections. There isn't much to do; however, the college towns of Champaign–Urbana and West Lafayette, Indiana (Purdue University), 50 miles east, provide some amenities. Chicago is a fairly long and not a direct haul of 170 miles. At 76.1, the Cost of Living Index is predictably low, and median home prices are lowest in the country at a rock-bottom $65,200, driven in part by the loss of population. The Vermilion River, Lake Vermilion, and Kickapoo State Park provide some minor recreation opportunities and more scenic interest than found in other areas of eastern Illinois.

Danville is located along the Vermilion River near its confluence with the Wabash. Surrounding terrain is mostly flat and agricultural but becomes slightly rolling and wooded near the river valleys. The climate is typical for the region, with warm, humid, and variable summers with thundershowers, and winters with a mix of rain and snow. Snow cover is common but its duration varies year to year. First freeze is late October; last is late April.

DEMOGRAPHICS	AREA	U.S. AVG	ETHNIC COMPOSITION	AREA	U.S. AVG	RESIDENT PROFILE	AREA	U.S. AVG
Population	82,333		White	85.1%	79.0%	Single	30.0%	32.4%
Population density per sq. mile	91.6	358.5	Black	11.0%	10.5%	Married	52.4%	52.7%
Population growth	-6.7%	21.1%	Asian	0.6%	2.7%	Divorced/separated	17.6%	14.9%
Median age	38.3	36.1	Hispanic	3.5%	10.6%	Married with children	19.8%	23.7%
Percent Democrat	43.7%	44.5%	Religious observance	39.9%	48.9%	Single with children	10.1%	9.1%
Percent Republican	55.6%	54.5%	Diversity measure	31.3	40.1	Percent over age 65	16.4%	12.9%

Population

INCOME	AREA	U.S. AVG	EMPLOYMENT	AREA	U.S. AVG	EMPLOYING INDUSTRIES	AREA	U.S. AVG
Per capita income	$18,785	$23,235	Unemployment rate	6.6%	4.7%	Largest: Manufacturing		
Household income	$37,595	$46,414	Recent job growth	2.9%	1.3%			
Household income < $25K	32.0%	26.2%	Projected future job growth	0.9%	11.5%	Percent manufacturing	23.1%	15.4%
Household income > $75K	15.5%	25.4%	White collar	48.4%	57.8%	Percent public sector	14.8%	15.7%
Household income growth	10.3%	13.6%	Blue collar	33.2%	25.2%	Percent construction	10.1%	9.9%

Economy & Jobs
Score: 33.2
Rank: 250

INDEXES & TAXES	AREA	U.S. AVG	HOUSING	AREA	U.S. AVG	NECESSITIES	AREA	U.S. AVG
Cost of Living Index	76.1	100.0	Median home price	$65,200	$220,000	Food Index	95.4	100.0
Buying Power Index	110.7	100.0	Home price appreciation	26.5%	10.1%	Housing Index	33.8	100.0
Income tax rate	3.00%	4.70%	Median rent	$539	$709	Utilities Index	123.6	100.0
Sales tax rate	6.50%	6.58%	Homes owned	66.1%	62.3%	Transportation Index	108.7	100.0
Property tax rate	$15.55	$12.00	Home price ratio	1.7	4.2	Healthcare Index	92.5	100.0
						Miscellaneous Cost Index	101.0	100.0

Cost of Living
Score: 97.1
Rank: 11

TEMPERATURE	AREA	U.S. AVG	PRECIPITATION	AREA	U.S. AVG	COMFORTS & HAZARDS	AREA	U.S. AVG
Average January low	18.0	26.2	Annual inches precipitation	40.2	37.7	July relative humidity	59%	66%
Average July high	85.0	87.4	Annual inches snowfall	25.0	7.0	Annual days mostly sunny	198	208
Annual days > 90°F	15	38	Annual days precipitation	127	109	Annual days with thunderstorms	49	39
Annual days < 32°F	122	89	Annual days rain > 0.5 inches	24	22	Tornado risk score	30	18
Annual days < 0°F	7	6	Annual days snow > 1.5 inches	5	6	Hurricane risk score	2	13

Climate
Score: 42.8
Rank: 213

TEMPERATURE

PRECIPITATION

DAYS OF CLOUDS & PRECIPITATION

ACHIEVEMENT	AREA	U.S. AVG	PUBLIC SCHOOLS	AREA	U.S. AVG	HIGHER EDUCATION	AREA	U.S. AVG
High school degree	78.7%	82.7%	Expenditures per pupil	$4,685	$5,686	No. 2-year colleges	2	4
2-year college degree	7.1%	6.4%	Student/teacher ratio	13.9	16.7	No. 4-year colleges/universities	1	6
4-year college degree	8.2%	15.7%	Attending public school	91.7%	90.1%	No. highly ranked universities	0	1
Graduate/professional degree	4.1%	8.9%	State SAT score	1200	1021			
			State ACT score	20.5*	20.9			

Education
Score: 13.4
Rank: 322

HAZARDS & ILLNESSES	AREA	U.S. AVG	HEALTHCARE	AREA	U.S. AVG	CRIME	AREA	U.S. AVG
Air-quality score	44	37	Physicians per capita	152.2	244.2	Violent crime rate	581.0	465.5
Water-quality score	36	52	Hospital beds per capita	502.8	420.0	Change in violent crime rate	-16.4%	-2.2%
Pollen/allergy score	60	61	No. teaching hospitals	0	3	Property crime rate	3,811.0	3,517.1
Cancer mortality per capita	218.7	201.9	Cost per doctor visit	$62	$77	Change in property crime rate	1.6%	-2.1%
Depression days per month	3.0	3.5	Cost per dental visit	$62	$70			
Stress score	68	50						

Health & Healthcare
Score: 55.1
Rank: 168

Crime
Score: 16.6
Rank: 312

COMMUTE	AREA	U.S. AVG	INTERCITY SERVICES	AREA	U.S. AVG	AUTOMOTIVE	AREA	U.S. AVG
Average commute time	22.0	27.4	Major airports within 60 miles	1	1	Insurance, annual premium	$953	$1,432
Percent commutes > 60 mins.	4.1%	5.9%	Size of regional airport	Medium	Large	Gas, cost per gallon	$2.50	$2.49
Commute by auto	81.7%	78.9%	Daily airline activity	319	686	Daily vehicle miles per capita	22.7	24.0
Commute by mass transit	0.6%	1.9%	Amtrak service	No	No			
Work at home	3.0%	3.1%						
Mass transit miles per capita	0.64	1.87						

Transportation
Score: 52.4
Rank: 179

Leisure Score: 2.1 Rank: 364	DINING & SHOPPING	AREA	U.S. AVG	ENTERTAINMENT	AREA	U.S. AVG	OUTDOOR ACTIVITIES	AREA	U.S. AVG
	Restaurant rating	1	2	Professional sports rating	1	4	Golf-course rating	2	4
	Outlet mall score	26	42	College sports rating	2	4	Ski-area rating	1	3
	No. Starbucks	0	13	Zoo/aquarium rating	1	3	Sq. miles inland water	3	4
	No. warehouse clubs	0	2	Amusement park rating	1	3	Miles of coastline	0.0	10.7
				Botanical garden/ arboretum rating	1	4	National Park rating	1	3

Arts & Culture Score: 15.8 Rank: 314	MEDIA & LIBRARIES	AREA	U.S. AVG	PERFORMING ARTS	AREA	U.S. AVG	MUSEUMS	AREA	U.S. AVG
	Arts radio rating	1	3	Classical music rating	2	4	Overall museum rating	1	5
	No. public libraries	10	27	Ballet/dance rating	1	3	Art museum rating	1	5
	Library volumes per capita	4.37	2.78	Professional theater rating	1	3	Science museum rating	1	5
				University arts programs rating	1	5	Children's museum rating	1	3

Danville, VA

Score: 34.6   Rank: 325   2004 rank: 298

Profile: Small city
Location: Extreme south-central Virginia at North Carolina border
Elevation: 500 feet
Time zone: Eastern Standard Time

PRO	CON
Cost of living	Declining economy
Attractive setting	Low educational attainment
Historic interest	Entertainment

Danville, located in what is referred to as the "southside" part of the state, remains today a depressed center for the tobacco and textile industries. Textile giant Dan River Corporation makes its home there, and the atmosphere is generally business-friendly. However, the current employment and job-prospect figures reflect the poor economic state of the dominant industries. Physically, the downtown area is a mix of historic and small-scale, modern buildings. The Millionaire's Row section of Main Street is listed on the National Register of Historic Places, and there are a few minor cultural assets. But the rest of the area reflects its depressed and largely working-class climate, with older, uninteresting residential areas, some in poor shape, dotting the hillsides

surrounding the city. The city has the lowest home prices and cost of living among Virginia's metropolitan areas, but the declining economy and lack of intellectual stimulation gives the area a notably low rank for the state. We don't see much change going forward.

The Dan River bisects the city on a rolling and wooded plain. Hilly, mostly wooded areas surround the city. Danville enjoys four distinct seasons with warm summers and crisp but moderate winters. Precipitation is spread evenly through the year, occurring mainly as summer thunderstorms and periods of fall and winter rain, with occasional snow and freezing rain. First freeze is mid-October; last is late April.

Population	DEMOGRAPHICS	AREA	U.S. AVG	ETHNIC COMPOSITION	AREA	U.S. AVG	RESIDENT PROFILE	AREA	U.S. AVG
	Population	107,592		White	65.3%	79.0%	Single	32.3%	32.4%
	Population density per sq. mile	106.1	358.5	Black	33.0%	10.5%	Married	51.7%	52.7%
	Population growth	0.3%	21.1%	Asian	0.4%	2.7%	Divorced/separated	16.0%	14.9%
	Median age	40.8	36.1	Hispanic	1.6%	10.6%	Married with children	18.8%	23.7%
	Percent Democrat	40.5%	44.5%	Religious observance	47.0%	48.9%	Single with children	9.7%	9.1%
	Percent Republican	57.9%	54.5%	Diversity measure	45.8	40.1	Percent over age 65	16.9%	12.9%

Economy & Jobs Score: 0.3 Rank: 372	INCOME	AREA	U.S. AVG	EMPLOYMENT	AREA	U.S. AVG	EMPLOYING INDUSTRIES	AREA	U.S. AVG
	Per capita income	$19,117	$23,235	Unemployment rate	8.6%	4.7%	Largest: Manufacturing		
	Household income	$34,654	$46,414	Recent job growth	-1.2%	1.3%			
	Household income < $25K	36.4%	26.2%	Projected future job growth	-5.5%	11.5%	Percent manufacturing	28.5%	15.4%
	Household income > $75K	14.3%	25.4%	White collar	44.9%	57.8%	Percent public sector	12.3%	15.7%
	Household income growth	9.8%	13.6%	Blue collar	39.6%	25.2%	Percent construction	11.1%	9.9%

Cost of Living Score: 99.5 Rank: 3	INDEXES & TAXES	AREA	U.S. AVG	HOUSING	AREA	U.S. AVG	NECESSITIES	AREA	U.S. AVG
	Cost of Living Index	73.4	100.0	Median home price	$92,200	$220,000	Food Index	95.4	100.0
	Buying Power Index	105.8	100.0	Home price appreciation	18.1%	10.1%	Housing Index	67.7	100.0
	Income tax rate	5.75%	4.70%	Median rent	$523	$709	Utilities Index	81.6	100.0
	Sales tax rate	5.00%	6.58%	Homes owned	62.7%	62.3%	Transportation Index	87.0	100.0
	Property tax rate	$5.82	$12.00	Home price ratio	2.7	4.2	Healthcare Index	95.6	100.0
							Miscellaneous Cost Index	95.9	100.0

Climate
Score: 60.4
Rank: 147

TEMPERATURE	AREA	U.S. AVG
Average January low	28.5	26.2
Average July high	87.5	87.4
Annual days > 90°F	28	38
Annual days < 32°F	85	89
Annual days < 0°F	0	6

PRECIPITATION	AREA	U.S. AVG
Annual inches precipitation	41.4	37.7
Annual inches snowfall	8.7	7.0
Annual days precipitation	121	109
Annual days rain > 0.5 inches	27	22
Annual days snow > 1.5 inches	2	6

COMFORTS & HAZARDS	AREA	U.S. AVG
July relative humidity	72%	66%
Annual days mostly sunny	217	208
Annual days with thunderstorms	46	39
Tornado risk score	2	18
Hurricane risk score	19	13

TEMPERATURE

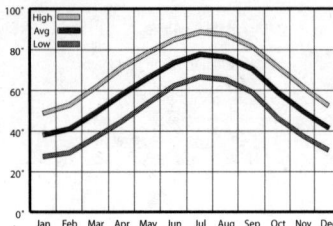

PRECIPITATION

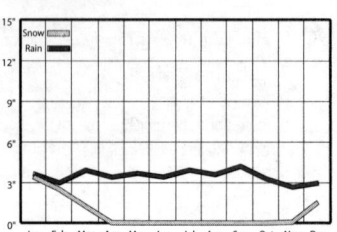

DAYS OF CLOUDS & PRECIPITATION

Education
Score: 2.4
Rank: 364

ACHIEVEMENT	AREA	U.S. AVG
High school degree	67.8%	82.7%
2-year college degree	5.4%	6.4%
4-year college degree	7.0%	15.7%
Graduate/professional degree	4.1%	8.9%

PUBLIC SCHOOLS	AREA	U.S. AVG
Expenditures per pupil	$4,684	$5,686
Student/teacher ratio	14.5	16.7
Attending public school	89.4%	90.1%
State SAT score	1025*	1021
State ACT score	21.1	20.9

HIGHER EDUCATION	AREA	U.S. AVG
No. 2-year colleges	2	4
No. 4-year colleges/universities	1	6
No. highly ranked universities	0	1

Health & Healthcare
Score: 88.0
Rank: 46

HAZARDS & ILLNESSES	AREA	U.S. AVG
Air-quality score	71	37
Water-quality score	69	52
Pollen/allergy score	61	61
Cancer mortality per capita	196.7	201.9
Depression days per month	3.3	3.5
Stress score	82	50

HEALTHCARE	AREA	U.S. AVG
Physicians per capita	160.1	244.2
Hospital beds per capita	385.7	420.0
No. teaching hospitals	0	3
Cost per doctor visit	$63	$77
Cost per dental visit	$59	$70

Crime
Score: 80.7
Rank: 73

CRIME	AREA	U.S. AVG
Violent crime rate	291.7	465.5
Change in violent crime rate	-16.4%	-2.2%
Property crime rate	2,506.3	3,517.1
Change in property crime rate	-2.3%	-2.1%

Transportation
Score: 38.5
Rank: 231

COMMUTE	AREA	U.S. AVG
Average commute time	24.6	27.4
Percent commutes > 60 mins.	5.9%	5.9%
Commute by auto	81.1%	78.9%
Commute by mass transit	1.0%	1.9%
Work at home	1.9%	3.1%
Mass transit miles per capita	1.01	1.87

INTERCITY SERVICES	AREA	U.S. AVG
Major airports within 60 miles	1	1
Size of regional airport	Medium	Large
Daily airline activity	525	686
Amtrak service	Yes	No

AUTOMOTIVE	AREA	U.S. AVG
Insurance, annual premium	$926	$1,432
Gas, cost per gallon	$2.38	$2.49
Daily vehicle miles per capita	23.5	24.0

Leisure
Score: 3.2
Rank: 361

DINING & SHOPPING	AREA	U.S. AVG
Restaurant rating	1	2
Outlet mall score	0	42
No. Starbucks	0	13
No. warehouse clubs	0	2

ENTERTAINMENT	AREA	U.S. AVG
Professional sports rating	2	4
College sports rating	1	4
Zoo/aquarium rating	1	3
Amusement park rating	1	3
Botanical garden/ arboretum rating	1	4

OUTDOOR ACTIVITIES	AREA	U.S. AVG
Golf-course rating	2	4
Ski-area rating	2	3
Sq. miles inland water	2	4
Miles of coastline	0.0	10.7
National Park rating	1	3

Arts & Culture
Score: 36.4
Rank: 238

MEDIA & LIBRARIES	AREA	U.S. AVG
Arts radio rating	1	3
No. public libraries	6	27
Library volumes per capita	2.09	2.78

PERFORMING ARTS	AREA	U.S. AVG
Classical music rating	6	4
Ballet/dance rating	1	3
Professional theater rating	1	3
University arts programs rating	2	5

MUSEUMS	AREA	U.S. AVG
Overall museum rating	2	5
Art museum rating	3	5
Science museum rating	4	5
Children's museum rating	1	3

Davenport–Moline–Rock Island, IA-IL   Score: 52.8   Rank: 233   2004 rank: 150

Profile: Small-city complex
Location: Northwest Illinois straddling Mississippi River at Iowa border, 175 miles west of Chicago
Elevation: 594 feet
Time zone: Central Standard Time

PRO	CON
Small-town atmosphere	Violent crime rate
Cost of living	Economic cycles
Air service	Flood risk

The "Quad Cities" span the Mississippi River and the Illinois-Iowa border. Davenport and Bettendorf form the Iowa component, and Moline and Rock Island are on the Illinois side. The area, also called the "Breadbasket of America," is a center for agriculture, particularly known as the headquarters of machinery manufacturer John Deere (in Moline), and the heart of the Corn Belt. Highlights include an attractive setting in the Mississippi Valley, a slow pace, and friendly people. Cost of living is below Iowa and Illinois averages, but violent crime rates are surprisingly high, and the economy is strongly connected to the farming industry. The downtown areas are plain and uninspiring but functional, with some historic interest and attractive river waterfront areas. The Illinois side is more industrial, although the Deere presence has left some positive imprints on Moline. These cities have experienced some flooding problems and are taking steps to prevent them in the future. There are some minor entertainment and cultural amenities and two large annual music festivals, but overall the area offers little to do. The area does have good regional air service to connect it to bigger cities.

The river-valley setting is distinct with low bluffs rising on both sides. Rolling prairie and occasional wooded areas lie beyond the bluffs. Periods of intense summer heat and humidity and subzero winter temperatures are common. There may be 50 to 60 days over 90°F each summer. Precipitation is well distributed annually, with most arriving in summer. The low flood plain location and the confluence of the Rock and Mississippi rivers can produce flooding, most recently in 1993. First freeze is late September; last is late May.

DEMOGRAPHICS	AREA	U.S. AVG	ETHNIC COMPOSITION	AREA	U.S. AVG	RESIDENT PROFILE	AREA	U.S. AVG
Population	374,905		White	87.6%	79.0%	Single	31.4%	32.4%
Population density per sq. mile	165.2	358.5	Black	6.0%	10.5%	Married	54.7%	52.7%
Population growth	1.9%	21.1%	Asian	1.4%	2.7%	Divorced/separated	13.9%	14.9%
Median age	37.8	36.1	Hispanic	6.3%	10.6%	Married with children	22.1%	23.7%
Percent Democrat	52.8%	44.5%	Religious observance	50.5%	48.9%	Single with children	9.0%	9.1%
Percent Republican	46.6%	54.5%	Diversity measure	31.2	40.1	Percent over age 65	14.2%	12.9%

Economy & Jobs
Score: 35.6
Rank: 241

INCOME	AREA	U.S. AVG	EMPLOYMENT	AREA	U.S. AVG	EMPLOYING INDUSTRIES	AREA	U.S. AVG
Per capita income	$23,270	$23,235	Unemployment rate	4.4%	4.7%	Largest: Manufacturing		
Household income	$45,819	$46,414	Recent job growth	0.8%	1.3%			
Household income < $25K	25.3%	26.2%	Projected future job growth	4.5%	11.5%	Percent manufacturing	18.2%	15.4%
Household income > $75K	24.4%	25.4%	White collar	55.7%	57.8%	Percent public sector	12.0%	15.7%
Household income growth	12.7%	13.6%	Blue collar	27.0%	25.2%	Percent construction	8.9%	9.9%

Cost of Living
Score: 39.6
Rank: 226

INDEXES & TAXES	AREA	U.S. AVG	HOUSING	AREA	U.S. AVG	NECESSITIES	AREA	U.S. AVG
Cost of Living Index	83.8	100.0	Median home price	$118,500	$220,000	Food Index	97.5	100.0
Buying Power Index	122.6	100.0	Home price appreciation	26.5%	10.1%	Housing Index	42.2	100.0
Income tax rate	8.41%	4.70%	Median rent	$592	$709	Utilities Index	124.3	100.0
Sales tax rate	6.57%	6.58%	Homes owned	68.1%	62.3%	Transportation Index	102.6	100.0
Property tax rate	$15.59	$12.00	Home price ratio	2.6	4.2	Healthcare Index	101.0	100.0
						Miscellaneous Cost Index	96.3	100.0

Climate
Score: 14.4
Rank: 319

TEMPERATURE	AREA	U.S. AVG	PRECIPITATION	AREA	U.S. AVG	COMFORTS & HAZARDS	AREA	U.S. AVG
Average January low	13.0	26.2	Annual inches precipitation	36.0	37.7	July relative humidity	70%	66%
Average July high	85.2	87.4	Annual inches snowfall	30.0	7.0	Annual days mostly sunny	202	208
Annual days > 90°F	22	38	Annual days precipitation	112	109	Annual days with thunderstorms	47	39
Annual days < 32°F	136	89	Annual days rain > 0.5 inches	25	22	Tornado risk score	32	18
Annual days < 0°F	16	6	Annual days snow > 1.5 inches	9	6	Hurricane risk score	0	13

TEMPERATURE

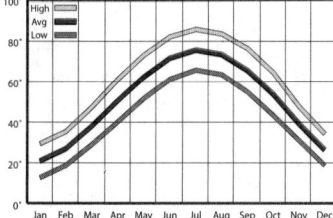

PRECIPITATION

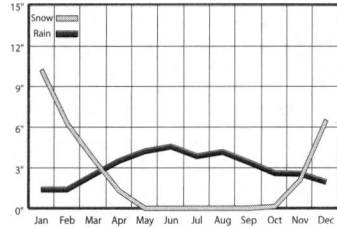

DAYS OF CLOUDS & PRECIPITATION

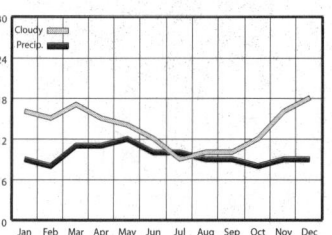

ACHIEVEMENT	AREA	U.S. AVG	PUBLIC SCHOOLS	AREA	U.S. AVG	HIGHER EDUCATION	AREA	U.S. AVG
High school degree	84.6%	82.7%	Expenditures per pupil	$5,182	$5,686	No. 2-year colleges	5	4
2-year college degree	7.2%	6.4%	Student/teacher ratio	16.2	16.7	No. 4-year colleges/universities	6	6
4-year college degree	13.6%	15.7%	Attending public school	91.5%	90.1%	No. highly ranked universities	1	1
Graduate/professional degree	6.5%	8.9%	State SAT score	1215	1021			
			State ACT score	22.1*	20.9			

Education
Score: 53.5
Rank: 173

HAZARDS & ILLNESSES	AREA	U.S. AVG	HEALTHCARE	AREA	U.S. AVG	CRIME	AREA	U.S. AVG
Air-quality score	45	37	Physicians per capita	179.5	244.2	Violent crime rate	633.1	465.5
Water-quality score	51	52	Hospital beds per capita	401.7	420.0	Change in violent crime rate	3.2%	-2.2%
Pollen/allergy score	48	61	No. teaching hospitals	4	3	Property crime rate	3,866.7	3,517.1
Cancer mortality per capita	213.6	201.9	Cost per doctor visit	$73	$77	Change in property crime rate	-0.3%	-2.1%
Depression days per month	2.7	3.5	Cost per dental visit	$61	$70			
Stress score	27	50						

Health & Healthcare
Score: 59.6
Rank: 152

Crime
Score: 22.5
Rank: 290

COMMUTE	AREA	U.S. AVG	INTERCITY SERVICES	AREA	U.S. AVG	AUTOMOTIVE	AREA	U.S. AVG
Average commute time	21.2	27.4	Major airports within 60 miles	0	1	Insurance, annual premium	$1,020	$1,432
Percent commutes > 60 mins.	3.4%	5.9%	Size of regional airport	Small	Large	Gas, cost per gallon	$2.47	$2.49
Commute by auto	83.7%	78.9%	Daily airline activity	58	686	Daily vehicle miles per capita	23.3	24.0
Commute by mass transit	0.9%	1.9%	Amtrak service	Yes	No			
Work at home	3.0%	3.1%						
Mass transit miles per capita	0.87	1.87						

Transportation
Score: 34.8
Rank: 245

DINING & SHOPPING	AREA	U.S. AVG	ENTERTAINMENT	AREA	U.S. AVG	OUTDOOR ACTIVITIES	AREA	U.S. AVG
Restaurant rating	1	2	Professional sports rating	3	4	Golf-course rating	4	4
Outlet mall score	12	42	College sports rating	2	4	Ski-area rating	2	3
No. Starbucks	3	13	Zoo/aquarium rating	2	3	Sq. miles inland water	4	4
No. warehouse clubs	0	2	Amusement park rating	1	3	Miles of coastline	0.0	10.7
			Botanical garden/ arboretum rating	1	4	National Park rating	2	3

Leisure
Score: 37.2
Rank: 232

MEDIA & LIBRARIES	AREA	U.S. AVG	PERFORMING ARTS	AREA	U.S. AVG	MUSEUMS	AREA	U.S. AVG
Arts radio rating	1	3	Classical music rating	4	4	Overall museum rating	6	5
No. public libraries	40	27	Ballet/dance rating	1	3	Art museum rating	6	5
Library volumes per capita	4.01	2.78	Professional theater rating	1	3	Science museum rating	5	5
			University arts programs rating	6	5	Children's museum rating	6	3

Arts & Culture
Score: 61.8
Rank: 143

Dayton, OH

Score: 71.0   **Rank:** 84   **2004 rank:** 41

Profile: Mid-size city
Location: West-central Ohio at crossroads of north–south I-75 and east–west I-70
Elevation: 757 feet
Time zone: Eastern Standard Time

PRO
Diverse economy
Nearby cities
Cost of living and housing

CON
Recent unemployment
Entertainment
Arts and culture

Dayton, at the crossroads of southwestern Ohio's major transportation routes, has a distinct industrial heritage. Local NCR Corporation, formerly the National Cash Register Corporation, is a leader in retail information technology and ATMs. The area has a strong heritage of innovation, and has attracted a number of other high-tech businesses in recent years. An assortment of other manufacturing and service activities, some tied to the auto and paper industry, round out the diverse economy. An old GM site along the river is being repurposed, with the help of state funds, into a "Tech Town" high-tech campus—interesting, if it works out. The more attractive residential areas are in the wooded hills to the southeast in Kettering and other areas along State Route 48, with classic Midwest-style neighborhoods, lots of trees, well-laid-out roads and shopping areas, and good home values. Areas north are more industrial. The downtown area is fairly plain and largely not an attraction. Although there is some new development, including an ice rink and farmer's market along the waterfront, there isn't much to do. But excellent cultural amenities and entertainment can be found in Cincinnati, 50 miles to the south. The Wright-Patterson Air Force Base brings a military presence, economic influence, and a first-class aviation museum. The University of Dayton adds some college-town amenities and sports excitement. The area has notably good air service. On the whole, Dayton doesn't excel in any area but offers a good balance.

Dayton is located near the center of the Miami River Valley, a nearly flat plain below the general elevation of the adjacent rolling country. Land to the north is open and slopes gradually upward to Indian Lake, near the highest point in the state at 1,500 feet. To the south is a mix of rolling farmland and deciduous wooded hills, sloping generally downward towards the Ohio River. Summers are warm, calm, and humid.

Winters are cold and changeable with below-zero temperatures every 4 in 5 years. Precipitation appears mostly as spring and summer showers and thunderstorms, with periods of winter rain. Snowfall is light to moderate, with frequent winter snow flurries. First freeze is late October; last is mid-April.

Population

DEMOGRAPHICS	AREA	U.S. AVG
Population	846,389	
Population density per sq. mile	495.4	358.5
Population growth	0.7%	21.1%
Median age	37.4	36.1
Percent Democrat	45.6%	44.5%
Percent Republican	53.9%	54.5%

ETHNIC COMPOSITION	AREA	U.S. AVG
White	81.5%	79.0%
Black	14.4%	10.5%
Asian	1.7%	2.7%
Hispanic	1.2%	10.6%
Religious observance	40.4%	48.9%
Diversity measure	31.7	40.1

RESIDENT PROFILE	AREA	U.S. AVG
Single	32.2%	32.4%
Married	52.7%	52.7%
Divorced/separated	15.1%	14.9%
Married with children	21.3%	23.7%
Single with children	9.3%	9.1%
Percent over age 65	13.8%	12.9%

Economy & Jobs
Score: 13.1
Rank: 323

INCOME	AREA	U.S. AVG
Per capita income	$24,610	$23,235
Household income	$47,096	$46,414
Household income < $25K	24.4%	26.2%
Household income > $75K	26.1%	25.4%
Household income growth	11.4%	13.6%

EMPLOYMENT	AREA	U.S. AVG
Unemployment rate	6.0%	4.7%
Recent job growth	-0.2%	1.3%
Projected future job growth	1.1%	11.5%
White collar	59.7%	57.8%
Blue collar	25.4%	25.2%

EMPLOYING INDUSTRIES	AREA	U.S. AVG
Largest: Manufacturing		
Percent manufacturing	17.6%	15.4%
Percent public sector	14.2%	15.7%
Percent construction	7.8%	9.9%

Cost of Living
Score: 34.2
Rank: 246

INDEXES & TAXES	AREA	U.S. AVG
Cost of Living Index	82.2	100.0
Buying Power Index	128.4	100.0
Income tax rate	7.09%	4.70%
Sales tax rate	7.35%	6.58%
Property tax rate	$13.90	$12.00

HOUSING	AREA	U.S. AVG
Median home price	$120,600	$220,000
Home price appreciation	16.8%	10.1%
Median rent	$632	$709
Homes owned	62.9%	62.3%
Home price ratio	2.6	4.2

NECESSITIES	AREA	U.S. AVG
Food Index	95.9	100.0
Housing Index	51.5	100.0
Utilities Index	98.4	100.0
Transportation Index	103.5	100.0
Healthcare Index	96.5	100.0
Miscellaneous Cost Index	96.7	100.0

Climate
Score: 46.5
Rank: 199

TEMPERATURE	AREA	U.S. AVG
Average January low	20.4	26.2
Average July high	84.7	87.4
Annual days > 90°F	17	38
Annual days < 32°F	117	89
Annual days < 0°F	6	6

PRECIPITATION	AREA	U.S. AVG
Annual inches precipitation	34.4	37.7
Annual inches snowfall	28.6	7.0
Annual days precipitation	130	109
Annual days rain > 0.5 inches	22	22
Annual days snow > 1.5 inches	6	6

COMFORTS & HAZARDS	AREA	U.S. AVG
July relative humidity	70%	66%
Annual days mostly sunny	182	208
Annual days with thunderstorms	40	39
Tornado risk score	43	18
Hurricane risk score	4	13

TEMPERATURE

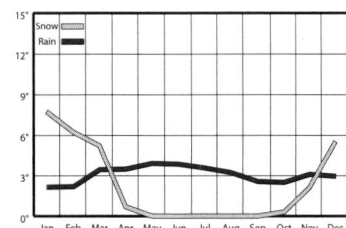

PRECIPITATION

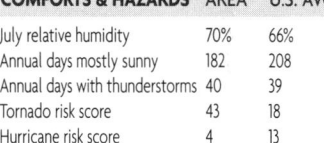

DAYS OF CLOUDS & PRECIPITATION

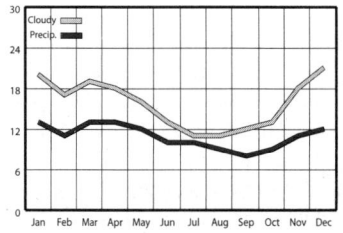

Education
Score: 63.9
Rank: 136

ACHIEVEMENT	AREA	U.S. AVG
High school degree	84.3%	82.7%
2-year college degree	7.0%	6.4%
4-year college degree	14.2%	15.7%
Graduate/professional degree	8.9%	8.9%

PUBLIC SCHOOLS	AREA	U.S. AVG
Expenditures per pupil	$5,727	$5,686
Student/teacher ratio	18.5	16.7
Attending public school	86.8%	90.1%
State SAT score	1079	1021
State ACT score	21.5*	20.9

HIGHER EDUCATION	AREA	U.S. AVG
No. 2-year colleges	16	4
No. 4-year colleges/universities	11	6
No. highly ranked universities	2	1

Health & Healthcare
Score: 40.9
Rank: 220

HAZARDS & ILLNESSES	AREA	U.S. AVG
Air-quality score	34	37
Water-quality score	31	52
Pollen/allergy score	60	61
Cancer mortality per capita	220.4	201.9
Depression days per month	4.2	3.5
Stress score	69	50

HEALTHCARE	AREA	U.S. AVG
Physicians per capita	277.1	244.2
Hospital beds per capita	410.6	420.0
No. teaching hospitals	8	3
Cost per doctor visit	$69	$77
Cost per dental visit	$59	$70

Crime
Score: 52.4
Rank: 177

CRIME	AREA	U.S. AVG
Violent crime rate	305.1	465.5
Change in violent crime rate	-1.3%	-2.2%
Property crime rate	3,777.2	3,517.1
Change in property crime rate	-7.2%	-2.1%

Transportation Score: 89.8 Rank: 39	COMMUTE	AREA	U.S. AVG	INTERCITY SERVICES	AREA	U.S. AVG	AUTOMOTIVE	AREA	U.S. AVG
	Average commute time	23.0	27.4	Major airports within 60 miles	2	1	Insurance, annual premium	$1,559	$1,432
	Percent commutes > 60 mins.	3.9%	5.9%	Size of regional airport	Large	Large	Gas, cost per gallon	$2.47	$2.49
	Commute by auto	84.3%	78.9%	Daily airline activity	1235	686	Daily vehicle miles per capita	25.6	24.0
	Commute by mass transit	1.8%	1.9%	Amtrak service	No	No			
	Work at home	2.5%	3.1%						
	Mass transit miles per capita	1.81	1.87						

Leisure Score: 54.3 Rank: 171	DINING & SHOPPING	AREA	U.S. AVG	ENTERTAINMENT	AREA	U.S. AVG	OUTDOOR ACTIVITIES	AREA	U.S. AVG
	Restaurant rating	3	2	Professional sports rating	4	4	Golf-course rating	6	4
	Outlet mall score	18	42	College sports rating	3	4	Ski-area rating	2	3
	No. Starbucks	5	13	Zoo/aquarium rating	4	3	Sq. miles inland water	2	4
	No. warehouse clubs	2	2	Amusement park rating	1	3	Miles of coastline	0.0	10.7
				Botanical garden/ arboretum rating	9	4	National Park rating	1	3

Arts & Culture Score: 91.4 Rank: 33	MEDIA & LIBRARIES	AREA	U.S. AVG	PERFORMING ARTS	AREA	U.S. AVG	MUSEUMS	AREA	U.S. AVG
	Arts radio rating	8	3	Classical music rating	6	4	Overall museum rating	9	5
	No. public libraries	49	27	Ballet/dance rating	7	3	Art museum rating	7	5
	Library volumes per capita	5.34	2.78	Professional theater rating	1	3	Science museum rating	9	5
				University arts programs rating	7	5	Children's museum rating	8	3

Decatur, AL

Score: 23.8 Rank: 347 2004 rank: 209

Profile: Small industrial city
Location: Extreme northern Alabama along the Tennessee River
Elevation: 590 feet
Time zone: Central Standard Time

PRO	CON
Cost of living	Summer heat and humidity
Nearby water recreation	Arts and culture
Low crime rate	Low educational attainment

Decatur is a northern Alabama transportation hub and manufacturing center for a variety of goods. The strategic location on the Tennessee River and key railroads brought Northern industrial interests following the Civil War, leaving the city with a strong imprint of fine older Victorian homes and some attractive parks. The Cost of Living Index of 82 is attractive, and crime rates are low for the state and region. The Tennessee River provides some recreational opportunities, but the immediate area has few other leisure or arts amenities. That isn't all bad, for the Decatur area lies only 25 miles west of Huntsville, a booming commercial and high-tech center with plenty of amenities, plenty of jobs, and plenty to do. The location and good labor force have attracted a strong and diverse industrial base with some high-tech spillover from the Huntsville direction. The list of employers is long, and everything from rocket engines to cat food is manufactured locally.

The town lies on a river plain on the southwest bank of the dammed-up Tennessee River. Land rises gently to the southwest into the William Bankhead National Forest, with hills to 1,100 feet. The climate features long, hot, muggy summers, and variable, wet winters with occasional snow.

Population	DEMOGRAPHICS	AREA	U.S. AVG	ETHNIC COMPOSITION	AREA	U.S. AVG	RESIDENT PROFILE	AREA	U.S. AVG
	Population	148,042		White	82.7%	79.0%	Single	26.3%	32.4%
	Population density per sq. mile	116.1	358.5	Black	11.9%	10.5%	Married	60.4%	52.7%
	Population growth	12.6%	21.1%	Asian	0.6%	2.7%	Divorced/separated	13.3%	14.9%
	Median age	37.8	36.1	Hispanic	3.7%	10.6%	Married with children	25.5%	23.7%
	Percent Democrat	33.3%	44.5%	Religious observance	57.1%	48.9%	Single with children	8.1%	9.1%
	Percent Republican	65.9%	54.5%	Diversity measure	35.1	40.1	Percent over age 65	13.1%	12.9%

Economy & Jobs Score: 31.8 Rank: 255	INCOME	AREA	U.S. AVG	EMPLOYMENT	AREA	U.S. AVG	EMPLOYING INDUSTRIES	AREA	U.S. AVG
	Per capita income	$20,803	$23,235	Unemployment rate	5.1%	4.7%	Largest: Manufacturing		
	Household income	$40,428	$46,414	Recent job growth	0.7%	1.3%			
	Household income < $25K	30.9%	26.2%	Projected future job growth	6.4%	11.5%	Percent manufacturing	25.4%	15.4%
	Household income > $75K	20.3%	25.4%	White collar	47.6%	57.8%	Percent public sector	12.2%	15.7%
	Household income growth	11.3%	13.6%	Blue collar	38.1%	25.2%	Percent construction	12.7%	9.9%

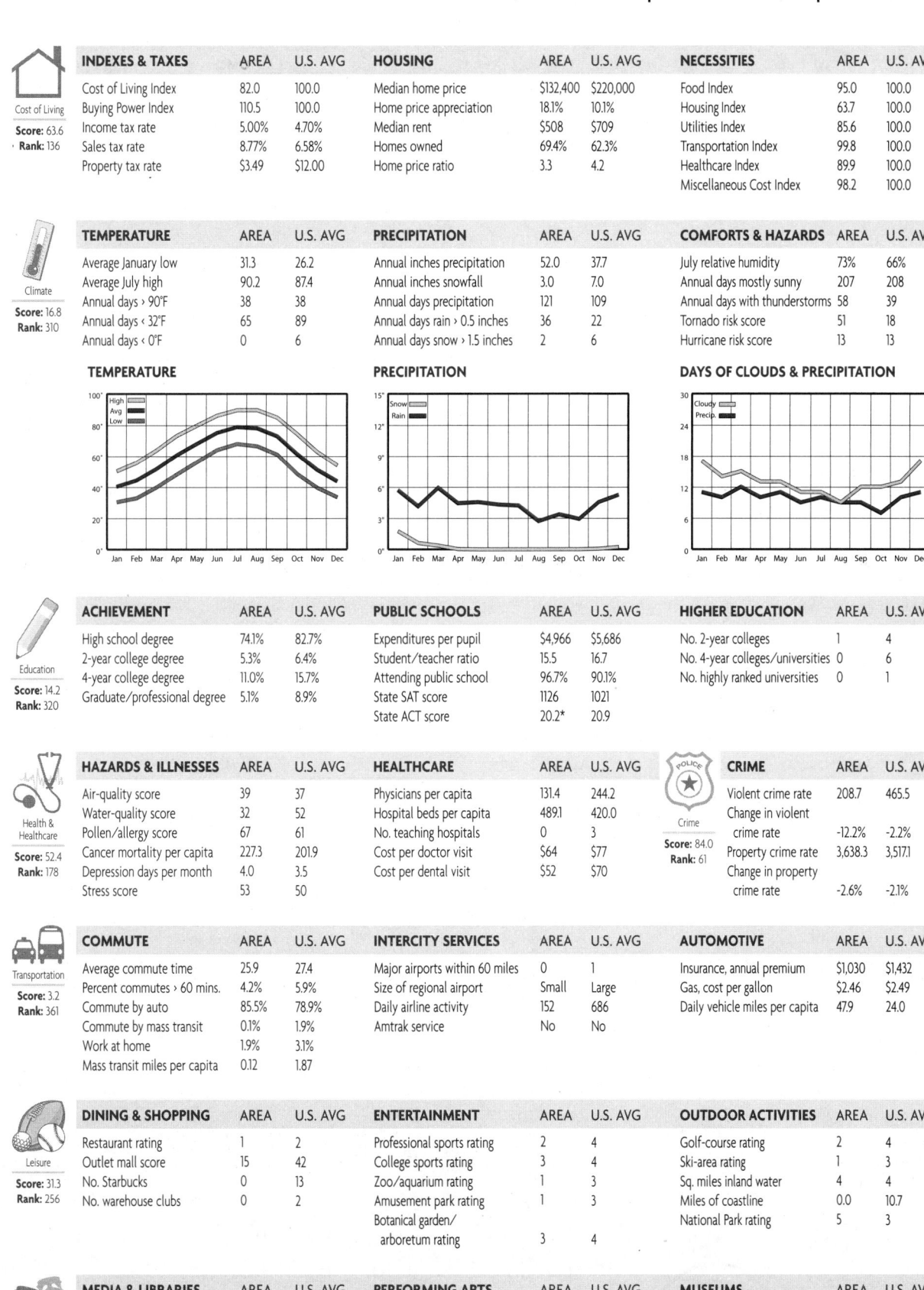

Cost of Living
Score: 63.6
Rank: 136

INDEXES & TAXES	AREA	U.S. AVG	HOUSING	AREA	U.S. AVG	NECESSITIES	AREA	U.S. AVG
Cost of Living Index	82.0	100.0	Median home price	$132,400	$220,000	Food Index	95.0	100.0
Buying Power Index	110.5	100.0	Home price appreciation	18.1%	10.1%	Housing Index	63.7	100.0
Income tax rate	5.00%	4.70%	Median rent	$508	$709	Utilities Index	85.6	100.0
Sales tax rate	8.77%	6.58%	Homes owned	69.4%	62.3%	Transportation Index	99.8	100.0
Property tax rate	$3.49	$12.00	Home price ratio	3.3	4.2	Healthcare Index	89.9	100.0
						Miscellaneous Cost Index	98.2	100.0

Climate
Score: 16.8
Rank: 310

TEMPERATURE	AREA	U.S. AVG	PRECIPITATION	AREA	U.S. AVG	COMFORTS & HAZARDS	AREA	U.S. AVG
Average January low	31.3	26.2	Annual inches precipitation	52.0	37.7	July relative humidity	73%	66%
Average July high	90.2	87.4	Annual inches snowfall	3.0	7.0	Annual days mostly sunny	207	208
Annual days > 90°F	38	38	Annual days precipitation	121	109	Annual days with thunderstorms	58	39
Annual days < 32°F	65	89	Annual days rain > 0.5 inches	36	22	Tornado risk score	51	18
Annual days < 0°F	0	6	Annual days snow > 1.5 inches	2	6	Hurricane risk score	13	13

TEMPERATURE

PRECIPITATION

DAYS OF CLOUDS & PRECIPITATION

Education
Score: 14.2
Rank: 320

ACHIEVEMENT	AREA	U.S. AVG	PUBLIC SCHOOLS	AREA	U.S. AVG	HIGHER EDUCATION	AREA	U.S. AVG
High school degree	74.1%	82.7%	Expenditures per pupil	$4,966	$5,686	No. 2-year colleges	1	4
2-year college degree	5.3%	6.4%	Student/teacher ratio	15.5	16.7	No. 4-year colleges/universities	0	6
4-year college degree	11.0%	15.7%	Attending public school	96.7%	90.1%	No. highly ranked universities	0	1
Graduate/professional degree	5.1%	8.9%	State SAT score	1126	1021			
			State ACT score	20.2*	20.9			

Health & Healthcare
Score: 52.4
Rank: 178

HAZARDS & ILLNESSES	AREA	U.S. AVG	HEALTHCARE	AREA	U.S. AVG	CRIME	AREA	U.S. AVG
Air-quality score	39	37	Physicians per capita	131.4	244.2	Violent crime rate	208.7	465.5
Water-quality score	32	52	Hospital beds per capita	489.1	420.0	Change in violent crime rate	-12.2%	-2.2%
Pollen/allergy score	67	61	No. teaching hospitals	0	3	Property crime rate	3,638.3	3,517.1
Cancer mortality per capita	227.3	201.9	Cost per doctor visit	$64	$77	Change in property crime rate	-2.6%	-2.1%
Depression days per month	4.0	3.5	Cost per dental visit	$52	$70			
Stress score	53	50						

Crime
Score: 84.0
Rank: 61

Transportation
Score: 3.2
Rank: 361

COMMUTE	AREA	U.S. AVG	INTERCITY SERVICES	AREA	U.S. AVG	AUTOMOTIVE	AREA	U.S. AVG
Average commute time	25.9	27.4	Major airports within 60 miles	0	1	Insurance, annual premium	$1,030	$1,432
Percent commutes > 60 mins.	4.2%	5.9%	Size of regional airport	Small	Large	Gas, cost per gallon	$2.46	$2.49
Commute by auto	85.5%	78.9%	Daily airline activity	152	686	Daily vehicle miles per capita	47.9	24.0
Commute by mass transit	0.1%	1.9%	Amtrak service	No	No			
Work at home	1.9%	3.1%						
Mass transit miles per capita	0.12	1.87						

Leisure
Score: 31.3
Rank: 256

DINING & SHOPPING	AREA	U.S. AVG	ENTERTAINMENT	AREA	U.S. AVG	OUTDOOR ACTIVITIES	AREA	U.S. AVG
Restaurant rating	1	2	Professional sports rating	2	4	Golf-course rating	2	4
Outlet mall score	15	42	College sports rating	3	4	Ski-area rating	1	3
No. Starbucks	0	13	Zoo/aquarium rating	1	3	Sq. miles inland water	4	4
No. warehouse clubs	0	2	Amusement park rating	1	3	Miles of coastline	0.0	10.7
			Botanical garden/arboretum rating	3	4	National Park rating	5	3

Arts & Culture
Score: 3.2
Rank: 361

MEDIA & LIBRARIES	AREA	U.S. AVG	PERFORMING ARTS	AREA	U.S. AVG	MUSEUMS	AREA	U.S. AVG
Arts radio rating	1	3	Classical music rating	3	4	Overall museum rating	3	5
No. public libraries	7	27	Ballet/dance rating	1	3	Art museum rating	4	5
Library volumes per capita	1.00	2.78	Professional theater rating	1	3	Science museum rating	1	5
			University arts programs rating	1	5	Children's museum rating	1	3

Decatur, IL

Profile: Small agricultural/industrial town
Location: East-central Illinois, 30 miles east of Springfield
Elevation: 613 feet
Time zone: Central Standard Time

PRO	CON
Small-town atmosphere	Entertainment
Cost of living and	Arts and culture
housing	Low future job growth
Stable employment	

Decatur forms the bottom point of a 90-mile-wide, 40-mile-tall diamond formed by Springfield to the west, Bloomington–Normal to the north, and Champaign–Urbana to the east. Common to the area, agriculture dominates the commercial activity and the local landscape. Agricultural processing giant Archer-Daniels-Midland (ADM) has its headquarters in Decatur, and Caterpillar and agricultural processor Tate & Lyle also operate large plants. ADM in particular provides a stable employment base, but the area is still suffering the effects of a 2001 Firestone plant closing. Employment and income-growth projections are among the lowest in the state. On the flip side, cost of living and home prices especially are among the lowest in the region and the U.S., and as measured by the Home Price Ratio, home prices are a bar-

gain relative to local incomes. The crime rate, high for the region, bears watching. The city is fairly plain and doesn't offer much in terms of entertainment or cultural amenities, but it does have a historic district with a mix of older homes, including some designed by Frank Lloyd Wright, and some Abraham Lincoln and Civil War sites.

The terrain is level and agricultural. Summers are typically warm and humid with periods of mainly afternoon showers and thundershowers, and a few cooler, drier spells. Precipitation is more or less evenly distributed through the year. Spring and fall are typical for the region, with windy, changeable springs and relatively calm autumns with periods of warm, dry Indian summers. First freeze is mid-October; last is mid-April.

Population

DEMOGRAPHICS	AREA	U.S. AVG	ETHNIC COMPOSITION	AREA	U.S. AVG	RESIDENT PROFILE	AREA	U.S. AVG
Population	109,589		White	82.4%	79.0%	Single	31.0%	32.4%
Population density per sq. mile	188.8	358.5	Black	14.5%	10.5%	Married	53.0%	52.7%
Population growth	-6.5%	21.1%	Asian	0.9%	2.7%	Divorced/separated	16.0%	14.9%
Median age	38.9	36.1	Hispanic	1.2%	10.6%	Married with children	19.7%	23.7%
Percent Democrat	45.1%	44.5%	Religious observance	49.8%	48.9%	Single with children	9.7%	9.1%
Percent Republican	54.3%	54.5%	Diversity measure	31.6	40.1	Percent over age 65	15.9%	12.9%

Economy & Jobs
Score: 59.9
Rank: 151

INCOME	AREA	U.S. AVG	EMPLOYMENT	AREA	U.S. AVG	EMPLOYING INDUSTRIES	AREA	U.S. AVG
Per capita income	$22,137	$23,235	Unemployment rate	6.3%	4.7%	Largest: Manufacturing		
Household income	$41,497	$46,414	Recent job growth	3.4%	1.3%			
Household income < $25K	29.5%	26.2%	Projected future job growth	4.0%	11.5%	Percent manufacturing	19.5%	15.4%
Household income > $75K	20.8%	25.4%	White collar	54.3%	57.8%	Percent public sector	11.1%	15.7%
Household income growth	9.6%	13.6%	Blue collar	29.2%	25.2%	Percent construction	9.7%	9.9%

Cost of Living
Score: 96.5
Rank: 13

INDEXES & TAXES	AREA	U.S. AVG	HOUSING	AREA	U.S. AVG	NECESSITIES	AREA	U.S. AVG
Cost of Living Index	74.3	100.0	Median home price	$85,300	$220,000	Food Index	93.1	100.0
Buying Power Index	125.2	100.0	Home price appreciation	21.7%	10.1%	Housing Index	39.5	100.0
Income tax rate	3.00%	4.70%	Median rent	$550	$709	Utilities Index	94.4	100.0
Sales tax rate	6.50%	6.58%	Homes owned	66.6%	62.3%	Transportation Index	100.0	100.0
Property tax rate	$17.84	$12.00	Home price ratio	2.1	4.2	Healthcare Index	86.9	100.0
						Miscellaneous Cost Index	96.3	100.0

Climate
Score: 37.4
Rank: 233

TEMPERATURE	AREA	U.S. AVG	PRECIPITATION	AREA	U.S. AVG	COMFORTS & HAZARDS	AREA	U.S. AVG
Average January low	18.6	26.2	Annual inches precipitation	35.0	37.7	July relative humidity	71%	66%
Average July high	86.6	87.4	Annual inches snowfall	22.0	7.0	Annual days mostly sunny	200	208
Annual days > 90°F	28	38	Annual days precipitation	112	109	Annual days with thunderstorms	50	39
Annual days < 32°F	119	89	Annual days rain > 0.5 inches	22	22	Tornado risk score	28	18
Annual days < 0°F	8	6	Annual days snow > 1.5 inches	5	6	Hurricane risk score	3	13

TEMPERATURE

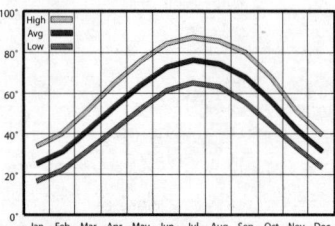

PRECIPITATION

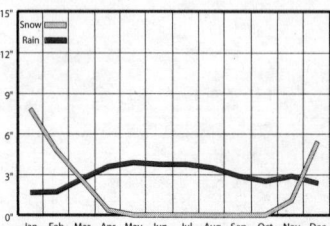

DAYS OF CLOUDS & PRECIPITATION

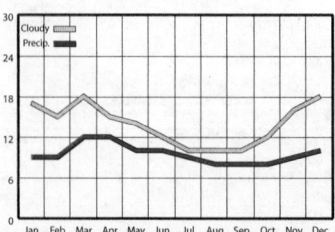

Education
Score: 16.3
Rank: 312

ACHIEVEMENT	AREA	U.S. AVG	PUBLIC SCHOOLS	AREA	U.S. AVG	HIGHER EDUCATION	AREA	U.S. AVG
High school degree	83.1%	82.7%	Expenditures per pupil	$4,300	$5,686	No. 2-year colleges	2	4
2-year college degree	5.6%	6.4%	Student/teacher ratio	18.8	16.7	No. 4-year colleges/universities	1	6
4-year college degree	11.4%	15.7%	Attending public school	88.5%	90.1%	No. highly ranked universities	0	1
Graduate/professional degree	5.6%	8.9%	State SAT score	1200	1021			
			State ACT score	20.5*	20.9			

Health & Healthcare
Score: 61.8
Rank: 143

HAZARDS & ILLNESSES	AREA	U.S. AVG	HEALTHCARE	AREA	U.S. AVG	CRIME	AREA	U.S. AVG
Air-quality score	41	37	Physicians per capita	199.7	244.2	Violent crime rate	700.1	465.5
Water-quality score	20	52	Hospital beds per capita	468.1	420.0	Change in violent crime rate	24.8%	-2.2%
Pollen/allergy score	49	61	No. teaching hospitals	2	3	Property crime rate	4,316.1	3,517.1
Cancer mortality per capita	203.5	201.9	Cost per doctor visit	$82	$77	Change in property crime rate	6.3%	-2.1%
Depression days per month	5.8	3.5	Cost per dental visit	$74	$70			
Stress score	70	50						

Crime — **Score: 34.5** **Rank: 245**

Transportation
Score: 46.8
Rank: 200

COMMUTE	AREA	U.S. AVG	INTERCITY SERVICES	AREA	U.S. AVG	AUTOMOTIVE	AREA	U.S. AVG
Average commute time	20.0	27.4	Major airports within 60 miles	0	1	Insurance, annual premium	$1,088	$1,432
Percent commutes > 60 mins.	3.8%	5.9%	Size of regional airport	None	Large	Gas, cost per gallon	$2.45	$2.49
Commute by auto	84.5%	78.9%	Daily airline activity	8	686	Daily vehicle miles per capita	18.9	24.0
Commute by mass transit	0.9%	1.9%	Amtrak service	No	No			
Work at home	2.5%	3.1%						
Mass transit miles per capita	0.87	1.87						

Leisure
Score: 9.6
Rank: 337

DINING & SHOPPING	AREA	U.S. AVG	ENTERTAINMENT	AREA	U.S. AVG	OUTDOOR ACTIVITIES	AREA	U.S. AVG
Restaurant rating	1	2	Professional sports rating	2	4	Golf-course rating	2	4
Outlet mall score	30	42	College sports rating	3	4	Ski-area rating	1	3
No. Starbucks	0	13	Zoo/aquarium rating	1	3	Sq. miles inland water	2	4
No. warehouse clubs	0	2	Amusement park rating	1	3	Miles of coastline	0.0	10.7
			Botanical garden/ arboretum rating	1	4	National Park rating	1	3

Arts & Culture
Score: 29.4
Rank: 263

MEDIA & LIBRARIES	AREA	U.S. AVG	PERFORMING ARTS	AREA	U.S. AVG	MUSEUMS	AREA	U.S. AVG
Arts radio rating	1	3	Classical music rating	2	4	Overall museum rating	2	5
No. public libraries	9	27	Ballet/dance rating	1	3	Art museum rating	3	5
Library volumes per capita	3.76	2.78	Professional theater rating	1	3	Science museum rating	1	5
			University arts programs rating	3	5	Children's museum rating	1	3

Deltona–Daytona Beach–Ormond Beach, FL

Score: 72.3   Rank: 75   2004 rank: 66

Profile: Beach-city/suburban complex
Location: Atlantic Coast, 90 miles south of Jacksonville
Elevation: 31 feet
Time zone: Eastern Standard Time

PRO
Auto racing
Water recreation
Strong employment trends

CON
Long commutes
Growth and sprawl
Healthcare

On the map, Daytona Beach is a typical Florida East Coast city, with a barrier island, wide beaches, and an inland town and residential area, known for its motor sports, beach racing, and the world-famous Daytona International Speedway. But this metro area starts with the name "Deltona," a city not familiar to many outside the state but actually the largest of the three cities in this metro area. Deltona is located some 25 miles inland along Interstate 4 about halfway between Daytona and the booming metropolis of Orlando. Having incorporated in 1995, it serves mainly as a bedroom community for both Daytona and Orlando, with affordable housing, much of it in planned communities and developments, and a high percentage of permanent residents. It is

not a tourist place, and in fact, seems to hide behind lakes and woods from touristy Orlando and from the coast. The more famous Daytona has distinguished itself as the "birthplace of speed." Upholding a long tradition, one can still drive on the beach where land speed records were once set—however, speed limits are now in effect. Good arts and culture amenities and the usual assortment of watersports are on hand. Ormond Beach has a similar profile—minus the auto sports—to Daytona. Some commute 50 miles to Orlando or to other coastal cities, explaining in part the recent uplift in employment figures. Cost of living, once a big plus for the area, and home prices in particular, have risen rapidly, but the area is still relatively more affordable than most Florida East Coast areas.

Wide, white sandy beaches dominate the coastline. Summer temperatures, while reaching 90°F or above during the late morning or early afternoon, tend to diminish in the afternoon with sea breezes and frequent afternoon thundershowers, both lowering temperatures into the 80s. Winters are mild with a few cold-air invasions. Long periods of cloudiness and rain are infrequent. While hurricanes do occur, they are not considered a great threat at this latitude.

Population

DEMOGRAPHICS	AREA	U.S. AVG
Population	481,398	
Population density per sq. mile	436.3	358.5
Population growth	29.9%	21.1%
Median age	42.8	36.1
Percent Democrat	50.5%	44.5%
Percent Republican	48.9%	54.5%

ETHNIC COMPOSITION	AREA	U.S. AVG
White	84.6%	79.0%
Black	10.0%	10.5%
Asian	1.2%	2.7%
Hispanic	8.4%	10.6%
Religious observance	37.5%	48.9%
Diversity measure	38.5	40.1

RESIDENT PROFILE	AREA	U.S. AVG
Single	29.8%	32.4%
Married	52.9%	52.7%
Divorced/separated	17.4%	14.9%
Married with children	16.2%	23.7%
Single with children	7.6%	9.1%
Percent over age 65	21.6%	12.9%

Economy & Jobs
Score: 85.8
Rank: 54

INCOME	AREA	U.S. AVG
Per capita income	$22,608	$23,235
Household income	$40,526	$46,414
Household income ‹ $25K	28.7%	26.2%
Household income › $75K	19.5%	25.4%
Household income growth	15.1%	13.6%

EMPLOYMENT	AREA	U.S. AVG
Unemployment rate	3.8%	4.7%
Recent job growth	4.4%	1.3%
Projected future job growth	18.2%	11.5%
White collar	57.9%	57.8%
Blue collar	23.4%	25.2%

EMPLOYING INDUSTRIES	AREA	U.S. AVG
Largest: Healthcare & Social Assistance		
Percent manufacturing	11.6%	15.4%
Percent public sector	13.3%	15.7%
Percent construction	11.7%	9.9%

Cost of Living
Score: 68.4
Rank: 119

INDEXES & TAXES	AREA	U.S. AVG
Cost of Living Index	97.5	100.0
Buying Power Index	93.2	100.0
Income tax rate	0.00%	4.70%
Sales tax rate	6.50%	6.58%
Property tax rate	$13.97	$12.00

HOUSING	AREA	U.S. AVG
Median home price	$214,400	$220,000
Home price appreciation	122.7%	10.1%
Median rent	$730	$709
Homes owned	66.4%	62.3%
Home price ratio	5.3	4.2

NECESSITIES	AREA	U.S. AVG
Food Index	101.0	100.0
Housing Index	65.5	100.0
Utilities Index	101.1	100.0
Transportation Index	101.9	100.0
Healthcare Index	105.2	100.0
Miscellaneous Cost Index	94.6	100.0

Climate
Score: 78.1
Rank: 82

TEMPERATURE	AREA	U.S. AVG
Average January low	47.6	26.2
Average July high	89.6	87.4
Annual days > 90°F	54	38
Annual days > 32°F	5	89
Annual days < 0°F	0	6

PRECIPITATION	AREA	U.S. AVG
Annual inches precipitation	50.2	37.7
Annual inches snowfall	0.1	7.0
Annual days precipitation	115	109
Annual days rain > 0.5 inches	30	22
Annual days snow > 1.5 inches	0	6

COMFORTS & HAZARDS	AREA	U.S. AVG
July relative humidity	78%	66%
Annual days mostly sunny	229	208
Annual days with thunderstorms	79	39
Tornado risk score	26	18
Hurricane risk score	75	13

TEMPERATURE

PRECIPITATION

DAYS OF CLOUDS & PRECIPITATION

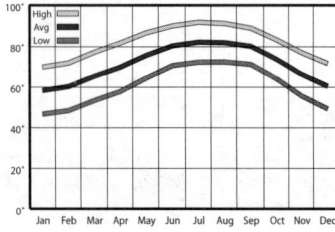

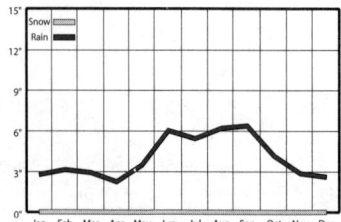

Education
Score: 38.2
Rank: 232

ACHIEVEMENT	AREA	U.S. AVG
High school degree	82.3%	82.7%
2-year college degree	8.0%	6.4%
4-year college degree	11.7%	15.7%
Graduate/professional degree	6.1%	8.9%

PUBLIC SCHOOLS	AREA	U.S. AVG
Expenditures per pupil	$4,796	$5,686
Student/teacher ratio	15.4	16.7
Attending public school	91.3%	90.1%
State SAT score	993*	1021
State ACT score	20.3	20.9

HIGHER EDUCATION	AREA	U.S. AVG
No. 2-year colleges	1	4
No. 4-year colleges/universities	4	6
No. highly ranked universities	0	1

Health & Healthcare
Score: 2.1
Rank: 365

HAZARDS & ILLNESSES	AREA	U.S. AVG
Air-quality score	15	37
Water-quality score	35	52
Pollen/allergy score	76	61
Cancer mortality per capita	271.4	201.9
Depression days per month	3.5	3.5
Stress score	73	50

HEALTHCARE	AREA	U.S. AVG
Physicians per capita	175.2	244.2
Hospital beds per capita	319.9	420.0
No. teaching hospitals	2	3
Cost per doctor visit	$65	$77
Cost per dental visit	$67	$70

Crime
Score: 38.0
Rank: 232

CRIME	AREA	U.S. AVG
Violent crime rate	568.2	465.5
Change in violent crime rate	-9.3%	-2.2%
Property crime rate	3,513.2	3,517.1
Change in property crime rate	-7.2%	-2.1%

Transportation
Score: 28.9
Rank: 267

COMMUTE	AREA	U.S. AVG	INTERCITY SERVICES	AREA	U.S. AVG	AUTOMOTIVE	AREA	U.S. AVG
Average commute time	27.3	27.4	Major airports within 60 miles	2	1	Insurance, annual premium	$1,798	$1,432
Percent commutes › 60 mins.	8.3%	5.9%	Size of regional airport	Large	Large	Gas, cost per gallon	$2.62	$2.49
Commute by auto	79.1%	78.9%	Daily airline activity	697	686	Daily vehicle miles per capita	28.6	24.0
Commute by mass transit	0.9%	1.9%	Amtrak service	No	No			
Work at home	3.0%	3.1%						
Mass transit miles per capita	0.94	1.87						

Leisure
Score: 63.9
Rank: 135

DINING & SHOPPING	AREA	U.S. AVG	ENTERTAINMENT	AREA	U.S. AVG	OUTDOOR ACTIVITIES	AREA	U.S. AVG
Restaurant rating	1	2	Professional sports rating	2	4	Golf-course rating	3	4
Outlet mall score	123	42	College sports rating	4	4	Ski-area rating	1	3
No. Starbucks	3	13	Zoo/aquarium rating	1	3	Sq. miles inland water	8	4
No. warehouse clubs	0	2	Amusement park rating	1	3	Miles of coastline	50.3	10.7
			Botanical garden/ arboretum rating	4	4	National Park rating	4	3

Arts & Culture
Score: 41.2
Rank: 220

MEDIA & LIBRARIES	AREA	U.S. AVG	PERFORMING ARTS	AREA	U.S. AVG	MUSEUMS	AREA	U.S. AVG
Arts radio rating	1	3	Classical music rating	1	4	Overall museum rating	6	5
No. public libraries	15	27	Ballet/dance rating	1	3	Art museum rating	8	5
Library volumes per capita	1.84	2.78	Professional theater rating	1	3	Science museum rating	6	5
			University arts programs rating	6	5	Children's museum rating	1	3

Denver–Aurora, CO

Score: 63.1   Rank: 150   2004 rank: 60

Profile: Regional center/capital city
Location: North-central Colorado at the base of the Rocky Mountain Front Range
Elevation: 5,280 feet
Time zone: Mountain Standard Time

PRO
Attractive downtown
Arts and culture
Nearby mountains

CON
Growth and sprawl
Commute times
Air quality

Denver is the commercial, financial, industrial, and government center for Colorado and a seven-state region of Rocky Mountain and western Plains states. The city and its surrounding area continue to be one of our favorite large cities, and the list of reasons is large; however, crowding and growth are taking their toll.

The downtown area is vibrant, functional, and attractive, one of the best downtowns in the country in our view as a business center, an attraction for local residents, and a place to live. More than most U.S. cities today, people want to live close to downtown, and good city neighborhoods combine with new housing in former industrial areas adjacent to downtown and the South Platte River to make it possible. The "LoDo," or Lower Downtown, area just to the northwest of the main downtown features renovated late-19th-century commercial and factory buildings repurposed into small business, entertainment, and shopping venues, accessible, walkable, and livable at all times. This area is anchored by the nicely restored Denver Union Station rail terminal, and the crown jewel is the industrial revival–style Coors Field ballpark. It is one of the finest urban-core restorations in the country. South of this area, also along the water, are new museums, a new convention center, excellent performing arts venues, and new sports facilities adding to the life and utility of the downtown area. Beyond downtown and mainly east and south is a patchwork of older neighborhoods with desirable early-20th-century housing, mixed with a few well-spaced high-rises. The city spreads into suburbs in all directions and especially east and south with varying living environments, but most suburban areas are attractive and well connected to downtown. All of this, of course, is in view of the main Rocky Mountain ridges, bringing picture postcard vistas on most days, except when smog and haze occasionally take over.

All services and amenities are of the first order. Air service at the Denver International Airport, the hub of discount carrier Frontier Airlines, is plentiful, although the facility is not conveniently located for most local residents. The old Stapleton Airport 5 miles east of downtown is undergoing a massive residential and commercial redevelopment and may turn out to be another area crown jewel. The Rockies to the west offer unlimited recreational opportunities, including skiing, hiking, fishing, and watersports. A unique "Snow Train" service takes skiers to Winter Park and other resorts. Museums, performing arts, libraries, bookstores, and professional sports are abundant and more accessible than in comparable places. The historical heritage of the city and region is interesting and well preserved. New gambling venues have revived such mining ghost towns to the west as Central City and Blackhawk; whether this is a tasteful use of historic sites brings different opinions.

Suburbs offer a lot of attractive living choices and environments in all price ranges. Many have good town centers of their own and plenty of local employment, especially those near the Denver Tech Center to the south. Close to the city, the Cherry Creek area and the Park Hill neighborhood east of the large "City Park" offer excellent living just a few miles from the downtown core. South of town the large suburbs of Littleton and Centennial offer good schools and housing, and still farther south Castle Rock offers family living in more of a country setting, though growth in this direction has been maybe a little *too* rapid. Aurora, to the east, is very large but rather featureless, as is Lakewood to the west. The other more attractive suburbs lie to the northwest towards Boulder—Arvada, Westminster, Lafayette, and Louisville. The latter two are in Boulder County and we discuss them in the earlier narrative for

Boulder (p. 229). These suburbs are self-contained towns with a strong country feel and plenty of local employment.

Denver's many attractions continue to lure new residents. Population growth is showing no signs of slowing. The impact is starting to show in cost of living, now at a borderline high 107.8. The good news: Costs have stayed relatively constant, given this pressure, compared especially to other large cities and other Western locations. Despite persistent efforts to keep the downtown attractive, urban sprawl has generated traffic, long commute times, and smog, particularly in summer and along the Interstate 25 corridor. The economic picture is still favorable but not without risk, and the area is stimulating and relatively affordable for a big city. The downsides of commutes, air quality, and some cost factors brought a drop in ranking, but we like Denver more than the figure indicates.

The city lies at the western edge of the undulating high prairie that extends east towards Kansas. The front wall of the Rockies rises abruptly west of town with numerous stream valleys and canyons converging in the South Platte River. Denver enjoys low relative humidity, light precipitation, and abundant sunshine. Summer days are warm with occasional thundershowers and cool evenings. Severe weather is usually confined to areas farther east. The mountains shelter the area from the strongest winter storms and cold air blasts, but fall and spring usually bring at least one snowstorm. Spring is the cloudiest and wettest season. First freeze is early October; last is late May.

Population

DEMOGRAPHICS	AREA	U.S. AVG	ETHNIC COMPOSITION	AREA	U.S. AVG	RESIDENT PROFILE	AREA	U.S. AVG
Population	2,350,559		White	77.7%	79.0%	Single	30.9%	32.4%
Population density per sq. mile	280.7	358.5	Black	5.5%	10.5%	Married	53.5%	52.7%
Population growth	61.8%	21.1%	Asian	3.6%	2.7%	Divorced/separated	15.6%	14.9%
Median age	34.8	36.1	Hispanic	21.1%	10.6%	Married with children	25.4%	23.7%
Percent Democrat	51.3%	44.5%	Religious observance	37.6%	48.9%	Single with children	8.2%	9.1%
Percent Republican	47.4%	54.5%	Diversity measure	54.4	40.1	Percent over age 65	9.2%	12.9%

Economy & Jobs
Score: 56.4
Rank: 163

INCOME	AREA	U.S. AVG	EMPLOYMENT	AREA	U.S. AVG	EMPLOYING INDUSTRIES	AREA	U.S. AVG
Per capita income	$30,599	$23,235	Unemployment rate	5.3%	4.7%	Largest: Healthcare & Social Assistance		
Household income	$61,777	$46,414	Recent job growth	0.9%	1.3%			
Household income < $25K	15.6%	26.2%	Projected future job growth	16.4%	11.5%	Percent manufacturing	10.0%	15.4%
Household income > $75K	38.5%	25.4%	White collar	67.6%	57.8%	Percent public sector	12.3%	15.7%
Household income growth	16.1%	13.6%	Blue collar	19.9%	25.2%	Percent construction	9.8%	9.9%

Cost of Living
Score: 15.2
Rank: 316

INDEXES & TAXES	AREA	U.S. AVG	HOUSING	AREA	U.S. AVG	NECESSITIES	AREA	U.S. AVG
Cost of Living Index	107.8	100.0	Median home price	$255,200	$220,000	Food Index	111.0	100.0
Buying Power Index	128.5	100.0	Home price appreciation	20.7%	10.1%	Housing Index	99.9	100.0
Income tax rate	5.00%	4.70%	Median rent	$909	$709	Utilities Index	96.7	100.0
Sales tax rate	7.85%	6.58%	Homes owned	65.9%	62.3%	Transportation Index	107.1	100.0
Property tax rate	$7.54	$12.00	Home price ratio	4.1	4.2	Healthcare Index	125.3	100.0
						Miscellaneous Cost Index	97.4	100.0

Climate
Score: 54.0
Rank: 171

TEMPERATURE	AREA	U.S. AVG	PRECIPITATION	AREA	U.S. AVG	COMFORTS & HAZARDS	AREA	U.S. AVG
Average January low	16.2	26.2	Annual inches precipitation	16.0	37.7	July relative humidity	53%	66%
Average July high	87.4	87.4	Annual inches snowfall	60.0	7.0	Annual days mostly sunny	246	208
Annual days > 90°F	32	38	Annual days precipitation	88	109	Annual days with thunderstorms	41	39
Annual days < 32°F	163	89	Annual days rain > 0.5 inches	7	22	Tornado risk score	52	18
Annual days < 0°F	10	6	Annual days snow > 1.5 inches	14	6	Hurricane risk score	0	13

TEMPERATURE

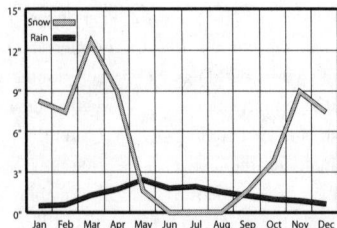

PRECIPITATION

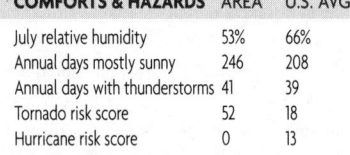

DAYS OF CLOUDS & PRECIPITATION

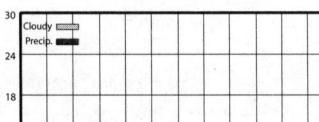

Education
Score: 94.7
Rank: 21

ACHIEVEMENT	AREA	U.S. AVG	PUBLIC SCHOOLS	AREA	U.S. AVG	HIGHER EDUCATION	AREA	U.S. AVG
High school degree	86.9%	82.7%	Expenditures per pupil	$5,419	$5,686	No. 2-year colleges	16	4
2-year college degree	6.8%	6.4%	Student/teacher ratio	19.1	16.7	No. 4-year colleges/universities	28	6
4-year college degree	23.3%	15.7%	Attending public school	91.6%	90.1%	No. highly ranked universities	3	1
Graduate/professional degree	11.1%	8.9%	State SAT score	1122	1021			
			State ACT score	20.3*	20.9			

HAZARDS & ILLNESSES	AREA	U.S. AVG	HEALTHCARE	AREA	U.S. AVG	CRIME	AREA	U.S. AVG
Air-quality score	27	37	Physicians per capita	253.0	244.2	Violent crime rate	444.3	465.5
Water-quality score	87	52	Hospital beds per capita	236.1	420.0	Change in violent		
Pollen/allergy score	85	61	No. teaching hospitals	18	3	crime rate	2.4%	-2.2%
Cancer mortality per capita	146.0	201.9	Cost per doctor visit	$82	$77	Property crime rate	4,457.7	3,517.1
Depression days per month	3.1	3.5	Cost per dental visit	$74	$70	Change in property		
Stress score	92	50				crime rate	4.0%	-2.1%

Health & Healthcare — Score: 18.2 — Rank: 305

Crime — Score: 42.2 — Rank: 216

COMMUTE	AREA	U.S. AVG	INTERCITY SERVICES	AREA	U.S. AVG	AUTOMOTIVE	AREA	U.S. AVG
Average commute time	29.3	27.4	Major airports within 60 miles	2	1	Insurance, annual premium	$2,113	$1,432
Percent commutes > 60 mins.	6.6%	5.9%	Size of regional airport	Large	Large	Gas, cost per gallon	$2.45	$2.49
Commute by auto	76.2%	78.9%	Daily airline activity	887	686	Daily vehicle miles per capita	24.1	24.0
Commute by mass transit	4.3%	1.9%	Amtrak service	Yes	No			
Work at home	4.7%	3.1%						
Mass transit miles per capita	4.34	1.87						

Transportation — Score: 32.4 — Rank: 253

DINING & SHOPPING	AREA	U.S. AVG	ENTERTAINMENT	AREA	U.S. AVG	OUTDOOR ACTIVITIES	AREA	U.S. AVG
Restaurant rating	3	2	Professional sports rating	9	4	Golf-course rating	7	4
Outlet mall score	217	42	College sports rating	5	4	Ski-area rating	10	3
No. Starbucks	85	13	Zoo/aquarium rating	7	3	Sq. miles inland water	3	4
No. warehouse clubs	10	2	Amusement park rating	7	3	Miles of coastline	0.0	10.7
			Botanical garden/ arboretum rating	10	4	National Park rating	3	3

Leisure — Score: 93.0 — Rank: 27

MEDIA & LIBRARIES	AREA	U.S. AVG	PERFORMING ARTS	AREA	U.S. AVG	MUSEUMS	AREA	U.S. AVG
Arts radio rating	9	3	Classical music rating	9	4	Overall museum rating	9	5
No. public libraries	74	27	Ballet/dance rating	9	3	Art museum rating	9	5
Library volumes per capita	2.59	2.78	Professional theater rating	10	3	Science museum rating	9	5
			University arts programs rating	9	5	Children's museum rating	8	3

Arts & Culture — Score: 95.2 — Rank: 19

Des Moines—West Des Moines, IA   Score: 79.7   Rank: 46   2004 rank: 52

Profile: Capital city
Location: Just south of geographic center of Iowa
Elevation: 963 feet
Time zone: Central Standard Time

PRO	CON
Attractive downtown	Entertainment
Capital city amenities	Air service
Stable economy	Harsh winters

As the cultural and economic heart of Iowa, Des Moines is headquarters to nearly 60 companies and most notably a center for the insurance industry as well as many agriculture-related businesses. Many characterize it as a "gentle" big city, retaining a small-town feel with larger-city amenities, but some also complain of a lack of entertainment and nightlife. It is quintessentially Midwestern with a clean but plain downtown with mostly rectangular tree-lined streets. The wealthier and more educated suburbs and most parks and recreational amenities lie west of town, the largest being West Des Moines, while the east is more industrial. The area contains about 400 factories, many processing food or manufacturing farming products. The city has an assortment of parks, museums, zoos, gardens, and historic attractions. Des Moines is large enough to have a good symphony and ballet and a large, concert venue, but small enough to be a "15-minute city"—15 minutes gets you about anywhere in town. With a 140-year tradition, the Iowa State Fair matches most people's image of a classic American fair. For a larger capital city, air service is relatively lacking and ethnic diversity is low, but cost of living at 88.4 is quite reasonable for what is available and for a capital city. As a place with strengths in all categories, Des Moines continues to do well in the rankings.

The gently rolling terrain sits in the shallow valley of the Des Moines River and its tributaries. The summer season is warm and humid with prevailing southerly winds and precipitation falling mainly as showers and thunderstorms, some heavy. Autumn is characteristically sunny with diminishing precipitation. Winter brings cold dry air, sometimes below 0°F, interrupted by occasional, short snowstorms. Extensive drifting snow can impede transportation. First freeze is early October; last is early May.

DEMOGRAPHICS	AREA	U.S. AVG	ETHNIC COMPOSITION	AREA	U.S. AVG	RESIDENT PROFILE	AREA	U.S. AVG
Population	512,416		White	88.9%	79.0%	Single	29.4%	32.4%
Population density per sq. mile	178.0	358.5	Black	3.8%	10.5%	Married	56.4%	52.7%
Population growth	24.1%	21.1%	Asian	2.8%	2.7%	Divorced/separated	14.2%	14.9%
Median age	36.0	36.1	Hispanic	4.7%	10.6%	Married with children	25.3%	23.7%
Percent Democrat	50.0%	44.5%	Religious observance	47.2%	48.9%	Single with children	7.8%	9.1%
Percent Republican	49.2%	54.5%	Diversity measure	27.3	40.1	Percent over age 65	11.5%	12.9%

Population

Economy & Jobs
Score: 76.5
Rank: 88

INCOME	AREA	U.S. AVG
Per capita income	$26,594	$23,235
Household income	$52,466	$46,414
Household income < $25K	19.6%	26.2%
Household income > $75K	30.1%	25.4%
Household income growth	13.2%	13.6%

EMPLOYMENT	AREA	U.S. AVG
Unemployment rate	3.7%	4.7%
Recent job growth	1.9%	1.3%
Projected future job growth	12.5%	11.5%
White collar	66.1%	57.8%
Blue collar	19.5%	25.2%

EMPLOYING INDUSTRIES	AREA	U.S. AVG
Largest: Finance & Insurance		
Percent manufacturing	11.4%	15.4%
Percent public sector	13.0%	15.7%
Percent construction	8.0%	9.9%

Cost of Living
Score: 25.1
Rank: 279

INDEXES & TAXES	AREA	U.S. AVG
Cost of Living Index	88.4	100.0
Buying Power Index	133.0	100.0
Income tax rate	8.72%	4.70%
Sales tax rate	6.03%	6.58%
Property tax rate	$15.15	$12.00

HOUSING	AREA	U.S. AVG
Median home price	$147,800	$220,000
Home price appreciation	28.8%	10.1%
Median rent	$689	$709
Homes owned	68.3%	62.3%
Home price ratio	2.8	4.2

NECESSITIES	AREA	U.S. AVG
Food Index	89.7	100.0
Housing Index	56.9	100.0
Utilities Index	130.2	100.0
Transportation Index	96.5	100.0
Healthcare Index	106.3	100.0
Miscellaneous Cost Index	98.5	100.0

Climate
Score: 22.2
Rank: 290

TEMPERATURE	AREA	U.S. AVG
Average January low	11.3	26.2
Average July high	84.9	87.4
Annual days > 90°F	21	38
Annual days < 32°F	137	89
Annual days < 0°F	16	6

PRECIPITATION	AREA	U.S. AVG
Annual inches precipitation	31.0	37.7
Annual inches snowfall	33.0	7.0
Annual days precipitation	106	109
Annual days rain > 0.5 inches	21	22
Annual days snow > 1.5 inches	10	6

COMFORTS & HAZARDS	AREA	U.S. AVG
July relative humidity	69%	66%
Annual days mostly sunny	199	208
Annual days with thunderstorms	50	39
Tornado risk score	36	18
Hurricane risk score	1	13

TEMPERATURE

PRECIPITATION

DAYS OF CLOUDS & PRECIPITATION

Education
Score: 84.8
Rank: 58

ACHIEVEMENT	AREA	U.S. AVG
High school degree	89.0%	82.7%
2-year college degree	7.5%	6.4%
4-year college degree	20.8%	15.7%
Graduate/professional degree	8.3%	8.9%

PUBLIC SCHOOLS	AREA	U.S. AVG
Expenditures per pupil	$5,700	$5,686
Student/teacher ratio	15.8	16.7
Attending public school	92.6%	90.1%
State SAT score	1215	1021
State ACT score	22.1*	20.9

HIGHER EDUCATION	AREA	U.S. AVG
No. 2-year colleges	7	4
No. 4-year colleges/universities	7	6
No. highly ranked universities	1	1

Health & Healthcare
Score: 49.5
Rank: 190

HAZARDS & ILLNESSES	AREA	U.S. AVG
Air-quality score	34	37
Water-quality score	61	52
Pollen/allergy score	40	61
Cancer mortality per capita	229.9	201.9
Depression days per month	2.8	3.5
Stress score	14	50

HEALTHCARE	AREA	U.S. AVG
Physicians per capita	244.9	244.2
Hospital beds per capita	377.2	420.0
No. teaching hospitals	5	3
Cost per doctor visit	$77	$77
Cost per dental visit	$60	$70

Crime
Score: 61.5
Rank: 145

CRIME	AREA	U.S. AVG
Violent crime rate	332.3	465.5
Change in violent crime rate	31.3%	-2.2%
Property crime rate	4,189.2	3,517.1
Change in property crime rate	5.7%	-2.1%

Transportation
Score: 37.4
Rank: 234

COMMUTE	AREA	U.S. AVG
Average commute time	21.6	27.4
Percent commutes > 60 mins.	2.6%	5.9%
Commute by auto	81.9%	78.9%
Commute by mass transit	1.4%	1.9%
Work at home	3.6%	3.1%
Mass transit miles per capita	1.43	1.87

INTERCITY SERVICES	AREA	U.S. AVG
Major airports within 60 miles	0	1
Size of regional airport	Small	Large
Daily airline activity	106	686
Amtrak service	No	No

AUTOMOTIVE	AREA	U.S. AVG
Insurance, annual premium	$1,132	$1,432
Gas, cost per gallon	$2.41	$2.49
Daily vehicle miles per capita	25.2	24.0

Leisure
Score: 40.6
Rank: 221

DINING & SHOPPING	AREA	U.S. AVG
Restaurant rating	1	2
Outlet mall score	17	42
No. Starbucks	6	13
No. warehouse clubs	2	2

ENTERTAINMENT	AREA	U.S. AVG
Professional sports rating	3	4
College sports rating	3	4
Zoo/aquarium rating	3	3
Amusement park rating	1	3
Botanical garden/arboretum rating	9	4

OUTDOOR ACTIVITIES	AREA	U.S. AVG
Golf-course rating	4	4
Ski-area rating	4	3
Sq. miles inland water	2	4
Miles of coastline	0.0	10.7
National Park rating	1	3

Arts & Culture
Score: 69.3
Rank: 115

MEDIA & LIBRARIES	AREA	U.S. AVG	PERFORMING ARTS	AREA	U.S. AVG	MUSEUMS	AREA	U.S. AVG
Arts radio rating	1	3	Classical music rating	6	4	Overall museum rating	7	5
No. public libraries	46	27	Ballet/dance rating	1	3	Art museum rating	8	5
Library volumes per capita	3.55	2.78	Professional theater rating	1	3	Science museum rating	7	5
			University arts programs rating	6	5	Children's museum rating	8	3

Detroit–Livonia–Dearborn

Score: 24.8   **Rank:** 344   **2004 rank:** 263

Profile: Large city
Location: Southeast Michigan, along the Detroit River, across the border from Windsor, Ontario
Elevation: 664 feet
Time zone: Eastern Standard Time

PRO	CON
Arts and culture	Economy
Professional sports	Violent crime
Cost of living	Urban decay

Detroit is a lesson in the evolution of urban America. Originally a Great Lakes transportation center, it rapidly became an industrial center thanks to its location between ore resources to the north and energy resources to the south. The transportation industry, the origin of the nickname "Motor City," began with carriages, bicycles, and other steel products, and blossomed with Henry Ford and his auto manufacturing empire. The industrial base continued to evolve through World War II with the production of military equipment and other manufactured goods. The large number of unskilled jobs attracted immigrants and U.S. migrants, particularly from the South, creating an ethnically mixed, working-class population. The industrial and commercial activity generated a great deal of wealth as well. Today Detroit retains a diverse socioeconomic character and a variety of neighborhoods, but also has a mixed economic outlook.

Detroit became one of the first cities to experience suburban flight and urban sprawl. The urban area deteriorated quickly (and ironically) with the advent of automobile transportation, and today's downtown area is still trying to rebuild with only modest success. Areas immediately surrounding downtown are still in considerable disrepair and an estimated 14,000 buildings are slated for destruction. One journalist described the city as a place that "looks like it had been punched in the face." Where did everybody go? To the suburbs, mainly west and north. The Detroit metropolitan area is a quilt of perfectly rectangular suburbs of varying socioeconomic status, separated by a grid of roads with names like Seven Mile, Eight Mile, and Ten Mile. Suburbs along the north shore and a few inland areas are more upscale, but, in general, suburbs are middle class. The stronger and more rapidly growing suburbs are to the northwest in Oakland County. These more affluent northern suburbs have been split off the primary Detroit metro area and are now covered in this book as the Warren–Troy–Farmington Hills metro area (p. 776). The adverse effects of urban sprawl include traffic, poor air quality, and unattractive development—characteristics that have long defined the city. Many Detroiters haven't been to the central city in years.

Dearborn is the traditional industrial capital of the Ford Motor empire. It is a mixed bag as a place to live but does have features of considerable interest, including the Henry Ford Museum and the Ford River Rouge plant and its tour. The area has a heavy immigrant flavor. Livonia is one of the more livable suburbs on the west side, and areas west of there, along the Interstate 275 beltway including Novi and Northville, are commercially strong centers with some of the higher-paying jobs in the area. Romulus and Inkster are very middle class and near the airport to the south.

The Detroit area does have some positives. There is enough local wealth and civic pride to attract an excellent set of arts and culture amenities, spearheaded by museums and performing arts. Sports are a local obsession, and everybody either watches or plays them, and the teams (except the NFL Lions) have improved in recent years. There are excellent recreational areas, and those wishing a getaway can head in several directions, including north or to Ann Arbor or Lake Huron. Intercity transportation services are excellent. The cost of living at 91.4 is definitely a plus, hard to match for a big city. But as a place to live, Detroit as a whole is a gamble. Whether it can recover from its longstanding urban problems is yet unknown. Several good qualities accompany the bad, and for those with patience, the city could eventually pay off, but today's ranking, lowest for a large city, is justified.

Detroit and its immediate western suburbs occupy a large area approximately spread about 25 miles from the city center. Nearly flat land slopes up gently from the water's edge and becomes almost completely flat moving west. Winter storms can bring combinations of rain, snow, freezing rain, and sleet with the possibility of heavy snowfall. In summer, most storms pass to the north allowing for intervals of warm, humid, sunny skies, and occasional thunderstorms followed by days of mild, dry, and fair weather. Lake breezes cool some parts of the city. Summer temperatures reach 90°F or higher. First freeze is late October; last is late April.

Population

DEMOGRAPHICS	AREA	U.S. AVG	ETHNIC COMPOSITION	AREA	U.S. AVG	RESIDENT PROFILE	AREA	U.S. AVG
Population	2,014,262		White	50.8%	79.0%	Single	41.2%	32.4%
Population density per sq. mile	3279.5	358.5	Black	42.1%	10.5%	Married	42.2%	52.7%
Population growth	-4.6%	21.1%	Asian	2.2%	2.7%	Divorced/separated	16.6%	14.9%
Median age	35.4	36.1	Hispanic	4.4%	10.6%	Married with children	19.1%	23.7%
Percent Democrat	69.4%	44.5%	Religious observance	37.7%	48.9%	Single with children	13.5%	9.1%
Percent Republican	29.8%	54.5%	Diversity measure	60.0%	40.1%	Percent over age 65	11.8%	12.9%

Economy & Jobs
Score: 0.0
Rank: 373

INCOME	AREA	U.S. AVG	EMPLOYMENT	AREA	U.S. AVG	EMPLOYING INDUSTRIES	AREA	U.S. AVG
Per capita income	$22,574	$23,235	Unemployment rate	9.9%	4.7%	Largest: Manufacturing		
Household income	$45,454	$46,414	Recent job growth	-0.6%	1.3%			
Household income ‹ $25K	28.2%	26.2%	Projected future job growth	-5.0%	11.5%	Percent manufacturing	19.4%	15.4%
Household income › $75K	27.2%	25.4%	White collar	55.3%	57.8%	Percent public sector	12.1%	15.7%
Household income growth	11.5%	13.6%	Blue collar	28.1%	25.2%	Percent construction	8.7%	9.9%

Cost of Living
Score: 14.4
Rank: 319

INDEXES & TAXES	AREA	U.S. AVG	HOUSING	AREA	U.S. AVG	NECESSITIES	AREA	U.S. AVG
Cost of Living Index	91.4	100.0	Median home price	$155,700	$220,000	Food Index	108.7	100.0
Buying Power Index	111.5	100.0	Home price appreciation	20.8%	10.1%	Housing Index	48.2	100.0
Income tax rate	7.40%	4.70%	Median rent	$793	$709	Utilities Index	103.6	100.0
Sales tax rate	6.00%	6.58%	Homes owned	62.4%	62.3%	Transportation Index	101.8	100.0
Property tax rate	$16.29	$12.00	Home price ratio	3.4	4.2	Healthcare Index	112.0	100.0
						Miscellaneous Cost Index	99.3	100.0

Climate
Score: 39.8
Rank: 224

TEMPERATURE	AREA	U.S. AVG	PRECIPITATION	AREA	U.S. AVG	COMFORTS & HAZARDS	AREA	U.S. AVG
Average January low	17.3	26.2	Annual inches precipitation	32.0	37.7	July relative humidity	72%	66%
Average July high	83.4	87.4	Annual inches snowfall	39.0	7.0	Annual days mostly sunny	185	208
Annual days › 90°F	11	38	Annual days precipitation	133	109	Annual days with thunderstorms	33	39
Annual days ‹ 32°F	139	89	Annual days rain › 0.5 inches	19	22	Tornado risk score	23	18
Annual days ‹ 0°F	7	6	Annual days snow › 1.5 inches	9	6	Hurricane risk score	2	13

TEMPERATURE

PRECIPITATION

DAYS OF CLOUDS & PRECIPITATION

Education
Score: 29.1
Rank: 265

ACHIEVEMENT	AREA	U.S. AVG	PUBLIC SCHOOLS	AREA	U.S. AVG	HIGHER EDUCATION	AREA	U.S. AVG
High school degree	77.2%	82.7%	Expenditures per pupil	$6,795	$5,686	No. 2-year colleges	7	4
2-year college degree	5.9%	6.4%	Student/teacher ratio	20.7	16.7	No. 4-year colleges/universities	10	6
4-year college degree	11.0%	15.7%	Attending public school	92.5%	90.1%	No. highly ranked universities	1	1
Graduate/professional degree	6.5%	8.9%	State SAT score	1151	1021			
			State ACT score	21.5*	20.9			

Health & Healthcare
Score: 4.0
Rank: 358

Crime
Score: 5.9
Rank: 351

HAZARDS & ILLNESSES	AREA	U.S. AVG	HEALTHCARE	AREA	U.S. AVG	CRIME	AREA	U.S. AVG
Air-quality score	1	37	Physicians per capita	225.1	244.2	Violent crime rate	1,250.7	465.5
Water-quality score	36	52	Hospital beds per capita	434.4	420.0	Change in violent crime rate	26.1%	-2.2%
Pollen/allergy score	63	61	No. teaching hospitals	21	3	Property crime rate	4,514.2	3,517.1
Cancer mortality per capita	224.1	201.9	Cost per doctor visit	$69	$77	Change in property crime rate	-1.2%	-2.1%
Depression days per month	4.0	3.5	Cost per dental visit	$70	$70			
Stress score	99	50						

Transportation
Score: 36.1
Rank: 237

COMMUTE	AREA	U.S. AVG	INTERCITY SERVICES	AREA	U.S. AVG	AUTOMOTIVE	AREA	U.S. AVG
Average commute time	27.5	27.4	Major airports within 60 miles	1	1	Insurance, annual premium	$4,213	$1,432
Percent commutes › 60 mins.	5.7%	5.9%	Size of regional airport	Large	Large	Gas, cost per gallon	$2.49	$2.49
Commute by auto	80.5%	78.9%	Daily airline activity	846	686	Daily vehicle miles per capita	26.0	24.0
Commute by mass transit	3.7%	1.9%	Amtrak service	Yes	No			
Work at home	1.8%	3.1%						
Mass transit miles per capita	3.65	1.87						

Leisure
Score: 90.6
Rank: 36

DINING & SHOPPING	AREA	U.S. AVG	ENTERTAINMENT	AREA	U.S. AVG	OUTDOOR ACTIVITIES	AREA	U.S. AVG
Restaurant rating	3	2	Professional sports rating	9	4	Golf-course rating	10	4
Outlet mall score	170	42	College sports rating	3	4	Ski-area rating	5	3
No. Starbucks	15	13	Zoo/aquarium rating	8	3	Sq. miles inland water	6	4
No. warehouse clubs	2	2	Amusement park rating	2	3	Miles of coastline	47.4	10.7
			Botanical garden/arboretum rating	8	4	National Park rating	1	3

Arts & Culture
Score: 94.1
Rank: 23

MEDIA & LIBRARIES	AREA	U.S. AVG	PERFORMING ARTS	AREA	U.S. AVG	MUSEUMS	AREA	U.S. AVG
Arts radio rating	6	3	Classical music rating	10	4	Overall museum rating	9	5
No. public libraries	61	27	Ballet/dance rating	6	3	Art museum rating	10	5
Library volumes per capita	2.71	2.78	Professional theater rating	1	3	Science museum rating	9	5
			University arts programs rating	10	5	Children's museum rating	6	3

Dothan, AL

Score: 23.8   **Rank:** 352   **2004 rank:** 256

Profile: Small agricultural city
Location: Extreme southeast Alabama near the Florida and Georgia borders
Elevation: 370 feet
Time zone: Central Standard Time

PRO	CON
Small-town atmosphere	Summer heat and humidity
Healthcare	Isolation
Cost of living	Entertainment

Dothan is a quiet but prosperous town serving a large agricultural area specializing in peanuts and other nuts but also rich in cotton and poultry. Industries include food processing and a relatively broad assortment of others, including Michelin Tire, Sony, GE, International Paper, and Pemco (aircraft). Dothan is central to other southeastern markets and thus acts as a transportation, mostly trucking, hub. The city has a low cost of living (83.0) and a few minor entertainment amenities and a good parks and recreation system, but on the whole there isn't a lot to do. With more than 70 90°F-plus days each year, Dothan is the hottest place in Alabama by far. For a Southern city, Dothan is relatively far away from big cities and big-city amenities, but it does have an unusually strong healthcare presence: The largest employer at 2,200 employees is the Southeast Alabama Medical Center, and a second hospital employs 1,200, very large for a town of this size.

The surrounding area is flat to gently rolling with pine forests and agricultural land spaces. Summers are long and hot, while winters are mild and wet and only subject to occasional freezes.

Population

DEMOGRAPHICS	AREA	U.S. AVG	ETHNIC COMPOSITION	AREA	U.S. AVG	RESIDENT PROFILE	AREA	U.S. AVG
Population	134,931		White	74.0%	79.0%	Single	28.1%	32.4%
Population density per sq. mile	78.5	358.5	Black	23.6%	10.5%	Married	56.3%	52.7%
Population growth	12.2%	21.1%	Asian	0.5%	2.7%	Divorced/separated	15.6%	14.9%
Median age	38.4	36.1	Hispanic	1.6%	10.6%	Married with children	22.4%	23.7%
Percent Democrat	25.3%	44.5%	Religious observance	66.5%	48.9%	Single with children	9.7%	9.1%
Percent Republican	74.2%	54.5%	Diversity measure	40.7	40.1	Percent over age 65	15.0%	12.9%

Economy & Jobs
Score: 62.3
Rank: 142

INCOME	AREA	U.S. AVG	EMPLOYMENT	AREA	U.S. AVG	EMPLOYING INDUSTRIES	AREA	U.S. AVG
Per capita income	$20,491	$23,235	Unemployment rate	3.6%	4.7%	Largest: Healthcare & Social Assistance		
Household income	$36,843	$46,414	Recent job growth	2.6%	1.3%			
Household income < $25K	35.6%	26.2%	Projected future job growth	10.3%	11.5%	Percent manufacturing	18.7%	15.4%
Household income > $75K	18.0%	25.4%	White collar	53.0%	57.8%	Percent public sector	13.2%	15.7%
Household income growth	13.6%	13.6%	Blue collar	30.6%	25.2%	Percent construction	11.9%	9.9%

Cost of Living
Score: 73.8
Rank: 98

INDEXES & TAXES	AREA	U.S. AVG	HOUSING	AREA	U.S. AVG	NECESSITIES	AREA	U.S. AVG
Cost of Living Index	83.0	100.0	Median home price	$136,900	$220,000	Food Index	97.9	100.0
Buying Power Index	99.5	100.0	Home price appreciation	27.0%	10.1%	Housing Index	57.1	100.0
Income tax rate	5.00%	4.70%	Median rent	$465	$709	Utilities Index	77.7	100.0
Sales tax rate	8.00%	6.58%	Homes owned	64.7%	62.3%	Transportation Index	92.2	100.0
Property tax rate	$3.24	$12.00	Home price ratio	3.7	4.2	Healthcare Index	88.7	100.0
						Miscellaneous Cost Index	102.1	100.0

Climate
Score: 47.3
Rank: 196

TEMPERATURE	AREA	U.S. AVG
Average January low	35.9	26.2
Average July high	90.8	87.4
Annual days > 90°F	74	38
Annual days < 32°F	46	89
Annual days < 0°F	0	6

PRECIPITATION	AREA	U.S. AVG
Annual inches precipitation	51.0	37.7
Annual inches snowfall	0.5	7.0
Annual days precipitation	111	109
Annual days rain > 0.5 inches	37	22
Annual days snow > 1.5 inches	1	6

COMFORTS & HAZARDS	AREA	U.S. AVG
July relative humidity	73%	66%
Annual days mostly sunny	216	208
Annual days with thunderstorms	58	39
Tornado risk score	25	18
Hurricane risk score	41	13

TEMPERATURE

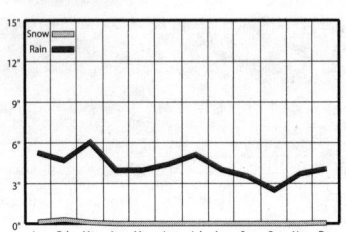

PRECIPITATION

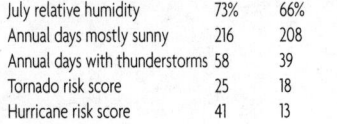
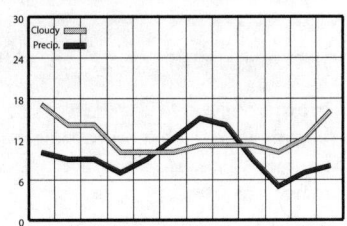

DAYS OF CLOUDS & PRECIPITATION

Education
Score: 6.7
Rank: 348

ACHIEVEMENT	AREA	U.S. AVG
High school degree	73.6%	82.7%
2-year college degree	6.0%	6.4%
4-year college degree	10.7%	15.7%
Graduate/professional degree	5.6%	8.9%

PUBLIC SCHOOLS	AREA	U.S. AVG
Expenditures per pupil	$4,913	$5,686
Student/teacher ratio	16.6	16.7
Attending public school	88.3%	90.1%
State SAT score	1126	1021
State ACT score	20.2*	20.9

HIGHER EDUCATION	AREA	U.S. AVG
No. 2-year colleges	1	4
No. 4-year colleges/universities	0	6
No. highly ranked universities	0	1

Health &
Healthcare
Score: 97.6
Rank: 10

HAZARDS & ILLNESSES	AREA	U.S. AVG
Air-quality score	53	37
Water-quality score	97	52
Pollen/allergy score	59	61
Cancer mortality per capita	210.5	201.9
Depression days per month	3.8	3.5
Stress score	28	50

HEALTHCARE	AREA	U.S. AVG
Physicians per capita	231.9	244.2
Hospital beds per capita	832.3	420.0
No. teaching hospitals	0	3
Cost per doctor visit	$58	$77
Cost per dental visit	$44	$70

Crime
Score: 54.3
Rank: 172

CRIME	AREA	U.S. AVG
Violent crime rate	369.7	465.5
Change in violent crime rate	9.8%	-2.2%
Property crime rate	3,872.3	3,517.1
Change in property crime rate	11.7%	-2.1%

Transportation
Score: 16.0
Rank: 314

COMMUTE	AREA	U.S. AVG
Average commute time	23.4	27.4
Percent commutes > 60 mins.	4.6%	5.9%
Commute by auto	84.8%	78.9%
Commute by mass transit	0.4%	1.9%
Work at home	2.0%	3.1%
Mass transit miles per capita	0.39	1.87

INTERCITY SERVICES	AREA	U.S. AVG
Major airports within 60 miles	0	1
Size of regional airport	Small	Large
Daily airline activity	69	686
Amtrak service	No	No

AUTOMOTIVE	AREA	U.S. AVG
Insurance, annual premium	$1,047	$1,432
Gas, cost per gallon	$2.40	$2.49
Daily vehicle miles per capita	36.5	24.0

Leisure
Score: 1.9
Rank: 366

DINING & SHOPPING	AREA	U.S. AVG
Restaurant rating	1	2
Outlet mall score	30	42
No. Starbucks	0	13
No. warehouse clubs	0	2

ENTERTAINMENT	AREA	U.S. AVG
Professional sports rating	2	4
College sports rating	2	4
Zoo/aquarium rating	1	3
Amusement park rating	1	3
Botanical garden/ arboretum rating	2	4

OUTDOOR ACTIVITIES	AREA	U.S. AVG
Golf-course rating	1	4
Ski-area rating	1	3
Sq. miles inland water	2	4
Miles of coastline	0.0	10.7
National Park rating	1	3

Arts & Culture
Score: 7.8
Rank: 344

MEDIA & LIBRARIES	AREA	U.S. AVG
Arts radio rating	1	3
No. public libraries	9	27
Library volumes per capita	2.97	2.78

PERFORMING ARTS	AREA	U.S. AVG
Classical music rating	1	4
Ballet/dance rating	3	3
Professional theater rating	1	3
University arts programs rating	1	5

MUSEUMS	AREA	U.S. AVG
Overall museum rating	2	5
Art museum rating	3	5
Science museum rating	4	5
Children's museum rating	1	3

Dover, DE

Score: 85.1   **Rank:** 21   **2004 rank:** 25

Profile: Small capital city
Location: Central Delaware, 5 miles inland from the Delaware Bay
Elevation: 74 feet
Time zone: Eastern Standard Time

PRO	CON
Small-town atmosphere	Violent crime
Capital-city amenities	Educational attainment
Nearby recreation	Healthcare

Dover is one of those pleasant "small city" capitals, with a stable economic base and a rich history. The setting in a flat, mostly agricultural area is idyllic without being too far removed from larger Northeastern cities. The nearby Delaware Bay and its beaches and wildlife areas provide ample recreational opportunities. The Dover International Speedway (NASCAR) and the Dover Downs harness racecourse add to entertainment options. Aside from the state government, Dover Air Force Base is a major employer, as is rubber and plastic apparel manufacturer Playtex. Aside from a few other mostly defense-related industries, there isn't much private sector employment. The area is growing as people mainly from more crowded East Coast cities seek a slower and less expensive pace of life. Cost of living is attractive at 97.1, and the Delaware tax climate is favorable especially for the East. Reducing the city's ranking somewhat is a high violent crime rate, and educational attainment is not as strong as seen in other capital cities. There are no standout categories, but Dover does well in the rankings because of consistency across all categories.

Dover lies in a flat plain separated from the Delaware Bay but has areas of level marshland. To the west and south are areas of level to gently rolling terrain used mostly for agriculture and dairy farming. Summers are warm and humid but with maximum temperatures seldom exceeding 80°F. Clouds are common, and humidity and moist Delaware Bay winds can cause fog year-round. Winters are usually mild, with temperatures seldom dropping to 0°F. Most winter precipitation occurs as rain or a mix of rain, sleet, and snow. Summer thunderstorms are common; occasional downpours from Atlantic hurricanes can cause lowland flooding. First freeze is late October; last is mid-April.

Population

DEMOGRAPHICS	AREA	U.S. AVG	ETHNIC COMPOSITION	AREA	U.S. AVG	RESIDENT PROFILE	AREA	U.S. AVG
Population	138,324		White	73.4%	79.0%	Single	32.2%	32.4%
Population density per sq. mile	234.6	358.5	Black	20.2%	10.5%	Married	52.9%	52.7%
Population growth	24.6%	21.1%	Asian	1.9%	2.7%	Divorced/separated	14.9%	14.9%
Median age	35.1	36.1	Hispanic	3.6%	10.6%	Married with children	23.8%	23.7%
Percent Democrat	42.6%	44.5%	Religious observance	32.1%	48.9%	Single with children	11.6%	9.1%
Percent Republican	56.4%	54.5%	Diversity measure	45.8	40.1	Percent over age 65	12.3%	12.9%

Economy & Jobs
Score: 85.3
Rank: 56

INCOME	AREA	U.S. AVG	EMPLOYMENT	AREA	U.S. AVG	EMPLOYING INDUSTRIES	AREA	U.S. AVG
Per capita income	$21,409	$23,235	Unemployment rate	3.8%	4.7%	Largest: Manufacturing		
Household income	$45,937	$46,414	Recent job growth	3.5%	1.3%			
Household income < $25K	24.6%	26.2%	Projected future job growth	15.1%	11.5%	Percent manufacturing	15.5%	15.4%
Household income > $75K	23.7%	25.4%	White collar	54.2%	57.8%	Percent public sector	22.2%	15.7%
Household income growth	12.2%	13.6%	Blue collar	27.2%	25.2%	Percent construction	11.7%	9.9%

Cost of Living
Score: 82.4
Rank: 65

INDEXES & TAXES	AREA	U.S. AVG	HOUSING	AREA	U.S. AVG	NECESSITIES	AREA	U.S. AVG
Cost of Living Index	97.1	100.0	Median home price	$200,000	$220,000	Food Index	106.4	100.0
Buying Power Index	106.0	100.0	Home price appreciation	65.2%	10.1%	Housing Index	67.9	100.0
Income tax rate	8.15%	4.70%	Median rent	$709	$709	Utilities Index	119.7	100.0
Sales tax rate	0.00%	6.58%	Homes owned	66.1%	62.3%	Transportation Index	96.8	100.0
Property tax rate	$6.14	$12.00	Home price ratio	4.4	4.2	Healthcare Index	95.6	100.0
						Miscellaneous Cost Index	97.7	100.0

Climate
Score: 60.2
Rank: 148

TEMPERATURE	AREA	U.S. AVG	PRECIPITATION	AREA	U.S. AVG	COMFORTS & HAZARDS	AREA	U.S. AVG
Average January low	23.8	26.2	Annual inches precipitation	40.3	37.7	July relative humidity	70%	66%
Average July high	85.5	87.4	Annual inches snowfall	20.8	7.0	Annual days mostly sunny	201	208
Annual days > 90°F	18	38	Annual days precipitation	123	109	Annual days with thunderstorms	31	39
Annual days < 32°F	102	89	Annual days rain > 0.5 inches	26	22	Tornado risk score	13	18
Annual days < 0°F	0	6	Annual days snow > 1.5 inches	5	6	Hurricane risk score	15	13

TEMPERATURE

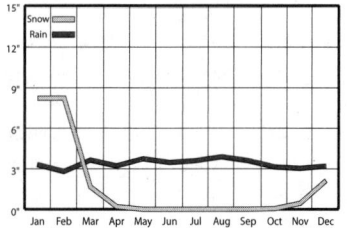

PRECIPITATION

DAYS OF CLOUDS & PRECIPITATION

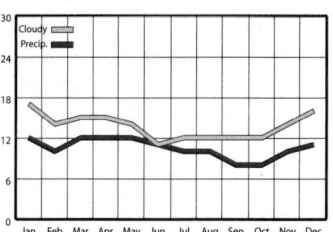

Education
Score: 21.4
Rank: 293

ACHIEVEMENT	AREA	U.S. AVG	PUBLIC SCHOOLS	AREA	U.S. AVG	HIGHER EDUCATION	AREA	U.S. AVG
High school degree	79.2%	82.7%	Expenditures per pupil	$6,328	$5,686	No. 2-year colleges	1	4
2-year college degree	6.5%	6.4%	Student/teacher ratio	22.0	16.7	No. 4-year colleges/universities	2	6
4-year college degree	11.5%	15.7%	Attending public school	90.7%	90.1%	No. highly ranked universities	0	1
Graduate/professional degree	6.9%	8.9%	State SAT score	995*	1021			
			State ACT score	21.4	20.9			

Health & Healthcare
Score: 40.1
Rank: 223

HAZARDS & ILLNESSES	AREA	U.S. AVG	HEALTHCARE	AREA	U.S. AVG	CRIME	AREA	U.S. AVG
Air-quality score	47	37	Physicians per capita	160.7	244.2	Violent crime rate	605.2	465.5
Water-quality score	32	52	Hospital beds per capita	175.0	420.0	Change in violent crime rate	-8.8%	-2.2%
Pollen/allergy score	51	61	No. teaching hospitals	0	3	Property crime rate	3,008.1	3,517.1
Cancer mortality per capita	219.5	201.9	Cost per doctor visit	$83	$77	Change in property crime rate	-8.8%	-2.1%
Depression days per month	3.6	3.5	Cost per dental visit	$81	$70			
Stress score	38	50						

Crime Score: 43.6 **Rank:** 211

Transportation
Score: 91.4
Rank: 33

COMMUTE	AREA	U.S. AVG	INTERCITY SERVICES	AREA	U.S. AVG	AUTOMOTIVE	AREA	U.S. AVG
Average commute time	24.8	27.4	Major airports within 60 miles	3	1	Insurance, annual premium	$1,420	$1,432
Percent commutes > 60 mins.	7.5%	5.9%	Size of regional airport	Large	Large	Gas, cost per gallon	$2.40	$2.49
Commute by auto	79.7%	78.9%	Daily airline activity	1591	686	Daily vehicle miles per capita	34.1	24.0
Commute by mass transit	0.8%	1.9%	Amtrak service	No	No			
Work at home	3.1%	3.1%						
Mass transit miles per capita	0.80	1.87						

Leisure
Score: 55.1
Rank: 168

DINING & SHOPPING	AREA	U.S. AVG	ENTERTAINMENT	AREA	U.S. AVG	OUTDOOR ACTIVITIES	AREA	U.S. AVG
Restaurant rating	1	2	Professional sports rating	4	4	Golf-course rating	4	4
Outlet mall score	109	42	College sports rating	2	4	Ski-area rating	3	3
No. Starbucks	0	13	Zoo/aquarium rating	1	3	Sq. miles inland water	5	4
No. warehouse clubs	1	2	Amusement park rating	1	3	Miles of coastline	0.0	10.7
			Botanical garden/ arboretum rating	1	4	National Park rating	2	3

Arts & Culture
Score: 21.9
Rank: 291

MEDIA & LIBRARIES	AREA	U.S. AVG	PERFORMING ARTS	AREA	U.S. AVG	MUSEUMS	AREA	U.S. AVG
Arts radio rating	1	3	Classical music rating	4	4	Overall museum rating	4	5
No. public libraries	4	27	Ballet/dance rating	1	3	Art museum rating	2	5
Library volumes per capita	1.15	2.78	Professional theater rating	6	3	Science museum rating	4	5
			University arts programs rating	5	5	Children's museum rating	1	3

Dubuque, IA
Score: 32.6 **Rank:** 339 **2004 rank:** 311

Profile: Small industrial town
Location: Extreme eastern Iowa along Mississippi River at Illinois border
Elevation: 798 feet
Time zone: Central Standard Time

PRO
Historic interest
Small-town atmosphere
Cost of living

CON
Economy
Harsh climate
Low ethnic diversity

Dubuque is an upper Mississippi River town and old industrial center. The city retains a rich historic core with old Victorian brick buildings rising gradually away from the Mississippi waterfront. The town and its buildings have frequently served as a movie set. The waterfront has seen some new investments, including a new aquarium and a convention center. Economically, Dubuque is supported by a large John Deere plant and A. Y. McDonald, a producer of brass fittings, plumbing, and heavy pipe works, as well as an Andersen Windows plant and several smaller manufacturing facilities. Although rated low statistically on a national scale, Dubuque has a few culture and entertainment amenities good for a town of its size, including a symphony and theater company. Cost of living and housing are quite reasonable. The area has extremely low ethnic diversity and is geographically isolated from many big-city amenities, but is probably a better place to live than the numbers indicate.

The Mississippi River is shallow and about ¼-mile wide at Dubuque. The surrounding terrain varies from gently rolling to the south and west to steep hills and bluffs around the city and along the Mississippi. Summers have frequent change between hot, humid days with thunderstorms and cool, comfortable northerly air. Winters are quite variable with cold snaps driving temperatures well below zero. Historic temperatures range from −32°F to 110°F. Most precipitation occurs during spring and fall seasons, with snow falling as late as May and as early as September. First freeze is early October; last is late April.

DEMOGRAPHICS	AREA	U.S. AVG	ETHNIC COMPOSITION	AREA	U.S. AVG	RESIDENT PROFILE	AREA	U.S. AVG
Population	90,696		White	96.2%	79.0%	Single	32.8%	32.4%
Population density per sq. mile	149.1	358.5	Black	1.1%	10.5%	Married	56.7%	52.7%
Population growth	5.0%	21.1%	Asian	1.0%	2.7%	Divorced/separated	10.5%	14.9%
Median age	37.8	36.1	Hispanic	1.3%	10.6%	Married with children	26.1%	23.7%
Percent Democrat	56.5%	44.5%	Religious observance	78.3%	48.9%	Single with children	6.9%	9.1%
Percent Republican	42.7%	54.5%	Diversity measure	9.8	40.1	Percent over age 65	15.1%	12.9%

Economy & Jobs
Score: 50.3
Rank: 187

INCOME	AREA	U.S. AVG	EMPLOYMENT	AREA	U.S. AVG	EMPLOYING INDUSTRIES	AREA	U.S. AVG
Per capita income	$22,604	$23,235	Unemployment rate	4.0%	4.7%	Largest: Manufacturing		
Household income	$44,917	$46,414	Recent job growth	1.9%	1.3%			
Household income < $25K	23.7%	26.2%	Projected future job growth	5.1%	11.5%	Percent manufacturing	19.5%	15.4%
Household income > $75K	21.6%	25.4%	White collar	54.6%	57.8%	Percent public sector	8.5%	15.7%
Household income growth	13.5%	13.6%	Blue collar	27.0%	25.2%	Percent construction	7.5%	9.9%

Cost of Living
Score: 47.1
Rank: 198

INDEXES & TAXES	AREA	U.S. AVG	HOUSING	AREA	U.S. AVG	NECESSITIES	AREA	U.S. AVG
Cost of Living Index	84.4	100.0	Median home price	$121,800	$220,000	Food Index	94.1	100.0
Buying Power Index	119.3	100.0	Home price appreciation	28.2%	10.1%	Housing Index	46.6	100.0
Income tax rate	7.67%	4.70%	Median rent	$542	$709	Utilities Index	134.5	100.0
Sales tax rate	7.00%	6.58%	Homes owned	70.7%	62.3%	Transportation Index	98.5	100.0
Property tax rate	$12.13	$12.00	Home price ratio	2.7	4.2	Healthcare Index	96.5	100.0
						Miscellaneous Cost Index	98.3	100.0

Climate
Score: 3.7
Rank: 359

TEMPERATURE	AREA	U.S. AVG	PRECIPITATION	AREA	U.S. AVG	COMFORTS & HAZARDS	AREA	U.S. AVG
Average January low	9.0	26.2	Annual inches precipitation	38.0	37.7	July relative humidity	71%	66%
Average July high	82.0	87.4	Annual inches snowfall	62.0	7.0	Annual days mostly sunny	201	208
Annual days > 90°F	9	38	Annual days precipitation	118	109	Annual days with thunderstorms	35	39
Annual days < 32°F	150	89	Annual days rain > 0.5 inches	25	22	Tornado risk score	23	18
Annual days < 0°F	18	6	Annual days snow > 1.5 inches	10	6	Hurricane risk score	0	13

TEMPERATURE

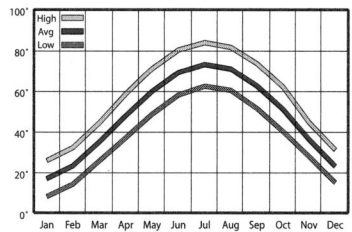

PRECIPITATION

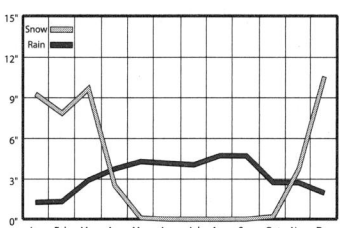

DAYS OF CLOUDS & PRECIPITATION

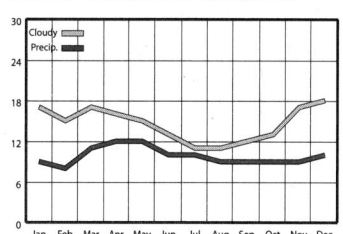

Education
Score: 20.3
Rank: 297

ACHIEVEMENT	AREA	U.S. AVG	PUBLIC SCHOOLS	AREA	U.S. AVG	HIGHER EDUCATION	AREA	U.S. AVG
High school degree	85.5%	82.7%	Expenditures per pupil	$5,416	$5,686	No. 2-year colleges	1	4
2-year college degree	5.6%	6.4%	Student/teacher ratio	18.5	16.7	No. 4-year colleges/universities	6	6
4-year college degree	14.9%	15.7%	Attending public school	75.0%	90.1%	No. highly ranked universities	0	1
Graduate/professional degree	6.9%	8.9%	State SAT score	1215	1021			
			State ACT score	22.1*	20.9			

Health & Healthcare
Score: 80.7
Rank: 72

HAZARDS & ILLNESSES	AREA	U.S. AVG	HEALTHCARE	AREA	U.S. AVG	CRIME	AREA	U.S. AVG
Air-quality score	44	37	Physicians per capita	219.9	244.2	Violent crime rate	406.1	465.5
Water-quality score	50	52	Hospital beds per capita	662.7	420.0	Change in violent crime rate	35.9%	-2.2%
Pollen/allergy score	41	61	No. teaching hospitals	0	3	Property crime rate	2,286.4	3,517.1
Cancer mortality per capita	220.6	201.9	Cost per doctor visit	$74	$77	Change in property crime rate	-8.2%	-2.1%
Depression days per month	2.3	3.5	Cost per dental visit	$63	$70			
Stress score	2	50						

Crime
Score: 92.5
Rank: 29

Transportation
Score: 74.9
Rank: 94

COMMUTE	AREA	U.S. AVG	INTERCITY SERVICES	AREA	U.S. AVG	AUTOMOTIVE	AREA	U.S. AVG
Average commute time	17.2	27.4	Major airports within 60 miles	0	1	Insurance, annual premium	$885	$1,432
Percent commutes > 60 mins.	2.3%	5.9%	Size of regional airport	Small	Large	Gas, cost per gallon	$2.50	$2.49
Commute by auto	82.2%	78.9%	Daily airline activity	107	686	Daily vehicle miles per capita	17.8	24.0
Commute by mass transit	0.6%	1.9%	Amtrak service	No	No			
Work at home	4.1%	3.1%						
Mass transit miles per capita	0.56	1.87						

DINING & SHOPPING	AREA	U.S. AVG	ENTERTAINMENT	AREA	U.S. AVG	OUTDOOR ACTIVITIES	AREA	U.S. AVG
Restaurant rating	1	2	Professional sports rating	2	4	Golf-course rating	2	4
Outlet mall score	12	42	College sports rating	1	4	Ski-area rating	3	3
No. Starbucks	0	13	Zoo/aquarium rating	1	3	Sq. miles inland water	2	4
No. warehouse clubs	0	2	Amusement park rating	1	3	Miles of coastline	0.0	10.7
			Botanical garden/			National Park rating	2	3
			arboretum rating	4	4			

Leisure
Score: 12.0
Rank: 328

MEDIA & LIBRARIES	AREA	U.S. AVG	PERFORMING ARTS	AREA	U.S. AVG	MUSEUMS	AREA	U.S. AVG
Arts radio rating	1	3	Classical music rating	1	4	Overall museum rating	4	5
No. public libraries	5	27	Ballet/dance rating	1	3	Art museum rating	2	5
Library volumes per capita	3.94	2.78	Professional theater rating	1	3	Science museum rating	5	5
			University arts programs rating	3	5	Children's museum rating	1	3

Arts & Culture
Score: 18.2
Rank: 305

Duluth, MN-WI

Score: 53.3   **Rank:** 229   **2004 rank:** 148

Profile: Small-port-city complex
Location: Northeastern Minnesota at western end of Lake Superior
Elevation: 1,417 feet
Time zone: Central Standard Time

PRO	CON
Nearby outdoor recreation	Winter climate
	Isolation
Historic preservation	Low job growth
Attractive setting	

Duluth is the world's third-largest inland port, located about as far as possible from an ocean on the North American continent. Superior, Wisconsin, sits to the south on the other side of the harbor. Shipping, mainly grain and, to a lesser extent, iron ore, is an important part of the economy. Some of the former heavy industry is gone today but the town still retains a decidedly commercial and industrial character. The city has taken effective steps to turn potential decay into an attractive preservation of its heritage, and downtown today is clean and interesting and in an attractive waterfront setting. Many classic industrial buildings and features have been renovated and some house entertainment and nightlife venues in a waterfront area known as Canal Park. Outdoor recreational opportunities abound in the lake and forest country to the north, and Duluth serves as a gateway to these areas. Winters are extreme and the area is far from major air transport and other services.

Duluth in total is about 20 miles long and lies at the base of a range of hills and bluffs that rise abruptly 600 feet to 800 feet above lake level. Summer days are warm, sometimes with clouds from the lake, and evenings are cool. Winters are cold and bitter when Lake Superior doesn't moderate temperatures. The area averages 51 below-zero days a year, making it the fourth coldest in the nation. Easterly winds, the major weather modifier, occur almost 50% of the time in summer and up to 25% in winter. Snow is dry, significant, and persistent, and ice may form in the harbor from November through April. First freeze is late September; last is mid-May.

DEMOGRAPHICS	AREA	U.S. AVG	ETHNIC COMPOSITION	AREA	U.S. AVG	RESIDENT PROFILE	AREA	U.S. AVG
Population	274,430		White	94.2%	79.0%	Single	33.9%	32.4%
Population density per sq. mile	32.7	358.5	Black	0.9%	10.5%	Married	51.9%	52.7%
Population growth	2.2%	21.1%	Asian	0.8%	2.7%	Divorced/separated	14.2%	14.9%
Median age	39.3	36.1	Hispanic	0.8%	10.6%	Married with children	20.0%	23.7%
Percent Democrat	64.9%	44.5%	Religious observance	52.9%	48.9%	Single with children	8.2%	9.1%
Percent Republican	33.9%	54.5%	Diversity measure	12.4	40.1	Percent over age 65	15.7%	12.9%

Population

INCOME	AREA	U.S. AVG	EMPLOYMENT	AREA	U.S. AVG	EMPLOYING INDUSTRIES	AREA	U.S. AVG
Per capita income	$21,663	$23,235	Unemployment rate	4.2%	4.7%	Largest: Healthcare & Social Assistance		
Household income	$41,562	$46,414	Recent job growth	0.6%	1.3%			
Household income < $25K	29.8%	26.2%	Projected future job growth	1.9%	11.5%	Percent manufacturing	14.0%	15.4%
Household income > $75K	20.4%	25.4%	White collar	55.2%	57.8%	Percent public sector	16.7%	15.7%
Household income growth	13.6%	13.6%	Blue collar	25.6%	25.2%	Percent construction	11.6%	9.9%

Economy & Jobs
Score: 18.4
Rank: 305

INDEXES & TAXES	AREA	U.S. AVG	HOUSING	AREA	U.S. AVG	NECESSITIES	AREA	U.S. AVG
Cost of Living Index	88.3	100.0	Median home price	$115,700	$220,000	Food Index	99.0	100.0
Buying Power Index	105.5	100.0	Home price appreciation	56.7%	10.1%	Housing Index	49.3	100.0
Income tax rate	7.51%	4.70%	Median rent	$555	$709	Utilities Index	142.1	100.0
Sales tax rate	6.34%	6.58%	Homes owned	65.5%	62.3%	Transportation Index	107.4	100.0
Property tax rate	$10.88	$12.00	Home price ratio	2.8	4.2	Healthcare Index	119.0	100.0
						Miscellaneous Cost Index	102.5	100.0

Cost of Living
Score: 46.3
Rank: 201

Climate
Score: 3.2
Rank: 361

TEMPERATURE	AREA	U.S. AVG
Average January low	-0.6	26.2
Average July high	76.4	87.4
Annual days > 90°F	2	38
Annual days < 32°F	187	89
Annual days < 0°F	51	6

PRECIPITATION	AREA	U.S. AVG
Annual inches precipitation	30.0	37.7
Annual inches snowfall	78.0	7.0
Annual days precipitation	135	109
Annual days rain > 0.5 inches	18	22
Annual days snow > 1.5 inches	15	6

COMFORTS & HAZARDS	AREA	U.S. AVG
July relative humidity	71%	66%
Annual days mostly sunny	180	208
Annual days with thunderstorms	35	39
Tornado risk score	3	18
Hurricane risk score	0	13

TEMPERATURE

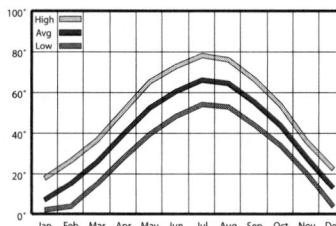

PRECIPITATION

DAYS OF CLOUDS & PRECIPITATION

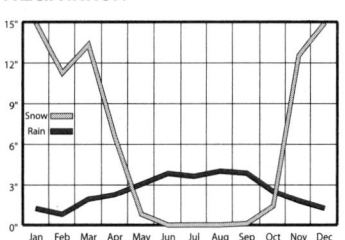

Education
Score: 71.1
Rank: 109

ACHIEVEMENT	AREA	U.S. AVG
High school degree	86.7%	82.7%
2-year college degree	8.2%	6.4%
4-year college degree	14.4%	15.7%
Graduate/professional degree	6.3%	8.9%

PUBLIC SCHOOLS	AREA	U.S. AVG
Expenditures per pupil	$6,627	$5,686
Student/teacher ratio	13.7	16.7
Attending public school	95.1%	90.1%
State SAT score	1191	1021
State ACT score	22.3*	20.9

HIGHER EDUCATION	AREA	U.S. AVG
No. 2-year colleges	5	4
No. 4-year colleges/universities	4	6
No. highly ranked universities	1	1

Health & Healthcare
Score: 69.5
Rank: 115

HAZARDS & ILLNESSES	AREA	U.S. AVG
Air-quality score	27	37
Water-quality score	66	52
Pollen/allergy score	44	61
Cancer mortality per capita	205.7	201.9
Depression days per month	2.9	3.5
Stress score	37	50

HEALTHCARE	AREA	U.S. AVG
Physicians per capita	246.6	244.2
Hospital beds per capita	617.6	420.0
No. teaching hospitals	2	3
Cost per doctor visit	$85	$77
Cost per dental visit	$69	$70

Crime
Score: 77.8
Rank: 82

CRIME	AREA	U.S. AVG
Violent crime rate	259.9	465.5
Change in violent crime rate	19.8%	-2.2%
Property crime rate	3,180.1	3,517.1
Change in property crime rate	-12.1%	-2.1%

Transportation
Score: 33.4
Rank: 250

COMMUTE	AREA	U.S. AVG
Average commute time	21.5	27.4
Percent commutes > 60 mins.	4.2%	5.9%
Commute by auto	79.2%	78.9%
Commute by mass transit	1.8%	1.9%
Work at home	3.4%	3.1%
Mass transit miles per capita	1.81	1.87

INTERCITY SERVICES	AREA	U.S. AVG
Major airports within 60 miles	0	1
Size of regional airport	None	Large
Daily airline activity	22	686
Amtrak service	No	No

AUTOMOTIVE	AREA	U.S. AVG
Insurance, annual premium	$1,201	$1,432
Gas, cost per gallon	$2.47	$2.49
Daily vehicle miles per capita	22.2	24.0

Leisure
Score: 74.9
Rank: 94

DINING & SHOPPING	AREA	U.S. AVG
Restaurant rating	1	2
Outlet mall score	0	42
No. Starbucks	2	13
No. warehouse clubs	1	2

ENTERTAINMENT	AREA	U.S. AVG
Professional sports rating	2	4
College sports rating	4	4
Zoo/aquarium rating	3	3
Amusement park rating	1	3
Botanical garden/ arboretum rating	1	4

OUTDOOR ACTIVITIES	AREA	U.S. AVG
Golf-course rating	2	4
Ski-area rating	4	3
Sq. miles inland water	10	4
Miles of coastline	36.0	10.7
National Park rating	10	3

Arts & Culture
Score: 58.6
Rank: 155

MEDIA & LIBRARIES	AREA	U.S. AVG
Arts radio rating	1	3
No. public libraries	22	27
Library volumes per capita	2.27	2.78

PERFORMING ARTS	AREA	U.S. AVG
Classical music rating	3	4
Ballet/dance rating	3	3
Professional theater rating	1	3
University arts programs rating	5	5

MUSEUMS	AREA	U.S. AVG
Overall museum rating	7	5
Art museum rating	7	5
Science museum rating	3	5
Children's museum rating	5	3

Durham, NC

Score: 87.2   Rank: 15   2004 rank: 13

Profile: College town/mid-size-city complex
Location: Northeast-central North Carolina, 40 miles south of Virginia border
Elevation: 441 feet
Time zone: Eastern Standard Time

PRO	CON
College-town amenities	Home prices
Attractive residential areas	Crime rates
Strong economy	Hot, humid summers

Previously, Durham was part of the larger Research Triangle triumvirate of Raleigh–Durham–Chapel Hill. Now Raleigh and the large suburban enclave of Cary have been split off into a metro area of that name (p. 640), leaving this western half of area. The Durham area includes Chapel Hill, so on the surface, the two major cities in the area are both college towns—Durham is home to Duke University, while Chapel Hill is home to the University of North Carolina. But that's where the similarities end. Durham is an old tobacco town, not too prosperous, not too interesting, but livable. Some of the old tobacco processing plants in town add some historic interest. Chapel Hill, on the other hand, is a model college town, with the nice small-shop and restaurant-oriented downtown, plenty of trees, and a vibrant, moderately upscale feel. Homes in the Chapel Hill area are set on large wooded lots and are noticeably more expensive. Employment is strong and stable throughout the area, anchored by the immense and unique Research Triangle Park business and technology complex that actually straddles the line between the Durham and Raleigh–Cary areas. The Durham side is more peaceful with a slower pace and relatively easier commutes to the center, and is somewhat less affected by urban sprawl. While cost of living is low on a national scale, it is relatively high for the region. Home prices for the area in general are reasonable, though prospective residents will find prices in Chapel Hill much higher. Balanced positives across all ranking categories help drive the high ranking.

Durham and Chapel Hill are located in a transitional zone between the Coastal Plain and the Piedmont Plateau. The surrounding terrain is rolling and heavily wooded and becomes more so in Chapel Hill and west. The central location between the mountains and coast means a favorable climate aside from some summer heat. The mountains form a partial barrier to cold-air masses, resulting in few winter days with temperatures below 20°F. During summer, tropical air is present over eastern and central sections of North Carolina, producing warm temperatures and high humidity. While snow and sleet usually occur each year, excessive accumulations are rare.

DEMOGRAPHICS	AREA	U.S. AVG	ETHNIC COMPOSITION	AREA	U.S. AVG	RESIDENT PROFILE	AREA	U.S. AVG
Population	456,036		White	61.0%	79.0%	Single	39.3%	32.4%
Population density per sq. mile	258.3	358.5	Black	28.3%	10.5%	Married	46.3%	52.7%
Population growth	32.6%	21.1%	Asian	3.8%	2.7%	Divorced/separated	14.4%	14.9%
Median age	34.3	36.1	Hispanic	8.6%	10.6%	Married with children	20.0%	23.7%
Percent Democrat	63.1%	44.5%	Religious observance	37.3%	48.9%	Single with children	8.9%	9.1%
Percent Republican	36.3%	54.5%	Diversity measure	58.4	40.1	Percent over age 65	10.4%	12.9%

INCOME	AREA	U.S. AVG	EMPLOYMENT	AREA	U.S. AVG	EMPLOYING INDUSTRIES	AREA	U.S. AVG
Per capita income	$26,783	$23,235	Unemployment rate	4.9%	4.7%	Largest: Professional, Scientific & Technical Services		
Household income	$49,095	$46,414	Recent job growth	1.4%	1.3%			
Household income < $25K	24.6%	26.2%	Projected future job growth	15.1%	11.5%	Percent manufacturing	10.8%	15.4%
Household income > $75K	29.7%	25.4%	White collar	66.7%	57.8%	Percent public sector	20.3%	15.7%
Household income growth	15.5%	13.6%	Blue collar	19.7%	25.2%	Percent construction	8.9%	9.9%

Economy & Jobs — Score: 58.6 Rank: 155

INDEXES & TAXES	AREA	U.S. AVG	HOUSING	AREA	U.S. AVG	NECESSITIES	AREA	U.S. AVG
Cost of Living Index	91.9	100.0	Median home price	$177,900	$220,000	Food Index	101.0	100.0
Buying Power Index	119.7	100.0	Home price appreciation	23.7%	10.1%	Housing Index	85.2	100.0
Income tax rate	7.00%	4.70%	Median rent	$766	$709	Utilities Index	92.3	100.0
Sales tax rate	7.00%	6.58%	Homes owned	55.5%	62.3%	Transportation Index	94.9	100.0
Property tax rate	$10.07	$12.00	Home price ratio	3.6	4.2	Healthcare Index	104.4	100.0
						Miscellaneous Cost Index	107.2	100.0

Cost of Living — Score: 28.6 Rank: 267

Climate
Score: 63.6
Rank: 135

TEMPERATURE	AREA	U.S. AVG	PRECIPITATION	AREA	U.S. AVG	COMFORTS & HAZARDS	AREA	U.S. AVG
Average January low	30.0	26.2	Annual inches precipitation	43.0	37.7	July relative humidity	71%	66%
Average July high	87.7	87.4	Annual inches snowfall	7.0	7.0	Annual days mostly sunny	220	208
Annual days > 90°F	25	38	Annual days precipitation	112	109	Annual days with thunderstorms	46	39
Annual days < 32°F	82	89	Annual days rain > 0.5 inches	29	22	Tornado risk score	13	18
Annual days < 0°F	0	6	Annual days snow > 1.5 inches	3	6	Hurricane risk score	29	13

TEMPERATURE

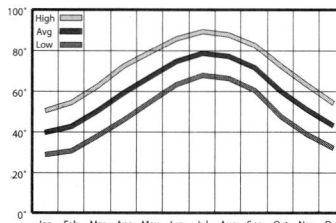

PRECIPITATION

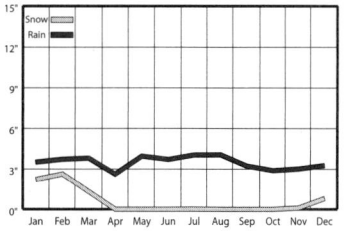

DAYS OF CLOUDS & PRECIPITATION

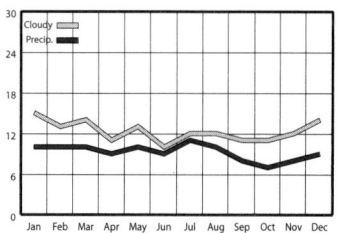

Education
Score: 90.9
Rank: 35

ACHIEVEMENT	AREA	U.S. AVG	PUBLIC SCHOOLS	AREA	U.S. AVG	HIGHER EDUCATION	AREA	U.S. AVG
High school degree	83.3%	82.7%	Expenditures per pupil	$5,488	$5,686	No. 2-year colleges	3	4
2-year college degree	5.9%	6.4%	Student/teacher ratio	13.4	16.7	No. 4-year colleges/universities	4	6
4-year college degree	21.8%	15.7%	Attending public school	88.9%	90.1%	No. highly ranked universities	2	1
Graduate/professional degree	18.4%	8.9%	State SAT score	1008*	1021			
			State ACT score	20.5	20.9			

Health & Healthcare
Score: 94.1
Rank: 23

HAZARDS & ILLNESSES	AREA	U.S. AVG	HEALTHCARE	AREA	U.S. AVG	CRIME	AREA	U.S. AVG
Air-quality score	46	37	Physicians per capita	857.2	244.2	Violent crime rate	497.7	465.5
Water-quality score	79	52	Hospital beds per capita	484.4	420.0	Change in violent crime rate	-4.0%	-2.2%
Pollen/allergy score	65	61	No. teaching hospitals	4	3	Property crime rate	4,492.3	3,517.1
Cancer mortality per capita	203.2	201.9	Cost per doctor visit	$80	$77	Change in property crime rate	-6.2%	-2.1%
Depression days per month	3.0	3.5	Cost per dental visit	$62	$70			
Stress score	31	50						

Crime (Score: 22.2, Rank: 291)

Transportation
Score: 38.2
Rank: 232

COMMUTE	AREA	U.S. AVG	INTERCITY SERVICES	AREA	U.S. AVG	AUTOMOTIVE	AREA	U.S. AVG
Average commute time	24.9	27.4	Major airports within 60 miles	1	1	Insurance, annual premium	$1,211	$1,432
Percent commutes > 60 mins.	4.2%	5.9%	Size of regional airport	Medium	Large	Gas, cost per gallon	$2.53	$2.49
Commute by auto	74.6%	78.9%	Daily airline activity	461	686	Daily vehicle miles per capita	30.1	24.0
Commute by mass transit	2.6%	1.9%	Amtrak service	Yes	No			
Work at home	3.4%	3.1%						
Mass transit miles per capita	2.63	1.87						

Leisure
Score: 66.3
Rank: 126

DINING & SHOPPING	AREA	U.S. AVG	ENTERTAINMENT	AREA	U.S. AVG	OUTDOOR ACTIVITIES	AREA	U.S. AVG
Restaurant rating	3	2	Professional sports rating	5	4	Golf-course rating	6	4
Outlet mall score	0	42	College sports rating	10	4	Ski-area rating	1	3
No. Starbucks	4	13	Zoo/aquarium rating	4	3	Sq. miles inland water	2	4
No. warehouse clubs	1	2	Amusement park rating	1	3	Miles of coastline	0.0	10.7
			Botanical garden/ arboretum rating	9	4	National Park rating	1	3

Arts & Culture
Score: 84.5
Rank: 59

MEDIA & LIBRARIES	AREA	U.S. AVG	PERFORMING ARTS	AREA	U.S. AVG	MUSEUMS	AREA	U.S. AVG
Arts radio rating	8	3	Classical music rating	7	4	Overall museum rating	7	5
No. public libraries	13	27	Ballet/dance rating	3	3	Art museum rating	6	5
Library volumes per capita	2.13	2.78	Professional theater rating	6	3	Science museum rating	8	5
			University arts programs rating	8	5	Children's museum rating	3	3

Eau Claire, WI

Score: 54.1   **Rank:** 225   **2004 rank:** 135

Profile: Small city
Location: Northwest Wisconsin
Elevation: 838 feet
Time zone: Central Standard Time

PRO	CON
Attractive setting	Harsh winters
Low crime	Recent economic weakness
Healthcare	Low ethnic diversity

Eau Claire lies along Interstate 94 about 60 miles east of the Minnesota border and Mississippi River and 80 miles east of Minneapolis–St. Paul. A former logging town with more diversified industry today, Eau Claire is a gateway to wilderness and recreation areas to the north and northeast. The attractive town has older buildings and shady streets along a graceful bend in the Chippewa River. The University of Wisconsin–Eau Claire adds about 10,000 students and some college-town flavor. The outskirts, mostly above the valley, are quite spread out with a number of retail developments and light manufacturing firms mainly south and east of downtown. Suburbs spread mainly north towards Chippewa Falls, a nice mainly residential small town with some higher-end developments about 5 miles away. Typical of a small Wisconsin town are the low cost of living and crime, and clean, attractive surroundings, but the area has somewhat more of a sprawly feel than many Wisconsin towns, and recent weakness in job statistics has hurt the ranking. The small-town atmosphere close to Minneapolis–St. Paul is a plus.

Eau Claire sits in the scenic Chippewa Valley at the convergence of the Chippewa and Eau Claire rivers. The immediate terrain is level with wooded hills rising in all directions from town. The landscape flattens to the west toward the Mississippi River and many lakes are to the north. Summers are warm with moderate humidity and periods of warmer weather. Winters are cold with varying humidity and outbreaks of bitter cold following storm systems arriving from the west. Summer precipitation occurs mainly as thunderstorms, while snowfall and snow cover persists all winter. The city's position to the west of the Great Lakes means more sunny days than other Wisconsin cities. First freeze is late September; last is mid-May.

Population

DEMOGRAPHICS	AREA	U.S. AVG	ETHNIC COMPOSITION	AREA	U.S. AVG	RESIDENT PROFILE	AREA	U.S. AVG
Population	153,621		White	95.5%	79.0%	Single	35.3%	32.4%
Population density per sq. mile	93.2	358.5	Black	0.4%	10.5%	Married	53.3%	52.7%
Population growth	11.7%	21.1%	Asian	2.2%	2.7%	Divorced/separated	11.3%	14.9%
Median age	35.5	36.1	Hispanic	0.8%	10.6%	Married with children	23.8%	23.7%
Percent Democrat	52.0%	44.5%	Religious observance	56.6%	48.9%	Single with children	7.4%	9.1%
Percent Republican	46.8%	54.5%	Diversity measure	10.2	40.1	Percent over age 65	13.1%	12.9%

Economy & Jobs
Score: 13.6
Rank: 321

INCOME	AREA	U.S. AVG	EMPLOYMENT	AREA	U.S. AVG	EMPLOYING INDUSTRIES	AREA	U.S. AVG
Per capita income	$22,115	$23,235	Unemployment rate	4.1%	4.7%	Largest: Healthcare & Social Assistance		
Household income	$44,857	$46,414	Recent job growth	-1.6%	1.3%			
Household income < $25K	24.5%	26.2%	Projected future job growth	6.7%	11.5%	Percent manufacturing	18.1%	15.4%
Household income > $75K	21.9%	25.4%	White collar	54.1%	57.8%	Percent public sector	13.4%	15.7%
Household income growth	14.0%	13.6%	Blue collar	26.8%	25.2%	Percent construction	8.7%	9.9%

Cost of Living
Score: 45.5
Rank: 204

INDEXES & TAXES	AREA	U.S. AVG	HOUSING	AREA	U.S. AVG	NECESSITIES	AREA	U.S. AVG
Cost of Living Index	86.4	100.0	Median home price	$121,800	$220,000	Food Index	98.4	100.0
Buying Power Index	116.4	100.0	Home price appreciation	31.5%	10.1%	Housing Index	52.0	100.0
Income tax rate	6.93%	4.70%	Median rent	$558	$709	Utilities Index	132.5	100.0
Sales tax rate	5.50%	6.58%	Homes owned	65.7%	62.3%	Transportation Index	101.5	100.0
Property tax rate	$17.99	$12.00	Home price ratio	2.7	4.2	Healthcare Index	109.1	100.0
						Miscellaneous Cost Index	99.2	100.0

Climate
Score: 9.4
Rank: 338

TEMPERATURE	AREA	U.S. AVG	PRECIPITATION	AREA	U.S. AVG	COMFORTS & HAZARDS	AREA	U.S. AVG
Average January low	3.2	26.2	Annual inches precipitation	26.0	37.7	July relative humidity	69%	66%
Average July high	82.4	87.4	Annual inches snowfall	46.0	7.0	Annual days mostly sunny	200	208
Annual days > 90°F	15	38	Annual days precipitation	113	109	Annual days with thunderstorms	36	39
Annual days < 32°F	158	89	Annual days rain > 0.5 inches	15	22	Tornado risk score	24	18
Annual days < 0°F	34	6	Annual days snow > 1.5 inches	11	6	Hurricane risk score	0	13

TEMPERATURE

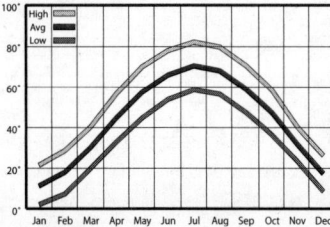

PRECIPITATION

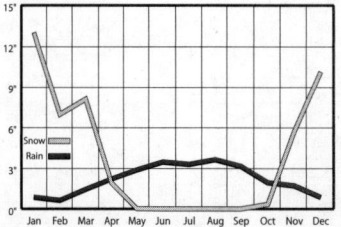

DAYS OF CLOUDS & PRECIPITATION

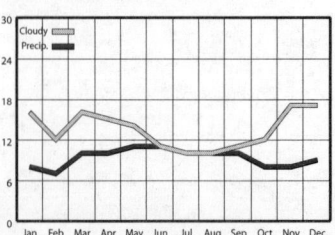

ACHIEVEMENT	AREA	U.S. AVG	PUBLIC SCHOOLS	AREA	U.S. AVG	HIGHER EDUCATION	AREA	U.S. AVG
High school degree	87.2%	82.7%	Expenditures per pupil	$6,576	$5,686	No. 2-year colleges	2	4
2-year college degree	9.5%	6.4%	Student/teacher ratio	15.2	16.7	No. 4-year colleges/universities	2	6
4-year college degree	15.4%	15.7%	Attending public school	88.2%	90.1%	No. highly ranked universities	0	1
Graduate/professional degree	7.0%	8.9%	State SAT score	1188	1021			
			State ACT score	22.2*	20.9			

Education
Score: 62.6
Rank: 141

HAZARDS & ILLNESSES	AREA	U.S. AVG	HEALTHCARE	AREA	U.S. AVG	CRIME	AREA	U.S. AVG
Air-quality score	56	37	Physicians per capita	281.3	244.2	Violent crime rate	125.4	465.5
Water-quality score	48	52	Hospital beds per capita	511.0	420.0	Change in violent crime rate	-15.7%	-2.2%
Pollen/allergy score	44	61	No. teaching hospitals	2	3	Property crime rate	2,279.3	3,517.1
Cancer mortality per capita	189.3	201.9	Cost per doctor visit	$107	$77	Change in property crime rate	-12.9%	-2.1%
Depression days per month	3.2	3.5	Cost per dental visit	$63	$70			
Stress score	15	50						

Health & Healthcare
Score: 92.0
Rank: 30

Crime
Score: 73.8
Rank: 99

COMMUTE	AREA	U.S. AVG	INTERCITY SERVICES	AREA	U.S. AVG	AUTOMOTIVE	AREA	U.S. AVG
Average commute time	20.4	27.4	Major airports within 60 miles	1	1	Insurance, annual premium	$925	$1,432
Percent commutes > 60 mins.	3.8%	5.9%	Size of regional airport	Large	Large	Gas, cost per gallon	$2.57	$2.49
Commute by auto	80.7%	78.9%	Daily airline activity	624	686	Daily vehicle miles per capita	23.6	24.0
Commute by mass transit	1.0%	1.9%	Amtrak service	No	No			
Work at home	4.4%	3.1%						
Mass transit miles per capita	0.97	1.87						

Transportation
Score: 82.4
Rank: 67

DINING & SHOPPING	AREA	U.S. AVG	ENTERTAINMENT	AREA	U.S. AVG	OUTDOOR ACTIVITIES	AREA	U.S. AVG
Restaurant rating	1	2	Professional sports rating	2	4	Golf-course rating	1	4
Outlet mall score	6	42	College sports rating	5	4	Ski-area rating	2	3
No. Starbucks	1	13	Zoo/aquarium rating	1	3	Sq. miles inland water	4	4
No. warehouse clubs	0	2	Amusement park rating	1	3	Miles of coastline	0.0	10.7
			Botanical garden/ arboretum rating	2	4	National Park rating	1	3

Leisure
Score: 26.5
Rank: 273

MEDIA & LIBRARIES	AREA	U.S. AVG	PERFORMING ARTS	AREA	U.S. AVG	MUSEUMS	AREA	U.S. AVG
Arts radio rating	1	3	Classical music rating	3	4	Overall museum rating	2	5
No. public libraries	10	27	Ballet/dance rating	1	3	Art museum rating	2	5
Library volumes per capita	3.67	2.78	Professional theater rating	1	3	Science museum rating	1	5
			University arts programs rating	4	5	Children's museum rating	1	3

Arts & Culture
Score: 29.1
Rank: 265

Edison, NJ

Score: 61.4   **Rank:** 161   **2004 rank:** 73

Profile: Suburban complex
Location: East-central New Jersey, mainly south of Newark and southwest of New York City
Elevation: 72 feet
Time zone: Eastern Standard Time

PRO
Strong and diverse economy
Close to New York City
Educated population

CON
Cost of living
Long commutes
Crowding and sprawl

The so-called Edison metro area is much more complex than it sounds. Edison itself is a mid-size suburban town of no particular distinction and a population of about 100,000. Federal OMB experts chose the city's name to apply to a vast and enormously complex four-county New Jersey metro area spread around the southwest flank of the New York area, including Middlesex, Somerset, Monmouth, and Ocean counties. These counties spread south along the shore two-thirds of the way down the state, and southwest across almost two-thirds of the state towards Trenton. It is one of the most complex and diverse metro areas we cover.

Middlesex County is farthest north and the most built-up of the four counties, containing such cities as the Brunswicks (North, East, and New Burnswick), the Amboys (Perth and South), Piscataway, and a num-

ber of smaller towns located mainly up the shallow valley of the Raritan River. The county rounds the coastal "notch" below Staten Island, and then becomes Monmouth County with a series of mostly grown-together smaller suburban towns like Red Bank and Matawan. Turning south around the "horn" gets you to Long Branch and the more famous Asbury Park along the shore, classic if slightly older beach towns known for music and entertainment. (Bruce Springsteen is one favorite son; Bon Jovi is another.) Somerset County spreads west up the Raritan River Valley with mostly smaller towns and suburbs.

These communities are defined in part by their New Jersey Transit and Northeast Corridor rail-commute corridors toward Newark, Hoboken, and ultimately Manhattan. Many cities, such as New Brunswick and Edison, lie along the rail lines, while other suburban communities are a short drive or connecting bus ride away. The percentage of residents commuting to New York is high—as high as 50% from many of these communities—and the rail corridors are lifelines; a breakdown is a major news event. Typical Manhattan commute times run 45 minutes to an hour from most suburban locations, not bad considering the distance, but some 17% of commutes take longer than an hour. Monmouth and Ocean county commuters can also take a ferry to Manhattan—a faster but more expensive choice.

Like many areas in northeast New Jersey, the area is a mix of heavy industry, commercial and corporate research and headquarters activity, and a patchwork of residential towns and villages. Most of the heavy industry is near the mouth of the Raritan River, near Perth Amboy and South Amboy. The area has a strong corporate pedigree, with headquarters of such Fortune 500 companies as Merck & Co., Johnson & Johnson, Pharmacia/Upjohn, American Standard, Chubb, Foster Wheeler, Engelhard, and Supermarkets General in the Middlesex area, while AT&T and Lucent Technologies among others have a large presence in Monmouth County. Farther south, Fort Dix is a large Ocean County employer, and tourism is big along the coast. The rest of the area is a livable balance of commercial, residential, and rural activity, and although urban sprawl is an issue, the state's rigorous efforts to contain development in the south and west portions of the region have paid off. The area is home to Rutgers University, the state's major public university, at New Brunswick. Educational attainment is high, and the crime rate is the lowest in the state. Residential areas vary and are mostly middle to upper-middle class with attractive if expensive housing, but some blighted and industrial areas exist particularly near the northern lowlands near the Amboys. Some of the beach towns in Monmouth and Ocean counties are better than others, and some of the suburbs away from the beaches are in a rebuilding mode as more seek the area as an alternative to more crowded locations north. Notably, Monmouth County has 50 towns and villages but only 2 with population above 20,000. Summing up, this dense area has a bit of everything and, of course, excellent access to the amenities of New York, but it comes at the price of crowding, high living costs, and long commutes.

Coastal areas are flat and mainly built up. Inland sections are mainly level valleys among low rolling hills, with some wooded areas and open farmland. Summers are warm, hazy, and humid, with a few hot spells and frequent afternoon thundershowers, particularly inland. Winters are an East Coast mix, typically with clouds, rain, and snow, and varying temperatures frequently fluctuating above and below freezing. First freeze is mid-October; last is late April.

Population

DEMOGRAPHICS	AREA	U.S. AVG	ETHNIC COMPOSITION	AREA	U.S. AVG	RESIDENT PROFILE	AREA	U.S. AVG
Population	2,313,085		White	77.5%	79.0%	Single	32.3%	32.4%
Population density per sq. mile	1342.8	358.5	Black	7.4%	10.5%	Married	56.1%	52.7%
Population growth	22.2%	21.1%	Asian	9.0%	2.7%	Divorced/separated	11.6%	14.9%
Median age	38.6	36.1	Hispanic	10.5%	10.6%	Married with children	27.2%	23.7%
Percent Democrat	47.6%	44.5%	Religious observance	60.2%	48.9%	Single with children	6.1%	9.1%
Percent Republican	51.5%	54.5%	Diversity measure	47.2	40.1	Percent over age 65	14.4%	12.9%

Economy & Jobs
Score: 55.6
Rank: 166

INCOME	AREA	U.S. AVG	EMPLOYMENT	AREA	U.S. AVG	EMPLOYING INDUSTRIES	AREA	U.S. AVG
Per capita income	$32,805	$23,235	Unemployment rate	4.2%	4.7%	Largest: Wholesale Trade		
Household income	$69,206	$46,414	Recent job growth	2.1%	1.3%			
Household income < $25K	15.6%	26.2%	Projected future job growth	10.4%	11.5%	Percent manufacturing	10.6%	15.4%
Household income > $75K	45.1%	25.4%	White collar	68.6%	57.8%	Percent public sector	14.0%	15.7%
Household income growth	14.0%	13.6%	Blue collar	18.8%	25.2%	Percent construction	8.3%	9.9%

Cost of Living
Score: 6.1
Rank: 350

INDEXES & TAXES	AREA	U.S. AVG	HOUSING	AREA	U.S. AVG	NECESSITIES	AREA	U.S. AVG
Cost of Living Index	136.8	100.0	Median home price	$393,600	$220,000	Food Index	116.5	100.0
Buying Power Index	113.4	100.0	Home price appreciation	92.9%	10.1%	Housing Index	114.1	100.0
Income tax rate	2.45%	4.70%	Median rent	$1,212	$709	Utilities Index	129.8	100.0
Sales tax rate	6.00%	6.58%	Homes owned	68.1%	62.3%	Transportation Index	117.8	100.0
Property tax rate	$22.49	$12.00	Home price ratio	5.7	4.2	Healthcare Index	127.7	100.0
						Miscellaneous Cost Index	117.1	100.0

Climate
Score: 59.1
Rank: 152

TEMPERATURE	AREA	U.S. AVG	PRECIPITATION	AREA	U.S. AVG	COMFORTS & HAZARDS	AREA	U.S. AVG
Average January low	25.3	26.2	Annual inches precipitation	40.2	37.7	July relative humidity	67%	66%
Average July high	84.9	87.4	Annual inches snowfall	23.4	7.0	Annual days mostly sunny	216	208
Annual days > 90°F	17	38	Annual days precipitation	128	109	Annual days with thunderstorms	33	39
Annual days < 32°F	88	89	Annual days rain > 0.5 inches	27	22	Tornado risk score	13	18
Annual days < 0°F	0	6	Annual days snow > 1.5 inches	5	6	Hurricane risk score	17	13

TEMPERATURE

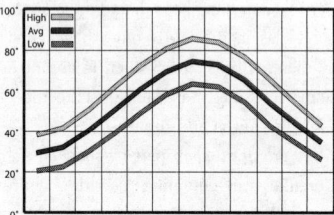

PRECIPITATION

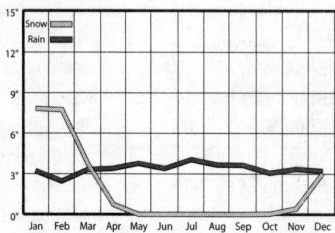

DAYS OF CLOUDS & PRECIPITATION

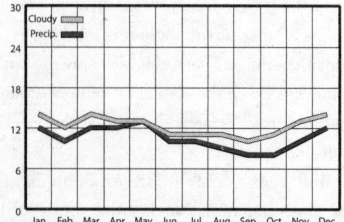

Education
Score: 89.6
Rank: 39

ACHIEVEMENT	AREA	U.S. AVG	PUBLIC SCHOOLS	AREA	U.S. AVG	HIGHER EDUCATION	AREA	U.S. AVG
High school degree	85.7%	82.7%	Expenditures per pupil	$8,864	$5,686	No. 2-year colleges	8	4
2-year college degree	5.7%	6.4%	Student/teacher ratio	15.0	16.7	No. 4-year colleges/universities	8	6
4-year college degree	20.1%	15.7%	Attending public school	84.2%	90.1%	No. highly ranked universities	5	1
Graduate/professional degree	12.0%	8.9%	State SAT score	1011*	1021			
			State ACT score	21.8	20.9			

Health & Healthcare
Score: 7.2
Rank: 346

HAZARDS & ILLNESSES	AREA	U.S. AVG	HEALTHCARE	AREA	U.S. AVG	CRIME	AREA	U.S. AVG
Air-quality score	28	37	Physicians per capita	294.8	244.2	Violent crime rate	172.4	465.5
Water-quality score	14	52	Hospital beds per capita	302.2	420.0	Change in violent crime rate	-7.3%	-2.2%
Pollen/allergy score	62	61	No. teaching hospitals	9	3	Property crime rate	1,875.7	3,517.1
Cancer mortality per capita	216.8	201.9	Cost per doctor visit	$69	$77	Change in property crime rate	-0.8%	-2.1%
Depression days per month	3.0	3.5	Cost per dental visit	$92	$70			
Stress score	19	50						

Crime
Score: 95.7
Rank: 17

Transportation
Score: 90.1
Rank: 38

COMMUTE	AREA	U.S. AVG	INTERCITY SERVICES	AREA	U.S. AVG	AUTOMOTIVE	AREA	U.S. AVG
Average commute time	34.6	27.4	Major airports within 60 miles	4	1	Insurance, annual premium	$2,596	$1,432
Percent commutes > 60 mins.	17.3%	5.9%	Size of regional airport	Large	Large	Gas, cost per gallon	$2.33	$2.49
Commute by auto	77.8%	78.9%	Daily airline activity	2696	686	Daily vehicle miles per capita	25.3	24.0
Commute by mass transit	6.5%	1.9%	Amtrak service	Yes	No			
Work at home	2.7%	3.1%						
Mass transit miles per capita	6.46	1.87						

Leisure
Score: 92.2
Rank: 30

DINING & SHOPPING	AREA	U.S. AVG	ENTERTAINMENT	AREA	U.S. AVG	OUTDOOR ACTIVITIES	AREA	U.S. AVG
Restaurant rating	1	2	Professional sports rating	10	4	Golf-course rating	9	4
Outlet mall score	3	42	College sports rating	8	4	Ski-area rating	4	3
No. Starbucks	24	13	Zoo/aquarium rating	4	3	Sq. miles inland water	8	4
No. warehouse clubs	9	2	Amusement park rating	8	3	Miles of coastline	45.2	10.7
			Botanical garden/ arboretum rating	8	4	National Park rating	4	3

Arts & Culture
Score: 79.4
Rank: 77

MEDIA & LIBRARIES	AREA	U.S. AVG	PERFORMING ARTS	AREA	U.S. AVG	MUSEUMS	AREA	U.S. AVG
Arts radio rating	4	3	Classical music rating	7	4	Overall museum rating	9	5
No. public libraries	106	27	Ballet/dance rating	6	3	Art museum rating	8	5
Library volumes per capita	3.46	2.78	Professional theater rating	8	3	Science museum rating	10	5
			University arts programs rating	6	5	Children's museum rating	8	3

El Centro, CA

Score: 13.6   **Rank:** 365   **2004 rank:** not ranked

Profile: Small agricultural city
Location: Southern California, near the Mexican border
Elevation: −45 feet
Time zone: Pacific Standard Time

PRO	CON
Pleasant winters	Summer heat
Cultural diversity	Low educational attainment
Future job growth	Isolation

As we look closer at this isolated deep-desert irrigation-supported agricultural community, there seems to be some hope for strong future employment, but there isn't a lot else to cheer about in El Centro. El Centro is a dry, dusty, agricultural center in the vast Imperial Valley, which is irrigated by the Colorado River. Although the name in Spanish translates to "the center," El Centro isn't in the center of very much except for several hundred square miles of flat irrigated agricultural land and surrounding desert. The city is 115 miles east of San Diego and only 12 miles north of the Mexican border. Employment is dominated by agriculture, agricultural transportation, and some government jobs; farm workers make up a sizeable portion of the population. Combined educational attainment is lowest in the country. There have been mostly unsuccessful attempts to establish retirement communities in the area, but the valley is physically unattractive, has extreme unemployment, and little to do for retirees or those in the workforce. Points scored for future employment, winter climate, and a relatively low reported crime rate for the region probably kept El Centro off the bottom of our list.

The southerly latitude and negative elevation give important clues as to the climate of El Centro—hot. In fact, temperatures over 90°F are experienced during more than half the days each year. Warm air is trapped and compressed in this mountain-surrounded valley, and the results can be made more uncomfortable by irrigation-sourced humidity. Winter weather, on the other hand, is pleasant, with days in the moderately warm 70s and 80s and desert-cool evenings.

Population

DEMOGRAPHICS	AREA	U.S. AVG	ETHNIC COMPOSITION	AREA	U.S. AVG	RESIDENT PROFILE	AREA	U.S. AVG
Population	153,881		White	48.4%	79.0%	Single	33.0%	32.4%
Population density per sq. mile	36.9	358.5	Black	3.7%	10.5%	Married	46.5%	52.7%
Population growth	40.8%	21.1%	Asian	1.8%	2.7%	Divorced/separated	20.5%	14.9%
Median age	31.1	36.1	Hispanic	75.7%	10.6%	Married with children	33.7%	23.7%
Percent Democrat	52.4%	44.5%	Religious observance	62.6%	48.9%	Single with children	13.2%	9.1%
Percent Republican	46.4%	54.5%	Diversity measure	74.5	40.1	Percent over age 65	10.4%	12.9%

Economy & Jobs
Score: 74.1
Rank: 98

INCOME	AREA	U.S. AVG	EMPLOYMENT	AREA	U.S. AVG	EMPLOYING INDUSTRIES	AREA	U.S. AVG
Per capita income	$14,969	$23,235	Unemployment rate	17.3%	4.7%	Largest: Retail Trade		
Household income	$36,919	$46,414	Recent job growth	9.0%	1.3%			
Household income < $25K	35.2%	26.2%	Projected future job growth	34.5%	11.5%	Percent manufacturing	11.6%	15.4%
Household income > $75K	19.7%	25.4%	White collar	49.9%	57.8%	Percent public sector	28.0%	15.7%
Household income growth	15.8%	13.6%	Blue collar	20.3%	25.2%	Percent construction	8.8%	9.9%

Cost of Living
Score: 8.6
Rank: 341

INDEXES & TAXES	AREA	U.S. AVG	HOUSING	AREA	U.S. AVG	NECESSITIES	AREA	U.S. AVG
Cost of Living Index	128.4	100.0	Median home price	$355,700	$220,000	Food Index	110.8	100.0
Buying Power Index	64.4	100.0	Home price appreciation	102.9%	10.1%	Housing Index	77.6	100.0
Income tax rate	6.00%	4.70%	Median rent	$680	$709	Utilities Index	128.7	100.0
Sales tax rate	7.75%	6.58%	Homes owned	52.7%	62.3%	Transportation Index	110.4	100.0
Property tax rate	$9.50	$12.00	Home price ratio	9.6	4.2	Healthcare Index	128.8	100.0
						Miscellaneous Cost Index	101.2	100.0

Climate
Score: 69.0
Rank: 115

TEMPERATURE	AREA	U.S. AVG	PRECIPITATION	AREA	U.S. AVG	COMFORTS & HAZARDS	AREA	U.S. AVG
Average January low	44.0	26.2	Annual inches precipitation	3.0	37.7	July relative humidity	20%	66%
Average July high	107.0	87.4	Annual inches snowfall	0.1	7.0	Annual days mostly sunny	277	208
Annual days > 90°F	179	38	Annual days precipitation	16	109	Annual days with thunderstorms	19	39
Annual days < 32°F	2	89	Annual days rain > 0.5 inches	2	22	Tornado risk score	4	18
Annual days < 0°F	0	6	Annual days snow > 1.5 inches	0	6	Hurricane risk score	0	13

TEMPERATURE

PRECIPITATION

DAYS OF CLOUDS & PRECIPITATION

Education
Score: 0.5
Rank: 371

ACHIEVEMENT	AREA	U.S. AVG	PUBLIC SCHOOLS	AREA	U.S. AVG	HIGHER EDUCATION	AREA	U.S. AVG
High school degree	58.8%	82.7%	Expenditures per pupil	$4,999	$5,686	No. 2-year colleges	1	4
2-year college degree	6.1%	6.4%	Student/teacher ratio	20.6	16.7	No. 4-year colleges/universities	1	6
4-year college degree	6.7%	15.7%	Attending public school	94.4%	90.1%	No. highly ranked universities	0	1
Graduate/professional degree	3.7%	8.9%	State SAT score	1019*	1021			
			State ACT score	21.6	20.9			

Health & Healthcare
Score: 8.0
Rank: 343

HAZARDS & ILLNESSES	AREA	U.S. AVG	HEALTHCARE	AREA	U.S. AVG	CRIME	AREA	U.S. AVG
Air-quality score	34	37	Physicians per capita	73.7	244.2	Violent crime rate	511.5	465.5
Water-quality score	30	52	Hospital beds per capita	139.7	420.0	Change in violent crime rate	12.4%	-2.2%
Pollen/allergy score	65	61	No. teaching hospitals	0	3	Property crime rate	4,059.0	3,517.1
Cancer mortality per capita	158.5	201.9	Cost per doctor visit	$90	$77	Change in property crime rate	9.0%	-2.1%
Depression days per month	3.7	3.5	Cost per dental visit	$76	$70			
Stress score	40	50						

Crime
Score: 71.1
Rank: 109

Transportation
Score: 63.1
Rank: 139

COMMUTE	AREA	U.S. AVG	INTERCITY SERVICES	AREA	U.S. AVG	AUTOMOTIVE	AREA	U.S. AVG
Average commute time	21.4	27.4	Major airports within 60 miles	1	1	Insurance, annual premium	$1,625	$1,432
Percent commutes > 60 mins.	5.1%	5.9%	Size of regional airport	Large	Large	Gas, cost per gallon	$2.46	$2.49
Commute by auto	72.7%	78.9%	Daily airline activity	350	686	Daily vehicle miles per capita	15.4	24.0
Commute by mass transit	1.7%	1.9%	Amtrak service	No	No			
Work at home	3.0%	3.1%						
Mass transit miles per capita	1.74	1.87						

DINING & SHOPPING	AREA	U.S. AVG	ENTERTAINMENT	AREA	U.S. AVG	OUTDOOR ACTIVITIES	AREA	U.S. AVG
Restaurant rating	1	2	Professional sports rating	1	4	Golf-course rating	2	4
Outlet mall score	22	42	College sports rating	1	4	Ski-area rating	1	3
No. Starbucks	3	13	Zoo/aquarium rating	1	3	Sq. miles inland water	1	4
No. warehouse clubs	1	2	Amusement park rating	1	3	Miles of coastline	0.0	10.7
			Botanical garden/			National Park rating	3	3
			arboretum rating	1	4			

Leisure
Score: 0.3
Rank: 372

MEDIA & LIBRARIES	AREA	U.S. AVG	PERFORMING ARTS	AREA	U.S. AVG	MUSEUMS	AREA	U.S. AVG
Arts radio rating	1	3	Classical music rating	1	4	Overall museum rating	1	5
No. public libraries	14	27	Ballet/dance rating	1	3	Art museum rating	1	5
Library volumes per capita	2.08	2.78	Professional theater rating	1	3	Science museum rating	1	5
			University arts programs rating	1	5	Children's museum rating	1	3

Arts & Culture
Score: 1.9
Rank: 366

Elizabethtown, KY

Score: 43.8   Rank: 297   2004 rank: not ranked

Profile: Small town
Location: West-central Kentucky, 45 miles south of Louisville
Elevation: 708 feet
Time zone: Eastern Standard Time

PRO	CON
Cost of living	Entertainment
Central location	Educational attainment
Low crime rates	Economic cycles

Elizabethtown, or "E-town," is a small transportation and commercial/industrial center located at the junction of the north–south Interstate 65 and east–west Western Kentucky Parkway, a short drive south of Louisville. There is a notable historic district in the small and otherwise nondescript downtown. The central location brings a diverse base of mostly light to medium manufacturing concerns, many tied to the automotive and machinery industries. Larger names include Dana Corporation, Dow Corning, Gates Rubber, and Remington (firearms), and UPS operates a logistics center here. Cost of living and housing are quite reasonable. A 300-bed hospital anchors the healthcare scene. Besides Louisville, the area is close to Fort Knox to the north, Mammoth Cave to the south, and Bardstown to the east.

Terrain is flat to gently rolling with mixed agricultural and other uses. Summers are hot and humid, punctuated by thunderstorms. Winters are an unpredictable mix with rain and occasional periods of heavy snow. Spring may bring strong storms, while fall seasons are relatively dry and pleasant. First freeze is mid- to late October; last is mid-April.

DEMOGRAPHICS	AREA	U.S. AVG	ETHNIC COMPOSITION	AREA	U.S. AVG	RESIDENT PROFILE	AREA	U.S. AVG
Population	110,153		White	81.9%	79.0%	Single	27.0%	32.4%
Population density per sq. mile	123.6	358.5	Black	11.4%	10.5%	Married	58.2%	52.7%
Population growth	9.2%	21.1%	Asian	2.2%	2.7%	Divorced/separated	14.9%	14.9%
Median age	35.3	36.1	Hispanic	2.9%	10.6%	Married with children	27.4%	23.7%
Percent Democrat	31.5%	44.5%	Religious observance	54.3%	48.9%	Single with children	9.8%	9.1%
Percent Republican	67.7%	54.5%	Diversity measure	34.8	40.1	Percent over age 65	11.2%	12.9%

Population

INCOME	AREA	U.S. AVG	EMPLOYMENT	AREA	U.S. AVG	EMPLOYING INDUSTRIES	AREA	U.S. AVG
Per capita income	$20,358	$23,235	Unemployment rate	6.2%	4.7%	Largest: Manufacturing		
Household income	$43,038	$46,414	Recent job growth	0.5%	1.3%			
Household income < $25K	26.6%	26.2%	Projected future job growth	6.2%	11.5%	Percent manufacturing	21.5%	15.4%
Household income > $75K	21.0%	25.4%	White collar	50.6%	57.8%	Percent public sector	18.3%	15.7%
Household income growth	16.2%	13.6%	Blue collar	31.9%	25.2%	Percent construction	10.4%	9.9%

Economy & Jobs
Score: 12.6
Rank: 326

INDEXES & TAXES	AREA	U.S. AVG	HOUSING	AREA	U.S. AVG	NECESSITIES	AREA	U.S. AVG
Cost of Living Index	83.7	100.0	Median home price	$131,000	$220,000	Food Index	100.3	100.0
Buying Power Index	115.3	100.0	Home price appreciation	30.2%	10.1%	Housing Index	57.5	100.0
Income tax rate	6.00%	4.70%	Median rent	$507	$709	Utilities Index	98.2	100.0
Sales tax rate	6.00%	6.58%	Homes owned	63.5%	62.3%	Transportation Index	98.4	100.0
Property tax rate	$6.75	$12.00	Home price ratio	3.0	4.2	Healthcare Index	89.3	100.0
						Miscellaneous Cost Index	97.6	100.0

Cost of Living
Score: 73.5
Rank: 100

Climate
Score: 21.1
Rank: 294

TEMPERATURE	AREA	U.S. AVG
Average January low	25.0	26.2
Average July high	88.0	87.4
Annual days > 90°F	35	38
Annual days < 32°F	90	89
Annual days < 0°F	2	6

PRECIPITATION	AREA	U.S. AVG
Annual inches precipitation	43.9	37.7
Annual inches snowfall	17.0	7.0
Annual days precipitation	125	109
Annual days rain > 0.5 inches	28	22
Annual days snow > 1.5 inches	4	6

COMFORTS & HAZARDS	AREA	U.S. AVG
July relative humidity	58%	66%
Annual days mostly sunny	190	208
Annual days with thunderstorms	45	39
Tornado risk score	2	18
Hurricane risk score	1	13

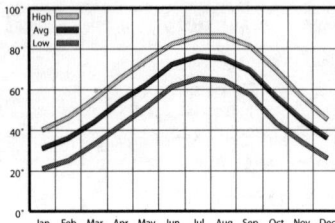

TEMPERATURE

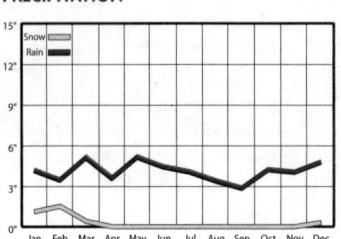

PRECIPITATION

DAYS OF CLOUDS & PRECIPITATION

Education
Score: 21.1
Rank: 294

ACHIEVEMENT	AREA	U.S. AVG
High school degree	80.9%	82.7%
2-year college degree	7.2%	6.4%
4-year college degree	8.4%	15.7%
Graduate/professional degree	6.4%	8.9%

PUBLIC SCHOOLS	AREA	U.S. AVG
Expenditures per pupil	$5,258	$5,686
Student/teacher ratio	20.8	16.7
Attending public school	93.8%	90.1%
State SAT score	1124	1021
State ACT score	20.6*	20.9

HIGHER EDUCATION	AREA	U.S. AVG
No. 2-year colleges	5	4
No. 4-year colleges/universities	0	6
No. highly ranked universities	0	1

Health & Healthcare
Score: 61.0
Rank: 147

HAZARDS & ILLNESSES	AREA	U.S. AVG
Air-quality score	60	37
Water-quality score	48	52
Pollen/allergy score	85	61
Cancer mortality per capita	234.1	201.9
Depression days per month	4.7	3.5
Stress score	58	50

HEALTHCARE	AREA	U.S. AVG
Physicians per capita	190.1	244.2
Hospital beds per capita	393.1	420.0
No. teaching hospitals	0	3
Cost per doctor visit	$68	$77
Cost per dental visit	$59	$70

Crime
Score: 89.3
Rank: 41

CRIME	AREA	U.S. AVG
Violent crime rate	160.5	465.5
Change in violent crime rate	1.1%	-2.2%
Property crime rate	1,859.9	3,517.1
Change in property crime rate	-9.8%	-2.1%

Transportation
Score: 17.9
Rank: 308

COMMUTE	AREA	U.S. AVG
Average commute time	25.4	27.4
Percent commutes > 60 mins.	7.7%	5.9%
Commute by auto	79.9%	78.9%
Commute by mass transit	0.6%	1.9%
Work at home	3.5%	3.1%
Mass transit miles per capita	0.64	1.87

INTERCITY SERVICES	AREA	U.S. AVG
Major airports within 60 miles	1	1
Size of regional airport	Medium	Large
Daily airline activity	280	686
Amtrak service	No	No

AUTOMOTIVE	AREA	U.S. AVG
Insurance, annual premium	$1,029	$1,432
Gas, cost per gallon	$2.44	$2.49
Daily vehicle miles per capita	22.4	24.0

Leisure
Score: 46.5
Rank: 199

DINING & SHOPPING	AREA	U.S. AVG
Restaurant rating	1	2
Outlet mall score	12	42
No. Starbucks	0	13
No. warehouse clubs	0	2

ENTERTAINMENT	AREA	U.S. AVG
Professional sports rating	3	4
College sports rating	6	4
Zoo/aquarium rating	6	3
Amusement park rating	1	3
Botanical garden/ arboretum rating	6	4

OUTDOOR ACTIVITIES	AREA	U.S. AVG
Golf-course rating	5	4
Ski-area rating	1	3
Sq. miles inland water	2	4
Miles of coastline	0.0	10.7
National Park rating	1	3

Arts & Culture
Score: 58.8
Rank: 154

MEDIA & LIBRARIES	AREA	U.S. AVG
Arts radio rating	1	3
No. public libraries	3	27
Library volumes per capita	1.09	2.78

PERFORMING ARTS	AREA	U.S. AVG
Classical music rating	4	4
Ballet/dance rating	3	3
Professional theater rating	1	3
University arts programs rating	8	5

MUSEUMS	AREA	U.S. AVG
Overall museum rating	7	5
Art museum rating	3	5
Science museum rating	3	5
Children's museum rating	1	3

Elkhart–Goshen, IN

Score: 44.2   **Rank:** 291   **2004 rank:** 272

Profile: Small manufacturing town complex
Location: Extreme northern Indiana at Michigan border, 15 miles east of South Bend
Elevation: 700 feet
Time zone: Eastern Standard Time

PRO	CON
Small-town atmosphere	Harsh winters
Cost of housing	Economic cycles
Nearby college town	Low educational attainment

Elkhart, a small industrial town, has a diversified manufacturing base. A typical small Midwestern town, Goshen, to the southeast, has an agricultural base, an extension of some Elkhart manufacturing, and Goshen College. The industrial base has some unique components. Elkhart is the U.S. center for the manufacture of recreational vehicles, marching band and other musical instruments, and firefighting equipment. Among other areas with this profile, Elkhart and Goshen have a better-than-average set of museums. A large Amish and Mennonite community resides east of Goshen. Even with the economic diversity, the area is vulnerable to economic cycles, particularly in the RV industry. The area is close enough to South Bend to share many of its amenities and services. Cost of living and housing cost profiles are very low; homes are affordable and quality is high. Locally, educational attainment and future job-growth projections are low.

Most of the area is a level glacial plain with mixed agriculture and wooded areas. Summers are warm and humid but subject to cooling breezes off nearby Lake Michigan. The lake moderates temperatures somewhat but creates high humidity, frequent cloudiness, and heavy winter snows. First freeze is early October; last is early May.

Population

DEMOGRAPHICS	AREA	U.S. AVG	ETHNIC COMPOSITION	AREA	U.S. AVG	RESIDENT PROFILE	AREA	U.S. AVG
Population	191,890		White	84.6%	79.0%	Single	28.5%	32.4%
Population density per sq. mile	413.7	358.5	Black	4.9%	10.5%	Married	57.4%	52.7%
Population growth	22.8%	21.1%	Asian	1.1%	2.7%	Divorced/separated	14.2%	14.9%
Median age	33.4	36.1	Hispanic	11.4%	10.6%	Married with children	26.7%	23.7%
Percent Democrat	29.3%	44.5%	Religious observance	38.4%	48.9%	Single with children	9.5%	9.1%
Percent Republican	70.0%	54.5%	Diversity measure	42.2	40.1	Percent over age 65	11.0%	12.9%

Economy
& Jobs

Score: 46.8
Rank: 200

INCOME	AREA	U.S. AVG	EMPLOYMENT	AREA	U.S. AVG	EMPLOYING INDUSTRIES	AREA	U.S. AVG
Per capita income	$22,143	$23,235	Unemployment rate	5.0%	4.7%	Largest: Manufacturing		
Household income	$48,526	$46,414	Recent job growth	0.6%	1.3%			
Household income < $25K	21.1%	26.2%	Projected future job growth	5.4%	11.5%	Percent manufacturing	32.6%	15.4%
Household income > $75K	24.1%	25.4%	White collar	46.2%	57.8%	Percent public sector	6.6%	15.7%
Household income growth	9.1%	13.6%	Blue collar	41.4%	25.2%	Percent construction	8.9%	9.9%

Cost of Living

Score: 78.6
Rank: 80

INDEXES & TAXES	AREA	U.S. AVG	HOUSING	AREA	U.S. AVG	NECESSITIES	AREA	U.S. AVG
Cost of Living Index	82.8	100.0	Median home price	$127,200	$220,000	Food Index	94.1	100.0
Buying Power Index	131.4	100.0	Home price appreciation	21.0%	10.1%	Housing Index	54.6	100.0
Income tax rate	4.31%	4.70%	Median rent	$660	$709	Utilities Index	109.8	100.0
Sales tax rate	6.00%	6.58%	Homes owned	69.3%	62.3%	Transportation Index	94.2	100.0
Property tax rate	$10.41	$12.00	Home price ratio	2.6	4.2	Healthcare Index	95.3	100.0
						Miscellaneous Cost Index	96.6	100.0

Climate

Score: 24.3
Rank: 282

TEMPERATURE	AREA	U.S. AVG	PRECIPITATION	AREA	U.S. AVG	COMFORTS & HAZARDS	AREA	U.S. AVG
Average January low	17.5	26.2	Annual inches precipitation	35.0	37.7	July relative humidity	72%	66%
Average July high	84.0	87.4	Annual inches snowfall	35.0	7.0	Annual days mostly sunny	182	208
Annual days > 90°F	14	38	Annual days precipitation	131	109	Annual days with thunderstorms	41	39
Annual days < 32°F	134	89	Annual days rain > 0.5 inches	22	22	Tornado risk score	100	18
Annual days < 0°F	10	6	Annual days snow > 1.5 inches	12	6	Hurricane risk score	2	13

TEMPERATURE

PRECIPITATION

DAYS OF CLOUDS & PRECIPITATION

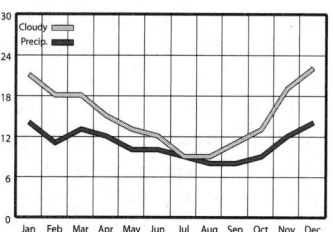

ACHIEVEMENT	AREA	U.S. AVG	PUBLIC SCHOOLS	AREA	U.S. AVG	HIGHER EDUCATION	AREA	U.S. AVG
High school degree	75.6%	82.7%	Expenditures per pupil	$5,552	$5,686	No. 2-year colleges	0	4
2-year college degree	4.5%	6.4%	Student/teacher ratio	18.6	16.7	No. 4-year colleges/universities	2	6
4-year college degree	9.8%	15.7%	Attending public school	90.0%	90.1%	No. highly ranked universities	0	1
Graduate/professional degree	5.5%	8.9%	State SAT score	1007*	1021			
			State ACT score	21.7	20.9			

Education
Score: 4.8
Rank: 355

HAZARDS & ILLNESSES	AREA	U.S. AVG	HEALTHCARE	AREA	U.S. AVG	CRIME	AREA	U.S. AVG
Air-quality score	35	37	Physicians per capita	128.7	244.2	Violent crime rate	177.9	465.5
Water-quality score	60	52	Hospital beds per capita	260.6	420.0	Change in violent crime rate	-3.4%	-2.2%
Pollen/allergy score	56	61	No. teaching hospitals	0	3	Property crime rate	3,742.8	3,517.1
Cancer mortality per capita	195.2	201.9	Cost per doctor visit	$71	$77	Change in property crime rate	-6.1%	-2.1%
Depression days per month	3.3	3.5	Cost per dental visit	$73	$70			
Stress score	10	50						

Health & Healthcare
Score: 44.4
Rank: 208

Crime
Score: 79.4
Rank: 77

COMMUTE	AREA	U.S. AVG	INTERCITY SERVICES	AREA	U.S. AVG	AUTOMOTIVE	AREA	U.S. AVG
Average commute time	20.2	27.4	Major airports within 60 miles	1	1	Insurance, annual premium	$1,216	$1,432
Percent commutes > 60 mins.	2.4%	5.9%	Size of regional airport	Medium	Large	Gas, cost per gallon	$2.48	$2.49
Commute by auto	79.4%	78.9%	Daily airline activity	608	686	Daily vehicle miles per capita	30.1	24.0
Commute by mass transit	0.4%	1.9%	Amtrak service	Yes	No			
Work at home	3.5%	3.1%						
Mass transit miles per capita	0.44	1.87						

Transportation
Score: 81.3
Rank: 70

DINING & SHOPPING	AREA	U.S. AVG	ENTERTAINMENT	AREA	U.S. AVG	OUTDOOR ACTIVITIES	AREA	U.S. AVG
Restaurant rating	1	2	Professional sports rating	2	4	Golf-course rating	2	4
Outlet mall score	31	42	College sports rating	2	4	Ski-area rating	1	3
No. Starbucks	0	13	Zoo/aquarium rating	1	3	Sq. miles inland water	2	4
No. warehouse clubs	0	2	Amusement park rating	1	3	Miles of coastline	0.0	10.7
			Botanical garden/ arboretum rating	1	4	National Park rating	1	3

Leisure
Score: 5.1
Rank: 354

MEDIA & LIBRARIES	AREA	U.S. AVG	PERFORMING ARTS	AREA	U.S. AVG	MUSEUMS	AREA	U.S. AVG
Arts radio rating	1	3	Classical music rating	4	4	Overall museum rating	2	5
No. public libraries	9	27	Ballet/dance rating	1	3	Art museum rating	3	5
Library volumes per capita	4.74	2.78	Professional theater rating	1	3	Science museum rating	1	5
			University arts programs rating	8	5	Children's museum rating	1	3

Arts & Culture
Score: 51.1
Rank: 183

Elmira, NY

Score: 23.8   Rank: 360   2004 rank: 288

Profile: Small town
Location: Western New York along Pennsylvania border, south of the Finger Lakes region
Elevation: 903 feet
Time zone: Eastern Standard Time

PRO
Cost of living
Nearby recreation
Attractive setting

CON
Winter climate
Economy
Arts and culture

Elmira is a quiet, nondescript town in the hills of southwestern New York with a fairly diverse, if cyclical, economic base. The biggest industrial landmark is Corning Glass Works, 14 miles west in Corning, which benefited from the 1990s fiber optic boom, fell on hard times, then picked up again with the growing flat-panel-display business. Such cycles, though not as sharp, have hurt other area businesses, and employment and income levels have had their bumps. For better or for worse, the area has two correctional facilities and a psychiatric facility; at least these provide employment. There isn't much to do and the area is somewhat geographically isolated from other cities, but the popular Finger Lakes region and well-known Watkins Glen International Speedway are nearby. The Cost of Living Index at 77.2 is lowest in the state by a large margin and extremely low for the region. Although the location is far enough south to escape the worst lake effects in winter, that season is still harsh.

The city sits in a creek valley surrounded by hills with hardwood forests. Summer temperatures are pleasant with only a few days above 90°F, but humidity is high and the valleys trap both warm and cold air. Winters are cold and variable with periods of clouds, rain, snow squalls, and heavier snows. While wind and snowfall are slightly less than areas near the Great Lakes, below-zero temperatures are common. First freeze is October 1; last is early May.

DEMOGRAPHICS	AREA	U.S. AVG	ETHNIC COMPOSITION	AREA	U.S. AVG	RESIDENT PROFILE	AREA	U.S. AVG
Population	90,057		White	89.7%	79.0%	Single	33.5%	32.4%
Population density per sq. mile	220.6	358.5	Black	6.6%	10.5%	Married	49.6%	52.7%
Population growth	-5.4%	21.1%	Asian	1.1%	2.7%	Divorced/separated	16.9%	14.9%
Median age	38.9	36.1	Hispanic	2.4%	10.6%	Married with children	20.6%	23.7%
Percent Democrat	43.7%	44.5%	Religious observance	46.8%	48.9%	Single with children	10.2%	9.1%
Percent Republican	54.6%	54.5%	Diversity measure	22.8	40.1	Percent over age 65	15.7%	12.9%

INCOME	AREA	U.S. AVG	EMPLOYMENT	AREA	U.S. AVG	EMPLOYING INDUSTRIES	AREA	U.S. AVG
Per capita income	$20,953	$23,235	Unemployment rate	5.2%	4.7%	Largest: Manufacturing		
Household income	$40,842	$46,414	Recent job growth	-1.3%	1.3%			
Household income < $25K	29.5%	26.2%	Projected future job growth	-5.9%	11.5%	Percent manufacturing	15.8%	15.4%
Household income > $75K	19.5%	25.4%	White collar	57.2%	57.8%	Percent public sector	18.1%	15.7%
Household income growth	12.2%	13.6%	Blue collar	23.3%	25.2%	Percent construction	7.4%	9.9%

Economy & Jobs
Score: 1.9
Rank: 366

INDEXES & TAXES	AREA	U.S. AVG	HOUSING	AREA	U.S. AVG	NECESSITIES	AREA	U.S. AVG
Cost of Living Index	77.2	100.0	Median home price	$87,300	$220,000	Food Index	95.6	100.0
Buying Power Index	118.6	100.0	Home price appreciation	24.1%	10.1%	Housing Index	34.3	100.0
Income tax rate	7.13%	4.70%	Median rent	$630	$709	Utilities Index	115.5	100.0
Sales tax rate	8.25%	6.58%	Homes owned	64.7%	62.3%	Transportation Index	96.1	100.0
Property tax rate	$25.96	$12.00	Home price ratio	2.1	4.2	Healthcare Index	89.5	100.0
						Miscellaneous Cost Index	100.3	100.0

Cost of Living
Score: 25.7
Rank: 277

TEMPERATURE	AREA	U.S. AVG	PRECIPITATION	AREA	U.S. AVG	COMFORTS & HAZARDS	AREA	U.S. AVG
Average January low	15.0	26.2	Annual inches precipitation	37.0	37.7	July relative humidity	75%	66%
Average July high	79.0	87.4	Annual inches snowfall	82.0	7.0	Annual days mostly sunny	151	208
Annual days > 90°F	3	38	Annual days precipitation	159	109	Annual days with thunderstorms	29	39
Annual days < 32°F	145	89	Annual days rain > 0.5 inches	22	22	Tornado risk score	2	18
Annual days < 0°F	8	6	Annual days snow > 1.5 inches	15	6	Hurricane risk score	5	13

Climate
Score: 5.1
Rank: 354

TEMPERATURE

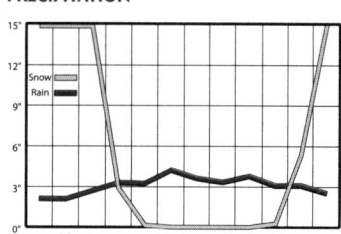

PRECIPITATION

DAYS OF CLOUDS & PRECIPITATION

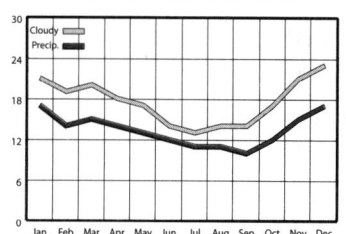

ACHIEVEMENT	AREA	U.S. AVG	PUBLIC SCHOOLS	AREA	U.S. AVG	HIGHER EDUCATION	AREA	U.S. AVG
High school degree	82.1%	82.7%	Expenditures per pupil	$8,013	$5,686	No. 2-year colleges	3	4
2-year college degree	8.9%	6.4%	Student/teacher ratio	16.2	16.7	No. 4-year colleges/universities	1	6
4-year college degree	10.5%	15.7%	Attending public school	90.4%	90.1%	No. highly ranked universities	1	1
Graduate/professional degree	8.2%	8.9%	State SAT score	1003*	1021			
			State ACT score	22.6	20.9			

Education
Score: 51.1
Rank: 184

HAZARDS & ILLNESSES	AREA	U.S. AVG	HEALTHCARE	AREA	U.S. AVG	CRIME	AREA	U.S. AVG
Air-quality score	62	37	Physicians per capita	252.2	244.2	Violent crime rate	231.9	465.5
Water-quality score	67	52	Hospital beds per capita	801.7	420.0	Change in violent crime rate	0.7%	-2.2%
Pollen/allergy score	57	61	No. teaching hospitals	0	3	Property crime rate	2,919.7	3,517.1
Cancer mortality per capita	230.6	201.9	Cost per doctor visit	$73	$77	Change in property crime rate	11.7%	-2.1%
Depression days per month	3.1	3.5	Cost per dental visit	$65	$70			
Stress score	17	50						

Health & Healthcare
Score: 96.8
Rank: 13

Crime
Score: 56.1
Rank: 165

COMMUTE	AREA	U.S. AVG	INTERCITY SERVICES	AREA	U.S. AVG	AUTOMOTIVE	AREA	U.S. AVG
Average commute time	21.0	27.4	Major airports within 60 miles	0	1	Insurance, annual premium	$1,524	$1,432
Percent commutes > 60 mins.	3.9%	5.9%	Size of regional airport	Small	Large	Gas, cost per gallon	$2.56	$2.49
Commute by auto	81.4%	78.9%	Daily airline activity	271	686	Daily vehicle miles per capita	25.9	24.0
Commute by mass transit	1.1%	1.9%	Amtrak service	No	No			
Work at home	2.3%	3.1%						
Mass transit miles per capita	1.09	1.87						

Transportation
Score: 51.6
Rank: 182

DINING & SHOPPING	AREA	U.S. AVG	ENTERTAINMENT	AREA	U.S. AVG	OUTDOOR ACTIVITIES	AREA	U.S. AVG
Restaurant rating	1	2	Professional sports rating	3	4	Golf-course rating	2	4
Outlet mall score	0	42	College sports rating	1	4	Ski-area rating	1	3
No. Starbucks	0	13	Zoo/aquarium rating	1	3	Sq. miles inland water	1	4
No. warehouse clubs	2	2	Amusement park rating	1	3	Miles of coastline	0.0	10.7
			Botanical garden/ arboretum rating	1	4	National Park rating	1	3

Leisure
Score: 3.5
Rank: 360

MEDIA & LIBRARIES	AREA	U.S. AVG	PERFORMING ARTS	AREA	U.S. AVG	MUSEUMS	AREA	U.S. AVG
Arts radio rating	1	3	Classical music rating	1	4	Overall museum rating	3	5
No. public libraries	7	27	Ballet/dance rating	1	3	Art museum rating	2	5
Library volumes per capita	3.22	2.78	Professional theater rating	1	3	Science museum rating	5	5
			University arts programs rating	2	5	Children's museum rating	2	3

Arts & Culture
Score: 16.6
Rank: 310

El Paso, TX

Score: 61.2   Rank: 165   2004 rank: 225

Profile: Mid-size city
Location: Extreme west Texas on the Rio Grande at the Mexico–New Mexico border
Elevation: 3,700 feet
Time zone: Mountain Standard Time

PRO
Cost of living
Dry climate
Mild winters

CON
Isolation
Violent crime
Low educational attainment

El Paso is a unique American city rather like an island in the sea. Self-sufficient and surprisingly large, the city has a modern downtown, with a commercial district and low skyscrapers, and development spreading mostly to the north and east. Because of its isolation, large industry has never taken root, but the area does have some agriculture, ranching, mining, oil, and *maquiladora* (border zone) industry powered by low-cost labor from Mexico. Fort Bliss brings a military presence to the economic and social base, and the recent base realignments have helped by locating more facilities and personnel there. There is an assortment of small museums mostly commemorating the history of the area, and the University of Texas at El Paso adds 16,000 students, a nice campus, and some sports amenities. Nearby geologic areas and the Franklin Mountains State Park offer some outdoor recreational opportunities. The climate, low cost of living, and the "get-away-from-it-all" isolation have made it a popular retirement location. The area is hundreds of miles from a city of any size, but the independent spirit and the availability of low-cost airline flights makes the area less isolated than geography may imply. A sizeable drop in the rate for violent crime helped the overall ranking.

The city is located in a flat valley among dry hills. The Rio Grande flows along the southwest border of the city. The Franklin Mountains begin within the city limits and extend northward with peaks up to 7,200 feet. Daytime summer temperatures are frequently above 90°F, and occasionally above 100°F, but with very low humidity, and nights are usually comfortable. Winter daytime temperatures are mild with freezing night temperatures common during mid-winter. Rainfall throughout the year is light and insufficient for any growth except desert vegetation. Dry periods lasting several months are not unusual. Most precipitation occurs July through September from brief but often heavy thunderstorms. Spring dust storms and sandstorms can occur.

DEMOGRAPHICS	AREA	U.S. AVG	ETHNIC COMPOSITION	AREA	U.S. AVG	RESIDENT PROFILE	AREA	U.S. AVG
Population	719,377		White	73.9%	79.0%	Single	31.9%	32.4%
Population density per sq. mile	710.1	358.5	Black	2.4%	10.5%	Married	51.8%	52.7%
Population growth	21.6%	21.1%	Asian	0.9%	2.7%	Divorced/separated	16.3%	14.9%
Median age	30.6	36.1	Hispanic	82.3%	10.6%	Married with children	32.8%	23.7%
Percent Democrat	56.1%	44.5%	Religious observance	63.4%	48.9%	Single with children	12.4%	9.1%
Percent Republican	43.2%	54.5%	Diversity measure	58.7	40.1	Percent over age 65	10.1%	12.9%

Population

INCOME	AREA	U.S. AVG	EMPLOYMENT	AREA	U.S. AVG	EMPLOYING INDUSTRIES	AREA	U.S. AVG
Per capita income	$15,351	$23,235	Unemployment rate	7.0%	4.7%	Largest: Healthcare & Social Assistance		
Household income	$35,116	$46,414	Recent job growth	2.8%	1.3%			
Household income < $25K	35.7%	26.2%	Projected future job growth	20.4%	11.5%	Percent manufacturing	16.8%	15.4%
Household income > $75K	17.1%	25.4%	White collar	57.4%	57.8%	Percent public sector	20.1%	15.7%
Household income growth	13.1%	13.6%	Blue collar	25.4%	25.2%	Percent construction	8.6%	9.9%

Economy & Jobs
Score: 67.1
Rank: 124

INDEXES & TAXES	AREA	U.S. AVG	HOUSING	AREA	U.S. AVG	NECESSITIES	AREA	U.S. AVG
Cost of Living Index	82.8	100.0	Median home price	$126,700	$220,000	Food Index	102.8	100.0
Buying Power Index	95.1	100.0	Home price appreciation	34.3%	10.1%	Housing Index	42.2	100.0
Income tax rate	0.00%	4.70%	Median rent	$587	$709	Utilities Index	96.0	100.0
Sales tax rate	8.25%	6.58%	Homes owned	60.8%	62.3%	Transportation Index	103.7	100.0
Property tax rate	$21.35	$12.00	Home price ratio	3.6	4.2	Healthcare Index	95.4	100.0
						Miscellaneous Cost Index	93.2	100.0

Cost of Living
Score: 73.8
Rank: 99

Climate
Score: 88.2
Rank: 45

TEMPERATURE	AREA	U.S. AVG
Average January low	30.2	26.2
Average July high	94.9	87.4
Annual days > 90°F	103	38
Annual days < 32°F	64	89
Annual days < 0°F	0	6

PRECIPITATION	AREA	U.S. AVG
Annual inches precipitation	8.0	37.7
Annual inches snowfall	5.0	7.0
Annual days precipitation	45	109
Annual days rain > 0.5 inches	6	22
Annual days snow > 1.5 inches	2	6

COMFORTS & HAZARDS	AREA	U.S. AVG
July relative humidity	39%	66%
Annual days mostly sunny	294	208
Annual days with thunderstorms	36	39
Tornado risk score	3	18
Hurricane risk score	2	13

TEMPERATURE

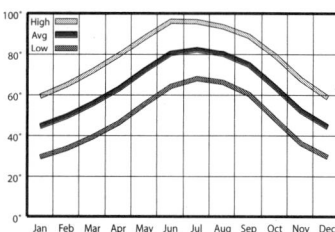

PRECIPITATION

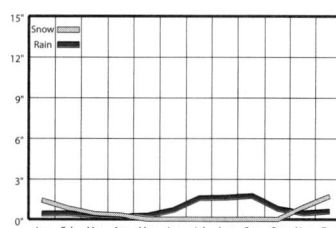

DAYS OF CLOUDS & PRECIPITATION

Education
Score: 5.9
Rank: 351

ACHIEVEMENT	AREA	U.S. AVG
High school degree	66.2%	82.7%
2-year college degree	5.0%	6.4%
4-year college degree	11.2%	15.7%
Graduate/professional degree	5.6%	8.9%

PUBLIC SCHOOLS	AREA	U.S. AVG
Expenditures per pupil	$4,973	$5,686
Student/teacher ratio	15.3	16.7
Attending public school	95.1%	90.1%
State SAT score	997*	1021
State ACT score	20.3	20.9

HIGHER EDUCATION	AREA	U.S. AVG
No. 2-year colleges	5	4
No. 4-year colleges/universities	1	6
No. highly ranked universities	0	1

Health & Healthcare
Score: 42.8
Rank: 213

HAZARDS & ILLNESSES	AREA	U.S. AVG
Air-quality score	29	37
Water-quality score	60	52
Pollen/allergy score	69	61
Cancer mortality per capita	143.3	201.9
Depression days per month	3.4	3.5
Stress score	51	50

HEALTHCARE	AREA	U.S. AVG
Physicians per capita	172.7	244.2
Hospital beds per capita	315.8	420.0
No. teaching hospitals	3	3
Cost per doctor visit	$64	$77
Cost per dental visit	$78	$70

Crime
Score: 29.9
Rank: 262

CRIME	AREA	U.S. AVG
Violent crime rate	408.9	465.5
Change in violent crime rate	-19.3%	-2.2%
Property crime rate	3,102.5	3,517.1
Change in property crime rate	-5.8%	-2.1%

Transportation
Score: 20.1
Rank: 299

COMMUTE	AREA	U.S. AVG
Average commute time	24.8	27.4
Percent commutes > 60 mins.	3.5%	5.9%
Commute by auto	76.4%	78.9%
Commute by mass transit	2.0%	1.9%
Work at home	2.2%	3.1%
Mass transit miles per capita	2.04	1.87

INTERCITY SERVICES	AREA	U.S. AVG
Major airports within 60 miles	1	1
Size of regional airport	Medium	Large
Daily airline activity	115	686
Amtrak service	Yes	No

AUTOMOTIVE	AREA	U.S. AVG
Insurance, annual premium	$1,223	$1,432
Gas, cost per gallon	$2.44	$2.49
Daily vehicle miles per capita	19.3	24.0

Leisure
Score: 27.5
Rank: 270

DINING & SHOPPING	AREA	U.S. AVG
Restaurant rating	1	2
Outlet mall score	0	42
No. Starbucks	8	13
No. warehouse clubs	2	2

ENTERTAINMENT	AREA	U.S. AVG
Professional sports rating	2	4
College sports rating	4	4
Zoo/aquarium rating	5	3
Amusement park rating	4	3
Botanical garden/ arboretum rating	1	4

OUTDOOR ACTIVITIES	AREA	U.S. AVG
Golf-course rating	2	4
Ski-area rating	1	3
Sq. miles inland water	1	4
Miles of coastline	0.0	10.7
National Park rating	1	3

Arts & Culture
Score: 52.4
Rank: 178

MEDIA & LIBRARIES	AREA	U.S. AVG
Arts radio rating	5	3
No. public libraries	13	27
Library volumes per capita	1.14	2.78

PERFORMING ARTS	AREA	U.S. AVG
Classical music rating	4	4
Ballet/dance rating	3	3
Professional theater rating	1	3
University arts programs rating	4	5

MUSEUMS	AREA	U.S. AVG
Overall museum rating	7	5
Art museum rating	6	5
Science museum rating	7	5
Children's museum rating	5	3

Erie, PA

Score: 51.9   Rank: 240   2004 rank: 309

Profile: Small industrial city
Location: Extreme northwest Pennsylvania along south shore of Lake Erie
Elevation: 731 feet
Time zone: Eastern Standard Time

PRO	CON
Cost of living	Economy
Nearby recreation	Entertainment
Central location	Wet climate

Erie, Pennsylvania's third-largest city, is a major port and industrial center in the northwest corner of the state. Located between Cleveland, Ohio, and Buffalo, New York, about 75 miles from each, Erie has a pleasant if somewhat declining small-town feel and many historic sites. Its role as a shipping point for the steel industry has been declining for years, but is being replaced by plastics and some high value-added manufacturing activities. Still, overall employment trends are far from encouraging. Lake Erie is a popular destination for fishing and boating, and Presque Isle State Park, Pennsylvania's largest state park, offers water recreation and good beaches. The downtown area is plain and uninspiring but a new waterfront redevelopment project is taking root with a new convention center, park facilities, and removal of some old industrial eyesores. The city has some minor cultural amenities and museums and a minor-league baseball team. The location with respect to Lake Erie makes it one of the cloudiest, rainiest, and snowiest places in the country (188 days of precipitation per year, every other day on average, is highest in the country). A clear day in Erie is to be celebrated indeed.

The area is located on the southeast shore of Lake Erie. The terrain rises gradually away from the shoreline in a series of ridges. Cool lake breezes, which may reach several miles inland, temper summer heat waves, and days with temperatures above 90°F are infrequent. Autumn, with long dry periods and abundant sunshine, is usually the most pleasant season. The area's 84 inches of annual snow is by far the most in the state and ranks ninth in the country. First freeze is mid-October; last is early May.

Population

DEMOGRAPHICS	AREA	U.S. AVG	ETHNIC COMPOSITION	AREA	U.S. AVG	RESIDENT PROFILE	AREA	U.S. AVG
Population	279,563		White	90.5%	79.0%	Single	35.7%	32.4%
Population density per sq. mile	348.6	358.5	Black	6.2%	10.5%	Married	50.1%	52.7%
Population growth	1.4%	21.1%	Asian	0.8%	2.7%	Divorced/separated	14.3%	14.9%
Median age	37.1	36.1	Hispanic	2.2%	10.6%	Married with children	22.0%	23.7%
Percent Democrat	53.9%	44.5%	Religious observance	58.8%	48.9%	Single with children	9.5%	9.1%
Percent Republican	45.6%	54.5%	Diversity measure	21.2	40.1	Percent over age 65	14.4%	12.9%

Economy & Jobs
Score: 34.8
Rank: 244

INCOME	AREA	U.S. AVG	EMPLOYMENT	AREA	U.S. AVG	EMPLOYING INDUSTRIES	AREA	U.S. AVG
Per capita income	$20,036	$23,235	Unemployment rate	5.8%	4.7%	Largest: Manufacturing		
Household income	$40,094	$46,414	Recent job growth	1.6%	1.3%			
Household income < $25K	30.2%	26.2%	Projected future job growth	3.2%	11.5%	Percent manufacturing	20.5%	15.4%
Household income > $75K	18.7%	25.4%	White collar	54.4%	57.8%	Percent public sector	10.0%	15.7%
Household income growth	9.5%	13.6%	Blue collar	28.4%	25.2%	Percent construction	7.9%	9.9%

Cost of Living
Score: 84.0
Rank: 61

INDEXES & TAXES	AREA	U.S. AVG	HOUSING	AREA	U.S. AVG	NECESSITIES	AREA	U.S. AVG
Cost of Living Index	80.4	100.0	Median home price	$102,300	$220,000	Food Index	104.7	100.0
Buying Power Index	111.8	100.0	Home price appreciation	18.4%	10.1%	Housing Index	49.8	100.0
Income tax rate	3.80%	4.70%	Median rent	$594	$709	Utilities Index	122.8	100.0
Sales tax rate	6.00%	6.58%	Homes owned	64.6%	62.3%	Transportation Index	92.1	100.0
Property tax rate	$17.49	$12.00	Home price ratio	2.6	4.2	Healthcare Index	94.9	100.0
						Miscellaneous Cost Index	93.7	100.0

Climate
Score: 8.8
Rank: 340

TEMPERATURE	AREA	U.S. AVG	PRECIPITATION	AREA	U.S. AVG	COMFORTS & HAZARDS	AREA	U.S. AVG
Average January low	18.5	26.2	Annual inches precipitation	38.2	37.7	July relative humidity	74%	66%
Average July high	77.4	87.4	Annual inches snowfall	83.6	7.0	Annual days mostly sunny	161	208
Annual days > 90°F	1	38	Annual days precipitation	188	109	Annual days with thunderstorms	38	39
Annual days < 32°F	134	89	Annual days rain > 0.5 inches	23	22	Tornado risk score	4	18
Annual days < 0°F	5	6	Annual days snow > 1.5 inches	17	6	Hurricane risk score	3	13

TEMPERATURE

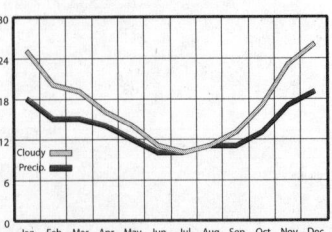

PRECIPITATION

DAYS OF CLOUDS & PRECIPITATION

ACHIEVEMENT	AREA	U.S. AVG	PUBLIC SCHOOLS	AREA	U.S. AVG	HIGHER EDUCATION	AREA	U.S. AVG
High school degree	84.5%	82.7%	Expenditures per pupil	$5,637	$5,686	No. 2-year colleges	5	4
2-year college degree	5.4%	6.4%	Student/teacher ratio	18.2	16.7	No. 4-year colleges/universities	6	6
4-year college degree	13.2%	15.7%	Attending public school	83.2%	90.1%	No. highly ranked universities	2	1
Graduate/professional degree	7.6%	8.9%	State SAT score	993*	1021			
			State ACT score	21.8	20.9			

Education
Score: 40.1
Rank: 225

HAZARDS & ILLNESSES	AREA	U.S. AVG	HEALTHCARE	AREA	U.S. AVG	CRIME	AREA	U.S. AVG
Air-quality score	34	37	Physicians per capita	242.9	244.2	Violent crime rate	260.5	465.5
Water-quality score	80	52	Hospital beds per capita	540.1	420.0	Change in violent crime rate	1.0%	-2.2%
Pollen/allergy score	32	61	No. teaching hospitals	4	3	Property crime rate	2,013.9	3,517.1
Cancer mortality per capita	258.0	201.9	Cost per doctor visit	$74	$77	Change in property crime rate	-13.2%	-2.1%
Depression days per month	3.6	3.5	Cost per dental visit	$72	$70			
Stress score	20	50						

Health & Healthcare
Score: 81.3
Rank: 71

Crime
Score: 77.5
Rank: 85

COMMUTE	AREA	U.S. AVG	INTERCITY SERVICES	AREA	U.S. AVG	AUTOMOTIVE	AREA	U.S. AVG
Average commute time	20.4	27.4	Major airports within 60 miles	1	1	Insurance, annual premium	$1,170	$1,432
Percent commutes > 60 mins.	2.6%	5.9%	Size of regional airport	Medium	Large	Gas, cost per gallon	$2.52	$2.49
Commute by auto	79.9%	78.9%	Daily airline activity	155	686	Daily vehicle miles per capita	17.1	24.0
Commute by mass transit	1.4%	1.9%	Amtrak service	Yes	No			
Work at home	2.3%	3.1%						
Mass transit miles per capita	1.38	1.87						

Transportation
Score: 61.5
Rank: 145

DINING & SHOPPING	AREA	U.S. AVG	ENTERTAINMENT	AREA	U.S. AVG	OUTDOOR ACTIVITIES	AREA	U.S. AVG
Restaurant rating	1	2	Professional sports rating	2	4	Golf-course rating	3	4
Outlet mall score	0	42	College sports rating	5	4	Ski-area rating	3	3
No. Starbucks	3	13	Zoo/aquarium rating	4	3	Sq. miles inland water	2	4
No. warehouse clubs	0	2	Amusement park rating	4	3	Miles of coastline	0.0	10.7
			Botanical garden/arboretum rating	6	4	National Park rating	1	3

Leisure
Score: 38.2
Rank: 230

MEDIA & LIBRARIES	AREA	U.S. AVG	PERFORMING ARTS	AREA	U.S. AVG	MUSEUMS	AREA	U.S. AVG
Arts radio rating	5	3	Classical music rating	3	4	Overall museum rating	6	5
No. public libraries	14	27	Ballet/dance rating	1	3	Art museum rating	4	5
Library volumes per capita	2.35	2.78	Professional theater rating	1	3	Science museum rating	7	5
			University arts programs rating	8	5	Children's museum rating	3	3

Arts & Culture
Score: 60.7
Rank: 147

Essex County, MA

Score: 48.7   Rank: 253   2004 rank: 326

Profile: Small-town/suburban complex
Location: Northeast corner of Massachusetts
Elevation: 50 feet
Time zone: Eastern Standard Time

PRO
Attractive setting
Close to Boston
Nearby coastline

CON
Long commutes
Cost of living
Some urban blight

Essex County spreads from the near northern suburbs of Boston, including such known names as Peabody, Lynn, Beverly, and Salem; northward into the mixed woods, towns, and agricultural areas along Interstate 95; and eastward into the picture-postcard maritime enclaves of Cape May. It also includes the older, somewhat depressed mill town of Lawrence just south of the New Hampshire border. The northeast suburbs range from upscale enclaves such as Marblehead along the shore to more middle-class and working-class areas along U.S. 1 somewhat inland. Rail-commute service is excellent and forms a lifeline for the many residents working in downtown Boston. As typical in the Boston area, there are mostly well-kept downtown areas, older homes, and some areas of greater historic interest, as found in downtown Salem. These suburbs enjoy the extensive and unique collection of cultural amenities offered in the Boston area. The Cape May area farther out, including seaport towns of Gloucester and Rockport, is more expensive but not out of sight for the region. Rail service practically extends to water's edge in Rockport, and although the commute to downtown takes slightly over an hour, it's a nice trade-off for the pastoral, cool, and refreshing living environment. Some of the nearby inland towns, such as Ipswich and Essex, provide the same access as well as the meticulously kept New England feel at a more moderate price with excellent home choices and little, if any, sprawl. This inland area and the South Shore area south of Boston are two of the gems that value-oriented residents should seek. Areas along Interstate 93 toward Lawrence are more plain but also a good value. A few areas along the U.S. 1 corridor and in Lawrence are a bit run-down and lack Boston's usual high level of educational attainment. The Cost of Living Index (116.6) is high on a national scale but reasonable for the Boston area.

The terrain is mainly level to low rolling hills with dense forests, becoming more sparsely forested on the exposed Cape May. Summers are moderate with an occasional hot, humid spell and thundershowers, but remain cool and sometimes windy on Cape May. Winters have frequent cold snaps and snow, although low temperatures may be moderated somewhat by water and wind. Occasional heavy "noreaster" storms can move up the Atlantic Coast, resulting in considerable snow cover. First freeze is mid-October; last is late April.

Population

DEMOGRAPHICS	AREA	U.S. AVG	ETHNIC COMPOSITION	AREA	U.S. AVG	RESIDENT PROFILE	AREA	U.S. AVG
Population	742,291		White	83.3%	79.0%	Single	35.0%	32.4%
Population density per sq. mile	1482.5	358.5	Black	3.0%	10.5%	Married	51.3%	52.7%
Population growth	10.8%	21.1%	Asian	2.8%	2.7%	Divorced/separated	13.7%	14.9%
Median age	38.2	36.1	Hispanic	14.0%	10.6%	Married with children	23.8%	23.7%
Percent Democrat	58.2%	44.5%	Religious observance	64.5%	48.9%	Single with children	8.8%	9.1%
Percent Republican	40.5%	54.5%	Diversity measure	46.7	40.1	Percent over age 65	13.6%	12.9%

Economy & Jobs
Score: 7.5
Rank: 345

INCOME	AREA	U.S. AVG	EMPLOYMENT	AREA	U.S. AVG	EMPLOYING INDUSTRIES	AREA	U.S. AVG
Per capita income	$30,932	$23,235	Unemployment rate	5.3%	4.7%	Largest: Manufacturing		
Household income	$60,491	$46,414	Recent job growth	0.2%	1.3%			
Household income < $25K	20.9%	26.2%	Projected future job growth	2.7%	11.5%	Percent manufacturing	12.4%	15.4%
Household income > $75K	39.3%	25.4%	White collar	66.3%	57.8%	Percent public sector	13.0%	15.7%
Household income growth	17.3%	13.6%	Blue collar	19.7%	25.2%	Percent construction	7.3%	9.9%

Cost of Living
Score: 13.4
Rank: 323

INDEXES & TAXES	AREA	U.S. AVG	HOUSING	AREA	U.S. AVG	NECESSITIES	AREA	U.S. AVG
Cost of Living Index	116.6	100.0	Median home price	$277,300	$220,000	Food Index	108.4	100.0
Buying Power Index	116.3	100.0	Home price appreciation	48.6%	10.1%	Housing Index	121.1	100.0
Income tax rate	5.95%	4.70%	Median rent	$1,259	$709	Utilities Index	136.7	100.0
Sales tax rate	5.00%	6.58%	Homes owned	61.0%	62.3%	Transportation Index	109.3	100.0
Property tax rate	$12.15	$12.00	Home price ratio	4.6	4.2	Healthcare Index	118.2	100.0
						Miscellaneous Cost Index	108.4	100.0

Climate
Score: 31.0
Rank: 257

TEMPERATURE	AREA	U.S. AVG	PRECIPITATION	AREA	U.S. AVG	COMFORTS & HAZARDS	AREA	U.S. AVG
Average January low	22.5	26.2	Annual inches precipitation	43.0	37.7	July relative humidity	67%	66%
Average July high	81.4	87.4	Annual inches snowfall	42.0	7.0	Annual days mostly sunny	205	208
Annual days > 90°F	12	38	Annual days precipitation	128	109	Annual days with thunderstorms	22	39
Annual days < 32°F	99	89	Annual days rain > 0.5 inches	28	22	Tornado risk score	10	18
Annual days < 0°F	1	6	Annual days snow > 1.5 inches	19	6	Hurricane risk score	19	13

TEMPERATURE

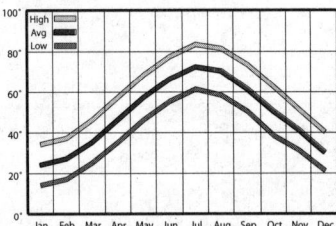

PRECIPITATION

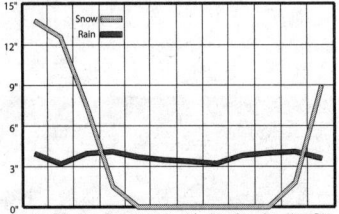

DAYS OF CLOUDS & PRECIPITATION

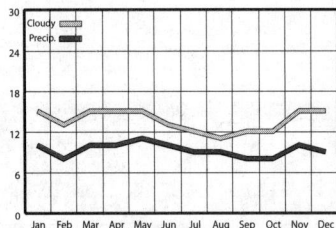

Education
Score: 88.0
Rank: 45

ACHIEVEMENT	AREA	U.S. AVG	PUBLIC SCHOOLS	AREA	U.S. AVG	HIGHER EDUCATION	AREA	U.S. AVG
High school degree	84.3%	82.7%	Expenditures per pupil	$6,587	$5,686	No. 2-year colleges	3	4
2-year college degree	7.6%	6.4%	Student/teacher ratio	0.0	16.7	No. 4-year colleges/universities	7	6
4-year college degree	19.4%	15.7%	Attending public school	85.8%	90.1%	No. highly ranked universities	1	1
Graduate/professional degree	11.6%	8.9%	State SAT score	1037*	1021			
			State ACT score	23	20.9			

Health & Healthcare
Score: 5.3
Rank: 353

Crime
Score: 73.3
Rank: 101

HAZARDS & ILLNESSES	AREA	U.S. AVG	HEALTHCARE	AREA	U.S. AVG	CRIME	AREA	U.S. AVG
Air-quality score	21	37	Physicians per capita	208.9	244.2	Violent crime rate	393.0	465.5
Water-quality score	13	52	Hospital beds per capita	278.3	420.0	Change in violent crime rate	14.0%	-2.2%
Pollen/allergy score	65	61	No. teaching hospitals	5	3	Property crime rate	2,101.7	3,517.1
Cancer mortality per capita	225.9	201.9	Cost per doctor visit	$100	$77	Change in property crime rate	0.0%	-2.1%
Depression days per month	3.4	3.5	Cost per dental visit	$89	$70			
Stress score	34	50						

Transportation
Score: 56.1
Rank: 165

COMMUTE	AREA	U.S. AVG
Average commute time	29.5	27.4
Percent commutes > 60 mins.	10.8%	5.9%
Commute by auto	78.8%	78.9%
Commute by mass transit	4.9%	1.9%
Work at home	3.3%	3.1%
Mass transit miles per capita	4.88	1.87

INTERCITY SERVICES	AREA	U.S. AVG
Major airports within 60 miles	2	1
Size of regional airport	Large	Large
Daily airline activity	1278	686
Amtrak service	Yes	No

AUTOMOTIVE	AREA	U.S. AVG
Insurance, annual premium	$2,253	$1,432
Gas, cost per gallon	$2.43	$2.49
Daily vehicle miles per capita	20.1	24.0

Leisure
Score: 96.3
Rank: 15

DINING & SHOPPING	AREA	U.S. AVG
Restaurant rating	6	2
Outlet mall score	21	42
No. Starbucks	11	13
No. warehouse clubs	2	2

ENTERTAINMENT	AREA	U.S. AVG
Professional sports rating	9	4
College sports rating	10	4
Zoo/aquarium rating	8	3
Amusement park rating	7	3
Botanical garden/ arboretum rating	7	4

OUTDOOR ACTIVITIES	AREA	U.S. AVG
Golf-course rating	9	4
Ski-area rating	7	3
Sq. miles inland water	7	4
Miles of coastline	39.8	10.7
National Park rating	2	3

Arts & Culture
Score: 98.9
Rank: 5

MEDIA & LIBRARIES	AREA	U.S. AVG
Arts radio rating	10	3
No. public libraries	43	27
Library volumes per capita	4.30	2.78

PERFORMING ARTS	AREA	U.S. AVG
Classical music rating	10	4
Ballet/dance rating	8	3
Professional theater rating	10	3
University arts programs rating	10	5

MUSEUMS	AREA	U.S. AVG
Overall museum rating	9	5
Art museum rating	8	5
Science museum rating	10	5
Children's museum rating	6	3

Eugene–Springfield, OR

Score: 73.7   Rank: 68   2004 rank: 21

Profile: College-town complex
Location: West-central Oregon at the south end of Willamette River Valley
Elevation: 373 feet
Time zone: Pacific Standard Time

PRO	CON
College-town feel	Recent unemployment
Attractive downtown	Wet winters
Nearby mountains	High property-crime rate

Eugene and Springfield sit across from one another on the Willamette River. The area has a large timber industry and is a transportation hub for routes south into California. The setting is attractive, and clean and prosperous downtown Eugene, which is home to the University of Oregon, has the kind of shops and restaurants one would expect in a college town. The park system is excellent, most particularly a waterfront park along the river. Good growth management has minimized sprawl effects, though there is a new and modern mall along Interstate 5 northeast of town. Most good residential areas lie west and south of the downtown and campus. The university and its attendees leave a distinctly liberal, folksy imprint on the otherwise conservative region. The slowing timber industry has brought some unemployment, which is projected to improve over time as other businesses locate there. Excellent state-subsidized rail service connects the area with other cities

north, and the area has a nice airport with good, if not cheap, service. The area has a nice mix of setting, climate, and small-town feel and a fairly low cost of living by Oregon standards.

Eugene is located at the southern end of the fertile Willamette Valley. The Cascade Mountains to the east, Coast Range to the west, and low hills to the south surround the valley, while the level valley floor broadens to the north. Foothills to the east obscure the snow-covered Cascade peaks, some 75 miles away. The Pacific Coast is 50 miles west. Forested areas lie in every direction except north. Summers are dry and warm with an occasional hot spell up to 95°F and cool evenings. Winter days are cool and damp with highs in the 50s, lows in the 30s, and occasional dips into the 20s. Rain is highly seasonal, starting in September and lasting through May, with sometimes heavy winter rains. Snow is rare and usually melts on contact. First freeze is late October; last is late April.

Population

DEMOGRAPHICS	AREA	U.S. AVG
Population	334,865	
Population density per sq. mile	73.5	358.5
Population growth	18.4%	21.1%
Median age	37.4	36.1
Percent Democrat	58.0%	44.5%
Percent Republican	40.4%	54.5%

ETHNIC COMPOSITION	AREA	U.S. AVG
White	89.4%	79.0%
Black	0.8%	10.5%
Asian	2.7%	2.7%
Hispanic	5.3%	10.6%
Religious observance	24.5%	48.9%
Diversity measure	27.8	40.1

RESIDENT PROFILE	AREA	U.S. AVG
Single	33.5%	32.4%
Married	51.0%	52.7%
Divorced/separated	15.5%	14.9%
Married with children	19.6%	23.7%
Single with children	8.8%	9.1%
Percent over age 65	13.7%	12.9%

Economy & Jobs
Score: 39.6
Rank: 225

INCOME	AREA	U.S. AVG
Per capita income	$22,429	$23,235
Household income	$41,785	$46,414
Household income < $25K	29.2%	26.2%
Household income > $75K	20.9%	25.4%
Household income growth	13.1%	13.6%

EMPLOYMENT	AREA	U.S. AVG
Unemployment rate	6.5%	4.7%
Recent job growth	2.3%	1.3%
Projected future job growth	11.8%	11.5%
White collar	57.9%	57.8%
Blue collar	24.8%	25.2%

EMPLOYING INDUSTRIES	AREA	U.S. AVG
Largest: Manufacturing		
Percent manufacturing	15.5%	15.4%
Percent public sector	16.0%	15.7%
Percent construction	9.3%	9.9%

Cost of Living

Score: 51.3
Rank: 181

INDEXES & TAXES	AREA	U.S. AVG
Cost of Living Index	102.4	100.0
Buying Power Index	91.5	100.0
Income tax rate	9.00%	4.70%
Sales tax rate	0.00%	6.58%
Property tax rate	$9.56	$12.00

HOUSING	AREA	U.S. AVG
Median home price	$227,600	$220,000
Home price appreciation	53.4%	10.1%
Median rent	$735	$709
Homes owned	58.8%	62.3%
Home price ratio	5.4	4.2

NECESSITIES	AREA	U.S. AVG
Food Index	103.8	100.0
Housing Index	77.8	100.0
Utilities Index	79.0	100.0
Transportation Index	103.9	100.0
Healthcare Index	121.7	100.0
Miscellaneous Cost Index	106.0	100.0

Climate

Score: 65.2
Rank: 129

TEMPERATURE	AREA	U.S. AVG
Average January low	33.1	26.2
Average July high	82.6	87.4
Annual days > 90°F	15	38
Annual days < 32°F	54	89
Annual days < 0°F	0	6

PRECIPITATION	AREA	U.S. AVG
Annual inches precipitation	43.0	37.7
Annual inches snowfall	7.0	7.0
Annual days precipitation	137	109
Annual days rain > 0.5 inches	30	22
Annual days snow > 1.5 inches	1	6

COMFORTS & HAZARDS	AREA	U.S. AVG
July relative humidity	72%	66%
Annual days mostly sunny	158	208
Annual days with thunderstorms	5	39
Tornado risk score	2	18
Hurricane risk score	0	13

TEMPERATURE

PRECIPITATION

DAYS OF CLOUDS & PRECIPITATION

Education

Score: 68.7
Rank: 118

ACHIEVEMENT	AREA	U.S. AVG
High school degree	87.6%	82.7%
2-year college degree	7.3%	6.4%
4-year college degree	15.7%	15.7%
Graduate/professional degree	10.0%	8.9%

PUBLIC SCHOOLS	AREA	U.S. AVG
Expenditures per pupil	$6,468	$5,686
Student/teacher ratio	18.6	16.7
Attending public school	93.7%	90.1%
State SAT score	1052*	1021
State ACT score	22.4	20.9

HIGHER EDUCATION	AREA	U.S. AVG
No. 2-year colleges	2	4
No. 4-year colleges/universities	3	6
No. highly ranked universities	0	1

Health & Healthcare

Score: 7.5
Rank: 345

HAZARDS & ILLNESSES	AREA	U.S. AVG
Air-quality score	15	37
Water-quality score	60	52
Pollen/allergy score	64	61
Cancer mortality per capita	206.8	201.9
Depression days per month	3.7	3.5
Stress score	85	50

HEALTHCARE	AREA	U.S. AVG
Physicians per capita	218.1	244.2
Hospital beds per capita	203.4	420.0
No. teaching hospitals	0	3
Cost per doctor visit	$105	$77
Cost per dental visit	$79	$70

Crime

Score: 65.5
Rank: 130

CRIME	AREA	U.S. AVG
Violent crime rate	247.4	465.5
Change in violent crime rate	-4.0%	-2.2%
Property crime rate	5,501.4	3,517.1
Change in property crime rate	12.1%	-2.1%

Transportation

Score: 70.9
Rank: 110

COMMUTE	AREA	U.S. AVG
Average commute time	21.7	27.4
Percent commutes > 60 mins.	4.5%	5.9%
Commute by auto	71.9%	78.9%
Commute by mass transit	3.2%	1.9%
Work at home	5.1%	3.1%
Mass transit miles per capita	3.20	1.87

INTERCITY SERVICES	AREA	U.S. AVG
Major airports within 60 miles	1	1
Size of regional airport	Medium	Large
Daily airline activity	484	686
Amtrak service	Yes	No

AUTOMOTIVE	AREA	U.S. AVG
Insurance, annual premium	$1,463	$1,432
Gas, cost per gallon	$2.49	$2.49
Daily vehicle miles per capita	18.2	24.0

Leisure

Score: 67.1
Rank: 123

DINING & SHOPPING	AREA	U.S. AVG
Restaurant rating	1	2
Outlet mall score	0	42
No. Starbucks	8	13
No. warehouse clubs	1	2

ENTERTAINMENT	AREA	U.S. AVG
Professional sports rating	2	4
College sports rating	6	4
Zoo/aquarium rating	1	3
Amusement park rating	1	3
Botanical garden/ arboretum rating	6	4

OUTDOOR ACTIVITIES	AREA	U.S. AVG
Golf-course rating	2	4
Ski-area rating	8	3
Sq. miles inland water	4	4
Miles of coastline	30.4	10.7
National Park rating	8	3

Arts & Culture

Score: 49.7
Rank: 187

MEDIA & LIBRARIES	AREA	U.S. AVG
Arts radio rating	1	3
No. public libraries	8	27
Library volumes per capita	2.55	2.78

PERFORMING ARTS	AREA	U.S. AVG
Classical music rating	4	4
Ballet/dance rating	6	3
Professional theater rating	1	3
University arts programs rating	6	5

MUSEUMS	AREA	U.S. AVG
Overall museum rating	5	5
Art museum rating	6	5
Science museum rating	6	5
Children's museum rating	1	3

Evansville, IN-KY

Score: 79.0   **Rank:** 50   **2004 rank:** 47

Profile: Small city complex
Location: Southwestern Indiana along the Ohio River on the Kentucky border
Elevation: 388 feet
Time zone: Central Standard Time

PRO	CON
Cost of living	Isolation
Low crime rates	Entertainment
Healthcare	Summer heat and humidity

Evansville is located in the far southwest portion of the state. This Ohio River port is the commercial and cultural hub of southwest Indiana and the nearby regions of Illinois and Kentucky. Downtown is modern and attractive with historic areas and a pedestrian mall near the waterfront. Most growth is spreading northeast along the Interstate 164 connector to the east–west Interstate 64. Evansville is one of the larger cities not to be directly served by an east–west or north–south interstate, with some good and some bad consequences. However, while new such construction is unusual, an extension of the north–south Interstate 69 from Indianapolis is on the drawing board to connect Michigan with Texas and Mexico through Evansville, which should make Evansville's location much more strategic, especially to markets to the south. Today the economy is supported by a varied mix of manufacturing and service businesses; there is no "heavyweight" employer. Crime and cost of living in particular are low. Evansville is a fairly quiet, sort of "all-American" place, used a lot by test marketers. There are some arts amenities, but downsides include isolation (Louisville is 100 miles east) and a general lack of things to do.

Located along the Ohio River, the terrain ranges from level to areas of rolling land and low hills near the river. The city itself is located on a flat valley sloping gently down to the river. Summers are hot and humid. Both summer and winter are highly variable. Storms and weather transitions bring high winds in all seasons and strong thunderstorms in summer. Snow does occur but Evansville is far enough south to make heavy accumulations uncommon. First freeze is late October; last is early April.

Population

DEMOGRAPHICS	AREA	U.S. AVG
Population	347,584	
Population density per sq. mile	151.7	358.5
Population growth	7.5%	21.1%
Median age	37.6	36.1
Percent Democrat	39.2%	44.5%
Percent Republican	60.2%	54.5%

ETHNIC COMPOSITION	AREA	U.S. AVG
White	91.9%	79.0%
Black	5.6%	10.5%
Asian	0.9%	2.7%
Hispanic	1.1%	10.6%
Religious observance	50.0%	48.9%
Diversity measure	16.9	40.1

RESIDENT PROFILE	AREA	U.S. AVG
Single	29.2%	32.4%
Married	56.2%	52.7%
Divorced/separated	14.6%	14.9%
Married with children	23.3%	23.7%
Single with children	8.2%	9.1%
Percent over age 65	14.0%	12.9%

Economy & Jobs
Score: 30.5
Rank: 259

INCOME	AREA	U.S. AVG
Per capita income	$23,022	$23,235
Household income	$44,368	$46,414
Household income < $25K	26.9%	26.2%
Household income > $75K	23.2%	25.4%
Household income growth	13.6%	13.6%

EMPLOYMENT	AREA	U.S. AVG
Unemployment rate	4.9%	4.7%
Recent job growth	0.7%	1.3%
Projected future job growth	4.2%	11.5%
White collar	53.4%	57.8%
Blue collar	31.0%	25.2%

EMPLOYING INDUSTRIES	AREA	U.S. AVG
Largest: Manufacturing		
Percent manufacturing	20.2%	15.4%
Percent public sector	9.8%	15.7%
Percent construction	10.8%	9.9%

Cost of Living
Score: 96.5
Rank: 14

INDEXES & TAXES	AREA	U.S. AVG
Cost of Living Index	76.0	100.0
Buying Power Index	130.9	100.0
Income tax rate	3.50%	4.70%
Sales tax rate	6.00%	6.58%
Property tax rate	$9.45	$12.00

HOUSING	AREA	U.S. AVG
Median home price	$104,300	$220,000
Home price appreciation	20.3%	10.1%
Median rent	$556	$709
Homes owned	67.4%	62.3%
Home price ratio	2.4	4.2

NECESSITIES	AREA	U.S. AVG
Food Index	93.7	100.0
Housing Index	46.1	100.0
Utilities Index	85.5	100.0
Transportation Index	95.0	100.0
Healthcare Index	92.6	100.0
Miscellaneous Cost Index	95.2	100.0

Climate
Score: 36.4
Rank: 237

TEMPERATURE	AREA	U.S. AVG
Average January low	23.7	26.2
Average July high	88.9	87.4
Annual days > 90°F	29	38
Annual days < 32°F	103	89
Annual days < 0°F	3	6

PRECIPITATION	AREA	U.S. AVG
Annual inches precipitation	42.0	37.7
Annual inches snowfall	13.0	7.0
Annual days precipitation	114	109
Annual days rain > 0.5 inches	27	22
Annual days snow > 1.5 inches	6	6

COMFORTS & HAZARDS	AREA	U.S. AVG
July relative humidity	70%	66%
Annual days mostly sunny	203	208
Annual days with thunderstorms	45	39
Tornado risk score	19	18
Hurricane risk score	5	13

TEMPERATURE

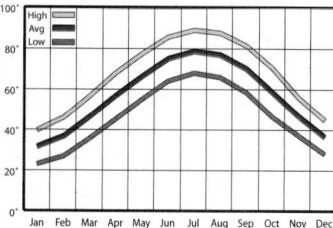

PRECIPITATION

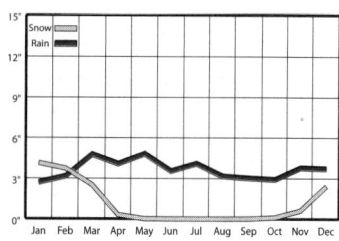

DAYS OF CLOUDS & PRECIPITATION

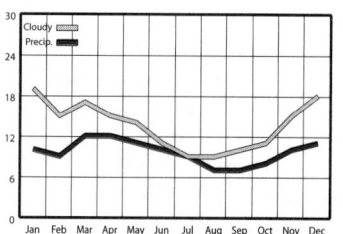

ACHIEVEMENT	AREA	U.S. AVG	PUBLIC SCHOOLS	AREA	U.S. AVG	HIGHER EDUCATION	AREA	U.S. AVG
High school degree	82.5%	82.7%	Expenditures per pupil	$5,935	$5,686	No. 2-year colleges	4	4
2-year college degree	6.9%	6.4%	Student/teacher ratio	17.1	16.7	No. 4-year colleges/universities	5	6
4-year college degree	11.2%	15.7%	Attending public school	85.3%	90.1%	No. highly ranked universities	1	1
Graduate/professional degree	6.4%	8.9%	State SAT score	1007*	1021			
			State ACT score	21.7	20.9			

Education
Score: 32.9
Rank: 252

HAZARDS & ILLNESSES	AREA	U.S. AVG	HEALTHCARE	AREA	U.S. AVG	CRIME	AREA	U.S. AVG
Air-quality score	40	37	Physicians per capita	229.3	244.2	Violent crime rate	232.6	465.5
Water-quality score	34	52	Hospital beds per capita	513.5	420.0	Change in violent crime rate	3.7%	-2.2%
Pollen/allergy score	69	61	No. teaching hospitals	3	3	Property crime rate	2,856.4	3,517.1
Cancer mortality per capita	216.3	201.9	Cost per doctor visit	$73	$77	Change in property crime rate	0.4%	-2.1%
Depression days per month	4.2	3.5	Cost per dental visit	$61	$70			
Stress score	56	50						

Health & Healthcare
Score: 54.5
Rank: 171

Crime
Score: 82.1
Rank: 68

COMMUTE	AREA	U.S. AVG	INTERCITY SERVICES	AREA	U.S. AVG	AUTOMOTIVE	AREA	U.S. AVG
Average commute time	22.8	27.4	Major airports within 60 miles	1	1	Insurance, annual premium	$1,082	$1,432
Percent commutes > 60 mins.	3.8%	5.9%	Size of regional airport	Medium	Large	Gas, cost per gallon	$2.50	$2.49
Commute by auto	84.7%	78.9%	Daily airline activity	228	686	Daily vehicle miles per capita	24.1	24.0
Commute by mass transit	0.7%	1.9%	Amtrak service	No	No			
Work at home	2.4%	3.1%						
Mass transit miles per capita	0.70	1.87						

Transportation
Score: 39.6
Rank: 227

DINING & SHOPPING	AREA	U.S. AVG	ENTERTAINMENT	AREA	U.S. AVG	OUTDOOR ACTIVITIES	AREA	U.S. AVG
Restaurant rating	1	2	Professional sports rating	2	4	Golf-course rating	3	4
Outlet mall score	6	42	College sports rating	4	4	Ski-area rating	1	3
No. Starbucks	5	13	Zoo/aquarium rating	3	3	Sq. miles inland water	4	4
No. warehouse clubs	0	2	Amusement park rating	1	3	Miles of coastline	0.0	10.7
			Botanical garden/ arboretum rating	1	4	National Park rating	1	3

Leisure
Score: 30.7
Rank: 258

MEDIA & LIBRARIES	AREA	U.S. AVG	PERFORMING ARTS	AREA	U.S. AVG	MUSEUMS	AREA	U.S. AVG
Arts radio rating	1	3	Classical music rating	4	4	Overall museum rating	6	5
No. public libraries	26	27	Ballet/dance rating	3	3	Art museum rating	6	5
Library volumes per capita	3.22	2.78	Professional theater rating	1	3	Science museum rating	6	5
			University arts programs rating	7	5	Children's museum rating	1	3

Arts & Culture
Score: 63.6
Rank: 136

Fairbanks, AK

Score: 33.6   **Rank:** 331   **2004 rank:** not ranked

Profile: Frontier town
Location: East-central Alaska, north of the Alaska Range
Elevation: 418 feet
Time zone: Alaska Standard Time

PRO
Attractive setting
Nearby recreation
Educated population

CON
Bitter winters
Isolation
Entertainment

Fairbanks, a low, sprawling frontier town along the Chena River, supports a huge land area. As a crossroads of major highways and the northern terminus of the Alaska Railroad, Fairbanks plays a significant role as a transportation center and commerce headquarters for most of the northern half of the state. Additionally, the area serves as a military, education, and health center for the region; the University of Alaska-Fairbanks is a large employer. Mining, forest products, the Alaska Pipeline, and tourism drive the economy, and recent job growth has been fairly healthy. Due to its isolation and the obvious effects of climate, the area not surprisingly has a strong sense of community, but there isn't a lot of outside stimulus or entertainment. The downtown area is clean and mostly modern. As with all of Alaska, cost of living is high. The summer climate and nearby recreation are exceptional, but winters are equally extraordinary with depressing darkness and below-zero temperatures almost daily.

Fairbanks is located in the Tanana Valley and experiences extreme temperature variations most of the year. Because of its location just 200 miles south of the Arctic Circle, summer days are 18 to 21 hours long, and solar heating can produce pleasant 80°F readings. Unbelievably for the latitude, the record high was 99°F, recorded in July 1919. Winter daylight, however, ranges from 4 to 10 hours per day, with prevalent below-zero temperatures, reaching −40°F or lower each winter. Winter temperatures, in fact, can range from +45°F to −65°F, with summer temperatures ranging from +30°F to +90°F. Snow cover persists from October to April, although cold air and mountain protection limits days with heavy snows to a minimum, and blizzards are seldom seen. Cold air trapped in the valley produces occasional ice fog. Occasional summer showers and thunderstorms, especially in nearby mountains, round out the precipitation picture.

Population

DEMOGRAPHICS	AREA	U.S. AVG	ETHNIC COMPOSITION	AREA	U.S. AVG	RESIDENT PROFILE	AREA	U.S. AVG
Population	84,771		White	75.5%	79.0%	Single	30.2%	32.4%
Population density per sq. mile	11.5	358.5	Black	6.7%	10.5%	Married	54.1%	52.7%
Population growth	9.1%	21.1%	Asian	2.2%	2.7%	Divorced/separated	15.7%	14.9%
Median age	30.8	36.1	Hispanic	5.0%	10.6%	Married with children	30.5%	23.7%
Percent Democrat	32.9%	44.5%	Religious observance	34.3%	48.9%	Single with children	10.4%	9.1%
Percent Republican	63.6%	54.5%	Diversity measure	47.0	40.1	Percent over age 65	5.4%	12.9%

Economy & Jobs
Score: 58.6
Rank: 156

INCOME	AREA	U.S. AVG	EMPLOYMENT	AREA	U.S. AVG	EMPLOYING INDUSTRIES	AREA	U.S. AVG
Per capita income	$25,044	$23,235	Unemployment rate	5.1%	4.7%	Largest: Healthcare & Social Assistance		
Household income	$55,569	$46,414	Recent job growth	3.3%	1.3%			
Household income < $25K	18.6%	26.2%	Projected future job growth	8.6%	11.5%	Percent manufacturing	9.7%	15.4%
Household income > $75K	33.5%	25.4%	White collar	61.0%	57.8%	Percent public sector	30.7%	15.7%
Household income growth	13.2%	13.6%	Blue collar	23.3%	25.2%	Percent construction	13.6%	9.9%

Cost of Living
Score: 81.8
Rank: 69

INDEXES & TAXES	AREA	U.S. AVG	HOUSING	AREA	U.S. AVG	NECESSITIES	AREA	U.S. AVG
Cost of Living Index	118.0	100.0	Median home price	$224,500	$220,000	Food Index	117.0	100.0
Buying Power Index	105.6	100.0	Home price appreciation	40.4%	10.1%	Housing Index	71.8	100.0
Income tax rate	0.00%	4.70%	Median rent	$859	$709	Utilities Index	177.1	100.0
Sales tax rate	0.00%	6.58%	Homes owned	49.1%	62.3%	Transportation Index	112.8	100.0
Property tax rate	$16.89	$12.00	Home price ratio	4.0	4.2	Healthcare Index	165.4	100.0
						Miscellaneous Cost Index	117.0	100.0

Climate
Score: 29.1
Rank: 264

TEMPERATURE	AREA	U.S. AVG	PRECIPITATION	AREA	U.S. AVG	COMFORTS & HAZARDS	AREA	U.S. AVG
Average January low	-19.3	26.2	Annual inches precipitation	10.8	37.7	July relative humidity	49%	66%
Average July high	72.4	87.4	Annual inches snowfall	67.8	7.0	Annual days mostly sunny	125	208
Annual days > 90°F	0	38	Annual days precipitation	108	109	Annual days with thunderstorms	7	39
Annual days < 32°F	225	89	Annual days rain > 0.5 inches	5	22	Tornado risk score	0	18
Annual days < 0°F	116	6	Annual days snow > 1.5 inches	15	6	Hurricane risk score	0	13

TEMPERATURE

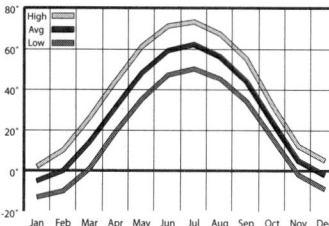

PRECIPITATION

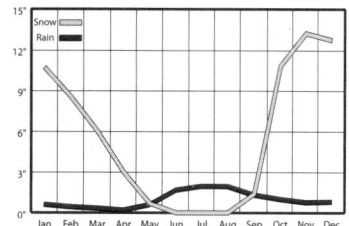

DAYS OF CLOUDS & PRECIPITATION

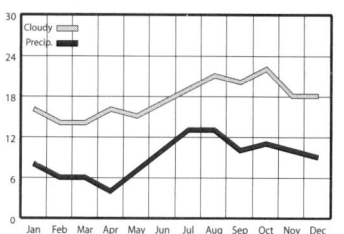

Education
Score: 80.5
Rank: 74

ACHIEVEMENT	AREA	U.S. AVG	PUBLIC SCHOOLS	AREA	U.S. AVG	HIGHER EDUCATION	AREA	U.S. AVG
High school degree	91.8%	82.7%	Expenditures per pupil	$7,804	$5,686	No. 2-year colleges	0	4
2-year college degree	7.5%	6.4%	Student/teacher ratio	19.0	16.7	No. 4-year colleges/universities	1	6
4-year college degree	16.4%	15.7%	Attending public school	95.9%	90.1%	No. highly ranked universities	0	1
Graduate/professional degree	10.7%	8.9%	State SAT score	1034*	1021			
			State ACT score	21.1	20.9			

Health & Healthcare
Score: 11.8
Rank: 329

HAZARDS & ILLNESSES	AREA	U.S. AVG	HEALTHCARE	AREA	U.S. AVG	CRIME	AREA	U.S. AVG
Air-quality score	31	37	Physicians per capita	210.5	244.2	Violent crime rate	960.1	465.5
Water-quality score	50	52	Hospital beds per capita	252.4	420.0	Change in violent crime rate	28.1%	-2.2%
Pollen/allergy score	57	61	No. teaching hospitals	0	3	Property crime rate	5,557.4	3,517.1
Cancer mortality per capita	103.6	201.9	Cost per doctor visit	$109	$77	Change in property crime rate	5.5%	-2.1%
Depression days per month	3.2	3.5	Cost per dental visit	$116	$70			
Stress score	75	50						

Crime
Score: 17.9
Rank: 307

Transportation
Score: 56.4
Rank: 163

COMMUTE	AREA	U.S. AVG	INTERCITY SERVICES	AREA	U.S. AVG	AUTOMOTIVE	AREA	U.S. AVG
Average commute time	19.3	27.4	Major airports within 60 miles	0	1	Insurance, annual premium	$1,413	$1,432
Percent commutes > 60 mins.	2.4%	5.9%	Size of regional airport	Small	Large	Gas, cost per gallon	$2.42	$2.49
Commute by auto	72.9%	78.9%	Daily airline activity	64	686	Daily vehicle miles per capita	21.2	24.0
Commute by mass transit	0.7%	1.9%	Amtrak service	No	No			
Work at home	3.8%	3.1%						
Mass transit miles per capita	0.71	1.87						

DINING & SHOPPING	AREA	U.S. AVG	ENTERTAINMENT	AREA	U.S. AVG	OUTDOOR ACTIVITIES	AREA	U.S. AVG
Restaurant rating	1	2	Professional sports rating	1	4	Golf-course rating	1	4
Outlet mall score	0	42	College sports rating	3	4	Ski-area rating	3	3
No. Starbucks	0	13	Zoo/aquarium rating	1	3	Sq. miles inland water	4	4
No. warehouse clubs	1	2	Amusement park rating	1	3	Miles of coastline	0.0	10.7
			Botanical garden/			National Park rating	10	3
			arboretum rating	1	4			

Leisure
Score: 42.2
Rank: 215

MEDIA & LIBRARIES	AREA	U.S. AVG	PERFORMING ARTS	AREA	U.S. AVG	MUSEUMS	AREA	U.S. AVG
Arts radio rating	1	3	Classical music rating	2	4	Overall museum rating	3	5
No. public libraries	2	27	Ballet/dance rating	1	3	Art museum rating	5	5
Library volumes per capita	2.45	2.78	Professional theater rating	1	3	Science museum rating	5	5
			University arts programs rating	1	5	Children's museum rating	1	3

Arts & Culture
Score: 11.5
Rank: 330

Fargo, ND-MN

Score: 80.8   **Rank:** 40   **2004 rank:** 87

Profile: Small city
Location: Extreme eastern North Dakota at the Minnesota border
Elevation: 899 feet
Time zone: Central Standard Time

PRO	CON
College-town element	Cold winters
Cool summers	Isolation
Educated population	Low ethnic diversity

Fargo, the largest city in North Dakota, lies alongside the Red River in the southeast part of the state near the Minnesota border. Located along east–west Interstate 94, it is an agricultural, commercial, and transportation center with the strongest economy in the state. Fargo is home to North Dakota State University, while Moorhead, Minnesota, across the river, has Moorhead State University and Concordia College, bringing some college-town amenities to the area. The well-preserved downtown district is classic mid-America with a mix of modern buildings and clean older brick structures. Waterfront areas along the Red River contain well-kept parks. The area is known for being friendly and having a strong community feel, and it has a strong Scandinavian influence. The economy is healthy and diversified, with an assortment of farm equipment manufacturers, food processors, and similar industries, some of which are in more innovative segments of their industries. Fargo currently has the lowest unemployment rate in the country at 2.5%. The area's central location relative to world markets, low costs, and free-trade-zone facilities have caused it to grow into a leading air cargo hub.

Cost of living is an attractive 85.5 and housing values are excellent. In part because of the university, there is plenty to do. Winters are a challenge, but most residents find things to do, for instance, making use of local high school swimming pools, which are open to the public. This clean and small city brings a well-balanced lifestyle with only winter climate as a significant negative, hence the high ranking.

The Red River flows northward between the two cities (one of few northbound rivers), and is a part of the Hudson Bay drainage area. The surrounding terrain is flat and open prairie. Summers are generally comfortable with few hot, humid days, and cool, comfortable nights. Winters are cold and dry with daytime temperatures rising above freezing only 6 days per month on average with lows dipping below 0°F half the time. Three-quarters of precipitation occurs from April to September, often as thunderstorms, some heavy. Heavy winter snowfall is the exception rather than the rule, however; low terrain and high winds lead to the legendary Dakota blizzards and even light snow can drift. First freeze is late September; last is mid-May.

DEMOGRAPHICS	AREA	U.S. AVG	ETHNIC COMPOSITION	AREA	U.S. AVG	RESIDENT PROFILE	AREA	U.S. AVG
Population	181,586		White	94.0%	79.0%	Single	37.8%	32.4%
Population density per sq. mile	64.6	358.5	Black	1.1%	10.5%	Married	51.0%	52.7%
Population growth	19.3%	21.1%	Asian	1.5%	2.7%	Divorced/separated	11.2%	14.9%
Median age	33.2	36.1	Hispanic	1.8%	10.6%	Married with children	23.9%	23.7%
Percent Democrat	41.2%	44.5%	Religious observance	59.1%	48.9%	Single with children	7.2%	9.1%
Percent Republican	57.2%	54.5%	Diversity measure	14.7	40.1	Percent over age 65	10.7%	12.9%

Population

INCOME	AREA	U.S. AVG	EMPLOYMENT	AREA	U.S. AVG	EMPLOYING INDUSTRIES	AREA	U.S. AVG
Per capita income	$23,332	$23,235	Unemployment rate	2.5%	4.7%	Largest: Healthcare & Social Assistance		
Household income	$43,601	$46,414	Recent job growth	0.8%	1.3%			
Household income ‹ $25K	27.0%	26.2%	Projected future job growth	14.2%	11.5%	Percent manufacturing	12.4%	15.4%
Household income › $75K	22.2%	25.4%	White collar	62.1%	57.8%	Percent public sector	13.9%	15.7%
Household income growth	14.5%	13.6%	Blue collar	21.0%	25.2%	Percent construction	8.6%	9.9%

Economy & Jobs
Score: 65.5
Rank: 130

Cost of Living
Score: 79.7
Rank: 77

INDEXES & TAXES	AREA	U.S. AVG
Cost of Living Index	85.5	100.0
Buying Power Index	114.3	100.0
Income tax rate	3.92%	4.70%
Sales tax rate	5.43%	6.58%
Property tax rate	$15.07	$12.00

HOUSING	AREA	U.S. AVG
Median home price	$137,200	$220,000
Home price appreciation	40.9%	10.1%
Median rent	$580	$709
Homes owned	57.0%	62.3%
Home price ratio	3.1	4.2

NECESSITIES	AREA	U.S. AVG
Food Index	99.6	100.0
Housing Index	50.2	100.0
Utilities Index	95.1	100.0
Transportation Index	96.9	100.0
Healthcare Index	98.6	100.0
Miscellaneous Cost Index	100.9	100.0

Climate
Score: 35.3
Rank: 241

TEMPERATURE	AREA	U.S. AVG
Average January low	-3.6	26.2
Average July high	82.8	87.4
Annual days > 90°F	12	38
Annual days < 32°F	181	89
Annual days < 0°F	54	6

PRECIPITATION	AREA	U.S. AVG
Annual inches precipitation	20.0	37.7
Annual inches snowfall	35.0	7.0
Annual days precipitation	102	109
Annual days rain > 0.5 inches	11	22
Annual days snow > 1.5 inches	8	6

COMFORTS & HAZARDS	AREA	U.S. AVG
July relative humidity	71%	66%
Annual days mostly sunny	199	208
Annual days with thunderstorms	33	39
Tornado risk score	31	18
Hurricane risk score	0	13

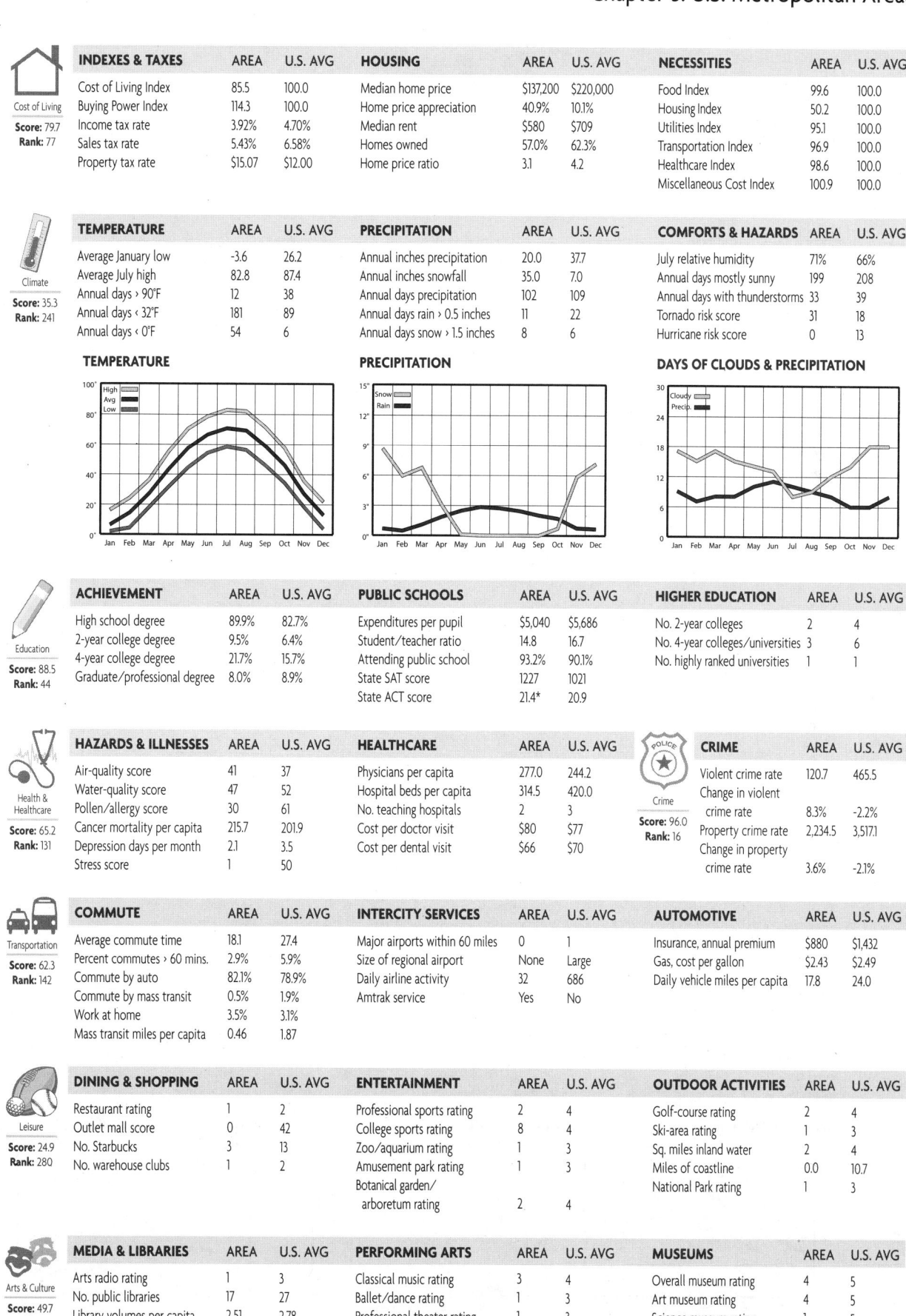

TEMPERATURE

PRECIPITATION

DAYS OF CLOUDS & PRECIPITATION

Education
Score: 88.5
Rank: 44

ACHIEVEMENT	AREA	U.S. AVG
High school degree	89.9%	82.7%
2-year college degree	9.5%	6.4%
4-year college degree	21.7%	15.7%
Graduate/professional degree	8.0%	8.9%

PUBLIC SCHOOLS	AREA	U.S. AVG
Expenditures per pupil	$5,040	$5,686
Student/teacher ratio	14.8	16.7
Attending public school	93.2%	90.1%
State SAT score	1227	1021
State ACT score	21.4*	20.9

HIGHER EDUCATION	AREA	U.S. AVG
No. 2-year colleges	2	4
No. 4-year colleges/universities	3	6
No. highly ranked universities	1	1

Health & Healthcare
Score: 65.2
Rank: 131

HAZARDS & ILLNESSES	AREA	U.S. AVG
Air-quality score	41	37
Water-quality score	47	52
Pollen/allergy score	30	61
Cancer mortality per capita	215.7	201.9
Depression days per month	2.1	3.5
Stress score	1	50

HEALTHCARE	AREA	U.S. AVG
Physicians per capita	277.0	244.2
Hospital beds per capita	314.5	420.0
No. teaching hospitals	2	3
Cost per doctor visit	$80	$77
Cost per dental visit	$66	$70

Crime
Score: 96.0
Rank: 16

CRIME	AREA	U.S. AVG
Violent crime rate	120.7	465.5
Change in violent crime rate	8.3%	-2.2%
Property crime rate	2,234.5	3,517.1
Change in property crime rate	3.6%	-2.1%

Transportation
Score: 62.3
Rank: 142

COMMUTE	AREA	U.S. AVG
Average commute time	18.1	27.4
Percent commutes > 60 mins.	2.9%	5.9%
Commute by auto	82.1%	78.9%
Commute by mass transit	0.5%	1.9%
Work at home	3.5%	3.1%
Mass transit miles per capita	0.46	1.87

INTERCITY SERVICES	AREA	U.S. AVG
Major airports within 60 miles	0	1
Size of regional airport	None	Large
Daily airline activity	32	686
Amtrak service	Yes	No

AUTOMOTIVE	AREA	U.S. AVG
Insurance, annual premium	$880	$1,432
Gas, cost per gallon	$2.43	$2.49
Daily vehicle miles per capita	17.8	24.0

Leisure
Score: 24.9
Rank: 280

DINING & SHOPPING	AREA	U.S. AVG
Restaurant rating	1	2
Outlet mall score	0	42
No. Starbucks	3	13
No. warehouse clubs	1	2

ENTERTAINMENT	AREA	U.S. AVG
Professional sports rating	2	4
College sports rating	8	4
Zoo/aquarium rating	1	3
Amusement park rating	1	3
Botanical garden/arboretum rating	2	4

OUTDOOR ACTIVITIES	AREA	U.S. AVG
Golf-course rating	2	4
Ski-area rating	1	3
Sq. miles inland water	2	4
Miles of coastline	0.0	10.7
National Park rating	1	3

Arts & Culture
Score: 49.7
Rank: 188

MEDIA & LIBRARIES	AREA	U.S. AVG
Arts radio rating	1	3
No. public libraries	17	27
Library volumes per capita	2.51	2.78

PERFORMING ARTS	AREA	U.S. AVG
Classical music rating	3	4
Ballet/dance rating	1	3
Professional theater rating	1	3
University arts programs rating	8	5

MUSEUMS	AREA	U.S. AVG
Overall museum rating	4	5
Art museum rating	4	5
Science museum rating	1	5
Children's museum rating	2	3

Farmington, NM

Score: 12.5 **Rank:** 368 **2004 rank:** not ranked

Profile: Small city
Location: Northwest corner of New Mexico along U.S. 64
Elevation: 5,590 feet
Time zone: Mountain Standard Time

PRO	CON
Nearby mountains	Entertainment
Cultural interest	Educational attainment
Pleasant, dry climate	Isolation

Farmington is located in the high San Juan Plateau, along the San Juan River near the Four Corners at the edge of the large Navajo reservation that spreads west into Arizona. The town itself is fairly plain, but areas to the north and east into Durango, Colorado; the Colorado San Juan Mountains; Mesa Verde National Park; and the Santa Fe National Forest offer excellent mountain recreation. The city serves as a trading post and cultural center for the Navajo nation. The reservation and a moderate oil, gas, and coal industry support the local economy, and as reflected in job statistics, natural resource industries bring strong growth projections. Living costs are reasonable compared to Durango and San Juan Mountain areas just north but are a bit high for the region. There is local commuter air service, but for bigger city services, Albuquerque is 180 fairly challenging miles southeast.

Farmington is in a relatively flat high desert valley, greened by the San Juan River and irrigation, inside a zone of sparse vegetation, erosion, and abundant rock outcroppings. The climate and terrain are typical of the high-desert location, with large variations in daily and evening temperatures and sparse precipitation. Summer days are sunny and warm but usually not too hot due to the altitude, while evenings cool considerably. Winters are mild and fairly dry with most nights below freezing, and occasional colder periods with snow as fronts pass through from the north.

Population

DEMOGRAPHICS	AREA	U.S. AVG	ETHNIC COMPOSITION	AREA	U.S. AVG	RESIDENT PROFILE	AREA	U.S. AVG
Population	126,259		White	48.9%	79.0%	Single	32.9%	32.4%
Population density per sq. mile	22.9	358.5	Black	0.5%	10.5%	Married	52.9%	52.7%
Population growth	37.8%	21.1%	Asian	0.4%	2.7%	Divorced/separated	14.2%	14.9%
Median age	31.3	36.1	Hispanic	15.5%	10.6%	Married with children	28.8%	23.7%
Percent Democrat	33.0%	44.5%	Religious observance	40.3%	48.9%	Single with children	13.0%	9.1%
Percent Republican	65.6%	54.5%	Diversity measure	70.1	40.1	Percent over age 65	9.5%	12.9%

Economy & Jobs
Score: 88.5
Rank: 44

INCOME	AREA	U.S. AVG	EMPLOYMENT	AREA	U.S. AVG	EMPLOYING INDUSTRIES	AREA	U.S. AVG
Per capita income	$16,845	$23,235	Unemployment rate	6.7%	4.7%	Largest: Mining		
Household income	$39,141	$46,414	Recent job growth	4.5%	1.3%			
Household income < $25K	32.2%	26.2%	Projected future job growth	27.8%	11.5%	Percent manufacturing	14.5%	15.4%
Household income > $75K	19.4%	25.4%	White collar	50.7%	57.8%	Percent public sector	19.9%	15.7%
Household income growth	15.9%	13.6%	Blue collar	31.8%	25.2%	Percent construction	17.3%	9.9%

Cost of Living
Score: 39.0
Rank: 228

INDEXES & TAXES	AREA	U.S. AVG	HOUSING	AREA	U.S. AVG	NECESSITIES	AREA	U.S. AVG
Cost of Living Index	94.3	100.0	Median home price	$177,100	$220,000	Food Index	112.9	100.0
Buying Power Index	93.0	100.0	Home price appreciation	56.7%	10.1%	Housing Index	58.9	100.0
Income tax rate	7.10%	4.70%	Median rent	$571	$709	Utilities Index	106.1	100.0
Sales tax rate	6.06%	6.58%	Homes owned	66.0%	62.3%	Transportation Index	101.2	100.0
Property tax rate	$9.35	$12.00	Home price ratio	4.5	4.2	Healthcare Index	101.6	100.0
						Miscellaneous Cost Index	97.0	100.0

Climate
Score: 73.0
Rank: 100

TEMPERATURE	AREA	U.S. AVG	PRECIPITATION	AREA	U.S. AVG	COMFORTS & HAZARDS	AREA	U.S. AVG
Average January low	16.8	26.2	Annual inches precipitation	8.2	37.7	July relative humidity	29%	66%
Average July high	91.7	87.4	Annual inches snowfall	13.6	7.0	Annual days mostly sunny	276	208
Annual days > 90°F	58	38	Annual days precipitation	73	109	Annual days with thunderstorms	55	39
Annual days < 32°F	152	89	Annual days rain > 0.5 inches	5	22	Tornado risk score	1	18
Annual days < 0°F	8	6	Annual days snow > 1.5 inches	10	6	Hurricane risk score	0	13

TEMPERATURE

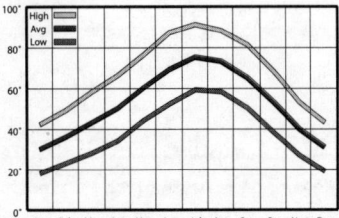

PRECIPITATION

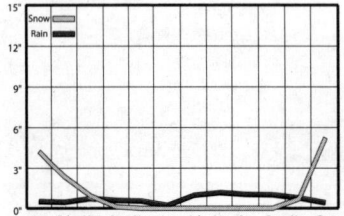

DAYS OF CLOUDS & PRECIPITATION

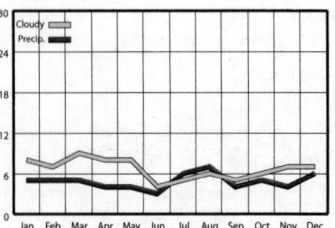

ACHIEVEMENT	AREA	U.S. AVG	PUBLIC SCHOOLS	AREA	U.S. AVG	HIGHER EDUCATION	AREA	U.S. AVG
High school degree	76.9%	82.7%	Expenditures per pupil	$4,509	$5,686	No. 2-year colleges	1	4
2-year college degree	6.7%	6.4%	Student/teacher ratio	15.8	16.7	No. 4-year colleges/universities	0	6
4-year college degree	8.7%	15.7%	Attending public school	97.5%	90.1%	No. highly ranked universities	0	1
Graduate/professional degree	4.8%	8.9%	State SAT score	1106	1021			
			State ACT score	20.1*	20.9			

Education Score: 16.6 Rank: 310

HAZARDS & ILLNESSES	AREA	U.S. AVG	HEALTHCARE	AREA	U.S. AVG	CRIME	AREA	U.S. AVG
Air-quality score	1	37	Physicians per capita	140.7	244.2	Violent crime rate	635.2	465.5
Water-quality score	43	52	Hospital beds per capita	137.0	420.0	Change in violent crime rate	-6.9%	-2.2%
Pollen/allergy score	68	61	No. teaching hospitals	0	3	Property crime rate	2,649.4	3,517.1
Cancer mortality per capita	170.9	201.9	Cost per doctor visit	$79	$77	Change in property crime rate	0.5%	-2.1%
Depression days per month	4.2	3.5	Cost per dental visit	$67	$70			
Stress score	87	50						

Health & Healthcare Score: 2.9 Rank: 362

Crime Score: 46.5 Rank: 200

COMMUTE	AREA	U.S. AVG	INTERCITY SERVICES	AREA	U.S. AVG	AUTOMOTIVE	AREA	U.S. AVG
Average commute time	25.2	27.4	Major airports within 60 miles	0	1	Insurance, annual premium	$1,162	$1,432
Percent commutes > 60 mins.	7.7%	5.9%	Size of regional airport	None	Large	Gas, cost per gallon	$2.54	$2.49
Commute by auto	78.7%	78.9%	Daily airline activity	20	686	Daily vehicle miles per capita	24.4	24.0
Commute by mass transit	0.1%	1.9%	Amtrak service	No	No			
Work at home	3.0%	3.1%						
Mass transit miles per capita	0.13	1.87						

Transportation Score: 2.1 Rank: 364

DINING & SHOPPING	AREA	U.S. AVG	ENTERTAINMENT	AREA	U.S. AVG	OUTDOOR ACTIVITIES	AREA	U.S. AVG
Restaurant rating	1	2	Professional sports rating	1	4	Golf-course rating	3	4
Outlet mall score	0	42	College sports rating	1	4	Ski-area rating	2	3
No. Starbucks	0	13	Zoo/aquarium rating	1	3	Sq. miles inland water	1	4
No. warehouse clubs	1	2	Amusement park rating	1	3	Miles of coastline	0.0	10.7
			Botanical garden/ arboretum rating	1	4	National Park rating	7	3

Leisure Score: 14.4 Rank: 319

MEDIA & LIBRARIES	AREA	U.S. AVG	PERFORMING ARTS	AREA	U.S. AVG	MUSEUMS	AREA	U.S. AVG
Arts radio rating	1	3	Classical music rating	2	4	Overall museum rating	4	5
No. public libraries	4	27	Ballet/dance rating	1	3	Art museum rating	1	5
Library volumes per capita	2.34	2.78	Professional theater rating	1	3	Science museum rating	6	5
			University arts programs rating	1	5	Children's museum rating	4	3

Arts & Culture Score: 6.1 Rank: 349

Fayetteville, NC

Score: 46.3   Rank: 273   2004 rank: 250

Profile: Mid-size city/military town
Location: South-central North Carolina, along Cape Fear River, 90 miles south of Raleigh-Durham
Elevation: 96 feet
Time zone: Eastern Standard Time

PRO
Attractive downtown
Low home prices
Outdoor recreation

CON
Entertainment
Dependence on military
Hot, humid summers

Once an important inland port on the Cape Fear River, Fayetteville houses two large military installations, Fort Bragg and Pope Air Force Base. The two facilities provide the city's main economic base. The clean, attractive, and walkable downtown contains numerous historic buildings and favorably reflects the results of an extensive revitalization program. Median home prices of just over $127,000 represent a good value, and there are appealing developments of homes and golf courses as the area becomes more desirable as a retirement destination. The city is well planned for the most part and sprawl is under control. There are some local arts and culture amenities, but overall the town is quiet. Scoring and ranking data don't reflect many of the area's qualities, particularly recent changes to the city's infrastructure. Particularly for those who don't mind a strong military presence, Fayetteville may be a pleasant surprise.

The area at the edge of the Coastal Plain begins to rise into the Carolina Piedmont Plateau. Surrounding terrain is level to gently rolling with agricultural land and mixed forests of pine and hardwood. Afternoon temperatures frequently reach the 90s, with high humidity and frequent afternoon thundershowers. Coastal storms produce rain year-round. Low temperatures are seldom below 20°F. There may be some snow and sleet, but most winter precipitation is rain.

Population

DEMOGRAPHICS	AREA	U.S. AVG	ETHNIC COMPOSITION	AREA	U.S. AVG	RESIDENT PROFILE	AREA	U.S. AVG
Population	344,757		White	51.4%	79.0%	Single	31.5%	32.4%
Population density per sq. mile	330.3	358.5	Black	37.4%	10.5%	Married	51.0%	52.7%
Population growth	18.3%	21.1%	Asian	2.3%	2.7%	Divorced/separated	17.5%	14.9%
Median age	30.5	36.1	Hispanic	5.6%	10.6%	Married with children	26.9%	23.7%
Percent Democrat	48.6%	44.5%	Religious observance	33.4%	48.9%	Single with children	12.5%	9.1%
Percent Republican	51.1%	54.5%	Diversity measure	63.3	40.1	Percent over age 65	8.5%	12.9%

Economy & Jobs
Score: 3.7
Rank: 359

INCOME	AREA	U.S. AVG	EMPLOYMENT	AREA	U.S. AVG	EMPLOYING INDUSTRIES	AREA	U.S. AVG
Per capita income	$19,754	$23,235	Unemployment rate	6.8%	4.7%	Largest: Healthcare & Social Assistance		
Household income	$42,893	$46,414	Recent job growth	0.9%	1.3%			
Household income < $25K	26.4%	26.2%	Projected future job growth	-0.3%	11.5%	Percent manufacturing	17.6%	15.4%
Household income > $75K	19.9%	25.4%	White collar	54.1%	57.8%	Percent public sector	23.3%	15.7%
Household income growth	16.0%	13.6%	Blue collar	28.4%	25.2%	Percent construction	10.8%	9.9%

Cost of Living
Score: 41.4
Rank: 219

INDEXES & TAXES	AREA	U.S. AVG	HOUSING	AREA	U.S. AVG	NECESSITIES	AREA	U.S. AVG
Cost of Living Index	85.9	100.0	Median home price	$127,300	$220,000	Food Index	103.1	100.0
Buying Power Index	111.9	100.0	Home price appreciation	22.5%	10.1%	Housing Index	53.6	100.0
Income tax rate	7.00%	4.70%	Median rent	$607	$709	Utilities Index	96.5	100.0
Sales tax rate	7.00%	6.58%	Homes owned	56.1%	62.3%	Transportation Index	97.4	100.0
Property tax rate	$11.24	$12.00	Home price ratio	3.0	4.2	Healthcare Index	98.4	100.0
						Miscellaneous Cost Index	105.2	100.0

Climate
Score: 61.2
Rank: 144

TEMPERATURE	AREA	U.S. AVG	PRECIPITATION	AREA	U.S. AVG	COMFORTS & HAZARDS	AREA	U.S. AVG
Average January low	30.0	26.2	Annual inches precipitation	43.0	37.7	July relative humidity	71%	66%
Average July high	87.7	87.4	Annual inches snowfall	7.0	7.0	Annual days mostly sunny	220	208
Annual days > 90°F	25	38	Annual days precipitation	112	109	Annual days with thunderstorms	46	39
Annual days < 32°F	82	89	Annual days rain > 0.5 inches	28	22	Tornado risk score	26	18
Annual days < 0°F	0	6	Annual days snow > 1.5 inches	2	6	Hurricane risk score	41	13

TEMPERATURE

PRECIPITATION

DAYS OF CLOUDS & PRECIPITATION

Education
Score: 48.7
Rank: 193

ACHIEVEMENT	AREA	U.S. AVG	PUBLIC SCHOOLS	AREA	U.S. AVG	HIGHER EDUCATION	AREA	U.S. AVG
High school degree	83.8%	82.7%	Expenditures per pupil	$4,601	$5,686	No. 2-year colleges	1	4
2-year college degree	9.0%	6.4%	Student/teacher ratio	14.2	16.7	No. 4-year colleges/universities	2	6
4-year college degree	12.5%	15.7%	Attending public school	94.1%	90.1%	No. highly ranked universities	0	1
Graduate/professional degree	5.6%	8.9%	State SAT score	1008*	1021			
			State ACT score	20.5	20.9			

Health & Healthcare
Score: 32.6
Rank: 251

HAZARDS & ILLNESSES	AREA	U.S. AVG	HEALTHCARE	AREA	U.S. AVG	CRIME	AREA	U.S. AVG
Air-quality score	37	37	Physicians per capita	190.0	244.2	Violent crime rate	581.8	465.5
Water-quality score	69	52	Hospital beds per capita	222.8	420.0	Change in violent crime rate	-4.5%	-2.2%
Pollen/allergy score	65	61	No. teaching hospitals	1	3	Property crime rate	5,560.4	3,517.1
Cancer mortality per capita	212.6	201.9	Cost per doctor visit	$76	$77	Change in property crime rate	0.6%	-2.1%
Depression days per month	3.5	3.5	Cost per dental visit	$67	$70			
Stress score	77	50						

Crime
Score: 18.7
Rank: 303

Transportation
Score: 42.8
Rank: 215

COMMUTE	AREA	U.S. AVG	INTERCITY SERVICES	AREA	U.S. AVG	AUTOMOTIVE	AREA	U.S. AVG
Average commute time	24.1	27.4	Major airports within 60 miles	1	1	Insurance, annual premium	$1,197	$1,432
Percent commutes > 60 mins.	5.0%	5.9%	Size of regional airport	Medium	Large	Gas, cost per gallon	$2.54	$2.49
Commute by auto	77.2%	78.9%	Daily airline activity	512	686	Daily vehicle miles per capita	21.9	24.0
Commute by mass transit	0.7%	1.9%	Amtrak service	Yes	No			
Work at home	2.2%	3.1%						
Mass transit miles per capita	0.68	1.87						

Leisure
Score: 8.0
Rank: 342

DINING & SHOPPING	AREA	U.S. AVG	ENTERTAINMENT	AREA	U.S. AVG	OUTDOOR ACTIVITIES	AREA	U.S. AVG
Restaurant rating	1	2	Professional sports rating	2	4	Golf-course rating	2	4
Outlet mall score	0	42	College sports rating	3	4	Ski-area rating	1	3
No. Starbucks	0	13	Zoo/aquarium rating	1	3	Sq. miles inland water	2	4
No. warehouse clubs	0	2	Amusement park rating	2	3	Miles of coastline	0.0	10.7
			Botanical garden/ arboretum rating	1	4	National Park rating	1	3

Arts & Culture
Score: 40.1
Rank: 224

MEDIA & LIBRARIES	AREA	U.S. AVG	PERFORMING ARTS	AREA	U.S. AVG	MUSEUMS	AREA	U.S. AVG
Arts radio rating	1	3	Classical music rating	2	4	Overall museum rating	6	5
No. public libraries	7	27	Ballet/dance rating	1	3	Art museum rating	7	5
Library volumes per capita	2.40	2.78	Professional theater rating	1	3	Science museum rating	1	5
			University arts programs rating	5	5	Children's museum rating	1	3

Fayetteville–Springdale–Rogers, AR   **Score: 71.8 Rank: 79 2004 rank: 27**

Profile: Small-city complex/college town
Location: Extreme northwest Arkansas in Ozark foothills
Elevation: 1,263 feet
Time zone: Central Standard Time

PRO	CON
Strong economy	Isolation
Variety	Growth and sprawl
Cost of living	Hot, humid summers

The northwest Arkansas region is one of the fastest growing in the country, and the three named cities, Rogers, Springdale, and Fayetteville, plus the elephant-in-the-room Bentonville represent an interesting mix of small cities that all work together and all offer something. The three named cities are located in a north–south line roughly 10 miles apart, while Bentonville lies 5 miles west of Rogers. Each of these towns brings something different to the area, and the mix works well. Fayetteville is home to the University of Arkansas and has an attractive campus, historic buildings, a progressive feel, and the usual college-town amenities. Springdale is more Old South as a center of light manufacturing, trucking, and agricultural processing, anchored by the headquarters and major operations of poultry processor Tyson. Rogers was once a sleepy nondescript Southern town but has boomed as a hot family-oriented residential area. One of the reasons why is Bentonville, and for those who don't recognize the name, it is the headquarters for retail giant Wal-Mart. Wal-Mart earns superlatives all over the country, but no single employer wields the economic influence that Wal-Mart has in Bentonville and the surrounding area. The headquarters employs some 13,000, and that is not the whole story, as scores of other companies supplying everything from product to marketing to legal services make the area their home. And there's a steady stream of business travelers calling on the nation's no. 1 retailer as well. All of this leads to

a booming economy and plenty of air service. The founding Walton family and the Jones family of trucking industry lineage have left a strong cultural imprint on the area as well. The Walton family has endowed a large performing arts center and a $50-million Walton family–supported art museum is scheduled to open in 2009. The Jones family has endowed the Jones Center for Families among other assets. There are plenty of water and outdoor recreation opportunities in nearby lakes and mountain areas, but some might feel a bit isolated from other "city" activities (the closest big city is Kansas City 175 miles north) and there is some growth-related strain. Living costs are low (85.0), and substantial employment and income growth bring strong buying power. Crime rates are notably low for the region. This area has been a rising star and offers a lot of variety and opportunity, but some might find it a bit conservative and dominated by Wal-Mart culture for their tastes, and growth pressures are starting to take their toll.

The area contains a mix of farmland, nearby lakes, and rolling, wooded hills. Climate is continental and typical of the region, with a strong Gulf influence particularly in summer. However, the elevation and nearby mountains keep temperatures a few degrees cooler than many other parts of the state. Winters are generally mild, with occasional cold spells.

Population

DEMOGRAPHICS	AREA	U.S. AVG	ETHNIC COMPOSITION	AREA	U.S. AVG	RESIDENT PROFILE	AREA	U.S. AVG
Population	392,659		White	87.8%	79.0%	Single	26.6%	32.4%
Population density per sq. mile	123.8	358.5	Black	1.6%	10.5%	Married	58.2%	52.7%
Population growth	66.3%	21.1%	Asian	1.9%	2.7%	Divorced/separated	15.2%	14.9%
Median age	33.9	36.1	Hispanic	10.3%	10.6%	Married with children	26.1%	23.7%
Percent Democrat	36.2%	44.5%	Religious observance	50.5%	48.9%	Single with children	7.8%	9.1%
Percent Republican	62.6%	54.5%	Diversity measure	36.7	40.1	Percent over age 65	11.7%	12.9%

Economy & Jobs
Score: 98.9
Rank: 4

INCOME	AREA	U.S. AVG	EMPLOYMENT	AREA	U.S. AVG	EMPLOYING INDUSTRIES	AREA	U.S. AVG
Per capita income	$20,929	$23,235	Unemployment rate	3.3%	4.7%	Largest: Manufacturing		
Household income	$42,209	$46,414	Recent job growth	6.5%	1.3%			
Household income < $25K	27.6%	26.2%	Projected future job growth	32.9%	11.5%	Percent manufacturing	19.5%	15.4%
Household income > $75K	20.1%	25.4%	White collar	54.5%	57.8%	Percent public sector	11.0%	15.7%
Household income growth	15.4%	13.6%	Blue collar	29.3%	25.2%	Percent construction	9.9%	9.9%

Cost of Living
Score: 31.8
Rank: 255

INDEXES & TAXES	AREA	U.S. AVG	HOUSING	AREA	U.S. AVG	NECESSITIES	AREA	U.S. AVG
Cost of Living Index	85.0	100.0	Median home price	$168,400	$220,000	Food Index	89.3	100.0
Buying Power Index	111.3	100.0	Home price appreciation	44.3%	10.1%	Housing Index	67.6	100.0
Income tax rate	6.94%	4.70%	Median rent	$570	$709	Utilities Index	82.3	100.0
Sales tax rate	8.92%	6.58%	Homes owned	60.7%	62.3%	Transportation Index	91.6	100.0
Property tax rate	$7.82	$12.00	Home price ratio	4.0	4.2	Healthcare Index	92.2	100.0
						Miscellaneous Cost Index	94.3	100.0

Climate
Score: 53.2
Rank: 174

TEMPERATURE	AREA	U.S. AVG	PRECIPITATION	AREA	U.S. AVG	COMFORTS & HAZARDS	AREA	U.S. AVG
Average January low	27.0	26.2	Annual inches precipitation	42.0	37.7	July relative humidity	70%	66%
Average July high	91.8	87.4	Annual inches snowfall	6.0	7.0	Annual days mostly sunny	220	208
Annual days > 90°F	60	38	Annual days precipitation	96	109	Annual days with thunderstorms	57	39
Annual days < 32°F	90	89	Annual days rain > 0.5 inches	26	22	Tornado risk score	17	18
Annual days < 0°F	0	6	Annual days snow > 1.5 inches	3	6	Hurricane risk score	4	13

TEMPERATURE

PRECIPITATION

DAYS OF CLOUDS & PRECIPITATION

Education
Score: 23.5
Rank: 286

ACHIEVEMENT	AREA	U.S. AVG	PUBLIC SCHOOLS	AREA	U.S. AVG	HIGHER EDUCATION	AREA	U.S. AVG
High school degree	79.0%	82.7%	Expenditures per pupil	$4,303	$5,686	No. 2-year colleges	2	4
2-year college degree	4.0%	6.4%	Student/teacher ratio	22.2	16.7	No. 4-year colleges/universities	2	6
4-year college degree	14.0%	15.7%	Attending public school	95.8%	90.1%	No. highly ranked universities	0	1
Graduate/professional degree	7.3%	8.9%	State SAT score	1142	1021			
			State ACT score	20.6*	20.9			

Health & Healthcare
Score: 61.5
Rank: 145

HAZARDS & ILLNESSES	AREA	U.S. AVG	HEALTHCARE	AREA	U.S. AVG	CRIME	AREA	U.S. AVG
Air-quality score	41	37	Physicians per capita	156.5	244.2	Violent crime rate	292.9	465.5
Water-quality score	67	52	Hospital beds per capita	308.4	420.0	Change in violent crime rate	21.7%	-2.2%
Pollen/allergy score	54	61	No. teaching hospitals	3	3	Property crime rate	3,087.4	3,517.1
Cancer mortality per capita	214.2	201.9	Cost per doctor visit	$72	$77	Change in property crime rate	11.8%	-2.1%
Depression days per month	3.2	3.5	Cost per dental visit	$63	$70			
Stress score	15	50						

Crime
Score: 77.8
Rank: 83

Transportation
Score: 40.4
Rank: 224

COMMUTE	AREA	U.S. AVG	INTERCITY SERVICES	AREA	U.S. AVG	AUTOMOTIVE	AREA	U.S. AVG
Average commute time	22.2	27.4	Major airports within 60 miles	1	1	Insurance, annual premium	$1,086	$1,432
Percent commutes > 60 mins.	3.6%	5.9%	Size of regional airport	Medium	Large	Gas, cost per gallon	$2.46	$2.49
Commute by auto	79.0%	78.9%	Daily airline activity	160	686	Daily vehicle miles per capita	20.6	24.0
Commute by mass transit	0.3%	1.9%	Amtrak service	No	No			
Work at home	3.7%	3.1%						
Mass transit miles per capita	0.33	1.87						

Leisure
Score: 21.4
Rank: 293

DINING & SHOPPING	AREA	U.S. AVG	ENTERTAINMENT	AREA	U.S. AVG	OUTDOOR ACTIVITIES	AREA	U.S. AVG
Restaurant rating	1	2	Professional sports rating	2	4	Golf-course rating	1	4
Outlet mall score	0	42	College sports rating	6	4	Ski-area rating	1	3
No. Starbucks	1	13	Zoo/aquarium rating	1	3	Sq. miles inland water	2	4
No. warehouse clubs	1	2	Amusement park rating	1	3	Miles of coastline	0.0	10.7
			Botanical garden/arboretum rating	2	4	National Park rating	3	3

Arts & Culture
Score: 14.2
Rank: 320

MEDIA & LIBRARIES	AREA	U.S. AVG	PERFORMING ARTS	AREA	U.S. AVG	MUSEUMS	AREA	U.S. AVG
Arts radio rating	1	3	Classical music rating	4	4	Overall museum rating	5	5
No. public libraries	14	27	Ballet/dance rating	1	3	Art museum rating	1	5
Library volumes per capita	2.23	2.78	Professional theater rating	1	3	Science museum rating	4	5
			University arts programs rating	4	5	Children's museum rating	1	3

Flagstaff, AZ

Score: 85.7 Rank: 18 2004 rank: 244

Profile: Small mountain city
Location: North-central Arizona, 50 miles south of Grand Canyon National Park
Elevation: 6,993 feet
Time zone: Mountain Standard Time (no daylight saving time)

PRO	CON
Nearby mountains	Rising living costs
Low heat and humidity	Growth and sprawl
Attractive setting	Some winter cold

Flagstaff is an old Route 66 railroad town, located in the high plateau of the San Francisco Mountains. The city has the second-highest altitude among metropolitan areas, and thus escapes the desert heat associated with much of Arizona. Serving as a gateway for the Grand Canyon National Park, as well as an oasis and junction on east–west Interstate 40, the city's predominant industry is tourism, supported by some relatively unattractive motel and restaurant strips. Downtown is clean with a strong Western feel. Downsides include a fairly undiversified economy, but the area's recent popularity as a Sun Belt alternative has brought new business, and Flagstaff has completely reversed its previous negative economic trends. Unfortunately, this growth has brought with it higher living costs. Northern Arizona University adds a college-town flavor, the population is the best educated in the state, and there's an overall youthful spirit. The area, with its pleasant, healthy climate most seasons, has become more of a retirement destination as well.

Home prices, while reasonable for the region in general, have risen fast as they have through most of Arizona. The area represents a good blend of lifestyle features, hence the dramatic jump in rankings. The negatives of growth and cost, however, bear watching.

The highest mountains in Arizona surround Flagstaff. Local vegetation is mainly desert scrub, grasses, and small trees, with coniferous forests in the nearby mountains. Cold nights prevail year-round—at 210 days per year, Flagstaff drops below freezing more often than any other metropolitan area in the continental U.S. Summers are mild and pleasantly cool with moderate humidity, although temperatures often rise above 80°F and may reach 95°F. Winters bring snow cover, clear skies, and below-zero temperatures. Two distinct precipitation seasons occur in winter and late summer. First freeze is late September; last is mid-June.

Population

DEMOGRAPHICS	AREA	U.S. AVG	ETHNIC COMPOSITION	AREA	U.S. AVG	RESIDENT PROFILE	AREA	U.S. AVG
Population	128,963		White	59.3%	79.0%	Single	39.0%	32.4%
Population density per sq. mile	6.9	358.5	Black	0.9%	10.5%	Married	47.4%	52.7%
Population growth	33.5%	21.1%	Asian	1.0%	2.7%	Divorced/separated	13.7%	14.9%
Median age	30.8	36.1	Hispanic	11.2%	10.6%	Married with children	24.1%	23.7%
Percent Democrat	55.8%	44.5%	Religious observance	30.9%	48.9%	Single with children	10.5%	9.1%
Percent Republican	43.0%	54.5%	Diversity measure	63.4	40.1	Percent over age 65	7.7%	12.9%

Economy & Jobs
Score: 66.3
Rank: 127

INCOME	AREA	U.S. AVG	EMPLOYMENT	AREA	U.S. AVG	EMPLOYING INDUSTRIES	AREA	U.S. AVG
Per capita income	$20,658	$23,235	Unemployment rate	5.6%	4.7%	Largest: Healthcare & Social Assistance		
Household income	$44,534	$46,414	Recent job growth	1.8%	1.3%			
Household income ‹ $25K	26.9%	26.2%	Projected future job growth	22.2%	11.5%	Percent manufacturing	9.8%	15.4%
Household income › $75K	24.6%	25.4%	White collar	60.7%	57.8%	Percent public sector	28.0%	15.7%
Household income growth	16.4%	13.6%	Blue collar	19.7%	25.2%	Percent construction	9.9%	9.9%

Cost of Living
Score: 61.0
Rank: 145

INDEXES & TAXES	AREA	U.S. AVG	HOUSING	AREA	U.S. AVG	NECESSITIES	AREA	U.S. AVG
Cost of Living Index	118.4	100.0	Median home price	$335,300	$220,000	Food Index	108.7	100.0
Buying Power Index	84.3	100.0	Home price appreciation	95.1%	10.1%	Housing Index	79.7	100.0
Income tax rate	3.90%	4.70%	Median rent	$939	$709	Utilities Index	81.4	100.0
Sales tax rate	6.53%	6.58%	Homes owned	46.4%	62.3%	Transportation Index	107.7	100.0
Property tax rate	$6.73	$12.00	Home price ratio	7.5	4.2	Healthcare Index	107.4	100.0
						Miscellaneous Cost Index	99.7	100.0

Climate
Score: 63.9
Rank: 134

TEMPERATURE	AREA	U.S. AVG	PRECIPITATION	AREA	U.S. AVG	COMFORTS & HAZARDS	AREA	U.S. AVG
Average January low	15.0	26.2	Annual inches precipitation	21.6	37.7	July relative humidity	36%	66%
Average July high	82.0	87.4	Annual inches snowfall	99.0	7.0	Annual days mostly sunny	290	208
Annual days > 90°F	3	38	Annual days precipitation	140	109	Annual days with thunderstorms	62	39
Annual days < 32°F	210	89	Annual days rain > 0.5 inches	11	22	Tornado risk score	1	18
Annual days < 0°F	13	6	Annual days snow > 1.5 inches	18	6	Hurricane risk score	0	13

TEMPERATURE

PRECIPITATION

DAYS OF CLOUDS & PRECIPITATION

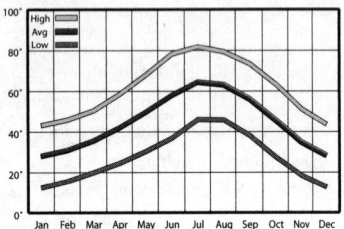
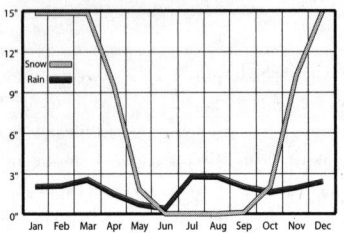
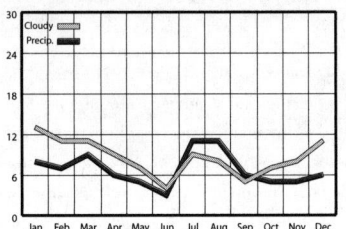

Education
Score: 73.5
Rank: 100

ACHIEVEMENT	AREA	U.S. AVG	PUBLIC SCHOOLS	AREA	U.S. AVG	HIGHER EDUCATION	AREA	U.S. AVG
High school degree	84.2%	82.7%	Expenditures per pupil	$4,936	$5,686	No. 2-year colleges	2	4
2-year college degree	6.0%	6.4%	Student/teacher ratio	16.9	16.7	No. 4-year colleges/universities	1	6
4-year college degree	19.1%	15.7%	Attending public school	97.4%	90.1%	No. highly ranked universities	0	1
Graduate/professional degree	11.4%	8.9%	State SAT score	1049	1021			
			State ACT score	21.6*	20.9			

Health & Healthcare
Score: 25.1
Rank: 279

Crime
Score: 27.0
Rank: 273

HAZARDS & ILLNESSES	AREA	U.S. AVG	HEALTHCARE	AREA	U.S. AVG	CRIME	AREA	U.S. AVG
Air-quality score	18	37	Physicians per capita	230.8	244.2	Violent crime rate	588.5	465.5
Water-quality score	57	52	Hospital beds per capita	177.6	420.0	Change in violent crime rate	14.4%	-2.2%
Pollen/allergy score	70	61	No. teaching hospitals	0	3	Property crime rate	4,764.0	3,517.1
Cancer mortality per capita	159.4	201.9	Cost per doctor visit	$73	$77	Change in property crime rate	-2.0%	-2.1%
Depression days per month	3.0	3.5	Cost per dental visit	$80	$70			
Stress score	58	50						

Transportation
Score: 54.8
Rank: 169

COMMUTE	AREA	U.S. AVG	INTERCITY SERVICES	AREA	U.S. AVG	AUTOMOTIVE	AREA	U.S. AVG
Average commute time	20.1	27.4	Major airports within 60 miles	0	1	Insurance, annual premium	$1,340	$1,432
Percent commutes > 60 mins.	5.6%	5.9%	Size of regional airport	Small	Large	Gas, cost per gallon	$2.58	$2.49
Commute by auto	68.6%	78.9%	Daily airline activity	168	686	Daily vehicle miles per capita	26.4	24.0
Commute by mass transit	0.7%	1.9%	Amtrak service	Yes	No			
Work at home	3.8%	3.1%						
Mass transit miles per capita	0.72	1.87						

Leisure
Score: 57.5
Rank: 159

DINING & SHOPPING	AREA	U.S. AVG	ENTERTAINMENT	AREA	U.S. AVG	OUTDOOR ACTIVITIES	AREA	U.S. AVG
Restaurant rating	1	2	Professional sports rating	2	4	Golf-course rating	6	4
Outlet mall score	8	42	College sports rating	5	4	Ski-area rating	4	3
No. Starbucks	1	13	Zoo/aquarium rating	1	3	Sq. miles inland water	2	4
No. warehouse clubs	1	2	Amusement park rating	1	3	Miles of coastline	0.0	10.7
			Botanical garden/arboretum rating	2	4	National Park rating	10	3

Arts & Culture
Score: 43.6
Rank: 211

MEDIA & LIBRARIES	AREA	U.S. AVG	PERFORMING ARTS	AREA	U.S. AVG	MUSEUMS	AREA	U.S. AVG
Arts radio rating	1	3	Classical music rating	3	4	Overall museum rating	9	5
No. public libraries	8	27	Ballet/dance rating	1	3	Art museum rating	7	5
Library volumes per capita	2.61	2.78	Professional theater rating	1	3	Science museum rating	9	5
			University arts programs rating	4	5	Children's museum rating	1	3

Flint, MI

Score: 33.3 Rank: 335 2004 rank: 234

Profile: Mid-size industrial city
Location: Eastern Michigan, 65 miles northwest of Detroit
Elevation: 771 feet
Time zone: Eastern Standard Time

PRO	CON
Cost of living	Economic cycles
Urban revitalization	Industrial flavor
Arts and culture	Violent crime rate

Flint is the birthplace of General Motors and is second only to Detroit in auto production. Though it works hard to deal with the effects, it continues to see its fortunes rise and fall with the auto industry, and recent problems at GM and parts maker Delphi have weighed down the modest resurgence the city saw in the past few years. The city's lowest point, in the 1980s, was the focus of the documentary film *Roger & Me*, which depicted the effects of 30,000 lost jobs on the local economy and social fabric. The city itself re-emerged from receivership in 2004, but the fact that the first link on the city's website is to its "Accounts Payable Inquiry System" (yes, it's alphabetical, but most cities don't have such a link prominently displayed) is not a positive sign. Flint continues to work to build a broader economic base. There is a small but proud base of cultural attractions including an

orchestra and other performing arts, plus a few quality museums. Cost of living and housing are understandably low; housing affordability as measured by our home price ratio (1.8) is second best in the country. Flint is a case study in city rebirth after an economic disaster but is far from out of the woods. It may work some day for more intrepid migrants.

The city is located in the Flint River Valley in the center of Genesee County. The surrounding terrain is generally level with some hills 15 miles southeast of the city. The wettest periods normally occur in the late spring, early summer, and early fall. Winter is normally the driest season. Although snowfall is occasionally heavy, most occurs as frequent light flurries. Winter months are marked by considerable cloudiness and high humidity, while summer humidity is usually not excessive and sunshine is plentiful. Weather changes are frequent. First freeze is early October; last is early May.

DEMOGRAPHICS	AREA	U.S. AVG	ETHNIC COMPOSITION	AREA	U.S. AVG	RESIDENT PROFILE	AREA	U.S. AVG
Population	444,915		White	75.2%	79.0%	Single	34.0%	32.4%
Population density per sq. mile	695.6	358.5	Black	20.1%	10.5%	Married	50.5%	52.7%
Population growth	3.4%	21.1%	Asian	1.0%	2.7%	Divorced/separated	15.5%	14.9%
Median age	36.1	36.1	Hispanic	2.4%	10.6%	Married with children	21.0%	23.7%
Percent Democrat	60.0%	44.5%	Religious observance	37.0%	48.9%	Single with children	12.5%	9.1%
Percent Republican	39.2%	54.5%	Diversity measure	42.1	40.1	Percent over age 65	12.1%	12.9%

Economy & Jobs
Score: 16.8
Rank: 311

INCOME	AREA	U.S. AVG	EMPLOYMENT	AREA	U.S. AVG	EMPLOYING INDUSTRIES	AREA	U.S. AVG
Per capita income	$23,031	$23,235	Unemployment rate	9.5%	4.7%	Largest: Manufacturing		
Household income	$45,519	$46,414	Recent job growth	1.2%	1.3%			
Household income < $25K	27.1%	26.2%	Projected future job growth	3.0%	11.5%	Percent manufacturing	21.2%	15.4%
Household income > $75K	25.9%	25.4%	White collar	51.7%	57.8%	Percent public sector	9.6%	15.7%
Household income growth	8.5%	13.6%	Blue collar	31.9%	25.2%	Percent construction	10.7%	9.9%

Cost of Living
Score: 56.7
Rank: 162

INDEXES & TAXES	AREA	U.S. AVG	HOUSING	AREA	U.S. AVG	NECESSITIES	AREA	U.S. AVG
Cost of Living Index	76.2	100.0	Median home price	$82,500	$220,000	Food Index	104.7	100.0
Buying Power Index	133.9	100.0	Home price appreciation	21.4%	10.1%	Housing Index	50.3	100.0
Income tax rate	5.49%	4.70%	Median rent	$649	$709	Utilities Index	82.2	100.0
Sales tax rate	6.00%	6.58%	Homes owned	68.4%	62.3%	Transportation Index	99.9	100.0
Property tax rate	$13.56	$12.00	Home price ratio	1.8	4.2	Healthcare Index	106.6	100.0
						Miscellaneous Cost Index	96.6	100.0

Climate
Score: 23.5
Rank: 285

TEMPERATURE	AREA	U.S. AVG	PRECIPITATION	AREA	U.S. AVG	COMFORTS & HAZARDS	AREA	U.S. AVG
Average January low	14.6	26.2	Annual inches precipitation	29.8	37.7	July relative humidity	71%	66%
Average July high	81.2	87.4	Annual inches snowfall	45.4	7.0	Annual days mostly sunny	174	208
Annual days > 90°F	5	38	Annual days precipitation	132	109	Annual days with thunderstorms	33	39
Annual days < 32°F	139	89	Annual days rain > 0.5 inches	17	22	Tornado risk score	24	18
Annual days < 0°F	10	6	Annual days snow > 1.5 inches	10	6	Hurricane risk score	3	13

TEMPERATURE

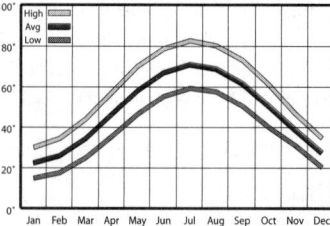

PRECIPITATION

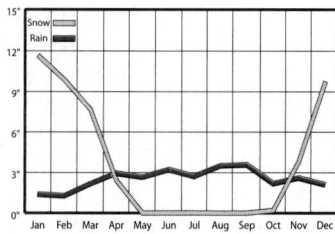

DAYS OF CLOUDS & PRECIPITATION

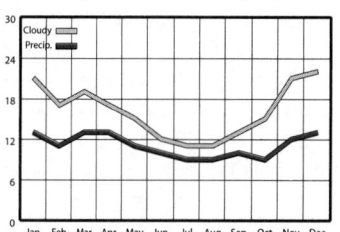

Education	ACHIEVEMENT	AREA	U.S. AVG	PUBLIC SCHOOLS	AREA	U.S. AVG	HIGHER EDUCATION	AREA	U.S. AVG
	High school degree	83.6%	82.7%	Expenditures per pupil	$6,002	$5,686	No. 2-year colleges	2	4
Score: 43.3	2-year college degree	8.0%	6.4%	Student/teacher ratio	20.0	16.7	No. 4-year colleges/universities	5	6
Rank: 213	4-year college degree	10.8%	15.7%	Attending public school	93.2%	90.1%	No. highly ranked universities	1	1
	Graduate/professional degree	5.8%	8.9%	State SAT score	1151	1021			
				State ACT score	21.5*	20.9			

Health & Healthcare	HAZARDS & ILLNESSES	AREA	U.S. AVG	HEALTHCARE	AREA	U.S. AVG		CRIME	AREA	U.S. AVG
	Air-quality score	25	37	Physicians per capita	238.3	244.2		Violent crime rate	859.1	465.5
	Water-quality score	20	52	Hospital beds per capita	383.2	420.0		Change in violent crime rate	11.8%	-2.2%
	Pollen/allergy score	53	61	No. teaching hospitals	5	3	Crime	Property crime rate	4,070.1	3,517.1
Score: 18.7	Cancer mortality per capita	220.7	201.9	Cost per doctor visit	$71	$77	Score: 17.6	Change in property crime rate	0.8%	-2.1%
Rank: 303	Depression days per month	3.8	3.5	Cost per dental visit	$68	$70	Rank: 308			
	Stress score	99	50							

Transportation	COMMUTE	AREA	U.S. AVG	INTERCITY SERVICES	AREA	U.S. AVG	AUTOMOTIVE	AREA	U.S. AVG
	Average commute time	27.8	27.4	Major airports within 60 miles	1	1	Insurance, annual premium	$2,060	$1,432
Score: 29.1	Percent commutes > 60 mins.	9.4%	5.9%	Size of regional airport	Large	Large	Gas, cost per gallon	$2.52	$2.49
Rank: 266	Commute by auto	84.7%	78.9%	Daily airline activity	956	686	Daily vehicle miles per capita	29.7	24.0
	Commute by mass transit	1.2%	1.9%	Amtrak service	Yes	No			
	Work at home	2.1%	3.1%						
	Mass transit miles per capita	1.15	1.87						

Leisure	DINING & SHOPPING	AREA	U.S. AVG	ENTERTAINMENT	AREA	U.S. AVG	OUTDOOR ACTIVITIES	AREA	U.S. AVG
	Restaurant rating	1	2	Professional sports rating	8	4	Golf-course rating	7	4
Score: 76.2	Outlet mall score	208	42	College sports rating	6	4	Ski-area rating	4	3
Rank: 89	No. Starbucks	3	13	Zoo/aquarium rating	2	3	Sq. miles inland water	3	4
	No. warehouse clubs	0	2	Amusement park rating	2	3	Miles of coastline	0.0	10.7
				Botanical garden/ arboretum rating	6	4	National Park rating	1	3

Arts & Culture	MEDIA & LIBRARIES	AREA	U.S. AVG	PERFORMING ARTS	AREA	U.S. AVG	MUSEUMS	AREA	U.S. AVG
	Arts radio rating	4	3	Classical music rating	4	4	Overall museum rating	9	5
Score: 64.7	No. public libraries	23	27	Ballet/dance rating	4	3	Art museum rating	7	5
Rank: 132	Library volumes per capita	2.72	2.78	Professional theater rating	1	3	Science museum rating	7	5
				University arts programs rating	6	5	Children's museum rating	6	3

Florence, SC

Score: 23.8   Rank: 359   2004 rank: 268

Profile: Small city
Location: Northeast South Carolina, 50 miles from the North Carolina border
Elevation: 225 feet
Time zone: Eastern Standard Time

PRO	CON
Diverse economy	Isolation
Healthcare	Entertainment
Cost of living	Crime rates

Florence has a thriving economy as a transportation and distribution center with manufacturing and agriculture added to the mix. The main transportation routes from the north and east split at this point, continuing inland to Atlanta and down the coast to Savannah and into Florida. Manufacturers include Honda, GE, Maytag, DuPont, and Southeastern Steel. The town is typically Southern with a simple grace and slow pace. The downtown business district is plain and unremarkable but clean, is well utilized, and has some historic interest. While it's far from big-city services and amenities, the town does have a modest set of local arts assets. The McLeod Regional Medical Center adds a significant healthcare presence. Darlington Raceway, 5 miles north, is an active NASCAR track, and a series of state parks offer some recreation in the piney hills to the northwest. The area is strong financially with an attractive Cost of Living Index of 84.7 and healthy recent job growth, but it may be too "deep South" for some.

Florence is at the edge of the Coastal Plain, where the land begins to rise to a wooded, rolling terrain. Predominant vegetation is pine forest with sections cleared for agriculture. Warm, moist air and low elevation keep summers hot, sticky, and wet. Winter weather is typically cool and damp but not excessively cold, although nighttime lows frequently drop below zero.

DEMOGRAPHICS	AREA	U.S. AVG	ETHNIC COMPOSITION	AREA	U.S. AVG	RESIDENT PROFILE	AREA	U.S. AVG
Population	198,117		White	56.6%	79.0%	Single	34.7%	32.4%
Population density per sq. mile	145.6	358.5	Black	41.4%	10.5%	Married	49.3%	52.7%
Population growth	12.5%	21.1%	Asian	0.7%	2.7%	Divorced/separated	16.1%	14.9%
Median age	36.7	36.1	Hispanic	1.1%	10.6%	Married with children	21.4%	23.7%
Percent Democrat	44.4%	44.5%	Religious observance	44.1%	48.9%	Single with children	11.7%	9.1%
Percent Republican	54.8%	54.5%	Diversity measure	51.8	40.1	Percent over age 65	12.6%	12.9%

Economy & Jobs
Score: 60.7
Rank: 148

INCOME	AREA	U.S. AVG	EMPLOYMENT	AREA	U.S. AVG	EMPLOYING INDUSTRIES	AREA	U.S. AVG
Per capita income	$20,148	$23,235	Unemployment rate	7.9%	4.7%	Largest: Healthcare & Social Assistance		
Household income	$38,443	$46,414	Recent job growth	4.0%	1.3%			
Household income < $25K	33.6%	26.2%	Projected future job growth	15.0%	11.5%	Percent manufacturing	20.5%	15.4%
Household income > $75K	19.3%	25.4%	White collar	52.6%	57.8%	Percent public sector	14.6%	15.7%
Household income growth	13.9%	13.6%	Blue collar	31.4%	25.2%	Percent construction	10.9%	9.9%

Cost of Living
Score: 59.6
Rank: 150

INDEXES & TAXES	AREA	U.S. AVG	HOUSING	AREA	U.S. AVG	NECESSITIES	AREA	U.S. AVG
Cost of Living Index	84.7	100.0	Median home price	$139,600	$220,000	Food Index	101.0	100.0
Buying Power Index	101.7	100.0	Home price appreciation	24.9%	10.1%	Housing Index	58.7	100.0
Income tax rate	6.48%	4.70%	Median rent	$503	$709	Utilities Index	91.8	100.0
Sales tax rate	6.34%	6.58%	Homes owned	67.5%	62.3%	Transportation Index	94.1	100.0
Property tax rate	$5.41	$12.00	Home price ratio	3.6	4.2	Healthcare Index	97.0	100.0
						Miscellaneous Cost Index	99.6	100.0

Climate
Score: 34.2
Rank: 245

TEMPERATURE	AREA	U.S. AVG	PRECIPITATION	AREA	U.S. AVG	COMFORTS & HAZARDS	AREA	U.S. AVG
Average January low	33.9	26.2	Annual inches precipitation	46.0	37.7	July relative humidity	73%	66%
Average July high	92.0	87.4	Annual inches snowfall	2.0	7.0	Annual days mostly sunny	223	208
Annual days > 90°F	64	38	Annual days precipitation	111	109	Annual days with thunderstorms	54	39
Annual days < 32°F	60	89	Annual days rain > 0.5 inches	31	22	Tornado risk score	15	18
Annual days < 0°F	0	6	Annual days snow > 1.5 inches	1	6	Hurricane risk score	42	13

TEMPERATURE	PRECIPITATION	DAYS OF CLOUDS & PRECIPITATION
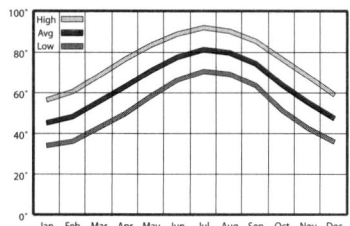	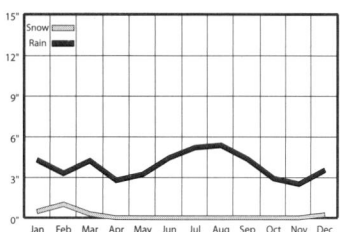	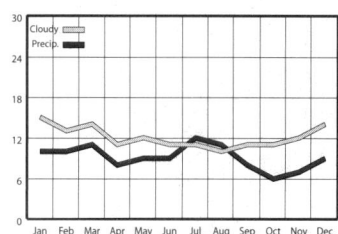

Education
Score: 9.4
Rank: 338

ACHIEVEMENT	AREA	U.S. AVG	PUBLIC SCHOOLS	AREA	U.S. AVG	HIGHER EDUCATION	AREA	U.S. AVG
High school degree	71.9%	82.7%	Expenditures per pupil	$5,125	$5,686	No. 2-year colleges	1	4
2-year college degree	6.1%	6.4%	Student/teacher ratio	14.9	16.7	No. 4-year colleges/universities	3	6
4-year college degree	11.4%	15.7%	Attending public school	89.3%	90.1%	No. highly ranked universities	0	1
Graduate/professional degree	5.4%	8.9%	State SAT score	985*	1021			
			State ACT score	19.5	20.9			

Health & Healthcare
Score: 67.6
Rank: 122

HAZARDS & ILLNESSES	AREA	U.S. AVG	HEALTHCARE	AREA	U.S. AVG	CRIME	AREA	U.S. AVG
Air-quality score	45	37	Physicians per capita	222.4	244.2	Violent crime rate	1,286.4	465.5
Water-quality score	45	52	Hospital beds per capita	599.1	420.0	Change in violent crime rate	13.7%	-2.2%
Pollen/allergy score	67	61	No. teaching hospitals	1	3	Property crime rate	5,733.4	3,517.1
Cancer mortality per capita	220.4	201.9	Cost per doctor visit	$83	$77	Change in property crime rate	-6.5%	-2.1%
Depression days per month	3.7	3.5	Cost per dental visit	$60	$70			
Stress score	81	50						

Crime
Score: 0.5
Rank: 371

Transportation
Score: 54.8
Rank: 170

COMMUTE	AREA	U.S. AVG	INTERCITY SERVICES	AREA	U.S. AVG	AUTOMOTIVE	AREA	U.S. AVG
Average commute time	24.9	27.4	Major airports within 60 miles	1	1	Insurance, annual premium	$1,333	$1,432
Percent commutes > 60 mins.	6.0%	5.9%	Size of regional airport	Large	Large	Gas, cost per gallon	$2.42	$2.49
Commute by auto	80.7%	78.9%	Daily airline activity	846	686	Daily vehicle miles per capita	18.9	24.0
Commute by mass transit	1.0%	1.9%	Amtrak service	Yes	No			
Work at home	1.6%	3.1%						
Mass transit miles per capita	0.96	1.87						

Leisure
Score: 7.8
Rank: 344

DINING & SHOPPING	AREA	U.S. AVG	ENTERTAINMENT	AREA	U.S. AVG	OUTDOOR ACTIVITIES	AREA	U.S. AVG
Restaurant rating	1	2	Professional sports rating	3	4	Golf-course rating	2	4
Outlet mall score	0	42	College sports rating	3	4	Ski-area rating	1	3
No. Starbucks	0	13	Zoo/aquarium rating	1	3	Sq. miles inland water	1	4
No. warehouse clubs	0	2	Amusement park rating	1	3	Miles of coastline	0.0	10.7
			Botanical garden/ arboretum rating	1	4	National Park rating	1	3

Arts & Culture
Score: 12.8
Rank: 325

MEDIA & LIBRARIES	AREA	U.S. AVG	PERFORMING ARTS	AREA	U.S. AVG	MUSEUMS	AREA	U.S. AVG
Arts radio rating	1	3	Classical music rating	3	4	Overall museum rating	5	5
No. public libraries	10	27	Ballet/dance rating	1	3	Art museum rating	3	5
Library volumes per capita	1.85	2.78	Professional theater rating	1	3	Science museum rating	3	5
			University arts programs rating	1	5	Children's museum rating	1	3

Florence–Muscle Shoals, AL

Score: 23.8 **Rank:** 357 **2004 rank:** 269

Profile: Small city
Location: Extreme northwest Alabama along the Tennessee River
Elevation: 540 feet
Time zone: Central Standard Time

PRO	CON
Cost of living	Isolation
Low crime rate	Economic cycles
Entertainment	Arts and culture

Florence is the center of the shoals area of the Tennessee Valley and is adjacent to the more well-known and colorfully named town of Muscle Shoals. The area is business friendly, and located here are several manufacturing industries, including aluminum, rubber, and steel, but the job base has declined from its strongest years. The Cost of Living Index is attractive at 79.1 and home prices are enviable. Crime rates are low for the region. Downtown Florence is typically Southern, attractive, and full of historic interest. The entertainment scene is diverse and is bolstered by its blues roots, brought to life by the W. C. Handy Blues Festival and several recording studios in Muscle Shoals; there is considerable cultural interest here for those who like traditional Southern culture with a mildly funky flair.

The town straddles the Tennessee River in a broad river valley, with low hills to the north and south. The climate is a mix of humid subtropical and continental types, with four seasons; long, warm humid summers; and mild but variable winters.

Population

DEMOGRAPHICS	AREA	U.S. AVG	ETHNIC COMPOSITION	AREA	U.S. AVG	RESIDENT PROFILE	AREA	U.S. AVG
Population	141,063		White	85.6%	79.0%	Single	28.1%	32.4%
Population density per sq. mile	111.6	358.5	Black	12.5%	10.5%	Married	58.3%	52.7%
Population growth	7.4%	21.1%	Asian	0.4%	2.7%	Divorced/separated	13.5%	14.9%
Median age	39.3	36.1	Hispanic	1.1%	10.6%	Married with children	22.6%	23.7%
Percent Democrat	41.3%	44.5%	Religious observance	60.6%	48.9%	Single with children	7.7%	9.1%
Percent Republican	57.9%	54.5%	Diversity measure	26.6	40.1	Percent over age 65	15.9%	12.9%

Economy & Jobs
Score: 44.4
Rank: 209

INCOME	AREA	U.S. AVG	EMPLOYMENT	AREA	U.S. AVG	EMPLOYING INDUSTRIES	AREA	U.S. AVG
Per capita income	$20,503	$23,235	Unemployment rate	4.9%	4.7%	Largest: Manufacturing		
Household income	$36,749	$46,414	Recent job growth	1.9%	1.3%			
Household income < $25K	34.9%	26.2%	Projected future job growth	7.5%	11.5%	Percent manufacturing	22.1%	15.4%
Household income > $75K	18.0%	25.4%	White collar	50.9%	57.8%	Percent public sector	15.9%	15.7%
Household income growth	12.0%	13.6%	Blue collar	34.2%	25.2%	Percent construction	12.1%	9.9%

Cost of Living
Score: 77.5
Rank: 85

INDEXES & TAXES	AREA	U.S. AVG	HOUSING	AREA	U.S. AVG	NECESSITIES	AREA	U.S. AVG
Cost of Living Index	79.1	100.0	Median home price	$126,400	$220,000	Food Index	92.7	100.0
Buying Power Index	104.1	100.0	Home price appreciation	21.2%	10.1%	Housing Index	55.0	100.0
Income tax rate	5.00%	4.70%	Median rent	$506	$709	Utilities Index	86.0	100.0
Sales tax rate	8.19%	6.58%	Homes owned	66.5%	62.3%	Transportation Index	91.7	100.0
Property tax rate	$3.96	$12.00	Home price ratio	3.4	4.2	Healthcare Index	88.0	100.0
						Miscellaneous Cost Index	96.3	100.0

Climate
Score: 17.1
Rank: 309

TEMPERATURE	AREA	U.S. AVG
Average January low	31.3	26.2
Average July high	90.2	87.4
Annual days > 90°F	38	38
Annual days < 32°F	65	89
Annual days < 0°F	0	6

PRECIPITATION	AREA	U.S. AVG
Annual inches precipitation	52.0	37.7
Annual inches snowfall	3.0	7.0
Annual days precipitation	121	109
Annual days rain > 0.5 inches	36	22
Annual days snow > 1.5 inches	2	6

COMFORTS & HAZARDS	AREA	U.S. AVG
July relative humidity	73%	66%
Annual days mostly sunny	207	208
Annual days with thunderstorms	58	39
Tornado risk score	19	18
Hurricane risk score	12	13

TEMPERATURE

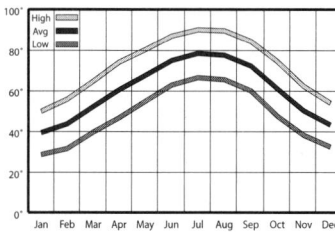

PRECIPITATION

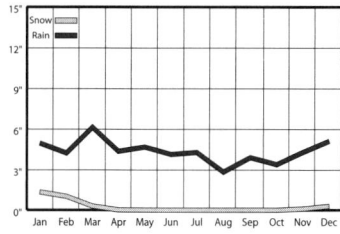

DAYS OF CLOUDS & PRECIPITATION

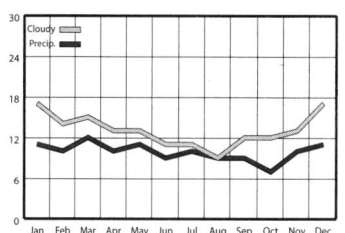

Education
Score: 11.5
Rank: 330

ACHIEVEMENT	AREA	U.S. AVG
High school degree	75.4%	82.7%
2-year college degree	4.6%	6.4%
4-year college degree	10.9%	15.7%
Graduate/professional degree	6.1%	8.9%

PUBLIC SCHOOLS	AREA	U.S. AVG
Expenditures per pupil	$5,025	$5,686
Student/teacher ratio	16.0	16.7
Attending public school	92.7%	90.1%
State SAT score	1126	1021
State ACT score	20.2*	20.9

HIGHER EDUCATION	AREA	U.S. AVG
No. 2-year colleges	1	4
No. 4-year colleges/universities	2	6
No. highly ranked universities	0	1

Health & Healthcare
Score: 73.0
Rank: 102

HAZARDS & ILLNESSES	AREA	U.S. AVG
Air-quality score	43	37
Water-quality score	48	52
Pollen/allergy score	67	61
Cancer mortality per capita	217.7	201.9
Depression days per month	4.7	3.5
Stress score	51	50

HEALTHCARE	AREA	U.S. AVG
Physicians per capita	175.3	244.2
Hospital beds per capita	713.9	420.0
No. teaching hospitals	0	3
Cost per doctor visit	$53	$77
Cost per dental visit	$55	$70

Crime
Score: 80.2
Rank: 75

CRIME	AREA	U.S. AVG
Violent crime rate	375.2	465.5
Change in violent crime rate	31.3%	-2.2%
Property crime rate	2,980.9	3,517.1
Change in property crime rate	-9.5%	-2.1%

Transportation
Score: 7.8
Rank: 345

COMMUTE	AREA	U.S. AVG
Average commute time	25.3	27.4
Percent commutes > 60 mins.	6.2%	5.9%
Commute by auto	86.0%	78.9%
Commute by mass transit	0.2%	1.9%
Work at home	1.7%	3.1%
Mass transit miles per capita	0.17	1.87

INTERCITY SERVICES	AREA	U.S. AVG
Major airports within 60 miles	0	1
Size of regional airport	Small	Large
Daily airline activity	152	686
Amtrak service	No	No

AUTOMOTIVE	AREA	U.S. AVG
Insurance, annual premium	$945	$1,432
Gas, cost per gallon	$2.46	$2.49
Daily vehicle miles per capita	28.2	24.0

Leisure
Score: 33.7
Rank: 247

DINING & SHOPPING	AREA	U.S. AVG
Restaurant rating	1	2
Outlet mall score	10	42
No. Starbucks	0	13
No. warehouse clubs	1	2

ENTERTAINMENT	AREA	U.S. AVG
Professional sports rating	2	4
College sports rating	3	4
Zoo/aquarium rating	1	3
Amusement park rating	1	3
Botanical garden/ arboretum rating	1	4

OUTDOOR ACTIVITIES	AREA	U.S. AVG
Golf-course rating	2	4
Ski-area rating	1	3
Sq. miles inland water	6	4
Miles of coastline	0.0	10.7
National Park rating	2	3

Arts & Culture
Score: 13.4
Rank: 323

MEDIA & LIBRARIES	AREA	U.S. AVG
Arts radio rating	1	3
No. public libraries	9	27
Library volumes per capita	2.05	2.78

PERFORMING ARTS	AREA	U.S. AVG
Classical music rating	1	4
Ballet/dance rating	1	3
Professional theater rating	1	3
University arts programs rating	4	5

MUSEUMS	AREA	U.S. AVG
Overall museum rating	3	5
Art museum rating	3	5
Science museum rating	1	5
Children's museum rating	1	3

Fond du Lac, WI

Score: 65.5 Rank: 136 2004 rank: not ranked

Profile: Small industrial town
Location: East-central Wisconsin, at the south end of Lake Winnebago
Elevation: 750 feet
Time zone: Central Standard Time

PRO	CON
Nearby recreation	Entertainment
Small-town feel	Low ethnic diversity
Diverse economy	Harsh winters

Along with its agricultural and recreational base, Fond du Lac is an industrial town specializing in forest products, machine tools, and boat motors. It is one of several typically Wisconsin towns on Lake Winnebago in the attractive and prosperous Fox River Valley (Oshkosh–Neenah [p. 597] and Appleton [p. 175] are others listed in this book), and reflects a strong 19th-century heritage with a few historic neighborhoods displaying early wealth. Downtown is clean and typically Midwestern, with lots of trees and a mix of older and modern structures. The University of Wisconsin operates a Fond du Lac campus, offering 4-year degree programs and feeding the larger UW system. Nearby areas offer abundant summer and winter recreation.

The area immediately surrounding the glacial Lake Winnebago is mostly flat and wooded with some agricultural areas, becoming hillier towards the south. Summers are cool and pleasant—becoming humid on occasion—normally with cool evenings. Most summer precipitation occurs as thunderstorms. Winters can be rigorous with periods of bitter cold, although these periods are dry and often accompanied by sunshine. Snow and snow cover are abundant. First freeze is early October; last is mid-May.

DEMOGRAPHICS	AREA	U.S. AVG	ETHNIC COMPOSITION	AREA	U.S. AVG	RESIDENT PROFILE	AREA	U.S. AVG
Population	98,791		White	95.7%	79.0%	Single	30.8%	32.4%
Population density per sq. mile	136.7	358.5	Black	1.1%	10.5%	Married	56.8%	52.7%
Population growth	9.7%	21.1%	Asian	0.9%	2.7%	Divorced/separated	12.4%	14.9%
Median age	38.2	36.1	Hispanic	2.6%	10.6%	Married with children	25.7%	23.7%
Percent Democrat	36.2%	44.5%	Religious observance	67.7%	48.9%	Single with children	6.8%	9.1%
Percent Republican	62.8%	54.5%	Diversity measure	13.0	40.1	Percent over age 65	14.4%	12.9%

Economy & Jobs
Score: 34.2
Rank: 246

INCOME	AREA	U.S. AVG	EMPLOYMENT	AREA	U.S. AVG	EMPLOYING INDUSTRIES	AREA	U.S. AVG
Per capita income	$23,386	$23,235	Unemployment rate	4.4%	4.7%	Largest: Manufacturing		
Household income	$51,308	$46,414	Recent job growth	0.1%	1.3%			
Household income < $25K	20.8%	26.2%	Projected future job growth	3.9%	11.5%	Percent manufacturing	25.1%	15.4%
Household income > $75K	24.9%	25.4%	White collar	46.8%	57.8%	Percent public sector	10.7%	15.7%
Household income growth	12.6%	13.6%	Blue collar	34.5%	25.2%	Percent construction	9.4%	9.9%

Cost of Living
Score: 50.5
Rank: 185

INDEXES & TAXES	AREA	U.S. AVG	HOUSING	AREA	U.S. AVG	NECESSITIES	AREA	U.S. AVG
Cost of Living Index	83.8	100.0	Median home price	$131,500	$220,000	Food Index	98.1	100.0
Buying Power Index	137.2	100.0	Home price appreciation	24.7%	10.1%	Housing Index	62.4	100.0
Income tax rate	6.93%	4.70%	Median rent	$584	$709	Utilities Index	99.3	100.0
Sales tax rate	5.00%	6.58%	Homes owned	68.9%	62.3%	Transportation Index	101.1	100.0
Property tax rate	$16.70	$12.00	Home price ratio	2.6	4.2	Healthcare Index	102.6	100.0
						Miscellaneous Cost Index	93.9	100.0

Climate
Score: 26.2
Rank: 275

TEMPERATURE	AREA	U.S. AVG	PRECIPITATION	AREA	U.S. AVG	COMFORTS & HAZARDS	AREA	U.S. AVG
Average January low	7.9	26.2	Annual inches precipitation	28.3	37.7	July relative humidity	62%	66%
Average July high	82.0	87.4	Annual inches snowfall	36.0	7.0	Annual days mostly sunny	195	208
Annual days > 90°F	7	38	Annual days precipitation	120	109	Annual days with thunderstorms	35	39
Annual days < 32°F	163	89	Annual days rain > 0.5 inches	16	22	Tornado risk score	3	18
Annual days < 0°F	25	6	Annual days snow > 1.5 inches	11	6	Hurricane risk score	1	13

TEMPERATURE

PRECIPITATION

DAYS OF CLOUDS & PRECIPITATION

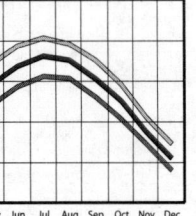

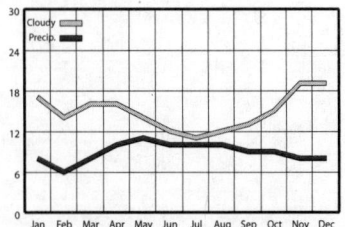

ACHIEVEMENT	AREA	U.S. AVG	PUBLIC SCHOOLS	AREA	U.S. AVG	HIGHER EDUCATION	AREA	U.S. AVG
High school degree	84.3%	82.7%	Expenditures per pupil	$5,942	$5,686	No. 2-year colleges	1	4
2-year college degree	8.3%	6.4%	Student/teacher ratio	14.1	16.7	No. 4-year colleges/universities	2	6
4-year college degree	12.1%	15.7%	Attending public school	84.2%	90.1%	No. highly ranked universities	0	1
Graduate/professional degree	5.0%	8.9%	State SAT score	1188	1021			
			State ACT score	22.2*	20.9			

Education
Score: 33.7
Rank: 248

HAZARDS & ILLNESSES	AREA	U.S. AVG	HEALTHCARE	AREA	U.S. AVG	CRIME	AREA	U.S. AVG
Air-quality score	52	37	Physicians per capita	157.4	244.2	Violent crime rate	126.1	465.5
Water-quality score	23	52	Hospital beds per capita	269.3	420.0	Change in violent crime rate	26.7%	-2.2%
Pollen/allergy score	36	61	No. teaching hospitals	0	3	Property crime rate	1,824.5	3,517.1
Cancer mortality per capita	197.0	201.9	Cost per doctor visit	$88	$77	Change in property crime rate	-7.7%	-2.1%
Depression days per month	2.2	3.5	Cost per dental visit	$58	$70			
Stress score	20	50						

Health & Healthcare
Score: 78.3
Rank: 82

Crime
Score: 96.3
Rank: 15

COMMUTE	AREA	U.S. AVG	INTERCITY SERVICES	AREA	U.S. AVG	AUTOMOTIVE	AREA	U.S. AVG
Average commute time	20.6	27.4	Major airports within 60 miles	1	1	Insurance, annual premium	$930	$1,432
Percent commutes > 60 mins.	3.9%	5.9%	Size of regional airport	Medium	Large	Gas, cost per gallon	$2.55	$2.49
Commute by auto	80.9%	78.9%	Daily airline activity	373	686	Daily vehicle miles per capita	17.8	24.0
Commute by mass transit	0.5%	1.9%	Amtrak service	No	No			
Work at home	3.5%	3.1%						
Mass transit miles per capita	0.47	1.87						

Transportation
Score: 66.3
Rank: 127

DINING & SHOPPING	AREA	U.S. AVG	ENTERTAINMENT	AREA	U.S. AVG	OUTDOOR ACTIVITIES	AREA	U.S. AVG
Restaurant rating	1	2	Professional sports rating	1	4	Golf-course rating	1	4
Outlet mall score	18	42	College sports rating	1	4	Ski-area rating	4	3
No. Starbucks	0	13	Zoo/aquarium rating	1	3	Sq. miles inland water	4	4
No. warehouse clubs	0	2	Amusement park rating	1	3	Miles of coastline	0.0	10.7
			Botanical garden/ arboretum rating	2	4	National Park rating	4	3

Leisure
Score: 25.1
Rank: 279

MEDIA & LIBRARIES	AREA	U.S. AVG	PERFORMING ARTS	AREA	U.S. AVG	MUSEUMS	AREA	U.S. AVG
Arts radio rating	1	3	Classical music rating	1	4	Overall museum rating	2	5
No. public libraries	6	27	Ballet/dance rating	1	3	Art museum rating	1	5
Library volumes per capita	3.84	2.78	Professional theater rating	1	3	Science museum rating	4	5
			University arts programs rating	1	5	Children's museum rating	1	3

Arts & Culture
Score: 5.9
Rank: 351

Fort Collins–Loveland, CO

Score: 89.8   **Rank:** 8   **2004 rank:** 128

Profile: Small town complex/college town
Location: Northern Colorado along the Front Range, 25 miles south of the Wyoming border
Elevation: 5,004 feet
Time zone: Mountain Standard Time

PRO
Attractive downtown
Nearby mountains
Educated population

CON
Home prices
Economic cycles
Cold winters

Fort Collins is an agricultural and high-tech center and college town at the northern end of Colorado's Front Range. Colorado State University, a diversified university with an agricultural base, provides some amenities, a nice campus, and ethnic diversity, but overall the town is more conservative than nearby Boulder. The downtown is a model college town with well-kept Victorian-era structures, a lively entertainment scene, and plenty to do. A significant high-tech base, led by Hewlett-Packard but with many smaller players, lies mostly east of town, while attractive residential neighborhoods lie mostly west. All have a view of the main Rocky Mountain ridges west, and with the exception of a few winter blasts, the climate goes well with the attractive outdoor setting. Recent consolidations at HP and Eastman Kodak have

led to some job dislocations, but overall the economy is healthy and high-paying jobs are numerous. Housing and living costs, while on the rise, are still attractive. The area is increasingly well rounded, intellectually stimulating, and close enough to Denver that new migrants don't feel too disconnected from big-city life and services. Currently the area is absorbing considerable growth and, so far, doing it fairly well.

Fort Collins isn't the whole story—Loveland to the south is quieter but prosperous and features an excellent downtown area and surrounding inner neighborhoods. The base is also a typical northern Colorado mix of high tech and agriculture. Housing is somewhat less expensive and residents of Loveland have convenient access to Fort Collins 10 miles north. The Rocky Mountain National Park and Estes Park (a town, not a park) to the west provide ample recreational opportunities. As a whole, the Fort Collins–Loveland area offers a nice package with no strong negatives, hence the strong and improved ranking.

Fort Collins is at the western edge of the high prairie grassland just against the base of the Front Range of the Rockies. The western horizon is spectacular with steep creek and river valleys descending into the area. Summer days are warm and evenings are cool, thanks to the mountain elevation. Winters can be quite cold, with temperatures well below zero with strong inflows of Canadian air; wind makes the air seem colder. First freeze is early October; last is late May.

Population

DEMOGRAPHICS	AREA	U.S. AVG	ETHNIC COMPOSITION	AREA	U.S. AVG	RESIDENT PROFILE	AREA	U.S. AVG
Population	270,414		White	90.1%	79.0%	Single	33.2%	32.4%
Population density per sq. mile	104.0	358.5	Black	0.9%	10.5%	Married	54.7%	52.7%
Population growth	45.3%	21.1%	Asian	1.9%	2.7%	Divorced/separated	12.0%	14.9%
Median age	34.1	36.1	Hispanic	9.2%	10.6%	Married with children	24.7%	23.7%
Percent Democrat	46.6%	44.5%	Religious observance	39.3%	48.9%	Single with children	7.0%	9.1%
Percent Republican	51.8%	54.5%	Diversity measure	32.1	40.1	Percent over age 65	9.9%	12.9%

Economy & Jobs
Score: 75.4
Rank: 93

INCOME	AREA	U.S. AVG	EMPLOYMENT	AREA	U.S. AVG	EMPLOYING INDUSTRIES	AREA	U.S. AVG
Per capita income	$28,302	$23,235	Unemployment rate	4.4%	4.7%	Largest: Manufacturing		
Household income	$57,558	$46,414	Recent job growth	1.0%	1.3%			
Household income ‹ $25K	18.7%	26.2%	Projected future job growth	22.9%	11.5%	Percent manufacturing	11.3%	15.4%
Household income › $75K	35.1%	25.4%	White collar	64.9%	57.8%	Percent public sector	16.0%	15.7%
Household income growth	18.3%	13.6%	Blue collar	20.7%	25.2%	Percent construction	9.4%	9.9%

Cost of Living
Score: 33.2
Rank: 248

INDEXES & TAXES	AREA	U.S. AVG	HOUSING	AREA	U.S. AVG	NECESSITIES	AREA	U.S. AVG
Cost of Living Index	102.8	100.0	Median home price	$237,500	$220,000	Food Index	108.1	100.0
Buying Power Index	125.5	100.0	Home price appreciation	26.2%	10.1%	Housing Index	86.2	100.0
Income tax rate	5.00%	4.70%	Median rent	$802	$709	Utilities Index	95.6	100.0
Sales tax rate	6.70%	6.58%	Homes owned	63.3%	62.3%	Transportation Index	101.0	100.0
Property tax rate	$6.97	$12.00	Home price ratio	4.1	4.2	Healthcare Index	107.8	100.0
						Miscellaneous Cost Index	97.0	100.0

Climate
Score: 54.8
Rank: 168

TEMPERATURE	AREA	U.S. AVG	PRECIPITATION	AREA	U.S. AVG	COMFORTS & HAZARDS	AREA	U.S. AVG
Average January low	16.2	26.2	Annual inches precipitation	16.0	37.7	July relative humidity	53%	66%
Average July high	87.4	87.4	Annual inches snowfall	60.0	7.0	Annual days mostly sunny	246	208
Annual days › 90°F	32	38	Annual days precipitation	88	109	Annual days with thunderstorms	41	39
Annual days ‹ 32°F	163	89	Annual days rain › 0.5 inches	7	22	Tornado risk score	25	18
Annual days ‹ 0°F	10	6	Annual days snow › 1.5 inches	13	6	Hurricane risk score	0	13

TEMPERATURE

PRECIPITATION

DAYS OF CLOUDS & PRECIPITATION

Education
Score: 93.9
Rank: 24

ACHIEVEMENT	AREA	U.S. AVG	PUBLIC SCHOOLS	AREA	U.S. AVG	HIGHER EDUCATION	AREA	U.S. AVG
High school degree	92.5%	82.7%	Expenditures per pupil	$4,890	$5,686	No. 2-year colleges	1	4
2-year college degree	7.2%	6.4%	Student/teacher ratio	18.6	16.7	No. 4-year colleges/universities	1	6
4-year college degree	25.5%	15.7%	Attending public school	92.8%	90.1%	No. highly ranked universities	1	1
Graduate/professional degree	14.6%	8.9%	State SAT score	1122	1021			
			State ACT score	20.3*	20.9			

Health & Healthcare
Score: 47.1
Rank: 199

Crime
Score: 88.5
Rank: 44

HAZARDS & ILLNESSES	AREA	U.S. AVG	HEALTHCARE	AREA	U.S. AVG	CRIME	AREA	U.S. AVG
Air-quality score	34	37	Physicians per capita	202.5	244.2	Violent crime rate	241.4	465.5
Water-quality score	99	52	Hospital beds per capita	186.4	420.0	Change in violent crime rate	12.8%	-2.2%
Pollen/allergy score	80	61	No. teaching hospitals	1	3	Property crime rate	3,006.3	3,517.1
Cancer mortality per capita	137.2	201.9	Cost per doctor visit	$77	$77	Change in property crime rate	-7.9%	-2.1%
Depression days per month	2.9	3.5	Cost per dental visit	$74	$70			
Stress score	23	50						

COMMUTE	AREA	U.S. AVG	INTERCITY SERVICES	AREA	U.S. AVG	AUTOMOTIVE	AREA	U.S. AVG
Average commute time	23.3	27.4	Major airports within 60 miles	1	1	Insurance, annual premium	$1,323	$1,432
Percent commutes > 60 mins.	6.0%	5.9%	Size of regional airport	Large	Large	Gas, cost per gallon	$2.46	$2.49
Commute by auto	77.9%	78.9%	Daily airline activity	812	686	Daily vehicle miles per capita	21.5	24.0
Commute by mass transit	0.8%	1.9%	Amtrak service	No	No			
Work at home	5.2%	3.1%						
Mass transit miles per capita	0.79	1.87						

Transportation
Score: 65.2
Rank: 131

DINING & SHOPPING	AREA	U.S. AVG	ENTERTAINMENT	AREA	U.S. AVG	OUTDOOR ACTIVITIES	AREA	U.S. AVG
Restaurant rating	1	2	Professional sports rating	4	4	Golf-course rating	2	4
Outlet mall score	101	42	College sports rating	4	4	Ski-area rating	10	3
No. Starbucks	9	13	Zoo/aquarium rating	1	3	Sq. miles inland water	4	4
No. warehouse clubs	1	2	Amusement park rating	1	3	Miles of coastline	0.0	10.7
			Botanical garden/ arboretum rating	1	4	National Park rating	10	3

Leisure
Score: 75.7
Rank: 91

MEDIA & LIBRARIES	AREA	U.S. AVG	PERFORMING ARTS	AREA	U.S. AVG	MUSEUMS	AREA	U.S. AVG
Arts radio rating	1	3	Classical music rating	3	4	Overall museum rating	9	5
No. public libraries	7	27	Ballet/dance rating	3	3	Art museum rating	4	5
Library volumes per capita	3.03	2.78	Professional theater rating	1	3	Science museum rating	8	5
			University arts programs rating	5	5	Children's museum rating	1	3

Arts & Culture
Score: 38.0
Rank: 232

Fort Lauderdale–Pompano Beach–Deerfield, FL

Score: 61.8   **Rank:** 158   **2004 rank:** 57

Profile: Large-city complex
Location: South Atlantic Coast of Florida, 25 miles north of Miami
Elevation: 12 feet
Time zone: Eastern Standard Time

PRO
Entertainment
Diverse economy
Winter climate

CON
Cost of living
Crowding and sprawl
Tourist impact

Fort Lauderdale is a large, cosmopolitan city on the southern Atlantic Coast long famous as a destination for tourists and college students, although the annual college spring-break migration has started to go elsewhere. Broad sandy beaches and high-rise complexes line the coast and barrier islands. Stretching to the edge of the Everglades are miles of inland sections containing residential areas mixed with diversified industry and commerce centered on tourism and the boating industry, but also with a considerable manufacturing and commercial presence. There are some corporate headquarters operations, including AutoNation, Office Depot, and DHL. The economy is diverse for the state. Although there are no major universities, there are many elements of college-town life, especially nightlife. Nearby Miami has more amenities, but Fort Lauderdale has a few of its own, including the Florida Panthers hockey team and a full-scale commercial airport. The Cost of Living Index of 129.4 has risen substantially and is third highest in the state, although in typical Florida fashion, costs vary considerably by location within the area. There are some excellent planned developments to the west, such as the planned community of Weston, and many larger middle-class enclaves such as Coral Springs and Sunrise, with extensive home and retail development, in which some might feel a bit lost. Downtown Fort Lauderdale features modern high-rise towers and some older typical Florida Art Deco structures, and it has experienced a residential boom, now slowing, with a number of high-rise condo developments. Pompano Beach, to the north, is a typical mid-size Florida beach town that had seen better days but has re-emerged as a hot real estate market with new developments along the coast; inland areas, like many such cities, lag. Deerfield (actually Deerfield Beach) fits a similar profile, although it is just south of the far more conspicuous and upscale Boca Raton. Urban sprawl has consumed most of the available land and led to such problems as traffic and air quality. More than many other Florida coastal cities, the entire area has a prosperous and middle-class feel, with more money being earned locally than brought in from somewhere else. It is a fun place to live if one can accept the downsides.

The terrain is typical for a city on Florida's east coast: Broad, flat, sandy barrier islands and level terrain give way to tropical forests and inland marshes. Palm trees are abundant. A system of rivers, inlets, and small bays—more inland waterways than any other Florida city—divides the area and provides interesting settings for homes and attractions. Residents expect a long, warm summer and abundant rainfall followed by a mild, dry winter. Inland locations are hotter in summer. Strong thunderstorms are frequent and hurricanes are a significant risk.

Population

DEMOGRAPHICS	AREA	U.S. AVG	ETHNIC COMPOSITION	AREA	U.S. AVG	RESIDENT PROFILE	AREA	U.S. AVG
Population	1,750,486		White	65.4%	79.0%	Single	33.8%	32.4%
Population density per sq. mile	1452.2	358.5	Black	23.7%	10.5%	Married	49.1%	52.7%
Population growth	39.4%	21.1%	Asian	2.8%	2.7%	Divorced/separated	17.1%	14.9%
Median age	38.4	36.1	Hispanic	21.5%	10.6%	Married with children	20.4%	23.7%
Percent Democrat	64.2%	44.5%	Religious observance	45.9%	48.9%	Single with children	9.0%	9.1%
Percent Republican	34.6%	54.5%	Diversity measure	67.7	40.1	Percent over age 65	14.7%	12.9%

Economy & Jobs
Score: 83.2
Rank: 64

INCOME	AREA	U.S. AVG	EMPLOYMENT	AREA	U.S. AVG	EMPLOYING INDUSTRIES	AREA	U.S. AVG
Per capita income	$26,151	$23,235	Unemployment rate	3.8%	4.7%	Largest: Healthcare & Social Assistance		
Household income	$47,167	$46,414	Recent job growth	4.2%	1.3%			
Household income < $25K	25.2%	26.2%	Projected future job growth	17.4%	11.5%	Percent manufacturing	9.2%	15.4%
Household income > $75K	28.4%	25.4%	White collar	64.9%	57.8%	Percent public sector	11.8%	15.7%
Household income growth	13.1%	13.6%	Blue collar	18.7%	25.2%	Percent construction	9.5%	9.9%

Cost of Living
Score: 11.2
Rank: 331

INDEXES & TAXES	AREA	U.S. AVG	HOUSING	AREA	U.S. AVG	NECESSITIES	AREA	U.S. AVG
Cost of Living Index	129.4	100.0	Median home price	$379,200	$220,000	Food Index	107.9	100.0
Buying Power Index	81.7	100.0	Home price appreciation	145.7%	10.1%	Housing Index	124.5	100.0
Income tax rate	0.00%	4.70%	Median rent	$1,054	$709	Utilities Index	100.3	100.0
Sales tax rate	6.00%	6.58%	Homes owned	61.8%	62.3%	Transportation Index	110.4	100.0
Property tax rate	$16.65	$12.00	Home price ratio	8.0	4.2	Healthcare Index	115.7	100.0
						Miscellaneous Cost Index	107.0	100.0

Climate
Score: 80.5
Rank: 74

TEMPERATURE	AREA	U.S. AVG	PRECIPITATION	AREA	U.S. AVG	COMFORTS & HAZARDS	AREA	U.S. AVG
Average January low	58.7	26.2	Annual inches precipitation	60.0	37.7	July relative humidity	75%	66%
Average July high	89.9	87.4	Annual inches snowfall	0.0	7.0	Annual days mostly sunny	248	208
Annual days > 90°F	30	38	Annual days precipitation	129	109	Annual days with thunderstorms	75	39
Annual days < 32°F	0	89	Annual days rain > 0.5 inches	32	22	Tornado risk score	61	18
Annual days < 0°F	0	6	Annual days snow > 1.5 inches	0	6	Hurricane risk score	100	13

TEMPERATURE

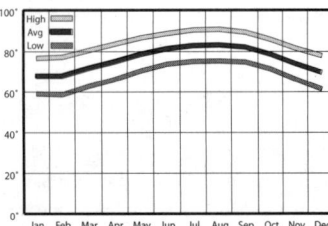

PRECIPITATION

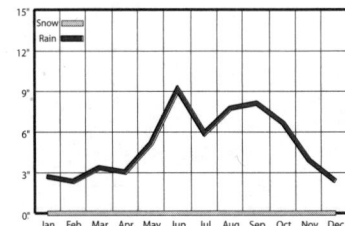

DAYS OF CLOUDS & PRECIPITATION

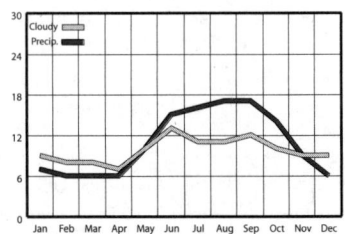

Education
Score: 50.0
Rank: 188

ACHIEVEMENT	AREA	U.S. AVG	PUBLIC SCHOOLS	AREA	U.S. AVG	HIGHER EDUCATION	AREA	U.S. AVG
High school degree	82.2%	82.7%	Expenditures per pupil	$5,227	$5,686	No. 2-year colleges	9	4
2-year college degree	7.5%	6.4%	Student/teacher ratio	21.5	16.7	No. 4-year colleges/universities	9	6
4-year college degree	16.1%	15.7%	Attending public school	87.3%	90.1%	No. highly ranked universities	0	1
Graduate/professional degree	8.9%	8.9%	State SAT score	993*	1021			
			State ACT score	20.3	20.9			

Health & Healthcare
Score: 8.3
Rank: 342

HAZARDS & ILLNESSES	AREA	U.S. AVG	HEALTHCARE	AREA	U.S. AVG	CRIME	AREA	U.S. AVG
Air-quality score	8	37	Physicians per capita	223.9	244.2	Violent crime rate	590.5	465.5
Water-quality score	50	52	Hospital beds per capita	418.6	420.0	Change in violent crime rate	-0.6%	-2.2%
Pollen/allergy score	49	61	No. teaching hospitals	7	3	Property crime rate	3,651.7	3,517.1
Cancer mortality per capita	239.8	201.9	Cost per doctor visit	$92	$77	Change in property crime rate	1.0%	-2.1%
Depression days per month	3.4	3.5	Cost per dental visit	$90	$70			
Stress score	69	50						

Crime
Score: 36.4
Rank: 238

Transportation
Score: 59.9
Rank: 151

COMMUTE	AREA	U.S. AVG	INTERCITY SERVICES	AREA	U.S. AVG	AUTOMOTIVE	AREA	U.S. AVG
Average commute time	29.9	27.4	Major airports within 60 miles	4	1	Insurance, annual premium	$2,305	$1,432
Percent commutes > 60 mins.	7.2%	5.9%	Size of regional airport	Large	Large	Gas, cost per gallon	$2.62	$2.49
Commute by auto	80.2%	78.9%	Daily airline activity	1262	686	Daily vehicle miles per capita	26.3	24.0
Commute by mass transit	2.2%	1.9%	Amtrak service	Yes	No			
Work at home	3.0%	3.1%						
Mass transit miles per capita	2.23	1.87						

Leisure Score: 82.4 Rank: 66	DINING & SHOPPING	AREA	U.S. AVG	ENTERTAINMENT	AREA	U.S. AVG	OUTDOOR ACTIVITIES	AREA	U.S. AVG
	Restaurant rating	1	2	Professional sports rating	8	4	Golf-course rating	8	4
	Outlet mall score	267	42	College sports rating	3	4	Ski-area rating	1	3
	No. Starbucks	28	13	Zoo/aquarium rating	2	3	Sq. miles inland water	3	4
	No. warehouse clubs	7	2	Amusement park rating	3	3	Miles of coastline	24.8	10.7
				Botanical garden/ arboretum rating	1	4	National Park rating	5	3

Arts & Culture Score: 67.4 Rank: 122	MEDIA & LIBRARIES	AREA	U.S. AVG	PERFORMING ARTS	AREA	U.S. AVG	MUSEUMS	AREA	U.S. AVG
	Arts radio rating	3	3	Classical music rating	6	4	Overall museum rating	7	5
	No. public libraries	41	27	Ballet/dance rating	3	3	Art museum rating	7	5
	Library volumes per capita	1.61	2.78	Professional theater rating	3	3	Science museum rating	7	5
				University arts programs rating	6	5	Children's museum rating	5	3

Fort Smith, AR-OK

Score: 34.2   Rank: 326   2004 rank: 322

Profile: Mid-size city
Location: Extreme western Arkansas at Oklahoma border in Arkansas River Valley
Elevation: 463 feet
Time zone: Central Standard Time

PRO	CON
Cost of living	Isolation
Nearby mountains	Arts and culture
Air quality	Low educational attainment

Fort Smith is a small town with Old West flavor located in a flat valley along the Arkansas River. Major industries include light manufacturing and natural gas, and major employers include the nearby Fort Chaffee military installation. The economy is steady with somewhat above-average job-growth prospects, and the Cost of Living Index (76.2) and median home price ($111,600) are probably among the biggest attractions. The downtown has some historic sites and districts. However, there isn't much to do. The town, like many in the region, mixes a Southern and Western feel and culture. Aside from outdoor recreation in the Ozarks just to the north, most amenities and city services are available in Tulsa, 120 miles to the west, and a variety of services and activities are available in the Fayetteville–Springdale–Rogers area 50 miles north.

Local terrain is hilly with flat, fertile rivers and creek bottoms. The Ozarks rise to 1,500 feet in the north and 3,000 feet in the south with areas of national forest and mountain lakes. The warm summers are suitable for growing fruit and wine grapes. Winters are mild with average daytime temperatures above freezing.

Population	DEMOGRAPHICS	AREA	U.S. AVG	ETHNIC COMPOSITION	AREA	U.S. AVG	RESIDENT PROFILE	AREA	U.S. AVG
	Population	282,729		White	81.6%	79.0%	Single	26.0%	32.4%
	Population density per sq. mile	70.7	358.5	Black	3.7%	10.5%	Married	57.6%	52.7%
	Population growth	21.1%	21.1%	Asian	2.1%	2.7%	Divorced/separated	16.4%	14.9%
	Median age	36.3	36.1	Hispanic	5.6%	10.6%	Married with children	24.9%	23.7%
	Percent Democrat	37.3%	44.5%	Religious observance	59.1%	48.9%	Single with children	9.0%	9.1%
	Percent Republican	61.9%	54.5%	Diversity measure	38.5	40.1	Percent over age 65	13.3%	12.9%

Economy & Jobs Score: 71.7 Rank: 107	INCOME	AREA	U.S. AVG	EMPLOYMENT	AREA	U.S. AVG	EMPLOYING INDUSTRIES	AREA	U.S. AVG
	Per capita income	$18,436	$23,235	Unemployment rate	4.5%	4.7%	Largest: Manufacturing		
	Household income	$36,179	$46,414	Recent job growth	3.0%	1.3%			
	Household income < $25K	34.5%	26.2%	Projected future job growth	15.6%	11.5%	Percent manufacturing	25.7%	15.4%
	Household income > $75K	15.5%	25.4%	White collar	47.2%	57.8%	Percent public sector	12.9%	15.7%
	Household income growth	15.1%	13.6%	Blue collar	36.3%	25.2%	Percent construction	10.6%	9.9%

Cost of Living Score: 55.1 Rank: 168	INDEXES & TAXES	AREA	U.S. AVG	HOUSING	AREA	U.S. AVG	NECESSITIES	AREA	U.S. AVG
	Cost of Living Index	76.2	100.0	Median home price	$111,600	$220,000	Food Index	89.3	100.0
	Buying Power Index	106.4	100.0	Home price appreciation	23.3%	10.1%	Housing Index	47.0	100.0
	Income tax rate	7.00%	4.70%	Median rent	$488	$709	Utilities Index	87.3	100.0
	Sales tax rate	8.64%	6.58%	Homes owned	64.2%	62.3%	Transportation Index	93.1	100.0
	Property tax rate	$7.24	$12.00	Home price ratio	3.1	4.2	Healthcare Index	85.7	100.0
							Miscellaneous Cost Index	95.7	100.0

Climate

Score: 47.9
Rank: 194

TEMPERATURE	AREA	U.S. AVG
Average January low	28.0	26.2
Average July high	93.8	87.4
Annual days > 90°F	65	38
Annual days < 32°F	80	89
Annual days < 0°F	0	6

PRECIPITATION	AREA	U.S. AVG
Annual inches precipitation	42.0	37.7
Annual inches snowfall	6.0	7.0
Annual days precipitation	96	109
Annual days rain > 0.5 inches	26	22
Annual days snow > 1.5 inches	3	6

COMFORTS & HAZARDS	AREA	U.S. AVG
July relative humidity	68%	66%
Annual days mostly sunny	220	208
Annual days with thunderstorms	57	39
Tornado risk score	33	18
Hurricane risk score	5	13

TEMPERATURE

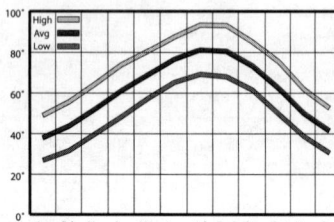

PRECIPITATION

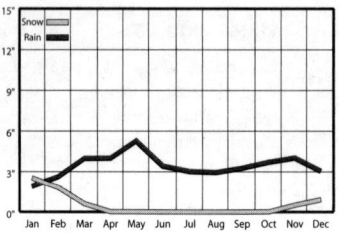

DAYS OF CLOUDS & PRECIPITATION

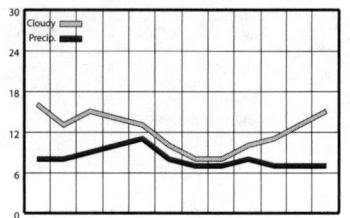

Education

Score: 4.5
Rank: 356

ACHIEVEMENT	AREA	U.S. AVG
High school degree	73.2%	82.7%
2-year college degree	5.7%	6.4%
4-year college degree	8.5%	15.7%
Graduate/professional degree	4.6%	8.9%

PUBLIC SCHOOLS	AREA	U.S. AVG
Expenditures per pupil	$4,656	$5,686
Student/teacher ratio	19.6	16.7
Attending public school	94.6%	90.1%
State SAT score	1142	1021
State ACT score	20.6*	20.9

HIGHER EDUCATION	AREA	U.S. AVG
No. 2-year colleges	4	4
No. 4-year colleges/universities	1	6
No. highly ranked universities	0	1

Health &
Healthcare

Score: 70.6
Rank: 111

HAZARDS & ILLNESSES	AREA	U.S. AVG
Air-quality score	52	37
Water-quality score	47	52
Pollen/allergy score	64	61
Cancer mortality per capita	243.7	201.9
Depression days per month	4.2	3.5
Stress score	74	50

HEALTHCARE	AREA	U.S. AVG
Physicians per capita	174.1	244.2
Hospital beds per capita	438.2	420.0
No. teaching hospitals	1	3
Cost per doctor visit	$82	$77
Cost per dental visit	$74	$70

Crime

Score: 34.0
Rank: 247

CRIME	AREA	U.S. AVG
Violent crime rate	550.9	465.5
Change in violent crime rate	7.4%	-2.2%
Property crime rate	3,415.9	3,517.1
Change in property crime rate	-5.2%	-2.1%

Transportation

Score: 10.7
Rank: 333

COMMUTE	AREA	U.S. AVG
Average commute time	24.0	27.4
Percent commutes > 60 mins.	4.9%	5.9%
Commute by auto	80.2%	78.9%
Commute by mass transit	0.4%	1.9%
Work at home	2.3%	3.1%
Mass transit miles per capita	0.45	1.87

INTERCITY SERVICES	AREA	U.S. AVG
Major airports within 60 miles	0	1
Size of regional airport	None	Large
Daily airline activity	24	686
Amtrak service	No	No

AUTOMOTIVE	AREA	U.S. AVG
Insurance, annual premium	$1,106	$1,432
Gas, cost per gallon	$2.39	$2.49
Daily vehicle miles per capita	23.5	24.0

Leisure

Score: 24.3
Rank: 282

DINING & SHOPPING	AREA	U.S. AVG
Restaurant rating	1	2
Outlet mall score	0	42
No. Starbucks	1	13
No. warehouse clubs	0	2

ENTERTAINMENT	AREA	U.S. AVG
Professional sports rating	2	4
College sports rating	1	4
Zoo/aquarium rating	1	3
Amusement park rating	1	3
Botanical garden/ arboretum rating	1	4

OUTDOOR ACTIVITIES	AREA	U.S. AVG
Golf-course rating	2	4
Ski-area rating	1	3
Sq. miles inland water	4	4
Miles of coastline	0.0	10.7
National Park rating	5	3

Arts & Culture

Score: 10.2
Rank: 335

MEDIA & LIBRARIES	AREA	U.S. AVG
Arts radio rating	1	3
No. public libraries	14	27
Library volumes per capita	2.35	2.78

PERFORMING ARTS	AREA	U.S. AVG
Classical music rating	4	4
Ballet/dance rating	1	3
Professional theater rating	1	3
University arts programs rating	1	5

MUSEUMS	AREA	U.S. AVG
Overall museum rating	5	5
Art museum rating	2	5
Science museum rating	3	5
Children's museum rating	1	3

Fort Walton Beach–Crestview–Destin, FL   Score: 47.5   Rank: 261   2004 rank: 152

Profile: Beach city/military town
Location: Florida Panhandle, on the Gulf Coast, 40 miles east of Pensacola
Elevation: 112 feet
Time zone: Eastern Standard Time

PRO	CON
Beaches	Arts and culture
Strong economy	Tourist sprawl
Cost of living	Air service

Fort Walton Beach is located at the head of the Choctawhatchee Bay. The city itself is primarily a tourist destination popular especially with residents of other parts of the South, with a long, built-up strip of beachside high-rise hotels. The beaches and ocean waters are particularly attractive and good places for fishing and other water activities, but the physical infrastructure and land assets aren't the best in the state. The resort community of Destin, on the barrier island sheltering the bay, has become the more up-and-coming tourist magnet. Nearby Eglin Air Force Base rounds out the economic picture, and Crestview, 15 miles inland, supports this installation and is located along Interstate 10, the major east–west transportation corridor. Fort Walton Beach is one of the strongest Florida areas in job-growth terms. The area took a fairly hard hit from Hurricane Ivan in 2004, and though most modern buildings survived intact, it did some damage to residential areas and tourist attractions. Downsides include the lack of cultural amenities, air service, and the steady flow of tourists and some ugly infrastructure set up to cater to their needs.

Sandy coastal areas rise slightly inland, where forests of pine and live oak begin, but the area is mostly open and level. The Gulf of Mexico moderates winter cold and creates cool, refreshing daytime breezes in summer. Summer temperatures are in the 80s and 90s; temperatures may rise if sea breezes diminish. Winter highs are usually in the 50s. There may be freezing temperatures, but extended cold waves are infrequent. Although distributed year-round, most rainfall occurs in July and August. Gulf hurricanes are a risk from early July to mid-October.

DEMOGRAPHICS	AREA	U.S. AVG	ETHNIC COMPOSITION	AREA	U.S. AVG	RESIDENT PROFILE	AREA	U.S. AVG
Population	183,733		White	82.5%	79.0%	Single	26.8%	32.4%
Population density per sq. mile	196.4	358.5	Black	9.2%	10.5%	Married	56.9%	52.7%
Population growth	27.8%	21.1%	Asian	2.9%	2.7%	Divorced/separated	16.3%	14.9%
Median age	36.7	36.1	Hispanic	4.3%	10.6%	Married with children	24.4%	23.7%
Percent Democrat	21.6%	44.5%	Religious observance	43.8%	48.9%	Single with children	8.6%	9.1%
Percent Republican	77.6%	54.5%	Diversity measure	36.6	40.1	Percent over age 65	13.1%	12.9%

Economy & Jobs
Score: 98.1
Rank: 8

INCOME	AREA	U.S. AVG	EMPLOYMENT	AREA	U.S. AVG	EMPLOYING INDUSTRIES	AREA	U.S. AVG
Per capita income	$24,535	$23,235	Unemployment rate	2.8%	4.7%	Largest: Professional, Scientific & Technical Services		
Household income	$47,936	$46,414	Recent job growth	5.8%	1.3%			
Household income < $25K	20.9%	26.2%	Projected future job growth	23.7%	11.5%	Percent manufacturing	9.2%	15.4%
Household income > $75K	25.7%	25.4%	White collar	59.0%	57.8%	Percent public sector	20.1%	15.7%
Household income growth	15.6%	13.6%	Blue collar	21.5%	25.2%	Percent construction	12.3%	9.9%

Cost of Living
Score: 100.0
Rank: 1

INDEXES & TAXES	AREA	U.S. AVG	HOUSING	AREA	U.S. AVG	NECESSITIES	AREA	U.S. AVG
Cost of Living Index	102.1	100.0	Median home price	$247,000	$220,000	Food Index	93.0	100.0
Buying Power Index	105.2	100.0	Home price appreciation	125.7%	10.1%	Housing Index	83.4	100.0
Income tax rate	0.00%	4.70%	Median rent	$653	$709	Utilities Index	83.1	100.0
Sales tax rate	6.00%	6.58%	Homes owned	56.2%	62.3%	Transportation Index	100.2	100.0
Property tax rate	$8.73	$12.00	Home price ratio	5.2	4.2	Healthcare Index	106.7	100.0
						Miscellaneous Cost Index	103.5	100.0

Climate
Score: 70.9
Rank: 108

TEMPERATURE	AREA	U.S. AVG	PRECIPITATION	AREA	U.S. AVG	COMFORTS & HAZARDS	AREA	U.S. AVG
Average January low	43.0	26.2	Annual inches precipitation	64.2	37.7	July relative humidity	74%	66%
Average July high	89.7	87.4	Annual inches snowfall	0.3	7.0	Annual days mostly sunny	220	208
Annual days > 90°F	55	38	Annual days precipitation	114	109	Annual days with thunderstorms	75	39
Annual days < 32°F	16	89	Annual days rain > 0.5 inches	37	22	Tornado risk score	38	18
Annual days < 0°F	0	6	Annual days snow > 1.5 inches	0	6	Hurricane risk score	58	13

TEMPERATURE

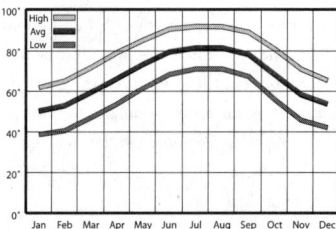

PRECIPITATION

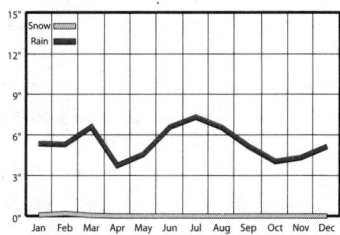

DAYS OF CLOUDS & PRECIPITATION

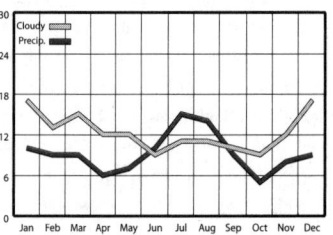

ACHIEVEMENT	AREA	U.S. AVG	PUBLIC SCHOOLS	AREA	U.S. AVG	HIGHER EDUCATION	AREA	U.S. AVG
High school degree	88.0%	82.7%	Expenditures per pupil	$4,517	$5,686	No. 2-year colleges	1	4
2-year college degree	9.0%	6.4%	Student/teacher ratio	18.1	16.7	No. 4-year colleges/universities	1	6
4-year college degree	15.0%	15.7%	Attending public school	93.2%	90.1%	No. highly ranked universities	0	1
Graduate/professional degree	9.3%	8.9%	State SAT score	993*	1021			
			State ACT score	20.3	20.9			

Education
Score: 67.4
Rank: 123

HAZARDS & ILLNESSES	AREA	U.S. AVG	HEALTHCARE	AREA	U.S. AVG	CRIME	AREA	U.S. AVG
Air-quality score	45	37	Physicians per capita	226.3	244.2	Violent crime rate	317.4	465.5
Water-quality score	90	52	Hospital beds per capita	283.6	420.0	Change in violent crime rate	-1.6%	-2.2%
Pollen/allergy score	63	61	No. teaching hospitals	0	3	Property crime rate	2,898.3	3,517.1
Cancer mortality per capita	282.7	201.9	Cost per doctor visit	$72	$77	Change in property crime rate	0.9%	-2.1%
Depression days per month	3.1	3.5	Cost per dental visit	$59	$70			
Stress score	24	50						

Health & Healthcare
Score: 44.1
Rank: 209

Crime
Score: 82.6
Rank: 66

COMMUTE	AREA	U.S. AVG	INTERCITY SERVICES	AREA	U.S. AVG	AUTOMOTIVE	AREA	U.S. AVG
Average commute time	23.8	27.4	Major airports within 60 miles	0	1	Insurance, annual premium	$1,389	$1,432
Percent commutes > 60 mins.	4.6%	5.9%	Size of regional airport	Small	Large	Gas, cost per gallon	$2.54	$2.49
Commute by auto	82.9%	78.9%	Daily airline activity	53	686	Daily vehicle miles per capita	29.5	24.0
Commute by mass transit	0.3%	1.9%	Amtrak service	Yes	No			
Work at home	2.1%	3.1%						
Mass transit miles per capita	0.30	1.87						

Transportation
Score: 13.4
Rank: 325

DINING & SHOPPING	AREA	U.S. AVG	ENTERTAINMENT	AREA	U.S. AVG	OUTDOOR ACTIVITIES	AREA	U.S. AVG
Restaurant rating	1	2	Professional sports rating	2	4	Golf-course rating	3	4
Outlet mall score	128	42	College sports rating	1	4	Ski-area rating	1	3
No. Starbucks	1	13	Zoo/aquarium rating	1	3	Sq. miles inland water	5	4
No. warehouse clubs	0	2	Amusement park rating	1	3	Miles of coastline	24.4	10.7
			Botanical garden/ arboretum rating	1	4	National Park rating	3	3

Leisure
Score: 41.2
Rank: 219

MEDIA & LIBRARIES	AREA	U.S. AVG	PERFORMING ARTS	AREA	U.S. AVG	MUSEUMS	AREA	U.S. AVG
Arts radio rating	1	3	Classical music rating	4	4	Overall museum rating	3	5
No. public libraries	6	27	Ballet/dance rating	3	3	Art museum rating	1	5
Library volumes per capita	1.19	2.78	Professional theater rating	1	3	Science museum rating	3	5
			University arts programs rating	1	5	Children's museum rating	1	3

Arts & Culture
Score: 7.0
Rank: 347

Fort Wayne, IN

Score: 67.2   Rank: 117   2004 rank: 102

Profile: Small city
Location: Northeastern Indiana, 15 miles from Ohio border
Elevation: 828 feet
Time zone: Eastern Standard Time

PRO
Diversified economy
Small town atmosphere
Arts and culture

CON
Entertainment
Low job-growth projections
Winter climate

Fort Wayne is a business center and the second-largest city in Indiana. Located in the northeast corner of the state at the confluence of three rivers, it is a diverse industrial and commercial center with an attractive downtown and a friendly, small-town feel for a city its size. Its industrial base has recovered from the 1980s decline of International Harvester and includes electronics manufacturer Motorola and other high-tech, electric motor, and automotive suppliers, as well as the headquarters of Fortune 500 member Lincoln National Life Insurance. Despite the vulnerability of these industries, employment has held steady thanks to the area's economic diversity. The Cost of Living Index is low at 79.9 although matched by several Indiana cities. Housing is a good value at a median home price just over $100,000; good value is received per dollar spent. The area has a better-than-average collection of small-scale arts-and-culture amenities for the type of town and some recreation in surrounding areas, but there isn't a lot to do. There is a strong community pride and sense of resilience to economic setbacks and to the occasional Fort Wayne joke heard from residents of nearby cities. While Fort Wayne has no outstanding draws, it also has no severe drawbacks, hence the relatively high ranking.

The surrounding area is generally level south and east of the city, rolling to the southwest, and quite hilly to the north and northwest. Summers are warm and humid. Winters are cool and cloudy, and occasionally very cold and windy. Annual precipitation is well distributed with somewhat larger amounts falling in late spring and early summer. Snow squalls and winter snow cover are common, but blizzards are infrequent. Summer thunderstorms are common and occasionally severe. The river confluence and low elevation have produced some severe floods. First freeze is mid-October; last is late April.

Population

DEMOGRAPHICS	AREA	U.S. AVG	ETHNIC COMPOSITION	AREA	U.S. AVG	RESIDENT PROFILE	AREA	U.S. AVG
Population	404,263		White	84.3%	79.0%	Single	31.2%	32.4%
Population density per sq. mile	296.7	358.5	Black	9.6%	10.5%	Married	55.0%	52.7%
Population growth	14.1%	21.1%	Asian	1.6%	2.7%	Divorced/separated	13.8%	14.9%
Median age	34.9	36.1	Hispanic	4.4%	10.6%	Married with children	24.7%	23.7%
Percent Democrat	34.7%	44.5%	Religious observance	50.3%	48.9%	Single with children	9.3%	9.1%
Percent Republican	64.6%	54.5%	Diversity measure	33.2	40.1	Percent over age 65	11.7%	12.9%

Economy & Jobs
Score: 53.2
Rank: 176

INCOME	AREA	U.S. AVG	EMPLOYMENT	AREA	U.S. AVG	EMPLOYING INDUSTRIES	AREA	U.S. AVG
Per capita income	$23,442	$23,235	Unemployment rate	5.1%	4.7%	Largest: Manufacturing		
Household income	$47,181	$46,414	Recent job growth	1.3%	1.3%			
Household income < $25K	22.9%	26.2%	Projected future job growth	5.5%	11.5%	Percent manufacturing	20.5%	15.4%
Household income > $75K	24.9%	25.4%	White collar	57.3%	57.8%	Percent public sector	8.4%	15.7%
Household income growth	9.8%	13.6%	Blue collar	29.3%	25.2%	Percent construction	8.9%	9.9%

Cost of Living
Score: 87.7
Rank: 47

INDEXES & TAXES	AREA	U.S. AVG	HOUSING	AREA	U.S. AVG	NECESSITIES	AREA	U.S. AVG
Cost of Living Index	79.9	100.0	Median home price	$103,700	$220,000	Food Index	97.5	100.0
Buying Power Index	132.4	100.0	Home price appreciation	16.7%	10.1%	Housing Index	43.9	100.0
Income tax rate	4.38%	4.70%	Median rent	$610	$709	Utilities Index	105.1	100.0
Sales tax rate	6.00%	6.58%	Homes owned	68.0%	62.3%	Transportation Index	100.3	100.0
Property tax rate	$9.74	$12.00	Home price ratio	2.2	4.2	Healthcare Index	95.4	100.0
						Miscellaneous Cost Index	99.4	100.0

Climate
Score: 41.2
Rank: 219

TEMPERATURE	AREA	U.S. AVG	PRECIPITATION	AREA	U.S. AVG	COMFORTS & HAZARDS	AREA	U.S. AVG
Average January low	17.9	26.2	Annual inches precipitation	36.0	37.7	July relative humidity	72%	66%
Average July high	83.6	87.4	Annual inches snowfall	31.0	7.0	Annual days mostly sunny	182	208
Annual days > 90°F	14	38	Annual days precipitation	131	109	Annual days with thunderstorms	41	39
Annual days < 32°F	134	89	Annual days rain > 0.5 inches	22	22	Tornado risk score	20	18
Annual days < 0°F	10	6	Annual days snow > 1.5 inches	9	6	Hurricane risk score	3	13

TEMPERATURE

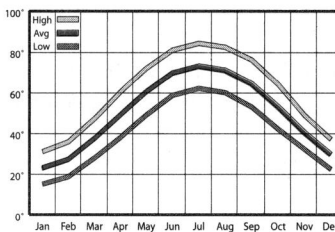

PRECIPITATION

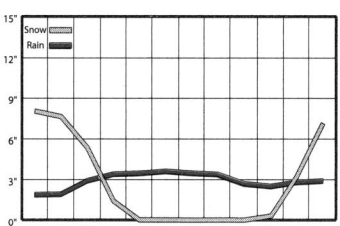

DAYS OF CLOUDS & PRECIPITATION

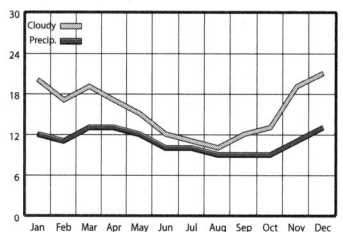

Education
Score: 43.9
Rank: 211

ACHIEVEMENT	AREA	U.S. AVG	PUBLIC SCHOOLS	AREA	U.S. AVG	HIGHER EDUCATION	AREA	U.S. AVG
High school degree	85.8%	82.7%	Expenditures per pupil	$5,951	$5,686	No. 2-year colleges	4	4
2-year college degree	7.9%	6.4%	Student/teacher ratio	19.4	16.7	No. 4-year colleges/universities	8	6
4-year college degree	14.1%	15.7%	Attending public school	83.5%	90.1%	No. highly ranked universities	0	1
Graduate/professional degree	7.2%	8.9%	State SAT score	1007*	1021			
			State ACT score	21.7	20.9			

Health & Healthcare
Score: 46.5
Rank: 201

HAZARDS & ILLNESSES	AREA	U.S. AVG	HEALTHCARE	AREA	U.S. AVG	CRIME	AREA	U.S. AVG
Air-quality score	34	37	Physicians per capita	225.4	244.2	Violent crime rate	228.5	465.5
Water-quality score	24	52	Hospital beds per capita	385.6	420.0	Change in violent crime rate	7.4%	-2.2%
Pollen/allergy score	57	61	No. teaching hospitals	2	3	Property crime rate	3,289.6	3,517.1
Cancer mortality per capita	202.2	201.9	Cost per doctor visit	$64	$77	Change in property crime rate	-3.2%	-2.1%
Depression days per month	3.3	3.5	Cost per dental visit	$60	$70			
Stress score	39	50						

Crime
Score: 59.4
Rank: 153

Transportation
Score: 32.9
Rank: 251

COMMUTE	AREA	U.S. AVG	INTERCITY SERVICES	AREA	U.S. AVG	AUTOMOTIVE	AREA	U.S. AVG
Average commute time	22.7	27.4	Major airports within 60 miles	0	1	Insurance, annual premium	$1,204	$1,432
Percent commutes > 60 mins.	3.3%	5.9%	Size of regional airport	Small	Large	Gas, cost per gallon	$2.51	$2.49
Commute by auto	84.3%	78.9%	Daily airline activity	303	686	Daily vehicle miles per capita	25.2	24.0
Commute by mass transit	0.7%	1.9%	Amtrak service	No	No			
Work at home	2.8%	3.1%						
Mass transit miles per capita	0.70	1.87						

DINING & SHOPPING	AREA	U.S. AVG	ENTERTAINMENT	AREA	U.S. AVG	OUTDOOR ACTIVITIES	AREA	U.S. AVG
Restaurant rating	1	2	Professional sports rating	3	4	Golf-course rating	4	4
Outlet mall score	40	42	College sports rating	2	4	Ski-area rating	2	3
No. Starbucks	6	13	Zoo/aquarium rating	6	3	Sq. miles inland water	2	4
No. warehouse clubs	0	2	Amusement park rating	1	3	Miles of coastline	0.0	10.7
			Botanical garden/ arboretum rating	2	4	National Park rating	1	3

Leisure
Score: 38.5
Rank: 229

MEDIA & LIBRARIES	AREA	U.S. AVG	PERFORMING ARTS	AREA	U.S. AVG	MUSEUMS	AREA	U.S. AVG
Arts radio rating	1	3	Classical music rating	7	4	Overall museum rating	7	5
No. public libraries	21	27	Ballet/dance rating	3	3	Art museum rating	5	5
Library volumes per capita	6.99	2.78	Professional theater rating	1	3	Science museum rating	1	5
			University arts programs rating	8	5	Children's museum rating	1	3

Arts & Culture
Score: 76.5
Rank: 88

Fort Worth–Arlington, TX

Score: 65.8   Rank: 133   2004 rank: 36

Profile: Large-city/suburban complex
Location: Northeast Texas, 30 miles west of Dallas
Elevation: 551 feet
Time zone: Central Standard Time

PRO	CON
Attractive downtown	Growth and sprawl
Arts and culture	Unattractive setting
Cost of living	Heat and humidity

Although just west of Dallas, the origins and character of Fort Worth are quite different. The city started as a livestock center, and has grown into a large and modern city without much of the glamour and glitz of its eastern neighbor. Arlington sits between Fort Worth and Dallas, a mega-suburb-slash-small-city covering some 12 zip codes lying mainly southeast of downtown Fort Worth, and the actual home of Major League Baseball's Texas Rangers and some Texas-size parks and amusement facilities among the wide assortment of commercial activities within city limits. Farther east lies a large, mostly developed area of suburbs blending into the fringes of Dallas, including Irving and Grand Prairie and the more upscale Grapevine somewhat north. Commutes carry residents across a grid network of freeways among and between all of these suburbs as well as the downtown areas, and traffic can be a challenge, especially heading to and from the Arlington area.

Today, Fort Worth is a commercial and industrial center with a user-friendly downtown, and a few nice and a few not-so-nice suburbs close to the city core. In the mid–20th century, money from the emerging oil industry endowed an assortment of quality cultural assets, including world-class museums and interesting architecture concentrated in a so-called "Cultural District." Overall the downtown is far more of an attraction than neighboring Dallas and is considered by many to be the finest downtown core in Texas. Lake Worth, a large reservoir within the city limits, offers a parklike setting and excellent watersports for beating the summer heat. Statistically, the Fort Worth–Arlington metro area city compares favorably to its larger Dallas–Plano–Irving brother (p. 298): Fort Worth has half the population, 10% lower cost of living, 30% lower median housing prices, two-thirds the crime and air pollution, and a higher job-growth rate while sharing all of the amenities—air transport, sports, shopping, and entertainment. Fort Worth residents consider the distinction from Dallas important, and bristle at an outsider's notion that they are "from Dallas." A slight uptick in crime rates and some weakness in healthcare and air-quality statistics knocked Fort Worth out of the top 10% of our rankings, but for most the area is probably better than the rank suggests.

The area contains mostly flat to rolling hills that begin to rise higher to the west of town. Tree cover is prevalent within the city but not in the surrounding area. Summer hot spells are broken by thunderstorm activity into 3- to 5-day periods. Summer daytime temperatures frequently exceed 100°F with occasional nights above 80°F. Winters are mild with sudden temperature changes and short periods of extreme cold. Most annual precipitation comes from thunderstorm activity with occasional heavy downpours, especially in the spring. Snowfall is rare.

DEMOGRAPHICS	AREA	U.S. AVG	ETHNIC COMPOSITION	AREA	U.S. AVG	RESIDENT PROFILE	AREA	U.S. AVG
Population	1,913,563		White	71.8%	79.0%	Single	28.6%	32.4%
Population density per sq. mile	562.6	358.5	Black	11.4%	10.5%	Married	55.4%	52.7%
Population growth	40.3%	21.1%	Asian	3.5%	2.7%	Divorced/separated	16.0%	14.9%
Median age	33.3	36.1	Hispanic	21.7%	10.6%	Married with children	28.0%	23.7%
Percent Democrat	35.0%	44.5%	Religious observance	51.7%	48.9%	Single with children	9.3%	9.1%
Percent Republican	64.4%	54.5%	Diversity measure	62.9	40.1	Percent over age 65	8.8%	12.9%

Population

INCOME	AREA	U.S. AVG	EMPLOYMENT	AREA	U.S. AVG	EMPLOYING INDUSTRIES	AREA	U.S. AVG
Per capita income	$25,044	$23,235	Unemployment rate	5.0%	4.7%	Largest: Manufacturing		
Household income	$52,130	$46,414	Recent job growth	2.7%	1.3%			
Household income < $25K	20.4%	26.2%	Projected future job growth	21.4%	11.5%	Percent manufacturing	13.8%	15.4%
Household income > $75K	31.2%	25.4%	White collar	63.0%	57.8%	Percent public sector	11.3%	15.7%
Household income growth	13.6%	13.6%	Blue collar	24.0%	25.2%	Percent construction	10.2%	9.9%

Economy & Jobs
Score: 91.4
Rank: 33

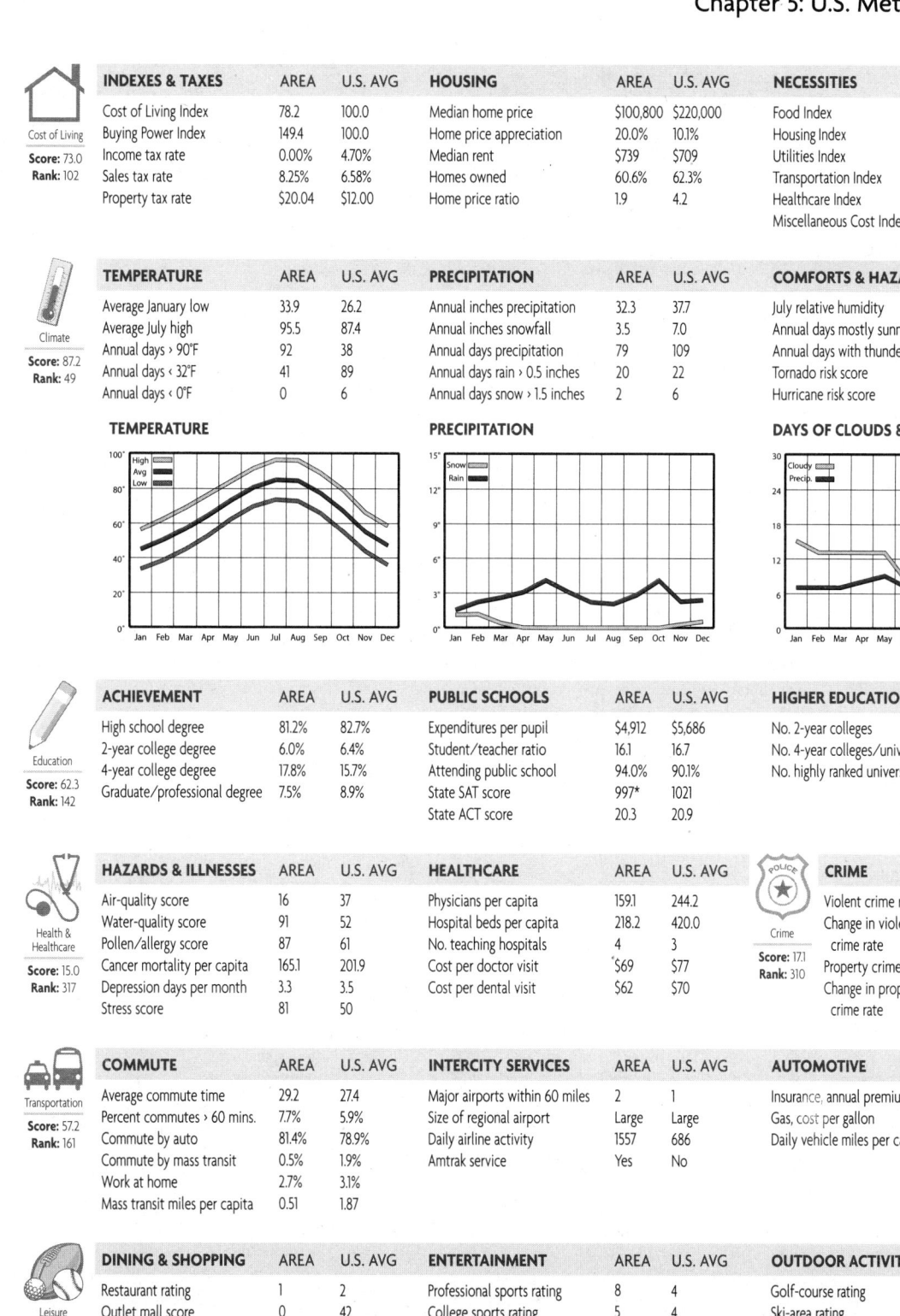

Cost of Living
Score: 73.0
Rank: 102

INDEXES & TAXES	AREA	U.S. AVG
Cost of Living Index	78.2	100.0
Buying Power Index	149.4	100.0
Income tax rate	0.00%	4.70%
Sales tax rate	8.25%	6.58%
Property tax rate	$20.04	$12.00

HOUSING	AREA	U.S. AVG
Median home price	$100,800	$220,000
Home price appreciation	20.0%	10.1%
Median rent	$739	$709
Homes owned	60.6%	62.3%
Home price ratio	1.9	4.2

NECESSITIES	AREA	U.S. AVG
Food Index	93.2	100.0
Housing Index	48.6	100.0
Utilities Index	93.3	100.0
Transportation Index	97.1	100.0
Healthcare Index	100.6	100.0
Miscellaneous Cost Index	99.7	100.0

Climate
Score: 87.2
Rank: 49

TEMPERATURE	AREA	U.S. AVG
Average January low	33.9	26.2
Average July high	95.5	87.4
Annual days > 90°F	92	38
Annual days < 32°F	41	89
Annual days < 0°F	0	6

PRECIPITATION	AREA	U.S. AVG
Annual inches precipitation	32.3	37.7
Annual inches snowfall	3.5	7.0
Annual days precipitation	79	109
Annual days rain > 0.5 inches	20	22
Annual days snow > 1.5 inches	2	6

COMFORTS & HAZARDS	AREA	U.S. AVG
July relative humidity	67%	66%
Annual days mostly sunny	234	208
Annual days with thunderstorms	45	39
Tornado risk score	48	18
Hurricane risk score	10	13

TEMPERATURE
PRECIPITATION
DAYS OF CLOUDS & PRECIPITATION

Education
Score: 62.3
Rank: 142

ACHIEVEMENT	AREA	U.S. AVG
High school degree	81.2%	82.7%
2-year college degree	6.0%	6.4%
4-year college degree	17.8%	15.7%
Graduate/professional degree	7.5%	8.9%

PUBLIC SCHOOLS	AREA	U.S. AVG
Expenditures per pupil	$4,912	$5,686
Student/teacher ratio	16.1	16.7
Attending public school	94.0%	90.1%
State SAT score	997*	1021
State ACT score	20.3	20.9

HIGHER EDUCATION	AREA	U.S. AVG
No. 2-year colleges	9	4
No. 4-year colleges/universities	8	6
No. highly ranked universities	1	1

Health & Healthcare
Score: 15.0
Rank: 317

HAZARDS & ILLNESSES	AREA	U.S. AVG
Air-quality score	16	37
Water-quality score	91	52
Pollen/allergy score	87	61
Cancer mortality per capita	165.1	201.9
Depression days per month	3.3	3.5
Stress score	81	50

HEALTHCARE	AREA	U.S. AVG
Physicians per capita	159.1	244.2
Hospital beds per capita	218.2	420.0
No. teaching hospitals	4	3
Cost per doctor visit	$69	$77
Cost per dental visit	$62	$70

Crime
Score: 17.1
Rank: 310

CRIME	AREA	U.S. AVG
Violent crime rate	469.8	465.5
Change in violent crime rate	8.0%	-2.2%
Property crime rate	4,756.0	3,517.1
Change in property crime rate	-2.9%	-2.1%

Transportation
Score: 57.2
Rank: 161

COMMUTE	AREA	U.S. AVG
Average commute time	29.2	27.4
Percent commutes > 60 mins.	7.7%	5.9%
Commute by auto	81.4%	78.9%
Commute by mass transit	0.5%	1.9%
Work at home	2.7%	3.1%
Mass transit miles per capita	0.51	1.87

INTERCITY SERVICES	AREA	U.S. AVG
Major airports within 60 miles	2	1
Size of regional airport	Large	Large
Daily airline activity	1557	686
Amtrak service	Yes	No

AUTOMOTIVE	AREA	U.S. AVG
Insurance, annual premium	$1,402	$1,432
Gas, cost per gallon	$2.50	$2.49
Daily vehicle miles per capita	25.9	24.0

Leisure
Score: 80.5
Rank: 73

DINING & SHOPPING	AREA	U.S. AVG
Restaurant rating	1	2
Outlet mall score	0	42
No. Starbucks	40	13
No. warehouse clubs	7	2

ENTERTAINMENT	AREA	U.S. AVG
Professional sports rating	8	4
College sports rating	5	4
Zoo/aquarium rating	7	3
Amusement park rating	9	3
Botanical garden/ arboretum rating	9	4

OUTDOOR ACTIVITIES	AREA	U.S. AVG
Golf-course rating	7	4
Ski-area rating	1	3
Sq. miles inland water	4	4
Miles of coastline	0.0	10.7
National Park rating	1	3

Arts & Culture
Score: 81.0
Rank: 72

MEDIA & LIBRARIES	AREA	U.S. AVG
Arts radio rating	5	3
No. public libraries	57	27
Library volumes per capita	2.23	2.78

PERFORMING ARTS	AREA	U.S. AVG
Classical music rating	6	4
Ballet/dance rating	7	3
Professional theater rating	9	3
University arts programs rating	8	5

MUSEUMS	AREA	U.S. AVG
Overall museum rating	9	5
Art museum rating	9	5
Science museum rating	9	5
Children's museum rating	10	3

Fresno, CA

Score: 36.4	**Rank:** 317	**2004 rank:** 116

Profile: Mid-size city
Location: Central California, center of San Joaquin Valley along State Route 99
Elevation: 327 feet
Time zone: Pacific Standard Time

PRO	CON
Winter climate	Summer heat
Nearby national parks	High unemployment
College-town amenities	Unattractive sprawl

Fresno is an agricultural and minor banking and financial center for the San Joaquin Valley, the southern half of California's famed agricultural Central Valley. Some light manufacturing rounds out the private employment picture. The California State University at Fresno, or more commonly known as Fresno State, adds some college-town life including sports and arts activities, but it doesn't have much influence on the look or atmosphere of the town. The city core, once neglected, has been renovated and some projects are still underway. A few nice older neighborhoods spread north, but much of the rest of the area could be described as "functional" and not very interesting, and some are downright gritty. Like many towns in this valley, large populations of uneducated and immigrant farm workers bring down average income levels, and the relatively low cost of housing versus the rest of California bring in economically disadvantaged individuals; these forces together have created some zones of poverty and areas of rather unattractive expansion. This said, the city is working hard to improve its image, education, and facilities. The Sierra Nevadas and the twin national parks Sequoia and Kings Canyon provide abundant outdoor recreation activities nearby. Crime rates—particularly violent crime—are a concern. Cost of living at 120.8 is fairly reasonable for a California city but it is hardly a bargain considering what you get, and housing prices have risen substantially. Air quality is poor and often obscures the mountains in what would otherwise be a more attractive setting. The negatives have grown; hence the drop in ranking.

The San Joaquin Valley is generally flat and agricultural. About 15 miles east of Fresno, the terrain slopes upward with the foothills of the Sierra Nevada, rapidly rising to more than 14,000 feet. The lower Coastal Range rises 45 miles to the west. The Mediterranean climate of the Central Valley is hot and dry in summer, with normally pleasant evenings, and mild in winter. Temperatures may reach the low 100s in summer but 90s are more common and rain is almost nonexistent. Winters are moist and heavy fogs may persist. Almost all rainfall occurs in winter.

DEMOGRAPHICS	AREA	U.S. AVG	ETHNIC COMPOSITION	AREA	U.S. AVG	RESIDENT PROFILE	AREA	U.S. AVG
Population	866,531		White	52.5%	79.0%	Single	35.0%	32.4%
Population density per sq. mile	145.3	358.5	Black	5.3%	10.5%	Married	48.5%	52.7%
Population growth	29.8%	21.1%	Asian	8.3%	2.7%	Divorced/separated	16.5%	14.9%
Median age	30.7	36.1	Hispanic	46.8%	10.6%	Married with children	28.3%	23.7%
Percent Democrat	41.7%	44.5%	Religious observance	47.6%	48.9%	Single with children	12.8%	9.1%
Percent Republican	57.4%	54.5%	Diversity measure	81.8	40.1	Percent over age 65	9.8%	12.9%

INCOME	AREA	U.S. AVG	EMPLOYMENT	AREA	U.S. AVG	EMPLOYING INDUSTRIES	AREA	U.S. AVG
Per capita income	$17,415	$23,235	Unemployment rate	7.9%	4.7%	Largest: Healthcare & Social Assistance		
Household income	$40,047	$46,414	Recent job growth	2.7%	1.3%			
Household income < $25K	31.3%	26.2%	Projected future job growth	16.7%	11.5%	Percent manufacturing	13.3%	15.4%
Household income > $75K	21.8%	25.4%	White collar	54.3%	57.8%	Percent public sector	19.7%	15.7%
Household income growth	15.3%	13.6%	Blue collar	21.7%	25.2%	Percent construction	8.5%	9.9%

Score: 31.3
Rank: 257

INDEXES & TAXES	AREA	U.S. AVG	HOUSING	AREA	U.S. AVG	NECESSITIES	AREA	U.S. AVG
Cost of Living Index	120.8	100.0	Median home price	$303,500	$220,000	Food Index	116.0	100.0
Buying Power Index	74.3	100.0	Home price appreciation	164.9%	10.1%	Housing Index	124.6	100.0
Income tax rate	6.00%	4.70%	Median rent	$726	$709	Utilities Index	121.1	100.0
Sales tax rate	7.98%	6.58%	Homes owned	53.0%	62.3%	Transportation Index	111.8	100.0
Property tax rate	$9.12	$12.00	Home price ratio	7.6	4.2	Healthcare Index	123.4	100.0
						Miscellaneous Cost Index	104.3	100.0

Score: 11.5
Rank: 330

Climate
Score: 89.8
Rank: 39

TEMPERATURE	AREA	U.S. AVG
Average January low	35.8	26.2
Average July high	98.2	87.4
Annual days > 90°F	107	38
Annual days < 32°F	29	89
Annual days < 0°F	0	6

PRECIPITATION	AREA	U.S. AVG
Annual inches precipitation	10.0	37.7
Annual inches snowfall	0.0	7.0
Annual days precipitation	44	109
Annual days rain > 0.5 inches	6	22
Annual days snow > 1.5 inches	0	6

COMFORTS & HAZARDS	AREA	U.S. AVG
July relative humidity	61%	66%
Annual days mostly sunny	271	208
Annual days with thunderstorms	6	39
Tornado risk score	8	18
Hurricane risk score	0	13

TEMPERATURE
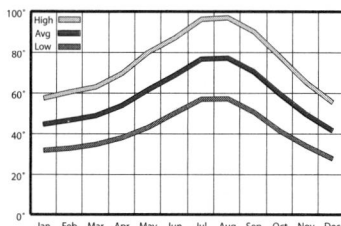

PRECIPITATION
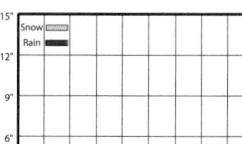

DAYS OF CLOUDS & PRECIPITATION
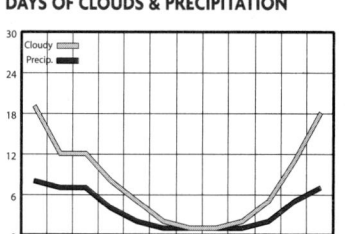

Education
Score: 17.9
Rank: 306

ACHIEVEMENT	AREA	U.S. AVG
High school degree	67.2%	82.7%
2-year college degree	6.5%	6.4%
4-year college degree	12.0%	15.7%
Graduate/professional degree	5.5%	8.9%

PUBLIC SCHOOLS	AREA	U.S. AVG
Expenditures per pupil	$5,107	$5,686
Student/teacher ratio	19.9	16.7
Attending public school	96.5%	90.1%
State SAT score	1019*	1021
State ACT score	21.6	20.9

HIGHER EDUCATION	AREA	U.S. AVG
No. 2-year colleges	7	4
No. 4-year colleges/universities	7	6
No. highly ranked universities	1	1

Health & Healthcare
Score: 7.0
Rank: 347

HAZARDS & ILLNESSES	AREA	U.S. AVG
Air-quality score	13	37
Water-quality score	22	52
Pollen/allergy score	60	61
Cancer mortality per capita	157.8	201.9
Depression days per month	3.9	3.5
Stress score	70	50

HEALTHCARE	AREA	U.S. AVG
Physicians per capita	178.4	244.2
Hospital beds per capita	200.6	420.0
No. teaching hospitals	2	3
Cost per doctor visit	$83	$77
Cost per dental visit	$77	$70

Crime
Score: 22.7
Rank: 289

CRIME	AREA	U.S. AVG
Violent crime rate	638.8	465.5
Change in violent crime rate	6.3%	-2.2%
Property crime rate	4,801.0	3,517.1
Change in property crime rate	-2.1%	-2.1%

Transportation
Score: 16.6
Rank: 313

COMMUTE	AREA	U.S. AVG
Average commute time	23.9	27.4
Percent commutes > 60 mins.	5.3%	5.9%
Commute by auto	74.3%	78.9%
Commute by mass transit	1.7%	1.9%
Work at home	3.0%	3.1%
Mass transit miles per capita	1.70	1.87

INTERCITY SERVICES	AREA	U.S. AVG
Major airports within 60 miles	0	1
Size of regional airport	Small	Large
Daily airline activity	75	686
Amtrak service	Yes	No

AUTOMOTIVE	AREA	U.S. AVG
Insurance, annual premium	$1,906	$1,432
Gas, cost per gallon	$2.69	$2.49
Daily vehicle miles per capita	20.7	24.0

Leisure
Score: 78.9
Rank: 79

DINING & SHOPPING	AREA	U.S. AVG
Restaurant rating	3	2
Outlet mall score	22	42
No. Starbucks	34	13
No. warehouse clubs	5	2

ENTERTAINMENT	AREA	U.S. AVG
Professional sports rating	3	4
College sports rating	5	4
Zoo/aquarium rating	5	3
Amusement park rating	8	3
Botanical garden/arboretum rating	3	4

OUTDOOR ACTIVITIES	AREA	U.S. AVG
Golf-course rating	3	4
Ski-area rating	5	3
Sq. miles inland water	4	4
Miles of coastline	0.0	10.7
National Park rating	10	3

Arts & Culture
Score: 43.9
Rank: 210

MEDIA & LIBRARIES	AREA	U.S. AVG
Arts radio rating	5	3
No. public libraries	35	27
Library volumes per capita	1.09	2.78

PERFORMING ARTS	AREA	U.S. AVG
Classical music rating	4	4
Ballet/dance rating	3	3
Professional theater rating	1	3
University arts programs rating	1	5

MUSEUMS	AREA	U.S. AVG
Overall museum rating	6	5
Art museum rating	5	5
Science museum rating	4	5
Children's museum rating	2	3

Gadsden, AL

Score: 33.3   Rank: 334   2004 rank: 324

Profile: Small industrial town
Location: Northeast Alabama, between Birmingham and Chattanooga, Tennessee
Elevation: 624 feet
Time zone: Central Standard Time

PRO	CON
Cost of living	Economy and jobs
Attractive setting	Entertainment
Nearby water recreation	Low educational attainment

Gadsden is historically one of the state's largest industrial centers, producing steel, rubber, fabricated metal, and electronic equipment in an almost early-20th-century, company-town environment. The steel and rubber factories, led by Goodyear and Republic Steel, mostly went away in the 1980s, leaving a fairly gritty and impoverished industrial landscape. The city worked hard through the 1990s to reverse the tide with redevelopment investments with some success, but today Gadsden is still a mixed bag with unemployment, crime, and education issues. The setting, along the Coosa River and near the main southern Appalachian ridge is fairly attractive, and the nearby dammed-up portions of the Coosa River provide some entertainment. There are some new arts amenities and a new cultural arts center in a cleaned-up downtown area. The Cost of Living Index at 77.2 is attractive and the median home price of $115,000 is once again lowest in the state, but educational attainment is also the lowest in the state. Bottom line: Gadsden has probably seen its worst days, has prettied itself up, and is working to attract new businesses and employment, but it's a long recovery path.

Gadsden is in the Coosa River Valley surrounded by hilly terrain with mixed forest, and is located at the south end of the long mountain ridge known as Lookout Mountain. There are four seasons with long, hot humid summers and mild winters. The orientation of nearby ridges blocks some cold air from the north but funnels in humid air from the southwest.

Population

DEMOGRAPHICS	AREA	U.S. AVG
Population	103,134	
Population density per sq. mile	192.8	358.5
Population growth	3.3%	21.1%
Median age	39.0	36.1
Percent Democrat	35.9%	44.5%
Percent Republican	63.3%	54.5%

ETHNIC COMPOSITION	AREA	U.S. AVG
White	82.7%	79.0%
Black	14.7%	10.5%
Asian	0.5%	2.7%
Hispanic	2.1%	10.6%
Religious observance	68.3%	48.9%
Diversity measure	32.4	40.1

RESIDENT PROFILE	AREA	U.S. AVG
Single	28.7%	32.4%
Married	55.7%	52.7%
Divorced/separated	15.7%	14.9%
Married with children	21.4%	23.7%
Single with children	8.3%	9.1%
Percent over age 65	16.2%	12.9%

Economy & Jobs
Score: 9.6
Rank: 337

INCOME	AREA	U.S. AVG
Per capita income	$19,193	$23,235
Household income	$34,883	$46,414
Household income ‹ $25K	36.4%	26.2%
Household income › $75K	16.4%	25.4%
Household income growth	11.9%	13.6%

EMPLOYMENT	AREA	U.S. AVG
Unemployment rate	4.4%	4.7%
Recent job growth	-0.6%	1.3%
Projected future job growth	2.4%	11.5%
White collar	50.1%	57.8%
Blue collar	35.2%	25.2%

EMPLOYING INDUSTRIES	AREA	U.S. AVG
Largest: Manufacturing		
Percent manufacturing	22.9%	15.4%
Percent public sector	12.8%	15.7%
Percent construction	12.3%	9.9%

Cost of Living
Score: 69.5
Rank: 114

INDEXES & TAXES	AREA	U.S. AVG
Cost of Living Index	77.2	100.0
Buying Power Index	101.3	100.0
Income tax rate	5.10%	4.70%
Sales tax rate	9.00%	6.58%
Property tax rate	$4.25	$12.00

HOUSING	AREA	U.S. AVG
Median home price	$115,000	$220,000
Home price appreciation	35.0%	10.1%
Median rent	$504	$709
Homes owned	68.1%	62.3%
Home price ratio	3.3	4.2

NECESSITIES	AREA	U.S. AVG
Food Index	93.2	100.0
Housing Index	51.6	100.0
Utilities Index	89.8	100.0
Transportation Index	84.8	100.0
Healthcare Index	83.6	100.0
Miscellaneous Cost Index	97.5	100.0

Climate
Score: 23.0
Rank: 287

TEMPERATURE	AREA	U.S. AVG
Average January low	34.1	26.2
Average July high	90.3	87.4
Annual days › 90°F	39	38
Annual days ‹ 32°F	60	89
Annual days ‹ 0°F	0	6

PRECIPITATION	AREA	U.S. AVG
Annual inches precipitation	53.0	37.7
Annual inches snowfall	1.0	7.0
Annual days precipitation	118	109
Annual days rain › 0.5 inches	36	22
Annual days snow › 1.5 inches	2	6

COMFORTS & HAZARDS	AREA	U.S. AVG
July relative humidity	72%	66%
Annual days mostly sunny	210	208
Annual days with thunderstorms	58	39
Tornado risk score	23	18
Hurricane risk score	18	13

TEMPERATURE

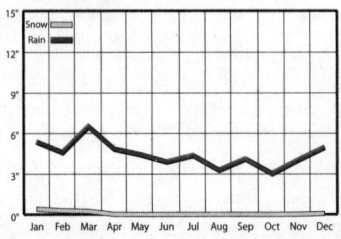

PRECIPITATION

DAYS OF CLOUDS & PRECIPITATION

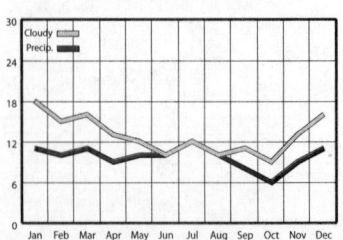

Education Score: 7.0 Rank: 347	ACHIEVEMENT	AREA	U.S. AVG	PUBLIC SCHOOLS	AREA	U.S. AVG	HIGHER EDUCATION	AREA	U.S. AVG
	High school degree	74.4%	82.7%	Expenditures per pupil	$4,640	$5,686	No. 2-year colleges	1	4
	2-year college degree	6.7%	6.4%	Student/teacher ratio	16.4	16.7	No. 4-year colleges/universities	0	6
	4-year college degree	8.2%	15.7%	Attending public school	91.6%	90.1%	No. highly ranked universities	0	1
	Graduate/professional degree	5.4%	8.9%	State SAT score	1126	1021			
				State ACT score	20.2*	20.9			

Health & Healthcare Score: 82.4 Rank: 67	HAZARDS & ILLNESSES	AREA	U.S. AVG	HEALTHCARE	AREA	U.S. AVG	CRIME Score: 41.2 Rank: 220	CRIME	AREA	U.S. AVG
	Air-quality score	43	37	Physicians per capita	183.4	244.2		Violent crime rate	417.8	465.5
	Water-quality score	85	52	Hospital beds per capita	614.7	420.0		Change in violent crime rate	-7.6%	-2.2%
	Pollen/allergy score	66	61	No. teaching hospitals	0	3		Property crime rate	4,502.3	3,517.1
	Cancer mortality per capita	226.5	201.9	Cost per doctor visit	$57	$77		Change in property crime rate	-5.8%	-2.1%
	Depression days per month	5.0	3.5	Cost per dental visit	$51	$70				
	Stress score	76	50							

Transportation Score: 76.7 Rank: 87	COMMUTE	AREA	U.S. AVG	INTERCITY SERVICES	AREA	U.S. AVG	AUTOMOTIVE	AREA	U.S. AVG
	Average commute time	25.8	27.4	Major airports within 60 miles	1	1	Insurance, annual premium	$1,250	$1,432
	Percent commutes > 60 mins.	8.2%	5.9%	Size of regional airport	Large	Large	Gas, cost per gallon	$2.45	$2.49
	Commute by auto	84.5%	78.9%	Daily airline activity	1575	686	Daily vehicle miles per capita	37.7	24.0
	Commute by mass transit	0.1%	1.9%	Amtrak service	No	No			
	Work at home	2.0%	3.1%						
	Mass transit miles per capita	0.10	1.87						

Leisure Score: 1.3 Rank: 368	DINING & SHOPPING	AREA	U.S. AVG	ENTERTAINMENT	AREA	U.S. AVG	OUTDOOR ACTIVITIES	AREA	U.S. AVG
	Restaurant rating	1	2	Professional sports rating	2	4	Golf-course rating	1	4
	Outlet mall score	50	42	College sports rating	1	4	Ski-area rating	1	3
	No. Starbucks	0	13	Zoo/aquarium rating	1	3	Sq. miles inland water	2	4
	No. warehouse clubs	0	2	Amusement park rating	1	3	Miles of coastline	0.0	10.7
				Botanical garden/ arboretum rating	1	4	National Park rating	1	3

Arts & Culture Score: 26.5 Rank: 275	MEDIA & LIBRARIES	AREA	U.S. AVG	PERFORMING ARTS	AREA	U.S. AVG	MUSEUMS	AREA	U.S. AVG
	Arts radio rating	1	3	Classical music rating	1	4	Overall museum rating	4	5
	No. public libraries	8	27	Ballet/dance rating	1	3	Art museum rating	7	5
	Library volumes per capita	2.90	2.78	Professional theater rating	1	3	Science museum rating	5	5
				University arts programs rating	1	5	Children's museum rating	6	3

Gainesville, FL

Score: 100.0   Rank: 1   2004 rank: 56

Profile: College town
Location: North-central Florida, 60 miles south of Georgia border
Elevation: 96 feet
Time zone: Eastern Standard Time

PRO	CON
College-town amenities	Summer heat
Performing arts	Violent crime rate
Healthcare	Air service

A Florida place that many across the country haven't heard of or thought about a lot, Gainesville has quietly but steadily marched to the head of the class. Gainesville is a right-sized college town centered on the 36,000-student University of Florida. The university is the area's largest employer, and the economic picture, recently mixed, has recovered well to become one of the strongest and most diverse economies in the state. Located away from the coast, the area has more of a small Southern town demeanor; it is not a touristy coastal city. The university has made Gainesville a center for the arts, particularly the performing arts, and the city has excellent arts venues. College sports are an obsession particularly during fall football season. The economy has diversified far beyond the university, attracting research and high tech, along with a large medical center and Veterans Administration hospital. The population has a strong concentration of young people and active retirees seeking the energy of a college town. The expression "I retired in Gainesville while my parents retired in St. Pete" says a lot. Gainesville has gained popularity among northern migrants seeking a Florida climate and intellectual stimulation without the high prices, tourist bustle, and stigma most commonly associated with the state. Not only attractive as a lifestyle destination, Gainesville has also become an attractive place to start small businesses. The area is also important as a nature and wildlife-viewing center, and nearby natural springs offer good recreational opportunities. A relatively high rate for violent crime and long, hot, sticky summers with more than 100 days over 90°F are negatives, but many like the small-town feel and find Gainesville one of the most livable cities in the state—and, as we've ranked it, in the nation.

The terrain is fairly level with forests of live oak and southern pine within the city and nearby. There are several nearby lakes to the east and south. The central location away from water causes more persistent heat. Winters are mild, with minimum temperatures averaging 44°F, although occasional freezing does occur, with record lows in the teens. Rainfall is appreciable in every month but is most abundant from summer showers and thunderstorms. August, which averages 8 inches of rainfall, is the wettest month. Because of its inland location, Gainesville does not have serious problems with hurricanes.

Population

DEMOGRAPHICS	AREA	U.S. AVG	ETHNIC COMPOSITION	AREA	U.S. AVG	RESIDENT PROFILE	AREA	U.S. AVG
Population	247,579		White	72.4%	79.0%	Single	44.8%	32.4%
Population density per sq. mile	202.4	358.5	Black	20.1%	10.5%	Married	40.9%	52.7%
Population growth	30.0%	21.1%	Asian	3.7%	2.7%	Divorced/separated	14.3%	14.9%
Median age	31.6	36.1	Hispanic	5.7%	10.6%	Married with children	17.0%	23.7%
Percent Democrat	54.4%	44.5%	Religious observance	34.1%	48.9%	Single with children	8.6%	9.1%
Percent Republican	44.7%	54.5%	Diversity measure	49.1	40.1	Percent over age 65	10.3%	12.9%

Economy & Jobs
Score: 83.7
Rank: 60

INCOME	AREA	U.S. AVG	EMPLOYMENT	AREA	U.S. AVG	EMPLOYING INDUSTRIES	AREA	U.S. AVG
Per capita income	$21,336	$23,235	Unemployment rate	3.1%	4.7%	Largest: Healthcare & Social Assistance		
Household income	$35,575	$46,414	Recent job growth	3.8%	1.3%			
Household income ‹ $25K	36.7%	26.2%	Projected future job growth	16.5%	11.5%	Percent manufacturing	7.2%	15.4%
Household income › $75K	20.2%	25.4%	White collar	68.7%	57.8%	Percent public sector	31.1%	15.7%
Household income growth	13.5%	13.6%	Blue collar	14.0%	25.2%	Percent construction	6.9%	9.9%

Cost of Living
Score: 80.5
Rank: 74

INDEXES & TAXES	AREA	U.S. AVG	HOUSING	AREA	U.S. AVG	NECESSITIES	AREA	U.S. AVG
Cost of Living Index	97.6	100.0	Median home price	$224,300	$220,000	Food Index	101.7	100.0
Buying Power Index	81.7	100.0	Home price appreciation	77.1%	10.1%	Housing Index	61.4	100.0
Income tax rate	0.00%	4.70%	Median rent	$651	$709	Utilities Index	88.8	100.0
Sales tax rate	6.30%	6.58%	Homes owned	53.0%	62.3%	Transportation Index	98.2	100.0
Property tax rate	$13.30	$12.00	Home price ratio	6.3	4.2	Healthcare Index	89.2	100.0
						Miscellaneous Cost Index	97.2	100.0

Climate
Score: 84.5
Rank: 59

TEMPERATURE	AREA	U.S. AVG	PRECIPITATION	AREA	U.S. AVG	COMFORTS & HAZARDS	AREA	U.S. AVG
Average January low	50.0	26.2	Annual inches precipitation	51.0	37.7	July relative humidity	74%	66%
Average July high	90.0	87.4	Annual inches snowfall	0.0	7.0	Annual days mostly sunny	242	208
Annual days › 90°F	104	38	Annual days precipitation	116	109	Annual days with thunderstorms	81	39
Annual days › 32°F	2	89	Annual days rain › 0.5 inches	32	22	Tornado risk score	21	18
Annual days ‹ 0°F	0	6	Annual days snow › 1.5 inches	0	6	Hurricane risk score	63	13

TEMPERATURE

PRECIPITATION

DAYS OF CLOUDS & PRECIPITATION

Education
Score: 93.0
Rank: 27

ACHIEVEMENT	AREA	U.S. AVG	PUBLIC SCHOOLS	AREA	U.S. AVG	HIGHER EDUCATION	AREA	U.S. AVG
High school degree	87.4%	82.7%	Expenditures per pupil	$4,949	$5,686	No. 2-year colleges	1	4
2-year college degree	9.5%	6.4%	Student/teacher ratio	16.4	16.7	No. 4-year colleges/universities	2	6
4-year college degree	19.4%	15.7%	Attending public school	90.0%	90.1%	No. highly ranked universities	1	1
Graduate/professional degree	18.3%	8.9%	State SAT score	993*	1021			
			State ACT score	20.3	20.9			

Health & Healthcare
Score: 70.9
Rank: 110

Crime
Score: 32.1
Rank: 254

HAZARDS & ILLNESSES	AREA	U.S. AVG	HEALTHCARE	AREA	U.S. AVG	CRIME	AREA	U.S. AVG
Air-quality score	40	37	Physicians per capita	668.5	244.2	Violent crime rate	867.4	465.5
Water-quality score	47	52	Hospital beds per capita	530.3	420.0	Change in violent crime rate	10.1%	-2.2%
Pollen/allergy score	68	61	No. teaching hospitals	2	3	Property crime rate	4,120.9	3,517.1
Cancer mortality per capita	273.3	201.9	Cost per doctor visit	$85	$77	Change in property crime rate	4.2%	-2.1%
Depression days per month	3.4	3.5	Cost per dental visit	$64	$70			
Stress score	40	50						

COMMUTE	AREA	U.S. AVG	INTERCITY SERVICES	AREA	U.S. AVG	AUTOMOTIVE	AREA	U.S. AVG
Average commute time	23.8	27.4	Major airports within 60 miles	1	1	Insurance, annual premium	$1,558	$1,432
Percent commutes > 60 mins.	4.5%	5.9%	Size of regional airport	Medium	Large	Gas, cost per gallon	$2.60	$2.49
Commute by auto	75.3%	78.9%	Daily airline activity	156	686	Daily vehicle miles per capita	23.5	24.0
Commute by mass transit	2.2%	1.9%	Amtrak service	Yes	No			
Work at home	3.3%	3.1%						
Mass transit miles per capita	2.19	1.87						

Transportation
Score: 29.9
Rank: 263

DINING & SHOPPING	AREA	U.S. AVG	ENTERTAINMENT	AREA	U.S. AVG	OUTDOOR ACTIVITIES	AREA	U.S. AVG
Restaurant rating	1	2	Professional sports rating	2	4	Golf-course rating	1	4
Outlet mall score	44	42	College sports rating	9	4	Ski-area rating	1	3
No. Starbucks	6	13	Zoo/aquarium rating	2	3	Sq. miles inland water	5	4
No. warehouse clubs	1	2	Amusement park rating	1	3	Miles of coastline	0.0	10.7
			Botanical garden/ arboretum rating	2	4	National Park rating	1	3

Leisure
Score: 44.4
Rank: 207

MEDIA & LIBRARIES	AREA	U.S. AVG	PERFORMING ARTS	AREA	U.S. AVG	MUSEUMS	AREA	U.S. AVG
Arts radio rating	5	3	Classical music rating	4	4	Overall museum rating	4	5
No. public libraries	11	27	Ballet/dance rating	1	3	Art museum rating	5	5
Library volumes per capita	3.69	2.78	Professional theater rating	6	3	Science museum rating	6	5
			University arts programs rating	5	5	Children's museum rating	2	3

Arts & Culture
Score: 66.0
Rank: 127

Gainesville, GA

Score: 58.6   Rank: 184   2004 rank: not ranked

Profile: Small city
Location: Northeast Georgia, 50 miles northeast of Atlanta
Elevation: 1,249 feet
Time zone: Eastern Standard Time

PRO	CON
Nearby recreation	Entertainment
Diverse economy	Rising living costs
Moderate climate	Arts and culture

Gainesville is a prosperous industrial, agricultural, and recreational center located along Lake Lanier. The area combines a Southern small-town feel with such advantages as excellent water recreation, proximity to Atlanta (50 miles to the southwest), and a relatively pleasant climate. Downtown is clean with a prominent town square and a number of historic homes and buildings nearby. The lake brings considerable tourism and weekend traffic from Atlanta. Some, not needing to be in Atlanta every day, are using Gainesville as a place to telecommute or run independent businesses. The high growth rate attests to the area's emerging popularity and has brought some "city"

elements, but that said, the area is far from becoming an Atlanta suburb. Cost of living is a bit high for the region.

Gainesville is located in the foothills of the Blue Ridge Mountains, a southern Appalachian extension rising to higher elevations in the northeast corner of the state. The gently rolling terrain is mainly covered with pine forests and becomes hillier to the north and northeast. Summers are moderated by elevation, but may bring periods of prolonged heat especially in late summer. Spring is wet with thunderstorms, some severe, until July, when it tends to dry out. Most winter precipitation is rain but with occasional snowfall or ice storms. First freeze is early November; last is late March.

DEMOGRAPHICS	AREA	U.S. AVG	ETHNIC COMPOSITION	AREA	U.S. AVG	RESIDENT PROFILE	AREA	U.S. AVG
Population	163,158		White	79.3%	79.0%	Single	28.3%	32.4%
Population density per sq. mile	414.4	358.5	Black	6.6%	10.5%	Married	55.9%	52.7%
Population growth	71.0%	21.1%	Asian	1.7%	2.7%	Divorced/separated	15.8%	14.9%
Median age	32.3	36.1	Hispanic	23.8%	10.6%	Married with children	28.7%	23.7%
Percent Democrat	21.1%	44.5%	Religious observance	46.9%	48.9%	Single with children	8.3%	9.1%
Percent Republican	78.2%	54.5%	Diversity measure	59.0	40.1	Percent over age 65	9.5%	12.9%

Population

INCOME	AREA	U.S. AVG	EMPLOYMENT	AREA	U.S. AVG	EMPLOYING INDUSTRIES	AREA	U.S. AVG
Per capita income	$21,697	$23,235	Unemployment rate	4.8%	4.7%	Largest: Manufacturing		
Household income	$49,740	$46,414	Recent job growth	2.6%	1.3%			
Household income < $25K	21.9%	26.2%	Projected future job growth	21.4%	11.5%	Percent manufacturing	23.9%	15.4%
Household income > $75K	28.0%	25.4%	White collar	49.9%	57.8%	Percent public sector	11.9%	15.7%
Household income growth	10.8%	13.6%	Blue collar	36.5%	25.2%	Percent construction	12.7%	9.9%

Economy & Jobs
Score: 90.1
Rank: 38

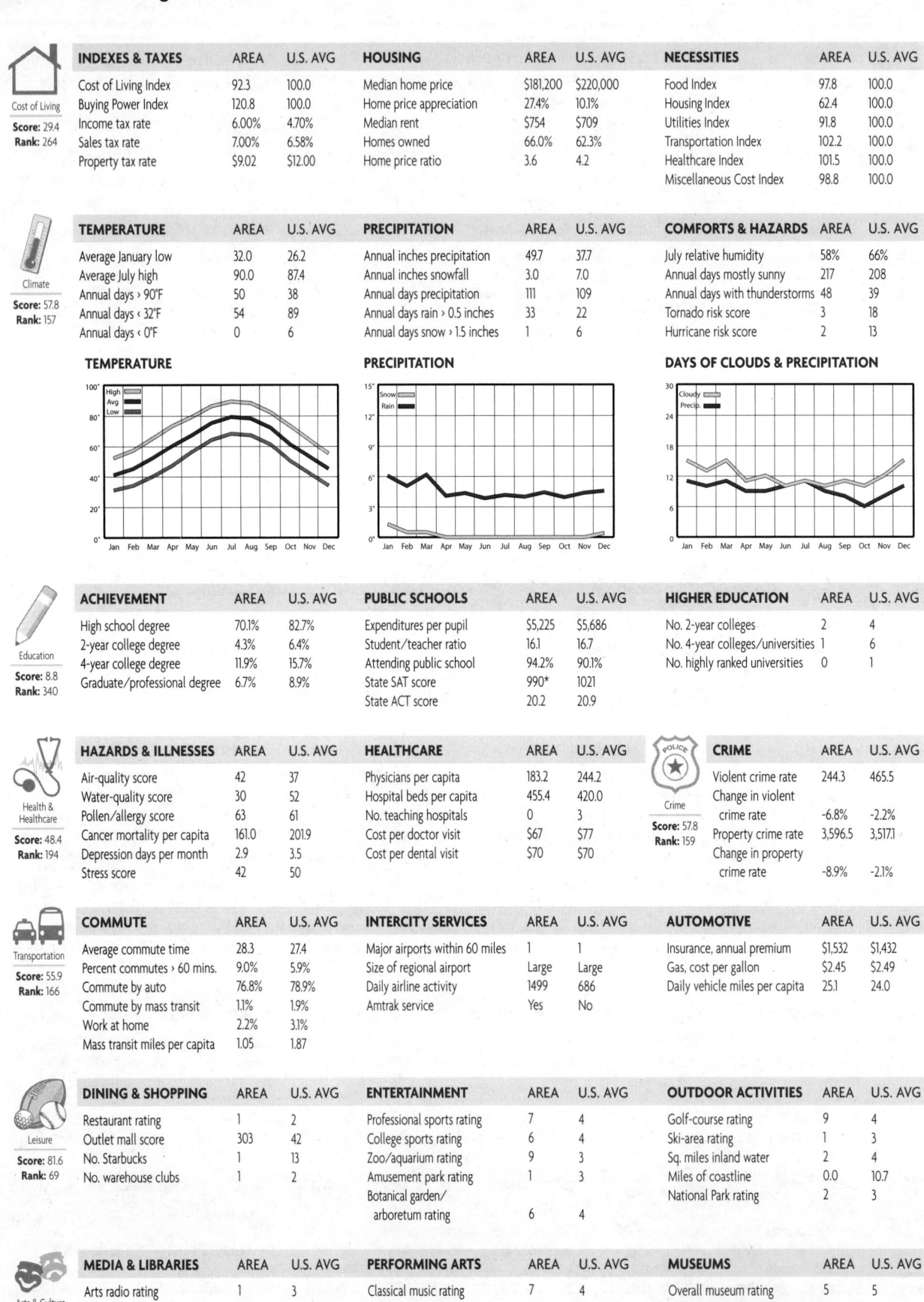

Cost of Living
Score: 29.4
Rank: 264

INDEXES & TAXES	AREA	U.S. AVG
Cost of Living Index	92.3	100.0
Buying Power Index	120.8	100.0
Income tax rate	6.00%	4.70%
Sales tax rate	7.00%	6.58%
Property tax rate	$9.02	$12.00

HOUSING	AREA	U.S. AVG
Median home price	$181,200	$220,000
Home price appreciation	27.4%	10.1%
Median rent	$754	$709
Homes owned	66.0%	62.3%
Home price ratio	3.6	4.2

NECESSITIES	AREA	U.S. AVG
Food Index	97.8	100.0
Housing Index	62.4	100.0
Utilities Index	91.8	100.0
Transportation Index	102.2	100.0
Healthcare Index	101.5	100.0
Miscellaneous Cost Index	98.8	100.0

Climate
Score: 57.8
Rank: 157

TEMPERATURE	AREA	U.S. AVG
Average January low	32.0	26.2
Average July high	90.0	87.4
Annual days > 90°F	50	38
Annual days < 32°F	54	89
Annual days < 0°F	0	6

PRECIPITATION	AREA	U.S. AVG
Annual inches precipitation	49.7	37.7
Annual inches snowfall	3.0	7.0
Annual days precipitation	111	109
Annual days rain > 0.5 inches	33	22
Annual days snow > 1.5 inches	1	6

COMFORTS & HAZARDS	AREA	U.S. AVG
July relative humidity	58%	66%
Annual days mostly sunny	217	208
Annual days with thunderstorms	48	39
Tornado risk score	3	18
Hurricane risk score	2	13

TEMPERATURE

PRECIPITATION

DAYS OF CLOUDS & PRECIPITATION

Education
Score: 8.8
Rank: 340

ACHIEVEMENT	AREA	U.S. AVG
High school degree	70.1%	82.7%
2-year college degree	4.3%	6.4%
4-year college degree	11.9%	15.7%
Graduate/professional degree	6.7%	8.9%

PUBLIC SCHOOLS	AREA	U.S. AVG
Expenditures per pupil	$5,225	$5,686
Student/teacher ratio	16.1	16.7
Attending public school	94.2%	90.1%
State SAT score	990*	1021
State ACT score	20.2	20.9

HIGHER EDUCATION	AREA	U.S. AVG
No. 2-year colleges	2	4
No. 4-year colleges/universities	1	6
No. highly ranked universities	0	1

Health & Healthcare
Score: 48.4
Rank: 194

HAZARDS & ILLNESSES	AREA	U.S. AVG
Air-quality score	42	37
Water-quality score	30	52
Pollen/allergy score	63	61
Cancer mortality per capita	161.0	201.9
Depression days per month	2.9	3.5
Stress score	42	50

HEALTHCARE	AREA	U.S. AVG
Physicians per capita	183.2	244.2
Hospital beds per capita	455.4	420.0
No. teaching hospitals	0	3
Cost per doctor visit	$67	$77
Cost per dental visit	$70	$70

Crime
Score: 57.8
Rank: 159

CRIME	AREA	U.S. AVG
Violent crime rate	244.3	465.5
Change in violent crime rate	-6.8%	-2.2%
Property crime rate	3,596.5	3,517.1
Change in property crime rate	-8.9%	-2.1%

Transportation
Score: 55.9
Rank: 166

COMMUTE	AREA	U.S. AVG
Average commute time	28.3	27.4
Percent commutes > 60 mins.	9.0%	5.9%
Commute by auto	76.8%	78.9%
Commute by mass transit	1.1%	1.9%
Work at home	2.2%	3.1%
Mass transit miles per capita	1.05	1.87

INTERCITY SERVICES	AREA	U.S. AVG
Major airports within 60 miles	1	1
Size of regional airport	Large	Large
Daily airline activity	1499	686
Amtrak service	Yes	No

AUTOMOTIVE	AREA	U.S. AVG
Insurance, annual premium	$1,532	$1,432
Gas, cost per gallon	$2.45	$2.49
Daily vehicle miles per capita	25.1	24.0

Leisure
Score: 81.6
Rank: 69

DINING & SHOPPING	AREA	U.S. AVG
Restaurant rating	1	2
Outlet mall score	303	42
No. Starbucks	1	13
No. warehouse clubs	1	2

ENTERTAINMENT	AREA	U.S. AVG
Professional sports rating	7	4
College sports rating	6	4
Zoo/aquarium rating	9	3
Amusement park rating	1	3
Botanical garden/arboretum rating	6	4

OUTDOOR ACTIVITIES	AREA	U.S. AVG
Golf-course rating	9	4
Ski-area rating	1	3
Sq. miles inland water	2	4
Miles of coastline	0.0	10.7
National Park rating	2	3

Arts & Culture
Score: 78.3
Rank: 81

MEDIA & LIBRARIES	AREA	U.S. AVG
Arts radio rating	1	3
No. public libraries	5	27
Library volumes per capita	1.58	2.78

PERFORMING ARTS	AREA	U.S. AVG
Classical music rating	7	4
Ballet/dance rating	9	3
Professional theater rating	1	3
University arts programs rating	10	5

MUSEUMS	AREA	U.S. AVG
Overall museum rating	5	5
Art museum rating	6	5
Science museum rating	7	5
Children's museum rating	6	3

Gary, IN

Profile: Industrial city
Location: Extreme northwest Indiana at Illinois border along Lake Michigan, 30 miles southeast of Chicago
Elevation: 623 feet
Time zone: Central Standard Time

PRO	CON
Proximity to Chicago	Industrial setting
Nearby beach areas	Economic cycles
Redevelopment effort	Harsh winters

Gary just celebrated its centennial, and used the event to kick off what will hopefully be a more progressive and successful second 100 years. The location, midway between deposits of iron ore in the upper Great Lakes and coal and limestone resources to the south, made it a major 20th-century center for steel and heavy industry. Although the steel industry has declined (there is one major US Steel mill left), the city's heavy industrial character remains. The landscape remains blighted with abandoned sites and lots around the city that the city has vowed to bring back to life. Some stronger middle-class suburbs and suburban towns are to the south, notably Merrillville. Two casinos opened in the late 1990s to add some economic vitality, but it's only a small start and may not be the right long-term direction. There is a sense of humor and perhaps a bit of pride about its role and plight; the aptly named minor league Gary Steelheads (basketball) and Gary SouthShore Railcats (baseball) bring some entertainment. Chicago to the northwest and the Indiana Dunes National Lakeshore and Michigan Dunes areas to the east provide considerable recreation and entertainment to those willing to travel short distances. Not surprisingly, cost of living and housing compare very favorably to the rest of the Chicagoland area, a fact not lost on redevelopment leaders. Commuter rail service along the old South Shore line reaches downtown Chicago in a little less than an hour and still less to some of the redeveloping areas south of downtown. The city will need heavy investment to capitalize on its location at the shore and near Chicago to make it work, but we like the strength of the commitment, and it's a definite wait-and-see.

Gary lies on a level plain spreading south from the Lake Michigan shore. The landscape is highly industrial with areas of trees and agriculture to the south and southeast. Like Chicago, weather is highly variable, with warm, humid summers and blustery, variable winters. However, Gary is downwind from northerly lake winds, so the area gets stronger lake-effect winds and snows compared to Chicago. That said, the lake does moderate temperatures more than comparable inland locations. First freeze is mid-October; last is late April.

DEMOGRAPHICS	AREA	U.S. AVG	ETHNIC COMPOSITION	AREA	U.S. AVG	RESIDENT PROFILE	AREA	U.S. AVG
Population	690,812		White	74.7%	79.0%	Single	34.3%	32.4%
Population density per sq. mile	368.1	358.5	Black	18.1%	10.5%	Married	52.3%	52.7%
Population growth	8.0%	21.1%	Asian	1.0%	2.7%	Divorced/separated	13.4%	14.9%
Median age	36.6	36.1	Hispanic	10.4%	10.6%	Married with children	23.5%	23.7%
Percent Democrat	55.6%	44.5%	Religious observance	43.9%	48.9%	Single with children	9.8%	9.1%
Percent Republican	43.6%	54.5%	Diversity measure	48.2	40.1	Percent over age 65	12.8%	12.9%

INCOME	AREA	U.S. AVG	EMPLOYMENT	AREA	U.S. AVG	EMPLOYING INDUSTRIES	AREA	U.S. AVG
Per capita income	$23,133	$23,235	Unemployment rate	5.5%	4.7%	Largest: Manufacturing		
Household income	$49,281	$46,414	Recent job growth	0.0%	1.3%			
Household income < $25K	24.1%	26.2%	Projected future job growth	5.0%	11.5%	Percent manufacturing	18.9%	15.4%
Household income > $75K	27.5%	25.4%	White collar	53.3%	57.8%	Percent public sector	11.3%	15.7%
Household income growth	11.0%	13.6%	Blue collar	31.0%	25.2%	Percent construction	12.1%	9.9%

Score: 26.7
Rank: 274

INDEXES & TAXES	AREA	U.S. AVG	HOUSING	AREA	U.S. AVG	NECESSITIES	AREA	U.S. AVG
Cost of Living Index	87.4	100.0	Median home price	$128,400	$220,000	Food Index	104.8	100.0
Buying Power Index	126.4	100.0	Home price appreciation	26.2%	10.1%	Housing Index	50.8	100.0
Income tax rate	3.40%	4.70%	Median rent	$749	$709	Utilities Index	106.2	100.0
Sales tax rate	6.00%	6.58%	Homes owned	67.3%	62.3%	Transportation Index	122.1	100.0
Property tax rate	$11.59	$12.00	Home price ratio	2.6	4.2	Healthcare Index	118.8	100.0
						Miscellaneous Cost Index	106.6	100.0

Score: 70.3
Rank: 112

Climate
Score: 25.7
Rank: 277

TEMPERATURE	AREA	U.S. AVG	PRECIPITATION	AREA	U.S. AVG	COMFORTS & HAZARDS	AREA	U.S. AVG
Average January low	17.0	26.2	Annual inches precipitation	34.0	37.7	July relative humidity	67%	66%
Average July high	84.4	87.4	Annual inches snowfall	40.0	7.0	Annual days mostly sunny	197	208
Annual days > 90°F	21	38	Annual days precipitation	123	109	Annual days with thunderstorms	40	39
Annual days < 32°F	119	89	Annual days rain > 0.5 inches	23	22	Tornado risk score	24	18
Annual days < 0°F	7	6	Annual days snow > 1.5 inches	18	6	Hurricane risk score	2	13

TEMPERATURE

PRECIPITATION

DAYS OF CLOUDS & PRECIPITATION

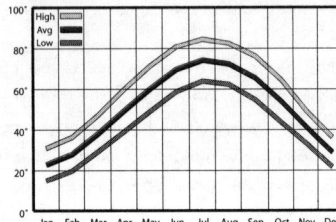
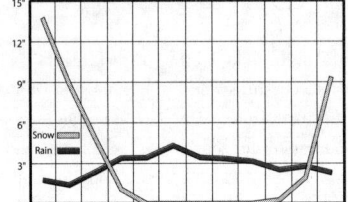

Education
Score: 31.6
Rank: 257

ACHIEVEMENT	AREA	U.S. AVG	PUBLIC SCHOOLS	AREA	U.S. AVG	HIGHER EDUCATION	AREA	U.S. AVG
High school degree	82.7%	82.7%	Expenditures per pupil	$6,098	$5,686	No. 2-year colleges	5	4
2-year college degree	5.3%	6.4%	Student/teacher ratio	19.4	16.7	No. 4-year colleges/universities	6	6
4-year college degree	11.3%	15.7%	Attending public school	90.6%	90.1%	No. highly ranked universities	1	1
Graduate/professional degree	6.3%	8.9%	State SAT score	1007*	1021			
			State ACT score	21.7	20.9			

Health & Healthcare
Score: 11.2
Rank: 330

Crime
Score: 57.5
Rank: 160

HAZARDS & ILLNESSES	AREA	U.S. AVG	HEALTHCARE	AREA	U.S. AVG	CRIME	AREA	U.S. AVG
Air-quality score	23	37	Physicians per capita	173.7	244.2	Violent crime rate	460.2	465.5
Water-quality score	34	52	Hospital beds per capita	418.5	420.0	Change in violent crime rate	6.7%	-2.2%
Pollen/allergy score	57	61	No. teaching hospitals	4	3	Property crime rate	3,876.1	3,517.1
Cancer mortality per capita	227.3	201.9	Cost per doctor visit	$68	$77	Change in property crime rate	4.4%	-2.1%
Depression days per month	3.6	3.5	Cost per dental visit	$74	$70			
Stress score	93	50						

Transportation
Score: 89.3
Rank: 41

COMMUTE	AREA	U.S. AVG	INTERCITY SERVICES	AREA	U.S. AVG	AUTOMOTIVE	AREA	U.S. AVG
Average commute time	29.2	27.4	Major airports within 60 miles	3	1	Insurance, annual premium	$1,647	$1,432
Percent commutes > 60 mins.	10.0%	5.9%	Size of regional airport	Large	Large	Gas, cost per gallon	$2.44	$2.49
Commute by auto	82.1%	78.9%	Daily airline activity	2083	686	Daily vehicle miles per capita	22.4	24.0
Commute by mass transit	2.5%	1.9%	Amtrak service	Yes	No			
Work at home	2.3%	3.1%						
Mass transit miles per capita	2.53	1.87						

Leisure
Score: 75.4
Rank: 92

DINING & SHOPPING	AREA	U.S. AVG	ENTERTAINMENT	AREA	U.S. AVG	OUTDOOR ACTIVITIES	AREA	U.S. AVG
Restaurant rating	1	2	Professional sports rating	8	4	Golf-course rating	7	4
Outlet mall score	103	42	College sports rating	2	4	Ski-area rating	4	3
No. Starbucks	5	13	Zoo/aquarium rating	2	3	Sq. miles inland water	2	4
No. warehouse clubs	2	2	Amusement park rating	3	3	Miles of coastline	32.9	10.7
			Botanical garden/ arboretum rating	6	4	National Park rating	3	3

Arts & Culture
Score: 76.2
Rank: 89

MEDIA & LIBRARIES	AREA	U.S. AVG	PERFORMING ARTS	AREA	U.S. AVG	MUSEUMS	AREA	U.S. AVG
Arts radio rating	4	3	Classical music rating	5	4	Overall museum rating	9	5
No. public libraries	50	27	Ballet/dance rating	4	3	Art museum rating	8	5
Library volumes per capita	5.88	2.78	Professional theater rating	5	3	Science museum rating	6	5
			University arts programs rating	8	5	Children's museum rating	6	3

Glens Falls, NY

Score: 50.7   Rank: 245   2004 rank: 285

Profile: Small city
Location: East-central New York at southeast edge of Adirondacks, 60 miles north of Albany
Elevation: 292 feet
Time zone: Eastern Standard Time

PRO	CON
Nearby mountains	Isolation
Nearby recreation	Future job growth
Small-town atmosphere	Harsh winters

Glens Falls is a minor industrial center and gateway to the Adirondack region to the north. It is located just to the north of the Albany–Schenectady–Troy area along the Hudson River. The town is quiet and boasts a pleasant small-town feel with low crime, moderate living costs, and good air quality, but there isn't much to do in the immediate town. As is typical with the region, economic prospects are not strong. The more well-known Saratoga Springs is 15 miles south and offers a number of cultural amenities in an attractive and historic setting. Lake George to the immediate north offers recreational opportunities and the Lake George Opera Festival. The Adirondacks offer numerous outdoor activities, including Lake Placid of Olympic Winter Games fame, 85 miles north.

The town is located in a small valley at a sharp bend in the Hudson River. It is surrounded by wooded hills, which become larger to the north, rising eventually to 5,300 feet in the heavily wooded Adirondacks. Summer days are warm and sunny and sometimes humid, but evening temperatures fall quickly. Hot, sticky weather occurs most summers, and most precipitation comes from summer thunderstorms. Winters are cold, frequently dropping below 10°F and even 0°F, with heavy and persistent snow during many winters. First freeze is end of September; last is mid-May.

Population

DEMOGRAPHICS	AREA	U.S. AVG	ETHNIC COMPOSITION	AREA	U.S. AVG	RESIDENT PROFILE	AREA	U.S. AVG
Population	127,879		White	95.9%	79.0%	Single	31.8%	32.4%
Population density per sq. mile	75.0	358.5	Black	2.0%	10.5%	Married	53.7%	52.7%
Population growth	8.0%	21.1%	Asian	0.5%	2.7%	Divorced/separated	14.5%	14.9%
Median age	39.7	36.1	Hispanic	2.0%	10.6%	Married with children	22.8%	23.7%
Percent Democrat	42.8%	44.5%	Religious observance	45.3%	48.9%	Single with children	8.9%	9.1%
Percent Republican	54.9%	54.5%	Diversity measure	11.6	40.1	Percent over age 65	15.0%	12.9%

Economy & Jobs
Score: 33.7
Rank: 248

INCOME	AREA	U.S. AVG	EMPLOYMENT	AREA	U.S. AVG	EMPLOYING INDUSTRIES	AREA	U.S. AVG
Per capita income	$22,202	$23,235	Unemployment rate	3.9%	4.7%	Largest: Manufacturing		
Household income	$43,506	$46,414	Recent job growth	1.7%	1.3%			
Household income < $25K	25.8%	26.2%	Projected future job growth	3.7%	11.5%	Percent manufacturing	16.7%	15.4%
Household income > $75K	21.0%	25.4%	White collar	53.6%	57.8%	Percent public sector	17.3%	15.7%
Household income growth	13.2%	13.6%	Blue collar	26.9%	25.2%	Percent construction	10.2%	9.9%

Cost of Living
Score: 21.4
Rank: 293

INDEXES & TAXES	AREA	U.S. AVG	HOUSING	AREA	U.S. AVG	NECESSITIES	AREA	U.S. AVG
Cost of Living Index	96.8	100.0	Median home price	$158,700	$220,000	Food Index	108.1	100.0
Buying Power Index	100.7	100.0	Home price appreciation	71.1%	10.1%	Housing Index	81.4	100.0
Income tax rate	7.13%	4.70%	Median rent	$662	$709	Utilities Index	141.8	100.0
Sales tax rate	7.25%	6.58%	Homes owned	57.3%	62.3%	Transportation Index	105.2	100.0
Property tax rate	$18.85	$12.00	Home price ratio	3.6	4.2	Healthcare Index	99.3	100.0
						Miscellaneous Cost Index	100.0	100.0

Climate
Score: 2.9
Rank: 362

TEMPERATURE	AREA	U.S. AVG	PRECIPITATION	AREA	U.S. AVG	COMFORTS & HAZARDS	AREA	U.S. AVG
Average January low	12.5	26.2	Annual inches precipitation	33.0	37.7	July relative humidity	71%	66%
Average July high	83.9	87.4	Annual inches snowfall	71.0	7.0	Annual days mostly sunny	182	208
Annual days > 90°F	8	38	Annual days precipitation	135	109	Annual days with thunderstorms	28	39
Annual days < 32°F	155	89	Annual days rain > 0.5 inches	23	22	Tornado risk score	4	18
Annual days < 0°F	17	6	Annual days snow > 1.5 inches	13	6	Hurricane risk score	6	13

TEMPERATURE

PRECIPITATION

DAYS OF CLOUDS & PRECIPITATION

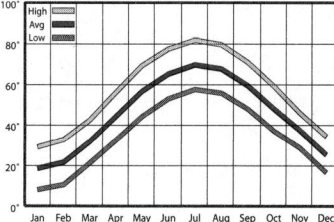

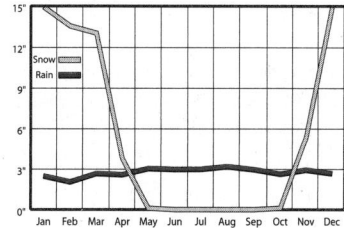

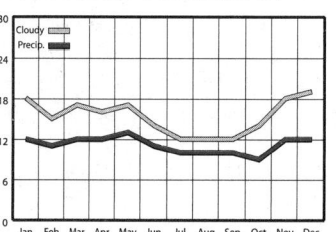

ACHIEVEMENT	AREA	U.S. AVG	PUBLIC SCHOOLS	AREA	U.S. AVG	HIGHER EDUCATION	AREA	U.S. AVG
High school degree	82.1%	82.7%	Expenditures per pupil	$9,372	$5,686	No. 2-year colleges	2	4
2-year college degree	8.8%	6.4%	Student/teacher ratio	14.8	16.7	No. 4-year colleges/universities	0	6
4-year college degree	11.2%	15.7%	Attending public school	97.2%	90.1%	No. highly ranked universities	0	1
Graduate/professional degree	7.8%	8.9%	State SAT score	1003*	1021			
			State ACT score	22.6	20.9			

Education
Score: 60.2
Rank: 150

HAZARDS & ILLNESSES	AREA	U.S. AVG	HEALTHCARE	AREA	U.S. AVG	CRIME	AREA	U.S. AVG
Air-quality score	61	37	Physicians per capita	187.5	244.2	Violent crime rate	247.3	465.5
Water-quality score	53	52	Hospital beds per capita	448.9	420.0	Change in violent crime rate	23.4%	-2.2%
Pollen/allergy score	44	61	No. teaching hospitals	0	3	Property crime rate	2,298.0	3,517.1
Cancer mortality per capita	218.6	201.9	Cost per doctor visit	$68	$77	Change in property crime rate	41.1%	-2.1%
Depression days per month	3.5	3.5	Cost per dental visit	$63	$70			
Stress score	17	50						

Health & Healthcare
Score: 81.8
Rank: 69

Crime
Score: 81.8
Rank: 69

COMMUTE	AREA	U.S. AVG	INTERCITY SERVICES	AREA	U.S. AVG	AUTOMOTIVE	AREA	U.S. AVG
Average commute time	24.8	27.4	Major airports within 60 miles	0	1	Insurance, annual premium	$1,401	$1,432
Percent commutes > 60 mins.	7.4%	5.9%	Size of regional airport	Small	Large	Gas, cost per gallon	$2.62	$2.49
Commute by auto	80.0%	78.9%	Daily airline activity	200	686	Daily vehicle miles per capita	27.7	24.0
Commute by mass transit	0.9%	1.9%	Amtrak service	Yes	No			
Work at home	3.9%	3.1%						
Mass transit miles per capita	0.85	1.87						

Transportation
Score: 13.6
Rank: 324

DINING & SHOPPING	AREA	U.S. AVG	ENTERTAINMENT	AREA	U.S. AVG	OUTDOOR ACTIVITIES	AREA	U.S. AVG
Restaurant rating	1	2	Professional sports rating	3	4	Golf-course rating	2	4
Outlet mall score	11	42	College sports rating	2	4	Ski-area rating	8	3
No. Starbucks	1	13	Zoo/aquarium rating	1	3	Sq. miles inland water	5	4
No. warehouse clubs	0	2	Amusement park rating	4	3	Miles of coastline	0.0	10.7
			Botanical garden/arboretum rating	4	4	National Park rating	1	3

Leisure
Score: 55.3
Rank: 167

MEDIA & LIBRARIES	AREA	U.S. AVG	PERFORMING ARTS	AREA	U.S. AVG	MUSEUMS	AREA	U.S. AVG
Arts radio rating	1	3	Classical music rating	3	4	Overall museum rating	4	5
No. public libraries	20	27	Ballet/dance rating	1	3	Art museum rating	7	5
Library volumes per capita	5.18	2.78	Professional theater rating	1	3	Science museum rating	4	5
			University arts programs rating	1	5	Children's museum rating	3	3

Arts & Culture
Score: 35.3
Rank: 242

Goldsboro, NC

Score: 54.7 **Rank:** 222 **2004 rank:** 86

Profile: Small town
Location: East-central North Carolina, 55 miles southeast of Raleigh
Elevation: 121 feet
Time zone: Eastern Standard Time

PRO
Cost of living
Close to Raleigh–Durham
Diverse economy

CON
Low educational attainment
Unattractive downtown
Hot, humid summers

Goldsboro is a Southern town with a diversified economy consisting of several small manufacturers, which make everything from roofing and mechanical pumps to slippers, and a larger Georgia-Pacific plywood mill. There is some agriculture and a major poultry processing plant. Most industry, as well as the Seymour Johnson Air Force Base, are outside of town. The downtown area, once a bright spot, has deteriorated considerably and reflects neglect and economic malaise. There isn't much to do. However, the cost of living is the lowest in the state, and the town is close enough to Raleigh and the Durham area (55 miles) and the coast (75 miles) to take advantage of amenities there.

Proximity to these areas has affected scores and ranks, yet most will find the area less attractive than the numbers indicate even with the drop in ranking since 2004.

Goldsboro is located in a mostly level coastal plain with deciduous wooded areas. Tropical air makes for hot, muggy summers with occasional thundershowers and steady rains from storms moving up the coast. Mountain protection and the coastal influence make winters fairly mild, with most precipitation as rain, although an occasional dusting of snow or sleet occurs.

Population

DEMOGRAPHICS	AREA	U.S. AVG
Population	113,261	
Population density per sq. mile	205.0	358.5
Population growth	8.2%	21.1%
Median age	35.5	36.1
Percent Democrat	37.6%	44.5%
Percent Republican	62.1%	54.5%

ETHNIC COMPOSITION	AREA	U.S. AVG
White	60.0%	79.0%
Black	33.6%	10.5%
Asian	1.1%	2.7%
Hispanic	5.7%	10.6%
Religious observance	37.3%	48.9%
Diversity measure	57.6	40.1

RESIDENT PROFILE	AREA	U.S. AVG
Single	32.0%	32.4%
Married	52.0%	52.7%
Divorced/separated	16.1%	14.9%
Married with children	23.2%	23.7%
Single with children	11.3%	9.1%
Percent over age 65	12.3%	12.9%

Economy & Jobs
Score: 12.3
Rank: 327

INCOME	AREA	U.S. AVG
Per capita income	$19,794	$23,235
Household income	$39,848	$46,414
Household income < $25K	29.6%	26.2%
Household income > $75K	18.4%	25.4%
Household income growth	17.4%	13.6%

EMPLOYMENT	AREA	U.S. AVG
Unemployment rate	6.5%	4.7%
Recent job growth	1.1%	1.3%
Projected future job growth	5.3%	11.5%
White collar	51.3%	57.8%
Blue collar	30.3%	25.2%

EMPLOYING INDUSTRIES	AREA	U.S. AVG
Largest: Manufacturing		
Percent manufacturing	18.7%	15.4%
Percent public sector	21.5%	15.7%
Percent construction	11.6%	9.9%

Cost of Living
Score: 65.2
Rank: 130

INDEXES & TAXES	AREA	U.S. AVG
Cost of Living Index	77.1	100.0
Buying Power Index	115.8	100.0
Income tax rate	7.00%	4.70%
Sales tax rate	7.00%	6.58%
Property tax rate	$8.15	$12.00

HOUSING	AREA	U.S. AVG
Median home price	$108,600	$220,000
Home price appreciation	18.5%	10.1%
Median rent	$544	$709
Homes owned	59.6%	62.3%
Home price ratio	2.7	4.2

NECESSITIES	AREA	U.S. AVG
Food Index	94.4	100.0
Housing Index	48.1	100.0
Utilities Index	92.9	100.0
Transportation Index	88.9	100.0
Healthcare Index	86.8	100.0
Miscellaneous Cost Index	97.6	100.0

Climate
Score: 61.5
Rank: 143

TEMPERATURE	AREA	U.S. AVG
Average January low	30.0	26.2
Average July high	87.7	87.4
Annual days > 90°F	25	38
Annual days < 32°F	82	89
Annual days < 0°F	0	6

PRECIPITATION	AREA	U.S. AVG
Annual inches precipitation	43.0	37.7
Annual inches snowfall	7.0	7.0
Annual days precipitation	112	109
Annual days rain > 0.5 inches	27	22
Annual days snow > 1.5 inches	2	6

COMFORTS & HAZARDS	AREA	U.S. AVG
July relative humidity	71%	66%
Annual days mostly sunny	220	208
Annual days with thunderstorms	46	39
Tornado risk score	30	18
Hurricane risk score	47	13

TEMPERATURE

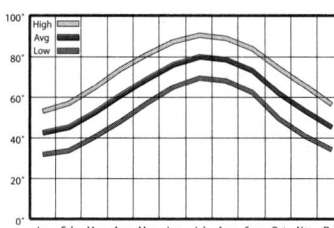

PRECIPITATION

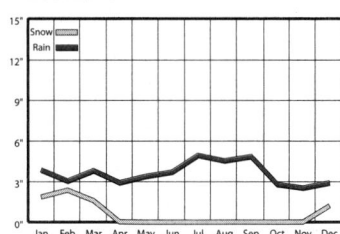

DAYS OF CLOUDS & PRECIPITATION

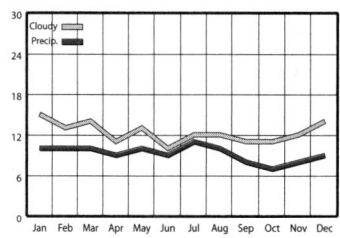

Education
Score: 22.2
Rank: 290

ACHIEVEMENT	AREA	U.S. AVG
High school degree	77.4%	82.7%
2-year college degree	7.8%	6.4%
4-year college degree	10.3%	15.7%
Graduate/professional degree	4.9%	8.9%

PUBLIC SCHOOLS	AREA	U.S. AVG
Expenditures per pupil	$4,672	$5,686
Student/teacher ratio	14.7	16.7
Attending public school	91.7%	90.1%
State SAT score	1008*	1021
State ACT score	20.5	20.9

HIGHER EDUCATION	AREA	U.S. AVG
No. 2-year colleges	1	4
No. 4-year colleges/universities	1	6
No. highly ranked universities	0	1

Health & Healthcare
Score: 66.3
Rank: 127

HAZARDS & ILLNESSES	AREA	U.S. AVG
Air-quality score	38	37
Water-quality score	70	52
Pollen/allergy score	65	61
Cancer mortality per capita	219.6	201.9
Depression days per month	3.2	3.5
Stress score	25	50

HEALTHCARE	AREA	U.S. AVG
Physicians per capita	158.3	244.2
Hospital beds per capita	879.4	420.0
No. teaching hospitals	1	3
Cost per doctor visit	$77	$77
Cost per dental visit	$68	$70

Crime
Score: 23.8
Rank: 285

CRIME	AREA	U.S. AVG
Violent crime rate	452.0	465.5
Change in violent crime rate	-8.4%	-2.2%
Property crime rate	4,287.7	3,517.1
Change in property crime rate	-2.2%	-2.1%

Transportation
Score: 41.7
Rank: 218

COMMUTE	AREA	U.S. AVG
Average commute time	23.2	27.4
Percent commutes > 60 mins.	6.1%	5.9%
Commute by auto	80.7%	78.9%
Commute by mass transit	0.4%	1.9%
Work at home	1.9%	3.1%
Mass transit miles per capita	0.42	1.87

INTERCITY SERVICES	AREA	U.S. AVG
Major airports within 60 miles	1	1
Size of regional airport	Medium	Large
Daily airline activity	352	686
Amtrak service	No	No

AUTOMOTIVE	AREA	U.S. AVG
Insurance, annual premium	$1,059	$1,432
Gas, cost per gallon	$2.53	$2.49
Daily vehicle miles per capita	30.9	24.0

DINING & SHOPPING	AREA	U.S. AVG	ENTERTAINMENT	AREA	U.S. AVG	OUTDOOR ACTIVITIES	AREA	U.S. AVG
Restaurant rating	1	2	Professional sports rating	2	4	Golf-course rating	6	4
Outlet mall score	0	42	College sports rating	4	4	Ski-area rating	1	3
No. Starbucks	0	13	Zoo/aquarium rating	1	3	Sq. miles inland water	3	4
No. warehouse clubs	0	2	Amusement park rating	1	3	Miles of coastline	0.0	10.7
			Botanical garden/			National Park rating	1	3
			arboretum rating	1	4			

Leisure
Score: 28.3
Rank: 267

MEDIA & LIBRARIES	AREA	U.S. AVG	PERFORMING ARTS	AREA	U.S. AVG	MUSEUMS	AREA	U.S. AVG
Arts radio rating	1	3	Classical music rating	6	4	Overall museum rating	2	5
No. public libraries	7	27	Ballet/dance rating	1	3	Art museum rating	1	5
Library volumes per capita	0.83	2.78	Professional theater rating	6	3	Science museum rating	5	5
			University arts programs rating	2	5	Children's museum rating	1	3

Arts & Culture
Score: 21.4
Rank: 293

Grand Forks, ND-MN

Score: 67.5 **Rank:** 113 **2004 rank:** 259

Profile: Small town/college town
Location: Extreme eastern North Dakota along Red River, 60 miles south of Canadian border
Elevation: 840 feet
Time zone: Central Standard Time

PRO	CON
Small-town atmosphere	Cold winters
Cool summers	Isolation
Cost of living	Future job growth

Grand Forks is located along the U.S. 2 east–west highway corridor at the Minnesota border. It is the home of the University of North Dakota, the state's oldest and largest institute of higher learning. The downtown area is typically Midwestern, with small shops and an assortment of mostly brick commercial buildings. Primary industries are related to the university or agriculture—the Red River Valley location contains some of the most fertile land in the world—and the Grand Forks Air Force Base adds to the economy. Some new high-tech and research organizations are mainly connected with the university. Employment is steady but not projected to grow rapidly. A devastating flood in 1997 and the gradual economic and population decline of the region as a whole hurt the economy, and prior to the flood, outward migration to suburbs primarily south and west were also taking a toll on downtown. But subsequent rebuilding did bring some life back into the city. A just-completed massive new dike system eliminated some older more vulnerable neighborhoods and provided plenty of new waterfront open space, and some repurposed older buildings and new high-rises are bringing in new commercial and residential activity. A few college-town amenities lie mostly west of town near the campus, but the closest big city is across the border in Winnipeg. Because of its northern Great Plains location and lack of moderating land features, Grand Forks has 55 days below zero—the second highest in the nation. Aside from weather, the absence of strong negatives brings a relatively healthy ranking.

Grand Forks and its sister city East Grand Forks, Minnesota, straddle the northward-flowing Red River, which divides North Dakota and Minnesota. The Red River Valley is flat and shallow, windswept year-round, subject to frequent spring flooding, and vulnerable to arctic outbreaks in winter. Snow covers the ground from mid-December through late March. Average winter snowfall is 38 inches. Summer months are typically warm—but not hot—and humid with frequent thunderstorms. Most precipitation occurs in the late spring through mid-summer thunderstorm season. Annual temperature variations are dramatic, with record lows below –40°F and record highs of 110°F. First freeze is late September; last is early May.

DEMOGRAPHICS	AREA	U.S. AVG	ETHNIC COMPOSITION	AREA	U.S. AVG	RESIDENT PROFILE	AREA	U.S. AVG
Population	95,087		White	92.6%	79.0%	Single	39.0%	32.4%
Population density per sq. mile	27.9	358.5	Black	1.3%	10.5%	Married	50.8%	52.7%
Population growth	-7.8%	21.1%	Asian	1.2%	2.7%	Divorced/separated	10.2%	14.9%
Median age	33.9	36.1	Hispanic	2.7%	10.6%	Married with children	24.2%	23.7%
Percent Democrat	42.0%	44.5%	Religious observance	64.9%	48.9%	Single with children	7.9%	9.1%
Percent Republican	56.4%	54.5%	Diversity measure	18.6	40.1	Percent over age 65	12.3%	12.9%

Population

INCOME	AREA	U.S. AVG	EMPLOYMENT	AREA	U.S. AVG	EMPLOYING INDUSTRIES	AREA	U.S. AVG
Per capita income	$20,822	$23,235	Unemployment rate	3.3%	4.7%	Largest: Healthcare & Social Assistance		
Household income	$41,355	$46,414	Recent job growth	1.2%	1.3%			
Household income ‹ $25K	28.1%	26.2%	Projected future job growth	0.6%	11.5%	Percent manufacturing	12.3%	15.4%
Household income › $75K	19.3%	25.4%	White collar	54.5%	57.8%	Percent public sector	20.1%	15.7%
Household income growth	16.3%	13.6%	Blue collar	22.8%	25.2%	Percent construction	10.6%	9.9%

Economy & Jobs
Score: 22.7
Rank: 289

Cost of Living
Score: 82.4
Rank: 66

INDEXES & TAXES	AREA	U.S. AVG
Cost of Living Index	82.0	100.0
Buying Power Index	113.0	100.0
Income tax rate	3.92%	4.70%
Sales tax rate	5.49%	6.58%
Property tax rate	$16.51	$12.00

HOUSING	AREA	U.S. AVG
Median home price	$133,000	$220,000
Home price appreciation	42.1%	10.1%
Median rent	$576	$709
Homes owned	54.9%	62.3%
Home price ratio	3.2	4.2

NECESSITIES	AREA	U.S. AVG
Food Index	95.8	100.0
Housing Index	54.4	100.0
Utilities Index	89.4	100.0
Transportation Index	90.7	100.0
Healthcare Index	95.5	100.0
Miscellaneous Cost Index	95.1	100.0

Climate
Score: 35.6
Rank: 240

TEMPERATURE	AREA	U.S. AVG
Average January low	-3.0	26.2
Average July high	83.0	87.4
Annual days > 90°F	13	38
Annual days < 32°F	180	89
Annual days < 0°F	55	6

PRECIPITATION	AREA	U.S. AVG
Annual inches precipitation	19.0	37.7
Annual inches snowfall	38.0	7.0
Annual days precipitation	100	109
Annual days rain > 0.5 inches	10	22
Annual days snow > 1.5 inches	8	6

COMFORTS & HAZARDS	AREA	U.S. AVG
July relative humidity	70%	66%
Annual days mostly sunny	198	208
Annual days with thunderstorms	31	39
Tornado risk score	9	18
Hurricane risk score	0	13

TEMPERATURE

PRECIPITATION

DAYS OF CLOUDS & PRECIPITATION

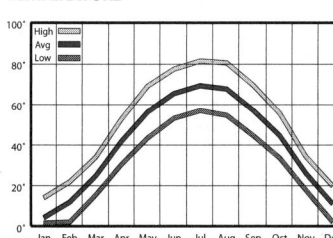 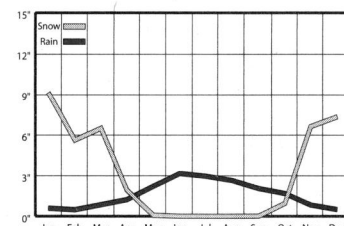 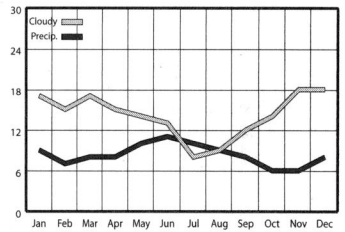

Education
Score: 73.0
Rank: 102

ACHIEVEMENT	AREA	U.S. AVG
High school degree	86.8%	82.7%
2-year college degree	9.0%	6.4%
4-year college degree	16.8%	15.7%
Graduate/professional degree	8.0%	8.9%

PUBLIC SCHOOLS	AREA	U.S. AVG
Expenditures per pupil	$4,961	$5,686
Student/teacher ratio	15.5	16.7
Attending public school	94.4%	90.1%
State SAT score	1227	1021
State ACT score	21.4*	20.9

HIGHER EDUCATION	AREA	U.S. AVG
No. 2-year colleges	1	4
No. 4-year colleges/universities	2	6
No. highly ranked universities	0	1

Health & Healthcare
Score: 97.1
Rank: 12

HAZARDS & ILLNESSES	AREA	U.S. AVG
Air-quality score	46	37
Water-quality score	58	52
Pollen/allergy score	31	61
Cancer mortality per capita	226.6	201.9
Depression days per month	2.9	3.5
Stress score	6	50

HEALTHCARE	AREA	U.S. AVG
Physicians per capita	261.3	244.2
Hospital beds per capita	764.6	420.0
No. teaching hospitals	1	3
Cost per doctor visit	$92	$77
Cost per dental visit	$56	$70

Crime
Score: 54.5
Rank: 171

CRIME	AREA	U.S. AVG
Violent crime rate	148.2	465.5
Change in violent crime rate	4.6%	-2.2%
Property crime rate	3,352.1	3,517.1
Change in property crime rate	7.4%	-2.1%

Transportation
Score: 73.5
Rank: 100

COMMUTE	AREA	U.S. AVG
Average commute time	16.8	27.4
Percent commutes > 60 mins.	2.6%	5.9%
Commute by auto	79.3%	78.9%
Commute by mass transit	0.8%	1.9%
Work at home	4.0%	3.1%
Mass transit miles per capita	0.76	1.87

INTERCITY SERVICES	AREA	U.S. AVG
Major airports within 60 miles	0	1
Size of regional airport	None	Large
Daily airline activity	15	686
Amtrak service	Yes	No

AUTOMOTIVE	AREA	U.S. AVG
Insurance, annual premium	$894	$1,432
Gas, cost per gallon	$2.46	$2.49
Daily vehicle miles per capita	14.0	24.0

Leisure
Score: 15.2
Rank: 316

DINING & SHOPPING	AREA	U.S. AVG
Restaurant rating	1	2
Outlet mall score	0	42
No. Starbucks	2	13
No. warehouse clubs	1	2

ENTERTAINMENT	AREA	U.S. AVG
Professional sports rating	2	4
College sports rating	6	4
Zoo/aquarium rating	1	3
Amusement park rating	1	3
Botanical garden/ arboretum rating	1	4

OUTDOOR ACTIVITIES	AREA	U.S. AVG
Golf-course rating	2	4
Ski-area rating	1	3
Sq. miles inland water	1	4
Miles of coastline	0.0	10.7
National Park rating	2	3

Arts & Culture
Score: 41.4
Rank: 218

MEDIA & LIBRARIES	AREA	U.S. AVG
Arts radio rating	1	3
No. public libraries	3	27
Library volumes per capita	4.16	2.78

PERFORMING ARTS	AREA	U.S. AVG
Classical music rating	3	4
Ballet/dance rating	1	3
Professional theater rating	1	3
University arts programs rating	4	5

MUSEUMS	AREA	U.S. AVG
Overall museum rating	2	5
Art museum rating	4	5
Science museum rating	3	5
Children's museum rating	1	3

Grand Junction, CO

Score: 75.1   **Rank:** 66   **2004 rank:** 62

Profile: Small city
Location: Western edge of Colorado, 25 miles from Utah
Elevation: 4,899 feet
Time zone: Mountain Standard Time

PRO	CON
Attractive setting	Isolation
Year-round climate	Growth and sprawl
Air quality	Arts and culture

Grand Junction is a small but rapidly growing town on the western desert slopes of the Rockies. It has become "discovered," first as a pleasant alternative to Colorado Front Range hustle and bustle, particularly for retirees, and more recently by migrants from all over the West. The climate is sunnier, drier, and generally more pleasant than other Colorado metropolitan areas and it has a well-preserved, Western-town flavor. Growth has pushed some suburbs north and west into the agricultural valleys toward the aptly named Fruita, with some high-end individual homes and developments. That the area now touts itself as "Colorado's Wine Country" says something about the climate and setting as well as the arriving city-refugee population. The air-quality score is the best in the state, and healthcare services are above average. Employment has been bolstered by the oil industry and construction and other services serving new arrivals. Cost of living has risen and is now about on par with local and national averages. The main downside is isolation—good air service or cultural amenities are located 250 miles east in Denver or 280 miles west in Salt Lake City, Utah, although local air service is improving. Grand Junction does not excel in any category but does consistently well in all of them, hence the favorable rank. We are concerned about the long-term effects of growth and sprawl on air quality and general quality of life, and that Grand Junction could become another of those "loved to death" Western towns like Reno and Boise, but it seems in check for now.

The town is located at the junction of the Colorado and Gunnison rivers in a large mountain valley on the west slope of the Rockies. Distant mountains on all sides reach heights of 9,000 feet to 12,000 feet from the valley floor, while low red-rock bluffs dominate the landscape closer in. The surrounding mountains block severe weather changes. Summer days are warm, usually in the 90s, but with very low humidity and an occasional thundershower. Long periods of winter cold can occur when cold air gets trapped in the valley. Sudden winter storms are infrequent and winter snows are light. First freeze is mid-September; last is late May.

DEMOGRAPHICS	AREA	U.S. AVG	ETHNIC COMPOSITION	AREA	U.S. AVG	RESIDENT PROFILE	AREA	U.S. AVG
Population	126,685		White	92.2%	79.0%	Single	27.5%	32.4%
Population density per sq. mile	38.1	358.5	Black	0.5%	10.5%	Married	57.5%	52.7%
Population growth	36.0%	21.1%	Asian	0.7%	2.7%	Divorced/separated	15.1%	14.9%
Median age	37.5	36.1	Hispanic	10.4%	10.6%	Married with children	22.8%	23.7%
Percent Democrat	31.6%	44.5%	Religious observance	28.6%	48.9%	Single with children	8.4%	9.1%
Percent Republican	67.1%	54.5%	Diversity measure	30.6	40.1	Percent over age 65	15.4%	12.9%

INCOME	AREA	U.S. AVG	EMPLOYMENT	AREA	U.S. AVG	EMPLOYING INDUSTRIES	AREA	U.S. AVG
Per capita income	$21,691	$23,235	Unemployment rate	4.9%	4.7%	Largest: Healthcare & Social Assistance		
Household income	$41,399	$46,414	Recent job growth	0.0%	1.3%			
Household income < $25K	27.9%	26.2%	Projected future job growth	15.4%	11.5%	Percent manufacturing	12.7%	15.4%
Household income > $75K	19.7%	25.4%	White collar	56.8%	57.8%	Percent public sector	14.1%	15.7%
Household income growth	15.4%	13.6%	Blue collar	24.5%	25.2%	Percent construction	11.7%	9.9%

Score: 30.5
Rank: 260

INDEXES & TAXES	AREA	U.S. AVG	HOUSING	AREA	U.S. AVG	NECESSITIES	AREA	U.S. AVG
Cost of Living Index	97.5	100.0	Median home price	$192,700	$220,000	Food Index	106.0	100.0
Buying Power Index	95.2	100.0	Home price appreciation	50.0%	10.1%	Housing Index	80.1	100.0
Income tax rate	5.00%	4.70%	Median rent	$602	$709	Utilities Index	101.3	100.0
Sales tax rate	4.90%	6.58%	Homes owned	69.9%	62.3%	Transportation Index	109.7	100.0
Property tax rate	$6.54	$12.00	Home price ratio	4.7	4.2	Healthcare Index	114.7	100.0
						Miscellaneous Cost Index	99.1	100.0

Score: 52.4
Rank: 176

Climate
Score: 71.7
Rank: 105

TEMPERATURE	AREA	U.S. AVG	PRECIPITATION	AREA	U.S. AVG	COMFORTS & HAZARDS	AREA	U.S. AVG
Average January low	16.0	26.2	Annual inches precipitation	9.0	37.7	July relative humidity	47%	66%
Average July high	93.0	87.4	Annual inches snowfall	26.0	7.0	Annual days mostly sunny	260	208
Annual days > 90°F	62	38	Annual days precipitation	70	109	Annual days with thunderstorms	36	39
Annual days < 32°F	134	89	Annual days rain > 0.5 inches	4	22	Tornado risk score	0	18
Annual days < 0°F	4	6	Annual days snow > 1.5 inches	7	6	Hurricane risk score	0	13

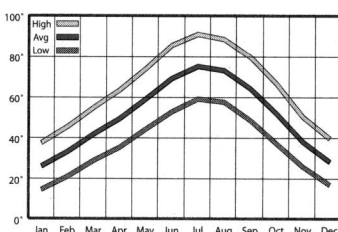

TEMPERATURE

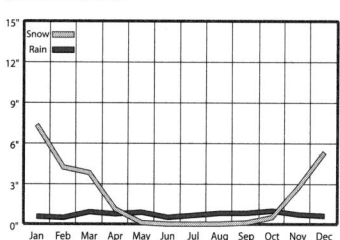

PRECIPITATION

DAYS OF CLOUDS & PRECIPITATION

Education
Score: 51.3
Rank: 183

ACHIEVEMENT	AREA	U.S. AVG	PUBLIC SCHOOLS	AREA	U.S. AVG	HIGHER EDUCATION	AREA	U.S. AVG
High school degree	85.1%	82.7%	Expenditures per pupil	$5,063	$5,686	No. 2-year colleges	1	4
2-year college degree	7.1%	6.4%	Student/teacher ratio	17.7	16.7	No. 4-year colleges/universities	1	6
4-year college degree	14.6%	15.7%	Attending public school	94.6%	90.1%	No. highly ranked universities	0	1
Graduate/professional degree	7.3%	8.9%	State SAT score	1122	1021			
			State ACT score	20.3*	20.9			

Health & Healthcare
Score: 92.8
Rank: 28

HAZARDS & ILLNESSES	AREA	U.S. AVG	HEALTHCARE	AREA	U.S. AVG	CRIME	AREA	U.S. AVG
Air-quality score	45	37	Physicians per capita	265.5	244.2	Violent crime rate	271.3	465.5
Water-quality score	87	52	Hospital beds per capita	599.1	420.0	Change in violent crime rate	-6.0%	-2.2%
Pollen/allergy score	60	61	No. teaching hospitals	2	3	Property crime rate	4,117.3	3,517.1
Cancer mortality per capita	153.9	201.9	Cost per doctor visit	$81	$77	Change in property crime rate	5.0%	-2.1%
Depression days per month	3.2	3.5	Cost per dental visit	$69	$70			
Stress score	30	50						

Crime
Score: 58.6
Rank: 155

Transportation
Score: 44.7
Rank: 208

COMMUTE	AREA	U.S. AVG	INTERCITY SERVICES	AREA	U.S. AVG	AUTOMOTIVE	AREA	U.S. AVG
Average commute time	20.0	27.4	Major airports within 60 miles	0	1	Insurance, annual premium	$1,376	$1,432
Percent commutes > 60 mins.	4.2%	5.9%	Size of regional airport	None	Large	Gas, cost per gallon	$2.45	$2.49
Commute by auto	77.3%	78.9%	Daily airline activity	36	686	Daily vehicle miles per capita	19.4	24.0
Commute by mass transit	0.5%	1.9%	Amtrak service	Yes	No			
Work at home	5.4%	3.1%						
Mass transit miles per capita	0.49	1.87						

Leisure
Score: 51.3
Rank: 180

DINING & SHOPPING	AREA	U.S. AVG	ENTERTAINMENT	AREA	U.S. AVG	OUTDOOR ACTIVITIES	AREA	U.S. AVG
Restaurant rating	1	2	Professional sports rating	2	4	Golf-course rating	1	4
Outlet mall score	0	42	College sports rating	3	4	Ski-area rating	10	3
No. Starbucks	0	13	Zoo/aquarium rating	1	3	Sq. miles inland water	4	4
No. warehouse clubs	0	2	Amusement park rating	1	3	Miles of coastline	0.0	10.7
			Botanical garden/ arboretum rating	1	4	National Park rating	3	3

Arts & Culture
Score: 16.3
Rank: 312

MEDIA & LIBRARIES	AREA	U.S. AVG	PERFORMING ARTS	AREA	U.S. AVG	MUSEUMS	AREA	U.S. AVG
Arts radio rating	1	3	Classical music rating	1	4	Overall museum rating	6	5
No. public libraries	9	27	Ballet/dance rating	1	3	Art museum rating	4	5
Library volumes per capita	2.27	2.78	Professional theater rating	1	3	Science museum rating	7	5
			University arts programs rating	3	5	Children's museum rating	2	3

Grand Rapids–Wyoming, MI   Score: 55.9   Rank: 213   2004 rank: 157

Profile: Mid-size city
Location: West-central Michigan, 25 miles inland from Lake Michigan
Elevation: 803 feet
Time zone: Eastern Standard Time

PRO	CON
Cultural amenities	Cold, cloudy winters
Diverse economy	Some urban decay
Attractive downtown	Isolation

Grand Rapids is the primary cultural and business hub of western Michigan. Nearby hardwood forests made the city a notable furniture-producing center in the 19th and early 20th centuries. That industry continues today but has transitioned somewhat toward high-tech office furniture, serving as headquarters for such names as Steelcase and Herman Miller. The area is far less vulnerable to the ups and downs of the auto industry than most of Michigan. The surrounding area is agricultural and interesting. The tempering effect of Lake Michigan promotes a greater agricultural variety than otherwise found in many Midwestern locations, with berries, lettuce, flowers, and such fruit trees as apple, peach, and cherry. Cultural and recreational amenities are above average with a strong performing arts component and abundant outdoor activities, including nearby beaches to the west. In part because of the agricultural environment, the area was attractive to 19th-century Dutch settlers, some of whom started large, successful businesses. The Meijer (groceries) and Van Andel and De Vos families (Amway, now known as Alticor) have left large endowments and a large imprint on the city—the Van Andel Museum Center (a gem), the Van Andel Arena, the De Vos Performance Hall, and Meijer Gardens, to name a few. As a result, the city has an outstanding set of performing and visual arts amenities for a city its size, as well as good minor league sports and other entertainment. Downtown is clean and typically Midwestern and even slightly European in appearance where the Grand River flows through. West of the Grand lies an attractive redevelopment zone, home of the Van Andel Museum. Some areas of town, particularly south, remain gritty and industrial, but nice suburbs that spread toward Hudsonville (southwest), Ada (more upscale and east), and Wyoming (west) offer a lot of choices. At 150 miles from Detroit and 175 miles from Chicago, the location is relatively isolated from big-city amenities and services. High incomes and low living costs bring a strong Buying Power Index (129.2), making this area is a good value for those who can take some dreary weather mainly in winter.

Grand Rapids is located in the Grand River Valley, with high hills rising on either side to 1,020 feet. In comparison to other Midwestern locations, springs are cooler and later while falls are longer and warmer. Summer days are pleasantly warm with about 3 weeks of hot, humid weather. Most summer nights are comfortable. Winters are very cloudy, with numerous snow flurries and strong westerly winds. Prolonged cold waves are infrequent, but below-zero temperatures and continuous snow cover are common. First freeze is early October; last is May 1.

Population

DEMOGRAPHICS	AREA	U.S. AVG	ETHNIC COMPOSITION	AREA	U.S. AVG	RESIDENT PROFILE	AREA	U.S. AVG
Population	770,802		White	84.2%	79.0%	Single	32.8%	32.4%
Population density per sq. mile	272.6	358.5	Black	7.7%	10.5%	Married	54.2%	52.7%
Population growth	19.4%	21.1%	Asian	1.8%	2.7%	Divorced/separated	13.0%	14.9%
Median age	34.2	36.1	Hispanic	7.3%	10.6%	Married with children	26.4%	23.7%
Percent Democrat	39.8%	44.5%	Religious observance	47.7%	48.9%	Single with children	9.2%	9.1%
Percent Republican	59.2%	54.5%	Diversity measure	37.1	40.1	Percent over age 65	10.7%	12.9%

Economy & Jobs
Score: 61.8
Rank: 144

INCOME	AREA	U.S. AVG	EMPLOYMENT	AREA	U.S. AVG	EMPLOYING INDUSTRIES	AREA	U.S. AVG
Per capita income	$23,711	$23,235	Unemployment rate	6.9%	4.7%	Largest: Manufacturing		
Household income	$50,252	$46,414	Recent job growth	2.4%	1.3%			
Household income < $25K	21.3%	26.2%	Projected future job growth	11.0%	11.5%	Percent manufacturing	21.6%	15.4%
Household income > $75K	27.8%	25.4%	White collar	55.3%	57.8%	Percent public sector	8.6%	15.7%
Household income growth	11.1%	13.6%	Blue collar	30.4%	25.2%	Percent construction	8.7%	9.9%

Cost of Living
Score: 53.5
Rank: 174

INDEXES & TAXES	AREA	U.S. AVG	HOUSING	AREA	U.S. AVG	NECESSITIES	AREA	U.S. AVG
Cost of Living Index	87.2	100.0	Median home price	$136,400	$220,000	Food Index	104.7	100.0
Buying Power Index	129.2	100.0	Home price appreciation	23.5%	10.1%	Housing Index	59.9	100.0
Income tax rate	5.21%	4.70%	Median rent	$670	$709	Utilities Index	89.4	100.0
Sales tax rate	6.00%	6.58%	Homes owned	68.4%	62.3%	Transportation Index	112.7	100.0
Property tax rate	$12.99	$12.00	Home price ratio	2.7	4.2	Healthcare Index	98.1	100.0
						Miscellaneous Cost Index	106.0	100.0

Climate
Score: 7.5
Rank: 344

TEMPERATURE	AREA	U.S. AVG
Average January low	16.0	26.2
Average July high	83.3	87.4
Annual days › 90°F	11	38
Annual days ‹ 32°F	149	89
Annual days ‹ 0°F	8	6

PRECIPITATION	AREA	U.S. AVG
Annual inches precipitation	32.0	37.7
Annual inches snowfall	77.0	7.0
Annual days precipitation	144	109
Annual days rain › 0.5 inches	20	22
Annual days snow › 1.5 inches	20	6

COMFORTS & HAZARDS	AREA	U.S. AVG
July relative humidity	73%	66%
Annual days mostly sunny	163	208
Annual days with thunderstorms	37	39
Tornado risk score	23	18
Hurricane risk score	1	13

TEMPERATURE

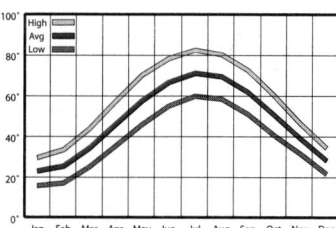

PRECIPITATION

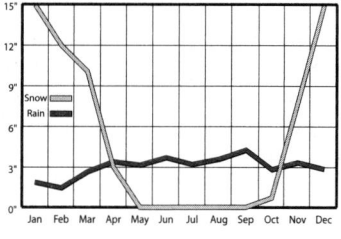

DAYS OF CLOUDS & PRECIPITATION

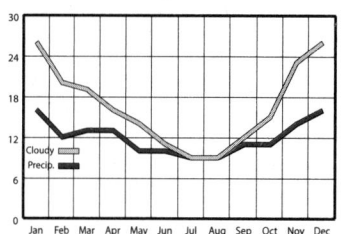

Education
Score: 48.1
Rank: 195

ACHIEVEMENT	AREA	U.S. AVG
High school degree	84.4%	82.7%
2-year college degree	7.5%	6.4%
4-year college degree	15.5%	15.7%
Graduate/professional degree	7.3%	8.9%

PUBLIC SCHOOLS	AREA	U.S. AVG
Expenditures per pupil	$6,126	$5,686
Student/teacher ratio	18.3	16.7
Attending public school	86.7%	90.1%
State SAT score	1151	1021
State ACT score	21.5*	20.9

HIGHER EDUCATION	AREA	U.S. AVG
No. 2-year colleges	2	4
No. 4-year colleges/universities	9	6
No. highly ranked universities	0	1

Health & Healthcare
Score: 45.5
Rank: 205

HAZARDS & ILLNESSES	AREA	U.S. AVG
Air-quality score	32	37
Water-quality score	41	52
Pollen/allergy score	49	61
Cancer mortality per capita	193.5	201.9
Depression days per month	3.6	3.5
Stress score	60	50

HEALTHCARE	AREA	U.S. AVG
Physicians per capita	232.7	244.2
Hospital beds per capita	310.3	420.0
No. teaching hospitals	4	3
Cost per doctor visit	$69	$77
Cost per dental visit	$68	$70

Crime
Score: 67.6
Rank: 122

CRIME	AREA	U.S. AVG
Violent crime rate	447.0	465.5
Change in violent crime rate	-2.1%	-2.2%
Property crime rate	3,124.5	3,517.1
Change in property crime rate	-0.6%	-2.1%

Transportation
Score: 17.1
Rank: 311

COMMUTE	AREA	U.S. AVG
Average commute time	24.4	27.4
Percent commutes › 60 mins.	4.6%	5.9%
Commute by auto	83.1%	78.9%
Commute by mass transit	0.9%	1.9%
Work at home	3.3%	3.1%
Mass transit miles per capita	0.87	1.87

INTERCITY SERVICES	AREA	U.S. AVG
Major airports within 60 miles	0	1
Size of regional airport	Small	Large
Daily airline activity	229	686
Amtrak service	Yes	No

AUTOMOTIVE	AREA	U.S. AVG
Insurance, annual premium	$1,582	$1,432
Gas, cost per gallon	$2.54	$2.49
Daily vehicle miles per capita	25.6	24.0

Leisure
Score: 71.7
Rank: 106

DINING & SHOPPING	AREA	U.S. AVG
Restaurant rating	1	2
Outlet mall score	51	42
No. Starbucks	5	13
No. warehouse clubs	3	2

ENTERTAINMENT	AREA	U.S. AVG
Professional sports rating	3	4
College sports rating	5	4
Zoo/aquarium rating	5	3
Amusement park rating	7	3
Botanical garden/ arboretum rating	4	4

OUTDOOR ACTIVITIES	AREA	U.S. AVG
Golf-course rating	7	4
Ski-area rating	5	3
Sq. miles inland water	3	4
Miles of coastline	23.4	10.7
National Park rating	1	3

Arts & Culture
Score: 83.2
Rank: 64

MEDIA & LIBRARIES	AREA	U.S. AVG
Arts radio rating	10	3
No. public libraries	47	27
Library volumes per capita	3.84	2.78

PERFORMING ARTS	AREA	U.S. AVG
Classical music rating	5	4
Ballet/dance rating	3	3
Professional theater rating	1	3
University arts programs rating	8	5

MUSEUMS	AREA	U.S. AVG
Overall museum rating	8	5
Art museum rating	7	5
Science museum rating	7	5
Children's museum rating	8	3

Great Falls, MT

Score: 65.6 Rank: 134 2004 rank: 212

Profile: Small town
Location: North-central Montana along the upper Missouri River
Elevation: 3,670 feet
Time zone: Mountain Standard Time

PRO	CON
Nearby mountains	Harsh winters
Pleasant summers	Isolation
Small-town atmosphere	Arts and culture

Great Falls is an agricultural and commercial center located at the foot of the Rockies and the western terminus of the Great Plains. The wilderness of the Lewis and Clark National Forest to the west and Glacier National Park to the northwest provides excellent recreational opportunities. Helena, the state capital, lies 90 miles to the south. The area is quiet and attractive, but is isolated geographically and doesn't benefit from the tourism that bolsters the economy of other Montana cities. Current employment is steady but future growth projections are only moderate. Downtown is clean and attractive, with a nice partially redeveloped Missouri River waterfront. The Malmstrom Air Force Base and other national defense installations provide some employment, and there are a few small manufacturers and a new call center. The area does feature attractive housing prices for a Western city.

The city is located along the main stem of the Missouri River at its confluence with the Sun River in a valley surrounded by plateaus and hills. Except to the north and northeast, it is encircled by mountain ranges. Summertime is pleasant, with cool nights; moderately warm, sunny days; and little hot, humid weather. Winters are not as cold as might be expected for the location because of warming, downslope winds from the mountains, which can raise temperatures by 40°F in 24 hours. While subzero weather is common, the coldest weather seldom lasts more than a few days, and snow rarely lingers. Freezing temperatures normally occur any time of year except July and August.

Population

DEMOGRAPHICS	AREA	U.S. AVG	ETHNIC COMPOSITION	AREA	U.S. AVG	RESIDENT PROFILE	AREA	U.S. AVG
Population	79,448		White	89.0%	79.0%	Single	28.5%	32.4%
Population density per sq. mile	29.4	358.5	Black	1.5%	10.5%	Married	55.5%	52.7%
Population growth	2.3%	21.1%	Asian	1.1%	2.7%	Divorced/separated	16.0%	14.9%
Median age	38.0	36.1	Hispanic	2.7%	10.6%	Married with children	22.8%	23.7%
Percent Democrat	40.9%	44.5%	Religious observance	43.3%	48.9%	Single with children	8.9%	9.1%
Percent Republican	56.9%	54.5%	Diversity measure	24.6	40.1	Percent over age 65	14.8%	12.9%

Economy
& Jobs
Score: 73.0
Rank: 102

INCOME	AREA	U.S. AVG	EMPLOYMENT	AREA	U.S. AVG	EMPLOYING INDUSTRIES	AREA	U.S. AVG
Per capita income	$20,166	$23,235	Unemployment rate	3.9%	4.7%	Largest: Healthcare & Social Assistance		
Household income	$37,332	$46,414	Recent job growth	4.1%	1.3%			
Household income < $25K	32.8%	26.2%	Projected future job growth	9.1%	11.5%	Percent manufacturing	10.4%	15.4%
Household income > $75K	15.5%	25.4%	White collar	59.1%	57.8%	Percent public sector	17.1%	15.7%
Household income growth	13.2%	13.6%	Blue collar	20.3%	25.2%	Percent construction	10.0%	9.9%

Cost of Living
Score: 86.4
Rank: 52

INDEXES & TAXES	AREA	U.S. AVG	HOUSING	AREA	U.S. AVG	NECESSITIES	AREA	U.S. AVG
Cost of Living Index	80.8	100.0	Median home price	$108,800	$220,000	Food Index	107.0	100.0
Buying Power Index	103.6	100.0	Home price appreciation	30.6%	10.1%	Housing Index	48.9	100.0
Income tax rate	10.00%	4.70%	Median rent	$550	$709	Utilities Index	89.2	100.0
Sales tax rate	0.00%	6.58%	Homes owned	60.9%	62.3%	Transportation Index	95.9	100.0
Property tax rate	$12.44	$12.00	Home price ratio	2.9	4.2	Healthcare Index	97.1	100.0
						Miscellaneous Cost Index	99.1	100.0

Climate
Score: 11.8
Rank: 329

TEMPERATURE	AREA	U.S. AVG	PRECIPITATION	AREA	U.S. AVG	COMFORTS & HAZARDS	AREA	U.S. AVG
Average January low	11.0	26.2	Annual inches precipitation	15.0	37.7	July relative humidity	58%	66%
Average July high	83.0	87.4	Annual inches snowfall	63.0	7.0	Annual days mostly sunny	187	208
Annual days > 90°F	18	38	Annual days precipitation	103	109	Annual days with thunderstorms	25	39
Annual days < 32°F	155	89	Annual days rain > 0.5 inches	9	22	Tornado risk score	7	18
Annual days < 0°F	28	6	Annual days snow > 1.5 inches	15	6	Hurricane risk score	0	13

TEMPERATURE

PRECIPITATION

DAYS OF CLOUDS & PRECIPITATION

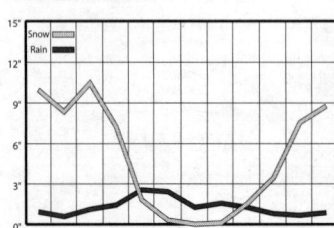

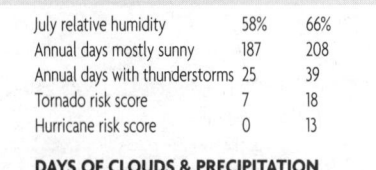

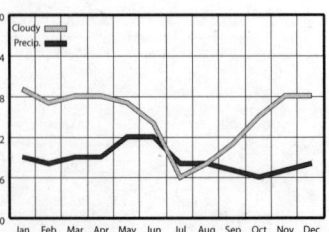

Education
Score: 57.0
Rank: 162

ACHIEVEMENT	AREA	U.S. AVG
High school degree	87.2%	82.7%
2-year college degree	6.8%	6.4%
4-year college degree	15.0%	15.7%
Graduate/professional degree	6.8%	8.9%

PUBLIC SCHOOLS	AREA	U.S. AVG
Expenditures per pupil	$5,577	$5,686
Student/teacher ratio	15.0	16.7
Attending public school	93.5%	90.1%
State SAT score	1083	1021
State ACT score	21.9*	20.9

HIGHER EDUCATION	AREA	U.S. AVG
No. 2-year colleges	2	4
No. 4-year colleges/universities	1	6
No. highly ranked universities	0	1

Health & Healthcare
Score: 87.2
Rank: 49

HAZARDS & ILLNESSES	AREA	U.S. AVG
Air-quality score	41	37
Water-quality score	31	52
Pollen/allergy score	38	61
Cancer mortality per capita	214.5	201.9
Depression days per month	3.0	3.5
Stress score	29	50

HEALTHCARE	AREA	U.S. AVG
Physicians per capita	261.4	244.2
Hospital beds per capita	998.1	420.0
No. teaching hospitals	0	3
Cost per doctor visit	$98	$77
Cost per dental visit	$69	$70

Crime
Score: 35.8
Rank: 240

CRIME	AREA	U.S. AVG
Violent crime rate	256.8	465.5
Change in violent crime rate	-21.2%	-2.2%
Property crime rate	4,690.6	3,517.1
Change in property crime rate	-12.4%	-2.1%

Transportation
Score: 66.6
Rank: 126

COMMUTE	AREA	U.S. AVG
Average commute time	17.7	27.4
Percent commutes > 60 mins.	2.4%	5.9%
Commute by auto	80.5%	78.9%
Commute by mass transit	0.8%	1.9%
Work at home	3.9%	3.1%
Mass transit miles per capita	0.79	1.87

INTERCITY SERVICES	AREA	U.S. AVG
Major airports within 60 miles	0	1
Size of regional airport	None	Large
Daily airline activity	38	686
Amtrak service	No	No

AUTOMOTIVE	AREA	U.S. AVG
Insurance, annual premium	$1,066	$1,432
Gas, cost per gallon	$2.32	$2.49
Daily vehicle miles per capita	14.6	24.0

Leisure
Score: 47.6
Rank: 193

DINING & SHOPPING	AREA	U.S. AVG
Restaurant rating	1	2
Outlet mall score	0	42
No. Starbucks	1	13
No. warehouse clubs	1	2

ENTERTAINMENT	AREA	U.S. AVG
Professional sports rating	2	4
College sports rating	1	4
Zoo/aquarium rating	1	3
Amusement park rating	1	3
Botanical garden/arboretum rating	1	4

OUTDOOR ACTIVITIES	AREA	U.S. AVG
Golf-course rating	1	4
Ski-area rating	7	3
Sq. miles inland water	3	4
Miles of coastline	0.0	10.7
National Park rating	8	3

Arts & Culture
Score: 34.0
Rank: 247

MEDIA & LIBRARIES	AREA	U.S. AVG
Arts radio rating	1	3
No. public libraries	3	27
Library volumes per capita	1.93	2.78

PERFORMING ARTS	AREA	U.S. AVG
Classical music rating	3	4
Ballet/dance rating	1	3
Professional theater rating	1	3
University arts programs rating	2	5

MUSEUMS	AREA	U.S. AVG
Overall museum rating	4	5
Art museum rating	7	5
Science museum rating	1	5
Children's museum rating	1	3

Greeley, CO

Score: 71.8   **Rank:** 80   **2004 rank:** 89

Profile: Mid-size agricultural city/college town
Location: North-central Colorado, 55 miles north of Denver
Elevation: 4,715 feet
Time zone: Mountain Standard Time

PRO	CON
Small-town atmosphere	Rising crime rate
Nearby mountains	Long commutes
Cost of living	Healthcare

Historically and in its base form, Greeley is largely an agricultural center—livestock, meat-packing, and sugar beets and related processing activities remain extensive today. Local feedlots can bring strong agricultural "fragrances," largely imperceptible to long-time residents. More recently the area has become the eastern flank of a large high-tech and light-manufacturing belt centered in nearby Windsor and anchored by Fort Collins and Loveland to the west. The University of Northern Colorado with some 13,000 students adds a light college-town accent. The area is close enough to the Rocky Mountains to benefit from its recreational opportunities. Many residents commute to the more commercialized Fort Collins or Loveland to the west, resulting in average commute times of almost 24 minutes. Greeley is also a 45-mile straight shot south to Denver International Airport, making it a good location for frequent business travelers looking for more of a small-town lifestyle.

Denver itself is close enough to share many of its amenities. Because incomes are relatively high compared to cost of living, the Buying Power Index is favorable (121.0), and the cost profile is strong for Colorado and even compared to the highly ranked Fort Collins–Loveland metro area. On the whole, Greeley is slower paced and some may not find enough to do, but there's a lot nearby. Although it doesn't excel in any category, Greeley scores consistently well in most, resulting in a favorable ranking.

The town is located among rolling grassland plains in a shallow valley at the confluence of the Cache La Poudre and South Platte rivers. Locals call the area the "Kansas part of Colorado," accurately depicting both landscape and climate. Warm, dry spring and summer days are punctuated by occasional heavy thunderstorms. Winters are variable with alternating cold spells and mild periods. Wind chill can make all winter weather more severe. First freeze is at the end of September; last is mid-May.

DEMOGRAPHICS	AREA	U.S. AVG	ETHNIC COMPOSITION	AREA	U.S. AVG	RESIDENT PROFILE	AREA	U.S. AVG
Population	221,957		White	79.5%	79.0%	Single	29.4%	32.4%
Population density per sq. mile	55.6	358.5	Black	0.7%	10.5%	Married	57.1%	52.7%
Population growth	68.4%	21.1%	Asian	1.1%	2.7%	Divorced/separated	13.5%	14.9%
Median age	31.2	36.1	Hispanic	30.7%	10.6%	Married with children	28.8%	23.7%
Percent Democrat	35.9%	44.5%	Religious observance	36.8%	48.9%	Single with children	8.2%	9.1%
Percent Republican	62.7%	54.5%	Diversity measure	62.3	40.1	Percent over age 65	8.4%	12.9%

Population

INCOME	AREA	U.S. AVG	EMPLOYMENT	AREA	U.S. AVG	EMPLOYING INDUSTRIES	AREA	U.S. AVG
Per capita income	$21,773	$23,235	Unemployment rate	5.1%	4.7%	Largest: Construction		
Household income	$48,704	$46,414	Recent job growth	2.3%	1.3%			
Household income < $25K	23.2%	26.2%	Projected future job growth	19.4%	11.5%	Percent manufacturing	15.6%	15.4%
Household income > $75K	27.3%	25.4%	White collar	53.7%	57.8%	Percent public sector	14.8%	15.7%
Household income growth	15.1%	13.6%	Blue collar	28.4%	25.2%	Percent construction	12.8%	9.9%

Economy & Jobs
Score: 79.1
Rank: 79

INDEXES & TAXES	AREA	U.S. AVG	HOUSING	AREA	U.S. AVG	NECESSITIES	AREA	U.S. AVG
Cost of Living Index	90.2	100.0	Median home price	$151,700	$220,000	Food Index	110.6	100.0
Buying Power Index	121.0	100.0	Home price appreciation	24.4%	10.1%	Housing Index	66.8	100.0
Income tax rate	5.00%	4.70%	Median rent	$690	$709	Utilities Index	95.2	100.0
Sales tax rate	2.90%	6.58%	Homes owned	67.9%	62.3%	Transportation Index	101.4	100.0
Property tax rate	$7.53	$12.00	Home price ratio	3.1	4.2	Healthcare Index	116.3	100.0
						Miscellaneous Cost Index	97.9	100.0

Cost of Living
Score: 84.2
Rank: 60

TEMPERATURE	AREA	U.S. AVG	PRECIPITATION	AREA	U.S. AVG	COMFORTS & HAZARDS	AREA	U.S. AVG
Average January low	16.2	26.2	Annual inches precipitation	16.0	37.7	July relative humidity	53%	66%
Average July high	87.4	87.4	Annual inches snowfall	60.0	7.0	Annual days mostly sunny	246	208
Annual days > 90°F	32	38	Annual days precipitation	88	109	Annual days with thunderstorms	41	39
Annual days < 32°F	163	89	Annual days rain > 0.5 inches	7	22	Tornado risk score	49	18
Annual days < 0°F	10	6	Annual days snow > 1.5 inches	13	6	Hurricane risk score	0	13

Climate
Score: 54.3
Rank: 170

TEMPERATURE

PRECIPITATION

DAYS OF CLOUDS & PRECIPITATION

ACHIEVEMENT	AREA	U.S. AVG	PUBLIC SCHOOLS	AREA	U.S. AVG	HIGHER EDUCATION	AREA	U.S. AVG
High school degree	80.5%	82.7%	Expenditures per pupil	$5,630	$5,686	No. 2-year colleges	1	4
2-year college degree	7.4%	6.4%	Student/teacher ratio	15.5	16.7	No. 4-year colleges/universities	1	6
4-year college degree	14.9%	15.7%	Attending public school	97.9%	90.1%	No. highly ranked universities	0	1
Graduate/professional degree	7.1%	8.9%	State SAT score	1122	1021			
			State ACT score	20.3*	20.9			

Education
Score: 54.3
Rank: 172

HAZARDS & ILLNESSES	AREA	U.S. AVG	HEALTHCARE	AREA	U.S. AVG	CRIME	AREA	U.S. AVG
Air-quality score	24	37	Physicians per capita	133.0	244.2	Violent crime rate	440.4	465.5
Water-quality score	84	52	Hospital beds per capita	117.1	420.0	Change in violent crime rate	15.6%	-2.2%
Pollen/allergy score	81	61	No. teaching hospitals	1	3	Property crime rate	4,433.7	3,517.1
Cancer mortality per capita	143.7	201.9	Cost per doctor visit	$92	$77	Change in property crime rate	6.3%	-2.1%
Depression days per month	2.5	3.5	Cost per dental visit	$68	$70			
Stress score	42	50						

Health & Healthcare
Score: 9.6
Rank: 337

Crime
Score: 21.7
Rank: 292

COMMUTE	AREA	U.S. AVG	INTERCITY SERVICES	AREA	U.S. AVG	AUTOMOTIVE	AREA	U.S. AVG
Average commute time	25.6	27.4	Major airports within 60 miles	1	1	Insurance, annual premium	$1,509	$1,432
Percent commutes > 60 mins.	6.9%	5.9%	Size of regional airport	Large	Large	Gas, cost per gallon	$2.43	$2.49
Commute by auto	79.1%	78.9%	Daily airline activity	812	686	Daily vehicle miles per capita	17.0	24.0
Commute by mass transit	0.4%	1.9%	Amtrak service	No	No			
Work at home	4.3%	3.1%						
Mass transit miles per capita	0.38	1.87						

Transportation
Score: 43.9
Rank: 211

DINING & SHOPPING	AREA	U.S. AVG	ENTERTAINMENT	AREA	U.S. AVG	OUTDOOR ACTIVITIES	AREA	U.S. AVG
Restaurant rating	1	2	Professional sports rating	8	4	Golf-course rating	3	4
Outlet mall score	130	42	College sports rating	3	4	Ski-area rating	10	3
No. Starbucks	4	13	Zoo/aquarium rating	2	3	Sq. miles inland water	4	4
No. warehouse clubs	0	2	Amusement park rating	2	3	Miles of coastline	0.0	10.7
			Botanical garden/ arboretum rating	1	4	National Park rating	3	3

Leisure
Score: 78.3
Rank: 81

MEDIA & LIBRARIES	AREA	U.S. AVG	PERFORMING ARTS	AREA	U.S. AVG	MUSEUMS	AREA	U.S. AVG
Arts radio rating	4	3	Classical music rating	4	4	Overall museum rating	2	5
No. public libraries	11	27	Ballet/dance rating	4	3	Art museum rating	2	5
Library volumes per capita	2.47	2.78	Professional theater rating	3	3	Science museum rating	3	5
			University arts programs rating	4	5	Children's museum rating	1	3

Arts & Culture
Score: 46.3
Rank: 201

Green Bay, WI

Score: 45.0 **Rank:** 283 **2004 rank:** 108

Profile: Mid-size city
Location: Northeastern Wisconsin, at the head of Green Bay
Elevation: 702 feet
Time zone: Central Standard Time

PRO	CON
Small-town atmosphere	Winter climate
Professional football	Isolation
Outdoor recreation	Recent job weakness

Green Bay is a mostly quiet paper, manufacturing, agriculture, and dairy town with a good labor force and a hardworking character. Quiet, that is, except during the fall, when the legendary NFL Green Bay Packers become a local obsession. The duration and success of the Packers in such a small, out-of-the-way market is unequaled in all professional sports. The downtown area is clean and anchored by new convention facilities along the waterfront, spreading south and west with nice city neighborhoods close in and prosperous suburbs especially northwest. There are some grittier areas east of town, and a new casino has arrived on the scene adjacent to the airport. The Packers add to an already-strong community spirit; residents are proud to be from Green Bay and don't bristle at the term "cheesehead" one bit. Aside from football, Green Bay residents enjoy a traditional small-town way of life with ample nearby recreation, including the offerings of Door Peninsula (the "thumb" of Wisconsin), a New England–like area of farms, small towns, and islands. There are considerable recreational areas to the north and west. The area has a complement of local museums and a few performing arts activities. Cost of living is moderate but employment prospects have faded a bit recently. Access to other amenities and services means a long trek to Milwaukee or Chicago. Recent employment weakness hurt the ranking; the area is better than the numbers look for hardier souls who can endure the winters and economic cycles.

The city is in the Fox River Valley, where the river empties into the bay, surrounded by slightly higher ground and mostly wooded terrain. Skies are frequently cloudy, causing further temperature moderation. Most precipitation normally falls from May through September as thunderstorms. Winter snowfall is less than in nearby communities where the ground is slightly higher. Bitter cold periods occur, but they are shorter than those of other inland areas at this latitude. First freeze is early October; last is mid-May.

DEMOGRAPHICS	AREA	U.S. AVG	ETHNIC COMPOSITION	AREA	U.S. AVG	RESIDENT PROFILE	AREA	U.S. AVG
Population	295,898		White	91.3%	79.0%	Single	32.0%	32.4%
Population density per sq. mile	158.3	358.5	Black	1.2%	10.5%	Married	55.7%	52.7%
Population growth	21.5%	21.1%	Asian	2.0%	2.7%	Divorced/separated	12.3%	14.9%
Median age	36.3	36.1	Hispanic	3.9%	10.6%	Married with children	25.8%	23.7%
Percent Democrat	44.5%	44.5%	Religious observance	71.8%	48.9%	Single with children	7.8%	9.1%
Percent Republican	54.5%	54.5%	Diversity measure	22.4	40.1	Percent over age 65	11.7%	12.9%

Population

INCOME	AREA	U.S. AVG	EMPLOYMENT	AREA	U.S. AVG	EMPLOYING INDUSTRIES	AREA	U.S. AVG
Per capita income	$24,587	$23,235	Unemployment rate	4.2%	4.7%	Largest: Manufacturing		
Household income	$51,507	$46,414	Recent job growth	-2.2%	1.3%			
Household income < $25K	20.5%	26.2%	Projected future job growth	6.2%	11.5%	Percent manufacturing	20.2%	15.4%
Household income > $75K	27.6%	25.4%	White collar	55.0%	57.8%	Percent public sector	9.6%	15.7%
Household income growth	13.0%	13.6%	Blue collar	30.1%	25.2%	Percent construction	9.8%	9.9%

Economy & Jobs
Score: 16.3
Rank: 313

INDEXES & TAXES	AREA	U.S. AVG	HOUSING	AREA	U.S. AVG	NECESSITIES	AREA	U.S. AVG
Cost of Living Index	89.0	100.0	Median home price	$152,600	$220,000	Food Index	96.2	100.0
Buying Power Index	129.7	100.0	Home price appreciation	28.7%	10.1%	Housing Index	49.6	100.0
Income tax rate	6.93%	4.70%	Median rent	$597	$709	Utilities Index	110.2	100.0
Sales tax rate	5.47%	6.58%	Homes owned	64.1%	62.3%	Transportation Index	101.0	100.0
Property tax rate	$19.48	$12.00	Home price ratio	3.0	4.2	Healthcare Index	100.4	100.0
						Miscellaneous Cost Index	99.6	100.0

Cost of Living
Score: 30.7
Rank: 259

Climate
Score: 13.4
Rank: 323

TEMPERATURE	AREA	U.S. AVG
Average January low	6.9	26.2
Average July high	80.7	87.4
Annual days > 90°F	7	38
Annual days < 32°F	163	89
Annual days < 0°F	29	6

PRECIPITATION	AREA	U.S. AVG
Annual inches precipitation	27.0	37.7
Annual inches snowfall	43.0	7.0
Annual days precipitation	120	109
Annual days rain > 0.5 inches	16	22
Annual days snow > 1.5 inches	10	6

COMFORTS & HAZARDS	AREA	U.S. AVG
July relative humidity	73%	66%
Annual days mostly sunny	192	208
Annual days with thunderstorms	35	39
Tornado risk score	14	18
Hurricane risk score	0	13

TEMPERATURE

PRECIPITATION

DAYS OF CLOUDS & PRECIPITATION

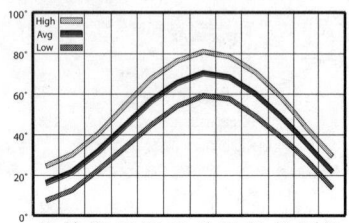
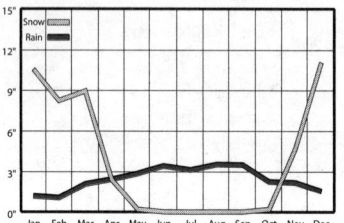
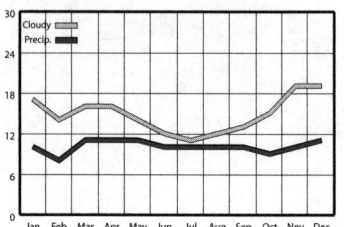

Education
Score: 52.4
Rank: 179

ACHIEVEMENT	AREA	U.S. AVG
High school degree	85.6%	82.7%
2-year college degree	8.6%	6.4%
4-year college degree	15.0%	15.7%
Graduate/professional degree	5.2%	8.9%

PUBLIC SCHOOLS	AREA	U.S. AVG
Expenditures per pupil	$6,116	$5,686
Student/teacher ratio	17.0	16.7
Attending public school	86.2%	90.1%
State SAT score	1188	1021
State ACT score	22.2*	20.9

HIGHER EDUCATION	AREA	U.S. AVG
No. 2-year colleges	4	4
No. 4-year colleges/universities	4	6
No. highly ranked universities	1	1

Health & Healthcare
Score: 78.1
Rank: 83

HAZARDS & ILLNESSES	AREA	U.S. AVG
Air-quality score	40	37
Water-quality score	28	52
Pollen/allergy score	28	61
Cancer mortality per capita	193.3	201.9
Depression days per month	2.5	3.5
Stress score	13	50

HEALTHCARE	AREA	U.S. AVG
Physicians per capita	195.7	244.2
Hospital beds per capita	365.7	420.0
No. teaching hospitals	2	3
Cost per doctor visit	$91	$77
Cost per dental visit	$63	$70

Crime
Score: 88.2
Rank: 45

CRIME	AREA	U.S. AVG
Violent crime rate	198.7	465.5
Change in violent crime rate	-10.0%	-2.2%
Property crime rate	2,340.6	3,517.1
Change in property crime rate	-2.0%	-2.1%

Transportation
Score: 39.8
Rank: 226

COMMUTE	AREA	U.S. AVG
Average commute time	20.7	27.4
Percent commutes > 60 mins.	3.4%	5.9%
Commute by auto	83.4%	78.9%
Commute by mass transit	0.7%	1.9%
Work at home	3.4%	3.1%
Mass transit miles per capita	0.71	1.87

INTERCITY SERVICES	AREA	U.S. AVG
Major airports within 60 miles	0	1
Size of regional airport	Small	Large
Daily airline activity	39	686
Amtrak service	No	No

AUTOMOTIVE	AREA	U.S. AVG
Insurance, annual premium	$1,050	$1,432
Gas, cost per gallon	$2.55	$2.49
Daily vehicle miles per capita	27.8	24.0

Leisure
Score: 43.3
Rank: 211

DINING & SHOPPING	AREA	U.S. AVG
Restaurant rating	1	2
Outlet mall score	0	42
No. Starbucks	1	13
No. warehouse clubs	0	2

ENTERTAINMENT	AREA	U.S. AVG
Professional sports rating	6	4
College sports rating	3	4
Zoo/aquarium rating	1	3
Amusement park rating	1	3
Botanical garden/ arboretum rating	1	4

OUTDOOR ACTIVITIES	AREA	U.S. AVG
Golf-course rating	2	4
Ski-area rating	2	3
Sq. miles inland water	2	4
Miles of coastline	17.9	10.7
National Park rating	1	3

Arts & Culture
Score: 17.1
Rank: 308

MEDIA & LIBRARIES	AREA	U.S. AVG
Arts radio rating	1	3
No. public libraries	19	27
Library volumes per capita	2.21	2.78

PERFORMING ARTS	AREA	U.S. AVG
Classical music rating	2	4
Ballet/dance rating	3	3
Professional theater rating	1	3
University arts programs rating	6	5

MUSEUMS	AREA	U.S. AVG
Overall museum rating	5	5
Art museum rating	1	5
Science museum rating	3	5
Children's museum rating	2	3

Greensboro–Winston-Salem–High Point, NC

Score: 83.0 Rank: 31 2004 rank: 81

Profile: Mid-size-city complex
Location: Northwest-central North Carolina, 30 miles south of the Virginia border
Elevation: 897 feet
Time zone: Eastern Standard Time

PRO	CON
Cost of living	Declining industries
Attractive downtown areas	Growth and sprawl
Some college presence	Summer heat and humidity

The Greensboro–Winston-Salem–High Point complex occupies two counties and is sometimes called the Piedmont Triad. In comparison to the state's better-known triad of Raleigh–Durham–Chapel Hill, the economy and lifestyle is more industrial and working class, although there is a strong university presence and a high level of educational attainment. The economy has an interesting mix of declining and emerging industries, but employment overall has been relatively stable. Winston-Salem, as the name suggests, has been a center for the tobacco industry. (The cigarettes are named after the town, not vice versa.) Winston-Salem is also home to Wake Forest University, some affiliated high-tech business, a collection of banking centers, Krispy Kreme donuts, and a new Dell Computer plant. High Point is a world trade center for furniture manufacturing. Unfortunately, the dislocation of that industry offshore, particularly to China, is having an impact on its manufacturing base. Downtown High Point is a fascinating collection of commercial, warehouse, and showroom facilities centered on this industry. Greensboro is the triad's financial center and is the most prosperous of the three cities, with high tech, light manufacturing, and a large campus of the University of North Carolina. The nicest suburbs in the area spread northwest of Greensboro toward the Piedmont Triad International Airport, which brings unusually good air service to the area. Bottom line: Greensboro is up and coming, Winston-Salem epitomizes the shift from older economy to new economy, and High Point is an industry town shifting emphasis from manufacturing to becoming a trade and design center. The Cost of Living Index at 84.3 is attractive for what the triad offers. Good scores in all ranking categories and the lack of major downsides bring a strong ranking, and the amenities of the Raleigh and Durham areas, about 80 miles east, are close enough for residents to benefit.

The city complex is located in northern Piedmont in an area of transition between the eastern coastal plain and mountains to the west. The immediate landscape is slightly rolling with woodlands and open country. Summers are generally mild to warm and humid, with varying temperatures. Most summer precipitation occurs as localized thunderstorms. Late summer and fall hurricanes bring heavy rain. Winter temperatures and rainfall are modified somewhat by the mountain barrier. Snow flurries may occur. First freeze is late October; last is mid-April.

Population

DEMOGRAPHICS	AREA	U.S. AVG	ETHNIC COMPOSITION	AREA	U.S. AVG	RESIDENT PROFILE	AREA	U.S. AVG
Population	1,253,347		White	71.2%	79.0%	Single	31.0%	32.4%
Population density per sq. mile	321.8	358.5	Black	21.9%	10.5%	Married	53.7%	52.7%
Population growth	24.4%	21.1%	Asian	1.7%	2.7%	Divorced/separated	15.4%	14.9%
Median age	36.8	36.1	Hispanic	6.8%	10.6%	Married with children	21.9%	23.7%
Percent Democrat	41.8%	44.5%	Religious observance	45.2%	48.9%	Single with children	9.1%	9.1%
Percent Republican	57.8%	54.5%	Diversity measure	49.6	40.1	Percent over age 65	13.0%	12.9%

Economy & Jobs
Score: 67.9
Rank: 121

INCOME	AREA	U.S. AVG	EMPLOYMENT	AREA	U.S. AVG	EMPLOYING INDUSTRIES	AREA	U.S. AVG
Per capita income	$23,965	$23,235	Unemployment rate	5.8%	4.7%	Largest: Manufacturing		
Household income	$45,110	$46,414	Recent job growth	2.5%	1.3%			
Household income < $25K	25.7%	26.2%	Projected future job growth	12.4%	11.5%	Percent manufacturing	20.0%	15.4%
Household income > $75K	23.9%	25.4%	White collar	57.0%	57.8%	Percent public sector	11.5%	15.7%
Household income growth	11.1%	13.6%	Blue collar	30.0%	25.2%	Percent construction	10.0%	9.9%

Cost of Living
Score: 42.2
Rank: 216

INDEXES & TAXES	AREA	U.S. AVG	HOUSING	AREA	U.S. AVG	NECESSITIES	AREA	U.S. AVG
Cost of Living Index	84.3	100.0	Median home price	$150,100	$220,000	Food Index	94.6	100.0
Buying Power Index	119.9	100.0	Home price appreciation	18.0%	10.1%	Housing Index	59.2	100.0
Income tax rate	7.00%	4.70%	Median rent	$669	$709	Utilities Index	89.1	100.0
Sales tax rate	7.00%	6.58%	Homes owned	64.0%	62.3%	Transportation Index	95.5	100.0
Property tax rate	$8.17	$12.00	Home price ratio	3.3	4.2	Healthcare Index	95.3	100.0
						Miscellaneous Cost Index	97.4	100.0

Climate
Score: 59.4
Rank: 151

TEMPERATURE	AREA	U.S. AVG
Average January low	28.5	26.2
Average July high	87.5	87.4
Annual days > 90°F	28	38
Annual days < 32°F	85	89
Annual days < 0°F	0	6

PRECIPITATION	AREA	U.S. AVG
Annual inches precipitation	41.4	37.7
Annual inches snowfall	8.7	7.0
Annual days precipitation	121	109
Annual days rain > 0.5 inches	29	22
Annual days snow > 1.5 inches	3	6

COMFORTS & HAZARDS	AREA	U.S. AVG
July relative humidity	72%	66%
Annual days mostly sunny	217	208
Annual days with thunderstorms	46	39
Tornado risk score	11	18
Hurricane risk score	21	13

TEMPERATURE

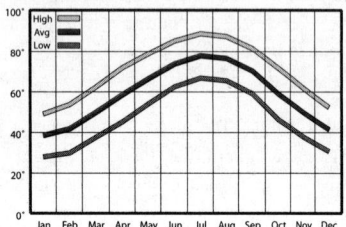

PRECIPITATION

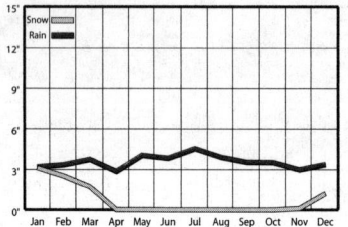

DAYS OF CLOUDS & PRECIPITATION

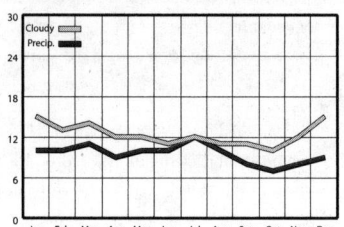

Education
Score: 56.7
Rank: 163

ACHIEVEMENT	AREA	U.S. AVG
High school degree	78.8%	82.7%
2-year college degree	6.2%	6.4%
4-year college degree	16.3%	15.7%
Graduate/professional degree	7.1%	8.9%

PUBLIC SCHOOLS	AREA	U.S. AVG
Expenditures per pupil	$5,189	$5,686
Student/teacher ratio	15.5	16.7
Attending public school	92.0%	90.1%
State SAT score	1008*	1021
State ACT score	20.5	20.9

HIGHER EDUCATION	AREA	U.S. AVG
No. 2-year colleges	5	4
No. 4-year colleges/universities	15	6
No. highly ranked universities	1	1

Health & Healthcare
Score: 53.2
Rank: 176

HAZARDS & ILLNESSES	AREA	U.S. AVG
Air-quality score	37	37
Water-quality score	78	52
Pollen/allergy score	65	61
Cancer mortality per capita	199.5	201.9
Depression days per month	3.5	3.5
Stress score	46	50

HEALTHCARE	AREA	U.S. AVG
Physicians per capita	259.0	244.2
Hospital beds per capita	368.5	420.0
No. teaching hospitals	3	3
Cost per doctor visit	$76	$77
Cost per dental visit	$72	$70

Crime
Score: 45.7
Rank: 203

CRIME	AREA	U.S. AVG
Violent crime rate	506.0	465.5
Change in violent crime rate	14.8%	-2.2%
Property crime rate	4,320.9	3,517.1
Change in property crime rate	1.5%	-2.1%

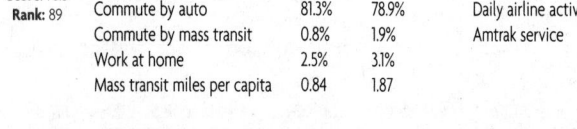

Transportation
Score: 76.5
Rank: 89

COMMUTE	AREA	U.S. AVG
Average commute time	24.4	27.4
Percent commutes > 60 mins.	4.4%	5.9%
Commute by auto	81.3%	78.9%
Commute by mass transit	0.8%	1.9%
Work at home	2.5%	3.1%
Mass transit miles per capita	0.84	1.87

INTERCITY SERVICES	AREA	U.S. AVG
Major airports within 60 miles	2	1
Size of regional airport	Large	Large
Daily airline activity	1091	686
Amtrak service	Yes	No

AUTOMOTIVE	AREA	U.S. AVG
Insurance, annual premium	$1,141	$1,432
Gas, cost per gallon	$2.51	$2.49
Daily vehicle miles per capita	35.3	24.0

Leisure
Score: 62.6
Rank: 139

DINING & SHOPPING	AREA	U.S. AVG
Restaurant rating	1	2
Outlet mall score	0	42
No. Starbucks	13	13
No. warehouse clubs	4	2

ENTERTAINMENT	AREA	U.S. AVG
Professional sports rating	3	4
College sports rating	6	4
Zoo/aquarium rating	6	3
Amusement park rating	1	3
Botanical garden/ arboretum rating	8	4

OUTDOOR ACTIVITIES	AREA	U.S. AVG
Golf-course rating	7	4
Ski-area rating	2	3
Sq. miles inland water	3	4
Miles of coastline	0.0	10.7
National Park rating	3	3

Arts & Culture
Score: 69.8
Rank: 113

MEDIA & LIBRARIES	AREA	U.S. AVG
Arts radio rating	1	3
No. public libraries	45	27
Library volumes per capita	2.29	2.78

PERFORMING ARTS	AREA	U.S. AVG
Classical music rating	5	4
Ballet/dance rating	5	3
Professional theater rating	6	3
University arts programs rating	9	5

MUSEUMS	AREA	U.S. AVG
Overall museum rating	8	5
Art museum rating	8	5
Science museum rating	8	5
Children's museum rating	9	3

Greenville, NC

Score: 67.9 Rank: 111 2004 rank: 180

Profile: Small city
Location: Eastern North Carolina, 80 miles east of Raleigh–Durham
Elevation: 40 feet
Time zone: Eastern Standard Time

PRO	CON
Nearby coastline	Crime rates
Cost of living	Hot, humid summers
Economic turnaround	Arts and culture

Greenville is a gateway to the eastern third of North Carolina and is mainly an agricultural and trading center with a strong tobacco presence. Some employment categories have declined, partially due to cutbacks in the tobacco industry, but the economy is in transition and the future job-growth projection at 20.5% is second highest in the state. A wide assortment of other manufacturing activity, from pharmaceuticals to material handling equipment, is located in the area. While East Carolina University provides a regional medical center and raises the level of educational attainment, most cultural amenities and services are found in Raleigh to the west. Greenville does have a strong local parks and recreation infrastructure. The area is a gateway to the coastal areas of the Outer Banks and Cape Hatteras, 100-plus miles to the east.

Greenville is located just above sea level on a flat coastal plain along the banks of the Tar River. Surrounding areas are agricultural with deciduous woods and tidewater marshes to the east. Summer is sunny, hot, and humid, with more 90°F-plus days than most towns in North Carolina. Winters are cool and fairly wet, but the area is close enough to the ocean and sheltered enough by the Appalachians to escape extreme cold; however, temperatures drop below freezing 45 times each winter. Annual rainfall is high, but snow is rare. First freeze is late October; last is mid-April.

DEMOGRAPHICS	AREA	U.S. AVG	ETHNIC COMPOSITION	AREA	U.S. AVG	RESIDENT PROFILE	AREA	U.S. AVG
Population	161,770		White	59.5%	79.0%	Single	41.0%	32.4%
Population density per sq. mile	176.4	358.5	Black	35.0%	10.5%	Married	44.4%	52.7%
Population growth	31.2%	21.1%	Asian	1.0%	2.7%	Divorced/separated	14.6%	14.9%
Median age	32.2	36.1	Hispanic	4.8%	10.6%	Married with children	19.9%	23.7%
Percent Democrat	45.8%	44.5%	Religious observance	31.4%	48.9%	Single with children	10.5%	9.1%
Percent Republican	54.0%	54.5%	Diversity measure	56.3	40.1	Percent over age 65	10.1%	12.9%

Economy & Jobs
Score: 52.9
Rank: 177

INCOME	AREA	U.S. AVG	EMPLOYMENT	AREA	U.S. AVG	EMPLOYING INDUSTRIES	AREA	U.S. AVG
Per capita income	$20,573	$23,235	Unemployment rate	6.9%	4.7%	Largest: Healthcare & Social Assistance		
Household income	$37,766	$46,414	Recent job growth	1.6%	1.3%			
Household income < $25K	34.7%	26.2%	Projected future job growth	20.5%	11.5%	Percent manufacturing	15.7%	15.4%
Household income > $75K	20.0%	25.4%	White collar	57.3%	57.8%	Percent public sector	20.0%	15.7%
Household income growth	15.2%	13.6%	Blue collar	25.3%	25.2%	Percent construction	9.6%	9.9%

Cost of Living
Score: 42.8
Rank: 214

INDEXES & TAXES	AREA	U.S. AVG	HOUSING	AREA	U.S. AVG	NECESSITIES	AREA	U.S. AVG
Cost of Living Index	85.5	100.0	Median home price	$144,800	$220,000	Food Index	98.2	100.0
Buying Power Index	99.0	100.0	Home price appreciation	20.6%	10.1%	Housing Index	58.7	100.0
Income tax rate	7.00%	4.70%	Median rent	$571	$709	Utilities Index	115.0	100.0
Sales tax rate	7.00%	6.58%	Homes owned	53.8%	62.3%	Transportation Index	93.1	100.0
Property tax rate	$8.95	$12.00	Home price ratio	3.8	4.2	Healthcare Index	96.3	100.0
						Miscellaneous Cost Index	93.9	100.0

Climate
Score: 52.7
Rank: 176

TEMPERATURE	AREA	U.S. AVG	PRECIPITATION	AREA	U.S. AVG	COMFORTS & HAZARDS	AREA	U.S. AVG
Average January low	36.2	26.2	Annual inches precipitation	54.0	37.7	July relative humidity	75%	66%
Average July high	88.8	87.4	Annual inches snowfall	1.8	7.0	Annual days mostly sunny	219	208
Annual days > 90°F	45	38	Annual days precipitation	117	109	Annual days with thunderstorms	46	39
Annual days < 32°F	45	89	Annual days rain > 0.5 inches	32	22	Tornado risk score	28	18
Annual days < 0°F	0	6	Annual days snow > 1.5 inches	1	6	Hurricane risk score	49	13

TEMPERATURE

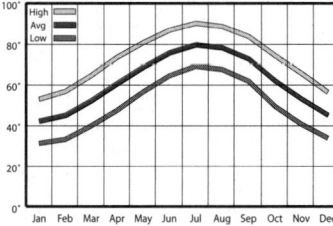

PRECIPITATION

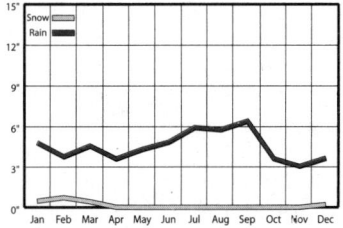

DAYS OF CLOUDS & PRECIPITATION

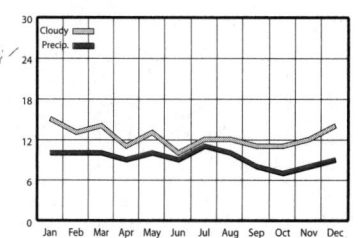

ACHIEVEMENT	AREA	U.S. AVG	PUBLIC SCHOOLS	AREA	U.S. AVG	HIGHER EDUCATION	AREA	U.S. AVG
High school degree	78.9%	82.7%	Expenditures per pupil	$4,857	$5,686	No. 2-year colleges	1	4
2-year college degree	7.5%	6.4%	Student/teacher ratio	14.0	16.7	No. 4-year colleges/universities	1	6
4-year college degree	16.2%	15.7%	Attending public school	91.3%	90.1%	No. highly ranked universities	0	1
Graduate/professional degree	8.8%	8.9%	State SAT score	1008*	1021			
			State ACT score	20.5	20.9			

Education
Score: 50.8
Rank: 185

HAZARDS & ILLNESSES	AREA	U.S. AVG	HEALTHCARE	AREA	U.S. AVG	CRIME	AREA	U.S. AVG
Air-quality score	50	37	Physicians per capita	491.6	244.2	Violent crime rate	559.1	465.5
Water-quality score	67	52	Hospital beds per capita	463.6	420.0	Change in violent crime rate	-3.2%	-2.2%
Pollen/allergy score	66	61	No. teaching hospitals	1	3	Property crime rate	4,429.9	3,517.1
Cancer mortality per capita	218.0	201.9	Cost per doctor visit	$73	$77	Change in property crime rate	-7.7%	-2.1%
Depression days per month	2.8	3.5	Cost per dental visit	$65	$70			
Stress score	49	50						

Health & Healthcare
Score: 74.1
Rank: 98

Crime
Score: 26.5
Rank: 275

COMMUTE	AREA	U.S. AVG	INTERCITY SERVICES	AREA	U.S. AVG	AUTOMOTIVE	AREA	U.S. AVG
Average commute time	23.0	27.4	Major airports within 60 miles	1	1	Insurance, annual premium	$1,022	$1,432
Percent commutes > 60 mins.	5.2%	5.9%	Size of regional airport	Medium	Large	Gas, cost per gallon	$2.53	$2.49
Commute by auto	80.5%	78.9%	Daily airline activity	352	686	Daily vehicle miles per capita	20.4	24.0
Commute by mass transit	0.8%	1.9%	Amtrak service	No	No			
Work at home	2.0%	3.1%						
Mass transit miles per capita	0.75	1.87						

Transportation
Score: 45.5
Rank: 205

DINING & SHOPPING	AREA	U.S. AVG	ENTERTAINMENT	AREA	U.S. AVG	OUTDOOR ACTIVITIES	AREA	U.S. AVG
Restaurant rating	1	2	Professional sports rating	2	4	Golf-course rating	1	4
Outlet mall score	0	42	College sports rating	3	4	Ski-area rating	1	3
No. Starbucks	2	13	Zoo/aquarium rating	1	3	Sq. miles inland water	3	4
No. warehouse clubs	1	2	Amusement park rating	1	3	Miles of coastline	29.4	10.7
			Botanical garden/ arboretum rating	2	4	National Park rating	1	3

Leisure
Score: 17.1
Rank: 309

MEDIA & LIBRARIES	AREA	U.S. AVG	PERFORMING ARTS	AREA	U.S. AVG	MUSEUMS	AREA	U.S. AVG
Arts radio rating	1	3	Classical music rating	3	4	Overall museum rating	1	5
No. public libraries	6	27	Ballet/dance rating	1	3	Art museum rating	3	5
Library volumes per capita	2.06	2.78	Professional theater rating	1	3	Science museum rating	2	5
			University arts programs rating	4	5	Children's museum rating	1	3

Arts & Culture
Score: 22.7
Rank: 288

Greenville, SC

Score: 69.6   **Rank:** 94   **2004 rank:** 80

Profile: Mid-size city
Location: Northwest South Carolina near North Carolina border, 75 miles southwest of Charlotte, NC
Elevation: 1,040 feet
Time zone: Eastern Standard Time

PRO
Attractive downtown
Strong economy
Arts and culture

CON
Hot, humid summers
Traffic and sprawl
Violent crime rate

Greenville is the cultural center among the triad of cities formerly grouped into the Greenville–Spartanburg–Anderson metro area. (We now cover each of these areas separately.) Located in the center of an old textile and agricultural region in the mountainous northwest part of the state, known by some as "upstate" South Carolina, Greenville is the most livable city in the triad. The relatively high altitude and view of the Appalachians to the northwest gave early Greenville regional status as a health destination, and to this day, it retains a clean and comfortable presence. The population is well educated for the region. Downtown is well maintained, vibrant, functional, historic, and—of course, in a place called Greenville—lined with trees. Not surprisingly, it won a 2003 Great American Main Street award from the National Trust for Historic Preservation. Arts amenities are abundant and accessible; performing arts include a recognized symphony, ballet, and theater performance venue at the new Peace Center for the Performing Arts. Many older mill buildings have been successfully repurposed into other uses, and there is abundant quality housing close to the city, mainly north and east. Automaker BMW located its plant in nearby Greer, 7 miles east, bringing a strong economic base and making Greer an up-and-coming family community, albeit with some growth and sprawl issues. The community is enjoying a vibrant economy and plenty of new infrastructure, and living costs are still very low (85.6). Outdoor activities are plentiful, particularly in the Blue Ridge Mountains to the north and lakes to the west. The town of Clemson 25 miles west, home of Clemson University, offers college-town amenities for those interested.

Located on the eastern slope of the Southern Appalachian Mountains, Greenville is in rolling country about 20 miles from the first mountain ridge and 55 miles northwest of the main ridge. Summers are warm and humid with thunderstorms. The elevation provides relatively cool nights during the summer months. Winters are pleasant, with below-freezing daytime temperatures only a few times a year. Rainfall is abundant and spread throughout the year. There are usually two to three small snowstorms and one to two episodes of freezing rain in winter.

Population

DEMOGRAPHICS	AREA	U.S. AVG
Population	586,800	
Population density per sq. mile	293.1	358.5
Population growth	24.3%	21.1%
Median age	36.3	36.1
Percent Democrat	32.1%	44.5%
Percent Republican	66.8%	54.5%

ETHNIC COMPOSITION	AREA	U.S. AVG
White	77.9%	79.0%
Black	17.5%	10.5%
Asian	1.5%	2.7%
Hispanic	4.3%	10.6%
Religious observance	55.6%	48.9%
Diversity measure	40.6	40.1

RESIDENT PROFILE	AREA	U.S. AVG
Single	31.1%	32.4%
Married	53.7%	52.7%
Divorced/separated	15.2%	14.9%
Married with children	23.1%	23.7%
Single with children	8.7%	9.1%
Percent over age 65	12.3%	12.9%

Economy & Jobs
Score: 83.4
Rank: 63

INCOME	AREA	U.S. AVG
Per capita income	$23,126	$23,235
Household income	$44,165	$46,414
Household income < $25K	27.1%	26.2%
Household income > $75K	23.8%	25.4%
Household income growth	12.3%	13.6%

EMPLOYMENT	AREA	U.S. AVG
Unemployment rate	5.5%	4.7%
Recent job growth	3.3%	1.3%
Projected future job growth	17.7%	11.5%
White collar	56.5%	57.8%
Blue collar	29.9%	25.2%

EMPLOYING INDUSTRIES	AREA	U.S. AVG
Largest: Manufacturing		
Percent manufacturing	19.3%	15.4%
Percent public sector	10.5%	15.7%
Percent construction	10.6%	9.9%

Cost of Living
Score: 58.3
Rank: 156

INDEXES & TAXES	AREA	U.S. AVG
Cost of Living Index	85.6	100.0
Buying Power Index	115.6	100.0
Income tax rate	6.88%	4.70%
Sales tax rate	5.31%	6.58%
Property tax rate	$6.23	$12.00

HOUSING	AREA	U.S. AVG
Median home price	$151,400	$220,000
Home price appreciation	19.4%	10.1%
Median rent	$612	$709
Homes owned	64.5%	62.3%
Home price ratio	3.4	4.2

NECESSITIES	AREA	U.S. AVG
Food Index	100.2	100.0
Housing Index	56.8	100.0
Utilities Index	83.6	100.0
Transportation Index	99.1	100.0
Healthcare Index	95.5	100.0
Miscellaneous Cost Index	96.9	100.0

Climate
Score: 50.3
Rank: 185

TEMPERATURE	AREA	U.S. AVG
Average January low	33.0	26.2
Average July high	87.6	87.4
Annual days > 90°F	29	38
Annual days < 32°F	68	89
Annual days < 0°F	0	6

PRECIPITATION	AREA	U.S. AVG
Annual inches precipitation	48.0	37.7
Annual inches snowfall	6.0	7.0
Annual days precipitation	119	109
Annual days rain > 0.5 inches	37	22
Annual days snow > 1.5 inches	2	6

COMFORTS & HAZARDS	AREA	U.S. AVG
July relative humidity	70%	66%
Annual days mostly sunny	221	208
Annual days with thunderstorms	44	39
Tornado risk score	18	18
Hurricane risk score	17	13

TEMPERATURE

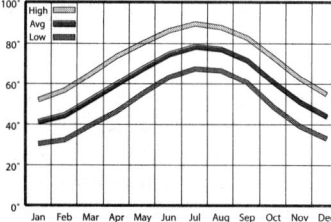

PRECIPITATION

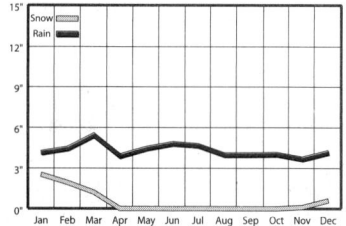

DAYS OF CLOUDS & PRECIPITATION

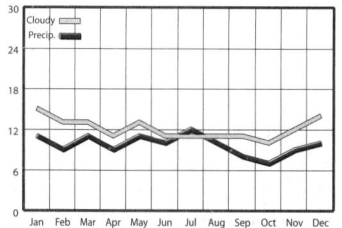

Education
Score: 53.2
Rank: 176

ACHIEVEMENT	AREA	U.S. AVG
High school degree	77.4%	82.7%
2-year college degree	7.0%	6.4%
4-year college degree	15.8%	15.7%
Graduate/professional degree	7.7%	8.9%

PUBLIC SCHOOLS	AREA	U.S. AVG
Expenditures per pupil	$4,612	$5,686
Student/teacher ratio	16.2	16.7
Attending public school	87.8%	90.1%
State SAT score	985*	1021
State ACT score	19.5	20.9

HIGHER EDUCATION	AREA	U.S. AVG
No. 2-year colleges	1	4
No. 4-year colleges/universities	7	6
No. highly ranked universities	3	1

Health & Healthcare
Score: 50.0
Rank: 188

HAZARDS & ILLNESSES	AREA	U.S. AVG
Air-quality score	33	37
Water-quality score	45	52
Pollen/allergy score	56	61
Cancer mortality per capita	189.8	201.9
Depression days per month	3.5	3.5
Stress score	83	50

HEALTHCARE	AREA	U.S. AVG
Physicians per capita	234.1	244.2
Hospital beds per capita	309.8	420.0
No. teaching hospitals	1	3
Cost per doctor visit	$72	$77
Cost per dental visit	$66	$70

Crime
Score: 10.4
Rank: 334

CRIME	AREA	U.S. AVG
Violent crime rate	705.6	465.5
Change in violent crime rate	2.7%	-2.2%
Property crime rate	4,044.3	3,517.1
Change in property crime rate	2.1%	-2.1%

TRANSPORTATION								
COMMUTE	AREA	U.S. AVG	**INTERCITY SERVICES**	AREA	U.S. AVG	**AUTOMOTIVE**	AREA	U.S. AVG
Average commute time	24.3	27.4	Major airports within 60 miles	1	1	Insurance, annual premium	$1,385	$1,432
Percent commutes > 60 mins.	4.0%	5.9%	Size of regional airport	Large	Large	Gas, cost per gallon	$2.36	$2.49
Commute by auto	81.6%	78.9%	Daily airline activity	806	686	Daily vehicle miles per capita	22.3	24.0
Commute by mass transit	0.4%	1.9%	Amtrak service	Yes	No			
Work at home	2.3%	3.1%						
Mass transit miles per capita	0.36	1.87						

Transportation
Score: 55.6
Rank: 167

LEISURE								
DINING & SHOPPING	AREA	U.S. AVG	**ENTERTAINMENT**	AREA	U.S. AVG	**OUTDOOR ACTIVITIES**	AREA	U.S. AVG
Restaurant rating	1	2	Professional sports rating	3	4	Golf-course rating	5	4
Outlet mall score	19	42	College sports rating	5	4	Ski-area rating	1	3
No. Starbucks	3	13	Zoo/aquarium rating	3	3	Sq. miles inland water	2	4
No. warehouse clubs	2	2	Amusement park rating	1	3	Miles of coastline	0.0	10.7
			Botanical garden/ arboretum rating	9	4	National Park rating	1	3

Leisure
Score: 38.0
Rank: 231

ARTS & CULTURE								
MEDIA & LIBRARIES	AREA	U.S. AVG	**PERFORMING ARTS**	AREA	U.S. AVG	**MUSEUMS**	AREA	U.S. AVG
Arts radio rating	1	3	Classical music rating	6	4	Overall museum rating	7	5
No. public libraries	18	27	Ballet/dance rating	3	3	Art museum rating	7	5
Library volumes per capita	2.20	2.78	Professional theater rating	1	3	Science museum rating	7	5
			University arts programs rating	3	5	Children's museum rating	1	3

Arts & Culture
Score: 54.0
Rank: 172

Hagerstown–Martinsburg, MD-WV

Score: 69.6 Rank: 95 2004 rank: 184

Profile: Small-city complex
Location: North-central Maryland near the Pennsylvania border
Elevation: 547 feet
Time zone: Eastern Standard Time

PRO	CON
Small-town atmosphere	Arts and culture
Historic interest	Low educational attainment
Attractive setting	Air service

Hagerstown lies at the gateway to the western Maryland region and the Shenandoah Valley to the south. Historically, it was an important transportation center because of its location along major east–west and north–south routes and near a passage west through the Cumberland Gap. Today, Hagerstown is a pleasant mix of old and new, with a notable downtown historic area and an unusually large concentration of pre–Civil War row homes not unlike nearby Baltimore's famous row houses. There are some attractive new suburbs mostly northeast and some gritty working-class areas close to the main city. Entertainment includes minor-league baseball, the Hagerstown Speedway, and the nation's oldest farmer's market. The area is a bit isolated from other East Coast cities, and educational attainment is low, but cost of living is very attractive for the region. Martinsburg is another historic transportation hub just across the border in the West Virginia panhandle toward

Virginia's Shenandoah Valley. Because of its strategic location, good labor force, and tax incentives, the area has developed a good base of light and medium industry. Remarkably the Maryland Transit Authority runs "MARC" commuter train service all the way to Martinsburg; commutes to Washington D.C. are 2 hours but many D.C. northern suburbs can be reached in a little over an hour.

The area is located in a broad, flat agricultural extension of Virginia's famed Shenandoah Valley. The surroundings, particularly to the northwest and southeast, are hilly and wooded with deciduous trees. Summers are warm, calm, and humid, with occasional thunderstorms. Winters are cold but severe effects are moderated by the mountains, which block many heavy storms and cold-air blasts. Occasional heavy snow occurs when storms originating on the Atlantic or from the southwest hit the area. Spring and fall are pleasant. First freeze is late October; last is mid-April.

POPULATION								
DEMOGRAPHICS	AREA	U.S. AVG	**ETHNIC COMPOSITION**	AREA	U.S. AVG	**RESIDENT PROFILE**	AREA	U.S. AVG
Population	245,404		White	90.6%	79.0%	Single	27.9%	32.4%
Population density per sq. mile	243.4	358.5	Black	6.5%	10.5%	Married	55.0%	52.7%
Population growth	29.5%	21.1%	Asian	0.8%	2.7%	Divorced/separated	17.2%	14.9%
Median age	37.6	36.1	Hispanic	1.5%	10.6%	Married with children	22.7%	23.7%
Percent Democrat	35.5%	44.5%	Religious observance	40.2%	48.9%	Single with children	9.0%	9.1%
Percent Republican	63.6%	54.5%	Diversity measure	19.7	40.1	Percent over age 65	13.3%	12.9%

ECONOMY & JOBS								
INCOME	AREA	U.S. AVG	**EMPLOYMENT**	AREA	U.S. AVG	**EMPLOYING INDUSTRIES**	AREA	U.S. AVG
Per capita income	$22,357	$23,235	Unemployment rate	4.3%	4.7%	Largest: Manufacturing		
Household income	$45,504	$46,414	Recent job growth	1.7%	1.3%			
Household income < $25K	25.0%	26.2%	Projected future job growth	12.7%	11.5%	Percent manufacturing	19.7%	15.4%
Household income > $75K	22.9%	25.4%	White collar	52.1%	57.8%	Percent public sector	16.6%	15.7%
Household income growth	15.0%	13.6%	Blue collar	32.1%	25.2%	Percent construction	12.4%	9.9%

Economy & Jobs
Score: 54.8
Rank: 170

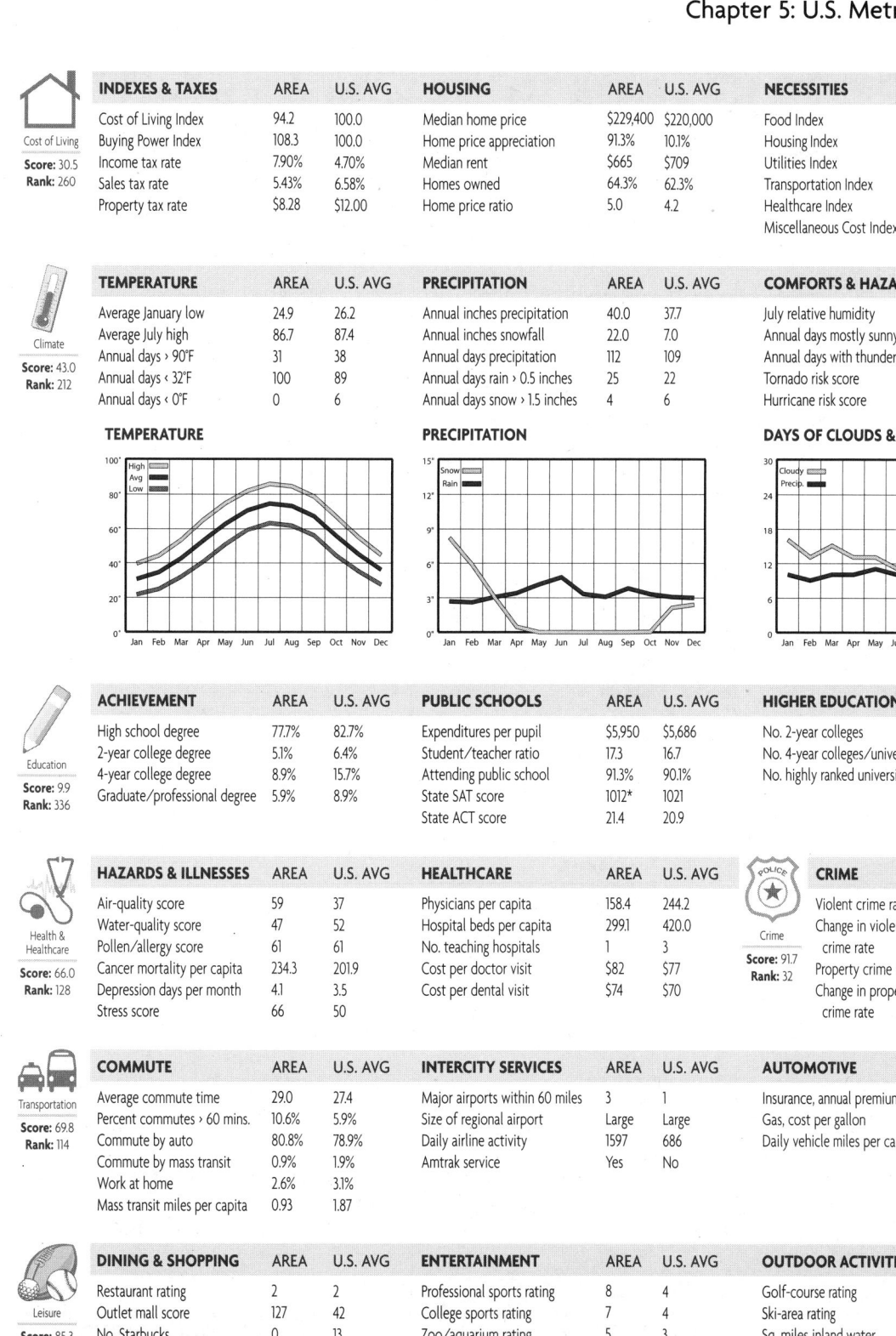

Cost of Living
Score: 30.5
Rank: 260

INDEXES & TAXES	AREA	U.S. AVG
Cost of Living Index	94.2	100.0
Buying Power Index	108.3	100.0
Income tax rate	7.90%	4.70%
Sales tax rate	5.43%	6.58%
Property tax rate	$8.28	$12.00

HOUSING	AREA	U.S. AVG
Median home price	$229,400	$220,000
Home price appreciation	91.3%	10.1%
Median rent	$665	$709
Homes owned	64.3%	62.3%
Home price ratio	5.0	4.2

NECESSITIES	AREA	U.S. AVG
Food Index	88.1	100.0
Housing Index	77.1	100.0
Utilities Index	97.0	100.0
Transportation Index	88.9	100.0
Healthcare Index	89.3	100.0
Miscellaneous Cost Index	91.1	100.0

Climate
Score: 43.0
Rank: 212

TEMPERATURE	AREA	U.S. AVG
Average January low	24.9	26.2
Average July high	86.7	87.4
Annual days > 90°F	31	38
Annual days < 32°F	100	89
Annual days < 0°F	0	6

PRECIPITATION	AREA	U.S. AVG
Annual inches precipitation	40.0	37.7
Annual inches snowfall	22.0	7.0
Annual days precipitation	112	109
Annual days rain > 0.5 inches	25	22
Annual days snow > 1.5 inches	4	6

COMFORTS & HAZARDS	AREA	U.S. AVG
July relative humidity	67%	66%
Annual days mostly sunny	205	208
Annual days with thunderstorms	26	39
Tornado risk score	6	18
Hurricane risk score	10	13

TEMPERATURE

PRECIPITATION

DAYS OF CLOUDS & PRECIPITATION

Education
Score: 9.9
Rank: 336

ACHIEVEMENT	AREA	U.S. AVG
High school degree	77.7%	82.7%
2-year college degree	5.1%	6.4%
4-year college degree	8.9%	15.7%
Graduate/professional degree	5.9%	8.9%

PUBLIC SCHOOLS	AREA	U.S. AVG
Expenditures per pupil	$5,950	$5,686
Student/teacher ratio	17.3	16.7
Attending public school	91.3%	90.1%
State SAT score	1012*	1021
State ACT score	21.4	20.9

HIGHER EDUCATION	AREA	U.S. AVG
No. 2-year colleges	5	4
No. 4-year colleges/universities	0	6
No. highly ranked universities	0	1

Health & Healthcare
Score: 66.0
Rank: 128

HAZARDS & ILLNESSES	AREA	U.S. AVG
Air-quality score	59	37
Water-quality score	47	52
Pollen/allergy score	61	61
Cancer mortality per capita	234.3	201.9
Depression days per month	4.1	3.5
Stress score	66	50

HEALTHCARE	AREA	U.S. AVG
Physicians per capita	158.4	244.2
Hospital beds per capita	299.1	420.0
No. teaching hospitals	1	3
Cost per doctor visit	$82	$77
Cost per dental visit	$74	$70

Crime
Score: 91.7
Rank: 32

CRIME	AREA	U.S. AVG
Violent crime rate	302.5	465.5
Change in violent crime rate	-4.3%	-2.2%
Property crime rate	2,263.5	3,517.1
Change in property crime rate	3.8%	-2.1%

Transportation
Score: 69.8
Rank: 114

COMMUTE	AREA	U.S. AVG
Average commute time	29.0	27.4
Percent commutes > 60 mins.	10.6%	5.9%
Commute by auto	80.8%	78.9%
Commute by mass transit	0.9%	1.9%
Work at home	2.6%	3.1%
Mass transit miles per capita	0.93	1.87

INTERCITY SERVICES	AREA	U.S. AVG
Major airports within 60 miles	3	1
Size of regional airport	Large	Large
Daily airline activity	1597	686
Amtrak service	Yes	No

AUTOMOTIVE	AREA	U.S. AVG
Insurance, annual premium	$1,313	$1,432
Gas, cost per gallon	$2.47	$2.49
Daily vehicle miles per capita	21.2	24.0

Leisure
Score: 85.3
Rank: 55

DINING & SHOPPING	AREA	U.S. AVG
Restaurant rating	2	2
Outlet mall score	127	42
No. Starbucks	0	13
No. warehouse clubs	0	2

ENTERTAINMENT	AREA	U.S. AVG
Professional sports rating	8	4
College sports rating	7	4
Zoo/aquarium rating	5	3
Amusement park rating	2	3
Botanical garden/ arboretum rating	1	4

OUTDOOR ACTIVITIES	AREA	U.S. AVG
Golf-course rating	7	4
Ski-area rating	4	3
Sq. miles inland water	6	4
Miles of coastline	0.0	10.7
National Park rating	3	3

Arts & Culture
Score: 78.1
Rank: 82

MEDIA & LIBRARIES	AREA	U.S. AVG
Arts radio rating	7	3
No. public libraries	13	27
Library volumes per capita	2.71	2.78

PERFORMING ARTS	AREA	U.S. AVG
Classical music rating	6	4
Ballet/dance rating	6	3
Professional theater rating	7	3
University arts programs rating	5	5

MUSEUMS	AREA	U.S. AVG
Overall museum rating	8	5
Art museum rating	8	5
Science museum rating	3	5
Children's museum rating	1	3

Hanford–Corcoran, CA

Score: 23.8 Rank: 362 2004 rank: not ranked

Profile: Small-agricultural-town complex
Location: Central California, 35 miles southeast of Fresno
Elevation: 248 feet
Time zone: Pacific Standard Time

PRO	CON
Nearby mountains	Unemployment
Mild winters	Educational attainment
Future job growth	Entertainment

Located in the southern San Joaquin Valley not far from Fresno, Hanford is a rather dull town supporting a wide variety of agriculture, while Corcoran is a similar but smaller town farther into the flatlands to the west. Areas to the east produce citrus crops. Many of the farms are prosperous, but the workers and many of the industries supporting them are economically challenged. The Sierra Nevada and its national parks begin their rise 20 miles east, with Sequoia and Kings Canyon national parks a windy 50-mile drive northeast. Downtown Hanford is plain and uninteresting, and there is little to do and little cultural interest except for some notable elements of migrant heritage brought by early California railroad and agricultural history. The mountains can be seen on a clear day, but immediate surroundings are pancake-flat, treeless,

irrigated agricultural land, and distance from the mountains and typical valley haze reduce the appeal of the setting. Unemployment is high and combined educational attainment is second lowest in the U.S; these don't mix well with a Cost of Living Index of 126.1.

The southern San Joaquin Valley is flat and dry with significant haze most times obscuring the dramatic mountains rising both east and west. Summers are extremely dry and sometimes unbearably hot, with temperatures usually exceeding 90 and often exceeding 100°F. Evening cooling may occur with mountain air or breezes from the northwest—but often there is no breeze at all and it remains hot. There is almost no precipitation May through October. Winters are cool and moist but almost always above freezing.

Population

DEMOGRAPHICS	AREA	U.S. AVG	ETHNIC COMPOSITION	AREA	U.S. AVG	RESIDENT PROFILE	AREA	U.S. AVG
Population	140,941		White	52.6%	79.0%	Single	27.5%	32.4%
Population density per sq. mile	101.3	358.5	Black	8.3%	10.5%	Married	43.1%	52.7%
Population growth	38.9%	21.1%	Asian	3.2%	2.7%	Divorced/separated	29.4%	14.9%
Median age	30.7	36.1	Hispanic	46.2%	10.6%	Married with children	32.8%	23.7%
Percent Democrat	33.7%	44.5%	Religious observance	39.9%	48.9%	Single with children	13.5%	9.1%
Percent Republican	65.4%	54.5%	Diversity measure	81.1	40.1	Percent over age 65	7.5%	12.9%

Economy
& Jobs
Score: 26.2
Rank: 276

INCOME	AREA	U.S. AVG	EMPLOYMENT	AREA	U.S. AVG	EMPLOYING INDUSTRIES	AREA	U.S. AVG
Per capita income	$17,528	$23,235	Unemployment rate	8.3%	4.7%	Largest: Manufacturing		
Household income	$42,031	$46,414	Recent job growth	2.0%	1.3%			
Household income < $25K	27.8%	26.2%	Projected future job growth	20.2%	11.5%	Percent manufacturing	13.6%	15.4%
Household income > $75K	22.1%	25.4%	White collar	46.4%	57.8%	Percent public sector	26.8%	15.7%
Household income growth	17.6%	13.6%	Blue collar	22.1%	25.2%	Percent construction	8.5%	9.9%

Cost of Living
Score: 10.2
Rank: 335

INDEXES & TAXES	AREA	U.S. AVG	HOUSING	AREA	U.S. AVG	NECESSITIES	AREA	U.S. AVG
Cost of Living Index	126.1	100.0	Median home price	$345,900	$220,000	Food Index	109.2	100.0
Buying Power Index	74.7	100.0	Home price appreciation	134.8%	10.1%	Housing Index	71.4	100.0
Income tax rate	6.00%	4.70%	Median rent	$633	$709	Utilities Index	120.6	100.0
Sales tax rate	7.25%	6.58%	Homes owned	52.8%	62.3%	Transportation Index	112.3	100.0
Property tax rate	$9.14	$12.00	Home price ratio	8.2	4.2	Healthcare Index	112.1	100.0
						Miscellaneous Cost Index	103.8	100.0

Climate
Score: 89.6
Rank: 40

TEMPERATURE	AREA	U.S. AVG	PRECIPITATION	AREA	U.S. AVG	COMFORTS & HAZARDS	AREA	U.S. AVG
Average January low	36.0	26.2	Annual inches precipitation	7.4	37.7	July relative humidity	24%	66%
Average July high	98.0	87.4	Annual inches snowfall	0.1	7.0	Annual days mostly sunny	264	208
Annual days > 90°F	111	38	Annual days precipitation	43	109	Annual days with thunderstorms	6	39
Annual days < 32°F	30	89	Annual days rain > 0.5 inches	6	22	Tornado risk score	4	18
Annual days < 0°F	0	6	Annual days snow > 1.5 inches	0	6	Hurricane risk score	0	13

TEMPERATURE

PRECIPITATION

DAYS OF CLOUDS & PRECIPITATION

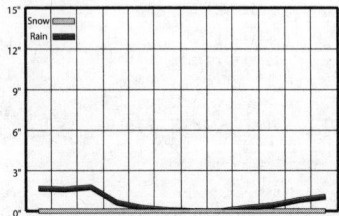

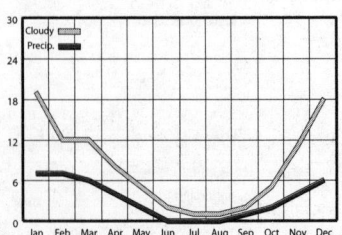

ACHIEVEMENT	AREA	U.S. AVG	PUBLIC SCHOOLS	AREA	U.S. AVG	HIGHER EDUCATION	AREA	U.S. AVG
High school degree	68.9%	82.7%	Expenditures per pupil	$5,251	$5,686	No. 2-year colleges	0	4
2-year college degree	7.9%	6.4%	Student/teacher ratio	20.6	16.7	No. 4-year colleges/universities	0	6
4-year college degree	7.8%	15.7%	Attending public school	95.7%	90.1%	No. highly ranked universities	0	1
Graduate/professional degree	2.8%	8.9%	State SAT score	1019*	1021			
			State ACT score	21.6	20.9			

Education
Score: 3.2
Rank: 361

HAZARDS & ILLNESSES	AREA	U.S. AVG	HEALTHCARE	AREA	U.S. AVG	CRIME	AREA	U.S. AVG
Air-quality score	38	37	Physicians per capita	81.6	244.2	Violent crime rate	381.2	465.5
Water-quality score	1	52	Hospital beds per capita	118.5	420.0	Change in violent crime rate	15.7%	-2.2%
Pollen/allergy score	60	61	No. teaching hospitals	0	3	Property crime rate	2,770.6	3,517.1
Cancer mortality per capita	152.0	201.9	Cost per doctor visit	$87	$77	Change in property crime rate	0.3%	-2.1%
Depression days per month	3.9	3.5	Cost per dental visit	$80	$70			
Stress score	41	50						

Health & Healthcare
Score: 21.9
Rank: 291

Crime
Score: 63.9
Rank: 136

COMMUTE	AREA	U.S. AVG	INTERCITY SERVICES	AREA	U.S. AVG	AUTOMOTIVE	AREA	U.S. AVG
Average commute time	22.8	27.4	Major airports within 60 miles	0	1	Insurance, annual premium	$1,423	$1,432
Percent commutes > 60 mins.	4.5%	5.9%	Size of regional airport	Small	Large	Gas, cost per gallon	$2.70	$2.49
Commute by auto	73.5%	78.9%	Daily airline activity	75	686	Daily vehicle miles per capita	16.3	24.0
Commute by mass transit	1.6%	1.9%	Amtrak service	Yes	No			
Work at home	2.6%	3.1%						
Mass transit miles per capita	1.58	1.87						

Transportation
Score: 25.7
Rank: 279

DINING & SHOPPING	AREA	U.S. AVG	ENTERTAINMENT	AREA	U.S. AVG	OUTDOOR ACTIVITIES	AREA	U.S. AVG
Restaurant rating	1	2	Professional sports rating	1	4	Golf-course rating	2	4
Outlet mall score	45	42	College sports rating	1	4	Ski-area rating	2	3
No. Starbucks	2	13	Zoo/aquarium rating	1	3	Sq. miles inland water	1	4
No. warehouse clubs	0	2	Amusement park rating	1	3	Miles of coastline	0.0	10.7
			Botanical garden/ arboretum rating	1	4	National Park rating	5	3

Leisure
Score: 8.6
Rank: 341

MEDIA & LIBRARIES	AREA	U.S. AVG	PERFORMING ARTS	AREA	U.S. AVG	MUSEUMS	AREA	U.S. AVG
Arts radio rating	1	3	Classical music rating	1	4	Overall museum rating	1	5
No. public libraries	7	27	Ballet/dance rating	1	3	Art museum rating	1	5
Library volumes per capita	1.44	2.78	Professional theater rating	1	3	Science museum rating	4	5
			University arts programs rating	1	5	Children's museum rating	1	3

Arts & Culture
Score: 0.5
Rank: 371

Harrisburg–Carlisle, PA

Score: 68.3   Rank: 107   2004 rank: 46

Profile: Capital-city complex
Location: Southeast-central Pennsylvania along the Susquehanna River
Elevation: 351 feet
Time zone: Eastern Standard Time

PRO
Capital-city amenities
Central location
Nearby mountains

CON
Entertainment
Air service
Dull infrastructure

Harrisburg, Pennsylvania's state capital, features a nondescript, fairly unattractive downtown for a capital city. A couple of pluses include an assortment of historic museums and a nice waterfront strip along the Susquehanna River. Beyond downtown, residential and industrial areas spread across the river into Camp Hill and Mechanicsburg to the west. The economy isn't spectacular but is projected to grow because of the area's relatively low cost of doing business and the strategic central location along key surface transportation routes within the eastern United States. The city has some minor-league sports and other recreational amenities, but overall is quieter with less to do than many capital cities of its size. Carlisle is a satellite town 12 miles west, a fairly nondescript but growing retail, commercial, and residen-

tial center. It also serves as a trucking hub at the junction of the northeast–southwest Interstate 81 and the east–west Pennsylvania Turnpike. The Cost of Living Index at 87.6 is low for a capital city, especially in this region.

Harrisburg is in the Great Valley of the eastern foothills of the Allegheny Mountains. The landscape rises rapidly to the west into the main Allegheny ridge and becomes rolling to more level to the east. Summers are warm and humid as landforms allow warm, moist air to invade from the southwest. The city receives substantial precipitation. Occasional late summer and fall hurricanes produce downpours, notably the 15 inches dropped in 3 days by Hurricane Agnes in 1972. First freeze is late October; last is late April.

Population

DEMOGRAPHICS	AREA	U.S. AVG	ETHNIC COMPOSITION	AREA	U.S. AVG	RESIDENT PROFILE	AREA	U.S. AVG
Population	521,971		White	85.4%	79.0%	Single	32.6%	32.4%
Population density per sq. mile	320.4	358.5	Black	9.5%	10.5%	Married	53.4%	52.7%
Population growth	10.2%	21.1%	Asian	2.2%	2.7%	Divorced/separated	14.0%	14.9%
Median age	39.3	36.1	Hispanic	2.7%	10.6%	Married with children	21.7%	23.7%
Percent Democrat	39.9%	44.5%	Religious observance	50.8%	48.9%	Single with children	8.0%	9.1%
Percent Republican	59.6%	54.5%	Diversity measure	28.2	40.1	Percent over age 65	14.6%	12.9%

Economy & Jobs
Score: 55.6
Rank: 167

INCOME	AREA	U.S. AVG	EMPLOYMENT	AREA	U.S. AVG	EMPLOYING INDUSTRIES	AREA	U.S. AVG
Per capita income	$25,698	$23,235	Unemployment rate	4.3%	4.7%	Largest: Healthcare & Social Assistance		
Household income	$49,454	$46,414	Recent job growth	1.2%	1.3%			
Household income < $25K	21.8%	26.2%	Projected future job growth	9.6%	11.5%	Percent manufacturing	14.9%	15.4%
Household income > $75K	27.6%	25.4%	White collar	62.6%	57.8%	Percent public sector	18.3%	15.7%
Household income growth	13.0%	13.6%	Blue collar	22.9%	25.2%	Percent construction	8.0%	9.9%

Cost of Living
Score: 74.6
Rank: 96

INDEXES & TAXES	AREA	U.S. AVG	HOUSING	AREA	U.S. AVG	NECESSITIES	AREA	U.S. AVG
Cost of Living Index	87.6	100.0	Median home price	$143,600	$220,000	Food Index	92.9	100.0
Buying Power Index	126.5	100.0	Home price appreciation	37.6%	10.1%	Housing Index	60.7	100.0
Income tax rate	2.80%	4.70%	Median rent	$728	$709	Utilities Index	111.4	100.0
Sales tax rate	6.00%	6.58%	Homes owned	65.7%	62.3%	Transportation Index	104.7	100.0
Property tax rate	$14.54	$12.00	Home price ratio	2.9	4.2	Healthcare Index	92.6	100.0
						Miscellaneous Cost Index	102.0	100.0

Climate
Score: 33.2
Rank: 249

TEMPERATURE	AREA	U.S. AVG	PRECIPITATION	AREA	U.S. AVG	COMFORTS & HAZARDS	AREA	U.S. AVG
Average January low	22.5	26.2	Annual inches precipitation	36.0	37.7	July relative humidity	67%	66%
Average July high	86.8	87.4	Annual inches snowfall	35.0	7.0	Annual days mostly sunny	193	208
Annual days > 90°F	24	38	Annual days precipitation	125	109	Annual days with thunderstorms	33	39
Annual days < 32°F	107	89	Annual days rain > 0.5 inches	25	22	Tornado risk score	13	18
Annual days < 0°F	1	6	Annual days snow > 1.5 inches	7	6	Hurricane risk score	10	13

TEMPERATURE

PRECIPITATION

DAYS OF CLOUDS & PRECIPITATION

Education
Score: 58.3
Rank: 157

ACHIEVEMENT	AREA	U.S. AVG	PUBLIC SCHOOLS	AREA	U.S. AVG	HIGHER EDUCATION	AREA	U.S. AVG
High school degree	84.3%	82.7%	Expenditures per pupil	$6,252	$5,686	No. 2-year colleges	5	4
2-year college degree	6.2%	6.4%	Student/teacher ratio	17.1	16.7	No. 4-year colleges/universities	7	6
4-year college degree	15.6%	15.7%	Attending public school	88.5%	90.1%	No. highly ranked universities	1	1
Graduate/professional degree	8.8%	8.9%	State SAT score	993*	1021			
			State ACT score	21.8	20.9			

Health & Healthcare
Score: 76.7
Rank: 88

HAZARDS & ILLNESSES	AREA	U.S. AVG	HEALTHCARE	AREA	U.S. AVG	CRIME	AREA	U.S. AVG
Air-quality score	43	37	Physicians per capita	346.5	244.2	Violent crime rate	350.6	465.5
Water-quality score	55	52	Hospital beds per capita	459.4	420.0	Change in violent crime rate	14.4%	-2.2%
Pollen/allergy score	45	61	No. teaching hospitals	5	3	Property crime rate	2,421.1	3,517.1
Cancer mortality per capita	239.2	201.9	Cost per doctor visit	$65	$77	Change in property crime rate	5.4%	-2.1%
Depression days per month	3.0	3.5	Cost per dental visit	$50	$70			
Stress score	12	50						

Crime
Score: 93.6
Rank: 25

Transportation
Score: 98.4
Rank: 7

COMMUTE	AREA	U.S. AVG	INTERCITY SERVICES	AREA	U.S. AVG	AUTOMOTIVE	AREA	U.S. AVG
Average commute time	24.1	27.4	Major airports within 60 miles	4	1	Insurance, annual premium	$1,213	$1,432
Percent commutes > 60 mins.	4.5%	5.9%	Size of regional airport	Large	Large	Gas, cost per gallon	$2.46	$2.49
Commute by auto	80.2%	78.9%	Daily airline activity	2329	686	Daily vehicle miles per capita	29.1	24.0
Commute by mass transit	1.4%	1.9%	Amtrak service	Yes	No			
Work at home	2.9%	3.1%						
Mass transit miles per capita	1.40	1.87						

DINING & SHOPPING	AREA	U.S. AVG	ENTERTAINMENT	AREA	U.S. AVG	OUTDOOR ACTIVITIES	AREA	U.S. AVG
Restaurant rating	1	2	Professional sports rating	3	4	Golf-course rating	5	4
Outlet mall score	54	42	College sports rating	5	4	Ski-area rating	4	3
No. Starbucks	3	13	Zoo/aquarium rating	6	3	Sq. miles inland water	4	4
No. warehouse clubs	2	2	Amusement park rating	10	3	Miles of coastline	0.0	10.7
			Botanical garden/ arboretum rating	9	4	National Park rating	2	3

Leisure
Score: 71.4
Rank: 107

MEDIA & LIBRARIES	AREA	U.S. AVG	PERFORMING ARTS	AREA	U.S. AVG	MUSEUMS	AREA	U.S. AVG
Arts radio rating	8	3	Classical music rating	3	4	Overall museum rating	8	5
No. public libraries	23	27	Ballet/dance rating	3	3	Art museum rating	6	5
Library volumes per capita	1.75	2.78	Professional theater rating	1	3	Science museum rating	9	5
			University arts programs rating	3	5	Children's museum rating	1	3

Arts & Culture
Score: 64.2
Rank: 133

Harrisonburg, VA

Score: 68.4 **Rank:** 105 **2004 rank:** not ranked

Profile: Small town/college town
Location: Western Virginia, center of the Shenandoah Valley
Elevation: 1,352 feet
Time zone: Eastern Standard Time

PRO	CON
Nearby recreation	Entertainment
Small-town feel	Cost of housing
Attractive setting	Air service

Harrisonburg is a small, pleasant town in the heart of the Shenandoah Valley. The downtown area is attractive and historic, particularly in the core area near James Madison University. The university brings 16,000 students and some minor local arts amenities, and the nearby Blue Ridge and Appalachian mountains offer plenty of recreation and outdoor interest. In addition to the university, agriculture, agricultural processing, and other light industries are the economy's main supports. The city and university have a jointly developed technology zone and incubator. Partly due to the mountain alignment, larger cities to the east are somewhat difficult to access for big-city services, but the area has a pleasant atmosphere and appearance, and crime is very low. Charlottesville and its services are 55 miles away across the

Blue Ridge. Cost of living is a challenging 107.7 and housing costs are high and rising fast for this type of locale, as more people from other areas in the East discover the quality of life.

Harrisonburg is beautifully set in the center of the broad Shenandoah Valley. The immediate area around the town is flat and wooded, giving way to agricultural land all around and heavily forested Blue Ridge to the east and Appalachian mountains to the west in plain view of the city. Summers are warm, still, and humid with periodic thunderstorms, and the higher elevation gives cooler evenings than some other parts of Virginia. Winters are cold but not severe. Heavy snow may occur with storms moving up the Atlantic Coast or from the Carolinas. Spring is pleasant and fall is gorgeous. First freeze is late October; last is mid-April.

Population

DEMOGRAPHICS	AREA	U.S. AVG	ETHNIC COMPOSITION	AREA	U.S. AVG	RESIDENT PROFILE	AREA	U.S. AVG
Population	113,343		White	91.1%	79.0%	Single	38.5%	32.4%
Population density per sq. mile	130.5	358.5	Black	3.3%	10.5%	Married	48.3%	52.7%
Population growth	28.9%	21.1%	Asian	1.5%	2.7%	Divorced/separated	13.2%	14.9%
Median age	33.2	36.1	Hispanic	6.8%	10.6%	Married with children	22.4%	23.7%
Percent Democrat	31.6%	44.5%	Religious observance	46.3%	48.9%	Single with children	6.8%	9.1%
Percent Republican	67.5%	54.5%	Diversity measure	25.9	40.1	Percent over age 65	12.3%	12.9%

Economy & Jobs
Score: 90.9
Rank: 35

INCOME	AREA	U.S. AVG	EMPLOYMENT	AREA	U.S. AVG	EMPLOYING INDUSTRIES	AREA	U.S. AVG
Per capita income	$19,391	$23,235	Unemployment rate	2.9%	4.7%	Largest: Manufacturing		
Household income	$40,856	$46,414	Recent job growth	4.7%	1.3%			
Household income < $25K	29.1%	26.2%	Projected future job growth	15.1%	11.5%	Percent manufacturing	20.8%	15.4%
Household income > $75K	19.7%	25.4%	White collar	49.8%	57.8%	Percent public sector	15.5%	15.7%
Household income growth	11.0%	13.6%	Blue collar	30.9%	25.2%	Percent construction	10.1%	9.9%

Cost of Living
Score: 37.4
Rank: 234

INDEXES & TAXES	AREA	U.S. AVG	HOUSING	AREA	U.S. AVG	NECESSITIES	AREA	U.S. AVG
Cost of Living Index	107.7	100.0	Median home price	$294,500	$220,000	Food Index	96.5	100.0
Buying Power Index	85.0	100.0	Home price appreciation	61.8%	10.1%	Housing Index	88.7	100.0
Income tax rate	5.75%	4.70%	Median rent	$610	$709	Utilities Index	88.5	100.0
Sales tax rate	5.00%	6.58%	Homes owned	59.4%	62.3%	Transportation Index	96.8	100.0
Property tax rate	$6.74	$12.00	Home price ratio	7.2	4.2	Healthcare Index	94.7	100.0
						Miscellaneous Cost Index	98.4	100.0

Climate

Score: 17.9
Rank: 306

TEMPERATURE	AREA	U.S. AVG
Average January low	18.0	26.2
Average July high	81.0	87.4
Annual days > 90°F	2	38
Annual days < 32°F	145	89
Annual days < 0°F	0	6

PRECIPITATION	AREA	U.S. AVG
Annual inches precipitation	44.5	37.7
Annual inches snowfall	71.0	7.0
Annual days precipitation	174	109
Annual days rain > 0.5 inches	28	22
Annual days snow > 1.5 inches	3	6

COMFORTS & HAZARDS	AREA	U.S. AVG
July relative humidity	59%	66%
Annual days mostly sunny	215	208
Annual days with thunderstorms	41	39
Tornado risk score	1	18
Hurricane risk score	1	13

TEMPERATURE
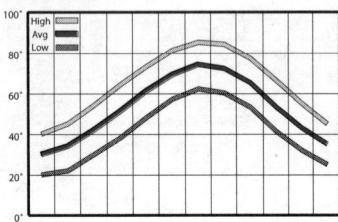

PRECIPITATION
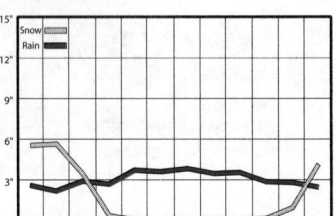

DAYS OF CLOUDS & PRECIPITATION

Education

Score: 36.4
Rank: 239

ACHIEVEMENT	AREA	U.S. AVG
High school degree	74.3%	82.7%
2-year college degree	4.3%	6.4%
4-year college degree	14.4%	15.7%
Graduate/professional degree	8.4%	8.9%

PUBLIC SCHOOLS	AREA	U.S. AVG
Expenditures per pupil	$5,204	$5,686
Student/teacher ratio	12.2	16.7
Attending public school	93.0%	90.1%
State SAT score	1025*	1021
State ACT score	21.1	20.9

HIGHER EDUCATION	AREA	U.S. AVG
No. 2-year colleges	0	4
No. 4-year colleges/universities	3	6
No. highly ranked universities	1	1

Health & Healthcare

Score: 74.3
Rank: 97

HAZARDS & ILLNESSES	AREA	U.S. AVG
Air-quality score	60	37
Water-quality score	65	52
Pollen/allergy score	61	61
Cancer mortality per capita	172.4	201.9
Depression days per month	3.9	3.5
Stress score	1	50

HEALTHCARE	AREA	U.S. AVG
Physicians per capita	171.7	244.2
Hospital beds per capita	259.4	420.0
No. teaching hospitals	0	3
Cost per doctor visit	$70	$77
Cost per dental visit	$60	$70

Crime

Score: 58.6
Rank: 156

CRIME	AREA	U.S. AVG
Violent crime rate	117.8	465.5
Change in violent crime rate	-16.7%	-2.2%
Property crime rate	1,559.0	3,517.1
Change in property crime rate	-11.1%	-2.1%

Transportation

Score: 81.8
Rank: 69

COMMUTE	AREA	U.S. AVG
Average commute time	21.3	27.4
Percent commutes > 60 mins.	4.0%	5.9%
Commute by auto	76.4%	78.9%
Commute by mass transit	1.4%	1.9%
Work at home	4.6%	3.1%
Mass transit miles per capita	1.43	1.87

INTERCITY SERVICES	AREA	U.S. AVG
Major airports within 60 miles	1	1
Size of regional airport	Medium	Large
Daily airline activity	739	686
Amtrak service	No	No

AUTOMOTIVE	AREA	U.S. AVG
Insurance, annual premium	$994	$1,432
Gas, cost per gallon	$2.46	$2.49
Daily vehicle miles per capita	24.1	24.0

Leisure

Score: 24.6
Rank: 281

DINING & SHOPPING	AREA	U.S. AVG
Restaurant rating	1	2
Outlet mall score	0	42
No. Starbucks	0	13
No. warehouse clubs	1	2

ENTERTAINMENT	AREA	U.S. AVG
Professional sports rating	1	4
College sports rating	6	4
Zoo/aquarium rating	1	3
Amusement park rating	1	3
Botanical garden/arboretum rating	1	4

OUTDOOR ACTIVITIES	AREA	U.S. AVG
Golf-course rating	3	4
Ski-area rating	2	3
Sq. miles inland water	2	4
Miles of coastline	0.0	10.7
National Park rating	3	3

Arts & Culture

Score: 28.9
Rank: 266

MEDIA & LIBRARIES	AREA	U.S. AVG
Arts radio rating	2	3
No. public libraries	7	27
Library volumes per capita	1.40	2.78

PERFORMING ARTS	AREA	U.S. AVG
Classical music rating	3	4
Ballet/dance rating	1	3
Professional theater rating	1	3
University arts programs rating	5	5

MUSEUMS	AREA	U.S. AVG
Overall museum rating	1	5
Art museum rating	2	5
Science museum rating	3	5
Children's museum rating	1	3

Hartford—West Hartford—East Hartford, CT

Profile: Capital city
Location: North-central Connecticut along the Connecticut River, 40 miles from the Long Island Sound
Elevation: 179 feet
Time zone: Eastern Standard Time

PRO	CON
Stable economy	Low job growth
Arts and culture	Cost of living
Cultural diversity	Harsh winters

As a state capital and center for the insurance industry, Hartford has a long and colorful history as a colonial center and prosperous industrial-era city. The first insurance company was established here in the late 1700s, and the Hartford Steam Boiler Inspection and Insurance Company, established in 1866, charted the course for industrial safety. Today Hartford is home to 35 insurance companies, including AETNA and The Hartford, which provide stable employment. The area is also headquarters to conglomerate United Technologies, but most manufacturing has disappeared from the Hartford landscape and it has become a center for "knowledge" industries By the 1870s, Hartford was home to many of the country's leading philanthropists and literary figures, including Mark Twain and Harriet Beecher Stowe. The old city center is located on the Connecticut River with a modern downtown sprinkled with older historic buildings and nicer suburbs spreading into the wooded areas in the west. Areas north are commercial and somewhat run-down while ethnic neighborhoods spread south. East Hartford, across the Connecticut River, is headquarters to Pratt & Whitney and has more of a blue-collar feel, but is currently developing a large downtown commercial/retail/hospitality center along the waterfront. West Hartford is a more upscale residential area. The philanthropic heritage leaves Hartford well stocked with museums, activities, and special events. The area's ethnic, economic, and educational diversity are noteworthy.

Hartford is located in the broad Connecticut River Valley with low north–south mountain ranges on both sides of the city. In winter, Hartford receives polar air masses from the north and moist, tropical air from the south, resulting in variable weather and strong winter storms. Cold air trapped in the river valley can produce freezing rain and ice storms. In summer, the climate is usually warm and pleasant with occasional thunderstorms. First freeze is early October; last is late April.

DEMOGRAPHICS	AREA	U.S. AVG	ETHNIC COMPOSITION	AREA	U.S. AVG	RESIDENT PROFILE	AREA	U.S. AVG
Population	1,192,119		White	79.2%	79.0%	Single	34.1%	32.4%
Population density per sq. mile	787.0	358.5	Black	10.0%	10.5%	Married	51.3%	52.7%
Population growth	6.3%	21.1%	Asian	2.9%	2.7%	Divorced/separated	14.6%	14.9%
Median age	38.8	36.1	Hispanic	10.0%	10.6%	Married with children	22.5%	23.7%
Percent Democrat	57.8%	44.5%	Religious observance	55.7%	48.9%	Single with children	8.7%	9.1%
Percent Republican	40.4%	54.5%	Diversity measure	45.8	40.1	Percent over age 65	14.0%	12.9%

Economy & Jobs
Score: 13.6
Rank: 322

INCOME	AREA	U.S. AVG	EMPLOYMENT	AREA	U.S. AVG	EMPLOYING INDUSTRIES	AREA	U.S. AVG
Per capita income	$30,028	$23,235	Unemployment rate	5.6%	4.7%	Largest: Finance & Insurance		
Household income	$59,265	$46,414	Recent job growth	0.1%	1.3%			
Household income < $25K	19.4%	26.2%	Projected future job growth	0.9%	11.5%	Percent manufacturing	12.0%	15.4%
Household income > $75K	37.9%	25.4%	White collar	66.6%	57.8%	Percent public sector	14.9%	15.7%
Household income growth	11.9%	13.6%	Blue collar	19.3%	25.2%	Percent construction	7.3%	9.9%

Cost of Living
Score: 15.0
Rank: 317

INDEXES & TAXES	AREA	U.S. AVG	HOUSING	AREA	U.S. AVG	NECESSITIES	AREA	U.S. AVG
Cost of Living Index	111.6	100.0	Median home price	$256,600	$220,000	Food Index	115.0	100.0
Buying Power Index	119.0	100.0	Home price appreciation	54.7%	10.1%	Housing Index	92.8	100.0
Income tax rate	4.50%	4.70%	Median rent	$1,030	$709	Utilities Index	119.3	100.0
Sales tax rate	6.00%	6.58%	Homes owned	63.0%	62.3%	Transportation Index	108.1	100.0
Property tax rate	$19.01	$12.00	Home price ratio	4.3	4.2	Healthcare Index	111.0	100.0
						Miscellaneous Cost Index	106.4	100.0

Climate
Score: 1.3
Rank: 367

TEMPERATURE	AREA	U.S. AVG
Average January low	16.1	26.2
Average July high	84.1	87.4
Annual days > 90°F	20	38
Annual days < 32°F	137	89
Annual days < 0°F	6	6

PRECIPITATION	AREA	U.S. AVG
Annual inches precipitation	43.0	37.7
Annual inches snowfall	53.0	7.0
Annual days precipitation	128	109
Annual days rain > 0.5 inches	26	22
Annual days snow > 1.5 inches	9	6

COMFORTS & HAZARDS	AREA	U.S. AVG
July relative humidity	68%	66%
Annual days mostly sunny	188	208
Annual days with thunderstorms	22	39
Tornado risk score	9	18
Hurricane risk score	19	13

TEMPERATURE

PRECIPITATION

DAYS OF CLOUDS & PRECIPITATION

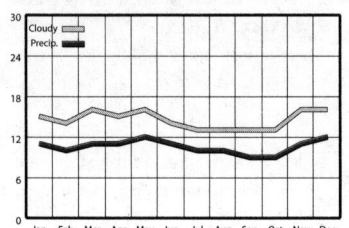

Education
Score: 89.3
Rank: 41

ACHIEVEMENT	AREA	U.S. AVG
High school degree	84.0%	82.7%
2-year college degree	7.0%	6.4%
4-year college degree	18.0%	15.7%
Graduate/professional degree	12.5%	8.9%

PUBLIC SCHOOLS	AREA	U.S. AVG
Expenditures per pupil	$8,265	$5,686
Student/teacher ratio	14.6	16.7
Attending public school	90.8%	90.1%
State SAT score	1028*	1021
State ACT score	23.1	20.9

HIGHER EDUCATION	AREA	U.S. AVG
No. 2-year colleges	8	4
No. 4-year colleges/universities	12	6
No. highly ranked universities	3	1

Health &
Healthcare
Score: 38.8
Rank: 228

HAZARDS & ILLNESSES	AREA	U.S. AVG
Air-quality score	27	37
Water-quality score	53	52
Pollen/allergy score	53	61
Cancer mortality per capita	208.3	201.9
Depression days per month	3.0	3.5
Stress score	22	50

HEALTHCARE	AREA	U.S. AVG
Physicians per capita	312.5	244.2
Hospital beds per capita	385.1	420.0
No. teaching hospitals	6	3
Cost per doctor visit	$99	$77
Cost per dental visit	$85	$70

Crime
Score: 39.6
Rank: 226

CRIME	AREA	U.S. AVG
Violent crime rate	294.9	465.5
Change in violent crime rate	-6.6%	-2.2%
Property crime rate	3,212.5	3,517.1
Change in property crime rate	6.4%	-2.1%

Transportation
Score: 95.2
Rank: 19

COMMUTE	AREA	U.S. AVG
Average commute time	24.7	27.4
Percent commutes > 60 mins.	4.4%	5.9%
Commute by auto	82.7%	78.9%
Commute by mass transit	2.9%	1.9%
Work at home	2.6%	3.1%
Mass transit miles per capita	2.87	1.87

INTERCITY SERVICES	AREA	U.S. AVG
Major airports within 60 miles	3	1
Size of regional airport	Large	Large
Daily airline activity	1969	686
Amtrak service	Yes	No

AUTOMOTIVE	AREA	U.S. AVG
Insurance, annual premium	$2,059	$1,432
Gas, cost per gallon	$2.57	$2.49
Daily vehicle miles per capita	25.0	24.0

Leisure
Score: 65.0
Rank: 131

DINING & SHOPPING	AREA	U.S. AVG
Restaurant rating	1	2
Outlet mall score	119	42
No. Starbucks	22	13
No. warehouse clubs	3	2

ENTERTAINMENT	AREA	U.S. AVG
Professional sports rating	3	4
College sports rating	6	4
Zoo/aquarium rating	2	3
Amusement park rating	1	3
Botanical garden/ arboretum rating	8	4

OUTDOOR ACTIVITIES	AREA	U.S. AVG
Golf-course rating	6	4
Ski-area rating	6	3
Sq. miles inland water	3	4
Miles of coastline	0.0	10.7
National Park rating	1	3

Arts & Culture
Score: 94.7
Rank: 21

MEDIA & LIBRARIES	AREA	U.S. AVG
Arts radio rating	5	3
No. public libraries	88	27
Library volumes per capita	4.07	2.78

PERFORMING ARTS	AREA	U.S. AVG
Classical music rating	10	4
Ballet/dance rating	5	3
Professional theater rating	8	3
University arts programs rating	9	5

MUSEUMS	AREA	U.S. AVG
Overall museum rating	8	5
Art museum rating	9	5
Science museum rating	8	5
Children's museum rating	10	3

Hattiesburg, MS

Score: 23.8 **Rank:** 349 **2004 rank:** 300

Profile: Small city
Location: Southeast Mississippi, about midway between Jackson and the Gulf Coast
Elevation: 150 feet
Time zone: Central Standard Time

PRO	CON
Historic interest	Summer heat
Cost of living	Arts and culture
Healthcare	Air service

Hattiesburg, the state's second-largest city, is definitely Old South, with well-preserved historic homes and a typical Southern town core with shaded streets. The economy is tied to the forest-products industry, and although it has diversified somewhat from that base with a variety of manufacturing activities, employment is still a concern. The University of Southern Mississippi and William Carey College lend some college-town flavor. The city is also positioning itself, with some success, as a good retirement destination. The cost of living is low (80.9) and crime is fairly low for the region. Many big-city amenities and services are absent, but Hattiesburg is centrally located between New Orleans; Mobile, Alabama; and Jackson, Mississippi, each about 90 miles away. Those who don't mind this shortcoming and who can tolerate the steamy summers may find Hattiesburg a better place than the ranking indicates.

The area mainly contains gently rolling and heavily wooded hills. Summers are consistently warm and humid, with 90°F days prevailing and frequent cooling afternoon thunderstorms. Winters are short and mild but some days can warm into the 80s. Cold spells bring temperatures briefly below freezing, but snow and hard freezes are uncommon. Subzero temperatures rarely occur. Fall is warm and relatively dry; spring is variable with more severe storms.

Population

DEMOGRAPHICS	AREA	U.S. AVG	ETHNIC COMPOSITION	AREA	U.S. AVG	RESIDENT PROFILE	AREA	U.S. AVG
Population	130,920		White	71.0%	79.0%	Single	36.4%	32.4%
Population density per sq. mile	81.3	358.5	Black	26.6%	10.5%	Married	49.2%	52.7%
Population growth	21.1%	21.1%	Asian	0.9%	2.7%	Divorced/separated	14.4%	14.9%
Median age	32.4	36.1	Hispanic	1.3%	10.6%	Married with children	23.3%	23.7%
Percent Democrat	30.7%	44.5%	Religious observance	63.2%	48.9%	Single with children	10.6%	9.1%
Percent Republican	68.6%	54.5%	Diversity measure	42.0	40.1	Percent over age 65	11.0%	12.9%

Economy & Jobs
Score: 15.5
Rank: 314

INCOME	AREA	U.S. AVG	EMPLOYMENT	AREA	U.S. AVG	EMPLOYING INDUSTRIES	AREA	U.S. AVG
Per capita income	$18,809	$23,235	Unemployment rate	5.8%	4.7%	Largest: Healthcare & Social Assistance		
Household income	$35,826	$46,414	Recent job growth	0.5%	1.3%			
Household income < $25K	36.8%	26.2%	Projected future job growth	9.1%	11.5%	Percent manufacturing	14.9%	15.4%
Household income > $75K	17.7%	25.4%	White collar	57.6%	57.8%	Percent public sector	18.4%	15.7%
Household income growth	16.1%	13.6%	Blue collar	25.2%	25.2%	Percent construction	10.4%	9.9%

Cost of Living
Score: 72.2
Rank: 105

INDEXES & TAXES	AREA	U.S. AVG	HOUSING	AREA	U.S. AVG	NECESSITIES	AREA	U.S. AVG
Cost of Living Index	80.9	100.0	Median home price	$123,700	$220,000	Food Index	91.4	100.0
Buying Power Index	99.3	100.0	Home price appreciation	24.3%	10.1%	Housing Index	53.8	100.0
Income tax rate	5.00%	4.70%	Median rent	$549	$709	Utilities Index	109.5	100.0
Sales tax rate	7.00%	6.58%	Homes owned	61.8%	62.3%	Transportation Index	91.7	100.0
Property tax rate	$7.45	$12.00	Home price ratio	3.5	4.2	Healthcare Index	86.5	100.0
						Miscellaneous Cost Index	98.0	100.0

Climate
Score: 62.0
Rank: 141

TEMPERATURE	AREA	U.S. AVG	PRECIPITATION	AREA	U.S. AVG	COMFORTS & HAZARDS	AREA	U.S. AVG
Average January low	35.0	26.2	Annual inches precipitation	49.0	37.7	July relative humidity	75%	66%
Average July high	90.0	87.4	Annual inches snowfall	1.0	7.0	Annual days mostly sunny	217	208
Annual days > 90°F	70	38	Annual days precipitation	100	109	Annual days with thunderstorms	70	39
Annual days < 32°F	40	89	Annual days rain > 0.5 inches	36	22	Tornado risk score	26	18
Annual days < 0°F	0	6	Annual days snow > 1.5 inches	0	6	Hurricane risk score	41	13

TEMPERATURE

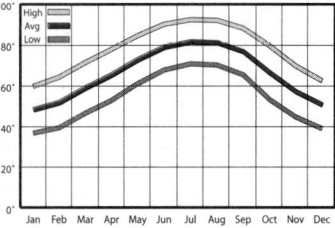

PRECIPITATION

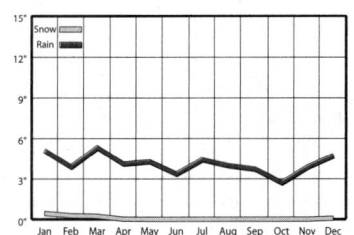

DAYS OF CLOUDS & PRECIPITATION

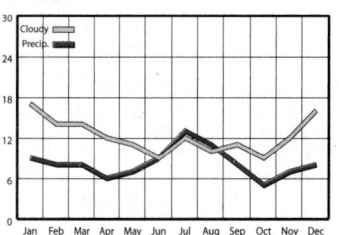

Education

Score: 41.2
Rank: 221

ACHIEVEMENT	AREA	U.S. AVG	PUBLIC SCHOOLS	AREA	U.S. AVG	HIGHER EDUCATION	AREA	U.S. AVG
High school degree	80.3%	82.7%	Expenditures per pupil	$4,024	$5,686	No. 2-year colleges	1	4
2-year college degree	5.9%	6.4%	Student/teacher ratio	15.4	16.7	No. 4-year colleges/universities	2	6
4-year college degree	14.9%	15.7%	Attending public school	92.3%	90.1%	No. highly ranked universities	0	1
Graduate/professional degree	8.5%	8.9%	State SAT score	1097	1021			
			State ACT score	18.8*	20.9			

Health & Healthcare

Score: 72.7
Rank: 103

HAZARDS & ILLNESSES	AREA	U.S. AVG	HEALTHCARE	AREA	U.S. AVG
Air-quality score	46	37	Physicians per capita	278.0	244.2
Water-quality score	42	52	Hospital beds per capita	638.6	420.0
Pollen/allergy score	73	61	No. teaching hospitals	0	3
Cancer mortality per capita	210.8	201.9	Cost per doctor visit	$67	$77
Depression days per month	4.4	3.5	Cost per dental visit	$74	$70
Stress score	54	50			

Crime

Score: 63.1
Rank: 138

CRIME	AREA	U.S. AVG
Violent crime rate	323.5	465.5
Change in violent crime rate	21.4%	-2.2%
Property crime rate	3,843.0	3,517.1
Change in property crime rate	-4.0%	-2.1%

Transportation

Score: 10.7
Rank: 334

COMMUTE	AREA	U.S. AVG	INTERCITY SERVICES	AREA	U.S. AVG	AUTOMOTIVE	AREA	U.S. AVG
Average commute time	24.5	27.4	Major airports within 60 miles	0	1	Insurance, annual premium	$1,135	$1,432
Percent commutes > 60 mins.	7.3%	5.9%	Size of regional airport	Small	Large	Gas, cost per gallon	$2.48	$2.49
Commute by auto	81.3%	78.9%	Daily airline activity	88	686	Daily vehicle miles per capita	29.8	24.0
Commute by mass transit	0.4%	1.9%	Amtrak service	Yes	No			
Work at home	2.3%	3.1%						
Mass transit miles per capita	0.44	1.87						

Leisure

Score: 13.6
Rank: 322

DINING & SHOPPING	AREA	U.S. AVG	ENTERTAINMENT	AREA	U.S. AVG	OUTDOOR ACTIVITIES	AREA	U.S. AVG
Restaurant rating	1	2	Professional sports rating	2	4	Golf-course rating	2	4
Outlet mall score	11	42	College sports rating	1	4	Ski-area rating	1	3
No. Starbucks	1	13	Zoo/aquarium rating	1	3	Sq. miles inland water	3	4
No. warehouse clubs	1	2	Amusement park rating	1	3	Miles of coastline	0.0	10.7
			Botanical garden/ arboretum rating	1	4	National Park rating	3	3

Arts & Culture

Score: 17.6
Rank: 307

MEDIA & LIBRARIES	AREA	U.S. AVG	PERFORMING ARTS	AREA	U.S. AVG	MUSEUMS	AREA	U.S. AVG
Arts radio rating	1	3	Classical music rating	1	4	Overall museum rating	1	5
No. public libraries	17	27	Ballet/dance rating	1	3	Art museum rating	1	5
Library volumes per capita	1.90	2.78	Professional theater rating	1	3	Science museum rating	1	5
			University arts programs rating	6	5	Children's museum rating	1	3

Hickory–Lenoir–Morganton, NC

Score: 57.6 **Rank:** 195 **2004 rank:** 254

Profile: Small-town complex
Location: Western North Carolina halfway between Winston-Salem and Asheville
Elevation: 897 feet
Time zone: Eastern Standard Time

PRO	CON
Nearby mountains	Employment
Cost of living	Arts and culture
Small-town feel	Low ethnic diversity

This interesting tri-city area is located in the broad Catawba Valley at the eastern base of the Blue Ridge Mountains. As the name Hickory implies, this is an area of hardwood forests, the original resource for Hickory's active furniture-making industry. According to local sources, 60% of the furniture manufactured in the United States is made within 200 miles of Hickory, and names such as Broyhill, Drexel Heritage, and Henredon among many others are headquartered locally. Furniture factory outlets draw people from miles around. The area is also home to the one of the country's largest fiber-optic cable plants operated by Corning. The downtown areas of Morganton and Hickory are small but clean and exceptionally authentic examples of the Southern small

town. There are some recreational opportunities in the nearby mountains to the west and large Lake Norman to the southeast. The area is in the heart of the Bible Belt, evidence of which is all around. Cost of living is low and crime is among the lowest in the state. Some may not find enough in the way of intellectual stimulation, including cultural amenities and higher education. There are lingering questions around the long-term viability of the furniture industry as more comes from offshore, and white-collar jobs in particular may be hard to find, but this area is authentic Southern small-town America at its best.

The terrain is mostly hilly and wooded. The Catawba River runs through the area and turns south into Lake Norman at the east edge of the county, where the land begins to flatten out into the Carolina Piedmont. Summers are warm with frequent 90°F days and thundershowers. Winters are cool but not excessively so. Winter temperatures frequently touch freezing, but seldom go far below. Snow and snow accumulations are rare. Rainfall is evenly distributed through the year, with fall being the driest.

Population

DEMOGRAPHICS	AREA	U.S. AVG
Population	353,336	
Population density per sq. mile	215.6	358.5
Population growth	21.1%	21.1%
Median age	37.7	36.1
Percent Democrat	33.4%	44.5%
Percent Republican	66.2%	54.5%

ETHNIC COMPOSITION	AREA	U.S. AVG
White	86.8%	79.0%
Black	6.7%	10.5%
Asian	2.6%	2.7%
Hispanic	5.4%	10.6%
Religious observance	61.2%	48.9%
Diversity measure	31.6	40.1

RESIDENT PROFILE	AREA	U.S. AVG
Single	27.5%	32.4%
Married	56.9%	52.7%
Divorced/separated	15.7%	14.9%
Married with children	23.1%	23.7%
Single with children	8.2%	9.1%
Percent over age 65	13.5%	12.9%

Economy & Jobs

Score: 27.8
Rank: 270

INCOME	AREA	U.S. AVG
Per capita income	$20,785	$23,235
Household income	$41,985	$46,414
Household income ‹ $25K	26.9%	26.2%
Household income › $75K	18.3%	25.4%
Household income growth	10.4%	13.6%

EMPLOYMENT	AREA	U.S. AVG
Unemployment rate	8.3%	4.7%
Recent job growth	1.0%	1.3%
Projected future job growth	9.5%	11.5%
White collar	43.8%	57.8%
Blue collar	43.5%	25.2%

EMPLOYING INDUSTRIES	AREA	U.S. AVG
Largest: Manufacturing		
Percent manufacturing	34.2%	15.4%
Percent public sector	11.4%	15.7%
Percent construction	9.4%	9.9%

Cost of Living

Score: 60.4
Rank: 148

INDEXES & TAXES	AREA	U.S. AVG
Cost of Living Index	80.6	100.0
Buying Power Index	116.8	100.0
Income tax rate	7.00%	4.70%
Sales tax rate	7.00%	6.58%
Property tax rate	$6.43	$12.00

HOUSING	AREA	U.S. AVG
Median home price	$121,700	$220,000
Home price appreciation	21.7%	10.1%
Median rent	$552	$709
Homes owned	69.0%	62.3%
Home price ratio	2.9	4.2

NECESSITIES	AREA	U.S. AVG
Food Index	97.9	100.0
Housing Index	53.4	100.0
Utilities Index	92.6	100.0
Transportation Index	91.0	100.0
Healthcare Index	89.4	100.0
Miscellaneous Cost Index	99.3	100.0

Climate

Score: 59.9
Rank: 149

TEMPERATURE	AREA	U.S. AVG
Average January low	28.5	26.2
Average July high	87.5	87.4
Annual days › 90°F	28	38
Annual days ‹ 32°F	85	89
Annual days ‹ 0°F	0	6

PRECIPITATION	AREA	U.S. AVG
Annual inches precipitation	41.4	37.7
Annual inches snowfall	8.7	7.0
Annual days precipitation	121	109
Annual days rain › 0.5 inches	29	22
Annual days snow › 1.5 inches	3	6

COMFORTS & HAZARDS	AREA	U.S. AVG
July relative humidity	72%	66%
Annual days mostly sunny	217	208
Annual days with thunderstorms	46	39
Tornado risk score	10	18
Hurricane risk score	14	13

TEMPERATURE

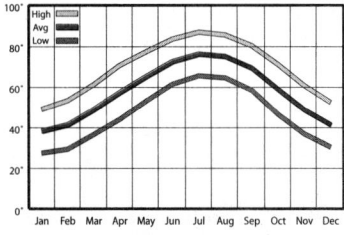

PRECIPITATION

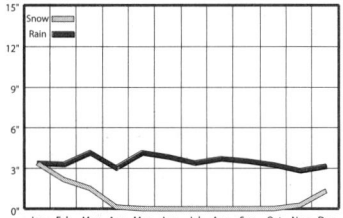

DAYS OF CLOUDS & PRECIPITATION

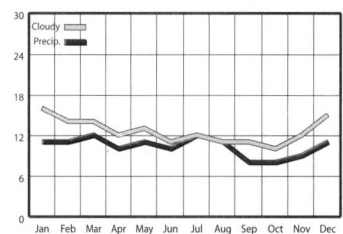

Education

Score: 8.3
Rank: 342

ACHIEVEMENT	AREA	U.S. AVG
High school degree	70.4%	82.7%
2-year college degree	6.6%	6.4%
4-year college degree	9.7%	15.7%
Graduate/professional degree	3.9%	8.9%

PUBLIC SCHOOLS	AREA	U.S. AVG
Expenditures per pupil	$4,764	$5,686
Student/teacher ratio	15.9	16.7
Attending public school	96.6%	90.1%
State SAT score	1008*	1021
State ACT score	20.5	20.9

HIGHER EDUCATION	AREA	U.S. AVG
No. 2-year colleges	3	4
No. 4-year colleges/universities	1	6
No. highly ranked universities	0	1

Health & Healthcare

Score: 73.5
Rank: 100

HAZARDS & ILLNESSES	AREA	U.S. AVG
Air-quality score	44	37
Water-quality score	65	52
Pollen/allergy score	64	61
Cancer mortality per capita	197.0	201.9
Depression days per month	3.4	3.5
Stress score	63	50

HEALTHCARE	AREA	U.S. AVG
Physicians per capita	174.2	244.2
Hospital beds per capita	587.5	420.0
No. teaching hospitals	1	3
Cost per doctor visit	$85	$77
Cost per dental visit	$64	$70

Crime

Score: 37.2
Rank: 235

CRIME	AREA	U.S. AVG
Violent crime rate	283.3	465.5
Change in violent crime rate	17.3%	-2.2%
Property crime rate	3,621.3	3,517.1
Change in property crime rate	10.3%	-2.1%

COMMUTE	AREA	U.S. AVG	INTERCITY SERVICES	AREA	U.S. AVG	AUTOMOTIVE	AREA	U.S. AVG
Average commute time	23.0	27.4	Major airports within 60 miles	1	1	Insurance, annual premium	$972	$1,432
Percent commutes > 60 mins.	4.2%	5.9%	Size of regional airport	Large	Large	Gas, cost per gallon	$2.49	$2.49
Commute by auto	81.3%	78.9%	Daily airline activity	822	686	Daily vehicle miles per capita	42.0	24.0
Commute by mass transit	0.2%	1.9%	Amtrak service	No	No			
Work at home	1.8%	3.1%						
Mass transit miles per capita	0.18	1.87						

Transportation
Score: 66.0
Rank: 128

DINING & SHOPPING	AREA	U.S. AVG	ENTERTAINMENT	AREA	U.S. AVG	OUTDOOR ACTIVITIES	AREA	U.S. AVG
Restaurant rating	1	2	Professional sports rating	4	4	Golf-course rating	3	4
Outlet mall score	0	42	College sports rating	1	4	Ski-area rating	2	3
No. Starbucks	0	13	Zoo/aquarium rating	1	3	Sq. miles inland water	3	4
No. warehouse clubs	1	2	Amusement park rating	1	3	Miles of coastline	0.0	10.7
			Botanical garden/			National Park rating	1	3
			arboretum rating	1	4			

Leisure
Score: 29.4
Rank: 263

MEDIA & LIBRARIES	AREA	U.S. AVG	PERFORMING ARTS	AREA	U.S. AVG	MUSEUMS	AREA	U.S. AVG
Arts radio rating	1	3	Classical music rating	2	4	Overall museum rating	4	5
No. public libraries	15	27	Ballet/dance rating	1	3	Art museum rating	4	5
Library volumes per capita	1.90	2.78	Professional theater rating	1	3	Science museum rating	6	5
			University arts programs rating	2	5	Children's museum rating	1	3

Arts & Culture
Score: 16.0
Rank: 313

Hinesville–Fort Stewart, GA

Score: 56.2 **Rank:** 204 **2004 rank:** not ranked

Profile: Military town
Location: Southeastern Georgia, southwest of Savannah
Elevation: 48 feet
Time zone: Eastern Standard Time

PRO	CON
Close to Savannah	Low educational attainment
Cost of living and	Summer heat
housing	Arts and culture
Mild winters	

Hinesville is a small, out-of-the-way military town mainly supporting—and supported by—the large military installation at Fort Stewart, home to the U.S. Third Infantry. There is some agriculture, timber, and turpentine processing, but not a lot else in the way of economic activity. The physical setting and infrastructure are nondescript and there is little of interest in the immediate area. Coastal areas 30 miles to the east offer some recreation while Savannah, 40 miles to the northeast, makes a more complete offering. Cost of living is quite low with a COL index of 81.6 and affordable homes. Educational attainment is low and the area is fairly isolated from other larger urban areas.

The Hinesville area sits in a mainly level coastal plain with areas of pine forest areas nearby. Summers are hot, sticky, and often breezeless, with most precipitation arriving as thunderstorms. Winters are mild. Persistent rainy periods and some tropical storms may affect the area.

DEMOGRAPHICS	AREA	U.S. AVG	ETHNIC COMPOSITION	AREA	U.S. AVG	RESIDENT PROFILE	AREA	U.S. AVG
Population	68,159		White	53.7%	79.0%	Single	30.3%	32.4%
Population density per sq. mile	74.1	358.5	Black	35.6%	10.5%	Married	54.1%	52.7%
Population growth	19.4%	21.1%	Asian	2.2%	2.7%	Divorced/separated	15.7%	14.9%
Median age	25.7	36.1	Hispanic	6.4%	10.6%	Married with children	35.5%	23.7%
Percent Democrat	48.9%	44.5%	Religious observance	23.1%	48.9%	Single with children	13.5%	9.1%
Percent Republican	50.7%	54.5%	Diversity measure	62.5	40.1	Percent over age 65	5.0%	12.9%

Population

INCOME	AREA	U.S. AVG	EMPLOYMENT	AREA	U.S. AVG	EMPLOYING INDUSTRIES	AREA	U.S. AVG
Per capita income	$15,554	$23,235	Unemployment rate	6.9%	4.7%	Largest: Healthcare & Social Assistance		
Household income	$37,915	$46,414	Recent job growth	2.1%	1.3%			
Household income < $25K	29.4%	26.2%	Projected future job growth	8.9%	11.5%	Percent manufacturing	16.3%	15.4%
Household income > $75K	14.1%	25.4%	White collar	50.0%	57.8%	Percent public sector	28.2%	15.7%
Household income growth	14.8%	13.6%	Blue collar	29.3%	25.2%	Percent construction	12.9%	9.9%

Economy & Jobs
Score: 28.6
Rank: 267

Cost of Living
Score: 66.8
Rank: 124

INDEXES & TAXES	AREA	U.S. AVG
Cost of Living Index	81.6	100.0
Buying Power Index	104.1	100.0
Income tax rate	6.00%	4.70%
Sales tax rate	7.00%	6.58%
Property tax rate	$9.62	$12.00

HOUSING	AREA	U.S. AVG
Median home price	$118,000	$220,000
Home price appreciation	44.3%	10.1%
Median rent	$536	$709
Homes owned	47.9%	62.3%
Home price ratio	3.1	4.2

NECESSITIES	AREA	U.S. AVG
Food Index	102.4	100.0
Housing Index	42.9	100.0
Utilities Index	92.6	100.0
Transportation Index	94.1	100.0
Healthcare Index	93.0	100.0
Miscellaneous Cost Index	101.6	100.0

Climate
Score: 70.1
Rank: 111

TEMPERATURE	AREA	U.S. AVG
Average January low	38.0	26.2
Average July high	91.0	87.4
Annual days > 90°F	69	38
Annual days < 32°F	31	89
Annual days < 0°F	0	6

PRECIPITATION	AREA	U.S. AVG
Annual inches precipitation	49.2	37.7
Annual inches snowfall	0.1	7.0
Annual days precipitation	111	109
Annual days rain > 0.5 inches	31	22
Annual days snow > 1.5 inches	1	6

COMFORTS & HAZARDS	AREA	U.S. AVG
July relative humidity	57%	66%
Annual days mostly sunny	212	208
Annual days with thunderstorms	64	39
Tornado risk score	1	18
Hurricane risk score	6	13

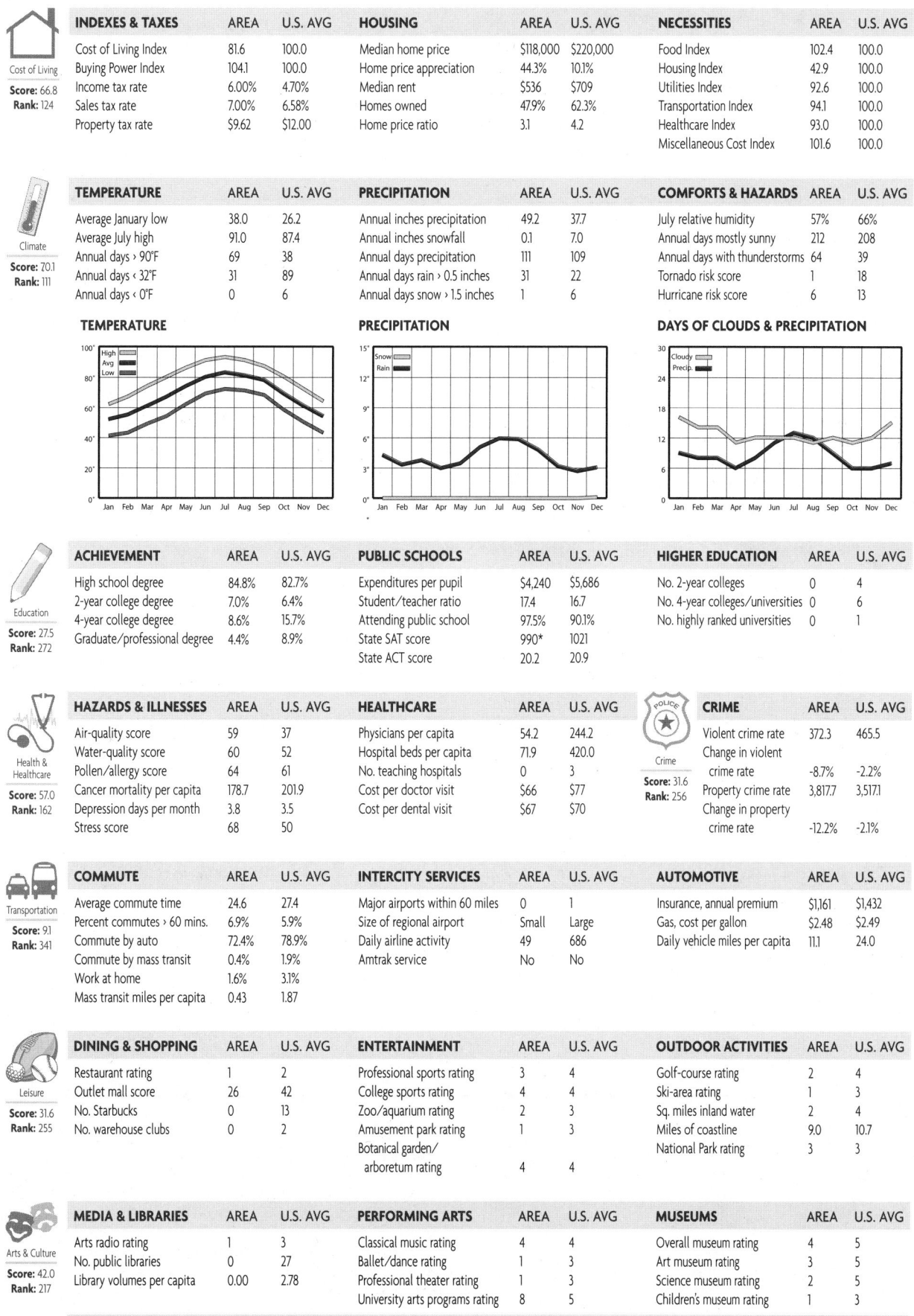

Education
Score: 27.5
Rank: 272

ACHIEVEMENT	AREA	U.S. AVG
High school degree	84.8%	82.7%
2-year college degree	7.0%	6.4%
4-year college degree	8.6%	15.7%
Graduate/professional degree	4.4%	8.9%

PUBLIC SCHOOLS	AREA	U.S. AVG
Expenditures per pupil	$4,240	$5,686
Student/teacher ratio	17.4	16.7
Attending public school	97.5%	90.1%
State SAT score	990*	1021
State ACT score	20.2	20.9

HIGHER EDUCATION	AREA	U.S. AVG
No. 2-year colleges	0	4
No. 4-year colleges/universities	0	6
No. highly ranked universities	0	1

Health & Healthcare
Score: 57.0
Rank: 162

HAZARDS & ILLNESSES	AREA	U.S. AVG
Air-quality score	59	37
Water-quality score	60	52
Pollen/allergy score	64	61
Cancer mortality per capita	178.7	201.9
Depression days per month	3.8	3.5
Stress score	68	50

HEALTHCARE	AREA	U.S. AVG
Physicians per capita	54.2	244.2
Hospital beds per capita	71.9	420.0
No. teaching hospitals	0	3
Cost per doctor visit	$66	$77
Cost per dental visit	$67	$70

Crime
Score: 31.6
Rank: 256

CRIME	AREA	U.S. AVG
Violent crime rate	372.3	465.5
Change in violent crime rate	-8.7%	-2.2%
Property crime rate	3,817.7	3,517.1
Change in property crime rate	-12.2%	-2.1%

Transportation
Score: 9.1
Rank: 341

COMMUTE	AREA	U.S. AVG
Average commute time	24.6	27.4
Percent commutes > 60 mins.	6.9%	5.9%
Commute by auto	72.4%	78.9%
Commute by mass transit	0.4%	1.9%
Work at home	1.6%	3.1%
Mass transit miles per capita	0.43	1.87

INTERCITY SERVICES	AREA	U.S. AVG
Major airports within 60 miles	0	1
Size of regional airport	Small	Large
Daily airline activity	49	686
Amtrak service	No	No

AUTOMOTIVE	AREA	U.S. AVG
Insurance, annual premium	$1,161	$1,432
Gas, cost per gallon	$2.48	$2.49
Daily vehicle miles per capita	11.1	24.0

Leisure
Score: 31.6
Rank: 255

DINING & SHOPPING	AREA	U.S. AVG
Restaurant rating	1	2
Outlet mall score	26	42
No. Starbucks	0	13
No. warehouse clubs	0	2

ENTERTAINMENT	AREA	U.S. AVG
Professional sports rating	3	4
College sports rating	4	4
Zoo/aquarium rating	2	3
Amusement park rating	1	3
Botanical garden/ arboretum rating	4	4

OUTDOOR ACTIVITIES	AREA	U.S. AVG
Golf-course rating	2	4
Ski-area rating	1	3
Sq. miles inland water	2	4
Miles of coastline	9.0	10.7
National Park rating	3	3

Arts & Culture
Score: 42.0
Rank: 217

MEDIA & LIBRARIES	AREA	U.S. AVG
Arts radio rating	1	3
No. public libraries	0	27
Library volumes per capita	0.00	2.78

PERFORMING ARTS	AREA	U.S. AVG
Classical music rating	4	4
Ballet/dance rating	1	3
Professional theater rating	1	3
University arts programs rating	8	5

MUSEUMS	AREA	U.S. AVG
Overall museum rating	4	5
Art museum rating	3	5
Science museum rating	2	5
Children's museum rating	1	3

Holland–Grand Haven, MI

Score: 65.2   **Rank:** 140   **2004 rank:** 157

Profile: Small-agricultural-city complex
Location: Southwestern Lake Michigan shore
Elevation: 610 feet
Time zone: Eastern Standard Time

PRO	CON
Attractive setting	Economic cycles
Historic interest	Cold, cloudy winters
Cost of living	Healthcare

Holland and Ottawa County sit in an attractive and historic agricultural area adjacent to the western Michigan shore of Lake Michigan. Religious oppression, good soil, and a moderating lake influence attracted Dutch settlers in the mid–19th century. Fruit and vegetables are grown in the area, but it is most known for its tulips. The annual Tulip Time Festival in May is a world attraction, and the fact that the local airport is named the Tulip City Airport gives a clue to the importance of this product. The town developed as a prosperous, well-kept Victorian-era farming community, and retains a lot of historic interest with a downtown on the National Register of Historic Interest and many fine period homes. The Dutch influence—the population was estimated at over 60% Dutch in the early 20th century—is unmistakable. Today Holland's economy is propelled by tourism, agriculture, small businesses, and an assortment of larger manufacturers making everything from pickles to plastics to pharmaceuticals. Two small colleges add some college amenities. Several beaches and state parks line the Lake Michigan coast. Grand Rapids, 20 miles northeast, is the closest cultural center, while Chicago is 2½ hours southwest. Cost of living is a reasonable 87.4 and healthy incomes bring a strong Buying Power Index of 147.0, fifth best in the country. A better climate and stronger healthcare resources would have brought a higher ranking.

Holland is located on a flat, fertile coastal and agricultural plain. Lake Michigan heavily influences the continental climate, moderating temperatures in summer and winter and prolonging both spring and fall seasons. Summers are pleasant with frequent lake breezes and comfortable evenings. Winters are very cloudy, with numerous snow flurries and strong westerly winds. Below-zero temperatures occur occasionally but not for prolonged periods, and continuous snow cover is common. First freeze is early October; last is early May.

DEMOGRAPHICS	AREA	U.S. AVG	ETHNIC COMPOSITION	AREA	U.S. AVG	RESIDENT PROFILE	AREA	U.S. AVG
Population	253,985		White	90.5%	79.0%	Single	29.6%	32.4%
Population density per sq. mile	449.0	358.5	Black	1.2%	10.5%	Married	60.3%	52.7%
Population growth	35.3%	21.1%	Asian	2.4%	2.7%	Divorced/separated	10.1%	14.9%
Median age	33.4	36.1	Hispanic	7.6%	10.6%	Married with children	32.6%	23.7%
Percent Democrat	27.6%	44.5%	Religious observance	56.0%	48.9%	Single with children	6.7%	9.1%
Percent Republican	71.6%	54.5%	Diversity measure	29.4	40.1	Percent over age 65	10.6%	12.9%

Population

INCOME	AREA	U.S. AVG	EMPLOYMENT	AREA	U.S. AVG	EMPLOYING INDUSTRIES	AREA	U.S. AVG
Per capita income	$24,004	$23,235	Unemployment rate	5.9%	4.7%	Largest: Manufacturing		
Household income	$57,310	$46,414	Recent job growth	0.7%	1.3%			
Household income < $25K	15.8%	26.2%	Projected future job growth	15.6%	11.5%	Percent manufacturing	21.6%	15.4%
Household income > $75K	32.0%	25.4%	White collar	56.0%	57.8%	Percent public sector	8.2%	15.7%
Household income growth	9.5%	13.6%	Blue collar	29.6%	25.2%	Percent construction	8.0%	9.9%

Economy & Jobs
Score: 74.9
Rank: 95

INDEXES & TAXES	AREA	U.S. AVG	HOUSING	AREA	U.S. AVG	NECESSITIES	AREA	U.S. AVG
Cost of Living Index	87.4	100.0	Median home price	$140,900	$220,000	Food Index	106.1	100.0
Buying Power Index	147.0	100.0	Home price appreciation	22.3%	10.1%	Housing Index	51.1	100.0
Income tax rate	5.40%	4.70%	Median rent	$669	$709	Utilities Index	83.4	100.0
Sales tax rate	6.00%	6.58%	Homes owned	75.9%	62.3%	Transportation Index	109.1	100.0
Property tax rate	$11.78	$12.00	Home price ratio	2.5	4.2	Healthcare Index	92.7	100.0
						Miscellaneous Cost Index	103.0	100.0

Cost of Living
Score: 54.3
Rank: 170

Climate
Score: 8.0
Rank: 343

TEMPERATURE	AREA	U.S. AVG
Average January low	16.0	26.2
Average July high	83.3	87.4
Annual days > 90°F	11	38
Annual days < 32°F	149	89
Annual days < 0°F	8	6

PRECIPITATION	AREA	U.S. AVG
Annual inches precipitation	32.0	37.7
Annual inches snowfall	77.0	7.0
Annual days precipitation	144	109
Annual days rain > 0.5 inches	20	22
Annual days snow > 1.5 inches	20	6

COMFORTS & HAZARDS	AREA	U.S. AVG
July relative humidity	73%	66%
Annual days mostly sunny	163	208
Annual days with thunderstorms	37	39
Tornado risk score	23	18
Hurricane risk score	1	13

TEMPERATURE

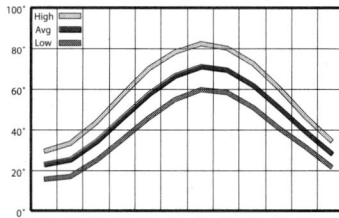

PRECIPITATION

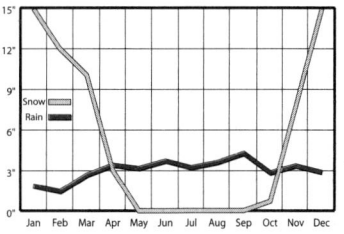

DAYS OF CLOUDS & PRECIPITATION

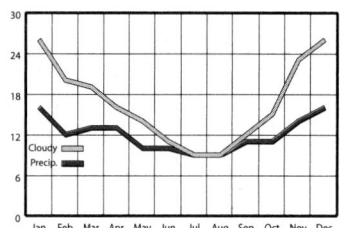

Education
Score: 60.7
Rank: 148

ACHIEVEMENT	AREA	U.S. AVG
High school degree	86.6%	82.7%
2-year college degree	7.5%	6.4%
4-year college degree	18.0%	15.7%
Graduate/professional degree	7.9%	8.9%

PUBLIC SCHOOLS	AREA	U.S. AVG
Expenditures per pupil	$5,703	$5,686
Student/teacher ratio	18.7	16.7
Attending public school	86.5%	90.1%
State SAT score	1151	1021
State ACT score	21.5*	20.9

HIGHER EDUCATION	AREA	U.S. AVG
No. 2-year colleges	0	4
No. 4-year colleges/universities	3	6
No. highly ranked universities	1	1

Health & Healthcare
Score: 34.2
Rank: 244

HAZARDS & ILLNESSES	AREA	U.S. AVG
Air-quality score	26	37
Water-quality score	36	52
Pollen/allergy score	49	61
Cancer mortality per capita	166.8	201.9
Depression days per month	2.5	3.5
Stress score	6	50

HEALTHCARE	AREA	U.S. AVG
Physicians per capita	126.7	244.2
Hospital beds per capita	157.9	420.0
No. teaching hospitals	0	3
Cost per doctor visit	$72	$77
Cost per dental visit	$67	$70

Crime
Score: 92.8
Rank: 28

CRIME	AREA	U.S. AVG
Violent crime rate	194.4	465.5
Change in violent crime rate	-1.9%	-2.2%
Property crime rate	1,906.9	3,517.1
Change in property crime rate	-8.4%	-2.1%

Transportation
Score: 67.9
Rank: 120

COMMUTE	AREA	U.S. AVG
Average commute time	21.2	27.4
Percent commutes > 60 mins.	2.5%	5.9%
Commute by auto	86.0%	78.9%
Commute by mass transit	0.5%	1.9%
Work at home	3.1%	3.1%
Mass transit miles per capita	0.51	1.87

INTERCITY SERVICES	AREA	U.S. AVG
Major airports within 60 miles	1	1
Size of regional airport	Medium	Large
Daily airline activity	514	686
Amtrak service	Yes	No

AUTOMOTIVE	AREA	U.S. AVG
Insurance, annual premium	$1,416	$1,432
Gas, cost per gallon	$2.54	$2.49
Daily vehicle miles per capita	18.2	24.0

Leisure
Score: 69.5
Rank: 114

DINING & SHOPPING	AREA	U.S. AVG
Restaurant rating	1	2
Outlet mall score	42	42
No. Starbucks	2	13
No. warehouse clubs	0	2

ENTERTAINMENT	AREA	U.S. AVG
Professional sports rating	3	4
College sports rating	5	4
Zoo/aquarium rating	5	3
Amusement park rating	7	3
Botanical garden/ arboretum rating	4	4

OUTDOOR ACTIVITIES	AREA	U.S. AVG
Golf-course rating	7	4
Ski-area rating	5	3
Sq. miles inland water	3	4
Miles of coastline	23.4	10.7
National Park rating	1	3

Arts & Culture
Score: 81.8
Rank: 69

MEDIA & LIBRARIES	AREA	U.S. AVG
Arts radio rating	10	3
No. public libraries	12	27
Library volumes per capita	3.15	2.78

PERFORMING ARTS	AREA	U.S. AVG
Classical music rating	5	4
Ballet/dance rating	3	3
Professional theater rating	1	3
University arts programs rating	8	5

MUSEUMS	AREA	U.S. AVG
Overall museum rating	6	5
Art museum rating	6	5
Science museum rating	3	5
Children's museum rating	5	3

Honolulu, HI

Score: 70.3   **Rank:** 89   **2004 rank:** 5

Profile: Large capital city/resort city
Location: Southern coast, Island of Oahu
Elevation: 15 feet
Time zone: Hawaii Standard Time

PRO	CON
Year-round climate	Cost of living
Attractive setting	Traffic and sprawl
Recreation	Tourist impact

Often called the "Crossroads of the Pacific," Honolulu is the capital of the multi-island state and port of entry for most of the state's millions of visitors. The city is a diverse commercial, industrial, and economic center for the entire Pacific and a center for tourism and recreation. The Waikiki beachfront area bustles with shopping, nightlife, and active sports. The rest of the city is a mix of residential, commercial, and industrial activity. Most of the city was built in the 1960s. There are large areas of plain and unattractive concrete structures, and there is less historic preservation than one might expect in such a destination.

Honolulu has significant traffic problems. While the city boasts the only interstate highways in Hawaii, there is considerable congestion, especially at rush hour. Public-transportation facilities are well developed. The downtown core is focused on government facilities, performing arts venues, and historic sites, gently transitioning to commercial and tourist areas east and some rather unattractive commercial, shipping, and industrial areas west. It looks and feels crowded. The nicer residential areas are found in the hills northeast of the central city but there isn't much land available for building. Several pleasant communities also exist along the Interstate H-1 highway north from the city, within commuting distance. As a rule, although most tourist activity is centered in the Waikiki area, avoiding tourists and their impact is difficult. The city has a strong military presence.

The climate is one of the best in the world. The economy is robust although vulnerable to tourism-driven cycles and the state of the Asian—and particularly the Japanese—economy. The big negative is cost of living and housing. The oppressive Cost of Living Index of 177.5 has risen 25 points since 2004 and is driven in a large part by housing—average home prices are among the country's highest. Because of the isolation from national markets for staples such as food and energy, prices for these items are high. Aside from cost, isolation from the mainland may reduce the appeal for some residents, although most urban amenities are available in abundance. Arts amenities of a high quality and entertainment is ubiquitous—but it must all be shared with tourists. The surge in living costs is the biggest factor behind the ranking drop.

Honolulu is located on a broad coastal plain of Oahu, the third largest of the Hawaiian Islands. The Koolau Range, at an average elevation of 2,000 feet, parallels the northeastern coast. The Waianae Mountains, somewhat higher in elevation, parallel the west coast. Most of the eastern half of the coastal plain is built up. The Hawaiian climate is unusually pleasant for the Tropics. Outstanding features are the persistent northeasterly trade winds, remarkable variance in rainfall over short distances, sunny leeward lowlands with persistent cloudiness over nearby mountain crests, equable temperature, and infrequency of severe storms. The city sits mostly in the lee (downwind) direction of the Koolau Range, which blocks heavier rains at most times of the year. The mountain range is low enough that clouds spill over it, allowing for occasional light rain and drizzle even as the overhead sun shines—an effect known locally as "liquid sunshine." Trade winds—and associated showers—are more prevalent in summer. Temperatures and humidity are generally comfortable, less than 90°F and more than 50°F. But when trade winds subside and tropical weather emerges, hot, humid periods can occur. There may be more intense winter storms and heavy downpours associated with nearby tropical storms, but few of them strike directly.

DEMOGRAPHICS	AREA	U.S. AVG	ETHNIC COMPOSITION	AREA	U.S. AVG	RESIDENT PROFILE	AREA	U.S. AVG
Population	917,158		White	20.2%	79.0%	Single	36.4%	32.4%
Population density per sq. mile	1529.1	358.5	Black	3.2%	10.5%	Married	49.1%	52.7%
Population growth	9.7%	21.1%	Asian	55.1%	2.7%	Divorced/separated	14.5%	14.9%
Median age	37.4	36.1	Hispanic	6.9%	10.6%	Married with children	24.7%	23.7%
Percent Democrat	51.1%	44.5%	Religious observance	33.3%	48.9%	Single with children	7.2%	9.1%
Percent Republican	48.3%	54.5%	Diversity measure	73.3	40.1	Percent over age 65	13.9%	12.9%

INCOME	AREA	U.S. AVG	EMPLOYMENT	AREA	U.S. AVG	EMPLOYING INDUSTRIES	AREA	U.S. AVG
Per capita income	$24,757	$23,235	Unemployment rate	2.9%	4.7%	Largest: Healthcare & Social Assistance		
Household income	$57,827	$46,414	Recent job growth	3.9%	1.3%			
Household income < $25K	19.1%	26.2%	Projected future job growth	10.3%	11.5%	Percent manufacturing	8.8%	15.4%
Household income > $75K	36.5%	25.4%	White collar	62.6%	57.8%	Percent public sector	22.6%	15.7%
Household income growth	11.4%	13.6%	Blue collar	16.9%	25.2%	Percent construction	8.1%	9.9%

Score: 71.4   **Rank:** 108   (Economy & Jobs)

INDEXES & TAXES	AREA	U.S. AVG	HOUSING	AREA	U.S. AVG	NECESSITIES	AREA	U.S. AVG
Cost of Living Index	177.5	100.0	Median home price	$640,000	$220,000	Food Index	124.3	100.0
Buying Power Index	73.0	100.0	Home price appreciation	99.4%	10.1%	Housing Index	201.1	100.0
Income tax rate	10.00%	4.70%	Median rent	$1,279	$709	Utilities Index	82.9.	100.0
Sales tax rate	4.00%	6.58%	Homes owned	49.8%	62.3%	Transportation Index	123.2	100.0
Property tax rate	$3.36	$12.00	Home price ratio	11.1	4.2	Healthcare Index	118.4	100.0
						Miscellaneous Cost Index	121.4	100.0

Score: 1.9   **Rank:** 366   (Cost of Living)

Climate
Score: 98.4
Rank: 7

TEMPERATURE	AREA	U.S. AVG
Average January low	65.3	26.2
Average July high	87.4	87.4
Annual days > 90°F	9	38
Annual days < 32°F	0	89
Annual days < 0°F	0	6

PRECIPITATION	AREA	U.S. AVG
Annual inches precipitation	23.0	37.7
Annual inches snowfall	0.0	7.0
Annual days precipitation	102	109
Annual days rain > 0.5 inches	12	22
Annual days snow > 1.5 inches	0	6

COMFORTS & HAZARDS	AREA	U.S. AVG
July relative humidity	67%	66%
Annual days mostly sunny	264	208
Annual days with thunderstorms	7	39
Tornado risk score	0	18
Hurricane risk score	3	13

TEMPERATURE

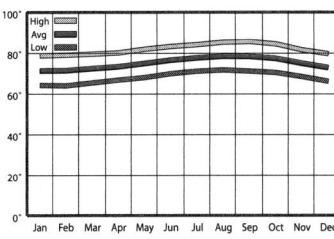

PRECIPITATION

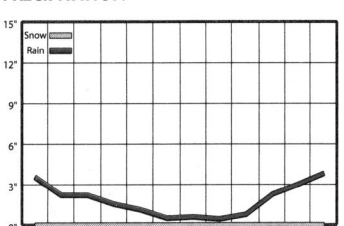

DAYS OF CLOUDS & PRECIPITATION

Education
Score: 67.1
Rank: 124

ACHIEVEMENT	AREA	U.S. AVG
High school degree	84.9%	82.7%
2-year college degree	7.9%	6.4%
4-year college degree	19.0%	15.7%
Graduate/professional degree	8.9%	8.9%

PUBLIC SCHOOLS	AREA	U.S. AVG
Expenditures per pupil	$5,909	$5,686
Student/teacher ratio	17.6	16.7
Attending public school	81.0%	90.1%
State SAT score	991*	1021
State ACT score	21.9	20.9

HIGHER EDUCATION	AREA	U.S. AVG
No. 2-year colleges	7	4
No. 4-year colleges/universities	11	6
No. highly ranked universities	1	1

Health & Healthcare
Score: 24.3
Rank: 282

HAZARDS & ILLNESSES	AREA	U.S. AVG
Air-quality score	19	37
Water-quality score	48	52
Pollen/allergy score	62	61
Cancer mortality per capita	159.8	201.9
Depression days per month	2.7	3.5
Stress score	24	50

HEALTHCARE	AREA	U.S. AVG
Physicians per capita	321.5	244.2
Hospital beds per capita	325.7	420.0
No. teaching hospitals	7	3
Cost per doctor visit	$80	$77
Cost per dental visit	$73	$70

Crime
Score: 38.5
Rank: 230

CRIME	AREA	U.S. AVG
Violent crime rate	282.9	465.5
Change in violent crime rate	2.3%	-2.2%
Property crime rate	4,665.1	3,517.1
Change in property crime rate	-4.1%	-2.1%

Transportation
Score: 9.4
Rank: 340

COMMUTE	AREA	U.S. AVG
Average commute time	30.1	27.4
Percent commutes > 60 mins.	9.1%	5.9%
Commute by auto	61.5%	78.9%
Commute by mass transit	8.3%	1.9%
Work at home	2.8%	3.1%
Mass transit miles per capita	8.27	1.87

INTERCITY SERVICES	AREA	U.S. AVG
Major airports within 60 miles	1	1
Size of regional airport	Large	Large
Daily airline activity	326	686
Amtrak service	No	No

AUTOMOTIVE	AREA	U.S. AVG
Insurance, annual premium	$2,367	$1,432
Gas, cost per gallon	$2.81	$2.49
Daily vehicle miles per capita	20.0	24.0

Leisure
Score: 67.6
Rank: 121

DINING & SHOPPING	AREA	U.S. AVG
Restaurant rating	1	2
Outlet mall score	0	42
No. Starbucks	0	13
No. warehouse clubs	4	2

ENTERTAINMENT	AREA	U.S. AVG
Professional sports rating	2	4
College sports rating	5	4
Zoo/aquarium rating	6	3
Amusement park rating	1	3
Botanical garden/ arboretum rating	7	4

OUTDOOR ACTIVITIES	AREA	U.S. AVG
Golf-course rating	5	4
Ski-area rating	1	3
Sq. miles inland water	3	4
Miles of coastline	137.8	10.7
National Park rating	2	3

Arts & Culture
Score: 88.0
Rank: 46

MEDIA & LIBRARIES	AREA	U.S. AVG
Arts radio rating	7	3
No. public libraries	50	27
Library volumes per capita	2.89	2.78

PERFORMING ARTS	AREA	U.S. AVG
Classical music rating	7	4
Ballet/dance rating	6	3
Professional theater rating	8	3
University arts programs rating	8	5

MUSEUMS	AREA	U.S. AVG
Overall museum rating	9	5
Art museum rating	8	5
Science museum rating	9	5
Children's museum rating	1	3

Hot Springs, AR

Score: 34.7   **Rank:** 322   **2004 rank:** not ranked

Profile: Small resort town
Location: West-central Arkansas, 50 miles southwest of Little Rock
Elevation: 632 feet
Time zone: Central Standard Time

PRO
Recreation
Cost of living
Attractive setting

CON
Tourist impact
Narrow employment base
Arts and culture

Hot Springs is a spa and resort town at the base of the Ouachita Mountains southwest of Little Rock. The area boasts 47 natural hot springs as well as the boyhood home of Bill Clinton. Surrounding the unusual Hot Springs National Park are several resorts, some tacky tourist sprawl, and a few historic sites. Downtown is clean, with a substantial historic district containing the historic Bathhouse Row preserved and repurposed by the National Park Service. The area is touristy with some minor performing arts and lots to do for everyone, but may be more of a place to visit than a place to live. Those looking beyond tourist attractions for something to do will find themselves enjoying outdoor recreation in the national forest or nearby lakes. Most employment is related to the tourist, hospitality, and convention industry. For a tourist destination, cost of living is reasonable.

Hot Springs is in a hilly, wooded area at the base of the large Ouachita National Forest and mountain range of the same name. The setting is attractive and known for beautiful spring and autumn seasons. But the climate becomes more humid in summer, giving warm and sticky days. Winters are fairly mild with outbreaks of cold, snow, and occasional ice storms. Precipitation is evenly distributed through the year, coming mainly as thunderstorms in summer. First freeze is early November; last is late March.

Population

DEMOGRAPHICS	AREA	U.S. AVG	ETHNIC COMPOSITION	AREA	U.S. AVG	RESIDENT PROFILE	AREA	U.S. AVG
Population	92,752		White	88.1%	79.0%	Single	25.7%	32.4%
Population density per sq. mile	137.0	358.5	Black	8.2%	10.5%	Married	56.9%	52.7%
Population growth	26.4%	21.1%	Asian	0.7%	2.7%	Divorced/separated	17.5%	14.9%
Median age	42.3	36.1	Hispanic	2.8%	10.6%	Married with children	17.4%	23.7%
Percent Democrat	44.9%	44.5%	Religious observance	59.7%	48.9%	Single with children	7.6%	9.1%
Percent Republican	54.1%	54.5%	Diversity measure	25.9	40.1	Percent over age 65	21.0%	12.9%

Economy & Jobs

Score: 95.2
Rank: 19

INCOME	AREA	U.S. AVG	EMPLOYMENT	AREA	U.S. AVG	EMPLOYING INDUSTRIES	AREA	U.S. AVG
Per capita income	$21,204	$23,235	Unemployment rate	5.0%	4.7%	Largest: Healthcare & Social Assistance		
Household income	$36,267	$46,414	Recent job growth	6.6%	1.3%			
Household income ‹ $25K	33.9%	26.2%	Projected future job growth	22.2%	11.5%	Percent manufacturing	14.8%	15.4%
Household income › $75K	16.9%	25.4%	White collar	52.2%	57.8%	Percent public sector	12.1%	15.7%
Household income growth	14.3%	13.6%	Blue collar	27.3%	25.2%	Percent construction	12.5%	9.9%

Cost of Living

Score: 65.0
Rank: 132

INDEXES & TAXES	AREA	U.S. AVG	HOUSING	AREA	U.S. AVG	NECESSITIES	AREA	U.S. AVG
Cost of Living Index	81.1	100.0	Median home price	$114,300	$220,000	Food Index	99.8	100.0
Buying Power Index	100.2	100.0	Home price appreciation	41.2%	10.1%	Housing Index	62.5	100.0
Income tax rate	7.00%	4.70%	Median rent	$575	$709	Utilities Index	104.9	100.0
Sales tax rate	6.50%	6.58%	Homes owned	60.2%	62.3%	Transportation Index	89.8	100.0
Property tax rate	$6.64	$12.00	Home price ratio	3.2	4.2	Healthcare Index	91.4	100.0
						Miscellaneous Cost Index	100.9	100.0

Climate

Score: 53.5
Rank: 173

TEMPERATURE	AREA	U.S. AVG	PRECIPITATION	AREA	U.S. AVG	COMFORTS & HAZARDS	AREA	U.S. AVG
Average January low	30.0	26.2	Annual inches precipitation	51.3	37.7	July relative humidity	56%	66%
Average July high	92.0	87.4	Annual inches snowfall	7.0	7.0	Annual days mostly sunny	216	208
Annual days › 90°F	62	38	Annual days precipitation	111	109	Annual days with thunderstorms	57	39
Annual days ‹ 32°F	51	89	Annual days rain › 0.5 inches	32	22	Tornado risk score	30	18
Annual days ‹ 0°F	0	6	Annual days snow › 1.5 inches	2	6	Hurricane risk score	9	13

TEMPERATURE

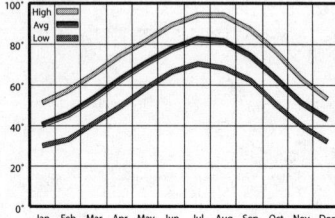

PRECIPITATION

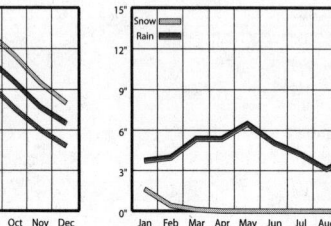

DAYS OF CLOUDS & PRECIPITATION

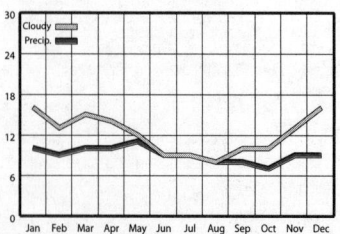

ACHIEVEMENT	AREA	U.S. AVG	PUBLIC SCHOOLS	AREA	U.S. AVG	HIGHER EDUCATION	AREA	U.S. AVG
High school degree	78.3%	82.7%	Expenditures per pupil	$4,175	$5,686	No. 2-year colleges	2	4
2-year college degree	4.4%	6.4%	Student/teacher ratio	22.5	16.7	No. 4-year colleges/universities	0	6
4-year college degree	11.6%	15.7%	Attending public school	94.8%	90.1%	No. highly ranked universities	0	1
Graduate/professional degree	6.3%	8.9%	State SAT score	1142	1021			
			State ACT score	20.6*	20.9			

Education
Score: 11.0
Rank: 331

HAZARDS & ILLNESSES	AREA	U.S. AVG	HEALTHCARE	AREA	U.S. AVG	CRIME	AREA	U.S. AVG
Air-quality score	54	37	Physicians per capita	261.0	244.2	Violent crime rate	663.2	465.5
Water-quality score	100	52	Hospital beds per capita	670.6	420.0	Change in violent crime rate	6.4%	-2.2%
Pollen/allergy score	63	61	No. teaching hospitals	0	3	Property crime rate	7,601.9	3,517.1
Cancer mortality per capita	213.2	201.9	Cost per doctor visit	$62	$77	Change in property crime rate	-12.6%	-2.1%
Depression days per month	3.0	3.5	Cost per dental visit	$48	$70			
Stress score	96	50						

Health & Healthcare
Score: 97.9
Rank: 9

Crime
Score: 0.0
Rank: 373

COMMUTE	AREA	U.S. AVG	INTERCITY SERVICES	AREA	U.S. AVG	AUTOMOTIVE	AREA	U.S. AVG
Average commute time	23.1	27.4	Major airports within 60 miles	0	1	Insurance, annual premium	$1,519	$1,432
Percent commutes > 60 mins.	5.7%	5.9%	Size of regional airport	Small	Large	Gas, cost per gallon	$2.45	$2.49
Commute by auto	78.9%	78.9%	Daily airline activity	96	686	Daily vehicle miles per capita	20.1	24.0
Commute by mass transit	1.0%	1.9%	Amtrak service	No	No			
Work at home	2.7%	3.1%						
Mass transit miles per capita	0.95	1.87						

Transportation
Score: 21.9
Rank: 293

DINING & SHOPPING	AREA	U.S. AVG	ENTERTAINMENT	AREA	U.S. AVG	OUTDOOR ACTIVITIES	AREA	U.S. AVG
Restaurant rating	1	2	Professional sports rating	1	4	Golf-course rating	3	4
Outlet mall score	0	42	College sports rating	1	4	Ski-area rating	1	3
No. Starbucks	1	13	Zoo/aquarium rating	1	3	Sq. miles inland water	3	4
No. warehouse clubs	0	2	Amusement park rating	1	3	Miles of coastline	0.0	10.7
			Botanical garden/ arboretum rating	1	4	National Park rating	3	3

Leisure
Score: 7.0
Rank: 347

MEDIA & LIBRARIES	AREA	U.S. AVG	PERFORMING ARTS	AREA	U.S. AVG	MUSEUMS	AREA	U.S. AVG
Arts radio rating	1	3	Classical music rating	2	4	Overall museum rating	5	5
No. public libraries	4	27	Ballet/dance rating	1	3	Art museum rating	1	5
Library volumes per capita	1.70	2.78	Professional theater rating	1	3	Science museum rating	7	5
			University arts programs rating	1	5	Children's museum rating	1	3

Arts & Culture
Score: 6.1
Rank: 350

Houma–Bayou Cane–Thibodaux, LA

Score: 23.8   **Rank:** 351   **2004 rank:** 320

Profile: Small-town complex
Location: Southeast Louisiana on the Mississippi Delta, 35 miles south of New Orleans
Elevation: 30 feet
Time zone: Central Standard Time

PRO
Water recreation
Wildlife viewing
Cultural interest

CON
Hurricane dislocations
Heat and humidity
Low educational attainment

Houma is the commercial and cultural center for a two-parish area comprising much of the Mississippi Delta extension south into the Gulf of Mexico south of the Mississippi River itself. Houma is deep in the marshlands just a few miles from the Gulf of Mexico and about 40 miles southwest of New Orleans. The swampy lowlands create the Venice-like canals and bayous for which the area is known. Bayou Cane and Thibodaux are smaller towns to the northwest of no particular interest, but their names suggest the rich Cajun cultural heritage abundant throughout the area. Coastal and marshland wildlife is a major attraction. Economically the area is supported by the oil industry, fishing, and shrimp and oyster harvesting. The area took a hard but not devastating hit from the 2005 Hurricane Katrina. While the headlines centered on New Orleans, there was extensive damage, flooding, and business disruption here as well; some estimate 99% of the oyster beds were destroyed. The area wasn't very prosperous economically nor rich in amenities to begin with, and like most hurricane-damaged Gulf cities, we consider the region a wait-and-see. Crime is fairly high for a small town.

The terrain is completely flat with wet marshland, slow-moving creeks (called bayous), and some wooded areas. The climate is governed by the Gulf of Mexico. Summers are wet, hot, and humid. Winters are cool but not cold and fairly wet.

Population

DEMOGRAPHICS	AREA	U.S. AVG	ETHNIC COMPOSITION	AREA	U.S. AVG	RESIDENT PROFILE	AREA	U.S. AVG
Population	199,005		White	77.3%	79.0%	Single	31.7%	32.4%
Population density per sq. mile	85.1	358.5	Black	15.8%	10.5%	Married	55.2%	52.7%
Population growth	8.9%	21.1%	Asian	0.9%	2.7%	Divorced/separated	13.1%	14.9%
Median age	34.7	36.1	Hispanic	1.7%	10.6%	Married with children	28.3%	23.7%
Percent Democrat	35.7%	44.5%	Religious observance	75.1%	48.9%	Single with children	10.2%	9.1%
Percent Republican	62.7%	54.5%	Diversity measure	39.4	40.1	Percent over age 65	11.1%	12.9%

Economy & Jobs
Score: 26.5
Rank: 275

INCOME	AREA	U.S. AVG	EMPLOYMENT	AREA	U.S. AVG	EMPLOYING INDUSTRIES	AREA	U.S. AVG
Per capita income	$19,287	$23,235	Unemployment rate	5.1%	4.7%	Largest: Manufacturing		
Household income	$41,833	$46,414	Recent job growth	2.0%	1.3%			
Household income < $25K	31.0%	26.2%	Projected future job growth	7.9%	11.5%	Percent manufacturing	18.9%	15.4%
Household income > $75K	21.4%	25.4%	White collar	51.3%	57.8%	Percent public sector	14.6%	15.7%
Household income growth	19.2%	13.6%	Blue collar	33.1%	25.2%	Percent construction	14.2%	9.9%

Cost of Living
Score: 70.1
Rank: 113

INDEXES & TAXES	AREA	U.S. AVG	HOUSING	AREA	U.S. AVG	NECESSITIES	AREA	U.S. AVG
Cost of Living Index	86.4	100.0	Median home price	$124,600	$220,000	Food Index	104.3	100.0
Buying Power Index	108.5	100.0	Home price appreciation	30.9%	10.1%	Housing Index	53.6	100.0
Income tax rate	4.00%	4.70%	Median rent	$541	$709	Utilities Index	114.7	100.0
Sales tax rate	8.59%	6.58%	Homes owned	70.1%	62.3%	Transportation Index	104.5	100.0
Property tax rate	$3.28	$12.00	Home price ratio	3.0	4.2	Healthcare Index	100.4	100.0
						Miscellaneous Cost Index	102.3	100.0

Climate
Score: 73.3
Rank: 99

TEMPERATURE	AREA	U.S. AVG	PRECIPITATION	AREA	U.S. AVG	COMFORTS & HAZARDS	AREA	U.S. AVG
Average January low	43.5	26.2	Annual inches precipitation	57.0	37.7	July relative humidity	77%	66%
Average July high	90.6	87.4	Annual inches snowfall	0.2	7.0	Annual days mostly sunny	229	208
Annual days > 90°F	67	38	Annual days precipitation	113	109	Annual days with thunderstorms	68	39
Annual days > 32°F	13	89	Annual days rain > 0.5 inches	37	22	Tornado risk score	20	18
Annual days < 0°F	0	6	Annual days snow > 1.5 inches	1	6	Hurricane risk score	67	13

TEMPERATURE

PRECIPITATION

DAYS OF CLOUDS & PRECIPITATION

Education
Score: 0.3
Rank: 372

ACHIEVEMENT	AREA	U.S. AVG	PUBLIC SCHOOLS	AREA	U.S. AVG	HIGHER EDUCATION	AREA	U.S. AVG
High school degree	67.1%	82.7%	Expenditures per pupil	$4,342	$5,686	No. 2-year colleges	2	4
2-year college degree	2.9%	6.4%	Student/teacher ratio	15.6	16.7	No. 4-year colleges/universities	1	6
4-year college degree	8.7%	15.7%	Attending public school	85.6%	90.1%	No. highly ranked universities	0	1
Graduate/professional degree	3.8%	8.9%	State SAT score	1141	1021			
			State ACT score	20.1*	20.9			

Health & Healthcare
Score: 46.3
Rank: 202

HAZARDS & ILLNESSES	AREA	U.S. AVG	HEALTHCARE	AREA	U.S. AVG	CRIME	AREA	U.S. AVG
Air-quality score	43	37	Physicians per capita	136.8	244.2	Violent crime rate	459.2	465.5
Water-quality score	49	52	Hospital beds per capita	443.7	420.0	Change in violent crime rate	-16.4%	-2.2%
Pollen/allergy score	79	61	No. teaching hospitals	1	3	Property crime rate	3,669.4	3,517.1
Cancer mortality per capita	217.5	201.9	Cost per doctor visit	$75	$77	Change in property crime rate	-15.6%	-2.1%
Depression days per month	3.6	3.5	Cost per dental visit	$66	$70			
Stress score	39	50						

Crime
Score: 19.5
Rank: 301

Transportation
Score: 12.6
Rank: 328

COMMUTE	AREA	U.S. AVG	INTERCITY SERVICES	AREA	U.S. AVG	AUTOMOTIVE	AREA	U.S. AVG
Average commute time	26.2	27.4	Major airports within 60 miles	1	1	Insurance, annual premium	$1,486	$1,432
Percent commutes > 60 mins.	9.4%	5.9%	Size of regional airport	Medium	Large	Gas, cost per gallon	$2.49	$2.49
Commute by auto	79.4%	78.9%	Daily airline activity	259	686	Daily vehicle miles per capita	24.8	24.0
Commute by mass transit	0.7%	1.9%	Amtrak service	Yes	No			
Work at home	2.0%	3.1%						
Mass transit miles per capita	0.75	1.87						

	DINING & SHOPPING	AREA	U.S. AVG		ENTERTAINMENT	AREA	U.S. AVG		OUTDOOR ACTIVITIES	AREA	U.S. AVG
Leisure	Restaurant rating	1	2		Professional sports rating	2	4		Golf-course rating	1	4
Score: 54.8	Outlet mall score	21	42		College sports rating	1	4		Ski-area rating	1	3
Rank: 169	No. Starbucks	1	13		Zoo/aquarium rating	1	3		Sq. miles inland water	10	4
	No. warehouse clubs	0	2		Amusement park rating	1	3		Miles of coastline	78.8	10.7
					Botanical garden/ arboretum rating	1	4		National Park rating	1	3

	MEDIA & LIBRARIES	AREA	U.S. AVG		PERFORMING ARTS	AREA	U.S. AVG		MUSEUMS	AREA	U.S. AVG
Arts & Culture	Arts radio rating	1	3		Classical music rating	1	4		Overall museum rating	1	5
Score: 1.6	No. public libraries	14	27		Ballet/dance rating	1	3		Art museum rating	1	5
Rank: 367	Library volumes per capita	1.98	2.78		Professional theater rating	1	3		Science museum rating	1	5
					University arts programs rating	1	5		Children's museum rating	1	3

Houston–Sugar Land–Baytown, TX   Score: 48.4   Rank: 256   2004 rank: 158

Profile: Large-city complex
Location: Southeast Texas, 50 miles inland from the Gulf Coast
Elevation: 108 feet
Time zone: Central Standard Time

PRO	CON
Diverse economy	Growth and sprawl
Entertainment	Hot, humid summers
Cost of living	Unattractive setting

Big—*huge*—and getting bigger. The rapidly growing Houston area continues to rank as the fourth-largest metro area in the United States—behind New York, Los Angeles, and Chicago—and the 5-year growth rate of 11% places it closer to the top three in that category. Not only is the population huge, but the area includes 10 counties covering some 900 square miles and spreads some 50 miles in each direction. As if it weren't big enough already, the OMB combined two other smaller metro areas, Galveston–Texas City to the southeast and the so-called "Brazoria" (Brazoria County), into the metro complex in 2005.

Houston is a national and world center for the petroleum and petrochemical industry, but also shines as a general corporate center, despite the Enron debacle that gave the city and its freewheeling pro-business ways a bit of a black eye. Local companies include Continental Airlines, Browning Ferris Industries, Waste Management, Minute Maid (owned by Coca-Cola), and American General (insurance). There is a considerable amount of banking and general commerce and trade in the area, driven in part by the large port facility and the petrochemical industry.

The city grew in a fairly haphazard manner, with skyscraper complexes downtown and satellite corporate centers on the periphery. To the west along the Interstate 610 inner beltway, the commercial center and satellite downtown area known as the Galleria contain large office complexes and a gigantic mall with more than 300 stores. Both of these core areas feature a very modern skyline and the latest in transportation conveyances. Together, downtown and the Galleria contain 6½ miles of underground tunnels and malls, and a new light rail system just opened to primarily serve the downtown area. So much commercial activity is actually done on the periphery that downtown—if you can get there—is relatively pleasant, uncrowded, and attractive.

Suburban growth has enjoyed no finer hour than it has in the Houston area, and so have growth, sprawl, and its related problems. Growth has spread in all directions, and traffic on the area's web of freeways, many undergoing their second reconstruction, can slow to a crawl anywhere, anytime. Air quality is among the country's worst. Areas southeast are older, more built up, industrial, and constrained by Galveston Bay. Sugar Land is the emblematic Houston suburb with gigantic new planned subdivisions and a planned town center developed in an old sugar company town long since overtaken by the advancing sprawl. The population of Sugar Land has doubled in 15 years to some 80,000; residents enjoy high incomes, excellent schools and home values, and plenty of retail and other infrastructure seemingly tailored for family life.

The story is repeated elsewhere in Katy, some 25 miles west with 175,000 residents, and in North Houston to the northwest, as well as in other areas far north near the George Bush Intercontinental Airport. For the most part, the area has filled in between these nodes with endless suburbs, retail and commercial, and some industrial centers. The heavier industry is east and southeast in a 25-mile industrial corridor towards Texas City. Baytown, to the east and at the head of Galveston Bay, is a major oil refining and petrochemical center dominated by Exxon-Mobil. Nearby Galveston offers an interesting mix of antebellum commercial history and beach resort on Galveston Island just southeast of Texas City, and is a favored weekend getaway in an area that doesn't have very many. Farther west along the coast lies the industrial center of Freeport in Brazoria County, an enormous petrochemical and mineral processing center, with numerous beach houses built up on stilts up and down the coast and a corridor of small towns and residential areas spread back north towards Houston.

Cultural amenities are excellent and include performing arts, museums, and a variety of entertainment options from the sophisticated to the bawdy. With the Houston Texans (NFL), the Houston Astros (MLB), the Houston Rockets (NBA), and the University of Houston and Rice University teams, the city offers a full slate of sports entertainment. The Texas Medical Center is a leading-edge facility including 39 centers and employing 50,000 healthcare professionals. Although there are some lakes and the Gulf is 50 miles away, the area is notably lacking in outdoor recreational opportunities and the landscape is relatively featureless. Cost of living at 86.3 is a notably low for a big city, and excellent housing is available, with good family homes in the low $200s in the best suburbs. It is little wonder that the area became a favorite refuge for Hurricane Katrina refugees (by one research report, some 150,000 new residents came to the area), but they got their scare when Rita roared onshore mainly east of town a few weeks later.

Bottom line: Residents trade off some major downsides—congestion, long commutes, summer heat, high crime, and limited outdoor recreation—for a low cost of living, good housing values, strong buying power, career opportunities, plenty to do (mostly indoors), and mild winters. The negatives have gotten stronger, and the employment picture has weakened somewhat, hence the diminished ranking.

The Houston landscape mainly is a flat, treeless plain crossed by several small streams and rivers, with a little more relief and some wooded areas to the north and northeast. Summers are hot and sultry with daytime temperatures in the 90s and occasionally over 100°F. High relative humidity makes these temperatures uncomfortable—air-conditioning is a must. Winters are cloudy and mild with abundant rainfall. Clear dry days are most common in the fall. Heavy thunderstorms and tropical storms occasionally pass through the area.

Population

DEMOGRAPHICS	AREA	U.S. AVG	ETHNIC COMPOSITION	AREA	U.S. AVG	RESIDENT PROFILE	AREA	U.S. AVG
Population	5,239,517		White	61.0%	79.0%	Single	31.0%	32.4%
Population density per sq. mile	586.9	358.5	Black	16.3%	10.5%	Married	53.3%	52.7%
Population growth	42.4%	21.1%	Asian	5.5%	2.7%	Divorced/separated	15.7%	14.9%
Median age	32.8	36.1	Hispanic	32.0%	10.6%	Married with children	29.1%	23.7%
Percent Democrat	41.4%	44.5%	Religious observance	49.8%	48.9%	Single with children	9.7%	9.1%
Percent Republican	57.9%	54.5%	Diversity measure	74.1	40.1	Percent over age 65	8.1%	12.9%

Economy & Jobs
Score: 82.6
Rank: 65

INCOME	AREA	U.S. AVG	EMPLOYMENT	AREA	U.S. AVG	EMPLOYING INDUSTRIES	AREA	U.S. AVG
Per capita income	$24,850	$23,235	Unemployment rate	5.3%	4.7%	Largest: Professional, Scientific & Technical Services		
Household income	$51,735	$46,414	Recent job growth	2.6%	1.3%			
Household income < $25K	22.5%	26.2%	Projected future job growth	18.5%	11.5%	Percent manufacturing	12.4%	15.4%
Household income > $75K	32.5%	25.4%	White collar	63.0%	57.8%	Percent public sector	12.2%	15.7%
Household income growth	14.5%	13.6%	Blue collar	23.3%	25.2%	Percent construction	10.9%	9.9%

Cost of Living
Score: 61.0
Rank: 146

INDEXES & TAXES	AREA	U.S. AVG	HOUSING	AREA	U.S. AVG	NECESSITIES	AREA	U.S. AVG
Cost of Living Index	86.3	100.0	Median home price	$152,700	$220,000	Food Index	94.4	100.0
Buying Power Index	134.4	100.0	Home price appreciation	24.9%	10.1%	Housing Index	54.2	100.0
Income tax rate	0.00%	4.70%	Median rent	$762	$709	Utilities Index	96.1	100.0
Sales tax rate	8.21%	6.58%	Homes owned	57.4%	62.3%	Transportation Index	103.2	100.0
Property tax rate	$19.93	$12.00	Home price ratio	3.0	4.2	Healthcare Index	106.7	100.0
						Miscellaneous Cost Index	97.1	100.0

Climate
Score: 56.1
Rank: 163

TEMPERATURE	AREA	U.S. AVG	PRECIPITATION	AREA	U.S. AVG	COMFORTS & HAZARDS	AREA	U.S. AVG
Average January low	41.5	26.2	Annual inches precipitation	48.0	37.7	July relative humidity	77%	66%
Average July high	94.3	87.4	Annual inches snowfall	0.0	7.0	Annual days mostly sunny	203	208
Annual days > 90°F	81	38	Annual days precipitation	107	109	Annual days with thunderstorms	69	39
Annual days < 32°F	24	89	Annual days rain > 0.5 inches	28	22	Tornado risk score	41	18
Annual days < 0°F	1	6	Annual days snow > 1.5 inches	0	6	Hurricane risk score	66	13

TEMPERATURE

PRECIPITATION

DAYS OF CLOUDS & PRECIPITATION

Education
Score: 78.1
Rank: 83

ACHIEVEMENT	AREA	U.S. AVG	PUBLIC SCHOOLS	AREA	U.S. AVG	HIGHER EDUCATION	AREA	U.S. AVG
High school degree	76.8%	82.7%	Expenditures per pupil	$5,016	$5,686	No. 2-year colleges	22	4
2-year college degree	5.1%	6.4%	Student/teacher ratio	16.5	16.7	No. 4-year colleges/universities	22	6
4-year college degree	18.0%	15.7%	Attending public school	93.3%	90.1%	No. highly ranked universities	3	1
Graduate/professional degree	8.8%	8.9%	State SAT score	997*	1021			
			State ACT score	20.3	20.9			

HAZARDS & ILLNESSES	AREA	U.S. AVG	HEALTHCARE	AREA	U.S. AVG	CRIME	AREA	U.S. AVG
Air-quality score	8	37	Physicians per capita	247.2	244.2	Violent crime rate	712.6	465.5
Water-quality score	42	52	Hospital beds per capita	305.1	420.0	Change in violent crime rate	-1.5%	-2.2%
Pollen/allergy score	70	61	No. teaching hospitals	21	3	Property crime rate	4,220.5	3,517.1
Cancer mortality per capita	167.8	201.9	Cost per doctor visit	$84	$77	Change in property crime rate	-3.4%	-2.1%
Depression days per month	3.0	3.5	Cost per dental visit	$66	$70			
Stress score	92	50						

Health & Healthcare — Score: 10.7 Rank: 333
Crime — Score: 15.0 Rank: 316

COMMUTE	AREA	U.S. AVG	INTERCITY SERVICES	AREA	U.S. AVG	AUTOMOTIVE	AREA	U.S. AVG
Average commute time	31.6	27.4	Major airports within 60 miles	2	1	Insurance, annual premium	$1,468	$1,432
Percent commutes > 60 mins.	9.6%	5.9%	Size of regional airport	Large	Large	Gas, cost per gallon	$2.49	$2.49
Commute by auto	77.5%	78.9%	Daily airline activity	963	686	Daily vehicle miles per capita	35.2	24.0
Commute by mass transit	3.1%	1.9%	Amtrak service	Yes	No			
Work at home	2.5%	3.1%						
Mass transit miles per capita	3.13	1.87						

Transportation — Score: 15.0 Rank: 319

DINING & SHOPPING	AREA	U.S. AVG	ENTERTAINMENT	AREA	U.S. AVG	OUTDOOR ACTIVITIES	AREA	U.S. AVG
Restaurant rating	4	2	Professional sports rating	8	4	Golf-course rating	8	4
Outlet mall score	0	42	College sports rating	6	4	Ski-area rating	1	3
No. Starbucks	99	13	Zoo/aquarium rating	6	3	Sq. miles inland water	6	4
No. warehouse clubs	5	2	Amusement park rating	8	3	Miles of coastline	3.2	10.7
			Botanical garden/ arboretum rating	4	4	National Park rating	4	3

Leisure — Score: 86.9 Rank: 49

MEDIA & LIBRARIES	AREA	U.S. AVG	PERFORMING ARTS	AREA	U.S. AVG	MUSEUMS	AREA	U.S. AVG
Arts radio rating	8	3	Classical music rating	7	4	Overall museum rating	10	5
No. public libraries	121	27	Ballet/dance rating	7	3	Art museum rating	10	5
Library volumes per capita	1.70	2.78	Professional theater rating	9	3	Science museum rating	10	5
			University arts programs rating	9	5	Children's museum rating	9	3

Arts & Culture — Score: 87.2 Rank: 49

Huntington—Ashland, WV-KY-OH Score: 23.8 Rank: 340 2004 rank: 228

Profile: Small river cities
Location: Extreme western West Virginia along the Ohio River
Elevation: 565 feet
Time zone: Eastern Standard Time

PRO	CON
Cost of living	Entertainment
Small-town atmosphere	Low educational attainment
Revitalizing downtown	Isolation

Industrial Huntington, located along the Ohio River, is a transport center for traffic between Ohio, the Great Lakes, Kentucky, and points east of the Appalachians. The diverse industrial base includes chemicals, metal products, and glass and glass products manufacturing. The smaller Ashland, in Kentucky 10 miles downriver, plays a similar role. The area has a low Cost of Living Index at 79.2, but low incomes give it relatively low buying power. Downtown renewal has brought more life to the area, centered on a retail, commercial, and entertainment complex known as "Superblock," and there is a new waterfront park. The 16,000-student Marshall University brings a strong college presence to the area and a lot of sports interest. The area is isolated by distance and geography from larger cities, but some might find the area a good future bet for those looking for a small-town climate.

Huntington is at the confluence of the Ohio and Big Sandy rivers across from the southern tip of Ohio. The city is located in a flat valley, with rounded, wooded Appalachian foothills rising on all sides. Summers are moderately warm and humid with valley locations considerably warmer and more humid than the hilltops. Winter months are moderately cold, with an occasional severe cold wave lasting a few days. The four seasons are nearly equal in length and autumn is the most pleasant. The heaviest rainfall occurs in July and August mostly as thunderstorms, and flash floods are common. Winter rainfall occurs mostly with a frontal passage and frequently lasts from 2 to 4 days, possibly causing stream flooding. Snow seldom remains more than 2 days in the valleys, but can linger on hilltops.

DEMOGRAPHICS	AREA	U.S. AVG	ETHNIC COMPOSITION	AREA	U.S. AVG	RESIDENT PROFILE	AREA	U.S. AVG
Population	286,119		White	95.6%	79.0%	Single	29.6%	32.4%
Population density per sq. mile	163.6	358.5	Black	2.4%	10.5%	Married	56.1%	52.7%
Population growth	-0.7%	21.1%	Asian	0.6%	2.7%	Divorced/separated	14.3%	14.9%
Median age	39.2	36.1	Hispanic	0.7%	10.6%	Married with children	21.1%	23.7%
Percent Democrat	44.8%	44.5%	Religious observance	39.1%	48.9%	Single with children	7.8%	9.1%
Percent Republican	54.5%	54.5%	Diversity measure	9.7	40.1	Percent over age 65	15.7%	12.9%

Economy & Jobs
Score: 7.2
Rank: 346

INCOME	AREA	U.S. AVG	EMPLOYMENT	AREA	U.S. AVG	EMPLOYING INDUSTRIES	AREA	U.S. AVG
Per capita income	$18,825	$23,235	Unemployment rate	5.4%	4.7%	Largest: Healthcare & Social Assistance		
Household income	$33,432	$46,414	Recent job growth	0.1%	1.3%			
Household income < $25K	38.8%	26.2%	Projected future job growth	2.3%	11.5%	Percent manufacturing	15.8%	15.4%
Household income > $75K	15.3%	25.4%	White collar	56.0%	57.8%	Percent public sector	16.2%	15.7%
Household income growth	12.7%	13.6%	Blue collar	26.8%	25.2%	Percent construction	11.0%	9.9%

Cost of Living
Score: 76.7
Rank: 88

INDEXES & TAXES	AREA	U.S. AVG	HOUSING	AREA	U.S. AVG	NECESSITIES	AREA	U.S. AVG
Cost of Living Index	79.2	100.0	Median home price	$107,200	$220,000	Food Index	103.7	100.0
Buying Power Index	94.6	100.0	Home price appreciation	29.4%	10.1%	Housing Index	50.2	100.0
Income tax rate	5.98%	4.70%	Median rent	$519	$709	Utilities Index	77.6	100.0
Sales tax rate	6.33%	6.58%	Homes owned	66.0%	62.3%	Transportation Index	100.0	100.0
Property tax rate	$8.19	$12.00	Home price ratio	3.2	4.2	Healthcare Index	93.3	100.0
						Miscellaneous Cost Index	99.0	100.0

Climate
Score: 81.0
Rank: 72

TEMPERATURE	AREA	U.S. AVG	PRECIPITATION	AREA	U.S. AVG	COMFORTS & HAZARDS	AREA	U.S. AVG
Average January low	25.6	26.2	Annual inches precipitation	38.9	37.7	July relative humidity	71%	66%
Average July high	85.7	87.4	Annual inches snowfall	25.6	7.0	Annual days mostly sunny	166	208
Annual days > 90°F	17	38	Annual days precipitation	139	109	Annual days with thunderstorms	44	39
Annual days > 32°F	23	89	Annual days rain > 0.5 inches	27	22	Tornado risk score	9	18
Annual days < 0°F	2	6	Annual days snow > 1.5 inches	7	6	Hurricane risk score	5	13

TEMPERATURE

PRECIPITATION

DAYS OF CLOUDS & PRECIPITATION

Education
Score: 15.8
Rank: 314

ACHIEVEMENT	AREA	U.S. AVG	PUBLIC SCHOOLS	AREA	U.S. AVG	HIGHER EDUCATION	AREA	U.S. AVG
High school degree	76.7%	82.7%	Expenditures per pupil	$5,567	$5,686	No. 2-year colleges	8	4
2-year college degree	5.0%	6.4%	Student/teacher ratio	17.0	16.7	No. 4-year colleges/universities	3	6
4-year college degree	8.7%	15.7%	Attending public school	95.7%	90.1%	No. highly ranked universities	0	1
Graduate/professional degree	6.1%	8.9%	State SAT score	1029	1021			
			State ACT score	20.6*	20.9			

Health & Healthcare
Score: 83.4
Rank: 63

HAZARDS & ILLNESSES	AREA	U.S. AVG	HEALTHCARE	AREA	U.S. AVG	CRIME	AREA	U.S. AVG
Air-quality score	57	37	Physicians per capita	293.7	244.2	Violent crime rate	208.2	465.5
Water-quality score	51	52	Hospital beds per capita	665.5	420.0	Change in violent crime rate	1.9%	-2.2%
Pollen/allergy score	60	61	No. teaching hospitals	2	3	Property crime rate	3,007.8	3,517.1
Cancer mortality per capita	262.4	201.9	Cost per doctor visit	$73	$77	Change in property crime rate	2.0%	-2.1%
Depression days per month	5.0	3.5	Cost per dental visit	$83	$70			
Stress score	65	50						

Crime
Score: 62.8
Rank: 140

Transportation
Score: 6.7
Rank: 349

COMMUTE	AREA	U.S. AVG	INTERCITY SERVICES	AREA	U.S. AVG	AUTOMOTIVE	AREA	U.S. AVG
Average commute time	24.7	27.4	Major airports within 60 miles	0	1	Insurance, annual premium	$1,278	$1,432
Percent commutes > 60 mins.	6.0%	5.9%	Size of regional airport	None	Large	Gas, cost per gallon	$2.47	$2.49
Commute by auto	84.3%	78.9%	Daily airline activity	19	686	Daily vehicle miles per capita	21.4	24.0
Commute by mass transit	0.6%	1.9%	Amtrak service	Yes	No			
Work at home	2.0%	3.1%						
Mass transit miles per capita	0.61	1.87						

Leisure
Score: 15.0
Rank: 317

DINING & SHOPPING	AREA	U.S. AVG	ENTERTAINMENT	AREA	U.S. AVG	OUTDOOR ACTIVITIES	AREA	U.S. AVG
Restaurant rating	1	2	Professional sports rating	2	4	Golf-course rating	3	4
Outlet mall score	0	42	College sports rating	3	4	Ski-area rating	1	3
No. Starbucks	2	13	Zoo/aquarium rating	1	3	Sq. miles inland water	3	4
No. warehouse clubs	0	2	Amusement park rating	1	3	Miles of coastline	0.0	10.7
			Botanical garden/arboretum rating	3	4	National Park rating	1	3

MEDIA & LIBRARIES	AREA	U.S. AVG	PERFORMING ARTS	AREA	U.S. AVG	MUSEUMS	AREA	U.S. AVG
Arts radio rating	1	3	Classical music rating	4	4	Overall museum rating	2	5
No. public libraries	22	27	Ballet/dance rating	1	3	Art museum rating	3	5
Library volumes per capita	2.74	2.78	Professional theater rating	1	3	Science museum rating	4	5
			University arts programs rating	4	5	Children's museum rating	2	3

Arts & Culture
Score: 36.1
Rank: 239

Huntsville, AL

Score: 55.9   Rank: 211   2004 rank: 226

Profile: Mid-size city
Location: Extreme northern Alabama, 15 miles south of Tennessee border
Elevation: 644 feet
Time zone: Central Standard Time

PRO	CON
Strong economy	Isolation
Low unemployment	Infrastructure
Educated population	Hot, humid summers

Huntsville is a surprising and up-and-coming research, technology, and high-tech manufacturing center in extreme north Alabama. Known as the "Space Capital of America," a role that started in the 1940s when a U.S. senator brought famed German scientists, including Dr. Wernher von Braun, to a local U.S. Army arsenal to continue their work. Today, NASA operates the George C. Marshall Space Flight Center, and numerous technology and aerospace names such as Boeing, Teledyne, Lockheed Martin Northrup, LG Electronics, DirecTV, Sanmina, and Intergraph have large operations there. These industries have created a stable economy attracting a well-educated and well-paid workforce, and the business and population base have naturally attracted a strong set of cultural and entertainment amenities. The city itself is quite attractive, with mostly modern buildings in a wooded mountainous setting. Good neighborhoods spread south and into neighboring towns to the west, notably Madison. There are some older unattractive commercial strips belying its older-South heritage to the north, but generally, the area is prosperous and it shows. Geographically the area is fairly isolated, but air service is improving. Some have complained that local infrastructure—roads, schools, hospitals—haven't kept up well with growth, a predictable downside to the state of Alabama's relatively low taxes and especially property taxes. The area, especially for the long term, is probably better than the ranking indicates.

Surrounded by Appalachian foothills and 1,200-foot to 1,400-foot mountains, Huntsville is about 7 miles north of the Tennessee River Valley. Summers are warm, still, and humid with thunderstorms every 1 in 3 days. Winters are cool with cold snaps alternating with warmer moist periods and occasional snow.

Population

DEMOGRAPHICS	AREA	U.S. AVG	ETHNIC COMPOSITION	AREA	U.S. AVG	RESIDENT PROFILE	AREA	U.S. AVG
Population	365,076		White	73.0%	79.0%	Single	28.0%	32.4%
Population density per sq. mile	265.9	358.5	Black	21.5%	10.5%	Married	56.7%	52.7%
Population growth	24.6%	21.1%	Asian	2.1%	2.7%	Divorced/separated	15.3%	14.9%
Median age	36.8	36.1	Hispanic	2.2%	10.6%	Married with children	24.9%	23.7%
Percent Democrat	38.5%	44.5%	Religious observance	54.8%	48.9%	Single with children	8.5%	9.1%
Percent Republican	60.6%	54.5%	Diversity measure	44.1	40.1	Percent over age 65	11.9%	12.9%

Economy & Jobs
Score: 75.9
Rank: 91

INCOME	AREA	U.S. AVG	EMPLOYMENT	AREA	U.S. AVG	EMPLOYING INDUSTRIES	AREA	U.S. AVG
Per capita income	$25,490	$23,235	Unemployment rate	3.5%	4.7%	Largest: Professional, Scientific & Technical Services		
Household income	$48,846	$46,414	Recent job growth	1.8%	1.3%			
Household income < $25K	24.7%	26.2%	Projected future job growth	13.6%	11.5%	Percent manufacturing	14.6%	15.4%
Household income > $75K	29.5%	25.4%	White collar	64.3%	57.8%	Percent public sector	18.7%	15.7%
Household income growth	12.8%	13.6%	Blue collar	23.1%	25.2%	Percent construction	8.4%	9.9%

Cost of Living
Score: 50.0
Rank: 187

INDEXES & TAXES	AREA	U.S. AVG	HOUSING	AREA	U.S. AVG	NECESSITIES	AREA	U.S. AVG
Cost of Living Index	88.0	100.0	Median home price	$168,800	$220,000	Food Index	96.8	100.0
Buying Power Index	124.4	100.0	Home price appreciation	25.3%	10.1%	Housing Index	72.6	100.0
Income tax rate	5.00%	4.70%	Median rent	$560	$709	Utilities Index	81.9	100.0
Sales tax rate	8.00%	6.58%	Homes owned	65.7%	62.3%	Transportation Index	98.6	100.0
Property tax rate	$3.99	$12.00	Home price ratio	3.5	4.2	Healthcare Index	89.6	100.0
						Miscellaneous Cost Index	100.1	100.0

Climate
Score: 16.6
Rank: 311

TEMPERATURE	AREA	U.S. AVG
Average January low	31.3	26.2
Average July high	90.2	87.4
Annual days > 90°F	38	38
Annual days < 32°F	65	89
Annual days < 0°F	0	6

PRECIPITATION	AREA	U.S. AVG
Annual inches precipitation	52.0	37.7
Annual inches snowfall	3.0	7.0
Annual days precipitation	121	109
Annual days rain > 0.5 inches	40	22
Annual days snow > 1.5 inches	2	6

COMFORTS & HAZARDS	AREA	U.S. AVG
July relative humidity	73%	66%
Annual days mostly sunny	207	208
Annual days with thunderstorms	58	39
Tornado risk score	61	18
Hurricane risk score	12	13

TEMPERATURE

PRECIPITATION

DAYS OF CLOUDS & PRECIPITATION

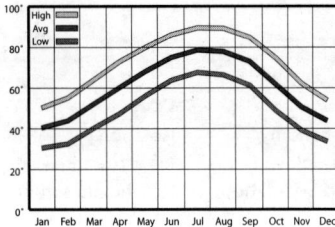

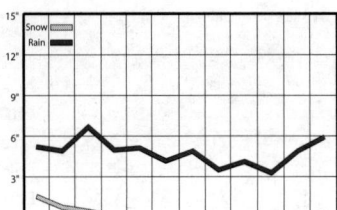

Education
Score: 72.5
Rank: 104

ACHIEVEMENT	AREA	U.S. AVG
High school degree	83.7%	82.7%
2-year college degree	5.9%	6.4%
4-year college degree	21.1%	15.7%
Graduate/professional degree	10.5%	8.9%

PUBLIC SCHOOLS	AREA	U.S. AVG
Expenditures per pupil	$4,774	$5,686
Student/teacher ratio	16.1	16.7
Attending public school	88.9%	90.1%
State SAT score	1126	1021
State ACT score	20.2*	20.9

HIGHER EDUCATION	AREA	U.S. AVG
No. 2-year colleges	2	4
No. 4-year colleges/universities	5	6
No. highly ranked universities	1	1

Health & Healthcare
Score: 24.6
Rank: 281

HAZARDS & ILLNESSES	AREA	U.S. AVG
Air-quality score	35	37
Water-quality score	6	52
Pollen/allergy score	67	61
Cancer mortality per capita	205.9	201.9
Depression days per month	3.0	3.5
Stress score	30	50

HEALTHCARE	AREA	U.S. AVG
Physicians per capita	206.3	244.2
Hospital beds per capita	301.3	420.0
No. teaching hospitals	1	3
Cost per doctor visit	$62	$77
Cost per dental visit	$58	$70

Crime
Score: 51.3
Rank: 183

CRIME	AREA	U.S. AVG
Violent crime rate	488.7	465.5
Change in violent crime rate	22.5%	-2.2%
Property crime rate	4,838.6	3,517.1
Change in property crime rate	19.8%	-2.1%

Transportation
Score: 37.4
Rank: 235

COMMUTE	AREA	U.S. AVG
Average commute time	23.8	27.4
Percent commutes > 60 mins.	3.0%	5.9%
Commute by auto	84.2%	78.9%
Commute by mass transit	0.3%	1.9%
Work at home	2.3%	3.1%
Mass transit miles per capita	0.32	1.87

INTERCITY SERVICES	AREA	U.S. AVG
Major airports within 60 miles	1	1
Size of regional airport	Medium	Large
Daily airline activity	416	686
Amtrak service	No	No

AUTOMOTIVE	AREA	U.S. AVG
Insurance, annual premium	$1,272	$1,432
Gas, cost per gallon	$2.46	$2.49
Daily vehicle miles per capita	24.6	24.0

Leisure
Score: 16.6
Rank: 311

DINING & SHOPPING	AREA	U.S. AVG
Restaurant rating	1	2
Outlet mall score	28	42
No. Starbucks	3	13
No. warehouse clubs	2	2

ENTERTAINMENT	AREA	U.S. AVG
Professional sports rating	2	4
College sports rating	3	4
Zoo/aquarium rating	1	3
Amusement park rating	2	3
Botanical garden/ arboretum rating	3	4

OUTDOOR ACTIVITIES	AREA	U.S. AVG
Golf-course rating	2	4
Ski-area rating	1	3
Sq. miles inland water	2	4
Miles of coastline	0.0	10.7
National Park rating	2	3

Arts & Culture
Score: 37.4
Rank: 234

MEDIA & LIBRARIES	AREA	U.S. AVG
Arts radio rating	1	3
No. public libraries	14	27
Library volumes per capita	2.04	2.78

PERFORMING ARTS	AREA	U.S. AVG
Classical music rating	3	4
Ballet/dance rating	1	3
Professional theater rating	1	3
University arts programs rating	3	5

MUSEUMS	AREA	U.S. AVG
Overall museum rating	7	5
Art museum rating	7	5
Science museum rating	8	5
Children's museum rating	1	3

Idaho Falls, ID

Score: 54.2   **Rank:** 224   **2004 rank:** not ranked

Profile: Small agricultural town
Location: Eastern Idaho, 45 miles northeast of Pocatello
Elevation: 4,710 feet
Time zone: Mountain Standard Time

PRO	CON
Nearby national parks	Entertainment
Nearby recreation	Arts and culture
Small-town feel	Narrow employment base

Idaho Falls is situated on the northeast portion of the Snake River Plain, at the edge of a large agricultural area. It is mainly an agricultural center but also serves as a gateway to Yellowstone National Park and the Grand Tetons to the northeast and east, respectively. It is a center for the Idaho branch of the Mormon culture, clear from the enormous temple visible for miles around. The town itself is nondescript and has little to offer, but the setting is attractive and the summer climate is pleasant. A small historic district with some arts venues lies along an attractive Snake River waterfront and most residential areas are quiet and concentrated to the south and east. Educational attainment is fairly high while cost of living is moderately low at 83.4. The area is attractive for outdoors-oriented residents and is gaining interest among retirees, especially in Rexburg and areas northeast toward Yellowstone.

The broad, flat, treeless Snake River Plain surrounds Idaho Falls; the larger Rockies and Grand Tetons to the east and the foothills of the Sawtooth Mountains to the west can be seen at a distance. The high elevation usually moderates summer temperatures giving warm but not hot, dry days and cool evenings, some requiring a jacket. Precipitation mainly occurs as occasional thundershowers. Winter moves back and forth between mild, wet periods and colder, harsher periods, sometimes driving temperatures below zero. Spring is wet; fall is most pleasant. First freeze is late September; last is late May.

Population

DEMOGRAPHICS	AREA	U.S. AVG	ETHNIC COMPOSITION	AREA	U.S. AVG	RESIDENT PROFILE	AREA	U.S. AVG
Population	110,220		White	91.3%	79.0%	Single	26.2%	32.4%
Population density per sq. mile	37.2	358.5	Black	0.5%	10.5%	Married	61.7%	52.7%
Population growth	24.2%	21.1%	Asian	0.9%	2.7%	Divorced/separated	12.1%	14.9%
Median age	31.8	36.1	Hispanic	8.8%	10.6%	Married with children	34.1%	23.7%
Percent Democrat	19.7%	44.5%	Religious observance	76.6%	48.9%	Single with children	7.7%	9.1%
Percent Republican	79.0%	54.5%	Diversity measure	29.9	40.1	Percent over age 65	10.4%	12.9%

Economy & Jobs
Score: 98.7
Rank: 6

INCOME	AREA	U.S. AVG	EMPLOYMENT	AREA	U.S. AVG	EMPLOYING INDUSTRIES	AREA	U.S. AVG
Per capita income	$20,377	$23,235	Unemployment rate	2.8%	4.7%	Largest: Professional, Scientific & Technical Services		
Household income	$46,808	$46,414	Recent job growth	6.6%	1.3%			
Household income < $25K	24.1%	26.2%	Projected future job growth	24.8%	11.5%	Percent manufacturing	11.9%	15.4%
Household income > $75K	24.9%	25.4%	White collar	60.8%	57.8%	Percent public sector	17.9%	15.7%
Household income growth	14.1%	13.6%	Blue collar	20.9%	25.2%	Percent construction	9.0%	9.9%

Cost of Living
Score: 48.4
Rank: 192

INDEXES & TAXES	AREA	U.S. AVG	HOUSING	AREA	U.S. AVG	NECESSITIES	AREA	U.S. AVG
Cost of Living Index	83.4	100.0	Median home price	$128,400	$220,000	Food Index	97.6	100.0
Buying Power Index	125.8	100.0	Home price appreciation	36.8%	10.1%	Housing Index	59.5	100.0
Income tax rate	8.20%	4.70%	Median rent	$568	$709	Utilities Index	86.6	100.0
Sales tax rate	6.00%	6.58%	Homes owned	73.4%	62.3%	Transportation Index	95.5	100.0
Property tax rate	$10.32	$12.00	Home price ratio	2.7	4.2	Healthcare Index	103.8	100.0
						Miscellaneous Cost Index	103.4	100.0

Climate
Score: 7.2
Rank: 346

TEMPERATURE	AREA	U.S. AVG	PRECIPITATION	AREA	U.S. AVG	COMFORTS & HAZARDS	AREA	U.S. AVG
Average January low	14.0	26.2	Annual inches precipitation	11.3	37.7	July relative humidity	26%	66%
Average July high	88.0	87.4	Annual inches snowfall	43.0	7.0	Annual days mostly sunny	197	208
Annual days > 90°F	33	38	Annual days precipitation	94	109	Annual days with thunderstorms	24	39
Annual days < 32°F	166	89	Annual days rain > 0.5 inches	4	22	Tornado risk score	1	18
Annual days < 0°F	15	6	Annual days snow > 1.5 inches	9	6	Hurricane risk score	0	13

TEMPERATURE

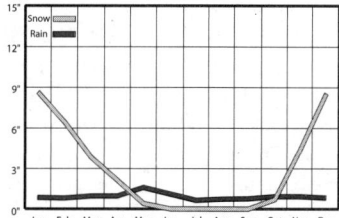

PRECIPITATION

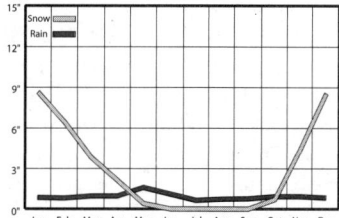

DAYS OF CLOUDS & PRECIPITATION

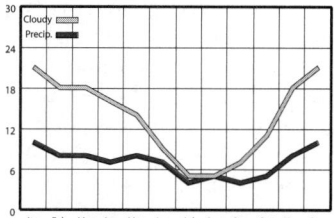

Education
Score: 72.2
Rank: 105

ACHIEVEMENT	AREA	U.S. AVG	PUBLIC SCHOOLS	AREA	U.S. AVG	HIGHER EDUCATION	AREA	U.S. AVG
High school degree	87.5%	82.7%	Expenditures per pupil	$4,484	$5,686	No. 2-year colleges	1	4
2-year college degree	9.2%	6.4%	Student/teacher ratio	19.1	16.7	No. 4-year colleges/universities	0	6
4-year college degree	16.5%	15.7%	Attending public school	97.7%	90.1%	No. highly ranked universities	0	1
Graduate/professional degree	8.0%	8.9%	State SAT score	1088	1021			
			State ACT score	21.4*	20.9			

Health & Healthcare
Score: 55.9
Rank: 166

HAZARDS & ILLNESSES	AREA	U.S. AVG	HEALTHCARE	AREA	U.S. AVG	CRIME	AREA	U.S. AVG
Air-quality score	46	37	Physicians per capita	177.2	244.2	Violent crime rate	211.9	465.5
Water-quality score	39	52	Hospital beds per capita	283.1	420.0	Change in violent crime rate	11.9%	-2.2%
Pollen/allergy score	53	61	No. teaching hospitals	0	3	Property crime rate	2,621.9	3,517.1
Cancer mortality per capita	138.3	201.9	Cost per doctor visit	$66	$77	Change in property crime rate	-8.0%	-2.1%
Depression days per month	3.3	3.5	Cost per dental visit	$64	$70			
Stress score	6	50						

Crime
Score: 75.9
Rank: 91

Transportation
Score: 36.1
Rank: 238

COMMUTE	AREA	U.S. AVG	INTERCITY SERVICES	AREA	U.S. AVG	AUTOMOTIVE	AREA	U.S. AVG
Average commute time	22.6	27.4	Major airports within 60 miles	0	1	Insurance, annual premium	$881	$1,432
Percent commutes > 60 mins.	8.7%	5.9%	Size of regional airport	None	Large	Gas, cost per gallon	$2.24	$2.49
Commute by auto	76.8%	78.9%	Daily airline activity	24	686	Daily vehicle miles per capita	19.7	24.0
Commute by mass transit	5.4%	1.9%	Amtrak service	No	No			
Work at home	5.0%	3.1%						
Mass transit miles per capita	5.37	1.87						

Leisure
Score: 41.7
Rank: 217

DINING & SHOPPING	AREA	U.S. AVG	ENTERTAINMENT	AREA	U.S. AVG	OUTDOOR ACTIVITIES	AREA	U.S. AVG
Restaurant rating	1	2	Professional sports rating	1	4	Golf-course rating	1	4
Outlet mall score	0	42	College sports rating	1	4	Ski-area rating	6	3
No. Starbucks	0	13	Zoo/aquarium rating	1	3	Sq. miles inland water	4	4
No. warehouse clubs	1	2	Amusement park rating	1	3	Miles of coastline	0.0	10.7
			Botanical garden/ arboretum rating	2	4	National Park rating	8	3

Arts & Culture
Score: 2.9
Rank: 362

MEDIA & LIBRARIES	AREA	U.S. AVG	PERFORMING ARTS	AREA	U.S. AVG	MUSEUMS	AREA	U.S. AVG
Arts radio rating	1	3	Classical music rating	1	4	Overall museum rating	1	5
No. public libraries	8	27	Ballet/dance rating	1	3	Art museum rating	1	5
Library volumes per capita	3.42	2.78	Professional theater rating	1	3	Science museum rating	1	5
			University arts programs rating	1	5	Children's museum rating	1	3

Indianapolis–Carmel, IN

Score: 85.4   Rank: 19   2004 rank: 79

Profile: Capital city
Location: Geographic center of Indiana
Elevation: 808 feet
Time zone: Eastern Standard Time

PRO	CON
Revitalized downtown	Growth and sprawl
Sports and recreation	Crime rates
Strong buying power	Air quality

Indianapolis, once a poster child for blighted Midwestern old-economy cities, is now a showcase for publicly coordinated and funded urban renewal. The 5-year growth rate of 7.5% is one of the Midwest's highest. The city features a city/county "Unigov" government system, which has worked well for coordinated planning and public-redevelopment efforts. Cost of living at 81.5 is very attractive for this type of city, but stops far short of telling the whole story. The vastly renewed downtown core boasts attractive new buildings, pedestrian zones, and Conseco Fieldhouse, a state-of-the-art sports arena, anchored by the 1990s Canal and White River State Park redevelopments. The area has a diverse industrial base of high-tech and agricultural industries, and serves as headquarters to pharmaceutical and research giant Eli Lilly along with a strong presence of financial services, publishing, industrial automation, and software companies. Spectator sports, including the NBA Pacers, 2007 Super Bowl Champion NFL Colts, and a few minor league franchises, are a huge draw. The venerable Indianapolis Motor Speedway hosts the Indianapolis 500 (IndyCar series), the Brickyard 400 (NASCAR), and the U.S. Grand Prix (Formula One). Pro and college sports—particularly basketball—get enormous attention. The NCAA Hall of Fame is located downtown, and the city frequently hosts portions of the NCAA basketball tournament. "Indy" boasts a well-rounded arts and cultural scene and the educational opportunities of the nearby Indiana-Purdue joint campus (IUPUI) and Butler University.

Access and transportation around the city are aided by a grid with radiating spokes and a circular beltway (I-465). Residential neighborhoods spread out in all directions, with the fashionable and attractive Carmel, Fishers, and Noblesville towards the north. Sections immediately south are more commercial and industrial, while areas farther to the south contain recreational opportunities at Brown County State Park and the nearby wooded and hilly town of Nashville. In part because of Southwest Airlines, air service features some of the best discounts in the Midwest. The low living costs combined with strong incomes produce a Buying Power Index of 148.9, fourth best in the country. Some traffic problems have emerged on commute corridors particularly in the north,

and the area has experienced some effects of the decline in the auto industry. Crime rates run a bit above average and air quality is somewhat worse. But these are minor issues; overall, Indy is one of the brighter spots in today's Midwest.

The surrounding terrain is mainly flat with small wooded areas dotting a largely agricultural landscape. The climate is continental with warm, humid summers, but without a dry season and little extreme heat. Precipitation is evenly distributed throughout the year, and winters are cold and variable with intermittent rain and snow. Snowfalls of 3 inches or more occur on average of two to three times each winter. First freeze is mid- to late October; last is late April.

Population

DEMOGRAPHICS	AREA	U.S. AVG
Population	1,626,173	
Population density per sq. mile	420.9	358.5
Population growth	33.3%	21.1%
Median age	35.1	36.1
Percent Democrat	39.1%	44.5%
Percent Republican	60.2%	54.5%

ETHNIC COMPOSITION	AREA	U.S. AVG
White	80.4%	79.0%
Black	14.3%	10.5%
Asian	1.7%	2.7%
Hispanic	3.5%	10.6%
Religious observance	40.8%	48.9%
Diversity measure	34.1	40.1

RESIDENT PROFILE	AREA	U.S. AVG
Single	30.8%	32.4%
Married	54.2%	52.7%
Divorced/separated	15.0%	14.9%
Married with children	24.9%	23.7%
Single with children	9.4%	9.1%
Percent over age 65	10.7%	12.9%

Economy & Jobs
Score: 59.4
Rank: 152

INCOME	AREA	U.S. AVG
Per capita income	$26,927	$23,235
Household income	$54,142	$46,414
Household income < $25K	20.4%	26.2%
Household income > $75K	31.7%	25.4%
Household income growth	12.4%	13.6%

EMPLOYMENT	AREA	U.S. AVG
Unemployment rate	4.6%	4.7%
Recent job growth	0.4%	1.3%
Projected future job growth	9.8%	11.5%
White collar	62.4%	57.8%
Blue collar	24.0%	25.2%

EMPLOYING INDUSTRIES	AREA	U.S. AVG
Largest: Manufacturing		
Percent manufacturing	14.7%	15.4%
Percent public sector	10.5%	15.7%
Percent construction	9.3%	9.9%

Cost of Living
Score: 74.9
Rank: 93

INDEXES & TAXES	AREA	U.S. AVG
Cost of Living Index	81.5	100.0
Buying Power Index	148.9	100.0
Income tax rate	4.07%	4.70%
Sales tax rate	6.00%	6.58%
Property tax rate	$10.64	$12.00

HOUSING	AREA	U.S. AVG
Median home price	$122,400	$220,000
Home price appreciation	19.6%	10.1%
Median rent	$691	$709
Homes owned	64.3%	62.3%
Home price ratio	2.3	4.2

NECESSITIES	AREA	U.S. AVG
Food Index	96.3	100.0
Housing Index	51.8	100.0
Utilities Index	98.2	100.0
Transportation Index	94.2	100.0
Healthcare Index	99.7	100.0
Miscellaneous Cost Index	94.9	100.0

Climate
Score: 48.4
Rank: 192

TEMPERATURE	AREA	U.S. AVG
Average January low	19.7	26.2
Average July high	85.4	87.4
Annual days > 90°F	15	38
Annual days < 32°F	122	89
Annual days < 0°F	7	6

PRECIPITATION	AREA	U.S. AVG
Annual inches precipitation	39.0	37.7
Annual inches snowfall	21.0	7.0
Annual days precipitation	122	109
Annual days rain > 0.5 inches	27	22
Annual days snow > 1.5 inches	6	6

COMFORTS & HAZARDS	AREA	U.S. AVG
July relative humidity	73%	66%
Annual days mostly sunny	191	208
Annual days with thunderstorms	45	39
Tornado risk score	33	18
Hurricane risk score	4	13

TEMPERATURE

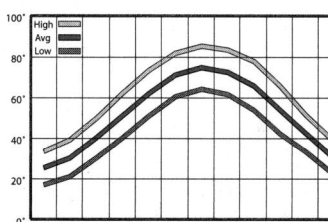

PRECIPITATION

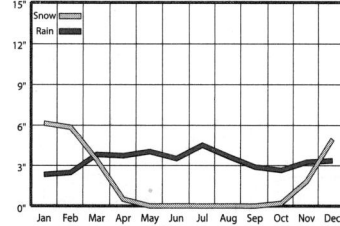

DAYS OF CLOUDS & PRECIPITATION

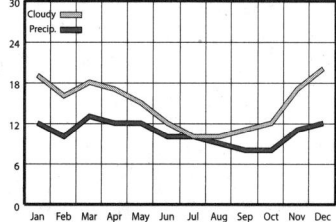

Education
Score: 73.3
Rank: 101

ACHIEVEMENT	AREA	U.S. AVG
High school degree	84.8%	82.7%
2-year college degree	6.0%	6.4%
4-year college degree	18.2%	15.7%
Graduate/professional degree	9.1%	8.9%

PUBLIC SCHOOLS	AREA	U.S. AVG
Expenditures per pupil	$6,211	$5,686
Student/teacher ratio	17.8	16.7
Attending public school	88.4%	90.1%
State SAT score	1007*	1021
State ACT score	21.7	20.9

HIGHER EDUCATION	AREA	U.S. AVG
No. 2-year colleges	7	4
No. 4-year colleges/universities	11	6
No. highly ranked universities	2	1

Health & Healthcare
Score: 23.3
Rank: 286

HAZARDS & ILLNESSES	AREA	U.S. AVG	HEALTHCARE	AREA	U.S. AVG	CRIME	AREA	U.S. AVG
Air-quality score	29	37	Physicians per capita	326.0	244.2	Violent crime rate	574.4	465.5
Water-quality score	10	52	Hospital beds per capita	357.0	420.0	Change in violent crime rate	7.7%	-2.2%
Pollen/allergy score	73	61	No. teaching hospitals	9	3	Property crime rate	4,224.8	3,517.1
Cancer mortality per capita	214.9	201.9	Cost per doctor visit	$69	$77	Change in property crime rate	3.3%	-2.1%
Depression days per month	3.6	3.5	Cost per dental visit	$62	$70			
Stress score	79	50						

Crime — **Score:** 46.0 **Rank:** 201

Transportation
Score: 65.8
Rank: 129

COMMUTE	AREA	U.S. AVG	INTERCITY SERVICES	AREA	U.S. AVG	AUTOMOTIVE	AREA	U.S. AVG
Average commute time	26.1	27.4	Major airports within 60 miles	2	1	Insurance, annual premium	$1,840	$1,432
Percent commutes > 60 mins.	4.6%	5.9%	Size of regional airport	Large	Large	Gas, cost per gallon	$2.46	$2.49
Commute by auto	83.1%	78.9%	Daily airline activity	1123	686	Daily vehicle miles per capita	33.5	24.0
Commute by mass transit	1.3%	1.9%	Amtrak service	Yes	No			
Work at home	3.1%	3.1%						
Mass transit miles per capita	1.27	1.87						

Leisure
Score: 74.3
Rank: 96

DINING & SHOPPING	AREA	U.S. AVG	ENTERTAINMENT	AREA	U.S. AVG	OUTDOOR ACTIVITIES	AREA	U.S. AVG
Restaurant rating	1	2	Professional sports rating	7	4	Golf-course rating	7	4
Outlet mall score	40	42	College sports rating	5	4	Ski-area rating	4	3
No. Starbucks	47	13	Zoo/aquarium rating	7	3	Sq. miles inland water	2	4
No. warehouse clubs	3	2	Amusement park rating	1	3	Miles of coastline	0.0	10.7
			Botanical garden/ arboretum rating	9	4	National Park rating	1	3

Arts & Culture
Score: 89.6
Rank: 39

MEDIA & LIBRARIES	AREA	U.S. AVG	PERFORMING ARTS	AREA	U.S. AVG	MUSEUMS	AREA	U.S. AVG
Arts radio rating	7	3	Classical music rating	7	4	Overall museum rating	9	5
No. public libraries	65	27	Ballet/dance rating	6	3	Art museum rating	9	5
Library volumes per capita	3.45	2.78	Professional theater rating	8	3	Science museum rating	10	5
			University arts programs rating	8	5	Children's museum rating	9	3

Iowa City, IA

Score: 82.5　**Rank:** 32　**2004 rank:** 191

Profile: College town
Location: Eastern Iowa along I-80
Elevation: 708 feet
Time zone: Central Standard Time

PRO
College-town amenities
Diverse economy
Educated population

CON
Harsh winters
Cost of housing
Outdoor recreation

Once the capital of the state, Iowa City is both home of the University of Iowa and a livable city boasting a diverse cultural environment, attractive downtown, and historic campus buildings. True to college-town form, the area has the highest housing costs in the state and one of the highest levels of educational attainment in the country. The city is well educated, progressive, and active, and has a strong community feel. An assortment of shops, restaurants, and entertainment venues in a lively downtown and Iowa River riverfront setting are anchored by a large pedestrian mall. The economic base, aside from the university, is a mix of agricultural, light manufacturing, high-tech, and biotech businesses. Good older tree-lined city neighborhoods lie mostly east and south of downtown, with more suburban environments lying northeast and west towards the small town of Coralville. Large retail developments are confined mainly to the Interstate 80 corridor, and growth and sprawl issues are modest. Although the area is isolated from big-city services (110 miles away in Des Moines), an improved recognition of its economic status and cultural assets has produced a higher ranking in this edition.

A scenic mix of flat river valleys and wooded undulating hills dominate the landscape. Summers are warm and humid, punctuated by frequent thunderstorms, although nearby hills may lessen the severity. Winters are cold and variable, although the hills again shelter the area from some northern fronts. That said, below-zero evening temperatures are fairly common, and blizzards do occur. First freeze is mid-October; last is late April.

DEMOGRAPHICS	AREA	U.S. AVG	ETHNIC COMPOSITION	AREA	U.S. AVG	RESIDENT PROFILE	AREA	U.S. AVG
Population	138,941		White	89.1%	79.0%	Single	42.2%	32.4%
Population density per sq. mile	117.4	358.5	Black	2.8%	10.5%	Married	46.6%	52.7%
Population growth	20.2%	21.1%	Asian	5.0%	2.7%	Divorced/separated	11.2%	14.9%
Median age	32.5	36.1	Hispanic	2.7%	10.6%	Married with children	21.6%	23.7%
Percent Democrat	60.8%	44.5%	Religious observance	40.1%	48.9%	Single with children	5.7%	9.1%
Percent Republican	38.0%	54.5%	Diversity measure	24.3	40.1	Percent over age 65	9.2%	12.9%

Economy & Jobs
Score: 89.8
Rank: 39

INCOME	AREA	U.S. AVG
Per capita income	$25,223	$23,235
Household income	$45,946	$46,414
Household income < $25K	26.5%	26.2%
Household income > $75K	26.8%	25.4%
Household income growth	15.1%	13.6%

EMPLOYMENT	AREA	U.S. AVG
Unemployment rate	2.7%	4.7%
Recent job growth	4.0%	1.3%
Projected future job growth	14.3%	11.5%
White collar	65.7%	57.8%
Blue collar	17.0%	25.2%

EMPLOYING INDUSTRIES	AREA	U.S. AVG
Largest: Healthcare & Social Assistance		
Percent manufacturing	10.3%	15.4%
Percent public sector	29.5%	15.7%
Percent construction	6.7%	9.9%

Cost of Living
Score: 49.7
Rank: 188

INDEXES & TAXES	AREA	U.S. AVG
Cost of Living Index	96.5	100.0
Buying Power Index	106.7	100.0
Income tax rate	7.75%	4.70%
Sales tax rate	5.31%	6.58%
Property tax rate	$12.45	$12.00

HOUSING	AREA	U.S. AVG
Median home price	$206,700	$220,000
Home price appreciation	27.9%	10.1%
Median rent	$657	$709
Homes owned	58.0%	62.3%
Home price ratio	4.5	4.2

NECESSITIES	AREA	U.S. AVG
Food Index	89.4	100.0
Housing Index	55.3	100.0
Utilities Index	133.5	100.0
Transportation Index	97.4	100.0
Healthcare Index	92.0	100.0
Miscellaneous Cost Index	99.0	100.0

Climate
Score: 23.8
Rank: 284

TEMPERATURE	AREA	U.S. AVG
Average January low	5.0	26.2
Average July high	84.0	87.4
Annual days > 90°F	16	38
Annual days < 32°F	157	89
Annual days < 0°F	29	6

PRECIPITATION	AREA	U.S. AVG
Annual inches precipitation	34.0	37.7
Annual inches snowfall	32.0	7.0
Annual days precipitation	107	109
Annual days rain > 0.5 inches	24	22
Annual days snow > 1.5 inches	9	6

COMFORTS & HAZARDS	AREA	U.S. AVG
July relative humidity	73%	66%
Annual days mostly sunny	194	208
Annual days with thunderstorms	41	39
Tornado risk score	22	18
Hurricane risk score	0	13

TEMPERATURE

PRECIPITATION

DAYS OF CLOUDS & PRECIPITATION

Education
Score: 96.5
Rank: 14

ACHIEVEMENT	AREA	U.S. AVG
High school degree	92.0%	82.7%
2-year college degree	7.4%	6.4%
4-year college degree	24.1%	15.7%
Graduate/professional degree	18.9%	8.9%

PUBLIC SCHOOLS	AREA	U.S. AVG
Expenditures per pupil	$5,442	$5,686
Student/teacher ratio	16.1	16.7
Attending public school	90.9%	90.1%
State SAT score	1215	1021
State ACT score	22.1*	20.9

HIGHER EDUCATION	AREA	U.S. AVG
No. 2-year colleges	1	4
No. 4-year colleges/universities	1	6
No. highly ranked universities	1	1

Health & Healthcare
Score: 99.7
Rank: 2

HAZARDS & ILLNESSES	AREA	U.S. AVG
Air-quality score	51	37
Water-quality score	71	52
Pollen/allergy score	46	61
Cancer mortality per capita	223.8	201.9
Depression days per month	2.5	3.5
Stress score	1	50

HEALTHCARE	AREA	U.S. AVG
Physicians per capita	927.8	244.2
Hospital beds per capita	778.0	420.0
No. teaching hospitals	2	3
Cost per doctor visit	$72	$77
Cost per dental visit	$60	$70

Crime
Score: 86.9
Rank: 49

CRIME	AREA	U.S. AVG
Violent crime rate	242.1	465.5
Change in violent crime rate	-18.7%	-2.2%
Property crime rate	2,165.3	3,517.1
Change in property crime rate	-11.5%	-2.1%

Transportation
Score: 61.2
Rank: 146

COMMUTE	AREA	U.S. AVG
Average commute time	20.2	27.4
Percent commutes > 60 mins.	2.5%	5.9%
Commute by auto	69.4%	78.9%
Commute by mass transit	4.4%	1.9%
Work at home	4.1%	3.1%
Mass transit miles per capita	4.43	1.87

INTERCITY SERVICES	AREA	U.S. AVG
Major airports within 60 miles	0	1
Size of regional airport	Small	Large
Daily airline activity	58	686
Amtrak service	No	No

AUTOMOTIVE	AREA	U.S. AVG
Insurance, annual premium	$825	$1,432
Gas, cost per gallon	$2.50	$2.49
Daily vehicle miles per capita	21.6	24.0

Leisure
Score: 22.2
Rank: 290

DINING & SHOPPING	AREA	U.S. AVG
Restaurant rating	1	2
Outlet mall score	58	42
No. Starbucks	2	13
No. warehouse clubs	0	2

ENTERTAINMENT	AREA	U.S. AVG
Professional sports rating	2	4
College sports rating	6	4
Zoo/aquarium rating	1	3
Amusement park rating	1	3
Botanical garden/arboretum rating	1	4

OUTDOOR ACTIVITIES	AREA	U.S. AVG
Golf-course rating	2	4
Ski-area rating	1	3
Sq. miles inland water	2	4
Miles of coastline	0.0	10.7
National Park rating	1	3

MEDIA & LIBRARIES	AREA	U.S. AVG	PERFORMING ARTS	AREA	U.S. AVG	MUSEUMS	AREA	U.S. AVG
Arts radio rating	7	3	Classical music rating	1	4	Overall museum rating	4	5
No. public libraries	8	27	Ballet/dance rating	1	3	Art museum rating	5	5
Library volumes per capita	3.61	2.78	Professional theater rating	1	3	Science museum rating	6	5
			University arts programs rating	5	5	Children's museum rating	1	3

Arts & Culture
Score: 59.4
Rank: 152

Ithaca, NY

Score: 57.4   **Rank:** 197   **2004 rank:** not ranked

Profile: College town
Location: Central upstate New York, 60 miles southwest of Syracuse
Elevation: 836 feet
Time zone: Eastern Standard Time

PRO	CON
Attractive downtown	Clouds and rain
College-town amenities	Harsh winters
Educated population	Isolation

Ithaca is most noted as home to Cornell University. As might be expected, the town is attractive and progressive, arts and culture activities are plentiful, and educational attainment is high. Additionally, the location, at the south end of the Finger Lakes region, affords access to nearby outdoor recreation, interesting landscapes, and a number of wineries. The economy is one of the few in central New York that is growing—albeit slowly—bolstered by the Ivy League university and the many small new-economy businesses it attracts. Downtown is clean and prosperous, although a recent shift toward large retailers on the outskirts has some locals concerned. Cost of living is reasonable for the region. Larger cities, such as Syracuse, can be hard to get to in bad weather, but Ithaca has good air service for its size. Ithaca loses ranking points due to climate, a soft job-growth picture, and cost of living, but for those who can navigate the climate and economic challenges, it is better than the ranking suggests.

Ithaca sits at the southern tip of Cayuga Lake in a hilly area of central New York. The city itself is located on a flat to moderately rising shoreline area, growing into the dense deciduous-wooded surrounding hills. The Lake Ontario–influenced climate produces frequent precipitation—almost 1 day in 2 on average year-round. Summers are warm but seldom oppressive, with typically cool evenings when breezes come off the lake. Winters are cold, long, and dreary, with only a few subzero readings each year. Snowfall is moderate but may become heavy at times, and snow cover persists most of the winter, especially in the hills. First freeze is early October; last is in early May.

Population

DEMOGRAPHICS	AREA	U.S. AVG	ETHNIC COMPOSITION	AREA	U.S. AVG	RESIDENT PROFILE	AREA	U.S. AVG
Population	103,641		White	82.2%	79.0%	Single	46.5%	32.4%
Population density per sq. mile	217.7	358.5	Black	4.0%	10.5%	Married	38.8%	52.7%
Population growth	10.1%	21.1%	Asian	9.5%	2.7%	Divorced/separated	14.7%	14.9%
Median age	30.8	36.1	Hispanic	3.8%	10.6%	Married with children	18.2%	23.7%
Percent Democrat	64.2%	44.5%	Religious observance	26.5%	48.9%	Single with children	7.4%	9.1%
Percent Republican	33.0%	54.5%	Diversity measure	36.3	40.1	Percent over age 65	9.6%	12.9%

Economy & Jobs
Score: 39.6
Rank: 226

INCOME	AREA	U.S. AVG	EMPLOYMENT	AREA	U.S. AVG	EMPLOYING INDUSTRIES	AREA	U.S. AVG
Per capita income	$23,018	$23,235	Unemployment rate	3.4%	4.7%	Largest: Manufacturing		
Household income	$42,359	$46,414	Recent job growth	1.9%	1.3%			
Household income < $25K	30.9%	26.2%	Projected future job growth	6.4%	11.5%	Percent manufacturing	7.5%	15.4%
Household income > $75K	24.0%	25.4%	White collar	71.1%	57.8%	Percent public sector	14.8%	15.7%
Household income growth	13.6%	13.6%	Blue collar	12.9%	25.2%	Percent construction	5.5%	9.9%

Cost of Living
Score: 11.0
Rank: 332

INDEXES & TAXES	AREA	U.S. AVG	HOUSING	AREA	U.S. AVG	NECESSITIES	AREA	U.S. AVG
Cost of Living Index	101.4	100.0	Median home price	$220,900	$220,000	Food Index	104.0	100.0
Buying Power Index	93.6	100.0	Home price appreciation	55.3%	10.1%	Housing Index	68.8	100.0
Income tax rate	7.13%	4.70%	Median rent	$773	$709	Utilities Index	133.2	100.0
Sales tax rate	8.25%	6.58%	Homes owned	51.1%	62.3%	Transportation Index	100.6	100.0
Property tax rate	$22.09	$12.00	Home price ratio	5.2	4.2	Healthcare Index	96.6	100.0
						Miscellaneous Cost Index	96.5	100.0

Climate
Score: 9.1
Rank: 339

TEMPERATURE	AREA	U.S. AVG
Average January low	15.0	26.2
Average July high	82.0	87.4
Annual days > 90°F	9	38
Annual days < 32°F	136	89
Annual days < 0°F	8	6

PRECIPITATION	AREA	U.S. AVG
Annual inches precipitation	38.5	37.7
Annual inches snowfall	107.0	7.0
Annual days precipitation	170	109
Annual days rain > 0.5 inches	22	22
Annual days snow > 1.5 inches	15	6

COMFORTS & HAZARDS	AREA	U.S. AVG
July relative humidity	59%	66%
Annual days mostly sunny	164	208
Annual days with thunderstorms	29	39
Tornado risk score	1	18
Hurricane risk score	1	13

TEMPERATURE
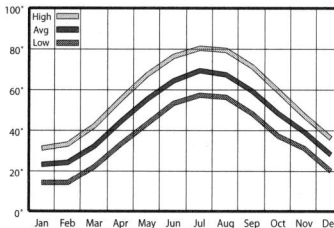

PRECIPITATION
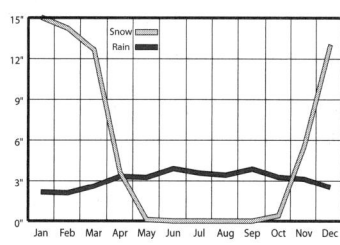

DAYS OF CLOUDS & PRECIPITATION

Education
Score: 99.7
Rank: 2

ACHIEVEMENT	AREA	U.S. AVG
High school degree	91.5%	82.7%
2-year college degree	7.6%	6.4%
4-year college degree	21.3%	15.7%
Graduate/professional degree	27.5%	8.9%

PUBLIC SCHOOLS	AREA	U.S. AVG
Expenditures per pupil	$10,189	$5,686
Student/teacher ratio	14.0	16.7
Attending public school	97.0%	90.1%
State SAT score	1003*	1021
State ACT score	22.6	20.9

HIGHER EDUCATION	AREA	U.S. AVG
No. 2-year colleges	1	4
No. 4-year colleges/universities	2	6
No. highly ranked universities	2	1

Health & Healthcare
Score: 72.2
Rank: 105

HAZARDS & ILLNESSES	AREA	U.S. AVG
Air-quality score	55	37
Water-quality score	69	52
Pollen/allergy score	56	61
Cancer mortality per capita	180.9	201.9
Depression days per month	3.3	3.5
Stress score	3	50

HEALTHCARE	AREA	U.S. AVG
Physicians per capita	208.1	244.2
Hospital beds per capita	218.1	420.0
No. teaching hospitals	0	3
Cost per doctor visit	$78	$77
Cost per dental visit	$69	$70

Crime
Score: 99.7
Rank: 2

CRIME	AREA	U.S. AVG
Violent crime rate	115.9	465.5
Change in violent crime rate	18.9%	-2.2%
Property crime rate	2,145.3	3,517.1
Change in property crime rate	22.3%	-2.1%

Transportation
Score: 74.3
Rank: 97

COMMUTE	AREA	U.S. AVG
Average commute time	19.8	27.4
Percent commutes > 60 mins.	3.0%	5.9%
Commute by auto	60.4%	78.9%
Commute by mass transit	4.8%	1.9%
Work at home	5.1%	3.1%
Mass transit miles per capita	4.77	1.87

INTERCITY SERVICES	AREA	U.S. AVG
Major airports within 60 miles	0	1
Size of regional airport	Small	Large
Daily airline activity	271	686
Amtrak service	No	No

AUTOMOTIVE	AREA	U.S. AVG
Insurance, annual premium	$1,483	$1,432
Gas, cost per gallon	$2.56	$2.49
Daily vehicle miles per capita	14.9	24.0

Leisure
Score: 48.4
Rank: 192

DINING & SHOPPING	AREA	U.S. AVG
Restaurant rating	1	2
Outlet mall score	0	42
No. Starbucks	0	13
No. warehouse clubs	0	2

ENTERTAINMENT	AREA	U.S. AVG
Professional sports rating	1	4
College sports rating	5	4
Zoo/aquarium rating	1	3
Amusement park rating	1	3
Botanical garden/ arboretum rating	7	4

OUTDOOR ACTIVITIES	AREA	U.S. AVG
Golf-course rating	2	4
Ski-area rating	4	3
Sq. miles inland water	6	4
Miles of coastline	0.0	10.7
National Park rating	5	3

Arts & Culture
Score: 42.5
Rank: 215

MEDIA & LIBRARIES	AREA	U.S. AVG
Arts radio rating	2	3
No. public libraries	5	27
Library volumes per capita	2.06	2.78

PERFORMING ARTS	AREA	U.S. AVG
Classical music rating	3	4
Ballet/dance rating	1	3
Professional theater rating	3	3
University arts programs rating	6	5

MUSEUMS	AREA	U.S. AVG
Overall museum rating	5	5
Art museum rating	5	5
Science museum rating	6	5
Children's museum rating	3	3

Jackson, MI

Score: 51.2   **Rank:** 242   **2004 rank:** 245

Profile: Small city
Location: South-central Michigan, 75 miles west of Detroit
Elevation: 841 feet
Time zone: Eastern Standard Time

PRO	CON
Cost of living	Entertainment
Low property crime	Economy
Central location	Winter climate

Jackson, in the central-southern part of the state, is a diversified commercial and manufacturing center with some ties to the auto industry. The biggest private employer is regional utility CMS Energy, which makes its headquarters in the city. Cost of living is moderately low, air quality is good, and it has a smaller feel than most other Michigan industrial centers. Downtown is plain but clean by regional standards. Nearby Michigan International Speedway is an attraction, as are numerous festivals through the year, including a monthlong Shakespeare festival. The city benefits from college-town amenities in nearby Ann Arbor and Lansing–East Lansing, and Detroit is 75 miles west.

The area sits at the confluence of several creeks into the Kalamazoo River. The surrounding terrain is rolling and wooded with many small lakes nearby. Summers are hot and humid, and winter temperatures are among the coldest in the state. Strong winds and storm fronts bring a variety of clouds, precipitation, and winter wind chill. Snowfall is moderate, and clouds and snow cover are common during winter. First freeze is early October; last is early May.

Population

DEMOGRAPHICS	AREA	U.S. AVG	ETHNIC COMPOSITION	AREA	U.S. AVG	RESIDENT PROFILE	AREA	U.S. AVG
Population	164,114		White	88.4%	79.0%	Single	28.7%	32.4%
Population density per sq. mile	232.3	358.5	Black	7.8%	10.5%	Married	52.7%	52.7%
Population growth	9.6%	21.1%	Asian	0.7%	2.7%	Divorced/separated	18.7%	14.9%
Median age	37.3	36.1	Hispanic	2.5%	10.6%	Married with children	22.9%	23.7%
Percent Democrat	43.2%	44.5%	Religious observance	35.2%	48.9%	Single with children	10.2%	9.1%
Percent Republican	55.8%	54.5%	Diversity measure	25.0	40.1	Percent over age 65	12.8%	12.9%

Economy & Jobs
Score: 49.5
Rank: 189

INCOME	AREA	U.S. AVG	EMPLOYMENT	AREA	U.S. AVG	EMPLOYING INDUSTRIES	AREA	U.S. AVG
Per capita income	$22,571	$23,235	Unemployment rate	7.4%	4.7%	Largest: Manufacturing		
Household income	$47,696	$46,414	Recent job growth	2.3%	1.3%			
Household income < $25K	23.9%	26.2%	Projected future job growth	7.3%	11.5%	Percent manufacturing	21.5%	15.4%
Household income > $75K	25.6%	25.4%	White collar	51.8%	57.8%	Percent public sector	12.0%	15.7%
Household income growth	10.5%	13.6%	Blue collar	30.9%	25.2%	Percent construction	9.5%	9.9%

Cost of Living
Score: 74.9
Rank: 94

INDEXES & TAXES	AREA	U.S. AVG	HOUSING	AREA	U.S. AVG	NECESSITIES	AREA	U.S. AVG
Cost of Living Index	82.1	100.0	Median home price	$120,500	$220,000	Food Index	100.7	100.0
Buying Power Index	130.2	100.0	Home price appreciation	28.8%	10.1%	Housing Index	51.1	100.0
Income tax rate	4.40%	4.70%	Median rent	$606	$709	Utilities Index	86.4	100.0
Sales tax rate	6.00%	6.58%	Homes owned	71.3%	62.3%	Transportation Index	100.6	100.0
Property tax rate	$12.60	$12.00	Home price ratio	2.5	4.2	Healthcare Index	98.6	100.0
						Miscellaneous Cost Index	99.0	100.0

Climate
Score: 5.9
Rank: 351

TEMPERATURE	AREA	U.S. AVG	PRECIPITATION	AREA	U.S. AVG	COMFORTS & HAZARDS	AREA	U.S. AVG
Average January low	15.3	26.2	Annual inches precipitation	30.4	37.7	July relative humidity	74%	66%
Average July high	82.6	87.4	Annual inches snowfall	49.0	7.0	Annual days mostly sunny	179	208
Annual days > 90°F	12	38	Annual days precipitation	156	109	Annual days with thunderstorms	34	39
Annual days > 32°F	151	89	Annual days rain > 0.5 inches	18	22	Tornado risk score	20	18
Annual days < 0°F	13	6	Annual days snow > 1.5 inches	11	6	Hurricane risk score	2	13

TEMPERATURE

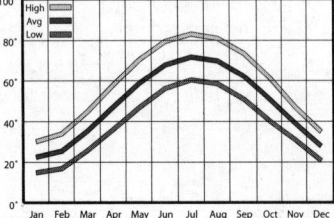

PRECIPITATION

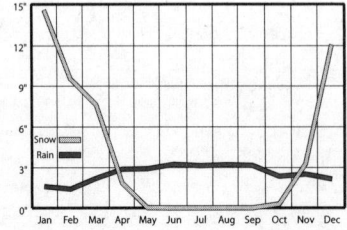

DAYS OF CLOUDS & PRECIPITATION

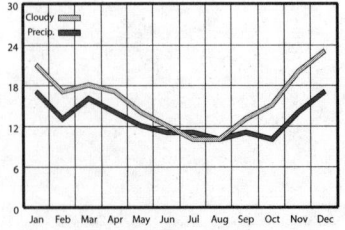

ACHIEVEMENT	AREA	U.S. AVG	PUBLIC SCHOOLS	AREA	U.S. AVG	HIGHER EDUCATION	AREA	U.S. AVG
High school degree	84.4%	82.7%	Expenditures per pupil	$5,564	$5,686	No. 2-year colleges	1	4
2-year college degree	8.0%	6.4%	Student/teacher ratio	19.6	16.7	No. 4-year colleges/universities	2	6
4-year college degree	11.3%	15.7%	Attending public school	91.0%	90.1%	No. highly ranked universities	0	1
Graduate/professional degree	5.1%	8.9%	State SAT score	1151	1021			
			State ACT score	21.5*	20.9			

Education
Score: 33.4
Rank: 250

HAZARDS & ILLNESSES	AREA	U.S. AVG	HEALTHCARE	AREA	U.S. AVG	CRIME	AREA	U.S. AVG
Air-quality score	45	37	Physicians per capita	123.2	244.2	Violent crime rate	390.5	465.5
Water-quality score	50	52	Hospital beds per capita	335.7	420.0	Change in violent crime rate	-6.4%	-2.2%
Pollen/allergy score	37	61	No. teaching hospitals	0	3	Property crime rate	2,939.2	3,517.1
Cancer mortality per capita	209.4	201.9	Cost per doctor visit	$68	$77	Change in property crime rate	6.8%	-2.1%
Depression days per month	4.0	3.5	Cost per dental visit	$66	$70			
Stress score	90	50						

Health & Healthcare
Score: 56.7
Rank: 163

Crime
Score: 61.2
Rank: 146

COMMUTE	AREA	U.S. AVG	INTERCITY SERVICES	AREA	U.S. AVG	AUTOMOTIVE	AREA	U.S. AVG
Average commute time	25.0	27.4	Major airports within 60 miles	1	1	Insurance, annual premium	$1,392	$1,432
Percent commutes > 60 mins.	6.2%	5.9%	Size of regional airport	Large	Large	Gas, cost per gallon	$2.54	$2.49
Commute by auto	83.7%	78.9%	Daily airline activity	1044	686	Daily vehicle miles per capita	25.5	24.0
Commute by mass transit	0.5%	1.9%	Amtrak service	Yes	No			
Work at home	2.8%	3.1%						
Mass transit miles per capita	0.49	1.87						

Transportation
Score: 61.0
Rank: 147

DINING & SHOPPING	AREA	U.S. AVG	ENTERTAINMENT	AREA	U.S. AVG	OUTDOOR ACTIVITIES	AREA	U.S. AVG
Restaurant rating	1	2	Professional sports rating	2	4	Golf-course rating	3	4
Outlet mall score	100	42	College sports rating	1	4	Ski-area rating	4	3
No. Starbucks	0	13	Zoo/aquarium rating	1	3	Sq. miles inland water	3	4
No. warehouse clubs	1	2	Amusement park rating	1	3	Miles of coastline	0.0	10.7
			Botanical garden/ arboretum rating	1	4	National Park rating	1	3

Leisure
Score: 32.1
Rank: 253

MEDIA & LIBRARIES	AREA	U.S. AVG	PERFORMING ARTS	AREA	U.S. AVG	MUSEUMS	AREA	U.S. AVG
Arts radio rating	1	3	Classical music rating	4	4	Overall museum rating	1	5
No. public libraries	13	27	Ballet/dance rating	1	3	Art museum rating	3	5
Library volumes per capita	2.90	2.78	Professional theater rating	1	3	Science museum rating	1	5
			University arts programs rating	3	5	Children's museum rating	1	3

Arts & Culture
Score: 31.6
Rank: 256

Jackson, MS

Score: 69.1   Rank: 98   2004 rank: 178

Profile: Capital city
Location: West-central Mississippi
Elevation: 331 feet
Time zone: Central Standard Time

PRO	CON
Cost of living	Summer heat
Arts and culture	Economy
Healthcare	Air service

Jackson is Mississippi's largest city and a hub of government, commerce, and manufacturing for the state. Civil War fires wiped out much of the town's antebellum feel and downtown isn't much of an attraction, although a new convention center is under development. There are several points of historic interest, including the capitol building, and some attractive older city neighborhoods close in. Some new development is moving to the north toward Canton, home of a new Nissan plant. The Ross Barnett Reservoir offers water recreation, and historic country drives radiate in all directions, notably north on the Natchez Trace to Canton and beyond. The University of Mississippi Medical Center adds to a strong network of healthcare facilities. There are several smaller colleges, and the area has a stronger arts presence than one might expect for such a city. At 81.0, the Cost of Living Index is among the lowest of capital cities. The city calls itself "The Best in the New South," but the economy doesn't really live up to this claim. The area is making progress but still has room for improvement.

The city is located in a wide river plain surrounded by gently rolling terrain and pine forests. The climate is significantly humid most of the year, with short mild winters that include frequent cold spells. Summer temperatures reach 90°F or higher every 2 out of 3 days, though extended periods of very hot weather are rare. Rainfall is abundant and well distributed throughout the year. Thunderstorms are common, occurring 1 out of 3 days during summer. Fall is typically the driest season. Winter snow is minimal, and ice storms occur occasionally.

Population

DEMOGRAPHICS	AREA	U.S. AVG	ETHNIC COMPOSITION	AREA	U.S. AVG	RESIDENT PROFILE	AREA	U.S. AVG
Population	516,783		White	51.5%	79.0%	Single	36.8%	32.4%
Population density per sq. mile	138.7	358.5	Black	46.3%	10.5%	Married	47.5%	52.7%
Population growth	20.4%	21.1%	Asian	0.9%	2.7%	Divorced/separated	15.7%	14.9%
Median age	34.2	36.1	Hispanic	1.1%	10.6%	Married with children	22.9%	23.7%
Percent Democrat	43.3%	44.5%	Religious observance	52.4%	48.9%	Single with children	12.4%	9.1%
Percent Republican	55.9%	54.5%	Diversity measure	45.8	40.1	Percent over age 65	10.9%	12.9%

Economy & Jobs
Score: 25.9
Rank: 277

INCOME	AREA	U.S. AVG	EMPLOYMENT	AREA	U.S. AVG	EMPLOYING INDUSTRIES	AREA	U.S. AVG
Per capita income	$21,368	$23,235	Unemployment rate	5.8%	4.7%	Largest: Healthcare & Social Assistance		
Household income	$42,820	$46,414	Recent job growth	-0.2%	1.3%			
Household income ‹ $25K	29.7%	26.2%	Projected future job growth	8.2%	11.5%	Percent manufacturing	13.2%	15.4%
Household income › $75K	23.5%	25.4%	White collar	62.7%	57.8%	Percent public sector	20.4%	15.7%
Household income growth	12.5%	13.6%	Blue collar	22.6%	25.2%	Percent construction	9.3%	9.9%

Cost of Living
Score: 70.9
Rank: 110

INDEXES & TAXES	AREA	U.S. AVG	HOUSING	AREA	U.S. AVG	NECESSITIES	AREA	U.S. AVG
Cost of Living Index	81.0	100.0	Median home price	$149,300	$220,000	Food Index	85.9	100.0
Buying Power Index	118.5	100.0	Home price appreciation	24.4%	10.1%	Housing Index	52.7	100.0
Income tax rate	5.00%	4.70%	Median rent	$629	$709	Utilities Index	83.6	100.0
Sales tax rate	7.00%	6.58%	Homes owned	65.1%	62.3%	Transportation Index	97.2	100.0
Property tax rate	$7.22	$12.00	Home price ratio	3.5	4.2	Healthcare Index	83.0	100.0
						Miscellaneous Cost Index	92.4	100.0

Climate
Score: 51.3
Rank: 181

TEMPERATURE	AREA	U.S. AVG	PRECIPITATION	AREA	U.S. AVG	COMFORTS & HAZARDS	AREA	U.S. AVG
Average January low	35.8	26.2	Annual inches precipitation	49.0	37.7	July relative humidity	75%	66%
Average July high	92.7	87.4	Annual inches snowfall	1.0	7.0	Annual days mostly sunny	217	208
Annual days › 90°F	78	38	Annual days precipitation	112	109	Annual days with thunderstorms	65	39
Annual days ‹ 32°F	47	89	Annual days rain › 0.5 inches	37	22	Tornado risk score	92	18
Annual days ‹ 0°F	0	6	Annual days snow › 1.5 inches	1	6	Hurricane risk score	25	13

TEMPERATURE

PRECIPITATION

DAYS OF CLOUDS & PRECIPITATION

Education
Score: 55.9
Rank: 166

ACHIEVEMENT	AREA	U.S. AVG	PUBLIC SCHOOLS	AREA	U.S. AVG	HIGHER EDUCATION	AREA	U.S. AVG
High school degree	80.2%	82.7%	Expenditures per pupil	$3,848	$5,686	No. 2-year colleges	6	4
2-year college degree	6.4%	6.4%	Student/teacher ratio	16.7	16.7	No. 4-year colleges/universities	8	6
4-year college degree	17.5%	15.7%	Attending public school	84.8%	90.1%	No. highly ranked universities	2	1
Graduate/professional degree	9.0%	8.9%	State SAT score	1097	1021			
			State ACT score	18.8*	20.9			

Health & Healthcare
Score: 76.5
Rank: 89

HAZARDS & ILLNESSES	AREA	U.S. AVG	HEALTHCARE	AREA	U.S. AVG	CRIME	AREA	U.S. AVG
Air-quality score	42	37	Physicians per capita	352.7	244.2	Violent crime rate	362.9	465.5
Water-quality score	25	52	Hospital beds per capita	579.4	420.0	Change in violent crime rate	-3.7%	-2.2%
Pollen/allergy score	71	61	No. teaching hospitals	2	3	Property crime rate	3,846.7	3,517.1
Cancer mortality per capita	214.2	201.9	Cost per doctor visit	$63	$77	Change in property crime rate	-4.2%	-2.1%
Depression days per month	3.7	3.5	Cost per dental visit	$83	$70			
Stress score	76	50						

Crime
Score: 51.6
Rank: 182

Transportation
Score: 3.5
Rank: 360

COMMUTE	AREA	U.S. AVG
Average commute time	25.6	27.4
Percent commutes > 60 mins.	4.8%	5.9%
Commute by auto	80.8%	78.9%
Commute by mass transit	0.6%	1.9%
Work at home	2.1%	3.1%
Mass transit miles per capita	0.61	1.87

INTERCITY SERVICES	AREA	U.S. AVG
Major airports within 60 miles	0	1
Size of regional airport	Small	Large
Daily airline activity	59	686
Amtrak service	Yes	No

AUTOMOTIVE	AREA	U.S. AVG
Insurance, annual premium	$1,459	$1,432
Gas, cost per gallon	$2.42	$2.49
Daily vehicle miles per capita	44.7	24.0

Leisure
Score: 20.6
Rank: 296

DINING & SHOPPING	AREA	U.S. AVG
Restaurant rating	1	2
Outlet mall score	11	42
No. Starbucks	2	13
No. warehouse clubs	0	2

ENTERTAINMENT	AREA	U.S. AVG
Professional sports rating	2	4
College sports rating	2	4
Zoo/aquarium rating	4	3
Amusement park rating	1	3
Botanical garden/ arboretum rating	2	4

OUTDOOR ACTIVITIES	AREA	U.S. AVG
Golf-course rating	3	4
Ski-area rating	1	3
Sq. miles inland water	2	4
Miles of coastline	0.0	10.7
National Park rating	2	3

Arts & Culture
Score: 74.9
Rank: 94

MEDIA & LIBRARIES	AREA	U.S. AVG
Arts radio rating	7	3
No. public libraries	43	27
Library volumes per capita	2.16	2.78

PERFORMING ARTS	AREA	U.S. AVG
Classical music rating	4	4
Ballet/dance rating	3	3
Professional theater rating	6	3
University arts programs rating	8	5

MUSEUMS	AREA	U.S. AVG
Overall museum rating	7	5
Art museum rating	7	5
Science museum rating	7	5
Children's museum rating	1	3

Jackson, TN

Score: 23.8   Rank: 355   2004 rank: 304

Profile: Small city
Location: West-central Tennessee
Elevation: 412 feet
Time zone: Central Standard Time

PRO	CON
Small-town feel	Crime rates
Cost of living	Entertainment
Diverse economy	Arts and culture

Jackson is a transportation center serving the agriculture industry, with cotton being a significant crop. The city is also a diverse manufacturing center for companies such as Procter & Gamble and toolmaker Porter-Cable. The town has a typical Southern-town feel with historic buildings and a vintage 1950s bus station often used as a movie set. Cost of living is low and the job base is expected to improve, as the area has received recent accolades for the quality of workforce and growth potential, though it hasn't yet shown up in the numbers. There is a popular minor league baseball team and a few other community events, but otherwise the town has little to do and little cultural interest. Until the future brings better amenities, Memphis with its big-city activities lies 90 miles west.

The surrounding countryside is flat with sections of slightly rolling farmland and deciduous woods. Summers have frequent thundershowers with regular temperatures above 90°F. Winters are changeable with periods of mild weather alternating with cool northerly air. Although temperatures below zero seldom occur, cold snaps and passing storms can deliver significant snowfall. The spring storm-track location brings occasional severe weather such as destructive tornadoes. First freeze is late October; last is April 1.

Population

DEMOGRAPHICS	AREA	U.S. AVG
Population	110,597	
Population density per sq. mile	130.8	358.5
Population growth	21.8%	21.1%
Median age	35.3	36.1
Percent Democrat	42.4%	44.5%
Percent Republican	57.2%	54.5%

ETHNIC COMPOSITION	AREA	U.S. AVG
White	67.1%	79.0%
Black	30.1%	10.5%
Asian	0.8%	2.7%
Hispanic	1.9%	10.6%
Religious observance	54.1%	48.9%
Diversity measure	46.3	40.1

RESIDENT PROFILE	AREA	U.S. AVG
Single	32.7%	32.4%
Married	51.8%	52.7%
Divorced/separated	15.5%	14.9%
Married with children	22.7%	23.7%
Single with children	10.7%	9.1%
Percent over age 65	12.5%	12.9%

Economy & Jobs
Score: 3.5
Rank: 360

INCOME	AREA	U.S. AVG
Per capita income	$21,816	$23,235
Household income	$41,957	$46,414
Household income < $25K	29.5%	26.2%
Household income > $75K	22.1%	25.4%
Household income growth	14.7%	13.6%

EMPLOYMENT	AREA	U.S. AVG
Unemployment rate	5.6%	4.7%
Recent job growth	-1.9%	1.3%
Projected future job growth	5.3%	11.5%
White collar	56.3%	57.8%
Blue collar	29.4%	25.2%

EMPLOYING INDUSTRIES	AREA	U.S. AVG
Largest: Manufacturing		
Percent manufacturing	19.8%	15.4%
Percent public sector	14.2%	15.7%
Percent construction	9.6%	9.9%

Cost of Living
Score: 89.8
Rank: 39

INDEXES & TAXES	AREA	U.S. AVG	HOUSING	AREA	U.S. AVG	NECESSITIES	AREA	U.S. AVG
Cost of Living Index	82.6	100.0	Median home price	$122,300	$220,000	Food Index	105.3	100.0
Buying Power Index	113.9	100.0	Home price appreciation	18.4%	10.1%	Housing Index	56.2	100.0
Income tax rate	0.00%	4.70%	Median rent	$617	$709	Utilities Index	77.9	100.0
Sales tax rate	9.75%	6.58%	Homes owned	64.0%	62.3%	Transportation Index	96.6	100.0
Property tax rate	$6.31	$12.00	Home price ratio	2.9	4.2	Healthcare Index	88.8	100.0
						Miscellaneous Cost Index	103.5	100.0

Climate
Score: 35.8
Rank: 239

TEMPERATURE	AREA	U.S. AVG	PRECIPITATION	AREA	U.S. AVG	COMFORTS & HAZARDS	AREA	U.S. AVG
Average January low	32.0	26.2	Annual inches precipitation	47.0	37.7	July relative humidity	70%	66%
Average July high	89.0	87.4	Annual inches snowfall	8.0	7.0	Annual days mostly sunny	209	208
Annual days > 90°F	42	38	Annual days precipitation	111	109	Annual days with thunderstorms	53	39
Annual days < 32°F	65	89	Annual days rain > 0.5 inches	34	22	Tornado risk score	16	18
Annual days < 0°F	0	6	Annual days snow > 1.5 inches	2	6	Hurricane risk score	10	13

TEMPERATURE

PRECIPITATION

DAYS OF CLOUDS & PRECIPITATION

Education
Score: 44.4
Rank: 208

ACHIEVEMENT	AREA	U.S. AVG	PUBLIC SCHOOLS	AREA	U.S. AVG	HIGHER EDUCATION	AREA	U.S. AVG
High school degree	77.9%	82.7%	Expenditures per pupil	$4,982	$5,686	No. 2-year colleges	2	4
2-year college degree	5.0%	6.4%	Student/teacher ratio	0.0	16.7	No. 4-year colleges/universities	4	6
4-year college degree	13.5%	15.7%	Attending public school	82.7%	90.1%	No. highly ranked universities	2	1
Graduate/professional degree	7.2%	8.9%	State SAT score	1142	1021			
			State ACT score	20.7*	20.9			

Health & Healthcare
Score: 91.4
Rank: 33

Crime
Score: 1.3
Rank: 368

HAZARDS & ILLNESSES	AREA	U.S. AVG	HEALTHCARE	AREA	U.S. AVG	CRIME	AREA	U.S. AVG
Air-quality score	57	37	Physicians per capita	323.9	244.2	Violent crime rate	989.0	465.5
Water-quality score	45	52	Hospital beds per capita	809.2	420.0	Change in violent crime rate	11.2%	-2.2%
Pollen/allergy score	66	61	No. teaching hospitals	1	3	Property crime rate	5,607.8	3,517.1
Cancer mortality per capita	215.6	201.9	Cost per doctor visit	$76	$77	Change in property crime rate	-1.0%	-2.1%
Depression days per month	2.5	3.5	Cost per dental visit	$55	$70			
Stress score	71	50						

Transportation
Score: 62.6
Rank: 141

COMMUTE	AREA	U.S. AVG	INTERCITY SERVICES	AREA	U.S. AVG	AUTOMOTIVE	AREA	U.S. AVG
Average commute time	21.8	27.4	Major airports within 60 miles	1	1	Insurance, annual premium	$845	$1,432
Percent commutes > 60 mins.	4.0%	5.9%	Size of regional airport	Medium	Large	Gas, cost per gallon	$2.46	$2.49
Commute by auto	83.8%	78.9%	Daily airline activity	500	686	Daily vehicle miles per capita	33.1	24.0
Commute by mass transit	0.7%	1.9%	Amtrak service	No	No			
Work at home	2.0%	3.1%						
Mass transit miles per capita	0.65	1.87						

Leisure
Score: 0.0
Rank: 373

DINING & SHOPPING	AREA	U.S. AVG	ENTERTAINMENT	AREA	U.S. AVG	OUTDOOR ACTIVITIES	AREA	U.S. AVG
Restaurant rating	1	2	Professional sports rating	2	4	Golf-course rating	1	4
Outlet mall score	2	42	College sports rating	1	4	Ski-area rating	1	3
No. Starbucks	1	13	Zoo/aquarium rating	1	3	Sq. miles inland water	1	4
No. warehouse clubs	0	2	Amusement park rating	1	3	Miles of coastline	0.0	10.7
			Botanical garden/arboretum rating	2	4	National Park rating	1	3

Arts & Culture
Score: 11.8
Rank: 329

MEDIA & LIBRARIES	AREA	U.S. AVG	PERFORMING ARTS	AREA	U.S. AVG	MUSEUMS	AREA	U.S. AVG
Arts radio rating	1	3	Classical music rating	3	4	Overall museum rating	3	5
No. public libraries	2	27	Ballet/dance rating	1	3	Art museum rating	1	5
Library volumes per capita	1.46	2.78	Professional theater rating	1	3	Science museum rating	5	5
			University arts programs rating	5	5	Children's museum rating	1	3

Jacksonville, FL

Score: 48.9   Rank: 252   2004 rank: 82

Profile: Large city
Location: Extreme northern Atlantic Coast of Florida, 20 miles inland along the St. Johns River
Elevation: 31 feet
Time zone: Eastern Standard Time

PRO	CON
Attractive downtown	Crime rates
Economy	Growth and sprawl
Arts and culture	Long commutes

Jacksonville is a large commercial and financial center with the most "northern" feel among large cities in Florida. Modern skyscrapers line a well-defined downtown and waterfront area, and the city spreads in all directions, especially south and west, from there. It is ultimately a mix of Northern, Southern, and Florida cities, prosperous and water-loving and culturally conscious but not too tourism-dependent. The economy is diverse, with an assortment of banking and financial institutions, a bustling port, and large corporations such as BellSouth and CSX. Sprawling and some fairly unattractive residential areas surround downtown, and the population has relatively low educational attainment. The best suburbs lie south toward Orange Park and east toward the coast. There is plenty to do in town and nearby along the coast 20 miles east, including the world-class beaches, golf courses, and resort areas of Amelia Island to the northeast and the historic area of St. Augustine to the southeast. Although healthcare statistics are low in general, they are enhanced by the presence of a Mayo Clinic. Home prices have escalated rapidly, as they have in most of Florida, but remain reasonable on a state and national scale. Although costs have escalated and the area does score poorly in some categories, we think the city is better than the score indicates.

The terrain surrounding Jacksonville is level. Summers are long, warm, and relatively humid. Inland summer temperatures frequently exceed 90°F while remaining in the 80s at the beach. Summer thunderstorms are common, occurring every other day. The area is vulnerable to hurricanes, but is far enough north so that most of them lose strength before reaching the area. Winters are mild.

Population

DEMOGRAPHICS	AREA	U.S. AVG	ETHNIC COMPOSITION	AREA	U.S. AVG	RESIDENT PROFILE	AREA	U.S. AVG
Population	1,243,108		White	70.8%	79.0%	Single	30.0%	32.4%
Population density per sq. mile	386.0	358.5	Black	22.8%	10.5%	Married	52.6%	52.7%
Population growth	36.6%	21.1%	Asian	2.7%	2.7%	Divorced/separated	17.4%	14.9%
Median age	36.1	36.1	Hispanic	4.3%	10.6%	Married with children	23.3%	23.7%
Percent Democrat	36.7%	44.5%	Religious observance	43.0%	48.9%	Single with children	10.4%	9.1%
Percent Republican	62.7%	54.5%	Diversity measure	46.5	40.1	Percent over age 65	11.3%	12.9%

Economy & Jobs
Score: 93.3
Rank: 26

INCOME	AREA	U.S. AVG	EMPLOYMENT	AREA	U.S. AVG	EMPLOYING INDUSTRIES	AREA	U.S. AVG
Per capita income	$24,895	$23,235	Unemployment rate	4.2%	4.7%	Largest: Finance & Insurance		
Household income	$48,810	$46,414	Recent job growth	4.1%	1.3%			
Household income < $25K	22.9%	26.2%	Projected future job growth	21.6%	11.5%	Percent manufacturing	11.8%	15.4%
Household income > $75K	27.2%	25.4%	White collar	63.3%	57.8%	Percent public sector	14.0%	15.7%
Household income growth	13.0%	13.6%	Blue collar	21.9%	25.2%	Percent construction	10.2%	9.9%

Cost of Living
Score: 80.2
Rank: 75

INDEXES & TAXES	AREA	U.S. AVG	HOUSING	AREA	U.S. AVG	NECESSITIES	AREA	U.S. AVG
Cost of Living Index	96.1	100.0	Median home price	$213,000	$220,000	Food Index	100.6	100.0
Buying Power Index	113.8	100.0	Home price appreciation	78.1%	10.1%	Housing Index	75.6	100.0
Income tax rate	0.00%	4.70%	Median rent	$774	$709	Utilities Index	87.5	100.0
Sales tax rate	6.88%	6.58%	Homes owned	62.3%	62.3%	Transportation Index	98.5	100.0
Property tax rate	$11.69	$12.00	Home price ratio	4.4	4.2	Healthcare Index	88.3	100.0
						Miscellaneous Cost Index	98.7	100.0

Climate
Score: 74.1
Rank: 97

TEMPERATURE	AREA	U.S. AVG	PRECIPITATION	AREA	U.S. AVG	COMFORTS & HAZARDS	AREA	U.S. AVG
Average January low	44.5	26.2	Annual inches precipitation	54.0	37.7	July relative humidity	75%	66%
Average July high	90.0	87.4	Annual inches snowfall	0.0	7.0	Annual days mostly sunny	226	208
Annual days > 90°F	82	38	Annual days precipitation	116	109	Annual days with thunderstorms	64	39
Annual days < 32°F	12	89	Annual days rain > 0.5 inches	30	22	Tornado risk score	14	18
Annual days < 0°F	0	6	Annual days snow > 1.5 inches	0	6	Hurricane risk score	63	13

TEMPERATURE

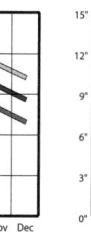

PRECIPITATION

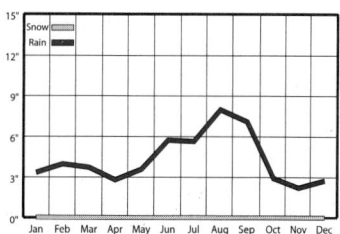

DAYS OF CLOUDS & PRECIPITATION

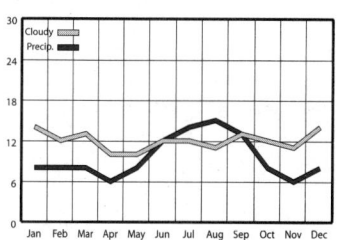

ACHIEVEMENT	AREA	U.S. AVG
High school degree	83.7%	82.7%
2-year college degree	7.6%	6.4%
4-year college degree	15.5%	15.7%
Graduate/professional degree	7.3%	8.9%

Education
Score: 59.9
Rank: 151

PUBLIC SCHOOLS	AREA	U.S. AVG
Expenditures per pupil	$4,691	$5,686
Student/teacher ratio	18.4	16.7
Attending public school	86.4%	90.1%
State SAT score	993*	1021
State ACT score	20.3	20.9

HIGHER EDUCATION	AREA	U.S. AVG
No. 2-year colleges	6	4
No. 4-year colleges/universities	12	6
No. highly ranked universities	2	1

HAZARDS & ILLNESSES	AREA	U.S. AVG
Air-quality score	24	37
Water-quality score	28	52
Pollen/allergy score	65	61
Cancer mortality per capita	289.0	201.9
Depression days per month	3.5	3.5
Stress score	88	50

Health & Healthcare
Score: 11.0
Rank: 332

HEALTHCARE	AREA	U.S. AVG
Physicians per capita	257.3	244.2
Hospital beds per capita	353.5	420.0
No. teaching hospitals	6	3
Cost per doctor visit	$63	$77
Cost per dental visit	$67	$70

Crime
Score: 11.0
Rank: 332

CRIME	AREA	U.S. AVG
Violent crime rate	741.9	465.5
Change in violent crime rate	1.5%	-2.2%
Property crime rate	4,511.9	3,517.1
Change in property crime rate	0.4%	-2.1%

COMMUTE	AREA	U.S. AVG
Average commute time	28.7	27.4
Percent commutes > 60 mins.	6.1%	5.9%
Commute by auto	80.6%	78.9%
Commute by mass transit	1.4%	1.9%
Work at home	2.3%	3.1%
Mass transit miles per capita	1.39	1.87

Transportation
Score: 0.8
Rank: 370

INTERCITY SERVICES	AREA	U.S. AVG
Major airports within 60 miles	1	1
Size of regional airport	Medium	Large
Daily airline activity	156	686
Amtrak service	Yes	No

AUTOMOTIVE	AREA	U.S. AVG
Insurance, annual premium	$2,005	$1,432
Gas, cost per gallon	$2.55	$2.49
Daily vehicle miles per capita	33.5	24.0

DINING & SHOPPING	AREA	U.S. AVG
Restaurant rating	3	2
Outlet mall score	75	42
No. Starbucks	26	13
No. warehouse clubs	5	2

Leisure
Score: 86.4
Rank: 51

ENTERTAINMENT	AREA	U.S. AVG
Professional sports rating	6	4
College sports rating	5	4
Zoo/aquarium rating	8	3
Amusement park rating	1	3
Botanical garden/ arboretum rating	3	4

OUTDOOR ACTIVITIES	AREA	U.S. AVG
Golf-course rating	6	4
Ski-area rating	1	3
Sq. miles inland water	10	4
Miles of coastline	79.9	10.7
National Park rating	2	3

MEDIA & LIBRARIES	AREA	U.S. AVG
Arts radio rating	1	3
No. public libraries	27	27
Library volumes per capita	2.66	2.78

Arts & Culture
Score: 65.2
Rank: 129

PERFORMING ARTS	AREA	U.S. AVG
Classical music rating	5	4
Ballet/dance rating	1	3
Professional theater rating	1	3
University arts programs rating	7	5

MUSEUMS	AREA	U.S. AVG
Overall museum rating	9	5
Art museum rating	8	5
Science museum rating	8	5
Children's museum rating	1	3

Jacksonville, NC

Score: 44.6   **Rank:** 287   **2004 rank:** 318

Profile: Military town
Location: Southeast North Carolina near Atlantic Coast 60 miles north of Wilmington
Elevation: 30 feet
Time zone: Eastern Standard Time

PRO
Nearby coastal areas
Low crime rates
Cost of living

CON
Arts and culture
Isolation
Economy

Jacksonville is located near the Atlantic Coast at the mouth of the New River. The 153,000-acre Camp Lejeune Marine base is the mainstay of the local economy and lifestyle, and accounts for about half of the 70,000 Jacksonville city residents. The military presence gives a stable economy but little growth opportunity. The area is also known for boating and watersports. Cost of living is quite low (79.5) and the winter climate is attractive, but the economy isn't very diverse and the area has few cultural and service amenities. It is quite isolated by geography, road structure, and distance from other North Carolina cities; Raleigh is about 130 miles northwest.

Jacksonville is located at the head of a bay formed by the New River, in a mostly level, often marshy coastal plain. Summers days are warm and very humid, and are sometimes cooled by marine breezes depending on the prevailing winds. High temperatures of 90°F are reached every other day in summer, but 100°F heat is rare. Winters are cool and wet but seldom cold. The area gets significant rain in all seasons, with peaks during summer thunderstorms and coastal storms.

DEMOGRAPHICS

DEMOGRAPHICS	AREA	U.S. AVG
Population	145,656	
Population density per sq. mile	190.0	358.5
Population growth	-2.8%	21.1%
Median age	25.0	36.1
Percent Democrat	30.2%	44.5%
Percent Republican	69.5%	54.5%

ETHNIC COMPOSITION	AREA	U.S. AVG
White	72.2%	79.0%
Black	17.7%	10.5%
Asian	2.5%	2.7%
Hispanic	5.3%	10.6%
Religious observance	25.8%	48.9%
Diversity measure	50.1	40.1

RESIDENT PROFILE	AREA	U.S. AVG
Single	34.4%	32.4%
Married	51.2%	52.7%
Divorced/separated	14.5%	14.9%
Married with children	32.4%	23.7%
Single with children	10.1%	9.1%
Percent over age 65	7.3%	12.9%

Economy & Jobs
Score: 17.1
Rank: 309

INCOME	AREA	U.S. AVG
Per capita income	$17,267	$23,235
Household income	$39,335	$46,414
Household income < $25K	28.1%	26.2%
Household income > $75K	15.5%	25.4%
Household income growth	16.5%	13.6%

EMPLOYMENT	AREA	U.S. AVG
Unemployment rate	6.1%	4.7%
Recent job growth	2.0%	1.3%
Projected future job growth	2.7%	11.5%
White collar	53.7%	57.8%
Blue collar	25.4%	25.2%

EMPLOYING INDUSTRIES	AREA	U.S. AVG
Largest: Retail Trade		
Percent manufacturing	11.4%	15.4%
Percent public sector	25.6%	15.7%
Percent construction	14.0%	9.9%

Cost of Living
Score: 66.8
Rank: 125

INDEXES & TAXES	AREA	U.S. AVG
Cost of Living Index	79.5	100.0
Buying Power Index	110.9	100.0
Income tax rate	7.00%	4.70%
Sales tax rate	7.00%	6.58%
Property tax rate	$7.44	$12.00

HOUSING	AREA	U.S. AVG
Median home price	$116,300	$220,000
Home price appreciation	44.4%	10.1%
Median rent	$557	$709
Homes owned	50.4%	62.3%
Home price ratio	3.0	4.2

NECESSITIES	AREA	U.S. AVG
Food Index	96.6	100.0
Housing Index	48.7	100.0
Utilities Index	106.1	100.0
Transportation Index	83.7	100.0
Healthcare Index	90.0	100.0
Miscellaneous Cost Index	98.6	100.0

Climate
Score: 52.4
Rank: 177

TEMPERATURE	AREA	U.S. AVG
Average January low	36.2	26.2
Average July high	88.8	87.4
Annual days > 90°F	45	38
Annual days < 32°F	45	89
Annual days < 0°F	0	6

PRECIPITATION	AREA	U.S. AVG
Annual inches precipitation	54.0	37.7
Annual inches snowfall	1.8	7.0
Annual days precipitation	117	109
Annual days rain > 0.5 inches	33	22
Annual days snow > 1.5 inches	1	6

COMFORTS & HAZARDS	AREA	U.S. AVG
July relative humidity	75%	66%
Annual days mostly sunny	219	208
Annual days with thunderstorms	46	39
Tornado risk score	18	18
Hurricane risk score	70	13

TEMPERATURE

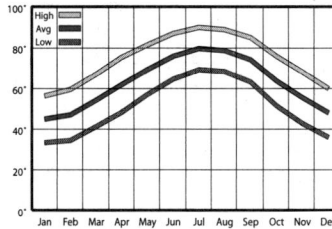

PRECIPITATION

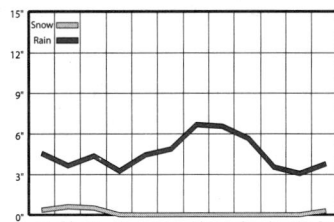

DAYS OF CLOUDS & PRECIPITATION

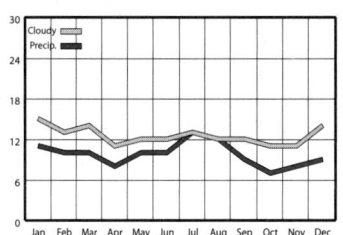

Education
Score: 22.7
Rank: 289

ACHIEVEMENT	AREA	U.S. AVG
High school degree	84.4%	82.7%
2-year college degree	8.1%	6.4%
4-year college degree	10.3%	15.7%
Graduate/professional degree	4.4%	8.9%

PUBLIC SCHOOLS	AREA	U.S. AVG
Expenditures per pupil	$4,146	$5,686
Student/teacher ratio	27.4	16.7
Attending public school	96.3%	90.1%
State SAT score	1008*	1021
State ACT score	20.5	20.9

HIGHER EDUCATION	AREA	U.S. AVG
No. 2-year colleges	1	4
No. 4-year colleges/universities	0	6
No. highly ranked universities	0	1

Health & Healthcare
Score: 55.1
Rank: 169

HAZARDS & ILLNESSES	AREA	U.S. AVG
Air-quality score	51	37
Water-quality score	86	52
Pollen/allergy score	65	61
Cancer mortality per capita	215.9	201.9
Depression days per month	3.7	3.5
Stress score	7	50

HEALTHCARE	AREA	U.S. AVG
Physicians per capita	134.2	244.2
Hospital beds per capita	161.3	420.0
No. teaching hospitals	0	3
Cost per doctor visit	$64	$77
Cost per dental visit	$56	$70

Crime
Score: 98.7
Rank: 6

CRIME	AREA	U.S. AVG
Violent crime rate	147.3	465.5
Change in violent crime rate	-10.3%	-2.2%
Property crime rate	2,128.8	3,517.1
Change in property crime rate	-8.8%	-2.1%

Transportation
Score: 21.1
Rank: 296

COMMUTE	AREA	U.S. AVG	INTERCITY SERVICES	AREA	U.S. AVG	AUTOMOTIVE	AREA	U.S. AVG
Average commute time	22.6	27.4	Major airports within 60 miles	0	1	Insurance, annual premium	$1,038	$1,432
Percent commutes › 60 mins.	5.0%	5.9%	Size of regional airport	None	Large	Gas, cost per gallon	$2.51	$2.49
Commute by auto	66.0%	78.9%	Daily airline activity	10	686	Daily vehicle miles per capita	14.6	24.0
Commute by mass transit	0.8%	1.9%	Amtrak service	No	No			
Work at home	2.5%	3.1%						
Mass transit miles per capita	0.81	1.87						

Leisure
Score: 21.7
Rank: 292

DINING & SHOPPING	AREA	U.S. AVG	ENTERTAINMENT	AREA	U.S. AVG	OUTDOOR ACTIVITIES	AREA	U.S. AVG
Restaurant rating	1	2	Professional sports rating	2	4	Golf-course rating	1	4
Outlet mall score	0	42	College sports rating	1	4	Ski-area rating	1	3
No. Starbucks	0	13	Zoo/aquarium rating	1	3	Sq. miles inland water	5	4
No. warehouse clubs	0	2	Amusement park rating	1	3	Miles of coastline	29.3	10.7
			Botanical garden/ arboretum rating	1	4	National Park rating	1	3

Arts & Culture
Score: 0.3
Rank: 372

MEDIA & LIBRARIES	AREA	U.S. AVG	PERFORMING ARTS	AREA	U.S. AVG	MUSEUMS	AREA	U.S. AVG
Arts radio rating	1	3	Classical music rating	1	4	Overall museum rating	1	5
No. public libraries	4	27	Ballet/dance rating	1	3	Art museum rating	1	5
Library volumes per capita	0.95	2.78	Professional theater rating	1	3	Science museum rating	1	5
			University arts programs rating	1	5	Children's museum rating	1	3

Janesville, WI

Score: 54.0   **Rank:** 227   **2004 rank:** 131

Profile: Small-town complex
Location: Extreme south-central Wisconsin at the Illinois border
Elevation: 803 feet
Time zone: Central Standard Time

PRO	CON
Small-town atmosphere	Cold winters
Attractive setting	Economic cycles
Close to Chicago	Arts and culture

Janesville and its smaller satellite city of Beloit are located about 15 miles apart in extreme south-central Wisconsin, with Beloit abutting the Illinois border. Both are small industrial towns with a large General Motors plant in Janesville and a variety of businesses, notably food processing and distribution, in Beloit. The GM plant is tied to pickup and SUV products, but is producing some of GM's newer products and has been relatively immune to the large-vehicle cycle so far. Predictably, the strong auto industry ties give the area a cyclical economy overall. The area was once home to Parker Pen but that business was absorbed by Gillette and the plant was closed. The downtown areas

are pretty much the clean and small townscapes we're used to seeing in Wisconsin. The somewhat more "hip" Beloit is home to Beloit College, a well-acclaimed small college, as well as historic districts and a few minor cultural assets. The area is about 100 miles north of Chicago and that city's vast resources. Cost of living is reasonable for the region.

Both towns are located in the broad, fertile agricultural valley of the Rock River. Summers are warm and humid with occasional hot, muggy spells and frequent afternoon thunderstorms. Winters are generally cold with most precipitation falling as snow and remaining as snow cover. First freeze is mid-October; last is late April.

Population

DEMOGRAPHICS	AREA	U.S. AVG	ETHNIC COMPOSITION	AREA	U.S. AVG	RESIDENT PROFILE	AREA	U.S. AVG
Population	155,268		White	90.3%	79.0%	Single	30.0%	32.4%
Population density per sq. mile	215.5	358.5	Black	4.5%	10.5%	Married	55.3%	52.7%
Population growth	11.3%	21.1%	Asian	1.1%	2.7%	Divorced/separated	14.6%	14.9%
Median age	37.0	36.1	Hispanic	4.7%	10.6%	Married with children	23.7%	23.7%
Percent Democrat	57.9%	44.5%	Religious observance	51.3%	48.9%	Single with children	9.7%	9.1%
Percent Republican	41.2%	54.5%	Diversity measure	25.5	40.1	Percent over age 65	13.0%	12.9%

Economy & Jobs
Score: 14.4
Rank: 318

INCOME	AREA	U.S. AVG	EMPLOYMENT	AREA	U.S. AVG	EMPLOYING INDUSTRIES	AREA	U.S. AVG
Per capita income	$23,609	$23,235	Unemployment rate	8.5%	4.7%	Largest: Manufacturing		
Household income	$49,833	$46,414	Recent job growth	-0.3%	1.3%			
Household income ‹ $25K	20.6%	26.2%	Projected future job growth	6.3%	11.5%	Percent manufacturing	26.4%	15.4%
Household income › $75K	26.5%	25.4%	White collar	48.4%	57.8%	Percent public sector	10.9%	15.7%
Household income growth	9.5%	13.6%	Blue collar	36.1%	25.2%	Percent construction	9.6%	9.9%

Cost of Living
Score: 40.9
Rank: 221

INDEXES & TAXES	AREA	U.S. AVG
Cost of Living Index	87.8	100.0
Buying Power Index	127.2	100.0
Income tax rate	6.93%	4.70%
Sales tax rate	5.00%	6.58%
Property tax rate	$20.89	$12.00

HOUSING	AREA	U.S. AVG
Median home price	$126,100	$220,000
Home price appreciation	28.5%	10.1%
Median rent	$646	$709
Homes owned	67.5%	62.3%
Home price ratio	2.5	4.2

NECESSITIES	AREA	U.S. AVG
Food Index	103.7	100.0
Housing Index	53.0	100.0
Utilities Index	131.5	100.0
Transportation Index	104.5	100.0
Healthcare Index	105.1	100.0
Miscellaneous Cost Index	97.2	100.0

Climate
Score: 21.4
Rank: 293

TEMPERATURE	AREA	U.S. AVG
Average January low	8.2	26.2
Average July high	81.4	87.4
Annual days > 90°F	12	38
Annual days < 32°F	164	89
Annual days < 0°F	25	6

PRECIPITATION	AREA	U.S. AVG
Annual inches precipitation	30.0	37.7
Annual inches snowfall	39.0	7.0
Annual days precipitation	117	109
Annual days rain > 0.5 inches	18	22
Annual days snow > 1.5 inches	10	6

COMFORTS & HAZARDS	AREA	U.S. AVG
July relative humidity	73%	66%
Annual days mostly sunny	190	208
Annual days with thunderstorms	40	39
Tornado risk score	13	18
Hurricane risk score	1	13

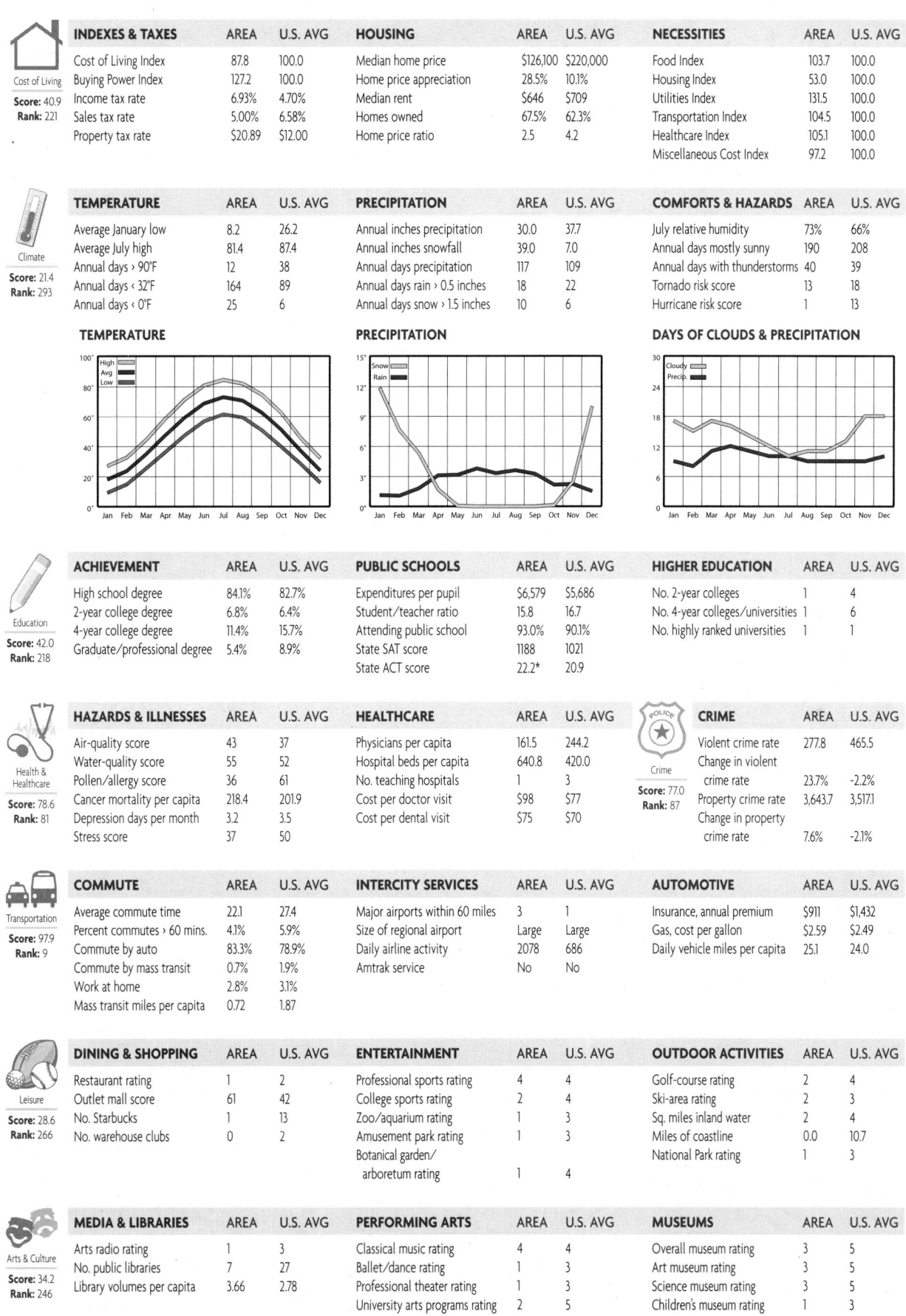

TEMPERATURE

PRECIPITATION

DAYS OF CLOUDS & PRECIPITATION

Education
Score: 42.0
Rank: 218

ACHIEVEMENT	AREA	U.S. AVG
High school degree	84.1%	82.7%
2-year college degree	6.8%	6.4%
4-year college degree	11.4%	15.7%
Graduate/professional degree	5.4%	8.9%

PUBLIC SCHOOLS	AREA	U.S. AVG
Expenditures per pupil	$6,579	$5,686
Student/teacher ratio	15.8	16.7
Attending public school	93.0%	90.1%
State SAT score	1188	1021
State ACT score	22.2*	20.9

HIGHER EDUCATION	AREA	U.S. AVG
No. 2-year colleges	1	4
No. 4-year colleges/universities	1	6
No. highly ranked universities	1	1

Health & Healthcare
Score: 78.6
Rank: 81

HAZARDS & ILLNESSES	AREA	U.S. AVG
Air-quality score	43	37
Water-quality score	55	52
Pollen/allergy score	36	61
Cancer mortality per capita	218.4	201.9
Depression days per month	3.2	3.5
Stress score	37	50

HEALTHCARE	AREA	U.S. AVG
Physicians per capita	161.5	244.2
Hospital beds per capita	640.8	420.0
No. teaching hospitals	1	3
Cost per doctor visit	$98	$77
Cost per dental visit	$75	$70

Crime
Score: 77.0
Rank: 87

CRIME	AREA	U.S. AVG
Violent crime rate	277.8	465.5
Change in violent crime rate	23.7%	-2.2%
Property crime rate	3,643.7	3,517.1
Change in property crime rate	7.6%	-2.1%

Transportation
Score: 97.9
Rank: 9

COMMUTE	AREA	U.S. AVG
Average commute time	22.1	27.4
Percent commutes > 60 mins.	4.1%	5.9%
Commute by auto	83.3%	78.9%
Commute by mass transit	0.7%	1.9%
Work at home	2.8%	3.1%
Mass transit miles per capita	0.72	1.87

INTERCITY SERVICES	AREA	U.S. AVG
Major airports within 60 miles	3	1
Size of regional airport	Large	Large
Daily airline activity	2078	686
Amtrak service	No	No

AUTOMOTIVE	AREA	U.S. AVG
Insurance, annual premium	$911	$1,432
Gas, cost per gallon	$2.59	$2.49
Daily vehicle miles per capita	25.1	24.0

Leisure
Score: 28.6
Rank: 266

DINING & SHOPPING	AREA	U.S. AVG
Restaurant rating	1	2
Outlet mall score	61	42
No. Starbucks	1	13
No. warehouse clubs	0	2

ENTERTAINMENT	AREA	U.S. AVG
Professional sports rating	4	4
College sports rating	2	4
Zoo/aquarium rating	1	3
Amusement park rating	1	3
Botanical garden/ arboretum rating	1	4

OUTDOOR ACTIVITIES	AREA	U.S. AVG
Golf-course rating	2	4
Ski-area rating	2	3
Sq. miles inland water	2	4
Miles of coastline	0.0	10.7
National Park rating	1	3

Arts & Culture
Score: 34.2
Rank: 246

MEDIA & LIBRARIES	AREA	U.S. AVG
Arts radio rating	1	3
No. public libraries	7	27
Library volumes per capita	3.66	2.78

PERFORMING ARTS	AREA	U.S. AVG
Classical music rating	4	4
Ballet/dance rating	1	3
Professional theater rating	1	3
University arts programs rating	2	5

MUSEUMS	AREA	U.S. AVG
Overall museum rating	3	5
Art museum rating	3	5
Science museum rating	3	5
Children's museum rating	1	3

Jefferson City, MO

Score: 33.7   **Rank:** 329   **2004 rank:** not ranked

Profile: Capital city
Location: East-central Missouri, 30 miles south of Columbia and I-70
Elevation: 600 feet
Time zone: Central Standard Time

PRO	CON
Cost of living	Entertainment
Capital-city amenities	Isolation
Historic interest	Arts and culture

Jefferson City, along the Missouri River near the center of the state, is an uninspiring capital somewhat off the beaten path. There are some capital-city amenities and a number of historic buildings and sites especially near the riverfront. Nearby water and state parks provide some outdoor recreation, most notably the Lake of the Ozarks State Park 40 miles south. But there is little to do overall. Reportedly, the state had to pass a law requiring state officials to live there. The economy is largely tied to the state government. The COL Index at 84.6 is low for a capital city. Most culture and entertainment is found in Columbia to the north, home of the University of Missouri. The town is isolated from air service, found mainly in St. Louis, 100 miles east.

The area consists of gently rolling and partially wooded hills and plains located along the Missouri River Valley. The climate features moderately cold winters and hot, muggy summers with daytime temperatures in the 90s and occasionally over 100°F. Rain and thunderstorms are frequent in spring and early summer. Winter weather varies, with occasional cold spells alternating with mild days and temperatures sometimes in the 60s. Below-zero temperatures occur, but not every winter. Snow falls every winter but snow cover does not persist for long. First freeze is mid-October; last is mid-April.

Population

DEMOGRAPHICS	AREA	U.S. AVG	ETHNIC COMPOSITION	AREA	U.S. AVG	RESIDENT PROFILE	AREA	U.S. AVG
Population	144,081		White	90.0%	79.0%	Single	30.8%	32.4%
Population density per sq. mile	64.0	358.5	Black	7.2%	10.5%	Married	52.8%	52.7%
Population growth	19.8%	21.1%	Asian	0.8%	2.7%	Divorced/separated	16.4%	14.9%
Median age	36.1	36.1	Hispanic	1.4%	10.6%	Married with children	25.6%	23.7%
Percent Democrat	32.5%	44.5%	Religious observance	62.6%	48.9%	Single with children	8.7%	9.1%
Percent Republican	67.0%	54.5%	Diversity measure	20.4	40.1	Percent over age 65	11.8%	12.9%

Economy & Jobs
Score: 29.4
Rank: 264

INCOME	AREA	U.S. AVG	EMPLOYMENT	AREA	U.S. AVG	EMPLOYING INDUSTRIES	AREA	U.S. AVG
Per capita income	$21,550	$23,235	Unemployment rate	4.8%	4.7%	Largest: Healthcare & Social Assistance		
Household income	$45,896	$46,414	Recent job growth	0.1%	1.3%			
Household income < $25K	24.5%	26.2%	Projected future job growth	5.9%	11.5%	Percent manufacturing	14.5%	15.4%
Household income > $75K	22.7%	25.4%	White collar	58.4%	57.8%	Percent public sector	29.6%	15.7%
Household income growth	12.2%	13.6%	Blue collar	25.2%	25.2%	Percent construction	10.7%	9.9%

Cost of Living
Score: 67.4
Rank: 123

INDEXES & TAXES	AREA	U.S. AVG	HOUSING	AREA	U.S. AVG	NECESSITIES	AREA	U.S. AVG
Cost of Living Index	84.6	100.0	Median home price	$139,100	$220,000	Food Index	92.7	100.0
Buying Power Index	121.6	100.0	Home price appreciation	22.1%	10.1%	Housing Index	55.7	100.0
Income tax rate	6.00%	4.70%	Median rent	$517	$709	Utilities Index	93.5	100.0
Sales tax rate	6.22%	6.58%	Homes owned	66.7%	62.3%	Transportation Index	108.6	100.0
Property tax rate	$7.81	$12.00	Home price ratio	3.0	4.2	Healthcare Index	92.1	100.0
						Miscellaneous Cost Index	98.3	100.0

Climate
Score: 19.5
Rank: 300

TEMPERATURE	AREA	U.S. AVG	PRECIPITATION	AREA	U.S. AVG	COMFORTS & HAZARDS	AREA	U.S. AVG
Average January low	18.0	26.2	Annual inches precipitation	39.9	37.7	July relative humidity	62%	66%
Average July high	89.0	87.4	Annual inches snowfall	27.0	7.0	Annual days mostly sunny	211	208
Annual days > 90°F	37	38	Annual days precipitation	110	109	Annual days with thunderstorms	51	39
Annual days < 32°F	108	89	Annual days rain > 0.5 inches	26	22	Tornado risk score	2	18
Annual days < 0°F	7	6	Annual days snow > 1.5 inches	6	6	Hurricane risk score	1	13

TEMPERATURE

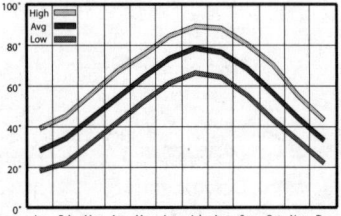

PRECIPITATION

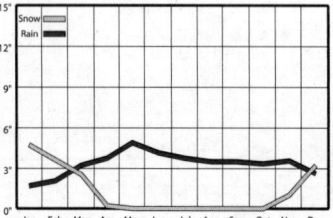

DAYS OF CLOUDS & PRECIPITATION

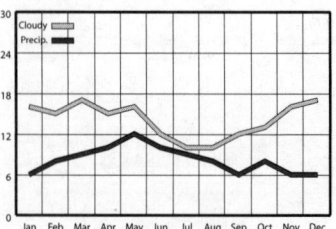

ACHIEVEMENT	AREA	U.S. AVG	PUBLIC SCHOOLS	AREA	U.S. AVG	HIGHER EDUCATION	AREA	U.S. AVG
High school degree	81.7%	82.7%	Expenditures per pupil	$4,730	$5,686	No. 2-year colleges	2	4
2-year college degree	4.8%	6.4%	Student/teacher ratio	13.4	16.7	No. 4-year colleges/universities	3	6
4-year college degree	14.2%	15.7%	Attending public school	80.4%	90.1%	No. highly ranked universities	1	1
Graduate/professional degree	6.9%	8.9%	State SAT score	1178	1021			
			State ACT score	21.6*	20.9			

Education
Score: 25.1
Rank: 280

HAZARDS & ILLNESSES	AREA	U.S. AVG	HEALTHCARE	AREA	U.S. AVG	CRIME	AREA	U.S. AVG
Air-quality score	56	37	Physicians per capita	163.4	244.2	Violent crime rate	342.7	465.5
Water-quality score	81	52	Hospital beds per capita	603.1	420.0	Change in violent crime rate	22.5%	-2.2%
Pollen/allergy score	55	61	No. teaching hospitals	2	3	Property crime rate	2,654.3	3,517.1
Cancer mortality per capita	220.4	201.9	Cost per doctor visit	$75	$77	Change in property crime rate	14.2%	-2.1%
Depression days per month	2.9	3.5	Cost per dental visit	$64	$70			
Stress score	25	50						

Health & Healthcare
Score: 90.1
Rank: 38

Crime
Score: 95.2
Rank: 19

COMMUTE	AREA	U.S. AVG	INTERCITY SERVICES	AREA	U.S. AVG	AUTOMOTIVE	AREA	U.S. AVG
Average commute time	22.5	27.4	Major airports within 60 miles	1	1	Insurance, annual premium	$987	$1,432
Percent commutes > 60 mins.	3.9%	5.9%	Size of regional airport	Large	Large	Gas, cost per gallon	$2.33	$2.49
Commute by auto	77.8%	78.9%	Daily airline activity	731	686	Daily vehicle miles per capita	24.1	24.0
Commute by mass transit	0.6%	1.9%	Amtrak service	Yes	No			
Work at home	3.3%	3.1%						
Mass transit miles per capita	0.60	1.87						

Transportation
Score: 66.8
Rank: 123

DINING & SHOPPING	AREA	U.S. AVG	ENTERTAINMENT	AREA	U.S. AVG	OUTDOOR ACTIVITIES	AREA	U.S. AVG
Restaurant rating	1	2	Professional sports rating	2	4	Golf-course rating	3	4
Outlet mall score	0	42	College sports rating	1	4	Ski-area rating	1	3
No. Starbucks	0	13	Zoo/aquarium rating	1	3	Sq. miles inland water	2	4
No. warehouse clubs	0	2	Amusement park rating	1	3	Miles of coastline	0.0	10.7
			Botanical garden/ arboretum rating	1	4	National Park rating	2	3

Leisure
Score: 5.6
Rank: 352

MEDIA & LIBRARIES	AREA	U.S. AVG	PERFORMING ARTS	AREA	U.S. AVG	MUSEUMS	AREA	U.S. AVG
Arts radio rating	1	3	Classical music rating	2	4	Overall museum rating	5	5
No. public libraries	3	27	Ballet/dance rating	1	3	Art museum rating	1	5
Library volumes per capita	2.70	2.78	Professional theater rating	1	3	Science museum rating	1	5
			University arts programs rating	1	5	Children's museum rating	1	3

Arts & Culture
Score: 3.5
Rank: 360

Johnson City, TN

Score: 57.8   Rank: 191   2004 rank: 77

Profile: Small city/college town
Location: Northeastern tip of Tennessee
Elevation: 1,662 feet
Time zone: Eastern Standard Time

PRO	CON
Cost of living	Isolation
College-town amenities	Low ethnic diversity
Healthcare	Arts and culture

In the very northeast tip of Tennessee lies a group of three smaller cities about 20 miles apart known locally as the Tri-Cities—Kingsport, Bristol, and Johnson City. Previously, the OMB considered these three together as a metro area but in their most recent designation, Johnson City, the largest and most unique of the three, has been split off as a metro area of its own. Long a major rail junction and shipping point for traffic crossing the Appalachians from the Midwest into the eastern seaboard, Johnson City is most known today as the home of East Tennessee State University, a school of 12,000 students and a major medical school and teaching hospital. Companies such as Siemens, Eastman Chemical, and American Water Heater have operations in the area, but Kingsport and Bristol are far more noted for their industry. Downtown is clean and attractively set against the Appalachian backdrop but is otherwise unremarkable. The city serves as a gateway to important mountain and lake recreation areas nearby. Johnson City is 110 miles east of Knoxville, and is accessible to other amenities in Virginia at Roanoke (150 miles) and northeast from there. As such it is isolated from many city services, particularly air service. Cost of living is a very attractive 76.3.

Johnson City is located in the upper East Tennessee Valley against the main ridge of the Appalachian Mountains. Immediate terrain is gently rolling to the north and west and very hilly and wooded, rising to 4,000 to 6,000 feet to the south and east. Summers are generally warm and humid, although the high elevation brings some cooling, especially in evenings. Summer thunderstorms are frequent, with the most rain occurring in July. Atlantic Coast storms can bring heavy winter precipitation. Normally only the mountains receive snow.

Population

DEMOGRAPHICS	AREA	U.S. AVG
Population	189,188	
Population density per sq. mile	221.7	358.5
Population growth	18.1%	21.1%
Median age	39.1	36.1
Percent Democrat	31.6%	44.5%
Percent Republican	67.6%	54.5%

ETHNIC COMPOSITION	AREA	U.S. AVG
White	94.7%	79.0%
Black	2.9%	10.5%
Asian	0.7%	2.7%
Hispanic	1.5%	10.6%
Religious observance	54.8%	48.9%
Diversity measure	12.9	40.1

RESIDENT PROFILE	AREA	U.S. AVG
Single	29.1%	32.4%
Married	55.5%	52.7%
Divorced/separated	15.4%	14.9%
Married with children	20.7%	23.7%
Single with children	7.3%	9.1%
Percent over age 65	15.1%	12.9%

Economy & Jobs
Score: 20.9
Rank: 295

INCOME	AREA	U.S. AVG
Per capita income	$20,016	$23,235
Household income	$35,321	$46,414
Household income < $25K	35.9%	26.2%
Household income > $75K	15.4%	25.4%
Household income growth	13.9%	13.6%

EMPLOYMENT	AREA	U.S. AVG
Unemployment rate	4.9%	4.7%
Recent job growth	-0.4%	1.3%
Projected future job growth	9.1%	11.5%
White collar	53.9%	57.8%
Blue collar	30.0%	25.2%

EMPLOYING INDUSTRIES	AREA	U.S. AVG
Largest: Healthcare & Social Assistance		
Percent manufacturing	19.0%	15.4%
Percent public sector	15.2%	15.7%
Percent construction	10.9%	9.9%

Cost of Living
Score: 97.6
Rank: 10

INDEXES & TAXES	AREA	U.S. AVG
Cost of Living Index	76.3	100.0
Buying Power Index	103.8	100.0
Income tax rate	0.00%	4.70%
Sales tax rate	9.44%	6.58%
Property tax rate	$6.63	$12.00

HOUSING	AREA	U.S. AVG
Median home price	$108,900	$220,000
Home price appreciation	29.8%	10.1%
Median rent	$521	$709
Homes owned	65.5%	62.3%
Home price ratio	3.1	4.2

NECESSITIES	AREA	U.S. AVG
Food Index	91.8	100.0
Housing Index	47.0	100.0
Utilities Index	101.8	100.0
Transportation Index	86.4	100.0
Healthcare Index	84.6	100.0
Miscellaneous Cost Index	90.7	100.0

Climate
Score: 56.4
Rank: 162

TEMPERATURE	AREA	U.S. AVG
Average January low	26.7	26.2
Average July high	85.9	87.4
Annual days > 90°F	13	38
Annual days < 32°F	96	89
Annual days < 0°F	1	6

PRECIPITATION	AREA	U.S. AVG
Annual inches precipitation	41.0	37.7
Annual inches snowfall	16.0	7.0
Annual days precipitation	134	109
Annual days rain > 0.5 inches	25	22
Annual days snow > 1.5 inches	4	6

COMFORTS & HAZARDS	AREA	U.S. AVG
July relative humidity	72%	66%
Annual days mostly sunny	202	208
Annual days with thunderstorms	45	39
Tornado risk score	3	18
Hurricane risk score	7	13

TEMPERATURE

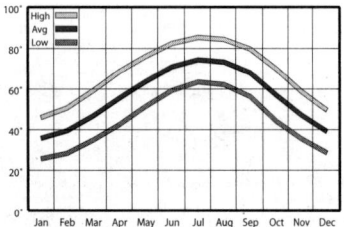

PRECIPITATION

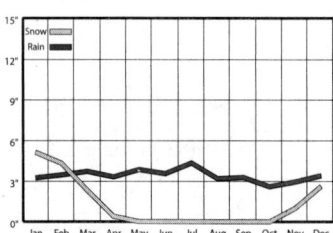

DAYS OF CLOUDS & PRECIPITATION

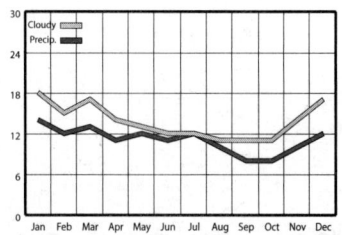

Education
Score: 23.3
Rank: 287

ACHIEVEMENT	AREA	U.S. AVG
High school degree	74.0%	82.7%
2-year college degree	4.6%	6.4%
4-year college degree	12.1%	15.7%
Graduate/professional degree	6.7%	8.9%

PUBLIC SCHOOLS	AREA	U.S. AVG
Expenditures per pupil	$4,472	$5,686
Student/teacher ratio	16.5	16.7
Attending public school	96.4%	90.1%
State SAT score	1142	1021
State ACT score	20.7*	20.9

HIGHER EDUCATION	AREA	U.S. AVG
No. 2-year colleges	0	4
No. 4-year colleges/universities	3	6
No. highly ranked universities	1	1

Health & Healthcare
Score: 99.2
Rank: 4

HAZARDS & ILLNESSES	AREA	U.S. AVG
Air-quality score	59	37
Water-quality score	93	52
Pollen/allergy score	60	61
Cancer mortality per capita	213.6	201.9
Depression days per month	4.8	3.5
Stress score	84	50

HEALTHCARE	AREA	U.S. AVG
Physicians per capita	397.9	244.2
Hospital beds per capita	524.9	420.0
No. teaching hospitals	1	3
Cost per doctor visit	$77	$77
Cost per dental visit	$50	$70

Crime
Score: 69.5
Rank: 112

CRIME	AREA	U.S. AVG
Violent crime rate	431.6	465.5
Change in violent crime rate	21.1%	-2.2%
Property crime rate	3,753.0	3,517.1
Change in property crime rate	-6.6%	-2.1%

COMMUTE	AREA	U.S. AVG	INTERCITY SERVICES	AREA	U.S. AVG	AUTOMOTIVE	AREA	U.S. AVG
Average commute time	23.3	27.4	Major airports within 60 miles	0	1	Insurance, annual premium	$903	$1,432
Percent commutes > 60 mins.	3.7%	5.9%	Size of regional airport	Small	Large	Gas, cost per gallon	$2.47	$2.49
Commute by auto	84.3%	78.9%	Daily airline activity	89	686	Daily vehicle miles per capita	27.6	24.0
Commute by mass transit	0.4%	1.9%	Amtrak service	No	No			
Work at home	2.0%	3.1%						
Mass transit miles per capita	0.35	1.87						

Transportation
Score: 17.4
Rank: 309

DINING & SHOPPING	AREA	U.S. AVG	ENTERTAINMENT	AREA	U.S. AVG	OUTDOOR ACTIVITIES	AREA	U.S. AVG
Restaurant rating	1	2	Professional sports rating	2	4	Golf-course rating	3	4
Outlet mall score	0	42	College sports rating	3	4	Ski-area rating	2	3
No. Starbucks	1	13	Zoo/aquarium rating	1	3	Sq. miles inland water	4	4
No. warehouse clubs	0	2	Amusement park rating	1	3	Miles of coastline	0.0	10.7
			Botanical garden/ arboretum rating	3	4	National Park rating	8	3

Leisure
Score: 43.9
Rank: 209

MEDIA & LIBRARIES	AREA	U.S. AVG	PERFORMING ARTS	AREA	U.S. AVG	MUSEUMS	AREA	U.S. AVG
Arts radio rating	1	3	Classical music rating	4	4	Overall museum rating	2	5
No. public libraries	5	27	Ballet/dance rating	3	3	Art museum rating	4	5
Library volumes per capita	1.31	2.78	Professional theater rating	8	3	Science museum rating	4	5
			University arts programs rating	6	5	Children's museum rating	4	3

Arts & Culture
Score: 39.8
Rank: 225

Johnstown, PA

Score: 55.6   Rank: 217   2004 rank: 187

Profile: Small city
Location: West-central Pennsylvania, 70 miles east of Pittsburgh
Elevation: 1,223 feet
Time zone: Eastern Standard Time

PRO	CON
Cost of living	Economy
Low crime rate	Low educational attainment
Attractive setting	Low ethnic diversity

Johnstown is a small city located just west of the main ridge of the Alleghenies. To most outsiders it is associated with four historic and devastating floods, the most recent in 1977. Today, the city has a mixed and somewhat depressed economy and a slow pace of life, but at one time it was a major steel producing center. The tight valley-floor geography and relative distance to resources compared to other steel towns led to a long decline that climaxed with the 1977 flood. There are still some steel fabrication industries, but heavy industry and manufacturing are largely a thing of the past, and the city struggles to reinvent itself today as a service and minor high-tech player. One theme is to become the healthcare and education center for a large portion of west-central Pennsylvania. Spurred by aggressive local business-development incentives, another is to bring in small firms looking for low costs,

and both themes have borne some fruit. Local amenities focus on museums that commemorate the floods and a historic incline railway, and arts amenities are on the upswing. There is good outdoor recreation in the area. The low cost of living, very affordable housing, and small-town environment are the main attractions. There isn't much employment security, much to do, or much intellectual stimulation, but all are on a slow rise and the area is clearly a wait-and-see.

The immediate area around downtown is located on a flat floodplain of the Conemaugh River. Several creeks converge on the plain, with a long, deep gorge to the west and an arrangement of mountains catching moisture flow from the south, creating ideal flood conditions. Summers are warm and humid, influenced by Gulf air from the south. Winters are cloudy and cool with mixed precipitation but infrequent severe cold.

DEMOGRAPHICS	AREA	U.S. AVG	ETHNIC COMPOSITION	AREA	U.S. AVG	RESIDENT PROFILE	AREA	U.S. AVG
Population	148,204		White	95.5%	79.0%	Single	36.4%	32.4%
Population density per sq. mile	215.4	358.5	Black	3.1%	10.5%	Married	51.5%	52.7%
Population growth	-9.1%	21.1%	Asian	0.5%	2.7%	Divorced/separated	12.2%	14.9%
Median age	42.3	36.1	Hispanic	1.0%	10.6%	Married with children	20.2%	23.7%
Percent Democrat	48.7%	44.5%	Religious observance	81.6%	48.9%	Single with children	6.7%	9.1%
Percent Republican	50.8%	54.5%	Diversity measure	10.5	40.1	Percent over age 65	19.6%	12.9%

Population

INCOME	AREA	U.S. AVG	EMPLOYMENT	AREA	U.S. AVG	EMPLOYING INDUSTRIES	AREA	U.S. AVG
Per capita income	$18,352	$23,235	Unemployment rate	6.6%	4.7%	Largest: Healthcare & Social Assistance		
Household income	$33,828	$46,414	Recent job growth	1.9%	1.3%			
Household income < $25K	36.5%	26.2%	Projected future job growth	5.2%	11.5%	Percent manufacturing	17.2%	15.4%
Household income > $75K	13.6%	25.4%	White collar	53.2%	57.8%	Percent public sector	14.9%	15.7%
Household income growth	12.1%	13.6%	Blue collar	27.5%	25.2%	Percent construction	10.3%	9.9%

Economy & Jobs
Score: 23.5
Rank: 286

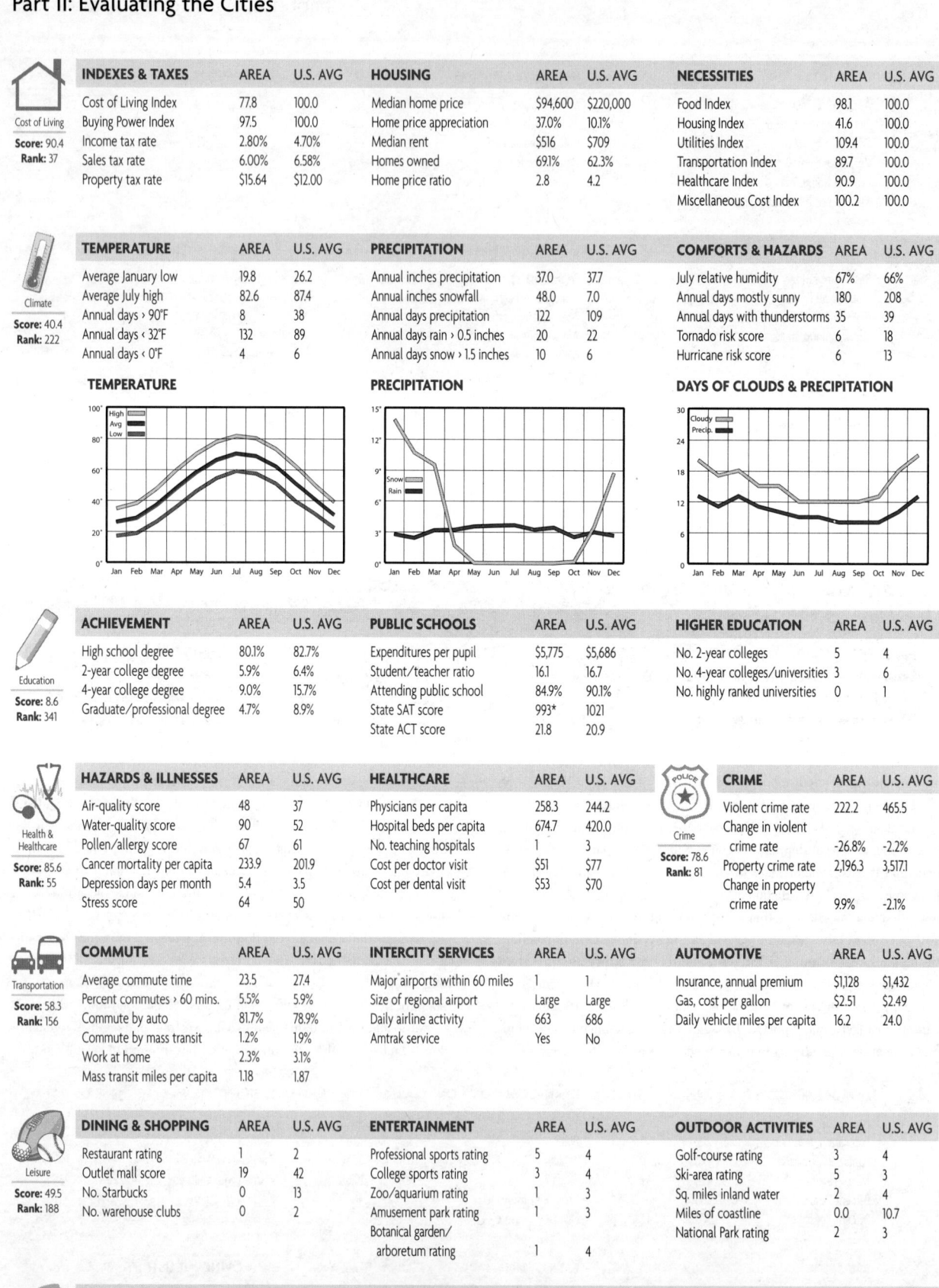

Cost of Living
Score: 90.4
Rank: 37

INDEXES & TAXES	AREA	U.S. AVG
Cost of Living Index	77.8	100.0
Buying Power Index	97.5	100.0
Income tax rate	2.80%	4.70%
Sales tax rate	6.00%	6.58%
Property tax rate	$15.64	$12.00

HOUSING	AREA	U.S. AVG
Median home price	$94,600	$220,000
Home price appreciation	37.0%	10.1%
Median rent	$516	$709
Homes owned	69.1%	62.3%
Home price ratio	2.8	4.2

NECESSITIES	AREA	U.S. AVG
Food Index	98.1	100.0
Housing Index	41.6	100.0
Utilities Index	109.4	100.0
Transportation Index	89.7	100.0
Healthcare Index	90.9	100.0
Miscellaneous Cost Index	100.2	100.0

Climate
Score: 40.4
Rank: 222

TEMPERATURE	AREA	U.S. AVG
Average January low	19.8	26.2
Average July high	82.6	87.4
Annual days > 90°F	8	38
Annual days < 32°F	132	89
Annual days < 0°F	4	6

PRECIPITATION	AREA	U.S. AVG
Annual inches precipitation	37.0	37.7
Annual inches snowfall	48.0	7.0
Annual days precipitation	122	109
Annual days rain > 0.5 inches	20	22
Annual days snow > 1.5 inches	10	6

COMFORTS & HAZARDS	AREA	U.S. AVG
July relative humidity	67%	66%
Annual days mostly sunny	180	208
Annual days with thunderstorms	35	39
Tornado risk score	6	18
Hurricane risk score	6	13

TEMPERATURE

PRECIPITATION

DAYS OF CLOUDS & PRECIPITATION

Education
Score: 8.6
Rank: 341

ACHIEVEMENT	AREA	U.S. AVG
High school degree	80.1%	82.7%
2-year college degree	5.9%	6.4%
4-year college degree	9.0%	15.7%
Graduate/professional degree	4.7%	8.9%

PUBLIC SCHOOLS	AREA	U.S. AVG
Expenditures per pupil	$5,775	$5,686
Student/teacher ratio	16.1	16.7
Attending public school	84.9%	90.1%
State SAT score	993*	1021
State ACT score	21.8	20.9

HIGHER EDUCATION	AREA	U.S. AVG
No. 2-year colleges	5	4
No. 4-year colleges/universities	3	6
No. highly ranked universities	0	1

Health & Healthcare
Score: 85.6
Rank: 55

HAZARDS & ILLNESSES	AREA	U.S. AVG
Air-quality score	48	37
Water-quality score	90	52
Pollen/allergy score	67	61
Cancer mortality per capita	233.9	201.9
Depression days per month	5.4	3.5
Stress score	64	50

HEALTHCARE	AREA	U.S. AVG
Physicians per capita	258.3	244.2
Hospital beds per capita	674.7	420.0
No. teaching hospitals	1	3
Cost per doctor visit	$51	$77
Cost per dental visit	$53	$70

Crime
Score: 78.6
Rank: 81

CRIME	AREA	U.S. AVG
Violent crime rate	222.2	465.5
Change in violent crime rate	-26.8%	-2.2%
Property crime rate	2,196.3	3,517.1
Change in property crime rate	9.9%	-2.1%

Transportation
Score: 58.3
Rank: 156

COMMUTE	AREA	U.S. AVG
Average commute time	23.5	27.4
Percent commutes > 60 mins.	5.5%	5.9%
Commute by auto	81.7%	78.9%
Commute by mass transit	1.2%	1.9%
Work at home	2.3%	3.1%
Mass transit miles per capita	1.18	1.87

INTERCITY SERVICES	AREA	U.S. AVG
Major airports within 60 miles	1	1
Size of regional airport	Large	Large
Daily airline activity	663	686
Amtrak service	Yes	No

AUTOMOTIVE	AREA	U.S. AVG
Insurance, annual premium	$1,128	$1,432
Gas, cost per gallon	$2.51	$2.49
Daily vehicle miles per capita	16.2	24.0

Leisure
Score: 49.5
Rank: 188

DINING & SHOPPING	AREA	U.S. AVG
Restaurant rating	1	2
Outlet mall score	19	42
No. Starbucks	0	13
No. warehouse clubs	0	2

ENTERTAINMENT	AREA	U.S. AVG
Professional sports rating	5	4
College sports rating	3	4
Zoo/aquarium rating	1	3
Amusement park rating	1	3
Botanical garden/arboretum rating	1	4

OUTDOOR ACTIVITIES	AREA	U.S. AVG
Golf-course rating	3	4
Ski-area rating	5	3
Sq. miles inland water	2	4
Miles of coastline	0.0	10.7
National Park rating	2	3

Arts & Culture
Score: 34.5
Rank: 245

MEDIA & LIBRARIES	AREA	U.S. AVG
Arts radio rating	1	3
No. public libraries	15	27
Library volumes per capita	2.07	2.78

PERFORMING ARTS	AREA	U.S. AVG
Classical music rating	3	4
Ballet/dance rating	1	3
Professional theater rating	1	3
University arts programs rating	3	5

MUSEUMS	AREA	U.S. AVG
Overall museum rating	5	5
Art museum rating	6	5
Science museum rating	1	5
Children's museum rating	1	3

Jonesboro, AR

Score: 45.2   Rank: 282   2004 rank: 257

Profile: Small town/college town
Location: Northeast Arkansas, about 50 miles northwest of Memphis, Tennessee
Elevation: 333
Time zone: Central Standard Time

PRO	CON
Cost of living	Hot, humid summers
Future job growth	Low educational attainment
Healthcare	Recreation

Jonesboro, home to Arkansas State University, is a fairly nondescript town with a few college-town amenities and a large agricultural and agricultural processing base. Crops grown nearby include cotton and rice in addition to standards such as corn and soybeans. "A State" is the state "ag" school, bringing in 16,500 students and a modern college-town presence superimposed on this rather typical Southern small town. But for a college town, Jonesboro has a low level of educational attainment. Jonesboro features a low cost of living (80.9) and better-than-average healthcare facilities designed to serve the much larger northeast

Arkansas and southeast Missouri regions. Arts and culture and recreational amenities are limited except for those associated with the school, but there is a new regional shopping mall and the drive to nearby Memphis fills the gap.

Jonesboro is located in a level area of gently rolling, mostly agricultural land. Summers are hot and sticky. Winters are mild with occasional cold snaps. Jonesboro gets more snow (8 inches) than any other metropolitan area in Arkansas. First freeze is late October; last is April 1.

Population

DEMOGRAPHICS	AREA	U.S. AVG	ETHNIC COMPOSITION	AREA	U.S. AVG	RESIDENT PROFILE	AREA	U.S. AVG
Population	111,174		White	87.8%	79.0%	Single	29.9%	32.4%
Population density per sq. mile	75.7	358.5	Black	9.2%	10.5%	Married	54.8%	52.7%
Population growth	19.5%	21.1%	Asian	0.6%	2.7%	Divorced/separated	15.3%	14.9%
Median age	34.8	36.1	Hispanic	2.2%	10.6%	Married with children	23.5%	23.7%
Percent Democrat	47.4%	44.5%	Religious observance	65.5%	48.9%	Single with children	8.7%	9.1%
Percent Republican	51.5%	54.5%	Diversity measure	25.4	40.1	Percent over age 65	12.6%	12.9%

Economy
& Jobs
Score: 82.1
Rank: 68

INCOME	AREA	U.S. AVG	EMPLOYMENT	AREA	U.S. AVG	EMPLOYING INDUSTRIES	AREA	U.S. AVG
Per capita income	$18,542	$23,235	Unemployment rate	5.1%	4.7%	Largest: Healthcare & Social Assistance		
Household income	$34,589	$46,414	Recent job growth	4.2%	1.3%			
Household income < $25K	36.9%	26.2%	Projected future job growth	15.7%	11.5%	Percent manufacturing	22.7%	15.4%
Household income > $75K	15.8%	25.4%	White collar	50.0%	57.8%	Percent public sector	13.5%	15.7%
Household income growth	11.2%	13.6%	Blue collar	33.1%	25.2%	Percent construction	10.4%	9.9%

Cost of Living
Score: 37.2
Rank: 235

INDEXES & TAXES	AREA	U.S. AVG	HOUSING	AREA	U.S. AVG	NECESSITIES	AREA	U.S. AVG
Cost of Living Index	80.9	100.0	Median home price	$145,200	$220,000	Food Index	90.9	100.0
Buying Power Index	95.8	100.0	Home price appreciation	16.1%	10.1%	Housing Index	69.2	100.0
Income tax rate	7.00%	4.70%	Median rent	$512	$709	Utilities Index	82.3	100.0
Sales tax rate	7.29%	6.58%	Homes owned	59.7%	62.3%	Transportation Index	86.3	100.0
Property tax rate	$7.61	$12.00	Home price ratio	4.2	4.2	Healthcare Index	89.1	100.0
						Miscellaneous Cost Index	92.6	100.0

Climate
Score: 46.8
Rank: 198

TEMPERATURE	AREA	U.S. AVG	PRECIPITATION	AREA	U.S. AVG	COMFORTS & HAZARDS	AREA	U.S. AVG
Average January low	31.6	26.2	Annual inches precipitation	47.0	37.7	July relative humidity	69%	66%
Average July high	91.6	87.4	Annual inches snowfall	8.0	7.0	Annual days mostly sunny	217	208
Annual days > 90°F	63	38	Annual days precipitation	104	109	Annual days with thunderstorms	54	39
Annual days < 32°F	60	89	Annual days rain > 0.5 inches	32	22	Tornado risk score	47	18
Annual days < 0°F	0	6	Annual days snow > 1.5 inches	3	6	Hurricane risk score	8	13

TEMPERATURE

PRECIPITATION

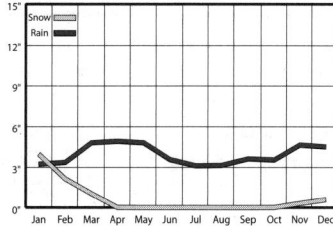

DAYS OF CLOUDS & PRECIPITATION

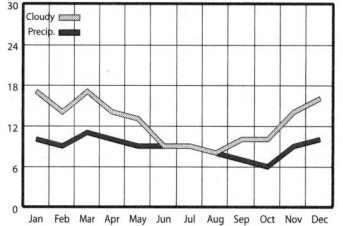

ACHIEVEMENT	AREA	U.S. AVG	PUBLIC SCHOOLS	AREA	U.S. AVG	HIGHER EDUCATION	AREA	U.S. AVG
High school degree	74.1%	82.7%	Expenditures per pupil	$4,339	$5,686	No. 2-year colleges	0	4
2-year college degree	3.3%	6.4%	Student/teacher ratio	21.0	16.7	No. 4-year colleges/universities	1	6
4-year college degree	11.5%	15.7%	Attending public school	96.8%	90.1%	No. highly ranked universities	0	1
Graduate/professional degree	6.4%	8.9%	State SAT score	1142	1021			
			State ACT score	20.6*	20.9			

Education
Score: 6.1
Rank: 350

HAZARDS & ILLNESSES	AREA	U.S. AVG	HEALTHCARE	AREA	U.S. AVG	CRIME	AREA	U.S. AVG
Air-quality score	53	37	Physicians per capita	228.0	244.2	Violent crime rate	604.8	465.5
Water-quality score	92	52	Hospital beds per capita	509.1	420.0	Change in violent crime rate	15.3%	-2.2%
Pollen/allergy score	64	61	No. teaching hospitals	2	3	Property crime rate	4,894.1	3,517.1
Cancer mortality per capita	226.8	201.9	Cost per doctor visit	$68	$77	Change in property crime rate	17.9%	-2.1%
Depression days per month	4.0	3.5	Cost per dental visit	$50	$70			
Stress score	79	50						

Health & Healthcare
Score: 92.0
Rank: 31

Crime
Score: 53.7
Rank: 174

COMMUTE	AREA	U.S. AVG	INTERCITY SERVICES	AREA	U.S. AVG	AUTOMOTIVE	AREA	U.S. AVG
Average commute time	21.3	27.4	Major airports within 60 miles	1	1	Insurance, annual premium	$1,068	$1,432
Percent commutes > 60 mins.	5.1%	5.9%	Size of regional airport	Medium	Large	Gas, cost per gallon	$2.46	$2.49
Commute by auto	82.6%	78.9%	Daily airline activity	500	686	Daily vehicle miles per capita	23.9	24.0
Commute by mass transit	0.1%	1.9%	Amtrak service	No	No			
Work at home	2.4%	3.1%						
Mass transit miles per capita	0.11	1.87						

Transportation
Score: 65.5
Rank: 130

DINING & SHOPPING	AREA	U.S. AVG	ENTERTAINMENT	AREA	U.S. AVG	OUTDOOR ACTIVITIES	AREA	U.S. AVG
Restaurant rating	1	2	Professional sports rating	2	4	Golf-course rating	1	4
Outlet mall score	6	42	College sports rating	4	4	Ski-area rating	1	3
No. Starbucks	0	13	Zoo/aquarium rating	1	3	Sq. miles inland water	1	4
No. warehouse clubs	0	2	Amusement park rating	1	3	Miles of coastline	0.0	10.7
			Botanical garden/ arboretum rating	2	4	National Park rating	1	3

Leisure
Score: 1.6
Rank: 367

MEDIA & LIBRARIES	AREA	U.S. AVG	PERFORMING ARTS	AREA	U.S. AVG	MUSEUMS	AREA	U.S. AVG
Arts radio rating	5	3	Classical music rating	1	4	Overall museum rating	2	5
No. public libraries	9	27	Ballet/dance rating	1	3	Art museum rating	2	5
Library volumes per capita	1.43	2.78	Professional theater rating	1	3	Science museum rating	1	5
			University arts programs rating	4	5	Children's museum rating	1	3

Arts & Culture
Score: 22.2
Rank: 290

Joplin, MO

Score: 42.8   Rank: 305   2004 rank: 306

Profile: Small city
Location: Southwest corner of Missouri, 6 miles from Kansas border
Elevation: 980 feet
Time zone: Central Standard Time

PRO
Cost of living
Nearby mountains
Small-town atmosphere

CON
Economy
Entertainment
Hot, humid summers

This old zinc mining and Route 66 town until recently had the lowest living and housing costs in the country. Reaching its heyday in the early 20th century, the city and area had a long period of decline. Led by some diversified manufacturing, including bedding manufacturer Leggett & Platt, and some trucking industries favoring the central U.S. location, the economy is improving. The area does serve as a regional center for healthcare and education, with the small Missouri Southern State University. But the downtown infrastructure, aside from a few historic sites, is old and dull, and there simply isn't a lot to do. Those who do find good jobs will prosper economically because of the area's low costs. Tulsa is 90 miles to the southwest.

The town is located near the foothills of the Ozarks, which rise to the southeast. Large agricultural areas surround the city. Summers are warm and sticky with little relief outside of the occasional thundershower. Winters are cool and variable, with snow and rain-snow mixes and periods of cold alternating with warmer weather. First freeze is mid-October; last is mid-April.

Population

DEMOGRAPHICS	AREA	U.S. AVG
Population	164,801	
Population density per sq. mile	130.2	358.5
Population growth	22.2%	21.1%
Median age	35.7	36.1
Percent Democrat	28.4%	44.5%
Percent Republican	71.1%	54.5%

ETHNIC COMPOSITION	AREA	U.S. AVG
White	92.0%	79.0%
Black	1.3%	10.5%
Asian	0.9%	2.7%
Hispanic	3.9%	10.6%
Religious observance	53.8%	48.9%
Diversity measure	21.7	40.1

RESIDENT PROFILE	AREA	U.S. AVG
Single	26.9%	32.4%
Married	57.1%	52.7%
Divorced/separated	15.9%	14.9%
Married with children	23.4%	23.7%
Single with children	8.7%	9.1%
Percent over age 65	13.7%	12.9%

Economy & Jobs
Score: 28.1
Rank: 269

INCOME	AREA	U.S. AVG
Per capita income	$18,702	$23,235
Household income	$36,557	$46,414
Household income < $25K	32.5%	26.2%
Household income > $75K	15.0%	25.4%
Household income growth	12.3%	13.6%

EMPLOYMENT	AREA	U.S. AVG
Unemployment rate	5.1%	4.7%
Recent job growth	-0.1%	1.3%
Projected future job growth	9.5%	11.5%
White collar	50.2%	57.8%
Blue collar	33.5%	25.2%

EMPLOYING INDUSTRIES	AREA	U.S. AVG
Largest: Manufacturing		
Percent manufacturing	23.7%	15.4%
Percent public sector	9.5%	15.7%
Percent construction	9.9%	9.9%

Cost of Living
Score: 79.9
Rank: 76

INDEXES & TAXES	AREA	U.S. AVG
Cost of Living Index	76.5	100.0
Buying Power Index	107.1	100.0
Income tax rate	6.00%	4.70%
Sales tax rate	6.42%	6.58%
Property tax rate	$6.86	$12.00

HOUSING	AREA	U.S. AVG
Median home price	$119,900	$220,000
Home price appreciation	28.0%	10.1%
Median rent	$520	$709
Homes owned	64.8%	62.3%
Home price ratio	3.3	4.2

NECESSITIES	AREA	U.S. AVG
Food Index	90.9	100.0
Housing Index	50.9	100.0
Utilities Index	79.7	100.0
Transportation Index	79.7	100.0
Healthcare Index	99.6	100.0
Miscellaneous Cost Index	94.0	100.0

Climate
Score: 27.0
Rank: 272

TEMPERATURE	AREA	U.S. AVG
Average January low	22.6	26.2
Average July high	91.0	87.4
Annual days > 90°F	40	38
Annual days < 32°F	105	89
Annual days < 0°F	3	6

PRECIPITATION	AREA	U.S. AVG
Annual inches precipitation	40.0	37.7
Annual inches snowfall	15.0	7.0
Annual days precipitation	107	109
Annual days rain > 0.5 inches	27	22
Annual days snow > 1.5 inches	5	6

COMFORTS & HAZARDS	AREA	U.S. AVG
July relative humidity	70%	66%
Annual days mostly sunny	216	208
Annual days with thunderstorms	58	39
Tornado risk score	35	18
Hurricane risk score	3	13

TEMPERATURE

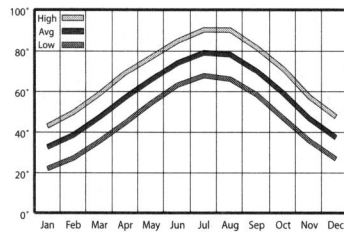

PRECIPITATION

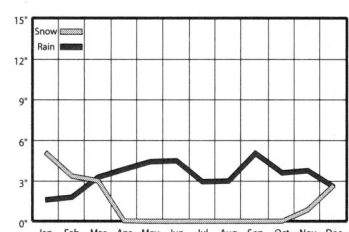

DAYS OF CLOUDS & PRECIPITATION

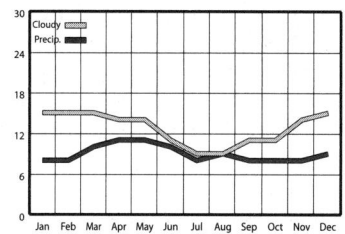

Education
Score: 20.6
Rank: 295

ACHIEVEMENT	AREA	U.S. AVG
High school degree	79.6%	82.7%
2-year college degree	5.1%	6.4%
4-year college degree	11.0%	15.7%
Graduate/professional degree	5.4%	8.9%

PUBLIC SCHOOLS	AREA	U.S. AVG
Expenditures per pupil	$4,343	$5,686
Student/teacher ratio	14.9	16.7
Attending public school	94.0%	90.1%
State SAT score	1178	1021
State ACT score	21.6*	20.9

HIGHER EDUCATION	AREA	U.S. AVG
No. 2-year colleges	2	4
No. 4-year colleges/universities	3	6
No. highly ranked universities	0	1

Health & Healthcare
Score: 63.9
Rank: 136

HAZARDS & ILLNESSES	AREA	U.S. AVG
Air-quality score	41	37
Water-quality score	62	52
Pollen/allergy score	54	61
Cancer mortality per capita	221.0	201.9
Depression days per month	2.5	3.5
Stress score	37	50

HEALTHCARE	AREA	U.S. AVG
Physicians per capita	201.0	244.2
Hospital beds per capita	493.3	420.0
No. teaching hospitals	1	3
Cost per doctor visit	$54	$77
Cost per dental visit	$68	$70

Crime
Score: 43.0
Rank: 213

CRIME	AREA	U.S. AVG
Violent crime rate	388.4	465.5
Change in violent crime rate	13.7%	-2.2%
Property crime rate	4,846.0	3,517.1
Change in property crime rate	3.1%	-2.1%

Transportation
Score: 35.0
Rank: 243

COMMUTE	AREA	U.S. AVG
Average commute time	20.9	27.4
Percent commutes > 60 mins.	3.6%	5.9%
Commute by auto	81.7%	78.9%
Commute by mass transit	0.2%	1.9%
Work at home	3.0%	3.1%
Mass transit miles per capita	0.20	1.87

INTERCITY SERVICES	AREA	U.S. AVG
Major airports within 60 miles	0	1
Size of regional airport	Small	Large
Daily airline activity	56	686
Amtrak service	No	No

AUTOMOTIVE	AREA	U.S. AVG
Insurance, annual premium	$1,272	$1,432
Gas, cost per gallon	$2.46	$2.49
Daily vehicle miles per capita	30.0	24.0

Leisure
Score: 6.7
Rank: 348

DINING & SHOPPING	AREA	U.S. AVG	ENTERTAINMENT	AREA	U.S. AVG	OUTDOOR ACTIVITIES	AREA	U.S. AVG
Restaurant rating	1	2	Professional sports rating	2	4	Golf-course rating	2	4
Outlet mall score	0	42	College sports rating	4	4	Ski-area rating	1	3
No. Starbucks	1	13	Zoo/aquarium rating	1	3	Sq. miles inland water	1	4
No. warehouse clubs	0	2	Amusement park rating	1	3	Miles of coastline	0.0	10.7
			Botanical garden/			National Park rating	2	3
			arboretum rating	1	4			

Arts & Culture
Score: 19.3
Rank: 301

MEDIA & LIBRARIES	AREA	U.S. AVG	PERFORMING ARTS	AREA	U.S. AVG	MUSEUMS	AREA	U.S. AVG
Arts radio rating	3	3	Classical music rating	2	4	Overall museum rating	5	5
No. public libraries	6	27	Ballet/dance rating	1	3	Art museum rating	2	5
Library volumes per capita	2.29	2.78	Professional theater rating	1	3	Science museum rating	5	5
			University arts programs rating	4	5	Children's museum rating	1	3

Kalamazoo–Portage, MI

Score: 52.6   **Rank:** 234   **2004 rank:** 237

Profile: Mid-size city
Location: Southwestern Michigan, midway between Detroit and Chicago along I-94
Elevation: 803 feet
Time zone: Eastern Standard Time

PRO
Cost of living
Educated population
College-town amenities

CON
Clouds and rain
Economic cycles
Winter climate

Although some discrepancy exists regarding the origin of "Kalamazoo," a colorful name that often appears in poems and children's stories, it is almost certainly Native American, and few city names are as memorable. Despite its exotic name, Kalamazoo is a rather plain industrial and commercial center with a bit of a college-town flair thanks to Western Michigan University and Kalamazoo College. Diverse industry and the university give Kalamazoo some employment stability; however, current unemployment is high. Industries include general manufacturing, some of which is auto-industry related, with plastics, pharmaceuticals and pharmaceutical research, and food flavorings businesses added to the mix. Some of these industries have replaced other noted names that started locally but have declined or moved elsewhere, such as Gibson guitars and Checker cabs. Pfizer employs some 6,000 in a former Upjohn facility in Portage, a growing suburban town to the south. Downtown is unremarkable, although there is a better-than-average concentration of shopping and small businesses. The university brings some college-town amenities and minor arts and cultural resources. A new anonymously funded tuition grant providing free Michigan state higher education tuition for graduates of Kalamazoo schools, called the Kalamazoo Promise, has brought some life and interest to the area. While Kalamazoo is centrally located among Chicago, Detroit, South Bend, and Grand Rapids, none of these places are close enough to take advantage of on a regular basis.

The terrain is flat to gently rolling, with more significant hills (including a ski area) to the northwest. Summers are warm but not too hot and moderately humid. Winters are cold, wet, and snowy with the most extreme cold tempered by Lake Michigan and the harshest winds moderated by the hills to the northwest. Still, prevailing winds bring significant cloudiness and precipitation. Warmth from the lake and local hardwood forests create attractive autumns, with some periods of clouds and rain. Winter snow cover is common. First freeze is mid-October; last is late April.

Population

DEMOGRAPHICS	AREA	U.S. AVG	ETHNIC COMPOSITION	AREA	U.S. AVG	RESIDENT PROFILE	AREA	U.S. AVG
Population	323,306		White	84.6%	79.0%	Single	34.8%	32.4%
Population density per sq. mile	275.7	358.5	Black	8.6%	10.5%	Married	50.6%	52.7%
Population growth	10.2%	21.1%	Asian	1.8%	2.7%	Divorced/separated	14.7%	14.9%
Median age	34.7	36.1	Hispanic	4.2%	10.6%	Married with children	22.1%	23.7%
Percent Democrat	50.3%	44.5%	Religious observance	34.2%	48.9%	Single with children	9.2%	9.1%
Percent Republican	48.7%	54.5%	Diversity measure	33.3	40.1	Percent over age 65	11.8%	12.9%

Economy & Jobs
Score: 60.4
Rank: 149

INCOME	AREA	U.S. AVG	EMPLOYMENT	AREA	U.S. AVG	EMPLOYING INDUSTRIES	AREA	U.S. AVG
Per capita income	$23,397	$23,235	Unemployment rate	6.3%	4.7%	Largest: Manufacturing		
Household income	$45,763	$46,414	Recent job growth	2.2%	1.3%			
Household income < $25K	26.0%	26.2%	Projected future job growth	9.8%	11.5%	Percent manufacturing	17.5%	15.4%
Household income > $75K	25.1%	25.4%	White collar	57.2%	57.8%	Percent public sector	11.8%	15.7%
Household income growth	10.7%	13.6%	Blue collar	26.2%	25.2%	Percent construction	8.7%	9.9%

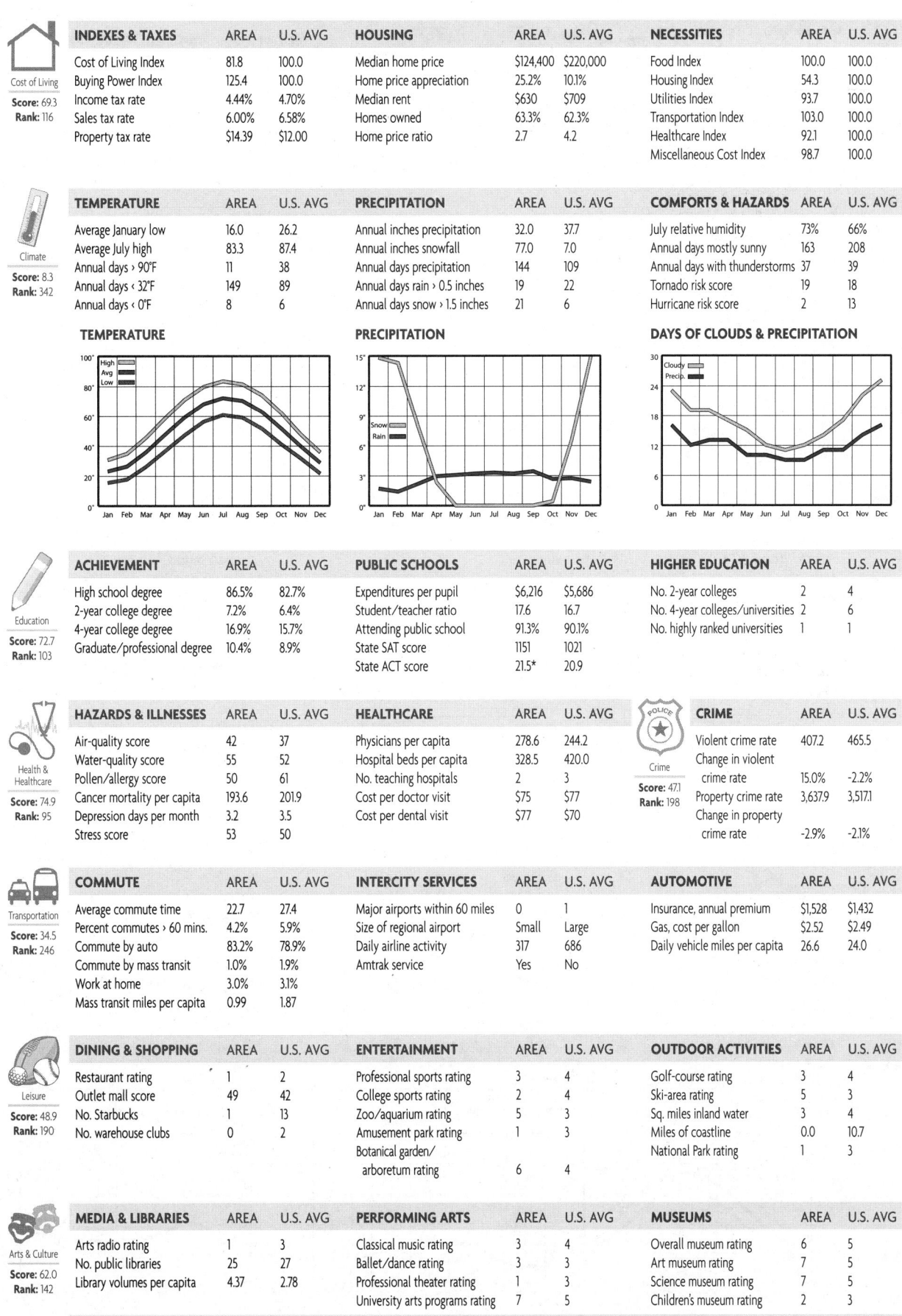

Cost of Living
Score: 69.3
Rank: 116

INDEXES & TAXES	AREA	U.S. AVG	HOUSING	AREA	U.S. AVG	NECESSITIES	AREA	U.S. AVG
Cost of Living Index	81.8	100.0	Median home price	$124,400	$220,000	Food Index	100.0	100.0
Buying Power Index	125.4	100.0	Home price appreciation	25.2%	10.1%	Housing Index	54.3	100.0
Income tax rate	4.44%	4.70%	Median rent	$630	$709	Utilities Index	93.7	100.0
Sales tax rate	6.00%	6.58%	Homes owned	63.3%	62.3%	Transportation Index	103.0	100.0
Property tax rate	$14.39	$12.00	Home price ratio	2.7	4.2	Healthcare Index	92.1	100.0
						Miscellaneous Cost Index	98.7	100.0

Climate
Score: 8.3
Rank: 342

TEMPERATURE	AREA	U.S. AVG	PRECIPITATION	AREA	U.S. AVG	COMFORTS & HAZARDS	AREA	U.S. AVG
Average January low	16.0	26.2	Annual inches precipitation	32.0	37.7	July relative humidity	73%	66%
Average July high	83.3	87.4	Annual inches snowfall	77.0	7.0	Annual days mostly sunny	163	208
Annual days > 90°F	11	38	Annual days precipitation	144	109	Annual days with thunderstorms	37	39
Annual days < 32°F	149	89	Annual days rain > 0.5 inches	19	22	Tornado risk score	19	18
Annual days < 0°F	8	6	Annual days snow > 1.5 inches	21	6	Hurricane risk score	2	13

TEMPERATURE

PRECIPITATION

DAYS OF CLOUDS & PRECIPITATION

Education
Score: 72.7
Rank: 103

ACHIEVEMENT	AREA	U.S. AVG	PUBLIC SCHOOLS	AREA	U.S. AVG	HIGHER EDUCATION	AREA	U.S. AVG
High school degree	86.5%	82.7%	Expenditures per pupil	$6,216	$5,686	No. 2-year colleges	2	4
2-year college degree	7.2%	6.4%	Student/teacher ratio	17.6	16.7	No. 4-year colleges/universities	2	6
4-year college degree	16.9%	15.7%	Attending public school	91.3%	90.1%	No. highly ranked universities	1	1
Graduate/professional degree	10.4%	8.9%	State SAT score	1151	1021			
			State ACT score	21.5*	20.9			

Health & Healthcare
Score: 74.9
Rank: 95

HAZARDS & ILLNESSES	AREA	U.S. AVG	HEALTHCARE	AREA	U.S. AVG	CRIME	AREA	U.S. AVG
Air-quality score	42	37	Physicians per capita	278.6	244.2	Violent crime rate	407.2	465.5
Water-quality score	55	52	Hospital beds per capita	328.5	420.0	Change in violent crime rate	15.0%	-2.2%
Pollen/allergy score	50	61	No. teaching hospitals	2	3	Property crime rate	3,637.9	3,517.1
Cancer mortality per capita	193.6	201.9	Cost per doctor visit	$75	$77	Change in property crime rate	-2.9%	-2.1%
Depression days per month	3.2	3.5	Cost per dental visit	$77	$70			
Stress score	53	50						

Crime
Score: 47.1
Rank: 198

Transportation
Score: 34.5
Rank: 246

COMMUTE	AREA	U.S. AVG	INTERCITY SERVICES	AREA	U.S. AVG	AUTOMOTIVE	AREA	U.S. AVG
Average commute time	22.7	27.4	Major airports within 60 miles	0	1	Insurance, annual premium	$1,528	$1,432
Percent commutes > 60 mins.	4.2%	5.9%	Size of regional airport	Small	Large	Gas, cost per gallon	$2.52	$2.49
Commute by auto	83.2%	78.9%	Daily airline activity	317	686	Daily vehicle miles per capita	26.6	24.0
Commute by mass transit	1.0%	1.9%	Amtrak service	Yes	No			
Work at home	3.0%	3.1%						
Mass transit miles per capita	0.99	1.87						

Leisure
Score: 48.9
Rank: 190

DINING & SHOPPING	AREA	U.S. AVG	ENTERTAINMENT	AREA	U.S. AVG	OUTDOOR ACTIVITIES	AREA	U.S. AVG
Restaurant rating	1	2	Professional sports rating	3	4	Golf-course rating	3	4
Outlet mall score	49	42	College sports rating	2	4	Ski-area rating	5	3
No. Starbucks	1	13	Zoo/aquarium rating	5	3	Sq. miles inland water	3	4
No. warehouse clubs	0	2	Amusement park rating	1	3	Miles of coastline	0.0	10.7
			Botanical garden/ arboretum rating	6	4	National Park rating	1	3

Arts & Culture
Score: 62.0
Rank: 142

MEDIA & LIBRARIES	AREA	U.S. AVG	PERFORMING ARTS	AREA	U.S. AVG	MUSEUMS	AREA	U.S. AVG
Arts radio rating	1	3	Classical music rating	3	4	Overall museum rating	6	5
No. public libraries	25	27	Ballet/dance rating	3	3	Art museum rating	7	5
Library volumes per capita	4.37	2.78	Professional theater rating	1	3	Science museum rating	7	5
			University arts programs rating	7	5	Children's museum rating	2	3

Kankakee–Bradley, IL

Score: 41.9   **Rank:** 310   **2004 rank:** 327

Profile: Small-town complex
Location: Northeast Illinois, 55 miles south of Chicago
Elevation: 632
Time zone: Central Standard Time

PRO	CON
Small-town atmosphere	Entertainment
Close to Chicago	Low educational attainment
Air quality	Cost of living

Kankakee and Bradley are adjacent and fairly typical small Illinois towns. The older Kankakee has industrial elements with an older central business district with classic brick buildings, a riverfront park, and abundant surrounding agricultural land. Sections of downtown have been turned into a retail antiques center, but the attempt to draw visitors and stimulate the economy has not been overwhelmingly successful. Kankakee is closer to Chicago's industrial areas than to its attractive ones. Reaching Chicago's O'Hare International Airport can take 90 minutes or more depending on traffic. Of the two cities, Bradley is where the stronger growth is occurring, with new housing and shopping developments. Cost of living is moderate and crime is a bit high for an area with this profile. Recent job growth has turned positive.

Proximity to Chicago holds the best chance for the area's future; there is talk of more commercial and industrial migration from Chicago and even a third Chicago airport in the area.

Kankakee sits in a flat agricultural plain bisected by the Kankakee River; Bradley lies 2 miles north. Cornfields and other agriculture spread across the horizon in all directions. Climate is similar to Chicago to the north, but with diminished lake effects, bringing more harsh weather at times. Summers are variable but mostly warm and humid, with occasional afternoon showers and thundershowers. Winter is cold and variable, with bitter cold snaps and periods of snow accumulation. First freeze is late September; last is early May.

Population

DEMOGRAPHICS	AREA	U.S. AVG	ETHNIC COMPOSITION	AREA	U.S. AVG	RESIDENT PROFILE	AREA	U.S. AVG
Population	106,591		White	78.7%	79.0%	Single	33.6%	32.4%
Population density per sq. mile	157.5	358.5	Black	15.5%	10.5%	Married	52.4%	52.7%
Population growth	10.7%	21.1%	Asian	0.8%	2.7%	Divorced/separated	14.0%	14.9%
Median age	35.4	36.1	Hispanic	6.3%	10.6%	Married with children	23.9%	23.7%
Percent Democrat	44.4%	44.5%	Religious observance	47.5%	48.9%	Single with children	10.2%	9.1%
Percent Republican	54.9%	54.5%	Diversity measure	43.2	40.1	Percent over age 65	13.0%	12.9%

Economy
& Jobs
Score: 50.0
Rank: 188

INCOME	AREA	U.S. AVG	EMPLOYMENT	AREA	U.S. AVG	EMPLOYING INDUSTRIES	AREA	U.S. AVG
Per capita income	$22,116	$23,235	Unemployment rate	6.0%	4.7%	Largest: Manufacturing		
Household income	$47,347	$46,414	Recent job growth	2.2%	1.3%			
Household income < $25K	24.6%	26.2%	Projected future job growth	9.9%	11.5%	Percent manufacturing	20.7%	15.4%
Household income > $75K	25.7%	25.4%	White collar	52.1%	57.8%	Percent public sector	12.9%	15.7%
Household income growth	14.0%	13.6%	Blue collar	31.2%	25.2%	Percent construction	10.5%	9.9%

Cost of Living
Score: 76.5
Rank: 89

INDEXES & TAXES	AREA	U.S. AVG	HOUSING	AREA	U.S. AVG	NECESSITIES	AREA	U.S. AVG
Cost of Living Index	91.7	100.0	Median home price	$134,900	$220,000	Food Index	106.9	100.0
Buying Power Index	115.7	100.0	Home price appreciation	31.5%	10.1%	Housing Index	60.9	100.0
Income tax rate	3.00%	4.70%	Median rent	$705	$709	Utilities Index	106.1	100.0
Sales tax rate	6.25%	6.58%	Homes owned	65.8%	62.3%	Transportation Index	119.5	100.0
Property tax rate	$17.50	$12.00	Home price ratio	2.8	4.2	Healthcare Index	117.7	100.0
						Miscellaneous Cost Index	107.0	100.0

Climate
Score: 6.1
Rank: 350

TEMPERATURE	AREA	U.S. AVG	PRECIPITATION	AREA	U.S. AVG	COMFORTS & HAZARDS	AREA	U.S. AVG
Average January low	10.0	26.2	Annual inches precipitation	37.0	37.7	July relative humidity	72%	66%
Average July high	84.0	87.4	Annual inches snowfall	37.0	7.0	Annual days mostly sunny	196	208
Annual days > 90°F	15	38	Annual days precipitation	117	109	Annual days with thunderstorms	43	39
Annual days < 32°F	145	89	Annual days rain > 0.5 inches	23	22	Tornado risk score	20	18
Annual days < 0°F	14	6	Annual days snow > 1.5 inches	12	6	Hurricane risk score	2	13

TEMPERATURE

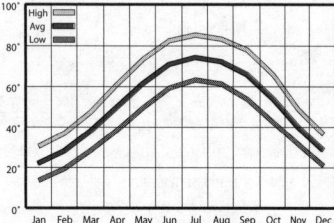

PRECIPITATION

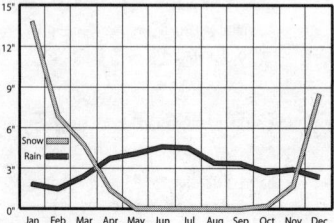

DAYS OF CLOUDS & PRECIPITATION

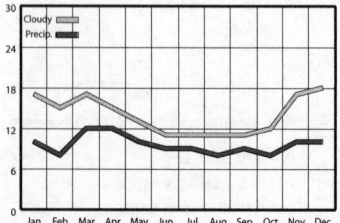

Education
Score: 12.8
Rank: 325

ACHIEVEMENT	AREA	U.S. AVG	PUBLIC SCHOOLS	AREA	U.S. AVG	HIGHER EDUCATION	AREA	U.S. AVG
High school degree	79.9%	82.7%	Expenditures per pupil	$4,927	$5,686	No. 2-year colleges	1	4
2-year college degree	6.3%	6.4%	Student/teacher ratio	16.3	16.7	No. 4-year colleges/universities	1	6
4-year college degree	9.4%	15.7%	Attending public school	88.8%	90.1%	No. highly ranked universities	0	1
Graduate/professional degree	5.6%	8.9%	State SAT score	1200	1021			
			State ACT score	20.5*	20.9			

Health & Healthcare
Score: 41.7
Rank: 217

Crime
Score: 68.4
Rank: 119

HAZARDS & ILLNESSES	AREA	U.S. AVG	HEALTHCARE	AREA	U.S. AVG	CRIME	AREA	U.S. AVG
Air-quality score	48	37	Physicians per capita	147.7	244.2	Violent crime rate	392.8	465.5
Water-quality score	60	52	Hospital beds per capita	463.5	420.0	Change in violent crime rate	4.6%	-2.2%
Pollen/allergy score	56	61	No. teaching hospitals	0	3	Property crime rate	3,037.7	3,517.1
Cancer mortality per capita	239.7	201.9	Cost per doctor visit	$60	$77	Change in property crime rate	-2.0%	-2.1%
Depression days per month	3.3	3.5	Cost per dental visit	$64	$70			
Stress score	60	50						

Transportation
Score: 90.9
Rank: 35

COMMUTE	AREA	U.S. AVG	INTERCITY SERVICES	AREA	U.S. AVG	AUTOMOTIVE	AREA	U.S. AVG
Average commute time	25.3	27.4	Major airports within 60 miles	2	1	Insurance, annual premium	$1,046	$1,432
Percent commutes > 60 mins.	9.1%	5.9%	Size of regional airport	Large	Large	Gas, cost per gallon	$2.44	$2.49
Commute by auto	81.4%	78.9%	Daily airline activity	1798	686	Daily vehicle miles per capita	22.6	24.0
Commute by mass transit	1.0%	1.9%	Amtrak service	Yes	No			
Work at home	2.6%	3.1%						
Mass transit miles per capita	1.04	1.87						

Leisure
Score: 68.2
Rank: 119

DINING & SHOPPING	AREA	U.S. AVG	ENTERTAINMENT	AREA	U.S. AVG	OUTDOOR ACTIVITIES	AREA	U.S. AVG
Restaurant rating	1	2	Professional sports rating	8	4	Golf-course rating	6	4
Outlet mall score	106	42	College sports rating	4	4	Ski-area rating	1	3
No. Starbucks	1	13	Zoo/aquarium rating	3	3	Sq. miles inland water	2	4
No. warehouse clubs	0	2	Amusement park rating	3	3	Miles of coastline	0.0	10.7
			Botanical garden/ arboretum rating	6	4	National Park rating	2	3

Arts & Culture
Score: 39.3
Rank: 227

MEDIA & LIBRARIES	AREA	U.S. AVG	PERFORMING ARTS	AREA	U.S. AVG	MUSEUMS	AREA	U.S. AVG
Arts radio rating	4	3	Classical music rating	4	4	Overall museum rating	7	5
No. public libraries	8	27	Ballet/dance rating	4	3	Art museum rating	6	5
Library volumes per capita	3.53	2.78	Professional theater rating	5	3	Science museum rating	6	5
			University arts programs rating	2	5	Children's museum rating	8	3

Kansas City, MO-KS

Score: 57.1 **Rank:** 199 **2004 rank:** 130

Profile: Large-city complex
Location: Missouri-Kansas border, on the Missouri River
Elevation: 1,014 feet
Time zone: Central Standard Time

PRO
Diverse economy
Entertainment
Attractive downtown

CON
Growth and sprawl
Uninteresting physical setting
Crime rates

Kansas City is a large, prosperous, self-sufficient, and culturally rich combined city located astride the Missouri River. The downtown area and most of the population are on the older Missouri side, filled with shaded neighborhoods and mixed development. For the past 20 years the big growth has been on the Kansas side to the southwest in suburbs such as Overland Park, Lenexa, and Shawnee. Once grittier and more industrial, the Kansas or "KCK" side is changing its image fast. The combined city grew up as an agricultural center that provided commercial and industrial support to the vast agricultural area to the west. Food processing is still a major industry, but diverse industries such as greeting cards (Hallmark), telecommunications, publishing, and automobile manufacturers have also set up shop. The area is centrally located to all U.S. markets and has an attractive business climate.

Although not a boom economy, economic growth projections are moderate, incomes are high, and buying power is strong. The Cost of Living Index is 87.7; the Buying Power Index is 135.7.

The attractive downtown boasts museums and architectural attractions, including modern buildings and restorations of older sites such as the 1914 Union Station. More recently, a major urban redevelopment and renewal effort has taken hold, anchored by a new Federal Reserve and IRS complex expected to employ 7,000 and a new headquarters for financial services giant H&R Block, plus a new entertainment district. These developments and more renovations of attractive older buildings are adding life to the area, and there is also a significant push towards residential units in the city, which earned an All-America City Award in 2006. The city reports that almost 40% of new apartment construction over the next 2 years is slated for downtown.

Kansas City has a cultural history more interesting than most: A mix of migrated workers from the Southeast and local customs led to fame in barbecue ribs and blues music, both available in abundance. Although well known for its restaurants, clubs, and live music, professional sports, particularly the NFL Chiefs and the MLB Royals, are also important. Locals share a strong sense of civic pride and the belief that the area is a well-kept secret. On the downside, "Westward expansion" takes on a whole new meaning here. One estimate holds that the average person has more "room"—over 85,000 square feet—in this metropolitan area than anywhere else in the country. Availability of cheap land, particularly to the west, and few geographic barriers have created some sprawl problems. The highway system is extensive but generally adequate and commute times are acceptable so far, but the future bears watching.

Intercity transport benefits from the presence of discount airlines and the central location. Home prices are moderate, and excellent values and family-style living can be found in older city neighborhoods and in suburbs to the west.

The area is located on a broad river plain at the confluence of the Missouri and Kansas rivers. Surrounding terrain is flat to gently rolling with mixed deciduous woods around the city center and open prairie to the west. Summer has warm days and mild nights with moderate humidity; occasional heat waves bring higher temperatures and humidity for a week or two each summer. Winters are not severely cold but occasional cold snaps do occur. Heavy snowfalls are uncommon. Spring is wet with rapid weather fluctuations and autumn is mild and sunny. First freeze is mid-October; last is mid-April.

Population

DEMOGRAPHICS	AREA	U.S. AVG	ETHNIC COMPOSITION	AREA	U.S. AVG	RESIDENT PROFILE	AREA	U.S. AVG
Population	1,934,400		White	80.0%	79.0%	Single	30.1%	32.4%
Population density per sq. mile	246.2	358.5	Black	12.6%	10.5%	Married	54.9%	52.7%
Population growth	20.7%	21.1%	Asian	2.2%	2.7%	Divorced/separated	15.0%	14.9%
Median age	36.0	36.1	Hispanic	6.0%	10.6%	Married with children	24.6%	23.7%
Percent Democrat	48.3%	44.5%	Religious observance	48.1%	48.9%	Single with children	8.9%	9.1%
Percent Republican	50.9%	54.5%	Diversity measure	38.1	40.1	Percent over age 65	11.5%	12.9%

Economy & Jobs

Score: 42.0
Rank: 217

INCOME	AREA	U.S. AVG	EMPLOYMENT	AREA	U.S. AVG	EMPLOYING INDUSTRIES	AREA	U.S. AVG
Per capita income	$26,523	$23,235	Unemployment rate	5.8%	4.7%	Largest: Healthcare & Social Assistance		
Household income	$53,112	$46,414	Recent job growth	0.7%	1.3%			
Household income < $25K	20.4%	26.2%	Projected future job growth	8.5%	11.5%	Percent manufacturing	12.8%	15.4%
Household income > $75K	30.7%	25.4%	White collar	63.8%	57.8%	Percent public sector	12.6%	15.7%
Household income growth	13.1%	13.6%	Blue collar	22.1%	25.2%	Percent construction	9.3%	9.9%

Cost of Living

Score: 26.2
Rank: 275

INDEXES & TAXES	AREA	U.S. AVG	HOUSING	AREA	U.S. AVG	NECESSITIES	AREA	U.S. AVG
Cost of Living Index	87.7	100.0	Median home price	$158,800	$220,000	Food Index	98.4	100.0
Buying Power Index	135.7	100.0	Home price appreciation	29.1%	10.1%	Housing Index	56.0	100.0
Income tax rate	6.97%	4.70%	Median rent	$710	$709	Utilities Index	100.3	100.0
Sales tax rate	7.40%	6.58%	Homes owned	64.8%	62.3%	Transportation Index	102.0	100.0
Property tax rate	$12.08	$12.00	Home price ratio	3.0	4.2	Healthcare Index	96.0	100.0
						Miscellaneous Cost Index	100.1	100.0

Climate

Score: 18.4
Rank: 304

TEMPERATURE	AREA	U.S. AVG	PRECIPITATION	AREA	U.S. AVG	COMFORTS & HAZARDS	AREA	U.S. AVG
Average January low	18.4	26.2	Annual inches precipitation	37.0	37.7	July relative humidity	69%	66%
Average July high	88.0	87.4	Annual inches snowfall	20.0	7.0	Annual days mostly sunny	213	208
Annual days > 90°F	40	38	Annual days precipitation	102	109	Annual days with thunderstorms	53	39
Annual days < 32°F	106	89	Annual days rain > 0.5 inches	24	22	Tornado risk score	49	18
Annual days < 0°F	9	6	Annual days snow > 1.5 inches	5	6	Hurricane risk score	2	13

TEMPERATURE

PRECIPITATION

DAYS OF CLOUDS & PRECIPITATION

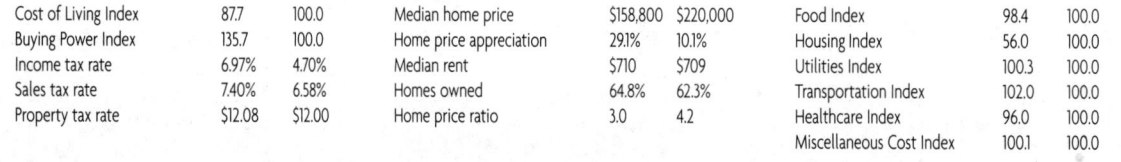

Education

Score: 88.0
Rank: 46

ACHIEVEMENT	AREA	U.S. AVG	PUBLIC SCHOOLS	AREA	U.S. AVG	HIGHER EDUCATION	AREA	U.S. AVG
High school degree	86.9%	82.7%	Expenditures per pupil	$5,673	$5,686	No. 2-year colleges	17	4
2-year college degree	5.9%	6.4%	Student/teacher ratio	15.2	16.7	No. 4-year colleges/universities	29	6
4-year college degree	19.1%	15.7%	Attending public school	89.8%	90.1%	No. highly ranked universities	2	1
Graduate/professional degree	9.5%	8.9%	State SAT score	1178	1021			
			State ACT score	21.6*	20.9			

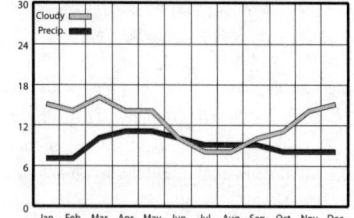

Health & Healthcare
Score: 35.8
Rank: 239

HAZARDS & ILLNESSES	AREA	U.S. AVG	HEALTHCARE	AREA	U.S. AVG
Air-quality score	30	37	Physicians per capita	263.3	244.2
Water-quality score	33	52	Hospital beds per capita	400.8	420.0
Pollen/allergy score	74	61	No. teaching hospitals	15	3
Cancer mortality per capita	211.0	201.9	Cost per doctor visit	$71	$77
Depression days per month	2.9	3.5	Cost per dental visit	$63	$70
Stress score	87	50			

Crime
Score: 11.2
Rank: 331

CRIME	AREA	U.S. AVG
Violent crime rate	614.7	465.5
Change in violent crime rate	3.2%	-2.2%
Property crime rate	4,676.7	3,517.1
Change in property crime rate	-2.7%	-2.1%

Transportation
Score: 22.5
Rank: 291

COMMUTE	AREA	U.S. AVG	INTERCITY SERVICES	AREA	U.S. AVG
Average commute time	25.3	27.4	Major airports within 60 miles	1	1
Percent commutes > 60 mins.	4.1%	5.9%	Size of regional airport	Medium	Large
Commute by auto	82.7%	78.9%	Daily airline activity	328	686
Commute by mass transit	1.2%	1.9%	Amtrak service	Yes	No
Work at home	3.5%	3.1%			
Mass transit miles per capita	1.21	1.87			

AUTOMOTIVE	AREA	U.S. AVG
Insurance, annual premium	$1,756	$1,432
Gas, cost per gallon	$2.35	$2.49
Daily vehicle miles per capita	28.7	24.0

Leisure
Score: 77.3
Rank: 85

DINING & SHOPPING	AREA	U.S. AVG	ENTERTAINMENT	AREA	U.S. AVG
Restaurant rating	4	2	Professional sports rating	6	4
Outlet mall score	46	42	College sports rating	2	4
No. Starbucks	20	13	Zoo/aquarium rating	7	3
No. warehouse clubs	7	2	Amusement park rating	4	3
			Botanical garden/ arboretum rating	2	4

OUTDOOR ACTIVITIES	AREA	U.S. AVG
Golf-course rating	8	4
Ski-area rating	2	3
Sq. miles inland water	4	4
Miles of coastline	0.0	10.7
National Park rating	1	3

Arts & Culture
Score: 92.5
Rank: 29

MEDIA & LIBRARIES	AREA	U.S. AVG	PERFORMING ARTS	AREA	U.S. AVG
Arts radio rating	5	3	Classical music rating	9	4
No. public libraries	92	27	Ballet/dance rating	3	3
Library volumes per capita	6.92	2.78	Professional theater rating	8	3
			University arts programs rating	8	5

MUSEUMS	AREA	U.S. AVG
Overall museum rating	9	5
Art museum rating	9	5
Science museum rating	7	5
Children's museum rating	9	3

Kennewick–Richland–Pasco, WA

Score: 56.0   **Rank:** 207   **2004 rank:** 114

Profile: Small-town complex
Location: Southeastern Washington at the confluence of the Snake and Columbia rivers
Elevation: 360 feet
Time zone: Pacific Standard Time

PRO	CON
Small-town atmosphere	Isolation
Future job growth	Entertainment
Water recreation	Harsh climate

This Tri-Cities area along the Snake-Columbia river confluence is agricultural, with irrigated vegetables, fruits, grains, seeds, and livestock, and then an assortment of industrial and government-related activities mixed in. The towns, which are separated by a few miles, are clean, plain, and simple, with low crime and a relative lack of historic and cultural amenities. Pasco in particular serves as a major Columbia River port for agricultural products, paper, and forest products; boats and metal fabrication are also a significant part of the economic base. Richland, 6 miles downriver, plays a major role as a commercial, research, and administrative center for the vast Hanford Site, a U.S. Department of Energy nuclear waste and research facility. Richland also has the strongest healthcare facilities and the strongest base of high-paying jobs. Kennewick is more residential and retail-commercial, and is the largest and most family-oriented of the three. The Columbia River and some of the vast outdoor spaces nearby provide some recreation, but relatively dry topography surrounding the area contradicts the usual image of lush, green forests often attached to the Washington and the Pacific Northwest. The area has become more noted as a wine-growing region. Walla Walla, a college town 40 miles east, offers some amenities in a more attractive and more wooded mountainous setting. The isolation and lack of things to do brought a lower ranking this time.

The area is in a broad, flat, agricultural valley. Dry, grassy hills rise to the south and east toward Walla Walla and the Blue Mountains of Washington and northeast Oregon. The climate features low rainfall, dry air, and large diurnal temperature ranges. Summer hot spells are common when the westerly airflow subsides; temperatures of 100°F are common. Cold spells occur when frigid Canadian air enters the valley. Strong winds can stir up dust. Occasional air stagnation may result from the valley location.

DEMOGRAPHICS	AREA	U.S. AVG	ETHNIC COMPOSITION	AREA	U.S. AVG	RESIDENT PROFILE	AREA	U.S. AVG
Population	216,153		White	78.3%	79.0%	Single	28.6%	32.4%
Population density per sq. mile	73.4	358.5	Black	1.4%	10.5%	Married	57.5%	52.7%
Population growth	44.3%	21.1%	Asian	2.3%	2.7%	Divorced/separated	14.0%	14.9%
Median age	33.2	36.1	Hispanic	23.7%	10.6%	Married with children	29.7%	23.7%
Percent Democrat	32.2%	44.5%	Religious observance	43.5%	48.9%	Single with children	10.1%	9.1%
Percent Republican	66.4%	54.5%	Diversity measure	53.5	40.1	Percent over age 65	9.8%	12.9%

Population

INCOME	AREA	U.S. AVG	EMPLOYMENT	AREA	U.S. AVG	EMPLOYING INDUSTRIES	AREA	U.S. AVG
Per capita income	$22,675	$23,235	Unemployment rate	5.6%	4.7%	Largest: Professional, Scientific & Technical Services		
Household income	$51,711	$46,414	Recent job growth	2.4%	1.3%			
Household income < $25K	22.1%	26.2%	Projected future job growth	18.9%	11.5%	Percent manufacturing	12.9%	15.4%
Household income > $75K	30.7%	25.4%	White collar	56.4%	57.8%	Percent public sector	17.4%	15.7%
Household income growth	15.1%	13.6%	Blue collar	22.7%	25.2%	Percent construction	9.8%	9.9%

Economy & Jobs
Score: 78.6
Rank: 80

INDEXES & TAXES	AREA	U.S. AVG	HOUSING	AREA	U.S. AVG	NECESSITIES	AREA	U.S. AVG
Cost of Living Index	89.8	100.0	Median home price	$157,100	$220,000	Food Index	103.6	100.0
Buying Power Index	129.1	100.0	Home price appreciation	29.0%	10.1%	Housing Index	55.2	100.0
Income tax rate	0.00%	4.70%	Median rent	$647	$709	Utilities Index	75.8	100.0
Sales tax rate	8.14%	6.58%	Homes owned	64.8%	62.3%	Transportation Index	104.5	100.0
Property tax rate	$11.85	$12.00	Home price ratio	3.0	4.2	Healthcare Index	123.1	100.0
						Miscellaneous Cost Index	99.7	100.0

Cost of Living
Score: 78.6
Rank: 81

TEMPERATURE	AREA	U.S. AVG	PRECIPITATION	AREA	U.S. AVG	COMFORTS & HAZARDS	AREA	U.S. AVG
Average January low	18.6	26.2	Annual inches precipitation	8.0	37.7	July relative humidity	60%	66%
Average July high	88.1	87.4	Annual inches snowfall	25.0	7.0	Annual days mostly sunny	202	208
Annual days > 90°F	33	38	Annual days precipitation	67	109	Annual days with thunderstorms	7	39
Annual days < 32°F	150	89	Annual days rain > 0.5 inches	5	22	Tornado risk score	0	18
Annual days < 0°F	4	6	Annual days snow > 1.5 inches	7	6	Hurricane risk score	0	13

Climate
Score: 33.7
Rank: 247

TEMPERATURE

PRECIPITATION

DAYS OF CLOUDS & PRECIPITATION

ACHIEVEMENT	AREA	U.S. AVG	PUBLIC SCHOOLS	AREA	U.S. AVG	HIGHER EDUCATION	AREA	U.S. AVG
High school degree	79.2%	82.7%	Expenditures per pupil	$5,800	$5,686	No. 2-year colleges	2	4
2-year college degree	8.7%	6.4%	Student/teacher ratio	19.0	16.7	No. 4-year colleges/universities	1	6
4-year college degree	14.6%	15.7%	Attending public school	94.3%	90.1%	No. highly ranked universities	0	1
Graduate/professional degree	8.6%	8.9%	State SAT score	1059*	1021			
			State ACT score	22.9	20.9			

Education
Score: 52.1
Rank: 180

HAZARDS & ILLNESSES	AREA	U.S. AVG	HEALTHCARE	AREA	U.S. AVG	CRIME	AREA	U.S. AVG
Air-quality score	49	37	Physicians per capita	150.5	244.2	Violent crime rate	238.1	465.5
Water-quality score	30	52	Hospital beds per capita	206.8	420.0	Change in violent crime rate	-8.1%	-2.2%
Pollen/allergy score	46	61	No. teaching hospitals	0	3	Property crime rate	3,725.2	3,517.1
Cancer mortality per capita	193.3	201.9	Cost per doctor visit	$84	$77	Change in property crime rate	1.1%	-2.1%
Depression days per month	3.0	3.5	Cost per dental visit	$90	$70			
Stress score	46	50						

Health & Healthcare
Score: 45.7
Rank: 204

Crime
Score: 83.2
Rank: 64

COMMUTE	AREA	U.S. AVG	INTERCITY SERVICES	AREA	U.S. AVG	AUTOMOTIVE	AREA	U.S. AVG
Average commute time	23.3	27.4	Major airports within 60 miles	0	1	Insurance, annual premium	$1,202	$1,432
Percent commutes > 60 mins.	4.7%	5.9%	Size of regional airport	None	Large	Gas, cost per gallon	$2.52	$2.49
Commute by auto	77.5%	78.9%	Daily airline activity	47	686	Daily vehicle miles per capita	19.0	24.0
Commute by mass transit	1.0%	1.9%	Amtrak service	Yes	No			
Work at home	3.8%	3.1%						
Mass transit miles per capita	0.98	1.87						

Transportation
Score: 15.8
Rank: 316

Leisure Score: 26.5 Rank: 274	DINING & SHOPPING	AREA	U.S. AVG	ENTERTAINMENT	AREA	U.S. AVG	OUTDOOR ACTIVITIES	AREA	U.S. AVG
	Restaurant rating	1	2	Professional sports rating	3	4	Golf-course rating	2	4
	Outlet mall score	0	42	College sports rating	1	4	Ski-area rating	1	3
	No. Starbucks	7	13	Zoo/aquarium rating	1	3	Sq. miles inland water	5	4
	No. warehouse clubs	1	2	Amusement park rating	1	3	Miles of coastline	0.0	10.7
				Botanical garden/ arboretum rating	1	4	National Park rating	1	3

Arts & Culture Score: 18.7 Rank: 303	MEDIA & LIBRARIES	AREA	U.S. AVG	PERFORMING ARTS	AREA	U.S. AVG	MUSEUMS	AREA	U.S. AVG
	Arts radio rating	5	3	Classical music rating	1	4	Overall museum rating	1	5
	No. public libraries	12	27	Ballet/dance rating	3	3	Art museum rating	1	5
	Library volumes per capita	3.31	2.78	Professional theater rating	1	3	Science museum rating	3	5
				University arts programs rating	1	5	Children's museum rating	1	3

Killeen–Temple–Fort Hood, TX   Score: 46.2   Rank: 274   2004 rank: 154

Profile: Military town/small-city complex
Location: East-central Texas along I-35 between Dallas and Austin
Elevation: 833 feet
Time zone: Central Standard Time

PRO	CON
Cost of living	Entertainment
Stable economy	Arts and culture
Healthcare	Summer heat

Temple is a small Texas town with a transportation heritage starting with the 19th-century Chisholm Trail and continuing today with distribution facilities strategically located to maximize trade with Mexico and proximity to other cities in the state. Headquartered there are McLane Company, Inc., the nation's largest convenience store supplier now owned by Wal-Mart, and Wilsonart International, a maker of plastic laminates. Temple's nondescript downtown is currently undergoing a renovation with focus on points of historic interest. Temple is home to the Scott and White Memorial Hospital and Clinic, a large regional teaching hospital with some 500 beds and a similar number of physicians. Killeen, 20 miles to the west, serves the massive Fort Hood military installation. Not surprisingly, the area has a very low cost-of-living

profile, one of the best for Texas outside of border towns. But there isn't much to do nor is there much intellectual stimulation. The area is known for spring wildflowers in the Grand Prairie to the west.

Temple and Killeen sit at the border between the Blackland Prairie agricultural area to the east and the Grand Prairie dry hills to the west. The area around both cities is mostly level to gently rolling. July and August days are particularly hot, with clear skies and relatively low humidity. Spring can be quite wet and stormy, and mild winters are punctuated by windy, cold-air invasions from the north. Winter precipitation may be a mix of snow, rain, sleet, and freezing rain, but snow accumulation is usually minimal.

Population	DEMOGRAPHICS	AREA	U.S. AVG	ETHNIC COMPOSITION	AREA	U.S. AVG	RESIDENT PROFILE	AREA	U.S. AVG
	Population	348,803		White	65.0%	79.0%	Single	26.9%	32.4%
	Population density per sq. mile	123.5	358.5	Black	17.9%	10.5%	Married	54.5%	52.7%
	Population growth	30.3%	21.1%	Asian	2.7%	2.7%	Divorced/separated	18.6%	14.9%
	Median age	30.2	36.1	Hispanic	17.7%	10.6%	Married with children	30.9%	23.7%
	Percent Democrat	32.3%	44.5%	Religious observance	45.9%	48.9%	Single with children	10.5%	9.1%
	Percent Republican	67.2%	54.5%	Diversity measure	66.5	40.1	Percent over age 65	8.9%	12.9%

Economy & Jobs Score: 66.8 Rank: 125	INCOME	AREA	U.S. AVG	EMPLOYMENT	AREA	U.S. AVG	EMPLOYING INDUSTRIES	AREA	U.S. AVG
	Per capita income	$19,388	$23,235	Unemployment rate	5.2%	4.7%	Largest: Healthcare & Social Assistance		
	Household income	$42,871	$46,414	Recent job growth	3.1%	1.3%			
	Household income < $25K	24.6%	26.2%	Projected future job growth	13.5%	11.5%	Percent manufacturing	13.5%	15.4%
	Household income > $75K	19.9%	25.4%	White collar	56.4%	57.8%	Percent public sector	24.4%	15.7%
	Household income growth	17.0%	13.6%	Blue collar	24.4%	25.2%	Percent construction	10.9%	9.9%

Cost of Living Score: 95.2 Rank: 17	INDEXES & TAXES	AREA	U.S. AVG	HOUSING	AREA	U.S. AVG	NECESSITIES	AREA	U.S. AVG
	Cost of Living Index	76.5	100.0	Median home price	$107,600	$220,000	Food Index	84.2	100.0
	Buying Power Index	125.6	100.0	Home price appreciation	30.0%	10.1%	Housing Index	47.5	100.0
	Income tax rate	0.00%	4.70%	Median rent	$621	$709	Utilities Index	93.2	100.0
	Sales tax rate	8.25%	6.58%	Homes owned	52.9%	62.3%	Transportation Index	95.5	100.0
	Property tax rate	$14.73	$12.00	Home price ratio	2.5	4.2	Healthcare Index	99.7	100.0
							Miscellaneous Cost Index	97.7	100.0

Climate
Score: 69.8
Rank: 112

TEMPERATURE	AREA	U.S. AVG
Average January low	29.4	26.2
Average July high	99.2	87.4
Annual days > 90°F	106	38
Annual days > 32°F	70	89
Annual days < 0°F	0	6

PRECIPITATION	AREA	U.S. AVG
Annual inches precipitation	31.3	37.7
Annual inches snowfall	1.5	7.0
Annual days precipitation	78	109
Annual days rain > 0.5 inches	18	22
Annual days snow > 1.5 inches	1	6

COMFORTS & HAZARDS	AREA	U.S. AVG
July relative humidity	67%	66%
Annual days mostly sunny	231	208
Annual days with thunderstorms	49	39
Tornado risk score	20	18
Hurricane risk score	15	13

TEMPERATURE

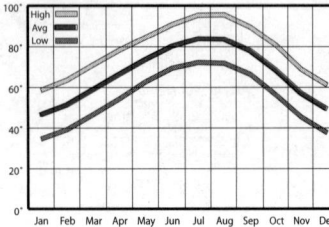

PRECIPITATION

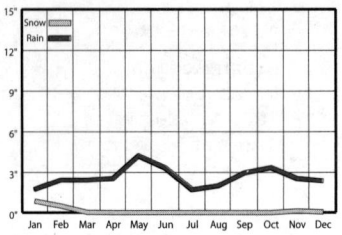

DAYS OF CLOUDS & PRECIPITATION

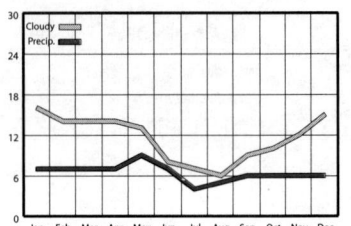

Education
Score: 53.5
Rank: 174

ACHIEVEMENT	AREA	U.S. AVG
High school degree	84.0%	82.7%
2-year college degree	8.6%	6.4%
4-year college degree	12.3%	15.7%
Graduate/professional degree	5.8%	8.9%

PUBLIC SCHOOLS	AREA	U.S. AVG
Expenditures per pupil	$5,216	$5,686
Student/teacher ratio	14.3	16.7
Attending public school	97.1%	90.1%
State SAT score	997*	1021
State ACT score	20.3	20.9

HIGHER EDUCATION	AREA	U.S. AVG
No. 2-year colleges	2	4
No. 4-year colleges/universities	1	6
No. highly ranked universities	0	1

Health & Healthcare
Score: 52.1
Rank: 180

HAZARDS & ILLNESSES	AREA	U.S. AVG
Air-quality score	43	37
Water-quality score	82	52
Pollen/allergy score	78	61
Cancer mortality per capita	179.0	201.9
Depression days per month	3.4	3.5
Stress score	52	50

HEALTHCARE	AREA	U.S. AVG
Physicians per capita	304.7	244.2
Hospital beds per capita	252.9	420.0
No. teaching hospitals	1	3
Cost per doctor visit	$64	$77
Cost per dental visit	$60	$70

Crime
Score: 52.4
Rank: 178

CRIME	AREA	U.S. AVG
Violent crime rate	381.2	465.5
Change in violent crime rate	-0.2%	-2.2%
Property crime rate	3,680.7	3,517.1
Change in property crime rate	7.4%	-2.1%

Transportation
Score: 30.2
Rank: 262

COMMUTE	AREA	U.S. AVG
Average commute time	23.1	27.4
Percent commutes > 60 mins.	6.3%	5.9%
Commute by auto	77.0%	78.9%
Commute by mass transit	0.2%	1.9%
Work at home	1.8%	3.1%
Mass transit miles per capita	0.25	1.87

INTERCITY SERVICES	AREA	U.S. AVG
Major airports within 60 miles	1	1
Size of regional airport	Medium	Large
Daily airline activity	183	686
Amtrak service	Yes	No

AUTOMOTIVE	AREA	U.S. AVG
Insurance, annual premium	$1,032	$1,432
Gas, cost per gallon	$2.44	$2.49
Daily vehicle miles per capita	23.7	24.0

Leisure
Score: 6.1
Rank: 350

DINING & SHOPPING	AREA	U.S. AVG
Restaurant rating	1	2
Outlet mall score	0	42
No. Starbucks	3	13
No. warehouse clubs	1	2

ENTERTAINMENT	AREA	U.S. AVG
Professional sports rating	2	4
College sports rating	1	4
Zoo/aquarium rating	1	3
Amusement park rating	1	3
Botanical garden/ arboretum rating	1	4

OUTDOOR ACTIVITIES	AREA	U.S. AVG
Golf-course rating	2	4
Ski-area rating	1	3
Sq. miles inland water	3	4
Miles of coastline	0.0	10.7
National Park rating	1	3

Arts & Culture
Score: 2.4
Rank: 364

MEDIA & LIBRARIES	AREA	U.S. AVG
Arts radio rating	1	3
No. public libraries	10	27
Library volumes per capita	1.92	2.78

PERFORMING ARTS	AREA	U.S. AVG
Classical music rating	1	4
Ballet/dance rating	1	3
Professional theater rating	1	3
University arts programs rating	3	5

MUSEUMS	AREA	U.S. AVG
Overall museum rating	3	5
Art museum rating	1	5
Science museum rating	1	5
Children's museum rating	1	3

Kingsport–Bristol–Bristol, TN-VA   Score: 58.3   Rank: 187   2004 rank: 77

Profile: Small-city complex
Location: Northeastern tip of Tennessee at the Virginia border
Elevation: 1,259 feet
Time zone: Eastern Standard Time

PRO	CON
Cost of living	Employment
Nearby recreation	Isolation
Diverse economy	Low educational attainment

The OMB recently split off Johnson City from this Tri-Cities metro area, although the remaining area still has three names, with Bristol listed twice because it straddles the Tennessee-Virginia line. Kingsport and Bristol, 20 miles separated, are typical small Southern centers supporting an assortment of industrial and agricultural activities. Chemicals, forest products, glass, textiles, and metal products are produced in the area. Bristol is a center for small business and industry, and Kingsport holds the largest single industrial employer in the state, Eastman Chemical. Kingsport is a planned city with ample parkland and greenbelts and the downtown is fairly attractive. All the cities have an assortment of arts and recreational activities, as well as access to the nearby Tennessee Valley Authority lakes. The rolling terrain north into Virginia is beautiful, especially in spring and fall. The

Bristol Motor Speedway is an important NASCAR track. Cost of living is very low (75.4) and the economy, while diverse, is going through some obvious adjustments. The area is geographically isolated from larger cities. Additional services are usually found in Virginia or in Knoxville 120 miles west, but it is a long drive.

The Tri-Cities area is located in the upper East Tennessee Valley. The immediate terrain is gently rolling on the east and south to very hilly on the west and north. Mountain ranges rise 4,000 to 6,000 feet farther across the valley to the southeast. Summer thunderstorms are frequent, with the most rain occurring in July. Atlantic Coast storms can bring heavy winter precipitation. Only the higher mountains typically receive snow.

Population

DEMOGRAPHICS	AREA	U.S. AVG
Population	301,138	
Population density per sq. mile	149.7	358.5
Population growth	9.9%	21.1%
Median age	41.2	36.1
Percent Democrat	32.3%	44.5%
Percent Republican	66.8%	54.5%

ETHNIC COMPOSITION	AREA	U.S. AVG
White	96.5%	79.0%
Black	2.0%	10.5%
Asian	0.5%	2.7%
Hispanic	0.8%	10.6%
Religious observance	51.6%	48.9%
Diversity measure	8.2	40.1

RESIDENT PROFILE	AREA	U.S. AVG
Single	25.8%	32.4%
Married	60.2%	52.7%
Divorced/separated	14.0%	14.9%
Married with children	21.9%	23.7%
Single with children	6.6%	9.1%
Percent over age 65	16.6%	12.9%

Economy & Jobs
Score: 5.6
Rank: 352

INCOME	AREA	U.S. AVG
Per capita income	$20,492	$23,235
Household income	$36,436	$46,414
Household income < $25K	34.3%	26.2%
Household income > $75K	16.4%	25.4%
Household income growth	13.4%	13.6%

EMPLOYMENT	AREA	U.S. AVG
Unemployment rate	5.5%	4.7%
Recent job growth	-0.4%	1.3%
Projected future job growth	0.9%	11.5%
White collar	51.6%	57.8%
Blue collar	33.9%	25.2%

EMPLOYING INDUSTRIES	AREA	U.S. AVG
Largest: Manufacturing		
Percent manufacturing	22.7%	15.4%
Percent public sector	11.4%	15.7%
Percent construction	11.2%	9.9%

Cost of Living
Score: 99.2
Rank: 4

INDEXES & TAXES	AREA	U.S. AVG
Cost of Living Index	75.4	100.0
Buying Power Index	108.3	100.0
Income tax rate	0.13%	4.70%
Sales tax rate	8.04%	6.58%
Property tax rate	$7.75	$12.00

HOUSING	AREA	U.S. AVG
Median home price	$109,600	$220,000
Home price appreciation	31.5%	10.1%
Median rent	$502	$709
Homes owned	69.6%	62.3%
Home price ratio	3.0	4.2

NECESSITIES	AREA	U.S. AVG
Food Index	91.7	100.0
Housing Index	51.1	100.0
Utilities Index	94.5	100.0
Transportation Index	88.8	100.0
Healthcare Index	86.3	100.0
Miscellaneous Cost Index	90.5	100.0

Climate
Score: 56.7
Rank: 161

TEMPERATURE	AREA	U.S. AVG
Average January low	26.7	26.2
Average July high	85.9	87.4
Annual days > 90°F	13	38
Annual days < 32°F	96	89
Annual days < 0°F	1	6

PRECIPITATION	AREA	U.S. AVG
Annual inches precipitation	41.0	37.7
Annual inches snowfall	16.0	7.0
Annual days precipitation	134	109
Annual days rain > 0.5 inches	25	22
Annual days snow > 1.5 inches	4	6

COMFORTS & HAZARDS	AREA	U.S. AVG
July relative humidity	72%	66%
Annual days mostly sunny	202	208
Annual days with thunderstorms	45	39
Tornado risk score	3	18
Hurricane risk score	7	13

TEMPERATURE

PRECIPITATION

DAYS OF CLOUDS & PRECIPITATION

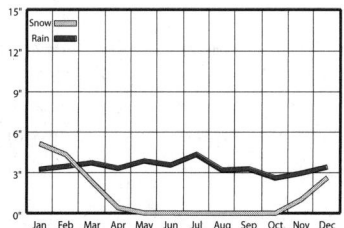

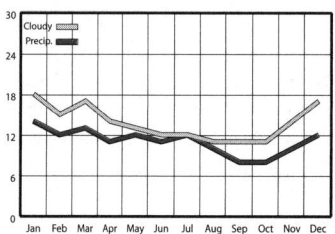

ACHIEVEMENT	AREA	U.S. AVG	PUBLIC SCHOOLS	AREA	U.S. AVG	HIGHER EDUCATION	AREA	U.S. AVG
High school degree	73.1%	82.7%	Expenditures per pupil	$5,272	$5,686	No. 2-year colleges	2	4
2-year college degree	5.5%	6.4%	Student/teacher ratio	13.8	16.7	No. 4-year colleges/universities	3	6
4-year college degree	10.3%	15.7%	Attending public school	95.6%	90.1%	No. highly ranked universities	1	1
Graduate/professional degree	5.2%	8.9%	State SAT score	1142	1021			
			State ACT score	20.7*	20.9			

Education Score: 20.1 Rank: 298

HAZARDS & ILLNESSES	AREA	U.S. AVG	HEALTHCARE	AREA	U.S. AVG	CRIME	AREA	U.S. AVG
Air-quality score	41	37	Physicians per capita	242.0	244.2	Violent crime rate	447.4	465.5
Water-quality score	92	52	Hospital beds per capita	393.2	420.0	Change in violent crime rate	0.6%	-2.2%
Pollen/allergy score	61	61	No. teaching hospitals	2	3	Property crime rate	3,488.9	3,517.1
Cancer mortality per capita	211.4	201.9	Cost per doctor visit	$82	$77	Change in property crime rate	-2.6%	-2.1%
Depression days per month	3.3	3.5	Cost per dental visit	$52	$70			
Stress score	82	50						

Health & Healthcare Score: 80.7 Rank: 73
Crime Score: 73.5 Rank: 100

COMMUTE	AREA	U.S. AVG	INTERCITY SERVICES	AREA	U.S. AVG	AUTOMOTIVE	AREA	U.S. AVG
Average commute time	24.6	27.4	Major airports within 60 miles	0	1	Insurance, annual premium	$912	$1,432
Percent commutes > 60 mins.	4.9%	5.9%	Size of regional airport	None	Large	Gas, cost per gallon	$2.47	$2.49
Commute by auto	85.4%	78.9%	Daily airline activity	37	686	Daily vehicle miles per capita	35.0	24.0
Commute by mass transit	0.3%	1.9%	Amtrak service	No	No			
Work at home	2.4%	3.1%						
Mass transit miles per capita	0.27	1.87						

Transportation Score: 7.0 Rank: 347

DINING & SHOPPING	AREA	U.S. AVG	ENTERTAINMENT	AREA	U.S. AVG	OUTDOOR ACTIVITIES	AREA	U.S. AVG
Restaurant rating	1	2	Professional sports rating	2	4	Golf-course rating	3	4
Outlet mall score	0	42	College sports rating	3	4	Ski-area rating	2	3
No. Starbucks	0	13	Zoo/aquarium rating	1	3	Sq. miles inland water	4	4
No. warehouse clubs	1	2	Amusement park rating	1	3	Miles of coastline	0.0	10.7
			Botanical garden/arboretum rating	3	4	National Park rating	8	3

Leisure Score: 44.9 Rank: 205

MEDIA & LIBRARIES	AREA	U.S. AVG	PERFORMING ARTS	AREA	U.S. AVG	MUSEUMS	AREA	U.S. AVG
Arts radio rating	1	3	Classical music rating	4	4	Overall museum rating	2	5
No. public libraries	20	27	Ballet/dance rating	3	3	Art museum rating	4	5
Library volumes per capita	2.14	2.78	Professional theater rating	8	3	Science museum rating	1	5
			University arts programs rating	6	5	Children's museum rating	3	3

Arts & Culture Score: 43.0 Rank: 213

Kingston, NY

Score: 53.1   Rank: 232   2004 rank: not ranked

Profile: Small town
Location: Hudson River Valley, 60 miles south of Albany
Elevation: 295 feet
Time zone: Eastern Standard Time

PRO
Historic interest
Educated population
Attractive setting

CON
Economic cycles
Entertainment
Harsh winters

Kingston is a pleasant but nondescript town in the Hudson River Valley south of Albany and 100 miles north of New York City. As the first capital of New York, the town contains some sites of historic interest enhanced by the nearby mansions of 19th-century tycoons such as the Vanderbilts. The setting is attractive, and nearby Catskill Mountains ski areas and the Ashokan Reservoir provide some recreation. The economy is a mixed bag. Like most Hudson River regions, Kingston and Ulster County have undergone a transition from a declining old-economy base to, with the help of New York State Economic Development Zone status, an attractive location for emerging businesses. Lower costs of doing business in the form of labor, real estate, and taxes are luring some businesses to the area from more expensive areas in the region. Crime is low, and the Cost of Living Index (117.0) is moderate for the region but high on a national scale, as are median home prices.

Kingston is located in an area of flat to gently wooded landscape on the Hudson River, with a mix of agricultural and wooded areas surrounding the town. The Catskills rise to over 4,000 feet to the northwest. Summer days are warm and usually humid but may be cooled by mountain breezes at night. Winters are cold and harsh with frequent lows below 10°F. Precipitation is frequent, 1 day in 3, and made up of summer thunderstorms, spring and fall rainy periods, and winter snows, some heavy. First freeze is early October; last is early May.

Population

DEMOGRAPHICS	AREA	U.S. AVG	ETHNIC COMPOSITION	AREA	U.S. AVG	RESIDENT PROFILE	AREA	U.S. AVG
Population	182,812		White	87.6%	79.0%	Single	35.1%	32.4%
Population density per sq. mile	162.3	358.5	Black	6.2%	10.5%	Married	48.2%	52.7%
Population growth	10.6%	21.1%	Asian	1.5%	2.7%	Divorced/separated	16.7%	14.9%
Median age	39.2	36.1	Hispanic	7.3%	10.6%	Married with children	21.8%	23.7%
Percent Democrat	54.3%	44.5%	Religious observance	50.6%	48.9%	Single with children	8.8%	9.1%
Percent Republican	43.1%	54.5%	Diversity measure	33.2	40.1	Percent over age 65	13.5%	12.9%

Economy & Jobs
Score: 37.2
Rank: 235

INCOME	AREA	U.S. AVG	EMPLOYMENT	AREA	U.S. AVG	EMPLOYING INDUSTRIES	AREA	U.S. AVG
Per capita income	$24,182	$23,235	Unemployment rate	4.3%	4.7%	Largest: Healthcare & Social Assistance		
Household income	$47,919	$46,414	Recent job growth	2.4%	1.3%			
Household income < $25K	24.6%	26.2%	Projected future job growth	5.1%	11.5%	Percent manufacturing	12.1%	15.4%
Household income > $75K	27.3%	25.4%	White collar	60.4%	57.8%	Percent public sector	20.2%	15.7%
Household income growth	12.6%	13.6%	Blue collar	22.0%	25.2%	Percent construction	10.0%	9.9%

Cost of Living
Score: 7.5
Rank: 345

INDEXES & TAXES	AREA	U.S. AVG	HOUSING	AREA	U.S. AVG	NECESSITIES	AREA	U.S. AVG
Cost of Living Index	117.0	100.0	Median home price	$248,600	$220,000	Food Index	116.0	100.0
Buying Power Index	91.8	100.0	Home price appreciation	90.7%	10.1%	Housing Index	71.0	100.0
Income tax rate	7.13%	4.70%	Median rent	$805	$709	Utilities Index	137.5	100.0
Sales tax rate	8.25%	6.58%	Homes owned	59.4%	62.3%	Transportation Index	113.0	100.0
Property tax rate	$21.64	$12.00	Home price ratio	5.2	4.2	Healthcare Index	129.6	100.0
						Miscellaneous Cost Index	119.0	100.0

Climate
Score: 7.0
Rank: 347

TEMPERATURE	AREA	U.S. AVG	PRECIPITATION	AREA	U.S. AVG	COMFORTS & HAZARDS	AREA	U.S. AVG
Average January low	13.0	26.2	Annual inches precipitation	35.8	37.7	July relative humidity	57%	66%
Average July high	83.0	87.4	Annual inches snowfall	63.0	7.0	Annual days mostly sunny	179	208
Annual days > 90°F	11	38	Annual days precipitation	133	109	Annual days with thunderstorms	28	39
Annual days < 32°F	150	89	Annual days rain > 0.5 inches	23	22	Tornado risk score	1	18
Annual days < 0°F	15	6	Annual days snow > 1.5 inches	13	6	Hurricane risk score	1	13

TEMPERATURE
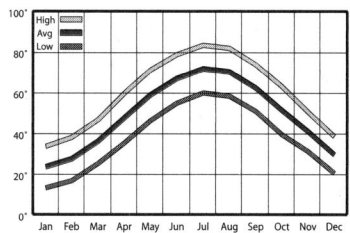

PRECIPITATION
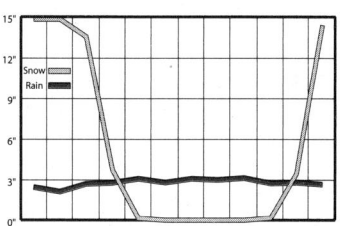

DAYS OF CLOUDS & PRECIPITATION
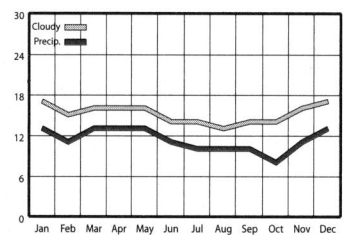

Education
Score: 77.3
Rank: 86

ACHIEVEMENT	AREA	U.S. AVG	PUBLIC SCHOOLS	AREA	U.S. AVG	HIGHER EDUCATION	AREA	U.S. AVG
High school degree	81.8%	82.7%	Expenditures per pupil	$10,495	$5,686	No. 2-year colleges	1	4
2-year college degree	8.3%	6.4%	Student/teacher ratio	15.0	16.7	No. 4-year colleges/universities	1	6
4-year college degree	13.8%	15.7%	Attending public school	95.2%	90.1%	No. highly ranked universities	1	1
Graduate/professional degree	11.2%	8.9%	State SAT score	1003*	1021			
			State ACT score	22.6	20.9			

Health & Healthcare
Score: 34.2
Rank: 245

Crime
Score: 74.3
Rank: 97

HAZARDS & ILLNESSES	AREA	U.S. AVG	HEALTHCARE	AREA	U.S. AVG	CRIME	AREA	U.S. AVG
Air-quality score	50	37	Physicians per capita	177.8	244.2	Violent crime rate	313.1	465.5
Water-quality score	52	52	Hospital beds per capita	254.9	420.0	Change in violent crime rate	20.1%	-2.2%
Pollen/allergy score	48	61	No. teaching hospitals	2	3	Property crime rate	1,974.3	3,517.1
Cancer mortality per capita	228.2	201.9	Cost per doctor visit	$75	$77	Change in property crime rate	1.5%	-2.1%
Depression days per month	4.7	3.5	Cost per dental visit	$67	$70			
Stress score	35	50						

Transportation
Score: 84.2
Rank: 60

COMMUTE	AREA	U.S. AVG	INTERCITY SERVICES	AREA	U.S. AVG	AUTOMOTIVE	AREA	U.S. AVG
Average commute time	28.4	27.4	Major airports within 60 miles	3	1	Insurance, annual premium	$1,492	$1,432
Percent commutes > 60 mins.	9.6%	5.9%	Size of regional airport	Large	Large	Gas, cost per gallon	$2.63	$2.49
Commute by auto	78.2%	78.9%	Daily airline activity	1695	686	Daily vehicle miles per capita	21.1	24.0
Commute by mass transit	2.2%	1.9%	Amtrak service	Yes	No			
Work at home	4.8%	3.1%						
Mass transit miles per capita	2.21	1.87						

Leisure
Score: 79.4
Rank: 77

DINING & SHOPPING	AREA	U.S. AVG	ENTERTAINMENT	AREA	U.S. AVG	OUTDOOR ACTIVITIES	AREA	U.S. AVG
Restaurant rating	1	2	Professional sports rating	10	4	Golf-course rating	9	4
Outlet mall score	34	42	College sports rating	4	4	Ski-area rating	5	3
No. Starbucks	1	13	Zoo/aquarium rating	5	3	Sq. miles inland water	2	4
No. warehouse clubs	0	2	Amusement park rating	1	3	Miles of coastline	0.0	10.7
			Botanical garden/ arboretum rating	6	4	National Park rating	3	3

Arts & Culture
Score: 79.9
Rank: 75

MEDIA & LIBRARIES	AREA	U.S. AVG	PERFORMING ARTS	AREA	U.S. AVG	MUSEUMS	AREA	U.S. AVG
Arts radio rating	1	3	Classical music rating	8	4	Overall museum rating	7	5
No. public libraries	22	27	Ballet/dance rating	6	3	Art museum rating	7	5
Library volumes per capita	3.96	2.78	Professional theater rating	1	3	Science museum rating	10	5
			University arts programs rating	8	5	Children's museum rating	6	3

Knoxville, TN

Score: 69.1   Rank: 99   2004 rank: 103

Profile: Mid-size city/college town
Location: East-central Tennessee near base of Appalachian range
Elevation: 980 feet
Time zone: Eastern Standard Time

PRO	CON
College-town amenities	Some downtown blight
Nearby mountains and national park	Weak recent job growth
Rebuilding downtown	Air service

Knoxville, the largest city in eastern Tennessee and home to the University of Tennessee, serves as a gateway to the tourist and recreation destinations of the Great Smoky Mountain National Park to the southeast. The 400-acre university campus with its 26,000 students is located along the waterfront just to the southwest of downtown, and adds a notable college-town element, particularly during football season. The economic base is a mix of the active university and Tennessee Valley Authority, which has its headquarters in Oak Ridge about 20 miles northwest. The manufacturing base has declined but the university, related healthcare facilities, the TVA, and a few large corporate employers such as Alcoa and Kimberly Clark have brought economic stability to the area. Downtown did not fare well for years, especially for a university town, but a renewal effort, kicked off by the 1982 World's Fair, has brought new life, particularly along the Tennessee River waterfront. There are nice older neighborhoods across the river from downtown to the south, and good suburbs mainly west along Fort Loudoun Lake. These suburbs, Farragut being one, offer a good family lifestyle and convenience both to Knoxville itself and to the energy research labs of the TVA. Costs of living and housing values are an attraction. Crime, once a negative, has improved. For a city its size, Knoxville has a number of quality museums, excellent mountain and water recreation, and established golf courses.

Knoxville is located in a broad valley between the Cumberland Mountains northwest and the Great Smoky Mountains to the southeast. Mountain air keeps summer nights comfortable. Most precipitation occurs in the winter with another peak period in the late spring and summer; frequent afternoon thunderstorms are common in summer. Snow does occur but seldom remains for more than a week. Fall is the driest period. The mountains typically shelter the area from strong winds and severe storms.

Population

DEMOGRAPHICS	AREA	U.S. AVG	ETHNIC COMPOSITION	AREA	U.S. AVG	RESIDENT PROFILE	AREA	U.S. AVG
Population	647,044		White	90.2%	79.0%	Single	29.7%	32.4%
Population density per sq. mile	348.4	358.5	Black	6.3%	10.5%	Married	55.5%	52.7%
Population growth	21.6%	21.1%	Asian	1.4%	2.7%	Divorced/separated	14.8%	14.9%
Median age	38.3	36.1	Hispanic	1.4%	10.6%	Married with children	21.6%	23.7%
Percent Democrat	35.8%	44.5%	Religious observance	62.2%	48.9%	Single with children	7.4%	9.1%
Percent Republican	63.3%	54.5%	Diversity measure	20.2	40.1	Percent over age 65	13.9%	12.9%

Economy & Jobs
Score: 22.5
Rank: 290

INCOME	AREA	U.S. AVG	EMPLOYMENT	AREA	U.S. AVG	EMPLOYING INDUSTRIES	AREA	U.S. AVG
Per capita income	$24,043	$23,235	Unemployment rate	4.1%	4.7%	Largest: Healthcare & Social Assistance		
Household income	$42,571	$46,414	Recent job growth	-1.0%	1.3%			
Household income < $25K	29.1%	26.2%	Projected future job growth	8.6%	11.5%	Percent manufacturing	14.5%	15.4%
Household income > $75K	23.3%	25.4%	White collar	61.1%	57.8%	Percent public sector	15.7%	15.7%
Household income growth	14.4%	13.6%	Blue collar	24.1%	25.2%	Percent construction	9.5%	9.9%

Cost of Living
Score: 88.2
Rank: 45

INDEXES & TAXES	AREA	U.S. AVG	HOUSING	AREA	U.S. AVG	NECESSITIES	AREA	U.S. AVG
Cost of Living Index	84.5	100.0	Median home price	$152,900	$220,000	Food Index	95.1	100.0
Buying Power Index	112.9	100.0	Home price appreciation	33.9%	10.1%	Housing Index	52.1	100.0
Income tax rate	0.00%	4.70%	Median rent	$592	$709	Utilities Index	93.3	100.0
Sales tax rate	9.29%	6.58%	Homes owned	65.1%	62.3%	Transportation Index	90.6	100.0
Property tax rate	$8.70	$12.00	Home price ratio	3.6	4.2	Healthcare Index	89.1	100.0
						Miscellaneous Cost Index	96.1	100.0

Climate
Score: 36.6
Rank: 236

TEMPERATURE	AREA	U.S. AVG
Average January low	32.2	26.2
Average July high	88.0	87.4
Annual days › 90°F	19	38
Annual days ‹ 32°F	71	89
Annual days ‹ 0°F	1	6

PRECIPITATION	AREA	U.S. AVG
Annual inches precipitation	46.0	37.7
Annual inches snowfall	12.0	7.0
Annual days precipitation	128	109
Annual days rain › 0.5 inches	35	22
Annual days snow › 1.5 inches	2	6

COMFORTS & HAZARDS	AREA	U.S. AVG
July relative humidity	71%	66%
Annual days mostly sunny	202	208
Annual days with thunderstorms	47	39
Tornado risk score	9	18
Hurricane risk score	6	13

TEMPERATURE

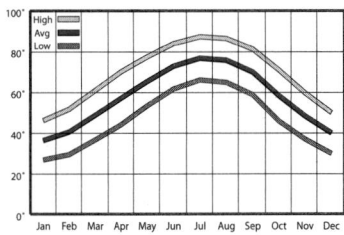

PRECIPITATION

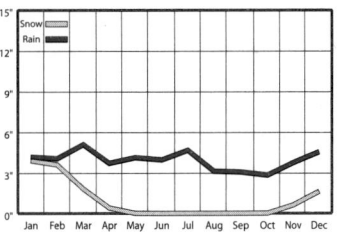

DAYS OF CLOUDS & PRECIPITATION

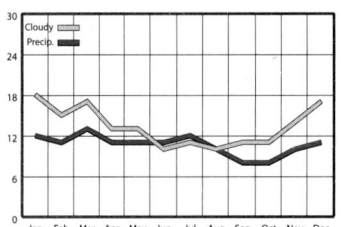

Education
Score: 70.3
Rank: 112

ACHIEVEMENT	AREA	U.S. AVG
High school degree	80.4%	82.7%
2-year college degree	5.4%	6.4%
4-year college degree	15.7%	15.7%
Graduate/professional degree	9.3%	8.9%

PUBLIC SCHOOLS	AREA	U.S. AVG
Expenditures per pupil	$4,720	$5,686
Student/teacher ratio	0.0	16.7
Attending public school	92.3%	90.1%
State SAT score	1142	1021
State ACT score	20.7*	20.9

HIGHER EDUCATION	AREA	U.S. AVG
No. 2-year colleges	1	4
No. 4-year colleges/universities	5	6
No. highly ranked universities	1	1

Health & Healthcare
Score: 57.5
Rank: 160

HAZARDS & ILLNESSES	AREA	U.S. AVG
Air-quality score	36	37
Water-quality score	60	52
Pollen/allergy score	61	61
Cancer mortality per capita	213.2	201.9
Depression days per month	2.9	3.5
Stress score	69	50

HEALTHCARE	AREA	U.S. AVG
Physicians per capita	303.4	244.2
Hospital beds per capita	429.3	420.0
No. teaching hospitals	1	3
Cost per doctor visit	$73	$77
Cost per dental visit	$58	$70

Crime
Score: 45.5
Rank: 204

CRIME	AREA	U.S. AVG
Violent crime rate	482.9	465.5
Change in violent crime rate	-0.8%	-2.2%
Property crime rate	3,806.3	3,517.1
Change in property crime rate	-4.1%	-2.1%

Transportation
Score: 8.6
Rank: 342

COMMUTE	AREA	U.S. AVG
Average commute time	24.9	27.4
Percent commutes › 60 mins.	3.8%	5.9%
Commute by auto	84.8%	78.9%
Commute by mass transit	0.5%	1.9%
Work at home	2.7%	3.1%
Mass transit miles per capita	0.48	1.87

INTERCITY SERVICES	AREA	U.S. AVG
Major airports within 60 miles	0	1
Size of regional airport	Small	Large
Daily airline activity	89	686
Amtrak service	No	No

AUTOMOTIVE	AREA	U.S. AVG
Insurance, annual premium	$964	$1,432
Gas, cost per gallon	$2.43	$2.49
Daily vehicle miles per capita	32.7	24.0

Leisure
Score: 76.5
Rank: 88

DINING & SHOPPING	AREA	U.S. AVG
Restaurant rating	1	2
Outlet mall score	6	42
No. Starbucks	5	13
No. warehouse clubs	0	2

ENTERTAINMENT	AREA	U.S. AVG
Professional sports rating	2	4
College sports rating	7	4
Zoo/aquarium rating	5	3
Amusement park rating	8	3
Botanical garden/ arboretum rating	6	4

OUTDOOR ACTIVITIES	AREA	U.S. AVG
Golf-course rating	5	4
Ski-area rating	3	3
Sq. miles inland water	8	4
Miles of coastline	0.0	10.7
National Park rating	8	3

Arts & Culture
Score: 70.6
Rank: 110

MEDIA & LIBRARIES	AREA	U.S. AVG
Arts radio rating	1	3
No. public libraries	32	27
Library volumes per capita	2.17	2.78

PERFORMING ARTS	AREA	U.S. AVG
Classical music rating	5	4
Ballet/dance rating	5	3
Professional theater rating	1	3
University arts programs rating	8	5

MUSEUMS	AREA	U.S. AVG
Overall museum rating	7	5
Art museum rating	9	5
Science museum rating	8	5
Children's museum rating	8	3

Kokomo, IN

Score: 57.6   **Rank:** 194   **2004 rank:** 101

Profile: Small industrial town
Location: North-central Indiana, 60 miles north of Indianapolis
Elevation: 808 feet
Time zone: Eastern Standard Time

PRO	CON
Cost of living	Educational attainment
Small-town atmosphere	Economic cycles
Air quality	Entertainment

Kokomo, an important industrial center mainly tied to the automotive industry, supplies automotive parts for assembly plants nationwide. DaimlerChrysler and the troubled Delphi are the two largest private employers. The city has a long history of auto innovation dating back to the creation of the first American automobile in Kokomo in 1894. Today the area is known on the world stage for having a prime business, manufacturing, and labor climate. Kokomo has a friendly small-town feel with a typically Midwestern downtown, boasts considerable local pride, and is unusually clean and attractive for a town with such a strong industrial presence. Mississinewa Lake to the northeast offers recreational opportunities. Living and especially housing costs are very attractive, and relatively high incomes give strong buying power, as measured by the Buying Power Index at 139.9. There is some college presence with local campuses of Indiana, Purdue, and Indiana Wesleyan universities. While somewhat economically diversified, the area is still tied to the fortunes of the auto industry. Indianapolis is an hour south.

The town is located on a primarily level, agricultural plain extending north to Lake Michigan. To the northeast lies an area of low wooded hills. The climate offers four distinct seasons, including warm humid summers and variably cold winters. Weather changes are frequent, and winter and summer alike have rainy periods. Winters also bring windy, snowy days partly arising from Lake Michigan to the north. First freeze is mid-October; last is late April.

Population

DEMOGRAPHICS	AREA	U.S. AVG	ETHNIC COMPOSITION	AREA	U.S. AVG	RESIDENT PROFILE	AREA	U.S. AVG
Population	101,258		White	90.6%	79.0%	Single	27.7%	32.4%
Population density per sq. mile	182.9	358.5	Black	5.8%	10.5%	Married	57.3%	52.7%
Population growth	4.5%	21.1%	Asian	1.0%	2.7%	Divorced/separated	15.0%	14.9%
Median age	37.8	36.1	Hispanic	1.7%	10.6%	Married with children	22.3%	23.7%
Percent Democrat	33.9%	44.5%	Religious observance	47.2%	48.9%	Single with children	8.8%	9.1%
Percent Republican	65.2%	54.5%	Diversity measure	20.1	40.1	Percent over age 65	14.1%	12.9%

Economy & Jobs
Score: 99.5
Rank: 3

INCOME	AREA	U.S. AVG	EMPLOYMENT	AREA	U.S. AVG	EMPLOYING INDUSTRIES	AREA	U.S. AVG
Per capita income	$24,115	$23,235	Unemployment rate	5.8%	4.7%	Largest: Manufacturing		
Household income	$47,984	$46,414	Recent job growth	8.6%	1.3%			
Household income < $25K	24.6%	26.2%	Projected future job growth	18.9%	11.5%	Percent manufacturing	26.8%	15.4%
Household income > $75K	26.5%	25.4%	White collar	46.0%	57.8%	Percent public sector	9.3%	15.7%
Household income growth	8.3%	13.6%	Blue collar	37.2%	25.2%	Percent construction	10.4%	9.9%

Cost of Living
Score: 93.3
Rank: 26

INDEXES & TAXES	AREA	U.S. AVG	HOUSING	AREA	U.S. AVG	NECESSITIES	AREA	U.S. AVG
Cost of Living Index	76.9	100.0	Median home price	$103,600	$220,000	Food Index	93.1	100.0
Buying Power Index	139.9	100.0	Home price appreciation	15.7%	10.1%	Housing Index	48.4	100.0
Income tax rate	3.40%	4.70%	Median rent	$620	$709	Utilities Index	97.9	100.0
Sales tax rate	6.00%	6.58%	Homes owned	68.1%	62.3%	Transportation Index	97.7	100.0
Property tax rate	$10.78	$12.00	Home price ratio	2.2	4.2	Healthcare Index	94.2	100.0
						Miscellaneous Cost Index	92.5	100.0

Climate
Score: 48.9
Rank: 190

TEMPERATURE	AREA	U.S. AVG	PRECIPITATION	AREA	U.S. AVG	COMFORTS & HAZARDS	AREA	U.S. AVG
Average January low	19.7	26.2	Annual inches precipitation	39.0	37.7	July relative humidity	73%	66%
Average July high	85.4	87.4	Annual inches snowfall	21.0	7.0	Annual days mostly sunny	191	208
Annual days > 90°F	15	38	Annual days precipitation	122	109	Annual days with thunderstorms	45	39
Annual days < 32°F	122	89	Annual days rain > 0.5 inches	26	22	Tornado risk score	35	18
Annual days < 0°F	7	6	Annual days snow > 1.5 inches	7	6	Hurricane risk score	3	13

TEMPERATURE

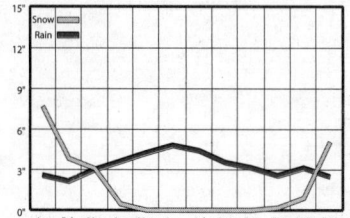

PRECIPITATION

DAYS OF CLOUDS & PRECIPITATION

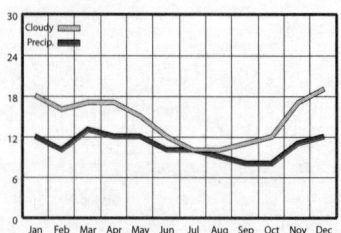

ACHIEVEMENT	AREA	U.S. AVG	PUBLIC SCHOOLS	AREA	U.S. AVG	HIGHER EDUCATION	AREA	U.S. AVG
High school degree	83.5%	82.7%	Expenditures per pupil	$6,062	$5,686	No. 2-year colleges	1	4
2-year college degree	6.0%	6.4%	Student/teacher ratio	16.7	16.7	No. 4-year colleges/universities	0	6
4-year college degree	10.8%	15.7%	Attending public school	94.3%	90.1%	No. highly ranked universities	0	1
Graduate/professional degree	6.6%	8.9%	State SAT score	1007*	1021			
			State ACT score	21.7	20.9			

Education
Score: 34.2
Rank: 247

HAZARDS & ILLNESSES	AREA	U.S. AVG	HEALTHCARE	AREA	U.S. AVG	CRIME	AREA	U.S. AVG
Air-quality score	55	37	Physicians per capita	155.1	244.2	Violent crime rate	294.8	465.5
Water-quality score	44	52	Hospital beds per capita	477.0	420.0	Change in violent crime rate	-1.4%	-2.2%
Pollen/allergy score	69	61	No. teaching hospitals	0	3	Property crime rate	4,210.1	3,517.1
Cancer mortality per capita	220.7	201.9	Cost per doctor visit	$71	$77	Change in property crime rate	13.4%	-2.1%
Depression days per month	3.7	3.5	Cost per dental visit	$72	$70			
Stress score	48	50						

Health & Healthcare
Score: 80.2
Rank: 75

Crime
Score: 48.4
Rank: 193

COMMUTE	AREA	U.S. AVG	INTERCITY SERVICES	AREA	U.S. AVG	AUTOMOTIVE	AREA	U.S. AVG
Average commute time	20.2	27.4	Major airports within 60 miles	1	1	Insurance, annual premium	$1,071	$1,432
Percent commutes > 60 mins.	4.4%	5.9%	Size of regional airport	Medium	Large	Gas, cost per gallon	$2.46	$2.49
Commute by auto	85.2%	78.9%	Daily airline activity	461	686	Daily vehicle miles per capita	20.6	24.0
Commute by mass transit	0.3%	1.9%	Amtrak service	No	No			
Work at home	2.3%	3.1%						
Mass transit miles per capita	0.34	1.87						

Transportation
Score: 73.0
Rank: 102

DINING & SHOPPING	AREA	U.S. AVG	ENTERTAINMENT	AREA	U.S. AVG	OUTDOOR ACTIVITIES	AREA	U.S. AVG
Restaurant rating	1	2	Professional sports rating	2	4	Golf-course rating	2	4
Outlet mall score	38	42	College sports rating	1	4	Ski-area rating	2	3
No. Starbucks	1	13	Zoo/aquarium rating	1	3	Sq. miles inland water	2	4
No. warehouse clubs	1	2	Amusement park rating	1	3	Miles of coastline	0.0	10.7
			Botanical garden/ arboretum rating	2	4	National Park rating	1	3

Leisure
Score: 9.1
Rank: 339

MEDIA & LIBRARIES	AREA	U.S. AVG	PERFORMING ARTS	AREA	U.S. AVG	MUSEUMS	AREA	U.S. AVG
Arts radio rating	1	3	Classical music rating	3	4	Overall museum rating	1	5
No. public libraries	7	27	Ballet/dance rating	1	3	Art museum rating	3	5
Library volumes per capita	4.13	2.78	Professional theater rating	1	3	Science museum rating	1	5
			University arts programs rating	3	5	Children's museum rating	1	3

Arts & Culture
Score: 35.0
Rank: 243

La Crosse, WI-MN

Score: 44.1   Rank: 294   2004 rank: 115

Profile: Small city
Location: Extreme southwest Wisconsin along Mississippi River and I-90, 60 miles east of Rochester, Minnesota
Elevation: 838 feet
Time zone: Central Standard Time

PRO
Attractive setting
Small-town atmosphere
Low crime rate

CON
Recent job declines
Harsh winters
Isolation

Eighteenth-century European travelers and trappers founded La Crosse as a crossing point over the Mississippi River. Today's balanced economic base includes mixed agriculture, orchards, and dairy farms alongside businesses in manufacturing, furniture, mail-order, and food distribution, but recently the employment picture has turned negative. The G. Heilemann Brewery, fronted by a giant six-pack of beer, gives a hint at the good-natured character of the town. The river setting is attractive, with scenic, wooded bluffs on both sides of the river. There are some localized arts and museum amenities, and the town has a number of historic buildings and several pubs. It won a 2002 National Trust for Historic Preservation Great American Main Street Award, and downtown is generally attractive and livable as is typical for the region. Costs of living and housing are reasonable. A large Lutheran hospital and a

Mayo Clinic affiliate bring a strong healthcare presence, in the shadow of healthcare giant Rochester, Minnesota, which also adds some services and amenities not available locally. The area is one of the coldest in Wisconsin and the country. The ranking took a hit from the recent economic speed-bump but the area is probably better for most than the figures indicate.

The city of La Crosse sits on the east bank of the Mississippi River at the confluence of the Mississippi, Black, and La Crosse rivers. Bluffs rise 500 feet above the valley floor. Heavily wooded, steep-sided hills with narrow valleys are characteristic of the region. Summers are warm with moderate humidity and periods of weeklong heat. Summer precipitation arrives as scattered thunderstorms, some severe. Winters are cold and variably humid. Snow is frequent, occasionally heavy, and is the prominent form of winter precipitation. First freeze is mid-October; last is late April.

Population

DEMOGRAPHICS	AREA	U.S. AVG	ETHNIC COMPOSITION	AREA	U.S. AVG	RESIDENT PROFILE	AREA	U.S. AVG
Population	129,118		White	94.2%	79.0%	Single	37.1%	32.4%
Population density per sq. mile	127.7	358.5	Black	0.9%	10.5%	Married	51.7%	52.7%
Population growth	10.9%	21.1%	Asian	3.0%	2.7%	Divorced/separated	11.2%	14.9%
Median age	35.5	36.1	Hispanic	0.9%	10.6%	Married with children	23.3%	23.7%
Percent Democrat	52.5%	44.5%	Religious observance	66.6%	48.9%	Single with children	7.2%	9.1%
Percent Republican	46.3%	54.5%	Diversity measure	12.6	40.1	Percent over age 65	13.2%	12.9%

Economy & Jobs
Score: 11.2
Rank: 331

INCOME	AREA	U.S. AVG	EMPLOYMENT	AREA	U.S. AVG	EMPLOYING INDUSTRIES	AREA	U.S. AVG
Per capita income	$22,973	$23,235	Unemployment rate	3.7%	4.7%	Largest: Healthcare & Social Assistance		
Household income	$45,330	$46,414	Recent job growth	-1.1%	1.3%			
Household income < $25K	24.7%	26.2%	Projected future job growth	2.9%	11.5%	Percent manufacturing	16.8%	15.4%
Household income > $75K	23.1%	25.4%	White collar	56.7%	57.8%	Percent public sector	12.9%	15.7%
Household income growth	14.3%	13.6%	Blue collar	24.9%	25.2%	Percent construction	8.1%	9.9%

Cost of Living
Score: 43.0
Rank: 213

INDEXES & TAXES	AREA	U.S. AVG	HOUSING	AREA	U.S. AVG	NECESSITIES	AREA	U.S. AVG
Cost of Living Index	86.8	100.0	Median home price	$127,200	$220,000	Food Index	97.4	100.0
Buying Power Index	117.1	100.0	Home price appreciation	34.5%	10.1%	Housing Index	53.5	100.0
Income tax rate	6.85%	4.70%	Median rent	$570	$709	Utilities Index	125.2	100.0
Sales tax rate	5.65%	6.58%	Homes owned	64.9%	62.3%	Transportation Index	100.9	100.0
Property tax rate	$17.52	$12.00	Home price ratio	2.8	4.2	Healthcare Index	107.7	100.0
						Miscellaneous Cost Index	98.4	100.0

Climate
Score: 10.2
Rank: 335

TEMPERATURE	AREA	U.S. AVG	PRECIPITATION	AREA	U.S. AVG	COMFORTS & HAZARDS	AREA	U.S. AVG
Average January low	3.2	26.2	Annual inches precipitation	26.0	37.7	July relative humidity	69%	66%
Average July high	82.4	87.4	Annual inches snowfall	46.0	7.0	Annual days mostly sunny	200	208
Annual days > 90°F	15	38	Annual days precipitation	113	109	Annual days with thunderstorms	36	39
Annual days < 32°F	158	89	Annual days rain > 0.5 inches	15	22	Tornado risk score	13	18
Annual days < 0°F	34	6	Annual days snow > 1.5 inches	9	6	Hurricane risk score	0	13

TEMPERATURE

PRECIPITATION

DAYS OF CLOUDS & PRECIPITATION

Education
Score: 74.1
Rank: 98

ACHIEVEMENT	AREA	U.S. AVG	PUBLIC SCHOOLS	AREA	U.S. AVG	HIGHER EDUCATION	AREA	U.S. AVG
High school degree	89.1%	82.7%	Expenditures per pupil	$6,282	$5,686	No. 2-year colleges	1	4
2-year college degree	10.5%	6.4%	Student/teacher ratio	13.5	16.7	No. 4-year colleges/universities	2	6
4-year college degree	16.1%	15.7%	Attending public school	85.7%	90.1%	No. highly ranked universities	0	1
Graduate/professional degree	8.6%	8.9%	State SAT score	1188	1021			
			State ACT score	22.2*	20.9			

Health & Healthcare
Score: 92.5
Rank: 29

HAZARDS & ILLNESSES	AREA	U.S. AVG	HEALTHCARE	AREA	U.S. AVG	CRIME	AREA	U.S. AVG
Air-quality score	55	37	Physicians per capita	379.7	244.2	Violent crime rate	147.7	465.5
Water-quality score	45	52	Hospital beds per capita	645.9	420.0	Change in violent crime rate	-5.3%	-2.2%
Pollen/allergy score	41	61	No. teaching hospitals	2	3	Property crime rate	2,324.0	3,517.1
Cancer mortality per capita	194.7	201.9	Cost per doctor visit	$91	$77	Change in property crime rate	7.1%	-2.1%
Depression days per month	3.0	3.5	Cost per dental visit	$60	$70			
Stress score	4	50						

Crime
Score: 90.4
Rank: 37

Transportation
Score: 50.3
Rank: 187

COMMUTE	AREA	U.S. AVG	INTERCITY SERVICES	AREA	U.S. AVG	AUTOMOTIVE	AREA	U.S. AVG
Average commute time	19.7	27.4	Major airports within 60 miles	0	1	Insurance, annual premium	$910	$1,432
Percent commutes > 60 mins.	3.1%	5.9%	Size of regional airport	None	Large	Gas, cost per gallon	$2.56	$2.49
Commute by auto	80.5%	78.9%	Daily airline activity	18	686	Daily vehicle miles per capita	24.1	24.0
Commute by mass transit	1.0%	1.9%	Amtrak service	Yes	No			
Work at home	3.9%	3.1%						
Mass transit miles per capita	1.04	1.87						

	DINING & SHOPPING	AREA	U.S. AVG	ENTERTAINMENT	AREA	U.S. AVG	OUTDOOR ACTIVITIES	AREA	U.S. AVG
Leisure	Restaurant rating	1	2	Professional sports rating	2	4	Golf-course rating	1	4
Score: 18.2	Outlet mall score	0	42	College sports rating	5	4	Ski-area rating	2	3
Rank: 305	No. Starbucks	0	13	Zoo/aquarium rating	1	3	Sq. miles inland water	3	4
	No. warehouse clubs	0	2	Amusement park rating	1	3	Miles of coastline	0.0	10.7
				Botanical garden/ arboretum rating	1	4	National Park rating	1	3

	MEDIA & LIBRARIES	AREA	U.S. AVG	PERFORMING ARTS	AREA	U.S. AVG	MUSEUMS	AREA	U.S. AVG
Arts & Culture	Arts radio rating	1	3	Classical music rating	3	4	Overall museum rating	2	5
Score: 37.7	No. public libraries	11	27	Ballet/dance rating	1	3	Art museum rating	2	5
Rank: 233	Library volumes per capita	3.67	2.78	Professional theater rating	1	3	Science museum rating	4	5
				University arts programs rating	6	5	Children's museum rating	1	3

Lafayette, IN

Score: 84.3   Rank: 25   2004 rank: 23

Profile: College town/mid-size-city complex
Location: Northwest Indiana along I-65 between Indianapolis and Chicago
Elevation: 808 feet
Time zone: Eastern Standard Time

PRO	CON
College-town atmosphere	Growth and sprawl
Cost of living and housing	Winter climate
Educated population	Low recent job growth

Lafayette is a fairly typical prosperous Midwestern agricultural and manufacturing center on the southeast bank of the Wabash River, across from the vibrant and dynamic college town of West Lafayette. West Lafayette is home to the 40,000-student engineering- and agriculture-rooted Purdue University. The combination of cities provides a diverse economy and a lot of interest compared to most metro areas in the region. Lafayette is home to the likes of Caterpillar, agricultural processor Tate & Lyle (formerly A. E. Staley), Alcoa, and a large Subaru plant, which just recently became an assembly plant for Toyota. The university brings a strong complement of research and technology firms, and employment and incomes especially on the west side of the river are strong and living standards are high. The university brings plenty to do for students, families, and some retirees alike. The sports teams of the Purdue Boilermakers, a mascot celebrating the area's role as a center of industrial and agricultural technology, are a local obsession. Downtown Lafayette, tucked neatly into the Wabash valley, has some charm and a slightly European look from a distance, with unattractive commercial sprawl spreading mostly north and east. West Lafayette, atop a bluff to the west of the river, is more modern and has a typical college-town look. Town highlights include a low cost of living and especially housing for a major university town, good air quality, and high educational attainment. Downsides are a somewhat cyclical economy and some sprawl issues, and the northern Indiana climate can be harsh in winter. Strengths outweigh weaknesses in all categories, hence the high ranking.

Both cities lie along the shallow wooded valley of the Wabash River. To the north is a flat agricultural plain; to the south is a mix of level and gently rolling terrain. Most of the outlying area is agricultural. The climate is continental with four distinct seasons, including warm humid summers and variably cold winters. Wide temperature fluctuations and rainy periods are frequent. Precipitation is evenly distributed throughout the year, with occasionally heavy thunderstorms in spring and summer. Winters can bring windy, snowy periods partly arising from Lake Michigan to the north. First freeze is mid-October; last is late April.

	DEMOGRAPHICS	AREA	U.S. AVG	ETHNIC COMPOSITION	AREA	U.S. AVG	RESIDENT PROFILE	AREA	U.S. AVG
Population	Population	187,749		White	88.9%	79.0%	Single	39.2%	32.4%
	Population density per sq. mile	146.9	358.5	Black	2.2%	10.5%	Married	47.1%	52.7%
	Population growth	18.6%	21.1%	Asian	4.7%	2.7%	Divorced/separated	13.8%	14.9%
	Median age	30.7	36.1	Hispanic	5.3%	10.6%	Married with children	22.3%	23.7%
	Percent Democrat	38.3%	44.5%	Religious observance	38.6%	48.9%	Single with children	7.0%	9.1%
	Percent Republican	60.5%	54.5%	Diversity measure	28.4	40.1	Percent over age 65	10.0%	12.9%

	INCOME	AREA	U.S. AVG	EMPLOYMENT	AREA	U.S. AVG	EMPLOYING INDUSTRIES	AREA	U.S. AVG
Economy & Jobs	Per capita income	$21,985	$23,235	Unemployment rate	4.5%	4.7%	Largest: Manufacturing		
	Household income	$43,767	$46,414	Recent job growth	0.0%	1.3%			
Score: 35.3	Household income < $25K	27.5%	26.2%	Projected future job growth	6.0%	11.5%	Percent manufacturing	18.4%	15.4%
Rank: 242	Household income > $75K	23.5%	25.4%	White collar	56.6%	57.8%	Percent public sector	18.6%	15.7%
	Household income growth	11.8%	13.6%	Blue collar	26.1%	25.2%	Percent construction	7.7%	9.9%

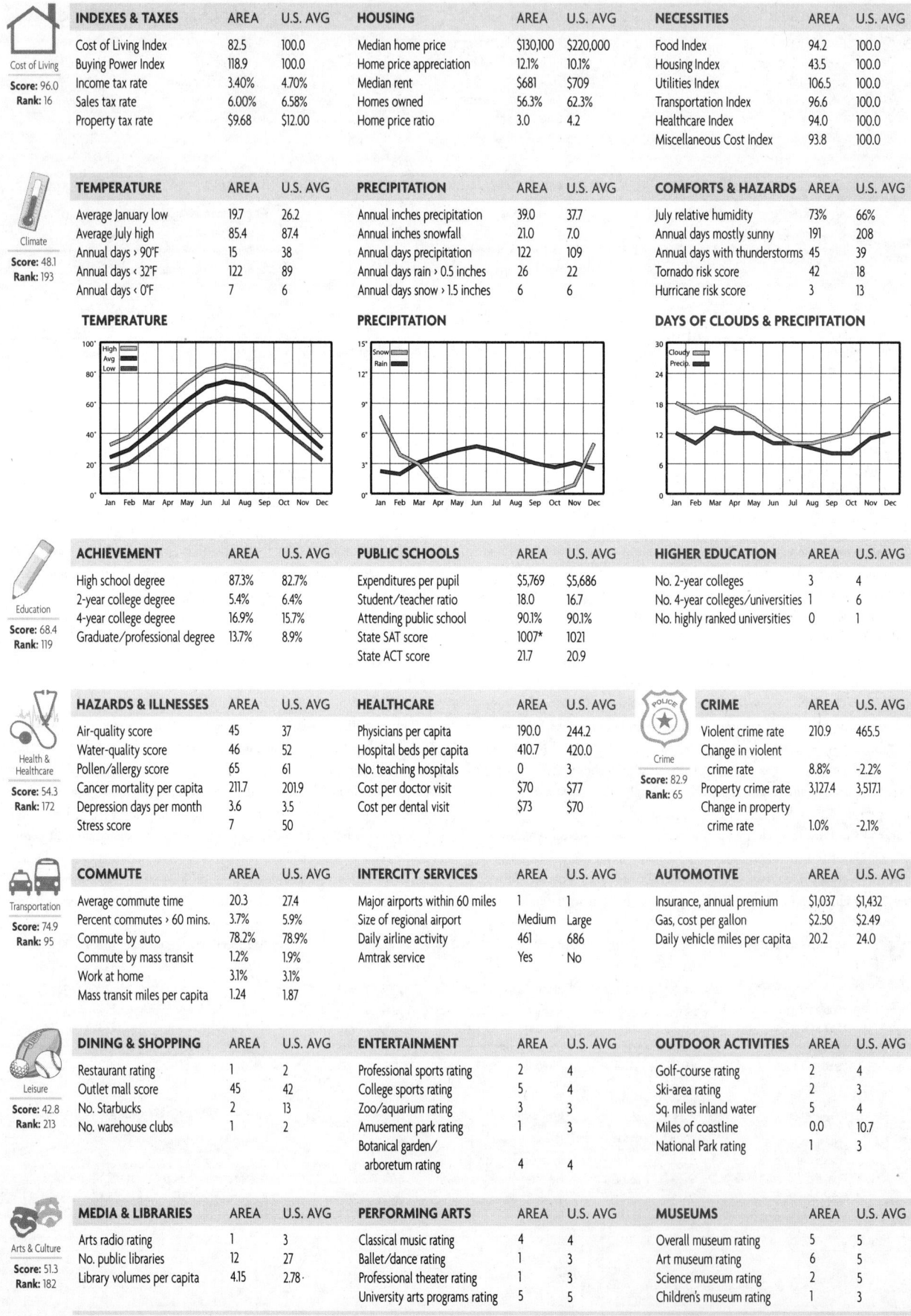

Cost of Living
Score: 96.0
Rank: 16

INDEXES & TAXES	AREA	U.S. AVG
Cost of Living Index	82.5	100.0
Buying Power Index	118.9	100.0
Income tax rate	3.40%	4.70%
Sales tax rate	6.00%	6.58%
Property tax rate	$9.68	$12.00

HOUSING	AREA	U.S. AVG
Median home price	$130,100	$220,000
Home price appreciation	12.1%	10.1%
Median rent	$681	$709
Homes owned	56.3%	62.3%
Home price ratio	3.0	4.2

NECESSITIES	AREA	U.S. AVG
Food Index	94.2	100.0
Housing Index	43.5	100.0
Utilities Index	106.5	100.0
Transportation Index	96.6	100.0
Healthcare Index	94.0	100.0
Miscellaneous Cost Index	93.8	100.0

Climate
Score: 48.1
Rank: 193

TEMPERATURE	AREA	U.S. AVG
Average January low	19.7	26.2
Average July high	85.4	87.4
Annual days > 90°F	15	38
Annual days < 32°F	122	89
Annual days < 0°F	7	6

PRECIPITATION	AREA	U.S. AVG
Annual inches precipitation	39.0	37.7
Annual inches snowfall	21.0	7.0
Annual days precipitation	122	109
Annual days rain > 0.5 inches	26	22
Annual days snow > 1.5 inches	6	6

COMFORTS & HAZARDS	AREA	U.S. AVG
July relative humidity	73%	66%
Annual days mostly sunny	191	208
Annual days with thunderstorms	45	39
Tornado risk score	42	18
Hurricane risk score	3	13

TEMPERATURE

PRECIPITATION

DAYS OF CLOUDS & PRECIPITATION

Education
Score: 68.4
Rank: 119

ACHIEVEMENT	AREA	U.S. AVG
High school degree	87.3%	82.7%
2-year college degree	5.4%	6.4%
4-year college degree	16.9%	15.7%
Graduate/professional degree	13.7%	8.9%

PUBLIC SCHOOLS	AREA	U.S. AVG
Expenditures per pupil	$5,769	$5,686
Student/teacher ratio	18.0	16.7
Attending public school	90.1%	90.1%
State SAT score	1007*	1021
State ACT score	21.7	20.9

HIGHER EDUCATION	AREA	U.S. AVG
No. 2-year colleges	3	4
No. 4-year colleges/universities	1	6
No. highly ranked universities	0	1

Health & Healthcare
Score: 54.3
Rank: 172

HAZARDS & ILLNESSES	AREA	U.S. AVG
Air-quality score	45	37
Water-quality score	46	52
Pollen/allergy score	65	61
Cancer mortality per capita	211.7	201.9
Depression days per month	3.6	3.5
Stress score	7	50

HEALTHCARE	AREA	U.S. AVG
Physicians per capita	190.0	244.2
Hospital beds per capita	410.7	420.0
No. teaching hospitals	0	3
Cost per doctor visit	$70	$77
Cost per dental visit	$73	$70

Crime
Score: 82.9
Rank: 65

CRIME	AREA	U.S. AVG
Violent crime rate	210.9	465.5
Change in violent crime rate	8.8%	-2.2%
Property crime rate	3,127.4	3,517.1
Change in property crime rate	1.0%	-2.1%

Transportation
Score: 74.9
Rank: 95

COMMUTE	AREA	U.S. AVG
Average commute time	20.3	27.4
Percent commutes > 60 mins.	3.7%	5.9%
Commute by auto	78.2%	78.9%
Commute by mass transit	1.2%	1.9%
Work at home	3.1%	3.1%
Mass transit miles per capita	1.24	1.87

INTERCITY SERVICES	AREA	U.S. AVG
Major airports within 60 miles	1	1
Size of regional airport	Medium	Large
Daily airline activity	461	686
Amtrak service	Yes	No

AUTOMOTIVE	AREA	U.S. AVG
Insurance, annual premium	$1,037	$1,432
Gas, cost per gallon	$2.50	$2.49
Daily vehicle miles per capita	20.2	24.0

Leisure
Score: 42.8
Rank: 213

DINING & SHOPPING	AREA	U.S. AVG
Restaurant rating	1	2
Outlet mall score	45	42
No. Starbucks	2	13
No. warehouse clubs	1	2

ENTERTAINMENT	AREA	U.S. AVG
Professional sports rating	2	4
College sports rating	5	4
Zoo/aquarium rating	3	3
Amusement park rating	1	3
Botanical garden/ arboretum rating	4	4

OUTDOOR ACTIVITIES	AREA	U.S. AVG
Golf-course rating	2	4
Ski-area rating	2	3
Sq. miles inland water	5	4
Miles of coastline	0.0	10.7
National Park rating	1	3

Arts & Culture
Score: 51.3
Rank: 182

MEDIA & LIBRARIES	AREA	U.S. AVG
Arts radio rating	1	3
No. public libraries	12	27
Library volumes per capita	4.15	2.78

PERFORMING ARTS	AREA	U.S. AVG
Classical music rating	4	4
Ballet/dance rating	1	3
Professional theater rating	1	3
University arts programs rating	5	5

MUSEUMS	AREA	U.S. AVG
Overall museum rating	5	5
Art museum rating	6	5
Science museum rating	2	5
Children's museum rating	1	3

Lafayette, LA

Score: 12.7 **Rank:** 367 **2004 rank:** 297

Profile: Small city
Location: South-central Louisiana, 130 miles west of New Orleans
Elevation: 64 feet
Time zone: Central Standard Time

PRO	CON
Cost of living	Hot, humid summers
Possible future growth	Crime rates
Winter climate	Isolation

Lafayette is a small city in south-central Louisiana, and like many small Southern cities, it has a modest downtown area with patches of decline and renewal, and a fair amount of sprawl along major arteries. Oil and gas are the main industries, but the University of Louisiana has a 17,000-student campus in town that adds some vitality. The heart of Cajun country, Lafayette is the center for the flavors, sounds, and history of that colorful culture—a fact earning the place a few recreation and culture points, but there isn't much intellectual stimulation or much to do. However, while the area offers some activities and amenities, it is isolated, especially with Hurricane Katrina's devastation of New Orleans. Lafayette did suffer minor hurricane-related damage but it was spared the devastation of cities southeast and southwest. Regional dislocations from hurricanes Katrina and Rita to the west have sent some migrants to Lafayette's slightly higher ground, but also hit the

area's tourist industry, as Lafayette was a base and jumping-off point for areas south. Now it has become more of a base for hurricane relief and reconstruction. The area is eligible for federal incentives, and there will likely be some long-term economic, physical, and cultural growth from the storms, but the exact nature of it is a wait-and-see.

Typical of Louisiana, the level terrain is a mix of open land and wooded areas, with many slow-moving creeks called "bayous." The climate is humid subtropical with a modest Gulf influence, which moderates heat extremes but feeds the almost tropical humidity through the summer. Winters are mild with an occasional colder spell. Rainfall is substantial in all seasons, with most precipitation arriving in spring and summer. Severe local storms occur most frequently in spring with hurricanes and tropical rains possible in late summer and fall. Nonetheless, the best seasons are spring and fall, which are mostly mild, dry, and sunny.

Population

DEMOGRAPHICS	AREA	U.S. AVG	ETHNIC COMPOSITION	AREA	U.S. AVG	RESIDENT PROFILE	AREA	U.S. AVG
Population	246,790		White	70.8%	79.0%	Single	34.4%	32.4%
Population density per sq. mile	244.4	358.5	Black	26.1%	10.5%	Married	50.6%	52.7%
Population growth	18.3%	21.1%	Asian	1.3%	2.7%	Divorced/separated	15.0%	14.9%
Median age	33.8	36.1	Hispanic	1.7%	10.6%	Married with children	25.3%	23.7%
Percent Democrat	36.9%	44.5%	Religious observance	80.8%	48.9%	Single with children	11.6%	9.1%
Percent Republican	61.9%	54.5%	Diversity measure	44.8	40.1	Percent over age 65	10.1%	12.9%

Economy & Jobs
Score: 43.0
Rank: 214

INCOME	AREA	U.S. AVG	EMPLOYMENT	AREA	U.S. AVG	EMPLOYING INDUSTRIES	AREA	U.S. AVG
Per capita income	$21,650	$23,235	Unemployment rate	5.0%	4.7%	Largest: Healthcare & Social Assistance		
Household income	$41,547	$46,414	Recent job growth	1.6%	1.3%			
Household income < $25K	31.3%	26.2%	Projected future job growth	12.9%	11.5%	Percent manufacturing	13.5%	15.4%
Household income > $75K	22.9%	25.4%	White collar	59.7%	57.8%	Percent public sector	13.1%	15.7%
Household income growth	17.6%	13.6%	Blue collar	25.0%	25.2%	Percent construction	11.5%	9.9%

Cost of Living
Score: 73.3
Rank: 101

INDEXES & TAXES	AREA	U.S. AVG	HOUSING	AREA	U.S. AVG	NECESSITIES	AREA	U.S. AVG
Cost of Living Index	83.7	100.0	Median home price	$131,200	$220,000	Food Index	94.0	100.0
Buying Power Index	111.3	100.0	Home price appreciation	33.9%	10.1%	Housing Index	65.2	100.0
Income tax rate	4.00%	4.70%	Median rent	$570	$709	Utilities Index	92.1	100.0
Sales tax rate	7.90%	6.58%	Homes owned	63.4%	62.3%	Transportation Index	101.6	100.0
Property tax rate	$3.82	$12.00	Home price ratio	3.2	4.2	Healthcare Index	92.1	100.0
						Miscellaneous Cost Index	99.1	100.0

Climate
Score: 73.8
Rank: 98

TEMPERATURE	AREA	U.S. AVG	PRECIPITATION	AREA	U.S. AVG	COMFORTS & HAZARDS	AREA	U.S. AVG
Average January low	40.5	26.2	Annual inches precipitation	54.1	37.7	July relative humidity	74%	66%
Average July high	91.2	87.4	Annual inches snowfall	1.8	7.0	Annual days mostly sunny	218	208
Annual days > 90°F	83	38	Annual days precipitation	108	109	Annual days with thunderstorms	70	39
Annual days < 32°F	25	89	Annual days rain > 0.5 inches	35	22	Tornado risk score	42	18
Annual days < 0°F	0	6	Annual days snow > 1.5 inches	1	6	Hurricane risk score	45	13

TEMPERATURE

PRECIPITATION

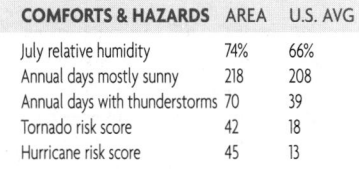

DAYS OF CLOUDS & PRECIPITATION

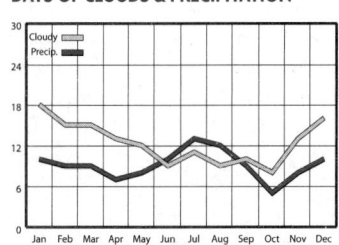

Education
Score: 7.2
Rank: 346

ACHIEVEMENT	AREA	U.S. AVG	PUBLIC SCHOOLS	AREA	U.S. AVG	HIGHER EDUCATION	AREA	U.S. AVG
High school degree	76.5%	82.7%	Expenditures per pupil	$4,325	$5,686	No. 2-year colleges	5	4
2-year college degree	3.5%	6.4%	Student/teacher ratio	16.5	16.7	No. 4-year colleges/universities	1	6
4-year college degree	15.4%	15.7%	Attending public school	80.9%	90.1%	No. highly ranked universities	0	1
Graduate/professional degree	6.7%	8.9%	State SAT score	1141	1021			
			State ACT score	20.1*	20.9			

Health & Healthcare
Score: 64.7
Rank: 133

Crime
Score: 18.4
Rank: 305

HAZARDS & ILLNESSES	AREA	U.S. AVG	HEALTHCARE	AREA	U.S. AVG	CRIME	AREA	U.S. AVG
Air-quality score	44	37	Physicians per capita	245.3	244.2	Violent crime rate	634.3	465.5
Water-quality score	12	52	Hospital beds per capita	528.8	420.0	Change in violent crime rate	-2.6%	-2.2%
Pollen/allergy score	72	61	No. teaching hospitals	1	3	Property crime rate	4,238.2	3,517.1
Cancer mortality per capita	224.2	201.9	Cost per doctor visit	$79	$77	Change in property crime rate	-15.7%	-2.1%
Depression days per month	3.1	3.5	Cost per dental visit	$82	$70			
Stress score	47	50						

Transportation
Score: 4.3
Rank: 357

COMMUTE	AREA	U.S. AVG	INTERCITY SERVICES	AREA	U.S. AVG	AUTOMOTIVE	AREA	U.S. AVG
Average commute time	25.4	27.4	Major airports within 60 miles	0	1	Insurance, annual premium	$1,845	$1,432
Percent commutes > 60 mins.	7.0%	5.9%	Size of regional airport	Small	Large	Gas, cost per gallon	$2.46	$2.49
Commute by auto	82.9%	78.9%	Daily airline activity	41	686	Daily vehicle miles per capita	28.5	24.0
Commute by mass transit	1.0%	1.9%	Amtrak service	Yes	No			
Work at home	2.5%	3.1%						
Mass transit miles per capita	0.97	1.87						

Leisure
Score: 18.7
Rank: 303

DINING & SHOPPING	AREA	U.S. AVG	ENTERTAINMENT	AREA	U.S. AVG	OUTDOOR ACTIVITIES	AREA	U.S. AVG
Restaurant rating	1	2	Professional sports rating	3	4	Golf-course rating	1	4
Outlet mall score	10	42	College sports rating	5	4	Ski-area rating	1	3
No. Starbucks	1	13	Zoo/aquarium rating	1	3	Sq. miles inland water	2	4
No. warehouse clubs	1	2	Amusement park rating	1	3	Miles of coastline	0.0	10.7
			Botanical garden/ arboretum rating	2	4	National Park rating	1	3

Arts & Culture
Score: 12.0
Rank: 328

MEDIA & LIBRARIES	AREA	U.S. AVG	PERFORMING ARTS	AREA	U.S. AVG	MUSEUMS	AREA	U.S. AVG
Arts radio rating	1	3	Classical music rating	1	4	Overall museum rating	3	5
No. public libraries	15	27	Ballet/dance rating	1	3	Art museum rating	3	5
Library volumes per capita	1.96	2.78	Professional theater rating	1	3	Science museum rating	5	5
			University arts programs rating	4	5	Children's museum rating	1	3

Lake Charles, LA

Score: 23.8   **Rank:** 348   **2004 rank:** 248

Profile: Small industrial city
Location: Southwest Louisiana, 30 miles west of Texas border
Elevation: 9 feet
Time zone: Central Standard Time

PRO
Cost of living
Recent job growth
Entertainment

CON
Hurricane dislocation
Low educational attainment
Hot, humid summers

Lake Charles is a deepwater port and center for the lumber and petrochemical industries. It suffered considerable damage in the 2005 Hurricane Rita. Prior to the storm, the city had a mostly industrial small-town feel with some historic areas, including the Victorian-era Charpentier District and a nice boardwalk area. Some casinos had arrived on the waterfront, including the large L'Auberge du Lac resort and casino. The hurricane wrecked the waterfront, electrical grid, and a large amount of housing. Basic services have recovered and the L'Auberge operation has actually announced expansion plans and an additional new casino, but a recent tax measure to fund housing and other redevelopment failed. The coastal marshlands in the Sabine National and Rockefeller State wildlife refuges to the south offer excellent wildlife viewing. Major air service and city amenities are distant—Houston, 150 miles west, or Baton Rouge, 130 miles east, are the choices. Long-term prospects and livability are a question mark.

The terrain is a flat, level plain. Extensive marshes begin to the south and extend to the coast. Elevations range from near sea level to about 25 feet above sea level. Winter months are normally mild with brief cold spells. Temperatures of 20°F or below rarely occur. Rainfall is substantial in all seasons, most arriving as brief showers and thundershowers. Spring and fall are mild and pleasant, usually dry and sunny. Severe local storms occur most frequently in spring with hurricanes in late summer and fall.

DEMOGRAPHICS	AREA	U.S. AVG	ETHNIC COMPOSITION	AREA	U.S. AVG	RESIDENT PROFILE	AREA	U.S. AVG
Population	194,173		White	73.4%	79.0%	Single	30.9%	32.4%
Population density per sq. mile	81.4	358.5	Black	23.8%	10.5%	Married	53.4%	52.7%
Population growth	9.5%	21.1%	Asian	0.8%	2.7%	Divorced/separated	15.8%	14.9%
Median age	35.3	36.1	Hispanic	1.6%	10.6%	Married with children	24.9%	23.7%
Percent Democrat	40.7%	44.5%	Religious observance	65.4%	48.9%	Single with children	10.8%	9.1%
Percent Republican	58.4%	54.5%	Diversity measure	41.8	40.1	Percent over age 65	12.3%	12.9%

Economy & Jobs
Score: 73.5
Rank: 100

INCOME	AREA	U.S. AVG	EMPLOYMENT	AREA	U.S. AVG	EMPLOYING INDUSTRIES	AREA	U.S. AVG
Per capita income	$20,385	$23,235	Unemployment rate	5.9%	4.7%	Largest: Manufacturing		
Household income	$40,366	$46,414	Recent job growth	4.0%	1.3%			
Household income < $25K	32.1%	26.2%	Projected future job growth	14.4%	11.5%	Percent manufacturing	15.2%	15.4%
Household income > $75K	21.6%	25.4%	White collar	52.3%	57.8%	Percent public sector	14.4%	15.7%
Household income growth	14.3%	13.6%	Blue collar	29.1%	25.2%	Percent construction	13.9%	9.9%

Cost of Living
Score: 71.7
Rank: 107

INDEXES & TAXES	AREA	U.S. AVG	HOUSING	AREA	U.S. AVG	NECESSITIES	AREA	U.S. AVG
Cost of Living Index	82.2	100.0	Median home price	$132,800	$220,000	Food Index	90.5	100.0
Buying Power Index	110.1	100.0	Home price appreciation	28.7%	10.1%	Housing Index	58.2	100.0
Income tax rate	4.00%	4.70%	Median rent	$577	$709	Utilities Index	90.1	100.0
Sales tax rate	8.28%	6.58%	Homes owned	64.9%	62.3%	Transportation Index	99.5	100.0
Property tax rate	$3.51	$12.00	Home price ratio	3.3	4.2	Healthcare Index	96.1	100.0
						Miscellaneous Cost Index	97.9	100.0

Climate
Score: 67.1
Rank: 122

TEMPERATURE	AREA	U.S. AVG	PRECIPITATION	AREA	U.S. AVG	COMFORTS & HAZARDS	AREA	U.S. AVG
Average January low	42.9	26.2	Annual inches precipitation	55.5	37.7	July relative humidity	78%	66%
Average July high	91.2	87.4	Annual inches snowfall	0.3	7.0	Annual days mostly sunny	215	208
Annual days > 90°F	71	38	Annual days precipitation	97	109	Annual days with thunderstorms	76	39
Annual days < 32°F	14	89	Annual days rain > 0.5 inches	32	22	Tornado risk score	33	18
Annual days < 0°F	0	6	Annual days snow > 1.5 inches	1	6	Hurricane risk score	47	13

TEMPERATURE

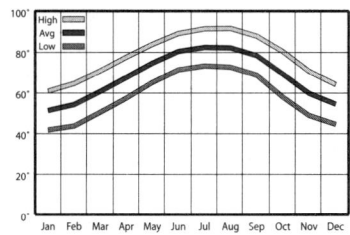

PRECIPITATION

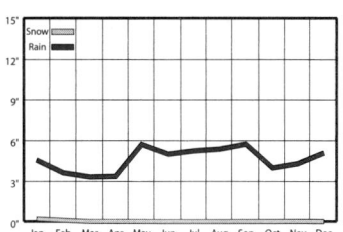

DAYS OF CLOUDS & PRECIPITATION

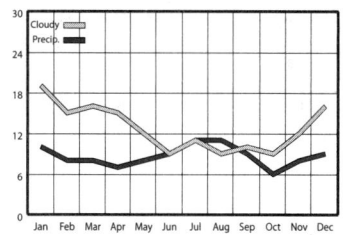

Education
Score: 6.4
Rank: 349

ACHIEVEMENT	AREA	U.S. AVG	PUBLIC SCHOOLS	AREA	U.S. AVG	HIGHER EDUCATION	AREA	U.S. AVG
High school degree	76.7%	82.7%	Expenditures per pupil	$4,566	$5,686	No. 2-year colleges	2	4
2-year college degree	4.0%	6.4%	Student/teacher ratio	15.6	16.7	No. 4-year colleges/universities	1	6
4-year college degree	11.5%	15.7%	Attending public school	88.7%	90.1%	No. highly ranked universities	0	1
Graduate/professional degree	5.1%	8.9%	State SAT score	1141	1021			
			State ACT score	20.1*	20.9			

Health & Healthcare
Score: 51.9
Rank: 181

HAZARDS & ILLNESSES	AREA	U.S. AVG	HEALTHCARE	AREA	U.S. AVG	CRIME	AREA	U.S. AVG
Air-quality score	24	37	Physicians per capita	166.4	244.2	Violent crime rate	591.9	465.5
Water-quality score	40	52	Hospital beds per capita	618.0	420.0	Change in violent crime rate	8.5%	-2.2%
Pollen/allergy score	70	61	No. teaching hospitals	2	3	Property crime rate	4,644.6	3,517.1
Cancer mortality per capita	217.5	201.9	Cost per doctor visit	$75	$77	Change in property crime rate	-7.4%	-2.1%
Depression days per month	3.0	3.5	Cost per dental visit	$55	$70			
Stress score	57	50						

Crime
Score: 16.0
Rank: 314

Transportation
Score: 24.3
Rank: 284

COMMUTE	AREA	U.S. AVG	INTERCITY SERVICES	AREA	U.S. AVG	AUTOMOTIVE	AREA	U.S. AVG
Average commute time	22.1	27.4	Major airports within 60 miles	0	1	Insurance, annual premium	$1,536	$1,432
Percent commutes > 60 mins.	4.4%	5.9%	Size of regional airport	None	Large	Gas, cost per gallon	$2.45	$2.49
Commute by auto	83.7%	78.9%	Daily airline activity	25	686	Daily vehicle miles per capita	26.7	24.0
Commute by mass transit	0.4%	1.9%	Amtrak service	Yes	No			
Work at home	1.8%	3.1%						
Mass transit miles per capita	0.40	1.87						

DINING & SHOPPING	AREA	U.S. AVG	ENTERTAINMENT	AREA	U.S. AVG	OUTDOOR ACTIVITIES	AREA	U.S. AVG
Restaurant rating	1	2	Professional sports rating	2	4	Golf-course rating	2	4
Outlet mall score	7	42	College sports rating	2	4	Ski-area rating	1	3
No. Starbucks	1	13	Zoo/aquarium rating	1	3	Sq. miles inland water	3	4
No. warehouse clubs	0	2	Amusement park rating	1	3	Miles of coastline	0.0	10.7
			Botanical garden/ arboretum rating	2	4	National Park rating	1	3

Leisure
Score: 9.4
Rank: 338

MEDIA & LIBRARIES	AREA	U.S. AVG	PERFORMING ARTS	AREA	U.S. AVG	MUSEUMS	AREA	U.S. AVG
Arts radio rating	1	3	Classical music rating	3	4	Overall museum rating	1	5
No. public libraries	15	27	Ballet/dance rating	3	3	Art museum rating	2	5
Library volumes per capita	2.16	2.78	Professional theater rating	1	3	Science museum rating	1	5
			University arts programs rating	3	5	Children's museum rating	2	3

Arts & Culture
Score: 19.8
Rank: 299

Lake County–Kenosha County, IL-WI

Score: 80.8 Rank: 41 2004 rank: 224

Profile: Small-town/suburban complex
Location: Along Lake Michigan between Milwaukee and Chicago
Elevation: 693 feet
Time zone: Central Standard Time

PRO	CON
Small-town atmosphere	Winter climate
Close to larger cities	Cost of living
Lakefront	Long commutes

This small but diverse metro area was recently created by combining the southeasternmost county of Wisconsin (Kenosha County) with the northeasternmost Lake County of Illinois. The result is a complex cluster of habitats and countryside with two major influences in common: Lake Michigan and the large metropolises of Milwaukee and Chicago north and south. Kenosha's heritage is mainly as an industrial center and port. The industrial highlight, until the 1980s, was American Motors and its predecessors, but that declining automaker was subsequently bought by DaimlerChrysler and the facilities absorbed and repurposed. That company kept one of the two plants going as an engine plant; the other was torn down in favor of a waterfront park, a welcome change. Other industries include machine tools and textile maker Jockey International. Kenosha is pleasant but uninteresting with tree-shaded streets and improving waterfront areas, and is used as a commute base to Milwaukee and the northern Chicago suburbs. It is much more white-collar than it was years ago. On the Illinois side lie an assortment of small towns and more upscale Chicago commuter suburbs such as the inland Lake Zurich and Fox Lake, and Lake Forest and Highland Park along the shore. Other shoreline communities, such as Waukegan and North Chicago, are more manufacturing oriented and of varying quality. All waterfront communities take advantage of their lakefront location and convenient commuter access. Wilmot Mountain ski area lies 15 miles west of Kenosha. Chicago provides many services and amenities, and Milwaukee is on the upswing, and both are close enough to unfavorably influence cost of living and housing, which are already high in the choicest locations.

The town sits on a coastal plain on the western shore of Lake Michigan. Wooded hills rise to the west. The warm summers are influenced both by the lake and the inflow of Gulf moisture from the south. Winter is often humid with frequent snow and cold snaps. Snow can remain on the ground for long periods. Winds off the lake may moderate temperature but add a wind chill. Summer precipitation is mainly thundershowers; spring and fall are variable with alternating pleasant dry days and rainy periods. First freeze is mid-October; last is mid-April.

DEMOGRAPHICS	AREA	U.S. AVG	ETHNIC COMPOSITION	AREA	U.S. AVG	RESIDENT PROFILE	AREA	U.S. AVG
Population	859,472		White	78.6%	79.0%	Single	29.1%	32.4%
Population density per sq. mile	1193.0	358.5	Black	6.7%	10.5%	Married	58.2%	52.7%
Population growth	33.5%	21.1%	Asian	4.6%	2.7%	Divorced/separated	12.7%	14.9%
Median age	34.6	36.1	Hispanic	15.7%	10.6%	Married with children	32.8%	23.7%
Percent Democrat	49.5%	44.5%	Religious observance	57.2%	48.9%	Single with children	7.7%	9.1%
Percent Republican	49.8%	54.5%	Diversity measure	53.0	40.1	Percent over age 65	9.4%	12.9%

Population

INCOME	AREA	U.S. AVG	EMPLOYMENT	AREA	U.S. AVG	EMPLOYING INDUSTRIES	AREA	U.S. AVG
Per capita income	$33,414	$23,235	Unemployment rate	4.6%	4.7%	Largest: Manufacturing		
Household income	$70,676	$46,414	Recent job growth	3.2%	1.3%			
Household income < $25K	13.7%	26.2%	Projected future job growth	19.4%	11.5%	Percent manufacturing	13.1%	15.4%
Household income > $75K	46.3%	25.4%	White collar	66.9%	57.8%	Percent public sector	10.4%	15.7%
Household income growth	11.8%	13.6%	Blue collar	21.1%	25.2%	Percent construction	8.1%	9.9%

Economy & Jobs
Score: 94.7
Rank: 21

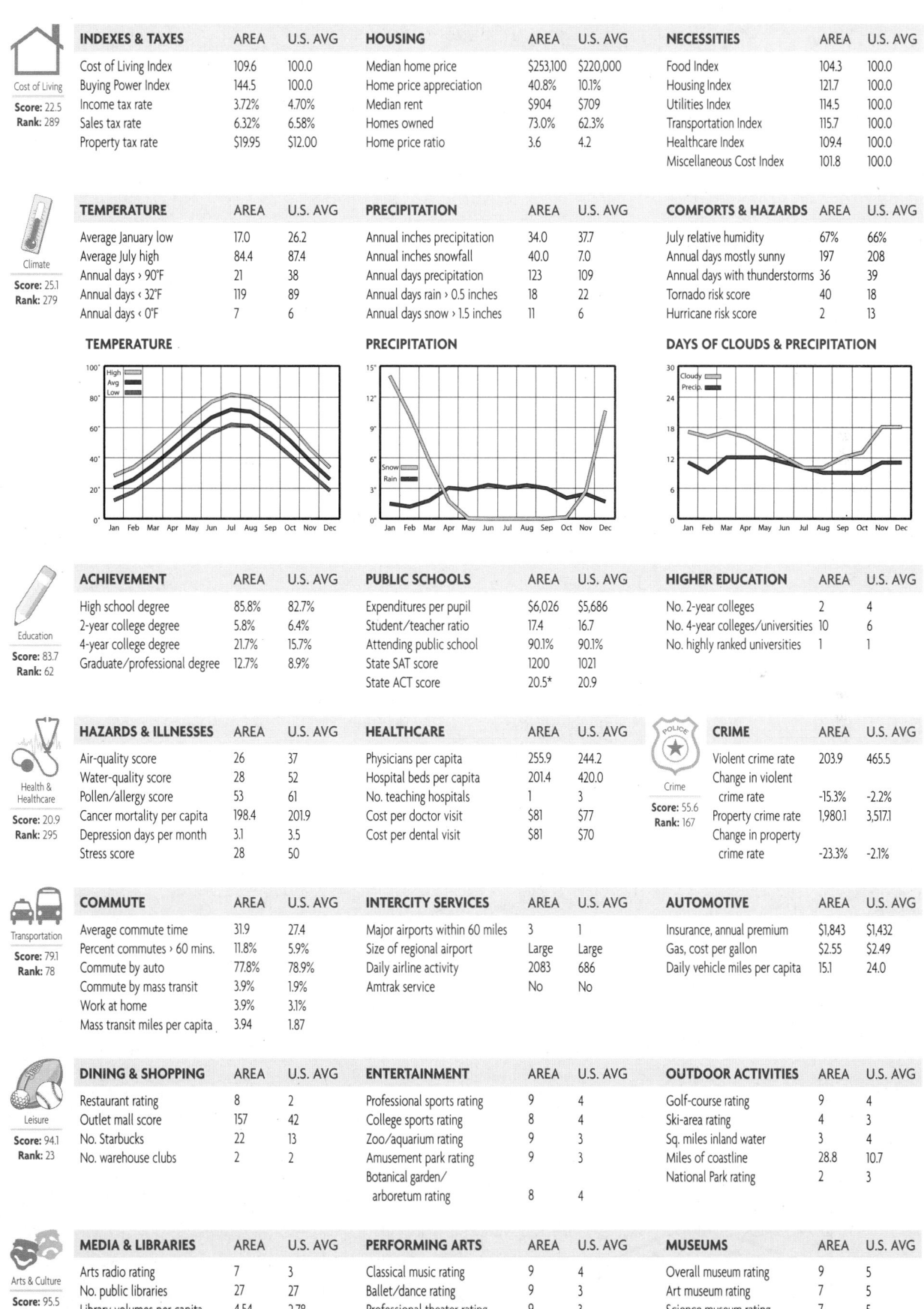

Cost of Living
Score: 22.5
Rank: 289

INDEXES & TAXES	AREA	U.S. AVG
Cost of Living Index	109.6	100.0
Buying Power Index	144.5	100.0
Income tax rate	3.72%	4.70%
Sales tax rate	6.32%	6.58%
Property tax rate	$19.95	$12.00

HOUSING	AREA	U.S. AVG
Median home price	$253,100	$220,000
Home price appreciation	40.8%	10.1%
Median rent	$904	$709
Homes owned	73.0%	62.3%
Home price ratio	3.6	4.2

NECESSITIES	AREA	U.S. AVG
Food Index	104.3	100.0
Housing Index	121.7	100.0
Utilities Index	114.5	100.0
Transportation Index	115.7	100.0
Healthcare Index	109.4	100.0
Miscellaneous Cost Index	101.8	100.0

Climate
Score: 25.1
Rank: 279

TEMPERATURE	AREA	U.S. AVG
Average January low	17.0	26.2
Average July high	84.4	87.4
Annual days > 90°F	21	38
Annual days < 32°F	119	89
Annual days < 0°F	7	6

PRECIPITATION	AREA	U.S. AVG
Annual inches precipitation	34.0	37.7
Annual inches snowfall	40.0	7.0
Annual days precipitation	123	109
Annual days rain > 0.5 inches	18	22
Annual days snow > 1.5 inches	11	6

COMFORTS & HAZARDS	AREA	U.S. AVG
July relative humidity	67%	66%
Annual days mostly sunny	197	208
Annual days with thunderstorms	36	39
Tornado risk score	40	18
Hurricane risk score	2	13

TEMPERATURE

PRECIPITATION

DAYS OF CLOUDS & PRECIPITATION

Education
Score: 83.7
Rank: 62

ACHIEVEMENT	AREA	U.S. AVG
High school degree	85.8%	82.7%
2-year college degree	5.8%	6.4%
4-year college degree	21.7%	15.7%
Graduate/professional degree	12.7%	8.9%

PUBLIC SCHOOLS	AREA	U.S. AVG
Expenditures per pupil	$6,026	$5,686
Student/teacher ratio	17.4	16.7
Attending public school	90.1%	90.1%
State SAT score	1200	1021
State ACT score	20.5*	20.9

HIGHER EDUCATION	AREA	U.S. AVG
No. 2-year colleges	2	4
No. 4-year colleges/universities	10	6
No. highly ranked universities	1	1

Health & Healthcare
Score: 20.9
Rank: 295

HAZARDS & ILLNESSES	AREA	U.S. AVG
Air-quality score	26	37
Water-quality score	28	52
Pollen/allergy score	53	61
Cancer mortality per capita	198.4	201.9
Depression days per month	3.1	3.5
Stress score	28	50

HEALTHCARE	AREA	U.S. AVG
Physicians per capita	255.9	244.2
Hospital beds per capita	201.4	420.0
No. teaching hospitals	1	3
Cost per doctor visit	$81	$77
Cost per dental visit	$81	$70

Crime
Score: 55.6
Rank: 167

CRIME	AREA	U.S. AVG
Violent crime rate	203.9	465.5
Change in violent crime rate	-15.3%	-2.2%
Property crime rate	1,980.1	3,517.1
Change in property crime rate	-23.3%	-2.1%

Transportation
Score: 79.1
Rank: 78

COMMUTE	AREA	U.S. AVG
Average commute time	31.9	27.4
Percent commutes > 60 mins.	11.8%	5.9%
Commute by auto	77.8%	78.9%
Commute by mass transit	3.9%	1.9%
Work at home	3.9%	3.1%
Mass transit miles per capita	3.94	1.87

INTERCITY SERVICES	AREA	U.S. AVG
Major airports within 60 miles	3	1
Size of regional airport	Large	Large
Daily airline activity	2083	686
Amtrak service	No	No

AUTOMOTIVE	AREA	U.S. AVG
Insurance, annual premium	$1,843	$1,432
Gas, cost per gallon	$2.55	$2.49
Daily vehicle miles per capita	15.1	24.0

Leisure
Score: 94.1
Rank: 23

DINING & SHOPPING	AREA	U.S. AVG
Restaurant rating	8	2
Outlet mall score	157	42
No. Starbucks	22	13
No. warehouse clubs	2	2

ENTERTAINMENT	AREA	U.S. AVG
Professional sports rating	9	4
College sports rating	8	4
Zoo/aquarium rating	9	3
Amusement park rating	9	3
Botanical garden/ arboretum rating	8	4

OUTDOOR ACTIVITIES	AREA	U.S. AVG
Golf-course rating	9	4
Ski-area rating	4	3
Sq. miles inland water	3	4
Miles of coastline	28.8	10.7
National Park rating	2	3

Arts & Culture
Score: 95.5
Rank: 18

MEDIA & LIBRARIES	AREA	U.S. AVG
Arts radio rating	7	3
No. public libraries	27	27
Library volumes per capita	4.54	2.78

PERFORMING ARTS	AREA	U.S. AVG
Classical music rating	9	4
Ballet/dance rating	9	3
Professional theater rating	9	3
University arts programs rating	9	5

MUSEUMS	AREA	U.S. AVG
Overall museum rating	9	5
Art museum rating	7	5
Science museum rating	7	5
Children's museum rating	7	3

Lakeland, FL

Score: 62.3   **Rank:** 156   **2004 rank:** 126

Profile: Mid-size city/resort city
Location: Central Florida, 25 miles inland from the Tampa Bay area
Elevation: 214 feet
Time zone: Eastern Standard Time

PRO	CON
Leisure activities	Growth and sprawl
Cost of living	Low educational attainment
Attractive setting	Summer heat and humidity

Lakeland historically has been a major agricultural center with citrus growing, processing, and distribution, and a large phosphate mining industry mainly to the west. Winter Haven is a rapidly growing resort area to the east, and both places, taking advantage of a strategic location between major Florida centers of Tampa Bay and Orlando and relatively low housing costs, are becoming retirement and family living destinations. The supermarket chain Publix is the largest private employer, and generates employment through a number of its suppliers. There is also a large hospital and healthcare complex. Not surprisingly from the area's name, nearby lakes provide an assortment of watersports, and the region has a growing number of golf-course communities. Baseball spring training camps round out the entertainment options. Florida Southern University brings a small college-town element and features the largest collection of buildings by Frank Lloyd

Wright in one place. The walkable downtown Lakeland is on the rebound, with renewal projects and some new residential construction along a small lakefront. Cost of living and especially housing have grown but remain reasonable by Florida standards, but downsides include areas of overdevelopment and a surprisingly low educational attainment. As reflected in commute statistics, some do commute to the Tampa Bay area.

The area has a level landscape with a mix of open agricultural, orchard, and wooded areas of stately cypress tress. The humid subtropical climate creates very warm, humid, summer days with highs in the 90s, lows in the upper 60s and 70s, and frequent afternoon showers and thundershowers. Winters are mild with a few days of below-freezing temperatures each year, but lingering cold weather seldom occurs. The inland location prevents major damage from hurricanes.

DEMOGRAPHICS	AREA	U.S. AVG	ETHNIC COMPOSITION	AREA	U.S. AVG	RESIDENT PROFILE	AREA	U.S. AVG
Population	523,502		White	77.1%	79.0%	Single	28.8%	32.4%
Population density per sq. mile	279.3	358.5	Black	14.5%	10.5%	Married	55.2%	52.7%
Population growth	29.1%	21.1%	Asian	1.2%	2.7%	Divorced/separated	16.0%	14.9%
Median age	38.3	36.1	Hispanic	12.1%	10.6%	Married with children	19.4%	23.7%
Percent Democrat	40.8%	44.5%	Religious observance	41.9%	48.9%	Single with children	9.0%	9.1%
Percent Republican	58.6%	54.5%	Diversity measure	51.3	40.1	Percent over age 65	18.0%	12.9%

Population

INCOME	AREA	U.S. AVG	EMPLOYMENT	AREA	U.S. AVG	EMPLOYING INDUSTRIES	AREA	U.S. AVG
Per capita income	$20,864	$23,235	Unemployment rate	4.5%	4.7%	Largest: Healthcare & Social Assistance		
Household income	$40,960	$46,414	Recent job growth	4.6%	1.3%			
Household income < $25K	28.2%	26.2%	Projected future job growth	13.6%	11.5%	Percent manufacturing	15.9%	15.4%
Household income > $75K	19.5%	25.4%	White collar	53.4%	57.8%	Percent public sector	12.9%	15.7%
Household income growth	13.7%	13.6%	Blue collar	27.5%	25.2%	Percent construction	11.6%	9.9%

Economy & Jobs
Score: 81.8
Rank: 69

INDEXES & TAXES	AREA	U.S. AVG	HOUSING	AREA	U.S. AVG	NECESSITIES	AREA	U.S. AVG
Cost of Living Index	93.9	100.0	Median home price	$184,200	$220,000	Food Index	100.8	100.0
Buying Power Index	97.8	100.0	Home price appreciation	85.5%	10.1%	Housing Index	60.2	100.0
Income tax rate	0.00%	4.70%	Median rent	$594	$709	Utilities Index	99.1	100.0
Sales tax rate	7.00%	6.58%	Homes owned	61.5%	62.3%	Transportation Index	99.3	100.0
Property tax rate	$12.13	$12.00	Home price ratio	4.5	4.2	Healthcare Index	102.1	100.0
						Miscellaneous Cost Index	102.1	100.0

Cost of Living
Score: 86.1
Rank: 53

TEMPERATURE	AREA	U.S. AVG	PRECIPITATION	AREA	U.S. AVG	COMFORTS & HAZARDS	AREA	U.S. AVG
Average January low	51.0	26.2	Annual inches precipitation	49.4	37.7	July relative humidity	74%	66%
Average July high	90.4	87.4	Annual inches snowfall	0.1	7.0	Annual days mostly sunny	259	208
Annual days > 90°F	83	38	Annual days precipitation	120	109	Annual days with thunderstorms	100	39
Annual days < 32°F	2	89	Annual days rain > 0.5 inches	29	22	Tornado risk score	69	18
Annual days < 0°F	0	6	Annual days snow > 1.5 inches	0	6	Hurricane risk score	76	13

Climate
Score: 79.1
Rank: 79

TEMPERATURE

PRECIPITATION

DAYS OF CLOUDS & PRECIPITATION

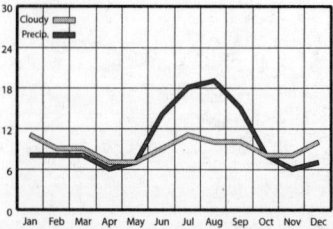

Education	ACHIEVEMENT	AREA	U.S. AVG	PUBLIC SCHOOLS	AREA	U.S. AVG	HIGHER EDUCATION	AREA	U.S. AVG
Score: 13.9 Rank: 321	High school degree	75.0%	82.7%	Expenditures per pupil	$5,014	$5,686	No. 2-year colleges	3	4
	2-year college degree	5.8%	6.4%	Student/teacher ratio	17.4	16.7	No. 4-year colleges/universities	6	6
	4-year college degree	10.1%	15.7%	Attending public school	91.0%	90.1%	No. highly ranked universities	1	1
	Graduate/professional degree	4.9%	8.9%	State SAT score	993*	1021			
				State ACT score	20.3	20.9			

Health & Healthcare	HAZARDS & ILLNESSES	AREA	U.S. AVG	HEALTHCARE	AREA	U.S. AVG	CRIME	AREA	U.S. AVG
Score: 2.4 Rank: 364	Air-quality score	18	37	Physicians per capita	143.4	244.2	Violent crime rate	493.4	465.5
	Water-quality score	46	52	Hospital beds per capita	301.2	420.0	Change in violent crime rate	2.9%	-2.2%
	Pollen/allergy score	81	61	No. teaching hospitals	0	3	Property crime rate	4,068.1	3,517.1
	Cancer mortality per capita	250.6	201.9	Cost per doctor visit	$60	$77	Change in property crime rate	0.0%	-2.1%
	Depression days per month	3.4	3.5	Cost per dental visit	$70	$70			
	Stress score	59	50						

Crime Score: 33.7 Rank: 248

Transportation	COMMUTE	AREA	U.S. AVG	INTERCITY SERVICES	AREA	U.S. AVG	AUTOMOTIVE	AREA	U.S. AVG
Score: 47.3 Rank: 198	Average commute time	27.2	27.4	Major airports within 60 miles	2	1	Insurance, annual premium	$1,590	$1,432
	Percent commutes > 60 mins.	7.1%	5.9%	Size of regional airport	Large	Large	Gas, cost per gallon	$2.55	$2.49
	Commute by auto	80.1%	78.9%	Daily airline activity	984	686	Daily vehicle miles per capita	28.0	24.0
	Commute by mass transit	0.7%	1.9%	Amtrak service	Yes	No			
	Work at home	2.1%	3.1%						
	Mass transit miles per capita	0.70	1.87						

Leisure	DINING & SHOPPING	AREA	U.S. AVG	ENTERTAINMENT	AREA	U.S. AVG	OUTDOOR ACTIVITIES	AREA	U.S. AVG
Score: 58.6 Rank: 155	Restaurant rating	1	2	Professional sports rating	2	4	Golf-course rating	4	4
	Outlet mall score	126	42	College sports rating	1	4	Ski-area rating	1	3
	No. Starbucks	3	13	Zoo/aquarium rating	1	3	Sq. miles inland water	10	4
	No. warehouse clubs	0	2	Amusement park rating	5	3	Miles of coastline	0.0	10.7
				Botanical garden/ arboretum rating	6	4	National Park rating	1	3

Arts & Culture	MEDIA & LIBRARIES	AREA	U.S. AVG	PERFORMING ARTS	AREA	U.S. AVG	MUSEUMS	AREA	U.S. AVG
Score: 46.0 Rank: 202	Arts radio rating	1	3	Classical music rating	6	4	Overall museum rating	6	5
	No. public libraries	16	27	Ballet/dance rating	1	3	Art museum rating	7	5
	Library volumes per capita	1.44	2.78	Professional theater rating	1	3	Science museum rating	7	5
				University arts programs rating	2	5	Children's museum rating	2	3

Lancaster, PA

Score: 69.5   Rank: 96   2004 rank: 186

Profile: Small city
Location: Southeastern Pennsylvania, 80 miles west Philadelphia
Elevation: 351 feet
Time zone: Eastern Standard Time

PRO	CON
Historic interest	Economic cycles
Cost of living	Entertainment
Central location	Low educational attainment

Lancaster is a manufacturing and commercial center in the heart of Pennsylvania's Amish country. The city has dealt with unemployment issues at times, as some of its manufacturing base has disappeared, but a large hospitality industry and a diversified food processing industry remain. Downtown is older but has some historic interest and is being cleaned up. The area has also been helped by location, as it is close enough to major East Coast cities, particularly Philadelphia, Baltimore, Harrisburg, and even Washington, D.C., and New York, to attract small businesses, the self-employed, and telecommuters looking for lower living costs, a small-town lifestyle, and occasional access to these markets. Surrounding areas are generally prosperous and economically diversified with light manufacturing of consumer and industrial staples, such as lighting and clothing products. The purest agrarian Pennsylvania Dutch communities lie immediately east within an attractive countryside dotted by old farms and picturesque barns. While they also support a sometimes-gaudy tourism industry, they add some entertainment value and cultural and historic interest. Amenities lacking in this region are available in Philadelphia, Baltimore, and Harrisburg, all less than 100 miles away. As one might expect, crime rates are low, but locally practiced culture also reduces educational attainment and brings values too traditional for some. Cost of living has been rising slowly, but incomes are keeping up and buying power is high. As with other areas of Amish influence, modern agricultural economics challenge the sustainability of small family farms.

The area contains mainly level to gentle rolling hills with fertile soil. Summers are warm and humid with occasional thunderstorms. Winters are not too rigorous. With the exception of occasional long warm spells in summer and fall, the weather is variable. First freeze is late October; last is mid-April.

Population

DEMOGRAPHICS	AREA	U.S. AVG	ETHNIC COMPOSITION	AREA	U.S. AVG	RESIDENT PROFILE	AREA	U.S. AVG
Population	488,738		White	90.6%	79.0%	Single	30.9%	32.4%
Population density per sq. mile	514.9	358.5	Black	2.9%	10.5%	Married	58.2%	52.7%
Population growth	15.6%	21.1%	Asian	1.7%	2.7%	Divorced/separated	10.9%	14.9%
Median age	37.0	36.1	Hispanic	6.1%	10.6%	Married with children	26.5%	23.7%
Percent Democrat	33.6%	44.5%	Religious observance	48.4%	48.9%	Single with children	7.0%	9.1%
Percent Republican	65.8%	54.5%	Diversity measure	27.1	40.1	Percent over age 65	14.3%	12.9%

Economy & Jobs

Score: 51.3
Rank: 183

INCOME	AREA	U.S. AVG	EMPLOYMENT	AREA	U.S. AVG	EMPLOYING INDUSTRIES	AREA	U.S. AVG
Per capita income	$23,163	$23,235	Unemployment rate	4.0%	4.7%	Largest: Manufacturing		
Household income	$50,271	$46,414	Recent job growth	0.6%	1.3%			
Household income < $25K	19.7%	26.2%	Projected future job growth	7.0%	11.5%	Percent manufacturing	21.9%	15.4%
Household income > $75K	26.7%	25.4%	White collar	51.6%	57.8%	Percent public sector	7.2%	15.7%
Household income growth	10.5%	13.6%	Blue collar	32.0%	25.2%	Percent construction	10.1%	9.9%

Cost of Living

Score: 63.9
Rank: 135

INDEXES & TAXES	AREA	U.S. AVG	HOUSING	AREA	U.S. AVG	NECESSITIES	AREA	U.S. AVG
Cost of Living Index	90.8	100.0	Median home price	$167,100	$220,000	Food Index	91.0	100.0
Buying Power Index	124.1	100.0	Home price appreciation	49.7%	10.1%	Housing Index	69.6	100.0
Income tax rate	2.80%	4.70%	Median rent	$704	$709	Utilities Index	112.4	100.0
Sales tax rate	6.00%	6.58%	Homes owned	68.2%	62.3%	Transportation Index	107.5	100.0
Property tax rate	$14.29	$12.00	Home price ratio	3.3	4.2	Healthcare Index	93.8	100.0
						Miscellaneous Cost Index	99.4	100.0

Climate

Score: 32.6
Rank: 251

TEMPERATURE	AREA	U.S. AVG	PRECIPITATION	AREA	U.S. AVG	COMFORTS & HAZARDS	AREA	U.S. AVG
Average January low	22.5	26.2	Annual inches precipitation	36.0	37.7	July relative humidity	67%	66%
Average July high	86.8	87.4	Annual inches snowfall	35.0	7.0	Annual days mostly sunny	193	208
Annual days > 90°F	24	38	Annual days precipitation	125	109	Annual days with thunderstorms	33	39
Annual days < 32°F	107	89	Annual days rain > 0.5 inches	25	22	Tornado risk score	14	18
Annual days < 0°F	1	6	Annual days snow > 1.5 inches	8	6	Hurricane risk score	11	13

TEMPERATURE

PRECIPITATION

DAYS OF CLOUDS & PRECIPITATION

Education

Score: 21.7
Rank: 292

ACHIEVEMENT	AREA	U.S. AVG	PUBLIC SCHOOLS	AREA	U.S. AVG	HIGHER EDUCATION	AREA	U.S. AVG
High school degree	77.4%	82.7%	Expenditures per pupil	$6,048	$5,686	No. 2-year colleges	5	4
2-year college degree	4.5%	6.4%	Student/teacher ratio	18.5	16.7	No. 4-year colleges/universities	6	6
4-year college degree	13.8%	15.7%	Attending public school	81.7%	90.1%	No. highly ranked universities	2	1
Graduate/professional degree	6.7%	8.9%	State SAT score	993*	1021			
			State ACT score	21.8	20.9			

Health & Healthcare

Score: 12.3
Rank: 327

Crime

Score: 83.7
Rank: 62

HAZARDS & ILLNESSES	AREA	U.S. AVG	HEALTHCARE	AREA	U.S. AVG	CRIME	AREA	U.S. AVG
Air-quality score	20	37	Physicians per capita	181.7	244.2	Violent crime rate	172.2	465.5
Water-quality score	20	52	Hospital beds per capita	235.3	420.0	Change in violent crime rate	-4.9%	-2.2%
Pollen/allergy score	52	61	No. teaching hospitals	2	3	Property crime rate	2,223.3	3,517.1
Cancer mortality per capita	229.0	201.9	Cost per doctor visit	$73	$77	Change in property crime rate	-4.0%	-2.1%
Depression days per month	3.2	3.5	Cost per dental visit	$64	$70			
Stress score	4	50						

Transportation

Score: 98.9
Rank: 5

COMMUTE	AREA	U.S. AVG	INTERCITY SERVICES	AREA	U.S. AVG	AUTOMOTIVE	AREA	U.S. AVG
Average commute time	23.5	27.4	Major airports within 60 miles	4	1	Insurance, annual premium	$1,300	$1,432
Percent commutes > 60 mins.	4.8%	5.9%	Size of regional airport	Large	Large	Gas, cost per gallon	$2.42	$2.49
Commute by auto	78.5%	78.9%	Daily airline activity	2329	686	Daily vehicle miles per capita	20.3	24.0
Commute by mass transit	1.1%	1.9%	Amtrak service	Yes	No			
Work at home	4.9%	3.1%						
Mass transit miles per capita	1.12	1.87						

DINING & SHOPPING	AREA	U.S. AVG	ENTERTAINMENT	AREA	U.S. AVG	OUTDOOR ACTIVITIES	AREA	U.S. AVG
Restaurant rating	1	2	Professional sports rating	4	4	Golf-course rating	3	4
Outlet mall score	67	42	College sports rating	5	4	Ski-area rating	4	3
No. Starbucks	1	13	Zoo/aquarium rating	1	3	Sq. miles inland water	3	4
No. warehouse clubs	2	2	Amusement park rating	3	3	Miles of coastline	0.0	10.7
			Botanical garden/			National Park rating	1	3
			arboretum rating	2	4			

Leisure
Score: 53.2
Rank: 175

MEDIA & LIBRARIES	AREA	U.S. AVG	PERFORMING ARTS	AREA	U.S. AVG	MUSEUMS	AREA	U.S. AVG
Arts radio rating	1	3	Classical music rating	1	4	Overall museum rating	6	5
No. public libraries	17	27	Ballet/dance rating	1	3	Art museum rating	5	5
Library volumes per capita	1.56	2.78	Professional theater rating	1	3	Science museum rating	4	5
			University arts programs rating	6	5	Children's museum rating	3	3

Arts & Culture
Score: 21.7
Rank: 292

Lansing–East Lansing, MI   Score: 52.4   Rank: 237   2004 rank: 162

Profile: Capital city/college town
Location: Central Michigan along I-96 halfway between Detroit and Grand Rapids
Elevation: 841 feet
Time zone: Eastern Standard Time

PRO
College-town atmosphere
Capital-city amenities
Stable employers

CON
Economic cycles
Winter climate
Cloudy skies

Lansing is the state capital, and East Lansing is home to Michigan State University. Together the two places form the second-most-populated area in Michigan, but individually, they are quite different. Downtown Lansing is plain and generally uninteresting, mainly anchored by the state government. A large GM assembly plant just west of town was recently replaced by a more modern plant farther out. Area employment has three distinct bases: government, the university, and GM. While government and the university create a stabilizing influence, GM and the rest of the industrial mix and economy have been anything but. The effects of GM's downsizing and recent buyout programs on the area economy and demographics are still unfolding, but recent unemployment is high and home sales are very slow. There are some interesting museums and other facilities typical of a capital city. Entertainment is provided by popular and aptly named Lansing Lugnuts minor league baseball team, and for most other entertainment activities, residents look east. East Lansing, the more attractive of the two cities, contains the usual college-town amenities, restaurants, and nightlife, and has a stronger employment base. Areas west along a major strip are generally unattractive, while pleasant suburbs and small suburban towns surround the area north, east, and south. Okemos, east of East Lansing, is one of the largest and more upscale examples and has a small base of high-tech employment. Small towns such as Williamston to the southeast and Owosso to the northeast offer an attractive small-town lifestyle with access to city employment. The cost of living is very attractive for a capital city and college town, but the economy, and certainly the dreary central Michigan climate, are issues to contend with.

Terrain is generally a mix of farmland and deciduous forest. The climate alternates between continental and semi-marine, based on the force and direction of the wind and storms. When there is little wind, the weather becomes continental with pronounced fluctuations in temperature. A strong lake wind may temper winter cold and summer heat, albeit with heightened wind chill factors in winter. Precipitation is evenly distributed throughout the year. Snowfall is moderate. First freeze is end of September; last is mid-May.

DEMOGRAPHICS	AREA	U.S. AVG	ETHNIC COMPOSITION	AREA	U.S. AVG	RESIDENT PROFILE	AREA	U.S. AVG
Population	459,398		White	83.0%	79.0%	Single	37.0%	32.4%
Population density per sq. mile	269.1	358.5	Black	8.5%	10.5%	Married	49.7%	52.7%
Population growth	6.8%	21.1%	Asian	3.2%	2.7%	Divorced/separated	13.3%	14.9%
Median age	34.2	36.1	Hispanic	4.9%	10.6%	Married with children	22.4%	23.7%
Percent Democrat	52.4%	44.5%	Religious observance	37.5%	48.9%	Single with children	9.2%	9.1%
Percent Republican	46.6%	54.5%	Diversity measure	35.7	40.1	Percent over age 65	10.6%	12.9%

Population

INCOME	AREA	U.S. AVG	EMPLOYMENT	AREA	U.S. AVG	EMPLOYING INDUSTRIES	AREA	U.S. AVG
Per capita income	$24,770	$23,235	Unemployment rate	7.0%	4.7%	Largest: Manufacturing		
Household income	$49,719	$46,414	Recent job growth	1.7%	1.3%			
Household income < $25K	23.1%	26.2%	Projected future job growth	8.0%	11.5%	Percent manufacturing	14.3%	15.4%
Household income > $75K	28.7%	25.4%	White collar	61.4%	57.8%	Percent public sector	20.4%	15.7%
Household income growth	11.3%	13.6%	Blue collar	22.5%	25.2%	Percent construction	8.2%	9.9%

Economy & Jobs
Score: 47.9
Rank: 196

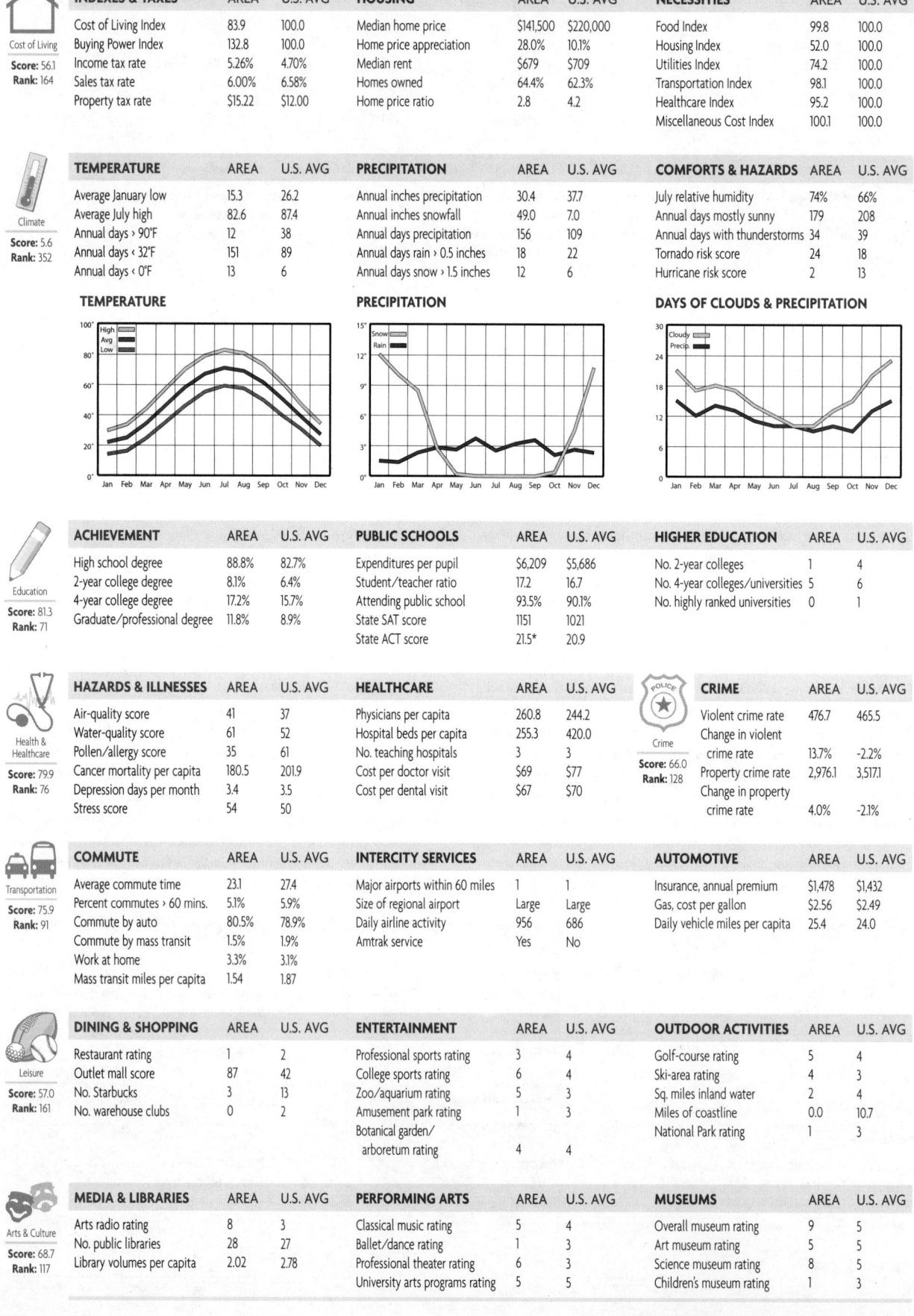

Cost of Living
Score: 56.1
Rank: 164

INDEXES & TAXES	AREA	U.S. AVG
Cost of Living Index	83.9	100.0
Buying Power Index	132.8	100.0
Income tax rate	5.26%	4.70%
Sales tax rate	6.00%	6.58%
Property tax rate	$15.22	$12.00

HOUSING	AREA	U.S. AVG
Median home price	$141,500	$220,000
Home price appreciation	28.0%	10.1%
Median rent	$679	$709
Homes owned	64.4%	62.3%
Home price ratio	2.8	4.2

NECESSITIES	AREA	U.S. AVG
Food Index	99.8	100.0
Housing Index	52.0	100.0
Utilities Index	74.2	100.0
Transportation Index	98.1	100.0
Healthcare Index	95.2	100.0
Miscellaneous Cost Index	100.1	100.0

Climate
Score: 5.6
Rank: 352

TEMPERATURE	AREA	U.S. AVG
Average January low	15.3	26.2
Average July high	82.6	87.4
Annual days > 90°F	12	38
Annual days < 32°F	151	89
Annual days < 0°F	13	6

PRECIPITATION	AREA	U.S. AVG
Annual inches precipitation	30.4	37.7
Annual inches snowfall	49.0	7.0
Annual days precipitation	156	109
Annual days rain > 0.5 inches	18	22
Annual days snow > 1.5 inches	12	6

COMFORTS & HAZARDS	AREA	U.S. AVG
July relative humidity	74%	66%
Annual days mostly sunny	179	208
Annual days with thunderstorms	34	39
Tornado risk score	24	18
Hurricane risk score	2	13

TEMPERATURE

PRECIPITATION

DAYS OF CLOUDS & PRECIPITATION

Education
Score: 81.3
Rank: 71

ACHIEVEMENT	AREA	U.S. AVG
High school degree	88.8%	82.7%
2-year college degree	8.1%	6.4%
4-year college degree	17.2%	15.7%
Graduate/professional degree	11.8%	8.9%

PUBLIC SCHOOLS	AREA	U.S. AVG
Expenditures per pupil	$6,209	$5,686
Student/teacher ratio	17.2	16.7
Attending public school	93.5%	90.1%
State SAT score	1151	1021
State ACT score	21.5*	20.9

HIGHER EDUCATION	AREA	U.S. AVG
No. 2-year colleges	1	4
No. 4-year colleges/universities	5	6
No. highly ranked universities	0	1

Health & Healthcare
Score: 79.9
Rank: 76

HAZARDS & ILLNESSES	AREA	U.S. AVG
Air-quality score	41	37
Water-quality score	61	52
Pollen/allergy score	35	61
Cancer mortality per capita	180.5	201.9
Depression days per month	3.4	3.5
Stress score	54	50

HEALTHCARE	AREA	U.S. AVG
Physicians per capita	260.8	244.2
Hospital beds per capita	255.3	420.0
No. teaching hospitals	3	3
Cost per doctor visit	$69	$77
Cost per dental visit	$67	$70

Crime
Score: 66.0
Rank: 128

CRIME	AREA	U.S. AVG
Violent crime rate	476.7	465.5
Change in violent crime rate	13.7%	-2.2%
Property crime rate	2,976.1	3,517.1
Change in property crime rate	4.0%	-2.1%

Transportation
Score: 75.9
Rank: 91

COMMUTE	AREA	U.S. AVG
Average commute time	23.1	27.4
Percent commutes > 60 mins.	5.1%	5.9%
Commute by auto	80.5%	78.9%
Commute by mass transit	1.5%	1.9%
Work at home	3.3%	3.1%
Mass transit miles per capita	1.54	1.87

INTERCITY SERVICES	AREA	U.S. AVG
Major airports within 60 miles	1	1
Size of regional airport	Large	Large
Daily airline activity	956	686
Amtrak service	Yes	No

AUTOMOTIVE	AREA	U.S. AVG
Insurance, annual premium	$1,478	$1,432
Gas, cost per gallon	$2.56	$2.49
Daily vehicle miles per capita	25.4	24.0

Leisure
Score: 57.0
Rank: 161

DINING & SHOPPING	AREA	U.S. AVG
Restaurant rating	1	2
Outlet mall score	87	42
No. Starbucks	3	13
No. warehouse clubs	0	2

ENTERTAINMENT	AREA	U.S. AVG
Professional sports rating	3	4
College sports rating	6	4
Zoo/aquarium rating	5	3
Amusement park rating	1	3
Botanical garden/ arboretum rating	4	4

OUTDOOR ACTIVITIES	AREA	U.S. AVG
Golf-course rating	5	4
Ski-area rating	4	3
Sq. miles inland water	2	4
Miles of coastline	0.0	10.7
National Park rating	1	3

Arts & Culture
Score: 68.7
Rank: 117

MEDIA & LIBRARIES	AREA	U.S. AVG
Arts radio rating	8	3
No. public libraries	28	27
Library volumes per capita	2.02	2.78

PERFORMING ARTS	AREA	U.S. AVG
Classical music rating	5	4
Ballet/dance rating	1	3
Professional theater rating	6	3
University arts programs rating	5	5

MUSEUMS	AREA	U.S. AVG
Overall museum rating	9	5
Art museum rating	5	5
Science museum rating	8	5
Children's museum rating	1	3

Laredo, TX

Score: 23.8   **Rank:** 341   **2004 rank:** 331

Profile: Small border city
Location: South Texas along the Rio Grande and Mexican border, 200 miles inland from the Gulf of Mexico
Elevation: 438 feet
Time zone: Central Standard Time

PRO	CON
Cost of living	Unattractive and industrial areas
Strong job growth	Low educational attainment
Historic core	Hot climate

Once the classic Old West town, modern Laredo is now the largest and most active port of entry to the United States in the Rio Grande Valley. Numerous border-zone manufacturing plants have sprung up since the North American Free Trade Agreement (NAFTA) came about in the early 1990s. The four border-crossing bridges are busy with truck and container traffic to Nuevo Laredo in Mexico, and rail and air cargo carriers have extensive operations. The area is known for having a pro-business environment. Laredo has a dominant Hispanic influence with a large middle class and a much larger working class, but many have low incomes and there is considerable poverty or near-poverty conditions in and especially outside the city. The Spanish-colonial city center has been reinvigorated following a commercial boom, and there are some minor league sports teams and some events of cultural interest, but overall there is little to do. At 111 days per year above 90°F, the city is one of the hottest in the United States. The Cost of Living Index is not surprisingly low at 75.3, but the city's constant bustle, lack of intellectual stimulation, poverty, high crime rate, and heat will try most anyone's patience.

Laredo sits far enough west of the Gulf Coastal Plain to be in a zone of dry, rolling hills and plains, supporting scrub vegetation, small cacti, and oak trees. Summers are hot with most days over 90°F, but humidity is lower than areas on the Gulf Coast. Most rain occurs in summer as thundershowers. Winters are mild and dry with many days in the 70s and 80s; evening lows dip below freezing occasionally.

Population

DEMOGRAPHICS	AREA	U.S. AVG	ETHNIC COMPOSITION	AREA	U.S. AVG	RESIDENT PROFILE	AREA	U.S. AVG
Population	223,790		White	82.1%	79.0%	Single	32.6%	32.4%
Population density per sq. mile	66.7	358.5	Black	0.3%	10.5%	Married	53.2%	52.7%
Population growth	68.0%	21.1%	Asian	0.4%	2.7%	Divorced/separated	14.2%	14.9%
Median age	26.5	36.1	Hispanic	95.4%	10.6%	Married with children	41.8%	23.7%
Percent Democrat	56.9%	44.5%	Religious observance	73.6%	48.9%	Single with children	11.9%	9.1%
Percent Republican	42.7%	54.5%	Diversity measure	36.5	40.1	Percent over age 65	7.6%	12.9%

Economy & Jobs
Score: 89.3
Rank: 41

INCOME	AREA	U.S. AVG	EMPLOYMENT	AREA	U.S. AVG	EMPLOYING INDUSTRIES	AREA	U.S. AVG
Per capita income	$12,431	$23,235	Unemployment rate	6.2%	4.7%	Largest: Transportation & Warehousing		
Household income	$32,731	$46,414	Recent job growth	3.7%	1.3%			
Household income < $25K	39.1%	26.2%	Projected future job growth	29.9%	11.5%	Percent manufacturing	14.6%	15.4%
Household income > $75K	16.4%	25.4%	White collar	56.0%	57.8%	Percent public sector	20.0%	15.7%
Household income growth	16.5%	13.6%	Blue collar	25.8%	25.2%	Percent construction	11.2%	9.9%

Cost of Living
Score: 91.4
Rank: 33

INDEXES & TAXES	AREA	U.S. AVG	HOUSING	AREA	U.S. AVG	NECESSITIES	AREA	U.S. AVG
Cost of Living Index	75.3	100.0	Median home price	$105,900	$220,000	Food Index	82.9	100.0
Buying Power Index	97.4	100.0	Home price appreciation	25.3%	10.1%	Housing Index	45.4	100.0
Income tax rate	0.00%	4.70%	Median rent	$573	$709	Utilities Index	87.2	100.0
Sales tax rate	8.25%	6.58%	Homes owned	61.8%	62.3%	Transportation Index	89.7	100.0
Property tax rate	$16.65	$12.00	Home price ratio	3.2	4.2	Healthcare Index	98.9	100.0
						Miscellaneous Cost Index	97.6	100.0

Climate
Score: 89.3
Rank: 41

TEMPERATURE	AREA	U.S. AVG	PRECIPITATION	AREA	U.S. AVG	COMFORTS & HAZARDS	AREA	U.S. AVG
Average January low	39.8	26.2	Annual inches precipitation	28.0	37.7	July relative humidity	67%	66%
Average July high	95.9	87.4	Annual inches snowfall	0.5	7.0	Annual days mostly sunny	227	208
Annual days > 90°F	111	38	Annual days precipitation	81	109	Annual days with thunderstorms	36	39
Annual days < 32°F	22	89	Annual days rain > 0.5 inches	18	22	Tornado risk score	2	18
Annual days < 0°F	0	6	Annual days snow > 1.5 inches	0	6	Hurricane risk score	14	13

TEMPERATURE

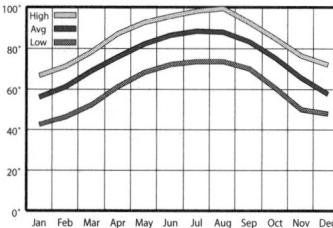

PRECIPITATION

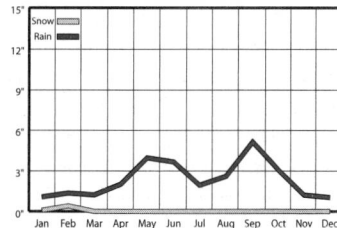

DAYS OF CLOUDS & PRECIPITATION

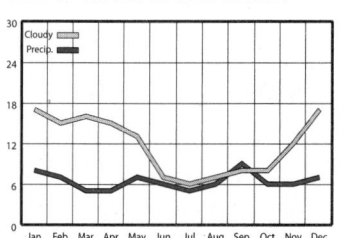

ACHIEVEMENT	AREA	U.S. AVG
High school degree	53.7%	82.7%
2-year college degree	5.3%	6.4%
4-year college degree	8.9%	15.7%
Graduate/professional degree	5.5%	8.9%

Education
Score: 1.9
Rank: 366

PUBLIC SCHOOLS	AREA	U.S. AVG
Expenditures per pupil	$6,692	$5,686
Student/teacher ratio	14.3	16.7
Attending public school	96.0%	90.1%
State SAT score	997*	1021
State ACT score	20.3	20.9

HIGHER EDUCATION	AREA	U.S. AVG
No. 2-year colleges	1	4
No. 4-year colleges/universities	1	6
No. highly ranked universities	0	1

HAZARDS & ILLNESSES	AREA	U.S. AVG
Air-quality score	47	37
Water-quality score	90	52
Pollen/allergy score	87	61
Cancer mortality per capita	121.4	201.9
Depression days per month	4.2	3.5
Stress score	54	50

Health & Healthcare
Score: 50.3
Rank: 187

HEALTHCARE	AREA	U.S. AVG
Physicians per capita	94.6	244.2
Hospital beds per capita	202.0	420.0
No. teaching hospitals	1	3
Cost per doctor visit	$71	$77
Cost per dental visit	$64	$70

Crime
Score: 26.2
Rank: 276

CRIME	AREA	U.S. AVG
Violent crime rate	502.5	465.5
Change in violent crime rate	-5.7%	-2.2%
Property crime rate	5,767.6	3,517.1
Change in property crime rate	-9.1%	-2.1%

COMMUTE	AREA	U.S. AVG
Average commute time	23.5	27.4
Percent commutes > 60 mins.	4.0%	5.9%
Commute by auto	72.1%	78.9%
Commute by mass transit	2.4%	1.9%
Work at home	2.9%	3.1%
Mass transit miles per capita	2.41	1.87

Transportation
Score: 19.0
Rank: 304

INTERCITY SERVICES	AREA	U.S. AVG
Major airports within 60 miles	0	1
Size of regional airport	None	Large
Daily airline activity	32	686
Amtrak service	No	No

AUTOMOTIVE	AREA	U.S. AVG
Insurance, annual premium	$1,315	$1,432
Gas, cost per gallon	$2.39	$2.49
Daily vehicle miles per capita	12.5	24.0

DINING & SHOPPING	AREA	U.S. AVG
Restaurant rating	1	2
Outlet mall score	0	42
No. Starbucks	2	13
No. warehouse clubs	1	2

Leisure
Score: 4.3
Rank: 357

ENTERTAINMENT	AREA	U.S. AVG
Professional sports rating	3	4
College sports rating	1	4
Zoo/aquarium rating	1	3
Amusement park rating	1	3
Botanical garden/ arboretum rating	1	4

OUTDOOR ACTIVITIES	AREA	U.S. AVG
Golf-course rating	1	4
Ski-area rating	1	3
Sq. miles inland water	2	4
Miles of coastline	0.0	10.7
National Park rating	1	3

MEDIA & LIBRARIES	AREA	U.S. AVG
Arts radio rating	1	3
No. public libraries	4	27
Library volumes per capita	0.97	2.78

Arts & Culture
Score: 0.0
Rank: 373

PERFORMING ARTS	AREA	U.S. AVG
Classical music rating	1	4
Ballet/dance rating	1	3
Professional theater rating	1	3
University arts programs rating	1	5

MUSEUMS	AREA	U.S. AVG
Overall museum rating	1	5
Art museum rating	1	5
Science museum rating	1	5
Children's museum rating	1	3

Las Cruces, NM

Score: 62.9   Rank: 151   2004 rank: 39

Profile: Small city/college town
Location: South-central New Mexico along Rio Grande Valley, 45 miles north of El Paso, Texas
Elevation: 3,881 feet
Time zone: Mountain Standard Time

PRO
Pleasant winters
Future job growth
Historic interest

CON
Isolation
Air quality
Growth and sprawl

Las Cruces is a small agricultural and transportation center and home to 17,000 New Mexico State University students. It is also the gateway to historic, geologic, and recreational sites, including White Sands National Monument to the northeast. The downtown is small, clean, and quiet, with an Old West–style historic district converted to a pedestrian mall. The campus lies south of downtown with commercial/retail areas just east. Large employers include the university; the White Sands Missile Range, which still employs about 3,000; a NASA test center; and various government and healthcare institutions. There are some manufacturers and high-tech firms but the employment base is small and unemployment levels have risen. Although the area is fairly close to El Paso and it has reasonably good air service for the size

of town, these don't relieve the feeling of isolation. The area is starting to pick up some of the sprawl and bustle found elsewhere in the Southwest; it may no longer be the small, quiet desert city some might have been seeking.

Las Cruces is located in the broad, flat Mesilla Valley, a grazing area with desert hills and mountains on both sides. The southerly desert climate allows an abundance of sunshine year-round; hot, dry summer days; and cool evenings. Limited precipitation falls in summer as thundershowers. Winters are mild, sunny, and dry, although below-freezing temperatures happen about once every 3 days. First freeze is mid-December; last is mid-February.

Population

DEMOGRAPHICS	AREA	U.S. AVG	ETHNIC COMPOSITION	AREA	U.S. AVG	RESIDENT PROFILE	AREA	U.S. AVG
Population	186,522		White	66.8%	79.0%	Single	34.9%	32.4%
Population density per sq. mile	49.0	358.5	Black	1.6%	10.5%	Married	50.4%	52.7%
Population growth	37.6%	21.1%	Asian	1.0%	2.7%	Divorced/separated	14.7%	14.9%
Median age	31.3	36.1	Hispanic	65.5%	10.6%	Married with children	25.9%	23.7%
Percent Democrat	51.3%	44.5%	Religious observance	77.4%	48.9%	Single with children	12.3%	9.1%
Percent Republican	47.7%	54.5%	Diversity measure	71.8	40.1	Percent over age 65	11.4%	12.9%

Economy & Jobs

Score: 83.7
Rank: 61

INCOME	AREA	U.S. AVG	EMPLOYMENT	AREA	U.S. AVG	EMPLOYING INDUSTRIES	AREA	U.S. AVG
Per capita income	$16,187	$23,235	Unemployment rate	6.9%	4.7%	Largest: Healthcare & Social Assistance		
Household income	$34,143	$46,414	Recent job growth	4.0%	1.3%			
Household income ‹ $25K	37.5%	26.2%	Projected future job growth	26.1%	11.5%	Percent manufacturing	11.7%	15.4%
Household income › $75K	16.8%	25.4%	White collar	56.5%	57.8%	Percent public sector	25.4%	15.7%
Household income growth	14.5%	13.6%	Blue collar	22.6%	25.2%	Percent construction	11.0%	9.9%

Cost of Living

Score: 57.2
Rank: 160

INDEXES & TAXES	AREA	U.S. AVG	HOUSING	AREA	U.S. AVG	NECESSITIES	AREA	U.S. AVG
Cost of Living Index	87.2	100.0	Median home price	$155,000	$220,000	Food Index	101.7	100.0
Buying Power Index	87.8	100.0	Home price appreciation	49.4%	10.1%	Housing Index	64.5	100.0
Income tax rate	7.10%	4.70%	Median rent	$521	$709	Utilities Index	92.1	100.0
Sales tax rate	5.81%	6.58%	Homes owned	62.1%	62.3%	Transportation Index	97.5	100.0
Property tax rate	$7.90	$12.00	Home price ratio	4.5	4.2	Healthcare Index	95.2	100.0
						Miscellaneous Cost Index	95.2	100.0

Climate

Score: 92.2
Rank: 30

TEMPERATURE	AREA	U.S. AVG	PRECIPITATION	AREA	U.S. AVG	COMFORTS & HAZARDS	AREA	U.S. AVG
Average January low	26.5	26.2	Annual inches precipitation	8.0	37.7	July relative humidity	49%	66%
Average July high	93.5	87.4	Annual inches snowfall	11.0	7.0	Annual days mostly sunny	287	208
Annual days › 90°F	70	38	Annual days precipitation	53	109	Annual days with thunderstorms	34	39
Annual days ‹ 32°F	15	89	Annual days rain › 0.5 inches	2	22	Tornado risk score	1	18
Annual days ‹ 0°F	6	6	Annual days snow › 1.5 inches	3	6	Hurricane risk score	2	13

TEMPERATURE

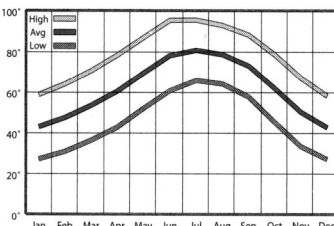

PRECIPITATION

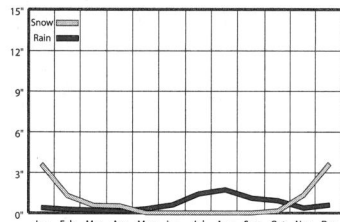

DAYS OF CLOUDS & PRECIPITATION

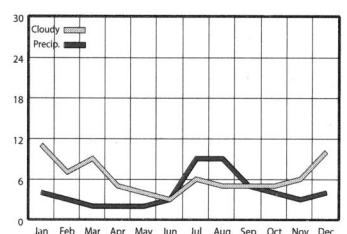

Education

Score: 26.7
Rank: 275

ACHIEVEMENT	AREA	U.S. AVG	PUBLIC SCHOOLS	AREA	U.S. AVG	HIGHER EDUCATION	AREA	U.S. AVG
High school degree	70.2%	82.7%	Expenditures per pupil	$4,701	$5,686	No. 2-year colleges	1	4
2-year college degree	5.4%	6.4%	Student/teacher ratio	16.4	16.7	No. 4-year colleges/universities	1	6
4-year college degree	13.2%	15.7%	Attending public school	97.3%	90.1%	No. highly ranked universities	0	1
Graduate/professional degree	9.4%	8.9%	State SAT score	1106	1021			
			State ACT score	20.1*	20.9			

Health & Healthcare

Score: 13.4
Rank: 323

Crime

Score: 60.2
Rank: 150

HAZARDS & ILLNESSES	AREA	U.S. AVG	HEALTHCARE	AREA	U.S. AVG	CRIME	AREA	U.S. AVG
Air-quality score	9	37	Physicians per capita	138.9	244.2	Violent crime rate	425.4	465.5
Water-quality score	40	52	Hospital beds per capita	250.4	420.0	Change in violent crime rate	3.5%	-2.2%
Pollen/allergy score	69	61	No. teaching hospitals	1	3	Property crime rate	3,206.6	3,517.1
Cancer mortality per capita	162.9	201.9	Cost per doctor visit	$65	$77	Change in property crime rate	-21.8%	-2.1%
Depression days per month	3.3	3.5	Cost per dental visit	$68	$70			
Stress score	46	50						

Transportation

Score: 25.9
Rank: 278

COMMUTE	AREA	U.S. AVG	INTERCITY SERVICES	AREA	U.S. AVG	AUTOMOTIVE	AREA	U.S. AVG
Average commute time	23.5	27.4	Major airports within 60 miles	1	1	Insurance, annual premium	$1,112	$1,432
Percent commutes › 60 mins.	4.8%	5.9%	Size of regional airport	Medium	Large	Gas, cost per gallon	$2.49	$2.49
Commute by auto	77.2%	78.9%	Daily airline activity	115	686	Daily vehicle miles per capita	34.8	24.0
Commute by mass transit	0.5%	1.9%	Amtrak service	No	No			
Work at home	3.5%	3.1%						
Mass transit miles per capita	0.45	1.87						

DINING & SHOPPING	AREA	U.S. AVG	ENTERTAINMENT	AREA	U.S. AVG	OUTDOOR ACTIVITIES	AREA	U.S. AVG
Restaurant rating	1	2	Professional sports rating	2	4	Golf-course rating	2	4
Outlet mall score	0	42	College sports rating	3	4	Ski-area rating	3	3
No. Starbucks	1	13	Zoo/aquarium rating	1	3	Sq. miles inland water	1	4
No. warehouse clubs	1	2	Amusement park rating	1	3	Miles of coastline	0.0	10.7
			Botanical garden/ arboretum rating	1	4	National Park rating	4	3

Leisure
Score: 21.1
Rank: 294

MEDIA & LIBRARIES	AREA	U.S. AVG	PERFORMING ARTS	AREA	U.S. AVG	MUSEUMS	AREA	U.S. AVG
Arts radio rating	5	3	Classical music rating	3	4	Overall museum rating	4	5
No. public libraries	3	27	Ballet/dance rating	1	3	Art museum rating	6	5
Library volumes per capita	0.94	2.78	Professional theater rating	1	3	Science museum rating	6	5
			University arts programs rating	4	5	Children's museum rating	1	3

Arts & Culture
Score: 44.7
Rank: 207

Las Vegas–Paradise, NV

Score: 62.5   **Rank:** 154   **2004 rank:** 129

Profile: Large resort city
Location: Southern Nevada near Colorado River
Elevation: 2,180 feet
Time zone: Pacific Standard Time

PRO
Desert climate
Job growth
Air service

CON
Summer heat
Rising home prices
Tourist impact

The unique and booming desert metropolis of Las Vegas continues to be a curiosity among today's U.S. cities. Las Vegas is known for its famous Strip, an adult Disneyland attracting visitors worldwide to its gaudy hotel-casino reproductions of famous world places, such as King Tut's tomb or downtown New York or Paris. In fact, most sites on the Strip are second generation, with older hotels being torn down and replaced with new fantasies apparently purposed as much to outdo each other as to entertain visitors. The reality: There is some one-upmanship going on, but it's also an attempt on the industry's part to keep Vegas in the forefront of the gambling/entertainment tourist's mind with the sprouting of tribal casinos, riverboats, and other legalized gaming forms all over the country. The Strip is actually the "Paradise" in the metro area name, stretching south along Las Vegas Boulevard from a not-too-interesting real downtown area and has resisted annexation from the city proper. That's probably okay; this area flourishes on its own and doesn't get much attention in real life from local residents, except those who work there.

Stripping away tourism and entertainment still reveals a hot, dry, desert town exploding with growth. Las Vegas has the highest growth rate among larger metropolitan areas, and naturally the sprawl problems that accompany it. The economy is highly tied to the tourist trade and more recently the construction trade, as housing construction, some speculative, is booming. Residential high-rises are sprouting all over, though some projects have recently been cancelled. Home prices have skyrocketed in recent years. The area has become quite popular with wealthy individuals and especially business owners looking for a favorable income and inheritance tax climate, and is also gaining ground as an escape destination from pricier West Coast locations and is picking up a number of overseas immigrants also bypassing the more expensive larger coast cities. The economy has traditionally been a "barbell" type, with a group of wealthy individuals and a much larger group of workers supporting them and the casino and hospitality trade, with not much in between. This is changing slowly as some companies are starting to move facilities into the area—again from expensive West Coast locations. The middle class is growing, but is still less evident than in most American cities.

As mentioned, the Strip, while near the center of town, is fairly self-contained with little spreading away from its central core. Sprouting up outside the city in most directions are suburbs and self-contained communities, particularly to the northwest, west, and southeast, for many miles. A few high-end community developments lie to the northwest, while Spring Valley to the west is middle class and one of the more family-oriented communities. The strongest growth is occurring south and east in Henderson, now a booming commercial and retail center and location of most of the heavier industry in the area. Finally, not inconsistent with other parts of the area, the posh resort area Lake Las Vegas just northeast of Henderson is a man-made re-creation of a Mediterranean villa.

The University of Nevada at Las Vegas adds a college presence and sports entertainment, and is a significant employer, as are local health-care providers. The tourist industry brings excellent air service to all parts of the country at reasonable prices. The surrounding mountainous terrain offers hiking and rock-climbing opportunities and winter skiing. Bottom line: Upsides include economic growth, albeit coming in a cyclically riskier form than most places; a pleasant winter climate; and attractive housing especially for more upscale buyers. Downsides include heat, desert monotony, high violent-crime rates, high home prices, dependence on tourism, and the constant influx of tourists.

Las Vegas is situated near the center of a broad desert valley surrounded by mountains rising 2,000 to 10,000 feet. Maximum summer temperatures are in the 100°F range. Mountain proximity contributes to relatively cool (mid-70s) summer nights. Winters on the whole are mild and pleasant; daytime temperatures average near 60°F with mostly clear skies. Spring and fall seasons are generally the most pleasant, although sharp temperature changes can occur during these months. The city is the driest and sunniest in the United States, with cloudy days averaging about 2 per month and rainy days less than 1 per month year-round. Snow rarely falls.

Population

DEMOGRAPHICS	AREA	U.S. AVG
Population	1,667,216	
Population density per sq. mile	210.8	358.5
Population growth	124.9%	21.1%
Median age	34.7	36.1
Percent Democrat	51.7%	44.5%
Percent Republican	46.8%	54.5%

ETHNIC COMPOSITION	AREA	U.S. AVG
White	70.1%	79.0%
Black	8.6%	10.5%
Asian	5.8%	2.7%
Hispanic	25.4%	10.6%
Religious observance	36.3%	48.9%
Diversity measure	68.1	40.1

RESIDENT PROFILE	AREA	U.S. AVG
Single	30.1%	32.4%
Married	50.7%	52.7%
Divorced/separated	19.2%	14.9%
Married with children	21.9%	23.7%
Single with children	9.4%	9.1%
Percent over age 65	11.1%	12.9%

Economy & Jobs
Score: 98.9
Rank: 5

INCOME	AREA	U.S. AVG
Per capita income	$23,864	$23,235
Household income	$49,312	$46,414
Household income < $25K	21.5%	26.2%
Household income > $75K	28.0%	25.4%
Household income growth	10.5%	13.6%

EMPLOYMENT	AREA	U.S. AVG
Unemployment rate	4.3%	4.7%
Recent job growth	4.5%	1.3%
Projected future job growth	41.0%	11.5%
White collar	53.9%	57.8%
Blue collar	20.0%	25.2%

EMPLOYING INDUSTRIES	AREA	U.S. AVG
Largest: Accommodations & Food Services		
Percent manufacturing	9.1%	15.4%
Percent public sector	11.1%	15.7%
Percent construction	10.9%	9.9%

Cost of Living
Score: 24.9
Rank: 280

INDEXES & TAXES	AREA	U.S. AVG
Cost of Living Index	117.1	100.0
Buying Power Index	94.4	100.0
Income tax rate	0.00%	4.70%
Sales tax rate	7.50%	6.58%
Property tax rate	$8.93	$12.00

HOUSING	AREA	U.S. AVG
Median home price	$319,100	$220,000
Home price appreciation	116.3%	10.1%
Median rent	$891	$709
Homes owned	57.0%	62.3%
Home price ratio	6.5	4.2

NECESSITIES	AREA	U.S. AVG
Food Index	110.7	100.0
Housing Index	120.7	100.0
Utilities Index	82.7	100.0
Transportation Index	110.0	100.0
Healthcare Index	112.5	100.0
Miscellaneous Cost Index	98.7	100.0

Climate
Score: 79.9
Rank: 76

TEMPERATURE	AREA	U.S. AVG
Average January low	32.6	26.2
Average July high	103.9	87.4
Annual days > 90°F	131	38
Annual days < 32°F	41	89
Annual days < 0°F	0	6

PRECIPITATION	AREA	U.S. AVG
Annual inches precipitation	4.0	37.7
Annual inches snowfall	1.5	7.0
Annual days precipitation	24	109
Annual days rain > 0.5 inches	4	22
Annual days snow > 1.5 inches	1	6

COMFORTS & HAZARDS	AREA	U.S. AVG
July relative humidity	29%	66%
Annual days mostly sunny	300	208
Annual days with thunderstorms	15	39
Tornado risk score	2	18
Hurricane risk score	0	13

TEMPERATURE

PRECIPITATION

DAYS OF CLOUDS & PRECIPITATION

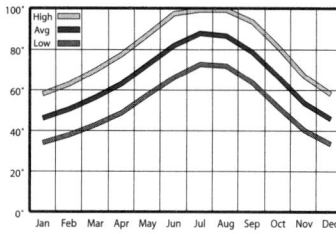
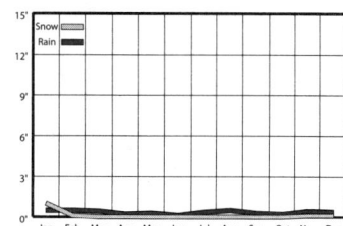
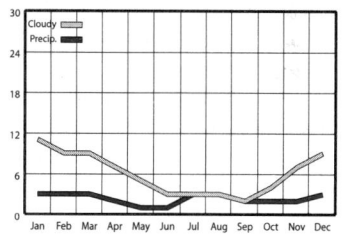

Education
Score: 36.1
Rank: 240

ACHIEVEMENT	AREA	U.S. AVG
High school degree	80.8%	82.7%
2-year college degree	6.0%	6.4%
4-year college degree	12.4%	15.7%
Graduate/professional degree	6.2%	8.9%

PUBLIC SCHOOLS	AREA	U.S. AVG
Expenditures per pupil	$5,051	$5,686
Student/teacher ratio	18.8	16.7
Attending public school	94.1%	90.1%
State SAT score	1006*	1021
State ACT score	21.5	20.9

HIGHER EDUCATION	AREA	U.S. AVG
No. 2-year colleges	8	4
No. 4-year colleges/universities	7	6
No. highly ranked universities	0	1

Health & Healthcare
Score: 6.4
Rank: 349

HAZARDS & ILLNESSES	AREA	U.S. AVG
Air-quality score	12	37
Water-quality score	70	52
Pollen/allergy score	71	61
Cancer mortality per capita	189.1	201.9
Depression days per month	3.7	3.5
Stress score	93	50

HEALTHCARE	AREA	U.S. AVG
Physicians per capita	166.6	244.2
Hospital beds per capita	188.9	420.0
No. teaching hospitals	2	3
Cost per doctor visit	$89	$77
Cost per dental visit	$73	$70

Crime
Score: 14.4
Rank: 319

CRIME	AREA	U.S. AVG
Violent crime rate	674.9	465.5
Change in violent crime rate	-2.7%	-2.2%
Property crime rate	4,613.1	3,517.1
Change in property crime rate	1.4%	-2.1%

Transportation
Score: 31.8
Rank: 256

COMMUTE	AREA	U.S. AVG
Average commute time	26.4	27.4
Percent commutes > 60 mins.	4.8%	5.9%
Commute by auto	75.8%	78.9%
Commute by mass transit	3.9%	1.9%
Work at home	2.5%	3.1%
Mass transit miles per capita	3.90	1.87

INTERCITY SERVICES	AREA	U.S. AVG
Major airports within 60 miles	1	1
Size of regional airport	Large	Large
Daily airline activity	545	686
Amtrak service	No	No

AUTOMOTIVE	AREA	U.S. AVG
Insurance, annual premium	$2,354	$1,432
Gas, cost per gallon	$2.49	$2.49
Daily vehicle miles per capita	31.4	24.0

DINING & SHOPPING	AREA	U.S. AVG	ENTERTAINMENT	AREA	U.S. AVG	OUTDOOR ACTIVITIES	AREA	U.S. AVG
Restaurant rating	1	2	Professional sports rating	3	4	Golf-course rating	3	4
Outlet mall score	0	42	College sports rating	5	4	Ski-area rating	6	3
No. Starbucks	66	13	Zoo/aquarium rating	2	3	Sq. miles inland water	10	4
No. warehouse clubs	6	2	Amusement park rating	1	3	Miles of coastline	0.0	10.7
			Botanical garden/ arboretum rating	6	4	National Park rating	10	3

Leisure
Score: 80.2
Rank: 74

MEDIA & LIBRARIES	AREA	U.S. AVG	PERFORMING ARTS	AREA	U.S. AVG	MUSEUMS	AREA	U.S. AVG
Arts radio rating	10	3	Classical music rating	3	4	Overall museum rating	7	5
No. public libraries	29	27	Ballet/dance rating	6	3	Art museum rating	6	5
Library volumes per capita	2.05	2.78	Professional theater rating	1	3	Science museum rating	8	5
			University arts programs rating	4	5	Children's museum rating	7	3

Arts & Culture
Score: 69.5
Rank: 114

Lawrence, KS

Score: 68.9   Rank: 100   2004 rank: 194

Profile: College town
Location: Northeast Kansas, 40 miles west of Kansas City
Elevation: 939 feet
Time zone: Central Standard Time

PRO	CON
College-town amenities	Harsh winters
Attractive downtown	Home prices
Educated population	Growth pressure

Home to the University of Kansas, Lawrence is considered one of the more progressive and attractive cities in the state. It is a classic college town with a typical layout and set of college-town amenities, including a pleasant self-contained campus high up on a hill overlooking downtown, plenty of entertainment, and a handful of interesting museums. The Kansas Jayhawks basketball team, perennially one of the best, provides a great deal of winter and early spring excitement. To the southwest, man-made Clinton Lake provides recreational opportunities—in fact, recreational assets are probably better than the statistics indicate. The university has some related research and medical facilities, and employment is fairly strong. The area has become attractive to professionals willing to commute the 30 miles or so east to the suburbs of Kansas City, Kansas, home to numerous corporate enterprises. These commutes take 30 minutes to an hour depending on location, and those who do it experience the best of both worlds—high incomes while living in a classic small-town environment. That said, home prices exceed state averages but are attractive on a national scale and are affordable for most. The area is battling growth pressure, especially on the east side of town, nearest to Kansas City.

The land rises into gently rolling prairie, mostly given to agriculture. Summer conditions vary, but may include prolonged periods with temperatures over 100°F. Winters are cold with frequent wind and snow. Spring can be windy and stormy mixed with periods of pleasant weather. Strong storms and severe weather generally happen during spring and summer. First freeze is mid-October; last is late April.

DEMOGRAPHICS	AREA	U.S. AVG	ETHNIC COMPOSITION	AREA	U.S. AVG	RESIDENT PROFILE	AREA	U.S. AVG
Population	104,295		White	85.4%	79.0%	Single	45.3%	32.4%
Population density per sq. mile	228.3	358.5	Black	3.9%	10.5%	Married	43.2%	52.7%
Population growth	27.5%	21.1%	Asian	3.8%	2.7%	Divorced/separated	11.5%	14.9%
Median age	29.7	36.1	Hispanic	3.7%	10.6%	Married with children	20.3%	23.7%
Percent Democrat	57.1%	44.5%	Religious observance	29.1%	48.9%	Single with children	7.2%	9.1%
Percent Republican	41.0%	54.5%	Diversity measure	31.8	40.1	Percent over age 65	8.2%	12.9%

Population

INCOME	AREA	U.S. AVG	EMPLOYMENT	AREA	U.S. AVG	EMPLOYING INDUSTRIES	AREA	U.S. AVG
Per capita income	$23,463	$23,235	Unemployment rate	4.3%	4.7%	Largest: Healthcare & Social Assistance		
Household income	$44,040	$46,414	Recent job growth	1.5%	1.3%			
Household income ‹ $25K	28.3%	26.2%	Projected future job growth	11.4%	11.5%	Percent manufacturing	10.0%	15.4%
Household income › $75K	25.0%	25.4%	White collar	65.3%	57.8%	Percent public sector	23.2%	15.7%
Household income growth	17.3%	13.6%	Blue collar	17.7%	25.2%	Percent construction	7.7%	9.9%

Economy & Jobs
Score: 44.7
Rank: 208

INDEXES & TAXES	AREA	U.S. AVG	HOUSING	AREA	U.S. AVG	NECESSITIES	AREA	U.S. AVG
Cost of Living Index	87.1	100.0	Median home price	$151,900	$220,000	Food Index	94.5	100.0
Buying Power Index	113.3	100.0	Home price appreciation	32.5%	10.1%	Housing Index	63.8	100.0
Income tax rate	6.38%	4.70%	Median rent	$659	$709	Utilities Index	111.6	100.0
Sales tax rate	7.30%	6.58%	Homes owned	50.7%	62.3%	Transportation Index	97.6	100.0
Property tax rate	$11.05	$12.00	Home price ratio	3.4	4.2	Healthcare Index	91.0	100.0
						Miscellaneous Cost Index	98.3	100.0

Cost of Living
Score: 38.0
Rank: 231

Climate
Score: 31.8
Rank: 254

TEMPERATURE	AREA	U.S. AVG
Average January low	17.0	26.2
Average July high	89.0	87.4
Annual days > 90°F	45	38
Annual days < 32°F	123	89
Annual days < 0°F	5	6

PRECIPITATION	AREA	U.S. AVG
Annual inches precipitation	34.0	37.7
Annual inches snowfall	21.0	7.0
Annual days precipitation	96	109
Annual days rain > 0.5 inches	23	22
Annual days snow > 1.5 inches	5	6

COMFORTS & HAZARDS	AREA	U.S. AVG
July relative humidity	68%	66%
Annual days mostly sunny	205	208
Annual days with thunderstorms	58	39
Tornado risk score	30	18
Hurricane risk score	2	13

TEMPERATURE

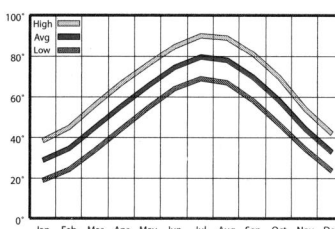

PRECIPITATION

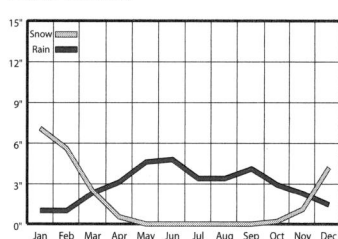

DAYS OF CLOUDS & PRECIPITATION

Education
Score: 95.5
Rank: 18

ACHIEVEMENT	AREA	U.S. AVG
High school degree	92.6%	82.7%
2-year college degree	4.8%	6.4%
4-year college degree	25.0%	15.7%
Graduate/professional degree	18.6%	8.9%

PUBLIC SCHOOLS	AREA	U.S. AVG
Expenditures per pupil	$5,643	$5,686
Student/teacher ratio	14.6	16.7
Attending public school	94.3%	90.1%
State SAT score	1172	1021
State ACT score	21.8*	20.9

HIGHER EDUCATION	AREA	U.S. AVG
No. 2-year colleges	0	4
No. 4-year colleges/universities	3	6
No. highly ranked universities	0	1

Health & Healthcare
Score: 30.5
Rank: 259

HAZARDS & ILLNESSES	AREA	U.S. AVG
Air-quality score	40	37
Water-quality score	45	52
Pollen/allergy score	74	61
Cancer mortality per capita	196.3	201.9
Depression days per month	2.9	3.5
Stress score	5	50

HEALTHCARE	AREA	U.S. AVG
Physicians per capita	180.6	244.2
Hospital beds per capita	174.5	420.0
No. teaching hospitals	0	3
Cost per doctor visit	$74	$77
Cost per dental visit	$64	$70

Crime
Score: 43.3
Rank: 212

CRIME	AREA	U.S. AVG
Violent crime rate	310.3	465.5
Change in violent crime rate	-24.1%	-2.2%
Property crime rate	4,040.5	3,517.1
Change in property crime rate	-15.1%	-2.1%

Transportation
Score: 57.8
Rank: 159

COMMUTE	AREA	U.S. AVG
Average commute time	21.6	27.4
Percent commutes > 60 mins.	3.1%	5.9%
Commute by auto	77.5%	78.9%
Commute by mass transit	0.9%	1.9%
Work at home	3.7%	3.1%
Mass transit miles per capita	0.93	1.87

INTERCITY SERVICES	AREA	U.S. AVG
Major airports within 60 miles	1	1
Size of regional airport	Medium	Large
Daily airline activity	328	686
Amtrak service	Yes	No

AUTOMOTIVE	AREA	U.S. AVG
Insurance, annual premium	$1,101	$1,432
Gas, cost per gallon	$2.42	$2.49
Daily vehicle miles per capita	17.4	24.0

Leisure
Score: 16.0
Rank: 313

DINING & SHOPPING	AREA	U.S. AVG
Restaurant rating	1	2
Outlet mall score	46	42
No. Starbucks	1	13
No. warehouse clubs	0	2

ENTERTAINMENT	AREA	U.S. AVG
Professional sports rating	2	4
College sports rating	4	4
Zoo/aquarium rating	1	3
Amusement park rating	1	3
Botanical garden/ arboretum rating	1	4

OUTDOOR ACTIVITIES	AREA	U.S. AVG
Golf-course rating	1	4
Ski-area rating	1	3
Sq. miles inland water	3	4
Miles of coastline	0.0	10.7
National Park rating	1	3

Arts & Culture
Score: 50.8
Rank: 184

MEDIA & LIBRARIES	AREA	U.S. AVG
Arts radio rating	1	3
No. public libraries	3	27
Library volumes per capita	3.25	2.78

PERFORMING ARTS	AREA	U.S. AVG
Classical music rating	3	4
Ballet/dance rating	3	3
Professional theater rating	1	3
University arts programs rating	7	5

MUSEUMS	AREA	U.S. AVG
Overall museum rating	5	5
Art museum rating	5	5
Science museum rating	6	5
Children's museum rating	1	3

Lawton, OK

Score: 57.7   **Rank:** 192   **2004 rank:** 159

Profile: Military town
Location: Southwest Oklahoma, 40 miles north of Texas border
Elevation: 994 feet
Time zone: Central Standard Time

PRO	CON
Cost of living	Entertainment
Small-town atmosphere	Isolation
Stable economy	Summer heat

Lawton, once a center of the Oklahoma land rush and now a military town, is neat and clean but fairly nondescript. Fort Sill, the area's main economic base, lies just outside of town. Outside of Fort Sill, government, healthcare, education, and a Goodyear plant, there is little private employment. Lawton sits at the edge of the Wichita Mountains, a mostly worn-down series of low hills and bluffs and home to the 60,000-acre Wichita Mountains Wildlife Refuge. There are some minor arts amenities and family-oriented activities, including a 16,000-square-foot, kid-designed, volunteer-built play structure. Military ties result in the low population, economic growth, and cost of living, including a COL Index of 80.1 and median home prices of $109,200. Oklahoma City is 90 miles northeast and the Dallas–Fort Worth metroplex is 190 miles southeast.

Lawton sits on level, dry, grassland at the edge of the southern Great Plains. Summers are hot and fairly humid, with average July temperatures of 99°F, placing the city among the top 10 hottest places in the United States. The area gets plenty of sunshine. Winters are generally mild. Spring and summer precipitation is mostly thundershowers and winter receives a mix with mostly rain.

Population

DEMOGRAPHICS	AREA	U.S. AVG	ETHNIC COMPOSITION	AREA	U.S. AVG	RESIDENT PROFILE	AREA	U.S. AVG
Population	114,348		White	62.7%	79.0%	Single	30.8%	32.4%
Population density per sq. mile	106.9	358.5	Black	20.6%	10.5%	Married	50.9%	52.7%
Population growth	2.6%	21.1%	Asian	2.7%	2.7%	Divorced/separated	18.3%	14.9%
Median age	31.0	36.1	Hispanic	6.9%	10.6%	Married with children	27.1%	23.7%
Percent Democrat	36.2%	44.5%	Religious observance	56.7%	48.9%	Single with children	11.7%	9.1%
Percent Republican	63.8%	54.5%	Diversity measure	61.4	40.1	Percent over age 65	10.3%	12.9%

Economy
& Jobs
Score: 52.4
Rank: 179

INCOME	AREA	U.S. AVG	EMPLOYMENT	AREA	U.S. AVG	EMPLOYING INDUSTRIES	AREA	U.S. AVG
Per capita income	$18,283	$23,235	Unemployment rate	4.4%	4.7%	Largest: Healthcare & Social Assistance		
Household income	$39,489	$46,414	Recent job growth	3.0%	1.3%			
Household income < $25K	30.9%	26.2%	Projected future job growth	8.3%	11.5%	Percent manufacturing	14.0%	15.4%
Household income > $75K	17.8%	25.4%	White collar	54.2%	57.8%	Percent public sector	26.7%	15.7%
Household income growth	16.6%	13.6%	Blue collar	24.3%	25.2%	Percent construction	10.3%	9.9%

Cost of Living
Score: 56.4
Rank: 163

INDEXES & TAXES	AREA	U.S. AVG	HOUSING	AREA	U.S. AVG	NECESSITIES	AREA	U.S. AVG
Cost of Living Index	80.1	100.0	Median home price	$109,200	$220,000	Food Index	96.8	100.0
Buying Power Index	110.5	100.0	Home price appreciation	30.6%	10.1%	Housing Index	45.2	100.0
Income tax rate	7.00%	4.70%	Median rent	$516	$709	Utilities Index	90.7	100.0
Sales tax rate	8.25%	6.58%	Homes owned	53.1%	62.3%	Transportation Index	100.8	100.0
Property tax rate	$7.41	$12.00	Home price ratio	2.8	4.2	Healthcare Index	93.4	100.0
						Miscellaneous Cost Index	101.3	100.0

Climate
Score: 77.3
Rank: 85

TEMPERATURE	AREA	U.S. AVG	PRECIPITATION	AREA	U.S. AVG	COMFORTS & HAZARDS	AREA	U.S. AVG
Average January low	29.4	26.2	Annual inches precipitation	27.2	37.7	July relative humidity	66%	66%
Average July high	99.1	87.4	Annual inches snowfall	6.0	7.0	Annual days mostly sunny	241	208
Annual days > 90°F	55	38	Annual days precipitation	71	109	Annual days with thunderstorms	49	39
Annual days < 32°F	70	89	Annual days rain > 0.5 inches	21	22	Tornado risk score	32	18
Annual days < 0°F	0	6	Annual days snow > 1.5 inches	3	6	Hurricane risk score	3	13

TEMPERATURE

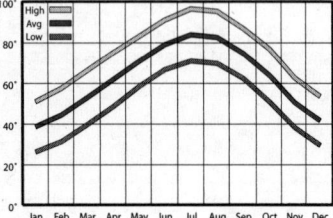

PRECIPITATION

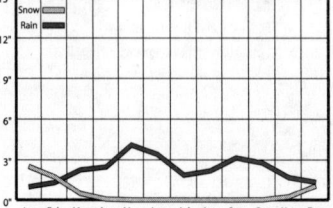

DAYS OF CLOUDS & PRECIPITATION

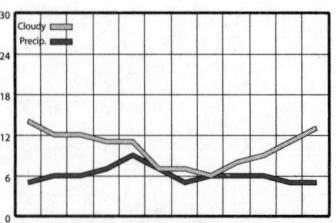

ACHIEVEMENT	AREA	U.S. AVG	PUBLIC SCHOOLS	AREA	U.S. AVG	HIGHER EDUCATION	AREA	U.S. AVG
High school degree	85.3%	82.7%	Expenditures per pupil	$4,869	$5,686	No. 2-year colleges	1	4
2-year college degree	5.6%	6.4%	Student/teacher ratio	16.1	16.7	No. 4-year colleges/universities	1	6
4-year college degree	13.1%	15.7%	Attending public school	98.7%	90.1%	No. highly ranked universities	0	1
Graduate/professional degree	6.1%	8.9%	State SAT score	1150	1021			
			State ACT score	20.5*	20.9			

Education
Score: 44.9
Rank: 207

HAZARDS & ILLNESSES	AREA	U.S. AVG	HEALTHCARE	AREA	U.S. AVG	CRIME	AREA	U.S. AVG
Air-quality score	44	37	Physicians per capita	194.0	244.2	Violent crime rate	647.9	465.5
Water-quality score	44	52	Hospital beds per capita	479.2	420.0	Change in violent crime rate	-5.6%	-2.2%
Pollen/allergy score	87	61	No. teaching hospitals	0	3	Property crime rate	4,471.7	3,517.1
Cancer mortality per capita	228.5	201.9	Cost per doctor visit	$85	$77	Change in property crime rate	-8.4%	-2.1%
Depression days per month	4.2	3.5	Cost per dental visit	$59	$70			
Stress score	46	50						

Health & Healthcare
Score: 43.9
Rank: 210

Crime
Score: 12.8
Rank: 325

COMMUTE	AREA	U.S. AVG	INTERCITY SERVICES	AREA	U.S. AVG	AUTOMOTIVE	AREA	U.S. AVG
Average commute time	18.6	27.4	Major airports within 60 miles	1	1	Insurance, annual premium	$1,134	$1,432
Percent commutes > 60 mins.	3.4%	5.9%	Size of regional airport	Medium	Large	Gas, cost per gallon	$2.35	$2.49
Commute by auto	73.6%	78.9%	Daily airline activity	102	686	Daily vehicle miles per capita	22.9	24.0
Commute by mass transit	0.9%	1.9%	Amtrak service	No	No			
Work at home	2.3%	3.1%						
Mass transit miles per capita	0.94	1.87						

Transportation
Score: 72.2
Rank: 105

DINING & SHOPPING	AREA	U.S. AVG	ENTERTAINMENT	AREA	U.S. AVG	OUTDOOR ACTIVITIES	AREA	U.S. AVG
Restaurant rating	1	2	Professional sports rating	2	4	Golf-course rating	1	4
Outlet mall score	0	42	College sports rating	6	4	Ski-area rating	1	3
No. Starbucks	0	13	Zoo/aquarium rating	1	3	Sq. miles inland water	2	4
No. warehouse clubs	0	2	Amusement park rating	2	3	Miles of coastline	0.0	10.7
			Botanical garden/arboretum rating	1	4	National Park rating	4	3

Leisure
Score: 25.7
Rank: 277

MEDIA & LIBRARIES	AREA	U.S. AVG	PERFORMING ARTS	AREA	U.S. AVG	MUSEUMS	AREA	U.S. AVG
Arts radio rating	5	3	Classical music rating	3	4	Overall museum rating	4	5
No. public libraries	3	27	Ballet/dance rating	3	3	Art museum rating	1	5
Library volumes per capita	1.46	2.78	Professional theater rating	1	3	Science museum rating	1	5
			University arts programs rating	3	5	Children's museum rating	1	3

Arts & Culture
Score: 23.8
Rank: 284

Lebanon, PA

Score: 58.2   Rank: 188   2004 rank: not ranked

Profile: Small city
Location: East-central Pennsylvania, 40 miles east of Harrisburg
Elevation: 460 feet
Time zone: Eastern Standard Time

PRO
Small-town feel
Cost of living
Central location

CON
Economy
Low educational attainment
Low ethnic diversity

Lebanon is an old transportation and minor industrial center located on the route of the original canal through the region. The area once had a steel mill. Bypassed by modern transport routes Interstate 78 and the Pennsylvania Turnpike, this quiet town with a typical core is centrally located between Harrisburg, Hershey, Lancaster, and Reading. Annville, a minor college town 5 miles west, is attractive but areas of Lebanon itself have a somewhat old, gritty, and working-class feel. There are a number of historic structures in the town, some of which are being nicely repurposed into small businesses and residential refurbishments. Economically, the area is attempting to make the transition into more of a new-economy, small-business center with a lot of state and local help.

It's unclear how it will work out. The city has also invested a lot in parks and recreation centers, and crime rates are low.

Lebanon sits in a flat to slightly rolling area consisting mainly of farmland. The main Allegheny Ridge lies in sight to the northwest, and protects the area somewhat from harsh weather arriving from that direction. The climate is pleasant for the region, with warm, humid summers and variable winters with relatively less snow and bitter cold than other areas in the northeast. Precipitation is frequent and can become heavy when storms move up the Atlantic Coast or when hurricane remnants stall over the area.

Population

DEMOGRAPHICS	AREA	U.S. AVG	ETHNIC COMPOSITION	AREA	U.S. AVG	RESIDENT PROFILE	AREA	U.S. AVG
Population	124,033		White	94.1%	79.0%	Single	30.4%	32.4%
Population density per sq. mile	342.7	358.5	Black	1.3%	10.5%	Married	57.0%	52.7%
Population growth	9.0%	21.1%	Asian	0.9%	2.7%	Divorced/separated	12.6%	14.9%
Median age	40.0	36.1	Hispanic	5.3%	10.6%	Married with children	23.0%	23.7%
Percent Democrat	32.5%	44.5%	Religious observance	48.7%	48.9%	Single with children	7.2%	9.1%
Percent Republican	66.6%	54.5%	Diversity measure	20.3	40.1	Percent over age 65	16.7%	12.9%

Economy & Jobs
Score: 34.0
Rank: 247

INCOME	AREA	U.S. AVG	EMPLOYMENT	AREA	U.S. AVG	EMPLOYING INDUSTRIES	AREA	U.S. AVG
Per capita income	$22,574	$23,235	Unemployment rate	3.8%	4.7%	Largest: Manufacturing		
Household income	$45,866	$46,414	Recent job growth	0.7%	1.3%			
Household income < $25K	23.3%	26.2%	Projected future job growth	3.2%	11.5%	Percent manufacturing	23.2%	15.4%
Household income > $75K	23.1%	25.4%	White collar	47.8%	57.8%	Percent public sector	11.0%	15.7%
Household income growth	12.3%	13.6%	Blue collar	33.7%	25.2%	Percent construction	10.5%	9.9%

Cost of Living
Score: 82.4
Rank: 67

INDEXES & TAXES	AREA	U.S. AVG	HOUSING	AREA	U.S. AVG	NECESSITIES	AREA	U.S. AVG
Cost of Living Index	82.8	100.0	Median home price	$125,400	$220,000	Food Index	91.4	100.0
Buying Power Index	124.2	100.0	Home price appreciation	28.1%	10.1%	Housing Index	65.6	100.0
Income tax rate	2.80%	4.70%	Median rent	$608	$709	Utilities Index	101.5	100.0
Sales tax rate	6.00%	6.58%	Homes owned	69.3%	62.3%	Transportation Index	107.5	100.0
Property tax rate	$13.91	$12.00	Home price ratio	2.7	4.2	Healthcare Index	93.3	100.0
						Miscellaneous Cost Index	100.1	100.0

Climate
Score: 57.0
Rank: 160

TEMPERATURE	AREA	U.S. AVG	PRECIPITATION	AREA	U.S. AVG	COMFORTS & HAZARDS	AREA	U.S. AVG
Average January low	22.5	26.2	Annual inches precipitation	36.0	37.7	July relative humidity	53%	66%
Average July high	86.8	87.4	Annual inches snowfall	35.0	7.0	Annual days mostly sunny	193	208
Annual days > 90°F	24	38	Annual days precipitation	125	109	Annual days with thunderstorms	33	39
Annual days < 32°F	107	89	Annual days rain > 0.5 inches	25	22	Tornado risk score	13	18
Annual days < 0°F	1	6	Annual days snow > 1.5 inches	8	6	Hurricane risk score	10	13

TEMPERATURE

PRECIPITATION

DAYS OF CLOUDS & PRECIPITATION

Education
Score: 12.0
Rank: 328

ACHIEVEMENT	AREA	U.S. AVG	PUBLIC SCHOOLS	AREA	U.S. AVG	HIGHER EDUCATION	AREA	U.S. AVG
High school degree	78.4%	82.7%	Expenditures per pupil	$6,175	$5,686	No. 2-year colleges	1	4
2-year college degree	4.5%	6.4%	Student/teacher ratio	18.0	16.7	No. 4-year colleges/universities	2	6
4-year college degree	9.4%	15.7%	Attending public school	90.8%	90.1%	No. highly ranked universities	1	1
Graduate/professional degree	5.9%	8.9%	State SAT score	993*	1021			
			State ACT score	21.8	20.9			

Health & Healthcare
Score: 60.2
Rank: 150

HAZARDS & ILLNESSES	AREA	U.S. AVG	HEALTHCARE	AREA	U.S. AVG	CRIME	AREA	U.S. AVG
Air-quality score	52	37	Physicians per capita	210.4	244.2	Violent crime rate	331.9	465.5
Water-quality score	35	52	Hospital beds per capita	225.7	420.0	Change in violent crime rate	8.3%	-2.2%
Pollen/allergy score	47	61	No. teaching hospitals	1	3	Property crime rate	2,123.1	3,517.1
Cancer mortality per capita	224.7	201.9	Cost per doctor visit	$61	$77	Change in property crime rate	-3.8%	-2.1%
Depression days per month	3.3	3.5	Cost per dental visit	$51	$70			
Stress score	11	50						

Crime
Score: 68.7
Rank: 118

Transportation
Score: 85.6
Rank: 55

COMMUTE	AREA	U.S. AVG	INTERCITY SERVICES	AREA	U.S. AVG	AUTOMOTIVE	AREA	U.S. AVG
Average commute time	24.0	27.4	Major airports within 60 miles	2	1	Insurance, annual premium	$1,187	$1,432
Percent commutes > 60 mins.	4.0%	5.9%	Size of regional airport	Large	Large	Gas, cost per gallon	$2.42	$2.49
Commute by auto	81.1%	78.9%	Daily airline activity	1244	686	Daily vehicle miles per capita	12.9	24.0
Commute by mass transit	0.6%	1.9%	Amtrak service	No	No			
Work at home	4.1%	3.1%						
Mass transit miles per capita	0.57	1.87						

DINING & SHOPPING	AREA	U.S. AVG	ENTERTAINMENT	AREA	U.S. AVG	OUTDOOR ACTIVITIES	AREA	U.S. AVG
Restaurant rating	1	2	Professional sports rating	3	4	Golf-course rating	5	4
Outlet mall score	54	42	College sports rating	5	4	Ski-area rating	4	3
No. Starbucks	0	13	Zoo/aquarium rating	6	3	Sq. miles inland water	4	4
No. warehouse clubs	0	2	Amusement park rating	10	3	Miles of coastline	0.0	10.7
			Botanical garden/ arboretum rating	6	4	National Park rating	2	3

Leisure
Score: 70.6
Rank: 110

MEDIA & LIBRARIES	AREA	U.S. AVG	PERFORMING ARTS	AREA	U.S. AVG	MUSEUMS	AREA	U.S. AVG
Arts radio rating	8	3	Classical music rating	3	4	Overall museum rating	3	5
No. public libraries	6	27	Ballet/dance rating	3	3	Art museum rating	3	5
Library volumes per capita	2.04	2.78	Professional theater rating	1	3	Science museum rating	4	5
			University arts programs rating	3	5	Children's museum rating	1	3

Arts & Culture
Score: 65.2
Rank: 130

Lewiston, ID-WA

Score: 73.5   **Rank:** 69   **2004 rank:** not ranked

Profile: Small town/college town
Location: Northwestern Idaho, along the Snake River
Elevation: 738 feet
Time zone: Pacific Standard Time

PRO
Nearby outdoor recreation
Mild winters
Small-town feel

CON
Isolation
Economic cycles
Arts and culture

Lewiston, in a deep canyon at the confluence of the Snake and Clearwater rivers, has a distinctly Old West feel. Forest products mills and a few other industries are the economic mainstays, with Potlatch operating the largest of these mills, giving an unpleasant odor at times. Moscow, 20 miles northwest, home to the University of Idaho, is a pleasant small, college town offering some entertainment and college amenities. The nearby terrain is rugged and varied and offers plenty of outdoor and water recreation. The area is isolated; Boise to the south and Spokane to the northwest are both difficult trips over windy two-lane roads. Strong current economic readings, low crime, a pleasant climate, and a lack of significant negatives contribute to a relatively high ranking.

The deep, narrow valley, in which Lewiston is located is studded with fruit and cottonwood trees and surrounded by dry grassland hills ranging from 700 to 1,300 feet above the valley. Lower Granite Dam creates a 32-mile-long lake on the Snake River just below the city. Although quite far north, at the same latitude as Duluth, Minnesota, winters are mild as they are influenced by Pacific air masses. Occasional cold snaps do occur as continental air masses move in from the north, but the valley location provides some protection. The valley location also shelters the immediate area from precipitation, and the prevailing climate is dry year-round. Summers are generally dry and pleasant, but heat can build especially in the valley and 100-plus temperatures are not uncommon.

DEMOGRAPHICS	AREA	U.S. AVG	ETHNIC COMPOSITION	AREA	U.S. AVG	RESIDENT PROFILE	AREA	U.S. AVG
Population	58,928		White	92.9%	79.0%	Single	29.4%	32.4%
Population density per sq. mile	39.7	358.5	Black	0.3%	10.5%	Married	54.6%	52.7%
Population growth	14.8%	21.1%	Asian	0.8%	2.7%	Divorced/separated	16.0%	14.9%
Median age	39.6	36.1	Hispanic	1.9%	10.6%	Married with children	20.3%	23.7%
Percent Democrat	37.0%	44.5%	Religious observance	39.5%	48.9%	Single with children	9.2%	9.1%
Percent Republican	61.6%	54.5%	Diversity measure	16.7	40.1	Percent over age 65	17.3%	12.9%

Population

INCOME	AREA	U.S. AVG	EMPLOYMENT	AREA	U.S. AVG	EMPLOYING INDUSTRIES	AREA	U.S. AVG
Per capita income	$20,991	$23,235	Unemployment rate	5.0%	4.7%	Largest: Manufacturing		
Household income	$40,157	$46,414	Recent job growth	2.3%	1.3%			
Household income < $25K	30.0%	26.2%	Projected future job growth	16.7%	11.5%	Percent manufacturing	16.9%	15.4%
Household income > $75K	18.9%	25.4%	White collar	52.4%	57.8%	Percent public sector	17.0%	15.7%
Household income growth	13.7%	13.6%	Blue collar	27.2%	25.2%	Percent construction	10.4%	9.9%

Economy & Jobs
Score: 65.8
Rank: 129

INDEXES & TAXES	AREA	U.S. AVG	HOUSING	AREA	U.S. AVG	NECESSITIES	AREA	U.S. AVG
Cost of Living Index	90.6	100.0	Median home price	$159,000	$220,000	Food Index	101.8	100.0
Buying Power Index	99.3	100.0	Home price appreciation	47.0%	10.1%	Housing Index	67.2	100.0
Income tax rate	5.32%	4.70%	Median rent	$570	$709	Utilities Index	82.1	100.0
Sales tax rate	6.75%	6.58%	Homes owned	64.1%	62.3%	Transportation Index	103.3	100.0
Property tax rate	$11.42	$12.00	Home price ratio	4.0	4.2	Healthcare Index	115.5	100.0
						Miscellaneous Cost Index	104.8	100.0

Cost of Living
Score: 49.5
Rank: 189

Climate
Score: 70.3
Rank: 110

TEMPERATURE	AREA	U.S. AVG
Average January low	26.0	26.2
Average July high	89.0	87.4
Annual days > 90°F	40	38
Annual days < 32°F	89	89
Annual days < 0°F	0	6

PRECIPITATION	AREA	U.S. AVG
Annual inches precipitation	12.6	37.7
Annual inches snowfall	15.0	7.0
Annual days precipitation	101	109
Annual days rain > 0.5 inches	7	22
Annual days snow > 1.5 inches	13	6

COMFORTS & HAZARDS	AREA	U.S. AVG
July relative humidity	29%	66%
Annual days mostly sunny	200	208
Annual days with thunderstorms	11	39
Tornado risk score	1	18
Hurricane risk score	0	13

TEMPERATURE

PRECIPITATION

DAYS OF CLOUDS & PRECIPITATION

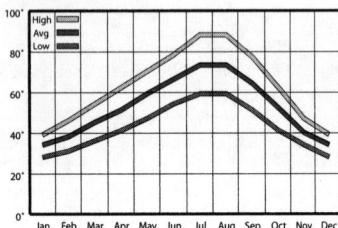

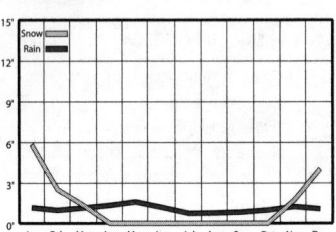

Education
Score: 49.5
Rank: 190

ACHIEVEMENT	AREA	U.S. AVG
High school degree	85.6%	82.7%
2-year college degree	7.9%	6.4%
4-year college degree	12.8%	15.7%
Graduate/professional degree	6.0%	8.9%

PUBLIC SCHOOLS	AREA	U.S. AVG
Expenditures per pupil	$5,894	$5,686
Student/teacher ratio	15.6	16.7
Attending public school	94.1%	90.1%
State SAT score	1088	1021
State ACT score	21.4*	20.9

HIGHER EDUCATION	AREA	U.S. AVG
No. 2-year colleges	2	4
No. 4-year colleges/universities	1	6
No. highly ranked universities	0	1

Health & Healthcare
Score: 86.9
Rank: 50

HAZARDS & ILLNESSES	AREA	U.S. AVG
Air-quality score	62	37
Water-quality score	31	52
Pollen/allergy score	43	61
Cancer mortality per capita	179.1	201.9
Depression days per month	3.4	3.5
Stress score	30	50

HEALTHCARE	AREA	U.S. AVG
Physicians per capita	205.9	244.2
Hospital beds per capita	356.4	420.0
No. teaching hospitals	0	3
Cost per doctor visit	$68	$77
Cost per dental visit	$67	$70

Crime
Score: 85.8
Rank: 54

CRIME	AREA	U.S. AVG
Violent crime rate	146.9	465.5
Change in violent crime rate	2.5%	-2.2%
Property crime rate	3,638.9	3,517.1
Change in property crime rate	-3.1%	-2.1%

Transportation
Score: 78.3
Rank: 82

COMMUTE	AREA	U.S. AVG
Average commute time	17.8	27.4
Percent commutes > 60 mins.	2.9%	5.9%
Commute by auto	83.2%	78.9%
Commute by mass transit	0.4%	1.9%
Work at home	3.3%	3.1%
Mass transit miles per capita	0.38	1.87

INTERCITY SERVICES	AREA	U.S. AVG
Major airports within 60 miles	1	1
Size of regional airport	Medium	Large
Daily airline activity	115	686
Amtrak service	No	No

AUTOMOTIVE	AREA	U.S. AVG
Insurance, annual premium	$955	$1,432
Gas, cost per gallon	$2.48	$2.49
Daily vehicle miles per capita	13.3	24.0

Leisure
Score: 34.0
Rank: 246

DINING & SHOPPING	AREA	U.S. AVG
Restaurant rating	1	2
Outlet mall score	4	42
No. Starbucks	1	13
No. warehouse clubs	1	2

ENTERTAINMENT	AREA	U.S. AVG
Professional sports rating	1	4
College sports rating	1	4
Zoo/aquarium rating	1	3
Amusement park rating	1	3
Botanical garden/ arboretum rating	1	4

OUTDOOR ACTIVITIES	AREA	U.S. AVG
Golf-course rating	2	4
Ski-area rating	6	3
Sq. miles inland water	3	4
Miles of coastline	0.0	10.7
National Park rating	5	3

Arts & Culture
Score: 18.4
Rank: 304

MEDIA & LIBRARIES	AREA	U.S. AVG
Arts radio rating	1	3
No. public libraries	11	27
Library volumes per capita	3.78	2.78

PERFORMING ARTS	AREA	U.S. AVG
Classical music rating	2	4
Ballet/dance rating	1	3
Professional theater rating	1	3
University arts programs rating	1	5

MUSEUMS	AREA	U.S. AVG
Overall museum rating	1	5
Art museum rating	2	5
Science museum rating	1	5
Children's museum rating	1	3

Lewiston–Auburn, ME

Score: 40.8 **Rank:** 312 **2004 rank:** 313

Profile: Small city complex
Location: Southern Maine, 30 miles north and inland from Portland
Elevation: 340 feet
Time zone: Eastern Standard Time

PRO	CON
Attractive setting	Harsh winters
Low crime rates	Low future job growth
Outdoor recreation	Low educational attainment

Lewiston, the second-largest city in the state, lies across the Androscoggin River from its twin city, Auburn. Once a large textile center, Lewiston and Auburn are currently reinventing themselves as manufacturing and service centers with high-tech businesses, but the transition is far from complete. This is an oft-repeated story in Maine, and some towns are doing better than others: Portland south and Waterville 50 miles north are doing much better, while Augusta, the state capital 25 miles north, remains surprisingly depressed. The area does have two small colleges and a large medical centers, adding some employment and interest to the area, but educational attainment is notably low for New England. The two cities have a small-town feel with a strong French presence, which remains from the 19th century when French Canadians migrated into the area for factory work. An ambitious new downtown revitalization effort was kicked off in Lewiston in 2004. As is also true for most of Maine, there is an abundance of outdoor recreation nearby, and a closely knit laid-back community feel contrasting with the bustle farther south and especially at the Massachusetts border.

The area is located in the Androscoggin River Valley in an area of forested hills and lakes. Summers are warm and pleasant with cool evenings. Winters are cold with frequent thaws, while springs are wet and variable. Autumn is the most pleasant season. Temperatures well below zero are recorded frequently each winter, and strong winter winds are common. The White Mountains block some snow and cold from the northwest, but snow is common, often arriving with Atlantic Coast "nore-aster" storms. First freeze is early October; last is early May.

Population

DEMOGRAPHICS	AREA	U.S. AVG	ETHNIC COMPOSITION	AREA	U.S. AVG	RESIDENT PROFILE	AREA	U.S. AVG
Population	107,449		White	96.0%	79.0%	Single	32.0%	32.4%
Population density per sq. mile	228.5	358.5	Black	1.1%	10.5%	Married	52.0%	52.7%
Population growth	2.1%	21.1%	Asian	0.8%	2.7%	Divorced/separated	16.0%	14.9%
Median age	38.8	36.1	Hispanic	1.1%	10.6%	Married with children	20.6%	23.7%
Percent Democrat	54.4%	44.5%	Religious observance	49.8%	48.9%	Single with children	10.1%	9.1%
Percent Republican	43.7%	54.5%	Diversity measure	9.9	40.1	Percent over age 65	14.4%	12.9%

Economy & Jobs
Score: 20.3
Rank: 298

INCOME	AREA	U.S. AVG	EMPLOYMENT	AREA	U.S. AVG	EMPLOYING INDUSTRIES	AREA	U.S. AVG
Per capita income	$21,619	$23,235	Unemployment rate	4.8%	4.7%	Largest: Healthcare & Social Assistance		
Household income	$40,894	$46,414	Recent job growth	1.3%	1.3%			
Household income ‹ $25K	29.5%	26.2%	Projected future job growth	3.4%	11.5%	Percent manufacturing	18.9%	15.4%
Household income › $75K	18.6%	25.4%	White collar	54.6%	57.8%	Percent public sector	11.2%	15.7%
Household income growth	14.3%	13.6%	Blue collar	29.9%	25.2%	Percent construction	11.0%	9.9%

Cost of Living
Score: 30.2
Rank: 261

INDEXES & TAXES	AREA	U.S. AVG	HOUSING	AREA	U.S. AVG	NECESSITIES	AREA	U.S. AVG
Cost of Living Index	93.1	100.0	Median home price	$142,400	$220,000	Food Index	101.3	100.0
Buying Power Index	98.5	100.0	Home price appreciation	62.7%	10.1%	Housing Index	56.7	100.0
Income tax rate	8.50%	4.70%	Median rent	$596	$709	Utilities Index	151.1	100.0
Sales tax rate	5.00%	6.58%	Homes owned	58.5%	62.3%	Transportation Index	104.7	100.0
Property tax rate	$17.47	$12.00	Home price ratio	3.5	4.2	Healthcare Index	106.4	100.0
						Miscellaneous Cost Index	103.7	100.0

Climate
Score: 0.3
Rank: 372

TEMPERATURE	AREA	U.S. AVG	PRECIPITATION	AREA	U.S. AVG	COMFORTS & HAZARDS	AREA	U.S. AVG
Average January low	11.0	26.2	Annual inches precipitation	45.1	37.7	July relative humidity	73%	66%
Average July high	78.0	87.4	Annual inches snowfall	71.0	7.0	Annual days mostly sunny	203	208
Annual days › 90°F	3	38	Annual days precipitation	129	109	Annual days with thunderstorms	30	39
Annual days ‹ 32°F	147	89	Annual days rain › 0.5 inches	29	22	Tornado risk score	0	18
Annual days ‹ 0°F	18	6	Annual days snow › 1.5 inches	15	6	Hurricane risk score	15	13

TEMPERATURE

PRECIPITATION

DAYS OF CLOUDS & PRECIPITATION

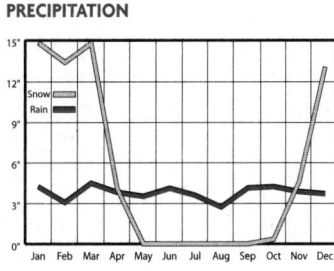

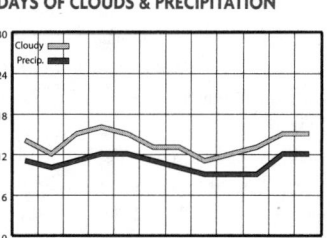

Education
Score: 26.2
Rank: 277

ACHIEVEMENT	AREA	U.S. AVG	PUBLIC SCHOOLS	AREA	U.S. AVG	HIGHER EDUCATION	AREA	U.S. AVG
High school degree	79.9%	82.7%	Expenditures per pupil	$5,948	$5,686	No. 2-year colleges	3	4
2-year college degree	6.7%	6.4%	Student/teacher ratio	14.6	16.7	No. 4-year colleges/universities	1	6
4-year college degree	9.9%	15.7%	Attending public school	91.1%	90.1%	No. highly ranked universities	1	1
Graduate/professional degree	4.5%	8.9%	State SAT score	1002*	1021			
			State ACT score	22.3	20.9			

Health & Healthcare
Score: 52.4
Rank: 179

Crime
Score: 94.7
Rank: 21

HAZARDS & ILLNESSES	AREA	U.S. AVG	HEALTHCARE	AREA	U.S. AVG	CRIME	AREA	U.S. AVG
Air-quality score	40	37	Physicians per capita	231.8	244.2	Violent crime rate	122.0	465.5
Water-quality score	66	52	Hospital beds per capita	474.6	420.0	Change in violent crime rate	6.2%	-2.2%
Pollen/allergy score	47	61	No. teaching hospitals	1	3	Property crime rate	2,684.3	3,517.1
Cancer mortality per capita	245.4	201.9	Cost per doctor visit	$81	$77	Change in property crime rate	0.3%	-2.1%
Depression days per month	4.1	3.5	Cost per dental visit	$72	$70			
Stress score	35	50						

Transportation
Score: 7.0
Rank: 348

COMMUTE	AREA	U.S. AVG	INTERCITY SERVICES	AREA	U.S. AVG	AUTOMOTIVE	AREA	U.S. AVG
Average commute time	25.2	27.4	Major airports within 60 miles	0	1	Insurance, annual premium	$921	$1,432
Percent commutes > 60 mins.	5.7%	5.9%	Size of regional airport	Small	Large	Gas, cost per gallon	$2.48	$2.49
Commute by auto	78.3%	78.9%	Daily airline activity	73	686	Daily vehicle miles per capita	20.3	24.0
Commute by mass transit	0.9%	1.9%	Amtrak service	No	No			
Work at home	2.6%	3.1%						
Mass transit miles per capita	0.91	1.87						

Leisure
Score: 36.1
Rank: 238

DINING & SHOPPING	AREA	U.S. AVG	ENTERTAINMENT	AREA	U.S. AVG	OUTDOOR ACTIVITIES	AREA	U.S. AVG
Restaurant rating	1	2	Professional sports rating	2	4	Golf-course rating	2	4
Outlet mall score	62	42	College sports rating	1	4	Ski-area rating	7	3
No. Starbucks	1	13	Zoo/aquarium rating	1	3	Sq. miles inland water	3	4
No. warehouse clubs	1	2	Amusement park rating	1	3	Miles of coastline	0.0	10.7
			Botanical garden/arboretum rating	3	4	National Park rating	1	3

Arts & Culture
Score: 13.1
Rank: 324

MEDIA & LIBRARIES	AREA	U.S. AVG	PERFORMING ARTS	AREA	U.S. AVG	MUSEUMS	AREA	U.S. AVG
Arts radio rating	1	3	Classical music rating	1	4	Overall museum rating	3	5
No. public libraries	11	27	Ballet/dance rating	1	3	Art museum rating	6	5
Library volumes per capita	3.33	2.78	Professional theater rating	1	3	Science museum rating	1	5
			University arts programs rating	2	5	Children's museum rating	3	3

Lexington–Fayette, KY

Score: 84.3   Rank: 24   2004 rank: 91

Profile: Mid-size city/college town
Location: Central Kentucky, 80 miles south of Cincinnati and 75 miles east of Louisville
Elevation: 989 feet
Time zone: Eastern Standard Time

PRO
Historic interest
College-town amenities
Attractive countryside

CON
Growth and sprawl
Entertainment
Air service

Situated in the heart of bluegrass country, Lexington is Kentucky's second-largest city. It is the world capital of the horse industry and a cultural hub of the state. In many ways it's just the right size, not too big to abandon the small-town lifestyle, but large enough to have urban amenities and employment opportunities. Future economic indicators are positive. Tech giant Lexmark and a major Toyota assembly plant in Georgetown are just north of the city and smaller businesses have found the area attractive, while university, healthcare, and public sector employment are strong. The impressive horse farms in the surrounding countryside and the historic downtown and other exceptional historic districts make Lexington visually attractive. The University of Kentucky just south of downtown adds a strong college-town element

and set of amenities, including the area's secular religion of basketball. University-related healthcare facilities are excellent. Good suburbs lie mainly south, southeast, and west, although longtime locals are alarmed at the recent spread, especially north into Georgetown and south and east into the area's fabled horse country. Interesting small-town alternatives lie west in the historic capital city of Frankfort and southwest in the historic Harrodsburg and the college town of Danville, although the physical geography gives Frankfort the only practical commute. Fayette is actually the name of the county; Lexington and Fayette County are merged into a unitary government, hence the metro area name. Although air service has traditionally been dependent on the proximity to Cincinnati and Louisville, an airport expansion has allowed better air service into the city; schedules and availability of discount carriers will take time. For other cultural and service amenities, Cincinnati and Louisville are reasonably convenient. Daniel Boone National Forest and Lake Cumberland to the south and southeast provide outdoor recreation. Home prices are moderate on a regional and national scale, and value received is good for the money. Lexington is an easy place to live with friendly people in an unusually attractive and prosperous environment for the region, and has few negatives.

Lexington sits on a gently rolling plateau with a mix of open grassland and deciduous wooded forests. The grassland areas typically contain horse farms surrounded by miles of attractive fencing. To the southeast, terrain becomes hillier and more wooded near the foothills of the Appalachian Mountains. Summers are warm and humid, but seldom extremely hot. Winter is typical for the latitude, with alternating mild and cold periods. Below-zero temperatures are relatively rare. Precipitation is evenly distributed throughout winter, spring, and summer. Snowfall amounts are variable and seldom remain for more than a few days. First freeze is late October; last is mid-April.

Population

DEMOGRAPHICS	AREA	U.S. AVG	ETHNIC COMPOSITION	AREA	U.S. AVG	RESIDENT PROFILE	AREA	U.S. AVG
Population	429,410		White	83.9%	79.0%	Single	33.2%	32.4%
Population density per sq. mile	290.4	358.5	Black	10.6%	10.5%	Married	51.3%	52.7%
Population growth	24.5%	21.1%	Asian	2.3%	2.7%	Divorced/separated	15.6%	14.9%
Median age	35.1	36.1	Hispanic	3.7%	10.6%	Married with children	22.2%	23.7%
Percent Democrat	42.2%	44.5%	Religious observance	49.3%	48.9%	Single with children	8.4%	9.1%
Percent Republican	56.9%	54.5%	Diversity measure	32.7	40.1	Percent over age 65	10.6%	12.9%

Economy & Jobs

Score: 69.0
Rank: 117

INCOME	AREA	U.S. AVG	EMPLOYMENT	AREA	U.S. AVG	EMPLOYING INDUSTRIES	AREA	U.S. AVG
Per capita income	$25,328	$23,235	Unemployment rate	4.5%	4.7%	Largest: Manufacturing		
Household income	$45,968	$46,414	Recent job growth	2.1%	1.3%			
Household income ‹ $25K	26.7%	26.2%	Projected future job growth	13.2%	11.5%	Percent manufacturing	14.3%	15.4%
Household income › $75K	26.5%	25.4%	White collar	61.4%	57.8%	Percent public sector	16.3%	15.7%
Household income growth	12.6%	13.6%	Blue collar	22.3%	25.2%	Percent construction	8.0%	9.9%

Cost of Living

Score: 37.7
Rank: 233

INDEXES & TAXES	AREA	U.S. AVG	HOUSING	AREA	U.S. AVG	NECESSITIES	AREA	U.S. AVG
Cost of Living Index	87.8	100.0	Median home price	$150,000	$220,000	Food Index	104.4	100.0
Buying Power Index	117.4	100.0	Home price appreciation	28.6%	10.1%	Housing Index	55.6	100.0
Income tax rate	7.94%	4.70%	Median rent	$647	$709	Utilities Index	98.4	100.0
Sales tax rate	6.00%	6.58%	Homes owned	57.2%	62.3%	Transportation Index	96.5	100.0
Property tax rate	$8.16	$12.00	Home price ratio	3.3	4.2	Healthcare Index	98.9	100.0
						Miscellaneous Cost Index	98.4	100.0

Climate

Score: 37.7
Rank: 232

TEMPERATURE	AREA	U.S. AVG	PRECIPITATION	AREA	U.S. AVG	COMFORTS & HAZARDS	AREA	U.S. AVG
Average January low	24.5	26.2	Annual inches precipitation	50.0	37.7	July relative humidity	70%	66%
Average July high	86.4	87.4	Annual inches snowfall	16.0	7.0	Annual days mostly sunny	197	208
Annual days › 90°F	16	38	Annual days precipitation	130	109	Annual days with thunderstorms	47	39
Annual days ‹ 32°F	97	89	Annual days rain › 0.5 inches	32	22	Tornado risk score	17	18
Annual days ‹ 0°F	2	6	Annual days snow › 1.5 inches	4	6	Hurricane risk score	6	13

TEMPERATURE

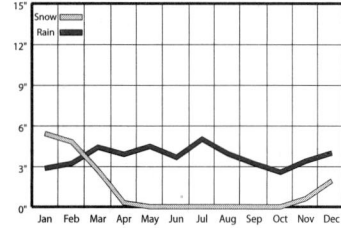

PRECIPITATION

DAYS OF CLOUDS & PRECIPITATION

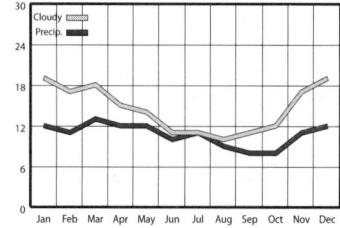

Education

Score: 79.1
Rank: 78

ACHIEVEMENT	AREA	U.S. AVG	PUBLIC SCHOOLS	AREA	U.S. AVG	HIGHER EDUCATION	AREA	U.S. AVG
High school degree	83.7%	82.7%	Expenditures per pupil	$5,735	$5,686	No. 2-year colleges	6	4
2-year college degree	6.1%	6.4%	Student/teacher ratio	20.7	16.7	No. 4-year colleges/universities	7	6
4-year college degree	18.1%	15.7%	Attending public school	85.8%	90.1%	No. highly ranked universities	4	1
Graduate/professional degree	12.2%	8.9%	State SAT score	1124	1021			
			State ACT score	20.6*	20.9			

HAZARDS & ILLNESSES	AREA	U.S. AVG	HEALTHCARE	AREA	U.S. AVG	CRIME	AREA	U.S. AVG
Air-quality score	49	37	Physicians per capita	425.2	244.2	Violent crime rate	403.5	465.5
Water-quality score	64	52	Hospital beds per capita	594.8	420.0	Change in violent crime rate	9.1%	-2.2%
Pollen/allergy score	62	61	No. teaching hospitals	4	3	Property crime rate	3,564.6	3,517.1
Cancer mortality per capita	223.8	201.9	Cost per doctor visit	$65	$77	Change in property crime rate	2.2%	-2.1%
Depression days per month	4.0	3.5	Cost per dental visit	$71	$70			
Stress score	47	50						

Health & Healthcare
Score: 88.5
Rank: 44

Crime
Score: 42.0
Rank: 217

COMMUTE	AREA	U.S. AVG	INTERCITY SERVICES	AREA	U.S. AVG	AUTOMOTIVE	AREA	U.S. AVG
Average commute time	22.9	27.4	Major airports within 60 miles	2	1	Insurance, annual premium	$1,413	$1,432
Percent commutes > 60 mins.	3.5%	5.9%	Size of regional airport	Large	Large	Gas, cost per gallon	$2.43	$2.49
Commute by auto	80.7%	78.9%	Daily airline activity	996	686	Daily vehicle miles per capita	18.7	24.0
Commute by mass transit	0.8%	1.9%	Amtrak service	No	No			
Work at home	2.8%	3.1%						
Mass transit miles per capita	0.83	1.87						

Transportation
Score: 85.3
Rank: 56

DINING & SHOPPING	AREA	U.S. AVG	ENTERTAINMENT	AREA	U.S. AVG	OUTDOOR ACTIVITIES	AREA	U.S. AVG
Restaurant rating	1	2	Professional sports rating	3	4	Golf-course rating	4	4
Outlet mall score	29	42	College sports rating	5	4	Ski-area rating	1	3
No. Starbucks	4	13	Zoo/aquarium rating	1	3	Sq. miles inland water	2	4
No. warehouse clubs	1	2	Amusement park rating	1	3	Miles of coastline	0.0	10.7
			Botanical garden/ arboretum rating	4	4	National Park rating	1	3

Leisure
Score: 30.5
Rank: 259

MEDIA & LIBRARIES	AREA	U.S. AVG	PERFORMING ARTS	AREA	U.S. AVG	MUSEUMS	AREA	U.S. AVG
Arts radio rating	8	3	Classical music rating	3	4	Overall museum rating	6	5
No. public libraries	10	27	Ballet/dance rating	3	3	Art museum rating	8	5
Library volumes per capita	2.20	2.78	Professional theater rating	1	3	Science museum rating	5	5
			University arts programs rating	8	5	Children's museum rating	6	3

Arts & Culture
Score: 75.9
Rank: 90

Lima, OH

Score: 33.1   Rank: 336   2004 rank: 276

Profile: Small city
Location: Northwest Ohio along I-75 between Dayton and Toledo
Elevation: 880 feet
Time zone: Eastern Standard Time

PRO
Cost of living
Small-town flavor
Air quality

CON
Economic decline
Low educational attainment
Industrial landscape

Lima is at a crossroads geographically between several Midwestern cities as well as metaphorically in its evolution. It has a robust past as a manufacturing center of automotive parts, neon signs, and steam locomotives, but those industries are in obvious decline, and the city has followed suit. A strong oil and gas industry tied to local production and reserves does give some vitality to the economy, although it doesn't bring a large number of jobs. The downtown area, which is Midwestern in character, is struggling and unattractive, and many residential areas aren't much better off. The area was the subject of a major PBS documentary on the decline of middle-American towns. Cost of living and housing are among the lowest in the region, and commutes and general stresses are low. The city knows its problems and is working to resolve them, but the jury is still out on whether revitalization will be successful. The energy industry, its central location to many markets, and an ambitious city government may indicate a favorable future.

Lima lies in the level, glaciated plain south of the Lake Erie shore. Most nearby land is agricultural. Summers are warm and humid with frequent afternoon showers and thunderstorms. Winters are cool and humid with considerable cloudiness and an occasional blast of cold air from the north. Snowfall is generally light to moderate but can be heavy. Alternating freezes and thaws are common, with the first freeze arriving in mid-October and the last occurring in late April.

DEMOGRAPHICS	AREA	U.S. AVG	ETHNIC COMPOSITION	AREA	U.S. AVG	RESIDENT PROFILE	AREA	U.S. AVG
Population	108,317		White	84.5%	79.0%	Single	33.3%	32.4%
Population density per sq. mile	267.8	358.5	Black	12.1%	10.5%	Married	52.4%	52.7%
Population growth	-1.3%	21.1%	Asian	0.9%	2.7%	Divorced/separated	14.2%	14.9%
Median age	36.6	36.1	Hispanic	1.5%	10.6%	Married with children	22.6%	23.7%
Percent Democrat	33.4%	44.5%	Religious observance	54.5%	48.9%	Single with children	10.0%	9.1%
Percent Republican	66.1%	54.5%	Diversity measure	29.2	40.1	Percent over age 65	14.1%	12.9%

Population

Economy & Jobs
Score: 23.3
Rank: 287

INCOME	AREA	U.S. AVG	EMPLOYMENT	AREA	U.S. AVG	EMPLOYING INDUSTRIES	AREA	U.S. AVG
Per capita income	$19,968	$23,235	Unemployment rate	5.9%	4.7%	Largest: Manufacturing		
Household income	$40,927	$46,414	Recent job growth	1.4%	1.3%			
Household income < $25K	29.6%	26.2%	Projected future job growth	1.2%	11.5%	Percent manufacturing	25.4%	15.4%
Household income > $75K	19.2%	25.4%	White collar	48.1%	57.8%	Percent public sector	11.6%	15.7%
Household income growth	10.5%	13.6%	Blue collar	34.5%	25.2%	Percent construction	9.1%	9.9%

Cost of Living
Score: 66.0
Rank: 128

INDEXES & TAXES	AREA	U.S. AVG	HOUSING	AREA	U.S. AVG	NECESSITIES	AREA	U.S. AVG
Cost of Living Index	84.4	100.0	Median home price	$116,800	$220,000	Food Index	101.8	100.0
Buying Power Index	108.7	100.0	Home price appreciation	24.6%	10.1%	Housing Index	47.8	100.0
Income tax rate	4.99%	4.70%	Median rent	$538	$709	Utilities Index	118.3	100.0
Sales tax rate	7.00%	6.58%	Homes owned	66.8%	62.3%	Transportation Index	100.8	100.0
Property tax rate	$11.16	$12.00	Home price ratio	2.9	4.2	Healthcare Index	91.9	100.0
						Miscellaneous Cost Index	100.4	100.0

Climate
Score: 20.1
Rank: 298

TEMPERATURE	AREA	U.S. AVG	PRECIPITATION	AREA	U.S. AVG	COMFORTS & HAZARDS	AREA	U.S. AVG
Average January low	20.7	26.2	Annual inches precipitation	33.7	37.7	July relative humidity	73%	66%
Average July high	83.7	87.4	Annual inches snowfall	42.2	7.0	Annual days mostly sunny	173	208
Annual days > 90°F	7	38	Annual days precipitation	152	109	Annual days with thunderstorms	39	39
Annual days < 32°F	127	89	Annual days rain > 0.5 inches	23	22	Tornado risk score	23	18
Annual days < 0°F	7	6	Annual days snow > 1.5 inches	9	6	Hurricane risk score	3	13

TEMPERATURE

PRECIPITATION

DAYS OF CLOUDS & PRECIPITATION

Education
Score: 15.0
Rank: 317

ACHIEVEMENT	AREA	U.S. AVG	PUBLIC SCHOOLS	AREA	U.S. AVG	HIGHER EDUCATION	AREA	U.S. AVG
High school degree	82.7%	82.7%	Expenditures per pupil	$4,762	$5,686	No. 2-year colleges	2	4
2-year college degree	7.9%	6.4%	Student/teacher ratio	18.6	16.7	No. 4-year colleges/universities	3	6
4-year college degree	8.6%	15.7%	Attending public school	86.1%	90.1%	No. highly ranked universities	0	1
Graduate/professional degree	5.1%	8.9%	State SAT score	1079	1021			
			State ACT score	21.5*	20.9			

Health & Healthcare
Score: 59.4
Rank: 153

HAZARDS & ILLNESSES	AREA	U.S. AVG	HEALTHCARE	AREA	U.S. AVG
Air-quality score	44	37	Physicians per capita	224.5	244.2
Water-quality score	35	52	Hospital beds per capita	667.5	420.0
Pollen/allergy score	58	61	No. teaching hospitals	0	3
Cancer mortality per capita	234.4	201.9	Cost per doctor visit	$69	$77
Depression days per month	3.0	3.5	Cost per dental visit	$55	$70
Stress score	33	50			

Crime
Score: 13.6
Rank: 322

CRIME	AREA	U.S. AVG
Violent crime rate	501.3	465.5
Change in violent crime rate	0.3%	-2.2%
Property crime rate	4,336.9	3,517.1
Change in property crime rate	5.4%	-2.1%

Transportation
Score: 78.1
Rank: 83

COMMUTE	AREA	U.S. AVG	INTERCITY SERVICES	AREA	U.S. AVG	AUTOMOTIVE	AREA	U.S. AVG
Average commute time	20.2	27.4	Major airports within 60 miles	1	1	Insurance, annual premium	$1,045	$1,432
Percent commutes > 60 mins.	3.4%	5.9%	Size of regional airport	Medium	Large	Gas, cost per gallon	$2.51	$2.49
Commute by auto	85.1%	78.9%	Daily airline activity	519	686	Daily vehicle miles per capita	22.9	24.0
Commute by mass transit	0.7%	1.9%	Amtrak service	No	No			
Work at home	2.1%	3.1%						
Mass transit miles per capita	0.74	1.87						

Leisure
Score: 13.1
Rank: 324

DINING & SHOPPING	AREA	U.S. AVG	ENTERTAINMENT	AREA	U.S. AVG	OUTDOOR ACTIVITIES	AREA	U.S. AVG
Restaurant rating	1	2	Professional sports rating	2	4	Golf-course rating	3	4
Outlet mall score	13	42	College sports rating	2	4	Ski-area rating	2	3
No. Starbucks	0	13	Zoo/aquarium rating	1	3	Sq. miles inland water	2	4
No. warehouse clubs	1	2	Amusement park rating	1	3	Miles of coastline	0.0	10.7
			Botanical garden/arboretum rating	2	4	National Park rating	1	3

MEDIA & LIBRARIES	AREA	U.S. AVG	PERFORMING ARTS	AREA	U.S. AVG	MUSEUMS	AREA	U.S. AVG
Arts radio rating	5	3	Classical music rating	3	4	Overall museum rating	2	5
No. public libraries	8	27	Ballet/dance rating	1	3	Art museum rating	1	5
Library volumes per capita	3.92	2.78	Professional theater rating	1	3	Science museum rating	1	5
			University arts programs rating	2	5	Children's museum rating	1	3

Arts & Culture
Score: 38.8
Rank: 228

Lincoln, NE

Score: 65.3   Rank: 139   2004 rank: 223

Profile: Capital city/college town
Location: Southeast Nebraska along I-80, 60 miles southwest of Omaha
Elevation: 1,189 feet
Time zone: Central Standard Time

PRO	CON
College-town amenities	Harsh climate
Educated population	Crime rates
Stable economy	Outdoor recreation

As the capital and higher education center of the state, Lincoln is a livable, small city with a diverse economy. The largest employers include state government, the University of Nebraska, Goodyear, and smaller businesses in printing, insurance, and pharmaceutical manufacturing. The university dominates the landscape and the economy, adding 22,000 students and a healthy set of college-town amenities. It is a major sports draw for the entire state and a larger region of the Midwest, particularly during football season. The city is home to two other small private colleges. The downtown is clean but fairly ordinary. According to some, the area has more parks per capita than any other metropolitan area, but otherwise recreational opportunities are relatively scarce. Crime rates are a bit high for the region and type of place. The best residential areas are southwest, but some are

moving 25 miles north up U.S. 77 toward Wahoo, a small Scandinavian farming community offering access to Lincoln and Omaha to the east.

The western edge of the city is in a flat valley. The surrounding area is level to gently rolling open prairie, with deep, rich, fertile soil. Areas north of downtown become somewhat hillier and more wooded. Summer brings sunny days and moderate to low humidity. Warm spells can exceed 100°F. Winter cold outbreaks can drive temperatures below zero for consecutive days. High winds add to discomfort in all seasons. Summer thunderstorms, particularly in late spring and early summer, can produce heavy rains and damaging hail, and often occur at night. Most snow is light and melts rapidly, but occasional heavy snows do occur. The first freeze is mid-October; last is mid-April.

Population

DEMOGRAPHICS	AREA	U.S. AVG	ETHNIC COMPOSITION	AREA	U.S. AVG	RESIDENT PROFILE	AREA	U.S. AVG
Population	283,001		White	89.2%	79.0%	Single	36.0%	32.4%
Population density per sq. mile	200.2	358.5	Black	2.7%	10.5%	Married	50.8%	52.7%
Population growth	23.7%	21.1%	Asian	3.4%	2.7%	Divorced/separated	13.2%	14.9%
Median age	33.4	36.1	Hispanic	3.6%	10.6%	Married with children	23.0%	23.7%
Percent Democrat	41.5%	44.5%	Religious observance	46.7%	48.9%	Single with children	7.4%	9.1%
Percent Republican	56.9%	54.5%	Diversity measure	25.6	40.1	Percent over age 65	10.6%	12.9%

Economy & Jobs
Score: 78.6
Rank: 81

INCOME	AREA	U.S. AVG	EMPLOYMENT	AREA	U.S. AVG	EMPLOYING INDUSTRIES	AREA	U.S. AVG
Per capita income	$24,255	$23,235	Unemployment rate	3.8%	4.7%	Largest: Healthcare & Social Assistance		
Household income	$47,358	$46,414	Recent job growth	2.6%	1.3%			
Household income < $25K	23.2%	26.2%	Projected future job growth	13.0%	11.5%	Percent manufacturing	13.3%	15.4%
Household income > $75K	25.5%	25.4%	White collar	62.2%	57.8%	Percent public sector	19.6%	15.7%
Household income growth	13.0%	13.6%	Blue collar	21.8%	25.2%	Percent construction	8.5%	9.9%

Cost of Living
Score: 29.1
Rank: 265

INDEXES & TAXES	AREA	U.S. AVG	HOUSING	AREA	U.S. AVG	NECESSITIES	AREA	U.S. AVG
Cost of Living Index	87.9	100.0	Median home price	$138,700	$220,000	Food Index	100.4	100.0
Buying Power Index	120.8	100.0	Home price appreciation	22.0%	10.1%	Housing Index	64.7	100.0
Income tax rate	6.68%	4.70%	Median rent	$608	$709	Utilities Index	122.0	100.0
Sales tax rate	6.91%	6.58%	Homes owned	59.0%	62.3%	Transportation Index	99.4	100.0
Property tax rate	$17.12	$12.00	Home price ratio	2.9	4.2	Healthcare Index	96.3	100.0
						Miscellaneous Cost Index	101.7	100.0

Climate
Score: 10.4
Rank: 333

TEMPERATURE	AREA	U.S. AVG
Average January low	11.7	26.2
Average July high	88.9	87.4
Annual days > 90°F	43	38
Annual days < 32°F	146	89
Annual days < 0°F	17	6

PRECIPITATION	AREA	U.S. AVG
Annual inches precipitation	29.0	37.7
Annual inches snowfall	26.0	7.0
Annual days precipitation	88	109
Annual days rain > 0.5 inches	18	22
Annual days snow > 1.5 inches	7	6

COMFORTS & HAZARDS	AREA	U.S. AVG
July relative humidity	68%	66%
Annual days mostly sunny	212	208
Annual days with thunderstorms	9	39
Tornado risk score	20	18
Hurricane risk score	0	13

TEMPERATURE

PRECIPITATION

DAYS OF CLOUDS & PRECIPITATION

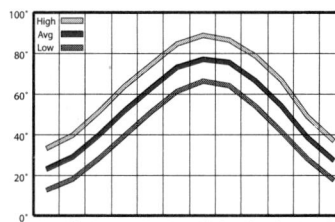

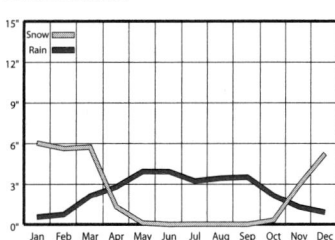

Education
Score: 86.1
Rank: 53

ACHIEVEMENT	AREA	U.S. AVG
High school degree	90.4%	82.7%
2-year college degree	8.9%	6.4%
4-year college degree	21.6%	15.7%
Graduate/professional degree	10.8%	8.9%

PUBLIC SCHOOLS	AREA	U.S. AVG
Expenditures per pupil	$6,076	$5,686
Student/teacher ratio	13.1	16.7
Attending public school	85.7%	90.1%
State SAT score	1159	1021
State ACT score	21.9*	20.9

HIGHER EDUCATION	AREA	U.S. AVG
No. 2-year colleges	4	4
No. 4-year colleges/universities	6	6
No. highly ranked universities	0	1

Health &
Healthcare
Score: 54.8
Rank: 170

HAZARDS & ILLNESSES	AREA	U.S. AVG
Air-quality score	35	37
Water-quality score	31	52
Pollen/allergy score	50	61
Cancer mortality per capita	208.8	201.9
Depression days per month	2.8	3.5
Stress score	8	50

HEALTHCARE	AREA	U.S. AVG
Physicians per capita	219.8	244.2
Hospital beds per capita	488.7	420.0
No. teaching hospitals	3	3
Cost per doctor visit	$80	$77
Cost per dental visit	$59	$70

Crime
Score: 32.6
Rank: 252

CRIME	AREA	U.S. AVG
Violent crime rate	501.0	465.5
Change in violent crime rate	10.0%	-2.2%
Property crime rate	4,888.5	3,517.1
Change in property crime rate	-4.8%	-2.1%

Transportation
Score: 64.7
Rank: 133

COMMUTE	AREA	U.S. AVG
Average commute time	19.8	27.4
Percent commutes > 60 mins.	3.1%	5.9%
Commute by auto	80.6%	78.9%
Commute by mass transit	1.1%	1.9%
Work at home	3.3%	3.1%
Mass transit miles per capita	1.05	1.87

INTERCITY SERVICES	AREA	U.S. AVG
Major airports within 60 miles	1	1
Size of regional airport	Medium	Large
Daily airline activity	136	686
Amtrak service	Yes	No

AUTOMOTIVE	AREA	U.S. AVG
Insurance, annual premium	$1,045	$1,432
Gas, cost per gallon	$2.49	$2.49
Daily vehicle miles per capita	20.3	24.0

Leisure
Score: 35.3
Rank: 241

DINING & SHOPPING	AREA	U.S. AVG
Restaurant rating	1	2
Outlet mall score	0	42
No. Starbucks	2	13
No. warehouse clubs	0	2

ENTERTAINMENT	AREA	U.S. AVG
Professional sports rating	2	4
College sports rating	9	4
Zoo/aquarium rating	3	3
Amusement park rating	1	3
Botanical garden/ arboretum rating	6	4

OUTDOOR ACTIVITIES	AREA	U.S. AVG
Golf-course rating	2	4
Ski-area rating	2	3
Sq. miles inland water	2	4
Miles of coastline	0.0	10.7
National Park rating	1	3

Arts & Culture
Score: 70.9
Rank: 109

MEDIA & LIBRARIES	AREA	U.S. AVG
Arts radio rating	1	3
No. public libraries	10	27
Library volumes per capita	3.49	2.78

PERFORMING ARTS	AREA	U.S. AVG
Classical music rating	6	4
Ballet/dance rating	1	3
Professional theater rating	1	3
University arts programs rating	8	5

MUSEUMS	AREA	U.S. AVG
Overall museum rating	7	5
Art museum rating	8	5
Science museum rating	7	5
Children's museum rating	5	3

Little Rock–North Little Rock, AR   Score: 57.6   Rank: 196   2004 rank: 99

Profile: Capital-city complex
Location: Center of the state along the Arkansas River
Elevation: 265 feet
Time zone: Central Standard Time

PRO	CON
Capital-city amenities	Crime rates
Cost of living	Air service
Healthcare	Hot, humid summers

Little Rock is the steady but unremarkable capital of Arkansas. Typical of mid-America, the downtown area is laid out on a rectangular grid with mostly average modern architecture, a sprinkling of older historic structures, and a waterfront park along the Arkansas River. North Little Rock is a growing, business-friendly, and mainly progressive middle-class center across the river. The area's economy is supported by the state government, a very large teaching hospital associated with the University of Arkansas, and a smattering of private employers mainly in the service sector, including retail and direct marketing with a modest amount of high-tech presence. Notable attributes include the low cost of living for a capital city and state center and the availability of healthcare resources. There is a small assortment of cultural assets, mostly local in character. Recreation consists mainly of college sports, a few minor league teams, and nearby watersports. For a capital city, incomes are relatively high especially in relation to the low cost of living, resulting in a desirable Buying Power Index of 121.7. Also in comparison to other capitals, housing costs are particularly low, but air service is lacking and recent violent crime has been enough of an issue to garner some unwanted journalistic attention.

Little Rock is situated between the Ouachita Mountains to the west and the flat Mississippi River Valley lowlands to the east. Hilly residential areas west of the city rise to 600 feet. Summers are warm and humid. Winters are mild, but outbreaks of cold air are common. Precipitation is fairly well distributed throughout the year with the majority arriving in summer as thunderstorms. Snow is negligible but occasional ice storms can be severe. First freeze is early November; last is late March.

Population

DEMOGRAPHICS	AREA	U.S. AVG	ETHNIC COMPOSITION	AREA	U.S. AVG	RESIDENT PROFILE	AREA	U.S. AVG
Population	636,868		White	73.3%	79.0%	Single	29.3%	32.4%
Population density per sq. mile	155.7	358.5	Black	22.7%	10.5%	Married	54.5%	52.7%
Population growth	22.6%	21.1%	Asian	1.2%	2.7%	Divorced/separated	16.3%	14.9%
Median age	35.8	36.1	Hispanic	2.1%	10.6%	Married with children	23.1%	23.7%
Percent Democrat	47.4%	44.5%	Religious observance	57.6%	48.9%	Single with children	9.8%	9.1%
Percent Republican	51.6%	54.5%	Diversity measure	39.0	40.1	Percent over age 65	11.8%	12.9%

Economy & Jobs
Score: 69.3
Rank: 114

INCOME	AREA	U.S. AVG	EMPLOYMENT	AREA	U.S. AVG	EMPLOYING INDUSTRIES	AREA	U.S. AVG
Per capita income	$23,439	$23,235	Unemployment rate	4.7%	4.7%	Largest: Healthcare & Social Assistance		
Household income	$44,426	$46,414	Recent job growth	2.6%	1.3%			
Household income < $25K	26.4%	26.2%	Projected future job growth	13.2%	11.5%	Percent manufacturing	13.6%	15.4%
Household income > $75K	23.5%	25.4%	White collar	62.1%	57.8%	Percent public sector	18.2%	15.7%
Household income growth	14.5%	13.6%	Blue collar	23.7%	25.2%	Percent construction	10.0%	9.9%

Cost of Living
Score: 47.3
Rank: 197

INDEXES & TAXES	AREA	U.S. AVG	HOUSING	AREA	U.S. AVG	NECESSITIES	AREA	U.S. AVG
Cost of Living Index	81.8	100.0	Median home price	$128,200	$220,000	Food Index	96.8	100.0
Buying Power Index	121.7	100.0	Home price appreciation	28.1%	10.1%	Housing Index	50.1	100.0
Income tax rate	7.00%	4.70%	Median rent	$611	$709	Utilities Index	102.1	100.0
Sales tax rate	7.49%	6.58%	Homes owned	62.0%	62.3%	Transportation Index	91.1	100.0
Property tax rate	$9.27	$12.00	Home price ratio	2.9	4.2	Healthcare Index	92.8	100.0
						Miscellaneous Cost Index	95.4	100.0

Climate
Score: 43.6
Rank: 210

TEMPERATURE	AREA	U.S. AVG	PRECIPITATION	AREA	U.S. AVG	COMFORTS & HAZARDS	AREA	U.S. AVG
Average January low	28.9	26.2	Annual inches precipitation	49.0	37.7	July relative humidity	70%	66%
Average July high	92.6	87.4	Annual inches snowfall	5.0	7.0	Annual days mostly sunny	220	208
Annual days > 90°F	70	38	Annual days precipitation	104	109	Annual days with thunderstorms	57	39
Annual days < 32°F	63	89	Annual days rain > 0.5 inches	32	22	Tornado risk score	36	18
Annual days < 0°F	0	6	Annual days snow > 1.5 inches	2	6	Hurricane risk score	8	13

TEMPERATURE

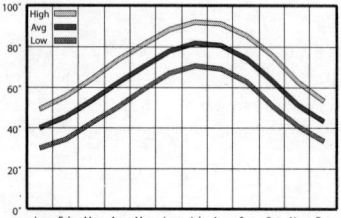

PRECIPITATION

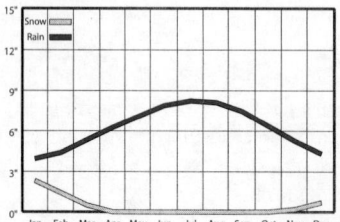

DAYS OF CLOUDS & PRECIPITATION

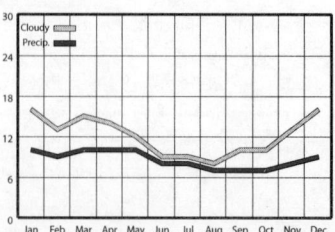

EDUCATION									
ACHIEVEMENT	AREA	U.S. AVG	**PUBLIC SCHOOLS**	AREA	U.S. AVG	**HIGHER EDUCATION**	AREA	U.S. AVG	
High school degree	83.2%	82.7%	Expenditures per pupil	$5,064	$5,686	No. 2-year colleges	3	4	
2-year college degree	4.7%	6.4%	Student/teacher ratio	21.8	16.7	No. 4-year colleges/universities	9	6	
4-year college degree	15.9%	15.7%	Attending public school	87.6%	90.1%	No. highly ranked universities	2	1	
Graduate/professional degree	8.5%	8.9%	State SAT score	1142	1021				
			State ACT score	20.6*	20.9				

Education
Score: 45.7
Rank: 204

HAZARDS & ILLNESSES	AREA	U.S. AVG	**HEALTHCARE**	AREA	U.S. AVG	**CRIME**	AREA	U.S. AVG
Air-quality score	37	37	Physicians per capita	375.9	244.2	Violent crime rate	863.5	465.5
Water-quality score	87	52	Hospital beds per capita	620.1	420.0	Change in violent crime rate	6.0%	-2.2%
Pollen/allergy score	58	61	No. teaching hospitals	5	3	Property crime rate	5,767.2	3,517.1
Cancer mortality per capita	222.0	201.9	Cost per doctor visit	$61	$77	Change in property crime rate	1.6%	-2.1%
Depression days per month	3.6	3.5	Cost per dental visit	$55	$70			
Stress score	95	50						

Health & Healthcare
Score: 85.0
Rank: 57

Crime
Score: 5.3
Rank: 353

COMMUTE	AREA	U.S. AVG	**INTERCITY SERVICES**	AREA	U.S. AVG	**AUTOMOTIVE**	AREA	U.S. AVG
Average commute time	25.3	27.4	Major airports within 60 miles	0	1	Insurance, annual premium	$1,274	$1,432
Percent commutes > 60 mins.	4.5%	5.9%	Size of regional airport	Small	Large	Gas, cost per gallon	$2.45	$2.49
Commute by auto	81.6%	78.9%	Daily airline activity	96	686	Daily vehicle miles per capita	31.3	24.0
Commute by mass transit	0.8%	1.9%	Amtrak service	Yes	No			
Work at home	2.3%	3.1%						
Mass transit miles per capita	0.79	1.87						

Transportation
Score: 6.1
Rank: 351

DINING & SHOPPING	AREA	U.S. AVG	**ENTERTAINMENT**	AREA	U.S. AVG	**OUTDOOR ACTIVITIES**	AREA	U.S. AVG
Restaurant rating	1	2	Professional sports rating	2	4	Golf-course rating	5	4
Outlet mall score	0	42	College sports rating	3	4	Ski-area rating	1	3
No. Starbucks	3	13	Zoo/aquarium rating	4	3	Sq. miles inland water	5	4
No. warehouse clubs	0	2	Amusement park rating	1	3	Miles of coastline	0.0	10.7
			Botanical garden/ arboretum rating	3	4	National Park rating	4	3

Leisure
Score: 47.6
Rank: 194

MEDIA & LIBRARIES	AREA	U.S. AVG	**PERFORMING ARTS**	AREA	U.S. AVG	**MUSEUMS**	AREA	U.S. AVG
Arts radio rating	7	3	Classical music rating	5	4	Overall museum rating	7	5
No. public libraries	29	27	Ballet/dance rating	3	3	Art museum rating	7	5
Library volumes per capita	2.19	2.78	Professional theater rating	6	3	Science museum rating	8	5
			University arts programs rating	4	5	Children's museum rating	5	3

Arts & Culture
Score: 73.3
Rank: 100

Logan, UT-ID

Score: 88.9 **Rank:** 12 **2004 rank:** not ranked

Profile: College town
Location: Extreme northern Utah, near Idaho border
Elevation: 4,507 feet
Time zone: Mountain Standard Time

PRO	CON
Attractive setting	Isolation
Nearby recreation	Arts and culture
Diverse economy	Entertainment

Logan, located at the south end of the Cache Valley against the Wasatch Range and the dramatic Wellsville Mountains to the west, is an attractive Western-style college town, well known for its scenic beauty and recreation. It is home to Utah State University and a center of Mormon culture and history. The economic base extends well beyond the university; a diverse set of businesses have discovered the area's pleasant surroundings, good labor force, and low operating costs. Industries include high tech, biomedical research, food processing, printing, and call centers with names such as Pepperidge Farms, RR Donnelly, Herff Jones (yearbooks and other educational products), and Convergys present. The downtown area is attractive and walkable with wide streets and independently owned businesses, spreading mostly east into the hills with traditional homes, trees, and several parks. Cost of living is reasonable for the type of area and crime rates are extremely low, but geography makes Ogden and especially Salt Lake City to the south a fairly long trip across a mountain pass that may be difficult at times in winter.

The Cache Valley is flat and dry and mostly grassland or agricultural. Logan is tucked into the south end of the valley with wooded mountains rising on three sides and especially to the south. The climate is generally dry and pleasant with lots of sun, warm days, and cool evenings in summer, with infrequent rain arriving mostly as thundershowers. Winter is mostly dry and fairly mild with a few blasts of rigorous weather each year, bringing snow, a few below-zero days, and a dusting to a moderate accumulation of snow.

Population

DEMOGRAPHICS	AREA	U.S. AVG	ETHNIC COMPOSITION	AREA	U.S. AVG	RESIDENT PROFILE	AREA	U.S. AVG
Population	110,632		White	91.3%	79.0%	Single	35.1%	32.4%
Population density per sq. mile	60.5	358.5	Black	0.5%	10.5%	Married	57.7%	52.7%
Population growth	39.4%	21.1%	Asian	2.0%	2.7%	Divorced/separated	7.1%	14.9%
Median age	26.2	36.1	Hispanic	7.7%	10.6%	Married with children	38.4%	23.7%
Percent Democrat	15.3%	44.5%	Religious observance	85.6%	48.9%	Single with children	5.6%	9.1%
Percent Republican	82.6%	54.5%	Diversity measure	28.3	40.1	Percent over age 65	7.8%	12.9%

Economy & Jobs
Score: 96.3
Rank: 15

INCOME	AREA	U.S. AVG	EMPLOYMENT	AREA	U.S. AVG	EMPLOYING INDUSTRIES	AREA	U.S. AVG
Per capita income	$17,103	$23,235	Unemployment rate	4.0%	4.7%	Largest: Manufacturing		
Household income	$44,505	$46,414	Recent job growth	4.1%	1.3%			
Household income < $25K	23.5%	26.2%	Projected future job growth	28.5%	11.5%	Percent manufacturing	19.1%	15.4%
Household income > $75K	21.0%	25.4%	White collar	54.5%	57.8%	Percent public sector	19.6%	15.7%
Household income growth	13.2%	13.6%	Blue collar	27.7%	25.2%	Percent construction	8.6%	9.9%

Cost of Living
Score: 51.3
Rank: 182

INDEXES & TAXES	AREA	U.S. AVG	HOUSING	AREA	U.S. AVG	NECESSITIES	AREA	U.S. AVG
Cost of Living Index	87.0	100.0	Median home price	$158,700	$220,000	Food Index	101.1	100.0
Buying Power Index	114.7	100.0	Home price appreciation	21.8%	10.1%	Housing Index	66.5	100.0
Income tax rate	7.13%	4.70%	Median rent	$615	$709	Utilities Index	81.7	100.0
Sales tax rate	6.31%	6.58%	Homes owned	63.5%	62.3%	Transportation Index	101.9	100.0
Property tax rate	$5.56	$12.00	Home price ratio	3.6	4.2	Healthcare Index	90.3	100.0
						Miscellaneous Cost Index	95.1	100.0

Climate
Score: 64.2
Rank: 133

TEMPERATURE	AREA	U.S. AVG	PRECIPITATION	AREA	U.S. AVG	COMFORTS & HAZARDS	AREA	U.S. AVG
Average January low	15.9	26.2	Annual inches precipitation	17.6	37.7	July relative humidity	24%	66%
Average July high	87.0	87.4	Annual inches snowfall	57.5	7.0	Annual days mostly sunny	234	208
Annual days > 90°F	23	38	Annual days precipitation	94	109	Annual days with thunderstorms	35	39
Annual days < 32°F	145	89	Annual days rain > 0.5 inches	7	22	Tornado risk score	1	18
Annual days < 0°F	7	6	Annual days snow > 1.5 inches	14	6	Hurricane risk score	0	13

TEMPERATURE

PRECIPITATION

DAYS OF CLOUDS & PRECIPITATION

Education
Score: 82.1
Rank: 67

ACHIEVEMENT	AREA	U.S. AVG	PUBLIC SCHOOLS	AREA	U.S. AVG	HIGHER EDUCATION	AREA	U.S. AVG
High school degree	90.4%	82.7%	Expenditures per pupil	$3,713	$5,686	No. 2-year colleges	1	4
2-year college degree	7.0%	6.4%	Student/teacher ratio	19.9	16.7	No. 4-year colleges/universities	2	6
4-year college degree	19.9%	15.7%	Attending public school	99.6%	90.1%	No. highly ranked universities	0	1
Graduate/professional degree	10.1%	8.9%	State SAT score	1117	1021			
			State ACT score	21.7*	20.9			

Health & Healthcare
Score: 84.2
Rank: 60

Crime
Score: 99.5
Rank: 3

HAZARDS & ILLNESSES	AREA	U.S. AVG	HEALTHCARE	AREA	U.S. AVG	CRIME	AREA	U.S. AVG
Air-quality score	51	37	Physicians per capita	134.9	244.2	Violent crime rate	67.1	465.5
Water-quality score	45	52	Hospital beds per capita	226.9	420.0	Change in violent crime rate	4.8%	-2.2%
Pollen/allergy score	60	61	No. teaching hospitals	0	3	Property crime rate	1,854.9	3,517.1
Cancer mortality per capita	98.2	201.9	Cost per doctor visit	$66	$77	Change in property crime rate	3.5%	-2.1%
Depression days per month	2.7	3.5	Cost per dental visit	$57	$70			
Stress score	1	50						

Transportation
Score: 83.7
Rank: 62

COMMUTE	AREA	U.S. AVG	INTERCITY SERVICES	AREA	U.S. AVG	AUTOMOTIVE	AREA	U.S. AVG
Average commute time	19.4	27.4	Major airports within 60 miles	1	1	Insurance, annual premium	$946	$1,432
Percent commutes > 60 mins.	4.9%	5.9%	Size of regional airport	Large	Large	Gas, cost per gallon	$2.24	$2.49
Commute by auto	73.5%	78.9%	Daily airline activity	452	686	Daily vehicle miles per capita	20.5	24.0
Commute by mass transit	1.2%	1.9%	Amtrak service	No	No			
Work at home	5.1%	3.1%						
Mass transit miles per capita	1.17	1.87						

DINING & SHOPPING	AREA	U.S. AVG	ENTERTAINMENT	AREA	U.S. AVG	OUTDOOR ACTIVITIES	AREA	U.S. AVG
Restaurant rating	1	2	Professional sports rating	1	4	Golf-course rating	2	4
Outlet mall score	0	42	College sports rating	4	4	Ski-area rating	5	3
No. Starbucks	0	13	Zoo/aquarium rating	2	3	Sq. miles inland water	3	4
No. warehouse clubs	1	2	Amusement park rating	1	3	Miles of coastline	0.0	10.7
			Botanical garden/ arboretum rating	1	4	National Park rating	7	3

Leisure
Score: 44.7
Rank: 206

MEDIA & LIBRARIES	AREA	U.S. AVG	PERFORMING ARTS	AREA	U.S. AVG	MUSEUMS	AREA	U.S. AVG
Arts radio rating	1	3	Classical music rating	2	4	Overall museum rating	2	5
No. public libraries	8	27	Ballet/dance rating	1	3	Art museum rating	3	5
Library volumes per capita	3.15	2.78	Professional theater rating	1	3	Science museum rating	1	5
			University arts programs rating	4	5	Children's museum rating	1	3

Arts & Culture
Score: 20.3
Rank: 297

Longview, TX

Score: 35.4   Rank: 319   2004 rank: 143

Profile: Small-city complex
Location: Northeast Texas, 30 miles from Louisiana border
Elevation: 259 feet
Time zone: Central Standard Time

PRO	CON
Cost of living	Entertainment
Historic interest	Violent crime rate
Nearby recreation	Summer heat

Longview is a small city in eastern Texas about 130 miles east of Dallas. Originally a transportation center for nearby agriculture and timber industries, this area prospered from the oil booms of the 1920s and 1930s, and Longview has a sizable downtown historic area ("One Hundred Acres of History"). Today's Longview still has a manufacturing and basic industrial economy but also supports a large region of East Texas with retail, healthcare, and other services. The largest employers are Eastman Chemical and the Good Shepard Health System, and there is an assortment of smaller manufacturers in recreational vehicles, heavy equipment, railroad cars, and fabricated parts. Contrary to the popular Texas stereotype of endless dry Western prairie, Longview and East Texas in general are known as the "piney woods" part of the state, and large trees and forests dominate the landscape where they weren't cleared for cotton growing and other agricultural interests. It is more Deep South than West, and that doesn't just apply to the physical landscape but also the culture. The most notable of the area's many lakes is Lake of the Pines to the north. While Shreveport to the east provides some amenities including air service, the area is fairly isolated and offers little to do. The low Cost of Living Index of 74.4 is one of the area's biggest attractions.

The city sits on level to gently rolling land with pine forests and intermittent agriculture. Summer months are hot and fairly humid. Winters are mild with a few short periods of cold temperatures. Rainfall occurs as steady winter rains or as spring and summer thundershowers. Storms may be strong, particularly in the spring.

DEMOGRAPHICS	AREA	U.S. AVG	ETHNIC COMPOSITION	AREA	U.S. AVG	RESIDENT PROFILE	AREA	U.S. AVG
Population	199,966		White	74.7%	79.0%	Single	27.6%	32.4%
Population density per sq. mile	112.0	358.5	Black	17.7%	10.5%	Married	54.9%	52.7%
Population growth	11.2%	21.1%	Asian	0.6%	2.7%	Divorced/separated	17.5%	14.9%
Median age	36.1	36.1	Hispanic	9.7%	10.6%	Married with children	23.8%	23.7%
Percent Democrat	28.5%	44.5%	Religious observance	65.9%	48.9%	Single with children	9.2%	9.1%
Percent Republican	71.1%	54.5%	Diversity measure	50.3	40.1	Percent over age 65	13.9%	12.9%

Population

INCOME	AREA	U.S. AVG	EMPLOYMENT	AREA	U.S. AVG	EMPLOYING INDUSTRIES	AREA	U.S. AVG
Per capita income	$20,287	$23,235	Unemployment rate	5.2%	4.7%	Largest: Manufacturing		
Household income	$39,747	$46,414	Recent job growth	3.6%	1.3%			
Household income < $25K	31.1%	26.2%	Projected future job growth	14.3%	11.5%	Percent manufacturing	18.6%	15.4%
Household income > $75K	20.1%	25.4%	White collar	52.7%	57.8%	Percent public sector	12.0%	15.7%
Household income growth	16.3%	13.6%	Blue collar	31.4%	25.2%	Percent construction	12.8%	9.9%

Economy & Jobs
Score: 72.5
Rank: 103

INDEXES & TAXES	AREA	U.S. AVG	HOUSING	AREA	U.S. AVG	NECESSITIES	AREA	U.S. AVG
Cost of Living Index	74.4	100.0	Median home price	$103,400	$220,000	Food Index	88.5	100.0
Buying Power Index	119.7	100.0	Home price appreciation	29.0%	10.1%	Housing Index	45.5	100.0
Income tax rate	0.00%	4.70%	Median rent	$547	$709	Utilities Index	79.2	100.0
Sales tax rate	7.77%	6.58%	Homes owned	64.3%	62.3%	Transportation Index	87.9	100.0
Property tax rate	$13.31	$12.00	Home price ratio	2.6	4.2	Healthcare Index	93.2	100.0
						Miscellaneous Cost Index	95.5	100.0

Cost of Living
Score: 97.1
Rank: 12

Climate
Score: 75.4
Rank: 92

TEMPERATURE	AREA	U.S. AVG	PRECIPITATION	AREA	U.S. AVG	COMFORTS & HAZARDS	AREA	U.S. AVG
Average January low	37.8	26.2	Annual inches precipitation	45.0	37.7	July relative humidity	71%	66%
Average July high	93.8	87.4	Annual inches snowfall	1.0	7.0	Annual days mostly sunny	217	208
Annual days > 90°F	87	38	Annual days precipitation	97	109	Annual days with thunderstorms	54	39
Annual days < 32°F	1	89	Annual days rain > 0.5 inches	23	22	Tornado risk score	31	18
Annual days < 0°F	0	6	Annual days snow > 1.5 inches	1	6	Hurricane risk score	14	13

TEMPERATURE

PRECIPITATION

DAYS OF CLOUDS & PRECIPITATION

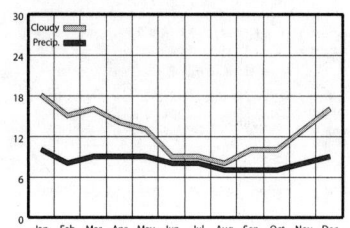

Education
Score: 32.1
Rank: 255

ACHIEVEMENT	AREA	U.S. AVG	PUBLIC SCHOOLS	AREA	U.S. AVG	HIGHER EDUCATION	AREA	U.S. AVG
High school degree	77.5%	82.7%	Expenditures per pupil	$5,217	$5,686	No. 2-year colleges	1	4
2-year college degree	6.2%	6.4%	Student/teacher ratio	14.0	16.7	No. 4-year colleges/universities	1	6
4-year college degree	10.9%	15.7%	Attending public school	96.3%	90.1%	No. highly ranked universities	1	1
Graduate/professional degree	5.4%	8.9%	State SAT score	997*	1021			
			State ACT score	20.3	20.9			

Health & Healthcare
Score: 59.9
Rank: 151

HAZARDS & ILLNESSES	AREA	U.S. AVG	HEALTHCARE	AREA	U.S. AVG
Air-quality score	40	37	Physicians per capita	162.2	244.2
Water-quality score	49	52	Hospital beds per capita	384.1	420.0
Pollen/allergy score	65	61	No. teaching hospitals	0	3
Cancer mortality per capita	183.2	201.9	Cost per doctor visit	$90	$77
Depression days per month	3.4	3.5	Cost per dental visit	$87	$70
Stress score	85	50			

Crime
Score: 6.7
Rank: 348

CRIME	AREA	U.S. AVG
Violent crime rate	662.7	465.5
Change in violent crime rate	-1.7%	-2.2%
Property crime rate	4,762.9	3,517.1
Change in property crime rate	1.0%	-2.1%

Transportation
Score: 15.2
Rank: 318

COMMUTE	AREA	U.S. AVG	INTERCITY SERVICES	AREA	U.S. AVG	AUTOMOTIVE	AREA	U.S. AVG
Average commute time	23.5	27.4	Major airports within 60 miles	0	1	Insurance, annual premium	$1,254	$1,432
Percent commutes > 60 mins.	4.8%	5.9%	Size of regional airport	Small	Large	Gas, cost per gallon	$2.43	$2.49
Commute by auto	82.5%	78.9%	Daily airline activity	66	686	Daily vehicle miles per capita	20.4	24.0
Commute by mass transit	0.2%	1.9%	Amtrak service	Yes	No			
Work at home	2.4%	3.1%						
Mass transit miles per capita	0.17	1.87						

Leisure
Score: 3.7
Rank: 359

DINING & SHOPPING	AREA	U.S. AVG	ENTERTAINMENT	AREA	U.S. AVG	OUTDOOR ACTIVITIES	AREA	U.S. AVG
Restaurant rating	1	2	Professional sports rating	2	4	Golf-course rating	2	4
Outlet mall score	2	42	College sports rating	2	4	Ski-area rating	1	3
No. Starbucks	1	13	Zoo/aquarium rating	1	3	Sq. miles inland water	2	4
No. warehouse clubs	1	2	Amusement park rating	1	3	Miles of coastline	0.0	10.7
			Botanical garden/ arboretum rating	2	4	National Park rating	1	3

Arts & Culture
Score: 20.9
Rank: 295

MEDIA & LIBRARIES	AREA	U.S. AVG	PERFORMING ARTS	AREA	U.S. AVG	MUSEUMS	AREA	U.S. AVG
Arts radio rating	1	3	Classical music rating	3	4	Overall museum rating	2	5
No. public libraries	10	27	Ballet/dance rating	1	3	Art museum rating	2	5
Library volumes per capita	1.88	2.78	Professional theater rating	1	3	Science museum rating	4	5
			University arts programs rating	3	5	Children's museum rating	2	3

Longview, WA

Score: 47.1   **Rank:** 263   **2004 rank:** not ranked

Profile: Industrial-town/port-town complex
Location: Southwest Washington, about 50 miles north of Portland, Oregon
Elevation: 26 feet
Time zone: Pacific Standard Time

PRO	CON
Nearby mountains	Unattractive downtown
Close to Portland	Economic cycles
Pleasant climate	Property crime rate

Longview and its sister city Kelso make up a grain-loading and forest-products center serving ocean traffic coming up the Columbia River. The area contains a complex of grain elevators and mills, an outdated urban core and set of working-class neighborhoods, and unattractive urban sprawl uncharacteristic of most Pacific Northwest towns. The area is close to Portland, 50 miles to the south, and is a western gateway to the Mount St. Helens area. There are some new industrial parks working to attract more light manufacturing and new-economy businesses, and town leaders are aware of the area's shortcomings and are working to deal with them. The strategic location on transportation routes between Portland and Seattle, good labor force, Columbia River

frontage, and nice surroundings make us think this area could be due for a rebound if it plays its cards right. And some economic statistics point that way, but it's a long haul. Cost of living is high for the type of area but low for the region, a possible long-term plus.

The terrain is generally hilly with wooded hilltops and broad, flat, mostly agricultural valleys away from industrial areas. The wooded hilltops give way to dense forests and Alpine climates 30 to 50 miles east in the main Cascade Range. The climate brings relatively warm, dry, sunny summers and cool, wet periods most of the rest of the year. The area is sheltered from severe weather, and snow, while it does occur, is uncommon.

Population

DEMOGRAPHICS	AREA	U.S. AVG	ETHNIC COMPOSITION	AREA	U.S. AVG	RESIDENT PROFILE	AREA	U.S. AVG
Population	96,262		White	91.2%	79.0%	Single	27.1%	32.4%
Population density per sq. mile	84.5	358.5	Black	0.7%	10.5%	Married	56.6%	52.7%
Population growth	17.2%	21.1%	Asian	1.4%	2.7%	Divorced/separated	16.4%	14.9%
Median age	37.5	36.1	Hispanic	5.5%	10.6%	Married with children	22.4%	23.7%
Percent Democrat	50.8%	44.5%	Religious observance	31.9%	48.9%	Single with children	10.3%	9.1%
Percent Republican	47.6%	54.5%	Diversity measure	25.4	40.1	Percent over age 65	13.8%	12.9%

Economy & Jobs
Score: 80.7
Rank: 73

INCOME	AREA	U.S. AVG	EMPLOYMENT	AREA	U.S. AVG	EMPLOYING INDUSTRIES	AREA	U.S. AVG
Per capita income	$20,881	$23,235	Unemployment rate	6.9%	4.7%	Largest: Manufacturing		
Household income	$44,094	$46,414	Recent job growth	3.6%	1.3%			
Household income < $25K	27.9%	26.2%	Projected future job growth	18.9%	11.5%	Percent manufacturing	21.1%	15.4%
Household income > $75K	21.6%	25.4%	White collar	46.8%	57.8%	Percent public sector	13.9%	15.7%
Household income growth	10.8%	13.6%	Blue collar	33.5%	25.2%	Percent construction	12.4%	9.9%

Cost of Living
Score: 64.7
Rank: 133

INDEXES & TAXES	AREA	U.S. AVG	HOUSING	AREA	U.S. AVG	NECESSITIES	AREA	U.S. AVG
Cost of Living Index	95.3	100.0	Median home price	$190,600	$220,000	Food Index	104.6	100.0
Buying Power Index	103.7	100.0	Home price appreciation	36.0%	10.1%	Housing Index	80.9	100.0
Income tax rate	0.00%	4.70%	Median rent	$609	$709	Utilities Index	72.5	100.0
Sales tax rate	7.60%	6.58%	Homes owned	63.0%	62.3%	Transportation Index	107.2	100.0
Property tax rate	$10.20	$12.00	Home price ratio	4.3	4.2	Healthcare Index	124.0	100.0
						Miscellaneous Cost Index	102.6	100.0

Climate
Score: 80.2
Rank: 75

TEMPERATURE	AREA	U.S. AVG	PRECIPITATION	AREA	U.S. AVG	COMFORTS & HAZARDS	AREA	U.S. AVG
Average January low	33.7	26.2	Annual inches precipitation	48.1	37.7	July relative humidity	47%	66%
Average July high	77.7	87.4	Annual inches snowfall	5.0	7.0	Annual days mostly sunny	152	208
Annual days > 90°F	6	38	Annual days precipitation	174	109	Annual days with thunderstorms	7	39
Annual days < 32°F	57	89	Annual days rain > 0.5 inches	23	22	Tornado risk score	1	18
Annual days < 0°F	0	6	Annual days snow > 1.5 inches	1	6	Hurricane risk score	0	13

TEMPERATURE

PRECIPITATION

DAYS OF CLOUDS & PRECIPITATION

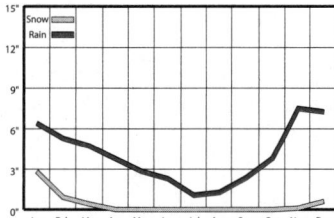

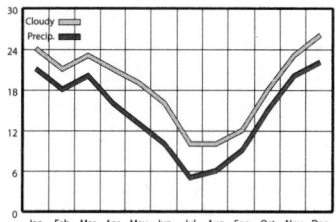

Education
Score: 25.9
Rank: 278

ACHIEVEMENT	AREA	U.S. AVG	PUBLIC SCHOOLS	AREA	U.S. AVG	HIGHER EDUCATION	AREA	U.S. AVG
High school degree	83.0%	82.7%	Expenditures per pupil	$5,791	$5,686	No. 2-year colleges	1	4
2-year college degree	8.3%	6.4%	Student/teacher ratio	20.6	16.7	No. 4-year colleges/universities	0	6
4-year college degree	8.3%	15.7%	Attending public school	95.2%	90.1%	No. highly ranked universities	0	1
Graduate/professional degree	4.8%	8.9%	State SAT score	1059*	1021			
			State ACT score	22.9	20.9			

Health & Healthcare
Score: 33.4
Rank: 248

Crime
Score: 24.1
Rank: 283

HAZARDS & ILLNESSES	AREA	U.S. AVG	HEALTHCARE	AREA	U.S. AVG	CRIME	AREA	U.S. AVG
Air-quality score	38	37	Physicians per capita	189.2	244.2	Violent crime rate	315.9	465.5
Water-quality score	60	52	Hospital beds per capita	205.7	420.0	Change in violent crime rate	-14.8%	-2.2%
Pollen/allergy score	37	61	No. teaching hospitals	0	3	Property crime rate	6,087.7	3,517.1
Cancer mortality per capita	205.8	201.9	Cost per doctor visit	$82	$77	Change in property crime rate	0.9%	-2.1%
Depression days per month	3.9	3.5	Cost per dental visit	$92	$70			
Stress score	89	50						

Transportation
Score: 85.8
Rank: 54

COMMUTE	AREA	U.S. AVG	INTERCITY SERVICES	AREA	U.S. AVG	AUTOMOTIVE	AREA	U.S. AVG
Average commute time	23.2	27.4	Major airports within 60 miles	2	1	Insurance, annual premium	$1,572	$1,432
Percent commutes > 60 mins.	6.5%	5.9%	Size of regional airport	Large	Large	Gas, cost per gallon	$2.45	$2.49
Commute by auto	81.6%	78.9%	Daily airline activity	1131	686	Daily vehicle miles per capita	22.2	24.0
Commute by mass transit	0.4%	1.9%	Amtrak service	Yes	No			
Work at home	2.9%	3.1%						
Mass transit miles per capita	0.39	1.87						

Leisure
Score: 8.0
Rank: 343

DINING & SHOPPING	AREA	U.S. AVG	ENTERTAINMENT	AREA	U.S. AVG	OUTDOOR ACTIVITIES	AREA	U.S. AVG
Restaurant rating	1	2	Professional sports rating	1	4	Golf-course rating	2	4
Outlet mall score	0	42	College sports rating	1	4	Ski-area rating	2	3
No. Starbucks	1	13	Zoo/aquarium rating	1	3	Sq. miles inland water	3	4
No. warehouse clubs	0	2	Amusement park rating	1	3	Miles of coastline	0.0	10.7
			Botanical garden/ arboretum rating	1	4	National Park rating	3	3

Arts & Culture
Score: 14.4
Rank: 319

MEDIA & LIBRARIES	AREA	U.S. AVG	PERFORMING ARTS	AREA	U.S. AVG	MUSEUMS	AREA	U.S. AVG
Arts radio rating	2	3	Classical music rating	2	4	Overall museum rating	1	5
No. public libraries	4	27	Ballet/dance rating	1	3	Art museum rating	2	5
Library volumes per capita	4.44	2.78	Professional theater rating	1	3	Science museum rating	1	5
			University arts programs rating	1	5	Children's museum rating	1	3

Los Angeles–Long Beach–Glendale, CA   Score: 69.8   Rank: 93   2004 rank: 54

Profile: National center complex
Location: Southern California Coast, south and west of the San Bernardino Mountains
Elevation: 104 feet
Time zone: Pacific Standard Time

PRO
Entertainment
Coastline and beach areas
Big-city amenities

CON
Overcrowding
Air quality
Cost of living

In the mid–20th century, the complex Los Angeles–Long Beach–Glendale area started as a warm-weather paradise with a strong economic base and the attraction of cosmopolitan adventure. But so many people migrated there from all over the world that much of the original attraction has been lost. The area is huge. Because of earthquake risk and the increasing importance of the automobile, the city built outward—into every nook and cranny of available level land for miles—rather than upward. Surrounding a network of city cores, the sprawl of low buildings extends 80 miles on a near-perfect grid from the beach at Santa Monica west of downtown east toward San Bernardino (the metro area itself actually extends about 40 miles east to Pomona; the rest is part of the Riverside–San Bernardino metro area, see p. 650). The L.A. metro area extends north into the San Fernando Valley, including Burbank and Glendale in another large sprawling panorama, and extends south to the busy port of Long Beach, a revitalizing area with grittier neighborhoods inland. Flying into Los Angeles International for the first time, the view of the sprawling cityscape is stunning—if one can see through the smog.

That isn't to say that everything is the same throughout the area. "L.A." includes some of the nicer places to live in the world, such as Beverly Hills, Malibu, San Marino, and the seemingly endless beach communities that stretch south from Santa Monica toward Long Beach. Pasadena to the northeast has a marvelous "old California" feel, as do areas of Santa Monica and some of the beach communities. But without extensive financial resources, these communities are all but inaccessible, and those who cannot afford them feel the full impact of the overcrowded landscape. "Middle class" often equates to "poor" in this area.

That said, the area has some of the best weather in the world. Warm sunny days, cool evenings, low morning clouds and fog, and sea breezes are the norm. Rain only falls in the winter, and seldom at that. Museums, performing arts, professional sports, boating, and beach recreation are among the world's best. All imaginable services—higher education, healthcare, transportation—are available in abundance. As the area is more economically diverse and less dependent on high-tech industry than northern California, the economy continues to be relatively strong for California.

The downsides of living in L.A. are legendary. Most are caused by overcrowding and sprawl. Traffic and air-pollution problems are extreme. Reported commute times are long but not worst in the U.S. as many might expect—but reality could be worse as many of those surveyed are retired or don't commute on a daily basis. Those who do face daily frustration, with freeways seldom moving at full speed at any time of the day. Air quality is the worst in the nation *by far*, to the extent that only two other U.S. cities are within 50% of L.A.'s pollution level. A brown cloud hovers over the city, particularly inland, most months of the year. Violent crime is twice the U.S. average, but property crime is surprisingly moderate. The Cost of Living Index is an oppressive 163.2, not

the state's highest but high enough. The median home price of $576,300 has escalated rapidly in recent years and doesn't buy much. A nice home or one in a favorable location for commuting costs *much* more.

Recently, the area has attempted to reduce dependence on the automobile by improving mass transit. And the 40-year campaign to reduce auto smog has definitely helped. However, the growing number of cars and miles driven have mitigated these effects. The area ranks in the Top 100 because of the outstanding climate, economy, services, and amenities. For those who can take the bad with the good, or who can afford one of the nicer areas near the beach or in the surrounding hills, L.A. can be a nice place to live. Otherwise, be warned. Those of average means should probably look elsewhere, and if Southern California is the destination, Riverside–San Bernardino, Santa Ana–Anaheim–Irvine (p. 695), or Oxnard–Thousand Oaks–Ventura (p. 600) are worth a look.

Los Angeles proper is located in a level coastal basin extending eastward from the Pacific Ocean. To the north and northwest lie areas of hills and coastal mountains separating the city proper from the flat San Fernando Valley. To the northeast lie the much higher San Bernardino Mountains, rising up to 7,000 feet above the valley floor. Temperatures above 80°F are observed every month of the year. Like other Pacific Coast areas, rainfall comes in winter, with 85% of precipitation occurring November through March. Rainfall totals increase in foothill areas, and flash floods and mudslides are common in canyon areas. At times, the lack of air movement, combined with a frequent and persistent air inversion (aloft warm, dry, desert air trapping slightly cooler and more moist Pacific air) brings considerable air pollution in the basin, causing health problems for some and reducing or even eliminating visibility of the nearby mountains.

DEMOGRAPHICS	AREA	U.S. AVG	ETHNIC COMPOSITION	AREA	U.S. AVG	RESIDENT PROFILE	AREA	U.S. AVG
Population	10,088,274		White	47.5%	79.0%	Single	39.5%	32.4%
Population density per sq. mile	2484.2	358.5	Black	9.3%	10.5%	Married	44.3%	52.7%
Population growth	13.8%	21.1%	Asian	12.7%	2.7%	Divorced/separated	16.3%	14.9%
Median age	33.5	36.1	Hispanic	47.1%	10.6%	Married with children	25.7%	23.7%
Percent Democrat	63.1%	44.5%	Religious observance	58.1%	48.9%	Single with children	10.9%	9.1%
Percent Republican	35.6%	54.5%	Diversity measure	84.2	40.1	Percent over age 65	10.0%	12.9%

Population

INCOME	AREA	U.S. AVG	EMPLOYMENT	AREA	U.S. AVG	EMPLOYING INDUSTRIES	AREA	U.S. AVG
Per capita income	$22,727	$23,235	Unemployment rate	5.7%	4.7%	Largest: Manufacturing		
Household income	$47,275	$46,414	Recent job growth	3.1%	1.3%			
Household income < $25K	26.7%	26.2%	Projected future job growth	6.7%	11.5%	Percent manufacturing	15.6%	15.4%
Household income > $75K	29.8%	25.4%	White collar	61.6%	57.8%	Percent public sector	12.6%	15.7%
Household income growth	12.1%	13.6%	Blue collar	23.4%	25.2%	Percent construction	7.8%	9.9%

Economy & Jobs
Score: 28.9
Rank: 266

INDEXES & TAXES	AREA	U.S. AVG	HOUSING	AREA	U.S. AVG	NECESSITIES	AREA	U.S. AVG
Cost of Living Index	163.2	100.0	Median home price	$576,300	$220,000	Food Index	113.4	100.0
Buying Power Index	64.9	100.0	Home price appreciation	150.2%	10.1%	Housing Index	219.7	100.0
Income tax rate	6.00%	4.70%	Median rent	$1,269	$709	Utilities Index	116.5	100.0
Sales tax rate	8.25%	6.58%	Homes owned	45.4%	62.3%	Transportation Index	108.0	100.0
Property tax rate	$8.38	$12.00	Home price ratio	12.2	4.2	Healthcare Index	118.7	100.0
						Miscellaneous Cost Index	106.7	100.0

Cost of Living
Score: 2.4
Rank: 364

Climate
Score: 97.9
Rank: 9

TEMPERATURE	AREA	U.S. AVG
Average January low	45.4	26.2
Average July high	75.8	87.4
Annual days > 90°F	5	38
Annual days < 32°F	0	89
Annual days < 0°F	0	6

PRECIPITATION	AREA	U.S. AVG
Annual inches precipitation	12.0	37.7
Annual inches snowfall	0.0	7.0
Annual days precipitation	35	109
Annual days rain > 0.5 inches	9	22
Annual days snow > 1.5 inches	0	6

COMFORTS & HAZARDS	AREA	U.S. AVG
July relative humidity	71%	66%
Annual days mostly sunny	258	208
Annual days with thunderstorms	3	39
Tornado risk score	13	18
Hurricane risk score	1	13

TEMPERATURE

PRECIPITATION

DAYS OF CLOUDS & PRECIPITATION

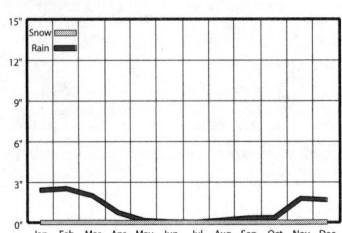
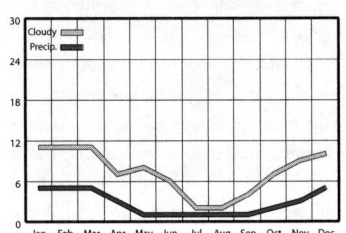

Education
Score: 98.4
Rank: 7

ACHIEVEMENT	AREA	U.S. AVG
High school degree	69.4%	82.7%
2-year college degree	6.2%	6.4%
4-year college degree	15.9%	15.7%
Graduate/professional degree	8.6%	8.9%

PUBLIC SCHOOLS	AREA	U.S. AVG
Expenditures per pupil	$5,203	$5,686
Student/teacher ratio	21.7	16.7
Attending public school	88.4%	90.1%
State SAT score	1019*	1021
State ACT score	21.6	20.9

HIGHER EDUCATION	AREA	U.S. AVG
No. 2-year colleges	40	4
No. 4-year colleges/universities	71	6
No. highly ranked universities	14	1

Health & Healthcare
Score: 15.8
Rank: 314

HAZARDS & ILLNESSES	AREA	U.S. AVG
Air-quality score	1	37
Water-quality score	52	52
Pollen/allergy score	41	61
Cancer mortality per capita	152.8	201.9
Depression days per month	3.6	3.5
Stress score	49	50

HEALTHCARE	AREA	U.S. AVG
Physicians per capita	243.5	244.2
Hospital beds per capita	307.4	420.0
No. teaching hospitals	48	3
Cost per doctor visit	$111	$77
Cost per dental visit	$81	$70

Crime
Score: 39.3
Rank: 227

CRIME	AREA	U.S. AVG
Violent crime rate	663.3	465.5
Change in violent crime rate	-13.6%	-2.2%
Property crime rate	2,860.6	3,517.1
Change in property crime rate	-4.0%	-2.1%

Transportation
Score: 78.6
Rank: 80

COMMUTE	AREA	U.S. AVG
Average commute time	31.8	27.4
Percent commutes > 60 mins.	11.0%	5.9%
Commute by auto	70.3%	78.9%
Commute by mass transit	6.6%	1.9%
Work at home	3.5%	3.1%
Mass transit miles per capita	6.61	1.87

INTERCITY SERVICES	AREA	U.S. AVG
Major airports within 60 miles	4	1
Size of regional airport	Large	Large
Daily airline activity	1697	686
Amtrak service	Yes	No

AUTOMOTIVE	AREA	U.S. AVG
Insurance, annual premium	$3,345	$1,432
Gas, cost per gallon	$2.74	$2.49
Daily vehicle miles per capita	23.3	24.0

Leisure
Score: 100.0
Rank: 1

DINING & SHOPPING	AREA	U.S. AVG
Restaurant rating	8	2
Outlet mall score	184	42
No. Starbucks	328	13
No. warehouse clubs	24	2

ENTERTAINMENT	AREA	U.S. AVG
Professional sports rating	10	4
College sports rating	10	4
Zoo/aquarium rating	10	3
Amusement park rating	10	3
Botanical garden/ arboretum rating	10	4

OUTDOOR ACTIVITIES	AREA	U.S. AVG
Golf-course rating	10	4
Ski-area rating	10	3
Sq. miles inland water	4	4
Miles of coastline	55.1	10.7
National Park rating	10	3

Arts & Culture
Score: 97.9
Rank: 9

MEDIA & LIBRARIES	AREA	U.S. AVG
Arts radio rating	10	3
No. public libraries	238	27
Library volumes per capita	2.24	2.78

PERFORMING ARTS	AREA	U.S. AVG
Classical music rating	10	4
Ballet/dance rating	10	3
Professional theater rating	10	3
University arts programs rating	10	5

MUSEUMS	AREA	U.S. AVG
Overall museum rating	10	5
Art museum rating	10	5
Science museum rating	10	5
Children's museum rating	10	3

Louisville–Jefferson County, KY

Score: 79.7   **Rank: 44**   **2004 rank: 167**

Profile: Mid-size city
Location: Northern Kentucky along the Ohio River at the Indiana border, 100 miles southwest of Cincinnati
Elevation: 488 feet
Time zone: Eastern Standard Time

PRO	CON
Cost of living	Economic cycles
Arts and culture	High pollen/allergy score
Attractive historic districts	Commute times

Louisville (pronounced "lou-*ah*-vul" locally) is an industrial, shipping, and commercial center. It has a prosperous river-town character with a distinct Southern accent. Following the lead of nearby Lexington, Louisville recently merged its government with Jefferson County, and the results of that merger will be interesting to watch (such mergers have done well for Lexington and northern neighbor Indianapolis). Downtown contains a few modern buildings, but the skyline is indistinct overall. The shady historic districts east and south of town with gracious Southern-style, Victorian-era homes are far more interesting. Areas farther south are more blue-collar, while the west side of town is a mixed bag. The first Saturday of every May, Louisville becomes the center of the sports world with the running of the Kentucky Derby, a major local event. The city is known for production of autos, appliances, baseball bats, and healthcare management; is home to the University of Louisville; and is a busy air cargo hub. Nationally, the city's air service and spectator sports have become more important in recent years. The Ohio River offers some recreational opportunities, and the city is known for its excellent park system, with some new downtown and waterfront facilities under development. The historically and culturally interesting bourbon country lies 50 miles south in Bardstown, making a nice weekend trip. Downsides include a low enrollment in public schools, a high pollen/allergy score, congestion, and fairly long commute times for the type of area. But negatives are fairly minor and overall, Louisville offers a complete and improving package, hence the higher ranking.

The city is divided into two portions with different topographies. The east is rolling hillsides with mostly residential areas, while the west is a flat flood plain containing industry. Summers are usually warm and humid. Winters are moderately cold though hills to the north in Indiana block polar air. Snow may be observed on those hills while absent in the city and river valley. Spring and summer thunderstorms are common, often producing heavy amounts. Fall is normally the driest season. First freeze is late October; last is mid-April.

DEMOGRAPHICS	AREA	U.S. AVG	ETHNIC COMPOSITION	AREA	U.S. AVG	RESIDENT PROFILE	AREA	U.S. AVG
Population	1,203,842		White	82.8%	79.0%	Single	31.1%	32.4%
Population density per sq. mile	291.1	358.5	Black	13.3%	10.5%	Married	53.2%	52.7%
Population growth	16.4%	21.1%	Asian	1.3%	2.7%	Divorced/separated	15.7%	14.9%
Median age	37.2	36.1	Hispanic	2.1%	10.6%	Married with children	22.8%	23.7%
Percent Democrat	44.5%	44.5%	Religious observance	53.2%	48.9%	Single with children	9.5%	9.1%
Percent Republican	54.8%	54.5%	Diversity measure	31.1	40.1	Percent over age 65	12.4%	12.9%

Economy & Jobs
Score: 36.6
Rank: 237

INCOME	AREA	U.S. AVG	EMPLOYMENT	AREA	U.S. AVG	EMPLOYING INDUSTRIES	AREA	U.S. AVG
Per capita income	$24,792	$23,235	Unemployment rate	5.7%	4.7%	Largest: Manufacturing		
Household income	$46,980	$46,414	Recent job growth	1.1%	1.3%			
Household income < $25K	25.2%	26.2%	Projected future job growth	8.3%	11.5%	Percent manufacturing	18.4%	15.4%
Household income > $75K	26.2%	25.4%	White collar	57.5%	57.8%	Percent public sector	11.8%	15.7%
Household income growth	13.7%	13.6%	Blue collar	28.1%	25.2%	Percent construction	9.7%	9.9%

Cost of Living
Score: 42.0
Rank: 217

INDEXES & TAXES	AREA	U.S. AVG	HOUSING	AREA	U.S. AVG	NECESSITIES	AREA	U.S. AVG
Cost of Living Index	85.2	100.0	Median home price	$138,100	$220,000	Food Index	97.3	100.0
Buying Power Index	123.6	100.0	Home price appreciation	24.5%	10.1%	Housing Index	56.2	100.0
Income tax rate	7.71%	4.70%	Median rent	$579	$709	Utilities Index	101.3	100.0
Sales tax rate	6.00%	6.58%	Homes owned	66.6%	62.3%	Transportation Index	104.6	100.0
Property tax rate	$8.97	$12.00	Home price ratio	2.9	4.2	Healthcare Index	90.2	100.0
						Miscellaneous Cost Index	98.0	100.0

Climate
Score: 45.2
Rank: 204

TEMPERATURE	AREA	U.S. AVG
Average January low	24.5	26.2
Average July high	87.3	87.4
Annual days > 90°F	24	38
Annual days < 32°F	92	89
Annual days < 0°F	2	6

PRECIPITATION	AREA	U.S. AVG
Annual inches precipitation	43.0	37.7
Annual inches snowfall	17.0	7.0
Annual days precipitation	124	109
Annual days rain > 0.5 inches	28	22
Annual days snow > 1.5 inches	4	6

COMFORTS & HAZARDS	AREA	U.S. AVG
July relative humidity	69%	66%
Annual days mostly sunny	197	208
Annual days with thunderstorms	45	39
Tornado risk score	17	18
Hurricane risk score	6	13

TEMPERATURE

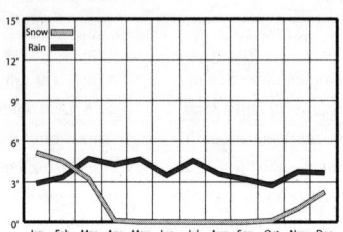

PRECIPITATION

DAYS OF CLOUDS & PRECIPITATION

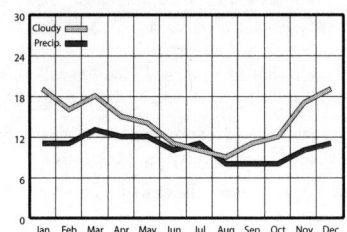

Education
Score: 34.5
Rank: 246

ACHIEVEMENT	AREA	U.S. AVG
High school degree	81.1%	82.7%
2-year college degree	5.8%	6.4%
4-year college degree	13.2%	15.7%
Graduate/professional degree	8.1%	8.9%

PUBLIC SCHOOLS	AREA	U.S. AVG
Expenditures per pupil	$5,975	$5,686
Student/teacher ratio	22.0	16.7
Attending public school	81.7%	90.1%
State SAT score	1124	1021
State ACT score	20.6*	20.9

HIGHER EDUCATION	AREA	U.S. AVG
No. 2-year colleges	16	4
No. 4-year colleges/universities	12	6
No. highly ranked universities	1	1

Health & Healthcare
Score: 21.1
Rank: 294

HAZARDS & ILLNESSES	AREA	U.S. AVG
Air-quality score	33	37
Water-quality score	17	52
Pollen/allergy score	87	61
Cancer mortality per capita	236.4	201.9
Depression days per month	4.2	3.5
Stress score	93	50

HEALTHCARE	AREA	U.S. AVG
Physicians per capita	276.1	244.2
Hospital beds per capita	435.8	420.0
No. teaching hospitals	6	3
Cost per doctor visit	$73	$77
Cost per dental visit	$69	$70

Crime
Score: 79.1
Rank: 79

CRIME	AREA	U.S. AVG
Violent crime rate	412.6	465.5
Change in violent crime rate	14.5%	-2.2%
Property crime rate	3,489.2	3,517.1
Change in property crime rate	3.4%	-2.1%

Transportation
Score: 66.8
Rank: 124

COMMUTE	AREA	U.S. AVG
Average commute time	25.5	27.4
Percent commutes > 60 mins.	4.4%	5.9%
Commute by auto	82.0%	78.9%
Commute by mass transit	1.9%	1.9%
Work at home	2.6%	3.1%
Mass transit miles per capita	1.91	1.87

INTERCITY SERVICES	AREA	U.S. AVG
Major airports within 60 miles	2	1
Size of regional airport	Large	Large
Daily airline activity	996	686
Amtrak service	No	No

AUTOMOTIVE	AREA	U.S. AVG
Insurance, annual premium	$1,762	$1,432
Gas, cost per gallon	$2.44	$2.49
Daily vehicle miles per capita	27.5	24.0

Leisure
Score: 65.8
Rank: 128

DINING & SHOPPING	AREA	U.S. AVG
Restaurant rating	3	2
Outlet mall score	26	42
No. Starbucks	10	13
No. warehouse clubs	0	2

ENTERTAINMENT	AREA	U.S. AVG
Professional sports rating	3	4
College sports rating	6	4
Zoo/aquarium rating	6	3
Amusement park rating	9	3
Botanical garden/ arboretum rating	9	4

OUTDOOR ACTIVITIES	AREA	U.S. AVG
Golf-course rating	5	4
Ski-area rating	1	3
Sq. miles inland water	3	4
Miles of coastline	0.0	10.7
National Park rating	1	3

Arts & Culture
Score: 71.7
Rank: 106

MEDIA & LIBRARIES	AREA	U.S. AVG
Arts radio rating	5	3
No. public libraries	44	27
Library volumes per capita	2.00	2.78

PERFORMING ARTS	AREA	U.S. AVG
Classical music rating	4	4
Ballet/dance rating	3	3
Professional theater rating	10	3
University arts programs rating	8	5

MUSEUMS	AREA	U.S. AVG
Overall museum rating	9	5
Art museum rating	8	5
Science museum rating	8	5
Children's museum rating	1	3

Lubbock, TX

Score: 61.0   **Rank:** 168   **2004 rank:** 120

Profile: Small city
Location: Southern edge of Texas Panhandle
Elevation: 3,241 feet
Time zone: Central Standard Time

PRO	CON
Cost of living	Crime rates
College influence	Isolation
Healthcare	Recreation

Lubbock is the commercial, educational, and cultural center for the southern part of the Texas Panhandle known as the South Plains. The economic base is a mix of industry, agriculture, government, and healthcare. There is a small high-tech industry but most employment is provided by agriculture-related businesses, healthcare, and education. The 28,000-student Texas Tech University provides a strong economic and cultural influence, as well as a college-town element with more than the usual nightlife and live music. The isolated location is 120 miles from the nearest metro area (Amarillo) and 320 miles from the Dallas–Fort Worth metroplex. The flat, monotonous landscape outside of town offers little to do. Predictably, cost of living (80.8) and housing

(median home price $116,800) are low. Discount air service is very important to Lubbock residents.

Lubbock is located in the South Plains region, which is predominately flat but with numerous, small, mostly dry, stream valleys. Summer temperatures are pleasant with low humidity on the hottest days; tropical air invades occasionally bringing heavy afternoon thunderstorms. Winters are variable and can become cold due to altitude and northerly cold-air invasions. Snowfall is generally light and unlikely to remain on the ground beyond a few days. Prolonged, sometimes dusty winds in excess of 25 mph may occur in late winter and spring. First freeze is early November; last is late April.

Population

DEMOGRAPHICS	AREA	U.S. AVG
Population	259,577	
Population density per sq. mile	144.3	358.5
Population growth	13.0%	21.1%
Median age	31.7	36.1
Percent Democrat	24.2%	44.5%
Percent Republican	75.2%	54.5%

ETHNIC COMPOSITION	AREA	U.S. AVG
White	72.9%	79.0%
Black	7.5%	10.5%
Asian	1.2%	2.7%
Hispanic	30.2%	10.6%
Religious observance	60.3%	48.9%
Diversity measure	67.3	40.1

RESIDENT PROFILE	AREA	U.S. AVG
Single	35.4%	32.4%
Married	49.5%	52.7%
Divorced/separated	15.0%	14.9%
Married with children	22.2%	23.7%
Single with children	9.5%	9.1%
Percent over age 65	11.3%	12.9%

Economy & Jobs
Score: 49.5
Rank: 190

INCOME	AREA	U.S. AVG
Per capita income	$19,459	$23,235
Household income	$35,758	$46,414
Household income < $25K	35.7%	26.2%
Household income > $75K	17.9%	25.4%
Household income growth	11.7%	13.6%

EMPLOYMENT	AREA	U.S. AVG
Unemployment rate	4.3%	4.7%
Recent job growth	2.3%	1.3%
Projected future job growth	6.8%	11.5%
White collar	61.7%	57.8%
Blue collar	20.2%	25.2%

EMPLOYING INDUSTRIES	AREA	U.S. AVG
Largest: Healthcare & Social Assistance		
Percent manufacturing	10.8%	15.4%
Percent public sector	19.9%	15.7%
Percent construction	9.4%	9.9%

Cost of Living
Score: 87.2
Rank: 49

INDEXES & TAXES	AREA	U.S. AVG
Cost of Living Index	80.8	100.0
Buying Power Index	99.2	100.0
Income tax rate	0.00%	4.70%
Sales tax rate	8.25%	6.58%
Property tax rate	$16.94	$12.00

HOUSING	AREA	U.S. AVG
Median home price	$116,800	$220,000
Home price appreciation	25.9%	10.1%
Median rent	$618	$709
Homes owned	55.0%	62.3%
Home price ratio	3.3	4.2

NECESSITIES	AREA	U.S. AVG
Food Index	93.1	100.0
Housing Index	50.0	100.0
Utilities Index	100.7	100.0
Transportation Index	102.6	100.0
Healthcare Index	102.5	100.0
Miscellaneous Cost Index	96.2	100.0

Climate
Score: 86.4
Rank: 52

TEMPERATURE	AREA	U.S. AVG
Average January low	24.8	26.2
Average July high	92.4	87.4
Annual days > 90°F	77	38
Annual days < 32°F	98	89
Annual days < 0°F	0	6

PRECIPITATION	AREA	U.S. AVG
Annual inches precipitation	18.0	37.7
Annual inches snowfall	9.6	7.0
Annual days precipitation	60	109
Annual days rain > 0.5 inches	10	22
Annual days snow > 1.5 inches	1	6

COMFORTS & HAZARDS	AREA	U.S. AVG
July relative humidity	56%	66%
Annual days mostly sunny	267	208
Annual days with thunderstorms	45	39
Tornado risk score	73	18
Hurricane risk score	0	13

TEMPERATURE

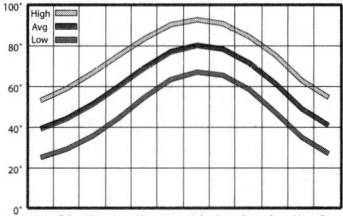

PRECIPITATION

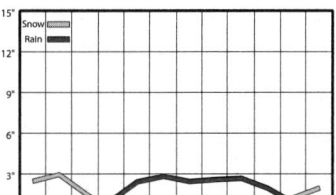

DAYS OF CLOUDS & PRECIPITATION

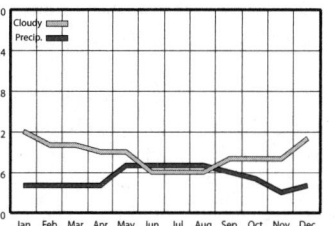

ACHIEVEMENT	AREA	U.S. AVG	PUBLIC SCHOOLS	AREA	U.S. AVG	HIGHER EDUCATION	AREA	U.S. AVG
High school degree	78.6%	82.7%	Expenditures per pupil	$5,301	$5,686	No. 2-year colleges	2	4
2-year college degree	4.6%	6.4%	Student/teacher ratio	13.4	16.7	No. 4-year colleges/universities	3	6
4-year college degree	16.1%	15.7%	Attending public school	95.5%	90.1%	No. highly ranked universities	1	1
Graduate/professional degree	8.4%	8.9%	State SAT score	997*	1021			
			State ACT score	20.3	20.9			

Education
Score: 51.6
Rank: 182

HAZARDS & ILLNESSES	AREA	U.S. AVG	HEALTHCARE	AREA	U.S. AVG	CRIME	AREA	U.S. AVG
Air-quality score	30	37	Physicians per capita	368.9	244.2	Violent crime rate	904.5	465.5
Water-quality score	60	52	Hospital beds per capita	970.4	420.0	Change in violent crime rate	0.7%	-2.2%
Pollen/allergy score	69	61	No. teaching hospitals	3	3	Property crime rate	5,509.7	3,517.1
Cancer mortality per capita	155.9	201.9	Cost per doctor visit	$83	$77	Change in property crime rate	-2.2%	-2.1%
Depression days per month	3.9	3.5	Cost per dental visit	$66	$70			
Stress score	53	50						

Health & Healthcare
Score: 88.2
Rank: 45

Crime
Score: 4.8
Rank: 355

COMMUTE	AREA	U.S. AVG	INTERCITY SERVICES	AREA	U.S. AVG	AUTOMOTIVE	AREA	U.S. AVG
Average commute time	18.9	27.4	Major airports within 60 miles	0	1	Insurance, annual premium	$1,221	$1,432
Percent commutes > 60 mins.	2.7%	5.9%	Size of regional airport	Small	Large	Gas, cost per gallon	$2.43	$2.49
Commute by auto	80.8%	78.9%	Daily airline activity	60	686	Daily vehicle miles per capita	20.8	24.0
Commute by mass transit	0.8%	1.9%	Amtrak service	No	No			
Work at home	2.5%	3.1%						
Mass transit miles per capita	0.83	1.87						

Transportation
Score: 60.2
Rank: 150

DINING & SHOPPING	AREA	U.S. AVG	ENTERTAINMENT	AREA	U.S. AVG	OUTDOOR ACTIVITIES	AREA	U.S. AVG
Restaurant rating	1	2	Professional sports rating	3	4	Golf-course rating	2	4
Outlet mall score	0	42	College sports rating	4	4	Ski-area rating	1	3
No. Starbucks	3	13	Zoo/aquarium rating	1	3	Sq. miles inland water	2	4
No. warehouse clubs	0	2	Amusement park rating	4	3	Miles of coastline	0.0	10.7
			Botanical garden/ arboretum rating	2	4	National Park rating	2	3

Leisure
Score: 27.8
Rank: 269

MEDIA & LIBRARIES	AREA	U.S. AVG	PERFORMING ARTS	AREA	U.S. AVG	MUSEUMS	AREA	U.S. AVG
Arts radio rating	1	3	Classical music rating	4	4	Overall museum rating	5	5
No. public libraries	10	27	Ballet/dance rating	1	3	Art museum rating	1	5
Library volumes per capita	1.69	2.78	Professional theater rating	1	3	Science museum rating	5	5
			University arts programs rating	7	5	Children's museum rating	1	3

Arts & Culture
Score: 26.2
Rank: 276

Lynchburg, VA

Score: 59.4   **Rank:** 179   **2004 rank:** 15

Profile: Small city
Location: West-central Virginia along James River, 50 miles east of Roanoke
Elevation: 648 feet
Time zone: Eastern Standard Time

PRO	CON
Historic interest	Growth and sprawl
Cost of living	Air service
Low crime rates	Arts and culture

Lynchburg is a small Virginia city with an Old South feel and views of the Blue Ridge and Appalachian mountains. Downtown is a mix of old and new, and the city is known for the historic districts of refined homes on the surrounding hilltops. Five of these districts are included in the National Register of Historic Districts. Additionally, five small colleges give a minor college town feel. The area has a few good museums and modest entertainment assets. Mountains to the west and Smith Mountain Lake to the south offer above-average outdoor recreation. Cost of living and housing are moderate among Virginia's metropolitan areas. The economy is not among Virginia's best, but not the worst either, supported by steel pipe and furniture manufacturing, healthcare, and an assortment of smaller businesses. The city has had problems with urban sprawl, particularly to the southeast and in the downtown area, to the extent that it became a court battleground for the sprawl-producing practice of annexation. Downtown is on the mend, and the city won a 2006 National Trust for Historic Preservation Great American Main Street Award, but there are still areas of neglect.

Lynchburg is situated in the James River Valley at the eastern edge of the Blue Ridge Mountains. Nearby terrain is hilly with deciduous forest and sheltered valleys. Summers are warm and fairly humid with cool evening breezes and cooler conditions in nearby hills. Rainfall is evenly distributed throughout the year with frequent summer thunderstorms. Fall brings periods of cloudy, cool weather with high humidity and light rain or drizzle. Winter cold fronts bring dry, invigorating air with clear skies. There are snow showers, but the mountains to the west block many storms, high winds, and blasts of bitter cold. First freeze is late October; last is mid-April.

Population

DEMOGRAPHICS	AREA	U.S. AVG	ETHNIC COMPOSITION	AREA	U.S. AVG	RESIDENT PROFILE	AREA	U.S. AVG
Population	232,081		White	79.1%	79.0%	Single	30.7%	32.4%
Population density per sq. mile	109.3	358.5	Black	18.3%	10.5%	Married	54.6%	52.7%
Population growth	14.2%	21.1%	Asian	0.8%	2.7%	Divorced/separated	14.7%	14.9%
Median age	38.6	36.1	Hispanic	1.0%	10.6%	Married with children	21.6%	23.7%
Percent Democrat	35.3%	44.5%	Religious observance	56.4%	48.9%	Single with children	8.7%	9.1%
Percent Republican	63.7%	54.5%	Diversity measure	33.5	40.1	Percent over age 65	15.2%	12.9%

Economy & Jobs
Score: 64.7
Rank: 132

INCOME	AREA	U.S. AVG	EMPLOYMENT	AREA	U.S. AVG	EMPLOYING INDUSTRIES	AREA	U.S. AVG
Per capita income	$21,182	$23,235	Unemployment rate	4.0%	4.7%	Largest: Manufacturing		
Household income	$40,996	$46,414	Recent job growth	2.7%	1.3%			
Household income < $25K	29.3%	26.2%	Projected future job growth	8.5%	11.5%	Percent manufacturing	19.6%	15.4%
Household income > $75K	19.6%	25.4%	White collar	54.5%	57.8%	Percent public sector	12.7%	15.7%
Household income growth	10.3%	13.6%	Blue collar	30.3%	25.2%	Percent construction	10.7%	9.9%

Cost of Living
Score: 68.7
Rank: 117

INDEXES & TAXES	AREA	U.S. AVG	HOUSING	AREA	U.S. AVG	NECESSITIES	AREA	U.S. AVG
Cost of Living Index	83.0	100.0	Median home price	$148,900	$220,000	Food Index	97.6	100.0
Buying Power Index	110.7	100.0	Home price appreciation	39.3%	10.1%	Housing Index	82.6	100.0
Income tax rate	5.75%	4.70%	Median rent	$556	$709	Utilities Index	74.2	100.0
Sales tax rate	5.00%	6.58%	Homes owned	68.2%	62.3%	Transportation Index	88.8	100.0
Property tax rate	$6.57	$12.00	Home price ratio	3.6	4.2	Healthcare Index	98.2	100.0
						Miscellaneous Cost Index	96.8	100.0

Climate
Score: 71.9
Rank: 104

TEMPERATURE	AREA	U.S. AVG	PRECIPITATION	AREA	U.S. AVG	COMFORTS & HAZARDS	AREA	U.S. AVG
Average January low	27.3	26.2	Annual inches precipitation	38.3	37.7	July relative humidity	70%	66%
Average July high	86.1	87.4	Annual inches snowfall	18.2	7.0	Annual days mostly sunny	218	208
Annual days > 90°F	19	38	Annual days precipitation	125	109	Annual days with thunderstorms	41	39
Annual days < 32°F	94	89	Annual days rain > 0.5 inches	28	22	Tornado risk score	2	18
Annual days < 0°F	1	6	Annual days snow > 1.5 inches	4	6	Hurricane risk score	14	13

TEMPERATURE

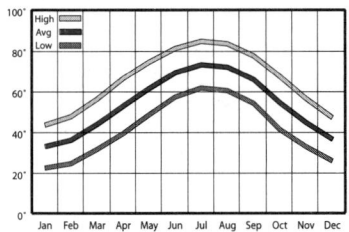

PRECIPITATION

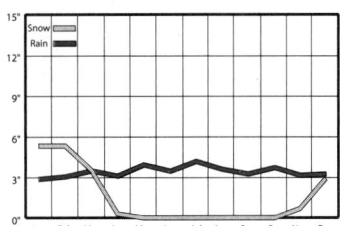

DAYS OF CLOUDS & PRECIPITATION

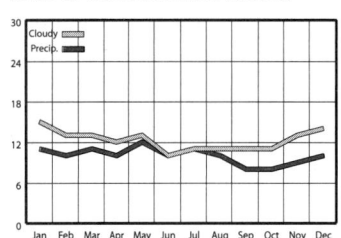

Education
Score: 36.6
Rank: 238

ACHIEVEMENT	AREA	U.S. AVG	PUBLIC SCHOOLS	AREA	U.S. AVG	HIGHER EDUCATION	AREA	U.S. AVG
High school degree	76.0%	82.7%	Expenditures per pupil	$4,794	$5,686	No. 2-year colleges	3	4
2-year college degree	5.6%	6.4%	Student/teacher ratio	14.2	16.7	No. 4-year colleges/universities	4	6
4-year college degree	12.3%	15.7%	Attending public school	93.6%	90.1%	No. highly ranked universities	2	1
Graduate/professional degree	6.5%	8.9%	State SAT score	1025*	1021			
			State ACT score	21.1	20.9			

Health & Healthcare
Score: 97.3
Rank: 11

HAZARDS & ILLNESSES	AREA	U.S. AVG	HEALTHCARE	AREA	U.S. AVG	CRIME	AREA	U.S. AVG
Air-quality score	70	37	Physicians per capita	176.2	244.2	Violent crime rate	202.2	465.5
Water-quality score	93	52	Hospital beds per capita	1023.3	420.0	Change in violent crime rate	2.6%	-2.2%
Pollen/allergy score	56	61	No. teaching hospitals	2	3	Property crime rate	2,002.6	3,517.1
Cancer mortality per capita	202.0	201.9	Cost per doctor visit	$65	$77	Change in property crime rate	0.1%	-2.1%
Depression days per month	2.7	3.5	Cost per dental visit	$60	$70			
Stress score	16	50						

Crime
Score: 81.6
Rank: 70

Transportation
Score: 13.1
Rank: 326

COMMUTE	AREA	U.S. AVG	INTERCITY SERVICES	AREA	U.S. AVG	AUTOMOTIVE	AREA	U.S. AVG
Average commute time	24.8	27.4	Major airports within 60 miles	0	1	Insurance, annual premium	$986	$1,432
Percent commutes > 60 mins.	4.8%	5.9%	Size of regional airport	Small	Large	Gas, cost per gallon	$2.38	$2.49
Commute by auto	81.5%	78.9%	Daily airline activity	173	686	Daily vehicle miles per capita	25.3	24.0
Commute by mass transit	1.1%	1.9%	Amtrak service	Yes	No			
Work at home	2.6%	3.1%						
Mass transit miles per capita	1.09	1.87						

DINING & SHOPPING	AREA	U.S. AVG	ENTERTAINMENT	AREA	U.S. AVG	OUTDOOR ACTIVITIES	AREA	U.S. AVG
Restaurant rating	1	2	Professional sports rating	2	4	Golf-course rating	2	4
Outlet mall score	0	42	College sports rating	3	4	Ski-area rating	4	3
No. Starbucks	2	13	Zoo/aquarium rating	1	3	Sq. miles inland water	2	4
No. warehouse clubs	1	2	Amusement park rating	1	3	Miles of coastline	0.0	10.7
			Botanical garden/ arboretum rating	1	4	National Park rating	4	3

Leisure
Score: 29.9
Rank: 261

MEDIA & LIBRARIES	AREA	U.S. AVG	PERFORMING ARTS	AREA	U.S. AVG	MUSEUMS	AREA	U.S. AVG
Arts radio rating	1	3	Classical music rating	2	4	Overall museum rating	2	5
No. public libraries	15	27	Ballet/dance rating	3	3	Art museum rating	3	5
Library volumes per capita	2.67	2.78	Professional theater rating	1	3	Science museum rating	1	5
			University arts programs rating	7	5	Children's museum rating	1	3

Arts & Culture
Score: 35.6
Rank: 241

Macon–Warner Robins, GA

Score: 67.4   **Rank:** 116   **2004 rank:** 302

Profile: Small city/military town
Location: Central Georgia, 80 miles southeast of Atlanta
Elevation: 354 feet
Time zone: Eastern Standard Time

PRO
Cost of living and
housing
Historic interest
Healthcare

CON
Summer heat
Property crime
Entertainment

Macon is a typical mid-size Southern city in both appearance and feel, with roots as a textile mill town. The downtown area is a mixed bag but has a large and well-used riverfront park, and the city has more entries on the National Register of Historic Places than any other city in Georgia. The area has a richer cultural and art presence than many others of its type. The Georgia Music Hall of Fame highlights state music achievements, and the city is well known for Southern-style music, food, and restaurants. Three hospitals add a strong healthcare presence. The central location and a business-friendly environment have attracted an assortment of manufacturers and distributors, including automotive and aerospace firms. Warner Robins is a military town 15 miles south supporting the large Warner Robins Air Force Base. Area downsides include high property crime, low educational attainment, and relatively few entertainment options. The area is close, but not that close, to Atlanta, and the part it is closest to, the south side, is least attractive. That said, convenience to Atlanta and its Hartsfield International Airport does offer some advantages. Bottom line: Macon offers small-town advantages in the shadow of a big city in a genuine Southern setting,

The city sits where the Piedmont plateau meets the broad coastal plain, giving some hills to the west and broad, flat forests; farmland; and wetlands to the southeast. In summer, warm, humid periods are cooled by dry northwesterly winds as well as by showers and thunderstorms. Some storms are severe, with tornadoes observed every year in adjacent counties. The Appalachians block some cold air in the winter. Snow occurs occasionally especially in surrounding hilly areas, but amounts are usually small. First freeze is early November; last is mid-March.

DEMOGRAPHICS	AREA	U.S. AVG	ETHNIC COMPOSITION	AREA	U.S. AVG	RESIDENT PROFILE	AREA	U.S. AVG
Population	353,400		White	60.4%	79.0%	Single	32.2%	32.4%
Population density per sq. mile	168.2	358.5	Black	36.0%	10.5%	Married	51.4%	52.7%
Population growth	22.1%	21.1%	Asian	1.4%	2.7%	Divorced/separated	16.4%	14.9%
Median age	35.0	36.1	Hispanic	1.9%	10.6%	Married with children	23.2%	23.7%
Percent Democrat	41.7%	44.5%	Religious observance	45.0%	48.9%	Single with children	11.9%	9.1%
Percent Republican	57.7%	54.5%	Diversity measure	49.4	40.1	Percent over age 65	11.3%	12.9%

Population

INCOME	AREA	U.S. AVG	EMPLOYMENT	AREA	U.S. AVG	EMPLOYING INDUSTRIES	AREA	U.S. AVG
Per capita income	$21,815	$23,235	Unemployment rate	5.8%	4.7%	Largest: Healthcare & Social Assistance		
Household income	$44,136	$46,414	Recent job growth	1.5%	1.3%			
Household income < $25K	28.1%	26.2%	Projected future job growth	8.8%	11.5%	Percent manufacturing	14.3%	15.4%
Household income > $75K	24.2%	25.4%	White collar	58.0%	57.8%	Percent public sector	22.1%	15.7%
Household income growth	12.9%	13.6%	Blue collar	26.4%	25.2%	Percent construction	12.0%	9.9%

Economy & Jobs
Score: 41.2
Rank: 219

INDEXES & TAXES	AREA	U.S. AVG	HOUSING	AREA	U.S. AVG	NECESSITIES	AREA	U.S. AVG
Cost of Living Index	83.3	100.0	Median home price	$126,800	$220,000	Food Index	99.0	100.0
Buying Power Index	118.8	100.0	Home price appreciation	24.9%	10.1%	Housing Index	58.6	100.0
Income tax rate	6.00%	4.70%	Median rent	$582	$709	Utilities Index	101.2	100.0
Sales tax rate	6.56%	6.58%	Homes owned	61.8%	62.3%	Transportation Index	95.4	100.0
Property tax rate	$9.66	$12.00	Home price ratio	2.9	4.2	Healthcare Index	93.1	100.0
						Miscellaneous Cost Index	100.2	100.0

Cost of Living
Score: 50.8
Rank: 184

Climate
Score: 50.5
Rank: 184

TEMPERATURE	AREA	U.S. AVG
Average January low	36.9	26.2
Average July high	92.1	87.4
Annual days > 90°F	78	38
Annual days < 32°F	51	89
Annual days < 0°F	0	6

PRECIPITATION	AREA	U.S. AVG
Annual inches precipitation	44.5	37.7
Annual inches snowfall	0.9	7.0
Annual days precipitation	111	109
Annual days rain > 0.5 inches	28	22
Annual days snow > 1.5 inches	1	6

COMFORTS & HAZARDS	AREA	U.S. AVG
July relative humidity	72%	66%
Annual days mostly sunny	217	208
Annual days with thunderstorms	56	39
Tornado risk score	19	18
Hurricane risk score	28	13

TEMPERATURE

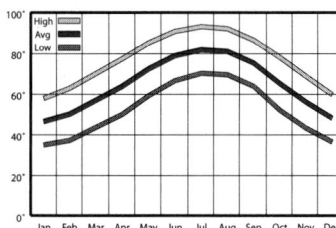

PRECIPITATION

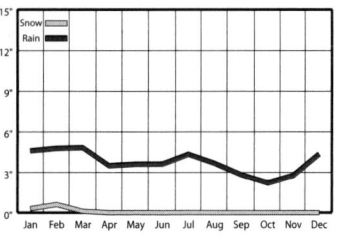

DAYS OF CLOUDS & PRECIPITATION

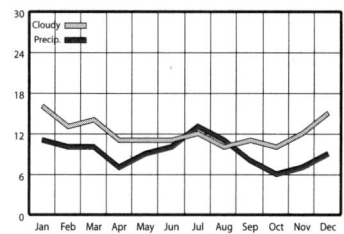

Education
Score: 24.3
Rank: 283

ACHIEVEMENT	AREA	U.S. AVG
High school degree	79.4%	82.7%
2-year college degree	5.3%	6.4%
4-year college degree	12.1%	15.7%
Graduate/professional degree	7.2%	8.9%

PUBLIC SCHOOLS	AREA	U.S. AVG
Expenditures per pupil	$5,247	$5,686
Student/teacher ratio	15.1	16.7
Attending public school	88.7%	90.1%
State SAT score	990*	1021
State ACT score	20.2	20.9

HIGHER EDUCATION	AREA	U.S. AVG
No. 2-year colleges	3	4
No. 4-year colleges/universities	3	6
No. highly ranked universities	0	1

Health & Healthcare
Score: 84.8
Rank: 58

HAZARDS & ILLNESSES	AREA	U.S. AVG
Air-quality score	45	37
Water-quality score	60	52
Pollen/allergy score	63	61
Cancer mortality per capita	168.9	201.9
Depression days per month	3.8	3.5
Stress score	73	50

HEALTHCARE	AREA	U.S. AVG
Physicians per capita	243.6	244.2
Hospital beds per capita	435.2	420.0
No. teaching hospitals	1	3
Cost per doctor visit	$71	$77
Cost per dental visit	$61	$70

Crime
Score: 44.9
Rank: 206

CRIME	AREA	U.S. AVG
Violent crime rate	416.0	465.5
Change in violent crime rate	16.3%	-2.2%
Property crime rate	4,947.4	3,517.1
Change in property crime rate	-5.2%	-2.1%

Transportation
Score: 82.9
Rank: 63

COMMUTE	AREA	U.S. AVG
Average commute time	24.6	27.4
Percent commutes > 60 mins.	4.5%	5.9%
Commute by auto	82.2%	78.9%
Commute by mass transit	0.9%	1.9%
Work at home	1.8%	3.1%
Mass transit miles per capita	0.90	1.87

INTERCITY SERVICES	AREA	U.S. AVG
Major airports within 60 miles	1	1
Size of regional airport	Large	Large
Daily airline activity	1423	686
Amtrak service	No	No

AUTOMOTIVE	AREA	U.S. AVG
Insurance, annual premium	$1,715	$1,432
Gas, cost per gallon	$2.43	$2.49
Daily vehicle miles per capita	30.6	24.0

Leisure
Score: 25.9
Rank: 276

DINING & SHOPPING	AREA	U.S. AVG
Restaurant rating	1	2
Outlet mall score	77	42
No. Starbucks	1	13
No. warehouse clubs	1	2

ENTERTAINMENT	AREA	U.S. AVG
Professional sports rating	2	4
College sports rating	2	4
Zoo/aquarium rating	1	3
Amusement park rating	1	3
Botanical garden/ arboretum rating	2	4

OUTDOOR ACTIVITIES	AREA	U.S. AVG
Golf-course rating	3	4
Ski-area rating	1	3
Sq. miles inland water	2	4
Miles of coastline	0.0	10.7
National Park rating	4	3

Arts & Culture
Score: 49.2
Rank: 190

MEDIA & LIBRARIES	AREA	U.S. AVG
Arts radio rating	1	3
No. public libraries	18	27
Library volumes per capita	1.81	2.78

PERFORMING ARTS	AREA	U.S. AVG
Classical music rating	3	4
Ballet/dance rating	1	3
Professional theater rating	1	3
University arts programs rating	7	5

MUSEUMS	AREA	U.S. AVG
Overall museum rating	7	5
Art museum rating	7	5
Science museum rating	8	5
Children's museum rating	1	3

Madera, CA

Profile: Small city
Location: California's San Joaquin Valley, 20 miles northwest of Fresno
Elevation: 272 feet
Time zone: Pacific Standard Time

PRO	CON
Nearby mountains	High home prices
Mild winters	Low educational attainment
Diverse economy	Arts and culture

Madera means "lumber" in Spanish. However, you won't find many naturally occurring trees or much of a timber industry in this mostly agricultural San Joaquin Valley town. It is located smack in the center of California's broad, flat, agricultural Central Valley. The name dates back to the 1870s when loggers built a flume to bring logs from the vast Sierra to the east to a railroad loading point. The Madera economy is driven by agriculture including wine growing and fruit and nut orchards, but also by a variety of manufacturing businesses including glass and plastic products, farm equipment, and machinery. These businesses enjoy relatively low costs, a good labor force, transportation, access to California markets, and Fresno services. Some preferring a small-town lifestyle live here and commute to Fresno. However, perhaps because of proximity to Fresno, the area has a higher cost of living and housing profile than many other valley towns. There are some good healthcare facilities, notably a large children's hospital, but most go to Fresno for city services. Like all Central Valley towns, access to Sierra recreation, and particularly Yosemite, Sequoia, and Kings Canyon national parks, is a plus. But home prices are sky high for what you get and there isn't a lot to do in the immediate vicinity.

As with most Central Valley towns, the terrain is completely flat and treeless (save for the numerous orchards), with mountains rising sharply to the east and less dramatically to the west but only visible on clear days. Summers are hot and completely dry with pleasant evenings if breezes are right (or even exist); winters are mild. Almost all precipitation falls in winter, and temperatures remain in a 35°F to 60°F range with persistent fog at times.

Population

DEMOGRAPHICS	AREA	U.S. AVG	ETHNIC COMPOSITION	AREA	U.S. AVG	RESIDENT PROFILE	AREA	U.S. AVG
Population	136,880		White	60.8%	79.0%	Single	32.1%	32.4%
Population density per sq. mile	64.1	358.5	Black	3.6%	10.5%	Married	50.8%	52.7%
Population growth	55.4%	21.1%	Asian	1.6%	2.7%	Divorced/separated	17.1%	14.9%
Median age	32.3	36.1	Hispanic	48.4%	10.6%	Married with children	29.2%	23.7%
Percent Democrat	34.7%	44.5%	Religious observance	31.6%	48.9%	Single with children	10.7%	9.1%
Percent Republican	64.0%	54.5%	Diversity measure	77.7	40.1	Percent over age 65	10.9%	12.9%

Economy & Jobs
Score: 64.4
Rank: 134

INCOME	AREA	U.S. AVG	EMPLOYMENT	AREA	U.S. AVG	EMPLOYING INDUSTRIES	AREA	U.S. AVG
Per capita income	$16,357	$23,235	Unemployment rate	7.0%	4.7%	Largest: Healthcare & Social Assistance		
Household income	$41,426	$46,414	Recent job growth	3.2%	1.3%			
Household income < $25K	30.1%	26.2%	Projected future job growth	22.6%	11.5%	Percent manufacturing	15.3%	15.4%
Household income > $75K	20.9%	25.4%	White collar	46.2%	57.8%	Percent public sector	17.9%	15.7%
Household income growth	14.2%	13.6%	Blue collar	25.5%	25.2%	Percent construction	10.2%	9.9%

Cost of Living
Score: 12.0
Rank: 328

INDEXES & TAXES	AREA	U.S. AVG	HOUSING	AREA	U.S. AVG	NECESSITIES	AREA	U.S. AVG
Cost of Living Index	119.7	100.0	Median home price	$299,000	$220,000	Food Index	113.5	100.0
Buying Power Index	77.6	100.0	Home price appreciation	143.7%	10.1%	Housing Index	142.0	100.0
Income tax rate	6.00%	4.70%	Median rent	$687	$709	Utilities Index	124.7	100.0
Sales tax rate	7.75%	6.58%	Homes owned	59.5%	62.3%	Transportation Index	113.4	100.0
Property tax rate	$9.87	$12.00	Home price ratio	7.2	4.2	Healthcare Index	117.1	100.0
						Miscellaneous Cost Index	106.8	100.0

Climate
Score: 94.7
Rank: 21

TEMPERATURE	AREA	U.S. AVG	PRECIPITATION	AREA	U.S. AVG	COMFORTS & HAZARDS	AREA	U.S. AVG
Average January low	37.0	26.2	Annual inches precipitation	10.6	37.7	July relative humidity	24%	66%
Average July high	98.0	87.4	Annual inches snowfall	0.0	7.0	Annual days mostly sunny	271	208
Annual days > 90°F	107	38	Annual days precipitation	45	109	Annual days with thunderstorms	6	39
Annual days < 32°F	29	89	Annual days rain > 0.5 inches	6	22	Tornado risk score	8	18
Annual days < 0°F	0	6	Annual days snow > 1.5 inches	0	6	Hurricane risk score	0	13

TEMPERATURE

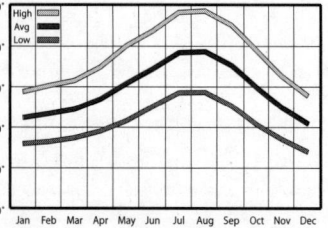

PRECIPITATION

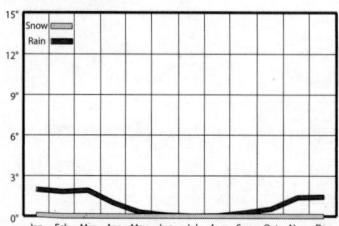

DAYS OF CLOUDS & PRECIPITATION

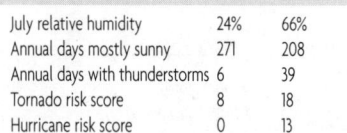
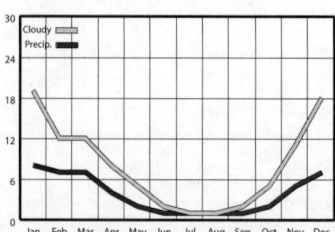

ACHIEVEMENT	AREA	U.S. AVG	PUBLIC SCHOOLS	AREA	U.S. AVG	HIGHER EDUCATION	AREA	U.S. AVG
High school degree	64.9%	82.7%	Expenditures per pupil	$5,375	$5,686	No. 2-year colleges	0	4
2-year college degree	5.7%	6.4%	Student/teacher ratio	20.4	16.7	No. 4-year colleges/universities	0	6
4-year college degree	8.1%	15.7%	Attending public school	98.4%	90.1%	No. highly ranked universities	0	1
Graduate/professional degree	3.8%	8.9%	State SAT score	1019*	1021			
			State ACT score	21.6	20.9			

Education Score: 2.7 Rank: 363

HAZARDS & ILLNESSES	AREA	U.S. AVG	HEALTHCARE	AREA	U.S. AVG	CRIME	AREA	U.S. AVG
Air-quality score	44	37	Physicians per capita	89.9	244.2	Violent crime rate	522.6	465.5
Water-quality score	16	52	Hospital beds per capita	244.7	420.0	Change in violent crime rate	-2.4%	-2.2%
Pollen/allergy score	60	61	No. teaching hospitals	1	3	Property crime rate	2,942.6	3,517.1
Cancer mortality per capita	154.7	201.9	Cost per doctor visit	$91	$77	Change in property crime rate	0.7%	-2.1%
Depression days per month	3.8	3.5	Cost per dental visit	$79	$70			
Stress score	88	50						

Health & Healthcare Score: 35.6 Rank: 240

Crime Score: 77.3 Rank: 86

COMMUTE	AREA	U.S. AVG	INTERCITY SERVICES	AREA	U.S. AVG	AUTOMOTIVE	AREA	U.S. AVG
Average commute time	27.7	27.4	Major airports within 60 miles	0	1	Insurance, annual premium	$1,555	$1,432
Percent commutes > 60 mins.	9.0%	5.9%	Size of regional airport	Small	Large	Gas, cost per gallon	$2.69	$2.49
Commute by auto	73.1%	78.9%	Daily airline activity	75	686	Daily vehicle miles per capita	14.8	24.0
Commute by mass transit	0.7%	1.9%	Amtrak service	Yes	No			
Work at home	4.2%	3.1%						
Mass transit miles per capita	0.73	1.87						

Transportation Score: 0.3 Rank: 372

DINING & SHOPPING	AREA	U.S. AVG	ENTERTAINMENT	AREA	U.S. AVG	OUTDOOR ACTIVITIES	AREA	U.S. AVG
Restaurant rating	3	2	Professional sports rating	3	4	Golf-course rating	3	4
Outlet mall score	40	42	College sports rating	5	4	Ski-area rating	5	3
No. Starbucks	3	13	Zoo/aquarium rating	5	3	Sq. miles inland water	4	4
No. warehouse clubs	0	2	Amusement park rating	8	3	Miles of coastline	0.0	10.7
			Botanical garden/arboretum rating	3	4	Miles of coastline		
						National Park rating	10	3

Leisure Score: 76.7 Rank: 87

MEDIA & LIBRARIES	AREA	U.S. AVG	PERFORMING ARTS	AREA	U.S. AVG	MUSEUMS	AREA	U.S. AVG
Arts radio rating	5	3	Classical music rating	4	4	Overall museum rating	3	5
No. public libraries	5	27	Ballet/dance rating	3	3	Art museum rating	2	5
Library volumes per capita	1.42	2.78	Professional theater rating	1	3	Science museum rating	1	5
			University arts programs rating	1	5	Children's museum rating	1	3

Arts & Culture Score: 44.9 Rank: 205

Madison, WI

Score: 71.9   Rank: 78   2004 rank: 37

Profile: Capital city/college town
Location: South-central Wisconsin
Elevation: 863 feet
Time zone: Central Standard Time

PRO	CON
Attractive downtown	Cold winters
College-town amenities	Cost of living
Architectural interest	Recent employment declines

Madison is a perennial contender for the top spot in *Cities Ranked & Rated* and most other comparative studies of places to live and work; if it weren't for the winters and cost of living it would be a stronger challenger. The state capital and home to the University of Wisconsin, Madison is clean, attractive, progressive, and well planned. The city itself surrounds a pair of lakes—Lake Mendota and Lake Monona—both of which provide recreation and attractive views from many city business and residential locations. The downtown is exceptionally clean and gives strong evidence of its twin roles as state government center and college town, and is one of the most walkable downtown cores we know of. The area boasts many buildings of architectural interest, most particularly those designed by Frank Lloyd Wright, including the spectacular Monona Terrace convention center on the Lake Monona shore. The surrounding countryside is beautiful and includes an assortment of outdoor recreation areas and attractions such as Taliesin, Wright's former home and studio, and the Wisconsin Dells, a collection of good but somewhat touristy family attractions. The economy is anchored by the university and state government but also is supported by a number of small new-economy firms mainly in biotech and software. East of town is a more traditional commercial complex with distribution centers and light manufacturing. However, employment trends have softened recently. Excellent albeit expensive residential areas lie all around the town, with more middle-class neighborhoods southwest and northeast toward the small town of DeForest. More upscale areas lie along the Lake Mendota lakefront north. Educational attainment is high, and college-town amenities abound, but one pays the price literally in housing and figuratively in winter chill. For those who can accept these negatives, the area is hard to beat.

The downtown sits on a narrow isthmus of land between Lake Mendota and Lake Monona. Madison has a continental climate with an extreme temperature range, historically—from 110°F to –40°F—and frequent temperature changes. Madison lies in the path of frequent storm systems during fall, winter, and spring. Winters are cloudy with occasional outbreaks of cold arctic air, and many days below freezing. Summers are pleasant with only occasional periods of extreme heat or high humidity. Summer months are prone to thunderstorms, and winter precipitation is lighter but lasts longer. Snow cover is common in the winter months. First freeze is early October; last is late April.

Population

DEMOGRAPHICS	AREA	U.S. AVG	ETHNIC COMPOSITION	AREA	U.S. AVG	RESIDENT PROFILE	AREA	U.S. AVG
Population	534,567		White	88.7%	79.0%	Single	36.7%	32.4%
Population density per sq. mile	195.2	358.5	Black	3.6%	10.5%	Married	50.7%	52.7%
Population growth	23.7%	21.1%	Asian	3.9%	2.7%	Divorced/separated	12.6%	14.9%
Median age	35.3	36.1	Hispanic	3.5%	10.6%	Married with children	22.6%	23.7%
Percent Democrat	63.8%	44.5%	Religious observance	54.2%	48.9%	Single with children	6.9%	9.1%
Percent Republican	35.2%	54.5%	Diversity measure	26.1	40.1	Percent over age 65	10.2%	12.9%

Economy & Jobs
Score: 31.0
Rank: 258

INCOME	AREA	U.S. AVG	EMPLOYMENT	AREA	U.S. AVG	EMPLOYING INDUSTRIES	AREA	U.S. AVG
Per capita income	$28,757	$23,235	Unemployment rate	3.2%	4.7%	Largest: Healthcare & Social Assistance		
Household income	$55,976	$46,414	Recent job growth	-0.6%	1.3%			
Household income < $25K	18.5%	26.2%	Projected future job growth	7.8%	11.5%	Percent manufacturing	11.4%	15.4%
Household income > $75K	33.0%	25.4%	White collar	66.9%	57.8%	Percent public sector	21.9%	15.7%
Household income growth	15.4%	13.6%	Blue collar	18.8%	25.2%	Percent construction	7.4%	9.9%

Cost of Living
Score: 18.7
Rank: 303

INDEXES & TAXES	AREA	U.S. AVG	HOUSING	AREA	U.S. AVG	NECESSITIES	AREA	U.S. AVG
Cost of Living Index	99.7	100.0	Median home price	$221,400	$220,000	Food Index	99.0	100.0
Buying Power Index	125.8	100.0	Home price appreciation	41.0%	10.1%	Housing Index	71.4	100.0
Income tax rate	6.93%	4.70%	Median rent	$754	$709	Utilities Index	116.7	100.0
Sales tax rate	5.50%	6.58%	Homes owned	57.4%	62.3%	Transportation Index	100.8	100.0
Property tax rate	$20.80	$12.00	Home price ratio	4.0	4.2	Healthcare Index	105.1	100.0
						Miscellaneous Cost Index	94.5	100.0

Climate
Score: 20.9
Rank: 295

TEMPERATURE	AREA	U.S. AVG	PRECIPITATION	AREA	U.S. AVG	COMFORTS & HAZARDS	AREA	U.S. AVG
Average January low	8.2	26.2	Annual inches precipitation	30.0	37.7	July relative humidity	73%	66%
Average July high	81.4	87.4	Annual inches snowfall	39.0	7.0	Annual days mostly sunny	190	208
Annual days > 90°F	12	38	Annual days precipitation	117	109	Annual days with thunderstorms	40	39
Annual days < 32°F	164	89	Annual days rain > 0.5 inches	18	22	Tornado risk score	24	18
Annual days < 0°F	25	6	Annual days snow > 1.5 inches	10	6	Hurricane risk score	1	13

TEMPERATURE

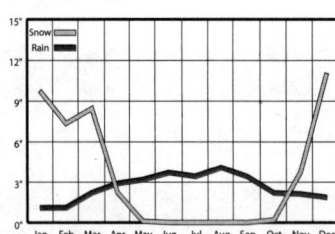

PRECIPITATION

DAYS OF CLOUDS & PRECIPITATION

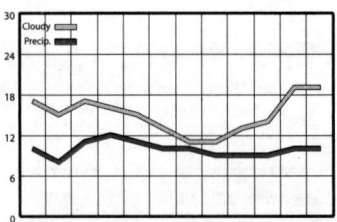

Education
Score: 95.7
Rank: 17

ACHIEVEMENT	AREA	U.S. AVG	PUBLIC SCHOOLS	AREA	U.S. AVG	HIGHER EDUCATION	AREA	U.S. AVG
High school degree	91.5%	82.7%	Expenditures per pupil	$7,016	$5,686	No. 2-year colleges	4	4
2-year college degree	8.8%	6.4%	Student/teacher ratio	15.0	16.7	No. 4-year colleges/universities	3	6
4-year college degree	23.3%	15.7%	Attending public school	91.1%	90.1%	No. highly ranked universities	1	1
Graduate/professional degree	14.5%	8.9%	State SAT score	1188	1021			
			State ACT score	22.2*	20.9			

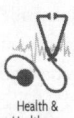

Health & Healthcare
Score: 65.5
Rank: 130

Crime
Score: 94.4
Rank: 22

HAZARDS & ILLNESSES	AREA	U.S. AVG	HEALTHCARE	AREA	U.S. AVG	CRIME	AREA	U.S. AVG
Air-quality score	29	37	Physicians per capita	421.6	244.2	Violent crime rate	229.4	465.5
Water-quality score	47	52	Hospital beds per capita	364.0	420.0	Change in violent crime rate	-0.4%	-2.2%
Pollen/allergy score	34	61	No. teaching hospitals	3	3	Property crime rate	2,843.6	3,517.1
Cancer mortality per capita	192.7	201.9	Cost per doctor visit	$87	$77	Change in property crime rate	3.4%	-2.1%
Depression days per month	3.4	3.5	Cost per dental visit	$62	$70			
Stress score	13	50						

Transportation **Score:** 59.1 **Rank:** 154	COMMUTE	AREA	U.S. AVG	INTERCITY SERVICES	AREA	U.S. AVG	AUTOMOTIVE	AREA	U.S. AVG
	Average commute time	22.5	27.4	Major airports within 60 miles	1	1	Insurance, annual premium	$972	$1,432
	Percent commutes > 60 mins.	3.6%	5.9%	Size of regional airport	Medium	Large	Gas, cost per gallon	$2.59	$2.49
	Commute by auto	75.3%	78.9%	Daily airline activity	334	686	Daily vehicle miles per capita	22.1	24.0
	Commute by mass transit	3.4%	1.9%	Amtrak service	Yes	No			
	Work at home	4.2%	3.1%						
	Mass transit miles per capita	3.40	1.87						

Leisure **Score:** 50.3 **Rank:** 185	DINING & SHOPPING	AREA	U.S. AVG	ENTERTAINMENT	AREA	U.S. AVG	OUTDOOR ACTIVITIES	AREA	U.S. AVG
	Restaurant rating	1	2	Professional sports rating	2	4	Golf-course rating	3	4
	Outlet mall score	26	42	College sports rating	7	4	Ski-area rating	2	3
	No. Starbucks	10	13	Zoo/aquarium rating	6	3	Sq. miles inland water	4	4
	No. warehouse clubs	0	2	Amusement park rating	1	3	Miles of coastline	0.0	10.7
				Botanical garden/ arboretum rating	9	4	National Park rating	1	3

Arts & Culture **Score:** 58.3 **Rank:** 156	MEDIA & LIBRARIES	AREA	U.S. AVG	PERFORMING ARTS	AREA	U.S. AVG	MUSEUMS	AREA	U.S. AVG
	Arts radio rating	1	3	Classical music rating	4	4	Overall museum rating	8	5
	No. public libraries	38	27	Ballet/dance rating	6	3	Art museum rating	7	5
	Library volumes per capita	3.75	2.78	Professional theater rating	1	3	Science museum rating	9	5
				University arts programs rating	2	5	Children's museum rating	6	3

Manchester–Nashua, NH   **Score: 73.4   Rank: 71   2004 rank: 151**

Profile: Small cities
Location: Southern New Hampshire along U.S. 3 corridor
Elevation: 130 feet
Time zone: Eastern Standard Time

PRO	CON
Educated population	Harsh winters
Attractive downtowns	Long commutes
Favorable tax climate	Low ethnic diversity

Sometimes the Office of Management and Budget (OMB) reconfigures metro areas and combines them for the sake of simplicity and to describe a larger "whole" with more synergy and more in common. The small cities of Manchester and Nashua were combined in late 2005, but we don't see the commonality normally associated with such combinations. Manchester and Nashua do share a common history: Both are Industrial Revolution textile-milling towns located on the Merrimack River with trademark New England downtowns dotted with large old mill buildings, many still abandoned, and considerable historic interest. However, the two cities, located only 20 miles apart, have grown to serve different purposes.

Nashua has grown up and prospered as a commuter suburb to Boston and its prosperous northern suburbs, offering the best of small-city living, tax climate, and considerably cheaper homes at the expense of long commutes across the Massachusetts border. The lack of a sales tax brings shoppers across the border from northern Massachusetts, leading to a larger retail infrastructure than one might expect. A new commuter rail service will strengthen Nashua's role as a bedroom community. The story isn't all about commuters—there is a considerable business presence in the area, with corporate names such as Oracle, Hewlett-Packard, Nashua Corporation (office machines), and Lockheed Martin operating large facilities. Workers at these facilities will find commutes a nonissue. Educated, higher-income professionals have flocked to the area's excellent homes mainly to the south and west, and have supported a strong downtown revitalization creating a very walkable core with plenty to do. Cost of living is low for the region but is rising and bears watching. The area still has some post-industrial blight and crime issues, and rapid growth plus low taxes equals some lag in creating public infrastructure and services, but it's generally far forward on the upward path.

Manchester may be on the same path toward reversal of prior industrial decline, but it isn't as far along. It also has the typical older downtown with several mill sites along the river, but the economy has been more depressed and for a longer period of time. However, signs of progress are starting to show; some of the mills in town have been attractively repurposed for new-economy businesses, and a few, such as Autodesk and Texas Instruments, recognizing low costs of doing business, have started to appear. The area has made a concerted effort to attract new business, and attractive new residential areas are starting to spring up especially to the north. Discount air carriers have discovered Manchester and have made it a jumping-off point for all of New England. Low living costs compared to Nashua and especially for the region, an attractive setting, and proximity to the Boston area and other prime New England spots should make the turnaround work, but Manchester today lacks many of the entertainment and arts amenities of its southern neighbors, and has a less educated population. It is more of a "diamond in the rough" than Nashua.

Both towns lie in the valley of the Merrimack River, and both are surrounded by low, rolling, wooded hills. Downtown Nashua lies on the west bank of the river and most growth is toward the southwest, which becomes hilly at the town's outskirts. The river valley at Manchester is more narrow but opens to the north and east into more level terrain. Summers are moderately warm and humid with occasional spells of hotter, stickier weather, and thundershowers alternating with pleasantly cool, drier periods. Fall seasons are classic and colorful, while spring is a mixed bag. Winters are cold with prevailing northwesterly winds bringing waves of cold, dry air. Snow is common and becomes heavy when "noreaster" storms move up the Atlantic Coast. Winter snow cover is prevalent December through March. First freeze is late September; last is late May.

Population

DEMOGRAPHICS	AREA	U.S. AVG	ETHNIC COMPOSITION	AREA	U.S. AVG	RESIDENT PROFILE	AREA	U.S. AVG
Population	399,781		White	92.4%	79.0%	Single	30.6%	32.4%
Population density per sq. mile	456.2	358.5	Black	1.6%	10.5%	Married	56.0%	52.7%
Population growth	19.0%	21.1%	Asian	2.7%	2.7%	Divorced/separated	13.4%	14.9%
Median age	37.7	36.1	Hispanic	3.8%	10.6%	Married with children	26.9%	23.7%
Percent Democrat	48.2%	44.5%	Religious observance	58.1%	48.9%	Single with children	8.0%	9.1%
Percent Republican	51.0%	54.5%	Diversity measure	20.8	40.1	Percent over age 65	10.9%	12.9%

Economy & Jobs
Score: 72.5
Rank: 104

INCOME	AREA	U.S. AVG	EMPLOYMENT	AREA	U.S. AVG	EMPLOYING INDUSTRIES	AREA	U.S. AVG
Per capita income	$29,004	$23,235	Unemployment rate	3.6%	4.7%	Largest: Manufacturing		
Household income	$60,837	$46,414	Recent job growth	2.7%	1.3%			
Household income < $25K	16.9%	26.2%	Projected future job growth	10.0%	11.5%	Percent manufacturing	14.7%	15.4%
Household income > $75K	37.6%	25.4%	White collar	64.8%	57.8%	Percent public sector	10.7%	15.7%
Household income growth	14.0%	13.6%	Blue collar	23.1%	25.2%	Percent construction	8.4%	9.9%

Cost of Living
Score: 75.7
Rank: 91

INDEXES & TAXES	AREA	U.S. AVG	HOUSING	AREA	U.S. AVG	NECESSITIES	AREA	U.S. AVG
Cost of Living Index	107.7	100.0	Median home price	$237,400	$220,000	Food Index	103.3	100.0
Buying Power Index	126.6	100.0	Home price appreciation	70.0%	10.1%	Housing Index	95.4	100.0
Income tax rate	0.18%	4.70%	Median rent	$1,050	$709	Utilities Index	133.2	100.0
Sales tax rate	0.00%	6.58%	Homes owned	63.3%	62.3%	Transportation Index	103.2	100.0
Property tax rate	$24.01	$12.00	Home price ratio	3.9	4.2	Healthcare Index	111.0	100.0
						Miscellaneous Cost Index	107.1	100.0

Climate
Score: 6.4
Rank: 349

TEMPERATURE	AREA	U.S. AVG	PRECIPITATION	AREA	U.S. AVG	COMFORTS & HAZARDS	AREA	U.S. AVG
Average January low	18.2	26.2	Annual inches precipitation	45.2	37.7	July relative humidity	68%	66%
Average July high	81.4	87.4	Annual inches snowfall	50.0	7.0	Annual days mostly sunny	197	208
Annual days > 90°F	15	38	Annual days precipitation	137	109	Annual days with thunderstorms	22	39
Annual days < 32°F	120	89	Annual days rain > 0.5 inches	30	22	Tornado risk score	13	18
Annual days < 0°F	5	6	Annual days snow > 1.5 inches	19	6	Hurricane risk score	18	13

TEMPERATURE

PRECIPITATION

DAYS OF CLOUDS & PRECIPITATION

Education
Score: 76.5
Rank: 88

ACHIEVEMENT	AREA	U.S. AVG	PUBLIC SCHOOLS	AREA	U.S. AVG	HIGHER EDUCATION	AREA	U.S. AVG
High school degree	87.0%	82.7%	Expenditures per pupil	$5,813	$5,686	No. 2-year colleges	1	4
2-year college degree	9.0%	6.4%	Student/teacher ratio	17.5	16.7	No. 4-year colleges/universities	7	6
4-year college degree	20.1%	15.7%	Attending public school	85.2%	90.1%	No. highly ranked universities	0	1
Graduate/professional degree	10.0%	8.9%	State SAT score	1044*	1021			
			State ACT score	22.6	20.9			

Health & Healthcare
Score: 33.7
Rank: 246

HAZARDS & ILLNESSES	AREA	U.S. AVG	HEALTHCARE	AREA	U.S. AVG	CRIME	AREA	U.S. AVG
Air-quality score	28	37	Physicians per capita	204.0	244.2	Violent crime rate	153.8	465.5
Water-quality score	60	52	Hospital beds per capita	272.1	420.0	Change in violent crime rate	-14.6%	-2.2%
Pollen/allergy score	48	61	No. teaching hospitals	1	3	Property crime rate	2,036.0	3,517.1
Cancer mortality per capita	199.0	201.9	Cost per doctor visit	$93	$77	Change in property crime rate	8.7%	-2.1%
Depression days per month	3.2	3.5	Cost per dental visit	$67	$70			
Stress score	25	50						

Crime **Score:** 81.0 **Rank:** 72

Transportation
Score: 55.3
Rank: 168

COMMUTE	AREA	U.S. AVG	INTERCITY SERVICES	AREA	U.S. AVG	AUTOMOTIVE	AREA	U.S. AVG
Average commute time	28.1	27.4	Major airports within 60 miles	2	1	Insurance, annual premium	$1,368	$1,432
Percent commutes > 60 mins.	9.6%	5.9%	Size of regional airport	Large	Large	Gas, cost per gallon	$2.39	$2.49
Commute by auto	83.4%	78.9%	Daily airline activity	1278	686	Daily vehicle miles per capita	23.7	24.0
Commute by mass transit	0.9%	1.9%	Amtrak service	No	No			
Work at home	3.6%	3.1%						
Mass transit miles per capita	0.87	1.87						

Leisure
Score: 79.9
Rank: 75

DINING & SHOPPING	AREA	U.S. AVG	ENTERTAINMENT	AREA	U.S. AVG	OUTDOOR ACTIVITIES	AREA	U.S. AVG
Restaurant rating	1	2	Professional sports rating	8	4	Golf-course rating	5	4
Outlet mall score	21	42	College sports rating	6	4	Ski-area rating	7	3
No. Starbucks	3	13	Zoo/aquarium rating	3	3	Sq. miles inland water	4	4
No. warehouse clubs	4	2	Amusement park rating	5	3	Miles of coastline	0.0	10.7
			Botanical garden/			National Park rating	2	3
			arboretum rating	6	4			

Arts & Culture
Score: 73.0
Rank: 101

MEDIA & LIBRARIES	AREA	U.S. AVG	PERFORMING ARTS	AREA	U.S. AVG	MUSEUMS	AREA	U.S. AVG
Arts radio rating	4	3	Classical music rating	4	4	Overall museum rating	8	5
No. public libraries	33	27	Ballet/dance rating	5	3	Art museum rating	8	5
Library volumes per capita	3.48	2.78	Professional theater rating	8	3	Science museum rating	8	5
			University arts programs rating	8	5	Children's museum rating	6	3

Mansfield, OH

Score: 44.2   Rank: 290   2004 rank: 61

Profile: Small town
Location: Northeast Ohio along I-71 about halfway between Cleveland and Columbus
Elevation: 1,230 feet
Time zone: Eastern Standard Time

PRO	CON
Cost of living and housing	Declining industry
Small-town flavor	Low educational attainment
Low violent crime rate	Cloudy, wet winters

Mansfield is a mid-size, mostly industrial town in north-central Ohio. The dominant Rust Belt industries, including heavy equipment, steel auto, farm machinery, and metallurgical industries have declined in a pattern consistent with much of the region. The downtown core has some historic interest and won a 2001 National Trust for Historic Preservation Great American Main Street Award. The rest of the city is plain, ordinary, and lacking in new vitality. New retail, commercial, and residential areas have grown out mainly to the west in Ontario. Although there isn't much to do in the immediate area, the area brings a low cost of living (81.1); a notably low cost of housing, especially for the quality; and a low violent-crime rate. The city is located between Cleveland and Columbus, about 70 miles from each, giving access to their amenities and services. Employment decline is the largest contributor to the lower ranking.

Mansfield is surrounded by rolling, open farmland. The terrain slopes gently downward toward Lake Erie, 38 miles to the north, while the Appalachian foothills start close by to the east. Lake breezes moderate the hot, humid summers, but temperatures rarely rise above 90°F. Most summer precipitation comes as thundershowers. Persistent cold northerly winds produce considerable winter snowfall and cloudy skies. Consistent snow cover occurs from December through March, and spring is short. First freeze is mid-October; last is late April.

Population

DEMOGRAPHICS	AREA	U.S. AVG	ETHNIC COMPOSITION	AREA	U.S. AVG	RESIDENT PROFILE	AREA	U.S. AVG
Population	128,231		White	87.9%	79.0%	Single	30.1%	32.4%
Population density per sq. mile	258.1	358.5	Black	9.4%	10.5%	Married	54.1%	52.7%
Population growth	1.7%	21.1%	Asian	0.7%	2.7%	Divorced/separated	15.8%	14.9%
Median age	38.6	36.1	Hispanic	0.9%	10.6%	Married with children	21.8%	23.7%
Percent Democrat	39.8%	44.5%	Religious observance	38.6%	48.9%	Single with children	8.8%	9.1%
Percent Republican	59.6%	54.5%	Diversity measure	23.2	40.1	Percent over age 65	15.0%	12.9%

Economy & Jobs
Score: 12.8
Rank: 325

INCOME	AREA	U.S. AVG	EMPLOYMENT	AREA	U.S. AVG	EMPLOYING INDUSTRIES	AREA	U.S. AVG
Per capita income	$21,038	$23,235	Unemployment rate	6.3%	4.7%	Largest: Manufacturing		
Household income	$42,081	$46,414	Recent job growth	0.1%	1.3%			
Household income < $25K	28.1%	26.2%	Projected future job growth	4.0%	11.5%	Percent manufacturing	25.9%	15.4%
Household income > $75K	20.4%	25.4%	White collar	47.9%	57.8%	Percent public sector	11.8%	15.7%
Household income growth	12.5%	13.6%	Blue collar	35.4%	25.2%	Percent construction	9.4%	9.9%

Cost of Living
Score: 66.6
Rank: 126

INDEXES & TAXES	AREA	U.S. AVG	HOUSING	AREA	U.S. AVG	NECESSITIES	AREA	U.S. AVG
Cost of Living Index	81.1	100.0	Median home price	$104,700	$220,000	Food Index	103.3	100.0
Buying Power Index	116.3	100.0	Home price appreciation	23.1%	10.1%	Housing Index	46.7	100.0
Income tax rate	4.99%	4.70%	Median rent	$544	$709	Utilities Index	127.7	100.0
Sales tax rate	7.25%	6.58%	Homes owned	67.2%	62.3%	Transportation Index	96.4	100.0
Property tax rate	$12.19	$12.00	Home price ratio	2.5	4.2	Healthcare Index	90.6	100.0
						Miscellaneous Cost Index	95.8	100.0

Climate
Score: 20.6
Rank: 296

TEMPERATURE	AREA	U.S. AVG
Average January low	20.7	26.2
Average July high	83.7	87.4
Annual days > 90°F	7	38
Annual days < 32°F	127	89
Annual days < 0°F	7	6

PRECIPITATION	AREA	U.S. AVG
Annual inches precipitation	33.7	37.7
Annual inches snowfall	42.2	7.0
Annual days precipitation	152	109
Annual days rain > 0.5 inches	23	22
Annual days snow > 1.5 inches	8	6

COMFORTS & HAZARDS	AREA	U.S. AVG
July relative humidity	73%	66%
Annual days mostly sunny	173	208
Annual days with thunderstorms	39	39
Tornado risk score	22	18
Hurricane risk score	2	13

TEMPERATURE

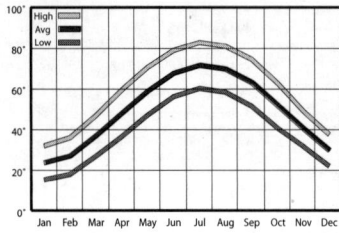

PRECIPITATION

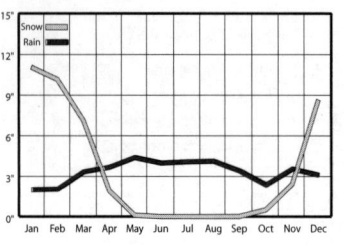

DAYS OF CLOUDS & PRECIPITATION

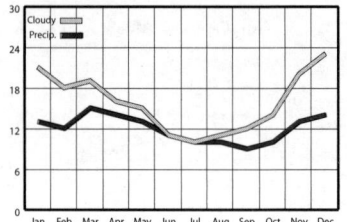

Education
Score: 9.6
Rank: 337

ACHIEVEMENT	AREA	U.S. AVG
High school degree	80.2%	82.7%
2-year college degree	6.1%	6.4%
4-year college degree	8.7%	15.7%
Graduate/professional degree	4.0%	8.9%

PUBLIC SCHOOLS	AREA	U.S. AVG
Expenditures per pupil	$5,425	$5,686
Student/teacher ratio	16.8	16.7
Attending public school	90.0%	90.1%
State SAT score	1079	1021
State ACT score	21.5*	20.9

HIGHER EDUCATION	AREA	U.S. AVG
No. 2-year colleges	1	4
No. 4-year colleges/universities	2	6
No. highly ranked universities	0	1

Health & Healthcare
Score: 76.2
Rank: 90

HAZARDS & ILLNESSES	AREA	U.S. AVG
Air-quality score	48	37
Water-quality score	32	52
Pollen/allergy score	58	61
Cancer mortality per capita	206.7	201.9
Depression days per month	2.4	3.5
Stress score	62	50

HEALTHCARE	AREA	U.S. AVG
Physicians per capita	164.5	244.2
Hospital beds per capita	476.5	420.0
No. teaching hospitals	0	3
Cost per doctor visit	$67	$77
Cost per dental visit	$56	$70

Crime
Score: 66.3
Rank: 127

CRIME	AREA	U.S. AVG
Violent crime rate	180.3	465.5
Change in violent crime rate	3.9%	-2.2%
Property crime rate	4,509.5	3,517.1
Change in property crime rate	0.0%	-2.1%

Transportation
Score: 82.9
Rank: 64

COMMUTE	AREA	U.S. AVG
Average commute time	21.9	27.4
Percent commutes > 60 mins.	5.6%	5.9%
Commute by auto	84.8%	78.9%
Commute by mass transit	0.7%	1.9%
Work at home	2.9%	3.1%
Mass transit miles per capita	0.67	1.87

INTERCITY SERVICES	AREA	U.S. AVG
Major airports within 60 miles	2	1
Size of regional airport	Medium	Large
Daily airline activity	757	686
Amtrak service	No	No

AUTOMOTIVE	AREA	U.S. AVG
Insurance, annual premium	$1,054	$1,432
Gas, cost per gallon	$2.48	$2.49
Daily vehicle miles per capita	21.2	24.0

Leisure
Score: 15.5
Rank: 315

DINING & SHOPPING	AREA	U.S. AVG
Restaurant rating	1	2
Outlet mall score	5	42
No. Starbucks	1	13
No. warehouse clubs	1	2

ENTERTAINMENT	AREA	U.S. AVG
Professional sports rating	1	4
College sports rating	5	4
Zoo/aquarium rating	1	3
Amusement park rating	1	3
Botanical garden/ arboretum rating	9	4

OUTDOOR ACTIVITIES	AREA	U.S. AVG
Golf-course rating	2	4
Ski-area rating	3	3
Sq. miles inland water	2	4
Miles of coastline	0.0	10.7
National Park rating	1	3

Arts & Culture
Score: 48.9
Rank: 191

MEDIA & LIBRARIES	AREA	U.S. AVG
Arts radio rating	5	3
No. public libraries	11	27
Library volumes per capita	4.35	2.78

PERFORMING ARTS	AREA	U.S. AVG
Classical music rating	3	4
Ballet/dance rating	1	3
Professional theater rating	1	3
University arts programs rating	3	5

MUSEUMS	AREA	U.S. AVG
Overall museum rating	6	5
Art museum rating	2	5
Science museum rating	6	5
Children's museum rating	1	3

McAllen–Edinburg–Mission, TX

Score: 23.8   **Rank:** 342   **2004 rank:** 317

Profile: Mid-size-border-city complex
Location: Extreme south Texas along the Rio Grande and Mexican border, 80 miles inland from the Gulf of Mexico
Elevation: 104 feet
Time zone: Central Standard Time

PRO	CON
Cost of living	Growth and sprawl
Economic growth	Low educational attainment
Pleasant winters	Crime rates

The McAllen area is dominated by local agriculture, border-zone factories, and commerce related to the port of entry at Reynosa into Mexico. Like other border towns, the area has a dominant Hispanic heritage, high growth rate, and a low cost of living. McAllen is in the center of a broad, flat agricultural area known locally as "The Valley," dotted with vegetable and citrus growing interspersed with small towns and expanding suburbs. The more middle-class Edinburg, 5 miles north, is home to the University of Texas–Pan American campus, the largest higher-education facility in south Texas. Mission is an agricultural center. McAllen, which has a reputation for being quieter than the border towns of Brownsville and Laredo, has a nice downtown area and is nicknamed "City of Palms." The area serves many needs, including shopping of wealthy Mexican residents from northern Mexico as far south as Monterrey, giving a strong retail presence for the type of area. There are many new businesses run by Mexicans. The area does pick up a tourist trade, particularly with winter migrants heading south. Median home prices are just over $92,000. But while the manufacturing and agricultural sectors are healthy, there are more workers than there are jobs, giving high unemployment and poor residential areas around the city. Cultural and recreational amenities are minor and locally focused.

The flat Rio Grande Valley gives way to low hills and desert sage and chaparral vegetation to the northwest. Summers are hot with periods of rain and stronger storms—most days are over 90°F. Although not quite as humid year-round as Texas cities to the east, summers are humid and uncomfortable. Winters are mild, with maybe one or two below-freezing spells, and the very occasional dusting of snow, usually in January.

Population

DEMOGRAPHICS	AREA	U.S. AVG	ETHNIC COMPOSITION	AREA	U.S. AVG	RESIDENT PROFILE	AREA	U.S. AVG
Population	666,049		White	77.4%	79.0%	Single	31.1%	32.4%
Population density per sq. mile	424.3	358.5	Black	0.5%	10.5%	Married	55.9%	52.7%
Population growth	73.7%	21.1%	Asian	0.7%	2.7%	Divorced/separated	13.0%	14.9%
Median age	27.3	36.1	Hispanic	89.5%	10.6%	Married with children	39.0%	23.7%
Percent Democrat	54.9%	44.5%	Religious observance	50.4%	48.9%	Single with children	10.9%	9.1%
Percent Republican	44.8%	54.5%	Diversity measure	48.4	40.1	Percent over age 65	9.3%	12.9%

Economy & Jobs
Score: 93.6
Rank: 25

INCOME	AREA	U.S. AVG	EMPLOYMENT	AREA	U.S. AVG	EMPLOYING INDUSTRIES	AREA	U.S. AVG
Per capita income	$11,482	$23,235	Unemployment rate	7.7%	4.7%	Largest: Healthcare & Social Assistance		
Household income	$28,677	$46,414	Recent job growth	5.7%	1.3%			
Household income ‹ $25K	44.8%	26.2%	Projected future job growth	33.2%	11.5%	Percent manufacturing	14.4%	15.4%
Household income › $75K	12.9%	25.4%	White collar	51.5%	57.8%	Percent public sector	19.2%	15.7%
Household income growth	15.3%	13.6%	Blue collar	26.9%	25.2%	Percent construction	12.5%	9.9%

Cost of Living
Score: 88.8
Rank: 43

INDEXES & TAXES	AREA	U.S. AVG	HOUSING	AREA	U.S. AVG	NECESSITIES	AREA	U.S. AVG
Cost of Living Index	74.9	100.0	Median home price	$92,200	$220,000	Food Index	81.6	100.0
Buying Power Index	85.8	100.0	Home price appreciation	25.4%	10.1%	Housing Index	40.4	100.0
Income tax rate	0.00%	4.70%	Median rent	$635	$709	Utilities Index	95.8	100.0
Sales tax rate	8.25%	6.58%	Homes owned	60.1%	62.3%	Transportation Index	93.8	100.0
Property tax rate	$19.45	$12.00	Home price ratio	3.2	4.2	Healthcare Index	108.3	100.0
						Miscellaneous Cost Index	101.0	100.0

Climate
Score: 78.6
Rank: 81

TEMPERATURE	AREA	U.S. AVG	PRECIPITATION	AREA	U.S. AVG	COMFORTS & HAZARDS	AREA	U.S. AVG
Average January low	43.6	26.2	Annual inches precipitation	34.3	37.7	July relative humidity	74%	66%
Average July high	93.4	87.4	Annual inches snowfall	0.2	7.0	Annual days mostly sunny	204	208
Annual days › 90°F	101	38	Annual days precipitation	88	109	Annual days with thunderstorms	48	39
Annual days ‹ 32°F	12	89	Annual days rain › 0.5 inches	19	22	Tornado risk score	14	18
Annual days ‹ 0°F	0	6	Annual days snow › 1.5 inches	0	6	Hurricane risk score	37	13

TEMPERATURE

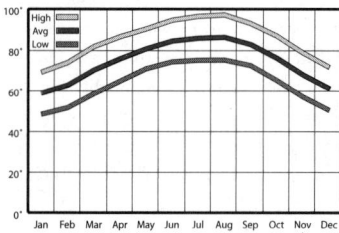

PRECIPITATION

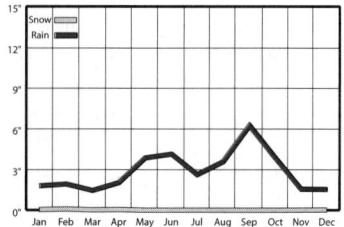

DAYS OF CLOUDS & PRECIPITATION

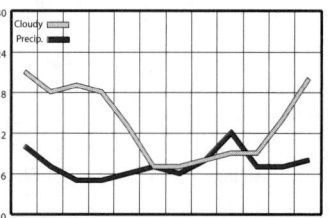

ACHIEVEMENT	AREA	U.S. AVG	PUBLIC SCHOOLS	AREA	U.S. AVG	HIGHER EDUCATION	AREA	U.S. AVG
High school degree	50.6%	82.7%	Expenditures per pupil	$5,642	$5,686	No. 2-year colleges	1	4
2-year college degree	2.9%	6.4%	Student/teacher ratio	15.8	16.7	No. 4-year colleges/universities	1	6
4-year college degree	8.4%	15.7%	Attending public school	97.9%	90.1%	No. highly ranked universities	0	1
Graduate/professional degree	4.6%	8.9%	State SAT score	997*	1021			
			State ACT score	20.3	20.9			

Education
Score: 0.0
Rank: 373

HAZARDS & ILLNESSES	AREA	U.S. AVG	HEALTHCARE	AREA	U.S. AVG	CRIME	AREA	U.S. AVG
Air-quality score	19	37	Physicians per capita	102.1	244.2	Violent crime rate	463.8	465.5
Water-quality score	60	52	Hospital beds per capita	203.1	420.0	Change in violent crime rate	-9.8%	-2.2%
Pollen/allergy score	83	61	No. teaching hospitals	1	3	Property crime rate	5,252.0	3,517.1
Cancer mortality per capita	116.0	201.9	Cost per doctor visit	$62	$77	Change in property crime rate	-6.9%	-2.1%
Depression days per month	2.6	3.5	Cost per dental visit	$79	$70			
Stress score	42	50						

Health & Healthcare
Score: 12.0
Rank: 328

Crime
Score: 28.3
Rank: 266

COMMUTE	AREA	U.S. AVG	INTERCITY SERVICES	AREA	U.S. AVG	AUTOMOTIVE	AREA	U.S. AVG
Average commute time	22.7	27.4	Major airports within 60 miles	0	1	Insurance, annual premium	$1,340	$1,432
Percent commutes > 60 mins.	3.6%	5.9%	Size of regional airport	Small	Large	Gas, cost per gallon	$2.39	$2.49
Commute by auto	73.9%	78.9%	Daily airline activity	28	686	Daily vehicle miles per capita	22.4	24.0
Commute by mass transit	0.3%	1.9%	Amtrak service	No	No			
Work at home	2.2%	3.1%						
Mass transit miles per capita	0.31	1.87						

Transportation
Score: 19.8
Rank: 301

DINING & SHOPPING	AREA	U.S. AVG	ENTERTAINMENT	AREA	U.S. AVG	OUTDOOR ACTIVITIES	AREA	U.S. AVG
Restaurant rating	1	2	Professional sports rating	2	4	Golf-course rating	2	4
Outlet mall score	0	42	College sports rating	3	4	Ski-area rating	1	3
No. Starbucks	3	13	Zoo/aquarium rating	1	3	Sq. miles inland water	3	4
No. warehouse clubs	0	2	Amusement park rating	1	3	Miles of coastline	0.0	10.7
			Botanical garden/ arboretum rating	2	4	National Park rating	2	3

Leisure
Score: 14.7
Rank: 318

MEDIA & LIBRARIES	AREA	U.S. AVG	PERFORMING ARTS	AREA	U.S. AVG	MUSEUMS	AREA	U.S. AVG
Arts radio rating	1	3	Classical music rating	3	4	Overall museum rating	3	5
No. public libraries	12	27	Ballet/dance rating	1	3	Art museum rating	6	5
Library volumes per capita	1.46	2.78	Professional theater rating	1	3	Science museum rating	6	5
			University arts programs rating	4	5	Children's museum rating	1	3

Arts & Culture
Score: 30.2
Rank: 261

Medford, OR

Score: 82.3   Rank: 34   2004 rank: 72

Profile: Small-town complex
Location: Southern Oregon along I-5, 30 miles north of the California border
Elevation: 1,298 feet
Time zone: Pacific Standard Time

PRO	CON
Nearby recreation	Growth and sprawl
Attractive setting	Air quality
College-town element	Low ethnic diversity

Medford is historically an agricultural and timber processing center also known for fruit growing, particularly for its pears. More recently it has evolved as a cultural and residential crossroads between California and the Pacific Northwest. The city itself is fairly nondescript but has undergone some renewal, and its full complement of shopping and retail establishments are popular with locals and Californians passing through to avoid sales tax. The timber industry is active but in long-term decline. Skiing, watersports, mountain biking, rafting, and hiking opportunities are abundant in the nearby mountains and Rogue River Valley. Ashland, 10 miles south, is a cute college town and arts community anchored by Southern Oregon State University and a renowned annual Shakespeare festival. Ashland is particularly popular as a destination for California migrants, which has had the predictable effect on home prices, which are far higher than most of Oregon. That effect has also come to Medford and surrounding small towns but not to the same degree. High-paying jobs remain scarce, and a number of migrants are retirees or self-employed individuals capable of working remotely. The entire area is growing rapidly as more seek its attractive climate and surroundings and proximity to California features south and Pacific Northwest features north. It's worth watching the long-term effects of migration on costs, sprawl, and air quality, but for now, the area offers an attractive mix.

The Medford area is located in a mountain valley formed by the Rogue River and one of its tributaries. The valley is mainly farmland with tree-covered foothills and mountains. Late fall, winter, and early spring are damp, cloudy, and cool under a marine influence. The rest of the year is sunny, warm, and dry. Summer high temperatures are around 90°F with low humidity and nights cooled by mountain air. There are occasional hot spells with dry heat in the 100s. Heavy winter snowfall in the surrounding mountains provides excellent skiing, but there is little snowfall in the valley.

DEMOGRAPHICS	AREA	U.S. AVG	ETHNIC COMPOSITION	AREA	U.S. AVG	RESIDENT PROFILE	AREA	U.S. AVG
Population	194,365		White	90.8%	79.0%	Single	28.3%	32.4%
Population density per sq. mile	69.8	358.5	Black	0.5%	10.5%	Married	55.0%	52.7%
Population growth	32.8%	21.1%	Asian	1.3%	2.7%	Divorced/separated	16.7%	14.9%
Median age	39.4	36.1	Hispanic	7.7%	10.6%	Married with children	21.1%	23.7%
Percent Democrat	43.4%	44.5%	Religious observance	22.2%	48.9%	Single with children	9.1%	9.1%
Percent Republican	55.3%	54.5%	Diversity measure	29.1	40.1	Percent over age 65	16.1%	12.9%

Population

INCOME	AREA	U.S. AVG	EMPLOYMENT	AREA	U.S. AVG	EMPLOYING INDUSTRIES	AREA	U.S. AVG
Per capita income	$22,459	$23,235	Unemployment rate	6.5%	4.7%	Largest: Healthcare & Social Assistance		
Household income	$42,141	$46,414	Recent job growth	2.7%	1.3%			
Household income < $25K	28.3%	26.2%	Projected future job growth	21.5%	11.5%	Percent manufacturing	14.5%	15.4%
Household income > $75K	22.1%	25.4%	White collar	56.7%	57.8%	Percent public sector	13.7%	15.7%
Household income growth	15.6%	13.6%	Blue collar	24.0%	25.2%	Percent construction	9.6%	9.9%

Economy & Jobs
Score: 63.6
Rank: 137

INDEXES & TAXES	AREA	U.S. AVG	HOUSING	AREA	U.S. AVG	NECESSITIES	AREA	U.S. AVG
Cost of Living Index	112.1	100.0	Median home price	$294,800	$220,000	Food Index	106.9	100.0
Buying Power Index	84.3	100.0	Home price appreciation	98.0%	10.1%	Housing Index	86.6	100.0
Income tax rate	9.00%	4.70%	Median rent	$703	$709	Utilities Index	72.6	100.0
Sales tax rate	0.00%	6.58%	Homes owned	63.3%	62.3%	Transportation Index	103.5	100.0
Property tax rate	$10.42	$12.00	Home price ratio	7.0	4.2	Healthcare Index	111.4	100.0
						Miscellaneous Cost Index	103.9	100.0

Cost of Living
Score: 54.8
Rank: 169

TEMPERATURE	AREA	U.S. AVG	PRECIPITATION	AREA	U.S. AVG	COMFORTS & HAZARDS	AREA	U.S. AVG
Average January low	29.0	26.2	Annual inches precipitation	21.0	37.7	July relative humidity	67%	66%
Average July high	89.5	87.4	Annual inches snowfall	8.0	7.0	Annual days mostly sunny	196	208
Annual days > 90°F	54	38	Annual days precipitation	101	109	Annual days with thunderstorms	9	39
Annual days > 32°F	90	89	Annual days rain > 0.5 inches	8	22	Tornado risk score	0	18
Annual days < 0°F	0	6	Annual days snow > 1.5 inches	1	6	Hurricane risk score	0	13

Climate
Score: 58.0
Rank: 156

TEMPERATURE

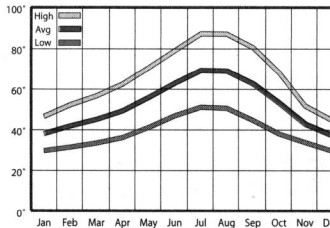

PRECIPITATION

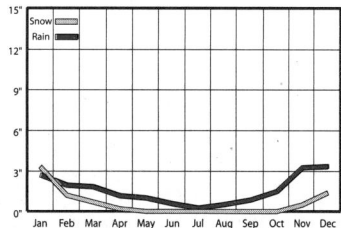

DAYS OF CLOUDS & PRECIPITATION

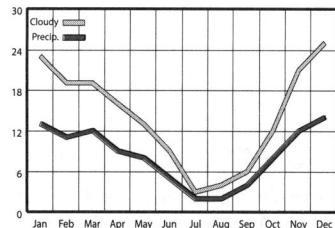

ACHIEVEMENT	AREA	U.S. AVG	PUBLIC SCHOOLS	AREA	U.S. AVG	HIGHER EDUCATION	AREA	U.S. AVG
High school degree	85.0%	82.7%	Expenditures per pupil	$5,787	$5,686	No. 2-year colleges	1	4
2-year college degree	5.8%	6.4%	Student/teacher ratio	18.9	16.7	No. 4-year colleges/universities	1	6
4-year college degree	14.4%	15.7%	Attending public school	93.6%	90.1%	No. highly ranked universities	0	1
Graduate/professional degree	7.7%	8.9%	State SAT score	1052*	1021			
			State ACT score	22.4	20.9			

Education
Score: 45.2
Rank: 206

HAZARDS & ILLNESSES	AREA	U.S. AVG	HEALTHCARE	AREA	U.S. AVG	CRIME	AREA	U.S. AVG
Air-quality score	24	37	Physicians per capita	237.8	244.2	Violent crime rate	302.8	465.5
Water-quality score	60	52	Hospital beds per capita	233.6	420.0	Change in violent crime rate	-4.4%	-2.2%
Pollen/allergy score	62	61	No. teaching hospitals	1	3	Property crime rate	3,885.7	3,517.1
Cancer mortality per capita	206.9	201.9	Cost per doctor visit	$88	$77	Change in property crime rate	-5.5%	-2.1%
Depression days per month	3.6	3.5	Cost per dental visit	$72	$70			
Stress score	78	50						

Health & Healthcare
Score: 20.6
Rank: 296

Crime
Score: 72.7
Rank: 102

Transportation
Score: 42.2
Rank: 217

COMMUTE	AREA	U.S. AVG	INTERCITY SERVICES	AREA	U.S. AVG	AUTOMOTIVE	AREA	U.S. AVG
Average commute time	20.4	27.4	Major airports within 60 miles	0	1	Insurance, annual premium	$1,127	$1,432
Percent commutes › 60 mins.	3.1%	5.9%	Size of regional airport	None	Large	Gas, cost per gallon	$2.61	$2.49
Commute by auto	77.8%	78.9%	Daily airline activity	35	686	Daily vehicle miles per capita	20.8	24.0
Commute by mass transit	0.7%	1.9%	Amtrak service	No	No			
Work at home	5.6%	3.1%						
Mass transit miles per capita	0.65	1.87						

Leisure
Score: 25.4
Rank: 278

DINING & SHOPPING	AREA	U.S. AVG	ENTERTAINMENT	AREA	U.S. AVG	OUTDOOR ACTIVITIES	AREA	U.S. AVG
Restaurant rating	1	2	Professional sports rating	2	4	Golf-course rating	1	4
Outlet mall score	0	42	College sports rating	1	4	Ski-area rating	7	3
No. Starbucks	5	13	Zoo/aquarium rating	1	3	Sq. miles inland water	2	4
No. warehouse clubs	1	2	Amusement park rating	1	3	Miles of coastline	0.0	10.7
			Botanical garden/ arboretum rating	1	4	National Park rating	1	3

Arts & Culture
Score: 20.6
Rank: 296

MEDIA & LIBRARIES	AREA	U.S. AVG	PERFORMING ARTS	AREA	U.S. AVG	MUSEUMS	AREA	U.S. AVG
Arts radio rating	1	3	Classical music rating	4	4	Overall museum rating	5	5
No. public libraries	15	27	Ballet/dance rating	3	3	Art museum rating	3	5
Library volumes per capita	2.77	2.78	Professional theater rating	10	3	Science museum rating	1	5
			University arts programs rating	1	5	Children's museum rating	8	3

Memphis, TN-MS-AR

Score: 45.6   **Rank:** 278   **2004 rank:** 109

Profile: Large city
Location: Extreme southwest Tennessee along the Mississippi River and Arkansas and Mississippi border
Elevation: 284 feet
Time zone: Central Standard Time

PRO
Entertainment
Cultural interest
Cost of living

CON
Crime rates
Recent employment
    declines
Hot, humid summers

Sultry, soulful Memphis is an interesting and vivid place, located along the Mississippi River at the Arkansas border. The largest city in Tennessee, Memphis has a history of dramatic highs and lows: antebellum cotton-trading prosperity, Civil War destruction and reconstruction, yellow-fever epidemics, resurgence as a lumber and (again) cotton-trading center, and post–World War II decline. The low point was Martin Luther King's assassination in 1968. Today the city is on an upswing, thanks to recognition of its unique cultural assets and urban renewal. As the hometown of the blues and Elvis Presley (who was actually born in Tupelo, Mississippi), the city left its mark on the history of music, and a general resurgence in the popularity of blues has brought new life to Memphis as a tourist attraction. The historic Beale Street neighborhood provides music and entertainment opportunities for residents and tourists. The city is a patchwork of redevelopment, preservation, and decay, but downtown is generally becoming a more habitable place. The area spreads in all directions including across the Mississippi into the gritty West Memphis, Arkansas, and south into Mississippi. Bartlett to the north is a more upscale suburb, while Germantown and Collierville to the southeast are undergoing the strongest growth and are also more upscale. The NBA Memphis Grizzlies add a spark to the area and there are several minor league and collegiate sports attractions.

The economic base is diverse and its status as a good business base is on the rise—the city is headquarters for retailer AutoZone, and International Paper is relocating its headquarters from Connecticut. It is also known as a good base for smaller and especially minority-owned businesses. FedEx operates mainly at the Memphis Airport, which is the largest air cargo hub in the world, south of town, but the company also has a large research facility in Collierville. Healthcare resources are strong, in particular the well-known St. Jude Children's Research Hospital. There are a few specialized small colleges, but Memphis is generally not a higher-education destination. Status as hub for FedEx and Northwest Airlines says something of its central geographic location. Cost of living, at 83.2, is low for a large city; the biggest downsides are a very high crime rate and oppressive summers, and more recently, employment trends have softened.

The city lies along the Mississippi River with a level landscape to the west in Arkansas and a level to slightly rolling landscape into Tennessee and northern Mississippi. Summers have periods of warm, steamy weather with thundershowers. Winters are cool with a few periods of freezing temperatures. At 50 inches per year, Memphis is comparatively wet with precipitation spread evenly throughout the year. Extreme temperatures are rare.

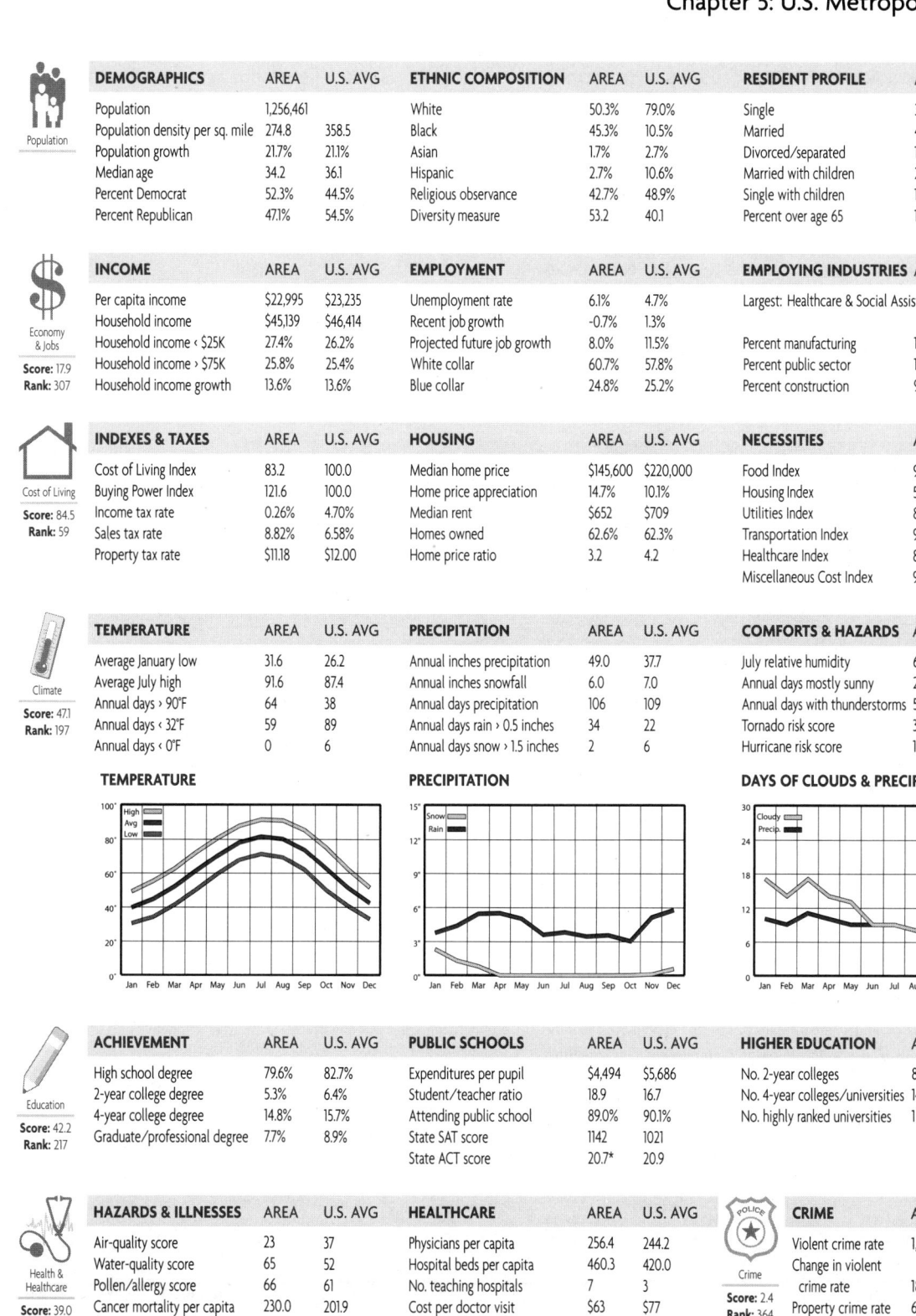

Population

DEMOGRAPHICS	AREA	U.S. AVG	ETHNIC COMPOSITION	AREA	U.S. AVG	RESIDENT PROFILE	AREA	U.S. AVG
Population	1,256,461		White	50.3%	79.0%	Single	35.6%	32.4%
Population density per sq. mile	274.8	358.5	Black	45.3%	10.5%	Married	47.6%	52.7%
Population growth	21.7%	21.1%	Asian	1.7%	2.7%	Divorced/separated	16.8%	14.9%
Median age	34.2	36.1	Hispanic	2.7%	10.6%	Married with children	22.1%	23.7%
Percent Democrat	52.3%	44.5%	Religious observance	42.7%	48.9%	Single with children	12.9%	9.1%
Percent Republican	47.1%	54.5%	Diversity measure	53.2	40.1	Percent over age 65	10.1%	12.9%

Economy & Jobs
Score: 17.9
Rank: 307

INCOME	AREA	U.S. AVG	EMPLOYMENT	AREA	U.S. AVG	EMPLOYING INDUSTRIES	AREA	U.S. AVG
Per capita income	$22,995	$23,235	Unemployment rate	6.1%	4.7%	Largest: Healthcare & Social Assistance		
Household income	$45,139	$46,414	Recent job growth	-0.7%	1.3%			
Household income < $25K	27.4%	26.2%	Projected future job growth	8.0%	11.5%	Percent manufacturing	15.6%	15.4%
Household income > $75K	25.8%	25.4%	White collar	60.7%	57.8%	Percent public sector	14.6%	15.7%
Household income growth	13.6%	13.6%	Blue collar	24.8%	25.2%	Percent construction	9.2%	9.9%

Cost of Living
Score: 84.5
Rank: 59

INDEXES & TAXES	AREA	U.S. AVG	HOUSING	AREA	U.S. AVG	NECESSITIES	AREA	U.S. AVG
Cost of Living Index	83.2	100.0	Median home price	$145,600	$220,000	Food Index	95.7	100.0
Buying Power Index	121.6	100.0	Home price appreciation	14.7%	10.1%	Housing Index	56.3	100.0
Income tax rate	0.26%	4.70%	Median rent	$652	$709	Utilities Index	84.3	100.0
Sales tax rate	8.82%	6.58%	Homes owned	62.6%	62.3%	Transportation Index	97.8	100.0
Property tax rate	$11.18	$12.00	Home price ratio	3.2	4.2	Healthcare Index	87.7	100.0
						Miscellaneous Cost Index	92.3	100.0

Climate
Score: 47.1
Rank: 197

TEMPERATURE	AREA	U.S. AVG	PRECIPITATION	AREA	U.S. AVG	COMFORTS & HAZARDS	AREA	U.S. AVG
Average January low	31.6	26.2	Annual inches precipitation	49.0	37.7	July relative humidity	69%	66%
Average July high	91.6	87.4	Annual inches snowfall	6.0	7.0	Annual days mostly sunny	217	208
Annual days > 90°F	64	38	Annual days precipitation	106	109	Annual days with thunderstorms	53	39
Annual days < 32°F	59	89	Annual days rain > 0.5 inches	34	22	Tornado risk score	38	18
Annual days < 0°F	0	6	Annual days snow > 1.5 inches	2	6	Hurricane risk score	12	13

TEMPERATURE

PRECIPITATION

DAYS OF CLOUDS & PRECIPITATION

Education
Score: 42.2
Rank: 217

ACHIEVEMENT	AREA	U.S. AVG	PUBLIC SCHOOLS	AREA	U.S. AVG	HIGHER EDUCATION	AREA	U.S. AVG
High school degree	79.6%	82.7%	Expenditures per pupil	$4,494	$5,686	No. 2-year colleges	8	4
2-year college degree	5.3%	6.4%	Student/teacher ratio	18.9	16.7	No. 4-year colleges/universities	14	6
4-year college degree	14.8%	15.7%	Attending public school	89.0%	90.1%	No. highly ranked universities	1	1
Graduate/professional degree	7.7%	8.9%	State SAT score	1142	1021			
			State ACT score	20.7*	20.9			

Health & Healthcare
Score: 39.0
Rank: 226

HAZARDS & ILLNESSES	AREA	U.S. AVG	HEALTHCARE	AREA	U.S. AVG	CRIME	AREA	U.S. AVG
Air-quality score	23	37	Physicians per capita	256.4	244.2	Violent crime rate	1,196.8	465.5
Water-quality score	65	52	Hospital beds per capita	460.3	420.0	Change in violent crime rate	18.6%	-2.2%
Pollen/allergy score	66	61	No. teaching hospitals	7	3	Property crime rate	6,085.8	3,517.1
Cancer mortality per capita	230.0	201.9	Cost per doctor visit	$63	$77	Change in property crime rate	2.2%	-2.1%
Depression days per month	3.6	3.5	Cost per dental visit	$64	$70			
Stress score	97	50						

Crime
Score: 2.4
Rank: 364

Transportation
Score: 18.4
Rank: 306

COMMUTE	AREA	U.S. AVG	INTERCITY SERVICES	AREA	U.S. AVG	AUTOMOTIVE	AREA	U.S. AVG
Average commute time	26.8	27.4	Major airports within 60 miles	1	1	Insurance, annual premium	$1,244	$1,432
Percent commutes > 60 mins.	4.7%	5.9%	Size of regional airport	Medium	Large	Gas, cost per gallon	$2.46	$2.49
Commute by auto	81.1%	78.9%	Daily airline activity	500	686	Daily vehicle miles per capita	26.9	24.0
Commute by mass transit	1.5%	1.9%	Amtrak service	Yes	No			
Work at home	2.2%	3.1%						
Mass transit miles per capita	1.50	1.87						

Leisure Score: 73.0 Rank: 101	DINING & SHOPPING	AREA	U.S. AVG	ENTERTAINMENT	AREA	U.S. AVG	OUTDOOR ACTIVITIES	AREA	U.S. AVG
	Restaurant rating	1	2	Professional sports rating	6	4	Golf-course rating	5	4
	Outlet mall score	21	42	College sports rating	4	4	Ski-area rating	1	3
	No. Starbucks	17	13	Zoo/aquarium rating	6	3	Sq. miles inland water	6	4
	No. warehouse clubs	6	2	Amusement park rating	3	3	Miles of coastline	0.0	10.7
				Botanical garden/ arboretum rating	5	4	National Park rating	2	3

Arts & Culture Score: 70.3 Rank: 111	MEDIA & LIBRARIES	AREA	U.S. AVG	PERFORMING ARTS	AREA	U.S. AVG	MUSEUMS	AREA	U.S. AVG
	Arts radio rating	5	3	Classical music rating	5	4	Overall museum rating	9	5
	No. public libraries	44	27	Ballet/dance rating	3	3	Art museum rating	8	5
	Library volumes per capita	2.13	2.78	Professional theater rating	6	3	Science museum rating	8	5
				University arts programs rating	6	5	Children's museum rating	6	3

Merced, CA

Score: 11.7   **Rank:** 370   **2004 rank:** 328

Profile: Small city
Location: Central California, mid-Central Valley, 80 miles south of Sacramento
Elevation: 22 feet
Time zone: Pacific Standard Time

PRO	CON
Emerging college town	Current unemployment
Nearby national parks	Cost of living
Future job growth	Low educational attainment

Merced has played a role, for the past 125 years, as a sleepy agricultural and transportation center and a travel gateway to Yosemite National Park. But in 2005, the long-awaited University of California Merced campus was finally opened, which should over time greatly influence the city's role and character and bring positive growth. Aside from the University and its 2,100-acre campus northeast of town, Merced is a typical Central Valley town, with a pleasant if somewhat mundane to run-down character in some areas. The downtown core is nicely laid out but not that attractive as it stands today; future renewal as a college town gives it potential. Retail and residential growth are well planned and attractive so far. As with most California Valley towns, it is plagued by an unusually high cost of living for the lifestyle and amenities offered, and a rather uneducated population and high crime until this point. At 128.5 and at $349,600 respectively, the Cost of Living Index and median home prices are extreme, especially given local incomes. Those willing to pay these prices are clearly betting on the future; and if Merced grows up to be another Davis, home of the University of California campus of that name and an excellent college-town example, things should work out well. Unfortunately, enrollment has been weak so far, as the university has been slow to build its base of majors, and its first session had only 500 students. Bottom line: It may take a while, but Merced is definitely on an upward path and offers potential not found in other Valley towns. This potential is clearly not shown in today's numbers.

The immediate area is level and mainly agricultural. Just to the east, the Sierra Nevada foothills rise into an oak-studded grassland, giving way to the central Sierra, with mountains approaching 13,500 feet. Coastal mountains rise to the west to 4,000 feet, providing a dramatic landscape on all but the most dusty or hazy valley days. Climate is typical for the Central Valley—hot, dry summers and mild winters with frequent valley fog and about 90% of the year's annual rain.

Population	DEMOGRAPHICS	AREA	U.S. AVG	ETHNIC COMPOSITION	AREA	U.S. AVG	RESIDENT PROFILE	AREA	U.S. AVG
	Population	236,401		White	53.7%	79.0%	Single	33.1%	32.4%
	Population density per sq. mile	122.6	358.5	Black	3.7%	10.5%	Married	52.2%	52.7%
	Population growth	32.5%	21.1%	Asian	6.1%	2.7%	Divorced/separated	14.7%	14.9%
	Median age	29.3	36.1	Hispanic	51.0%	10.6%	Married with children	32.5%	23.7%
	Percent Democrat	42.3%	44.5%	Religious observance	50.4%	48.9%	Single with children	12.8%	9.1%
	Percent Republican	56.5%	54.5%	Diversity measure	80.9	40.1	Percent over age 65	9.1%	12.9%

Economy & Jobs Score: 2.9 Rank: 362	INCOME	AREA	U.S. AVG	EMPLOYMENT	AREA	U.S. AVG	EMPLOYING INDUSTRIES	AREA	U.S. AVG
	Per capita income	$15,951	$23,235	Unemployment rate	9.2%	4.7%	Largest: Manufacturing		
	Household income	$40,471	$46,414	Recent job growth	1.0%	1.3%			
	Household income < $25K	29.7%	26.2%	Projected future job growth	9.6%	11.5%	Percent manufacturing	17.7%	15.4%
	Household income > $75K	20.5%	25.4%	White collar	44.8%	57.8%	Percent public sector	16.7%	15.7%
	Household income growth	13.9%	13.6%	Blue collar	28.4%	25.2%	Percent construction	10.7%	9.9%

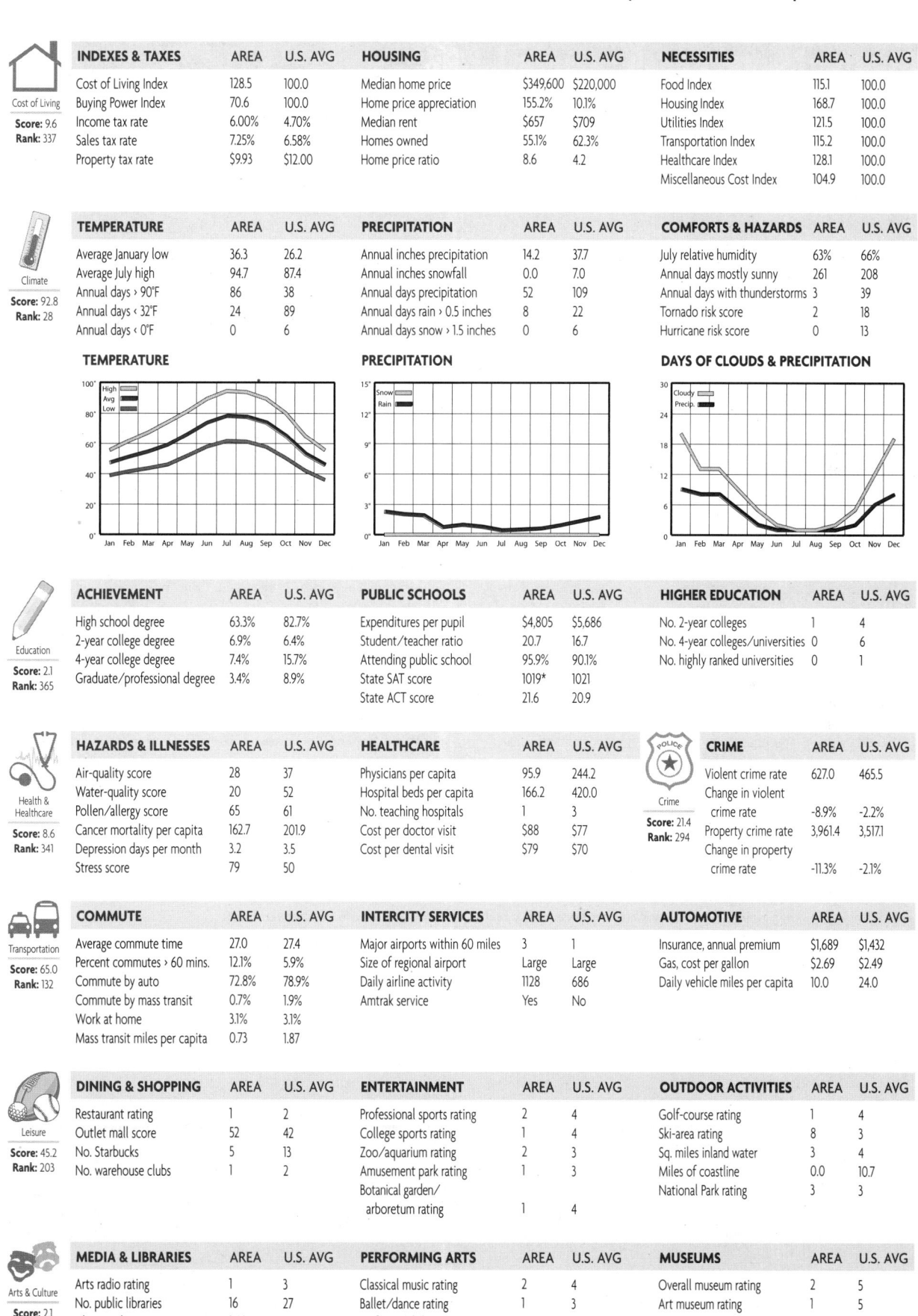

Cost of Living
Score: 9.6
Rank: 337

INDEXES & TAXES	AREA	U.S. AVG	HOUSING	AREA	U.S. AVG	NECESSITIES	AREA	U.S. AVG
Cost of Living Index	128.5	100.0	Median home price	$349,600	$220,000	Food Index	115.1	100.0
Buying Power Index	70.6	100.0	Home price appreciation	155.2%	10.1%	Housing Index	168.7	100.0
Income tax rate	6.00%	4.70%	Median rent	$657	$709	Utilities Index	121.5	100.0
Sales tax rate	7.25%	6.58%	Homes owned	55.1%	62.3%	Transportation Index	115.2	100.0
Property tax rate	$9.93	$12.00	Home price ratio	8.6	4.2	Healthcare Index	128.1	100.0
						Miscellaneous Cost Index	104.9	100.0

Climate
Score: 92.8
Rank: 28

TEMPERATURE	AREA	U.S. AVG	PRECIPITATION	AREA	U.S. AVG	COMFORTS & HAZARDS	AREA	U.S. AVG
Average January low	36.3	26.2	Annual inches precipitation	14.2	37.7	July relative humidity	63%	66%
Average July high	94.7	87.4	Annual inches snowfall	0.0	7.0	Annual days mostly sunny	261	208
Annual days > 90°F	86	38	Annual days precipitation	52	109	Annual days with thunderstorms	3	39
Annual days < 32°F	24	89	Annual days rain > 0.5 inches	8	22	Tornado risk score	2	18
Annual days < 0°F	0	6	Annual days snow > 1.5 inches	0	6	Hurricane risk score	0	13

TEMPERATURE   **PRECIPITATION**   **DAYS OF CLOUDS & PRECIPITATION**

Education
Score: 2.1
Rank: 365

ACHIEVEMENT	AREA	U.S. AVG	PUBLIC SCHOOLS	AREA	U.S. AVG	HIGHER EDUCATION	AREA	U.S. AVG
High school degree	63.3%	82.7%	Expenditures per pupil	$4,805	$5,686	No. 2-year colleges	1	4
2-year college degree	6.9%	6.4%	Student/teacher ratio	20.7	16.7	No. 4-year colleges/universities	0	6
4-year college degree	7.4%	15.7%	Attending public school	95.9%	90.1%	No. highly ranked universities	0	1
Graduate/professional degree	3.4%	8.9%	State SAT score	1019*	1021			
			State ACT score	21.6	20.9			

Health & Healthcare
Score: 8.6
Rank: 341

HAZARDS & ILLNESSES	AREA	U.S. AVG	HEALTHCARE	AREA	U.S. AVG	CRIME	AREA	U.S. AVG
Air-quality score	28	37	Physicians per capita	95.9	244.2	Violent crime rate	627.0	465.5
Water-quality score	20	52	Hospital beds per capita	166.2	420.0	Change in violent crime rate	-8.9%	-2.2%
Pollen/allergy score	65	61	No. teaching hospitals	1	3	Property crime rate	3,961.4	3,517.1
Cancer mortality per capita	162.7	201.9	Cost per doctor visit	$88	$77	Change in property crime rate	-11.3%	-2.1%
Depression days per month	3.2	3.5	Cost per dental visit	$79	$70			
Stress score	79	50						

Crime Score: 21.4 Rank: 294

Transportation
Score: 65.0
Rank: 132

COMMUTE	AREA	U.S. AVG	INTERCITY SERVICES	AREA	U.S. AVG	AUTOMOTIVE	AREA	U.S. AVG
Average commute time	27.0	27.4	Major airports within 60 miles	3	1	Insurance, annual premium	$1,689	$1,432
Percent commutes > 60 mins.	12.1%	5.9%	Size of regional airport	Large	Large	Gas, cost per gallon	$2.69	$2.49
Commute by auto	72.8%	78.9%	Daily airline activity	1128	686	Daily vehicle miles per capita	10.0	24.0
Commute by mass transit	0.7%	1.9%	Amtrak service	Yes	No			
Work at home	3.1%	3.1%						
Mass transit miles per capita	0.73	1.87						

Leisure
Score: 45.2
Rank: 203

DINING & SHOPPING	AREA	U.S. AVG	ENTERTAINMENT	AREA	U.S. AVG	OUTDOOR ACTIVITIES	AREA	U.S. AVG
Restaurant rating	1	2	Professional sports rating	2	4	Golf-course rating	1	4
Outlet mall score	52	42	College sports rating	1	4	Ski-area rating	8	3
No. Starbucks	5	13	Zoo/aquarium rating	2	3	Sq. miles inland water	3	4
No. warehouse clubs	1	2	Amusement park rating	1	3	Miles of coastline	0.0	10.7
			Botanical garden/arboretum rating	1	4	National Park rating	3	3

Arts & Culture
Score: 2.1
Rank: 365

MEDIA & LIBRARIES	AREA	U.S. AVG	PERFORMING ARTS	AREA	U.S. AVG	MUSEUMS	AREA	U.S. AVG
Arts radio rating	1	3	Classical music rating	2	4	Overall museum rating	2	5
No. public libraries	16	27	Ballet/dance rating	1	3	Art museum rating	1	5
Library volumes per capita	1.46	2.78	Professional theater rating	1	3	Science museum rating	4	5
			University arts programs rating	1	5	Children's museum rating	1	3

Miami–Miami Beach–Kendall, FL

Score: 49.0　　**Rank:** 250　　**2004 rank:** 125

Profile: Regional center
Location: South Atlantic Coast near the southern tip of the Florida Peninsula
Elevation: 12 feet
Time zone: Eastern Standard Time

PRO	CON
Entertainment	Crime rates
Beaches and water recreation	Cost of living
Cultural diversity	Hurricane risk

Miami has always been the commercial and cultural center for Florida and the nearby Caribbean, but in the past 30 years it has emerged as a world-class international hub and a gateway for all of Latin America. In many ways it serves as the central logistical and cultural hub of the entire Western Hemisphere. The inevitable result is a diverse and invigorating Latin culture superimposed upon what was already a major commercial, resort, and retirement area dating back to the 1920s. Many think of it as a tourist center, but import/export and international financial trade with Latin countries make up a far larger part of the economy. These activities bring a large banking industry as well as cargo transport and warehousing; the manufacturing and corporate headquarters rosters are also growing. The city is busy—in many ways stressful—and the mix of cultures, heat, and poverty has occasionally boiled over into ethnic and civil strife. But the city is fun and undeniably alive.

Downtown is fairly average with the usual glass skyscrapers. Inland to the west, the area sprawls with low to mid-size commercial buildings and housing for miles with a mix of neighborhoods, until ending abruptly at the Everglades. Wealthy retirees and others escaping the northeast winters have established themselves on Miami Beach, the high-rise-studded barrier island to the east, or to Coral Gables and Kendall just to the south. The planned Coral Gables is quite upscale, while Kendall is more middle class, and all suburbs to the south are a rich and unusual combination of wealthy and middle-class U. S. migrants and retirees mixed in with similar strata from all over Latin America. Inland areas are much warmer and less comfortable. Covering almost all buildable land, the vast and mostly middle-class residential areas continue to sprawl 25 miles to the south to Homestead. Hurricane Andrew, one of the most devastating hurricanes on record, made a nearly successful attempt to reclaim Homestead and surrounding areas for nature in 1992. That hurricane still has Miami residents back on their heels, and it and

other hurricanes have had major effects on property insurance premiums and availability. To the north, residential and light-commercial developments merge with Fort Lauderdale and its suburbs to the west.

There is no shortage of things to do in Miami—indoors or outdoors. The South Beach section of Miami Beach houses a historic district lined with pastel-colored, Art Deco buildings from the '20s and '30s, now filled with restaurants and clubs active throughout the day and evening. Water and beach recreation are superb, and Latin-accented nightlife goes on everywhere. Professional and college sports are a passion. There is a good assortment of museums and performing arts amenities. Air service is excellent everywhere, particularly to international destinations. The Cost of Living Index at 130.0 is uncomfortably high and growing as home prices rise, but varies considerably by location within the area. A recent speculative boom, particularly centered in the condominium market, has caused real estate price dislocations, and the future direction of home prices is uncertain. Crime rates are among the highest in the nation for a big city. Average commute times—almost 33 minutes—are the worst in Florida. Only Fort Lauderdale and West Palm Beach—both just to the north—have a higher hurricane risk. Taken together, the city offers world-class activities and an interesting cultural mix at the expense of cost, crowding, and crime safety. Some of the negatives have gotten worse, hence the ranking decline.

Miami lies on a level coastal plain. The surrounding countryside is level and sparsely wooded with areas of water and swampland approaching the Everglades to the west. The climate is subtropical marine with long, warm, humid summers and abundant rainfall, followed by mild, dry winters. Sea breezes from the east and southeast may cause year-round temperature differences of 15°F or more from inland locations. Freezing conditions occur occasionally in the western suburbs. Strong thunderstorms with dangerous lightning can occur year-round, and hurricanes are a risk in late summer and fall.

DEMOGRAPHICS	AREA	U.S. AVG	ETHNIC COMPOSITION	AREA	U.S. AVG	RESIDENT PROFILE	AREA	U.S. AVG
Population	2,378,142		White	69.9%	79.0%	Single	35.4%	32.4%
Population density per sq. mile	1222.0	358.5	Black	19.7%	10.5%	Married	44.8%	52.7%
Population growth	22.8%	21.1%	Asian	1.3%	2.7%	Divorced/separated	19.8%	14.9%
Median age	37.2	36.1	Hispanic	61.7%	10.6%	Married with children	22.7%	23.7%
Percent Democrat	52.9%	44.5%	Religious observance	39.6%	48.9%	Single with children	11.1%	9.1%
Percent Republican	46.6%	54.5%	Diversity measure	72.0	40.1	Percent over age 65	13.8%	12.9%

INCOME	AREA	U.S. AVG	EMPLOYMENT	AREA	U.S. AVG	EMPLOYING INDUSTRIES	AREA	U.S. AVG
Per capita income	$20,510	$23,235	Unemployment rate	5.0%	4.7%	Largest: Healthcare & Social Assistance		
Household income	$40,519	$46,414	Recent job growth	4.1%	1.3%			
Household income < $25K	32.1%	26.2%	Projected future job growth	13.4%	11.5%	Percent manufacturing	11.7%	15.4%
Household income > $75K	23.4%	25.4%	White collar	61.3%	57.8%	Percent public sector	12.8%	15.7%
Household income growth	12.7%	13.6%	Blue collar	21.2%	25.2%	Percent construction	9.4%	9.9%

Population

Economy & Jobs
Score: 63.1
Rank: 139

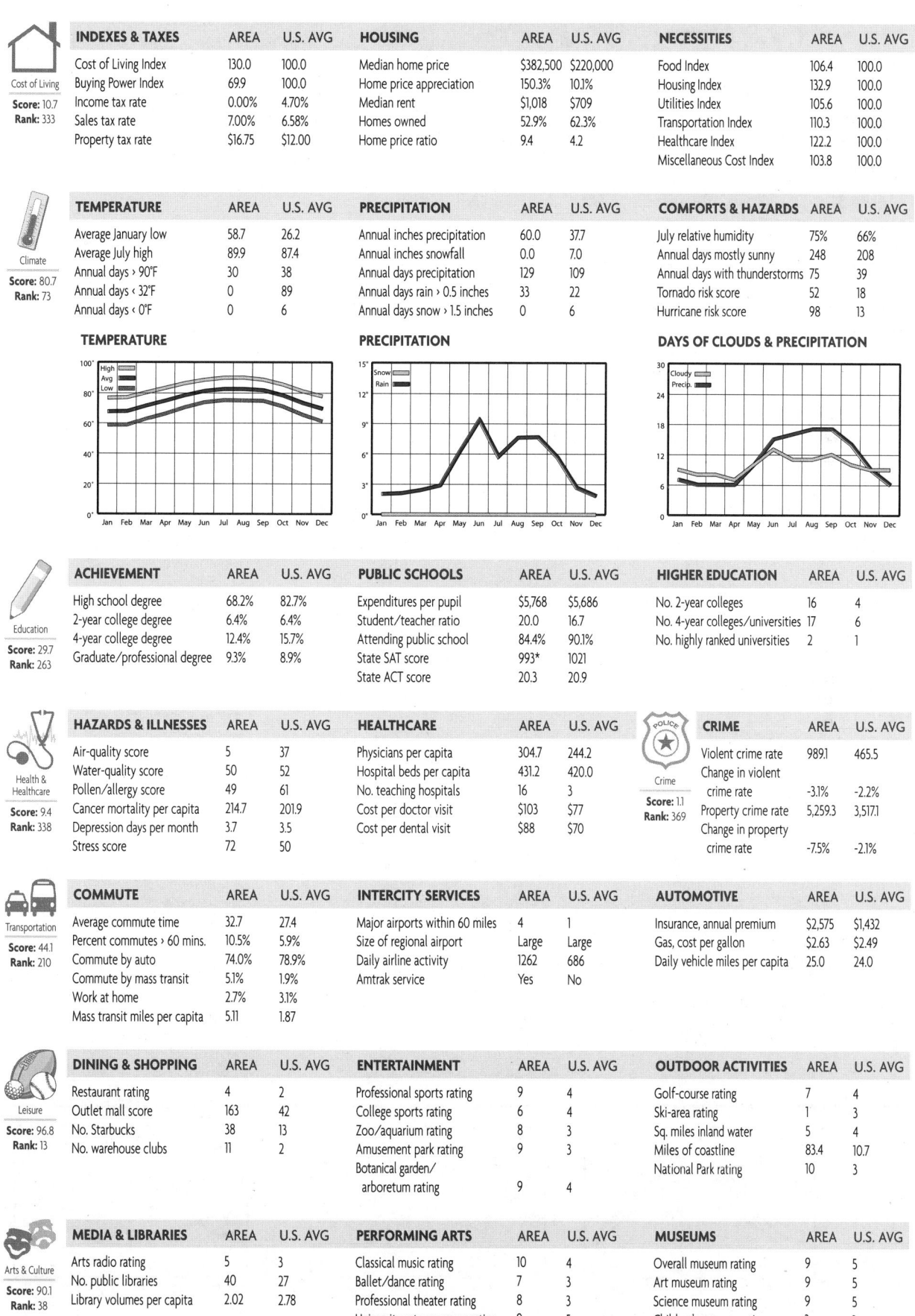

Cost of Living
Score: 10.7
Rank: 333

INDEXES & TAXES	AREA	U.S. AVG	HOUSING	AREA	U.S. AVG	NECESSITIES	AREA	U.S. AVG
Cost of Living Index	130.0	100.0	Median home price	$382,500	$220,000	Food Index	106.4	100.0
Buying Power Index	69.9	100.0	Home price appreciation	150.3%	10.1%	Housing Index	132.9	100.0
Income tax rate	0.00%	4.70%	Median rent	$1,018	$709	Utilities Index	105.6	100.0
Sales tax rate	7.00%	6.58%	Homes owned	52.9%	62.3%	Transportation Index	110.3	100.0
Property tax rate	$16.75	$12.00	Home price ratio	9.4	4.2	Healthcare Index	122.2	100.0
						Miscellaneous Cost Index	103.8	100.0

Climate
Score: 80.7
Rank: 73

TEMPERATURE	AREA	U.S. AVG	PRECIPITATION	AREA	U.S. AVG	COMFORTS & HAZARDS	AREA	U.S. AVG
Average January low	58.7	26.2	Annual inches precipitation	60.0	37.7	July relative humidity	75%	66%
Average July high	89.9	87.4	Annual inches snowfall	0.0	7.0	Annual days mostly sunny	248	208
Annual days > 90°F	30	38	Annual days precipitation	129	109	Annual days with thunderstorms	75	39
Annual days < 32°F	0	89	Annual days rain > 0.5 inches	33	22	Tornado risk score	52	18
Annual days < 0°F	0	6	Annual days snow > 1.5 inches	0	6	Hurricane risk score	98	13

TEMPERATURE

PRECIPITATION

DAYS OF CLOUDS & PRECIPITATION

Education
Score: 29.7
Rank: 263

ACHIEVEMENT	AREA	U.S. AVG	PUBLIC SCHOOLS	AREA	U.S. AVG	HIGHER EDUCATION	AREA	U.S. AVG
High school degree	68.2%	82.7%	Expenditures per pupil	$5,768	$5,686	No. 2-year colleges	16	4
2-year college degree	6.4%	6.4%	Student/teacher ratio	20.0	16.7	No. 4-year colleges/universities	17	6
4-year college degree	12.4%	15.7%	Attending public school	84.4%	90.1%	No. highly ranked universities	2	1
Graduate/professional degree	9.3%	8.9%	State SAT score	993*	1021			
			State ACT score	20.3	20.9			

Health & Healthcare
Score: 9.4
Rank: 338

Crime
Score: 1.1
Rank: 369

HAZARDS & ILLNESSES	AREA	U.S. AVG	HEALTHCARE	AREA	U.S. AVG	CRIME	AREA	U.S. AVG
Air-quality score	5	37	Physicians per capita	304.7	244.2	Violent crime rate	989.1	465.5
Water-quality score	50	52	Hospital beds per capita	431.2	420.0	Change in violent crime rate	-3.1%	-2.2%
Pollen/allergy score	49	61	No. teaching hospitals	16	3	Property crime rate	5,259.3	3,517.1
Cancer mortality per capita	214.7	201.9	Cost per doctor visit	$103	$77	Change in property crime rate	-7.5%	-2.1%
Depression days per month	3.7	3.5	Cost per dental visit	$88	$70			
Stress score	72	50						

Transportation
Score: 44.1
Rank: 210

COMMUTE	AREA	U.S. AVG	INTERCITY SERVICES	AREA	U.S. AVG	AUTOMOTIVE	AREA	U.S. AVG
Average commute time	32.7	27.4	Major airports within 60 miles	4	1	Insurance, annual premium	$2,575	$1,432
Percent commutes > 60 mins.	10.5%	5.9%	Size of regional airport	Large	Large	Gas, cost per gallon	$2.63	$2.49
Commute by auto	74.0%	78.9%	Daily airline activity	1262	686	Daily vehicle miles per capita	25.0	24.0
Commute by mass transit	5.1%	1.9%	Amtrak service	Yes	No			
Work at home	2.7%	3.1%						
Mass transit miles per capita	5.11	1.87						

Leisure
Score: 96.8
Rank: 13

DINING & SHOPPING	AREA	U.S. AVG	ENTERTAINMENT	AREA	U.S. AVG	OUTDOOR ACTIVITIES	AREA	U.S. AVG
Restaurant rating	4	2	Professional sports rating	9	4	Golf-course rating	7	4
Outlet mall score	163	42	College sports rating	6	4	Ski-area rating	1	3
No. Starbucks	38	13	Zoo/aquarium rating	8	3	Sq. miles inland water	5	4
No. warehouse clubs	11	2	Amusement park rating	9	3	Miles of coastline	83.4	10.7
			Botanical garden/ arboretum rating	9	4	National Park rating	10	3

Arts & Culture
Score: 90.1
Rank: 38

MEDIA & LIBRARIES	AREA	U.S. AVG	PERFORMING ARTS	AREA	U.S. AVG	MUSEUMS	AREA	U.S. AVG
Arts radio rating	5	3	Classical music rating	10	4	Overall museum rating	9	5
No. public libraries	40	27	Ballet/dance rating	7	3	Art museum rating	9	5
Library volumes per capita	2.02	2.78	Professional theater rating	8	3	Science museum rating	9	5
			University arts programs rating	9	5	Children's museum rating	3	3

Michigan City–La Porte, IN

Score: 56.0   **Rank:** 209   **2004 rank:** not ranked

Profile: Small-town complex
Location: Extreme northern Indiana, at the Michigan border
Elevation: 608 feet
Time zone: Central Standard Time

PRO	CON
Nearby recreation	Economic cycles
Close to Chicago	Harsh winters
Cost of living and housing	Low educational attainment

It's kind of hard to call any place in Indiana a "beach town," but Michigan City probably comes the closest to earning this designation. Located right on Lake Michigan and almost adjacent to the Indiana Dunes National Seashore, the area picks up its share of tourist activity from Chicago and all over the Midwest in the late spring, summer, and fall. Otherwise, both Michigan City and La Porte have a strong industrial heritage, with an important but somewhat declining old-economy manufacturing base. Michigan City in particular has the well-preserved markings of a typical Midwestern industrial melting-pot city. Downtown is clean and features a number of places of historic interest. There are some minor arts and culture amenities, including museums, theater, and waterfront performances. Cost of living is low, and median home prices are under $100,000. Chicago, 60 miles to the west, is relatively close and can be reached by commuter rail services.

Northern Indiana is generally flat, and if anything, it gets flatter as you approach the Lake Michigan shore. The continental climate is pleasant in summer, but proximity to the lake causes high winter winds and substantial precipitation, while also moderating extreme cold. Cloudy days are common. First freeze is early October; last is early May.

Population

DEMOGRAPHICS	AREA	U.S. AVG	ETHNIC COMPOSITION	AREA	U.S. AVG	RESIDENT PROFILE	AREA	U.S. AVG
Population	109,665		White	86.2%	79.0%	Single	29.7%	32.4%
Population density per sq. mile	183.3	358.5	Black	9.9%	10.5%	Married	52.5%	52.7%
Population growth	2.4%	21.1%	Asian	0.4%	2.7%	Divorced/separated	17.8%	14.9%
Median age	37.6	36.1	Hispanic	3.7%	10.6%	Married with children	22.6%	23.7%
Percent Democrat	49.6%	44.5%	Religious observance	44.9%	48.9%	Single with children	9.0%	9.1%
Percent Republican	49.1%	54.5%	Diversity measure	30.0	40.1	Percent over age 65	13.7%	12.9%

Economy & Jobs
Score: 23.8
Rank: 285

INCOME	AREA	U.S. AVG	EMPLOYMENT	AREA	U.S. AVG	EMPLOYING INDUSTRIES	AREA	U.S. AVG
Per capita income	$21,106	$23,235	Unemployment rate	5.4%	4.7%	Largest: Manufacturing		
Household income	$45,578	$46,414	Recent job growth	-0.1%	1.3%			
Household income < $25K	24.6%	26.2%	Projected future job growth	2.0%	11.5%	Percent manufacturing	23.4%	15.4%
Household income > $75K	22.4%	25.4%	White collar	48.0%	57.8%	Percent public sector	11.4%	15.7%
Household income growth	10.0%	13.6%	Blue collar	35.2%	25.2%	Percent construction	11.9%	9.9%

Cost of Living
Score: 94.9
Rank: 20

INDEXES & TAXES	AREA	U.S. AVG	HOUSING	AREA	U.S. AVG	NECESSITIES	AREA	U.S. AVG
Cost of Living Index	79.1	100.0	Median home price	$97,900	$220,000	Food Index	94.6	100.0
Buying Power Index	129.2	100.0	Home price appreciation	26.8%	10.1%	Housing Index	50.1	100.0
Income tax rate	3.40%	4.70%	Median rent	$610	$709	Utilities Index	105.1	100.0
Sales tax rate	6.00%	6.58%	Homes owned	68.3%	62.3%	Transportation Index	104.2	100.0
Property tax rate	$9.72	$12.00	Home price ratio	2.1	4.2	Healthcare Index	99.3	100.0
						Miscellaneous Cost Index	96.6	100.0

Climate
Score: 24.1
Rank: 283

TEMPERATURE	AREA	U.S. AVG	PRECIPITATION	AREA	U.S. AVG	COMFORTS & HAZARDS	AREA	U.S. AVG
Average January low	13.0	26.2	Annual inches precipitation	35.4	37.7	July relative humidity	57%	66%
Average July high	84.0	87.4	Annual inches snowfall	39.0	7.0	Annual days mostly sunny	191	208
Annual days > 90°F	17	38	Annual days precipitation	125	109	Annual days with thunderstorms	41	39
Annual days < 32°F	132	89	Annual days rain > 0.5 inches	23	22	Tornado risk score	3	18
Annual days < 0°F	12	6	Annual days snow > 1.5 inches	16	6	Hurricane risk score	1	13

TEMPERATURE

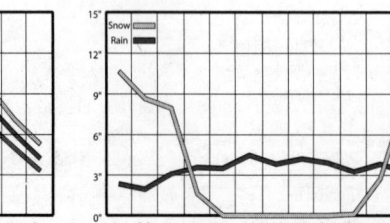

PRECIPITATION

DAYS OF CLOUDS & PRECIPITATION

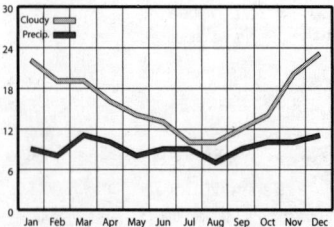

Education
Score: 10.4
Rank: 334

ACHIEVEMENT	AREA	U.S. AVG	PUBLIC SCHOOLS	AREA	U.S. AVG	HIGHER EDUCATION	AREA	U.S. AVG
High school degree	80.6%	82.7%	Expenditures per pupil	$5,782	$5,686	No. 2-year colleges	1	4
2-year college degree	5.5%	6.4%	Student/teacher ratio	16.7	16.7	No. 4-year colleges/universities	1	6
4-year college degree	8.9%	15.7%	Attending public school	89.3%	90.1%	No. highly ranked universities	0	1
Graduate/professional degree	5.0%	8.9%	State SAT score	1007*	1021			
			State ACT score	21.7	20.9			

Health & Healthcare
Score: 70.3
Rank: 112

HAZARDS & ILLNESSES	AREA	U.S. AVG	HEALTHCARE	AREA	U.S. AVG	CRIME	AREA	U.S. AVG
Air-quality score	44	37	Physicians per capita	163.8	244.2	Violent crime rate	203.0	465.5
Water-quality score	33	52	Hospital beds per capita	617.3	420.0	Change in violent crime rate	-1.5%	-2.2%
Pollen/allergy score	56	61	No. teaching hospitals	1	3	Property crime rate	3,867.3	3,517.1
Cancer mortality per capita	221.0	201.9	Cost per doctor visit	$69	$77	Change in property crime rate	5.8%	-2.1%
Depression days per month	3.2	3.5	Cost per dental visit	$74	$70			
Stress score	72	50						

Crime **Score:** 57.0 **Rank:** 162

Transportation
Score: 93.6
Rank: 25

COMMUTE	AREA	U.S. AVG	INTERCITY SERVICES	AREA	U.S. AVG	AUTOMOTIVE	AREA	U.S. AVG
Average commute time	23.9	27.4	Major airports within 60 miles	2	1	Insurance, annual premium	$1,105	$1,432
Percent commutes > 60 mins.	5.9%	5.9%	Size of regional airport	Large	Large	Gas, cost per gallon	$2.52	$2.49
Commute by auto	83.7%	78.9%	Daily airline activity	1886	686	Daily vehicle miles per capita	23.3	24.0
Commute by mass transit	1.0%	1.9%	Amtrak service	Yes	No			
Work at home	2.7%	3.1%						
Mass transit miles per capita	0.96	1.87						

Leisure
Score: 82.6
Rank: 65

DINING & SHOPPING	AREA	U.S. AVG	ENTERTAINMENT	AREA	U.S. AVG	OUTDOOR ACTIVITIES	AREA	U.S. AVG
Restaurant rating	1	2	Professional sports rating	9	4	Golf-course rating	8	4
Outlet mall score	161	42	College sports rating	7	4	Ski-area rating	4	3
No. Starbucks	1	13	Zoo/aquarium rating	7	3	Sq. miles inland water	3	4
No. warehouse clubs	0	2	Amusement park rating	1	3	Miles of coastline	8.0	10.7
			Botanical garden/arboretum rating	6	4	National Park rating	2	3

Arts & Culture
Score: 81.6
Rank: 70

MEDIA & LIBRARIES	AREA	U.S. AVG	PERFORMING ARTS	AREA	U.S. AVG	MUSEUMS	AREA	U.S. AVG
Arts radio rating	1	3	Classical music rating	7	4	Overall museum rating	8	5
No. public libraries	11	27	Ballet/dance rating	7	3	Art museum rating	8	5
Library volumes per capita	5.07	2.78	Professional theater rating	1	3	Science museum rating	7	5
			University arts programs rating	8	5	Children's museum rating	6	3

Midland–Odessa, TX

Score: 48.6   Rank: 255   2004 rank: 283

Profile: Small cities
Location: West Texas high country near southeast corner of New Mexico
Elevation: 2,851 feet
Time zone: Central Standard Time

PRO
Cost of living
Small-town atmosphere
Dry climate

CON
Entertainment
Unattractive setting
Economic cycles

Midland was so named as the midpoint in an otherwise empty trip between Dallas and El Paso, while Odessa received its name from homesick Russian railroad laborers in the 1880s. The economic base is concentrated mainly in the oil and gas industry and employment prospects are up and down with that industry. Odessa has two higher-education facilities: a small University of Texas campus with 3,500 students and a health science center run by Texas Tech. Midland is the county seat and more of a commercial center, and oil money brought an unusually attractive, skyscraper-centered downtown given its size and location. The area's real story is low cost of living and affordable housing. Diversions include the Permian Basin Petroleum Museum and the Confederate Air Force, the largest owner and operator of vintage aircraft from World War II. Otherwise, the area is dry, dusty, and flat, with little physical or cultural interest.

The Midland–Odessa region is on a relatively high southern extension of the Great Plains. The terrain is level with slight undulations. Summer daytime temperatures are hot but with a large diurnal range and most nights are comfortable. Humidity is low. Winters are characterized by frequent cold periods followed by rapid warming. Cloudiness is minimal. Summer showers are common and most of the annual precipitation comes from violent spring and early summer thunderstorms. Due to the flat nature of the countryside, local flooding and blowing dust may occur.

Population

DEMOGRAPHICS	AREA	U.S. AVG	ETHNIC COMPOSITION	AREA	U.S. AVG	RESIDENT PROFILE	AREA	U.S. AVG
Population	244,036		White	74.0%	79.0%	Single	27.7%	32.4%
Population density per sq. mile	135.5	358.5	Black	5.4%	10.5%	Married	56.8%	52.7%
Population growth	8.3%	21.1%	Asian	0.8%	2.7%	Divorced/separated	15.5%	14.9%
Median age	33.2	36.1	Hispanic	40.1%	10.6%	Married with children	28.2%	23.7%
Percent Democrat	20.8%	44.5%	Religious observance	57.8%	48.9%	Single with children	10.4%	9.1%
Percent Republican	78.6%	54.5%	Diversity measure	69.2	40.1	Percent over age 65	11.5%	12.9%

Economy & Jobs
Score: 57.0
Rank: 162

INCOME	AREA	U.S. AVG	EMPLOYMENT	AREA	U.S. AVG	EMPLOYING INDUSTRIES	AREA	U.S. AVG
Per capita income	$20,315	$23,235	Unemployment rate	4.3%	4.7%	Largest: Mining		
Household income	$40,126	$46,414	Recent job growth	2.5%	1.3%			
Household income < $25K	30.9%	26.2%	Projected future job growth	8.8%	11.5%	Percent manufacturing	13.4%	15.4%
Household income > $75K	20.8%	25.4%	White collar	57.9%	57.8%	Percent public sector	14.1%	15.7%
Household income growth	14.7%	13.6%	Blue collar	25.9%	25.2%	Percent construction	12.6%	9.9%

Cost of Living
Score: 88.5
Rank: 44

INDEXES & TAXES	AREA	U.S. AVG	HOUSING	AREA	U.S. AVG	NECESSITIES	AREA	U.S. AVG
Cost of Living Index	78.6	100.0	Median home price	$104,300	$220,000	Food Index	88.2	100.0
Buying Power Index	114.4	100.0	Home price appreciation	35.7%	10.1%	Housing Index	44.6	100.0
Income tax rate	0.00%	4.70%	Median rent	$531	$709	Utilities Index	104.6	100.0
Sales tax rate	8.25%	6.58%	Homes owned	61.3%	62.3%	Transportation Index	95.7	100.0
Property tax rate	$19.91	$12.00	Home price ratio	2.6	4.2	Healthcare Index	98.2	100.0
						Miscellaneous Cost Index	101.3	100.0

Climate
Score: 88.5
Rank: 44

TEMPERATURE	AREA	U.S. AVG	PRECIPITATION	AREA	U.S. AVG	COMFORTS & HAZARDS	AREA	U.S. AVG
Average January low	29.4	26.2	Annual inches precipitation	13.5	37.7	July relative humidity	53%	66%
Average July high	95.0	87.4	Annual inches snowfall	3.5	7.0	Annual days mostly sunny	263	208
Annual days > 90°F	92	38	Annual days precipitation	53	109	Annual days with thunderstorms	36	39
Annual days < 32°F	64	89	Annual days rain > 0.5 inches	7	22	Tornado risk score	26	18
Annual days < 0°F	0	6	Annual days snow > 1.5 inches	1	6	Hurricane risk score	1	13

TEMPERATURE

PRECIPITATION

DAYS OF CLOUDS & PRECIPITATION

Education
Score: 16.6
Rank: 311

ACHIEVEMENT	AREA	U.S. AVG	PUBLIC SCHOOLS	AREA	U.S. AVG	HIGHER EDUCATION	AREA	U.S. AVG
High school degree	73.5%	82.7%	Expenditures per pupil	$4,540	$5,686	No. 2-year colleges	2	4
2-year college degree	5.8%	6.4%	Student/teacher ratio	16.6	16.7	No. 4-year colleges/universities	1	6
4-year college degree	13.5%	15.7%	Attending public school	93.9%	90.1%	No. highly ranked universities	0	1
Graduate/professional degree	4.9%	8.9%	State SAT score	997*	1021			
			State ACT score	20.3	20.9			

Health & Healthcare
Score: 64.4
Rank: 134

HAZARDS & ILLNESSES	AREA	U.S. AVG	HEALTHCARE	AREA	U.S. AVG	CRIME	AREA	U.S. AVG
Air-quality score	46	37	Physicians per capita	178.2	244.2	Violent crime rate	434.1	465.5
Water-quality score	50	52	Hospital beds per capita	401.2	420.0	Change in violent crime rate	-11.9%	-2.2%
Pollen/allergy score	71	61	No. teaching hospitals	2	3	Property crime rate	3,711.4	3,517.1
Cancer mortality per capita	166.6	201.9	Cost per doctor visit	$70	$77	Change in property crime rate	-9.8%	-2.1%
Depression days per month	2.2	3.5	Cost per dental visit	$61	$70			
Stress score	25	50						

Crime
Score: 64.2
Rank: 134

Transportation
Score: 46.3
Rank: 201

COMMUTE	AREA	U.S. AVG	INTERCITY SERVICES	AREA	U.S. AVG	AUTOMOTIVE	AREA	U.S. AVG
Average commute time	20.0	27.4	Major airports within 60 miles	0	1	Insurance, annual premium	$1,008	$1,432
Percent commutes > 60 mins.	4.0%	5.9%	Size of regional airport	Small	Large	Gas, cost per gallon	$2.43	$2.49
Commute by auto	82.6%	78.9%	Daily airline activity	40	686	Daily vehicle miles per capita	20.3	24.0
Commute by mass transit	0.2%	1.9%	Amtrak service	No	No			
Work at home	2.4%	3.1%						
Mass transit miles per capita	0.16	1.87						

Leisure
Score: 2.1
Rank: 365

DINING & SHOPPING	AREA	U.S. AVG	ENTERTAINMENT	AREA	U.S. AVG	OUTDOOR ACTIVITIES	AREA	U.S. AVG
Restaurant rating	1	2	Professional sports rating	3	4	Golf-course rating	1	4
Outlet mall score	0	42	College sports rating	2	4	Ski-area rating	1	3
No. Starbucks	2	13	Zoo/aquarium rating	1	3	Sq. miles inland water	1	4
No. warehouse clubs	1	2	Amusement park rating	1	3	Miles of coastline	0.0	10.7
			Botanical garden/ arboretum rating	2	4	National Park rating	1	3

Arts & Culture
Score: 23.0
Rank: 287

MEDIA & LIBRARIES	AREA	U.S. AVG	PERFORMING ARTS	AREA	U.S. AVG	MUSEUMS	AREA	U.S. AVG
Arts radio rating	1	3	Classical music rating	3	4	Overall museum rating	4	5
No. public libraries	3	27	Ballet/dance rating	1	3	Art museum rating	6	5
Library volumes per capita	1.50	2.78	Professional theater rating	1	3	Science museum rating	6	5
			University arts programs rating	1	5	Children's museum rating	5	3

Milwaukee–Waukesha–West Allis, WI   **Score:** 45.4   **Rank:** 280   **2004 rank:** 198

Profile: Large-city/suburban complex
Location: Extreme southeast Wisconsin along Lake Michigan, 40 miles north of Illinois border
Elevation: 693 feet
Time zone: Central Standard Time

PRO	CON
Downtown revitalization	Winter climate
Arts and culture	Economic cycles
Close to Chicago	Some gritty areas

Somewhat in the economic and cultural shadow of Chicago, 90 miles south, Milwaukee is nevertheless a self-sufficient city, as well as a commercial and cultural center for Wisconsin and particularly its more populous southeastern portions. A melting pot for 19th-century immigrants from northern Europe, the city has kept up old-world traditions, most notably the brewing (and consumption) of beer. Following a period of industrial decline—including the brewing industry—the city has revitalized some areas, particularly downtown, and created an area of lakefront parks and museums, in modest imitation of Chicago. The business picture has changed to include more financial services and retailing companies along with the traditional base of metal products, electrical equipment, and machine tools. The area is headquarters to a surprising list of mid-size corporations, including Briggs & Stratton, Harley-Davidson, Allen-Bradley, Rockwell Automation, and Johnson Controls, which operate plants in the vicinity, and service players such as Manpower, Inc., Northwestern Mutual, and retailer Kohl's.

Milwaukee has a full complement of cultural, performing arts, and recreational amenities, including a world-class art museum. Chicago is close enough to add to the cultural mix on occasion. The city has good transportation services, thanks to airlines choosing to avoid Chicago and good rail service arteries emanating from the Windy City. Suburbs have a true neighborhood feel, often with a strong ethnic character and

substantial historic preservation. The city won a National Trust for Historic Preservation "Dozen Distinctive Locations" award for 2006. Waukesha, a few miles to the west, is a large satellite with a small college presence and strong family-oriented residential areas. West Allis is a large and fairly nondescript older suburb west of Milwaukee between the downtown core and Waukesha. A bit surprising considering proximity to Chicago is the city's strong complement of major-league sports, including the NBA's Bucks and the MLB's Brewers. The economy has been affected by the slowdown in manufacturing, and employment trends continue to be weak and should soon hit bottom. Cost of living and housing are a bit high on a Wisconsin scale but attractive nationally and considering proximity to Chicago. The area has a strong community pride and residents have a reputation for having fun.

The city is located on a shore plain where the Menomonee River flows into Lake Michigan. Terrain is generally flat near the lake, giving way to rolling hills inland with mixed farmland and woodland. Summer temperatures reach into the 80s and 90s with occasional warmer and humid spells. Winter precipitation is usually of long duration and low intensity in the form of snow or mixed rain and snow. Occasional severe winter storms can drop an excess of 10 inches of snow and deliver frigid Canadian air. Winds from Lake Michigan can generate significant wind chills. First freeze is early October; last is early May.

Population

DEMOGRAPHICS	AREA	U.S. AVG	ETHNIC COMPOSITION	AREA	U.S. AVG	RESIDENT PROFILE	AREA	U.S. AVG
Population	1,518,832		White	75.1%	79.0%	Single	36.4%	32.4%
Population density per sq. mile	1040.4	358.5	Black	16.5%	10.5%	Married	50.5%	52.7%
Population growth	7.6%	21.1%	Asian	2.6%	2.7%	Divorced/separated	13.1%	14.9%
Median age	36.6	36.1	Hispanic	7.1%	10.6%	Married with children	22.2%	23.7%
Percent Democrat	50.1%	44.5%	Religious observance	54.9%	48.9%	Single with children	9.6%	9.1%
Percent Republican	49.1%	54.5%	Diversity measure	43.3	40.1	Percent over age 65	12.5%	12.9%

$ Economy & Jobs
Score: 15.5
Rank: 315

INCOME	AREA	U.S. AVG	EMPLOYMENT	AREA	U.S. AVG	EMPLOYING INDUSTRIES	AREA	U.S. AVG
Per capita income	$26,701	$23,235	Unemployment rate	5.1%	4.7%	Largest: Manufacturing		
Household income	$53,034	$46,414	Recent job growth	-0.2%	1.3%			
Household income < $25K	21.7%	26.2%	Projected future job growth	2.2%	11.5%	Percent manufacturing	17.0%	15.4%
Household income > $75K	31.0%	25.4%	White collar	62.1%	57.8%	Percent public sector	11.3%	15.7%
Household income growth	12.6%	13.6%	Blue collar	24.1%	25.2%	Percent construction	7.1%	9.9%

Cost of Living
Score: 15.8
Rank: 314

INDEXES & TAXES	AREA	U.S. AVG	HOUSING	AREA	U.S. AVG	NECESSITIES	AREA	U.S. AVG
Cost of Living Index	101.5	100.0	Median home price	$227,700	$220,000	Food Index	100.5	100.0
Buying Power Index	117.1	100.0	Home price appreciation	44.1%	10.1%	Housing Index	72.3	100.0
Income tax rate	6.93%	4.70%	Median rent	$726	$709	Utilities Index	125.3	100.0
Sales tax rate	5.48%	6.58%	Homes owned	59.1%	62.3%	Transportation Index	104.3	100.0
Property tax rate	$23.54	$12.00	Home price ratio	4.3	4.2	Healthcare Index	99.0	100.0
						Miscellaneous Cost Index	97.0	100.0

Climate
Score: 12.3
Rank: 327

TEMPERATURE	AREA	U.S. AVG	PRECIPITATION	AREA	U.S. AVG	COMFORTS & HAZARDS	AREA	U.S. AVG
Average January low	11.4	26.2	Annual inches precipitation	29.0	37.7	July relative humidity	73%	66%
Average July high	80.4	87.4	Annual inches snowfall	45.0	7.0	Annual days mostly sunny	195	208
Annual days > 90°F	9	38	Annual days precipitation	122	109	Annual days with thunderstorms	36	39
Annual days < 32°F	146	89	Annual days rain > 0.5 inches	20	22	Tornado risk score	19	18
Annual days < 0°F	16	6	Annual days snow > 1.5 inches	11	6	Hurricane risk score	1	13

TEMPERATURE

PRECIPITATION

DAYS OF CLOUDS & PRECIPITATION

Education
Score: 71.7
Rank: 107

ACHIEVEMENT	AREA	U.S. AVG	PUBLIC SCHOOLS	AREA	U.S. AVG	HIGHER EDUCATION	AREA	U.S. AVG
High school degree	84.5%	82.7%	Expenditures per pupil	$7,247	$5,686	No. 2-year colleges	5	4
2-year college degree	6.8%	6.4%	Student/teacher ratio	17.4	16.7	No. 4-year colleges/universities	21	6
4-year college degree	18.3%	15.7%	Attending public school	81.1%	90.1%	No. highly ranked universities	2	1
Graduate/professional degree	8.7%	8.9%	State SAT score	1188	1021			
			State ACT score	22.2*	20.9			

Health & Healthcare
Score: 43.0
Rank: 212

Crime
Score: 44.1
Rank: 209

HAZARDS & ILLNESSES	AREA	U.S. AVG	HEALTHCARE	AREA	U.S. AVG	CRIME	AREA	U.S. AVG
Air-quality score	23	37	Physicians per capita	323.6	244.2	Violent crime rate	457.9	465.5
Water-quality score	25	52	Hospital beds per capita	365.8	420.0	Change in violent crime rate	9.9%	-2.2%
Pollen/allergy score	42	61	No. teaching hospitals	14	3	Property crime rate	3,521.5	3,517.1
Cancer mortality per capita	215.7	201.9	Cost per doctor visit	$92	$77	Change in property crime rate	-10.2%	-2.1%
Depression days per month	3.7	3.5	Cost per dental visit	$60	$70			
Stress score	62	50						

Transportation
Score: 97.6
Rank: 10

COMMUTE	AREA	U.S. AVG	INTERCITY SERVICES	AREA	U.S. AVG	AUTOMOTIVE	AREA	U.S. AVG
Average commute time	24.0	27.4	Major airports within 60 miles	3	1	Insurance, annual premium	$1,877	$1,432
Percent commutes > 60 mins.	3.7%	5.9%	Size of regional airport	Large	Large	Gas, cost per gallon	$2.55	$2.49
Commute by auto	79.6%	78.9%	Daily airline activity	2117	686	Daily vehicle miles per capita	24.9	24.0
Commute by mass transit	4.4%	1.9%	Amtrak service	Yes	No			
Work at home	2.6%	3.1%						
Mass transit miles per capita	4.39	1.87						

Leisure
Score: 80.7
Rank: 72

DINING & SHOPPING	AREA	U.S. AVG	ENTERTAINMENT	AREA	U.S. AVG	OUTDOOR ACTIVITIES	AREA	U.S. AVG
Restaurant rating	4	2	Professional sports rating	6	4	Golf-course rating	7	4
Outlet mall score	78	42	College sports rating	3	4	Ski-area rating	3	3
No. Starbucks	33	13	Zoo/aquarium rating	7	3	Sq. miles inland water	4	4
No. warehouse clubs	2	2	Amusement park rating	1	3	Miles of coastline	48.1	10.7
			Botanical garden/ arboretum rating	9	4	National Park rating	1	3

Arts & Culture	MEDIA & LIBRARIES	AREA	U.S. AVG	PERFORMING ARTS	AREA	U.S. AVG	MUSEUMS	AREA	U.S. AVG
Score: 93.0	Arts radio rating	7	3	Classical music rating	9	4	Overall museum rating	9	5
Rank: 27	No. public libraries	53	27	Ballet/dance rating	5	3	Art museum rating	9	5
	Library volumes per capita	4.02	2.78	Professional theater rating	9	3	Science museum rating	8	5
				University arts programs rating	7	5	Children's museum rating	7	3

Minneapolis–St. Paul–Bloomington, MN   Score: 47.2   Rank: 262   2004 rank: 24

Profile: Regional-center complex/capital city
Location: Southeast Minnesota along upper Mississippi River, 20 miles west of Wisconsin border
Elevation: 838 feet
Time zone: Central Standard Time

PRO	CON
Education	Harsh winters
Attractive neighborhoods	Cost of living
Attractive downtown	Growth and sprawl

The "twin cities" serve as a regional center for the upper Midwest and northern Great Plains as far as the Rocky Mountains. The fully cosmopolitan area is a balanced industrial, commercial, educational, and cultural center, and functions much as one city. The area is one of the most economically diverse in the country, serving as headquarters to large firms in agriculture, food, banking, technology, retailing, healthcare, and transportation. A few of the well-known companies include General Mills, 3M, US Bancorp, United Healthcare, and retailers Target and Best Buy. Job growth is still fairly modest, but overall, the Twin Cities have a strong and prosperous feel.

The twin downtown areas sit on either side of the Mississippi River. Both are modern with attractive buildings, clean streets, entertainment, nightlife, parks, museums, and other first-class arts and cultural amenities. Minneapolis is more progressive, energetic, and cosmopolitan, while St. Paul is the smaller, quieter, and more traditional of the two. Both downtowns are well used and aided by a network of elevated interior walkways called "skyways" that connect buildings and attractions—a feature necessitated by the harsh winter climate. According to one source, the area has more theaters, dance companies, and classical concerts per capita than any city outside of New York. Because Minneapolis–St. Paul is not a tourist destination, the local population enjoys these amenities almost exclusively. The population is highly educated, schools have an excellent reputation, and there is an abundant intellectual energy among the area's citizens. The city ranked no. 1 in the Central Connecticut State University annual Most Literate Cities study as recently as 2004, but dropped to no. 2 behind Seattle in 2005—not a major change.

For those not interested in the arts and downtown scene, there is still plenty to do. Sports are a big attraction—the city has a full assortment of major and minor league sports teams. On the south side of Minneapolis in Bloomington, the Mall of America—with 400 stores—is the largest mall in the U.S. and is as much an amusement park as a mall. Such indoor facilities are particularly attractive given the winter climate. Summer recreation includes outdoor activities on the many surrounding lakes and wildlife viewing. Winter-sports enthusiasts enjoy ice-skating and hockey, snowmobiling, and cross-country and downhill skiing at nearby facilities. For those wishing to get away, air service is excellent, although the dominance of Northwest Airlines can mean higher fares.

The downtown area is surrounded by a patchwork of residential and commercial neighborhoods which are on the whole more attractive than most other cities of the size. Some of the better suburbs lie south and west of Minneapolis. The more upscale Edina and Eden Prairie are comfortable and well planned, and some of Edina has an older tree-lined dignity interspersed with high-end retail developments. Bloomington and Richfield are more middle class, with substantial commercial and retail development. Large super-suburbs, including Lakeville and Apple Valley across the Minnesota River to the south, offer excellent family settings. Farther west, Minnetonka, the small upscale lakefront Wayzata, and the booming Maple Grove to the northwest offer an excellent set of residential choices, with considerable employment nearby. Commutes are busy and getting busier, but the variety of neighborhoods and location of commercial and industrial areas makes it possible for residents to choose their commute. Not to leave St. Paul out, Woodbury, Maplewood, and White Bear Lake are excellent suburbs, each with its own collection of quality employment in commercial areas nearby.

Cost, climate, and commutes hurt the ranking statistically, but we feel the area is much better than the numbers suggest. Winters are long and hard, with many days below zero. Cost of living has traditionally been high by national, and particularly regional, standards, but the rest of the nation is catching up. That said, the more expensive areas are far more expensive, especially on a Midwest scale, and Minnesota taxes are relatively high compared to other states. For those willing to wear warm clothes and sacrifice a little financially, the Twin Cities have a lot to offer. The ranking misses many of the subtle and unmeasurable qualities of the place, and shouldn't be taken too literally.

Terrain around the Twin Cities is flat or gently rolling, with a mix of open and densely wooded areas. Dotting the surrounding landscape are numerous lakes, the largest being Lake Minnetonka, 15 miles west. Most lakes are relatively small and shallow and freeze in winter. Seasonal temperatures vary from −30°F or lower to over 100°F. Summers can be warm and humid, but are usually pleasant. Winters are cold, with days ranging from cloudy near freezing to clear, bitter cold, and windy. The area averages 34 nights per year below zero, far more than any other large American city. Severe storms, including blizzards, freezing rain, tornadoes, wind, and hailstorms occur. Most precipitation occurs during the summer period, and snow cover is persistent through the winter, averaging 6 to 8 inches in the city and 8 to 10 inches in the suburbs. First freeze is October 1; last is early May.

Population

DEMOGRAPHICS	AREA	U.S. AVG	ETHNIC COMPOSITION	AREA	U.S. AVG	RESIDENT PROFILE	AREA	U.S. AVG
Population	3,138,324		White	84.3%	79.0%	Single	33.5%	32.4%
Population density per sq. mile	517.6	358.5	Black	5.8%	10.5%	Married	54.4%	52.7%
Population growth	27.8%	21.1%	Asian	4.9%	2.7%	Divorced/separated	12.1%	14.9%
Median age	35.6	36.1	Hispanic	4.0%	10.6%	Married with children	26.8%	23.7%
Percent Democrat	53.0%	44.5%	Religious observance	56.3%	48.9%	Single with children	8.0%	9.1%
Percent Republican	45.9%	54.5%	Diversity measure	32.6	40.1	Percent over age 65	9.9%	12.9%

Economy & Jobs
Score: 71.9
Rank: 106

INCOME	AREA	U.S. AVG	EMPLOYMENT	AREA	U.S. AVG	EMPLOYING INDUSTRIES	AREA	U.S. AVG
Per capita income	$30,504	$23,235	Unemployment rate	3.3%	4.7%	Largest: Finance & Insurance		
Household income	$62,776	$46,414	Recent job growth	1.4%	1.3%			
Household income < $25K	15.3%	26.2%	Projected future job growth	14.5%	11.5%	Percent manufacturing	12.9%	15.4%
Household income > $75K	39.6%	25.4%	White collar	66.7%	57.8%	Percent public sector	11.7%	15.7%
Household income growth	14.7%	13.6%	Blue collar	20.5%	25.2%	Percent construction	7.6%	9.9%

Cost of Living
Score: 12.3
Rank: 327

INDEXES & TAXES	AREA	U.S. AVG	HOUSING	AREA	U.S. AVG	NECESSITIES	AREA	U.S. AVG
Cost of Living Index	109.6	100.0	Median home price	$233,000	$220,000	Food Index	99.3	100.0
Buying Power Index	128.4	100.0	Home price appreciation	51.5%	10.1%	Housing Index	72.1	100.0
Income tax rate	7.96%	4.70%	Median rent	$858	$709	Utilities Index	148.3	100.0
Sales tax rate	6.78%	6.58%	Homes owned	72.0%	62.3%	Transportation Index	113.0	100.0
Property tax rate	$13.24	$12.00	Home price ratio	3.7	4.2	Healthcare Index	129.6	100.0
						Miscellaneous Cost Index	108.1	100.0

Climate
Score: 9.9
Rank: 336

TEMPERATURE	AREA	U.S. AVG	PRECIPITATION	AREA	U.S. AVG	COMFORTS & HAZARDS	AREA	U.S. AVG
Average January low	3.2	26.2	Annual inches precipitation	26.0	37.7	July relative humidity	69%	66%
Average July high	82.4	87.4	Annual inches snowfall	46.0	7.0	Annual days mostly sunny	200	208
Annual days > 90°F	15	38	Annual days precipitation	113	109	Annual days with thunderstorms	36	39
Annual days < 32°F	158	89	Annual days rain > 0.5 inches	16	22	Tornado risk score	20	18
Annual days < 0°F	34	6	Annual days snow > 1.5 inches	11	6	Hurricane risk score	0	13

TEMPERATURE

PRECIPITATION

DAYS OF CLOUDS & PRECIPITATION

Education
Score: 97.9
Rank: 9

ACHIEVEMENT	AREA	U.S. AVG	PUBLIC SCHOOLS	AREA	U.S. AVG	HIGHER EDUCATION	AREA	U.S. AVG
High school degree	90.7%	82.7%	Expenditures per pupil	$6,333	$5,686	No. 2-year colleges	19	4
2-year college degree	7.7%	6.4%	Student/teacher ratio	16.0	16.7	No. 4-year colleges/universities	40	6
4-year college degree	23.0%	15.7%	Attending public school	88.8%	90.1%	No. highly ranked universities	4	1
Graduate/professional degree	9.9%	8.9%	State SAT score	1191	1021			
			State ACT score	22.3*	20.9			

Health & Healthcare
Score: 14.7
Rank: 318

HAZARDS & ILLNESSES	AREA	U.S. AVG	HEALTHCARE	AREA	U.S. AVG	CRIME	AREA	U.S. AVG
Air-quality score	29	37	Physicians per capita	241.9	244.2	Violent crime rate	371.2	465.5
Water-quality score	23	52	Hospital beds per capita	265.6	420.0	Change in violent crime rate	9.6%	-2.2%
Pollen/allergy score	47	61	No. teaching hospitals	16	3	Property crime rate	3,809.3	3,517.1
Cancer mortality per capita	191.7	201.9	Cost per doctor visit	$84	$77	Change in property crime rate	12.5%	-2.1%
Depression days per month	3.2	3.5	Cost per dental visit	$70	$70			
Stress score	22	50						

Crime
Score: 48.9
Rank: 191

Transportation
Score: 43.0
Rank: 214

COMMUTE	AREA	U.S. AVG	INTERCITY SERVICES	AREA	U.S. AVG	AUTOMOTIVE	AREA	U.S. AVG
Average commute time	26.1	27.4	Major airports within 60 miles	1	1	Insurance, annual premium	$1,956	$1,432
Percent commutes > 60 mins.	4.4%	5.9%	Size of regional airport	Large	Large	Gas, cost per gallon	$2.48	$2.49
Commute by auto	78.7%	78.9%	Daily airline activity	624	686	Daily vehicle miles per capita	25.4	24.0
Commute by mass transit	4.2%	1.9%	Amtrak service	Yes	No			
Work at home	3.8%	3.1%						
Mass transit miles per capita	4.20	1.87						

DINING & SHOPPING	AREA	U.S. AVG	ENTERTAINMENT	AREA	U.S. AVG	OUTDOOR ACTIVITIES	AREA	U.S. AVG
Restaurant rating	1	2	Professional sports rating	7	4	Golf-course rating	9	4
Outlet mall score	69	42	College sports rating	8	4	Ski-area rating	5	3
No. Starbucks	58	13	Zoo/aquarium rating	9	3	Sq. miles inland water	10	4
No. warehouse clubs	12	2	Amusement park rating	10	3	Miles of coastline	0.0	10.7
			Botanical garden/ arboretum rating	9	4	National Park rating	3	3

Leisure
Score: 93.9
Rank: 24

MEDIA & LIBRARIES	AREA	U.S. AVG	PERFORMING ARTS	AREA	U.S. AVG	MUSEUMS	AREA	U.S. AVG
Arts radio rating	10	3	Classical music rating	9	4	Overall museum rating	10	5
No. public libraries	132	27	Ballet/dance rating	7	3	Art museum rating	10	5
Library volumes per capita	3.54	2.78	Professional theater rating	10	3	Science museum rating	10	5
			University arts programs rating	10	5	Children's museum rating	9	3

Arts & Culture
Score: 97.1
Rank: 12

Missoula, MT

Score: 70.3   Rank: 88   2004 rank: 96

Profile: College town
Location: Western Montana, 25 miles from Idaho border
Elevation: 3,361 feet
Time zone: Mountain Standard Time

PRO	CON
Attractive setting	Harsh winters
Outdoor recreation	Cost of housing
College-town amenities	Isolation

Missoula, located in the extreme west-central part of the state, is a youthful and progressive college town with an unusual mix of students, ranchers, jet-setters, and nature lovers, set among a beautiful backdrop of mountains and scenic valleys. The city is home to the University of Montana, and the area is an outdoor paradise, with national forests, ski areas, raging rivers, and excellent fishing and bicycling. Missoula has become a sort of northerly Jackson Hole with a Boulder, Colorado, accent. Naturally that brings relatively high living and high housing costs for the region, but it is still reasonably attractive on a national scale. The university and a large National Forest Service office are economic mainstays; the decline of the forest products industry has left private employment hard to find but has also left cleaner skies. Those looking to Missoula should prepare to contend with long,

cold winters and long trips, especially in winter, to reach bigger-city amenities; Spokane is closest at 200 miles away.

The town is situated in the heart of the Montana Rockies in the extreme north portion of the Bitterroot Valley. The Bitterroot Range rises 5,000 to 7,000 feet above the valley floor just 20 miles to the southwest. The main ridge of the Rockies and Continental Divide rise to the east and northeast. Summers are dry with moderate temperatures and cool nights. Some cold waves produce blizzard conditions as air funnels through the narrow valleys. This cold air can settle in the valley for long periods, especially in December and January, and bring cloudy conditions as well. Most precipitation occurs in May and early June as showers and thundershowers. First freeze is late September; last is mid-May.

DEMOGRAPHICS	AREA	U.S. AVG	ETHNIC COMPOSITION	AREA	U.S. AVG	RESIDENT PROFILE	AREA	U.S. AVG
Population	99,890		White	93.0%	79.0%	Single	37.0%	32.4%
Population density per sq. mile	38.4	358.5	Black	0.4%	10.5%	Married	48.2%	52.7%
Population growth	26.9%	21.1%	Asian	1.4%	2.7%	Divorced/separated	14.8%	14.9%
Median age	35.1	36.1	Hispanic	1.7%	10.6%	Married with children	20.9%	23.7%
Percent Democrat	51.4%	44.5%	Religious observance	32.4%	48.9%	Single with children	8.2%	9.1%
Percent Republican	45.7%	54.5%	Diversity measure	16.2	40.1	Percent over age 65	10.5%	12.9%

Population

INCOME	AREA	U.S. AVG	EMPLOYMENT	AREA	U.S. AVG	EMPLOYING INDUSTRIES	AREA	U.S. AVG
Per capita income	$21,137	$23,235	Unemployment rate	3.7%	4.7%	Largest: Healthcare & Social Assistance		
Household income	$40,184	$46,414	Recent job growth	2.8%	1.3%			
Household income < $25K	31.2%	26.2%	Projected future job growth	18.9%	11.5%	Percent manufacturing	10.7%	15.4%
Household income > $75K	19.6%	25.4%	White collar	60.6%	57.8%	Percent public sector	17.1%	15.7%
Household income growth	16.6%	13.6%	Blue collar	20.3%	25.2%	Percent construction	9.6%	9.9%

Economy & Jobs
Score: 78.3
Rank: 82

INDEXES & TAXES	AREA	U.S. AVG	HOUSING	AREA	U.S. AVG	NECESSITIES	AREA	U.S. AVG
Cost of Living Index	98.9	100.0	Median home price	$210,300	$220,000	Food Index	109.2	100.0
Buying Power Index	91.1	100.0	Home price appreciation	63.1%	10.1%	Housing Index	57.1	100.0
Income tax rate	10.00%	4.70%	Median rent	$668	$709	Utilities Index	83.7	100.0
Sales tax rate	0.00%	6.58%	Homes owned	57.7%	62.3%	Transportation Index	99.0	100.0
Property tax rate	$10.56	$12.00	Home price ratio	5.2	4.2	Healthcare Index	102.1	100.0
						Miscellaneous Cost Index	104.7	100.0

Cost of Living
Score: 79.4
Rank: 78

Climate
Score: 18.7
Rank: 303

TEMPERATURE	AREA	U.S. AVG
Average January low	17.1	26.2
Average July high	82.7	87.4
Annual days > 90°F	19	38
Annual days < 32°F	167	89
Annual days < 0°F	24	6

PRECIPITATION	AREA	U.S. AVG
Annual inches precipitation	16.0	37.7
Annual inches snowfall	51.4	7.0
Annual days precipitation	124	109
Annual days rain > 0.5 inches	5	22
Annual days snow > 1.5 inches	10	6

COMFORTS & HAZARDS	AREA	U.S. AVG
July relative humidity	56%	66%
Annual days mostly sunny	158	208
Annual days with thunderstorms	35	39
Tornado risk score	9	18
Hurricane risk score	0	13

TEMPERATURE

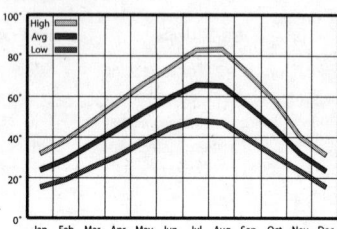

PRECIPITATION

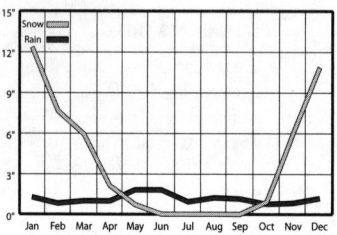

DAYS OF CLOUDS & PRECIPITATION

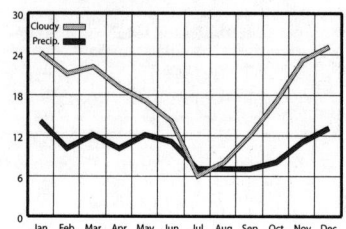

Education
Score: 81.0
Rank: 72

ACHIEVEMENT	AREA	U.S. AVG
High school degree	91.0%	82.7%
2-year college degree	4.9%	6.4%
4-year college degree	22.6%	15.7%
Graduate/professional degree	10.9%	8.9%

PUBLIC SCHOOLS	AREA	U.S. AVG
Expenditures per pupil	$5,211	$5,686
Student/teacher ratio	14.9	16.7
Attending public school	91.1%	90.1%
State SAT score	1083	1021
State ACT score	21.9*	20.9

HIGHER EDUCATION	AREA	U.S. AVG
No. 2-year colleges	1	4
No. 4-year colleges/universities	1	6
No. highly ranked universities	0	1

Health &
Healthcare
Score: 73.3
Rank: 101

HAZARDS & ILLNESSES	AREA	U.S. AVG
Air-quality score	42	37
Water-quality score	45	52
Pollen/allergy score	45	61
Cancer mortality per capita	198.7	201.9
Depression days per month	3.3	3.5
Stress score	27	50

HEALTHCARE	AREA	U.S. AVG
Physicians per capita	328.5	244.2
Hospital beds per capita	349.4	420.0
No. teaching hospitals	0	3
Cost per doctor visit	$96	$77
Cost per dental visit	$70	$70

Crime
Score: 55.3
Rank: 168

CRIME	AREA	U.S. AVG
Violent crime rate	321.1	465.5
Change in violent crime rate	4.5%	-2.2%
Property crime rate	4,550.9	3,517.1
Change in property crime rate	50.2%	-2.1%

Transportation
Score: 58.8
Rank: 155

COMMUTE	AREA	U.S. AVG
Average commute time	18.9	27.4
Percent commutes > 60 mins.	3.1%	5.9%
Commute by auto	73.5%	78.9%
Commute by mass transit	1.3%	1.9%
Work at home	4.6%	3.1%
Mass transit miles per capita	1.30	1.87

INTERCITY SERVICES	AREA	U.S. AVG
Major airports within 60 miles	0	1
Size of regional airport	None	Large
Daily airline activity	26	686
Amtrak service	No	No

AUTOMOTIVE	AREA	U.S. AVG
Insurance, annual premium	$1,061	$1,432
Gas, cost per gallon	$2.37	$2.49
Daily vehicle miles per capita	16.8	24.0

Leisure
Score: 46.0
Rank: 201

DINING & SHOPPING	AREA	U.S. AVG
Restaurant rating	1	2
Outlet mall score	0	42
No. Starbucks	2	13
No. warehouse clubs	1	2

ENTERTAINMENT	AREA	U.S. AVG
Professional sports rating	2	4
College sports rating	3	4
Zoo/aquarium rating	1	3
Amusement park rating	1	3
Botanical garden/ arboretum rating	1	4

OUTDOOR ACTIVITIES	AREA	U.S. AVG
Golf-course rating	2	4
Ski-area rating	7	3
Sq. miles inland water	2	4
Miles of coastline	0.0	10.7
National Park rating	6	3

Arts & Culture
Score: 25.1
Rank: 279

MEDIA & LIBRARIES	AREA	U.S. AVG
Arts radio rating	1	3
No. public libraries	3	27
Library volumes per capita	2.26	2.78

PERFORMING ARTS	AREA	U.S. AVG
Classical music rating	2	4
Ballet/dance rating	1	3
Professional theater rating	1	3
University arts programs rating	4	5

MUSEUMS	AREA	U.S. AVG
Overall museum rating	2	5
Art museum rating	4	5
Science museum rating	1	5
Children's museum rating	1	3

Mobile, AL

Score: 34.6   Rank: 323   2004 rank: 174

Profile: Mid-size port city
Location: Southern tip of Alabama near the Gulf Coast
Elevation: 221 feet
Time zone: Central Standard Time

PRO	CON
Historic interest	Wet climate
Winter climate	Crime rates
Arts and culture	Hurricane risk

Mobile is a major port and shipbuilding and commercial center at the head of Mobile Bay on the Gulf Coast. The area has a rich history as an antebellum seaport, and parts of the city reflect this heritage, as well as its Spanish and French colonial and cultural history. For many, Mobile offers what New Orleans offers without many of its problems. There is some tourism, and manufacturing industries include paper, aerospace, and automotive. The area has grown considerably as a port facility, in part because of the growth of Asian-owned auto plants upland in Alabama and other parts of the South. Employment has been a mixed bag, with high-paying jobs in short supply, but that may be changing. Downtown isn't exceptional, but has an assortment of new buildings and a nice historic district. The best suburbs are to the west near the airport and a few smaller towns surrounding Mobile Bay to the east. The area has a relatively strong assortment of recreation, arts, and cultural assets, and the University of Mobile and the relatively new University of South Alabama bring a college presence. Crime has traditionally been a problem, but recent statistics show improvement. It is the wettest city in the United States with 67 inches of rain per year, although much arrives in short downpours as the city also rates as one of the sunniest in the state. The relatively high hurricane and tropical storm risk was confirmed in 2005 by Hurricane Katrina, which mainly caused wind damage to trees and a few structures and disrupted port operations, but did not create the storm surge and flooding experienced in areas to the west. That storm did bring many migrants, 50,000 by one estimate, into the Mobile area, but also caused employment dislocations for some, particularly on the west side of the city, who worked in Pascagoula, Misisstpp, and areas along the Gulf Coast. (Today, however, a number of workers are prospering on the reconstruction effort.) The long-term Katrina impact remains to be seen, but is likely to be positive.

Mobile is located 30 miles north of the Gulf of Mexico on a mainly level coastal plain. Coastal marshes and sandy beaches lie near the bay, while coniferous forests extend inland. Summers are consistently warm, but temperatures are seldom as high as farther inland. Summer days are in the 90s but often cooled by an afternoon breeze, and evenings are warm and muggy. Winter is mild with one or two cooler snaps and an occasional frost. Summer thundershowers may occur every other day.

DEMOGRAPHICS	AREA	U.S. AVG	ETHNIC COMPOSITION	AREA	U.S. AVG	RESIDENT PROFILE	AREA	U.S. AVG
Population	399,938		White	61.2%	79.0%	Single	33.4%	32.4%
Population density per sq. mile	324.3	358.5	Black	34.7%	10.5%	Married	50.7%	52.7%
Population growth	5.6%	21.1%	Asian	1.8%	2.7%	Divorced/separated	15.8%	14.9%
Median age	35.3	36.1	Hispanic	1.2%	10.6%	Married with children	22.6%	23.7%
Percent Democrat	40.7%	44.5%	Religious observance	53.3%	48.9%	Single with children	11.7%	9.1%
Percent Republican	58.7%	54.5%	Diversity measure	51.6	40.1	Percent over age 65	12.4%	12.9%

INCOME	AREA	U.S. AVG	EMPLOYMENT	AREA	U.S. AVG	EMPLOYING INDUSTRIES	AREA	U.S. AVG
Per capita income	$19,440	$23,235	Unemployment rate	4.6%	4.7%	Largest: Healthcare & Social Assistance		
Household income	$38,000	$46,414	Recent job growth	2.8%	1.3%			
Household income < $25K	34.3%	26.2%	Projected future job growth	10.0%	11.5%	Percent manufacturing	16.1%	15.4%
Household income > $75K	18.9%	25.4%	White collar	56.0%	57.8%	Percent public sector	14.1%	15.7%
Household income growth	12.7%	13.6%	Blue collar	28.3%	25.2%	Percent construction	12.2%	9.9%

Economy & Jobs — Score: 60.2 Rank: 150

INDEXES & TAXES	AREA	U.S. AVG	HOUSING	AREA	U.S. AVG	NECESSITIES	AREA	U.S. AVG
Cost of Living Index	83.5	100.0	Median home price	$138,200	$220,000	Food Index	92.0	100.0
Buying Power Index	102.0	100.0	Home price appreciation	28.4%	10.1%	Housing Index	49.3	100.0
Income tax rate	5.00%	4.70%	Median rent	$590	$709	Utilities Index	105.5	100.0
Sales tax rate	9.00%	6.58%	Homes owned	63.3%	62.3%	Transportation Index	96.8	100.0
Property tax rate	$4.51	$12.00	Home price ratio	3.6	4.2	Healthcare Index	84.4	100.0
						Miscellaneous Cost Index	97.3	100.0

Cost of Living — Score: 52.4 Rank: 177

Climate
Score: 60.7
Rank: 146

TEMPERATURE	AREA	U.S. AVG
Average January low	41.3	26.2
Average July high	90.6	87.4
Annual days > 90°F	81	38
Annual days < 32°F	19	89
Annual days < 0°F	0	6

PRECIPITATION	AREA	U.S. AVG
Annual inches precipitation	67.0	37.7
Annual inches snowfall	0.4	7.0
Annual days precipitation	124	109
Annual days rain > 0.5 inches	40	22
Annual days snow > 1.5 inches	1	6

COMFORTS & HAZARDS	AREA	U.S. AVG
July relative humidity	73%	66%
Annual days mostly sunny	217	208
Annual days with thunderstorms	80	39
Tornado risk score	33	18
Hurricane risk score	58	13

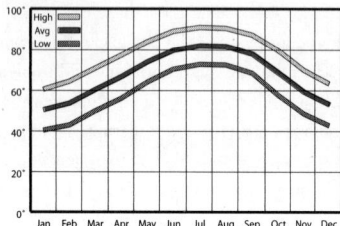

TEMPERATURE

PRECIPITATION

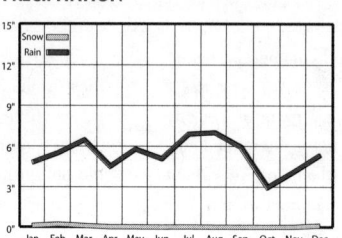

DAYS OF CLOUDS & PRECIPITATION

Education
Score: 7.8
Rank: 344

ACHIEVEMENT	AREA	U.S. AVG
High school degree	76.9%	82.7%
2-year college degree	5.3%	6.4%
4-year college degree	12.3%	15.7%
Graduate/professional degree	6.5%	8.9%

PUBLIC SCHOOLS	AREA	U.S. AVG
Expenditures per pupil	$4,323	$5,686
Student/teacher ratio	16.3	16.7
Attending public school	81.8%	90.1%
State SAT score	1126	1021
State ACT score	20.2*	20.9

HIGHER EDUCATION	AREA	U.S. AVG
No. 2-year colleges	2	4
No. 4-year colleges/universities	4	6
No. highly ranked universities	0	1

Health & Healthcare
Score: 29.9
Rank: 260

HAZARDS & ILLNESSES	AREA	U.S. AVG
Air-quality score	12	37
Water-quality score	60	52
Pollen/allergy score	70	61
Cancer mortality per capita	243.9	201.9
Depression days per month	4.1	3.5
Stress score	59	50

HEALTHCARE	AREA	U.S. AVG
Physicians per capita	264.9	244.2
Hospital beds per capita	545.8	420.0
No. teaching hospitals	5	3
Cost per doctor visit	$54	$77
Cost per dental visit	$44	$70

Crime
Score: 10.2
Rank: 335

CRIME	AREA	U.S. AVG
Violent crime rate	397.1	465.5
Change in violent crime rate	-14.0%	-2.2%
Property crime rate	4,656.2	3,517.1
Change in property crime rate	-19.1%	-2.1%

Transportation
Score: 1.1
Rank: 369

COMMUTE	AREA	U.S. AVG
Average commute time	26.8	27.4
Percent commutes > 60 mins.	5.6%	5.9%
Commute by auto	82.9%	78.9%
Commute by mass transit	0.7%	1.9%
Work at home	1.9%	3.1%
Mass transit miles per capita	0.72	1.87

INTERCITY SERVICES	AREA	U.S. AVG
Major airports within 60 miles	0	1
Size of regional airport	Small	Large
Daily airline activity	82	686
Amtrak service	Yes	No

AUTOMOTIVE	AREA	U.S. AVG
Insurance, annual premium	$1,398	$1,432
Gas, cost per gallon	$2.49	$2.49
Daily vehicle miles per capita	27.9	24.0

Leisure
Score: 59.1
Rank: 153

DINING & SHOPPING	AREA	U.S. AVG
Restaurant rating	1	2
Outlet mall score	70	42
No. Starbucks	2	13
No. warehouse clubs	1	2

ENTERTAINMENT	AREA	U.S. AVG
Professional sports rating	2	4
College sports rating	4	4
Zoo/aquarium rating	1	3
Amusement park rating	1	3
Botanical garden/ arboretum rating	9	4

OUTDOOR ACTIVITIES	AREA	U.S. AVG
Golf-course rating	3	4
Ski-area rating	1	3
Sq. miles inland water	8	4
Miles of coastline	52.5	10.7
National Park rating	2	3

Arts & Culture
Score: 41.4
Rank: 219

MEDIA & LIBRARIES	AREA	U.S. AVG
Arts radio rating	1	3
No. public libraries	14	27
Library volumes per capita	1.56	2.78

PERFORMING ARTS	AREA	U.S. AVG
Classical music rating	1	4
Ballet/dance rating	1	3
Professional theater rating	1	3
University arts programs rating	8	5

MUSEUMS	AREA	U.S. AVG
Overall museum rating	7	5
Art museum rating	6	5
Science museum rating	8	5
Children's museum rating	1	3

Modesto, CA

Score: 0.0   **Rank:** 373   **2004 rank:** 316

Profile: Small, agricultural town
Location: Central California, in the Central Valley, 80 miles southeast of Sacramento and 70 miles east of the Bay Area
Elevation: 22 feet
Time zone: Pacific Standard Time

PRO	CON
Winter climate	Crime rates
Small-town atmosphere	Unemployment
Nearby national parks	Low educational attainment

Mainly agricultural in character, Modesto is a "modest" Central Valley town—so named because the dignitary the town intended to name itself after refused the honor out of modesty. The unremarkable downtown has enough of a small-town feel to be the subject of the movie *American Graffiti* (although the actual filming was done in Marin County north of San Francisco). But there isn't much to do and unemployment is high. Worse, crime continues to be a real as well as an image problem, with well-publicized and high-profile crimes giving the area more of a black eye than it probably deserves. However, it was recently noted as having the highest auto theft rate in the nation. Modesto isn't as gritty as these events make it sound, but it does have its problems. While the cost of living is fairly modest on a California scale,

it is still high—and housing prices are extremely high—for what's available. Incredibly, some people make the 2- to 3-hour commute into the San Francisco Bay Area. Yosemite National Park, 80 miles east, provides some recreational fulfillment. But the strong negatives combined with high costs create little appeal for prospective residents; Modesto draws the bottom spot on our ranking list.

Modesto is located in a completely flat area of agriculture and orchards along the Tuolumne River. Just 15 miles to the east, the Sierra foothills begin their persistent rise into the main Sierra Ridge. Typical for the region, summer offers warm to blistering hot, dry days and pleasant to somewhat warm nights. Winter brings mild temperatures and valley fog. Almost all rain falls in winter.

Population

DEMOGRAPHICS	AREA	U.S. AVG
Population	504,411	
Population density per sq. mile	337.7	358.5
Population growth	36.1%	21.1%
Median age	31.9	36.1
Percent Democrat	40.4%	44.5%
Percent Republican	58.6%	54.5%

ETHNIC COMPOSITION	AREA	U.S. AVG
White	65.4%	79.0%
Black	2.9%	10.5%
Asian	4.6%	2.7%
Hispanic	37.6%	10.6%
Religious observance	43.7%	48.9%
Diversity measure	74.9	40.1

RESIDENT PROFILE	AREA	U.S. AVG
Single	31.3%	32.4%
Married	52.5%	52.7%
Divorced/separated	16.3%	14.9%
Married with children	29.8%	23.7%
Single with children	11.5%	9.1%
Percent over age 65	10.0%	12.9%

Economy & Jobs
Score: 17.6
Rank: 308

INCOME	AREA	U.S. AVG
Per capita income	$18,922	$23,235
Household income	$45,245	$46,414
Household income < $25K	26.5%	26.2%
Household income > $75K	24.7%	25.4%
Household income growth	12.8%	13.6%

EMPLOYMENT	AREA	U.S. AVG
Unemployment rate	7.7%	4.7%
Recent job growth	1.9%	1.3%
Projected future job growth	10.3%	11.5%
White collar	51.1%	57.8%
Blue collar	28.9%	25.2%

EMPLOYING INDUSTRIES	AREA	U.S. AVG
Largest: Manufacturing		
Percent manufacturing	17.5%	15.4%
Percent public sector	14.7%	15.7%
Percent construction	11.4%	9.9%

Cost of Living
Score: 6.7
Rank: 348

INDEXES & TAXES	AREA	U.S. AVG
Cost of Living Index	137.1	100.0
Buying Power Index	74.0	100.0
Income tax rate	6.00%	4.70%
Sales tax rate	7.38%	6.58%
Property tax rate	$9.81	$12.00

HOUSING	AREA	U.S. AVG
Median home price	$398,900	$220,000
Home price appreciation	155.5%	10.1%
Median rent	$760	$709
Homes owned	59.9%	62.3%
Home price ratio	8.8	4.2

NECESSITIES	AREA	U.S. AVG
Food Index	117.9	100.0
Housing Index	170.0	100.0
Utilities Index	112.6	100.0
Transportation Index	114.5	100.0
Healthcare Index	135.5	100.0
Miscellaneous Cost Index	104.9	100.0

Climate
Score: 93.0
Rank: 27

TEMPERATURE	AREA	U.S. AVG
Average January low	36.3	26.2
Average July high	94.7	87.4
Annual days > 90°F	86	38
Annual days < 32°F	24	89
Annual days < 0°F	0	6

PRECIPITATION	AREA	U.S. AVG
Annual inches precipitation	14.2	37.7
Annual inches snowfall	0.0	7.0
Annual days precipitation	52	109
Annual days rain > 0.5 inches	8	22
Annual days snow > 1.5 inches	0	6

COMFORTS & HAZARDS	AREA	U.S. AVG
July relative humidity	63%	66%
Annual days mostly sunny	261	208
Annual days with thunderstorms	3	39
Tornado risk score	2	18
Hurricane risk score	0	13

TEMPERATURE

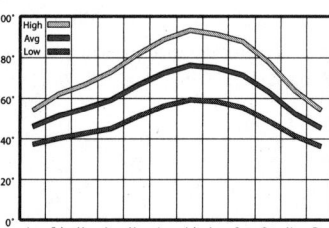

PRECIPITATION

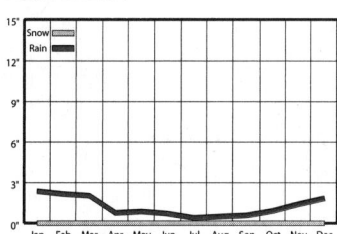

DAYS OF CLOUDS & PRECIPITATION

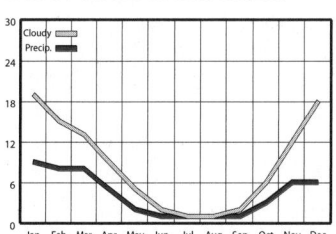

ACHIEVEMENT	AREA	U.S. AVG	PUBLIC SCHOOLS	AREA	U.S. AVG	HIGHER EDUCATION	AREA	U.S. AVG
High school degree	70.2%	82.7%	Expenditures per pupil	$4,517	$5,686	No. 2-year colleges	2	4
2-year college degree	6.6%	6.4%	Student/teacher ratio	22.0	16.7	No. 4-year colleges/universities	1	6
4-year college degree	9.6%	15.7%	Attending public school	94.9%	90.1%	No. highly ranked universities	0	1
Graduate/professional degree	4.4%	8.9%	State SAT score	1019*	1021			
			State ACT score	21.6	20.9			

Education
Score: 4.3
Rank: 357

HAZARDS & ILLNESSES	AREA	U.S. AVG	HEALTHCARE	AREA	U.S. AVG	CRIME	AREA	U.S. AVG
Air-quality score	23	37	Physicians per capita	146.3	244.2	Violent crime rate	614.0	465.5
Water-quality score	34	52	Hospital beds per capita	295.6	420.0	Change in violent crime rate	6.4%	-2.2%
Pollen/allergy score	72	61	No. teaching hospitals	3	3	Property crime rate	5,418.0	3,517.1
Cancer mortality per capita	172.8	201.9	Cost per doctor visit	$87	$77	Change in property crime rate	-10.7%	-2.1%
Depression days per month	3.7	3.5	Cost per dental visit	$75	$70			
Stress score	98	50						

Health & Healthcare
Score: 4.3
Rank: 357

Crime
Score: 17.4
Rank: 309

COMMUTE	AREA	U.S. AVG	INTERCITY SERVICES	AREA	U.S. AVG	AUTOMOTIVE	AREA	U.S. AVG
Average commute time	27.9	27.4	Major airports within 60 miles	4	1	Insurance, annual premium	$2,384	$1,432
Percent commutes › 60 mins.	11.5%	5.9%	Size of regional airport	Large	Large	Gas, cost per gallon	$2.60	$2.49
Commute by auto	77.0%	78.9%	Daily airline activity	1272	686	Daily vehicle miles per capita	15.6	24.0
Commute by mass transit	0.9%	1.9%	Amtrak service	Yes	No			
Work at home	3.1%	3.1%						
Mass transit miles per capita	0.94	1.87						

Transportation
Score: 71.7
Rank: 107

DINING & SHOPPING	AREA	U.S. AVG	ENTERTAINMENT	AREA	U.S. AVG	OUTDOOR ACTIVITIES	AREA	U.S. AVG
Restaurant rating	1	2	Professional sports rating	4	4	Golf-course rating	2	4
Outlet mall score	72	42	College sports rating	4	4	Ski-area rating	9	3
No. Starbucks	18	13	Zoo/aquarium rating	1	3	Sq. miles inland water	2	4
No. warehouse clubs	2	2	Amusement park rating	1	3	Miles of coastline	0.0	10.7
			Botanical garden/ arboretum rating	1	4	National Park rating	1	3

Leisure
Score: 57.8
Rank: 157

MEDIA & LIBRARIES	AREA	U.S. AVG	PERFORMING ARTS	AREA	U.S. AVG	MUSEUMS	AREA	U.S. AVG
Arts radio rating	1	3	Classical music rating	4	4	Overall museum rating	1	5
No. public libraries	13	27	Ballet/dance rating	3	3	Art museum rating	2	5
Library volumes per capita	1.48	2.78	Professional theater rating	1	3	Science museum rating	3	5
			University arts programs rating	3	5	Children's museum rating	1	3

Arts & Culture
Score: 19.0
Rank: 302

Monroe, LA

Score: 12.4   Rank: 369   2004 rank: 247

Profile: Small city
Location: Northeast Louisiana along I-20
Elevation: 259 feet
Time zone: Central Standard Time

PRO	CON
Nearby water recreation	Crime rates
Nature areas	Heat and humidity
Educated population	Isolation

Located along the Ouachita River, Monroe is the commercial and cultural center for northeast Louisiana. An early-20th-century oil and gas boom has subsided, but modestly sized commercial and industrial activities, including agricultural processing and distribution, forest products, and papermaking remain. The area has started up the knowledge-economy path as headquarters for CenturyTel, a large telecommunications provider, and regional headquarters for insurer State Farm. The University of Louisiana at Monroe adds some 10,000 students, some college-town amenities, and an excellent affiliated public radio station, and brings a relatively well-educated population for the type of town. There is an assortment of amenities, small but beyond what

one might expect, including a good art museum, a zoo, and a good parks and recreation system. But the area has the highest crime rate in a high-crime state, the overall employment picture looks bad, and it is fairly isolated from big-city amenities, hence the low ranking.

The terrain is level to gently rolling, with areas of agriculture and pine forest. Summers are consistently warm and humid with ample precipitation and thunderstorms, especially in early summer. Winters are mild but with occasional below-freezing temperatures, a few ice storms, and an infrequent light snow. First freeze is early November; last is late March.

Population

DEMOGRAPHICS	AREA	U.S. AVG	ETHNIC COMPOSITION	AREA	U.S. AVG	RESIDENT PROFILE	AREA	U.S. AVG
Population	171,870		White	64.2%	79.0%	Single	34.5%	32.4%
Population density per sq. mile	115.5	358.5	Black	33.5%	10.5%	Married	49.5%	52.7%
Population growth	5.6%	21.1%	Asian	0.8%	2.7%	Divorced/separated	16.0%	14.9%
Median age	33.8	36.1	Hispanic	1.5%	10.6%	Married with children	21.4%	23.7%
Percent Democrat	33.4%	44.5%	Religious observance	58.8%	48.9%	Single with children	12.2%	9.1%
Percent Republican	65.4%	54.5%	Diversity measure	49.0	40.1	Percent over age 65	12.5%	12.9%

Economy & Jobs
Score: 14.4
Rank: 319

INCOME	AREA	U.S. AVG	EMPLOYMENT	AREA	U.S. AVG	EMPLOYING INDUSTRIES	AREA	U.S. AVG
Per capita income	$19,638	$23,235	Unemployment rate	6.2%	4.7%	Largest: Healthcare & Social Assistance		
Household income	$36,484	$46,414	Recent job growth	0.9%	1.3%			
Household income < $25K	35.6%	26.2%	Projected future job growth	7.8%	11.5%	Percent manufacturing	13.9%	15.4%
Household income > $75K	19.6%	25.4%	White collar	58.3%	57.8%	Percent public sector	17.5%	15.7%
Household income growth	15.3%	13.6%	Blue collar	24.7%	25.2%	Percent construction	10.8%	9.9%

Cost of Living
Score: 55.6
Rank: 165

INDEXES & TAXES	AREA	U.S. AVG	HOUSING	AREA	U.S. AVG	NECESSITIES	AREA	U.S. AVG
Cost of Living Index	83.2	100.0	Median home price	$125,300	$220,000	Food Index	90.6	100.0
Buying Power Index	98.3	100.0	Home price appreciation	25.9%	10.1%	Housing Index	57.9	100.0
Income tax rate	4.00%	4.70%	Median rent	$538	$709	Utilities Index	117.6	100.0
Sales tax rate	9.72%	6.58%	Homes owned	60.3%	62.3%	Transportation Index	99.7	100.0
Property tax rate	$3.77	$12.00	Home price ratio	3.4	4.2	Healthcare Index	89.7	100.0
						Miscellaneous Cost Index	103.0	100.0

Climate
Score: 75.7
Rank: 91

TEMPERATURE	AREA	U.S. AVG	PRECIPITATION	AREA	U.S. AVG	COMFORTS & HAZARDS	AREA	U.S. AVG
Average January low	37.8	26.2	Annual inches precipitation	45.0	37.7	July relative humidity	71%	66%
Average July high	93.8	87.4	Annual inches snowfall	1.0	7.0	Annual days mostly sunny	217	208
Annual days > 90°F	87	38	Annual days precipitation	97	109	Annual days with thunderstorms	54	39
Annual days < 32°F	1	89	Annual days rain > 0.5 inches	29	22	Tornado risk score	26	18
Annual days < 0°F	0	6	Annual days snow > 1.5 inches	0	6	Hurricane risk score	15	13

TEMPERATURE

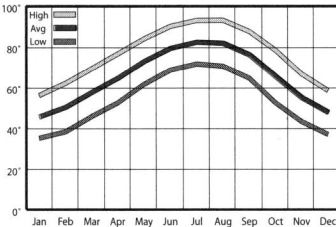

PRECIPITATION

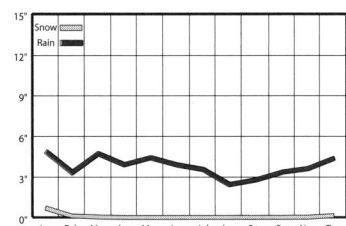

DAYS OF CLOUDS & PRECIPITATION

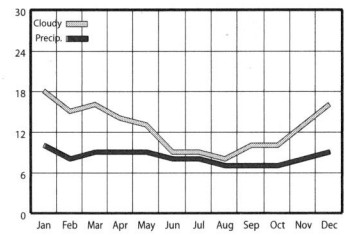

Education
Score: 17.4
Rank: 308

ACHIEVEMENT	AREA	U.S. AVG	PUBLIC SCHOOLS	AREA	U.S. AVG	HIGHER EDUCATION	AREA	U.S. AVG
High school degree	77.9%	82.7%	Expenditures per pupil	$4,237	$5,686	No. 2-year colleges	4	4
2-year college degree	2.8%	6.4%	Student/teacher ratio	16.5	16.7	No. 4-year colleges/universities	1	6
4-year college degree	13.9%	15.7%	Attending public school	91.7%	90.1%	No. highly ranked universities	0	1
Graduate/professional degree	7.4%	8.9%	State SAT score	1141	1021			
			State ACT score	20.1*	20.9			

Health & Healthcare
Score: 93.9
Rank: 24

HAZARDS & ILLNESSES	AREA	U.S. AVG	HEALTHCARE	AREA	U.S. AVG	CRIME	AREA	U.S. AVG
Air-quality score	40	37	Physicians per capita	237.6	244.2	Violent crime rate	602.2	465.5
Water-quality score	53	52	Hospital beds per capita	788.4	420.0	Change in violent crime rate	-25.0%	-2.2%
Pollen/allergy score	66	61	No. teaching hospitals	1	3	Property crime rate	5,048.2	3,517.1
Cancer mortality per capita	202.0	201.9	Cost per doctor visit	$76	$77	Change in property crime rate	-5.8%	-2.1%
Depression days per month	2.9	3.5	Cost per dental visit	$68	$70			
Stress score	46	50						

Crime
Score: 7.5
Rank: 345

Transportation
Score: 19.5
Rank: 302

COMMUTE	AREA	U.S. AVG	INTERCITY SERVICES	AREA	U.S. AVG	AUTOMOTIVE	AREA	U.S. AVG
Average commute time	23.2	27.4	Major airports within 60 miles	0	1	Insurance, annual premium	$1,534	$1,432
Percent commutes > 60 mins.	3.9%	5.9%	Size of regional airport	Small	Large	Gas, cost per gallon	$2.43	$2.49
Commute by auto	81.8%	78.9%	Daily airline activity	66	686	Daily vehicle miles per capita	26.4	24.0
Commute by mass transit	1.1%	1.9%	Amtrak service	No	No			
Work at home	1.7%	3.1%						
Mass transit miles per capita	1.10	1.87						

Leisure

Score: 11.0
Rank: 332

DINING & SHOPPING	AREA	U.S. AVG	ENTERTAINMENT	AREA	U.S. AVG	OUTDOOR ACTIVITIES	AREA	U.S. AVG
Restaurant rating	1	2	Professional sports rating	2	4	Golf-course rating	1	4
Outlet mall score	10	42	College sports rating	4	4	Ski-area rating	1	3
No. Starbucks	0	13	Zoo/aquarium rating	1	3	Sq. miles inland water	2	4
No. warehouse clubs	1	2	Amusement park rating	1	3	Miles of coastline	0.0	10.7
			Botanical garden/ arboretum rating	4	4	National Park rating	2	3

Arts & Culture

Score: 30.5
Rank: 260

MEDIA & LIBRARIES	AREA	U.S. AVG	PERFORMING ARTS	AREA	U.S. AVG	MUSEUMS	AREA	U.S. AVG
Arts radio rating	1	3	Classical music rating	3	4	Overall museum rating	2	5
No. public libraries	6	27	Ballet/dance rating	3	3	Art museum rating	3	5
Library volumes per capita	2.50	2.78	Professional theater rating	1	3	Science museum rating	3	5
			University arts programs rating	4	5	Children's museum rating	1	3

Monroe, MI

Score: 46.5   Rank: 270   2004 rank: not ranked

Profile: Small port city
Location: Southeastern Michigan along Lake Erie between Detroit and Toledo
Elevation: 593 feet
Time zone: Eastern Standard Time

PRO	CON
Small-town feel	Entertainment
Historic interest	Economic cycles
Low crime rates	Winter climate

Monroe is an old manufacturing and port city along the western shore of Lake Erie between Detroit and Toledo, Ohio. The setting is flat and uninteresting. However, this typically Midwestern town contains numerous early-20th-century homes on shaded streets and some historic attractions related to earlier French settlement and the former residence of General George A. Custer. It is quiet with plenty of water recreation but not much else to do. The economy is diverse, with the headquarters of furniture giant La-Z-Boy and plants of the Monroe Auto Equipment Company (maker of Monroe shocks and struts, now a division of Tenneco) among the mainstays. The cost of living profile is a bit high for the type of town and region, and educational attainment is low. Detroit is 40 miles north and Toledo is 25 miles south, offering amenities missing locally.

The area is mainly level, with areas of deciduous woods away from shore mixed with farmland. Summers are warm and humid but are cooled by lake breezes. The lake location brings considerable cloudiness in all seasons and especially in winter. First freeze is mid-October; last is late April.

Population

DEMOGRAPHICS	AREA	U.S. AVG	ETHNIC COMPOSITION	AREA	U.S. AVG	RESIDENT PROFILE	AREA	U.S. AVG
Population	152,801		White	94.9%	79.0%	Single	28.8%	32.4%
Population density per sq. mile	277.3	358.5	Black	2.0%	10.5%	Married	59.6%	52.7%
Population growth	14.4%	21.1%	Asian	0.7%	2.7%	Divorced/separated	11.7%	14.9%
Median age	37.2	36.1	Hispanic	2.3%	10.6%	Married with children	27.6%	23.7%
Percent Democrat	48.7%	44.5%	Religious observance	53.6%	48.9%	Single with children	8.1%	9.1%
Percent Republican	50.5%	54.5%	Diversity measure	13.8	40.1	Percent over age 65	11.8%	12.9%

Economy & Jobs

Score: 54.5
Rank: 171

INCOME	AREA	U.S. AVG	EMPLOYMENT	AREA	U.S. AVG	EMPLOYING INDUSTRIES	AREA	U.S. AVG
Per capita income	$25,313	$23,235	Unemployment rate	7.7%	4.7%	Largest: Manufacturing		
Household income	$56,835	$46,414	Recent job growth	1.2%	1.3%			
Household income < $25K	19.4%	26.2%	Projected future job growth	12.5%	11.5%	Percent manufacturing	24.1%	15.4%
Household income > $75K	34.2%	25.4%	White collar	48.2%	57.8%	Percent public sector	8.9%	15.7%
Household income growth	9.8%	13.6%	Blue collar	37.0%	25.2%	Percent construction	12.9%	9.9%

Cost of Living

Score: 27.0
Rank: 272

INDEXES & TAXES	AREA	U.S. AVG	HOUSING	AREA	U.S. AVG	NECESSITIES	AREA	U.S. AVG
Cost of Living Index	93.2	100.0	Median home price	$172,000	$220,000	Food Index	106.0	100.0
Buying Power Index	136.7	100.0	Home price appreciation	23.8%	10.1%	Housing Index	53.3	100.0
Income tax rate	7.21%	4.70%	Median rent	$745	$709	Utilities Index	107.7	100.0
Sales tax rate	6.00%	6.58%	Homes owned	77.5%	62.3%	Transportation Index	101.1	100.0
Property tax rate	$11.44	$12.00	Home price ratio	3.0	4.2	Healthcare Index	108.4	100.0
						Miscellaneous Cost Index	98.7	100.0

Climate

Score: 55.6
Rank: 165

TEMPERATURE	AREA	U.S. AVG
Average January low	17.3	26.2
Average July high	83.4	87.4
Annual days > 90°F	11	38
Annual days < 32°F	139	89
Annual days < 0°F	7	6

PRECIPITATION	AREA	U.S. AVG
Annual inches precipitation	32.0	37.7
Annual inches snowfall	39.0	7.0
Annual days precipitation	133	109
Annual days rain > 0.5 inches	20	22
Annual days snow > 1.5 inches	9	6

COMFORTS & HAZARDS	AREA	U.S. AVG
July relative humidity	55%	66%
Annual days mostly sunny	185	208
Annual days with thunderstorms	40	39
Tornado risk score	23	18
Hurricane risk score	2	13

TEMPERATURE

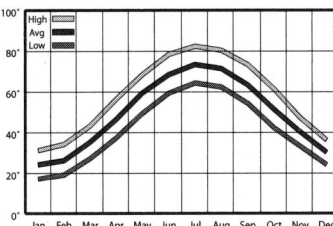

PRECIPITATION

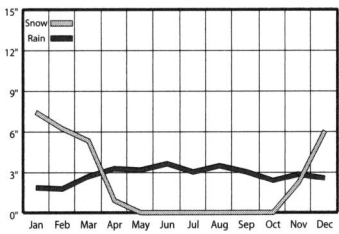

DAYS OF CLOUDS & PRECIPITATION

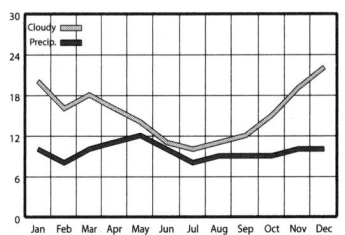

Education

Score: 17.6
Rank: 307

ACHIEVEMENT	AREA	U.S. AVG
High school degree	83.2%	82.7%
2-year college degree	7.3%	6.4%
4-year college degree	9.6%	15.7%
Graduate/professional degree	4.7%	8.9%

PUBLIC SCHOOLS	AREA	U.S. AVG
Expenditures per pupil	$5,545	$5,686
Student/teacher ratio	20.7	16.7
Attending public school	89.8%	90.1%
State SAT score	1151	1021
State ACT score	21.5*	20.9

HIGHER EDUCATION	AREA	U.S. AVG
No. 2-year colleges	1	4
No. 4-year colleges/universities	0	6
No. highly ranked universities	0	1

Health & Healthcare

Score: 4.8
Rank: 355

HAZARDS & ILLNESSES	AREA	U.S. AVG
Air-quality score	21	37
Water-quality score	28	52
Pollen/allergy score	54	61
Cancer mortality per capita	219.4	201.9
Depression days per month	4.0	3.5
Stress score	82	50

HEALTHCARE	AREA	U.S. AVG
Physicians per capita	85.6	244.2
Hospital beds per capita	126.3	420.0
No. teaching hospitals	0	3
Cost per doctor visit	$69	$77
Cost per dental visit	$69	$70

Crime

Score: 88.8
Rank: 43

CRIME	AREA	U.S. AVG
Violent crime rate	211.6	465.5
Change in violent crime rate	4.5%	-2.2%
Property crime rate	2,366.4	3,517.1
Change in property crime rate	5.5%	-2.1%

Transportation

Score: 71.1
Rank: 109

COMMUTE	AREA	U.S. AVG
Average commute time	26.2	27.4
Percent commutes > 60 mins.	5.5%	5.9%
Commute by auto	88.2%	78.9%
Commute by mass transit	0.4%	1.9%
Work at home	1.8%	3.1%
Mass transit miles per capita	0.42	1.87

INTERCITY SERVICES	AREA	U.S. AVG
Major airports within 60 miles	2	1
Size of regional airport	Large	Large
Daily airline activity	1333	686
Amtrak service	No	No

AUTOMOTIVE	AREA	U.S. AVG
Insurance, annual premium	$1,414	$1,432
Gas, cost per gallon	$2.46	$2.49
Daily vehicle miles per capita	32.6	24.0

Leisure

Score: 87.4
Rank: 47

DINING & SHOPPING	AREA	U.S. AVG
Restaurant rating	3	2
Outlet mall score	67	42
No. Starbucks	0	13
No. warehouse clubs	0	2

ENTERTAINMENT	AREA	U.S. AVG
Professional sports rating	9	4
College sports rating	3	4
Zoo/aquarium rating	8	3
Amusement park rating	2	3
Botanical garden/ arboretum rating	6	4

OUTDOOR ACTIVITIES	AREA	U.S. AVG
Golf-course rating	10	4
Ski-area rating	5	3
Sq. miles inland water	6	4
Miles of coastline	47.4	10.7
National Park rating	1	3

Arts & Culture

Score: 94.4
Rank: 22

MEDIA & LIBRARIES	AREA	U.S. AVG
Arts radio rating	6	3
No. public libraries	17	27
Library volumes per capita	3.04	2.78

PERFORMING ARTS	AREA	U.S. AVG
Classical music rating	10	4
Ballet/dance rating	6	3
Professional theater rating	1	3
University arts programs rating	10	5

MUSEUMS	AREA	U.S. AVG
Overall museum rating	6	5
Art museum rating	6	5
Science museum rating	4	5
Children's museum rating	6	3

Montgomery, AL

Score: 57.1   **Rank:** 200   **2004 rank:** 258

Profile: Capital city
Location: South-central Alabama
Elevation: 202 feet
Time zone: Central Standard Time

PRO	CON
Historic interest	Crime rates
Strengthening economy	Summer heat and humidity
Cost of living	Air service

Montgomery is a steamy old Southern town with a strong legacy as the first Confederate capital, and later, as a center of civil rights struggles and their resolution in the mid–20th century. While some cities might shy away from this legacy, Montgomery honors it with considerable pride and dignity. It remains a state capital today, but offers only modest amenities for a capital its size. Economy and employment have been relatively strong in keeping with the region. Korean automaker Hyundai opened its only North American plant in the area in 2005 and is scheduled to grow to 300,000 vehicles per year. It employs about 2,700 but is expected to create thousands of jobs in its wake through suppliers and affiliated industries. The area has good historical exhibits and museums celebrating its unique heritage, including a new Rosa Parks Library and Museum. There are a few other quality arts amenities and a Shakespeare festival. Downsides include crime, air service, and health resources, which are low by capital city standards, but the recent economic boost will probably help with these issues. Crime rates are among the highest in the state.

This gently rolling area of Alabama has no significant topographic features and is a mix of open agricultural land and pine forest. Summers are warm, still, and humid with little change from day to day. Winter shifts between mild and moist. Temperature and precipitation are about average for the state.

Population

DEMOGRAPHICS	AREA	U.S. AVG	ETHNIC COMPOSITION	AREA	U.S. AVG	RESIDENT PROFILE	AREA	U.S. AVG
Population	355,235		White	55.6%	79.0%	Single	33.4%	32.4%
Population density per sq. mile	130.4	358.5	Black	41.6%	10.5%	Married	49.8%	52.7%
Population growth	19.0%	21.1%	Asian	1.0%	2.7%	Divorced/separated	16.8%	14.9%
Median age	34.9	36.1	Hispanic	1.3%	10.6%	Married with children	22.8%	23.7%
Percent Democrat	41.8%	44.5%	Religious observance	49.7%	48.9%	Single with children	11.4%	9.1%
Percent Republican	57.7%	54.5%	Diversity measure	47.8	40.1	Percent over age 65	11.7%	12.9%

Economy & Jobs
Score: 52.7
Rank: 178

INCOME	AREA	U.S. AVG	EMPLOYMENT	AREA	U.S. AVG	EMPLOYING INDUSTRIES	AREA	U.S. AVG
Per capita income	$21,847	$23,235	Unemployment rate	4.2%	4.7%	Largest: Healthcare & Social Assistance		
Household income	$42,875	$46,414	Recent job growth	1.7%	1.3%			
Household income < $25K	28.9%	26.2%	Projected future job growth	10.4%	11.5%	Percent manufacturing	13.7%	15.4%
Household income > $75K	23.1%	25.4%	White collar	62.3%	57.8%	Percent public sector	22.4%	15.7%
Household income growth	14.8%	13.6%	Blue collar	22.5%	25.2%	Percent construction	8.9%	9.9%

Cost of Living
Score: 54.3
Rank: 171

INDEXES & TAXES	AREA	U.S. AVG	HOUSING	AREA	U.S. AVG	NECESSITIES	AREA	U.S. AVG
Cost of Living Index	87.6	100.0	Median home price	$150,700	$220,000	Food Index	95.5	100.0
Buying Power Index	109.7	100.0	Home price appreciation	24.9%	10.1%	Housing Index	52.5	100.0
Income tax rate	5.00%	4.70%	Median rent	$623	$709	Utilities Index	106.8	100.0
Sales tax rate	8.98%	6.58%	Homes owned	63.7%	62.3%	Transportation Index	101.8	100.0
Property tax rate	$3.22	$12.00	Home price ratio	3.5	4.2	Healthcare Index	94.0	100.0
						Miscellaneous Cost Index	98.1	100.0

Climate
Score: 55.3
Rank: 166

TEMPERATURE	AREA	U.S. AVG	PRECIPITATION	AREA	U.S. AVG	COMFORTS & HAZARDS	AREA	U.S. AVG
Average January low	37.1	26.2	Annual inches precipitation	50.0	37.7	July relative humidity	73%	66%
Average July high	90.7	87.4	Annual inches snowfall	0.2	7.0	Annual days mostly sunny	216	208
Annual days > 90°F	66	38	Annual days precipitation	109	109	Annual days with thunderstorms	62	39
Annual days < 32°F	39	89	Annual days rain > 0.5 inches	33	22	Tornado risk score	21	18
Annual days < 0°F	0	6	Annual days snow > 1.5 inches	1	6	Hurricane risk score	28	13

TEMPERATURE

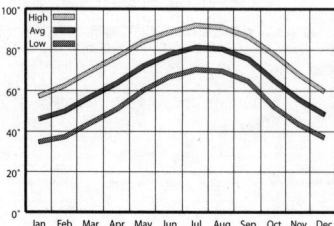

PRECIPITATION

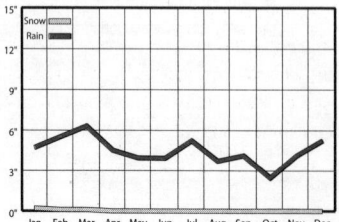

DAYS OF CLOUDS & PRECIPITATION

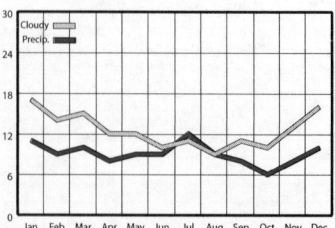

ACHIEVEMENT	AREA	U.S. AVG	PUBLIC SCHOOLS	AREA	U.S. AVG	HIGHER EDUCATION	AREA	U.S. AVG
High school degree	79.8%	82.7%	Expenditures per pupil	$4,293	$5,686	No. 2-year colleges	3	4
2-year college degree	5.1%	6.4%	Student/teacher ratio	16.6	16.7	No. 4-year colleges/universities	6	6
4-year college degree	15.5%	15.7%	Attending public school	85.2%	90.1%	No. highly ranked universities	1	1
Graduate/professional degree	9.6%	8.9%	State SAT score	1126	1021			
			State ACT score	20.2*	20.9			

Education
Score: 39.6
Rank: 227

HAZARDS & ILLNESSES	AREA	U.S. AVG	HEALTHCARE	AREA	U.S. AVG	CRIME	AREA	U.S. AVG
Air-quality score	41	37	Physicians per capita	187.2	244.2	Violent crime rate	565.0	465.5
Water-quality score	86	52	Hospital beds per capita	337.0	420.0	Change in violent crime rate	11.3%	-2.2%
Pollen/allergy score	57	61	No. teaching hospitals	1	3	Property crime rate	4,809.3	3,517.1
Cancer mortality per capita	226.5	201.9	Cost per doctor visit	$71	$77	Change in property crime rate	-9.1%	-2.1%
Depression days per month	3.3	3.5	Cost per dental visit	$49	$70			
Stress score	44	50						

Health & Healthcare
Score: 67.4
Rank: 123

Crime
Score: 29.7
Rank: 263

COMMUTE	AREA	U.S. AVG	INTERCITY SERVICES	AREA	U.S. AVG	AUTOMOTIVE	AREA	U.S. AVG
Average commute time	25.1	27.4	Major airports within 60 miles	0	1	Insurance, annual premium	$1,305	$1,432
Percent commutes › 60 mins.	4.4%	5.9%	Size of regional airport	Small	Large	Gas, cost per gallon	$2.46	$2.49
Commute by auto	83.1%	78.9%	Daily airline activity	111	686	Daily vehicle miles per capita	32.4	24.0
Commute by mass transit	0.5%	1.9%	Amtrak service	No	No			
Work at home	1.9%	3.1%						
Mass transit miles per capita	0.52	1.87						

Transportation
Score: 8.0
Rank: 344

DINING & SHOPPING	AREA	U.S. AVG	ENTERTAINMENT	AREA	U.S. AVG	OUTDOOR ACTIVITIES	AREA	U.S. AVG
Restaurant rating	1	2	Professional sports rating	2	4	Golf-course rating	3	4
Outlet mall score	12	42	College sports rating	4	4	Ski-area rating	1	3
No. Starbucks	3	13	Zoo/aquarium rating	4	3	Sq. miles inland water	4	4
No. warehouse clubs	2	2	Amusement park rating	1	3	Miles of coastline	0.0	10.7
			Botanical garden/ arboretum rating	2	4	National Park rating	1	3

Leisure
Score: 35.6
Rank: 240

MEDIA & LIBRARIES	AREA	U.S. AVG	PERFORMING ARTS	AREA	U.S. AVG	MUSEUMS	AREA	U.S. AVG
Arts radio rating	7	3	Classical music rating	3	4	Overall museum rating	6	5
No. public libraries	19	27	Ballet/dance rating	5	3	Art museum rating	7	5
Library volumes per capita	2.45	2.78	Professional theater rating	1	3	Science museum rating	4	5
			University arts programs rating	8	5	Children's museum rating	1	3

Arts & Culture
Score: 72.5
Rank: 103

Morgantown, WV

Score: 44.4 **Rank:** 288 **2004 rank:** not ranked

Profile: College town
Location: Extreme northern West Virginia
Elevation: 823 feet
Time zone: Eastern Standard Time

PRO	CON
College-town amenities	Cloudy, wet weather
Low crime rates	Isolation
Steady employment	Arts and culture

Morgantown, along the Monongahela River, is home to the 26,000-student West Virginia University. The area has a selection of typical West Virginia businesses including chemicals and forest products, but has emerged into a diversified business center with research and high-tech industries and a strong employment base. There is plenty of recreation in the nearby mountains and rivers, and Pittsburgh is 70 miles to the north. The university brings above-average healthcare and educational resources to the area. The downtown area is interesting, well preserved, and livable with a few minor cultural amenities. Cost of living and housing are moderate especially for a college town. The area is probably better than the ranking indicates.

Morgantown is located in an attractive hilly, deciduous-wooded region extending for miles in all directions. The climate is a humid continental type, alternately pleasant and hot and humid in summer with occasional thundershowers. Winter weather is variable and the location on storm tracks and downwind of Lake Erie brings periods of wet or snowy weather in winter and clouds at all times of year.

Population

DEMOGRAPHICS	AREA	U.S. AVG	ETHNIC COMPOSITION	AREA	U.S. AVG	RESIDENT PROFILE	AREA	U.S. AVG
Population	115,519		White	93.1%	79.0%	Single	40.2%	32.4%
Population density per sq. mile	114.4	358.5	Black	2.7%	10.5%	Married	48.2%	52.7%
Population growth	10.7%	21.1%	Asian	2.4%	2.7%	Divorced/separated	11.5%	14.9%
Median age	34.4	36.1	Hispanic	0.9%	10.6%	Married with children	19.9%	23.7%
Percent Democrat	43.8%	44.5%	Religious observance	29.8%	48.9%	Single with children	6.1%	9.1%
Percent Republican	55.2%	54.5%	Diversity measure	14.5	40.1	Percent over age 65	11.9%	12.9%

Economy & Jobs
Score: 35.0
Rank: 243

INCOME	AREA	U.S. AVG	EMPLOYMENT	AREA	U.S. AVG	EMPLOYING INDUSTRIES	AREA	U.S. AVG
Per capita income	$19,305	$23,235	Unemployment rate	3.6%	4.7%	Largest: Healthcare & Social Assistance		
Household income	$32,712	$46,414	Recent job growth	1.3%	1.3%			
Household income < $25K	40.0%	26.2%	Projected future job growth	10.9%	11.5%	Percent manufacturing	12.6%	15.4%
Household income > $75K	16.3%	25.4%	White collar	59.1%	57.8%	Percent public sector	25.3%	15.7%
Household income growth	15.0%	13.6%	Blue collar	23.1%	25.2%	Percent construction	10.5%	9.9%

Cost of Living
Score: 68.2
Rank: 120

INDEXES & TAXES	AREA	U.S. AVG	HOUSING	AREA	U.S. AVG	NECESSITIES	AREA	U.S. AVG
Cost of Living Index	89.2	100.0	Median home price	$141,900	$220,000	Food Index	99.8	100.0
Buying Power Index	82.2	100.0	Home price appreciation	51.6%	10.1%	Housing Index	59.8	100.0
Income tax rate	6.00%	4.70%	Median rent	$533	$709	Utilities Index	139.5	100.0
Sales tax rate	6.00%	6.58%	Homes owned	59.8%	62.3%	Transportation Index	98.6	100.0
Property tax rate	$6.17	$12.00	Home price ratio	4.3	4.2	Healthcare Index	92.8	100.0
						Miscellaneous Cost Index	104.5	100.0

Climate
Score: 28.1
Rank: 268

TEMPERATURE	AREA	U.S. AVG	PRECIPITATION	AREA	U.S. AVG	COMFORTS & HAZARDS	AREA	U.S. AVG
Average January low	20.8	26.2	Annual inches precipitation	37.1	37.7	July relative humidity	60%	66%
Average July high	83.0	87.4	Annual inches snowfall	43.0	7.0	Annual days mostly sunny	185	208
Annual days > 90°F	8	38	Annual days precipitation	154	109	Annual days with thunderstorms	36	39
Annual days < 32°F	121	89	Annual days rain > 0.5 inches	27	22	Tornado risk score	1	18
Annual days < 0°F	5	6	Annual days snow > 1.5 inches	11	6	Hurricane risk score	1	13

TEMPERATURE

PRECIPITATION

DAYS OF CLOUDS & PRECIPITATION

Education
Score: 52.9
Rank: 177

ACHIEVEMENT	AREA	U.S. AVG	PUBLIC SCHOOLS	AREA	U.S. AVG	HIGHER EDUCATION	AREA	U.S. AVG
High school degree	81.3%	82.7%	Expenditures per pupil	$5,839	$5,686	No. 2-year colleges	3	4
2-year college degree	3.5%	6.4%	Student/teacher ratio	14.8	16.7	No. 4-year colleges/universities	2	6
4-year college degree	13.2%	15.7%	Attending public school	94.4%	90.1%	No. highly ranked universities	0	1
Graduate/professional degree	14.4%	8.9%	State SAT score	1029	1021			
			State ACT score	20.6*	20.9			

Health & Healthcare
Score: 96.0
Rank: 16

HAZARDS & ILLNESSES	AREA	U.S. AVG	HEALTHCARE	AREA	U.S. AVG	CRIME	AREA	U.S. AVG
Air-quality score	47	37	Physicians per capita	660.3	244.2	Violent crime rate	253.8	465.5
Water-quality score	46	52	Hospital beds per capita	754.0	420.0	Change in violent crime rate	3.8%	-2.2%
Pollen/allergy score	69	61	No. teaching hospitals	3	3	Property crime rate	2,380.8	3,517.1
Cancer mortality per capita	260.1	201.9	Cost per doctor visit	$72	$77	Change in property crime rate	4.2%	-2.1%
Depression days per month	4.0	3.5	Cost per dental visit	$87	$70			
Stress score	24	50						

Crime
Score: 94.9
Rank: 20

Transportation
Score: 46.0
Rank: 203

COMMUTE	AREA	U.S. AVG	INTERCITY SERVICES	AREA	U.S. AVG	AUTOMOTIVE	AREA	U.S. AVG
Average commute time	24.7	27.4	Major airports within 60 miles	1	1	Insurance, annual premium	$1,130	$1,432
Percent commutes > 60 mins.	6.0%	5.9%	Size of regional airport	Large	Large	Gas, cost per gallon	$2.51	$2.49
Commute by auto	76.3%	78.9%	Daily airline activity	663	686	Daily vehicle miles per capita	3.8	24.0
Commute by mass transit	0.7%	1.9%	Amtrak service	No	No			
Work at home	3.2%	3.1%						
Mass transit miles per capita	0.72	1.87						

DINING & SHOPPING	AREA	U.S. AVG	ENTERTAINMENT	AREA	U.S. AVG	OUTDOOR ACTIVITIES	AREA	U.S. AVG
Restaurant rating	1	2	Professional sports rating	1	4	Golf-course rating	2	4
Outlet mall score	0	42	College sports rating	3	4	Ski-area rating	2	3
No. Starbucks	1	13	Zoo/aquarium rating	1	3	Sq. miles inland water	2	4
No. warehouse clubs	0	2	Amusement park rating	1	3	Miles of coastline	0.0	10.7
			Botanical garden/ arboretum rating	3	4	National Park rating	3	3

Leisure
Score: 10.2
Rank: 335

MEDIA & LIBRARIES	AREA	U.S. AVG	PERFORMING ARTS	AREA	U.S. AVG	MUSEUMS	AREA	U.S. AVG
Arts radio rating	1	3	Classical music rating	2	4	Overall museum rating	2	5
No. public libraries	6	27	Ballet/dance rating	1	3	Art museum rating	1	5
Library volumes per capita	2.39	2.78	Professional theater rating	1	3	Science museum rating	4	5
			University arts programs rating	3	5	Children's museum rating	1	3

Arts & Culture
Score: 10.7
Rank: 333

Morristown, TN

Score: 23.8   **Rank:** 345   **2004 rank:** not ranked

Profile: Small town
Location: Eastern Tennessee, 50 miles east of Knoxville
Elevation: 1,283 feet
Time zone: Eastern Standard Time

PRO	CON
Cost of living	Low educational attainment
Nearby recreation	Isolation
Small-town feel	Arts and culture

Morristown is a nondescript town located along Interstate 81, a major transportation route, at the northwestern base of the Great Smoky Mountains east of Knoxville. Owing to a low-cost workforce and a central location relative to U.S. markets, the town has a diverse, but slightly declining industrial base of auto parts, furniture, office supplies, and other manufacturing. Downtown is small, original, and has some historic interest. An overhead sidewalk and "Skymart" was built in the late 1960s, an unusual feature for this size of town, and currently, another renewal project is under way. Recreational opportunities center on the large Cherokee Lake to the west and the Great Smoky

Mountains National Park to the east. Knoxville provides some city amenities and services not available locally. Cost of living and housing are the biggest attraction.

Morristown is located in a relatively flat, green valley nestled between the southwest-to-northeast Appalachians to the east and Clinch Mountain to the west. The valley is a mix of open agricultural land and deciduous forest. Summers are variable with periods of heat and humidity. The elevation and nearby mountain air keeps evenings relatively cool. Winters are cool and variable, with some periods of snow but accumulations seldom last.

DEMOGRAPHICS	AREA	U.S. AVG	ETHNIC COMPOSITION	AREA	U.S. AVG	RESIDENT PROFILE	AREA	U.S. AVG
Population	129,332		White	92.7%	79.0%	Single	25.6%	32.4%
Population density per sq. mile	180.8	358.5	Black	2.8%	10.5%	Married	59.5%	52.7%
Population growth	29.9%	21.1%	Asian	0.7%	2.7%	Divorced/separated	14.9%	14.9%
Median age	38.1	36.1	Hispanic	4.8%	10.6%	Married with children	23.2%	23.7%
Percent Democrat	32.9%	44.5%	Religious observance	59.4%	48.9%	Single with children	7.4%	9.1%
Percent Republican	66.5%	54.5%	Diversity measure	20.9	40.1	Percent over age 65	14.0%	12.9%

Population

INCOME	AREA	U.S. AVG	EMPLOYMENT	AREA	U.S. AVG	EMPLOYING INDUSTRIES	AREA	U.S. AVG
Per capita income	$19,046	$23,235	Unemployment rate	5.6%	4.7%	Largest: Manufacturing		
Household income	$36,473	$46,414	Recent job growth	1.1%	1.3%			
Household income < $25K	33.7%	26.2%	Projected future job growth	15.5%	11.5%	Percent manufacturing	29.5%	15.4%
Household income > $75K	14.9%	25.4%	White collar	43.7%	57.8%	Percent public sector	11.3%	15.7%
Household income growth	14.7%	13.6%	Blue collar	41.1%	25.2%	Percent construction	11.6%	9.9%

Economy & Jobs
Score: 47.3
Rank: 197

INDEXES & TAXES	AREA	U.S. AVG	HOUSING	AREA	U.S. AVG	NECESSITIES	AREA	U.S. AVG
Cost of Living Index	76.0	100.0	Median home price	$99,600	$220,000	Food Index	96.4	100.0
Buying Power Index	107.6	100.0	Home price appreciation	31.6%	10.1%	Housing Index	50.7	100.0
Income tax rate	0.00%	4.70%	Median rent	$492	$709	Utilities Index	87.1	100.0
Sales tax rate	9.45%	6.58%	Homes owned	69.5%	62.3%	Transportation Index	94.1	100.0
Property tax rate	$5.65	$12.00	Home price ratio	2.7	4.2	Healthcare Index	85.0	100.0
						Miscellaneous Cost Index	97.4	100.0

Cost of Living
Score: 98.7
Rank: 6

Climate
Score: 26.7
Rank: 273

TEMPERATURE	AREA	U.S. AVG
Average January low	26.0	26.2
Average July high	87.0	87.4
Annual days > 90°F	27	38
Annual days < 32°F	91	89
Annual days < 0°F	0	6

PRECIPITATION	AREA	U.S. AVG
Annual inches precipitation	53.2	37.7
Annual inches snowfall	10.0	7.0
Annual days precipitation	128	109
Annual days rain > 0.5 inches	35	22
Annual days snow > 1.5 inches	2	6

COMFORTS & HAZARDS	AREA	U.S. AVG
July relative humidity	60%	66%
Annual days mostly sunny	205	208
Annual days with thunderstorms	47	39
Tornado risk score	1	18
Hurricane risk score	1	13

TEMPERATURE

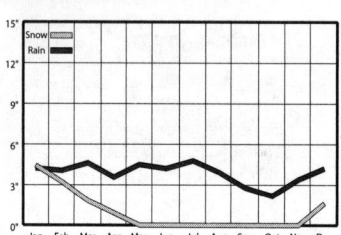

PRECIPITATION

DAYS OF CLOUDS & PRECIPITATION

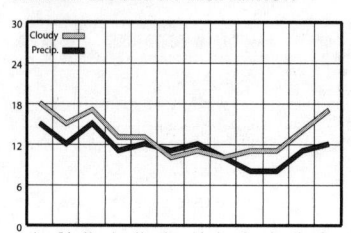

Education
Score: 14.4
Rank: 319

ACHIEVEMENT	AREA	U.S. AVG
High school degree	68.5%	82.7%
2-year college degree	4.4%	6.4%
4-year college degree	7.7%	15.7%
Graduate/professional degree	4.4%	8.9%

PUBLIC SCHOOLS	AREA	U.S. AVG
Expenditures per pupil	$4,305	$5,686
Student/teacher ratio	0.0	16.7
Attending public school	97.6%	90.1%
State SAT score	1142	1021
State ACT score	20.7*	20.9

HIGHER EDUCATION	AREA	U.S. AVG
No. 2-year colleges	1	4
No. 4-year colleges/universities	1	6
No. highly ranked universities	1	1

Health & Healthcare
Score: 86.6
Rank: 51

HAZARDS & ILLNESSES	AREA	U.S. AVG
Air-quality score	62	37
Water-quality score	90	52
Pollen/allergy score	61	61
Cancer mortality per capita	219.0	201.9
Depression days per month	3.0	3.5
Stress score	91	50

HEALTHCARE	AREA	U.S. AVG
Physicians per capita	136.9	244.2
Hospital beds per capita	265.2	420.0
No. teaching hospitals	0	3
Cost per doctor visit	$72	$77
Cost per dental visit	$57	$70

Crime
Score: 49.7
Rank: 189

CRIME	AREA	U.S. AVG
Violent crime rate	418.8	465.5
Change in violent crime rate	14.3%	-2.2%
Property crime rate	3,401.2	3,517.1
Change in property crime rate	-5.0%	-2.1%

Transportation
Score: 1.6
Rank: 367

COMMUTE	AREA	U.S. AVG
Average commute time	25.9	27.4
Percent commutes > 60 mins.	6.0%	5.9%
Commute by auto	83.4%	78.9%
Commute by mass transit	0.2%	1.9%
Work at home	2.1%	3.1%
Mass transit miles per capita	0.24	1.87

INTERCITY SERVICES	AREA	U.S. AVG
Major airports within 60 miles	0	1
Size of regional airport	Small	Large
Daily airline activity	89	686
Amtrak service	No	No

AUTOMOTIVE	AREA	U.S. AVG
Insurance, annual premium	$911	$1,432
Gas, cost per gallon	$2.43	$2.49
Daily vehicle miles per capita	30.0	24.0

Leisure
Score: 9.9
Rank: 336

DINING & SHOPPING	AREA	U.S. AVG
Restaurant rating	1	2
Outlet mall score	0	42
No. Starbucks	0	13
No. warehouse clubs	0	2

ENTERTAINMENT	AREA	U.S. AVG
Professional sports rating	1	4
College sports rating	1	4
Zoo/aquarium rating	1	3
Amusement park rating	1	3
Botanical garden/ arboretum rating	2	4

OUTDOOR ACTIVITIES	AREA	U.S. AVG
Golf-course rating	2	4
Ski-area rating	2	3
Sq. miles inland water	2	4
Miles of coastline	0.0	10.7
National Park rating	5	3

Arts & Culture
Score: 4.0
Rank: 358

MEDIA & LIBRARIES	AREA	U.S. AVG
Arts radio rating	1	3
No. public libraries	10	27
Library volumes per capita	1.59	2.78

PERFORMING ARTS	AREA	U.S. AVG
Classical music rating	2	4
Ballet/dance rating	1	3
Professional theater rating	1	3
University arts programs rating	1	5

MUSEUMS	AREA	U.S. AVG
Overall museum rating	2	5
Art museum rating	4	5
Science museum rating	1	5
Children's museum rating	1	3

Mount Vernon–Anacortes, WA

Score: 66.7   **Rank:** 123   **2004 rank:** not ranked

Profile: Small-town complex
Location: Northwest Washington, along Puget Sound
Elevation: 23 feet
Time zone: Pacific Standard Time

PRO	CON
Attractive setting	Economy
Mild year-round climate	Some unattractive sprawl
Central location	Property crime rate

In an area of uncommon scenic beauty, Mount Vernon is adjacent to a vast river delta that stretches west to the Puget Sound but is otherwise surrounded by mountains. Anacortes is a main port gateway to the San Juan Islands and an oil terminal and refining center. The river delta supports a magnificent area of farmland, settled by Swedes and later by the Dutch, bringing visitors worldwide during the annual Skagit Valley Tulip Festival in spring. The economy, currently weak, is a mix of farming, forest products, fishing, tourism, and some industry. The area is located centrally between Seattle, Bellingham, and Vancouver, British Columbia, with easy access to all three. There is a strong and mostly successful effort to preserve the farmland, but areas of unattractive commercial sprawl spread north along Interstate 5 toward the towns of Burlington and Sedro Wooley. Attractive new subdivisions are appearing east of town among the coniferous forests, populated in part by people working in northern Seattle suburbs. The area works for telecommuters or occasional commuters needing a big city at times, and transportation links, including Amtrak "Cascade" service, are effective.

Mount Vernon itself is located along Interstate 5 just east of the delta farmland, with wooded Cascade foothills rising just to the east and views of the San Juans to the northwest and the Olympic Mountains farther southwest. The marine climate gives very pleasant and mostly dry summers, while winters are cool, wet, and variable, but not as wet as the latitude might suggest due to the shadowing effects of the Olympics to the southwest. That said, occasional snows and strong windy Pacific storms can occur.

Population

DEMOGRAPHICS	AREA	U.S. AVG	ETHNIC COMPOSITION	AREA	U.S. AVG	RESIDENT PROFILE	AREA	U.S. AVG
Population	110,809		White	85.1%	79.0%	Single	28.0%	32.4%
Population density per sq. mile	63.9	358.5	Black	0.5%	10.5%	Married	56.4%	52.7%
Population growth	39.3%	21.1%	Asian	1.9%	2.7%	Divorced/separated	15.6%	14.9%
Median age	37.3	36.1	Hispanic	13.0%	10.6%	Married with children	23.8%	23.7%
Percent Democrat	48.1%	44.5%	Religious observance	43.5%	48.9%	Single with children	8.9%	9.1%
Percent Republican	50.0%	54.5%	Diversity measure	43.4	40.1	Percent over age 65	14.4%	12.9%

Economy & Jobs
Score: 87.7
Rank: 47

INCOME	AREA	U.S. AVG	EMPLOYMENT	AREA	U.S. AVG	EMPLOYING INDUSTRIES	AREA	U.S. AVG
Per capita income	$23,748	$23,235	Unemployment rate	5.4%	4.7%	Largest: Manufacturing		
Household income	$48,384	$46,414	Recent job growth	3.9%	1.3%			
Household income < $25K	22.4%	26.2%	Projected future job growth	22.2%	11.5%	Percent manufacturing	15.7%	15.4%
Household income > $75K	26.8%	25.4%	White collar	52.5%	57.8%	Percent public sector	15.7%	15.7%
Household income growth	14.2%	13.6%	Blue collar	27.2%	25.2%	Percent construction	11.5%	9.9%

Cost of Living
Score: 47.6
Rank: 196

INDEXES & TAXES	AREA	U.S. AVG	HOUSING	AREA	U.S. AVG	NECESSITIES	AREA	U.S. AVG
Cost of Living Index	102.5	100.0	Median home price	$234,700	$220,000	Food Index	102.3	100.0
Buying Power Index	105.8	100.0	Home price appreciation	56.1%	10.1%	Housing Index	82.3	100.0
Income tax rate	0.00%	4.70%	Median rent	$820	$709	Utilities Index	66.9	100.0
Sales tax rate	7.90%	6.58%	Homes owned	63.5%	62.3%	Transportation Index	111.8	100.0
Property tax rate	$10.69	$12.00	Home price ratio	4.9	4.2	Healthcare Index	118.0	100.0
						Miscellaneous Cost Index	102.7	100.0

Climate
Score: 91.7
Rank: 32

TEMPERATURE	AREA	U.S. AVG	PRECIPITATION	AREA	U.S. AVG	COMFORTS & HAZARDS	AREA	U.S. AVG
Average January low	33.6	26.2	Annual inches precipitation	32.6	37.7	July relative humidity	51%	66%
Average July high	73.7	87.4	Annual inches snowfall	3.8	7.0	Annual days mostly sunny	133	208
Annual days > 90°F	1	38	Annual days precipitation	155	109	Annual days with thunderstorms	7	39
Annual days < 32°F	56	89	Annual days rain > 0.5 inches	24	22	Tornado risk score	1	18
Annual days < 0°F	0	6	Annual days snow > 1.5 inches	2	6	Hurricane risk score	0	13

TEMPERATURE

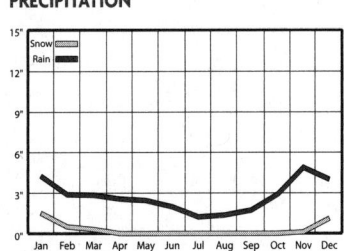

PRECIPITATION

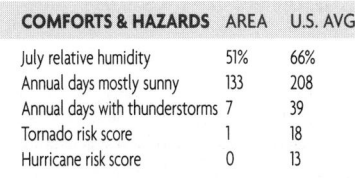

DAYS OF CLOUDS & PRECIPITATION

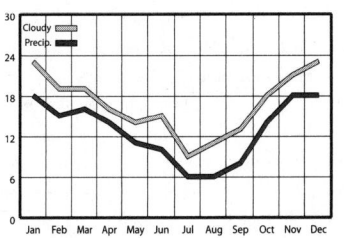

Education
Score: 51.9
Rank: 181

ACHIEVEMENT	AREA	U.S. AVG	PUBLIC SCHOOLS	AREA	U.S. AVG	HIGHER EDUCATION	AREA	U.S. AVG
High school degree	83.7%	82.7%	Expenditures per pupil	$5,302	$5,686	No. 2-year colleges	2	4
2-year college degree	8.7%	6.4%	Student/teacher ratio	18.9	16.7	No. 4-year colleges/universities	0	6
4-year college degree	13.6%	15.7%	Attending public school	95.7%	90.1%	No. highly ranked universities	0	1
Graduate/professional degree	6.9%	8.9%	State SAT score	1059*	1021			
			State ACT score	22.9	20.9			

Health & Healthcare
Score: 50.8
Rank: 185

HAZARDS & ILLNESSES	AREA	U.S. AVG	HEALTHCARE	AREA	U.S. AVG	CRIME	AREA	U.S. AVG
Air-quality score	43	37	Physicians per capita	233.4	244.2	Violent crime rate	214.1	465.5
Water-quality score	52	52	Hospital beds per capita	255.4	420.0	Change in violent crime rate	-15.8%	-2.2%
Pollen/allergy score	48	61	No. teaching hospitals	0	3	Property crime rate	7,469.3	3,517.1
Cancer mortality per capita	187.6	201.9	Cost per doctor visit	$86	$77	Change in property crime rate	10.4%	-2.1%
Depression days per month	3.0	3.5	Cost per dental visit	$89	$70			
Stress score	94	50						

Crime
Score: 20.1
Rank: 298

Transportation
Score: 27.3
Rank: 272

COMMUTE	AREA	U.S. AVG	INTERCITY SERVICES	AREA	U.S. AVG	AUTOMOTIVE	AREA	U.S. AVG
Average commute time	26.6	27.4	Major airports within 60 miles	1	1	Insurance, annual premium	$1,374	$1,432
Percent commutes > 60 mins.	9.6%	5.9%	Size of regional airport	Large	Large	Gas, cost per gallon	$2.70	$2.49
Commute by auto	77.3%	78.9%	Daily airline activity	698	686	Daily vehicle miles per capita	20.7	24.0
Commute by mass transit	1.0%	1.9%	Amtrak service	Yes	No			
Work at home	4.6%	3.1%						
Mass transit miles per capita	1.02	1.87						

Leisure
Score: 14.2
Rank: 320

DINING & SHOPPING	AREA	U.S. AVG	ENTERTAINMENT	AREA	U.S. AVG	OUTDOOR ACTIVITIES	AREA	U.S. AVG
Restaurant rating	1	2	Professional sports rating	1	4	Golf-course rating	2	4
Outlet mall score	0	42	College sports rating	1	4	Ski-area rating	3	3
No. Starbucks	4	13	Zoo/aquarium rating	1	3	Sq. miles inland water	2	4
No. warehouse clubs	1	2	Amusement park rating	1	3	Miles of coastline	9.0	10.7
			Botanical garden/ arboretum rating	1	4	National Park rating	4	3

Arts & Culture
Score: 6.7
Rank: 348

MEDIA & LIBRARIES	AREA	U.S. AVG	PERFORMING ARTS	AREA	U.S. AVG	MUSEUMS	AREA	U.S. AVG
Arts radio rating	1	3	Classical music rating	2	4	Overall museum rating	2	5
No. public libraries	6	27	Ballet/dance rating	1	3	Art museum rating	3	5
Library volumes per capita	4.24	2.78	Professional theater rating	1	3	Science museum rating	3	5
			University arts programs rating	1	5	Children's museum rating	1	3

Muncie, IN

Score: 45.6   Rank: 279   2004 rank: 90

Profile: Small town/college town
Location: Northeast Indiana, about 60 miles northeast of Indianapolis
Elevation: 700 feet
Time zone: Eastern Standard Time

PRO
College-town amenities
Small-town atmosphere
Cost of living and housing

CON
Employment
Low educational attainment
Winter climate

Muncie is an agricultural center with a college-town element and a variety of industry. In the 19th century, the Ball family started manufacturing canning jars, and Ball jars are still the world standard. The family business endowed Ball State University, a mid-size school with an attractive campus and an above-average reputation. The college-town influence and private endowments bring above-average healthcare and a few arts amenities. The Cost of Living Index at 75.7 is second lowest in the state and a good value for what's available. Housing is also very reasonable, with a median home price of $96,500. The city has long served as a model "mid-America" town for sociological and marketing studies starting in the 1920s and continuing into the present. Negatives include a harsh winter climate and somewhat lower educational attainment than would be expected in a college town. Recent and

projected future employment trends are very weak. That said, student loan funder Sallie Mae recently announced a new facility bringing 700 jobs, and recent redevelopment efforts have brought new streetscapes, parks, and some national recognition. We see Muncie as a good value and the future may be better than the ranking suggests, and it doesn't hurt to be only 60 miles from Indianapolis and closer to its prosperous northeast suburbs.

The town is located in a mainly level agricultural plain with a few rolling hills to the south and areas of deciduous trees. Summers are warm and humid with thundershowers but extreme heat is rare. Winters are cold and variable with occasional blasts of cold polar air and snow. Snowfalls of 3 inches or more occur on average of two to three times each winter. First freeze is mid- to late October; the last is late April.

Population

DEMOGRAPHICS	AREA	U.S. AVG
Population	116,688	
Population density per sq. mile	296.7	358.5
Population growth	-2.5%	21.1%
Median age	34.3	36.1
Percent Democrat	42.6%	44.5%
Percent Republican	56.5%	54.5%

ETHNIC COMPOSITION	AREA	U.S. AVG
White	90.5%	79.0%
Black	6.6%	10.5%
Asian	0.9%	2.7%
Hispanic	1.1%	10.6%
Religious observance	27.3%	48.9%
Diversity measure	19.4	40.1

RESIDENT PROFILE	AREA	U.S. AVG
Single	35.4%	32.4%
Married	49.6%	52.7%
Divorced/separated	15.0%	14.9%
Married with children	19.1%	23.7%
Single with children	8.6%	9.1%
Percent over age 65	13.8%	12.9%

Economy & Jobs
Score: 1.1
Rank: 369

INCOME	AREA	U.S. AVG
Per capita income	$21,409	$23,235
Household income	$39,180	$46,414
Household income < $25K	31.8%	26.2%
Household income > $75K	20.4%	25.4%
Household income growth	13.0%	13.6%

EMPLOYMENT	AREA	U.S. AVG
Unemployment rate	6.7%	4.7%
Recent job growth	-1.4%	1.3%
Projected future job growth	-2.4%	11.5%
White collar	56.4%	57.8%
Blue collar	25.6%	25.2%

EMPLOYING INDUSTRIES	AREA	U.S. AVG
Largest: Manufacturing		
Percent manufacturing	17.5%	15.4%
Percent public sector	15.9%	15.7%
Percent construction	8.1%	9.9%

Cost of Living
Score: 94.7
Rank: 21

INDEXES & TAXES	AREA	U.S. AVG
Cost of Living Index	75.7	100.0
Buying Power Index	116.0	100.0
Income tax rate	3.40%	4.70%
Sales tax rate	6.00%	6.58%
Property tax rate	$11.46	$12.00

HOUSING	AREA	U.S. AVG
Median home price	$96,500	$220,000
Home price appreciation	19.4%	10.1%
Median rent	$616	$709
Homes owned	62.6%	62.3%
Home price ratio	2.5	4.2

NECESSITIES	AREA	U.S. AVG
Food Index	92.6	100.0
Housing Index	42.5	100.0
Utilities Index	93.6	100.0
Transportation Index	100.9	100.0
Healthcare Index	93.0	100.0
Miscellaneous Cost Index	93.4	100.0

Climate
Score: 49.7
Rank: 187

TEMPERATURE	AREA	U.S. AVG
Average January low	19.7	26.2
Average July high	85.4	87.4
Annual days > 90°F	15	38
Annual days < 32°F	122	89
Annual days < 0°F	7	6

PRECIPITATION	AREA	U.S. AVG
Annual inches precipitation	39.0	37.7
Annual inches snowfall	21.0	7.0
Annual days precipitation	122	109
Annual days rain > 0.5 inches	27	22
Annual days snow > 1.5 inches	7	6

COMFORTS & HAZARDS	AREA	U.S. AVG
July relative humidity	73%	66%
Annual days mostly sunny	191	208
Annual days with thunderstorms	45	39
Tornado risk score	20	18
Hurricane risk score	4	13

TEMPERATURE

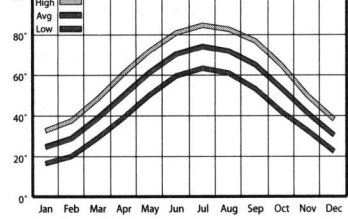

PRECIPITATION

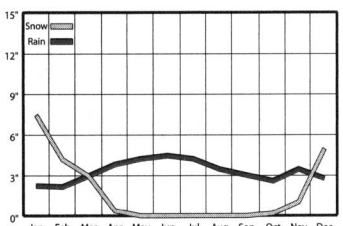

DAYS OF CLOUDS & PRECIPITATION

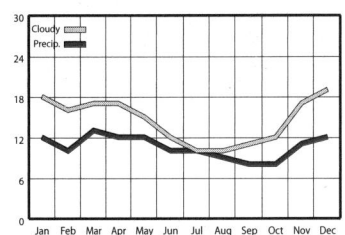

Education
Score: 38.0
Rank: 233

ACHIEVEMENT	AREA	U.S. AVG
High school degree	81.9%	82.7%
2-year college degree	4.7%	6.4%
4-year college degree	11.1%	15.7%
Graduate/professional degree	9.8%	8.9%

PUBLIC SCHOOLS	AREA	U.S. AVG
Expenditures per pupil	$5,888	$5,686
Student/teacher ratio	15.7	16.7
Attending public school	94.6%	90.1%
State SAT score	1007*	1021
State ACT score	21.7	20.9

HIGHER EDUCATION	AREA	U.S. AVG
No. 2-year colleges	3	4
No. 4-year colleges/universities	1	6
No. highly ranked universities	0	1

Health & Healthcare
Score: 34.8
Rank: 243

HAZARDS & ILLNESSES	AREA	U.S. AVG
Air-quality score	44	37
Water-quality score	10	52
Pollen/allergy score	65	61
Cancer mortality per capita	220.7	201.9
Depression days per month	2.7	3.5
Stress score	51	50

HEALTHCARE	AREA	U.S. AVG
Physicians per capita	260.5	244.2
Hospital beds per capita	338.5	420.0
No. teaching hospitals	1	3
Cost per doctor visit	$69	$77
Cost per dental visit	$72	$70

Crime
Score: 77.8
Rank: 84

CRIME	AREA	U.S. AVG
Violent crime rate	292.2	465.5
Change in violent crime rate	-16.1%	-2.2%
Property crime rate	3,164.9	3,517.1
Change in property crime rate	-9.1%	-2.1%

Transportation
Score: 92.5
Rank: 29

COMMUTE	AREA	U.S. AVG
Average commute time	21.7	27.4
Percent commutes > 60 mins.	5.7%	5.9%
Commute by auto	81.3%	78.9%
Commute by mass transit	1.1%	1.9%
Work at home	2.7%	3.1%
Mass transit miles per capita	1.11	1.87

INTERCITY SERVICES	AREA	U.S. AVG
Major airports within 60 miles	2	1
Size of regional airport	Large	Large
Daily airline activity	1284	686
Amtrak service	No	No

AUTOMOTIVE	AREA	U.S. AVG
Insurance, annual premium	$1,100	$1,432
Gas, cost per gallon	$2.46	$2.49
Daily vehicle miles per capita	19.3	24.0

Leisure
Score: 11.8
Rank: 329

DINING & SHOPPING	AREA	U.S. AVG	ENTERTAINMENT	AREA	U.S. AVG	OUTDOOR ACTIVITIES	AREA	U.S. AVG
Restaurant rating	1	2	Professional sports rating	2	4	Golf-course rating	2	4
Outlet mall score	22	42	College sports rating	3	4	Ski-area rating	2	3
No. Starbucks	1	13	Zoo/aquarium rating	1	3	Sq. miles inland water	2	4
No. warehouse clubs	0	2	Amusement park rating	1	3	Miles of coastline	0.0	10.7
			Botanical garden/ arboretum rating	2	4	National Park rating	1	3

Arts & Culture
Score: 53.5
Rank: 174

MEDIA & LIBRARIES	AREA	U.S. AVG	PERFORMING ARTS	AREA	U.S. AVG	MUSEUMS	AREA	U.S. AVG
Arts radio rating	1	3	Classical music rating	3	4	Overall museum rating	4	5
No. public libraries	6	27	Ballet/dance rating	1	3	Art museum rating	7	5
Library volumes per capita	3.63	2.78	Professional theater rating	1	3	Science museum rating	6	5
			University arts programs rating	7	5	Children's museum rating	3	3

Muskegon–Norton Shores, MI

Score: 63.6   **Rank:** 146   **2004 rank:** 157

Profile: Small city
Location: Central Lake Michigan shore
Elevation: 620 feet
Time zone: Eastern Standard Time

PRO	CON
Nearby recreation	Cold, cloudy winters
Arts and culture	Educational attainment
Pleasant summers	Current unemployment

Strategically located on Michigan's west shoreline, Muskegon is an old economic powerhouse dating back to the mid–19th century. The economic strength was then driven by lumber and shipping, and as the 20th century unfolded, lumber declined and was replaced by diverse manufacturing, with good access to auto markets to the east and a number of major manufacturing markets across Lake Michigan. As a manufacturing center specializing in foundries and machining, the area declined somewhat in the last half of the 20th century but has enjoyed a resurgence due to its attractive summer climate and extensive water and beach amenities both north and south of town. It has attracted families and retirees alike, and is currently working to capitalize on old legacies and endowments, a revitalizing downtown, and the waterfront and nearby beaches. Tourism is big. Developmental zones and new industrial parks have attracted some new business to the area, and employment is on the way up. The new prosperity has brought improvements to the schools and downtown. Endowments have supported some above-average arts amenities. Michigan's Adventure, supposedly the largest amusement park in the state, adds entertainment and tourist appeal. The area is on the upswing and the cost of living is low, but some may not like the climate. Additional city services are available in Grand Rapids 30 miles southeast or in Chicago 3½ hours southwest, but Milwaukee and Chicago are also accessible by the Lake Express high-speed ferry, a nice but expensive 2½-hour ride. Norton Shores is a mainly residential shore community with some industry and agriculture presence 5 miles southwest.

Muskegon is located on the Lake Michigan shore at the mouth of the Muskegon River about 100 miles north of the southern tip of the lake. The area is flat with coastal grasslands, marshes, and sand dunes giving way to forested hills especially to the north. Summer days are mostly cool and breezy with pleasant evenings and some thunderstorms. The lake effect prolongs spring and fall, giving gorgeous fall seasons especially in the hardwood forests to the north. The location along the lake brings frequent clouds, winds, snow and snow cover, squalls and flurries, although bitter cold outbreaks are less frequent than in Wisconsin or central parts of Michigan. Persistent clouds may break for days at a time when cool, dry air arrives from the north. First freeze is early October; last is May 1.

Population

DEMOGRAPHICS	AREA	U.S. AVG	ETHNIC COMPOSITION	AREA	U.S. AVG	RESIDENT PROFILE	AREA	U.S. AVG
Population	174,431		White	81.1%	79.0%	Single	32.0%	32.4%
Population density per sq. mile	342.6	358.5	Black	14.0%	10.5%	Married	51.7%	52.7%
Population growth	9.7%	21.1%	Asian	0.5%	2.7%	Divorced/separated	16.4%	14.9%
Median age	36.1	36.1	Hispanic	3.9%	10.6%	Married with children	22.8%	23.7%
Percent Democrat	55.1%	44.5%	Religious observance	35.0%	48.9%	Single with children	11.5%	9.1%
Percent Republican	44.0%	54.5%	Diversity measure	37.3	40.1	Percent over age 65	12.8%	12.9%

Economy & Jobs
Score: 51.9
Rank: 181

INCOME	AREA	U.S. AVG	EMPLOYMENT	AREA	U.S. AVG	EMPLOYING INDUSTRIES	AREA	U.S. AVG
Per capita income	$20,336	$23,235	Unemployment rate	8.0%	4.7%	Largest: Manufacturing		
Household income	$42,817	$46,414	Recent job growth	3.4%	1.3%			
Household income < $25K	28.1%	26.2%	Projected future job growth	11.2%	11.5%	Percent manufacturing	25.7%	15.4%
Household income > $75K	20.5%	25.4%	White collar	49.3%	57.8%	Percent public sector	9.7%	15.7%
Household income growth	12.7%	13.6%	Blue collar	34.6%	25.2%	Percent construction	8.8%	9.9%

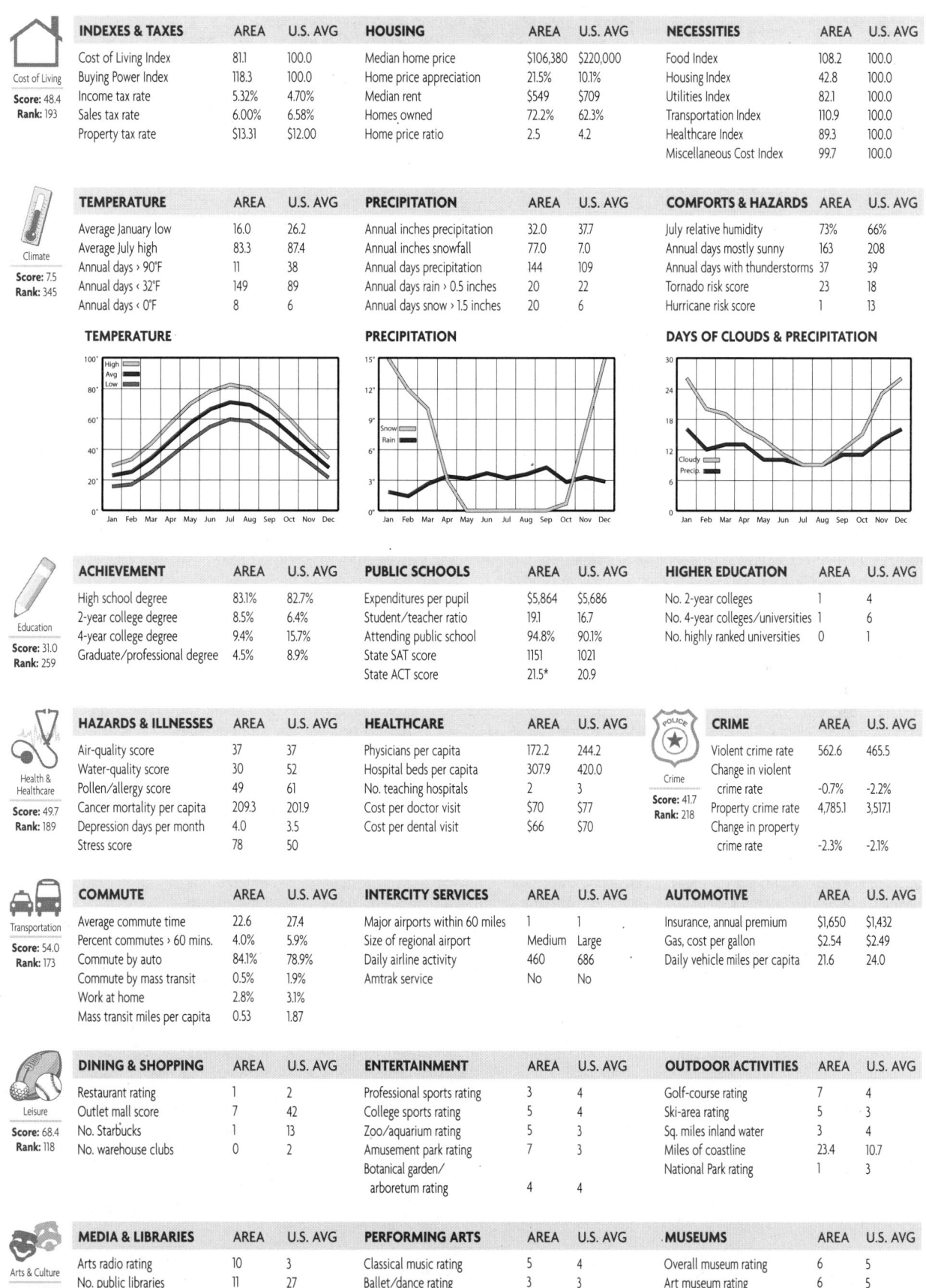

Cost of Living
Score: 48.4
Rank: 193

INDEXES & TAXES	AREA	U.S. AVG
Cost of Living Index	81.1	100.0
Buying Power Index	118.3	100.0
Income tax rate	5.32%	4.70%
Sales tax rate	6.00%	6.58%
Property tax rate	$13.31	$12.00

HOUSING	AREA	U.S. AVG
Median home price	$106,380	$220,000
Home price appreciation	21.5%	10.1%
Median rent	$549	$709
Homes owned	72.2%	62.3%
Home price ratio	2.5	4.2

NECESSITIES	AREA	U.S. AVG
Food Index	108.2	100.0
Housing Index	42.8	100.0
Utilities Index	82.1	100.0
Transportation Index	110.9	100.0
Healthcare Index	89.3	100.0
Miscellaneous Cost Index	99.7	100.0

Climate
Score: 7.5
Rank: 345

TEMPERATURE	AREA	U.S. AVG
Average January low	16.0	26.2
Average July high	83.3	87.4
Annual days > 90°F	11	38
Annual days < 32°F	149	89
Annual days < 0°F	8	6

PRECIPITATION	AREA	U.S. AVG
Annual inches precipitation	32.0	37.7
Annual inches snowfall	77.0	7.0
Annual days precipitation	144	109
Annual days rain > 0.5 inches	20	22
Annual days snow > 1.5 inches	20	6

COMFORTS & HAZARDS	AREA	U.S. AVG
July relative humidity	73%	66%
Annual days mostly sunny	163	208
Annual days with thunderstorms	37	39
Tornado risk score	23	18
Hurricane risk score	1	13

TEMPERATURE

PRECIPITATION

DAYS OF CLOUDS & PRECIPITATION

Education
Score: 31.0
Rank: 259

ACHIEVEMENT	AREA	U.S. AVG
High school degree	83.1%	82.7%
2-year college degree	8.5%	6.4%
4-year college degree	9.4%	15.7%
Graduate/professional degree	4.5%	8.9%

PUBLIC SCHOOLS	AREA	U.S. AVG
Expenditures per pupil	$5,864	$5,686
Student/teacher ratio	19.1	16.7
Attending public school	94.8%	90.1%
State SAT score	1151	1021
State ACT score	21.5*	20.9

HIGHER EDUCATION	AREA	U.S. AVG
No. 2-year colleges	1	4
No. 4-year colleges/universities	1	6
No. highly ranked universities	0	1

Health & Healthcare
Score: 49.7
Rank: 189

HAZARDS & ILLNESSES	AREA	U.S. AVG
Air-quality score	37	37
Water-quality score	30	52
Pollen/allergy score	49	61
Cancer mortality per capita	209.3	201.9
Depression days per month	4.0	3.5
Stress score	78	50

HEALTHCARE	AREA	U.S. AVG
Physicians per capita	172.2	244.2
Hospital beds per capita	307.9	420.0
No. teaching hospitals	2	3
Cost per doctor visit	$70	$77
Cost per dental visit	$66	$70

Crime
Score: 41.7
Rank: 218

CRIME	AREA	U.S. AVG
Violent crime rate	562.6	465.5
Change in violent crime rate	-0.7%	-2.2%
Property crime rate	4,785.1	3,517.1
Change in property crime rate	-2.3%	-2.1%

Transportation
Score: 54.0
Rank: 173

COMMUTE	AREA	U.S. AVG
Average commute time	22.6	27.4
Percent commutes > 60 mins.	4.0%	5.9%
Commute by auto	84.1%	78.9%
Commute by mass transit	0.5%	1.9%
Work at home	2.8%	3.1%
Mass transit miles per capita	0.53	1.87

INTERCITY SERVICES	AREA	U.S. AVG
Major airports within 60 miles	1	1
Size of regional airport	Medium	Large
Daily airline activity	460	686
Amtrak service	No	No

AUTOMOTIVE	AREA	U.S. AVG
Insurance, annual premium	$1,650	$1,432
Gas, cost per gallon	$2.54	$2.49
Daily vehicle miles per capita	21.6	24.0

Leisure
Score: 68.4
Rank: 118

DINING & SHOPPING	AREA	U.S. AVG
Restaurant rating	1	2
Outlet mall score	7	42
No. Starbucks	1	13
No. warehouse clubs	0	2

ENTERTAINMENT	AREA	U.S. AVG
Professional sports rating	3	4
College sports rating	5	4
Zoo/aquarium rating	5	3
Amusement park rating	7	3
Botanical garden/ arboretum rating	4	4

OUTDOOR ACTIVITIES	AREA	U.S. AVG
Golf-course rating	7	4
Ski-area rating	5	3
Sq. miles inland water	3	4
Miles of coastline	23.4	10.7
National Park rating	1	3

Arts & Culture
Score: 80.5
Rank: 74

MEDIA & LIBRARIES	AREA	U.S. AVG
Arts radio rating	10	3
No. public libraries	11	27
Library volumes per capita	2.42	2.78

PERFORMING ARTS	AREA	U.S. AVG
Classical music rating	5	4
Ballet/dance rating	3	3
Professional theater rating	1	3
University arts programs rating	8	5

MUSEUMS	AREA	U.S. AVG
Overall museum rating	6	5
Art museum rating	6	5
Science museum rating	5	5
Children's museum rating	7	3

Myrtle Beach–Conway–North Myrtle Beach, SC

Score: 44.0   Rank: 295   2004 rank: 266

Profile: Beach-city complex/college town
Location: Northeast South Carolina on Atlantic Coast, 20 miles from North Carolina border
Elevation: 30 feet
Time zone: Eastern Standard Time

PRO	CON
Entertainment	Crime rates
Beaches and recreation	Arts and culture
Job growth	Tourist sprawl

Myrtle Beach might be called the "northernmost city in Florida." The wide, white, sandy beaches lined with high-rise hotels and residences look just like a beach resort city in Florida—and functionally and financially, that is what Myrtle Beach is. The area is a center for tourism, attracting some 15 million tourists per year, mainly from the Southeast and from the North during spring break. Serving this market are vast developments of chain restaurants, amusement parks, miniature golf courses, and a variety of local events. Other amenities include more than 100 golf courses and some country-and-western–themed museums and entertainment—making Myrtle Beach an emerging Branson. People also come to the area to shop, and a large new mall and outlet mall anchor a diverse shopping scene. The springtime Canadian-American Days festival (or "Can-Am") draws thousands from north of the U.S. border. The vast majority of employment is tied to the tourist, entertainment, and retail industries. Conway is a more family-oriented small town with a nice historic district and the small public Coastal Carolina University some 12 miles inland, while North Myrtle Beach is a more family-oriented beach town 10 miles north almost at the North Carolina border. For Myrtle Beach itself, some areas close to the beach are moderately attractive but on the whole, the area, much of it overbuilt and unattractive, has a gaudy, commercial feel and an exceptionally high crime rate.

The city sits on a sandy barrier island in extreme northeastern South Carolina. Areas of level plain and low sand hills and pine trees cover the island and inland sections. Summer days are warm and humid but moderated along the coast by sea breezes. Winters are very mild, although temperatures do drop below freezing. Skies are sunny every 2 in 3 days, but plenty of rain falls year-round. The area is vulnerable to Atlantic hurricanes, although it's slightly north of the main hazard area.

DEMOGRAPHICS	AREA	U.S. AVG	ETHNIC COMPOSITION	AREA	U.S. AVG	RESIDENT PROFILE	AREA	U.S. AVG
Population	217,547		White	79.8%	79.0%	Single	30.2%	32.4%
Population density per sq. mile	191.9	358.5	Black	16.0%	10.5%	Married	53.7%	52.7%
Population growth	51.0%	21.1%	Asian	1.0%	2.7%	Divorced/separated	16.1%	14.9%
Median age	39.1	36.1	Hispanic	3.3%	10.6%	Married with children	17.6%	23.7%
Percent Democrat	36.3%	44.5%	Religious observance	42.3%	48.9%	Single with children	8.5%	9.1%
Percent Republican	62.0%	54.5%	Diversity measure	38.0	40.1	Percent over age 65	16.0%	12.9%

INCOME	AREA	U.S. AVG	EMPLOYMENT	AREA	U.S. AVG	EMPLOYING INDUSTRIES	AREA	U.S. AVG
Per capita income	$22,765	$23,235	Unemployment rate	4.3%	4.7%	Largest: Retail trade		
Household income	$41,374	$46,414	Recent job growth	2.7%	1.3%			
Household income < $25K	26.7%	26.2%	Projected future job growth	23.3%	11.5%	Percent manufacturing	9.9%	15.4%
Household income > $75K	19.2%	25.4%	White collar	55.7%	57.8%	Percent public sector	11.5%	15.7%
Household income growth	13.4%	13.6%	Blue collar	23.1%	25.2%	Percent construction	13.2%	9.9%

Economy & Jobs — Score: 85.6   Rank: 55

INDEXES & TAXES	AREA	U.S. AVG	HOUSING	AREA	U.S. AVG	NECESSITIES	AREA	U.S. AVG
Cost of Living Index	95.0	100.0	Median home price	$199,600	$220,000	Food Index	102.3	100.0
Buying Power Index	97.6	100.0	Home price appreciation	51.4%	10.1%	Housing Index	81.8	100.0
Income tax rate	6.93%	4.70%	Median rent	$712	$709	Utilities Index	90.3	100.0
Sales tax rate	5.00%	6.58%	Homes owned	49.1%	62.3%	Transportation Index	95.1	100.0
Property tax rate	$5.05	$12.00	Home price ratio	4.8	4.2	Healthcare Index	96.1	100.0
						Miscellaneous Cost Index	101.3	100.0

Cost of Living — Score: 39.8   Rank: 225

Climate
Score: 51.9
Rank: 179

TEMPERATURE	AREA	U.S. AVG
Average January low	36.2	26.2
Average July high	88.8	87.4
Annual days > 90°F	45	38
Annual days < 32°F	45	89
Annual days < 0°F	0	6

PRECIPITATION	AREA	U.S. AVG
Annual inches precipitation	54.0	37.7
Annual inches snowfall	1.8	7.0
Annual days precipitation	117	109
Annual days rain > 0.5 inches	31	22
Annual days snow > 1.5 inches	1	6

COMFORTS & HAZARDS	AREA	U.S. AVG
July relative humidity	75%	66%
Annual days mostly sunny	219	208
Annual days with thunderstorms	46	39
Tornado risk score	15	18
Hurricane risk score	65	13

TEMPERATURE

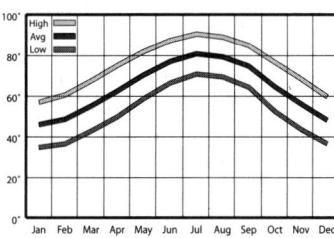

PRECIPITATION

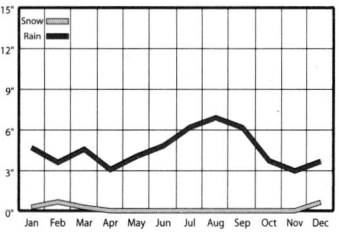

DAYS OF CLOUDS & PRECIPITATION

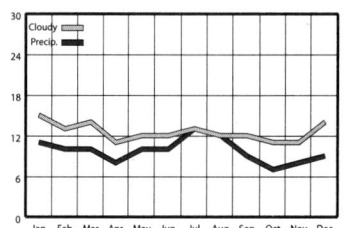

Education
Score: 42.5
Rank: 215

ACHIEVEMENT	AREA	U.S. AVG
High school degree	81.4%	82.7%
2-year college degree	6.9%	6.4%
4-year college degree	12.9%	15.7%
Graduate/professional degree	5.9%	8.9%

PUBLIC SCHOOLS	AREA	U.S. AVG
Expenditures per pupil	$5,362	$5,686
Student/teacher ratio	15.0	16.7
Attending public school	95.5%	90.1%
State SAT score	985*	1021
State ACT score	19.5	20.9

HIGHER EDUCATION	AREA	U.S. AVG
No. 2-year colleges	2	4
No. 4-year colleges/universities	2	6
No. highly ranked universities	0	1

Health &
Healthcare
Score: 35.3
Rank: 241

HAZARDS & ILLNESSES	AREA	U.S. AVG
Air-quality score	38	37
Water-quality score	28	52
Pollen/allergy score	68	61
Cancer mortality per capita	200.3	201.9
Depression days per month	3.7	3.5
Stress score	94	50

HEALTHCARE	AREA	U.S. AVG
Physicians per capita	163.7	244.2
Hospital beds per capita	304.8	420.0
No. teaching hospitals	0	3
Cost per doctor visit	$70	$77
Cost per dental visit	$63	$70

Crime
Score: 1.6
Rank: 367

CRIME	AREA	U.S. AVG
Violent crime rate	860.5	465.5
Change in violent crime rate	-1.6%	-2.2%
Property crime rate	6,862.0	3,517.1
Change in property crime rate	-10.0%	-2.1%

Transportation
Score: 7.5
Rank: 346

COMMUTE	AREA	U.S. AVG
Average commute time	25.3	27.4
Percent commutes > 60 mins.	5.4%	5.9%
Commute by auto	79.0%	78.9%
Commute by mass transit	0.5%	1.9%
Work at home	2.7%	3.1%
Mass transit miles per capita	0.52	1.87

INTERCITY SERVICES	AREA	U.S. AVG
Major airports within 60 miles	0	1
Size of regional airport	Small	Large
Daily airline activity	116	686
Amtrak service	No	No

AUTOMOTIVE	AREA	U.S. AVG
Insurance, annual premium	$1,637	$1,432
Gas, cost per gallon	$2.42	$2.49
Daily vehicle miles per capita	20.2	24.0

Leisure
Score: 32.9
Rank: 250

DINING & SHOPPING	AREA	U.S. AVG
Restaurant rating	1	2
Outlet mall score	0	42
No. Starbucks	1	13
No. warehouse clubs	2	2

ENTERTAINMENT	AREA	U.S. AVG
Professional sports rating	2	4
College sports rating	3	4
Zoo/aquarium rating	1	3
Amusement park rating	6	3
Botanical garden/ arboretum rating	2	4

OUTDOOR ACTIVITIES	AREA	U.S. AVG
Golf-course rating	2	4
Ski-area rating	1	3
Sq. miles inland water	3	4
Miles of coastline	26.7	10.7
National Park rating	1	3

Arts & Culture
Score: 24.6
Rank: 281

MEDIA & LIBRARIES	AREA	U.S. AVG
Arts radio rating	1	3
No. public libraries	9	27
Library volumes per capita	1.74	2.78

PERFORMING ARTS	AREA	U.S. AVG
Classical music rating	4	4
Ballet/dance rating	1	3
Professional theater rating	1	3
University arts programs rating	3	5

MUSEUMS	AREA	U.S. AVG
Overall museum rating	2	5
Art museum rating	3	5
Science museum rating	4	5
Children's museum rating	2	3

Napa, CA

Profile: Small city
Location: Northern California, 10 miles north of San Francisco Bay
Elevation: 17 feet
Time zone: Pacific Standard Time

PRO	CON
Year-round climate	Cost of living
Attractive setting	Cost of housing
Entertainment	Tourist impact

Napa is a small town located at the base of California's famed Napa Valley, a Mediterranean-like wine-growing region extending 30 miles northwest. Once largely agricultural in form and purpose, Napa has become a commercial and residential center serving the region, and also houses some commuters heading south into the San Francisco Bay Area. The town itself is unremarkable, and fortunately, growth controls have preserved its modest size. The wine-growing areas north are beautiful, and the fortunate arrangement of mountains and the bay has created one of the most appealing micro-climates in the world. The wine-growing region is not only prosperous and acclaimed worldwide for its product, but also the wineries themselves create quite a tourist attraction. The area is close enough to the bustling Bay Area to pick up quite an influx of weekend tourists to add to regular tourist flows occurring mainly in summer and fall; the main roads and amenities can become quite crowded at times. But tight growth controls throughout the valley have preserved much of the agricultural look and feel, and the climate and physical beauty make the valley starting just north of Napa a special spot. Naturally, as a result, home prices have gone through the roof; the area has the most expensive housing we saw for a smaller city. The median price of $538,700 buys a tiny two- or three-bedroom bungalow or a small ranch—if you can find one. But the area is very nice for those who can afford it.

Napa Valley is a deep, flat, fertile valley surrounded by wooded Coastal Range mountains on both sides rising to 1,500 feet above the valley floor. South of Napa the valley turns into marshland on approach to the San Pablo Bay extension of the San Francisco Bay. Summer days are pleasantly warm and almost completely dry; evenings are cool. Winters are cool and cloudy with daytime highs in the 50s and 60s and only occasional readings below freezing. Most precipitation falls in winter as light to moderate rain, although some periods of persistent rain can cause flooding in Napa River.

DEMOGRAPHICS	AREA	U.S. AVG	ETHNIC COMPOSITION	AREA	U.S. AVG	RESIDENT PROFILE	AREA	U.S. AVG
Population	133,051		White	75.6%	79.0%	Single	31.9%	32.4%
Population density per sq. mile	176.5	358.5	Black	1.8%	10.5%	Married	51.5%	52.7%
Population growth	20.1%	21.1%	Asian	4.8%	2.7%	Divorced/separated	16.6%	14.9%
Median age	38.3	36.1	Hispanic	27.7%	10.6%	Married with children	23.2%	23.7%
Percent Democrat	59.5%	44.5%	Religious observance	37.8%	48.9%	Single with children	8.0%	9.1%
Percent Republican	39.0%	54.5%	Diversity measure	64.5	40.1	Percent over age 65	14.6%	12.9%

INCOME	AREA	U.S. AVG	EMPLOYMENT	AREA	U.S. AVG	EMPLOYING INDUSTRIES	AREA	U.S. AVG
Per capita income	$30,474	$23,235	Unemployment rate	4.0%	4.7%	Largest: Manufacturing		
Household income	$61,155	$46,414	Recent job growth	1.4%	1.3%			
Household income < $25K	16.4%	26.2%	Projected future job growth	10.0%	11.5%	Percent manufacturing	11.5%	15.4%
Household income > $75K	39.3%	25.4%	White collar	57.2%	57.8%	Percent public sector	14.1%	15.7%
Household income growth	18.2%	13.6%	Blue collar	20.9%	25.2%	Percent construction	9.5%	9.9%

Score: 24.1
Rank: 283

INDEXES & TAXES	AREA	U.S. AVG	HOUSING	AREA	U.S. AVG	NECESSITIES	AREA	U.S. AVG
Cost of Living Index	163.8	100.0	Median home price	$538,700	$220,000	Food Index	120.5	100.0
Buying Power Index	83.7	100.0	Home price appreciation	98.6%	10.1%	Housing Index	256.1	100.0
Income tax rate	6.00%	4.70%	Median rent	$1,112	$709	Utilities Index	128.1	100.0
Sales tax rate	7.75%	6.58%	Homes owned	61.5%	62.3%	Transportation Index	123.0	100.0
Property tax rate	$7.40	$12.00	Home price ratio	8.8	4.2	Healthcare Index	161.8	100.0
						Miscellaneous Cost Index	107.4	100.0

Score: 3.7
Rank: 359

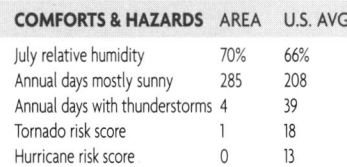

Climate
Score: 95.5
Rank: 18

TEMPERATURE	AREA	U.S. AVG
Average January low	35.7	26.2
Average July high	83.6	87.4
Annual days > 90°F	33	38
Annual days < 32°F	43	89
Annual days < 0°F	0	6

PRECIPITATION	AREA	U.S. AVG
Annual inches precipitation	30.0	37.7
Annual inches snowfall	0.0	7.0
Annual days precipitation	47	109
Annual days rain > 0.5 inches	20	22
Annual days snow > 1.5 inches	0	6

COMFORTS & HAZARDS	AREA	U.S. AVG
July relative humidity	70%	66%
Annual days mostly sunny	285	208
Annual days with thunderstorms	4	39
Tornado risk score	1	18
Hurricane risk score	0	13

TEMPERATURE

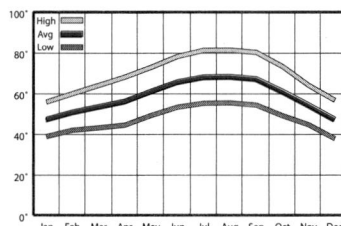

PRECIPITATION

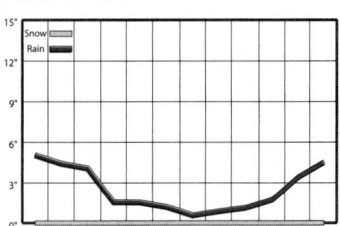

DAYS OF CLOUDS & PRECIPITATION

Education
Score: 49.2
Rank: 191

ACHIEVEMENT	AREA	U.S. AVG
High school degree	80.2%	82.7%
2-year college degree	8.0%	6.4%
4-year college degree	16.6%	15.7%
Graduate/professional degree	9.1%	8.9%

PUBLIC SCHOOLS	AREA	U.S. AVG
Expenditures per pupil	$5,033	$5,686
Student/teacher ratio	18.9	16.7
Attending public school	86.6%	90.1%
State SAT score	1019*	1021
State ACT score	21.6	20.9

HIGHER EDUCATION	AREA	U.S. AVG
No. 2-year colleges	1	4
No. 4-year colleges/universities	1	6
No. highly ranked universities	1	1

Health & Healthcare
Score: 77.0
Rank: 87

HAZARDS & ILLNESSES	AREA	U.S. AVG
Air-quality score	53	37
Water-quality score	27	52
Pollen/allergy score	90	61
Cancer mortality per capita	172.7	201.9
Depression days per month	4.3	3.5
Stress score	31	50

HEALTHCARE	AREA	U.S. AVG
Physicians per capita	306.2	244.2
Hospital beds per capita	2359.2	420.0
No. teaching hospitals	0	3
Cost per doctor visit	$102	$77
Cost per dental visit	$84	$70

Crime
Score: 65.8
Rank: 129

CRIME	AREA	U.S. AVG
Violent crime rate	358.1	465.5
Change in violent crime rate	5.7%	-2.2%
Property crime rate	2,456.1	3,517.1
Change in property crime rate	-12.2%	-2.1%

Transportation
Score: 82.9
Rank: 65

COMMUTE	AREA	U.S. AVG
Average commute time	26.5	27.4
Percent commutes > 60 mins.	9.5%	5.9%
Commute by auto	72.9%	78.9%
Commute by mass transit	1.4%	1.9%
Work at home	5.0%	3.1%
Mass transit miles per capita	1.42	1.87

INTERCITY SERVICES	AREA	U.S. AVG
Major airports within 60 miles	4	1
Size of regional airport	Large	Large
Daily airline activity	1197	686
Amtrak service	No	No

AUTOMOTIVE	AREA	U.S. AVG
Insurance, annual premium	$1,361	$1,432
Gas, cost per gallon	$2.58	$2.49
Daily vehicle miles per capita	14.3	24.0

Leisure
Score: 94.7
Rank: 21

DINING & SHOPPING	AREA	U.S. AVG
Restaurant rating	5	2
Outlet mall score	192	42
No. Starbucks	4	13
No. warehouse clubs	0	2

ENTERTAINMENT	AREA	U.S. AVG
Professional sports rating	9	4
College sports rating	7	4
Zoo/aquarium rating	7	3
Amusement park rating	9	3
Botanical garden/ arboretum rating	7	4

OUTDOOR ACTIVITIES	AREA	U.S. AVG
Golf-course rating	5	4
Ski-area rating	9	3
Sq. miles inland water	8	4
Miles of coastline	0.0	10.7
National Park rating	3	3

Arts & Culture
Score: 60.2
Rank: 149

MEDIA & LIBRARIES	AREA	U.S. AVG
Arts radio rating	4	3
No. public libraries	5	27
Library volumes per capita	1.94	2.78

PERFORMING ARTS	AREA	U.S. AVG
Classical music rating	5	4
Ballet/dance rating	5	3
Professional theater rating	6	3
University arts programs rating	2	5

MUSEUMS	AREA	U.S. AVG
Overall museum rating	7	5
Art museum rating	8	5
Science museum rating	10	5
Children's museum rating	6	3

Naples–Marco Island, FL

Score: 78.5   **Rank:** 52   **2004 rank:** 53

Profile: Beach/resort town
Location: South Gulf coast, 40 miles south of Fort Myers, on the western edge of the Everglades
Elevation: 15 feet
Time zone: Eastern Standard Time

PRO	CON
Winter climate	Cost of living
Job growth	Air service
Attractive setting	Hurricane risk

Naples, an upscale residential enclave with beaches and a variety of activities, serves more year-round and winter residents than vacationing tourists. There are many golf courses and golf-course developments with upscale housing and shopping areas. The area has a full set of performing arts and a number of galleries and other presentations of visual arts. It is generally attractive and has a relaxed, modern feel, not unlike Hilton Head Island, South Carolina. Job growth is the highest in the state and educational attainment is among the best, but commercial activity is mainly related to supporting the area's residents and some hospitality and convention business. There are plenty of parks, excellent beaches, and outstanding nature preserves inland. With these attributes come a high cost of living and housing; the Cost of Living Index of 138.5 makes Naples the most expensive metro area in Florida. Commercial air service is still undeveloped, and air travel usu-

ally requires a 75-mile trip across the Everglades to Miami or Fort Lauderdale, or north to Fort Myers for more limited service. Marco Island is a large planned community 15 miles south on the northernmost of Florida's "Ten Thousand Islands" chain. The median age for the area gives a hint to its lead role as a retirement community.

Naples is level and near the southernmost point of habitable land where the Everglades begin to drain into the ocean. Beaches give way to cypress and mangrove forests, and natural, undeveloped areas to the south. The Everglades marshes begin just to the east of town. Summers are warm and humid with some sea breeze; winters are mild and relatively dry with temperatures mainly in the 70s and 80s. Afternoon thunderstorms are common in summer. Winter freezes, particularly near shore, are extremely rare.

Population

DEMOGRAPHICS	AREA	U.S. AVG	ETHNIC COMPOSITION	AREA	U.S. AVG	RESIDENT PROFILE	AREA	U.S. AVG
Population	307,487		White	83.5%	79.0%	Single	25.3%	32.4%
Population density per sq. mile	151.8	358.5	Black	5.2%	10.5%	Married	59.6%	52.7%
Population growth	102.2%	21.1%	Asian	0.9%	2.7%	Divorced/separated	15.1%	14.9%
Median age	43.4	36.1	Hispanic	24.7%	10.6%	Married with children	16.5%	23.7%
Percent Democrat	34.1%	44.5%	Religious observance	36.8%	48.9%	Single with children	5.9%	9.1%
Percent Republican	65.0%	54.5%	Diversity measure	55.7	40.1	Percent over age 65	24.1%	12.9%

Economy & Jobs
Score: 97.6
Rank: 10

INCOME	AREA	U.S. AVG	EMPLOYMENT	AREA	U.S. AVG	EMPLOYING INDUSTRIES	AREA	U.S. AVG
Per capita income	$34,473	$23,235	Unemployment rate	3.7%	4.7%	Largest: Construction		
Household income	$55,488	$46,414	Recent job growth	5.6%	1.3%			
Household income < $25K	18.2%	26.2%	Projected future job growth	32.7%	11.5%	Percent manufacturing	7.9%	15.4%
Household income > $75K	34.7%	25.4%	White collar	57.0%	57.8%	Percent public sector	9.4%	15.7%
Household income growth	14.9%	13.6%	Blue collar	20.4%	25.2%	Percent construction	12.6%	9.9%

Cost of Living
Score: 7.8
Rank: 344

INDEXES & TAXES	AREA	U.S. AVG	HOUSING	AREA	U.S. AVG	NECESSITIES	AREA	U.S. AVG
Cost of Living Index	138.5	100.0	Median home price	$451,100	$220,000	Food Index	105.0	100.0
Buying Power Index	89.8	100.0	Home price appreciation	149.0%	10.1%	Housing Index	123.5	100.0
Income tax rate	0.00%	4.70%	Median rent	$896	$709	Utilities Index	102.5	100.0
Sales tax rate	6.00%	6.58%	Homes owned	54.7%	62.3%	Transportation Index	109.5	100.0
Property tax rate	$10.00	$12.00	Home price ratio	8.1	4.2	Healthcare Index	109.1	100.0
						Miscellaneous Cost Index	99.5	100.0

Climate
Score: 83.7
Rank: 62

TEMPERATURE	AREA	U.S. AVG	PRECIPITATION	AREA	U.S. AVG	COMFORTS & HAZARDS	AREA	U.S. AVG
Average January low	52.3	26.2	Annual inches precipitation	54.0	37.7	July relative humidity	76%	66%
Average July high	91.5	87.4	Annual inches snowfall	0.0	7.0	Annual days mostly sunny	264	208
Annual days > 90°F	106	38	Annual days precipitation	112	109	Annual days with thunderstorms	93	39
Annual days < 32°F	1	89	Annual days rain > 0.5 inches	32	22	Tornado risk score	20	18
Annual days < 0°F	0	6	Annual days snow > 1.5 inches	0	6	Hurricane risk score	83	13

TEMPERATURE

PRECIPITATION

DAYS OF CLOUDS & PRECIPITATION

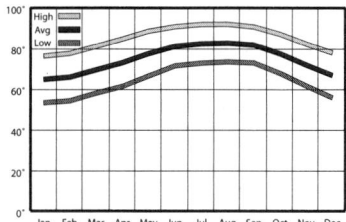

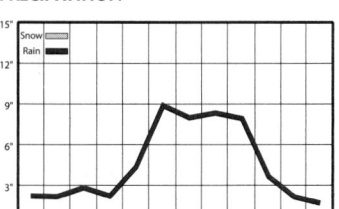

Education
Score: 57.2
Rank: 161

ACHIEVEMENT	AREA	U.S. AVG	PUBLIC SCHOOLS	AREA	U.S. AVG	HIGHER EDUCATION	AREA	U.S. AVG
High school degree	82.5%	82.7%	Expenditures per pupil	$5,889	$5,686	No. 2-year colleges	0	4
2-year college degree	5.8%	6.4%	Student/teacher ratio	17.6	16.7	No. 4-year colleges/universities	1	6
4-year college degree	18.6%	15.7%	Attending public school	90.2%	90.1%	No. highly ranked universities	0	1
Graduate/professional degree	10.1%	8.9%	State SAT score	993*	1021			
			State ACT score	20.3	20.9			

Health & Healthcare
Score: 29.7
Rank: 262

HAZARDS & ILLNESSES	AREA	U.S. AVG	HEALTHCARE	AREA	U.S. AVG	CRIME	AREA	U.S. AVG
Air-quality score	42	37	Physicians per capita	228.9	244.2	Violent crime rate	442.7	465.5
Water-quality score	53	52	Hospital beds per capita	179.5	420.0	Change in violent crime rate	-1.5%	-2.2%
Pollen/allergy score	63	61	No. teaching hospitals	0	3	Property crime rate	2,110.9	3,517.1
Cancer mortality per capita	192.1	201.9	Cost per doctor visit	$76	$77	Change in property crime rate	-9.5%	-2.1%
Depression days per month	2.7	3.5	Cost per dental visit	$72	$70			
Stress score	28	50						

Crime
Score: 65.2
Rank: 131

Transportation
Score: 76.7
Rank: 88

COMMUTE	AREA	U.S. AVG	INTERCITY SERVICES	AREA	U.S. AVG	AUTOMOTIVE	AREA	U.S. AVG
Average commute time	26.0	27.4	Major airports within 60 miles	3	1	Insurance, annual premium	$1,330	$1,432
Percent commutes > 60 mins.	5.5%	5.9%	Size of regional airport	Large	Large	Gas, cost per gallon	$2.62	$2.49
Commute by auto	75.4%	78.9%	Daily airline activity	1149	686	Daily vehicle miles per capita	26.5	24.0
Commute by mass transit	1.7%	1.9%	Amtrak service	No	No			
Work at home	4.9%	3.1%						
Mass transit miles per capita	1.68	1.87						

Leisure
Score: 74.1
Rank: 97

DINING & SHOPPING	AREA	U.S. AVG	ENTERTAINMENT	AREA	U.S. AVG	OUTDOOR ACTIVITIES	AREA	U.S. AVG
Restaurant rating	1	2	Professional sports rating	2	4	Golf-course rating	5	4
Outlet mall score	168	42	College sports rating	1	4	Ski-area rating	1	3
No. Starbucks	6	13	Zoo/aquarium rating	1	3	Sq. miles inland water	7	4
No. warehouse clubs	2	2	Amusement park rating	4	3	Miles of coastline	66.6	10.7
			Botanical garden/arboretum rating	3	4	National Park rating	10	3

Arts & Culture
Score: 24.1
Rank: 283

MEDIA & LIBRARIES	AREA	U.S. AVG	PERFORMING ARTS	AREA	U.S. AVG	MUSEUMS	AREA	U.S. AVG
Arts radio rating	1	3	Classical music rating	1	4	Overall museum rating	5	5
No. public libraries	8	27	Ballet/dance rating	1	3	Art museum rating	7	5
Library volumes per capita	1.52	2.78	Professional theater rating	1	3	Science museum rating	4	5
			University arts programs rating	2	5	Children's museum rating	1	3

Nashville–Davidson–Murfreesboro, TN

Score: 45.3   Rank: 281   2004 rank: 206

Profile: Capital city
Location: North-central Tennessee along the Cumberland River
Elevation: 605 feet
Time zone: Central Standard Time

PRO	CON
Entertainment	Crime rates
Expanding amenities	Growth and sprawl
Cost of living	Hot, humid summers

Nashville is the capital and second-largest city in Tennessee. Known worldwide as the center of country music, it has long been a destination for music-related tourism, and that is what most outsiders know it for. However, the area has blossomed into a full-fledged major league city on several fronts. The city has been working for some time to renovate its downtown area and attract first-class amenities. Areas of downtown, notably the District, have stylish older buildings repurposed into shopping and nightlife areas. Nashville is a big sports town: The Tennessee Titans are the state's first NFL team, the NHL is represented by the Nashville Predators, and there are minor league or secondary league teams in just about every sport. Vanderbilt University, Fisk University, and an assortment of smaller colleges add a higher-education dimension with the expected amenities. Beyond tourism and music, the economic base encompasses government, banking, finance, and insurance, and more recently, it has become a center for a modern automotive industry. In the early 1990s, General Motors located Saturn in Spring Hill, some 30 miles southwest. Later, Nissan set up its U.S. assembly plant in Smyrna, and must have liked how that worked out, for they moved their North American headquarters to the area from Southern California in 2006. The Nashville area is also a center for the national healthcare industry and is headquarters for Caremark Rx and HCA, a hospital administrator. A center of the Bible Belt, the city is sometimes called the "Protestant Vatican," and it doesn't take too long to be reminded that you're in the Bible Belt even though Nashville has grown into a large and relatively progressive metro area.

For a big city Nashville has an attractive cost-of-living profile. There are growth and sprawl issues and related problems with traffic and air quality. Some of the better neighborhoods lie east and south. In particular we like the historic town of Franklin, and Murfreesboro is a college town southeast, home to the large Middle Tennessee State University. Murfreesboro has some characteristics of a Nashville exurb, being close enough for some residents to commute to the city's prosperous southeastern suburbs, but it has its own identity and economy. Incidentally, there is no "Davidson" save for Davidson County; Nashville merged into the county government in the early 1960s. Bottom line: Job-growth projections have tapered off, growth effects are being felt, and crime rates remain stubbornly high, all of which affected the ranking. The area is better than the figure indicates for those favoring a rising star.

Nashville is in a river valley along the edge of the Highland Rim, which rises 300 to 400 feet above the basin forming an amphitheater about the city from the southwest to the southeast. The climate is typical for the region with warm, humid summers and alternating periods of cool and cold in the winter. Summer thunderstorms are sometimes severe. Periods of winter precipitation are common with an occasional stronger winter storm.

DEMOGRAPHICS	AREA	U.S. AVG	ETHNIC COMPOSITION	AREA	U.S. AVG	RESIDENT PROFILE	AREA	U.S. AVG
Population	1,398,214		White	79.1%	79.0%	Single	30.7%	32.4%
Population density per sq. mile	245.9	358.5	Black	15.0%	10.5%	Married	53.5%	52.7%
Population growth	38.4%	21.1%	Asian	2.0%	2.7%	Divorced/separated	15.8%	14.9%
Median age	35.8	36.1	Hispanic	4.0%	10.6%	Married with children	24.4%	23.7%
Percent Democrat	43.8%	44.5%	Religious observance	47.1%	48.9%	Single with children	8.8%	9.1%
Percent Republican	55.5%	54.5%	Diversity measure	37.0	40.1	Percent over age 65	10.6%	12.9%

Population

INCOME	AREA	U.S. AVG	EMPLOYMENT	AREA	U.S. AVG	EMPLOYING INDUSTRIES	AREA	U.S. AVG
Per capita income	$25,727	$23,235	Unemployment rate	4.3%	4.7%	Largest: Healthcare & Social Assistance		
Household income	$51,096	$46,414	Recent job growth	-0.7%	1.3%			
Household income ‹ $25K	22.4%	26.2%	Projected future job growth	10.3%	11.5%	Percent manufacturing	15.3%	15.4%
Household income › $75K	28.6%	25.4%	White collar	61.6%	57.8%	Percent public sector	12.0%	15.7%
Household income growth	13.4%	13.6%	Blue collar	25.2%	25.2%	Percent construction	9.9%	9.9%

Economy & Jobs
Score: 38.8
Rank: 229

INDEXES & TAXES	AREA	U.S. AVG	HOUSING	AREA	U.S. AVG	NECESSITIES	AREA	U.S. AVG
Cost of Living Index	88.2	100.0	Median home price	$177,900	$220,000	Food Index	99.8	100.0
Buying Power Index	129.9	100.0	Home price appreciation	29.1%	10.1%	Housing Index	65.4	100.0
Income tax rate	0.00%	4.70%	Median rent	$684	$709	Utilities Index	86.7	100.0
Sales tax rate	9.37%	6.58%	Homes owned	64.1%	62.3%	Transportation Index	95.2	100.0
Property tax rate	$7.91	$12.00	Home price ratio	3.5	4.2	Healthcare Index	82.7	100.0
						Miscellaneous Cost Index	95.9	100.0

Cost of Living
Score: 80.7
Rank: 73

Climate
Score: 17.6
Rank: 307

TEMPERATURE	AREA	U.S. AVG
Average January low	29.0	26.2
Average July high	90.2	87.4
Annual days > 90°F	37	38
Annual days < 32°F	75	89
Annual days < 0°F	1	6

PRECIPITATION	AREA	U.S. AVG
Annual inches precipitation	46.0	37.7
Annual inches snowfall	10.7	7.0
Annual days precipitation	119	109
Annual days rain > 0.5 inches	32	22
Annual days snow > 1.5 inches	3	6

COMFORTS & HAZARDS	AREA	U.S. AVG
July relative humidity	71%	66%
Annual days mostly sunny	210	208
Annual days with thunderstorms	55	39
Tornado risk score	16	18
Hurricane risk score	8	13

TEMPERATURE

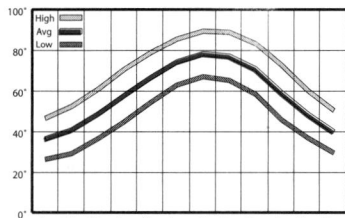

PRECIPITATION

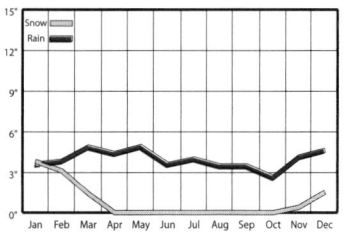

DAYS OF CLOUDS & PRECIPITATION

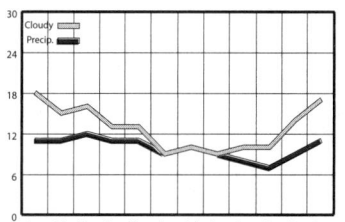

Education
Score: 78.3
Rank: 82

ACHIEVEMENT	AREA	U.S. AVG
High school degree	80.7%	82.7%
2-year college degree	5.0%	6.4%
4-year college degree	17.6%	15.7%
Graduate/professional degree	8.2%	8.9%

PUBLIC SCHOOLS	AREA	U.S. AVG
Expenditures per pupil	$4,831	$5,686
Student/teacher ratio	0.0	16.7
Attending public school	89.1%	90.1%
State SAT score	1142	1021
State ACT score	20.7*	20.9

HIGHER EDUCATION	AREA	U.S. AVG
No. 2-year colleges	11	4
No. 4-year colleges/universities	19	6
No. highly ranked universities	1	1

Health & Healthcare
Score: 71.4
Rank: 108

HAZARDS & ILLNESSES	AREA	U.S. AVG
Air-quality score	40	37
Water-quality score	77	52
Pollen/allergy score	68	61
Cancer mortality per capita	215.1	201.9
Depression days per month	3.1	3.5
Stress score	90	50

HEALTHCARE	AREA	U.S. AVG
Physicians per capita	299.6	244.2
Hospital beds per capita	419.7	420.0
No. teaching hospitals	5	3
Cost per doctor visit	$71	$77
Cost per dental visit	$59	$70

Crime
Score: 12.3
Rank: 327

CRIME	AREA	U.S. AVG
Violent crime rate	894.1	465.5
Change in violent crime rate	2.5%	-2.2%
Property crime rate	4,135.5	3,517.1
Change in property crime rate	-0.8%	-2.1%

Transportation
Score: 1.3
Rank: 368

COMMUTE	AREA	U.S. AVG
Average commute time	28.4	27.4
Percent commutes > 60 mins.	6.4%	5.9%
Commute by auto	80.7%	78.9%
Commute by mass transit	0.8%	1.9%
Work at home	3.2%	3.1%
Mass transit miles per capita	0.85	1.87

INTERCITY SERVICES	AREA	U.S. AVG
Major airports within 60 miles	1	1
Size of regional airport	Medium	Large
Daily airline activity	264	686
Amtrak service	No	No

AUTOMOTIVE	AREA	U.S. AVG
Insurance, annual premium	$980	$1,432
Gas, cost per gallon	$2.47	$2.49
Daily vehicle miles per capita	32.4	24.0

Leisure
Score: 69.0
Rank: 116

DINING & SHOPPING	AREA	U.S. AVG
Restaurant rating	1	2
Outlet mall score	1	42
No. Starbucks	22	13
No. warehouse clubs	4	2

ENTERTAINMENT	AREA	U.S. AVG
Professional sports rating	7	4
College sports rating	5	4
Zoo/aquarium rating	5	3
Amusement park rating	1	3
Botanical garden/ arboretum rating	8	4

OUTDOOR ACTIVITIES	AREA	U.S. AVG
Golf-course rating	5	4
Ski-area rating	1	3
Sq. miles inland water	4	4
Miles of coastline	0.0	10.7
National Park rating	2	3

Arts & Culture
Score: 86.1
Rank: 53

MEDIA & LIBRARIES	AREA	U.S. AVG
Arts radio rating	8	3
No. public libraries	52	27
Library volumes per capita	1.80	2.78

PERFORMING ARTS	AREA	U.S. AVG
Classical music rating	7	4
Ballet/dance rating	3	3
Professional theater rating	1	3
University arts programs rating	9	5

MUSEUMS	AREA	U.S. AVG
Overall museum rating	8	5
Art museum rating	8	5
Science museum rating	9	5
Children's museum rating	1	3

Nassau–Suffolk, NY

Score: 70.2   **Rank:** 90   **2004 rank:** 19

Profile: Suburban complex
Location: Long Island
Elevation: 13 feet
Time zone: Eastern Standard Time

PRO	CON
Close to New York	Long commutes
Attractive suburbs	Cost of living
Low crime rates	Future job growth

Nassau and Suffolk counties occupy the eastern four-fifths of Long Island, east of New York City. The western two-thirds of the island, which stretches a total of 120 miles, consists of residential communities, shopping malls, and commercial districts that mainly support Manhattan commuters, although the area has a vibrant commercial, industrial, and service economy of its own. The built-up sections are a patchwork of small- and medium-size suburban towns, connected by the Long Island Rail Road (LIRR) to each other and, more importantly, New York City to the west. The LIRR is a lifeline for this area. The list of communities, located mainly along LIRR corridors—is almost endless—Hempstead, Brentwood, Deer Park, Levittown, Hicksville, and Plainview along central corridors; Merrick, Massapequa, Babylon, the Islips, and numerous others along the south shore; and Great Neck, Glen Cove, and Stony Brook to the north along the Long Island Sound. Most of these communities are quite middle class in character, each reflecting the middle-class suburban housing of the time, from early-20th-century row houses to Cape Cods to small ranches to larger ranches to more contemporary homes—depending on the age of the suburb. Most communities have attractive downtowns, ample park space, and other recreational amenities. Few clues—except the local accents and the pervasive LIRR facilities—tell you that you're so close, 10 to 50 miles, from Manhattan. This is suburban America at its best: mostly quiet places with convenient services and amenities insulated from the stress of the big city while still giving access to it when needed or desired. Although the area is spread out but does not exhibit the overgrown leapfrog sprawl feel of many American suburbs, it does feel crowded at times.

Naturally several communities have a more upscale feel, particularly north along the Long Island Sound, and as you go east beyond normal commute distances, the wealthy enclaves and former whaling towns of the Hamptons—Southhampton, East Hampton, West Hampton—mix with other small communities to provide weekend retreats and good telecommute spots, as well as plenty for the lifestyles of the rich and famous. We think some of the south-shore neighborhoods, such as Bay Shore, East Islip, and West Sayville, offer some of the best values, with reasonable home prices for the region, plenty of New-England style charm, and access to beach and recreational areas.

Cost of living and particularly housing costs are high, although there is substantial variation across the island, with coastal areas being more expensive. New York City commutes are long, typically 45 minutes or more, but the LIRR works well, is reliable, and is well regarded by most locals. Local amenities and entertainment include plenty of shopping and restaurants, good parks, the New York Islanders hockey team, low-cost air service to Islip by Southwest Airlines, and plenty of beach and water recreation. Barrier-island beach areas provide excellent short getaways but can become crowded on hot summer days. Long Island provides the amenities and benefits of New York City without many of the big-city problems.

Long Island is the terminal moraine marking the southernmost advance of an ice sheet along the Atlantic Coast during the last ice age. The terrain is generally flat with only a gradual rise in elevation toward the center from Long Island Sound on the northern shore and from the Atlantic Ocean on the southern shore. Cool, summer sea breezes alleviate afternoon heat and moderate coastal temperatures. Tropical weather systems moving along the Atlantic Coast can produce episodes of heavy rain and strong winds in the late summer or fall. The winter season is relatively mild. Below-zero temperatures are only reported 1 or 2 days every other winter. Coastal low-pressure systems called "noreasters" are the principal source of snow, but snow totals are less than the rest of the state and rain is more likely. First freeze is mid-October; last is late April.

DEMOGRAPHICS	AREA	U.S. AVG	ETHNIC COMPOSITION	AREA	U.S. AVG	RESIDENT PROFILE	AREA	U.S. AVG
Population	2,828,933		White	78.6%	79.0%	Single	32.7%	32.4%
Population density per sq. mile	2359.6	358.5	Black	9.5%	10.5%	Married	56.1%	52.7%
Population growth	8.6%	21.1%	Asian	4.7%	2.7%	Divorced/separated	11.1%	14.9%
Median age	38.9	36.1	Hispanic	12.8%	10.6%	Married with children	30.0%	23.7%
Percent Democrat	50.8%	44.5%	Religious observance	71.8%	48.9%	Single with children	5.9%	9.1%
Percent Republican	47.6%	54.5%	Diversity measure	50.8	40.1	Percent over age 65	13.7%	12.9%

INCOME	AREA	U.S. AVG	EMPLOYMENT	AREA	U.S. AVG	EMPLOYING INDUSTRIES	AREA	U.S. AVG
Per capita income	$33,324	$23,235	Unemployment rate	4.5%	4.7%	Largest: Healthcare & Social Assistance		
Household income	$77,691	$46,414	Recent job growth	1.2%	1.3%			
Household income ‹ $25K	12.9%	26.2%	Projected future job growth	4.1%	11.5%	Percent manufacturing	9.3%	15.4%
Household income › $75K	51.5%	25.4%	White collar	67.8%	57.8%	Percent public sector	17.6%	15.7%
Household income growth	13.4%	13.6%	Blue collar	18.0%	25.2%	Percent construction	8.7%	9.9%

Score: 29.9
Rank: 262

INDEXES & TAXES	AREA	U.S. AVG	HOUSING	AREA	U.S. AVG	NECESSITIES	AREA	U.S. AVG
Cost of Living Index	157.1	100.0	Median home price	$478,000	$220,000	Food Index	131.7	100.0
Buying Power Index	110.8	100.0	Home price appreciation	90.6%	10.1%	Housing Index	175.7	100.0
Income tax rate	7.13%	4.70%	Median rent	$1,356	$709	Utilities Index	152.2	100.0
Sales tax rate	8.75%	6.58%	Homes owned	75.0%	62.3%	Transportation Index	115.0	100.0
Property tax rate	$21.51	$12.00	Home price ratio	6.2	4.2	Healthcare Index	162.9	100.0
						Miscellaneous Cost Index	128.6	100.0

Score: 2.7
Rank: 363

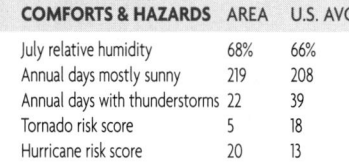

Climate
Score: 77.5
Rank: 84

TEMPERATURE	AREA	U.S. AVG
Average January low	24.8	26.2
Average July high	83.2	87.4
Annual days > 90°F	10	38
Annual days < 32°F	85	89
Annual days < 0°F	0	6

PRECIPITATION	AREA	U.S. AVG
Annual inches precipitation	41.5	37.7
Annual inches snowfall	24.9	7.0
Annual days precipitation	125	109
Annual days rain > 0.5 inches	30	22
Annual days snow > 1.5 inches	4	6

COMFORTS & HAZARDS	AREA	U.S. AVG
July relative humidity	68%	66%
Annual days mostly sunny	219	208
Annual days with thunderstorms	22	39
Tornado risk score	5	18
Hurricane risk score	20	13

TEMPERATURE

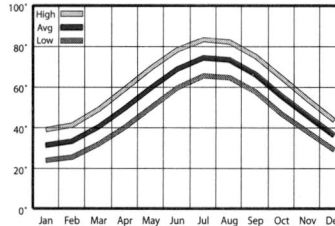

PRECIPITATION

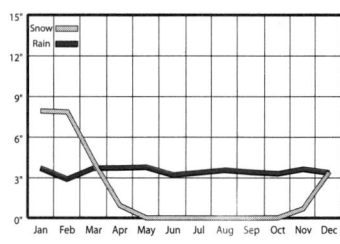

DAYS OF CLOUDS & PRECIPITATION

Education
Score: 94.1
Rank: 23

ACHIEVEMENT	AREA	U.S. AVG
High school degree	86.3%	82.7%
2-year college degree	7.5%	6.4%
4-year college degree	17.5%	15.7%
Graduate/professional degree	13.6%	8.9%

PUBLIC SCHOOLS	AREA	U.S. AVG
Expenditures per pupil	$11,864	$5,686
Student/teacher ratio	14.8	16.7
Attending public school	88.8%	90.1%
State SAT score	1003*	1021
State ACT score	22.6	20.9

HIGHER EDUCATION	AREA	U.S. AVG
No. 2-year colleges	8	4
No. 4-year colleges/universities	21	6
No. highly ranked universities	3	1

Health & Healthcare
Score: 4.5
Rank: 356

HAZARDS & ILLNESSES	AREA	U.S. AVG
Air-quality score	14	37
Water-quality score	61	52
Pollen/allergy score	60	61
Cancer mortality per capita	202.9	201.9
Depression days per month	3.4	3.5
Stress score	14	50

HEALTHCARE	AREA	U.S. AVG
Physicians per capita	427.4	244.2
Hospital beds per capita	471.0	420.0
No. teaching hospitals	20	3
Cost per doctor visit	$93	$77
Cost per dental visit	$88	$70

Crime
Score: 96.8
Rank: 13

CRIME	AREA	U.S. AVG
Violent crime rate	201.7	465.5
Change in violent crime rate	6.0%	-2.2%
Property crime rate	1,680.2	3,517.1
Change in property crime rate	-3.4%	-2.1%

Transportation
Score: 92.8
Rank: 28

COMMUTE	AREA	U.S. AVG
Average commute time	35.2	27.4
Percent commutes > 60 mins.	18.4%	5.9%
Commute by auto	74.0%	78.9%
Commute by mass transit	11.0%	1.9%
Work at home	2.8%	3.1%
Mass transit miles per capita	11.03	1.87

INTERCITY SERVICES	AREA	U.S. AVG
Major airports within 60 miles	4	1
Size of regional airport	Large	Large
Daily airline activity	2696	686
Amtrak service	No	No

AUTOMOTIVE	AREA	U.S. AVG
Insurance, annual premium	$1,786	$1,432
Gas, cost per gallon	$2.63	$2.49
Daily vehicle miles per capita	23.1	24.0

Leisure
Score: 98.1
Rank: 8

DINING & SHOPPING	AREA	U.S. AVG
Restaurant rating	1	2
Outlet mall score	23	42
No. Starbucks	64	13
No. warehouse clubs	13	2

ENTERTAINMENT	AREA	U.S. AVG
Professional sports rating	10	4
College sports rating	6	4
Zoo/aquarium rating	7	3
Amusement park rating	6	3
Botanical garden/ arboretum rating	10	4

OUTDOOR ACTIVITIES	AREA	U.S. AVG
Golf-course rating	10	4
Ski-area rating	2	3
Sq. miles inland water	9	4
Miles of coastline	172.5	10.7
National Park rating	4	3

Arts & Culture
Score: 92.8
Rank: 28

MEDIA & LIBRARIES	AREA	U.S. AVG
Arts radio rating	4	3
No. public libraries	126	27
Library volumes per capita	6.26	2.78

PERFORMING ARTS	AREA	U.S. AVG
Classical music rating	8	4
Ballet/dance rating	8	3
Professional theater rating	9	3
University arts programs rating	10	5

MUSEUMS	AREA	U.S. AVG
Overall museum rating	9	5
Art museum rating	9	5
Science museum rating	9	5
Children's museum rating	9	3

Newark–Union, NJ

Score: 59.2   **Rank:** 180   **2004 rank:** 261

Profile: Large-city/suburban complex
Location: Northern New Jersey near the lower Hudson River, west of New York City
Elevation: 10 feet
Time zone: Eastern Standard Time

PRO	CON
Close to New York City	Cost of living and housing
Diverse economy	Some industrial areas
Educated population	Future job growth

The Newark area is a diverse patchwork of communities including downtown Newark and a series of small cities, towns, and residential suburbs lying across the Hudson River from New York City extending to the Pennsylvania border. The six-county area includes Middlesex, Hunterdon, Morris, Sussex, Union, and Pike counties, and covers a list of well-known town names that wouldn't fit on this page. Most of these cities and towns could exist quite well on their own, but in this case are usually tied by commute routes to New York or other more commercial and industrial parts of New Jersey. Some of the more well-known and larger names include Parsippany, Morristown, Livingston, the Oranges (East, West, South, and Orange itself), Union, Plainfield, and Rockaway, to name a few. Tight land-use controls have prevented these suburbs from extending west indefinitely; west of Parsippany and Morristown the area has a decidedly country feel, although considerable research and technology in areas such as Basking Ridge along Interstate 287 south of Morristown and rail commute corridors do extend this far out.

Closer in, Newark itself is a large downtown and industrial center with a poor reputation and a gritty recent past, but its geographic position near New York and the presence of transportation networks and modernizing industries are helping to generate a rebound. Areas to the north and south of the downtown, such as Elizabeth and Bayonne, and Jersey City to the east, are some of the most industrial in the country with oil refineries, chemical plants, port facilities, and other monuments to heavy industry. The aforementioned suburbs have become major corporate centers, and headquarters to such giants as Lucent Technologies, American Home Products, Prudential, and drug giants Warner Lambert

and Schering-Plough—in all, home to nine Fortune 500 companies and many of their research facilities. To the northwest, the towns of Montclair and Cedar Grove, nestled up against the large ridge known as First Mountain, are excellent middle- and upper-class areas with shady streets, traditional housing, and reasonable commutes to Newark, Hoboken, and New York City. Along the Hudson, Hoboken is re-emerging as sort of a "sixth borough" for New York, and is a very popular residential and commercial area. The area has plenty of restaurants, nightlife, working singles, and young couples, and has become a chief hub and gateway for New Jersey Transit rail lines headed in all directions, but homes, mainly in restored 19th-century city buildings, are expensive. The restored Newark Penn Station is also a transportation hub for the state and the Northeast Corridor, and Newark Airport is a major hub for the New York area. The employment picture is mixed, and projected employment growth is one-third the U.S. average. The Cost of Living Index is high at 144.5 and housing costs and property taxes are notoriously high. But the area has a lot to offer for the price, and its value is getting more recognition.

The natural terrain—what little there is—is mostly flat and marshy. To the northwest are wooded ridges oriented roughly in a southwest-to-northeast direction. Summers are hot and muggy when winds are from the west or southwest but can be 15°F cooler when from the south or southeast. Winters are cool and wet. Passing "noreaster" storms typically produce 1 to 2 inches of precipitation as rain or snow. Snowfalls of 8 inches or more occur every other year. Snow is heavier to the west of the city. Cold polar air does invade, and below-zero temperatures occur one winter out of four. First freeze is late October; last is mid-April.

DEMOGRAPHICS	AREA	U.S. AVG	ETHNIC COMPOSITION	AREA	U.S. AVG	RESIDENT PROFILE	AREA	U.S. AVG
Population	2,159,686		White	65.6%	79.0%	Single	36.1%	32.4%
Population density per sq. mile	983.2	358.5	Black	21.6%	10.5%	Married	50.8%	52.7%
Population growth	11.6%	21.1%	Asian	4.4%	2.7%	Divorced/separated	13.0%	14.9%
Median age	37.5	36.1	Hispanic	14.9%	10.6%	Married with children	25.7%	23.7%
Percent Democrat	55.8%	44.5%	Religious observance	57.1%	48.9%	Single with children	8.9%	9.1%
Percent Republican	43.4%	54.5%	Diversity measure	56.6	40.1	Percent over age 65	12.2%	12.9%

Population

INCOME	AREA	U.S. AVG	EMPLOYMENT	AREA	U.S. AVG	EMPLOYING INDUSTRIES	AREA	U.S. AVG
Per capita income	$32,938	$23,235	Unemployment rate	4.7%	4.7%	Largest: Manufacturing		
Household income	$66,398	$46,414	Recent job growth	1.4%	1.3%			
Household income < $25K	18.7%	26.2%	Projected future job growth	3.9%	11.5%	Percent manufacturing	12.1%	15.4%
Household income > $75K	43.9%	25.4%	White collar	66.9%	57.8%	Percent public sector	13.4%	15.7%
Household income growth	13.6%	13.6%	Blue collar	19.6%	25.2%	Percent construction	7.5%	9.9%

Economy & Jobs
Score: 24.9
Rank: 281

INDEXES & TAXES	AREA	U.S. AVG	HOUSING	AREA	U.S. AVG	NECESSITIES	AREA	U.S. AVG
Cost of Living Index	144.5	100.0	Median home price	$443,800	$220,000	Food Index	111.6	100.0
Buying Power Index	103.0	100.0	Home price appreciation	86.8%	10.1%	Housing Index	143.2	100.0
Income tax rate	2.57%	4.70%	Median rent	$1,071	$709	Utilities Index	121.3	100.0
Sales tax rate	6.00%	6.58%	Homes owned	58.5%	62.3%	Transportation Index	118.5	100.0
Property tax rate	$23.61	$12.00	Home price ratio	6.7	4.2	Healthcare Index	118.0	100.0
						Miscellaneous Cost Index	111.8	100.0

Cost of Living
Score: 4.8
Rank: 355

Climate
Score: 58.8
Rank: 153

TEMPERATURE	AREA	U.S. AVG
Average January low	25.3	26.2
Average July high	84.9	87.4
Annual days > 90°F	17	38
Annual days < 32°F	88	89
Annual days < 0°F	0	6

PRECIPITATION	AREA	U.S. AVG
Annual inches precipitation	40.2	37.7
Annual inches snowfall	23.4	7.0
Annual days precipitation	128	109
Annual days rain > 0.5 inches	26	22
Annual days snow > 1.5 inches	5	6

COMFORTS & HAZARDS	AREA	U.S. AVG
July relative humidity	67%	66%
Annual days mostly sunny	216	208
Annual days with thunderstorms	25	39
Tornado risk score	13	18
Hurricane risk score	17	13

TEMPERATURE
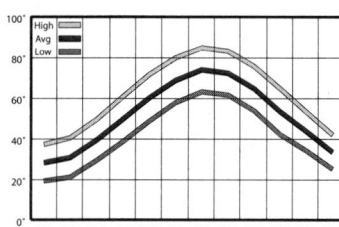

PRECIPITATION
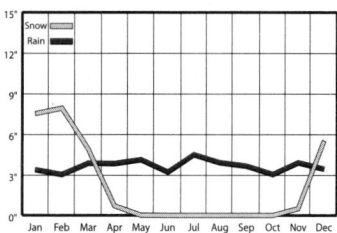

DAYS OF CLOUDS & PRECIPITATION
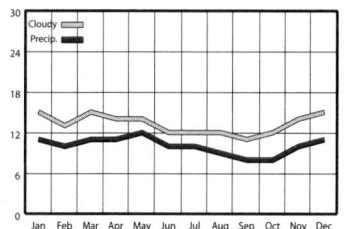

Education
Score: 85.8
Rank: 54

ACHIEVEMENT	AREA	U.S. AVG
High school degree	81.8%	82.7%
2-year college degree	5.0%	6.4%
4-year college degree	19.5%	15.7%
Graduate/professional degree	12.1%	8.9%

PUBLIC SCHOOLS	AREA	U.S. AVG
Expenditures per pupil	$9,590	$5,686
Student/teacher ratio	15.2	16.7
Attending public school	86.0%	90.1%
State SAT score	1011*	1021
State ACT score	21.8	20.9

HIGHER EDUCATION	AREA	U.S. AVG
No. 2-year colleges	12	4
No. 4-year colleges/universities	12	6
No. highly ranked universities	4	1

Health &
Healthcare
Score: 17.6
Rank: 307

HAZARDS & ILLNESSES	AREA	U.S. AVG
Air-quality score	29	37
Water-quality score	16	52
Pollen/allergy score	62	61
Cancer mortality per capita	218.8	201.9
Depression days per month	3.1	3.5
Stress score	40	50

HEALTHCARE	AREA	U.S. AVG
Physicians per capita	323.6	244.2
Hospital beds per capita	454.7	420.0
No. teaching hospitals	15	3
Cost per doctor visit	$67	$77
Cost per dental visit	$85	$70

Crime
Score: 53.2
Rank: 176

CRIME	AREA	U.S. AVG
Violent crime rate	428.7	465.5
Change in violent crime rate	-2.3%	-2.2%
Property crime rate	2,509.6	3,517.1
Change in property crime rate	-4.6%	-2.1%

Transportation
Score: 94.7
Rank: 21

COMMUTE	AREA	U.S. AVG
Average commute time	33.7	27.4
Percent commutes > 60 mins.	14.5%	5.9%
Commute by auto	71.5%	78.9%
Commute by mass transit	10.7%	1.9%
Work at home	3.1%	3.1%
Mass transit miles per capita	10.73	1.87

INTERCITY SERVICES	AREA	U.S. AVG
Major airports within 60 miles	4	1
Size of regional airport	Large	Large
Daily airline activity	2696	686
Amtrak service	Yes	No

AUTOMOTIVE	AREA	U.S. AVG
Insurance, annual premium	$3,412	$1,432
Gas, cost per gallon	$2.34	$2.49
Daily vehicle miles per capita	24.2	24.0

Leisure
Score: 90.9
Rank: 35

DINING & SHOPPING	AREA	U.S. AVG
Restaurant rating	1	2
Outlet mall score	3	42
No. Starbucks	21	13
No. warehouse clubs	7	2

ENTERTAINMENT	AREA	U.S. AVG
Professional sports rating	10	4
College sports rating	4	4
Zoo/aquarium rating	8	3
Amusement park rating	7	3
Botanical garden/ arboretum rating	10	4

OUTDOOR ACTIVITIES	AREA	U.S. AVG
Golf-course rating	10	4
Ski-area rating	5	3
Sq. miles inland water	7	4
Miles of coastline	0.4	10.7
National Park rating	4	3

Arts & Culture
Score: 93.6
Rank: 25

MEDIA & LIBRARIES	AREA	U.S. AVG
Arts radio rating	4	3
No. public libraries	118	27
Library volumes per capita	3.82	2.78

PERFORMING ARTS	AREA	U.S. AVG
Classical music rating	9	4
Ballet/dance rating	8	3
Professional theater rating	10	3
University arts programs rating	10	5

MUSEUMS	AREA	U.S. AVG
Overall museum rating	9	5
Art museum rating	9	5
Science museum rating	9	5
Children's museum rating	9	3

New Haven–Milford, CT

Score: 61.3   **Rank:** 164   **2004 rank:** 149

Profile: Large industrial city/college town
Location: South coast along Long Island Sound, 75 miles northeast of New York City
Elevation: 7 feet
Time zone: Eastern Standard Time

PRO	CON
Historic downtown core	Cost of housing
College-town amenities	Low job growth
Healthcare	Areas of urban decay

A city of contrasts, New Haven is a mix of colonial history, Ivy League college town, and a past-its-prime industrial center. Once an important manufacturing center, it is known today as the home of prestigious Yale University. The first planned city in the American Colonies, New Haven was laid out in 1638 in nine equal squares. The New Haven Green, a square reserved for the public, is now a pedestrian area surrounded by stately trees, the Yale campus, and an assortment of museums and architecturally significant homes and churches. Between the Yale campus and a series of modern buildings in the core, the downtown is generally clean and attractive and known for its large number of trees. The area has a history of good planning and urban consciousness, which continues today in a number of redevelopment projects. The university provides substantial arts and culture and entertainment amenities. Healthcare resources are the best in the state. Aside from the university and some service industries, there is a new high-tech and biotech presence with ties to the university, but it hasn't had a favorable impact on job-growth projections as yet. New Haven is too far for a practical commute to New York, but some commute by an old railroad right-of-way to corporate centers in Bridgeport and other areas west along the shore. Although not bad on a state scale, cost of living is high and much higher than reported in nicer areas of town. Milford is a rapidly growing, up-and-coming coastal town to the west along the Long Island Sound. The metro area was recently expanded to include Waterbury and a number of small towns, some industrial but most more residential, upstate from New Haven's shore location.

New Haven is located on a mostly level plain at the head of New Haven Harbor. Several creeks and small rivers enter the Long Island Sound through the New Haven area. Densely wooded hills and ridges rise to the north and northwest. Summers are warm and humid. Winters are cool with occasional cold blasts. Summer thunderstorms are common, as is winter snow. Stronger storms are brought by coastal "noreasters" and late summer hurricane remnants. First freeze is mid-October; last is late April.

Population

DEMOGRAPHICS	AREA	U.S. AVG	ETHNIC COMPOSITION	AREA	U.S. AVG	RESIDENT PROFILE	AREA	U.S. AVG
Population	850,873		White	77.3%	79.0%	Single	36.4%	32.4%
Population density per sq. mile	1405.0	358.5	Black	11.9%	10.5%	Married	49.9%	52.7%
Population growth	5.8%	21.1%	Asian	3.0%	2.7%	Divorced/separated	13.7%	14.9%
Median age	38.2	36.1	Hispanic	11.4%	10.6%	Married with children	21.5%	23.7%
Percent Democrat	54.3%	44.5%	Religious observance	53.7%	48.9%	Single with children	9.5%	9.1%
Percent Republican	43.8%	54.5%	Diversity measure	50.9	40.1	Percent over age 65	14.0%	12.9%

Economy & Jobs
Score: 5.3
Rank: 353

INCOME	AREA	U.S. AVG	EMPLOYMENT	AREA	U.S. AVG	EMPLOYING INDUSTRIES	AREA	U.S. AVG
Per capita income	$27,668	$23,235	Unemployment rate	5.9%	4.7%	Largest: Healthcare & Social Assistance		
Household income	$54,196	$46,414	Recent job growth	0.0%	1.3%			
Household income ‹ $25K	22.8%	26.2%	Projected future job growth	-0.7%	11.5%	Percent manufacturing	13.6%	15.4%
Household income › $75K	34.0%	25.4%	White collar	63.6%	57.8%	Percent public sector	14.0%	15.7%
Household income growth	11.0%	13.6%	Blue collar	21.7%	25.2%	Percent construction	8.1%	9.9%

Cost of Living
Score: 8.0
Rank: 343

INDEXES & TAXES	AREA	U.S. AVG	HOUSING	AREA	U.S. AVG	NECESSITIES	AREA	U.S. AVG
Cost of Living Index	118.5	100.0	Median home price	$292,600	$220,000	Food Index	111.1	100.0
Buying Power Index	102.5	100.0	Home price appreciation	69.7%	10.1%	Housing Index	83.9	100.0
Income tax rate	4.50%	4.70%	Median rent	$1,007	$709	Utilities Index	128.7	100.0
Sales tax rate	6.00%	6.58%	Homes owned	59.4%	62.3%	Transportation Index	105.3	100.0
Property tax rate	$19.22	$12.00	Home price ratio	5.4	4.2	Healthcare Index	107.0	100.0
						Miscellaneous Cost Index	111.1	100.0

Climate
Score: 75.9
Rank: 90

TEMPERATURE	AREA	U.S. AVG	PRECIPITATION	AREA	U.S. AVG	COMFORTS & HAZARDS	AREA	U.S. AVG
Average January low	23.4	26.2	Annual inches precipitation	38.6	37.7	July relative humidity	70%	66%
Average July high	81.5	87.4	Annual inches snowfall	27.7	7.0	Annual days mostly sunny	208	208
Annual days > 90°F	6	38	Annual days precipitation	126	109	Annual days with thunderstorms	21	39
Annual days < 32°F	102	89	Annual days rain > 0.5 inches	24	22	Tornado risk score	7	18
Annual days < 0°F	0	6	Annual days snow > 1.5 inches	5	6	Hurricane risk score	19	13

TEMPERATURE

PRECIPITATION

DAYS OF CLOUDS & PRECIPITATION

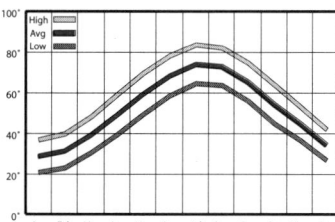

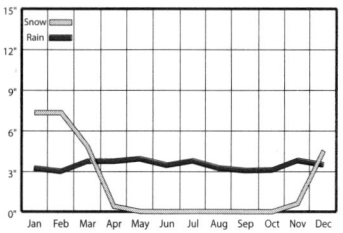

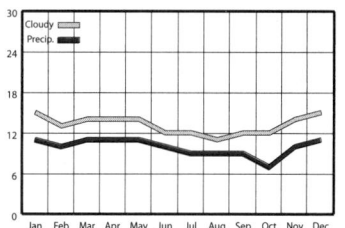

Education
Score: 69.8
Rank: 114

ACHIEVEMENT	AREA	U.S. AVG	PUBLIC SCHOOLS	AREA	U.S. AVG	HIGHER EDUCATION	AREA	U.S. AVG
High school degree	82.9%	82.7%	Expenditures per pupil	$7,851	$5,686	No. 2-year colleges	2	4
2-year college degree	6.4%	6.4%	Student/teacher ratio	15.3	16.7	No. 4-year colleges/universities	9	6
4-year college degree	15.2%	15.7%	Attending public school	88.6%	90.1%	No. highly ranked universities	1	1
Graduate/professional degree	12.3%	8.9%	State SAT score	1028*	1021			
			State ACT score	23.1	20.9			

Health & Healthcare
Score: 31.6
Rank: 255

Crime
Score: 79.9
Rank: 76

HAZARDS & ILLNESSES	AREA	U.S. AVG	HEALTHCARE	AREA	U.S. AVG	CRIME	AREA	U.S. AVG
Air-quality score	22	37	Physicians per capita	412.2	244.2	Violent crime rate	260.5	465.5
Water-quality score	44	52	Hospital beds per capita	353.8	420.0	Change in violent crime rate	-5.2%	-2.2%
Pollen/allergy score	54	61	No. teaching hospitals	8	3	Property crime rate	2,160.6	3,517.1
Cancer mortality per capita	222.2	201.9	Cost per doctor visit	$84	$77	Change in property crime rate	-3.0%	-2.1%
Depression days per month	3.4	3.5	Cost per dental visit	$105	$70			
Stress score	19	50						

Transportation
Score: 98.1
Rank: 8

COMMUTE	AREA	U.S. AVG	INTERCITY SERVICES	AREA	U.S. AVG	AUTOMOTIVE	AREA	U.S. AVG
Average commute time	25.2	27.4	Major airports within 60 miles	4	1	Insurance, annual premium	$2,143	$1,432
Percent commutes > 60 mins.	5.8%	5.9%	Size of regional airport	Large	Large	Gas, cost per gallon	$2.56	$2.49
Commute by auto	80.8%	78.9%	Daily airline activity	2329	686	Daily vehicle miles per capita	22.6	24.0
Commute by mass transit	3.2%	1.9%	Amtrak service	Yes	No			
Work at home	2.5%	3.1%						
Mass transit miles per capita	3.17	1.87						

Leisure
Score: 91.2
Rank: 34

DINING & SHOPPING	AREA	U.S. AVG	ENTERTAINMENT	AREA	U.S. AVG	OUTDOOR ACTIVITIES	AREA	U.S. AVG
Restaurant rating	1	2	Professional sports rating	10	4	Golf-course rating	8	4
Outlet mall score	135	42	College sports rating	5	4	Ski-area rating	6	3
No. Starbucks	8	13	Zoo/aquarium rating	8	3	Sq. miles inland water	6	4
No. warehouse clubs	6	2	Amusement park rating	5	3	Miles of coastline	16.7	10.7
			Botanical garden/ arboretum rating	7	4	National Park rating	3	3

Arts & Culture
Score: 83.7
Rank: 62

MEDIA & LIBRARIES	AREA	U.S. AVG	PERFORMING ARTS	AREA	U.S. AVG	MUSEUMS	AREA	U.S. AVG
Arts radio rating	4	3	Classical music rating	7	4	Overall museum rating	8	5
No. public libraries	39	27	Ballet/dance rating	6	3	Art museum rating	10	5
Library volumes per capita	3.57	2.78	Professional theater rating	8	3	Science museum rating	10	5
			University arts programs rating	8	5	Children's museum rating	6	3

New Orleans–Metairie–Kenner, LA

Profile: Large-city complex
Location: Southeast Louisiana on the Mississippi Delta south of Lake Pontchartrain
Elevation: 30 feet
Time zone: Central Standard Time

PRO	CON
Entertainment	Hurricane dislocations
Arts and culture	Crime rate
Historic interest	Flood risk

Due to the August 2005 Hurricane Katrina disaster, we cannot verify the effects of that disaster on our fact base, and much is unclear about the current and future state of the area. Therefore, we cannot rank the New Orleans area for this edition.

To be sure, New Orleans had its difficulties prior to the hurricane. Long a complex multicultural city crossing a wide range of socioeconomic strata, the pre-2005 New Orleans had its share of problems with crime, education, social infrastructure, and economic health. At the same time, the city exuded a unique cross-cultural charm, making it a favorite tourist spot as well as a proud home to many enjoying its arts, its unique entertainment profile, and its French-accented Southern grace and way of life.

The hurricane devastated some neighborhoods, most particularly and visibly the flooded Lower Ninth Ward area east of downtown and along one of the city's key canal infrastructures. This area is not yet completely open, and its future is still uncertain. Other areas of the city have erratic utility services and need of extensive reconstruction. The downtown and some of the tourist areas fared relatively well. But the tourist economy has not recovered. On the other hand, most of the industrial economy, including a large petrochemical industry and port and transportation infrastructure, has. Job dislocations are still prevalent. Some jobs have gone away, probably forever, while for some others there aren't enough workers available, and there have been reports of very high wages paid even for fast-food workers.

The population has clearly contracted. Estimates vary, but as many as half of the more than 400,000-plus residents of New Orleans itself have left for higher ground in Baton Rouge, Alexandria, and other points north in Louisiana; east toward Mobile, Alabama; west toward Houston; and elsewhere. Louisiana license plates are seen frequently throughout the U.S. Because many people still give a New Orleans address, even when temporarily living elsewhere, the current population status is unclear, but some estimates have the current population somewhere around 225,000. The long-term effects on demographic and socioeconomic mix are also far from clear. Many very poor residents don't have the wherewithal or the welcoming destination to leave, while perhaps only the wealthier will be able to afford to return and rebuild. Along with the rest of the mainstream economy, much of the tax base has also

suffered, and while federal aid is certainly a help, it is unclear whether infrastructure and services, like schools, will return in poorer or even possibly in better shape than they were before. It depends not only on how much money is available and when but also on how effective state and local leaders are in spending it. The long-term future also depends on whether solutions can be found—and funded—for the city's precarious existence on a soft, soggy river delta below sea level.

Regardless of the outcome, New Orleans is and will always be a unique and diverse city. For arts, culture, entertainment, music, food, history, and architecture, there was hardly a better place to live before Katrina's destruction. It is probably the most right-brained city in the country. Things get done, but at a relaxed, leisurely pace, generally with an element of artistic expression and fun. The local phrase *laissez les bon temps rouler*, or "let the good times roll," sums it up. Residents need a laid-back attitude to prosper because the city can push an impatient person to the limit. Old infrastructures and geographic limitations have left the city with narrow streets and underdeveloped transportation routes. Before the hurricane, traffic problems were extreme; whether these issues can be solved by new infrastructure and a declining population remains to be seen. The summer climate is generally uncomfortable, and heavy downpours occur with almost no notice. Tourists were everywhere before the storm, and will likely be back. The crime rate was and continues to be notoriously high, improving a bit before the storm but relapsing into chaotic periods that still go on. Metairie is a more family-oriented commercial unincorporated area to the west of downtown. Kenner is a suburb farther west and is the location of the international airport. Both suburbs fared better in the hurricane than the city itself.

The New Orleans metro area is virtually surrounded by water. Lake Pontchartrain, some 610 square miles in area, borders the city on the north and the Mississippi River flows along the southern edge. In other directions, there are bayous, lakes, and marshlands. Elevations vary from a few feet *below* sea level (protected by massive levees) to a few feet above. Floods are a persistent hazard. Summers are persistently warm and humid with almost daily showers and thundershowers. Winter is mild, with steady rains from December through March. Nearby water can produce dense fog. Late spring and late fall are the driest seasons.

Population

DEMOGRAPHICS	AREA	U.S. AVG	ETHNIC COMPOSITION	AREA	U.S. AVG	RESIDENT PROFILE	AREA	U.S. AVG
Population	1,321,402		White	56.3%	79.0%	Single	38.1%	32.4%
Population density per sq. mile	419.0	358.5	Black	37.8%	10.5%	Married	45.6%	52.7%
Population growth	7.4%	21.1%	Asian	2.6%	2.7%	Divorced/separated	16.2%	14.9%
Median age	35.8	36.1	Hispanic	4.8%	10.6%	Married with children	21.0%	23.7%
Percent Democrat	49.6%	44.5%	Religious observance	52.5%	48.9%	Single with children	12.2%	9.1%
Percent Republican	49.5%	54.5%	Diversity measure	48.6	40.1	Percent over age 65	11.7%	12.9%

Economy & Jobs
Score: -
Rank: -

INCOME	AREA	U.S. AVG	EMPLOYMENT	AREA	U.S. AVG	EMPLOYING INDUSTRIES	AREA	U.S. AVG
Per capita income	$22,223	$23,235	Unemployment rate	5.6%	4.7%	Largest: Healthcare & Social Assistance		
Household income	$41,733	$46,414	Recent job growth	2.7%	1.3%			
Household income < $25K	31.2%	26.2%	Projected future job growth	10.5%	11.5%	Percent manufacturing	11.3%	15.4%
Household income > $75K	23.7%	25.4%	White collar	60.9%	57.8%	Percent public sector	16.3%	15.7%
Household income growth	15.6%	13.6%	Blue collar	21.2%	25.2%	Percent construction	9.9%	9.9%

Cost of Living
Score: -
Rank: -

INDEXES & TAXES	AREA	U.S. AVG	HOUSING	AREA	U.S. AVG	NECESSITIES	AREA	U.S. AVG
Cost of Living Index	95.1	100.0	Median home price	$178,000	$220,000	Food Index	107.6	100.0
Buying Power Index	98.4	100.0	Home price appreciation	42.9%	10.1%	Housing Index	66.1	100.0
Income tax rate	4.00%	4.70%	Median rent	$978	$709	Utilities Index	104.5	100.0
Sales tax rate	8.82%	6.58%	Homes owned	57.4%	62.3%	Transportation Index	106.9	100.0
Property tax rate	$5.36	$12.00	Home price ratio	4.3	4.2	Healthcare Index	105.9	100.0
						Miscellaneous Cost Index	98.6	100.0

Climate
Score: -
Rank: -

TEMPERATURE	AREA	U.S. AVG	PRECIPITATION	AREA	U.S. AVG	COMFORTS & HAZARDS	AREA	U.S. AVG
Average January low	43.5	26.2	Annual inches precipitation	57.0	37.7	July relative humidity	77%	66%
Average July high	90.6	87.4	Annual inches snowfall	0.2	7.0	Annual days mostly sunny	229	208
Annual days > 90°F	67	38	Annual days precipitation	113	109	Annual days with thunderstorms	68	39
Annual days < 32°F	13	89	Annual days rain > 0.5 inches	38	22	Tornado risk score	25	18
Annual days < 0°F	0	6	Annual days snow > 1.5 inches	1	6	Hurricane risk score	58	13

TEMPERATURE

PRECIPITATION

DAYS OF CLOUDS & PRECIPITATION

Education
Score: -
Rank: -

ACHIEVEMENT	AREA	U.S. AVG	PUBLIC SCHOOLS	AREA	U.S. AVG	HIGHER EDUCATION	AREA	U.S. AVG
High school degree	77.8%	82.7%	Expenditures per pupil	$4,780	$5,686	No. 2-year colleges	14	4
2-year college degree	4.2%	6.4%	Student/teacher ratio	16.5	16.7	No. 4-year colleges/universities	16	6
4-year college degree	14.6%	15.7%	Attending public school	74.5%	90.1%	No. highly ranked universities	1	1
Graduate/professional degree	8.1%	8.9%	State SAT score	1141	1021			
			State ACT score	20.1*	20.9			

Health & Healthcare
Score: -
Rank: -

HAZARDS & ILLNESSES	AREA	U.S. AVG	HEALTHCARE	AREA	U.S. AVG	CRIME	AREA	U.S. AVG
Air-quality score	31	37	Physicians per capita	393.5	244.2	Violent crime rate	612.0	465.5
Water-quality score	40	52	Hospital beds per capita	544.9	420.0	Change in violent crime rate	-9.1%	-2.2%
Pollen/allergy score	80	61	No. teaching hospitals	14	3	Property crime rate	3,613.2	3,517.1
Cancer mortality per capita	222.1	201.9	Cost per doctor visit	$60	$77	Change in property crime rate	-18.4%	-2.1%
Depression days per month	3.0	3.5	Cost per dental visit	$68	$70			
Stress score	100	50						

Transportation
Score: -
Rank: -

COMMUTE	AREA	U.S. AVG	INTERCITY SERVICES	AREA	U.S. AVG	AUTOMOTIVE	AREA	U.S. AVG
Average commute time	28.8	27.4	Major airports within 60 miles	1	1	Insurance, annual premium	$2,344	$1,432
Percent commutes > 60 mins.	8.2%	5.9%	Size of regional airport	Medium	Large	Gas, cost per gallon	$2.49	$2.49
Commute by auto	72.6%	78.9%	Daily airline activity	259	686	Daily vehicle miles per capita	16.6	24.0
Commute by mass transit	5.8%	1.9%	Amtrak service	Yes	No			
Work at home	2.4%	3.1%						
Mass transit miles per capita	5.78	1.87						

Leisure
Score: -
Rank: -

DINING & SHOPPING	AREA	U.S. AVG	ENTERTAINMENT	AREA	U.S. AVG	OUTDOOR ACTIVITIES	AREA	U.S. AVG
Restaurant rating	7	2	Professional sports rating	6	4	Golf-course rating	5	4
Outlet mall score	19	42	College sports rating	4	4	Ski-area rating	1	3
No. Starbucks	13	13	Zoo/aquarium rating	8	3	Sq. miles inland water	10	4
No. warehouse clubs	2	2	Amusement park rating	1	3	Miles of coastline	76.3	10.7
			Botanical garden/arboretum rating	10	4	National Park rating	4	3

Arts & Culture
Score: -
Rank: -

MEDIA & LIBRARIES	AREA	U.S. AVG	PERFORMING ARTS	AREA	U.S. AVG	MUSEUMS	AREA	U.S. AVG
Arts radio rating	5	3	Classical music rating	7	4	Overall museum rating	9	5
No. public libraries	54	27	Ballet/dance rating	5	3	Art museum rating	8	5
Library volumes per capita	2.11	2.78	Professional theater rating	1	3	Science museum rating	9	5
			University arts programs rating	9	5	Children's museum rating	7	3

New York–White Plains, NY

Score: 49.0   **Rank:** 251   **2004 rank:** 40

Profile: National center
Location: Southeast corner of New York State, at mouth of Hudson River
Elevation: 87 feet
Time zone: Eastern Standard Time

PRO
Arts and culture
Economic center
Education

CON
Cost of living and housing
Crowded lifestyle
Weak future job growth

New York is the largest metro area in the United States. It includes the island of Manhattan, an eight-county area immediately north, western Long Island, and Staten Island. The metro area could be much larger if nearby suburbs of New Jersey and Connecticut were also included. (Actually, as defined by the OMB, the New York area now includes Bergen County in northern New Jersey. We felt it enough different to keep separate—see p. 207.) New York is the fourth largest city in the world behind Tokyo, Mexico City, and Sao Paulo, Brazil. Regardless of how the area is defined, New York is among the richest and most complex places to live in America.

Boroughs, districts, and neighborhoods define the city. The borough of Manhattan, a 10-mile-long, 2-mile-wide island, is the financial, commercial, and entertainment core. Much of Lower Manhattan consists of narrow, haphazard streets, dating back to the city's earliest days as a Dutch colony. With the exception of older areas, such as Greenwich Village, the rest of the city follows an orderly grid pattern of avenues and streets laid out in 1811. (Broadway, another exception, moves at a gentle diagonal across the city.) Filling out the island are distinct districts. Lower Manhattan contains the Financial District. Midtown is the commercial center, with corporate headquarters, various media businesses, and world-class shopping along Fifth Avenue. Large skyscrapers dominate Lower Manhattan, retreat as does the hard bedrock to build on in those areas, and then re-emerge in Midtown. The in-between area is dominated by older ethnic enclaves such as Chinatown and Koreatown and the more famous artsy areas of Greenwich and Soho. "Hip" residential areas lie east and west, mainly popular with young single professionals. North and west is Hells Kitchen; in the "40s" (most Manhattan area locations are so approximated by their east–west numbered streets) is an old ethnic area and warehouse district enjoying a residential renaissance, to be aided soon by an elevated bikeway and commercial corridor along an old rail line. Times Square and the Theater District just west of Midtown contain the world-famous theaters and numerous restaurants. Surrounding Central Park, the Upper West and Upper East sides are predominantly residential, although both contain ample dining and shopping. The Upper East Side also contains posh enclaves unaffordable for most, outstanding museums, and the designer boutiques of Madison Avenue. The Upper West Side is dotted with large apartment buildings and is a favorite for working professionals and families. Farther north above Central Park, neighborhoods start to decline, although Harlem is undergoing a rebirth.

The boroughs of Brooklyn, Queens, and the Bronx are a patchwork of residential and commercial areas and parks. They have large industrial areas with a predominant blue-collar feel containing manufacturing and freight distribution centers for the area. All are close to the city and offer relatively more living space, and all are experiencing varying degrees of economic and residential revival. Ethnic diversity is strong in all boroughs, while Queens is reputedly the most ethnically diverse area in the country. Brooklyn is large and diverse enough to function as a stand-alone city, with large and some upscale residential areas with a modern downtown and substantial commercial and retail offerings areas. Brooklyn is known for its large Olmstead-designed (of Central Park fame) Prospect Park. Brooklyn shares the western end of Long Island with Queens, with excellent transportation service into the city by rail and subway and numerous beaches, parks, and residential neighborhoods south and east towards the large JFK airport. Brooklyn is socioeconomically very diverse, with a mix of upscale, middle-class, and poorer areas, while Queens is more clearly identifiable as middle class. The Bronx area, on the mainland to the north of Manhattan, is the grittiest of the three areas, although its strategic location between the city and to better areas north is starting to bring some interest. Staten Island, a mainly residential borough to the south, is connected to Manhattan by ferries and the Verrazano Narrows Bridge.

Finally, the New York metro area, as defined, includes northern suburbs stretching up into Westchester County between the east bank of the north–south Hudson River and the Connecticut border, and Rockland County on the west bank of the river. Westchester County is generally upscale and expensive, with spread-out towns and a predominant country setting. White Plains is the largest city and a modern corporate center with large facilities for IBM and a number of companies relocating north from Manhattan. Smaller but very upscale areas lie east along the Long Island Sound, Rye being an example, and north along the Hudson, such as the smaller towns of Tarrytown, Ossining, and Croton-on-Hudson. Rockland County is more middle class with some working-class areas. West Nyack is a large family-oriented, middle-class area with reputedly the second-largest mall in the U.S.; other suburbs give workers access to New York by freeway or by meeting rail commute lines across the Hudson or to employment in northern New Jersey, which lies just south. Readers thinking that these areas are complex, defined by major commute routes, and out of the price range of many Americans are getting the idea. The New York area offers a rich assortment of amenities, with world-class dining, shopping, and performing arts including theater, symphony, opera, and live music. Museums and architectural attractions, large and small, draw global audiences. Numerous major league teams play in the area, including the MLB Yankees and Mets, NBA Knicks and Nets, NFL Giants and Jets, and NHL Rangers. An extensive public transit system with subways and buses serves the urban core and links the boroughs. A suburban rail and ferry network services surrounding communities in Connecticut, Long Island, and New Jersey, while rail lines on the Northeast Corridor make such cities as Boston and Washington, D.C., easily accessible. Only 51% of

New York commuters commute by auto—by far the lowest percentage in the nation. Many residents don't own cars and choose to depend on public transit or an occasional car rental. Three major airports—La Guardia, JFK, and nearby Newark—provide air service domestically and abroad. Surrounding the city are numerous recreation areas: Long Island beaches, the Poconos, the Hudson Valley, and the Jersey Shore, to name only a few.

The downsides are significant. The city is crowded and stressful, and some neighborhoods are run-down. Violent-crime rates are high, although not as bad as the stereotype. Cost of living is high in all categories and is rising, with a Cost of Living Index at 177.6. Median home prices of $549,200 don't buy much, especially in Manhattan, where prices can be five to six times higher for comparable properties in surrounding boroughs. Income differentials between wealthy workers and others are high, and overall the Buying Power Index of 60.7, worst in the country, suggests incomes aren't keeping up with costs. Cost

increases, reduced job-growth projections, and crime hurt the rankings, which are otherwise stellar in most categories. New York is a great place—if you like the lifestyle and can make ends meet.

The New York City area exceeds 300 square miles and is located mostly on islands, with elevations ranging from less than 50 feet over most of Manhattan, Brooklyn, and Queens to several hundred feet in northern Manhattan, the Bronx, and Staten Island. Summers are hot and humid with occasional long periods of discomfort. Sea breezes occasionally moderate summer heat and winter cold in Lower Manhattan. Manhattan and the inner boroughs are more likely to receive rain in winter while outlying areas get snow. Precipitation is distributed fairly evenly throughout the year. Summer rainfall is mainly from thunderstorms usually of brief duration. Late summer and fall rains associated with tropical storms may occur. Coastal "noreaster" storms can produce significant snow. First freeze is mid-November; last is early April.

Population

DEMOGRAPHICS	AREA	U.S. AVG	ETHNIC COMPOSITION	AREA	U.S. AVG	RESIDENT PROFILE	AREA	U.S. AVG
Population	9,456,583		White	46.8%	79.0%	Single	42.9%	32.4%
Population density per sq. mile	8283.6	358.5	Black	24.3%	10.5%	Married	40.1%	52.7%
Population growth	10.8%	21.1%	Asian	10.2%	2.7%	Divorced/separated	17.0%	14.9%
Median age	36.1	36.1	Hispanic	26.9%	10.6%	Married with children	19.4%	23.7%
Percent Democrat	72.0%	44.5%	Religious observance	61.7%	48.9%	Single with children	11.7%	9.1%
Percent Republican	27.0%	54.5%	Diversity measure	76.0	40.1	Percent over age 65	12.4%	12.9%

Economy & Jobs
Score: 9.1
Rank: 338

INCOME	AREA	U.S. AVG	EMPLOYMENT	AREA	U.S. AVG	EMPLOYING INDUSTRIES	AREA	U.S. AVG
Per capita income	$26,788	$23,235	Unemployment rate	5.6%	4.7%	Largest: Finance & Insurance		
Household income	$48,120	$46,414	Recent job growth	1.7%	1.3%			
Household income < $25K	29.8%	26.2%	Projected future job growth	3.8%	11.5%	Percent manufacturing	10.5%	15.4%
Household income > $75K	30.1%	25.4%	White collar	64.2%	57.8%	Percent public sector	16.4%	15.7%
Household income growth	13.9%	13.6%	Blue collar	17.3%	25.2%	Percent construction	6.7%	9.9%

Cost of Living
Score: 3.5
Rank: 360

INDEXES & TAXES	AREA	U.S. AVG	HOUSING	AREA	U.S. AVG	NECESSITIES	AREA	U.S. AVG
Cost of Living Index	177.6	100.0	Median home price	$549,200	$220,000	Food Index	136.7	100.0
Buying Power Index	60.7	100.0	Home price appreciation	93.7%	10.1%	Housing Index	203.3	100.0
Income tax rate	10.53%	4.70%	Median rent	$1,210	$709	Utilities Index	156.7	100.0
Sales tax rate	8.48%	6.58%	Homes owned	34.1%	62.3%	Transportation Index	118.9	100.0
Property tax rate	$12.85	$12.00	Home price ratio	11.4	4.2	Healthcare Index	177.9	100.0
						Miscellaneous Cost Index	134.9	100.0

Climate
Score: 45.7
Rank: 202

TEMPERATURE	AREA	U.S. AVG	PRECIPITATION	AREA	U.S. AVG	COMFORTS & HAZARDS	AREA	U.S. AVG
Average January low	24.3	26.2	Annual inches precipitation	41.5	37.7	July relative humidity	65%	66%
Average July high	85.6	87.4	Annual inches snowfall	28.4	7.0	Annual days mostly sunny	207	208
Annual days > 90°F	20	38	Annual days precipitation	129	109	Annual days with thunderstorms	25	39
Annual days < 32°F	87	89	Annual days rain > 0.5 inches	26	22	Tornado risk score	14	18
Annual days < 0°F	0	6	Annual days snow > 1.5 inches	5	6	Hurricane risk score	17	13

TEMPERATURE

PRECIPITATION

DAYS OF CLOUDS & PRECIPITATION

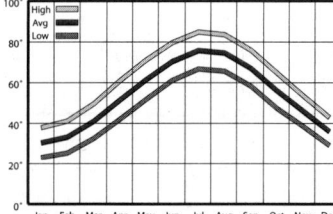
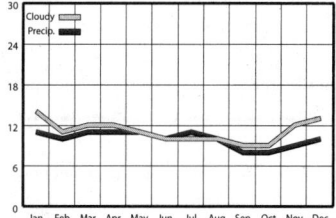

Education
Score: 100.0
Rank: 1

ACHIEVEMENT	AREA	U.S. AVG	PUBLIC SCHOOLS	AREA	U.S. AVG	HIGHER EDUCATION	AREA	U.S. AVG
High school degree	73.5%	82.7%	Expenditures per pupil	$8,311	$5,686	No. 2-year colleges	47	4
2-year college degree	5.4%	6.4%	Student/teacher ratio	17.1	16.7	No. 4-year colleges/universities	126	6
4-year college degree	16.2%	15.7%	Attending public school	81.0%	90.1%	No. highly ranked universities	11	1
Graduate/professional degree	12.2%	8.9%	State SAT score	1003*	1021			
			State ACT score	22.6	20.9			

Health & Healthcare
Score: 2.7
Rank: 363

HAZARDS & ILLNESSES	AREA	U.S. AVG
Air-quality score	19	37
Water-quality score	42	52
Pollen/allergy score	63	61
Cancer mortality per capita	183.2	201.9
Depression days per month	3.5	3.5
Stress score	43	50

HEALTHCARE	AREA	U.S. AVG
Physicians per capita	390.6	244.2
Hospital beds per capita	474.9	420.0
No. teaching hospitals	64	3
Cost per doctor visit	$100	$77
Cost per dental visit	$94	$70

Crime
Score: 50.0
Rank: 188

CRIME	AREA	U.S. AVG
Violent crime rate	576.1	465.5
Change in violent crime rate	-1.1%	-2.2%
Property crime rate	1,967.9	3,517.1
Change in property crime rate	-5.9%	-2.1%

Transportation
Score: 99.2
Rank: 4

COMMUTE	AREA	U.S. AVG
Average commute time	42.4	27.4
Percent commutes > 60 mins.	24.2%	5.9%
Commute by auto	31.2%	78.9%
Commute by mass transit	47.6%	1.9%
Work at home	2.9%	3.1%
Mass transit miles per capita	42.28	1.87

INTERCITY SERVICES	AREA	U.S. AVG
Major airports within 60 miles	4	1
Size of regional airport	Large	Large
Daily airline activity	2696	686
Amtrak service	Yes	No

AUTOMOTIVE	AREA	U.S. AVG
Insurance, annual premium	$2,711	$1,432
Gas, cost per gallon	$2.68	$2.49
Daily vehicle miles per capita	16.8	24.0

Leisure
Score: 99.7
Rank: 2

DINING & SHOPPING	AREA	U.S. AVG
Restaurant rating	10	2
Outlet mall score	23	42
No. Starbucks	213	13
No. warehouse clubs	13	2

ENTERTAINMENT	AREA	U.S. AVG
Professional sports rating	10	4
College sports rating	6	4
Zoo/aquarium rating	10	3
Amusement park rating	6	3
Botanical garden/ arboretum rating	10	4

OUTDOOR ACTIVITIES	AREA	U.S. AVG
Golf-course rating	10	4
Ski-area rating	5	3
Sq. miles inland water	10	4
Miles of coastline	26.5	10.7
National Park rating	4	3

Arts & Culture
Score: 99.7
Rank: 2

MEDIA & LIBRARIES	AREA	U.S. AVG
Arts radio rating	9	3
No. public libraries	279	27
Library volumes per capita	5.14	2.78

PERFORMING ARTS	AREA	U.S. AVG
Classical music rating	10	4
Ballet/dance rating	10	3
Professional theater rating	10	3
University arts programs rating	10	5

MUSEUMS	AREA	U.S. AVG
Overall museum rating	10	5
Art museum rating	10	5
Science museum rating	10	5
Children's museum rating	10	3

Niles–Benton Harbor, MI

Score: 63.4   **Rank:** 147   **2004 rank:** 299

Profile: Small-city complex
Location: Southwestern Michigan along the Lake Michigan shore and Indiana border
Elevation: 623 feet
Time zone: Eastern Standard Time

PRO
Nearby beaches
Cost of living
Healthcare

CON
Unemployment
Blighted areas
Arts and culture

Southwestern Michigan is known for excellent agriculture with fruit, vegetable, and flower growing and a notable Dutch influence. It is also known for its Lake Michigan shore beaches, dunes, and state parks. These beach areas are known around the Midwest for their sandy, almost Southern California–like beaches and summer recreation. But the cities of Niles, Benton Harbor, and its twin city St. Joseph generally do not fit the area's mold. Niles is a small and fairly nondescript light manufacturing town 3 miles north of the Indiana border and only 15 miles from South Bend, and along the South Shore line to Chicago (but too far to commute regularly downtown for work). Benton Harbor and St. Joseph were originally an agricultural port for the area but have become somewhat declining industrial and commercial cities with considerable poverty and decay, particularly on the Benton Harbor side of the St. Joseph River. There were some well-documented racial tensions in

2003, and it is clear that the river is not only a physical but also a notable socioeconomic dividing line between the two cities. On the positive side, Benton Harbor is home to Whirlpool Corporation, and that company just announced a 400-job expansion in the area related to its acquisition of Maytag. Tourism is a plus for the area as a whole. Cost of living is very reasonable. On the whole, the area has a number of positives but also some rough edges.

The area contains mostly level to gently rolling terrain inland with areas of deciduous forest. Summer days are pleasantly warm, with lake breezes and a few weeks of hot, humid weather. Most summer nights are comfortable. Winters are cloudy with strong northwesterly winds and occasional heavy lake-effect snows. Prolonged cold waves are infrequent but below-zero temperatures are fairly common First freeze is early October; last is late April.

DEMOGRAPHICS	AREA	U.S. AVG
Population	163,121	
Population density per sq. mile	285.7	358.5
Population growth	1.1%	21.1%
Median age	38.1	36.1
Percent Democrat	44.0%	44.5%
Percent Republican	55.0%	54.5%

ETHNIC COMPOSITION	AREA	U.S. AVG
White	79.4%	79.0%
Black	15.5%	10.5%
Asian	1.5%	2.7%
Hispanic	3.5%	10.6%
Religious observance	46.9%	48.9%
Diversity measure	38.9	40.1

RESIDENT PROFILE	AREA	U.S. AVG
Single	32.8%	32.4%
Married	52.9%	52.7%
Divorced/separated	14.3%	14.9%
Married with children	20.8%	23.7%
Single with children	10.1%	9.1%
Percent over age 65	14.7%	12.9%

Economy & Jobs
Score: 28.3
Rank: 268

INCOME	AREA	U.S. AVG
Per capita income	$22,543	$23,235
Household income	$42,828	$46,414
Household income ‹ $25K	28.9%	26.2%
Household income › $75K	22.8%	25.4%
Household income growth	11.0%	13.6%

EMPLOYMENT	AREA	U.S. AVG
Unemployment rate	7.8%	4.7%
Recent job growth	2.1%	1.3%
Projected future job growth	4.4%	11.5%
White collar	52.7%	57.8%
Blue collar	30.1%	25.2%

EMPLOYING INDUSTRIES	AREA	U.S. AVG
Largest: Manufacturing		
Percent manufacturing	21.2%	15.4%
Percent public sector	9.2%	15.7%
Percent construction	9.0%	9.9%

Cost of Living
Score: 74.9
Rank: 95

INDEXES & TAXES	AREA	U.S. AVG
Cost of Living Index	81.0	100.0
Buying Power Index	118.5	100.0
Income tax rate	4.40%	4.70%
Sales tax rate	6.00%	6.58%
Property tax rate	$11.81	$12.00

HOUSING	AREA	U.S. AVG
Median home price	$136,000	$220,000
Home price appreciation	36.9%	10.1%
Median rent	$584	$709
Homes owned	62.9%	62.3%
Home price ratio	3.2	4.2

NECESSITIES	AREA	U.S. AVG
Food Index	90.0	100.0
Housing Index	56.6	100.0
Utilities Index	89.9	100.0
Transportation Index	97.7	100.0
Healthcare Index	93.1	100.0
Miscellaneous Cost Index	93.4	100.0

Climate
Score: 25.4
Rank: 278

TEMPERATURE	AREA	U.S. AVG
Average January low	17.0	26.2
Average July high	84.4	87.4
Annual days › 90°F	21	38
Annual days ‹ 32°F	119	89
Annual days ‹ 0°F	7	6

PRECIPITATION	AREA	U.S. AVG
Annual inches precipitation	34.0	37.7
Annual inches snowfall	40.0	7.0
Annual days precipitation	123	109
Annual days rain › 0.5 inches	20	22
Annual days snow › 1.5 inches	9	6

COMFORTS & HAZARDS	AREA	U.S. AVG
July relative humidity	67%	66%
Annual days mostly sunny	197	208
Annual days with thunderstorms	40	39
Tornado risk score	28	18
Hurricane risk score	2	13

TEMPERATURE

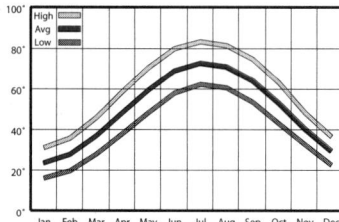

PRECIPITATION

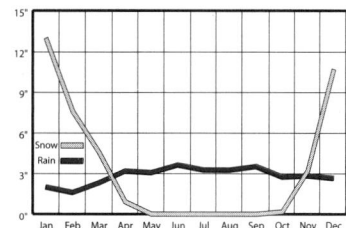

DAYS OF CLOUDS & PRECIPITATION

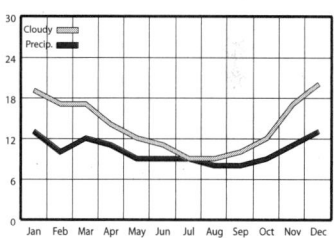

Education
Score: 39.3
Rank: 228

ACHIEVEMENT	AREA	U.S. AVG
High school degree	82.0%	82.7%
2-year college degree	7.7%	6.4%
4-year college degree	12.3%	15.7%
Graduate/professional degree	7.4%	8.9%

PUBLIC SCHOOLS	AREA	U.S. AVG
Expenditures per pupil	$6,038	$5,686
Student/teacher ratio	15.5	16.7
Attending public school	89.0%	90.1%
State SAT score	1151	1021
State ACT score	21.5*	20.9

HIGHER EDUCATION	AREA	U.S. AVG
No. 2-year colleges	1	4
No. 4-year colleges/universities	1	6
No. highly ranked universities	0	1

Health & Healthcare
Score: 68.4
Rank: 118

HAZARDS & ILLNESSES	AREA	U.S. AVG
Air-quality score	40	37
Water-quality score	36	52
Pollen/allergy score	56	61
Cancer mortality per capita	194.6	201.9
Depression days per month	2.6	3.5
Stress score	61	50

HEALTHCARE	AREA	U.S. AVG
Physicians per capita	164.7	244.2
Hospital beds per capita	644.9	420.0
No. teaching hospitals	0	3
Cost per doctor visit	$69	$77
Cost per dental visit	$66	$70

Crime
Score: 36.9
Rank: 236

CRIME	AREA	U.S. AVG
Violent crime rate	487.0	465.5
Change in violent crime rate	-7.5%	-2.2%
Property crime rate	3,172.9	3,517.1
Change in property crime rate	3.8%	-2.1%

Transportation
Score: 97.1
Rank: 12

COMMUTE	AREA	U.S. AVG
Average commute time	21.4	27.4
Percent commutes › 60 mins.	4.4%	5.9%
Commute by auto	81.7%	78.9%
Commute by mass transit	0.6%	1.9%
Work at home	3.3%	3.1%
Mass transit miles per capita	0.62	1.87

INTERCITY SERVICES	AREA	U.S. AVG
Major airports within 60 miles	2	1
Size of regional airport	Large	Large
Daily airline activity	1996	686
Amtrak service	Yes	No

AUTOMOTIVE	AREA	U.S. AVG
Insurance, annual premium	$1,431	$1,432
Gas, cost per gallon	$2.52	$2.49
Daily vehicle miles per capita	32.3	24.0

DINING & SHOPPING	AREA	U.S. AVG	ENTERTAINMENT	AREA	U.S. AVG	OUTDOOR ACTIVITIES	AREA	U.S. AVG
Restaurant rating	1	2	Professional sports rating	2	4	Golf-course rating	3	4
Outlet mall score	104	42	College sports rating	1	4	Ski-area rating	5	3
No. Starbucks	0	13	Zoo/aquarium rating	1	3	Sq. miles inland water	2	4
No. warehouse clubs	0	2	Amusement park rating	1	3	Miles of coastline	44.2	10.7
			Botanical garden/ arboretum rating	4	4	National Park rating	1	3

MEDIA & LIBRARIES	AREA	U.S. AVG	PERFORMING ARTS	AREA	U.S. AVG	MUSEUMS	AREA	U.S. AVG
Arts radio rating	1	3	Classical music rating	1	4	Overall museum rating	4	5
No. public libraries	14	27	Ballet/dance rating	1	3	Art museum rating	3	5
Library volumes per capita	4.86	2.78	Professional theater rating	1	3	Science museum rating	5	5
			University arts programs rating	2	5	Children's museum rating	4	3

Norwich–New London, CT

Score: 32.9   Rank: 338   2004 rank: 67

Profile: Small-city complex
Location: Eastern Connecticut along the Long Island Sound to 15 miles north along the Thames River
Elevation: 7 feet
Time zone: Eastern Standard Time

PRO	CON
Attractive setting	Weak job growth
Historic interest	Some urban decay
Central location	Harsh winters

New London is located—not surprisingly—where the broad Thames River empties into the Long Island Sound. Norwich lies about 13 miles upriver. New London has a rich maritime history and is now home to the U.S. Coast Guard Academy. Norwich is an early industrial center, where the first paper and iron nails were made in the mid-1700s. Both cities remain fairly industrial but have modestly attractive downtown cores with areas of historic buildings but also some areas of decay. New London is also home to two small colleges. Norwich has some local arts amenities but is also transforming itself into a regional weekend tourist destination, first with two large casinos nearby, and more recently with more upscale hotels and spas, one connected with one of the casinos. The central location to New England and New York just might make this work. New London made national news in 2005 with a landmark Supreme Court case allowing the city to use eminent domain to seize property for a large commercial development deemed to be in the public interest. Since then this notion has been tested and rejected in many parts of the U.S., most recently the Ohio Supreme Court, and is likely to get U.S. Supreme Court attention again. We believe a sustained decision would be a disaster for U.S. cities, causing more yielding to large developer interests than already goes on today. We applaud the small group of citizens in New London who fought this. Air and many other services are available in Providence, 60 miles northeast. Employment projections have declined. Cost of living, while high, is moderate on a Connecticut scale. Employment declines and a few "just misses" in other categories hurt the ranking; the area is probably better than the figure indicates.

Level terrain with marshes and beach at the coast give way to rolling and wooded terrain to the north. Summers are warm and humid but with refreshing sea breezes. The inland Norwich area is typically warmer in summer and colder in winter. Winters are cold and wet with occasional periods of more extreme cold. Since the area lies east of the main part of Long Island, coastal "noreaster" storms are strong and can produce significant rain and snow. First freeze is late October; last is late April.

DEMOGRAPHICS	AREA	U.S. AVG	ETHNIC COMPOSITION	AREA	U.S. AVG	RESIDENT PROFILE	AREA	U.S. AVG
Population	266,582		White	85.3%	79.0%	Single	31.8%	32.4%
Population density per sq. mile	400.3	358.5	Black	5.8%	10.5%	Married	52.2%	52.7%
Population growth	4.6%	21.1%	Asian	2.8%	2.7%	Divorced/separated	16.0%	14.9%
Median age	38.3	36.1	Hispanic	5.6%	10.6%	Married with children	23.3%	23.7%
Percent Democrat	55.8%	44.5%	Religious observance	45.4%	48.9%	Single with children	8.9%	9.1%
Percent Republican	42.2%	54.5%	Diversity measure	34.4	40.1	Percent over age 65	13.3%	12.9%

INCOME	AREA	U.S. AVG	EMPLOYMENT	AREA	U.S. AVG	EMPLOYING INDUSTRIES	AREA	U.S. AVG
Per capita income	$28,438	$23,235	Unemployment rate	4.9%	4.7%	Largest: Manufacturing		
Household income	$57,866	$46,414	Recent job growth	1.2%	1.3%			
Household income < $25K	18.1%	26.2%	Projected future job growth	1.0%	11.5%	Percent manufacturing	10.8%	15.4%
Household income > $75K	35.3%	25.4%	White collar	59.7%	57.8%	Percent public sector	15.2%	15.7%
Household income growth	14.3%	13.6%	Blue collar	19.7%	25.2%	Percent construction	8.9%	9.9%

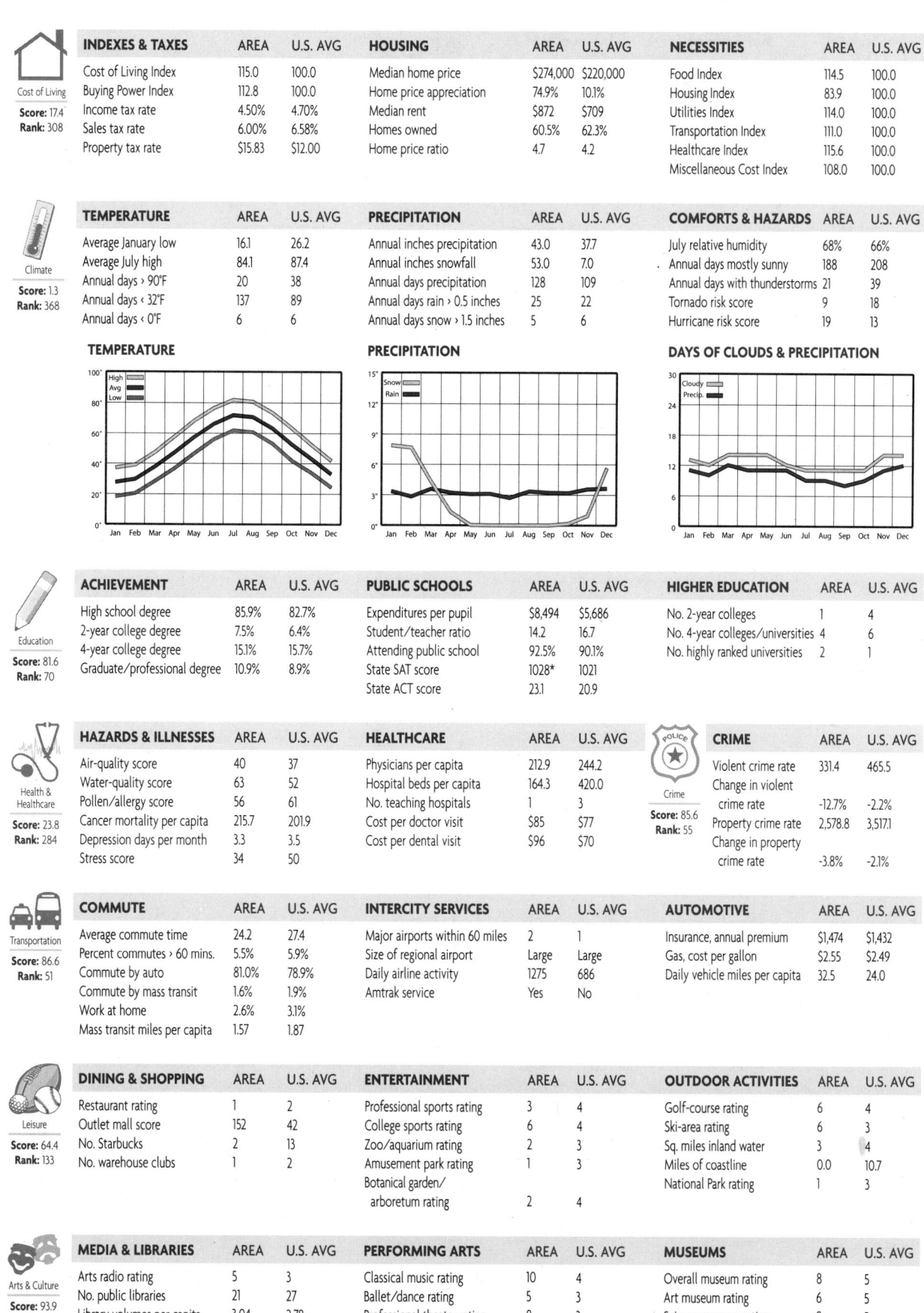

Cost of Living
Score: 17.4
Rank: 308

INDEXES & TAXES	AREA	U.S. AVG	HOUSING	AREA	U.S. AVG	NECESSITIES	AREA	U.S. AVG
Cost of Living Index	115.0	100.0	Median home price	$274,000	$220,000	Food Index	114.5	100.0
Buying Power Index	112.8	100.0	Home price appreciation	74.9%	10.1%	Housing Index	83.9	100.0
Income tax rate	4.50%	4.70%	Median rent	$872	$709	Utilities Index	114.0	100.0
Sales tax rate	6.00%	6.58%	Homes owned	60.5%	62.3%	Transportation Index	111.0	100.0
Property tax rate	$15.83	$12.00	Home price ratio	4.7	4.2	Healthcare Index	115.6	100.0
						Miscellaneous Cost Index	108.0	100.0

Climate
Score: 1.3
Rank: 368

TEMPERATURE	AREA	U.S. AVG	PRECIPITATION	AREA	U.S. AVG	COMFORTS & HAZARDS	AREA	U.S. AVG
Average January low	16.1	26.2	Annual inches precipitation	43.0	37.7	July relative humidity	68%	66%
Average July high	84.1	87.4	Annual inches snowfall	53.0	7.0	Annual days mostly sunny	188	208
Annual days > 90°F	20	38	Annual days precipitation	128	109	Annual days with thunderstorms	21	39
Annual days < 32°F	137	89	Annual days rain > 0.5 inches	25	22	Tornado risk score	9	18
Annual days < 0°F	6	6	Annual days snow > 1.5 inches	5	6	Hurricane risk score	19	13

Education
Score: 81.6
Rank: 70

ACHIEVEMENT	AREA	U.S. AVG	PUBLIC SCHOOLS	AREA	U.S. AVG	HIGHER EDUCATION	AREA	U.S. AVG
High school degree	85.9%	82.7%	Expenditures per pupil	$8,494	$5,686	No. 2-year colleges	1	4
2-year college degree	7.5%	6.4%	Student/teacher ratio	14.2	16.7	No. 4-year colleges/universities	4	6
4-year college degree	15.1%	15.7%	Attending public school	92.5%	90.1%	No. highly ranked universities	2	1
Graduate/professional degree	10.9%	8.9%	State SAT score	1028*	1021			
			State ACT score	23.1	20.9			

Health & Healthcare
Score: 23.8
Rank: 284

HAZARDS & ILLNESSES	AREA	U.S. AVG	HEALTHCARE	AREA	U.S. AVG	CRIME	AREA	U.S. AVG
Air-quality score	40	37	Physicians per capita	212.9	244.2	Violent crime rate	331.4	465.5
Water-quality score	63	52	Hospital beds per capita	164.3	420.0	Change in violent crime rate	-12.7%	-2.2%
Pollen/allergy score	56	61	No. teaching hospitals	1	3	Property crime rate	2,578.8	3,517.1
Cancer mortality per capita	215.7	201.9	Cost per doctor visit	$85	$77	Change in property crime rate	-3.8%	-2.1%
Depression days per month	3.3	3.5	Cost per dental visit	$96	$70			
Stress score	34	50						

Crime
Score: 85.6
Rank: 55

Transportation
Score: 86.6
Rank: 51

COMMUTE	AREA	U.S. AVG	INTERCITY SERVICES	AREA	U.S. AVG	AUTOMOTIVE	AREA	U.S. AVG
Average commute time	24.2	27.4	Major airports within 60 miles	2	1	Insurance, annual premium	$1,474	$1,432
Percent commutes > 60 mins.	5.5%	5.9%	Size of regional airport	Large	Large	Gas, cost per gallon	$2.55	$2.49
Commute by auto	81.0%	78.9%	Daily airline activity	1275	686	Daily vehicle miles per capita	32.5	24.0
Commute by mass transit	1.6%	1.9%	Amtrak service	Yes	No			
Work at home	2.6%	3.1%						
Mass transit miles per capita	1.57	1.87						

Leisure
Score: 64.4
Rank: 133

DINING & SHOPPING	AREA	U.S. AVG	ENTERTAINMENT	AREA	U.S. AVG	OUTDOOR ACTIVITIES	AREA	U.S. AVG
Restaurant rating	1	2	Professional sports rating	3	4	Golf-course rating	6	4
Outlet mall score	152	42	College sports rating	6	4	Ski-area rating	6	3
No. Starbucks	2	13	Zoo/aquarium rating	2	3	Sq. miles inland water	3	4
No. warehouse clubs	1	2	Amusement park rating	1	3	Miles of coastline	0.0	10.7
			Botanical garden/arboretum rating	2	4	National Park rating	1	3

Arts & Culture
Score: 93.9
Rank: 24

MEDIA & LIBRARIES	AREA	U.S. AVG	PERFORMING ARTS	AREA	U.S. AVG	MUSEUMS	AREA	U.S. AVG
Arts radio rating	5	3	Classical music rating	10	4	Overall museum rating	8	5
No. public libraries	21	27	Ballet/dance rating	5	3	Art museum rating	6	5
Library volumes per capita	3.04	2.78	Professional theater rating	8	3	Science museum rating	8	5
			University arts programs rating	9	5	Children's museum rating	6	3

TEMPERATURE

PRECIPITATION

DAYS OF CLOUDS & PRECIPITATION

Oakland–Fremont–Hayward, CA

Score: 69.2   **Rank:** 97   **2004 rank:** 165

Profile: Large-city/suburban complex
Location: Northern California, on the east shore of San Francisco Bay
Elevation: 6 feet
Time zone: Pacific Standard Time

PRO	CON
Year-round climate	Cost of living and housing
Entertainment	Crowding and sprawl
Close to San Francisco	Long commutes

The Oakland–Fremont–Hayward area covers most of the inhabitable land along the east shore of the San Francisco Bay and east along the Suisun Bay, and is known locally as the "East Bay." It is made up of two counties, Alameda and Contra Costa. The more level areas close to water have been developed into a mix of industrial, commercial, and port areas, while residential, retail, and light manufacturing cover most level land up to the limits of the steep Diablo Range that sits behind the area. Oakland itself has a large and fairly modern but wholly uninteresting downtown, especially compared to its more famous neighbor across the Bay. Areas of small older California-style homes spread east toward the East Bay Hills, and the more upscale communities of Orinda and Moraga line the State Route 24 corridor, a major pass through the mountains. But gritty industrial and lower-class residential areas surround the downtown, except for the attractive Jack London Square commercial and entertainment district at the water. Alameda Island, just west across a narrow estuary and once mainly industrial, is starting to attract some new high-density residences to take advantage of the prime bayside location, but with few exceptions, Oakland itself isn't a particularly desirable place to live.

Smaller cities and suburban towns fill the rail and highway corridors north and south of Oakland and turning east along the Suisun Bay. The list of residential areas is long. Berkeley to the north is the famous college town and home to the largest University of California campus. It has a strong multicultural flavor and excellent homes especially in the hills near campus, but is expensive and a bit weird for some people. Between Oakland and Berkeley is the once-industrial Emeryville, now reclaimed with excellent new high-density housing, shopping, hospitality centers, and loft-style offices surrounding a recently completed main rail and regional transit hub for the Bay Area. Richmond and San Pablo, north of Berkeley, are very gritty industrial port and former Navy areas. New homes, some in planned communities with pleasing architectural and design setups, are emerging in Pinole, with nice views of the Bay in one direction and oil refineries in Hercules in another. Martinez is another refinery town but has some older charm and is on the upswing. The more affordable and family-oriented suburban developments are in Contra Costa County, including Concord, Pittsburg, and Antioch. These communities offer extensive newer California-style home choices and good local amenities, but naturally, commutes aren't easy. Many commute to large commercial centers in Walnut Creek, Danville, San Ramon, and Pleasanton along the Interstate 680 corridor, where the area's fastest growth is occurring. These communities also have attractive residential and retail areas but show many of the usual signs of having grown too fast.

Hayward, Fremont, and Union City are among the larger communities spreading south from Oakland along the Bay and Interstate 880.

They have grown together into one sprawling city-suburb. Hayward is older and not particularly interesting, but does have some new high-tech industry and convenient access to the San Francisco Peninsula across the San Mateo Bridge. There is also a California State University campus. Union City, despite the name, is mainly residential, while Fremont is the newest city in the area, with newer housing and a larger high-tech presence as it starts to blend into the Silicon Valley areas in San Jose and Santa Clara County to the south. It also has a major auto assembly plant.

Be warned: These areas are almost all crowded, stressful, and expensive. But relative to other areas in the San Francisco Bay area, some find them a bargain, and some of the more family-oriented communities are in this area, particularly in Contra Costa County. Job growth is strong, and the industrial base is more diverse than either San Francisco or the Silicon Valley. The area has a full set of amenities, including air and rail transportation, healthcare, education, arts, and entertainment amenities, and that which isn't found in the immediate vicinity is available in San Francisco or other parts of the Bay Area. The excellent Mediterranean climate is a big plus. But there are more gritty areas than elsewhere in the Bay Area, and neighborhoods must be chosen carefully. The area's ethnicities, appearance, and amenities are characterized by diversity. Commutes are complex and long, but the Bay Area Rapid Transit system (BART) makes commuting easier, especially to San Francisco. Many outlying valleys contain unattractive areas of commercial and residential sprawl, exemplified by Walnut Creek and Pleasanton, with accompanying commute, air-quality, crowding, and aesthetic issues.

Cost of living and commute times are the main negatives for the area. The Cost of Living Index of 171.9 is high by any standard, and median home prices are probably understated due to the abundance of low-end housing in industrial areas. The reported 35-minute commute time is the worst on the West Coast. Crime is high, but has improved somewhat in recent years. The area, like many in California, has a lot to offer, but also a lot to watch out for.

Oakland and many of the towns to the north and south are located on a mostly level coastal plain west of the 4,000-foot Diablo Range. Remaining natural vegetation is grassland with a few oak and coniferous trees. The marine air cools the area in summer and keeps it relatively mild in winter. Low stratus clouds, known locally as "fog," frequently blow in from the Pacific, particularly along the east shore of the bay, and may burn off or may linger all day. When the fog dissipates, expect sunny, mild weather in all seasons, except when winter rainstorms are present. Summer temperatures seldom reach the 90s along the bay, but can be warmer inland. Winter temperatures are seldom below freezing. Most rain occurs in winter.

Population

DEMOGRAPHICS	AREA	U.S. AVG	ETHNIC COMPOSITION	AREA	U.S. AVG	RESIDENT PROFILE	AREA	U.S. AVG
Population	2,500,934		White	52.5%	79.0%	Single	34.9%	32.4%
Population density per sq. mile	1715.9	358.5	Black	11.8%	10.5%	Married	49.2%	52.7%
Population growth	20.3%	21.1%	Asian	19.2%	2.7%	Divorced/separated	15.9%	14.9%
Median age	36.7	36.1	Hispanic	20.8%	10.6%	Married with children	24.8%	23.7%
Percent Democrat	69.9%	44.5%	Religious observance	36.6%	48.9%	Single with children	8.9%	9.1%
Percent Republican	28.6%	54.5%	Diversity measure	76.7	40.1	Percent over age 65	10.9%	12.9%

Economy & Jobs

Score: 46.0
Rank: 203

INCOME	AREA	U.S. AVG	EMPLOYMENT	AREA	U.S. AVG	EMPLOYING INDUSTRIES	AREA	U.S. AVG
Per capita income	$33,012	$23,235	Unemployment rate	5.1%	4.7%	Largest: Manufacturing		
Household income	$69,319	$46,414	Recent job growth	2.9%	1.3%			
Household income < $25K	16.2%	26.2%	Projected future job growth	12.6%	11.5%	Percent manufacturing	10.5%	15.4%
Household income > $75K	45.9%	25.4%	White collar	68.6%	57.8%	Percent public sector	14.5%	15.7%
Household income growth	17.4%	13.6%	Blue collar	18.6%	25.2%	Percent construction	8.1%	9.9%

Cost of Living

Score: 1.6
Rank: 367

INDEXES & TAXES	AREA	U.S. AVG	HOUSING	AREA	U.S. AVG	NECESSITIES	AREA	U.S. AVG
Cost of Living Index	171.9	100.0	Median home price	$572,400	$220,000	Food Index	119.8	100.0
Buying Power Index	90.4	100.0	Home price appreciation	76.6%	10.1%	Housing Index	251.8	100.0
Income tax rate	6.00%	4.70%	Median rent	$1,250	$709	Utilities Index	127.0	100.0
Sales tax rate	8.55%	6.58%	Homes owned	58.6%	62.3%	Transportation Index	122.5	100.0
Property tax rate	$8.21	$12.00	Home price ratio	8.3	4.2	Healthcare Index	153.4	100.0
						Miscellaneous Cost Index	107.5	100.0

Climate

Score: 99.2
Rank: 4

TEMPERATURE	AREA	U.S. AVG	PRECIPITATION	AREA	U.S. AVG	COMFORTS & HAZARDS	AREA	U.S. AVG
Average January low	42.7	26.2	Annual inches precipitation	18.7	37.7	July relative humidity	76%	66%
Average July high	69.7	87.4	Annual inches snowfall	0.0	7.0	Annual days mostly sunny	260	208
Annual days > 90°F	2	38	Annual days precipitation	63	109	Annual days with thunderstorms	2	39
Annual days < 32°F	1	89	Annual days rain > 0.5 inches	12	22	Tornado risk score	2	18
Annual days < 0°F	0	6	Annual days snow > 1.5 inches	0	6	Hurricane risk score	0	13

TEMPERATURE

PRECIPITATION

DAYS OF CLOUDS & PRECIPITATION

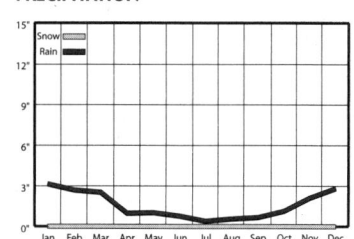

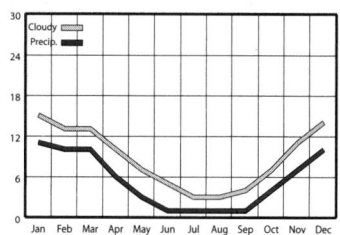

Education

Score: 90.6
Rank: 36

ACHIEVEMENT	AREA	U.S. AVG	PUBLIC SCHOOLS	AREA	U.S. AVG	HIGHER EDUCATION	AREA	U.S. AVG
High school degree	83.9%	82.7%	Expenditures per pupil	$5,221	$5,686	No. 2-year colleges	17	4
2-year college degree	7.2%	6.4%	Student/teacher ratio	20.7	16.7	No. 4-year colleges/universities	29	6
4-year college degree	21.7%	15.7%	Attending public school	88.1%	90.1%	No. highly ranked universities	2	1
Graduate/professional degree	12.8%	8.9%	State SAT score	1019*	1021			
			State ACT score	21.6	20.9			

Health & Healthcare

Score: 0.0
Rank: 373

Crime

Score: 35.0
Rank: 243

HAZARDS & ILLNESSES	AREA	U.S. AVG	HEALTHCARE	AREA	U.S. AVG	CRIME	AREA	U.S. AVG
Air-quality score	14	37	Physicians per capita	240.9	244.2	Violent crime rate	574.9	465.5
Water-quality score	33	52	Hospital beds per capita	230.0	420.0	Change in violent crime rate	8.8%	-2.2%
Pollen/allergy score	93	61	No. teaching hospitals	8	3	Property crime rate	4,119.0	3,517.1
Cancer mortality per capita	163.8	201.9	Cost per doctor visit	$86	$77	Change in property crime rate	-4.7%	-2.1%
Depression days per month	3.7	3.5	Cost per dental visit	$86	$70			
Stress score	69	50						

COMMUTE	AREA	U.S. AVG	INTERCITY SERVICES	AREA	U.S. AVG	AUTOMOTIVE	AREA	U.S. AVG
Average commute time	35.3	27.4	Major airports within 60 miles	4	1	Insurance, annual premium	$2,312	$1,432
Percent commutes > 60 mins.	16.3%	5.9%	Size of regional airport	Large	Large	Gas, cost per gallon	$2.66	$2.49
Commute by auto	68.1%	78.9%	Daily airline activity	1197	686	Daily vehicle miles per capita	14.4	24.0
Commute by mass transit	9.8%	1.9%	Amtrak service	Yes	No			
Work at home	3.8%	3.1%						
Mass transit miles per capita	9.84	1.87						

Transportation **Score:** 30.5 **Rank:** 260

DINING & SHOPPING	AREA	U.S. AVG	ENTERTAINMENT	AREA	U.S. AVG	OUTDOOR ACTIVITIES	AREA	U.S. AVG
Restaurant rating	1	2	Professional sports rating	10	4	Golf-course rating	7	4
Outlet mall score	88	42	College sports rating	9	4	Ski-area rating	9	3
No. Starbucks	112	13	Zoo/aquarium rating	5	3	Sq. miles inland water	10	4
No. warehouse clubs	9	2	Amusement park rating	5	3	Miles of coastline	0.0	10.7
			Botanical garden/ arboretum rating	8	4	National Park rating	4	3

Leisure **Score:** 96.5 **Rank:** 14

MEDIA & LIBRARIES	AREA	U.S. AVG	PERFORMING ARTS	AREA	U.S. AVG	MUSEUMS	AREA	U.S. AVG
Arts radio rating	4	3	Classical music rating	8	4	Overall museum rating	10	5
No. public libraries	69	27	Ballet/dance rating	10	3	Art museum rating	9	5
Library volumes per capita	2.20	2.78	Professional theater rating	9	3	Science museum rating	9	5
			University arts programs rating	10	5	Children's museum rating	10	3

Arts & Culture **Score:** 89.0 **Rank:** 42

Ocala, FL

Score: 61.4   Rank: 162   2004 rank: 58

Profile: Small city
Location: Central Florida, 60 miles east of Daytona Beach
Elevation: 75 feet
Time zone: Eastern Standard Time

PRO	CON
Economy	Hot, humid summers
Attractive downtown	Isolation
Nearby recreation	Violent crime

Ocala, a small agricultural and manufacturing center, is about halfway between Gainesville to the north and Orlando to the southeast. With its attractive tree-lined streets and Old South–style homes, it more resembles a typical Southern city than a Florida city or beach town. Ocala is the capital of Florida's thoroughbred industry, and ranching and horse-breeding are popular. Just east of town is the Ocala National Forest, a preserve of Florida pines, cypress, and hardwood trees with water and plenty of recreation. The area has above-average historic and natural interest. Manufacturing is mostly light, with household goods, auto parts, and some electronics manufacturing, and recent employment trends are favorable. Cost of living and housing prices, following Florida trends, have grown and are partly responsible for the lower ranking this time. The location is a bit isolated from Orlando's services and amenities, 75 miles away.

The level area is characterized by a mix of open land and areas of medium-size trees, some tropical in nature. Summers are warm and humid with maximum temperatures averaging a little more than 90°F. Winters are mild with daytime temperatures in the 60s and 70s but with some occasional freezing. Rainfall is appreciable in every month but most comes from summer afternoon showers and thunderstorms. Ocala does not have a serious hurricane risk because of its inland location.

DEMOGRAPHICS	AREA	U.S. AVG	ETHNIC COMPOSITION	AREA	U.S. AVG	RESIDENT PROFILE	AREA	U.S. AVG
Population	291,640		White	83.2%	79.0%	Single	26.1%	32.4%
Population density per sq. mile	184.7	358.5	Black	11.9%	10.5%	Married	58.1%	52.7%
Population growth	49.7%	21.1%	Asian	0.9%	2.7%	Divorced/separated	15.8%	14.9%
Median age	43.6	36.1	Hispanic	7.3%	10.6%	Married with children	15.9%	23.7%
Percent Democrat	41.0%	44.5%	Religious observance	34.4%	48.9%	Single with children	7.8%	9.1%
Percent Republican	58.2%	54.5%	Diversity measure	38.9	40.1	Percent over age 65	24.2%	12.9%

Population

INCOME	AREA	U.S. AVG	EMPLOYMENT	AREA	U.S. AVG	EMPLOYING INDUSTRIES	AREA	U.S. AVG
Per capita income	$20,233	$23,235	Unemployment rate	3.9%	4.7%	Largest: Healthcare & Social Assistance		
Household income	$36,373	$46,414	Recent job growth	4.1%	1.3%			
Household income < $25K	32.5%	26.2%	Projected future job growth	22.9%	11.5%	Percent manufacturing	14.5%	15.4%
Household income > $75K	15.2%	25.4%	White collar	54.1%	57.8%	Percent public sector	13.4%	15.7%
Household income growth	13.9%	13.6%	Blue collar	26.4%	25.2%	Percent construction	12.0%	9.9%

Economy & Jobs **Score:** 90.6 **Rank:** 36

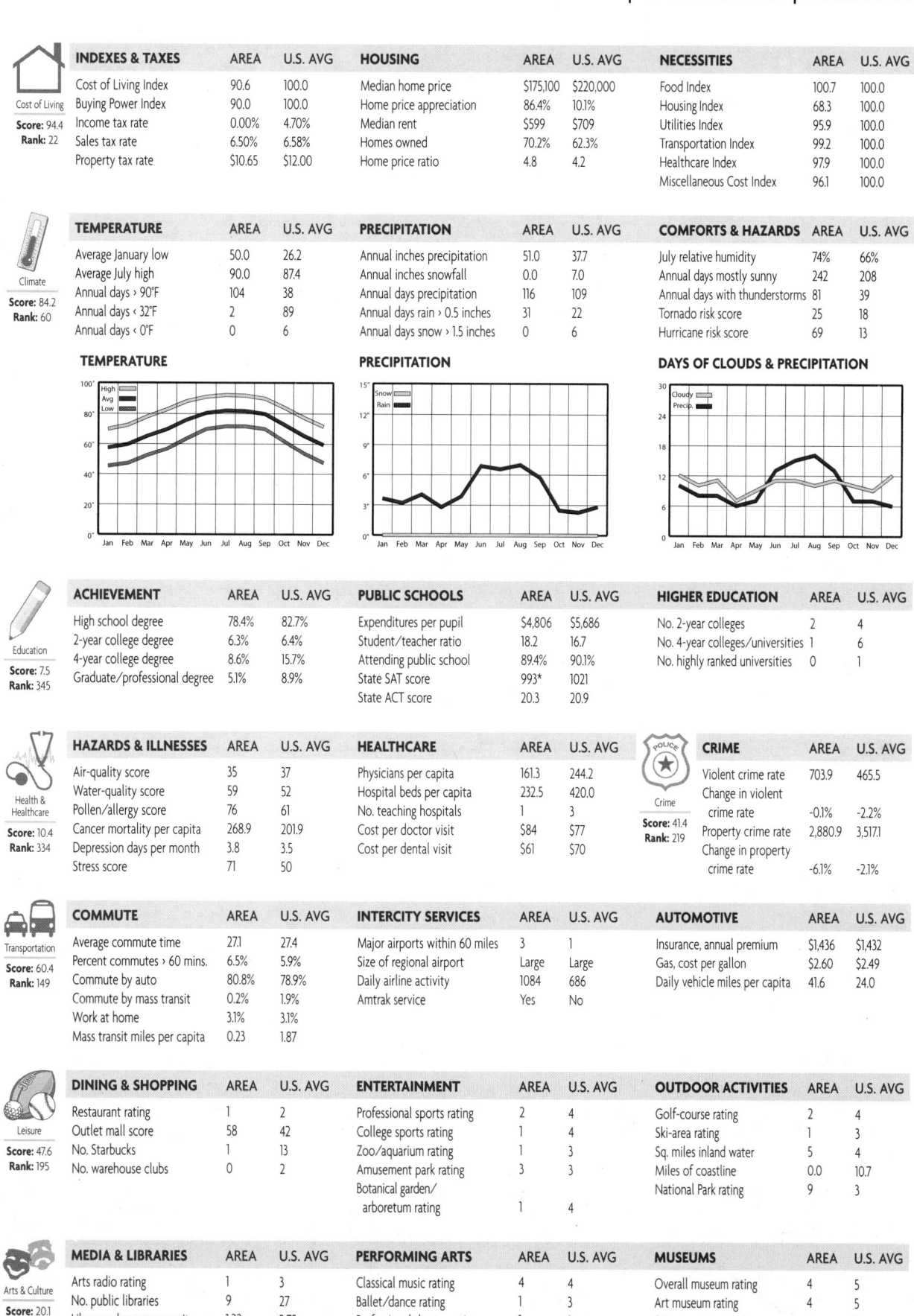

Cost of Living
Score: 94.4
Rank: 22

INDEXES & TAXES	AREA	U.S. AVG
Cost of Living Index	90.6	100.0
Buying Power Index	90.0	100.0
Income tax rate	0.00%	4.70%
Sales tax rate	6.50%	6.58%
Property tax rate	$10.65	$12.00

HOUSING	AREA	U.S. AVG
Median home price	$175,100	$220,000
Home price appreciation	86.4%	10.1%
Median rent	$599	$709
Homes owned	70.2%	62.3%
Home price ratio	4.8	4.2

NECESSITIES	AREA	U.S. AVG
Food Index	100.7	100.0
Housing Index	68.3	100.0
Utilities Index	95.9	100.0
Transportation Index	99.2	100.0
Healthcare Index	97.9	100.0
Miscellaneous Cost Index	96.1	100.0

Climate
Score: 84.2
Rank: 60

TEMPERATURE	AREA	U.S. AVG
Average January low	50.0	26.2
Average July high	90.0	87.4
Annual days > 90°F	104	38
Annual days < 32°F	2	89
Annual days < 0°F	0	6

PRECIPITATION	AREA	U.S. AVG
Annual inches precipitation	51.0	37.7
Annual inches snowfall	0.0	7.0
Annual days precipitation	116	109
Annual days rain > 0.5 inches	31	22
Annual days snow > 1.5 inches	0	6

COMFORTS & HAZARDS	AREA	U.S. AVG
July relative humidity	74%	66%
Annual days mostly sunny	242	208
Annual days with thunderstorms	81	39
Tornado risk score	25	18
Hurricane risk score	69	13

TEMPERATURE — High / Avg / Low

PRECIPITATION — Snow / Rain

DAYS OF CLOUDS & PRECIPITATION — Cloudy / Precip.

Education
Score: 7.5
Rank: 345

ACHIEVEMENT	AREA	U.S. AVG
High school degree	78.4%	82.7%
2-year college degree	6.3%	6.4%
4-year college degree	8.6%	15.7%
Graduate/professional degree	5.1%	8.9%

PUBLIC SCHOOLS	AREA	U.S. AVG
Expenditures per pupil	$4,806	$5,686
Student/teacher ratio	18.2	16.7
Attending public school	89.4%	90.1%
State SAT score	993*	1021
State ACT score	20.3	20.9

HIGHER EDUCATION	AREA	U.S. AVG
No. 2-year colleges	2	4
No. 4-year colleges/universities	1	6
No. highly ranked universities	0	1

Health & Healthcare
Score: 10.4
Rank: 334

HAZARDS & ILLNESSES	AREA	U.S. AVG
Air-quality score	35	37
Water-quality score	59	52
Pollen/allergy score	76	61
Cancer mortality per capita	268.9	201.9
Depression days per month	3.8	3.5
Stress score	71	50

HEALTHCARE	AREA	U.S. AVG
Physicians per capita	161.3	244.2
Hospital beds per capita	232.5	420.0
No. teaching hospitals	1	3
Cost per doctor visit	$84	$77
Cost per dental visit	$61	$70

Crime
Score: 41.4
Rank: 219

CRIME	AREA	U.S. AVG
Violent crime rate	703.9	465.5
Change in violent crime rate	-0.1%	-2.2%
Property crime rate	2,880.9	3,517.1
Change in property crime rate	-6.1%	-2.1%

Transportation
Score: 60.4
Rank: 149

COMMUTE	AREA	U.S. AVG
Average commute time	27.1	27.4
Percent commutes > 60 mins.	6.5%	5.9%
Commute by auto	80.8%	78.9%
Commute by mass transit	0.2%	1.9%
Work at home	3.1%	3.1%
Mass transit miles per capita	0.23	1.87

INTERCITY SERVICES	AREA	U.S. AVG
Major airports within 60 miles	3	1
Size of regional airport	Large	Large
Daily airline activity	1084	686
Amtrak service	Yes	No

AUTOMOTIVE	AREA	U.S. AVG
Insurance, annual premium	$1,436	$1,432
Gas, cost per gallon	$2.60	$2.49
Daily vehicle miles per capita	41.6	24.0

Leisure
Score: 47.6
Rank: 195

DINING & SHOPPING	AREA	U.S. AVG
Restaurant rating	1	2
Outlet mall score	58	42
No. Starbucks	1	13
No. warehouse clubs	0	2

ENTERTAINMENT	AREA	U.S. AVG
Professional sports rating	2	4
College sports rating	1	4
Zoo/aquarium rating	1	3
Amusement park rating	3	3
Botanical garden/ arboretum rating	1	4

OUTDOOR ACTIVITIES	AREA	U.S. AVG
Golf-course rating	2	4
Ski-area rating	1	3
Sq. miles inland water	5	4
Miles of coastline	0.0	10.7
National Park rating	9	3

Arts & Culture
Score: 20.1
Rank: 298

MEDIA & LIBRARIES	AREA	U.S. AVG
Arts radio rating	1	3
No. public libraries	9	27
Library volumes per capita	1.22	2.78

PERFORMING ARTS	AREA	U.S. AVG
Classical music rating	4	4
Ballet/dance rating	1	3
Professional theater rating	1	3
University arts programs rating	1	5

MUSEUMS	AREA	U.S. AVG
Overall museum rating	4	5
Art museum rating	4	5
Science museum rating	4	5
Children's museum rating	2	3

Ocean City, NJ

Score: 79.7   **Rank:** 45   **2004 rank:** not ranked

Profile: Beach resort town
Location: Southeastern New Jersey, 10 miles south of Atlantic City
Elevation: 19 feet
Time zone: Eastern Standard Time

PRO
Beach areas
Calm ambience
Pleasant summers

CON
Dependence on tourism
Tourist impact
Cost of living

When you think of Ocean City, you really think of the 45-mile stretch of shoreline and barrier islands between Cape May at the southernmost tip and Ocean City, just south of the bustling and quite-different Atlantic City. This area, really defined as Cape May County, has been an established family-oriented resort and tourist destination for years. Unlike Atlantic City, it isn't on the national and international radar but is enjoyed mostly by vacationers from nearby East Coast cities, the nearest of which is Philadelphia. Ocean City itself sits on an easily accessed barrier island, and is clean and mainly tourist-oriented and has a waterfront boardwalk characteristic of the region. Boating, beach, and water activities dominate, and music and live entertainment is usually readily available. Although having the infrastructure and flavor typical of nearby beach towns, it has resisted the development of ugly sprawl, high-rise buildings, and in-your-face beach tourism common in many other so-called "beach towns."

Cost of living and especially housing are high but not unreasonable for a coastal area, and in keeping with the low-growth character of the area, future job growth is fairly weak while current employment is healthy.

Surrounding terrain is mainly flat and treeless and sandy near the shore, with numerous tidal marshes. Most vegetation consists of grass and low underbrush, transitioning to farmland and some wooded areas away from shore. For the region, the year-round climate is quite pleasant, with Atlantic waters moderating both summer heat and winter cold. Sea breezes keep summer morning and afternoon temperatures in the 80s. Precipitation is evenly distributed through the year, but there is some hurricane and tropical storm risk in late summer and fall. "Noreasters" traveling up the coast can bring heavy rain all seasons and some rain-snow mix or heavy snow. Snow accumulations are far more likely inland. First freeze is late October; last is mid-April.

Population

DEMOGRAPHICS	AREA	U.S. AVG
Population	101,848	
Population density per sq. mile	399.1	358.5
Population growth	7.1%	21.1%
Median age	43.3	36.1
Percent Democrat	42.3%	44.5%
Percent Republican	56.8%	54.5%

ETHNIC COMPOSITION	AREA	U.S. AVG
White	92.1%	79.0%
Black	4.7%	10.5%
Asian	0.6%	2.7%
Hispanic	3.7%	10.6%
Religious observance	46.5%	48.9%
Diversity measure	21.0	40.1

RESIDENT PROFILE	AREA	U.S. AVG
Single	32.9%	32.4%
Married	53.7%	52.7%
Divorced/separated	13.5%	14.9%
Married with children	18.4%	23.7%
Single with children	7.4%	9.1%
Percent over age 65	20.6%	12.9%

Economy & Jobs
Score: 19.3
Rank: 302

INCOME	AREA	U.S. AVG
Per capita income	$28,363	$23,235
Household income	$48,213	$46,414
Household income < $25K	23.9%	26.2%
Household income > $75K	29.6%	25.4%
Household income growth	15.9%	13.6%

EMPLOYMENT	AREA	U.S. AVG
Unemployment rate	3.9%	4.7%
Recent job growth	1.1%	1.3%
Projected future job growth	3.0%	11.5%
White collar	58.6%	57.8%
Blue collar	19.2%	25.2%

EMPLOYING INDUSTRIES	AREA	U.S. AVG
Largest: Retail trade		
Percent manufacturing	8.0%	15.4%
Percent public sector	19.9%	15.7%
Percent construction	11.2%	9.9%

Cost of Living
Score: 25.4
Rank: 278

INDEXES & TAXES	AREA	U.S. AVG
Cost of Living Index	123.9	100.0
Buying Power Index	87.2	100.0
Income tax rate	2.45%	4.70%
Sales tax rate	6.00%	6.58%
Property tax rate	$16.33	$12.00

HOUSING	AREA	U.S. AVG
Median home price	$357,900	$220,000
Home price appreciation	145.4%	10.1%
Median rent	$834	$709
Homes owned	34.4%	62.3%
Home price ratio	7.4	4.2

NECESSITIES	AREA	U.S. AVG
Food Index	103.4	100.0
Housing Index	83.0	100.0
Utilities Index	124.1	100.0
Transportation Index	98.8	100.0
Healthcare Index	95.5	100.0
Miscellaneous Cost Index	101.3	100.0

Climate
Score: 93.3
Rank: 26

TEMPERATURE	AREA	U.S. AVG
Average January low	22.0	26.2
Average July high	84.0	87.4
Annual days > 90°F	16	38
Annual days < 32°F	15	89
Annual days < 0°F	1	6

PRECIPITATION	AREA	U.S. AVG
Annual inches precipitation	40.7	37.7
Annual inches snowfall	18.0	7.0
Annual days precipitation	111	109
Annual days rain > 0.5 inches	26	22
Annual days snow > 1.5 inches	4	6

COMFORTS & HAZARDS	AREA	U.S. AVG
July relative humidity	57%	66%
Annual days mostly sunny	204	208
Annual days with thunderstorms	25	39
Tornado risk score	5	18
Hurricane risk score	25	13

TEMPERATURE

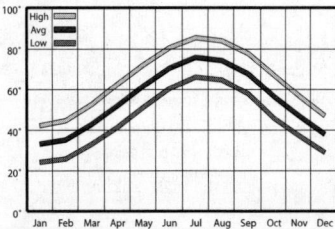

PRECIPITATION

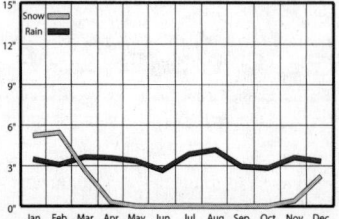

DAYS OF CLOUDS & PRECIPITATION

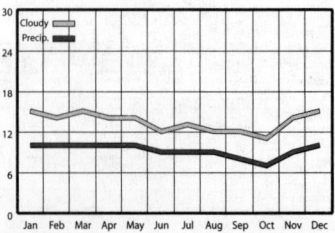

ACHIEVEMENT	AREA	U.S. AVG	PUBLIC SCHOOLS	AREA	U.S. AVG	HIGHER EDUCATION	AREA	U.S. AVG
High school degree	81.9%	82.7%	Expenditures per pupil	$10,496	$5,686	No. 2-year colleges	0	4
2-year college degree	5.3%	6.4%	Student/teacher ratio	11.7	16.7	No. 4-year colleges/universities	0	6
4-year college degree	15.5%	15.7%	Attending public school	89.1%	90.1%	No. highly ranked universities	0	1
Graduate/professional degree	6.6%	8.9%	State SAT score	1011*	1021			
			State ACT score	21.8	20.9			

Education
Score: 46.5
Rank: 201

HAZARDS & ILLNESSES	AREA	U.S. AVG	HEALTHCARE	AREA	U.S. AVG	CRIME	AREA	U.S. AVG
Air-quality score	51	37	Physicians per capita	175.8	244.2	Violent crime rate	307.0	465.5
Water-quality score	20	52	Hospital beds per capita	253.3	420.0	Change in violent crime rate	-15.6%	-2.2%
Pollen/allergy score	58	61	No. teaching hospitals	0	3	Property crime rate	4,438.5	3,517.1
Cancer mortality per capita	231.7	201.9	Cost per doctor visit	$69	$77	Change in property crime rate	0.2%	-2.1%
Depression days per month	3.6	3.5	Cost per dental visit	$85	$70			
Stress score	44	50						

Health & Healthcare
Score: 37.2
Rank: 234

Crime
Score: 40.9
Rank: 221

COMMUTE	AREA	U.S. AVG	INTERCITY SERVICES	AREA	U.S. AVG	AUTOMOTIVE	AREA	U.S. AVG
Average commute time	25.0	27.4	Major airports within 60 miles	1	1	Insurance, annual premium	$1,788	$1,432
Percent commutes > 60 mins.	8.4%	5.9%	Size of regional airport	Large	Large	Gas, cost per gallon	$2.32	$2.49
Commute by auto	80.2%	78.9%	Daily airline activity	669	686	Daily vehicle miles per capita	18.1	24.0
Commute by mass transit	1.8%	1.9%	Amtrak service	No	No			
Work at home	2.8%	3.1%						
Mass transit miles per capita	1.80	1.87						

Transportation
Score: 47.1
Rank: 199

DINING & SHOPPING	AREA	U.S. AVG	ENTERTAINMENT	AREA	U.S. AVG	OUTDOOR ACTIVITIES	AREA	U.S. AVG
Restaurant rating	1	2	Professional sports rating	8	4	Golf-course rating	6	4
Outlet mall score	82	42	College sports rating	3	4	Ski-area rating	3	3
No. Starbucks	0	13	Zoo/aquarium rating	8	3	Sq. miles inland water	6	4
No. warehouse clubs	0	2	Amusement park rating	6	3	Miles of coastline	53.2	10.7
			Botanical garden/ arboretum rating	9	4	National Park rating	3	3

Leisure
Score: 84.8
Rank: 57

MEDIA & LIBRARIES	AREA	U.S. AVG	PERFORMING ARTS	AREA	U.S. AVG	MUSEUMS	AREA	U.S. AVG
Arts radio rating	8	3	Classical music rating	7	4	Overall museum rating	7	5
No. public libraries	9	27	Ballet/dance rating	5	3	Art museum rating	1	5
Library volumes per capita	4.77	2.78	Professional theater rating	5	3	Science museum rating	8	5
			University arts programs rating	3	5	Children's museum rating	1	3

Arts & Culture
Score: 85.6
Rank: 55

Ogden–Clearfield, UT

Score: 92.8   Rank: 6   2004 rank: 84

Profile: Mid-size city/suburban complex
Location: North-central Utah, 40 miles north of Salt Lake City
Elevation: 4,300 feet
Time zone: Mountain Standard Time

PRO	CON
Attractive setting	Growth and sprawl
Nearby recreation	Air quality
Climate	Nightlife

The Salt Lake Valley, anchored by the political and Mormon community capital Salt Lake City, is a prosperous, rapidly growing, energetic, and physically attractive region of the country. At a point just north of Salt Lake City, the valley narrows, then widens out again giving a flat plain bounded by the Wasatch Mountains suitable for agriculture and urban development. Ogden is at the center of that flat plain, with clean and attractive family-friendly suburban communities spreading south, including Clearfield, Layton, Kaysville, and Farmington. Ogden is sort of the unassuming, shy, but quietly prosperous little sister of the booming Salt Lake City and Provo to the south. The large Hill Air Force Base is a major employer, and the area also hosts a number of mostly technology-oriented manufacturers, large and small, including Thiokol, Iomega, and Levelor, and a large processing center for the IRS. The area is a freight transportation hub, as goods arrive by road and rail through canyons to the east and are rerouted to all points west. Suburbs are plain, clean, well laid out, and affordable. Homes are high quality, with large lots and comfortable neighborhoods with a traditional feel. In part because of the Mormon influence, the area has a strong community feel, with excellent education and healthcare facilities. The Mormon influence also brings conservative social norms and traditions. The Wasatch provide not only an excellent view but also a source of almost limitless mountain recreation, and the rest of the state is a recreational paradise also. Most arts and big-city amenities are found south in Salt Lake City, and many commute that direction to work, although traffic is becoming more of a problem. Cost of living, though growing, is reasonable at 91.0, and median home prices of $171,700 represent a bargain considering the quality of homes in the area. The Ogden area has a lot of strengths and few notable weaknesses, hence the high ranking.

Ogden is located in a 15-mile wide flat valley defined by the Great Salt Lake to the west and the Wasatch Mountains to the east, which rise to peaks exceeding 12,000 feet. The valley rises gradually towards the base of the mountains, with few natural trees until higher elevations are reached in the mountains. The peaks are snowcapped much of the year, providing a stunning scenic backdrop for much of the area. Summers are hot and dry but generally tolerable because of low humidity and cool nights. Winters are cold but usually not severe. Average annual snowfall is under 60 inches in the valley but much higher in the mountains. The lake and mountains together create summer breezes and more precipitation than would otherwise occur in this high-desert environment. Heavy precipitation comes from Pacific storms in spring. First freeze is mid-October; last is late April.

Population

DEMOGRAPHICS	AREA	U.S. AVG	ETHNIC COMPOSITION	AREA	U.S. AVG	RESIDENT PROFILE	AREA	U.S. AVG
Population	476,959		White	89.2%	79.0%	Single	28.6%	32.4%
Population density per sq. mile	320.3	358.5	Black	1.3%	10.5%	Married	59.8%	52.7%
Population growth	35.7%	21.1%	Asian	1.9%	2.7%	Divorced/separated	11.5%	14.9%
Median age	28.8	36.1	Hispanic	9.6%	10.6%	Married with children	37.7%	23.7%
Percent Democrat	22.6%	44.5%	Religious observance	74.9%	48.9%	Single with children	8.0%	9.1%
Percent Republican	75.3%	54.5%	Diversity measure	33.3	40.1	Percent over age 65	8.8%	12.9%

Economy & Jobs
Score: 92.5
Rank: 29

INCOME	AREA	U.S. AVG	EMPLOYMENT	AREA	U.S. AVG	EMPLOYING INDUSTRIES	AREA	U.S. AVG
Per capita income	$22,011	$23,235	Unemployment rate	4.8%	4.7%	Largest: Manufacturing		
Household income	$57,064	$46,414	Recent job growth	3.1%	1.3%			
Household income < $25K	15.6%	26.2%	Projected future job growth	22.7%	11.5%	Percent manufacturing	13.8%	15.4%
Household income > $75K	33.2%	25.4%	White collar	61.9%	57.8%	Percent public sector	20.5%	15.7%
Household income growth	15.3%	13.6%	Blue collar	24.6%	25.2%	Percent construction	10.8%	9.9%

Cost of Living
Score: 33.2
Rank: 249

INDEXES & TAXES	AREA	U.S. AVG	HOUSING	AREA	U.S. AVG	NECESSITIES	AREA	U.S. AVG
Cost of Living Index	91.0	100.0	Median home price	$171,700	$220,000	Food Index	109.7	100.0
Buying Power Index	140.6	100.0	Home price appreciation	17.4%	10.1%	Housing Index	54.1	100.0
Income tax rate	7.00%	4.70%	Median rent	$639	$709	Utilities Index	83.8	100.0
Sales tax rate	6.54%	6.58%	Homes owned	73.8%	62.3%	Transportation Index	100.6	100.0
Property tax rate	$6.82	$12.00	Home price ratio	3.0	4.2	Healthcare Index	92.5	100.0
						Miscellaneous Cost Index	99.3	100.0

Climate
Score: 29.7
Rank: 262

TEMPERATURE	AREA	U.S. AVG	PRECIPITATION	AREA	U.S. AVG	COMFORTS & HAZARDS	AREA	U.S. AVG
Average January low	18.5	26.2	Annual inches precipitation	15.0	37.7	July relative humidity	54%	66%
Average July high	92.8	87.4	Annual inches snowfall	58.0	7.0	Annual days mostly sunny	232	208
Annual days > 90°F	58	38	Annual days precipitation	88	109	Annual days with thunderstorms	35	39
Annual days < 32°F	134	89	Annual days rain > 0.5 inches	7	22	Tornado risk score	6	18
Annual days < 0°F	3	6	Annual days snow > 1.5 inches	14	6	Hurricane risk score	0	13

TEMPERATURE

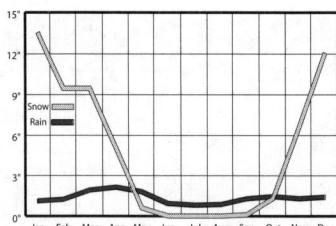

PRECIPITATION

DAYS OF CLOUDS & PRECIPITATION

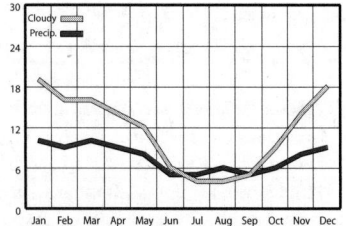

Education
Score: 71.4
Rank: 108

ACHIEVEMENT	AREA	U.S. AVG	PUBLIC SCHOOLS	AREA	U.S. AVG	HIGHER EDUCATION	AREA	U.S. AVG
High school degree	89.5%	82.7%	Expenditures per pupil	$3,785	$5,686	No. 2-year colleges	5	4
2-year college degree	8.2%	6.4%	Student/teacher ratio	20.9	16.7	No. 4-year colleges/universities	2	6
4-year college degree	17.9%	15.7%	Attending public school	97.2%	90.1%	No. highly ranked universities	0	1
Graduate/professional degree	7.1%	8.9%	State SAT score	1117	1021			
			State ACT score	21.7*	20.9			

Health & Healthcare
Score: 71.1
Rank: 109

Crime
Score: 93.3
Rank: 26

HAZARDS & ILLNESSES	AREA	U.S. AVG	HEALTHCARE	AREA	U.S. AVG	CRIME	AREA	U.S. AVG
Air-quality score	39	37	Physicians per capita	139.8	244.2	Violent crime rate	174.2	465.5
Water-quality score	60	52	Hospital beds per capita	273.6	420.0	Change in violent crime rate	-1.5%	-2.2%
Pollen/allergy score	60	61	No. teaching hospitals	2	3			
Cancer mortality per capita	104.8	201.9	Cost per doctor visit	$70	$77	Property crime rate	3,128.9	3,517.1
Depression days per month	3.3	3.5	Cost per dental visit	$56	$70	Change in property crime rate	-2.6%	-2.1%
Stress score	16	50						

Transportation
Score: 41.2
Rank: 220

COMMUTE	AREA	U.S. AVG	INTERCITY SERVICES	AREA	U.S. AVG	AUTOMOTIVE	AREA	U.S. AVG
Average commute time	24.3	27.4	Major airports within 60 miles	1	1	Insurance, annual premium	$1,328	$1,432
Percent commutes > 60 mins.	6.0%	5.9%	Size of regional airport	Large	Large	Gas, cost per gallon	$2.24	$2.49
Commute by auto	78.9%	78.9%	Daily airline activity	452	686	Daily vehicle miles per capita	22.0	24.0
Commute by mass transit	1.8%	1.9%	Amtrak service	No	No			
Work at home	3.7%	3.1%						
Mass transit miles per capita	1.77	1.87						

Leisure
Score: 89.6
Rank: 40

DINING & SHOPPING	AREA	U.S. AVG	ENTERTAINMENT	AREA	U.S. AVG	OUTDOOR ACTIVITIES	AREA	U.S. AVG
Restaurant rating	1	2	Professional sports rating	6	4	Golf-course rating	5	4
Outlet mall score	0	42	College sports rating	6	4	Ski-area rating	10	3
No. Starbucks	1	13	Zoo/aquarium rating	7	3	Sq. miles inland water	10	4
No. warehouse clubs	4	2	Amusement park rating	3	3	Miles of coastline	0.0	10.7
			Botanical garden/ arboretum rating	6	4	National Park rating	8	3

Arts & Culture
Score: 79.7
Rank: 76

MEDIA & LIBRARIES	AREA	U.S. AVG	PERFORMING ARTS	AREA	U.S. AVG	MUSEUMS	AREA	U.S. AVG
Arts radio rating	9	3	Classical music rating	6	4	Overall museum rating	8	5
No. public libraries	11	27	Ballet/dance rating	5	3	Art museum rating	6	5
Library volumes per capita	1.99	2.78	Professional theater rating	9	3	Science museum rating	6	5
			University arts programs rating	4	5	Children's museum rating	3	3

Oklahoma City, OK

Score: 58.6   Rank: 185   2004 rank: 161

Profile: Capital city
Location: Center of Oklahoma
Elevation: 1,304 feet
Time zone: Central Standard Time

PRO	CON
Cost of living	Growth and sprawl
Revitalizing economy	Crime rates
Attractive downtown	Severe storms and heat

Oklahoma City, the capital and largest city in the state, is a major center for the oil industry and related manufacturing. The city has a boomtown past reflected in its infrastructure—with patches of prosperity mixed in with expanses of dull, haphazard, oil-well-studded growth, much of which became run-down during its downturns. For most of its life, Oklahoma City, known locally as "OKC," has been considered a fairly dull city located in a dull part of the country, but that is changing. The last oil bust in the 1990s and the 1995 Murrah Federal Building bombing tragedy seemed to spark something in the city, and it has undergone a major renaissance, particularly in its downtown areas funded in part by a well-supported sales tax initiative. Downtown is now clean and modern with unusually attractive parks and a nicely restored "Bricktown" historic residential and entertainment district with a canal and promenade. A new art museum, library, and performing arts center, and new sports facilities dot the area, and the area also has a noted zoo and science museum. There is a strong set of minor league sports, and recent experience as temporary host for the displaced New Orleans Hornets may help OKC to be a major league city

some day. The University of Oklahoma in suburban Norman south of town brings a college-town element. The oil industry still dominates the local economy, but the state government and an increasing base of small manufacturers and service businesses are starting to balance things out. The Cost of Living Index of 81.9 is a big attraction. Crime rates are a negative, but overall this friendly city seems to be better than its old reputation and seems to be headed for better times.

The area is located along the frequently dry North Canadian River. The surrounding country contains the gently rolling Arbuckle Mountains, 80 miles south. Summers are long and usually hot. Temperatures reach 100°F about 10 times a year, but can last 50 days or more. Breezes and relatively low humidity temper the heat somewhat. Winters are comparatively mild and short with one winter in three having temperatures below zero. Frequently located on the boundary of major air masses, spring and summer storms can be severe, spawning tornadoes and large hail, and winter "mixes" of sleet and freezing rain. First freeze is November 1; last is early April.

Population

DEMOGRAPHICS	AREA	U.S. AVG	ETHNIC COMPOSITION	AREA	U.S. AVG	RESIDENT PROFILE	AREA	U.S. AVG
Population	1,150,837		White	74.5%	79.0%	Single	30.8%	32.4%
Population density per sq. mile	208.6	358.5	Black	10.9%	10.5%	Married	52.8%	52.7%
Population growth	18.9%	21.1%	Asian	3.1%	2.7%	Divorced/separated	16.4%	14.9%
Median age	35.0	36.1	Hispanic	7.7%	10.6%	Married with children	23.0%	23.7%
Percent Democrat	33.5%	44.5%	Religious observance	58.8%	48.9%	Single with children	9.6%	9.1%
Percent Republican	66.5%	54.5%	Diversity measure	49.3	40.1	Percent over age 65	11.6%	12.9%

Economy & Jobs
Score: 66.6
Rank: 126

INCOME	AREA	U.S. AVG	EMPLOYMENT	AREA	U.S. AVG	EMPLOYING INDUSTRIES	AREA	U.S. AVG
Per capita income	$22,410	$23,235	Unemployment rate	4.0%	4.7%	Largest: Healthcare & Social Assistance		
Household income	$42,701	$46,414	Recent job growth	2.8%	1.3%			
Household income ‹ $25K	28.0%	26.2%	Projected future job growth	10.9%	11.5%	Percent manufacturing	13.0%	15.4%
Household income › $75K	22.4%	25.4%	White collar	60.6%	57.8%	Percent public sector	18.0%	15.7%
Household income growth	15.0%	13.6%	Blue collar	23.6%	25.2%	Percent construction	10.6%	9.9%

Cost of Living
Score: 36.6
Rank: 237

INDEXES & TAXES	AREA	U.S. AVG	HOUSING	AREA	U.S. AVG	NECESSITIES	AREA	U.S. AVG
Cost of Living Index	81.9	100.0	Median home price	$125,400	$220,000	Food Index	91.3	100.0
Buying Power Index	116.9	100.0	Home price appreciation	32.1%	10.1%	Housing Index	48.0	100.0
Income tax rate	7.00%	4.70%	Median rent	$579	$709	Utilities Index	107.1	100.0
Sales tax rate	8.38%	6.58%	Homes owned	60.0%	62.3%	Transportation Index	94.4	100.0
Property tax rate	$8.74	$12.00	Home price ratio	2.9	4.2	Healthcare Index	93.4	100.0
						Miscellaneous Cost Index	100.1	100.0

Climate
Score: 72.7
Rank: 101

TEMPERATURE	AREA	U.S. AVG	PRECIPITATION	AREA	U.S. AVG	COMFORTS & HAZARDS	AREA	U.S. AVG
Average January low	26.0	26.2	Annual inches precipitation	33.0	37.7	July relative humidity	65%	66%
Average July high	92.6	87.4	Annual inches snowfall	9.0	7.0	Annual days mostly sunny	237	208
Annual days › 90°F	64	38	Annual days precipitation	81	109	Annual days with thunderstorms	51	39
Annual days ‹ 32°F	80	89	Annual days rain › 0.5 inches	23	22	Tornado risk score	62	18
Annual days ‹ 0°F	0	6	Annual days snow › 1.5 inches	3	6	Hurricane risk score	2	13

TEMPERATURE

PRECIPITATION

DAYS OF CLOUDS & PRECIPITATION

Education
Score: 65.0
Rank: 132

ACHIEVEMENT	AREA	U.S. AVG	PUBLIC SCHOOLS	AREA	U.S. AVG	HIGHER EDUCATION	AREA	U.S. AVG
High school degree	83.8%	82.7%	Expenditures per pupil	$4,428	$5,686	No. 2-year colleges	10	4
2-year college degree	5.3%	6.4%	Student/teacher ratio	16.0	16.7	No. 4-year colleges/universities	14	6
4-year college degree	16.2%	15.7%	Attending public school	93.9%	90.1%	No. highly ranked universities	1	1
Graduate/professional degree	8.4%	8.9%	State SAT score	1150	1021			
			State ACT score	20.5*	20.9			

Health & Healthcare
Score: 26.2
Rank: 275

Crime
Score: 9.4
Rank: 338

HAZARDS & ILLNESSES	AREA	U.S. AVG	HEALTHCARE	AREA	U.S. AVG	CRIME	AREA	U.S. AVG
Air-quality score	26	37	Physicians per capita	257.4	244.2	Violent crime rate	532.7	465.5
Water-quality score	50	52	Hospital beds per capita	444.1	420.0	Change in violent crime rate	1.7%	-2.2%
Pollen/allergy score	92	61	No. teaching hospitals	8	3	Property crime rate	5,345.4	3,517.1
Cancer mortality per capita	209.8	201.9	Cost per doctor visit	$72	$77	Change in property crime rate	-6.5%	-2.1%
Depression days per month	3.6	3.5	Cost per dental visit	$70	$70			
Stress score	61	50						

Transportation
Score: 20.1
Rank: 300

COMMUTE	AREA	U.S. AVG	INTERCITY SERVICES	AREA	U.S. AVG	AUTOMOTIVE	AREA	U.S. AVG
Average commute time	24.2	27.4	Major airports within 60 miles	1	1	Insurance, annual premium	$1,616	$1,432
Percent commutes › 60 mins.	3.9%	5.9%	Size of regional airport	Medium	Large	Gas, cost per gallon	$2.35	$2.49
Commute by auto	81.7%	78.9%	Daily airline activity	102	686	Daily vehicle miles per capita	31.6	24.0
Commute by mass transit	0.6%	1.9%	Amtrak service	Yes	No			
Work at home	3.0%	3.1%						
Mass transit miles per capita	0.58	1.87						

Leisure
Score: 61.5
Rank: 144

DINING & SHOPPING	AREA	U.S. AVG	ENTERTAINMENT	AREA	U.S. AVG	OUTDOOR ACTIVITIES	AREA	U.S. AVG
Restaurant rating	1	2	Professional sports rating	3	4	Golf-course rating	5	4
Outlet mall score	0	42	College sports rating	8	4	Ski-area rating	1	3
No. Starbucks	11	13	Zoo/aquarium rating	6	3	Sq. miles inland water	4	4
No. warehouse clubs	1	2	Amusement park rating	4	3	Miles of coastline	0.0	10.7
			Botanical garden/arboretum rating	9	4	National Park rating	1	3

MEDIA & LIBRARIES	AREA	U.S. AVG	PERFORMING ARTS	AREA	U.S. AVG	MUSEUMS	AREA	U.S. AVG
Arts radio rating	1	3	Classical music rating	4	4	Overall museum rating	8	5
No. public libraries	41	27	Ballet/dance rating	6	3	Art museum rating	8	5
Library volumes per capita	1.47	2.78	Professional theater rating	1	3	Science museum rating	9	5
			University arts programs rating	8	5	Children's museum rating	2	3

Olympia, WA

Score: 86.8   Rank: 16   2004 rank: 16

Profile: Capital city
Location: West-central Washington at the south end of Puget Sound
Elevation: 100 feet
Time zone: Pacific Standard Time

PRO	CON
Attractive setting	Cloudy, wet winters
Nearby national parks	Cost of living
Educated population	Narrow job base

Olympia is one of the more attractive capital cities in the United States. While there is heavy industry to the north toward Tacoma, Olympia is a clean, mid-size capital city with a distinctively Pacific Northwest small-town feel. Outdoor recreational opportunities are abundant with national forests, the Olympic Peninsula and Olympic National Park, Mount Rainier National Park, and the Washington coast all within a day's drive. Excellent city amenities and services are available in Seattle, 60 miles to the north, although traffic particularly in the Tacoma area can make the drive challenging. The population is highly educated and most of the area has a well-kept appearance. The clean, quiet, small waterfront downtown is well used and inner neighborhoods are livable. As with much of the Northwest, large, unattractive expanses of residential sprawl aren't found; most residential areas feature individual homes or small single-street developments set among the woods. The small, progressive Evergreen State College adds a college presence, and there is abundant local music and entertainment. Outside of the state government, healthcare, and education, employment is a bit of a challenge but current trends and projections are strong. There are two military installations just north of town and some employment in basic industries related to forest products, fishing, and shipping is in decline. Many commute north toward Tacoma or Seattle. The area's lush greenery owes its existence to the marine climate, which brings a downside—the area is the sixth cloudiest city in the nation and one of the rainiest, although rain is seasonal and seldom heavy. Nearby hydroelectric power brings among the lowest utility costs in the country.

Local terrain is hilly and wooded with tall coniferous trees and low mountains to the west, high mountains (the Cascades) to the east, and gradually flattening forest and farmland to the south and east. The marine climate is characterized by mild, generally dry summers and wet, mild winters. Autumn rains from frequent Pacific weather systems usually begin about mid-October. Rains continue with few interruptions through spring. Pacific storms can be strong but the Coast Range moderates winds. Summer highs are a comfortable 70°F to 80°F with clear skies 2 out of every 3 days. Winter daytime temperatures are in the 40s and low 50s with nighttime temperatures in the 30s. Occasional blasts of Canadian air drop temperatures into the 10s and 20s. Snow accumulations sufficient to disrupt traffic occur infrequently. There is some fog mainly in spring and fall.

DEMOGRAPHICS	AREA	U.S. AVG	ETHNIC COMPOSITION	AREA	U.S. AVG	RESIDENT PROFILE	AREA	U.S. AVG
Population	224,064		White	84.7%	79.0%	Single	29.5%	32.4%
Population density per sq. mile	308.2	358.5	Black	2.6%	10.5%	Married	54.5%	52.7%
Population growth	39.0%	21.1%	Asian	5.2%	2.7%	Divorced/separated	16.1%	14.9%
Median age	37.2	36.1	Hispanic	4.9%	10.6%	Married with children	23.6%	23.7%
Percent Democrat	55.5%	44.5%	Religious observance	27.4%	48.9%	Single with children	9.3%	9.1%
Percent Republican	42.6%	54.5%	Diversity measure	34.4	40.1	Percent over age 65	11.7%	12.9%

INCOME	AREA	U.S. AVG	EMPLOYMENT	AREA	U.S. AVG	EMPLOYING INDUSTRIES	AREA	U.S. AVG
Per capita income	$26,385	$23,235	Unemployment rate	5.0%	4.7%	Largest: Healthcare & Social Assistance		
Household income	$54,417	$46,414	Recent job growth	4.4%	1.3%			
Household income < $25K	19.1%	26.2%	Projected future job growth	25.5%	11.5%	Percent manufacturing	10.1%	15.4%
Household income > $75K	31.2%	25.4%	White collar	64.1%	57.8%	Percent public sector	32.3%	15.7%
Household income growth	15.8%	13.6%	Blue collar	19.1%	25.2%	Percent construction	9.0%	9.9%

INDEXES & TAXES	AREA	U.S. AVG	HOUSING	AREA	U.S. AVG	NECESSITIES	AREA	U.S. AVG
Cost of Living Index	99.1	100.0	Median home price	$199,900	$220,000	Food Index	110.0	100.0
Buying Power Index	123.1	100.0	Home price appreciation	64.5%	10.1%	Housing Index	82.0	100.0
Income tax rate	0.00%	4.70%	Median rent	$763	$709	Utilities Index	78.6	100.0
Sales tax rate	8.40%	6.58%	Homes owned	63.3%	62.3%	Transportation Index	106.9	100.0
Property tax rate	$12.57	$12.00	Home price ratio	3.7	4.2	Healthcare Index	126.4	100.0
						Miscellaneous Cost Index	102.2	100.0

Climate
Score: 44.4
Rank: 207

TEMPERATURE	AREA	U.S. AVG
Average January low	30.4	26.2
Average July high	78.4	87.4
Annual days > 90°F	6	38
Annual days < 32°F	89	89
Annual days < 0°F	0	6

PRECIPITATION	AREA	U.S. AVG
Annual inches precipitation	51.0	37.7
Annual inches snowfall	19.0	7.0
Annual days precipitation	163	109
Annual days rain > 0.5 inches	34	22
Annual days snow > 1.5 inches	5	6

COMFORTS & HAZARDS	AREA	U.S. AVG
July relative humidity	71%	66%
Annual days mostly sunny	137	208
Annual days with thunderstorms	5	39
Tornado risk score	0	18
Hurricane risk score	0	13

TEMPERATURE

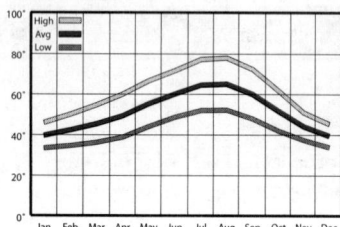

PRECIPITATION

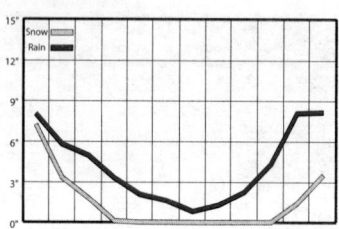

DAYS OF CLOUDS & PRECIPITATION

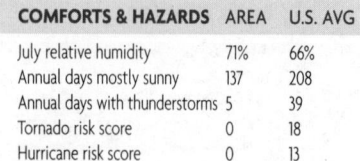

Education
Score: 80.7
Rank: 73

ACHIEVEMENT	AREA	U.S. AVG
High school degree	89.4%	82.7%
2-year college degree	8.0%	6.4%
4-year college degree	18.7%	15.7%
Graduate/professional degree	11.1%	8.9%

PUBLIC SCHOOLS	AREA	U.S. AVG
Expenditures per pupil	$5,768	$5,686
Student/teacher ratio	20.4	16.7
Attending public school	94.8%	90.1%
State SAT score	1059*	1021
State ACT score	22.9	20.9

HIGHER EDUCATION	AREA	U.S. AVG
No. 2-year colleges	2	4
No. 4-year colleges/universities	2	6
No. highly ranked universities	0	1

Health & Healthcare
Score: 31.3
Rank: 256

HAZARDS & ILLNESSES	AREA	U.S. AVG
Air-quality score	40	37
Water-quality score	50	52
Pollen/allergy score	47	61
Cancer mortality per capita	199.7	201.9
Depression days per month	3.5	3.5
Stress score	86	50

HEALTHCARE	AREA	U.S. AVG
Physicians per capita	231.6	244.2
Hospital beds per capita	198.2	420.0
No. teaching hospitals	1	3
Cost per doctor visit	$80	$77
Cost per dental visit	$93	$70

Crime
Score: 63.6
Rank: 137

CRIME	AREA	U.S. AVG
Violent crime rate	261.7	465.5
Change in violent crime rate	-0.7%	-2.2%
Property crime rate	3,772.3	3,517.1
Change in property crime rate	2.5%	-2.1%

Transportation
Score: 30.5
Rank: 261

COMMUTE	AREA	U.S. AVG
Average commute time	26.6	27.4
Percent commutes > 60 mins.	7.7%	5.9%
Commute by auto	77.4%	78.9%
Commute by mass transit	2.1%	1.9%
Work at home	3.9%	3.1%
Mass transit miles per capita	2.05	1.87

INTERCITY SERVICES	AREA	U.S. AVG
Major airports within 60 miles	1	1
Size of regional airport	Large	Large
Daily airline activity	698	686
Amtrak service	Yes	No

AUTOMOTIVE	AREA	U.S. AVG
Insurance, annual premium	$1,350	$1,432
Gas, cost per gallon	$2.56	$2.49
Daily vehicle miles per capita	26.4	24.0

Leisure
Score: 82.1
Rank: 67

DINING & SHOPPING	AREA	U.S. AVG
Restaurant rating	1	2
Outlet mall score	0	42
No. Starbucks	8	13
No. warehouse clubs	2	2

ENTERTAINMENT	AREA	U.S. AVG
Professional sports rating	7	4
College sports rating	3	4
Zoo/aquarium rating	3	3
Amusement park rating	3	3
Botanical garden/ arboretum rating	6	4

OUTDOOR ACTIVITIES	AREA	U.S. AVG
Golf-course rating	3	4
Ski-area rating	9	3
Sq. miles inland water	6	4
Miles of coastline	10.1	10.7
National Park rating	7	3

Arts & Culture
Score: 55.9
Rank: 164

MEDIA & LIBRARIES	AREA	U.S. AVG
Arts radio rating	3	3
No. public libraries	27	27
Library volumes per capita	2.69	2.78

PERFORMING ARTS	AREA	U.S. AVG
Classical music rating	3	4
Ballet/dance rating	4	3
Professional theater rating	3	3
University arts programs rating	5	5

MUSEUMS	AREA	U.S. AVG
Overall museum rating	7	5
Art museum rating	6	5
Science museum rating	5	5
Children's museum rating	7	3

Omaha–Council Bluffs, NE-IA

Score: 66.5   **Rank:** 127   **2004 rank:** 201

Profile: Mid-size-city complex
Location: Extreme eastern Nebraska along Missouri River at Iowa border
Elevation: 982 feet
Time zone: Central Standard Time

PRO	CON
Stable economy	Harsh winters
Cost of living	Outdoor recreation
Arts and culture	Entertainment

This metropolitan area includes Omaha, Nebraska's largest city, and Council Bluffs, a more industrial city on the east (Iowa) bank of the Missouri River. As a gateway to the Great Plains, Omaha is historically a world-class livestock, meatpacking, and grain-shipping city. The city has always been a gateway and transportation center, starting with the Lewis and Clark expedition and continuing as the eastern terminus of the transcontinental Union Pacific Railroad. Today the city's diverse economy includes food production and insurance. Mutual of Omaha, ConAgra, and Warren Buffett's Berkshire Hathaway Company have headquarters here. Led by Mr. Buffett, Omaha reportedly has more millionaires per capita than any other U.S. city.

Typically Midwestern, the city is well kept, generally clean, and not flashy in any way. The downtown is clean and modern with attractive redevelopment in former railyards along the Missouri River waterfront. There is a new convention and performing arts center and attractive new high-rise residential developments along the waterfront and a nice historic district; the city core is much more interesting than in the past and surpasses its reputation. Shaded streets and older suburbs cover the hills north and immediately west of town, while newer development lies in the flatter areas to the west along Interstate 80 and Interstate 680.

Attractive, well-spaced suburbs lead into the country through Boys Town (named after the major facility of that name), Papillion to the south, Elkhorn to the west in the North Platte Valley, all the way to Wahoo, a small Scandinavian farming community starting to grow as a nice rural alternative with access to Lincoln to the south. Housing values throughout the area are excellent.

The Strategic Air Command headquarters and nearby Offutt Air Force Base provide a sizable military presence, and Creighton University brings a college-town element. The harsh climate holds the area back from a higher ranking, and crime rates are a little high for the region.

Omaha is situated on the west bank of the Missouri River. The narrow river valley gives way to hills and ridges rising about 350 feet above the valley. Lush deciduous trees cover the hills, especially to the north, while the land to the west and south is more level and open as prairie and farmland. The climate is typically continental with relatively warm summers and cold, dry winters. Most precipitation falls during strong summer showers or thunderstorms mainly in the evening or nighttime. Although winters are relatively cold, precipitation is light. Wind can be significant, particularly to the west. First freeze is mid-October; last is late April.

Population

DEMOGRAPHICS	AREA	U.S. AVG
Population	806,108	
Population density per sq. mile	184.8	358.5
Population growth	18.0%	21.1%
Median age	34.8	36.1
Percent Democrat	37.5%	44.5%
Percent Republican	61.2%	54.5%

ETHNIC COMPOSITION	AREA	U.S. AVG
White	85.0%	79.0%
Black	7.7%	10.5%
Asian	2.0%	2.7%
Hispanic	6.0%	10.6%
Religious observance	50.9%	48.9%
Diversity measure	34.0	40.1

RESIDENT PROFILE	AREA	U.S. AVG
Single	32.0%	32.4%
Married	54.3%	52.7%
Divorced/separated	13.7%	14.9%
Married with children	25.6%	23.7%
Single with children	8.6%	9.1%
Percent over age 65	11.0%	12.9%

Economy & Jobs
Score: 69.3
Rank: 115

INCOME	AREA	U.S. AVG
Per capita income	$25,251	$23,235
Household income	$50,939	$46,414
Household income < $25K	20.6%	26.2%
Household income > $75K	29.1%	25.4%
Household income growth	13.8%	13.6%

EMPLOYMENT	AREA	U.S. AVG
Unemployment rate	4.6%	4.7%
Recent job growth	1.9%	1.3%
Projected future job growth	12.8%	11.5%
White collar	64.4%	57.8%
Blue collar	21.0%	25.2%

EMPLOYING INDUSTRIES	AREA	U.S. AVG
Largest: Finance & Insurance		
Percent manufacturing	12.3%	15.4%
Percent public sector	11.8%	15.7%
Percent construction	8.7%	9.9%

Cost of Living
Score: 26.5
Rank: 274

INDEXES & TAXES	AREA	U.S. AVG
Cost of Living Index	86.9	100.0
Buying Power Index	131.4	100.0
Income tax rate	6.68%	4.70%
Sales tax rate	6.62%	6.58%
Property tax rate	$17.39	$12.00

HOUSING	AREA	U.S. AVG
Median home price	$142,900	$220,000
Home price appreciation	23.4%	10.1%
Median rent	$680	$709
Homes owned	64.4%	62.3%
Home price ratio	2.8	4.2

NECESSITIES	AREA	U.S. AVG
Food Index	92.1	100.0
Housing Index	58.2	100.0
Utilities Index	125.4	100.0
Transportation Index	100.4	100.0
Healthcare Index	97.7	100.0
Miscellaneous Cost Index	97.0	100.0

Climate
Score: 14.7
Rank: 318

TEMPERATURE	AREA	U.S. AVG
Average January low	12.4	26.2
Average July high	88.6	87.4
Annual days > 90°F	38	38
Annual days < 32°F	138	89
Annual days < 0°F	13	6

PRECIPITATION	AREA	U.S. AVG
Annual inches precipitation	30.0	37.7
Annual inches snowfall	32.0	7.0
Annual days precipitation	99	109
Annual days rain > 0.5 inches	18	22
Annual days snow > 1.5 inches	6	6

COMFORTS & HAZARDS	AREA	U.S. AVG
July relative humidity	68%	66%
Annual days mostly sunny	220	208
Annual days with thunderstorms	48	39
Tornado risk score	23	18
Hurricane risk score	1	13

TEMPERATURE

PRECIPITATION

DAYS OF CLOUDS & PRECIPITATION

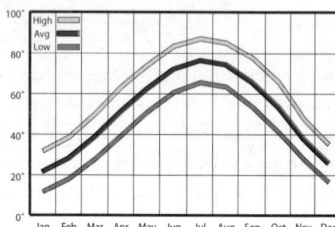

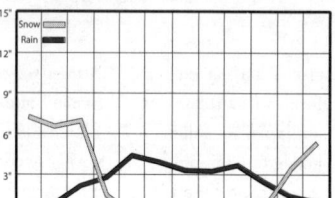

Education
Score: 77.8
Rank: 84

ACHIEVEMENT	AREA	U.S. AVG
High school degree	88.2%	82.7%
2-year college degree	6.8%	6.4%
4-year college degree	19.5%	15.7%
Graduate/professional degree	8.5%	8.9%

PUBLIC SCHOOLS	AREA	U.S. AVG
Expenditures per pupil	$5,311	$5,686
Student/teacher ratio	15.5	16.7
Attending public school	86.4%	90.1%
State SAT score	1159	1021
State ACT score	21.9*	20.9

HIGHER EDUCATION	AREA	U.S. AVG
No. 2-year colleges	8	4
No. 4-year colleges/universities	13	6
No. highly ranked universities	1	1

Health & Healthcare
Score: 58.0
Rank: 158

HAZARDS & ILLNESSES	AREA	U.S. AVG
Air-quality score	34	37
Water-quality score	54	52
Pollen/allergy score	50	61
Cancer mortality per capita	222.7	201.9
Depression days per month	2.8	3.5
Stress score	14	50

HEALTHCARE	AREA	U.S. AVG
Physicians per capita	315.0	244.2
Hospital beds per capita	485.2	420.0
No. teaching hospitals	7	3
Cost per doctor visit	$83	$77
Cost per dental visit	$61	$70

Crime
Score: 44.4
Rank: 208

CRIME	AREA	U.S. AVG
Violent crime rate	430.4	465.5
Change in violent crime rate	-6.3%	-2.2%
Property crime rate	4,175.8	3,517.1
Change in property crime rate	-4.2%	-2.1%

Transportation
Score: 48.1
Rank: 195

COMMUTE	AREA	U.S. AVG
Average commute time	21.7	27.4
Percent commutes > 60 mins.	2.7%	5.9%
Commute by auto	83.0%	78.9%
Commute by mass transit	1.0%	1.9%
Work at home	3.2%	3.1%
Mass transit miles per capita	1.00	1.87

INTERCITY SERVICES	AREA	U.S. AVG
Major airports within 60 miles	1	1
Size of regional airport	Medium	Large
Daily airline activity	136	686
Amtrak service	Yes	No

AUTOMOTIVE	AREA	U.S. AVG
Insurance, annual premium	$1,735	$1,432
Gas, cost per gallon	$2.52	$2.49
Daily vehicle miles per capita	22.7	24.0

Leisure
Score: 64.7
Rank: 132

DINING & SHOPPING	AREA	U.S. AVG
Restaurant rating	1	2
Outlet mall score	0	42
No. Starbucks	10	13
No. warehouse clubs	2	2

ENTERTAINMENT	AREA	U.S. AVG
Professional sports rating	3	4
College sports rating	5	4
Zoo/aquarium rating	8	3
Amusement park rating	1	3
Botanical garden/ arboretum rating	4	4

OUTDOOR ACTIVITIES	AREA	U.S. AVG
Golf-course rating	5	4
Ski-area rating	4	3
Sq. miles inland water	4	4
Miles of coastline	0.0	10.7
National Park rating	2	3

Arts & Culture
Score: 77.0
Rank: 86

MEDIA & LIBRARIES	AREA	U.S. AVG
Arts radio rating	5	3
No. public libraries	48	27
Library volumes per capita	2.93	2.78

PERFORMING ARTS	AREA	U.S. AVG
Classical music rating	6	4
Ballet/dance rating	1	3
Professional theater rating	8	3
University arts programs rating	8	5

MUSEUMS	AREA	U.S. AVG
Overall museum rating	8	5
Art museum rating	7	5
Science museum rating	7	5
Children's museum rating	6	3

Orlando–Kissimmee, FL

Score: 62.3   **Rank:** 155   **2004 rank:** 134

Profile: Diverse resort city
Location: East-central Florida, about 25 miles from the Atlantic Coast
Elevation: 106 feet
Time zone: Eastern Standard Time

PRO	CON
Entertainment	Tourist impact
Outdoor recreation	Hot, humid summers
Strong job growth	Growth and sprawl

Before Walt Disney World came to the area in the 1970s, Orlando was a sleepy town with an economy based on citrus and cattle. Not any more. Starting with the clandestine 1965 purchase of 43 square miles of farmland southwest of the city and the opening of Walt Disney World in 1971, the city has become a major tourist destination and entertainment center. It is so much a tourist attraction, and known so well for its tourist venues, that evaluating it as a place to live is a challenge.

A variety of activities and attractions have been built around the Disney complex, and in areas nearby mostly south of town. While some of them, like the many restaurants and golf courses, are likely to be used by local residents, many are not. The area plays host to some 50 million tourists each year, and has also developed a convention industry second only to Las Vegas. The good news is that most of the tourist activity is confined to the south and southwestern portion of the city. Kissimmee, a former agriculture center, is part of this explosion south, and is strongly connected to the tourist industries but has a nice small and historic downtown area. Downtown Orlando and areas north and east of the city support a fairly normal sun-drenched Florida way of life, with lots of retirees, families, and working professionals gravitating towards Winter Park, Maitland, and other suburbs north. The employment base in the area, outside of tourism, is relatively strong, with a large high-tech and military high-tech presence; notables include IBM, Siemens, Veritas, Electronic Arts, General Dynamics, and Northrup/Grumman. The area has also become a popular headquarters location for service businesses, including Darden, Hard Rock Cafe, and Ruth's Chris Steakhouse, and,

not surprisingly, some hospitality businesses. Overall, the employment base is becoming more diverse.

The cost of living (105.3) and cost of housing have risen considerably in recent years, but they're considered by many to be reasonable for a place with so many amenities. The central location and transportation network give excellent access to other areas in Florida, and not surprisingly, air service is excellent. Orlando has grown very rapidly since Disney arrived, resulting in considerable sprawl and a homogeneous look to development unpleasant for those who don't like that look. In 1998, the Sierra Club listed Orlando as the no. 1 sprawl-threatened city for a place its size. The area continues to grow to the northeast toward Sanford and Deltona. Traffic can be bad and commute times long. The crime rate is also one of the state's highest. Because of its inland location the Orlando area is generally thought to have less hurricane risk, however, Hurricane Charley in 2004 brought a wake-up call and moderate damage. Bottom line: For those who like the entertainment, Florida climate, and diverse economic prosperity away from the beaches and can tolerate or avoid the tourist stampede, Orlando works.

The flat area is a mix of open land and mostly deciduous woods surrounded by lakes. The fertile terrain is suitable for orchards and citrus crops. Summers are warm and humid but temperatures over 95°F are rare and breezes provide comfort. The rainy season extends from June through September, with scattered showers almost daily and thunderstorms. Winters are mild with light rainfall. Although not a great threat because of the inland location, hurricanes can create heavy rains.

DEMOGRAPHICS	AREA	U.S. AVG	ETHNIC COMPOSITION	AREA	U.S. AVG	RESIDENT PROFILE	AREA	U.S. AVG
Population	1,894,018		White	71.5%	79.0%	Single	32.1%	32.4%
Population density per sq. mile	542.6	358.5	Black	15.1%	10.5%	Married	52.0%	52.7%
Population growth	57.0%	21.1%	Asian	3.2%	2.7%	Divorced/separated	15.9%	14.9%
Median age	36.3	36.1	Hispanic	20.0%	10.6%	Married with children	22.5%	23.7%
Percent Democrat	46.2%	44.5%	Religious observance	38.1%	48.9%	Single with children	9.5%	9.1%
Percent Republican	53.2%	54.5%	Diversity measure	61.1	40.1	Percent over age 65	12.5%	12.9%

INCOME	AREA	U.S. AVG	EMPLOYMENT	AREA	U.S. AVG	EMPLOYING INDUSTRIES	AREA	U.S. AVG
Per capita income	$23,950	$23,235	Unemployment rate	3.7%	4.7%	Largest: Healthcare & Social Assistance		
Household income	$47,492	$46,414	Recent job growth	5.5%	1.3%			
Household income < $25K	22.8%	26.2%	Projected future job growth	26.0%	11.5%	Percent manufacturing	10.2%	15.4%
Household income > $75K	26.0%	25.4%	White collar	62.0%	57.8%	Percent public sector	10.9%	15.7%
Household income growth	12.9%	13.6%	Blue collar	19.8%	25.2%	Percent construction	9.5%	9.9%

Economy & Jobs — **Score:** 96.8 — **Rank:** 13

INDEXES & TAXES	AREA	U.S. AVG	HOUSING	AREA	U.S. AVG	NECESSITIES	AREA	U.S. AVG
Cost of Living Index	105.3	100.0	Median home price	$256,900	$220,000	Food Index	100.3	100.0
Buying Power Index	101.1	100.0	Home price appreciation	109.6%	10.1%	Housing Index	92.4	100.0
Income tax rate	0.00%	4.70%	Median rent	$814	$709	Utilities Index	102.3	100.0
Sales tax rate	6.73%	6.58%	Homes owned	60.8%	62.3%	Transportation Index	97.2	100.0
Property tax rate	$12.79	$12.00	Home price ratio	5.4	4.2	Healthcare Index	106.2	100.0
						Miscellaneous Cost Index	99.0	100.0

Cost of Living — **Score:** 40.1 — **Rank:** 224

Climate
Score: 83.4
Rank: 63

TEMPERATURE	AREA	U.S. AVG
Average January low	50.0	26.2
Average July high	90.0	87.4
Annual days > 90°F	104	38
Annual days < 32°F	2	89
Annual days < 0°F	0	6

PRECIPITATION	AREA	U.S. AVG
Annual inches precipitation	51.0	37.7
Annual inches snowfall	0.0	7.0
Annual days precipitation	116	109
Annual days rain > 0.5 inches	31	22
Annual days snow > 1.5 inches	0	6

COMFORTS & HAZARDS	AREA	U.S. AVG
July relative humidity	74%	66%
Annual days mostly sunny	242	208
Annual days with thunderstorms	81	39
Tornado risk score	42	18
Hurricane risk score	75	13

TEMPERATURE

PRECIPITATION

DAYS OF CLOUDS & PRECIPITATION

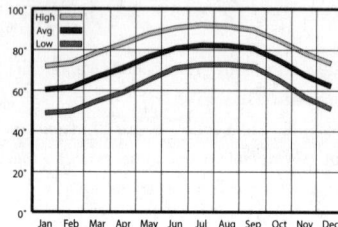

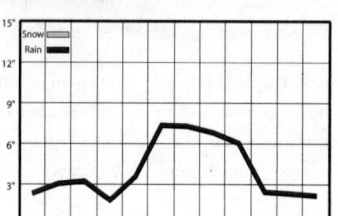

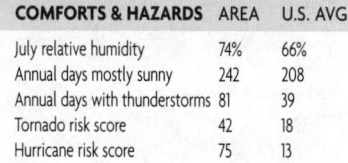

Education
Score: 74.9
Rank: 95

ACHIEVEMENT	AREA	U.S. AVG
High school degree	82.9%	82.7%
2-year college degree	8.0%	6.4%
4-year college degree	17.2%	15.7%
Graduate/professional degree	7.6%	8.9%

PUBLIC SCHOOLS	AREA	U.S. AVG
Expenditures per pupil	$4,854	$5,686
Student/teacher ratio	17.8	16.7
Attending public school	88.7%	90.1%
State SAT score	993*	1021
State ACT score	20.3	20.9

HIGHER EDUCATION	AREA	U.S. AVG
No. 2-year colleges	15	4
No. 4-year colleges/universities	15	6
No. highly ranked universities	2	1

Health & Healthcare
Score: 5.6
Rank: 352

HAZARDS & ILLNESSES	AREA	U.S. AVG
Air-quality score	24	37
Water-quality score	61	52
Pollen/allergy score	78	61
Cancer mortality per capita	252.9	201.9
Depression days per month	3.6	3.5
Stress score	63	50

HEALTHCARE	AREA	U.S. AVG
Physicians per capita	193.7	244.2
Hospital beds per capita	272.2	420.0
No. teaching hospitals	2	3
Cost per doctor visit	$70	$77
Cost per dental visit	$68	$70

Crime
Score: 18.2
Rank: 306

CRIME	AREA	U.S. AVG
Violent crime rate	821.4	465.5
Change in violent crime rate	8.9%	-2.2%
Property crime rate	4,314.0	3,517.1
Change in property crime rate	1.8%	-2.1%

Transportation
Score: 27.3
Rank: 273

COMMUTE	AREA	U.S. AVG
Average commute time	29.2	27.4
Percent commutes > 60 mins.	6.3%	5.9%
Commute by auto	80.6%	78.9%
Commute by mass transit	1.6%	1.9%
Work at home	2.9%	3.1%
Mass transit miles per capita	1.58	1.87

INTERCITY SERVICES	AREA	U.S. AVG
Major airports within 60 miles	2	1
Size of regional airport	Large	Large
Daily airline activity	951	686
Amtrak service	Yes	No

AUTOMOTIVE	AREA	U.S. AVG
Insurance, annual premium	$2,073	$1,432
Gas, cost per gallon	$2.55	$2.49
Daily vehicle miles per capita	30.4	24.0

Leisure
Score: 85.6
Rank: 54

DINING & SHOPPING	AREA	U.S. AVG
Restaurant rating	3	2
Outlet mall score	251	42
No. Starbucks	29	13
No. warehouse clubs	11	2

ENTERTAINMENT	AREA	U.S. AVG
Professional sports rating	4	4
College sports rating	4	4
Zoo/aquarium rating	4	3
Amusement park rating	10	3
Botanical garden/arboretum rating	7	4

OUTDOOR ACTIVITIES	AREA	U.S. AVG
Golf-course rating	7	4
Ski-area rating	1	3
Sq. miles inland water	10	4
Miles of coastline	0.0	10.7
National Park rating	1	3

Arts & Culture
Score: 68.4
Rank: 118

MEDIA & LIBRARIES	AREA	U.S. AVG
Arts radio rating	7	3
No. public libraries	41	27
Library volumes per capita	1.86	2.78

PERFORMING ARTS	AREA	U.S. AVG
Classical music rating	4	4
Ballet/dance rating	3	3
Professional theater rating	1	3
University arts programs rating	1	5

MUSEUMS	AREA	U.S. AVG
Overall museum rating	8	5
Art museum rating	8	5
Science museum rating	7	5
Children's museum rating	1	3

Oshkosh–Neenah, WI

Score: 64.7   **Rank:** 142   **2004 rank:** 117

Profile: Small-city complex
Location: Northeastern Wisconsin along the shore of
Lake Winnebago
Elevation: 755 feet
Time zone: Central Standard Time

PRO	CON
Cost of living	Cold winters
Outdoor recreation	Arts and culture
Low crime rates	Low ethnic diversity

Known in a larger sense as the Fox Cities for their location in the Fox River Valley, the cities of Appleton (p. 175), Oshkosh, Neenah, and Fond du Lac (p. 362) surround Lake Winnebago, the source of the Fox River. Lumber and paper production form much of the area's economic base, led by paper products giant Kimberly-Clark, which once made its headquarters in Neenah but moved to Dallas, affecting the local white-collar employment base, but still has a number of local operations. Neenah also has a substantial iron and steel foundry and commercial printing industry. While the area sounds overly dominated by industry, the industrial areas are confined to a small part of town along the lakefront, and Neenah enjoys strong endowments from its industrial legacy. It has a nice small-town center with good parks and inner residential neighborhoods. Oshkosh has a similar legacy but is larger and more economically diverse. Most famous is the Oshkosh clothing name (OshKosh B'Gosh), but there is a substantial forest products industry and the area is also a producer of emergency vehicles and specialized trucks. Beyond these industries, both cities have the usual Wisconsin assortment of dairy products, agriculture, and light manufacturing. Oshkosh is home to the 9,000-student University of Wisconsin-Oshkosh campus. The cities have a distinct, clean, small-town feel with lots of trees and historic buildings, and residents have an uncommon pride for the area. Outdoor recreation is abundant, highlighted by watersports in summer and snowmobiling in winter. Crime rates are very low, and living costs are reasonable relative to incomes, giving a high Buying Power Index of 133.5. The overall rating would probably be higher if the winters weren't so harsh.

The Fox Cities sit in a mostly level valley plain surrounded by areas of low rolling and densely wooded hills. The decidedly continental climate receives the full effects of continental air masses, particularly in winter. Summers are pleasantly warm and sometimes humid, with occasional hot spells and cool evenings. Most precipitation arrives as thunderstorms from May through September. Winters are harsh and cold, although the coldest days are often sunny and dry. Most winter precipitation comes as snow with persistent snow cover. First freeze is early October; last is mid-May

DEMOGRAPHICS	AREA	U.S. AVG	ETHNIC COMPOSITION	AREA	U.S. AVG	RESIDENT PROFILE	AREA	U.S. AVG
Population	159,972		White	94.4%	79.0%	Single	32.5%	32.4%
Population density per sq. mile	364.7	358.5	Black	1.2%	10.5%	Married	53.5%	52.7%
Population growth	14.0%	21.1%	Asian	2.1%	2.7%	Divorced/separated	14.0%	14.9%
Median age	36.8	36.1	Hispanic	2.1%	10.6%	Married with children	23.5%	23.7%
Percent Democrat	46.2%	44.5%	Religious observance	57.4%	48.9%	Single with children	7.2%	9.1%
Percent Republican	52.5%	54.5%	Diversity measure	14.5	40.1	Percent over age 65	12.7%	12.9%

Score: 50.8
Rank: 185

INCOME	AREA	U.S. AVG	EMPLOYMENT	AREA	U.S. AVG	EMPLOYING INDUSTRIES	AREA	U.S. AVG
Per capita income	$24,729	$23,235	Unemployment rate	4.2%	4.7%	Largest: Manufacturing		
Household income	$50,041	$46,414	Recent job growth	0.8%	1.3%			
Household income < $25K	20.1%	26.2%	Projected future job growth	7.1%	11.5%	Percent manufacturing	22.3%	15.4%
Household income > $75K	26.1%	25.4%	White collar	54.7%	57.8%	Percent public sector	12.4%	15.7%
Household income growth	12.6%	13.6%	Blue collar	29.9%	25.2%	Percent construction	7.6%	9.9%

Score: 43.6
Rank: 211

INDEXES & TAXES	AREA	U.S. AVG	HOUSING	AREA	U.S. AVG	NECESSITIES	AREA	U.S. AVG
Cost of Living Index	84.0	100.0	Median home price	$131,600	$220,000	Food Index	96.6	100.0
Buying Power Index	133.5	100.0	Home price appreciation	26.1%	10.1%	Housing Index	53.9	100.0
Income tax rate	6.93%	4.70%	Median rent	$583	$709	Utilities Index	99.1	100.0
Sales tax rate	5.00%	6.58%	Homes owned	64.9%	62.3%	Transportation Index	98.2	100.0
Property tax rate	$20.34	$12.00	Home price ratio	2.6	4.2	Healthcare Index	102.1	100.0
						Miscellaneous Cost Index	98.3	100.0

Climate

Score: 12.8
Rank: 324

TEMPERATURE	AREA	U.S. AVG
Average January low	6.9	26.2
Average July high	80.7	87.4
Annual days > 90°F	7	38
Annual days < 32°F	163	89
Annual days < 0°F	29	6

PRECIPITATION	AREA	U.S. AVG
Annual inches precipitation	27.0	37.7
Annual inches snowfall	43.0	7.0
Annual days precipitation	120	109
Annual days rain > 0.5 inches	16	22
Annual days snow > 1.5 inches	11	6

COMFORTS & HAZARDS	AREA	U.S. AVG
July relative humidity	73%	66%
Annual days mostly sunny	192	208
Annual days with thunderstorms	35	39
Tornado risk score	16	18
Hurricane risk score	0	13

TEMPERATURE

PRECIPITATION

DAYS OF CLOUDS & PRECIPITATION

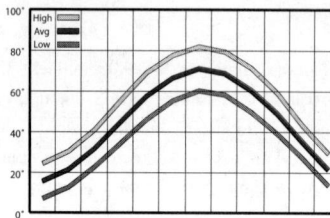
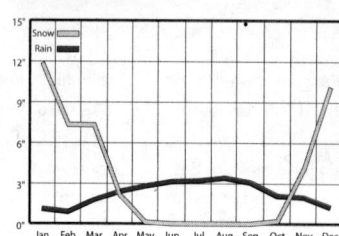

Education

Score: 48.9
Rank: 192

ACHIEVEMENT	AREA	U.S. AVG
High school degree	86.4%	82.7%
2-year college degree	6.8%	6.4%
4-year college degree	16.3%	15.7%
Graduate/professional degree	6.5%	8.9%

PUBLIC SCHOOLS	AREA	U.S. AVG
Expenditures per pupil	$6,119	$5,686
Student/teacher ratio	17.1	16.7
Attending public school	89.0%	90.1%
State SAT score	1188	1021
State ACT score	22.2*	20.9

HIGHER EDUCATION	AREA	U.S. AVG
No. 2-year colleges	1	4
No. 4-year colleges/universities	1	6
No. highly ranked universities	0	1

Health & Healthcare

Score: 73.8
Rank: 99

HAZARDS & ILLNESSES	AREA	U.S. AVG
Air-quality score	43	37
Water-quality score	25	52
Pollen/allergy score	31	61
Cancer mortality per capita	198.9	201.9
Depression days per month	3.2	3.5
Stress score	19	50

HEALTHCARE	AREA	U.S. AVG
Physicians per capita	246.7	244.2
Hospital beds per capita	479.5	420.0
No. teaching hospitals	1	3
Cost per doctor visit	$87	$77
Cost per dental visit	$61	$70

Crime
Score: 85.0
Rank: 57

CRIME	AREA	U.S. AVG
Violent crime rate	190.9	465.5
Change in violent crime rate	30.8%	-2.2%
Property crime rate	2,122.1	3,517.1
Change in property crime rate	-8.6%	-2.1%

Transportation

Score: 75.7
Rank: 92

COMMUTE	AREA	U.S. AVG
Average commute time	19.6	27.4
Percent commutes > 60 mins.	3.2%	5.9%
Commute by auto	84.7%	78.9%
Commute by mass transit	0.8%	1.9%
Work at home	2.7%	3.1%
Mass transit miles per capita	0.75	1.87

INTERCITY SERVICES	AREA	U.S. AVG
Major airports within 60 miles	1	1
Size of regional airport	Medium	Large
Daily airline activity	373	686
Amtrak service	No	No

AUTOMOTIVE	AREA	U.S. AVG
Insurance, annual premium	$901	$1,432
Gas, cost per gallon	$2.55	$2.49
Daily vehicle miles per capita	20.9	24.0

Leisure

Score: 63.1
Rank: 138

DINING & SHOPPING	AREA	U.S. AVG
Restaurant rating	1	2
Outlet mall score	0	42
No. Starbucks	1	13
No. warehouse clubs	0	2

ENTERTAINMENT	AREA	U.S. AVG
Professional sports rating	4	4
College sports rating	4	4
Zoo/aquarium rating	1	3
Amusement park rating	1	3
Botanical garden/ arboretum rating	7	4

OUTDOOR ACTIVITIES	AREA	U.S. AVG
Golf-course rating	4	4
Ski-area rating	2	3
Sq. miles inland water	10	4
Miles of coastline	0.0	10.7
National Park rating	1	3

Arts & Culture

Score: 38.2
Rank: 231

MEDIA & LIBRARIES	AREA	U.S. AVG
Arts radio rating	1	3
No. public libraries	5	27
Library volumes per capita	4.11	2.78

PERFORMING ARTS	AREA	U.S. AVG
Classical music rating	2	4
Ballet/dance rating	1	3
Professional theater rating	1	3
University arts programs rating	2	5

MUSEUMS	AREA	U.S. AVG
Overall museum rating	4	5
Art museum rating	5	5
Science museum rating	6	5
Children's museum rating	1	3

Owensboro, KY

Score: 34.0   Rank: 328   2004 rank: 303

Profile: Small river town
Location: Northwestern Kentucky along the Ohio River, 100 miles west of Louisville
Elevation: 406 feet
Time zone: Eastern Standard Time

PRO	CON
Cost of living	Entertainment
Low crime rate	Arts and culture
Small-town feel	Isolation

An industrial and agricultural center on the Ohio River, Owensboro is the third-largest city in Kentucky, and serves the retail and service needs for a large part of western Kentucky. It is known for a favorable small-business and manufacturing climate. Isolation is an issue, but a planned cross-river highway connection to Interstate 64, a major east–west artery, will improve access to both Louisville and Evansville, Indiana. The city has a diverse industrial base, strong employment, and reasonably high income relative to the low cost of living, giving moderately high buying power. In 2006, the University of Louisville announced a new biomed research center. The downtown area has a nicely refreshed historic feel, and there is a new riverfront redevelopment in progress. But despite some locally flavored amenities—a bluegrass music museum and an annual barbecue festival—there isn't much to do.

Owensboro is located on a river plain of the Ohio River, with mostly level terrain of mixed agriculture and wooded areas. Summers are hot and humid. Both summer and winter are highly variable, with alternations between cold northwesterly winds and warm southerly ones. Storms and weather transitions bring high winds in all seasons and strong thunderstorms in summer. Snow does occur, but large and lengthy accumulations are uncommon. First freeze is late October; last is early April.

DEMOGRAPHICS	AREA	U.S. AVG	ETHNIC COMPOSITION	AREA	U.S. AVG	RESIDENT PROFILE	AREA	U.S. AVG
Population	111,518		White	94.0%	79.0%	Single	28.1%	32.4%
Population density per sq. mile	123.2	358.5	Black	3.9%	10.5%	Married	57.3%	52.7%
Population growth	6.6%	21.1%	Asian	0.5%	2.7%	Divorced/separated	14.7%	14.9%
Median age	37.4	36.1	Hispanic	1.1%	10.6%	Married with children	24.3%	23.7%
Percent Democrat	38.7%	44.5%	Religious observance	71.9%	48.9%	Single with children	8.7%	9.1%
Percent Republican	60.6%	54.5%	Diversity measure	13.4	40.1	Percent over age 65	13.9%	12.9%

Score: 43.9
Rank: 211

INCOME	AREA	U.S. AVG	EMPLOYMENT	AREA	U.S. AVG	EMPLOYING INDUSTRIES	AREA	U.S. AVG
Per capita income	$21,096	$23,235	Unemployment rate	5.9%	4.7%	Largest: Manufacturing		
Household income	$41,130	$46,414	Recent job growth	1.9%	1.3%			
Household income < $25K	30.4%	26.2%	Projected future job growth	8.4%	11.5%	Percent manufacturing	21.4%	15.4%
Household income > $75K	19.7%	25.4%	White collar	49.1%	57.8%	Percent public sector	11.8%	15.7%
Household income growth	13.6%	13.6%	Blue collar	33.7%	25.2%	Percent construction	12.3%	9.9%

Score: 83.7
Rank: 62

INDEXES & TAXES	AREA	U.S. AVG	HOUSING	AREA	U.S. AVG	NECESSITIES	AREA	U.S. AVG
Cost of Living Index	77.1	100.0	Median home price	$107,900	$220,000	Food Index	95.5	100.0
Buying Power Index	119.6	100.0	Home price appreciation	18.4%	10.1%	Housing Index	49.0	100.0
Income tax rate	6.00%	4.70%	Median rent	$534	$709	Utilities Index	80.3	100.0
Sales tax rate	6.00%	6.58%	Homes owned	67.3%	62.3%	Transportation Index	96.2	100.0
Property tax rate	$7.76	$12.00	Home price ratio	2.6	4.2	Healthcare Index	90.5	100.0
						Miscellaneous Cost Index	95.7	100.0

Score: 37.2
Rank: 234

TEMPERATURE	AREA	U.S. AVG	PRECIPITATION	AREA	U.S. AVG	COMFORTS & HAZARDS	AREA	U.S. AVG
Average January low	18.0	26.2	Annual inches precipitation	40.0	37.7	July relative humidity	70%	66%
Average July high	85.0	87.4	Annual inches snowfall	25.0	7.0	Annual days mostly sunny	205	208
Annual days > 90°F	19	38	Annual days precipitation	127	109	Annual days with thunderstorms	43	39
Annual days < 32°F	119	89	Annual days rain > 0.5 inches	27	22	Tornado risk score	10	18
Annual days < 0°F	3	6	Annual days snow > 1.5 inches	4	6	Hurricane risk score	5	13

TEMPERATURE

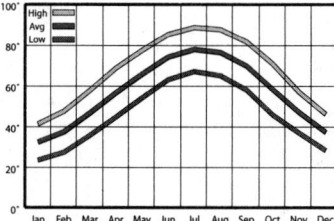

PRECIPITATION

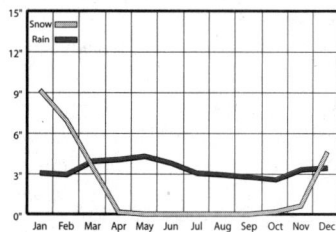

DAYS OF CLOUDS & PRECIPITATION

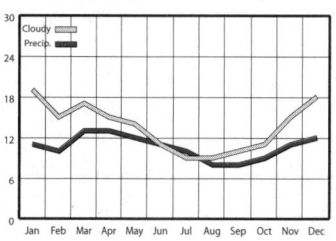

ACHIEVEMENT	AREA	U.S. AVG	PUBLIC SCHOOLS	AREA	U.S. AVG	HIGHER EDUCATION	AREA	U.S. AVG
High school degree	79.9%	82.7%	Expenditures per pupil	$5,440	$5,686	No. 2-year colleges	3	4
2-year college degree	5.6%	6.4%	Student/teacher ratio	24.0	16.7	No. 4-year colleges/universities	2	6
4-year college degree	10.1%	15.7%	Attending public school	91.7%	90.1%	No. highly ranked universities	2	1
Graduate/professional degree	5.7%	8.9%	State SAT score	1124	1021			
			State ACT score	20.6*	20.9			

Education
Score: 18.7
Rank: 303

HAZARDS & ILLNESSES	AREA	U.S. AVG	HEALTHCARE	AREA	U.S. AVG	CRIME	AREA	U.S. AVG
Air-quality score	48	37	Physicians per capita	175.3	244.2	Violent crime rate	172.7	465.5
Water-quality score	72	52	Hospital beds per capita	520.1	420.0	Change in violent crime rate	-1.1%	-2.2%
Pollen/allergy score	72	61	No. teaching hospitals	0	3	Property crime rate	2,338.9	3,517.1
Cancer mortality per capita	233.3	201.9	Cost per doctor visit	$72	$77	Change in property crime rate	-11.5%	-2.1%
Depression days per month	4.0	3.5	Cost per dental visit	$62	$70			
Stress score	67	50						

Health & Healthcare
Score: 57.8
Rank: 159

Crime
Score: 96.5
Rank: 14

COMMUTE	AREA	U.S. AVG	INTERCITY SERVICES	AREA	U.S. AVG	AUTOMOTIVE	AREA	U.S. AVG
Average commute time	22.5	27.4	Major airports within 60 miles	1	1	Insurance, annual premium	$1,078	$1,432
Percent commutes > 60 mins.	4.6%	5.9%	Size of regional airport	Medium	Large	Gas, cost per gallon	$2.41	$2.49
Commute by auto	85.3%	78.9%	Daily airline activity	228	686	Daily vehicle miles per capita	18.5	24.0
Commute by mass transit	0.3%	1.9%	Amtrak service	No	No			
Work at home	2.0%	3.1%						
Mass transit miles per capita	0.27	1.87						

Transportation
Score: 40.9
Rank: 222

DINING & SHOPPING	AREA	U.S. AVG	ENTERTAINMENT	AREA	U.S. AVG	OUTDOOR ACTIVITIES	AREA	U.S. AVG
Restaurant rating	1	2	Professional sports rating	2	4	Golf-course rating	2	4
Outlet mall score	5	42	College sports rating	1	4	Ski-area rating	1	3
No. Starbucks	0	13	Zoo/aquarium rating	1	3	Sq. miles inland water	3	4
No. warehouse clubs	0	2	Amusement park rating	1	3	Miles of coastline	0.0	10.7
			Botanical garden/arboretum rating	1	4	National Park rating	1	3

Leisure
Score: 4.5
Rank: 356

MEDIA & LIBRARIES	AREA	U.S. AVG	PERFORMING ARTS	AREA	U.S. AVG	MUSEUMS	AREA	U.S. AVG
Arts radio rating	1	3	Classical music rating	1	4	Overall museum rating	3	5
No. public libraries	3	27	Ballet/dance rating	1	3	Art museum rating	5	5
Library volumes per capita	2.14	2.78	Professional theater rating	1	3	Science museum rating	3	5
			University arts programs rating	2	5	Children's museum rating	1	3

Arts & Culture
Score: 16.6
Rank: 311

Oxnard–Thousand Oaks–Ventura, CA   Score: 85.1   Rank: 22   2004 rank: 147

Profile: Beach-town/suburban complex
Location: Southern California in the Santa Clara River coastal area and inland valley northwest of Los Angeles
Elevation: 49 feet
Time zone: Pacific Standard Time

PRO
Year-round climate
Attractive setting
Low crime rates

CON
Cost of living
Growth and sprawl
Long commutes

The inhabited portion of Ventura County consists of Ventura, a medium-size city at the coast, and numerous towns, including Oxnard, Simi Valley, Thousand Oaks, and Santa Paula, spreading south and inland into the valley defined by the Santa Clara River. Ventura is a beach town along the original Pacific Coast Highway (U.S. 101). Aside from Ventura and its beaches, the area is a mix of agriculture, small industry, and residential areas. Oxnard is set along the coast in a broad, mainly agricultural plain dotted with subdivisions. The city is the area's industrial center, with Procter & Gamble and food processor Sysco among others operating plants in the area. There is a small high-tech industry, and shipping and import-export companies are tied to a small port and naval facility just south of town. While most of the area is prosperous and attractive, Oxnard has some gritty areas largely absent in the nearby towns. Thousand Oaks is a mostly residential and family-oriented community in the valley 20 miles inland, and has been a leader among the region in controlled growth practice with mixed results, as growth pressure in this ideally located town is very high. The Cost of Living Index at 175.0 is high and rising but the area has the lowest crime rates in the state and a high level of educational attainment. The location is isolated by mountains and long freeway drives—Los Angeles is too far for a practical commute but some may commute to its northern areas in or near the San Fernando Valley. Public transportation facilities are lacking for an area its size. The coast and Channel Islands ("America's Galapagos") offer plenty of recreational opportunities.

While costs are rising, the rest of the package is complete and on the upswing, hence the high ranking.

The east–west running valley is flat to gently rolling with a gradual slope toward the coast. The inhabited area is bounded by two coastal ranges rising 4,000 feet. The mountains are dry and covered with oaks at lower elevations and some coniferous trees at higher ones. Clear, sunny days are the rule in summer, with occasional incursions of coastal low clouds called "fog" locally. Excessive heat is rare but may occur, especially inland.

Population

DEMOGRAPHICS	AREA	U.S. AVG	ETHNIC COMPOSITION	AREA	U.S. AVG	RESIDENT PROFILE	AREA	U.S. AVG
Population	806,367		White	68.0%	79.0%	Single	30.9%	32.4%
Population density per sq. mile	437.0	358.5	Black	1.9%	10.5%	Married	53.2%	52.7%
Population growth	20.5%	21.1%	Asian	5.9%	2.7%	Divorced/separated	15.9%	14.9%
Median age	35.3	36.1	Hispanic	36.0%	10.6%	Married with children	31.0%	23.7%
Percent Democrat	47.5%	44.5%	Religious observance	44.6%	48.9%	Single with children	8.7%	9.1%
Percent Republican	51.2%	54.5%	Diversity measure	72.8	40.1	Percent over age 65	10.7%	12.9%

Economy
& Jobs
Score: 52.1
Rank: 180

INCOME	AREA	U.S. AVG	EMPLOYMENT	AREA	U.S. AVG	EMPLOYING INDUSTRIES	AREA	U.S. AVG
Per capita income	$28,367	$23,235	Unemployment rate	4.9%	4.7%	Largest: Manufacturing		
Household income	$68,144	$46,414	Recent job growth	2.3%	1.3%			
Household income < $25K	14.7%	26.2%	Projected future job growth	13.9%	11.5%	Percent manufacturing	11.5%	15.4%
Household income > $75K	44.6%	25.4%	White collar	63.4%	57.8%	Percent public sector	14.3%	15.7%
Household income growth	14.2%	13.6%	Blue collar	19.6%	25.2%	Percent construction	8.2%	9.9%

Cost of Living
Score: 1.3
Rank: 368

INDEXES & TAXES	AREA	U.S. AVG	HOUSING	AREA	U.S. AVG	NECESSITIES	AREA	U.S. AVG
Cost of Living Index	175.0	100.0	Median home price	$660,900	$220,000	Food Index	111.0	100.0
Buying Power Index	87.3	100.0	Home price appreciation	128.8%	10.1%	Housing Index	266.1	100.0
Income tax rate	6.00%	4.70%	Median rent	$1,471	$709	Utilities Index	111.9	100.0
Sales tax rate	7.25%	6.58%	Homes owned	65.3%	62.3%	Transportation Index	106.7	100.0
Property tax rate	$8.28	$12.00	Home price ratio	9.7	4.2	Healthcare Index	116.6	100.0
						Miscellaneous Cost Index	105.1	100.0

Climate
Score: 97.6
Rank: 10

TEMPERATURE	AREA	U.S. AVG	PRECIPITATION	AREA	U.S. AVG	COMFORTS & HAZARDS	AREA	U.S. AVG
Average January low	45.4	26.2	Annual inches precipitation	12.0	37.7	July relative humidity	71%	66%
Average July high	75.8	87.4	Annual inches snowfall	0.0	7.0	Annual days mostly sunny	258	208
Annual days > 90°F	5	38	Annual days precipitation	35	109	Annual days with thunderstorms	3	39
Annual days < 32°F	0	89	Annual days rain > 0.5 inches	7	22	Tornado risk score	1	18
Annual days < 0°F	0	6	Annual days snow > 1.5 inches	0	6	Hurricane risk score	1	13

TEMPERATURE

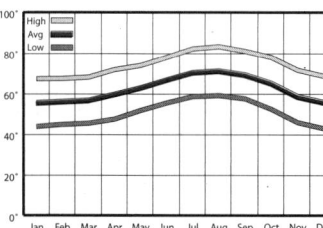

PRECIPITATION

DAYS OF CLOUDS & PRECIPITATION

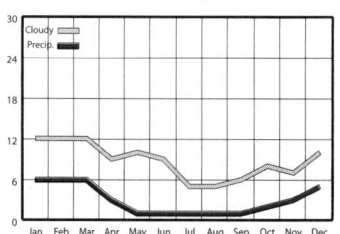

Education
Score: 57.5
Rank: 160

ACHIEVEMENT	AREA	U.S. AVG	PUBLIC SCHOOLS	AREA	U.S. AVG	HIGHER EDUCATION	AREA	U.S. AVG
High school degree	79.5%	82.7%	Expenditures per pupil	$4,718	$5,686	No. 2-year colleges	4	4
2-year college degree	7.8%	6.4%	Student/teacher ratio	21.8	16.7	No. 4-year colleges/universities	6	6
4-year college degree	17.3%	15.7%	Attending public school	90.5%	90.1%	No. highly ranked universities	1	1
Graduate/professional degree	9.4%	8.9%	State SAT score	1019*	1021			
			State ACT score	21.6	20.9			

Health &
Healthcare
Score: 28.9
Rank: 265

HAZARDS & ILLNESSES	AREA	U.S. AVG	HEALTHCARE	AREA	U.S. AVG		CRIME	AREA	U.S. AVG
Air-quality score	20	37	Physicians per capita	188.8	244.2		Violent crime rate	259.4	465.5
Water-quality score	44	52	Hospital beds per capita	226.0	420.0		Change in violent crime rate	9.4%	-2.2%
Pollen/allergy score	42	61	No. teaching hospitals	1	3		Property crime rate	2,083.1	3,517.1
Cancer mortality per capita	156.1	201.9	Cost per doctor visit	$103	$77		Change in property crime rate	-4.9%	-2.1%
Depression days per month	3.2	3.5	Cost per dental visit	$84	$70				
Stress score	26	50							

Crime
Score: 89.8
Rank: 39

Transportation
Score: 88.8
Rank: 43

COMMUTE	AREA	U.S. AVG
Average commute time	27.5	27.4
Percent commutes > 60 mins.	8.4%	5.9%
Commute by auto	75.8%	78.9%
Commute by mass transit	1.1%	1.9%
Work at home	4.2%	3.1%
Mass transit miles per capita	1.07	1.87

INTERCITY SERVICES	AREA	U.S. AVG
Major airports within 60 miles	4	1
Size of regional airport	Large	Large
Daily airline activity	1692	686
Amtrak service	Yes	No

AUTOMOTIVE	AREA	U.S. AVG
Insurance, annual premium	$1,688	$1,432
Gas, cost per gallon	$2.71	$2.49
Daily vehicle miles per capita	22.1	24.0

Leisure
Score: 91.4
Rank: 33

DINING & SHOPPING	AREA	U.S. AVG
Restaurant rating	1	2
Outlet mall score	143	42
No. Starbucks	31	13
No. warehouse clubs	3	2

ENTERTAINMENT	AREA	U.S. AVG
Professional sports rating	9	4
College sports rating	6	4
Zoo/aquarium rating	2	3
Amusement park rating	5	3
Botanical garden/ arboretum rating	7	4

OUTDOOR ACTIVITIES	AREA	U.S. AVG
Golf-course rating	7	4
Ski-area rating	10	3
Sq. miles inland water	3	4
Miles of coastline	35.9	10.7
National Park rating	10	3

Arts & Culture
Score: 71.4
Rank: 107

MEDIA & LIBRARIES	AREA	U.S. AVG
Arts radio rating	5	3
No. public libraries	22	27
Library volumes per capita	2.05	2.78

PERFORMING ARTS	AREA	U.S. AVG
Classical music rating	6	4
Ballet/dance rating	6	3
Professional theater rating	5	3
University arts programs rating	3	5

MUSEUMS	AREA	U.S. AVG
Overall museum rating	9	5
Art museum rating	8	5
Science museum rating	10	5
Children's museum rating	6	3

Palm Bay–Melbourne–Titusville, FL   Score: 75.0   Rank: 67   2004 rank: 64

Profile: Beach-city complex
Location: Central Atlantic coast, 50 miles east/southeast of Orlando
Elevation: 31 feet
Time zone: Eastern Standard Time

PRO	CON
Climate	Violent crime rate
Water recreation	Rising living costs
Cost of living	Arts and culture

Palm Bay, Melbourne, and Titusville anchor a large, complex, and spread-out area of barrier islands and beach and coastal communities comprising an area known as the "Space Coast." Cape Canaveral and the John F. Kennedy Space Center are located on the northernmost large barrier islands, adding considerable interest and economic benefit to the area. There are fine beaches on the barrier islands, while the coast cities tend to carry most of the commercial, residential, and agricultural activity. Driven in part by the NASA facilities, there are a number of high-tech firms in the area, especially in Melbourne and Titusville, while the more family-oriented Palm Bay is the most populous of the three. Melbourne is home to the 3,000-student Florida Institute of Technology. Titusville has most of the museums and amenities tied to space and space technology and some noted wildlife viewing areas. Long a fairly quiet and inexpensive area, this city complex is only 30 miles due east of Orlando, giving access to bigger-city amenities but also staying away from the bustle of that city. As a result, the area has grown rapidly, and home price appreciation is second highest in the state. The area is popular for families and retirees alike, and generally speaking, except at major space launches, these aren't big tourist areas, a fact appreciated by most locals. Some arts and culture amenities are absent. The area ranks high because of climate, recreation, and overall quality of life and the lack of strong negatives.

The narrow barrier islands are mainly sand and palm trees, becoming wider toward Cape Canaveral. Inland is a mix of agriculture and marshland with a few inland lakes. Summer temperatures, while reaching 90°F or above during the late morning or early afternoon, tend to diminish in the afternoon due to sea breezes and frequent afternoon thundershowers. Winters are relatively mild. Summer is the rainy season with thunderstorms, many quite heavy.

Population

DEMOGRAPHICS	AREA	U.S. AVG
Population	520,207	
Population density per sq. mile	510.9	358.5
Population growth	30.4%	21.1%
Median age	42.6	36.1
Percent Democrat	41.6%	44.5%
Percent Republican	57.7%	54.5%

ETHNIC COMPOSITION	AREA	U.S. AVG
White	85.6%	79.0%
Black	9.0%	10.5%
Asian	1.8%	2.7%
Hispanic	5.5%	10.6%
Religious observance	39.2%	48.9%
Diversity measure	33.5	40.1

RESIDENT PROFILE	AREA	U.S. AVG
Single	27.6%	32.4%
Married	56.2%	52.7%
Divorced/separated	16.1%	14.9%
Married with children	18.5%	23.7%
Single with children	7.7%	9.1%
Percent over age 65	20.3%	12.9%

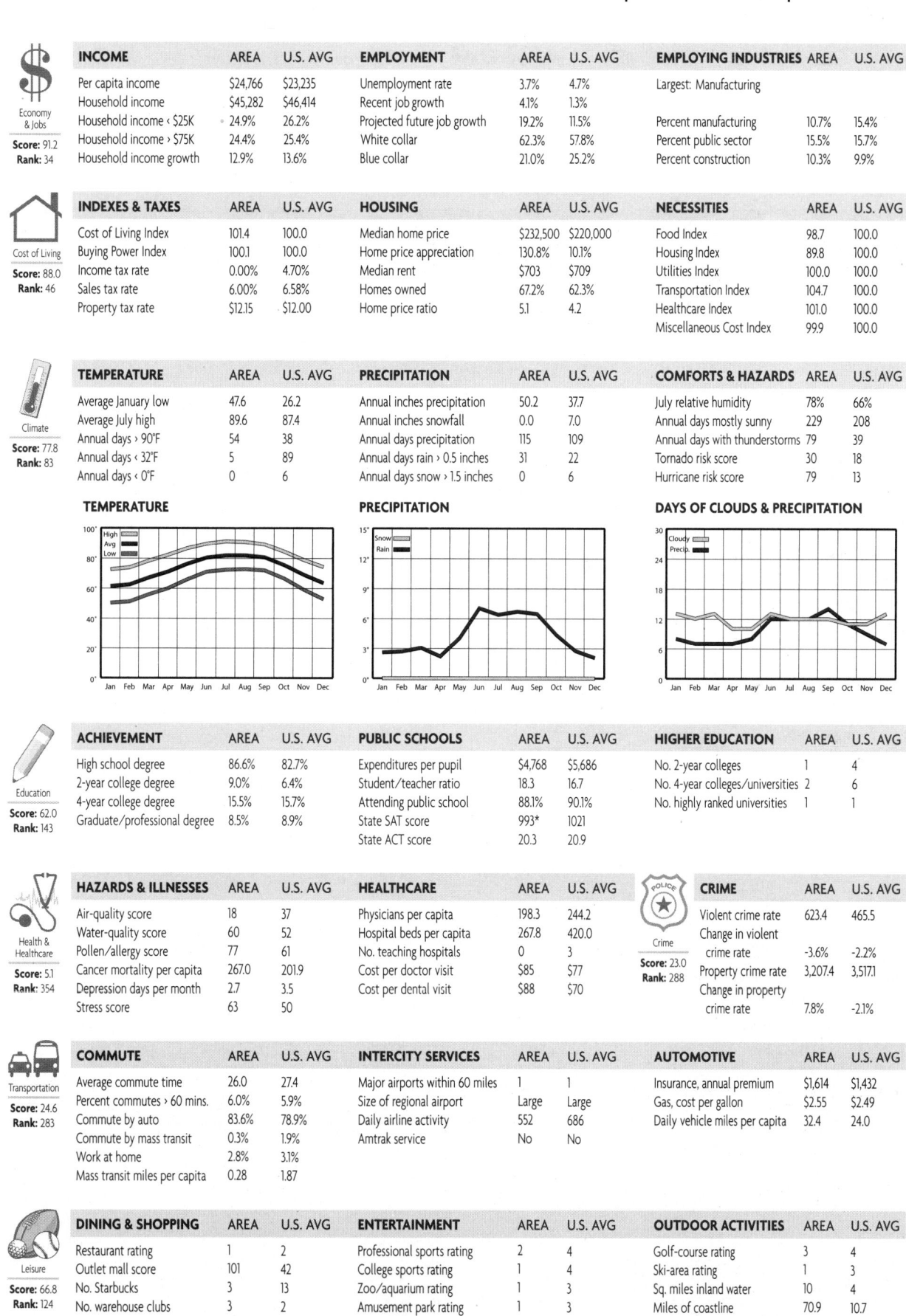

INCOME

	AREA	U.S. AVG
Per capita income	$24,766	$23,235
Household income	$45,282	$46,414
Household income < $25K	24.9%	26.2%
Household income > $75K	24.4%	25.4%
Household income growth	12.9%	13.6%

Economy & Jobs
Score: 91.2
Rank: 34

EMPLOYMENT

	AREA	U.S. AVG
Unemployment rate	3.7%	4.7%
Recent job growth	4.1%	1.3%
Projected future job growth	19.2%	11.5%
White collar	62.3%	57.8%
Blue collar	21.0%	25.2%

EMPLOYING INDUSTRIES

	AREA	U.S. AVG
Largest: Manufacturing		
Percent manufacturing	10.7%	15.4%
Percent public sector	15.5%	15.7%
Percent construction	10.3%	9.9%

INDEXES & TAXES

	AREA	U.S. AVG
Cost of Living Index	101.4	100.0
Buying Power Index	100.1	100.0
Income tax rate	0.00%	4.70%
Sales tax rate	6.00%	6.58%
Property tax rate	$12.15	$12.00

Cost of Living
Score: 88.0
Rank: 46

HOUSING

	AREA	U.S. AVG
Median home price	$232,500	$220,000
Home price appreciation	130.8%	10.1%
Median rent	$703	$709
Homes owned	67.2%	62.3%
Home price ratio	5.1	4.2

NECESSITIES

	AREA	U.S. AVG
Food Index	98.7	100.0
Housing Index	89.8	100.0
Utilities Index	100.0	100.0
Transportation Index	104.7	100.0
Healthcare Index	101.0	100.0
Miscellaneous Cost Index	99.9	100.0

TEMPERATURE

	AREA	U.S. AVG
Average January low	47.6	26.2
Average July high	89.6	87.4
Annual days > 90°F	54	38
Annual days < 32°F	5	89
Annual days < 0°F	0	6

Climate
Score: 77.8
Rank: 83

PRECIPITATION

	AREA	U.S. AVG
Annual inches precipitation	50.2	37.7
Annual inches snowfall	0.0	7.0
Annual days precipitation	115	109
Annual days rain > 0.5 inches	31	22
Annual days snow > 1.5 inches	0	6

COMFORTS & HAZARDS

	AREA	U.S. AVG
July relative humidity	78%	66%
Annual days mostly sunny	229	208
Annual days with thunderstorms	79	39
Tornado risk score	30	18
Hurricane risk score	79	13

TEMPERATURE

PRECIPITATION

DAYS OF CLOUDS & PRECIPITATION

ACHIEVEMENT

	AREA	U.S. AVG
High school degree	86.6%	82.7%
2-year college degree	9.0%	6.4%
4-year college degree	15.5%	15.7%
Graduate/professional degree	8.5%	8.9%

Education
Score: 62.0
Rank: 143

PUBLIC SCHOOLS

	AREA	U.S. AVG
Expenditures per pupil	$4,768	$5,686
Student/teacher ratio	18.3	16.7
Attending public school	88.1%	90.1%
State SAT score	993*	1021
State ACT score	20.3	20.9

HIGHER EDUCATION

	AREA	U.S. AVG
No. 2-year colleges	1	4
No. 4-year colleges/universities	2	6
No. highly ranked universities	1	1

HAZARDS & ILLNESSES

	AREA	U.S. AVG
Air-quality score	18	37
Water-quality score	60	52
Pollen/allergy score	77	61
Cancer mortality per capita	267.0	201.9
Depression days per month	2.7	3.5
Stress score	63	50

Health & Healthcare
Score: 5.1
Rank: 354

HEALTHCARE

	AREA	U.S. AVG
Physicians per capita	198.3	244.2
Hospital beds per capita	267.8	420.0
No. teaching hospitals	0	3
Cost per doctor visit	$85	$77
Cost per dental visit	$88	$70

CRIME

	AREA	U.S. AVG
Violent crime rate	623.4	465.5
Change in violent crime rate	-3.6%	-2.2%
Property crime rate	3,207.4	3,517.1
Change in property crime rate	7.8%	-2.1%

Crime
Score: 23.0
Rank: 288

COMMUTE

	AREA	U.S. AVG
Average commute time	26.0	27.4
Percent commutes > 60 mins.	6.0%	5.9%
Commute by auto	83.6%	78.9%
Commute by mass transit	0.3%	1.9%
Work at home	2.8%	3.1%
Mass transit miles per capita	0.28	1.87

Transportation
Score: 24.6
Rank: 283

INTERCITY SERVICES

	AREA	U.S. AVG
Major airports within 60 miles	1	1
Size of regional airport	Large	Large
Daily airline activity	552	686
Amtrak service	No	No

AUTOMOTIVE

	AREA	U.S. AVG
Insurance, annual premium	$1,614	$1,432
Gas, cost per gallon	$2.55	$2.49
Daily vehicle miles per capita	32.4	24.0

DINING & SHOPPING

	AREA	U.S. AVG
Restaurant rating	1	2
Outlet mall score	101	42
No. Starbucks	3	13
No. warehouse clubs	3	2

Leisure
Score: 66.8
Rank: 124

ENTERTAINMENT

	AREA	U.S. AVG
Professional sports rating	2	4
College sports rating	1	4
Zoo/aquarium rating	1	3
Amusement park rating	1	3
Botanical garden/ arboretum rating	1	4

OUTDOOR ACTIVITIES

	AREA	U.S. AVG
Golf-course rating	3	4
Ski-area rating	1	3
Sq. miles inland water	10	4
Miles of coastline	70.9	10.7
National Park rating	4	3

Arts & Culture
Score: 31.3
Rank: 257

MEDIA & LIBRARIES	AREA	U.S. AVG	PERFORMING ARTS	AREA	U.S. AVG	MUSEUMS	AREA	U.S. AVG
Arts radio rating	1	3	Classical music rating	4	4	Overall museum rating	2	5
No. public libraries	17	27	Ballet/dance rating	1	3	Art museum rating	4	5
Library volumes per capita	2.43	2.78	Professional theater rating	1	3	Science museum rating	5	5
			University arts programs rating	2	5	Children's museum rating	2	3

Panama City–Lynn Haven, FL   Score: 46.2   Rank: 275   2004 rank: 252

Profile: Beach town/military town
Location: Florida Panhandle on the Gulf Coast
Elevation: 112 feet
Time zone: Eastern Standard Time

PRO	CON
Attractive beaches	Crime rates
Future job growth	Isolation
Water recreation	Tourist sprawl

Panama City is one of the more popular beach cities in the Florida Panhandle. The area has large, white, sandy beaches, particularly to the northwest in Panama City Beach, a separate city. Panama City Beach is a spring-break destination with a substantial tourist-oriented infrastructure including amusement parks; its older, 1950s-style, oft-tacky beach strip appearance reflects its mostly lower-middle-class clientele. But the beaches themselves and the water are very attractive and create a prime destination for watersports enthusiasts. Nearby ocean currents support abundant marine life, and fishing and diving are popular. The relatively more complete and purposeful Panama City has a modest industrial base and some historic interest. Lynn Haven is a mainly residential community with an interesting history as a planned residential "haven" for elderly Civil War veterans

developed by W. H. Lynn, a New York senator just before World War I. Aside from tourism, the largest employer is the Tyndall Air Force Base. Cost of living and especially housing are reasonable for a Florida beach town, but both are on the rise. High crime rates, isolation from cultural and air service amenities, and tourist impact are the main downsides.

Panama City sits in an area of beaches, coastal dunes, and wet low-land. The interior contains numerous creeks and bays, and forested swampland with a rich assortment of live oaks, magnolia, cypress, and pine. The Gulf moderates summer heat. Average annual rainfall is high at 64 inches but monthly and yearly totals vary widely. Thunderstorms occur year-round, but most arrive in summer. Tropical storms occasionally affect the area.

Population

DEMOGRAPHICS	AREA	U.S. AVG	ETHNIC COMPOSITION	AREA	U.S. AVG	RESIDENT PROFILE	AREA	U.S. AVG
Population	158,050		White	83.6%	79.0%	Single	27.3%	32.4%
Population density per sq. mile	207.0	358.5	Black	11.1%	10.5%	Married	54.3%	52.7%
Population growth	24.5%	21.1%	Asian	1.9%	2.7%	Divorced/separated	18.4%	14.9%
Median age	38.3	36.1	Hispanic	2.0%	10.6%	Married with children	20.7%	23.7%
Percent Democrat	28.1%	44.5%	Religious observance	41.5%	48.9%	Single with children	9.6%	9.1%
Percent Republican	71.2%	54.5%	Diversity measure	31.6	40.1	Percent over age 65	14.4%	12.9%

Economy & Jobs
Score: 94.4
Rank: 22

INCOME	AREA	U.S. AVG	EMPLOYMENT	AREA	U.S. AVG	EMPLOYING INDUSTRIES	AREA	U.S. AVG
Per capita income	$21,797	$23,235	Unemployment rate	3.5%	4.7%	Largest: Healthcare & Social Assistance		
Household income	$41,466	$46,414	Recent job growth	5.7%	1.3%			
Household income < $25K	28.7%	26.2%	Projected future job growth	22.9%	11.5%	Percent manufacturing	10.8%	15.4%
Household income > $75K	20.0%	25.4%	White collar	56.6%	57.8%	Percent public sector	17.7%	15.7%
Household income growth	14.9%	13.6%	Blue collar	23.2%	25.2%	Percent construction	12.4%	9.9%

Cost of Living
Score: 60.2
Rank: 149

INDEXES & TAXES	AREA	U.S. AVG	HOUSING	AREA	U.S. AVG	NECESSITIES	AREA	U.S. AVG
Cost of Living Index	98.8	100.0	Median home price	$220,100	$220,000	Food Index	104.3	100.0
Buying Power Index	94.1	100.0	Home price appreciation	102.7%	10.1%	Housing Index	74.0	100.0
Income tax rate	0.00%	4.70%	Median rent	$618	$709	Utilities Index	87.5	100.0
Sales tax rate	6.50%	6.58%	Homes owned	52.6%	62.3%	Transportation Index	105.0	100.0
Property tax rate	$10.06	$12.00	Home price ratio	5.3	4.2	Healthcare Index	102.7	100.0
						Miscellaneous Cost Index	97.3	100.0

Climate
Score: 71.1
Rank: 107

TEMPERATURE	AREA	U.S. AVG	PRECIPITATION	AREA	U.S. AVG	COMFORTS & HAZARDS	AREA	U.S. AVG
Average January low	43.0	26.2	Annual inches precipitation	64.2	37.7	July relative humidity	74%	66%
Average July high	89.7	87.4	Annual inches snowfall	0.3	7.0	Annual days mostly sunny	220	208
Annual days > 90°F	55	38	Annual days precipitation	114	109	Annual days with thunderstorms	76	39
Annual days < 32°F	16	89	Annual days rain > 0.5 inches	37	22	Tornado risk score	28	18
Annual days < 0°F	0	6	Annual days snow > 1.5 inches	0	6	Hurricane risk score	60	13

TEMPERATURE

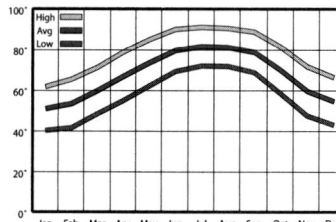

PRECIPITATION

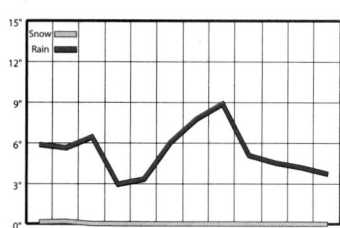

DAYS OF CLOUDS & PRECIPITATION

Education
Score: 38.8
Rank: 230

ACHIEVEMENT	AREA	U.S. AVG	PUBLIC SCHOOLS	AREA	U.S. AVG	HIGHER EDUCATION	AREA	U.S. AVG
High school degree	81.3%	82.7%	Expenditures per pupil	$5,106	$5,686	No. 2-year colleges	2	4
2-year college degree	7.8%	6.4%	Student/teacher ratio	17.3	16.7	No. 4-year colleges/universities	1	6
4-year college degree	11.2%	15.7%	Attending public school	95.4%	90.1%	No. highly ranked universities	0	1
Graduate/professional degree	6.7%	8.9%	State SAT score	993*	1021			
			State ACT score	20.3	20.9			

Health & Healthcare
Score: 31.8
Rank: 254

HAZARDS & ILLNESSES	AREA	U.S. AVG	HEALTHCARE	AREA	U.S. AVG	CRIME	AREA	U.S. AVG
Air-quality score	32	37	Physicians per capita	198.5	244.2	Violent crime rate	661.2	465.5
Water-quality score	100	52	Hospital beds per capita	384.1	420.0	Change in violent crime rate	-4.2%	-2.2%
Pollen/allergy score	61	61	No. teaching hospitals	0	3	Property crime rate	4,181.7	3,517.1
Cancer mortality per capita	291.8	201.9	Cost per doctor visit	$74	$77	Change in property crime rate	-13.2%	-2.1%
Depression days per month	3.7	3.5	Cost per dental visit	$67	$70			
Stress score	54	50						

Crime
Score: 14.2
Rank: 320

Transportation
Score: 20.9
Rank: 297

COMMUTE	AREA	U.S. AVG	INTERCITY SERVICES	AREA	U.S. AVG	AUTOMOTIVE	AREA	U.S. AVG
Average commute time	23.1	27.4	Major airports within 60 miles	0	1	Insurance, annual premium	$1,544	$1,432
Percent commutes > 60 mins.	4.3%	5.9%	Size of regional airport	Small	Large	Gas, cost per gallon	$2.57	$2.49
Commute by auto	81.2%	78.9%	Daily airline activity	122	686	Daily vehicle miles per capita	30.2	24.0
Commute by mass transit	0.3%	1.9%	Amtrak service	No	No			
Work at home	2.3%	3.1%						
Mass transit miles per capita	0.31	1.87						

Leisure
Score: 46.8
Rank: 198

DINING & SHOPPING	AREA	U.S. AVG	ENTERTAINMENT	AREA	U.S. AVG	OUTDOOR ACTIVITIES	AREA	U.S. AVG
Restaurant rating	1	2	Professional sports rating	2	4	Golf-course rating	2	4
Outlet mall score	22	42	College sports rating	1	4	Ski-area rating	1	3
No. Starbucks	1	13	Zoo/aquarium rating	1	3	Sq. miles inland water	7	4
No. warehouse clubs	1	2	Amusement park rating	5	3	Miles of coastline	44.0	10.7
			Botanical garden/ arboretum rating	1	4	National Park rating	1	3

Arts & Culture
Score: 15.2
Rank: 316

MEDIA & LIBRARIES	AREA	U.S. AVG	PERFORMING ARTS	AREA	U.S. AVG	MUSEUMS	AREA	U.S. AVG
Arts radio rating	1	3	Classical music rating	3	4	Overall museum rating	2	5
No. public libraries	8	27	Ballet/dance rating	1	3	Art museum rating	4	5
Library volumes per capita	1.19	2.78	Professional theater rating	1	3	Science museum rating	3	5
			University arts programs rating	1	5	Children's museum rating	5	3

Parkersburg–Marietta–Vienna, WV-OH

Score: 44.3   **Rank: 289**   **2004 rank: 193**

Profile: Small industrial river towns
Location: Northwestern West Virginia along the Ohio River
Elevation: 649 feet
Time zone: Eastern Standard Time

PRO	CON
Cost of living	Economy
Attractive setting	Isolation
Water recreation	Low ethnic diversity

Parkersburg is a small town on the Ohio River with a primarily industrial heritage, while also serving as a transportation gateway between the eastern seaboard and the Midwest and Great Lakes regions. Marietta, located across the river, is another industrial town with more of a historic flavor, while Vienna, West Virginia, is a suburb just north of Parkersburg. Both, aside from a few historic attractions, have relatively plain downtown and residential areas. Nearby oil and gas fields supply resources to local chemical, plastics, and glass companies. DuPont, Borg-Warner, Ashland, Goodyear, Shell, and Union Carbide all produce plastics nearby. Significant numbers of smaller companies engage in glassmaking, both for commercial and artistic purposes. The cyclical economic base is diversifying somewhat with clothing and food distribution, as large companies begin to recognize the area's suitable location for access to the East Coast, Midwest, and South. But the area still suffers from economic cycles, an industrial landscape, and little to do.

Parkersburg is located at the confluence of the Little Kanawha and Ohio rivers. A series of wooded ridges parallel the rivers and rise as much as 150 feet above the valley floor. Summers are warm and humid; the ridges can block wind creating muggy conditions, but prolonged hot or cold weather is infrequent. Rain occurs year-round and snowfall varies greatly from year to year. First freeze is mid-October; last is late April.

Population

DEMOGRAPHICS	AREA	U.S. AVG	ETHNIC COMPOSITION	AREA	U.S. AVG	RESIDENT PROFILE	AREA	U.S. AVG
Population	162,558		White	97.1%	79.0%	Single	27.9%	32.4%
Population density per sq. mile	119.0	358.5	Black	1.0%	10.5%	Married	57.9%	52.7%
Population growth	0.4%	21.1%	Asian	0.7%	2.7%	Divorced/separated	14.3%	14.9%
Median age	40.4	36.1	Hispanic	0.5%	10.6%	Married with children	22.5%	23.7%
Percent Democrat	38.0%	44.5%	Religious observance	42.5%	48.9%	Single with children	7.6%	9.1%
Percent Republican	61.3%	54.5%	Diversity measure	6.7	40.1	Percent over age 65	15.9%	12.9%

Economy
& Jobs
Score: 13.1
Rank: 324

INCOME	AREA	U.S. AVG	EMPLOYMENT	AREA	U.S. AVG	EMPLOYING INDUSTRIES	AREA	U.S. AVG
Per capita income	$20,519	$23,235	Unemployment rate	5.7%	4.7%	Largest: Manufacturing		
Household income	$38,285	$46,414	Recent job growth	0.9%	1.3%			
Household income < $25K	31.9%	26.2%	Projected future job growth	3.8%	11.5%	Percent manufacturing	19.5%	15.4%
Household income > $75K	18.4%	25.4%	White collar	55.3%	57.8%	Percent public sector	13.2%	15.7%
Household income growth	14.1%	13.6%	Blue collar	29.3%	25.2%	Percent construction	9.8%	9.9%

Cost of Living
Score: 63.4
Rank: 137

INDEXES & TAXES	AREA	U.S. AVG	HOUSING	AREA	U.S. AVG	NECESSITIES	AREA	U.S. AVG
Cost of Living Index	83.7	100.0	Median home price	$121,100	$220,000	Food Index	103.1	100.0
Buying Power Index	102.5	100.0	Home price appreciation	20.4%	10.1%	Housing Index	55.8	100.0
Income tax rate	6.00%	4.70%	Median rent	$519	$709	Utilities Index	116.6	100.0
Sales tax rate	6.58%	6.58%	Homes owned	68.1%	62.3%	Transportation Index	99.7	100.0
Property tax rate	$7.78	$12.00	Home price ratio	3.2	4.2	Healthcare Index	90.0	100.0
						Miscellaneous Cost Index	99.3	100.0

Climate
Score: 45.5
Rank: 203

TEMPERATURE	AREA	U.S. AVG	PRECIPITATION	AREA	U.S. AVG	COMFORTS & HAZARDS	AREA	U.S. AVG
Average January low	24.4	26.2	Annual inches precipitation	38.4	37.7	July relative humidity	71%	66%
Average July high	85.6	87.4	Annual inches snowfall	24.2	7.0	Annual days mostly sunny	212	208
Annual days > 90°F	22	38	Annual days precipitation	150	109	Annual days with thunderstorms	44	39
Annual days < 32°F	98	89	Annual days rain > 0.5 inches	26	22	Tornado risk score	3	18
Annual days < 0°F	2	6	Annual days snow > 1.5 inches	7	6	Hurricane risk score	5	13

TEMPERATURE

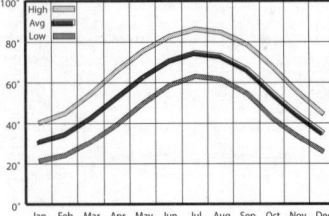

PRECIPITATION

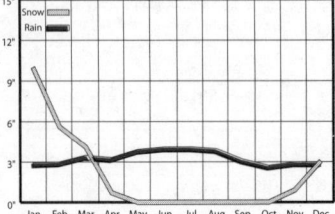

DAYS OF CLOUDS & PRECIPITATION

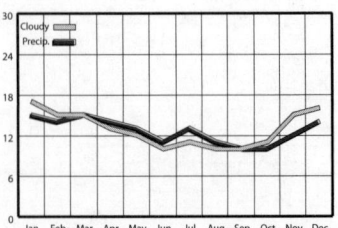

Education
Score: 27.8
Rank: 271

ACHIEVEMENT	AREA	U.S. AVG	PUBLIC SCHOOLS	AREA	U.S. AVG	HIGHER EDUCATION	AREA	U.S. AVG
High school degree	82.2%	82.7%	Expenditures per pupil	$5,541	$5,686	No. 2-year colleges	4	4
2-year college degree	6.4%	6.4%	Student/teacher ratio	17.4	16.7	No. 4-year colleges/universities	3	6
4-year college degree	9.3%	15.7%	Attending public school	94.9%	90.1%	No. highly ranked universities	0	1
Graduate/professional degree	5.4%	8.9%	State SAT score	1029	1021			
			State ACT score	20.6*	20.9			

Health & Healthcare
Score: 58.8
Rank: 155

HAZARDS & ILLNESSES	AREA	U.S. AVG	HEALTHCARE	AREA	U.S. AVG	CRIME	AREA	U.S. AVG
Air-quality score	39	37	Physicians per capita	180.3	244.2	Violent crime rate	269.8	465.5
Water-quality score	36	52	Hospital beds per capita	548.7	420.0	Change in violent crime rate	-18.5%	-2.2%
Pollen/allergy score	60	61	No. teaching hospitals	1	3	Property crime rate	2,515.6	3,517.1
Cancer mortality per capita	232.2	201.9	Cost per doctor visit	$66	$77	Change in property crime rate	19.9%	-2.1%
Depression days per month	4.3	3.5	Cost per dental visit	$62	$70			
Stress score	43	50						

Crime **Score:** 72.7 **Rank:** 103

Transportation
Score: 33.7
Rank: 248

COMMUTE	AREA	U.S. AVG	INTERCITY SERVICES	AREA	U.S. AVG	AUTOMOTIVE	AREA	U.S. AVG
Average commute time	23.2	27.4	Major airports within 60 miles	1	1	Insurance, annual premium	$1,175	$1,432
Percent commutes > 60 mins.	4.5%	5.9%	Size of regional airport	Medium	Large	Gas, cost per gallon	$2.49	$2.49
Commute by auto	84.2%	78.9%	Daily airline activity	270	686	Daily vehicle miles per capita	16.1	24.0
Commute by mass transit	0.5%	1.9%	Amtrak service	No	No			
Work at home	2.2%	3.1%						
Mass transit miles per capita	0.47	1.87						

Leisure
Score: 4.0
Rank: 358

DINING & SHOPPING	AREA	U.S. AVG	ENTERTAINMENT	AREA	U.S. AVG	OUTDOOR ACTIVITIES	AREA	U.S. AVG
Restaurant rating	1	2	Professional sports rating	2	4	Golf-course rating	2	4
Outlet mall score	0	42	College sports rating	1	4	Ski-area rating	2	3
No. Starbucks	0	13	Zoo/aquarium rating	1	3	Sq. miles inland water	2	4
No. warehouse clubs	1	2	Amusement park rating	1	3	Miles of coastline	0.0	10.7
			Botanical garden/ arboretum rating	1	4	National Park rating	1	3

Arts & Culture
Score: 37.2
Rank: 235

MEDIA & LIBRARIES	AREA	U.S. AVG	PERFORMING ARTS	AREA	U.S. AVG	MUSEUMS	AREA	U.S. AVG
Arts radio rating	1	3	Classical music rating	1	4	Overall museum rating	3	5
No. public libraries	12	27	Ballet/dance rating	3	3	Art museum rating	5	5
Library volumes per capita	3.16	2.78	Professional theater rating	1	3	Science museum rating	1	5
			University arts programs rating	6	5	Children's museum rating	1	3

Pensacola–Ferry Pass–Brent, FL

Score: 59.0 **Rank:** 182 **2004 rank:** 239

Profile: Beach city/military town
Location: Western tip of Florida Panhandle on Pensacola Bay along the Gulf Coast
Elevation: 112 feet
Time zone: Eastern Standard Time

PRO	CON
Nearby beaches and water	Growth and sprawl
Historic interest	Arts and culture
Cost of living	Hurricane risk

Because of the strategic location and harbor protection, Pensacola has a rich and varied history, having "changed hands" among nations 13 times, with periods of French, British, and Spanish occupation. A lumber boom in the late 1800s also left its mark on architectural and historic sites. Today, the city has a strong military presence with the Pensacola Naval Air Station, the headquarters of the Blue Angels. Educational attainment is fairly high for a town of this type, although the 9,000-student University of West Florida adds a college-town element. Santa Rosa Island, a barrier island containing the white-sand beaches of the Gulf Island National Seashore, is a major draw for beach and watersports. The area's beaches and water, once a draw mainly for Southern visitors and local military families, have expanded their tourist reach, although at the price of some unattractive development. The area has a distinct Southern flavor, and many refer to the entire Florida Panhandle as "LA"—Lower Alabama. Ferry Pass and Brent are suburbs north of downtown Pensacola, Ferry Pass being the larger and more prosperous of the two. Hurricane Ivan in 2004, and to lesser extent, Hurricane Dennis in 2005, caused extensive damage in the area, particularly to the area's housing and some bridges and highways. Cost of living and home prices are among the lowest in the state, especially for a beach area, and economic figures have turned up somewhat.

Pensacola is situated on a sandy slope bordering the Pensacola Bay breakwater. The Gulf of Mexico moderates the climate year-round. Summer temperatures are in the 80s and 90s, with an occasional 100°F day if sea breezes diminish. Winter highs are usually in the 50s. Freezing temperatures may occur December through February but extended cold waves are infrequent. Rainfall is usually well distributed through the year, but is heaviest in July and August. Fall is relatively dry. Summer rain comes as thunderstorms while winter rains are lighter but occur over longer periods. Snow is observed in 3 out of 10 winters but measurable amounts are rare. Gulf hurricanes are a risk from early July to mid-October.

DEMOGRAPHICS	AREA	U.S. AVG	ETHNIC COMPOSITION	AREA	U.S. AVG	RESIDENT PROFILE	AREA	U.S. AVG
Population	438,226		White	75.8%	79.0%	Single	31.1%	32.4%
Population density per sq. mile	261.0	358.5	Black	17.9%	10.5%	Married	50.7%	52.7%
Population growth	31.2%	21.1%	Asian	2.3%	2.7%	Divorced/separated	18.1%	14.9%
Median age	36.1	36.1	Hispanic	2.1%	10.6%	Married with children	21.9%	23.7%
Percent Democrat	30.0%	44.5%	Religious observance	45.6%	48.9%	Single with children	10.0%	9.1%
Percent Republican	69.1%	54.5%	Diversity measure	40.0	40.1	Percent over age 65	13.5%	12.9%

Economy & Jobs
Score: 82.4
Rank: 67

INCOME	AREA	U.S. AVG	EMPLOYMENT	AREA	U.S. AVG	EMPLOYING INDUSTRIES	AREA	U.S. AVG
Per capita income	$21,990	$23,235	Unemployment rate	4.0%	4.7%	Largest: Healthcare & Social Assistance		
Household income	$42,723	$46,414	Recent job growth	3.3%	1.3%			
Household income ‹ $25K	27.5%	26.2%	Projected future job growth	17.5%	11.5%	Percent manufacturing	11.5%	15.4%
Household income › $75K	21.9%	25.4%	White collar	59.0%	57.8%	Percent public sector	18.0%	15.7%
Household income growth	14.5%	13.6%	Blue collar	23.5%	25.2%	Percent construction	11.9%	9.9%

Cost of Living
Score: 92.8
Rank: 28

INDEXES & TAXES	AREA	U.S. AVG	HOUSING	AREA	U.S. AVG	NECESSITIES	AREA	U.S. AVG
Cost of Living Index	90.6	100.0	Median home price	$174,200	$220,000	Food Index	95.7	100.0
Buying Power Index	105.7	100.0	Home price appreciation	82.7%	10.1%	Housing Index	63.7	100.0
Income tax rate	0.00%	4.70%	Median rent	$602	$709	Utilities Index	91.8	100.0
Sales tax rate	7.19%	6.58%	Homes owned	64.0%	62.3%	Transportation Index	100.7	100.0
Property tax rate	$9.22	$12.00	Home price ratio	4.1	4.2	Healthcare Index	99.6	100.0
						Miscellaneous Cost Index	99.9	100.0

Climate
Score: 70.6
Rank: 109

TEMPERATURE	AREA	U.S. AVG	PRECIPITATION	AREA	U.S. AVG	COMFORTS & HAZARDS	AREA	U.S. AVG
Average January low	43.0	26.2	Annual inches precipitation	64.2	37.7	July relative humidity	74%	66%
Average July high	89.7	87.4	Annual inches snowfall	0.3	7.0	Annual days mostly sunny	220	208
Annual days › 90°F	55	38	Annual days precipitation	114	109	Annual days with thunderstorms	76	39
Annual days ‹ 32°F	16	89	Annual days rain › 0.5 inches	38	22	Tornado risk score	75	18
Annual days ‹ 0°F	0	6	Annual days snow › 1.5 inches	0	6	Hurricane risk score	60	13

TEMPERATURE

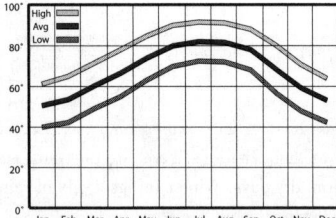

PRECIPITATION

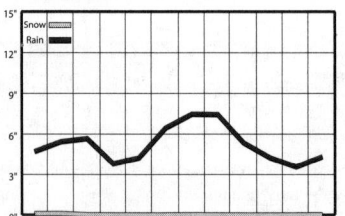

DAYS OF CLOUDS & PRECIPITATION

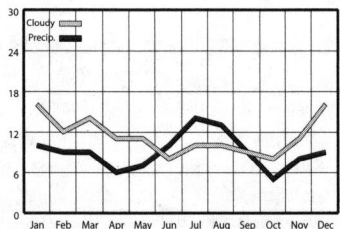

Education
Score: 48.4
Rank: 194

ACHIEVEMENT	AREA	U.S. AVG	PUBLIC SCHOOLS	AREA	U.S. AVG	HIGHER EDUCATION	AREA	U.S. AVG
High school degree	83.5%	82.7%	Expenditures per pupil	$4,890	$5,686	No. 2-year colleges	5	4
2-year college degree	8.5%	6.4%	Student/teacher ratio	17.6	16.7	No. 4-year colleges/universities	1	6
4-year college degree	14.3%	15.7%	Attending public school	89.8%	90.1%	No. highly ranked universities	0	1
Graduate/professional degree	7.6%	8.9%	State SAT score	993*	1021			
			State ACT score	20.3	20.9			

Health & Healthcare
Score: 23.5
Rank: 285

Crime
Score: 47.6
Rank: 195

HAZARDS & ILLNESSES	AREA	U.S. AVG	HEALTHCARE	AREA	U.S. AVG	CRIME	AREA	U.S. AVG
Air-quality score	25	37	Physicians per capita	239.9	244.2	Violent crime rate	609.2	465.5
Water-quality score	79	52	Hospital beds per capita	411.2	420.0	Change in violent crime rate	8.1%	-2.2%
Pollen/allergy score	65	61	No. teaching hospitals	1	3	Property crime rate	3,167.1	3,517.1
Cancer mortality per capita	270.9	201.9	Cost per doctor visit	$61	$77	Change in property crime rate	3.9%	-2.1%
Depression days per month	3.7	3.5	Cost per dental visit	$61	$70			
Stress score	63	50						

Transportation
Score: 2.9
Rank: 362

COMMUTE	AREA	U.S. AVG
Average commute time	25.9	27.4
Percent commutes > 60 mins.	5.8%	5.9%
Commute by auto	78.4%	78.9%
Commute by mass transit	1.0%	1.9%
Work at home	2.6%	3.1%
Mass transit miles per capita	0.95	1.87

INTERCITY SERVICES	AREA	U.S. AVG
Major airports within 60 miles	0	1
Size of regional airport	Small	Large
Daily airline activity	82	686
Amtrak service	Yes	No

AUTOMOTIVE	AREA	U.S. AVG
Insurance, annual premium	$1,504	$1,432
Gas, cost per gallon	$2.54	$2.49
Daily vehicle miles per capita	36.9	24.0

Leisure
Score: 69.8
Rank: 113

DINING & SHOPPING	AREA	U.S. AVG
Restaurant rating	1	2
Outlet mall score	111	42
No. Starbucks	2	13
No. warehouse clubs	0	2

ENTERTAINMENT	AREA	U.S. AVG
Professional sports rating	3	4
College sports rating	5	4
Zoo/aquarium rating	3	3
Amusement park rating	1	3
Botanical garden/ arboretum rating	6	4

OUTDOOR ACTIVITIES	AREA	U.S. AVG
Golf-course rating	3	4
Ski-area rating	1	3
Sq. miles inland water	10	4
Miles of coastline	42.7	10.7
National Park rating	1	3

Arts & Culture
Score: 30.7
Rank: 259

MEDIA & LIBRARIES	AREA	U.S. AVG
Arts radio rating	1	3
No. public libraries	8	27
Library volumes per capita	0.89	2.78

PERFORMING ARTS	AREA	U.S. AVG
Classical music rating	4	4
Ballet/dance rating	1	3
Professional theater rating	1	3
University arts programs rating	3	5

MUSEUMS	AREA	U.S. AVG
Overall museum rating	7	5
Art museum rating	6	5
Science museum rating	7	5
Children's museum rating	1	3

Peoria, IL

Score: 66.6　Rank: 125　2004 rank: 51

Profile: Mid-size city
Location: North-central Illinois, 135 miles southwest of Chicago
Elevation: 662 feet
Time zone: Central Standard Time

PRO
Cost of living
Healthcare
Attractive residential
　areas

CON
Economic cycles
Entertainment
Air service

Peoria is a pleasant, small community that, while not outstanding in any category, does okay in most. One of the oldest cities in the state, it is a business, industrial, and agricultural center known as the headquarters for Caterpillar, Inc., and the heavy-equipment industry. It is also home to the U.S. Agricultural Research Laboratory. Consistent with its mainstream Midwestern stereotype, life in Peoria is generally quiet. Downtown is clean and unremarkable but has some new entertainment venues and is undergoing some redevelopment, including a new museum center, civic center, and high-rise residential units. The Illinois River waterfront is nice. Attractive older residential areas surround the city in the nearby hills. Cost of living and especially home prices and values are attractive on a national scale. The nature of Caterpillar and the equipment business suggests economic cycles.

There have been periods of extended economic malaise, but the industrial/commercial base is growing and diversifying. Peoria is home to the 6,000-student Bradley University, and educational attainment is high. The city is also home to a strong healthcare sector, including three hospitals and the University of Illinois College of Medicine. Obviously, bigger-city amenities can be found in Chicago.

Peoria is situated next to the Illinois River in a shallow river valley surrounded by level and gently rolling terrain. Summer is generally pleasant, with some humid periods midseason. Most precipitation falls in summer, mainly as thunderstorms. Falls are pleasant, with frequent periods of long, warm, dry days. Winter brings a mix of rain and snow. First freeze is late October; last is late April.

Population

DEMOGRAPHICS	AREA	U.S. AVG
Population	366,035	
Population density per sq. mile	148.2	358.5
Population growth	2.2%	21.1%
Median age	37.7	36.1
Percent Democrat	44.6%	44.5%
Percent Republican	54.7%	54.5%

ETHNIC COMPOSITION	AREA	U.S. AVG
White	87.4%	79.0%
Black	8.8%	10.5%
Asian	1.4%	2.7%
Hispanic	1.9%	10.6%
Religious observance	48.9%	48.9%
Diversity measure	23.9	40.1

RESIDENT PROFILE	AREA	U.S. AVG
Single	30.8%	32.4%
Married	55.6%	52.7%
Divorced/separated	13.6%	14.9%
Married with children	22.6%	23.7%
Single with children	8.3%	9.1%
Percent over age 65	14.9%	12.9%

Economy & Jobs
Score: 77.0
Rank: 87

INCOME	AREA	U.S. AVG
Per capita income	$24,061	$23,235
Household income	$47,978	$46,414
Household income < $25K	23.9%	26.2%
Household income > $75K	26.2%	25.4%
Household income growth	11.7%	13.6%

EMPLOYMENT	AREA	U.S. AVG
Unemployment rate	4.8%	4.7%
Recent job growth	3.1%	1.3%
Projected future job growth	9.8%	11.5%
White collar	58.6%	57.8%
Blue collar	24.6%	25.2%

EMPLOYING INDUSTRIES	AREA	U.S. AVG
Largest: Healthcare & Social Assistance		
Percent manufacturing	15.9%	15.4%
Percent public sector	10.5%	15.7%
Percent construction	8.7%	9.9%

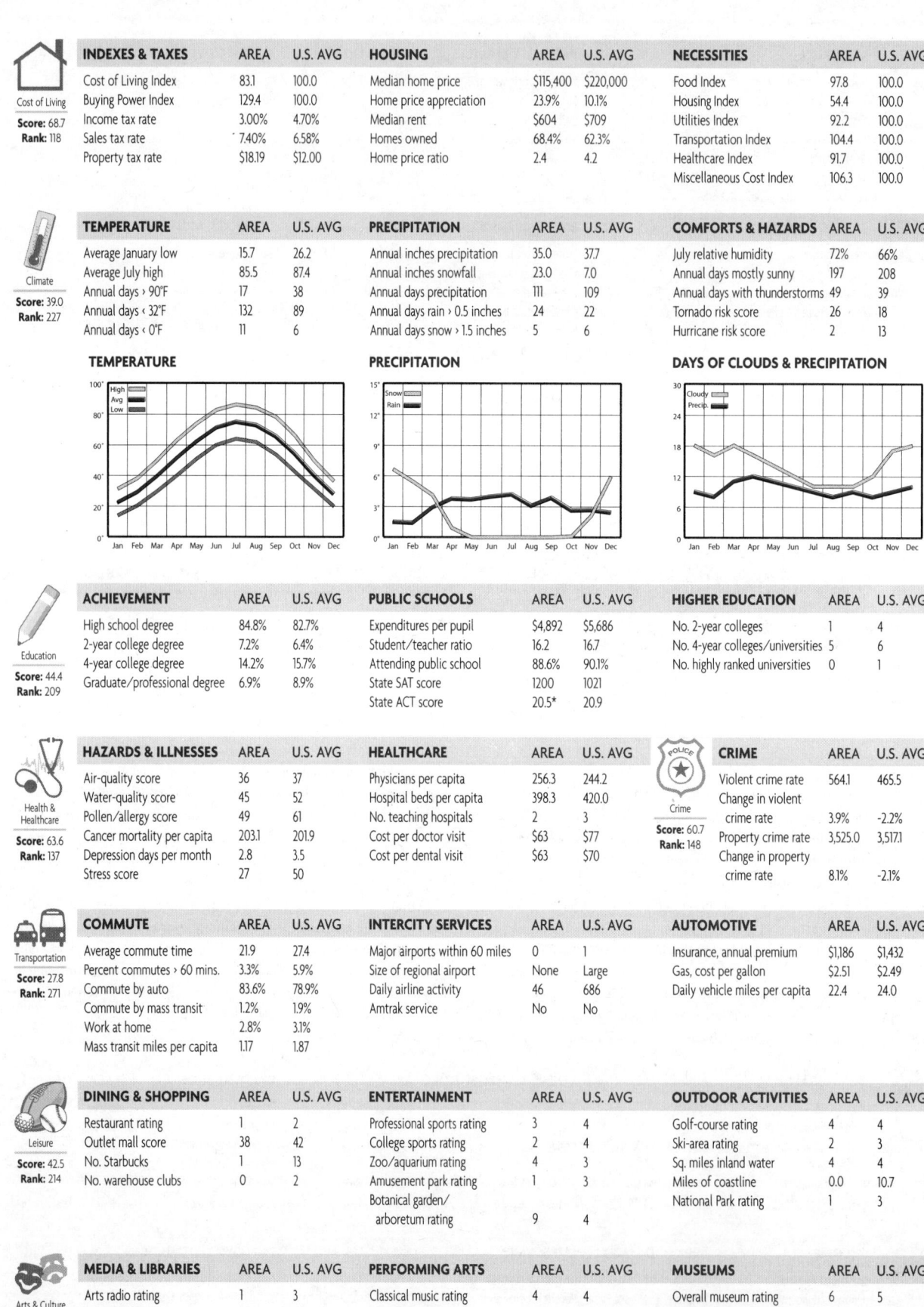

Cost of Living
Score: 68.7
Rank: 118

INDEXES & TAXES	AREA	U.S. AVG
Cost of Living Index	83.1	100.0
Buying Power Index	129.4	100.0
Income tax rate	3.00%	4.70%
Sales tax rate	7.40%	6.58%
Property tax rate	$18.19	$12.00

HOUSING	AREA	U.S. AVG
Median home price	$115,400	$220,000
Home price appreciation	23.9%	10.1%
Median rent	$604	$709
Homes owned	68.4%	62.3%
Home price ratio	2.4	4.2

NECESSITIES	AREA	U.S. AVG
Food Index	97.8	100.0
Housing Index	54.4	100.0
Utilities Index	92.2	100.0
Transportation Index	104.4	100.0
Healthcare Index	91.7	100.0
Miscellaneous Cost Index	106.3	100.0

Climate
Score: 39.0
Rank: 227

TEMPERATURE	AREA	U.S. AVG
Average January low	15.7	26.2
Average July high	85.5	87.4
Annual days > 90°F	17	38
Annual days < 32°F	132	89
Annual days < 0°F	11	6

PRECIPITATION	AREA	U.S. AVG
Annual inches precipitation	35.0	37.7
Annual inches snowfall	23.0	7.0
Annual days precipitation	111	109
Annual days rain > 0.5 inches	24	22
Annual days snow > 1.5 inches	5	6

COMFORTS & HAZARDS	AREA	U.S. AVG
July relative humidity	72%	66%
Annual days mostly sunny	197	208
Annual days with thunderstorms	49	39
Tornado risk score	26	18
Hurricane risk score	2	13

Education
Score: 44.4
Rank: 209

ACHIEVEMENT	AREA	U.S. AVG
High school degree	84.8%	82.7%
2-year college degree	7.2%	6.4%
4-year college degree	14.2%	15.7%
Graduate/professional degree	6.9%	8.9%

PUBLIC SCHOOLS	AREA	U.S. AVG
Expenditures per pupil	$4,892	$5,686
Student/teacher ratio	16.2	16.7
Attending public school	88.6%	90.1%
State SAT score	1200	1021
State ACT score	20.5*	20.9

HIGHER EDUCATION	AREA	U.S. AVG
No. 2-year colleges	1	4
No. 4-year colleges/universities	5	6
No. highly ranked universities	0	1

Health & Healthcare
Score: 63.6
Rank: 137

HAZARDS & ILLNESSES	AREA	U.S. AVG
Air-quality score	36	37
Water-quality score	45	52
Pollen/allergy score	49	61
Cancer mortality per capita	203.1	201.9
Depression days per month	2.8	3.5
Stress score	27	50

HEALTHCARE	AREA	U.S. AVG
Physicians per capita	256.3	244.2
Hospital beds per capita	398.3	420.0
No. teaching hospitals	2	3
Cost per doctor visit	$63	$77
Cost per dental visit	$63	$70

Crime
Score: 60.7
Rank: 148

CRIME	AREA	U.S. AVG
Violent crime rate	564.1	465.5
Change in violent crime rate	3.9%	-2.2%
Property crime rate	3,525.0	3,517.1
Change in property crime rate	8.1%	-2.1%

Transportation
Score: 27.8
Rank: 271

COMMUTE	AREA	U.S. AVG
Average commute time	21.9	27.4
Percent commutes > 60 mins.	3.3%	5.9%
Commute by auto	83.6%	78.9%
Commute by mass transit	1.2%	1.9%
Work at home	2.8%	3.1%
Mass transit miles per capita	1.17	1.87

INTERCITY SERVICES	AREA	U.S. AVG
Major airports within 60 miles	0	1
Size of regional airport	None	Large
Daily airline activity	46	686
Amtrak service	No	No

AUTOMOTIVE	AREA	U.S. AVG
Insurance, annual premium	$1,186	$1,432
Gas, cost per gallon	$2.51	$2.49
Daily vehicle miles per capita	22.4	24.0

Leisure
Score: 42.5
Rank: 214

DINING & SHOPPING	AREA	U.S. AVG
Restaurant rating	1	2
Outlet mall score	38	42
No. Starbucks	1	13
No. warehouse clubs	0	2

ENTERTAINMENT	AREA	U.S. AVG
Professional sports rating	3	4
College sports rating	2	4
Zoo/aquarium rating	4	3
Amusement park rating	1	3
Botanical garden/ arboretum rating	9	4

OUTDOOR ACTIVITIES	AREA	U.S. AVG
Golf-course rating	4	4
Ski-area rating	2	3
Sq. miles inland water	4	4
Miles of coastline	0.0	10.7
National Park rating	1	3

Arts & Culture
Score: 61.0
Rank: 146

MEDIA & LIBRARIES	AREA	U.S. AVG
Arts radio rating	1	3
No. public libraries	43	27
Library volumes per capita	6.12	2.78

PERFORMING ARTS	AREA	U.S. AVG
Classical music rating	4	4
Ballet/dance rating	3	3
Professional theater rating	1	3
University arts programs rating	3	5

MUSEUMS	AREA	U.S. AVG
Overall museum rating	6	5
Art museum rating	6	5
Science museum rating	7	5
Children's museum rating	1	3

Philadelphia, PA

Score: 62.8   **Rank:** 153   **2004 rank:** 76

Profile: Large city
Location: Extreme southeastern Pennsylvania along the Delaware River at the New Jersey border
Elevation: 28 feet
Time zone: Eastern Standard Time

PRO	CON
Arts and culture	Low economic growth
Education	Some urban decay
Historic interest	Violent crime

The "City of Brotherly Love," a direct translation of the city's name from the Greek language, is the seventh-largest metropolitan area in the United States. Philadelphia served as the nation's first capital and cultural center before being replaced in these roles by Washington, D.C., and New York City, respectively. Since the Industrial Revolution, the city has prospered as an important port and manufacturing center. Today, it's part of an economic corridor of large cities stretching down the East Coast from Boston to Washington, D.C. The metro area includes five counties in southeastern Pennsylvania; for the New Jersey side, see the narrative for Camden on p. 245.

"Philly" offers a full set of big-city amenities comparable to those of most major cities. In the late 17th century, William Penn laid out the city on a grid, one of the nation's first. Today, the modern downtown is adjacent to a large historic district anchored by Independence Hall and the waterfront. The majority of the land between the historic district and the Schuylkill River to the west resembles a typical large U.S. city with a mix of old and new structures. Large Fairmount Park contains many of the area's museums and historic buildings. Across the Schuylkill in University Park, a college town within the city, are the University of Pennsylvania and Drexel University. With these two schools and nearby Temple University and Villanova, the area offers more than its share of quality higher education. Some of the city's strong traditions, such as its major league sports teams and Philly cheesesteaks, are nationally famous. Because of its history, museums, and top-of-the-line performing arts, the city gets a top score for arts and culture.

Philadelphia is a city of neighborhoods. South Philadelphia has a mainly immigrant, working-class population, while North Philadelphia and areas west of University Park are rough and somewhat run-down. Some of the best older suburbs lie along the old Pennsylvania Railroad Main Line running to the west. These have spacious, shady neighborhoods with historic homes situated around small-town cores and railroad stations. These suburbs line the tracks well west into suburban towns such as Paoli, Malvern, and Exton. These towns and many nearby have considerable historic interest, attractive topography, and excellent housing values, especially compared to other Northeastern cities. Some towns off the line, such as West Chester and areas south toward the Delaware border, are very livable with considerable local and nearby employment, excellent schools, and family amenities. Some of Philly's growth has also extended northwest to formerly placid areas such as Valley Forge, with a mix of commercial and residential development resulting in some sprawl issues, but these areas are more attractive than comparable rapid-growth areas in other cities. To the north, the suburbs of Hatboro, Warminster, and Doylestown along former Reading Railroad lines offer good residential values as well, although these areas have also been cited for sprawl issues and long commutes. Transportation services, both within the metro area and between Philly and other places, are generally excellent; the Philadelphia International Airport is less crowded than most and served well by discount carriers.

The economy is diverse. Although not known for steel production like many of its Pennsylvania neighbors, the area is a center for several industries, most notably the chemical industry and financial services. While employment has been fairly steady, except for certain pockets of manufacturing that have declined nationally, future job-growth projections are low. Violent crime is high and summers can be uncomfortably warm and humid. However, the Cost of Living Index of 109.6, highest in the state, is low by regional standards, especially for an East Coast city. Although location within the city is important, the outstanding cultural amenities, cost of living, and central East Coast location make Philly attractive and a good value overall, and better for many than the ranking indicates.

The downtown area is in a broad, flat valley. Rolling, hilly countryside stretches to the north and west. The Appalachian Mountains to the west and the Atlantic Ocean to the east moderate the otherwise continental climate. Weather is variable and extreme temperatures seldom last for more than 3 or 4 days. In summer, high humidity can add discomfort to seasonally warm temperatures, while stagnant maritime air can engulf the area. Precipitation is fairly evenly distributed throughout the year, with maximum amounts in late summer as thunderstorms. Snowfall is more abundant in the northern suburbs, while precipitation may arrive as rain rather than snow within the city. Coastal storms produce heavy snowfalls every few years.

DEMOGRAPHICS	AREA	U.S. AVG	ETHNIC COMPOSITION	AREA	U.S. AVG	RESIDENT PROFILE	AREA	U.S. AVG
Population	3,888,163		White	69.3%	79.0%	Single	38.8%	32.4%
Population density per sq. mile	1795.3	358.5	Black	21.8%	10.5%	Married	47.5%	52.7%
Population growth	5.6%	21.1%	Asian	4.4%	2.7%	Divorced/separated	13.6%	14.9%
Median age	37.6	36.1	Hispanic	5.0%	10.6%	Married with children	21.8%	23.7%
Percent Democrat	63.5%	44.5%	Religious observance	59.8%	48.9%	Single with children	9.2%	9.1%
Percent Republican	36.1%	54.5%	Diversity measure	43.8	40.1	Percent over age 65	13.8%	12.9%

INCOME	AREA	U.S. AVG	EMPLOYMENT	AREA	U.S. AVG	EMPLOYING INDUSTRIES	AREA	U.S. AVG
Per capita income	$27,813	$23,235	Unemployment rate	5.3%	4.7%	Largest: Healthcare & Social Assistance		
Household income	$54,558	$46,414	Recent job growth	1.3%	1.3%			
Household income < $25K	23.7%	26.2%	Projected future job growth	2.0%	11.5%	Percent manufacturing	11.2%	15.4%
Household income > $75K	33.7%	25.4%	White collar	66.8%	57.8%	Percent public sector	11.7%	15.7%
Household income growth	12.7%	13.6%	Blue collar	18.5%	25.2%	Percent construction	7.3%	9.9%

Population

Economy & Jobs
Score: 24.1
Rank: 284

Cost of Living
Score: 12.6
Rank: 326

INDEXES & TAXES	AREA	U.S. AVG
Cost of Living Index	109.6	100.0
Buying Power Index	111.6	100.0
Income tax rate	7.65%	4.70%
Sales tax rate	6.38%	6.58%
Property tax rate	$16.79	$12.00

HOUSING	AREA	U.S. AVG
Median home price	$235,100	$220,000
Home price appreciation	73.5%	10.1%
Median rent	$923	$709
Homes owned	64.7%	62.3%
Home price ratio	4.3	4.2

NECESSITIES	AREA	U.S. AVG
Food Index	106.2	100.0
Housing Index	95.0	100.0
Utilities Index	126.0	100.0
Transportation Index	114.3	100.0
Healthcare Index	104.8	100.0
Miscellaneous Cost Index	109.9	100.0

Climate
Score: 64.7
Rank: 131

TEMPERATURE	AREA	U.S. AVG
Average January low	24.4	26.2
Average July high	86.8	87.4
Annual days > 90°F	19	38
Annual days < 32°F	101	89
Annual days < 0°F	0	6

PRECIPITATION	AREA	U.S. AVG
Annual inches precipitation	40.0	37.7
Annual inches snowfall	20.0	7.0
Annual days precipitation	116	109
Annual days rain > 0.5 inches	28	22
Annual days snow > 1.5 inches	6	6

COMFORTS & HAZARDS	AREA	U.S. AVG
July relative humidity	67%	66%
Annual days mostly sunny	205	208
Annual days with thunderstorms	27	39
Tornado risk score	20	18
Hurricane risk score	16	13

TEMPERATURE

PRECIPITATION

DAYS OF CLOUDS & PRECIPITATION

Education
Score: 97.3
Rank: 11

ACHIEVEMENT	AREA	U.S. AVG
High school degree	81.8%	82.7%
2-year college degree	5.5%	6.4%
4-year college degree	17.5%	15.7%
Graduate/professional degree	11.4%	8.9%

PUBLIC SCHOOLS	AREA	U.S. AVG
Expenditures per pupil	$7,022	$5,686
Student/teacher ratio	18.1	16.7
Attending public school	77.1%	90.1%
State SAT score	993*	1021
State ACT score	21.8	20.9

HIGHER EDUCATION	AREA	U.S. AVG
No. 2-year colleges	39	4
No. 4-year colleges/universities	60	6
No. highly ranked universities	10	1

Health & Healthcare
Score: 12.8
Rank: 324

HAZARDS & ILLNESSES	AREA	U.S. AVG
Air-quality score	18	37
Water-quality score	7	52
Pollen/allergy score	62	61
Cancer mortality per capita	266.6	201.9
Depression days per month	3.8	3.5
Stress score	66	50

HEALTHCARE	AREA	U.S. AVG
Physicians per capita	419.1	244.2
Hospital beds per capita	444.0	420.0
No. teaching hospitals	44	3
Cost per doctor visit	$85	$77
Cost per dental visit	$87	$70

Crime
Score: 48.7
Rank: 192

CRIME	AREA	U.S. AVG
Violent crime rate	720.3	465.5
Change in violent crime rate	6.4%	-2.2%
Property crime rate	2,734.6	3,517.1
Change in property crime rate	-2.1%	-2.1%

Transportation
Score: 99.5
Rank: 3

COMMUTE	AREA	U.S. AVG
Average commute time	31.5	27.4
Percent commutes > 60 mins.	10.3%	5.9%
Commute by auto	68.5%	78.9%
Commute by mass transit	12.3%	1.9%
Work at home	3.0%	3.1%
Mass transit miles per capita	12.29	1.87

INTERCITY SERVICES	AREA	U.S. AVG
Major airports within 60 miles	5	1
Size of regional airport	Large	Large
Daily airline activity	3044	686
Amtrak service	Yes	No

AUTOMOTIVE	AREA	U.S. AVG
Insurance, annual premium	$3,124	$1,432
Gas, cost per gallon	$2.51	$2.49
Daily vehicle miles per capita	20.0	24.0

Leisure
Score: 94.9
Rank: 20

DINING & SHOPPING	AREA	U.S. AVG
Restaurant rating	8	2
Outlet mall score	62	42
No. Starbucks	62	13
No. warehouse clubs	10	2

ENTERTAINMENT	AREA	U.S. AVG
Professional sports rating	10	4
College sports rating	6	4
Zoo/aquarium rating	8	3
Amusement park rating	6	3
Botanical garden/arboretum rating	10	4

OUTDOOR ACTIVITIES	AREA	U.S. AVG
Golf-course rating	10	4
Ski-area rating	4	3
Sq. miles inland water	5	4
Miles of coastline	0.0	10.7
National Park rating	3	3

Arts & Culture
Score: 98.1
Rank: 8

MEDIA & LIBRARIES	AREA	U.S. AVG
Arts radio rating	10	3
No. public libraries	150	27
Library volumes per capita	2.85	2.78

PERFORMING ARTS	AREA	U.S. AVG
Classical music rating	10	4
Ballet/dance rating	9	3
Professional theater rating	10	3
University arts programs rating	10	5

MUSEUMS	AREA	U.S. AVG
Overall museum rating	10	5
Art museum rating	10	5
Science museum rating	10	5
Children's museum rating	9	3

Phoenix–Mesa–Scottsdale, AZ

Score: 37.6   **Rank:** 314   **2004 rank:** 273

Profile: Regional center/capital city
Location: South-central Arizona in a low desert valley
Elevation: 1,107 feet
Time zone: Mountain Standard Time (no daylight saving time)

PRO	CON
Pleasant winters	Intense summer heat
Entertainment	Growth and sprawl
Air service	Rapidly rising home prices

Originally a resort city, Phoenix has grown phenomenally in the past 40 years into a full-scale urban center, largely made possible by the advent of air-conditioning. The Phoenix metropolitan area covers over 1,000 square miles. Downtown, which is fairly modest for a city its size, features a few skyscrapers, the capitol, government offices, and a few quality museums. Surrounding downtown are several large and fairly distinct city-suburbs, mostly built on a sprawling grid, in some cases separated by low hills. These include the large middle-class suburbs of Peoria, Mesa, Chandler, and Glendale; upscale Scottsdale; and the college area of Tempe that serves as home to Arizona State University. All areas are modern and generally lacking in historic interest, but keep in mind that Phoenix had only 100,000 residents in 1950.

As best exemplified by its temperatures, Phoenix is a city of extremes. It has the highest average July temperature of any U.S. metropolitan area—almost 105°F. Many days are over 115°F, and temperatures exceeding 120°F occur occasionally. Even though this is "dry" heat, it is still oppressive. At 164, the area has the second-most days of any metropolitan area over 90°F. In 2003, a record nighttime *low* temperature of 96°F was recorded, and nighttime temperatures in the 90s happen frequently. Getting into a car that has been sitting outside in summer can be a memorable experience for outsiders. Winters, on the other hand, are quite pleasant, with daytime highs in the 60s and 70s and only a few evenings below freezing, and no snow. It is little wonder that wealthy "snowbirds" from other parts of the country have used Phoenix as a winter hangout for years.

The low ranking is mainly the result of summer heat, air quality, crime, increasing costs, and home prices, and, except for museums, a relatively weak collection of arts and culture amenities for a city this size. Phoenix is currently in an economic boom cycle, but to be sure it has been prone to boom-bust cycles in the past. The economy has been driven in part by high-tech companies relocating from California, particularly in semiconductor, software, and defense fields, and these companies recently have been doing fairly well. Moreover, the area is seen as a good escape route from the expense and crowding of California. It is also becoming a "first destination" for Asian immigrants and has always been popular with middle-class Mexican immigrants. The result is a strong population inflow, which of course drives up prices and causes many of the same problems people are trying to get away from.

The area, trapped in a geographic bowl and dominated by long automobile trips, has the fifth-poorest air quality in the United States. Agriculture and green spaces have actually elevated pollen counts to the point where Phoenix is in the worst 20% nationwide for the pollen/allergy score. Average commute times of 29 minutes are probably worse than the data indicates due to the large number of retirees who don't commute. On the plus side, Phoenix is a hub for US Airways (recently merged with America West Airlines) and a regional hub for Southwest Airlines, producing an abundance of air choices and reasonable fares. Major league teams for football (Cardinals), baseball (Diamondbacks), basketball (Suns), and hockey (Coyotes) all play in the area; and Arizona State University brings additional sports excitement. There is plenty of entertainment and restaurants in the area's seemingly endless strip malls. Golf amenities are excellent with nationally recognized golf resorts mainly west of town. You find little nightlife in the downtown, but plenty in the suburbs in Tempe, Scottsdale, and elsewhere, and an effort is underway to bring more back into the city center, but we have our doubts—Phoenicians are by nature suburban animals. Weekend getaways can take residents north into the mountains and even to Alpine climates toward Sedona and Flagstaff for a nice "cool" summer break or winter ski outing. Shorter afternoon or evening getaways in the posh and relatively lush Scottsdale can also bring relief from the stress and the heat of this expansive desert city.

Phoenix is located in the Salt River Valley, a broad, desert valley surrounded by low desert mountains as high as the Superstition Mountains to the east at 5,000 feet. Natural vegetation is sparse to nonexistent; uncultivated freeway medians remain as plain dirt. Not surprisingly, the climate is considered arid. Rain usually arrives in June as "monsoons"—tropical moisture flows from the south, which triggers large thunderstorms and raises humidity. Some Pacific storms get through mainly in March and April. Annual precipitation of 7 inches, annual rain days of 34, and annual cloud days of 70 are all among the lowest in the country.

DEMOGRAPHICS	AREA	U.S. AVG	ETHNIC COMPOSITION	AREA	U.S. AVG	RESIDENT PROFILE	AREA	U.S. AVG
Population	3,730,550		White	74.0%	79.0%	Single	31.0%	32.4%
Population density per sq. mile	256.0	358.5	Black	3.8%	10.5%	Married	53.2%	52.7%
Population growth	66.7%	21.1%	Asian	2.5%	2.7%	Divorced/separated	15.8%	14.9%
Median age	33.3	36.1	Hispanic	29.2%	10.6%	Married with children	24.0%	23.7%
Percent Democrat	42.3%	44.5%	Religious observance	39.3%	48.9%	Single with children	8.9%	9.1%
Percent Republican	57.0%	54.5%	Diversity measure	66.5	40.1	Percent over age 65	11.5%	12.9%

INCOME	AREA	U.S. AVG	EMPLOYMENT	AREA	U.S. AVG	EMPLOYING INDUSTRIES	AREA	U.S. AVG
Per capita income	$24,919	$23,235	Unemployment rate	4.3%	4.7%	Largest: Healthcare & Social Assistance		
Household income	$50,834	$46,414	Recent job growth	2.1%	1.3%			
Household income ‹ $25K	21.1%	26.2%	Projected future job growth	22.9%	11.5%	Percent manufacturing	11.1%	15.4%
Household income › $75K	30.1%	25.4%	White collar	62.9%	57.8%	Percent public sector	12.7%	15.7%
Household income growth	13.5%	13.6%	Blue collar	21.7%	25.2%	Percent construction	10.5%	9.9%

Population

Economy & Jobs
Score: 84.5
Rank: 59

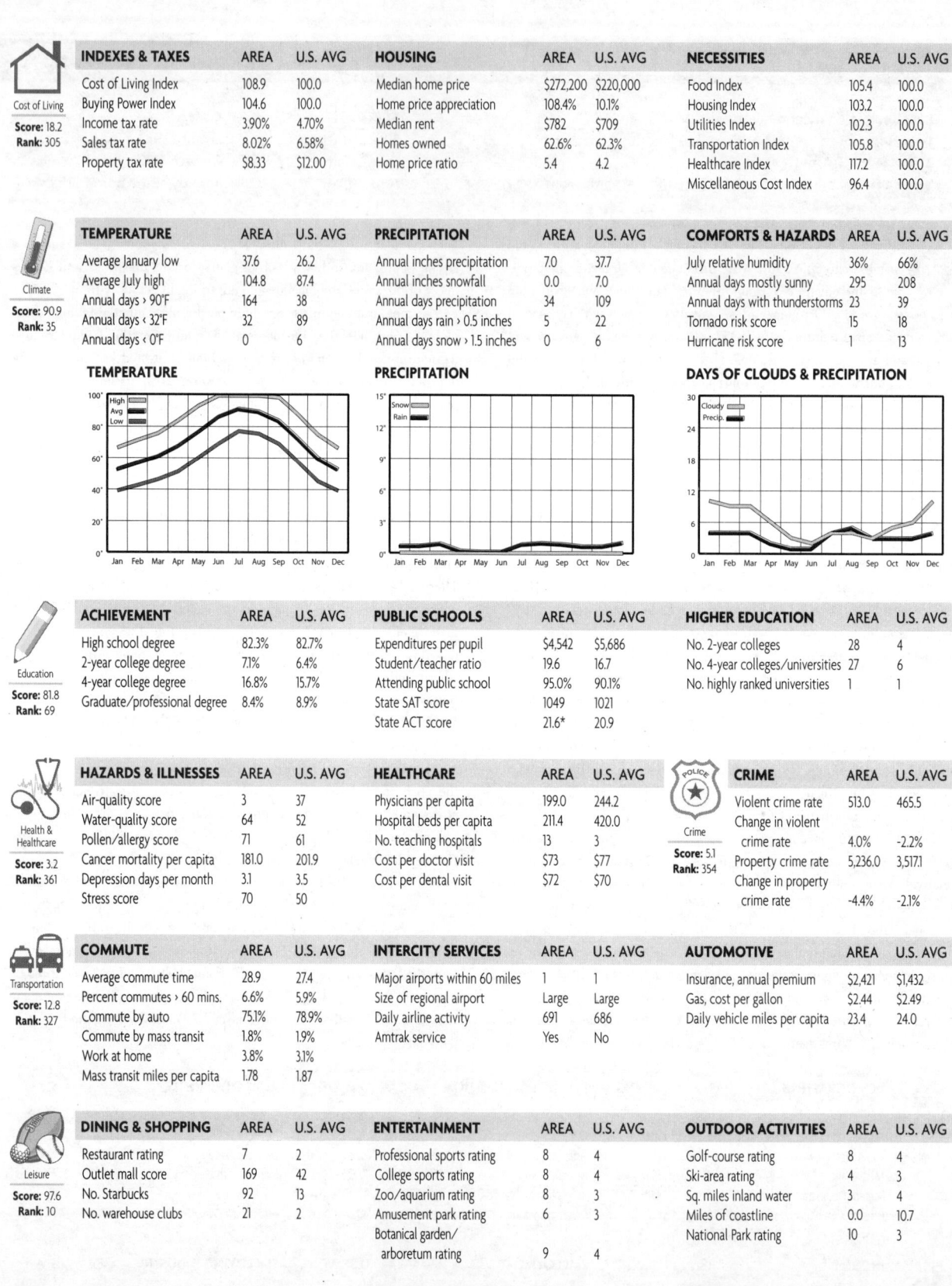

Cost of Living
Score: 18.2
Rank: 305

INDEXES & TAXES	AREA	U.S. AVG	HOUSING	AREA	U.S. AVG	NECESSITIES	AREA	U.S. AVG
Cost of Living Index	108.9	100.0	Median home price	$272,200	$220,000	Food Index	105.4	100.0
Buying Power Index	104.6	100.0	Home price appreciation	108.4%	10.1%	Housing Index	103.2	100.0
Income tax rate	3.90%	4.70%	Median rent	$782	$709	Utilities Index	102.3	100.0
Sales tax rate	8.02%	6.58%	Homes owned	62.6%	62.3%	Transportation Index	105.8	100.0
Property tax rate	$8.33	$12.00	Home price ratio	5.4	4.2	Healthcare Index	117.2	100.0
						Miscellaneous Cost Index	96.4	100.0

Climate
Score: 90.9
Rank: 35

TEMPERATURE	AREA	U.S. AVG	PRECIPITATION	AREA	U.S. AVG	COMFORTS & HAZARDS	AREA	U.S. AVG
Average January low	37.6	26.2	Annual inches precipitation	7.0	37.7	July relative humidity	36%	66%
Average July high	104.8	87.4	Annual inches snowfall	0.0	7.0	Annual days mostly sunny	295	208
Annual days > 90°F	164	38	Annual days precipitation	34	109	Annual days with thunderstorms	23	39
Annual days < 32°F	32	89	Annual days rain > 0.5 inches	5	22	Tornado risk score	15	18
Annual days < 0°F	0	6	Annual days snow > 1.5 inches	0	6	Hurricane risk score	1	13

TEMPERATURE   **PRECIPITATION**   **DAYS OF CLOUDS & PRECIPITATION**

Education
Score: 81.8
Rank: 69

ACHIEVEMENT	AREA	U.S. AVG	PUBLIC SCHOOLS	AREA	U.S. AVG	HIGHER EDUCATION	AREA	U.S. AVG
High school degree	82.3%	82.7%	Expenditures per pupil	$4,542	$5,686	No. 2-year colleges	28	4
2-year college degree	7.1%	6.4%	Student/teacher ratio	19.6	16.7	No. 4-year colleges/universities	27	6
4-year college degree	16.8%	15.7%	Attending public school	95.0%	90.1%	No. highly ranked universities	1	1
Graduate/professional degree	8.4%	8.9%	State SAT score	1049	1021			
			State ACT score	21.6*	20.9			

Health & Healthcare
Score: 3.2
Rank: 361

Crime
Score: 5.1
Rank: 354

HAZARDS & ILLNESSES	AREA	U.S. AVG	HEALTHCARE	AREA	U.S. AVG	CRIME	AREA	U.S. AVG
Air-quality score	3	37	Physicians per capita	199.0	244.2	Violent crime rate	513.0	465.5
Water-quality score	64	52	Hospital beds per capita	211.4	420.0	Change in violent crime rate	4.0%	-2.2%
Pollen/allergy score	71	61	No. teaching hospitals	13	3	Property crime rate	5,236.0	3,517.1
Cancer mortality per capita	181.0	201.9	Cost per doctor visit	$73	$77	Change in property crime rate	-4.4%	-2.1%
Depression days per month	3.1	3.5	Cost per dental visit	$72	$70			
Stress score	70	50						

Transportation
Score: 12.8
Rank: 327

COMMUTE	AREA	U.S. AVG	INTERCITY SERVICES	AREA	U.S. AVG	AUTOMOTIVE	AREA	U.S. AVG
Average commute time	28.9	27.4	Major airports within 60 miles	1	1	Insurance, annual premium	$2,421	$1,432
Percent commutes > 60 mins.	6.6%	5.9%	Size of regional airport	Large	Large	Gas, cost per gallon	$2.44	$2.49
Commute by auto	75.1%	78.9%	Daily airline activity	691	686	Daily vehicle miles per capita	23.4	24.0
Commute by mass transit	1.8%	1.9%	Amtrak service	Yes	No			
Work at home	3.8%	3.1%						
Mass transit miles per capita	1.78	1.87						

Leisure
Score: 97.6
Rank: 10

DINING & SHOPPING	AREA	U.S. AVG	ENTERTAINMENT	AREA	U.S. AVG	OUTDOOR ACTIVITIES	AREA	U.S. AVG
Restaurant rating	7	2	Professional sports rating	8	4	Golf-course rating	8	4
Outlet mall score	169	42	College sports rating	8	4	Ski-area rating	4	3
No. Starbucks	92	13	Zoo/aquarium rating	8	3	Sq. miles inland water	3	4
No. warehouse clubs	21	2	Amusement park rating	6	3	Miles of coastline	0.0	10.7
			Botanical garden/arboretum rating	9	4	National Park rating	10	3

Arts & Culture
Score: 82.1
Rank: 68

MEDIA & LIBRARIES	AREA	U.S. AVG	PERFORMING ARTS	AREA	U.S. AVG	MUSEUMS	AREA	U.S. AVG
Arts radio rating	7	3	Classical music rating	6	4	Overall museum rating	9	5
No. public libraries	60	27	Ballet/dance rating	5	3	Art museum rating	9	5
Library volumes per capita	1.96	2.78	Professional theater rating	1	3	Science museum rating	9	5
			University arts programs rating	7	5	Children's museum rating	4	3

Pine Bluff, AR

Score: 23.8   **Rank:** 361   **2004 rank:** 325

Profile: Small city
Location: Southeast, 40 miles from Little Rock, along the Arkansas River
Elevation: 219 feet
Time zone: Central Standard Time

PRO	CON
Home prices	Crime rates
Cost of living	Low educational attainment
Healthcare	High unemployment

Pine Bluff, the second-oldest city in Arkansas, is a small working-class agricultural, industrial, and railroad town with some antebellum and Civil War history. Cotton, rice, and poultry are grown and processed locally, and the assortment of manufacturing includes papermaking, steel and wire, and electrical distribution products. The area is a major hub and service location on the Union Pacific Railroad, and the Pine Bluff Arsenal provides some military-related employment. Some water and outdoor recreation is available nearby on the partially dammed Arkansas River and in wooded areas nearby. Overshadowing positive qualities is a high violent-crime rate (worst in the U.S.), and the likely contributing factors of low educational attainment and high unemployment. On the positive side, housing costs are the eighth-lowest in the country.

The area around Pine Bluff is mostly level, especially along the broad Arkansas Valley. As the name suggests, Pine Bluff is known for its large pine trees. Summer has prolonged periods of warm and humid weather. Winters are mild with some cold spells. Most precipitation is in summer as thunderstorms with a dry period in late summer and fall. Snow is negligible, but the city is located in an area of relatively frequent ice storms.

Population

DEMOGRAPHICS	AREA	U.S. AVG
Population	105,528	
Population density per sq. mile	51.6	358.5
Population growth	-1.1%	21.1%
Median age	35.7	36.1
Percent Democrat	60.9%	44.5%
Percent Republican	37.3%	54.5%

ETHNIC COMPOSITION	AREA	U.S. AVG
White	50.8%	79.0%
Black	47.0%	10.5%
Asian	0.7%	2.7%
Hispanic	1.2%	10.6%
Religious observance	47.8%	48.9%
Diversity measure	50.4	40.1

RESIDENT PROFILE	AREA	U.S. AVG
Single	33.2%	32.4%
Married	46.9%	52.7%
Divorced/separated	19.9%	14.9%
Married with children	21.1%	23.7%
Single with children	12.2%	9.1%
Percent over age 65	13.0%	12.9%

Economy & Jobs
Score: 47.3
Rank: 198

INCOME	AREA	U.S. AVG
Per capita income	$17,168	$23,235
Household income	$35,380	$46,414
Household income < $25K	36.8%	26.2%
Household income > $75K	17.0%	25.4%
Household income growth	13.4%	13.6%

EMPLOYMENT	AREA	U.S. AVG
Unemployment rate	7.3%	4.7%
Recent job growth	4.4%	1.3%
Projected future job growth	8.0%	11.5%
White collar	49.9%	57.8%
Blue collar	32.4%	25.2%

EMPLOYING INDUSTRIES	AREA	U.S. AVG
Largest: Manufacturing		
Percent manufacturing	22.2%	15.4%
Percent public sector	21.3%	15.7%
Percent construction	10.2%	9.9%

Cost of Living
Score: 36.4
Rank: 238

INDEXES & TAXES	AREA	U.S. AVG
Cost of Living Index	77.4	100.0
Buying Power Index	102.5	100.0
Income tax rate	7.00%	4.70%
Sales tax rate	8.41%	6.58%
Property tax rate	$9.95	$12.00

HOUSING	AREA	U.S. AVG
Median home price	$86,800	$220,000
Home price appreciation	26.4%	10.1%
Median rent	$547	$709
Homes owned	61.2%	62.3%
Home price ratio	2.5	4.2

NECESSITIES	AREA	U.S. AVG
Food Index	102.0	100.0
Housing Index	51.9	100.0
Utilities Index	110.8	100.0
Transportation Index	97.4	100.0
Healthcare Index	97.7	100.0
Miscellaneous Cost Index	96.9	100.0

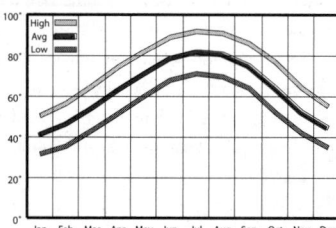
Climate
Score: 44.7
Rank: 206

TEMPERATURE	AREA	U.S. AVG
Average January low	28.9	26.2
Average July high	92.6	87.4
Annual days > 90°F	70	38
Annual days < 32°F	63	89
Annual days < 0°F	0	6

PRECIPITATION	AREA	U.S. AVG
Annual inches precipitation	49.0	37.7
Annual inches snowfall	5.0	7.0
Annual days precipitation	104	109
Annual days rain > 0.5 inches	31	22
Annual days snow > 1.5 inches	2	6

COMFORTS & HAZARDS	AREA	U.S. AVG
July relative humidity	70%	66%
Annual days mostly sunny	220	208
Annual days with thunderstorms	57	39
Tornado risk score	11	18
Hurricane risk score	10	13

TEMPERATURE

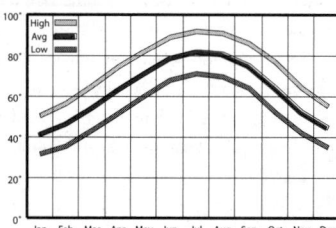

PRECIPITATION

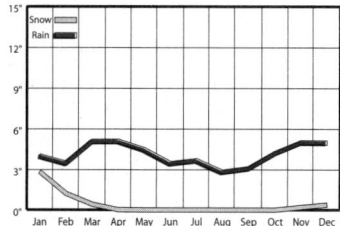

DAYS OF CLOUDS & PRECIPITATION

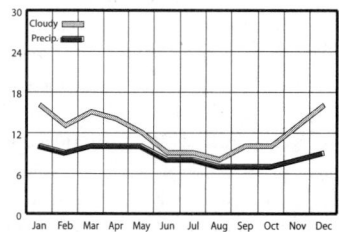

ACHIEVEMENT	AREA	U.S. AVG	PUBLIC SCHOOLS	AREA	U.S. AVG	HIGHER EDUCATION	AREA	U.S. AVG
High school degree	73.5%	82.7%	Expenditures per pupil	$4,825	$5,686	No. 2-year colleges	2	4
2-year college degree	3.3%	6.4%	Student/teacher ratio	20.3	16.7	No. 4-year colleges/universities	1	6
4-year college degree	9.8%	15.7%	Attending public school	96.1%	90.1%	No. highly ranked universities	0	1
Graduate/professional degree	4.3%	8.9%	State SAT score	1142	1021			
			State ACT score	20.6*	20.9			

Education
Score: 3.5
Rank: 360

HAZARDS & ILLNESSES	AREA	U.S. AVG	HEALTHCARE	AREA	U.S. AVG	CRIME	AREA	U.S. AVG
Air-quality score	42	37	Physicians per capita	145.1	244.2	Violent crime rate	799.9	465.5
Water-quality score	65	52	Hospital beds per capita	450.1	420.0	Change in violent crime rate	18.3%	-2.2%
Pollen/allergy score	59	61	No. teaching hospitals	1	3	Property crime rate	5,518.1	3,517.1
Cancer mortality per capita	239.8	201.9	Cost per doctor visit	$66	$77	Change in property crime rate	2.7%	-2.1%
Depression days per month	4.1	3.5	Cost per dental visit	$51	$70			
Stress score	97	50						

Health & Healthcare
Score: 40.6
Rank: 221

Crime
Score: 3.2
Rank: 361

COMMUTE	AREA	U.S. AVG	INTERCITY SERVICES	AREA	U.S. AVG	AUTOMOTIVE	AREA	U.S. AVG
Average commute time	24.7	27.4	Major airports within 60 miles	0	1	Insurance, annual premium	$1,132	$1,432
Percent commutes > 60 mins.	5.9%	5.9%	Size of regional airport	Small	Large	Gas, cost per gallon	$2.46	$2.49
Commute by auto	79.9%	78.9%	Daily airline activity	96	686	Daily vehicle miles per capita	23.8	24.0
Commute by mass transit	0.4%	1.9%	Amtrak service	No	No			
Work at home	1.9%	3.1%						
Mass transit miles per capita	0.40	1.87						

Transportation
Score: 9.6
Rank: 339

DINING & SHOPPING	AREA	U.S. AVG	ENTERTAINMENT	AREA	U.S. AVG	OUTDOOR ACTIVITIES	AREA	U.S. AVG
Restaurant rating	1	2	Professional sports rating	2	4	Golf-course rating	1	4
Outlet mall score	6	42	College sports rating	1	4	Ski-area rating	1	3
No. Starbucks	0	13	Zoo/aquarium rating	1	3	Sq. miles inland water	4	4
No. warehouse clubs	0	2	Amusement park rating	1	3	Miles of coastline	0.0	10.7
			Botanical garden/ arboretum rating	3	4	National Park rating	1	3

Leisure
Score: 7.5
Rank: 345

MEDIA & LIBRARIES	AREA	U.S. AVG	PERFORMING ARTS	AREA	U.S. AVG	MUSEUMS	AREA	U.S. AVG
Arts radio rating	1	3	Classical music rating	3	4	Overall museum rating	4	5
No. public libraries	4	27	Ballet/dance rating	1	3	Art museum rating	6	5
Library volumes per capita	1.93	2.78	Professional theater rating	1	3	Science museum rating	4	5
			University arts programs rating	3	5	Children's museum rating	2	3

Arts & Culture
Score: 23.5
Rank: 285

Pittsburgh, PA

Score: 72.5   Rank: 74   2004 rank: 28

Profile: Large city
Location: West-central Pennsylvania at the confluence of the Allegheny and Monongahela rivers into the Ohio River
Elevation: 760 feet
Time zone: Eastern Standard Time

PRO
Arts and culture
Attractive downtown
Cost of living

CON
Low job-growth projections
Clouds and rain
Commute times

Once a rough and gritty center for the steel-making industry, Pittsburgh is now home to one lone blast furnace and a wide assortment of other industries. Remarkably, for a city of its size and location removed from major transportation routes and large cities, Pittsburgh has a tremendous base of headquarters operations for U.S. and some foreign companies in a variety of industries from banking to food processing to steel and heavy manufactured goods to pharmaceuticals. Names include Alcoa, HJ Heinz, PNC Bank, PPG Industries, Mellon Bank, US Steel, Allegheny Technologies, Wesco, Bayer North America, GlaxoSmithKline, American Eagle Outfitters, General Nutrition Centers, and more. The former grime and smoke have largely blown away, leaving a livable city with historic and revitalized neighborhoods and plenty to do. Employment is shifting from blue-collar to

professional jobs, although there have been some dislocations in recent years due to mergers and acquisitions and general corporate downsizing.

Pittsburgh is a city of neighborhoods. Steep hills rise on all sides of town; some neighborhoods can be reached by a 19th-century incline tram from the central city. The neighborhoods have unique identity and personality, and the city's planning department recognizes more than 90 neighborhoods in all. The population is ethnically diverse. The downtown area is vibrant and active with nightlife along the river and downtown shopping. Excellent residential neighborhoods and suburban towns extend in all directions, especially west, north, and south. The Moon Township area west above the river town of Coraopolis and near the airport is the fastest growing and one of the best family areas, while older suburbs such as Mt. Lebanon and Bethel Park to the south and McCandless and

Allison Park to the north are all worth a look. These areas have generously spaced, high-quality housing, with a median home price just over $120,000 and typically under $200,000 even in the better neighborhoods.

The area is well known for its sports, education, and cultural amenities. Pittsburgh has major league teams in football (Steelers), hockey (Penguins), and baseball (Pirates). Fan support and interest, particularly for the Steelers football team, is legendary. The new Heinz Field and PNC Park are attractive, accessible sports venues. Educational opportunities are excellent, particularly at the highest level with Duquesne and Carnegie-Mellon universities and the University of Pittsburgh. The city has excellent public transportation facilities especially for neighborhoods closer to downtown. It is the major hub for US Airways, which for years gave good if not price-competitive air service, but now with that company's acquisition of discounter America West, fares should become more attractive. Early industrial wealth endowed the city with numerous cultural assets. The Carnegie-endowed museums, the Pittsburgh Symphony, and the Pittsburgh Zoo & PPG Aquarium are all noted in their fields. For all of this, the Cost of Living Index of 85.4 is a bargain. Crime is also

lower than expected given the area's gritty industrial history. The area is an excellent place for corporate professionals or small businesses supporting corporations, and is an excellent place to raise a family, but it does take a few hits as being a bit dull for singles. Other than that, the main downsides are weather (cloudy and variable), employment shifts, and some decayed areas.

Downtown Pittsburgh sits at the confluence of the "Three Rivers" (Allegheny, Monongahela, and Ohio), about 100 miles south of Lake Erie. Most of Pittsburgh lies in a narrow valley, with high, wooded bluffs surrounding the city. Summers are warm, still, and humid with periodic thunderstorms and occasional cooling from the northwest. Winters are cool and variable with intermittent periods of freezing and thawing. Precipitation is distributed evenly throughout the year. Cool northwest winds deliver moisture from the Great Lakes creating persistent cloudy conditions and showers especially in winter. The area has the most cloudy days in the state, the 15th cloudiest in the country. Fog may persist in the valleys during colder months. First freeze is mid-October; last is end of April.

Population

DEMOGRAPHICS	AREA	U.S. AVG	ETHNIC COMPOSITION	AREA	U.S. AVG	RESIDENT PROFILE	AREA	U.S. AVG
Population	2,402,483		White	89.3%	79.0%	Single	34.9%	32.4%
Population density per sq. mile	455.1	358.5	Black	8.0%	10.5%	Married	52.6%	52.7%
Population growth	-2.2%	21.1%	Asian	1.4%	2.7%	Divorced/separated	12.5%	14.9%
Median age	41.3	36.1	Hispanic	0.7%	10.6%	Married with children	20.5%	23.7%
Percent Democrat	51.6%	44.5%	Religious observance	66.2%	48.9%	Single with children	7.2%	9.1%
Percent Republican	47.8%	54.5%	Diversity measure	20.1	40.1	Percent over age 65	17.6%	12.9%

Economy & Jobs
Score: 17.1
Rank: 310

INCOME	AREA	U.S. AVG	EMPLOYMENT	AREA	U.S. AVG	EMPLOYING INDUSTRIES	AREA	U.S. AVG
Per capita income	$23,957	$23,235	Unemployment rate	5.5%	4.7%	Largest: Healthcare & Social Assistance		
Household income	$42,483	$46,414	Recent job growth	0.9%	1.3%			
Household income < $25K	29.3%	26.2%	Projected future job growth	1.8%	11.5%	Percent manufacturing	13.8%	15.4%
Household income > $75K	23.2%	25.4%	White collar	61.0%	57.8%	Percent public sector	9.8%	15.7%
Household income growth	13.6%	13.6%	Blue collar	22.8%	25.2%	Percent construction	9.1%	9.9%

Cost of Living
Score: 48.9
Rank: 191

INDEXES & TAXES	AREA	U.S. AVG	HOUSING	AREA	U.S. AVG	NECESSITIES	AREA	U.S. AVG
Cost of Living Index	85.4	100.0	Median home price	$120,300	$220,000	Food Index	101.4	100.0
Buying Power Index	111.5	100.0	Home price appreciation	25.5%	10.1%	Housing Index	48.1	100.0
Income tax rate	4.56%	4.70%	Median rent	$741	$709	Utilities Index	137.9	100.0
Sales tax rate	6.52%	6.58%	Homes owned	66.5%	62.3%	Transportation Index	97.9	100.0
Property tax rate	$19.73	$12.00	Home price ratio	2.8	4.2	Healthcare Index	93.2	100.0
						Miscellaneous Cost Index	101.6	100.0

Climate
Score: 27.3
Rank: 271

TEMPERATURE	AREA	U.S. AVG	PRECIPITATION	AREA	U.S. AVG	COMFORTS & HAZARDS	AREA	U.S. AVG
Average January low	20.8	26.2	Annual inches precipitation	36.0	37.7	July relative humidity	68%	66%
Average July high	82.5	87.4	Annual inches snowfall	45.0	7.0	Annual days mostly sunny	161	208
Annual days > 90°F	7	38	Annual days precipitation	152	109	Annual days with thunderstorms	36	39
Annual days < 32°F	124	89	Annual days rain > 0.5 inches	22	22	Tornado risk score	14	18
Annual days < 0°F	5	6	Annual days snow > 1.5 inches	9	6	Hurricane risk score	4	13

TEMPERATURE

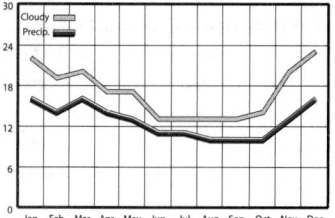

PRECIPITATION

DAYS OF CLOUDS & PRECIPITATION

ACHIEVEMENT	AREA	U.S. AVG	PUBLIC SCHOOLS	AREA	U.S. AVG	HIGHER EDUCATION	AREA	U.S. AVG
High school degree	85.0%	82.7%	Expenditures per pupil	$6,809	$5,686	No. 2-year colleges	43	4
2-year college degree	7.0%	6.4%	Student/teacher ratio	17.7	16.7	No. 4-year colleges/universities	27	6
4-year college degree	15.0%	15.7%	Attending public school	87.6%	90.1%	No. highly ranked universities	5	1
Graduate/professional degree	8.6%	8.9%	State SAT score	993*	1021			
			State ACT score	21.8	20.9			

Education
Score: 91.4
Rank: 33

HAZARDS & ILLNESSES	AREA	U.S. AVG	HEALTHCARE	AREA	U.S. AVG	CRIME	AREA	U.S. AVG
Air-quality score	23	37	Physicians per capita	335.5	244.2	Violent crime rate	360.5	465.5
Water-quality score	51	52	Hospital beds per capita	529.7	420.0	Change in violent crime rate	-2.2%	-2.2%
Pollen/allergy score	72	61	No. teaching hospitals	18	3	Property crime rate	2,433.8	3,517.1
Cancer mortality per capita	252.0	201.9	Cost per doctor visit	$65	$77	Change in property crime rate	2.7%	-2.1%
Depression days per month	3.7	3.5	Cost per dental visit	$53	$70			
Stress score	65	50						

Health & Healthcare
Score: 30.7
Rank: 258

Crime
Score: 84.8
Rank: 58

COMMUTE	AREA	U.S. AVG	INTERCITY SERVICES	AREA	U.S. AVG	AUTOMOTIVE	AREA	U.S. AVG
Average commute time	27.5	27.4	Major airports within 60 miles	1	1	Insurance, annual premium	$1,604	$1,432
Percent commutes > 60 mins.	7.0%	5.9%	Size of regional airport	Large	Large	Gas, cost per gallon	$2.50	$2.49
Commute by auto	77.9%	78.9%	Daily airline activity	663	686	Daily vehicle miles per capita	21.7	24.0
Commute by mass transit	5.8%	1.9%	Amtrak service	Yes	No			
Work at home	2.5%	3.1%						
Mass transit miles per capita	5.78	1.87						

Transportation
Score: 33.7
Rank: 249

DINING & SHOPPING	AREA	U.S. AVG	ENTERTAINMENT	AREA	U.S. AVG	OUTDOOR ACTIVITIES	AREA	U.S. AVG
Restaurant rating	1	2	Professional sports rating	7	4	Golf-course rating	9	4
Outlet mall score	0	42	College sports rating	6	4	Ski-area rating	5	3
No. Starbucks	36	13	Zoo/aquarium rating	8	3	Sq. miles inland water	4	4
No. warehouse clubs	2	2	Amusement park rating	6	3	Miles of coastline	0.0	10.7
			Botanical garden/ arboretum rating	9	4	National Park rating	2	3

Leisure
Score: 83.2
Rank: 63

MEDIA & LIBRARIES	AREA	U.S. AVG	PERFORMING ARTS	AREA	U.S. AVG	MUSEUMS	AREA	U.S. AVG
Arts radio rating	8	3	Classical music rating	9	4	Overall museum rating	10	5
No. public libraries	131	27	Ballet/dance rating	7	3	Art museum rating	10	5
Library volumes per capita	2.74	2.78	Professional theater rating	10	3	Science museum rating	10	5
			University arts programs rating	10	5	Children's museum rating	6	3

Arts & Culture
Score: 95.7
Rank: 17

Pittsfield, MA

Score: 51.2   Rank: 243   2004 rank: 243

Profile: Small city
Location: Extreme western Massachusetts in the Berkshires, 7 miles east of the New York border
Elevation: 1,158 feet
Time zone: Eastern Standard Time

PRO
Nearby mountains
Outdoor recreation
Low property crime

CON
Economy
Isolation
Harsh winters

An old agricultural and minor industrial center, Pittsfield has evolved into a gateway to the Berkshires. Nearby ski resorts, particularly to the north, draw winter visitors. To the south, are the Tanglewood performing arts center in Lenox and the Norman Rockwell Museum in Stockbridge. The town itself is quiet, nondescript, and fairly isolated from big-city amenities especially in winter, but Albany, New York, is about 40 miles west. A small assortment of corporate employers centers in the plastics and printing industries, but this is not a growth area—future projected job growth is the lowest in the state and fifth-lowest in the country. Crime, however, is also among the lowest in the state.

The city is located in a relatively level section of a mostly hilly, wooded region. The surrounding mountains rise to 2,300 feet. Summers are warm and humid with mostly pleasant evenings. Winters are variable with frequent cold snaps and heavy snows, although the mountains block some of the strongest weather. First freeze is late September; last is early May.

Population

DEMOGRAPHICS	AREA	U.S. AVG	ETHNIC COMPOSITION	AREA	U.S. AVG	RESIDENT PROFILE	AREA	U.S. AVG
Population	132,926		White	94.5%	79.0%	Single	34.5%	32.4%
Population density per sq. mile	142.7	358.5	Black	2.2%	10.5%	Married	50.1%	52.7%
Population growth	-4.6%	21.1%	Asian	1.2%	2.7%	Divorced/separated	15.4%	14.9%
Median age	41.7	36.1	Hispanic	2.2%	10.6%	Married with children	18.8%	23.7%
Percent Democrat	73.1%	44.5%	Religious observance	67.1%	48.9%	Single with children	8.5%	9.1%
Percent Republican	25.7%	54.5%	Diversity measure	14.5	40.1	Percent over age 65	18.1%	12.9%

Economy & Jobs
Score: 1.3
Rank: 368

INCOME	AREA	U.S. AVG	EMPLOYMENT	AREA	U.S. AVG	EMPLOYING INDUSTRIES	AREA	U.S. AVG
Per capita income	$25,435	$23,235	Unemployment rate	4.0%	4.7%	Largest: Healthcare & Social Assistance		
Household income	$44,622	$46,414	Recent job growth	-0.7%	1.3%			
Household income < $25K	27.7%	26.2%	Projected future job growth	-4.2%	11.5%	Percent manufacturing	11.9%	15.4%
Household income > $75K	24.6%	25.4%	White collar	59.9%	57.8%	Percent public sector	13.1%	15.7%
Household income growth	14.3%	13.6%	Blue collar	20.7%	25.2%	Percent construction	8.8%	9.9%

Cost of Living
Score: 23.0
Rank: 287

INDEXES & TAXES	AREA	U.S. AVG	HOUSING	AREA	U.S. AVG	NECESSITIES	AREA	U.S. AVG
Cost of Living Index	110.6	100.0	Median home price	$213,800	$220,000	Food Index	119.6	100.0
Buying Power Index	90.4	100.0	Home price appreciation	65.3%	10.1%	Housing Index	90.9	100.0
Income tax rate	5.95%	4.70%	Median rent	$692	$709	Utilities Index	129.7	100.0
Sales tax rate	5.00%	6.58%	Homes owned	56.7%	62.3%	Transportation Index	112.0	100.0
Property tax rate	$12.35	$12.00	Home price ratio	4.8	4.2	Healthcare Index	132.5	100.0
						Miscellaneous Cost Index	115.2	100.0

Climate
Score: 2.4
Rank: 364

TEMPERATURE	AREA	U.S. AVG	PRECIPITATION	AREA	U.S. AVG	COMFORTS & HAZARDS	AREA	U.S. AVG
Average January low	13.0	26.2	Annual inches precipitation	33.0	37.7	July relative humidity	70%	66%
Average July high	84.0	87.4	Annual inches snowfall	73.0	7.0	Annual days mostly sunny	184	208
Annual days > 90°F	10	38	Annual days precipitation	137	109	Annual days with thunderstorms	28	39
Annual days < 32°F	155	89	Annual days rain > 0.5 inches	27	22	Tornado risk score	7	18
Annual days < 0°F	16	6	Annual days snow > 1.5 inches	20	6	Hurricane risk score	13	13

TEMPERATURE **PRECIPITATION** **DAYS OF CLOUDS & PRECIPITATION**

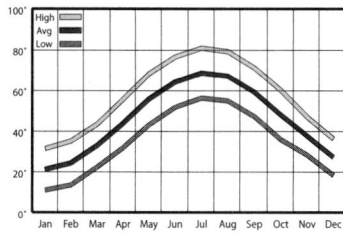 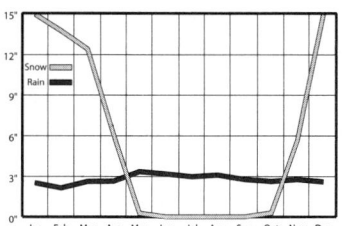 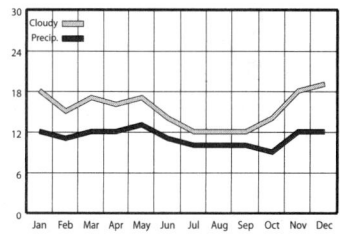

Education
Score: 76.5
Rank: 89

ACHIEVEMENT	AREA	U.S. AVG	PUBLIC SCHOOLS	AREA	U.S. AVG	HIGHER EDUCATION	AREA	U.S. AVG
High school degree	85.0%	82.7%	Expenditures per pupil	$7,975	$5,686	No. 2-year colleges	1	4
2-year college degree	7.1%	6.4%	Student/teacher ratio	11.0	16.7	No. 4-year colleges/universities	3	6
4-year college degree	15.0%	15.7%	Attending public school	87.7%	90.1%	No. highly ranked universities	2	1
Graduate/professional degree	10.9%	8.9%	State SAT score	1037*	1021			
			State ACT score	23	20.9			

Health & Healthcare
Score: 66.6
Rank: 126

Crime
Score: 94.1
Rank: 23

HAZARDS & ILLNESSES	AREA	U.S. AVG	HEALTHCARE	AREA	U.S. AVG	CRIME	AREA	U.S. AVG
Air-quality score	47	37	Physicians per capita	329.3	244.2	Violent crime rate	430.7	465.5
Water-quality score	50	52	Hospital beds per capita	482.2	420.0	Change in violent crime rate	29.3%	-2.2%
Pollen/allergy score	44	61	No. teaching hospitals	1	3	Property crime rate	1,969.4	3,517.1
Cancer mortality per capita	212.0	201.9	Cost per doctor visit	$83	$77	Change in property crime rate	11.3%	-2.1%
Depression days per month	3.6	3.5	Cost per dental visit	$75	$70			
Stress score	21	50						

Transportation
Score: 73.3
Rank: 101

COMMUTE	AREA	U.S. AVG	INTERCITY SERVICES	AREA	U.S. AVG	AUTOMOTIVE	AREA	U.S. AVG
Average commute time	21.0	27.4	Major airports within 60 miles	1	1	Insurance, annual premium	$1,419	$1,432
Percent commutes > 60 mins.	4.5%	5.9%	Size of regional airport	Medium	Large	Gas, cost per gallon	$2.42	$2.49
Commute by auto	79.2%	78.9%	Daily airline activity	532	686	Daily vehicle miles per capita	19.6	24.0
Commute by mass transit	1.5%	1.9%	Amtrak service	Yes	No			
Work at home	3.7%	3.1%						
Mass transit miles per capita	1.45	1.87						

Leisure
Score: 53.7
Rank: 173

DINING & SHOPPING	AREA	U.S. AVG	ENTERTAINMENT	AREA	U.S. AVG	OUTDOOR ACTIVITIES	AREA	U.S. AVG
Restaurant rating	4	2	Professional sports rating	2	4	Golf-course rating	3	4
Outlet mall score	111	42	College sports rating	1	4	Ski-area rating	8	3
No. Starbucks	1	13	Zoo/aquarium rating	2	3	Sq. miles inland water	2	4
No. warehouse clubs	0	2	Amusement park rating	1	3	Miles of coastline	0.0	10.7
			Botanical garden/ arboretum rating	2	4	National Park rating	1	3

Arts & Culture
Score: 55.9
Rank: 165

MEDIA & LIBRARIES	AREA	U.S. AVG	PERFORMING ARTS	AREA	U.S. AVG	MUSEUMS	AREA	U.S. AVG
Arts radio rating	1	3	Classical music rating	1	4	Overall museum rating	7	5
No. public libraries	31	27	Ballet/dance rating	5	3	Art museum rating	8	5
Library volumes per capita	5.56	2.78	Professional theater rating	6	3	Science museum rating	5	5
			University arts programs rating	1	5	Children's museum rating	2	3

Pocatello, ID

Score: 51.8 **Rank:** 241 **2004 rank:** 279

Profile: Small town/college town
Location: Southeastern Idaho at the upper end of the Snake River Valley
Elevation: 4,680 feet
Time zone: Mountain Standard Time

PRO
Nearby outdoor recreation
Strong economy
Small-town feel

CON
Isolation
Harsh climate
Arts and culture

Pocatello is a major transportation, agricultural, and education center for southeast Idaho. It lies at the convergence of the irrigated Snake River Valley and major transportation routes between the Pacific Northwest and the rest of the country through the Salt Lake area. Local Idaho State University provides some college-town flavor, 13,000 students, and 3,300 jobs. But the town is for the most part nondescript with an unattractive strip of trucking and agriculture-related industries spreading for miles northwest of town. This plus the low dry mountain backdrop gives a less attractive setting than one might expect for the region, but there are more attractive physical landscapes nearby. Large employers include the Union Pacific Railroad, potato processors J.R. Simplot and Heinz Frozen Foods, and Convergys (call centers). Nearby fishing streams, the American Falls Reservoir, and Yellowstone National Park and the Grand Tetons less than 100 miles to the northeast are important attractions. By most standards, the area is isolated from urban services and amenities but the town is self-contained enough to provide a reasonable lifestyle.

The Snake River Plain is a desert composed of sand and lava rock extending to the west, a large portion of which is covered with irrigated farming. To the east the ground rises steadily toward the crests of the Continental Divide and the Grand Tetons. The climate is variable, invigorating, and by some standards harsh. Cloudy and unsettled weather prevails through the winter with measurable precipitation every 1 in 3 days, and occasional large snowfalls. Cold snaps drive temperatures below zero. Summer evenings can be quite cool with temperatures in the 40s. Occasional summer thunderstorms and hail occur during the otherwise dry summer. Dry heat waves in July and August can drive temperatures into the 90s or even low 100s. First freeze is end of September; last is late May.

Population

DEMOGRAPHICS	AREA	U.S. AVG	ETHNIC COMPOSITION	AREA	U.S. AVG	RESIDENT PROFILE	AREA	U.S. AVG
Population	82,874		White	89.4%	79.0%	Single	29.8%	32.4%
Population density per sq. mile	32.9	358.5	Black	0.6%	10.5%	Married	56.3%	52.7%
Population growth	13.5%	21.1%	Asian	1.2%	2.7%	Divorced/separated	13.9%	14.9%
Median age	31.9	36.1	Hispanic	7.0%	10.6%	Married with children	28.2%	23.7%
Percent Democrat	36.2%	44.5%	Religious observance	63.0%	48.9%	Single with children	8.5%	9.1%
Percent Republican	62.5%	54.5%	Diversity measure	29.3	40.1	Percent over age 65	10.7%	12.9%

Economy & Jobs
Score: 93.9
Rank: 24

INCOME	AREA	U.S. AVG	EMPLOYMENT	AREA	U.S. AVG	EMPLOYING INDUSTRIES	AREA	U.S. AVG
Per capita income	$19,576	$23,235	Unemployment rate	4.0%	4.7%	Largest: Healthcare & Social Assistance		
Household income	$41,956	$46,414	Recent job growth	4.6%	1.3%			
Household income ‹ $25K	29.2%	26.2%	Projected future job growth	23.5%	11.5%	Percent manufacturing	13.7%	15.4%
Household income › $75K	21.3%	25.4%	White collar	58.4%	57.8%	Percent public sector	21.0%	15.7%
Household income growth	15.6%	13.6%	Blue collar	23.5%	25.2%	Percent construction	9.8%	9.9%

Cost of Living
Score: 51.1
Rank: 183

INDEXES & TAXES	AREA	U.S. AVG	HOUSING	AREA	U.S. AVG	NECESSITIES	AREA	U.S. AVG
Cost of Living Index	82.8	100.0	Median home price	$121,200	$220,000	Food Index	99.6	100.0
Buying Power Index	113.6	100.0	Home price appreciation	32.1%	10.1%	Housing Index	53.7	100.0
Income tax rate	8.20%	4.70%	Median rent	$545	$709	Utilities Index	87.2	100.0
Sales tax rate	6.00%	6.58%	Homes owned	66.9%	62.3%	Transportation Index	99.3	100.0
Property tax rate	$10.22	$12.00	Home price ratio	2.9	4.2	Healthcare Index	99.9	100.0
						Miscellaneous Cost Index	101.8	100.0

Climate
Score: 1.9
Rank: 366

TEMPERATURE	AREA	U.S. AVG	PRECIPITATION	AREA	U.S. AVG	COMFORTS & HAZARDS	AREA	U.S. AVG
Average January low	14.0	26.2	Annual inches precipitation	12.0	37.7	July relative humidity	62%	66%
Average July high	88.0	87.4	Annual inches snowfall	43.0	7.0	Annual days mostly sunny	205	208
Annual days > 90°F	33	38	Annual days precipitation	94	109	Annual days with thunderstorms	24	39
Annual days < 32°F	166	89	Annual days rain > 0.5 inches	4	22	Tornado risk score	6	18
Annual days < 0°F	15	6	Annual days snow > 1.5 inches	9	6	Hurricane risk score	0	13

TEMPERATURE

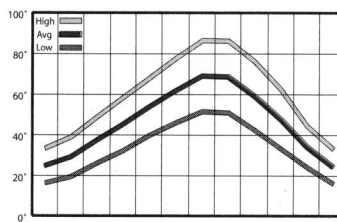

PRECIPITATION

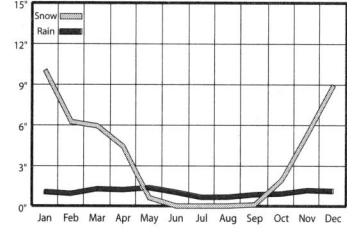

DAYS OF CLOUDS & PRECIPITATION

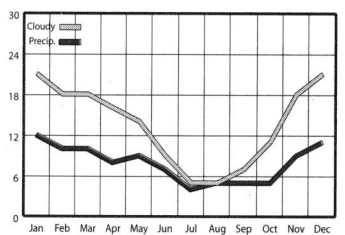

Education
Score: 61.0
Rank: 147

ACHIEVEMENT	AREA	U.S. AVG	PUBLIC SCHOOLS	AREA	U.S. AVG	HIGHER EDUCATION	AREA	U.S. AVG
High school degree	86.6%	82.7%	Expenditures per pupil	$4,567	$5,686	No. 2-year colleges	1	4
2-year college degree	7.3%	6.4%	Student/teacher ratio	18.2	16.7	No. 4-year colleges/universities	1	6
4-year college degree	16.1%	15.7%	Attending public school	95.2%	90.1%	No. highly ranked universities	0	1
Graduate/professional degree	8.3%	8.9%	State SAT score	1088	1021			
			State ACT score	21.4*	20.9			

Health & Healthcare
Score: 94.7
Rank: 21

HAZARDS & ILLNESSES	AREA	U.S. AVG	HEALTHCARE	AREA	U.S. AVG	CRIME	AREA	U.S. AVG
Air-quality score	51	37	Physicians per capita	197.7	244.2	Violent crime rate	303.7	465.5
Water-quality score	20	52	Hospital beds per capita	590.1	420.0	Change in violent crime rate	8.0%	-2.2%
Pollen/allergy score	56	61	No. teaching hospitals	2	3	Property crime rate	3,102.2	3,517.1
Cancer mortality per capita	154.0	201.9	Cost per doctor visit	$68	$77	Change in property crime rate	-14.6%	-2.1%
Depression days per month	4.1	3.5	Cost per dental visit	$66	$70			
Stress score	12	50						

Crime
Score: 81.3
Rank: 71

Transportation
Score: 59.6
Rank: 152

COMMUTE	AREA	U.S. AVG	INTERCITY SERVICES	AREA	U.S. AVG	AUTOMOTIVE	AREA	U.S. AVG
Average commute time	19.0	27.4	Major airports within 60 miles	0	1	Insurance, annual premium	$906	$1,432
Percent commutes > 60 mins.	4.9%	5.9%	Size of regional airport	None	Large	Gas, cost per gallon	$2.24	$2.49
Commute by auto	78.3%	78.9%	Daily airline activity	26	686	Daily vehicle miles per capita	19.5	24.0
Commute by mass transit	1.5%	1.9%	Amtrak service	No	No			
Work at home	3.1%	3.1%						
Mass transit miles per capita	1.54	1.87						

Leisure
Score: 41.4
Rank: 218

DINING & SHOPPING	AREA	U.S. AVG	ENTERTAINMENT	AREA	U.S. AVG	OUTDOOR ACTIVITIES	AREA	U.S. AVG
Restaurant rating	1	2	Professional sports rating	2	4	Golf-course rating	1	4
Outlet mall score	0	42	College sports rating	2	4	Ski-area rating	10	3
No. Starbucks	0	13	Zoo/aquarium rating	1	3	Sq. miles inland water	2	4
No. warehouse clubs	0	2	Amusement park rating	1	3	Miles of coastline	0.0	10.7
			Botanical garden/ arboretum rating	1	4	National Park rating	3	3

Arts & Culture
Score: 8.6
Rank: 341

MEDIA & LIBRARIES	AREA	U.S. AVG	PERFORMING ARTS	AREA	U.S. AVG	MUSEUMS	AREA	U.S. AVG
Arts radio rating	1	3	Classical music rating	1	4	Overall museum rating	2	5
No. public libraries	6	27	Ballet/dance rating	1	3	Art museum rating	1	5
Library volumes per capita	2.95	2.78	Professional theater rating	1	3	Science museum rating	4	5
			University arts programs rating	4	5	Children's museum rating	1	3

Portland–South Portland–Biddeford, ME   Score: 53.3 Rank: 231 2004 rank: 236

Profile: Mid-size coastal-city/town complex
Location: Southern Maine on the Atlantic Coast at Casco Bay
Elevation: 63 feet
Time zone: Eastern Standard Time

PRO	CON
Historic interest	Harsh winters
Attractive towns	Home prices
Educated population	Low ethnic diversity

Portland is Maine's largest city and cultural center. It is a New England classic, with shipping, commercial fishing, and a quaint historic core known as the Old Port. After suffering an extensive urban decline in the 1970s, locals realized what they had and restored much of the downtown core commercially and aesthetically, and the result is an excellent example for other cities to follow. Today the Old Port area is an active commercial and entertainment district, with some excellent seafood restaurants. The rest of the downtown area is clean, attractive, and functional, and the entire city has a slow pace and small-town, New England feel. Portland suburbs, especially across the small Back Cove inlet, are very attractive. Excellent suburban and small-town environments are found inland and up and down the coast, through Yarmouth to the unique, stylish, and prosperous town of Freeport to the north, home of famed clothing purveyor L.L. Bean. Freeport has grown up into a major retail outlet center, but it isn't what you would think—these mostly high-end outlets are located in old New England homes and storefronts giving a most pleasant downtown streetscape. South Portland is more commercial and industrial, but the nice towns pick up again in the South Coast area through Old Orchard Beach, Biddeford, Kennebunk, Kennebunkport, and Kittery to the Massachusetts border. Biddeford in particular is growing rapidly as home to the University of New England. Generally the area has a highly educated population and professional workforce and a lot of people who seem to care about where they live and it shows. Employment, always an issue in Maine, is stronger and steadier in Portland, which is less dependent on manufacturing and basic industries than many of its Maine neighbors. Crime is very low. There are plenty of outdoor activities for all seasons. Homes are expensive in New England fashion, but not as expensive as south in Massachusetts, and value is good for what is paid. Auto commutes to the north Boston suburbs are possible but not really practical, but commuter rail service is good and expanding. The area is ideal for the self-employed and telecommuters needing access to the Boston area only occasionally. Portland would rate much higher if it weren't for the harsh New England winters and a high cost of living. The city is much better than ranked for those tolerant of those issues.

The coastline around Portland is rugged and attractive. The surrounding country is mostly rolling with a mix of open and wooded land. The 44-square-mile Sebago Lake is 15 miles to the northwest and the White Mountains are 45 miles beyond that. Portland has pleasant summers and falls, cold winters with frequent thaws, and disagreeable springs. Summer nights are cool and comfortable for sleeping. Winters are quite severe but begin late and then extend deep into the normal springtime. Temperatures well below zero are recorded frequently each winter. Cold waves sometimes come with strong winds, but extremely low temperatures generally come with light winds. Climate inland from the city is more extreme, as much as 10° to 15° cooler just a few miles inland. First freeze is late September; last is mid-May.

DEMOGRAPHICS	AREA	U.S. AVG	ETHNIC COMPOSITION	AREA	U.S. AVG	RESIDENT PROFILE	AREA	U.S. AVG
Population	513,373		White	95.9%	79.0%	Single	31.0%	32.4%
Population density per sq. mile	246.8	358.5	Black	0.9%	10.5%	Married	54.8%	52.7%
Population growth	16.6%	21.1%	Asian	1.4%	2.7%	Divorced/separated	14.1%	14.9%
Median age	39.8	36.1	Hispanic	1.0%	10.6%	Married with children	23.0%	23.7%
Percent Democrat	55.9%	44.5%	Religious observance	38.3%	48.9%	Single with children	8.0%	9.1%
Percent Republican	42.4%	54.5%	Diversity measure	9.8	40.1	Percent over age 65	13.6%	12.9%

INCOME	AREA	U.S. AVG	EMPLOYMENT	AREA	U.S. AVG	EMPLOYING INDUSTRIES	AREA	U.S. AVG
Per capita income	$26,461	$23,235	Unemployment rate	3.7%	4.7%	Largest: Healthcare & Social Assistance		
Household income	$49,569	$46,414	Recent job growth	1.2%	1.3%			
Household income < $25K	22.1%	26.2%	Projected future job growth	6.8%	11.5%	Percent manufacturing	13.5%	15.4%
Household income > $75K	27.6%	25.4%	White collar	62.1%	57.8%	Percent public sector	12.7%	15.7%
Household income growth	13.4%	13.6%	Blue collar	22.7%	25.2%	Percent construction	9.1%	9.9%

Economy & Jobs
Score: 37.4
Rank: 234

INDEXES & TAXES	AREA	U.S. AVG	HOUSING	AREA	U.S. AVG	NECESSITIES	AREA	U.S. AVG
Cost of Living Index	109.5	100.0	Median home price	$242,700	$220,000	Food Index	101.6	100.0
Buying Power Index	101.5	100.0	Home price appreciation	70.1%	10.1%	Housing Index	90.1	100.0
Income tax rate	7.77%	4.70%	Median rent	$880	$709	Utilities Index	151.3	100.0
Sales tax rate	5.00%	6.58%	Homes owned	59.0%	62.3%	Transportation Index	106.2	100.0
Property tax rate	$14.24	$12.00	Home price ratio	4.9	4.2	Healthcare Index	107.8	100.0
						Miscellaneous Cost Index	105.2	100.0

Cost of Living
Score: 17.9
Rank: 306

Climate
Score: 0.5
Rank: 371

TEMPERATURE	AREA	U.S. AVG
Average January low	11.7	26.2
Average July high	79.1	87.4
Annual days > 90°F	5	38
Annual days < 32°F	160	89
Annual days < 0°F	15	6

PRECIPITATION	AREA	U.S. AVG
Annual inches precipitation	41.0	37.7
Annual inches snowfall	74.0	7.0
Annual days precipitation	127	109
Annual days rain > 0.5 inches	29	22
Annual days snow > 1.5 inches	15	6

COMFORTS & HAZARDS	AREA	U.S. AVG
July relative humidity	74%	66%
Annual days mostly sunny	205	208
Annual days with thunderstorms	18	39
Tornado risk score	0	18
Hurricane risk score	16	13

TEMPERATURE

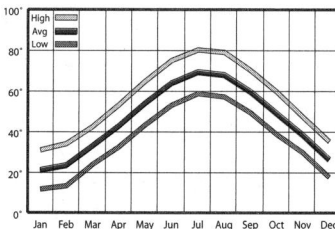

PRECIPITATION

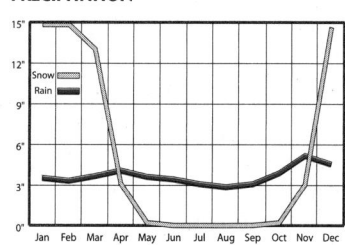

DAYS OF CLOUDS & PRECIPITATION

Education
Score: 84.2
Rank: 60

ACHIEVEMENT	AREA	U.S. AVG
High school degree	88.5%	82.7%
2-year college degree	8.2%	6.4%
4-year college degree	18.8%	15.7%
Graduate/professional degree	10.1%	8.9%

PUBLIC SCHOOLS	AREA	U.S. AVG
Expenditures per pupil	$6,591	$5,686
Student/teacher ratio	15.7	16.7
Attending public school	90.7%	90.1%
State SAT score	1002*	1021
State ACT score	22.3	20.9

HIGHER EDUCATION	AREA	U.S. AVG
No. 2-year colleges	5	4
No. 4-year colleges/universities	6	6
No. highly ranked universities	1	1

Health & Healthcare
Score: 41.2
Rank: 219

HAZARDS & ILLNESSES	AREA	U.S. AVG
Air-quality score	26	37
Water-quality score	61	52
Pollen/allergy score	50	61
Cancer mortality per capita	243.3	201.9
Depression days per month	3.4	3.5
Stress score	22	50

HEALTHCARE	AREA	U.S. AVG
Physicians per capita	333.1	244.2
Hospital beds per capita	298.4	420.0
No. teaching hospitals	3	3
Cost per doctor visit	$84	$77
Cost per dental visit	$67	$70

Crime
Score: 98.4
Rank: 7

CRIME	AREA	U.S. AVG
Violent crime rate	139.5	465.5
Change in violent crime rate	13.0%	-2.2%
Property crime rate	2,446.3	3,517.1
Change in property crime rate	4.7%	-2.1%

Transportation
Score: 53.7
Rank: 174

COMMUTE	AREA	U.S. AVG
Average commute time	25.4	27.4
Percent commutes > 60 mins.	5.7%	5.9%
Commute by auto	80.0%	78.9%
Commute by mass transit	1.2%	1.9%
Work at home	4.3%	3.1%
Mass transit miles per capita	1.17	1.87

INTERCITY SERVICES	AREA	U.S. AVG
Major airports within 60 miles	1	1
Size of regional airport	Large	Large
Daily airline activity	913	686
Amtrak service	Yes	No

AUTOMOTIVE	AREA	U.S. AVG
Insurance, annual premium	$937	$1,432
Gas, cost per gallon	$2.45	$2.49
Daily vehicle miles per capita	25.0	24.0

Leisure
Score: 72.5
Rank: 103

DINING & SHOPPING	AREA	U.S. AVG
Restaurant rating	1	2
Outlet mall score	69	42
No. Starbucks	10	13
No. warehouse clubs	2	2

ENTERTAINMENT	AREA	U.S. AVG
Professional sports rating	3	4
College sports rating	4	4
Zoo/aquarium rating	1	3
Amusement park rating	4	3
Botanical garden/ arboretum rating	3	4

OUTDOOR ACTIVITIES	AREA	U.S. AVG
Golf-course rating	3	4
Ski-area rating	7	3
Sq. miles inland water	7	4
Miles of coastline	35.7	10.7
National Park rating	2	3

Arts & Culture
Score: 56.4
Rank: 163

MEDIA & LIBRARIES	AREA	U.S. AVG
Arts radio rating	1	3
No. public libraries	77	27
Library volumes per capita	4.10	2.78

PERFORMING ARTS	AREA	U.S. AVG
Classical music rating	4	4
Ballet/dance rating	1	3
Professional theater rating	6	3
University arts programs rating	4	5

MUSEUMS	AREA	U.S. AVG
Overall museum rating	6	5
Art museum rating	8	5
Science museum rating	3	5
Children's museum rating	6	3

Portland–Vancouver–Beaverton, OR-WA

Score: 95.0 **Rank:** 3 **2004 rank:** 12

Profile: Large-city complex
Location: Northwest Oregon along the Columbia River and Oregon-Washington border
Elevation: 39 feet
Time zone: Pacific Standard Time

PRO	CON
Attractive downtown	Economic cycles
Arts and culture	Cost of living
Educated population	Clouds and rain

Today's Portland area is a wonderfully well-evolved, progressive, and cosmopolitan Pacific Northwest center located at the junction of the Willamette and Columbia rivers. Originally founded as a trading center, Portland first grew during local gold rushes before developing first into a forest- and food-products processing and shipping point, and now more recently into a center for the knowledge economy. The greater Portland area includes Vancouver, Washington, across the Columbia River. South of the Columbia, numerous neighborhoods and communities spread east, south along the Willamette River, and west up into wooded plateaus west of downtown.

Downtown Portland is almost a perfect model for what today's larger city should look like. Set along the banks of the Willamette, the downtown core is clean and modern with a financial district, well-patronized downtown shopping, and several parks. Just north is the more historic Pearl District, anchored by the restored Portland Union Station rail hub and its famous "Go By Train" neon sign at the top. The surrounding streets are studded with small restaurants and businesses in well-maintained older brick buildings. The downtown population is steadily growing with new riverfront highrise units and a number of Pearl District residential developments. The city has excellent destination museums, cultural amenities, and entertainment venues in an interesting blend of modern and historic facilities. As a rule, this city is quite comfortable both with its past and its present, and it shows.

Likewise, many of the neighborhoods radiating from the city's core and especially south and east maintain this good balance of old and new. Areas close in are gentrifying and becoming more expensive, causing some dislocations among long-time residents. Older tree-lined streets and boulevards are framed with well-kept late Victorian and early-20th-century bungalow-style homes and plenty of small street-corner restaurants and businesses; most of these neighborhoods are set up well for walking and using the area's good public transportation facilities. Farther away from downtown, suburbia has emerged, but to a lesser degree than many other cities. There is a well-enforced "urban growth boundary" prohibiting much of the sprawling development seen in other U.S. cities. Beaverton and Tigard are middle-class suburbs up on the plateau west of town, featuring some of the area's larger employers, led by Intel and Nike. With no Washington income tax and no Oregon sales tax, many residents choose to live in Vancouver and work and shop in Portland. Vancouver also has an excellent supply of family homes, good jobs, and schools.

Once heavily dependent on the forest products industry, the economy has diversified and now includes a strong high-tech and creative employment presence, earning Portland the nickname "Silicon Forest." While there is still significant blue-collar employment mainly in forest product mills and transportation, today the workforce is slanted toward executive and professional positions. Job growth has picked up again, as Portland continues to be a desirable place for business, and transitions from basic industries move forward.

Although average commute times are long, the area has good public transit with a light-rail system among the nation's best. Excellent intercity rail service is also present mainly in the form of the Amtrak Cascades, connecting Eugene, Oregon, to Portland, Seattle, and ultimately Vancouver, British Columbia. Recreation and outdoor activities abound at the coast, 60 miles west, and the Oregon Cascades and Mount Hood ski area, 50 miles east. Rugged and interesting Cascade mountain areas northeast and southeast offer plenty of outdoor recreation and skiing, and the Columbia River is well known for watersports, especially windsurfing.

The urban growth boundary has kept the urban and suburban landscape attractive and livable, but also, with the mentioned gentrification and a steady stream of migrants from other parts of the country, has pushed up home prices considerably. Many locals feel that, while things are good today, Portland may succumb to some of the overcrowding and cost issues pressuring many other cities along the West Coast. Although high on a national scale, cost of living is moderate among West Coast cities. Aside from rising costs, economic cycles, and wet weather, the city has a lot to offer for all lifestyles and interests; the area has strong cultural amenities and a highly educated population for a big city. We applaud Portland's no. 3 ranking and status as the top *large* city.

Portland is situated midway between a low coastal range to the west and the higher Cascade range to the east, each starting their rise about 30 miles from the city. The natural landscape is heavily forested with large, coniferous trees. Almost 90% of annual precipitation occurs October through May. Summer produces pleasantly mild temperatures, northwesterly winds, and very little precipitation. Winter is characterized by mild temperatures, cloudy skies, and rain; measurable snow is recorded only 5 days each year. First freeze is early November; last is early May.

DEMOGRAPHICS	AREA	U.S. AVG	ETHNIC COMPOSITION	AREA	U.S. AVG	RESIDENT PROFILE	AREA	U.S. AVG
Population	2,082,023		White	82.4%	79.0%	Single	31.4%	32.4%
Population density per sq. mile	311.5	358.5	Black	2.8%	10.5%	Married	53.1%	52.7%
Population growth	39.3%	21.1%	Asian	5.6%	2.7%	Divorced/separated	15.5%	14.9%
Median age	35.9	36.1	Hispanic	9.1%	10.6%	Married with children	24.3%	23.7%
Percent Democrat	56.5%	44.5%	Religious observance	33.0%	48.9%	Single with children	8.4%	9.1%
Percent Republican	42.2%	54.5%	Diversity measure	41.9	40.1	Percent over age 65	10.4%	12.9%

INCOME	AREA	U.S. AVG	EMPLOYMENT	AREA	U.S. AVG	EMPLOYING INDUSTRIES	AREA	U.S. AVG
Per capita income	$26,668	$23,235	Unemployment rate	6.2%	4.7%	Largest: Healthcare & Social Assistance		
Household income	$53,876	$46,414	Recent job growth	2.4%	1.3%			
Household income < $25K	19.5%	26.2%	Projected future job growth	21.1%	11.5%	Percent manufacturing	14.3%	15.4%
Household income > $75K	31.6%	25.4%	White collar	62.2%	57.8%	Percent public sector	11.6%	15.7%
Household income growth	14.0%	13.6%	Blue collar	23.2%	25.2%	Percent construction	8.9%	9.9%

Population

Economy & Jobs
Score: 75.7
Rank: 92

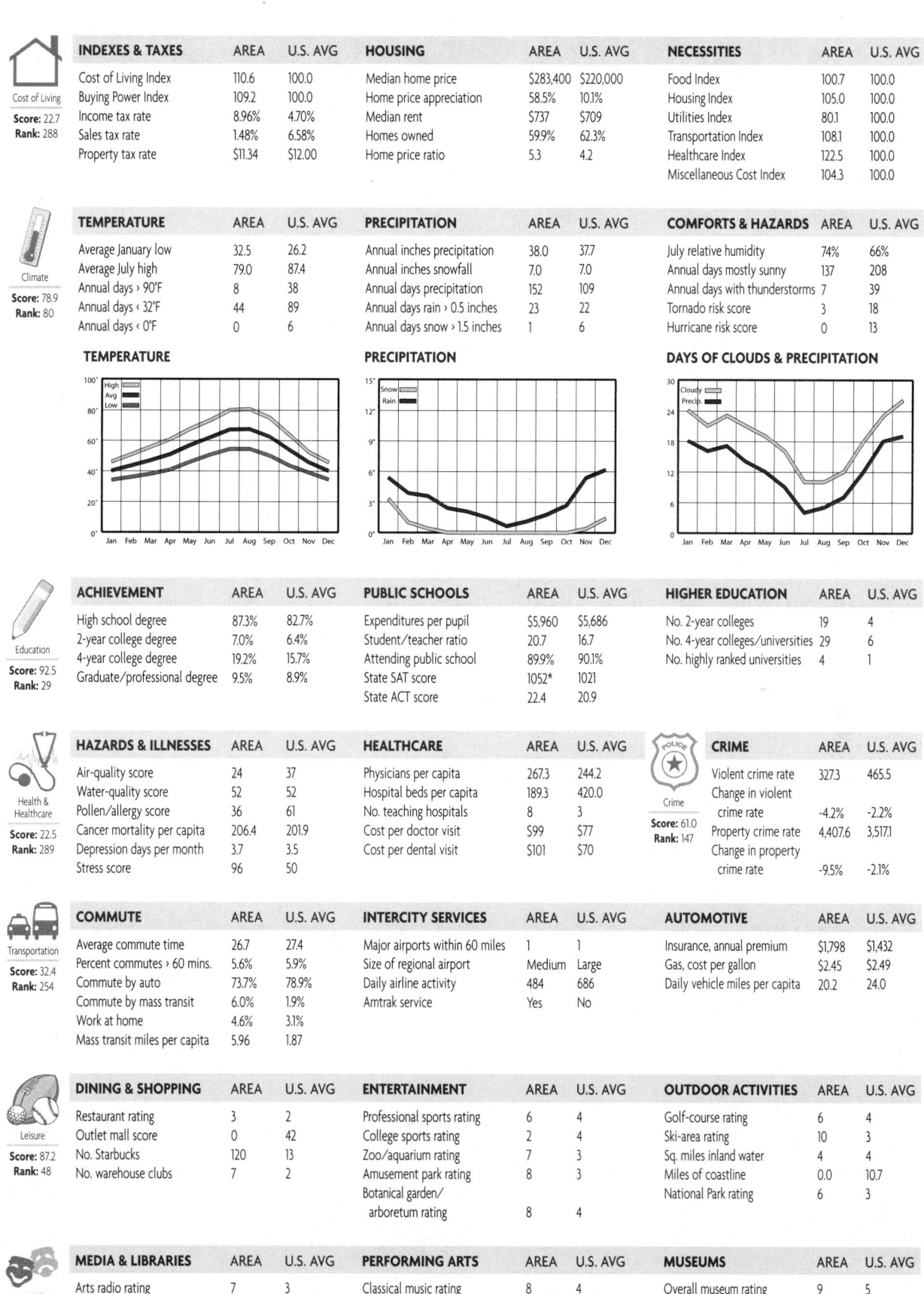

Cost of Living
Score: 22.7
Rank: 288

INDEXES & TAXES	AREA	U.S. AVG	HOUSING	AREA	U.S. AVG	NECESSITIES	AREA	U.S. AVG
Cost of Living Index	110.6	100.0	Median home price	$283,400	$220,000	Food Index	100.7	100.0
Buying Power Index	109.2	100.0	Home price appreciation	58.5%	10.1%	Housing Index	105.0	100.0
Income tax rate	8.96%	4.70%	Median rent	$737	$709	Utilities Index	80.1	100.0
Sales tax rate	1.48%	6.58%	Homes owned	59.9%	62.3%	Transportation Index	108.1	100.0
Property tax rate	$11.34	$12.00	Home price ratio	5.3	4.2	Healthcare Index	122.5	100.0
						Miscellaneous Cost Index	104.3	100.0

Climate
Score: 78.9
Rank: 80

TEMPERATURE	AREA	U.S. AVG	PRECIPITATION	AREA	U.S. AVG	COMFORTS & HAZARDS	AREA	U.S. AVG
Average January low	32.5	26.2	Annual inches precipitation	38.0	37.7	July relative humidity	74%	66%
Average July high	79.0	87.4	Annual inches snowfall	7.0	7.0	Annual days mostly sunny	137	208
Annual days > 90°F	8	38	Annual days precipitation	152	109	Annual days with thunderstorms	7	39
Annual days < 32°F	44	89	Annual days rain > 0.5 inches	23	22	Tornado risk score	3	18
Annual days < 0°F	0	6	Annual days snow > 1.5 inches	1	6	Hurricane risk score	0	13

TEMPERATURE **PRECIPITATION** **DAYS OF CLOUDS & PRECIPITATION**

Education
Score: 92.5
Rank: 29

ACHIEVEMENT	AREA	U.S. AVG	PUBLIC SCHOOLS	AREA	U.S. AVG	HIGHER EDUCATION	AREA	U.S. AVG
High school degree	87.3%	82.7%	Expenditures per pupil	$5,960	$5,686	No. 2-year colleges	19	4
2-year college degree	7.0%	6.4%	Student/teacher ratio	20.7	16.7	No. 4-year colleges/universities	29	6
4-year college degree	19.2%	15.7%	Attending public school	89.9%	90.1%	No. highly ranked universities	4	1
Graduate/professional degree	9.5%	8.9%	State SAT score	1052*	1021			
			State ACT score	22.4	20.9			

Health & Healthcare
Score: 22.5
Rank: 289

Crime
Score: 61.0
Rank: 147

HAZARDS & ILLNESSES	AREA	U.S. AVG	HEALTHCARE	AREA	U.S. AVG	CRIME	AREA	U.S. AVG
Air-quality score	24	37	Physicians per capita	267.3	244.2	Violent crime rate	327.3	465.5
Water-quality score	52	52	Hospital beds per capita	189.3	420.0	Change in violent crime rate	-4.2%	-2.2%
Pollen/allergy score	36	61	No. teaching hospitals	8	3	Property crime rate	4,407.6	3,517.1
Cancer mortality per capita	206.4	201.9	Cost per doctor visit	$99	$77	Change in property crime rate	-9.5%	-2.1%
Depression days per month	3.7	3.5	Cost per dental visit	$101	$70			
Stress score	96	50						

Transportation
Score: 32.4
Rank: 254

COMMUTE	AREA	U.S. AVG	INTERCITY SERVICES	AREA	U.S. AVG	AUTOMOTIVE	AREA	U.S. AVG
Average commute time	26.7	27.4	Major airports within 60 miles	1	1	Insurance, annual premium	$1,798	$1,432
Percent commutes > 60 mins.	5.6%	5.9%	Size of regional airport	Medium	Large	Gas, cost per gallon	$2.45	$2.49
Commute by auto	73.7%	78.9%	Daily airline activity	484	686	Daily vehicle miles per capita	20.2	24.0
Commute by mass transit	6.0%	1.9%	Amtrak service	Yes	No			
Work at home	4.6%	3.1%						
Mass transit miles per capita	5.96	1.87						

Leisure
Score: 87.2
Rank: 48

DINING & SHOPPING	AREA	U.S. AVG	ENTERTAINMENT	AREA	U.S. AVG	OUTDOOR ACTIVITIES	AREA	U.S. AVG
Restaurant rating	3	2	Professional sports rating	6	4	Golf-course rating	6	4
Outlet mall score	0	42	College sports rating	2	4	Ski-area rating	10	3
No. Starbucks	120	13	Zoo/aquarium rating	7	3	Sq. miles inland water	4	4
No. warehouse clubs	7	2	Amusement park rating	8	3	Miles of coastline	0.0	10.7
			Botanical garden/ arboretum rating	8	4	National Park rating	6	3

Arts & Culture
Score: 89.6
Rank: 40

MEDIA & LIBRARIES	AREA	U.S. AVG	PERFORMING ARTS	AREA	U.S. AVG	MUSEUMS	AREA	U.S. AVG
Arts radio rating	7	3	Classical music rating	8	4	Overall museum rating	9	5
No. public libraries	65	27	Ballet/dance rating	6	3	Art museum rating	9	5
Library volumes per capita	2.48	2.78	Professional theater rating	7	3	Science museum rating	9	5
			University arts programs rating	9	5	Children's museum rating	5	3

Port St. Lucie–Fort Pierce, FL

Score: 60.3 Rank: 176 2004 rank: 163

Profile: Beach-city complex
Location: Central Atlantic coast between Melbourne and West Palm Beach, 125 miles north of Miami
Elevation: 11 feet
Time zone: Eastern Standard Time

PRO	CON
Attractive setting	Isolation
Strong job growth	Arts and culture
Water recreation	Hurricane risk

The towns of Port St. Lucie and Fort Pierce are among several that make up the south end of the so-called "Treasure Coast," named for old Spanish shipwrecks lying off the coast, but for many residents, the phrase conjures a more contemporary meaning. Compared to larger cities and resort areas to the south, these are smaller, comfortable, more laid-back residential communities than the bustling beach cities farther south. The north end of the Treasure Coast is comprised of the Sebastian–Vero Beach metro area (p. 712). Port St. Lucie is a small, business-friendly, but largely nondescript community just south and inland from Fort Pierce along U.S. 1. Growth is rapid, as is redevelopment as the town makes the transition from a sleepy backwater to a preferred small-town destination. Employers include QVC, Tropicana, and a Wal-Mart distribution center, but the area in general doesn't have a lot of high-paying jobs for new entrants. Fort Pierce shares the story with a little more historic interest and typical beachfront amenities.

Entertainment is provided by baseball spring-training camps, golf, watersports, and the study and viewing of wildlife. The area is still less crowded and affected by sprawl problems than those areas to the south, but it's also far from services such as healthcare and air transportation. The long commute times reflect distances from jobs rather than congestion.

The landscape consists of a barrier island and coastal plain—topography typical of Florida's coastal cities. There is extensive agriculture, tropical trees, and vegetation inland. Lake Okeechobee is 40 miles to the southwest. Summer temperatures are tempered by ocean breezes and by the frequent formation of afternoon cumulus clouds and showers. Temperatures of 90°F have occurred in all months but seldom reach 100°F. There is some hurricane risk and the area was hit by some of the recent Florida storms, but the area is north of the major hurricane tracks.

Population

DEMOGRAPHICS	AREA	U.S. AVG	ETHNIC COMPOSITION	AREA	U.S. AVG	RESIDENT PROFILE	AREA	U.S. AVG
Population	360,929		White	81.7%	79.0%	Single	26.7%	32.4%
Population density per sq. mile	319.9	358.5	Black	12.0%	10.5%	Married	58.4%	52.7%
Population growth	44.0%	21.1%	Asian	1.0%	2.7%	Divorced/separated	15.0%	14.9%
Median age	44.0	36.1	Hispanic	10.0%	10.6%	Married with children	17.0%	23.7%
Percent Democrat	47.9%	44.5%	Religious observance	41.9%	48.9%	Single with children	7.2%	9.1%
Percent Republican	51.2%	54.5%	Diversity measure	43.4	40.1	Percent over age 65	24.1%	12.9%

Economy & Jobs
Score: 91.7
Rank: 31

INCOME	AREA	U.S. AVG	EMPLOYMENT	AREA	U.S. AVG	EMPLOYING INDUSTRIES	AREA	U.S. AVG
Per capita income	$25,875	$23,235	Unemployment rate	4.8%	4.7%	Largest: Healthcare & Social Assistance		
Household income	$44,221	$46,414	Recent job growth	5.3%	1.3%			
Household income < $25K	25.6%	26.2%	Projected future job growth	22.1%	11.5%	Percent manufacturing	10.5%	15.4%
Household income > $75K	23.6%	25.4%	White collar	56.9%	57.8%	Percent public sector	12.5%	15.7%
Household income growth	13.6%	13.6%	Blue collar	23.0%	25.2%	Percent construction	12.4%	9.9%

Cost of Living
Score: 35.0
Rank: 243

INDEXES & TAXES	AREA	U.S. AVG	HOUSING	AREA	U.S. AVG	NECESSITIES	AREA	U.S. AVG
Cost of Living Index	108.7	100.0	Median home price	$260,100	$220,000	Food Index	102.9	100.0
Buying Power Index	91.2	100.0	Home price appreciation	153.5%	10.1%	Housing Index	92.1	100.0
Income tax rate	0.00%	4.70%	Median rent	$734	$709	Utilities Index	96.5	100.0
Sales tax rate	6.31%	6.58%	Homes owned	67.3%	62.3%	Transportation Index	110.7	100.0
Property tax rate	$14.76	$12.00	Home price ratio	5.9	4.2	Healthcare Index	102.1	100.0
						Miscellaneous Cost Index	106.0	100.0

Climate
Score: 66.0
Rank: 126

TEMPERATURE	AREA	U.S. AVG
Average January low	55.9	26.2
Average July high	89.6	87.4
Annual days > 90°F	55	38
Annual days < 32°F	1	89
Annual days < 0°F	.0	6

PRECIPITATION	AREA	U.S. AVG
Annual inches precipitation	62.1	37.7
Annual inches snowfall	0.0	7.0
Annual days precipitation	131	109
Annual days rain > 0.5 inches	37	22
Annual days snow > 1.5 inches	0	6

COMFORTS & HAZARDS	AREA	U.S. AVG
July relative humidity	73%	66%
Annual days mostly sunny	228	208
Annual days with thunderstorms	79	39
Tornado risk score	25	18
Hurricane risk score	87	13

TEMPERATURE

PRECIPITATION

DAYS OF CLOUDS & PRECIPITATION

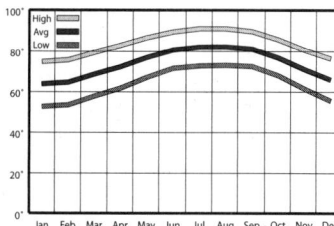

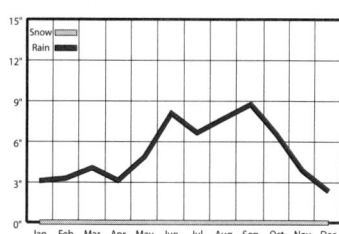

Education
Score: 30.2
Rank: 262

ACHIEVEMENT	AREA	U.S. AVG
High school degree	81.3%	82.7%
2-year college degree	6.9%	6.4%
4-year college degree	13.0%	15.7%
Graduate/professional degree	6.8%	8.9%

PUBLIC SCHOOLS	AREA	U.S. AVG
Expenditures per pupil	$5,294	$5,686
Student/teacher ratio	18.6	16.7
Attending public school	89.5%	90.1%
State SAT score	993*	1021
State ACT score	20.3	20.9

HIGHER EDUCATION	AREA	U.S. AVG
No. 2-year colleges	1	4
No. 4-year colleges/universities	1	6
No. highly ranked universities	0	1

Health & Healthcare
Score: 29.9
Rank: 261

HAZARDS & ILLNESSES	AREA	U.S. AVG
Air-quality score	47	37
Water-quality score	51	52
Pollen/allergy score	64	61
Cancer mortality per capita	245.7	201.9
Depression days per month	3.1	3.5
Stress score	66	50

HEALTHCARE	AREA	U.S. AVG
Physicians per capita	179.9	244.2
Hospital beds per capita	264.9	420.0
No. teaching hospitals	0	3
Cost per doctor visit	$83	$77
Cost per dental visit	$84	$70

Crime
Score: 64.2
Rank: 135

CRIME	AREA	U.S. AVG
Violent crime rate	537.8	465.5
Change in violent crime rate	2.4%	-2.2%
Property crime rate	2,951.2	3,517.1
Change in property crime rate	-10.4%	-2.1%

Transportation
Score: 16.0
Rank: 315

COMMUTE	AREA	U.S. AVG
Average commute time	27.7	27.4
Percent commutes > 60 mins.	7.2%	5.9%
Commute by auto	80.2%	78.9%
Commute by mass transit	0.7%	1.9%
Work at home	3.5%	3.1%
Mass transit miles per capita	0.70	1.87

INTERCITY SERVICES	AREA	U.S. AVG
Major airports within 60 miles	2	1
Size of regional airport	Medium	Large
Daily airline activity	484	686
Amtrak service	No	No

AUTOMOTIVE	AREA	U.S. AVG
Insurance, annual premium	$1,519	$1,432
Gas, cost per gallon	$2.66	$2.49
Daily vehicle miles per capita	35.6	24.0

Leisure
Score: 42.0
Rank: 216

DINING & SHOPPING	AREA	U.S. AVG
Restaurant rating	1	2
Outlet mall score	58	42
No. Starbucks	1	13
No. warehouse clubs	1	2

ENTERTAINMENT	AREA	U.S. AVG
Professional sports rating	2	4
College sports rating	1	4
Zoo/aquarium rating	1	3
Amusement park rating	1	3
Botanical garden/ arboretum rating	2	4

OUTDOOR ACTIVITIES	AREA	U.S. AVG
Golf-course rating	4	4
Ski-area rating	1	3
Sq. miles inland water	5	4
Miles of coastline	45.1	10.7
National Park rating	2	3

Arts & Culture
Score: 19.5
Rank: 300

MEDIA & LIBRARIES	AREA	U.S. AVG
Arts radio rating	5	3
No. public libraries	12	27
Library volumes per capita	1.84	2.78

PERFORMING ARTS	AREA	U.S. AVG
Classical music rating	1	4
Ballet/dance rating	1	3
Professional theater rating	1	3
University arts programs rating	1	5

MUSEUMS	AREA	U.S. AVG
Overall museum rating	3	5
Art museum rating	3	5
Science museum rating	5	5
Children's museum rating	2	3

Poughkeepsie–Newburgh–Middletown, NY   Score: 42.2 Rank: 308 2004 rank: 329

Profile: Small-city complex
Location: Southern New York along the Hudson River
Elevation: 292 feet
Time zone: Eastern Standard Time

PRO	CON
Close to New York City	Cost of living and housing
Attractive setting	Economic cycles
Low crime rates	Long commutes

This complex metro area, which includes Dutchess and Orange counties, spans the Hudson River above New York City and the more upscale suburban cities and towns of Westchester County. Newburgh is located 70 miles north of New York City on the west bank of the Hudson just north of the West Point Military Academy, while Middletown is located in the southern Catskill Mountains about 20 miles west. Poughkeepsie is on the east bank of the Hudson 20 miles north of Newburgh. Numerous small towns fill the valleys in between. The two counties stretch from the Connecticut border east to New Jersey to the west.

Poughkeepsie is perhaps the best-known town in the area, if for no other reason than its name and the large IBM complex in the town. It is also home to the well-regarded Vassar College, and is probably the most culturally rich town in this part of the Hudson Valley. Commuter rail service runs up this side of the Hudson, although the town is a bit far for daily commutes into Manhattan but can be used occasionally for business or pleasure visits. The downtown area is fairly nondescript but significant investments are being made in the Hudson waterfront. The once-prosperous industrial center of Newburgh has fallen on hard times, as a diverse core of manufacturing has largely left the city and little has replaced it; some renewal initiatives have since failed and the area remains depressed. Whether historic preservation interests and state economic development initiatives can improve this city remains to be seen. The story of Middletown is similar. Both cities are starting to get some interest from residents farther south looking for less expensive housing, but that said, the area's East Coast location and proximity to New York City bring high costs on a national scale. If the right economic circumstances come together, the physical setting, nearby Catskill recreation, and proximity to New York promise a better future, but there's a long way to go.

The area is mainly hilly and wooded with deciduous trees. The east bank of the Hudson is a narrow, flat valley with hills rising to the east, while the west bank consists of high rocky bluffs, especially near West Point, with hills to the west. Summers are warm and frequently muggy, with evenings occasionally cooled by breezes from all directions. Summer showers and thundershowers are common. Winters are cold and fairly wet with snow common even as New York City receives rain. Periods of bitter cold with below-zero nighttime temperatures occur, although the Hudson Valley and hills shelter the area from the strongest winds and harshest cold. First freeze is late September; last is late April.

DEMOGRAPHICS	AREA	U.S. AVG	ETHNIC COMPOSITION	AREA	U.S. AVG	RESIDENT PROFILE	AREA	U.S. AVG
Population	668,899		White	80.2%	79.0%	Single	32.8%	32.4%
Population density per sq. mile	413.4	358.5	Black	10.0%	10.5%	Married	53.6%	52.7%
Population growth	18.1%	21.1%	Asian	2.7%	2.7%	Divorced/separated	13.6%	14.9%
Median age	36.4	36.1	Hispanic	12.4%	10.6%	Married with children	29.0%	23.7%
Percent Democrat	45.2%	44.5%	Religious observance	60.9%	48.9%	Single with children	8.2%	9.1%
Percent Republican	53.1%	54.5%	Diversity measure	48.4	40.1	Percent over age 65	11.2%	12.9%

Population

INCOME	AREA	U.S. AVG	EMPLOYMENT	AREA	U.S. AVG	EMPLOYING INDUSTRIES	AREA	U.S. AVG
Per capita income	$26,002	$23,235	Unemployment rate	4.2%	4.7%	Largest: Manufacturing		
Household income	$60,490	$46,414	Recent job growth	1.6%	1.3%			
Household income < $25K	18.4%	26.2%	Projected future job growth	7.6%	11.5%	Percent manufacturing	11.2%	15.4%
Household income > $75K	38.1%	25.4%	White collar	61.8%	57.8%	Percent public sector	19.5%	15.7%
Household income growth	15.2%	13.6%	Blue collar	21.4%	25.2%	Percent construction	10.2%	9.9%

Economy & Jobs
Score: 44.1
Rank: 210

INDEXES & TAXES	AREA	U.S. AVG	HOUSING	AREA	U.S. AVG	NECESSITIES	AREA	U.S. AVG
Cost of Living Index	122.5	100.0	Median home price	$288,300	$220,000	Food Index	117.0	100.0
Buying Power Index	110.7	100.0	Home price appreciation	91.1%	10.1%	Housing Index	151.7	100.0
Income tax rate	7.13%	4.70%	Median rent	$1,060	$709	Utilities Index	133.7	100.0
Sales tax rate	8.25%	6.58%	Homes owned	64.1%	62.3%	Transportation Index	115.9	100.0
Property tax rate	$22.29	$12.00	Home price ratio	4.8	4.2	Healthcare Index	130.8	100.0
						Miscellaneous Cost Index	115.9	100.0

Cost of Living
Score: 8.3
Rank: 342

Climate
Score: 2.1
Rank: 365

TEMPERATURE	AREA	U.S. AVG
Average January low	12.5	26.2
Average July high	83.9	87.4
Annual days > 90°F	8	38
Annual days < 32°F	155	89
Annual days < 0°F	17	6

PRECIPITATION	AREA	U.S. AVG
Annual inches precipitation	33.0	37.7
Annual inches snowfall	71.0	7.0
Annual days precipitation	135	109
Annual days rain > 0.5 inches	20	22
Annual days snow > 1.5 inches	13	6

COMFORTS & HAZARDS	AREA	U.S. AVG
July relative humidity	71%	66%
Annual days mostly sunny	182	208
Annual days with thunderstorms	28	39
Tornado risk score	11	18
Hurricane risk score	12	13

TEMPERATURE

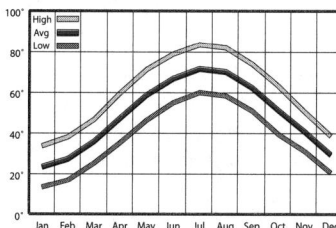

PRECIPITATION

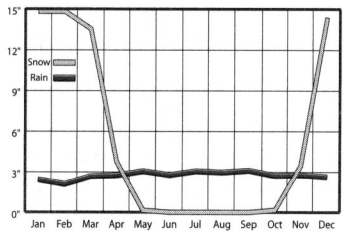

DAYS OF CLOUDS & PRECIPITATION

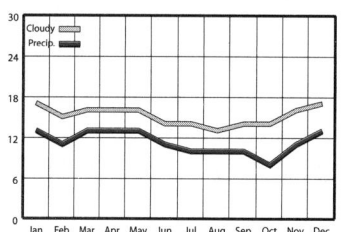

Education
Score: 82.1
Rank: 68

ACHIEVEMENT	AREA	U.S. AVG
High school degree	82.7%	82.7%
2-year college degree	8.6%	6.4%
4-year college degree	14.3%	15.7%
Graduate/professional degree	10.4%	8.9%

PUBLIC SCHOOLS	AREA	U.S. AVG
Expenditures per pupil	$8,542	$5,686
Student/teacher ratio	16.5	16.7
Attending public school	89.9%	90.1%
State SAT score	1003*	1021
State ACT score	22.6	20.9

HIGHER EDUCATION	AREA	U.S. AVG
No. 2-year colleges	2	4
No. 4-year colleges/universities	6	6
No. highly ranked universities	4	1

Health & Healthcare
Score: 20.1
Rank: 298

HAZARDS & ILLNESSES	AREA	U.S. AVG
Air-quality score	35	37
Water-quality score	42	52
Pollen/allergy score	56	61
Cancer mortality per capita	214.2	201.9
Depression days per month	3.7	3.5
Stress score	21	50

HEALTHCARE	AREA	U.S. AVG
Physicians per capita	206.3	244.2
Hospital beds per capita	380.6	420.0
No. teaching hospitals	2	3
Cost per doctor visit	$72	$77
Cost per dental visit	$63	$70

Crime
Score: 97.6
Rank: 10

CRIME	AREA	U.S. AVG
Violent crime rate	274.3	465.5
Change in violent crime rate	4.9%	-2.2%
Property crime rate	1,880.1	3,517.1
Change in property crime rate	5.3%	-2.1%

Transportation
Score: 87.4
Rank: 48

COMMUTE	AREA	U.S. AVG
Average commute time	33.0	27.4
Percent commutes > 60 mins.	16.4%	5.9%
Commute by auto	77.4%	78.9%
Commute by mass transit	4.5%	1.9%
Work at home	3.0%	3.1%
Mass transit miles per capita	4.47	1.87

INTERCITY SERVICES	AREA	U.S. AVG
Major airports within 60 miles	4	1
Size of regional airport	Large	Large
Daily airline activity	2367	686
Amtrak service	Yes	No

AUTOMOTIVE	AREA	U.S. AVG
Insurance, annual premium	$1,693	$1,432
Gas, cost per gallon	$2.63	$2.49
Daily vehicle miles per capita	40.3	24.0

Leisure
Score: 87.7
Rank: 46

DINING & SHOPPING	AREA	U.S. AVG
Restaurant rating	2	2
Outlet mall score	34	42
No. Starbucks	4	13
No. warehouse clubs	4	2

ENTERTAINMENT	AREA	U.S. AVG
Professional sports rating	10	4
College sports rating	4	4
Zoo/aquarium rating	5	3
Amusement park rating	5	3
Botanical garden/ arboretum rating	7	4

OUTDOOR ACTIVITIES	AREA	U.S. AVG
Golf-course rating	9	4
Ski-area rating	5	3
Sq. miles inland water	8	4
Miles of coastline	0.0	10.7
National Park rating	3	3

Arts & Culture
Score: 82.4
Rank: 67

MEDIA & LIBRARIES	AREA	U.S. AVG
Arts radio rating	4	3
No. public libraries	44	27
Library volumes per capita	3.20	2.78

PERFORMING ARTS	AREA	U.S. AVG
Classical music rating	8	4
Ballet/dance rating	5	3
Professional theater rating	8	3
University arts programs rating	8	5

MUSEUMS	AREA	U.S. AVG
Overall museum rating	10	5
Art museum rating	10	5
Science museum rating	10	5
Children's museum rating	7	3

Prescott, AZ

Score: 69.9 **Rank:** 92 **2004 rank:** not ranked

Profile: Small city
Location: Northwest Arizona, south end of Chino Valley
Elevation: 5,354 feet
Time zone: Mountain Standard Time (no daylight saving time)

PRO	CON
Attractive downtown	Home prices
Historic interest	Entertainment
Pleasant climate	Water shortages

Prescott is a pleasant, prosperous, and historic desert mountain city located about 90 miles northwest of Phoenix, 100 miles south of Flagstaff, and 60 miles south of Sedona, a popular arts and retirement community. Downtown is clean, quiet, and a mix of Old West and Midwest with a number of historic structures. Older homes, mostly of Victorian vintage, are nicely kept and restored, due in part to preservation incentives. More than 700 structures are listed in the National Register of Historic Places, and the city won a 2006 National Trust for Historic Preservation "Dozen Distinctive Locations" award. Numerous newer homes and developments lie outside of Prescott and in neighboring areas, including Prescott Valley and Chino Valley. Many are upscale and targeted to wealthy retirees. There are some minor arts and cultural

assets, and recreation is plentiful in nearby mountains, small lakes, and the area's many nice golf courses. The area does not get a lot of rainfall nor does it have an extensive water infrastructure, so water availability and conservation are an ongoing concern. Home prices have grown rapidly as the area attracts retirees and other migrants from the West Coast.

The valley location is characterized by low rolling desert studded with rocks, scrub pine, and intermittent green, becoming more densely forested with Ponderosa pine as you move into higher mountains both west and east of Prescott. The year-round, high-desert climate is pleasant and dry, although given to frequent below-freezing nights. Many like the area because it has four seasons, low humidity, and lots of sunshine, and its elevation is ideal to avoid Phoenix valley heat and Flagstaff cold.

Population

DEMOGRAPHICS	AREA	U.S. AVG	ETHNIC COMPOSITION	AREA	U.S. AVG	RESIDENT PROFILE	AREA	U.S. AVG
Population	192,353		White	91.3%	79.0%	Single	25.5%	32.4%
Population density per sq. mile	23.7	358.5	Black	0.4%	10.5%	Married	58.3%	52.7%
Population growth	78.6%	21.1%	Asian	0.6%	2.7%	Divorced/separated	16.2%	14.9%
Median age	44.8	36.1	Hispanic	10.8%	10.6%	Married with children	16.8%	23.7%
Percent Democrat	37.8%	44.5%	Religious observance	29.7%	48.9%	Single with children	6.8%	9.1%
Percent Republican	61.0%	54.5%	Diversity measure	32.5	40.1	Percent over age 65	22.1%	12.9%

Economy & Jobs
Score: 86.1
Rank: 53

INCOME	AREA	U.S. AVG	EMPLOYMENT	AREA	U.S. AVG	EMPLOYING INDUSTRIES	AREA	U.S. AVG
Per capita income	$23,087	$23,235	Unemployment rate	4.2%	4.7%	Largest: Healthcare & Social Assistance		
Household income	$40,004	$46,414	Recent job growth	2.0%	1.3%			
Household income < $25K	29.1%	26.2%	Projected future job growth	30.8%	11.5%	Percent manufacturing	11.6%	15.4%
Household income > $75K	19.7%	25.4%	White collar	55.0%	57.8%	Percent public sector	14.4%	15.7%
Household income growth	14.6%	13.6%	Blue collar	24.8%	25.2%	Percent construction	13.2%	9.9%

Cost of Living
Score: 21.9
Rank: 291

INDEXES & TAXES	AREA	U.S. AVG	HOUSING	AREA	U.S. AVG	NECESSITIES	AREA	U.S. AVG
Cost of Living Index	121.7	100.0	Median home price	$345,300	$220,000	Food Index	109.4	100.0
Buying Power Index	73.7	100.0	Home price appreciation	98.0%	10.1%	Housing Index	82.9	100.0
Income tax rate	3.90%	4.70%	Median rent	$744	$709	Utilities Index	91.1	100.0
Sales tax rate	6.35%	6.58%	Homes owned	63.6%	62.3%	Transportation Index	108.7	100.0
Property tax rate	$7.14	$12.00	Home price ratio	8.6	4.2	Healthcare Index	119.6	100.0
						Miscellaneous Cost Index	97.5	100.0

Climate
Score: 97.1
Rank: 12

TEMPERATURE	AREA	U.S. AVG	PRECIPITATION	AREA	U.S. AVG	COMFORTS & HAZARDS	AREA	U.S. AVG
Average January low	15.0	26.2	Annual inches precipitation	21.6	37.7	July relative humidity	33%	66%
Average July high	82.0	87.4	Annual inches snowfall	21.0	7.0	Annual days mostly sunny	293	208
Annual days > 90°F	3	38	Annual days precipitation	82	109	Annual days with thunderstorms	62	39
Annual days < 32°F	210	89	Annual days rain > 0.5 inches	11	22	Tornado risk score	3	18
Annual days < 0°F	0	6	Annual days snow > 1.5 inches	18	6	Hurricane risk score	0	13

TEMPERATURE

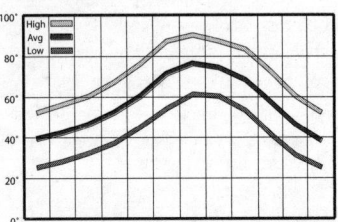

PRECIPITATION

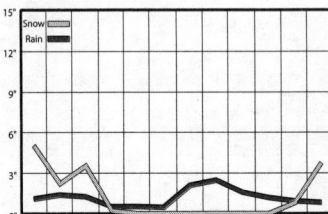

DAYS OF CLOUDS & PRECIPITATION

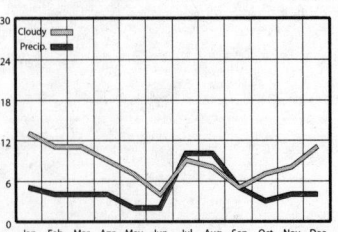

ACHIEVEMENT	AREA	U.S. AVG	PUBLIC SCHOOLS	AREA	U.S. AVG	HIGHER EDUCATION	AREA	U.S. AVG
High school degree	84.9%	82.7%	Expenditures per pupil	$4,856	$5,686	No. 2-year colleges	1	4
2-year college degree	6.7%	6.4%	Student/teacher ratio	17.7	16.7	No. 4-year colleges/universities	3	6
4-year college degree	13.1%	15.7%	Attending public school	96.3%	90.1%	No. highly ranked universities	0	1
Graduate/professional degree	8.1%	8.9%	State SAT score	1049	1021			
			State ACT score	21.6*	20.9			

Education
Score: 49.7
Rank: 189

HAZARDS & ILLNESSES	AREA	U.S. AVG	HEALTHCARE	AREA	U.S. AVG	CRIME	AREA	U.S. AVG
Air-quality score	38	37	Physicians per capita	169.7	244.2	Violent crime rate	353.1	465.5
Water-quality score	61	52	Hospital beds per capita	110.2	420.0	Change in violent crime rate	3.1%	-2.2%
Pollen/allergy score	70	61	No. teaching hospitals	0	3	Property crime rate	2,985.1	3,517.1
Cancer mortality per capita	175.4	201.9	Cost per doctor visit	$82	$77	Change in property crime rate	-10.2%	-2.1%
Depression days per month	3.5	3.5	Cost per dental visit	$73	$70			
Stress score	52	50						

Health & Healthcare
Score: 19.0
Rank: 302

Crime
Score: 79.4
Rank: 78

COMMUTE	AREA	U.S. AVG	INTERCITY SERVICES	AREA	U.S. AVG	AUTOMOTIVE	AREA	U.S. AVG
Average commute time	23.8	27.4	Major airports within 60 miles	1	1	Insurance, annual premium	$1,308	$1,432
Percent commutes > 60 mins.	6.6%	5.9%	Size of regional airport	Large	Large	Gas, cost per gallon	$2.58	$2.49
Commute by auto	75.3%	78.9%	Daily airline activity	859	686	Daily vehicle miles per capita	24.1	24.0
Commute by mass transit	0.3%	1.9%	Amtrak service	No	No			
Work at home	5.9%	3.1%						
Mass transit miles per capita	0.31	1.87						

Transportation
Score: 61.8
Rank: 144

DINING & SHOPPING	AREA	U.S. AVG	ENTERTAINMENT	AREA	U.S. AVG	OUTDOOR ACTIVITIES	AREA	U.S. AVG
Restaurant rating	1	2	Professional sports rating	1	4	Golf-course rating	5	4
Outlet mall score	39	42	College sports rating	1	4	Ski-area rating	3	3
No. Starbucks	3	13	Zoo/aquarium rating	2	3	Sq. miles inland water	1	4
No. warehouse clubs	1	2	Amusement park rating	1	3	Miles of coastline	0.0	10.7
			Botanical garden/ arboretum rating	1	4	National Park rating	3	3

Leisure
Score: 20.1
Rank: 298

MEDIA & LIBRARIES	AREA	U.S. AVG	PERFORMING ARTS	AREA	U.S. AVG	MUSEUMS	AREA	U.S. AVG
Arts radio rating	1	3	Classical music rating	2	4	Overall museum rating	4	5
No. public libraries	18	27	Ballet/dance rating	1	3	Art museum rating	2	5
Library volumes per capita	3.19	2.78	Professional theater rating	2	3	Science museum rating	6	5
			University arts programs rating	1	5	Children's museum rating	1	3

Arts & Culture
Score: 12.6
Rank: 326

Providence–New Bedford–Fall River, RI-MA   Score: 46.7   Rank: 266   2004 rank: 173

Profile: Capital-city complex
Location: Eastern edge of Rhode Island at the head of Narragansett Bay
Elevation: 51 feet
Time zone: Eastern Standard Time

PRO	CON
Educated population	Cost of living and housing
Arts and culture	Economy
Attractive downtown	Depressed areas

Providence is the capital and primary commercial, industrial, and residential area for this small New England state. Established as an enclave of religious tolerance and resident American rights in pre-Revolutionary times, it remains a center of liberal intellectual thought. But it is also an old manufacturing and typically New England–style old textile milling center. With its surrounding communities of New Bedford and Fall River, Providence has borne the brunt of considerable economic dislocation, and it shows in many parts of this area. The metro area covers the state of Rhode Island and spreads eastward into Bristol County, Massachusetts, where New Bedford and Fall River are located.

While surrounding areas are somewhat depressed and nondescript, downtown Providence itself has undergone quite a renaissance, and is one of the better examples of urban redevelopment we've seen. Older historic buildings have been cleaned up and restored and attractive parks and a "River Walk" line the Providence River as it descends into the bay. A shopping complex, convention center, and new residential developments have brought residents downtown seeking a relatively more affordable East Coast–city environment. New office complexes host banking and financial institutions, and the historic Ivy League Brown University campus lies just east of the downtown.

Suburban Providence is a mixed bag, with older industrial and working-class suburbs lying in all directions, including Cranston, Warwick, Pawtucket, and East Providence. Of these, Pawtucket is probably in the best shape. Nicer suburbs lie farther southwest and across the Massachusetts border towards Attleboro. Newport, 25 miles south at the head of the bay, is a world-famous historic and present-day playground for the wealthy with more connection to New York and Boston than Providence. New Bedford is an old whaling town trying to capitalize on tourism in its old historic district, recently made into a national park, but it has a long way to go.

Providence has a laid-back character despite its capital-city status. Brown University adds to the intellectual and cultural landscape. Many are capitalizing on the area's central location relative to other East Coast cities, and while many living costs and especially housing are reasonable by East Coast standards, property taxes are quite high. The city has become an air gateway to New England, with a small, manageable airport and discount carrier service. Statistically, the area suffered in ranking by the recent inclusion of the New Bedford and Fall River areas, and the economy shows relatively low future employment prospects. With a better financial picture, the area would rank much higher.

Providence is located at a point where numerous streams flow into the Narragansett Bay. Typical of eastern lowlands, the terrain is flat to slightly rolling, with heavy deciduous tree cover away from the water. In summer, refreshing sea breezes often cool the otherwise uncomfortable days. Measurable precipitation occurs about 1 day in 3 and is evenly distributed throughout the year. Most summer rainfall comes as thunderstorms. Late summer and fall tropical storms can hit, and the area is prone to coastal "noreaster" storms year-round. Winter temperatures and snowfall are moderate; snow cover does not remain for long periods. First freeze is late October; last is mid-April.

Population

DEMOGRAPHICS	AREA	U.S. AVG	ETHNIC COMPOSITION	AREA	U.S. AVG	RESIDENT PROFILE	AREA	U.S. AVG
Population	1,641,304		White	85.3%	79.0%	Single	36.1%	32.4%
Population density per sq. mile	1025.2	358.5	Black	4.1%	10.5%	Married	50.1%	52.7%
Population growth	8.8%	21.1%	Asian	2.3%	2.7%	Divorced/separated	13.8%	14.9%
Median age	37.8	36.1	Hispanic	8.1%	10.6%	Married with children	21.7%	23.7%
Percent Democrat	61.1%	44.5%	Religious observance	62.3%	48.9%	Single with children	9.5%	9.1%
Percent Republican	37.3%	54.5%	Diversity measure	35.0	40.1	Percent over age 65	14.0%	12.9%

Economy
& Jobs

Score: 7.0
Rank: 347

INCOME	AREA	U.S. AVG	EMPLOYMENT	AREA	U.S. AVG	EMPLOYING INDUSTRIES	AREA	U.S. AVG
Per capita income	$25,015	$23,235	Unemployment rate	5.5%	4.7%	Largest: Manufacturing		
Household income	$49,053	$46,414	Recent job growth	1.1%	1.3%			
Household income < $25K	26.5%	26.2%	Projected future job growth	1.7%	11.5%	Percent manufacturing	16.2%	15.4%
Household income > $75K	29.1%	25.4%	White collar	59.5%	57.8%	Percent public sector	13.6%	15.7%
Household income growth	14.8%	13.6%	Blue collar	24.5%	25.2%	Percent construction	8.3%	9.9%

Cost of Living

Score: 8.8
Rank: 340

INDEXES & TAXES	AREA	U.S. AVG	HOUSING	AREA	U.S. AVG	NECESSITIES	AREA	U.S. AVG
Cost of Living Index	118.8	100.0	Median home price	$291,100	$220,000	Food Index	111.8	100.0
Buying Power Index	92.6	100.0	Home price appreciation	96.0%	10.1%	Housing Index	86.8	100.0
Income tax rate	7.03%	4.70%	Median rent	$995	$709	Utilities Index	115.8	100.0
Sales tax rate	6.33%	6.58%	Homes owned	56.8%	62.3%	Transportation Index	116.5	100.0
Property tax rate	$16.63	$12.00	Home price ratio	5.9	4.2	Healthcare Index	134.6	100.0
						Miscellaneous Cost Index	107.1	100.0

Climate

Score: 31.3
Rank: 256

TEMPERATURE	AREA	U.S. AVG	PRECIPITATION	AREA	U.S. AVG	COMFORTS & HAZARDS	AREA	U.S. AVG
Average January low	20.6	26.2	Annual inches precipitation	42.8	37.7	July relative humidity	68%	66%
Average July high	81.1	87.4	Annual inches snowfall	39.2	7.0	Annual days mostly sunny	205	208
Annual days > 90°F	8	38	Annual days precipitation	134	109	Annual days with thunderstorms	20	39
Annual days < 32°F	123	89	Annual days rain > 0.5 inches	29	22	Tornado risk score	3	18
Annual days < 0°F	2	6	Annual days snow > 1.5 inches	6	6	Hurricane risk score	22	13

TEMPERATURE

PRECIPITATION

DAYS OF CLOUDS & PRECIPITATION

Education

Score: 65.5
Rank: 130

ACHIEVEMENT	AREA	U.S. AVG	PUBLIC SCHOOLS	AREA	U.S. AVG	HIGHER EDUCATION	AREA	U.S. AVG
High school degree	76.1%	82.7%	Expenditures per pupil	$6,986	$5,686	No. 2-year colleges	5	4
2-year college degree	7.1%	6.4%	Student/teacher ratio	14.2	16.7	No. 4-year colleges/universities	16	6
4-year college degree	14.9%	15.7%	Attending public school	85.8%	90.1%	No. highly ranked universities	4	1
Graduate/professional degree	8.5%	8.9%	State SAT score	997*	1021			
			State ACT score	21.2	20.9			

Health & Healthcare	HAZARDS & ILLNESSES	AREA	U.S. AVG	HEALTHCARE	AREA	U.S. AVG	Crime	CRIME	AREA	U.S. AVG
Score: 12.6 Rank: 326	Air-quality score	36	37	Physicians per capita	262.7	244.2	Score: 76.2 Rank: 90	Violent crime rate	388.2	465.5
	Water-quality score	49	52	Hospital beds per capita	326.3	420.0		Change in violent crime rate	8.6%	-2.2%
	Pollen/allergy score	61	61	No. teaching hospitals	9	3		Property crime rate	2,581.7	3,517.1
	Cancer mortality per capita	230.9	201.9	Cost per doctor visit	$108	$77		Change in property crime rate	-7.6%	-2.1%
	Depression days per month	3.7	3.5	Cost per dental visit	$82	$70				
	Stress score	51	50							

Transportation	COMMUTE	AREA	U.S. AVG	INTERCITY SERVICES	AREA	U.S. AVG		AUTOMOTIVE	AREA	U.S. AVG
Score: 77.5 Rank: 84	Average commute time	25.7	27.4	Major airports within 60 miles	2	1		Insurance, annual premium	$2,004	$1,432
	Percent commutes > 60 mins.	7.0%	5.9%	Size of regional airport	Large	Large		Gas, cost per gallon	$2.46	$2.49
	Commute by auto	80.7%	78.9%	Daily airline activity	1205	686		Daily vehicle miles per capita	21.2	24.0
	Commute by mass transit	2.5%	1.9%	Amtrak service	Yes	No				
	Work at home	2.2%	3.1%							
	Mass transit miles per capita	2.54	1.87							

Leisure	DINING & SHOPPING	AREA	U.S. AVG	ENTERTAINMENT	AREA	U.S. AVG		OUTDOOR ACTIVITIES	AREA	U.S. AVG
Score: 89.0 Rank: 42	Restaurant rating	3	2	Professional sports rating	6	4		Golf-course rating	6	4
	Outlet mall score	187	42	College sports rating	7	4		Ski-area rating	7	3
	No. Starbucks	13	13	Zoo/aquarium rating	7	3		Sq. miles inland water	7	4
	No. warehouse clubs	8	2	Amusement park rating	4	3		Miles of coastline	23.2	10.7
				Botanical garden/ arboretum rating	3	4		National Park rating	1	3

Arts & Culture	MEDIA & LIBRARIES	AREA	U.S. AVG	PERFORMING ARTS	AREA	U.S. AVG		MUSEUMS	AREA	U.S. AVG
Score: 90.9 Rank: 35	Arts radio rating	4	3	Classical music rating	9	4		Overall museum rating	9	5
	No. public libraries	102	27	Ballet/dance rating	7	3		Art museum rating	9	5
	Library volumes per capita	3.41	2.78	Professional theater rating	9	3		Science museum rating	6	5
				University arts programs rating	9	5		Children's museum rating	7	3

Provo–Orem, UT

Score: 88.5   Rank: 13   2004 rank: 146

Profile: Small-city complex/college town
Location: North-central Utah at the south end of the greater Salt Lake City area
Elevation: 4,227 feet
Time zone: Mountain Standard Time

PRO	CON
Attractive setting	Growth and sprawl
Educated population	Some air quality issues
Future job growth	Rising cost of living

Provo is at the south end of a long complex of cities, towns, and suburbs extending in both directions from Salt Lake City. Home to Brigham Young University, with 32,000 students, Provo has a strong college-town feel. Orem, just north, is a suburban family community, and there is some older infrastructure north of there in Lehi. Other towns are smaller, and all are somewhat run together. Provo and Orem are clean and relatively modern in look and feel but traditional in values and culture. There is some industry and commercial development in the immediate area, mostly high-tech and service firms; Novell (software) is one local name. Considerable employment opportunities exist at the university and in areas north towards Salt Lake, and while crowded, commutes are manageable. There is plenty to do in Provo with more options available in the cities along the Wasatch front to the north. The high population and job-growth rate combined with a limited geography threaten the city's pleasant atmosphere, and growth and sprawl continue to be an issue to contend with. For now, the area is clean and crime is low. Robert Redford's Sundance resort to the east up Provo Canyon adds tourist traffic to the area, and Provo also serves as a gateway to considerable scenic and recreational country southeast and southwest. Cost of living and housing are moderate by national and regional standards, but living costs overall have been on the rise. The area is strong in all categories and deserves the high ranking, but too much of a good thing could cause problems longer term.

The area is located in a narrow plain between Lake Bonneville and the front range of the Wasatch. The immediate area is built up with grassland and a few trees to the west. Toward Heber City to the east is steep terrain and dense coniferous Alpine forests. Summers have hot, dry weather but low humidity and occasional cooling breezes from the mountains. Winters are mostly dry and cold with occasional light rain and infrequent but sometimes heavy snow. Summer thunderstorms occur, but they're usually not severe. The valley location can cause air stagnation and quality issues especially in summer. First freeze is mid-October; last is late April.

Population

DEMOGRAPHICS	AREA	U.S. AVG	ETHNIC COMPOSITION	AREA	U.S. AVG	RESIDENT PROFILE	AREA	U.S. AVG
Population	424,127		White	91.4%	79.0%	Single	34.0%	32.4%
Population density per sq. mile	78.7	358.5	Black	0.3%	10.5%	Married	57.7%	52.7%
Population growth	57.4%	21.1%	Asian	1.8%	2.7%	Divorced/separated	8.4%	14.9%
Median age	24.9	36.1	Hispanic	7.8%	10.6%	Married with children	43.2%	23.7%
Percent Democrat	11.8%	44.5%	Religious observance	89.8%	48.9%	Single with children	5.7%	9.1%
Percent Republican	85.8%	54.5%	Diversity measure	28.2	40.1	Percent over age 65	6.5%	12.9%

Economy & Jobs
Score: 97.9
Rank: 9

INCOME	AREA	U.S. AVG	EMPLOYMENT	AREA	U.S. AVG	EMPLOYING INDUSTRIES	AREA	U.S. AVG
Per capita income	$17,935	$23,235	Unemployment rate	4.5%	4.7%	Largest: Healthcare & Social Assistance		
Household income	$52,279	$46,414	Recent job growth	4.6%	1.3%			
Household income < $25K	18.5%	26.2%	Projected future job growth	32.0%	11.5%	Percent manufacturing	11.5%	15.4%
Household income > $75K	29.2%	25.4%	White collar	63.6%	57.8%	Percent public sector	12.2%	15.7%
Household income growth	14.5%	13.6%	Blue collar	21.9%	25.2%	Percent construction	10.4%	9.9%

Cost of Living
Score: 47.9
Rank: 195

INDEXES & TAXES	AREA	U.S. AVG	HOUSING	AREA	U.S. AVG	NECESSITIES	AREA	U.S. AVG
Cost of Living Index	107.2	100.0	Median home price	$265,600	$220,000	Food Index	111.9	100.0
Buying Power Index	109.3	100.0	Home price appreciation	19.7%	10.1%	Housing Index	68.4	100.0
Income tax rate	7.00%	4.70%	Median rent	$675	$709	Utilities Index	87.0	100.0
Sales tax rate	6.24%	6.58%	Homes owned	66.1%	62.3%	Transportation Index	100.2	100.0
Property tax rate	$5.59	$12.00	Home price ratio	5.1	4.2	Healthcare Index	88.3	100.0
						Miscellaneous Cost Index	98.8	100.0

Climate
Score: 55.1
Rank: 167

TEMPERATURE	AREA	U.S. AVG	PRECIPITATION	AREA	U.S. AVG	COMFORTS & HAZARDS	AREA	U.S. AVG
Average January low	18.5	26.2	Annual inches precipitation	15.0	37.7	July relative humidity	54%	66%
Average July high	82.8	87.4	Annual inches snowfall	58.0	7.0	Annual days mostly sunny	232	208
Annual days > 90°F	58	38	Annual days precipitation	88	109	Annual days with thunderstorms	35	39
Annual days < 32°F	134	89	Annual days rain > 0.5 inches	7	22	Tornado risk score	4	18
Annual days < 0°F	3	6	Annual days snow > 1.5 inches	13	6	Hurricane risk score	0	13

TEMPERATURE

PRECIPITATION

DAYS OF CLOUDS & PRECIPITATION

Education
Score: 90.1
Rank: 38

ACHIEVEMENT	AREA	U.S. AVG	PUBLIC SCHOOLS	AREA	U.S. AVG	HIGHER EDUCATION	AREA	U.S. AVG
High school degree	91.0%	82.7%	Expenditures per pupil	$3,728	$5,686	No. 2-year colleges	3	4
2-year college degree	9.8%	6.4%	Student/teacher ratio	20.4	16.7	No. 4-year colleges/universities	3	6
4-year college degree	21.5%	15.7%	Attending public school	98.6%	90.1%	No. highly ranked universities	1	1
Graduate/professional degree	9.6%	8.9%	State SAT score	1117	1021			
			State ACT score	21.7*	20.9			

Health & Healthcare
Score: 61.8
Rank: 144

HAZARDS & ILLNESSES	AREA	U.S. AVG	HEALTHCARE	AREA	U.S. AVG	CRIME	AREA	U.S. AVG
Air-quality score	29	37	Physicians per capita	130.3	244.2	Violent crime rate	110.7	465.5
Water-quality score	52	52	Hospital beds per capita	252.8	420.0	Change in violent crime rate	5.2%	-2.2%
Pollen/allergy score	60	61	No. teaching hospitals	1	3	Property crime rate	3,078.1	3,517.1
Cancer mortality per capita	100.2	201.9	Cost per doctor visit	$70	$77	Change in property crime rate	-16.1%	-2.1%
Depression days per month	3.4	3.5	Cost per dental visit	$60	$70			
Stress score	2	50						

Crime
Score: 69.5
Rank: 113

Transportation
Score: 64.2
Rank: 135

COMMUTE	AREA	U.S. AVG	INTERCITY SERVICES	AREA	U.S. AVG	AUTOMOTIVE	AREA	U.S. AVG
Average commute time	21.7	27.4	Major airports within 60 miles	1	1	Insurance, annual premium	$1,117	$1,432
Percent commutes > 60 mins.	4.5%	5.9%	Size of regional airport	Large	Large	Gas, cost per gallon	$2.28	$2.49
Commute by auto	73.0%	78.9%	Daily airline activity	452	686	Daily vehicle miles per capita	22.3	24.0
Commute by mass transit	1.3%	1.9%	Amtrak service	Yes	No			
Work at home	5.1%	3.1%						
Mass transit miles per capita	1.33	1.87						

DINING & SHOPPING	AREA	U.S. AVG	ENTERTAINMENT	AREA	U.S. AVG	OUTDOOR ACTIVITIES	AREA	U.S. AVG
Restaurant rating	1	2	Professional sports rating	2	4	Golf-course rating	2	4
Outlet mall score	0	42	College sports rating	9	4	Ski-area rating	10	3
No. Starbucks	2	13	Zoo/aquarium rating	1	3	Sq. miles inland water	8	4
No. warehouse clubs	2	2	Amusement park rating	1	3	Miles of coastline	0.0	10.7
			Botanical garden/ arboretum rating	1	4	National Park rating	10	3

Leisure
Score: 78.1
Rank: 82

MEDIA & LIBRARIES	AREA	U.S. AVG	PERFORMING ARTS	AREA	U.S. AVG	MUSEUMS	AREA	U.S. AVG
Arts radio rating	1	3	Classical music rating	4	4	Overall museum rating	6	5
No. public libraries	11	27	Ballet/dance rating	1	3	Art museum rating	7	5
Library volumes per capita	2.17	2.78	Professional theater rating	1	3	Science museum rating	7	5
			University arts programs rating	5	5	Children's museum rating	1	3

Arts & Culture
Score: 52.1
Rank: 179

Pueblo, CO

Score: 72.3 Rank: 76 2004 rank: 20

Profile: Small city
Location: South-central Colorado along the Arkansas River near the Front Range, 110 miles south of Denver
Elevation: 4,684 feet
Time zone: Mountain Standard Time

PRO	CON
Year-round climate	Economy
Cost of living	Isolation
Healthcare	Crime rates

Twenty-five years ago, the massive Colorado Fuel & Iron plant closed, changing Pueblo forever. Once a gritty steel town, Pueblo has been in transition ever since. Ranching and irrigated farming are economic mainstays, and there is still some metal-products industries in the area. The real attractions now are the quiet, small-town life and a pleasant climate. As part of the effort to transition the economy, the city has spent a lot for revitalization and waterfront restoration along the Arkansas River waterfront, and some of the steel mill facilities may be preserved as a historic site. The area is home to large medical facilities and a state mental health center, a Colorado State University campus, and an assortment of smaller employers. The mountains and Royal Gorge area to the west provide extensive outdoor recreation. The unemployment rate of 7% is highest in the state. The city is a bit isolated but many services and amenities are available in Colorado Springs, 25 miles north, which

also provides jobs for some Pueblo residents who commute there. Cost of living is moderate and attractive relative to other Colorado cities. On the downside, there are some areas of unattractive growth outside of town.

Lake Pueblo, the largest body of water in southern Colorado, is located 7 miles west of the city and provides a variety of watersports, fishing, and picnicking, and has a wildlife preserve. The surrounding countryside consists of rolling plains, broken by normally dry arroyos, and is covered mainly with sparse bunchgrass and occasional cacti. Summer days reach 90°F about half the time, but low humidity means reasonable comfort. Mountain breezes keep summer nights cool. Winter is comparatively mild due to abundant sunshine and mountain protection. Cold spells are usually broken by warm, dry, chinook winds coming down the mountains. Summer rains occur as sporadic afternoon thunderstorms. Winter precipitation is usually light. First freeze is early October; last is early May.

DEMOGRAPHICS	AREA	U.S. AVG	ETHNIC COMPOSITION	AREA	U.S. AVG	RESIDENT PROFILE	AREA	U.S. AVG
Population	150,748		White	78.7%	79.0%	Single	31.2%	32.4%
Population density per sq. mile	63.1	358.5	Black	2.0%	10.5%	Married	52.0%	52.7%
Population growth	22.5%	21.1%	Asian	0.8%	2.7%	Divorced/separated	16.8%	14.9%
Median age	35.9	36.1	Hispanic	39.8%	10.6%	Married with children	21.1%	23.7%
Percent Democrat	52.6%	44.5%	Religious observance	56.5%	48.9%	Single with children	10.4%	9.1%
Percent Republican	46.3%	54.5%	Diversity measure	66.7	40.1	Percent over age 65	14.7%	12.9%

INCOME	AREA	U.S. AVG	EMPLOYMENT	AREA	U.S. AVG	EMPLOYING INDUSTRIES	AREA	U.S. AVG
Per capita income	$19,723	$23,235	Unemployment rate	7.0%	4.7%	Largest: Healthcare & Social Assistance		
Household income	$38,411	$46,414	Recent job growth	0.8%	1.3%			
Household income < $25K	32.2%	26.2%	Projected future job growth	10.9%	11.5%	Percent manufacturing	13.2%	15.4%
Household income > $75K	18.2%	25.4%	White collar	56.2%	57.8%	Percent public sector	18.6%	15.7%
Household income growth	17.2%	13.6%	Blue collar	24.9%	25.2%	Percent construction	11.7%	9.9%

Economy & Jobs
Score: 15.0
Rank: 317

INDEXES & TAXES	AREA	U.S. AVG	HOUSING	AREA	U.S. AVG	NECESSITIES	AREA	U.S. AVG
Cost of Living Index	84.4	100.0	Median home price	$134,700	$220,000	Food Index	109.4	100.0
Buying Power Index	102.0	100.0	Home price appreciation	22.6%	10.1%	Housing Index	58.9	100.0
Income tax rate	5.00%	4.70%	Median rent	$652	$709	Utilities Index	89.4	100.0
Sales tax rate	7.40%	6.58%	Homes owned	66.2%	62.3%	Transportation Index	95.9	100.0
Property tax rate	$7.83	$12.00	Home price ratio	3.5	4.2	Healthcare Index	103.0	100.0
						Miscellaneous Cost Index	94.1	100.0

Cost of Living
Score: 58.8
Rank: 154

Climate
Score: 68.4
Rank: 117

TEMPERATURE	AREA	U.S. AVG
Average January low	14.7	26.2
Average July high	91.1	87.4
Annual days > 90°F	64	38
Annual days < 32°F	153	89
Annual days < 0°F	8	6

PRECIPITATION	AREA	U.S. AVG
Annual inches precipitation	11.9	37.7
Annual inches snowfall	30.8	7.0
Annual days precipitation	78	109
Annual days rain > 0.5 inches	4	22
Annual days snow > 1.5 inches	6	6

COMFORTS & HAZARDS	AREA	U.S. AVG
July relative humidity	50%	66%
Annual days mostly sunny	261	208
Annual days with thunderstorms	40	39
Tornado risk score	4	18
Hurricane risk score	0	13

TEMPERATURE

PRECIPITATION

DAYS OF CLOUDS & PRECIPITATION

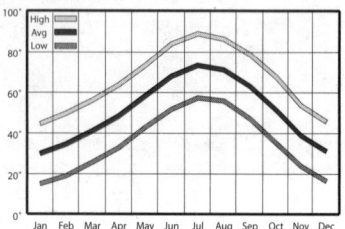
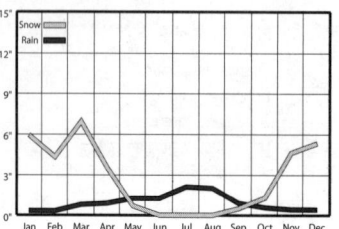
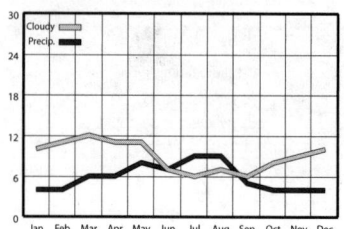

Education
Score: 42.5
Rank: 216

ACHIEVEMENT	AREA	U.S. AVG
High school degree	81.8%	82.7%
2-year college degree	8.0%	6.4%
4-year college degree	12.2%	15.7%
Graduate/professional degree	6.5%	8.9%

PUBLIC SCHOOLS	AREA	U.S. AVG
Expenditures per pupil	$4,679	$5,686
Student/teacher ratio	17.9	16.7
Attending public school	96.4%	90.1%
State SAT score	1122	1021
State ACT score	20.3*	20.9

HIGHER EDUCATION	AREA	U.S. AVG
No. 2-year colleges	1	4
No. 4-year colleges/universities	1	6
No. highly ranked universities	0	1

Health & Healthcare
Score: 87.4
Rank: 48

HAZARDS & ILLNESSES	AREA	U.S. AVG
Air-quality score	43	37
Water-quality score	100	52
Pollen/allergy score	65	61
Cancer mortality per capita	150.7	201.9
Depression days per month	3.6	3.5
Stress score	96	50

HEALTHCARE	AREA	U.S. AVG
Physicians per capita	242.7	244.2
Hospital beds per capita	758.2	420.0
No. teaching hospitals	1	3
Cost per doctor visit	$74	$77
Cost per dental visit	$59	$70

Crime
Score: 27.5
Rank: 270

CRIME	AREA	U.S. AVG
Violent crime rate	483.4	465.5
Change in violent crime rate	2.0%	-2.2%
Property crime rate	5,674.8	3,517.1
Change in property crime rate	18.8%	-2.1%

Transportation
Score: 28.3
Rank: 269

COMMUTE	AREA	U.S. AVG
Average commute time	23.0	27.4
Percent commutes > 60 mins.	5.2%	5.9%
Commute by auto	79.6%	78.9%
Commute by mass transit	0.7%	1.9%
Work at home	3.4%	3.1%
Mass transit miles per capita	0.71	1.87

INTERCITY SERVICES	AREA	U.S. AVG
Major airports within 60 miles	1	1
Size of regional airport	Medium	Large
Daily airline activity	75	686
Amtrak service	No	No

AUTOMOTIVE	AREA	U.S. AVG
Insurance, annual premium	$1,444	$1,432
Gas, cost per gallon	$2.51	$2.49
Daily vehicle miles per capita	20.0	24.0

Leisure
Score: 40.9
Rank: 220

DINING & SHOPPING	AREA	U.S. AVG
Restaurant rating	1	2
Outlet mall score	17	42
No. Starbucks	2	13
No. warehouse clubs	1	2

ENTERTAINMENT	AREA	U.S. AVG
Professional sports rating	2	4
College sports rating	2	4
Zoo/aquarium rating	2	3
Amusement park rating	1	3
Botanical garden/ arboretum rating	1	4

OUTDOOR ACTIVITIES	AREA	U.S. AVG
Golf-course rating	1	4
Ski-area rating	10	3
Sq. miles inland water	2	4
Miles of coastline	0.0	10.7
National Park rating	1	3

Arts & Culture
Score: 67.9
Rank: 120

MEDIA & LIBRARIES	AREA	U.S. AVG
Arts radio rating	8	3
No. public libraries	4	27
Library volumes per capita	2.89	2.78

PERFORMING ARTS	AREA	U.S. AVG
Classical music rating	3	4
Ballet/dance rating	1	3
Professional theater rating	1	3
University arts programs rating	3	5

MUSEUMS	AREA	U.S. AVG
Overall museum rating	5	5
Art museum rating	7	5
Science museum rating	5	5
Children's museum rating	7	3

Punta Gorda, FL

Score: 75.3 Rank: 65 2004 rank: 49

Profile: Small-city complex
Location: Gulf Coast, 25 miles north of Fort Myers along I-75
Elevation: 15 feet
Time zone: Eastern Standard Time

PRO	CON
Pleasant winter climate	Arts and culture
Future job growth	Transportation services
Small-town feel	Entertainment

Charlotte County is a mainly agricultural and residential area, with the towns of Punta Gorda and Port Charlotte located at the head of Charlotte Bay along Florida's Gulf Coast. Punta Gorda has the character of a small port town while neighboring Port Charlotte is a large planned community. Both towns are quiet and residential with a substantial percentage of retirees and winter residents. Compared to other Gulf Coast cities, they are not particularly touristy. Local activities include boating and golf, and the more complete and culturally diverse city of Ft. Myers is 25 miles south. The area was hit hard by Hurricane Charley in 2004 and is still recovering. The area has the highest future job-growth expectations in the state. While hospital services are better than average, the area is lacking in other services and arts and entertainment amenities.

The terrain is level with residential areas close to the water and agriculture mixed with cypress forests and swampland farther inland. Summer temperatures are in the 80s or low 90s with humidity, some Gulf breezes, and frequent late-afternoon thunderstorms. Winters are very pleasant, with bright, sunny, relatively dry days in the 60s and 70s. Gulf hurricanes and tropical storms can bring heavy downpours, especially in late summer and fall.

DEMOGRAPHICS	AREA	U.S. AVG	ETHNIC COMPOSITION	AREA	U.S. AVG	RESIDENT PROFILE	AREA	U.S. AVG
Population	157,503		White	92.0%	79.0%	Single	23.7%	32.4%
Population density per sq. mile	227.1	358.5	Black	4.8%	10.5%	Married	63.7%	52.7%
Population growth	41.9%	21.1%	Asian	1.1%	2.7%	Divorced/separated	12.6%	14.9%
Median age	53.9	36.1	Hispanic	4.1%	10.6%	Married with children	12.0%	23.7%
Percent Democrat	42.9%	44.5%	Religious observance	35.8%	48.9%	Single with children	5.0%	9.1%
Percent Republican	55.7%	54.5%	Diversity measure	21.8	40.1	Percent over age 65	34.5%	12.9%

INCOME	AREA	U.S. AVG	EMPLOYMENT	AREA	U.S. AVG	EMPLOYING INDUSTRIES	AREA	U.S. AVG
Per capita income	$25,162	$23,235	Unemployment rate	3.8%	4.7%	Largest: Healthcare & Social Assistance		
Household income	$41,963	$46,414	Recent job growth	5.4%	1.3%			
Household income < $25K	26.5%	26.2%	Projected future job growth	30.8%	11.5%	Percent manufacturing	9.1%	15.4%
Household income > $75K	19.6%	25.4%	White collar	57.2%	57.8%	Percent public sector	12.6%	15.7%
Household income growth	15.3%	13.6%	Blue collar	21.6%	25.2%	Percent construction	12.5%	9.9%

Score: 96.5
Rank: 14

INDEXES & TAXES	AREA	U.S. AVG	HOUSING	AREA	U.S. AVG	NECESSITIES	AREA	U.S. AVG
Cost of Living Index	102.1	100.0	Median home price	$230,100	$220,000	Food Index	102.3	100.0
Buying Power Index	92.1	100.0	Home price appreciation	148.3%	10.1%	Housing Index	83.4	100.0
Income tax rate	0.00%	4.70%	Median rent	$701	$709	Utilities Index	101.9	100.0
Sales tax rate	7.00%	6.58%	Homes owned	67.4%	62.3%	Transportation Index	109.7	100.0
Property tax rate	$12.80	$12.00	Home price ratio	5.5	4.2	Healthcare Index	98.6	100.0
						Miscellaneous Cost Index	97.7	100.0

Score: 57.0
Rank: 161

TEMPERATURE	AREA	U.S. AVG	PRECIPITATION	AREA	U.S. AVG	COMFORTS & HAZARDS	AREA	U.S. AVG
Average January low	52.3	26.2	Annual inches precipitation	54.0	37.7	July relative humidity	76%	66%
Average July high	91.5	87.4	Annual inches snowfall	0.0	7.0	Annual days mostly sunny	264	208
Annual days > 90°F	106	38	Annual days precipitation	112	109	Annual days with thunderstorms	93	39
Annual days < 32°F	1	89	Annual days rain > 0.5 inches	30	22	Tornado risk score	31	18
Annual days < 0°F	0	6	Annual days snow > 1.5 inches	0	6	Hurricane risk score	77	13

Score: 84.0
Rank: 61

TEMPERATURE

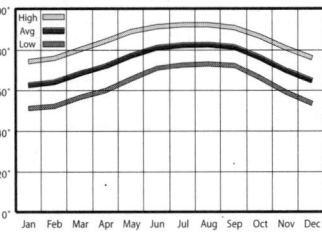

PRECIPITATION

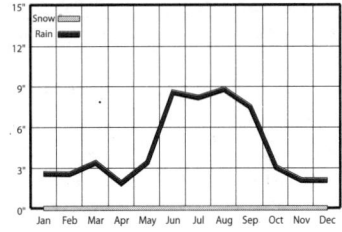

DAYS OF CLOUDS & PRECIPITATION

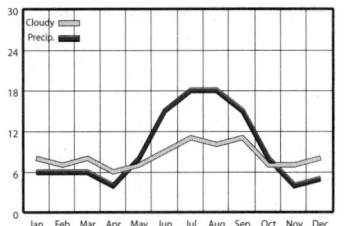

Education
Score: 26.5
Rank: 276

ACHIEVEMENT	AREA	U.S. AVG
High school degree	82.5%	82.7%
2-year college degree	5.9%	6.4%
4-year college degree	11.2%	15.7%
Graduate/professional degree	6.8%	8.9%

PUBLIC SCHOOLS	AREA	U.S. AVG
Expenditures per pupil	$5,151	$5,686
Student/teacher ratio	20.3	16.7
Attending public school	94.0%	90.1%
State SAT score	993*	1021
State ACT score	20.3	20.9

HIGHER EDUCATION	AREA	U.S. AVG
No. 2-year colleges	1	4
No. 4-year colleges/universities	0	6
No. highly ranked universities	0	1

Health & Healthcare
Score: 52.9
Rank: 177

HAZARDS & ILLNESSES	AREA	U.S. AVG
Air-quality score	56	37
Water-quality score	50	52
Pollen/allergy score	80	61
Cancer mortality per capita	223.5	201.9
Depression days per month	3.2	3.5
Stress score	40	50

HEALTHCARE	AREA	U.S. AVG
Physicians per capita	214.5	244.2
Hospital beds per capita	498.4	420.0
No. teaching hospitals	1	3
Cost per doctor visit	$76	$77
Cost per dental visit	$79	$70

Crime
Score: 68.2
Rank: 120

CRIME	AREA	U.S. AVG
Violent crime rate	456.8	465.5
Change in violent crime rate	13.3%	-2.2%
Property crime rate	3,080.0	3,517.1
Change in property crime rate	3.7%	-2.1%

Transportation
Score: 38.8
Rank: 229

COMMUTE	AREA	U.S. AVG
Average commute time	25.2	27.4
Percent commutes > 60 mins.	6.6%	5.9%
Commute by auto	81.8%	78.9%
Commute by mass transit	0.2%	1.9%
Work at home	3.3%	3.1%
Mass transit miles per capita	0.23	1.87

INTERCITY SERVICES	AREA	U.S. AVG
Major airports within 60 miles	2	1
Size of regional airport	Large	Large
Daily airline activity	524	686
Amtrak service	No	No

AUTOMOTIVE	AREA	U.S. AVG
Insurance, annual premium	$1,403	$1,432
Gas, cost per gallon	$2.62	$2.49
Daily vehicle miles per capita	34.7	24.0

Leisure
Score: 45.7
Rank: 202

DINING & SHOPPING	AREA	U.S. AVG
Restaurant rating	1	2
Outlet mall score	131	42
No. Starbucks	0	13
No. warehouse clubs	0	2

ENTERTAINMENT	AREA	U.S. AVG
Professional sports rating	2	4
College sports rating	1	4
Zoo/aquarium rating	1	3
Amusement park rating	1	3
Botanical garden/ arboretum rating	1	4

OUTDOOR ACTIVITIES	AREA	U.S. AVG
Golf-course rating	4	4
Ski-area rating	1	3
Sq. miles inland water	5	4
Miles of coastline	37.3	10.7
National Park rating	2	3

Arts & Culture
Score: 2.7
Rank: 363

MEDIA & LIBRARIES	AREA	U.S. AVG
Arts radio rating	1	3
No. public libraries	5	27
Library volumes per capita	1.03	2.78

PERFORMING ARTS	AREA	U.S. AVG
Classical music rating	3	4
Ballet/dance rating	1	3
Professional theater rating	1	3
University arts programs rating	1	5

MUSEUMS	AREA	U.S. AVG
Overall museum rating	1	5
Art museum rating	1	5
Science museum rating	3	5
Children's museum rating	1	3

Racine, WI

Score: 43.5   **Rank:** 302   **2004 rank:** 307

Profile: Small industrial city
Location: Southeast Wisconsin along Lake Michigan between Milwaukee and Chicago
Elevation: 693 feet
Time zone: Central Standard Time

PRO	CON
Architectural interest	Winter climate
Waterfront	Economy
Central location	Some urban decay

Racine is an industrial center located 30 miles south of Milwaukee and 50 miles north of downtown Chicago. Local businesses include J.I. Case, a manufacturer of farm equipment, and the S.C. Johnson Co. of Johnson Wax and Windex fame. The Frank Lloyd Wright–designed Johnson's headquarters is one of the most famous commercial buildings in the country, and there are four other Wright buildings in town. Despite the steady employment brought by S.C. Johnson and its headquarters and factory operations, most of the rest of the economy has been in the doldrums, and recently elected leadership is working hard to bring new business to the area. Aside from the Johnson headquarters and some attractive renewal on the city's main street, there is little of architectural or physical interest. The city has recognized its waterfront as a valuable asset, and has done a good job revitalizing it and adding parks and open areas. A few minor cultural amenities exist, with additional options in nearby Milwaukee and Chicago. The Cost of Living Index (89.3) is attractively low given its proximity to Milwaukee and Chicago, and housing is particularly affordable. Racine might be a diamond in the rough as the economy improves and as people recognize its strategic location.

The Root River bisects Racine before entering Lake Michigan, providing settings for riverfront parks. The surrounding terrain is mainly level and built up or cleared for agriculture. Summers are warm and often humid, although cooling afternoon breezes occur near shore. Winter brings storms and occasionally severe, dropping snow and temperature readings. Snow can remain on the ground for weeks. Winds off the lake moderate temperature but increase windchill factor. Summer precipitation is mainly thundershowers; spring and fall are variable with pleasant dry days alternating with rainy periods.

DEMOGRAPHICS	AREA	U.S. AVG	ETHNIC COMPOSITION	AREA	U.S. AVG	RESIDENT PROFILE	AREA	U.S. AVG
Population	192,488		White	81.8%	79.0%	Single	30.6%	32.4%
Population density per sq. mile	577.9	358.5	Black	10.8%	10.5%	Married	54.8%	52.7%
Population growth	10.0%	21.1%	Asian	1.0%	2.7%	Divorced/separated	14.6%	14.9%
Median age	37.1	36.1	Hispanic	8.9%	10.6%	Married with children	24.2%	23.7%
Percent Democrat	47.5%	44.5%	Religious observance	60.0%	48.9%	Single with children	9.9%	9.1%
Percent Republican	51.6%	54.5%	Diversity measure	42.8	40.1	Percent over age 65	12.4%	12.9%

Economy & Jobs
Score: 8.0
Rank: 343

INCOME	AREA	U.S. AVG	EMPLOYMENT	AREA	U.S. AVG	EMPLOYING INDUSTRIES	AREA	U.S. AVG
Per capita income	$25,034	$23,235	Unemployment rate	5.9%	4.7%	Largest: Manufacturing		
Household income	$54,084	$46,414	Recent job growth	-1.3%	1.3%			
Household income < $25K	20.3%	26.2%	Projected future job growth	1.6%	11.5%	Percent manufacturing	21.1%	15.4%
Household income > $75K	30.8%	25.4%	White collar	56.2%	57.8%	Percent public sector	10.8%	15.7%
Household income growth	12.5%	13.6%	Blue collar	30.1%	25.2%	Percent construction	9.1%	9.9%

Cost of Living
Score: 34.0
Rank: 247

INDEXES & TAXES	AREA	U.S. AVG	HOUSING	AREA	U.S. AVG	NECESSITIES	AREA	U.S. AVG
Cost of Living Index	89.3	100.0	Median home price	$147,500	$220,000	Food Index	99.2	100.0
Buying Power Index	135.8	100.0	Home price appreciation	46.0%	10.1%	Housing Index	58.9	100.0
Income tax rate	6.93%	4.70%	Median rent	$695	$709	Utilities Index	127.8	100.0
Sales tax rate	5.10%	6.58%	Homes owned	67.4%	62.3%	Transportation Index	104.0	100.0
Property tax rate	$20.62	$12.00	Home price ratio	2.7	4.2	Healthcare Index	98.3	100.0
						Miscellaneous Cost Index	98.0	100.0

Climate
Score: 13.6
Rank: 322

TEMPERATURE	AREA	U.S. AVG	PRECIPITATION	AREA	U.S. AVG	COMFORTS & HAZARDS	AREA	U.S. AVG
Average January low	11.4	26.2	Annual inches precipitation	29.0	37.7	July relative humidity	73%	66%
Average July high	80.4	87.4	Annual inches snowfall	45.0	7.0	Annual days mostly sunny	195	208
Annual days > 90°F	9	38	Annual days precipitation	122	109	Annual days with thunderstorms	36	39
Annual days < 32°F	146	89	Annual days rain > 0.5 inches	19	22	Tornado risk score	8	18
Annual days < 0°F	16	6	Annual days snow > 1.5 inches	11	6	Hurricane risk score	1	13

TEMPERATURE

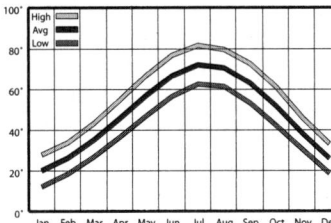

PRECIPITATION

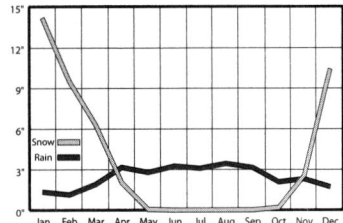

DAYS OF CLOUDS & PRECIPITATION

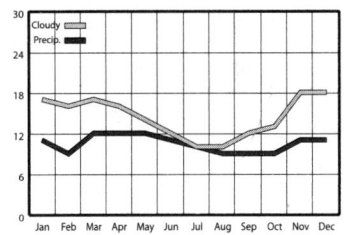

Education
Score: 34.8
Rank: 245

ACHIEVEMENT	AREA	U.S. AVG	PUBLIC SCHOOLS	AREA	U.S. AVG	HIGHER EDUCATION	AREA	U.S. AVG
High school degree	83.0%	82.7%	Expenditures per pupil	$6,048	$5,686	No. 2-year colleges	0	4
2-year college degree	7.4%	6.4%	Student/teacher ratio	16.3	16.7	No. 4-year colleges/universities	1	6
4-year college degree	14.0%	15.7%	Attending public school	85.0%	90.1%	No. highly ranked universities	0	1
Graduate/professional degree	6.3%	8.9%	State SAT score	1188	1021			
			State ACT score	22.2*	20.9			

Health & Healthcare
Score: 61.2
Rank: 146

Crime
Score: 74.1
Rank: 98

HAZARDS & ILLNESSES	AREA	U.S. AVG	HEALTHCARE	AREA	U.S. AVG	CRIME	AREA	U.S. AVG
Air-quality score	47	37	Physicians per capita	162.8	244.2	Violent crime rate	229.6	465.5
Water-quality score	30	52	Hospital beds per capita	308.1	420.0	Change in violent crime rate	12.2%	-2.2%
Pollen/allergy score	43	61	No. teaching hospitals	2	3	Property crime rate	3,510.7	3,517.1
Cancer mortality per capita	204.0	201.9	Cost per doctor visit	$88	$77	Change in property crime rate	-1.9%	-2.1%
Depression days per month	3.9	3.5	Cost per dental visit	$62	$70			
Stress score	72	50						

Transportation
Score: 96.3
Rank: 15

COMMUTE	AREA	U.S. AVG	INTERCITY SERVICES	AREA	U.S. AVG	AUTOMOTIVE	AREA	U.S. AVG
Average commute time	24.0	27.4	Major airports within 60 miles	3	1	Insurance, annual premium	$1,146	$1,432
Percent commutes > 60 mins.	5.0%	5.9%	Size of regional airport	Large	Large	Gas, cost per gallon	$2.55	$2.49
Commute by auto	83.8%	78.9%	Daily airline activity	2078	686	Daily vehicle miles per capita	13.5	24.0
Commute by mass transit	1.5%	1.9%	Amtrak service	Yes	No			
Work at home	2.3%	3.1%						
Mass transit miles per capita	1.53	1.87						

DINING & SHOPPING	AREA	U.S. AVG	ENTERTAINMENT	AREA	U.S. AVG	OUTDOOR ACTIVITIES	AREA	U.S. AVG
Restaurant rating	1	2	Professional sports rating	5	4	Golf-course rating	3	4
Outlet mall score	157	42	College sports rating	3	4	Ski-area rating	3	3
No. Starbucks	1	13	Zoo/aquarium rating	5	3	Sq. miles inland water	2	4
No. warehouse clubs	0	2	Amusement park rating	1	3	Miles of coastline	11.8	10.7
			Botanical garden/ arboretum rating	6	4	National Park rating	1	3

Leisure
Score: 59.4
Rank: 152

MEDIA & LIBRARIES	AREA	U.S. AVG	PERFORMING ARTS	AREA	U.S. AVG	MUSEUMS	AREA	U.S. AVG
Arts radio rating	3	3	Classical music rating	3	4	Overall museum rating	6	5
No. public libraries	5	27	Ballet/dance rating	3	3	Art museum rating	7	5
Library volumes per capita	2.15	2.78	Professional theater rating	3	3	Science museum rating	5	5
			University arts programs rating	6	5	Children's museum rating	3	3

Arts & Culture
Score: 51.9
Rank: 180

Raleigh–Cary, NC

Score: 75.9 Rank: 63 2004 rank: 13

Profile: Mid-size-city complex
Location: Northeast-central North Carolina, 40 miles south of Virginia border
Elevation: 363 feet
Time zone: Eastern Standard Time

PRO	CON
Strong economy	Growth and sprawl
Attractive residential areas	Long commutes
Educated population	Hot, humid summers

The Raleigh–Durham–Chapel Hill triad, sometimes referred to as the Research Triangle, is a multifaceted commercial center and capital city. Raleigh, and the rapidly growing suburban community of Cary just west, form the eastern corner of the triangle. (See p. 326 for information about the western two-thirds of the triangle, Durham and Chapel Hill, better known as college towns with the presence of Duke University and the University of North Carolina.)

Taken together, the Triangle is the educational, intellectual, and high-tech center of North Carolina and a large area of the South. Highlights include a solid, growing economic base; high degree of livability; and impressive amenities mostly related to local universities. Raleigh has a college presence, too, with a North Carolina State University branch campus, but its main role is as a capital city, with the jobs and cultural interest that typically accompany that role. The city itself is plain and relatively uninteresting as capital cities go, with nondescript government buildings, a few historic sites, and nicer residential areas near the N.C. State campus to the southwest towards Cary. The immense 6,800-acre Research Triangle Park, the area's economic crown jewel, contains major corporate offices and extensive research facilities. The Research Triangle Park isn't the only game in town; Cary itself has an extensive base of light manufacturing and new-economy businesses. Although the area is well kept and growth between the cities is fairly well managed, sprawl is an ever-present issue, and commutes from the Raleigh and Cary areas to the Research Triangle are crowded. The area as a whole and Cary in particular have experienced phenomenal growth, with a large community especially from the Northeast having settled in the area, attracted by relatively low living costs, attractive housing, climate, and laid-back lifestyle. More recently, a large number have migrated north from Florida in response to the threat of hurricanes. While costs are very attractive compared to the coasts, they are relatively high for North Carolina and most of the South.

Raleigh and Cary are located in a transitional zone between the Coastal Plain and the Piedmont Plateau. The surrounding terrain is gently rolling and heavily wooded. The central location between the mountains and coast brings favorable climate with the exception of some summer heat. Rainfall is well distributed year-round with most occurring in summers as thunderstorms, some of which can be intense. The area is far enough inland to reduce the effects of coastal storms. While snow and sleet usually occur each year, excessive accumulations are rare.

DEMOGRAPHICS	AREA	U.S. AVG	ETHNIC COMPOSITION	AREA	U.S. AVG	RESIDENT PROFILE	AREA	U.S. AVG
Population	922,315		White	70.7%	79.0%	Single	31.4%	32.4%
Population density per sq. mile	435.9	358.5	Black	19.9%	10.5%	Married	54.5%	52.7%
Population growth	70.7%	21.1%	Asian	3.5%	2.7%	Divorced/separated	14.1%	14.9%
Median age	34.0	36.1	Hispanic	7.5%	10.6%	Married with children	26.5%	23.7%
Percent Democrat	45.8%	44.5%	Religious observance	42.0%	48.9%	Single with children	7.8%	9.1%
Percent Republican	53.7%	54.5%	Diversity measure	53.2	40.1	Percent over age 65	8.2%	12.9%

Population

INCOME	AREA	U.S. AVG	EMPLOYMENT	AREA	U.S. AVG	EMPLOYING INDUSTRIES	AREA	U.S. AVG
Per capita income	$28,820	$23,235	Unemployment rate	4.6%	4.7%	Largest: Professional, Scientific & Technical Services		
Household income	$59,460	$46,414	Recent job growth	2.2%	1.3%			
Household income < $25K	17.8%	26.2%	Projected future job growth	20.3%	11.5%	Percent manufacturing	9.9%	15.4%
Household income > $75K	36.7%	25.4%	White collar	69.0%	57.8%	Percent public sector	16.0%	15.7%
Household income growth	14.6%	13.6%	Blue collar	19.3%	25.2%	Percent construction	9.4%	9.9%

Economy & Jobs
Score: 86.4
Rank: 52

Cost of Living
Score: 23.5
Rank: 285

INDEXES & TAXES	AREA	U.S. AVG
Cost of Living Index	98.1	100.0
Buying Power Index	135.9	100.0
Income tax rate	7.00%	4.70%
Sales tax rate	7.00%	6.58%
Property tax rate	$8.41	$12.00

HOUSING	AREA	U.S. AVG
Median home price	$207,700	$220,000
Home price appreciation	18.7%	10.1%
Median rent	$850	$709
Homes owned	63.3%	62.3%
Home price ratio	3.5	4.2

NECESSITIES	AREA	U.S. AVG
Food Index	102.3	100.0
Housing Index	86.0	100.0
Utilities Index	95.0	100.0
Transportation Index	100.4	100.0
Healthcare Index	104.3	100.0
Miscellaneous Cost Index	105.4	100.0

Climate
Score: 63.4
Rank: 136

TEMPERATURE	AREA	U.S. AVG
Average January low	30.0	26.2
Average July high	87.7	87.4
Annual days > 90°F	25	38
Annual days < 32°F	82	89
Annual days < 0°F	0	6

PRECIPITATION	AREA	U.S. AVG
Annual inches precipitation	43.0	37.7
Annual inches snowfall	7.0	7.0
Annual days precipitation	112	109
Annual days rain > 0.5 inches	29	22
Annual days snow > 1.5 inches	3	6

COMFORTS & HAZARDS	AREA	U.S. AVG
July relative humidity	71%	66%
Annual days mostly sunny	220	208
Annual days with thunderstorms	46	39
Tornado risk score	13	18
Hurricane risk score	29	13

TEMPERATURE **PRECIPITATION** **DAYS OF CLOUDS & PRECIPITATION**

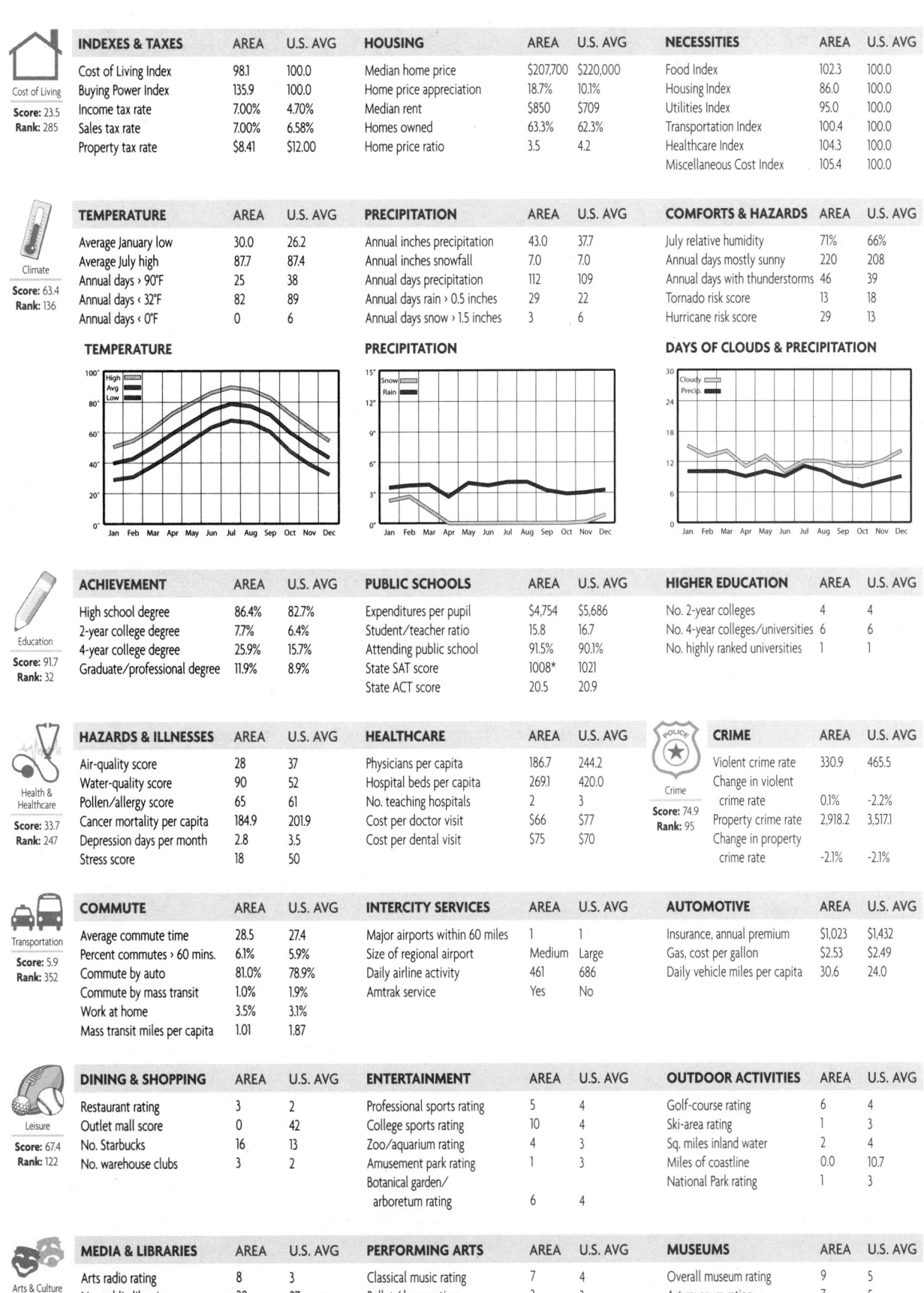

Education
Score: 91.7
Rank: 32

ACHIEVEMENT	AREA	U.S. AVG
High school degree	86.4%	82.7%
2-year college degree	7.7%	6.4%
4-year college degree	25.9%	15.7%
Graduate/professional degree	11.9%	8.9%

PUBLIC SCHOOLS	AREA	U.S. AVG
Expenditures per pupil	$4,754	$5,686
Student/teacher ratio	15.8	16.7
Attending public school	91.5%	90.1%
State SAT score	1008*	1021
State ACT score	20.5	20.9

HIGHER EDUCATION	AREA	U.S. AVG
No. 2-year colleges	4	4
No. 4-year colleges/universities	6	6
No. highly ranked universities	1	1

Health & Healthcare
Score: 33.7
Rank: 247

HAZARDS & ILLNESSES	AREA	U.S. AVG
Air-quality score	28	37
Water-quality score	90	52
Pollen/allergy score	65	61
Cancer mortality per capita	184.9	201.9
Depression days per month	2.8	3.5
Stress score	18	50

HEALTHCARE	AREA	U.S. AVG
Physicians per capita	186.7	244.2
Hospital beds per capita	269.1	420.0
No. teaching hospitals	2	3
Cost per doctor visit	$66	$77
Cost per dental visit	$75	$70

Crime
Score: 74.9
Rank: 95

CRIME	AREA	U.S. AVG
Violent crime rate	330.9	465.5
Change in violent crime rate	0.1%	-2.2%
Property crime rate	2,918.2	3,517.1
Change in property crime rate	-2.1%	-2.1%

Transportation
Score: 5.9
Rank: 352

COMMUTE	AREA	U.S. AVG
Average commute time	28.5	27.4
Percent commutes > 60 mins.	6.1%	5.9%
Commute by auto	81.0%	78.9%
Commute by mass transit	1.0%	1.9%
Work at home	3.5%	3.1%
Mass transit miles per capita	1.01	1.87

INTERCITY SERVICES	AREA	U.S. AVG
Major airports within 60 miles	1	1
Size of regional airport	Medium	Large
Daily airline activity	461	686
Amtrak service	Yes	No

AUTOMOTIVE	AREA	U.S. AVG
Insurance, annual premium	$1,023	$1,432
Gas, cost per gallon	$2.53	$2.49
Daily vehicle miles per capita	30.6	24.0

Leisure
Score: 67.4
Rank: 122

DINING & SHOPPING	AREA	U.S. AVG
Restaurant rating	3	2
Outlet mall score	0	42
No. Starbucks	16	13
No. warehouse clubs	3	2

ENTERTAINMENT	AREA	U.S. AVG
Professional sports rating	5	4
College sports rating	10	4
Zoo/aquarium rating	4	3
Amusement park rating	1	3
Botanical garden/arboretum rating	6	4

OUTDOOR ACTIVITIES	AREA	U.S. AVG
Golf-course rating	6	4
Ski-area rating	1	3
Sq. miles inland water	2	4
Miles of coastline	0.0	10.7
National Park rating	1	3

Arts & Culture
Score: 84.8
Rank: 58

MEDIA & LIBRARIES	AREA	U.S. AVG
Arts radio rating	8	3
No. public libraries	28	27
Library volumes per capita	2.25	2.78

PERFORMING ARTS	AREA	U.S. AVG
Classical music rating	7	4
Ballet/dance rating	3	3
Professional theater rating	6	3
University arts programs rating	8	5

MUSEUMS	AREA	U.S. AVG
Overall museum rating	9	5
Art museum rating	7	5
Science museum rating	6	5
Children's museum rating	7	3

Rapid City, SD

Score: 62.1 Rank: 157 2004 rank: 284

Profile: Small city
Location: Western South Dakota at the edge of the Black Hills
Elevation: 3,505 feet
Time zone: Mountain Standard Time

PRO	CON
Nearby mountains	Isolation
Attractive downtown	Tourist impact
Cost of living	Harsh climate

Rapid City is a gateway to the Black Hills of southwest South Dakota. Originally a center for the mining and timber industries, this clean, small city today is more reliant on light industry, tourism, and the large Ellsworth Air Force Base nearby. That base narrowly escaped closure recently, but the prospect of future closure hangs over the area's employment picture. The downtown core is a Western classic, with a broad main street featuring a mix of traditional small-town commercial establishments and some more oriented toward tourists. Surrounding towns, particularly Keystone and others along main routes into the Black Hills, are intensely tourist-oriented, and summer tourist impact is strong enough to be a negative. That said, the impressive Mt. Rushmore memorial and the Black Hills beyond feature extensive beauty and recreation and, apart from the summer tourist crowds, afford an excellent playground for Rapid City residents. Local museums and performing arts amenities are small but high quality. Cost of living is attractive with a COL Index of 87.3; however, the mountain base location has drawn some vacation home investment, which has pushed home prices up a bit. The location is very isolated; Denver, the nearest city with significant services and amenities, is 400 miles to the southwest. The rumble heard from 25 miles north every August comes from half a million Harley-Davidson motorcycles attending the annual Sturgis Rally.

Rapid City is located in an area of creek valleys and mostly coniferous wooded hills. To the west, the Black Hills rise to 3,000 feet into an Alpine terrain. Summers are warm and fairly dry with low humidity and cool, comfortable evenings. However, strong chinook winds off the mountains to the west can produce temperatures over 100°F. Most precipitation comes as summer thunderstorms and winter snows, some heavy. The city averages 31 days a year with below-zero readings *and* 32 days a year above 90°F, the only city with such a climate profile. First freeze is late September; last is mid-May.

Population

DEMOGRAPHICS	AREA	U.S. AVG
Population	118,211	
Population density per sq. mile	18.9	358.5
Population growth	14.5%	21.1%
Median age	35.1	36.1
Percent Democrat	30.3%	44.5%
Percent Republican	67.9%	54.5%

ETHNIC COMPOSITION	AREA	U.S. AVG
White	87.7%	79.0%
Black	1.4%	10.5%
Asian	1.1%	2.7%
Hispanic	2.5%	10.6%
Religious observance	57.9%	48.9%
Diversity measure	26.3	40.1

RESIDENT PROFILE	AREA	U.S. AVG
Single	29.6%	32.4%
Married	55.7%	52.7%
Divorced/separated	14.7%	14.9%
Married with children	24.6%	23.7%
Single with children	10.1%	9.1%
Percent over age 65	12.2%	12.9%

Economy & Jobs
Score: 80.2
Rank: 75

INCOME	AREA	U.S. AVG
Per capita income	$21,626	$23,235
Household income	$42,337	$46,414
Household income < $25K	25.8%	26.2%
Household income > $75K	19.5%	25.4%
Household income growth	13.3%	13.6%

EMPLOYMENT	AREA	U.S. AVG
Unemployment rate	3.3%	4.7%
Recent job growth	2.8%	1.3%
Projected future job growth	14.4%	11.5%
White collar	57.5%	57.8%
Blue collar	22.9%	25.2%

EMPLOYING INDUSTRIES	AREA	U.S. AVG
Largest: Healthcare & Social Assistance		
Percent manufacturing	12.7%	15.4%
Percent public sector	15.6%	15.7%
Percent construction	10.3%	9.9%

Cost of Living
Score: 90.6
Rank: 36

INDEXES & TAXES	AREA	U.S. AVG
Cost of Living Index	87.3	100.0
Buying Power Index	108.7	100.0
Income tax rate	0.00%	4.70%
Sales tax rate	5.58%	6.58%
Property tax rate	$18.99	$12.00

HOUSING	AREA	U.S. AVG
Median home price	$143,900	$220,000
Home price appreciation	36.9%	10.1%
Median rent	$650	$709
Homes owned	61.7%	62.3%
Home price ratio	3.4	4.2

NECESSITIES	AREA	U.S. AVG
Food Index	105.3	100.0
Housing Index	57.7	100.0
Utilities Index	102.8	100.0
Transportation Index	95.4	100.0
Healthcare Index	91.1	100.0
Miscellaneous Cost Index	101.3	100.0

Climate
Score: 4.5
Rank: 356

TEMPERATURE	AREA	U.S. AVG
Average January low	10.0	26.2
Average July high	87.0	87.4
Annual days > 90°F	32	38
Annual days < 32°F	169	89
Annual days < 0°F	31	6

PRECIPITATION	AREA	U.S. AVG
Annual inches precipitation	16.0	37.7
Annual inches snowfall	40.0	7.0
Annual days precipitation	96	109
Annual days rain > 0.5 inches	10	22
Annual days snow > 1.5 inches	9	6

COMFORTS & HAZARDS	AREA	U.S. AVG
July relative humidity	71%	66%
Annual days mostly sunny	205	208
Annual days with thunderstorms	40	39
Tornado risk score	18	18
Hurricane risk score	0	13

TEMPERATURE

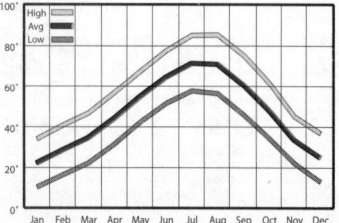

PRECIPITATION

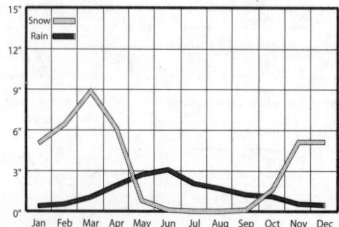

DAYS OF CLOUDS & PRECIPITATION

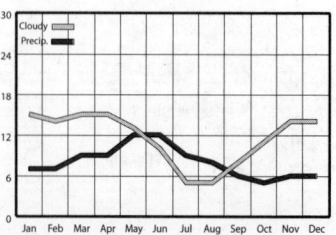

ACHIEVEMENT	AREA	U.S. AVG	PUBLIC SCHOOLS	AREA	U.S. AVG	HIGHER EDUCATION	AREA	U.S. AVG
High school degree	87.7%	82.7%	Expenditures per pupil	$4,679	$5,686	No. 2-year colleges	3	4
2-year college degree	7.9%	6.4%	Student/teacher ratio	12.3	16.7	No. 4-year colleges/universities	3	6
4-year college degree	15.8%	15.7%	Attending public school	92.5%	90.1%	No. highly ranked universities	0	1
Graduate/professional degree	7.2%	8.9%	State SAT score	1194	1021			
			State ACT score	21.8*	20.9			

Education
Score: 66.3
Rank: 127

HAZARDS & ILLNESSES	AREA	U.S. AVG	HEALTHCARE	AREA	U.S. AVG	CRIME	AREA	U.S. AVG
Air-quality score	47	37	Physicians per capita	278.0	244.2	Violent crime rate	319.6	465.5
Water-quality score	39	52	Hospital beds per capita	418.7	420.0	Change in violent crime rate	8.6%	-2.2%
Pollen/allergy score	52	61	No. teaching hospitals	1	3	Property crime rate	3,028.2	3,517.1
Cancer mortality per capita	220.0	201.9	Cost per doctor visit	$68	$77	Change in property crime rate	-2.6%	-2.1%
Depression days per month	2.9	3.5	Cost per dental visit	$53	$70			
Stress score	8	50						

Health & Healthcare
Score: 68.2
Rank: 120

Crime
Score: 69.5
Rank: 114

COMMUTE	AREA	U.S. AVG	INTERCITY SERVICES	AREA	U.S. AVG	AUTOMOTIVE	AREA	U.S. AVG
Average commute time	19.2	27.4	Major airports within 60 miles	0	1	Insurance, annual premium	$901	$1,432
Percent commutes > 60 mins.	2.9%	5.9%	Size of regional airport	None	Large	Gas, cost per gallon	$2.44	$2.49
Commute by auto	82.0%	78.9%	Daily airline activity	25	686	Daily vehicle miles per capita	25.8	24.0
Commute by mass transit	0.4%	1.9%	Amtrak service	No	No			
Work at home	3.8%	3.1%						
Mass transit miles per capita	0.44	1.87						

Transportation
Score: 52.7
Rank: 177

DINING & SHOPPING	AREA	U.S. AVG	ENTERTAINMENT	AREA	U.S. AVG	OUTDOOR ACTIVITIES	AREA	U.S. AVG
Restaurant rating	1	2	Professional sports rating	2	4	Golf-course rating	2	4
Outlet mall score	0	42	College sports rating	1	4	Ski-area rating	2	3
No. Starbucks	1	13	Zoo/aquarium rating	5	3	Sq. miles inland water	2	4
No. warehouse clubs	1	2	Amusement park rating	1	3	Miles of coastline	0.0	10.7
			Botanical garden/ arboretum rating	1	4	National Park rating	10	3

Leisure
Score: 44.1
Rank: 208

MEDIA & LIBRARIES	AREA	U.S. AVG	PERFORMING ARTS	AREA	U.S. AVG	MUSEUMS	AREA	U.S. AVG
Arts radio rating	1	3	Classical music rating	3	4	Overall museum rating	8	5
No. public libraries	6	27	Ballet/dance rating	1	3	Art museum rating	6	5
Library volumes per capita	1.79	2.78	Professional theater rating	1	3	Science museum rating	8	5
			University arts programs rating	2	5	Children's museum rating	1	3

Arts & Culture
Score: 26.7
Rank: 274

Reading, PA

Score: 67.2   Rank: 118   2004 rank: 122

Profile: Small city
Location: East-central Pennsylvania, 60 miles northwest of Philadelphia
Elevation: 260 feet
Time zone: Eastern Standard Time

PRO
Historic interest
Attractive setting
Strategic location

CON
Economy
Low educational attainment
Entertainment

Reading is a declining industrial center in southwest Pennsylvania originally built on heavy industry, textiles, and anthracite coal. The heavy industry and Victorian wealth have left an imprint on the town, which has done a good job preserving its historic heritage. The city reached its nadir in the early 1970s, first with industrial and downtown commercial closures and then with flooding from Hurricane Agnes in 1972. Among the first steps in recovery was the creation of a large outlet mall, supposedly among the first in the country, for which the area is well known today. More recently the area has gained ground as a strategic location relative to larger East Coast areas, notably Philadelphia and, farther away, New Jersey and even New York. Reading is attracting migrants, particularly those not needing to make a daily commute, who seek a small-town feel, an attractive setting, a moderate cost of living, and proximity to Philadelphia and its amenities. Like many cities in southeast Pennsylvania, this trend brings a strong sense of upside to the future. Still, some concerns linger about the economy, although it has shown signs of improvement, as has educational attainment as more migrate to the area. Outside of some local cultural and minor league sports activities, there isn't a lot to do in the immediate area.

The area is characterized by large, wooded hills surrounding flat mostly agricultural valleys. Summers are warm, still, and humid with occasional thunderstorms. Winters are fairly mild for the latitude. The area may receive snow while Philadelphia is getting rain or a mix. Snow amounts are variable and freezing rain occurs occasionally. First freeze is mid-October; last is late April.

DEMOGRAPHICS	AREA	U.S. AVG	ETHNIC COMPOSITION	AREA	U.S. AVG	RESIDENT PROFILE	AREA	U.S. AVG
Population	390,857		White	86.9%	79.0%	Single	31.7%	32.4%
Population density per sq. mile	455.1	358.5	Black	3.9%	10.5%	Married	54.8%	52.7%
Population growth	16.1%	21.1%	Asian	1.2%	2.7%	Divorced/separated	13.6%	14.9%
Median age	38.2	36.1	Hispanic	10.9%	10.6%	Married with children	23.7%	23.7%
Percent Democrat	46.4%	44.5%	Religious observance	53.9%	48.9%	Single with children	7.8%	9.1%
Percent Republican	53.0%	54.5%	Diversity measure	38.7	40.1	Percent over age 65	14.6%	12.9%

Population

INCOME	AREA	U.S. AVG	EMPLOYMENT	AREA	U.S. AVG	EMPLOYING INDUSTRIES	AREA	U.S. AVG
Per capita income	$23,747	$23,235	Unemployment rate	5.1%	4.7%	Largest: Manufacturing		
Household income	$49,450	$46,414	Recent job growth	2.0%	1.3%			
Household income < $25K	22.6%	26.2%	Projected future job growth	6.6%	11.5%	Percent manufacturing	21.1%	15.4%
Household income > $75K	27.6%	25.4%	White collar	55.1%	57.8%	Percent public sector	9.0%	15.7%
Household income growth	10.6%	13.6%	Blue collar	30.2%	25.2%	Percent construction	9.1%	9.9%

Economy & Jobs
Score: 55.3
Rank: 168

INDEXES & TAXES	AREA	U.S. AVG	HOUSING	AREA	U.S. AVG	NECESSITIES	AREA	U.S. AVG
Cost of Living Index	89.9	100.0	Median home price	$141,900	$220,000	Food Index	101.0	100.0
Buying Power Index	123.3	100.0	Home price appreciation	50.1%	10.1%	Housing Index	66.4	100.0
Income tax rate	3.91%	4.70%	Median rent	$673	$709	Utilities Index	111.6	100.0
Sales tax rate	6.00%	6.58%	Homes owned	70.1%	62.3%	Transportation Index	107.5	100.0
Property tax rate	$19.02	$12.00	Home price ratio	2.9	4.2	Healthcare Index	102.5	100.0
						Miscellaneous Cost Index	106.4	100.0

Cost of Living
Score: 53.7
Rank: 173

TEMPERATURE	AREA	U.S. AVG	PRECIPITATION	AREA	U.S. AVG	COMFORTS & HAZARDS	AREA	U.S. AVG
Average January low	19.8	26.2	Annual inches precipitation	42.5	37.7	July relative humidity	71%	66%
Average July high	85.4	87.4	Annual inches snowfall	32.2	7.0	Annual days mostly sunny	206	208
Annual days > 90°F	16	38	Annual days precipitation	133	109	Annual days with thunderstorms	33	39
Annual days < 32°F	127	89	Annual days rain > 0.5 inches	26	22	Tornado risk score	7	18
Annual days < 0°F	2	6	Annual days snow > 1.5 inches	8	6	Hurricane risk score	11	13

Climate
Score: 32.9
Rank: 250

TEMPERATURE

PRECIPITATION

DAYS OF CLOUDS & PRECIPITATION

ACHIEVEMENT	AREA	U.S. AVG	PUBLIC SCHOOLS	AREA	U.S. AVG	HIGHER EDUCATION	AREA	U.S. AVG
High school degree	78.2%	82.7%	Expenditures per pupil	$6,486	$5,686	No. 2-year colleges	4	4
2-year college degree	5.8%	6.4%	Student/teacher ratio	18.9	16.7	No. 4-year colleges/universities	4	6
4-year college degree	12.2%	15.7%	Attending public school	91.4%	90.1%	No. highly ranked universities	0	1
Graduate/professional degree	6.5%	8.9%	State SAT score	993*	1021			
			State ACT score	21.8	20.9			

Education
Score: 24.9
Rank: 281

HAZARDS & ILLNESSES	AREA	U.S. AVG	HEALTHCARE	AREA	U.S. AVG	CRIME	AREA	U.S. AVG
Air-quality score	27	37	Physicians per capita	182.2	244.2	Violent crime rate	361.4	465.5
Water-quality score	40	52	Hospital beds per capita	376.9	420.0	Change in violent crime rate	-12.6%	-2.2%
Pollen/allergy score	54	61	No. teaching hospitals	3	3	Property crime rate	2,816.9	3,517.1
Cancer mortality per capita	236.4	201.9	Cost per doctor visit	$61	$77	Change in property crime rate	2.9%	-2.1%
Depression days per month	2.7	3.5	Cost per dental visit	$51	$70			
Stress score	30	50						

Health & Healthcare
Score: 19.3
Rank: 300

Crime
Score: 70.9
Rank: 110

COMMUTE	AREA	U.S. AVG	INTERCITY SERVICES	AREA	U.S. AVG	AUTOMOTIVE	AREA	U.S. AVG
Average commute time	24.5	27.4	Major airports within 60 miles	3	1	Insurance, annual premium	$1,524	$1,432
Percent commutes > 60 mins.	5.7%	5.9%	Size of regional airport	Large	Large	Gas, cost per gallon	$2.42	$2.49
Commute by auto	81.4%	78.9%	Daily airline activity	1938	686	Daily vehicle miles per capita	18.4	24.0
Commute by mass transit	1.6%	1.9%	Amtrak service	No	No			
Work at home	2.9%	3.1%						
Mass transit miles per capita	1.58	1.87						

Transportation
Score: 94.9
Rank: 20

Leisure
Score: 52.4
Rank: 177

DINING & SHOPPING	AREA	U.S. AVG	ENTERTAINMENT	AREA	U.S. AVG	OUTDOOR ACTIVITIES	AREA	U.S. AVG
Restaurant rating	1	2	Professional sports rating	5	4	Golf-course rating	4	4
Outlet mall score	39	42	College sports rating	4	4	Ski-area rating	4	3
No. Starbucks	1	13	Zoo/aquarium rating	1	3	Sq. miles inland water	2	4
No. warehouse clubs	2	2	Amusement park rating	1	3	Miles of coastline	0.0	10.7
			Botanical garden/ arboretum rating	1	4	National Park rating	2	3

Arts & Culture
Score: 48.4
Rank: 193

MEDIA & LIBRARIES	AREA	U.S. AVG	PERFORMING ARTS	AREA	U.S. AVG	MUSEUMS	AREA	U.S. AVG
Arts radio rating	1	3	Classical music rating	4	4	Overall museum rating	5	5
No. public libraries	24	27	Ballet/dance rating	1	3	Art museum rating	7	5
Library volumes per capita	1.60	2.78	Professional theater rating	1	3	Science museum rating	6	5
			University arts programs rating	6	5	Children's museum rating	1	3

Redding, CA

Score: 65.0 Rank: 141 2004 rank: 177

Profile: Small town
Location: Northern California, at the north end of the Central Valley
Elevation: 342 feet
Time zone: Pacific Standard Time

PRO	CON
Nearby outdoor recreation	Summer heat
Revitalizing economy	Educational attainment
Mild winters	Isolation

Redding is located along Interstate 5 between the Central Valley and the mountainous region to the north into Oregon. Although the nearby mountain ranges and hillier terrain give a different physical appearance from other valley towns, economically and otherwise, Redding shares many of the same concerns of the others—weak economy, high cost of living and especially housing, and little to do. But there are some signs of an upswing. The economy, traditionally based on declining forest products from the nearby mountains and some light manufacturing and food processing, had experienced some employment dislocations. More recently, Redding's role as a center for a large region of tourism and some retirement destinations has brought some renewed economic strength, but the area is far from a career-building destination. Outdoor recreational opportunities are abundant around Lake Shasta to the north, in Trinity Alps to the northwest, and in the Sierra/Cascades to the east. The town itself is nondescript and somewhat lacking in intellectual stimulation, and living costs, following most of California, have risen substantially. Redding is a long 3-hour drive from Sacramento, source of the nearest major air service and other amenities.

Low mountains surround Redding in three directions with higher mountains in the distance. Terrain is slightly undulating with typical California valley vegetation—grasses and occasional trees. Summers are consistently hot and completely dry, with trapped valley air and abundant sunshine leading to extreme heat with 98 days above 90°F, and readings of 105°F to 110°F not uncommon. The weather is pleasant the rest of the year. Winters are cool and wet but with little to no snow except in the surrounding mountains.

Population

DEMOGRAPHICS	AREA	U.S. AVG	ETHNIC COMPOSITION	AREA	U.S. AVG	RESIDENT PROFILE	AREA	U.S. AVG
Population	178,425		White	88.1%	79.0%	Single	28.2%	32.4%
Population density per sq. mile	47.1	358.5	Black	0.9%	10.5%	Married	54.0%	52.7%
Population growth	21.3%	21.1%	Asian	2.1%	2.7%	Divorced/separated	17.8%	14.9%
Median age	38.9	36.1	Hispanic	7.1%	10.6%	Married with children	21.0%	23.7%
Percent Democrat	31.3%	44.5%	Religious observance	23.9%	48.9%	Single with children	10.6%	9.1%
Percent Republican	67.2%	54.5%	Diversity measure	32.3	40.1	Percent over age 65	15.3%	12.9%

Economy & Jobs
Score: 58.3
Rank: 157

INCOME	AREA	U.S. AVG	EMPLOYMENT	AREA	U.S. AVG	EMPLOYING INDUSTRIES	AREA	U.S. AVG
Per capita income	$20,716	$23,235	Unemployment rate	6.6%	4.7%	Largest: Healthcare & Social Assistance		
Household income	$39,471	$46,414	Recent job growth	3.6%	1.3%			
Household income < $25K	31.8%	26.2%	Projected future job growth	18.2%	11.5%	Percent manufacturing	12.3%	15.4%
Household income > $75K	20.1%	25.4%	White collar	56.8%	57.8%	Percent public sector	18.4%	15.7%
Household income growth	15.0%	13.6%	Blue collar	22.1%	25.2%	Percent construction	9.8%	9.9%

Cost of Living
Score: 16.0
Rank: 313

INDEXES & TAXES	AREA	U.S. AVG	HOUSING	AREA	U.S. AVG	NECESSITIES	AREA	U.S. AVG
Cost of Living Index	112.7	100.0	Median home price	$280,800	$220,000	Food Index	113.0	100.0
Buying Power Index	78.5	100.0	Home price appreciation	123.8%	10.1%	Housing Index	109.8	100.0
Income tax rate	6.00%	4.70%	Median rent	$680	$709	Utilities Index	87.0	100.0
Sales tax rate	7.25%	6.58%	Homes owned	60.7%	62.3%	Transportation Index	108.0	100.0
Property tax rate	$8.50	$12.00	Home price ratio	7.1	4.2	Healthcare Index	119.5	100.0
						Miscellaneous Cost Index	103.2	100.0

Climate
Score: 96.5
Rank: 14

TEMPERATURE	AREA	U.S. AVG		PRECIPITATION	AREA	U.S. AVG		COMFORTS & HAZARDS	AREA	U.S. AVG
Average January low	36.7	26.2		Annual inches precipitation	22.1	37.7		July relative humidity	52%	66%
Average July high	98.0	87.4		Annual inches snowfall	2.4	7.0		Annual days mostly sunny	247	208
Annual days > 90°F	98	38		Annual days precipitation	71	109		Annual days with thunderstorms	10	39
Annual days < 32°F	22	89		Annual days rain > 0.5 inches	22	22		Tornado risk score	1	18
Annual days < 0°F	0	6		Annual days snow > 1.5 inches	1	6		Hurricane risk score	0	13

TEMPERATURE

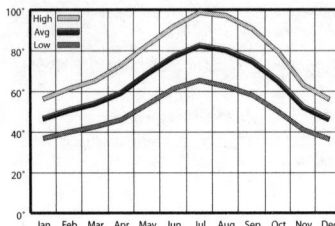

PRECIPITATION

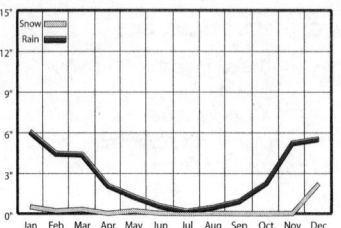

DAYS OF CLOUDS & PRECIPITATION

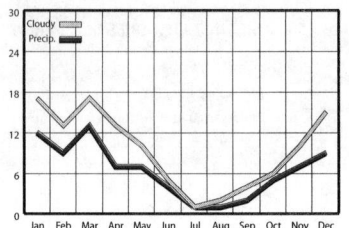

Education
Score: 38.5
Rank: 231

ACHIEVEMENT	AREA	U.S. AVG		PUBLIC SCHOOLS	AREA	U.S. AVG		HIGHER EDUCATION	AREA	U.S. AVG
High school degree	83.2%	82.7%		Expenditures per pupil	$5,404	$5,686		No. 2-year colleges	1	4
2-year college degree	9.2%	6.4%		Student/teacher ratio	18.2	16.7		No. 4-year colleges/universities	2	6
4-year college degree	11.3%	15.7%		Attending public school	91.8%	90.1%		No. highly ranked universities	0	1
Graduate/professional degree	5.3%	8.9%		State SAT score	1019*	1021				
				State ACT score	21.6	20.9				

Health & Healthcare
Score: 28.6
Rank: 266

HAZARDS & ILLNESSES	AREA	U.S. AVG		HEALTHCARE	AREA	U.S. AVG		CRIME	AREA	U.S. AVG
Air-quality score	27	37		Physicians per capita	249.9	244.2		Violent crime rate	475.4	465.5
Water-quality score	43	52		Hospital beds per capita	369.9	420.0		Change in violent crime rate	-7.1%	-2.2%
Pollen/allergy score	71	61		No. teaching hospitals	1	3		Property crime rate	3,366.0	3,517.1
Cancer mortality per capita	183.2	201.9		Cost per doctor visit	$83	$77		Change in property crime rate	3.2%	-2.1%
Depression days per month	3.9	3.5		Cost per dental visit	$75	$70				
Stress score	94	50								

Crime
Score: 69.0
Rank: 116

Transportation
Score: 28.6
Rank: 268

COMMUTE	AREA	U.S. AVG		INTERCITY SERVICES	AREA	U.S. AVG		AUTOMOTIVE	AREA	U.S. AVG
Average commute time	21.6	27.4		Major airports within 60 miles	0	1		Insurance, annual premium	$1,356	$1,432
Percent commutes > 60 mins.	5.5%	5.9%		Size of regional airport	None	Large		Gas, cost per gallon	$2.70	$2.49
Commute by auto	79.7%	78.9%		Daily airline activity	20	686		Daily vehicle miles per capita	26.5	24.0
Commute by mass transit	0.9%	1.9%		Amtrak service	Yes	No				
Work at home	4.1%	3.1%								
Mass transit miles per capita	0.88	1.87								

Leisure
Score: 51.3
Rank: 181

DINING & SHOPPING	AREA	U.S. AVG		ENTERTAINMENT	AREA	U.S. AVG		OUTDOOR ACTIVITIES	AREA	U.S. AVG
Restaurant rating	1	2		Professional sports rating	2	4		Golf-course rating	1	4
Outlet mall score	29	42		College sports rating	1	4		Ski-area rating	4	3
No. Starbucks	4	13		Zoo/aquarium rating	1	3		Sq. miles inland water	5	4
No. warehouse clubs	1	2		Amusement park rating	1	3		Miles of coastline	0.0	10.7
				Botanical garden/arboretum rating	4	4		National Park rating	10	3

Arts & Culture
Score: 27.8
Rank: 270

MEDIA & LIBRARIES	AREA	U.S. AVG		PERFORMING ARTS	AREA	U.S. AVG		MUSEUMS	AREA	U.S. AVG
Arts radio rating	1	3		Classical music rating	3	4		Overall museum rating	3	5
No. public libraries	3	27		Ballet/dance rating	1	3		Art museum rating	6	5
Library volumes per capita	1.10	2.78		Professional theater rating	1	3		Science museum rating	5	5
				University arts programs rating	2	5		Children's museum rating	1	3

Reno–Sparks, NV

Score: 75.4 Rank: 64 2004 rank: 9

Profile: Mid-size city
Location: Western Nevada, 15 miles east of the California border
Elevation: 4,400 feet
Time zone: Pacific Standard Time

PRO	CON
Nearby mountains	Growth and sprawl
Attractive setting	Rapid cost increases
Tax climate	Employment sustainability

The self-described "Biggest Little City in the World" is growing up to be a not-so-little city, combining its traditional heritage as a transportation, mining, and gambling center with distinct features of a California satellite. Rapid growth has brought a more diverse amenity base and family-friendly environment quite desirable for those willing to put up with its downsides. A favorable tax climate and strategic location as a distribution point to northern California have generated some commercial and industrial development. But much of the recent boom has derived from California migration, and we feel that some of the area's prosperity is driven by the resulting construction and may not be sustainable. The city has a lively but somewhat quirky downtown, mixing older casino and similar entertainment venues with modern commercial buildings, convention facilities, and a few modern casinos. Gambling and entertainment don't dominate as they do in Las Vegas to the south. Sparks to the east is a largely unattractive commercial and industrial center but is starting to grow as a less expensive suburban alternative. The Sierra Nevada and Lake Tahoe areas to the west offer a wide range of recreational opportunities, with national forests and world-class ski areas. The growth surge has led to considerable California-style sprawl into the desert mainly south and northwest. Commercial zones close to downtown and the airport are also crowded and unattractive. The more appealing residential areas lie in the rising Sierra foothills to the southwest. The negatives reflect the California influence, bringing rapidly increasing living and housing costs, as well as air-quality and traffic issues. Cost increases, crowding, and employment concerns have knocked Reno off its lofty 2004 no. 9 ranking perch.

Reno is located at the west edge of Truckee Meadows in a semiarid plateau lying in the lee of the Sierra Nevadas. To the immediate west, the Sierras rise to elevations of 9,000 to 11,000 feet. Desert hills to the east reach 6,000 to 7,000 feet. The Truckee River, flowing from the Sierras eastward through Reno, drains into Pyramid Lake, a remnant salt lake to the northeast. Landscape is primarily sagebrush desert with lush forests in the mountains to the west. The climate is high desert with daily temperature ranges often exceeding 45°F. While summer afternoon highs may exceed 90°F, a light jacket is often needed shortly after sunset. Nights with low temperatures above 60°F are rare. Winter afternoon temperatures are moderate. Most precipitation falls from December through March, mainly as mixed rain and snow. Brief late afternoon thunderstorms are common in summer. Sunshine is abundant in all seasons. First freeze is mid-September; last is early June.

Population

DEMOGRAPHICS	AREA	U.S. AVG	ETHNIC COMPOSITION	AREA	U.S. AVG	RESIDENT PROFILE	AREA	U.S. AVG
Population	388,876		White	79.6%	79.0%	Single	30.2%	32.4%
Population density per sq. mile	58.9	358.5	Black	1.6%	10.5%	Married	50.4%	52.7%
Population growth	51.2%	21.1%	Asian	4.3%	2.7%	Divorced/separated	19.3%	14.9%
Median age	36.1	36.1	Hispanic	19.2%	10.6%	Married with children	22.0%	23.7%
Percent Democrat	47.0%	44.5%	Religious observance	27.7%	48.9%	Single with children	9.0%	9.1%
Percent Republican	51.3%	54.5%	Diversity measure	55.4	40.1	Percent over age 65	11.2%	12.9%

Economy & Jobs

Score: 42.5
Rank: 216

INCOME	AREA	U.S. AVG	EMPLOYMENT	AREA	U.S. AVG	EMPLOYING INDUSTRIES	AREA	U.S. AVG
Per capita income	$26,921	$23,235	Unemployment rate	3.9%	4.7%	Largest: Healthcare & Social Assistance		
Household income	$52,315	$46,414	Recent job growth	1.4%	1.3%			
Household income < $25K	20.2%	26.2%	Projected future job growth	11.4%	11.5%	Percent manufacturing	12.0%	15.4%
Household income > $75K	30.9%	25.4%	White collar	58.9%	57.8%	Percent public sector	13.8%	15.7%
Household income growth	14.2%	13.6%	Blue collar	21.4%	25.2%	Percent construction	9.4%	9.9%

Cost of Living

Score: 16.8
Rank: 310

INDEXES & TAXES	AREA	U.S. AVG	HOUSING	AREA	U.S. AVG	NECESSITIES	AREA	U.S. AVG
Cost of Living Index	125.2	100.0	Median home price	$353,400	$220,000	Food Index	112.6	100.0
Buying Power Index	93.7	100.0	Home price appreciation	110.4%	10.1%	Housing Index	115.8	100.0
Income tax rate	0.00%	4.70%	Median rent	$911	$709	Utilities Index	85.5	100.0
Sales tax rate	7.37%	6.58%	Homes owned	55.5%	62.3%	Transportation Index	110.3	100.0
Property tax rate	$9.14	$12.00	Home price ratio	6.8	4.2	Healthcare Index	115.9	100.0
						Miscellaneous Cost Index	100.9	100.0

Climate
Score: 85.6
Rank: 55

TEMPERATURE	AREA	U.S. AVG
Average January low	18.3	26.2
Average July high	81.1	87.4
Annual days > 90°F	52	38
Annual days < 32°F	189	89
Annual days < 0°F	3	6

PRECIPITATION	AREA	U.S. AVG
Annual inches precipitation	7.0	37.7
Annual inches snowfall	27.0	7.0
Annual days precipitation	49	109
Annual days rain > 0.5 inches	1	22
Annual days snow > 1.5 inches	4	6

COMFORTS & HAZARDS	AREA	U.S. AVG
July relative humidity	50%	66%
Annual days mostly sunny	255	208
Annual days with thunderstorms	13	39
Tornado risk score	1	18
Hurricane risk score	0	13

TEMPERATURE

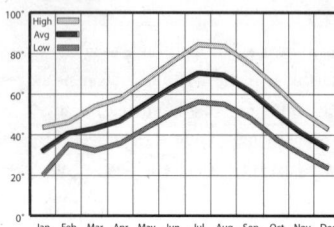

PRECIPITATION

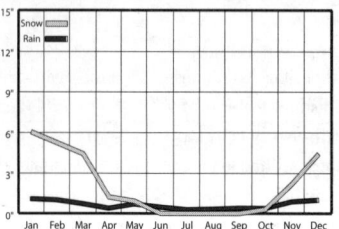

DAYS OF CLOUDS & PRECIPITATION

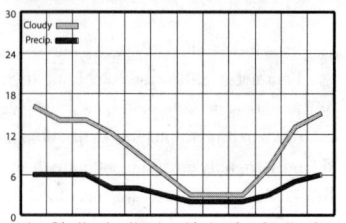

Education
Score: 55.3
Rank: 168

ACHIEVEMENT	AREA	U.S. AVG
High school degree	84.3%	82.7%
2-year college degree	7.1%	6.4%
4-year college degree	15.9%	15.7%
Graduate/professional degree	7.8%	8.9%

PUBLIC SCHOOLS	AREA	U.S. AVG
Expenditures per pupil	$5,082	$5,686
Student/teacher ratio	17.7	16.7
Attending public school	92.9%	90.1%
State SAT score	1006*	1021
State ACT score	21.5	20.9

HIGHER EDUCATION	AREA	U.S. AVG
No. 2-year colleges	2	4
No. 4-year colleges/universities	3	6
No. highly ranked universities	0	1

Health & Healthcare
Score: 29.1
Rank: 264

HAZARDS & ILLNESSES	AREA	U.S. AVG
Air-quality score	34	37
Water-quality score	40	52
Pollen/allergy score	63	61
Cancer mortality per capita	181.2	201.9
Depression days per month	3.7	3.5
Stress score	58	50

HEALTHCARE	AREA	U.S. AVG
Physicians per capita	269.3	244.2
Hospital beds per capita	292.1	420.0
No. teaching hospitals	1	3
Cost per doctor visit	$88	$77
Cost per dental visit	$96	$70

Crime
Score: 51.9
Rank: 181

CRIME	AREA	U.S. AVG
Violent crime rate	532.3	465.5
Change in violent crime rate	1.3%	-2.2%
Property crime rate	4,101.1	3,517.1
Change in property crime rate	1.1%	-2.1%

Transportation
Score: 57.5
Rank: 160

COMMUTE	AREA	U.S. AVG
Average commute time	21.3	27.4
Percent commutes > 60 mins.	3.3%	5.9%
Commute by auto	76.0%	78.9%
Commute by mass transit	3.0%	1.9%
Work at home	2.9%	3.1%
Mass transit miles per capita	2.97	1.87

INTERCITY SERVICES	AREA	U.S. AVG
Major airports within 60 miles	1	1
Size of regional airport	Medium	Large
Daily airline activity	123	686
Amtrak service	Yes	No

AUTOMOTIVE	AREA	U.S. AVG
Insurance, annual premium	$1,642	$1,432
Gas, cost per gallon	$2.62	$2.49
Daily vehicle miles per capita	21.2	24.0

Leisure
Score: 79.1
Rank: 78

DINING & SHOPPING	AREA	U.S. AVG
Restaurant rating	1	2
Outlet mall score	30	42
No. Starbucks	16	13
No. warehouse clubs	3	2

ENTERTAINMENT	AREA	U.S. AVG
Professional sports rating	2	4
College sports rating	4	4
Zoo/aquarium rating	1	3
Amusement park rating	5	3
Botanical garden/ arboretum rating	8	4

OUTDOOR ACTIVITIES	AREA	U.S. AVG
Golf-course rating	2	4
Ski-area rating	10	3
Sq. miles inland water	10	4
Miles of coastline	0.0	10.7
National Park rating	8	3

Arts & Culture
Score: 56.7
Rank: 162

MEDIA & LIBRARIES	AREA	U.S. AVG
Arts radio rating	1	3
No. public libraries	14	27
Library volumes per capita	2.31	2.78

PERFORMING ARTS	AREA	U.S. AVG
Classical music rating	6	4
Ballet/dance rating	5	3
Professional theater rating	1	3
University arts programs rating	5	5

MUSEUMS	AREA	U.S. AVG
Overall museum rating	6	5
Art museum rating	5	5
Science museum rating	5	5
Children's museum rating	4	3

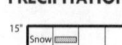

Richmond, VA

Score: 83.5 Rank: 30 2004 rank: 55

Profile: Capital-city complex
Location: East-central Virginia along the James River
Elevation: 177 feet
Time zone: Eastern Standard Time

PRO	CON
Historic interest	Growth and sprawl
Attractive housing	Entertainment
Strong economy	Air service

The former capital of the Confederacy, Richmond is an attractively sized, livable capital city with a strong sense of history. The downtown area mixes unremarkable modern buildings with some historic features; on the whole, the area has a considerable base of historic sites, museums, and neighborhoods. Outlying suburbs have sprawled concentrically, especially to the west along Patterson Avenue towards the Tuckahoe area and south toward Petersburg. Attractive and historic, more family-oriented suburbs line this western corridor north of the James River with a few excellent residential areas south of the river. Easy access to Washington, D.C., 100 miles north, and pleasant residential settings have attracted businesses, and future job growth is projected at a robust 16.4%, second highest in the state. Retailers Circuit City and CarMax and financial services giant Capital One make their headquarters in Richmond. The area is spread out and there are some traffic problems, but growth seems to attend to aesthetic considerations and most suburbs are more attractive than in other comparable areas. The University of Richmond adds a few college-town amenities, including sports. Richmond scores well in all categories and is generally on the rise, hence the high ranking.

Richmond is located along the James River in a mostly wooded area at the border of the Coastal Plain and Piedmont Hills. The Blue Ridge Mountains lie about 90 miles west and the Chesapeake Bay is 60 miles east. Summers are warm and humid, among the warmest in Virginia, and winters are generally mild. Precipitation is uniformly distributed through the year. Dry periods, especially in autumn, create periods of pleasant, mild weather. Snow usually remains on the ground only 1 to 2 days at a time and ice storms occur occasionally. Late summer and fall hurricanes along the coast can cause flooding.

DEMOGRAPHICS	AREA	U.S. AVG	ETHNIC COMPOSITION	AREA	U.S. AVG	RESIDENT PROFILE	AREA	U.S. AVG
Population	1,160,347		White	64.1%	79.0%	Single	33.0%	32.4%
Population density per sq. mile	203.1	358.5	Black	30.6%	10.5%	Married	51.4%	52.7%
Population growth	25.5%	21.1%	Asian	2.2%	2.7%	Divorced/separated	15.5%	14.9%
Median age	37.0	36.1	Hispanic	2.8%	10.6%	Married with children	23.5%	23.7%
Percent Democrat	45.5%	44.5%	Religious observance	42.5%	48.9%	Single with children	9.9%	9.1%
Percent Republican	53.9%	54.5%	Diversity measure	46.6	40.1	Percent over age 65	11.7%	12.9%

**Score: 92.8
Rank: 28**

INCOME	AREA	U.S. AVG	EMPLOYMENT	AREA	U.S. AVG	EMPLOYING INDUSTRIES	AREA	U.S. AVG
Per capita income	$26,653	$23,235	Unemployment rate	3.7%	4.7%	Largest: Finance & Insurance		
Household income	$53,369	$46,414	Recent job growth	4.2%	1.3%			
Household income < $25K	20.4%	26.2%	Projected future job growth	16.4%	11.5%	Percent manufacturing	12.7%	15.4%
Household income > $75K	31.4%	25.4%	White collar	63.7%	57.8%	Percent public sector	17.8%	15.7%
Household income growth	12.4%	13.6%	Blue collar	22.3%	25.2%	Percent construction	9.6%	9.9%

**Score: 46.8
Rank: 199**

INDEXES & TAXES	AREA	U.S. AVG	HOUSING	AREA	U.S. AVG	NECESSITIES	AREA	U.S. AVG
Cost of Living Index	99.1	100.0	Median home price	$227,300	$220,000	Food Index	95.4	100.0
Buying Power Index	120.7	100.0	Home price appreciation	59.3%	10.1%	Housing Index	74.7	100.0
Income tax rate	5.75%	4.70%	Median rent	$783	$709	Utilities Index	107.8	100.0
Sales tax rate	5.00%	6.58%	Homes owned	66.4%	62.3%	Transportation Index	103.1	100.0
Property tax rate	$9.92	$12.00	Home price ratio	4.3	4.2	Healthcare Index	89.5	100.0
						Miscellaneous Cost Index	95.4	100.0

**Score: 35.0
Rank: 242**

TEMPERATURE	AREA	U.S. AVG	PRECIPITATION	AREA	U.S. AVG	COMFORTS & HAZARDS	AREA	U.S. AVG
Average January low	27.6	26.2	Annual inches precipitation	43.0	37.7	July relative humidity	72%	66%
Average July high	88.2	87.4	Annual inches snowfall	14.0	7.0	Annual days mostly sunny	210	208
Annual days > 90°F	41	38	Annual days precipitation	113	109	Annual days with thunderstorms	37	39
Annual days < 32°F	85	89	Annual days rain > 0.5 inches	27	22	Tornado risk score	21	18
Annual days < 0°F	0	6	Annual days snow > 1.5 inches	3	6	Hurricane risk score	21	13

TEMPERATURE

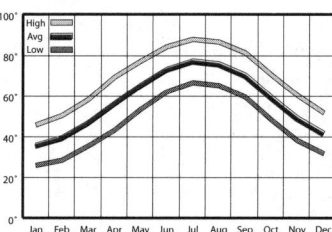

PRECIPITATION

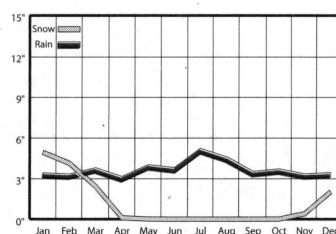

DAYS OF CLOUDS & PRECIPITATION

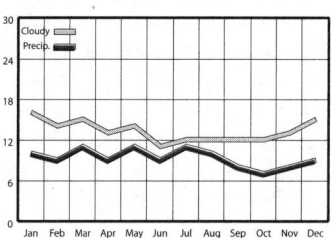

Education
Score: 69.3
Rank: 116

ACHIEVEMENT	AREA	U.S. AVG	PUBLIC SCHOOLS	AREA	U.S. AVG	HIGHER EDUCATION	AREA	U.S. AVG
High school degree	81.7%	82.7%	Expenditures per pupil	$5,549	$5,686	No. 2-year colleges	7	4
2-year college degree	5.2%	6.4%	Student/teacher ratio	15.8	16.7	No. 4-year colleges/universities	10	6
4-year college degree	18.6%	15.7%	Attending public school	93.8%	90.1%	No. highly ranked universities	1	1
Graduate/professional degree	9.2%	8.9%	State SAT score	1025*	1021			
			State ACT score	21.1	20.9			

Health & Healthcare
Score: 79.7
Rank: 77

HAZARDS & ILLNESSES	AREA	U.S. AVG	HEALTHCARE	AREA	U.S. AVG	CRIME	AREA	U.S. AVG
Air-quality score	49	37	Physicians per capita	287.9	244.2	Violent crime rate	406.0	465.5
Water-quality score	78	52	Hospital beds per capita	514.1	420.0	Change in violent crime rate	-6.0%	-2.2%
Pollen/allergy score	66	61	No. teaching hospitals	4	3	Property crime rate	3,501.9	3,517.1
Cancer mortality per capita	212.3	201.9	Cost per doctor visit	$70	$77	Change in property crime rate	-3.0%	-2.1%
Depression days per month	3.5	3.5	Cost per dental visit	$76	$70			
Stress score	43	50						

Crime **Score:** 28.3 **Rank:** 267

Transportation
Score: 67.9
Rank: 121

COMMUTE	AREA	U.S. AVG	INTERCITY SERVICES	AREA	U.S. AVG	AUTOMOTIVE	AREA	U.S. AVG
Average commute time	27.3	27.4	Major airports within 60 miles	2	1	Insurance, annual premium	$1,065	$1,432
Percent commutes > 60 mins.	5.6%	5.9%	Size of regional airport	Large	Large	Gas, cost per gallon	$2.47	$2.49
Commute by auto	81.6%	78.9%	Daily airline activity	1351	686	Daily vehicle miles per capita	28.7	24.0
Commute by mass transit	2.0%	1.9%	Amtrak service	Yes	No			
Work at home	2.7%	3.1%						
Mass transit miles per capita	1.98	1.87						

Leisure
Score: 62.6
Rank: 140

DINING & SHOPPING	AREA	U.S. AVG	ENTERTAINMENT	AREA	U.S. AVG	OUTDOOR ACTIVITIES	AREA	U.S. AVG
Restaurant rating	1	2	Professional sports rating	3	4	Golf-course rating	5	4
Outlet mall score	0	42	College sports rating	5	4	Ski-area rating	2	3
No. Starbucks	17	13	Zoo/aquarium rating	1	3	Sq. miles inland water	6	4
No. warehouse clubs	2	2	Amusement park rating	8	3	Miles of coastline	0.0	10.7
			Botanical garden/ arboretum rating	8	4	National Park rating	2	3

Arts & Culture
Score: 84.0
Rank: 61

MEDIA & LIBRARIES	AREA	U.S. AVG	PERFORMING ARTS	AREA	U.S. AVG	MUSEUMS	AREA	U.S. AVG
Arts radio rating	5	3	Classical music rating	7	4	Overall museum rating	9	5
No. public libraries	56	27	Ballet/dance rating	3	3	Art museum rating	8	5
Library volumes per capita	3.01	2.78	Professional theater rating	8	3	Science museum rating	9	5
			University arts programs rating	8	5	Children's museum rating	7	3

Riverside–San Bernardino–Ontario, CA   Score: 68.4   Rank: 106   2004 rank: 170

Profile: Suburban complex
Location: Southern California, 50 to 80 miles east of Los Angeles and Orange County
Elevation: 850 feet
Time zone: Pacific Standard Time

PRO
Year-round climate
Recreation
Diverse economy

CON
Growth and sprawl
Traffic and crowding
Air quality

Riverside County and San Bernardino County to the north form this metro area. Like many such metro areas in the Southwest, it extends far into uninhabited desert areas, in this case east through the Mojave Desert to the Nevada/Arizona border. Larger than nine U.S. states, it is often referred to as the Inland Empire. Cities in the western portion, including Riverside, San Bernardino, Ontario, and a patchwork of other communities, are developed suburbs of the Los Angeles area with a rapidly growing and increasingly self-sufficient economy. Suburbs along the Interstate 10 corridor, including Ontario, Rancho Cucamonga, Fontana, and Colton, tend to be more commercial, while others off the main roads and against the area's many mountain ranges, such as Loma Linda, Chino Hills, and many parts of Riverside, are more residential. Ontario is also the site of one of the L.A. area's best airports, with con-

siderable discount air service. Old mansions, public buildings, and packing sheds serve as evidence of the orange-growing industry that once dominated the area, but these have been long since surrounded by housing developments, industrial parks, and commercial/retail centers; areas of historic interest and strong "place" identity are few and far between. Farther east through a mountain gap lie the resort communities of Palm Springs and Palm Desert. Today the main economic activities include a host of diversified light manufacturing, international trade and offices of overseas companies, traditional services, and retail, with no real dominant employer. The projected 10-year job-growth rate remains among the highest in the state. Although rising rapidly, costs of living and housing remain *relatively* affordable for comparable areas in Los Angeles and Southern California. The area is now facing many of the same issues confronting Los Angeles as a whole—overcrowding, sprawl, poor air quality, and long freeway commutes. The average commute, while high at 33 minutes, has dropped somewhat since 2004, reflecting a greater abundance of local employment. Bottom line: This area offers many Southern California advantages while bringing the negatives in somewhat smaller doses.

The area is semiarid to arid with dry valleys surrounded by desert mountain ranges. Most of the valley floor to the west is built up. Moving east, coastal grasses and brush give way to desert foliage, including brush, creosote bush, and cactus. Summers are warm in the western portion of the counties to extremely hot and dry eastward. Evenings, consistent with the desert climate and with some marine cooling, are comfortable. Winters are mild and mostly dry, but most annual precipitation, including rainy spells, occurs during this season. There are a few days each winter with below-freezing temperatures, but many winters are frost-free. Snow is rare but can occur.

Population

DEMOGRAPHICS	AREA	U.S. AVG
Population	3,753,368	
Population density per sq. mile	137.7	358.5
Population growth	45.9%	21.1%
Median age	31.8	36.1
Percent Democrat	42.3%	44.5%
Percent Republican	56.6%	54.5%

ETHNIC COMPOSITION	AREA	U.S. AVG
White	59.2%	79.0%
Black	7.7%	10.5%
Asian	4.7%	2.7%
Hispanic	42.1%	10.6%
Religious observance	42.5%	48.9%
Diversity measure	78.8	40.1

RESIDENT PROFILE	AREA	U.S. AVG
Single	32.0%	32.4%
Married	51.9%	52.7%
Divorced/separated	16.1%	14.9%
Married with children	29.8%	23.7%
Single with children	11.4%	9.1%
Percent over age 65	10.1%	12.9%

Economy & Jobs
Score: 79.4
Rank: 77

INCOME	AREA	U.S. AVG
Per capita income	$19,807	$23,235
Household income	$47,829	$46,414
Household income < $25K	24.9%	26.2%
Household income > $75K	28.1%	25.4%
Household income growth	12.6%	13.6%

EMPLOYMENT	AREA	U.S. AVG
Unemployment rate	5.4%	4.7%
Recent job growth	3.1%	1.3%
Projected future job growth	22.5%	11.5%
White collar	55.1%	57.8%
Blue collar	27.0%	25.2%

EMPLOYING INDUSTRIES	AREA	U.S. AVG
Largest: Healthcare & Social Assistance		
Percent manufacturing	15.6%	15.4%
Percent public sector	16.7%	15.7%
Percent construction	11.4%	9.9%

Cost of Living
Score: 7.0
Rank: 347

INDEXES & TAXES	AREA	U.S. AVG
Cost of Living Index	134.1	100.0
Buying Power Index	79.9	100.0
Income tax rate	6.00%	4.70%
Sales tax rate	7.75%	6.58%
Property tax rate	$10.22	$12.00

HOUSING	AREA	U.S. AVG
Median home price	$395,700	$220,000
Home price appreciation	157.1%	10.1%
Median rent	$974	$709
Homes owned	58.4%	62.3%
Home price ratio	8.3	4.2

NECESSITIES	AREA	U.S. AVG
Food Index	111.9	100.0
Housing Index	170.9	100.0
Utilities Index	117.8	100.0
Transportation Index	107.3	100.0
Healthcare Index	127.9	100.0
Miscellaneous Cost Index	103.0	100.0

Climate
Score: 96.3
Rank: 15

TEMPERATURE	AREA	U.S. AVG
Average January low	44.4	26.2
Average July high	81.8	87.4
Annual days > 90°F	20	38
Annual days < 32°F	0	89
Annual days < 0°F	0	6

PRECIPITATION	AREA	U.S. AVG
Annual inches precipitation	12.0	37.7
Annual inches snowfall	0.0	7.0
Annual days precipitation	35	109
Annual days rain > 0.5 inches	2	22
Annual days snow > 1.5 inches	0	6

COMFORTS & HAZARDS	AREA	U.S. AVG
July relative humidity	69%	66%
Annual days mostly sunny	268	208
Annual days with thunderstorms	3	39
Tornado risk score	2	18
Hurricane risk score	2	13

TEMPERATURE

PRECIPITATION

DAYS OF CLOUDS & PRECIPITATION

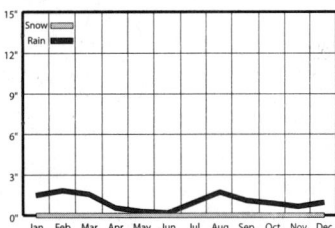

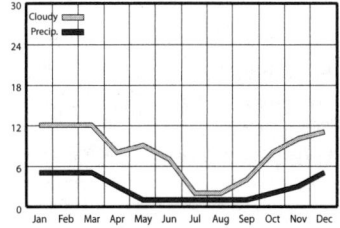

(Education icon)
Education
Score: 25.4
Rank: 279

ACHIEVEMENT	AREA	U.S. AVG
High school degree	74.5%	82.7%
2-year college degree	7.2%	6.4%
4-year college degree	10.6%	15.7%
Graduate/professional degree	5.7%	8.9%

PUBLIC SCHOOLS	AREA	U.S. AVG
Expenditures per pupil	$4,807	$5,686
Student/teacher ratio	20.9	16.7
Attending public school	94.0%	90.1%
State SAT score	1019*	1021
State ACT score	21.6	20.9

HIGHER EDUCATION	AREA	U.S. AVG
No. 2-year colleges	18	4
No. 4-year colleges/universities	9	6
No. highly ranked universities	0	1

Health & Healthcare
Score: 6.7
Rank: 348

HAZARDS & ILLNESSES	AREA	U.S. AVG	HEALTHCARE	AREA	U.S. AVG
Air-quality score	12	37	Physicians per capita	142.6	244.2
Water-quality score	49	52	Hospital beds per capita	197.0	420.0
Pollen/allergy score	55	61	No. teaching hospitals	9	3
Cancer mortality per capita	170.8	201.9	Cost per doctor visit	$70	$77
Depression days per month	3.6	3.5	Cost per dental visit	$81	$70
Stress score	71	50			

Crime
Score: 31.0
Rank: 257

CRIME	AREA	U.S. AVG
Violent crime rate	481.8	465.5
Change in violent crime rate	-3.4%	-2.2%
Property crime rate	3,683.6	3,517.1
Change in property crime rate	-0.7%	-2.1%

Transportation
Score: 72.5
Rank: 104

COMMUTE	AREA	U.S. AVG	INTERCITY SERVICES	AREA	U.S. AVG	AUTOMOTIVE	AREA	U.S. AVG
Average commute time	33.0	27.4	Major airports within 60 miles	5	1	Insurance, annual premium	$1,823	$1,432
Percent commutes › 60 mins.	15.7%	5.9%	Size of regional airport	Large	Large	Gas, cost per gallon	$2.74	$2.49
Commute by auto	73.6%	78.9%	Daily airline activity	1993	686	Daily vehicle miles per capita	21.0	24.0
Commute by mass transit	1.6%	1.9%	Amtrak service	Yes	No			
Work at home	3.5%	3.1%						
Mass transit miles per capita	1.64	1.87						

Leisure
Score: 97.3
Rank: 11

DINING & SHOPPING	AREA	U.S. AVG	ENTERTAINMENT	AREA	U.S. AVG	OUTDOOR ACTIVITIES	AREA	U.S. AVG
Restaurant rating	1	2	Professional sports rating	9	4	Golf-course rating	10	4
Outlet mall score	229	42	College sports rating	2	4	Ski-area rating	10	3
No. Starbucks	109	13	Zoo/aquarium rating	5	3	Sq. miles inland water	7	4
No. warehouse clubs	13	2	Amusement park rating	7	3	Miles of coastline	0.0	10.7
			Botanical garden/ arboretum rating	9	4	National Park rating	10	3

Arts & Culture
Score: 86.6
Rank: 51

MEDIA & LIBRARIES	AREA	U.S. AVG	PERFORMING ARTS	AREA	U.S. AVG	MUSEUMS	AREA	U.S. AVG
Arts radio rating	9	3	Classical music rating	7	4	Overall museum rating	9	5
No. public libraries	78	27	Ballet/dance rating	6	3	Art museum rating	9	5
Library volumes per capita	1.30	2.78	Professional theater rating	5	3	Science museum rating	10	5
			University arts programs rating	8	5	Children's museum rating	10	3

Roanoke, VA

Score: 76.8   **Rank:** 60   **2004 rank:** 11

Profile: Mid-size city
Location: Southwestern Virginia along the Blue Ridge Mountains
Elevation: 1,176 feet
Time zone: Eastern Standard Time

PRO
Nearby mountains
Attractive downtown
Pleasant climate

CON
Air service
Some industrial feel
Future job growth

Roanoke is a mid-size commercial and transportation center located between the Blue Ridge and Appalachian mountains in the western part of the state. The city area spreads through a narrow valley surrounded by hills and mountains, especially to the northwest and southwest. The downtown area itself is an American classic, compact and walkable with museums, performing-arts venues, shops, and a famous farmer's market in a lively historic central core known as Market Square. More modern commercial structures surround this core. On the whole, Roanoke is more Old than New South, but is bringing in a strong influx of northern migrants, evidenced among other things by a minor league hockey team. The relatively diverse economy includes an industrial base ranging from heavy steel products to textiles and electronics. Cultural amenities are varied and abundant for the town's size, and nearby mountains offer recreational opportunities. Cost of living is reasonable, the climate attractive, and healthcare excellent, anchored by the large Carilion Health Foundation medical complex just south of

town. Poor air quality can result from the valley location, and some parts of the area still have a bit of an industrial feel from its days as a rail center; however, it is largely clean and well kept. Local residents complain about air service and often must drive to the Washington, D.C., area or south to Greensboro, North Carolina, to get favorable selection and prices. A drop in job-growth projections is partly responsible for the lower ranking.

Roanoke sits at the point where the Blue Ridge Mountains pinch against the main ridge of the Appalachians. The surrounding terrain is hilly to mountainous and generally wooded. Numerous mountain creeks and small streams empty into the headwaters of the Roanoke River. The climate is relatively mild. The elevation usually produces cool summer nights. Extreme temperatures are rare. Rainfall is well apportioned throughout the year. Snow usually falls each winter, occasionally producing significant accumulations. The mountain stream convergence can produce damaging floods. First freeze is late October; last is mid-April.

Population

DEMOGRAPHICS	AREA	U.S. AVG	ETHNIC COMPOSITION	AREA	U.S. AVG	RESIDENT PROFILE	AREA	U.S. AVG
Population	292,443		White	84.4%	79.0%	Single	29.4%	32.4%
Population density per sq. mile	156.1	358.5	Black	12.5%	10.5%	Married	54.9%	52.7%
Population growth	10.3%	21.1%	Asian	1.2%	2.7%	Divorced/separated	15.6%	14.9%
Median age	40.5	36.1	Hispanic	1.5%	10.6%	Married with children	20.6%	23.7%
Percent Democrat	40.1%	44.5%	Religious observance	52.4%	48.9%	Single with children	8.0%	9.1%
Percent Republican	59.0%	54.5%	Diversity measure	26.9	40.1	Percent over age 65	15.9%	12.9%

Economy & Jobs
Score: 69.3
Rank: 116

INCOME	AREA	U.S. AVG	EMPLOYMENT	AREA	U.S. AVG	EMPLOYING INDUSTRIES	AREA	U.S. AVG
Per capita income	$24,049	$23,235	Unemployment rate	3.6%	4.7%	Largest: Healthcare & Social Assistance		
Household income	$44,391	$46,414	Recent job growth	3.2%	1.3%			
Household income < $25K	26.5%	26.2%	Projected future job growth	7.2%	11.5%	Percent manufacturing	16.2%	15.4%
Household income > $75K	22.7%	25.4%	White collar	59.3%	57.8%	Percent public sector	12.9%	15.7%
Household income growth	11.3%	13.6%	Blue collar	26.2%	25.2%	Percent construction	10.1%	9.9%

Cost of Living
Score: 49.2
Rank: 190

INDEXES & TAXES	AREA	U.S. AVG	HOUSING	AREA	U.S. AVG	NECESSITIES	AREA	U.S. AVG
Cost of Living Index	80.6	100.0	Median home price	$145,600	$220,000	Food Index	93.7	100.0
Buying Power Index	123.5	100.0	Home price appreciation	42.8%	10.1%	Housing Index	88.5	100.0
Income tax rate	5.75%	4.70%	Median rent	$594	$709	Utilities Index	72.0	100.0
Sales tax rate	5.00%	6.58%	Homes owned	66.1%	62.3%	Transportation Index	86.2	100.0
Property tax rate	$9.57	$12.00	Home price ratio	3.3	4.2	Healthcare Index	93.9	100.0
						Miscellaneous Cost Index	94.0	100.0

Climate
Score: 76.7
Rank: 87

TEMPERATURE	AREA	U.S. AVG	PRECIPITATION	AREA	U.S. AVG	COMFORTS & HAZARDS	AREA	U.S. AVG
Average January low	27.2	26.2	Annual inches precipitation	39.0	37.7	July relative humidity	65%	66%
Average July high	85.9	87.4	Annual inches snowfall	25.0	7.0	Annual days mostly sunny	217	208
Annual days > 90°F	20	38	Annual days precipitation	121	109	Annual days with thunderstorms	38	39
Annual days < 32°F	92	89	Annual days rain > 0.5 inches	26	22	Tornado risk score	1	18
Annual days < 0°F	0	6	Annual days snow > 1.5 inches	5	6	Hurricane risk score	10	13

TEMPERATURE

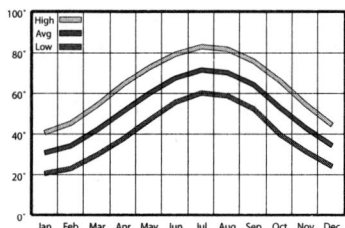

PRECIPITATION

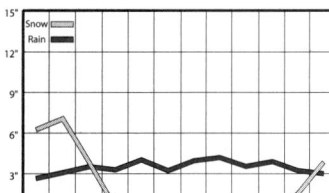

DAYS OF CLOUDS & PRECIPITATION

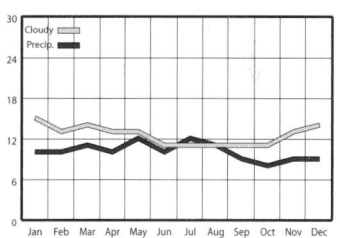

Education
Score: 47.3
Rank: 198

ACHIEVEMENT	AREA	U.S. AVG	PUBLIC SCHOOLS	AREA	U.S. AVG	HIGHER EDUCATION	AREA	U.S. AVG
High school degree	79.3%	82.7%	Expenditures per pupil	$5,680	$5,686	No. 2-year colleges	2	4
2-year college degree	6.8%	6.4%	Student/teacher ratio	14.7	16.7	No. 4-year colleges/universities	5	6
4-year college degree	13.8%	15.7%	Attending public school	96.6%	90.1%	No. highly ranked universities	0	1
Graduate/professional degree	7.1%	8.9%	State SAT score	1025*	1021			
			State ACT score	21.1	20.9			

Health & Healthcare
Score: 98.7
Rank: 6

HAZARDS & ILLNESSES	AREA	U.S. AVG	HEALTHCARE	AREA	U.S. AVG	CRIME	AREA	U.S. AVG
Air-quality score	66	37	Physicians per capita	335.1	244.2	Violent crime rate	421.6	465.5
Water-quality score	84	52	Hospital beds per capita	618.6	420.0	Change in violent crime rate	3.5%	-2.2%
Pollen/allergy score	53	61	No. teaching hospitals	2	3	Property crime rate	3,296.6	3,517.1
Cancer mortality per capita	182.0	201.9	Cost per doctor visit	$78	$77	Change in property crime rate	5.0%	-2.1%
Depression days per month	3.4	3.5	Cost per dental visit	$55	$70			
Stress score	36	50						

Crime
Score: 67.9
Rank: 121

Transportation
Score: 19.3
Rank: 303

COMMUTE	AREA	U.S. AVG	INTERCITY SERVICES	AREA	U.S. AVG	AUTOMOTIVE	AREA	U.S. AVG
Average commute time	23.9	27.4	Major airports within 60 miles	0	1	Insurance, annual premium	$934	$1,432
Percent commutes > 60 mins.	4.4%	5.9%	Size of regional airport	Small	Large	Gas, cost per gallon	$2.38	$2.49
Commute by auto	83.3%	78.9%	Daily airline activity	173	686	Daily vehicle miles per capita	25.3	24.0
Commute by mass transit	1.2%	1.9%	Amtrak service	No	No			
Work at home	2.5%	3.1%						
Mass transit miles per capita	1.16	1.87						

Leisure Score: 33.4 Rank: 248	DINING & SHOPPING	AREA	U.S. AVG	ENTERTAINMENT	AREA	U.S. AVG	OUTDOOR ACTIVITIES	AREA	U.S. AVG
	Restaurant rating	1	2	Professional sports rating	3	4	Golf-course rating	2	4
	Outlet mall score	0	42	College sports rating	1	4	Ski-area rating	4	3
	No. Starbucks	1	13	Zoo/aquarium rating	1	3	Sq. miles inland water	2	4
	No. warehouse clubs	0	2	Amusement park rating	1	3	Miles of coastline	0.0	10.7
				Botanical garden/ arboretum rating	1	4	National Park rating	5	3

Arts & Culture Score: 50.5 Rank: 185	MEDIA & LIBRARIES	AREA	U.S. AVG	PERFORMING ARTS	AREA	U.S. AVG	MUSEUMS	AREA	U.S. AVG
	Arts radio rating	1	3	Classical music rating	3	4	Overall museum rating	6	5
	No. public libraries	18	27	Ballet/dance rating	1	3	Art museum rating	6	5
	Library volumes per capita	3.63	2.78	Professional theater rating	1	3	Science museum rating	6	5
				University arts programs rating	6	5	Children's museum rating	1	3

Rochester, MN

Score: 66.0   Rank: 131   2004 rank: 144

Profile: Mid-size city
Location: Southeastern Minnesota, 45 miles west of Wisconsin and 35 miles north of Iowa
Elevation: 1,006 feet
Time zone: Central Standard Time

PRO	CON
Healthcare	Winter climate
Educated population	Entertainment
Nearby outdoor recreation	Arts and culture

Rochester is a livable mid-size commercial and agricultural center with a diverse economy. But its biggest claim to fame is the renowned Mayo Clinic medical research and practice center, which covers some 18 city blocks in the downtown core. Mayo is a major economic driver as well as a strong healthcare presence in the area, directly providing some 42,000 jobs and many more in serving and supporting the some 400,000 patients that come through each year. Not surprisingly, Mayo and related facilities give Rochester the best healthcare statistics and rating in the country, and bring a strong educational presence as well. Other notable employers include IBM and some agribusiness and food processing industries. Rochester has a small-town feel, and is known especially for its good park system and low crime rates. Missing amenities or services are available in Minneapolis–St Paul, 80 miles to the northwest. The nearby Dorer state forest, known for its hardwood forests, provides outdoor recreation, such as camping, picnicking, and hiking. Downsides include harsh winters, some unemployment outside the healthcare industry, and a general lack of entertainment and things to do.

Rochester, in the shallow Zumbro River Valley, is surrounded by rolling and wooded terrain ranging from 1,000 to 1,300 feet in elevation. Summers are pleasant but can be warm. Winters are cold and variable with periods of bitter cold and regular snow cover. Flooding can occur on the Zumbro River in spring and summer. First freeze is late September; last is early May.

Population	DEMOGRAPHICS	AREA	U.S. AVG	ETHNIC COMPOSITION	AREA	U.S. AVG	RESIDENT PROFILE	AREA	U.S. AVG
	Population	176,606		White	90.9%	79.0%	Single	29.0%	32.4%
	Population density per sq. mile	109.2	358.5	Black	2.3%	10.5%	Married	59.6%	52.7%
	Population growth	24.6%	21.1%	Asian	4.0%	2.7%	Divorced/separated	11.3%	14.9%
	Median age	36.4	36.1	Hispanic	2.4%	10.6%	Married with children	28.7%	23.7%
	Percent Democrat	46.0%	44.5%	Religious observance	65.2%	48.9%	Single with children	7.0%	9.1%
	Percent Republican	52.6%	54.5%	Diversity measure	20.9	40.1	Percent over age 65	11.9%	12.9%

Economy & Jobs Score: 78.1 Rank: 83	INCOME	AREA	U.S. AVG	EMPLOYMENT	AREA	U.S. AVG	EMPLOYING INDUSTRIES	AREA	U.S. AVG
	Per capita income	$28,173	$23,235	Unemployment rate	2.9%	4.7%	Largest: Healthcare & Social Assistance		
	Household income	$57,594	$46,414	Recent job growth	2.1%	1.3%			
	Household income < $25K	17.5%	26.2%	Projected future job growth	12.0%	11.5%	Percent manufacturing	11.8%	15.4%
	Household income > $75K	34.2%	25.4%	White collar	63.4%	57.8%	Percent public sector	9.5%	15.7%
	Household income growth	15.8%	13.6%	Blue collar	20.0%	25.2%	Percent construction	8.2%	9.9%

Cost of Living Score: 27.5 Rank: 270	INDEXES & TAXES	AREA	U.S. AVG	HOUSING	AREA	U.S. AVG	NECESSITIES	AREA	U.S. AVG
	Cost of Living Index	93.1	100.0	Median home price	$153,800	$220,000	Food Index	95.6	100.0
	Buying Power Index	138.7	100.0	Home price appreciation	30.3%	10.1%	Housing Index	65.3	100.0
	Income tax rate	7.04%	4.70%	Median rent	$723	$709	Utilities Index	136.0	100.0
	Sales tax rate	6.88%	6.58%	Homes owned	75.4%	62.3%	Transportation Index	107.0	100.0
	Property tax rate	$11.65	$12.00	Home price ratio	2.7	4.2	Healthcare Index	112.8	100.0
							Miscellaneous Cost Index	104.9	100.0

Climate
Score: 9.6
Rank: 337

TEMPERATURE	AREA	U.S. AVG
Average January low	3.2	26.2
Average July high	82.4	87.4
Annual days > 90°F	15	38
Annual days < 32°F	158	89
Annual days < 0°F	34	6

PRECIPITATION	AREA	U.S. AVG
Annual inches precipitation	26.0	37.7
Annual inches snowfall	46.0	7.0
Annual days precipitation	113	109
Annual days rain > 0.5 inches	18	22
Annual days snow > 1.5 inches	10	6

COMFORTS & HAZARDS	AREA	U.S. AVG
July relative humidity	69%	66%
Annual days mostly sunny	200	208
Annual days with thunderstorms	36	39
Tornado risk score	20	18
Hurricane risk score	0	13

TEMPERATURE

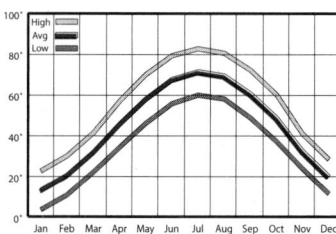

PRECIPITATION

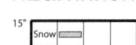
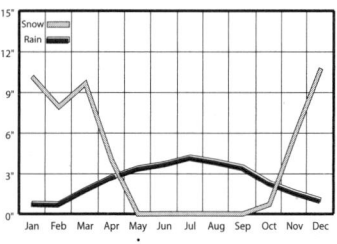

DAYS OF CLOUDS & PRECIPITATION

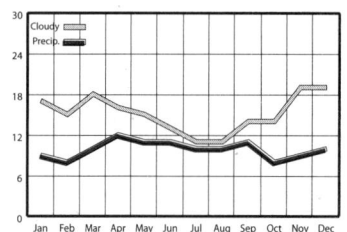

Education
Score: 85.3
Rank: 56

ACHIEVEMENT	AREA	U.S. AVG
High school degree	90.0%	82.7%
2-year college degree	9.7%	6.4%
4-year college degree	19.5%	15.7%
Graduate/professional degree	11.4%	8.9%

PUBLIC SCHOOLS	AREA	U.S. AVG
Expenditures per pupil	$5,589	$5,686
Student/teacher ratio	16.4	16.7
Attending public school	89.5%	90.1%
State SAT score	1191	1021
State ACT score	22.3*	20.9

HIGHER EDUCATION	AREA	U.S. AVG
No. 2-year colleges	1	4
No. 4-year colleges/universities	4	6
No. highly ranked universities	0	1

Health & Healthcare
Score: 100.0
Rank: 1

HAZARDS & ILLNESSES	AREA	U.S. AVG
Air-quality score	49	37
Water-quality score	22	52
Pollen/allergy score	46	61
Cancer mortality per capita	174.2	201.9
Depression days per month	1.9	3.5
Stress score	1	50

HEALTHCARE	AREA	U.S. AVG
Physicians per capita	1386.4	244.2
Hospital beds per capita	918.4	420.0
No. teaching hospitals	2	3
Cost per doctor visit	$103	$77
Cost per dental visit	$70	$70

Crime
Score: 62.0
Rank: 142

CRIME	AREA	U.S. AVG
Violent crime rate	181.3	465.5
Change in violent crime rate	6.5%	-2.2%
Property crime rate	1,966.5	3,517.1
Change in property crime rate	-10.7%	-2.1%

Transportation
Score: 88.2
Rank: 45

COMMUTE	AREA	U.S. AVG
Average commute time	19.6	27.4
Percent commutes > 60 mins.	3.2%	5.9%
Commute by auto	77.2%	78.9%
Commute by mass transit	2.6%	1.9%
Work at home	4.6%	3.1%
Mass transit miles per capita	2.61	1.87

INTERCITY SERVICES	AREA	U.S. AVG
Major airports within 60 miles	1	1
Size of regional airport	Large	Large
Daily airline activity	624	686
Amtrak service	No	No

AUTOMOTIVE	AREA	U.S. AVG
Insurance, annual premium	$1,143	$1,432
Gas, cost per gallon	$2.45	$2.49
Daily vehicle miles per capita	21.4	24.0

Leisure
Score: 62.0
Rank: 142

DINING & SHOPPING	AREA	U.S. AVG
Restaurant rating	1	2
Outlet mall score	36	42
No. Starbucks	0	13
No. warehouse clubs	1	2

ENTERTAINMENT	AREA	U.S. AVG
Professional sports rating	2	4
College sports rating	9	4
Zoo/aquarium rating	1	3
Amusement park rating	1	3
Botanical garden/ arboretum rating	1	4

OUTDOOR ACTIVITIES	AREA	U.S. AVG
Golf-course rating	9	4
Ski-area rating	5	3
Sq. miles inland water	2	4
Miles of coastline	0.0	10.7
National Park rating	3	3

Arts & Culture
Score: 35.8
Rank: 240

MEDIA & LIBRARIES	AREA	U.S. AVG
Arts radio rating	1	3
No. public libraries	8	27
Library volumes per capita	0.82	2.78

PERFORMING ARTS	AREA	U.S. AVG
Classical music rating	4	4
Ballet/dance rating	1	3
Professional theater rating	1	3
University arts programs rating	2	5

MUSEUMS	AREA	U.S. AVG
Overall museum rating	2	5
Art museum rating	4	5
Science museum rating	1	5
Children's museum rating	1	3

Rochester, NY

Score: 43.9   **Rank:** 296   **2004 rank:** 214

Profile: Large city
Location: Northwestern New York on Lake Ontario
Elevation: 547 feet
Time zone: Eastern Standard Time

PRO	CON
Arts and culture	Snow
Education	Clouds and rain
Cost of housing	Employment declines

Rochester is an important industrial and research center and Great Lakes shipping port. Commercial and industrial activity has a strong science and technology presence, led by the Eastman Kodak Company but also including Xerox, Bausch & Lomb, and even GM's hydrogen power research labs. The scientific and industrial legacy has strengthened a set of excellent arts, cultural, and educational assets, including the Rochester Institute of Technology and the University of Rochester. Scientists, aspiring scientists, and science buffs feel quite at home in the area. The news isn't all good, for technology transformations affecting Kodak, and Xerox to a lesser degree, have created a lot of employment dislocations. Whether or not Kodak's "retooling" as a digital media company is successful and leads to job growth once again is a wait-and-see, but job-growth projections are currently weak. A combination of soil, moisture, and lake warmth create a long growing season for the latitude and a favorable environment for fruits, vegetables, and wineries, and the Lake Ontario shore offers a number of parks and waterfront amenities. Together these assets provide plenty of day-trip opportunities. Climate is the main downside, with abundant clouds and rain and heavy lake-effect snows. The area is the fourth-rainiest place in the country. Cost of living and home values are quite attractive on a national and a New York scale. Perhaps somewhat strengthened by the adverse climate and common science denominator, the area has a strong community feel. Combined with the strong arts presence, these features make Rochester a good place for those adaptable to the employment and physical climates.

The area is located on a broad plain defined by Lake Ontario and the Genesee River Valley. Twenty miles south, low rolling hills begin to rise to 1,000 feet. Precipitation is evenly distributed throughout the year in quantity, but frequency is much higher during winter. Snowfall is heavy, but highly variable over short distances. Snow covers the ground from Christmas into early March. The lake modifies extreme cold, and below-zero temperatures are infrequent but do occur more inland. Summers are warm and sunny with intermittent rain or thundershowers. Temperatures seldom exceed 90°F. Spring comes slowly and fall is brief. First freeze is mid-October; last is early May.

Population

DEMOGRAPHICS	AREA	U.S. AVG	ETHNIC COMPOSITION	AREA	U.S. AVG	RESIDENT PROFILE	AREA	U.S. AVG
Population	1,043,266		White	81.6%	79.0%	Single	35.4%	32.4%
Population density per sq. mile	355.9	358.5	Black	11.6%	10.5%	Married	50.1%	52.7%
Population growth	4.1%	21.1%	Asian	2.3%	2.7%	Divorced/separated	14.5%	14.9%
Median age	37.8	36.1	Hispanic	5.4%	10.6%	Married with children	22.5%	23.7%
Percent Democrat	47.3%	44.5%	Religious observance	50.8%	48.9%	Single with children	9.8%	9.1%
Percent Republican	50.9%	54.5%	Diversity measure	37.8	40.1	Percent over age 65	13.2%	12.9%

Economy & Jobs

Score: 14.2
Rank: 320

INCOME	AREA	U.S. AVG	EMPLOYMENT	AREA	U.S. AVG	EMPLOYING INDUSTRIES	AREA	U.S. AVG
Per capita income	$24,466	$23,235	Unemployment rate	5.0%	4.7%	Largest: Manufacturing		
Household income	$48,836	$46,414	Recent job growth	-0.7%	1.3%			
Household income ‹ $25K	24.1%	26.2%	Projected future job growth	-0.3%	11.5%	Percent manufacturing	15.1%	15.4%
Household income › $75K	28.3%	25.4%	White collar	62.9%	57.8%	Percent public sector	13.0%	15.7%
Household income growth	10.2%	13.6%	Blue collar	22.1%	25.2%	Percent construction	7.0%	9.9%

Cost of Living

Score: 16.6
Rank: 311

INDEXES & TAXES	AREA	U.S. AVG	HOUSING	AREA	U.S. AVG	NECESSITIES	AREA	U.S. AVG
Cost of Living Index	87.1	100.0	Median home price	$115,300	$220,000	Food Index	111.8	100.0
Buying Power Index	125.7	100.0	Home price appreciation	24.0%	10.1%	Housing Index	51.1	100.0
Income tax rate	7.13%	4.70%	Median rent	$690	$709	Utilities Index	133.4	100.0
Sales tax rate	8.15%	6.58%	Homes owned	63.9%	62.3%	Transportation Index	104.8	100.0
Property tax rate	$27.66	$12.00	Home price ratio	2.4	4.2	Healthcare Index	102.7	100.0
						Miscellaneous Cost Index	97.9	100.0

Climate
Score: 11.0
Rank: 332

TEMPERATURE	AREA	U.S. AVG
Average January low	16.7	26.2
Average July high	82.2	87.4
Annual days > 90°F	11	38
Annual days < 32°F	135	89
Annual days < 0°F	6	6

PRECIPITATION	AREA	U.S. AVG
Annual inches precipitation	31.3	37.7
Annual inches snowfall	88.4	7.0
Annual days precipitation	182	109
Annual days rain > 0.5 inches	17	22
Annual days snow > 1.5 inches	19	6

COMFORTS & HAZARDS	AREA	U.S. AVG
July relative humidity	73%	66%
Annual days mostly sunny	170	208
Annual days with thunderstorms	29	39
Tornado risk score	1	18
Hurricane risk score	5	13

TEMPERATURE

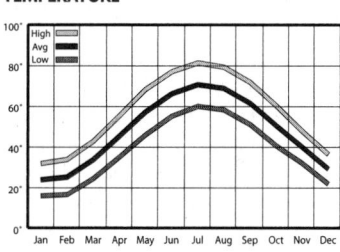

PRECIPITATION

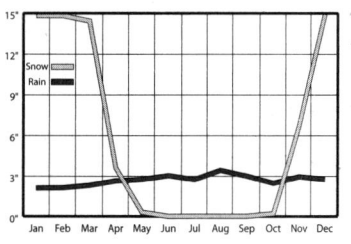

DAYS OF CLOUDS & PRECIPITATION

Education
Score: 93.3
Rank: 26

ACHIEVEMENT	AREA	U.S. AVG
High school degree	84.5%	82.7%
2-year college degree	10.0%	6.4%
4-year college degree	16.6%	15.7%
Graduate/professional degree	11.3%	8.9%

PUBLIC SCHOOLS	AREA	U.S. AVG
Expenditures per pupil	$8,254	$5,686
Student/teacher ratio	15.0	16.7
Attending public school	91.3%	90.1%
State SAT score	1003*	1021
State ACT score	22.6	20.9

HIGHER EDUCATION	AREA	U.S. AVG
No. 2-year colleges	5	4
No. 4-year colleges/universities	14	6
No. highly ranked universities	4	1

Health & Healthcare
Score: 37.4
Rank: 232

HAZARDS & ILLNESSES	AREA	U.S. AVG
Air-quality score	27	37
Water-quality score	50	52
Pollen/allergy score	67	61
Cancer mortality per capita	210.9	201.9
Depression days per month	3.0	3.5
Stress score	10	50

HEALTHCARE	AREA	U.S. AVG
Physicians per capita	320.3	244.2
Hospital beds per capita	478.8	420.0
No. teaching hospitals	7	3
Cost per doctor visit	$74	$77
Cost per dental visit	$66	$70

Crime
Score: 52.4
Rank: 179

CRIME	AREA	U.S. AVG
Violent crime rate	288.2	465.5
Change in violent crime rate	7.5%	-2.2%
Property crime rate	3,018.5	3,517.1
Change in property crime rate	-9.5%	-2.1%

Transportation
Score: 54.3
Rank: 172

COMMUTE	AREA	U.S. AVG
Average commute time	23.0	27.4
Percent commutes > 60 mins.	3.5%	5.9%
Commute by auto	81.9%	78.9%
Commute by mass transit	2.0%	1.9%
Work at home	2.9%	3.1%
Mass transit miles per capita	2.03	1.87

INTERCITY SERVICES	AREA	U.S. AVG
Major airports within 60 miles	1	1
Size of regional airport	Medium	Large
Daily airline activity	426	686
Amtrak service	Yes	No

AUTOMOTIVE	AREA	U.S. AVG
Insurance, annual premium	$1,977	$1,432
Gas, cost per gallon	$2.57	$2.49
Daily vehicle miles per capita	24.4	24.0

Leisure
Score: 77.0
Rank: 86

DINING & SHOPPING	AREA	U.S. AVG
Restaurant rating	1	2
Outlet mall score	0	42
No. Starbucks	13	13
No. warehouse clubs	4	2

ENTERTAINMENT	AREA	U.S. AVG
Professional sports rating	3	4
College sports rating	8	4
Zoo/aquarium rating	5	3
Amusement park rating	6	3
Botanical garden/ arboretum rating	10	4

OUTDOOR ACTIVITIES	AREA	U.S. AVG
Golf-course rating	7	4
Ski-area rating	4	3
Sq. miles inland water	4	4
Miles of coastline	88.7	10.7
National Park rating	1	3

Arts & Culture
Score: 82.9
Rank: 65

MEDIA & LIBRARIES	AREA	U.S. AVG
Arts radio rating	8	3
No. public libraries	71	27
Library volumes per capita	3.87	2.78

PERFORMING ARTS	AREA	U.S. AVG
Classical music rating	4	4
Ballet/dance rating	3	3
Professional theater rating	6	3
University arts programs rating	8	5

MUSEUMS	AREA	U.S. AVG
Overall museum rating	9	5
Art museum rating	8	5
Science museum rating	9	5
Children's museum rating	8	3

Rockford, IL

Score: 43.7   Rank: 299   2004 rank: 231

Profile: Small town
Location: North-central Illinois near the Wisconsin border, 80 miles west of Chicago
Elevation: 743 feet
Time zone: Central Standard Time

PRO	CON
Small-town atmosphere	Harsh climate
Cost of living	Crime rates
Access to Chicago	Entertainment

Despite its location in a largely agricultural region, Rockford has a strong heritage as an industrial center. The diverse manufacturing base partially transitioned away from its Rust Belt beginnings, and today's local industries include aviation, aerospace, precision tools, and medicine along with the mainstays of agriculture and agricultural machinery. The industrial transformation is being augmented by its not-too-distant location relative to suburban Chicago and new commuter rail service. The area still suffers the marks of economic decline, and the downtown area, passed by the Northwest Tollway, still shows signs of neglect. But the new commuter access, low housing costs, and some downtown and Rock River waterfront rehabilitation are bringing in residents and new facilities. There are good museums, and nearby Magic Waters is acclaimed to be the world's largest water park. Some recreational opportunities are available in Wisconsin to the north, but residents must travel to Chicago for many amenities. Overall prospects may be better than the ranking indicates.

Rockford is located along the Rock River in an area of level to gently rolling terrain and open farmland. Summers are hot and sticky while winters are typically cold and blustery. Precipitation is distributed evenly throughout the year, with slightly more arriving in summer, mainly as thunderstorms. Rockford is far enough north to have snow cover through the mid-winter months. First freeze is mid-October; last is late April.

Population

DEMOGRAPHICS	AREA	U.S. AVG	ETHNIC COMPOSITION	AREA	U.S. AVG	RESIDENT PROFILE	AREA	U.S. AVG
Population	336,260		White	81.1%	79.0%	Single	30.4%	32.4%
Population density per sq. mile	423.0	358.5	Black	9.6%	10.5%	Married	55.3%	52.7%
Population growth	20.1%	21.1%	Asian	1.9%	2.7%	Divorced/separated	14.3%	14.9%
Median age	36.2	36.1	Hispanic	10.2%	10.6%	Married with children	24.3%	23.7%
Percent Democrat	48.2%	44.5%	Religious observance	48.8%	48.9%	Single with children	9.4%	9.1%
Percent Republican	51.1%	54.5%	Diversity measure	45.2	40.1	Percent over age 65	12.5%	12.9%

Economy & Jobs
Score: 77.8
Rank: 84

INCOME	AREA	U.S. AVG	EMPLOYMENT	AREA	U.S. AVG	EMPLOYING INDUSTRIES	AREA	U.S. AVG
Per capita income	$23,483	$23,235	Unemployment rate	6.2%	4.7%	Largest: Manufacturing		
Household income	$48,845	$46,414	Recent job growth	3.0%	1.3%			
Household income < $25K	22.9%	26.2%	Projected future job growth	10.8%	11.5%	Percent manufacturing	22.3%	15.4%
Household income > $75K	26.5%	25.4%	White collar	55.4%	57.8%	Percent public sector	9.1%	15.7%
Household income growth	8.2%	13.6%	Blue collar	31.2%	25.2%	Percent construction	8.8%	9.9%

Cost of Living
Score: 52.4
Rank: 178

INDEXES & TAXES	AREA	U.S. AVG	HOUSING	AREA	U.S. AVG	NECESSITIES	AREA	U.S. AVG
Cost of Living Index	85.7	100.0	Median home price	$115,900	$220,000	Food Index	100.9	100.0
Buying Power Index	127.8	100.0	Home price appreciation	27.9%	10.1%	Housing Index	59.6	100.0
Income tax rate	3.00%	4.70%	Median rent	$635	$709	Utilities Index	126.2	100.0
Sales tax rate	7.18%	6.58%	Homes owned	67.4%	62.3%	Transportation Index	104.2	100.0
Property tax rate	$23.51	$12.00	Home price ratio	2.4	4.2	Healthcare Index	102.2	100.0
						Miscellaneous Cost Index	99.3	100.0

Climate
Score: 19.3
Rank: 301

TEMPERATURE	AREA	U.S. AVG	PRECIPITATION	AREA	U.S. AVG	COMFORTS & HAZARDS	AREA	U.S. AVG
Average January low	11.5	26.2	Annual inches precipitation	37.0	37.7	July relative humidity	72%	66%
Average July high	84.2	87.4	Annual inches snowfall	33.0	7.0	Annual days mostly sunny	196	208
Annual days > 90°F	13	38	Annual days precipitation	114	109	Annual days with thunderstorms	42	39
Annual days < 32°F	142	89	Annual days rain > 0.5 inches	25	22	Tornado risk score	20	18
Annual days < 0°F	16	6	Annual days snow > 1.5 inches	10	6	Hurricane risk score	1	13

TEMPERATURE

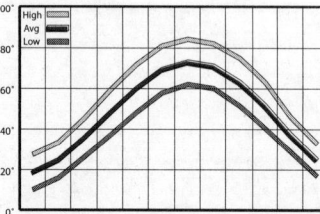

PRECIPITATION

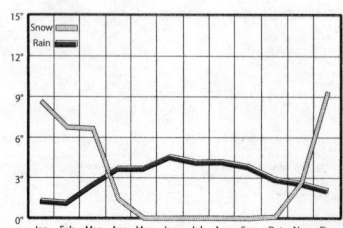

DAYS OF CLOUDS & PRECIPITATION

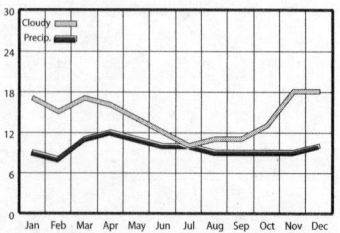

ACHIEVEMENT	AREA	U.S. AVG	PUBLIC SCHOOLS	AREA	U.S. AVG	HIGHER EDUCATION	AREA	U.S. AVG
High school degree	81.4%	82.7%	Expenditures per pupil	$5,665	$5,686	No. 2-year colleges	3	4
2-year college degree	6.3%	6.4%	Student/teacher ratio	19.2	16.7	No. 4-year colleges/universities	2	6
4-year college degree	12.4%	15.7%	Attending public school	84.5%	90.1%	No. highly ranked universities	0	1
Graduate/professional degree	6.4%	8.9%	State SAT score	1200	1021			
			State ACT score	20.5*	20.9			

Education
Score: 19.5
Rank: 299

HAZARDS & ILLNESSES	AREA	U.S. AVG	HEALTHCARE	AREA	U.S. AVG	CRIME	AREA	U.S. AVG
Air-quality score	38	37	Physicians per capita	218.0	244.2	Violent crime rate	569.1	465.5
Water-quality score	56	52	Hospital beds per capita	367.9	420.0	Change in violent crime rate	2.6%	-2.2%
Pollen/allergy score	39	61	No. teaching hospitals	1	3	Property crime rate	4,872.1	3,517.1
Cancer mortality per capita	206.9	201.9	Cost per doctor visit	$73	$77	Change in property crime rate	-6.3%	-2.1%
Depression days per month	3.8	3.5	Cost per dental visit	$73	$70			
Stress score	74	50						

Health & Healthcare
Score: 60.4
Rank: 149

Crime
Score: 31.0
Rank: 258

COMMUTE	AREA	U.S. AVG	INTERCITY SERVICES	AREA	U.S. AVG	AUTOMOTIVE	AREA	U.S. AVG
Average commute time	23.8	27.4	Major airports within 60 miles	3	1	Insurance, annual premium	$1,484	$1,432
Percent commutes > 60 mins.	6.1%	5.9%	Size of regional airport	Large	Large	Gas, cost per gallon	$2.53	$2.49
Commute by auto	83.3%	78.9%	Daily airline activity	2078	686	Daily vehicle miles per capita	24.7	24.0
Commute by mass transit	0.9%	1.9%	Amtrak service	No	No			
Work at home	2.7%	3.1%						
Mass transit miles per capita	0.94	1.87						

Transportation
Score: 96.0
Rank: 16

DINING & SHOPPING	AREA	U.S. AVG	ENTERTAINMENT	AREA	U.S. AVG	OUTDOOR ACTIVITIES	AREA	U.S. AVG
Restaurant rating	1	2	Professional sports rating	3	4	Golf-course rating	3	4
Outlet mall score	61	42	College sports rating	2	4	Ski-area rating	3	3
No. Starbucks	3	13	Zoo/aquarium rating	1	3	Sq. miles inland water	2	4
No. warehouse clubs	0	2	Amusement park rating	1	3	Miles of coastline	0.0	10.7
			Botanical garden/ arboretum rating	2	4	National Park rating	1	3

Leisure
Score: 28.9
Rank: 265

MEDIA & LIBRARIES	AREA	U.S. AVG	PERFORMING ARTS	AREA	U.S. AVG	MUSEUMS	AREA	U.S. AVG
Arts radio rating	1	3	Classical music rating	3	4	Overall museum rating	5	5
No. public libraries	14	27	Ballet/dance rating	1	3	Art museum rating	4	5
Library volumes per capita	4.21	2.78	Professional theater rating	6	3	Science museum rating	6	5
			University arts programs rating	1	5	Children's museum rating	6	3

Arts & Culture
Score: 28.1
Rank: 269

Rockingham County–Strafford County, NH   Score: 84.0   Rank: 28   2004 rank: 287

Profile: Small-city complex
Location: Southeastern New Hampshire along Maine border and Atlantic Coast
Elevation: 63 feet
Time zone: Eastern Standard Time

PRO	CON
Historic interest	Winter climate
Strategic location	Entertainment
Educated population	Long commutes

Known as the Seacoast Region of New Hampshire, this two-county area covers the small neck of land separating northern Massachusetts from Maine, and contains the cities of Portsmouth and Rochester and a number of smaller towns. Portsmouth is located along the Piscataqua River just inland from New Hampshire's 13-mile stretch of Atlantic Coast, while Rochester and the town of Dover lie farther upriver and inland. Not surprisingly, Portsmouth has a long history as a port and early manufacturing center, but much of the Industrial Age manufacturing boom migrated upriver, as well as up the nearby Merrimac River to Lowell and Lawrence in Massachusetts and Manchester and Nashua in New Hampshire. Portsmouth remained a shipbuilding and commercial center and home to wealthy merchant seamen. An early-19th-century fire and a subsequent rebuild in the classic Federal architectural style has left the area with a considerable collection of period residential architecture and an excellent downtown. The area has made the most of its heritage, while evolving into today's economy. Some Portsmouth residents commute south to the Boston area and particularly the northern suburbs, while enjoying the state's relatively favorable tax climate. The favorable business climate and an exemplary repurposing of a closed military base have attracted some new business interests, notably in technology and software. It has earned the nickname "eCoast." It is a favorite for telecommuters and work-at-home businesses requiring occasional access to the Boston area. Downtown Boston itself is about 65 miles south of Portsmouth and accessible by commuter rail. It also has access to good recreation and expanding commercial areas along the Maine coast to the north. The strategic location, attractive cost profile for the region, rock-bottom crime rates, and an expanded amenity base has brought a big jump in the rankings since 2004, as predicted in the last edition.

Portsmouth sits in a coastal tidewater area just inland from the Atlantic Coast. The surrounding landscape is mainly level and covered with deciduous trees. Summer days are pleasant and nights cool. Winters are cold, cloudy, and wet, with occasional blasts of cold air from the north, although the marine influence moderates the coldest air. Coastal "noreaster" storms bring heavy snow in winter and periods of heavy rain at other times of the year. Fall is crisp and pleasant. First freeze is late September; last is late May.

Population

DEMOGRAPHICS	AREA	U.S. AVG	ETHNIC COMPOSITION	AREA	U.S. AVG	RESIDENT PROFILE	AREA	U.S. AVG
Population	415,131		White	96.1%	79.0%	Single	30.1%	32.4%
Population density per sq. mile	390.3	358.5	Black	0.7%	10.5%	Married	57.0%	52.7%
Population growth	18.6%	21.1%	Asian	1.5%	2.7%	Divorced/separated	12.9%	14.9%
Median age	38.1	36.1	Hispanic	1.2%	10.6%	Married with children	27.4%	23.7%
Percent Democrat	49.8%	44.5%	Religious observance	49.8%	48.9%	Single with children	7.3%	9.1%
Percent Republican	49.3%	54.5%	Diversity measure	9.9	40.1	Percent over age 65	11.0%	12.9%

Economy & Jobs
Score: 81.6
Rank: 70

INCOME	AREA	U.S. AVG	EMPLOYMENT	AREA	U.S. AVG	EMPLOYING INDUSTRIES	AREA	U.S. AVG
Per capita income	$29,508	$23,235	Unemployment rate	3.8%	4.7%	Largest: Manufacturing		
Household income	$62,626	$46,414	Recent job growth	3.2%	1.3%			
Household income < $25K	15.5%	26.2%	Projected future job growth	13.8%	11.5%	Percent manufacturing	13.9%	15.4%
Household income > $75K	38.9%	25.4%	White collar	64.2%	57.8%	Percent public sector	12.8%	15.7%
Household income growth	15.3%	13.6%	Blue collar	22.9%	25.2%	Percent construction	9.0%	9.9%

Cost of Living
Score: 62.6
Rank: 140

INDEXES & TAXES	AREA	U.S. AVG	HOUSING	AREA	U.S. AVG	NECESSITIES	AREA	U.S. AVG
Cost of Living Index	110.8	100.0	Median home price	$242,200	$220,000	Food Index	103.6	100.0
Buying Power Index	126.7	100.0	Home price appreciation	59.5%	10.1%	Housing Index	98.6	100.0
Income tax rate	1.93%	4.70%	Median rent	$1,030	$709	Utilities Index	149.9	100.0
Sales tax rate	0.00%	6.58%	Homes owned	67.7%	62.3%	Transportation Index	107.3	100.0
Property tax rate	$20.80	$12.00	Home price ratio	3.9	4.2	Healthcare Index	111.7	100.0
						Miscellaneous Cost Index	107.0	100.0

Climate
Score: 29.9
Rank: 261

TEMPERATURE	AREA	U.S. AVG	PRECIPITATION	AREA	U.S. AVG	COMFORTS & HAZARDS	AREA	U.S. AVG
Average January low	22.5	26.2	Annual inches precipitation	43.0	37.7	July relative humidity	67%	66%
Average July high	81.4	87.4	Annual inches snowfall	42.0	7.0	Annual days mostly sunny	205	208
Annual days > 90°F	12	38	Annual days precipitation	128	109	Annual days with thunderstorms	18	39
Annual days < 32°F	99	89	Annual days rain > 0.5 inches	26	22	Tornado risk score	10	18
Annual days < 0°F	1	6	Annual days snow > 1.5 inches	15	6	Hurricane risk score	19	13

TEMPERATURE

PRECIPITATION

DAYS OF CLOUDS & PRECIPITATION

Education
Score: 83.2
Rank: 64

ACHIEVEMENT	AREA	U.S. AVG	PUBLIC SCHOOLS	AREA	U.S. AVG	HIGHER EDUCATION	AREA	U.S. AVG
High school degree	89.3%	82.7%	Expenditures per pupil	$6,449	$5,686	No. 2-year colleges	2	4
2-year college degree	9.4%	6.4%	Student/teacher ratio	16.7	16.7	No. 4-year colleges/universities	2	6
4-year college degree	19.9%	15.7%	Attending public school	85.0%	90.1%	No. highly ranked universities	1	1
Graduate/professional degree	10.3%	8.9%	State SAT score	1044*	1021			
			State ACT score	22.6	20.9			

Health & Healthcare
Score: 26.7
Rank: 273

Crime
Score: 95.5
Rank: 18

HAZARDS & ILLNESSES	AREA	U.S. AVG	HEALTHCARE	AREA	U.S. AVG	CRIME	AREA	U.S. AVG
Air-quality score	40	37	Physicians per capita	177.3	244.2	Violent crime rate	117.9	465.5
Water-quality score	20	52	Hospital beds per capita	199.9	420.0	Change in violent crime rate	-13.4%	-2.2%
Pollen/allergy score	52	61	No. teaching hospitals	0	3	Property crime rate	1,599.4	3,517.1
Cancer mortality per capita	209.8	201.9	Cost per doctor visit	$95	$77	Change in property crime rate	-10.3%	-2.1%
Depression days per month	3.3	3.5	Cost per dental visit	$65	$70			
Stress score	20	50						

Transportation
Score: 35.6
Rank: 242

COMMUTE	AREA	U.S. AVG	INTERCITY SERVICES	AREA	U.S. AVG	AUTOMOTIVE	AREA	U.S. AVG
Average commute time	29.7	27.4	Major airports within 60 miles	2	1	Insurance, annual premium	$1,118	$1,432
Percent commutes > 60 mins.	10.0%	5.9%	Size of regional airport	Large	Large	Gas, cost per gallon	$2.38	$2.49
Commute by auto	83.6%	78.9%	Daily airline activity	1278	686	Daily vehicle miles per capita	26.3	24.0
Commute by mass transit	0.8%	1.9%	Amtrak service	Yes	No			
Work at home	3.8%	3.1%						
Mass transit miles per capita	0.81	1.87						

Leisure
Score: 92.8
Rank: 28

DINING & SHOPPING	AREA	U.S. AVG	ENTERTAINMENT	AREA	U.S. AVG	OUTDOOR ACTIVITIES	AREA	U.S. AVG
Restaurant rating	5	2	Professional sports rating	9	4	Golf-course rating	8	4
Outlet mall score	42	42	College sports rating	8	4	Ski-area rating	7	3
No. Starbucks	1	13	Zoo/aquarium rating	7	3	Sq. miles inland water	6	4
No. warehouse clubs	3	2	Amusement park rating	6	3	Miles of coastline	35.9	10.7
			Botanical garden/ arboretum rating	7	4	National Park rating	2	3

Arts & Culture
Score: 94.9
Rank: 20

MEDIA & LIBRARIES	AREA	U.S. AVG	PERFORMING ARTS	AREA	U.S. AVG	MUSEUMS	AREA	U.S. AVG
Arts radio rating	8	3	Classical music rating	9	4	Overall museum rating	7	5
No. public libraries	51	27	Ballet/dance rating	7	3	Art museum rating	7	5
Library volumes per capita	3.66	2.78	Professional theater rating	9	3	Science museum rating	9	5
			University arts programs rating	8	5	Children's museum rating	8	3

Rocky Mount, NC

Score: 23.8   Rank: 353   2004 rank: 301

Profile: Small city
Location: Northeastern North Carolina along I-95 corridor, 55 miles east of Raleigh
Elevation: 150 feet
Time zone: Eastern Standard Time

PRO	CON
Small-town atmosphere	Declining industries
Historic interest	Low educational attainment
Close to Raleigh	Hot, humid summers

Rocky Mount is a typical small Old South city. Like many Carolina towns along transportation arteries, it started as an agricultural and tobacco center, and over time because of costs and availability of labor and location along key transportation routes, it developed a strong manufacturing and economic base. Such diverse companies as Abbott Laboratories, Honeywell, Sara Lee, Barcalounger (furniture), and QVC Network have facilities here, but employment has slowed dramatically in recent years and the current economic base is weak. Today the area is plagued with relatively high crime for the region and little to do. The town has a well-kept historic downtown. Most cultural and recreational amenities exist in the Raleigh area to the west and the Outer Banks to the east.

Rocky Mount is located on the eastern Carolina coastal plain. The surrounding terrain is mainly level with agriculture and deciduous woodland. Summers are warm and humid with frequent thundershowers. Winters are cool with below-freezing temperatures, snow, and freezing rain.

Population

DEMOGRAPHICS	AREA	U.S. AVG	ETHNIC COMPOSITION	AREA	U.S. AVG	RESIDENT PROFILE	AREA	U.S. AVG
Population	145,601		White	51.8%	79.0%	Single	34.0%	32.4%
Population density per sq. mile	139.3	358.5	Black	44.2%	10.5%	Married	50.4%	52.7%
Population growth	10.3%	21.1%	Asian	0.5%	2.7%	Divorced/separated	15.5%	14.9%
Median age	36.9	36.1	Hispanic	3.6%	10.6%	Married with children	21.4%	23.7%
Percent Democrat	49.0%	44.5%	Religious observance	40.7%	48.9%	Single with children	11.2%	9.1%
Percent Republican	50.8%	54.5%	Diversity measure	54.7	40.1	Percent over age 65	12.8%	12.9%

Economy & Jobs
Score: 2.7
Rank: 363

INCOME	AREA	U.S. AVG	EMPLOYMENT	AREA	U.S. AVG	EMPLOYING INDUSTRIES	AREA	U.S. AVG
Per capita income	$19,599	$23,235	Unemployment rate	7.9%	4.7%	Largest: Manufacturing		
Household income	$39,334	$46,414	Recent job growth	-0.5%	1.3%			
Household income < $25K	32.4%	26.2%	Projected future job growth	4.3%	11.5%	Percent manufacturing	23.5%	15.4%
Household income > $75K	18.7%	25.4%	White collar	49.7%	57.8%	Percent public sector	14.7%	15.7%
Household income growth	13.1%	13.6%	Blue collar	34.8%	25.2%	Percent construction	11.3%	9.9%

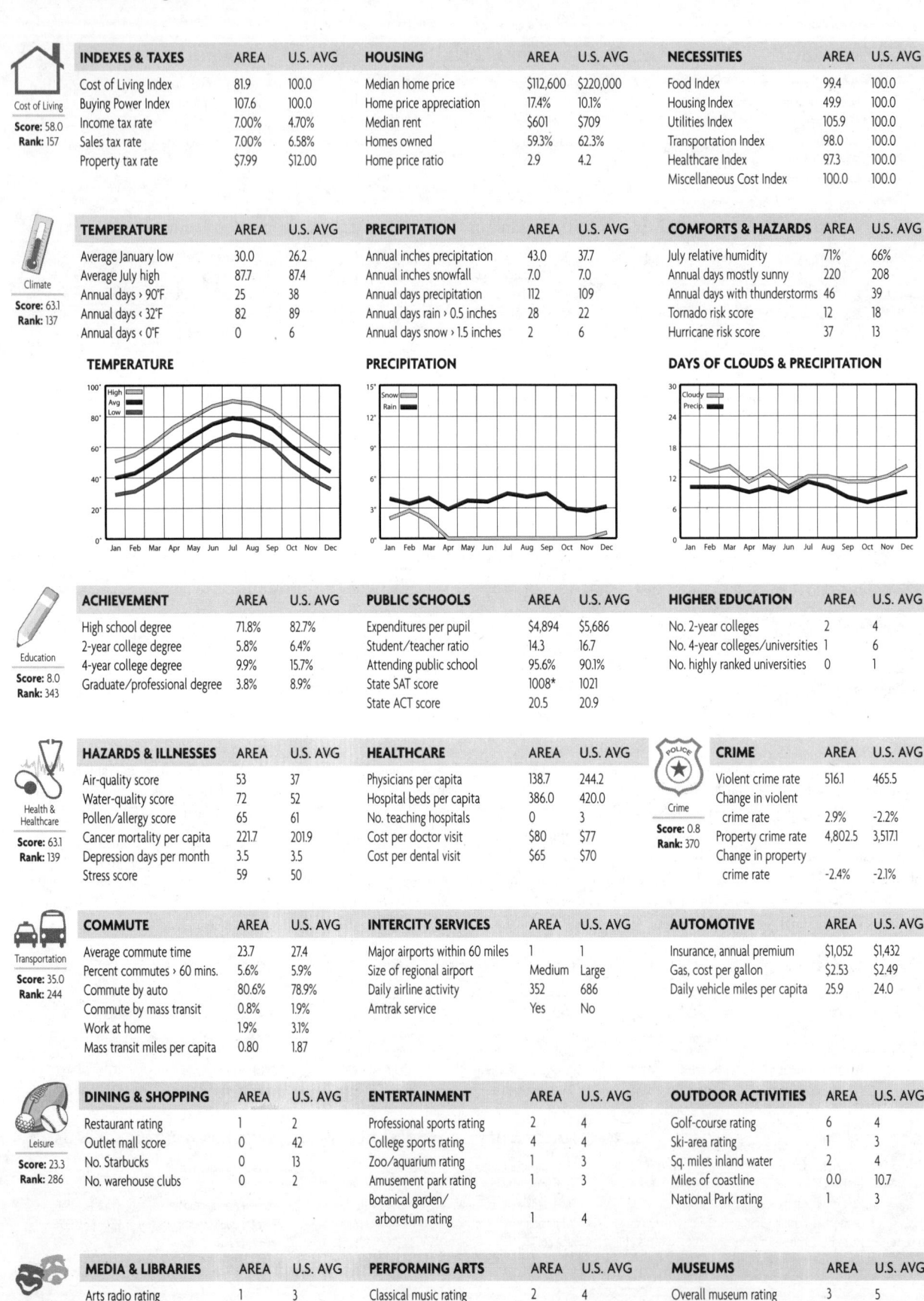

INDEXES & TAXES	AREA	U.S. AVG	HOUSING	AREA	U.S. AVG	NECESSITIES	AREA	U.S. AVG
Cost of Living Index	81.9	100.0	Median home price	$112,600	$220,000	Food Index	99.4	100.0
Buying Power Index	107.6	100.0	Home price appreciation	17.4%	10.1%	Housing Index	49.9	100.0
Income tax rate	7.00%	4.70%	Median rent	$601	$709	Utilities Index	105.9	100.0
Sales tax rate	7.00%	6.58%	Homes owned	59.3%	62.3%	Transportation Index	98.0	100.0
Property tax rate	$7.99	$12.00	Home price ratio	2.9	4.2	Healthcare Index	97.3	100.0
						Miscellaneous Cost Index	100.0	100.0

Cost of Living
Score: 58.0
Rank: 157

TEMPERATURE	AREA	U.S. AVG	PRECIPITATION	AREA	U.S. AVG	COMFORTS & HAZARDS	AREA	U.S. AVG
Average January low	30.0	26.2	Annual inches precipitation	43.0	37.7	July relative humidity	71%	66%
Average July high	87.7	87.4	Annual inches snowfall	7.0	7.0	Annual days mostly sunny	220	208
Annual days > 90°F	25	38	Annual days precipitation	112	109	Annual days with thunderstorms	46	39
Annual days < 32°F	82	89	Annual days rain > 0.5 inches	28	22	Tornado risk score	12	18
Annual days < 0°F	0	6	Annual days snow > 1.5 inches	2	6	Hurricane risk score	37	13

Climate
Score: 63.1
Rank: 137

TEMPERATURE

PRECIPITATION

DAYS OF CLOUDS & PRECIPITATION

ACHIEVEMENT	AREA	U.S. AVG	PUBLIC SCHOOLS	AREA	U.S. AVG	HIGHER EDUCATION	AREA	U.S. AVG
High school degree	71.8%	82.7%	Expenditures per pupil	$4,894	$5,686	No. 2-year colleges	2	4
2-year college degree	5.8%	6.4%	Student/teacher ratio	14.3	16.7	No. 4-year colleges/universities	1	6
4-year college degree	9.9%	15.7%	Attending public school	95.6%	90.1%	No. highly ranked universities	0	1
Graduate/professional degree	3.8%	8.9%	State SAT score	1008*	1021			
			State ACT score	20.5	20.9			

Education
Score: 8.0
Rank: 343

HAZARDS & ILLNESSES	AREA	U.S. AVG	HEALTHCARE	AREA	U.S. AVG	CRIME	AREA	U.S. AVG
Air-quality score	53	37	Physicians per capita	138.7	244.2	Violent crime rate	516.1	465.5
Water-quality score	72	52	Hospital beds per capita	386.0	420.0	Change in violent crime rate	2.9%	-2.2%
Pollen/allergy score	65	61	No. teaching hospitals	0	3	Property crime rate	4,802.5	3,517.1
Cancer mortality per capita	221.7	201.9	Cost per doctor visit	$80	$77	Change in property crime rate	-2.4%	-2.1%
Depression days per month	3.5	3.5	Cost per dental visit	$65	$70			
Stress score	59	50						

Health & Healthcare
Score: 63.1
Rank: 139

Crime
Score: 0.8
Rank: 370

COMMUTE	AREA	U.S. AVG	INTERCITY SERVICES	AREA	U.S. AVG	AUTOMOTIVE	AREA	U.S. AVG
Average commute time	23.7	27.4	Major airports within 60 miles	1	1	Insurance, annual premium	$1,052	$1,432
Percent commutes > 60 mins.	5.6%	5.9%	Size of regional airport	Medium	Large	Gas, cost per gallon	$2.53	$2.49
Commute by auto	80.6%	78.9%	Daily airline activity	352	686	Daily vehicle miles per capita	25.9	24.0
Commute by mass transit	0.8%	1.9%	Amtrak service	Yes	No			
Work at home	1.9%	3.1%						
Mass transit miles per capita	0.80	1.87						

Transportation
Score: 35.0
Rank: 244

DINING & SHOPPING	AREA	U.S. AVG	ENTERTAINMENT	AREA	U.S. AVG	OUTDOOR ACTIVITIES	AREA	U.S. AVG
Restaurant rating	1	2	Professional sports rating	2	4	Golf-course rating	6	4
Outlet mall score	0	42	College sports rating	4	4	Ski-area rating	1	3
No. Starbucks	0	13	Zoo/aquarium rating	1	3	Sq. miles inland water	2	4
No. warehouse clubs	0	2	Amusement park rating	1	3	Miles of coastline	0.0	10.7
			Botanical garden/arboretum rating	1	4	National Park rating	1	3

Leisure
Score: 23.3
Rank: 286

MEDIA & LIBRARIES	AREA	U.S. AVG	PERFORMING ARTS	AREA	U.S. AVG	MUSEUMS	AREA	U.S. AVG
Arts radio rating	1	3	Classical music rating	2	4	Overall museum rating	3	5
No. public libraries	4	27	Ballet/dance rating	1	3	Art museum rating	4	5
Library volumes per capita	1.59	2.78	Professional theater rating	1	3	Science museum rating	3	5
			University arts programs rating	2	5	Children's museum rating	3	3

Arts & Culture
Score: 15.0
Rank: 317

Rome, GA

Score: 44.2 **Rank:** 292 **2004 rank:** not ranked

Profile: Small Southern town
Location: Northwest Georgia, 65 miles northwest of Atlanta
Elevation: 603 feet
Time zone: Eastern Standard Time

PRO	CON
Attractive downtown	Low educational attainment
Cost of living	Property crime rate
Close to Atlanta	Arts and culture

Rome, a typical mid-size Southern town, is located near an attractive area of mountains, rivers, and lakes in northwest Georgia. A city of seven hills like its Italian namesake, Rome has roots in agriculture, textile, and carpet milling. There are some typical homes and landmarks of the 19th-century South, and Rome did win a 2003 National Trust for Historic Preservation Great American Main Street award for revamping its historic core. But for the most part the city is plain and unremarkable with some areas of unattractive sprawl. Most entertainment and leisure activity is connected to water and mountain areas nearby, although there are minor league sports and a few other amenities in town. The city lies 65 miles northwest of Atlanta, giving access to the many amenities of the sprawling Georgia capital. A few do commute the distance, at least to Atlanta's prosperous northern suburbs, accounting for the rather long average commute time. Cost of living at 80.9 and median home prices are attractive. Many of the area's traditional businesses are in decline, but low costs and central location among larger Southern cities are attracting some new business. The economy is moderately healthy. There are a few items of historic interest, but the town offers little entertainment or intellectual stimulation.

The area is located in a gently rolling to hilly area of woods and plains along the Coosa River, with a more mountainous southern extension of the Appalachian Range lying just north and west. Summers are warm and humid with most days in the 90s, a few into the 100s, and frequent thunderstorms. Occasional heavy rains originate from hurricanes in the Gulf of Mexico. Winters are mild with temperatures seldom below 20°F. Snow is rare. First freeze is early November; last is late March.

Population

DEMOGRAPHICS	AREA	U.S. AVG	ETHNIC COMPOSITION	AREA	U.S. AVG	RESIDENT PROFILE	AREA	U.S. AVG
Population	94,758		White	80.7%	79.0%	Single	30.3%	32.4%
Population density per sq. mile	184.7	358.5	Black	13.1%	10.5%	Married	53.8%	52.7%
Population growth	16.6%	21.1%	Asian	1.2%	2.7%	Divorced/separated	15.9%	14.9%
Median age	35.5	36.1	Hispanic	6.9%	10.6%	Married with children	23.0%	23.7%
Percent Democrat	31.7%	44.5%	Religious observance	65.4%	48.9%	Single with children	9.0%	9.1%
Percent Republican	67.7%	54.5%	Diversity measure	41.6	40.1	Percent over age 65	13.8%	12.9%

Economy & Jobs
Score: 51.1
Rank: 184

INCOME	AREA	U.S. AVG	EMPLOYMENT	AREA	U.S. AVG	EMPLOYING INDUSTRIES	AREA	U.S. AVG
Per capita income	$19,873	$23,235	Unemployment rate	5.7%	4.7%	Largest: Healthcare & Social Assistance		
Household income	$39,661	$46,414	Recent job growth	2.3%	1.3%			
Household income < $25K	30.6%	26.2%	Projected future job growth	8.2%	11.5%	Percent manufacturing	22.6%	15.4%
Household income > $75K	19.2%	25.4%	White collar	50.3%	57.8%	Percent public sector	14.0%	15.7%
Household income growth	11.4%	13.6%	Blue collar	33.7%	25.2%	Percent construction	11.2%	9.9%

Cost of Living
Score: 59.6
Rank: 151

INDEXES & TAXES	AREA	U.S. AVG	HOUSING	AREA	U.S. AVG	NECESSITIES	AREA	U.S. AVG
Cost of Living Index	80.9	100.0	Median home price	$124,200	$220,000	Food Index	94.3	100.0
Buying Power Index	109.9	100.0	Home price appreciation	28.2%	10.1%	Housing Index	61.0	100.0
Income tax rate	6.00%	4.70%	Median rent	$565	$709	Utilities Index	88.2	100.0
Sales tax rate	7.00%	6.58%	Homes owned	62.5%	62.3%	Transportation Index	90.9	100.0
Property tax rate	$9.65	$12.00	Home price ratio	3.1	4.2	Healthcare Index	97.3	100.0
						Miscellaneous Cost Index	101.2	100.0

Climate
Score: 44.9
Rank: 205

TEMPERATURE	AREA	U.S. AVG	PRECIPITATION	AREA	U.S. AVG	COMFORTS & HAZARDS	AREA	U.S. AVG
Average January low	29.0	26.2	Annual inches precipitation	53.3	37.7	July relative humidity	57%	66%
Average July high	90.0	87.4	Annual inches snowfall	4.0	7.0	Annual days mostly sunny	218	208
Annual days > 90°F	48	38	Annual days precipitation	120	109	Annual days with thunderstorms	58	39
Annual days < 32°F	73	89	Annual days rain > 0.5 inches	36	22	Tornado risk score	4	18
Annual days < 0°F	0	6	Annual days snow > 1.5 inches	2	6	Hurricane risk score	2	13

TEMPERATURE

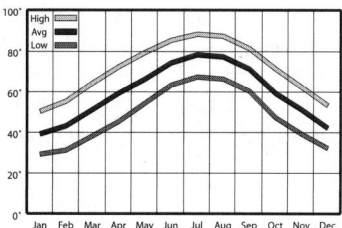

PRECIPITATION

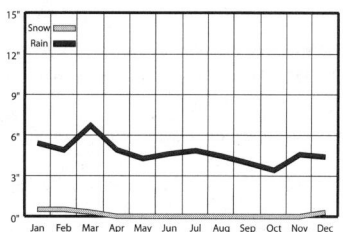

DAYS OF CLOUDS & PRECIPITATION

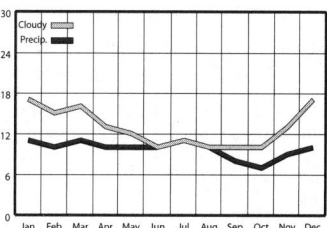

Education
Score: 5.3
Rank: 353

ACHIEVEMENT	AREA	U.S. AVG	PUBLIC SCHOOLS	AREA	U.S. AVG	HIGHER EDUCATION	AREA	U.S. AVG
High school degree	71.4%	82.7%	Expenditures per pupil	$5,140	$5,686	No. 2-year colleges	2	4
2-year college degree	4.0%	6.4%	Student/teacher ratio	15.8	16.7	No. 4-year colleges/universities	2	6
4-year college degree	10.0%	15.7%	Attending public school	90.9%	90.1%	No. highly ranked universities	1	1
Graduate/professional degree	5.8%	8.9%	State SAT score	990*	1021			
			State ACT score	20.2	20.9			

Health & Healthcare
Score: 90.9
Rank: 35

HAZARDS & ILLNESSES	AREA	U.S. AVG	HEALTHCARE	AREA	U.S. AVG	CRIME	AREA	U.S. AVG
Air-quality score	36	37	Physicians per capita	305.2	244.2	Violent crime rate	356.1	465.5
Water-quality score	73	52	Hospital beds per capita	975.1	420.0	Change in violent crime rate	-20.7%	-2.2%
Pollen/allergy score	63	61	No. teaching hospitals	1	3	Property crime rate	4,944.2	3,517.1
Cancer mortality per capita	175.4	201.9	Cost per doctor visit	$66	$77	Change in property crime rate	10.2%	-2.1%
Depression days per month	4.1	3.5	Cost per dental visit	$69	$70			
Stress score	77	50						

Crime
Score: 35.3
Rank: 242

Transportation
Score: 77.3
Rank: 86

COMMUTE	AREA	U.S. AVG	INTERCITY SERVICES	AREA	U.S. AVG	AUTOMOTIVE	AREA	U.S. AVG
Average commute time	25.3	27.4	Major airports within 60 miles	1	1	Insurance, annual premium	$1,317	$1,432
Percent commutes > 60 mins.	7.5%	5.9%	Size of regional airport	Large	Large	Gas, cost per gallon	$2.46	$2.49
Commute by auto	79.9%	78.9%	Daily airline activity	1464	686	Daily vehicle miles per capita	21.7	24.0
Commute by mass transit	0.4%	1.9%	Amtrak service	No	No			
Work at home	2.0%	3.1%						
Mass transit miles per capita	0.36	1.87						

Leisure
Score: 4.8
Rank: 355

DINING & SHOPPING	AREA	U.S. AVG	ENTERTAINMENT	AREA	U.S. AVG	OUTDOOR ACTIVITIES	AREA	U.S. AVG
Restaurant rating	1	2	Professional sports rating	1	4	Golf-course rating	2	4
Outlet mall score	60	42	College sports rating	1	4	Ski-area rating	1	3
No. Starbucks	0	13	Zoo/aquarium rating	1	3	Sq. miles inland water	2	4
No. warehouse clubs	1	2	Amusement park rating	1	3	Miles of coastline	0.0	10.7
			Botanical garden/ arboretum rating	1	4	National Park rating	3	3

Arts & Culture
Score: 22.5
Rank: 289

MEDIA & LIBRARIES	AREA	U.S. AVG	PERFORMING ARTS	AREA	U.S. AVG	MUSEUMS	AREA	U.S. AVG
Arts radio rating	1	3	Classical music rating	2	4	Overall museum rating	1	5
No. public libraries	4	27	Ballet/dance rating	1	3	Art museum rating	2	5
Library volumes per capita	3.69	2.78	Professional theater rating	1	3	Science museum rating	1	5
			University arts programs rating	1	5	Children's museum rating	1	3

Sacramento–Arden-Arcade–Roseville, CA   Score: 58.7   Rank: 183   2004 rank: 85

Profile: Capital-city/suburban complex
Location: Northern California, northern Central Valley at the base of the Sierra Nevada
Elevation: 25 feet
Time zone: Pacific Standard Time

PRO
Mild winters
Nearby recreation
Central location

CON
Growth and sprawl
Rising cost of living
Summer heat

Sacramento, the capital of California, has been a leading agricultural and transportation center for most of its history. In the past 15 years, as costs have escalated in California's coastal cities, thousands have migrated to the area for its reduced cost of living and proximity to San Francisco and Lake Tahoe. Now, as a result, costs in this area have escalated considerably, with median home prices rising some 70% since the last edition of this book (2004), and growth and traffic issues have become top-of-mind issues for the area. Downtown Sacramento is pleasant and attractive but somewhat lacking in entertainment and activities aside from the restored historic Old Sacramento riverfront downtown area. Most recent growth has occurred to the north, northeast, and south as typical California sprawl—freeways, strip malls,

and endless developments of tightly packed, cookie-cutter homes, some too close to freeways and lacking in appeal. Traffic and smog problems are on the increase, as the area's highway infrastructure, built mainly for intercity and interstate traffic, has bottlenecks and can't handle commute loads. Job-growth projections remain strong, although cutbacks in state government will affect this picture and the strong economic ties to real estate and construction are concerns for the long term.

The Sacramento area has a broad variety of recreational opportunities including water and mountain sports. Excellent skiing and many other recreational opportunities are a moderate day trip away. Professional sports teams, such as the NBA Kings, add to the recreation and the overall economy, and the arts and culture scene is on the upswing and is respectable for a city of this size. A downtown railyard conversion in final planning stages will strengthen the downtown area's role beyond today's fairly bland government and commercial mix. The climate through most of the year is an advantage, although summers can be uncomfortably hot. At 133.6, the Cost of Living Index is high for what's available and is increasing. While growth is an issue, the area is more family-friendly than most California cities and does have several attractive family neighborhoods, particularly along the U.S. 50 corridor. Lincoln, formerly a sleepy agricultural town to the northeast, has become a booming family and retirement center, and home to one of the two large Del Webb "Sun City" active senior complexes. Roseville is an overbuilt suburban town and hub to the rapidly growing northeastern suburbs in southwestern Placer County, while Arden-Arcade is an older inner suburb and commercial area a few miles east of downtown. The metro area now also includes Yolo County, site of the excellent college town of Davis and the growing small residential towns of Woodland and Dixon. Stronger negatives hurt the area's ranking this time around.

At Sacramento, located along the banks of the Sacramento River, the Central Valley is approximately 50 miles wide. The terrain is completely flat. A few miles to the east, rolling terrain rises gradually to the 8,000- to 10,000-foot Sierra Nevada crest. Local natural vegetation is grassland; deciduous trees have been planted in the inhabited area. Summer is dry with warm to hot afternoons and mostly mild nights. "Delta breezes" from the Bay Area cool the region. Most rain falls from November through March. Heavy snowfall and torrential winter rains fall on the western Sierra slopes and may produce flood conditions along the Sacramento River and its tributaries. Winter brings sometimes heavy and persistent ground fog.

Population

DEMOGRAPHICS	AREA	U.S. AVG	ETHNIC COMPOSITION	AREA	U.S. AVG	RESIDENT PROFILE	AREA	U.S. AVG
Population	2,023,535		White	67.2%	79.0%	Single	33.0%	32.4%
Population density per sq. mile	397.2	358.5	Black	7.2%	10.5%	Married	50.5%	52.7%
Population growth	38.0%	21.1%	Asian	10.4%	2.7%	Divorced/separated	16.5%	14.9%
Median age	35.0	36.1	Hispanic	17.4%	10.6%	Married with children	23.8%	23.7%
Percent Democrat	47.4%	44.5%	Religious observance	35.7%	48.9%	Single with children	10.3%	9.1%
Percent Republican	51.3%	54.5%	Diversity measure	64.0	40.1	Percent over age 65	11.3%	12.9%

Economy & Jobs

Score: 68.4
Rank: 119

INCOME	AREA	U.S. AVG	EMPLOYMENT	AREA	U.S. AVG	EMPLOYING INDUSTRIES	AREA	U.S. AVG
Per capita income	$25,765	$23,235	Unemployment rate	4.7%	4.7%	Largest: Healthcare & Social Assistance		
Household income	$53,087	$46,414	Recent job growth	2.8%	1.3%			
Household income < $25K	21.3%	26.2%	Projected future job growth	18.6%	11.5%	Percent manufacturing	9.8%	15.4%
Household income > $75K	32.5%	25.4%	White collar	66.0%	57.8%	Percent public sector	22.5%	15.7%
Household income growth	14.8%	13.6%	Blue collar	18.6%	25.2%	Percent construction	8.8%	9.9%

Cost of Living

Score: 6.4
Rank: 349

INDEXES & TAXES	AREA	U.S. AVG	HOUSING	AREA	U.S. AVG	NECESSITIES	AREA	U.S. AVG
Cost of Living Index	133.6	100.0	Median home price	$380,600	$220,000	Food Index	121.2	100.0
Buying Power Index	89.1	100.0	Home price appreciation	131.5%	10.1%	Housing Index	185.0	100.0
Income tax rate	6.00%	4.70%	Median rent	$984	$709	Utilities Index	109.7	100.0
Sales tax rate	7.59%	6.58%	Homes owned	57.4%	62.3%	Transportation Index	113.8	100.0
Property tax rate	$8.62	$12.00	Home price ratio	7.2	4.2	Healthcare Index	150.3	100.0
						Miscellaneous Cost Index	102.5	100.0

Climate

Score: 94.1
Rank: 23

TEMPERATURE	AREA	U.S. AVG	PRECIPITATION	AREA	U.S. AVG	COMFORTS & HAZARDS	AREA	U.S. AVG
Average January low	37.1	26.2	Annual inches precipitation	17.0	37.7	July relative humidity	66%	66%
Average July high	92.9	87.4	Annual inches snowfall	0.1	7.0	Annual days mostly sunny	265	208
Annual days > 90°F	77	38	Annual days precipitation	57	109	Annual days with thunderstorms	5	39
Annual days < 32°F	17	89	Annual days rain > 0.5 inches	14	22	Tornado risk score	3	18
Annual days < 0°F	0	6	Annual days snow > 1.5 inches	0	6	Hurricane risk score	0	13

TEMPERATURE

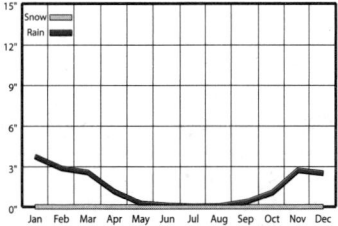

PRECIPITATION

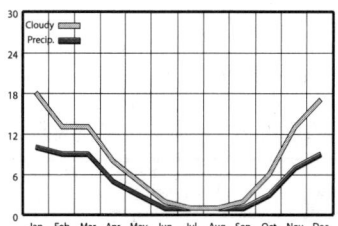

DAYS OF CLOUDS & PRECIPITATION

Education

Score: 77.5
Rank: 85

ACHIEVEMENT	AREA	U.S. AVG	PUBLIC SCHOOLS	AREA	U.S. AVG	HIGHER EDUCATION	AREA	U.S. AVG
High school degree	84.5%	82.7%	Expenditures per pupil	$5,017	$5,686	No. 2-year colleges	15	4
2-year college degree	8.8%	6.4%	Student/teacher ratio	20.5	16.7	No. 4-year colleges/universities	6	6
4-year college degree	17.7%	15.7%	Attending public school	92.4%	90.1%	No. highly ranked universities	1	1
Graduate/professional degree	9.1%	8.9%	State SAT score	1019*	1021			
			State ACT score	21.6	20.9			

Health & Healthcare
Score: 1.3
Rank: 368

HAZARDS & ILLNESSES	AREA	U.S. AVG	HEALTHCARE	AREA	U.S. AVG
Air-quality score	21	37	Physicians per capita	230.8	244.2
Water-quality score	43	52	Hospital beds per capita	195.5	420.0
Pollen/allergy score	74	61	No. teaching hospitals	8	3
Cancer mortality per capita	172.0	201.9	Cost per doctor visit	$79	$77
Depression days per month	3.9	3.5	Cost per dental visit	$79	$70
Stress score	83	50			

Crime
Score: 13.9
Rank: 321

CRIME	AREA	U.S. AVG
Violent crime rate	570.4	465.5
Change in violent crime rate	0.8%	-2.2%
Property crime rate	4,063.9	3,517.1
Change in property crime rate	-7.3%	-2.1%

Transportation
Score: 79.1
Rank: 79

COMMUTE	AREA	U.S. AVG	INTERCITY SERVICES	AREA	U.S. AVG	AUTOMOTIVE	AREA	U.S. AVG
Average commute time	27.5	27.4	Major airports within 60 miles	4	1	Insurance, annual premium	$2,397	$1,432
Percent commutes > 60 mins.	6.7%	5.9%	Size of regional airport	Large	Large	Gas, cost per gallon	$2.58	$2.49
Commute by auto	75.6%	78.9%	Daily airline activity	1197	686	Daily vehicle miles per capita	19.5	24.0
Commute by mass transit	2.7%	1.9%	Amtrak service	Yes	No			
Work at home	4.0%	3.1%						
Mass transit miles per capita	2.66	1.87						

Leisure
Score: 91.7
Rank: 32

DINING & SHOPPING	AREA	U.S. AVG	ENTERTAINMENT	AREA	U.S. AVG	OUTDOOR ACTIVITIES	AREA	U.S. AVG
Restaurant rating	1	2	Professional sports rating	6	4	Golf-course rating	6	4
Outlet mall score	135	42	College sports rating	2	4	Ski-area rating	10	3
No. Starbucks	101	13	Zoo/aquarium rating	5	3	Sq. miles inland water	9	4
No. warehouse clubs	8	2	Amusement park rating	8	3	Miles of coastline	0.0	10.7
			Botanical garden/ arboretum rating	10	4	National Park rating	10	3

Arts & Culture
Score: 75.1
Rank: 93

MEDIA & LIBRARIES	AREA	U.S. AVG	PERFORMING ARTS	AREA	U.S. AVG	MUSEUMS	AREA	U.S. AVG
Arts radio rating	9	3	Classical music rating	6	4	Overall museum rating	9	5
No. public libraries	50	27	Ballet/dance rating	4	3	Art museum rating	8	5
Library volumes per capita	1.68	2.78	Professional theater rating	8	3	Science museum rating	8	5
			University arts programs rating	5	5	Children's museum rating	3	3

Saginaw–Saginaw Township North, MI   Score: 43.0   Rank: 304   2004 rank: 219

Profile: Small-industrial-city complex
Location: Eastern Michigan near the head of Saginaw Bay
Elevation: 595 feet
Time zone: Eastern Standard Time

PRO
Cost of living and housing
Nearby recreation
Healthcare

CON
Economic cycles
Unattractive downtown
Clouds and rain

Saginaw is a middle-of-the-road industrial city and gateway to recreational areas in northern Michigan. Once an important forest products processor, that industry has declined somewhat and the area now has more general industry and agricultural processing. Downtown is uninteresting and has been in decline for years, although there is a small Old Town entertainment district across the Saginaw River. Today, unemployment is a problem in the area, crime rates are high, and the weak economy has driven housing prices down to the point where they make national news for how low they are. As a gateway to the region, Saginaw does have a good balance of services and facilities for a city of its size and profile, including higher education, healthcare, air service, and some cultural amenities.

This tri-city area of Saginaw, Bay City (p. 200), and Midland sits on Saginaw Bay, which forms Michigan's "thumb." Saginaw itself sits about 12 miles up the Saginaw River. The area is mostly flat coastal plain, dotted by agriculture and densely forested land moving away from the cities. Summers are humid but moderate in temperature, with most days below 90°F. Winters are cold with frequent snow and rain/snow mixes. Lake moisture produces significant snows and snow cover is prevalent through winter. First freeze is early October; last is early May.

Population

DEMOGRAPHICS	AREA	U.S. AVG	ETHNIC COMPOSITION	AREA	U.S. AVG	RESIDENT PROFILE	AREA	U.S. AVG
Population	209,037		White	74.1%	79.0%	Single	35.0%	32.4%
Population density per sq. mile	258.4	358.5	Black	19.3%	10.5%	Married	51.4%	52.7%
Population growth	-1.4%	21.1%	Asian	1.0%	2.7%	Divorced/separated	13.7%	14.9%
Median age	37.2	36.1	Hispanic	6.9%	10.6%	Married with children	20.9%	23.7%
Percent Democrat	53.4%	44.5%	Religious observance	49.5%	48.9%	Single with children	11.5%	9.1%
Percent Republican	45.9%	54.5%	Diversity measure	48.8	40.1	Percent over age 65	13.8%	12.9%

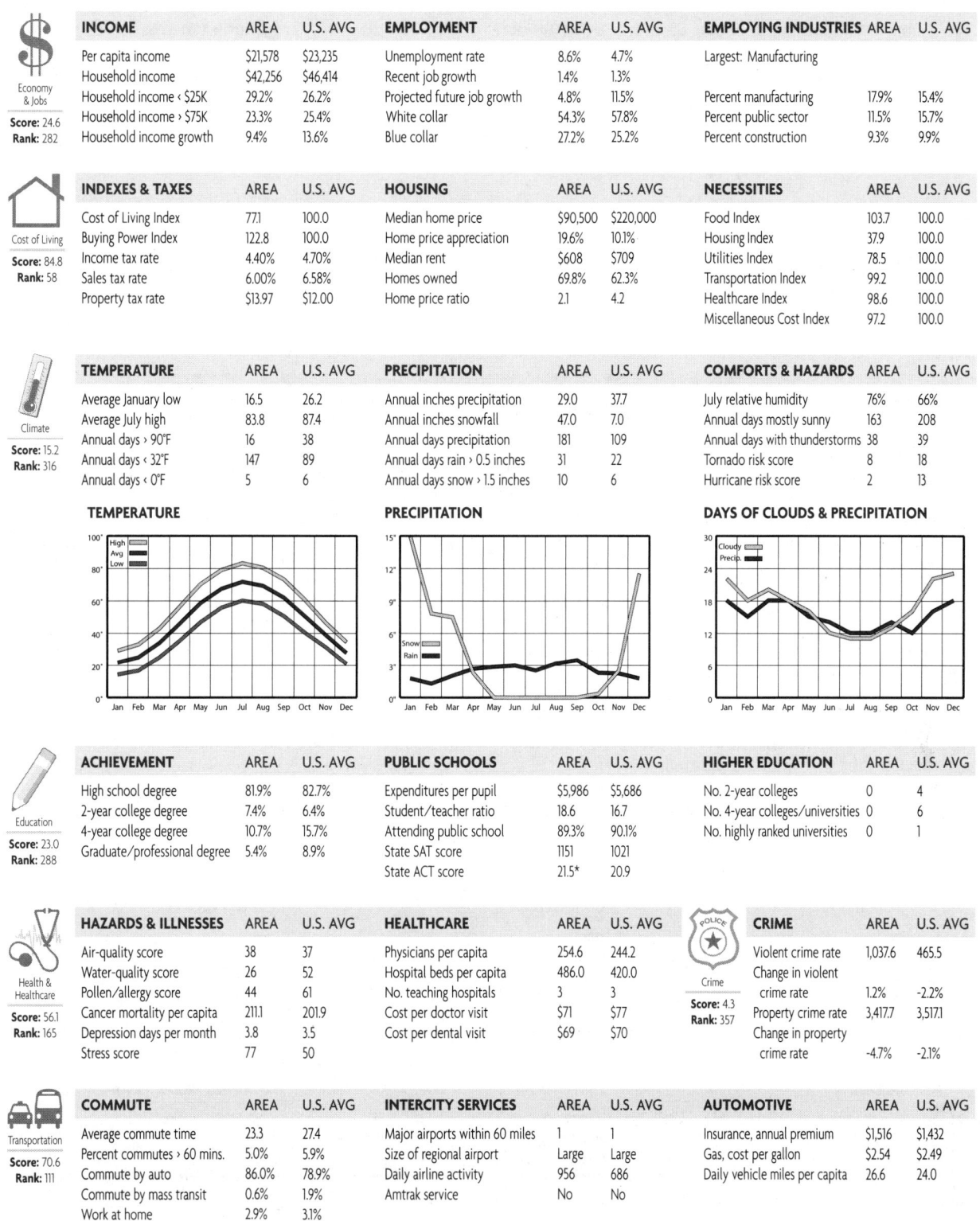

Economy & Jobs
Score: 24.6
Rank: 282

INCOME	AREA	U.S. AVG
Per capita income	$21,578	$23,235
Household income	$42,256	$46,414
Household income ‹ $25K	29.2%	26.2%
Household income › $75K	23.3%	25.4%
Household income growth	9.4%	13.6%

EMPLOYMENT	AREA	U.S. AVG
Unemployment rate	8.6%	4.7%
Recent job growth	1.4%	1.3%
Projected future job growth	4.8%	11.5%
White collar	54.3%	57.8%
Blue collar	27.2%	25.2%

EMPLOYING INDUSTRIES	AREA	U.S. AVG
Largest: Manufacturing		
Percent manufacturing	17.9%	15.4%
Percent public sector	11.5%	15.7%
Percent construction	9.3%	9.9%

Cost of Living
Score: 84.8
Rank: 58

INDEXES & TAXES	AREA	U.S. AVG
Cost of Living Index	77.1	100.0
Buying Power Index	122.8	100.0
Income tax rate	4.40%	4.70%
Sales tax rate	6.00%	6.58%
Property tax rate	$13.97	$12.00

HOUSING	AREA	U.S. AVG
Median home price	$90,500	$220,000
Home price appreciation	19.6%	10.1%
Median rent	$608	$709
Homes owned	69.8%	62.3%
Home price ratio	2.1	4.2

NECESSITIES	AREA	U.S. AVG
Food Index	103.7	100.0
Housing Index	37.9	100.0
Utilities Index	78.5	100.0
Transportation Index	99.2	100.0
Healthcare Index	98.6	100.0
Miscellaneous Cost Index	97.2	100.0

Climate
Score: 15.2
Rank: 316

TEMPERATURE	AREA	U.S. AVG
Average January low	16.5	26.2
Average July high	83.8	87.4
Annual days › 90°F	16	38
Annual days ‹ 32°F	147	89
Annual days ‹ 0°F	5	6

PRECIPITATION	AREA	U.S. AVG
Annual inches precipitation	29.0	37.7
Annual inches snowfall	47.0	7.0
Annual days precipitation	181	109
Annual days rain › 0.5 inches	31	22
Annual days snow › 1.5 inches	10	6

COMFORTS & HAZARDS	AREA	U.S. AVG
July relative humidity	76%	66%
Annual days mostly sunny	163	208
Annual days with thunderstorms	38	39
Tornado risk score	8	18
Hurricane risk score	2	13

TEMPERATURE   PRECIPITATION   DAYS OF CLOUDS & PRECIPITATION

Education
Score: 23.0
Rank: 288

ACHIEVEMENT	AREA	U.S. AVG
High school degree	81.9%	82.7%
2-year college degree	7.4%	6.4%
4-year college degree	10.7%	15.7%
Graduate/professional degree	5.4%	8.9%

PUBLIC SCHOOLS	AREA	U.S. AVG
Expenditures per pupil	$5,986	$5,686
Student/teacher ratio	18.6	16.7
Attending public school	89.3%	90.1%
State SAT score	1151	1021
State ACT score	21.5*	20.9

HIGHER EDUCATION	AREA	U.S. AVG
No. 2-year colleges	0	4
No. 4-year colleges/universities	0	6
No. highly ranked universities	0	1

Health & Healthcare
Score: 56.1
Rank: 165

HAZARDS & ILLNESSES	AREA	U.S. AVG
Air-quality score	38	37
Water-quality score	26	52
Pollen/allergy score	44	61
Cancer mortality per capita	211.1	201.9
Depression days per month	3.8	3.5
Stress score	77	50

HEALTHCARE	AREA	U.S. AVG
Physicians per capita	254.6	244.2
Hospital beds per capita	486.0	420.0
No. teaching hospitals	3	3
Cost per doctor visit	$71	$77
Cost per dental visit	$69	$70

Crime
Score: 4.3
Rank: 357

CRIME	AREA	U.S. AVG
Violent crime rate	1,037.6	465.5
Change in violent crime rate	1.2%	-2.2%
Property crime rate	3,417.7	3,517.1
Change in property crime rate	-4.7%	-2.1%

Transportation
Score: 70.6
Rank: 111

COMMUTE	AREA	U.S. AVG
Average commute time	23.3	27.4
Percent commutes › 60 mins.	5.0%	5.9%
Commute by auto	86.0%	78.9%
Commute by mass transit	0.6%	1.9%
Work at home	2.9%	3.1%
Mass transit miles per capita	0.57	1.87

INTERCITY SERVICES	AREA	U.S. AVG
Major airports within 60 miles	1	1
Size of regional airport	Large	Large
Daily airline activity	956	686
Amtrak service	No	No

AUTOMOTIVE	AREA	U.S. AVG
Insurance, annual premium	$1,516	$1,432
Gas, cost per gallon	$2.54	$2.49
Daily vehicle miles per capita	26.6	24.0

Leisure
Score: 56.4
Rank: 163

DINING & SHOPPING	AREA	U.S. AVG	ENTERTAINMENT	AREA	U.S. AVG	OUTDOOR ACTIVITIES	AREA	U.S. AVG
Restaurant rating	1	2	Professional sports rating	2	4	Golf-course rating	5	4
Outlet mall score	158	42	College sports rating	4	4	Ski-area rating	4	3
No. Starbucks	1	13	Zoo/aquarium rating	2	3	Sq. miles inland water	2	4
No. warehouse clubs	1	2	Amusement park rating	1	3	Miles of coastline	39.9	10.7
			Botanical garden/ arboretum rating	3	4	National Park rating	2	3

Arts & Culture
Score: 52.7
Rank: 177

MEDIA & LIBRARIES	AREA	U.S. AVG	PERFORMING ARTS	AREA	U.S. AVG	MUSEUMS	AREA	U.S. AVG
Arts radio rating	1	3	Classical music rating	4	4	Overall museum rating	3	5
No. public libraries	14	27	Ballet/dance rating	1	3	Art museum rating	2	5
Library volumes per capita	3.77	2.78	Professional theater rating	1	3	Science museum rating	1	5
			University arts programs rating	3	5	Children's museum rating	1	3

St. Cloud, MN

Score: 64.6   **Rank:** 143   **2004 rank:** 136

Profile: Small city
Location: Central Minnesota, 60 miles northwest of Minneapolis–St. Paul along the upper Mississippi
Elevation: 1,028 feet
Time zone: Central Standard Time

PRO
Cost of living
Small-town atmosphere
Nearby outdoor recreation

CON
Winter climate
Low job growth
Low ethnic diversity

The name and geographic position of St. Cloud suggests a small, quiet Heartland agricultural center, and that isn't too far from reality. Today's St. Cloud is more of a "small town grown into a large town," with a friendly Midwestern feel but an expanding role as a commercial and educational center and commuter suburb to the northwestern reaches of Minneapolis–St. Paul. The downtown is clean and in good shape if not especially exciting. Five small private colleges and the larger St. Cloud State University bring some college-town feel and cultural diversity. The area serves as a gateway to wilderness lakes and parks to the north. The city has a number of its own amenities and is close enough to share those of Minneapolis–St. Paul while being almost 20% lower on the cost-of-living scale. Proximity to the Twin Cities area is a plus, and suburban development southeast of town is springing up to take advantage of it. There is talk of commuter rail service, which will work to further connect the two metro areas.

The terrain is flat to gently rolling with numerous lakes and wooded areas. Spring, summer, and fall are pleasant, with moderate temperatures and low humidity. Prolonged periods of hot, humid weather are infrequent. Thunderstorms are the principal source of rainfall and severe storms are common. Winters are cold with low humidity. On average in winter, 5 to 10 days reach temperatures between –20°F and –30°F. Heavy snowfalls occur, but they are less frequent than in Minnesota cities to the south. Snow generally remains on the ground throughout winter. First freeze is late September; last is mid-May.

Population

DEMOGRAPHICS	AREA	U.S. AVG	ETHNIC COMPOSITION	AREA	U.S. AVG	RESIDENT PROFILE	AREA	U.S. AVG
Population	177,225		White	95.0%	79.0%	Single	37.6%	32.4%
Population density per sq. mile	101.1	358.5	Black	1.3%	10.5%	Married	53.4%	52.7%
Population growth	19.1%	21.1%	Asian	1.7%	2.7%	Divorced/separated	8.9%	14.9%
Median age	32.9	36.1	Hispanic	1.5%	10.6%	Married with children	27.9%	23.7%
Percent Democrat	43.3%	44.5%	Religious observance	68.4%	48.9%	Single with children	7.1%	9.1%
Percent Republican	55.1%	54.5%	Diversity measure	12.3	40.1	Percent over age 65	11.1%	12.9%

Economy & Jobs
Score: 39.0
Rank: 228

INCOME	AREA	U.S. AVG	EMPLOYMENT	AREA	U.S. AVG	EMPLOYING INDUSTRIES	AREA	U.S. AVG
Per capita income	$22,542	$23,235	Unemployment rate	3.3%	4.7%	Largest: Manufacturing		
Household income	$48,438	$46,414	Recent job growth	0.4%	1.3%			
Household income < $25K	22.5%	26.2%	Projected future job growth	7.4%	11.5%	Percent manufacturing	19.3%	15.4%
Household income > $75K	25.3%	25.4%	White collar	53.6%	57.8%	Percent public sector	11.6%	15.7%
Household income growth	14.4%	13.6%	Blue collar	28.6%	25.2%	Percent construction	9.2%	9.9%

Cost of Living
Score: 35.3
Rank: 242

INDEXES & TAXES	AREA	U.S. AVG	HOUSING	AREA	U.S. AVG	NECESSITIES	AREA	U.S. AVG
Cost of Living Index	89.8	100.0	Median home price	$132,900	$220,000	Food Index	98.9	100.0
Buying Power Index	120.9	100.0	Home price appreciation	49.5%	10.1%	Housing Index	55.0	100.0
Income tax rate	7.82%	4.70%	Median rent	$582	$709	Utilities Index	134.4	100.0
Sales tax rate	6.50%	6.58%	Homes owned	69.8%	62.3%	Transportation Index	106.2	100.0
Property tax rate	$11.40	$12.00	Home price ratio	2.7	4.2	Healthcare Index	108.6	100.0
						Miscellaneous Cost Index	103.0	100.0

Climate

Score: 12.8
Rank: 325

TEMPERATURE	AREA	U.S. AVG
Average January low	-1.4	26.2
Average July high	81.8	87.4
Annual days > 90°F	11	38
Annual days < 32°F	178	89
Annual days < 0°F	46	6

PRECIPITATION	AREA	U.S. AVG
Annual inches precipitation	26.8	37.7
Annual inches snowfall	43.1	7.0
Annual days precipitation	122	109
Annual days rain > 0.5 inches	17	22
Annual days snow > 1.5 inches	9	6

COMFORTS & HAZARDS	AREA	U.S. AVG
July relative humidity	71%	66%
Annual days mostly sunny	197	208
Annual days with thunderstorms	36	39
Tornado risk score	16	18
Hurricane risk score	0	13

TEMPERATURE

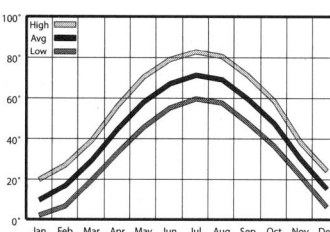

PRECIPITATION

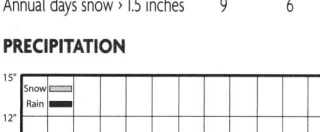

DAYS OF CLOUDS & PRECIPITATION

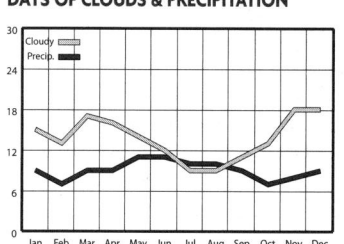

Education

Score: 56.1
Rank: 165

ACHIEVEMENT	AREA	U.S. AVG
High school degree	86.2%	82.7%
2-year college degree	7.3%	6.4%
4-year college degree	14.6%	15.7%
Graduate/professional degree	6.7%	8.9%

PUBLIC SCHOOLS	AREA	U.S. AVG
Expenditures per pupil	$5,357	$5,686
Student/teacher ratio	14.3	16.7
Attending public school	85.3%	90.1%
State SAT score	1191	1021
State ACT score	22.3*	20.9

HIGHER EDUCATION	AREA	U.S. AVG
No. 2-year colleges	2	4
No. 4-year colleges/universities	3	6
No. highly ranked universities	2	1

Health & Healthcare

Score: 75.1
Rank: 94

HAZARDS & ILLNESSES	AREA	U.S. AVG
Air-quality score	40	37
Water-quality score	47	52
Pollen/allergy score	46	61
Cancer mortality per capita	182.2	201.9
Depression days per month	2.7	3.5
Stress score	2	50

HEALTHCARE	AREA	U.S. AVG
Physicians per capita	217.1	244.2
Hospital beds per capita	535.5	420.0
No. teaching hospitals	1	3
Cost per doctor visit	$88	$77
Cost per dental visit	$64	$70

Crime

Score: 86.9
Rank: 50

CRIME	AREA	U.S. AVG
Violent crime rate	194.7	465.5
Change in violent crime rate	-3.8%	-2.2%
Property crime rate	2,553.9	3,517.1
Change in property crime rate	-4.1%	-2.1%

Transportation

Score: 71.4
Rank: 108

COMMUTE	AREA	U.S. AVG
Average commute time	21.6	27.4
Percent commutes > 60 mins.	5.7%	5.9%
Commute by auto	78.6%	78.9%
Commute by mass transit	1.1%	1.9%
Work at home	5.5%	3.1%
Mass transit miles per capita	1.13	1.87

INTERCITY SERVICES	AREA	U.S. AVG
Major airports within 60 miles	1	1
Size of regional airport	Large	Large
Daily airline activity	624	686
Amtrak service	Yes	No

AUTOMOTIVE	AREA	U.S. AVG
Insurance, annual premium	$1,099	$1,432
Gas, cost per gallon	$2.43	$2.49
Daily vehicle miles per capita	18.8	24.0

Leisure

Score: 50.5
Rank: 184

DINING & SHOPPING	AREA	U.S. AVG
Restaurant rating	1	2
Outlet mall score	54	42
No. Starbucks	0	13
No. warehouse clubs	1	2

ENTERTAINMENT	AREA	U.S. AVG
Professional sports rating	2	4
College sports rating	5	4
Zoo/aquarium rating	1	3
Amusement park rating	1	3
Botanical garden/ arboretum rating	6	4

OUTDOOR ACTIVITIES	AREA	U.S. AVG
Golf-course rating	2	4
Ski-area rating	4	3
Sq. miles inland water	5	4
Miles of coastline	0.0	10.7
National Park rating	4	3

Arts & Culture

Score: 45.7
Rank: 203

MEDIA & LIBRARIES	AREA	U.S. AVG
Arts radio rating	1	3
No. public libraries	31	27
Library volumes per capita	1.96	2.78

PERFORMING ARTS	AREA	U.S. AVG
Classical music rating	3	4
Ballet/dance rating	1	3
Professional theater rating	1	3
University arts programs rating	8	5

MUSEUMS	AREA	U.S. AVG
Overall museum rating	5	5
Art museum rating	4	5
Science museum rating	4	5
Children's museum rating	4	3

St. George, UT

Score: 73.3   **Rank:** 72   **2004 rank:** not ranked

Profile: Small resort town
Location: Extreme southwest Utah, near Arizona and Nevada borders
Elevation: 2,880 feet
Time zone: Mountain Standard Time

PRO	CON
Nearby national parks	Rapid growth and sprawl
Dry climate	Isolation
Employment growth	Summer heat

St. George, 8 miles from the Arizona border along Interstate 15, is a small city and popular retirement area adjacent to some of the most attractive mountain and recreational areas in the country. The surrounding red-rock terrain is stunning, and Zion National Park is 30 miles to the northeast. Surrounding areas offer extensive recreation opportunities, including golf, hiking, and skiing. The town itself is uninteresting, and the rapid 127% 15-year growth rate has produced some unattractive sprawl. Employment is hard to find outside of the large and growing construction, retail, and service sectors, and for such an isolated small city, living and housing costs are uncomfortably high. The city would like to attract business and industry to supplement its retirement population with an active middle class, but it hasn't happened yet. The area is 115 miles northeast of Las Vegas, the nearest major city with services. The future direction of this rapidly evolving city is far from clear.

The St. George area is located in an area of undulating arid hills and red-rock bluffs south of the more heavily forested areas of the Dixie National Forest to the north and Zion to the east. Summers are warm to uncomfortably hot with frequent 100°F-plus weather, although temperatures in nearby mountains can be much cooler. There are occasional summer thunderstorms particularly during the June "monsoon" season, though rain is much more likely in nearby mountains. Winter nights average just below freezing, with daytime highs in the 50s and 60s and occasional cold snaps and dry snow but little to no accumulation.

Population

DEMOGRAPHICS	AREA	U.S. AVG	ETHNIC COMPOSITION	AREA	U.S. AVG	RESIDENT PROFILE	AREA	U.S. AVG
Population	110,515		White	92.8%	79.0%	Single	25.7%	32.4%
Population density per sq. mile	45.5	358.5	Black	0.3%	10.5%	Married	63.6%	52.7%
Population growth	127.6%	21.1%	Asian	1.0%	2.7%	Divorced/separated	10.7%	14.9%
Median age	30.1	36.1	Hispanic	5.9%	10.6%	Married with children	30.4%	23.7%
Percent Democrat	17.1%	44.5%	Religious observance	75.1%	48.9%	Single with children	6.4%	9.1%
Percent Republican	81.0%	54.5%	Diversity measure	23.4	40.1	Percent over age 65	16.5%	12.9%

Economy & Jobs
Score: 100.0
Rank: 1

INCOME	AREA	U.S. AVG	EMPLOYMENT	AREA	U.S. AVG	EMPLOYING INDUSTRIES	AREA	U.S. AVG
Per capita income	$18,634	$23,235	Unemployment rate	3.9%	4.7%	Largest: Healthcare & Social Assistance		
Household income	$43,133	$46,414	Recent job growth	8.2%	1.3%			
Household income < $25K	24.6%	26.2%	Projected future job growth	52.9%	11.5%	Percent manufacturing	13.0%	15.4%
Household income > $75K	20.5%	25.4%	White collar	54.5%	57.8%	Percent public sector	13.5%	15.7%
Household income growth	15.9%	13.6%	Blue collar	26.7%	25.2%	Percent construction	13.7%	9.9%

Cost of Living
Score: 38.0
Rank: 232

INDEXES & TAXES	AREA	U.S. AVG	HOUSING	AREA	U.S. AVG	NECESSITIES	AREA	U.S. AVG
Cost of Living Index	100.5	100.0	Median home price	$229,400	$220,000	Food Index	112.7	100.0
Buying Power Index	96.2	100.0	Home price appreciation	71.6%	10.1%	Housing Index	67.7	100.0
Income tax rate	7.00%	4.70%	Median rent	$650	$709	Utilities Index	78.4	100.0
Sales tax rate	6.00%	6.58%	Homes owned	61.7%	62.3%	Transportation Index	98.8	100.0
Property tax rate	$5.59	$12.00	Home price ratio	5.3	4.2	Healthcare Index	96.2	100.0
						Miscellaneous Cost Index	98.2	100.0

Climate
Score: 55.9
Rank: 164

TEMPERATURE	AREA	U.S. AVG	PRECIPITATION	AREA	U.S. AVG	COMFORTS & HAZARDS	AREA	U.S. AVG
Average January low	25.8	26.2	Annual inches precipitation	8.4	37.7	July relative humidity	19%	66%
Average July high	101.6	87.4	Annual inches snowfall	3.5	7.0	Annual days mostly sunny	230	208
Annual days > 90°F	113	38	Annual days precipitation	65	109	Annual days with thunderstorms	15	39
Annual days < 32°F	90	89	Annual days rain > 0.5 inches	4	22	Tornado risk score	1	18
Annual days < 0°F	0	6	Annual days snow > 1.5 inches	1	6	Hurricane risk score	0	13

TEMPERATURE

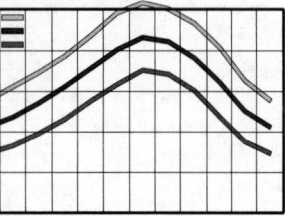

PRECIPITATION

DAYS OF CLOUDS & PRECIPITATION

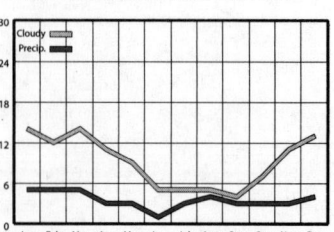

ACHIEVEMENT	AREA	U.S. AVG	PUBLIC SCHOOLS	AREA	U.S. AVG	HIGHER EDUCATION	AREA	U.S. AVG
High school degree	87.8%	82.7%	Expenditures per pupil	$3,444	$5,686	No. 2-year colleges	2	4
2-year college degree	8.2%	6.4%	Student/teacher ratio	21.7	16.7	No. 4-year colleges/universities	1	6
4-year college degree	14.0%	15.7%	Attending public school	96.8%	90.1%	No. highly ranked universities	0	1
Graduate/professional degree	7.1%	8.9%	State SAT score	1117	1021			
			State ACT score	21.7*	20.9			

Education
Score: 54.8
Rank: 170

HAZARDS & ILLNESSES	AREA	U.S. AVG	HEALTHCARE	AREA	U.S. AVG	CRIME	AREA	U.S. AVG
Air-quality score	59	37	Physicians per capita	148.8	244.2	Violent crime rate	249.1	465.5
Water-quality score	73	52	Hospital beds per capita	138.4	420.0	Change in violent crime rate	-4.3%	-2.2%
Pollen/allergy score	68	61	No. teaching hospitals	0	3	Property crime rate	2,374.4	3,517.1
Cancer mortality per capita	98.2	201.9	Cost per doctor visit	$66	$77	Change in property crime rate	-5.3%	-2.1%
Depression days per month	3.5	3.5	Cost per dental visit	$55	$70			
Stress score	4	50						

Health & Healthcare
Score: 82.6
Rank: 66

Crime
Score: 100.0
Rank: 1

COMMUTE	AREA	U.S. AVG	INTERCITY SERVICES	AREA	U.S. AVG	AUTOMOTIVE	AREA	U.S. AVG
Average commute time	18.7	27.4	Major airports within 60 miles	0	1	Insurance, annual premium	$925	$1,432
Percent commutes > 60 mins.	3.2%	5.9%	Size of regional airport	None	Large	Gas, cost per gallon	$2.49	$2.49
Commute by auto	76.3%	78.9%	Daily airline activity	11	686	Daily vehicle miles per capita	21.1	24.0
Commute by mass transit	0.2%	1.9%	Amtrak service	No	No			
Work at home	5.0%	3.1%						
Mass transit miles per capita	0.16	1.87						

Transportation
Score: 56.4
Rank: 164

DINING & SHOPPING	AREA	U.S. AVG	ENTERTAINMENT	AREA	U.S. AVG	OUTDOOR ACTIVITIES	AREA	U.S. AVG
Restaurant rating	1	2	Professional sports rating	1	4	Golf-course rating	5	4
Outlet mall score	0	42	College sports rating	2	4	Ski-area rating	3	3
No. Starbucks	1	13	Zoo/aquarium rating	1	3	Sq. miles inland water	1	4
No. warehouse clubs	1	2	Amusement park rating	1	3	Miles of coastline	0.0	10.7
			Botanical garden/ arboretum rating	1	4	National Park rating	8	3

Leisure
Score: 32.6
Rank: 251

MEDIA & LIBRARIES	AREA	U.S. AVG	PERFORMING ARTS	AREA	U.S. AVG	MUSEUMS	AREA	U.S. AVG
Arts radio rating	1	3	Classical music rating	2	4	Overall museum rating	2	5
No. public libraries	4	27	Ballet/dance rating	1	3	Art museum rating	1	5
Library volumes per capita	1.88	2.78	Professional theater rating	2	3	Science museum rating	1	5
			University arts programs rating	1	5	Children's museum rating	1	3

Arts & Culture
Score: 3.7
Rank: 359

St. Joseph, MO-KS

Score: 23.8   Rank: 346   2004 rank: 213

Profile: Small city
Location: Northeast Missouri along the Missouri River at the Kansas border
Elevation: 894 feet
Time zone: Central Standard Time

PRO
Cost of living
Historic interest
Close to Kansas City

CON
Economy
Entertainment
Harsh climate

St. Joseph, once the eastern terminus of the Pony Express, is a former frontier and meatpacking center that has today evolved into more of a mixed agricultural and industrial center. The diverse economy ranges from fence wire to Stetson hats to Sara Lee baked goods, but the economic outlook is uncertain and job-growth projections are weak. The future depends on the city's ability to attract businesses looking for an alternative to Kansas City. As reflected by relatively long average commute times, some do commute towards K.C. There are some minor cultural amenities and the area has considerable historic interest as a key hub in the Old West with several museums and historic buildings and homes. The attractive downtown, small-town feel, very low living costs, and a short, 50-mile drive to the K.C. area are among the area's principal draws.

The city sits in the broad, flat Missouri Valley in a mainly agricultural area. Summer brings warm days and mild nights with moderate humidity. Winters are not severely cold but have cold snaps. Falls are usually mild and pleasant. Spring is the stormiest season—in 2003, St. Joseph was the center of a tornado outbreak that devastated several nearby towns. First freeze is mid-October; last is mid-April.

Population

DEMOGRAPHICS	AREA	U.S. AVG	ETHNIC COMPOSITION	AREA	U.S. AVG	RESIDENT PROFILE	AREA	U.S. AVG
Population	122,675		White	92.8%	79.0%	Single	31.1%	32.4%
Population density per sq. mile	73.8	358.5	Black	4.3%	10.5%	Married	52.0%	52.7%
Population growth	6.7%	21.1%	Asian	0.5%	2.7%	Divorced/separated	16.9%	14.9%
Median age	37.1	36.1	Hispanic	2.0%	10.6%	Married with children	22.4%	23.7%
Percent Democrat	43.3%	44.5%	Religious observance	53.1%	48.9%	Single with children	8.8%	9.1%
Percent Republican	55.8%	54.5%	Diversity measure	17.0	40.1	Percent over age 65	14.7%	12.9%

Economy & Jobs
Score: 9.1
Rank: 339

INCOME	AREA	U.S. AVG	EMPLOYMENT	AREA	U.S. AVG	EMPLOYING INDUSTRIES	AREA	U.S. AVG
Per capita income	$19,905	$23,235	Unemployment rate	5.8%	4.7%	Largest: Manufacturing		
Household income	$39,960	$46,414	Recent job growth	0.3%	1.3%			
Household income < $25K	30.4%	26.2%	Projected future job growth	1.7%	11.5%	Percent manufacturing	18.0%	15.4%
Household income > $75K	18.1%	25.4%	White collar	52.1%	57.8%	Percent public sector	14.1%	15.7%
Household income growth	13.9%	13.6%	Blue collar	28.6%	25.2%	Percent construction	10.6%	9.9%

Cost of Living
Score: 79.1
Rank: 79

INDEXES & TAXES	AREA	U.S. AVG	HOUSING	AREA	U.S. AVG	NECESSITIES	AREA	U.S. AVG
Cost of Living Index	77.2	100.0	Median home price	$105,400	$220,000	Food Index	88.3	100.0
Buying Power Index	116.0	100.0	Home price appreciation	26.7%	10.1%	Housing Index	44.4	100.0
Income tax rate	6.03%	4.70%	Median rent	$527	$709	Utilities Index	93.0	100.0
Sales tax rate	6.92%	6.58%	Homes owned	65.0%	62.3%	Transportation Index	94.7	100.0
Property tax rate	$7.98	$12.00	Home price ratio	2.6	4.2	Healthcare Index	95.8	100.0
						Miscellaneous Cost Index	98.9	100.0

Climate
Score: 19.0
Rank: 302

TEMPERATURE	AREA	U.S. AVG	PRECIPITATION	AREA	U.S. AVG	COMFORTS & HAZARDS	AREA	U.S. AVG
Average January low	18.4	26.2	Annual inches precipitation	37.0	37.7	July relative humidity	69%	66%
Average July high	88.0	87.4	Annual inches snowfall	20.0	7.0	Annual days mostly sunny	213	208
Annual days > 90°F	40	38	Annual days precipitation	102	109	Annual days with thunderstorms	53	39
Annual days > 32°F	106	89	Annual days rain > 0.5 inches	25	22	Tornado risk score	25	18
Annual days > 0°F	9	6	Annual days snow > 1.5 inches	6	6	Hurricane risk score	1	13

TEMPERATURE

PRECIPITATION

DAYS OF CLOUDS & PRECIPITATION

Education
Score: 19.5
Rank: 300

ACHIEVEMENT	AREA	U.S. AVG	PUBLIC SCHOOLS	AREA	U.S. AVG	HIGHER EDUCATION	AREA	U.S. AVG
High school degree	81.6%	82.7%	Expenditures per pupil	$4,988	$5,686	No. 2-year colleges	3	4
2-year college degree	4.1%	6.4%	Student/teacher ratio	13.4	16.7	No. 4-year colleges/universities	1	6
4-year college degree	11.3%	15.7%	Attending public school	91.5%	90.1%	No. highly ranked universities	0	1
Graduate/professional degree	5.3%	8.9%	State SAT score	1178	1021			
			State ACT score	21.6*	20.9			

Health & Healthcare
Score: 60.7
Rank: 148

HAZARDS & ILLNESSES	AREA	U.S. AVG	HEALTHCARE	AREA	U.S. AVG	CRIME	AREA	U.S. AVG
Air-quality score	57	37	Physicians per capita	142.8	244.2	Violent crime rate	244.4	465.5
Water-quality score	73	52	Hospital beds per capita	525.8	420.0	Change in violent crime rate	20.7%	-2.2%
Pollen/allergy score	71	61	No. teaching hospitals	0	3	Property crime rate	4,144.8	3,517.1
Cancer mortality per capita	233.9	201.9	Cost per doctor visit	$42	$77	Change in property crime rate	-13.4%	-2.1%
Depression days per month	4.1	3.5	Cost per dental visit	$95	$70			
Stress score	47	50						

Crime
Score: 57.2
Rank: 161

Transportation
Score: 49.7
Rank: 189

COMMUTE	AREA	U.S. AVG	INTERCITY SERVICES	AREA	U.S. AVG	AUTOMOTIVE	AREA	U.S. AVG
Average commute time	22.4	27.4	Major airports within 60 miles	1	1	Insurance, annual premium	$1,146	$1,432
Percent commutes > 60 mins.	6.1%	5.9%	Size of regional airport	Medium	Large	Gas, cost per gallon	$2.37	$2.49
Commute by auto	81.7%	78.9%	Daily airline activity	328	686	Daily vehicle miles per capita	21.8	24.0
Commute by mass transit	0.6%	1.9%	Amtrak service	No	No			
Work at home	3.4%	3.1%						
Mass transit miles per capita	0.57	1.87						

DINING & SHOPPING	AREA	U.S. AVG	ENTERTAINMENT	AREA	U.S. AVG	OUTDOOR ACTIVITIES	AREA	U.S. AVG
Restaurant rating	1	2	Professional sports rating	2	4	Golf-course rating	1	4
Outlet mall score	9	42	College sports rating	2	4	Ski-area rating	1	3
No. Starbucks	1	13	Zoo/aquarium rating	1	3	Sq. miles inland water	2	4
No. warehouse clubs	0	2	Amusement park rating	1	3	Miles of coastline	0.0	10.7
			Botanical garden/ arboretum rating	1	4	National Park rating	1	3

Leisure
Score: 0.8
Rank: 370

MEDIA & LIBRARIES	AREA	U.S. AVG	PERFORMING ARTS	AREA	U.S. AVG	MUSEUMS	AREA	U.S. AVG
Arts radio rating	1	3	Classical music rating	3	4	Overall museum rating	3	5
No. public libraries	10	27	Ballet/dance rating	1	3	Art museum rating	3	5
Library volumes per capita	4.27	2.78	Professional theater rating	1	3	Science museum rating	4	5
			University arts programs rating	3	5	Children's museum rating	1	3

Arts & Culture
Score: 32.6
Rank: 252

St. Louis, MO-IL

Score: 82.1   Rank: 35   2004 rank: 97

Profile: Large city
Location: Missouri-Illinois border along the Mississippi River
Elevation: 570 feet
Time zone: Central Standard Time

PRO	CON
Cost of living	Growth and sprawl
Educated population	Employment concerns
Arts and culture	Hot, humid summers

Known since the early days as the "Gateway City" because of its access to transportation routes in all directions, St. Louis continues to be an important center of commerce and culture for the Mississippi River Basin. The area includes a broad assortment of mostly residential neighborhoods to the west and the more industrial East St. Louis and several agricultural counties on the Illinois side of the river. For years the downtown area had few highlights outside of the landmark Gateway Arch and the restored Union Station. The population of the city itself had declined gradually for decades, and most of the infrastructure had declined in sympathy as people moved into the suburbs or away altogether. But more recently, after some failed attempts, the downtown has started to come back, with new residential facilities and reclaimed warehouse lofts downtown anchored by new sports venues. Similar restorations are going on in other important inner neighborhoods.

The St. Louis area is known for its parks, and the flagship is Forest Park, the 1,300-acre site of the 1904 World's Fair, now the location of several high-quality museums. To the west lies a patchwork of mostly quiet, shady neighborhoods, including the University City area, home to the highly rated Washington University. Grittier neighborhoods lie to the north of the city, and good family neighborhoods lie along the Interstate 70 corridor to the northwest across the Missouri River and around the Interstate 270 beltway. St. Louis offers plenty of urban and suburban living choices, and home prices and living costs are quite reasonable for this type of city. The diverse economy is led by such companies as Anheuser-Busch, McDonnell-Douglas (now a part of Boeing), Monsanto,

and a number of other manufacturing, distribution, and service firms. Due to acquisitions and some relocations, the area is less prominent as a corporate headquarters than in the past, and projected job growth is modest. There is some concern about the auto industry in particular; there are four auto assembly plants in the area.

The St. Louis area has a very strong base of cultural and entertainment amenities for a city its size. A number of amenities are directed at children, and St. Louis in general is considered a good place to raise a family. Other advantages include a highly educated population for a large city and popular professional sports teams—MLB Cardinals, NFL Rams, and NHL Blues—which are accessible and inexpensive by national standards. Rates for violent crime have dropped significantly from earlier years but are still an issue. Some may not like the hot, humid summer weather, and air quality could be better. The high ranking reflects the full plate of big-city benefits at an attractive price without some of the typical big-city downsides.

The city is located on a plain on the west bank of the Mississippi River with gently rolling hills and undulating plains rising to the west, and mostly level terrain to the east. Hilly areas are wooded and level areas are mainly farmland. During summer, Gulf air tends to dominate, producing warm, humid conditions. Temperatures of 90°F or higher are common. Winters are brisk and stimulating, but prolonged periods of extreme cold are rare. Temperatures of zero or below are infrequent. Summer thunderstorms are common and sometimes severe. Spring is the wettest season. Snow is infrequent, with measurable snowfall on 5 to 10 days in most years. First freeze is mid-October; last is mid-April.

DEMOGRAPHICS	AREA	U.S. AVG	ETHNIC COMPOSITION	AREA	U.S. AVG	RESIDENT PROFILE	AREA	U.S. AVG
Population	2,754,233		White	77.8%	79.0%	Single	33.4%	32.4%
Population density per sq. mile	318.4	358.5	Black	18.1%	10.5%	Married	52.3%	52.7%
Population growth	10.1%	21.1%	Asian	1.8%	2.7%	Divorced/separated	14.3%	14.9%
Median age	37.1	36.1	Hispanic	1.7%	10.6%	Married with children	23.6%	23.7%
Percent Democrat	53.8%	44.5%	Religious observance	51.1%	48.9%	Single with children	9.6%	9.1%
Percent Republican	45.6%	54.5%	Diversity measure	33.0	40.1	Percent over age 65	13.0%	12.9%

Population

Economy & Jobs
Score: 32.6
Rank: 252

INCOME	AREA	U.S. AVG	EMPLOYMENT	AREA	U.S. AVG	EMPLOYING INDUSTRIES	AREA	U.S. AVG
Per capita income	$25,820	$23,235	Unemployment rate	6.1%	4.7%	Largest: Healthcare & Social Assistance		
Household income	$50,994	$46,414	Recent job growth	0.9%	1.3%			
Household income ‹ $25K	22.5%	26.2%	Projected future job growth	6.0%	11.5%	Percent manufacturing	14.0%	15.4%
Household income › $75K	29.4%	25.4%	White collar	61.4%	57.8%	Percent public sector	10.9%	15.7%
Household income growth	13.2%	13.6%	Blue collar	23.1%	25.2%	Percent construction	9.0%	9.9%

Cost of Living
Score: 32.1
Rank: 254

INDEXES & TAXES	AREA	U.S. AVG	HOUSING	AREA	U.S. AVG	NECESSITIES	AREA	U.S. AVG
Cost of Living Index	87.6	100.0	Median home price	$153,000	$220,000	Food Index	95.1	100.0
Buying Power Index	130.5	100.0	Home price appreciation	39.6%	10.1%	Housing Index	61.8	100.0
Income tax rate	6.85%	4.70%	Median rent	$664	$709	Utilities Index	89.9	100.0
Sales tax rate	7.19%	6.58%	Homes owned	68.0%	62.3%	Transportation Index	105.2	100.0
Property tax rate	$12.76	$12.00	Home price ratio	3.0	4.2	Healthcare Index	103.0	100.0
						Miscellaneous Cost Index	101.0	100.0

Climate
Score: 36.1
Rank: 238

TEMPERATURE	AREA	U.S. AVG	PRECIPITATION	AREA	U.S. AVG	COMFORTS & HAZARDS	AREA	U.S. AVG
Average January low	22.6	26.2	Annual inches precipitation	36.0	37.7	July relative humidity	70%	66%
Average July high	88.4	87.4	Annual inches snowfall	18.0	7.0	Annual days mostly sunny	206	208
Annual days › 90°F	37	38	Annual days precipitation	108	109	Annual days with thunderstorms	45	39
Annual days ‹ 32°F	107	89	Annual days rain › 0.5 inches	22	22	Tornado risk score	44	18
Annual days ‹ 0°F	3	6	Annual days snow › 1.5 inches	5	6	Hurricane risk score	4	13

TEMPERATURE

PRECIPITATION

DAYS OF CLOUDS & PRECIPITATION

Education
Score: 85.0
Rank: 57

ACHIEVEMENT	AREA	U.S. AVG	PUBLIC SCHOOLS	AREA	U.S. AVG	HIGHER EDUCATION	AREA	U.S. AVG
High school degree	83.3%	82.7%	Expenditures per pupil	$5,446	$5,686	No. 2-year colleges	21	4
2-year college degree	6.2%	6.4%	Student/teacher ratio	16.1	16.7	No. 4-year colleges/universities	34	6
4-year college degree	15.8%	15.7%	Attending public school	83.2%	90.1%	No. highly ranked universities	5	1
Graduate/professional degree	8.9%	8.9%	State SAT score	1178	1021			
			State ACT score	21.6*	20.9			

Health & Healthcare
Score: 28.3
Rank: 267

Crime
Score: 46.0
Rank: 202

HAZARDS & ILLNESSES	AREA	U.S. AVG	HEALTHCARE	AREA	U.S. AVG	CRIME	AREA	U.S. AVG
Air-quality score	25	37	Physicians per capita	284.9	244.2	Violent crime rate	544.4	465.5
Water-quality score	47	52	Hospital beds per capita	466.8	420.0	Change in violent crime rate	11.1%	-2.2%
Pollen/allergy score	68	61	No. teaching hospitals	18	3	Property crime rate	3,643.3	3,517.1
Cancer mortality per capita	223.4	201.9	Cost per doctor visit	$74	$77	Change in property crime rate	0.1%	-2.1%
Depression days per month	3.4	3.5	Cost per dental visit	$72	$70			
Stress score	88	50						

Transportation
Score: 24.1
Rank: 285

COMMUTE	AREA	U.S. AVG	INTERCITY SERVICES	AREA	U.S. AVG	AUTOMOTIVE	AREA	U.S. AVG
Average commute time	27.9	27.4	Major airports within 60 miles	1	1	Insurance, annual premium	$1,976	$1,432
Percent commutes › 60 mins.	6.0%	5.9%	Size of regional airport	Large	Large	Gas, cost per gallon	$2.42	$2.49
Commute by auto	82.4%	78.9%	Daily airline activity	731	686	Daily vehicle miles per capita	31.0	24.0
Commute by mass transit	2.4%	1.9%	Amtrak service	Yes	No			
Work at home	2.9%	3.1%						
Mass transit miles per capita	2.38	1.87						

Leisure
Score: 85.0
Rank: 56

DINING & SHOPPING	AREA	U.S. AVG	ENTERTAINMENT	AREA	U.S. AVG	OUTDOOR ACTIVITIES	AREA	U.S. AVG
Restaurant rating	3	2	Professional sports rating	8	4	Golf-course rating	7	4
Outlet mall score	1	42	College sports rating	4	4	Ski-area rating	1	3
No. Starbucks	29	13	Zoo/aquarium rating	9	3	Sq. miles inland water	6	4
No. warehouse clubs	3	2	Amusement park rating	10	3	Miles of coastline	0.0	10.7
			Botanical garden/arboretum rating	10	4	National Park rating	2	3

Arts & Culture
Score: 96.3
Rank: 15

MEDIA & LIBRARIES	AREA	U.S. AVG	PERFORMING ARTS	AREA	U.S. AVG	MUSEUMS	AREA	U.S. AVG
Arts radio rating	7	3	Classical music rating	10	4	Overall museum rating	10	5
No. public libraries	128	27	Ballet/dance rating	5	3	Art museum rating	10	5
Library volumes per capita	4.46	2.78	Professional theater rating	8	3	Science museum rating	9	5
			University arts programs rating	10	5	Children's museum rating	10	3

Salem, OR

Score: 71.3   Rank: 82   2004 rank: 141

Profile: Capital city
Location: North-central Oregon in Willamette Valley, 50 miles south of Portland
Elevation: 196 feet
Time zone: Pacific Standard Time

PRO	CON
Small-town atmosphere	Clouds and rain
Nearby recreation	Crime
Close to Portland	Low ethnic diversity

Salem is the state capital and an agricultural center. State government buildings dominate a small but attractive and progressive downtown core. Surrounding built-up areas are unremarkable. Local agriculture includes orchards, fruits, grapes, nursery stock, and vegetables; the agriculture and rolling, moist terrain make for an attractive landscape. The area is close enough to Portland to enjoy some of its amenities and services while retaining a small-town flavor. Some residents commute north, particularly to high-tech sections south of Portland. While the state government lends some stability to the economy, and there is a trickle of new industry into the area, the economic outlook is not encouraging but has reversed declines in the past few years. While crime isn't a huge problem, crime rates are high for the type of area. The winter climate is gloomy.

Salem is located in the middle of Willamette Valley some 60 air miles east of the Pacific Ocean. The valley is approximately 50 miles wide with the city about equidistant from the Coast Range on the west and the Cascade Range on the east. Land is rolling with flat valleys and a mix of woods and farmland. Some of the heaviest yearly rainfall in the country, up to 170 inches, occurs in the mountains surrounding the city. The valley floor receives about 40 annual inches of rainfall, most occurring during winter. In the immediate area, measurable amounts of snow falls only 3 or 4 days a year. Summer days are typically sunny to partly cloudy and pleasant, while winter days are cold, cloudy, and damp, with few extremes in either season. First freeze is late October; last is early May.

Population

DEMOGRAPHICS	AREA	U.S. AVG	ETHNIC COMPOSITION	AREA	U.S. AVG	RESIDENT PROFILE	AREA	U.S. AVG
Population	369,411		White	80.6%	79.0%	Single	31.0%	32.4%
Population density per sq. mile	191.9	358.5	Black	0.9%	10.5%	Married	52.4%	52.7%
Population growth	32.9%	21.1%	Asian	2.1%	2.7%	Divorced/separated	16.6%	14.9%
Median age	34.4	36.1	Hispanic	18.7%	10.6%	Married with children	24.4%	23.7%
Percent Democrat	44.3%	44.5%	Religious observance	34.8%	48.9%	Single with children	9.4%	9.1%
Percent Republican	54.1%	54.5%	Diversity measure	53.0	40.1	Percent over age 65	12.6%	12.9%

Economy & Jobs
Score: 32.1
Rank: 253

INCOME	AREA	U.S. AVG	EMPLOYMENT	AREA	U.S. AVG	EMPLOYING INDUSTRIES	AREA	U.S. AVG
Per capita income	$20,805	$23,235	Unemployment rate	6.5%	4.7%	Largest: Healthcare & Social Assistance		
Household income	$45,636	$46,414	Recent job growth	0.2%	1.3%			
Household income < $25K	24.4%	26.2%	Projected future job growth	14.0%	11.5%	Percent manufacturing	15.1%	15.4%
Household income > $75K	23.3%	25.4%	White collar	54.7%	57.8%	Percent public sector	20.4%	15.7%
Household income growth	12.2%	13.6%	Blue collar	24.3%	25.2%	Percent construction	9.2%	9.9%

Cost of Living
Score: 48.1
Rank: 194

INDEXES & TAXES	AREA	U.S. AVG	HOUSING	AREA	U.S. AVG	NECESSITIES	AREA	U.S. AVG
Cost of Living Index	97.8	100.0	Median home price	$195,300	$220,000	Food Index	103.8	100.0
Buying Power Index	104.6	100.0	Home price appreciation	38.1%	10.1%	Housing Index	78.1	100.0
Income tax rate	9.00%	4.70%	Median rent	$634	$709	Utilities Index	88.8	100.0
Sales tax rate	0.00%	6.58%	Homes owned	60.2%	62.3%	Transportation Index	104.8	100.0
Property tax rate	$10.94	$12.00	Home price ratio	4.3	4.2	Healthcare Index	120.7	100.0
						Miscellaneous Cost Index	105.6	100.0

Climate
Score: 67.9
Rank: 119

TEMPERATURE	AREA	U.S. AVG
Average January low	32.2	26.2
Average July high	82.4	87.4
Annual days > 90°F	7	38
Annual days < 32°F	50	89
Annual days < 0°F	0	6

PRECIPITATION	AREA	U.S. AVG
Annual inches precipitation	41.1	37.7
Annual inches snowfall	7.0	7.0
Annual days precipitation	152	109
Annual days rain > 0.5 inches	25	22
Annual days snow > 1.5 inches	2	6

COMFORTS & HAZARDS	AREA	U.S. AVG
July relative humidity	74%	66%
Annual days mostly sunny	159	208
Annual days with thunderstorms	5	39
Tornado risk score	1	18
Hurricane risk score	0	13

TEMPERATURE

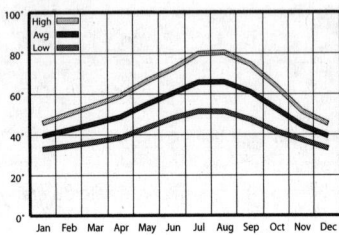

PRECIPITATION

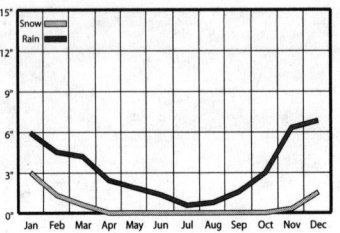

DAYS OF CLOUDS & PRECIPITATION

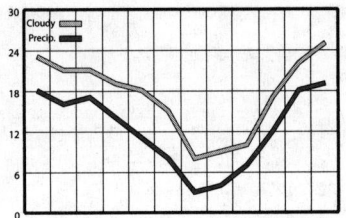

Education
Score: 45.5
Rank: 205

ACHIEVEMENT	AREA	U.S. AVG
High school degree	80.3%	82.7%
2-year college degree	6.7%	6.4%
4-year college degree	13.6%	15.7%
Graduate/professional degree	7.1%	8.9%

PUBLIC SCHOOLS	AREA	U.S. AVG
Expenditures per pupil	$5,710	$5,686
Student/teacher ratio	18.3	16.7
Attending public school	93.2%	90.1%
State SAT score	1052*	1021
State ACT score	22.4	20.9

HIGHER EDUCATION	AREA	U.S. AVG
No. 2-year colleges	6	4
No. 4-year colleges/universities	4	6
No. highly ranked universities	1	1

Health & Healthcare
Score: 19.3
Rank: 301

HAZARDS & ILLNESSES	AREA	U.S. AVG
Air-quality score	28	37
Water-quality score	60	52
Pollen/allergy score	44	61
Cancer mortality per capita	213.8	201.9
Depression days per month	3.6	3.5
Stress score	89	50

HEALTHCARE	AREA	U.S. AVG
Physicians per capita	157.1	244.2
Hospital beds per capita	207.4	420.0
No. teaching hospitals	0	3
Cost per doctor visit	$93	$77
Cost per dental visit	$80	$70

Crime
Score: 25.4
Rank: 279

CRIME	AREA	U.S. AVG
Violent crime rate	321.0	465.5
Change in violent crime rate	-1.2%	-2.2%
Property crime rate	4,605.3	3,517.1
Change in property crime rate	-7.5%	-2.1%

Transportation
Score: 31.6
Rank: 257

COMMUTE	AREA	U.S. AVG
Average commute time	25.3	27.4
Percent commutes > 60 mins.	6.9%	5.9%
Commute by auto	73.3%	78.9%
Commute by mass transit	1.9%	1.9%
Work at home	4.6%	3.1%
Mass transit miles per capita	1.85	1.87

INTERCITY SERVICES	AREA	U.S. AVG
Major airports within 60 miles	1	1
Size of regional airport	Medium	Large
Daily airline activity	484	686
Amtrak service	Yes	No

AUTOMOTIVE	AREA	U.S. AVG
Insurance, annual premium	$1,496	$1,432
Gas, cost per gallon	$2.39	$2.49
Daily vehicle miles per capita	18.8	24.0

Leisure
Score: 65.2
Rank: 130

DINING & SHOPPING	AREA	U.S. AVG
Restaurant rating	1	2
Outlet mall score	0	42
No. Starbucks	9	13
No. warehouse clubs	1	2

ENTERTAINMENT	AREA	U.S. AVG
Professional sports rating	3	4
College sports rating	3	4
Zoo/aquarium rating	2	3
Amusement park rating	3	3
Botanical garden/ arboretum rating	1	4

OUTDOOR ACTIVITIES	AREA	U.S. AVG
Golf-course rating	3	4
Ski-area rating	8	3
Sq. miles inland water	3	4
Miles of coastline	0.0	10.7
National Park rating	8	3

Arts & Culture
Score: 38.8
Rank: 229

MEDIA & LIBRARIES	AREA	U.S. AVG
Arts radio rating	3	3
No. public libraries	10	27
Library volumes per capita	2.17	2.78

PERFORMING ARTS	AREA	U.S. AVG
Classical music rating	2	4
Ballet/dance rating	3	3
Professional theater rating	3	3
University arts programs rating	3	5

MUSEUMS	AREA	U.S. AVG
Overall museum rating	4	5
Art museum rating	4	5
Science museum rating	5	5
Children's museum rating	5	3

Salinas, CA

Score: 38.4   Rank: 313   2004 rank: 153

Profile: Beach town/small city
Location: Northern California, on the south end of Monterey Bay, 110 miles south of San Francisco
Elevation: 267 feet
Time zone: Pacific Standard Time

PRO	CON
Attractive setting	Cost of living and housing
Year-round climate	Isolation
Recreation and entertainment	Tourist impact

This is probably the most inaptly named metro area in the book. Clearly there's more to this diverse metropolitan area than the plain, unremarkable inland agricultural town of Salinas. Monterey County includes the famous seaside cities of Monterey, Carmel, and Pacific Grove, established playgrounds for the wealthy and a steady stream of tourists arriving to enjoy the spectacular coastline, golf, shopping, entertainment, and climate. It would be an understatement to say that the area presents extreme contrasts. Agricultural Salinas was dubbed the "salad bowl of the nation" by John Steinbeck because of its lettuce crops. Salinas is affordable and small in comparison to the others, but has the character of a typical California Central Valley town—dry, dusty, functional, and with little intellectual stimulation. By contrast, Monterey, Carmel, and Pacific Grove are located on the coastal Monterey Peninsula; Carmel, a noted artist colony and Hollywood refuge, has controlled growth and maintains a charming village character with some exceptional residential properties; and Monterey is a more commercialized setup honoring its fishing village heritage for its many visitors. Pacific Grove, with its assortment of well-built Victorian- and Craftsman-era homes, is probably the most livable city on the peninsula. Not surprisingly, you'll need a large endowment to afford any of the coastal cities and particularly Carmel. The Cost of Living index of 191.5 and the median home price of $744,700 *for the entire area* say a lot. What's worse, you won't earn the money locally, for employment prospects, especially for high-paying jobs, are bleak. Crime rates are quite high for the type of area. Aside from these issues, the location is a bit isolated from big-city amenities and services, all of which are available to the north in San Francisco, which while not far is hard to get to. Bottom line: This is a magnificent area to live in *if* you can afford to live in the right parts of it.

Salinas sits in an agricultural valley. The peninsula cities are in an area of low hills with dense pine and cypress trees. Large sand dunes occur at the head of Monterey Bay. South of Carmel, hills grow larger and the coastline becomes rugged and elevated. Summer days, when clear, are invariably sunny, cool, and breezy, but can be warmer to quite hot at Salinas and inland. Winters are moderate with periods of Pacific rain. Heavy, low, stratus clouds, known locally as "fog," occur in all seasons.

DEMOGRAPHICS	AREA	U.S. AVG	ETHNIC COMPOSITION	AREA	U.S. AVG	RESIDENT PROFILE	AREA	U.S. AVG
Population	419,440		White	54.2%	79.0%	Single	32.9%	32.4%
Population density per sq. mile	126.3	358.5	Black	3.5%	10.5%	Married	47.5%	52.7%
Population growth	17.9%	21.1%	Asian	6.4%	2.7%	Divorced/separated	19.6%	14.9%
Median age	32.3	36.1	Hispanic	50.8%	10.6%	Married with children	29.8%	23.7%
Percent Democrat	60.4%	44.5%	Religious observance	45.0%	48.9%	Single with children	9.4%	9.1%
Percent Republican	38.4%	54.5%	Diversity measure	80.4	40.1	Percent over age 65	9.9%	12.9%

INCOME	AREA	U.S. AVG	EMPLOYMENT	AREA	U.S. AVG	EMPLOYING INDUSTRIES	AREA	U.S. AVG
Per capita income	$23,123	$23,235	Unemployment rate	5.4%	4.7%	Largest: Healthcare & Social Assistance		
Household income	$56,789	$46,414	Recent job growth	0.5%	1.3%			
Household income < $25K	18.5%	26.2%	Projected future job growth	5.3%	11.5%	Percent manufacturing	11.2%	15.4%
Household income > $75K	34.6%	25.4%	White collar	51.2%	57.8%	Percent public sector	16.2%	15.7%
Household income growth	17.6%	13.6%	Blue collar	19.7%	25.2%	Percent construction	8.5%	9.9%

Economy & Jobs — Score: 2.1 Rank: 365

INDEXES & TAXES	AREA	U.S. AVG	HOUSING	AREA	U.S. AVG	NECESSITIES	AREA	U.S. AVG
Cost of Living Index	191.5	100.0	Median home price	$744,700	$220,000	Food Index	115.4	100.0
Buying Power Index	66.5	100.0	Home price appreciation	121.5%	10.1%	Housing Index	270.7	100.0
Income tax rate	6.00%	4.70%	Median rent	$1,106	$709	Utilities Index	121.3	100.0
Sales tax rate	7.25%	6.58%	Homes owned	50.6%	62.3%	Transportation Index	114.6	100.0
Property tax rate	$7.12	$12.00	Home price ratio	13.1	4.2	Healthcare Index	126.7	100.0
						Miscellaneous Cost Index	104.0	100.0

Cost of Living — Score: 0.5 Rank: 371

Climate
Score: 100.0
Rank: 1

TEMPERATURE	AREA	U.S. AVG
Average January low	41.2	26.2
Average July high	73.6	87.4
Annual days > 90°F	1	38
Annual days < 32°F	0	89
Annual days < 0°F	0	6

PRECIPITATION	AREA	U.S. AVG
Annual inches precipitation	21.0	37.7
Annual inches snowfall	0.0	7.0
Annual days precipitation	67	109
Annual days rain > 0.5 inches	13	22
Annual days snow > 1.5 inches	0	6

COMFORTS & HAZARDS	AREA	U.S. AVG
July relative humidity	75%	66%
Annual days mostly sunny	265	208
Annual days with thunderstorms	2	39
Tornado risk score	3	18
Hurricane risk score	0	13

TEMPERATURE

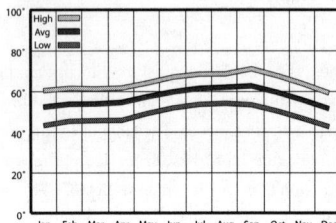

PRECIPITATION

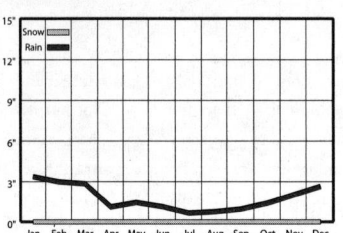

DAYS OF CLOUDS & PRECIPITATION

Education
Score: 19.3
Rank: 301

ACHIEVEMENT	AREA	U.S. AVG
High school degree	67.6%	82.7%
2-year college degree	6.4%	6.4%
4-year college degree	13.5%	15.7%
Graduate/professional degree	8.5%	8.9%

PUBLIC SCHOOLS	AREA	U.S. AVG
Expenditures per pupil	$5,718	$5,686
Student/teacher ratio	19.5	16.7
Attending public school	93.9%	90.1%
State SAT score	1019*	1021
State ACT score	21.6	20.9

HIGHER EDUCATION	AREA	U.S. AVG
No. 2-year colleges	3	4
No. 4-year colleges/universities	2	6
No. highly ranked universities	0	1

Health & Healthcare
Score: 3.5
Rank: 360

HAZARDS & ILLNESSES	AREA	U.S. AVG
Air-quality score	24	37
Water-quality score	30	52
Pollen/allergy score	83	61
Cancer mortality per capita	147.3	201.9
Depression days per month	3.3	3.5
Stress score	58	50

HEALTHCARE	AREA	U.S. AVG
Physicians per capita	167.7	244.2
Hospital beds per capita	167.1	420.0
No. teaching hospitals	1	3
Cost per doctor visit	$104	$77
Cost per dental visit	$76	$70

Crime
Score: 29.4
Rank: 264

CRIME	AREA	U.S. AVG
Violent crime rate	445.2	465.5
Change in violent crime rate	-11.0%	-2.2%
Property crime rate	3,502.3	3,517.1
Change in property crime rate	3.8%	-2.1%

Transportation
Score: 81.3
Rank: 71

COMMUTE	AREA	U.S. AVG
Average commute time	25.2	27.4
Percent commutes > 60 mins.	7.0%	5.9%
Commute by auto	68.6%	78.9%
Commute by mass transit	2.2%	1.9%
Work at home	3.6%	3.1%
Mass transit miles per capita	2.17	1.87

INTERCITY SERVICES	AREA	U.S. AVG
Major airports within 60 miles	3	1
Size of regional airport	Large	Large
Daily airline activity	1053	686
Amtrak service	Yes	No

AUTOMOTIVE	AREA	U.S. AVG
Insurance, annual premium	$1,499	$1,432
Gas, cost per gallon	$2.71	$2.49
Daily vehicle miles per capita	15.0	24.0

Leisure
Score: 81.3
Rank: 70

DINING & SHOPPING	AREA	U.S. AVG
Restaurant rating	1	2
Outlet mall score	102	42
No. Starbucks	14	13
No. warehouse clubs	3	2

ENTERTAINMENT	AREA	U.S. AVG
Professional sports rating	4	4
College sports rating	1	4
Zoo/aquarium rating	7	3
Amusement park rating	1	3
Botanical garden/ arboretum rating	4	4

OUTDOOR ACTIVITIES	AREA	U.S. AVG
Golf-course rating	4	4
Ski-area rating	8	3
Sq. miles inland water	2	4
Miles of coastline	84.0	10.7
National Park rating	9	3

Arts & Culture
Score: 47.1
Rank: 198

MEDIA & LIBRARIES	AREA	U.S. AVG
Arts radio rating	7	3
No. public libraries	24	27
Library volumes per capita	2.35	2.78

PERFORMING ARTS	AREA	U.S. AVG
Classical music rating	3	4
Ballet/dance rating	1	3
Professional theater rating	1	3
University arts programs rating	1	5

MUSEUMS	AREA	U.S. AVG
Overall museum rating	8	5
Art museum rating	4	5
Science museum rating	5	5
Children's museum rating	1	3

Salisbury, MD

Score: 36.5 **Rank:** 316 **2004 rank:** not ranked

Profile: Small town
Location: Delmarva Peninsula, 8 miles south of Delaware border
Elevation: 33 feet
Time zone: Eastern Standard Time

PRO	CON
Small-town feel	Entertainment
Nearby outdoor recreation	Violent crime
Moderate climate	Isolation

Salisbury is a quiet small town along the Wicomico River in an area known as Maryland's Eastern Shore, It has a history as a port and transportation center serving the agricultural "Delmarva" peninsula, incorporating eastern Maryland, Delaware, and a part of Virginia north of the Chesapeake Bay. The area is pleasant with few extremes because of the nearby waters of the Chesapeake Bay and Atlantic Ocean. Cost of living is reasonable for the region. The area has become a bit of a magnet for small businesses seeking to escape higher-cost East Coast cities. Although somewhat cut off by water, Salisbury is centrally located among Washington, D.C.; Philadelphia; Baltimore; and the Norfolk, Virginia, area. That said, it is still more than 100 miles to these cities, but they are close enough to provide the cultural amenities and services missing locally. Downtown is clean and well kept with some historic interest, and the city is a center for health and education for the southern Delmarva area. No doubt the reported crime rate, which may be an anomaly, hurt the ranking.

Salisbury lies in a mostly level plain about 12 miles from Chesapeake Bay. Surrounding land is mainly agricultural. Summers are warm and humid but with temperatures only occasionally exceeding 90°F. Cloudy days are common, and rain can come as persistent light drizzle or thundershowers with approaching cold fronts. Winters are also mild with only infrequent colder snaps. Winter precipitation is usually rain or a mix of rain and snow. Atlantic hurricanes and "noreasters" can bring heavier precipitation and lowland flooding is a risk. First freeze is late October; last is mid-April.

Population

DEMOGRAPHICS	AREA	U.S. AVG	ETHNIC COMPOSITION	AREA	U.S. AVG	RESIDENT PROFILE	AREA	U.S. AVG
Population	114,561		White	69.8%	79.0%	Single	37.1%	32.4%
Population density per sq. mile	162.6	358.5	Black	26.3%	10.5%	Married	46.3%	52.7%
Population growth	17.3%	21.1%	Asian	1.6%	2.7%	Divorced/separated	16.7%	14.9%
Median age	36.1	36.1	Hispanic	2.0%	10.6%	Married with children	20.0%	23.7%
Percent Democrat	41.4%	44.5%	Religious observance	43.8%	48.9%	Single with children	10.7%	9.1%
Percent Republican	57.7%	54.5%	Diversity measure	45.5	40.1	Percent over age 65	13.2%	12.9%

Economy & Jobs

Score: 36.1
Rank: 239

INCOME	AREA	U.S. AVG	EMPLOYMENT	AREA	U.S. AVG	EMPLOYING INDUSTRIES	AREA	U.S. AVG
Per capita income	$20,871	$23,235	Unemployment rate	4.5%	4.7%	Largest: Healthcare & Social Assistance		
Household income	$41,735	$46,414	Recent job growth	1.6%	1.3%			
Household income < $25K	29.7%	26.2%	Projected future job growth	7.6%	11.5%	Percent manufacturing	14.3%	15.4%
Household income > $75K	21.1%	25.4%	White collar	54.7%	57.8%	Percent public sector	20.5%	15.7%
Household income growth	12.9%	13.6%	Blue collar	24.6%	25.2%	Percent construction	10.3%	9.9%

Cost of Living

Score: 31.0
Rank: 258

INDEXES & TAXES	AREA	U.S. AVG	HOUSING	AREA	U.S. AVG	NECESSITIES	AREA	U.S. AVG
Cost of Living Index	99.2	100.0	Median home price	$212,800	$220,000	Food Index	103.5	100.0
Buying Power Index	94.3	100.0	Home price appreciation	76.2%	10.1%	Housing Index	69.6	100.0
Income tax rate	7.45%	4.70%	Median rent	$630	$709	Utilities Index	121.3	100.0
Sales tax rate	5.00%	6.58%	Homes owned	61.6%	62.3%	Transportation Index	95.8	100.0
Property tax rate	$9.37	$12.00	Home price ratio	5.1	4.2	Healthcare Index	94.4	100.0
						Miscellaneous Cost Index	98.7	100.0

Climate

Score: 84.8
Rank: 58

TEMPERATURE	AREA	U.S. AVG	PRECIPITATION	AREA	U.S. AVG	COMFORTS & HAZARDS	AREA	U.S. AVG
Average January low	29.0	26.2	Annual inches precipitation	41.9	37.7	July relative humidity	54%	66%
Average July high	86.0	87.4	Annual inches snowfall	14.0	7.0	Annual days mostly sunny	204	208
Annual days > 90°F	21	38	Annual days precipitation	113	109	Annual days with thunderstorms	31	39
Annual days < 32°F	67	89	Annual days rain > 0.5 inches	26	22	Tornado risk score	1	18
Annual days < 0°F	0	6	Annual days snow > 1.5 inches	5	6	Hurricane risk score	3	13

TEMPERATURE

PRECIPITATION

DAYS OF CLOUDS & PRECIPITATION

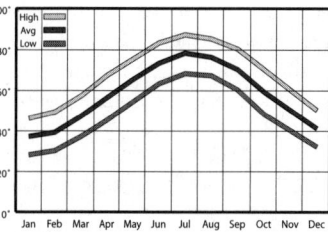

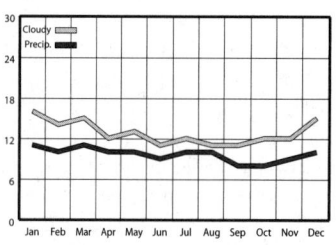

ACHIEVEMENT	AREA	U.S. AVG	PUBLIC SCHOOLS	AREA	U.S. AVG	HIGHER EDUCATION	AREA	U.S. AVG
High school degree	78.2%	82.7%	Expenditures per pupil	$6,233	$5,686	No. 2-year colleges	1	4
2-year college degree	4.7%	6.4%	Student/teacher ratio	17.8	16.7	No. 4-year colleges/universities	2	6
4-year college degree	12.4%	15.7%	Attending public school	86.2%	90.1%	No. highly ranked universities	0	1
Graduate/professional degree	7.4%	8.9%	State SAT score	1012*	1021			
			State ACT score	21.4	20.9			

Education
Score: 14.7
Rank: 318

HAZARDS & ILLNESSES	AREA	U.S. AVG	HEALTHCARE	AREA	U.S. AVG	CRIME	AREA	U.S. AVG
Air-quality score	62	37	Physicians per capita	266.4	244.2	Violent crime rate	906.4	465.5
Water-quality score	67	52	Hospital beds per capita	501.9	420.0	Change in violent crime rate	11.3%	-2.2%
Pollen/allergy score	61	61	No. teaching hospitals	0	3	Property crime rate	4,224.4	3,517.1
Cancer mortality per capita	222.2	201.9	Cost per doctor visit	$84	$77	Change in property crime rate	7.2%	-2.1%
Depression days per month	3.3	3.5	Cost per dental visit	$80	$70			
Stress score	41	50						

Health & Healthcare
Score: 93.6
Rank: 25

Crime
Score: 5.6
Rank: 352

COMMUTE	AREA	U.S. AVG	INTERCITY SERVICES	AREA	U.S. AVG	AUTOMOTIVE	AREA	U.S. AVG
Average commute time	23.2	27.4	Major airports within 60 miles	2	1	Insurance, annual premium	$1,262	$1,432
Percent commutes > 60 mins.	4.8%	5.9%	Size of regional airport	Large	Large	Gas, cost per gallon	$2.36	$2.49
Commute by auto	78.4%	78.9%	Daily airline activity	841	686	Daily vehicle miles per capita	25.2	24.0
Commute by mass transit	1.5%	1.9%	Amtrak service	No	No			
Work at home	3.3%	3.1%						
Mass transit miles per capita	1.45	1.87						

Transportation
Score: 77.5
Rank: 85

DINING & SHOPPING	AREA	U.S. AVG	ENTERTAINMENT	AREA	U.S. AVG	OUTDOOR ACTIVITIES	AREA	U.S. AVG
Restaurant rating	1	2	Professional sports rating	1	4	Golf-course rating	2	4
Outlet mall score	106	42	College sports rating	1	4	Ski-area rating	1	3
No. Starbucks	1	13	Zoo/aquarium rating	1	3	Sq. miles inland water	3	4
No. warehouse clubs	1	2	Amusement park rating	1	3	Miles of coastline	8.0	10.7
			Botanical garden/ arboretum rating	2	4	National Park rating	3	3

Leisure
Score: 16.8
Rank: 310

MEDIA & LIBRARIES	AREA	U.S. AVG	PERFORMING ARTS	AREA	U.S. AVG	MUSEUMS	AREA	U.S. AVG
Arts radio rating	1	3	Classical music rating	2	4	Overall museum rating	4	5
No. public libraries	5	27	Ballet/dance rating	1	3	Art museum rating	4	5
Library volumes per capita	2.08	2.78	Professional theater rating	1	3	Science museum rating	1	5
			University arts programs rating	1	5	Children's museum rating	1	3

Arts & Culture
Score: 4.8
Rank: 355

Salt Lake City, UT

Score: 84.1   Rank: 27   2004 rank: 84

Profile: Capital-city complex
Location: North-central Utah
Elevation: 4,260 feet
Time zone: Mountain Standard Time

PRO
Attractive downtown and setting
Economy
Nearby recreation

CON
Growth and sprawl
Long commutes
Nightlife

Salt Lake City, the cultural capital and headquarters for the Mormon community, is a self-contained, rapidly growing, cosmopolitan, and tradition-oriented city. Mormon settlers originally chose the location for its isolation and favorable agricultural resources. Today it serves as a major commercial and cultural center for the large intermountain U.S. west region, and is becoming increasingly popular as an alternative to crowded Pacific destinations. A favorable business climate has led to the development of a wide range of industries, from traditional manufactured goods to a growing base of new-economy products. The growth has attracted migrants from other places west, especially California, seeking less crowding, lower living cost, and employment opportunities in a pleasant climate. Proximity to outstanding outdoor recreation, including

skiing, rafting, and hiking in the Wasatch Mountains, is almost without comparison among large metropolitan areas. By contrast, the desert areas to the west offer little recreation or economic interest.

Downtown Salt Lake is beautiful, with boulevards originally designed by Mormons to be wide enough for wagons to make a U-turn. The city itself preserves a clean, dignified character enhanced by the capitol and government buildings and the various landmarks and sites of the Mormon Church. Extensive and mostly unattractive commercial and industrial areas spread south and west of Interstate 15. Aside from Ogden to the north (p. 587), most of the area's growth has spread south along a 40-mile stretch of relatively flat valley ending at Provo (p. 633). A string of attractive family-oriented suburbs starts about 5 miles south of downtown and east of Interstate 15 against the mountains; Sandy and Draper are the largest. Because of limited geography and high growth, the city is experiencing some crowding, traffic congestion, smog, and a rise in the cost of living, and without these negatives, the ranking would likely be still higher. But the economy is strong, there is plenty to do, the climate is generally pleasant, the population is educated, and good housing values can be found. A complete set of cultural amenities is available, and entertainment is wholesome if a little subdued. The Mormon community maintains a strong influence on state government; conservative policies on alcohol and other matters are uncomfortable for some.

Salt Lake City is located in a dramatic valley surrounded by high mountains on three sides and the Great Salt Lake to the northwest. The city center is flat but the Wasatch Mountains to the east have peaks to 12,000 feet. The dry Oquirrh Mountains to the southwest of the city have peaks to above 10,000 feet. Summers have hot, dry weather, but high temperatures are generally tolerable because of low humidity and cool nights. Winters are cold but usually not severe. Average annual snowfall is less than 60 inches at the airport but much higher in the mountains. Heavy fog can develop under temperature inversions in the winter and persist for several days. The lake and mountains together create summer breezes and more precipitation than would otherwise occur in this high-desert environment. First freeze is mid-October; last is late April.

DEMOGRAPHICS	AREA	U.S. AVG	ETHNIC COMPOSITION	AREA	U.S. AVG	RESIDENT PROFILE	AREA	U.S. AVG
Population	1,023,434		White	84.9%	79.0%	Single	31.8%	32.4%
Population density per sq. mile	107.3	358.5	Black	1.2%	10.5%	Married	55.1%	52.7%
Population growth	35.5%	21.1%	Asian	4.0%	2.7%	Divorced/separated	13.1%	14.9%
Median age	30.1	36.1	Hispanic	13.5%	10.6%	Married with children	32.7%	23.7%
Percent Democrat	37.2%	44.5%	Religious observance	67.7%	48.9%	Single with children	8.0%	9.1%
Percent Republican	60.0%	54.5%	Diversity measure	44.3	40.1	Percent over age 65	8.2%	12.9%

Economy & Jobs
Score: 91.7
Rank: 32

INCOME	AREA	U.S. AVG	EMPLOYMENT	AREA	U.S. AVG	EMPLOYING INDUSTRIES	AREA	U.S. AVG
Per capita income	$23,765	$23,235	Unemployment rate	4.7%	4.7%	Largest: Manufacturing		
Household income	$56,988	$46,414	Recent job growth	4.1%	1.3%			
Household income ‹ $25K	16.9%	26.2%	Projected future job growth	20.6%	11.5%	Percent manufacturing	13.0%	15.4%
Household income › $75K	33.5%	25.4%	White collar	63.7%	57.8%	Percent public sector	13.8%	15.7%
Household income growth	16.7%	13.6%	Blue collar	23.0%	25.2%	Percent construction	10.0%	9.9%

Cost of Living
Score: 26.7
Rank: 273

INDEXES & TAXES	AREA	U.S. AVG	HOUSING	AREA	U.S. AVG	NECESSITIES	AREA	U.S. AVG
Cost of Living Index	94.4	100.0	Median home price	$191,200	$220,000	Food Index	110.8	100.0
Buying Power Index	135.3	100.0	Home price appreciation	29.5%	10.1%	Housing Index	69.6	100.0
Income tax rate	7.00%	4.70%	Median rent	$721	$709	Utilities Index	85.6	100.0
Sales tax rate	6.55%	6.58%	Homes owned	66.2%	62.3%	Transportation Index	100.9	100.0
Property tax rate	$7.87	$12.00	Home price ratio	3.4	4.2	Healthcare Index	87.7	100.0
						Miscellaneous Cost Index	99.6	100.0

Climate
Score: 29.4
Rank: 263

TEMPERATURE	AREA	U.S. AVG	PRECIPITATION	AREA	U.S. AVG	COMFORTS & HAZARDS	AREA	U.S. AVG
Average January low	18.5	26.2	Annual inches precipitation	15.0	37.7	July relative humidity	54%	66%
Average July high	92.8	87.4	Annual inches snowfall	58.0	7.0	Annual days mostly sunny	232	208
Annual days › 90°F	58	38	Annual days precipitation	88	109	Annual days with thunderstorms	35	39
Annual days ‹ 32°F	134	89	Annual days rain › 0.5 inches	7	22	Tornado risk score	6	18
Annual days ‹ 0°F	3	6	Annual days snow › 1.5 inches	13	6	Hurricane risk score	0	13

TEMPERATURE 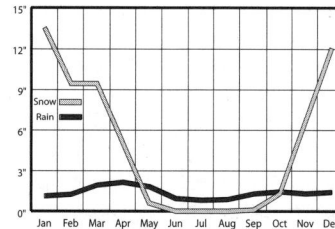 **PRECIPITATION** 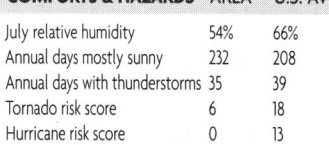 **DAYS OF CLOUDS & PRECIPITATION**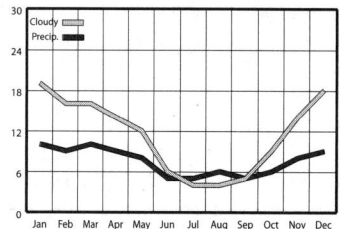

Education
Score: 74.3
Rank: 96

ACHIEVEMENT	AREA	U.S. AVG	PUBLIC SCHOOLS	AREA	U.S. AVG	HIGHER EDUCATION	AREA	U.S. AVG
High school degree	87.2%	82.7%	Expenditures per pupil	$3,920	$5,686	No. 2-year colleges	12	4
2-year college degree	7.6%	6.4%	Student/teacher ratio	19.9	16.7	No. 4-year colleges/universities	7	6
4-year college degree	18.5%	15.7%	Attending public school	93.6%	90.1%	No. highly ranked universities	0	1
Graduate/professional degree	9.0%	8.9%	State SAT score	1117	1021			
			State ACT score	21.7*	20.9			

Health & Healthcare
Score: 58.3
Rank: 157

HAZARDS & ILLNESSES	AREA	U.S. AVG
Air-quality score	16	37
Water-quality score	68	52
Pollen/allergy score	60	61
Cancer mortality per capita	108.5	201.9
Depression days per month	3.5	3.5
Stress score	37	50

HEALTHCARE	AREA	U.S. AVG
Physicians per capita	280.9	244.2
Hospital beds per capita	236.1	420.0
No. teaching hospitals	6	3
Cost per doctor visit	$96	$77
Cost per dental visit	$54	$70

Crime
Score: 20.1
Rank: 299

CRIME	AREA	U.S. AVG
Violent crime rate	332.3	465.5
Change in violent crime rate	-7.6%	-2.2%
Property crime rate	5,287.2	3,517.1
Change in property crime rate	-3.6%	-2.1%

Transportation
Score: 32.9
Rank: 252

COMMUTE	AREA	U.S. AVG
Average commute time	25.5	27.4
Percent commutes > 60 mins.	4.4%	5.9%
Commute by auto	76.2%	78.9%
Commute by mass transit	3.2%	1.9%
Work at home	4.1%	3.1%
Mass transit miles per capita	3.21	1.87

INTERCITY SERVICES	AREA	U.S. AVG
Major airports within 60 miles	1	1
Size of regional airport	Large	Large
Daily airline activity	452	686
Amtrak service	Yes	No

AUTOMOTIVE	AREA	U.S. AVG
Insurance, annual premium	$1,545	$1,432
Gas, cost per gallon	$2.24	$2.49
Daily vehicle miles per capita	22.8	24.0

Leisure
Score: 90.1
Rank: 38

DINING & SHOPPING	AREA	U.S. AVG
Restaurant rating	1	2
Outlet mall score	0	42
No. Starbucks	16	13
No. warehouse clubs	4	2

ENTERTAINMENT	AREA	U.S. AVG
Professional sports rating	6	4
College sports rating	6	4
Zoo/aquarium rating	7	3
Amusement park rating	3	3
Botanical garden/ arboretum rating	9	4

OUTDOOR ACTIVITIES	AREA	U.S. AVG
Golf-course rating	5	4
Ski-area rating	10	3
Sq. miles inland water	10	4
Miles of coastline	0.0	10.7
National Park rating	8	3

Arts & Culture
Score: 82.6
Rank: 66

MEDIA & LIBRARIES	AREA	U.S. AVG
Arts radio rating	9	3
No. public libraries	31	27
Library volumes per capita	2.96	2.78

PERFORMING ARTS	AREA	U.S. AVG
Classical music rating	6	4
Ballet/dance rating	5	3
Professional theater rating	9	3
University arts programs rating	4	5

MUSEUMS	AREA	U.S. AVG
Overall museum rating	9	5
Art museum rating	9	5
Science museum rating	8	5
Children's museum rating	7	3

San Angelo, TX

Score: 62.8 **Rank:** 152 **2004 rank:** 277

Profile: Small city
Location: West-central Texas, about 200 miles northwest of San Antonio
Elevation: 1,953 feet
Time zone: Central Standard Time

PRO	CON
Cost of living	Isolation
Small-town atmosphere	Entertainment
Historic interest	Summer heat

San Angelo is a quiet, agricultural and light manufacturing center in west-central Texas. Originally a frontier fort, the city retains some outpost character along with a Spanish/Mexican influence. Industries include ranching, cotton, pecans, and light manufacturing with some oil and gas development. The area has picked up some business activity migrating from bigger Texas cities looking for lower costs and the small-town lifestyle. The city is also a commercial, health, and minor cultural center for a 13-county area. Goodfellow Air Force Base adds a military and a strong economic influence. Highlights include a few minor cultural amenities, minor league sports, and Angelo State University with 6,000 students, but the area is isolated and some won't find enough to do.

San Angelo is located near the center of Texas at the northern edge of the Edwards Plateau. The landscape is level to slightly rolling with hills up to 2,700 feet. Warm, dry weather predominates, although changes may be rapid and frequent with the passage of northerly cold fronts. Summer high temperatures come with fair skies, southwest winds, and dry air. Rapid temperature drops occur after sunset, and most nights are pleasant with lows in the upper 60s and lower 70s. Temperatures can dip to zero or below. Heavy rainfall occurs in spring and fall and may occur in late summer months with tropical storms. Winds can be high and persistent for several days, carrying dust if conditions are dry.

Population

DEMOGRAPHICS	AREA	U.S. AVG
Population	105,367	
Population density per sq. mile	40.9	358.5
Population growth	5.3%	21.1%
Median age	34.3	36.1
Percent Democrat	24.0%	44.5%
Percent Republican	75.5%	54.5%

ETHNIC COMPOSITION	AREA	U.S. AVG
White	78.5%	79.0%
Black	3.3%	10.5%
Asian	0.9%	2.7%
Hispanic	33.8%	10.6%
Religious observance	60.3%	48.9%
Diversity measure	64.7	40.1

RESIDENT PROFILE	AREA	U.S. AVG
Single	30.5%	32.4%
Married	53.0%	52.7%
Divorced/separated	16.4%	14.9%
Married with children	23.4%	23.7%
Single with children	9.4%	9.1%
Percent over age 65	13.8%	12.9%

Economy & Jobs
Score: 70.9
Rank: 110

INCOME	AREA	U.S. AVG
Per capita income	$19,871	$23,235
Household income	$37,631	$46,414
Household income < $25K	32.6%	26.2%
Household income > $75K	17.1%	25.4%
Household income growth	13.3%	13.6%

EMPLOYMENT	AREA	U.S. AVG
Unemployment rate	4.3%	4.7%
Recent job growth	3.8%	1.3%
Projected future job growth	9.7%	11.5%
White collar	55.9%	57.8%
Blue collar	23.7%	25.2%

EMPLOYING INDUSTRIES	AREA	U.S. AVG
Largest: Healthcare & Social Assistance		
Percent manufacturing	13.1%	15.4%
Percent public sector	18.0%	15.7%
Percent construction	10.6%	9.9%

Cost of Living
Score: 95.2
Rank: 18

INDEXES & TAXES	AREA	U.S. AVG
Cost of Living Index	80.5	100.0
Buying Power Index	104.8	100.0
Income tax rate	0.00%	4.70%
Sales tax rate	8.23%	6.58%
Property tax rate	$12.73	$12.00

HOUSING	AREA	U.S. AVG
Median home price	$121,900	$220,000
Home price appreciation	31.8%	10.1%
Median rent	$578	$709
Homes owned	57.8%	62.3%
Home price ratio	3.2	4.2

NECESSITIES	AREA	U.S. AVG
Food Index	88.6	100.0
Housing Index	49.5	100.0
Utilities Index	82.1	100.0
Transportation Index	98.7	100.0
Healthcare Index	98.8	100.0
Miscellaneous Cost Index	103.0	100.0

Climate
Score: 93.6
Rank: 25

TEMPERATURE	AREA	U.S. AVG
Average January low	32.0	26.2
Average July high	95.0	87.4
Annual days > 90°F	109	38
Annual days < 32°F	50	89
Annual days < 0°F	0	6

PRECIPITATION	AREA	U.S. AVG
Annual inches precipitation	19.0	37.7
Annual inches snowfall	3.0	7.0
Annual days precipitation	58	109
Annual days rain > 0.5 inches	12	22
Annual days snow > 1.5 inches	2	6

COMFORTS & HAZARDS	AREA	U.S. AVG
July relative humidity	57%	66%
Annual days mostly sunny	254	208
Annual days with thunderstorms	37	39
Tornado risk score	20	18
Hurricane risk score	2	13

TEMPERATURE

PRECIPITATION

DAYS OF CLOUDS & PRECIPITATION

Education
Score: 35.0
Rank: 244

ACHIEVEMENT	AREA	U.S. AVG
High school degree	76.9%	82.7%
2-year college degree	5.2%	6.4%
4-year college degree	14.5%	15.7%
Graduate/professional degree	5.6%	8.9%

PUBLIC SCHOOLS	AREA	U.S. AVG
Expenditures per pupil	$6,661	$5,686
Student/teacher ratio	13.4	16.7
Attending public school	96.2%	90.1%
State SAT score	997*	1021
State ACT score	20.3	20.9

HIGHER EDUCATION	AREA	U.S. AVG
No. 2-year colleges	0	4
No. 4-year colleges/universities	1	6
No. highly ranked universities	0	1

Health & Healthcare
Score: 94.9
Rank: 20

HAZARDS & ILLNESSES	AREA	U.S. AVG
Air-quality score	48	37
Water-quality score	100	52
Pollen/allergy score	79	61
Cancer mortality per capita	152.9	201.9
Depression days per month	1.6	3.5
Stress score	45	50

HEALTHCARE	AREA	U.S. AVG
Physicians per capita	197.5	244.2
Hospital beds per capita	789.6	420.0
No. teaching hospitals	0	3
Cost per doctor visit	$78	$77
Cost per dental visit	$57	$70

Crime
Score: 28.1
Rank: 269

CRIME	AREA	U.S. AVG
Violent crime rate	373.9	465.5
Change in violent crime rate	-10.3%	-2.2%
Property crime rate	5,327.9	3,517.1
Change in property crime rate	-8.4%	-2.1%

Transportation
Score: 51.9
Rank: 181

COMMUTE	AREA	U.S. AVG
Average commute time	19.2	27.4
Percent commutes > 60 mins.	3.7%	5.9%
Commute by auto	79.5%	78.9%
Commute by mass transit	0.4%	1.9%
Work at home	2.2%	3.1%
Mass transit miles per capita	0.38	1.87

INTERCITY SERVICES	AREA	U.S. AVG
Major airports within 60 miles	0	1
Size of regional airport	None	Large
Daily airline activity	15	686
Amtrak service	No	No

AUTOMOTIVE	AREA	U.S. AVG
Insurance, annual premium	$1,066	$1,432
Gas, cost per gallon	$2.44	$2.49
Daily vehicle miles per capita	14.7	24.0

Leisure Score: 18.4 Rank: 304	DINING & SHOPPING	AREA	U.S. AVG	ENTERTAINMENT	AREA	U.S. AVG	OUTDOOR ACTIVITIES	AREA	U.S. AVG
	Restaurant rating	1	2	Professional sports rating	3	4	Golf-course rating	1	4
	Outlet mall score	0	42	College sports rating	4	4	Ski-area rating	1	3
	No. Starbucks	1	13	Zoo/aquarium rating	1	3	Sq. miles inland water	3	4
	No. warehouse clubs	0	2	Amusement park rating	1	3	Miles of coastline	0.0	10.7
				Botanical garden/ arboretum rating	1	4	National Park rating	1	3

Arts & Culture Score: 32.1 Rank: 254	MEDIA & LIBRARIES	AREA	U.S. AVG	PERFORMING ARTS	AREA	U.S. AVG	MUSEUMS	AREA	U.S. AVG
	Arts radio rating	1	3	Classical music rating	3	4	Overall museum rating	3	5
	No. public libraries	4	27	Ballet/dance rating	1	3	Art museum rating	4	5
	Library volumes per capita	2.85	2.78	Professional theater rating	1	3	Science museum rating	1	5
				University arts programs rating	3	5	Children's museum rating	2	3

San Antonio, TX

Score: 78.9 Rank: 51 2004 rank: 93

Profile: Large city
Location: South-central Texas
Elevation: 794 feet
Time zone: Central Standard Time

PRO	CON
Strong economy	Growth and sprawl
Attractive downtown	Crime rates
Entertainment	Summer heat

San Antonio, a modern city with a distinct cross-cultural and Hispanic influence, is the third-largest city in Texas and has grown to become the eighth largest in the United States. Most of the downtown area is attractive with modern skyscrapers intermingled with historic sites, including the Alamo and the Spanish Governors Palace. The Paseo del Rio, or River Walk, contains shops and sidewalk cafes along the San Antonio River, and downtown entertainment is lively and a popular destination. The winning of the Mexican War in the 19th century opened up large areas particularly north and east of town for agriculture and settlement, which at the time gave rise to such towns as New Braunfels and San Marcos, adding many European immigrants and especially Germans to the mix. The best suburbs spread in this direction from the center city, with excellent housing values, schools, and neighborhoods. These include Hollywood Park, the older and more upscale Hill Country Village, and numerous developments northeast of the State Route 1604 beltway. The sheer distance to some of these outer suburbs has brought some of the traffic and commute problems one might expect. Unfortunately, other inner neighborhoods and some suburbs extending in other directions have not fared as well economically and have a reputation for high crime.

Although the city has a laid-back character, there is a substantial business community that includes the headquarters of SBC Communications (AT&T), Valero Energy, Tesoro Petroleum (oil and gas), Clear Channel Communications, and a strong banking and financial presence. Future job-growth projections are strong at 21.5%. The South Texas Medical Center is one of the largest in the state, with a substantial medical and biotech research component. Four nearby Air Force facilities bring a strong military presence. The city has a full complement of museums and cultural assets, sports teams (notably the NBA San Antonio Spurs), transportation facilities, and entertainment venues. These advantages are accompanied by a strong economy, low cost of living (especially for a sizable and complete city), and a favorable winter climate. Better planning than most Texas cities has allowed San Antonio to avoid some growth-related issues, but it still faces challenges.

Located on the San Antonio River in a flat to gently rolling area, the city sits at the border of the coastal plain to the southeast and the hill country to the northwest. Temperatures are in the 50s in January, and above 90°F more than 80% of the time in midsummer. Precipitation is fairly well distributed throughout the year, with the heaviest amounts occurring from May to September. Summer rain usually occurs as thunderstorms and most winter precipitation occurs as light rain or drizzle. Measurable snow occurs only once every 3 or 4 years. Tropical storms occasionally affect the city.

Population	DEMOGRAPHICS	AREA	U.S. AVG	ETHNIC COMPOSITION	AREA	U.S. AVG	RESIDENT PROFILE	AREA	U.S. AVG
	Population	1,863,789		White	71.1%	79.0%	Single	31.6%	32.4%
	Population density per sq. mile	253.9	358.5	Black	5.8%	10.5%	Married	52.2%	52.7%
	Population growth	34.0%	21.1%	Asian	1.5%	2.7%	Divorced/separated	16.2%	14.9%
	Median age	33.4	36.1	Hispanic	52.8%	10.6%	Married with children	26.2%	23.7%
	Percent Democrat	40.9%	44.5%	Religious observance	62.6%	48.9%	Single with children	10.5%	9.1%
	Percent Republican	58.4%	54.5%	Diversity measure	71.0	40.1	Percent over age 65	10.9%	12.9%

Economy & Jobs Score: 87.2 Rank: 48	INCOME	AREA	U.S. AVG	EMPLOYMENT	AREA	U.S. AVG	EMPLOYING INDUSTRIES	AREA	U.S. AVG
	Per capita income	$21,278	$23,235	Unemployment rate	5.0%	4.7%	Largest: Healthcare & Social Assistance		
	Household income	$44,934	$46,414	Recent job growth	3.0%	1.3%			
	Household income < $25K	26.4%	26.2%	Projected future job growth	21.5%	11.5%	Percent manufacturing	10.9%	15.4%
	Household income > $75K	24.6%	25.4%	White collar	62.3%	57.8%	Percent public sector	16.6%	15.7%
	Household income growth	15.0%	13.6%	Blue collar	21.6%	25.2%	Percent construction	10.7%	9.9%

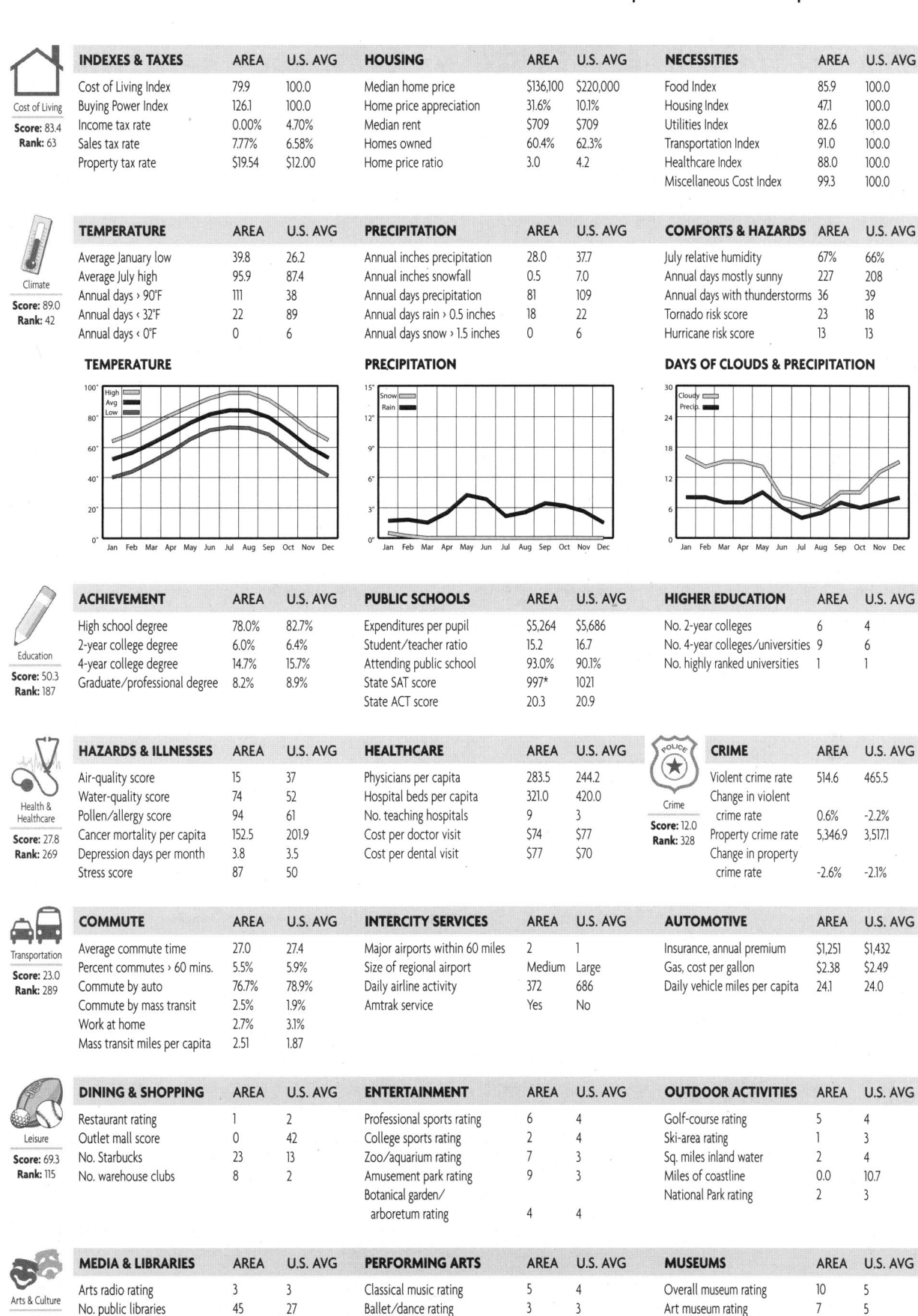

Cost of Living
Score: 83.4
Rank: 63

INDEXES & TAXES	AREA	U.S. AVG	HOUSING	AREA	U.S. AVG	NECESSITIES	AREA	U.S. AVG
Cost of Living Index	79.9	100.0	Median home price	$136,100	$220,000	Food Index	85.9	100.0
Buying Power Index	126.1	100.0	Home price appreciation	31.6%	10.1%	Housing Index	47.1	100.0
Income tax rate	0.00%	4.70%	Median rent	$709	$709	Utilities Index	82.6	100.0
Sales tax rate	7.77%	6.58%	Homes owned	60.4%	62.3%	Transportation Index	91.0	100.0
Property tax rate	$19.54	$12.00	Home price ratio	3.0	4.2	Healthcare Index	88.0	100.0
						Miscellaneous Cost Index	99.3	100.0

Climate
Score: 89.0
Rank: 42

TEMPERATURE	AREA	U.S. AVG	PRECIPITATION	AREA	U.S. AVG	COMFORTS & HAZARDS	AREA	U.S. AVG
Average January low	39.8	26.2	Annual inches precipitation	28.0	37.7	July relative humidity	67%	66%
Average July high	95.9	87.4	Annual inches snowfall	0.5	7.0	Annual days mostly sunny	227	208
Annual days > 90°F	111	38	Annual days precipitation	81	109	Annual days with thunderstorms	36	39
Annual days < 32°F	22	89	Annual days rain > 0.5 inches	18	22	Tornado risk score	23	18
Annual days < 0°F	0	6	Annual days snow > 1.5 inches	0	6	Hurricane risk score	13	13

TEMPERATURE

PRECIPITATION

DAYS OF CLOUDS & PRECIPITATION

Education
Score: 50.3
Rank: 187

ACHIEVEMENT	AREA	U.S. AVG	PUBLIC SCHOOLS	AREA	U.S. AVG	HIGHER EDUCATION	AREA	U.S. AVG
High school degree	78.0%	82.7%	Expenditures per pupil	$5,264	$5,686	No. 2-year colleges	6	4
2-year college degree	6.0%	6.4%	Student/teacher ratio	15.2	16.7	No. 4-year colleges/universities	9	6
4-year college degree	14.7%	15.7%	Attending public school	93.0%	90.1%	No. highly ranked universities	1	1
Graduate/professional degree	8.2%	8.9%	State SAT score	997*	1021			
			State ACT score	20.3	20.9			

Health & Healthcare
Score: 27.8
Rank: 269

Crime
Score: 12.0
Rank: 328

HAZARDS & ILLNESSES	AREA	U.S. AVG	HEALTHCARE	AREA	U.S. AVG	CRIME	AREA	U.S. AVG
Air-quality score	15	37	Physicians per capita	283.5	244.2	Violent crime rate	514.6	465.5
Water-quality score	74	52	Hospital beds per capita	321.0	420.0	Change in violent crime rate	0.6%	-2.2%
Pollen/allergy score	94	61	No. teaching hospitals	9	3	Property crime rate	5,346.9	3,517.1
Cancer mortality per capita	152.5	201.9	Cost per doctor visit	$74	$77	Change in property crime rate	-2.6%	-2.1%
Depression days per month	3.8	3.5	Cost per dental visit	$77	$70			
Stress score	87	50						

Transportation
Score: 23.0
Rank: 289

COMMUTE	AREA	U.S. AVG	INTERCITY SERVICES	AREA	U.S. AVG	AUTOMOTIVE	AREA	U.S. AVG
Average commute time	27.0	27.4	Major airports within 60 miles	2	1	Insurance, annual premium	$1,251	$1,432
Percent commutes > 60 mins.	5.5%	5.9%	Size of regional airport	Medium	Large	Gas, cost per gallon	$2.38	$2.49
Commute by auto	76.7%	78.9%	Daily airline activity	372	686	Daily vehicle miles per capita	24.1	24.0
Commute by mass transit	2.5%	1.9%	Amtrak service	Yes	No			
Work at home	2.7%	3.1%						
Mass transit miles per capita	2.51	1.87						

Leisure
Score: 69.3
Rank: 115

DINING & SHOPPING	AREA	U.S. AVG	ENTERTAINMENT	AREA	U.S. AVG	OUTDOOR ACTIVITIES	AREA	U.S. AVG
Restaurant rating	1	2	Professional sports rating	6	4	Golf-course rating	5	4
Outlet mall score	0	42	College sports rating	2	4	Ski-area rating	1	3
No. Starbucks	23	13	Zoo/aquarium rating	7	3	Sq. miles inland water	2	4
No. warehouse clubs	8	2	Amusement park rating	9	3	Miles of coastline	0.0	10.7
			Botanical garden/ arboretum rating	4	4	National Park rating	2	3

Arts & Culture
Score: 69.0
Rank: 116

MEDIA & LIBRARIES	AREA	U.S. AVG	PERFORMING ARTS	AREA	U.S. AVG	MUSEUMS	AREA	U.S. AVG
Arts radio rating	3	3	Classical music rating	5	4	Overall museum rating	10	5
No. public libraries	45	27	Ballet/dance rating	3	3	Art museum rating	7	5
Library volumes per capita	1.49	2.78	Professional theater rating	1	3	Science museum rating	8	5
			University arts programs rating	9	5	Children's museum rating	3	3

San Diego–Carlsbad–San Marcos, CA   Score: 71.1   Rank: 83   2004 rank: 74

Profile: Large-coastal-city complex
Location: Southern California coast, 120 miles south of Los Angeles and 20 miles north of Mexican border
Elevation: 28 feet
Time zone: Pacific Standard Time

PRO	CON
Year-round climate	Rapid cost increases
Recreation	Growth and sprawl
Attractive suburbs	Air quality

So far as evaluating cities goes, the complex San Diego area presents one of our greatest challenges. Those that have been there know—the endearing ocean-moderated Southern California climate is hard to beat and enables year-round enjoyment of the area's many outdoor amenities and activities. The economy has typically been strong, even against the backdrop of some of the high-tech and other woes facing California cities. The city is well endowed with arts and recreational amenities; those visiting wished they lived there just so they'd have time to take advantage of it all. So why isn't San Diego closer to the top of our list?

Inevitably that which makes the area nice has drawn the crowds—retirees, overseas and domestic migrants, migrants from other parts of California. Inevitably such an influx drives up prices and drives down quality of life—and nowhere have we seen this effect like we've seen it here. Median home prices have skyrocketed from $379,300 to $613,100 in just 3 years, and what you (don't) get for that price is shocking. The cost of living, once a relative bargain for a California coastal city, is no longer. Commute times have risen and air-quality problems have worsened. The future job-growth projection, once a big plus, has dropped 5% since our last edition as the cost of doing business escalates and more activity is moved to cheaper locations or offshore. The area has gained some notoriety for municipal government scandal and real estate speculation; it just isn't the quiet, prosperous seaside city it once was.

All this said, the San Diego area still has a lot to offer. Downtown is a mix of modern and old Mission-style architecture, pleasant but nondescript with a nice waterfront area dominated by hospitality activities. Balboa Park just to the north is an urban treasure. San Diego Bay and Mission Bay offer excellent boating and water recreation, and Sea World and the San Diego Zoo are nationally famous. Farther to the north along the coast, La Jolla is a classic and attractive if expensive beach enclave. Residential areas have grown to the north along State Route 163 and Interstate 15 in places such as Poway and Rancho Bernardo. Still farther north along the coast lies the entertainment, shopping, and retirement seaside town of Carlsbad, pleasant but expensive, and San Marcos lies inland near the more famous desert retirement enclave of Escondido. Most of these communities are very attractive, but demand and geographic limitations have raised prices considerably. A number of companies, particularly in high tech, have located facilities in these northern areas avoiding the need to commute downtown, or, worse, across the area's mountain ranges. Areas to the south toward Mexico have a working-class character. Cost of living is now 170.5, up from 157 3 years ago, and in the 110 to 120 range at the beginning of the decade. Travel downtown and to the airport is easy at all but the worst times, and suburban roadways are generally well planned and devoid of major traffic bottlenecks. As San Diego evolves, it offers a similar good-with-the-bad proposition—maybe just a bit more tilted towards good—as offered by California's other attractive places.

San Diego itself is located on a narrow coastal plain giving way to desert foothills to the east and north. Local vegetation is sparse coastal bush and grasses, with desert scrub inland. The strong Pacific influence creates cool summers and warm winters in comparison with other places at the same latitude. The climate varies according to proximity to the coast. Temperatures below freezing are rare, while desert-influenced temperatures above 90°F or even 100°F do occur, generally inland. Desert winds bring the highest temperatures during early fall. Most precipitation falls in winter but there may be an occasional thunderstorm or tropical rain. Morning ocean-borne low clouds (called "fog" or "June gloom" locally) occur in summer but usually dissipate by afternoon. Humidity is low and sunshine is plentiful for a marine location.

DEMOGRAPHICS	AREA	U.S. AVG	ETHNIC COMPOSITION	AREA	U.S. AVG	RESIDENT PROFILE	AREA	U.S. AVG
Population	2,998,625		White	64.8%	79.0%	Single	35.1%	32.4%
Population density per sq. mile	714.0	358.5	Black	5.4%	10.5%	Married	48.4%	52.7%
Population growth	20.0%	21.1%	Asian	9.7%	2.7%	Divorced/separated	16.5%	14.9%
Median age	34.4	36.1	Hispanic	29.5%	10.6%	Married with children	24.9%	23.7%
Percent Democrat	46.4%	44.5%	Religious observance	43.7%	48.9%	Single with children	8.9%	9.1%
Percent Republican	52.5%	54.5%	Diversity measure	73.5	40.1	Percent over age 65	11.0%	12.9%

INCOME	AREA	U.S. AVG	EMPLOYMENT	AREA	U.S. AVG	EMPLOYING INDUSTRIES	AREA	U.S. AVG
Per capita income	$26,675	$23,235	Unemployment rate	4.4%	4.7%	Largest: Professional, Scientific & Technical Services		
Household income	$55,170	$46,414	Recent job growth	3.0%	1.3%			
Household income < $25K	20.2%	26.2%	Projected future job growth	18.4%	11.5%	Percent manufacturing	9.8%	15.4%
Household income > $75K	34.6%	25.4%	White collar	65.1%	57.8%	Percent public sector	16.0%	15.7%
Household income growth	17.2%	13.6%	Blue collar	18.3%	25.2%	Percent construction	8.5%	9.9%

Economy & Jobs
Score: 58.0
Rank: 158

INDEXES & TAXES	AREA	U.S. AVG	HOUSING	AREA	U.S. AVG	NECESSITIES	AREA	U.S. AVG
Cost of Living Index	170.5	100.0	Median home price	$613,100	$220,000	Food Index	113.3	100.0
Buying Power Index	72.5	100.0	Home price appreciation	114.5%	10.1%	Housing Index	226.4	100.0
Income tax rate	6.00%	4.70%	Median rent	$1,205	$709	Utilities Index	126.3	100.0
Sales tax rate	7.75%	6.58%	Homes owned	53.0%	62.3%	Transportation Index	113.3	100.0
Property tax rate	$7.97	$12.00	Home price ratio	11.1	4.2	Healthcare Index	128.4	100.0
						Miscellaneous Cost Index	104.3	100.0

Cost of Living
Score: 1.1
Rank: 369

Climate
Score: 96.8
Rank: 13

TEMPERATURE	AREA	U.S. AVG
Average January low	45.8	26.2
Average July high	77.3	87.4
Annual days > 90°F	3	38
Annual days < 32°F	0	89
Annual days < 0°F	0	6

PRECIPITATION	AREA	U.S. AVG
Annual inches precipitation	9.0	37.7
Annual inches snowfall	0.0	7.0
Annual days precipitation	41	109
Annual days rain > 0.5 inches	5	22
Annual days snow > 1.5 inches	0	6

COMFORTS & HAZARDS	AREA	U.S. AVG
July relative humidity	68%	66%
Annual days mostly sunny	267	208
Annual days with thunderstorms	3	39
Tornado risk score	5	18
Hurricane risk score	3	13

TEMPERATURE

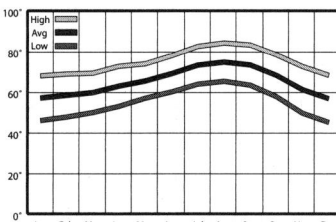

PRECIPITATION

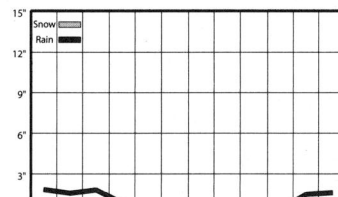

DAYS OF CLOUDS & PRECIPITATION

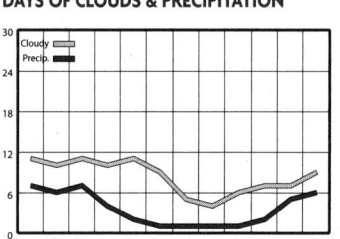

Education
Score: 85.6
Rank: 55

ACHIEVEMENT	AREA	U.S. AVG
High school degree	82.5%	82.7%
2-year college degree	7.6%	6.4%
4-year college degree	18.9%	15.7%
Graduate/professional degree	10.9%	8.9%

PUBLIC SCHOOLS	AREA	U.S. AVG
Expenditures per pupil	$5,444	$5,686
Student/teacher ratio	20.5	16.7
Attending public school	90.8%	90.1%
State SAT score	1019*	1021
State ACT score	21.6	20.9

HIGHER EDUCATION	AREA	U.S. AVG
No. 2-year colleges	18	4
No. 4-year colleges/universities	24	6
No. highly ranked universities	2	1

Health &
Healthcare
Score: 5.9
Rank: 351

HAZARDS & ILLNESSES	AREA	U.S. AVG
Air-quality score	1	37
Water-quality score	75	52
Pollen/allergy score	66	61
Cancer mortality per capita	161.8	201.9
Depression days per month	3.1	3.5
Stress score	43	50

HEALTHCARE	AREA	U.S. AVG
Physicians per capita	266.0	244.2
Hospital beds per capita	243.3	420.0
No. teaching hospitals	7	3
Cost per doctor visit	$84	$77
Cost per dental visit	$92	$70

POLICE
Crime
Score: 59.1
Rank: 154

CRIME	AREA	U.S. AVG
Violent crime rate	469.3	465.5
Change in violent crime rate	0.2%	-2.2%
Property crime rate	3,307.9	3,517.1
Change in property crime rate	0.7%	-2.1%

Transportation
Score: 48.4
Rank: 194

COMMUTE	AREA	U.S. AVG
Average commute time	27.4	27.4
Percent commutes > 60 mins.	6.4%	5.9%
Commute by auto	74.1%	78.9%
Commute by mass transit	3.3%	1.9%
Work at home	4.4%	3.1%
Mass transit miles per capita	3.34	1.87

INTERCITY SERVICES	AREA	U.S. AVG
Major airports within 60 miles	3	1
Size of regional airport	Large	Large
Daily airline activity	677	686
Amtrak service	Yes	No

AUTOMOTIVE	AREA	U.S. AVG
Insurance, annual premium	$2,780	$1,432
Gas, cost per gallon	$2.72	$2.49
Daily vehicle miles per capita	24.4	24.0

Leisure
Score: 95.5
Rank: 18

DINING & SHOPPING	AREA	U.S. AVG
Restaurant rating	1	2
Outlet mall score	196	42
No. Starbucks	149	13
No. warehouse clubs	11	2

ENTERTAINMENT	AREA	U.S. AVG
Professional sports rating	5	4
College sports rating	5	4
Zoo/aquarium rating	10	3
Amusement park rating	9	3
Botanical garden/ arboretum rating	10	4

OUTDOOR ACTIVITIES	AREA	U.S. AVG
Golf-course rating	7	4
Ski-area rating	9	3
Sq. miles inland water	5	4
Miles of coastline	54.1	10.7
National Park rating	9	3

Arts & Culture
Score: 87.4
Rank: 48

MEDIA & LIBRARIES	AREA	U.S. AVG
Arts radio rating	7	3
No. public libraries	80	27
Library volumes per capita	2.16	2.78

PERFORMING ARTS	AREA	U.S. AVG
Classical music rating	6	4
Ballet/dance rating	6	3
Professional theater rating	10	3
University arts programs rating	9	5

MUSEUMS	AREA	U.S. AVG
Overall museum rating	10	5
Art museum rating	9	5
Science museum rating	10	5
Children's museum rating	8	3

Sandusky, OH

Profile: Small port town
Location: Northern Ohio, along southern shore of Lake Erie
Elevation: 597 feet
Time zone: Eastern Standard Time

PRO
Recreational amenities
Central location
Diverse industry

CON
Industrial areas
Winter climate
Low educational attainment

Sandusky is an old port town on the southern shore of Lake Erie, traditionally with strong ties to the steel industry. The area has evolved into a major recreation and entertainment destination with offshore islands and bays and the famed Cedar Point amusement park. While there is still plenty of industry, not only related to steel but also manufacturing of machinery, paint, food processing, and plastics, the area has become more desirable and livable. Downtown has gone through considerable renewal and is attractive and clean with some historic interest. There is a new waterfront park and redevelopment zone.

At approximately 60 miles from both Cleveland to the east and Toledo to the west along the Ohio Turnpike, big city services are easy to access.

The area lies in mainly flat coastal plain with grassland and sparse trees along Lake Erie and Sandusky Bay, giving way to mostly agricultural land to the south. Lake Erie effects moderate the continental climate, but produce considerable clouds, and precipitation at all times of the year and especially in winter. Winter snows can also be heavy with the lake effect. Summers are normally pleasant with lake breezes, thundershowers, and periods of sticky humidity when the winds don't cooperate.

Population

DEMOGRAPHICS	AREA	U.S. AVG	ETHNIC COMPOSITION	AREA	U.S. AVG	RESIDENT PROFILE	AREA	U.S. AVG
Population	78,374		White	88.5%	79.0%	Single	30.0%	32.4%
Population density per sq. mile	307.5	358.5	Black	8.4%	10.5%	Married	56.4%	52.7%
Population growth	1.9%	21.1%	Asian	0.5%	2.7%	Divorced/separated	13.6%	14.9%
Median age	40.7	36.1	Hispanic	2.3%	10.6%	Married with children	21.4%	23.7%
Percent Democrat	53.4%	44.5%	Religious observance	53.5%	48.9%	Single with children	8.7%	9.1%
Percent Republican	46.4%	54.5%	Diversity measure	24.5	40.1	Percent over age 65	16.2%	12.9%

Economy & Jobs
Score: 27.0
Rank: 273

INCOME	AREA	U.S. AVG	EMPLOYMENT	AREA	U.S. AVG	EMPLOYING INDUSTRIES	AREA	U.S. AVG
Per capita income	$24,387	$23,235	Unemployment rate	5.2%	4.7%	Largest: Manufacturing		
Household income	$47,287	$46,414	Recent job growth	0.0%	1.3%			
Household income < $25K	23.8%	26.2%	Projected future job growth	3.2%	11.5%	Percent manufacturing	23.4%	15.4%
Household income > $75K	25.5%	25.4%	White collar	51.0%	57.8%	Percent public sector	12.3%	15.7%
Household income growth	10.6%	13.6%	Blue collar	32.1%	25.2%	Percent construction	8.8%	9.9%

Cost of Living
Score: 69.5
Rank: 115

INDEXES & TAXES	AREA	U.S. AVG	HOUSING	AREA	U.S. AVG	NECESSITIES	AREA	U.S. AVG
Cost of Living Index	82.3	100.0	Median home price	$102,600	$220,000	Food Index	104.7	100.0
Buying Power Index	128.8	100.0	Home price appreciation	20.9%	10.1%	Housing Index	60.6	100.0
Income tax rate	5.28%	4.70%	Median rent	$598	$709	Utilities Index	123.9	100.0
Sales tax rate	7.00%	6.58%	Homes owned	64.1%	62.3%	Transportation Index	101.6	100.0
Property tax rate	$11.64	$12.00	Home price ratio	2.2	4.2	Healthcare Index	95.5	100.0
						Miscellaneous Cost Index	97.6	100.0

Climate
Score: 51.1
Rank: 182

TEMPERATURE	AREA	U.S. AVG	PRECIPITATION	AREA	U.S. AVG	COMFORTS & HAZARDS	AREA	U.S. AVG
Average January low	18.1	26.2	Annual inches precipitation	32.6	37.7	July relative humidity	59%	66%
Average July high	81.3	87.4	Annual inches snowfall	37.0	7.0	Annual days mostly sunny	180	208
Annual days > 90°F	14	38	Annual days precipitation	135	109	Annual days with thunderstorms	39	39
Annual days < 32°F	141	89	Annual days rain > 0.5 inches	23	22	Tornado risk score	2	18
Annual days < 0°F	6	6	Annual days snow > 1.5 inches	8	6	Hurricane risk score	1	13

TEMPERATURE

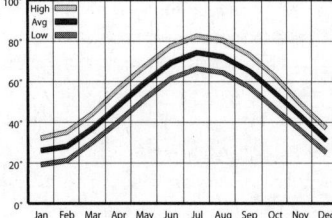

PRECIPITATION

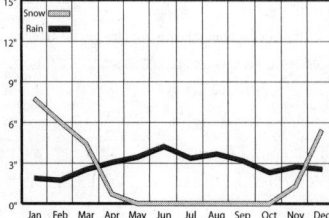

DAYS OF CLOUDS & PRECIPITATION

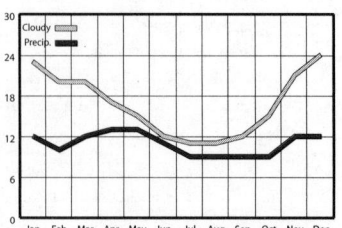

Education
Score: 32.4
Rank: 254

ACHIEVEMENT	AREA	U.S. AVG	PUBLIC SCHOOLS	AREA	U.S. AVG	HIGHER EDUCATION	AREA	U.S. AVG
High school degree	84.0%	82.7%	Expenditures per pupil	$7,203	$5,686	No. 2-year colleges	4	4
2-year college degree	5.9%	6.4%	Student/teacher ratio	18.8	16.7	No. 4-year colleges/universities	0	6
4-year college degree	11.1%	15.7%	Attending public school	93.8%	90.1%	No. highly ranked universities	0	1
Graduate/professional degree	5.7%	8.9%	State SAT score	1079	1021			
			State ACT score	21.5*	20.9			

Health & Healthcare
Score: 67.1
Rank: 124

HAZARDS & ILLNESSES	AREA	U.S. AVG	HEALTHCARE	AREA	U.S. AVG	CRIME	AREA	U.S. AVG
Air-quality score	49	37	Physicians per capita	235.0	244.2	Violent crime rate	294.8	465.5
Water-quality score	20	52	Hospital beds per capita	625.2	420.0	Change in violent crime rate	23.7%	-2.2%
Pollen/allergy score	58	61	No. teaching hospitals	1	3	Property crime rate	3,684.8	3,517.1
Cancer mortality per capita	226.3	201.9	Cost per doctor visit	$69	$77	Change in property crime rate	-5.2%	-2.1%
Depression days per month	3.7	3.5	Cost per dental visit	$61	$70			
Stress score	29	50						

Crime
Score: 70.6
Rank: 111

Transportation
Score: 96.5
Rank: 14

COMMUTE	AREA	U.S. AVG	INTERCITY SERVICES	AREA	U.S. AVG	AUTOMOTIVE	AREA	U.S. AVG
Average commute time	20.5	27.4	Major airports within 60 miles	3	1	Insurance, annual premium	$1,025	$1,432
Percent commutes › 60 mins.	4.0%	5.9%	Size of regional airport	Large	Large	Gas, cost per gallon	$2.46	$2.49
Commute by auto	88.2%	78.9%	Daily airline activity	1538	686	Daily vehicle miles per capita	15.8	24.0
Commute by mass transit	0.5%	1.9%	Amtrak service	Yes	No			
Work at home	2.4%	3.1%						
Mass transit miles per capita	0.48	1.87						

Leisure
Score: 2.7
Rank: 363

DINING & SHOPPING	AREA	U.S. AVG	ENTERTAINMENT	AREA	U.S. AVG	OUTDOOR ACTIVITIES	AREA	U.S. AVG
Restaurant rating	1	2	Professional sports rating	1	4	Golf-course rating	3	4
Outlet mall score	24	42	College sports rating	1	4	Ski-area rating	1	3
No. Starbucks	1	13	Zoo/aquarium rating	1	3	Sq. miles inland water	2	4
No. warehouse clubs	0	2	Amusement park rating	1	3	Miles of coastline	9.0	10.7
			Botanical garden/ arboretum rating	1	4	National Park rating	2	3

Arts & Culture
Score: 31.0
Rank: 258

MEDIA & LIBRARIES	AREA	U.S. AVG	PERFORMING ARTS	AREA	U.S. AVG	MUSEUMS	AREA	U.S. AVG
Arts radio rating	1	3	Classical music rating	2	4	Overall museum rating	2	5
No. public libraries	7	27	Ballet/dance rating	1	3	Art museum rating	1	5
Library volumes per capita	5.92	2.78	Professional theater rating	1	3	Science museum rating	1	5
			University arts programs rating	1	5	Children's museum rating	1	3

San Francisco–San Mateo– Redwood City, CA

Score: 72.8   Rank: 73   2004 rank: 107

Profile: Regional center
Location: Northern California coast at the head of San Francisco Bay
Elevation: 155 feet
Time zone: Pacific Standard Time

PRO
Attractive setting
Year-round climate
Arts and culture

CON
Extreme living costs
Crowding
Soft economy

A world-class city in every respect, the stunningly beautiful and culturally rich San Francisco is not only a unique place to visit but also to live. The area has a lot going for it: exceptional arts and cultural activities, plenty of history and sense of place, a strong commercial and financial core, and all the education and services anyone could want. The climate is one of the most unusual in the world, and the area is among the most ethnically and socially diverse in the country. The many world-famous tourist attractions—Fisherman's Wharf, Chinatown, the cable car system, hilltop residential enclaves, and the wine country to the north—mix with considerable local entertainment, culture, and streetscape interest to make the city one of the most interesting and fun places to live in the country.

But the city's narrow peninsula location presents an obvious problem upon a first look at a map: lack of space. There simply isn't enough room for all the people and commercial activity. The downtown area is dense, as one may expect, but the residential areas to the south are as tightly packed as any city in the United States. The result: San Francisco has the highest living and housing costs in the country. At 200.9, the Cost of Living Index is twice the national average, and median home price of $751,900 is extraordinary and almost 50% higher than 3 years ago. Many residents live in outlying areas, but these areas are still expensive and require long, difficult commutes. Fortunately, the area's excellent public transit system (spearheaded by the Bay Area Rapid Transit, or BART) helps soften the blow.

Residential communities lie mostly across the tightly packed southern hills and ridges in the city itself and in Daly City and South San Francisco, north across the Golden Gate in Marin County, east across the Bay Bridge, and south along the peninsula in such places as San Mateo, Redwood City, and Menlo Park. These "Bayshore" towns and commuter communities have built up and grown with the city, declined, and are growing again as driven by economics of the area. Foster City, located at the foot of the San Mateo Bridge commute route, is a mostly planned and new commercial and residential center built on reclaimed land, and is one of the newer and better residential areas close in. CalTrain has taken over the old Southern Pacific rail commute facilities; this route is a lifeline for these peninsula communities. Attractive urban living has emerged in a formerly waterfront industrial area just southeast of downtown near the new AT&T Park, home of the MLB San Francisco Giants. Anyone wanting to live in or near "the City" should expect a lengthy home-search process covering the many neighborhoods. Persistent job softness remains from the end of the dot-com era, and the more recent real estate boom has softened and may help bring real estate prices in line with economic opportunities. While this sounds scary, there are still plenty of career opportunities for high-paid professionals, but there is a lot of job competition. There are also plenty of other places in the Bay Area to live, but these are expensive too (see Oakland–Fremont–Hayward, p. 582; San Jose–Sunnyvale–Santa Clara, p. 692; and Santa Rosa–Petaluma, p. 703). The economy, high prices, and crowding may deter some, but those tolerant of these issues and prepared for a fascinating urban lifestyle among some of the best cultural amenities on the planet will love San Francisco.

The northern end of the peninsula containing downtown San Francisco is built up, giving away to lushly vegetated coastal mountains to the south. A long, narrow, mostly built-up plain extends along the east (bay) side of the peninsula toward San Jose. A similar topography extends north from the Golden Gate into Marin County. Geographic and strong marine influences result in the unusual climate. It is known as the "air-conditioned city" in summer, and heavy coats are worn frequently during summer in certain locations (hence the Mark Twain quip, "I spent the coldest winter of my life one summer in San Francisco"). Differences between ocean and inland temperatures and the resulting pressure gradient bring heavy sea fogs and low, ocean-born stratus clouds inland with strong sea breezes. The area probably has greater variability in temperature, cloudiness, and sunshine than any other similarly sized urban area in the country. In certain locations, hills block the fog; in others, it pours in freely, at times covering the entire area including San Jose 50 miles south. Although there is almost no summer rain, fogs often produce a chilly drizzle. Maximum summer temperatures frequently reach only the 50s. Spring and fall are relatively fog-free, and temperatures may rise into the 60s and 70s. Occasionally, early fall winds blowing from the deserts to the southeast block sea breezes and shoot temperatures into the 90s or even over 100°F. Winter temperatures are mild and consistent across the area. Eighty percent of precipitation occurs November through March. Snow may occur in the surrounding coastal mountains but melts quickly. Freezing temperatures in the city are rare.

DEMOGRAPHICS	AREA	U.S. AVG	ETHNIC COMPOSITION	AREA	U.S. AVG	RESIDENT PROFILE	AREA	U.S. AVG
Population	1,714,445		White	57.2%	79.0%	Single	41.4%	32.4%
Population density per sq. mile	1688.1	358.5	Black	4.8%	10.5%	Married	42.9%	52.7%
Population growth	6.9%	21.1%	Asian	25.1%	2.7%	Divorced/separated	15.7%	14.9%
Median age	40.0	36.1	Hispanic	17.2%	10.6%	Married with children	18.4%	23.7%
Percent Democrat	76.1%	44.5%	Religious observance	40.5%	48.9%	Single with children	5.6%	9.1%
Percent Republican	22.4%	54.5%	Diversity measure	69.6	40.1	Percent over age 65	13.9%	12.9%

Population

INCOME	AREA	U.S. AVG	EMPLOYMENT	AREA	U.S. AVG	EMPLOYING INDUSTRIES	AREA	U.S. AVG
Per capita income	$41,665	$23,235	Unemployment rate	4.6%	4.7%	Largest: Professional, Scientific & Technical Services		
Household income	$74,809	$46,414	Recent job growth	2.4%	1.3%			
Household income < $25K	15.5%	26.2%	Projected future job growth	8.3%	11.5%	Percent manufacturing	7.6%	15.4%
Household income > $75K	49.5%	25.4%	White collar	72.5%	57.8%	Percent public sector	11.3%	15.7%
Household income growth	17.4%	13.6%	Blue collar	13.4%	25.2%	Percent construction	5.9%	9.9%

Economy & Jobs
Score: 27.3
Rank: 272

INDEXES & TAXES	AREA	U.S. AVG	HOUSING	AREA	U.S. AVG	NECESSITIES	AREA	U.S. AVG
Cost of Living Index	200.9	100.0	Median home price	$751,900	$220,000	Food Index	121.3	100.0
Buying Power Index	83.5	100.0	Home price appreciation	46.7%	10.1%	Housing Index	333.6	100.0
Income tax rate	6.00%	4.70%	Median rent	$1,551	$709	Utilities Index	143.3	100.0
Sales tax rate	8.29%	6.58%	Homes owned	47.7%	62.3%	Transportation Index	129.6	100.0
Property tax rate	$5.84	$12.00	Home price ratio	10.1	4.2	Healthcare Index	166.9	100.0
						Miscellaneous Cost Index	110.2	100.0

Cost of Living
Score: 0.0
Rank: 373

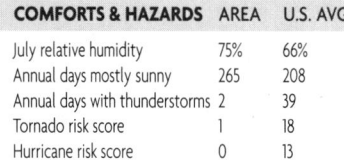

Climate
Score: 99.5
Rank: 3

TEMPERATURE	AREA	U.S. AVG	PRECIPITATION	AREA	U.S. AVG	COMFORTS & HAZARDS	AREA	U.S. AVG
Average January low	41.2	26.2	Annual inches precipitation	21.0	37.7	July relative humidity	75%	66%
Average July high	73.6	87.4	Annual inches snowfall	0.0	7.0	Annual days mostly sunny	265	208
Annual days > 90°F	1	38	Annual days precipitation	67	109	Annual days with thunderstorms	2	39
Annual days < 32°F	0	89	Annual days rain > 0.5 inches	14	22	Tornado risk score	1	18
Annual days < 0°F	0	6	Annual days snow > 1.5 inches	0	6	Hurricane risk score	0	13

TEMPERATURE

PRECIPITATION

DAYS OF CLOUDS & PRECIPITATION

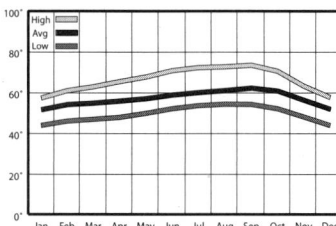

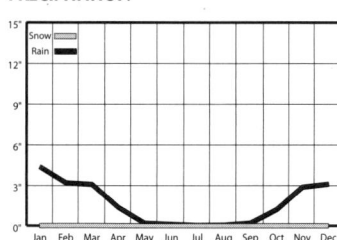

Education
Score: 92.0
Rank: 31

ACHIEVEMENT	AREA	U.S. AVG	PUBLIC SCHOOLS	AREA	U.S. AVG	HIGHER EDUCATION	AREA	U.S. AVG
High school degree	84.0%	82.7%	Expenditures per pupil	$5,661	$5,686	No. 2-year colleges	9	4
2-year college degree	6.3%	6.4%	Student/teacher ratio	18.8	16.7	No. 4-year colleges/universities	23	6
4-year college degree	27.0%	15.7%	Attending public school	77.3%	90.1%	No. highly ranked universities	2	1
Graduate/professional degree	16.0%	8.9%	State SAT score	1019*	1021			
			State ACT score	21.6	20.9			

Health & Healthcare
Score: 3.7
Rank: 359

Crime
Score: 36.6
Rank: 237

HAZARDS & ILLNESSES	AREA	U.S. AVG	HEALTHCARE	AREA	U.S. AVG	CRIME	AREA	U.S. AVG
Air-quality score	23	37	Physicians per capita	488.2	244.2	Violent crime rate	527.5	465.5
Water-quality score	45	52	Hospital beds per capita	446.0	420.0	Change in violent crime rate	7.1%	-2.2%
Pollen/allergy score	97	61	No. teaching hospitals	11	3	Property crime rate	3,523.3	3,517.1
Cancer mortality per capita	153.4	201.9	Cost per doctor visit	$94	$77	Change in property crime rate	-3.2%	-2.1%
Depression days per month	3.4	3.5	Cost per dental visit	$87	$70			
Stress score	55	50						

Transportation
Score: 87.2
Rank: 49

COMMUTE	AREA	U.S. AVG	INTERCITY SERVICES	AREA	U.S. AVG	AUTOMOTIVE	AREA	U.S. AVG
Average commute time	32.1	27.4	Major airports within 60 miles	4	1	Insurance, annual premium	$2,014	$1,432
Percent commutes > 60 mins.	10.6%	5.9%	Size of regional airport	Large	Large	Gas, cost per gallon	$2.71	$2.49
Commute by auto	57.0%	78.9%	Daily airline activity	1197	686	Daily vehicle miles per capita	22.3	24.0
Commute by mass transit	18.3%	1.9%	Amtrak service	No	No			
Work at home	4.8%	3.1%						
Mass transit miles per capita	18.33	1.87						

Leisure
Score: 98.9
Rank: 5

DINING & SHOPPING	AREA	U.S. AVG	ENTERTAINMENT	AREA	U.S. AVG	OUTDOOR ACTIVITIES	AREA	U.S. AVG
Restaurant rating	5	2	Professional sports rating	10	4	Golf-course rating	7	4
Outlet mall score	98	42	College sports rating	4	4	Ski-area rating	9	3
No. Starbucks	120	13	Zoo/aquarium rating	8	3	Sq. miles inland water	10	4
No. warehouse clubs	6	2	Amusement park rating	5	3	Miles of coastline	76.1	10.7
			Botanical garden/ arboretum rating	9	4	National Park rating	6	3

Arts & Culture
Score: 97.6
Rank: 10

MEDIA & LIBRARIES	AREA	U.S. AVG	PERFORMING ARTS	AREA	U.S. AVG	MUSEUMS	AREA	U.S. AVG
Arts radio rating	9	3	Classical music rating	10	4	Overall museum rating	10	5
No. public libraries	81	27	Ballet/dance rating	10	3.	Art museum rating	10	5
Library volumes per capita	2.95	2.78	Professional theater rating	10	3	Science museum rating	10	5
			University arts programs rating	9	5	Children's museum rating	9	3

San Jose–Sunnyvale–Santa Clara, CA

Score: 77.0   **Rank:** 58   **2004 rank:** 168

Profile: Large-city/suburban complex
Location: Northern California, on the south end of San Francisco Bay
Elevation: 67 feet
Time zone: Pacific Standard Time

PRO	CON
Year-round climate	Cost of living
Educated population	Economic cycles
Entertainment	Air quality

This large metro area covers the southern portion of the San Francisco Bay Area and is otherwise known as Santa Clara County, or more informally, as Silicon Valley. Once a quiet agricultural valley of orchards and small towns and anchored by the indistinct processing and shipping point of San Jose, the area has completely transformed over a period of 40 years into an economic and technology powerhouse and cultural crossroads between America and Asia. The small towns, which include the likes of Sunnyvale and Santa Clara, have completely grown together into a vast sprawl of residential and commercial spaces. Major high-tech manufacturers, research facilities, and an enormous array of supporting small- and medium-size businesses fill the valley, which is known for the emergence of the electronics industry and perfection of the semiconductor, the integrated circuit, the computer, and much of the software that runs on it. Several defense technology suppliers are also present. The area has a distinct high-tech culture with its own lingo and architectural style of endless long, low, glass-fronted buildings in some way mimicking the circuit boards they produce. An influx of educated workers from around the world, particularly Asia, has brought a highly diverse ethnic culture, but not all has moved in this direction. At one time, though there was hardly a smokestack visible, the area was one of the leading manufacturing centers in the country. But now the post-dot-com bust has brought a shakeout that continues to this day as manufacturing and even a lot of technology hardware and software development work has moved elsewhere—offshore in particular. While weak compared to the boom years, employment statistics have stabilized and there is even a bit of an upturn as the more successful technology companies, such as Yahoo!, eBay, Hewlett-Packard, Advanced Micro Devices, and Applied Materials, turn upward. Better focused and more successful ventures are starting to bring new capital and investment into the area after a long dot-com hangover, but all workers in the area are more sensitized to economic cycles than they were years ago.

Many settle in the area because of career opportunity and the excellent climate, and are rewarded so long as they are tolerant of crowding and high prices. Entertainment assets and cultural activities are abundant and varied, but some of the better activities fill quickly and are hard to get into. We applaud the revitalization of downtown San Jose and some if its surrounding neighborhoods. The Technology Museum of Innovation anchors the downtown core, once again a destination after years of neglect, but the demise of the San Jose Symphony suggests that all is not well. Like many recent-growth places in California, San Jose suffers from overcrowding and sprawl—in fact, neighborhoods cover buildable land in all directions and traffic along main commute corridors is horrible. Many neighborhoods built at the same time in the 1960s and 1970s are dull and uninteresting, and the abundance of rental housing has led to poor maintenance and upkeep. There is a "grinding sameness" to most of the area. That said, neighborhoods such as Los Gatos, Los Altos, and Palo Alto at the western edges adjacent to the Coastal Range foothills feature exceptional housing and appealing, small downtowns, but homes under $1 million are rare. Despite the tech-bubble contraction, costs of living and housing are still second highest in the nation. The area ranks highly because of solid assets in most ranking categories, but many of the downsides fall into the "intangibles" category, and especially for those of modest economic means, this area is probably worse than the ranking suggests.

The broad, flat valley narrows considerably but continues south toward Gilroy, which is becoming increasingly built up. Summers are clear, dry, and sunny, with normal daytime highs in the low 80s. In the evening, marine air often delivers low, stratus clouds, known locally as "fog," which typically burns off by mid-morning the next day. Light jackets are usually required in summer. The valley location and stable, summer air produce some hazy or smoggy days. Hot, desert winds sometimes blow in late summer and fall, but temperatures seldom reach 100°F. Winter is typically mild with days in the 60s and nights in the 40s, with occasional lows in the 30s or upper 20s. Winter is the rainy season; most precipitation falls when steady Pacific storms enter the area, but the coastal mountains reduce the impact.

Population

DEMOGRAPHICS	AREA	U.S. AVG	ETHNIC COMPOSITION	AREA	U.S. AVG	RESIDENT PROFILE	AREA	U.S. AVG
Population	1,764,054		White	50.4%	79.0%	Single	34.6%	32.4%
Population density per sq. mile	658.3	358.5	Black	2.5%	10.5%	Married	50.5%	52.7%
Population growth	15.3%	21.1%	Asian	28.6%	2.7%	Divorced/separated	14.9%	14.9%
Median age	36.2	36.1	Hispanic	25.6%	10.6%	Married with children	27.9%	23.7%
Percent Democrat	63.6%	44.5%	Religious observance	44.1%	48.9%	Single with children	7.2%	9.1%
Percent Republican	35.0%	54.5%	Diversity measure	77.8	40.1	Percent over age 65	10.3%	12.9%

Economy & Jobs

Score: 37.7
Rank: 233

INCOME	AREA	U.S. AVG	EMPLOYMENT	AREA	U.S. AVG	EMPLOYING INDUSTRIES	AREA	U.S. AVG
Per capita income	$36,761	$23,235	Unemployment rate	5.5%	4.7%	Largest: Manufacturing		
Household income	$84,618	$46,414	Recent job growth	1.7%	1.3%			
Household income < $25K	11.7%	26.2%	Projected future job growth	11.5%	11.5%	Percent manufacturing	11.4%	15.4%
Household income > $75K	55.6%	25.4%	White collar	70.4%	57.8%	Percent public sector	9.4%	15.7%
Household income growth	14.7%	13.6%	Blue collar	18.2%	25.2%	Percent construction	6.8%	9.9%

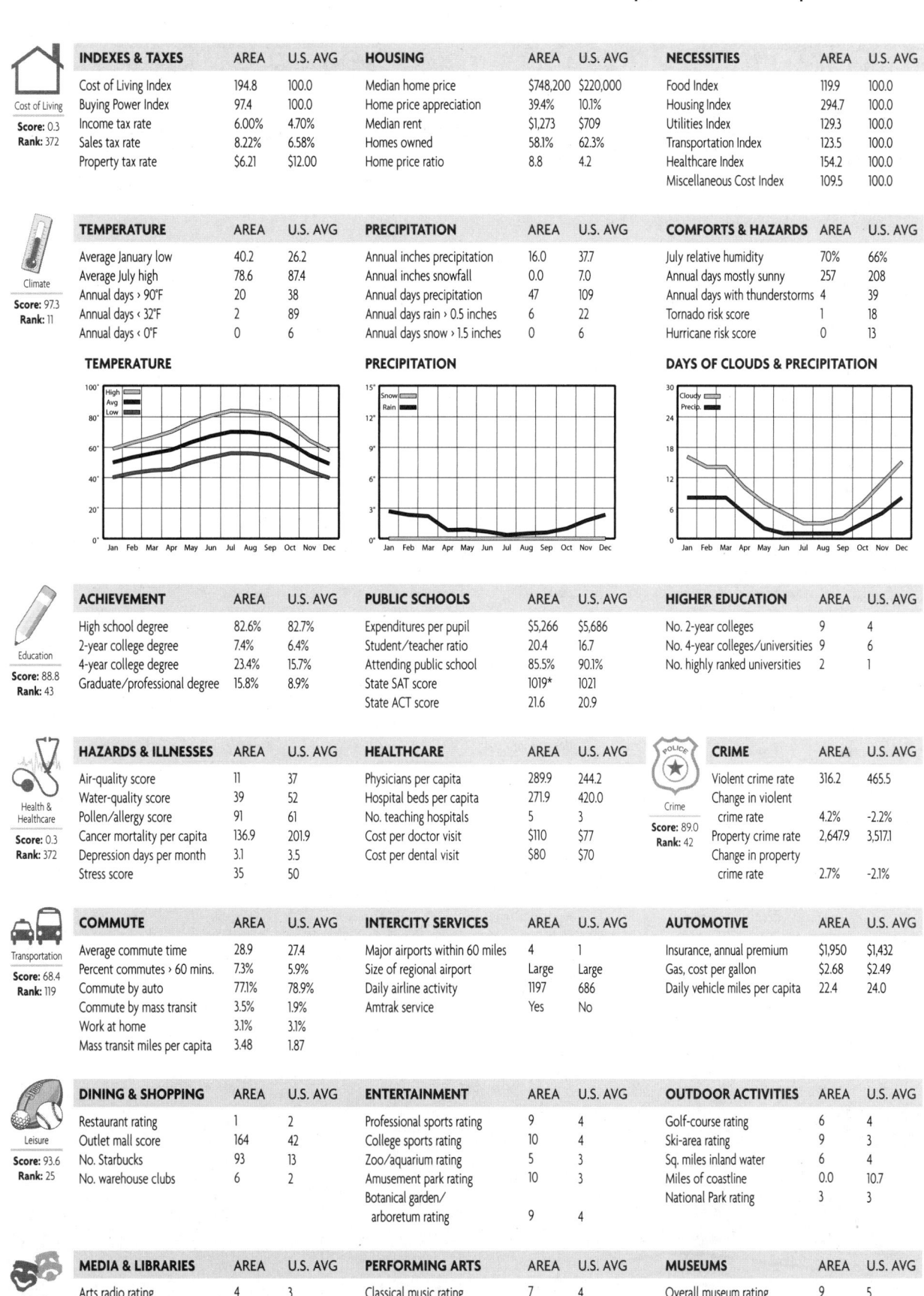

Cost of Living
Score: 0.3
Rank: 372

INDEXES & TAXES	AREA	U.S. AVG	HOUSING	AREA	U.S. AVG	NECESSITIES	AREA	U.S. AVG
Cost of Living Index	194.8	100.0	Median home price	$748,200	$220,000	Food Index	119.9	100.0
Buying Power Index	97.4	100.0	Home price appreciation	39.4%	10.1%	Housing Index	294.7	100.0
Income tax rate	6.00%	4.70%	Median rent	$1,273	$709	Utilities Index	129.3	100.0
Sales tax rate	8.22%	6.58%	Homes owned	58.1%	62.3%	Transportation Index	123.5	100.0
Property tax rate	$6.21	$12.00	Home price ratio	8.8	4.2	Healthcare Index	154.2	100.0
						Miscellaneous Cost Index	109.5	100.0

Climate
Score: 97.3
Rank: 11

TEMPERATURE	AREA	U.S. AVG	PRECIPITATION	AREA	U.S. AVG	COMFORTS & HAZARDS	AREA	U.S. AVG
Average January low	40.2	26.2	Annual inches precipitation	16.0	37.7	July relative humidity	70%	66%
Average July high	78.6	87.4	Annual inches snowfall	0.0	7.0	Annual days mostly sunny	257	208
Annual days > 90°F	20	38	Annual days precipitation	47	109	Annual days with thunderstorms	4	39
Annual days < 32°F	2	89	Annual days rain > 0.5 inches	6	22	Tornado risk score	1	18
Annual days < 0°F	0	6	Annual days snow > 1.5 inches	0	6	Hurricane risk score	0	13

TEMPERATURE

PRECIPITATION

DAYS OF CLOUDS & PRECIPITATION

Education
Score: 88.8
Rank: 43

ACHIEVEMENT	AREA	U.S. AVG	PUBLIC SCHOOLS	AREA	U.S. AVG	HIGHER EDUCATION	AREA	U.S. AVG
High school degree	82.6%	82.7%	Expenditures per pupil	$5,266	$5,686	No. 2-year colleges	9	4
2-year college degree	7.4%	6.4%	Student/teacher ratio	20.4	16.7	No. 4-year colleges/universities	9	6
4-year college degree	23.4%	15.7%	Attending public school	85.5%	90.1%	No. highly ranked universities	2	1
Graduate/professional degree	15.8%	8.9%	State SAT score	1019*	1021			
			State ACT score	21.6	20.9			

Health & Healthcare
Score: 0.3
Rank: 372

Crime
Score: 89.0
Rank: 42

HAZARDS & ILLNESSES	AREA	U.S. AVG	HEALTHCARE	AREA	U.S. AVG	CRIME	AREA	U.S. AVG
Air-quality score	11	37	Physicians per capita	289.9	244.2	Violent crime rate	316.2	465.5
Water-quality score	39	52	Hospital beds per capita	271.9	420.0	Change in violent crime rate	4.2%	-2.2%
Pollen/allergy score	91	61	No. teaching hospitals	5	3	Property crime rate	2,647.9	3,517.1
Cancer mortality per capita	136.9	201.9	Cost per doctor visit	$110	$77	Change in property crime rate	2.7%	-2.1%
Depression days per month	3.1	3.5	Cost per dental visit	$80	$70			
Stress score	35	50						

Transportation
Score: 68.4
Rank: 119

COMMUTE	AREA	U.S. AVG	INTERCITY SERVICES	AREA	U.S. AVG	AUTOMOTIVE	AREA	U.S. AVG
Average commute time	28.9	27.4	Major airports within 60 miles	4	1	Insurance, annual premium	$1,950	$1,432
Percent commutes > 60 mins.	7.3%	5.9%	Size of regional airport	Large	Large	Gas, cost per gallon	$2.68	$2.49
Commute by auto	77.1%	78.9%	Daily airline activity	1197	686	Daily vehicle miles per capita	22.4	24.0
Commute by mass transit	3.5%	1.9%	Amtrak service	Yes	No			
Work at home	3.1%	3.1%						
Mass transit miles per capita	3.48	1.87						

Leisure
Score: 93.6
Rank: 25

DINING & SHOPPING	AREA	U.S. AVG	ENTERTAINMENT	AREA	U.S. AVG	OUTDOOR ACTIVITIES	AREA	U.S. AVG
Restaurant rating	1	2	Professional sports rating	9	4	Golf-course rating	6	4
Outlet mall score	164	42	College sports rating	10	4	Ski-area rating	9	3
No. Starbucks	93	13	Zoo/aquarium rating	5	3	Sq. miles inland water	6	4
No. warehouse clubs	6	2	Amusement park rating	10	3	Miles of coastline	0.0	10.7
			Botanical garden/arboretum rating	9	4	National Park rating	3	3

Arts & Culture
Score: 84.2
Rank: 60

MEDIA & LIBRARIES	AREA	U.S. AVG	PERFORMING ARTS	AREA	U.S. AVG	MUSEUMS	AREA	U.S. AVG
Arts radio rating	4	3	Classical music rating	7	4	Overall museum rating	9	5
No. public libraries	35	27	Ballet/dance rating	9	3	Art museum rating	9	5
Library volumes per capita	2.44	2.78	Professional theater rating	9	3	Science museum rating	10	5
			University arts programs rating	8	5	Children's museum rating	9	3

San Luis Obispo–Paso Robles, CA

Score: 89.8   **Rank:** 9   **2004 rank:** 3

Profile: College town/small-town complex
Location: Central California, halfway between Los Angeles and San Francisco, 15 miles from the coast
Elevation: 238 feet
Time zone: Pacific Standard Time

PRO	CON
College-town atmosphere	Cost of living
Year-round climate	Isolation
Historic interest	Healthcare

San Luis Obispo is a charming and historic college town and home to the 18,000-student California Polytechnic University. It has resisted the development seen in other parts of the state and preserves a pleasant, off-the-beaten-path character. The interesting downtown is accessible by foot and is centered on the old Spanish mission dating from 1772. The university brings numerous arts and entertainment amenities, and the central California coastal climate is ideal. Predictably, cost of living is high, although not as high as other places in the state. The absence of a strong commercial economy makes jobs difficult to find and future job-growth projections are low but improving. While San Luis Obispo is more oriented toward students and some wealthier residents, Paso Robles and Atascadero, along U.S. 101 toward the north, are more family-oriented and not as closely tied to the university. Paso Robles is a nice old resort town and wine-growing area and a 2004 recipient of the Great American Main Street Award for its revitalization efforts. Location influences the rating positively and negatively—the town is isolated from big-city services but also big-city problems, and the area scores well in all categories except living costs and healthcare and is a continued favorite.

San Luis Obispo is located in the center of the narrow Los Osos Valley, which opens to the northwest onto scenic Morro Bay. The town is far enough inland to be warmer and drier than many coastal locations. The hills to the southwest tend to block some of the ocean-borne low, stratus clouds, resulting in mostly sunny and pleasant summer days. Very cold weather is unusual. Almost all precipitation falls in winter as rain.

Population

DEMOGRAPHICS	AREA	U.S. AVG	ETHNIC COMPOSITION	AREA	U.S. AVG	RESIDENT PROFILE	AREA	U.S. AVG
Population	257,154		White	83.9%	79.0%	Single	33.3%	32.4%
Population density per sq. mile	77.8	358.5	Black	2.0%	10.5%	Married	48.3%	52.7%
Population growth	18.5%	21.1%	Asian	2.8%	2.7%	Divorced/separated	18.5%	14.9%
Median age	37.8	36.1	Hispanic	17.7%	10.6%	Married with children	20.7%	23.7%
Percent Democrat	45.5%	44.5%	Religious observance	43.4%	48.9%	Single with children	7.4%	9.1%
Percent Republican	52.7%	54.5%	Diversity measure	49.7	40.1	Percent over age 65	14.5%	12.9%

Economy & Jobs
Score: 44.9
Rank: 205

INCOME	AREA	U.S. AVG	EMPLOYMENT	AREA	U.S. AVG	EMPLOYING INDUSTRIES	AREA	U.S. AVG
Per capita income	$25,942	$23,235	Unemployment rate	4.1%	4.7%	Largest: Healthcare & Social Assistance		
Household income	$49,528	$46,414	Recent job growth	2.4%	1.3%			
Household income < $25K	23.7%	26.2%	Projected future job growth	14.4%	11.5%	Percent manufacturing	9.8%	15.4%
Household income > $75K	30.0%	25.4%	White collar	58.5%	57.8%	Percent public sector	20.6%	15.7%
Household income growth	16.7%	13.6%	Blue collar	19.6%	25.2%	Percent construction	9.8%	9.9%

Cost of Living
Score: 4.3
Rank: 357

INDEXES & TAXES	AREA	U.S. AVG	HOUSING	AREA	U.S. AVG	NECESSITIES	AREA	U.S. AVG
Cost of Living Index	151.4	100.0	Median home price	$513,200	$220,000	Food Index	112.7	100.0
Buying Power Index	73.3	100.0	Home price appreciation	122.2%	10.1%	Housing Index	221.5	100.0
Income tax rate	6.00%	4.70%	Median rent	$955	$709	Utilities Index	114.8	100.0
Sales tax rate	7.25%	6.58%	Homes owned	56.1%	62.3%	Transportation Index	109.6	100.0
Property tax rate	$8.59	$12.00	Home price ratio	10.4	4.2	Healthcare Index	110.7	100.0
						Miscellaneous Cost Index	101.3	100.0

Climate
Score: 98.9
Rank: 5

TEMPERATURE	AREA	U.S. AVG	PRECIPITATION	AREA	U.S. AVG	COMFORTS & HAZARDS	AREA	U.S. AVG
Average January low	38.3	26.2	Annual inches precipitation	12.0	37.7	July relative humidity	74%	66%
Average July high	73.9	87.4	Annual inches snowfall	0.0	7.0	Annual days mostly sunny	285	208
Annual days > 90°F	6	38	Annual days precipitation	45	109	Annual days with thunderstorms	2	39
Annual days > 32°F	24	89	Annual days rain > 0.5 inches	8	22	Tornado risk score	0	18
Annual days < 0°F	0	6	Annual days snow > 1.5 inches	0	6	Hurricane risk score	0	13

TEMPERATURE

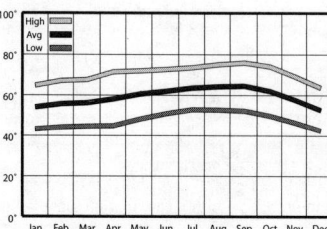

PRECIPITATION

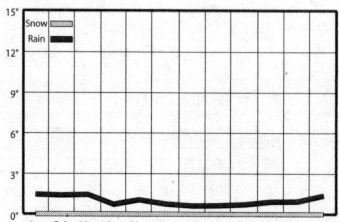

DAYS OF CLOUDS & PRECIPITATION

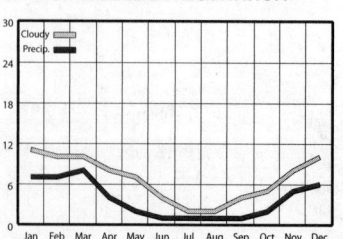

ACHIEVEMENT	AREA	U.S. AVG	PUBLIC SCHOOLS	AREA	U.S. AVG	HIGHER EDUCATION	AREA	U.S. AVG
High school degree	85.6%	82.7%	Expenditures per pupil	$5,108	$5,686	No. 2-year colleges	2	4
2-year college degree	9.2%	6.4%	Student/teacher ratio	19.4	16.7	No. 4-year colleges/universities	1	6
4-year college degree	17.4%	15.7%	Attending public school	92.6%	90.1%	No. highly ranked universities	1	1
Graduate/professional degree	9.3%	8.9%	State SAT score	1019*	1021			
			State ACT score	21.6	20.9			

Education
Score: 74.3
Rank: 97

HAZARDS & ILLNESSES	AREA	U.S. AVG	HEALTHCARE	AREA	U.S. AVG	CRIME	AREA	U.S. AVG
Air-quality score	31	37	Physicians per capita	244.9	244.2	Violent crime rate	296.6	465.5
Water-quality score	30	52	Hospital beds per capita	236.8	420.0	Change in violent crime rate	-2.3%	-2.2%
Pollen/allergy score	62	61	No. teaching hospitals	0	3	Property crime rate	2,508.0	3,517.1
Cancer mortality per capita	155.9	201.9	Cost per doctor visit	$98	$77	Change in property crime rate	-6.6%	-2.1%
Depression days per month	3.0	3.5	Cost per dental visit	$77	$70			
Stress score	21	50						

Health & Healthcare
Score: 38.0
Rank: 231

Crime
Score: 92.0
Rank: 30

COMMUTE	AREA	U.S. AVG	INTERCITY SERVICES	AREA	U.S. AVG	AUTOMOTIVE	AREA	U.S. AVG
Average commute time	22.4	27.4	Major airports within 60 miles	0	1	Insurance, annual premium	$1,176	$1,432
Percent commutes > 60 mins.	4.9%	5.9%	Size of regional airport	Small	Large	Gas, cost per gallon	$2.80	$2.49
Commute by auto	74.0%	78.9%	Daily airline activity	49	686	Daily vehicle miles per capita	17.9	24.0
Commute by mass transit	1.0%	1.9%	Amtrak service	Yes	No			
Work at home	5.7%	3.1%						
Mass transit miles per capita	0.97	1.87						

Transportation
Score: 25.4
Rank: 280

DINING & SHOPPING	AREA	U.S. AVG	ENTERTAINMENT	AREA	U.S. AVG	OUTDOOR ACTIVITIES	AREA	U.S. AVG
Restaurant rating	1	2	Professional sports rating	2	4	Golf-course rating	3	4
Outlet mall score	58	42	College sports rating	4	4	Ski-area rating	10	3
No. Starbucks	11	13	Zoo/aquarium rating	2	3	Sq. miles inland water	2	4
No. warehouse clubs	1	2	Amusement park rating	1	3	Miles of coastline	77.3	10.7
			Botanical garden/ arboretum rating	1	4	National Park rating	10	3

Leisure
Score: 75.1
Rank: 93

MEDIA & LIBRARIES	AREA	U.S. AVG	PERFORMING ARTS	AREA	U.S. AVG	MUSEUMS	AREA	U.S. AVG
Arts radio rating	5	3	Classical music rating	3	4	Overall museum rating	8	5
No. public libraries	16	27	Ballet/dance rating	1	3	Art museum rating	7	5
Library volumes per capita	2.14	2.78	Professional theater rating	1	3	Science museum rating	5	5
			University arts programs rating	5	5	Children's museum rating	1	3

Arts & Culture
Score: 70.1
Rank: 112

Santa Ana–Anaheim–Irvine, CA

Score: 76.8   Rank: 59   2004 rank: 65

Profile: Suburban complex
Location: Southern California coast, 30 miles south of Los Angeles
Elevation: 850 feet
Time zone: Pacific Standard Time

PRO
Year-round climate
Entertainment
Nearby beaches

CON
Growth and sprawl
Cost of living
Air quality

This large metro area south of Los Angeles is perhaps better known by the county it occupies: Orange County. Once primarily agricultural, the area is now a sprawling network of small cities and bedroom communities, mostly grown together to form an energetic and dynamic, if crowded, commercial and residential area. The area's explosive growth followed the opening of Disneyland in 1955 and has steadily built into more commerce, technology, international trade, and other primarily knowledge-oriented businesses. More established cities and towns include Anaheim, Costa Mesa, and Garden Grove, with downtown areas circled by "older" (meaning predominantly '50s, '60s, and '70s) residential neighborhoods. New mega-suburbs have evolved farther inland and against the bordering desert mountains, among them Mission Viejo, Rancho Santa Margarita, and Aliso Viejo. Irvine, located

adjacent to the John Wayne Airport, is probably the most modern and dominant commercial area, anchored by high-tech, banking, and similar businesses. The area also includes wealthy coastal enclaves of Huntington Beach and Newport Beach, offering plenty of weekend recreation and some employment. The area is socially and economically diverse, although to a lesser extent than Los Angeles to the north, and unlike its northern neighbor, it has a notably conservative political bent. Amenities include professional sports teams (MLB Los Angeles Angels of Anaheim and NHL Anaheim Ducks) and plenty of nightlife, restaurants, and full entertainment amenities one might expect in popular coastal areas. Over the years the area has developed its own economic base, but commuting to other parts of Los Angeles is still common, and commutes are long and complex for all but those who work in the

Irvine area. Growth and building patterns have brought unattractive cookie-cutter sprawl, and away from the coast, the area has a sameness that might get to some. Cost of living and housing costs are high even by California standards, but there is considerable variety within the area.

Most of Orange County is a broad, level coastal plain. Beaches are broad and oceans are calm and relatively warm due to the latitude and influence of Catalina Island to the west. The Santa Ana Mountains provide a dry mountainous backdrop to the east. Sea breezes keep summers pleasant, with temperatures rarely above 90°F and cool evenings. Winters are mild and mainly dry with occasional mild Pacific storms. Inland weather is more variable. Smog is persistent in summer and inland.

Population

DEMOGRAPHICS	AREA	U.S. AVG
Population	3,015,707	
Population density per sq. mile	3820.3	358.5
Population growth	25.1%	21.1%
Median age	35.0	36.1
Percent Democrat	39.0%	44.5%
Percent Republican	59.7%	54.5%

ETHNIC COMPOSITION	AREA	U.S. AVG
White	62.3%	79.0%
Black	1.7%	10.5%
Asian	15.4%	2.7%
Hispanic	32.6%	10.6%
Religious observance	44.8%	48.9%
Diversity measure	75.4	40.1

RESIDENT PROFILE	AREA	U.S. AVG
Single	33.1%	32.4%
Married	51.2%	52.7%
Divorced/separated	15.6%	14.9%
Married with children	29.0%	23.7%
Single with children	7.9%	9.1%
Percent over age 65	10.5%	12.9%

Economy & Jobs
Score: 67.4
Rank: 123

INCOME	AREA	U.S. AVG
Per capita income	$29,187	$23,235
Household income	$66,895	$46,414
Household income < $25K	14.9%	26.2%
Household income > $75K	43.7%	25.4%
Household income growth	13.7%	13.6%

EMPLOYMENT	AREA	U.S. AVG
Unemployment rate	3.9%	4.7%
Recent job growth	3.2%	1.3%
Projected future job growth	14.8%	11.5%
White collar	67.1%	57.8%
Blue collar	19.5%	25.2%

EMPLOYING INDUSTRIES	AREA	U.S. AVG
Largest: Manufacturing		
Percent manufacturing	12.3%	15.4%
Percent public sector	11.0%	15.7%
Percent construction	7.2%	9.9%

Cost of Living
Score: 0.8
Rank: 370

INDEXES & TAXES	AREA	U.S. AVG
Cost of Living Index	186.5	100.0
Buying Power Index	80.4	100.0
Income tax rate	6.00%	4.70%
Sales tax rate	7.75%	6.58%
Property tax rate	$8.28	$12.00

HOUSING	AREA	U.S. AVG
Median home price	$726,200	$220,000
Home price appreciation	130.8%	10.1%
Median rent	$1,485	$709
Homes owned	59.2%	62.3%
Home price ratio	10.9	4.2

NECESSITIES	AREA	U.S. AVG
Food Index	110.3	100.0
Housing Index	273.4	100.0
Utilities Index	112.6	100.0
Transportation Index	111.9	100.0
Healthcare Index	119.8	100.0
Miscellaneous Cost Index	105.7	100.0

Climate
Score: 98.1
Rank: 8

TEMPERATURE	AREA	U.S. AVG
Average January low	45.4	26.2
Average July high	75.8	87.4
Annual days > 90°F	5	38
Annual days < 32°F	0	89
Annual days < 0°F	0	6

PRECIPITATION	AREA	U.S. AVG
Annual inches precipitation	12.0	37.7
Annual inches snowfall	0.0	7.0
Annual days precipitation	40	109
Annual days rain > 0.5 inches	8	22
Annual days snow > 1.5 inches	0	6

COMFORTS & HAZARDS	AREA	U.S. AVG
July relative humidity	71%	66%
Annual days mostly sunny	258	208
Annual days with thunderstorms	3	39
Tornado risk score	16	18
Hurricane risk score	2	13

TEMPERATURE

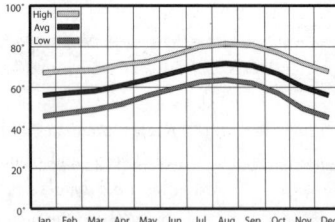

PRECIPITATION

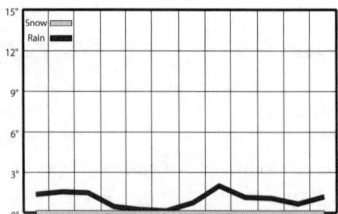

DAYS OF CLOUDS & PRECIPITATION

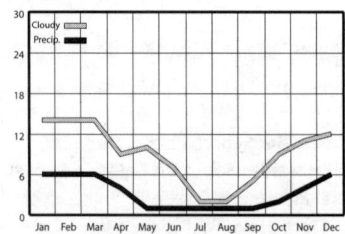

Education
Score: 79.1
Rank: 79

ACHIEVEMENT	AREA	U.S. AVG
High school degree	79.4%	82.7%
2-year college degree	7.8%	6.4%
4-year college degree	20.6%	15.7%
Graduate/professional degree	10.5%	8.9%

PUBLIC SCHOOLS	AREA	U.S. AVG
Expenditures per pupil	$4,847	$5,686
Student/teacher ratio	22.2	16.7
Attending public school	88.8%	90.1%
State SAT score	1019*	1021
State ACT score	21.6	20.9

HIGHER EDUCATION	AREA	U.S. AVG
No. 2-year colleges	14	4
No. 4-year colleges/universities	23	6
No. highly ranked universities	1	1

Health & Healthcare
Score: 16.6
Rank: 311

HAZARDS & ILLNESSES	AREA	U.S. AVG
Air-quality score	2	37
Water-quality score	65	52
Pollen/allergy score	46	61
Cancer mortality per capita	149.3	201.9
Depression days per month	3.1	3.5
Stress score	18	50

HEALTHCARE	AREA	U.S. AVG
Physicians per capita	263.2	244.2
Hospital beds per capita	264.5	420.0
No. teaching hospitals	7	3
Cost per doctor visit	$102	$77
Cost per dental visit	$73	$70

Crime
Score: 86.1
Rank: 53

CRIME	AREA	U.S. AVG
Violent crime rate	283.6	465.5
Change in violent crime rate	2.1%	-2.2%
Property crime rate	2,394.3	3,517.1
Change in property crime rate	-3.4%	-2.1%

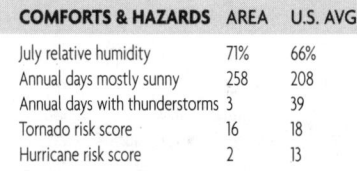

Transportation
Score: 84.0
Rank: 61

COMMUTE	AREA	U.S. AVG	INTERCITY SERVICES	AREA	U.S. AVG	AUTOMOTIVE	AREA	U.S. AVG
Average commute time	29.6	27.4	Major airports within 60 miles	4	1	Insurance, annual premium	$2,844	$1,432
Percent commutes › 60 mins.	8.5%	5.9%	Size of regional airport	Large	Large	Gas, cost per gallon	$2.70	$2.49
Commute by auto	76.6%	78.9%	Daily airline activity	1697	686	Daily vehicle miles per capita	22.5	24.0
Commute by mass transit	2.8%	1.9%	Amtrak service	Yes	No			
Work at home	3.8%	3.1%						
Mass transit miles per capita	2.78	1.87						

Leisure
Score: 98.7
Rank: 6

DINING & SHOPPING	AREA	U.S. AVG	ENTERTAINMENT	AREA	U.S. AVG	OUTDOOR ACTIVITIES	AREA	U.S. AVG
Restaurant rating	3	2	Professional sports rating	10	4	Golf-course rating	8	4
Outlet mall score	157	42	College sports rating	4	4	Ski-area rating	10	3
No. Starbucks	127	13	Zoo/aquarium rating	5	3	Sq. miles inland water	4	4
No. warehouse clubs	14	2	Amusement park rating	10	3	Miles of coastline	39.8	10.7
			Botanical garden/ arboretum rating	9	4	National Park rating	10	3

Arts & Culture
Score: 79.1
Rank: 78

MEDIA & LIBRARIES	AREA	U.S. AVG	PERFORMING ARTS	AREA	U.S. AVG	MUSEUMS	AREA	U.S. AVG
Arts radio rating	5	3	Classical music rating	5	4	Overall museum rating	10	5
No. public libraries	53	27	Ballet/dance rating	7	3	Art museum rating	9	5
Library volumes per capita	1.91	2.78	Professional theater rating	5	3	Science museum rating	10	5
			University arts programs rating	8	5	Children's museum rating	7	3

Santa Barbara–Santa Maria, CA   **Score:** 89.6   **Rank:** 11   **2004 rank:** 4

Profile: Small-city complex/college town
Location: Central California coast, 90 miles northwest of Los Angeles
Elevation: 238 feet
Time zone: Pacific Standard Time

PRO	CON
Year-round climate	Cost of living
Coastline	Home prices
Small-town atmosphere	Economy

The three major cities in Santa Barbara County, two named in the metro area, and the other one, Lompoc, no longer in the name, offer a highly contrasting set of places to live. Coastal Santa Barbara is the center of the "California Riviera"—an area of mild climate, beautiful coastline, Mediterranean architecture, laid-back ambience, and affluence. The University of California at Santa Barbara, about 10 miles north, brings a college-town element without dominating town life. Educational attainment is notably high. Santa Maria, 15 miles inland, is primarily agricultural but is growing as a residential and minor commercial center. Lompoc, on a hilly projection into the Pacific known as Point Conception, contains the Vandenberg Air Force Base, a major coastal military installation and testing facility. Lompoc has started to emerge as an attractive residential alternative to tony Santa Barbara. If it weren't for high cost of living and housing, the area would be difficult to beat in the rankings. The climate is exceptional, and the small-town ambience and attractiveness is well preserved compared to other California locations. The high Cost of Living Index of 149.9 and average home price of $499,700 statistically represent the whole county, but Santa Barbara is assuredly more expensive. Because of this, the other towns are more attractive to most migrating to the area. The location is a bit isolated, but most residents love the area if they can afford it.

Santa Barbara is on a narrow coastal plain that spreads east–west, while Santa Maria and Lompoc are located inland and to the north, respectively. Oak-studded hills surround all three. Temperatures are mild year-round, with those in summers tempered by sea breezes and cloudy mornings. Inland areas are warmer when breezes blow from the deserts to the southeast. The southerly orientation of Santa Barbara and the inland location of the other cities provide shelter from strong Pacific storms in winter. Santa Maria is far enough inland to experience temperatures of 32°F or lower several times in winter. Most precipitation occurs in winter.

Population

DEMOGRAPHICS	AREA	U.S. AVG	ETHNIC COMPOSITION	AREA	U.S. AVG	RESIDENT PROFILE	AREA	U.S. AVG
Population	408,425		White	71.6%	79.0%	Single	35.1%	32.4%
Population density per sq. mile	149.2	358.5	Black	2.1%	10.5%	Married	47.4%	52.7%
Population growth	10.4%	21.1%	Asian	4.2%	2.7%	Divorced/separated	17.5%	14.9%
Median age	34.4	36.1	Hispanic	36.9%	10.6%	Married with children	24.5%	23.7%
Percent Democrat	53.2%	44.5%	Religious observance	55.8%	48.9%	Single with children	7.9%	9.1%
Percent Republican	45.2%	54.5%	Diversity measure	70.9	40.1	Percent over age 65	12.8%	12.9%

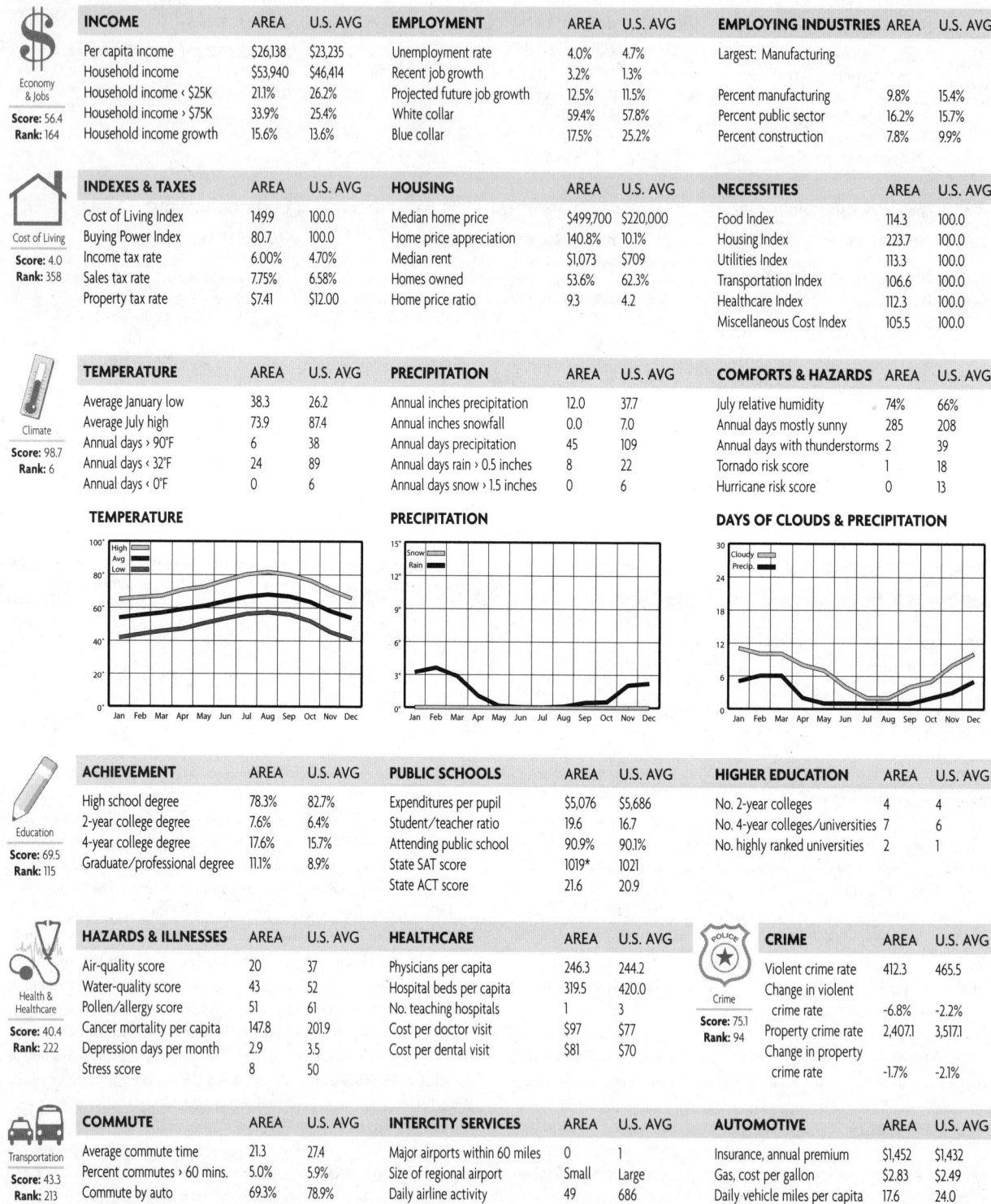

Economy & Jobs
Score: 56.4
Rank: 164

INCOME	AREA	U.S. AVG
Per capita income	$26,138	$23,235
Household income	$53,940	$46,414
Household income ‹ $25K	21.1%	26.2%
Household income › $75K	33.9%	25.4%
Household income growth	15.6%	13.6%

EMPLOYMENT	AREA	U.S. AVG
Unemployment rate	4.0%	4.7%
Recent job growth	3.2%	1.3%
Projected future job growth	12.5%	11.5%
White collar	59.4%	57.8%
Blue collar	17.5%	25.2%

EMPLOYING INDUSTRIES	AREA	U.S. AVG
Largest: Manufacturing		
Percent manufacturing	9.8%	15.4%
Percent public sector	16.2%	15.7%
Percent construction	7.8%	9.9%

Cost of Living
Score: 4.0
Rank: 358

INDEXES & TAXES	AREA	U.S. AVG
Cost of Living Index	149.9	100.0
Buying Power Index	80.7	100.0
Income tax rate	6.00%	4.70%
Sales tax rate	7.75%	6.58%
Property tax rate	$7.41	$12.00

HOUSING	AREA	U.S. AVG
Median home price	$499,700	$220,000
Home price appreciation	140.8%	10.1%
Median rent	$1,073	$709
Homes owned	53.6%	62.3%
Home price ratio	9.3	4.2

NECESSITIES	AREA	U.S. AVG
Food Index	114.3	100.0
Housing Index	223.7	100.0
Utilities Index	113.3	100.0
Transportation Index	106.6	100.0
Healthcare Index	112.3	100.0
Miscellaneous Cost Index	105.5	100.0

Climate
Score: 98.7
Rank: 6

TEMPERATURE	AREA	U.S. AVG
Average January low	38.3	26.2
Average July high	73.9	87.4
Annual days › 90°F	6	38
Annual days ‹ 32°F	24	89
Annual days ‹ 0°F	0	6

PRECIPITATION	AREA	U.S. AVG
Annual inches precipitation	12.0	37.7
Annual inches snowfall	0.0	7.0
Annual days precipitation	45	109
Annual days rain › 0.5 inches	8	22
Annual days snow › 1.5 inches	0	6

COMFORTS & HAZARDS	AREA	U.S. AVG
July relative humidity	74%	66%
Annual days mostly sunny	285	208
Annual days with thunderstorms	2	39
Tornado risk score	1	18
Hurricane risk score	0	13

TEMPERATURE

PRECIPITATION

DAYS OF CLOUDS & PRECIPITATION

Education
Score: 69.5
Rank: 115

ACHIEVEMENT	AREA	U.S. AVG
High school degree	78.3%	82.7%
2-year college degree	7.6%	6.4%
4-year college degree	17.6%	15.7%
Graduate/professional degree	11.1%	8.9%

PUBLIC SCHOOLS	AREA	U.S. AVG
Expenditures per pupil	$5,076	$5,686
Student/teacher ratio	19.6	16.7
Attending public school	90.9%	90.1%
State SAT score	1019*	1021
State ACT score	21.6	20.9

HIGHER EDUCATION	AREA	U.S. AVG
No. 2-year colleges	4	4
No. 4-year colleges/universities	7	6
No. highly ranked universities	2	1

Health & Healthcare
Score: 40.4
Rank: 222

HAZARDS & ILLNESSES	AREA	U.S. AVG
Air-quality score	20	37
Water-quality score	43	52
Pollen/allergy score	51	61
Cancer mortality per capita	147.8	201.9
Depression days per month	2.9	3.5
Stress score	8	50

HEALTHCARE	AREA	U.S. AVG
Physicians per capita	246.3	244.2
Hospital beds per capita	319.5	420.0
No. teaching hospitals	1	3
Cost per doctor visit	$97	$77
Cost per dental visit	$81	$70

Crime
Score: 75.1
Rank: 94

CRIME	AREA	U.S. AVG
Violent crime rate	412.3	465.5
Change in violent crime rate	-6.8%	-2.2%
Property crime rate	2,407.1	3,517.1
Change in property crime rate	-1.7%	-2.1%

Transportation
Score: 43.3
Rank: 213

COMMUTE	AREA	U.S. AVG
Average commute time	21.3	27.4
Percent commutes › 60 mins.	5.0%	5.9%
Commute by auto	69.3%	78.9%
Commute by mass transit	2.4%	1.9%
Work at home	4.6%	3.1%
Mass transit miles per capita	2.40	1.87

INTERCITY SERVICES	AREA	U.S. AVG
Major airports within 60 miles	0	1
Size of regional airport	Small	Large
Daily airline activity	49	686
Amtrak service	Yes	No

AUTOMOTIVE	AREA	U.S. AVG
Insurance, annual premium	$1,452	$1,432
Gas, cost per gallon	$2.83	$2.49
Daily vehicle miles per capita	17.6	24.0

Leisure Score: 77.5 Rank: 84	DINING & SHOPPING	AREA	U.S. AVG	ENTERTAINMENT	AREA	U.S. AVG	OUTDOOR ACTIVITIES	AREA	U.S. AVG
	Restaurant rating	1	2	Professional sports rating	2	4	Golf-course rating	3	4
	Outlet mall score	44	42	College sports rating	3	4	Ski-area rating	10	3
	No. Starbucks	14	13	Zoo/aquarium rating	6	3	Sq. miles inland water	2	4
	No. warehouse clubs	2	2	Amusement park rating	3	3	Miles of coastline	77.6	10.7
				Botanical garden/ arboretum rating	5	4	National Park rating	10	3

Arts & Culture Score: 66.8 Rank: 124	MEDIA & LIBRARIES	AREA	U.S. AVG	PERFORMING ARTS	AREA	U.S. AVG	MUSEUMS	AREA	U.S. AVG
	Arts radio rating	5	3	Classical music rating	3	4	Overall museum rating	7	5
	No. public libraries	15	27	Ballet/dance rating	5	3	Art museum rating	7	5
	Library volumes per capita	1.82	2.78	Professional theater rating	5	3	Science museum rating	8	5
				University arts programs rating	7	5	Children's museum rating	1	3

Santa Cruz–Watsonville, CA

Score: 55.6   Rank: 216   2004 rank: 124

Profile: Beach-town complex/small town
Location: Northern California on Pacific coast, 60 miles south of San Francisco
Elevation: 100 feet
Time zone: Pacific Standard Time

PRO	CON
Beaches and outdoor recreation	Cost of living
Year-round climate	Tourist impact
Educational attainment	Healthcare

Santa Cruz, a colorful mix of college town, beach town, and cultural center, is an attraction for hippies, yuppies, and families alike. The city is famous for its boardwalk, wide and sandy beaches, and beach amusements. Watsonville is an agricultural center inland, and Soquel and Capitola to the south are more sedate but very attractive beach towns. The University of California at Santa Cruz brings some college life, and the population in general is highly educated. Excellent outdoor recreation is available just to the north in the coastal forests and state parks of the Santa Cruz Mountains. The town of Santa Cruz itself has a nice downtown and offers plenty to do, and is a favorite weekend tourist destination for northern Californians and Bay Area residents in particular. Outside of tourism, the area has never really had a prosperous economy, and it continues to lag behind other California places.

Some make the commute over the mountains to the Bay Area, but this is a difficult commute and that economy hasn't prospered recently, either. Not surprisingly, as a coastal area, cost of living (index is 173.4) and housing ($601,500) are major downsides. Healthcare resources are sparse and expensive, but missing services are available to the north in San Jose and San Francisco.

The city lies on a narrow coastal plain at the foot of the Santa Cruz Mountains. Summers are cool and sunny when the area isn't blanketed by ocean-borne, low, stratus clouds, known locally as "fog." The area is breezy at all times, and the fog may create a chill on summer days. Spring and fall are mild and experience less fog. Winters bring a mix of fog; clear, mild days; and Pacific storms, which can be heavy.

Population	DEMOGRAPHICS	AREA	U.S. AVG	ETHNIC COMPOSITION	AREA	U.S. AVG	RESIDENT PROFILE	AREA	U.S. AVG
	Population	254,222		White	74.3%	79.0%	Single	38.0%	32.4%
	Population density per sq. mile	571.0	358.5	Black	0.9%	10.5%	Married	44.5%	52.7%
	Population growth	10.7%	21.1%	Asian	3.7%	2.7%	Divorced/separated	17.4%	14.9%
	Median age	36.6	36.1	Hispanic	28.0%	10.6%	Married with children	23.1%	23.7%
	Percent Democrat	73.0%	44.5%	Religious observance	34.5%	48.9%	Single with children	8.7%	9.1%
	Percent Republican	24.9%	54.5%	Diversity measure	65.4	40.1	Percent over age 65	10.2%	12.9%

Economy & Jobs Score: 18.7 Rank: 304	INCOME	AREA	U.S. AVG	EMPLOYMENT	AREA	U.S. AVG	EMPLOYING INDUSTRIES	AREA	U.S. AVG
	Per capita income	$30,873	$23,235	Unemployment rate	5.1%	4.7%	Largest: Healthcare & Social Assistance		
	Household income	$63,919	$46,414	Recent job growth	1.6%	1.3%			
	Household income < $25K	17.7%	26.2%	Projected future job growth	9.8%	11.5%	Percent manufacturing	9.0%	15.4%
	Household income > $75K	41.9%	25.4%	White collar	62.9%	57.8%	Percent public sector	15.4%	15.7%
	Household income growth	18.4%	13.6%	Blue collar	17.8%	25.2%	Percent construction	8.8%	9.9%

Cost of Living Score: 2.9 Rank: 362	INDEXES & TAXES	AREA	U.S. AVG	HOUSING	AREA	U.S. AVG	NECESSITIES	AREA	U.S. AVG
	Cost of Living Index	173.4	100.0	Median home price	$601,500	$220,000	Food Index	121.0	100.0
	Buying Power Index	82.6	100.0	Home price appreciation	65.6%	10.1%	Housing Index	311.8	100.0
	Income tax rate	6.00%	4.70%	Median rent	$1,359	$709	Utilities Index	129.6	100.0
	Sales tax rate	8.00%	6.58%	Homes owned	55.0%	62.3%	Transportation Index	122.6	100.0
	Property tax rate	$6.69	$12.00	Home price ratio	9.4	4.2	Healthcare Index	157.5	100.0
							Miscellaneous Cost Index	108.5	100.0

Climate
Score: 99.7
Rank: 2

TEMPERATURE	AREA	U.S. AVG
Average January low	41.2	26.2
Average July high	73.6	87.4
Annual days > 90°F	1	38
Annual days < 32°F	0	89
Annual days < 0°F	0	6

PRECIPITATION	AREA	U.S. AVG
Annual inches precipitation	21.0	37.7
Annual inches snowfall	0.0	7.0
Annual days precipitation	67	109
Annual days rain > 0.5 inches	15	22
Annual days snow > 1.5 inches	0	6

COMFORTS & HAZARDS	AREA	U.S. AVG
July relative humidity	75%	66%
Annual days mostly sunny	265	208
Annual days with thunderstorms	2	39
Tornado risk score	2	18
Hurricane risk score	0	13

TEMPERATURE

PRECIPITATION

DAYS OF CLOUDS & PRECIPITATION

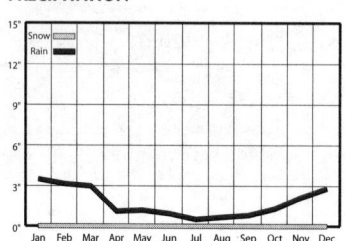
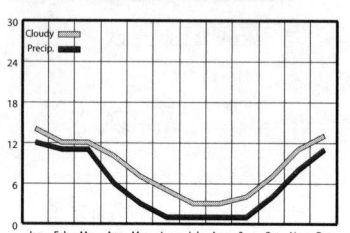

Education
Score: 77.0
Rank: 87

ACHIEVEMENT	AREA	U.S. AVG
High school degree	82.7%	82.7%
2-year college degree	7.3%	6.4%
4-year college degree	21.5%	15.7%
Graduate/professional degree	12.4%	8.9%

PUBLIC SCHOOLS	AREA	U.S. AVG
Expenditures per pupil	$4,971	$5,686
Student/teacher ratio	20.9	16.7
Attending public school	89.9%	90.1%
State SAT score	1019*	1021
State ACT score	21.6	20.9

HIGHER EDUCATION	AREA	U.S. AVG
No. 2-year colleges	1	4
No. 4-year colleges/universities	3	6
No. highly ranked universities	1	1

Health & Healthcare
Score: 1.9
Rank: 366

HAZARDS & ILLNESSES	AREA	U.S. AVG
Air-quality score	35	37
Water-quality score	29	52
Pollen/allergy score	88	61
Cancer mortality per capita	147.3	201.9
Depression days per month	2.8	3.5
Stress score	89	50

HEALTHCARE	AREA	U.S. AVG
Physicians per capita	241.7	244.2
Hospital beds per capita	159.3	420.0
No. teaching hospitals	0	3
Cost per doctor visit	$100	$77
Cost per dental visit	$76	$70

Crime
Score: 43.9
Rank: 210

CRIME	AREA	U.S. AVG
Violent crime rate	457.8	465.5
Change in violent crime rate	-2.8%	-2.2%
Property crime rate	4,064.7	3,517.1
Change in property crime rate	10.1%	-2.1%

Transportation
Score: 38.8
Rank: 230

COMMUTE	AREA	U.S. AVG
Average commute time	30.3	27.4
Percent commutes > 60 mins.	12.8%	5.9%
Commute by auto	69.3%	78.9%
Commute by mass transit	3.3%	1.9%
Work at home	5.3%	3.1%
Mass transit miles per capita	3.34	1.87

INTERCITY SERVICES	AREA	U.S. AVG
Major airports within 60 miles	3	1
Size of regional airport	Large	Large
Daily airline activity	1053	686
Amtrak service	No	No

AUTOMOTIVE	AREA	U.S. AVG
Insurance, annual premium	$1,556	$1,432
Gas, cost per gallon	$2.68	$2.49
Daily vehicle miles per capita	19.7	24.0

Leisure
Score: 89.3
Rank: 41

DINING & SHOPPING	AREA	U.S. AVG
Restaurant rating	1	2
Outlet mall score	186	42
No. Starbucks	7	13
No. warehouse clubs	1	2

ENTERTAINMENT	AREA	U.S. AVG
Professional sports rating	9	4
College sports rating	6	4
Zoo/aquarium rating	3	3
Amusement park rating	9	3
Botanical garden/ arboretum rating	9	4

OUTDOOR ACTIVITIES	AREA	U.S. AVG
Golf-course rating	4	4
Ski-area rating	8	3
Sq. miles inland water	6	4
Miles of coastline	40.5	10.7
National Park rating	3	3

Arts & Culture
Score: 75.4
Rank: 92

MEDIA & LIBRARIES	AREA	U.S. AVG
Arts radio rating	4	3
No. public libraries	12	27
Library volumes per capita	2.36	2.78

PERFORMING ARTS	AREA	U.S. AVG
Classical music rating	6	4
Ballet/dance rating	9	3
Professional theater rating	6	3
University arts programs rating	5	5

MUSEUMS	AREA	U.S. AVG
Overall museum rating	7	5
Art museum rating	7	5
Science museum rating	10	5
Children's museum rating	6	3

Santa Fe, NM

Score: 85.3   **Rank:** 20   **2004 rank:** 2

Profile: Capital city
Location: North-central New Mexico
Elevation: 7,710 feet
Time zone: Mountain Standard Time

PRO	CON
Climate and setting	Growth and sprawl
Arts and culture	Tourist impact
Historic interest	Cost of living

Santa Fe, established almost 400 years ago, is the capital of New Mexico; a crossroads of Spanish, European, and Native American cultures; and a tourist attraction. The area's distinct architecture, lifestyle, and food are unique among American cities. Over 250 art galleries and the recently opened Georgia O'Keeffe Museum attract visitors from around the world. The historic old town—with its plaza, Palace of the Governors, Navajo craft market, and restaurants—is a tourist favorite. In summer, it can be quite crowded. Many local buildings, including homes in wealthier residential areas in the hills to the north, are built in a distinct "Santa Fe" style, which resembles historic Spanish and Pueblo Indian adobe structures and blends nicely with the landscape. Growth and development to the south of the city has been dense and is, at best, a mixed bag. Surrounding the city are more than 1.5 million acres of national forest, stunning landscapes, downhill ski areas, and historic treasures, particularly to the north. Santa Fe has long been a haven for performing and visual artists. More recently an affluent population, many retired or self-employed, has been relocating to the area, although there is little industry or commercial employment thus far. As a whole, the population is educated and wealthy. At over 7,000 feet, the city is by far the highest capital and is also the highest metropolitan statistical area in the country. The elevation may cause health problems for some, and healthcare facilities are not extensive. The cost of living and housing has continued to rise, and while not exorbitant on a national scale, was enough to drop the city to a rank of 20 from 2 in the last edition. Aside from cost and a few other, minor downsides—a few cold winter days, tourist impact, and some growth issues—Santa Fe is a stimulating and aesthetically pleasing place to live.

The city is located on a high desert plateau at the foot of the Rocky Mountains. The terrain is rolling to hilly high desert, with scrub and sagebrush vegetation and dry creeks and washes. The landscape rises to scrub-pine covered hills in the north, then to the Sangre de Cristo Mountains to the northeast and Jemez Mountains to the northwest. To the south of the city, the land slopes gently down toward lower deserts and the Rio Grande Valley. Summers bring sunny, dry, pleasant days and cool evenings. Winters are dry with relatively mild days and cold nights with below-freezing temperatures. Most winter precipitation falls as dry snow, which is seldom heavy. Much heavier snows fall in the nearby mountains. First freeze is early October; last is mid-May.

Population

DEMOGRAPHICS	AREA	U.S. AVG	ETHNIC COMPOSITION	AREA	U.S. AVG	RESIDENT PROFILE	AREA	U.S. AVG
Population	139,921		White	73.1%	79.0%	Single	32.8%	32.4%
Population density per sq. mile	73.3	358.5	Black	0.7%	10.5%	Married	48.3%	52.7%
Population growth	41.4%	21.1%	Asian	1.2%	2.7%	Divorced/separated	18.9%	14.9%
Median age	39.6	36.1	Hispanic	49.6%	10.6%	Married with children	19.9%	23.7%
Percent Democrat	71.1%	44.5%	Religious observance	49.5%	48.9%	Single with children	10.6%	9.1%
Percent Republican	27.9%	54.5%	Diversity measure	71.6	40.1	Percent over age 65	12.0%	12.9%

Economy & Jobs
Score: 84.8
Rank: 57

INCOME	AREA	U.S. AVG	EMPLOYMENT	AREA	U.S. AVG	EMPLOYING INDUSTRIES	AREA	U.S. AVG
Per capita income	$28,175	$23,235	Unemployment rate	4.9%	4.7%	Largest: Healthcare & Social Assistance		
Household income	$49,119	$46,414	Recent job growth	3.3%	1.3%			
Household income < $25K	23.1%	26.2%	Projected future job growth	24.5%	11.5%	Percent manufacturing	6.5%	15.4%
Household income > $75K	30.4%	25.4%	White collar	66.6%	57.8%	Percent public sector	23.2%	15.7%
Household income growth	16.4%	13.6%	Blue collar	16.3%	25.2%	Percent construction	9.8%	9.9%

Cost of Living
Score: 14.7
Rank: 318

INDEXES & TAXES	AREA	U.S. AVG	HOUSING	AREA	U.S. AVG	NECESSITIES	AREA	U.S. AVG
Cost of Living Index	110.3	100.0	Median home price	$275,300	$220,000	Food Index	105.6	100.0
Buying Power Index	99.8	100.0	Home price appreciation	57.0%	10.1%	Housing Index	114.9	100.0
Income tax rate	7.10%	4.70%	Median rent	$872	$709	Utilities Index	91.6	100.0
Sales tax rate	7.31%	6.58%	Homes owned	62.3%	62.3%	Transportation Index	106.5	100.0
Property tax rate	$4.97	$12.00	Home price ratio	5.6	4.2	Healthcare Index	114.1	100.0
						Miscellaneous Cost Index	102.5	100.0

Climate
Score: 94.9
Rank: 20

TEMPERATURE	AREA	U.S. AVG
Average January low	19.9	26.2
Average July high	84.6	87.4
Annual days > 90°F	8	38
Annual days < 32°F	150	89
Annual days < 0°F	1	6

PRECIPITATION	AREA	U.S. AVG
Annual inches precipitation	14.6	37.7
Annual inches snowfall	33.0	7.0
Annual days precipitation	36	109
Annual days rain > 0.5 inches	5	22
Annual days snow > 1.5 inches	10	6

COMFORTS & HAZARDS	AREA	U.S. AVG
July relative humidity	53%	66%
Annual days mostly sunny	283	208
Annual days with thunderstorms	55	39
Tornado risk score	4	18
Hurricane risk score	0	13

TEMPERATURE

PRECIPITATION

DAYS OF CLOUDS & PRECIPITATION

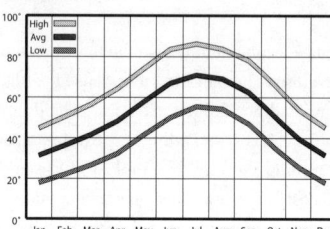
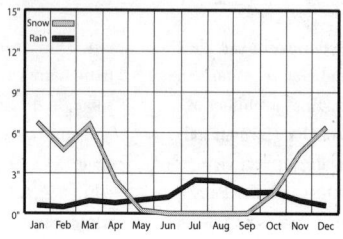
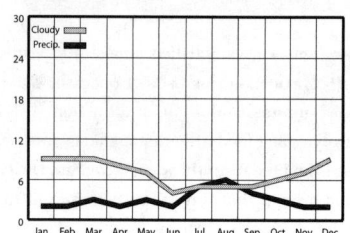

Education
Score: 75.1
Rank: 94

ACHIEVEMENT	AREA	U.S. AVG
High school degree	83.8%	82.7%
2-year college degree	5.7%	6.4%
4-year college degree	20.0%	15.7%
Graduate/professional degree	16.3%	8.9%

PUBLIC SCHOOLS	AREA	U.S. AVG
Expenditures per pupil	$4,598	$5,686
Student/teacher ratio	16.9	16.7
Attending public school	82.7%	90.1%
State SAT score	1106	1021
State ACT score	20.1*	20.9

HIGHER EDUCATION	AREA	U.S. AVG
No. 2-year colleges	1	4
No. 4-year colleges/universities	5	6
No. highly ranked universities	1	1

Health & Healthcare
Score: 26.5
Rank: 274

Crime
Score: 24.1
Rank: 284

HAZARDS & ILLNESSES	AREA	U.S. AVG
Air-quality score	21	37
Water-quality score	74	52
Pollen/allergy score	74	61
Cancer mortality per capita	131.3	201.9
Depression days per month	2.7	3.5
Stress score	64	50

HEALTHCARE	AREA	U.S. AVG
Physicians per capita	282.9	244.2
Hospital beds per capita	137.9	420.0
No. teaching hospitals	1	3
Cost per doctor visit	$76	$77
Cost per dental visit	$72	$70

CRIME	AREA	U.S. AVG
Violent crime rate	706.6	465.5
Change in violent crime rate	18.6%	-2.2%
Property crime rate	3,703.0	3,517.1
Change in property crime rate	-5.0%	-2.1%

Transportation
Score: 23.5
Rank: 287

COMMUTE	AREA	U.S. AVG
Average commute time	24.3	27.4
Percent commutes > 60 mins.	5.0%	5.9%
Commute by auto	71.6%	78.9%
Commute by mass transit	0.9%	1.9%
Work at home	7.3%	3.1%
Mass transit miles per capita	0.89	1.87

INTERCITY SERVICES	AREA	U.S. AVG
Major airports within 60 miles	1	1
Size of regional airport	Medium	Large
Daily airline activity	184	686
Amtrak service	Yes	No

AUTOMOTIVE	AREA	U.S. AVG
Insurance, annual premium	$1,271	$1,432
Gas, cost per gallon	$2.65	$2.49
Daily vehicle miles per capita	38.1	24.0

Leisure
Score: 55.9
Rank: 165

DINING & SHOPPING	AREA	U.S. AVG
Restaurant rating	1	2
Outlet mall score	0	42
No. Starbucks	3	13
No. warehouse clubs	1	2

ENTERTAINMENT	AREA	U.S. AVG
Professional sports rating	2	4
College sports rating	2	4
Zoo/aquarium rating	1	3
Amusement park rating	1	3
Botanical garden/ arboretum rating	2	4

OUTDOOR ACTIVITIES	AREA	U.S. AVG
Golf-course rating	1	4
Ski-area rating	10	3
Sq. miles inland water	2	4
Miles of coastline	0.0	10.7
National Park rating	9	3

Arts & Culture
Score: 59.6
Rank: 151

MEDIA & LIBRARIES	AREA	U.S. AVG
Arts radio rating	1	3
No. public libraries	5	27
Library volumes per capita	4.24	2.78

PERFORMING ARTS	AREA	U.S. AVG
Classical music rating	4	4
Ballet/dance rating	3	3
Professional theater rating	1	3
University arts programs rating	3	5

MUSEUMS	AREA	U.S. AVG
Overall museum rating	8	5
Art museum rating	10	5
Science museum rating	6	5
Children's museum rating	4	3

Santa Rosa–Petaluma, CA

Score: 68.0 **Rank:** 108 **2004 rank:** 166

Profile: Small-city/suburban complex
Location: Northern California, 40 miles north of San Francisco
Elevation: 167 feet
Time zone: Pacific Standard Time

PRO	CON
Year-round climate	Cost of living and housing
Nearby coastline	Long, crowded commutes
Close to San Francisco	Air quality

Santa Rosa, an area of rugged hills and valleys north of San Francisco, is the commercial center of a broad set of suburban communities and small towns making up Sonoma County. Geographically, this area is just north of Marin County, the relatively upscale set of San Francisco suburbs, and extends into open and unsettled areas far north of the city. Santa Rosa itself lies along U.S. 101 near the communities of Rohnert Park, home of a California State University campus and some high-tech industry, and Petaluma, a growing former agriculture center. Just east across a low mountain range is the wine-growing center of Sonoma, and west the area extends to the rugged Pacific coastline. Downtown Santa Rosa is modern and very pleasant, and has a surprisingly strong arts base considering its size and proximity to the San Francisco powerhouse. The area has a complex and mixed economy, partially self-sufficient and partially dependent on San Francisco and other Bay Area cities mainly south. Proximity to San Francisco and popular areas south, a relatively bucolic setting compared to those areas, and an excellent climate has brought considerable growth pressure, and that has been managed fairly well; the area has avoided some of the sprawl explosions seen in other parts of the region. Health statistics are affected by poor air quality and exorbitant healthcare costs, second highest in the U.S. behind New York City. Many parts of the area are quite rural in character. But of course that drives living and housing costs up. Finding local work is possible but challenging; many commute toward "the City." For those who can establish themselves economically and avoid the commutes, this area is one of California's best.

Valleys are attractive and mainly flat, and surrounded by low, forested hills near the coast. The region has consistently comfortable summer temperatures and cool summer evenings. Winters vary from pleasant and sunny to chilly and wet. Most rain falls during winter and can be heavy, although the mountains reduce the force of Pacific storms. Freezing weather occurs occasionally.

DEMOGRAPHICS	AREA	U.S. AVG	ETHNIC COMPOSITION	AREA	U.S. AVG	RESIDENT PROFILE	AREA	U.S. AVG
Population	472,121		White	78.9%	79.0%	Single	33.3%	32.4%
Population density per sq. mile	299.6	358.5	Black	1.4%	10.5%	Married	49.6%	52.7%
Population growth	21.6%	21.1%	Asian	3.7%	2.7%	Divorced/separated	17.1%	14.9%
Median age	38.4	36.1	Hispanic	20.7%	10.6%	Married with children	23.2%	23.7%
Percent Democrat	67.2%	44.5%	Religious observance	32.2%	48.9%	Single with children	8.7%	9.1%
Percent Republican	30.9%	54.5%	Diversity measure	57.3	40.1	Percent over age 65	12.7%	12.9%

INCOME	AREA	U.S. AVG	EMPLOYMENT	AREA	U.S. AVG	EMPLOYING INDUSTRIES	AREA	U.S. AVG
Per capita income	$30,551	$23,235	Unemployment rate	4.5%	4.7%	Largest: Manufacturing		
Household income	$63,178	$46,414	Recent job growth	1.9%	1.3%			
Household income ‹ $25K	16.1%	26.2%	Projected future job growth	13.2%	11.5%	Percent manufacturing	11.5%	15.4%
Household income › $75K	40.2%	25.4%	White collar	60.9%	57.8%	Percent public sector	13.5%	15.7%
Household income growth	19.0%	13.6%	Blue collar	21.7%	25.2%	Percent construction	10.2%	9.9%

Economy & Jobs
Score: 29.7
Rank: 263

INDEXES & TAXES	AREA	U.S. AVG	HOUSING	AREA	U.S. AVG	NECESSITIES	AREA	U.S. AVG
Cost of Living Index	176.5	100.0	Median home price	$603,000	$220,000	Food Index	121.2	100.0
Buying Power Index	80.2	100.0	Home price appreciation	79.9%	10.1%	Housing Index	244.1	100.0
Income tax rate	6.00%	4.70%	Median rent	$1,165	$709	Utilities Index	141.7	100.0
Sales tax rate	7.75%	6.58%	Homes owned	60.1%	62.3%	Transportation Index	129.1	100.0
Property tax rate	$7.53	$12.00	Home price ratio	9.5	4.2	Healthcare Index	169.6	100.0
						Miscellaneous Cost Index	110.7	100.0

Cost of Living
Score: 2.1
Rank: 365

Climate

Score: 95.2
Rank: 19

TEMPERATURE	AREA	U.S. AVG
Average January low	35.7	26.2
Average July high	83.6	87.4
Annual days > 90°F	33	38
Annual days < 32°F	43	89
Annual days < 0°F	0	6

PRECIPITATION	AREA	U.S. AVG
Annual inches precipitation	30.0	37.7
Annual inches snowfall	0.0	7.0
Annual days precipitation	47	109
Annual days rain > 0.5 inches	18	22
Annual days snow > 1.5 inches	0	6

COMFORTS & HAZARDS	AREA	U.S. AVG
July relative humidity	70%	66%
Annual days mostly sunny	285	208
Annual days with thunderstorms	4	39
Tornado risk score	4	18
Hurricane risk score	0	13

TEMPERATURE

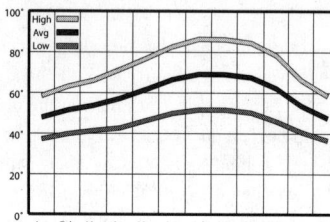

PRECIPITATION

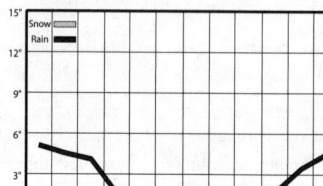

DAYS OF CLOUDS & PRECIPITATION

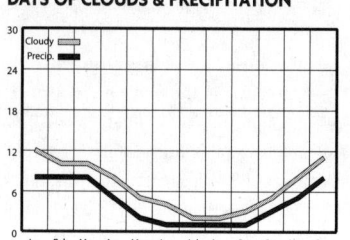

Education

Score: 70.1
Rank: 113

ACHIEVEMENT	AREA	U.S. AVG
High school degree	84.5%	82.7%
2-year college degree	8.9%	6.4%
4-year college degree	18.5%	15.7%
Graduate/professional degree	9.5%	8.9%

PUBLIC SCHOOLS	AREA	U.S. AVG
Expenditures per pupil	$5,549	$5,686
Student/teacher ratio	19.4	16.7
Attending public school	90.9%	90.1%
State SAT score	1019*	1021
State ACT score	21.6	20.9

HIGHER EDUCATION	AREA	U.S. AVG
No. 2-year colleges	3	4
No. 4-year colleges/universities	1	6
No. highly ranked universities	0	1

Health & Healthcare

Score: 0.5
Rank: 371

HAZARDS & ILLNESSES	AREA	U.S. AVG
Air-quality score	18	37
Water-quality score	30	52
Pollen/allergy score	93	61
Cancer mortality per capita	170.1	201.9
Depression days per month	4.5	3.5
Stress score	65	50

HEALTHCARE	AREA	U.S. AVG
Physicians per capita	239.1	244.2
Hospital beds per capita	509.0	420.0
No. teaching hospitals	2	3
Cost per doctor visit	$87	$77
Cost per dental visit	$78	$70

Crime

Score: 69.0
Rank: 117

CRIME	AREA	U.S. AVG
Violent crime rate	510.4	465.5
Change in violent crime rate	7.5%	-2.2%
Property crime rate	2,558.9	3,517.1
Change in property crime rate	-9.2%	-2.1%

Transportation

Score: 69.0
Rank: 117

COMMUTE	AREA	U.S. AVG
Average commute time	28.5	27.4
Percent commutes > 60 mins.	11.6%	5.9%
Commute by auto	74.8%	78.9%
Commute by mass transit	2.4%	1.9%
Work at home	5.4%	3.1%
Mass transit miles per capita	2.42	1.87

INTERCITY SERVICES	AREA	U.S. AVG
Major airports within 60 miles	4	1
Size of regional airport	Large	Large
Daily airline activity	1197	686
Amtrak service	No	No

AUTOMOTIVE	AREA	U.S. AVG
Insurance, annual premium	$1,427	$1,432
Gas, cost per gallon	$2.65	$2.49
Daily vehicle miles per capita	15.9	24.0

Leisure

Score: 88.0
Rank: 45

DINING & SHOPPING	AREA	U.S. AVG
Restaurant rating	1	2
Outlet mall score	146	42
No. Starbucks	22	13
No. warehouse clubs	2	2

ENTERTAINMENT	AREA	U.S. AVG
Professional sports rating	9	4
College sports rating	3	4
Zoo/aquarium rating	4	3
Amusement park rating	6	3
Botanical garden/ arboretum rating	9	4

OUTDOOR ACTIVITIES	AREA	U.S. AVG
Golf-course rating	5	4
Ski-area rating	9	3
Sq. miles inland water	6	4
Miles of coastline	45.0	10.7
National Park rating	3	3

MEDIA & LIBRARIES	AREA	U.S. AVG
Arts radio rating	4	3
No. public libraries	13	27
Library volumes per capita	1.52	2.78

PERFORMING ARTS	AREA	U.S. AVG
Classical music rating	6	4
Ballet/dance rating	6	3
Professional theater rating	6	3
University arts programs rating	3	5

MUSEUMS	AREA	U.S. AVG
Overall museum rating	9	5
Art museum rating	7	5
Science museum rating	9	5
Children's museum rating	8	3

Arts & Culture

Score: 61.2
Rank: 145

Sarasota–Bradenton–Venice, FL

Score: 63.2   Rank: 149   2004 rank: 43

Profile: Resort city complex
Location: Central Florida Gulf Coast, starting 25 miles south of the Tampa–St. Petersburg area
Elevation: 11 feet
Time zone: Eastern Standard Time

PRO	CON
Leisure activities	Cost of living
Attractive setting	Tourist impact
Historic interest	Crime rates

Sarasota is an affluent resort community with an interesting history to accompany the usual assortment of Florida beaches and watersports. In the late 1880s, golf was introduced to the area from Scotland, and today, there are more than 30 golf courses near downtown, and leftover Scottish influence defines the appearance of many buildings. Led in part by the Ringling family of circus fame, the area became a top resort and real estate investment attraction in the 1920s. The boom faded but left the area with a surprising assortment of arts, cultural amenities, and interesting buildings, especially in Sarasota itself. Today the area is booming once again as a pleasant Florida residential area and retirement destination—acknowledged by Sarasota's recognition as an All-American City, earned in 2006—and not surprisingly, this has had its impact on housing and living costs. Bradenton is more residential and close enough to the Tampa area that some make the commute, while also being close enough to that area that many weekenders make the trip south to enjoy Bradenton's beaches. Venice is a small coastal city some 12 miles south of Sarasota. The downtown areas of all three cities are pleasant and walkable, with plain, sprawling suburbs surrounding Bradenton and Sarasota towards the north–south Interstate 75 corridor. Although the economy in general and future job-growth projections are strong, this is not a great area for the career-minded to settle; much of the area's wealth and economic base are brought in from elsewhere, and employment is heavily centered on healthcare, government, and retail. There is plenty to do, and the area provides a smaller-city lifestyle while taking advantage of the greater set of city services available in the Tampa–St Petersburg area.

Located on the shore of Sarasota Bay, Sarasota sits on level, sandy terrain across from a long, narrow barrier island. There are areas of banyan trees and other tropical plants. Inland sections contain agriculture and orchards. Summers are long, warm, and humid, with afternoon highs of 90°F or more and warm evenings in the 70s. Afternoon sea breezes and frequent thunderstorms moderate temperatures. Winters are quite mild with temperatures in the 60s and 70s and lows rarely below 50°F. Invasions of cold northern air produce an occasional light frost and a cold winter morning or two.

Population

DEMOGRAPHICS	AREA	U.S. AVG	ETHNIC COMPOSITION	AREA	U.S. AVG	RESIDENT PROFILE	AREA	U.S. AVG
Population	654,397		White	88.3%	79.0%	Single	27.2%	32.4%
Population density per sq. mile	498.6	358.5	Black	6.5%	10.5%	Married	57.8%	52.7%
Population growth	33.9%	21.1%	Asian	1.1%	2.7%	Divorced/separated	15.1%	14.9%
Median age	47.0	36.1	Hispanic	8.4%	10.6%	Married with children	14.3%	23.7%
Percent Democrat	44.0%	44.5%	Religious observance	41.8%	48.9%	Single with children	6.0%	9.1%
Percent Republican	54.9%	54.5%	Diversity measure	33.0	40.1	Percent over age 65	27.2%	12.9%

Economy & Jobs
Score: 95.5
Rank: 18

INCOME	AREA	U.S. AVG	EMPLOYMENT	AREA	U.S. AVG	EMPLOYING INDUSTRIES	AREA	U.S. AVG
Per capita income	$29,526	$23,235	Unemployment rate	3.3%	4.7%	Largest: Healthcare & Social Assistance		
Household income	$46,573	$46,414	Recent job growth	5.8%	1.3%			
Household income < $25K	23.5%	26.2%	Projected future job growth	24.9%	11.5%	Percent manufacturing	10.7%	15.4%
Household income > $75K	26.0%	25.4%	White collar	59.9%	57.8%	Percent public sector	11.1%	15.7%
Household income growth	15.1%	13.6%	Blue collar	21.3%	25.2%	Percent construction	10.6%	9.9%

Cost of Living
Score: 16.3
Rank: 312

INDEXES & TAXES	AREA	U.S. AVG	HOUSING	AREA	U.S. AVG	NECESSITIES	AREA	U.S. AVG
Cost of Living Index	118.1	100.0	Median home price	$331,400	$220,000	Food Index	100.2	100.0
Buying Power Index	88.4	100.0	Home price appreciation	132.7%	10.1%	Housing Index	117.3	100.0
Income tax rate	0.00%	4.70%	Median rent	$857	$709	Utilities Index	102.9	100.0
Sales tax rate	6.77%	6.58%	Homes owned	63.2%	62.3%	Transportation Index	109.2	100.0
Property tax rate	$12.36	$12.00	Home price ratio	7.1	4.2	Healthcare Index	100.8	100.0
						Miscellaneous Cost Index	99.8	100.0

Climate
Score: 83.2
Rank: 64

TEMPERATURE	AREA	U.S. AVG
Average January low	50.1	26.2
Average July high	90.4	87.4
Annual days > 90°F	81	38
Annual days < 32°F	4	89
Annual days < 0°F	0	6

PRECIPITATION	AREA	U.S. AVG
Annual inches precipitation	49.0	37.7
Annual inches snowfall	0.0	7.0
Annual days precipitation	107	109
Annual days rain > 0.5 inches	28	22
Annual days snow > 1.5 inches	0	6

COMFORTS & HAZARDS	AREA	U.S. AVG
July relative humidity	74%	66%
Annual days mostly sunny	238	208
Annual days with thunderstorms	88	39
Tornado risk score	55	18
Hurricane risk score	75	13

TEMPERATURE

PRECIPITATION

DAYS OF CLOUDS & PRECIPITATION

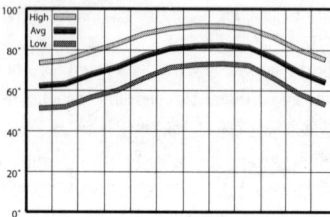

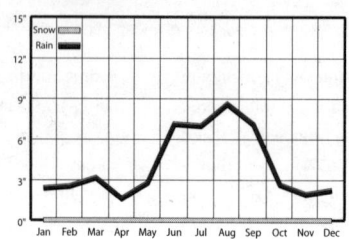

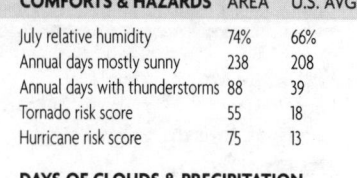

Education
Score: 56.4
Rank: 164

ACHIEVEMENT	AREA	U.S. AVG
High school degree	84.8%	82.7%
2-year college degree	6.3%	6.4%
4-year college degree	15.7%	15.7%
Graduate/professional degree	9.0%	8.9%

PUBLIC SCHOOLS	AREA	U.S. AVG
Expenditures per pupil	$5,810	$5,686
Student/teacher ratio	18.7	16.7
Attending public school	88.8%	90.1%
State SAT score	993*	1021
State ACT score	20.3	20.9

HIGHER EDUCATION	AREA	U.S. AVG
No. 2-year colleges	4	4
No. 4-year colleges/universities	4	6
No. highly ranked universities	1	1

Health &
Healthcare
Score: 13.9
Rank: 321

HAZARDS & ILLNESSES	AREA	U.S. AVG
Air-quality score	34	37
Water-quality score	36	52
Pollen/allergy score	85	61
Cancer mortality per capita	228.6	201.9
Depression days per month	3.4	3.5
Stress score	48	50

HEALTHCARE	AREA	U.S. AVG
Physicians per capita	255.9	244.2
Hospital beds per capita	368.3	420.0
No. teaching hospitals	0	3
Cost per doctor visit	$92	$77
Cost per dental visit	$72	$70

Crime
Score: 27.3
Rank: 272

CRIME	AREA	U.S. AVG
Violent crime rate	632.0	465.5
Change in violent crime rate	3.9%	-2.2%
Property crime rate	4,055.1	3,517.1
Change in property crime rate	-6.1%	-2.1%

Transportation
Score: 50.0
Rank: 188

COMMUTE	AREA	U.S. AVG
Average commute time	24.4	27.4
Percent commutes > 60 mins.	4.8%	5.9%
Commute by auto	80.4%	78.9%
Commute by mass transit	0.6%	1.9%
Work at home	4.2%	3.1%
Mass transit miles per capita	0.63	1.87

INTERCITY SERVICES	AREA	U.S. AVG
Major airports within 60 miles	2	1
Size of regional airport	Large	Large
Daily airline activity	524	686
Amtrak service	No	No

AUTOMOTIVE	AREA	U.S. AVG
Insurance, annual premium	$1,692	$1,432
Gas, cost per gallon	$2.59	$2.49
Daily vehicle miles per capita	25.7	24.0

Leisure
Score: 55.6
Rank: 166

DINING & SHOPPING	AREA	U.S. AVG
Restaurant rating	1	2
Outlet mall score	156	42
No. Starbucks	10	13
No. warehouse clubs	3	2

ENTERTAINMENT	AREA	U.S. AVG
Professional sports rating	2	4
College sports rating	1	4
Zoo/aquarium rating	6	3
Amusement park rating	1	3
Botanical garden/ arboretum rating	5	4

OUTDOOR ACTIVITIES	AREA	U.S. AVG
Golf-course rating	5	4
Ski-area rating	1	3
Sq. miles inland water	4	4
Miles of coastline	35.6	10.7
National Park rating	1	3

Arts & Culture
Score: 43.3
Rank: 212

MEDIA & LIBRARIES	AREA	U.S. AVG
Arts radio rating	1	3
No. public libraries	13	27
Library volumes per capita	1.89	2.78

PERFORMING ARTS	AREA	U.S. AVG
Classical music rating	3	4
Ballet/dance rating	3	3
Professional theater rating	8	3
University arts programs rating	3	5

MUSEUMS	AREA	U.S. AVG
Overall museum rating	8	5
Art museum rating	8	5
Science museum rating	8	5
Children's museum rating	2	3

Savannah, GA

Score: 70.1   **Rank:** 91   **2004 rank:** 156

Profile: Mid-size coastal city
Location: Southeast coast of Georgia at the mouth of the Savannah River along the South Carolina border
Elevation: 15 feet
Time zone: Eastern Standard Time

PRO	CON
Historic interest	Summer heat
Attractive downtown	Crime rates
Pleasant winters	Air service

Savannah is a beautiful coastal city known for its well-preserved historic core and laid-back Southern lifestyle. Its appeal was so strong that Gen. William T. Sherman spared the city from Civil War destruction in 1864. Today the Southern charm continues to radiate from old mansions; cobblestone, tree-shaded streets; and restored historic areas, such as the City Market and its nightlife and art galleries. However, the quality and appeal rapidly diminish away farther inland and away from the historic city center. Incomes are low, and expenses outside the historic center are also low, giving a COL Index of 89.7. But living in the historic or coastal areas to the east can be far more expensive. The port facilities have always been a primary economic driver, although some of this activity has shifted south toward Brunswick. Hospitality and tourism are important, and the area also has some paper, aerospace, and general industry, but not enough to drive strong employment numbers or extensive career opportunities. The economy, arts, and education are getting a boost by the many Northerners moving into the area. Coastal islands to the east, particularly Tybee Island, offer beaches, recreation, fine seafood restaurants, and local flavor.

Savannah is located on a coastal plain a few miles inland from the Atlantic along the Savannah River. Areas particularly to the north and east are flat with marshes. Land to the south and west is a mix of agriculture, woods, and swamps. Muggy conditions can occur in summer when sea breezes diminish. Most summer days are clear and pleasant. Winter temperatures are usually mild and snow is rare. Most precipitation comes as summer thunderstorms. Severe tropical storms affect the area about once every 10 years.

Population

DEMOGRAPHICS	AREA	U.S. AVG
Population	309,709	
Population density per sq. mile	227.9	358.5
Population growth	25.2%	21.1%
Median age	34.5	36.1
Percent Democrat	43.7%	44.5%
Percent Republican	55.8%	54.5%

ETHNIC COMPOSITION	AREA	U.S. AVG
White	62.0%	79.0%
Black	33.8%	10.5%
Asian	1.7%	2.7%
Hispanic	1.9%	10.6%
Religious observance	44.1%	48.9%
Diversity measure	49.2	40.1

RESIDENT PROFILE	AREA	U.S. AVG
Single	33.6%	32.4%
Married	50.3%	52.7%
Divorced/separated	16.1%	14.9%
Married with children	22.6%	23.7%
Single with children	11.0%	9.1%
Percent over age 65	11.6%	12.9%

Economy
& Jobs
Score: 64.7
Rank: 133

INCOME	AREA	U.S. AVG
Per capita income	$23,953	$23,235
Household income	$45,184	$46,414
Household income < $25K	27.9%	26.2%
Household income > $75K	26.5%	25.4%
Household income growth	13.0%	13.6%

EMPLOYMENT	AREA	U.S. AVG
Unemployment rate	4.9%	4.7%
Recent job growth	2.4%	1.3%
Projected future job growth	12.7%	11.5%
White collar	58.2%	57.8%
Blue collar	25.6%	25.2%

EMPLOYING INDUSTRIES	AREA	U.S. AVG
Largest: Healthcare & Social Assistance		
Percent manufacturing	13.8%	15.4%
Percent public sector	15.5%	15.7%
Percent construction	11.8%	9.9%

Cost of Living
Score: 39.3
Rank: 227

INDEXES & TAXES	AREA	U.S. AVG
Cost of Living Index	89.7	100.0
Buying Power Index	112.9	100.0
Income tax rate	6.00%	4.70%
Sales tax rate	6.24%	6.58%
Property tax rate	$13.10	$12.00

HOUSING	AREA	U.S. AVG
Median home price	$163,500	$220,000
Home price appreciation	52.2%	10.1%
Median rent	$703	$709
Homes owned	59.7%	62.3%
Home price ratio	3.6	4.2

NECESSITIES	AREA	U.S. AVG
Food Index	104.7	100.0
Housing Index	69.8	100.0
Utilities Index	91.7	100.0
Transportation Index	97.7	100.0
Healthcare Index	97.7	100.0
Miscellaneous Cost Index	101.5	100.0

Climate
Score: 61.0
Rank: 145

TEMPERATURE	AREA	U.S. AVG
Average January low	38.7	26.2
Average July high	90.8	87.4
Annual days > 90°F	54	38
Annual days < 32°F	35	89
Annual days < 0°F	0	6

PRECIPITATION	AREA	U.S. AVG
Annual inches precipitation	51.0	37.7
Annual inches snowfall	0.3	7.0
Annual days precipitation	112	109
Annual days rain > 0.5 inches	31	22
Annual days snow > 1.5 inches	1	6

COMFORTS & HAZARDS	AREA	U.S. AVG
July relative humidity	74%	66%
Annual days mostly sunny	217	208
Annual days with thunderstorms	64	39
Tornado risk score	16	18
Hurricane risk score	57	13

TEMPERATURE

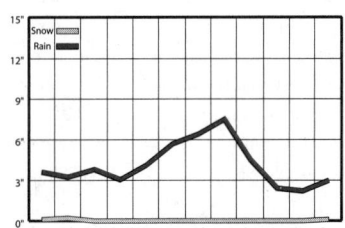

PRECIPITATION

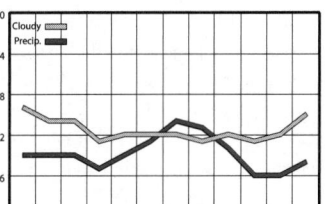

DAYS OF CLOUDS & PRECIPITATION

Education
Score: 29.7
Rank: 264

ACHIEVEMENT	AREA	U.S. AVG	PUBLIC SCHOOLS	AREA	U.S. AVG	HIGHER EDUCATION	AREA	U.S. AVG
High school degree	80.4%	82.7%	Expenditures per pupil	$5,203	$5,686	No. 2-year colleges	1	4
2-year college degree	5.3%	6.4%	Student/teacher ratio	17.6	16.7	No. 4-year colleges/universities	4	6
4-year college degree	15.6%	15.7%	Attending public school	85.9%	90.1%	No. highly ranked universities	0	1
Graduate/professional degree	7.7%	8.9%	State SAT score	990*	1021			
			State ACT score	20.2	20.9			

Health & Healthcare
Score: 51.6
Rank: 182

HAZARDS & ILLNESSES	AREA	U.S. AVG	HEALTHCARE	AREA	U.S. AVG	CRIME	AREA	U.S. AVG
Air-quality score	29	37	Physicians per capita	265.2	244.2	Violent crime rate	582.9	465.5
Water-quality score	48	52	Hospital beds per capita	506.3	420.0	Change in violent crime rate	-0.9%	-2.2%
Pollen/allergy score	64	61	No. teaching hospitals	1	3	Property crime rate	4,737.7	3,517.1
Cancer mortality per capita	170.9	201.9	Cost per doctor visit	$66	$77	Change in property crime rate	-6.3%	-2.1%
Depression days per month	3.2	3.5	Cost per dental visit	$66	$70			
Stress score	73	50						

Crime
Score: 23.3
Rank: 287

Transportation
Score: 5.6
Rank: 353

COMMUTE	AREA	U.S. AVG	INTERCITY SERVICES	AREA	U.S. AVG	AUTOMOTIVE	AREA	U.S. AVG
Average commute time	26.2	27.4	Major airports within 60 miles	0	1	Insurance, annual premium	$1,687	$1,432
Percent commutes > 60 mins.	5.0%	5.9%	Size of regional airport	Small	Large	Gas, cost per gallon	$2.48	$2.49
Commute by auto	78.2%	78.9%	Daily airline activity	114	686	Daily vehicle miles per capita	28.7	24.0
Commute by mass transit	2.4%	1.9%	Amtrak service	Yes	No			
Work at home	2.4%	3.1%						
Mass transit miles per capita	2.36	1.87						

Leisure
Score: 59.9
Rank: 150

DINING & SHOPPING	AREA	U.S. AVG	ENTERTAINMENT	AREA	U.S. AVG	OUTDOOR ACTIVITIES	AREA	U.S. AVG
Restaurant rating	3	2	Professional sports rating	3	4	Golf-course rating	2	4
Outlet mall score	52	42	College sports rating	4	4	Ski-area rating	1	3
No. Starbucks	4	13	Zoo/aquarium rating	2	3	Sq. miles inland water	5	4
No. warehouse clubs	1	2	Amusement park rating	3	3	Miles of coastline	29.2	10.7
			Botanical garden/ arboretum rating	5	4	National Park rating	3	3

Arts & Culture
Score: 54.5
Rank: 170

MEDIA & LIBRARIES	AREA	U.S. AVG	PERFORMING ARTS	AREA	U.S. AVG	MUSEUMS	AREA	U.S. AVG
Arts radio rating	1	3	Classical music rating	4	4	Overall museum rating	7	5
No. public libraries	19	27	Ballet/dance rating	1	3	Art museum rating	6	5
Library volumes per capita	2.20	2.78	Professional theater rating	1	3	Science museum rating	6	5
			University arts programs rating	8	5	Children's museum rating	1	3

Scranton–Wilkes-Barre, PA

Score: 43.4   Rank: 303   2004 rank: 271

Profile: Small-industrial-city complex
Location: Northeastern Pennsylvania, 40 miles from New York–New Jersey border
Elevation: 930 feet
Time zone: Eastern Standard Time

PRO
Nearby recreation
Cost of living
Historic interest

CON
Economy
Isolation
Arts and culture

In one 1975 episode of *All in the Family*, Archie Bunker quips, "The only way I'm going to Scranton is if some screwball hijacks the airplane." He may have had a point back then, as the city and most of the surrounding area were in the nadir of a 50-year decline from the glory years as an anthracite mining, manufacturing, and railroad center tied to the fortunes and energy needs of large East Coast cities. Things were bad in 1975 and aren't great now, as reflected in the weak employment stats and projections. But some modest industrial development and urban renewal have occurred, adding some key museums and slowly improving the aging downtown. The area is gaining some ground as a gateway to the Pocono Mountains, a recreational area to the north and east with skiing and watersports. Local museums focusing on the industrial heritage, such as the Anthracite Complex and the Steamtown National Historic Site, are excellent models of working historic preservation and education. The location is isolated from big-city amenities and services, but there is talk of reviving commuter rail passenger service into New Jersey, which could give the area a big boost as a residential area and base for telecommuters and small business. It will take some time, but perhaps the low cost of living and strategic location relative to major eastern markets will bring a long-awaited economic resurgence.

The city complex lies at the southwest end of the crescent-shaped Lackawanna River Valley where that river empties into the Susquehanna River. Surrounding the valley to the northwest and east, mountains provide protection from winds and influence temperature and precipitation during both summer and winter. Summers are relatively cool with frequent shower and thunderstorm activity. Winter temperatures are not severe, and most precipitation occurs as rain. However, when warm moist air from the valleys to the southwest collides with cold air from the north, snow and blizzards can occur. The area is cloudier and rainier than most areas of the state. First freeze is mid-October; last is late April.

Population

DEMOGRAPHICS	AREA	U.S. AVG	ETHNIC COMPOSITION	AREA	U.S. AVG	RESIDENT PROFILE	AREA	U.S. AVG
Population	549,430		White	96.2%	79.0%	Single	37.0%	32.4%
Population density per sq. mile	314.6	358.5	Black	1.7%	10.5%	Married	50.7%	52.7%
Population growth	-4.5%	21.1%	Asian	0.8%	2.7%	Divorced/separated	12.3%	14.9%
Median age	41.7	36.1	Hispanic	1.6%	10.6%	Married with children	19.9%	23.7%
Percent Democrat	52.5%	44.5%	Religious observance	61.7%	48.9%	Single with children	7.1%	9.1%
Percent Republican	46.3%	54.5%	Diversity measure	10.4	40.1	Percent over age 65	19.0%	12.9%

Economy & Jobs
Score: 6.1
Rank: 349

INCOME	AREA	U.S. AVG	EMPLOYMENT	AREA	U.S. AVG	EMPLOYING INDUSTRIES	AREA	U.S. AVG
Per capita income	$21,355	$23,235	Unemployment rate	5.8%	4.7%	Largest: Manufacturing		
Household income	$38,868	$46,414	Recent job growth	0.8%	1.3%			
Household income ‹ $25K	32.5%	26.2%	Projected future job growth	-1.4%	11.5%	Percent manufacturing	18.4%	15.4%
Household income › $75K	19.3%	25.4%	White collar	56.4%	57.8%	Percent public sector	11.9%	15.7%
Household income growth	13.8%	13.6%	Blue collar	27.8%	25.2%	Percent construction	9.4%	9.9%

Cost of Living
Score: 67.6
Rank: 122

INDEXES & TAXES	AREA	U.S. AVG	HOUSING	AREA	U.S. AVG	NECESSITIES	AREA	U.S. AVG
Cost of Living Index	81.6	100.0	Median home price	$113,100	$220,000	Food Index	96.0	100.0
Buying Power Index	106.8	100.0	Home price appreciation	36.3%	10.1%	Housing Index	50.2	100.0
Income tax rate	4.99%	4.70%	Median rent	$624	$709	Utilities Index	114.5	100.0
Sales tax rate	6.00%	6.58%	Homes owned	63.1%	62.3%	Transportation Index	96.7	100.0
Property tax rate	$15.50	$12.00	Home price ratio	2.9	4.2	Healthcare Index	90.6	100.0
						Miscellaneous Cost Index	99.8	100.0

Climate
Score: 15.8
Rank: 314

TEMPERATURE	AREA	U.S. AVG	PRECIPITATION	AREA	U.S. AVG	COMFORTS & HAZARDS	AREA	U.S. AVG
Average January low	18.4	26.2	Annual inches precipitation	34.8	37.7	July relative humidity	70%	66%
Average July high	83.0	87.4	Annual inches snowfall	51.3	7.0	Annual days mostly sunny	176	208
Annual days › 90°F	7	38	Annual days precipitation	153	109	Annual days with thunderstorms	31	39
Annual days ‹ 32°F	132	89	Annual days rain › 0.5 inches	22	22	Tornado risk score	7	18
Annual days ‹ 0°F	4	6	Annual days snow › 1.5 inches	11	6	Hurricane risk score	8	13

TEMPERATURE

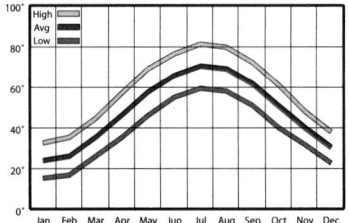

PRECIPITATION

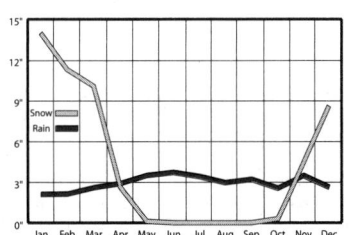

DAYS OF CLOUDS & PRECIPITATION

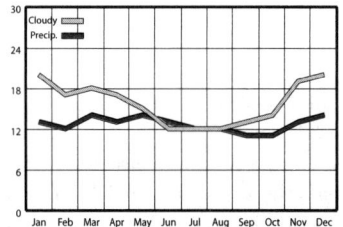

Education
Score: 24.1
Rank: 284

ACHIEVEMENT	AREA	U.S. AVG	PUBLIC SCHOOLS	AREA	U.S. AVG	HIGHER EDUCATION	AREA	U.S. AVG
High school degree	81.6%	82.7%	Expenditures per pupil	$6,494	$5,686	No. 2-year colleges	5	4
2-year college degree	6.8%	6.4%	Student/teacher ratio	19.1	16.7	No. 4-year colleges/universities	11	6
4-year college degree	11.2%	15.7%	Attending public school	82.6%	90.1%	No. highly ranked universities	0	1
Graduate/professional degree	6.4%	8.9%	State SAT score	993*	1021			
			State ACT score	21.8	20.9			

Health & Healthcare
Score: 78.9
Rank: 80

Crime
Score: 65.0
Rank: 132

HAZARDS & ILLNESSES	AREA	U.S. AVG	HEALTHCARE	AREA	U.S. AVG	CRIME	AREA	U.S. AVG
Air-quality score	43	37	Physicians per capita	246.8	244.2	Violent crime rate	323.4	465.5
Water-quality score	78	52	Hospital beds per capita	544.7	420.0	Change in violent crime rate	14.9%	-2.2%
Pollen/allergy score	55	61	No. teaching hospitals	6	3	Property crime rate	2,383.6	3,517.1
Cancer mortality per capita	249.2	201.9	Cost per doctor visit	$63	$77	Change in property crime rate	7.2%	-2.1%
Depression days per month	3.9	3.5	Cost per dental visit	$53	$70			
Stress score	48	50						

Transportation
Score: 71.9
Rank: 106

COMMUTE	AREA	U.S. AVG	INTERCITY SERVICES	AREA	U.S. AVG	AUTOMOTIVE	AREA	U.S. AVG
Average commute time	22.6	27.4	Major airports within 60 miles	1	1	Insurance, annual premium	$1,240	$1,432
Percent commutes > 60 mins.	4.8%	5.9%	Size of regional airport	Large	Large	Gas, cost per gallon	$2.48	$2.49
Commute by auto	81.5%	78.9%	Daily airline activity	838	686	Daily vehicle miles per capita	20.3	24.0
Commute by mass transit	0.9%	1.9%	Amtrak service	No	No			
Work at home	2.1%	3.1%						
Mass transit miles per capita	0.92	1.87						

Leisure
Score: 57.2
Rank: 160

DINING & SHOPPING	AREA	U.S. AVG	ENTERTAINMENT	AREA	U.S. AVG	OUTDOOR ACTIVITIES	AREA	U.S. AVG
Restaurant rating	1	2	Professional sports rating	3	4	Golf-course rating	7	4
Outlet mall score	0	42	College sports rating	5	4	Ski-area rating	5	3
No. Starbucks	1	13	Zoo/aquarium rating	1	3	Sq. miles inland water	4	4
No. warehouse clubs	0	2	Amusement park rating	1	3	Miles of coastline	0.0	10.7
			Botanical garden/ arboretum rating	1	4	National Park rating	2	3

Arts & Culture
Score: 42.8
Rank: 214

MEDIA & LIBRARIES	AREA	U.S. AVG	PERFORMING ARTS	AREA	U.S. AVG	MUSEUMS	AREA	U.S. AVG
Arts radio rating	1	3	Classical music rating	4	4	Overall museum rating	5	5
No. public libraries	30	27	Ballet/dance rating	1	3	Art museum rating	4	5
Library volumes per capita	1.92	2.78	Professional theater rating	7	3	Science museum rating	4	5
			University arts programs rating	6	5	Children's museum rating	2	3

Seattle–Bellevue–Everett, WA

Score: 66.3   Rank: 129   2004 rank: 88

Profile: Regional center
Location: East shore of Puget Sound in west-central Washington
Elevation: 125 feet
Time zone: Pacific Standard Time

PRO
Attractive setting and downtown
Arts and culture
Nearby recreation

CON
Sprawl and traffic
Clouds and rain
Cost of living

Seattle is a lively and cosmopolitan city beautifully set in a dramatic backdrop of water, forests, and mountains. The main downtown area sits on a narrow, hilly strip of land between Puget Sound to the west and Lake Washington to the east. Modern skyscrapers rise on high hills in the city center with residential units in lower areas along the water and north of downtown. To the south is the Pioneer Square Historic District, recalling late-19th-century commerce, and beyond are the attractive, new stadiums of the MLB Seattle Mariners and the NFL Seattle Seahawks. To the immediate north of downtown is the Seattle Center, site of the 1962 World's Fair punctuated by the landmark Space Needle and the recently completed Experience Music Project music history museum and complex. Seattle has one of the more culturally rich and fun downtowns, for work or play, found anywhere.

Most suburbs, some among the most attractive in the country, spread to the east across Lake Washington in such places as Bellevue, Redmond, and Issaquah. The University of Washington, nicknamed "U-Dub," has a large campus to the north of downtown and active sports and nightlife. Everett is a large suburban city/town to the north and site of an extensive Boeing manufacturing and test facility, and surrounded by attractive residential areas, especially adjacent to the Puget Sound. To the south lie industrial areas and the less appealing suburbs of Renton, Kent, and Auburn. The Seattle area goes on for miles in all directions and has a full complement of cultural, recreational, and transportation amenities. Local geography and policy have restrained growth to a degree but have also aggravated the traffic and congestion problems at Lake Washington crossings toward the east and along most north–south corridors.

From its origins as a center of the forest products industry and as a gateway to Alaska and the Yukon to the north, Seattle has become an important regional center with banking, high-tech companies, and consumer products. It retains its original character as a bustling seaport while also exuding an intelligence and sophistication commensurate with its prominent role in the knowledge economy. Some of the largest employers include Microsoft (in Redmond to the northeast), Amazon.com (downtown), Starbucks (in a redeveloped industrial zone south of downtown), and Boeing's labs and manufacturing facilities (in Everett and also south of downtown near the airport). The economy is robust although the aerospace and technology sectors make it more cyclical than that of other large cities. Cost of living and particularly housing have risen substantially in recent years. And the long stretches of cloudy days and rainy periods can be a significant downside. In general, the area represents the usual big-city trade-offs—excellent cultural and educational resources, plenty to do, and plenty of variety in exchange for high costs and crowding—but with the additional elements of natural beauty and climate to consider. The negatives have weighed down the ranking somewhat, but we think the area shouldn't be overlooked.

Along the edge of Puget Sound, the area is hilly and heavily forested where not completely built up. The Cascade Range rises to the east (with 14,000-foot Mount Rainier to the southeast) and the Olympic Mountains rise across the Sound to the west. Steady marine air keeps winters comparatively warm and summers cool. Temperature extremes are moderate and usually of short duration. Normal summers have fewer than 3 days above 90°F. Summer nights are invariably cool. Daily winter highs are almost always above freezing. Winters are wet but the annual total of 39 inches makes Seattle drier than many cities in the East and Midwest. Long stretches of cloudy days and rainy periods tend to occur in all seasons except summer. Only 20% of rainfall occurs during the April to September dry season. Seattle is far enough north to get winter snow, about 9 inches per year, but it seldom remains more than 2 days.

DEMOGRAPHICS	AREA	U.S. AVG	ETHNIC COMPOSITION	AREA	U.S. AVG	RESIDENT PROFILE	AREA	U.S. AVG
Population	2,444,743		White	75.6%	79.0%	Single	33.9%	32.4%
Population density per sq. mile	580.0	358.5	Black	4.8%	10.5%	Married	50.8%	52.7%
Population growth	24.6%	21.1%	Asian	11.4%	2.7%	Divorced/separated	15.3%	14.9%
Median age	37.3	36.1	Hispanic	6.4%	10.6%	Married with children	23.0%	23.7%
Percent Democrat	61.8%	44.5%	Religious observance	33.7%	48.9%	Single with children	7.7%	9.1%
Percent Republican	36.9%	54.5%	Diversity measure	48.0	40.1	Percent over age 65	10.4%	12.9%

Population

INCOME	AREA	U.S. AVG	EMPLOYMENT	AREA	U.S. AVG	EMPLOYING INDUSTRIES	AREA	U.S. AVG
Per capita income	$30,436	$23,235	Unemployment rate	4.7%	4.7%	Largest: Information		
Household income	$58,550	$46,414	Recent job growth	2.6%	1.3%			
Household income < $25K	17.7%	26.2%	Projected future job growth	15.6%	11.5%	Percent manufacturing	11.0%	15.4%
Household income > $75K	36.2%	25.4%	White collar	67.2%	57.8%	Percent public sector	13.0%	15.7%
Household income growth	10.2%	13.6%	Blue collar	19.4%	25.2%	Percent construction	8.4%	9.9%

Economy & Jobs
Score: 80.5
Rank: 74

INDEXES & TAXES	AREA	U.S. AVG	HOUSING	AREA	U.S. AVG	NECESSITIES	AREA	U.S. AVG
Cost of Living Index	120.3	100.0	Median home price	$340,000	$220,000	Food Index	108.9	100.0
Buying Power Index	109.1	100.0	Home price appreciation	49.3%	10.1%	Housing Index	137.0	100.0
Income tax rate	0.00%	4.70%	Median rent	$854	$709	Utilities Index	74.3	100.0
Sales tax rate	8.72%	6.58%	Homes owned	58.8%	62.3%	Transportation Index	108.3	100.0
Property tax rate	$10.84	$12.00	Home price ratio	5.8	4.2	Healthcare Index	125.8	100.0
						Miscellaneous Cost Index	100.5	100.0

Cost of Living
Score: 14.2
Rank: 320

TEMPERATURE	AREA	U.S. AVG	PRECIPITATION	AREA	U.S. AVG	COMFORTS & HAZARDS	AREA	U.S. AVG
Average January low	33.0	26.2	Annual inches precipitation	39.0	37.7	July relative humidity	74%	66%
Average July high	75.1	87.4	Annual inches snowfall	15.0	7.0	Annual days mostly sunny	136	208
Annual days > 90°F	3	38	Annual days precipitation	160	109	Annual days with thunderstorms	7	39
Annual days < 32°F	32	89	Annual days rain > 0.5 inches	24	22	Tornado risk score	0	18
Annual days < 0°F	0	6	Annual days snow > 1.5 inches	2	6	Hurricane risk score	0	13

Climate
Score: 81.8
Rank: 69

TEMPERATURE

PRECIPITATION

DAYS OF CLOUDS & PRECIPITATION

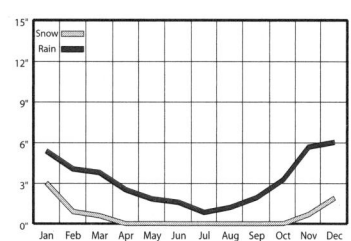

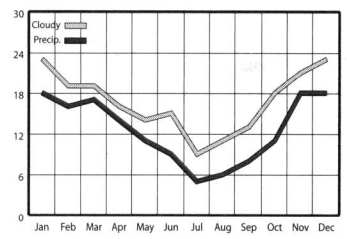

ACHIEVEMENT	AREA	U.S. AVG	PUBLIC SCHOOLS	AREA	U.S. AVG	HIGHER EDUCATION	AREA	U.S. AVG
High school degree	89.9%	82.7%	Expenditures per pupil	$5,890	$5,686	No. 2-year colleges	20	4
2-year college degree	8.0%	6.4%	Student/teacher ratio	21.6	16.7	No. 4-year colleges/universities	21	6
4-year college degree	24.2%	15.7%	Attending public school	89.0%	90.1%	No. highly ranked universities	2	1
Graduate/professional degree	11.5%	8.9%	State SAT score	1059*	1021			
			State ACT score	22.9	20.9			

Education
Score: 95.2
Rank: 19

HAZARDS & ILLNESSES	AREA	U.S. AVG	HEALTHCARE	AREA	U.S. AVG	CRIME	AREA	U.S. AVG
Air-quality score	9	37	Physicians per capita	317.9	244.2	Violent crime rate	363.0	465.5
Water-quality score	58	52	Hospital beds per capita	191.7	420.0	Change in violent crime rate	1.9%	-2.2%
Pollen/allergy score	48	61	No. teaching hospitals	9	3	Property crime rate	5,359.1	3,517.1
Cancer mortality per capita	175.7	201.9	Cost per doctor visit	$100	$77	Change in property crime rate	5.5%	-2.1%
Depression days per month	3.5	3.5	Cost per dental visit	$100	$70			
Stress score	80	50						

Health & Healthcare
Score: 11.2
Rank: 331

Crime
Score: 47.6
Rank: 196

COMMUTE	AREA	U.S. AVG	INTERCITY SERVICES	AREA	U.S. AVG	AUTOMOTIVE	AREA	U.S. AVG
Average commute time	29.8	27.4	Major airports within 60 miles	1	1	Insurance, annual premium	$1,877	$1,432
Percent commutes > 60 mins.	7.8%	5.9%	Size of regional airport	Large	Large	Gas, cost per gallon	$2.57	$2.49
Commute by auto	70.5%	78.9%	Daily airline activity	698	686	Daily vehicle miles per capita	23.5	24.0
Commute by mass transit	8.0%	1.9%	Amtrak service	Yes	No			
Work at home	4.3%	3.1%						
Mass transit miles per capita	7.97	1.87						

Transportation
Score: 24.9
Rank: 282

DINING & SHOPPING	AREA	U.S. AVG	ENTERTAINMENT	AREA	U.S. AVG	OUTDOOR ACTIVITIES	AREA	U.S. AVG
Restaurant rating	5	2	Professional sports rating	8	4	Golf-course rating	7	4
Outlet mall score	0	42	College sports rating	8	4	Ski-area rating	10	3
No. Starbucks	210	13	Zoo/aquarium rating	8	3	Sq. miles inland water	8	4
No. warehouse clubs	11	2	Amusement park rating	8	3	Miles of coastline	69.8	10.7
			Botanical garden/ arboretum rating	10	4	National Park rating	10	3

Leisure
Score: 99.5
Rank: 3

MEDIA & LIBRARIES	AREA	U.S. AVG	PERFORMING ARTS	AREA	U.S. AVG	MUSEUMS	AREA	U.S. AVG
Arts radio rating	5	3	Classical music rating	7	4	Overall museum rating	10	5
No. public libraries	89	27	Ballet/dance rating	8	3	Art museum rating	10	5
Library volumes per capita	2.94	2.78	Professional theater rating	10	3	Science museum rating	9	5
			University arts programs rating	9	5	Children's museum rating	10	3

Arts & Culture
Score: 88.5
Rank: 44

Sebastian–Vero Beach, FL

Score: 84.8   Rank: 23   2004 rank: not ranked

Profile: Beach-town complex
Location: Central Florida East Coast, between Melbourne and Fort Pierce
Elevation: 17 feet
Time zone: Eastern Standard Time

PRO
Beaches
Small-town atmosphere
Pleasant winters

CON
Entertainment
Hurricane risk
Cost of housing

Sebastian and Vero Beach are among the few remaining Florida East Coast places maintaining a small-town flavor not overly tilted toward tourists or retirees. They are attractive, quiet, and somewhat upscale communities with typical barrier islands, small downtown areas, a few subdivisions and resorts nearby, and wild marshlands to the west. Retirees, snowbirds, citrus agriculture, and fishing mainly support the area economy. There is a small amount of manufacturing, but future job-growth projections are only modest. The area comes with some of the traditional leisure amenities of a Florida coastal city, but compared to other places up and down the coast, there isn't much to do. That's the way many prefer it, and the high ranking results from strengths and the absence of strong negatives.

Like many Florida southeast coast cities, Sebastian and Vero Beach are separated from the Atlantic by a narrow barrier island and the Inland Waterway. Summers are warm and humid but moderated by the ocean with most days in the 90s. Winters are mild with lows generally above 50, although freezing temperatures may occur yearly. Rainfall is heaviest in summer with frequent thundershowers; summer precipitation is almost double that in winter. Hurricanes are a risk, but most going this far north actually swing farther north and up the Atlantic Coast.

DEMOGRAPHICS	AREA	U.S. AVG	ETHNIC COMPOSITION	AREA	U.S. AVG	RESIDENT PROFILE	AREA	U.S. AVG
Population	124,365		White	86.6%	79.0%	Single	26.6%	32.4%
Population density per sq. mile	247.1	358.5	Black	8.5%	10.5%	Married	58.5%	52.7%
Population growth	37.9%	21.1%	Asian	0.9%	2.7%	Divorced/separated	15.0%	14.9%
Median age	46.9	36.1	Hispanic	8.0%	10.6%	Married with children	15.1%	23.7%
Percent Democrat	39.0%	44.5%	Religious observance	50.8%	48.9%	Single with children	6.6%	9.1%
Percent Republican	60.1%	54.5%	Diversity measure	35.4	40.1	Percent over age 65	28.2%	12.9%

Population

INCOME	AREA	U.S. AVG	EMPLOYMENT	AREA	U.S. AVG	EMPLOYING INDUSTRIES	AREA	U.S. AVG
Per capita income	$30,789	$23,235	Unemployment rate	5.3%	4.7%	Largest: Healthcare & Social Assistance		
Household income	$45,449	$46,414	Recent job growth	2.5%	1.3%			
Household income < $25K	25.1%	26.2%	Projected future job growth	10.8%	11.5%	Percent manufacturing	9.5%	15.4%
Household income > $75K	25.9%	25.4%	White collar	54.5%	57.8%	Percent public sector	12.7%	15.7%
Household income growth	14.7%	13.6%	Blue collar	21.3%	25.2%	Percent construction	11.8%	9.9%

Economy & Jobs
Score: 46.3
Rank: 202

INDEXES & TAXES	AREA	U.S. AVG	HOUSING	AREA	U.S. AVG	NECESSITIES	AREA	U.S. AVG
Cost of Living Index	103.8	100.0	Median home price	$234,300	$220,000	Food Index	102.2	100.0
Buying Power Index	98.1	100.0	Home price appreciation	125.0%	10.1%	Housing Index	93.1	100.0
Income tax rate	0.00%	4.70%	Median rent	$734	$709	Utilities Index	99.6	100.0
Sales tax rate	7.00%	6.58%	Homes owned	66.3%	62.3%	Transportation Index	111.6	100.0
Property tax rate	$13.29	$12.00	Home price ratio	5.2	4.2	Healthcare Index	97.2	100.0
						Miscellaneous Cost Index	105.1	100.0

Cost of Living
Score: 58.6
Rank: 155

Climate
Score: 66.3
Rank: 125

TEMPERATURE	AREA	U.S. AVG
Average January low	56.0	26.2
Average July high	89.0	87.4
Annual days > 90°F	55	38
Annual days < 32°F	1	89
Annual days < 0°F	0	6

PRECIPITATION	AREA	U.S. AVG
Annual inches precipitation	62.0	37.7
Annual inches snowfall	0.0	7.0
Annual days precipitation	131	109
Annual days rain > 0.5 inches	37	22
Annual days snow > 1.5 inches	0	6

COMFORTS & HAZARDS	AREA	U.S. AVG
July relative humidity	73%	66%
Annual days mostly sunny	228	208
Annual days with thunderstorms	79	39
Tornado risk score	20	18
Hurricane risk score	88	13

TEMPERATURE

PRECIPITATION

DAYS OF CLOUDS & PRECIPITATION

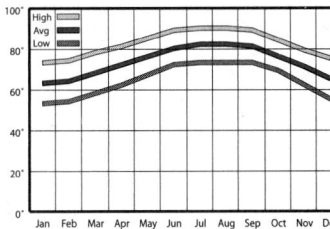

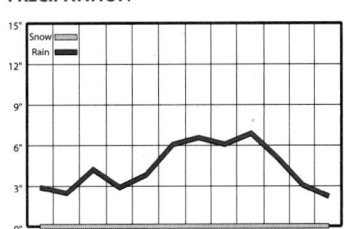

Education
Score: 37.4
Rank: 235

ACHIEVEMENT	AREA	U.S. AVG
High school degree	81.2%	82.7%
2-year college degree	6.1%	6.4%
4-year college degree	15.0%	15.7%
Graduate/professional degree	7.9%	8.9%

PUBLIC SCHOOLS	AREA	U.S. AVG
Expenditures per pupil	$5,558	$5,686
Student/teacher ratio	18.3	16.7
Attending public school	89.5%	90.1%
State SAT score	993*	1021
State ACT score	20.3	20.9

HIGHER EDUCATION	AREA	U.S. AVG
No. 2-year colleges	0	4
No. 4-year colleges/universities	3	6
No. highly ranked universities	0	1

Health & Healthcare
Score: 62.3
Rank: 141

HAZARDS & ILLNESSES	AREA	U.S. AVG
Air-quality score	55	37
Water-quality score	53	52
Pollen/allergy score	74	61
Cancer mortality per capita	248.6	201.9
Depression days per month	2.7	3.5
Stress score	28	50

HEALTHCARE	AREA	U.S. AVG
Physicians per capita	260.7	244.2
Hospital beds per capita	522.7	420.0
No. teaching hospitals	0	3
Cost per doctor visit	$69	$77
Cost per dental visit	$84	$70

Crime
Score: 38.2
Rank: 231

CRIME	AREA	U.S. AVG
Violent crime rate	352.2	465.5
Change in violent crime rate	-12.6%	-2.2%
Property crime rate	3,382.6	3,517.1
Change in property crime rate	4.3%	-2.1%

Transportation
Score: 78.6
Rank: 81

COMMUTE	AREA	U.S. AVG
Average commute time	21.9	27.4
Percent commutes > 60 mins.	4.1%	5.9%
Commute by auto	80.4%	78.9%
Commute by mass transit	0.4%	1.9%
Work at home	3.7%	3.1%
Mass transit miles per capita	0.38	1.87

INTERCITY SERVICES	AREA	U.S. AVG
Major airports within 60 miles	2	1
Size of regional airport	Large	Large
Daily airline activity	687	686
Amtrak service	No	No

AUTOMOTIVE	AREA	U.S. AVG
Insurance, annual premium	$1,419	$1,432
Gas, cost per gallon	$2.66	$2.49
Daily vehicle miles per capita	24.1	24.0

Leisure
Score: 29.7
Rank: 262

DINING & SHOPPING	AREA	U.S. AVG
Restaurant rating	1	2
Outlet mall score	85	42
No. Starbucks	0	13
No. warehouse clubs	1	2

ENTERTAINMENT	AREA	U.S. AVG
Professional sports rating	2	4
College sports rating	1	4
Zoo/aquarium rating	1	3
Amusement park rating	1	3
Botanical garden/ arboretum rating	2	4

OUTDOOR ACTIVITIES	AREA	U.S. AVG
Golf-course rating	3	4
Ski-area rating	1	3
Sq. miles inland water	3	4
Miles of coastline	10.0	10.7
National Park rating	4	3

Arts & Culture
Score: 23.3
Rank: 286

MEDIA & LIBRARIES	AREA	U.S. AVG
Arts radio rating	1	3
No. public libraries	3	27
Library volumes per capita	2.96	2.78

PERFORMING ARTS	AREA	U.S. AVG
Classical music rating	3	4
Ballet/dance rating	1	3
Professional theater rating	2	3
University arts programs rating	2	5

MUSEUMS	AREA	U.S. AVG
Overall museum rating	3	5
Art museum rating	6	5
Science museum rating	3	5
Children's museum rating	1	3

Sheboygan, WI

Score: 67.0   **Rank:** 121   **2004 rank:** 199

Profile: Small city
Location: Eastern Wisconsin on the Lake Michigan shore
Elevation: 693 feet
Time zone: Central Standard Time

PRO
Small-town atmosphere
Low crime rate
Nearby recreation

CON
Winter climate
Some employment
    dislocations
Low ethnic diversity

Sheboygan, located about halfway between Milwaukee and the Door Peninsula, or "thumb" of Wisconsin, is a clean, well-kept, and diversified port town and commercial center, which has grown up as a tourist and retirement destination attractive to residents of the larger cities to the south. The well-used small downtown area is a classic, with particularly pleasant city neighborhoods to the north along the shore. Major employers include plumbing products manufacturers Kohler and Bemis, both headquartered here, and food processing businesses specializing in cheese and sausage. The waterfront is attractive with a large resort and indoor water park complex south of town, and the area has noted golf courses, especially in the more upscale suburb of Kohler to the west. There is a notable collection of arts assets for the size of town, some endowed by the Kohler family. Manitowoc, 20 miles north, is a prosperous, clean, and rock-solid manufacturing center and terminus to the *Badger*, a ferry to Michigan. Additional amenities are available in Milwaukee, 60 miles south. Crime rate, cost of living, and general stresses of urban living are absent here; the chief negative is the rigorous climate. Current employment prospects are weak, with some manufacturing jobs in Sheboygan and nearby Manitowoc having left for overseas locations, but the area is starting to attract some knowledge-economy players. Once low, educational attainment figures will increase as retirees and other migrants find the area. Overall, the small-town environment and simplicity are hard to beat among metro-area-size small American cities.

Sheboygan sits at the mouth of the Sheboygan River along a Lake Michigan coastal plain with mixed deciduous forest and clear areas. Land becomes rolling to hilly to the west. Summers are pleasant with periods of warm weather; cooling lake breezes and afternoon thundershowers are common. Winters are vigorous but milder than inland locations. Periods of cool, cloudy weather alternate with crisp, cold weather when air masses invade from the northwest. Snow is common and may linger, although not in amounts seen to the east and south of the lake. The lake moderates the cold somewhat, although winds can be strong. First freeze is early October; last is early May.

DEMOGRAPHICS	AREA	U.S. AVG	ETHNIC COMPOSITION	AREA	U.S. AVG	RESIDENT PROFILE	AREA	U.S. AVG
Population	114,338		White	91.4%	79.0%	Single	29.5%	32.4%
Population density per sq. mile	222.6	358.5	Black	1.1%	10.5%	Married	58.5%	52.7%
Population growth	10.1%	21.1%	Asian	4.2%	2.7%	Divorced/separated	12.0%	14.9%
Median age	38.2	36.1	Hispanic	4.2%	10.6%	Married with children	25.6%	23.7%
Percent Democrat	44.1%	44.5%	Religious observance	72.3%	48.9%	Single with children	6.5%	9.1%
Percent Republican	55.0%	54.5%	Diversity measure	22.9	40.1	Percent over age 65	13.9%	12.9%

Population

INCOME	AREA	U.S. AVG	EMPLOYMENT	AREA	U.S. AVG	EMPLOYING INDUSTRIES	AREA	U.S. AVG
Per capita income	$24,710	$23,235	Unemployment rate	4.2%	4.7%	Largest: Manufacturing		
Household income	$52,032	$46,414	Recent job growth	-0.6%	1.3%			
Household income < $25K	18.8%	26.2%	Projected future job growth	2.8%	11.5%	Percent manufacturing	29.3%	15.4%
Household income > $75K	26.5%	25.4%	White collar	47.0%	57.8%	Percent public sector	8.9%	15.7%
Household income growth	12.5%	13.6%	Blue collar	37.7%	25.2%	Percent construction	8.4%	9.9%

Economy & Jobs
Score: 25.7
Rank: 278

INDEXES & TAXES	AREA	U.S. AVG	HOUSING	AREA	U.S. AVG	NECESSITIES	AREA	U.S. AVG
Cost of Living Index	85.2	100.0	Median home price	$132,000	$220,000	Food Index	96.9	100.0
Buying Power Index	136.9	100.0	Home price appreciation	28.4%	10.1%	Housing Index	54.7	100.0
Income tax rate	6.93%	4.70%	Median rent	$572	$709	Utilities Index	112.2	100.0
Sales tax rate	5.00%	6.58%	Homes owned	68.2%	62.3%	Transportation Index	105.6	100.0
Property tax rate	$20.34	$12.00	Home price ratio	2.5	4.2	Healthcare Index	100.0	100.0
						Miscellaneous Cost Index	94.6	100.0

Cost of Living
Score: 43.9
Rank: 209

Climate
Score: 14.2
Rank: 320

TEMPERATURE	AREA	U.S. AVG
Average January low	11.4	26.2
Average July high	80.4	87.4
Annual days > 90°F	9	38
Annual days < 32°F	146	89
Annual days < 0°F	16	6

PRECIPITATION	AREA	U.S. AVG
Annual inches precipitation	29.0	37.7
Annual inches snowfall	45.0	7.0
Annual days precipitation	122	109
Annual days rain > 0.5 inches	20	22
Annual days snow > 1.5 inches	11	6

COMFORTS & HAZARDS	AREA	U.S. AVG
July relative humidity	73%	66%
Annual days mostly sunny	195	208
Annual days with thunderstorms	36	39
Tornado risk score	4	18
Hurricane risk score	0	13

TEMPERATURE

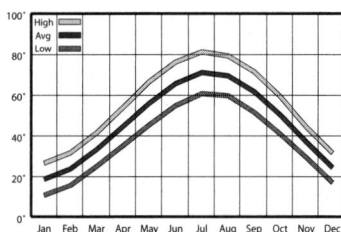

PRECIPITATION

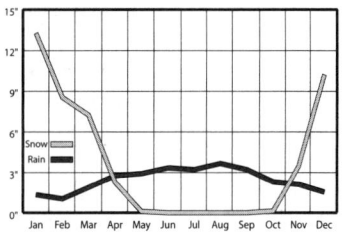

DAYS OF CLOUDS & PRECIPITATION

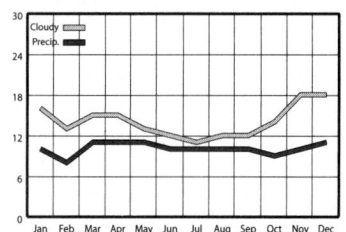

Education
Score: 32.6
Rank: 253

ACHIEVEMENT	AREA	U.S. AVG
High school degree	84.6%	82.7%
2-year college degree	7.0%	6.4%
4-year college degree	13.0%	15.7%
Graduate/professional degree	5.2%	8.9%

PUBLIC SCHOOLS	AREA	U.S. AVG
Expenditures per pupil	$6,613	$5,686
Student/teacher ratio	16.1	16.7
Attending public school	86.5%	90.1%
State SAT score	1188	1021
State ACT score	22.2*	20.9

HIGHER EDUCATION	AREA	U.S. AVG
No. 2-year colleges	0	4
No. 4-year colleges/universities	1	6
No. highly ranked universities	0	1

Health & Healthcare
Score: 59.1
Rank: 154

HAZARDS & ILLNESSES	AREA	U.S. AVG
Air-quality score	42	37
Water-quality score	20	52
Pollen/allergy score	37	61
Cancer mortality per capita	206.4	201.9
Depression days per month	3.9	3.5
Stress score	13	50

HEALTHCARE	AREA	U.S. AVG
Physicians per capita	153.5	244.2
Hospital beds per capita	307.9	420.0
No. teaching hospitals	0	3
Cost per doctor visit	$95	$77
Cost per dental visit	$63	$70

Crime
Score: 92.0
Rank: 31

CRIME	AREA	U.S. AVG
Violent crime rate	107.4	465.5
Change in violent crime rate	0.5%	-2.2%
Property crime rate	2,583.0	3,517.1
Change in property crime rate	3.1%	-2.1%

Transportation
Score: 84.8
Rank: 58

COMMUTE	AREA	U.S. AVG
Average commute time	18.6	27.4
Percent commutes > 60 mins.	3.5%	5.9%
Commute by auto	81.2%	78.9%
Commute by mass transit	0.8%	1.9%
Work at home	3.1%	3.1%
Mass transit miles per capita	0.76	1.87

INTERCITY SERVICES	AREA	U.S. AVG
Major airports within 60 miles	1	1
Size of regional airport	Medium	Large
Daily airline activity	373	686
Amtrak service	No	No

AUTOMOTIVE	AREA	U.S. AVG
Insurance, annual premium	$945	$1,432
Gas, cost per gallon	$2.55	$2.49
Daily vehicle miles per capita	14.9	24.0

Leisure
Score: 53.5
Rank: 174

DINING & SHOPPING	AREA	U.S. AVG
Restaurant rating	1	2
Outlet mall score	18	42
No. Starbucks	0	13
No. warehouse clubs	0	2

ENTERTAINMENT	AREA	U.S. AVG
Professional sports rating	2	4
College sports rating	8	4
Zoo/aquarium rating	1	3
Amusement park rating	1	3
Botanical garden/ arboretum rating	1	4

OUTDOOR ACTIVITIES	AREA	U.S. AVG
Golf-course rating	7	4
Ski-area rating	3	3
Sq. miles inland water	2	4
Miles of coastline	48.1	10.7
National Park rating	1	3

Arts & Culture
Score: 51.6
Rank: 181

MEDIA & LIBRARIES	AREA	U.S. AVG
Arts radio rating	1	3
No. public libraries	8	27
Library volumes per capita	4.43	2.78

PERFORMING ARTS	AREA	U.S. AVG
Classical music rating	3	4
Ballet/dance rating	1	3
Professional theater rating	1	3
University arts programs rating	3	5

MUSEUMS	AREA	U.S. AVG
Overall museum rating	4	5
Art museum rating	7	5
Science museum rating	3	5
Children's museum rating	1	3

Sherman–Denison, TX

Score: 61.1   **Rank:** 167   **2004 rank:** 221

Profile: Small-town complex
Location: Extreme northeast Texas, 90 miles north of Dallas and 15 miles south of the Oklahoma border
Elevation: 669 feet
Time zone: Central Standard Time

PRO	CON
Strong economy	Entertainment
Small-town atmosphere	Arts and culture
Close to Dallas–Ft. Worth	Summer heat

Sherman is a typical small Texas town on the southern extension of the Great Plains. Smaller Denison is about 6 miles north. Proximity to Dallas and Fort Worth, a central U.S. location, and the availability of a good labor force have allowed Sherman to grow into a mid-size manufacturing and industrial center with favorable prospects for future economic development. Sitting at the north end of the so-called North Texas Technology Corridor, the area includes plants for Procter & Gamble, Johnson & Johnson Medical, Kaiser Aluminum, Consolidated Container, Texas Instruments, and Raytheon. Aside from some recreational amenities on the Red River and Lake Texoma to the north, and the revitalized Denison downtown, there isn't much to do locally. However, additional amenities and big-city services can be found in the Dallas–Fort Worth metroplex to the south. The area has a reasonable cost of living and pleasant small-town prosperity.

The area sits on a broad, level plain with areas of deciduous trees, particularly around town. Summers are warm with occasional hot spells and thunderstorms. Winters are generally mild but with occasional cold snaps and snow as polar air invades from the north. Spring weather is changeable and severe weather is possible; the area is located close to "tornado alley."

Population

DEMOGRAPHICS	AREA	U.S. AVG	ETHNIC COMPOSITION	AREA	U.S. AVG	RESIDENT PROFILE	AREA	U.S. AVG
Population	118,041		White	86.4%	79.0%	Single	28.0%	32.4%
Population density per sq. mile	126.4	358.5	Black	5.4%	10.5%	Married	56.3%	52.7%
Population growth	24.2%	21.1%	Asian	0.6%	2.7%	Divorced/separated	15.7%	14.9%
Median age	37.0	36.1	Hispanic	8.5%	10.6%	Married with children	23.0%	23.7%
Percent Democrat	30.3%	44.5%	Religious observance	60.8%	48.9%	Single with children	8.7%	9.1%
Percent Republican	69.3%	54.5%	Diversity measure	36.6	40.1	Percent over age 65	14.8%	12.9%

Economy & Jobs
Score: 89.0
Rank: 42

INCOME	AREA	U.S. AVG	EMPLOYMENT	AREA	U.S. AVG	EMPLOYING INDUSTRIES	AREA	U.S. AVG
Per capita income	$21,400	$23,235	Unemployment rate	5.0%	4.7%	Largest: Manufacturing		
Household income	$42,344	$46,414	Recent job growth	4.8%	1.3%			
Household income ‹ $25K	28.9%	26.2%	Projected future job growth	15.4%	11.5%	Percent manufacturing	17.4%	15.4%
Household income › $75K	21.9%	25.4%	White collar	55.2%	57.8%	Percent public sector	11.9%	15.7%
Household income growth	13.9%	13.6%	Blue collar	29.1%	25.2%	Percent construction	11.7%	9.9%

Cost of Living
Score: 94.1
Rank: 23

INDEXES & TAXES	AREA	U.S. AVG	HOUSING	AREA	U.S. AVG	NECESSITIES	AREA	U.S. AVG
Cost of Living Index	78.4	100.0	Median home price	$101,100	$220,000	Food Index	90.1	100.0
Buying Power Index	121.1	100.0	Home price appreciation	24.0%	10.1%	Housing Index	44.5	100.0
Income tax rate	0.00%	4.70%	Median rent	$630	$709	Utilities Index	101.6	100.0
Sales tax rate	8.25%	6.58%	Homes owned	63.1%	62.3%	Transportation Index	104.7	100.0
Property tax rate	$14.50	$12.00	Home price ratio	2.4	4.2	Healthcare Index	99.0	100.0
						Miscellaneous Cost Index	98.7	100.0

Climate
Score: 88.0
Rank: 46

TEMPERATURE	AREA	U.S. AVG	PRECIPITATION	AREA	U.S. AVG	COMFORTS & HAZARDS	AREA	U.S. AVG
Average January low	33.9	26.2	Annual inches precipitation	32.0	37.7	July relative humidity	67%	66%
Average July high	96.1	87.4	Annual inches snowfall	3.0	7.0	Annual days mostly sunny	233	208
Annual days › 90°F	88	38	Annual days precipitation	79	109	Annual days with thunderstorms	46	39
Annual days ‹ 32°F	39	89	Annual days rain › 0.5 inches	19	22	Tornado risk score	33	18
Annual days ‹ 0°F	0	6	Annual days snow › 1.5 inches	1	6	Hurricane risk score	8	13

TEMPERATURE

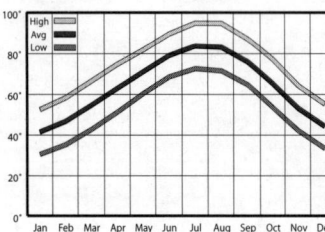

PRECIPITATION

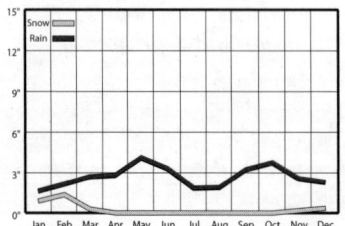

DAYS OF CLOUDS & PRECIPITATION

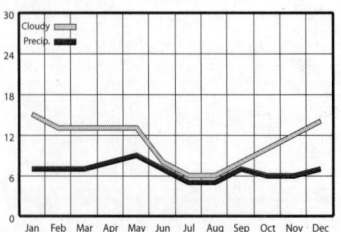

ACHIEVEMENT	AREA	U.S. AVG	PUBLIC SCHOOLS	AREA	U.S. AVG	HIGHER EDUCATION	AREA	U.S. AVG
High school degree	80.3%	82.7%	Expenditures per pupil	$5,426	$5,686	No. 2-year colleges	1	4
2-year college degree	7.6%	6.4%	Student/teacher ratio	13.3	16.7	No. 4-year colleges/universities	1	6
4-year college degree	11.2%	15.7%	Attending public school	97.1%	90.1%	No. highly ranked universities	1	1
Graduate/professional degree	6.0%	8.9%	State SAT score	997*	1021			
			State ACT score	20.3	20.9			

Education
Score: 46.0
Rank: 203

HAZARDS & ILLNESSES	AREA	U.S. AVG	HEALTHCARE	AREA	U.S. AVG	CRIME	AREA	U.S. AVG
Air-quality score	41	37	Physicians per capita	179.8	244.2	Violent crime rate	281.7	465.5
Water-quality score	79	52	Hospital beds per capita	522.7	420.0	Change in violent crime rate	-0.4%	-2.2%
Pollen/allergy score	85	61	No. teaching hospitals	0	3	Property crime rate	3,735.6	3,517.1
Cancer mortality per capita	168.6	201.9	Cost per doctor visit	$58	$77	Change in property crime rate	5.9%	-2.1%
Depression days per month	3.4	3.5	Cost per dental visit	$70	$70			
Stress score	85	50						

Health & Healthcare
Score: 69.8
Rank: 114

Crime
Score: 40.6
Rank: 222

COMMUTE	AREA	U.S. AVG	INTERCITY SERVICES	AREA	U.S. AVG	AUTOMOTIVE	AREA	U.S. AVG
Average commute time	26.9	27.4	Major airports within 60 miles	2	1	Insurance, annual premium	$1,021	$1,432
Percent commutes > 60 mins.	10.7%	5.9%	Size of regional airport	Large	Large	Gas, cost per gallon	$2.51	$2.49
Commute by auto	80.9%	78.9%	Daily airline activity	1557	686	Daily vehicle miles per capita	36.2	24.0
Commute by mass transit	0.2%	1.9%	Amtrak service	No	No			
Work at home	2.9%	3.1%						
Mass transit miles per capita	0.16	1.87						

Transportation
Score: 74.6
Rank: 96

DINING & SHOPPING	AREA	U.S. AVG	ENTERTAINMENT	AREA	U.S. AVG	OUTDOOR ACTIVITIES	AREA	U.S. AVG
Restaurant rating	1	2	Professional sports rating	5	4	Golf-course rating	2	4
Outlet mall score	0	42	College sports rating	1	4	Ski-area rating	1	3
No. Starbucks	1	13	Zoo/aquarium rating	1	3	Sq. miles inland water	4	4
No. warehouse clubs	1	2	Amusement park rating	1	3	Miles of coastline	0.0	10.7
			Botanical garden/ arboretum rating	1	4	National Park rating	1	3

Leisure
Score: 34.2
Rank: 245

MEDIA & LIBRARIES	AREA	U.S. AVG	PERFORMING ARTS	AREA	U.S. AVG	MUSEUMS	AREA	U.S. AVG
Arts radio rating	1	3	Classical music rating	1	4	Overall museum rating	1	5
No. public libraries	8	27	Ballet/dance rating	1	3	Art museum rating	1	5
Library volumes per capita	3.26	2.78	Professional theater rating	1	3	Science museum rating	1	5
			University arts programs rating	2	5	Children's museum rating	1	3

Arts & Culture
Score: 4.3
Rank: 357

Shreveport–Bossier City, LA

Score: 46.5   **Rank:** 271   **2004 rank:** 242

Profile: Mid-size city
Location: Northwest corner of Louisiana near Texas border
Elevation: 209 feet
Time zone: Central Standard Time

PRO	CON
Downtown renewal	Heat and humidity
Cost of living	Economy
Healthcare	Crime rates

Shreveport is a commercial and cultural center for northwest Louisiana, northeast Texas, and southern Arkansas. In the early 20th century, the area experienced a major oil boom, which then declined through the century. Recently, a new riverfront entertainment district with nightlife and casinos and a new convention center have revitalized downtown Shreveport. Bossier City, across the Red River, pronounced "*bo*-zure" and traditionally more depressed than Shreveport, has also emerged as a gambling center and more recently as a retail and entertainment hub with the large new Louisiana Boardwalk downtown complex. It might appear to some that the two cities are putting their downtown areas into competitive play, while not too much is happening to improve their outskirts. The abundance of casinos is also surprising given the area's strong Bible Belt roots. For better or worse, the area's economy got a shot in the arm from Hurricane Katrina evacuees, and has had some success luring business and manufacturers, including a new mill for steel products manufacturer Steelscape. The city's museums and cultural amenities are among the state's best outside of New Orleans and Baton Rouge. There is plenty of outdoor and water recreation nearby. Low living costs are an attraction, but employment prospects are still weak overall and crime is high. Downsides also include persistently hot summers and a degree of isolation, although the area does have commercial jet service.

The city sits on Red River bottomland with gently rolling terrain nearby especially to the west, with a mix of general agriculture, cotton plantations, and wooded areas throughout. At 209 feet, Shreveport is the highest city in the state. Summer months are consistently still, warm, and humid, with temperatures frequently above 95°F. Winters are mild with cold spells of short duration. Rainfall is abundant with greater amounts in late spring and less in late summer. Measurable snowfall occurs 1 in 2 years.

Population

DEMOGRAPHICS	AREA	U.S. AVG
Population	380,050	
Population density per sq. mile	146.3	358.5
Population growth	6.3%	21.1%
Median age	35.3	36.1
Percent Democrat	42.9%	44.5%
Percent Republican	56.5%	54.5%

ETHNIC COMPOSITION	AREA	U.S. AVG
White	57.6%	79.0%
Black	38.8%	10.5%
Asian	1.1%	2.7%
Hispanic	2.2%	10.6%
Religious observance	54.6%	48.9%
Diversity measure	51.7	40.1

RESIDENT PROFILE	AREA	U.S. AVG
Single	34.6%	32.4%
Married	47.7%	52.7%
Divorced/separated	17.7%	14.9%
Married with children	19.8%	23.7%
Single with children	12.7%	9.1%
Percent over age 65	13.1%	12.9%

Economy & Jobs
Score: 34.5
Rank: 245

INCOME	AREA	U.S. AVG
Per capita income	$20,498	$23,235
Household income	$38,022	$46,414
Household income < $25K	34.0%	26.2%
Household income > $75K	20.2%	25.4%
Household income growth	14.0%	13.6%

EMPLOYMENT	AREA	U.S. AVG
Unemployment rate	6.6%	4.7%
Recent job growth	2.5%	1.3%
Projected future job growth	7.4%	11.5%
White collar	55.5%	57.8%
Blue collar	25.5%	25.2%

EMPLOYING INDUSTRIES	AREA	U.S. AVG
Largest: Healthcare & Social Assistance		
Percent manufacturing	14.9%	15.4%
Percent public sector	17.9%	15.7%
Percent construction	10.5%	9.9%

Cost of Living
Score: 71.4
Rank: 108

INDEXES & TAXES	AREA	U.S. AVG
Cost of Living Index	80.1	100.0
Buying Power Index	106.4	100.0
Income tax rate	4.00%	4.70%
Sales tax rate	8.60%	6.58%
Property tax rate	$4.98	$12.00

HOUSING	AREA	U.S. AVG
Median home price	$136,100	$220,000
Home price appreciation	34.6%	10.1%
Median rent	$586	$709
Homes owned	60.0%	62.3%
Home price ratio	3.6	4.2

NECESSITIES	AREA	U.S. AVG
Food Index	88.1	100.0
Housing Index	44.0	100.0
Utilities Index	87.4	100.0
Transportation Index	93.7	100.0
Healthcare Index	91.1	100.0
Miscellaneous Cost Index	91.9	100.0

Climate
Score: 74.6
Rank: 95

TEMPERATURE	AREA	U.S. AVG
Average January low	37.8	26.2
Average July high	93.8	87.4
Annual days > 90°F	87	38
Annual days < 32°F	1	89
Annual days < 0°F	0	6

PRECIPITATION	AREA	U.S. AVG
Annual inches precipitation	45.0	37.7
Annual inches snowfall	1.0	7.0
Annual days precipitation	97	109
Annual days rain > 0.5 inches	29	22
Annual days snow > 1.5 inches	1	6

COMFORTS & HAZARDS	AREA	U.S. AVG
July relative humidity	71%	66%
Annual days mostly sunny	217	208
Annual days with thunderstorms	54	39
Tornado risk score	45	18
Hurricane risk score	15	13

TEMPERATURE

PRECIPITATION

DAYS OF CLOUDS & PRECIPITATION

Education
Score: 31.8
Rank: 256

ACHIEVEMENT	AREA	U.S. AVG
High school degree	79.4%	82.7%
2-year college degree	4.3%	6.4%
4-year college degree	12.7%	15.7%
Graduate/professional degree	6.6%	8.9%

PUBLIC SCHOOLS	AREA	U.S. AVG
Expenditures per pupil	$4,766	$5,686
Student/teacher ratio	16.2	16.7
Attending public school	94.0%	90.1%
State SAT score	1141	1021
State ACT score	20.1*	20.9

HIGHER EDUCATION	AREA	U.S. AVG
No. 2-year colleges	5	4
No. 4-year colleges/universities	3	6
No. highly ranked universities	1	1

Health & Healthcare
Score: 89.3
Rank: 41

HAZARDS & ILLNESSES	AREA	U.S. AVG
Air-quality score	40	37
Water-quality score	43	52
Pollen/allergy score	62	61
Cancer mortality per capita	215.4	201.9
Depression days per month	2.8	3.5
Stress score	65	50

HEALTHCARE	AREA	U.S. AVG
Physicians per capita	407.0	244.2
Hospital beds per capita	647.0	420.0
No. teaching hospitals	3	3
Cost per doctor visit	$79	$77
Cost per dental visit	$62	$70

Crime
Score: 7.2
Rank: 346

CRIME	AREA	U.S. AVG
Violent crime rate	1,078.5	465.5
Change in violent crime rate	-15.7%	-2.2%
Property crime rate	4,894.9	3,517.1
Change in property crime rate	-11.0%	-2.1%

COMMUTE	AREA	U.S. AVG	INTERCITY SERVICES	AREA	U.S. AVG	AUTOMOTIVE	AREA	U.S. AVG
Average commute time	23.7	27.4	Major airports within 60 miles	0	1	Insurance, annual premium	$1,836	$1,432
Percent commutes > 60 mins.	4.1%	5.9%	Size of regional airport	Small	Large	Gas, cost per gallon	$2.43	$2.49
Commute by auto	81.0%	78.9%	Daily airline activity	66	686	Daily vehicle miles per capita	27.9	24.0
Commute by mass transit	1.7%	1.9%	Amtrak service	No	No			
Work at home	1.7%	3.1%						
Mass transit miles per capita	1.69	1.87						

Transportation
Score: 17.4
Rank: 310

DINING & SHOPPING	AREA	U.S. AVG	ENTERTAINMENT	AREA	U.S. AVG	OUTDOOR ACTIVITIES	AREA	U.S. AVG
Restaurant rating	1	2	Professional sports rating	3	4	Golf-course rating	2	4
Outlet mall score	13	42	College sports rating	2	4	Ski-area rating	1	3
No. Starbucks	1	13	Zoo/aquarium rating	1	3	Sq. miles inland water	5	4
No. warehouse clubs	0	2	Amusement park rating	3	3	Miles of coastline	0.0	10.7
			Botanical garden/ arboretum rating	8	4	National Park rating	1	3

Leisure
Score: 32.4
Rank: 252

MEDIA & LIBRARIES	AREA	U.S. AVG	PERFORMING ARTS	AREA	U.S. AVG	MUSEUMS	AREA	U.S. AVG
Arts radio rating	1	3	Classical music rating	4	4	Overall museum rating	7	5
No. public libraries	31	27	Ballet/dance rating	5	3	Art museum rating	6	5
Library volumes per capita	2.48	2.78	Professional theater rating	1	3	Science museum rating	8	5
			University arts programs rating	5	5	Children's museum rating	1	3

Arts & Culture
Score: 50.3
Rank: 186

Sioux City, IA-NE-SD

Score: 54.0 Rank: 226 2004 rank: 270

Profile: Small agricultural city
Location: Extreme western Iowa at the Missouri River and Nebraska border
Elevation: 1,103 feet
Time zone: Central Standard Time

PRO	CON
Small-town atmosphere	Harsh winters
Cost of living	Entertainment
Arts and culture	Isolation

Sioux City, an important agricultural processing and shipping center on the Missouri River, serves the tristate area of northwest Iowa, northeast Nebraska, and South Dakota. This quiet but industrious city was once a major meatpacking and stockyards center, giving some interesting history but also leaving some neglected areas in its wake. Food processing is still a major economic activity, and leftover historic interest has been preserved and brought forward with a few good museums and historic areas. There are other small but notable arts amenities for a town this size. Cost of living and home prices are among the lowest in the state. The economy is stable but shows little sign of growth, and there isn't much to do in the area. Omaha is about 80 miles to the south, making Sioux City relatively less isolated than other towns in the upper Midwest and Great Plains region.

The city is located along the Missouri River in an area of flat river valleys and rolling, mostly agricultural land. The business district lies in the river valley and the residential sections, for the most part, spread over nearby hills, which rise 100 feet to 200 feet. Under normal conditions winters are cold and summers are warm and humid but not excessively hot. Most precipitation arrives from April to September. Temperature and precipitation fluctuate considerably by season and from year to year, as occurs elsewhere in the northern plains. First freeze is early October; last is late May.

DEMOGRAPHICS	AREA	U.S. AVG	ETHNIC COMPOSITION	AREA	U.S. AVG	RESIDENT PROFILE	AREA	U.S. AVG
Population	142,968		White	85.8%	79.0%	Single	32.6%	32.4%
Population density per sq. mile	69.0	358.5	Black	1.7%	10.5%	Married	54.7%	52.7%
Population growth	9.6%	21.1%	Asian	2.9%	2.7%	Divorced/separated	12.7%	14.9%
Median age	35.2	36.1	Hispanic	11.1%	10.6%	Married with children	25.2%	23.7%
Percent Democrat	46.9%	44.5%	Religious observance	57.1%	48.9%	Single with children	9.4%	9.1%
Percent Republican	52.4%	54.5%	Diversity measure	39.1	40.1	Percent over age 65	12.9%	12.9%

Population

INCOME	AREA	U.S. AVG	EMPLOYMENT	AREA	U.S. AVG	EMPLOYING INDUSTRIES	AREA	U.S. AVG
Per capita income	$21,151	$23,235	Unemployment rate	4.6%	4.7%	Largest: Healthcare & Social Assistance		
Household income	$43,876	$46,414	Recent job growth	0.5%	1.3%			
Household income < $25K	25.6%	26.2%	Projected future job growth	8.8%	11.5%	Percent manufacturing	20.2%	15.4%
Household income > $75K	21.4%	25.4%	White collar	53.4%	57.8%	Percent public sector	10.4%	15.7%
Household income growth	12.6%	13.6%	Blue collar	29.0%	25.2%	Percent construction	8.8%	9.9%

Economy & Jobs
Score: 40.9
Rank: 221

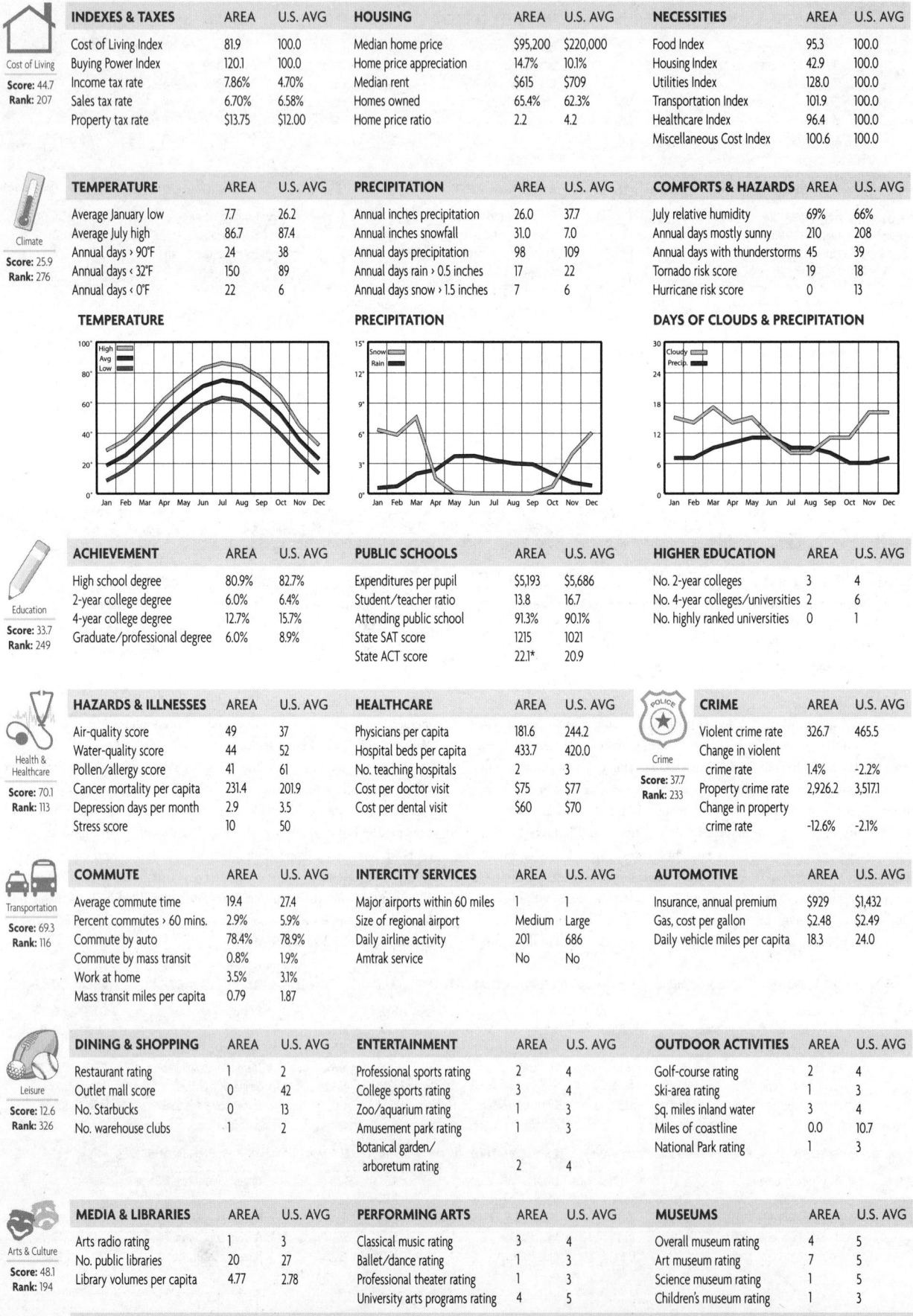

Cost of Living
Score: 44.7
Rank: 207

INDEXES & TAXES	AREA	U.S. AVG
Cost of Living Index	81.9	100.0
Buying Power Index	120.1	100.0
Income tax rate	7.86%	4.70%
Sales tax rate	6.70%	6.58%
Property tax rate	$13.75	$12.00

HOUSING	AREA	U.S. AVG
Median home price	$95,200	$220,000
Home price appreciation	14.7%	10.1%
Median rent	$615	$709
Homes owned	65.4%	62.3%
Home price ratio	2.2	4.2

NECESSITIES	AREA	U.S. AVG
Food Index	95.3	100.0
Housing Index	42.9	100.0
Utilities Index	128.0	100.0
Transportation Index	101.9	100.0
Healthcare Index	96.4	100.0
Miscellaneous Cost Index	100.6	100.0

Climate
Score: 25.9
Rank: 276

TEMPERATURE	AREA	U.S. AVG
Average January low	7.7	26.2
Average July high	86.7	87.4
Annual days > 90°F	24	38
Annual days < 32°F	150	89
Annual days < 0°F	22	6

PRECIPITATION	AREA	U.S. AVG
Annual inches precipitation	26.0	37.7
Annual inches snowfall	31.0	7.0
Annual days precipitation	98	109
Annual days rain > 0.5 inches	17	22
Annual days snow > 1.5 inches	7	6

COMFORTS & HAZARDS	AREA	U.S. AVG
July relative humidity	69%	66%
Annual days mostly sunny	210	208
Annual days with thunderstorms	45	39
Tornado risk score	19	18
Hurricane risk score	0	13

TEMPERATURE

PRECIPITATION

DAYS OF CLOUDS & PRECIPITATION

Education
Score: 33.7
Rank: 249

ACHIEVEMENT	AREA	U.S. AVG
High school degree	80.9%	82.7%
2-year college degree	6.0%	6.4%
4-year college degree	12.7%	15.7%
Graduate/professional degree	6.0%	8.9%

PUBLIC SCHOOLS	AREA	U.S. AVG
Expenditures per pupil	$5,193	$5,686
Student/teacher ratio	13.8	16.7
Attending public school	91.3%	90.1%
State SAT score	1215	1021
State ACT score	22.1*	20.9

HIGHER EDUCATION	AREA	U.S. AVG
No. 2-year colleges	3	4
No. 4-year colleges/universities	2	6
No. highly ranked universities	0	1

Health & Healthcare
Score: 70.1
Rank: 113

HAZARDS & ILLNESSES	AREA	U.S. AVG
Air-quality score	49	37
Water-quality score	44	52
Pollen/allergy score	41	61
Cancer mortality per capita	231.4	201.9
Depression days per month	2.9	3.5
Stress score	10	50

HEALTHCARE	AREA	U.S. AVG
Physicians per capita	181.6	244.2
Hospital beds per capita	433.7	420.0
No. teaching hospitals	2	3
Cost per doctor visit	$75	$77
Cost per dental visit	$60	$70

Crime
Score: 37.7
Rank: 233

CRIME	AREA	U.S. AVG
Violent crime rate	326.7	465.5
Change in violent crime rate	1.4%	-2.2%
Property crime rate	2,926.2	3,517.1
Change in property crime rate	-12.6%	-2.1%

Transportation
Score: 69.3
Rank: 116

COMMUTE	AREA	U.S. AVG
Average commute time	19.4	27.4
Percent commutes > 60 mins.	2.9%	5.9%
Commute by auto	78.4%	78.9%
Commute by mass transit	0.8%	1.9%
Work at home	3.5%	3.1%
Mass transit miles per capita	0.79	1.87

INTERCITY SERVICES	AREA	U.S. AVG
Major airports within 60 miles	1	1
Size of regional airport	Medium	Large
Daily airline activity	201	686
Amtrak service	No	No

AUTOMOTIVE	AREA	U.S. AVG
Insurance, annual premium	$929	$1,432
Gas, cost per gallon	$2.48	$2.49
Daily vehicle miles per capita	18.3	24.0

Leisure
Score: 12.6
Rank: 326

DINING & SHOPPING	AREA	U.S. AVG
Restaurant rating	1	2
Outlet mall score	0	42
No. Starbucks	0	13
No. warehouse clubs	1	2

ENTERTAINMENT	AREA	U.S. AVG
Professional sports rating	2	4
College sports rating	3	4
Zoo/aquarium rating	1	3
Amusement park rating	1	3
Botanical garden/arboretum rating	2	4

OUTDOOR ACTIVITIES	AREA	U.S. AVG
Golf-course rating	2	4
Ski-area rating	1	3
Sq. miles inland water	3	4
Miles of coastline	0.0	10.7
National Park rating	1	3

Arts & Culture
Score: 48.1
Rank: 194

MEDIA & LIBRARIES	AREA	U.S. AVG
Arts radio rating	1	3
No. public libraries	20	27
Library volumes per capita	4.77	2.78

PERFORMING ARTS	AREA	U.S. AVG
Classical music rating	3	4
Ballet/dance rating	1	3
Professional theater rating	1	3
University arts programs rating	4	5

MUSEUMS	AREA	U.S. AVG
Overall museum rating	4	5
Art museum rating	7	5
Science museum rating	1	5
Children's museum rating	1	3

Sioux Falls, SD

Score: 55.6　**Rank:** 215　**2004 rank:** 100

Profile: Small city
Location: Eastern South Dakota near the Iowa-Minnesota border at the junction of I-90 and I-29
Elevation: 1,427 feet
Time zone: Central Standard Time

PRO	CON
Small-town atmosphere	Cold winters
Diverse economy	Isolation
Cost of living	Low ethnic diversity

Sioux Falls is the state's largest city and most important commercial and cultural center. This fairly typical Midwestern city has a strong and diverse economy based not only on local activities like agriculture but also a significant presence in the service economy, especially banking and credit processing. Why? Because of low taxes, a good labor force, and business-friendly state laws. Wells Fargo, Citibank, HSBC, and others have large processing operations here and future job-growth projections are strong for the region. Sioux Falls is also a healthcare hub for a large region of South Dakota, Iowa, and Minnesota. The downtown area is clean but nondescript, as are most of the outlying suburbs. Aside from winter weather, the quality of life is high, with such attributes as low density, low crime, and an assortment of modest cultural amenities. For those seeking more, other cities are a long way away—Minneapolis–St. Paul is 270 miles east.

Sioux Falls is located in the Big Sioux River Valley in southeast South Dakota. The surrounding terrain is gently rolling grassland with some wooded areas. In fall and winter, cold air masses can move in rapidly, bringing gusty winds and temperature drops of 20°F to 30°F in 1 day. There are one or two heavy snowfalls each winter. Severe cold spells usually last only a few days, but long stretches of below-freezing weather can occur. Summers are warm but not excessively hot; temperatures above 100°F occur only 1 in 3 years. Summer nights are pleasant. Rainfall is heaviest in spring and summer, and rain and melting snow can cause some flooding in the lower areas. Strong winds occur in all seasons. First freeze is early October; last is mid-May.

Population

DEMOGRAPHICS	AREA	U.S. AVG	ETHNIC COMPOSITION	AREA	U.S. AVG	RESIDENT PROFILE	AREA	U.S. AVG
Population	203,375		White	92.6%	79.0%	Single	31.6%	32.4%
Population density per sq. mile	78.9	358.5	Black	1.7%	10.5%	Married	56.7%	52.7%
Population growth	37.3%	21.1%	Asian	1.2%	2.7%	Divorced/separated	11.6%	14.9%
Median age	34.9	36.1	Hispanic	2.0%	10.6%	Married with children	27.1%	23.7%
Percent Democrat	39.9%	44.5%	Religious observance	64.8%	48.9%	Single with children	7.9%	9.1%
Percent Republican	58.7%	54.5%	Diversity measure	17.4	40.1	Percent over age 65	11.5%	12.9%

Economy & Jobs
Score: 87.2
Rank: 49

INCOME	AREA	U.S. AVG	EMPLOYMENT	AREA	U.S. AVG	EMPLOYING INDUSTRIES	AREA	U.S. AVG
Per capita income	$23,629	$23,235	Unemployment rate	3.1%	4.7%	Largest: Healthcare & Social Assistance		
Household income	$48,933	$46,414	Recent job growth	2.6%	1.3%			
Household income < $25K	20.7%	26.2%	Projected future job growth	17.4%	11.5%	Percent manufacturing	14.3%	15.4%
Household income > $75K	24.9%	25.4%	White collar	61.7%	57.8%	Percent public sector	9.0%	15.7%
Household income growth	13.8%	13.6%	Blue collar	23.1%	25.2%	Percent construction	8.9%	9.9%

Cost of Living
Score: 90.1
Rank: 38

INDEXES & TAXES	AREA	U.S. AVG	HOUSING	AREA	U.S. AVG	NECESSITIES	AREA	U.S. AVG
Cost of Living Index	88.9	100.0	Median home price	$140,300	$220,000	Food Index	99.7	100.0
Buying Power Index	123.4	100.0	Home price appreciation	27.3%	10.1%	Housing Index	47.4	100.0
Income tax rate	0.00%	4.70%	Median rent	$640	$709	Utilities Index	137.7	100.0
Sales tax rate	5.94%	6.58%	Homes owned	65.9%	62.3%	Transportation Index	100.5	100.0
Property tax rate	$15.99	$12.00	Home price ratio	2.9	4.2	Healthcare Index	93.5	100.0
						Miscellaneous Cost Index	99.1	100.0

Climate
Score: 16.0
Rank: 313

TEMPERATURE	AREA	U.S. AVG	PRECIPITATION	AREA	U.S. AVG	COMFORTS & HAZARDS	AREA	U.S. AVG
Average January low	3.7	26.2	Annual inches precipitation	25.0	37.7	July relative humidity	69%	66%
Average July high	85.1	87.4	Annual inches snowfall	39.0	7.0	Annual days mostly sunny	210	208
Annual days > 90°F	28	38	Annual days precipitation	93	109	Annual days with thunderstorms	43	39
Annual days < 32°F	171	89	Annual days rain > 0.5 inches	14	22	Tornado risk score	19	18
Annual days < 0°F	33	6	Annual days snow > 1.5 inches	9	6	Hurricane risk score	0	13

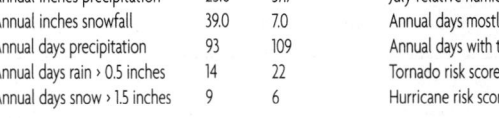

TEMPERATURE

PRECIPITATION

DAYS OF CLOUDS & PRECIPITATION

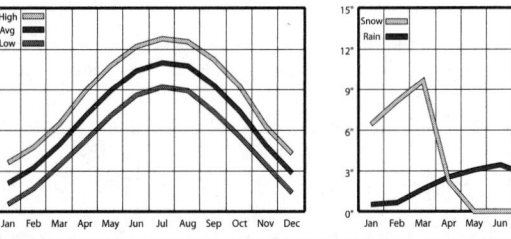

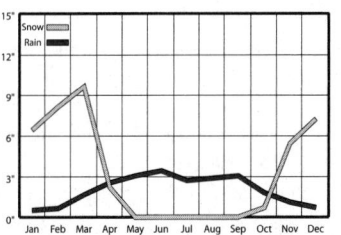

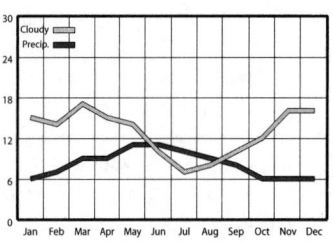

Education
Score: 67.6
Rank: 122

ACHIEVEMENT	AREA	U.S. AVG	PUBLIC SCHOOLS	AREA	U.S. AVG	HIGHER EDUCATION	AREA	U.S. AVG
High school degree	88.6%	82.7%	Expenditures per pupil	$4,492	$5,686	No. 2-year colleges	5	4
2-year college degree	8.1%	6.4%	Student/teacher ratio	19.9	16.7	No. 4-year colleges/universities	5	6
4-year college degree	19.2%	15.7%	Attending public school	87.2%	90.1%	No. highly ranked universities	1	1
Graduate/professional degree	6.7%	8.9%	State SAT score	1194	1021			
			State ACT score	21.8*	20.9			

Health & Healthcare
Score: 93.0
Rank: 27

HAZARDS & ILLNESSES	AREA	U.S. AVG	HEALTHCARE	AREA	U.S. AVG	CRIME	AREA	U.S. AVG
Air-quality score	48	37	Physicians per capita	342.0	244.2	Violent crime rate	261.4	465.5
Water-quality score	20	52	Hospital beds per capita	606.8	420.0	Change in violent crime rate	9.0%	-2.2%
Pollen/allergy score	37	61	No. teaching hospitals	2	3	Property crime rate	2,357.1	3,517.1
Cancer mortality per capita	217.6	201.9	Cost per doctor visit	$65	$77	Change in property crime rate	-9.9%	-2.1%
Depression days per month	2.5	3.5	Cost per dental visit	$53	$70			
Stress score	3	50						

Crime
Score: 76.5
Rank: 89

Transportation
Score: 52.7
Rank: 178

COMMUTE	AREA	U.S. AVG	INTERCITY SERVICES	AREA	U.S. AVG	AUTOMOTIVE	AREA	U.S. AVG
Average commute time	19.6	27.4	Major airports within 60 miles	0	1	Insurance, annual premium	$968	$1,432
Percent commutes > 60 mins.	3.0%	5.9%	Size of regional airport	Small	Large	Gas, cost per gallon	$2.49	$2.49
Commute by auto	83.1%	78.9%	Daily airline activity	65	686	Daily vehicle miles per capita	17.5	24.0
Commute by mass transit	0.6%	1.9%	Amtrak service	No	No			
Work at home	4.0%	3.1%						
Mass transit miles per capita	0.63	1.87						

Leisure
Score: 17.4
Rank: 308

DINING & SHOPPING	AREA	U.S. AVG	ENTERTAINMENT	AREA	U.S. AVG	OUTDOOR ACTIVITIES	AREA	U.S. AVG
Restaurant rating	1	2	Professional sports rating	2	4	Golf-course rating	2	4
Outlet mall score	0	42	College sports rating	1	4	Ski-area rating	2	3
No. Starbucks	2	13	Zoo/aquarium rating	3	3	Sq. miles inland water	2	4
No. warehouse clubs	1	2	Amusement park rating	4	3	Miles of coastline	0.0	10.7
			Botanical garden/ arboretum rating	1	4	National Park rating	1	3

Arts & Culture
Score: 48.7
Rank: 192

MEDIA & LIBRARIES	AREA	U.S. AVG	PERFORMING ARTS	AREA	U.S. AVG	MUSEUMS	AREA	U.S. AVG
Arts radio rating	1	3	Classical music rating	4	4	Overall museum rating	6	5
No. public libraries	21	27	Ballet/dance rating	1	3	Art museum rating	7	5
Library volumes per capita	3.05	2.78	Professional theater rating	1	3	Science museum rating	7	5
			University arts programs rating	4	5	Children's museum rating	6	3

South Bend–Mishawaka, IN-MI

Score: 78.3   Rank: 53   2004 rank: 132

Profile: Mid-size-city complex/college town
Location: Extreme northern Indiana at Michigan border
Elevation: 700 feet
Time zone: Eastern Standard Time

PRO
Cost of living
College-town amenities
Nearby recreation

CON
Harsh winters
Economic cycles
Crime rates

South Bend is located about 30 miles inland from where the Michigan-Indiana border intersects with the lower portion of Lake Michigan. The city has a well-balanced mix of industry, education, and cultural amenities, and has become an economic center for a large portion of northern Indiana and southern Michigan known locally as "Michiana." Once an automotive center and home to the Studebaker Motor Company, the South Bend area is still a manufacturing center for automotive and defense products. Much of this manufacturing actually occurs in Mishawaka, just east along the St. Joseph River. The 150-year-old Notre Dame University adds variety, college amenities, and a set of nationally followed sports programs, although the arts and culture influence is not as strong as in some large university towns. Aside from the Notre Dame campus, the downtown is fairly nondescript, but good local parks and the Lake Michigan shore provide recreation. Chicago is accessible by rail transit although it is too far for a regular commute.

Cost of living is remarkably low for the region and type of area, with a COL Index of 76.9, and housing is a bargain with the median home price just over $100,000. Problems in the auto industry have hurt employment prospects, and crime has been a problem in the past but is improving. The climate receives the full brunt of the Lake Michigan lake effect. But the area scores relatively well in all categories with no major negatives, hence the solid ranking.

The area sits on a level, glacial, coastal plain with gently rolling terrain mainly to the south and east. The downwind location from Lake Michigan effects summer and winter weather. The lake moderates temperatures in all seasons but produces periods of high humidity and extended cloudiness year-round and heavy snows in winter. Precipitation is fairly well distributed, with most occurring in the summer as thundershowers. First freeze is early October; last is early May.

Population

DEMOGRAPHICS	AREA	U.S. AVG	ETHNIC COMPOSITION	AREA	U.S. AVG	RESIDENT PROFILE	AREA	U.S. AVG
Population	318,102		White	82.7%	79.0%	Single	34.3%	32.4%
Population density per sq. mile	335.0	358.5	Black	10.4%	10.5%	Married	51.7%	52.7%
Population growth	7.3%	21.1%	Asian	1.5%	2.7%	Divorced/separated	14.0%	14.9%
Median age	35.7	36.1	Hispanic	4.8%	10.6%	Married with children	22.1%	23.7%
Percent Democrat	47.4%	44.5%	Religious observance	40.9%	48.9%	Single with children	9.5%	9.1%
Percent Republican	51.9%	54.5%	Diversity measure	36.5	40.1	Percent over age 65	13.4%	12.9%

Economy & Jobs
Score: 61.0
Rank: 147

INCOME	AREA	U.S. AVG	EMPLOYMENT	AREA	U.S. AVG	EMPLOYING INDUSTRIES	AREA	U.S. AVG
Per capita income	$22,480	$23,235	Unemployment rate	5.4%	4.7%	Largest: Manufacturing		
Household income	$45,466	$46,414	Recent job growth	2.0%	1.3%			
Household income < $25K	25.1%	26.2%	Projected future job growth	8.3%	11.5%	Percent manufacturing	19.8%	15.4%
Household income > $75K	24.0%	25.4%	White collar	56.7%	57.8%	Percent public sector	9.3%	15.7%
Household income growth	12.1%	13.6%	Blue collar	28.4%	25.2%	Percent construction	8.6%	9.9%

Cost of Living
Score: 95.2
Rank: 19

INDEXES & TAXES	AREA	U.S. AVG	HOUSING	AREA	U.S. AVG	NECESSITIES	AREA	U.S. AVG
Cost of Living Index	76.9	100.0	Median home price	$100,600	$220,000	Food Index	91.2	100.0
Buying Power Index	132.5	100.0	Home price appreciation	23.6%	10.1%	Housing Index	38.8	100.0
Income tax rate	3.56%	4.70%	Median rent	$623	$709	Utilities Index	107.6	100.0
Sales tax rate	6.00%	6.58%	Homes owned	67.6%	62.3%	Transportation Index	92.9	100.0
Property tax rate	$11.86	$12.00	Home price ratio	2.2	4.2	Healthcare Index	96.4	100.0
						Miscellaneous Cost Index	94.7	100.0

Climate
Score: 24.6
Rank: 281

TEMPERATURE	AREA	U.S. AVG	PRECIPITATION	AREA	U.S. AVG	COMFORTS & HAZARDS	AREA	U.S. AVG
Average January low	17.5	26.2	Annual inches precipitation	35.0	37.7	July relative humidity	72%	66%
Average July high	84.0	87.4	Annual inches snowfall	35.0	7.0	Annual days mostly sunny	182	208
Annual days > 90°F	14	38	Annual days precipitation	131	109	Annual days with thunderstorms	41	39
Annual days < 32°F	134	89	Annual days rain > 0.5 inches	23	22	Tornado risk score	74	18
Annual days < 0°F	10	6	Annual days snow > 1.5 inches	16	6	Hurricane risk score	2	13

TEMPERATURE

PRECIPITATION

DAYS OF CLOUDS & PRECIPITATION

Education
Score: 41.7
Rank: 219

ACHIEVEMENT	AREA	U.S. AVG	PUBLIC SCHOOLS	AREA	U.S. AVG	HIGHER EDUCATION	AREA	U.S. AVG
High school degree	82.1%	82.7%	Expenditures per pupil	$6,037	$5,686	No. 2-year colleges	3	4
2-year college degree	6.1%	6.4%	Student/teacher ratio	17.5	16.7	No. 4-year colleges/universities	6	6
4-year college degree	13.3%	15.7%	Attending public school	83.5%	90.1%	No. highly ranked universities	2	1
Graduate/professional degree	8.3%	8.9%	State SAT score	1007*	1021			
			State ACT score	21.7	20.9			

Health & Healthcare
Score: 49.2
Rank: 191

HAZARDS & ILLNESSES	AREA	U.S. AVG	HEALTHCARE	AREA	U.S. AVG	CRIME	AREA	U.S. AVG
Air-quality score	37	37	Physicians per capita	212.8	244.2	Violent crime rate	364.7	465.5
Water-quality score	49	52	Hospital beds per capita	293.0	420.0	Change in violent crime rate	-15.7%	-2.2%
Pollen/allergy score	56	61	No. teaching hospitals	4	3	Property crime rate	4,112.6	3,517.1
Cancer mortality per capita	209.6	201.9	Cost per doctor visit	$74	$77	Change in property crime rate	-2.4%	-2.1%
Depression days per month	3.1	3.5	Cost per dental visit	$62	$70			
Stress score	50	50						

Crime
Score: 55.9
Rank: 166

Transportation
Score: 95.5
Rank: 18

COMMUTE	AREA	U.S. AVG	INTERCITY SERVICES	AREA	U.S. AVG	AUTOMOTIVE	AREA	U.S. AVG
Average commute time	22.6	27.4	Major airports within 60 miles	2	1	Insurance, annual premium	$1,241	$1,432
Percent commutes > 60 mins.	3.7%	5.9%	Size of regional airport	Large	Large	Gas, cost per gallon	$2.48	$2.49
Commute by auto	81.6%	78.9%	Daily airline activity	1996	686	Daily vehicle miles per capita	21.7	24.0
Commute by mass transit	1.0%	1.9%	Amtrak service	Yes	No			
Work at home	2.8%	3.1%						
Mass transit miles per capita	1.04	1.87						

Leisure
Score: 47.1
Rank: 197

DINING & SHOPPING	AREA	U.S. AVG	ENTERTAINMENT	AREA	U.S. AVG	OUTDOOR ACTIVITIES	AREA	U.S. AVG
Restaurant rating	1	2	Professional sports rating	3	4	Golf-course rating	3	4
Outlet mall score	82	42	College sports rating	6	4	Ski-area rating	3	3
No. Starbucks	3	13	Zoo/aquarium rating	3	3	Sq. miles inland water	2	4
No. warehouse clubs	1	2	Amusement park rating	1	3	Miles of coastline	0.0	10.7
			Botanical garden/ arboretum rating	1	4	National Park rating	1	3

Arts & Culture
Score: 64.2
Rank: 134

MEDIA & LIBRARIES	AREA	U.S. AVG	PERFORMING ARTS	AREA	U.S. AVG	MUSEUMS	AREA	U.S. AVG
Arts radio rating	1	3	Classical music rating	4	4	Overall museum rating	6	5
No. public libraries	20	27	Ballet/dance rating	1	3	Art museum rating	7	5
Library volumes per capita	3.62	2.78	Professional theater rating	1	3	Science museum rating	3	5
			University arts programs rating	8	5	Children's museum rating	3	3

Spartanburg, SC

Score: 79.5   **Rank:** 48   **2004 rank:** 80

Profile: Mid-size city
Location: Northwest South Carolina near North Carolina border, 55 miles southwest of Charlotte
Elevation: 910 feet
Time zone: Eastern Standard Time

PRO
Diverse economy
Cost of living
Nearby recreation

CON
Hot, humid summers
Crime rates
Low educational attainment

Spartanburg is the prosperous business and commercial center of the old metro area triad Greenville–Spartanburg–Anderson. For many years mainly a textile milling and agriculture center, the economy has made the turn to bring in more new-economy businesses, as well as strengthen the old ones. Spartanburg is still a major center for agriculture processing and shipping, most particularly peaches and other orchard fruit. Most of the textile mills are gone, but it still remains the headquarters of textile leader Milliken, which also operates a research facility in the city. The addition of a BMW plant in nearby Greer brought a lot of smaller businesses supporting that operation, and a large Michelin plant has also located there. Spartanburg offers a business-friendly environment with skilled low-cost labor and a very low cost of living profile (COL Index is 80.8) and diverse but somewhat cyclical employment. Downtown is fairly plain but accessible; those looking for

a more interesting downtown experience might go to Greenville, 15 miles west. Greenville is also the entertainment and cultural center of the area. There is plenty of outdoor recreation in the mountains to the north and lake areas to the west, and Charlotte offers a lot that might not be present locally. The area has few strong downsides, hence the high ranking, which may be a bit higher than it should be.

The southern Appalachians rise gradually to the northwest of Spartanburg, which itself is in an area of flat to gently rolling agricultural land. Summers are warm and humid with thunderstorms; the elevation and mountains can provide some summer evening cooling. The mountains usually protect the area from the brunt of winter, giving only occasional below-freezing daytime temperatures. Rainfall is abundant and spread throughout the year. There are usually a few small snowfalls and an occasional ice storm or spell of freezing rain.

Population

DEMOGRAPHICS	AREA	U.S. AVG	ETHNIC COMPOSITION	AREA	U.S. AVG	RESIDENT PROFILE	AREA	U.S. AVG
Population	264,753		White	73.5%	79.0%	Single	30.9%	32.4%
Population density per sq. mile	326.5	358.5	Black	21.4%	10.5%	Married	54.0%	52.7%
Population growth	16.7%	21.1%	Asian	1.8%	2.7%	Divorced/separated	15.1%	14.9%
Median age	37.2	36.1	Hispanic	3.7%	10.6%	Married with children	22.5%	23.7%
Percent Democrat	34.8%	44.5%	Religious observance	58.9%	48.9%	Single with children	9.7%	9.1%
Percent Republican	64.1%	54.5%	Diversity measure	45.5	40.1	Percent over age 65	12.9%	12.9%

Economy & Jobs
Score: 54.0
Rank: 173

INCOME	AREA	U.S. AVG	EMPLOYMENT	AREA	U.S. AVG	EMPLOYING INDUSTRIES	AREA	U.S. AVG
Per capita income	$21,524	$23,235	Unemployment rate	7.2%	4.7%	Largest: Manufacturing		
Household income	$42,343	$46,414	Recent job growth	2.5%	1.3%			
Household income < $25K	28.7%	26.2%	Projected future job growth	12.4%	11.5%	Percent manufacturing	24.5%	15.4%
Household income > $75K	21.3%	25.4%	White collar	51.6%	57.8%	Percent public sector	10.9%	15.7%
Household income growth	12.7%	13.6%	Blue collar	35.5%	25.2%	Percent construction	11.0%	9.9%

Cost of Living
Score: 72.5
Rank: 103

INDEXES & TAXES	AREA	U.S. AVG	HOUSING	AREA	U.S. AVG	NECESSITIES	AREA	U.S. AVG
Cost of Living Index	80.8	100.0	Median home price	$132,300	$220,000	Food Index	96.9	100.0
Buying Power Index	117.5	100.0	Home price appreciation	21.4%	10.1%	Housing Index	52.3	100.0
Income tax rate	7.00%	4.70%	Median rent	$580	$709	Utilities Index	79.2	100.0
Sales tax rate	5.00%	6.58%	Homes owned	66.3%	62.3%	Transportation Index	92.3	100.0
Property tax rate	$7.70	$12.00	Home price ratio	3.1	4.2	Healthcare Index	96.5	100.0
						Miscellaneous Cost Index	93.5	100.0

Climate
Score: 50.8
Rank: 183

TEMPERATURE	AREA	U.S. AVG
Average January low	33.0	26.2
Average July high	87.6	87.4
Annual days > 90°F	29	38
Annual days < 32°F	68	89
Annual days < 0°F	0	6

PRECIPITATION	AREA	U.S. AVG
Annual inches precipitation	48.0	37.7
Annual inches snowfall	6.0	7.0
Annual days precipitation	119	109
Annual days rain > 0.5 inches	37	22
Annual days snow > 1.5 inches	2	6

COMFORTS & HAZARDS	AREA	U.S. AVG
July relative humidity	70%	66%
Annual days mostly sunny	221	208
Annual days with thunderstorms	44	39
Tornado risk score	18	18
Hurricane risk score	17	13

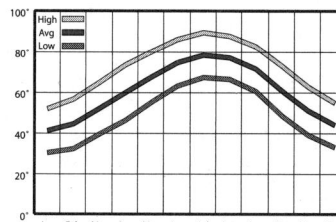

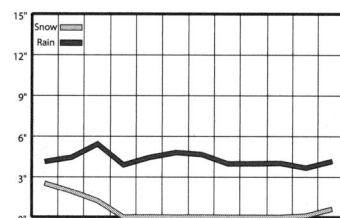

DAYS OF CLOUDS & PRECIPITATION

Education
Score: 28.9
Rank: 267

ACHIEVEMENT	AREA	U.S. AVG
High school degree	73.3%	82.7%
2-year college degree	6.7%	6.4%
4-year college degree	11.8%	15.7%
Graduate/professional degree	6.3%	8.9%

PUBLIC SCHOOLS	AREA	U.S. AVG
Expenditures per pupil	$5,449	$5,686
Student/teacher ratio	15.0	16.7
Attending public school	93.6%	90.1%
State SAT score	985*	1021
State ACT score	19.5	20.9

HIGHER EDUCATION	AREA	U.S. AVG
No. 2-year colleges	2	4
No. 4-year colleges/universities	4	6
No. highly ranked universities	1	1

Health & Healthcare
Score: 24.1
Rank: 283

HAZARDS & ILLNESSES	AREA	U.S. AVG
Air-quality score	30	37
Water-quality score	27	52
Pollen/allergy score	56	61
Cancer mortality per capita	217.0	201.9
Depression days per month	4.4	3.5
Stress score	92	50

HEALTHCARE	AREA	U.S. AVG
Physicians per capita	196.7	244.2
Hospital beds per capita	311.2	420.0
No. teaching hospitals	1	3
Cost per doctor visit	$68	$77
Cost per dental visit	$61	$70

Crime
Score: 28.3
Rank: 268

CRIME	AREA	U.S. AVG
Violent crime rate	649.3	465.5
Change in violent crime rate	-7.8%	-2.2%
Property crime rate	4,489.6	3,517.1
Change in property crime rate	0.4%	-2.1%

Transportation
Score: 57.0
Rank: 162

COMMUTE	AREA	U.S. AVG
Average commute time	24.2	27.4
Percent commutes > 60 mins.	3.9%	5.9%
Commute by auto	82.4%	78.9%
Commute by mass transit	0.5%	1.9%
Work at home	2.0%	3.1%
Mass transit miles per capita	0.51	1.87

INTERCITY SERVICES	AREA	U.S. AVG
Major airports within 60 miles	1	1
Size of regional airport	Large	Large
Daily airline activity	806	686
Amtrak service	Yes	No

AUTOMOTIVE	AREA	U.S. AVG
Insurance, annual premium	$1,425	$1,432
Gas, cost per gallon	$2.36	$2.49
Daily vehicle miles per capita	18.7	24.0

Leisure
Score: 36.9
Rank: 235

DINING & SHOPPING	AREA	U.S. AVG
Restaurant rating	1	2
Outlet mall score	19	42
No. Starbucks	0	13
No. warehouse clubs	1	2

ENTERTAINMENT	AREA	U.S. AVG
Professional sports rating	3	4
College sports rating	5	4
Zoo/aquarium rating	3	3
Amusement park rating	1	3
Botanical garden/ arboretum rating	6	4

OUTDOOR ACTIVITIES	AREA	U.S. AVG
Golf-course rating	5	4
Ski-area rating	1	3
Sq. miles inland water	2	4
Miles of coastline	0.0	10.7
National Park rating	1	3

Arts & Culture
Score: 60.4
Rank: 148

MEDIA & LIBRARIES	AREA	U.S. AVG
Arts radio rating	1	3
No. public libraries	10	27
Library volumes per capita	3.15	2.78

PERFORMING ARTS	AREA	U.S. AVG
Classical music rating	6	4
Ballet/dance rating	3	3
Professional theater rating	1	3
University arts programs rating	3	5

MUSEUMS	AREA	U.S. AVG
Overall museum rating	6	5
Art museum rating	7	5
Science museum rating	6	5
Children's museum rating	1	3

Spokane, WA

Profile: Mid-size city
Location: Extreme eastern Washington, 20 miles west of the Idaho border
Elevation: 1,880 feet
Time zone: Pacific Standard Time

PRO
Attractive setting and downtown
Educated population
Arts and culture

CON
Harsh winters
Property crime
Low ethnic diversity

Spokane is the financial, cultural, and retail center for a large area of Washington, Idaho, and western Montana known as the "Inland Northwest." The dry climate and relatively plain infrastructure differ from what one might picture for a Pacific Northwest city, but the area is on the upswing after years in the shadow of the larger Puget Sound cities west. The economy of agriculture, commerce, and industry is diverse and once again healthy, aided by a large migration from other points west for retirement and to escape more crowded and expensive coastal cities. Nearby outdoor and mountain recreation are excellent. The downtown area is clean, lively, and popular with attractive new and restored buildings. The notable 100-acre downtown Riverfront Park, once the 1974 World's Fair site, is an excellent urban park dotted with attractive cultural venues and recreation opportunities. The modest but diverse cultural amenities are noteworthy for a city with this size and location. Residential areas on the plateau to the south range from average to very attractive. The area to the east blends into Coeur d'Alene, Idaho, a growing recreation and retirement area (p. 279). The cost of living profile (COL Index is 93.7) remains attractive for the region, although recent migration has driven home prices up a bit. Southwest Airlines provides ample, inexpensive air service to other areas in the West. Except for rugged winters, some sprawl, and a relatively high property-crime rate for the region, Spokane is a balanced and attractive place to live.

The city sits on the eastern edge of the broad Columbia Basin, which is bounded by the Cascade Range to the west and the Rocky Mountains to the east. Spokane sits on the upper plateau where the long gradual slope from the Columbia River meets the sharp rise of the Rockies. Much of the urban area lies along both sides of the Spokane River with residential areas spreading to plateau crests 500 feet above the city. Rainfall is less than 50% of that directly west of the Cascades. However, the location receives more clouds and rain than most of eastern Washington. Continental air masses occasionally bring subzero winter temperatures. Summer weather is mild and arid while winter varies from coastal and wet to cold and dry. Like most of the Pacific Northwest, the majority of precipitation falls from October to April. Winter days are often cloudy or foggy with an occasional snowfall of several inches. First freeze is early October; last is early May.

DEMOGRAPHICS	AREA	U.S. AVG	ETHNIC COMPOSITION	AREA	U.S. AVG	RESIDENT PROFILE	AREA	U.S. AVG
Population	436,631		White	90.7%	79.0%	Single	31.0%	32.4%
Population density per sq. mile	247.6	358.5	Black	1.7%	10.5%	Married	52.0%	52.7%
Population growth	20.8%	21.1%	Asian	2.1%	2.7%	Divorced/separated	17.0%	14.9%
Median age	36.1	36.1	Hispanic	3.2%	10.6%	Married with children	22.6%	23.7%
Percent Democrat	43.2%	44.5%	Religious observance	36.1%	48.9%	Single with children	9.6%	9.1%
Percent Republican	55.1%	54.5%	Diversity measure	22.7	40.1	Percent over age 65	12.5%	12.9%

Population

INCOME	AREA	U.S. AVG	EMPLOYMENT	AREA	U.S. AVG	EMPLOYING INDUSTRIES	AREA	U.S. AVG
Per capita income	$21,869	$23,235	Unemployment rate	5.5%	4.7%	Largest: Healthcare & Social Assistance		
Household income	$42,419	$46,414	Recent job growth	3.1%	1.3%			
Household income < $25K	28.2%	26.2%	Projected future job growth	16.1%	11.5%	Percent manufacturing	12.5%	15.4%
Household income > $75K	21.8%	25.4%	White collar	61.5%	57.8%	Percent public sector	15.9%	15.7%
Household income growth	13.7%	13.6%	Blue collar	21.1%	25.2%	Percent construction	8.6%	9.9%

Economy & Jobs
Score: 70.3
Rank: 111

INDEXES & TAXES	AREA	U.S. AVG	HOUSING	AREA	U.S. AVG	NECESSITIES	AREA	U.S. AVG
Cost of Living Index	93.7	100.0	Median home price	$179,000	$220,000	Food Index	103.3	100.0
Buying Power Index	101.5	100.0	Home price appreciation	50.2%	10.1%	Housing Index	72.7	100.0
Income tax rate	0.00%	4.70%	Median rent	$656	$709	Utilities Index	74.8	100.0
Sales tax rate	8.50%	6.58%	Homes owned	61.7%	62.3%	Transportation Index	100.7	100.0
Property tax rate	$13.42	$12.00	Home price ratio	4.2	4.2	Healthcare Index	118.3	100.0
						Miscellaneous Cost Index	107.1	100.0

Cost of Living
Score: 66.3
Rank: 127

Climate
Score: 28.9
Rank: 265

TEMPERATURE	AREA	U.S. AVG
Average January low	19.6	26.2
Average July high	84.3	87.4
Annual days > 90°F	21	38
Annual days < 32°F	141	89
Annual days < 0°F	5	6

PRECIPITATION	AREA	U.S. AVG
Annual inches precipitation	17.0	37.7
Annual inches snowfall	53.0	7.0
Annual days precipitation	114	109
Annual days rain > 0.5 inches	7	22
Annual days snow > 1.5 inches	13	6

COMFORTS & HAZARDS	AREA	U.S. AVG
July relative humidity	63%	66%
Annual days mostly sunny	176	208
Annual days with thunderstorms	11	39
Tornado risk score	0	18
Hurricane risk score	0	13

TEMPERATURE

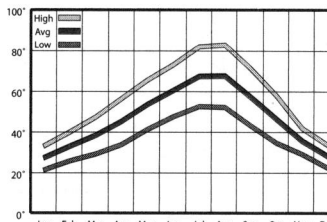

PRECIPITATION

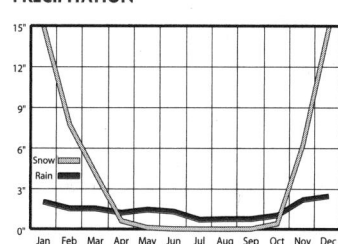

DAYS OF CLOUDS & PRECIPITATION

Education
Score: 80.2
Rank: 75

ACHIEVEMENT	AREA	U.S. AVG
High school degree	89.2%	82.7%
2-year college degree	10.1%	6.4%
4-year college degree	16.5%	15.7%
Graduate/professional degree	8.8%	8.9%

PUBLIC SCHOOLS	AREA	U.S. AVG
Expenditures per pupil	$5,771	$5,686
Student/teacher ratio	20.4	16.7
Attending public school	91.4%	90.1%
State SAT score	1059*	1021
State ACT score	22.9	20.9

HIGHER EDUCATION	AREA	U.S. AVG
No. 2-year colleges	4	4
No. 4-year colleges/universities	6	6
No. highly ranked universities	1	1

Health & Healthcare
Score: 35.0
Rank: 242

HAZARDS & ILLNESSES	AREA	U.S. AVG
Air-quality score	25	37
Water-quality score	38	52
Pollen/allergy score	42	61
Cancer mortality per capita	188.6	201.9
Depression days per month	3.6	3.5
Stress score	84	50

HEALTHCARE	AREA	U.S. AVG
Physicians per capita	266.1	244.2
Hospital beds per capita	371.5	420.0
No. teaching hospitals	3	3
Cost per doctor visit	$80	$77
Cost per dental visit	$83	$70

Crime
Score: 47.3
Rank: 197

CRIME	AREA	U.S. AVG
Violent crime rate	402.2	465.5
Change in violent crime rate	5.6%	-2.2%
Property crime rate	4,373.1	3,517.1
Change in property crime rate	-29.4%	-2.1%

Transportation
Score: 36.1
Rank: 239

COMMUTE	AREA	U.S. AVG
Average commute time	23.1	27.4
Percent commutes > 60 mins.	3.4%	5.9%
Commute by auto	76.9%	78.9%
Commute by mass transit	2.7%	1.9%
Work at home	4.2%	3.1%
Mass transit miles per capita	2.70	1.87

INTERCITY SERVICES	AREA	U.S. AVG
Major airports within 60 miles	1	1
Size of regional airport	Medium	Large
Daily airline activity	115	686
Amtrak service	Yes	No

AUTOMOTIVE	AREA	U.S. AVG
Insurance, annual premium	$1,511	$1,432
Gas, cost per gallon	$2.48	$2.49
Daily vehicle miles per capita	22.3	24.0

Leisure
Score: 56.1
Rank: 164

DINING & SHOPPING	AREA	U.S. AVG
Restaurant rating	1	2
Outlet mall score	18	42
No. Starbucks	20	13
No. warehouse clubs	2	2

ENTERTAINMENT	AREA	U.S. AVG
Professional sports rating	3	4
College sports rating	3	4
Zoo/aquarium rating	1	3
Amusement park rating	1	3
Botanical garden/ arboretum rating	2	4

OUTDOOR ACTIVITIES	AREA	U.S. AVG
Golf-course rating	2	4
Ski-area rating	9	3
Sq. miles inland water	3	4
Miles of coastline	0.0	10.7
National Park rating	3	3

Arts & Culture
Score: 47.3
Rank: 197

MEDIA & LIBRARIES	AREA	U.S. AVG
Arts radio rating	1	3
No. public libraries	16	27
Library volumes per capita	2.71	2.78

PERFORMING ARTS	AREA	U.S. AVG
Classical music rating	4	4
Ballet/dance rating	1	3
Professional theater rating	1	3
University arts programs rating	5	5

MUSEUMS	AREA	U.S. AVG
Overall museum rating	3	5
Art museum rating	5	5
Science museum rating	1	5
Children's museum rating	3	3

Springfield, IL

Score: 56.1   Rank: 205   2004 rank: 196

Profile: Small capital city
Location: Near the geographic center of Illinois
Elevation: 613 feet
Time zone: Central Standard Time

PRO	CON
Capital-city amenities	Recreation
Historic interest	Violent crime
Cost of living	Low ethnic diversity

Springfield, the state capital, is a quiet agricultural center with a strong government presence. This quiet town with a fairly well-educated population has a substantial heritage built around Abraham Lincoln's residence and activities. It is "altogether fitting" that the Lincoln memorabilia should be mixed into such a traditional, mid-American city. The low cost of living makes it that much more attractive. Healthcare facilities are above average, anchored by major branch campus medical and pharmacy schools. The employment scene is dominated by government and healthcare providers; employment is solid but not on a strong growth trajectory. Rates for violent crime are high, especially for the region, and aside from historic sites, there isn't much to do in the city or surrounding area.

Springfield is located in the middle of a vast agricultural plain with rolling terrain near the Sangamon River and Spring Creek. Summers bring sunny, clear, warm, and humid days with frequent afternoon thundershowers. Windy, changeable springs and relatively calm autumns with periods of warm, dry, Indian summers are typical. Winters are fairly cold. Precipitation is evenly spread throughout the year. First freeze is mid-October; last is mid-April.

Population

DEMOGRAPHICS	AREA	U.S. AVG	ETHNIC COMPOSITION	AREA	U.S. AVG	RESIDENT PROFILE	AREA	U.S. AVG
Population	205,571		White	86.8%	79.0%	Single	31.9%	32.4%
Population density per sq. mile	173.9	358.5	Black	9.8%	10.5%	Married	53.0%	52.7%
Population growth	8.5%	21.1%	Asian	1.4%	2.7%	Divorced/separated	15.1%	14.9%
Median age	38.2	36.1	Hispanic	1.3%	10.6%	Married with children	21.5%	23.7%
Percent Democrat	40.0%	44.5%	Religious observance	56.9%	48.9%	Single with children	9.2%	9.1%
Percent Republican	59.1%	54.5%	Diversity measure	25.6	40.1	Percent over age 65	13.5%	12.9%

Economy
& Jobs
Score: 81.0
Rank: 72

INCOME	AREA	U.S. AVG	EMPLOYMENT	AREA	U.S. AVG	EMPLOYING INDUSTRIES	AREA	U.S. AVG
Per capita income	$26,790	$23,235	Unemployment rate	4.7%	4.7%	Largest: Healthcare & Social Assistance		
Household income	$49,229	$46,414	Recent job growth	3.5%	1.3%			
Household income < $25K	22.3%	26.2%	Projected future job growth	10.4%	11.5%	Percent manufacturing	8.3%	15.4%
Household income > $75K	28.1%	25.4%	White collar	68.4%	57.8%	Percent public sector	29.8%	15.7%
Household income growth	14.0%	13.6%	Blue collar	16.2%	25.2%	Percent construction	7.9%	9.9%

Cost of Living
Score: 75.7
Rank: 92

INDEXES & TAXES	AREA	U.S. AVG	HOUSING	AREA	U.S. AVG	NECESSITIES	AREA	U.S. AVG
Cost of Living Index	79.1	100.0	Median home price	$112,100	$220,000	Food Index	94.5	100.0
Buying Power Index	139.5	100.0	Home price appreciation	17.0%	10.1%	Housing Index	49.2	100.0
Income tax rate	3.00%	4.70%	Median rent	$596	$709	Utilities Index	104.1	100.0
Sales tax rate	7.66%	6.58%	Homes owned	65.5%	62.3%	Transportation Index	98.1	100.0
Property tax rate	$17.56	$12.00	Home price ratio	2.3	4.2	Healthcare Index	98.4	100.0
						Miscellaneous Cost Index	92.6	100.0

Climate
Score: 36.9
Rank: 235

TEMPERATURE	AREA	U.S. AVG	PRECIPITATION	AREA	U.S. AVG	COMFORTS & HAZARDS	AREA	U.S. AVG
Average January low	18.6	26.2	Annual inches precipitation	35.0	37.7	July relative humidity	71%	66%
Average July high	86.6	87.4	Annual inches snowfall	22.0	7.0	Annual days mostly sunny	200	208
Annual days > 90°F	28	38	Annual days precipitation	112	109	Annual days with thunderstorms	50	39
Annual days < 32°F	119	89	Annual days rain > 0.5 inches	20	22	Tornado risk score	34	18
Annual days < 0°F	8	6	Annual days snow > 1.5 inches	5	6	Hurricane risk score	2	13

TEMPERATURE

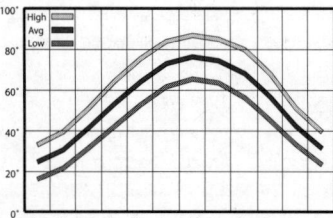

PRECIPITATION

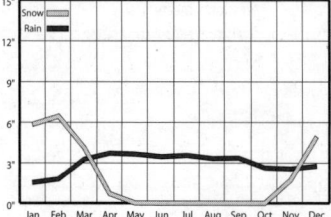

DAYS OF CLOUDS & PRECIPITATION

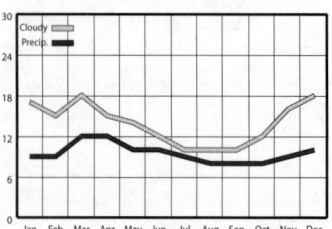

Education
Score: 61.8
Rank: 144

ACHIEVEMENT	AREA	U.S. AVG	PUBLIC SCHOOLS	AREA	U.S. AVG	HIGHER EDUCATION	AREA	U.S. AVG
High school degree	88.1%	82.7%	Expenditures per pupil	$4,578	$5,686	No. 2-year colleges	2	4
2-year college degree	6.7%	6.4%	Student/teacher ratio	17.6	16.7	No. 4-year colleges/universities	3	6
4-year college degree	18.1%	15.7%	Attending public school	86.6%	90.1%	No. highly ranked universities	0	1
Graduate/professional degree	10.1%	8.9%	State SAT score	1200	1021			
			State ACT score	20.5*	20.9			

Health & Healthcare
Score: 75.9
Rank: 91

HAZARDS & ILLNESSES	AREA	U.S. AVG	HEALTHCARE	AREA	U.S. AVG	CRIME	AREA	U.S. AVG
Air-quality score	36	37	Physicians per capita	429.5	244.2	Violent crime rate	917.2	465.5
Water-quality score	27	52	Hospital beds per capita	669.4	420.0	Change in violent crime rate	-2.0%	-2.2%
Pollen/allergy score	46	61	No. teaching hospitals	3	3	Property crime rate	4,442.1	3,517.1
Cancer mortality per capita	213.3	201.9	Cost per doctor visit	$79	$77	Change in property crime rate	-6.7%	-2.1%
Depression days per month	2.7	3.5	Cost per dental visit	$75	$70			
Stress score	44	50						

Crime
Score: 4.0
Rank: 358

Transportation
Score: 79.9
Rank: 76

COMMUTE	AREA	U.S. AVG	INTERCITY SERVICES	AREA	U.S. AVG	AUTOMOTIVE	AREA	U.S. AVG
Average commute time	21.5	27.4	Major airports within 60 miles	1	1	Insurance, annual premium	$1,177	$1,432
Percent commutes > 60 mins.	3.1%	5.9%	Size of regional airport	Large	Large	Gas, cost per gallon	$2.45	$2.49
Commute by auto	82.1%	78.9%	Daily airline activity	731	686	Daily vehicle miles per capita	29.2	24.0
Commute by mass transit	1.6%	1.9%	Amtrak service	Yes	No			
Work at home	2.8%	3.1%						
Mass transit miles per capita	1.56	1.87						

Leisure
Score: 10.4
Rank: 334

DINING & SHOPPING	AREA	U.S. AVG	ENTERTAINMENT	AREA	U.S. AVG	OUTDOOR ACTIVITIES	AREA	U.S. AVG
Restaurant rating	1	2	Professional sports rating	2	4	Golf-course rating	2	4
Outlet mall score	12	42	College sports rating	2	4	Ski-area rating	1	3
No. Starbucks	3	13	Zoo/aquarium rating	3	3	Sq. miles inland water	2	4
No. warehouse clubs	0	2	Amusement park rating	1	3	Miles of coastline	0.0	10.7
			Botanical garden/arboretum rating	6	4	National Park rating	1	3

Arts & Culture
Score: 46.8
Rank: 199

MEDIA & LIBRARIES	AREA	U.S. AVG	PERFORMING ARTS	AREA	U.S. AVG	MUSEUMS	AREA	U.S. AVG
Arts radio rating	1	3	Classical music rating	3	4	Overall museum rating	9	5
No. public libraries	16	27	Ballet/dance rating	1	3	Art museum rating	7	5
Library volumes per capita	4.90	2.78	Professional theater rating	1	3	Science museum rating	8	5
			University arts programs rating	1	5	Children's museum rating	2	3

Springfield, MA

Score: 41.0   **Rank:** 311   **2004 rank:** 251

Profile: Mid-size city
Location: Southwest Massachusetts, on the Connecticut River, 6 miles north of the Connecticut border
Elevation: 179 feet
Time zone: Eastern Standard Time

PRO	CON
Nearby mountains	Economy
Museums	Entertainment
Cost of living	Violent crime

Springfield, once a major center of industrial innovation, is the state's third-largest city and a regional health, retail, and financial center. Locals are credited with development of the Springfield rifle, the 1895 Duryea motorcar, and basketball (thanks to Dr. James Naismith, in 1891), and some credit the motorcycle to area inventors and the early Indian Manufacturing Company. At one time the area was a significant manufacturing center, but most have left the area, including most recently a forge that made Craftsman tools. Economic dislocation is evident everywhere. The downtown underwent an early renewal in the 1970s, and has declined from that point leaving an unfortunate modern but uninhabited look; there is a sprinkling of history through its museums, buildings, and historic sites including the Quadrangle cultural center and park, but downtown overall is not an attraction. The "five college" area to the north includes the University of Massachusetts in Amherst and colleges of Amherst, Holyoke, Smith, and Hampshire, and the Berkshire mountains to the north and west offer some recreation. The Cost of Living Index at 105.7 is no bargain, but on a Massachusetts scale it is attractive, particularly scaled against local incomes and projected income growth. The employment picture is currently very weak, and climate and crime further depress the ranking.

The area sits in a broad valley in the western part of Massachusetts. Thickly wooded hills rise immediately to the east and west of the valley. Bodies of water to the east and south have an effect. Summers are hot, humid, and calm with occasional thundershowers. Winters bring frequent cold snaps and snow, particularly generated by moist mid-Atlantic storms colliding with cold, northerly air masses. First freeze is mid-October; last is late April.

Population

DEMOGRAPHICS	AREA	U.S. AVG	ETHNIC COMPOSITION	AREA	U.S. AVG	RESIDENT PROFILE	AREA	U.S. AVG
Population	693,648		White	82.1%	79.0%	Single	39.1%	32.4%
Population density per sq. mile	375.0	358.5	Black	6.3%	10.5%	Married	46.4%	52.7%
Population growth	3.1%	21.1%	Asian	2.0%	2.7%	Divorced/separated	14.5%	14.9%
Median age	37.1	36.1	Hispanic	12.5%	10.6%	Married with children	20.0%	23.7%
Percent Democrat	63.6%	44.5%	Religious observance	58.5%	48.9%	Single with children	10.6%	9.1%
Percent Republican	35.0%	54.5%	Diversity measure	44.2	40.1	Percent over age 65	13.7%	12.9%

Economy & Jobs
Score: 4.3
Rank: 357

INCOME	AREA	U.S. AVG	EMPLOYMENT	AREA	U.S. AVG	EMPLOYING INDUSTRIES	AREA	U.S. AVG
Per capita income	$23,205	$23,235	Unemployment rate	5.4%	4.7%	Largest: Healthcare & Social Assistance		
Household income	$46,492	$46,414	Recent job growth	0.0%	1.3%			
Household income < $25K	27.1%	26.2%	Projected future job growth	-1.2%	11.5%	Percent manufacturing	15.7%	15.4%
Household income > $75K	26.3%	25.4%	White collar	59.6%	57.8%	Percent public sector	18.5%	15.7%
Household income growth	12.6%	13.6%	Blue collar	23.6%	25.2%	Percent construction	8.0%	9.9%

Cost of Living
Score: 20.1
Rank: 298

INDEXES & TAXES	AREA	U.S. AVG	HOUSING	AREA	U.S. AVG	NECESSITIES	AREA	U.S. AVG
Cost of Living Index	105.7	100.0	Median home price	$208,600	$220,000	Food Index	118.4	100.0
Buying Power Index	98.6	100.0	Home price appreciation	68.1%	10.1%	Housing Index	72.5	100.0
Income tax rate	5.95%	4.70%	Median rent	$828	$709	Utilities Index	108.3	100.0
Sales tax rate	5.00%	6.58%	Homes owned	59.8%	62.3%	Transportation Index	110.8	100.0
Property tax rate	$16.12	$12.00	Home price ratio	4.5	4.2	Healthcare Index	121.1	100.0
						Miscellaneous Cost Index	105.7	100.0

Climate
Score: 1.1
Rank: 369

TEMPERATURE	AREA	U.S. AVG	PRECIPITATION	AREA	U.S. AVG	COMFORTS & HAZARDS	AREA	U.S. AVG
Average January low	16.1	26.2	Annual inches precipitation	43.0	37.7	July relative humidity	68%	66%
Average July high	84.1	87.4	Annual inches snowfall	53.0	7.0	Annual days mostly sunny	188	208
Annual days > 90°F	20	38	Annual days precipitation	128	109	Annual days with thunderstorms	22	39
Annual days < 32°F	137	89	Annual days rain > 0.5 inches	26	22	Tornado risk score	19	18
Annual days < 0°F	6	6	Annual days snow > 1.5 inches	19	6	Hurricane risk score	16	13

TEMPERATURE

PRECIPITATION

DAYS OF CLOUDS & PRECIPITATION

Education
Score: 92.8
Rank: 28

ACHIEVEMENT	AREA	U.S. AVG	PUBLIC SCHOOLS	AREA	U.S. AVG	HIGHER EDUCATION	AREA	U.S. AVG
High school degree	82.2%	82.7%	Expenditures per pupil	$7,004	$5,686	No. 2-year colleges	3	4
2-year college degree	8.1%	6.4%	Student/teacher ratio	0.0	16.7	No. 4-year colleges/universities	13	6
4-year college degree	14.6%	15.7%	Attending public school	89.2%	90.1%	No. highly ranked universities	5	1
Graduate/professional degree	10.7%	8.9%	State SAT score	1037*	1021			
			State ACT score	23	20.9			

Health & Healthcare
Score: 41.4
Rank: 218

Crime
Score: 21.1
Rank: 295

HAZARDS & ILLNESSES	AREA	U.S. AVG	HEALTHCARE	AREA	U.S. AVG	CRIME	AREA	U.S. AVG
Air-quality score	38	37	Physicians per capita	259.5	244.2	Violent crime rate	644.3	465.5
Water-quality score	63	52	Hospital beds per capita	314.7	420.0	Change in violent crime rate	-7.3%	-2.2%
Pollen/allergy score	53	61	No. teaching hospitals	1	3	Property crime rate	3,080.6	3,517.1
Cancer mortality per capita	218.9	201.9	Cost per doctor visit	$87	$77	Change in property crime rate	-10.1%	-2.1%
Depression days per month	4.3	3.5	Cost per dental visit	$77	$70			
Stress score	61	50						

Transportation
Score: 90.4
Rank: 37

COMMUTE	AREA	U.S. AVG	INTERCITY SERVICES	AREA	U.S. AVG	AUTOMOTIVE	AREA	U.S. AVG
Average commute time	24.0	27.4	Major airports within 60 miles	2	1	Insurance, annual premium	$2,000	$1,432
Percent commutes > 60 mins.	4.8%	5.9%	Size of regional airport	Large	Large	Gas, cost per gallon	$2.41	$2.49
Commute by auto	79.7%	78.9%	Daily airline activity	1434	686	Daily vehicle miles per capita	24.2	24.0
Commute by mass transit	2.3%	1.9%	Amtrak service	Yes	No			
Work at home	2.9%	3.1%						
Mass transit miles per capita	2.32	1.87						

DINING & SHOPPING	AREA	U.S. AVG	ENTERTAINMENT	AREA	U.S. AVG	OUTDOOR ACTIVITIES	AREA	U.S. AVG
Restaurant rating	1	2	Professional sports rating	3	4	Golf-course rating	5	4
Outlet mall score	88	42	College sports rating	4	4	Ski-area rating	7	3
No. Starbucks	4	13	Zoo/aquarium rating	2	3	Sq. miles inland water	3	4
No. warehouse clubs	3	2	Amusement park rating	3	3	Miles of coastline	0.0	10.7
			Botanical garden/ arboretum rating	4	4	National Park rating	1	3

Leisure
Score: 62.3
Rank: 141

MEDIA & LIBRARIES	AREA	U.S. AVG	PERFORMING ARTS	AREA	U.S. AVG	MUSEUMS	AREA	U.S. AVG
Arts radio rating	1	3	Classical music rating	4	4	Overall museum rating	8	5
No. public libraries	92	27	Ballet/dance rating	5	3	Art museum rating	8	5
Library volumes per capita	4.53	2.78	Professional theater rating	6	3	Science museum rating	7	5
			University arts programs rating	9	5	Children's museum rating	7	3

Arts & Culture
Score: 74.3
Rank: 96

Springfield, MO

Score: 55.5   Rank: 218   2004 rank: 119

Profile: Small city
Location: Southwest Missouri at the foot of the Ozark Mountains
Elevation: 1,270 feet
Time zone: Central Standard Time

PRO
Nearby mountains
Nearby recreation
Cost of living

CON
Growth and sprawl
Economic concerns
Low ethnic diversity

Springfield, the state's third-largest city, serves as a commercial center and gateway to the Ozark Mountains. The town is an important crossroads and agricultural center for livestock and poultry production, and has grown rapidly in recent years, strengthening the economy but also bringing some unattractive sprawl and contentious growth-management issues. The former Southwest Missouri State University, recently renamed Missouri State, now brings some 18,000 students to town and some cultural and especially sports interest. The Ozark Mountains provide recreation, scenic attractions, and relief from summer heat. There is a strong Bible Belt influence. The large number of tourist attractions sometimes border on the tawdry. Branson, a glittery entertainment and recreation center aimed at country music fans, is 40 miles south. Branson's recent, rapid growth has helped the economy and put the area on the national map, but it has also brought some unwanted tourist impact; we're not sure the kind of economic growth found here is sustainable. The cost of living and housing cost profiles are, not surprisingly, attractive and consistent with the rest of the region.

The flat to gently rolling terrain, located on an Ozark Mountain plateau, contains areas of mixed deciduous forest and farmland. The higher Ozarks and numerous, wooded creek valleys extend to the south and west into Arkansas. Ozark winters are considerably milder and summers are appreciably cooler than conditions in nearby lower elevations. Hot, humid spells and cold can occur, but pockets of mountain air usually moderate them. First freeze is mid-October; last is mid-April.

DEMOGRAPHICS	AREA	U.S. AVG	ETHNIC COMPOSITION	AREA	U.S. AVG	RESIDENT PROFILE	AREA	U.S. AVG
Population	392,592		White	94.4%	79.0%	Single	29.1%	32.4%
Population density per sq. mile	130.4	358.5	Black	1.7%	10.5%	Married	55.9%	52.7%
Population growth	36.0%	21.1%	Asian	1.0%	2.7%	Divorced/separated	15.0%	14.9%
Median age	35.7	36.1	Hispanic	1.7%	10.6%	Married with children	23.4%	23.7%
Percent Democrat	34.7%	44.5%	Religious observance	51.6%	48.9%	Single with children	7.9%	9.1%
Percent Republican	64.7%	54.5%	Diversity measure	13.7	40.1	Percent over age 65	13.4%	12.9%

Population

INCOME	AREA	U.S. AVG	EMPLOYMENT	AREA	U.S. AVG	EMPLOYING INDUSTRIES	AREA	U.S. AVG
Per capita income	$20,735	$23,235	Unemployment rate	4.3%	4.7%	Largest: Healthcare & Social Assistance		
Household income	$38,798	$46,414	Recent job growth	1.3%	1.3%			
Household income < $25K	30.7%	26.2%	Projected future job growth	14.7%	11.5%	Percent manufacturing	16.7%	15.4%
Household income > $75K	17.9%	25.4%	White collar	56.5%	57.8%	Percent public sector	11.2%	15.7%
Household income growth	14.1%	13.6%	Blue collar	26.5%	25.2%	Percent construction	9.8%	9.9%

Economy & Jobs
Score: 59.4
Rank: 153

INDEXES & TAXES	AREA	U.S. AVG	HOUSING	AREA	U.S. AVG	NECESSITIES	AREA	U.S. AVG
Cost of Living Index	79.5	100.0	Median home price	$122,100	$220,000	Food Index	98.1	100.0
Buying Power Index	109.4	100.0	Home price appreciation	28.1%	10.1%	Housing Index	46.1	100.0
Income tax rate	6.00%	4.70%	Median rent	$533	$709	Utilities Index	77.7	100.0
Sales tax rate	6.38%	6.58%	Homes owned	63.7%	62.3%	Transportation Index	93.7	100.0
Property tax rate	$7.20	$12.00	Home price ratio	3.1	4.2	Healthcare Index	100.9	100.0
						Miscellaneous Cost Index	94.8	100.0

Cost of Living
Score: 78.1
Rank: 83

Climate
Score: 31.6
Rank: 255

TEMPERATURE	AREA	U.S. AVG
Average January low	22.6	26.2
Average July high	89.0	87.4
Annual days > 90°F	40	38
Annual days < 32°F	105	89
Annual days < 0°F	3	6

PRECIPITATION	AREA	U.S. AVG
Annual inches precipitation	40.0	37.7
Annual inches snowfall	15.0	7.0
Annual days precipitation	107	109
Annual days rain > 0.5 inches	27	22
Annual days snow > 1.5 inches	5	6

COMFORTS & HAZARDS	AREA	U.S. AVG
July relative humidity	70%	66%
Annual days mostly sunny	216	208
Annual days with thunderstorms	58	39
Tornado risk score	30	18
Hurricane risk score	3	13

TEMPERATURE

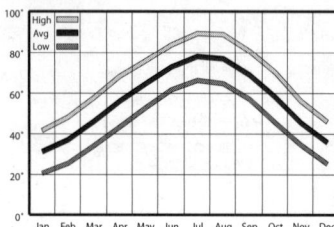

PRECIPITATION

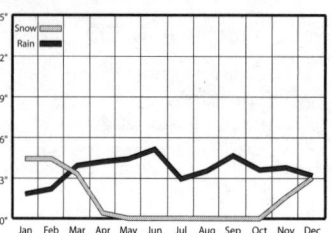

DAYS OF CLOUDS & PRECIPITATION

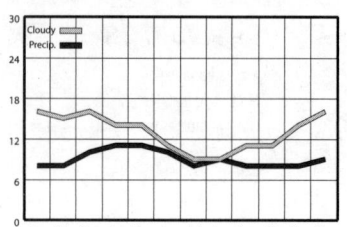

Education
Score: 57.8
Rank: 159

ACHIEVEMENT	AREA	U.S. AVG
High school degree	83.1%	82.7%
2-year college degree	4.6%	6.4%
4-year college degree	14.4%	15.7%
Graduate/professional degree	7.0%	8.9%

PUBLIC SCHOOLS	AREA	U.S. AVG
Expenditures per pupil	$4,355	$5,686
Student/teacher ratio	14.9	16.7
Attending public school	94.8%	90.1%
State SAT score	1178	1021
State ACT score	21.6*	20.9

HIGHER EDUCATION	AREA	U.S. AVG
No. 2-year colleges	6	4
No. 4-year colleges/universities	12	6
No. highly ranked universities	2	1

Health & Healthcare
Score: 77.8
Rank: 84

HAZARDS & ILLNESSES	AREA	U.S. AVG
Air-quality score	45	37
Water-quality score	86	52
Pollen/allergy score	42	61
Cancer mortality per capita	220.7	201.9
Depression days per month	3.9	3.5
Stress score	48	50

HEALTHCARE	AREA	U.S. AVG
Physicians per capita	235.5	244.2
Hospital beds per capita	490.6	420.0
No. teaching hospitals	1	3
Cost per doctor visit	$75	$77
Cost per dental visit	$66	$70

Crime
Score: 71.9
Rank: 106

CRIME	AREA	U.S. AVG
Violent crime rate	355.8	465.5
Change in violent crime rate	12.0%	-2.2%
Property crime rate	4,427.4	3,517.1
Change in property crime rate	0.6%	-2.1%

Transportation
Score: 14.2
Rank: 322

COMMUTE	AREA	U.S. AVG
Average commute time	23.8	27.4
Percent commutes > 60 mins.	4.3%	5.9%
Commute by auto	81.3%	78.9%
Commute by mass transit	0.6%	1.9%
Work at home	3.9%	3.1%
Mass transit miles per capita	0.56	1.87

INTERCITY SERVICES	AREA	U.S. AVG
Major airports within 60 miles	0	1
Size of regional airport	Small	Large
Daily airline activity	56	686
Amtrak service	No	No

AUTOMOTIVE	AREA	U.S. AVG
Insurance, annual premium	$1,220	$1,432
Gas, cost per gallon	$2.34	$2.49
Daily vehicle miles per capita	23.6	24.0

Leisure
Score: 23.5
Rank: 285

DINING & SHOPPING	AREA	U.S. AVG
Restaurant rating	1	2
Outlet mall score	0	42
No. Starbucks	3	13
No. warehouse clubs	0	2

ENTERTAINMENT	AREA	U.S. AVG
Professional sports rating	2	4
College sports rating	3	4
Zoo/aquarium rating	3	3
Amusement park rating	1	3
Botanical garden/ arboretum rating	1	4

OUTDOOR ACTIVITIES	AREA	U.S. AVG
Golf-course rating	2	4
Ski-area rating	1	3
Sq. miles inland water	2	4
Miles of coastline	0.0	10.7
National Park rating	4	3

Arts & Culture
Score: 61.5
Rank: 144

MEDIA & LIBRARIES	AREA	U.S. AVG
Arts radio rating	5	3
No. public libraries	14	27
Library volumes per capita	2.13	2.78

PERFORMING ARTS	AREA	U.S. AVG
Classical music rating	4	4
Ballet/dance rating	1	3
Professional theater rating	1	3
University arts programs rating	8	5

MUSEUMS	AREA	U.S. AVG
Overall museum rating	4	5
Art museum rating	4	5
Science museum rating	1	5
Children's museum rating	3	3

Springfield, OH

Score: 70.5   **Rank:** 87   **2004 rank:** 41

Profile: Small city
Location: West-central Ohio 30 miles northeast of Dayton and 45 miles west of Columbus
Elevation: 905 feet
Time zone: Eastern Standard Time

PRO	CON
Diverse economy	Economic cycles
Nearby cities	Entertainment
Cost of housing	Property crime

Springfield is strategically located between Dayton and Columbus on or near major east–west and north–south transportation routes through Ohio and serving the country. The city has a strong industrial heritage, at one time being a manufacturing center for automobiles and farm implements before that industry concentrated into just a few players. Big employers today include Navistar International and Honda and an assortment of smaller manufacturing, food processing, and distribution enterprises. Downtown is more interesting than some, with a number of historic buildings and an active preservation and redevelopment program. Springfield has nice inner neighborhoods with quality homes on densely wooded streets. The 2,100-student Wittenberg University adds a noticeable college-town element, and there are relatively strong arts amenities in general for this size of town. A new 45-acre community healthcare campus is scheduled to break ground in 2007. The area overall has a good balance of amenities and features for the price and an attractive central location relative to larger Ohio cities, hence the relatively high ranking.

Springfield is located in the small valley of Buck Creek in an area of gently rolling agricultural and wooded hills in west-central Ohio. The continental climate gives warm, calm, humid summers. Winters are cold and changeable with occasional below-zero temperatures, but highs in the 30s and 40s and lows in the 20s is the norm. Frequent air-mass collisions produce precipitation throughout the year, mostly as spring and summer showers and thunderstorms, with periods of winter rain. Snowfall is light to moderate, with frequent winter snow flurries. First freeze is late October; last is mid-April.

Population

DEMOGRAPHICS	AREA	U.S. AVG	ETHNIC COMPOSITION	AREA	U.S. AVG	RESIDENT PROFILE	AREA	U.S. AVG
Population	142,815		White	87.9%	79.0%	Single	30.9%	32.4%
Population density per sq. mile	357.1	358.5	Black	8.7%	10.5%	Married	54.3%	52.7%
Population growth	-3.2%	21.1%	Asian	0.7%	2.7%	Divorced/separated	14.8%	14.9%
Median age	38.4	36.1	Hispanic	1.4%	10.6%	Married with children	21.1%	23.7%
Percent Democrat	48.7%	44.5%	Religious observance	34.2%	48.9%	Single with children	9.9%	9.1%
Percent Republican	50.8%	54.5%	Diversity measure	24.1	40.1	Percent over age 65	15.1%	12.9%

Economy & Jobs
Score: 15.2
Rank: 316

INCOME	AREA	U.S. AVG	EMPLOYMENT	AREA	U.S. AVG	EMPLOYING INDUSTRIES	AREA	U.S. AVG
Per capita income	$21,935	$23,235	Unemployment rate	6.0%	4.7%	Largest: Manufacturing		
Household income	$44,259	$46,414	Recent job growth	0.2%	1.3%			
Household income < $25K	26.1%	26.2%	Projected future job growth	-0.1%	11.5%	Percent manufacturing	22.6%	15.4%
Household income > $75K	22.3%	25.4%	White collar	52.2%	57.8%	Percent public sector	13.7%	15.7%
Household income growth	9.7%	13.6%	Blue collar	31.9%	25.2%	Percent construction	9.3%	9.9%

Cost of Living
Score: 35.8
Rank: 240

INDEXES & TAXES	AREA	U.S. AVG	HOUSING	AREA	U.S. AVG	NECESSITIES	AREA	U.S. AVG
Cost of Living Index	83.3	100.0	Median home price	$120,600	$220,000	Food Index	98.1	100.0
Buying Power Index	119.1	100.0	Home price appreciation	16.2%	10.1%	Housing Index	47.2	100.0
Income tax rate	7.24%	4.70%	Median rent	$578	$709	Utilities Index	103.7	100.0
Sales tax rate	7.50%	6.58%	Homes owned	67.0%	62.3%	Transportation Index	103.3	100.0
Property tax rate	$11.72	$12.00	Home price ratio	2.7	4.2	Healthcare Index	97.6	100.0
						Miscellaneous Cost Index	98.4	100.0

Climate
Score: 46.3
Rank: 200

TEMPERATURE	AREA	U.S. AVG	PRECIPITATION	AREA	U.S. AVG	COMFORTS & HAZARDS	AREA	U.S. AVG
Average January low	20.4	26.2	Annual inches precipitation	34.4	37.7	July relative humidity	70%	66%
Average July high	84.7	87.4	Annual inches snowfall	28.6	7.0	Annual days mostly sunny	182	208
Annual days > 90°F	17	38	Annual days precipitation	130	109	Annual days with thunderstorms	40	39
Annual days < 32°F	117	89	Annual days rain > 0.5 inches	22	22	Tornado risk score	43	18
Annual days < 0°F	6	6	Annual days snow > 1.5 inches	6	6	Hurricane risk score	4	13

TEMPERATURE

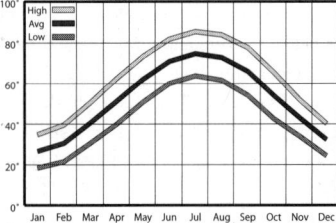

PRECIPITATION

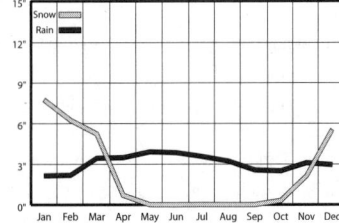

DAYS OF CLOUDS & PRECIPITATION

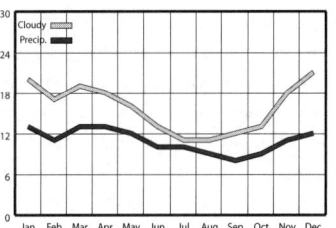

Education
Score: 28.1
Rank: 270

ACHIEVEMENT	AREA	U.S. AVG	PUBLIC SCHOOLS	AREA	U.S. AVG	HIGHER EDUCATION	AREA	U.S. AVG
High school degree	81.5%	82.7%	Expenditures per pupil	$4,951	$5,686	No. 2-year colleges	3	4
2-year college degree	6.2%	6.4%	Student/teacher ratio	17.2	16.7	No. 4-year colleges/universities	1	6
4-year college degree	9.6%	15.7%	Attending public school	93.9%	90.1%	No. highly ranked universities	1	1
Graduate/professional degree	5.5%	8.9%	State SAT score	1079	1021			
			State ACT score	21.5*	20.9			

Health & Healthcare
Score: 48.1
Rank: 195

Crime
Score: 63.1
Rank: 139

HAZARDS & ILLNESSES	AREA	U.S. AVG	HEALTHCARE	AREA	U.S. AVG	CRIME	AREA	U.S. AVG
Air-quality score	52	37	Physicians per capita	147.2	244.2	Violent crime rate	440.9	465.5
Water-quality score	36	52	Hospital beds per capita	399.1	420.0	Change in violent crime rate	8.4%	-2.2%
Pollen/allergy score	60	61	No. teaching hospitals	0	3	Property crime rate	6,031.1	3,517.1
Cancer mortality per capita	228.1	201.9	Cost per doctor visit	$71	$77	Change in property crime rate	0.1%	-2.1%
Depression days per month	4.2	3.5	Cost per dental visit	$61	$70			
Stress score	92	50						

Transportation
Score: 86.4
Rank: 52

COMMUTE	AREA	U.S. AVG	INTERCITY SERVICES	AREA	U.S. AVG	AUTOMOTIVE	AREA	U.S. AVG
Average commute time	23.4	27.4	Major airports within 60 miles	2	1	Insurance, annual premium	$1,365	$1,432
Percent commutes > 60 mins.	4.3%	5.9%	Size of regional airport	Large	Large	Gas, cost per gallon	$2.47	$2.49
Commute by auto	82.9%	78.9%	Daily airline activity	1147	686	Daily vehicle miles per capita	22.5	24.0
Commute by mass transit	1.0%	1.9%	Amtrak service	No	No			
Work at home	2.1%	3.1%						
Mass transit miles per capita	1.04	1.87						

Leisure
Score: 51.9
Rank: 179

DINING & SHOPPING	AREA	U.S. AVG	ENTERTAINMENT	AREA	U.S. AVG	OUTDOOR ACTIVITIES	AREA	U.S. AVG
Restaurant rating	3	2	Professional sports rating	4	4	Golf-course rating	6	4
Outlet mall score	4	42	College sports rating	3	4	Ski-area rating	2	3
No. Starbucks	0	13	Zoo/aquarium rating	4	3	Sq. miles inland water	2	4
No. warehouse clubs	0	2	Amusement park rating	1	3	Miles of coastline	0.0	10.7
			Botanical garden/ arboretum rating	6	4	National Park rating	1	3

Arts & Culture
Score: 87.7
Rank: 47

MEDIA & LIBRARIES	AREA	U.S. AVG	PERFORMING ARTS	AREA	U.S. AVG	MUSEUMS	AREA	U.S. AVG
Arts radio rating	8	3	Classical music rating	6	4	Overall museum rating	5	5
No. public libraries	6	27	Ballet/dance rating	7	3	Art museum rating	6	5
Library volumes per capita	3.36	2.78	Professional theater rating	1	3	Science museum rating	3	5
			University arts programs rating	7	5	Children's museum rating	3	3

State College, PA   Score: 79.5   Rank: 49   2004 rank: 31

Profile: College town
Location: Central Pennsylvania in the Nittany Valley at the central Allegheny ridge
Elevation: 1,200 feet
Time zone: Eastern Standard Time

PRO	CON
College-town amenities	Isolation
Educated population	Narrow employment base
Attractive setting	Low ethnic diversity

Not surprisingly, the name State College is fairly self-explanatory. The town is built around gigantic Penn State University, which provides the town with the usual college amenities, steady employment, and sports entertainment. At some 40,000 plus in number, the student body outnumbers the town's nonstudent population, which is highly educated, almost 40% possessing 4-year or graduate-level degrees. There are some small high-tech and defense-related industries in the area, but those looking for career employment might not find much here. In another name giveaway, the greater area is known informally as Happy Valley, indicating the area's notably low crime rates and low stress. The surrounding mountains provide some recreational opportunities, the setting is attractive, and the downtown is classic college town. Although the area is centrally located, the orientation of mountains and highway thoroughfares makes it relatively isolated from larger cities. Cost of living and housing are quite reasonable for such a college-town landscape.

The valley location, with its woods and rolling meadows, is green in summer and beautiful in fall. The Allegheny Plateau rises to the west. Summers are typically sunny and warm but less humid than other areas of the state; readings over 90°F are rare. Winters are fairly cold with most daytime lows below freezing and an occasional subzero reading. There is plenty of precipitation but less than in areas west of the Alleghenies, closer to Lake Erie. The mountains block the heaviest snows and coldest arctic air but the area receives significant snow and cloud cover. First freeze is early October; last is mid-May.

Population

DEMOGRAPHICS	AREA	U.S. AVG	ETHNIC COMPOSITION	AREA	U.S. AVG	RESIDENT PROFILE	AREA	U.S. AVG
Population	144,311		White	90.9%	79.0%	Single	46.3%	32.4%
Population density per sq. mile	130.3	358.5	Black	2.7%	10.5%	Married	43.9%	52.7%
Population growth	16.6%	21.1%	Asian	4.5%	2.7%	Divorced/separated	9.8%	14.9%
Median age	31.1	36.1	Hispanic	1.5%	10.6%	Married with children	20.8%	23.7%
Percent Democrat	47.8%	44.5%	Religious observance	42.8%	48.9%	Single with children	4.8%	9.1%
Percent Republican	51.6%	54.5%	Diversity measure	19.4	40.1	Percent over age 65	10.6%	12.9%

Economy & Jobs

Score: 33.4
Rank: 249

INCOME	AREA	U.S. AVG	EMPLOYMENT	AREA	U.S. AVG	EMPLOYING INDUSTRIES	AREA	U.S. AVG
Per capita income	$20,395	$23,235	Unemployment rate	4.2%	4.7%	Largest: Manufacturing		
Household income	$40,949	$46,414	Recent job growth	0.9%	1.3%			
Household income ‹ $25K	31.1%	26.2%	Projected future job growth	7.0%	11.5%	Percent manufacturing	11.1%	15.4%
Household income › $75K	21.7%	25.4%	White collar	64.7%	57.8%	Percent public sector	21.6%	15.7%
Household income growth	13.2%	13.6%	Blue collar	17.8%	25.2%	Percent construction	6.7%	9.9%

Cost of Living

Score: 77.0
Rank: 87

INDEXES & TAXES	AREA	U.S. AVG	HOUSING	AREA	U.S. AVG	NECESSITIES	AREA	U.S. AVG
Cost of Living Index	86.9	100.0	Median home price	$152,700	$220,000	Food Index	96.4	100.0
Buying Power Index	105.6	100.0	Home price appreciation	38.9%	10.1%	Housing Index	65.1	100.0
Income tax rate	2.80%	4.70%	Median rent	$742	$709	Utilities Index	108.4	100.0
Sales tax rate	6.00%	6.58%	Homes owned	56.3%	62.3%	Transportation Index	90.3	100.0
Property tax rate	$13.55	$12.00	Home price ratio	3.7	4.2	Healthcare Index	91.1	100.0
						Miscellaneous Cost Index	101.2	100.0

Climate

Score: 40.6
Rank: 221

TEMPERATURE	AREA	U.S. AVG	PRECIPITATION	AREA	U.S. AVG	COMFORTS & HAZARDS	AREA	U.S. AVG
Average January low	19.8	26.2	Annual inches precipitation	37.0	37.7	July relative humidity	67%	66%
Average July high	82.6	87.4	Annual inches snowfall	48.0	7.0	Annual days mostly sunny	180	208
Annual days › 90°F	8	38	Annual days precipitation	122	109	Annual days with thunderstorms	35	39
Annual days ‹ 32°F	132	89	Annual days rain › 0.5 inches	20	22	Tornado risk score	4	18
Annual days ‹ 0°F	4	6	Annual days snow › 1.5 inches	10	6	Hurricane risk score	6	13

TEMPERATURE

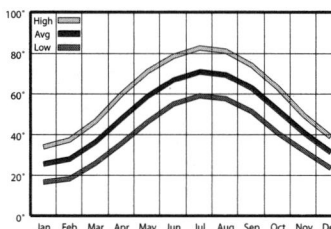

PRECIPITATION

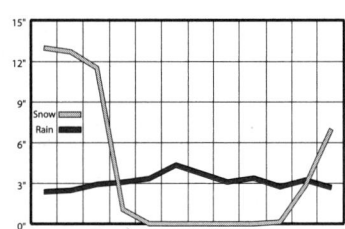

DAYS OF CLOUDS & PRECIPITATION

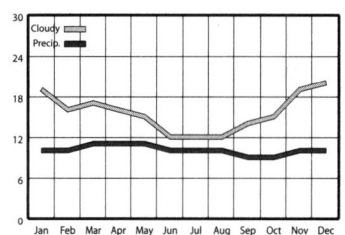

Education

Score: 86.6
Rank: 51

ACHIEVEMENT	AREA	U.S. AVG	PUBLIC SCHOOLS	AREA	U.S. AVG	HIGHER EDUCATION	AREA	U.S. AVG
High school degree	88.8%	82.7%	Expenditures per pupil	$6,645	$5,686	No. 2-year colleges	1	4
2-year college degree	4.7%	6.4%	Student/teacher ratio	17.7	16.7	No. 4-year colleges/universities	1	6
4-year college degree	19.6%	15.7%	Attending public school	90.9%	90.1%	No. highly ranked universities	1	1
Graduate/professional degree	18.7%	8.9%	State SAT score	993*	1021			
			State ACT score	21.8	20.9			

Health & Healthcare

Score: 88.8
Rank: 43

Crime

Score: 98.1
Rank: 8

HAZARDS & ILLNESSES	AREA	U.S. AVG	HEALTHCARE	AREA	U.S. AVG	CRIME	AREA	U.S. AVG
Air-quality score	52	37	Physicians per capita	187.8	244.2	Violent crime rate	108.0	465.5
Water-quality score	92	52	Hospital beds per capita	304.9	420.0	Change in violent crime rate	-7.0%	-2.2%
Pollen/allergy score	52	61	No. teaching hospitals	0	3	Property crime rate	2,000.9	3,517.1
Cancer mortality per capita	207.4	201.9	Cost per doctor visit	$62	$77	Change in property crime rate	1.2%	-2.1%
Depression days per month	4.2	3.5	Cost per dental visit	$52	$70			
Stress score	3	50						

Transportation

Score: 48.9
Rank: 191

COMMUTE	AREA	U.S. AVG	INTERCITY SERVICES	AREA	U.S. AVG	AUTOMOTIVE	AREA	U.S. AVG
Average commute time	21.4	27.4	Major airports within 60 miles	0	1	Insurance, annual premium	$1,021	$1,432
Percent commutes › 60 mins.	3.3%	5.9%	Size of regional airport	Small	Large	Gas, cost per gallon	$2.46	$2.49
Commute by auto	67.2%	78.9%	Daily airline activity	81	686	Daily vehicle miles per capita	16.3	24.0
Commute by mass transit	3.8%	1.9%	Amtrak service	No	No			
Work at home	4.1%	3.1%						
Mass transit miles per capita	3.78	1.87						

DINING & SHOPPING	AREA	U.S. AVG	ENTERTAINMENT	AREA	U.S. AVG	OUTDOOR ACTIVITIES	AREA	U.S. AVG
Restaurant rating	1	2	Professional sports rating	2	4	Golf-course rating	2	4
Outlet mall score	19	42	College sports rating	9	4	Ski-area rating	3	3
No. Starbucks	2	13	Zoo/aquarium rating	1	3	Sq. miles inland water	1	4
No. warehouse clubs	0	2	Amusement park rating	1	3	Miles of coastline	0.0	10.7
			Botanical garden/ arboretum rating	1	4	National Park rating	1	3

Leisure
Score: 30.2
Rank: 260

MEDIA & LIBRARIES	AREA	U.S. AVG	PERFORMING ARTS	AREA	U.S. AVG	MUSEUMS	AREA	U.S. AVG
Arts radio rating	1	3	Classical music rating	4	4	Overall museum rating	2	5
No. public libraries	5	27	Ballet/dance rating	3	3	Art museum rating	5	5
Library volumes per capita	2.01	2.78	Professional theater rating	1	3	Science museum rating	3	5
			University arts programs rating	5	5	Children's museum rating	1	3

Arts & Culture
Score: 44.1
Rank: 209

Stockton, CA

Score: 23.8   **Rank:** 350   **2004 rank:** 330

Profile: Small port/Industrial city
Location: Northern California, in Central Valley, 50 miles south of Sacramento
Elevation: 22 feet
Time zone: Pacific Standard Time

PRO	CON
Mild winters	Cost of living and housing
Close to Bay Area	Crime rates
Improving economy	Low educational attainment

Stockton, an inland port at the end of a ship channel accessing the San Francisco Bay, is a somewhat gritty central California transportation, distribution, and agricultural center. Despite an attempted comeback with some downtown renewal and public relations efforts, and pleasant suburbs near the University of the Pacific campus, the area remains generally unattractive and working class in character. These efforts, however, have lifted the area off of the bottom rung of the 2004 ranking, and as seen elsewhere, community leaders are responding to the area's problems and perceptions. Crime rates, particularly violent crime, remain very high, but the employment picture has improved somewhat. The strategic location at the crossroads of major north–south and east–west roads and rail routes into the Bay Area do add to the economy, especially in the commercial and industrial center of Lathrop to the south. Aside from recent renewal efforts, the downtown is nondescript and there isn't much to do. There is an active local symphony but other arts amenities are sparse. Another bright spot is the small agricultural town of Lodi 12 miles north, which is growing as a favored regional wine-growing and residential area. The bedroom community of Tracy farther south houses a large group of commuters willing to sacrifice a long, windy Bay Area commute for the privilege of owning a family home, though the Altamont Commuter Express rail service aids this commute somewhat. Winter climate and proximity to San Francisco are among the few positives, but ironically, the area may suffer from being a little too close to Sacramento and the Bay Area to develop its own amenities. Median home prices have skyrocketed to $461,500 from $216,000 in 2004, underscoring a common Central Valley problem of sparse amenities and economic and social problems, overlaid by high California costs.

Stockton is on the southeast corner of the broad delta formed by the confluence of the San Joaquin and Sacramento rivers. The surrounding terrain is flat, irrigated farm and orchard land, near sea level. The Sierra Nevada foothills rise about 25 miles to the east and northeast. The climate brings warm, dry days and relatively cool nights with clear skies and no rainfall. Winter brings mild temperatures with relatively light rain and frequent valley fog, which can last for 4 to 5 weeks. Most rain occurs in winter and snow is practically unknown.

DEMOGRAPHICS	AREA	U.S. AVG	ETHNIC COMPOSITION	AREA	U.S. AVG	RESIDENT PROFILE	AREA	U.S. AVG
Population	650,102		White	53.0%	79.0%	Single	31.6%	32.4%
Population density per sq. mile	464.6	358.5	Black	7.5%	10.5%	Married	51.1%	52.7%
Population growth	35.3%	21.1%	Asian	13.0%	2.7%	Divorced/separated	17.3%	14.9%
Median age	31.8	36.1	Hispanic	34.5%	10.6%	Married with children	29.1%	23.7%
Percent Democrat	45.8%	44.5%	Religious observance	38.2%	48.9%	Single with children	11.8%	9.1%
Percent Republican	53.2%	54.5%	Diversity measure	81.3	40.1	Percent over age 65	10.0%	12.9%

Population

INCOME	AREA	U.S. AVG	EMPLOYMENT	AREA	U.S. AVG	EMPLOYING INDUSTRIES	AREA	U.S. AVG
Per capita income	$19,661	$23,235	Unemployment rate	7.3%	4.7%	Largest: Healthcare & Social Assistance		
Household income	$46,689	$46,414	Recent job growth	2.8%	1.3%			
Household income < $25K	26.5%	26.2%	Projected future job growth	14.8%	11.5%	Percent manufacturing	16.8%	15.4%
Household income > $75K	27.4%	25.4%	White collar	53.8%	57.8%	Percent public sector	15.8%	15.7%
Household income growth	13.1%	13.6%	Blue collar	27.0%	25.2%	Percent construction	10.2%	9.9%

Economy & Jobs
Score: 36.4
Rank: 238

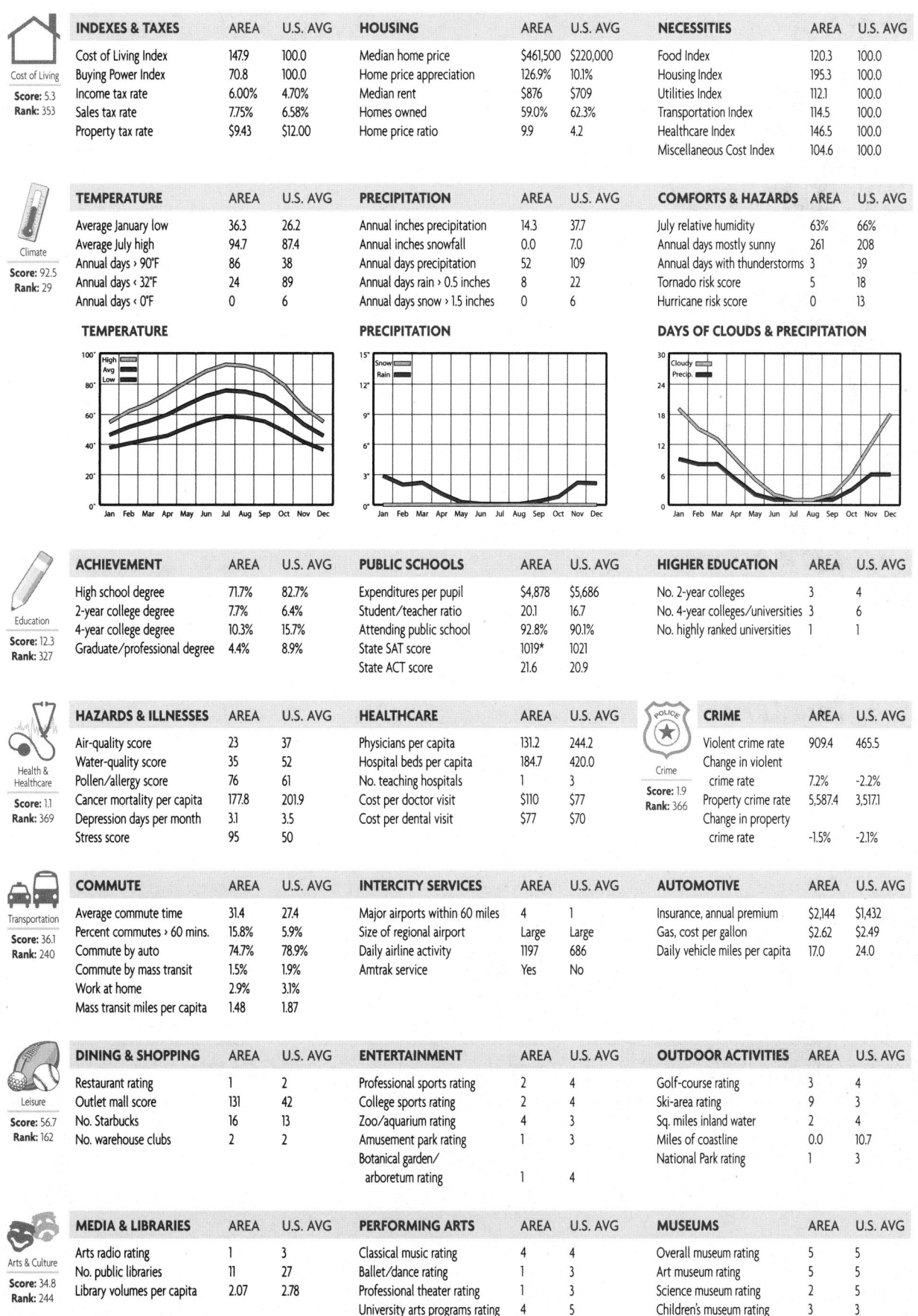

INDEXES & TAXES	AREA	U.S. AVG	HOUSING	AREA	U.S. AVG	NECESSITIES	AREA	U.S. AVG
Cost of Living Index	147.9	100.0	Median home price	$461,500	$220,000	Food Index	120.3	100.0
Buying Power Index	70.8	100.0	Home price appreciation	126.9%	10.1%	Housing Index	195.3	100.0
Income tax rate	6.00%	4.70%	Median rent	$876	$709	Utilities Index	112.1	100.0
Sales tax rate	7.75%	6.58%	Homes owned	59.0%	62.3%	Transportation Index	114.5	100.0
Property tax rate	$9.43	$12.00	Home price ratio	9.9	4.2	Healthcare Index	146.5	100.0
						Miscellaneous Cost Index	104.6	100.0

Cost of Living
Score: 5.3
Rank: 353

TEMPERATURE	AREA	U.S. AVG	PRECIPITATION	AREA	U.S. AVG	COMFORTS & HAZARDS	AREA	U.S. AVG
Average January low	36.3	26.2	Annual inches precipitation	14.3	37.7	July relative humidity	63%	66%
Average July high	94.7	87.4	Annual inches snowfall	0.0	7.0	Annual days mostly sunny	261	208
Annual days > 90°F	86	38	Annual days precipitation	52	109	Annual days with thunderstorms	3	39
Annual days < 32°F	24	89	Annual days rain > 0.5 inches	8	22	Tornado risk score	5	18
Annual days < 0°F	0	6	Annual days snow > 1.5 inches	0	6	Hurricane risk score	0	13

Climate
Score: 92.5
Rank: 29

ACHIEVEMENT	AREA	U.S. AVG	PUBLIC SCHOOLS	AREA	U.S. AVG	HIGHER EDUCATION	AREA	U.S. AVG
High school degree	71.7%	82.7%	Expenditures per pupil	$4,878	$5,686	No. 2-year colleges	3	4
2-year college degree	7.7%	6.4%	Student/teacher ratio	20.1	16.7	No. 4-year colleges/universities	3	6
4-year college degree	10.3%	15.7%	Attending public school	92.8%	90.1%	No. highly ranked universities	1	1
Graduate/professional degree	4.4%	8.9%	State SAT score	1019*	1021			
			State ACT score	21.6	20.9			

Education
Score: 12.3
Rank: 327

HAZARDS & ILLNESSES	AREA	U.S. AVG	HEALTHCARE	AREA	U.S. AVG	CRIME	AREA	U.S. AVG
Air-quality score	23	37	Physicians per capita	131.2	244.2	Violent crime rate	909.4	465.5
Water-quality score	35	52	Hospital beds per capita	184.7	420.0	Change in violent crime rate	7.2%	-2.2%
Pollen/allergy score	76	61	No. teaching hospitals	1	3	Property crime rate	5,587.4	3,517.1
Cancer mortality per capita	177.8	201.9	Cost per doctor visit	$110	$77	Change in property crime rate	-1.5%	-2.1%
Depression days per month	3.1	3.5	Cost per dental visit	$77	$70			
Stress score	95	50						

Health & Healthcare
Score: 1.1
Rank: 369

Crime
Score: 1.9
Rank: 366

COMMUTE	AREA	U.S. AVG	INTERCITY SERVICES	AREA	U.S. AVG	AUTOMOTIVE	AREA	U.S. AVG
Average commute time	31.4	27.4	Major airports within 60 miles	4	1	Insurance, annual premium	$2,144	$1,432
Percent commutes > 60 mins.	15.8%	5.9%	Size of regional airport	Large	Large	Gas, cost per gallon	$2.62	$2.49
Commute by auto	74.7%	78.9%	Daily airline activity	1197	686	Daily vehicle miles per capita	17.0	24.0
Commute by mass transit	1.5%	1.9%	Amtrak service	Yes	No			
Work at home	2.9%	3.1%						
Mass transit miles per capita	1.48	1.87						

Transportation
Score: 36.1
Rank: 240

DINING & SHOPPING	AREA	U.S. AVG	ENTERTAINMENT	AREA	U.S. AVG	OUTDOOR ACTIVITIES	AREA	U.S. AVG
Restaurant rating	1	2	Professional sports rating	2	4	Golf-course rating	3	4
Outlet mall score	131	42	College sports rating	2	4	Ski-area rating	9	3
No. Starbucks	16	13	Zoo/aquarium rating	4	3	Sq. miles inland water	2	4
No. warehouse clubs	2	2	Amusement park rating	1	3	Miles of coastline	0.0	10.7
			Botanical garden/ arboretum rating	1	4	National Park rating	1	3

Leisure
Score: 56.7
Rank: 162

MEDIA & LIBRARIES	AREA	U.S. AVG	PERFORMING ARTS	AREA	U.S. AVG	MUSEUMS	AREA	U.S. AVG
Arts radio rating	1	3	Classical music rating	4	4	Overall museum rating	5	5
No. public libraries	11	27	Ballet/dance rating	1	3	Art museum rating	5	5
Library volumes per capita	2.07	2.78	Professional theater rating	1	3	Science museum rating	2	5
			University arts programs rating	4	5	Children's museum rating	3	3

Arts & Culture
Score: 34.8
Rank: 244

Sumter, SC

Score: 14.4   **Rank:** 363   **2004 rank:** 274

Profile: Military town
Location: East-central South Carolina, 45 miles east of Columbia
Elevation: 225 feet
Time zone: Eastern Standard Time

PRO	CON
Small-town atmosphere	Crime
Cost of living	Economy
Central location	Hot, humid summers

Sumter, near the center of the state, is a small typically Southern town and county seat. Shaw Air Force Base and agriculture are the economic mainstays, but recent employment statistics and projections are weak. Downtown is nondescript but tidy with small areas of attractive housing mainly to the north. Outdoor recreation is available nearby, notably at large Marion Lake to the south. There is little in the way of cultural amenities, intellectual stimulation, or entertainment, but Sumter is 45 miles from Columbia and 100 miles from Charleston and Myrtle Beach. The area offers a low cost of living, a slow pace of life, and quality healthcare facilities, but not much else.

Sumter is located along the banks of the Pocotaligo River in an area of level and gently rolling terrain with pine forests and agricultural land. Summers are consistently warm and humid, and nearby swampy areas breed large insect populations. Winters are mild with brief cold outbreaks and rain. Fall is the most pleasant season.

Population

DEMOGRAPHICS	AREA	U.S. AVG	ETHNIC COMPOSITION	AREA	U.S. AVG	RESIDENT PROFILE	AREA	U.S. AVG
Population	106,986		White	47.1%	79.0%	Single	34.2%	32.4%
Population density per sq. mile	160.8	358.5	Black	49.5%	10.5%	Married	49.1%	52.7%
Population growth	4.2%	21.1%	Asian	1.1%	2.7%	Divorced/separated	16.6%	14.9%
Median age	34.3	36.1	Hispanic	1.5%	10.6%	Married with children	23.5%	23.7%
Percent Democrat	50.5%	44.5%	Religious observance	38.6%	48.9%	Single with children	12.7%	9.1%
Percent Republican	48.8%	54.5%	Diversity measure	54.7	40.1	Percent over age 65	12.0%	12.9%

Economy
& Jobs
Score: 3.2
Rank: 361

INCOME	AREA	U.S. AVG	EMPLOYMENT	AREA	U.S. AVG	EMPLOYING INDUSTRIES	AREA	U.S. AVG
Per capita income	$18,267	$23,235	Unemployment rate	8.5%	4.7%	Largest: Manufacturing		
Household income	$37,921	$46,414	Recent job growth	0.4%	1.3%			
Household income < $25K	32.9%	26.2%	Projected future job growth	5.0%	11.5%	Percent manufacturing	23.2%	15.4%
Household income > $75K	17.0%	25.4%	White collar	48.9%	57.8%	Percent public sector	18.5%	15.7%
Household income growth	14.0%	13.6%	Blue collar	34.6%	25.2%	Percent construction	11.4%	9.9%

Cost of Living
Score: 65.2
Rank: 131

INDEXES & TAXES	AREA	U.S. AVG	HOUSING	AREA	U.S. AVG	NECESSITIES	AREA	U.S. AVG
Cost of Living Index	82.2	100.0	Median home price	$125,400	$220,000	Food Index	101.0	100.0
Buying Power Index	103.4	100.0	Home price appreciation	28.9%	10.1%	Housing Index	52.6	100.0
Income tax rate	7.00%	4.70%	Median rent	$518	$709	Utilities Index	93.3	100.0
Sales tax rate	6.00%	6.58%	Homes owned	63.4%	62.3%	Transportation Index	92.1	100.0
Property tax rate	$7.00	$12.00	Home price ratio	3.3	4.2	Healthcare Index	93.8	100.0
						Miscellaneous Cost Index	98.5	100.0

Climate
Score: 34.5
Rank: 244

TEMPERATURE	AREA	U.S. AVG	PRECIPITATION	AREA	U.S. AVG	COMFORTS & HAZARDS	AREA	U.S. AVG
Average January low	33.9	26.2	Annual inches precipitation	46.0	37.7	July relative humidity	73%	66%
Average July high	92.0	87.4	Annual inches snowfall	2.0	7.0	Annual days mostly sunny	223	208
Annual days > 90°F	64	38	Annual days precipitation	111	109	Annual days with thunderstorms	54	39
Annual days < 32°F	60	89	Annual days rain > 0.5 inches	31	22	Tornado risk score	9	18
Annual days < 0°F	0	6	Annual days snow > 1.5 inches	1	6	Hurricane risk score	40	13

TEMPERATURE

PRECIPITATION

DAYS OF CLOUDS & PRECIPITATION

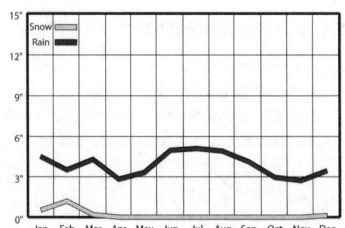

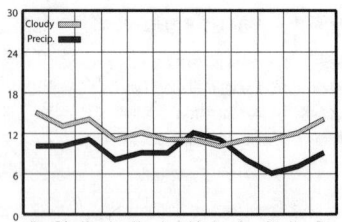

Education
Score: 13.4
Rank: 323

ACHIEVEMENT	AREA	U.S. AVG	PUBLIC SCHOOLS	AREA	U.S. AVG	HIGHER EDUCATION	AREA	U.S. AVG
High school degree	74.3%	82.7%	Expenditures per pupil	$4,606	$5,686	No. 2-year colleges	2	4
2-year college degree	7.2%	6.4%	Student/teacher ratio	15.3	16.7	No. 4-year colleges/universities	1	6
4-year college degree	10.6%	15.7%	Attending public school	91.2%	90.1%	No. highly ranked universities	0	1
Graduate/professional degree	5.0%	8.9%	State SAT score	985*	1021			
			State ACT score	19.5	20.9			

Health & Healthcare
Score: 37.4
Rank: 233

HAZARDS & ILLNESSES	AREA	U.S. AVG	HEALTHCARE	AREA	U.S. AVG	CRIME	AREA	U.S. AVG
Air-quality score	47	37	Physicians per capita	136.8	244.2	Violent crime rate	939.6	465.5
Water-quality score	60	52	Hospital beds per capita	285.1	420.0	Change in violent crime rate	-20.1%	-2.2%
Pollen/allergy score	67	61	No. teaching hospitals	0	3	Property crime rate	4,578.0	3,517.1
Cancer mortality per capita	233.5	201.9	Cost per doctor visit	$64	$77	Change in property crime rate	-15.3%	-2.1%
Depression days per month	3.6	3.5	Cost per dental visit	$61	$70			
Stress score	73	50						

Crime
Score: 0.3
Rank: 372

Transportation
Score: 66.8
Rank: 125

COMMUTE	AREA	U.S. AVG	INTERCITY SERVICES	AREA	U.S. AVG	AUTOMOTIVE	AREA	U.S. AVG
Average commute time	23.3	27.4	Major airports within 60 miles	1	1	Insurance, annual premium	$1,387	$1,432
Percent commutes > 60 mins.	5.9%	5.9%	Size of regional airport	Large	Large	Gas, cost per gallon	$2.38	$2.49
Commute by auto	80.5%	78.9%	Daily airline activity	846	686	Daily vehicle miles per capita	17.3	24.0
Commute by mass transit	0.8%	1.9%	Amtrak service	No	No			
Work at home	1.6%	3.1%						
Mass transit miles per capita	0.83	1.87						

Leisure
Score: 15.8
Rank: 314

DINING & SHOPPING	AREA	U.S. AVG	ENTERTAINMENT	AREA	U.S. AVG	OUTDOOR ACTIVITIES	AREA	U.S. AVG
Restaurant rating	1	2	Professional sports rating	2	4	Golf-course rating	3	4
Outlet mall score	0	42	College sports rating	3	4	Ski-area rating	1	3
No. Starbucks	0	13	Zoo/aquarium rating	1	3	Sq. miles inland water	2	4
No. warehouse clubs	0	2	Amusement park rating	1	3	Miles of coastline	0.0	10.7
			Botanical garden/arboretum rating	1	4	National Park rating	3	3

Arts & Culture
Score: 9.1
Rank: 339

MEDIA & LIBRARIES	AREA	U.S. AVG	PERFORMING ARTS	AREA	U.S. AVG	MUSEUMS	AREA	U.S. AVG
Arts radio rating	1	3	Classical music rating	3	4	Overall museum rating	1	5
No. public libraries	3	27	Ballet/dance rating	1	3	Art museum rating	2	5
Library volumes per capita	1.50	2.78	Professional theater rating	1	3	Science museum rating	1	5
			University arts programs rating	2	5	Children's museum rating	1	3

Syracuse, NY

Score: 45.9   Rank: 276   2004 rank: 246

Profile: Mid-size city
Location: North-central New York, 35 miles southeast of Lake Ontario's eastern shore
Elevation: 408 feet
Time zone: Eastern Standard Time

PRO	CON
Nearby recreation	Winter climate
College-town amenities	Economy
Central location	Entertainment

Syracuse is located along the old Erie Canal adjacent to the well-known Finger Lakes region. It is a commercial and transportation center at the crossroads of major north–south and east–west routes. Large industries once took advantage of the area's clean water and strategic location, but the decline of the manufacturing base has hurt the area and it faces difficulties attracting jobs, and for that matter, new residents to town. Syracuse University adds a college-town element and is the area's largest employer. The rest of the employment base is spread among a number of smaller employers and increasingly service-oriented businesses, healthcare, and public agencies. Canal parks and a museum preserve the city's Erie Canal heritage. The cityscape is fairly nondescript but attractive wooded neighborhoods surround the city. In fact, Syracuse is among the top five cities in the U.S. and Canada for trees per capita (see "Finding Refuge among the Trees" in chapter 3). There are minor league sports franchises, and the Syracuse basketball team is a local attraction. Oneida Lake nearby and Lake Ontario to the north provide recreational opportunities. However, Syracuse ties Utica to the east for the greatest annual snowfall in the country, and the area is in a belt of gloomy lake-driven weather year-round and especially in winter. For some, Syracuse is a good alternative to crowded and expensive areas farther east and south.

Gently rolling terrain stretches northward for about 30 miles to the eastern end of Lake Ontario. Hills rise to 1,500 feet about 5 miles south. To the west open land and woods cover rolling hills. The location near the St. Lawrence storm track makes for dynamic weather. Summer temperatures rise quickly, occasionally exceeding 90°F, and fall rapidly

after sunset. Hot, humid conditions happen only a few times a year. Winters are cold and somewhat severe. Temperatures average from the low 30s to the low teens. While Lake Ontario provides some moderation, below-zero temperatures do occur. Precipitation is evenly distributed year-round with thunderstorms in summer and frequent winter snow squalls fed by lake moisture. More than 100 inches of snow falls annually. First freeze is mid-October; last is late April.

Population

DEMOGRAPHICS	AREA	U.S. AVG
Population	656,857	
Population density per sq. mile	274.9	358.5
Population growth	-0.4%	21.1%
Median age	37.3	36.1
Percent Democrat	51.6%	44.5%
Percent Republican	46.3%	54.5%

ETHNIC COMPOSITION	AREA	U.S. AVG
White	86.8%	79.0%
Black	7.7%	10.5%
Asian	2.1%	2.7%
Hispanic	2.7%	10.6%
Religious observance	47.6%	48.9%
Diversity measure	27.3	40.1

RESIDENT PROFILE	AREA	U.S. AVG
Single	35.9%	32.4%
Married	50.3%	52.7%
Divorced/separated	13.8%	14.9%
Married with children	22.5%	23.7%
Single with children	9.9%	9.1%
Percent over age 65	13.3%	12.9%

Economy & Jobs
Score: 46.5
Rank: 201

INCOME	AREA	U.S. AVG
Per capita income	$23,117	$23,235
Household income	$44,893	$46,414
Household income < $25K	27.4%	26.2%
Household income > $75K	25.3%	25.4%
Household income growth	12.3%	13.6%

EMPLOYMENT	AREA	U.S. AVG
Unemployment rate	5.1%	4.7%
Recent job growth	2.4%	1.3%
Projected future job growth	4.8%	11.5%
White collar	61.9%	57.8%
Blue collar	22.5%	25.2%

EMPLOYING INDUSTRIES	AREA	U.S. AVG
Largest: Manufacturing		
Percent manufacturing	14.5%	15.4%
Percent public sector	16.2%	15.7%
Percent construction	8.0%	9.9%

Cost of Living
Score: 17.1
Rank: 309

INDEXES & TAXES	AREA	U.S. AVG
Cost of Living Index	87.2	100.0
Buying Power Index	115.4	100.0
Income tax rate	7.13%	4.70%
Sales tax rate	8.25%	6.58%
Property tax rate	$28.06	$12.00

HOUSING	AREA	U.S. AVG
Median home price	$116,800	$220,000
Home price appreciation	37.6%	10.1%
Median rent	$616	$709
Homes owned	61.4%	62.3%
Home price ratio	2.6	4.2

NECESSITIES	AREA	U.S. AVG
Food Index	107.4	100.0
Housing Index	53.3	100.0
Utilities Index	141.8	100.0
Transportation Index	104.7	100.0
Healthcare Index	100.2	100.0
Miscellaneous Cost Index	97.2	100.0

Climate
Score: 4.3
Rank: 357

TEMPERATURE	AREA	U.S. AVG
Average January low	15.8	26.2
Average July high	82.0	87.4
Annual days > 90°F	6	38
Annual days < 32°F	138	89
Annual days < 0°F	9	6

PRECIPITATION	AREA	U.S. AVG
Annual inches precipitation	36.0	37.7
Annual inches snowfall	109.0	7.0
Annual days precipitation	168	109
Annual days rain > 0.5 inches	21	22
Annual days snow > 1.5 inches	25	6

COMFORTS & HAZARDS	AREA	U.S. AVG
July relative humidity	73%	66%
Annual days mostly sunny	164	208
Annual days with thunderstorms	29	39
Tornado risk score	6	18
Hurricane risk score	4	13

TEMPERATURE

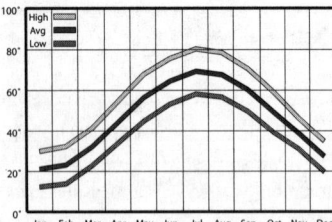

PRECIPITATION

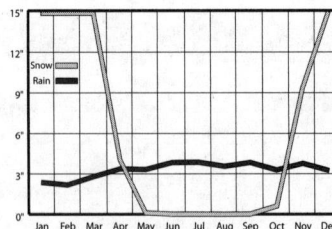

DAYS OF CLOUDS & PRECIPITATION

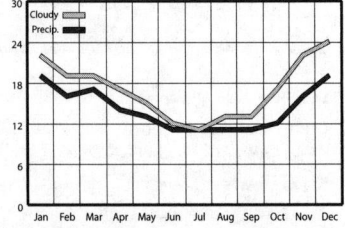

Education
Score: 89.6
Rank: 40

ACHIEVEMENT	AREA	U.S. AVG
High school degree	84.6%	82.7%
2-year college degree	9.7%	6.4%
4-year college degree	14.9%	15.7%
Graduate/professional degree	10.5%	8.9%

PUBLIC SCHOOLS	AREA	U.S. AVG
Expenditures per pupil	$7,818	$5,686
Student/teacher ratio	15.1	16.7
Attending public school	92.8%	90.1%
State SAT score	1003*	1021
State ACT score	22.6	20.9

HIGHER EDUCATION	AREA	U.S. AVG
No. 2-year colleges	7	4
No. 4-year colleges/universities	8	6
No. highly ranked universities	4	1

Health & Healthcare
Score: 53.7
Rank: 174

HAZARDS & ILLNESSES	AREA	U.S. AVG
Air-quality score	35	37
Water-quality score	67	52
Pollen/allergy score	57	61
Cancer mortality per capita	214.4	201.9
Depression days per month	2.7	3.5
Stress score	10	50

HEALTHCARE	AREA	U.S. AVG
Physicians per capita	342.8	244.2
Hospital beds per capita	417.4	420.0
No. teaching hospitals	5	3
Cost per doctor visit	$71	$77
Cost per dental visit	$65	$70

Crime
Score: 45.2
Rank: 205

CRIME	AREA	U.S. AVG
Violent crime rate	343.7	465.5
Change in violent crime rate	16.9%	-2.2%
Property crime rate	2,402.0	3,517.1
Change in property crime rate	-10.2%	-2.1%

COMMUTE	AREA	U.S. AVG	INTERCITY SERVICES	AREA	U.S. AVG	AUTOMOTIVE	AREA	U.S. AVG
Average commute time	22.5	27.4	Major airports within 60 miles	0	1	Insurance, annual premium	$1,826	$1,432
Percent commutes > 60 mins.	3.5%	5.9%	Size of regional airport	Small	Large	Gas, cost per gallon	$2.57	$2.49
Commute by auto	80.3%	78.9%	Daily airline activity	271	686	Daily vehicle miles per capita	25.2	24.0
Commute by mass transit	2.0%	1.9%	Amtrak service	Yes	No			
Work at home	2.9%	3.1%						
Mass transit miles per capita	1.98	1.87						

Transportation
Score: 40.6
Rank: 223

DINING & SHOPPING	AREA	U.S. AVG	ENTERTAINMENT	AREA	U.S. AVG	OUTDOOR ACTIVITIES	AREA	U.S. AVG
Restaurant rating	1	2	Professional sports rating	3	4	Golf-course rating	7	4
Outlet mall score	0	42	College sports rating	5	4	Ski-area rating	4	3
No. Starbucks	4	13	Zoo/aquarium rating	5	3	Sq. miles inland water	6	4
No. warehouse clubs	3	2	Amusement park rating	1	3	Miles of coastline	35.3	10.7
			Botanical garden/ arboretum rating	2	4	National Park rating	1	3

Leisure
Score: 70.9
Rank: 109

MEDIA & LIBRARIES	AREA	U.S. AVG	PERFORMING ARTS	AREA	U.S. AVG	MUSEUMS	AREA	U.S. AVG
Arts radio rating	9	3	Classical music rating	9	4	Overall museum rating	7	5
No. public libraries	49	27	Ballet/dance rating	1	3	Art museum rating	8	5
Library volumes per capita	2.32	2.78	Professional theater rating	1	3	Science museum rating	7	5
			University arts programs rating	8	5	Children's museum rating	2	3

Arts & Culture
Score: 89.3
Rank: 41

Tacoma, WA

Score: 46.3   Rank: 272   2004 rank: 59

Profile: Mid-size port city
Location: West-central Washington at the south end of Puget Sound and the Seattle area
Elevation: 125 feet
Time zone: Pacific Standard Time

PRO	CON
Revitalized downtown	Industrial setting
Close to Seattle	High crime rates
Nearby recreation	Clouds and rain

Tacoma has traditionally been the working-class, industrial heartland of the Puget Sound area with a central core dominated by shipping, paper and lumber mills, and other manufacturing industries. But while these activities continue and the city has grown to be one of the most important port complexes on the West Coast, it has evolved considerably beyond these roots. The city's progressive leadership has brought an extensive downtown revitalization, and downtown is once again attracting business, museums, and arts and entertainment activities. The city installed a high-speed fiber optic system, run by its local utility, making it one of the most "wired" cities in the U.S. The relative low cost of living (100.0) and housing for the Puget Sound area have also helped. Residential activity has returned downtown, and good residential areas also lie on the plateau south of town, along the Puget Sound shore west, and in the growing suburban town of Puyallup southeast. Recreational opportunities are abundant on the Puget Sound and in the national forests towards Mt. Rainier National Park, and Seattle is a treasure trove of arts, entertainment, and other amenities beyond what's found locally. On the downside, traffic in the commercial section along Interstate 5 can be horrendous, commutes can be long, and some of the sprawl along Interstate 5 south toward Olympia is unattractive. Crime rates remain high and educational attainment is fairly low. Despite the low ranking in this edition, we think that Tacoma is on the rise and might be a good bet for those with patience.

Downtown Tacoma sits on a mostly built-up coastal plain rising to a hilly, wooded plateau immediately to the south. Hills rise into the Mount Rainier area to the southeast, and a series of Puget Sound fjords and inlets gives way to the Olympic Mountains and peninsula to the west. The climate is marine, with persistent cloudy, cool, and wet weather from October through May and drier, pleasant days most of the summer. Winter temperatures usually hover above freezing into the 50s with an occasional colder period.

DEMOGRAPHICS	AREA	U.S. AVG	ETHNIC COMPOSITION	AREA	U.S. AVG	RESIDENT PROFILE	AREA	U.S. AVG
Population	756,177		White	76.8%	79.0%	Single	30.1%	32.4%
Population density per sq. mile	450.4	358.5	Black	7.1%	10.5%	Married	53.2%	52.7%
Population growth	29.0%	21.1%	Asian	6.2%	2.7%	Divorced/separated	16.8%	14.9%
Median age	34.8	36.1	Hispanic	6.6%	10.6%	Married with children	25.3%	23.7%
Percent Democrat	50.5%	44.5%	Religious observance	29.8%	48.9%	Single with children	10.5%	9.1%
Percent Republican	48.1%	54.5%	Diversity measure	47.2	40.1	Percent over age 65	10.4%	12.9%

Population

Economy & Jobs
Score: 82.6
Rank: 66

INCOME	AREA	U.S. AVG	EMPLOYMENT	AREA	U.S. AVG	EMPLOYING INDUSTRIES	AREA	U.S. AVG
Per capita income	$24,415	$23,235	Unemployment rate	6.0%	4.7%	Largest: Healthcare & Social Assistance		
Household income	$51,338	$46,414	Recent job growth	3.5%	1.3%			
Household income < $25K	20.7%	26.2%	Projected future job growth	19.6%	11.5%	Percent manufacturing	15.1%	15.4%
Household income > $75K	29.6%	25.4%	White collar	56.8%	57.8%	Percent public sector	17.6%	15.7%
Household income growth	13.6%	13.6%	Blue collar	26.5%	25.2%	Percent construction	11.3%	9.9%

Cost of Living
Score: 40.4
Rank: 223

INDEXES & TAXES	AREA	U.S. AVG	HOUSING	AREA	U.S. AVG	NECESSITIES	AREA	U.S. AVG
Cost of Living Index	100.0	100.0	Median home price	$214,200	$220,000	Food Index	107.6	100.0
Buying Power Index	115.1	100.0	Home price appreciation	53.8%	10.1%	Housing Index	87.7	100.0
Income tax rate	0.00%	4.70%	Median rent	$788	$709	Utilities Index	78.9	100.0
Sales tax rate	8.80%	6.58%	Homes owned	60.2%	62.3%	Transportation Index	103.3	100.0
Property tax rate	$13.00	$12.00	Home price ratio	4.2	4.2	Healthcare Index	126.3	100.0
						Miscellaneous Cost Index	101.1	100.0

Climate
Score: 82.1
Rank: 68

TEMPERATURE	AREA	U.S. AVG	PRECIPITATION	AREA	U.S. AVG	COMFORTS & HAZARDS	AREA	U.S. AVG
Average January low	33.0	26.2	Annual inches precipitation	38.8	37.7	July relative humidity	74%	66%
Average July high	75.1	87.4	Annual inches snowfall	14.3	7.0	Annual days mostly sunny	136	208
Annual days > 90°F	3	38	Annual days precipitation	164	109	Annual days with thunderstorms	7	39
Annual days < 32°F	31	89	Annual days rain > 0.5 inches	25	22	Tornado risk score	0	18
Annual days < 0°F	0	6	Annual days snow > 1.5 inches	1	6	Hurricane risk score	0	13

TEMPERATURE

PRECIPITATION

DAYS OF CLOUDS & PRECIPITATION

Education
Score: 67.9
Rank: 121

ACHIEVEMENT	AREA	U.S. AVG	PUBLIC SCHOOLS	AREA	U.S. AVG	HIGHER EDUCATION	AREA	U.S. AVG
High school degree	86.9%	82.7%	Expenditures per pupil	$5,810	$5,686	No. 2-year colleges	7	4
2-year college degree	8.1%	6.4%	Student/teacher ratio	19.4	16.7	No. 4-year colleges/universities	6	6
4-year college degree	13.6%	15.7%	Attending public school	93.7%	90.1%	No. highly ranked universities	2	1
Graduate/professional degree	6.8%	8.9%	State SAT score	1059*	1021			
			State ACT score	22.9	20.9			

Health & Healthcare
Score: 12.8
Rank: 325

HAZARDS & ILLNESSES	AREA	U.S. AVG	HEALTHCARE	AREA	U.S. AVG	CRIME	AREA	U.S. AVG
Air-quality score	20	37	Physicians per capita	222.7	244.2	Violent crime rate	543.3	465.5
Water-quality score	60	52	Hospital beds per capita	240.7	420.0	Change in violent crime rate	1.0%	-2.2%
Pollen/allergy score	48	61	No. teaching hospitals	3	3	Property crime rate	5,312.2	3,517.1
Cancer mortality per capita	195.7	201.9	Cost per doctor visit	$81	$77	Change in property crime rate	3.3%	-2.1%
Depression days per month	3.8	3.5	Cost per dental visit	$97	$70			
Stress score	100	50						

Crime Score: 16.8
Rank: 311

Transportation
Score: 1.9
Rank: 366

COMMUTE	AREA	U.S. AVG	INTERCITY SERVICES	AREA	U.S. AVG	AUTOMOTIVE	AREA	U.S. AVG
Average commute time	31.0	27.4	Major airports within 60 miles	1	1	Insurance, annual premium	$1,745	$1,432
Percent commutes > 60 mins.	11.1%	5.9%	Size of regional airport	Large	Large	Gas, cost per gallon	$2.50	$2.49
Commute by auto	76.6%	78.9%	Daily airline activity	698	686	Daily vehicle miles per capita	24.1	24.0
Commute by mass transit	2.6%	1.9%	Amtrak service	Yes	No			
Work at home	3.6%	3.1%						
Mass transit miles per capita	2.62	1.87						

Leisure
Score: 88.5
Rank: 44

DINING & SHOPPING	AREA	U.S. AVG	ENTERTAINMENT	AREA	U.S. AVG	OUTDOOR ACTIVITIES	AREA	U.S. AVG
Restaurant rating	1	2	Professional sports rating	7	4	Golf-course rating	5	4
Outlet mall score	0	42	College sports rating	3	4	Ski-area rating	10	3
No. Starbucks	33	13	Zoo/aquarium rating	6	3	Sq. miles inland water	8	4
No. warehouse clubs	3	2	Amusement park rating	3	3	Miles of coastline	15.3	10.7
			Botanical garden/arboretum rating	8	4	National Park rating	10	3

Arts & Culture
Score: 77.3
Rank: 85

MEDIA & LIBRARIES	AREA	U.S. AVG	PERFORMING ARTS	AREA	U.S. AVG	MUSEUMS	AREA	U.S. AVG
Arts radio rating	3	3	Classical music rating	5	4	Overall museum rating	9	5
No. public libraries	29	27	Ballet/dance rating	5	3	Art museum rating	9	5
Library volumes per capita	4.90	2.78	Professional theater rating	3	3	Science museum rating	9	5
			University arts programs rating	6	5	Children's museum rating	8	3

Tallahassee, FL

Score: 67.0   **Rank:** 122   **2004 rank:** 249

Profile: Capital city/college town
Location: Middle of Florida Panhandle, 30 miles north of the Gulf of Mexico and 20 miles from the Georgia border
Elevation: 68 feet
Time zone: Eastern Standard Time

PRO	CON
College-town amenities	Violent crime
Surrounding countryside	Air service
Educated population	Hot, humid summers

Tallahassee is a mid-size mix of several defining elements. It is the state's capital but bears little resemblance to the coastal cities more aligned with the Florida image. It is a college town, home to the 35,000-student Florida State University and the smaller Florida A&M, but doesn't come across as a typical college town. It is, both in character and appearance, more of a Southern city than a Florida one—laid-back, dignified buildings, and grid streets with canopies of large trees, and forests and cotton fields outside of town. The profile—and its attributes—are diverse, and its ranking has risen despite persistent crime issues, a lack of air service, and some other "big city" amenities that would bring it closer to center stage. Upsides include a few college-town amenities, particularly sports, nightlife, and healthcare facilities, high educational attainment, and the aforementioned Southern dignity. Home prices haven't escalated as much as in other Florida cities, and Tallahassee has good home values and neighborhoods. For that reason,

the area is starting to become more popular for retirees looking for a pleasant climate, less crowding, and some intellectual stimulation, and its ranking is on the rise. Outdoor recreation opportunities lie in the Apalachicola National Forest and beach areas just south of town. With 36 days below freezing, Tallahassee is by far the coldest metro area in Florida, although hardly cold by national standards.

Local terrain is rolling, with rich, red soil and forests of oak, live oak, pine, magnolia, and a variety of other subtropical vegetation. Numerous lakes surround the area, and the countryside is famous for its "canopy roads," long stretches of road completely sheltered by overhanging live oak trees. Winter brings considerable rain and cloudiness, with temperatures occasionally dropping into the teens. Summer is the least pleasant season: high temperatures and very high humidity cause considerable discomfort, and thunderstorms occur every other day.

Population

DEMOGRAPHICS	AREA	U.S. AVG	ETHNIC COMPOSITION	AREA	U.S. AVG	RESIDENT PROFILE	AREA	U.S. AVG
Population	340,298		White	62.4%	79.0%	Single	41.3%	32.4%
Population density per sq. mile	142.5	358.5	Black	33.2%	10.5%	Married	42.5%	52.7%
Population growth	33.2%	21.1%	Asian	1.7%	2.7%	Divorced/separated	16.2%	14.9%
Median age	33.1	36.1	Hispanic	4.0%	10.6%	Married with children	18.7%	23.7%
Percent Democrat	60.8%	44.5%	Religious observance	35.2%	48.9%	Single with children	10.2%	9.1%
Percent Republican	38.6%	54.5%	Diversity measure	51.4	40.1	Percent over age 65	9.7%	12.9%

Economy & Jobs
Score: 75.1
Rank: 94

INCOME	AREA	U.S. AVG	EMPLOYMENT	AREA	U.S. AVG	EMPLOYING INDUSTRIES	AREA	U.S. AVG
Per capita income	$22,642	$23,235	Unemployment rate	3.5%	4.7%	Largest: Professional, Scientific & Technical Services		
Household income	$41,179	$46,414	Recent job growth	2.9%	1.3%			
Household income < $25K	31.5%	26.2%	Projected future job growth	14.2%	11.5%	Percent manufacturing	7.2%	15.4%
Household income > $75K	23.0%	25.4%	White collar	69.0%	57.8%	Percent public sector	35.9%	15.7%
Household income growth	13.0%	13.6%	Blue collar	14.7%	25.2%	Percent construction	7.5%	9.9%

Cost of Living
Score: 81.3
Rank: 71

INDEXES & TAXES	AREA	U.S. AVG	HOUSING	AREA	U.S. AVG	NECESSITIES	AREA	U.S. AVG
Cost of Living Index	96.0	100.0	Median home price	$178,500	$220,000	Food Index	107.7	100.0
Buying Power Index	96.1	100.0	Home price appreciation	67.7%	10.1%	Housing Index	71.8	100.0
Income tax rate	0.00%	4.70%	Median rent	$705	$709	Utilities Index	108.0	100.0
Sales tax rate	7.37%	6.58%	Homes owned	57.9%	62.3%	Transportation Index	102.0	100.0
Property tax rate	$10.97	$12.00	Home price ratio	4.3	4.2	Healthcare Index	100.6	100.0
						Miscellaneous Cost Index	108.5	100.0

Climate
Score: 61.8
Rank: 142

TEMPERATURE	AREA	U.S. AVG
Average January low	41.0	26.2
Average July high	90.6	87.4
Annual days > 90°F	87	38
Annual days < 32°F	36	89
Annual days < 0°F	0	6

PRECIPITATION	AREA	U.S. AVG
Annual inches precipitation	62.0	37.7
Annual inches snowfall	0.0	7.0
Annual days precipitation	119	109
Annual days rain > 0.5 inches	38	22
Annual days snow > 1.5 inches	0	6

COMFORTS & HAZARDS	AREA	U.S. AVG
July relative humidity	76%	66%
Annual days mostly sunny	233	208
Annual days with thunderstorms	86	39
Tornado risk score	14	18
Hurricane risk score	50	13

TEMPERATURE

PRECIPITATION

DAYS OF CLOUDS & PRECIPITATION

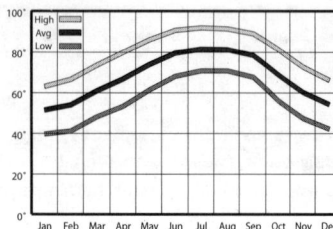
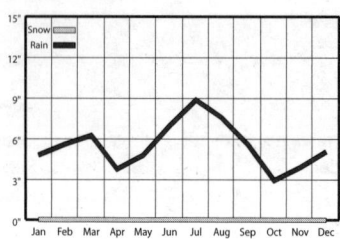
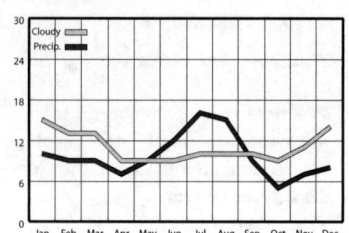

Education
Score: 84.0
Rank: 61

ACHIEVEMENT	AREA	U.S. AVG
High school degree	85.1%	82.7%
2-year college degree	7.3%	6.4%
4-year college degree	20.3%	15.7%
Graduate/professional degree	14.5%	8.9%

PUBLIC SCHOOLS	AREA	U.S. AVG
Expenditures per pupil	$5,368	$5,686
Student/teacher ratio	17.0	16.7
Attending public school	89.1%	90.1%
State SAT score	993*	1021
State ACT score	20.3	20.9

HIGHER EDUCATION	AREA	U.S. AVG
No. 2-year colleges	2	4
No. 4-year colleges/universities	3	6
No. highly ranked universities	1	1

Health & Healthcare
Score: 62.3
Rank: 142

HAZARDS & ILLNESSES	AREA	U.S. AVG
Air-quality score	48	37
Water-quality score	98	52
Pollen/allergy score	58	61
Cancer mortality per capita	272.0	201.9
Depression days per month	3.5	3.5
Stress score	36	50

HEALTHCARE	AREA	U.S. AVG
Physicians per capita	200.1	244.2
Hospital beds per capita	611.8	420.0
No. teaching hospitals	1	3
Cost per doctor visit	$74	$77
Cost per dental visit	$70	$70

Crime
Score: 27.5
Rank: 271

CRIME	AREA	U.S. AVG
Violent crime rate	819.7	465.5
Change in violent crime rate	7.4%	-2.2%
Property crime rate	3,968.5	3,517.1
Change in property crime rate	3.1%	-2.1%

Transportation
Score: 2.1
Rank: 365

COMMUTE	AREA	U.S. AVG
Average commute time	26.0	27.4
Percent commutes > 60 mins.	4.6%	5.9%
Commute by auto	78.7%	78.9%
Commute by mass transit	1.3%	1.9%
Work at home	2.5%	3.1%
Mass transit miles per capita	1.31	1.87

INTERCITY SERVICES	AREA	U.S. AVG
Major airports within 60 miles	0	1
Size of regional airport	Small	Large
Daily airline activity	69	686
Amtrak service	Yes	No

AUTOMOTIVE	AREA	U.S. AVG
Insurance, annual premium	$1,612	$1,432
Gas, cost per gallon	$2.57	$2.49
Daily vehicle miles per capita	28.9	24.0

Leisure
Score: 45.2
Rank: 204

DINING & SHOPPING	AREA	U.S. AVG
Restaurant rating	1	2
Outlet mall score	9	42
No. Starbucks	3	13
No. warehouse clubs	1	2

ENTERTAINMENT	AREA	U.S. AVG
Professional sports rating	2	4
College sports rating	6	4
Zoo/aquarium rating	3	3
Amusement park rating	1	3
Botanical garden/ arboretum rating	4	4

OUTDOOR ACTIVITIES	AREA	U.S. AVG
Golf-course rating	2	4
Ski-area rating	1	3
Sq. miles inland water	4	4
Miles of coastline	0.0	10.7
National Park rating	5	3

Arts & Culture
Score: 74.6
Rank: 95

MEDIA & LIBRARIES	AREA	U.S. AVG
Arts radio rating	7	3
No. public libraries	12	27
Library volumes per capita	2.20	2.78

PERFORMING ARTS	AREA	U.S. AVG
Classical music rating	4	4
Ballet/dance rating	3	3
Professional theater rating	1	3
University arts programs rating	8	5

MUSEUMS	AREA	U.S. AVG
Overall museum rating	6	5
Art museum rating	7	5
Science museum rating	7	5
Children's museum rating	1	3

Tampa–St. Petersburg–Clearwater, FL

Score: 54.8   **Rank:** 220   **2004 rank:** 48

Profile: Large-city complex
Location: Central Florida Gulf Coast at Tampa Bay
Elevation: 57 feet
Time zone: Eastern Standard Time

PRO	CON
Strengthening economy	Violent crime
Winter climate	Growth and sprawl
Attractive downtown areas	Hot, humid summers

This metropolitan area includes Tampa, St. Petersburg, and Clearwater, all of which surround Tampa Bay. The area is varied and cosmopolitan with a pleasant climate and balanced local economy less driven by tourism than many coastal Florida cities. A 1980s building boom brought downtown Tampa skyscrapers, a major airport renovation, and the development of a cruise-ship terminal. While soft in the early part of the decade, the economy has gained traction recently as the benefits of a business-friendly climate have paid off. Among other new-economy pursuits, the area has become a favorite as a secondary location for information processing for the financial industry. There are plenty of amusement parks, museums, outdoor activities, and major league professional sports, including baseball (Devil Rays), football (Buccaneers), and hockey (Lightning), and nearby beaches, especially those south near Bradenton, are attractions for locals and tourists alike. Transportation and air service are excellent. Beachside areas in Clearwater and St. Petersburg are tastefully developed, with palm tree–lined boulevards and pockets of interesting restaurants and shops. These areas tend to be more geared to retirees, especially coastal Clearwater, while more family-oriented suburbs and extensive commercial areas such as Brandon and Valrico are located east of Tampa. The cost of living is reasonable (100.5) for the type of area, but housing has followed the Florida boom and median home prices have doubled since the 2004 edition. Downsides include the stubbornly high rate of violent crime, and typical growth related to issues of traffic and poor air quality. The ranking has dropped from our last edition, but the area is probably better than the ranking indicates.

The flat, coastal plain has coastal grasses, palm trees, and white sand, and much of it has an elevation of less than 15 feet. Most of the city area and coast is built up, with coastal plain forests of pine and laurel mixed with orchards and other agricultural uses inland. The Pinellas Peninsula, separating Tampa Bay from the Gulf, is an area of broad, sandy beaches and palm trees. Clearwater and St. Petersburg are located here. Summers are long, warm, and humid. Afternoon highs reach 90°F, with moderating afternoon sea breezes and frequent thunderstorms, and warm evenings in the 70s. Lightning is abundant; in fact, "Tampa" is a misspelling of a Native American term for "sticks of fire," meaning lightning. Winters are mild with temperatures in the 60s and 70s, and lows rarely below 50°F.

DEMOGRAPHICS	AREA	U.S. AVG	ETHNIC COMPOSITION	AREA	U.S. AVG	RESIDENT PROFILE	AREA	U.S. AVG
Population	2,592,782		White	80.6%	79.0%	Single	31.0%	32.4%
Population density per sq. mile	1015.2	358.5	Black	11.2%	10.5%	Married	51.9%	52.7%
Population growth	26.8%	21.1%	Asian	2.3%	2.7%	Divorced/separated	17.1%	14.9%
Median age	40.7	36.1	Hispanic	12.7%	10.6%	Married with children	17.9%	23.7%
Percent Democrat	47.1%	44.5%	Religious observance	37.9%	48.9%	Single with children	8.3%	9.1%
Percent Republican	51.9%	54.5%	Diversity measure	45.9	40.1	Percent over age 65	18.2%	12.9%

INCOME	AREA	U.S. AVG	EMPLOYMENT	AREA	U.S. AVG	EMPLOYING INDUSTRIES	AREA	U.S. AVG
Per capita income	$25,008	$23,235	Unemployment rate	3.8%	4.7%	Largest: Healthcare & Social Assistance		
Household income	$43,561	$46,414	Recent job growth	4.1%	1.3%			
Household income ‹ $25K	26.6%	26.2%	Projected future job growth	18.4%	11.5%	Percent manufacturing	11.1%	15.4%
Household income › $75K	23.4%	25.4%	White collar	64.0%	57.8%	Percent public sector	12.1%	15.7%
Household income growth	15.5%	13.6%	Blue collar	20.2%	25.2%	Percent construction	9.2%	9.9%

Score: 84.8
Rank: 58

INDEXES & TAXES	AREA	U.S. AVG	HOUSING	AREA	U.S. AVG	NECESSITIES	AREA	U.S. AVG
Cost of Living Index	100.5	100.0	Median home price	$227,000	$220,000	Food Index	100.8	100.0
Buying Power Index	97.2	100.0	Home price appreciation	105.4%	10.1%	Housing Index	85.9	100.0
Income tax rate	0.00%	4.70%	Median rent	$817	$709	Utilities Index	102.0	100.0
Sales tax rate	6.97%	6.58%	Homes owned	62.6%	62.3%	Transportation Index	100.6	100.0
Property tax rate	$13.89	$12.00	Home price ratio	5.2	4.2	Healthcare Index	99.1	100.0
						Miscellaneous Cost Index	100.3	100.0

Score: 43.9
Rank: 210

Climate
Score: 82.6
Rank: 66

TEMPERATURE	AREA	U.S. AVG
Average January low	50.1	26.2
Average July high	90.4	87.4
Annual days > 90°F	81	38
Annual days < 32°F	4	89
Annual days < 0°F	0	6

PRECIPITATION	AREA	U.S. AVG
Annual inches precipitation	49.0	37.7
Annual inches snowfall	0.0	7.0
Annual days precipitation	107	109
Annual days rain > 0.5 inches	28	22
Annual days snow > 1.5 inches	0	6

COMFORTS & HAZARDS	AREA	U.S. AVG
July relative humidity	74%	66%
Annual days mostly sunny	238	208
Annual days with thunderstorms	88	39
Tornado risk score	85	18
Hurricane risk score	73	13

TEMPERATURE

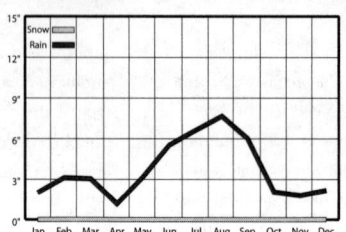

PRECIPITATION

DAYS OF CLOUDS & PRECIPITATION

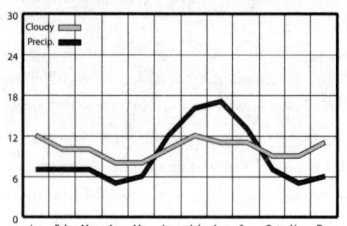

Education
Score: 60.4
Rank: 149

ACHIEVEMENT	AREA	U.S. AVG
High school degree	81.7%	82.7%
2-year college degree	7.4%	6.4%
4-year college degree	14.8%	15.7%
Graduate/professional degree	7.5%	8.9%

PUBLIC SCHOOLS	AREA	U.S. AVG
Expenditures per pupil	$5,186	$5,686
Student/teacher ratio	17.8	16.7
Attending public school	88.7%	90.1%
State SAT score	993*	1021
State ACT score	20.3	20.9

HIGHER EDUCATION	AREA	U.S. AVG
No. 2-year colleges	9	4
No. 4-year colleges/universities	21	6
No. highly ranked universities	1	1

Health &
Healthcare
Score: 6.1
Rank: 350

HAZARDS & ILLNESSES	AREA	U.S. AVG
Air-quality score	16	37
Water-quality score	44	52
Pollen/allergy score	86	61
Cancer mortality per capita	259.9	201.9
Depression days per month	4.0	3.5
Stress score	86	50

HEALTHCARE	AREA	U.S. AVG
Physicians per capita	250.8	244.2
Hospital beds per capita	401.5	420.0
No. teaching hospitals	11	3
Cost per doctor visit	$60	$77
Cost per dental visit	$69	$70

Crime
Score: 9.6
Rank: 337

CRIME	AREA	U.S. AVG
Violent crime rate	749.7	465.5
Change in violent crime rate	-4.6%	-2.2%
Property crime rate	4,163.0	3,517.1
Change in property crime rate	-8.8%	-2.1%

Transportation
Score: 39.3
Rank: 228

COMMUTE	AREA	U.S. AVG
Average commute time	28.0	27.4
Percent commutes > 60 mins.	6.8%	5.9%
Commute by auto	79.9%	78.9%
Commute by mass transit	1.3%	1.9%
Work at home	3.2%	3.1%
Mass transit miles per capita	1.30	1.87

INTERCITY SERVICES	AREA	U.S. AVG
Major airports within 60 miles	2	1
Size of regional airport	Large	Large
Daily airline activity	961	686
Amtrak service	Yes	No

AUTOMOTIVE	AREA	U.S. AVG
Insurance, annual premium	$2,606	$1,432
Gas, cost per gallon	$2.53	$2.49
Daily vehicle miles per capita	28.1	24.0

Leisure
Score: 86.6
Rank: 50

DINING & SHOPPING	AREA	U.S. AVG
Restaurant rating	1	2
Outlet mall score	95	42
No. Starbucks	39	13
No. warehouse clubs	6	2

ENTERTAINMENT	AREA	U.S. AVG
Professional sports rating	7	4
College sports rating	4	4
Zoo/aquarium rating	6	3
Amusement park rating	9	3
Botanical garden/ arboretum rating	1	4

OUTDOOR ACTIVITIES	AREA	U.S. AVG
Golf-course rating	9	4
Ski-area rating	1	3
Sq. miles inland water	7	4
Miles of coastline	76.5	10.7
National Park rating	2	3

Arts & Culture
Score: 67.6
Rank: 121

MEDIA & LIBRARIES	AREA	U.S. AVG
Arts radio rating	1	3
No. public libraries	62	27
Library volumes per capita	2.20	2.78

PERFORMING ARTS	AREA	U.S. AVG
Classical music rating	7	4
Ballet/dance rating	6	3
Professional theater rating	8	3
University arts programs rating	2	5

MUSEUMS	AREA	U.S. AVG
Overall museum rating	9	5
Art museum rating	9	5
Science museum rating	8	5
Children's museum rating	8	3

Terre Haute, IN

Score: 54.8   **Rank:** 221   **2004 rank:** 188

Profile: Small city
Location: Extreme west-central Indiana along the Wabash River, 10 miles from the Illinois border
Elevation: 808 feet
Time zone: Eastern Standard Time

PRO	CON
Cost of living	Economy
Historic interest	Recreation
College-town amenities	Isolation

Terre Haute, the so-called "Crossroads of America" for its location on the National Road (U.S. 40) and the major north–south U.S. 41, has a typically Midwestern mix of agriculture and industry with an added college-town influence. The city is home to Indiana State University, the Rose-Hulman Institute of Technology, and the historic Saint-Mary-of-the-Woods College. None of these schools are particularly large, but they add variety to the area. The downtown is somewhat typical for the region, though the 800 historic buildings in an 80-block area reflect earlier prosperity. Overall cost of living is low and the median home price of $81,600 remains lowest in the state and fourth lowest in the country. The economy, once more tied to manufacturing and coal mining, continues to lag behind other parts of Indiana. There isn't much to do locally, but Indianapolis (80 miles northeast) and Bloomington (60 miles southeast) help compensate for what's missing.

The Wabash Valley is broad and flat at this location. To the west lie the mainly flat, agricultural prairies of Illinois. Terrain is gently rolling to the east. Summers are warm and humid. Precipitation is evenly distributed throughout the year, with frequent spring and summer thunderstorms, some heavy. Winters offer variable temperatures and some periods of winter wind and snow. First freeze is mid-October; last is late April.

Population

DEMOGRAPHICS	AREA	U.S. AVG	ETHNIC COMPOSITION	AREA	U.S. AVG	RESIDENT PROFILE	AREA	U.S. AVG
Population	169,676		White	92.9%	79.0%	Single	32.7%	32.4%
Population density per sq. mile	115.8	358.5	Black	4.2%	10.5%	Married	51.2%	52.7%
Population growth	2.2%	21.1%	Asian	1.1%	2.7%	Divorced/separated	16.1%	14.9%
Median age	36.2	36.1	Hispanic	0.9%	10.6%	Married with children	21.8%	23.7%
Percent Democrat	43.3%	44.5%	Religious observance	34.6%	48.9%	Single with children	8.6%	9.1%
Percent Republican	55.9%	54.5%	Diversity measure	14.9	40.1	Percent over age 65	14.2%	12.9%

Economy & Jobs
Score: 8.8
Rank: 340

INCOME	AREA	U.S. AVG	EMPLOYMENT	AREA	U.S. AVG	EMPLOYING INDUSTRIES	AREA	U.S. AVG
Per capita income	$19,574	$23,235	Unemployment rate	6.3%	4.7%	Largest: Manufacturing		
Household income	$38,303	$46,414	Recent job growth	0.7%	1.3%			
Household income < $25K	32.0%	26.2%	Projected future job growth	1.8%	11.5%	Percent manufacturing	19.2%	15.4%
Household income > $75K	17.7%	25.4%	White collar	52.2%	57.8%	Percent public sector	14.7%	15.7%
Household income growth	13.0%	13.6%	Blue collar	29.4%	25.2%	Percent construction	10.2%	9.9%

Cost of Living
Score: 96.3
Rank: 15

INDEXES & TAXES	AREA	U.S. AVG	HOUSING	AREA	U.S. AVG	NECESSITIES	AREA	U.S. AVG
Cost of Living Index	78.4	100.0	Median home price	$81,600	$220,000	Food Index	99.8	100.0
Buying Power Index	109.5	100.0	Home price appreciation	20.9%	10.1%	Housing Index	37.8	100.0
Income tax rate	3.40%	4.70%	Median rent	$540	$709	Utilities Index	110.6	100.0
Sales tax rate	6.00%	6.58%	Homes owned	65.8%	62.3%	Transportation Index	106.6	100.0
Property tax rate	$10.33	$12.00	Home price ratio	2.1	4.2	Healthcare Index	96.6	100.0
						Miscellaneous Cost Index	101.3	100.0

Climate
Score: 49.5
Rank: 188

TEMPERATURE	AREA	U.S. AVG	PRECIPITATION	AREA	U.S. AVG	COMFORTS & HAZARDS	AREA	U.S. AVG
Average January low	19.7	26.2	Annual inches precipitation	39.0	37.7	July relative humidity	73%	66%
Average July high	85.4	87.4	Annual inches snowfall	21.0	7.0	Annual days mostly sunny	191	208
Annual days > 90°F	15	38	Annual days precipitation	122	109	Annual days with thunderstorms	45	39
Annual days < 32°F	122	89	Annual days rain > 0.5 inches	25	22	Tornado risk score	16	18
Annual days < 0°F	7	6	Annual days snow > 1.5 inches	6	6	Hurricane risk score	4	13

TEMPERATURE

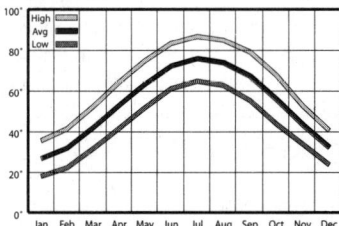

PRECIPITATION

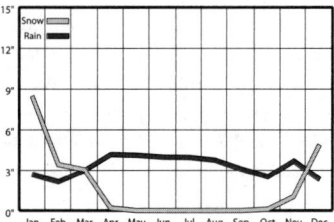

DAYS OF CLOUDS & PRECIPITATION

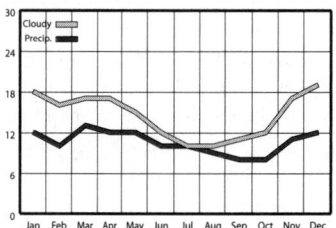

ACHIEVEMENT	AREA	U.S. AVG	PUBLIC SCHOOLS	AREA	U.S. AVG	HIGHER EDUCATION	AREA	U.S. AVG
High school degree	81.2%	82.7%	Expenditures per pupil	$5,536	$5,686	No. 2-year colleges	2	4
2-year college degree	5.9%	6.4%	Student/teacher ratio	16.7	16.7	No. 4-year colleges/universities	3	6
4-year college degree	9.7%	15.7%	Attending public school	96.2%	90.1%	No. highly ranked universities	1	1
Graduate/professional degree	7.6%	8.9%	State SAT score	1007*	1021			
			State ACT score	21.7	20.9			

Education
Score: 37.7
Rank: 234

HAZARDS & ILLNESSES	AREA	U.S. AVG	HEALTHCARE	AREA	U.S. AVG	CRIME	AREA	U.S. AVG
Air-quality score	42	37	Physicians per capita	190.0	244.2	Violent crime rate	151.2	465.5
Water-quality score	31	52	Hospital beds per capita	572.9	420.0	Change in violent crime rate	-18.2%	-2.2%
Pollen/allergy score	67	61	No. teaching hospitals	1	3	Property crime rate	4,567.7	3,517.1
Cancer mortality per capita	230.8	201.9	Cost per doctor visit	$80	$77	Change in property crime rate	0.4%	-2.1%
Depression days per month	4.0	3.5	Cost per dental visit	$88	$70			
Stress score	90	50						

Health & Healthcare
Score: 71.7
Rank: 106

Crime
Score: 21.7
Rank: 293

COMMUTE	AREA	U.S. AVG	INTERCITY SERVICES	AREA	U.S. AVG	AUTOMOTIVE	AREA	U.S. AVG
Average commute time	23.3	27.4	Major airports within 60 miles	1	1	Insurance, annual premium	$1,085	$1,432
Percent commutes › 60 mins.	5.3%	5.9%	Size of regional airport	Medium	Large	Gas, cost per gallon	$2.43	$2.49
Commute by auto	82.4%	78.9%	Daily airline activity	319	686	Daily vehicle miles per capita	31.6	24.0
Commute by mass transit	0.3%	1.9%	Amtrak service	No	No			
Work at home	2.3%	3.1%						
Mass transit miles per capita	0.29	1.87						

Transportation
Score: 38.0
Rank: 233

DINING & SHOPPING	AREA	U.S. AVG	ENTERTAINMENT	AREA	U.S. AVG	OUTDOOR ACTIVITIES	AREA	U.S. AVG
Restaurant rating	1	2	Professional sports rating	2	4	Golf-course rating	2	4
Outlet mall score	26	42	College sports rating	4	4	Ski-area rating	2	3
No. Starbucks	1	13	Zoo/aquarium rating	1	3	Sq. miles inland water	1	4
No. warehouse clubs	1	2	Amusement park rating	1	3	Miles of coastline	0.0	10.7
			Botanical garden/ arboretum rating	1	4	National Park rating	1	3

Leisure
Score: 11.2
Rank: 331

MEDIA & LIBRARIES	AREA	U.S. AVG	PERFORMING ARTS	AREA	U.S. AVG	MUSEUMS	AREA	U.S. AVG
Arts radio rating	1	3	Classical music rating	3	4	Overall museum rating	2	5
No. public libraries	20	27	Ballet/dance rating	1	3	Art museum rating	3	5
Library volumes per capita	3.51	2.78	Professional theater rating	1	3	Science museum rating	3	5
			University arts programs rating	8	5	Children's museum rating	1	3

Arts & Culture
Score: 44.4
Rank: 208

Texarkana, TX-AR

Score: 23.8   **Rank:** 343   **2004 rank:** 296

Profile: Small-town complex
Location: Extreme northeast Texas at the Texas-Arkansas border
Elevation: 259 feet
Time zone: Central Standard Time

PRO	CON
Cost of living	Low educational attainment
Nearby water recreation	Arts and culture
Recent job growth	Entertainment

This area straddles the Texas-Arkansas border with Texarkana, Texas, to the west and Texarkana, Arkansas, to the east. The twin cities are inseparable. In fact, the state line bisects the post office, which serves them both simultaneously. Typical for the region, both cities are plain and quiet but are business friendly. Low business costs and a strategic location bring a fairly large, albeit fairly low-tech, manufacturing base, including such items as tires, aluminum, cardboard, and pipe fittings. Recent employment trends have been strong. At 71.3, the area continues to have the lowest Cost of Living Index in the country. Recreation opportunities abound in nearby lakes and state parks,

but there isn't much to do in either town. There isn't much intellectual stimulation, and the low rating is consistent with the notion that there is more to life than jobs and low living costs.

The city sits in an area of level to gently rolling land with mixed agricultural areas, cotton plantations, and pine forests. Summer months are hot and fairly humid, but more pleasant than areas to the south near the Gulf. Winters are mild, with occasional, short periods of cold. Rainfall occurs as steady winter rains or as spring and summer thundershowers, which can be severe in spring.

Population

DEMOGRAPHICS	AREA	U.S. AVG	ETHNIC COMPOSITION	AREA	U.S. AVG	RESIDENT PROFILE	AREA	U.S. AVG
Population	133,977		White	72.4%	79.0%	Single	29.5%	32.4%
Population density per sq. mile	88.6	358.5	Black	24.0%	10.5%	Married	50.5%	52.7%
Population growth	11.5%	21.1%	Asian	0.6%	2.7%	Divorced/separated	20.0%	14.9%
Median age	36.2	36.1	Hispanic	3.7%	10.6%	Married with children	22.1%	23.7%
Percent Democrat	37.3%	44.5%	Religious observance	62.4%	48.9%	Single with children	11.1%	9.1%
Percent Republican	62.3%	54.5%	Diversity measure	45.9	40.1	Percent over age 65	13.5%	12.9%

Economy & Jobs
Score: 77.5
Rank: 85

INCOME	AREA	U.S. AVG	EMPLOYMENT	AREA	U.S. AVG	EMPLOYING INDUSTRIES	AREA	U.S. AVG
Per capita income	$19,534	$23,235	Unemployment rate	5.1%	4.7%	Largest: Healthcare & Social Assistance		
Household income	$37,004	$46,414	Recent job growth	4.5%	1.3%			
Household income < $25K	35.3%	26.2%	Projected future job growth	11.1%	11.5%	Percent manufacturing	17.5%	15.4%
Household income > $75K	18.6%	25.4%	White collar	53.8%	57.8%	Percent public sector	18.4%	15.7%
Household income growth	14.4%	13.6%	Blue collar	28.7%	25.2%	Percent construction	11.2%	9.9%

Cost of Living
Score: 98.1
Rank: 8

INDEXES & TAXES	AREA	U.S. AVG	HOUSING	AREA	U.S. AVG	NECESSITIES	AREA	U.S. AVG
Cost of Living Index	71.3	100.0	Median home price	$92,400	$220,000	Food Index	85.4	100.0
Buying Power Index	116.3	100.0	Home price appreciation	26.3%	10.1%	Housing Index	39.7	100.0
Income tax rate	0.56%	4.70%	Median rent	$546	$709	Utilities Index	85.4	100.0
Sales tax rate	8.33%	6.58%	Homes owned	63.1%	62.3%	Transportation Index	95.0	100.0
Property tax rate	$11.61	$12.00	Home price ratio	2.5	4.2	Healthcare Index	90.7	100.0
						Miscellaneous Cost Index	87.9	100.0

Climate
Score: 76.5
Rank: 88

TEMPERATURE	AREA	U.S. AVG	PRECIPITATION	AREA	U.S. AVG	COMFORTS & HAZARDS	AREA	U.S. AVG
Average January low	37.8	26.2	Annual inches precipitation	45.0	37.7	July relative humidity	71%	66%
Average July high	93.8	87.4	Annual inches snowfall	1.0	7.0	Annual days mostly sunny	217	208
Annual days > 90°F	87	38	Annual days precipitation	97	109	Annual days with thunderstorms	54	39
Annual days < 32°F	1	89	Annual days rain > 0.5 inches	23	22	Tornado risk score	20	18
Annual days < 0°F	0	6	Annual days snow > 1.5 inches	1	6	Hurricane risk score	11	13

TEMPERATURE

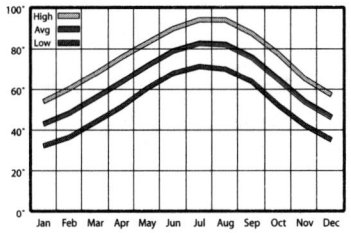

PRECIPITATION

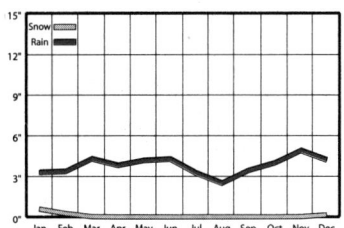

DAYS OF CLOUDS & PRECIPITATION

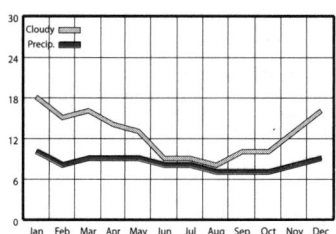

Education
Score: 12.6
Rank: 326

ACHIEVEMENT	AREA	U.S. AVG	PUBLIC SCHOOLS	AREA	U.S. AVG	HIGHER EDUCATION	AREA	U.S. AVG
High school degree	76.7%	82.7%	Expenditures per pupil	$4,941	$5,686	No. 2-year colleges	1	4
2-year college degree	4.8%	6.4%	Student/teacher ratio	16.1	16.7	No. 4-year colleges/universities	1	6
4-year college degree	9.8%	15.7%	Attending public school	96.1%	90.1%	No. highly ranked universities	0	1
Graduate/professional degree	5.4%	8.9%	State SAT score	997*	1021			
			State ACT score	20.3	20.9			

Health & Healthcare
Score: 96.5
Rank: 14

Crime
Score: 13.1
Rank: 324

HAZARDS & ILLNESSES	AREA	U.S. AVG	HEALTHCARE	AREA	U.S. AVG	CRIME	AREA	U.S. AVG
Air-quality score	49	37	Physicians per capita	227.9	244.2	Violent crime rate	847.6	465.5
Water-quality score	70	52	Hospital beds per capita	682.2	420.0	Change in violent crime rate	8.3%	-2.2%
Pollen/allergy score	64	61	No. teaching hospitals	3	3	Property crime rate	4,238.2	3,517.1
Cancer mortality per capita	206.4	201.9	Cost per doctor visit	$77	$77	Change in property crime rate	-2.4%	-2.1%
Depression days per month	3.2	3.5	Cost per dental visit	$74	$70			
Stress score	76	50						

Transportation
Score: 29.4
Rank: 265

COMMUTE	AREA	U.S. AVG	INTERCITY SERVICES	AREA	U.S. AVG	AUTOMOTIVE	AREA	U.S. AVG
Average commute time	21.6	27.4	Major airports within 60 miles	0	1	Insurance, annual premium	$1,091	$1,432
Percent commutes > 60 mins.	4.0%	5.9%	Size of regional airport	Small	Large	Gas, cost per gallon	$2.40	$2.49
Commute by auto	83.2%	78.9%	Daily airline activity	66	686	Daily vehicle miles per capita	29.6	24.0
Commute by mass transit	0.2%	1.9%	Amtrak service	Yes	No			
Work at home	2.0%	3.1%						
Mass transit miles per capita	0.23	1.87						

DINING & SHOPPING	AREA	U.S. AVG	ENTERTAINMENT	AREA	U.S. AVG	OUTDOOR ACTIVITIES	AREA	U.S. AVG
Restaurant rating	1	2	Professional sports rating	2	4	Golf-course rating	1	4
Outlet mall score	3	42	College sports rating	1	4	Ski-area rating	1	3
No. Starbucks	1	13	Zoo/aquarium rating	1	3	Sq. miles inland water	5	4
No. warehouse clubs	1	2	Amusement park rating	1	3	Miles of coastline	0.0	10.7
			Botanical garden/ arboretum rating	1	4	National Park rating	1	3

Leisure
Score: 13.9
Rank: 321

MEDIA & LIBRARIES	AREA	U.S. AVG	PERFORMING ARTS	AREA	U.S. AVG	MUSEUMS	AREA	U.S. AVG
Arts radio rating	1	3	Classical music rating	1	4	Overall museum rating	1	5
No. public libraries	5	27	Ballet/dance rating	1	3	Art museum rating	1	5
Library volumes per capita	3.83	2.78	Professional theater rating	1	3	Science museum rating	1	5
			University arts programs rating	1	5	Children's museum rating	2	3

Arts & Culture
Score: 1.1
Rank: 369

Toledo, OH

Score: 67.0 **Rank: 120** **2004 rank: 267**

Profile: Mid-size city
Location: Northwest Ohio at the western corner of Lake Erie at the Michigan border
Elevation: 692 feet
Time zone: Eastern Standard Time

PRO	CON
Central location	Weak employment
Cost of living	Industrial feel
Nearby water recreation	Gloomy winters

Toledo is a hard-working city that would like to outrun its image, and generally brings more to the table than meets the eye. It is a major Great Lakes port, transportation, and industrial center with concentrations in auto parts and glassmaking. While these businesses haven't fared well recently, Toledo has been spared some of the worst. The strategic central location among markets and major east–west and north–south routes has made it a favorite crossroads for transportation providers and global freight companies, including UPS and BAX, and the area is a popular residence for business travelers covering other parts of the East and Midwest. The downtown is unremarkable but improving slowly with some attractive new waterfront developments; there are some gritty areas particularly north of town. Good neighborhoods extend mainly south and west along the Anthony Wayne Parkway toward the airport, including the attractive suburbs of Perrysville and Maumee, the latter of which earned an All-American City Award in 2006. Prior industrial endowments have brought some better-than-average

museums and cultural amenities, and the venerable Toledo Mud Hens minor league baseball team and a good zoo are part of a healthy entertainment picture. Civic pride among local residents runs strong. Amenities and services missing locally are available in Detroit, 60 miles north, or Cleveland, 115 miles east, and Sandusky, 60 miles east, is an excellent recreation destination. The location on Lake Erie's western shore gives better winters than other parts of northern Ohio, but climate is hardly an attraction. Overall, Toledo has its problems but has some strengths in all ranking categories and isn't as bad as some think.

The city is located at the mouth of the Maumee River. Except for a 30-foot riverbank, the terrain is generally level with only a slight slope toward the river and Lake Erie. Summers are warm and humid while winters are cool and humid with considerable cloudiness. Winter sun is only 30% of daylight hours, with December and January only clear 16% of the time. Snowfall, on the other hand, is generally light. First freeze is mid-October; last is late April.

DEMOGRAPHICS	AREA	U.S. AVG	ETHNIC COMPOSITION	AREA	U.S. AVG	RESIDENT PROFILE	AREA	U.S. AVG
Population	661,740		White	82.4%	79.0%	Single	35.2%	32.4%
Population density per sq. mile	408.6	358.5	Black	12.0%	10.5%	Married	50.6%	52.7%
Population growth	1.4%	21.1%	Asian	1.3%	2.7%	Divorced/separated	14.2%	14.9%
Median age	35.9	36.1	Hispanic	4.6%	10.6%	Married with children	21.4%	23.7%
Percent Democrat	55.4%	44.5%	Religious observance	50.0%	48.9%	Single with children	9.9%	9.1%
Percent Republican	44.3%	54.5%	Diversity measure	35.4	40.1	Percent over age 65	12.8%	12.9%

Population

INCOME	AREA	U.S. AVG	EMPLOYMENT	AREA	U.S. AVG	EMPLOYING INDUSTRIES	AREA	U.S. AVG
Per capita income	$23,124	$23,235	Unemployment rate	6.7%	4.7%	Largest: Healthcare & Social Assistance		
Household income	$44,160	$46,414	Recent job growth	0.8%	1.3%			
Household income < $25K	27.4%	26.2%	Projected future job growth	3.7%	11.5%	Percent manufacturing	19.8%	15.4%
Household income > $75K	24.1%	25.4%	White collar	55.5%	57.8%	Percent public sector	12.4%	15.7%
Household income growth	10.5%	13.6%	Blue collar	28.6%	25.2%	Percent construction	8.8%	9.9%

Economy & Jobs
Score: 22.2
Rank: 291

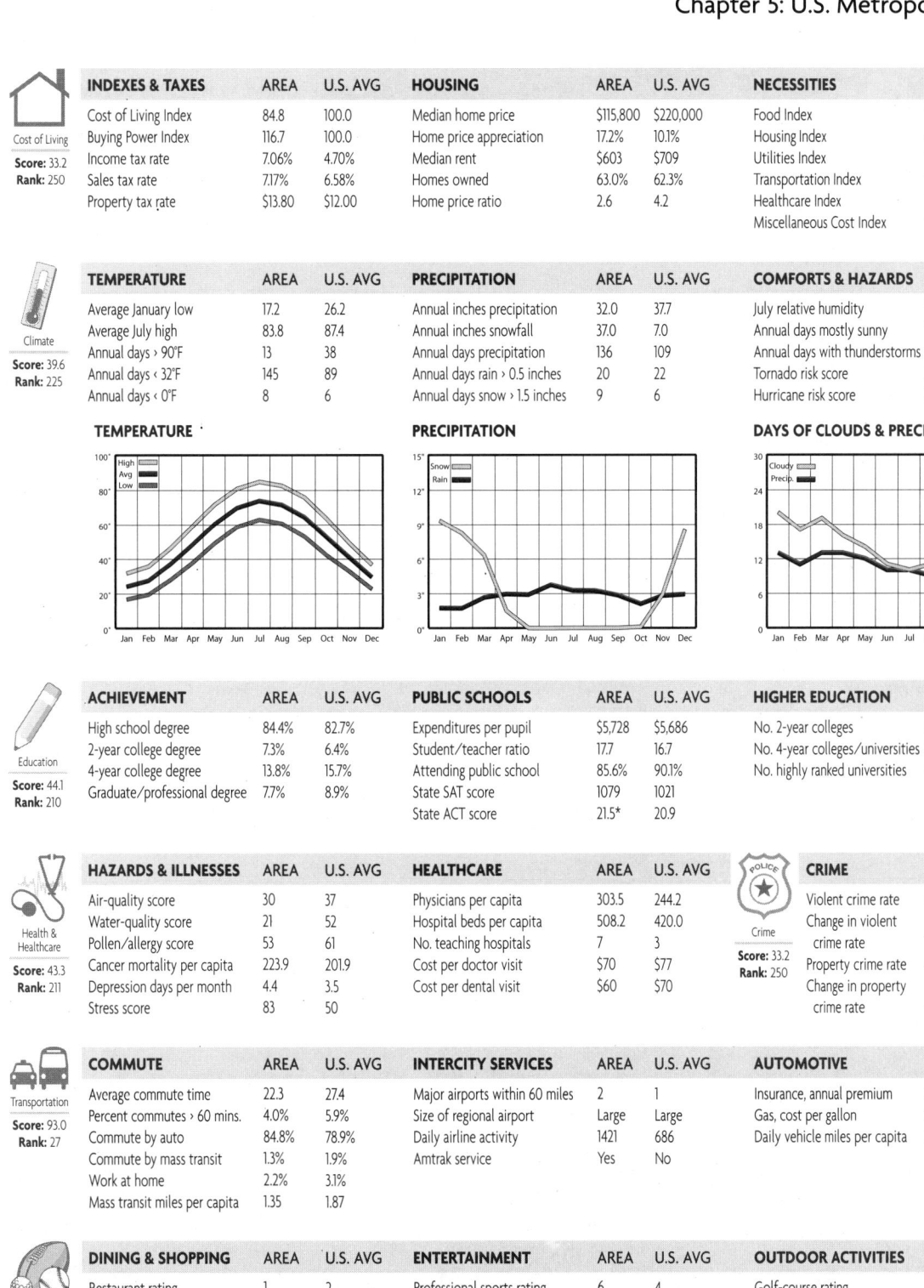

Cost of Living
Score: 33.2
Rank: 250

INDEXES & TAXES	AREA	U.S. AVG	HOUSING	AREA	U.S. AVG	NECESSITIES	AREA	U.S. AVG
Cost of Living Index	84.8	100.0	Median home price	$115,800	$220,000	Food Index	106.4	100.0
Buying Power Index	116.7	100.0	Home price appreciation	17.2%	10.1%	Housing Index	49.7	100.0
Income tax rate	7.06%	4.70%	Median rent	$603	$709	Utilities Index	122.0	100.0
Sales tax rate	7.17%	6.58%	Homes owned	63.0%	62.3%	Transportation Index	101.6	100.0
Property tax rate	$13.80	$12.00	Home price ratio	2.6	4.2	Healthcare Index	99.7	100.0
						Miscellaneous Cost Index	99.0	100.0

Climate
Score: 39.6
Rank: 225

TEMPERATURE	AREA	U.S. AVG	PRECIPITATION	AREA	U.S. AVG	COMFORTS & HAZARDS	AREA	U.S. AVG
Average January low	17.2	26.2	Annual inches precipitation	32.0	37.7	July relative humidity	72%	66%
Average July high	83.8	87.4	Annual inches snowfall	37.0	7.0	Annual days mostly sunny	181	208
Annual days > 90°F	13	38	Annual days precipitation	136	109	Annual days with thunderstorms	40	39
Annual days < 32°F	145	89	Annual days rain > 0.5 inches	20	22	Tornado risk score	23	18
Annual days < 0°F	8	6	Annual days snow > 1.5 inches	9	6	Hurricane risk score	3	13

TEMPERATURE · **PRECIPITATION** **DAYS OF CLOUDS & PRECIPITATION**

Education
Score: 44.1
Rank: 210

ACHIEVEMENT	AREA	U.S. AVG	PUBLIC SCHOOLS	AREA	U.S. AVG	HIGHER EDUCATION	AREA	U.S. AVG
High school degree	84.4%	82.7%	Expenditures per pupil	$5,728	$5,686	No. 2-year colleges	8	4
2-year college degree	7.3%	6.4%	Student/teacher ratio	17.7	16.7	No. 4-year colleges/universities	5	6
4-year college degree	13.8%	15.7%	Attending public school	85.6%	90.1%	No. highly ranked universities	0	1
Graduate/professional degree	7.7%	8.9%	State SAT score	1079	1021			
			State ACT score	21.5*	20.9			

Health & Healthcare
Score: 43.3
Rank: 211

Crime
Score: 33.2
Rank: 250

HAZARDS & ILLNESSES	AREA	U.S. AVG	HEALTHCARE	AREA	U.S. AVG	CRIME	AREA	U.S. AVG
Air-quality score	30	37	Physicians per capita	303.5	244.2	Violent crime rate	602.1	465.5
Water-quality score	21	52	Hospital beds per capita	508.2	420.0	Change in violent crime rate	10.7%	-2.2%
Pollen/allergy score	53	61	No. teaching hospitals	7	3	Property crime rate	4,766.1	3,517.1
Cancer mortality per capita	223.9	201.9	Cost per doctor visit	$70	$77	Change in property crime rate	-0.7%	-2.1%
Depression days per month	4.4	3.5	Cost per dental visit	$60	$70			
Stress score	83	50						

Transportation
Score: 93.0
Rank: 27

COMMUTE	AREA	U.S. AVG	INTERCITY SERVICES	AREA	U.S. AVG	AUTOMOTIVE	AREA	U.S. AVG
Average commute time	22.3	27.4	Major airports within 60 miles	2	1	Insurance, annual premium	$1,612	$1,432
Percent commutes > 60 mins.	4.0%	5.9%	Size of regional airport	Large	Large	Gas, cost per gallon	$2.46	$2.49
Commute by auto	84.8%	78.9%	Daily airline activity	1421	686	Daily vehicle miles per capita	25.3	24.0
Commute by mass transit	1.3%	1.9%	Amtrak service	Yes	No			
Work at home	2.2%	3.1%						
Mass transit miles per capita	1.35	1.87						

Leisure
Score: 68.7
Rank: 117

DINING & SHOPPING	AREA	U.S. AVG	ENTERTAINMENT	AREA	U.S. AVG	OUTDOOR ACTIVITIES	AREA	U.S. AVG
Restaurant rating	1	2	Professional sports rating	6	4	Golf-course rating	5	4
Outlet mall score	64	42	College sports rating	5	4	Ski-area rating	2	3
No. Starbucks	2	13	Zoo/aquarium rating	7	3	Sq. miles inland water	2	4
No. warehouse clubs	2	2	Amusement park rating	1	3	Miles of coastline	19.5	10.7
			Botanical garden/arboretum rating	2	4	National Park rating	2	3

Arts & Culture
Score: 83.4
Rank: 63

MEDIA & LIBRARIES	AREA	U.S. AVG	PERFORMING ARTS	AREA	U.S. AVG	MUSEUMS	AREA	U.S. AVG
Arts radio rating	5	3	Classical music rating	5	4	Overall museum rating	8	5
No. public libraries	44	27	Ballet/dance rating	3	3	Art museum rating	7	5
Library volumes per capita	5.47	2.78	Professional theater rating	1	3	Science museum rating	8	5
			University arts programs rating	7	5	Children's museum rating	1	3

Topeka, KS

Score: 48.4 Rank: 257 2004 rank: 197

Profile: Capital city
Location: Northeast Kansas, 60 miles west of Kansas City
Elevation: 877 feet
Time zone: Central Standard Time

PRO	CON
Capital-city amenities	Economy
Cost of living	Entertainment
Healthcare	Property crime

Topeka, the capital of Kansas, is also an agricultural, industrial, and transportation center serving a large portion of north and central Kansas. Highlights in the traditionally laid-out downtown include the statehouse, Kansas Museum of History, *Brown vs. Board of Education* historic site, and Heartland Park, a state-of-the-art motorsports complex. Costs of living and housing are low, particularly for a capital city. But rates for property crime are high for the region, and projected job and income growth are low. That said, a low cost of living brings a high Buying Power Index of 131.1. There isn't much to do, and the area has lagged behind other Kansas cities aesthetically, socially, and economically. Excellent entertainment and cultural amenities are available in the university town of Lawrence, 20 miles east and in the Kansas City area.

The city straddles the Kansas River in a valley, 2 to 4 miles wide, bordered by rolling prairie. Summers are usually hot with low relative humidity, persistent southerly winds, and, in some years, temperatures exceeding 100°F for 50 days or more. Frequent cold and snow characterize winter. Bitter cold spells are seldom prolonged. Spring is windy, while autumn brings warm days, cool nights, and relative dryness. Seventy percent of annual precipitation falls from April through September, the crop-growing months, predominantly as thunderstorms. Warm-season thunderstorms can deliver over 8 inches of rain in 24 hours. Tornadoes are a risk. First freeze is mid-October; last is late April.

Population

DEMOGRAPHICS	AREA	U.S. AVG	ETHNIC COMPOSITION	AREA	U.S. AVG	RESIDENT PROFILE	AREA	U.S. AVG
Population	227,273		White	85.1%	79.0%	Single	29.2%	32.4%
Population density per sq. mile	70.1	358.5	Black	7.0%	10.5%	Married	55.8%	52.7%
Population growth	8.2%	21.1%	Asian	1.0%	2.7%	Divorced/separated	15.0%	14.9%
Median age	37.9	36.1	Hispanic	6.7%	10.6%	Married with children	22.6%	23.7%
Percent Democrat	42.0%	44.5%	Religious observance	44.5%	48.9%	Single with children	8.9%	9.1%
Percent Republican	56.5%	54.5%	Diversity measure	35.0	40.1	Percent over age 65	14.1%	12.9%

Economy & Jobs
Score: 32.1
Rank: 254

INCOME	AREA	U.S. AVG	EMPLOYMENT	AREA	U.S. AVG	EMPLOYING INDUSTRIES	AREA	U.S. AVG
Per capita income	$23,173	$23,235	Unemployment rate	5.6%	4.7%	Largest: Healthcare & Social Assistance		
Household income	$46,271	$46,414	Recent job growth	0.8%	1.3%			
Household income < $25K	24.1%	26.2%	Projected future job growth	4.6%	11.5%	Percent manufacturing	13.2%	15.4%
Household income > $75K	23.8%	25.4%	White collar	60.5%	57.8%	Percent public sector	20.7%	15.7%
Household income growth	12.5%	13.6%	Blue collar	23.5%	25.2%	Percent construction	10.3%	9.9%

Cost of Living
Score: 55.6
Rank: 166

INDEXES & TAXES	AREA	U.S. AVG	HOUSING	AREA	U.S. AVG	NECESSITIES	AREA	U.S. AVG
Cost of Living Index	79.1	100.0	Median home price	$105,100	$220,000	Food Index	96.6	100.0
Buying Power Index	131.1	100.0	Home price appreciation	26.7%	10.1%	Housing Index	43.0	100.0
Income tax rate	6.25%	4.70%	Median rent	$585	$709	Utilities Index	106.0	100.0
Sales tax rate	7.20%	6.58%	Homes owned	66.4%	62.3%	Transportation Index	98.3	100.0
Property tax rate	$13.57	$12.00	Home price ratio	2.3	4.2	Healthcare Index	92.5	100.0
						Miscellaneous Cost Index	98.2	100.0

Climate
Score: 41.4
Rank: 218

TEMPERATURE	AREA	U.S. AVG	PRECIPITATION	AREA	U.S. AVG	COMFORTS & HAZARDS	AREA	U.S. AVG
Average January low	17.7	26.2	Annual inches precipitation	34.7	37.7	July relative humidity	69%	66%
Average July high	89.2	87.4	Annual inches snowfall	21.4	7.0	Annual days mostly sunny	208	208
Annual days > 90°F	40	38	Annual days precipitation	102	109	Annual days with thunderstorms	58	39
Annual days < 32°F	123	89	Annual days rain > 0.5 inches	24	22	Tornado risk score	61	18
Annual days < 0°F	5	6	Annual days snow > 1.5 inches	5	6	Hurricane risk score	2	13

TEMPERATURE

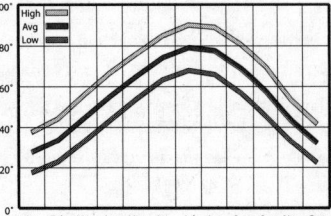

PRECIPITATION

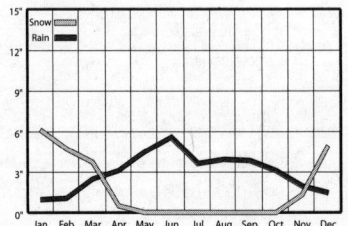

DAYS OF CLOUDS & PRECIPITATION

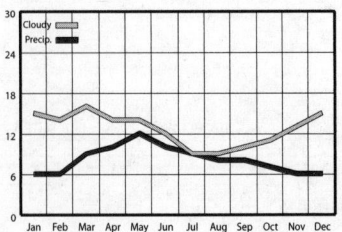

Education	Score: 47.9 Rank: 196									

ACHIEVEMENT	AREA	U.S. AVG	PUBLIC SCHOOLS	AREA	U.S. AVG	HIGHER EDUCATION	AREA	U.S. AVG
High school degree	88.1%	82.7%	Expenditures per pupil	$5,631	$5,686	No. 2-year colleges	0	4
2-year college degree	4.2%	6.4%	Student/teacher ratio	15.8	16.7	No. 4-year colleges/universities	2	6
4-year college degree	15.8%	15.7%	Attending public school	91.7%	90.1%	No. highly ranked universities	0	1
Graduate/professional degree	7.9%	8.9%	State SAT score	1172	1021			
			State ACT score	21.8*	20.9			

Health & Healthcare — Score: 68.4 Rank: 119

HAZARDS & ILLNESSES	AREA	U.S. AVG	HEALTHCARE	AREA	U.S. AVG	CRIME	AREA	U.S. AVG
Air-quality score	44	37	Physicians per capita	201.9	244.2	Violent crime rate	399.9	465.5
Water-quality score	40	52	Hospital beds per capita	527.1	420.0	Change in violent crime rate	8.8%	-2.2%
Pollen/allergy score	71	61	No. teaching hospitals	4	3	Property crime rate	5,467.1	3,517.1
Cancer mortality per capita	209.1	201.9	Cost per doctor visit	$66	$77	Change in property crime rate	8.7%	-2.1%
Depression days per month	3.2	3.5	Cost per dental visit	$62	$70			
Stress score	60	50						

Crime — Score: 42.8 Rank: 214

Transportation — Score: 47.9 Rank: 196

COMMUTE	AREA	U.S. AVG	INTERCITY SERVICES	AREA	U.S. AVG	AUTOMOTIVE	AREA	U.S. AVG
Average commute time	22.7	27.4	Major airports within 60 miles	1	1	Insurance, annual premium	$1,218	$1,432
Percent commutes > 60 mins.	4.5%	5.9%	Size of regional airport	Medium	Large	Gas, cost per gallon	$2.42	$2.49
Commute by auto	82.0%	78.9%	Daily airline activity	328	686	Daily vehicle miles per capita	20.6	24.0
Commute by mass transit	0.7%	1.9%	Amtrak service	Yes	No			
Work at home	3.1%	3.1%						
Mass transit miles per capita	0.74	1.87						

Leisure — Score: 19.5 Rank: 300

DINING & SHOPPING	AREA	U.S. AVG	ENTERTAINMENT	AREA	U.S. AVG	OUTDOOR ACTIVITIES	AREA	U.S. AVG
Restaurant rating	1	2	Professional sports rating	2	4	Golf-course rating	2	4
Outlet mall score	46	42	College sports rating	2	4	Ski-area rating	2	3
No. Starbucks	1	13	Zoo/aquarium rating	3	3	Sq. miles inland water	2	4
No. warehouse clubs	1	2	Amusement park rating	1	3	Miles of coastline	0.0	10.7
			Botanical garden/ arboretum rating	4	4	National Park rating	1	3

Arts & Culture — Score: 11.0 Rank: 332

MEDIA & LIBRARIES	AREA	U.S. AVG	PERFORMING ARTS	AREA	U.S. AVG	MUSEUMS	AREA	U.S. AVG
Arts radio rating	1	3	Classical music rating	1	4	Overall museum rating	6	5
No. public libraries	15	27	Ballet/dance rating	1	3	Art museum rating	2	5
Library volumes per capita	3.55	2.78	Professional theater rating	1	3	Science museum rating	7	5
			University arts programs rating	3	5	Children's museum rating	1	3

Trenton–Ewing, NJ

Score: 71.6 Rank: 81 2004 rank: 169

Profile: Capital city
Location: Western New Jersey along the Delaware River and Pennsylvania border, 40 miles north of Philadelphia
Elevation: 56 feet
Time zone: Eastern Standard Time

PRO
Nearby college town
Historic interest
Moderate living costs

CON
Economy
Long commutes
Low educational attainment

Trenton, the capital of New Jersey, contains a fairly typical mix of government activities with a strong complement of commercial and industrial activities typically found in mid-size Eastern cities. Unlike most New Jersey cities, it is more tied economically to the Delaware Valley and Philadelphia than it is to the New York area, but like many places in the state, the area is characterized by contrasts. Numerous well-preserved historic districts date back to the Revolutionary War. Impoverished areas are also present and there's a strong working-class element. In marked contrast to most of Trenton itself is Princeton, the college town 15 miles northeast with the Ivy League university of the same name. Princeton and some of the other communities along the U.S. 1 corridor have excellent residential areas, arts and culture amenities, and a highly educated, mostly upper-middle-class population. Princeton also serves as the outer edge of a residential area for commuters who endure a 1½-hour rail trip to New York City. Most don't do this commute, but a few do as reflected in commute time statistics. Cost of living is moderate for the region, and housing, while quite high in Princeton, is reasonable in other areas and buying power is high. Outside of Princeton, the economic outlook is mixed and educational attainment fairly low—again the contrast theme is evident—but the area as a whole scores well enough in all categories to receive a relatively high ranking.

Trenton lies in the Delaware River Valley with level and gently rolling, mostly wooded and agricultural terrain to the east and more significant hills to the north and west. The climate is variable, with periods of extreme temperatures seldom lasting for more than a few days. Precipitation is evenly distributed throughout the year with maximum amounts arriving in summer months. Winter is a mix of cool and colder periods, with rain or snow arriving from either the northwest-leading continental air masses or the south as coastal Atlantic storms. First freeze is mid-October; last is late April.

Population

DEMOGRAPHICS	AREA	U.S. AVG	ETHNIC COMPOSITION	AREA	U.S. AVG	RESIDENT PROFILE	AREA	U.S. AVG
Population	367,375		White	65.5%	79.0%	Single	36.5%	32.4%
Population density per sq. mile	1626.3	358.5	Black	20.0%	10.5%	Married	48.3%	52.7%
Population growth	12.8%	21.1%	Asian	6.8%	2.7%	Divorced/separated	15.3%	14.9%
Median age	36.9	36.1	Hispanic	11.4%	10.6%	Married with children	23.8%	23.7%
Percent Democrat	61.3%	44.5%	Religious observance	50.8%	48.9%	Single with children	9.0%	9.1%
Percent Republican	37.9%	54.5%	Diversity measure	62.0	40.1	Percent over age 65	12.4%	12.9%

Economy & Jobs
Score: 61.5
Rank: 145

INCOME	AREA	U.S. AVG	EMPLOYMENT	AREA	U.S. AVG	EMPLOYING INDUSTRIES	AREA	U.S. AVG
Per capita income	$32,519	$23,235	Unemployment rate	4.0%	4.7%	Largest: Professional, Scientific & Technical Services		
Household income	$65,719	$46,414	Recent job growth	2.7%	1.3%			
Household income < $25K	17.9%	26.2%	Projected future job growth	7.4%	11.5%	Percent manufacturing	9.6%	15.4%
Household income > $75K	43.3%	25.4%	White collar	70.1%	57.8%	Percent public sector	20.4%	15.7%
Household income growth	16.1%	13.6%	Blue collar	15.6%	25.2%	Percent construction	6.0%	9.9%

Cost of Living
Score: 13.1
Rank: 324

INDEXES & TAXES	AREA	U.S. AVG	HOUSING	AREA	U.S. AVG	NECESSITIES	AREA	U.S. AVG
Cost of Living Index	119.5	100.0	Median home price	$290,400	$220,000	Food Index	109.3	100.0
Buying Power Index	123.3	100.0	Home price appreciation	87.2%	10.1%	Housing Index	84.5	100.0
Income tax rate	2.45%	4.70%	Median rent	$1,084	$709	Utilities Index	126.8	100.0
Sales tax rate	6.00%	6.58%	Homes owned	63.4%	62.3%	Transportation Index	117.3	100.0
Property tax rate	$27.49	$12.00	Home price ratio	4.4	4.2	Healthcare Index	111.6	100.0
						Miscellaneous Cost Index	112.6	100.0

Climate
Score: 59.6
Rank: 150

TEMPERATURE	AREA	U.S. AVG	PRECIPITATION	AREA	U.S. AVG	COMFORTS & HAZARDS	AREA	U.S. AVG
Average January low	25.3	26.2	Annual inches precipitation	40.2	37.7	July relative humidity	67%	66%
Average July high	84.9	87.4	Annual inches snowfall	23.4	7.0	Annual days mostly sunny	216	208
Annual days > 90°F	17	38	Annual days precipitation	128	109	Annual days with thunderstorms	33	39
Annual days < 32°F	88	89	Annual days rain > 0.5 inches	28	22	Tornado risk score	17	18
Annual days < 0°F	0	6	Annual days snow > 1.5 inches	6	6	Hurricane risk score	15	13

TEMPERATURE

PRECIPITATION

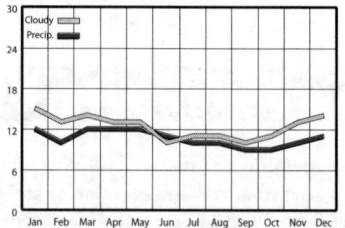

DAYS OF CLOUDS & PRECIPITATION

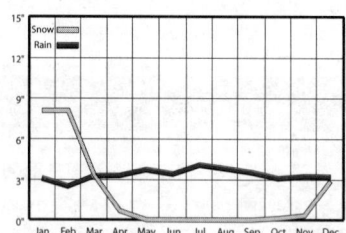

Education
Score: 78.6
Rank: 81

ACHIEVEMENT	AREA	U.S. AVG	PUBLIC SCHOOLS	AREA	U.S. AVG	HIGHER EDUCATION	AREA	U.S. AVG
High school degree	81.9%	82.7%	Expenditures per pupil	$9,513	$5,686	No. 2-year colleges	3	4
2-year college degree	5.4%	6.4%	Student/teacher ratio	14.4	16.7	No. 4-year colleges/universities	5	6
4-year college degree	18.6%	15.7%	Attending public school	81.2%	90.1%	No. highly ranked universities	2	1
Graduate/professional degree	15.6%	8.9%	State SAT score	1011*	1021			
			State ACT score	21.8	20.9			

Health & Healthcare
Score: 36.9
Rank: 235

Crime
Score: 39.8
Rank: 225

HAZARDS & ILLNESSES	AREA	U.S. AVG	HEALTHCARE	AREA	U.S. AVG	CRIME	AREA	U.S. AVG
Air-quality score	33	37	Physicians per capita	322.7	244.2	Violent crime rate	543.1	465.5
Water-quality score	27	52	Hospital beds per capita	533.0	420.0	Change in violent crime rate	11.1%	-2.2%
Pollen/allergy score	63	61	No. teaching hospitals	4	3	Property crime rate	2,523.3	3,517.1
Cancer mortality per capita	216.2	201.9	Cost per doctor visit	$67	$77	Change in property crime rate	-5.0%	-2.1%
Depression days per month	3.0	3.5	Cost per dental visit	$90	$70			
Stress score	31	50						

COMMUTE	AREA	U.S. AVG	INTERCITY SERVICES	AREA	U.S. AVG	AUTOMOTIVE	AREA	U.S. AVG
Average commute time	29.3	27.4	Major airports within 60 miles	4	1	Insurance, annual premium	$2,843	$1,432
Percent commutes › 60 mins.	11.6%	5.9%	Size of regional airport	Large	Large	Gas, cost per gallon	$2.35	$2.49
Commute by auto	73.5%	78.9%	Daily airline activity	2696	686	Daily vehicle miles per capita	24.7	24.0
Commute by mass transit	7.0%	1.9%	Amtrak service	Yes	No			
Work at home	3.2%	3.1%						
Mass transit miles per capita	7.01	1.87						

Transportation
Score: 97.3
Rank: 11

DINING & SHOPPING	AREA	U.S. AVG	ENTERTAINMENT	AREA	U.S. AVG	OUTDOOR ACTIVITIES	AREA	U.S. AVG
Restaurant rating	1	2	Professional sports rating	10	4	Golf-course rating	8	4
Outlet mall score	8	42	College sports rating	6	4	Ski-area rating	4	3
No. Starbucks	5	13	Zoo/aquarium rating	4	3	Sq. miles inland water	6	4
No. warehouse clubs	0	2	Amusement park rating	5	3	Miles of coastline	0.0	10.7
			Botanical garden/ arboretum rating	7	4	National Park rating	3	3

Leisure
Score: 84.2
Rank: 59

MEDIA & LIBRARIES	AREA	U.S. AVG	PERFORMING ARTS	AREA	U.S. AVG	MUSEUMS	AREA	U.S. AVG
Arts radio rating	6	3	Classical music rating	7	4	Overall museum rating	9	5
No. public libraries	18	27	Ballet/dance rating	6	3	Art museum rating	9	5
Library volumes per capita	4.24	2.78	Professional theater rating	9	3	Science museum rating	10	5
			University arts programs rating	8	5	Children's museum rating	7	3

Arts & Culture
Score: 88.8
Rank: 43

Tucson, AZ

Score: 55.9 Rank: 212 2004 rank: 70

Profile: Mid-size city/college town
Location: South-central Arizona, 60 miles north of the Mexican border
Elevation: 2,555 feet
Time zone: Mountain Standard Time (no daylight saving time)

PRO
High desert climate
Arts and culture
Attractive setting

CON
High crime rates
Growth and sprawl
Economic cycles

Tucson is a large and growing Sun Belt city known for its attractive setting, pleasant climate, and cosmopolitan nature. It attracts retirees and a younger crowd. The area consists of an attractive, modern downtown with a small historic district, surrounded by suburbs laid out in a grid. The University of Arizona, about a mile north of downtown, brings some college-town feel, particularly on football weekends and during the basketball season. Tall, forested mountains surround the city up to an elevation of 9,000 feet. Toward, and into, the mountains are numerous planned communities and higher-priced homes, many around golf courses, and some of which sustained damage in recent wildfires. The economy is mainly supported by the university, retirees, and high-tech industry. Several large companies have facilities in the area, including IBM, Raytheon, Intuit, and Texas Instruments, as do a number of smaller companies. Some of these businesses have proven to be cyclical in the past but are doing reasonably well now. The cost of living has been rising and is now above the U.S. average, and home prices have escalated rapidly. The climate is close to ideal: The high altitude moderates the desert heat while the southerly location and dry surroundings moderate winter influences and create a generally pleasant atmosphere. The arts and culture scene is strong for a city its size. On the downside, the crime rate is persistently high, and some sprawl issues including relatively long commutes, poor air quality, and areas of bland housing and commercial infrastructure are evident. These downsides were strong enough to pull it down in the rankings.

Located at the foot of the Catalina Mountains, Tucson lies in a broad, flat valley with many dry riverbeds and washes. The soil is sandy, and vegetation is mostly brush, cacti, and small trees. Temperatures above 90°F prevail from May through September, with 100°F-plus temperatures an average of 41 days per year. Humidity is low. Summer thunderstorms, which can flood otherwise dry washes, produce 50% of annual precipitation. Snow may fall in higher mountains, but is infrequent in the city. Clear, sunny days are commonplace with some dust and haze at times. First freeze is late November; last is late February.

DEMOGRAPHICS	AREA	U.S. AVG	ETHNIC COMPOSITION	AREA	U.S. AVG	RESIDENT PROFILE	AREA	U.S. AVG
Population	924,462		White	72.8%	79.0%	Single	33.4%	32.4%
Population density per sq. mile	100.6	358.5	Black	2.9%	10.5%	Married	50.6%	52.7%
Population growth	38.6%	21.1%	Asian	2.4%	2.7%	Divorced/separated	16.0%	14.9%
Median age	35.9	36.1	Hispanic	32.9%	10.6%	Married with children	19.8%	23.7%
Percent Democrat	52.6%	44.5%	Religious observance	44.9%	48.9%	Single with children	9.2%	9.1%
Percent Republican	46.6%	54.5%	Diversity measure	68.9	40.1	Percent over age 65	14.3%	12.9%

Population

INCOME

Economy & Jobs
Score: 44.9
Rank: 206

INCOME	AREA	U.S. AVG
Per capita income	$22,716	$23,235
Household income	$42,048	$46,414
Household income < $25K	28.5%	26.2%
Household income > $75K	22.5%	25.4%
Household income growth	14.4%	13.6%

EMPLOYMENT	AREA	U.S. AVG
Unemployment rate	4.8%	4.7%
Recent job growth	1.7%	1.3%
Projected future job growth	13.7%	11.5%
White collar	62.4%	57.8%
Blue collar	19.8%	25.2%

EMPLOYING INDUSTRIES	AREA	U.S. AVG
Largest: Healthcare & Social Assistance		
Percent manufacturing	9.2%	15.4%
Percent public sector	18.8%	15.7%
Percent construction	10.6%	9.9%

Cost of Living

Cost of Living
Score: 20.6
Rank: 296

INDEXES & TAXES	AREA	U.S. AVG
Cost of Living Index	105.2	100.0
Buying Power Index	89.6	100.0
Income tax rate	3.90%	4.70%
Sales tax rate	7.60%	6.58%
Property tax rate	$10.01	$12.00

HOUSING	AREA	U.S. AVG
Median home price	$247,300	$220,000
Home price appreciation	87.0%	10.1%
Median rent	$772	$709
Homes owned	59.3%	62.3%
Home price ratio	5.9	4.2

NECESSITIES	AREA	U.S. AVG
Food Index	104.3	100.0
Housing Index	85.8	100.0
Utilities Index	105.3	100.0
Transportation Index	104.7	100.0
Healthcare Index	110.0	100.0
Miscellaneous Cost Index	94.5	100.0

Climate

Climate
Score: 96.0
Rank: 16

TEMPERATURE	AREA	U.S. AVG
Average January low	38.2	26.2
Average July high	98.3	87.4
Annual days > 90°F	139	38
Annual days < 32°F	21	89
Annual days < 0°F	0	6

PRECIPITATION	AREA	U.S. AVG
Annual inches precipitation	11.0	37.7
Annual inches snowfall	2.0	7.0
Annual days precipitation	50	109
Annual days rain > 0.5 inches	7	22
Annual days snow > 1.5 inches	2	6

COMFORTS & HAZARDS	AREA	U.S. AVG
July relative humidity	38%	66%
Annual days mostly sunny	287	208
Annual days with thunderstorms	40	39
Tornado risk score	7	18
Hurricane risk score	3	13

TEMPERATURE

PRECIPITATION

DAYS OF CLOUDS & PRECIPITATION

Education

Education
Score: 65.8
Rank: 129

ACHIEVEMENT	AREA	U.S. AVG
High school degree	83.9%	82.7%
2-year college degree	6.8%	6.4%
4-year college degree	16.1%	15.7%
Graduate/professional degree	10.9%	8.9%

PUBLIC SCHOOLS	AREA	U.S. AVG
Expenditures per pupil	$4,526	$5,686
Student/teacher ratio	18.7	16.7
Attending public school	91.9%	90.1%
State SAT score	1049	1021
State ACT score	21.6*	20.9

HIGHER EDUCATION	AREA	U.S. AVG
No. 2-year colleges	5	4
No. 4-year colleges/universities	6	6
No. highly ranked universities	1	1

Health & Healthcare

Health & Healthcare
Score: 89.8
Rank: 39

HAZARDS & ILLNESSES	AREA	U.S. AVG
Air-quality score	89	37
Water-quality score	48	52
Pollen/allergy score	68	61
Cancer mortality per capita	178.4	201.9
Depression days per month	3.0	3.5
Stress score	90	50

HEALTHCARE	AREA	U.S. AVG
Physicians per capita	299.7	244.2
Hospital beds per capita	273.3	420.0
No. teaching hospitals	4	3
Cost per doctor visit	$73	$77
Cost per dental visit	$75	$70

Crime
Score: 9.1
Rank: 339

CRIME	AREA	U.S. AVG
Violent crime rate	649.7	465.5
Change in violent crime rate	1.5%	-2.2%
Property crime rate	5,229.8	3,517.1
Change in property crime rate	-24.6%	-2.1%

Transportation

Transportation
Score: 11.8
Rank: 331

COMMUTE	AREA	U.S. AVG
Average commute time	26.1	27.4
Percent commutes > 60 mins.	4.7%	5.9%
Commute by auto	74.5%	78.9%
Commute by mass transit	2.4%	1.9%
Work at home	3.7%	3.1%
Mass transit miles per capita	2.38	1.87

INTERCITY SERVICES	AREA	U.S. AVG
Major airports within 60 miles	1	1
Size of regional airport	Medium	Large
Daily airline activity	81	686
Amtrak service	Yes	No

AUTOMOTIVE	AREA	U.S. AVG
Insurance, annual premium	$1,989	$1,432
Gas, cost per gallon	$2.44	$2.49
Daily vehicle miles per capita	23.6	24.0

Leisure

Leisure
Score: 77.8
Rank: 83

DINING & SHOPPING	AREA	U.S. AVG
Restaurant rating	5	2
Outlet mall score	58	42
No. Starbucks	19	13
No. warehouse clubs	2	2

ENTERTAINMENT	AREA	U.S. AVG
Professional sports rating	3	4
College sports rating	9	4
Zoo/aquarium rating	5	3
Amusement park rating	2	3
Botanical garden/arboretum rating	6	4

OUTDOOR ACTIVITIES	AREA	U.S. AVG
Golf-course rating	4	4
Ski-area rating	4	3
Sq. miles inland water	2	4
Miles of coastline	0.0	10.7
National Park rating	10	3

MEDIA & LIBRARIES	AREA	U.S. AVG	PERFORMING ARTS	AREA	U.S. AVG	MUSEUMS	AREA	U.S. AVG
Arts radio rating	7	3	Classical music rating	5	4	Overall museum rating	8	5
No. public libraries	19	27	Ballet/dance rating	1	3	Art museum rating	8	5
Library volumes per capita	1.44	2.78	Professional theater rating	7	3	Science museum rating	9	5
			University arts programs rating	5	5	Children's museum rating	3	3

Arts & Culture
Score: 74.1
Rank: 97

Tulsa, OK

Score: 64.2 Rank: 144 2004 rank: 133

Profile: Mid-size city
Location: Northeastern Oklahoma along the Arkansas River
Elevation: 676 feet
Time zone: Central Standard Time

PRO	CON
Cost of living	Violent crime
Attractive downtown	Unattractive setting
Arts and culture	Summer heat

Tulsa, located along the Arkansas River in the northeast part of the state, is a commercial, industrial, and cultural center for a large agricultural and oil-producing region. Many say it is "where the South meets the West," mixing characteristics of a traditional, genteel, and historic Southern city with the ruggedness, ambitions, and appearances of the West. Not surprisingly, energy is the biggest industry, and several oil and gas companies make Tulsa their home, and some 1,000 more companies have energy-related operations here. This industry is on an uptrend and more recently the economic base has broadened into high-tech, telecommunications, banking, and financial services. The downtown area is prosperous and modern with parks, gardens, and attractive older areas, such as the oil-boom era Art Deco district. Although not the largest city in the state, Tulsa has a full set of performing arts and museums. Excellent suburbs lie east, northeast, and south,

and Tulsa is coming into its own as a good family city. The Cost of Living Index of 83.0 makes Tulsa a good value for what is available.

The city of Tulsa lies along the Arkansas River surrounded by gently rolling grassland and hardwood trees, mostly oaks. Tulsa is far enough north to escape long periods of heat in summer and far enough south to miss extreme winter cold. Summers are hot with frequent 100°F days, but occasional low humidity and southerly breezes can moderate temperatures. Winters are generally mild with temperatures occasionally falling below zero but only for a short time. Falls are long with pleasant, sunny days and cool nights. Precipitation occurs evenly throughout the year with spring being the wettest. Thunderstorms are common and occasionally severe. Snow is light and remains only for brief periods. First freeze is early November; last is late March.

DEMOGRAPHICS	AREA	U.S. AVG	ETHNIC COMPOSITION	AREA	U.S. AVG	RESIDENT PROFILE	AREA	U.S. AVG
Population	887,968		White	74.8%	79.0%	Single	28.2%	32.4%
Population density per sq. mile	141.4	358.5	Black	9.0%	10.5%	Married	56.2%	52.7%
Population growth	17.5%	21.1%	Asian	1.5%	2.7%	Divorced/separated	15.7%	14.9%
Median age	36.0	36.1	Hispanic	5.6%	10.6%	Married with children	24.3%	23.7%
Percent Democrat	35.8%	44.5%	Religious observance	52.6%	48.9%	Single with children	9.0%	9.1%
Percent Republican	64.2%	54.5%	Diversity measure	47.9	40.1	Percent over age 65	12.3%	12.9%

Population

INCOME	AREA	U.S. AVG	EMPLOYMENT	AREA	U.S. AVG	EMPLOYING INDUSTRIES	AREA	U.S. AVG
Per capita income	$22,730	$23,235	Unemployment rate	4.2%	4.7%	Largest: Manufacturing		
Household income	$43,395	$46,414	Recent job growth	2.0%	1.3%			
Household income < $25K	27.5%	26.2%	Projected future job growth	10.2%	11.5%	Percent manufacturing	14.2%	15.4%
Household income > $75K	23.3%	25.4%	White collar	60.1%	57.8%	Percent public sector	11.2%	15.7%
Household income growth	14.7%	13.6%	Blue collar	25.5%	25.2%	Percent construction	11.2%	9.9%

Economy & Jobs
Score: 59.1
Rank: 154

INDEXES & TAXES	AREA	U.S. AVG	HOUSING	AREA	U.S. AVG	NECESSITIES	AREA	U.S. AVG
Cost of Living Index	83.0	100.0	Median home price	$135,000	$220,000	Food Index	98.6	100.0
Buying Power Index	117.2	100.0	Home price appreciation	22.0%	10.1%	Housing Index	45.1	100.0
Income tax rate	7.00%	4.70%	Median rent	$619	$709	Utilities Index	98.6	100.0
Sales tax rate	8.75%	6.58%	Homes owned	63.2%	62.3%	Transportation Index	87.8	100.0
Property tax rate	$9.49	$12.00	Home price ratio	3.1	4.2	Healthcare Index	98.4	100.0
						Miscellaneous Cost Index	97.2	100.0

Cost of Living
Score: 32.4
Rank: 253

Climate
Score: 79.4
Rank: 78

TEMPERATURE	AREA	U.S. AVG
Average January low	26.1	26.2
Average July high	92.8	87.4
Annual days > 90°F	70	38
Annual days < 32°F	85	89
Annual days < 0°F	1	6

PRECIPITATION	AREA	U.S. AVG
Annual inches precipitation	37.0	37.7
Annual inches snowfall	9.0	7.0
Annual days precipitation	90	109
Annual days rain > 0.5 inches	25	22
Annual days snow > 1.5 inches	3	6

COMFORTS & HAZARDS	AREA	U.S. AVG
July relative humidity	52%	66%
Annual days mostly sunny	228	208
Annual days with thunderstorms	52	39
Tornado risk score	55	18
Hurricane risk score	2	13

TEMPERATURE

PRECIPITATION

DAYS OF CLOUDS & PRECIPITATION

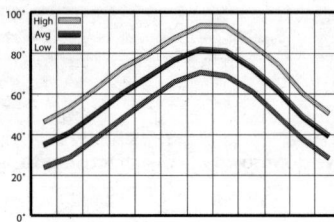
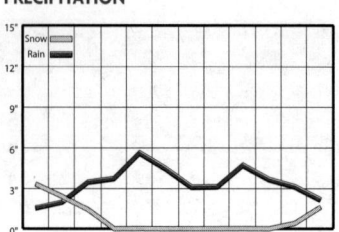

Education
Score: 59.4
Rank: 153

ACHIEVEMENT	AREA	U.S. AVG
High school degree	83.5%	82.7%
2-year college degree	7.0%	6.4%
4-year college degree	15.7%	15.7%
Graduate/professional degree	7.0%	8.9%

PUBLIC SCHOOLS	AREA	U.S. AVG
Expenditures per pupil	$4,585	$5,686
Student/teacher ratio	17.3	16.7
Attending public school	92.6%	90.1%
State SAT score	1150	1021
State ACT score	20.5*	20.9

HIGHER EDUCATION	AREA	U.S. AVG
No. 2-year colleges	6	4
No. 4-year colleges/universities	9	6
No. highly ranked universities	1	1

Health & Healthcare
Score: 31.0
Rank: 257

HAZARDS & ILLNESSES	AREA	U.S. AVG
Air-quality score	25	37
Water-quality score	62	52
Pollen/allergy score	72	61
Cancer mortality per capita	222.3	201.9
Depression days per month	3.6	3.5
Stress score	64	50

HEALTHCARE	AREA	U.S. AVG
Physicians per capita	227.1	244.2
Hospital beds per capita	325.2	420.0
No. teaching hospitals	6	3
Cost per doctor visit	$82	$77
Cost per dental visit	$64	$70

Crime
Score: 11.8
Rank: 329

CRIME	AREA	U.S. AVG
Violent crime rate	701.4	465.5
Change in violent crime rate	4.9%	-2.2%
Property crime rate	4,160.5	3,517.1
Change in property crime rate	-6.6%	-2.1%

Transportation
Score: 21.4
Rank: 295

COMMUTE	AREA	U.S. AVG
Average commute time	24.0	27.4
Percent commutes > 60 mins.	3.9%	5.9%
Commute by auto	81.1%	78.9%
Commute by mass transit	0.6%	1.9%
Work at home	3.2%	3.1%
Mass transit miles per capita	0.61	1.87

INTERCITY SERVICES	AREA	U.S. AVG
Major airports within 60 miles	1	1
Size of regional airport	Medium	Large
Daily airline activity	104	686
Amtrak service	No	No

AUTOMOTIVE	AREA	U.S. AVG
Insurance, annual premium	$1,701	$1,432
Gas, cost per gallon	$2.38	$2.49
Daily vehicle miles per capita	37.0	24.0

Leisure
Score: 60.4
Rank: 148

DINING & SHOPPING	AREA	U.S. AVG
Restaurant rating	1	2
Outlet mall score	0	42
No. Starbucks	6	13
No. warehouse clubs	0	2

ENTERTAINMENT	AREA	U.S. AVG
Professional sports rating	3	4
College sports rating	5	4
Zoo/aquarium rating	6	3
Amusement park rating	1	3
Botanical garden/ arboretum rating	10	4

OUTDOOR ACTIVITIES	AREA	U.S. AVG
Golf-course rating	5	4
Ski-area rating	1	3
Sq. miles inland water	7	4
Miles of coastline	0.0	10.7
National Park rating	1	3

Arts & Culture
Score: 57.8
Rank: 158

MEDIA & LIBRARIES	AREA	U.S. AVG
Arts radio rating	1	3
No. public libraries	43	27
Library volumes per capita	2.61	2.78

PERFORMING ARTS	AREA	U.S. AVG
Classical music rating	4	4
Ballet/dance rating	3	3
Professional theater rating	5	3
University arts programs rating	6	5

MUSEUMS	AREA	U.S. AVG
Overall museum rating	8	5
Art museum rating	7	5
Science museum rating	7	5
Children's museum rating	8	3

Tuscaloosa, AL

Score: 60.7 Rank: 170 2004 rank: 111

Profile: College town
Location: West-central Alabama along I-20/I-59, 60 miles west of Birmingham
Elevation: 160 feet
Time zone: Central Standard Time

PRO	CON
College-town amenities	Summer heat and humidity
Strong economy	Educational attainment
Healthcare	Isolation

Tuscaloosa is home to the University of Alabama, a large quality institution known among other things for its sports programs, notably football's Crimson Tide. The city has a strong college-town character with the usual entertainment and cultural amenities. For such a college town, the economy has always been fairly diverse, but more recently, the arrival of a Mercedes-Benz plant has done a lot for the city's economy as well as its image. As found elsewhere in the South, the new auto plant not only brings direct employment but also supports smaller businesses, further strengthening the economy, and that pattern is evident in the strong job statistics. The city scores well for cost of living at 87.2, especially for a college town, and also scores well for healthcare and overall quality of life. Climate, crime, and air service are among the negatives, although the crime issue has been improving over the years. Educational attainment is a bit weak for a college town. Tuscaloosa received a National Civic League All-America City Award in 2002. The area may be better than the ranking suggests.

The city is located in an area of level to low rolling hills on the banks of the Black Warrior River. Dams just to the northeast contain Lake Tuscaloosa and Bankhead Lake. Land cover is mainly agricultural and southern pine forests. Summers are long with temperatures in the 90s, persistent humidity, and frequent thunderstorms. Winters are mild with temperatures above freezing most days. Spring is variable, with strong storms. Fall is mild and pleasant with an occasional tropical downpour. First freeze is early November; last is late March.

Population

DEMOGRAPHICS	AREA	U.S. AVG	ETHNIC COMPOSITION	AREA	U.S. AVG	RESIDENT PROFILE	AREA	U.S. AVG
Population	195,626		White	62.0%	79.0%	Single	39.5%	32.4%
Population density per sq. mile	74.8	358.5	Black	35.4%	10.5%	Married	47.1%	52.7%
Population growth	11.2%	21.1%	Asian	0.9%	2.7%	Divorced/separated	13.4%	14.9%
Median age	33.7	36.1	Hispanic	1.3%	10.6%	Married with children	20.4%	23.7%
Percent Democrat	41.9%	44.5%	Religious observance	48.2%	48.9%	Single with children	10.5%	9.1%
Percent Republican	57.4%	54.5%	Diversity measure	47.1	40.1	Percent over age 65	11.7%	12.9%

Economy & Jobs
Score: 88.8
Rank: 43

INCOME	AREA	U.S. AVG	EMPLOYMENT	AREA	U.S. AVG	EMPLOYING INDUSTRIES	AREA	U.S. AVG
Per capita income	$20,670	$23,235	Unemployment rate	3.8%	4.7%	Largest: Manufacturing		
Household income	$37,826	$46,414	Recent job growth	5.0%	1.3%			
Household income < $25K	35.8%	26.2%	Projected future job growth	17.3%	11.5%	Percent manufacturing	17.9%	15.4%
Household income > $75K	20.2%	25.4%	White collar	56.8%	57.8%	Percent public sector	19.8%	15.7%
Household income growth	15.0%	13.6%	Blue collar	27.9%	25.2%	Percent construction	9.9%	9.9%

Cost of Living
Score: 62.3
Rank: 141

INDEXES & TAXES	AREA	U.S. AVG	HOUSING	AREA	U.S. AVG	NECESSITIES	AREA	U.S. AVG
Cost of Living Index	87.2	100.0	Median home price	$148,100	$220,000	Food Index	95.2	100.0
Buying Power Index	97.2	100.0	Home price appreciation	28.0%	10.1%	Housing Index	60.9	100.0
Income tax rate	5.00%	4.70%	Median rent	$610	$709	Utilities Index	100.3	100.0
Sales tax rate	7.95%	6.58%	Homes owned	58.2%	62.3%	Transportation Index	95.4	100.0
Property tax rate	$3.59	$12.00	Home price ratio	3.9	4.2	Healthcare Index	97.2	100.0
						Miscellaneous Cost Index	104.9	100.0

Climate
Score: 19.8
Rank: 299

TEMPERATURE	AREA	U.S. AVG	PRECIPITATION	AREA	U.S. AVG	COMFORTS & HAZARDS	AREA	U.S. AVG
Average January low	35.1	26.2	Annual inches precipitation	53.0	37.7	July relative humidity	72%	66%
Average July high	92.3	87.4	Annual inches snowfall	1.0	7.0	Annual days mostly sunny	210	208
Annual days > 90°F	39	38	Annual days precipitation	118	109	Annual days with thunderstorms	58	39
Annual days < 32°F	60	89	Annual days rain > 0.5 inches	36	22	Tornado risk score	18	18
Annual days < 0°F	0	6	Annual days snow > 1.5 inches	1	6	Hurricane risk score	19	13

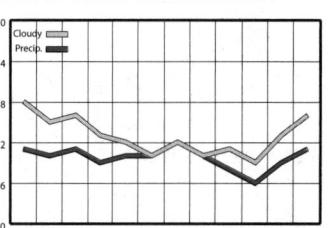

TEMPERATURE

PRECIPITATION

DAYS OF CLOUDS & PRECIPITATION

Education
Score: 33.2
Rank: 251

ACHIEVEMENT	AREA	U.S. AVG	PUBLIC SCHOOLS	AREA	U.S. AVG	HIGHER EDUCATION	AREA	U.S. AVG
High school degree	77.2%	82.7%	Expenditures per pupil	$4,736	$5,686	No. 2-year colleges	2	4
2-year college degree	5.3%	6.4%	Student/teacher ratio	15.4	16.7	No. 4-year colleges/universities	2	6
4-year college degree	13.6%	15.7%	Attending public school	91.5%	90.1%	No. highly ranked universities	0	1
Graduate/professional degree	9.0%	8.9%	State SAT score	1126	1021			
			State ACT score	20.2*	20.9			

Health & Healthcare
Score: 69.0
Rank: 117

HAZARDS & ILLNESSES	AREA	U.S. AVG	HEALTHCARE	AREA	U.S. AVG	CRIME	AREA	U.S. AVG
Air-quality score	41	37	Physicians per capita	214.4	244.2	Violent crime rate	494.5	465.5
Water-quality score	93	52	Hospital beds per capita	466.7	420.0	Change in violent crime rate	5.9%	-2.2%
Pollen/allergy score	67	61	No. teaching hospitals	1	3	Property crime rate	4,370.8	3,517.1
Cancer mortality per capita	237.6	201.9	Cost per doctor visit	$55	$77	Change in property crime rate	-0.5%	-2.1%
Depression days per month	4.2	3.5	Cost per dental visit	$72	$70			
Stress score	32	50						

Crime
Score: 56.7
Rank: 163

Transportation
Score: 12.0
Rank: 330

COMMUTE	AREA	U.S. AVG	INTERCITY SERVICES	AREA	U.S. AVG	AUTOMOTIVE	AREA	U.S. AVG
Average commute time	24.4	27.4	Major airports within 60 miles	0	1	Insurance, annual premium	$1,129	$1,432
Percent commutes > 60 mins.	5.9%	5.9%	Size of regional airport	Small	Large	Gas, cost per gallon	$2.48	$2.49
Commute by auto	83.0%	78.9%	Daily airline activity	111	686	Daily vehicle miles per capita	27.2	24.0
Commute by mass transit	0.5%	1.9%	Amtrak service	Yes	No			
Work at home	2.1%	3.1%						
Mass transit miles per capita	0.48	1.87						

Leisure
Score: 22.5
Rank: 289

DINING & SHOPPING	AREA	U.S. AVG	ENTERTAINMENT	AREA	U.S. AVG	OUTDOOR ACTIVITIES	AREA	U.S. AVG
Restaurant rating	1	2	Professional sports rating	2	4	Golf-course rating	2	4
Outlet mall score	16	42	College sports rating	6	4	Ski-area rating	1	3
No. Starbucks	0	13	Zoo/aquarium rating	1	3	Sq. miles inland water	2	4
No. warehouse clubs	1	2	Amusement park rating	1	3	Miles of coastline	0.0	10.7
			Botanical garden/ arboretum rating	2	4	National Park rating	2	3

Arts & Culture
Score: 44.9
Rank: 206

MEDIA & LIBRARIES	AREA	U.S. AVG	PERFORMING ARTS	AREA	U.S. AVG	MUSEUMS	AREA	U.S. AVG
Arts radio rating	5	3	Classical music rating	3	4	Overall museum rating	4	5
No. public libraries	8	27	Ballet/dance rating	1	3	Art museum rating	4	5
Library volumes per capita	0.74	2.78	Professional theater rating	1	3	Science museum rating	5	5
			University arts programs rating	6	5	Children's museum rating	4	3

Tyler, TX

Score: 35.5   Rank: 318   2004 rank: 138

Profile: Small city
Location: Northeast Texas, 100 miles east of Dallas
Elevation: 259 feet
Time zone: Central Standard Time

PRO	CON
Diverse economy	Arts and culture
Cost of living	Entertainment
Healthcare	Summer heat

Tyler is the commercial and cultural capital of the East Texas region, a large, state-sized area of piney woods and traditions more reminiscent of the South than the dry, dusty plains Texas is more famous for. The area came to prominence with the huge oil boom of the 1920s and 1930s, and that wealth and boomtime exuberance left an imprint on the city core still evident today. Although petroleum and related industries are still important, the city has diversified both commercially and culturally. Businesses in food processing, cotton and cottonseed oil, furniture, machining, forest products, and retail distribution have developed. More recently, the area has evolved into a healthcare and retail hub for the region; today the economy is relatively strong. The well-kept downtown area has historic homes and is surrounded by mostly wooded, residential neighborhoods spreading primarily south into newer areas toward the suburban town of Whitehouse. Tyler does have some small cultural amenities, but on the whole there isn't much to do. Outdoor recreation is available at nearby lakes and state parks. The most recent statistics show a rise in crime rate, which hurt the most recent ranking, but crime rates have steadied somewhat. On a Texas scale, the Dallas–Fort Worth metroplex isn't too far away, but the drive is long for some services and amenities.

The terrain is level to gently rolling with dense southern pine forests predominately and intermittent agricultural land. Summer months are hot and fairly humid, but more comfortable than areas to the south near the Gulf. Winters are mild, with occasional, short periods of cold. Rainfall occurs as steady winter rains or as spring and summer thundershowers, which can be severe, particularly in spring.

Population

DEMOGRAPHICS	AREA	U.S. AVG	ETHNIC COMPOSITION	AREA	U.S. AVG	RESIDENT PROFILE	AREA	U.S. AVG
Population	188,887		White	71.7%	79.0%	Single	28.0%	32.4%
Population density per sq. mile	203.5	358.5	Black	18.3%	10.5%	Married	56.0%	52.7%
Population growth	24.8%	21.1%	Asian	0.8%	2.7%	Divorced/separated	16.0%	14.9%
Median age	35.4	36.1	Hispanic	13.7%	10.6%	Married with children	24.0%	23.7%
Percent Democrat	27.1%	44.5%	Religious observance	65.3%	48.9%	Single with children	8.9%	9.1%
Percent Republican	72.5%	54.5%	Diversity measure	57.8	40.1	Percent over age 65	14.1%	12.9%

Economy & Jobs
Score: 70.3
Rank: 112

INCOME	AREA	U.S. AVG	EMPLOYMENT	AREA	U.S. AVG	EMPLOYING INDUSTRIES	AREA	U.S. AVG
Per capita income	$21,945	$23,235	Unemployment rate	5.3%	4.7%	Largest: Healthcare & Social Assistance		
Household income	$42,687	$46,414	Recent job growth	3.0%	1.3%			
Household income < $25K	28.4%	26.2%	Projected future job growth	14.1%	11.5%	Percent manufacturing	15.9%	15.4%
Household income > $75K	23.0%	25.4%	White collar	57.4%	57.8%	Percent public sector	12.3%	15.7%
Household income growth	14.9%	13.6%	Blue collar	26.5%	25.2%	Percent construction	10.6%	9.9%

Cost of Living
Score: 91.2
Rank: 34

INDEXES & TAXES	AREA	U.S. AVG	HOUSING	AREA	U.S. AVG	NECESSITIES	AREA	U.S. AVG
Cost of Living Index	79.5	100.0	Median home price	$129,100	$220,000	Food Index	90.8	100.0
Buying Power Index	120.4	100.0	Home price appreciation	32.5%	10.1%	Housing Index	54.0	100.0
Income tax rate	0.00%	4.70%	Median rent	$614	$709	Utilities Index	89.2	100.0
Sales tax rate	8.25%	6.58%	Homes owned	64.0%	62.3%	Transportation Index	88.8	100.0
Property tax rate	$13.35	$12.00	Home price ratio	3.0	4.2	Healthcare Index	93.4	100.0
						Miscellaneous Cost Index	96.0	100.0

Climate
Score: 75.1
Rank: 93

TEMPERATURE	AREA	U.S. AVG	PRECIPITATION	AREA	U.S. AVG	COMFORTS & HAZARDS	AREA	U.S. AVG
Average January low	37.8	26.2	Annual inches precipitation	45.0	37.7	July relative humidity	71%	66%
Average July high	93.8	87.4	Annual inches snowfall	1.0	7.0	Annual days mostly sunny	217	208
Annual days > 90°F	87	38	Annual days precipitation	97	109	Annual days with thunderstorms	54	39
Annual days < 32°F	1	89	Annual days rain > 0.5 inches	24	22	Tornado risk score	41	18
Annual days < 0°F	0	6	Annual days snow > 1.5 inches	1	6	Hurricane risk score	16	13

TEMPERATURE

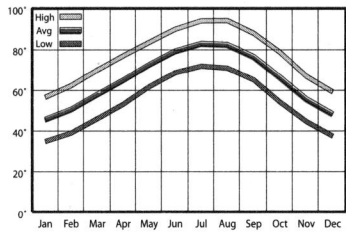

PRECIPITATION

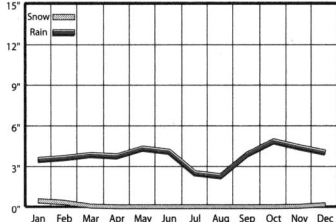

DAYS OF CLOUDS & PRECIPITATION

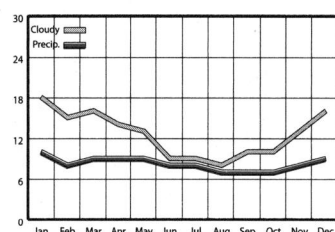

Education
Score: 52.7
Rank: 178

ACHIEVEMENT	AREA	U.S. AVG	PUBLIC SCHOOLS	AREA	U.S. AVG	HIGHER EDUCATION	AREA	U.S. AVG
High school degree	80.4%	82.7%	Expenditures per pupil	$4,613	$5,686	No. 2-year colleges	1	4
2-year college degree	7.5%	6.4%	Student/teacher ratio	14.6	16.7	No. 4-year colleges/universities	2	6
4-year college degree	15.4%	15.7%	Attending public school	95.3%	90.1%	No. highly ranked universities	0	1
Graduate/professional degree	7.3%	8.9%	State SAT score	997*	1021			
			State ACT score	20.3	20.9			

Health & Healthcare
Score: 77.5
Rank: 85

Crime
Score: 6.1
Rank: 350

HAZARDS & ILLNESSES	AREA	U.S. AVG	HEALTHCARE	AREA	U.S. AVG	CRIME	AREA	U.S. AVG
Air-quality score	27	37	Physicians per capita	331.0	244.2	Violent crime rate	496.6	465.5
Water-quality score	87	52	Hospital beds per capita	477.5	420.0	Change in violent crime rate	4.7%	-2.2%
Pollen/allergy score	76	61	No. teaching hospitals	2	3	Property crime rate	3,956.1	3,517.1
Cancer mortality per capita	164.8	201.9	Cost per doctor visit	$83	$77	Change in property crime rate	-1.0%	-2.1%
Depression days per month	3.9	3.5	Cost per dental visit	$66	$70			
Stress score	67	50						

Transportation
Score: 32.1
Rank: 255

COMMUTE	AREA	U.S. AVG	INTERCITY SERVICES	AREA	U.S. AVG	AUTOMOTIVE	AREA	U.S. AVG
Average commute time	23.7	27.4	Major airports within 60 miles	1	1	Insurance, annual premium	$1,120	$1,432
Percent commutes > 60 mins.	4.9%	5.9%	Size of regional airport	Medium	Large	Gas, cost per gallon	$2.51	$2.49
Commute by auto	82.0%	78.9%	Daily airline activity	313	686	Daily vehicle miles per capita	26.5	24.0
Commute by mass transit	0.3%	1.9%	Amtrak service	No	No			
Work at home	2.6%	3.1%						
Mass transit miles per capita	0.31	1.87						

DINING & SHOPPING	AREA	U.S. AVG	ENTERTAINMENT	AREA	U.S. AVG	OUTDOOR ACTIVITIES	AREA	U.S. AVG
Restaurant rating	1	2	Professional sports rating	2	4	Golf-course rating	2	4
Outlet mall score	2	42	College sports rating	1	4	Ski-area rating	1	3
No. Starbucks	2	13	Zoo/aquarium rating	6	3	Sq. miles inland water	2	4
No. warehouse clubs	0	2	Amusement park rating	1	3	Miles of coastline	0.0	10.7
			Botanical garden/			National Park rating	1	3
			arboretum rating	4	4			

MEDIA & LIBRARIES	AREA	U.S. AVG	PERFORMING ARTS	AREA	U.S. AVG	MUSEUMS	AREA	U.S. AVG
Arts radio rating	1	3	Classical music rating	3	4	Overall museum rating	6	5
No. public libraries	6	27	Ballet/dance rating	1	3	Art museum rating	3	5
Library volumes per capita	2.74	2.78	Professional theater rating	1	3	Science museum rating	3	5
			University arts programs rating	2	5	Children's museum rating	1	3

Utica–Rome, NY

Score: 35.0 Rank: 321 2004 rank: 289

Profile: Small-city complex
Location: Central New York, 50 miles east of Syracuse
Elevation: 706 feet
Time zone: Eastern Standard Time

PRO	CON
Nearby recreation	Economy
Low crime rates	Winter climate
Arts and culture	Entertainment

Utica and Rome, small towns separated by 16 miles, trace their origins to the Erie Canal. Both towns are hard-working and industrial in nature and are fairly lacking in small-town charm. However, nearby areas offer plentiful snow and winter sports, and the Adirondacks are a short distance to the northeast. Cooperstown, one of the most likeable small towns in the northeast and home to the National Baseball Hall of Fame, is on the shore of Lake Otsego, 40 miles southeast. Crime is low, but cost of living, while moderate on a New York/East Coast scale, is still a bit high for what's available. The economy, like most of upstate New York, is weak and appears to be getting weaker. There are some modest museums and cultural amenities, but overall there is little to do in the immediate area and winter weather is dreary. Utica has the dubious distinction of being tied with Syracuse for receiving the nation's highest annual snowfall among metro areas. The right

combination of economic incentives and investment might mix well with the area's location, cost profile, and recreational opportunities to bring a brighter future, but it's a long road forward.

Utica and Rome sit in a broad, relatively level Mohawk Valley, opening into Oneida Lake to the west. The landscape is mixed farmland and deciduous forest. The hilly Tug Hill Plateau rises to the north, and the mostly wooded Adirondack foothills rise to the northeast and east. Summer brings warm, sunny days and cool evenings and an occasional hot, sticky spell. Precipitation comes mainly in the form of afternoon thundershowers. Winters are harsh and snowy, as a rise in the terrain and the position with respect to storm tracks and Lake Ontario bring snow and snow squalls. Very heavy snows, as much as 200 inches per year, occur in some of the hills to the north.

DEMOGRAPHICS	AREA	U.S. AVG	ETHNIC COMPOSITION	AREA	U.S. AVG	RESIDENT PROFILE	AREA	U.S. AVG
Population	297,934		White	90.8%	79.0%	Single	36.0%	32.4%
Population density per sq. mile	113.5	358.5	Black	5.1%	10.5%	Married	49.4%	52.7%
Population growth	-5.9%	21.1%	Asian	1.4%	2.7%	Divorced/separated	14.7%	14.9%
Median age	39.5	36.1	Hispanic	3.5%	10.6%	Married with children	20.9%	23.7%
Percent Democrat	42.4%	44.5%	Religious observance	52.6%	48.9%	Single with children	9.3%	9.1%
Percent Republican	55.3%	54.5%	Diversity measure	22.5	40.1	Percent over age 65	16.3%	12.9%

INCOME	AREA	U.S. AVG	EMPLOYMENT	AREA	U.S. AVG	EMPLOYING INDUSTRIES	AREA	U.S. AVG
Per capita income	$20,484	$23,235	Unemployment rate	4.9%	4.7%	Largest: Healthcare & Social Assistance		
Household income	$39,918	$46,414	Recent job growth	0.3%	1.3%			
Household income < $25K	31.1%	26.2%	Projected future job growth	-2.8%	11.5%	Percent manufacturing	15.8%	15.4%
Household income > $75K	19.0%	25.4%	White collar	57.0%	57.8%	Percent public sector	18.9%	15.7%
Household income growth	13.2%	13.6%	Blue collar	23.6%	25.2%	Percent construction	7.8%	9.9%

INDEXES & TAXES	AREA	U.S. AVG	HOUSING	AREA	U.S. AVG	NECESSITIES	AREA	U.S. AVG
Cost of Living Index	88.7	100.0	Median home price	$121,000	$220,000	Food Index	107.4	100.0
Buying Power Index	100.9	100.0	Home price appreciation	38.5%	10.1%	Housing Index	42.9	100.0
Income tax rate	7.13%	4.70%	Median rent	$596	$709	Utilities Index	139.9	100.0
Sales tax rate	9.43%	6.58%	Homes owned	59.3%	62.3%	Transportation Index	103.9	100.0
Property tax rate	$23.56	$12.00	Home price ratio	3.0	4.2	Healthcare Index	100.3	100.0
						Miscellaneous Cost Index	99.7	100.0

Climate

Score: 4.0
Rank: 358

TEMPERATURE	AREA	U.S. AVG
Average January low	15.8	26.2
Average July high	82.0	87.4
Annual days > 90°F	6	38
Annual days < 32°F	138	89
Annual days < 0°F	9	6

PRECIPITATION	AREA	U.S. AVG
Annual inches precipitation	36.0	37.7
Annual inches snowfall	109.0	7.0
Annual days precipitation	168	109
Annual days rain > 0.5 inches	21	22
Annual days snow > 1.5 inches	26	6

COMFORTS & HAZARDS	AREA	U.S. AVG
July relative humidity	73%	66%
Annual days mostly sunny	164	208
Annual days with thunderstorms	29	39
Tornado risk score	6	18
Hurricane risk score	3	13

TEMPERATURE

PRECIPITATION

DAYS OF CLOUDS & PRECIPITATION

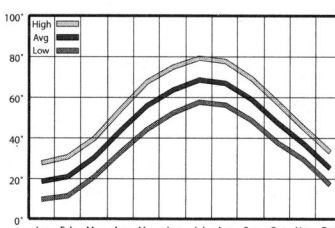

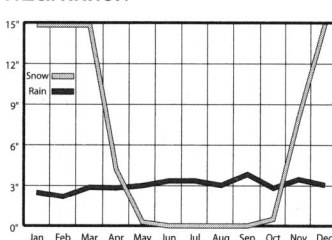

Education

Score: 58.6
Rank: 156

ACHIEVEMENT	AREA	U.S. AVG
High school degree	79.2%	82.7%
2-year college degree	9.6%	6.4%
4-year college degree	10.7%	15.7%
Graduate/professional degree	7.2%	8.9%

PUBLIC SCHOOLS	AREA	U.S. AVG
Expenditures per pupil	$7,984	$5,686
Student/teacher ratio	15.2	16.7
Attending public school	95.5%	90.1%
State SAT score	1003*	1021
State ACT score	22.6	20.9

HIGHER EDUCATION	AREA	U.S. AVG
No. 2-year colleges	6	4
No. 4-year colleges/universities	3	6
No. highly ranked universities	1	1

Health & Healthcare

Score: 71.7
Rank: 107

HAZARDS & ILLNESSES	AREA	U.S. AVG
Air-quality score	44	37
Water-quality score	87	52
Pollen/allergy score	55	61
Cancer mortality per capita	207.6	201.9
Depression days per month	3.3	3.5
Stress score	9	50

HEALTHCARE	AREA	U.S. AVG
Physicians per capita	183.6	244.2
Hospital beds per capita	468.2	420.0
No. teaching hospitals	1	3
Cost per doctor visit	$74	$77
Cost per dental visit	$64	$70

Crime

Score: 56.4
Rank: 164

CRIME	AREA	U.S. AVG
Violent crime rate	256.6	465.5
Change in violent crime rate	5.4%	-2.2%
Property crime rate	2,243.6	3,517.1
Change in property crime rate	-5.9%	-2.1%

Transportation

Score: 41.7
Rank: 219

COMMUTE	AREA	U.S. AVG
Average commute time	22.1	27.4
Percent commutes > 60 mins.	4.6%	5.9%
Commute by auto	79.8%	78.9%
Commute by mass transit	1.4%	1.9%
Work at home	2.7%	3.1%
Mass transit miles per capita	1.37	1.87

INTERCITY SERVICES	AREA	U.S. AVG
Major airports within 60 miles	0	1
Size of regional airport	Small	Large
Daily airline activity	260	686
Amtrak service	Yes	No

AUTOMOTIVE	AREA	U.S. AVG
Insurance, annual premium	$1,522	$1,432
Gas, cost per gallon	$2.59	$2.49
Daily vehicle miles per capita	28.2	24.0

Leisure

Score: 57.8
Rank: 158

DINING & SHOPPING	AREA	U.S. AVG
Restaurant rating	1	2
Outlet mall score	0	42
No. Starbucks	0	13
No. warehouse clubs	1	2

ENTERTAINMENT	AREA	U.S. AVG
Professional sports rating	2	4
College sports rating	3	4
Zoo/aquarium rating	2	3
Amusement park rating	6	3
Botanical garden/ arboretum rating	1	4

OUTDOOR ACTIVITIES	AREA	U.S. AVG
Golf-course rating	5	4
Ski-area rating	5	3
Sq. miles inland water	6	4
Miles of coastline	0.0	10.7
National Park rating	1	3

Arts & Culture

Score: 66.3
Rank: 126

MEDIA & LIBRARIES	AREA	U.S. AVG
Arts radio rating	7	3
No. public libraries	36	27
Library volumes per capita	4.31	2.78

PERFORMING ARTS	AREA	U.S. AVG
Classical music rating	3	4
Ballet/dance rating	1	3
Professional theater rating	1	3
University arts programs rating	4	5

MUSEUMS	AREA	U.S. AVG
Overall museum rating	6	5
Art museum rating	6	5
Science museum rating	5	5
Children's museum rating	2	3

Valdosta, GA

Score: 32.9 **Rank:** 337 **2004 rank:** not ranked

Profile: Small city
Location: Extreme southern Georgia, along I-75 16 miles north of the Florida border
Elevation: 215 feet
Time zone: Eastern Standard Time

PRO	CON
Cost of living	Arts and culture
Mild winters	Entertainment
Current employment	Hot, humid summers

Valdosta is a transportation gateway, agricultural and manufacturing center, and a favorite stop on the major Interstate 75 artery south into Florida. The location on the major north–south artery, major rail lines, and on or near major east–west highways has made it attractive as a manufacturing center and shipping point. Basic industries include wood products and turpentine manufacturing, food processing, and some tobacco, and there is considerable activity in the area's five industrial parks. The area lacks interest in general, but does have some history, historical homes and buildings, and a handful of performing arts and cultural amenities. A new theme park just opened to capitalize on the north–south leisure traffic. The cost of living is low at 80.6.

The surrounding terrain is flat, uninteresting, and mostly set up for agriculture. Summers are warm and sticky with occasional downpours. Winters are mild with cloudy, rainy periods. Total rainfall is fifth highest among U.S. metro areas. Freezing does occur in most winters, and many have at least some snow. First freeze is early December; last is mid-February.

DEMOGRAPHICS	AREA	U.S. AVG	ETHNIC COMPOSITION	AREA	U.S. AVG	RESIDENT PROFILE	AREA	U.S. AVG
Population	123,938		White	63.6%	79.0%	Single	35.3%	32.4%
Population density per sq. mile	78.0	358.5	Black	32.0%	10.5%	Married	46.5%	52.7%
Population growth	26.0%	21.1%	Asian	1.0%	2.7%	Divorced/separated	18.2%	14.9%
Median age	32.3	36.1	Hispanic	3.0%	10.6%	Married with children	23.3%	23.7%
Percent Democrat	39.2%	44.5%	Religious observance	43.3%	48.9%	Single with children	11.5%	9.1%
Percent Republican	60.3%	54.5%	Diversity measure	51.6	40.1	Percent over age 65	10.2%	12.9%

Economy & Jobs
Score: 48.9
Rank: 192

INCOME	AREA	U.S. AVG	EMPLOYMENT	AREA	U.S. AVG	EMPLOYING INDUSTRIES	AREA	U.S. AVG
Per capita income	$18,390	$23,235	Unemployment rate	4.6%	4.7%	Largest: Healthcare & Social Assistance		
Household income	$35,716	$46,414	Recent job growth	2.1%	1.3%			
Household income ‹ $25K	35.7%	26.2%	Projected future job growth	11.3%	11.5%	Percent manufacturing	16.9%	15.4%
Household income › $75K	17.3%	25.4%	White collar	52.7%	57.8%	Percent public sector	19.5%	15.7%
Household income growth	15.0%	13.6%	Blue collar	28.2%	25.2%	Percent construction	11.3%	9.9%

Cost of Living
Score: 65.8
Rank: 129

INDEXES & TAXES	AREA	U.S. AVG	HOUSING	AREA	U.S. AVG	NECESSITIES	AREA	U.S. AVG
Cost of Living Index	80.6	100.0	Median home price	$122,100	$220,000	Food Index	97.6	100.0
Buying Power Index	99.3	100.0	Home price appreciation	30.8%	10.1%	Housing Index	55.3	100.0
Income tax rate	6.00%	4.70%	Median rent	$557	$709	Utilities Index	90.5	100.0
Sales tax rate	7.00%	6.58%	Homes owned	57.3%	62.3%	Transportation Index	96.2	100.0
Property tax rate	$8.57	$12.00	Home price ratio	3.4	4.2	Healthcare Index	96.0	100.0
						Miscellaneous Cost Index	97.3	100.0

Climate
Score: 72.2
Rank: 103

TEMPERATURE	AREA	U.S. AVG	PRECIPITATION	AREA	U.S. AVG	COMFORTS & HAZARDS	AREA	U.S. AVG
Average January low	40.0	26.2	Annual inches precipitation	63.3	37.7	July relative humidity	59%	66%
Average July high	91.0	87.4	Annual inches snowfall	0.1	7.0	Annual days mostly sunny	219	208
Annual days › 90°F	86	38	Annual days precipitation	114	109	Annual days with thunderstorms	86	39
Annual days ‹ 32°F	31	89	Annual days rain › 0.5 inches	38	22	Tornado risk score	2	18
Annual days ‹ 0°F	0	6	Annual days snow › 1.5 inches	0	6	Hurricane risk score	5	13

TEMPERATURE

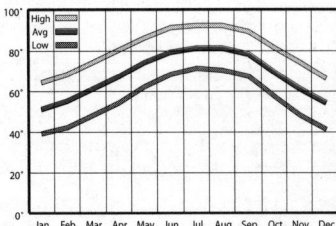

PRECIPITATION

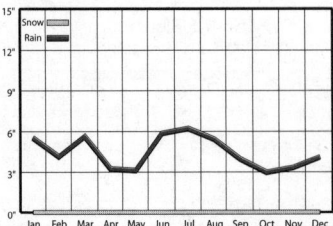

DAYS OF CLOUDS & PRECIPITATION

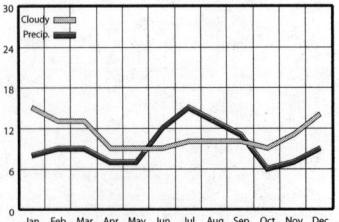

ACHIEVEMENT	AREA	U.S. AVG	**PUBLIC SCHOOLS**	AREA	U.S. AVG	**HIGHER EDUCATION**	AREA	U.S. AVG
High school degree	75.4%	82.7%	Expenditures per pupil	$4,923	$5,686	No. 2-year colleges	2	4
2-year college degree	5.5%	6.4%	Student/teacher ratio	15.0	16.7	No. 4-year colleges/universities	1	6
4-year college degree	11.2%	15.7%	Attending public school	91.5%	90.1%	No. highly ranked universities	0	1
Graduate/professional degree	6.4%	8.9%	State SAT score	990*	1021			
			State ACT score	20.2	20.9			

Education
Score: 16.0
Rank: 313

HAZARDS & ILLNESSES	AREA	U.S. AVG	**HEALTHCARE**	AREA	U.S. AVG	**CRIME**	AREA	U.S. AVG
Air-quality score	52	37	Physicians per capita	163.8	244.2	Violent crime rate	450.6	465.5
Water-quality score	75	52	Hospital beds per capita	546.2	420.0	Change in violent crime rate	-8.6%	-2.2%
Pollen/allergy score	62	61	No. teaching hospitals	0	3	Property crime rate	4,803.1	3,517.1
Cancer mortality per capita	178.2	201.9	Cost per doctor visit	$80	$77	Change in property crime rate	7.1%	-2.1%
Depression days per month	2.9	3.5	Cost per dental visit	$70	$70			
Stress score	23	50						

Health & Healthcare
Score: 95.7
Rank: 17

Crime
Score: 32.4
Rank: 253

COMMUTE	AREA	U.S. AVG	**INTERCITY SERVICES**	AREA	U.S. AVG	**AUTOMOTIVE**	AREA	U.S. AVG
Average commute time	21.6	27.4	Major airports within 60 miles	0	1	Insurance, annual premium	$1,255	$1,432
Percent commutes > 60 mins.	3.8%	5.9%	Size of regional airport	Small	Large	Gas, cost per gallon	$2.46	$2.49
Commute by auto	79.2%	78.9%	Daily airline activity	69	686	Daily vehicle miles per capita	24.9	24.0
Commute by mass transit	0.3%	1.9%	Amtrak service	No	No			
Work at home	1.8%	3.1%						
Mass transit miles per capita	0.30	1.87						

Transportation
Score: 29.7
Rank: 264

DINING & SHOPPING	AREA	U.S. AVG	**ENTERTAINMENT**	AREA	U.S. AVG	**OUTDOOR ACTIVITIES**	AREA	U.S. AVG
Restaurant rating	1	2	Professional sports rating	1	4	Golf-course rating	3	4
Outlet mall score	37	42	College sports rating	1	4	Ski-area rating	1	3
No. Starbucks	1	13	Zoo/aquarium rating	1	3	Sq. miles inland water	2	4
No. warehouse clubs	1	2	Amusement park rating	1	3	Miles of coastline	0.0	10.7
			Botanical garden/ arboretum rating	2	4	National Park rating	2	3

Leisure
Score: 2.9
Rank: 362

MEDIA & LIBRARIES	AREA	U.S. AVG	**PERFORMING ARTS**	AREA	U.S. AVG	**MUSEUMS**	AREA	U.S. AVG
Arts radio rating	1	3	Classical music rating	2	4	Overall museum rating	1	5
No. public libraries	9	27	Ballet/dance rating	1	3	Art museum rating	2	5
Library volumes per capita	2.15	2.78	Professional theater rating	1	3	Science museum rating	3	5
			University arts programs rating	1	5	Children's museum rating	1	3

Arts & Culture
Score: 5.6
Rank: 352

Vallejo–Fairfield, CA

Score: 35.1   Rank: 320   2004 rank: 78

Profile: Suburban complex
Location: Northern California, 30 to 50 miles northeast of San Francisco
Elevation: 15 feet
Time zone: Pacific Standard Time

PRO	CON
Year-round climate	Cost of living and housing
Strong economy	Growth and sprawl
Close to San Francisco	Long commutes

This area, known also as Solano County, is really a series of residential communities strung along Interstate 80 as it heads east from the San Francisco Bay Area. The string starts with Vallejo, once a gritty port and navy town now having been transformed as a result of Bay Area crowding and high home prices into a fairly desirable commuter community. East across a narrow range of mountains, the land flattens again into the towns of Cordelia, Suisun City, and the larger Fairfield and Vacaville. Fairfield was once primarily a military town supporting Travis Air Force Base, which is still an important part of the local economy. But a number of commercial and some industrial enterprises have spread into Fairfield and especially the Vacaville area to escape but still serve the Bay Area. These firms, from chemical to biotech to small manufacturers, have sprung up in the open valleys mainly in Vacaville and east, and have created a lot of employment. Taken together with those commuting into the Bay, incomes and employment for residents of the area are strong. Proximity to the Bay and geographic barriers (mountains and marshes) have restricted building somewhat, driving home prices upward. Most homes are modern California style—large homes, very small lots in tracts surrounded by high sound walls, a crowded feel even though there's an empty field or marsh adjacent to the tract. Schools, healthcare, shopping, and other facilities are new and modern. Entertainment and arts venues in the immediate area are modest, but the area has good access to San Francisco and to the college town of Davis to the east. The negatives (cost, commute, sprawl, and crime) are distinct, and the ranking suffered from the separation from the Napa metro area (p. 562), but the area is better for some than this figure suggests.

Vallejo, Fairfield, and Vacaville are built on narrow strips of flat, dry land between dry coastal mountains and the marshlands surrounding San Pablo and Suisun bays, eastern extensions of the San Francisco Bay. Farther east, the land spreads into prime agricultural land used mainly for orchards and vegetable growing. Summer days are pleasantly warm; evenings are cool. Most precipitation falls in winter as light to moderate rain, and temperatures seldom drop below freezing.

Population

DEMOGRAPHICS	AREA	U.S. AVG	ETHNIC COMPOSITION	AREA	U.S. AVG	RESIDENT PROFILE	AREA	U.S. AVG
Population	417,749		White	53.6%	79.0%	Single	31.0%	32.4%
Population density per sq. mile	503.8	358.5	Black	15.0%	10.5%	Married	51.3%	52.7%
Population growth	22.7%	21.1%	Asian	13.9%	2.7%	Divorced/separated	17.7%	14.9%
Median age	34.7	36.1	Hispanic	20.7%	10.6%	Married with children	28.4%	23.7%
Percent Democrat	57.2%	44.5%	Religious observance	37.4%	48.9%	Single with children	11.3%	9.1%
Percent Republican	41.9%	54.5%	Diversity measure	77.1	40.1	Percent over age 65	10.2%	12.9%

Economy & Jobs
Score: 53.7
Rank: 174

INCOME	AREA	U.S. AVG	EMPLOYMENT	AREA	U.S. AVG	EMPLOYING INDUSTRIES	AREA	U.S. AVG
Per capita income	$25,736	$23,235	Unemployment rate	5.5%	4.7%	Largest: Healthcare & Social Assistance		
Household income	$64,007	$46,414	Recent job growth	2.5%	1.3%			
Household income < $25K	15.4%	26.2%	Projected future job growth	19.9%	11.5%	Percent manufacturing	12.9%	15.4%
Household income > $75K	40.7%	25.4%	White collar	59.0%	57.8%	Percent public sector	20.4%	15.7%
Household income growth	18.3%	13.6%	Blue collar	23.8%	25.2%	Percent construction	10.9%	9.9%

Cost of Living
Score: 3.2
Rank: 361

INDEXES & TAXES	AREA	U.S. AVG	HOUSING	AREA	U.S. AVG	NECESSITIES	AREA	U.S. AVG
Cost of Living Index	163.1	100.0	Median home price	$534,800	$220,000	Food Index	120.9	100.0
Buying Power Index	88.0	100.0	Home price appreciation	118.1%	10.1%	Housing Index	197.5	100.0
Income tax rate	6.00%	4.70%	Median rent	$997	$709	Utilities Index	125.5	100.0
Sales tax rate	7.38%	6.58%	Homes owned	63.4%	62.3%	Transportation Index	123.4	100.0
Property tax rate	$8.24	$12.00	Home price ratio	8.4	4.2	Healthcare Index	161.6	100.0
						Miscellaneous Cost Index	107.1	100.0

Climate
Score: 95.7
Rank: 17

TEMPERATURE	AREA	U.S. AVG	PRECIPITATION	AREA	U.S. AVG	COMFORTS & HAZARDS	AREA	U.S. AVG
Average January low	35.7	26.2	Annual inches precipitation	30.0	37.7	July relative humidity	70%	66%
Average July high	83.6	87.4	Annual inches snowfall	0.0	7.0	Annual days mostly sunny	285	208
Annual days > 90°F	33	38	Annual days precipitation	47	109	Annual days with thunderstorms	4	39
Annual days < 32°F	43	89	Annual days rain > 0.5 inches	20	22	Tornado risk score	1	18
Annual days < 0°F	0	6	Annual days snow > 1.5 inches	0	6	Hurricane risk score	0	13

TEMPERATURE

PRECIPITATION

DAYS OF CLOUDS & PRECIPITATION

Education
Score: 46.8
Rank: 200

ACHIEVEMENT	AREA	U.S. AVG	PUBLIC SCHOOLS	AREA	U.S. AVG	HIGHER EDUCATION	AREA	U.S. AVG
High school degree	83.8%	82.7%	Expenditures per pupil	$4,858	$5,686	No. 2-year colleges	1	4
2-year college degree	8.9%	6.4%	Student/teacher ratio	20.7	16.7	No. 4-year colleges/universities	1	6
4-year college degree	15.2%	15.7%	Attending public school	91.7%	90.1%	No. highly ranked universities	0	1
Graduate/professional degree	6.4%	8.9%	State SAT score	1019*	1021			
			State ACT score	21.6	20.9			

Health & Healthcare
Score: 0.8
Rank: 370

Crime
Score: 9.9
Rank: 336

HAZARDS & ILLNESSES	AREA	U.S. AVG	HEALTHCARE	AREA	U.S. AVG	CRIME	AREA	U.S. AVG
Air-quality score	32	37	Physicians per capita	176.6	244.2	Violent crime rate	510.7	465.5
Water-quality score	33	52	Hospital beds per capita	162.3	420.0	Change in violent crime rate	-4.7%	-2.2%
Pollen/allergy score	84	61	No. teaching hospitals	1	3	Property crime rate	3,653.6	3,517.1
Cancer mortality per capita	174.3	201.9	Cost per doctor visit	$100	$77	Change in property crime rate	-2.7%	-2.1%
Depression days per month	3.9	3.5	Cost per dental visit	$82	$70			
Stress score	75	50						

Transportation
Score: 18.2
Rank: 307

COMMUTE	AREA	U.S. AVG	INTERCITY SERVICES	AREA	U.S. AVG	AUTOMOTIVE	AREA	U.S. AVG
Average commute time	34.0	27.4	Major airports within 60 miles	4	1	Insurance, annual premium	$1,805	$1,432
Percent commutes > 60 mins.	16.7%	5.9%	Size of regional airport	Large	Large	Gas, cost per gallon	$2.58	$2.49
Commute by auto	73.4%	78.9%	Daily airline activity	1197	686	Daily vehicle miles per capita	27.0	24.0
Commute by mass transit	2.6%	1.9%	Amtrak service	No	No			
Work at home	3.1%	3.1%						
Mass transit miles per capita	2.63	1.87						

Leisure
Score: 95.7
Rank: 17

DINING & SHOPPING	AREA	U.S. AVG	ENTERTAINMENT	AREA	U.S. AVG	OUTDOOR ACTIVITIES	AREA	U.S. AVG
Restaurant rating	5	2	Professional sports rating	9	4	Golf-course rating	5	4
Outlet mall score	171	42	College sports rating	7	4	Ski-area rating	9	3
No. Starbucks	17	13	Zoo/aquarium rating	7	3	Sq. miles inland water	8	4
No. warehouse clubs	4	2	Amusement park rating	9	3	Miles of coastline	0.0	10.7
			Botanical garden/ arboretum rating	6	4	National Park rating	3	3

Arts & Culture
Score: 58.0
Rank: 157

MEDIA & LIBRARIES	AREA	U.S. AVG	PERFORMING ARTS	AREA	U.S. AVG	MUSEUMS	AREA	U.S. AVG
Arts radio rating	4	3	Classical music rating	5	4	Overall museum rating	9	5
No. public libraries	8	27	Ballet/dance rating	5	3	Art museum rating	6	5
Library volumes per capita	1.76	2.78	Professional theater rating	6	3	Science museum rating	9	5
			University arts programs rating	2	5	Children's museum rating	6	3

Victoria, TX

Score: 23.8 Rank: 356 2004 rank: 290

Profile: Small city
Location: Southeast Texas, 40 miles inland from the Gulf Coast
Elevation: 91 feet
Time zone: Central Standard Time

PRO	CON
Cost of living	Entertainment
Diverse economy	Low educational attainment
Pleasant winter climate	Hot, humid summers

Victoria, a small agricultural and industrial center, resides in the middle of a triangle formed by Houston, San Antonio, and Corpus Christi on the coastal plain of southeast Texas. Located on transportation routes about 30 miles inland from the Gulf, Victoria is home to several petrochemical and plastics companies, including large Dow Chemical and DuPont plants and an assortment of other manufacturers. Ranching and meatpacking round out the economic picture. While employment prospects are moderate, the town has a very low cost of living profile and high incomes, giving a strong Buying Power Index (127.6). Victoria College and the University of Houston-Victoria provide some higher education but little in the way of college-town amenities or atmosphere. The city has a historic downtown district and a few small but good quality arts and cultural assets beyond what's found in most small Texas towns, including a ballet and symphony. Residents pride themselves on *not* having to travel to Houston or San Antonio for these experiences. Still, a 2-hour plus drive is required for other services.

The city of Victoria is in the south-central Texas Coastal Plain on the Guadalupe River. The landscape is flat with numerous small creeks, waterways, and trees. Summers are hot, usually in the 90s, with high humidity and occasional sea breezes. Winter conditions vary between clear, cold, dry periods and cloudy, mild, drizzly days. The area gets fewer freezing days than most other Texas cities. Occasional summer and fall tropical disturbances may produce torrential rains.

Population

DEMOGRAPHICS	AREA	U.S. AVG	ETHNIC COMPOSITION	AREA	U.S. AVG	RESIDENT PROFILE	AREA	U.S. AVG
Population	113,803		White	74.8%	79.0%	Single	28.5%	32.4%
Population density per sq. mile	50.6	358.5	Black	5.3%	10.5%	Married	57.2%	52.7%
Population growth	14.6%	21.1%	Asian	1.3%	2.7%	Divorced/separated	14.3%	14.9%
Median age	35.1	36.1	Hispanic	41.5%	10.6%	Married with children	26.6%	23.7%
Percent Democrat	30.8%	44.5%	Religious observance	67.7%	48.9%	Single with children	9.8%	9.1%
Percent Republican	68.7%	54.5%	Diversity measure	69.6	40.1	Percent over age 65	13.0%	12.9%

Economy & Jobs
Score: 83.7
Rank: 62

INCOME	AREA	U.S. AVG	EMPLOYMENT	AREA	U.S. AVG	EMPLOYING INDUSTRIES	AREA	U.S. AVG
Per capita income	$20,332	$23,235	Unemployment rate	4.9%	4.7%	Largest: Healthcare & Social Assistance		
Household income	$42,536	$46,414	Recent job growth	3.5%	1.3%			
Household income < $25K	28.4%	26.2%	Projected future job growth	13.2%	11.5%	Percent manufacturing	16.0%	15.4%
Household income > $75K	22.7%	25.4%	White collar	52.8%	57.8%	Percent public sector	14.3%	15.7%
Household income growth	12.2%	13.6%	Blue collar	30.3%	25.2%	Percent construction	14.2%	9.9%

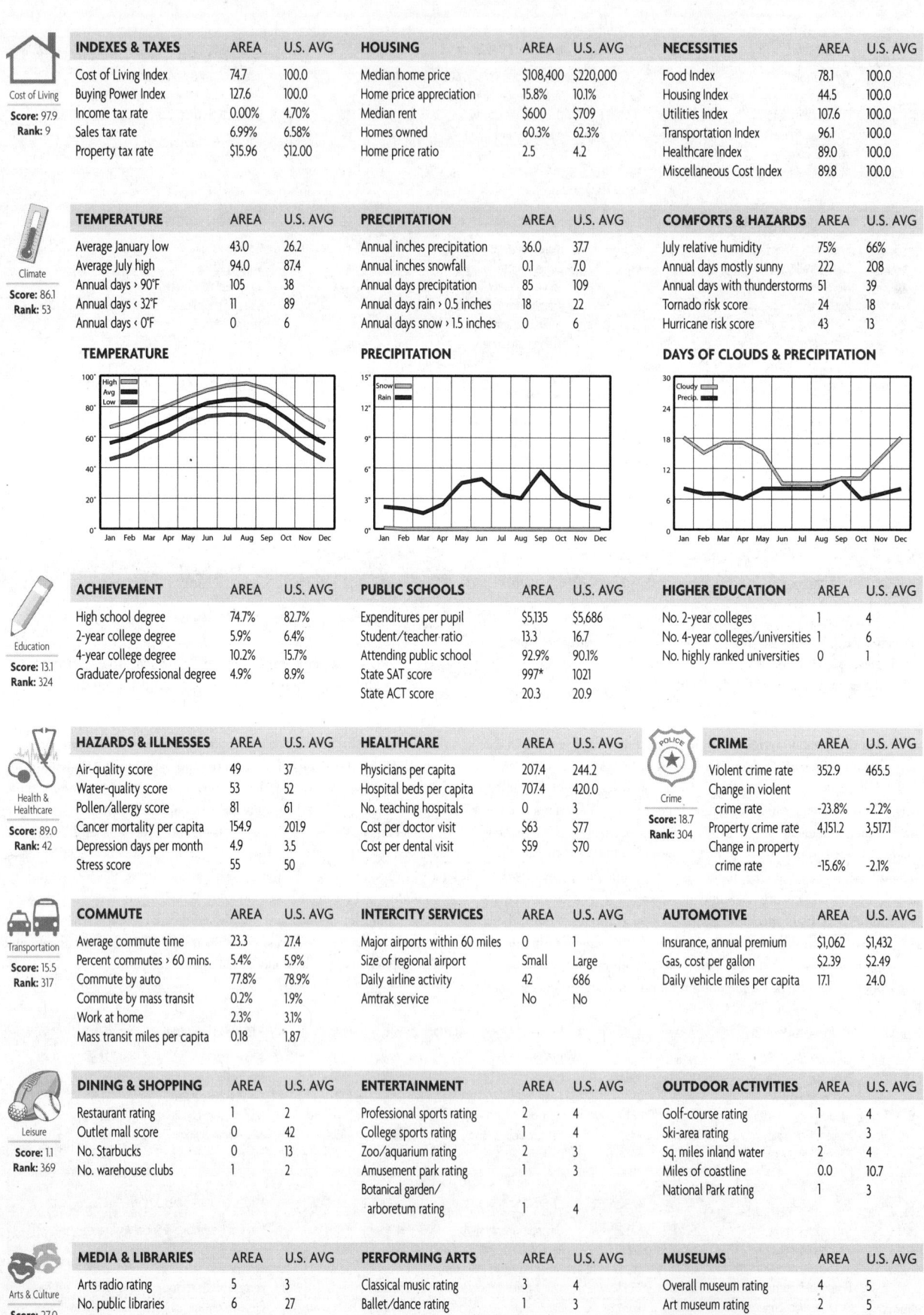

Cost of Living
Score: 97.9
Rank: 9

INDEXES & TAXES	AREA	U.S. AVG	HOUSING	AREA	U.S. AVG	NECESSITIES	AREA	U.S. AVG
Cost of Living Index	74.7	100.0	Median home price	$108,400	$220,000	Food Index	78.1	100.0
Buying Power Index	127.6	100.0	Home price appreciation	15.8%	10.1%	Housing Index	44.5	100.0
Income tax rate	0.00%	4.70%	Median rent	$600	$709	Utilities Index	107.6	100.0
Sales tax rate	6.99%	6.58%	Homes owned	60.3%	62.3%	Transportation Index	96.1	100.0
Property tax rate	$15.96	$12.00	Home price ratio	2.5	4.2	Healthcare Index	89.0	100.0
						Miscellaneous Cost Index	89.8	100.0

Climate
Score: 86.1
Rank: 53

TEMPERATURE	AREA	U.S. AVG	PRECIPITATION	AREA	U.S. AVG	COMFORTS & HAZARDS	AREA	U.S. AVG
Average January low	43.0	26.2	Annual inches precipitation	36.0	37.7	July relative humidity	75%	66%
Average July high	94.0	87.4	Annual inches snowfall	0.1	7.0	Annual days mostly sunny	222	208
Annual days > 90°F	105	38	Annual days precipitation	85	109	Annual days with thunderstorms	51	39
Annual days < 32°F	11	89	Annual days rain > 0.5 inches	18	22	Tornado risk score	24	18
Annual days < 0°F	0	6	Annual days snow > 1.5 inches	0	6	Hurricane risk score	43	13

TEMPERATURE

PRECIPITATION

DAYS OF CLOUDS & PRECIPITATION

Education
Score: 13.1
Rank: 324

ACHIEVEMENT	AREA	U.S. AVG	PUBLIC SCHOOLS	AREA	U.S. AVG	HIGHER EDUCATION	AREA	U.S. AVG
High school degree	74.7%	82.7%	Expenditures per pupil	$5,135	$5,686	No. 2-year colleges	1	4
2-year college degree	5.9%	6.4%	Student/teacher ratio	13.3	16.7	No. 4-year colleges/universities	1	6
4-year college degree	10.2%	15.7%	Attending public school	92.9%	90.1%	No. highly ranked universities	0	1
Graduate/professional degree	4.9%	8.9%	State SAT score	997*	1021			
			State ACT score	20.3	20.9			

Health & Healthcare
Score: 89.0
Rank: 42

Crime
Score: 18.7
Rank: 304

HAZARDS & ILLNESSES	AREA	U.S. AVG	HEALTHCARE	AREA	U.S. AVG	CRIME	AREA	U.S. AVG
Air-quality score	49	37	Physicians per capita	207.4	244.2	Violent crime rate	352.9	465.5
Water-quality score	53	52	Hospital beds per capita	707.4	420.0	Change in violent crime rate	-23.8%	-2.2%
Pollen/allergy score	81	61	No. teaching hospitals	0	3	Property crime rate	4,151.2	3,517.1
Cancer mortality per capita	154.9	201.9	Cost per doctor visit	$63	$77	Change in property crime rate	-15.6%	-2.1%
Depression days per month	4.9	3.5	Cost per dental visit	$59	$70			
Stress score	55	50						

Transportation
Score: 15.5
Rank: 317

COMMUTE	AREA	U.S. AVG	INTERCITY SERVICES	AREA	U.S. AVG	AUTOMOTIVE	AREA	U.S. AVG
Average commute time	23.3	27.4	Major airports within 60 miles	0	1	Insurance, annual premium	$1,062	$1,432
Percent commutes > 60 mins.	5.4%	5.9%	Size of regional airport	Small	Large	Gas, cost per gallon	$2.39	$2.49
Commute by auto	77.8%	78.9%	Daily airline activity	42	686	Daily vehicle miles per capita	17.1	24.0
Commute by mass transit	0.2%	1.9%	Amtrak service	No	No			
Work at home	2.3%	3.1%						
Mass transit miles per capita	0.18	1.87						

Leisure
Score: 1.1
Rank: 369

DINING & SHOPPING	AREA	U.S. AVG	ENTERTAINMENT	AREA	U.S. AVG	OUTDOOR ACTIVITIES	AREA	U.S. AVG
Restaurant rating	1	2	Professional sports rating	2	4	Golf-course rating	1	4
Outlet mall score	0	42	College sports rating	1	4	Ski-area rating	1	3
No. Starbucks	0	13	Zoo/aquarium rating	2	3	Sq. miles inland water	2	4
No. warehouse clubs	1	2	Amusement park rating	1	3	Miles of coastline	0.0	10.7
			Botanical garden/arboretum rating	1	4	National Park rating	1	3

Arts & Culture
Score: 27.0
Rank: 273

MEDIA & LIBRARIES	AREA	U.S. AVG	PERFORMING ARTS	AREA	U.S. AVG	MUSEUMS	AREA	U.S. AVG
Arts radio rating	5	3	Classical music rating	3	4	Overall museum rating	4	5
No. public libraries	6	27	Ballet/dance rating	1	3	Art museum rating	2	5
Library volumes per capita	2.14	2.78	Professional theater rating	1	3	Science museum rating	1	5
			University arts programs rating	1	5	Children's museum rating	1	3

Vineland–Millville–Bridgeton, NJ

Score: 61.5 Rank: 159 2004 rank: 222

Profile: Small-town complex
Location: Southern New Jersey, inland and 40 miles southeast of Philadelphia
Elevation: 10 feet
Time zone: Eastern Standard Time

PRO	CON
Small-town feel	Violent crime
Central location	Future job growth
Cost of living	Low educational attainment

Cumberland County, in the southerly tidewater area of the state, has a mainly rural character with the towns of Vineland and Millville serving as its center. While the area is somewhat economically tied to Philadelphia and Wilmington, Delaware, to the north and northwest, it's generally self-sufficient and most people work locally, primarily in glassmaking and agriculture. The area has a rich and well-preserved history from the colonial era and Revolutionary War. The economy is somewhat weak, although some new investment is attracting business and visitors into the downtown areas, notably Millville. Rates for violent crime remain surprisingly high for this type of area, and educational attainment

is low. The cost of living is the lowest by far among New Jersey metropolitan areas. Services and amenities are sparse locally, but the area is strategically located between the Delaware Valley and beaches to the east.

The flat coastal plain contains marshes and tidewater creeks, with areas of agriculture and mixed pine and deciduous forests inland. Summer days are usually pleasant, but hot, humid spells occur annually. Winters are cool, cloudy, and wet, a mix of rain and snow, with coastal "noreaster" storms moving up the coast from the south bringing heavy rains and winter snows. First freeze is late October; last is mid-April.

Population

DEMOGRAPHICS	AREA	U.S. AVG
Population	151,111	
Population density per sq. mile	308.8	358.5
Population growth	9.5%	21.1%
Median age	35.9	36.1
Percent Democrat	52.4%	44.5%
Percent Republican	45.8%	54.5%

ETHNIC COMPOSITION	AREA	U.S. AVG
White	64.2%	79.0%
Black	20.6%	10.5%
Asian	1.1%	2.7%
Hispanic	21.8%	10.6%
Religious observance	39.8%	48.9%
Diversity measure	69.3	40.1

RESIDENT PROFILE	AREA	U.S. AVG
Single	37.8%	32.4%
Married	43.0%	52.7%
Divorced/separated	19.2%	14.9%
Married with children	21.0%	23.7%
Single with children	12.9%	9.1%
Percent over age 65	12.8%	12.9%

Economy & Jobs
Score: 20.9
Rank: 296

INCOME	AREA	U.S. AVG
Per capita income	$19,764	$23,235
Household income	$43,817	$46,414
Household income ‹ $25K	28.2%	26.2%
Household income › $75K	23.7%	25.4%
Household income growth	11.9%	13.6%

EMPLOYMENT	AREA	U.S. AVG
Unemployment rate	6.2%	4.7%
Recent job growth	1.7%	1.3%
Projected future job growth	3.4%	11.5%
White collar	48.2%	57.8%
Blue collar	30.7%	25.2%

EMPLOYING INDUSTRIES	AREA	U.S. AVG
Largest: Manufacturing		
Percent manufacturing	20.9%	15.4%
Percent public sector	20.4%	15.7%
Percent construction	9.8%	9.9%

Cost of Living
Score: 24.1
Rank: 283

INDEXES & TAXES	AREA	U.S. AVG
Cost of Living Index	101.6	100.0
Buying Power Index	96.7	100.0
Income tax rate	2.93%	4.70%
Sales tax rate	6.00%	6.58%
Property tax rate	$24.23	$12.00

HOUSING	AREA	U.S. AVG
Median home price	$202,700	$220,000
Home price appreciation	76.4%	10.1%
Median rent	$889	$709
Homes owned	63.5%	62.3%
Home price ratio	4.6	4.2

NECESSITIES	AREA	U.S. AVG
Food Index	108.0	100.0
Housing Index	80.6	100.0
Utilities Index	122.7	100.0
Transportation Index	106.3	100.0
Healthcare Index	106.0	100.0
Miscellaneous Cost Index	104.6	100.0

Climate
Score: 85.0
Rank: 57

TEMPERATURE	AREA	U.S. AVG
Average January low	24.0	26.2
Average July high	84.7	87.4
Annual days › 90°F	16	38
Annual days ‹ 32°F	15	89
Annual days ‹ 0°F	1	6

PRECIPITATION	AREA	U.S. AVG
Annual inches precipitation	46.0	37.7
Annual inches snowfall	16.0	7.0
Annual days precipitation	112	109
Annual days rain › 0.5 inches	29	22
Annual days snow › 1.5 inches	5	6

COMFORTS & HAZARDS	AREA	U.S. AVG
July relative humidity	73%	66%
Annual days mostly sunny	204	208
Annual days with thunderstorms	25	39
Tornado risk score	10	18
Hurricane risk score	21	13

TEMPERATURE

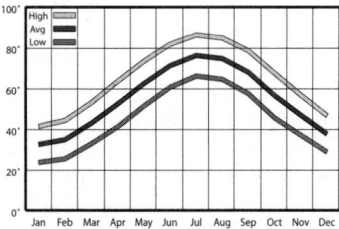

PRECIPITATION

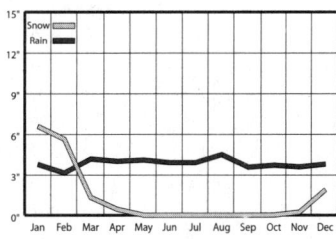

DAYS OF CLOUDS & PRECIPITATION

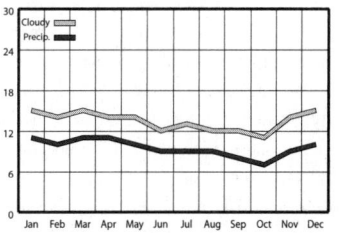

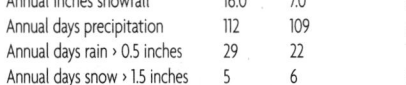

Education
Score: 2.9
Rank: 362

ACHIEVEMENT	AREA	U.S. AVG	PUBLIC SCHOOLS	AREA	U.S. AVG	HIGHER EDUCATION	AREA	U.S. AVG
High school degree	68.4%	82.7%	Expenditures per pupil	$9,030	$5,686	No. 2-year colleges	1	4
2-year college degree	4.7%	6.4%	Student/teacher ratio	13.1	16.7	No. 4-year colleges/universities	0	6
4-year college degree	8.0%	15.7%	Attending public school	90.9%	90.1%	No. highly ranked universities	0	1
Graduate/professional degree	3.7%	8.9%	State SAT score	1011*	1021			
			State ACT score	21.8	20.9			

Health & Healthcare
Score: 46.0
Rank: 203

HAZARDS & ILLNESSES	AREA	U.S. AVG	HEALTHCARE	AREA	U.S. AVG	CRIME	AREA	U.S. AVG
Air-quality score	54	37	Physicians per capita	148.7	244.2	Violent crime rate	899.6	465.5
Water-quality score	20	52	Hospital beds per capita	360.7	420.0	Change in violent crime rate	15.9%	-2.2%
Pollen/allergy score	54	61	No. teaching hospitals	0	3	Property crime rate	3,943.5	3,517.1
Cancer mortality per capita	236.8	201.9	Cost per doctor visit	$69	$77	Change in property crime rate	-6.7%	-2.1%
Depression days per month	3.8	3.5	Cost per dental visit	$90	$70			
Stress score	74	50						

Crime Score: 15.0
Rank: 317

Transportation
Score: 80.5
Rank: 74

COMMUTE	AREA	U.S. AVG	INTERCITY SERVICES	AREA	U.S. AVG	AUTOMOTIVE	AREA	U.S. AVG
Average commute time	25.0	27.4	Major airports within 60 miles	2	1	Insurance, annual premium	$1,862	$1,432
Percent commutes > 60 mins.	7.9%	5.9%	Size of regional airport	Large	Large	Gas, cost per gallon	$2.32	$2.49
Commute by auto	78.4%	78.9%	Daily airline activity	1163	686	Daily vehicle miles per capita	24.6	24.0
Commute by mass transit	2.2%	1.9%	Amtrak service	No	No			
Work at home	2.2%	3.1%						
Mass transit miles per capita	2.23	1.87						

Leisure
Score: 74.6
Rank: 95

DINING & SHOPPING	AREA	U.S. AVG	ENTERTAINMENT	AREA	U.S. AVG	OUTDOOR ACTIVITIES	AREA	U.S. AVG
Restaurant rating	1	2	Professional sports rating	8	4	Golf-course rating	5	4
Outlet mall score	86	42	College sports rating	3	4	Ski-area rating	3	3
No. Starbucks	1	13	Zoo/aquarium rating	2	3	Sq. miles inland water	4	4
No. warehouse clubs	1	2	Amusement park rating	4	3	Miles of coastline	30.3	10.7
			Botanical garden/ arboretum rating	6	4	National Park rating	2	3

Arts & Culture
Score: 63.4
Rank: 137

MEDIA & LIBRARIES	AREA	U.S. AVG	PERFORMING ARTS	AREA	U.S. AVG	MUSEUMS	AREA	U.S. AVG
Arts radio rating	5	3	Classical music rating	4	4	Overall museum rating	7	5
No. public libraries	4	27	Ballet/dance rating	4	3	Art museum rating	7	5
Library volumes per capita	2.88	2.78	Professional theater rating	5	3	Science museum rating	6	5
			University arts programs rating	1	5	Children's museum rating	4	3

Virginia Beach–Norfolk–Newport News, VA-NC

Score: 65.4   Rank: 137   2004 rank: 17

Profile: Large-city complex
Location: Southeast Virginia coast
Elevation: 30 feet
Time zone: Eastern Standard Time

PRO
Nearby water recreation
Educated population
Stable economy

CON
Growth and sprawl
Rising costs
Air service

This complex area straddles the waterway known as Hampton Roads, a large estuarine bay that empties into the Chesapeake Bay and Atlantic Ocean. It is the largest metropolitan area in the state in terms of population, and offers an interesting mix of urban, suburban, waterfront, and inland environments. The cities of Norfolk, Chesapeake, and Portsmouth are to the south of the waterway, with the large and rapidly growing Virginia Beach located a few miles to the east along the Atlantic shore. Hampton and Newport News lie to the north across a long bridge-tunnel connection. The natural harbor makes for one of the best ports on the East Coast, and shipping and shipbuilding activity are paramount, along with fishing and seaport-related commerce. Additionally, the area has a substantial Navy and Marine presence, with a sizable portion of the economy connected to these activities. Virginia Beach has grown rapidly and is an interesting mix of touristy beachfront and modern commercial and family residential areas, with the large Oceana Naval Air Station thrown into the mix for good measure. Of the three major cities, Virginia Beach is by far the most prosperous and fun, but it is suffering somewhat from the strains of growth, and some might find the tourist impact excessive. Farther north on the James Peninsula lies the excellent historic and upscale residential and commercial area of Williamsburg, perhaps the top choice among all parts of the area if affordable. Since 2004, job-growth projections have fallen off and home prices have risen some 76%; both factors have a lot to do with the drop in ranking.

The area has an assortment of museums, particularly related to its maritime history, and a good set of performing arts activities. For an area this size, there are relatively few sports teams and no major league teams, a complaint among some locals and particularly those (and there are a lot) who have migrated from larger East Coast cities. Other downsides include areas of overdone growth; traffic problems, especially at bridges and tunnels and along heavily traveled Virginia Beach corridors; and often-unattractive naval and port areas and gritty neighborhoods

nearby. Cost of living is moderate for an East Coast area of this size but has been on the rise as the area becomes a more popular destination. The marine climate is pleasant and there is plenty to do.

The city of Norfolk is almost surrounded by water, with the Chesapeake Bay immediately to the north, Hampton Roads and the James River to the west, and the Atlantic Ocean 18 miles east. Numerous rivers and waterways traverse the area. The land is low and level throughout the city. Cool Atlantic breezes frequently temper the long, warm summers. Extreme temperatures are infrequent. Winters are usually mild and may pass with no measurable snowfall.

Population

DEMOGRAPHICS	AREA	U.S. AVG	ETHNIC COMPOSITION	AREA	U.S. AVG	RESIDENT PROFILE	AREA	U.S. AVG
Population	1,645,236		White	61.0%	79.0%	Single	32.7%	32.4%
Population density per sq. mile	626.1	358.5	Black	31.8%	10.5%	Married	50.6%	52.7%
Population growth	16.7%	21.1%	Asian	2.9%	2.7%	Divorced/separated	16.7%	14.9%
Median age	34.6	36.1	Hispanic	3.2%	10.6%	Married with children	24.4%	23.7%
Percent Democrat	47.3%	44.5%	Religious observance	34.8%	48.9%	Single with children	11.2%	9.1%
Percent Republican	52.0%	54.5%	Diversity measure	51.7	40.1	Percent over age 65	10.7%	12.9%

Economy & Jobs
Score: 62.0
Rank: 143

INCOME	AREA	U.S. AVG	EMPLOYMENT	AREA	U.S. AVG	EMPLOYING INDUSTRIES	AREA	U.S. AVG
Per capita income	$23,521	$23,235	Unemployment rate	4.2%	4.7%	Largest: Healthcare & Social Assistance		
Household income	$49,335	$46,414	Recent job growth	2.2%	1.3%			
Household income < $25K	22.3%	26.2%	Projected future job growth	11.4%	11.5%	Percent manufacturing	12.0%	15.4%
Household income > $75K	26.7%	25.4%	White collar	61.1%	57.8%	Percent public sector	21.9%	15.7%
Household income growth	13.7%	13.6%	Blue collar	22.8%	25.2%	Percent construction	10.9%	9.9%

Cost of Living
Score: 31.3
Rank: 257

INDEXES & TAXES	AREA	U.S. AVG	HOUSING	AREA	U.S. AVG	NECESSITIES	AREA	U.S. AVG
Cost of Living Index	103.0	100.0	Median home price	$237,300	$220,000	Food Index	96.1	100.0
Buying Power Index	107.4	100.0	Home price appreciation	91.3%	10.1%	Housing Index	77.1	100.0
Income tax rate	5.75%	4.70%	Median rent	$844	$709	Utilities Index	138.3	100.0
Sales tax rate	5.03%	6.58%	Homes owned	59.5%	62.3%	Transportation Index	105.2	100.0
Property tax rate	$12.13	$12.00	Home price ratio	4.8	4.2	Healthcare Index	93.3	100.0
						Miscellaneous Cost Index	94.2	100.0

Climate
Score: 62.8
Rank: 138

TEMPERATURE	AREA	U.S. AVG	PRECIPITATION	AREA	U.S. AVG	COMFORTS & HAZARDS	AREA	U.S. AVG
Average January low	32.2	26.2	Annual inches precipitation	45.0	37.7	July relative humidity	71%	66%
Average July high	86.6	87.4	Annual inches snowfall	7.0	7.0	Annual days mostly sunny	212	208
Annual days > 90°F	30	38	Annual days precipitation	115	109	Annual days with thunderstorms	37	39
Annual days < 32°F	54	89	Annual days rain > 0.5 inches	27	22	Tornado risk score	14	18
Annual days < 0°F	0	6	Annual days snow > 1.5 inches	2	6	Hurricane risk score	41	13

TEMPERATURE

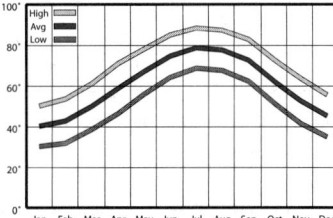

PRECIPITATION

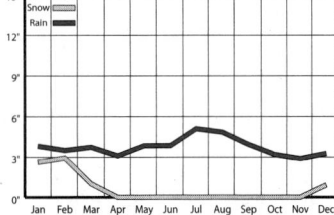

DAYS OF CLOUDS & PRECIPITATION

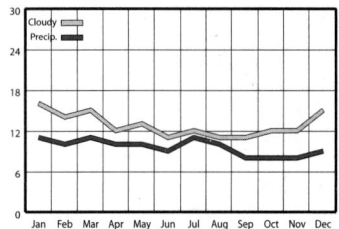

Education
Score: 66.0
Rank: 128

ACHIEVEMENT	AREA	U.S. AVG	PUBLIC SCHOOLS	AREA	U.S. AVG	HIGHER EDUCATION	AREA	U.S. AVG
High school degree	84.7%	82.7%	Expenditures per pupil	$5,122	$5,686	No. 2-year colleges	9	4
2-year college degree	6.8%	6.4%	Student/teacher ratio	16.0	16.7	No. 4-year colleges/universities	13	6
4-year college degree	15.4%	15.7%	Attending public school	90.5%	90.1%	No. highly ranked universities	1	1
Graduate/professional degree	8.4%	8.9%	State SAT score	1025*	1021			
			State ACT score	21.1	20.9			

Health & Healthcare
Score: 66.8
Rank: 125

HAZARDS & ILLNESSES	AREA	U.S. AVG
Air-quality score	56	37
Water-quality score	63	52
Pollen/allergy score	69	61
Cancer mortality per capita	207.9	201.9
Depression days per month	2.9	3.5
Stress score	26	50

HEALTHCARE	AREA	U.S. AVG
Physicians per capita	249.3	244.2
Hospital beds per capita	328.5	420.0
No. teaching hospitals	11	3
Cost per doctor visit	$67	$77
Cost per dental visit	$61	$70

Crime
Score: 40.1
Rank: 224

CRIME	AREA	U.S. AVG
Violent crime rate	470.3	465.5
Change in violent crime rate	9.6%	-2.2%
Property crime rate	3,683.0	3,517.1
Change in property crime rate	1.3%	-2.1%

Transportation
Score: 10.7
Rank: 335

COMMUTE	AREA	U.S. AVG
Average commute time	26.0	27.4
Percent commutes › 60 mins.	5.1%	5.9%
Commute by auto	78.9%	78.9%
Commute by mass transit	1.9%	1.9%
Work at home	2.7%	3.1%
Mass transit miles per capita	1.85	1.87

INTERCITY SERVICES	AREA	U.S. AVG
Major airports within 60 miles	0	1
Size of regional airport	Small	Large
Daily airline activity	266	686
Amtrak service	Yes	No

AUTOMOTIVE	AREA	U.S. AVG
Insurance, annual premium	$1,805	$1,432
Gas, cost per gallon	$2.45	$2.49
Daily vehicle miles per capita	23.7	24.0

Leisure
Score: 82.9
Rank: 64

DINING & SHOPPING	AREA	U.S. AVG
Restaurant rating	1	2
Outlet mall score	0	42
No. Starbucks	27	13
No. warehouse clubs	6	2

ENTERTAINMENT	AREA	U.S. AVG
Professional sports rating	3	4
College sports rating	5	4
Zoo/aquarium rating	8	3
Amusement park rating	9	3
Botanical garden/ arboretum rating	9	4

OUTDOOR ACTIVITIES	AREA	U.S. AVG
Golf-course rating	5	4
Ski-area rating	1	3
Sq. miles inland water	8	4
Miles of coastline	69.0	10.7
National Park rating	5	3

Arts & Culture
Score: 85.0
Rank: 57

MEDIA & LIBRARIES	AREA	U.S. AVG
Arts radio rating	8	3
No. public libraries	50	27
Library volumes per capita	2.84	2.78

PERFORMING ARTS	AREA	U.S. AVG
Classical music rating	6	4
Ballet/dance rating	8	3
Professional theater rating	6	3
University arts programs rating	5	5

MUSEUMS	AREA	U.S. AVG
Overall museum rating	10	5
Art museum rating	9	5
Science museum rating	10	5
Children's museum rating	10	3

Visalia–Porterville, CA

Score: 3.6   **Rank:** 372   **2004 rank:** 211

Profile: Small agricultural towns
Location: Central California, southeastern portion of the Central Valley at the foot of the Sierra Nevada
Elevation: 327 feet
Time zone: Pacific Standard Time

PRO	CON
Nearby national parks	Economy
Winter climate	Arts and culture
Small-town atmosphere	Isolation

This San Joaquin Valley agricultural area is one of the largest producers of oranges and citrus fruits in the world. The flat landscape rises dramatically from flat orchard land to Sequoia National Park, just 50 miles to the east. The downtown areas of both Visalia and Porterville are fairly neat and functional but lack interest. Once California's "bargain" metro area, the Cost of Living Index has risen to 108.4 from 95 just 3 years ago, and median home prices have risen from $114,000 to $243,400. Activities include outdoor recreation and some watersports. There is little in the way of entertainment or intellectual stimulation nearby. The increasing cost profile, lack of economic diversity, weak economic growth, and low educational attainment have driven the ranking down to second to last, but there is opportunity for improvement under the right set of circumstances. Fresno is 40 miles northwest, but bigger cities are all more than 100 miles distant.

Just to the east, the Sierra Nevada rises dramatically, first as oak-studded foothills and then as a high ridge of granite, with peaks over 14,000 feet. Winter snow cover on these peaks creates a dramatic landscape. The climate is generally pleasant except for summer hot spells. Summers are hot and dry and winters are mild and relatively wet with 90% of annual precipitation. Summer evenings may be cooled by mountain breezes. Dense ground fogs are common; freezes are not.

Population

DEMOGRAPHICS	AREA	U.S. AVG
Population	397,963	
Population density per sq. mile	82.5	358.5
Population growth	27.6%	21.1%
Median age	29.5	36.1
Percent Democrat	32.9%	44.5%
Percent Republican	66.2%	54.5%

ETHNIC COMPOSITION	AREA	U.S. AVG
White	55.7%	79.0%
Black	1.7%	10.5%
Asian	3.2%	2.7%
Hispanic	55.1%	10.6%
Religious observance	51.8%	48.9%
Diversity measure	78.5	40.1

RESIDENT PROFILE	AREA	U.S. AVG
Single	33.0%	32.4%
Married	51.4%	52.7%
Divorced/separated	15.5%	14.9%
Married with children	31.7%	23.7%
Single with children	13.0%	9.1%
Percent over age 65	9.5%	12.9%

Economy & Jobs
Score: 0.5
Rank: 371

INCOME	AREA	U.S. AVG
Per capita income	$15,809	$23,235
Household income	$39,157	$46,414
Household income < $25K	31.7%	26.2%
Household income > $75K	20.0%	25.4%
Household income growth	15.2%	13.6%

EMPLOYMENT	AREA	U.S. AVG
Unemployment rate	8.9%	4.7%
Recent job growth	-0.2%	1.3%
Projected future job growth	5.4%	11.5%
White collar	46.1%	57.8%
Blue collar	22.7%	25.2%

EMPLOYING INDUSTRIES	AREA	U.S. AVG
Largest: Healthcare & Social Assistance		
Percent manufacturing	14.3%	15.4%
Percent public sector	18.5%	15.7%
Percent construction	8.4%	9.9%

Cost of Living
Score: 23.8
Rank: 284

INDEXES & TAXES	AREA	U.S. AVG
Cost of Living Index	108.4	100.0
Buying Power Index	81.0	100.0
Income tax rate	6.00%	4.70%
Sales tax rate	7.25%	6.58%
Property tax rate	$8.28	$12.00

HOUSING	AREA	U.S. AVG
Median home price	$243,400	$220,000
Home price appreciation	138.4%	10.1%
Median rent	$647	$709
Homes owned	57.1%	62.3%
Home price ratio	6.2	4.2

NECESSITIES	AREA	U.S. AVG
Food Index	109.8	100.0
Housing Index	105.8	100.0
Utilities Index	114.4	100.0
Transportation Index	106.1	100.0
Healthcare Index	118.7	100.0
Miscellaneous Cost Index	102.8	100.0

Climate
Score: 90.1
Rank: 38

TEMPERATURE	AREA	U.S. AVG
Average January low	35.8	26.2
Average July high	98.2	87.4
Annual days > 90°F	107	38
Annual days < 32°F	29	89
Annual days < 0°F	0	6

PRECIPITATION	AREA	U.S. AVG
Annual inches precipitation	10.0	37.7
Annual inches snowfall	0.0	7.0
Annual days precipitation	44	109
Annual days rain > 0.5 inches	6	22
Annual days snow > 1.5 inches	0	6

COMFORTS & HAZARDS	AREA	U.S. AVG
July relative humidity	61%	66%
Annual days mostly sunny	271	208
Annual days with thunderstorms	6	39
Tornado risk score	3	18
Hurricane risk score	0	13

TEMPERATURE

PRECIPITATION

DAYS OF CLOUDS & PRECIPITATION

Education
Score: 1.6
Rank: 367

ACHIEVEMENT	AREA	U.S. AVG
High school degree	61.6%	82.7%
2-year college degree	6.3%	6.4%
4-year college degree	7.7%	15.7%
Graduate/professional degree	3.7%	8.9%

PUBLIC SCHOOLS	AREA	U.S. AVG
Expenditures per pupil	$4,965	$5,686
Student/teacher ratio	20.5	16.7
Attending public school	96.6%	90.1%
State SAT score	1019*	1021
State ACT score	21.6	20.9

HIGHER EDUCATION	AREA	U.S. AVG
No. 2-year colleges	3	4
No. 4-year colleges/universities	0	6
No. highly ranked universities	0	1

Health & Healthcare
Score: 19.8
Rank: 299

HAZARDS & ILLNESSES	AREA	U.S. AVG
Air-quality score	20	37
Water-quality score	30	52
Pollen/allergy score	60	61
Cancer mortality per capita	161.8	201.9
Depression days per month	5.1	3.5
Stress score	70	50

HEALTHCARE	AREA	U.S. AVG
Physicians per capita	108.8	244.2
Hospital beds per capita	554.3	420.0
No. teaching hospitals	0	3
Cost per doctor visit	$102	$77
Cost per dental visit	$82	$70

Crime
Score: 4.5
Rank: 356

CRIME	AREA	U.S. AVG
Violent crime rate	682.9	465.5
Change in violent crime rate	3.3%	-2.2%
Property crime rate	4,936.3	3,517.1
Change in property crime rate	-1.6%	-2.1%

Transportation
Score: 18.7
Rank: 305

COMMUTE	AREA	U.S. AVG
Average commute time	23.3	27.4
Percent commutes > 60 mins.	5.8%	5.9%
Commute by auto	72.4%	78.9%
Commute by mass transit	0.9%	1.9%
Work at home	3.5%	3.1%
Mass transit miles per capita	0.92	1.87

INTERCITY SERVICES	AREA	U.S. AVG
Major airports within 60 miles	0	1
Size of regional airport	Small	Large
Daily airline activity	75	686
Amtrak service	No	No

AUTOMOTIVE	AREA	U.S. AVG
Insurance, annual premium	$1,871	$1,432
Gas, cost per gallon	$2.70	$2.49
Daily vehicle miles per capita	16.0	24.0

Leisure
Score: 47.3
Rank: 196

DINING & SHOPPING	AREA	U.S. AVG
Restaurant rating	1	2
Outlet mall score	39	42
No. Starbucks	6	13
No. warehouse clubs	1	2

ENTERTAINMENT	AREA	U.S. AVG
Professional sports rating	2	4
College sports rating	1	4
Zoo/aquarium rating	1	3
Amusement park rating	1	3
Botanical garden/ arboretum rating	1	4

OUTDOOR ACTIVITIES	AREA	U.S. AVG
Golf-course rating	2	4
Ski-area rating	5	3
Sq. miles inland water	2	4
Miles of coastline	0.0	10.7
National Park rating	10	3

Arts & Culture
Score: 9.4
Rank: 338

MEDIA & LIBRARIES	AREA	U.S. AVG	PERFORMING ARTS	AREA	U.S. AVG	MUSEUMS	AREA	U.S. AVG
Arts radio rating	1	3	Classical music rating	1	4	Overall museum rating	3	5
No. public libraries	18	27	Ballet/dance rating	1	3	Art museum rating	2	5
Library volumes per capita	4.05	2.78	Professional theater rating	1	3	Science museum rating	3	5
			University arts programs rating	1	5	Children's museum rating	1	3

Waco, TX

Score: 43.5 Rank: 301 2004 rank: 227

Profile: Small city/college town
Location: East-central Texas along I-35, 100 miles south of Dallas
Elevation: 501 feet
Time zone: Central Standard Time

PRO	CON
Cost of living	Crime rates
College-town amenities	Low educational attainment
Historic interest	Summer heat

The typically Texas small city of Waco is an important commercial and transportation hub with an added college presence. The economic base consists of small to mid-size manufacturers in a variety of industries and a strong agricultural presence with ranching, poultry, and cotton. Another principal employer, Baylor University, brings 15,000 students and some college-town amenities; however, educational attainment is unusually low for a college town. Downtown is fairly modern but uninspiring with a small historic area; many older buildings were destroyed in a 1953 tornado. The city prides itself as a good filmmaking set because of its many neighborhood "looks" and varied terrain. Lakes within and outside the city provide watersports, but most other forms of recreation, entertainment, and cultural interest are in short supply. The biggest draw is cost of living and housing, quite reasonable especially for a place with a college presence.

Waco is located in the rich agricultural region of the Brazos River Valley. The gently rolling, agricultural Blackland Prairies spread to the east and the rolling to hilly Grand Prairie with sagebrush and cactus starts to the west—the contrast between the two areas is one feature that attracts filmmakers. Summer daytime temperatures are hot, especially in July and August. Highest temperatures are associated with fair skies, light winds, and comparatively low humidity. Winters are mild. Cold spells rarely last longer than 2 to 3 days. In an average year, April and May are the wettest months, while the July to August period is the driest. Most warm-season rainfall occurs from thunderstorm activity. Winter precipitation may arrive as rain, freezing rain, sleet, or snow, though most years have little snow.

Population

DEMOGRAPHICS	AREA	U.S. AVG	ETHNIC COMPOSITION	AREA	U.S. AVG	RESIDENT PROFILE	AREA	U.S. AVG
Population	222,521		White	70.9%	79.0%	Single	33.6%	32.4%
Population density per sq. mile	213.6	358.5	Black	14.8%	10.5%	Married	49.5%	52.7%
Population growth	17.7%	21.1%	Asian	1.2%	2.7%	Divorced/separated	16.9%	14.9%
Median age	32.2	36.1	Hispanic	20.5%	10.6%	Married with children	22.8%	23.7%
Percent Democrat	33.8%	44.5%	Religious observance	60.5%	48.9%	Single with children	10.1%	9.1%
Percent Republican	65.7%	54.5%	Diversity measure	63.9	40.1	Percent over age 65	12.6%	12.9%

Economy & Jobs
Score: 79.4
Rank: 78

INCOME	AREA	U.S. AVG	EMPLOYMENT	AREA	U.S. AVG	EMPLOYING INDUSTRIES	AREA	U.S. AVG
Per capita income	$19,382	$23,235	Unemployment rate	5.0%	4.7%	Largest: Manufacturing		
Household income	$37,840	$46,414	Recent job growth	3.9%	1.3%			
Household income ‹ $25K	33.8%	26.2%	Projected future job growth	12.9%	11.5%	Percent manufacturing	15.4%	15.4%
Household income › $75K	19.3%	25.4%	White collar	57.6%	57.8%	Percent public sector	14.6%	15.7%
Household income growth	12.8%	13.6%	Blue collar	25.8%	25.2%	Percent construction	10.4%	9.9%

Cost of Living
Score: 93.6
Rank: 25

INDEXES & TAXES	AREA	U.S. AVG	HOUSING	AREA	U.S. AVG	NECESSITIES	AREA	U.S. AVG
Cost of Living Index	76.6	100.0	Median home price	$101,000	$220,000	Food Index	86.8	100.0
Buying Power Index	110.7	100.0	Home price appreciation	32.8%	10.1%	Housing Index	45.5	100.0
Income tax rate	0.00%	4.70%	Median rent	$629	$709	Utilities Index	95.7	100.0
Sales tax rate	8.25%	6.58%	Homes owned	55.8%	62.3%	Transportation Index	96.3	100.0
Property tax rate	$14.42	$12.00	Home price ratio	2.7	4.2	Healthcare Index	98.0	100.0
						Miscellaneous Cost Index	100.4	100.0

Climate
Score: 87.7
Rank: 47

TEMPERATURE	AREA	U.S. AVG
Average January low	36.6	26.2
Average July high	96.2	87.4
Annual days > 90°F	105	38
Annual days < 32°F	35	89
Annual days < 0°F	0	6

PRECIPITATION	AREA	U.S. AVG
Annual inches precipitation	31.3	37.7
Annual inches snowfall	1.5	7.0
Annual days precipitation	78	109
Annual days rain > 0.5 inches	18	22
Annual days snow > 1.5 inches	1	6

COMFORTS & HAZARDS	AREA	U.S. AVG
July relative humidity	67%	66%
Annual days mostly sunny	231	208
Annual days with thunderstorms	45	39
Tornado risk score	28	18
Hurricane risk score	18	13

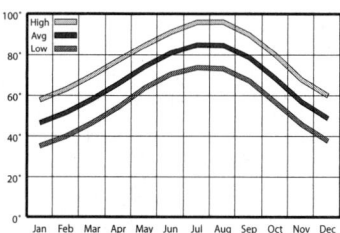

TEMPERATURE

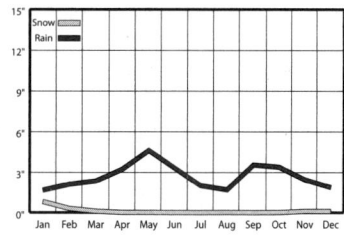

PRECIPITATION

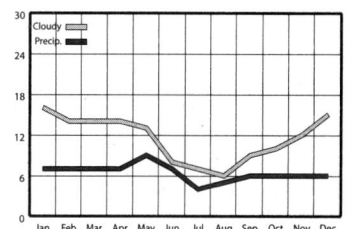

DAYS OF CLOUDS & PRECIPITATION

Education
Score: 43.6
Rank: 212

ACHIEVEMENT	AREA	U.S. AVG
High school degree	76.9%	82.7%
2-year college degree	7.1%	6.4%
4-year college degree	12.0%	15.7%
Graduate/professional degree	7.4%	8.9%

PUBLIC SCHOOLS	AREA	U.S. AVG
Expenditures per pupil	$6,504	$5,686
Student/teacher ratio	15.2	16.7
Attending public school	95.5%	90.1%
State SAT score	997*	1021
State ACT score	20.3	20.9

HIGHER EDUCATION	AREA	U.S. AVG
No. 2-year colleges	2	4
No. 4-year colleges/universities	1	6
No. highly ranked universities	1	1

Health & Healthcare
Score: 39.0
Rank: 227

HAZARDS & ILLNESSES	AREA	U.S. AVG
Air-quality score	30	37
Water-quality score	75	52
Pollen/allergy score	82	61
Cancer mortality per capita	176.5	201.9
Depression days per month	2.8	3.5
Stress score	35	50

HEALTHCARE	AREA	U.S. AVG
Physicians per capita	201.5	244.2
Hospital beds per capita	344.7	420.0
No. teaching hospitals	2	3
Cost per doctor visit	$72	$77
Cost per dental visit	$77	$70

Crime
Score: 8.8
Rank: 340

CRIME	AREA	U.S. AVG
Violent crime rate	552.0	465.5
Change in violent crime rate	-0.7%	-2.2%
Property crime rate	5,523.7	3,517.1
Change in property crime rate	-3.1%	-2.1%

Transportation
Score: 96.8
Rank: 13

COMMUTE	AREA	U.S. AVG
Average commute time	21.5	27.4
Percent commutes > 60 mins.	3.7%	5.9%
Commute by auto	79.2%	78.9%
Commute by mass transit	0.8%	1.9%
Work at home	2.6%	3.1%
Mass transit miles per capita	0.75	1.87

INTERCITY SERVICES	AREA	U.S. AVG
Major airports within 60 miles	3	1
Size of regional airport	Large	Large
Daily airline activity	1740	686
Amtrak service	Yes	No

AUTOMOTIVE	AREA	U.S. AVG
Insurance, annual premium	$1,228	$1,432
Gas, cost per gallon	$2.50	$2.49
Daily vehicle miles per capita	27.9	24.0

Leisure
Score: 19.3
Rank: 301

DINING & SHOPPING	AREA	U.S. AVG
Restaurant rating	1	2
Outlet mall score	0	42
No. Starbucks	3	13
No. warehouse clubs	0	2

ENTERTAINMENT	AREA	U.S. AVG
Professional sports rating	2	4
College sports rating	5	4
Zoo/aquarium rating	3	3
Amusement park rating	1	3
Botanical garden/ arboretum rating	2	4

OUTDOOR ACTIVITIES	AREA	U.S. AVG
Golf-course rating	2	4
Ski-area rating	1	3
Sq. miles inland water	2	4
Miles of coastline	0.0	10.7
National Park rating	1	3

Arts & Culture
Score: 33.4
Rank: 249

MEDIA & LIBRARIES	AREA	U.S. AVG
Arts radio rating	1	3
No. public libraries	8	27
Library volumes per capita	1.81	2.78

PERFORMING ARTS	AREA	U.S. AVG
Classical music rating	3	4
Ballet/dance rating	1	3
Professional theater rating	1	3
University arts programs rating	4	5

MUSEUMS	AREA	U.S. AVG
Overall museum rating	6	5
Art museum rating	6	5
Science museum rating	4	5
Children's museum rating	1	3

Warren–Troy–Farmington Hills, MI   Score: 57.8 Rank: 190 2004 rank: 263

Profile: Suburban complex
Location: Southeast Michigan in northern half of the suburban Detroit area
Elevation: 664 feet
Time zone: Eastern Standard Time

PRO	CON
Educated population	Winter climate
Buying power	Economic cycles
Strong community feel	Clouds and rain

Detroit's seemingly endless grid-patterned suburbs spread mainly west of town, and the northern half of this suburban cluster has been split off of the formerly singular Detroit metro area (p. 317). That northern half consists of the relatively new and prosperous suburbs spreading north into Oakland County, including not only the named places of Warren, Troy, and Farmington Hills but also such familiar names as Southfield, Pontiac, Royal Oak, Auburn Hills, and Bloomfield. These suburbs, located on once-agricultural land, are plain, business friendly, and mostly family friendly, and are the "where the puck is going" suburbs of the Detroit area if indeed there are any.

Troy has become a major business and commercial center, with a number of plants and headquarters operations. Many of the firms making a home there are well known in the automotive industry, including Altain Engineering, Budd Company, Delphi, and SAE International. Temporary employer Kelly Services and a couple of banks also call Troy home. The area suffered a bit of a blow with the bankruptcy of locally headquartered Kmart, and much of that operation has been moved, through merger, to Chicago. Like most of Detroit, and Michigan at large, the area is vulnerable to economic cycles. Troy and the other suburbs are mostly modern, with large commercial concrete and glass structures and attractive if plain housing. The area is known for its community feel and strength of community-sports programs. Warren is similar, and goes to market with the slogan "Small Town Lifestyle, Big City Commerce." Warren is home to the General Motors Technical Center and a series of U.S. Army technical and research facilities among other installations. A

number of Detroit suburbs are known for their lack of diversity; Warren is one of them. Finally, Farmington Hills is a mostly upscale residential suburb and shopping area with attractive housing developments spreading northward into West Bloomfield.

For the most part, these northern suburbs feature a strong community framework, modern amenities, and a comfortable if not showy suburban lifestyle. Detroit itself provides many city amenities and services not available locally. Main roads, laid out on a grid, make getting around fairly easy; while the area is spread out, traffic isn't much of an issue. Most work somewhere in the area; relatively few commute to Detroit. The airport is on the southwest side, a long drive around the Interstate 696/275 beltway. Large areas of outdoor recreation lie to the north and especially to the north of Saginaw Bay or east at Lake St. Clair. Cost of Living Index is a moderate 92.9, and homes, averaging $177,500, are good values for the money. The Buying Power Index, our measure of incomes relative to costs, is 154.1, strongest in the U.S. Nevertheless, climate and a dubious economy weigh on the ranking.

Detroit's northern suburbs occupy mainly flat to gently rolling agricultural terrain in the glacial plain spreading north into the state. Winter storms can bring combinations of rain, snow, freezing rain, and sleet with the possibility of heavy snowfall. In summer, most storms pass to the north allowing for intervals of warm, humid, sunny skies, and occasional thunderstorms followed by days of mild, dry, and fair weather. Summer temperatures can reach 90°F or higher. First freeze is late October; last is late April.

DEMOGRAPHICS	AREA	U.S. AVG	ETHNIC COMPOSITION	AREA	U.S. AVG	RESIDENT PROFILE	AREA	U.S. AVG
Population	2,481,882		White	86.0%	79.0%	Single	31.0%	32.4%
Population density per sq. mile	752.1	358.5	Black	7.3%	10.5%	Married	56.9%	52.7%
Population growth	16.9%	21.1%	Asian	3.7%	2.7%	Divorced/separated	12.0%	14.9%
Median age	38.1	36.1	Hispanic	2.3%	10.6%	Married with children	26.2%	23.7%
Percent Democrat	47.8%	44.5%	Religious observance	45.2%	48.9%	Single with children	6.6%	9.1%
Percent Republican	51.2%	54.5%	Diversity measure	28.1	40.1	Percent over age 65	12.2%	12.9%

INCOME	AREA	U.S. AVG	EMPLOYMENT	AREA	U.S. AVG	EMPLOYING INDUSTRIES	AREA	U.S. AVG
Per capita income	$32,054	$23,235	Unemployment rate	6.9%	4.7%	Largest: Professional, Scientific & Technical Services		
Household income	$63,871	$46,414	Recent job growth	-0.2%	1.3%			
Household income < $25K	16.1%	26.2%	Projected future job growth	9.2%	11.5%	Percent manufacturing	14.8%	15.4%
Household income > $75K	40.7%	25.4%	White collar	64.2%	57.8%	Percent public sector	8.7%	15.7%
Household income growth	10.8%	13.6%	Blue collar	23.7%	25.2%	Percent construction	8.9%	9.9%

Score: 41.2
Rank: 220

INDEXES & TAXES	AREA	U.S. AVG	HOUSING	AREA	U.S. AVG	NECESSITIES	AREA	U.S. AVG
Cost of Living Index	92.9	100.0	Median home price	$177,500	$220,000	Food Index	106.3	100.0
Buying Power Index	154.1	100.0	Home price appreciation	17.5%	10.1%	Housing Index	74.2	100.0
Income tax rate	7.08%	4.70%	Median rent	$798	$709	Utilities Index	87.9	100.0
Sales tax rate	6.00%	6.58%	Homes owned	74.7%	62.3%	Transportation Index	103.7	100.0
Property tax rate	$13.22	$12.00	Home price ratio	2.8	4.2	Healthcare Index	113.9	100.0
						Miscellaneous Cost Index	96.6	100.0

Cost of Living
Score: 20.9
Rank: 295

Climate
Score: 38.5
Rank: 229

TEMPERATURE	AREA	U.S. AVG
Average January low	17.3	26.2
Average July high	83.4	87.4
Annual days > 90°F	11	38
Annual days < 32°F	139	89
Annual days < 0°F	7	6

PRECIPITATION	AREA	U.S. AVG
Annual inches precipitation	32.0	37.7
Annual inches snowfall	39.0	7.0
Annual days precipitation	133	109
Annual days rain > 0.5 inches	19	22
Annual days snow > 1.5 inches	9	6

COMFORTS & HAZARDS	AREA	U.S. AVG
July relative humidity	72%	66%
Annual days mostly sunny	185	208
Annual days with thunderstorms	33	39
Tornado risk score	31	18
Hurricane risk score	3	13

TEMPERATURE

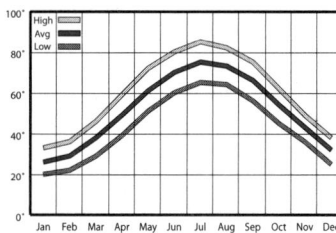

PRECIPITATION

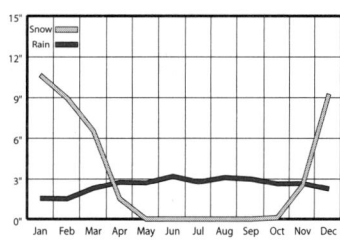

DAYS OF CLOUDS & PRECIPITATION

Education
Score: 76.2
Rank: 90

ACHIEVEMENT	AREA	U.S. AVG
High school degree	86.8%	82.7%
2-year college degree	7.4%	6.4%
4-year college degree	17.6%	15.7%
Graduate/professional degree	10.3%	8.9%

PUBLIC SCHOOLS	AREA	U.S. AVG
Expenditures per pupil	$7,036	$5,686
Student/teacher ratio	19.3	16.7
Attending public school	89.6%	90.1%
State SAT score	1151	1021
State ACT score	21.5*	20.9

HIGHER EDUCATION	AREA	U.S. AVG
No. 2-year colleges	8	4
No. 4-year colleges/universities	13	6
No. highly ranked universities	0	1

Health & Healthcare
Score: 15.5
Rank: 315

HAZARDS & ILLNESSES	AREA	U.S. AVG
Air-quality score	20	37
Water-quality score	37	52
Pollen/allergy score	63	61
Cancer mortality per capita	197.1	201.9
Depression days per month	3.6	3.5
Stress score	84	50

HEALTHCARE	AREA	U.S. AVG
Physicians per capita	323.3	244.2
Hospital beds per capita	294.3	420.0
No. teaching hospitals	18	3
Cost per doctor visit	$68	$77
Cost per dental visit	$67	$70

Crime
Score: 75.4
Rank: 93

CRIME	AREA	U.S. AVG
Violent crime rate	317.6	465.5
Change in violent crime rate	6.6%	-2.2%
Property crime rate	2,879.9	3,517.1
Change in property crime rate	1.4%	-2.1%

Transportation
Score: 10.4
Rank: 336

COMMUTE	AREA	U.S. AVG
Average commute time	29.8	27.4
Percent commutes > 60 mins.	7.4%	5.9%
Commute by auto	88.0%	78.9%
Commute by mass transit	0.4%	1.9%
Work at home	2.5%	3.1%
Mass transit miles per capita	0.43	1.87

INTERCITY SERVICES	AREA	U.S. AVG
Major airports within 60 miles	1	1
Size of regional airport	Large	Large
Daily airline activity	846	686
Amtrak service	Yes	No

AUTOMOTIVE	AREA	U.S. AVG
Insurance, annual premium	$2,635	$1,432
Gas, cost per gallon	$2.49	$2.49
Daily vehicle miles per capita	29.0	24.0

Leisure
Score: 92.0
Rank: 31

DINING & SHOPPING	AREA	U.S. AVG
Restaurant rating	3	2
Outlet mall score	202	42
No. Starbucks	40	13
No. warehouse clubs	12	2

ENTERTAINMENT	AREA	U.S. AVG
Professional sports rating	9	4
College sports rating	4	4
Zoo/aquarium rating	8	3
Amusement park rating	2	3
Botanical garden/ arboretum rating	6	4

OUTDOOR ACTIVITIES	AREA	U.S. AVG
Golf-course rating	10	4
Ski-area rating	5	3
Sq. miles inland water	6	4
Miles of coastline	44.0	10.7
National Park rating	1	3

Arts & Culture
Score: 92.2
Rank: 30

MEDIA & LIBRARIES	AREA	U.S. AVG
Arts radio rating	6	3
No. public libraries	93	27
Library volumes per capita	2.67	2.78

PERFORMING ARTS	AREA	U.S. AVG
Classical music rating	10	4
Ballet/dance rating	6	3
Professional theater rating	1	3
University arts programs rating	10	5

MUSEUMS	AREA	U.S. AVG
Overall museum rating	10	5
Art museum rating	9	5
Science museum rating	9	5
Children's museum rating	6	3

Washington–Arlington–Alexandria, DC-MD-VA-WV

Profile: National center
Location: Along the Potomac River between southern Maryland and northern Virginia, inland from Chesapeake Bay
Elevation: 26 feet
Time zone: Eastern Standard Time

PRO	CON
Uniquely attractive core	Growth and sprawl
Arts and culture	Cost of living
Historic interest	Summer heat

It would be an understatement to say that the nation's capital is a unique place. The centrally located National Mall is an urban planning gem, with excellent open spaces, walking paths, and major monuments in a classic architectural style. Lining the mall is the Smithsonian museum complex, probably the best set of museums in the world in a single location. In reality, the whole mall setup is a museum in and of itself and a major destination for locals and visitors alike. Numerous government offices and some first-class hospitality venues surround the mall. To the northwest of the mall, but still within the city limits, lies the upscale residential and commercial enclave of Georgetown, home to Georgetown University, George Washington Hospital, and a variety of entertainment and nightlife amenities. But not all of the D.C. central city glitters; to the north and east in particular lies a considerable expanse of socioeconomically mixed neighborhoods and areas of urban decay.

For most prospective residents, the real story of the D.C. area is the array of residential and commercial corridors surrounding the city on all sides. Just south across the Potomac in Virginia lies Fairfax County, a built-up area including the satellite city of Arlington and the larger suburbs of Alexandria, McLean, and the more upscale Fairfax. This is hardly the whole northern Virginia story—the sprawling D.C. suburbs spread for miles into the one-time countryside, south into Prince William County, and especially west into Loudoun County along the Dulles Airport corridor. The super-suburbs include such names as Reston, Herndon, and Ashburn, and extend even farther west to Leesburg, all very large and mostly new residential suburbs, some well planned and some not. Extensive commercial and corporate developments lie along the corridor with new-economy names such as AOL, Nextel, Siebel, Oracle, IBM, and Accenture mixed with numerous other businesses and government contractors. Employment in the greater D.C. area is strong in general and particularly strong in this zone. Many do commute to D.C. proper but more often commute to other places in the suburbs. The outlying northern Virginia suburbs in most ways meet the definition of exurbs, where people benefit economically from the city and may use its airport, but have little daily connection with it. There are museum-grade sprawl issues,

including traffic, air quality, and overbuilding—the latter of which has led to some significant real estate price dislocations. Areas east of the city are more industrial and generally uninspiring, while the Maryland suburbs along Interstate 270 northwest through Bethesda, Silver Spring, Rockville, and Gaithersburg have been split off into another metro area (p. 209).

The dominance of the U.S. government and its impact on the local economy and culture cannot be overstated. Not surprisingly, the area has a high percentage of well-educated citizens. But a significant number of educationally and economically disadvantaged people are also within its borders. Arts, entertainment, and cultural assets in total are among the best. At 140.6, the Cost of Living Index is high but not exorbitant for this type of area. Housing options and costs vary across the metropolitan area, and costs have escalated significantly in recent years, but there are signs of softening. Growth and sprawl is a major concern, with development and business activity flung farther out into the countryside and even across venerated Civil War historic sites. Public transportation works well as far out as Dulles Airport and northwest into Maryland, but whether it relieves traffic issues farther out is a wait-and-see.

Bottom line: Washington, D.C., and its Virginia suburbs stand alone as a U.S. city and metro area with unique beauty, plenty to see and do, a relatively active and intellectually stimulating lifestyle, and a wide variety of employment and living options. It does have downsides, and they are becoming strong enough even in the suburbs to negatively impact the ranking. The D.C. area isn't for everyone, but most who live there are glad they do.

Washington lies at the western edge of the mid-Atlantic Coastal Plain, about 50 miles east of the Blue Ridge Mountains and 35 miles west of Chesapeake Bay. The immediate area is flat with rolling hills starting just outside the city to the northwest and southwest. Summers are warm and humid with occasional hot, sticky spells and thunderstorms. Winters are cold but not severe. Precipitation is uniformly distributed throughout the year. Normal winter snowfall is 16 inches, but occasional heavy snows of 25 inches or more do occur. First freeze is early November; last is April 1.

DEMOGRAPHICS	AREA	U.S. AVG	ETHNIC COMPOSITION	AREA	U.S. AVG	RESIDENT PROFILE	AREA	U.S. AVG
Population	4,080,798		White	55.4%	79.0%	Single	36.1%	32.4%
Population density per sq. mile	913.2	358.5	Black	29.2%	10.5%	Married	49.1%	52.7%
Population growth	37.0%	21.1%	Asian	7.0%	2.7%	Divorced/separated	14.8%	14.9%
Median age	35.6	36.1	Hispanic	10.6%	10.6%	Married with children	24.8%	23.7%
Percent Democrat	62.2%	44.5%	Religious observance	43.2%	48.9%	Single with children	9.2%	9.1%
Percent Republican	37.0%	54.5%	Diversity measure	58.2	40.1	Percent over age 65	9.0%	12.9%

INCOME	AREA	U.S. AVG	EMPLOYMENT	AREA	U.S. AVG	EMPLOYING INDUSTRIES	AREA	U.S. AVG
Per capita income	$34,176	$23,235	Unemployment rate	3.6%	4.7%	Largest: Professional, Scientific & Technical Services		
Household income	$71,836	$46,414	Recent job growth	3.5%	1.3%			
Household income < $25K	13.0%	26.2%	Projected future job growth	16.8%	11.5%	Percent manufacturing	6.7%	15.4%
Household income > $75K	47.0%	25.4%	White collar	72.1%	57.8%	Percent public sector	24.6%	15.7%
Household income growth	13.9%	13.6%	Blue collar	14.4%	25.2%	Percent construction	7.6%	9.9%

Population

Economy & Jobs
Score: 88.2
Rank: 45

Cost of Living
Score: 5.9
Rank: 351

INDEXES & TAXES	AREA	U.S. AVG
Cost of Living Index	140.6	100.0
Buying Power Index	114.5	100.0
Income tax rate	9.50%	4.70%
Sales tax rate	5.11%	6.58%
Property tax rate	$11.23	$12.00

HOUSING	AREA	U.S. AVG
Median home price	$443,400	$220,000
Home price appreciation	121.3%	10.1%
Median rent	$1,273	$709
Homes owned	61.4%	62.3%
Home price ratio	6.2	4.2

NECESSITIES	AREA	U.S. AVG
Food Index	106.1	100.0
Housing Index	136.6	100.0
Utilities Index	93.7	100.0
Transportation Index	114.2	100.0
Healthcare Index	112.7	100.0
Miscellaneous Cost Index	105.1	100.0

Climate
Score: 42.2
Rank: 215

TEMPERATURE	AREA	U.S. AVG
Average January low	27.7	26.2
Average July high	88.2	87.4
Annual days > 90°F	37	38
Annual days < 32°F	75	89
Annual days < 0°F	0	6

PRECIPITATION	AREA	U.S. AVG
Annual inches precipitation	39.0	37.7
Annual inches snowfall	16.0	7.0
Annual days precipitation	111	109
Annual days rain > 0.5 inches	27	22
Annual days snow > 1.5 inches	4	6

COMFORTS & HAZARDS	AREA	U.S. AVG
July relative humidity	64%	66%
Annual days mostly sunny	207	208
Annual days with thunderstorms	29	39
Tornado risk score	12	18
Hurricane risk score	13	13

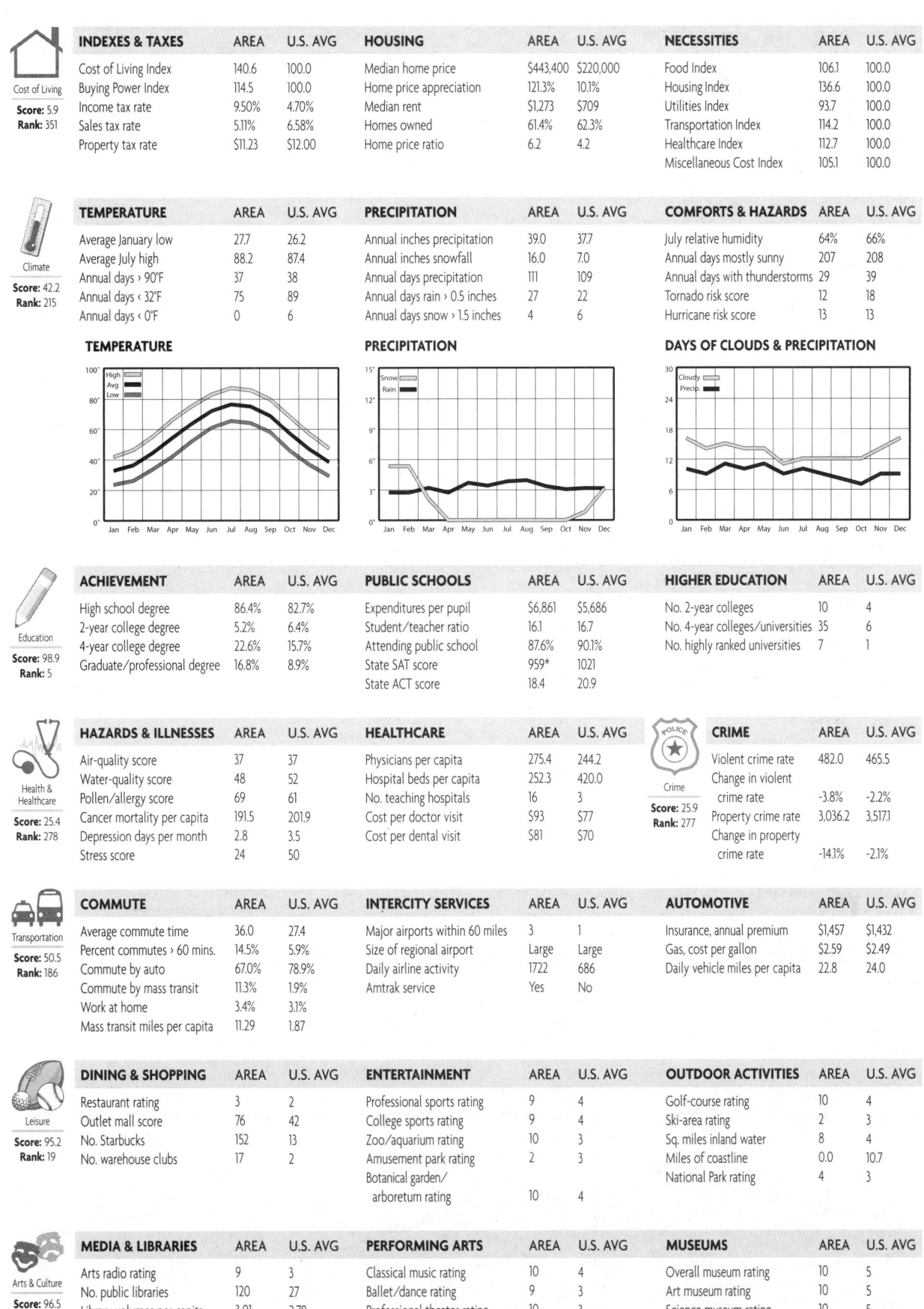

Education
Score: 98.9
Rank: 5

ACHIEVEMENT	AREA	U.S. AVG
High school degree	86.4%	82.7%
2-year college degree	5.2%	6.4%
4-year college degree	22.6%	15.7%
Graduate/professional degree	16.8%	8.9%

PUBLIC SCHOOLS	AREA	U.S. AVG
Expenditures per pupil	$6,861	$5,686
Student/teacher ratio	16.1	16.7
Attending public school	87.6%	90.1%
State SAT score	959*	1021
State ACT score	18.4	20.9

HIGHER EDUCATION	AREA	U.S. AVG
No. 2-year colleges	10	4
No. 4-year colleges/universities	35	6
No. highly ranked universities	7	1

Health & Healthcare
Score: 25.4
Rank: 278

HAZARDS & ILLNESSES	AREA	U.S. AVG
Air-quality score	37	37
Water-quality score	48	52
Pollen/allergy score	69	61
Cancer mortality per capita	191.5	201.9
Depression days per month	2.8	3.5
Stress score	24	50

HEALTHCARE	AREA	U.S. AVG
Physicians per capita	275.4	244.2
Hospital beds per capita	252.3	420.0
No. teaching hospitals	16	3
Cost per doctor visit	$93	$77
Cost per dental visit	$81	$70

Crime
Score: 25.9
Rank: 277

CRIME	AREA	U.S. AVG
Violent crime rate	482.0	465.5
Change in violent crime rate	-3.8%	-2.2%
Property crime rate	3,036.2	3,517.1
Change in property crime rate	-14.1%	-2.1%

Transportation
Score: 50.5
Rank: 186

COMMUTE	AREA	U.S. AVG
Average commute time	36.0	27.4
Percent commutes > 60 mins.	14.5%	5.9%
Commute by auto	67.0%	78.9%
Commute by mass transit	11.3%	1.9%
Work at home	3.4%	3.1%
Mass transit miles per capita	11.29	1.87

INTERCITY SERVICES	AREA	U.S. AVG
Major airports within 60 miles	3	1
Size of regional airport	Large	Large
Daily airline activity	1722	686
Amtrak service	Yes	No

AUTOMOTIVE	AREA	U.S. AVG
Insurance, annual premium	$1,457	$1,432
Gas, cost per gallon	$2.59	$2.49
Daily vehicle miles per capita	22.8	24.0

Leisure
Score: 95.2
Rank: 19

DINING & SHOPPING	AREA	U.S. AVG
Restaurant rating	3	2
Outlet mall score	76	42
No. Starbucks	152	13
No. warehouse clubs	17	2

ENTERTAINMENT	AREA	U.S. AVG
Professional sports rating	9	4
College sports rating	9	4
Zoo/aquarium rating	10	3
Amusement park rating	2	3
Botanical garden/ arboretum rating	10	4

OUTDOOR ACTIVITIES	AREA	U.S. AVG
Golf-course rating	10	4
Ski-area rating	2	3
Sq. miles inland water	8	4
Miles of coastline	0.0	10.7
National Park rating	4	3

Arts & Culture
Score: 96.5
Rank: 14

MEDIA & LIBRARIES	AREA	U.S. AVG
Arts radio rating	9	3
No. public libraries	120	27
Library volumes per capita	3.01	2.78

PERFORMING ARTS	AREA	U.S. AVG
Classical music rating	10	4
Ballet/dance rating	9	3
Professional theater rating	10	3
University arts programs rating	10	5

MUSEUMS	AREA	U.S. AVG
Overall museum rating	10	5
Art museum rating	10	5
Science museum rating	10	5
Children's museum rating	10	3

Waterloo–Cedar Falls, IA

Score: 66.6 **Rank:** 126 **2004 rank:** 113

Profile: Small-city complex
Location: Northeast Iowa along the Cedar River
Elevation: 868 feet
Time zone: Central Standard Time

PRO
Cost of living
Small-town lifestyle
Outdoor recreation

CON
Harsh winters
Economic cycles
Entertainment

The Waterloo–Cedar Falls area is a busy manufacturing and agricultural center dominated by such names as John Deere and Tyson Foods, among others. The downtown areas are typically Midwestern, functional, and an attractive mix of old and new. While entertainment and nightlife are minimal, there are waterfront parks, and a well-used bike trail runs 52 miles to Cedar Rapids on an old railroad grade. The area has two noted science museums. Cedar Falls lies 8 miles west of Waterloo and is home to the 13,000-student University of Northern Iowa. The area is vulnerable to the economic cycles of the farm industry, but has attractive housing costs and overall cost of living,

which at $108,200 and 80.3 respectively are among lowest in the state. Short commute times make it a stress-free place to live. Cedar Falls won a 2002 National Trust for Historic Preservation Great American Main Street Award.

Waterloo is situated on the banks of the Cedar River in northeast Iowa. The terrain is flat to gently rolling, mainly farmland. Summer is warm and humid, and receives most of the year's rainfall as thunderstorms. Winter is cold and dry with occasional snow. There is some bitter cold, with an average of 31 days per year with a high temperature below zero. First freeze is early October; last is late April.

Population

DEMOGRAPHICS	AREA	U.S. AVG	ETHNIC COMPOSITION	AREA	U.S. AVG	RESIDENT PROFILE	AREA	U.S. AVG
Population	161,638		White	89.8%	79.0%	Single	35.8%	32.4%
Population density per sq. mile	107.2	358.5	Black	6.4%	10.5%	Married	52.9%	52.7%
Population growth	1.9%	21.1%	Asian	1.2%	2.7%	Divorced/separated	11.3%	14.9%
Median age	36.6	36.1	Hispanic	1.7%	10.6%	Married with children	21.8%	23.7%
Percent Democrat	52.6%	44.5%	Religious observance	63.7%	48.9%	Single with children	7.9%	9.1%
Percent Republican	46.7%	54.5%	Diversity measure	21.3	40.1	Percent over age 65	15.0%	12.9%

Economy
& Jobs
Score: 51.6
Rank: 182

INCOME	AREA	U.S. AVG	EMPLOYMENT	AREA	U.S. AVG	EMPLOYING INDUSTRIES	AREA	U.S. AVG
Per capita income	$22,034	$23,235	Unemployment rate	3.9%	4.7%	Largest: Manufacturing		
Household income	$43,794	$46,414	Recent job growth	2.4%	1.3%			
Household income < $25K	25.7%	26.2%	Projected future job growth	5.1%	11.5%	Percent manufacturing	17.8%	15.4%
Household income > $75K	22.2%	25.4%	White collar	56.5%	57.8%	Percent public sector	14.4%	15.7%
Household income growth	15.4%	13.6%	Blue collar	26.1%	25.2%	Percent construction	8.3%	9.9%

Cost of Living
Score: 43.3
Rank: 212

INDEXES & TAXES	AREA	U.S. AVG	HOUSING	AREA	U.S. AVG	NECESSITIES	AREA	U.S. AVG
Cost of Living Index	80.3	100.0	Median home price	$108,200	$220,000	Food Index	89.5	100.0
Buying Power Index	122.2	100.0	Home price appreciation	33.3%	10.1%	Housing Index	38.6	100.0
Income tax rate	8.47%	4.70%	Median rent	$559	$709	Utilities Index	123.0	100.0
Sales tax rate	7.00%	6.58%	Homes owned	68.3%	62.3%	Transportation Index	99.8	100.0
Property tax rate	$12.97	$12.00	Home price ratio	2.5	4.2	Healthcare Index	92.6	100.0
						Miscellaneous Cost Index	99.0	100.0

Climate
Score: 28.6
Rank: 266

TEMPERATURE	AREA	U.S. AVG	PRECIPITATION	AREA	U.S. AVG	COMFORTS & HAZARDS	AREA	U.S. AVG
Average January low	6.9	26.2	Annual inches precipitation	34.0	37.7	July relative humidity	72%	66%
Average July high	83.6	87.4	Annual inches snowfall	31.0	7.0	Annual days mostly sunny	194	208
Annual days > 90°F	15	38	Annual days precipitation	99	109	Annual days with thunderstorms	43	39
Annual days > 32°F	159	89	Annual days rain > 0.5 inches	22	22	Tornado risk score	19	18
Annual days < 0°F	31	6	Annual days snow > 1.5 inches	6	6	Hurricane risk score	0	13

TEMPERATURE

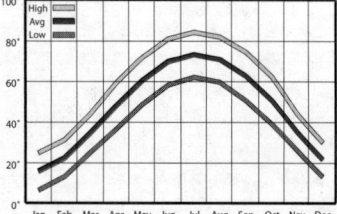

PRECIPITATION

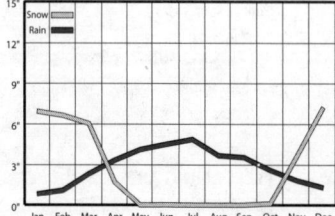

DAYS OF CLOUDS & PRECIPITATION

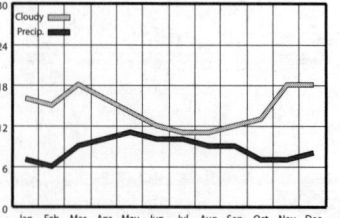

ACHIEVEMENT	AREA	U.S. AVG	PUBLIC SCHOOLS	AREA	U.S. AVG	HIGHER EDUCATION	AREA	U.S. AVG
High school degree	86.9%	82.7%	Expenditures per pupil	$4,741	$5,686	No. 2-year colleges	3	4
2-year college degree	7.7%	6.4%	Student/teacher ratio	16.8	16.7	No. 4-year colleges/universities	4	6
4-year college degree	14.7%	15.7%	Attending public school	88.0%	90.1%	No. highly ranked universities	1	1
Graduate/professional degree	8.3%	8.9%	State SAT score	1215	1021			
			State ACT score	22.1*	20.9			

Education
Score: 58.8
Rank: 155

HAZARDS & ILLNESSES	AREA	U.S. AVG	HEALTHCARE	AREA	U.S. AVG	CRIME	AREA	U.S. AVG
Air-quality score	49	37	Physicians per capita	195.4	244.2	Violent crime rate	321.7	465.5
Water-quality score	60	52	Hospital beds per capita	482.6	420.0	Change in violent crime rate	9.1%	-2.2%
Pollen/allergy score	43	61	No. teaching hospitals	2	3	Property crime rate	2,844.4	3,517.1
Cancer mortality per capita	217.4	201.9	Cost per doctor visit	$77	$77	Change in property crime rate	-8.4%	-2.1%
Depression days per month	2.8	3.5	Cost per dental visit	$53	$70			
Stress score	2	50						

Health & Healthcare
Score: 91.2
Rank: 34

Crime
Score: 75.7
Rank: 92

COMMUTE	AREA	U.S. AVG	INTERCITY SERVICES	AREA	U.S. AVG	AUTOMOTIVE	AREA	U.S. AVG
Average commute time	18.2	27.4	Major airports within 60 miles	0	1	Insurance, annual premium	$897	$1,432
Percent commutes > 60 mins.	2.8%	5.9%	Size of regional airport	Small	Large	Gas, cost per gallon	$2.40	$2.49
Commute by auto	82.0%	78.9%	Daily airline activity	164	686	Daily vehicle miles per capita	21.7	24.0
Commute by mass transit	0.7%	1.9%	Amtrak service	No	No			
Work at home	3.8%	3.1%						
Mass transit miles per capita	0.66	1.87						

Transportation
Score: 69.5
Rank: 115

DINING & SHOPPING	AREA	U.S. AVG	ENTERTAINMENT	AREA	U.S. AVG	OUTDOOR ACTIVITIES	AREA	U.S. AVG
Restaurant rating	1	2	Professional sports rating	2	4	Golf-course rating	3	4
Outlet mall score	14	42	College sports rating	4	4	Ski-area rating	3	3
No. Starbucks	1	13	Zoo/aquarium rating	1	3	Sq. miles inland water	1	4
No. warehouse clubs	1	2	Amusement park rating	1	3	Miles of coastline	0.0	10.7
			Botanical garden/ arboretum rating	1	4	National Park rating	1	3

Leisure
Score: 17.6
Rank: 307

MEDIA & LIBRARIES	AREA	U.S. AVG	PERFORMING ARTS	AREA	U.S. AVG	MUSEUMS	AREA	U.S. AVG
Arts radio rating	1	3	Classical music rating	4	4	Overall museum rating	5	5
No. public libraries	19	27	Ballet/dance rating	1	3	Art museum rating	7	5
Library volumes per capita	3.55	2.78	Professional theater rating	1	3	Science museum rating	5	5
			University arts programs rating	4	5	Children's museum rating	3	3

Arts & Culture
Score: 55.3
Rank: 167

Wausau, WI

Score: 52.2   Rank: 238   2004 rank: 208

Profile: Small city
Location: North-central Wisconsin
Elevation: 1,196 feet
Time zone: Central Standard Time

PRO
Small-town atmosphere
Outdoor recreation
Low crime rates

CON
Cold winters
Isolation
Recent economic weakness

Wausau is an agricultural center with diversified industry in forest products, paper, and food processing, and more recently insurance, financial services, and healthcare. The surrounding area is known for outdoor recreation, including watersports and hiking in summer and skiing and snowmobiling in winter. Some of the area's industries are clearly in transition as shown by the employment numbers, but we expect this area, which is gaining migrants from Chicago and other larger Wisconsin cities, to gain ground. The small downtown area underwent a recent renewal, and there is a large new hospital south of town. The railroad station bearing the Wausau name is an oft-seen insurance industry icon that exists in real life but is out of the way and not part of the downtown landscape. Wausau, like most small Wisconsin towns, has a strong and friendly community feel, good housing, and a family environment with a lot to offer for those tolerant of winter. The

climate and job questions hurt the ranking; long term, the area is probably better than the ranking indicates.

The area is the coldest in Wisconsin and one of the coldest in the nation. Wausau sits in a shallow valley along the upper reaches of the Wisconsin River. Areas to the east are rolling and mixed with woods and farmland. Agricultural areas to the west are more level. Farther to the north lie several areas of national and state forest. Summers are pleasant with only 4 days per year over 90°F. Spring and fall are variable with periods of pleasant dry weather, particularly in fall. Winters are harsh and cold as prevailing northwesterly winds deliver cold air. Lingering moisture from the south or from Lake Superior produces snow, sometimes heavy. Snow cover persists through the winter. First freeze is early October; last is mid-May.

Population

DEMOGRAPHICS	AREA	U.S. AVG	ETHNIC COMPOSITION	AREA	U.S. AVG	RESIDENT PROFILE	AREA	U.S. AVG
Population	128,677		White	92.9%	79.0%	Single	29.9%	32.4%
Population density per sq. mile	83.3	358.5	Black	0.4%	10.5%	Married	60.0%	52.7%
Population growth	11.5%	21.1%	Asian	5.2%	2.7%	Divorced/separated	10.1%	14.9%
Median age	37.8	36.1	Hispanic	1.0%	10.6%	Married with children	27.3%	23.7%
Percent Democrat	45.4%	44.5%	Religious observance	70.8%	48.9%	Single with children	6.5%	9.1%
Percent Republican	53.5%	54.5%	Diversity measure	15.0	40.1	Percent over age 65	13.3%	12.9%

Economy & Jobs
Score: 21.4
Rank: 294

INCOME	AREA	U.S. AVG	EMPLOYMENT	AREA	U.S. AVG	EMPLOYING INDUSTRIES	AREA	U.S. AVG
Per capita income	$24,140	$23,235	Unemployment rate	3.8%	4.7%	Largest: Manufacturing		
Household income	$51,282	$46,414	Recent job growth	-1.1%	1.3%			
Household income < $25K	19.7%	26.2%	Projected future job growth	2.9%	11.5%	Percent manufacturing	21.7%	15.4%
Household income > $75K	26.4%	25.4%	White collar	53.3%	57.8%	Percent public sector	9.4%	15.7%
Household income growth	13.5%	13.6%	Blue collar	30.6%	25.2%	Percent construction	8.8%	9.9%

Cost of Living
Score: 41.2
Rank: 220

INDEXES & TAXES	AREA	U.S. AVG	HOUSING	AREA	U.S. AVG	NECESSITIES	AREA	U.S. AVG
Cost of Living Index	85.3	100.0	Median home price	$132,700	$220,000	Food Index	97.0	100.0
Buying Power Index	134.8	100.0	Home price appreciation	32.5%	10.1%	Housing Index	56.0	100.0
Income tax rate	6.93%	4.70%	Median rent	$575	$709	Utilities Index	118.5	100.0
Sales tax rate	5.50%	6.58%	Homes owned	72.3%	62.3%	Transportation Index	100.2	100.0
Property tax rate	$19.31	$12.00	Home price ratio	2.6	4.2	Healthcare Index	107.2	100.0
						Miscellaneous Cost Index	95.6	100.0

Climate
Score: 13.9
Rank: 321

TEMPERATURE	AREA	U.S. AVG	PRECIPITATION	AREA	U.S. AVG	COMFORTS & HAZARDS	AREA	U.S. AVG
Average January low	3.1	26.2	Annual inches precipitation	29.0	37.7	July relative humidity	72%	66%
Average July high	77.0	87.4	Annual inches snowfall	55.0	7.0	Annual days mostly sunny	262	208
Annual days > 90°F	4	38	Annual days precipitation	185	109	Annual days with thunderstorms	40	39
Annual days < 32°F	170	89	Annual days rain > 0.5 inches	24	22	Tornado risk score	8	18
Annual days < 0°F	38	6	Annual days snow > 1.5 inches	13	6	Hurricane risk score	0	13

TEMPERATURE

PRECIPITATION

DAYS OF CLOUDS & PRECIPITATION

Education
Score: 40.9
Rank: 222

ACHIEVEMENT	AREA	U.S. AVG	PUBLIC SCHOOLS	AREA	U.S. AVG	HIGHER EDUCATION	AREA	U.S. AVG
High school degree	83.9%	82.7%	Expenditures per pupil	$6,157	$5,686	No. 2-year colleges	2	4
2-year college degree	9.3%	6.4%	Student/teacher ratio	15.8	16.7	No. 4-year colleges/universities	0	6
4-year college degree	12.7%	15.7%	Attending public school	86.5%	90.1%	No. highly ranked universities	0	1
Graduate/professional degree	5.6%	8.9%	State SAT score	1188	1021			
			State ACT score	22.2*	20.9			

Health & Healthcare
Score: 65.8
Rank: 129

Crime
Score: 90.1
Rank: 38

HAZARDS & ILLNESSES	AREA	U.S. AVG	HEALTHCARE	AREA	U.S. AVG	CRIME	AREA	U.S. AVG
Air-quality score	41	37	Physicians per capita	221.8	244.2	Violent crime rate	148.8	465.5
Water-quality score	50	52	Hospital beds per capita	484.9	420.0	Change in violent crime rate	2.4%	-2.2%
Pollen/allergy score	36	61	No. teaching hospitals	1	3	Property crime rate	1,880.6	3,517.1
Cancer mortality per capita	194.5	201.9	Cost per doctor visit	$103	$77	Change in property crime rate	-1.9%	-2.1%
Depression days per month	3.2	3.5	Cost per dental visit	$61	$70			
Stress score	5	50						

Transportation
Score: 48.9
Rank: 192

COMMUTE	AREA	U.S. AVG	INTERCITY SERVICES	AREA	U.S. AVG	AUTOMOTIVE	AREA	U.S. AVG
Average commute time	20.0	27.4	Major airports within 60 miles	0	1	Insurance, annual premium	$917	$1,432
Percent commutes > 60 mins.	3.1%	5.9%	Size of regional airport	Small	Large	Gas, cost per gallon	$2.55	$2.49
Commute by auto	81.3%	78.9%	Daily airline activity	39	686	Daily vehicle miles per capita	22.3	24.0
Commute by mass transit	0.9%	1.9%	Amtrak service	No	No			
Work at home	5.1%	3.1%						
Mass transit miles per capita	0.90	1.87						

DINING & SHOPPING	AREA	U.S. AVG	ENTERTAINMENT	AREA	U.S. AVG	OUTDOOR ACTIVITIES	AREA	U.S. AVG
Restaurant rating	1	2	Professional sports rating	2	4	Golf-course rating	1	4
Outlet mall score	0	42	College sports rating	1	4	Ski-area rating	2	3
No. Starbucks	1	13	Zoo/aquarium rating	1	3	Sq. miles inland water	3	4
No. warehouse clubs	0	2	Amusement park rating	1	3	Miles of coastline	0.0	10.7
			Botanical garden/ arboretum rating	2	4	National Park rating	1	3

Leisure Score: 5.3 Rank: 353

MEDIA & LIBRARIES	AREA	U.S. AVG	PERFORMING ARTS	AREA	U.S. AVG	MUSEUMS	AREA	U.S. AVG
Arts radio rating	1	3	Classical music rating	3	4	Overall museum rating	2	5
No. public libraries	8	27	Ballet/dance rating	1	3	Art museum rating	4	5
Library volumes per capita	2.69	2.78	Professional theater rating	1	3	Science museum rating	1	5
			University arts programs rating	1	5	Children's museum rating	1	3

Arts & Culture Score: 24.3 Rank: 282

Weirton–Steubenville, OH-WV

Score: 23.8 Rank: 358 2004 rank: 217

Profile: Small-town complex
Location: Southeast Ohio along the Ohio River at the West Virginia border
Elevation: 1,223 feet
Time zone: Eastern Standard Time

PRO	CON
Cost of living	Economic cycles
Attractive setting	Clouds and rain
Close to Pittsburgh	Entertainment

Weirton is one of the eastern Ohio Valley's region's many small steel towns, dominated by the large International Steel Group's Weirton works. That mill makes steel and steel products, and the fact that this industry is in a correction is hardly news. Steubenville, across the Ohio River also has a steel heritage but has begun to diversify. The decline of steel and its related industries has led to high unemployment, low job-growth prospects, and a significant population decline in recent years. But that trend has slowed and recent events position the area for a turnaround. A combination of low costs, local workforce, ground transport network, and strategic national location has brought a new Wal-Mart distribution facility, which reputedly covers more space and employs more people than the existing central business district. An additional economic boost should come from large Wal-Mart suppliers drawn to the area, but we don't think that effect is incorporated into the job-growth statistics, and prospects are probably better than the figures show. Pittsburgh and its amenities lie 50 miles to the east, and the otherwise physically attractive location may also turn out to be a strategic one if the economic cards fall right. But there isn't much to do and the weather can be dreary, and statistically the area is weak in many categories, leading to the low ranking. The economic promise and low cost of living, especially housing, make the area an interesting play for those with patience.

Steubenville is located on a level floodplain extending west from the Ohio River. Areas to the north and south are hilly with dense deciduous forests. Summers are warm and humid, while winters are fairly mild but subject to occasional cold snaps. Fall and spring are changeable. Long periods of cool, cloudy weather occur in all seasons. First freeze is late October; last is mid-April.

DEMOGRAPHICS	AREA	U.S. AVG	ETHNIC COMPOSITION	AREA	U.S. AVG	RESIDENT PROFILE	AREA	U.S. AVG
Population	127,280		White	94.4%	79.0%	Single	31.6%	32.4%
Population density per sq. mile	219.0	358.5	Black	4.0%	10.5%	Married	55.2%	52.7%
Population growth	-10.7%	21.1%	Asian	0.5%	2.7%	Divorced/separated	13.3%	14.9%
Median age	42.9	36.1	Hispanic	0.6%	10.6%	Married with children	19.2%	23.7%
Percent Democrat	51.0%	44.5%	Religious observance	44.8%	48.9%	Single with children	7.2%	9.1%
Percent Republican	48.3%	54.5%	Diversity measure	11.8	40.1	Percent over age 65	19.0%	12.9%

Population

INCOME	AREA	U.S. AVG	EMPLOYMENT	AREA	U.S. AVG	EMPLOYING INDUSTRIES	AREA	U.S. AVG
Per capita income	$19,445	$23,235	Unemployment rate	7.8%	4.7%	Largest: Manufacturing		
Household income	$36,036	$46,414	Recent job growth	-0.1%	1.3%			
Household income < $25K	34.1%	26.2%	Projected future job growth	-4.3%	11.5%	Percent manufacturing	21.2%	15.4%
Household income > $75K	14.8%	25.4%	White collar	49.0%	57.8%	Percent public sector	10.6%	15.7%
Household income growth	12.7%	13.6%	Blue collar	33.0%	25.2%	Percent construction	11.8%	9.9%

Economy & Jobs Score: 0.8 Rank: 370

INDEXES & TAXES	AREA	U.S. AVG	HOUSING	AREA	U.S. AVG	NECESSITIES	AREA	U.S. AVG
Cost of Living Index	79.7	100.0	Median home price	$88,100	$220,000	Food Index	100.9	100.0
Buying Power Index	101.3	100.0	Home price appreciation	30.3%	10.1%	Housing Index	37.8	100.0
Income tax rate	4.99%	4.70%	Median rent	$519	$709	Utilities Index	134.5	100.0
Sales tax rate	6.84%	6.58%	Homes owned	69.8%	62.3%	Transportation Index	94.2	100.0
Property tax rate	$8.52	$12.00	Home price ratio	2.4	4.2	Healthcare Index	90.0	100.0
						Miscellaneous Cost Index	98.2	100.0

Cost of Living Score: 85.3 Rank: 55

Climate
Score: 27.5
Rank: 270

TEMPERATURE	AREA	U.S. AVG	PRECIPITATION	AREA	U.S. AVG	COMFORTS & HAZARDS	AREA	U.S. AVG
Average January low	20.8	26.2	Annual inches precipitation	36.0	37.7	July relative humidity	68%	66%
Average July high	82.5	87.4	Annual inches snowfall	45.0	7.0	Annual days mostly sunny	161	208
Annual days > 90°F	7	38	Annual days precipitation	152	109	Annual days with thunderstorms	36	39
Annual days < 32°F	124	89	Annual days rain > 0.5 inches	27	22	Tornado risk score	3	18
Annual days < 0°F	5	6	Annual days snow > 1.5 inches	9	6	Hurricane risk score	3	13

TEMPERATURE

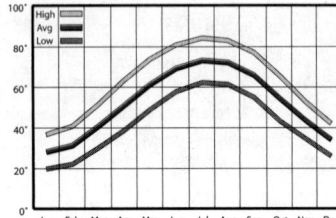

PRECIPITATION

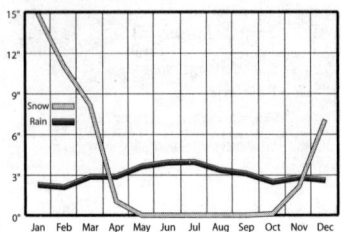

DAYS OF CLOUDS & PRECIPITATION

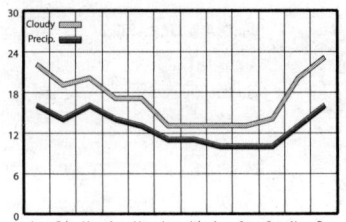

Education
Score: 11.0
Rank: 332

ACHIEVEMENT	AREA	U.S. AVG	PUBLIC SCHOOLS	AREA	U.S. AVG	HIGHER EDUCATION	AREA	U.S. AVG
High school degree	81.6%	82.7%	Expenditures per pupil	$5,475	$5,686	No. 2-year colleges	3	4
2-year college degree	6.2%	6.4%	Student/teacher ratio	16.8	16.7	No. 4-year colleges/universities	3	6
4-year college degree	8.0%	15.7%	Attending public school	89.6%	90.1%	No. highly ranked universities	0	1
Graduate/professional degree	4.0%	8.9%	State SAT score	1029	1021			
			State ACT score	20.6*	20.9			

Health & Healthcare
Score: 20.3
Rank: 297

HAZARDS & ILLNESSES	AREA	U.S. AVG	HEALTHCARE	AREA	U.S. AVG	CRIME	AREA	U.S. AVG
Air-quality score	29	37	Physicians per capita	139.9	244.2	Violent crime rate	212.4	465.5
Water-quality score	20	52	Hospital beds per capita	709.5	420.0	Change in violent crime rate	-4.0%	-2.2%
Pollen/allergy score	70	61	No. teaching hospitals	0	3	Property crime rate	1,889.2	3,517.1
Cancer mortality per capita	253.7	201.9	Cost per doctor visit	$74	$77	Change in property crime rate	6.8%	-2.1%
Depression days per month	3.7	3.5	Cost per dental visit	$78	$70			
Stress score	80	50						

Crime
Score: 97.1
Rank: 12

Transportation
Score: 82.6
Rank: 66

COMMUTE	AREA	U.S. AVG	INTERCITY SERVICES	AREA	U.S. AVG	AUTOMOTIVE	AREA	U.S. AVG
Average commute time	24.0	27.4	Major airports within 60 miles	2	1	Insurance, annual premium	$1,248	$1,432
Percent commutes > 60 mins.	5.7%	5.9%	Size of regional airport	Large	Large	Gas, cost per gallon	$2.47	$2.49
Commute by auto	85.4%	78.9%	Daily airline activity	1150	686	Daily vehicle miles per capita	22.4	24.0
Commute by mass transit	0.4%	1.9%	Amtrak service	No	No			
Work at home	1.9%	3.1%						
Mass transit miles per capita	0.42	1.87						

Leisure
Score: 6.4
Rank: 349

DINING & SHOPPING	AREA	U.S. AVG	ENTERTAINMENT	AREA	U.S. AVG	OUTDOOR ACTIVITIES	AREA	U.S. AVG
Restaurant rating	1	2	Professional sports rating	3	4	Golf-course rating	2	4
Outlet mall score	0	42	College sports rating	1	4	Ski-area rating	1	3
No. Starbucks	0	13	Zoo/aquarium rating	1	3	Sq. miles inland water	2	4
No. warehouse clubs	0	2	Amusement park rating	1	3	Miles of coastline	0.0	10.7
			Botanical garden/ arboretum rating	1	4	National Park rating	1	3

Arts & Culture
Score: 7.2
Rank: 346

MEDIA & LIBRARIES	AREA	U.S. AVG	PERFORMING ARTS	AREA	U.S. AVG	MUSEUMS	AREA	U.S. AVG
Arts radio rating	1	3	Classical music rating	1	4	Overall museum rating	1	5
No. public libraries	12	27	Ballet/dance rating	1	3	Art museum rating	1	5
Library volumes per capita	2.95	2.78	Professional theater rating	1	3	Science museum rating	1	5
			University arts programs rating	3	5	Children's museum rating	2	3

Wenatchee, WA

Score: 50.9 **Rank:** 244 **2004 rank:** not ranked

Profile: Small town
Location: Central Washington, east slope of Cascade Range
Elevation: 645 feet
Time zone: Pacific Standard Time

PRO	CON
Nearby mountains	Recent job declines
Year-round climate	Cost of housing
Attractive downtown	Isolation

Wenatchee is a mountain gateway between western Washington and the agricultural areas of the Columbia Plateau to the east. The economy is supported by agriculture and forest products and some retirees, but there have been some recent job dislocations. The physical setting is attractive and the original downtown area is pleasant (winning a National Trust for Historic Preservation 2003 Great American Main Street Award), but the geography doesn't support recent growth and ugly sprawl has emerged to the north of town. Still, on balance, the town is clean, quiet, and pleasant. Significant recreational opportunities are available in the Cascades to the west, starting with the funky European-style Leavenworth just 15 miles up the grade. Housing costs are high for the type of area. Wenatchee is a bit isolated; the northern suburbs of Seattle and Everett are 150 miles west, but it is a long haul across the 4,000-foot winter wonderland of Stevens Pass.

Wenatchee is located on a narrow Columbia River plain surrounded on all sides by mostly dry mountains and foothills of the Cascades. Elevations rise rapidly to 9,000 feet to the west, giving heavy forestation, but most of this is out of Wenatchee's view. The mountains create a deep rain shadow, giving plenty of sun and minimal precipitation, while the marine influence from the west creates a fairly stable and pleasant year-round climate.

Population

DEMOGRAPHICS	AREA	U.S. AVG	ETHNIC COMPOSITION	AREA	U.S. AVG	RESIDENT PROFILE	AREA	U.S. AVG
Population	103,216		White	83.3%	79.0%	Single	26.9%	32.4%
Population density per sq. mile	21.8	358.5	Black	0.3%	10.5%	Married	58.6%	52.7%
Population growth	31.6%	21.1%	Asian	0.8%	2.7%	Divorced/separated	14.5%	14.9%
Median age	36.8	36.1	Hispanic	20.7%	10.6%	Married with children	26.9%	23.7%
Percent Democrat	34.5%	44.5%	Religious observance	37.3%	48.9%	Single with children	8.6%	9.1%
Percent Republican	64.1%	54.5%	Diversity measure	52.3	40.1	Percent over age 65	13.9%	12.9%

Economy & Jobs
Score: 1.6
Rank: 367

INCOME	AREA	U.S. AVG	EMPLOYMENT	AREA	U.S. AVG	EMPLOYING INDUSTRIES	AREA	U.S. AVG
Per capita income	$21,470	$23,235	Unemployment rate	4.2%	4.7%	Largest: Healthcare & Social Assistance		
Household income	$43,980	$46,414	Recent job growth	-3.1%	1.3%			
Household income ‹ $25K	26.5%	26.2%	Projected future job growth	6.5%	11.5%	Percent manufacturing	12.3%	15.4%
Household income › $75K	23.6%	25.4%	White collar	51.3%	57.8%	Percent public sector	18.1%	15.7%
Household income growth	16.7%	13.6%	Blue collar	21.7%	25.2%	Percent construction	9.4%	9.9%

Cost of Living
Score: 57.8
Rank: 158

INDEXES & TAXES	AREA	U.S. AVG	HOUSING	AREA	U.S. AVG	NECESSITIES	AREA	U.S. AVG
Cost of Living Index	97.4	100.0	Median home price	$209,300	$220,000	Food Index	102.6	100.0
Buying Power Index	101.2	100.0	Home price appreciation	38.4%	10.1%	Housing Index	76.1	100.0
Income tax rate	0.00%	4.70%	Median rent	$650	$709	Utilities Index	50.2	100.0
Sales tax rate	7.87%	6.58%	Homes owned	57.2%	62.3%	Transportation Index	115.1	100.0
Property tax rate	$11.63	$12.00	Home price ratio	4.8	4.2	Healthcare Index	119.2	100.0
						Miscellaneous Cost Index	102.7	100.0

Climate
Score: 77.0
Rank: 86

TEMPERATURE	AREA	U.S. AVG	PRECIPITATION	AREA	U.S. AVG	COMFORTS & HAZARDS	AREA	U.S. AVG
Average January low	24.3	26.2	Annual inches precipitation	8.9	37.7	July relative humidity	28%	66%
Average July high	87.9	87.4	Annual inches snowfall	27.2	7.0	Annual days mostly sunny	202	208
Annual days › 90°F	33	38	Annual days precipitation	70	109	Annual days with thunderstorms	7	39
Annual days ‹ 32°F	115	89	Annual days rain › 0.5 inches	4	22	Tornado risk score	1	18
Annual days ‹ 0°F	2	6	Annual days snow › 1.5 inches	7	6	Hurricane risk score	0	13

TEMPERATURE

PRECIPITATION

DAYS OF CLOUDS & PRECIPITATION

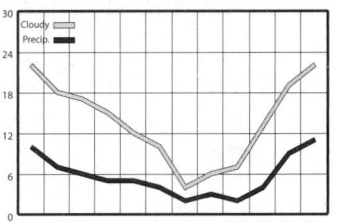

ACHIEVEMENT	AREA	U.S. AVG	PUBLIC SCHOOLS	AREA	U.S. AVG	HIGHER EDUCATION	AREA	U.S. AVG
High school degree	78.8%	82.7%	Expenditures per pupil	$6,340	$5,686	No. 2-year colleges	2	4
2-year college degree	7.2%	6.4%	Student/teacher ratio	18.2	16.7	No. 4-year colleges/universities	0	6
4-year college degree	13.6%	15.7%	Attending public school	97.5%	90.1%	No. highly ranked universities	0	1
Graduate/professional degree	6.6%	8.9%	State SAT score	1059*	1021			
			State ACT score	22.9	20.9			

Education
Score: 43.0
Rank: 214

HAZARDS & ILLNESSES	AREA	U.S. AVG	HEALTHCARE	AREA	U.S. AVG	CRIME	AREA	U.S. AVG
Air-quality score	62	37	Physicians per capita	205.2	244.2	Violent crime rate	208.0	465.5
Water-quality score	59	52	Hospital beds per capita	264.5	420.0	Change in violent crime rate	-1.8%	-2.2%
Pollen/allergy score	47	61	No. teaching hospitals	0	3	Property crime rate	4,058.6	3,517.1
Cancer mortality per capita	163.0	201.9	Cost per doctor visit	$86	$77	Change in property crime rate	-8.7%	-2.1%
Depression days per month	2.9	3.5	Cost per dental visit	$88	$70			
Stress score	9	50						

Health & Healthcare
Score: 86.4
Rank: 52

Crime
Score: 69.5
Rank: 115

COMMUTE	AREA	U.S. AVG	INTERCITY SERVICES	AREA	U.S. AVG	AUTOMOTIVE	AREA	U.S. AVG
Average commute time	19.7	27.4	Major airports within 60 miles	1	1	Insurance, annual premium	$1,160	$1,432
Percent commutes > 60 mins.	4.1%	5.9%	Size of regional airport	Large	Large	Gas, cost per gallon	$2.53	$2.49
Commute by auto	74.4%	78.9%	Daily airline activity	698	686	Daily vehicle miles per capita	16.5	24.0
Commute by mass transit	1.0%	1.9%	Amtrak service	Yes	No			
Work at home	5.1%	3.1%						
Mass transit miles per capita	0.97	1.87						

Transportation
Score: 86.9
Rank: 50

DINING & SHOPPING	AREA	U.S. AVG	ENTERTAINMENT	AREA	U.S. AVG	OUTDOOR ACTIVITIES	AREA	U.S. AVG
Restaurant rating	1	2	Professional sports rating	1	4	Golf-course rating	2	4
Outlet mall score	0	42	College sports rating	1	4	Ski-area rating	3	3
No. Starbucks	4	13	Zoo/aquarium rating	1	3	Sq. miles inland water	4	4
No. warehouse clubs	1	2	Amusement park rating	1	3	Miles of coastline	0.0	10.7
			Botanical garden/ arboretum rating	1	4	National Park rating	3	3

Leisure
Score: 19.8
Rank: 299

MEDIA & LIBRARIES	AREA	U.S. AVG	PERFORMING ARTS	AREA	U.S. AVG	MUSEUMS	AREA	U.S. AVG
Arts radio rating	1	3	Classical music rating	2	4	Overall museum rating	3	5
No. public libraries	27	27	Ballet/dance rating	1	3	Art museum rating	5	5
Library volumes per capita	3.68	2.78	Professional theater rating	1	3	Science museum rating	3	5
			University arts programs rating	1	5	Children's museum rating	1	3

Arts & Culture
Score: 40.9
Rank: 221

West Palm Beach–Boca Raton–Boynton Beach, FL

Score: 57.1   Rank: 198   2004 rank: 69

Profile: Large-beach-city complex
Location: Easternmost point of Florida Peninsula along south Atlantic Coast
Elevation: 18 feet
Time zone: Eastern Standard Time

PRO
Leisure activities
Arts and culture
Strong economy

CON
Growth and sprawl
Cost of living
High crime rates

West Palm Beach is a complex area with the typical Florida east coast arrangement of a barrier island and a series of inland communities. The barrier island of Palm Beach is an old-money, retirement, and snowbird enclave, while the series of communities along the inland coast, including West Palm Beach and Boynton Beach, contain a socioeconomic mix and are the more "real" places with ordinary residential and commercial development. Delray Beach and Boca Raton are along the coast further south, and Boca in particular is also more upscale. Boca has an interesting commercial history, once the main campus for IBM's mainframe computer and manufacturing operations, since sold off as a technology park. The city went through a period of decline and renewal, with tight planning standards giving a more-attractive-than-most streetscape. West Palm Beach is growing rapidly to the limits presented by swampland to the west and is experiencing the high-rise condo boom observed elsewhere in Florida. The region has leisure activities typical of a Florida tourist destination, and a number of quality museums, including the Norton Museum of Art, the largest such museum in Florida. Educational attainment is high and the economic picture is healthy relative to most of the state. The area has its own scheduled commercial jet service. Downsides include crowding and sprawl to the south and west, violent crime, some air-quality issues, and a cost of living and housing profile among the state's highest and growing rapidly.

Palm Beach is on a long, narrow, barrier island, separated by a narrow, coastal waterway from the mainland. Inland, a narrow, sandy, coastal plain includes land reclaimed from western swamps initially for agriculture and now for development. The Gulf Stream flows northward about 2 miles offshore, its nearest approach to the Florida coast, creating excellent ocean swimming and climate. Summers are warm and humid with sea breezes and afternoon showers. Winters are mild but can be quite warm.

Population

DEMOGRAPHICS	AREA	U.S. AVG
Population	1,250,845	
Population density per sq. mile	633.6	358.5
Population growth	44.9%	21.1%
Median age	42.2	36.1
Percent Democrat	60.4%	44.5%
Percent Republican	39.1%	54.5%

ETHNIC COMPOSITION	AREA	U.S. AVG
White	76.0%	79.0%
Black	15.4%	10.5%
Asian	1.9%	2.7%
Hispanic	15.8%	10.6%
Religious observance	55.9%	48.9%
Diversity measure	55.7	40.1

RESIDENT PROFILE	AREA	U.S. AVG
Single	30.5%	32.4%
Married	54.1%	52.7%
Divorced/separated	15.4%	14.9%
Married with children	17.6%	23.7%
Single with children	7.2%	9.1%
Percent over age 65	22.3%	12.9%

Economy & Jobs
Score: 86.6
Rank: 51

INCOME	AREA	U.S. AVG
Per capita income	$31,918	$23,235
Household income	$50,747	$46,414
Household income < $25K	22.3%	26.2%
Household income > $75K	31.8%	25.4%
Household income growth	12.6%	13.6%

EMPLOYMENT	AREA	U.S. AVG
Unemployment rate	4.5%	4.7%
Recent job growth	4.0%	1.3%
Projected future job growth	21.7%	11.5%
White collar	63.7%	57.8%
Blue collar	17.9%	25.2%

EMPLOYING INDUSTRIES	AREA	U.S. AVG
Largest: Healthcare & Social Assistance		
Percent manufacturing	8.3%	15.4%
Percent public sector	11.9%	15.7%
Percent construction	9.6%	9.9%

Cost of Living
Score: 9.4
Rank: 338

INDEXES & TAXES	AREA	U.S. AVG
Cost of Living Index	134.4	100.0
Buying Power Index	84.6	100.0
Income tax rate	0.00%	4.70%
Sales tax rate	6.50%	6.58%
Property tax rate	$16.75	$12.00

HOUSING	AREA	U.S. AVG
Median home price	$410,400	$220,000
Home price appreciation	141.2%	10.1%
Median rent	$1,057	$709
Homes owned	64.1%	62.3%
Home price ratio	8.1	4.2

NECESSITIES	AREA	U.S. AVG
Food Index	107.7	100.0
Housing Index	111.1	100.0
Utilities Index	96.8	100.0
Transportation Index	109.3	100.0
Healthcare Index	114.5	100.0
Miscellaneous Cost Index	106.7	100.0

Climate
Score: 65.8
Rank: 127

TEMPERATURE	AREA	U.S. AVG
Average January low	55.9	26.2
Average July high	89.6	87.4
Annual days > 90°F	55	38
Annual days < 32°F	1	89
Annual days < 0°F	0	6

PRECIPITATION	AREA	U.S. AVG
Annual inches precipitation	62.1	37.7
Annual inches snowfall	0.0	7.0
Annual days precipitation	131	109
Annual days rain > 0.5 inches	37	22
Annual days snow > 1.5 inches	0	6

COMFORTS & HAZARDS	AREA	U.S. AVG
July relative humidity	73%	66%
Annual days mostly sunny	228	208
Annual days with thunderstorms	79	39
Tornado risk score	37	18
Hurricane risk score	100	13

TEMPERATURE
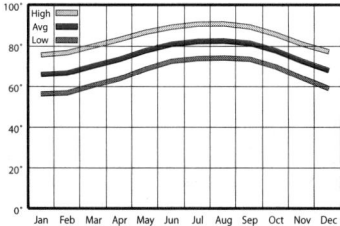

PRECIPITATION
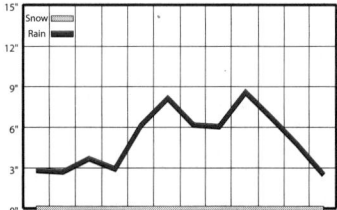

DAYS OF CLOUDS & PRECIPITATION
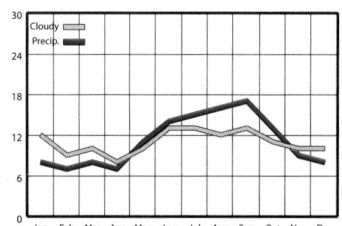

Education
Score: 59.6
Rank: 152

ACHIEVEMENT	AREA	U.S. AVG
High school degree	83.8%	82.7%
2-year college degree	6.7%	6.4%
4-year college degree	17.7%	15.7%
Graduate/professional degree	10.2%	8.9%

PUBLIC SCHOOLS	AREA	U.S. AVG
Expenditures per pupil	$5,300	$5,686
Student/teacher ratio	17.5	16.7
Attending public school	86.4%	90.1%
State SAT score	993*	1021
State ACT score	20.3	20.9

HIGHER EDUCATION	AREA	U.S. AVG
No. 2-year colleges	4	4
No. 4-year colleges/universities	8	6
No. highly ranked universities	0	1

Health & Healthcare
Score: 7.8
Rank: 344

HAZARDS & ILLNESSES	AREA	U.S. AVG
Air-quality score	11	37
Water-quality score	30	52
Pollen/allergy score	52	61
Cancer mortality per capita	229.3	201.9
Depression days per month	3.0	3.5
Stress score	66	50

HEALTHCARE	AREA	U.S. AVG
Physicians per capita	263.0	244.2
Hospital beds per capita	302.0	420.0
No. teaching hospitals	2	3
Cost per doctor visit	$87	$77
Cost per dental visit	$93	$70

Crime
Score: 20.9
Rank: 296

CRIME	AREA	U.S. AVG
Violent crime rate	669.4	465.5
Change in violent crime rate	-7.1%	-2.2%
Property crime rate	4,290.7	3,517.1
Change in property crime rate	-9.3%	-2.1%

Transportation
Score: 74.1
Rank: 98

COMMUTE	AREA	U.S. AVG	INTERCITY SERVICES	AREA	U.S. AVG	AUTOMOTIVE	AREA	U.S. AVG
Average commute time	27.7	27.4	Major airports within 60 miles	4	1	Insurance, annual premium	$2,010	$1,432
Percent commutes › 60 mins.	6.7%	5.9%	Size of regional airport	Large	Large	Gas, cost per gallon	$2.66	$2.49
Commute by auto	79.9%	78.9%	Daily airline activity	1262	686	Daily vehicle miles per capita	26.9	24.0
Commute by mass transit	1.3%	1.9%	Amtrak service	Yes	No			
Work at home	4.1%	3.1%						
Mass transit miles per capita	1.34	1.87						

Leisure
Score: 83.7
Rank: 61

DINING & SHOPPING	AREA	U.S. AVG	ENTERTAINMENT	AREA	U.S. AVG	OUTDOOR ACTIVITIES	AREA	U.S. AVG
Restaurant rating	5	2	Professional sports rating	3	4	Golf-course rating	10	4
Outlet mall score	104	42	College sports rating	3	4	Ski-area rating	1	3
No. Starbucks	24	13	Zoo/aquarium rating	5	3	Sq. miles inland water	10	4
No. warehouse clubs	6	2	Amusement park rating	1	3	Miles of coastline	45.7	10.7
			Botanical garden/ arboretum rating	6	4	National Park rating	2	3

Arts & Culture
Score: 73.8
Rank: 98

MEDIA & LIBRARIES	AREA	U.S. AVG	PERFORMING ARTS	AREA	U.S. AVG	MUSEUMS	AREA	U.S. AVG
Arts radio rating	5	3	Classical music rating	5	4	Overall museum rating	7	5
No. public libraries	25	27	Ballet/dance rating	5	3	Art museum rating	9	5
Library volumes per capita	1.62	2.78	Professional theater rating	7	3	Science museum rating	7	5
			University arts programs rating	6	5	Children's museum rating	9	3

Wheeling, WV-OH

Score: 56.0 Rank: 206 2004 rank: 305

Profile: Small city
Location: Northern West Virginia Panhandle along the Ohio River between the Ohio and Pennsylvania borders
Elevation: 645 feet
Time zone: Eastern Standard Time

PRO
Attractive setting
Historic interest
Close to Pittsburgh

CON
Clouds and rain
Industrial feel
Educational attainment

Once a gateway for travelers coming west across the National Road (U.S. 40), Wheeling remains a central point on transportation networks with good access to the Northeast and Midwest. The metro area includes Belmont County with Martins Ferry and a few other small towns in southeastern Ohio. The main industries are steel and metalworking. Wheeling-Pittsburgh Steel employs more than 4,000 people. The city has a well-preserved older section downtown and a few arts and entertainment amenities including a small but energetic symphony and two minor league sports teams. With Pittsburgh 60 miles to the northeast, big-city features aren't too far away. Downsides include low job-growth projections and a cloudy, wet climate. But many predict that the strategic location, low overall costs, and proximity to Pittsburgh will attract new businesses. These forces are already at work in nearby Steubenville, Ohio, but the area has low educational attainment and an aging blue-collar population mix; the transition will take time.

Wheeling sits on the east bank of the Ohio River in a narrow plain with steep, deciduous-wooded hills on all sides. Summers are warm and humid, particularly in the bottom of the valley. Winters are fairly mild, but are subject to occasional cold snaps. Fall and spring are changeable, with periods of cool, cloudy weather—making the area one of the cloudiest and rainiest in the country.

Population

DEMOGRAPHICS	AREA	U.S. AVG	ETHNIC COMPOSITION	AREA	U.S. AVG	RESIDENT PROFILE	AREA	U.S. AVG
Population	149,366		White	95.3%	79.0%	Single	32.2%	32.4%
Population density per sq. mile	157.1	358.5	Black	3.1%	10.5%	Married	53.5%	52.7%
Population growth	-6.1%	21.1%	Asian	0.5%	2.7%	Divorced/separated	14.3%	14.9%
Median age	41.9	36.1	Hispanic	0.5%	10.6%	Married with children	20.1%	23.7%
Percent Democrat	47.1%	44.5%	Religious observance	52.0%	48.9%	Single with children	7.6%	9.1%
Percent Republican	52.2%	54.5%	Diversity measure	9.9	40.1	Percent over age 65	18.2%	12.9%

Economy & Jobs
Score: 25.4
Rank: 279

INCOME	AREA	U.S. AVG	EMPLOYMENT	AREA	U.S. AVG	EMPLOYING INDUSTRIES	AREA	U.S. AVG
Per capita income	$19,152	$23,235	Unemployment rate	5.2%	4.7%	Largest: Healthcare & Social Assistance		
Household income	$34,195	$46,414	Recent job growth	2.1%	1.3%			
Household income ‹ $25K	37.4%	26.2%	Projected future job growth	3.7%	11.5%	Percent manufacturing	16.8%	15.4%
Household income › $75K	15.3%	25.4%	White collar	52.7%	57.8%	Percent public sector	14.0%	15.7%
Household income growth	12.7%	13.6%	Blue collar	28.5%	25.2%	Percent construction	11.7%	9.9%

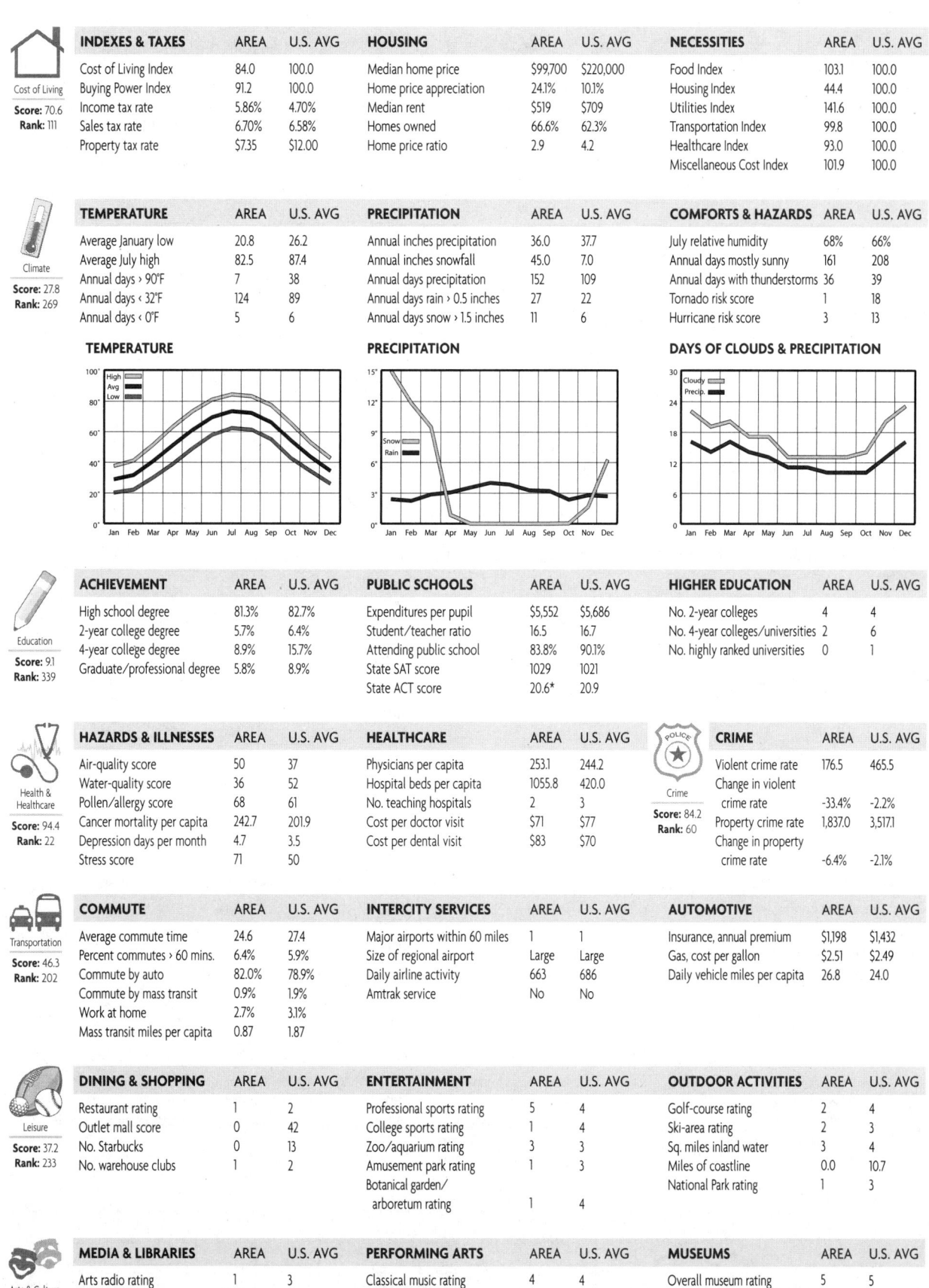

INDEXES & TAXES	AREA	U.S. AVG	HOUSING	AREA	U.S. AVG	NECESSITIES	AREA	U.S. AVG
Cost of Living Index	84.0	100.0	Median home price	$99,700	$220,000	Food Index	103.1	100.0
Buying Power Index	91.2	100.0	Home price appreciation	24.1%	10.1%	Housing Index	44.4	100.0
Income tax rate	5.86%	4.70%	Median rent	$519	$709	Utilities Index	141.6	100.0
Sales tax rate	6.70%	6.58%	Homes owned	66.6%	62.3%	Transportation Index	99.8	100.0
Property tax rate	$7.35	$12.00	Home price ratio	2.9	4.2	Healthcare Index	93.0	100.0
						Miscellaneous Cost Index	101.9	100.0

Cost of Living — Score: 70.6 — Rank: 111

TEMPERATURE	AREA	U.S. AVG	PRECIPITATION	AREA	U.S. AVG	COMFORTS & HAZARDS	AREA	U.S. AVG
Average January low	20.8	26.2	Annual inches precipitation	36.0	37.7	July relative humidity	68%	66%
Average July high	82.5	87.4	Annual inches snowfall	45.0	7.0	Annual days mostly sunny	161	208
Annual days > 90°F	7	38	Annual days precipitation	152	109	Annual days with thunderstorms	36	39
Annual days < 32°F	124	89	Annual days rain > 0.5 inches	27	22	Tornado risk score	1	18
Annual days < 0°F	5	6	Annual days snow > 1.5 inches	11	6	Hurricane risk score	3	13

Climate — Score: 27.8 — Rank: 269

TEMPERATURE / PRECIPITATION / DAYS OF CLOUDS & PRECIPITATION

ACHIEVEMENT	AREA	U.S. AVG	PUBLIC SCHOOLS	AREA	U.S. AVG	HIGHER EDUCATION	AREA	U.S. AVG
High school degree	81.3%	82.7%	Expenditures per pupil	$5,552	$5,686	No. 2-year colleges	4	4
2-year college degree	5.7%	6.4%	Student/teacher ratio	16.5	16.7	No. 4-year colleges/universities	2	6
4-year college degree	8.9%	15.7%	Attending public school	83.8%	90.1%	No. highly ranked universities	0	1
Graduate/professional degree	5.8%	8.9%	State SAT score	1029	1021			
			State ACT score	20.6*	20.9			

Education — Score: 9.1 — Rank: 339

HAZARDS & ILLNESSES	AREA	U.S. AVG	HEALTHCARE	AREA	U.S. AVG	CRIME	AREA	U.S. AVG
Air-quality score	50	37	Physicians per capita	253.1	244.2	Violent crime rate	176.5	465.5
Water-quality score	36	52	Hospital beds per capita	1055.8	420.0	Change in violent crime rate	-33.4%	-2.2%
Pollen/allergy score	68	61	No. teaching hospitals	2	3	Property crime rate	1,837.0	3,517.1
Cancer mortality per capita	242.7	201.9	Cost per doctor visit	$71	$77	Change in property crime rate	-6.4%	-2.1%
Depression days per month	4.7	3.5	Cost per dental visit	$83	$70			
Stress score	71	50						

Health & Healthcare — Score: 94.4 — Rank: 22. Crime — Score: 84.2 — Rank: 60

COMMUTE	AREA	U.S. AVG	INTERCITY SERVICES	AREA	U.S. AVG	AUTOMOTIVE	AREA	U.S. AVG
Average commute time	24.6	27.4	Major airports within 60 miles	1	1	Insurance, annual premium	$1,198	$1,432
Percent commutes > 60 mins.	6.4%	5.9%	Size of regional airport	Large	Large	Gas, cost per gallon	$2.51	$2.49
Commute by auto	82.0%	78.9%	Daily airline activity	663	686	Daily vehicle miles per capita	26.8	24.0
Commute by mass transit	0.9%	1.9%	Amtrak service	No	No			
Work at home	2.7%	3.1%						
Mass transit miles per capita	0.87	1.87						

Transportation — Score: 46.3 — Rank: 202

DINING & SHOPPING	AREA	U.S. AVG	ENTERTAINMENT	AREA	U.S. AVG	OUTDOOR ACTIVITIES	AREA	U.S. AVG
Restaurant rating	1	2	Professional sports rating	5	4	Golf-course rating	2	4
Outlet mall score	0	42	College sports rating	1	4	Ski-area rating	2	3
No. Starbucks	0	13	Zoo/aquarium rating	3	3	Sq. miles inland water	3	4
No. warehouse clubs	1	2	Amusement park rating	1	3	Miles of coastline	0.0	10.7
			Botanical garden/arboretum rating	1	4	National Park rating	1	3

Leisure — Score: 37.2 — Rank: 233

MEDIA & LIBRARIES	AREA	U.S. AVG	PERFORMING ARTS	AREA	U.S. AVG	MUSEUMS	AREA	U.S. AVG
Arts radio rating	1	3	Classical music rating	4	4	Overall museum rating	5	5
No. public libraries	17	27	Ballet/dance rating	1	3	Art museum rating	7	5
Library volumes per capita	3.78	2.78	Professional theater rating	1	3	Science museum rating	6	5
			University arts programs rating	4	5	Children's museum rating	1	3

Arts & Culture — Score: 57.5 — Rank: 159

Wichita, KS

Score: 80.0 **Rank:** 43 **2004 rank:** 35

Profile: Mid-size city
Location: South-central Kansas along the Arkansas River
Elevation: 1,340 feet
Time zone: Central Standard Time

PRO	CON
Cost of living	Harsh climate
Attractive downtown	Economic cycles
Arts and culture	Isolation

It may surprise some, but Wichita is the largest city in Kansas (remember, most of Kansas City is in Missouri). Surrounded by wheat fields and oil-industry facilities, this traditional Midwestern city has a diverse agricultural and industrial economy. In part because of its invulnerable central U.S. location, World War II aircraft design and production facilities were located in the area. Today, aviation firms such as Beech, Cessna (Raytheon), Stearman, Lear (Bombardier), and Boeing all have plants nearby, and there are numerous supporting precision parts and engineering firms in the area. That industry has been very cyclical, and has recently started to emerge from a down cycle, giving very slowly improving, but still weak, employment signals. Downtown Wichita has undergone renewal, and the city center has new and attractive parks and a new convention center along the Arkansas River among other attractions. Arts and entertainment facilities are stronger than one might expect for the type of city, and

community feel is strong. The workforce is relatively well educated and well paid, the Cost of Living Index is very reasonable at 80.8, and very good housing values can be found. With 170 miles to Tulsa and 190 miles to Kansas City, residents are mainly dependent on local features. The area ranks consistently well in most categories giving a high overall ranking.

Wichita is mainly flat with trees along the river and its tributaries. Summers are usually warm and humid, but can be extremely hot and dry. Winters are usually mild with brief periods of very cold weather and high windchill. Summer temperatures above 90°F are common, while winter below-zero highs occur about 2 days per year. Seventy percent of precipitation falls from April through September. The range of annual precipitation is notable, with over 50 inches in wet years and less than 15 in dry years. Thunderstorms occur mainly during spring and early summer with potential for damaging rain, hail, winds, and tornadoes.

Population

DEMOGRAPHICS	AREA	U.S. AVG	ETHNIC COMPOSITION	AREA	U.S. AVG	RESIDENT PROFILE	AREA	U.S. AVG
Population	587,939		White	80.7%	79.0%	Single	28.8%	32.4%
Population density per sq. mile	141.7	358.5	Black	7.7%	10.5%	Married	56.7%	52.7%
Population growth	15.3%	21.1%	Asian	3.2%	2.7%	Divorced/separated	14.5%	14.9%
Median age	35.0	36.1	Hispanic	8.5%	10.6%	Married with children	25.9%	23.7%
Percent Democrat	35.3%	44.5%	Religious observance	48.5%	48.9%	Single with children	8.7%	9.1%
Percent Republican	63.3%	54.5%	Diversity measure	43.2	40.1	Percent over age 65	12.0%	12.9%

Economy & Jobs

Score: 20.6
Rank: 297

INCOME	AREA	U.S. AVG	EMPLOYMENT	AREA	U.S. AVG	EMPLOYING INDUSTRIES	AREA	U.S. AVG
Per capita income	$23,196	$23,235	Unemployment rate	6.1%	4.7%	Largest: Manufacturing		
Household income	$47,582	$46,414	Recent job growth	-0.6%	1.3%			
Household income < $25K	23.3%	26.2%	Projected future job growth	4.8%	11.5%	Percent manufacturing	16.1%	15.4%
Household income > $75K	25.6%	25.4%	White collar	58.2%	57.8%	Percent public sector	12.1%	15.7%
Household income growth	11.7%	13.6%	Blue collar	27.3%	25.2%	Percent construction	11.2%	9.9%

Cost of Living

Score: 59.4
Rank: 152

INDEXES & TAXES	AREA	U.S. AVG	HOUSING	AREA	U.S. AVG	NECESSITIES	AREA	U.S. AVG
Cost of Living Index	80.8	100.0	Median home price	$111,500	$220,000	Food Index	96.8	100.0
Buying Power Index	132.0	100.0	Home price appreciation	20.2%	10.1%	Housing Index	41.1	100.0
Income tax rate	6.25%	4.70%	Median rent	$614	$709	Utilities Index	106.5	100.0
Sales tax rate	6.24%	6.58%	Homes owned	63.8%	62.3%	Transportation Index	94.3	100.0
Property tax rate	$13.08	$12.00	Home price ratio	2.3	4.2	Healthcare Index	99.2	100.0
						Miscellaneous Cost Index	99.0	100.0

Climate

Score: 58.6
Rank: 154

TEMPERATURE	AREA	U.S. AVG	PRECIPITATION	AREA	U.S. AVG	COMFORTS & HAZARDS	AREA	U.S. AVG
Average January low	21.2	26.2	Annual inches precipitation	31.0	37.7	July relative humidity	66%	66%
Average July high	91.7	87.4	Annual inches snowfall	16.0	7.0	Annual days mostly sunny	224	208
Annual days > 90°F	62	38	Annual days precipitation	84	109	Annual days with thunderstorms	55	39
Annual days < 32°F	114	89	Annual days rain > 0.5 inches	18	22	Tornado risk score	88	18
Annual days < 0°F	2	6	Annual days snow > 1.5 inches	5	6	Hurricane risk score	1	13

TEMPERATURE

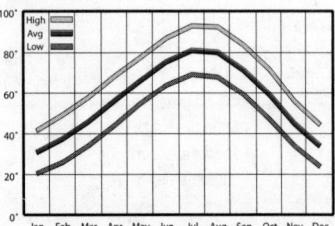

PRECIPITATION

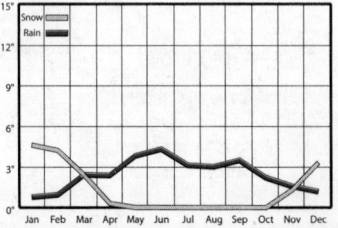

DAYS OF CLOUDS & PRECIPITATION

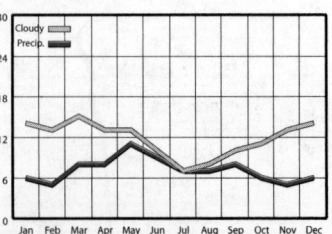

Education
Score: 53.5
Rank: 175

ACHIEVEMENT	AREA	U.S. AVG	PUBLIC SCHOOLS	AREA	U.S. AVG	HIGHER EDUCATION	AREA	U.S. AVG
High school degree	85.7%	82.7%	Expenditures per pupil	$5,265	$5,686	No. 2-year colleges	5	4
2-year college degree	5.5%	6.4%	Student/teacher ratio	16.8	16.7	No. 4-year colleges/universities	5	6
4-year college degree	17.0%	15.7%	Attending public school	90.1%	90.1%	No. highly ranked universities	0	1
Graduate/professional degree	7.8%	8.9%	State SAT score	1172	1021			
			State ACT score	21.8*	20.9			

Health & Healthcare
Score: 39.6
Rank: 225

HAZARDS & ILLNESSES	AREA	U.S. AVG	HEALTHCARE	AREA	U.S. AVG	CRIME	AREA	U.S. AVG
Air-quality score	24	37	Physicians per capita	235.5	244.2	Violent crime rate	602.4	465.5
Water-quality score	39	52	Hospital beds per capita	420.8	420.0	Change in violent crime rate	4.9%	-2.2%
Pollen/allergy score	58	61	No. teaching hospitals	4	3	Property crime rate	4,495.1	3,517.1
Cancer mortality per capita	216.3	201.9	Cost per doctor visit	$64	$77	Change in property crime rate	-5.5%	-2.1%
Depression days per month	3.2	3.5	Cost per dental visit	$60	$70			
Stress score	42	50						

Crime
Score: 24.6
Rank: 281

Transportation
Score: 34.2
Rank: 247

COMMUTE	AREA	U.S. AVG	INTERCITY SERVICES	AREA	U.S. AVG	AUTOMOTIVE	AREA	U.S. AVG
Average commute time	21.2	27.4	Major airports within 60 miles	0	1	Insurance, annual premium	$1,276	$1,432
Percent commutes > 60 mins.	2.3%	5.9%	Size of regional airport	Small	Large	Gas, cost per gallon	$2.40	$2.49
Commute by auto	84.6%	78.9%	Daily airline activity	74	686	Daily vehicle miles per capita	22.6	24.0
Commute by mass transit	0.5%	1.9%	Amtrak service	Yes	No			
Work at home	2.9%	3.1%						
Mass transit miles per capita	0.53	1.87						

Leisure
Score: 35.0
Rank: 242

DINING & SHOPPING	AREA	U.S. AVG	ENTERTAINMENT	AREA	U.S. AVG	OUTDOOR ACTIVITIES	AREA	U.S. AVG
Restaurant rating	1	2	Professional sports rating	3	4	Golf-course rating	3	4
Outlet mall score	16	42	College sports rating	2	4	Ski-area rating	1	3
No. Starbucks	7	13	Zoo/aquarium rating	5	3	Sq. miles inland water	2	4
No. warehouse clubs	1	2	Amusement park rating	4	3	Miles of coastline	0.0	10.7
			Botanical garden/arboretum rating	7	4	National Park rating	1	3

Arts & Culture
Score: 67.1
Rank: 123

MEDIA & LIBRARIES	AREA	U.S. AVG	PERFORMING ARTS	AREA	U.S. AVG	MUSEUMS	AREA	U.S. AVG
Arts radio rating	1	3	Classical music rating	6	4	Overall museum rating	7	5
No. public libraries	45	27	Ballet/dance rating	3	3	Art museum rating	8	5
Library volumes per capita	3.76	2.78	Professional theater rating	1	3	Science museum rating	7	5
			University arts programs rating	6	5	Children's museum rating	5	3

Wichita Falls, TX

Score: 46.8   **Rank:** 265   **2004 rank:** 294

Profile: Small city
Location: Extreme north-central Texas, 15 miles south of the Oklahoma border
Elevation: 994 feet
Time zone: Central Standard Time

PRO	CON
Cost of living	Isolation
Small-town atmosphere	High crime rates
Nearby water recreation	Summer heat

Wichita Falls, named for a 5-foot waterfall considered significant in these flat parts, is an agricultural and ranching center that boomed during the 1930s with the discovery of oil. Agriculture, petroleum, and some manufacturing of auto parts and aviation components are the economic mainstays; there is also a small Air Force base and a small 4-year college. Like many small Texas towns, Wichita Falls is plain, clean, and quiet. There is a small set of local amenities such as a symphony, ballet, theater, and art museum, and a number of lakes around the area, but on the whole, there isn't much to do. The crime rate is high, especially for the type of town. For big-city services and amenities, the Dallas–Fort Worth metroplex is 135 miles southeast.

The town is located in the North Central Plains of Texas, just south of the Red River separating Texas and Oklahoma. The topography is level to gently rolling agriculture and mesquite plain with few trees. Summers are warm to hot with low humidity and lots of sun and wind. Temperatures frequently exceed 100°F. Polar air masses moving down from the north during winter can drop temperatures 20°F to 30°F within an hour. While variable, winters are on the whole relatively mild with few subzero readings. Snow accumulation occurs only once or twice a year. Most rainfall comes from brief showers, and prolonged dry periods are common.

Population

DEMOGRAPHICS	AREA	U.S. AVG	ETHNIC COMPOSITION	AREA	U.S. AVG	RESIDENT PROFILE	AREA	U.S. AVG
Population	151,127		White	80.5%	79.0%	Single	28.4%	32.4%
Population density per sq. mile	57.3	358.5	Black	8.3%	10.5%	Married	52.9%	52.7%
Population growth	7.7%	21.1%	Asian	1.7%	2.7%	Divorced/separated	18.7%	14.9%
Median age	34.1	36.1	Hispanic	12.4%	10.6%	Married with children	24.4%	23.7%
Percent Democrat	27.4%	44.5%	Religious observance	63.6%	48.9%	Single with children	9.0%	9.1%
Percent Republican	72.1%	54.5%	Diversity measure	47.5	40.1	Percent over age 65	13.1%	12.9%

Economy & Jobs
Score: 64.2
Rank: 135

INCOME	AREA	U.S. AVG	EMPLOYMENT	AREA	U.S. AVG	EMPLOYING INDUSTRIES	AREA	U.S. AVG
Per capita income	$19,571	$23,235	Unemployment rate	4.6%	4.7%	Largest: Healthcare & Social Assistance		
Household income	$39,034	$46,414	Recent job growth	3.4%	1.3%			
Household income < $25K	29.9%	26.2%	Projected future job growth	9.0%	11.5%	Percent manufacturing	15.7%	15.4%
Household income > $75K	17.4%	25.4%	White collar	54.7%	57.8%	Percent public sector	19.4%	15.7%
Household income growth	14.1%	13.6%	Blue collar	25.9%	25.2%	Percent construction	10.2%	9.9%

Cost of Living
Score: 89.0
Rank: 42

INDEXES & TAXES	AREA	U.S. AVG	HOUSING	AREA	U.S. AVG	NECESSITIES	AREA	U.S. AVG
Cost of Living Index	78.1	100.0	Median home price	$104,600	$220,000	Food Index	92.9	100.0
Buying Power Index	112.0	100.0	Home price appreciation	26.6%	10.1%	Housing Index	45.5	100.0
Income tax rate	0.00%	4.70%	Median rent	$569	$709	Utilities Index	92.7	100.0
Sales tax rate	8.17%	6.58%	Homes owned	58.7%	62.3%	Transportation Index	98.3	100.0
Property tax rate	$17.31	$12.00	Home price ratio	2.7	4.2	Healthcare Index	99.8	100.0
						Miscellaneous Cost Index	99.2	100.0

Climate
Score: 79.7
Rank: 77

TEMPERATURE	AREA	U.S. AVG	PRECIPITATION	AREA	U.S. AVG	COMFORTS & HAZARDS	AREA	U.S. AVG
Average January low	29.4	26.2	Annual inches precipitation	27.2	37.7	July relative humidity	66%	66%
Average July high	99.2	87.4	Annual inches snowfall	2.0	7.0	Annual days mostly sunny	248	208
Annual days > 90°F	106	38	Annual days precipitation	71	109	Annual days with thunderstorms	49	39
Annual days < 32°F	70	89	Annual days rain > 0.5 inches	18	22	Tornado risk score	71	18
Annual days < 0°F	0	6	Annual days snow > 1.5 inches	1	6	Hurricane risk score	4	13

TEMPERATURE

PRECIPITATION

DAYS OF CLOUDS & PRECIPITATION

Education
Score: 39.8
Rank: 226

ACHIEVEMENT	AREA	U.S. AVG	PUBLIC SCHOOLS	AREA	U.S. AVG	HIGHER EDUCATION	AREA	U.S. AVG
High school degree	80.4%	82.7%	Expenditures per pupil	$5,151	$5,686	No. 2-year colleges	0	4
2-year college degree	5.7%	6.4%	Student/teacher ratio	13.8	16.7	No. 4-year colleges/universities	1	6
4-year college degree	14.2%	15.7%	Attending public school	96.9%	90.1%	No. highly ranked universities	0	1
Graduate/professional degree	5.5%	8.9%	State SAT score	997*	1021			
			State ACT score	20.3	20.9			

Health & Healthcare
Score: 89.6
Rank: 40

Crime
Score: 2.1
Rank: 365

HAZARDS & ILLNESSES	AREA	U.S. AVG	HEALTHCARE	AREA	U.S. AVG	CRIME	AREA	U.S. AVG
Air-quality score	48	37	Physicians per capita	217.1	244.2	Violent crime rate	523.8	465.5
Water-quality score	73	52	Hospital beds per capita	753.7	420.0	Change in violent crime rate	-24.4%	-2.2%
Pollen/allergy score	84	61	No. teaching hospitals	2	3	Property crime rate	5,723.5	3,517.1
Cancer mortality per capita	182.6	201.9	Cost per doctor visit	$65	$77	Change in property crime rate	-0.2%	-2.1%
Depression days per month	4.5	3.5	Cost per dental visit	$59	$70			
Stress score	50	50						

Transportation
Score: 48.7
Rank: 193

COMMUTE	AREA	U.S. AVG	INTERCITY SERVICES	AREA	U.S. AVG	AUTOMOTIVE	AREA	U.S. AVG
Average commute time	19.6	27.4	Major airports within 60 miles	0	1	Insurance, annual premium	$1,292	$1,432
Percent commutes > 60 mins.	3.4%	5.9%	Size of regional airport	None	Large	Gas, cost per gallon	$2.50	$2.49
Commute by auto	78.2%	78.9%	Daily airline activity	6	686	Daily vehicle miles per capita	21.0	24.0
Commute by mass transit	0.4%	1.9%	Amtrak service	No	No			
Work at home	2.2%	3.1%						
Mass transit miles per capita	0.40	1.87						

DINING & SHOPPING	AREA	U.S. AVG	ENTERTAINMENT	AREA	U.S. AVG	OUTDOOR ACTIVITIES	AREA	U.S. AVG
Restaurant rating	1	2	Professional sports rating	2	4	Golf-course rating	2	4
Outlet mall score	0	42	College sports rating	3	4	Ski-area rating	1	3
No. Starbucks	1	13	Zoo/aquarium rating	1	3	Sq. miles inland water	2	4
No. warehouse clubs	1	2	Amusement park rating	1	3	Miles of coastline	0.0	10.7
			Botanical garden/ arboretum rating	1	4	National Park rating	1	3

Leisure
Score: 7.2
Rank: 346

MEDIA & LIBRARIES	AREA	U.S. AVG	PERFORMING ARTS	AREA	U.S. AVG	MUSEUMS	AREA	U.S. AVG
Arts radio rating	1	3	Classical music rating	3	4	Overall museum rating	2	5
No. public libraries	6	27	Ballet/dance rating	1	3	Art museum rating	5	5
Library volumes per capita	1.82	2.78	Professional theater rating	1	3	Science museum rating	5	5
			University arts programs rating	3	5	Children's museum rating	2	3

Arts & Culture
Score: 24.9
Rank: 280

Williamsport, PA

Score: 33.5 Rank: 332 2004 rank: 216

Profile: Small town
Location: North-central Pennsylvania along the upper Susquehanna River
Elevation: 524 feet
Time zone: Eastern Standard Time

PRO	CON
Cost of living	Isolation
Small-town atmosphere	Economy
Low crime rates	Low ethnic diversity

Williamsport is an old lumber town still noted for production of hardwood lumber, particularly furniture-grade cherry. It's better known as the birthplace of Little League Baseball and the location of the Little League World Series every August—attracting considerable international attention during that time. The setting is attractive and the area has some well-preserved historic districts but is otherwise nondescript. The economy lags with high unemployment and relatively low job growth. The area is isolated geographically from major transportation links, a fact that doesn't help the economy. There are two small colleges but nearby amenities are thin and residents may have to travel to upstate New York to find what they need.

The town, in a narrow valley junction where the Lycoming River flows into the Susquehanna River, is surrounded by wooded hills and low mountains on all sides. In the summer, warm, humid air can be trapped in the valley, creating periods of discomfort. Winter extremes are moderated somewhat by the valley location and occasionally by warmer coastal weather, although deep fogs can occur. Snowfall varies and is much higher in the hills. First freeze is late October; last is late April.

DEMOGRAPHICS	AREA	U.S. AVG	ETHNIC COMPOSITION	AREA	U.S. AVG	RESIDENT PROFILE	AREA	U.S. AVG
Population	117,917		White	94.1%	79.0%	Single	31.6%	32.4%
Population density per sq. mile	95.5	358.5	Black	4.1%	10.5%	Married	53.0%	52.7%
Population growth	-0.7%	21.1%	Asian	0.5%	2.7%	Divorced/separated	15.4%	14.9%
Median age	39.7	36.1	Hispanic	0.6%	10.6%	Married with children	21.0%	23.7%
Percent Democrat	31.3%	44.5%	Religious observance	48.6%	48.9%	Single with children	8.6%	9.1%
Percent Republican	67.9%	54.5%	Diversity measure	12.4	40.1	Percent over age 65	16.4%	12.9%

Population

INCOME	AREA	U.S. AVG	EMPLOYMENT	AREA	U.S. AVG	EMPLOYING INDUSTRIES	AREA	U.S. AVG
Per capita income	$19,942	$23,235	Unemployment rate	5.5%	4.7%	Largest: Manufacturing		
Household income	$38,577	$46,414	Recent job growth	1.0%	1.3%			
Household income < $25K	31.0%	26.2%	Projected future job growth	0.2%	11.5%	Percent manufacturing	22.6%	15.4%
Household income > $75K	16.8%	25.4%	White collar	50.5%	57.8%	Percent public sector	11.2%	15.7%
Household income growth	13.4%	13.6%	Blue collar	32.4%	25.2%	Percent construction	9.8%	9.9%

Economy & Jobs
Score: 11.8
Rank: 329

INDEXES & TAXES	AREA	U.S. AVG	HOUSING	AREA	U.S. AVG	NECESSITIES	AREA	U.S. AVG
Cost of Living Index	79.6	100.0	Median home price	$116,400	$220,000	Food Index	94.4	100.0
Buying Power Index	108.6	100.0	Home price appreciation	28.6%	10.1%	Housing Index	49.4	100.0
Income tax rate	2.80%	4.70%	Median rent	$553	$709	Utilities Index	101.9	100.0
Sales tax rate	6.00%	6.58%	Homes owned	62.7%	62.3%	Transportation Index	92.0	100.0
Property tax rate	$14.60	$12.00	Home price ratio	3.0	4.2	Healthcare Index	88.2	100.0
						Miscellaneous Cost Index	99.6	100.0

Cost of Living
Score: 89.6
Rank: 40

Climate
Score: 10.4
Rank: 334

TEMPERATURE	AREA	U.S. AVG
Average January low	19.4	26.2
Average July high	84.4	87.4
Annual days > 90°F	13	38
Annual days < 32°F	129	89
Annual days < 0°F	4	6

PRECIPITATION	AREA	U.S. AVG
Annual inches precipitation	40.0	37.7
Annual inches snowfall	44.5	7.0
Annual days precipitation	156	109
Annual days rain > 0.5 inches	26	22
Annual days snow > 1.5 inches	9	6

COMFORTS & HAZARDS	AREA	U.S. AVG
July relative humidity	72%	66%
Annual days mostly sunny	181	208
Annual days with thunderstorms	34	39
Tornado risk score	11	18
Hurricane risk score	7	13

TEMPERATURE

PRECIPITATION

DAYS OF CLOUDS & PRECIPITATION

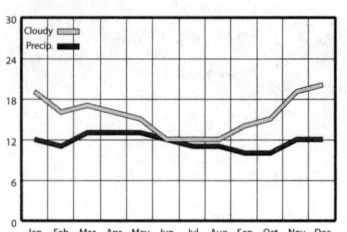

Education
Score: 29.1
Rank: 266

ACHIEVEMENT	AREA	U.S. AVG
High school degree	80.6%	82.7%
2-year college degree	8.0%	6.4%
4-year college degree	9.9%	15.7%
Graduate/professional degree	5.2%	8.9%

PUBLIC SCHOOLS	AREA	U.S. AVG
Expenditures per pupil	$6,386	$5,686
Student/teacher ratio	17.3	16.7
Attending public school	93.8%	90.1%
State SAT score	993*	1021
State ACT score	21.8	20.9

HIGHER EDUCATION	AREA	U.S. AVG
No. 2-year colleges	1	4
No. 4-year colleges/universities	2	6
No. highly ranked universities	0	1

Health & Healthcare
Score: 95.2
Rank: 19

HAZARDS & ILLNESSES	AREA	U.S. AVG
Air-quality score	52	37
Water-quality score	94	52
Pollen/allergy score	52	61
Cancer mortality per capita	222.5	201.9
Depression days per month	3.4	3.5
Stress score	16	50

HEALTHCARE	AREA	U.S. AVG
Physicians per capita	197.6	244.2
Hospital beds per capita	528.3	420.0
No. teaching hospitals	1	3
Cost per doctor visit	$65	$77
Cost per dental visit	$52	$70

Crime
Score: 87.7
Rank: 47

CRIME	AREA	U.S. AVG
Violent crime rate	193.7	465.5
Change in violent crime rate	3.7%	-2.2%
Property crime rate	2,131.9	3,517.1
Change in property crime rate	-4.8%	-2.1%

Transportation
Score: 44.9
Rank: 207

COMMUTE	AREA	U.S. AVG
Average commute time	21.0	27.4
Percent commutes > 60 mins.	3.9%	5.9%
Commute by auto	80.4%	78.9%
Commute by mass transit	1.1%	1.9%
Work at home	2.4%	3.1%
Mass transit miles per capita	1.05	1.87

INTERCITY SERVICES	AREA	U.S. AVG
Major airports within 60 miles	0	1
Size of regional airport	Small	Large
Daily airline activity	144	686
Amtrak service	No	No

AUTOMOTIVE	AREA	U.S. AVG
Insurance, annual premium	$1,077	$1,432
Gas, cost per gallon	$2.48	$2.49
Daily vehicle miles per capita	28.7	24.0

Leisure
Score: 23.0
Rank: 287

DINING & SHOPPING	AREA	U.S. AVG
Restaurant rating	1	2
Outlet mall score	0	42
No. Starbucks	0	13
No. warehouse clubs	0	2

ENTERTAINMENT	AREA	U.S. AVG
Professional sports rating	2	4
College sports rating	5	4
Zoo/aquarium rating	1	3
Amusement park rating	1	3
Botanical garden/ arboretum rating	2	4

OUTDOOR ACTIVITIES	AREA	U.S. AVG
Golf-course rating	1	4
Ski-area rating	4	3
Sq. miles inland water	2	4
Miles of coastline	0.0	10.7
National Park rating	1	3

Arts & Culture
Score: 17.1
Rank: 309

MEDIA & LIBRARIES	AREA	U.S. AVG
Arts radio rating	1	3
No. public libraries	6	27
Library volumes per capita	2.12	2.78

PERFORMING ARTS	AREA	U.S. AVG
Classical music rating	3	4
Ballet/dance rating	1	3
Professional theater rating	1	3
University arts programs rating	5	5

MUSEUMS	AREA	U.S. AVG
Overall museum rating	2	5
Art museum rating	1	5
Science museum rating	1	5
Children's museum rating	2	3

Wilmington, DE-MD-NJ

Score: 80.5 **Rank:** 42 **2004 rank:** 83

Profile: Mid-size-city complex
Location: Extreme northern Delaware along the Delaware River
Elevation: 120 feet
Time zone: Eastern Standard Time

PRO	CON
Central location	Industrial areas
Good housing values	Entertainment
Low taxes	Violent crime

In 1802, a young Frenchman by the name of Henry Francis du Pont started a gunpowder factory where the Brandywine River meets the Delaware River near the top of Delaware Bay, site of present-day Wilmington. Led by the chemical industry, northern Delaware became a prosperous industrial center and remains so today. But the financial services sector and a favorable legal climate for business have picked up where industry has left off and brought a relatively strong employment picture to the area. The downtown area is unremarkable but is undergoing some renewal. But by East Coast standards, Wilmington is manageably sized and has a number of big-city amenities, including some excellent historic sites and museums in the city and north of it. Its central location and access to large cities along the Northeast Corridor is a major advantage. Good rail service connects it to New York, Philadelphia, Baltimore, and Washington, D.C. Wilmington is also close to southern Delaware beach areas and the tranquil Pennsylvania Dutch country to the northwest. Cost of living is modest for a city in this region and taxes are low on an Eastern scale. Good family neighborhoods and housing values are found north of downtown up the Brandywine River

Valley and U.S. 202 towards Pennsylvania. Some commute from this area into southeastern Pennsylvania. Downsides include the heavy industrial feel in parts of the city and some crime issues (although recent trends are positive), and for some, less entertainment than they might be accustomed to for the region. But the area scores consistently well in all categories, a virtue in short supply in East Coast cities, and gets a high ranking as a result.

Wilmington is located on the flat and marshy Atlantic Coastal Plain. Low rolling hills extend to the north and northwest into Pennsylvania. Summers are warm and humid and winters are usually mild. Maximum summer temperatures are usually in the 80s, with 100°F readings occurring only once every 6 years. Zero-degree weather can be expected once every 4 years. Most winter precipitation occurs as rain or a rain/snow/sleet mix. Snow seldom remains on the ground for more than a few days. Summer thunderstorms are common, and occasional tropical downpours from Atlantic hurricanes may cause lowland flooding. First freeze is late October; last is mid-April.

Population

DEMOGRAPHICS	AREA	U.S. AVG	ETHNIC COMPOSITION	AREA	U.S. AVG	RESIDENT PROFILE	AREA	U.S. AVG
Population	683,379		White	75.3%	79.0%	Single	34.4%	32.4%
Population density per sq. mile	614.4	358.5	Black	17.7%	10.5%	Married	51.1%	52.7%
Population growth	18.7%	21.1%	Asian	2.8%	2.7%	Divorced/separated	14.5%	14.9%
Median age	36.5	36.1	Hispanic	5.3%	10.6%	Married with children	23.4%	23.7%
Percent Democrat	56.1%	44.5%	Religious observance	42.1%	48.9%	Single with children	9.7%	9.1%
Percent Republican	42.9%	54.5%	Diversity measure	44.8	40.1	Percent over age 65	11.8%	12.9%

Economy & Jobs

Score: 71.1
Rank: 109

INCOME	AREA	U.S. AVG	EMPLOYMENT	AREA	U.S. AVG	EMPLOYING INDUSTRIES	AREA	U.S. AVG
Per capita income	$28,089	$23,235	Unemployment rate	4.9%	4.7%	Largest: Finance & Insurance		
Household income	$59,171	$46,414	Recent job growth	2.8%	1.3%			
Household income < $25K	17.9%	26.2%	Projected future job growth	11.6%	11.5%	Percent manufacturing	12.5%	15.4%
Household income > $75K	36.6%	25.4%	White collar	64.2%	57.8%	Percent public sector	12.5%	15.7%
Household income growth	14.8%	13.6%	Blue collar	21.8%	25.2%	Percent construction	9.3%	9.9%

Cost of Living

Score: 53.2
Rank: 175

INDEXES & TAXES	AREA	U.S. AVG	HOUSING	AREA	U.S. AVG	NECESSITIES	AREA	U.S. AVG
Cost of Living Index	115.9	100.0	Median home price	$298,900	$220,000	Food Index	106.7	100.0
Buying Power Index	114.4	100.0	Home price appreciation	72.5%	10.1%	Housing Index	77.1	100.0
Income tax rate	8.11%	4.70%	Median rent	$923	$709	Utilities Index	119.9	100.0
Sales tax rate	0.99%	6.58%	Homes owned	67.1%	62.3%	Transportation Index	99.0	100.0
Property tax rate	$9.52	$12.00	Home price ratio	5.1	4.2	Healthcare Index	110.4	100.0
						Miscellaneous Cost Index	102.8	100.0

Climate
Score: 64.4
Rank: 132

TEMPERATURE	AREA	U.S. AVG	PRECIPITATION	AREA	U.S. AVG	COMFORTS & HAZARDS	AREA	U.S. AVG
Average January low	24.4	26.2	Annual inches precipitation	40.0	37.7	July relative humidity	67%	66%
Average July high	86.8	87.4	Annual inches snowfall	20.0	7.0	Annual days mostly sunny	205	208
Annual days > 90°F	19	38	Annual days precipitation	116	109	Annual days with thunderstorms	31	39
Annual days < 32°F	101	89	Annual days rain > 0.5 inches	26	22	Tornado risk score	20	18
Annual days < 0°F	0	6	Annual days snow > 1.5 inches	5	6	Hurricane risk score	16	13

TEMPERATURE

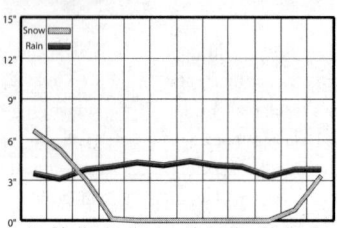

PRECIPITATION

DAYS OF CLOUDS & PRECIPITATION

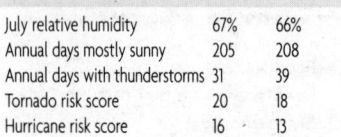
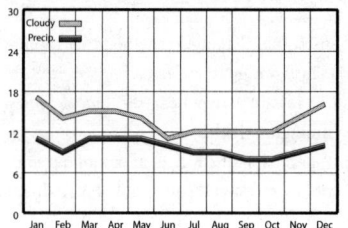

Education
Score: 50.5
Rank: 186

ACHIEVEMENT	AREA	U.S. AVG	PUBLIC SCHOOLS	AREA	U.S. AVG	HIGHER EDUCATION	AREA	U.S. AVG
High school degree	84.4%	82.7%	Expenditures per pupil	$7,004	$5,686	No. 2-year colleges	4	4
2-year college degree	6.7%	6.4%	Student/teacher ratio	17.4	16.7	No. 4-year colleges/universities	4	6
4-year college degree	16.8%	15.7%	Attending public school	79.1%	90.1%	No. highly ranked universities	1	1
Graduate/professional degree	9.5%	8.9%	State SAT score	995*	1021			
			State ACT score	21.4	20.9			

Health & Healthcare
Score: 21.7
Rank: 292

HAZARDS & ILLNESSES	AREA	U.S. AVG	HEALTHCARE	AREA	U.S. AVG		CRIME	AREA	U.S. AVG
Air-quality score	27	37	Physicians per capita	242.6	244.2		Violent crime rate	592.4	465.5
Water-quality score	15	52	Hospital beds per capita	342.0	420.0		Change in violent crime rate	-2.2%	-2.2%
Pollen/allergy score	45	61	No. teaching hospitals	5	3	**Crime**	Property crime rate	3,115.6	3,517.1
Cancer mortality per capita	219.2	201.9	Cost per doctor visit	$91	$77	**Score:** 62.0	Change in property crime rate	-6.2%	-2.1%
Depression days per month	3.6	3.5	Cost per dental visit	$88	$70	**Rank:** 143			
Stress score	57	50							

Transportation
Score: 100.0
Rank: 1

COMMUTE	AREA	U.S. AVG	INTERCITY SERVICES	AREA	U.S. AVG	AUTOMOTIVE	AREA	U.S. AVG
Average commute time	27.0	27.4	Major airports within 60 miles	5	1	Insurance, annual premium	$1,990	$1,432
Percent commutes > 60 mins.	6.6%	5.9%	Size of regional airport	Large	Large	Gas, cost per gallon	$2.44	$2.49
Commute by auto	80.2%	78.9%	Daily airline activity	3044	686	Daily vehicle miles per capita	32.4	24.0
Commute by mass transit	3.1%	1.9%	Amtrak service	Yes	No			
Work at home	2.6%	3.1%						
Mass transit miles per capita	3.06	1.87						

Leisure
Score: 81.0
Rank: 71

DINING & SHOPPING	AREA	U.S. AVG	ENTERTAINMENT	AREA	U.S. AVG	OUTDOOR ACTIVITIES	AREA	U.S. AVG
Restaurant rating	2	2	Professional sports rating	8	4	Golf-course rating	7	4
Outlet mall score	91	42	College sports rating	2	4	Ski-area rating	3	3
No. Starbucks	5	13	Zoo/aquarium rating	4	3	Sq. miles inland water	6	4
No. warehouse clubs	2	2	Amusement park rating	4	3	Miles of coastline	0.0	10.7
			Botanical garden/ arboretum rating	7	4	National Park rating	2	3

Arts & Culture
Score: 86.9
Rank: 50

MEDIA & LIBRARIES	AREA	U.S. AVG	PERFORMING ARTS	AREA	U.S. AVG	MUSEUMS	AREA	U.S. AVG
Arts radio rating	5	3	Classical music rating	8	4	Overall museum rating	9	5
No. public libraries	28	27	Ballet/dance rating	6	3	Art museum rating	10	5
Library volumes per capita	2.49	2.78	Professional theater rating	8	3	Science museum rating	7	5
			University arts programs rating	10	5	Children's museum rating	4	3

Wilmington, NC

Score: 57.6 **Rank:** 193 **2004 rank:** 172

Profile: Mid-size port city
Location: Southern North Carolina coast
Elevation: 30 feet
Time zone: Eastern Standard Time

PRO	CON
Historic downtown	Isolation
Nearby beaches	Cost of living
Mild winters	Crime rates

Wilmington is an old Colonial port city known for shipping, agricultural processing, and flowers. The historic town center and waterfront along the Cape Fear River are interesting and attractive, and it reminds many of Charleston, South Carolina, without its hoards of tourists and wealthy Northeast migrants. Due to its historic interest and its location on a peninsula formed by the Cape Fear River on the west and the Atlantic Intracoastal Waterway on the east, housing costs and cost of living tend to be higher than other small North Carolina cities. The median home price of $190,800 has grown rapidly and is second highest in the state. Employment growth is also very strong as more find the area. The area has a healthy mix of old- and new-economy employers, from International Paper and Louisiana Pacific to GE Nuclear Systems and Corning optical fiber, with a few pharmaceutical and biotech equipment firms thrown in. There is a large regional hospital and medical complex. Wilmington is isolated from many big-city amenities and services, but climate is pleasant and residential sections are attractive.

Because of the curvature of the Atlantic coastline, the ocean lies about 5 miles east and about 20 miles south. The surrounding terrain is typical of coastal Carolina, with low-lying, gently rolling land with rivers, creeks, and lakes with considerable swamp or marshland adjoining them. Large wooded areas alternate with cultivated fields. Summers are warm and humid, usually with cool afternoon breezes but without excessive heat. High temperatures of 90°F or more are reached about 1 day in 3 but 100°F is rare. Cold air from the north invades in winter and doesn't last, and the season is short and mild. On average, daytime temperatures stay below freezing only once a year. Rainfall is well distributed with most occurring during summer thunderstorms. The area is subject to coastal storms and hurricanes, with high winds, high tides, and heavy rain. Winter rain is more likely to be slow and steady and last 2 to 3 days.

Population

DEMOGRAPHICS	AREA	U.S. AVG	ETHNIC COMPOSITION	AREA	U.S. AVG	RESIDENT PROFILE	AREA	U.S. AVG
Population	301,847		White	80.3%	79.0%	Single	30.4%	32.4%
Population density per sq. mile	156.9	358.5	Black	16.0%	10.5%	Married	54.5%	52.7%
Population growth	51.6%	21.1%	Asian	0.7%	2.7%	Divorced/separated	15.1%	14.9%
Median age	38.5	36.1	Hispanic	2.9%	10.6%	Married with children	18.3%	23.7%
Percent Democrat	42.1%	44.5%	Religious observance	40.9%	48.9%	Single with children	8.1%	9.1%
Percent Republican	57.5%	54.5%	Diversity measure	36.5	40.1	Percent over age 65	14.9%	12.9%

Economy & Jobs

Score: 76.5
Rank: 89

INCOME	AREA	U.S. AVG	EMPLOYMENT	AREA	U.S. AVG	EMPLOYING INDUSTRIES	AREA	U.S. AVG
Per capita income	$25,086	$23,235	Unemployment rate	4.8%	4.7%	Largest: Healthcare & Social Assistance		
Household income	$44,263	$46,414	Recent job growth	2.2%	1.3%			
Household income ‹ $25K	27.3%	26.2%	Projected future job growth	22.2%	11.5%	Percent manufacturing	12.7%	15.4%
Household income › $75K	23.8%	25.4%	White collar	55.8%	57.8%	Percent public sector	14.0%	15.7%
Household income growth	15.5%	13.6%	Blue collar	26.5%	25.2%	Percent construction	13.8%	9.9%

Cost of Living

Score: 28.1
Rank: 269

INDEXES & TAXES	AREA	U.S. AVG	HOUSING	AREA	U.S. AVG	NECESSITIES	AREA	U.S. AVG
Cost of Living Index	94.8	100.0	Median home price	$190,800	$220,000	Food Index	105.8	100.0
Buying Power Index	104.7	100.0	Home price appreciation	50.5%	10.1%	Housing Index	77.6	100.0
Income tax rate	7.00%	4.70%	Median rent	$689	$709	Utilities Index	98.4	100.0
Sales tax rate	7.00%	6.58%	Homes owned	55.0%	62.3%	Transportation Index	90.3	100.0
Property tax rate	$8.17	$12.00	Home price ratio	4.3	4.2	Healthcare Index	93.6	100.0
						Miscellaneous Cost Index	103.5	100.0

Climate
Score: 52.1
Rank: 178

TEMPERATURE	AREA	U.S. AVG
Average January low	36.2	26.2
Average July high	88.8	87.4
Annual days > 90°F	45	38
Annual days < 32°F	45	89
Annual days < 0°F	0	6

PRECIPITATION	AREA	U.S. AVG
Annual inches precipitation	54.0	37.7
Annual inches snowfall	1.8	7.0
Annual days precipitation	117	109
Annual days rain > 0.5 inches	33	22
Annual days snow > 1.5 inches	1	6

COMFORTS & HAZARDS	AREA	U.S. AVG
July relative humidity	75%	66%
Annual days mostly sunny	219	208
Annual days with thunderstorms	46	39
Tornado risk score	6	18
Hurricane risk score	68	13

TEMPERATURE

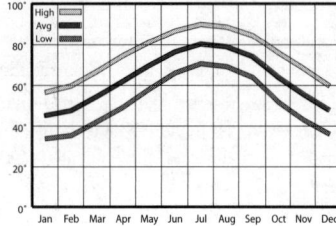

PRECIPITATION

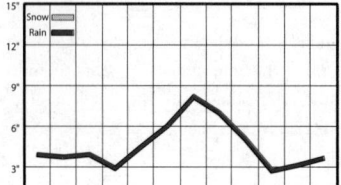

DAYS OF CLOUDS & PRECIPITATION

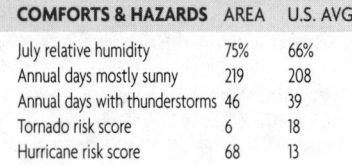

Education
Score: 63.6
Rank: 137

ACHIEVEMENT	AREA	U.S. AVG
High school degree	82.8%	82.7%
2-year college degree	7.3%	6.4%
4-year college degree	17.3%	15.7%
Graduate/professional degree	6.9%	8.9%

PUBLIC SCHOOLS	AREA	U.S. AVG
Expenditures per pupil	$4,959	$5,686
Student/teacher ratio	14.7	16.7
Attending public school	94.7%	90.1%
State SAT score	1008*	1021
State ACT score	20.5	20.9

HIGHER EDUCATION	AREA	U.S. AVG
No. 2-year colleges	3	4
No. 4-year colleges/universities	1	6
No. highly ranked universities	1	1

Health & Healthcare
Score: 65.0
Rank: 132

HAZARDS & ILLNESSES	AREA	U.S. AVG
Air-quality score	48	37
Water-quality score	63	52
Pollen/allergy score	66	61
Cancer mortality per capita	198.1	201.9
Depression days per month	3.2	3.5
Stress score	39	50

HEALTHCARE	AREA	U.S. AVG
Physicians per capita	229.7	244.2
Hospital beds per capita	298.5	420.0
No. teaching hospitals	1	3
Cost per doctor visit	$74	$77
Cost per dental visit	$91	$70

Crime
Score: 30.5
Rank: 260

CRIME	AREA	U.S. AVG
Violent crime rate	450.6	465.5
Change in violent crime rate	-3.0%	-2.2%
Property crime rate	4,833.5	3,517.1
Change in property crime rate	-3.4%	-2.1%

Transportation
Score: 9.9
Rank: 337

COMMUTE	AREA	U.S. AVG
Average commute time	24.6	27.4
Percent commutes > 60 mins.	5.0%	5.9%
Commute by auto	81.1%	78.9%
Commute by mass transit	0.7%	1.9%
Work at home	3.1%	3.1%
Mass transit miles per capita	0.70	1.87

INTERCITY SERVICES	AREA	U.S. AVG
Major airports within 60 miles	0	1
Size of regional airport	Small	Large
Daily airline activity	51	686
Amtrak service	No	No

AUTOMOTIVE	AREA	U.S. AVG
Insurance, annual premium	$1,253	$1,432
Gas, cost per gallon	$2.51	$2.49
Daily vehicle miles per capita	21.8	24.0

Leisure
Score: 37.2
Rank: 234

DINING & SHOPPING	AREA	U.S. AVG
Restaurant rating	1	2
Outlet mall score	0	42
No. Starbucks	4	13
No. warehouse clubs	1	2

ENTERTAINMENT	AREA	U.S. AVG
Professional sports rating	2	4
College sports rating	2	4
Zoo/aquarium rating	5	3
Amusement park rating	3	3
Botanical garden/ arboretum rating	1	4

OUTDOOR ACTIVITIES	AREA	U.S. AVG
Golf-course rating	2	4
Ski-area rating	1	3
Sq. miles inland water	4	4
Miles of coastline	25.4	10.7
National Park rating	1	3

Arts & Culture
Score: 29.4
Rank: 264

MEDIA & LIBRARIES	AREA	U.S. AVG
Arts radio rating	1	3
No. public libraries	11	27
Library volumes per capita	2.28	2.78

PERFORMING ARTS	AREA	U.S. AVG
Classical music rating	3	4
Ballet/dance rating	1	3
Professional theater rating	1	3
University arts programs rating	4	5

MUSEUMS	AREA	U.S. AVG
Overall museum rating	7	5
Art museum rating	4	5
Science museum rating	7	5
Children's museum rating	1	3

Winchester, VA-WV

Score: 79.7 **Rank:** 47 **2004 rank:** not ranked

Profile: Small town
Location: Northern Virginia, north end of Shenandoah Valley 7 miles south of the Maryland border
Elevation: 717 feet
Time zone: Eastern Standard Time

PRO	CON
Historic interest	Growth pressure
Central location	Housing costs
Pleasant climate	Entertainment

Winchester is a rising star in Virginia's Shenandoah Valley. For years it has been a stable, prosperous agricultural center and light manufacturing point in the center of a large area of good farm and orchard land. Now, it is just close enough to the ever-expanding D.C. area to support those tolerant of a long commute, especially to the suburbs around Dulles Airport and west. It has also become a favorite for telecommuters or entrepreneurs needing a city just once in awhile. The strategic location allows these individuals to also get to New York in 4 hours or just about any other major Eastern city. This geographic advantage isn't just a recent realization, as Winchester changed hands 72 times during the Civil War. As that might lead you to think, the town sits in the middle of an area of considerable historic interest. The downtown core with its historic buildings is attractive and interesting. The exceptional central historic district could be used almost as is for a 19th-century or Civil War movie set, and is now occupied by small

businesses, artisans, and minor entertainment venues. But growth pressure is strong and many long-time residents are concerned about Winchester's existence as a pleasant small town. Some unattractive sprawl has emerged outside of town, particularly to the south toward Interstate 66.

The immediate area around Winchester is a flat mix of typical agricultural and orchard land. Low, wooded foothills and mountains of the Blue Ridge and the main Appalachian range are visible to the east and west respectively. Summers are warm, mostly calm and humid with periodic rainy spells and thunderstorms. Winters are cold and can be wet, but severe effects of northwesterly cold blasts are moderated by the mountains. Periods of heavy rain or snow may occur with storms moving up off the Atlantic. Spring and especially fall are quite pleasant. First freeze is late October; last is mid-April.

Population

DEMOGRAPHICS	AREA	U.S. AVG	ETHNIC COMPOSITION	AREA	U.S. AVG	RESIDENT PROFILE	AREA	U.S. AVG
Population	113,613		White	91.7%	79.0%	Single	28.8%	32.4%
Population density per sq. mile	106.6	358.5	Black	4.3%	10.5%	Married	57.1%	52.7%
Population growth	36.3%	21.1%	Asian	0.8%	2.7%	Divorced/separated	14.1%	14.9%
Median age	37.4	36.1	Hispanic	3.9%	10.6%	Married with children	24.8%	23.7%
Percent Democrat	33.5%	44.5%	Religious observance	39.2%	48.9%	Single with children	8.2%	9.1%
Percent Republican	65.5%	54.5%	Diversity measure	20.8	40.1	Percent over age 65	12.9%	12.9%

Economy & Jobs
Score: 96.0
Rank: 16

INCOME	AREA	U.S. AVG	EMPLOYMENT	AREA	U.S. AVG	EMPLOYING INDUSTRIES	AREA	U.S. AVG
Per capita income	$23,155	$23,235	Unemployment rate	2.8%	4.7%	Largest: Healthcare & Social Assistance		
Household income	$47,448	$46,414	Recent job growth	5.7%	1.3%			
Household income < $25K	22.5%	26.2%	Projected future job growth	20.8%	11.5%	Percent manufacturing	20.3%	15.4%
Household income > $75K	24.5%	25.4%	White collar	52.4%	57.8%	Percent public sector	13.9%	15.7%
Household income growth	15.3%	13.6%	Blue collar	33.6%	25.2%	Percent construction	13.2%	9.9%

Cost of Living
Score: 50.3
Rank: 186

INDEXES & TAXES	AREA	U.S. AVG	HOUSING	AREA	U.S. AVG	NECESSITIES	AREA	U.S. AVG
Cost of Living Index	109.4	100.0	Median home price	$324,500	$220,000	Food Index	87.9	100.0
Buying Power Index	97.2	100.0	Home price appreciation	101.1%	10.1%	Housing Index	87.1	100.0
Income tax rate	5.83%	4.70%	Median rent	$673	$709	Utilities Index	93.9	100.0
Sales tax rate	5.19%	6.58%	Homes owned	65.5%	62.3%	Transportation Index	89.4	100.0
Property tax rate	$6.23	$12.00	Home price ratio	6.8	4.2	Healthcare Index	87.1	100.0
						Miscellaneous Cost Index	93.5	100.0

Climate
Score: 68.7
Rank: 116

TEMPERATURE	AREA	U.S. AVG
Average January low	21.0	26.2
Average July high	87.0	87.4
Annual days > 90°F	28	38
Annual days < 32°F	116	89
Annual days < 0°F	0	6

PRECIPITATION	AREA	U.S. AVG
Annual inches precipitation	40.4	37.7
Annual inches snowfall	23.0	7.0
Annual days precipitation	116	109
Annual days rain > 0.5 inches	24	22
Annual days snow > 1.5 inches	7	6

COMFORTS & HAZARDS	AREA	U.S. AVG
July relative humidity	55%	66%
Annual days mostly sunny	214	208
Annual days with thunderstorms	35	39
Tornado risk score	1	18
Hurricane risk score	1	13

TEMPERATURE

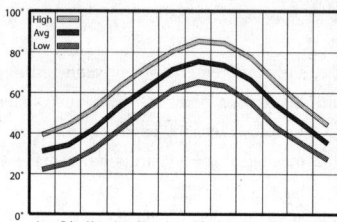

PRECIPITATION

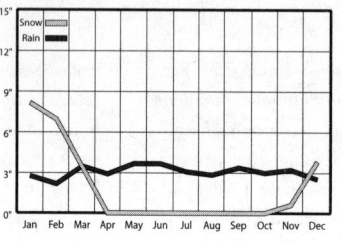

DAYS OF CLOUDS & PRECIPITATION

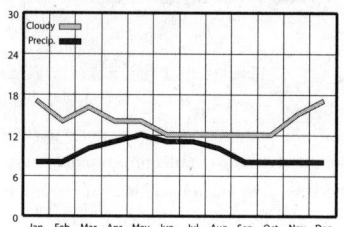

Education
Score: 20.6
Rank: 296

ACHIEVEMENT	AREA	U.S. AVG
High school degree	76.4%	82.7%
2-year college degree	4.7%	6.4%
4-year college degree	11.6%	15.7%
Graduate/professional degree	6.6%	8.9%

PUBLIC SCHOOLS	AREA	U.S. AVG
Expenditures per pupil	$5,388	$5,686
Student/teacher ratio	14.4	16.7
Attending public school	94.5%	90.1%
State SAT score	1025*	1021
State ACT score	21.1	20.9

HIGHER EDUCATION	AREA	U.S. AVG
No. 2-year colleges	1	4
No. 4-year colleges/universities	1	6
No. highly ranked universities	0	1

Health & Healthcare
Score: 91.7
Rank: 32

HAZARDS & ILLNESSES	AREA	U.S. AVG
Air-quality score	72	37
Water-quality score	53	52
Pollen/allergy score	63	61
Cancer mortality per capita	205.7	201.9
Depression days per month	2.2	3.5
Stress score	29	50

HEALTHCARE	AREA	U.S. AVG
Physicians per capita	261.3	244.2
Hospital beds per capita	423.4	420.0
No. teaching hospitals	1	3
Cost per doctor visit	$67	$77
Cost per dental visit	$62	$70

Crime
Score: 97.3
Rank: 11

CRIME	AREA	U.S. AVG
Violent crime rate	207.4	465.5
Change in violent crime rate	8.8%	-2.2%
Property crime rate	2,505.5	3,517.1
Change in property crime rate	-1.9%	-2.1%

Transportation
Score: 58.3
Rank: 157

COMMUTE	AREA	U.S. AVG
Average commute time	29.9	27.4
Percent commutes > 60 mins.	13.3%	5.9%
Commute by auto	78.3%	78.9%
Commute by mass transit	0.7%	1.9%
Work at home	2.9%	3.1%
Mass transit miles per capita	0.68	1.87

INTERCITY SERVICES	AREA	U.S. AVG
Major airports within 60 miles	3	1
Size of regional airport	Large	Large
Daily airline activity	1516	686
Amtrak service	No	No

AUTOMOTIVE	AREA	U.S. AVG
Insurance, annual premium	$976	$1,432
Gas, cost per gallon	$2.47	$2.49
Daily vehicle miles per capita	30.6	24.0

Leisure
Score: 84.0
Rank: 60

DINING & SHOPPING	AREA	U.S. AVG
Restaurant rating	1	2
Outlet mall score	64	42
No. Starbucks	0	13
No. warehouse clubs	1	2

ENTERTAINMENT	AREA	U.S. AVG
Professional sports rating	9	4
College sports rating	9	4
Zoo/aquarium rating	10	3
Amusement park rating	1	3
Botanical garden/arboretum rating	6	4

OUTDOOR ACTIVITIES	AREA	U.S. AVG
Golf-course rating	10	4
Ski-area rating	2	3
Sq. miles inland water	2	4
Miles of coastline	0.0	10.7
National Park rating	4	3

Arts & Culture
Score: 90.4
Rank: 37

MEDIA & LIBRARIES	AREA	U.S. AVG
Arts radio rating	2	3
No. public libraries	6	27
Library volumes per capita	1.76	2.78

PERFORMING ARTS	AREA	U.S. AVG
Classical music rating	10	4
Ballet/dance rating	9	3
Professional theater rating	1	3
University arts programs rating	10	5

MUSEUMS	AREA	U.S. AVG
Overall museum rating	7	5
Art museum rating	6	5
Science museum rating	8	5
Children's museum rating	6	3

Worcester, MA

Profile: Mid-size city
Location: Center of Massachusetts between Connecticut/Rhode Island and New Hampsire border
Elevation: 470 feet
Time zone: Eastern Standard Time

PRO	CON
Educated population	Economy
Local arts and culture	Harsh winters
Central location	Cost of living

Worcester is the second-largest city in Massachusetts. From its roots in the Industrial Revolution, it is evolving into a diverse research, manufacturing, and technology center, featuring a significant healthcare presence and a large biotechnology research park. The central location among other important New England markets helps the manufacturing cause, but current and future employment projections are still weak. The downtown is being gradually restored and modernized. Origins as a cultural center continue with the area's many small museums and colleges and a good set of small performing arts amenities. Mountain areas to the west and lakes mainly north offer good recreation opportunities. Cost of living is obviously influenced by more expensive areas east and is high for local income levels. Under the new OMB metro area alignment, this area has grown to include all of Worcester County, and thus the twin cities of Fitchburg and Leominster to the north, typical New England towns with similar economic challenges and transition efforts into the new economy. There is a strong sense of community pride, and the central location relative to Boston, discount air service, and other amenities in Providence and other points in New England make it attractive for those patient with its climate and economic prospects.

Worcester is located in a valley surrounded by hills and ridges rising from 500 feet above the city to over 1,000 feet 15 miles north. There are long valleys, some with reservoirs, between the nearby hills. Proximity to the Atlantic Ocean, Long Island Sound, and the Berkshire Hills to the west plays an important part in weather and climate. Summers are moderate. Winters are usually moderate for the latitude but have frequent cold snaps. Precipitation is spread evenly throughout the year, with summer thunderstorms developing over the mountains. First freeze is mid-October; last is late April.

Population

DEMOGRAPHICS	AREA	U.S. AVG	ETHNIC COMPOSITION	AREA	U.S. AVG	RESIDENT PROFILE	AREA	U.S. AVG
Population	787,489		White	87.5%	79.0%	Single	33.8%	32.4%
Population density per sq. mile	520.4	358.5	Black	3.4%	10.5%	Married	52.7%	52.7%
Population growth	11.0%	21.1%	Asian	3.5%	2.7%	Divorced/separated	13.5%	14.9%
Median age	37.2	36.1	Hispanic	7.6%	10.6%	Married with children	24.8%	23.7%
Percent Democrat	56.4%	44.5%	Religious observance	57.4%	48.9%	Single with children	8.7%	9.1%
Percent Republican	42.3%	54.5%	Diversity measure	33.8	40.1	Percent over age 65	12.6%	12.9%

Economy & Jobs
Score: 6.1
Rank: 350

INCOME	AREA	U.S. AVG	EMPLOYMENT	AREA	U.S. AVG	EMPLOYING INDUSTRIES	AREA	U.S. AVG
Per capita income	$27,009	$23,235	Unemployment rate	5.3%	4.7%	Largest: Manufacturing		
Household income	$55,153	$46,414	Recent job growth	0.1%	1.3%			
Household income < $25K	22.5%	26.2%	Projected future job growth	2.0%	11.5%	Percent manufacturing	14.6%	15.4%
Household income > $75K	34.4%	25.4%	White collar	63.1%	57.8%	Percent public sector	13.5%	15.7%
Household income growth	15.2%	13.6%	Blue collar	22.8%	25.2%	Percent construction	8.2%	9.9%

Cost of Living
Score: 12.8
Rank: 325

INDEXES & TAXES	AREA	U.S. AVG	HOUSING	AREA	U.S. AVG	NECESSITIES	AREA	U.S. AVG
Cost of Living Index	116.9	100.0	Median home price	$285,700	$220,000	Food Index	113.1	100.0
Buying Power Index	105.8	100.0	Home price appreciation	61.4%	10.1%	Housing Index	95.4	100.0
Income tax rate	5.95%	4.70%	Median rent	$896	$709	Utilities Index	108.4	100.0
Sales tax rate	5.00%	6.58%	Homes owned	61.5%	62.3%	Transportation Index	110.5	100.0
Property tax rate	$14.16	$12.00	Home price ratio	5.2	4.2	Healthcare Index	127.0	100.0
						Miscellaneous Cost Index	106.9	100.0

Climate
Score: 30.7
Rank: 258

TEMPERATURE	AREA	U.S. AVG
Average January low	22.5	26.2
Average July high	81.4	87.4
Annual days › 90°F	12	38
Annual days ‹ 32°F	99	89
Annual days ‹ 0°F	1	6

PRECIPITATION	AREA	U.S. AVG
Annual inches precipitation	43.0	37.7
Annual inches snowfall	42.0	7.0
Annual days precipitation	128	109
Annual days rain › 0.5 inches	27	22
Annual days snow › 1.5 inches	21	6

COMFORTS & HAZARDS	AREA	U.S. AVG
July relative humidity	67%	66%
Annual days mostly sunny	205	208
Annual days with thunderstorms	21	39
Tornado risk score	10	18
Hurricane risk score	19	13

TEMPERATURE

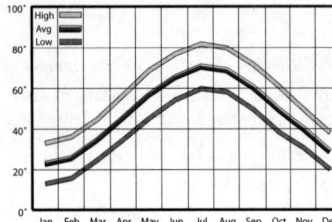

PRECIPITATION

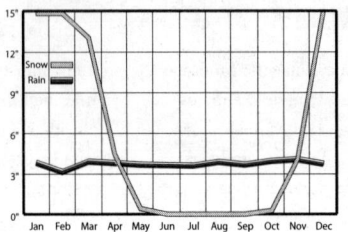

DAYS OF CLOUDS & PRECIPITATION

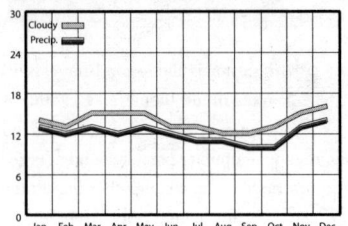

Education
Score: 84.5
Rank: 59

ACHIEVEMENT	AREA	U.S. AVG
High school degree	83.4%	82.7%
2-year college degree	7.9%	6.4%
4-year college degree	16.7%	15.7%
Graduate/professional degree	10.2%	8.9%

PUBLIC SCHOOLS	AREA	U.S. AVG
Expenditures per pupil	$6,329	$5,686
Student/teacher ratio	12.8	16.7
Attending public school	87.8%	90.1%
State SAT score	1037*	1021
State ACT score	23	20.9

HIGHER EDUCATION	AREA	U.S. AVG
No. 2-year colleges	2	4
No. 4-year colleges/universities	12	6
No. highly ranked universities	4	1

Health & Healthcare
Score: 17.9
Rank: 306

HAZARDS & ILLNESSES	AREA	U.S. AVG
Air-quality score	21	37
Water-quality score	52	52
Pollen/allergy score	57	61
Cancer mortality per capita	221.3	201.9
Depression days per month	3.8	3.5
Stress score	50	50

HEALTHCARE	AREA	U.S. AVG
Physicians per capita	311.9	244.2
Hospital beds per capita	347.7	420.0
No. teaching hospitals	7	3
Cost per doctor visit	$84	$77
Cost per dental visit	$75	$70

Crime
Score: 90.9
Rank: 35

CRIME	AREA	U.S. AVG
Violent crime rate	374.4	465.5
Change in violent crime rate	-3.9%	-2.2%
Property crime rate	2,004.4	3,517.1
Change in property crime rate	-4.3%	-2.1%

Transportation
Score: 52.1
Rank: 180

COMMUTE	AREA	U.S. AVG
Average commute time	28.2	27.4
Percent commutes › 60 mins.	8.7%	5.9%
Commute by auto	82.7%	78.9%
Commute by mass transit	1.6%	1.9%
Work at home	2.8%	3.1%
Mass transit miles per capita	1.63	1.87

INTERCITY SERVICES	AREA	U.S. AVG
Major airports within 60 miles	2	1
Size of regional airport	Large	Large
Daily airline activity	1205	686
Amtrak service	Yes	No

AUTOMOTIVE	AREA	U.S. AVG
Insurance, annual premium	$1,709	$1,432
Gas, cost per gallon	$2.41	$2.49
Daily vehicle miles per capita	27.0	24.0

Leisure
Score: 97.1
Rank: 12

DINING & SHOPPING	AREA	U.S. AVG
Restaurant rating	6	2
Outlet mall score	106	42
No. Starbucks	5	13
No. warehouse clubs	4	2

ENTERTAINMENT	AREA	U.S. AVG
Professional sports rating	9	4
College sports rating	10	4
Zoo/aquarium rating	8	3
Amusement park rating	7	3
Botanical garden/ arboretum rating	8	4

OUTDOOR ACTIVITIES	AREA	U.S. AVG
Golf-course rating	9	4
Ski-area rating	7	3
Sq. miles inland water	7	4
Miles of coastline	39.8	10.7
National Park rating	2	3

Arts & Culture
Score: 99.5
Rank: 3

MEDIA & LIBRARIES	AREA	U.S. AVG
Arts radio rating	10	3
No. public libraries	68	27
Library volumes per capita	4.48	2.78

PERFORMING ARTS	AREA	U.S. AVG
Classical music rating	10	4
Ballet/dance rating	8	3
Professional theater rating	10	3
University arts programs rating	10	5

MUSEUMS	AREA	U.S. AVG
Overall museum rating	9	5
Art museum rating	10	5
Science museum rating	9	5
Children's museum rating	6	3

Yakima, WA

Score: 45.8 **Rank:** 277 **2004 rank:** 265

Profile: Small agricultural city
Location: South-central Washington east of the Cascade Range
Elevation: 1,066 feet
Time zone: Pacific Standard Time

PRO	CON
Small-town atmosphere	Economy
Dry climate	Low educational
Nearby mountains	attainment
	Air quality

Agriculture is the dominating influence and raison dêtre for Yakima, located at the eastern base of the Cascade Range. Good soil, sunny days, and irrigation from the Yakima River support the area's many orchards, which produce apples, pears, peaches, and other fruits for the U.S. market. The city has a plain small-town character, although a large Hispanic population attracted by farm labor adds a hint of cultural diversity. The city is highly dependent on agriculture and currently has high unemployment and poor employment prospects. There isn't much to do. The downtown area has declined and redevelopment efforts to diversify the economy have proven unsuccessful thus far. Physically, Yakima is one of the country's best examples of the rain shadow effect: The city is one of the 10 driest in the nation with 8 inches of rain annually, while Seattle, less than 150 miles northwest, receives five times as much rain with three times as many cloudy days. Unfortunately, the city is also under an economic shadow, and the physical effects bring some air-quality problems at times. Aside from these issues, some like the dry climate, low cost of living, small-town lifestyle, and access to Puget Sound cities—although the latter means a rigorous mountain trip.

Yakima, located in a small east–west valley, resides in an area of complex topography with a number of minor valleys and ridges rising as much as 1,000 feet. The valley is mostly farm and orchard land while surrounding hills are dry and grass covered. Summers are dry and hot; afternoons can reach 100°F, but the dry air reduces the impact and leads to cool evenings usually in the 50s. Summer inversions trap air in the valley creating poor air quality. The maritime influence is strongest in winter, which is cloudy and cool with only light snowfall. Below-zero temperatures may occur. Most precipitation arrives in fall and winter. First freeze is early November; last is late March.

Population

DEMOGRAPHICS	AREA	U.S. AVG	ETHNIC COMPOSITION	AREA	U.S. AVG	RESIDENT PROFILE	AREA	U.S. AVG
Population	229,111		White	63.4%	79.0%	Single	31.3%	32.4%
Population density per sq. mile	53.3	358.5	Black	1.0%	10.5%	Married	53.7%	52.7%
Population growth	21.3%	21.1%	Asian	1.1%	2.7%	Divorced/separated	15.0%	14.9%
Median age	31.7	36.1	Hispanic	39.3%	10.6%	Married with children	27.8%	23.7%
Percent Democrat	39.1%	44.5%	Religious observance	38.9%	48.9%	Single with children	11.7%	9.1%
Percent Republican	59.6%	54.5%	Diversity measure	75.1	40.1	Percent over age 65	11.2%	12.9%

Economy & Jobs

Score: 2.4
Rank: 364

INCOME	AREA	U.S. AVG	EMPLOYMENT	AREA	U.S. AVG	EMPLOYING INDUSTRIES	AREA	U.S. AVG
Per capita income	$17,382	$23,235	Unemployment rate	6.7%	4.7%	Largest: Healthcare & Social Assistance		
Household income	$39,724	$46,414	Recent job growth	-1.7%	1.3%			
Household income < $25K	30.4%	26.2%	Projected future job growth	7.0%	11.5%	Percent manufacturing	16.6%	15.4%
Household income > $75K	19.5%	25.4%	White collar	48.1%	57.8%	Percent public sector	16.7%	15.7%
Household income growth	14.1%	13.6%	Blue collar	24.9%	25.2%	Percent construction	8.3%	9.9%

Cost of Living

Score: 85.3
Rank: 56

INDEXES & TAXES	AREA	U.S. AVG	HOUSING	AREA	U.S. AVG	NECESSITIES	AREA	U.S. AVG
Cost of Living Index	86.3	100.0	Median home price	$130,200	$220,000	Food Index	107.8	100.0
Buying Power Index	103.2	100.0	Home price appreciation	23.7%	10.1%	Housing Index	56.0	100.0
Income tax rate	0.00%	4.70%	Median rent	$684	$709	Utilities Index	76.2	100.0
Sales tax rate	7.90%	6.58%	Homes owned	60.4%	62.3%	Transportation Index	102.8	100.0
Property tax rate	$10.76	$12.00	Home price ratio	3.3	4.2	Healthcare Index	126.4	100.0
						Miscellaneous Cost Index	102.1	100.0

Climate
Score: 34.0
Rank: 246

TEMPERATURE	AREA	U.S. AVG
Average January low	18.6	26.2
Average July high	88.1	87.4
Annual days > 90°F	33	38
Annual days < 32°F	150	89
Annual days < 0°F	4	6

PRECIPITATION	AREA	U.S. AVG
Annual inches precipitation	8.0	37.7
Annual inches snowfall	25.0	7.0
Annual days precipitation	67	109
Annual days rain > 0.5 inches	4	22
Annual days snow > 1.5 inches	7	6

COMFORTS & HAZARDS	AREA	U.S. AVG
July relative humidity	60%	66%
Annual days mostly sunny	202	208
Annual days with thunderstorms	7	39
Tornado risk score	0	18
Hurricane risk score	0	13

TEMPERATURE

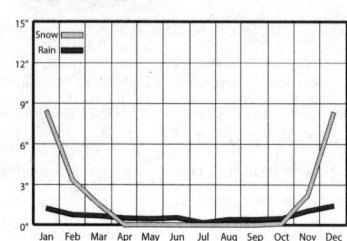

PRECIPITATION

DAYS OF CLOUDS & PRECIPITATION

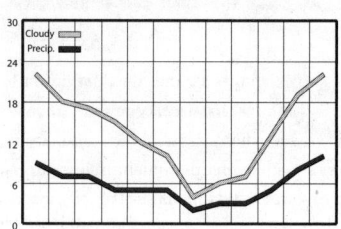

Education
Score: 4.0
Rank: 358

ACHIEVEMENT	AREA	U.S. AVG
High school degree	68.3%	82.7%
2-year college degree	5.2%	6.4%
4-year college degree	9.7%	15.7%
Graduate/professional degree	5.5%	8.9%

PUBLIC SCHOOLS	AREA	U.S. AVG
Expenditures per pupil	$5,548	$5,686
Student/teacher ratio	21.3	16.7
Attending public school	95.5%	90.1%
State SAT score	1059*	1021
State ACT score	22.9	20.9

HIGHER EDUCATION	AREA	U.S. AVG
No. 2-year colleges	4	4
No. 4-year colleges/universities	1	6
No. highly ranked universities	0	1

Health & Healthcare
Score: 32.4
Rank: 252

HAZARDS & ILLNESSES	AREA	U.S. AVG
Air-quality score	34	37
Water-quality score	53	52
Pollen/allergy score	46	61
Cancer mortality per capita	181.0	201.9
Depression days per month	3.6	3.5
Stress score	57	50

HEALTHCARE	AREA	U.S. AVG
Physicians per capita	170.2	244.2
Hospital beds per capita	230.9	420.0
No. teaching hospitals	2	3
Cost per doctor visit	$86	$77
Cost per dental visit	$88	$70

Crime
Score: 24.6
Rank: 282

CRIME	AREA	U.S. AVG
Violent crime rate	329.5	465.5
Change in violent crime rate	10.3%	-2.2%
Property crime rate	7,017.4	3,517.1
Change in property crime rate	15.7%	-2.1%

Transportation
Score: 31.3
Rank: 258

COMMUTE	AREA	U.S. AVG
Average commute time	21.2	27.4
Percent commutes > 60 mins.	3.9%	5.9%
Commute by auto	77.5%	78.9%
Commute by mass transit	0.5%	1.9%
Work at home	3.5%	3.1%
Mass transit miles per capita	0.53	1.87

INTERCITY SERVICES	AREA	U.S. AVG
Major airports within 60 miles	0	1
Size of regional airport	None	Large
Daily airline activity	25	686
Amtrak service	No	No

AUTOMOTIVE	AREA	U.S. AVG
Insurance, annual premium	$1,602	$1,432
Gas, cost per gallon	$2.53	$2.49
Daily vehicle miles per capita	20.0	24.0

Leisure
Score: 61.2
Rank: 145

DINING & SHOPPING	AREA	U.S. AVG
Restaurant rating	1	2
Outlet mall score	0	42
No. Starbucks	5	13
No. warehouse clubs	1	2

ENTERTAINMENT	AREA	U.S. AVG
Professional sports rating	2	4
College sports rating	5	4
Zoo/aquarium rating	1	3
Amusement park rating	1	3
Botanical garden/ arboretum rating	1	4

OUTDOOR ACTIVITIES	AREA	U.S. AVG
Golf-course rating	2	4
Ski-area rating	7	3
Sq. miles inland water	3	4
Miles of coastline	0.0	10.7
National Park rating	10	3

Arts & Culture
Score: 40.4
Rank: 223

MEDIA & LIBRARIES	AREA	U.S. AVG
Arts radio rating	7	3
No. public libraries	20	27
Library volumes per capita	2.71	2.78

PERFORMING ARTS	AREA	U.S. AVG
Classical music rating	3	4
Ballet/dance rating	1	3
Professional theater rating	1	3
University arts programs rating	1	5

MUSEUMS	AREA	U.S. AVG
Overall museum rating	3	5
Art museum rating	3	5
Science museum rating	5	5
Children's museum rating	2	3

York–Hanover, PA

Score: 56.9 Rank: 201 2004 rank: 260

Profile: Mid-size city
Location: Southeast Pennsylvania, 110 miles west of Philadelphia and 20 miles north of the Maryland border
Elevation: 351 feet
Time zone: Eastern Standard Time

PRO	CON
Central location	Economy
Cost of living	Educational attainment
Historic interest	Entertainment

Parts of York look much as they did in colonial times, with a downtown area of historic brick buildings and nearby factories, farmers' markets, and a large town square, which all suggest the city's importance before and during the Industrial Revolution. Today, aside from a large Harley-Davidson plant and climate-control maker York International, the area has a diverse base of mostly small manufacturers, and has a blue-collar feel with modest employment trends. There isn't much to do in the city, but the area is strategically located among an array of places providing employment and amenities. The proximity to larger East Coast cities, particularly Baltimore and Washington, D.C., south, is bringing in new residents, some of whom derive incomes from these cities and seek lower living costs and small-town living. These new residents are slowly improving the economic and educational landscape. Baltimore

is closest at 60 miles south. York also sits between historic Gettysburg to the west and the Pennsylvania Dutch country and Philadelphia areas east. Hanover is a nondescript small town 15 miles southwest that serves as a manufacturing and retail center. For those not seeking local employment and willing to travel for certain amenities and services, York has a pleasant small-town feel. If likely future growth is managed well, as predicted in 2004, York should continue to improve in the rankings.

The area has mostly rolling hills given to agricultural use with intermittent creek valleys and wooded areas. The hills become larger toward the south. Summers are warm and humid with frequent thunderstorms and an occasional hot spell. While most bitter cold weather avoids the area in winter, there is snow and snow accumulation. First freeze is mid-October; last is late April.

Population

DEMOGRAPHICS	AREA	U.S. AVG	ETHNIC COMPOSITION	AREA	U.S. AVG	RESIDENT PROFILE	AREA	U.S. AVG
Population	401,753		White	92.1%	79.0%	Single	28.4%	32.4%
Population density per sq. mile	444.2	358.5	Black	3.8%	10.5%	Married	58.7%	52.7%
Population growth	18.3%	21.1%	Asian	1.0%	2.7%	Divorced/separated	13.0%	14.9%
Median age	39.1	36.1	Hispanic	3.3%	10.6%	Married with children	24.6%	23.7%
Percent Democrat	35.5%	44.5%	Religious observance	45.0%	48.9%	Single with children	7.7%	9.1%
Percent Republican	63.7%	54.5%	Diversity measure	20.4	40.1	Percent over age 65	13.9%	12.9%

Economy
& Jobs

Score: 62.8
Rank: 140

INCOME	AREA	U.S. AVG	EMPLOYMENT	AREA	U.S. AVG	EMPLOYING INDUSTRIES	AREA	U.S. AVG
Per capita income	$23,872	$23,235	Unemployment rate	4.5%	4.7%	Largest: Manufacturing		
Household income	$49,723	$46,414	Recent job growth	1.7%	1.3%			
Household income < $25K	20.5%	26.2%	Projected future job growth	7.6%	11.5%	Percent manufacturing	22.5%	15.4%
Household income > $75K	25.4%	25.4%	White collar	54.3%	57.8%	Percent public sector	9.5%	15.7%
Household income growth	9.8%	13.6%	Blue collar	32.4%	25.2%	Percent construction	9.9%	9.9%

Cost of Living

Score: 77.8
Rank: 84

INDEXES & TAXES	AREA	U.S. AVG	HOUSING	AREA	U.S. AVG	NECESSITIES	AREA	U.S. AVG
Cost of Living Index	87.5	100.0	Median home price	$148,900	$220,000	Food Index	91.7	100.0
Buying Power Index	127.4	100.0	Home price appreciation	51.3%	10.1%	Housing Index	60.9	100.0
Income tax rate	2.80%	4.70%	Median rent	$671	$709	Utilities Index	113.3	100.0
Sales tax rate	6.00%	6.58%	Homes owned	72.6%	62.3%	Transportation Index	105.3	100.0
Property tax rate	$14.30	$12.00	Home price ratio	3.0	4.2	Healthcare Index	91.4	100.0
						Miscellaneous Cost Index	99.2	100.0

Climate

Score: 32.1
Rank: 253

TEMPERATURE	AREA	U.S. AVG	PRECIPITATION	AREA	U.S. AVG	COMFORTS & HAZARDS	AREA	U.S. AVG
Average January low	22.5	26.2	Annual inches precipitation	36.0	37.7	July relative humidity	67%	66%
Average July high	86.8	87.4	Annual inches snowfall	35.0	7.0	Annual days mostly sunny	193	208
Annual days > 90°F	24	38	Annual days precipitation	125	109	Annual days with thunderstorms	33	39
Annual days < 32°F	107	89	Annual days rain > 0.5 inches	25	22	Tornado risk score	14	18
Annual days < 0°F	1	6	Annual days snow > 1.5 inches	8	6	Hurricane risk score	12	13

TEMPERATURE

PRECIPITATION

DAYS OF CLOUDS & PRECIPITATION

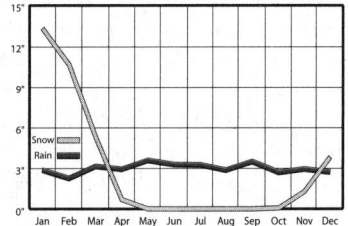
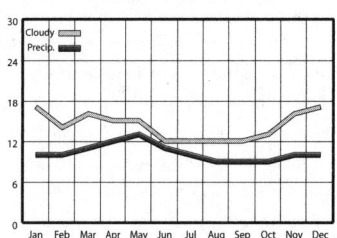

Education	ACHIEVEMENT	AREA	U.S. AVG	PUBLIC SCHOOLS	AREA	U.S. AVG	HIGHER EDUCATION	AREA	U.S. AVG
	High school degree	80.8%	82.7%	Expenditures per pupil	$5,729	$5,686	No. 2-year colleges	4	4
Score: 40.4	2-year college degree	5.8%	6.4%	Student/teacher ratio	18.5	16.7	No. 4-year colleges/universities	3	6
Rank: 224	4-year college degree	12.6%	15.7%	Attending public school	93.0%	90.1%	No. highly ranked universities	2	1
	Graduate/professional degree	5.9%	8.9%	State SAT score	993*	1021			
				State ACT score	21.8	20.9			

Health & Healthcare	HAZARDS & ILLNESSES	AREA	U.S. AVG	HEALTHCARE	AREA	U.S. AVG	CRIME	AREA	U.S. AVG
	Air-quality score	20	37	Physicians per capita	188.9	244.2	Violent crime rate	278.6	465.5
	Water-quality score	40	52	Hospital beds per capita	212.6	420.0	Change in violent crime rate	3.6%	-2.2%
Score: 16.8	Pollen/allergy score	50	61	No. teaching hospitals	2	3	Property crime rate	2,471.6	3,517.1
Rank: 310	Cancer mortality per capita	237.1	201.9	Cost per doctor visit	$64	$77	Change in property crime rate	-1.1%	-2.1%
	Depression days per month	3.9	3.5	Cost per dental visit	$60	$70			
	Stress score	33	50						

(Crime: Score: 85.3, Rank: 56)

Transportation	COMMUTE	AREA	U.S. AVG	INTERCITY SERVICES	AREA	U.S. AVG	AUTOMOTIVE	AREA	U.S. AVG
	Average commute time	26.1	27.4	Major airports within 60 miles	4	1	Insurance, annual premium	$1,254	$1,432
Score: 95.7	Percent commutes > 60 mins.	6.1%	5.9%	Size of regional airport	Large	Large	Gas, cost per gallon	$2.46	$2.49
Rank: 17	Commute by auto	84.4%	78.9%	Daily airline activity	2329	686	Daily vehicle miles per capita	20.6	24.0
	Commute by mass transit	0.6%	1.9%	Amtrak service	No	No			
	Work at home	2.7%	3.1%						
	Mass transit miles per capita	0.60	1.87						

Leisure	DINING & SHOPPING	AREA	U.S. AVG	ENTERTAINMENT	AREA	U.S. AVG	OUTDOOR ACTIVITIES	AREA	U.S. AVG
	Restaurant rating	1	2	Professional sports rating	4	4	Golf-course rating	3	4
Score: 46.3	Outlet mall score	62	42	College sports rating	2	4	Ski-area rating	5	3
Rank: 200	No. Starbucks	2	13	Zoo/aquarium rating	1	3	Sq. miles inland water	2	4
	No. warehouse clubs	2	2	Amusement park rating	1	3	Miles of coastline	0.0	10.7
				Botanical garden/ arboretum rating	4	4	National Park rating	2	3

Arts & Culture	MEDIA & LIBRARIES	AREA	U.S. AVG	PERFORMING ARTS	AREA	U.S. AVG	MUSEUMS	AREA	U.S. AVG
	Arts radio rating	1	3	Classical music rating	3	4	Overall museum rating	2	5
Score: 7.5	No. public libraries	15	27	Ballet/dance rating	5	3	Art museum rating	1	5
Rank: 345	Library volumes per capita	1.07	2.78	Professional theater rating	1	3	Science museum rating	1	5
				University arts programs rating	3	5	Children's museum rating	1	3

Youngstown–Warren–Boardman, OH-PA   Score: 46.6   Rank: 269   2004 rank: 291

Profile: Mid-size industrial-town complex
Location: Northeastern Ohio near the Pennsylvania border halfway between Cleveland and Pittsburgh
Elevation: 1,178 feet
Time zone: Eastern Standard Time

PRO
Small-town atmosphere
Cost of living
Proximity to larger cities

CON
Economic decline
Entertainment
Rugged winters

Youngstown's early prosperity and character emerged from the steel industry. Few places have seen a more pronounced decline in that industry than Youngstown, although steel and steel products manufacturing remain important to the local economy. Today the city struggles with some success to diversify into automobile assembly and other manufacturing mixed with a wide range of small businesses. A local business incubator has been set up to aid this effort. Youngstown also benefits from the 13,000-student Youngstown State University. Warren, to the north, also has an industrial character but with a bit of historic charm, and Boardman is an unremarkable middle-class suburb south of Youngstown. The metro area now includes Sharon, another struggling and small post-industrial city just across the Pennsylvania border. Youngstown's location midway between Cleveland and Pittsburgh, 80 miles from the center of each, is attractive for business and for those seeking a small-town lifestyle with access to big-city services and amenities. Not surprisingly, home prices and living costs are notably low. There are some attractive recreational areas in the nearby Appalachian foothills and in Pennsylvania to the east. On the whole, the area is down but not out; its strategic location and a successful economic turnaround may prove the area to be a good value, but it's a long path out of the woods.

The area mainly lies in a river valley surrounded by low wooded hills and ridges. The region has numerous streams and lakes, both natural and man-made. Summer is typically warm and humid with thundershowers and few temperature extremes. The lake effect from Lake Erie produces persistent cloudiness, snow flurries, and occasional heavier snows. The area has the highest cloudiness, days of precipitation, and total annual snowfall in the state. First freeze is mid-October; last is early May.

Population

DEMOGRAPHICS	AREA	U.S. AVG	ETHNIC COMPOSITION	AREA	U.S. AVG	RESIDENT PROFILE	AREA	U.S. AVG
Population	589,541		White	86.8%	79.0%	Single	32.9%	32.4%
Population density per sq. mile	346.1	358.5	Black	10.6%	10.5%	Married	52.7%	52.7%
Population growth	-3.9%	21.1%	Asian	0.6%	2.7%	Divorced/separated	14.4%	14.9%
Median age	40.3	36.1	Hispanic	1.7%	10.6%	Married with children	20.3%	23.7%
Percent Democrat	59.3%	44.5%	Religious observance	55.9%	48.9%	Single with children	8.6%	9.1%
Percent Republican	40.1%	54.5%	Diversity measure	25.5	40.1	Percent over age 65	17.2%	12.9%

Economy & Jobs
Score: 5.1
Rank: 354

INCOME	AREA	U.S. AVG	EMPLOYMENT	AREA	U.S. AVG	EMPLOYING INDUSTRIES	AREA	U.S. AVG
Per capita income	$20,826	$23,235	Unemployment rate	7.0%	4.7%	Largest: Manufacturing		
Household income	$40,303	$46,414	Recent job growth	-0.5%	1.3%			
Household income < $25K	30.2%	26.2%	Projected future job growth	-0.1%	11.5%	Percent manufacturing	22.5%	15.4%
Household income > $75K	19.4%	25.4%	White collar	52.1%	57.8%	Percent public sector	11.0%	15.7%
Household income growth	11.2%	13.6%	Blue collar	31.3%	25.2%	Percent construction	8.8%	9.9%

Cost of Living
Score: 72.5
Rank: 104

INDEXES & TAXES	AREA	U.S. AVG	HOUSING	AREA	U.S. AVG	NECESSITIES	AREA	U.S. AVG
Cost of Living Index	74.4	100.0	Median home price	$78,700	$220,000	Food Index	98.9	100.0
Buying Power Index	121.4	100.0	Home price appreciation	13.8%	10.1%	Housing Index	37.7	100.0
Income tax rate	6.14%	4.70%	Median rent	$559	$709	Utilities Index	122.8	100.0
Sales tax rate	6.40%	6.58%	Homes owned	69.1%	62.3%	Transportation Index	86.4	100.0
Property tax rate	$12.60	$12.00	Home price ratio	2.0	4.2	Healthcare Index	87.8	100.0
						Miscellaneous Cost Index	92.5	100.0

Climate
Score: 5.3
Rank: 353

TEMPERATURE	AREA	U.S. AVG	PRECIPITATION	AREA	U.S. AVG	COMFORTS & HAZARDS	AREA	U.S. AVG
Average January low	18.3	26.2	Annual inches precipitation	38.0	37.7	July relative humidity	74%	66%
Average July high	81.8	87.4	Annual inches snowfall	57.6	7.0	Annual days mostly sunny	164	208
Annual days > 90°F	7	38	Annual days precipitation	181	109	Annual days with thunderstorms	36	39
Annual days < 32°F	136	89	Annual days rain > 0.5 inches	22	22	Tornado risk score	35	18
Annual days < 0°F	6	6	Annual days snow > 1.5 inches	12	6	Hurricane risk score	3	13

TEMPERATURE

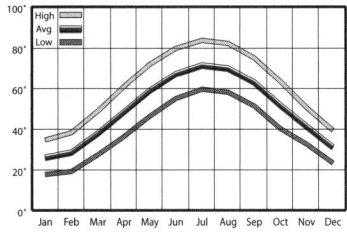

PRECIPITATION

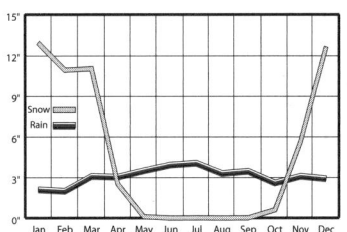

DAYS OF CLOUDS & PRECIPITATION

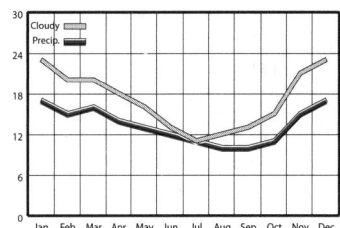

Education
Score: 28.3
Rank: 269

ACHIEVEMENT	AREA	U.S. AVG	PUBLIC SCHOOLS	AREA	U.S. AVG	HIGHER EDUCATION	AREA	U.S. AVG
High school degree	82.6%	82.7%	Expenditures per pupil	$5,389	$5,686	No. 2-year colleges	11	4
2-year college degree	5.1%	6.4%	Student/teacher ratio	18.4	16.7	No. 4-year colleges/universities	4	6
4-year college degree	11.1%	15.7%	Attending public school	90.4%	90.1%	No. highly ranked universities	1	1
Graduate/professional degree	5.3%	8.9%	State SAT score	1079	1021			
			State ACT score	21.5*	20.9			

Health & Healthcare
Score: 63.4
Rank: 138

HAZARDS & ILLNESSES	AREA	U.S. AVG	HEALTHCARE	AREA	U.S. AVG	CRIME	AREA	U.S. AVG
Air-quality score	37	37	Physicians per capita	228.3	244.2	Violent crime rate	413.9	465.5
Water-quality score	47	52	Hospital beds per capita	541.4	420.0	Change in violent crime rate	28.0%	-2.2%
Pollen/allergy score	59	61	No. teaching hospitals	6	3	Property crime rate	3,616.6	3,517.1
Cancer mortality per capita	221.6	201.9	Cost per doctor visit	$68	$77	Change in property crime rate	13.6%	-2.1%
Depression days per month	3.8	3.5	Cost per dental visit	$60	$70			
Stress score	62	50						

Crime
Score: 66.8
Rank: 125

Transportation
Score: 87.7
Rank: 47

COMMUTE	AREA	U.S. AVG	INTERCITY SERVICES	AREA	U.S. AVG	AUTOMOTIVE	AREA	U.S. AVG
Average commute time	22.7	27.4	Major airports within 60 miles	2	1	Insurance, annual premium	$1,170	$1,432
Percent commutes > 60 mins.	4.8%	5.9%	Size of regional airport	Large	Large	Gas, cost per gallon	$2.46	$2.49
Commute by auto	86.1%	78.9%	Daily airline activity	1150	686	Daily vehicle miles per capita	21.8	24.0
Commute by mass transit	0.5%	1.9%	Amtrak service	Yes	No			
Work at home	2.3%	3.1%						
Mass transit miles per capita	0.52	1.87						

Leisure
Score: 36.6
Rank: 236

DINING & SHOPPING	AREA	U.S. AVG	ENTERTAINMENT	AREA	U.S. AVG	OUTDOOR ACTIVITIES	AREA	U.S. AVG
Restaurant rating	1	2	Professional sports rating	3	4	Golf-course rating	5	4
Outlet mall score	0	42	College sports rating	3	4	Ski-area rating	3	3
No. Starbucks	3	13	Zoo/aquarium rating	1	3	Sq. miles inland water	3	4
No. warehouse clubs	3	2	Amusement park rating	1	3	Miles of coastline	0.0	10.7
			Botanical garden/ arboretum rating	2	4	National Park rating	1	3

Arts & Culture
Score: 54.3
Rank: 171

MEDIA & LIBRARIES	AREA	U.S. AVG	PERFORMING ARTS	AREA	U.S. AVG	MUSEUMS	AREA	U.S. AVG
Arts radio rating	1	3	Classical music rating	5	4	Overall museum rating	4	5
No. public libraries	36	27	Ballet/dance rating	1	3	Art museum rating	7	5
Library volumes per capita	2.93	2.78	Professional theater rating	1	3	Science museum rating	1	5
			University arts programs rating	5	5	Children's museum rating	1	3

Yuba City, CA

Score: 10.9 Rank: 371 2004 rank: 315

Profile: Small-town complex
Location: Northern California, northern part of Central Valley, 30 miles north of Sacramento
Elevation: 100 feet
Time zone: Pacific Standard Time

PRO	CON
Mild winters	Cost of living
Nearby recreation	Educational attainment
Close to Sacramento	Entertainment

Yuba City and Marysville are Central Valley cities separated by the Sacramento River at the junction of the Feather River. The local economy has traditionally been largely agricultural and working class in character. Local amenities are noticeably lacking and there is little in the way of attractive small-town flavor, although Marysville has accomplished a minor downtown renewal. Residential development is arriving in the southern portions of the county primarily connected to the Sacramento area, creating a construction boom but not doing a lot else, thus far, for the area. Proximity to Sacramento and the Lake Tahoe Region add to the list of available amenities, and for that reason the statistical rating probably underestimates reality—for those willing to drive 30 miles or more. The climate is pleasant particularly in winter, and

there is plenty of nearby recreation with water and wildlife-viewing areas. Employment prospects have improved since 2004 but still aren't great, and are probably distorted by the building boom. Cost of living is very high for what is available in the region, crime is fairly high, educational attainment is low, and there isn't much to do.

The immediate area is level with a mix of general agriculture and orchards. Both rivers are broad and slow moving. The Sierra Nevada rises to the east and northeast, with oak-studded foothills beginning just a few miles east of town. In summer, the Mediterranean valley climate produces hot, dry, clear days, with spells of oppressive 100°F-plus heat. Winters are mild and occasionally foggy, with a few freezing days but little chance for snow. Most of the year's rain arrives in winter.

Population

DEMOGRAPHICS	AREA	U.S. AVG	ETHNIC COMPOSITION	AREA	U.S. AVG	RESIDENT PROFILE	AREA	U.S. AVG
Population	150,706		White	67.1%	79.0%	Single	29.7%	32.4%
Population density per sq. mile	122.2	358.5	Black	2.5%	10.5%	Married	53.2%	52.7%
Population growth	24.0%	21.1%	Asian	9.5%	2.7%	Divorced/separated	17.0%	14.9%
Median age	33.3	36.1	Hispanic	23.2%	10.6%	Married with children	26.7%	23.7%
Percent Democrat	31.7%	44.5%	Religious observance	28.6%	48.9%	Single with children	11.0%	9.1%
Percent Republican	67.1%	54.5%	Diversity measure	68.8	40.1	Percent over age 65	11.5%	12.9%

Economy & Jobs
Score: 44.9
Rank: 207

INCOME	AREA	U.S. AVG	EMPLOYMENT	AREA	U.S. AVG	EMPLOYING INDUSTRIES	AREA	U.S. AVG
Per capita income	$17,908	$23,235	Unemployment rate	8.4%	4.7%	Largest: Healthcare & Social Assistance		
Household income	$39,750	$46,414	Recent job growth	3.6%	1.3%			
Household income < $25K	30.9%	26.2%	Projected future job growth	17.1%	11.5%	Percent manufacturing	16.0%	15.4%
Household income > $75K	20.4%	25.4%	White collar	49.1%	57.8%	Percent public sector	18.4%	15.7%
Household income growth	13.7%	13.6%	Blue collar	27.6%	25.2%	Percent construction	11.6%	9.9%

Cost of Living
Score: 15.5
Rank: 315

INDEXES & TAXES	AREA	U.S. AVG	HOUSING	AREA	U.S. AVG	NECESSITIES	AREA	U.S. AVG
Cost of Living Index	116.8	100.0	Median home price	$268,200	$220,000	Food Index	121.0	100.0
Buying Power Index	76.3	100.0	Home price appreciation	143.6%	10.1%	Housing Index	106.1	100.0
Income tax rate	6.00%	4.70%	Median rent	$627	$709	Utilities Index	111.6	100.0
Sales tax rate	7.25%	6.58%	Homes owned	54.9%	62.3%	Transportation Index	116.1	100.0
Property tax rate	$9.00	$12.00	Home price ratio	6.7	4.2	Healthcare Index	154.5	100.0
						Miscellaneous Cost Index	103.8	100.0

Climate
Score: 94.4
Rank: 22

TEMPERATURE	AREA	U.S. AVG
Average January low	36.0	26.2
Average July high	94.0	87.4
Annual days > 90°F	82	38
Annual days < 32°F	25	89
Annual days < 0°F	0	6

PRECIPITATION	AREA	U.S. AVG
Annual inches precipitation	30.0	37.7
Annual inches snowfall	0.5	7.0
Annual days precipitation	60	109
Annual days rain > 0.5 inches	19	22
Annual days snow > 1.5 inches	0	6

COMFORTS & HAZARDS	AREA	U.S. AVG
July relative humidity	67%	66%
Annual days mostly sunny	276	208
Annual days with thunderstorms	6	39
Tornado risk score	2	18
Hurricane risk score	0	13

TEMPERATURE

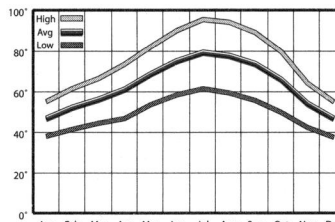

PRECIPITATION

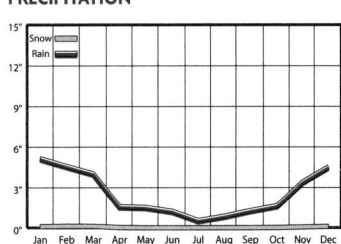

DAYS OF CLOUDS & PRECIPITATION

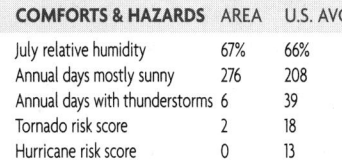

Education
Score: 10.2
Rank: 335

ACHIEVEMENT	AREA	U.S. AVG
High school degree	72.2%	82.7%
2-year college degree	8.9%	6.4%
4-year college degree	9.0%	15.7%
Graduate/professional degree	4.0%	8.9%

PUBLIC SCHOOLS	AREA	U.S. AVG
Expenditures per pupil	$4,889	$5,686
Student/teacher ratio	20.0	16.7
Attending public school	95.5%	90.1%
State SAT score	1019*	1021
State ACT score	21.6	20.9

HIGHER EDUCATION	AREA	U.S. AVG
No. 2-year colleges	1	4
No. 4-year colleges/universities	0	6
No. highly ranked universities	0	1

Health & Healthcare
Score: 9.9
Rank: 336

HAZARDS & ILLNESSES	AREA	U.S. AVG
Air-quality score	50	37
Water-quality score	60	52
Pollen/allergy score	74	61
Cancer mortality per capita	189.3	201.9
Depression days per month	3.9	3.5
Stress score	99	50

HEALTHCARE	AREA	U.S. AVG
Physicians per capita	167.5	244.2
Hospital beds per capita	216.3	420.0
No. teaching hospitals	0	3
Cost per doctor visit	$82	$77
Cost per dental visit	$79	$70

Crime
Score: 29.1
Rank: 265

CRIME	AREA	U.S. AVG
Violent crime rate	440.3	465.5
Change in violent crime rate	-11.9%	-2.2%
Property crime rate	3,855.7	3,517.1
Change in property crime rate	-2.8%	-2.1%

Transportation
Score: 9.9
Rank: 338

COMMUTE	AREA	U.S. AVG
Average commute time	27.6	27.4
Percent commutes > 60 mins.	9.7%	5.9%
Commute by auto	76.1%	78.9%
Commute by mass transit	0.7%	1.9%
Work at home	3.4%	3.1%
Mass transit miles per capita	0.66	1.87

INTERCITY SERVICES	AREA	U.S. AVG
Major airports within 60 miles	2	1
Size of regional airport	Medium	Large
Daily airline activity	267	686
Amtrak service	No	No

AUTOMOTIVE	AREA	U.S. AVG
Insurance, annual premium	$1,618	$1,432
Gas, cost per gallon	$2.66	$2.49
Daily vehicle miles per capita	13.3	24.0

Leisure
Score: 48.7
Rank: 191

DINING & SHOPPING	AREA	U.S. AVG
Restaurant rating	1	2
Outlet mall score	67	42
No. Starbucks	3	13
No. warehouse clubs	1	2

ENTERTAINMENT	AREA	U.S. AVG
Professional sports rating	2	4
College sports rating	1	4
Zoo/aquarium rating	1	3
Amusement park rating	1	3
Botanical garden/ arboretum rating	1	4

OUTDOOR ACTIVITIES	AREA	U.S. AVG
Golf-course rating	1	4
Ski-area rating	10	3
Sq. miles inland water	2	4
Miles of coastline	0.0	10.7
National Park rating	4	3

Arts & Culture
Score: 0.8
Rank: 370

MEDIA & LIBRARIES	AREA	U.S. AVG
Arts radio rating	1	3
No. public libraries	6	27
Library volumes per capita	1.77	2.78

PERFORMING ARTS	AREA	U.S. AVG
Classical music rating	1	4
Ballet/dance rating	1	3
Professional theater rating	1	3
University arts programs rating	1	5

MUSEUMS	AREA	U.S. AVG
Overall museum rating	1	5
Art museum rating	1	5
Science museum rating	1	5
Children's museum rating	1	3

Yuma, AZ

Profile: Small desert city
Location: Southwest corner of Arizona along the Colorado River and California border, 25 miles north of Mexican border
Elevation: 138
Time zone: Mountain Standard Time (no daylight saving time)

PRO	CON
Desert climate	Economy
Cost of living	Summer heat
Nearby recreation	Educational attainment

Yuma is located at the extreme southwest corner of Arizona where the state borders California just north of the Mexican border. A true oasis in the desert, Yuma was originally settled as a crossing point at the Colorado River for California settlers. Today, the dry desert climate is the main attraction. Yuma, one of the driest and sunniest places in the country, averages almost 300 days of sunshine each year. Retirees are attracted to the climate, access to California, and low cost of living and crime rate by regional standards. On the downside, educational attainment is very low, healthcare resources are weak, summers are oppressive, and the area features one of the worst current employment pictures in the country. Climate, cost of living, and some nearby desert and Colorado River recreation bring some positive ranking points

and have drawn a number of retirees, but we think the area faces many challenges and may fare more poorly than the ranking indicates.

Yuma is located in the Colorado River Valley, which narrows at this point with rugged, hilly, desert terrain on all sides. Green vegetation only grows at the river. The rest of the terrain has scant vegetation, mostly sagebrush, scrub, and short grasses. The climate is true desert. Summers bring dry and sometimes oppressive desert heat during the day followed by relatively cool evenings. *Average* high temperatures from June to September are over 100°F. During the short winter, daytime temperatures are mild, usually in the 70s, but nights can drop below freezing. Precipitation is minimal. First freeze is mid-December; last is early February.

Population

DEMOGRAPHICS	AREA	U.S. AVG	ETHNIC COMPOSITION	AREA	U.S. AVG	RESIDENT PROFILE	AREA	U.S. AVG
Population	177,838		White	66.1%	79.0%	Single	27.3%	32.4%
Population density per sq. mile	32.3	358.5	Black	1.8%	10.5%	Married	58.7%	52.7%
Population growth	66.4%	21.1%	Asian	1.1%	2.7%	Divorced/separated	14.1%	14.9%
Median age	33.5	36.1	Hispanic	55.8%	10.6%	Married with children	27.6%	23.7%
Percent Democrat	41.6%	44.5%	Religious observance	36.1%	48.9%	Single with children	9.6%	9.1%
Percent Republican	57.6%	54.5%	Diversity measure	74.3	40.1	Percent over age 65	17.1%	12.9%

Economy & Jobs

Score: 21.9
Rank: 292

INCOME	AREA	U.S. AVG	EMPLOYMENT	AREA	U.S. AVG	EMPLOYING INDUSTRIES	AREA	U.S. AVG
Per capita income	$17,330	$23,235	Unemployment rate	21.3%	4.7%	Largest: Healthcare & Social Assistance		
Household income	$37,997	$46,414	Recent job growth	6.6%	1.3%			
Household income < $25K	31.1%	26.2%	Projected future job growth	30.3%	11.5%	Percent manufacturing	12.2%	15.4%
Household income > $75K	17.7%	25.4%	White collar	52.1%	57.8%	Percent public sector	22.7%	15.7%
Household income growth	18.1%	13.6%	Blue collar	22.8%	25.2%	Percent construction	10.6%	9.9%

Cost of Living

Score: 45.7
Rank: 203

INDEXES & TAXES	AREA	U.S. AVG	HOUSING	AREA	U.S. AVG	NECESSITIES	AREA	U.S. AVG
Cost of Living Index	104.2	100.0	Median home price	$238,900	$220,000	Food Index	102.4	100.0
Buying Power Index	81.7	100.0	Home price appreciation	87.5%	10.1%	Housing Index	69.9	100.0
Income tax rate	3.90%	4.70%	Median rent	$695	$709	Utilities Index	122.8	100.0
Sales tax rate	8.80%	6.58%	Homes owned	53.5%	62.3%	Transportation Index	105.6	100.0
Property tax rate	$9.82	$12.00	Home price ratio	6.3	4.2	Healthcare Index	107.1	100.0
						Miscellaneous Cost Index	95.9	100.0

Climate

Score: 90.6
Rank: 36

TEMPERATURE	AREA	U.S. AVG	PRECIPITATION	AREA	U.S. AVG	COMFORTS & HAZARDS	AREA	U.S. AVG
Average January low	37.6	26.2	Annual inches precipitation	7.0	37.7	July relative humidity	36%	66%
Average July high	104.8	87.4	Annual inches snowfall	0.0	7.0	Annual days mostly sunny	295	208
Annual days > 90°F	164	38	Annual days precipitation	34	109	Annual days with thunderstorms	23	39
Annual days < 32°F	32	89	Annual days rain > 0.5 inches	2	22	Tornado risk score	4	18
Annual days < 0°F	0	6	Annual days snow > 1.5 inches	0	6	Hurricane risk score	3	13

TEMPERATURE

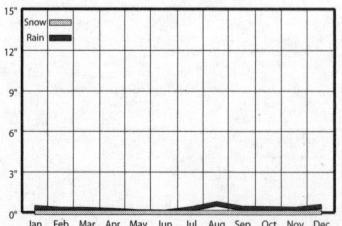

PRECIPITATION

DAYS OF CLOUDS & PRECIPITATION

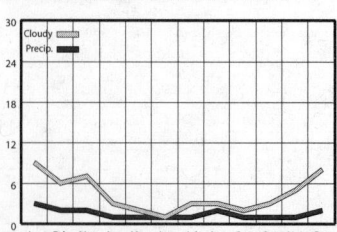

Education
Score: 0.8
Rank: 370

ACHIEVEMENT	AREA	U.S. AVG	PUBLIC SCHOOLS	AREA	U.S. AVG	HIGHER EDUCATION	AREA	U.S. AVG
High school degree	65.5%	82.7%	Expenditures per pupil	$5,740	$5,686	No. 2-year colleges	1	4
2-year college degree	5.0%	6.4%	Student/teacher ratio	29.3	16.7	No. 4-year colleges/universities	0	6
4-year college degree	7.3%	15.7%	Attending public school	96.5%	90.1%	No. highly ranked universities	0	1
Graduate/professional degree	4.7%	8.9%	State SAT score	1049	1021			
			State ACT score	21.6*	20.9			

Health & Healthcare
Score: 27.5
Rank: 270

HAZARDS & ILLNESSES	AREA	U.S. AVG	HEALTHCARE	AREA	U.S. AVG	CRIME	AREA	U.S. AVG
Air-quality score	45	37	Physicians per capita	104.0	244.2	Violent crime rate	487.7	465.5
Water-quality score	20	52	Hospital beds per capita	172.6	420.0	Change in violent crime rate	-16.8%	-2.2%
Pollen/allergy score	66	61	No. teaching hospitals	0	3	Property crime rate	3,671.0	3,517.1
Cancer mortality per capita	134.8	201.9	Cost per doctor visit	$87	$77	Change in property crime rate	0.3%	-2.1%
Depression days per month	2.8	3.5	Cost per dental visit	$72	$70			
Stress score	31	50						

Crime
Score: 39.0
Rank: 228

Transportation
Score: 41.2
Rank: 221

COMMUTE	AREA	U.S. AVG	INTERCITY SERVICES	AREA	U.S. AVG	AUTOMOTIVE	AREA	U.S. AVG
Average commute time	20.7	27.4	Major airports within 60 miles	0	1	Insurance, annual premium	$1,611	$1,432
Percent commutes > 60 mins.	4.0%	5.9%	Size of regional airport	None	Large	Gas, cost per gallon	$2.46	$2.49
Commute by auto	74.1%	78.9%	Daily airline activity	0	686	Daily vehicle miles per capita	18.3	24.0
Commute by mass transit	1.3%	1.9%	Amtrak service	Yes	No			
Work at home	1.9%	3.1%						
Mass transit miles per capita	1.31	1.87						

Leisure
Score: 61.0
Rank: 146

DINING & SHOPPING	AREA	U.S. AVG	ENTERTAINMENT	AREA	U.S. AVG	OUTDOOR ACTIVITIES	AREA	U.S. AVG
Restaurant rating	1	2	Professional sports rating	2	4	Golf-course rating	8	4
Outlet mall score	0	42	College sports rating	3	4	Ski-area rating	4	3
No. Starbucks	1	13	Zoo/aquarium rating	1	3	Sq. miles inland water	3	4
No. warehouse clubs	1	2	Amusement park rating	1	3	Miles of coastline	0.0	10.7
			Botanical garden/ arboretum rating	1	4	National Park rating	10	3

Arts & Culture
Score: 11.2
Rank: 331

MEDIA & LIBRARIES	AREA	U.S. AVG	PERFORMING ARTS	AREA	U.S. AVG	MUSEUMS	AREA	U.S. AVG
Arts radio rating	1	3	Classical music rating	3	4	Overall museum rating	3	5
No. public libraries	7	27	Ballet/dance rating	1	3	Art museum rating	3	5
Library volumes per capita	2.07	2.78	Professional theater rating	1	3	Science museum rating	1	5
			University arts programs rating	1	5	Children's museum rating	1	3

chapter

Canada Metropolitan Areas

As the world's second largest country in land area, Canada offers spectacular geography, rich cultures, and a fascinating assortment of cities. While just larger than the U.S. in land area, the official 2001 Canadian population of 31.4 million, which is estimated to have grown to just above 33 million in 2006, is just one-ninth of its bustling southern neighbor. That fact only begins the comparisons between U.S. and Canadian cities. With respect to their U.S. counterparts, Canadian cities are cleaner, generally more livable, and distinctly more international with pockets of strong European influence.

There is more to know about Canada and Canadian history than can possibly be presented here. The historic rivalry between the French and British, largely eliminated in the United States by the Louisiana Purchase, remains alive in Canada. French language and culture dominate Québec and influence other eastern provinces. In fact, upon arriving blindfolded in Québec City, especially in its wonderful historic core, you may insist you were in France—at least until the arrival of winter. Most of the remainder of the country exhibits an attenuated British influence in custom, infrastructure, and style of government. That influence becomes slightly more obvious in the Maritime provinces of the Atlantic and in British Columbia, most particularly in its English-style capital of Victoria.

Canada is a British-style constitutional monarchy with 10 self-governing provinces and three territories. That in itself doesn't influence its cities, but like much of Europe, Canada takes a more socialistic approach than the United States. The healthcare system is nationalized, and governments at all levels exert greater influence on social issues and city infrastructure. As a result, Canadian cities have a more planned look and feel, and are resistant to the anything-goes urban sprawl found in many U.S. equivalents. They are cleaner and generally lack the high crime rates and areas of urban blight found to the south. That isn't to say that Canadian cities don't have problems, but most people comparing the two countries notice these differences right away.

Immigration has been an important recent influence on Canadian cities, much as it was in U.S. cities in the late 19th century. Canada has generally more relaxed immigration policies than the United States. In the 1990s, immigration experienced a big surge, the numbers entering the country almost doubling in size from the previous decade. Because of the British influence, the country was particularly attractive to wealthy Hong Kong residents, and immigrants from Asia now comprise 60% of the quarter of a million immigrants arriving each year. The cities of Toronto and Vancouver in particular have large and growing Asian communities, which add a spark of diversity and a stronger international flavor but also aggravate growth-related problems already evident in those cities.

More recently, a combination of factors, including immigration, has brought the healthiest economy seen in Canada in years. A natural resource boom led by petroleum, improved government fiscal performance, and reduced separatist tension in French Canada has led to the strongest employment picture since 1974, some tax reductions, and a generally improved standard of living. Lower interest rates have sparked a housing boom much as in the U.S., and most parts of Canada, especially the west, have seen rapid economic expansion. As in the U.S., there are some doubts about the sustainability of the expansion, as some of it is dependent on construction and other boom-dependent industries, while the manufacturing sectors, particularly in Ontario, continue to suffer to a degree. How this will all play out is unclear, but Canada has a far more positive economic environment than even that of 3 years ago.

Ranking & Rating Canadian Cities

In this chapter, *Cities Ranked & Rated*, 2nd Edition, sets out to (1) compare Canadian cities with each other and (2) compare them with U.S. counterparts. As with the 375 U.S. government–defined Metropolitan Statistical Areas (MSAs) in chapter 5, the Canadian government has identified 27 Census Metropolitan Areas (CMAs) using a definition largely modeled after that of the United States. (See "Census Metropolitan Areas [CMAs]" in chapter 1 for a discussion of the definition.) The CMA list hasn't changed since 2004 except for a pair of name changes: the former Chicoutimi–Jonquière area in northern Québec now goes by the name of the region—Saguenay—as these

cities and two smaller villages merged into one, and the Ottawa–Hull region that straddles the Ontario and Québec borders is now called Ottawa–Gatineau, the result of a merger of five Québec cities. This chapter presents statistics for each CMA, along with a brief description of its character, topography, and climate.

Due to space and the unavailability of certain data comparable to the U.S. MSAs, the tables are abbreviated but retain important comparative statistics such as cost of living and climate. Eight of the U.S. ranking categories— Economy & Jobs, Cost of Living, Climate, Education, Crime, Transportation, Leisure, and Arts & Culture—are blended with a Quality of Life rating to achieve the Canada ranking on a scale from 1 to 27, 1 being the top city. Because of the smaller data sample and because each of the eight categories does not have a score calculated into the ranking, the approach is more qualitative than that used for U.S. metro areas in chapter 5.

Each city is then compared with a U.S. counterpart. Where possible, equivalent U.S. cities are identified based on

TABLE 6.1 CANADIAN CENSUS METROPOLITAN AREAS: RANKINGS & SELECTED STATISTICS BY CMA

CENSUS METROPOLITAN AREA	CANADA RANK	2004 CANADA RANK	COMPARABLE U.S. RANK	2001 POPULATION	1996–2001 POPULATION GROWTH	UNEMPLOYMENT RATE	COST OF LIVING INDEX	ANNUAL PRECIPITATION (MM./INCHES)	ANNUAL SNOWFALL (CM./INCHES)	DAYS BELOW -20°C/-4°F	UNIVERSITY DEGREE	CRIME (CANADA AVERAGE 100)	MUSEUM RATING	QUALITY OF LIFE RATING
Abbotsford, British Columbia	8	10	90	147,370	8.0%	5.0%	93.2	1,573.2/61.9	63.5/25.0	0.0	15.2%	n/a	3	7
Calgary, Alberta	7	6	60	951,395	15.8%	4.0%	114.8	412.6/16.2	126.7/49.9	26.0	27.4%	120	7	8
Edmonton, Alberta	9	8	100	937,845	8.7%	5.0%	103.9	476.9/18.8	123.5/48.6	28.1	21.3%	204	5	7
Halifax, Nova Scotia	12	13	130	359,183	4.7%	5.2%	92.8	1,508.0/59.4	151.8/59.8	0.9	27.9%	89	7	7
Hamilton, Ontario	22	20	250	662,401	6.1%	5.9%	83.6	910.0/35.8	151.8/59.8	3.4	20.0%	151	4	4
Kingston, Ontario	15	16	160	146,838	1.6%	6.3%	92.1	968.2/38.1	180.9/71.2	11.3	23.7%	138	7	6
Kitchener–Waterloo, Ontario	14	24	140	414,284	8.2%	5.5%	92.7	907.9/35.7	159.5/62.8	7.6	20.4%	114	5	7
London, Ontario	17	15	190	432,451	3.8%	6.6%	88.6	987.1/38.9	202.4/79.7	5.0	21.1%	144	8	6
Montréal, Québec	2	2	30	3,426,350	3.0%	8.9%	85.8	1,062.6/41.8	226.2/89.1	7.7	25.9%	188	10	9
Oshawa, Ontario	19	21	200	296,298	10.2%	6.2%	97.8	877.9/34.6	118.4/46.6	3.4	15.3%	215	5	5
Ottawa–Gatineau, Ontario	3	4	35	1,063,664	6.5%	6.7%	122.7	914.2/36.0	202.7/79.8	18.9	33.0%	95	10	9
Québec City, Québec	4	7	50	682,757	1.6%	5.7%	98.5	504.0/19.8	114.8/45.2	31.1	24.9%	149	9	8
Regina, Saskatchewan	18	18	195	192,800	-0.4%	5.2%	84.9	388.1/15.3	105.9/41.7	47.7	23.0%	223	5	4
Saguenay, Québec	27	26	320	154,938	-3.4%	11.2%	76.6	1,002.1/39.5	301.5/118.7	37.1	16.9%	n/a	2	2
St. Catharines–Niagara, Ontario	10	11	110	377,099	1.2%	7.9%	84.2	871.6/34.3	136.6/53.8	0.9	15.6%	71	5	7
Saint John, New Brunswick	24	25	290	122,678	-2.4%	8.4%	85.4	1,390.3/54.7	256.9/101.1	15.2	17.6%	238	3	3
St. John's, Newfoundland and Labrador	16	14	190	172,918	-0.7%	8.7%	87.1	1,513.7/59.6	322.3/126.9	1.0	22.7%	258	6	5
Saskatoon, Saskatchewan	13	12	140	225,927	3.1%	5.7%	95.9	350.0/13.8	97.2/38.3	52.1	23.8%	232	4	5
Sherbrooke, Québec	21	22	245	153,811	2.8%	7.2%	85.2	1,144.1/45.0	294.3/115.9	35.7	21.8%	n/a	4	4
Sudbury, Ontario	26	27	300	155,219	-6.1%	7.7%	76.4	899.3/35.4	274.4/108.0	36.4	14.9%	121	6	3
Thunder Bay, Ontario	20	17	240	121,986	-3.7%	6.4%	81.5	711.6/28.0	187.6/73.9	49.1	18.3%	n/a	3	3
Toronto, Ontario	6	5	50	4,682,897	9.8%	6.6%	120.3	834.0/32.8	133.1/52.4	1.4	30.8%	50	10	8
Trois-Rivières, Québec	25	19	290	137,507	-1.7%	8.0%	76.9	1,099.8/43.3	241.3/95.0	30.1	19.2%	140	4	3
Vancouver, British Columbia	1	1	20	1,986,965	8.5%	5.3%	108.3	1,474.9/58.1	43.6/17.2	0.0	28.7%	251	9	10
Victoria, British Columbia	5	3	50	311,902	2.5%	4.4%	96.0	686.1/27.0	12.5/4.9	0.0	26.6%	349	8	9
Windsor, Ontario	23	23	265	307,877	7.3%	7.5%	89.2	805.2/31.7	126.6/49.8	1.6	20.6%	164	4	4
Winnipeg, Manitoba	11	9	120	671,274	0.6%	5.0%	90.2	504.0/19.8	114.8/45.2	57.5	22.7%	205	7	7

Source: Statistics Canada; Environment Canada; *Canadian Global Almanac 2004*

TABLE 6.2 CANADIAN CENSUS METROPOLITAN AREAS: RANKINGS & SELECTED STATISTICS BY RANK

CENSUS METROPOLITAN AREA	CANADA RANK	2004 CANADA RANK	COMPARABLE U.S. RANK	2001 POPULATION	1996–2001 POPULATION GROWTH	UNEMPLOYMENT RATE	COST OF LIVING INDEX	ANNUAL PRECIPITATION (MM./INCHES)	ANNUAL SNOWFALL (CM./INCHES)	DAYS BELOW -20°C/-4°F	UNIVERSITY DEGREE	CRIME (CANADA AVERAGE 100)	MUSEUM RATING	QUALITY OF LIFE RATING
Vancouver, British Columbia	1	1	20	1,986,965	8.5%	5.3%	108.3	1,474.9/58.1	43.6/17.2	0.0	28.7%	251	9	10
Montréal, Québec	2	2	30	3,426,350	3.0%	8.9%	85.8	1,062.6/41.8	226.2/89.1	7.7	25.9%	188	10	9
Ottawa–Gatineau, Ontario	3	4	35	1,063,664	6.5%	6.7%	122.7	914.2/36.0	202.7/79.8	18.9	33.0%	95	10	9
Québec City, Québec	4	7	50	682,757	1.6%	5.7%	98.5	504.0/19.8	114.8/45.2	31.1	24.9%	149	9	8
Victoria, British Columbia	5	3	50	311,902	2.5%	4.4%	96.0	686.1/27.0	12.5/4.9	0.0	26.6%	349	8	9
Toronto, Ontario	6	5	50	4,682,897	9.8%	6.6%	120.3	834.0/32.8	133.1/52.4	1.4	30.8%	50	10	8
Calgary, Alberta	7	6	60	951,395	15.8%	4.0%	114.8	412.6/16.2	126.7/49.9	26.0	27.4%	120	7	8
Abbotsford, British Columbia	8	10	90	147,370	8.0%	5.0%	93.2	1,573.2/61.9	63.5/25.0	0.0	15.2%	n/a	3	7
Edmonton, Alberta	9	8	100	937,845	8.7%	5.0%	103.9	476.9/18.8	123.5/48.6	28.1	21.3%	204	5	7
St. Catharines–Niagara, Ontario	10	11	120	377,099	1.2%	7.9%	84.2	871.6/34.3	136.6/53.8	0.9	15.6%	71	5	7
Winnipeg, Manitoba	11	9	120	671,274	0.6%	5.0%	90.2	504.0/19.8	114.8/45.2	57.5	22.7%	205	7	7
Halifax, Nova Scotia	12	13	130	359,183	4.7%	5.7%	92.8	1,508.0/59.4	151.8/59.8	0.9	27.9%	89	7	7
Saskatoon, Saskatchewan	13	12	140	225,927	3.1%	5.7%	95.9	350.0/13.8	97.2/38.3	52.1	23.8%	232	4	5
Kitchener–Waterloo, Ontario	14	24	140	414,284	8.2%	5.5%	92.7	907.9/35.7	159.5/62.8	7.6	20.4%	114	5	7
Kingston, Ontario	15	16	160	146,838	1.6%	6.3%	92.1	968.2/38.1	180.9/71.2	11.3	23.7%	138	7	6
St. John's, Newfoundland and Labrador	16	14	190	172,918	-0.7%	8.7%	87.1	1,513.7/59.6	322.3/126.9	1.0	22.7%	258	6	5
London, Ontario	17	15	190	432,451	3.8%	6.6%	88.6	987.1/38.9	202.4/79.7	5.0	21.1%	144	8	6
Regina, Saskatchewan	18	18	195	192,800	-0.4%	5.2%	84.9	388.1/15.3	105.9/41.7	47.7	23.0%	223	5	4
Oshawa, Ontario	19	21	200	296,298	10.2%	6.2%	97.8	877.9/34.6	118.4/46.6	3.4	15.3%	215	5	5
Thunder Bay, Ontario	20	17	240	121,986	-3.7%	6.4%	81.5	711.6/28.0	187.6/73.9	49.1	18.3%	n/a	3	3
Sherbrooke, Québec	21	22	245	153,811	2.8%	7.2%	85.2	1,144.1/45.0	294.3/115.9	35.7	21.8%	n/a	4	4
Hamilton, Ontario	22	20	250	662,401	6.1%	5.9%	83.6	910.0/35.8	151.8/59.8	3.4	20.0%	151	4	4
Windsor, Ontario	23	23	265	307,877	7.3%	7.5%	89.2	805.2/31.7	126.6/49.8	1.6	20.6%	164	4	4
Saint John, New Brunswick	24	25	290	122,678	-2.4%	8.4%	85.4	1,390.3/54.7	256.9/101.1	15.2	17.6%	238	3	3
Trois-Rivières, Québec	25	19	280	137,507	-1.7%	8.0%	76.9	1,099.8/43.3	241.3/95.0	30.1	19.2%	140	4	3
Sudbury, Ontario	26	27	300	155,219	-6.1%	7.7%	76.4	899.3/35.4	274.4/108.0	36.4	14.9%	121	6	3
Saguenay, Québec	27	26	320	154,938	-3.4%	11.2%	76.6	1,002.1/39.5	301.5/118.7	37.1	16.9%	n/a	2	2

Source: Statistics Canada; Environment Canada; *Canadian Global Almanac 2004*

physical nature, function, or specific data attributes. These equivalencies may be close, as in the case of many U.S. Great Lakes and Canadian Prairie cities, or they may be hard to identify, as in the heavily French- and European-influenced cities of Québec and the east. Regardless, from facts and these equivalencies, *Cities Ranked & Rated* offers a comparable U.S. rank showing where the Canadian city might fall if the places in chapters 5 and 6 were ranked together.

For the Canadian city rankings with comparable U.S. rankings and summary facts, see tables 6.1 and 6.2, which show rankings and facts first in alphabetical order and then in rank sequence.

Data Sources

Sources for Canadian data are patterned after those collected for U.S. equivalents. However, subtle differences in collection and aggregation underlie certain items, including market baskets used for cost of living, averaging

approaches used for home prices, and the calculation of tax rates. While these items are close enough for reasonable comparison, this qualifier should be kept in mind.

Most data comes from the Canadian national government statistics and analysis agency, Statistics Canada (www.statcan.ca). Data for population and population trends, economy and jobs, education, crime, and transportation come from this source, most of which is updated through 2001, but unfortunately, not through 2006 (see "A Question of Timing," below). Climate data comes from Environment Canada Climate Normals (http://climate.weatheroffice.ec.gc.ca/climate_normals/index_e.html). Data relevant to the descriptive text comes from Transport Canada, Citizenship and Immigration Canada, Natural Resources Canada, and other agencies. The *Canadian Global Almanac 2004* (John Wiley & Sons Canada, 2004) organizes certain Canada government data for easy interpretation and provides broad, fact-based insight. A few local websites, notably the financial planning site Taxtips.ca, also provided valuable information.

A Question of Timing

Unfortunately, the production and press schedule for *Cities Ranked & Rated,* 2nd Edition, did not accommodate getting the latest update for many Canada facts and figures. Census Canada works on a 5-year schedule, processing a new census in years ending in "1" and "6." The 2006 Canada Census occurred on schedule, but to our disappointment the results aren't published until late spring 2007—too late to factor into this edition. Thus, many of our CMA-level facts and figures retain a 2001 vintage. Fortunately, we have timely updates for more dynamic factors such as employment, home prices, and living costs. We believe the facts, as collected and presented, still represent a good picture of Canadian CMAs.

Canadian city and provincial sites were used, as were a number of travel guides and publications. Finally, the authors used a network of Canadian contacts and local travel experience as a guide.

What follows is a discussion of the major data categories and their contents and insights.

Population

Ninety percent of Canada's population lies within 161 kilometers (100 miles) of the U.S. border, a fact driven not only by economic ties to the United States, but also by the obvious influence of climate. Two-thirds of the population live in Ontario or Québec, and about 65% live in Census Metropolitan Areas. This latter figure is lower than in the United States, where about 84% live in Metropolitan Statistical Areas. Note that Canada defines CMAs as having 100,000 or more people in the core city or cities while a U.S. MSA requires 50,000. A full 15% of Canada's population live in the Toronto CMA, a far greater dominance than the New York area in the U.S., which with all nearby metropolitan areas included represents only about 7% of the U.S. population.

Population statistics show total population, density, growth, and demographics. Similar to the United States, average population growth in all of Canada is about 1% per year. Calgary is the fastest growing at 15.3% per year, while Sudbury and other natural resource–based towns such as Saguenay are losing population. The "visible minority" is a self-explanatory and uniquely Canadian statistic, as are the numbers delineating the percentage using French or English as a primary language and those who are bilingual with both. All population statistics are sourced from Statistics Canada and are from the 2001 Census.

Economy & Jobs/Cost of Living

The Canadian economy is a mix of agriculture, natural resources, manufacturing, and general commerce. Vast areas of natural resources, particularly timber, petroleum, and mining products, have had strong influences on the economy. In fact, the country's economy in general and that of many cities are tied to these primary industries. This has led to strong boom and bust cycles, particularly in Alberta and the northern areas of Ontario and Québec. Canada's unemployment has historically been higher than that of the United States, ranging from 7.2% to 10.7% during the past 20 years. Currently, as mentioned at the outset, Canada is in the middle of one of the strongest employment cycles in recent years, and June 2006 unemployment was estimated at 6.1%, down from 8.0% as recently as 2004. A closer look reveals stronger employment in service sectors, with more part-timers going full-time and more women in the workforce. Outside of the oil-rich Rocky Mountain areas, unemployment continues to be a problem in natural resource–rich areas, and we have some concerns about the many areas dependent on forest products, as construction in both Canada and the U.S. slows—these areas weren't doing that well anyway. On the flip side, a relaxation of recent trade restrictions with the U.S. should help. Larger cities, particularly those dependent on auto and other manufacturing and those in the Great Lakes region, still have some employment concerns. Table 6.3 shows comparative 2001 and 2005 employment rates for each CMA.

The Cost of Living Index is calculated in a manner similar to that of the United States, and is basically comparable. That is to say, Ottawa, with the nation's highest COL Index at 122.7, is 22.7% higher than the Canadian average.

Housing prices, in sympathy with the U.S. and driven in part by increased immigration and lower interest rates,

TABLE 6.3 CANADIAN CMA UNEMPLOYMENT RATES, 2001 & 2005

CENSUS METROPOLITAN AREA	2005 UNEMPLOYMENT	2001 UNEMPLOYMENT	CHANGE
Abbotsford, British Columbia	5.0%	8.2%	–3.2%
St. John's, Newfoundland and Labrador	8.7%	11.3%	–2.6%
Thunder Bay, Ontario	6.4%	8.8%	–2.4%
Victoria, British Columbia	4.4%	6.6%	–2.2%
Halifax, Nova Scotia	5.2%	7.2%	–2.0%
Vancouver, British Columbia	5.3%	7.2%	–1.9%
Sudbury, Ontario	7.7%	9.1%	–1.4%
Québec City, Québec	5.7%	6.9%	–1.2%
Trois-Rivières, Québec	8.0%	9.2%	–1.2%
Saguenay, Québec	11.2%	12.4%	–1.2%
Saskatoon, Saskatchewan	5.7%	6.7%	–1.0%
Calgary, Alberta	4.0%	4.9%	–0.9%
Regina, Saskatchewan	5.2%	6%	–0.8%
Saint John, New Brunswick	8.4%	9.2%	–0.8%
Kingston, Ontario	6.3%	6.9%	–0.6%
Winnipeg, Manitoba	5.0%	5.6%	–0.6%
Edmonton, Alberta	5.0%	5.5%	–0.5%
London, Ontario	6.6%	6.7%	–0.1%
Kitchener–Waterloo, Ontario	5.5%	5.5%	0.0%
Hamilton, Ontario	5.9%	5.7%	0.2%
Oshawa, Ontario	6.2%	6%	0.2%
Sherbrooke, Québec	7.2%	6.9%	0.3%
Toronto, Ontario	6.6%	5.9%	0.7%
Ottawa–Gatineau, Ontario	6.7%	5.6%	1.1%
Windsor, Ontario	7.5%	6.3%	1.2%
Montréal, Québec	8.9%	7.5%	1.4%
St. Catharines–Niagara, Ontario	7.9%	6%	1.9%

Source: Statistics Canada

TABLE 6.4 CANADIAN CMA HOME PRICES, 2001 & 2006

CANADA AVERAGE HOUSING PRICES

Canadian Dollars, 2001 & 2006

CENSUS METROPOLITAN AREA	2006	2001	CHANGE 2001–2006
Vancouver, British Columbia	$518,176	$294,847	76%
Victoria, British Columbia	$515,755	$243,970	111%
Toronto, Ontario	$365,537	$273,397	34%
Calgary, Alberta	$350,000	$201,750	73%
Abbotsford, British Columbia	$343,352	$195,437	76%
Kingston, Ontario	$309,900	$156,445	98%
CANADA	$280,740	$205,174	37%
Ottawa–Gatineau, Ontario	$260,249	$173,610	50%
Kitchener–Waterloo, Ontario	$259,900	$172,550	51%
Windsor, Ontario	$259,900	$160,656	62%
Edmonton, Alberta	$249,900	$148,529	68%
Oshawa, Ontario	$245,000	$182,790	34%
St. Catharines–Niagara, Ontario	$229,000	$145,432	57%
Halifax, Nova Scotia	$224,900	$134,286	67%
Montréal, Québec	$219,433	$142,206	54%
London, Ontario	$209,900	$157,577	33%
Hamilton, Ontario	$189,000	$134,286	41%
Sherbrooke, Québec	$179,900	$99,458	81%
Saskatoon, Saskatchewan	$162,279	$128,335	26%
Winnipeg, Manitoba	$159,900	$104,331	53%
Thunder Bay, Ontario	$153,000	$129,161	18%
Québec City, Québec	$150,324	$101,520	48%
Trois-Rivières, Québec	$149,000	$82,942	80%
Sudbury, Ontario	$143,514	$121,671	18%
Regina, Saskatchewan	$142,147	$107,706	32%
St. John's, Newfoundland and Labrador	$135,100	$114,086	18%
Saint John, New Brunswick	$129,844	$99,483	31%
Saguenay, Québec	$124,856	$84,377	48%

Source: Statistics Canada; Canadian Real Estate Association

have shot up to an average just over C$280,740 (US$248,442) in 2006 versus US$231,000 in the U.S. for the same period. However, there are some differences in the way data is collected for Canadian home prices: The Canadian number is an average, not a mean, and is based on value, not price. Regardless of these differences, Canadian housing costs are slightly higher than the number indicates because of the nondeductibility of mortgage interest. More visibly, the Canadian dollar is now worth about 88.5 cents (C$1.13 = US$1), a major change since 2003, again affected by the strong economy. In 2003 the Canadian dollar was worth about 71 cents U.S. (C$1.41 = US$1). In Canadian dollar terms, housing prices have grown from C$205,174 in 2001 to C$280,740, a 37% increase. But in U.S. terms, home price growth is from US$145,513 in 2001 to US$238,442 in 2006—fully a 59% increase, more than the already-spectacular 44% U.S. increase. As in the United States, housing prices vary greatly depending on geographic location—home prices average C$124,856 (US$110,492) in Saguenay, Québec, and C$518,176 (US$367,501) in Vancouver, British Columbia. Table 6.4 has a full listing of average home prices in 2001 and 2006.

A comparison between the personal tax climates of Canada and the United States points to some important differences. As all Canadians will quickly tell you, taxes *are* higher in Canada, but government services are also broader and deeper, most notably in the provision of national health insurance. But when all is added up, Canadian taxes are not *that* much higher than those in the United States. For income tax, Canada citizens are taxed at the national and provincial level, with important differences from the United States, such as the nondeductibility of mortgage interest mentioned above. Combined national and provincial tax burden ranges from 29% to 35%, depending on the province, for a family income of C$100,000 (US$88,495). In the United States, this figure might run from 18% to 25%, depending on the state. There is a national pension payroll tax (Canada Pension Plan) comparable to U.S. Social Security/FICA, but it is only 4.95% compared to 7.15% for employees in the U.S., and applies only to the first $42,100 of gross income. Factoring in the larger U.S. FICA payroll tax (which funds

Social Security, Medicare, and other benefits), which rises to 15.3% for the self-employed, the combined final income tax rates are much closer. The data tables for each CMA show the highest *marginal* income tax rate for each province.

Sales taxes raise a distinct difference between the U.S. and Canada. Like most U.S. states, provinces collect a sales tax ranging in effect from zero (Alberta and the northern territories) to 8% (Ontario) and 10% (Prince Edward Island). But, additionally, with no comparable concept on the immediate U.S. horizon, there is a national 6% goods and services tax (GST), essentially a national sales tax. The good news: This tax was just lowered to 6% from 7% in July 2006—another sign of Canadian economic and fiscal health. But unlike U.S. state sales taxes, GST is collected not only on goods but also services, such as auto repair and hair styling. In some provinces, notably Québec, the provincial sales tax (PST) is levied on not only the price of the item but the price plus the GST, creating in essence a tax on a tax. It is worth noting that three provinces—Nova Scotia, Newfoundland and Labrador, and New Brunswick—have combined GST and PST into an HST (harmonized sales tax), but this combination doesn't affect the resulting burden. It's also worth noting that western provinces offer a better deal: Alberta has no PST, and British Columbia recently lowered its rate from 7.5% to 7%. Bottom line: For the most part sales/consumption taxes in Canada are decidedly higher.

Property taxes vary by locality, but are generally lower than in the United States. According to a Statistics Canada study, Canadians pay a tax on property values that ranges from 0.7% to 1.9%—generally on the higher side in Ontario and Québec. Higher property values may be causing Canadian property taxes to catch up with U.S. total tax burdens. But the system may still favor property owners, particularly those not holding large mortgages, at the expense of lower income residents who pay proportionately more GST/PST. When the government-provided healthcare services are factored in, tax payments in Canada and the United States start to look more comparable, but the comparison is by no means simple and varies according to the individual situation. For more detail on Canadian taxes, see Taxtips.ca (www.taxtips.ca).

Climate

That climate is a major player in the quality of life and livability of Canadian cities is no surprise to anyone. The country has one of the most interesting and dynamic climate profiles in the world, and climate patterns can produce weather ranging from exceptionally pleasant to literally dangerous. The mainly inhabited areas of Canada can be loosely divided into four climate zones:

- The Pacific region has a marine climate typical of the U.S. Pacific Northwest west of the Cascade Range. The marine influence moderates temperatures to give few extremes in summer or winter. Most of the abundant precipitation falls as rain, with almost continuous clouds and drizzle particularly in winter and little snow at lower elevations. This climate persists primarily west of the Rockies in British Columbia.

- The Prairie region is characterized by a strong continental climate with extreme seasonal and even daily variation, warm pleasant summers, and bitterly cold, windy winters. The region is the driest in Canada with intermittent summer rain as thundershowers and relatively light snow except in the strongest storms. The area gets the most sunshine in Canada. Alberta east of the Rockies, Saskatchewan, and Manitoba are in this region.

- The Great Lakes region is made up of the areas in Ontario surrounding (or surrounded by) lakes Superior, Huron, Erie, and Ontario and moves east into parts of Québec. As in the United States, the region is a highly seasonal, continental climate with a marine influence determined by location of water and prevailing winds. The area is far enough south and east to receive warm, moist Gulf of Mexico air in the summer, creating hot, sticky conditions with thundershowers and occasional severe weather interchanged with cooler, milder air from the north. Winter likewise is a mix with relatively mild air and some rain along with blasts of northerly cold and snow. The position of most Canadian cities to the north and west of water means they receive less snow than their U.S. equivalents to the south and east of the lakes. Nevertheless, temperatures below –20°C (–4 °F) are recorded nearly everywhere in winter and heavy snowfalls are common.

- The Maritime region is principally the provinces bordering the Atlantic and spreading into eastern Québec. Here alternating continental and marine influences produce a mix of weather with mostly pleasant summers and highly variable winters ranging from deep cold and heavy snow to mild periods with clouds and rain. Clouds, fog, and rain are almost constant in cities on the Atlantic, with St. John's, Newfoundland and Labrador, receiving precipitation 2 in 3 days each year. The so-called St. Lawrence storm track brings heavy weather, particularly in winter with heavy snows followed by intense cold as the storms pass.

The climate statistics in the tables represent average data collected by Environment Canada over a 30-year period.

Education, Crime & Transportation

This section represents a sampling of key data related mainly to the condition of public services in Canadian cities. For education, the level of attainment is shown with the double purpose of indicating systematic educational achievement and the level of education of the local population. U.S. readers need to understand the "college" and "university" terminology: "College" (*cégeps* in Québec) is basic post-high-school education, usually 1 to 3 years in duration. Curriculum is often geared to specific trades in arts, business, science, technology, or health but may also include basic university-level requirements. Certificates are awarded upon completion, and many students continue at the "university" level, another 1 to 4 years with higher-level academic, professional, and post-graduate training. The "college" system is somewhat comparable to the U.S. junior-college system, particularly in states such as California where many students complete basic requirements in a junior college before transferring to a state university. But a Canada college certificate usually carries more weight than a U.S. junior college or associate degree. University graduation rates in Canada are comparable to U.S. 4-year college graduation rates. Statistics shown for educational attainment are from the 2001 Canada Census.

Reported crime rates in Canada are considerably lower than in the U.S. Estimates show that U.S. homicide rates are as much as three times as high, while aggravated assault is almost twice as high. The gap between the two countries in property crime is less but still higher in the U.S., although Canada has a relatively high rate of auto theft and shoplifting. Overall, Canada has experienced a similar drop in crime rates as the U.S. through the early part of the decade. Recently, again following U.S. patterns, violent crime rates have turned slightly upward while property crime rates are steady to slightly lower. The CMA narratives in this chapter now show a locally calculated crime index known as the Relocation Crime Index (RCI), developed by an organization called the Relocation Crime Lab. The RCI estimates local crime rates per 100,000 population and calculates an index based on a national average of 100. As with U.S. crime rates, reported figures for large metro areas can occasionally appear low due to the large size of the denominator, as with New York City in the U.S. It doesn't necessarily mean that locals aren't fearful of crime. Likewise, areas with smaller populations may look more risky than they really are.

Data on public transportation in Canada varies considerably among cities, and is also from the 2001 Canada Census. Public transportation is generally considered excellent, especially in the larger cities, with a coordinated mix of bus and light- and heavy-rail systems. It has a well-deserved reputation for being clean, efficient, and timely. Although there have been cutbacks in recent years, intercity rail, as managed by the VIA Rail Canada system (comparable in purpose to Amtrak in the U.S.), is good and still serves such distant destinations as Saguenay, Québec; Prince Rupert, British Columbia; and even Churchill in remote northern Manitoba. Commercial air service is predictably good in the larger cities and is available in smaller CMAs. The statistics showing the number of passengers departing each day through local airports are sourced from the Airports Council International 2002 North America Passenger Traffic Report (www.aci-na.org).

Leisure/Arts & Culture

This section includes an abbreviated selection of leisure and arts and culture attributes. *Cities Ranked & Rated* assigns a 1 to 10 rating based on availability, quality, and access. Features with a national or international renown get the highest scores. Canada is a nation rich in recreational assets, particularly outdoor recreation with vast expanses of mountains, water, forests, parks, and coastline, as well as ample snow for winter sports. Entertainment is plentiful and quite multicultural in the big cities, while somewhat lacking in the mid-size cities and smaller towns. Spectator sports are big, with hockey and Canadian football (CFL) adding to the usual mix of baseball and basketball. Ice-skating, skiing, snowmobiling, and most watersports are abundant in Canada. Some of the country's arts and culture assets, particularly classical music and ballet, are world-renowned. Canada has always had a strong influence on the pop culture and music scene, bringing such diverse acts as Gordon Lightfoot, Bryan Adams, and Céline Dion, among others.

Cities Ranked & Rated, 2nd Edition, assigns a Quality of Life rating to each city. This number takes into consideration not only leisure and arts and culture assets but also economic opportunity, physical appearance, climate, heritage, and ease of living.

Abbotsford, British Columbia

Rank: 8 2004 rank: 10

Profile: Small city
Location: Along Fraser River and Highway 1, 56 kilometers (35 miles) southeast of Vancouver and 8 kilometers (5 miles) north of the U.S. border
Elevation: 58 meters/190 feet

PRO	CON
Strong economy	High home prices
Attractive setting	Growth and sprawl

Abbotsford is a rapidly growing small city and residential area just outside the outskirts of Vancouver. Once largely agricultural, the nearby U.S. border crossing, immigration, and the spread of commerce east from Vancouver have brought a growing and diversifying economic base. Aerospace and high-tech industries are important contributors. The rather nondescript town area is set on top of a wooded ridge between two agricultural valleys with residential areas extending along the ridge. The population is ethnically diverse, with many migrants from Asia and other parts of Canada. Most residents work in the area but 20% commute to Vancouver or, more likely, its outskirt cities of Surrey and Langley.

The area lies in the broad flat valley of the Fraser River surrounded by low, fir-forested mountains and several lakes. The climate is decidedly marine with cool pleasant summers and relatively mild winters. The annual precipitation total is among the highest in Canada.

Abbotsford compares to Everett, Washington, part of the Seattle–Bellevue–Everett MSA (no. 129), and has some similarities in size and look to Salem, Oregon (no. 82). The comparable U.S. rank is 90.

POPULATION

Population	147,370	Median age	35.4	Visible minorities	17.8%
Population density	653.9 sq. km/252.5 sq. miles	Average family size	3.2	English-speaking	n/a
Population growth	8.0%	Single	27.9%	French-speaking	n/a
		Married	55.7%	Bilingual	n/a

ECONOMY & JOBS

Household income	C$48,721/US$43,116
Unemployment rate	5.0%
White collar	66.0%
Blue collar	34.0%

COST OF LIVING

Cost of Living Index	93.2	Average home price	C$343,352/US$303,351
Provincial income tax	14.7%	Average rent	C$815/US$751
Provincial sales tax	7.0%	Homes owned	71%
		Homes rented	29%

CLIMATE

Average January low	−0.6°C/30.9 °F	Annual days › 30°C/86°F	0.44	Annual days precipitation	177.2
Average July high	23.4°C/74.1°F	Annual days ‹ 0°C/32°F	19.6	Annual days snowfall	13.8
Annual precipitation	1,573.2mm/61.9 in.	Annual days ‹ −20°C/−4°F	0	Annual sun hours	1,866
Annual snowfall	63.5cm/25.0 in.				

TEMPERATURE

PRECIPITATION

EDUCATION

High school degree	75%
Completed trade school	14%
College degree	17%
University degree	15.2%

CRIME

Violent crime rate	1,217
Change in violent crime rate	−2.8%
Property crime rate	3,762
Change in property crime rate	2.9%
Relocation Crime Index	n/a

TRANSPORTATION

Commute by auto	75.7%
Commute by mass transit	1.4%
Work at home	9.9%
Air service (passengers/day)	‹ 500

LEISURE

Restaurant rating	8	Spectator-sports rating	3
Golf-course rating	5	Inland water rating	9
Ski-area rating	8	Park rating	7
		Quality of life rating	7

ARTS & CULTURE

Library rating	8
Classical music rating	2
Ballet/dance rating	7
Museum rating	3

Calgary, Alberta

Rank: 7 2004 rank: 6

Profile: Large city
Location: Southern Alberta along Highway 1 at the foot of the Rocky Mountains
Elevation: 1,084 meters/3,556 feet

PRO
Nearby mountains
Strong economy

CON
Growth and sprawl
Cold winters

By a sizable margin, Calgary continues to be the fastest growing city in Canada. Located within sight of the Rocky Mountains, the city is modern and clean with a favorable business climate, no provincial sales taxes, and a strong oil industry. The economy has diversified, particularly with tourism, but the area has a boomtown feel and the lowest unemployment rate in Canada at 4.0%. There is plenty to do, both day and night, with mountain recreation opportunities and an active nightlife scene. While not as strong or renowned as larger Canadian cities, the local assortment of arts amenities is complete. The growth and boomtown climate have brought a high Cost of Living Index at 114.8, particularly high considering lower taxes and land availability.

The climate is northern Great Plains with some mountain influence including warming chinook winds in winter, but there is no shelter from advancing northerly cold and bitter cold temperatures are common.

Although a bit smaller, Calgary is similar to Denver, Colorado (no. 150), but ranks higher due to stronger employment, lower living costs, and fewer big-city problems. The comparable U.S. rank is 60.

POPULATION

Population	951,395	Median age	34.9	Visible minorities	17.5%
Population density	520 sq. km/200.8 sq. miles	Average family size	3.2	English-speaking	90.7%
Population growth	15.8%	Single	34.1%	French-speaking	0.1%
		Married	50.9%	Bilingual	7.3%

ECONOMY & JOBS

Household income	C$58,861/US$52,089
Unemployment rate	4.0%
White collar	80%
Blue collar	20%

COST OF LIVING

Cost of Living Index	114.8	Average home price	C$252,273/US$223,250
Provincial income tax	10.0%	Average rent	C$837/US$741
Provincial sales tax	0.0%	Homes owned	71%
		Homes rented	29%

CLIMATE

Average January low	−15.1°C/4.8°F	Annual days > 30°C/86°F	4.5	Annual days precipitation	113.6
Average July high	22.9°C/73.2°F	Annual days < 0°C/32°F	196	Annual days snowfall	56.8
Annual precipitation	412.6mm/16.2 in.	Annual days < −20°C/−4°F	26	Annual sun hours	2,395
Annual snowfall	126.7cm/49.9 in.				

TEMPERATURE

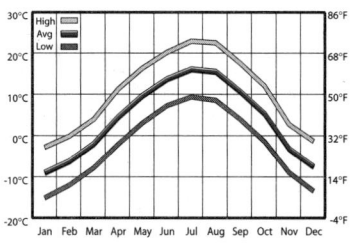

PRECIPITATION

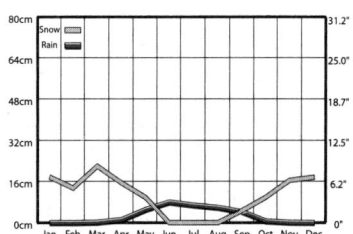

EDUCATION

High school degree	83%
Completed trade school	12%
College degree	19%
University degree	27.4%

CRIME

Violent crime rate	719
Change in violent crime rate	30.0%
Property crime rate	1,639
Change in property crime rate	−1.1%
Relocation Crime Index	120

TRANSPORTATION

Commute by auto	66.3%
Commute by mass transit	12.2%
Work at home	7.1%
Air service (passengers/day)	21,597

LEISURE

Restaurant rating	5
Golf-course rating	7
Ski-area rating	9

Spectator-sports rating	7
Inland water rating	4
Park rating	10
Quality of life rating	8

ARTS & CULTURE

Library rating	8
Classical music rating	7
Ballet/dance rating	5
Museum rating	7

Edmonton, Alberta

Profile: Large capital city
Location: Center of Alberta along Saskatchewan River
Elevation: 671 meters/2,201 feet

PRO	CON
Strong economy	Harsh climate
Capital-city amenities	Economic cycles

Edmonton, Alberta's capital, is Canada's sixth largest city, recently outgrown by Calgary, its southern neighbor. Along with Vancouver, Edmonton serves as the major economic and cultural center of western Canada. The area has a long history as an agricultural and transportation gateway between the Prairie provinces and the west. The oil industry has brought cyclical economic boosts during the last 60 years with explosive growth in the 1970s and a strong surge more recently related not only to natural resources but also to an increasingly diversified economy. The tax and business climate are among the best in Canada. The city is laid out in a grid with a mix of older and modern buildings and is, on the whole, attractive. There is a concentration of industrial areas to the north. Nicer residential sections lie to the west,

the location of the West Edmonton Mall, North America's largest and more of an amusement park than a mall. The Cost of Living Index at 103.9 is moderate for an area with a strong economy. The city has a complete set of leisure and arts amenities.

Edmonton, the most northerly Western Hemisphere city with a population exceeding 1 million (a figure that the 2006 Canada Census will more than likely confirm), has strong northern interior climate and a generally flat to gently rolling, treeless Prairie topography with the main ridge of the Rockies plainly visible to the west.

Like Calgary, Edmonton compares to Denver, Colorado (no. 150), economically and geographically. Winters are harsher but the economy is better and costs are lower; the area gets a comparable U.S. rank of 100.

POPULATION

Population	937,845	Median age	36.6	Visible minorities	14.6%
Population density	181.7 sq. km/70.2 sq. miles	Average family size	3.2	English-speaking	90.9%
Population growth	8.7%	Single	33.7%	French-speaking	0.1%
		Married	50.2%	Bilingual	7.5%

ECONOMY & JOBS

		COST OF LIVING			
Household income	C$51,685/US$45,739	Cost of Living Index	103.9	Average home price	C$249,900/US$221,150
Unemployment rate	5.0%	Provincial income tax	10.0%	Average rent	C$732/US$648
White collar	76%	Provincial sales tax	0.0%	Homes owned	66%
Blue collar	24%			Homes rented	34%

CLIMATE

Average January low	−16.0°C/3.2°F	Annual days > 30°C/86°F	3.2	Annual days precipitation	125.8
Average July high	22.8°C/73.0°F	Annual days < 0°C/32°F	178.6	Annual days snowfall	54.5
Annual precipitation	476.9mm/18.8 in.	Annual days < −20°C/−4°F	28.1	Annual sun hours	2,303
Annual snowfall	123.5cm/48.6 in.				

TEMPERATURE

PRECIPITATION

EDUCATION

High school degree	80%
Completed trade school	14%
College degree	19%
University degree	21.3%

CRIME

Violent crime rate	1,099
Change in violent crime rate	3.8%
Property crime rate	3,546
Change in property crime rate	10.3%
Relocation Crime Index	204

TRANSPORTATION

Commute by auto	72.4%
Commute by mass transit	8.1%
Work at home	6.4%
Air service (passengers/day)	10,330

LEISURE

Restaurant rating	7	Spectator-sports rating	8
Golf-course rating	6	Inland water rating	7
Ski-area rating	5	Park rating	8
		Quality of life rating	7

ARTS & CULTURE

Library rating	7
Classical music rating	3
Ballet/dance rating	5
Museum rating	5

Halifax, Nova Scotia

Rank: 12 2004 rank: 13

Profile: Large port city
Location: Central Nova Scotia on the Atlantic Coast
Elevation: 70 meters/230 feet

PRO	CON
Historic interest	Cloudy, wet climate
Educated population	Tourist impact

Halifax, a major port city on a natural harbor, is the only Canadian Atlantic port normally operational year-round. The area grew up as a shipping hub and a regional, naval, and governmental center, but has also become a tourist destination, and is today the largest city in Atlantic Canada. Its crowded waterfront, which has elements of Boston and San Francisco, contains a mix of modern and preserved historic buildings, entertainment, and tourist activity. This popular area can become crowded, particularly when cruise ships arrive. Most of the residential areas lie inland and to the southwest. Unemployment has dropped a full 2% from 2001 to 2005 and now stands at 5.2%. The tight geography and water barriers have made public transportation by necessity an important way to get around, and at 9.3% the area has one of the higher rates of public transport utilization in the country.

The terrain is rocky, hilly, and wooded, typical of the Atlantic Coast. The strong northern marine climate brings heavy clouds, fog, and rain year-round. Annual rainfall is just exceeded by Saint John, New Brunswick, to the northeast and by a handful of U.S. cities. The surrounding terrain is mostly hilly and heavily wooded.

Halifax compares with Portland, Maine (no. 231), although bitter cold is less common, and with Boston, Massachusetts (no. 160), but has fewer negatives. The comparable U.S. rank is 130.

POPULATION

Population	359,183	Median age	36.6	Visible minorities	7.0%
Population density	65.4 sq. km/40.6 sq. miles	Average family size	3.1	English-speaking	88.9%
Population growth	4.7%	Single	34.5%	French-speaking	0.1%
		Married	49.3%	Bilingual	10.7%

ECONOMY & JOBS

Household income	C$46,491/US$41,142
Unemployment rate	5.2%
White collar	84%
Blue collar	16%

COST OF LIVING

Cost of Living Index	92.8	Average home price	C$224,900/US$199,027
Provincial income tax	16.7%	Average rent	C$762/US$674
Provincial sales tax	7.5%	Homes owned	62%
		Homes rented	38%

CLIMATE

Average January low	−8.6°C/16.5°F	Annual days > 30°C/86°F	0.9	Annual days precipitation	151.6
Average July high	22.9°C/73.2°F	Annual days < 0°C/32°F	136.4	Annual days snowfall	24
Annual precipitation	1,508.0mm/59.4 in.	Annual days < −20°C/−4°F	0.9	Annual sun hours	1,949
Annual snowfall	151.8cm/59.8 in.				

TEMPERATURE

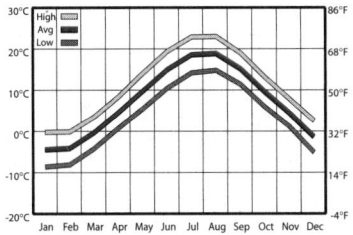

PRECIPITATION

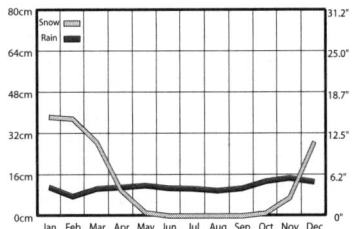

EDUCATION

High school degree	83%
Completed trade school	14%
College degree	19%
University degree	27.9%

CRIME

Violent crime	1,046
Change in violent crime rate	5.8%
Property crime rate	3,141
Change in property crime rate	4.8%
Relocation Crime Index	89

TRANSPORTATION

Commute by auto	63.5%
Commute by mass transit	9.3%
Work at home	5.9%
Air service (passengers/day)	8,393

LEISURE

Restaurant rating	5	Spectator-sports rating	2
Golf-course rating	2	Inland water rating	8
Ski-area rating	3	Park rating	6
		Quality of life rating	7

ARTS & CULTURE

Library rating	7
Classical music rating	3
Ballet/dance rating	3
Museum rating	7

Hamilton, Ontario

Rank: 22 2004 rank: 20

Profile: Mid-size industrial city
Location: Southwestern Ontario at the western corner of Lake Ontario, 81 kilometers (50 miles) west of Toronto
Elevation: 93 meters/305 feet

PRO	CON
Cost of living	Industrial feel
Close to Toronto	Clouds and rain

Hamilton sits in the strategic center of the "Golden Horseshoe" stretching from Toronto to the Niagara/Buffalo area along Lake Ontario. Hamilton is known to many Canadians as "Steeltown"—two large steel mills each employ more than 4,000 workers and are the area's two largest employers; a railcar manufacturer and several auto parts concerns round out the top six. Despite the heavy industry infrastructure, the town has modernized to a degree and has capitalized on its location and ability to offer a relatively attractive lifestyle for a reasonable price—and is marketing itself accordingly. Outside of professional sports, McMaster University, and a handful of museums, there are few local amenities, but the area is close enough to Toronto and Buffalo (106km/66 miles) to take advantage of their offerings. Cost of living and home prices are 30% to 40% lower than Toronto.

Physically, Hamilton surrounds the western corner of Lake Ontario. Much of the city is elevated on the Niagara Escarpment, which sits above lowlands containing the major industry and highways. Although the city is on the west (windward) side of Lake Ontario, it is close enough to Lake Huron to the northwest to pick up a wet and sometimes snowy climate.

Geographically, historically, industrially, and in its revitalization steps, the area is like Toledo, Ohio (no. 120), or nearby Buffalo (no. 300). The comparable U.S. rank is 250.

POPULATION

Population	662,401	Median age	37.8	Visible minorities	9.8%
Population density	1,341.4 sq. km/517.9 sq. miles	Average family size	3.2	English-speaking	91.7%
Population growth	6.1%	Single	29.4%	French-speaking	0.1%
		Married	53.5%	Bilingual	6.8%

ECONOMY & JOBS

Household income	C$52,786/US$46,713
Unemployment rate	5.9%
White collar	74%
Blue collar	26%

COST OF LIVING

Cost of Living Index	83.6	Average home price	C$189,000/US$167,267
Provincial income tax	11.2%	Average rent	C$731/US$647
Provincial sales tax	8.0%	Homes owned	68%
		Homes rented	32%

CLIMATE

Average January low	−9.7°C/14.5°F	Annual days > 30°C/86°F	9.1	Annual days precipitation	157.7
Average July high	26.3°C/79.3°F	Annual days < 0°C/32°F	142.1	Annual days snowfall	55.7
Annual precipitation	910.0mm/35.8 in.	Annual days < −20°C/−4°F	3.4	Annual sun hours	2,079
Annual snowfall	151.8cm/59.8 in.				

TEMPERATURE

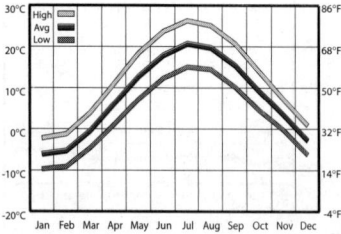

PRECIPITATION

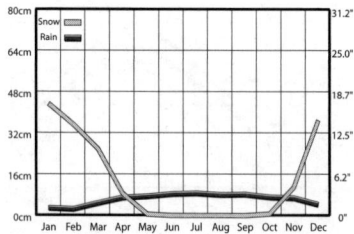

EDUCATION

High school degree	80%
Completed trade school	11%
College degree	21%
University degree	20%

CRIME

Violent crime rate	903
Change in violent crime rate	1.8%
Property crime rate	6,509
Change in property crime rate	1.6%
Relocation Crime Index	151

TRANSPORTATION

Commute by auto	73.2%
Commute by mass transit	7.5%
Work at home	6.0%
Air service (passengers/day)	2,318

LEISURE

Restaurant rating	5	Spectator-sports rating	7
Golf-course rating	5	Inland water rating	7
Ski-area rating	3	Park rating	5
		Quality of life rating	4

ARTS & CULTURE

Library rating	5
Classical music rating	5
Ballet/dance rating	4
Museum rating	4

Kingston, Ontario

Rank: 15 **2004 rank:** 16

Profile: Small city/university town
Location: Eastern Ontario along the St. Lawrence River, halfway between Toronto and Montréal
Elevation: 93 meters/305 feet

PRO	CON
Historic interest	Entertainment
Central location	Air service

Kingston, at one time the provincial capital of Canada under British rule, serves as a cultural hub in the Toronto–Montréal corridor. The location makes it a popular stopover on the Toronto-to-Montréal trip, and several businesses are located in the area to take advantage of this, although most employment comes from the public sector. The city has an attractive and historic downtown, and many preserved older buildings and military installations. The well-recognized Queens University adds a university-town element. Overall, Kingston has more of a European flair than most cities in the province. Beyond downtown are quiet areas of shaded streets and parks. The nearby Thousand Islands provide some recreational opportunities. However, the downtown core only has a few restaurants and the area is generally quiet with relatively little to do compared to other cities in the region.

The city sits on the north shore of the St. Lawrence River where it originates from Lake Ontario. Typical of the region, the climate is continental with a marine influence. Winters are fairly cold and wet.

Physically, Kingston is uniquely Canadian and comparable U.S. cities are hard to identify, but like its geography, it is statistically in the middle in many categories. The historic interest could remind one of Savannah, Georgia (no. 91), but it isn't a close comparison. The comparable U.S. rank is 160.

POPULATION

Population	146,838	Median age	38.1	Visible minorities	4.2%
Population density	213.9 sq. km/82.6 sq. miles	Average family size	3.0	English-speaking	87.6%
Population growth	1.6%	Single	32.0%	French-speaking	0.8%
		Married	49.9%	Bilingual	8.0%

ECONOMY & JOBS

Household income	C$47,979/US$42,459
Unemployment rate	6.3%
White collar	82%
Blue collar	18%

COST OF LIVING

Cost of Living Index	92.1	Average home price	C$309,900/US$274,248
Provincial income tax	11.2%	Average rent	C$805/US$712
Provincial sales tax	8.0%	Homes owned	64%
		Homes rented	36%

CLIMATE

Average January low	−12.2°C/10.0°F	Annual days > 30°C/86°F	2.4	Annual days precipitation	157.4
Average July high	24.8°C/76.6°F	Annual days < 0°C/32°F	145.7	Annual days snowfall	52.3
Annual precipitation	968.2mm/38.1 in.	Annual days < −20°C/−4°F	11.3	Annual sun hours	2,012
Annual snowfall	180.9cm/71.2 in.				

TEMPERATURE

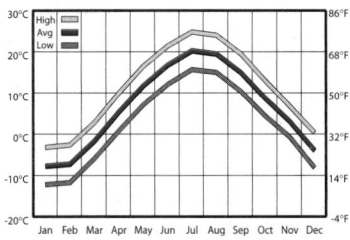

PRECIPITATION

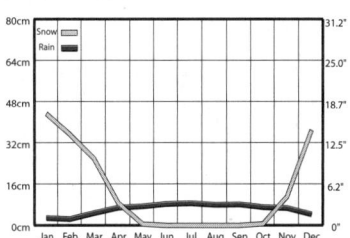

EDUCATION

High school degree	84%
Completed trade school	11%
College degree	22%
University degree	23.7%

CRIME

Violent crime rate	903
Change in violent crime rate	1.8%
Property crime rate	6,509
Change in property crime rate	1.6%
Relocation Crime Index	138

TRANSPORTATION

Commute by auto	68.3%
Commute by mass transit	3.3%
Work at home	7.5%
Air service (passengers/day)	< 500

LEISURE

Restaurant rating	7	Spectator-sports rating	2
Golf-course rating	5	Inland water rating	9
Ski-area rating	6	Park rating	7
		Quality of life rating	6

ARTS & CULTURE

Library rating	4
Classical music rating	3
Ballet/dance rating	3
Museum rating	7

Kitchener–Waterloo, Ontario

Profile: Mid-size city complex/university town
Location: Southwestern Ontario, 121 kilometers (75 miles) west of Toronto
Elevation: 371 meters/1,217 feet

PRO
Stable economy
University-town amenities

CON
Home prices
Harsh winters

Kitchener and Waterloo lie in a nondescript region of western Ontario. Both support a modest assortment of industry and agriculture in the nearby region, and Waterloo is home to the respected University of Waterloo and Wilfrid Laurier University. Of the two, Waterloo has a stronger university-town character, while Kitchener is more commercial and industrial. The area forms one corner of Ontario's so-called "Technology Triangle," and these new-economy industries are becoming more important. Adding character is a Mennonite community and a strong German influence. A growing number of residents seeking a quiet smaller-town lifestyle commute to the greater Toronto area, the fringes of which begin about 72 kilometers (45 miles) east. At closer look, "K-W" and its stable university-influenced lifestyle has led us to reappraise its qualities, and the area has jumped to no. 14 from no. 24 in our ranking.

The area, which sits on mostly level terrain, is more exposed to Lake Huron than most cities in Ontario. This results in colder winters and more rain and snow.

The adjacent university/industrial town structure and proximity to a large regional city remind us of Lafayette, Indiana (no. 25), but quieter with less activity and interest and more expensive housing. The Mennonite influence and city pairing also remind us of Elkhart–Goshen, Indiana (no. 291). The comparable U.S. rank is 140.

POPULATION

Population	414,284	Median age	35.3	Visible minorities	10.7%
Population density	1,391.7 sq. km/537.3 sq. miles	Average family size	3.2	English-speaking	91.4%
Population growth	8.2%	Single	30.4%	French-speaking	0.1%
		Married	53.9%	Bilingual	6.9%

ECONOMY & JOBS

Household income	C$55,528/US$49,140	Cost of Living Index	92.7	Average home price	C$259,900/US$230,000
Unemployment rate	5.7%	Provincial income tax	11.2%	Average rent	C$811/US$718
White collar	69.5%	Provincial sales tax	8.0%	Homes owned	67%
Blue collar	30.5%			Homes rented	33%

COST OF LIVING

(see above)

CLIMATE

Average January low	−11°C/12.2°F	Annual days › 30°C/86°F	6.9	Annual days precipitation	164.4
Average July high	25.9°C/78.6°F	Annual days ‹ 0°C/32°F	160.4	Annual days snowfall	96.6
Annual precipitation	907.9mm/35.7 in.	Annual days ‹ −20°C/−4°F	7.6	Annual sun hours	1,969
Annual snowfall	159.5cm/62.8 in.				

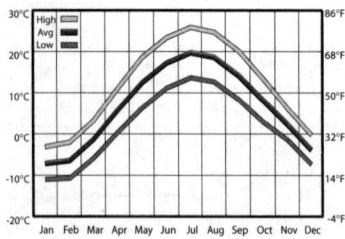

TEMPERATURE

PRECIPITATION

EDUCATION

High school degree	79%
Completed trade school	11%
College degree	19%
University degree	20.4%

CRIME

Violent crime rate	903
Change in violent crime rate	1.8%
Property crime rate	6,509
Change in property crime rate	1.6%
Relocation Crime Index	114

TRANSPORTATION

Commute by auto	76.4%
Commute by mass transit	3.7%
Work at home	5.7%
Air service (passengers/day)	‹ 500

LEISURE

Restaurant rating	7	Spectator-sports rating	2
Golf-course rating	6	Inland water rating	3
Ski-area rating	6	Park rating	4
		Quality of life rating	7

ARTS & CULTURE

Library rating	4
Classical music rating	3
Ballet/dance rating	1
Museum rating	5

London, Ontario

Rank: 17 **2004 rank:** 15

Profile: Mid-size city/university town
Location: Southwestern Ontario, 201 kilometers (125 miles) west of Toronto
Elevation: 278 meters/912 feet

PRO	CON
University-town amenities	Economic cycles
Small-town feel	Winter climate

London is a middle-of-the-road industrial and agricultural city known for its auto assembly plants, insurance company head offices, and the University of Western Ontario. It is fairly clean and quiet, with a few historic buildings downtown and modest areas of local entertainment. The university brings some amenities, most notably a good collection of museums. The location (west of Toronto and 145 kilometers/90 miles northeast of the Detroit/Windsor area) is a bit isolated from major-city amenities and air service.

The terrain is fairly nondescript. The climate is continental with a strong marine influence particularly from Lake Huron to the north, giving wetter and snowier winters than many other Ontario locations.

The city could be compared to Lansing–East Lansing, Michigan (no. 237), but is in better physical shape and has steadier employment. The comparable U.S. rank is 190.

POPULATION

Population	432,451	Median age	36.9	Visible minorities	9.0%
Population density	514.7 sq. km/198.7 sq. miles	Average family size	3.1	English-speaking	92.2%
Population growth	3.8%	Single	31.4%	French-speaking	0.0%
		Married	50.8%	Bilingual	6.6%

ECONOMY & JOBS

Household income	C$48,026/US$42,501
Unemployment rate	6.6%
White collar	75%
Blue collar	25%

COST OF LIVING

Cost of Living Index	88.6	Average home price	C$209,900/US$185,752
Provincial income tax	11.2%	Average rent	C$775/US$686
Provincial sales tax	8.0%	Homes owned	63%
		Homes rented	37%

CLIMATE

Average January low	−10.1°C/13.8°F	Annual days › 30°C/86°F	8.1	Annual days precipitation	170.4
Average July high	26.3°C/79.3°F	Annual days ‹ 0°C/32°F	148	Annual days snowfall	65.6
Annual precipitation	987.1mm/38.9 in.	Annual days ‹ −20°C/−4°F	5	Annual sun hours	1,858
Annual snowfall	202.4cm/79.7 in.				

TEMPERATURE

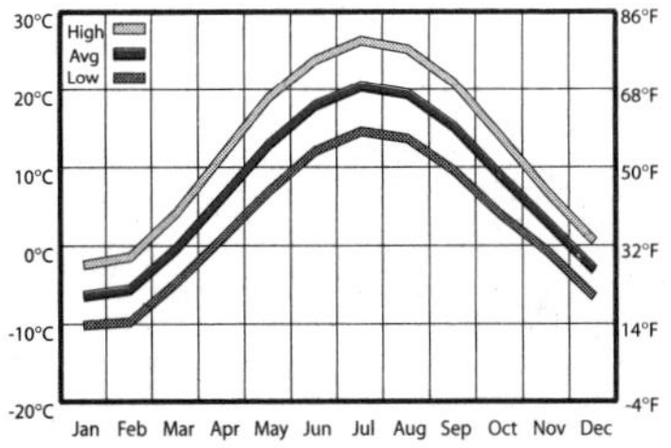

PRECIPITATION

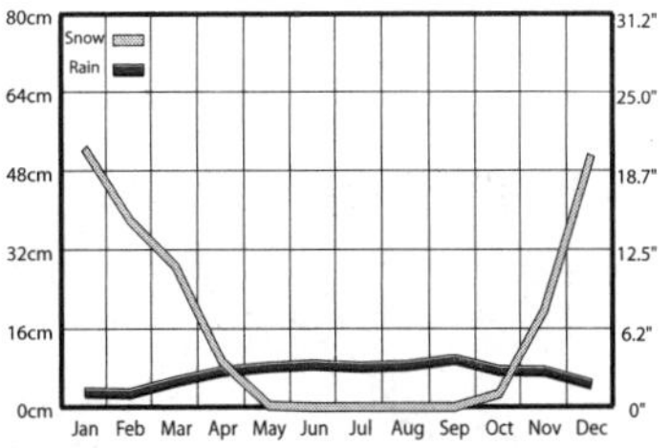

EDUCATION

High school degree	82%
Completed trade school	11%
College degree	22%
University degree	21.1%

CRIME

Violent crime rate	903
Change in violent crime rate	1.8%
Property crime rate	6,509
Change in property crime rate	1.6%
Relocation Crime Index	144

TRANSPORTATION

Commute by auto	72.3%
Commute by mass transit	5.6%
Work at home	6.8%
Air service (passengers/day)	‹ 500

LEISURE

Restaurant rating	5	Spectator-sports rating	2
Golf-course rating	6	Inland water rating	7
Ski-area rating	5	Park rating	4
		Quality of life rating	6

ARTS & CULTURE

Library rating	6
Classical music rating	6
Ballet/dance rating	4
Museum rating	8

Montréal, Québec

Rank: 2 **2004 rank:** 2

Profile: Regional center
Location: South-central Québec along the St. Lawrence River
Elevation: 371 meters/1,217 feet

PRO	CON
Arts and culture	Economic cycles
Attractive downtown	Harsh climate

A rich cosmopolitan city with a strong European accent, Montréal is the cultural and economic center of eastern Canada. Its diverse economic base includes manufacturing, service, financial, and government activities. The attractive downtown contains an extraordinary collection of old and modern buildings with a variety of urban settings. The suburbs are also appealing, and public transportation, a necessity, is excellent and includes a modern subway system. Public transport utilization of 20.5% is highest in Canada. While French language and culture dominate the city, many residents are bilingual and the primary language varies from neighborhood to neighborhood. The city is packed with cultural and entertainment amenities, including world-famous museums, restaurants, theater, and other performing arts. McGill University and the University of Montréal add to the educational and cultural mix. While hurt by the tax structure and the overhanging political uncertainty caused by the separatist movement, those concerns have subsided. However, going against Canadian trends, employment has deteriorated somewhat since 2001. At 85.8, the Cost of Living Index continues to be exceptionally low for a city that offers so much.

The city is along the main channel of the St. Lawrence River in rocky and somewhat hilly, wooded terrain. Climate is mainly continental with generally pleasant summers and brisk winters with considerable snow and occasional rain and freezing rain.

Montréal is truly unique against a U.S. background, but might compare to New Orleans (not ranked in this edition) culturally and geographically. However, in comparison to that U.S. city, Montréal's crime rate is much lower and the level of intellectual stimulation is much higher. Montréal gets a comparable U.S. rank of 30 and could be higher with a stronger employment picture and a more attractive climate.

POPULATION

Population	3,426,350	Median age	37.9	Visible minorities	13.6%
Population density	2,351.7 sq. km/908.0 sq. miles	Average family size	3.1	English-speaking	8.5%
Population growth	3.0%	Single	40.9%	French-speaking	39.8%
		Married	40.0%	Bilingual	49.7%

ECONOMY & JOBS

Household income	C$42,123/US$37,277
Unemployment rate	8.9%
White collar	79%
Blue collar	21%

COST OF LIVING

Cost of Living Index	85.8	Average home price	C$213,433/US$194,188
Provincial income tax	24.0%	Average rent	C$616/US$545
Provincial sales tax	7.5%	Homes owned	50%
		Homes rented	50%

CLIMATE

Average January low	−12.4°C/9.7°F	Annual days > 30°C/86°F	8.2	Annual days precipitation	163.9
Average July high	26.6°C/79.9°F	Annual days < 0°C/32°F	132.2	Annual days snowfall	53.9
Annual precipitation	1,062.6mm/41.8 in.	Annual days < −20°C/−4°F	7.7	Annual sun hours	2,015
Annual snowfall	226.2cm/89.1 in.				

TEMPERATURE

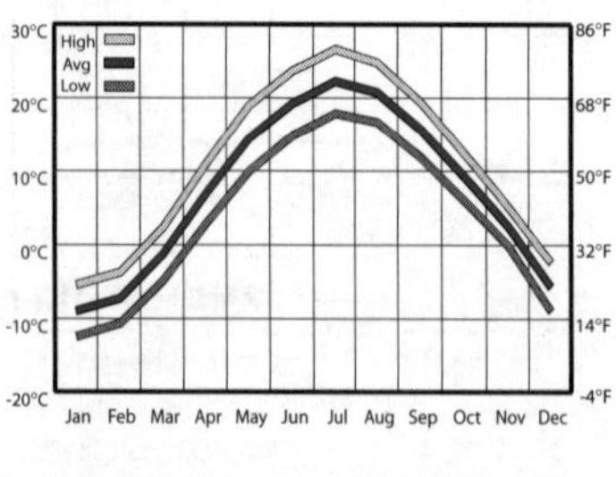

PRECIPITATION

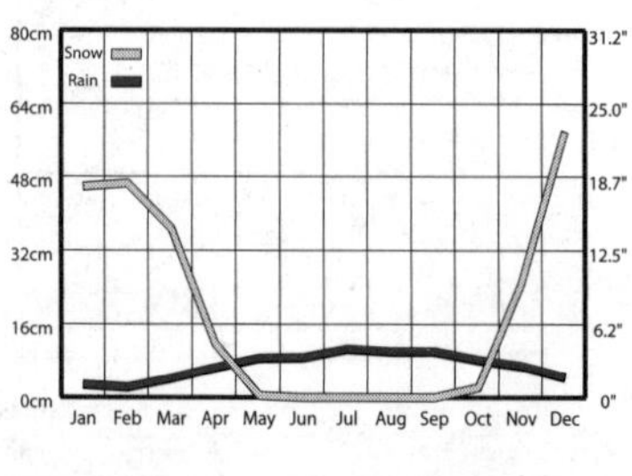

EDUCATION

High school degree	80%
Completed trade school	11%
College degree	18%
University degree	25.9%

CRIME

Violent crime rate	719
Change in violent crime rate	30.0%
Property crime rate	1,639
Change in property crime rate	−1.1%
Relocation Crime Index	188

TRANSPORTATION

Commute by auto	61.7%
Commute by mass transit	20.5%
Work at home	5.5%
Air service (passengers/day)	24,126

LEISURE

Restaurant rating	10	Spectator-sports rating	10
Golf-course rating	8	Inland water rating	5
Ski-area rating	9	Park rating	7
		Quality of life rating	9

ARTS & CULTURE

Library rating	10
Classical music rating	10
Ballet/dance rating	10
Museum rating	10

Oshawa, Ontario

Rank: 19 2004 rank: 21

Profile: Small industrial city
Location: Along Lake Ontario, 56 kilometers (35 miles) east of Toronto
Elevation: 84 meters/276 feet

PRO	CON
Close to Toronto	Industrial setting
Nearby water	Economic cycles

Oshawa, an outlying eastern suburb in the greater Toronto area, is known mostly as a center for automobile manufacturing and assembly. The area contains several auto plants and mostly middle-class neighborhoods arising from Toronto's suburban growth. There isn't much of interest in the immediate area. Economically, Oshawa is dependent on Toronto, and the many smaller suburbs between Oshawa and Toronto along Highway 401 give the area a feeling of being connected to the larger city; in fact, many residents commute to other Toronto suburbs along the 401. Suburbanization has hurt the downtown area, and much of it feels more like a bedroom community than a viable metro area. Most amenities and services are located in Toronto, and the Arts & Culture and Leisure ratings reflect the larger city's proximity. The economy has experienced large swings in the past, and has largely missed out on Canada's recent economic upswing. Cost of living is moderate on the greater Toronto scale.

The setting on a flat, coastal plain to the northwest of Lake Ontario receives relatively less harsh winters than its U.S. counterparts to the south in New York.

Oshawa compares to several towns in Michigan, with elements of Flint (no. 335) and the Warren–Troy–Farmington Hills area (no. 190) outside of Detroit. The comparable U.S. rank is 200.

POPULATION

Population	296,298	Median age	35.8	Visible minorities	7.0%
Population density	911.1 sq. km/351.8 sq. miles	Average family size	3.3	English-speaking	92.8%
Population growth	10.2%	Single	28.8%	French-speaking	0.1%
		Married	54.5%	Bilingual	6.7%

ECONOMY & JOBS

Household income	C$62,956/US$55,713
Unemployment rate	6.2%
White collar	72%
Blue collar	28%

COST OF LIVING

Cost of Living Index	97.8	Average home price	C$245,000/US$216,814
Provincial income tax	11.2%	Average rent	C$855/US$757
Provincial sales tax	8.0%	Homes owned	76%
		Homes rented	24%

CLIMATE

Average January low	−9.2°C/15.4°F	Annual days > 30°C/86°F	2.8	Annual days precipitation	142.1
Average July high	25.0°C/77.0°F	Annual days < 0°C/32°F	131.8	Annual days snowfall	28.5
Annual precipitation	877.9mm/34.6 in.	Annual days < −20°C/−4°F	3.4	Annual sun hours	2,025
Annual snowfall	118.4cm/46.6 in.				

TEMPERATURE

PRECIPITATION

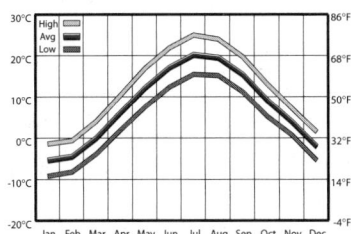

EDUCATION

High school degree	80%
Completed trade school	12%
College degree	23%
University degree	15.3%

CRIME

Violent crime rate	903
Change in violent crime rate	1.8%
Property crime rate	6,509
Change in property crime rate	1.6%
Relocation Crime Index	215

TRANSPORTATION

Commute by auto	75.8%
Commute by mass transit	6.7%
Work at home	5.2%
Air service (passengers/day)	< 500

LEISURE

Restaurant rating	5	Spectator-sports rating	5
Golf-course rating	3	Inland water rating	8
Ski-area rating	4	Park rating	4
		Quality of life rating	5

ARTS & CULTURE

Library rating	4
Classical music rating	5
Ballet/dance rating	5
Museum rating	5

Ottawa–Gatineau, Ontario-Québec

Rank: 3 2004 rank: 4

Profile: Capital-city complex
Location: Along Ottawa River at the Ontario-Québec border, 89 kilometers (55 miles) northwest of the St. Lawrence River
Elevation: 79 meters/259 feet

PRO	CON
Strong economic base	Cost of living
Attractive downtown	Cold winters

Ottawa is the capital of Canada and its downtown appearance reflects it in every way. The city has avoided tall buildings and skyscrapers in favor of a uniform and dignified historic appearance. Majestic Gothic government buildings dominate the downtown core, and the area as a whole is clean and inviting. The shady suburbs and parks surrounding the city are also most appealing. Gatineau is a quiet, French-speaking suburb across the Ottawa River. The area, known as "Silicon Valley North," gets a major boost from a broad assortment of technology and research entities, especially in the telecommunications sector, headed up by the large, but somewhat challenged, Nortel Networks. While Nortel has shed some 30,000 jobs since the tech bubble bust, others among the some 40 technology companies in the area have taken up most of the slack. That said, unemployment has bucked the Canada trend and is up slightly. The government provides a stable base behind the technology component, and Carleton University adds a university element. Not surprisingly, the cost of living is high, with a Cost of Living Index of 122.7.

The terrain is rolling with mostly deciduous trees that yield spectacular fall seasons. The great distance from large bodies of water makes the winter climate more severe than most places in eastern Canada.

Although much is different, Ottawa compares in some ways to Washington, D.C. (no. 130), but without many of its problems; some might find similarities with the Boston area or North Carolina's Research Triangle (Raleigh–Cary; no. 63) or Durham (no. 15) but no clear-cut comparison exists. We assign a comparable U.S. rank of 35.

POPULATION

Population	1,063,664	Median age	36.6	Visible minorities	14.1%
Population density	555.6 sq. km/214.5 sq. miles	Average family size	3.2	English-speaking	45.8%
Population growth	6.5%	Single	35.4%	French-speaking	9.0%
		Married	48.1%	Bilingual	44.0%

ECONOMY & JOBS · COST OF LIVING

Household income	C$59,009/US$52,220	Cost of Living Index	122.7	Average home price	C$260,249/US$230,309
Unemployment rate	6.7%	Provincial income tax	11.2%	Average rent	C$920/US$814
White collar	87%	Provincial sales tax	8.0%	Homes owned	62%
Blue collar	13%			Homes rented	38%

CLIMATE

Average January low	−14.8°C/5.4°F	Annual days > 30°C/86°F	10.3	Annual days precipitation	163.4
Average July high	26.4°C/79.5°F	Annual days < 0°C/32°F	153.4	Annual days snowfall	56.6
Annual precipitation	914.2mm/36.0 in.	Annual days < −20°C/−4°F	18.9	Annual sun hours	2,054
Annual snowfall	202.7cm/79.8 in.				

TEMPERATURE

PRECIPITATION

EDUCATION

High school degree	86%
Completed trade school	8%
College degree	19%
University degree	33%

CRIME

Violent crime rate	903
Change in violent crime rate	1.8%
Property crime rate	6,509
Change in property crime rate	1.6%
Relocation Crime Index	95

TRANSPORTATION

Commute by auto	60.4%
Commute by mass transit	17.3%
Work at home	6.1%
Air service (passengers/day)	8,811

LEISURE

Restaurant rating	9	Spectator-sports rating	6
Golf-course rating	8	Inland water rating	6
Ski-area rating	8	Park rating	8
		Quality of life rating	9

ARTS & CULTURE

Library rating	6
Classical music rating	7
Ballet/dance rating	7
Museum rating	10

Québec City, Québec

Rank: 4 2004 rank: 7

Profile: Capital city
Location: East-central Québec along the St. Lawrence River, 242 kilometers (150 miles) northeast of Montréal
Elevation: 74 meters/243 feet

PRO	CON
Attractive downtown	Tourist impact
Historic and cultural	Cold winters
interest	

Québec City, the capital of the province of Québec, is one of the oldest and most interesting cities in North America. The irregular cobblestone streets and stone buildings in the Old City surrounded by a perimeter wall add to the city's distinct European flavor. The economy is supported mainly by the Québec government and tourism. The city's atmosphere and amenities attract thousands of visitors each year. Some of the country's better museums, arts, and entertainment are located in and around the city. The largest ski area in eastern Canada is 16 kilometers (10 miles) north. The Old City is crowded and tight, so most residents live in the relatively nondescript suburbs outside the Old City walls to the west. Cost of living (with a COL Index of 98.5) and housing are reasonable for what's available, but household incomes are among the lowest in Canada.

The city is located in the St. Lawrence Valley with hilly to mountainous, wooded terrain, particularly to the north. The climate is continental with relatively severe winters due to latitude and distance from major bodies of water.

A comparable U.S. city is almost impossible to identify, although the historic roots and preservation recall Charlottesville, Virginia (no. 17), but the climate is harsh and the economy is less diverse. The comparable U.S. rank is 50.

POPULATION

Population	682,757	Median age	39.5	Visible minorities	1.6%
Population density	601.1 sq. km/232.1 sq. miles	Average family size	3.0	English-speaking	0.2%
Population growth	1.6%	Single	44.3%	French-speaking	69.6%
		Married	36.9%	Bilingual	30.0%

ECONOMY & JOBS

Household income	C$41,864/US$37,048
Unemployment rate	5.7%
White collar	83%
Blue collar	17%

COST OF LIVING

Cost of Living Index	98.5	Average home price	C$150,324/US$133,030
Provincial income tax	24.0%	Average rent	C$607/US$537
Provincial sales tax	7.5%	Homes owned	55.5%
		Homes rented	44.5%

CLIMATE

Average January low	−17.6°C/0.3°F	Annual days > 30°C/86°F	4.6	Annual days precipitation	181.9
Average July high	25.0°C/77.0°F	Annual days < 0°C/32°F	175.9	Annual days snowfall	148.9
Annual precipitation	1,230.3mm/48.4 in.	Annual days < −20°C/−4°F	31.1	Annual sun hours	1,910
Annual snowfall	315.9cm/124.4 in.				

TEMPERATURE

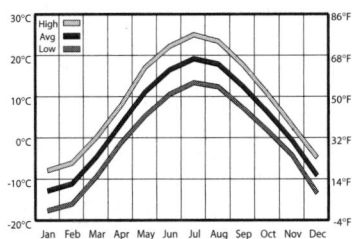

PRECIPITATION

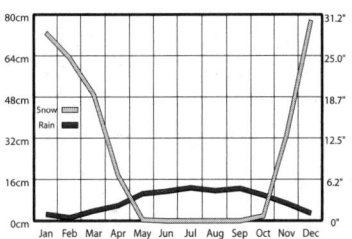

EDUCATION

High school degree	85%
Completed trade school	13%
College degree	22%
University degree	24.9%

CRIME

Violent crime rate	719
Change in violent crime rate	30.0%
Property crime rate	1,639
Change in property crime rate	−1.1%
Relocation Crime Index	149

TRANSPORTATION

Commute by auto	71.8%
Commute by mass transit	9.3%
Work at home	5.2%
Air service (passengers/day)	1,665

LEISURE

Restaurant rating	8
Golf-course rating	5
Ski-area rating	9

Spectator-sports rating	2
Inland water rating	4
Park rating	6
Quality of life rating	8

ARTS & CULTURE

Library rating	3
Classical music rating	7
Ballet/dance rating	5
Museum rating	9

Regina, Saskatchewan

Profile: Capital city
Location: Southeastern Saskatchewan along Highway 1
Elevation: 79 meters/259 feet

PRO	CON
Small-town feel	Entertainment
Attractive downtown	Cold winters

Regina, a small city rising above the seemingly endless prairie, is the capital of the province and a regional agricultural, commercial, and financial center. The city is clean, quiet, and traditional, but there isn't a whole lot to do, and the downtown area isn't as nice as many Canadian cities, particularly its provincial capitals. The few highlights include some worthwhile museums mostly of a local character, a few parks, a Canadian Football League team, and good air service to the rest of Canada.

Regina sits in a shallow creek valley on a treeless prairie. The continental climate is harsh and changeable with little to block northerly bitter cold and wind. There are 47 days each year with temperatures below −20°C (−4°F). On the positive side, the area is far enough north and away from water to be relatively dry and sunny compared to most Canadian cities.

Bismarck, North Dakota (no. 114), might be a good U.S. comparison, although that American city is in a more lush and protected river valley setting and offers more to do. The comparable U.S. rank is 195.

POPULATION

Population	192,800	Median age	35.9	Visible minorities	5.2%
Population density	157.2 sq. km/60.7 sq. miles	Average family size	3.1	English-speaking	93.9%
Population growth	-0.4%	Single	34.6%	French-speaking	0.1%
		Married	49.2%	Bilingual	5.6%

ECONOMY & JOBS

		COST OF LIVING			
Household income	C$47,757/US$42,263	Cost of Living Index	84.9	Average home price	C$142,147/US$125,794
Unemployment rate	5.2%	Provincial income tax	15.5%	Average rent	C$621/US$550
White collar	82%	Provincial sales tax	6.0%	Homes owned	68%
Blue collar	18%			Homes rented	32%

CLIMATE

Average January low	−21.6°C/−6.9°F	Annual days > 30°C/86°F	15.7	Annual days precipitation	114.5
Average July high	25.7°C/78.3°F	Annual days < 0°C/32°F	199.6	Annual days snowfall	57.2
Annual precipitation	388.1mm/15.3 in.	Annual days < −20°C/−4°F	47.7	Annual sun hours	2,365
Annual snowfall	105.9cm/41.7 in.				

TEMPERATURE

PRECIPITATION

EDUCATION

High school degree	80%
Completed trade school	13%
College degree	16%
University degree	23%

CRIME

Violent crime rate	1,802
Change in violent crime rate	8.0%
Property crime rate	5,793
Change in property crime rate	11.0%
Relocation Crime Index	223

TRANSPORTATION

Commute by auto	75.2%
Commute by mass transit	4.1%
Work at home	5.9%
Air service (passengers/day)	1,942

LEISURE

Restaurant rating	3	Spectator-sports rating	3
Golf-course rating	2	Inland water rating	5
Ski-area rating	2	Park rating	4
		Quality of life rating	4

ARTS & CULTURE

Library rating	7
Classical music rating	5
Ballet/dance rating	1
Museum rating	5

Saguenay, Québec

Rank: 27 2004 rank: 26

Profile: Small-city complex
Location: Northeastern Québec along the Saguenay River, 129 kilometers (80 miles) west of the St. Lawrence Seaway
Elevation: 6.4 meters/21 feet

PRO	CON
Attractive setting	Economy
Cost of living	Isolation

This renamed CMA was created by the merger of the twin cities of Chicoutimi–Jonquière and two smaller villages, and lies in the center of a large, forested wilderness in northeastern Québec. These centers developed economically as a major center for the pulp and paper industry, and greater efficiencies in that industry have led to employment difficulties, although the 11.2% unemployment rate—the highest among Canadian metro areas—has improved a bit from 12.4% in 2001. The attractive fjord setting and nearby recreation have brought some tourist trade, but there isn't much to do here overall. The area is separated from Québec City by 209 kilometers (130 miles) of wilderness, making access to most big-city amenities and services a challenge.

The area is located in a dramatic river valley setting surrounded by heavily wooded hills. The wet, northern climate, partly influenced by the Atlantic Ocean and St. Lawrence River, produces plenty of cold and the second highest snowfall in the country.

A comparable U.S. area might be Utica–Rome, New York (no. 321). We give the area a comparable U.S. rank of 320.

POPULATION

Population	154,938	Median age	39.8	Visible minorities	0.6%
Population density	245.6 sq. km/94.8 sq. miles	Average family size	3.1	English-speaking	0.1%
Population growth	-3.4%	Single	38.3%	French-speaking	82.5%
		Married	42.9%	Bilingual	17.4%

ECONOMY & JOBS

Household income	C$41,854/US$37,039
Unemployment rate	11.2%
White collar	73%
Blue collar	27%

COST OF LIVING

Cost of Living Index	76.6
Provincial income tax	24.0%
Provincial sales tax	7.5%

Average home price	C$124,856/US$110,482
Average rent	C$472/US$419
Homes owned	62%
Homes rented	38%

CLIMATE

Average January low	−19.5°C/−3.1°F	Annual days > 30°C/86°F	3.4	Annual days precipitation	150.2
Average July high	23.4°C/74.1°F	Annual days < 0°C/32°F	197.5	Annual days snowfall	167.4
Annual precipitation	1,002.1mm/39.5 in.	Annual days < −20°C/−4°F	37.2	Annual sun hours	1,676
Annual snowfall	301.5cm/118.7 in.				

TEMPERATURE

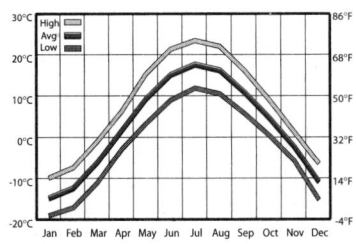

PRECIPITATION

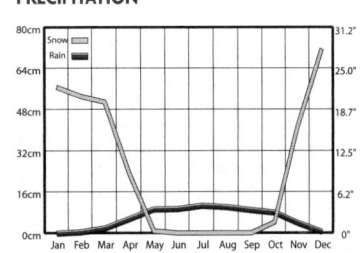

EDUCATION

High school degree	81%
Completed trade school	20%
College degree	20%
University degree	16.9%

CRIME

Violent crime rate	719
Change in violent crime rate	30.0%
Property crime rate	1,639
Change in property crime rate	−1.1%
Relocation Crime Index	n/a

TRANSPORTATION

Commute by auto	81.5%
Commute by mass transit	2.4%
Work at home	4.1%
Air service (passengers/day)	< 500

LEISURE

Restaurant rating	3
Golf-course rating	3
Ski-area rating	3

Spectator-sports rating	1
Inland water rating	9
Park rating	8
Quality of life rating	2

ARTS & CULTURE

Library rating	2
Classical music rating	1
Ballet/dance rating	1
Museum rating	2

St. Catharines–Niagara, Ontario

Rank: 10 **2004 rank:** 11

Profile: Small-city complex
Location: Niagara Peninsula, between Lake Erie and Lake Ontario near New York border
Elevation: 79 meters/259 feet

PRO	CON
Small-town feel	Low educational attainment
Relatively mild climate	Economic cycles

The St. Catharines–Niagara metropolitan area includes the small cities of St. Catharines and Niagara Falls, the more historic and upscale enclave of Niagara-on-the-Lake, and a few smaller towns. The area is well known for agriculture and as the gateway to Niagara Falls and Buffalo, New York, to the east. The local towns have a clean and attractive small-town feel. Only Niagara Falls itself suffers a bit from tourism and tourist sprawl; the impact is mainly felt in summer. Although the economy is diverse, with tourism, auto parts, and some other manufacturing concerns leading the way, employment actually has weakened during the Canada employment boom—more, in fact, than any other CMA (see Table 6.3). Were it not for that fact, this area might

have ranked higher. Bigger city amenities are available in Buffalo across the border and in Toronto, 145 kilometers (90 miles) around Lake Ontario to the north.

The influence from Lake Ontario brings extended warmth to the area, particularly in fall. However, the cities are far enough west to avoid the brunt of the lake-effect snows observed in upstate New York to the east. The resulting climate is excellent for fruit orchards and wine grapes—in fact, the area has some of the best wineries in Canada.

A direct U.S. comparison isn't easy, but St. Catharines–Niagara might compare with Sheboygan, Wisconsin (no. 121), and earns a comparable U.S. rank of 120.

POPULATION

Population	377,009	Median age	40.2	Visible minorities	4.5%
Population density	744.7 sq. km/287.5 sq. miles	Average family size	3.0	English-speaking	90.8%
Population growth	1.2%	Single	27.1%	French-speaking	0.2%
		Married	53.3%	Bilingual	8.3%

ECONOMY & JOBS

Household income	C$45,881/US$40,603
Unemployment rate	7.9%
White collar	71.5%
Blue collar	28.5%

COST OF LIVING

Cost of Living Index	84.2	Average home price	C$229,000/US$202,655
Provincial income tax	11.2%	Average rent	C$736/US$651
Provincial sales tax	8.0%	Homes owned	73%
		Homes rented	27%

CLIMATE

Average January low	−7.7°C/18.1°F	Annual days > 30°C/86°F	13.7	Annual days precipitation	151
Average July high	27.1°C/80.8°F	Annual days < 0°C/32°F	129.2	Annual days snowfall	44.6
Annual precipitation	871.6mm/34.3 in.	Annual days < −20°C/−4°F	0.9	Annual sun hours	2,079
Annual snowfall	136.6cm/53.8 in.				

TEMPERATURE

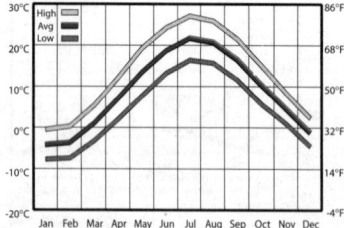

PRECIPITATION

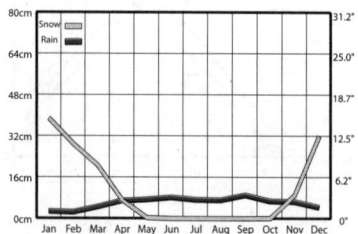

EDUCATION

High school degree	79%
Completed trade school	12%
College degree	20%
University degree	15.6%

CRIME

Violent crime rate	903
Change in violent crime rate	1.8%
Property crime rate	6,509
Change in property crime rate	1.6%
Relocation Crime Index	71

TRANSPORTATION

Commute by auto	78.0%
Commute by mass transit	1.9%
Work at home	5.7%
Air service (passengers/day)	< 500

LEISURE

Restaurant rating	4	Spectator-sports rating	3
Golf-course rating	5	Inland water rating	8
Ski-area rating	3	Park rating	8
		Quality of life rating	7

ARTS & CULTURE

Library rating	5
Classical music rating	3
Ballet/dance rating	3
Museum rating	5

Saint John, New Brunswick

Profile: Small port city
Location: Along southeast coast of New Brunswick, 97 kilometers (60 miles) northeast of the U.S. border at Calais, Maine
Elevation: 109 meters/358 feet

PRO	CON
Historic interest	Economic cycles
Nearby water recreation	Industrial feel

Saint John, originally a Loyalist colony, is a major shipping and industrial gateway for eastern Canada. Industries include shipbuilding, oil refining, pulp and paper, and shipping for a variety of bulk commodities. Parts of the city have a gritty industrial feel, and the city has felt the brunt of economic cycles in a number of these industries. Current unemployment is 8.4%, but cost of living and particularly housing are low on a Canadian scale. The downtown area has been revitalized and contains a number of historic buildings with interesting Victorian-era architectural ornamentation. However, the area isn't as interesting as Halifax to the east, and doesn't offer much to do.

The terrain is mostly low wooded hills and the climate is a rigorous mix of marine and continental. While the area gets a distinct marine influence with frequent Bay of Fundy fogs and precipitation, cold air still invades from the northwest, dropping temperatures below −20°C (−4°F) 15 times a year.

The area compares in some ways to Portland, Maine (no. 231), although behind in urban revitalization and intellectual stimulation, and gets a comparable U.S. rank of 290.

POPULATION

Population	122,678	Median age	37.9	Visible minorities	2.6%
Population density	101.4 sq. km/39.2 sq. miles	Average family size	3.1	English-speaking	87.5%
Population growth	-2.4%	Single	30.8%	French-speaking	0.1%
		Married	51.4%	Bilingual	12.3%

ECONOMY & JOBS

Household income	C$41,596/US$36,811
Unemployment rate	8.4%
White collar	78%
Blue collar	22%

COST OF LIVING

Cost of Living Index	85.4	Average home price	C$129,844/US$114,906
Provincial income tax	17.8%	Average rent	C$526/US$465
Provincial sales tax	7.5%	Homes owned	67%
		Homes rented	33%

CLIMATE

Average January low	−13.6°C/7.5°F	Annual days > 30°C/86°F	0.8	Annual days precipitation	162.3
Average July high	22.4°C/72.3°F	Annual days < 0°C/32°F	168.6	Annual days snowfall	55.7
Annual precipitation	1,390.3mm/54.7 in.	Annual days < −20°C/−4°F	15.2	Annual sun hours	1,950
Annual snowfall	256.9cm/101.1 in.				

TEMPERATURE

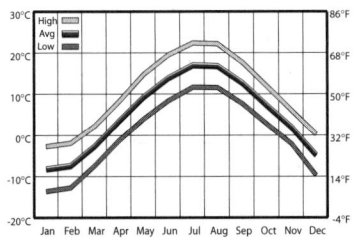

PRECIPITATION

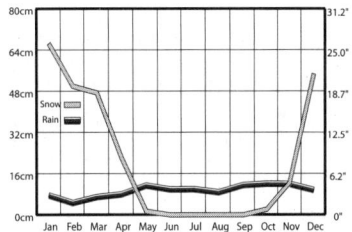

EDUCATION

High school degree	79%
Completed trade school	14%
College degree	18%
University degree	17.6%

CRIME

Violent crime rate	988
Change in violent crime rate	4.8%
Property crime rate	2,664
Change in property crime rate	−0.7%
Relocation Crime Index	238

TRANSPORTATION

Commute by auto	72.6%
Commute by mass transit	4.1%
Work at home	4.7%
Air service (passengers/day)	552

LEISURE

Restaurant rating	3	Spectator-sports rating	2
Golf-course rating	2	Inland water rating	9
Ski-area rating	1	Park rating	5
		Quality of life rating	3

ARTS & CULTURE

Library rating	5
Classical music rating	3
Ballet/dance rating	1
Museum rating	3

St. John's, Newfoundland and Labrador

Rank: 16 2004 rank: 14

Profile: Small port city
Location: Southwestern tip of Newfoundland
Elevation: 141 meters/462 feet

PRO	CON
Attractive setting	Cloudy, wet climate
Cost of living	Isolation

St. John's, the capital of Newfoundland and Labrador, is an old port city reputed to be the oldest city in North America. The natural harbor and central location for Atlantic shipping virtually guarantee its prominence as a shipping center and refueling stop, and as a hub for the fishing industry. The recent oil boom has added to the economy, and unemployment, while still high at 8.7%, is much lower than the 11.3% reported in 2001. The downtown area on the waterfront is fairly nondescript. The oil industry is financing some new construction, but not without controversy. Because of fires early in the city's history, many of the more interesting historic buildings are in the hills away from downtown. Many modest amenities are available in the area, but it's 940 miles by air or ferry to Halifax for any that aren't present.

Downsides include an unpleasant, Maritime climate with rain almost 2 in 3 days year-round and an inhospitable, rocky, hilly, mostly treeless landscape and seascape away from town.

Although economic statistics and especially living costs differ, Anchorage, Alaska (no. 228), is the most similar U.S. city. The comparable U.S. rank is 190.

POPULATION

Population	172,918	Median age	36.3	Visible minorities	1.4%
Population density	596.9 sq. km/230.5 sq. miles	Average family size	3.2	English-speaking	94.5%
Population growth	-0.7%	Single	35.1%	French-speaking	0.0%
		Married	51.0%	Bilingual	5.4%

ECONOMY & JOBS

Household income	C$45,675/US$40,420
Unemployment rate	8.7%
White collar	84%
Blue collar	16%

COST OF LIVING

Cost of Living Index	87.1	Average home price	C$135,100/US$119,558
Provincial income tax	18.0%	Average rent	C$634/US$581
Provincial sales tax	7.5%	Homes owned	69.5%
		Homes rented	30.5%

CLIMATE

Average January low	-8.6°C/16.5°F	Annual days > 30°C/86°F	0.2	Annual days precipitation	215.8
Average July high	20.3°C/68.5°F	Annual days < 0°C/32°F	174	Annual days snowfall	84.2
Annual precipitation	1,513.7mm/59.6 in.	Annual days < -20°C/-4°F	1	Annual sun hours	1,527
Annual snowfall	322.3cm/126.9 in.				

TEMPERATURE

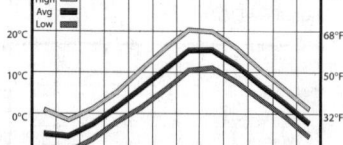

PRECIPITATION

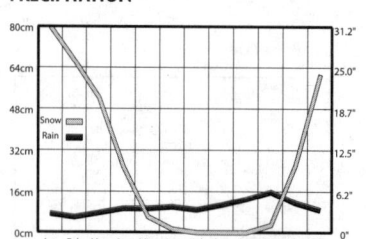

EDUCATION

High school degree	80%
Completed trade school	20%
College degree	17%
University degree	22.7%

CRIME

Violent crime rate	892
Change in violent crime rate	-1.4%
Property crime rate	2,459
Change in property crime rate	1.8%
Relocation Crime Index	258

TRANSPORTATION

Commute by auto	73.1%
Commute by mass transit	2.6%
Work at home	5.0%
Air service (passengers/day)	< 500

LEISURE

Restaurant rating	6	Spectator-sports rating	2
Golf-course rating	2	Inland water rating	8
Ski-area rating	2	Park rating	7
		Quality of life rating	5

ARTS & CULTURE

Library rating	3
Classical music rating	3
Ballet/dance rating	1
Museum rating	6

Saskatoon, Saskatchewan

Rank: 13 2004 rank: 12

Profile: Mid-size city
Location: Southwestern Saskatchewan along the South Saskatchewan River
Elevation: 504 meters/1,653 feet

PRO	CON
Diverse economy	Isolation
Educated population	Cold winters

Regina may be the provincial capital, but Saskatoon is stronger economically and culturally. Of the two Saskatchewan Prairie cities, Saskatoon is larger, more modern and progressive, and offers more to do. However, it's still fairly plain and quiet. Saskatoon is home to the University of Saskatchewan and serves as center to a large agricultural area and potash industry. The economy and employment picture is healthy and includes a diverse research and high-tech base in addition to these basic industries. The city has some modest cultural and entertainment amenities, but the real highlight is the vast outdoors and its recreational opportunities.

Although the city sits in more of a river valley than Regina or Winnipeg, the downtown is visible for miles across the prairie. The northern plains climate is pleasant in summer, but quite rugged the rest of the year. Saskatoon's winter cold is second only to Winnipeg in intensity.

Saskatoon compares somewhat to Fargo, North Dakota (no. 40), but the university presence and employment and cost-of-living profiles aren't as strong. The comparable U.S. rank is 140.

POPULATION

Population	225,927	Median age	34.4	Visible minorities	5.6%
Population density	120.8 sq. km/46.6 sq. miles	Average family size	3.3	English-speaking	92.9%
Population growth	3.1%	Single	34.8%	French-speaking	0.0%
		Married	49.5%	Bilingual	6.5%

ECONOMY & JOBS

		COST OF LIVING			
Household income	C$43,392/US$38,400	Cost of Living Index	95.9	Average home price	C$162,279/US$142,610
Unemployment rate	5.7%	Provincial income tax	15.5%	Average rent	C$584/US$517
White collar	76.5%	Provincial sales tax	6.0%	Homes owned	65%
Blue collar	23.5%			Homes rented	35%

CLIMATE

Average January low	−22.3°C/−8.1°F	Annual days > 30°C/86°F	11.3	Annual days precipitation	111.9
Average July high	24.9°C/76.8°F	Annual days < 0°C/32°F	198.9	Annual days snowfall	56.8
Annual precipitation	350mm/13.8 in.	Annual days < −20°C/−4°F	52.1	Annual sun hours	2,381
Annual snowfall	97.2cm/38.3 in.				

TEMPERATURE

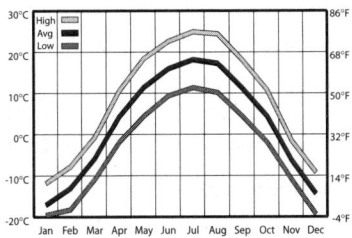

PRECIPITATION

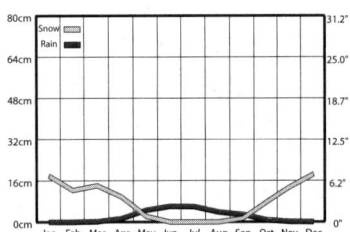

EDUCATION

High school degree	80%
Completed trade school	14%
College degree	17%
University degree	23.8%

CRIME

Violent crime rate	1,802
Change in violent crime rate	8.0%
Property crime rate	5,793
Change in property crime rate	11.0%
Relocation Crime Index	232

TRANSPORTATION

Commute by auto	73.7%
Commute by mass transit	3.8%
Work at home	7.2%
Air service (passengers/day)	2,089

LEISURE

Restaurant rating	2	Spectator-sports rating	1
Golf-course rating	3	Inland water rating	7
Ski-area rating	2	Park rating	7
		Quality of life rating	5

ARTS & CULTURE

Library rating	7
Classical music rating	4
Ballet/dance rating	1
Museum rating	4

Sherbrooke, Québec

Profile: Small city
Location: Southeastern Québec, 56 kilometers (35 miles) north of the U.S. border at Derby Line, Vermont
Elevation: 241 meters/790 feet

PRO	CON
Cost of living	Entertainment
Nearby outdoor recreation	Growth and sprawl

Sherbrooke is a bicultural former industrial center located at the edge of the mountainous area extending southward across the U.S. border into Vermont and New York. The city is fairly nondescript, with a small Victorian-era downtown core and a large and unattractive commercial strip extending west, with pockets of residential and commercial areas elsewhere. Manufacturing, once based on typical New England–style milling and forest products industries, has declined noticeably and the economy is still weak. Two small universities have brought some new economic life and a bit of cultural life, but there isn't much to do in town. Nearby mountains and lakes offer some quality recreational opportunities. The pace of life is slow and home prices are reasonable.

The surrounding terrain is mainly hilly and wooded and the area is far enough away from major bodies of water to experience harsh winters, but summers are quite pleasant.

The area might compare to Pittsfield, Massachusetts (no. 243), and the comparable U.S. rank is 245.

POPULATION

Population	153,811	Median age	38.1	Visible minorities	2.6%
Population density	385.6 sq. km/148.9 sq. miles	Average family size	3.0	English-speaking	1.9%
Population growth	2.8%	Single	42.8%	French-speaking	58.8%
		Married	36.4%	Bilingual	39.1%

ECONOMY & JOBS

Household income	C$36,744/US$32,517
Unemployment rate	7.2%
White collar	74%
Blue collar	26%

COST OF LIVING

Cost of Living Index	85.2	Average home price	C$179,900/US$159,204
Provincial income tax	24.0%	Average rent	C$505/US$447
Provincial sales tax	7.5%	Homes owned	52%
		Homes rented	48%

CLIMATE

Average January low	−18.0°C/−0.4°F	Annual days > 30°C/86°F	3.4	Annual days precipitation	192.2
Average July high	24.7°C/76.5°F	Annual days < 0°C/32°F	189	Annual days snowfall	79.4
Annual precipitation	1,144.1mm/45.0 in.	Annual days < −20°C/−4°F	35.7	Annual sun hours	1,901
Annual snowfall	294.3cm/115.9 in.				

TEMPERATURE

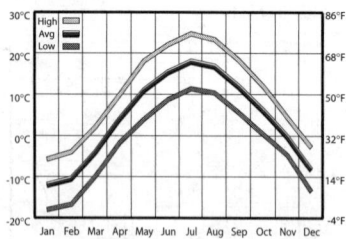

PRECIPITATION

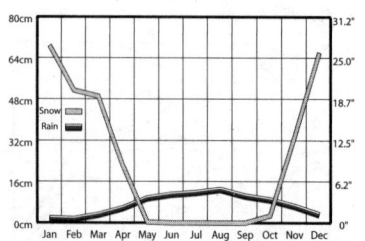

EDUCATION

High school degree	81%
Completed trade school	14%
College degree	20%
University degree	21.8%

CRIME

Violent crime rate	719
Change in violent crime rate	30.0%
Property crime rate	1,639
Change in property crime rate	−1.1%
Relocation Crime Index	n/a

TRANSPORTATION

Commute by auto	75.1%
Commute by mass transit	5.2%
Work at home	5.9%
Air service (passengers/day)	< 500

LEISURE

Restaurant rating	4	Spectator-sports rating	2
Golf-course rating	3	Inland water rating	8
Ski-area rating	7	Park rating	7
		Quality of life rating	4

ARTS & CULTURE

Library rating	3
Classical music rating	3
Ballet/dance rating	1
Museum rating	4

Sudbury, Ontario

Rank: 26 2004 rank: 27

Profile: Small city
Location: Northern Ontario, north of Lake Huron, 403 kilometers (250 miles) northwest of Toronto
Elevation: 347 meters/1,138 feet

PRO	CON
Nearby recreation	Isolation
Pleasant summers	Entertainment

Sudbury is a major mining center located in a unique geologic area known as the Precambrian or Canadian Shield. Enormous mines supplying most of the world's nickel have been the economic mainstay for years; other metals are mined as well. The area was once an environmental disaster with so much impact from mining and smelting that the astronauts used it for training in lunar exploration. Public and private sectors have worked together on what has turned out to be a very successful reclamation. The town itself lacks interest and doesn't have a lot to do, but there are some cultural amenities anchored by Science North, a well-known science museum. The area is extremely isolated from larger cities. It has a particularly strong community feel, and has accomplishments such as the installation of a fiber optic network for its citizens. While educational attainment remains low and unemployment is still an issue, the overall quality of life may be on the upswing. Outdoor recreational opportunities are plentiful, particularly in the Killarney Provincial Park to the south.

The terrain is rocky and rough—early railroad builders had a particularly difficult time cutting through it. The climate can bring protracted periods of deep winter cold and wind.

Sudbury compares with some differences to Butte, Montana, which is not a U.S. metropolitan area. The equivalent U.S. ranking is 300.

POPULATION

Population	155,219	Median age	38.9	Visible minorities	2.0%
Population density	128.6 sq. km/49.7 sq. miles	Average family size	3.0	English-speaking	58.0%
Population growth	-6.1%	Single	29.5%	French-speaking	1.5%
		Married	52.1%	Bilingual	40.1%

ECONOMY & JOBS

Household income	C$45,255/US$40,049				
Unemployment rate	7.7%				
White collar	76%				
Blue collar	24%				

COST OF LIVING

Cost of Living Index	76.4	Average home price	C$143,514/US$127,004
Provincial income tax	11.2%	Average rent	C$668/US$591
Provincial sales tax	8.0%	Homes owned	66%
		Homes rented	34%

CLIMATE

Average January low	−18.6°C/−1.5°F	Annual days > 30°C/86°F	5.4	Annual days precipitation	163.9
Average July high	24.8°C/76.6°F	Annual days < 0°C/32°F	182.3	Annual days snowfall	78.4
Annual precipitation	899.3mm/35.4 in.	Annual days < −20°C/−4°F	36.4	Annual sun hours	1,960
Annual snowfall	274.4cm/108.0 in.				

TEMPERATURE

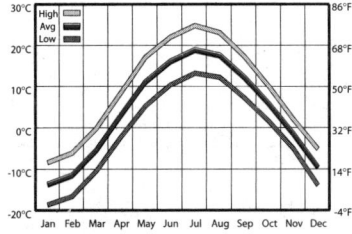

PRECIPITATION

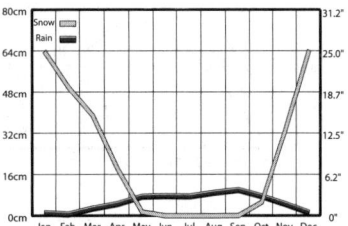

EDUCATION

High school degree	79%
Completed trade school	15%
College degree	21%
University degree	14.9%

CRIME

Violent crime rate	903
Change in violent crime rate	1.8%
Property crime rate	6,509
Change in property crime rate	1.6%
Relocation Crime Index	121

TRANSPORTATION

Commute by auto	74.7%
Commute by mass transit	4.7%
Work at home	4.3%
Air service (passengers/day)	< 500

LEISURE

Restaurant rating	2	Spectator-sports rating	1
Golf-course rating	2	Inland water rating	9
Ski-area rating	4	Park rating	7
		Quality of life rating	3

ARTS & CULTURE

Library rating	5
Classical music rating	1
Ballet/dance rating	1
Museum rating	6

Thunder Bay, Ontario

Rank: 20 2004 rank: 17

Profile: Small port city
Location: Northern Ontario on the west shore of Lake Superior, 48 kilometers (30 miles) from the U.S. border near Grand Portage, Minnesota
Elevation: 199 meters/653 feet

PRO	CON
Nearby outdoor recreation	Economic cycles
Pleasant summers	Entertainment

Thunder Bay, a major Great Lakes inland port, is mainly supported by the shipping of grain and agricultural products and, to a smaller extent, by mining products and manufactured goods. The waterfront is crowded with grain and other shipping terminals. The city was formed by merger of two small, nondescript downtown areas, which continue to show wear and tear from past economic cycles, although some renewal efforts are underway. The employment picture has improved somewhat, but there isn't much to draw people to the city. That said, Thunder Bay is the gateway to world-class lakes, parks, and fishing, making the city a popular summer destination.

The terrain is rocky, moderately hilly, and wooded with numerous lakes and streams. The climate is decidedly continental. Summers are pleasant and moderated by Lake Superior. Winters are bleak and cold with the third highest number of −20°C (−4°F) days in Canada.

The area compares to Duluth, Minnesota (no. 229), but has a less attractive downtown than that city to the south and lacks some of its entertainment. Thunder Bay gets a U.S. equivalent ranking of 240.

POPULATION

Population	121,986	Median age	39.1	Visible minorities	2.2%
Population density	133.1 sq. km/51.4 sq. miles	Average family size	3.1	English-speaking	91.7%
Population growth	-3.7%	Single	31.0%	French-speaking	0.1%
		Married	50.3%	Bilingual	7.4%

ECONOMY & JOBS

		COST OF LIVING			
Household income	C$47,489/US$42,026	Cost of Living Index	81.5	Average home price	C$153,000/US$135,398
Unemployment rate	6.4%	Provincial income tax	11.2%	Average rent	C$713/US$631
White collar	74%	Provincial sales tax	8.0%	Homes owned	72%
Blue collar	26%			Homes rented	28%

CLIMATE

Average January low	−21.1°C/−6.0°F	Annual days > 30°C/86°F	5.8	Annual days precipitation	139.5
Average July high	24.2°C/75.6°F	Annual days < 0°C/32°F	203.3	Annual days snowfall	61.3
Annual precipitation	711.6mm/28.0 in.	Annual days < −20°C/−4°F	49.1	Annual sun hours	2,183
Annual snowfall	187.6cm/73.9 in.				

TEMPERATURE

PRECIPITATION

EDUCATION

High school degree	80%
Completed trade school	14%
College degree	21%
University degree	18.3%

CRIME

Violent crime rate	903
Change in violent crime rate	1.8%
Property crime rate	6,509
Change in property crime rate	1.6%
Relocation Crime Index	n/a

TRANSPORTATION

Commute by auto	78.5%
Commute by mass transit	2.9%
Work at home	4.5%
Air service (passengers/day)	1,542

LEISURE

Restaurant rating	2
Golf-course rating	3
Ski-area rating	5

Spectator-sports rating	2
Inland water rating	10
Park rating	9
Quality of life rating	3

ARTS & CULTURE

Library rating	5
Classical music rating	3
Ballet/dance rating	1
Museum rating	3

Toronto, Ontario

	Rank: 6 2004 rank: 5

Profile: National center
Location: Northwest shore of Lake Ontario
Elevation: 113 meters/371 feet

PRO	**CON**
Attractive downtown	Cost of living
Entertainment, arts, culture	Crowding and sprawl

Toronto, a world-class city and cosmopolitan center, is the largest city in Canada, with almost 15% of the country's population. Set in a mostly flat plain north of Lake Ontario, the city has a modern and attractive downtown with a number of unique waterfront features including the CN Tower and Rogers Centre (formerly the Skydome). A mix of neighborhoods spreads in all directions. Recent immigration and a strong world presence give the city an international flavor that's reflected in most neighborhoods, restaurants, and the arts. There is no shortage of intellectual stimulation or things to do. Toronto has a strong, diverse economy as the transport, commercial, and financial hub for the country, and is also the provincial capital for Ontario. It is also home to York University and the University of Toronto. At 120.3, the Cost of Living Index is high but has finally been edged out by Ottawa for the top spot. While housing is expensive, it hasn't risen as much as in the U.S. counterparts. Traffic and sprawl are growing concerns, and recent employment hasn't followed suit with national trends, but Toronto is still an exciting and stimulating place to live.

The climate is continental with a lake influence. Summers are warm and humid, while winters are cold but not extreme. Its north shore location on Lake Ontario often means Toronto receives little or no snow from the same storm system that dumps as much as 2 feet of snow on Buffalo, Niagara Falls, and other areas of western New York.

New York City (no. 251) is the functional U.S. equivalent, but Toronto is cleaner and looks more like Chicago (no. 258). We give an equivalent U.S. ranking of 50.

POPULATION

Population	4,682,897	Median age	36.2	Visible minorities	36.8%
Population density	2,203.6 sq. km/850.8 sq. miles	Average family size	3.3	English-speaking	87.4%
Population growth	9.8%	Single	32.5%	French-speaking	0.1%
		Married	52.9%	Bilingual	8.0%

ECONOMY & JOBS

Household income	C$63,700/US$56,372	Cost of Living Index	120.3	Average home price	C$365,537/US$323,484
Unemployment rate	6.6%	Provincial income tax	11.2%	Average rent	C$1,052/US$931
White collar	80%	Provincial sales tax	8.0%	Homes owned	63%
Blue collar	20%			Homes rented	37%

COST OF LIVING

CLIMATE

Average January low	−7.3°C/18.9°F	Annual days > 30°C/86°F	9.5	Annual days precipitation	145
Average July high	26.4°C/79.5°F	Annual days < 0°C/32°F	106.6	Annual days snowfall	42
Annual precipitation	834.0mm/32.8 in.	Annual days < −20°C/−4°F	1.4	Annual sun hours	2,038
Annual snowfall	133.1cm/52.4 in.				

TEMPERATURE

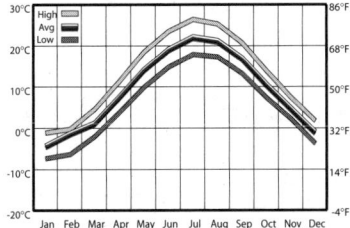

PRECIPITATION

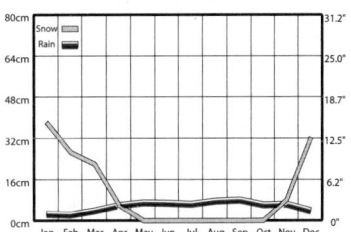

EDUCATION

High school degree	82%
Completed trade school	8%
College degree	17%
University degree	30.8%

CRIME

Violent crime rate	903
Change in violent crime rate	1.8%
Property crime rate	6,509
Change in property crime rate	1.6%
Relocation Crime Index	50

TRANSPORTATION

Commute by auto	60.3%
Commute by mass transit	20.9%
Work at home	6.3%
Air service (passengers/day)	71,402

LEISURE

Restaurant rating	10	Spectator-sports rating	10
Golf-course rating	8	Inland water rating	6
Ski-area rating	6	Park rating	8
		Quality of life rating	8

ARTS & CULTURE

Library rating	10
Classical music rating	10
Ballet/dance rating	10
Museum rating	10

Trois-Rivières, Québec

Rank: 25 2004 rank: 19

Profile: Small industrial town
Location: East-central Québec, along the St. Lawrence River
Elevation: 55 meters/180 feet

PRO	CON
Historic interest	Economy
Cost of living	Industrial feel

One of the oldest towns in North America, Trois-Rivières is a somewhat depressed industrial town mainly supported by pulp and paper manufacturing. Although the forest products industry dominates the town's economy and appearance, there is also a small historical presence with some interesting sites and museums. The setting is nondescript and other Québec cities offer much more in the way of appearance and cultural interest. Considerable outdoor recreation is available, particularly to the north. The decline in employment in the forest products industry has left its mark, but the cost of living is among the lowest in Canada.

The area sits in the mostly level and agricultural St. Lawrence Valley with wooded areas and hills to the north. The climate is typical for the region with pleasant summers and relatively cold winters. The area is far enough from large bodies of water to be drier and colder than many other places in eastern Canada.

Trois-Rivières has some similarities to the Wisconsin areas of Oshkosh–Neenah (no. 142) and Green Bay (no. 283), but has a weaker economy and a less attractive setting. The equivalent U.S. ranking is 280.

POPULATION

Population	137,507	Median age	41.2	Visible minorities	0.9%
Population density	433.9 sq. km/167.5 sq. miles	Average family size	2.9	English-speaking	0.1%
Population growth	-1.7%	Single	41.2%	French-speaking	75.4%
		Married	37.6%	Bilingual	24.4%

ECONOMY & JOBS

Household income	C$35,969/US$31,831
Unemployment rate	8.0%
White collar	73%
Blue collar	27%

COST OF LIVING

Cost of Living Index	76.9	Average home price	C$149,000/US$131,858
Provincial income tax	24.0%	Average rent	C$474/US$418
Provincial sales tax	7.5%	Homes owned	57%
		Homes rented	43%

CLIMATE

Average January low	-17.6°C/0.3°F	Annual days > 30°C/86°F	4.8	Annual days precipitation	116.6
Average July high	25.5°C/77.9°F	Annual days < 0°C/32°F	172.3	Annual days snowfall	48.7
Annual precipitation	1,099.8mm/43.3 in.	Annual days < -20°C/-4°F	30.1	Annual sun hours	1,910
Annual snowfall	241.3cm/95.0 in.				

TEMPERATURE

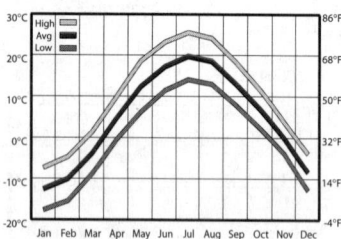

PRECIPITATION

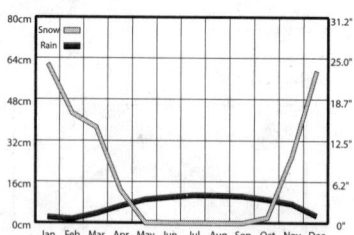

EDUCATION

High school degree	81%
Completed trade school	15%
College degree	19%
University degree	19.2%

CRIME

Violent crime rate	719
Change in violent crime rate	30.0%
Property crime rate	1,639
Change in property crime rate	-1.1%
Relocation Crime Index	140

TRANSPORTATION

Commute by auto	79.7%
Commute by mass transit	2.8%
Work at home	5.2%
Air service (passengers/day)	< 500

LEISURE

Restaurant rating	7	Spectator-sports rating	1
Golf-course rating	3	Inland water rating	6
Ski-area rating	7	Park rating	6
		Quality of life rating	3

ARTS & CULTURE

Library rating	3
Classical music rating	1
Ballet/dance rating	1
Museum rating	4

Vancouver, British Columbia

Rank: 1 **2004 rank:** 1

Profile: Regional center
Location: Southwest corner of British Columbia along the Straits of Georgia
Elevation: 86 meters/282 feet

PRO	CON
Attractive setting	Crowding and sprawl
Year-round climate	Cost of living

The rapidly growing and cosmopolitan Vancouver is the commercial, financial, industrial, and shipping center for the western half of Canada. The city is also a busy gateway to the world, particularly the Pacific Rim. Downtown is set on a beautiful natural harbor with forested mountains to the north. The core is attractive and modern with a number of historic districts and waterfront parks and beaches. Neighborhoods vary with some typical big-city suburbs spreading mainly east. The area has seen a large influx of Asian immigration, which, while adding a cultural dimension, has exacerbated some crowding and traffic problems already brought on by the constrained geography. The area has a full set of arts and entertainment amenities and the usual set of big-city services, and is home to Simon Fraser University. Recreational facilities are varied and excellent.

The climate is marine and considerably milder than most Canada cities, with persistent clouds and rain but few heavy rains, little snow, and no violent weather. Temperatures are confined to comfortable ranges; only 20 days per year are below freezing and there is no bitter cold. The climate, a major draw for Canadians, is generally regarded as the most pleasant in the country.

Vancouver compares with Portland, Oregon (no. 3), and Seattle, Washington (no. 129), to the south, but with less crowding (so far) and a more stable economy than Seattle. It's a bit congested, wet, and expensive, but excellence in other areas earns a comparable U.S. ranking of 20.

POPULATION

Population	1,986,965	Median age	37.4	Visible minorities	36.9%
Population density	1,917.5 sq. km/740.4 sq. miles	Average family size	3.2	English-speaking	87.9%
Population growth	8.5%	Single	33.9%	French-speaking	0.1%
		Married	50.1%	Bilingual	7.4%

ECONOMY & JOBS

Household income	C$49,940/US$44,195
Unemployment rate	5.3%
White collar	81.5%
Blue collar	18.5%

COST OF LIVING

Cost of Living Index	108.3	Average home price	C$518,176/US$456,563
Provincial income tax	14.7%	Average rent	C$1,004/US$888
Provincial sales tax	7.0%	Homes owned	61.5%
		Homes rented	38.5%

CLIMATE

Average January low	2.7°C/36.9°F	Annual days › 30°C/86°F	0.44	Annual days precipitation	169.1
Average July high	22°C/71.6°F	Annual days ‹ 0°C/32°F	19.6	Annual days snowfall	9.6
Annual precipitation	1,474.9mm/58.1 in.	Annual days ‹ –20°C/–4°F	0	Annual sun hours	1,919
Annual snowfall	43.6cm/17.2 in.				

TEMPERATURE

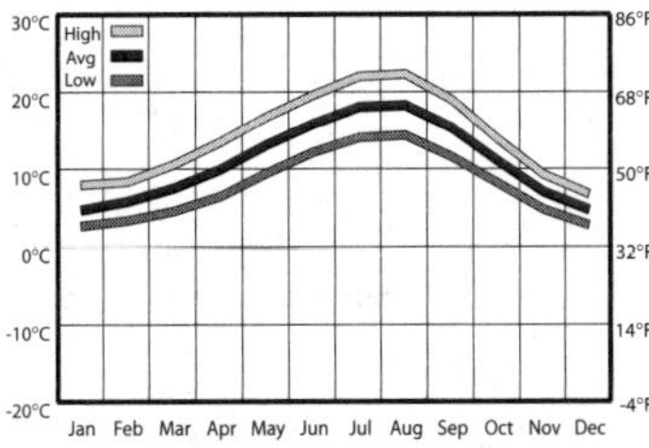

PRECIPITATION

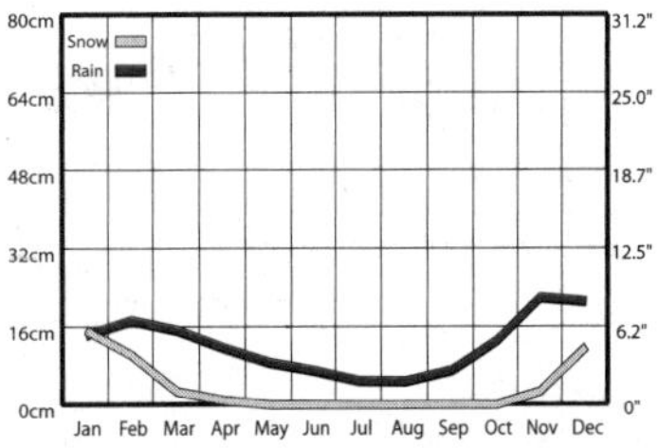

EDUCATION

High school degree	84%
Completed trade school	11%
College degree	18%
University degree	28.7%

CRIME

Violent crime rate	1,217
Change in violent crime rate	–2.8%
Property crime rate	3,762
Change in property crime rate	2.9%
Relocation Crime Index	251

TRANSPORTATION

Commute by auto	72.2%
Commute by mass transit	10.5%
Work at home	8.1%
Air service (passengers/day)	41,307

LEISURE

Restaurant rating	10	Spectator-sports rating	7
Golf-course rating	9	Inland water rating	9
Ski-area rating	10	Park rating	10
		Quality of life rating	10

ARTS & CULTURE

Library rating	10
Classical music rating	9
Ballet/dance rating	9
Museum rating	9

Victoria, British Columbia

Profile: Capital city
Location: Southern end of Vancouver Island
Elevation: 347 meters/1,138 feet

PRO	CON
Attractive downtown	High home prices
Year-round climate	Tourist impact

Victoria is a provincial capital and the cultural capital of "British" British Columbia. The city was once an important commercial center and port for distributing the natural resources of Vancouver Island and, to a lesser extent, for serving the mainland, but that role has diminished with the depletion of those resources and the emergence of Vancouver to the east. Today the area has turned its history, pleasant downtown, and strong British influence into a tourist attraction. Tourism is now the dominant industry, and the city is particularly crowded in summer. Nonetheless, Victoria is quiet and pleasant. The downtown, harbor area, and suburbs are particularly clean and attractive with a European flavor. The cultural and entertainment amenities are mainly of interest to tourists, but are of sufficient quality to benefit residents. Some services and amenities require a trip to Vancouver, usually a full-day excursion. Rapidly rising home prices (up 111% in 5 years) and a questionable crime score brought the ranking down a bit.

The area is surrounded by saltwater channels and islands. Wooded hills and mountains rise to the northwest. The Pacific marine climate is mild but wet with few temperature extremes. Summers are very pleasant.

A direct U.S. comparison doesn't really exist, but there are vague similarities to Olympia, Washington (no. 16). Victoria gets a comparable U.S. rank of 50.

POPULATION

Population	311,902	Median age	41	Visible minorities	8.9%
Population density	1,246.1 sq. km/481.1 sq. miles	Average family size	2.9	English-speaking	90.6%
Population growth	2.5%	Single	31.7%	French-speaking	0.0%
		Married	47.6%	Bilingual	8.6%

ECONOMY & JOBS

Household income	C$46,387/US$41,050
Unemployment rate	4.4%
White collar	85%
Blue collar	15%

COST OF LIVING

Cost of Living Index	96.0	Average home price	C$515,715/US$456,385
Provincial income tax	14.7%	Average rent	C$808/US$715
Provincial sales tax	7.0%	Homes owned	72%
		Homes rented	28%

CLIMATE

Average January low	7.2°C/45.0°F	Annual days > 30°C/86°F	0.05	Annual days precipitation	149.3
Average July high	20.1°C/68.2°F	Annual days < 0°C/32°F	10.3	Annual days snowfall	3.4
Annual precipitation	686.1mm/27.0 in.	Annual days < −20°C/−4°F	0	Annual sun hours	2,082
Annual snowfall	12.5cm/4.9 in.				

TEMPERATURE

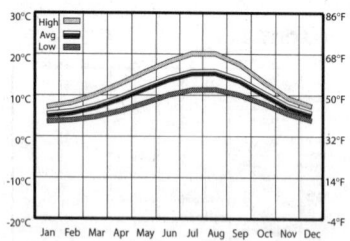

PRECIPITATION

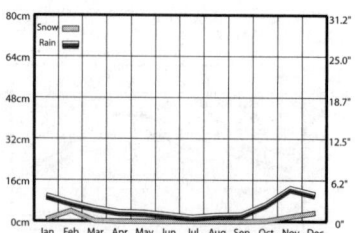

EDUCATION

High school degree	86%
Completed trade school	12%
College degree	20%
University degree	26.6%

CRIME

Violent crime rate	1,217
Change in violent crime rate	−2.8%
Property crime rate	3,762
Change in property crime rate	2.9%
Relocation Crime Index	349

TRANSPORTATION

Commute by auto	60.9%
Commute by mass transit	8.8%
Work at home	9.2%
Air service (passengers/day)	3,020

LEISURE

Restaurant rating	9	Spectator-sports rating	2
Golf-course rating	8	Inland water rating	5
Ski-area rating	5	Park rating	9
		Quality of life rating	9

ARTS & CULTURE

Library rating	8
Classical music rating	6
Ballet/dance rating	5
Museum rating	8

Windsor, Ontario

Rank: 23 **2004 rank:** 23

Profile: Mid-size city
Location: Southwestern Ontario across the Detroit River from Detroit, Michigan
Elevation: 176 meters/577 feet

PRO	CON
Entertainment	Industrial feel
Close to Detroit	Economic cycles

Windsor, essentially a border town with strong ties to Detroit, Michigan, is linked physically and metaphorically to the United States by the Ambassador Bridge. Like Detroit, the area's economy is driven by the auto industry and related manufacturing, but it also benefits from trade with the U.S. The revitalized downtown and attractive waterfront areas provide entertainment for Canadians and Americans alike. While entertainment is a plus, most arts, cultural activities, sports, and services are found in Detroit. There isn't as much in the way of historic interest or European flavor found in many other Canadian cities. Many areas of the city reflect its heavy industrial character, and recent employment statistics, influenced by the heavy auto industry presence, project a negative picture in contrast to the rest of Canada.

The terrain is mostly level coastal plain. The climate is Great Lakes marine, a continental type with relatively few extremes due to water moderation. Still, winters are cold and damp.

The area compares to the Michigan regions of Warren–Troy–Farmington Hills (no. 190) and Detroit (no. 344) without the big-city amenities, or many of its problems. The comparable U.S. rank is 265.

POPULATION

Population	307,877	Median age	39	Visible minorities	12.9%
Population density	836.4 sq. km/322.9 sq. miles	Average family size	3.2	English-speaking	87.8%
Population growth	7.3%	Single	30.8%	French-speaking	0.2%
		Married	49.3%	Bilingual	10.5%

ECONOMY & JOBS

Household income	C$54,542/US$48,267				
Unemployment rate	7.5%				
White collar	67%				
Blue collar	33%				

COST OF LIVING

Cost of Living Index	89.2	Average home price	C$259,900/US$230,000
Provincial income tax	11.2%	Average rent	C$780/US$690
Provincial sales tax	8.0%	Homes owned	72%
		Homes rented	28%

CLIMATE

Average January low	−4.5°C/23.9°F	Annual days > 30°C/86°F	20.7	Annual days precipitation	115.7
Average July high	27.9°C/82.2°F	Annual days < 0°C/32°F	122.8	Annual days snowfall	45
Annual precipitation	805.2mm/31.7 in.	Annual days < −20°C/−4°F	1.6	Annual sun hours	2,045
Annual snowfall	126.6cm/49.8 in.				

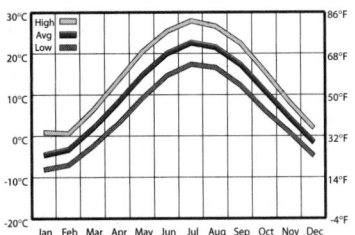

TEMPERATURE

PRECIPITATION

EDUCATION

High school degree	82%
Completed trade school	11%
College degree	17%
University degree	20.6%

CRIME

Violent crime rate	903
Change in violent crime rate	1.8%
Property crime rate	6,509
Change in property crime rate	1.6%
Relocation Crime Index	164

TRANSPORTATION

Commute by auto	77.0%
Commute by mass transit	2.8%
Work at home	3.5%
Air service (passengers/day)	< 500

LEISURE

Restaurant rating	7	Spectator-sports rating	5
Golf-course rating	5	Inland water rating	8
Ski-area rating	4	Park rating	7
		Quality of life rating	4

ARTS & CULTURE

Library rating	5
Classical music rating	5
Ballet/dance rating	3
Museum rating	4

Winnipeg, Manitoba

Profile: Mid-size capital city
Location: Southeastern Manitoba at the confluence of Red and Assiniboine rivers
Elevation: 239 meters/784 feet

PRO	CON
Attractive downtown	Severe winters
Arts and culture	Unattractive landscape

If it weren't for the climate, Winnipeg would be among the top cities in all of North America. The city serves as a transportation gateway and commercial center for a vast agricultural region, mainly to the west. The city itself is clean, well planned, and modern with attractive buildings and parks and never a feeling of crowding. The economic base is diverse and secure, and the surprising arts and culture establishment is among the best in Canada. The Royal Winnipeg Ballet has a global reputation and the other performing arts and museums complement it. The downside is climate, which is so severe that the city is the object of ridicule even from Canadians ("Winterpeg, Mani-snowba").

Winnipeg sits in the path of arctic air flow with no topographic protection. Winter cold can extend beyond unpleasant to plainly dangerous. Summers, in contrast, are pleasant to quite warm and dry. The city is the coldest but is also the sunniest in Canada.

The area is similar to Chicago, Illinois (no. 258), but not as big; Minneapolis-St. Paul, Minnesota (no. 262), but not as expensive; and St. Louis, Missouri (no. 35), but culturally stronger, and has fewer problems, climate aside, than all three, and retains its comparable U.S. rank of 120.

POPULATION

Population	671,274	Median age	37.3	Visible minorities	12.5%
Population density	161.7 sq. km/62.4 sq. miles	Average family size	3.1	English-speaking	87.9%
Population growth	0.6%	Single	33.1%	French-speaking	0.1%
		Married	49.3%	Bilingual	10.9%

ECONOMY & JOBS

Household income	C$44,562/US$39,435
Unemployment rate	5.0%
White collar	78%
Blue collar	22%

COST OF LIVING

Cost of Living Index	90.2	Average home price	C$159,900/US$141,504
Provincial income tax	17.4%	Average rent	C$683/US$604
Provincial sales tax	7.0%	Homes owned	65.5%
		Homes rented	34.5%

CLIMATE

Average January low	−23.6°C/−10.5°F	Annual days › 30°C/86°F	13.5	Annual days precipitation	123.5
Average July high	26.1°C/79.0°F	Annual days ‹ 0°C/32°F	194	Annual days snowfall	54.7
Annual precipitation	504.0mm/19.8 in.	Annual days ‹ −20°C/−4°F	57.5	Annual sun hours	2,577
Annual snowfall	114.8cm/45.2 in.				

TEMPERATURE

PRECIPITATION

EDUCATION

High school degree	78%
Completed trade school	12%
College degree	17%
University degree	22.7%

CRIME

Violent crime rate	1,620
Change in violent crime rate	−1.5%
Property crime rate	5,136
Change in property crime rate	11.5%
Relocation Crime Index	205

TRANSPORTATION

Commute by auto	70.0%
Commute by mass transit	14.3%
Work at home	5.6%
Air service (passengers/day)	7,351

LEISURE

Restaurant rating	8	Spectator-sports rating	5
Golf-course rating	6	Inland water rating	8
Ski-area rating	3	Park rating	5
		Quality of life rating	7

ARTS & CULTURE

Library rating	8
Classical music rating	8
Ballet/dance rating	10
Museum rating	7

index

U.S. & Canadian Cities